The Ox...
and Englis...

D0439050

The Oxford Dictionary and English Usage Guide

Oxford New York

OXFORD UNIVERSITY PRESS

1996

Oxford University Press, Walton Street, Oxford OX2 6DP

Oxford New York
Athens Auckland Bangkok Bombay
Calcutta Cape Town Dar es Salaam Delhi
Florence Hong Kong Istanbul Karachi
Kuala Lumpur Madras Madrid Melbourne
Mexico City Nairobi Paris Singapore
Taipei Tokyo Toronto

and associated companies in
Berlin Ibadan

Oxford is a trade mark of Oxford University Press

Published in the United States
by Oxford University Press Inc., New York

Compilation © Oxford University Press 1995
Usage Guide © Oxford University Press 1994
Dictionary text © Oxford University Press 1994
First published in paperback 1996

British Library Cataloguing in Publication Data
Data available

Library of Congress Cataloging in Publication Data
The Oxford dictionary and English usage guide /
Maurice Waite, Andrew Delahunty, Edmund Weiner, editors.
1. English language—Dictionaries.
2. English language—Usage—Dictionaries.
I. Waite, Maurice.   II. Delahunty, Andrew.   III. Weiner, E.S.C.
PE 1628.08647   1996   428.1—dc20   95-53794

ISBN 0-19-861325-3

10 9 8 7 6 5 4 3 2 1

Typeset by Latimer Trend & Company Ltd
in Monotype Nimrod
Printed in Great Britain
by Mackays PLC
Chatham, Kent

Contents

English Usage Guide

Dictionary

English Usage Guide

Introduction

The *English Usage Guide* aims to give guidance in as clear, concise, and systematic a manner as possible on matters of pronunciation, spelling, meaning, and grammar about which there is controversy or uncertainty. It has five special features:

1. *Layout.* In the *Guide* the subject of usage is divided into four fields: *word formation, pronunciation, vocabulary,* and *grammar.* Each field is covered by a separate section of the book, and each of the four sections has its own alphabetical arrangement of entries. Each entry is headed by its title in **bold type**. All the words that share a particular kind of spelling, sound, or construction can therefore be treated together. This makes for both economy and comprehensiveness of treatment.

2. *Explanation.* The explanations given in each entry are intended to be simple and straightforward, even where the subject is inevitably slightly complicated. They take into account the approaches developed by modern linguistic analysis, but employ the traditional terms of grammar as much as possible. (A glossary of all grammatical terms used in this book will be found on pp. 1–5 ff.) Technical symbols and abbreviations, and the phonetic alphabet, are not used at all.

3. *Exemplification.* Wherever appropriate, example sentences are given to illustrate the point being discussed. The majority of these are real examples, many drawn from the works of some of the best twentieth-century writers. Even informal or substandard usage has been illustrated in this way, taken, for example, from speeches in novels.

4. *Recommendation.* Recommendations are clearly set out. The blob ● is used to state a warning, restriction, or prohibition. The square □ is used, particularly in section I, where a recommendation is given alongside acceptable alternatives. The emphasis of the recommendations is on the degree of acceptability in standard English, rather than on a dogmatic distinction of right and wrong. Much that is condemned as 'bad English' is better regarded as appropriate in informal contexts but inappropriate in formal ones. The appropriateness of usage to context is indicated by the fairly rough categories 'formal' and 'informal', 'standard', 'regional', and 'non-standard', 'jocular', and so on. Some of the ways in which American usage differs from British are pointed out.

5. *Reference.* Ease of access is a priority of the *Guide.* Its four-part division means that (roughly speaking) only a quarter of the total range of pages need be looked through in order to find a particular entry. But this should rarely be necessary, since there is an index in which every subject and every word and affix covered by the *Guide* can be found. Within each section there are many cross-references to other entries; these are indicated by **bold type** and followed by the page number if necessary.

In addition to the four main sections described at 1 above, the *Guide* has two *appendices*: I is an outline of the principles of punctuation; and II lists some of the clichés and overworked diction most widely disliked at present.

Grammatical terms used in this book

Where an example is partly in italics and partly in roman type, it is the words in roman that exemplify the term being defined.

absolute used independently of its customary grammatical relationship or construction, e.g. Weather permitting, *I will come.*

acronym a word formed from the initial letters of other words, e.g. *NATO.*

active applied to a verb whose subject is also the source of the action of the verb, e.g. *We saw him*; opposite of **passive**.

adjective a word that names an attribute, used to describe a noun or pronoun, e.g. small *child*, *it is* small.

adverb a word that modifies an adjective, verb, or another adverb, expressing a relation of place, time, circumstance, manner, cause, degree, etc., e.g. *gently, accordingly, now, here, why.*

agent noun a noun denoting the doer of an action, e.g. *builder.*

agent suffix a suffix added to a verb to form an agent noun, e.g. *-er.*

agree to have the same grammatical number, gender, case, or person as another word.

analogy the formation of a word, derivative, or construction in imitation of an existing word or pattern.

animate denoting a living being.

antecedent a noun or phrase to which a relative pronoun refers back.

antepenultimate last but two.

antonym a word of contrary meaning to another.

apposition the placing of a word, especially a noun, syntactically parallel to another, e.g. *William the Conqueror.*

article *a/an* (**indefinite** article) or *the* (**definite** article).

attributive designating a noun, adjective, or phrase expressing an attribute, characteristically preceding the word it qualifies, e.g. *old* in *the old dog*; opposite of **predicative**.

auxiliary verb a verb used in forming tenses, moods, and voices of other verbs.

case the form (**subjective, objective, or possessive**) of a noun or pronoun, expressing relation to some other word.

clause a distinct part of a sentence including a **subject** (sometimes by implication) and **predicate**.

collective noun a singular noun denoting many individuals; see page 77.

collocation an expression consisting of two (or more) words frequently juxtaposed, especially adjective + noun, e.g. *derisory offer, heavy drinker.*

comparative the form of an adjective or adverb expressing a higher degree of a quality, e.g. *braver, worse.*

comparison the differentiation of the **comparative** and **superlative** degrees from the positive (basic) form of an adjective or adverb.

complement a word or words necessary to complete a grammatical construction: the complement of a clause, e.g. *John is* (a) thoughtful (man), *Solitude makes John* thoughtful; of an adjective, e.g. *John is glad* of your help; of a preposition, e.g. *I thought of* John.

compound preposition a preposition made up of more than one word, e.g. *with regard to.*

concord agreement between words in gender, number, or person, e.g. *the girl who* is *here, you who* are *alive,* Those *men* work.

conditional designating (1) a clause which expresses a condition, or (2) a mood of the verb used in the consequential clause of a conditional sentence, e.g. (1) *If he had come,* (2) *I* should have seen *him.*

consonant (1) a speech sound in which breath is at least partly obstructed, combining with a **vowel** to form a syllable; (2) a letter usually used to represent (1); e.g. *ewe* is written with vowel + consonant + vowel, but is pronounced as consonant (y) + vowel (oo).

coordination the linking of two or more parts of a compound sentence that are equal in importance, e.g. *He sang and she played the piano.*

correlative coordination coordination by means of pairs of corresponding words regularly used together, e.g. *either . . or.*

countable designating a noun that refers in the singular to one and in the plural to more than one, and can be qualified by *a, one, every,* etc. and *many, two, three,* etc.; opposite of **mass (noun)**.

diminutive denoting a word referring to a small, liked, or despised member of the class denoted by the corresponding root word, e.g. *ringlet, Johnny, princeling.*

diphthong: see **digraph,** p. 56.

direct object the **object** that expresses the primary object of the action of the verb, e.g. *He sent* a present *to his son.*

disyllabic having two syllables.

double passive: see p. 79 f.

elide to omit by **elision.**

elision the omission of a vowel or syllable in pronouncing, e.g. *let's.*

ellipsis the omission from a sentence of words needed to complete a construction or sense.

elliptical involving **ellipsis.**

feminine the gender to which words referring to female beings usually belong.

finite designating (part of) a verb limited by person and number, e.g. *I am, He* comes.

formal designating the type of English used publicly for some serious purpose, either in writing or in public speeches.

future the tense of a verb referring to an event yet to happen: **simple future,** e.g. *I shall go;* **future in the past,** referring to an event that was yet to happen at a time prior to the time of speaking, e.g. *He said he* would go.

gerund the part of the verb which can be used like a noun, ending in *-ing,* e.g. *What is the use of my* scolding *him?*

govern (said of a verb or preposition) to have (a noun or pronoun, or a case) dependent on it.

group possessive: see p. 81.

hard designating a letter, chiefly *c* or *g,* that indicates a guttural sound, as in *cot* or *got.*

if-**clause** a clause introduced by *if.*

imperative the mood of a verb expressing command, e.g. Come *here!*

inanimate opposite of **animate.**

indirect object the person or thing affected by the action of the verb but not primarily acted upon, e.g. *I gave* him *the book.*

infinitive the basic form of a verb that does not indicate a particular tense or number or person; the *to*-**infinitive,** used with preceding *to,* e.g. *I want* to know; the **bare infinitive,** without preceding *to,* e.g. *Help me* pack.

inflection a part of a word, usually a suffix, that expresses grammatical relationship, such as number, person, tense, etc.; also used to refer to the process by which this part is added.

informal designating the type of English used in private conversation, personal letters, and popular public communication.

intransitive designating a verb that does not take a direct object, e.g. *I must think.*

intrusive *r* : see p. 34.

linking *r* : see p. 34.

living designating a **prefix** or **suffix** that can be freely used to form new compounds.

loanword a word adopted by one language from another.

main clause the principal clause of a sentence.

masculine the gender to which words referring to male beings usually belong.

mass noun (or **uncountable noun**) a noun that refers to something regarded as grammatically indivisible, treated only as singular, and never qualified by *those, many, two, three,* etc.; opposite of **countable** noun.

modal relating to the **mood** of a verb; used to express mood.

mood form of a verb serving to indicate whether it is to express fact, command, permission, wish, etc.

monosyllabic having one syllable.

nominal designating a phrase or clause that is used like a noun, e.g. What you need *is a drink.*

nonce-word a word coined for one occasion.

non-finite designating (a part of) a verb not limited by person and number, e.g. the infinitive, gerund, or participle.

non-restrictive: see p. 89 f.

noun a word used to denote a person, place, or thing.

noun phrase a phrase functioning within the sentence as a noun, e.g. The one over there *is mine.*

object a noun or its equivalent governed by an active transitive verb, e.g. *I will take* that one.

objective the case of a pronoun typically used when the pronoun is the object of a verb or governed by a preposition, e.g. *me, him.*

paradigm the complete pattern of inflection of a noun, verb, etc.

participle the part of a verb used like an adjective but retaining some verbal qualities (tense and government of an object) and also used to form compound verb forms: the **present participle** ends in *-ing,* the **past participle** of regular verbs in *-ed,* e.g. *While* doing *her work she had* kept *the baby* amused.

passive designating a form of the verb by which the verbal action is attributed to the person or thing to whom it is actually directed (i.e. the logical object is the grammatical subject), e.g. *He was seen by us*; opposite of **active.**

past a tense expressing past action or state, e.g. *I arrived yesterday.*

past perfect a tense expressing action already completed prior to the time being spoken or written about, e.g. *I had arrived by then.*

pejorative disparaging, depreciatory.

penultimate last but one.

perfect a tense denoting completed action or action viewed in relation to the present; e.g. *I have finished now*; **perfect infinitive,** e.g. *He seems* to have finished *now.*

periphrasis a roundabout way of expressing something.

person one of the three classes of personal pronouns or verb-forms, denoting the person speaking (**first person**), the person spoken to (**second person**), and the person or thing spoken about (**third person**).

phrasal verb an expression consisting of a verb and an adverb (and preposition), e.g. *break down, look forward to.*

phrase a group of words without a predicate, functioning like an adjective, adverb, or noun.

plural denoting more than one.

polysyllabic having more than one syllable.

possessive the case of a noun or a pronoun indicating possession, e.g. *John's*; **possessive pronoun**, e.g. *my, his.*

predicate the part of a clause consisting of what is said of the subject, including verb + complement or object.

predicative designating (especially) an adjective that forms part or the whole of the predicate, e.g. *The dog is* old.

prefix a verbal element placed at the beginning of a word to qualify its meaning, e.g. *ex-, non-.*

preposition a word governing a noun or pronoun, expressing the relation of the latter to other words, e.g. *seated* at *the table.*

prepositional phrase a phrase consisting of a preposition and its complement, e.g. *I am surprised* at *your reaction.*

present a tense expressing action now going on or habitually performed in past and future, e.g. *He* commutes *daily.*

pronoun a word used instead of a noun to designate (without naming) a person or thing already known or indefinite, e.g. *I, you, he*, etc., *anyone, something*, etc.

proper name a name used to designate an individual person, animal, town, ship, etc.

qualify (of an adjective or adverb) to attribute some quality to (a noun or adjective/verb).

reflexive implying the subject's action on himself, herself, or itself; **reflexive pronoun**, e.g. *myself, yourself*, etc.

relative: see p. 89 f.

restrictive: see p. 89.

semi-vowel a sound intermediate between vowel and consonant, e.g. the sound of *y* and *w.*

sentence adverb an adverb that qualifies or comments on the whole sentence, not one of the elements in it, e.g. Unfortunately, *he missed his train.*

simple future: see **future**.

singular denoting a single person or thing.

soft designating a letter, chiefly *c* or *g*, that indicates a sibilant sound, as in *city* or *germ.*

split infinitive: see p. 91 f.

stem the essential part of a word to which inflections and other suffixes are added, e.g. *un*limit*ed.*

stress the especially heavy vocal emphasis falling on one (the **stressed**) syllable of a word more than on the others.

subject the element in a clause (usually a noun or its equivalent) about which something is predicated (the latter is the **predicate**).

subjective the case of a pronoun typically used when the pronoun is the subject of a clause.

subjunctive the mood of a verb denoting what is imagined, wished, or possible, e.g. *I insist that it* be *finished.*

subordinate clause a clause dependent on the main clause and functioning like a noun, adjective, or adverb within the sentence, e.g. *He said* that you had gone.

substitute verb the verb *do* used in place of another verb, e.g. '*He likes chocolate.*' 'Does *he*?'

suffix a verbal element added at the end of a word to form a derivative, e.g. *-ation, -ing, -itis, -ize.*

superlative the form of an adjective or adverb expressing the highest or a very high degree of a quality, e.g. *bravest, worst.*

synonym a word that means exactly or nearly the same as another.

transitive designating a verb that takes a direct object, e.g. *I said nothing.*

uncountable noun: see **mass noun**.

unreal condition (especially in a **conditional** sentence) a condition which will not be or has not been fulfilled.

unstressed designating a word, syllable, or vowel not having **stress**.

variant a form of a word etc. that differs in spelling or pronunciation from another (often the main or usual) form.

verb a part of speech that predicates.

vowel (1) an open speech sound made without audible friction and capable of forming a syllable with or without a consonant; (2) a letter usually used to represent (1), e.g. *a, e, i, o, u.*

wh-**question word** a convenient term for the interrogative and relative words, most beginning with *wh*: *what, when, where, whether, which, who, whom, whose, why, how.*

Abbreviations

Amer.	American
COD	*The Concise Oxford Dictionary* (edn. 8, Oxford, 1990)
Hart's Rules	*Hart's Rules for Compositors and Readers* (edn. 39, Oxford, 1983)
MEU	H. W. Fowler, *A Dictionary of Modern English Usage* (edn. 2, revised by Sir Ernest Gowers, Oxford, 1965)
OED	*The Oxford English Dictionary* (edn. 2, Oxford, 1989)
OWD	*The Oxford Writers' Dictionary* (Oxford, 1990)
TLS	*The Times Literary Supplement*

Word formation

This section deals with the forms of single words and word elements as regards spelling, including that of inflected and compounded forms and of those formed by adding prefixes and suffixes; little space has been given to meaning or use. There is some treatment of words requiring hyphens or capitals, but for a further discussion the reader is referred to the *Oxford Writers' Dictionary* and *Hart's Rules*. Some notes are added where the conventions of American spelling differ.

Where there is widespread variation in spelling, the spelling recommended is that preferred (as its 'house style') by Oxford University Press.

abbreviations

It is usual to indicate an abbreviation by placing a point (full stop) after it, e.g.

> *H. G. Wells, five miles S.* (= south), *p. 7* (= page 7).

However, no point is used:

1. With a sequence of capitals alone, e.g. *BBC*, AD (and not with acronyms, e.g. *Aslef, Naafi*).

2. With the numerical abbreviations *1st, 2nd*, etc.

3. With *C, F* (of temperature), chemical symbols, and measures of length, weight, time, etc., e.g. *cm, ft, cwt, lb, kg*.

4. After *Dr, Revd, Mr, Mrs, Ms, Mme, Mlle, St, Hants, Northants, p* (= penny or pence).

5. In colloquial abbreviations, e.g. *co-op, vac*.

-able and -ible

Adjectives ending in *-able* generally owe their form to the Latin termination *-abilis* or the Old French *-able* (or both), and those in *-ible* to the Latin *-ibilis*. The suffix *-able* is also added to words of 'distinctly French or English origin' (*OED*, s.v. *-ble*), and as a living element to English roots. Nouns in *-ability, -ibility* undergo the same changes.

A. Words ending in *-able*. The following alterations are made to the stem:

1. Silent final *-e* is dropped (see p. 10 f.).

Exceptions: words whose stem ends in *-ce, -ee, -ge*, and:

blameable	nameable
dyeable	rateable
giveable	ropeable
(but *forgivable*)	saleable
hireable	shareable
holeable	sizeable
likeable	tameable
liveable	unshakeable

● Amer. spelling tends to omit *-e-* in the words above.

2. Final *-y* becomes *-i-* (see p. 22).

Exception: *flyable*.

3. A final consonant may be doubled (see p. 10 f.).

Exceptions:

inferable	referable
preferable	transferable
(but *conferrable*)	

4. Most verbs of more than two syllables ending in *-ate* drop this ending before *-able*, e.g. *alienable, calculable*, etc. Verbs of two syllables ending in *-ate* form adjectives in *-able* regularly, e.g. *creatable, debatable*, etc.

B. Words ending in *-ible*. These are fewer, since *-ible* is not a living suffix (i.e. it cannot be freely used to form new words). Below is a list of the commonest. Almost all form their negative in *in-, il-*, etc.; the exceptions are indicated by (*un*).

accessible	comprehensible
adducible	contemptible
admissible	convertible
audible	corrigible
avertible	corruptible
collapsible	credible
combustible	defensible
compatible	destructible

digestible · ostensible
dirigible · perceptible
discernible · perfectible
divisible · permissible
edible · persuasible
eligible · plausible
exhaustible · possible
expressible · reducible
extensible · reprehensible
fallible · repressible
(un)feasible · reproducible
flexible · resistible
forcible · responsible
fusible · reversible
gullible · risible
horrible · sensible
indelible · (un)susceptible
(un)intelligible · tangible
irascible · terrible
legible · vincible
negligible · visible

ae and oe

In words derived from Latin and Greek, these are now always written as separate letters, not as the ligatures *ae*, *oe*, e.g. *aeon*, *gynaecology*; *amoeba*, *Oedipus*. The simple *e* is preferable in several words once commonly spelt with *ae*, *oe*, especially *medieval* and *ecology*, *ecumenical*.

● In Amer. spelling, *e* replaces *ae*, *oe* in many words, e.g. *gynecology*, *diarrhea*.

American spelling

Differences between Amer. and British spelling are mentioned at the following places: *-able* and *-ible* (p. 7); *ae* and *oe* (p. 8); *-ce* or *-se* (p. 9); **doubling of final consonant** (p. 10); **dropping of silent *-e*** (p. 11); **hyphens** (p. 14); *l* and *ll* (p. 15); *-oul-* (p. 16); *-our* or *-or* (p. 16); **past of verbs, formation of** (p. 16 f.); *-re* or *-er* (p. 20); *-yse* or *-yze* (p. 21).

See also **difficult and confusable spellings** (pp. 22 ff.) *passim*.

ante- and anti-

ante- (from Latin) = 'before'; *anti-* (from Greek) = 'against, opposite to'. Note especially *antechamber* and *antitype*.

-ant or -ent

-ant is the noun ending, *-ent* the adjective ending in:

dependant · dependent
descendant · descendent
pendant · pendent
propellant · propellent

independent is both adjective and noun; *dependence*, *independence* are the abstract nouns.

The following are correct spellings:

ascendant, -ncy · relevant, -nce
attendant, -nce · repellent, -nce, -ncy
contribuent · superintendent, -ncy
expellent · tendency
impellent · transcendent, -nce
intendant, -ncy

a or an

A. Before *h*.

1. Where *h* is pronounced, use *a*, e.g. *a harvest*, *hero*, *hope*.
2. Where *h* is silent, use *an*, e.g. *an heir*, *honour*, *honorarium*.
3. Where *h* is pronounced but the first syllable is unstressed, use *a*, e.g. *a hotel*.

● The older usage, e.g. *an hotel*, is now almost obsolete.

B. Before capital letter abbreviations, follow the pronunciation.

1. Where the abbreviation is pronounced as letter-names, e.g.

   a B road   *a UN resolution*

but

   an A road   *an MP*

2. Where the abbreviation is pronounced as a word, e.g.

   a RADA student   *a SABENA airline typist*

but

   an AIDS conference   *an OPEC minister*

But where the abbreviation would in speech be pronounced as a word, use *a* or *an* as appropriate, e.g. *a MS* 'a manuscript'.

-ative or -ive

Correct are:

(a) authoritative   qualitative
exploitative   quantitative
interpretative
(b) absorptive   preventive
assertive   supportive

The forms interpretive (which has a special computing meaning) and preventative also occur.

by- prefix

One word: bygone, byline, byname, bypass, bypath, byplay, byroad, bystander, byway, byword; the others (e.g. by-election, by-product) are hyphened.

● Bye (noun) in sport, bye-bye (= good-bye) take final -e.

c and ck

Words ending in -c interpose k before -ed, -er, -ing, -y, e.g.:

colicky   picnicked, -er, -ing
frolicked, -ing   plastic-macked
mimicked, -ing   tarmacked, -ing
panicky   trafficked, -ing

Exceptions: arced, -ing, zinced, zincify, zincing.

Before -ism, -ist, -ity, and -ize c remains and is pronounced soft, e.g. physicist, italicize.

capital or small initials

There are four classes of word that especially give trouble.

A. Compass points. Use capitals:

1. When abbreviated, e.g. NNE for north-north-east.
2. When denoting a region, e.g. unemployment in the North.
3. When part of a geographical name with recognized status, e.g. Northern Ireland, East Africa, Western Australia.
4. In bridge.

Otherwise use small initials, e.g. a south-easter.

B. Parties, denominations, and organizations.

'The general rule is: capitalization makes a word more specific and limited in its reference: contrast a Christian scientist (man of science) and a Christian Scientist (member of the Church of Christ Scientist).' (Hart's Rules, pp. 10–11.)

So, for example, Conservative, Democratic (names of parties); Roman Catholic, Congregational; but conservative, democratic (as normal adjectives), catholic sympathies, congregational singing.

C. Words derived from proper names.

When connection with the proper name is indirect or allusive, use a small initial letter, e.g.

jersey, platonic (love), pasteurize.

When the connection of a derived adjective or verb with a proper name is felt to be alive, use a capital, e.g.

Platonic (philosophy), Anglicize.

● Adjectives of nationality usually retain the capital even when used in transferred senses, e.g. Dutch courage, Turkish delight. The chief exceptions are arabic (numeral), roman (numeral, type).

D. Proprietary names.

The name of a product or process, if registered as a trade mark, is a proprietary name, and should be given a capital initial, e.g. Araldite, Coca-Cola, Marmite, Xerox.

-cede or -ceed

Exceed, proceed, succeed; the other similar verbs have -cede, e.g. concede, intercede, precede, recede. Note also supersede.

-ce or -se

Advice, device, licence, and practice are nouns; the related verbs are spelt with -se: advise, devise, license, practise. Similarly prophecy (noun), prophesy (verb).

● Amer. spelling favours license, practise for both noun and verb; but the nouns defence, offence, pretence are spelt with c in Britain, s in America.

co- prefix

Most words with this prefix have no hyphen. Those that are usually spelt with a hyphen are:

1. A few words with *o* following, e.g. *co-op*, *co-opt* (but *cooperate, uncooperative, coordinate*).

2. Words in which the hyphen preserves correct syllabication, so aiding recognition, e.g. *co-respondent* (distinguished from *correspondent*).

3. Words in which *co-* is a living prefix meaning 'fellow-', e.g. *co-author, co-star*.

doubling of final consonant

1. Before certain suffixes beginning with a vowel, the final consonant of the stem word is doubled:

> (*a*) if the preceding vowel is written with a single letter (or single letter preceded by *qu*) and
> (*b*) if that vowel bears the main stress (hence all monosyllables are included).

So *bed, bedding* but *head, heading*; *occúr, occúrred* but *óffer, óffered*; *befít, befítted* but *bénefit, bénefited*.

Suffixes which cause this doubling include:

(*a*) The verb inflections *-ed, -ing*, e.g.

> *begged, begging*   *revved, revving*
> *bussed, bussing*   *trekked, trekking*

(*b*) The suffixes *-able, -age, -en, -er, -ery, -est, -ish, -y*, e.g.

> *clubbable*   *waggery*
> *tonnage*   *saddest*
> *sadden*   *priggish*
> *trapper*   *shrubby*

2. Words of more than one syllable, not stressed on the last syllable, do not double the final consonant, unless it is *l*, when a suffix beginning with a vowel is added, e.g.

> *biased*   *gossipy*   *turbaned*
> *blossoming*   *lettered*   *wainscoted*
> *faceted*   *pilotage*   *wickedest*
> *focusing*   *targeted*   *womanish*

Exception: *worship* makes *worshipped, -ing*.

Note that some other words in which the final syllable has a full vowel (not obscure *e* or *i*) also double this consonant, e.g.

> *format*   *horsewhip*   *leap-frog*
> *handicap*   *humbug*   *sandbag*
> *hobnob*   *kidnap*   *zigzag*

● Amer. sometimes *kidnaped, kidnaping, worshiped, worshiping*.

3. Consonants that are never doubled are *c, h, w, x, y*.

4. When endings beginning with a vowel are added, *l* is *always* doubled after a single vowel wherever the stress falls, e.g.

> *controllable*   *jeweller*
> *flannelled*   *panelling*

Note also *woollen, woolly*.

Exceptions: *parallel* makes *paralleled, -ing*; *devil* makes *devilish*.

● In Amer. spelling *l* obeys the same rules as the other consonants (except *c, h, w, x, y*), e.g. *traveler*, but *pally*.

Note also Amer. *woolen* (but *woolly*).

5. A silent final consonant is not doubled. Endings are added as if the consonant were pronounced, e.g.

> *crocheted, -ing*   *rendezvouses* (third
> *pince-nezed*   person singular)
> *précised*   *rendezvousing*

dropping of silent -e

A. When a suffix beginning with a vowel (including *-y*) is added to a word ending in silent *-e* (including *e* following another vowel), the *-e* is dropped; e.g.

> *braver, bravery, bravest*   *hoed*
> *dyed, dyer*   *issued*
> *freer, freest*   *manoeuvred*

> *adorable*   *imaginable*
> *analysable*   *manoeuvrable*
> *bribable*   *usable*

> *cleavage*   *dotage*

> *centring*   *housing*
> *gluing*   *queuing*

> *whitish*   *mousy*

Exceptions:

(*a*) Words ending in *-ce* and *-ge* retain the *e* to indicate the softness of the consonant, e.g. *bridgeable*.

(b) In a number of -*able* adjectives, *e* is retained. See list on p. 7.

(c) The few -*able* adjectives formed on verbs ending in consonant + -*le*; e.g. *handleable.*

(d) *acreage, mileage.*

(e) *ee, oe,* and *ye* remain, e.g.

agreeing   dyeing   hoeing
canoeing   eyeing   shoeing

(f) *blueing, cueing.*

(g) *routeing, singeing, swingeing* are distinguished from *routing* 'putting to flight', *singing,* and *swinging.*

(h) *moreish, ogreish.*

(i) See -*y* or -*ey* adjectives, p. 21f. Both *stagy* and *stagey* are acceptable. For change of *i* to *y, dying, lying,* etc., see p. 15.

B. When a suffix beginning with a consonant is added to a word ending in silent -*e,* the -*e* is retained, e.g.

abridgement   houseful
acknowledgement judgement (judgment
awesome   often in legal works)
definitely   whiteness

Exceptions: *argument, awful, duly, eerily, eeriness, fledgling, truly, wholly.*

● In Amer. spelling *e* is dropped after *dg* and before a suffix beginning with a consonant, e.g. *abridgment, judgment.*

C. Final silent -*e* is often omitted in Amer. spelling, and so is final silent -*ue* in the endings -*gogue,* -*logue,* e.g.

ax   adz   program
analog epilog   pedagog

-efy or -ify

The chief words with -*efy* (-*efied,* -*efication,* etc.) are:

liquefy   rubefy   tumefy
putrefy   stupefy
rarefy   torrefy

All the others have -*ify* etc. See also -**ified** or -*yfied,* p. 14.

-ei- or -ie-

The rule '*i* before *e* except after *c*' holds good for nearly all words in which the vowel-sound is *ee,* as *Aries, hygienic, yield,* but *ceiling, deceit, receive.*

Exceptions: *prima facie, specie, species, superficies.*

The following words which are, or can be, pronounced with the *ee*-sound have *ei*:

caffeine   heinous   protein
casein   inveigle   seise
codeine   Madeira   seize
counterfeit neither   seizure
deceive   peripeteia weir
either   plebeian   weird

Note also *forfeit, surfeit,* and many proper names, e.g. *Keith, Leith, Neil, Reid, Sheila.*

en- or in-

The following pairs of words can give trouble:

encrust (verb)   *incrustation*
engrain (verb) to   *ingrain* (adjective)
 dye in the raw   dyed in the yarn
 state
                        ingrained deeply
                         rooted
enquire ask   *inquire* undertake a
                         formal investigation
enquiry question   *inquiry* official
                         investigation
ensure make sure   *insure* take out
                         insurance
                         (against risk: note
                         assurance of life)

Although *enquire, enquiry* and *inquire, inquiry* are used almost interchangeably by many people, they are usually used as above.

-er and -est

These suffixes of comparison may require:
1. Doubling of final consonant (see p. 10f.).
2. Dropping of silent -*e* (see p. 10f.).
3. Change of *y* to *i* (see p. 22).

-erous or -rous

The ending -*erous* is normal in adjectives related to nouns ending in -*er,* e.g. *murderous, thunderous.* But:

ambidextrous meandrous
cumbrous   monstrous
disastrous   wondrous
leprous

final vowels before suffixes

A. For treatment of final -*e* and -*y* before suffixes see **dropping of silent -*e*, p. 10f.,** and *y* **to *i*, p. 22.**

B. For treatment of final -*o* before -*s* (suffix), see **plural formation, p. 18** and **-*s* suffix, p. 20.**

C. In nearly all other cases, the final vowels -*a*, -*i*, -*o*, and -*u* are unaffected by suffixes and do not affect them:

skier	*vetoer*
cameras	(*he*) *rumbas*
corgis	(*she*) *skis*
emus	*taxis*
echoing	*skiing*
radioing	*taxiing*
baaed	*radioed*
concertinaed	*subpoenaed*
echoed	*taxied*
mascaraed	*tiaraed*
mustachioed	

The -*ed* spelling is preferable for this last group, but an -'*d* spelling is often acceptable, especially after the letter *a*, e.g. *rumba'd*. This spelling is preferable in *idea'd* (having ideas) and *ski'd* (from *ski*, contrasting with *skied* from *sky*).

D. Final -*é* in words taken from French is retained before all suffixes; the *e* of -*ed* is dropped after it, e.g.

appliquéd	*chasséing*
attachés	*communiqués*
cafés	*émigrés*
canapés	*soufflés*

for- and fore-

Note especially:

forbear refrain	*forebear* ancestor
forgather	*foreclose*
forgo abstain from	*forego* precede

f to v

Certain nouns that end in *f* or *f* followed by silent *e* change this *f* to *v* in some derivatives. In some cases, there is variation or uncertainty:

beef: plural *beeves* oxen, *beefs* kinds of beef.

calf (young animal): *calfish* calflike; *calves-foot jelly*.

calf (of leg): (*enormously*) *calved* having (enormous) calves.

corf (basket): plural *corves*.

dwarf: plural *dwarfs*. ● *Dwarves* is increasingly found.

elf: *elfish* and *elvish* are both acceptable; *elfin* but *elven* (in fantasy writings).

handkerchief: plural *handkerchiefs*.

hoof: plural usually *hooves*; the historic form *hoofs* is also common; adjective *hoofed* or *hooved*.

knife: verb *knife*.

leaf: *leaved* having leaves (*broad-leaved* etc.) but *leafed* as past of *leaf* (*through a book* etc.).

life: *lifelong* lasting a lifetime; *livelong* (*day* etc., poetic: the *i* is short); the plural of *still life* is *still lifes*.

oaf: plural *oafs*.

roof: plural *roofs*. ● *Rooves* is commonly heard and sometimes written, but the written use should be avoided.

scarf (garment): plural *scarves*; *scarfed* wearing a scarf.

scarf (joint): plural and verb keep *f*.

sheaf: plural *sheaves*; verb *sheaf* or *sheave*; *sheaved* made into a sheaf.

shelf: plural *shelves*; *shelvy* having sandbanks.

staff: plural *staffs* but archaic and musical *staves*.

turf: plural *turfs* or *turves*; verb *turf*; *turfy*.

wharf: plural *wharves* or *wharfs*.

wolf: *wolfish* of a wolf.

-ful suffix

The adjectival suffix -*ful* may require the following changes in spelling:

1. Change of *y* to *i* (see p. 22).

2. Simplification of -*ll* (see *l and ll*, p. 15).

hyphens

A. Hyphens are used to connect words that are more closely linked to each other than to the surrounding syntax. Unfortunately their use is not consistent. Some pairs or groups of words are written as a single word (e.g. *motorway*, *railwayman*), others, despite their equally close bond, as separate words (e.g. *motor cycle*, *pay slip*); very similar pairs may be found with a hyphen (e.g. *motor-cyclist*, *pay-bed*). There are no hard and fast rules that will predict whether a group of words should be written as one, with a hyphen, or separately. For individual items, consult the most recent edition of *COD*.

1. Groups consisting of attributive noun + noun are probably the most unpredictable. Such a group generally remains written as separate words until it is recognized as a lexical item with a special meaning, when it may receive a hyphen. Eventually it may be written as one word, but this usually happens when the two nouns are monosyllabic and there is no clash between the final letter of the first and the first letter of the second.

   This generalization is, however, a very weak guide to what happens in practice. Compare, for example, *coal tar*, *coal-sack*, *coalfield*; *oil well*, *oil-painting*, *oilfield*.

2. Nouns derived from phrasal verbs, consisting of verb + adverb, are slightly more predictable. They are either hyphened or written as one, e.g. *play-off*, *set-back*, *turn-out*; *feedback*, *layout*, *turnover*. Phrases consisting of *-er* + adverb are usually hyphened, e.g. *runner-up*; those consisting of *-ing* + adverb are usually left as two words, e.g. *Your coming back surprised me*, unless they have become a unit with a special meaning, e.g. *Gave him a going-over*.

3. Various collocations which are not otherwise hyphened are given hyphens before a noun, e.g.

   (*a*) adjective + noun: *a common-sense argument* (but *This is common sense*), *an open-air restaurant* (but *eating in the open air*).

   (*b*) preposition + noun: *an out-of-date aircraft* (but *This is out of date*), *an in-depth interview* (but *interviewing him in depth*).

   (*c*) participle + adverb: *a longed-for departure* (but *the departure greatly longed for*).

   (*d*) other syntactic groups used attributively, e.g. *An all-but-unbearable mixture* (Lynne Reid Banks).

4. Collocations of adverb + adjective (or participle) are usually written as two words, e.g. *a less interesting topic*, *an amazingly good performance*, but may very occasionally take a hyphen to avoid misunderstanding, e.g. *Sir Edgar, who had heard one or two more-sophisticated rumours* (Angus Wilson) (this does not mean 'one or two additional sophisticated rumours').

   See also **well**, p. 72.

5. When two words that form a close collocation but are not normally joined by a hyphen enter into combination with another word that requires a hyphen, it may be necessary to join them with a hyphen as well to avoid an awkward or even absurd result, e.g. *natural gas* needs no hyphen in *natural gas pipeline*, but *natural-gas-producer* may be preferred to the ambiguous *natural gas-producer*. Occasionally a real distinction in meaning may be indicated, e.g. *The non-German-speakers at the conference used interpreters* versus *The non-German speakers at the conference were all Austrians*.

6. A group of words forming a syntactic unit normally has hyphens, e.g. *court-martial* (verb), *happy-go-lucky* (adjective), *good-for-nothing*, *stick-in-the-mud*, *ne'er-do-well* (nouns).

7. A hyphen is used to indicate a common second element in all but the last word of a list, e.g. *two-*, *three-*, *or fourfold*.

B. With most prefixes and suffixes it is normal to write the whole compound as a single word; the use of the hyphen is exceptional, and the writing of prefix or suffix and stem as two words virtually unknown.

The hyphen is used in the following cases:

1. After a number of prefixes that can be freely used to form new compounds:

   ex- (= formerly), e.g. *ex-President*; *neo-* (denoting a revived movement), e.g. *neo-Nazism*; *non-*, e.g. *non-stick*;

pro- (= in favour of), e.g. *pro-marketeer*; *self-*, e.g. *self-destructive*.

Exceptions: *Neoplatonism* (*-ic*, etc.); *selfsame, unselfconscious*.

2. After a number of prefixes to aid recognition of the second element, e.g. *anti-g*, or to distinguish the compound from another word identically spelt, e.g. *un-ionized* (as against *unionized*); see also **co-** prefix, **re-** prefix.

3. Between a prefix ending with a vowel and a stem beginning with the same vowel, e.g. *de-escalate, pre-empt*; see also **co-** prefix, **re-** prefix.

4. Between a prefix and a stem beginning with a capital letter, e.g. *anti-Darwinian, hyper-Calvinism, Pre-Raphaelite*.

5. With some living suffixes forming specially coined compounds, e.g. *Mickey Mouse-like*; or still regarded to some extent as full words, such as *-wise* (= as regards ——), e.g. *Weather-wise we have had a good summer*.

6. In irregularly formed compounds, e.g. *unget-at-able*.

7. With the suffix *-like* after a stem ending in *-l*, e.g. *eel-like*, and when attached to a word of two or more syllables, e.g. *cabbage-like*; with the suffix *-less* after a stem ending in double *-l*, e.g. *bell-less, will-lessness*.

Note. In Amer. spelling there is a greater tendency than in British spelling to write compounds as one word, rather than hyphened, e.g. *nonplaying, nonprofit, roundhouse, runback*.

-ified or -yfied

-ified is usual, whatever the stem of the preceding element, e.g.

citified	*gentrified*
countrified	*sissified*
Frenchified	*yuppified*

But *ladyfied*.

in- or un-

There is no comprehensive set of rules, but the following guidelines are offered. Note that *in-* takes the form of *il-*, *im-*, or *ir-* before initial *l, m,* or *r*.

1. *in-* properly belongs to words derived from Latin, whereas *un-* combines with any English word. Hence

(a) *un-* may be expected to spread to words originally having *in-*. This has happened when the *in-* word has developed a sense more specific than merely the negative of the stem word:

unapt	*inept*
unartistic	*inartistic*
unhuman	*inhuman*
unmaterial	*immaterial*
unmoral	*immoral*
unreligious	*irreligious*
unsolvable	*insoluble*

(b) It is always possible to coin a nonce-word with *un-*:

> A small bullied-looking woman with unabundant brown hair (Kingsley Amis)

2. Adjectives and participles ending in *-ed* and *-ing* rarely accept *in-*.

Exception: *inexperienced*.

3. *in-* seems to be preferred before *ad-, co-* (*col-, com-, con-, cor-*), *de-, di(s)-, ex-, per-*. Important exceptions are:

unadventurous	*undeniable*
uncommunicative	*undesirable*
unconditional	*undetectable*
unconscionable	*unexceptionable*
unconscious	*unexceptional*
uncooperative	*unpersuasive*
undemonstrative	

4. *un-* is preferred before *em-, en-, im-, in-, inte(r)-*.

5. Adjectives ending in *-able* usually take *in-* if the stem preceding the suffix *-able* is not, by itself, an English word:

> *palpable*, stem *palp-*, negative *im-*

Exceptions: *unamenable, unamiable, unconscionable*.

They usually take *un-* if the stem is a short English word:

> *unbridgeable*   *unreadable*

Exceptions: *incurable, immovable, impass-able* (that cannot be traversed: but *im-passible* = unfeeling).

But no generalization covers those with a longer English stem:

> *illimitable*   *undeniable*
> *invariable*   *unmistakable*

Note: Rule 2 overrides rule 3 (e.g. *uncom-plaining, undisputed, unperturbed*) and rule 3 overrides rule 5 (*unconscionable*).

i to *y*

When the suffix *-ing* is added to words (chiefly verbs) that end in *-ie*, *e* is dropped (see **dropping of silent *-e*, p. 10), and *i* becomes *y*, e.g.

> *dying*   *tying*

Exceptions: *hie, sortie,* make *hieing, sor-tieing.* Both *stymieing* and *stymying* are acceptable.

-ize and *-ise*

-ize should be preferred to *-ise* as a verbal ending where both are in use, according to Oxford University Press house style, and is also usual in North America. Both spell-ings are common in the UK.

1. The choice arises only where the end-ing is pronounced *eyes*, not where it is *ice, iss,* or *eez.*

So: *precise, promise, chemise, expertise.*

2. The choice applies only to the verbal suffix with the sense 'make into, treat with, or act in the way of (the stem word)'.

Hence are eliminated

(a) nouns in *-ise*:

> *compromise*   *franchise*
> *demise*   *merchandise*
> *disguise*   *revise*
> *enterprise*   *surmise*
> *exercise*   *surprise*

(b) verbs corresponding to a noun which has *-is-* as a part of the stem, or ident-ical with a noun in *-ise*:

> *advertise*   *arise*
> *advise*   *chastise*
> *apprise*   *circumcise*

> *enfranchise*   *incise*
> *excise*   *premise*
> *improvise*   *prise* (*open*)
> *comprise*   *supervise*
> *despise*   *televise*
> *devise*

3. Most *-ize* verbs are formed on familiar English stems, e.g. *authorize, symbolize*; or with a slight alteration to the stem, e.g. *agonize, sterilize.* A few have no such im-mediate stem: *aggrandize* (cf. *aggrandize-ment*), *baptize* (cf. *baptism*), *catechize* (cf. *catechism*), *recognize* (cf. *recognition*); and *capsize.*

l and *ll*

Whether to write a single or double *l* can be a problem:

1. Where a suffix is added to single final *l*: see **doubling of final consonants, p. 10 f.

2. *l* is single when it is the last letter of the following verbs:

> *annul*   *enrol*   *fulfil*
> *appal*   *enthral*   *impel*
> *distil*   *extol*   *instil*

These double the *l* before a vowel (see p. 10 f.), but not before *-ment*:

> *enrolment   distillation   enthralling*

● In Amer. spelling *l* is usually double here except in *annul*(*ment*), *extol.*

3. Final *-ll* usually becomes *l* before a consonant, e.g.

> *almighty, almost,* etc.   *skilful*
> *chilblain*   *thraldom*
> *dully*   *wilful*

Exception: Before *-ness, -ll* remains in *dullness, fullness.*

● In Amer. spelling *ll* is usual in *skillful, thralldom, willful.*

-ly

The suffix *-ly* forms adjectives and ad-verbs, e.g. *earth, earthly; sad, sadly.* One of the following spelling changes may be re-quired:

1. If the word ends in double *ll*, add only *-y*, e.g. *fully, shrilly.*

2. If the word ends in consonant + *le*, change *e* to *y*, e.g. *ably, singly, subtly, supply, terribly*.

3. If the word ends in consonant + *y*, change *y* to *i* and add *-ly*, e.g. *drily, happily*.

Exceptions: *shyly, slyly, spryly, wryly*.

4. Unstressed *ey* changes to *i*, e.g. *matily*.

5. If the word ends in *-ic*, add *-ally*, e.g. *basically, scientifically*.

Exceptions: *politicly* (from *politic*, distinguished from *politically*, from *political*), *publicly*.

6. Final *-e* is dropped before *-ly* in *duly, eerily, truly, wholly*.

7. Final *-y* changes to *i* before *-ly* in *daily, gaily*.

-ness

It may require the change of *y* to *i*: see p. 22.

-or and -er

They both mean 'person or thing that performs (a verb)'. But:

1. *-er* is the living suffix, forming most agent nouns; but *-or* is common with words of Latin origin, e.g.

> *chopper, producer, avenger, qualifier, organizer, counsellor, carburettor, conqueror*.

2. *-or* follows *-at-* to form *-ator*, e.g. *duplicator, incubator*.

Exception: *debater*.

Note: nouns such as *idolater* do not contain the agent suffix.

3. Both suffixes are very common after *-s-*, *-ss-*, and *-t-* (apart from *-at-*). So *supervisor, prospector*, but *adviser, perfecter*. Only rough guidelines can be given: *-tor* usually follows *-c*, unstressed *i*, and *u*, e.g. *actor, compositor*; *-ter* usually follows *f, gh, l, r*, and *s*, e.g. *drifter, fighter*.

4. A functional distinction is made between *-or* and *-er* in the following:

accepter one who accepts	*acceptor* (in scientific use)
caster one who casts, casting machine	*castor* beaver; plant giving oil; sugar (sprinkler); wheel
censer for incense	*censor* official
resister one who resists	*resistor* electrical device
sailer ship of specified power	*sailor* seaman

5. A number of words have *-er* in normal use but *-or* in Law:

abetter	*mortgager*
accepter	*settler*
granter	*vender*

-oul-

In *mould, moulder, moult, smoulder*, Amer. spelling favours *o* alone instead of *ou*.

-our or -or

1. In agent nouns, only *-or* occurs as the ending (cf. *-or and -er*), e.g. *actor, counsellor*.

Exception: *saviour*.

2. In abstract nouns, *-our* is usual, e.g. *colour, favour, humour*. Only the following end in *-or*:

error	*pallor*	*terror*
horror	*squalor*	*torpor*
languor	*stupor*	*tremor*
liquor		

● In Amer. English *-or* is usual here except in *glamour*.

3. Nouns in *-our* change this to *-or* before the suffixes *-ation*, *-iferous*, *-ific*, *-ize*, and *-ous*, e.g.

> *coloration, humorous, soporific, vaporize*.

Exception: *colourize*.

But *-our* keeps the *u* before other suffixes, e.g.

> *armourer, behaviourism, colourful, favourite, honourable*.

Exceptions: *humorist, rigorist*.

past of verbs, formation of

A. Regular verbs add *-ed* for the past tense and past participle, and may make the following spelling changes:

1. Doubling of final consonant (see p. 10).
2. Dropping of silent -*e* (see p. 10 f.).
3. Change of *y* to *i* (see p. 22).

Note *laid*, *paid*, and *said* from *lay*, *pay*, and *say*.

B. A number of verbs vary between -*ed* and -*t* (and in some cases a different vowel-sound in the stem):

burned, burnt	learned, learnt
dreamed, dreamt	smelled, smelt
kneeled, knelt	spelled, spelt
leaned, leant	spilled, spilt
leaped, leapt	spoiled, spoilt

The -*t* form is usual in Received Pronunciation* and should be written by those who pronounce it. The regular form is usual in Amer. English.

Bereave is regular when the reference is to the loss of relatives by death; *bereft* is used for loss of possessions.

Cleave is a rare word with two opposite meanings: (i) = stick; *A man .. shall cleave unto his wife* (Genesis 2: 24) (regular). (ii) = split. The past tense *clave* is archaic; *clove*, *cleft*, and regular *cleaved* are all permissible, but *cleaved* is usual in scientific and technical contexts. The past participle varies in certain fixed expressions, *cloven-footed*, *cloven hoof*, *cleft palate*, *cleft stick*; *cleaved* is probably best used elsewhere.

C. A number of verbs vary in the past participle only between the regular form and one ending in -(*e*)*n*:

> *hew*, *mow*, *saw*, *sew*, *shear*, *show*, *sow*, *strew*, *swell*.

In most of these the latter form is to be preferred; in British English it is obligatory when the participle is used as an attributive adjective. So *new-mown hay*, *a sawn-off* (Amer. *sawed-off*) *shotgun*, *shorn* (not *sheared*) *of one's strength*, *a swollen gland*; *swollen* or *swelled head* (= conceit) is a colloquial exception.

D. The past tense has -*a*-, the past participle -*u*-, in

begin	shrink	stink
drink	sing	swim
ring	sink	

* See p. 55.

● It is an error to use *begun*, *drunk*, etc. for the past tense.

E. The following verbs can cause difficulty:

abide (*by*) makes *abided*

alight makes *alighted*

bet: *betted* is increasingly common beside *bet*

bid (make a bid): *bid*

bid (command; say (goodnight etc.)): *bid* is usual (*bade*, *bidden* are archaic)

broadcast unchanged in past tense and past participle

chide: *chided* is now usual (older *chid*)

forecast unchanged in past tense and past participle

hang: *hanged* for capital punishment; otherwise *hung*

highlight makes *highlighted*

knit: *knitted* is usual, but *knit* metaphorical

light makes *lit* but *lighted* attributively (*a lighted match*)

quit makes *quit*, but *quitted* is also occasionally found

reeve (nautical) makes *rove*

rid unchanged in past tense and past participle

speed makes *sped*, but *speeded* in the senses 'cause to go at (a certain) speed' and 'travel at illegal speed'

spit makes *spat* ● Amer. *spit*

spotlight makes *spotlighted*

stave: (to dent) *staved* or *stove*; (to ward off) *staved*

sweat makes *sweated* ● Amer. *sweat*

thrive: *thrived* is increasingly common beside *throve*, *thriven*

plural formation

Most nouns simply add -*s*, e.g. *cats*, *dogs*, *horses*, *cameras*.

A. The regular plural suffix -*s* is preceded by -*e*-:

1. After sibilant consonants, i.e. after

ch: e.g. *benches*, *coaches*, *matches* (but not *lochs*, *stomachs* where the *ch* has a different sound)

s: e.g. *buses*, *gases*, *pluses*, *yeses* (single *s* is not doubled)

sh: e.g. *ashes*, *bushes*

ss: e.g. *grasses, successes*

x: e.g. *boxes, sphinxes*

z: e.g. *buzzes, waltzes (fezzes, quizzes* have double *z*)

Proper names follow the same rule, e.g. *the Joneses, the Rogerses, the two Charleses.*

2. After *-y* (not preceded by a vowel), which changes to *i*, e.g. *ladies, soliloquies, spies.*

Exceptions: proper names, e.g. *the Willoughbys, the three Marys*; also *lay-bys, standbys, zlotys* (Polish currency).

3. After *-o* in certain words:

bravoes (= ruffians;	*mementoes*
bravos = shouts	*mosquitoes*
of 'bravo!')	*mottoes*
buffaloes	*Negroes*
calicoes	*noes*
cargoes	*peccadilloes*
dingoes	*porticoes*
dominoes	*potatoes*
echoes	*salvoes*
embargoes	*stuccoes*
goes	*tomatoes*
grottoes	*tornadoes*
haloes	*torpedoes*
heroes	*vetoes*
innuendoes	*volcanoes*
mangoes	

The forms *grottos, innuendos, mangos, mementos, porticos, salvos* also occur. Words not in the above list add only *-s*.

It is helpful to remember that *-e-* is never inserted:

(*a*) when the *o* follows another vowel, e.g. *cuckoos, ratios.*

(*b*) when the word is an abbreviation, e.g. *hippos, kilos.*

(*c*) with proper names, e.g. *Lotharios, Figaros, the Munros.*

4. With words which change final *f* to *v* (see p. 12 f.).

B. Plural of compound nouns.

1. Compounds made up of a noun followed by an adjective, prepositional phrase, or adverb attach *-s* to the noun, e.g.

(*a*) *courts martial   heirs presumptive*

But *brigadier-generals, lieutenant-colonels, sergeant-majors.*

(*b*) *sons-in-law   tugs of war*

(*c*) *hangers-on   passers-by*

Note: Informally, type (*a*) often pluralize the second word.

2. Compounds which contain no (apparent) noun add *-s* at the end. So also do nouns formed from phrasal verbs and compounds ending in *-ful*, e.g.

(*a*) *forget-me-nots   will-o'-the-wisps*

(*b*) *pullovers   set-ups*

(*c*) *handfuls   spoonfuls*

3. Compounds containing *man* or *woman* make both elements plural, e.g.

menservants   women doctors

C. The plural of these nouns in *-s* is unchanged:

biceps	*means*	*species*
congeries	*mews*	*superficies*
forceps	*series*	*thrips*
innings		

The following are mass nouns, not plurals:

bona fides (= 'good faith'), *kudos*

● The singulars *bona-fide* (as a noun; there is an adjective *bona-fide*), *congery, kudo*, sometimes seen, are erroneous.

D. Plural of nouns of foreign origin. The foreign patterns are given below, with the words that normally follow them. Elsewhere, it is recommended to use the regular *-s* plural, even though some words accept either plural.

1. *-a* (Latin and Greek) becomes *-ae*:

alga	*lamina*	*nebula*
alumna	*larva*	*papilla*

Note: *formula* has *-ae* in mathematical and scientific use.

2. *-eau, -eu* (French) add *-x*:

beau	*château*	*plateau*
bureau	*milieu*	*tableau*

But *beaus, bureaus, milieus, plateaus* are also acceptable.

3. *-ex, -ix* (Latin) become *-ices*:

appendix	*cortex*	*matrix*
codex	*helix*	*radix*

Note: *index, vortex* have *-ices* in mathematical and scientific use, and *appendixes* is common for the internal organ.

4. *-is* (Greek and Latin) becomes *-es* (pronounced *eez*):

> *amanuensis*   *hypothesis*
> *analysis*   *metamorphosis*
> *antithesis*   *oasis*
> *axis*   *parenthesis*
> *basis*   *synopsis*
> *crisis*   *thesis*
> *ellipsis*

5. *-o* (Italian) becomes *-i*:

> *concerto grosso (concerti grossi)*
>
> *graffito*   *ripieno*
> *maestro*   *virtuoso*

But *maestros*, *ripienos*, *virtuosos* are also acceptable, and *solo*, *soprano* may have *-i* in technical contexts.

6. *-on* (Greek) becomes *-a*:

> *criterion   parhelion   phenomenon*

Note: The plural of *automaton* is in *-a* when used collectively.

7. *-s* (French) is unchanged in the plural:

> *chamois*   *corps*   *fracas*
> *chassis*   *faux pas*   *patois*

Also (not a noun in French): *rendezvous*.

8. *-um* (Latin) becomes *-a*:

> *addendum*   *effluvium*
> *bacterium*   *emporium*
> *candelabrum*   *epithalamium*
> *compendium*   *erratum*
> *corrigendum*   *maximum*
> *cranium*   *minimum*
> *crematorium*   *quantum*
> *curriculum*   *scholium*
> *datum*   *spectrum*
> *desideratum*   *speculum*
> *dictum*   *stratum*

The forms *compendiums*, *emporiums*, *epithalamiums* are acceptable variants.

Note: *medium* in scientific use, and in the sense 'means of communication' has plural in *-a*; the collective plural of *memorandum* 'things to be noted' is in *-a*; *rostrum* and *vacuum* have *-a* in technical use.

9. *-us* (Latin) becomes *-i*:

> *alumnus*   *bronchus*   *calculus*
> *bacillus*   *cactus*   *fungus*

> *gladiolus*   *nucleus*   *stimulus*
> *locus*   *radius*   *terminus*
> *narcissus*

Note: *focus* has plural in *-i* in scientific use; genius has plural *genii* when used to mean 'guardian spirit'; *corpus*, *genus*, *opus* become *corpora*, *genera*, *opera* (or, to avoid confusion, *opuses*).

● The following are plural; they should normally not be construed as singulars (see also in section III):

> *bacteria*   *graffiti*   *phenomena*
> *candelabra*   *insignia*   *regalia*
> *criteria*   *media*   *strata*
> *data*

E. There is no need to use an apostrophe before *-s*:

1. After figures: *the 1890s*.
2. After abbreviations: *KOs*, *MPs*, *SOSs*.

But it is needed in: *dot the i's and cross the t's*, *do's and don'ts*.

possessive case

To form the possessive:

1. Add *-'s* to singulars, and to plurals not ending in *-s*, e.g.

Bill's book   *his master's voice*
children's   *Father Christmas's*
a fortnight's holiday

2. Add an apostrophe to *-s* plurals, e.g.

> *the Johnsons' dog*   *the octopuses'*
> *two weeks' holiday*   *tentacles*

French names ending in silent *s* or *x* add *-'s*, e.g. *Dumas's* (= Dumah's), *Crémieux's*.

Names ending in *-es* pronounced *iz* take only an apostrophe, e.g. *Bridges'*, *Moses'*.

Polysyllables not accented on the last or second last syllable can take the apostrophe alone, e.g. *Nicholas'* or *Nicholas's*.

It is the custom in classical works to use the apostrophe alone for ancient classical names ending in *-s*, e.g. *Ceres'*, *Mars'*.

Jesus' 'is an accepted liturgical archaism' (*Hart's Rules*, p. 31). But in non-liturgical use, *Jesus's* is acceptable.

Before the word *sake*, be guided by the pronunciation, e.g.

for goodness' but *for God's sake*
sake *for Charles's sake*

After -*x* and -*z*, use -'*s*, e.g. *Ajax's, Berlioz's*.

3. In *I'm going to the butcher's, to Brown's, to Susan's*, etc. the apostrophe signals an ellipsis of 'shop', 'business', or 'establishment'. But many businesses use the title *Browns, Greens*, etc., without an apostrophe (e.g. *Debenhams, Barclays Bank*). No apostrophe is necessary in a Debenhams store or in *go to the cleaners*.

4. The apostrophe must not be used:

(*a*) with the plural non-possessive -*s*: notices such as *TEA'S* are often seen, but are wrong.

(*b*) in the possessive pronouns *hers, its, ours, theirs, yours*; the possessive of *who* is *whose*.

● *it's* = *it is* or *it has*; *who's* = *who is* or *who has*.

● There are no words *her's, our's, their's, your's*.

-re or -er

The principal words in which the ending -*re* (with the unstressed *er* sound—there are others with the sound *ruh*, e.g. *macabre*, or *ray*, e.g. *padre*) is found are:

accoutre	*metre* (note *meter*
*acre	the measuring
amphitheatre	device)
*cadre	*mitre*
calibre	*nitre*
centre	*ochre*
*euchre	**ogre*
fibre	*philtre*
goitre	*reconnoitre*
litre	*sabre*
louvre	*sceptre*
*lucre	*sepulchre*
lustre	*sombre*
manoeuvre	*spectre*
*massacre	*theatre*
meagre	*titre*
*mediocre	**wiseacre*

● All but those marked * are spelt with -*er* in Amer. English.

re- prefix

This prefix is followed by a hyphen:

1. Before another *e*, e.g. *re-echo, re-entry*.

2. So as to distinguish the compound so formed from the more familiar identically spelt word written solid, e.g.

> *re-cover* (put new cover on): *recover*
> *re-form* (form again): *reform*
> *re-sign* (sign again): *resign*

silent final consonants

French words with silent final consonants give difficulty over plurals, possessives, and verbal inflections. See pp. 18 f, 10.

-s suffix

A. As the inflection of the plural of nouns: see **plural formation**.

B. As the inflection of the third person singular present indicative of verbs, it requires the insertion of -*e*-:

1. After sibilants (*ch, s, sh, x, z*), e.g. *catches, tosses, pushes, fixes, buzzes*; note that single *s* and *z* are subject to doubling of final consonant (see p. 10 f.), e.g. *nonplusses, quizzes, whizzes*.

2. After *y*, which may become *i* (see p. 22), e.g. *cries, copies*.

3. After *o*: *echo, go, torpedo, veto*, like the corresponding nouns, insert -*e*- before -*s*; *crescendo, radio, solo, zero* should have -*s* alone, but there is variation.

-xion or -ction

Complexion, crucifixion, effluxion, fluxion all have -*x*-; *connection, deflection, inflection, reflection* all have -*ct*-; both *genuflection* and *genuflexion* occur.

-y, -ey, or -ie nouns

The diminutive or pet form of nouns can be spelt -*y*, -*ey*, or -*ie*. Most nouns which end in the sound of -*y* are so spelt, e.g.

> *aunty* *baby* *nappy*

The following are the main diminutives spelt with -*ey* (-*ey* nouns of other kinds are excluded from the list):

goosey   matey
housey-housey   nursey
Limey   Sawney
lovey-dovey   slavey

The following list contains the diminutives in *-ie*, and many similar nouns. Most Scottish diminutives are spelt with *-ie*, e.g. *corbie*, *kiltie*.

beanie   goalie
birdie   junkie
bookie   Kewpie (doll)
brownie   laddie
budgie   lassie
caddie (golf; *tea   mealie (maize;
    caddy*)   *mealy* adjective)
chappie   Mountie
charlie   movie
clippie   nightie
cookie   oldie
coolie   pinkie (little finger)
dearie   pixie
doggie (noun;   quickie
    doggy adjective)   rookie
genie (spirit;   sheltie
    plural *genii*)   softie
Geordie   Tin Lizzie
gillie   walkie-talkie
girlie   zombie

Note: *bogie* (undercarriage), *bogey* (golf score, ghost).

-y or -ey adjectives

When *-y* is added to a word to form an adjective, the following changes in spelling occur:

1. Doubling of final consonant (see p. 10 f.).

2. Dropping of silent *-e* (see p. 10).

Exceptions:

(*a*) After *u*:

bluey   gluey
cliquey   tissuey

(*b*) Where the retention of *-e* helps to clarify the sense:

cagey   dicey   pacey
cakey   dikey   pricey
chocolatey   matey   smiley
cottagey   orangey   villagey

Note also *holey* (distinguished from *holy*); *phoney*.

3. Insertion of *-e-* when *-y* is also the final letter of the stem:

clayey   sprayey
skyey   wheyey

Also in *gooey*.

4. Adjectives ending in unstressed *-ey* (2 (*a*) and (*b*) and 3 above) change this *-ey* to *-i-* before the comparative and superlative suffixes *-er* and *-est* and the adverbial suffix *-ly*, e.g.

cagey: cagily   gooey: gooier
cliquey: cliquier   matey: matily
dicey: dicier   pricey: pricier

Before *-ness* there is variation, e.g.

cagey: cageyness,   wheyey:
    caginess   wheyiness
matey: mateyness,
    matiness

y or i

There is often uncertainty about whether *y* or *i* should be written in the following words:

Write *i* in:	Write *y* in:
cider	dyke
cipher	gypsy
Libya	lyke-wake
lich-gate	lynch law
linchpin	pygmy
sibyl (classical)	style (manner)
siphon	stylus
siren	stymie
stile (in fence)	Sybil (frequently as
timpani (drums)	Christian name)
tiro	syllabub
witch hazel	sylvan
	syrup
	tyke
	tympanum (ear-drum)
	tyre (of wheel)
	wych-elm

-yse or -yze

This verbal ending (e.g. in *analyse*, *paralyse*) should not be written with *z* (though *z* is normally used in such words in America).

y to i

A. Words that end in -y after a vowel retain the -y before certain suffixes.

So *enjoyable, conveyed, gayer, donkeys, buys, joyful, coyly*.

Exceptions: *daily, gaily*, and adjectives ending in unstressed -ey (see p. 21).

B. If the -y follows a consonant (or silent *u* after *g* or *q*), it changes to -i- before:

1. *-able*, e.g. *deniable*. (But *flyable*).
2. *-ed*, e.g. *carried*.
3. *-er, -est*, e.g. *carrier, driest*.

Exceptions: *fryer, shyer* (one that shies), *skyer* (in cricket). Both *flyer* and *flier* occur, as do *drier* (one that dries) and *dryer*.

4. *-es*, e.g. *ladies, carries*. (But see p. 18.)
5. *-ful* (adjectives), e.g. *beautiful*. (*Bellyful* is not an adjective.)
6. *-less* (adjectives), e.g. *merciless, remediless*.

Exceptions: some rare compounds, e.g. *countryless*.

7. *-ly* (adverbs), e.g. *drily, happily, plaguily*.

Exceptions: *shyly, slyly, spryly, wryly*.

8. *-ment* (nouns), e.g. *embodiment, merriment*.

9. *-ness* (nouns), e.g. *happiness, cliquiness*.

Exceptions: *dryness, flyness, shyness, slyness, spryness, wryness; busyness* (distinguished from *business*).

DIFFICULT AND CONFUSABLE SPELLINGS
(not covered earlier)

The list below contains words (i) which occasion difficulty in spelling; (ii) of which various spellings exist; or (iii) which need to be distinguished from other words spelt similarly. In each case the recommended form is given, and in some cases is followed by the mark □ and the rejected variant. Misspellings, and spellings which are essentially American, are preceded by the mark ●. Where the rejected variant is widely separated alphabetically from the recommended form, the former is preceded by the mark □ and followed by 'use' and the recommended form.

accommodation
adaptor
adviser
□ *aerie*: use *eyrie*
ait □ not *eyot*
align, alignment ● not *aline, alinement*
allege
alleluia □ not *alleluya*
almanac (*almanack* only in some titles)
aluminium ● Amer. *aluminum*
ambiance (term in art)
ambience surroundings
amok □ not *amuck*
ancillary ● not *ancilliary*
annex (verb)
annexe (noun)
any one (of a number)
anyone anybody
any time
any way any manner
anyway at all events
apophthegm ● Amer. *apothegm*
apostasy
archaeology
artefact □ not *artifact*
aubrietia □ not *aubretia*
aught anything □ not *ought*
autarchy despotism
autarky self-sufficiency
auxiliary
aye yes □ not *ay*
aye always
bail out obtain release □ not *bale out*
bale out from aircraft □ not *bail out*
balk (verb)
balmy like balm
barbecue ● not *barbeque*
barmy (informal) mad
baulk timber
behove ● Amer. *behoove*
bivouac (noun and verb)
bivouacked, bivouacking
blond (of man)
blonde (of woman)
born: *be born* (of child)

borne: carried or given birth to
brand-new
brier □ not *briar*
bur clinging seed □ not *burr*
burr rough edge, drill, rock, accent, etc.
□ not *bur*
caftan □ not *kaftan*
calendar almanac
calender press
caliph
calligraphy
calliper □ not *caliper*
callous (adjective)
callus (noun)
camellia shrub
canvas (noun) cloth
canvas (verb) cover with canvas (past
canvassed)
canvass (verb)
carcass □ not *carcase*
caviar □ not *caviare*
chameleon
chancellor
chaperon □ not *chaperone*
Charollais
cheque (bank)
chequer (noun) pattern (verb) variegate;
● Amer. *checker*
chilli pepper
chivvy, chivvied
choosy
chord (music; geometry)
chukker (polo)
clarinettist ● Amer. *clarinetist*
coco palm
cocoa chocolate
coconut
colander strainer
commit(ment)
committee
comparative
complement make complete
compliment praise
conjuror
connection
conscientious
consensus
cord string, flex, spinal or vocal *cord*, rib of
cloth
cornelian □ not *carnelian*
corslet armour, underwear □ not *corselet*
cosy ● Amer. *cozy*
council assembly
councillor member of council

counsel advice, barrister
counsellor adviser
court martial (noun)
court-martial (verb)
crape black fabric
crêpe thin fabric; rubber; pancake
crevasse large fissure in ice
crevice small fissure
crosier □ not *crozier*
crumby covered in crumbs
crummy (informal) dirty, inferior
curb restrain, restraint
curtsy □ not *curtsey*
□ *czar*: use *tsar*
dare say ● not *daresay*
debonair
descendant
desiccated
□ *despatch*: use *dispatch*
devest (only Law: general use *divest*)
dinghy boat
dingy grimy
disc ● Amer. *disk*
discreet judicious
discrete separate
disk (in computing)
dispatch □ not *despatch*
dissect
dissociate □ not *disassociate*
disyllable
doily □ not *doyley*
douse quench □ not *dowse*
dowse use divining rod
draft military party, money order, sketch
draftsman (documents)
draught act of drawing, act of drinking,
vessel's depth, current of air
● Amer. *draft*
draughtsman one who draws plans; piece
in game of draughts
ecology
ecstasy
ecumenical
educationist □ not *educationalist*
□ *eikon*: use *icon*
elegiac ● not *elegaic*
embarrassment
embed □ not *imbed*
employee (masculine and feminine; no
accent)
enclose
enclosure (but *Inclosure Acts*)
encyclopedia □ not *encyclopaedia*
envelop (verb)

envelope (noun)
erupt break out
espresso □ not *expresso*
ethereal □ not *etherial*
everlasting
every one (of a number)
everyone everybody
exalt raise, praise
expatriate ● not *expatriot*
exult rejoice
□ *eyot*: use *ait*
eyrie □ not *aerie*
faecal
faeces
fascia □ not *facia*
fee'd (*a fee'd lawyer*) □ not *feed*
feldspar □ not *felspar*
ferrule cap on stick
ferule cane
fetid □ not *foetid*
florescence flowering
flotation □ not *floatation*
flu □ not *'flu*
fluorescence light radiation
foetal, foetus □ Amer. and medicine, *fetal, fetus*
fogy □ not *fogey*
forbade □ not *forbad*
forestall
for ever for always
forever continually
forty
fount (typeface) ● Amer. *font*
furore ● Amer. *furor*
fusilier
fusillade
gaol (official use) □ Amer. *jail* (both forms used in Brit. English)
gaoler (as for *gaol*)
gauge measure
gazump ● not *gazoomph*, etc.
gibe jeer □ not *jibe*
gild make gold
□ *gild* association: use *guild*
glycerine
gormandize eat greedily
gormless
gourmand glutton
gram □ not *gramme*
grandad
granddaughter
grayling (fish, butterfly)
grey ● Amer. *gray*
griffin fabulous creature □ not *gryphon*

griffon vulture, dog
grisly terrible
grizzly grey-haired; bear
groin (anatomy; architecture)
groyne breakwater
guerrilla
guild association
gybe (nautical) ● Amer. *jibe*
haemo- (prefix = 'blood')
haemorrhage
haemorrhoids
hallelujah
harass
hark
harum-scarum
hearken
hiccup □ not *hiccough*
Hindu
homoeopathy
homogeneous all the same
homogenous having common descent
honorific
□ *hooping cough*: use *whooping cough*
horsy □ not *horsey*
hummus chick-pea spread
humous of humus
humus rich soil
hurrah, hurray ● not *hoorah, hooray*
hypocrisy
hypocrite
icon
idiosyncrasy
idyll
ignoramus plural *ignoramuses*
□ *imbed*: use *embed*
impostor
inadvisable
□ *inclose, inclosure*: use *en-*
inoculate
input, inputting
in so far
insomuch
inure
investor
irrupt enter violently
its of it
it's it is, it has
jail (see *gaol*)
jailor (see *gaol*)
jam pack tightly; conserve
jamb door-post
□ *jibe*: use *gibe, gybe*
 ● Amer. also = accord with
□ *kaftan*: use *caftan*

kerb pavement ● Amer. *curb*

ketchup

□ *khalif*: use *caliph*

kilogram

kilometre

Koran □ not *Qur'an*

labyrinth

lachrymal of tears

lachrymose tearful

lacquer

lacrimal (in science)

lacrimate, -ation, -atory (in science)

ledger account book

leger line (in music)

liaison

licence (noun)

license (verb)

licensee

□ *licorice*: use *liquorice*

lightening making light

lightning (with thunder)

linage number of lines

lineage ancestry

lineament feature

liniment embrocation

liqueur flavoured alcoholic liquor

liquor

liquorice □ not *licorice*

□ *litchi*: use *lychee*

literature

littérateur

littoral

loath(some) (adjectives)

loathe (verb)

lodestar

lodestone □ not *loadstone*

longevity

longitude ● not *longtitude*

lour frown □ not *lower*

lychee □ not *litchi*

Mac (prefix) spelling depends on the custom of the one bearing the name; in alphabetical arrangement, treat as Mac however spelt

mac (informal) mackintosh

mackintosh □ not *macintosh*

maharaja

maharanee

□ *Mahomet*: use *Muhammad*

mandolin

manikin dwarf, anatomical model

manila hemp, paper

manilla African bracelet

mannequin (live) model

manoeuvrable ● Amer. *maneuverable*

mantel(piece)

mantle cloak

marijuana □ not *marihuana*

marquis

marshal (noun and verb)

marten weasel

martial of war (*martial law*)

martin bird

matins □ not *mattins*

matt lustreless □ not *mat*

medieval ● not *mediaeval*

mendacity lying

mendicity being a beggar

millenary thousandth anniversary

millennium thousand years

milli- (prefix = one-thousandth)

millipede □ not *millepede*

milometer ● not *mileometer*

miniature

minuscule ● not *miniscule*

missis (slang) □ not *missus*

misspell

mistle thrush □ not *missel*

mizen (nautical)

mnemonic

moneyed

moneys □ not *monies*

mongoose (plural *mongooses*)

moustache ● Amer. *mustache*

mouth (verb) ● not *mouthe*

mucous (adjective)

mucus (noun)

Muhammad

Muslim ● not *Moslem*

naive, naivety □ not *naïve, naïvety, naïveté*

naught nothing

negligée □ not *negligee, négligé*

negligible

nerve-racking ● not *-wracking*

net not subject to deduction □ not *nett*

nonplussed

nonsuch unrivalled person or thing □ not *nonesuch*

no one nobody

nought the figure zero

numskull □ not *numbskull*

O used to form a vocative (*O Caesar*)

occurrence

● *of*: not to be written instead of *have* in, e.g., *'Did you go?' 'I would have, if it hadn't rained.'*

omelette □ not *omelet*

on to ● not *onto*
orangeade
orang-utan □ not *orang-outang*
outcast person cast out
outcaste casteless Hindu
oyez! □ not *oyes!*
paediatric
palaeo- (prefix = ancient)
palate roof of mouth
palette artist's board
pallet mattress, machine part, platform for
  loads
panda animal
pander pimp; to gratify
panellist ● Amer. *panelist*
paraffin
parallel, paralleled, paralleling
partisan □ not *partizan*
pastel (crayon)
pastille
pawpaw (fruit) □ not *papaw*
pedal (use) foot lever
peddle sell as pedlar
pederast
pedigreed
pedlar vendor of small wares
  ● Amer. *peddler*
Pekingese dog, inhabitant of Peking □ not
  Pekinese
peninsula (noun)
peninsular (adjective)
pennant (nautical) piece of rigging, flag
pennon (military) long narrow flag
peony
phone (informal) telephone □ not *'phone*
pi pious
pidgin simplified language
pie jumbled type
pigeon bird; *not one's pigeon* not one's
  affair
piggyback □ not *pickaback*
pilau □ not *pilaff, pilaw*
pimento aromatic spice
pimiento sweet pepper
plane (informal) aeroplane □ not *'plane*
plebeian
plenitude ● not *plentitude*
plimsoll □ not *plimsole*
plough ● Amer. *plow*
pommel knob, saddle-bow
pore (*over* e.g. a map)
practice (noun)
practise (verb)
precede come before

précised
predominant(ly) ● not *predominate(ly)*
premise say as introduction
premises foregoing matters,
  building
premiss (in logic) proposition
principal chief
principle truth, moral basis
prise force open
privilege
Privy Council
Privy Counsellor
proceed go on, continue
program (in computing) ● Amer. in all
  senses
programme (general use)
promoter
pukka
pummel pound with fists
pupillage □ not *pupilage*
putt (in golf)
pyjamas ● Amer. *pajamas*
quadraphony, quadraphonic □ not
  quadro- ● not *quadri-*
quatercentenary ● not *quarter-*
questionnaire
□ *Qur'an*: use Koran
rabbet groove in woodwork (also *rebate*)
racket (for ball games) □ not *racquet*
rackets game
racoon □ not *raccoon*
radical (chemistry)
radicle (botany)
raja □ not *rajah*
rarity
raze □ not *rase*
recompense
Renaissance ● not *Renascence*
renege □ not *renegue*
repairable (of material)
reparable (of loss)
restaurateur
reverend (deserving reverence; title of
  clergy)
reverent (showing reverence)
review survey, report
revue musical entertainment
rhyme ● not *rime*
riband (sport, heraldry)
ribbon
rigor (medical) shivering-fit
rigour severity ● Amer. *rigor*
rill stream
rille (on moon)

rime frost
role □ not *rôle*
Romania
rule the roost □ not *roast*
rumba □ not *rhumba*
saccharin (noun)
saccharine (adjective)
salutary beneficial
salutatory welcoming
sanatorium ● Amer. *sanitarium*
satire literary work
satiric(al) of satire
satyr woodland deity
satyric of satyrs
scallop □ not *scollop*
scallywag ● Amer. *scalawag*
sceptic ● Amer. *skeptic*
scrimmage tussle ● also term in Amer.
  football
scrummage (Rugby)
sear to scorch, wither(ed)
secrecy
selvage
separate
sere of gunlock; in ecology
sergeant (military, police)
serjeant (law)
sestet (in a sonnet)
□ *sett* (noun): use *set*
sextet (in music, etc.)
Shakespearian □ not *Shakespearean*
shanty hut, song
sharif Muslim leader □ not *sherif*
sheath (noun)
sheathe (verb)
sheikh
□ *sherif*: use *sharif*
sheriff county officer
Shia (branch of Islam)
show ● not *shew*
sibylline
Sinhalese □ not *Singhalese*
smart alec □ not *aleck*
smooth (adjective and verb) ● not *smoothe*
sobriquet □ not *soubriquet*
solemness
some time (come and see me some time)
sometime former, formerly
spinal cord □ not *chord*
spirituel having refinement of mind
sprightly ● not *spritely*
spurt □ not *spirt*
squirearchy □ not *squirarchy*
stanch (verb) stop a flow □ not *staunch*

State (capital S for the political unit)
stationary at rest
stationery paper, etc.
staunch loyal □ not *stanch*
step-parent
stoep (South Africa) veranda
storey division of building ● Amer. *story*
storeyed having storeys
storied celebrated in story
stoup for holy water, etc. □ not *stoop*
straight without curve
strait narrow
strait-jacket
sty for pigs; on eyelid ● not *stye*
subtlety
subtly ● not *subtlely*
sulphur ● Amer. *sulfur*
summons command to appear (plural
  summonses)
summons (verb inflected *summonsed*)
supersede ● not *supercede*
swap □ not *swop*
swat hit sharply
swot study hard
sycamore (member of maple genus)
synthesist, synthesize ● not *synthet-*
teasel (plant)
tee-hee (laugh)
teetotalism
teetotaller ● Amer. *teetotaler*
tell (archaeology)
template □ not *templet*
tenet principle
thank you ● not *thankyou*
thank-you (noun), *thank-you letter*
threshold
tic contraction of muscles
tick-tack semaphore □ not *tic-tac*
titbit ● Amer. *tidbit*
titillate excite
titivate □ not *tittivate*
today
tomorrow
tonight
tonsillar, tonsillitis
toupee
Trades Union Congress
trade union □ not *trades union*
traipse trudge □ not *trapes*
tranquillity, tranquillize
transferable
transonic □ not *transsonic*
transsexual □ not *transexual*
transship(ment) □ not *tranship(ment)*

trolley
troop (soldiers)
trooper member of troop
troupe (performers)
trouper member of troupe
tsar □ not *czar*
T-shirt
Turco- (combining form of Turkish)
tympanum ear-drum
tyre ● Amer. *tire*
'un (informal for *one*)
under way ● not *under weigh* or *underway*
valance curtain, drapery
valence (in chemistry)
veld □ not *veldt*
vendor
veranda □ not *verandah*
vermilion
vice tool ● Amer. *vise*
villain evil-doer
villein serf
visor □ not *vizor*

vocal cord □ not *chord*
wagon □ not *waggon*
waiver forgoing of right
wastable
waver be unsteady
weird
whiskey (Irish, Amer.)
whisky (Scotch)
Whit Monday, Sunday
whiz □ not *whizz*
whooping cough
who's who is, who has
whose of whom
wisteria □ not *wistaria*
withhold
woebegone
woeful ● not *woful*
wrath anger
wreath (noun)
wreathe (verb)
wroth angry
yoghurt □ not *yogurt*

Pronunciation

This section is in two parts: A, general points of pronunciation, and B, a list of preferred pronunciations.

The recommending of any one pronunciation naturally implies the existence of a standard. There are many varieties of spoken English, but the treatment here is based upon British Received Pronunciation (RP), the neutral national standard used in broadcasting and taught to foreigners.

A. GENERAL POINTS OF PRONUNCIATION

It is impossible to lay down hard and fast rules here, since pronunciation is continually changing, and at any time there is bound to be considerable variation. Uncertainty about pronunciation also arises from the irregularity of English spelling.

The entries are arranged in alphabetical order of individual letters, or sequences of letters, that repeatedly cause difficulty. There are also three other kinds of entry, which deal with (*a*) American pronunciation, (*b*) the reduction of common words in rapid speech, and (*c*) patterns of stress.

a

1. There is variation in the pronunciation of *a* between the sound heard in *calm*, *father* and that heard in *cat*, *fan*, in

(*a*) the suffix -*graph* (in *photograph*, *telegraph*, etc.), where the sound of *calm* is preferred except where -*ic* is added (e.g. in *photographic*) where only the *a* of *cat* is used.

(*b*) the prefix *trans-* (as in *transfer*, *translate*, etc.), where either kind of *a* is acceptable.

2. The word endings -*ada*, -*ade*, and -*ado* occasion difficulty.

(*a*) In -*ada* words, *a* is as in *calm*, e.g. in *armada*, *cicada*.

(*b*) In most -*ade* words, *a* is as in *made*, e.g. *barricade*.
Exceptions: *a* as in *calm* in

aubade	façade	promenade
ballade	gambade	roulade
charade	pomade	saccade

and in loan-words from French, e.g. *oeillade*.

(*c*) In most -*ado* words, *a* is as in *calm*, e.g. *bravado*.
Exceptions: *a* as in *made* in *bastinado*, *tornado*.

3. *a* in -*alia* is like *a* in *alien*, e.g. in *marginalia*.

4. *a* before *ls* and *lt* in many words is pronounced either like *aw* in *bawl* or *o* in *doll*, e.g. in

alter	palsy	waltz

The same variation occurs with *au* in *assault*, *fault*, *somersault*, *vault*.

Note: in several words *a* before *ls* and *lt* can only be pronounced like *a* in *sally*, e.g.

Alsatian	contralto	peristalsis
alto	Malthusian	saltation

5. The *a* in -*ata*, -*atum*, and -*atus* is usually pronounced as in *mate*, e.g. in *apparatus*. Exceptions: *cantata*, *cassata*, *chipolata*, *desideratum* (plural *desiderata*), *erratum* (plural *errata*), *serenata*, *sonata*, *toccata* with *a* as in *calm*; *stratum*, *stratus* with the *a* of *mate* or *calm*.

-age

The standard pronunciation of the following words of French origin ending in -*age* is with stress on the first syllable, *a* as in *calm*, and *g* as in *regime*.

arbitrage	dressage	mirage
barrage	fuselage	persiflage
camouflage	garage	sabotage
collage	massage	

Note that *montage* is stressed on the second syllable.

● The pronunciation of -age as in cabbage is non-standard in all of these words except for arbitrage. Amer. pronunciation stresses the final syllable in some of them.

□ It is acceptable to use the sound of g as in large in several of these, particularly garage.

American pronunciation

Where the American pronunciation of individual forms and words significantly differs from the British, this is indicated as part of the individual entries in this Section. Among the many constant features of 'General American'* pronunciation, such as the pronunciation of r wherever it occurs in the spelling (see r, p. 34), perhaps the most relevant here is a matter of stress. In words of four syllables and over, in which the main stress falls on the first or second syllable, there is a strong secondary stress on the last syllable but one, the vowel of which is fully enunciated, e.g. cóntemplàtive, térritòry.

-arily

In a few five-syllable adverbs ending with -arily, there is a tendency to stress the a for ease of pronunciation. Some in common use are:

arbitrarily ordinarily
momentarily temporarily
necessarily voluntarily

Rapid colloquial speech, probably under the influence of Amer. English (see **American pronunciation**, above), has adopted a pronunciation with the a sounding like e in verily, which it would be pedantic to censure.

The case of the word primarily is different. It contains only four syllables, which can be reduced to the easily pronounced spoken form prim'rily.

● There is therefore no need to pronounce the word with stress on the second syllable. Pronunciations like pri-merr-ily or pri-marr-ily are not acceptable in careful speech.

* 'A form of U.S. speech without marked dialectal or regional characteristics' (OED).

-ed

1. In the following adjectives the ending -ed is pronounced as a separate syllable:

accursed naked wicked
cragged rugged wretched
deuced sacred

Note: accursed and deuced can also be pronounced as one syllable.

2. The following words have different meanings according to whether -ed is pronounced as a separate syllable or not. In most cases the former pronunciation indicates an adjective (as with the list under 1 above), the latter part of a verb.

	(a) -ed as separate syllable	(b) -ed pronounced 'd
aged	= very old (he is very aged, an aged man)	= having the age of (one etc.) (a boy aged three); past of to age (he has aged greatly)
beloved	used before noun (beloved brethren); = beloved person (my beloved is mine)	used as predicate (he was beloved by all)
blessed	= fortunate, holy, sacred (blessed are the meek, the blessed saints)	part of to bless; sometimes also in senses listed in left-hand column
crabbed	= cross-grained, hard to follow, etc.	past of to crab
crooked	= not straight, dishonest	= having transverse handle (crooked stick); past of to crook

cursed

	before noun = damnable	past of *to curse*
dogged	= tenacious	past of *to dog*
jagged	= indented	past of *to jag*
learned	= erudite	past of *to learn* (usually *learnt*)
ragged	= rough, torn, etc.	past of *to rag*

-edly, -edness

When the further suffixes -*ly* and -*ness* are added to adjectives ending in -*ed*, an uncertainty arises about whether to pronounce this -*ed*- as a separate syllable. Such can be divided into three kinds.

1. Those in which -*ed* is already a separate syllable (*a*) because it is preceded by *d* or *t* or (*b*) because the adjective is one of those discussed in the entry for -*ed* above; e.g. *belated*, *wicked*. When either -*ly* or -*ness* are added, -*ed*- remains a separate syllable, e.g. (i) *belatedly*, *wickedly*; (ii) *belatedness*, *wickedness*.

2. Those in which the syllable preceding -*ed* is unstressed, i.e. if -(*e*)*d* is removed the word ends in an unstressed syllable, e.g. *embarrassed*, *self-centred*. When either -*ly* or -*ness* are added, -*ed*- remains non-syllabic (i.e. it sounds like 'd), e.g.

(i)	*abandonedly*	*self-centredly*
	embarrassedly	*variedly*
(ii)	*self-centredness* (= -center'dness)	*studiedness*

3. Those in which the syllable preceding -*ed* is stressed, i.e. if -(*e*)*d* is removed the word ends in a stressed syllable, or is a monosyllable, e.g. *assured*, *fixed*.

● (i) When -*ly* is added -*ed* becomes an extra syllable, e.g.

advisedly	*fixedly*
allegedly	*markedly*
assuredly	*professedly*
deservedly	*unfeignedly*

Exceptions:

There are a few exceptions to this rule, e.g. *subduedly*, *tiredly* (-*ed* is not a separate syllable). Some words show variation, e.g. *depressedly*, *shamefacedly*.

● Note that some adverbs formed on adjectives in -*ed* sound awkward whether -*ed*- is pronounced as a separate syllable or not. Because of this, some authorities discourage the formation of words like *boredly*, *discouragedly*.

(ii) When -*ness* is added, there is greater variation. In *COD* -*ed*- is an extra syllable in only the following:

concernedness	*mixedness*
deservedness	*preparedness*
fixedness	*unashamedness*
markedness	

while *informedness* has this pronunciation as an alternative.

Many other words are not specially marked, and it has probably become increasingly rare for -*ed*- to be separately sounded.

□ It is acceptable *not* to make -*ed*- a separate syllable in words of this type.

-ein(e)

The ending -*ein*(*e*) (originally two syllables) is now usually pronounced like -*ene* in *polythene* in

| *caffeine* | *codeine* |
| *casein* | *protein* |

Note: *casein* can also be pronounced with -*ein* disyllabic.

-eity

The traditional pronunciation of *e* in this termination is as in *me*, e.g. in

contemporaneity	*homogeneity*
deity	*simultaneity*
heterogeneity	*spontaneity*

There is increasingly a tendency to substitute the sound of *e* in *café*, *suede*, although some speakers pronounce the first two syllables of *deity* like *deer*, and so with the other words. The same variation is found in the sequence -*ei*- in the words *deism, deist, reify, reification* (but not *theism, theist*).

-eur

This termination, occurring in words originally taken from French, in which it is the agent suffix, normally carries the stress and sounds like *er* in *deter, refer*, e.g. in:

agent provocateur	*masseur*
coiffeur	*raconteur*
connoisseur	*restaurateur*
(con-a-*ser*)	*saboteur*
entrepreneur	*secateurs*

Stress is on the first syllable usually in

amateur (and *amateurish*: am-a-ter-ish)
chauffeur

Stress can also be on the second syllable in *chauffeur*.

Feminine nouns can be formed from some of these by the substitution of *-se* for *-r*: the resulting termination is pronounced like *urze* in *furze*, e.g. *coiffeuse, masseuse, saboteuse*.

liqueur is pronounced li-*cure* (Amer. li-*cur*).

g

A. In certain less familiar words there is often uncertainty as to whether *g* preceding *e, i,* and (especially) *y* is pronounced hard as in *get* or soft as in *gem*.

1. The prefix *gyn(o)-* meaning 'woman' now always has a hard *g*, as in *gynaecology, gynoecium*.

2. The element *-gyn-* with the same meaning, occurring inside the word, usually has a soft *g*, as in *androgynous, misogynist*.

3. The elements *gyr-* (from a root meaning 'ring') and *-gitis* (in names of diseases) always have a soft *g*, as in

gyrate	*gyro* (-*scope*,
gyre (poetic, =	-*compass*, etc.)
gyrate, gyration)	*laryngitis*

4. The following, among many other words, have a hard *g*:

gibbous	*gill* (fish's organ)
gig (all senses)	*gingham*

● *g* should be hard in *analogous*.

5. The following have a soft *g*:

gibber	*gypsophila*
gibe	*gypsum*
gill (measure)	*gyrfalcon*
gillyflower	*longevity*
giro (payment system)	*panegyric*
gybe	

6. The following can vary, but usually have a hard *g*:

demagogic, -y   *pedagogic, -y*

7. The following can vary, but usually have a soft *g*:

gibberish   *hegemony*

B. See *-age*, p. 29.

-gm

g is silent in the sequence *gm* at the end of the word:

diaphragm   *phlegm*

But the *g* is pronounced between vowels:

enigma   *phlegmatic*

h

1. Initial *h* is silent in *heir, honest, honour, hour*, and their derivatives; also in *honorarium*. It is sounded in *habitué*.
2. Initial *h* used commonly to be silent if the first syllable was unstressed, as in *habitual, hereditary, historic, hotel*. This pronunciation is now old-fashioned. (See also *a* or *an*, p. 8.)

-ies

The ending *-ies* is usually pronounced as one syllable (like *ies* in *diesel*) in:

caries	*rabies*
congeries	*scabies*
facies	

● The reduction of this ending to a sound like the ending of *armies, babies*, etc., should be avoided in careful speech.

Exceptions: *series* and *species* can have either pronunciation.

-ile

The ending -*ile* is normally pronounced like *isle*, e.g. in

> *docile   missile   sterile*

● The usual Amer. pronunciation in most words of this kind is with the sound of *il* in *daffodil* or *pencil*.

The pronunciation is like *eel* in:

> *automobile   -mobile* (suffix)
> *imbecile*

-*ile* forms two syllables in *campanile* (rhyming with *Ely*), *cantabile* (pronounced can-*tah*-bi-ly), and *sal volatile* (rhyming with *philately*).

ng

There is a distinction between *ng* representing a single sound and *ng* representing a compound consisting of this sound followed by the sound of hard *g*.

1. The single sound is the only one to occur at the end of a word, e.g. in *song*, *writing*.

2. The single sound also occurs in the middle of words, but usually in compounds of a word ending in -*ng* + a suffix, e.g.

> *bringing   kingly   stringy*
> *hanged   longish   wrongful*

3. The compound sound, *ng* + *g*, is otherwise normal in the middle of words, e.g. in *hungry*, *language*, and also, as an exception to rule 2, in *longer*, -*est*, *prolongation*, *stronger*, -*est*, *younger*, -*est*.

● 4. It is non-standard:

(*a*) To pronounce *bringing*, *writing*, etc. as bringin, writin.

(*b*) To use *n* for *ng* in *length*, *strength*. (The pronunciation lenkth, strenkth is acceptable.)

(*c*) To use *nk* for *ng* in *anything*, *everything*, *nothing*, *something*.

(*d*) To use *ng* + *g* in all cases of *ng*, i.e. in words covered by rules 1 and 2 as well as 3. This pronunciation is, however, normal in certain regional forms of English.

o

1. In many words the *u*-sound as in *butter* is spelt with *o*, e.g. *come*. There is an increasing tendency to pronounce a few such words with the sound of *o* in *body*.

(*a*) More usually with the *u*-sound:

> *accomplice   constable   mongrel*
> *accomplish   frontier*

(*b*) More usually with the *o*-sound:

> *combat   dromedary   pomegranate*
> *comrade   hovel   pommel* (noun)
> *conduit   hover   sojourn*

2. Before *ff*, *ft*, *ss*, *st*, and *th*, in certain words, there was formerly a variety of RP in which *o* was pronounced like *aw* in *law*, so that *off*, *often*, etc. sounded like *orf*, *orphan*, etc.

● This pronunciation is now non-standard.

3. Before double *ll*, *o* has the long sound (as in *pole*) in some words, and the short sound (as in *Polly*) in others.

(*a*) With the long sound:

> *boll   roll   toll*
> *droll   scroll   troll*
> *knoll   stroll   wholly*
> *poll* (vote, *swollen*
> head)

(*b*) With the short sound:

> *doll*, *loll*, *moll*, *poll* (parrot), and most words in which another syllable follows, e.g. *collar*, *holly*, *pollen*, etc.

4. Before *lt*, *o* is pronounced long, e.g. *bolt*, *revolt*.

● The substitution of short *o* in these words is non-standard.

5. Before *lv*, *o* is pronounced short, e.g.

> *absolve   involve   revolver*
> *dissolve   resolve   solve*

● The substitution of long *o* in these words is non-standard.

ough

Although most words with *ough* are familiar, difficulties may arise with the following:

brougham	(a kind of carriage) *broo*-am or broom
chough	(bird) chuff
clough	(ravine) cluff
hough	(animal's joint), same as, and sounds like, *hock*
slough	(swamp) rhymes with *plough*
slough	(snake's skin) sluff
sough	(sound) rhymes with *plough* (also *tough*)

phth

This sequence should sound like *fth* (in *fifth*, *twelfth*), e.g. in *diphtheria*, *diphthong*, *monophthong*, *naphtha*, *ophthalmic*.

● It is non-standard to pronounce these as if written *dip-theria* etc.

Initially, as in the words *phthisical*, *phthisis*, the *ph* can be silent; it is also usually silent in *apophthegm*.

pn-, ps-, pt-

In these sequences at the beginning of words, it is normal not to pronounce the *p-*. The exception is *psi* representing the name of a Greek letter, used, e.g., as a symbol.

r

1. When *r* is the last letter of a word or precedes 'silent' final *e*, it is normally silent in RP, e.g. in *four*, *here*, *runner*.

But when another word, beginning with a vowel sound, follows in the same sentence, it is normal to pronounce the final *r*, e.g. in *four hours*, *here it is*, *runner-up*.

This is called the 'linking *r*'.

● It is standard to use linking *r* and unnatural to try to avoid it.

2. A closely connected feature of the spoken language is what is called 'intrusive *r*'. This occurs when an *r*-sound is introduced where there is no letter *r* in the spelling:

(*a*) after a word such as *villa*, ending with the obscure *a*-sound:

a villa-r *in Italy*

Here it is acceptable in rapid, informal speech.

(*b*) after the sounds of *ah* and *aw*, and the *eu* of *milieu*, both between words and before endings:

The Shah-r *of Iran*	a milieu-r in which . . .
law-r *and order*	draw-r-*ing room*

● The use of intrusive *r* here is very widely unacceptable. Indeed, it should not be used anywhere in formal speech.

3. There is a tendency in certain words to drop *r* if it is closely followed (or in a few cases, preceded) by another *r* at the beginning of an unstressed syllable, e.g. in

deteriorate pronounced deteriate
February pronounced Febuary
honorary pronounced honary
(prefer hon'rary)
itinerary pronounced itinery
library pronounced lib'ry
secretary pronounced seketry or
seketerry
temporary pronounced tempary
(prefer temp'rary)

● This should be avoided, especially in formal speech.

reduced forms

In rapid speech, many shorter grammatical words, being lightly stressed, tend to be reduced either by the obscuring of their vowels or the loss of a consonant or both. They may even be attached to one another or to more prominent words. Similarly, some such words are in rapid speech omitted altogether, while longer but common words are shortened by the elision of unstressed syllables. Typical examples are:

gonna, wanna	= going to, want to
kinda, sorta	= kind of, sort of
gimme, lemme	= give me, let me
'snot	= it's not
innit, wannit	= isn't it, wasn't it
doncher, dunno	= don't you, I don't know

what's he say, where d'you find it, we done it, what you want it for?

'spect or *I'xpect*   = I expect
(*I*) *spose*   = I suppose
cos, course, on'y, praps, probly =
   because, of course, only, perhaps,
   probably

● Most of these reduced forms (with the possible exception of *innit, wannit*) are natural in informal RP, but should be avoided in formal contexts.

s, sh, z, and zh

In certain kinds of word, where the spelling is *ci, si,* or *ti,* or where it is *s* before long *u,* there is variation between two or more of the four sounds which may be represented as:

s as in *sun*   *zh* representing the
sh as in *ship*   sound of *s* in *leisure*
z as in *zone*   or *g* in *regime*

1. There is variation between *s* and *sh* in words such as:

    appreciate   *negotiate*
    associate   *omniscient*
    glacial   *sociology*

This variation does not occur in all words with a similar structure: only *s* is used in *glaciation, pronunciation* (= *-see-ay-*shon), and only *sh* in *partiality* (par-shee-*al-*ity). Only *sh* occurs in *initial, racial, sociable, spatial, special,* etc.

2. There is variation between *s* and *sh* in *sensual, sexual, issue, tissue,* and between *z* and *zh* in *casual, casuist, visual.*

3. There is variation between *sh* and *zh* in *aversion, equation, immersion, version.*

□ Either variant is acceptable in each of these kinds of word, although in all of them *sh* is the traditional pronunciation.

4. In the names of some countries and regions ending in *-sia,* and in the adjectives derived from them, there is variation between *sh* and *zh,* and in some cases *z(i)* and *s(i)* as well. So:

Asian   = *A-*shan or *A-*zhan
Asiatic   = A-shi-*at-*ic or
                     A-zhi-*at-*ic or
                     A-zi-*at-*ic or A-si-*at-*ic

Australasian   = Austral-*a-*zhan or -shan
Indonesian   = Indo-*nee-*shan or
                      -zhan or -zi-an or
                      -si-an
Persian   = *Per-*shan or *Per-*zhan

● The pronunciation with *sh* is the most widely acceptable. The pronunciation with *zh* is also generally acceptable.

5. There is variation between *zh* and *z(i)* in *artesian* (*well*), *Cartesian, Caucasian,* and *Friesian.*

□ Either variant is acceptable.

stress

1. The position of the stress accent is the key to the pronunciation of many English polysyllabic words, since unstressed vowels are subject to reduction in length, obscuration of quality, and, quite often, complete elision. Compare the sound of the stressed vowel in the words on the left with that of the same vowel, unstressed, in the words on the right:

a: humánity   húman
     monárchic   mónarch
     practicálity   práctically(-ic'ly)
     secretárial   sécretary(-t'ry)
e: presént (verb)   présent (noun)
     protést   protestátion
     mystérious   mýstery
                     (= myst'ry)
i: satírical   sátirist
     combíne   combinátion
     anxíety   ánxious
                     (= anksh'ous)
o: ecónomy   económic
     oppóse   ópposite
     históric   hístory (= hist'ry)
u: luxúrious   lúxury
     indústrial   índustry

Many of the most hotly disputed questions of pronunciation centre on the placing of the stress.

2. It is impossible to formulate rules accounting for the position of the stress in every English word, but two very general observations can be made.

(*a*) Although the stress can fall on any syllable, more than three unstressed syllables cannot easily be uttered in sequence. Hence, for example, five-syllable words with stress on the first or last syllable are rare. Very often in polysyllabic words at least one syllable bears a secondary stress, e.g. *cáterpìllar, còntrovèrtibílity.*

(b) Some patterns of stress are clearly associated with spelling or with grammatical function (or, especially, with variation of grammatical function in a single word). For example, almost all words ending in -ic and -ical are stressed on the syllable immediately preceding the suffix. There is only a handful of exceptions: *Arabic, arithmetic* (noun), *arsenic, catholic, choleric, heretic, lunatic, politic(s), rhetoric.*

Some general tendencies will now be described, and related to the existing canons of acceptability.

3. *Two-syllable words*

There is a fixed, although not invariable, pattern, by which nouns and adjectives are stressed on the first syllable, and verbs on the second, e.g.

accent	import	torment
conflict	present	transfer
fragment	suspect	

nouns: *climate*   verbs: *create*
      mandate   *dictate*

This pattern has recently exercised an influence over several other words not originally conforming to it. The words

ally	defect	rampage
combine	intern	

were all originally stressed on the second syllable; but as nouns, they are all usually stressed on the first. Exactly the same tendency has affected

      dispute   *research*
      recess   *romance*

but in these words, the stressing of the noun on the first syllable is rejected in good usage. The following nouns and adjectives (not corresponding to identically spelt verbs) show the same transference of stress: *adept, adult, chagrin, supine.*

In the verbs *combat, contact, harass,* and *traverse,* a tendency towards stress on the second syllable is discernible, but the new stress has been fully accepted only in the word *traverse.*

4. *Three-syllable words*

Of the three possible stress patterns in three-syllable words, that with stress on the first syllable is the best established.

(a) Words with stress on the final syllable are rare. In some, a stress on the first syllable is acceptable in RP, e.g. artisan, *commandant, confidant, partisan, promenade*; in others it is not, e.g. *cigarette, magazine.*

(b) Many words originally having stress on the second syllable now commonly have stress on the first, e.g.

abdomen	obdurate	remonstrate
albumen	precedent	secretive
composite	(noun)	subsidence

In some other words the pronunciation with stress on the first syllable has not been accepted as standard, e.g. in

      Byzantine   *contribute*
      clandestine   *distribute*

(c) There is a tendency in a few words to move the stress from the first to the second syllable. It is generally resisted in standard usage, e.g. in

combatant	exquisite	stigmata
deficit	patina	

all of which have stress on the first syllable. But it has prevailed in *aggrandize, chastisement, conversant, doctrinal, environs, pariah, urinal.*

5. *Four-syllable words*

Broadly speaking, it has been traditional in RP to favour stress on the first syllable of these, so that the shift to the second syllable has been strongly resisted in:

applicable	demonstrable
aristocrat	illustrative
capitalist	intricacy
contumacy	lamentable

With the words *controversy*, *formidable*, and *kilometre* in particular, a pronunciation with stress on the second syllable arouses strong disapproval on the part of many people.

In many words one of the two middle unstressed syllables is elided:

adversary	participle
comparable	preferable
migratory	primarily
momentary	promissory
necessary	voluntary

However, many words have been, or are being, adapted to the antepenultimate stress pattern, e.g.

centenary	miscellany
despicable	nomenclature
explicable	pejorative
hospitable	peremptory
metallurgy	transferable

Because antepenultimate stress has been accepted in most of these words, it is difficult to reject it elsewhere. Analogy is the obvious argument in some cases, i.e. the analogy of *capital*, *demonstrate*, *illustrate*, *intricate*, etc. for the words related to them, but this cannot be used everywhere.

6. *Five-syllable words*

Five-syllable words originally stressed on the first syllable have been affected by the difficulty of uttering more than three unstressed syllables in sequence (see 2(*a*) above). The stress has been shifted to the second syllable in *laboratory*, *obligatory*, whereas in *veterinary* the fourth syllable is elided, and usually the second as well. For *arbitrarily*, *momentarily*, etc., see *-arily*, p. 30.

t

1. In rapid speech, *t* is often dropped from the sequence *cts*, so that *acts*, *ducts*, *pacts* sound like *axe*, *ducks*, *packs*.

● This should be avoided in careful speech.

2. The sounding of *t* in *often* is a spelling pronunciation: the traditional form in RP rhymes with *soften*.

th

1. Monosyllabic nouns ending in -*th* after a vowel sound (or vowel + *r*) form the plural by adding -*s* in the usual way, but the resulting sequence *ths* may be voiceless as in *myths*, or voiced as in *mouths*.

(*a*) The following are like *myth*:

berth	fourth	moth
birth	girth	sleuth
breath	growth	sloth
death	hearth	smith
faith	heath	wraith

(*b*) The following are like *mouth*:

oath	sheath	wreath
path	truth	youth

bath, *cloth*, *lath*, *swath* vary, but are now commonly like *myth*.

2. Note that final *th* is like *th* in *bathe*, *father* in:

bequeath	booth
betroth	mouth (verb)

booth can also be pronounced to rhyme with *tooth*.

u

The sound of long *u*, as in *cube*, *cubic*, *cue*, *use* is also spelt *eu*, *ew*, and *ui*, as in *feud*, *few*, *pursuit*. It is properly a compound of two sounds, the semi-vowel *y* followed by the long vowel elsewhere written *oo*. Hence the word *you* (= y + oo) sounds like the name of the letter *U*, *ewe*, and *yew*.

After some consonants the *y* is lost, leaving only the *oo*-sound.

1. After *ch*, *j*, *r*, the sound of *sh*, and *l* following a consonant. So *brewed*, *chews*, *chute*, *Jules*, *rude*, sound like *brood*, *choose*, *shoot*, *joules*, *rood*, and *blew*, *glue*, etc. sound as if they were spelt *bloo*, *gloo*, etc.

2. In a stressed syllable after *l* not following a consonant. *COD* gives only the *oo* pronunciation in many words, e.g. *lubricate*, *lucid*, *ludicrous*, etc., and either pronunciation for others, e.g. *lunar*, *Lutheran*, *allude*, *voluminous*, and (with secondary stress) *absolute*, *interlude*. However, *lewd* and *lieu* are given only the *yoo* pronunciation.

□ In all syllables of these kinds, the *oo*-sound is probably the predominant type, but either is acceptable.

● In *unstressed* syllables, however, the *yoo*-sound is the only one possible, e.g. in

> deluge   soluble   value
> prelude   valuable   volume

Contrast *solute* (= *sol*-yoot) with *salute* (= sa-*loot*).

3. After *s*, there is variation. Most people now use *oo* in *Susan* and *Sue*, and where another vowel follows, as in *sewer* and *suicide*, but *yoo* in *pseudo-*, *assume*, and *pursue*.

In an unstressed syllable, the *y*-sound is kept:

> capsule   consular   peninsula

□ Apart from in *Susan* and *Sue*, and in an unstressed syllable, either pronunciation is acceptable.

4. After *d*, *n*, and *t*, the loss of the *y*-sound is non-standard, e.g. in *due*, *new*, *tune*.

Note: In Amer. English loss of the *y*-sound is normal after these consonants and *l* and *s*.

● The tendency to make *t* and *d* preceding this sound in stressed syllables sound like *ch* and *j*, e.g. *Tuesday*, *duel* as if *Choosday*, *jewel*, should be avoided in careful speech.

In unstressed syllables (e.g. in *picture*, *procedure*) it is normal.

ul

After *b*, *f*, and *p*, the sequence *ul* sounds like *ool* in *wool* in some words, e.g. in *bull*, *pull*, and like *ull* in *hull* in others, e.g. in *bulk*, *pulp*. In a few words there is uncertainty or variation.

(*a*) Normally with *u* as in *hull*:

> Bulgarian   effulgent   pullulate
> catapult   fulminate   pulmonary
> ebullient   fulvous   pulverize

(*b*) Normally with *u* as in *bull*:

> bulwark   fulmar   fulsome

(*c*) With variation: *fulcrum*.

urr

In Standard English the stressed vowel of *furry* and *occurring* is like that of *stirring*, not that of *hurry* and *occurrence*.

● The two sounds are identical in normal Amer. English.

wh

In some regions *wh* is preceded or accompanied by an *h*-sound.

□ This pronunciation is not standard in RP, but is acceptable to most RP-speakers.

B. PREFERRED PRONUNCIATIONS

The entries in this list are of three kinds. Some are words, mainly unusual ones, that have only one current pronunciation, which cannot be deduced with certainty from the spelling. Others have one pronunciation, which is slurred in rapid speech; these reduced forms are noted, with a warning against using them in careful speech. The third and largest group is of words with two or more current pronunciations. Both (or all) are given, with notes as to their acceptability.

The approach throughout is fairly flexible.

Where American pronunciations differ significantly, they are noted in brackets, or sometimes stand alone after the recommended one, implying that the use of the American form is incorrect in British speech.

The symbol ● is used to warn against forms especially to be avoided.

abdomen: stress on 1st syllable in general use; on 2nd in the speech of many members of the medical profession.

accomplice, accomplish: the pronunciation with 2nd syllable as *come* rather than as in *comma* is now predominant.

acoustic: 2nd syllable as *coo*, not *cow*.

acumen: stress on 1st syllable; the traditional pronunciation has stress on 2nd syllable.

adept (adjective): stress on 1st or 2nd syllable; (noun) on 1st syllable.

adult (adjective and noun): stress on 1st syllable.

adversary: stress on 1st syllable.

aficionado: a-fiss-eon-*ah*-do.

ague: two syllables.

albumen: stress on 1st syllable.

ally (noun): stress on 1st syllable; (verb) on 1st or 2nd syllable; **allied** preceding a noun is stressed on 1st syllable.

analogous: *g* as in *log*; not a-*na*-lo-jus.

Antarctic: ● do not drop the first *c*.

anti- (prefix): rhymes with *shanty*, not, as often Amer., *ant eye*.

apache (Indian): rhymes with *patchy*; (street ruffian) rhymes with *cash*.

apartheid: 3rd syllable like *hate*. ● Not *apart-ite* or *apart-hide*.

apophthegm: a-po-them.

apparatus: 3rd syllable like *rate*; not appar-*ah*-tus.

applicable: stress either on 1st syllable or on 2nd.

apposite: 3rd syllable like that of *opposite*.

arbitrarily: stress properly on 1st syllable, informally on 3rd.

Arctic: ● do not drop the first *c*.

Argentine: 3rd syllable as in *turpentine*.

argot: rhymes with *cargo*.

aristocrat: stress on 1st syllable. ● Not (except Amer.) a-*rist*-ocrat.

artisan: stress originally on 3rd syllable; Amer. pronunciation with stress on 1st syllable is now common in Britain.

aspirant: stress either on 1st syllable or on 2nd.

asthma: *ass*-ma is the familiar pronunciation; to sound the *th* is pedantic (Amer. *az*-ma).

ate: rhymes with *bet* or *bate* (also the Amer. pronunciation).

audacious: *au* as in *audience*, not as in *gaucho*.

auld lang syne: 3rd word like *sign*, not *zine*.

auxiliary: awg-*zil*-yer-ri.

azure: now usually *az*-yoor.

banal: 2nd syllable like that of *canal* or *morale* (Amer. rhymes with *anal*).

basalt: 1st *a* as in *gas*, 2nd as in *salt*; stress on either.

bathos: *a* as in *paper*.

bestial: 1st syllable like *best* not *beast*.

blackguard: *blagg*-ard.

bolero (dance): stress on 2nd syllable; (jacket) stress on 1st.

booth: rhymes with *smooth* or *tooth*.

bouquet: first syllable as *book*, not as *beau*.

Bourbon (dynasty): 1st syllable as *bourgeois*; (US whisky) as *bur*.

breeches: rhymes with *pitches*.

brochure: stress on 1st syllable.

brusque: should be Anglicized: broosk or brusk.

bureau: stress on 1st syllable.

burgh (in Scotland): sounds like *borough*.

Byzantine: stress on 2nd syllable (Amer. *biz*-en-teen).

cadaver: 2nd syllable as in *waver, average,* or *lava.*

cadaverous: 2nd syllable like 1st of *average.*

cadre: rhymes with *harder.*

caliph: rhymes with *bailiff,* or 1st syllable as in *pal.*

camellia: rhymes with *Amelia.*

canine: 1st syllable as *can* or *cane.*

canton (subdivision): 2nd syllable as 1st of *tonic*; (military, also in **cantonment**) 2nd syllable as that of *cartoon.*

capitalist: stress on 1st syllable.

Caribbean: stress on 3rd syllable more usual, but on 2nd is also acceptable.

carillon: rhymes with *trillion* (Amer. *carry*-lon).

caryatid: stress on 2nd *a.*

catacomb: 3rd syllable as *comb,* or rhyming with *tomb.*

catechumen: stress on 3rd syllable (catty-*cue*-men).

centenary: sen-*tee*-nary (Amer. *sen*-tenary).

cento: *c* as in *cent,* not *cello.*

centrifugal, centripetal: stress originally on 2nd syllable, but now usually on 3rd.

certification: stress on 1st and 4th syllables, not 2nd and 4th.

cervical: stress either on 1st syllable (with last two syllables as in *vertical*) or on 2nd (rhyming with *cycle*) (Amer. only the first pronunciation).

chaff: rhymes with *staff.*

chagrin: stress on 1st syllable; 2nd as *grin* (Amer. stress on 2nd syllable).

chamois (antelope): *sham*-wah; (leather) shammy.

chastisement: stress on 1st or 2nd syllable.

chimera: *ch* = k, not sh.

chiropodist: strictly *ch* = k, but as sh is common.

choleric: 1st two syllables like *collar.*

chutzpa: 1st syllable rhymes with p*uts*; the initial sound should properly be pronounced like the *ch* in *loch.*

cigarette: stress on 3rd syllable (Amer. on 1st).

clandestine: stress on 2nd syllable.

clangour: rhymes with *anger.*

clientele: kleeon-*tell.*

clique: rhymes with *leak,* not *lick.*

coccyx: *cc* = ks.

colander: 1st syllable as *cull.*

combat (verb), **combatant, -ive:** stress on 1st syllable (Amer. on 2nd).

combine (noun): stress on 1st syllable.

commandant: stress on 3rd syllable, or now often on 1st.

communal: stress on 1st syllable.

commune (noun): stress on 1st syllable.

comparable: stress on 1st syllable, not on 2nd.

compensatory: the older (and Amer.) pronunciation has stress on 2nd syllable, but stress on 3rd is now common.

compilation: 2nd syllable as *pill.*

composite: stress on 1st syllable; 3rd as that of *opposite* (Amer. stress on 2nd syllable).

conch: originally = *conk*; now often with *ch* as in *lunch.*

conduit: last three letters formerly like those of *circuit,* but now usually *con*-dew-it.

confidant(e): stress on 1st or on last syllable, which rhymes with *ant.*

congener: stress on 1st or 2nd syllable; *o* as *con*; *g* as in *gin.*

congeries: con-*jeer*-eez or con-*jeer*-y-eez.

congratulatory: stress on 2nd or 4th syllable.

conjugal: stress on 1st syllable.

consuetude: stress on 1st syllable; *sue* like *swi* in *swift.*

consummate (adjective): stress on 2nd syllable; (verb) on 1st syllable, 3rd syllable as *mate.*

contact (noun): stress on 1st syllable; (verb) stress on 1st or 2nd.

contemplative: stress on 2nd syllable.

contrarily (on the contrary): stress on 1st syllable; (perversely) stress on 2nd syllable.

contribute: stress on 2nd syllable. ● The pronunciation with stress on 1st syllable is not accepted as standard.

controversy: stress on 1st syllable. ● The now common pronunciation with stress on 2nd is strongly disapproved by many users of RP.

contumacy: stress on 1st syllable (Amer. on 2nd).

contumely: three syllables with stress on the 1st.

conversant: now usually stressed on 2nd syllable.

courier: *ou* as in *could*.

courteous: 1st syllable like *curt*.

courtesan: 1st syllable like *court*.

courtesy: 1st syllable like *curt*.

covert: 1st syllable like that of *cover*. ● The pronunciation *co*-vert is chiefly Amer.

cul-de-sac: 1st syllable may rhyme with *dull* or *full*.

culinary: *cul-* now usually as in *culprit*; formerly as in *peculiar*.

cyclical: 1st syllable like *cycle*, though *sick* is also common.

dais: originally one syllable; now only with two.

data: 1st syllable as *date*. ● Does not rhyme with *sonata*.

decade: stress on 1st syllable. ● The pronunciation with stress on 2nd syllable is not accepted as standard.

defect (noun): stress on 1st syllable is now usual.

deficit: stress on 1st syllable.

deify, deity: properly with *e* as in *me*; pronunciation with *e* as in *suede*, *fête* is increasingly common.

delirious: 2nd syllable as 1st of *lyrical*, not *Leary*.

demesne: 2nd syllable sounds like *main*.

demonstrable: stress now usually on the 2nd syllable.

deprivation: 1st two syllables like those of *deprecation*.

derisive, derisory: 2nd syllable like *rice*.

despicable: stress on 1st syllable; informally on 2nd.

desuetude: as for **consuetude**.

desultory: stress on 1st syllable.

deteriorate: ● do not drop 4th syllable, i.e. not deteri-ate.

detour: *dee*-tour not *day*-tour (Amer. de-*tour*).

deus ex machina: *day*-us ex *mak*-ina, not ma-*shee*-na.

dilemma: 1st syllable like *dill* or, now commonly, like *die*.

dinghy: either ding-gy or rhyming with *stringy*.

diphtheria, diphthong: *ph* = f not p.

disciplinary: the older (and Amer.) pronunciation has stress on 1st syllable, but it is now usually on the 3rd.

disputable: stress on 2nd syllable.

dispute (noun): stress on 2nd syllable, not on 1st.

dissect: 1st syllable as *Diss*. ● Does not rhyme with *bisect*.

distribute: stress on 2nd syllable. ● The pronunciation with stress on the 1st is considered incorrect by some people.

doctrinal: stress now usually on the 2nd syllable (with *i* as in *mine*).

dolorous, dolour: 1st syllable like *doll* (Amer. like *dole*).

dour: rhymes with *poor* not *power*.

dubiety: last three syllables like those of *anxiety*.

ducat: 1st syllable like *duck*.

dynastic, dynasty: 1st syllable like *din* (Amer. like *dine*).

ebullient: *u* as in *dull*, not as in *bull*.

economic: *e* as in *extra* or as in *equal*: both are current.

Edwardian: 2nd syllable as *ward*.

e'er (poetry, = *ever*): sounds like *air*.

efficacy: stress on 1st syllable, not 2nd.

ego: 1st syllable as that of *eager*.

egocentric, egoism, etc.: 1st syllable like *egg* (Amer. usually as **ego**).

either: *ei* as in *height* or *seize* (Amer. only the second).

elixir: rhymes with *licks ear*.

enclave: *en-* as in *end*, *a* as in *slave*.

entirety: now usually entire-ety; formerly entire-ty.

envelope: *en-* as in *end*; the pronunciation as in *on* is widespread but disliked by many RP speakers.

environs: rhymes with *sirens*.

epoxy: stress on 2nd syllable.

equerry: stress properly on 2nd syllable, but commonly on 1st.

espionage: now usually with *-age* as in *camouflage*.

et cetera: etsetera. ● Not eksetera.

explicable: stress originally on 1st syllable, now usually on 2nd.

exquisite: stress originally on 1st syllable, now usually on 2nd.

extraordinary: 1st *a* is silent.

fakir: sounds like *fake-*ear.

falcon: *a* as in *talk*, not as in *alcove*.

fascia: rhymes with *Alsatia*; in medicine, often like *fashion*.

fascism, fascist: 1st syllable like that of *fashion*.

February: ● do not drop the 1st r: feb-roor-y, not feb-yoor-y or feb-wa-ry or feb-yoo-erry (Amer. feb-roo-erry).

fetid, fetish: e as in fetter.

fifth: in careful speech, do not drop the 2nd f.

finance: stress on 1st syllable (only with i as in fine) or on 2nd (with i as in fin or fine).

flaccid: cc as in accident, or rhyming with acid.

forbade: 2nd syllable like bad.

formidable: stress on 1st syllable; informally, on 2nd.

forte (one's strong point): originally (and Amer.) like fort, but now usually like the musical term forte.

foyer: foy-ay or, less commonly, fwah-yay (Amer. foy-er).

fracas (singular): frack-ah, (plural) frack-ahz (Amer. frake-us).

fulminate: u as in dull.

fulsome: u formerly as in dull, now always as in full.

furore: three syllables (Amer. **furor** with two).

Gaelic: 1st syllable as gale.

gala: 1st a as in calm. ● The former pronunciation with a as in gale is still used in the North and US.

gallant: stress on 1st syllable; (polite to women) stress on 1st or 2nd.

garage: stress on 1st syllable, age as in camouflage (or rhyming with large). ● Pronunciation to rhyme with carriage is disapproved of by many RP speakers.

garrulity: stress on 2nd syllable, which sounds like rule.

garrulous: stress on 1st syllable.

gaseous: 1st syllable like gas.

genuine: ine as in engine.

genus: e as in genius; **genera** (plural) has e as in general.

gibber, gibberish: with g as in gin.

glacial: 1st a as in glade.

golf: o as in got. ● The pronunciation goff is old-fashioned.

gone: o as in on. ● The pronunciation gawn is non-standard.

government: ● In careful speech, do not drop the 1st n (or the whole 2nd syllable).

gratis: a as in grate; but grahtis and grattis are common.

greasy: s may be as in cease or easy.

grievous: ● does not rhyme with previous.

guacamole: gwark-er-mole-i.

gunwale: gunn'l.

half-past: ● In careful speech, avoid saying hah past or hoff posst.

hara-kiri: ● not harry-carry.

harass(ment): stress on 1st syllable. ● The pronunciation with stress on the 2nd is considered incorrect by some people.

have: in rapid speech, the weakly stressed have sounds like weakly stressed of. When stress is restored to it, it should become have, as in 'You couldn't 've done it', 'I could have' (not 'I could of').

hectare: 2nd syllable like tare or, less commonly, tar.

hegemony: stress on 2nd syllable, g as in get or (as also Amer.) as in gem.

Hegira: stress on 1st syllable, which is like hedge.

heinous: ei as in rein. ● The pronunciation rhyming with Venus is disliked by many RP speakers; that rhyming with genius is erroneous.

homo- (prefix = same): o now usually as in hoe.

homoeopath: 1st two syllables rhyme with Romeo.

homogeneous: last three syllables sound like genius.

honorarium: h silent, a as in rare.

hospitable: stress on 1st or 2nd syllable.

hotel: h to be pronounced.

housewifery: stress on 1st syllable, i as in whiff.

hovel, hover: o as in hot. ● Pronunciation with o as in love is now only Amer.

idyll, idyllic: i as in idiot.

illustrative: stress on 1st syllable (Amer. on 2nd).

imbroglio: g is silent; rhymes with folio.

impious: stress on 1st syllable; on 2nd in impiety.

importune: stress on 3rd syllable or (some speakers) on 2nd.

inchoate: stress on 1st syllable.

indict: c is silent; rhymes with incite.

indisputable: stress on 3rd syllable.

inexplicable: stress usually on 3rd syllable.

infamous: stress on 1st syllable.

inherent: 1st *e* as in *here* or *error*.

intaglio: *g* is silent, *a* as in *pal* or *pass*.

integral: stress on 1st syllable. ● The pronunciation with stress on the 2nd is considered incorrect by some people. The pronunciation *int*-re-gal is erroneous.

intern (verb): stress on 2nd syllable; (noun, Amer.) on 1st.

internecine: stress on 3rd syllable, last syllables like *knee sign*.

interstice: stress on 2nd syllable.

intestinal: the traditional pronunciation has stress on 2nd syllable, 3rd like *tin*; now commonly with stress on 3rd, pronounced *tine*.

intricacy: stress on 1st syllable.

invalid (sick person): stress on 1st syllable, 2nd *i* as in *lid* or *machine*; (verb) stress on 1st syllable, 2nd *i* as in *machine*; (not valid) stress on 2nd syllable.

inveigle: 2nd syllable as in *vague* or rhyming with *beagle*.

inventory: like *infantry* with *v* instead of *f*.

irrefragable: stress on 2nd syllable.

irreparable: stress on 2nd syllable.

irrevocable: stress on 2nd syllable.

issue: *ss* as in *mission*; but rhyming with *miss you* is common.

isthmus: in careful speech, do not drop the *th*.

January: *jan*-yoor-y (Amer. *jan*-yoo-erry).

jejune: stress on 2nd syllable.

jewellery: jewel-ry. ● Not jool-ery.

joule (unit): rhymes with *fool*.

jubilee: stress on 1st syllable. ● Not 3rd.

jugular: 1st syllable like *jug*: formerly as in *conjugal*.

junta: pronounce as written. ● Hoonta, an attempt to reproduce the Spanish, is the standard Amer. pronunciation.

karaoke: 1st two syllables properly like those of *caramel*, but (to avoid the awkward hiatus) often like *carry*.

kilometre: stress on 1st syllable. ● The pronunciation with stress on the 2nd is considered incorrect by many people.

knoll: *o* as in *no*.

laboratory: stress on 2nd syllable. ● The former pronunciation, with stress on 1st, is now chiefly Amer. (with *ory* as in *Tory*).

lamentable: stress on 1st syllable.

languor: as for **clangour**.

lasso: stress on 2nd syllable, *o* as in *do*.

lather: rhymes with *rather* or *gather*.

leeward (in general use): *lee*-ward; (nautical) like *lured*.

leisure: rhymes with *pleasure* (Amer. with *seizure*).

length: *ng* as in *long*. ● Not lenth.

levee (reception): like *levy*; (Amer., embankment) may be stressed on 2nd.

library: in careful speech avoid dropping the 2nd syllable (li-bry).

lichen: sounds like *liken*.

lieutenant: 1st syllable like *left* (Amer. like *loot*).

liquorice: licker-iss.

longevity: *ng* as in *lunge*.

longitude: *ng* as in *lunge* or as in *linger*. ● Not *longtitude*.

lour: rhymes with *hour*.

lugubrious: loo-*goo*-brious.

machete: *ch* as in *machine* or *attach*; rhymes with *Betty*.

machination: *ch* as in *mechanical*, but pronunciation as in *machine* is increasingly common.

machismo, macho: *ch* as in *attach*, not as in *mechanical*.

magazine: stress on 3rd syllable (Amer. has stress on 1st).

mandatory: stress on 1st syllable.

margarine: *g* as in *Margery*.

marital: stress on 1st syllable.

massage: stress on 1st syllable (Amer. on 2nd).

matrix: *a* as in *mate*; **matrices** the same, with stress on 1st.

medicine: two syllables (med-sin). ● The pronunciation with three syllables is normal in Scotland and the US, but is disapproved of by many users of RP.

mediocre: 1st syllable like *mead*.

metallurgy, -ist: stress on 2nd syllable. ● The older pronunciation with stress on 1st is now chiefly Amer.

metamorphosis: stress on 3rd syllable.

metope: two syllables.

midwifery: stress on 1st syllable, *i* as in *whiff*.

mien: sounds like *mean*.

migraine: 1st syllable like *me* (Amer. like *my*).

migratory: stress on 1st syllable.

millenary: stress on 2nd syllable, which is like *Len*.

miscellany: stress on 2nd syllable (Amer. on 1st).

mischievous: stress on 1st syllable. ● Not rhyming with *previous*.

misericord: stress on 2nd syllable.

mnemonic: stress on 2nd syllable, 1st like *nimble* not *Newman*.

mocha: like *mocker* (Amer. rhyming with *coca*).

momentary, -ily: stress on 1st syllable.

mullah: *u* as in *dull*.

municipal: stress on 2nd syllable.

nadir: *nay*-dear.

naive: nah-*Eve* or nigh-*Eve*.

naivety: has three syllables.

nascent: *a* as in *fascinate*.

necessarily: in formal speech, has stress on 1st syllable; informally stressed on 3rd (e.g. *not necess*arily!).

neither: as for **either**.

nephew: formerly with *ph* like *v*, but now usually *neff*-you.

nicety: has three syllables.

niche: nitch or neesh.

nomenclature: stress on 2nd syllable. The pronunciation with stress on 1st and 3rd syllables is now chiefly Amer.

nonchalant: stress on 1st syllable, *ch* as in *machine*.

nuclear: *newk*-lee-er. ● Not as if spelt *nucular*.

nucleic: stress on 2nd syllable, which has *e* as in *equal*.

obdurate: stress on 1st syllable.

obeisance: 2nd syllable like *base*.

obligatory: stress on 2nd syllable.

obscenity: *e* as in *scent*.

occurrence: 2nd syllable like the 1st in *current*.

oche (darts): rhymes with *hockey*.

o'er (poetry, = over): now usually rhyming with *goer*.

of: see **have**.

often: the traditional pronunciation has a silent *t*, as in *soften*; the sounding of the *t* is sometimes heard.

ominous: 1st syllable as that of *omelette*.

ophthalmic: *ph* = f not p.

opus: *o* as in *open*.

ormolu: *orm*-o-loo with weak 2nd *o* as in *Caroline*.

p (abbreviation for *penny, pence*): in formal context, say *penny* (after 1) or *pence*. ● 'Pee' is informal only.

pace (with all due respect to): like *pacey*.

paella: usually pie-*ell*-a rather than pah-*ell*-a.

panegyric: stress on 3rd syllable, *g* as in *gin*, *y* as in *lyric*.

paprika: stress on 1st syllable (Amer. on 2nd).

pariah: the older pronunciation rhymes with *carrier*; the pronunciation rhyming with *Isaiah* is now common (and normal Amer.).

participle: stress on 1st syllable; 1st *i* may be dropped. ● The stressing of 2nd syllable is not yet standard.

particularly: in careful speech, avoid saying particuly.

partisan: as **artisan**.

pasty (pie): *a* now usually as in *lass*.

patent: 1st syllable like *pate*. ● Some have 1st syllable like *pat* in *Patent Office*, *letters patent*.

pathos: as for **bathos**.

patina: stress on 1st syllable.

patriarch: 1st *a* as in *paper*.

patriot(ic): *a* as in *pat* or *paper*.

patron, patroness: *a* as in *paper*.

patronage, patronize: *a* as in *pat*.

pejorative: stress on 2nd syllable. ● The older pronunciation, with stress on 1st syllable, is now rare.

peremptory: stress on 2nd syllable (Amer. on 1st).

perhaps: in careful speech, two syllables with *h*, not *r*, sounded; informally praps.

pharmacopoeia: stress on *oe*; *-poeia* rhymes with *idea*.

philharmonic: 2nd *h* is traditionally silent.

phthisis: *ph* is silent.

pianist: stress on 1st *i*, *ia* as in *Ian*.

piano (instrument): *a* as in *man*; (= softly) *a* as in *calm*.

piazza: *zz* = ts.

pistachio: *a* as in *calm*, *ch* as in *machine*.

plaid, plait: rhyme with *lad, flat*.

plastic: now rhymes with *fantastic*, rather than with the *a* of *calm*.

plenty: ● *plenny* is non-standard.
pogrom: stress on the 1st syllable.
pomegranate: *pommy*-gran-it is now usual, rather than *pom*-gran-it.
porpoise: *oise* like *ose* in *purpose*.
posthumous: *h* is silent.
pot-pourri: stress on 2nd syllable (Amer. on 3rd), *pot-* like *Poe*.
precedence, precedent, precedented: stress on 1st syllable, which sounds like *press*; but on 2nd for *precedent* (adjective).
predilection: ● not as if spelt predeliction.
preferable: stress on 1st syllable.
premise (verb): stress on 2nd syllable, rhyming with *surmise*.
prestige: stress on 2nd syllable, *i* and *g* as in *regime*.
prestigious: rhymes with *religious*.
prima facie: *pry*-ma *fay*-shee.
primarily: stress on 1st syllable. ● The pronunciation with stress on the 2nd, used by some Americans, is disapproved of by many users of RP.
primer (school-book): *i* as in *prime*. ● The older pronunciation with *i* as in *prim* survives in New Zealand.
privacy: *i* as in *privet* or *private*; the latter is the older pronunciation.
probably: in careful speech, three syllables; informally often probbly.
proboscis: pro-*boss*-iss.
process (noun): *o* as in *probe*. ● An older pronunciation with *o* as in *profit* is now only Amer.
process (verb, to treat): like the noun; (to walk in procession) stress on 2nd syllable.
promissory: stress on 1st syllable.
pronunciation: 2nd syllable like *nun*. ● Not pro-*noun*-ciation.
prosody: 1st syllable like that of *prospect*.
protean: stress originally on 1st syllable, now commonly on 2nd.
protégé: 1st syllable like *protestant* (Amer. like *protest*).
proven: *o* as in *prove*, but pronunciation like *woven* is widespread.
proviso: 2nd syllable as that of *revise*.
puissance (show-jumping): pronounced with approximation to French, *pui* = pwi, *a* nasalized; (in poetry) may be *pwiss*-ance or *pew*-iss-ance, depending on scansion.

pursuivant: *Percy*-vant.
pyramidal: stress on 2nd syllable.
quaff: rhymes with *scoff*.
quagmire: *a* originally as in *wag*, now usually as in *quad*.
qualm: rhymes with *calm*; to rhyme with *shawm* is now rare.
quandary: stress on 1st syllable.
quasi: the vowels are like those in *wayside*.
quatercentenary: *kwatt*-er-, not *quarter-*.
questionnaire: 1st two syllables like *question*.
rabid: 1st syllable like that of *rabbit*.
rabies: 2nd syllable like *bees*, not like *babies*.
rampage (verb): stress on 2nd syllable; (noun) on 1st or 2nd.
rapport: stress on 2nd syllable, which sounds like *pore* (Amer. like *port*).
ratiocinate: 1st two syllables like *ratty*, stress on 3rd.
rationale: *ale* as in *morale*.
really: rhymes with *ideally*, *clearly*, not with *freely*.
recess (noun and verb): stress on 2nd syllable.
recognize: ● do not drop the *g*.
recondite: stress on 1st or 2nd syllable.
recuperate: 2nd syllable like the 1st of *Cupid*.
referable: stress on 2nd syllable.
remediable, -al: stress on 2nd syllable, *e* as in *medium*.
remonstrate: stress on 1st syllable.
Renaissance: stress on 2nd syllable, *ai* as in *plaice*.
renege: rhymes with *league* or *plague*. ● *g* as in *get*.
reportage: *age* as in *camouflage*, but with stress.
research (noun): stress on 2nd syllable. ● The Amer. pronunciation with stress on the 1st is now quite widespread in Britain, but is considered incorrect by some people.
respite: stress on 1st syllable, 2nd like *spite* (Amer. like *spit*).
restaurant: pronunciation with final *t* silent and second *a* nasalized is preferred by many, but that with *ant* = ont is now more common.
revanchism: *anch* as in *ranch*.
ribald: 1st syllable like *rib*.

risible: rhymes with *visible*.

risqué: *riss*-kay or riss-*kay*.

romance: stress on 2nd syllable. ● Pronunciation with stress on 1st syllable, usually in sense 'love affair, love story', is considered incorrect by some people.

Romany: 1st syllable as that of *romp* or *rope*.

rotatory: stress on 1st or 2nd syllable.

rowan: *ow* as in *low* or *cow*.

rowlock: rhymes with *Pollock*.

sacrilegious: now always rhymes with *religious*.

sahib: sounds like *Saab*.

salsify: *sal*-si-fee.

salve (noun, ointment; verb, soothe): properly rhymes with *halve*, but now usually with *valve* (Amer. with *have*).

salve (save ship): rhymes with *valve*.

satiety: as for **dubiety**.

Saudi: rhymes with *rowdy*, not *bawdy*.

scabies: as for **rabies**.

scabrous: *a* as in *skate* (Amer. as in *scab*).

scallop: rhymes with *wallop* or (Amer.) with *gallop*.

scarify (make an incision): rhymes with *clarify*. ● Not to be confused with slang *scarify* (terrify) pronounced *scare*-ify.

scenario: *sc* as in *scene*, *ario* as in *impresario* (Amer. with *a* as in *Mary*).

schedule: *sch* as in *Schubert* (Amer. as in *school*).

schism: properly, *ch* is silent (siz'm); but skiz'm is often heard.

schist (rock): *sch* as in *Schubert*.

schizo-: skitso.

scilicet: 1st syllable like that of *silent* or *silly*.

scone: traditionally rhymes with *on*.

second (to support): stress on 1st syllable; (to transfer) on 2nd.

secretary: *sek*-re-try. ● Not *sek*-e-try or *sek*-e-terry or (Amer.) *sek*-re-terry.

secretive: stress on 1st syllable.

segue: *seg*-way.

seise, seisin: *ei* as in *seize*.

seismic: 1st syllable like *size*.

seraglio: *g* silent, *a* as in *ask*.

shaman: 1st syllable like *sham*, not *shame*.

sheikh: sounds like *shake* (Amer. like *chic*).

simultaneous: *i* as in *simple* (Amer. as in *Simon*).

sinecure: properly, *i* as in *sign*, but *i* as in *sin* is common.

Sinhalese: sin-(h)al-*ese*.

Sioux: soo.

sisal: 1st syllable like the 2nd of *precise*.

sixth: in careful speech, avoid the pronunciation sikth.

slalom: *a* as in *spa*.

slaver (dribble): *a* as in *have*.

sleight: sounds like *slight*.

sloth: rhymes with *both*.

slough (bog): rhymes with *bough*; (to cast a skin) with *tough*.

sobriquet: 1st syllable like that of *sober*.

sojourn: 1st *o* as in *sob* (Amer. as in *sober*).

solder: *o* as in *sob* (Amer. pronunciation is sodder or sawder).

solecism: *o* as in *sob*.

solenoid: stress on 1st syllable, *o* as in *sober* or as in *sob*.

sonorous: stress on 1st syllable, 1st *o* as in *sob*.

soporific: 1st *o* now usually as in *sob*.

sough (rushing sound): rhymes with *plough*.

sovereignty: *sov*'renty. ● Not sov-*rain*-ity.

Soviet: *o* as in *sober* or *sob*.

species: *ci* as in *precious*. ● Not *spee*-seez.

spinet: may be stressed on either syllable.

spontaneity: as for **deify, deity**.

stalwart: 1st syllable like *stall*.

status: 1st syllable like *stay*. ● Not *statt*-us.

stigmata: stress on 1st syllable. ● Not with *ata* as in *sonata*.

strafe: rhymes with *staff*.

stratosphere: *a* as in *Stratford*.

stratum, strata: *a* of 1st syllable like 1st *a* of *sonata*.

strength: *ng* as in *strong*. ● Not *strenth*.

suave, suavity: *a* as 1st *a* in *lava*.

subsidence: stress originally on 2nd syllable with *i* as in *side*; now often with stress on 1st and *i* as in *sit*.

substantial: 1st *a* as in *ant*, not *aunt*.

substantive (in grammar): stress on 1st syllable; (separate, permanent) on 2nd.

suffragan: *g* as in *get*.

suit: now usually with *oo*, though *yoo* is common.

supererogatory: stress on 4th syllable.

superficies: super-*fish*-(i-)eez.

supine (adjective): stress on 1st syllable (Amer. on 2nd).

suppose: ● in careful speech, has two syllables.

surety: now usually *sure*-et-y; originally *sure*-ty.

surveillance: ● do not drop the *l*; = sur-*vey*-lance.

suzerain: *u* as in *Susan*.

swath: *a* as in *water* or to rhyme with *cloth*.

syndrome: two syllables (formerly three).

Taoiseach: *tee*-sh'kh, the last sound pronounced like *ch* in *loch*.

taxidermist: stress on 1st syllable.

temporarily: stress on 1st syllable: *temp*-ra-rily. ● Not tempo-*rar*-ily.

Tibetan: 2nd syllable like *bet*, not *beat*.

tirade: tie-*raid*.

tissue: as for **issue**.

tonne: sounds like *ton*. ● To avoid misunderstanding, *metric* can be prefixed; but in most spoken contexts the slight difference between the weights will not matter.

tortoise: as for **porpoise**.

tourniquet: 3rd syllable like *croquet* (Amer. turn-a-*kit*).

towards: the form with two syllables is now the most common; some speakers say tords.

trachea: stress on *e* (Amer. on 1st *a*, pronounced as in *trade*).

trait: 2nd *t* is silent (in Amer. pronunciation, it is sounded).

trajectory: stress on 1st syllable or (and Amer.) on 2nd.

transferable: stress on 2nd syllable.

transition: tran-*zish*-on. ● tran-*sizh*-on is now rare.

transparent: last two syllables like *apparent* or *parent*.

trauma, traumatic: *au* as in *cause* (Amer. as in *gaucho*).

traverse (noun): stress on 1st syllable; (verb) on 2nd syllable.

trefoil: stress on 1st syllable, *e* as in *even* or as in *ever*.

triumvir: 1st two syllables like those of *triumphant*.

troth: rhymes with *both* (Amer. with *cloth*).

trow: traditionally rhymes with *know*.

truculent: 1st *u* as in *truck*; formerly as in *true*.

turquoise: *tur*-kwoyz or *tur*-kwahz.

ululate: *yool*-yoo-late.

umbilical: stress on 2nd syllable.

unprecedented: 2nd syllable like *press*.

untoward: the older pronunciation rhymed with *lowered*, but the pronunciation with stress on the 3rd syllable is now usual.

Uranus: stress on 1st or 2nd syllable.

urinal: stress on 1st or 2nd syllable.

usual: in careful speech, avoid complete loss of *u* (*yoo*-zh'l).

uvula: *yoo*-vyoo-la.

uxorious: 1st *u* as *Uxbridge*.

vacuum: now frequently two, not three, syllables (*vak*-yoom).

vagary: now stressed on 1st, rather than 2nd, syllable.

vagina, vaginal: stress on 2nd syllable, *i* as in *china*.

valance: rhymes with *balance*.

valence, -cy (chemistry): *a* as in *ale*.

valet: those who employ them sound the *t*.

valeting: rhymes with **balloting**.

Valkyrie: stress on 1st syllable.

vase: *a* as in *dance* (Amer. rhymes with *face* or *phase*).

veld: sounds like *felt*.

venison: *ven*-i-z'n or *ven*-i-s'n are usual.

veterinary: stress on 1st syllable, with reduction (*vet*-rin-ry). ● Not *vet*-nary or (Amer.) *vet*-rin-ery.

vice (in *vice versa*): rhymes with *spicy*.

vicegerent: three syllables, 2nd *e* as in *errant*.

victualler, victuals: sound like *vitt*-ell-er, vittles.

viola (instrument): stress on 2nd syllable, *i* as in *Fiona*; (flower) stress on 1st syllable, *i* as in *vie*.

vitamin: *i* as in *hit* (Amer. as in *vital*).

viz. (= videlicet): in speech, it is customary to say *namely*.

voluntarily: stress on 1st syllable.

waistcoat: the older pronunciation was *wess*-kot (with 2nd syllable like *mascot*); but now usually as spelt.

walnut, walrus: ● do not drop the *l*.

werewolf: 1st syllable like *weir* or *wear*.

whoop (cry of excitement): = woop; (cough) = hoop; both rhyme with *loop*.

wrath: rhymes with *cloth* (Amer. with *hath*).

wroth: as for **troth**.

yoghurt: *yogg*-urt (Amer. *yoh*-gurt).

zoology: in careful speech, best pronounced with 1st *o* as in *zone*. ● The common pronunciation zoo-*ol*-ogy is considered incorrect by some people.

Vocabulary

This section is concerned with problems of meaning, construction, derivation, and diction. The main aim is to recommend the meaning or construction most appropriate for formal writing or speaking, but some attention is paid to informal and American usage.

aboriginal (noun) should be used in formal contexts as the singular of *aborigines*. However, when referring to the aboriginal inhabitants of Australia, *Aborigine* and *Aborigines* (with capitals) are now preferred.

account, to reckon, consider, is not followed by *as*, e.g. *Account him wise*.

affect, to have an influence on, e.g. *Hugh was immensely affected by the way Randall had put it* (Iris Murdoch).
  ● Do not confuse with *effect* to accomplish, e.g. *Effect changes.* ● There is a noun *effect* 'result, property', e.g. *to good effect, personal effects*; but no noun *affect* except in the specialized language of Psychology.

affinity *between* or *with*, not *to* or *for*, e.g. *Ann felt an affinity with them* (Iris Murdoch); *Points of affinity between Stephen and Bloom* (Anthony Burgess).

afflict: see **inflict.**

aftermath can be used of any after-effects, e.g. *The aftermath of war*. It is pedantic to object to the sense 'unpleasant consequences' on the ground of derivation.

agenda (from a Latin plural) is usually a singular noun (with plural *agendas*), e.g. *It's a short agenda, by the way* (Edward Hyams). But it is occasionally found as a plural meaning 'things to be done' (singular *agendum*).

aggravate (1) To make worse. (2) To annoy, exasperate.
  ● Sense (2) is regarded by some people as incorrect, but is common informally. The participial adjective *aggravating* is often used in sense (2) by good writers, e.g. *He had pronounced*

and aggravating views (Graham Greene).

ain't (= are not, is not, have not, has not) is not used in Standard English except in representations of dialect speech, or humorously. *Aren't* (= are not) is also a recognized colloquialism for *am not* in *aren't I*.

alibi, a claim that when an alleged act took place one was elsewhere.
  ● The sense 'an excuse' is unacceptable to some people, e.g. *Low spirits make you seem complaining .. I have an alibi because I'm going to have a baby* (L. P. Hartley).

all of (= the whole of, every one of) is usual before pronouns, e.g. *And so say all of us*, or often paralleling *none of* etc. before nouns, e.g. *Marshall Stone has all of the problems but none of the attributes of a star* (Frederic Raphael). Otherwise *all* + noun is normal, e.g. *All the King's men*.
  ● The general use of *all of* before nouns is Amer. only.

all right. This phrase is popularly thought of as a unit, e.g. *an all-right bloke*, but the expression remains largely an informal one.
  ● *Alright* remains non-standard, even where the standard spelling is cumbersome, as in: *I just wanted to make sure it was all all right* (Iris Murdoch).

allude means 'refer indirectly'; an *allusion* is 'an indirect reference', e.g. *He would allude to her .. but never mention her by name* (E. M. Forster).
  ● The words are not mere synonyms for *refer, reference*.

alternative (adjective and noun). The use of *alternative* with reference to more than two options, though sometimes criticized, is acceptable, e.g. *Many alternative methods.* ● Do not confuse with *alternate* happening or following in turns, e.g. *Alternate joy and misery*. The use of *alternate* for *alternative* is, however, acceptable in Amer. English:

Liaison and Reserve watched alternate exits in buildings (Norman Mailer).

altogether. ● Beware of using *altogether* (meaning 'in total') when *all together* (meaning 'all at once, all in one place') is meant, e.g. *They went up all together to the hotel and sat down to tea* (John Galsworthy). But *altogether* is correct in *There's too much going on altogether at the moment* (Evelyn Waugh).

amend, to alter to something better, e.g. *If you consider my expression inadequate I am willing to amend it* (G. B. Shaw); noun *amendment*.

● Do not confuse with *emend* to remove errors from (something written), e.g. *An instance of how the dictionary may be emended or censored* (Frederic Raphael); noun *emendation*. An *emendation* will almost always be an *amendment*, but the converse is not true.

analogous means 'similar in certain respects'. It is not a mere synonym for *similar*.

anticipate (1) To be aware of (something) in advance and take suitable action, to deal with (a thing) or perform (an action) in advance, e.g. *His power to .. anticipate every change of volume and tempo* (C. Day Lewis); *I shall anticipate any such opposition by tendering my resignation now* (Angus Wilson); *She had anticipated execution by suicide* (Robert Graves).

(2) To forestall (another person), e.g. *I'm sorry—do go on. I did not mean to anticipate you* (John le Carré).

(3) To expect, regard as probable (an event), e.g. *Serious writers .. anticipated that the detective story might supersede traditional fiction; Left-wing socialists really anticipated a Fascist dictatorship* (A. J. P. Taylor).

● Sense (3) is well established in informal use, but is regarded as incorrect by many people. Use *expect* in formal contexts. In any case, *anticipate* cannot be followed, as *expect* can, by the infinitive (*I expect to see him* or *him to come*) or a personal object (*I expect him today*) and cannot mean 'expect as one's due' (*I expect good behaviour from pupils*).

antithetical means 'contrasted, opposite', not merely 'opposed'.

appraise, to estimate the value or quality of, e.g. *I appraised her skills*.

● Do not confuse with *apprise*, to inform, e.g. *Apprised, sir, of my daughter's sudden flight .., I followed her at once* (Oscar Wilde).

approve (1) (Followed by direct object) authorize, e.g. *The naval plan was approved by the war council* (A. J. P. Taylor).

(2) (With *of*) consider good, e.g. *All the books approved of by young persons of cultivated taste* (C. P. Snow).

● *Approve* should not be used in sense (2) with a direct object, as (wrongly) in *Laziness, rudeness, and untidiness are not approved in this establishment* (correctly, *approved of*).

apt, followed by the *to*-infinitive, carries no implication that the state or action expressed by the verb is undesirable from the point of view of its grammatical subject (though it often is from that of the writer), e.g. *In weather like this he is apt to bowl at the batsman's head* (Robert Graves). It indicates that the subject has a habitual tendency, e.g. *Time was apt to become confusing* (Muriel Spark). Compare **liable**, which, however, is not complementary to *apt to*, but overlaps with it; *apt to*, followed by a verb with undesirable overtones, = 'habitually or customarily liable to'.

Arab is now the usual term for 'native of Arabia' or an Arabic-speaking country, not *Arabian*.

aren't: see **ain't**.

Argentine, Argentinian can be both noun (= a native of Argentina) and adjective (= belonging to Argentina).

● Only the former is used in *Argentine Republic*. It rhymes with *turpentine*.

artiste, a professional public performer of either sex.

as (1) = *that*, *which*, or *who* (relative) is now non-standard except after *same*, *such*, e.g. *Such countries as France*; but not *I know somebody who knows this kid as went blind* (Alan Sillitoe, representing regional speech).

(2) = *that* (conjunction), introducing a

noun clause, is now non-standard, e.g. in *I don't know as you'll like it.*

as from is used in formal dating to mean 'on and after' (a date), e.g. *As from 15 October. As of*, originally Amer., has the same meaning and use.

● *As of now, yesterday*, and the like, are informal only.

Asian (1) *Asian* is to be preferred when used of persons to *Asiatic*, which is now widely considered derogatory. *Asiatic* is acceptable in e.g. *Asiatic cholera.*

(2) In Britain an *Asian* is also a person who comes from (or whose parents come from) the Indian subcontinent.

aside from: Amer., = apart from, except for.

as if, as though (1) Followed by the past tense when the verb refers to an unreal possibility, e.g. *It's not as though he lived like a Milord* (Evelyn Waugh). (2) Followed by the present tense when the statement is true, or might be true, e.g. *I suppose you get on pretty well with your parents. You look as though you do* (Kingsley Amis).

attention. *Someone called it to my attention* (Alison Lurie) represents an illogical reversal of the idiom; *someone called* (or *drew*) *my attention to it* or *someone brought it to my attention* would be better in formal contexts.

author (verb) is a rarely required synonym for *write*; *co-author*, however, is acceptable as a verb.

avenge: one avenges an injured person or oneself *on* (occasionally *against*) an offender, or a wrong *on* an offender; the noun is *vengeance* (*on*), and the idea is usually of justifiable retribution, as distinct from **revenge**.

avert, to ward off (a danger), e.g. *Many disastrous sequels to depression might be averted if the victims received support* (William Styron).

● Do not confuse with *escape*, as this writer has done: *On a couple of occasions he only narrowly averted being arrested.*

aware is normally followed by an *of*-phrase or a *that*-clause, but can also be preceded by an adverb in the sense 'aware of, appreciative of (the subject indicated by the adverb)', a chiefly Amer. use, e.g. *The most technically aware* (W. S. Graham).

● In popular usage *aware* is sometimes used alone in the sense 'well-informed', e.g. *a very aware person.* This use should be avoided in formal contexts.

bacteria is the plural of *bacterium*, not a singular noun.

baluster, a short, fat pillar, especially in a balustrade; *banister*, an upright supporting a stair handrail (usually plural).

beg the question, to assume the truth of what is to be proved, e.g. *That pompous question-begging word 'Evolution'* (H. G. Wells). ● It does not mean (1) to avoid giving a straight answer; or (2) to invite the obvious question (that . .).

behalf: *on behalf of X* (= in X's interest, as X's representative) should not be confused with *on the part of X* (= done by X); *behalf* cannot replace *part* in *His death was due to panic on his part.*

benign (in Medicine) has *malignant* as its antonym.

beside (preposition) is used of spatial relationships, or in figurative adaptations of these, e.g. *Beside oneself with joy*; *Quite beside the point*; *besides* = in addition to, other than, e.g. *Eros includes other things besides sexual activity* (C. S. Lewis).

between. There is no objection to the use of *between* to express relations, actions, etc. involving more than two parties; *among* should not be substituted in, e.g., *Cordial relations between Britain, Greece, and Turkey.* See also **choose between**.

bi- (prefix). *Biannual* = appearing (etc.) twice a year; *biennial* = recurring (etc.) every two years. *Bimonthly, biweekly*, and *biyearly* mean either 'twice' or 'every two', and are therefore best avoided.

● Use *twice a month* or *semi-monthly, twice a week* or *semi-weekly*, and *twice a year* in the first sense, and *every two months, fortnightly* or *every two weeks*, and *every two years* in the second sense.

billion, etc. (1) Traditional British usage has a *billion* = a million million (1,000,000,000,000 = 10^{12}), a *trillion* = a million^3 (10^{18}), and a *quadrillion* = a million^4 (10^{24}).

(2) The US usage makes each 'step' from *million* to *quadrillion*, and beyond, a power of 1,000; i.e. *million* = 1000^2, *billion* = 1000^3, *trillion* = 1000^4, *quadrillion* = 1000^5.

(3) For the quantity 'thousand million' (1000^3 = 10^9), many people now use the American *billion*. Most British national newspapers have officially adopted it too.

● In general contexts it is probably safer to use *thousand million* (X,000 m.). But where the sense is vague, e.g. *A billion miles away*, *Billions of stars*, the exact value is immaterial. Note that American *trillion* (10^{12}) = traditional British *billion*.

but = 'except', followed by a pronoun: see p. 77.

candelabra is strictly speaking the plural of *candelabrum* and is best kept so in written English.

● *Candelabra* (singular), *candelabras* (plural) are often found in informal use.

censure, to criticize harshly and unfavourably. ● Do not confuse with *censor* to suppress (the whole or parts of books, plays, etc.).

centre about, (a)round, meaning (figuratively) 'to revolve around, have as its main centre' is criticized by many authorities, though used by good writers, e.g. *A rather restless, cultureless life, centring round tinned food*, Picture Post, *the radio and the internal combustion engine* (George Orwell). It can be avoided by using *to be centred in* or *on*.

century. Strictly, since the first century ran from the year 1 to the year 100, the first year of a given century should be that ending in the digits 01, and the last year of the preceding century should be the year before.

● In popular usage, understandably, the reference of these terms has been moved back, so that the twenty-first century will be regarded as running from 2000 to 2099. Beware of ambiguity here.

character. ● Avoid using adjective + *character* to replace an abstract noun, e.g. write *the antiquity of the fabric*, not *the ancient character of the fabric*.

charisma (1) Properly, a theological word (plural *charismata*) designating any of the gifts of the Holy Spirit. (2) In general use, the capacity to inspire followers with devotion and enthusiasm. The adjective is *charismatic*.

choose between: this construction, and *choice between,* are normally followed by *and* in written English but sometimes by *or,* e.g. *The poorest girl alive may not be able to choose between being Queen of England or Principal of Newnham; but she can choose between ragpicking and flowerselling* (G. B. Shaw).

chronic is used of a disease that is long-lasting, though perhaps intermittent (the opposite is *acute*); it is used similarly of other conditions, e.g. *The commodities of which there is a chronic shortage* (George Orwell). ● The sense 'objectionable, bad, severe' is very informal.

cohort properly means:
(1) an ancient Roman military unit, equal to $1/10$ of a legion; (2) a band of warriors; (3) a group of persons banded together in common cause; (4) a group of persons with a common statistical characteristic.

● The sense 'companion, ally', though quite common, especially in Amer. English, is much criticized and should be avoided.

comparable is followed by *with* in sense (1) of *compare* and by *to* in sense (2). The latter is much the more usual use, e.g. *The little wooden crib-figures* .. *were by no means comparable to the mass-produced figures* (Muriel Spark).

compare. In formal use, the following distinctions of sense are made: (1) 'Make a comparison of x with y', followed by *with,* e.g. *You've got to compare method with method, and ideal with ideal* (John le Carré).

(2) 'Say to be similar to, liken to', followed by *to,* e.g. *To call a bishop a*

mitred fool and compare him to a mouse (G. B. Shaw).
(3) Intransitively, = 'to stand comparison', followed by *with*, e.g. *The American hipsters' writings cannot begin to compare with the work of .. Celine and Genet* (Norman Mailer).

● *Compare with* is loosely used in sense (2), e.g. *How can you compare the Brigadier with my father?* (John Osborne). Conversely, in the separate clause (*as*) *compared with* or *to x, to* occurs as well as *with*, e.g. *Compared to Sarajevo, Belfast was paradise.*

comparison is usually followed by *with*, especially in *by* or *in comparison with*. It is followed by *to* when the sense is 'the action of likening (to)', e.g. *The comparison of philosophy to a yelping she-dog.*

complaisant, disposed to comply with others' wishes; noun *complaisance.*
● Do not confuse with *complacent* self-satisfied (noun *complacency*).

compose can mean 'constitute, make up' with the constituents as subject and the whole as object, e.g. *The tribes which composed the German nation.* In the passive, the whole is subject and the constituents object, e.g. *The German nation was composed of tribes.*

comprise. The proper constructions with **comprise** are the converse of those used with **compose.** (1) In the active, meaning 'consist of', with the whole as subject and the constituents as object, e.g. *The faculty comprises the following six departments.*
● In sense (1), *comprise* differs from *consist* in not being followed by *of*. Unlike *include, comprise* indicates a comprehensive statement of constituents.
(2) In the passive, meaning 'be embraced *in*', with the constituents as subject and the whole as object, e.g. *Fifty American dollars comprised in a single note* (Graham Greene).
● *Comprise* is often used as a synonym of **compose**, e.g. *The twenty-odd children who now comprise the school* (Miss Read). This is commonly regarded as incorrect, and is worse in the passive, since *comprise* is not followed by *of*; write *The faculty is*

composed (not *comprised*) *of six departments.*

condole, to express sympathy, is always followed by *with*, e.g. *Many .. had come .. to condole with them about their brother* (*Revised English Bible*).
● Do not confuse with *console* 'to comfort', followed by direct object.

conduce, to lead or contribute (to a result), is always followed by *to*; similarly *conducive* (adjective); e.g. *The enterprise .. conduced to cut-price jobs* (J. I. M. Stewart).

conform may be followed by *to* or *with*, e.g. *The United Nations .. conformed to Anglo-American plans* (A. J. P. Taylor); *Having himself no .. tastes he relied upon whatever conformed with those of his companion* (John le Carré).

congeries, a collection of things massed together, is a singular noun, unchanged in the plural. ● The form *congery*, formed in the misapprehension that *congeries* is plural only, is incorrect.

connote, denote. *Connote* means 'to imply in addition to the primary meaning, to imply as a consequence or condition', e.g. *To exploit all the connotations that lie latent in a word* (Anthony Burgess). *Denote* means 'to be the sign of, indicate, signify', e.g. *A proper name .. denotes a person* (Stephen Ullman).
● The two terms are kept rigidly distinct in Logic, but in popular usage *connote* frequently verges on the sense of *denote*. *Denote* cannot be used in the senses of *connote*, e.g. in *His silence does not connote hesitation* (Iris Murdoch).

consequent, following as a result, adverb *consequently*, e.g. *Two engaged in a common pursuit do not consequently share personal identity* (Muriel Spark). These are nearly always to be used rather than *consequential* 'following indirectly' and *consequentially*, which are more specialized.

consist: *consist of* = be made up of; *consist in* = have as its essence, e.g. *All enjoyment consists in undetected sinning* (G. B. Shaw).

continual, frequently recurring; *continuous*, uninterrupted; similarly the adverbs; e.g. *He was continually sending . . military advice* (Robert Graves); *There was a continuous rattle from the one-armed bandits* (Graham Greene).

continuance, continuation. The former relates mainly to the sense of *continue* 'to be still in existence', the latter to the sense 'to resume', e.g. *The great question of our continuance after death* (J. S. Huxley); *As if contemplating a continuation of her assault* (William Trevor).

cousin (1) The children of brothers or sisters are *first cousins* to each other. (2) The children of first cousins are *second cousins* to each other. (3) The child of one's first cousin, or the first cousin of one's parent, is one's *first cousin once removed*. (4) The grandchild of one's first cousin, or the first cousin of one's grandparent, is one's *first cousin twice removed*; and so on. (5) *Cousin-german* = first cousin.

credible, believable. ● Do not confuse with *credulous*, gullible, as e.g. in *Even if one is credible* (correctly *credulous*) *enough to believe in their ability*.

crescendo, used figuratively, means 'a progressive increase in force or effect'. Do not use it for *climax*, e.g. in *The storm reached a crescendo* (correctly *a climax*) *at midnight*.

criteria is the plural of *criterion*, not a singular noun.

crucial, decisive, critical, e.g. *His medical studies were not merely an episode in the development of his persona but crucial to it* (Frederic Raphael). ● The weakened sense 'important' is informal only.

data (1) In scientific, philosophical, and general use, usually treated as plural, e.g. *The optical data are incomplete* (*Nature*); the singular is *datum*. (2) In computing and allied fields it is treated as a mass noun (i.e. a collective item), and used with words like *this*, *that*, and *much*, and with singular verbs; it is sometimes so treated in general use. ● Some people object to use (2), though it is more common than use (1). ● *Data* cannot be preceded by *a*, *every*, *each*, *either*, *neither*, and cannot be given a plural form *datas*.

decidedly, decisively. *Decidedly*, undoubtedly, e.g. *The bungalow had a decidedly English appearance* (Muriel Spark). *Decisively* (1) conclusively, e.g. *The definition of 'capital' itself depends decisively on the level of technology employed* (E. F. Schumacher); (2) unhesitatingly, e.g. *The young lady . . decisively objected to him* (G. B. Shaw).

decimate (originally) to kill or destroy one in every ten of; (now usually) to destroy a large proportion of, e.g. *All my parents' friends, my friends' brothers were getting killed. Our circle was decimated* (Rosamond Lehmann). ● *Decimate* does not mean 'defeat utterly'.

decline (verb: to refuse) has no derived noun; we have to make do with *refusal* if *declining* cannot be used.

definitive, decisive, unconditional, final; (of an edition) authoritative; e.g. *The Gold Cup flat handicap, the official and definitive result of which he had read in the Evening Telegraph* (James Joyce). ● Do not use instead of *definite* (= distinct, precise). A *definite no* is a firm refusal. A *definitive no* is an authoritative decision that something is not the case.

delusion, illusion. A general distinction can be drawn, though it is not absolute. *Delusion* denotes a false belief held tenaciously, arising mainly from the internal workings of the mind; e.g. *He's been sent here for delusions. His most serious delusion is that he's a murderer* (Robert Graves). *Illusion* denotes a false impression derived either from the external world, e.g. *optical illusion*, or from faulty thinking, e.g. *I still imagine I could live in Rome, but it may be an illusion* (Iris Murdoch). It is in this second sense that *illusion* is almost equivalent to *delusion*; cf. *I have no delusions that knock-outs are likely* (Frederic Raphael). *Delusion* carries the sense of *being deluded* (by oneself or another), whereas no verb is implied in *illusion*; on the other hand, one can be said to be *disillusioned*, whereas *delusion* forms no such derivative.

demean (1) *Demean oneself* = behave (usually with adverbial expression), e.g. *He demeaned himself well*. This is now rare. (2) *Demean* (*someone* or *something*) = lower in status, especially with *oneself*, e.g. *Nor must you think that you demean yourself by treading the boards* (W. Somerset Maugham).

denote: see **connote**.

depend, to be controlled or determined by (a condition or cause), is followed by *on* or *upon*.

● The use of *it depends* followed, without *on* or *upon*, by an interrogative clause, is informal only, e.g. *It depends how you tackle the problem*.

depreciate, deprecate. *Depreciate* (1) to make or become lower in value; (2) to belittle, disparage, e.g. *To defend our record we seem forced to depreciate the Africans* (*Listener*); *To become a little more forthcoming and less self-depreciating* (Richard Adams).

Deprecate (1) (with a plan, purpose, etc. as the object) to deplore, e.g. *I deprecate this extreme course, because it is good neither for my pocket nor for their own souls* (G. B. Shaw). (2) (with a person as the object) to express disapproval of, disparage, e.g. *Anyone who has reprinted his reviews is in no position to deprecate our reprinter* (Christopher Ricks).

● Sense (2) of *deprecate* tends to take on the sense of *depreciate* (2), especially in conjunction with *self*. This use is frequently found in good writers, e.g. *A humorous self-deprecation about one's own advancing senility* (Aldous Huxley). It is, however, widely regarded as incorrect.

derisive = scoffing; *derisory* = (1) scoffing, (2) so small or unimportant as to be ridiculous (now the more usual sense), e.g. *The £40 . . you'll pay for any of the current sets is derisory compared with the £16.50 charged . . 39 years ago* (*Independent*).

dialect (form of speech) forms *dialectal* as its adjective; *dialectic* (form of reasoning) can be adjective as well as noun, or can have *dialectical* as its adjective.

dice is the normal singular as well as the plural; the old singular, *die*, is found only in *the die is cast, straight* (or *true*) *as a die*, and in mathematical contexts.

dichotomy in non-technical use means 'differentiation into two contrasting categories' and is frequently followed by *between*, e.g. *An absolute dichotomy between science on the one hand and faith on the other*.

● It does not mean *dilemma* or *ambivalence*.

die (noun): see **dice**.

different can be followed by *from, to,* or *than*.

(1) *Different from* is the most favoured by good writers, and is acceptable in all contexts, e.g. *It is also an 'important' book, in a sense different from the sense in which that word is generally used* (George Orwell).

(2) *Different to* is common informally. It sometimes sounds more natural than *different from*, e.g. when yoked with *similar* and followed by a phrase introduced by *to*: *His looks are neither especially similar nor markedly different to those of his twin brother*.

(3) *Different than* is established in Amer. English, but is not uncommon in British use, e.g. *Both came from a different world than the housing estate outside London* (Doris Lessing). *Different than* usefully avoids the repetition and the relative construction required after *different from* in sentences like *I was a very different man in 1935 from what I was in 1916* (Joyce Cary). This could be recast as *I was a very different man in 1935 than I was in 1916* or *than in 1916*. Compare *The American theatre, which is suffering from a different malaise than ours*, which is greatly preferable to *suffering from a different malaise from that which ours is suffering from*.

Uses (2) and (3) are long established, and are especially common when *different* is part of an adverbial clause (e.g. *in a different way*) or when the adverb *differently* is used, e.g. *Things were constructed very differently now than in former times* (Trollope); *Puts one in a different position to your own father* (John Osborne).

differential, a technical term in Mathematics, an abbreviation for *differential gear*, or a difference in wage between groups of workers. ● It is not a synonym for *difference*.

digraph = two letters standing for a single sound, e.g. *ea* in *head*, *gh* in *cough*; *ligature* = a typographical symbol consisting of two letters joined together, e.g. fi, fl, æ, œ. The term *diphthong* is best restricted to the sense 'a union of two vowels pronounced in one syllable', e.g. *i* in *find*, *ei* in *rein*, and *eau* in *bureau*.

dilemma (1) A choice between two (or more) undesirable alternatives, e.g. *The dilemma of cutting public services or increasing taxes* (*The Times*). (2) More loosely, a perplexing situation involving choice, e.g. *The dilemma of the 1960s about whether nice girls should sleep with men* (Alan Watkins). ● It is not merely a synonym for *problem*.

diphthong: see **digraph**.

direct is used as an adverb meaning: (1) straight, e.g. *Another door led direct to the house* (Evelyn Waugh); (2) without intermediaries, e.g. *I appeal now, over your head, .. direct to the august oracle* (G. B. Shaw).

directly is used in most of the main senses of the adjective, e.g. *Why don't you deal directly with the wholesalers?* (G. B. Shaw); *The wind is blowing directly on shore*; *directly opposite, opposed*.

● It is not usually used to mean 'straight', since it can also mean 'without delay', e.g. *Just a night in London—I'll be back directly* (Iris Murdoch).

discomfit, to thwart, disconcert; similarly *discomfiture*. ● Do not confuse with *discomfort* (now rare as a verb, = make uneasy).

disinterest, lack of interest, indifference, e.g. *Buried the world under a heavy snowfall of disinterest* (Christopher Fry).

● The use of *disinterest* in this sense may be objected to on the same grounds as sense (2) of **disinterested**;

but the word is rarely used in any other sense.

disinterested (1) Impartial, unbiased, e.g. *Thanks to his scientific mind he understood—a proof of disinterested intelligence which had pleased her* (Virginia Woolf). The noun is *disinterestedness*. (2) Uninterested, indifferent, e.g. *It is not that we are disinterested in these subjects, but that we are better qualified to talk about our own interests* (*The Times*). The noun is **disinterest**.

● Sense (2) is common, but is widely regarded as incorrect and is avoided by careful writers, who prefer *uninterested*.

disposal is the noun from *dispose of* (get off one's hands, deal with); *disposition* is from *dispose* (arrange, incline).

distinctive, characteristic, e.g. *A light, entirely distinctive smell* (Susan Hill).

● Do not confuse with *distinct*, separate, individual, definite, e.g. *Trying to put into words an impression that was not distinct in my own mind* (W. Somerset Maugham).

drunk, drunken. In older and literary usage, the predicative and attributive forms respectively; now usually meaning respectively 'intoxicated' and 'fond of drinking', e.g. *They were lazy, irresponsible, and drunken; but today they were not drunk. Drunken* also means 'exhibiting drunkenness', e.g. *a drunken brawl*.

due to (1) That ought to be given to, e.g. *The respect due to the boss's nephew* (Vladimir Nabokov). (2) To be ascribed to, e.g. *Half the diseases of modern civilization are due to starvation of the affections in the young* (G. B. Shaw). *Due* is here an adjective, which needs to be attached to a noun as complement (see example above), or as part of a verbless adjective clause, e.g. *A few days' temporary absence of mind due to sunstroke* (Muriel Spark). (3) = *owing to*. Good writers now not uncommonly use *due to* as a compound preposition, where no noun is involved, e.g. *It .. didn't begin until twenty past due to a hitch* (William Trevor).

● This third use of *due to* is widely regarded as unacceptable. It can often be avoided by the addition of the verb *to be* and *that*, e.g. It is *due to your provident care* that .. *improvements are being made* (*Revised English Bible*).

effect: see **affect**.

e.g., i.e.: *E.g.* (short for Latin *exempli gratia*) = for example: *Many countries of Asia, e.g. India, Indonesia, and Malaysia. I.e.* (short for Latin *id est*) = that is: *It was natural that the largest nation* (*i.e. India*) *should take the lead*.

egoism, -ist(ic), egotism, -ist(ic). *Egoism* denotes self-interest (often contrasted with *altruism*), e.g. *Egoistic instincts concerned with self-preservation or the good of the Ego* (Gilbert Murray). *Egotism* is the practice of talking or thinking excessively about oneself, self-centredness, e.g. *He is petty, selfish, vain, egotistical; he is spoilt; he is a tyrant* (Virginia Woolf).

● In practice the senses tend to overlap, e.g. *Human loves don't last, .. they are far too egoistic* (Iris Murdoch); *A complete egotist in all his dealings with women* (Joyce Cary).

egregious, flagrant, outrageous; used mainly with words like *ass, folly, waste*, e.g. *Wark tenderly forgives her most egregious clerical errors* (Martin Amis). It does not mean simply 'offending, errant' as in *If sanctuary officers spot a particularly egregious diver they will direct him to the surface*.

either (adjective and pronoun). (1) One or other of the two, e.g. *Simple explanations are for simple minds. I've no use for either* (Joe Orton). (2) Each of the two, e.g. *Every few kilometres on either side of the road, there were .. guardposts* (Graham Greene).

● *Either* is frequently used in sense (2), with reference to a thing that comes naturally in a pair, e.g. *end, hand, side*. This use is sometimes ignorantly condemned but is commonly found in good writers of all periods.

elder (adjective) the earlier-born (of two related or indicated persons), e.g. *The first and elder wife .. returned .. to Jericho* (Muriel Spark); *He is my elder by ten years. Eldest* first-born or oldest surviving (member of family etc.).

elusive (rather than *elusory*) is the usual adjective related to *elude*; *illusory* (rather than *illusive*) is that related to *illusion*.

enjoin: one can enjoin an action, etc., *on* someone, or enjoin someone *to* do something; e.g. *To .. enjoin celibacy on its .. clergy* and *That enables and enjoins the citizen to earn his own living* (G. B. Shaw). In legal writing, *to enjoin* (a person) *from* (doing something) is also found.

enormity (1) Great wickedness (of something), e.g. *Hugh was made entirely speechless .. by the enormity of the proposal* (Iris Murdoch); a serious offence, e.g. *To pass sentence on Wingfield for his enormities* (David Garnett). (2) Enormousness. ● Sense (2) is common, but is regarded by many people as incorrect.

enthuse, to show or fill with enthusiasm, is chiefly informal.

● **equally as** (+ adjective) should not be used for *equally*, e.g. in *How to apply it was equally as important*, or for *as*, e.g. *The Government are equally as guilty as the Opposition*.

event: *in the event of* is followed by a noun or gerund, e.g. *In the event of the earl's death, the title will lapse*.

● *In the event that*, used for *if*, is avoided by good writers; it is even less acceptable with *that* omitted, e.g. *In the event the car overturns*.

ever. When placed after a *wh*-question word, *ever* should be written separately, e.g. *Where ever have you been?, when ever is he coming?, who ever would have thought it?, why ever did you do it?, how ever shall I escape?* When used with a relative pronoun or adverb to give it force, *ever* is written as one word with it, e.g. *Wherever you go I'll follow; whenever he washes up he breaks something; there's a reward for whoever* (not *whomever*) *finds it; whatever else you do, don't get lost; however it's done, it's difficult.*

evidence, evince. *Evidence* (verb), to attest, e.g. *There was an innate refinement .. about Gerty which was* *unmistakably evidenced in her delicate hands* (James Joyce).

Evince, to show that one has (a quality), e.g. *Highly evolved sentiments and needs (sometimes said to be distinctively human, though birds and animals .. evince them)* (G. B. Shaw).

● *Evince* should not be confused with *evoke* to call up (a response, a feeling, etc.), e.g. *A timely and generous act which evoked a fresh outburst of emotion* (James Joyce).

exceedingly, extremely; *excessively,* beyond measure, immoderately.

excepting (preposition) is only used after *not* and *always*.

exceptionable, to which exception may be taken; *unexceptionable* with which no fault may be found, e.g. *The opposite claim would seem to him unexceptionable even if he disagreed with it* (George Orwell).

● Do not confuse with *(un)exceptional,* that is (not) unusual or outstanding.

excess. *In excess of.* ● Prefer *more than,* e.g. in *The Data Centre, which processes in excess of 1200 jobs per week.*

expect (1) in the sense 'suppose, think' is informal; (2) see **anticipate.**

explicit, express. *Explicit,* leaving nothing implied, e.g. *I had been too tactful, .. too vague .. But I now saw that I ought to have been more explicit* (Iris Murdoch); *express,* definite, unmistakable in import, e.g. *Idolatry fulsome enough to irritate Jonson into an express disavowal of it* (G. B. Shaw).

exposure (to) should not be used for *experience (of)*, e.g. in *Candidates who have had exposure to North American markets.*

express (adjective): see **explicit.**

facility in the sense 'ease in doing something', e.g. *I knew that I had a facility with words* (George Orwell), should not be confused with a similar sense of *faculty,* viz. 'specific ability', e.g. *Hess .. had that odd faculty, peculiar to lunatics, of falling into strained positions* (Rebecca West).

factious: see **fractious.**

factitious, not natural; artificial; e.g. *Factitious value. Fictitious,* simulated; imaginary, e.g. *Rumours of false*

accounting and fictitious loans (*The Economist*).

farther, farthest: though originally interchangeable with *further, furthest,* these words are now only used where the sense of 'distance' is involved, e.g. *The farther mysteries of the cosmos* (J. I. M. Stewart). ● Even in this sense many people prefer *further, furthest.*

feasible, capable of being done, e.g. *Young people believing that niceness and innocence are politically as well as morally feasible* (J. I. M. Stewart).

● It is sometimes used for 'possible' or 'probable', but whichever of these is appropriate should be used instead.

fewer: see **less.**

fictitious: see **factitious.**

flammable, easily set on fire; preferable as a warning of danger to *inflammable,* which may be mistaken for a negative. The real negatives are *non-flammable* and *non-inflammable.*

flaunt, to display ostentatiously, e.g. *He's unemployed by the way, so don't flaunt your fabulous wealth in front of him* (Joseph O'Connor).

● Do not confuse with *flout* 'to disobey openly and scornfully', e.g. *His deliberate flouting of one still supposedly iron rule* (Frederic Raphael): *flout* should have been used by the public figure reported as having said *Those wanting to flaunt the policy would recognize that public opinion was not behind them.*

following, consequent on, is used in two ways. (1) Properly, as an adjective, dependent on a preceding noun, e.g. *During demonstrations following the hanging of two British soldiers.* (2) By extension, as a quasi-preposition, e.g. *The prologue was written by the company following an incident witnessed by them.*

● Many people regard use (2) as erroneous (cf. **due to** (3)). It can also give rise to ambiguity, e.g. *Police arrested a man following the hunt.* In any case, *following* should not be used merely for *after* (e.g. *Following supper they went to bed*).

for . The subject of a clause of which the verb is the *to-* infinitive is normally preceded by *for*, e.g. *For him to stay elsewhere is unthinkable*. But if the clause is a direct object, *for* is omitted: hence *I could not bear for him to stay elsewhere* is non-standard.

forbid can be followed by a personal object and a *to*-infinitive, e.g. *My means forbade me to indulge in such delightful fantasies* (Lawrence Durrell) or by an *-ing* form (see p. 83 f.), e.g. *Politeness .. forbade my doubting them* (Dickens). ● Do not use with *from* as in *She has an injunction forbidding him from calling her on the telephone*.

forensic (1) of or used in courts of law, e.g. *forensic science*; (2) of or involving forensic science, e.g. *forensic examination*. ● Sense (2) is often deplored, but is widespread.

former (latter). When referring to the first (last) of three or more, *the first* (*the last*) should be used, not *the former* (*the latter*).

fortuitous means 'happening by chance', e.g. *His presence is not fortuitous. He has a role to play* (André Brink).

● It does not mean either 'fortunate' or 'timely', as (incorrectly) in *He could not believe it. It was too fortuitous to be chance.*

fractious, unruly; peevish. ● Do not confuse with *factious* 'given to, or proceeding from, faction', e.g. *A divisive past and a fractious* (correctly, *factious*) *present*.

fruition, fulfilment, especially in *be brought to, come to, grow to, reach*, etc. *fruition*, once stigmatized, is now standard.

fulsome is a pejorative term, applied to *flattery, praise, affection*, etc., and means 'cloying, disgusting by excess', e.g. *They listened to fulsome speeches* (Beryl Bainbridge). ● *Fulsome* is not now regarded as a synonym of *copious*, its original meaning.

further, furthest: see **farther, farthest**.

geriatric means 'pertaining to the health and welfare of the elderly'; it is very informal (and may be offensive) to use it for *old* or *outdated*, or as a noun meaning 'old, outdated, or senile person'.

gourmand, glutton; *gourmet*, connoisseur of good food.

graffiti is the plural of *graffito*. The use of *graffiti* as a singular or mass noun is regarded as incorrect by some people but is common, e.g. in *Graffiti is an eyesore*.

half. The use of *half* to mean *half-past* is indigenous to Britain and has been remarked on since the 1930s, e.g. *We'd easily get the half-five bus* (William Trevor); it remains non-standard.

hardly. (1) *Hardly* is not used with negative constructions.

● Expressions like *I couldn't hardly tell what he meant* (substitute *I could hardly tell . .*) are non-standard.

(2) *Hardly* and *scarcely* are followed by *when* or *before*, not *than*, e.g. *Hardly had Grimes left the house when a tall young man . . presented himself at the front door* (Evelyn Waugh).

heir apparent, one whose right of inheritance cannot be superseded by the birth of another heir; as opposed to an *heir presumptive*, whose right can be so superseded.

● *Heir apparent* does not mean 'seeming heir'.

help. *More than*, or *as little as*, one can help are illogical but established idioms, e.g. *They will not respect more than they can help treaties extracted from them under duress* (Winston Churchill).

hoi polloi can be preceded by *the*, even though *hoi* is the Greek *the*, e.g. *The screens with which working archaeologists baffle the* hoi polloi (Frederic Raphael).

● **homogenous** is a frequent error for *homogeneous*. A word *homogenous* exists, but only as a technical term in biology. *Homogeneous* means 'of the same kind, uniform', e.g. *The style throughout was homogeneous but the authors' names were multiform* (Evelyn Waugh).

hopefully, thankfully. These adverbs are used in two ways: (1) As adverbs of manner = 'in a hopeful/thankful way', e.g. *I moved to the East Coast, and in 1938 hopefully built another boat* (Arthur Ransome); *When it thankfully* *dawned on her that the travel agency . . would be open* (Muriel Spark). (2) As sentence adverbs, conveying the speaker's comment on the statement, e.g. *Hopefully they will be available in the autumn* (*Guardian*); *The editor, thankfully, has left them as they were written* (TLS).

● Use (2) is very common but regarded by many people as unacceptable. The main reason is that other commenting sentence adverbs, such as *regrettably*, can be converted to the form *it is regrettable that* —, but these are to be resolved as *it is to be hoped that*—and *one is thankful that* —. (The same objection could be, but is not, made to *happily* and *unhappily* which mean *one is* (*un*)*happy* not *it is* (*un*)*happy that* —, e.g. in *Unhappily children do hurt flies* (Jean Rhys).) A further objection is that ambiguity can arise from the interplay of senses (1) and (2), e.g. *Any decision to trust Egypt . . and move forward hopefully toward peace . . in the Middle East* (*Guardian Weekly*). It is recommended that sense (2) should be restricted to informal contexts.

how ever: see **ever**.

i.e.: see **e.g., i.e.**

if in certain constructions (usually linking two adjectives or adverbs) can be ambiguous, e.g. *A great play, if not the greatest, by this author.* ● It is best to paraphrase such sentences as, e.g., either *A great play, though not the greatest by this author* or *A great play, perhaps* (or *very nearly*) *the greatest by this author*.

ignorant is better followed by *of* than by *about*, e.g. *The residents are . . ignorant of their rights* (*Independent*).

ilk. *Of that ilk* is a Scots term, meaning 'of the same place or name', e.g. *Wemyss of that ilk* = Wemyss of Wemyss. ● By a misunderstanding *ilk* has come to mean 'sort, lot' (usually pejorative), e.g. *Joan Baez and other vocalists of that ilk* (David Lodge). This should be avoided in formal English.

ill used predicatively = 'unwell'; *sick* used predicatively = 'about to vomit, in the act of vomiting', e.g. *I felt sick*; *I was violently sick*; used attributively = 'un-

well', e.g. *a sick man*, except in collocations like *sick bay, sick leave*. ● It is non-standard to use *ill* for 'in the act of vomiting' or *sick* predicatively for 'unwell' (though the latter is standard Amer.), except in *off sick* 'away on sick leave'.

illusion: see **delusion**.

illusory: see **elusive**.

impact, used figuratively, is best confined to contexts of someone or something striking another, e.g. *The most dynamic colour combination if used too often loses its impact*. It is weakened if used as a mere synonym for *effect* or *influence*.

impedance, the resistance of an electric circuit to alternating current. ● Do not confuse with *impediment*, a hindrance, a defect (in speech etc.), e.g. *A serious impediment to his marriage* (Evelyn Waugh).

imply, infer. *Imply* (1) to involve the truth or existence of; (2) to express indirectly, insinuate, hint at. *Infer* to reach (an opinion), deduce, from facts and reasoning, e.g. *She left it to my intelligence to infer her meaning. I inferred it all right* (W. Somerset Maugham). ● *Infer* should not be used for sense (2) of *imply*, as in *I have inferred once, and I repeat, that Limehouse is the most overrated excitement in London* (H. V. Morton).

imprimatur, official licence to print. ● Do not confuse with *imprint*, the name of the publisher/printer, place of publication/printing, etc., on the verso of the title-page or at the end of a book.

inapt, inept. *Inapt* = 'not apt', 'unsuitable'; *inept* = (1) unskilful, e.g. *Foxtrots and quicksteps, at which he had been so inept* (David Lodge); (2) inappropriate, e.g. *ineptly dressed*; (3) absurd, silly.

inchoate means 'just begun, underdeveloped', e.g. *Trying to give his work a finished look—and all the time . . the stuff's fatally inchoate* (John Wain). ● It does not mean *chaotic* or *incoherent*.

include: see **comprise** (1).

infer: see **imply**.

inflammable: see **flammable**.

inflict, afflict. One *inflicts* something *on* someone or *afflicts* someone *with* something. ● Do not use *inflict with* where *afflict with* is meant, e.g. in *The miners are still out, and industry is inflicted* (correctly, *afflicted*) *with a kind of creeping paralysis.*

ingenious, clever at inventing, etc.; noun *ingenuity*; *ingenuous* open, frank, innocent; noun *ingenuousness.*

insignia is, in origin, a plural noun, e.g. *Fourteen different airline insignia* (David Lodge); its singular, rarely encountered, is *insigne.* ● Use as a countable noun is non-standard, e.g. in *The insignias that immune system cells use to tell friend from foe.*

intense, existing in a high degree, e.g. *The intense evening sunshine* (Iris Murdoch); *intensive* employing much effort, concentrated, e.g. *Intensive care.*

interface (noun) (1) A surface forming a common boundary, e.g. *The interfaces between solid and solid, solid and liquid.* (2) A piece of equipment in which interaction occurs between two systems, processes, etc., e.g. *Modular interfaces to adapt the general-purpose computer to the equipment.* (3) A point of interaction between two systems, organizations, or disciplines, e.g. *The interface between physics and music* (*Nature*).
● Sense (3) is deplored by many people, since it is often overused for *meeting-point, liaison, link,* etc., e.g. *The need for the interface of lecturer and student will diminish.*

interface (verb), to connect with (another piece of equipment) by an interface, e.g. *Using the Kontron image analyser interfaced to the computer* (*Brain*).
● *Interface* is nowadays regrettably overused as a synonym for *interact* (*with*), as, e.g., in *The ideal candidate will have the ability to interface effectively with other departments.*

internment, confinement (from verb *intern*).
● Do not confuse with *interment,* burial (from verb *inter*).

invite (noun = 'invitation') remains informal only.

ironic, ironical, ironically. The noun *irony* can mean (1) a way of speaking in which the intended meaning (for those with insight) is the opposite to, or very different from, that expressed by the words used; or (2) an ill-timed or perverse outcome.
The adjectives *ironic, ironical,* and the adverb *ironically* are commonly used in sense (1) of *irony,* e.g. *Ironical silent apology for the absence of naked women and tanks of gin from the amenities* (Kingsley Amis). They are also frequently found in sense (2), e.g. *The fact that after all she had been faithful to me was ironic* (Graham Greene). ● Some people object to this use, especially when *ironic* or *ironically* introduces a trivial oddity, e.g. *It was ironic that he thought himself locked out when the key was in his pocket all the time.*

kind of, sort of (1) *A kind of, a sort of* should not be followed by *a* before the noun, e.g. *a kind of shock,* not *a kind of a shock.* (2) *Kind of, sort of,* etc., followed by a plural noun, are often qualified by plural words like *these, those,* or followed by a plural verb, e.g. *They would be on those sort of terms* (Anthony Powell). This is widely regarded as incorrect except in informal use: substitute *that* (etc.) *kind* (or *sort*) *of* or *of that kind* (or *sort*), e.g. *this kind of car is unpopular* or *cars of this kind are unpopular.* (3) *Kind of, sort of* used adverbially, e.g. *I kind of expected it,* are informal only.

kudos is a mass noun like *glory* or *fame.*
● It is not a plural noun and there is no singular *kudo.*

latter: see **former.**

laudable, praiseworthy; *laudatory,* expressing praise.

lay (verb), past *laid,* = 'put down, arrange', etc. is only transitive, e.g. *Lay her on the bed*; *They laid her on the bed.* ● To use *lay* for 'lie', e.g. *She wants to lay down*; *She was laying on the bed,* is non-standard, even though fairly common in speech. Cf. **lie.**

leading question, in Law, is a question that prompts the desired answer, e.g. *The solicitor . . at once asked me some* *leading questions . . I had to try to be both forthcoming and discreet* (C. P. Snow).

● It does not mean a 'principal (or loaded or searching) question'.

learn with a person as the object, = 'teach', is non-standard, or occasionally jocular as in *I'll learn you.*

less (adjective) is the comparative of (*a*) *little*, and, like the latter, is used with mass nouns, e.g. *I owe him little duty and less love* (Shakespeare); *fewer* is the comparative of (*a*) *few*, and both are used with plurals, e.g. *Few people have their houses broken into; and fewer still have them burnt* (G. B. Shaw).

● *Less* is quite often used informally as the comparative of *few*, e.g. *Our copiers have less parts inside them so there's less to go wrong* (*Office Magazine*). This is regarded as incorrect in formal English.

● *Less* should not be used as the comparative of *small* (or some similar adjective such as *low*), e.g. *a lower price* not *a less price*.

lesser, not so great as the other or the rest e.g. *The lesser celandine.* ● *Lesser* should not be used for 'not so big' or 'not so large': its opposition to *greater* is essential. It cannot replace *smaller* in *A smaller prize will probably be offered.*

lest is very formal; it is followed by *should* or (in exalted style) the subjunctive, e.g. *Lest the eye wander aimlessly, a Doric temple stood by the water's edge* (Evelyn Waugh); *Lest some too sudden gesture or burst of emotion should turn the petals brown* (Patrick White).

let, to allow (followed by the bare infinitive) is rare in the passive: the effect is usually unidiomatic, e.g. *Halfdan's two sons . . are let owe their lives to a trick* (Gwyn Jones).

liable (1) can be followed by *to* + a noun or noun phrase in the sense 'subject to, likely to suffer from', or by an infinitive; (2) carries the implication that what is expressed is undesirable, e.g. *Receiving in the bedroom is liable to get a woman talked about* (Tom Stoppard);

(3) can indicate either the mere possibility, or the habituality, of what is expressed by the verb, e.g. *The kind of point that one is always liable to miss* (George Orwell).

● The sense 'likely to' is American, e.g. *Boston is liable to be the ultimate place for holding the convention.* Contrast **apt**.

lie (verb) past *lay, lain,* = 'recline', 'be situated', is only intransitive, e.g. *Lie down on the bed; The ship lay at anchor until yesterday; Her left arm, on which she had lain all night, was numb.* Although correct, *lain* can sound somewhat stilted, and *been lying* is often preferred.

● To use *lie* for 'lay', e.g. *Lie her on the bed,* is non-standard. The past *lay* and participle *lain* are quite often wrongly used for *laid* out of over-correctness, e.g. *He had lain this peer's honour in the dust.* Cf. **lay.**

ligature: see **digraph.**

like, indicating resemblance between two things: (1) It is normally used as an adjective followed by a noun, noun phrase, or pronoun (in the objective case), e.g. *There can't be many fellows about with brains like yours* (P. G. Wodehouse); *He loathes people like you and me* (not . . *and I*). It can be used to mean 'such as', e.g. *Good writers like Dickens.*

● In formal contexts some people prefer *such as* to be used if more than one example is mentioned, e.g. *He dealt in types, such as the rich bitch, the honest whore, the socializing snob* (*London Magazine*).

(2) It is often used as a conjunction with a dependent clause, e.g. *Everything went wrong . . like it does in dreams* (Iris Murdoch), or with an adverbial phrase, e.g. *It was as if I saw myself. Like in a looking-glass* (Jean Rhys). ● Although this use of *like* as a conjunction is not uncommon in formal writing, it is best avoided, except informally. Use *as*, e.g. *Do you mean to murder me as you murdered the Egyptian?* (*Revised English Bible*), or recast the sentence, e.g. *A costume like those that the others wore.*

(3) It is often informally used to mean 'as if', e.g. *You wake like someone hit you on the head* (T. S. Eliot). ● This use is very informal.

likely (adverb), in the sense 'probably', must be preceded by *more, most, quite,* or *very,* e.g. *Its inhabitants .. very likely do make that claim for it* (George Orwell).

● The use without the qualifying adverb is standard only in Amer. English, e.g. *They'll likely turn ugly* (Eugene O'Neill).

linguist means 'one whose subject is linguistics' as well as 'one skilled in the use of languages'; there is no other suitable term (*linguistician* exists but is not commonly used).

literally. In very informal speech, *literally* is used as an intensifying adverb without meaning apart from its emotive force.

● This use should be avoided in writing or formal speech, since it almost invariably involves absurdity, e.g. *The dwarfs mentioned here are literally within a stone's throw of the Milky Way* (*New Scientist*).

loan (verb) has some justification in financial contexts, e.g. *The gas industry is .. loaning money to Government* (*Observer*). It should not be used merely as a variant for *lend*.

locate can mean 'discover the exact position of', e.g. *She had located and could usefully excavate her Saharan highland emporium* (Margaret Drabble); it should not be used to mean merely 'find'.

lot. *A lot of,* though somewhat informal, is acceptable in serious writing; *lots of* is not.

luncheon is formal; *lunch* should normally be used, except in fixed expressions like *luncheon voucher*.

luxuriant, profuse in growth, prolific, e.g. *His hair .. does not seem to have been luxuriant even in its best days* (G. B. Shaw). ● Do not confuse with *luxurious* (the adjective from *luxury*), e.g. *The food, which had always been good, was now luxurious* (C. P. Snow).

majority can mean 'the greater number of a countable set', and is then followed by the plural, e.g. *The majority of the plays produced were failures* (G. B. Shaw).

● *Great* (or *huge, vast,* etc.) can precede *majority* in this sense, e.g. *The first thing you gather from the vast majority of the speakers* (C. S. Lewis); but not *greater, greatest.* ● *Majority* is not used to mean 'the greater part of a quantity', e.g. *I was doing most of the cooking* (not *the majority of the cooking*).

malignant: see **benign**.

masterful, domineering, e.g. *People might say she was tyrannical, domineering, masterful* (Virginia Woolf).

● Do not confuse with *masterly,* very skilful, e.g. *A masterly piece of work*.

maximize, to make as great as possible.

● It should not be used for 'to make as good, easy, etc. as possible' or 'to make the most of' as in *To maximize customer service*; *To maximize this situation*.

means (1) Money resources: a plural noun, e.g. *You might find out from Larry .. what his means are* (G. B. Shaw).

(2) That by which a result is brought about. It may be used either as a singular or as a plural, e.g. (singular) *The press was, at this time, the only means .. of influencing opinion* (A. J. P. Taylor); (plural) *All the time-honoured means of meeting the opposite sex* (Frederic Raphael).

● Beware of mixing singular and plural, as in *The right to resist by every* (singular) *means that are* (plural) *consonant with the law of God*.

media, agency, means (of communication etc.), is a plural noun, e.g. *The communication media inflate language because they dare not be honest* (Anthony Burgess). Its singular is *medium* (rare except in *mass medium*).

● Although *media* is commonly treated as a singular noun, this use should be avoided, as should the plural form *medias. Medium* (in Spiritualism) forms its plural in *-s*.

militate: see **mitigate**.

minimize, to reduce to, or estimate at, the minimum, e.g. *Each side was inclined*

to minimize its own losses in battle.
- It does not mean *lessen* and therefore cannot be qualified by adverbs like *greatly*.

minority. *Large, vast,* etc. *minority* can mean either 'almost half', or 'a number who are very much the minority': although it usually means the former, it is best to avoid the ambiguity.

mitigate, alleviate, moderate (usually transitive), e.g. *Its heat mitigated by the strong sea-wind* (Anthony Burgess).
- Do not confuse with *militate* (intransitive) *against*, to have effect against, e.g. *The very fact that Leamas was a professional could militate against his interests* (John le Carré).

momentum, impetus. • Do not confuse with *moment* 'importance', e.g. *An error of some moment* (not *momentum*).

more than one is followed by a singular verb and is referred back to by singular pronouns, e.g. *More than one popular dancing man inquired anxiously at his bank* (Evelyn Waugh).

motif, motive. *Motif* (1) theme in an artistic work, (2) decorative pattern, (3) ornament sewn on a garment. *Motive,* what induces a person to act in a particular way. *Motive* might have been a better choice in the following: *Fear of failure is a strong motif in men's lives.*

motivate, to be the motive of (a person, an action), e.g. *A .. tax grab motivated by the politics of envy* (*Daily Express*). • It does not mean 'justify', e.g. (wrongly) in *The publisher motivates the slim size of these volumes by claiming it makes them more likely to be read.*

mutual (1) Felt, done, etc., by each to(wards) the other, e.g. *mutual affection.* (2) Standing in a (specified) relation to each other, e.g. *mutual beneficiaries.* This sense is now rare. (3) Shared, e.g. *a mutual friend.* • Sense (3) is acceptable in a small number of collocations, such as that indicated, in which *common* might be ambiguous; cf. *They had already formed a small island of mutual Englishness* (Muriel Spark): *common Englishness* might imply vulgarity. Otherwise *common* is preferable, e.g.

in *By common* (rather than *mutual*) *agreement they finished the card-game at nine.*

naturalist, expert in natural history; *naturist,* nudist.

nature. • Avoid using adjective + *nature* as a periphrasis for an abstract noun, e.g. write *The dangerousness of the spot,* not *The dangerous nature of the spot.*

need (*this needs changing* etc.): see **want.**

neighbourhood. *In the neighbourhood of* is an unnecessarily cumbersome periphrasis for *round about, approximately.*

neither (adverb). • It is non-standard to use it instead of *either* to strengthen a preceding negative, e.g. *There were no books either* (not *neither*).

non-flammable: see **flammable.**

normalcy is chiefly Amer. • Prefer *normality.*

not only: see **only** (4).

no way (1) (Initially, followed by inversion of verb and subject) = 'not at all, by no means', e.g. *No way will you stop prices .. going up again* (James Callaghan). • Informal only. (2) = 'certainly not', e.g. *'Did you go up in the elevator?' 'No way.'* • Chiefly Amer.; informal only.

number. *A number* (*of*) takes the plural, *the number* (*of*) the singular, e.g. *A number of people around us were unashamedly staring* (Bruce Arnold); *The number of accidents has decreased.*

obligate (verb) is in Britain only used in Law. • There is no gain in using it (as often in Amer. usage) for *oblige.*

oblivious, in the sense 'unaware of', may be followed by *of* or *to,* e.g. *'When the summer comes,' said Lord Marchmain, oblivious of the deep corn .. outside his windows* (Evelyn Waugh); *Rose seemed oblivious to individuals* (Angus Wilson). • This sense is now fully established in the language.

obscene• Avoid using it as a general term of disapproval, e.g. *TV's claim to 'show it like it is' in 1990 appears as obscene as it did in the Falklands War.*

of used for *have*: see **of,** p. 25, and **have,** p. 42.

off of used for the preposition *off*, e.g. *Picked him off of the floor*, is non-standard.

one (pronoun) (1) = 'any person, people in general' has *one*, *one's*, and *oneself* as objective, possessive, and reflexive forms. ● These forms should point back to a previous use of *one*, e.g. *One always did, in foreign parts, become friendly with one's fellow-countrymen more quickly than one did at home* (Muriel Spark). *One* should not be mixed with *he* (*him*, *his*, etc.) (acceptable Amer. usage) or *we*, *you*, etc.

(2) = single thing or person, following *any*, *every*, and *some*; the resulting phrase is written as two words and is distinct from *anyone*, *everyone*, *someone*, e.g. *Any one* (*of these*) *will do.*

ongoing has a valid use meaning 'that is happening and will continue', e.g. *The refugee problem in our time is an ongoing problem* (Robert Kee). ● The vague or tautologous use of *ongoing* should be avoided, as in the cliché *ongoing situation.*

only (1) In spoken English, it is usual to place *only* between subject and verb, e.g. *He only saw Bill yesterday*: intonation shows whether *only* limits *he*, *saw*, *Bill*, or *yesterday*.

(2) It is an established idiom that, in a sentence containing *only* + verb + another item, in the absence of special intonation, *only* is understood as limiting that other item. *I only want some water* is the natural way of saying *I want only some water*. If there is more than one item following the verb, *only* often limits the item nearest the end of the sentence, e.g. *A type of mind that can only accept ideas if they are put in the language he would use himself* (Doris Lessing) (= only if . .); but not always, e.g. *The captain was a thin unapproachable man .. who only appeared once at table* (Graham Greene) (= only once).

(3) Despite the idiom described under (2), there are often sentences in which confusion can arise. If this is likely, *only* should be placed before the item which it limits, e.g. *The coalminer is second in importance only to the man who ploughs the soil* (George Orwell).

(4) *Not only* should not be placed in the position before the verb. This is a fairly common slip, e.g. *Katherine's marriage not only kept her away, but at least two of Mr. March's cousins* (C. P. Snow); *kept not only her* would be better. If placing it before the verb is inevitable, the verb should be repeated after *but* (*also*), e.g. *It not only brings the coal out but brings the roof down as well* (George Orwell).

ordinance (1) authoritative decree; (2) religious rite. ● Do not confuse with *ordnance*, (1) mounted guns, (2) government service dealing with military stores and materials. Note also *Ordnance Survey*.

orient, orientate. They are virtually synonymous. In general use, *orientate* seems to predominate, but either is acceptable.

other than can be used where *other* is an adjective or pronoun, e.g. *He was no other than the rightful lord*; *The acts of any person other than myself*. ● *Other* cannot be treated as an adverb: *otherwise* should be used instead, e.g. in *cannot react other than angrily.*

out used as a preposition instead of *out of*, e.g. *looked out the window*, is non-standard.

outside of (1) = 'apart from' is informal only, e.g. *The need of some big belief outside of art* (Roger Fry, in a letter).

(2) = beyond the limits of, e.g. *The most important such facility outside of Japan* (*Gramophone*). ● In sense (2) *outside* alone is preferable.

outstanding. ● Do not use in the sense 'remaining undetermined, unpaid, etc.' where ambiguity with the sense 'eminent, striking' can arise, e.g. *In a moment we'll give you the other outstanding results* (in a sports commentary).

overly, excessively, too, is still regarded as an Americanism, e.g. *overly cautious.*

● Use *excessively*, *too*, or *over*- instead; for *not overly*, *not very* or *none too* make satisfactory replacements.

overseas (adjective and adverb) is now more usual than *oversea*.

owing to, unlike **due to,** has for long been established as a compound preposition meaning 'because of ', e.g. *My rooms became uninhabitable, owing to a burst gas-pipe* (C. P. Snow). ● *Owing to the fact that* should be avoided: use a conjunction like *because.*

pace means 'despite (someone)'s opinion', e.g. *Our civilization, pace Chesterton, is founded on coal* (George Orwell).

● It does not mean 'according to (someone)' or 'notwithstanding (something)'.

parameter. (1) (In technical use) a quantity constant in the case considered, but varying in different cases. (2) A (measurable) defining characteristic, e.g. *The three major parameters of colour—brightness, hue, and saturation.* (3) (Loosely) a limit or boundary, e.g. *Within the parameters of the parole system* (*The Times*); an aspect or feature, e.g. *The main parameters of the problem.* ● Use (3) is a popular dilution of the word's meaning, probably influenced (at least in the first quotation) by *perimeter*; it should be avoided.

parricide refers to the killing of a near relative, especially of a parent; *patricide* only to the killing of one's father.

part (on the part of): see **behalf.**

partially, partly. Apart from the (rare) use of *partially* to mean 'in a partial or biased way', these two words are largely interchangeable; but *partly .. partly* is more usual than *partially .. partially*, e.g. *Partly in verse and partly in prose.*

peer, as in *to have no peer*, means 'equal', not 'superior'.

pence is sometimes informally used as a singular, *one pence.* ● Normally *penny* should be used in the singular.

perquisite (informal abbreviation *perk*) extra profit attached to employment, e.g. *The dead man's clothes are the perquisites of the layer-out* (Lawrence Durrell). ● Do not confuse with *prerequisite* 'something required as a precondition', e.g. *Her mere comforting presence .. was already a prerequisite to peaceful sleep* (Lynne Reid Banks).

persistency is limited in sense to 'perseverance', e.g. *They made repeated requests for compensation, but an official apology was the only reward for their persistency*; *persistence* is sometimes used in that sense, e.g. *Phil Davies' try .. was just reward for the flanker's persistence* (*Independent on Sunday*), but more often for 'continued existence', e.g. *The persistence of this primitive custom.*

perspicuous, easily understood; expressing things clearly; similarly *perspicuity*; e.g. *There is nothing more desirable in composition than perspicuity* (Southey).

● Do not confuse with *perspicacious*, having insight, and *perspicacity*, e.g. *Her perspicacity at having guessed his passion* (Vita Sackville-West).

petit bourgeois, **petty bourgeois.** The meaning is the same. If the former is used, the correct French inflections should be added: *petits bourgeois* (plural), *petite(s) bourgeoise(s)* (feminine (plural)); also *petite bourgeoisie.*

phenomena is the plural of *phenomenon.* ● It cannot be used as a singular and cannot form a plural *phenomenas.*

picaresque (of a style of fiction) dealing with the episodic adventures of rogues.

● It does not mean 'transitory' or 'roaming'.

pivotal, crucial, decisive, e.g. *The pardon of Richard Nixon was pivotal to those who made up their minds at the last minute.* ● Do not use it merely to mean *vital.*

plaid, shawl-like garment; *tartan,* woollen cloth with distinctive pattern; the pattern itself.

● **plus** (conjunction), = 'and in addition', is not generally acceptable in Standard English, e.g. *They arrived late, plus they were hungry.*

polity, a form of civil government, e.g. *A republican polity*; a state. ● It does not mean *policy* or *politics.*

portentous can mean: (1) Like a portent, ominous, e.g. *Fiery-eyed with a sense of portentous utterance* (Muriel Spark).

(2) Prodigious. (3) Solemn, pompous, e.g. *A portentous commentary on Holy Scripture* (Lord Hailsham).

● Sense (3) is sometimes criticized, but is an established, slightly jocular use.

● The form *portentious* (due to the influence of *pretentious*) is erroneous.

post, pre. Their use as full words (not prefixes) should be avoided, e.g. in *Post the Geneva meeting of Opec* (*Daily Telegraph*); *Pre my being in office* (Henry Kissinger).

practicable, practical. When applied to things, *practicable* means 'able to be done', e.g. (with the negative *impracticable*), *Schemes which look very fine on paper, but which, as we well know, are impracticable* (C. S. Lewis); *practical* 'suited to the conditions', e.g. *Having considered the problem, he came up with several practical suggestions.*

pre: see **post, pre.**

precipitous, like a precipice, e.g. *A precipitous marble staircase* (Evelyn Waugh). ● Do not confuse with *precipitate*, hasty, rash, e.g. *Precipitate departure.*

predicate (verb) (1) (Followed by *of*) to assert as a property of, e.g. *That easy Bohemianism—conventionally predicated of the 'artistic' temperament* (J. I. M. Stewart). (2) (Followed by *on*) to found or base (a statement etc.) on. ● Sense (2) tends to sound pretentious. Use *found*, or *base, on.*

pre-empt (1) To acquire in advance, e.g. *Contributions pre-empt a slice of incomes which would otherwise be available for saving* (Enoch Powell). (2) To preclude, forestall, e.g. *The Nazi régime by its own grotesque vileness pre-empted fictional effort* (Listener). ● Sense (2) is better expressed by *preclude* or *forestall*. ● *Pre-empt* is not a synonym for *prevent.*

prefer. The rejected alternative is introduced by *to*, e.g. *People preferred darkness to light* (*Revised English Bible*). But when the rejected alternative is an infinitive, it is preceded by *rather than* (not *than* alone), e.g. *I'd prefer to be stung to death rather than to wake up . . with half of me shot away* (John Osborne). ● *Prefer . . over* is chiefly Amer.

preferable to means 'more desirable than' and is therefore intensified by *far, greatly*, or *much*, not *more.*

preference. The alternatives are introduced by *for* and *over*, e.g. *The preference for a single word over a phrase or clause* (Anthony Burgess); but *in preference* is followed by *to.*

prejudice (1) = bias, is followed by *against* or *in favour of*; (2) = detriment, is followed by *to*; (3) = injury, is followed by *of* (in the phrase *to the prejudice of*).

prepared: *to be prepared to*, to be willing to, has been criticized, but is now established usage, e.g. *One should kill oneself, which, of course, I was not prepared to do* (Cyril Connolly).

prerequisite: see **perquisite.**

prescribe, to lay down as a rule to be followed; *proscribe*, to forbid by law.

presently (1) Soon, e.g. *Presently we left the table and sat in the garden-room* (Evelyn Waugh). (2) Now, e.g. *The praise presently being heaped upon him* (*The Economist*). ● Sense (2) (long current in Amer. English) is regarded as incorrect by some people but is widely used and often sounds more natural than *at present.*

prestigious (1) Characterized by magic, deceptive, e.g. *The prestigious balancing act which he was constantly obliged to perform* (TLS): now rare. (2) Having prestige, e.g. *A career in pure science is still more socially prestigious . . than one in engineering* (*The Times*): a fully acceptable sense.

prevaricate, to speak or act evasively or misleadingly; *procrastinate*, to postpone action.

prevent is followed by *from* + the gerund, or by the possessive case + the gerund, e.g. *prevent me from going* or *prevent my going*. ● *Prevent me going* is informal only.

● **pre-war** as an adverb, in, e.g., *Some time pre-war there was a large contract out for tender* (*Daily Telegraph*): prefer *before the war.*

pristine (1) Ancient, original. (2) Unspoilt, e.g. *Pristine snow reflects about 90 per cent of incident sunlight* (Fred Hoyle). ● *Pristine* does not mean 'spotless', 'pure', or 'fresh'.

procrastinate: see **prevaricate**.

prone (followed by *to*) is used like **liable**, but usually with a personal subject, e.g. *My literary temperament rendering me especially prone to 'all that kind of poisonous nonsense'* (Cyril Connolly).

proportion means 'a comparative part'; it is not a mere *part*.

proscribe: see **prescribe**.

protagonist, the leading character in a story or incident.

● In Greek drama there was only one protagonist, but this is no reason to debar the use of the word in the plural, e.g. *We .. sometimes mistook a mere supernumerary in a fine dress for one of the protagonists* (C. S. Lewis).

● Do not confuse with *proponent*: the word contains the Greek prefix *prot-* 'first', not the prefix *pro-* 'in favour of', and does not mean 'champion, advocate'.

protest (verb, transitive) to affirm solemnly, e.g. *He protested his innocence.*

● The sense 'object to', e.g. in *The residents have protested the sale*, is Amer. only.

proven. It is not the standard past participle of *prove* in British English (it is standard Scots and Amer.); it is, however, common attributively in expressions such as *of proven ability*.

provenance, origin, place of origin, is used in Britain; the form *provenience* is its usual Amer. equivalent.

prudent, careful, circumspect, e.g. *What is the difference in matrimonial affairs, between the mercenary and the prudent move?* (Jane Austen); *prudential*, involving or marked by prudence, e.g. *prudential motives.*

pry, to prise (open etc.): chiefly Amer., but occasionally in British literary use. The normal sense is 'peer' or 'inquire'.

quadrillion: see **billion**.

question: (1) *No question that* (or *but*), no doubt that, e.g. *There can be no question that the burning of Joan of Arc must have been a most instructive and interesting experiment* (G. B. Shaw).

(2) *No question of*, no possibility of, e.g. *There can be no question of tabulating successes and failures* (C. S. Lewis). See also **beg the question, leading question**.

quote (noun = quotation) is informal only (except in Printing and Commerce).

● **re** (in the matter of, referring to) is better avoided and should not be used for 'about, concerning'.

reason. *The reason (why) .. is ..* should be followed by *that*, not *because*.

recoup (1) (transitive) to reimburse, e.g. *Dixon felt he could recoup himself a little for the expensiveness of the drinks* (Kingsley Amis); also *to recoup one's losses*; (2) (intransitive) to make good one's loss, e.g. *I had .. so many debts that if I didn't return to England to recoup, we might have to run for it* (Chaim Bermant).

● This word is not synonymous with *recuperate*.

recuperate (1) (intransitive) to recover from ill-health, financial loss, etc., e.g. *I've got a good mind .. to put all my winnings on red and give him a chance to recuperate* (Graham Greene); (2) (transitive) to recover (health, a loss, material). In sense (2) *recover* is preferable.

redolent, smelling *of* something, e.g. *Corley's breath redolent of rotten cornjuice* (James Joyce); also 'strongly suggestive of', e.g. *The missive most redolent of money and sex* (Martin Amis).

referendum. ● The plural *referendums* is preferable to *referenda*.

refute, to disprove (a statement etc.), e.g. *The case against most of them must have been so easily refuted that they could hardly rank as suspects* (Rebecca West); to prove (a person) to be in error, e.g. *German scholars whose function is to be refuted in a footnote* (Frederic Raphael). ● *Refute* does not mean 'deny' or 'repudiate' (an allegation etc.).

regalia is a plural noun, meaning 'emblems of royalty or of an order'. It has no singular in ordinary English.

region: *in the region of*, an unwieldy periphrasis for *round about, approximately*, is better avoided.

register office is the official term for *registry office*.

regretfully, in a regretful manner; *regretably*, it is to be regretted (that).

● *Regretfully* should not be used where *regrettably* is intended: *The investigators, who must regretfully remain anonymous* (TLS), reads as a guess at the investigators' feelings instead of an expression of the writer's opinion, which was what was intended. Compare **hopefully** (2).

renege (intransitive), to fail to fulfil an undertaking, is usually constructed with *on*, e.g. *It . . reneged on Britain's commitment to the East African Asians* (*The Times*).

replace: see **substitute**.

resource is often confused with *recourse* and *resort*. *Resource* means (1) a reserve upon which one can draw (often used in the plural); (2) an expedient to which one can turn in difficulty; (3) mental capabilities for amusing oneself etc.; (4) ability to deal with a crisis, e.g. *A man of infinite resource*. *Recourse* means the action of turning to a possible source of help, e.g. *have recourse to, without recourse to*. *Resort* means (1) the action of turning to a possible source of help (= *recourse*); frequently in the phrase *in the last resort*, as a last expedient; (2) a thing to which one can turn in difficulty.

responsible for (1) Liable to be called to account for, e.g. *I'm not responsible for what uncle Percy does* (E. M. Forster).

(2) Obliged to take care of, e.g. *The Prime Minister was directly responsible for the security service* (Harold Wilson).

(3) Being the cause of, e.g. *A war-criminal responsible for so many unidentified deaths* (Graham Greene).

● Beware of using senses (1) or (2) where sense (3) can be understood, e.g. *Now, as Secretary for Trade, he is directly responsible for pollution* (*The Times*).

restive (1) Unmanageable, rejecting control, obstinate, e.g. *The I.L.P. . . had been increasingly restive during the second Labour government, and now . . voluntarily disaffiliated from the Labour party* (A. J. P. Taylor).

(2) Restless, fidgety, e.g. *The audiences were . . apt to be restive and noisy at the back* (J. B. Priestley). ● Sense (2) is objected to by some, but is quite commonly used by good writers.

revenge: one revenges oneself or a wrong (*on* an offender); one is revenged (*for* a wrong): the noun is *revenge* (*on*), and the idea is usually of retaliation. Cf. **avenge**.

reverend, deserving reverence; *reverent*, showing reverence.

(*The*) *Revd*, plural *Revds*, is the abbreviation of *Reverend* as a clergy title and should be used in preference to *Rev*.

reversal is the noun corresponding to the verb *reverse*; *reversion* is the noun corresponding to the verb *revert*.

same. ● It is non-standard to use *same as* for 'in the same way as', e.g. *But I shouldn't be able to serve them personally, same as I do now* (L. P. Hartley).

sanction (verb) to give approval to, to authorize. ● It does not mean 'impose sanctions on'.

sc. (short for Latin *scilicet* = to wit) introduces (1) a word to be supplied, e.g. *He asserted that he had met him* (*sc. the defendant*), or (2) a word to be substituted to render an expression intelligible, e.g. '*I wouldn't of* (*sc. have*) *done' was her answer*.

scabrous (1) Rough, scaly. (2) Risqué, indecent, e.g. *Silly and scabrous titters about Greek pederasty* (C. S. Lewis). ● *Scabrous* does not mean 'scathing, scurrilous'.

scarcely: see **hardly**.

scarify, to loosen or scratch the surface of.

● The verb *scarify* (pronounced scare-ify) 'scare, terrify' is informal only.

scenario (1) An outline of the plot of a play. (2) A detailed film script. (3) A postulated (usually future) sequence of events, e.g. *Several of the computer 'scenarios' include a catastrophic and sudden collapse of population* (*Observer*).

● Sense (3) is valid when a detailed narrative of events that might happen is denoted. The word should not be used loosely for *scene, situation, circumstance*, etc.

scilicet: see **sc.**

Scottish is now the usual adjective; *Scotch* is restricted to certain fixed expressions, e.g. *Scotch broth, egg, whisky; Scots* is used mainly for Scottish English, in the names of regiments, and in *Scotsman, Scotswoman* (*Scotchman, -woman* are old-fashioned). For the inhabitants of Scotland, the plural noun *Scots* is normal.

seasonable, suitable for the time or season, opportune; *unseasonable* occurring at the wrong time or season, e.g. *You are apt to be pressed to drink a glass of vinegary port at an unseasonable hour* (Somerset Maugham). ● Do not confuse with *seasonal*, occurring at a particular season, e.g. *There is a certain seasonal tendency to think better of the Government . . in spring* (*The Economist*).

senior, superior are followed by *to*. They contain the idea of 'more' and so cannot be constructed with *more . . than*, e.g. *There are several officers senior*, or *superior in rank, to him*, not *. . more senior*, or *more superior in rank, than him*.

sensibility, sensitiveness of feeling, e.g. *The man's moving fingers . . showed no sign of acute sensibility* (Graham Greene). ● *Sensibility* does not mean 'possession of good sense'.

sensual, fleshly; indulging oneself with physical pleasures, showing that one does this, e.g. *His sensual eye took in her slim feminine figure* (Angus Wilson); *sensuous*, appealing to the senses (without the pejorative implications of *sensual*), e.g. *I got up and ran about the . . meadow in my bare feet. I remember the sensuous pleasure of it* (C. Day Lewis); *sensory*, of sensation or the senses, e.g. *sensory experience*.

serendipity, the faculty of making pleasant discoveries by accident; the adjective is *serendipitous*. ● *Serendipitous* does not mean merely 'fortunate'.

sic (Latin for *thus*) is placed in brackets after a word to show that the word is quoted exactly as in the original, e.g. *Daisy Ashford's novel* The Young Visiters (*sic*).

sick: see **ill.**

similar should be followed by *to*, not *as*. The following is non-standard: *Wolverton Seconds showed similar form as their seniors in their two home games.*

● **sit, stand.** The use of the past participles *sat, stood* with the verb *to be*, meaning *to be sitting, standing*, is non-standard, e.g. *I'd be sat there falling asleep* (Kingsley Amis).

situation. A useful noun for 'state of affairs' which may validly be preceded by a defining adjective, e.g. *the financial, industrial, military situation.* ● The substitution of an attributive noun for an adjective before *situation* is often tautologous (e.g. *a crisis situation, people in work situations*: crises and *work* are themselves *situations*). The placing of an attributive phrase before *situation* should be avoided, e.g. *The deep space situation, a balance-of-terror situation.* ● Avoid the cliché **on-going** *situation.*

sled is Amer. for *sledge; sleigh* is a sledge for passengers that is drawn by horses (or reindeer).

so meaning 'therefore' may be preceded by *and* but need not be; e.g. *I had received no word from Martha all day, so I was drawn back to the casino* (Graham Greene).

so-called (1) has long been used in the sense 'called by this term, but not entitled to it'; (2) is now often used without implication of incorrectness, especially in Science.

sort of: see **kind of.**

specialty, except for its use in Law, is an equivalent of *speciality* restricted to North America.

spectate, to be a spectator, is informal only.
● *Watch* is usually an adequate substitute, e.g. in *A spectating, as opposed to a reading, audience* (*Listener*).

strata is the plural of *stratum.* ● It is incorrect to treat it as a singular noun, e.g. in *This strata.*

style. (1) Adjective + *-style* used to qualify a noun, e.g. *European-style clothing*, is acceptable.
(2) Adjective or noun + *-style*, forming an adverb, is somewhat informal,

e.g. *A revolution, British-style* (A. J. P. Taylor).

substantial, of real value; of solid material; having much property; in essentials; e.g. *substantial damages*; *a substantial house*, *yeoman*; *substantial agreement.* ● It is not merely a synonym of *large.*

substantive (adjective) is mainly technical; e.g. *substantive rank*, in the services, is permanent, not acting.

substitute (verb) to put (someone or something) in place of another: with *for*; e.g. *Substituted it for the broken one.*

● The sense 'replace (someone or something) *by* or *with* another' is incorrect, or at best highly informal, e.g. in *Having substituted her hat with a steel safety helmet, she toured the site* (better, *Having replaced her hat with . . or Having substituted a steel safety helmet for . .*).

such as: see **like.**

superior: see **senior.**

suppositious, hypothetical, e.g. *We might take a small cottage . . our suppositious cottage* (James Joyce); *supposititious*, fraudulently substituted, e.g. *Russia . . is the supposititious child of necessity in the household of theory* (H. G. Wells).

synchronize (transitive), to make simultaneous. ● It is not a synonym for *combine* or *coordinate.*

than: see **different, other than, prefer, senior.**

thankfully: see **hopefully.**

the (the article). When a name like *The Times* or *The Hague* is used attributively, *The* is dropped, e.g. *A* Times *correspondent, Last year's* Hague *conference.* If *the* precedes the name in such a construction, it is not part of the name, and is therefore not given a capital initial (or italics), e.g. *A report from the* Times *correspondent.*

the (adverb) with a comparative means 'thereby', e.g. *What student is the better for mastering these distinctions?* This combination can enter into such expressions as *The more the merrier.* It cannot be used with *than.* Avoid putting *any the more, none the less* for *any more, no less*, e.g. in *The intellectual*

release had been no less (not *none the less*) *marked than the physical.*

then may precede a noun as a neat alternative to *at that time*, e.g. *the then Prime Minister.* ● It should not be placed before the noun if it would sound equally well in its usual position, e.g. *Harold Macmillan was the then Prime Minister* could equally well be . . *was then the Prime Minister.* Rather than *The then existing constitution* write *The constitution then existing.*

there- adverbs, e.g. *therein, thereon, thereof*, etc., are mostly very formal and should be avoided in ordinary writing (apart from certain idiomatic adverbs, e.g. *thereabouts, thereby, thereupon*); e.g. *We did not question this reasoning, and there lay our mistake* (Evelyn Waugh): a lesser writer might have written *therein.*

through, up to and including, e.g. *Friday through Tuesday*, though useful, is Amer. only.

too followed by an adjective used attributively should be confined to special effects, e.g. *A small too-pretty house* (Graham Greene). ● In normal prose it is a clumsy construction, e.g. *The crash came during a too-tight loop.*

tooth-comb and *fine tooth-comb* are now established expressions whose illogicality it is pedantic to object to.

tortuous, torturous. Do not confuse: *tortuous* means (1) twisting, e.g. *A tortuous route*; (2) devious, e.g. *A tortuous mind. Torturous* means 'involving torture, excruciating'.

transcendent, surpassing others (e.g. *Of transcendent importance*), (of God) above and distinct from the universe; *transcendental*, visionary, beyond experience, etc. (Other more technical senses of each word are ignored here.)

transpire (figuratively): (1) To leak out, come to be known, e.g. *What had transpired concerning that father was not so reassuring* (John Galsworthy). (2) To occur, happen, e.g. *What transpired between them is unknown* (David Cecil). ● Sense (2) is regarded by many people as unacceptable, especially if the idea of something emerging from ignorance is absent: it should therefore not be used in sentences like *A storm transpired*.

trillion: see **billion**.

triumphal, of or celebrating a triumph, e.g. *A triumphal arch*; *triumphant*, victorious, exultant.

try (verb) in writing normally followed by the *to*-infinitive: *try and* + bare infinitive is informal. This latter construction is uncommon in negative contexts (except in the imperative, e.g. *Don't try and jump*), in the third person singular, and in the past tense.

turbid (1) muddy, thick; (2) confused, disordered. *Turgid* (1) swollen; (2) (of language) inflated, pompous.

underlay (verb) (past *underlaid*) to lay something under, e.g. *Underlaid the tiles with felt*; *underlie* (past tense *underlay*, past participle *underlain*) to lie under; to be the basis of; to exist beneath the surface of, e.g. *The arrogance that underlay their cool good manners* (Doris Lessing).

unequivocal, not ambiguous, unmistakable, e.g. *His refusal .. was unequivocal. 'Not in a million years' was the expression he used* (P. G. Wodehouse); similarly *unequivocally* adverb.
● The forms *unequivocable, -ably* are erroneous.

unexceptionable, -al: see **exceptionable**.

unique: (1) Being the only one of its kind, e.g. *This vase is considered unique*: in this sense *unique* cannot be qualified by adverbs like *most, so, thoroughly*, etc. (2) Unusual, remarkable, singular, e.g. *The most unique man I ever met*. ● Sense (2) is regarded by many people as incorrect. Substitute a suitable synonym.

unlike (adverb) may govern a noun, noun phrase, or pronoun, just as *like* may, e.g. *A sarcasm unlike ordinary sarcasm* (V. S. Pritchett). ● It may not govern a clause or adverbial phrase, e.g. *He was unlike he had ever been*; *Unlike in countries of lesser economic importance*.

● **various** cannot be followed by *of* (as, for example, *several* can), as (wrongly) in *Various of the Commonwealth representatives*.

venal, able to be bribed, influenced by bribery; *venial*, pardonable.

vengeance: see **avenge**.

verbal (1) of or in words; (2) of a verb; (3) spoken rather than written. ● Some people prefer *oral* for sense (3). However, *verbal* is the usual term in many idioms, such as *verbal communication*, *contract, evidence*.

verge (verb) in *verge on, upon*, to border on, e.g. *Verging on the ridiculous*, is in origin a different word from *verge* in *verge to, towards* to incline towards, approach, e.g. *Industrial disputes always verged towards violence* (A. J. P. Taylor). Both are acceptable.

vermin is usually treated as plural, e.g. *A lot of parasites, vermin who feed on God's love and charity* (Joyce Cary).

via (1) By way of (a place), e.g. *To London via Reading*. (2) Through the agency of, e.g. *They had sent a photo of Tina as a baby to the .. mother via a social worker* (*Independent*). ● Sense (2) is informal.

waive to refrain from insisting on, to dispense with, e.g. *To waive the formalities*. ● Do not confuse this with *wave*, chiefly with *aside, away*, as (wrongly) in *But the Earl simply waived the subject away with his hand* (Trollope).

want, need. ● The two legitimate constructions exemplified by *Your hair needs* or *wants cutting* and *We want* or *need this changed* are not correctly to be combined into *We want* or *need this changing*.

well is joined by a hyphen to a following participle before a noun, e.g. *A well-worn argument*. Predicatively a hyphen is not necessary unless the combination is to be distinguished in meaning from the two words written separately, e.g. *He is well-spoken* but *The words were well spoken*.

what ever, when ever, where ever: see **ever**.

whence meaning 'from where' need not be preceded by *from*.

who ever: see **ever**.

whoever, any one who, no matter who: use *whoever* for the objective case as well as the subjective, rather than the rather stilted *whomever*, e.g. *Whoever he painted now was transfigured into that image on the canvas* (Kathleen Jones). ● Beware of introducing the objective *whomever* incorrectly, as in *A black mark for whomever it was that ordered the verges to be shorn* (*Daily Telegraph*).

-**wise** (suffix) added to nouns (1) forming adverbs of manner, is very well established in fixed expressions like *clockwise*; (2) forming viewpoint adverbs (meaning 'as regards —'), e.g. *moneywise*. ● (2) should be restricted to informal contexts. ● Adverbs of type (2) are formed on nouns only: hence sentences like *The ratepayers would have to shoulder an extra burden financial-wise* are incorrect (substitute .. *burden finance-wise* or *financial burden*).

● **without** = 'unless' is non-standard, e.g. *Do not leave without you tell me.*

womankind is better than *womenkind* (cf. *mankind*).

worth while is usually written as two words predicatively, but as one attributively, e.g. *He thought it worth while*, or *a worthwhile undertaking, to publish the method.*

write with personal object, e.g. *I will write you about it*, is not acceptable British English (but is good Amer. English).

Grammar

This section deals with specific problems of grammar; it makes no attempt at a systematic exposition of English syntax.

Wherever possible, the headings chosen for the entries are the words or grammatical endings which actually cause problems (e.g. *as*, *may* or *might*, *-ing*). But inevitably many entries have had to be given abstract labels (e.g. *double passive*, *subjunctive*). To compensate for this, a number of cross-references are included. The aim throughout is to tackle a particular problem immediately and to give a recommendation as soon as the problem has been identified.

adverbial relative clauses

A relative clause, expressing time, manner, or place, can follow a noun governed by a preposition (*on the day* in the example below):

> The town was shelled by heavy guns on the day that we departed (Edmund Blunden)

It is possible for the relative clause to begin with the same preposition and *which*, e.g.

> On the day on which the books were opened *three hundred thousand pounds were subscribed* (Lord Macaulay)

But it is a perfectly acceptable idiom to use a relative clause introduced by *that*, or often omitting *that*, without repeating the preposition, especially after the nouns *day*, *morning*, *night*, *time*, *year*, etc., *manner*, *sense*, *way* (see p. 95), *place*, e.g.

> Envy in the consuming sense that certain persons display the trait (Anthony Powell)
> If he would take it in the sense she meant it (L. P. Hartley)

adverbs without *-ly*

Most adverbs consist of an adjective + the ending *-ly*, e.g. *badly*, *differently*. For the changes in spelling that the addition of *-ly* may require, see p. 15 f. Normally the use of the ordinary adjective as an adverb, without *-ly*, is non-standard, e.g.

> I was sent for special
> The Americans speak different from us

There are, however, a number of words which are both adjective and adverb and cannot add the adverbial ending *-ly*, e.g.

alone	fast	low
enough	little	much
far	long	still

Some other adjectives can be used as adverbs both with and without *-ly*. The two forms have different meanings, e.g.

deep	high	near
hard	late	

The forms without *-ly* are the adverbs more closely similar in meaning to the adjectives, as the following examples illustrate:

deep: He read deep into the night
hard: They hit me hard in the chest
      He lost his hard-earned money
high: It soared high above us
      Don't fix your hopes too high
late: I will stay up late to finish it
      A drawing dated as late as 1960
near: As near as makes no difference
      Near-famine conditions

The forms with *-ly* have meanings more remote from those of the adjectives:

deeply is chiefly figurative, e.g. *Deeply in love*
hardly = 'scarcely', e.g. *He hardly earned his money*
highly is chiefly figurative, e.g. *Highly amusing*
lately = 'recently', e.g. *I have been very tired lately*
nearly = 'almost', e.g. *We are nearly there*

• The forms with and without -ly should not be confused.

See also -lily adverbs.

article, omission of

To omit, or not to omit, a (an) and the?

Omission of the definite or indefinite article before a noun or noun phrase in apposition to a name is a journalistic device, e.g.

> Clarissa, American business woman, comes to England (Radio Times)
>
> Nansen, hero and humanitarian, moves among them (The Times)

It is more natural to write an American business woman, the hero and humanitarian.

Similarly, when the name follows the noun or noun phrase, the effect is of journalistic style, e.g.

> Best-selling novelist Barbara Cartland
> Unemployed labourer William Smith

Preferably write: The best-selling novelist, An unemployed labourer (with a comma before and after the name which follows).

After as it is possible to omit a or the, e.g.

> As manipulator of words, the author reminded me of X. Y.

It is preferable not to omit these words, however.

as, case following

In the following sentences, the pronoun is in the subjective case, because it would be the subject if a verb were supplied:

> I am, my lord, as well deriv'd as he (Shakespeare) (in full, as he is)
>
> Widmerpool . . might not have heard the motif so often as I (Anthony Powell) (in full, as I had)

Informal usage permits the objective case, e.g. You are just as intelligent as him.

Formal English uses the objective case only when the pronoun would be the object if a verb were supplied:

> I thought you preferred John to Mary, but I see that you like her just as much as him (= as much as you like him)

In real usage, sentences like this are not very natural. It is more usual for the verb to be included.

as if, as though

For the tense following these see p. 51.

auxiliary verbs

There are sixteen auxiliary verbs in English, three primary auxiliaries (used in the compounding of ordinary verbs) and thirteen modal auxiliaries (used to express mood, and, to some extent, tense).

Primary: be, do, have

Modal:	can	ought (to)
	could	shall
	dare	should
	may	used (to)
	might	will
	must	would
	need	

Auxiliaries differ from regular verbs in the following ways:

(1) They can precede the negative not, instead of taking the do not construction, e.g. I cannot but I do not know;
(2) They can precede the subject in questions, instead of taking do, e.g. Can you hear but Do you know.

The modal auxiliaries additionally differ from regular verbs in the following ways:

(3) They do not add -s for the third person present, and do not form a past tense in -ed; e.g. He must go; he must have seen it.
(4) They are usually followed by the bare infinitive; e.g. He will go, he can go (not 'to go' as with other verbs, e.g. He intends to go, he is able to go).

Use of auxiliaries

In reported speech and some other that-clauses can, may, shall, and will become could, might, should, and would for the past tense:

> He said that he could do it straight away
> I told you that I might arrive unexpectedly
> I knew that when I grew up I should be a writer (George Orwell)

Did you think that the money you brought would *be enough?*

In clauses of this kind, the auxiliaries *must*, *need*, and *ought* can also be used for the past tense:

> *This business .. meant that I* must *go to London* (Evelyn Waugh)
> *To go to church had made her feel she* need *not reproach herself for impropriety* (V. S. Pritchett)
> *She was quite aware that she* ought *not to quarter Freddy there* (G. B. Shaw)

Note that this use is restricted to *that*-clauses. It would not be permissible to use *must*, *need*, or *ought* for the past tense in a main sentence; one could not say: *Yesterday I must go.*

Further discussion of the use of auxiliary verbs will be found under **can and may, dare, have, need, ought, shall and will, should** and **would, used to, were or was**.

but, case following

The personal pronoun following *but* (= 'except') should be in the case it would have if a verb were supplied.

> *I walked through the mud .. Who but I?* (Kipling)
> *Our uneducated brethren who have, under God, no defence but us* (C. S. Lewis)

In the Kipling example *I* is used because it would be the subject of *I walked*. In the Lewis example *us* is used because it would be the object of *who have* (i.e. 'who have *us*').

can and may

The auxiliary verbs *can* and *may* are both used to express permission, but *may* is more formal and polite:

> *May I offer you a spot? .. I can recommend the Scotch*
> *Can I have a word with you? .. In private. Get lost, young Jane* (both examples from P. G. Wodehouse)

collective nouns

Collective nouns are singular words that denote many individuals, e.g.

audience	family	orchestra
board (of directors etc.)	fleet	parliament
	gang	squad
	government	staff
class	group	team
club	herd	tribe
committee	jury	union (i.e.
company	majority	trade
congregation	nation	union)
crowd		

the bourgeoisie	the nobility
the Cabinet	the public
the élite	the upper class
the intelligentsia	the working class

It is normal for collective nouns to be followed by singular verbs and pronouns:

> *The Government* is *determined to beat inflation, as* it has *promised*
> *Their family* is *huge:* it consists *of five boys and three girls*
> *The bourgeoisie* is *despised for not being proletarian* (C. S. Lewis)

The singular verb and pronouns are preferable unless the collective clearly refers to separate individuals, e.g.

> *The Cabinet has made* its *decision*, but
> *The Cabinet are resuming* their *places around the table*
> *The Brigade of Guards is on parade*, but
> *The Brigade of Guards are above average height*

The singular should always be used if the collective noun is qualified by a singular word like *this, that, every*, etc.:

> *This family* is *divided*
> *Every team* has *its chance to win*

If a relative clause follows, it must be *which* + singular verb or *who* + plural verb, e.g.

> *It was not the intelligentsia .. which was gathered there* (John Galsworthy)
> *The working party who had been preparing the decorations* (Evelyn Waugh)

● Do not mix singular and plural, as (wrongly) in

> *The congregation were now dispersing. It tended to form knots and groups*

comparison of adjectives and adverbs

Whether to use *-er*, *-est* or *more*, *most*.

The two ways are:

(*a*) The addition of the suffixes *-er* and *-est* (for spelling changes that may be required see p. 10 f.). Monosyllabic adjectives and adverbs almost always require these suffixes, e.g. *big* (*bigger*, *biggest*), *soon* (*sooner*, *soonest*), and so do many of two syllables, e.g. *narrow* (*narrower*, *narrowest*), *silly* (*sillier*, *silliest*).

(*b*) The placing of *more* and *most* before the adjective or adverb. These are used with adjectives of three syllables or more (e.g. *difficult*, *memorable*), participles (e.g. *bored*, *boring*), many adjectives of two syllables (e.g. *afraid*, *widespread*), adjectives containing any suffix except *-ly* or *-y* (e.g. *awful*, *childish*, *harmless*, *static*), and adverbs ending in *-ly* (e.g. *highly*, *slowly*).

Adjectives with two syllables vary in this matter.

There are many which never take the suffixes, e.g.

> *antique   devoid   steadfast*

There are also many adjectives which are acceptable with either, e.g.

> *clever   extreme   polite*
> *common   pleasant   solemn*

The choice is largely a matter of style.

Even monosyllabic adjectives can sometimes take *more* and *most*:

(i) When two adjectives are compared with each other, e.g.
> *More dead than alive*
> *More good than bad*
> *More well-known than popular*

This is standard (we would not say 'better than bad').

(ii) Occasionally, for stylistic reasons, e.g.
> *This was never more true than at present*

(iii) Thoughtlessly, e.g.
> *Facts that should be more well known*
> *The most well-dressed man in town*

> *Wimbledon will be yet more hot tomorrow*

● These are not acceptable: substitute *better known*, *best-dressed*, and *hotter*.

comparisons

Comparisons between two persons or things require the comparative (*-er* or *more*) in constructions like the following:

> *I cannot tell which of the two is the* elder (not *eldest*)
> *Which of the two is more likely to win?* (not *most likely*)
> *Of the two teams, they are the* slower-moving (not *slowest-moving*)

The superlative is of course used for more than two.

compound subject

A subject consisting of two singular nouns or noun phrases joined by *and* normally takes a plural verb:

> *My son and daughter* are *twins*
> *Where to go and what to see* were *my main concern*

If one half of the subject is *I* or *you*, and the other is a noun or *he*, *she*, or *it*, or if the subject is *you and I*, the verb must be plural.

> *He and I* are *good friends*
> *Do my sister and I look alike?*
> *You and your mother* have *similar talents*
> *You and I* are *hardly acquainted*

But if the compound represents a single item, it takes a singular verb:

> *The bread and butter* was *scattered on the floor* (W. Somerset Maugham)
> *The Stars and Stripes* was *flying at half-mast*

And similarly if the two parts of the subject refer to a single individual:

> *My son and heir* is *safe!*

See also **neither .. nor** and **subjects joined by (either . .) or**.

coordination

The linking of two main clauses by a comma alone, though sometimes said to be incorrect, is on occasion used by good writers. It should be regarded as acceptable if used sparingly.

> *The peasants possess no harrows, they merely plough the soil several times over* (George Orwell)
>
> *Charles carried a mackintosh over his arm, he was stooping a little* (C. P. Snow)

correlative conjunctions

The correct placing of the pairs

> *both . . and   neither . . nor*
> *either . . or   not only . . but (also)*

A sentence containing any of these pairs must be so constructed that the part introduced by the first member of the pair 'matches' the part introduced by the second member.

The rule is that if one covers up the two correlative words and all between them, the sentence should remain grammatical.

The following sentence illustrates this rule:

> *Candidates will have a background in* either commercial electronics or *university research*

Because *in* precedes *either*, it need not be repeated after *or*. If it had followed *either*, it would have had to be inserted after *or* as well.

In the following example the preposition *of* comes after *either* and must therefore be repeated after *or*:

> *He did not wish to pay the price either of peace or of war* (George Orwell)

This conforms with the rule stated above.

It is, however, not uncommon for the conjunctions to be placed so that the two halves are not quite parallel, even in the writings of careful authors, e.g.

> *I end neither with a death nor a marriage* (W. Somerset Maugham)

Here, *with* belongs to both halves and needs to be repeated after *nor*.

This is a fairly trivial slip that rarely causes difficulty (except in the case of *not only*: see p. 65).

● A more serious error is the placing of the first correlative conjunction too late, so that words belonging only to the first half are carried over to the second, e.g.

> *The other Exocet was either destroyed or blew up* (BBC News)

This should be carefully avoided.

dangling participles: see participles

dare

The verb *to dare* can be used either like a regular verb or like an auxiliary.

As an ordinary verb it forms such parts as:

I dare	*I do not dare*	*do I dare?*
he dares	*he did not dare*	*does he dare?*
he dared	*I have dared*	*did he dare?*

As an auxiliary verb it forms:

> *I dare not   he dared not*
> *he dare not   dared he?*
> *dare he?*

The first use, as an ordinary verb, is always acceptably followed by the *to*-infinitive, e.g.

> *I knew what I would find if I dared to look* (Jean Rhys)

But many of the forms can also be followed by the bare infinitive. This sometimes sounds more natural:

> *Don't you dare put that light on* (Shelagh Delaney)

The second use requires the bare infinitive, e.g.

> *How dare he keep secrets from me?* (G. B. Shaw)

double passive

The construction whereby a passive infinitive directly follows a passive verb is correctly used in the following:

> *The prisoners were ordered to be shot*

The rule is that if the subject and the first passive verb can be changed into the active, leaving the passive infinitive intact, the sentence is correctly formed. The example above (if a subject, say *he*, is supplied) can be changed back to:

> *He* ordered the prisoners *to be shot*

An active infinitive could equally well be part of the sentence, e.g.

The prisoners were ordered to march

The examples below violate the rule because both verbs have to be made active in order to form a grammatical sentence:

The order was attempted to be carried out (active: *He attempted to carry out the order*)

A new definition was sought to be inserted in the Bill (active: *He sought to insert a new definition in the Bill*)

This 'double passive' construction is unacceptable.

The passive of the verbs *to fear* and *to say* can be followed by either an active or a passive infinitive, e.g.

(i) *The passengers are feared* to have drowned

The escaped prisoner is said to be very dangerous

or

(ii) *The passengers are feared* to have been killed

The escaped prisoner is said to have been sighted

The construction at (ii) is entirely acceptable. Both constructions occur with other verbs of saying (e.g. *to allege, to assert, to imply*):

Morris demonstrated that Mr Elton was obviously implied to be impotent (David Lodge)

either . . or: see **subjects joined by (either . .) or.**

either (pronoun)

Either is a singular pronoun and requires a singular verb:

Enormous evils, either of which depends on somebody else's voice (Louis MacNeice)

In the following example the plural verb accords with the notional meaning 'both parents were not'.

It was improbable that either of our parents were *giving thought to the matter* (J. I. M. Stewart)

This is quite common, but should be avoided in formal prose.

gender of indefinite expressions

It is often uncertain what personal pronoun should be used to refer back to the following pronouns and adjectives:

any	*no* (+ noun)
anybody	*nobody*
anyone	*none*
each	*no one*
every (+ noun)	*some* (+ noun)
everybody	*somebody*
everyone	*someone*

and also to refer back to (a) *person*, used indefinitely, or a male and a female noun linked by (*either . .*) *or* or *neither . . nor*, e.g.

Has anybody eaten his/their *lunch yet?*
An angry person may vent his/their *feelings on* his/their *family*
Neither John nor Mary has a home of their/his or her *own*

If it is known that the individuals referred to are all of the same sex, there is no difficulty; use *he* or *she* as appropriate:

Everyone in the women's movement has had her *own experience of sexual discrimination*

If, however, the sex of those referred to is mixed or unknown, the difficulty arises that English has no singular pronoun to denote common gender.

The grammarians' recommendation has traditionally been that *he* (*him, himself, his*) should be used:

Everyone took his *place in a half-circle about the fire* (Malcolm Bradbury)
(The context shows that the company was mixed.)
The long street in which nobody knows his *neighbour* (G. B. Shaw)
Each person should give as he *has decided for* himself (*Revised English Bible*)

Popular usage, however, has for at least five centuries favoured the plural pronoun *they* (*them, themselves, their*):

It's the sort of thing any of us would dislike, wouldn't they? (C. P. Snow)

Delavacquerie allowed everyone to examine the proofs as long as they wished (Anthony Powell)

This is entirely acceptable in informal speech. It is becoming increasingly common, to avoid the perhaps inequitable use of *he* to include both sexes, but is not yet fully accepted in more formal contexts.

One can avoid the difficulty by writing *he or she*:

Nobody has room in his or her *life for more than one such relationship at a time* (G. B. Shaw)

But this grows unwieldy with repetition:

If I ever wished to disconcert anyone, all I had to do was to ask him (or her) *how many friends* he/she *had* (Frederic Raphael)

● The form *themself* is sometimes used as a singular pronoun: *I think somebody should immediately address themself to this problem* (Alice Thomas Ellis)

This use is not generally regarded as acceptable.

group possessive

The group possessive is the construction by which the ending ·'*s* is added to the last word of a noun phrase, e.g.

The king of Spain's daughter
John and Mary's baby
Somebody else's umbrella
A quarter of an hour's drive

Expressions like these are natural and acceptable.

Informal language, however, extends the construction to longer and more loosely connected phrases, often with ludicrous effect.

The people in the house opposite's geraniums
The woman I told you about on the phone yesterday's name is Thompson
The man who called last week's umbrella is still in the hall

● Expressions of this sort should not be used in serious prose. Substitute:

The geraniums of the people in the house opposite

The name of the woman I told you about on the phone yesterday is Thompson
The umbrella of the man who called last week is still in the hall

have

1. The verb *to have*, in some of its uses, can form its interrogative and negative either with or without the verb *to do*, e.g. *Do you have/have you?*, *You don't have/you haven't*.

In sentences like those below, *have* is a verb of event, meaning 'experience'. The interrogative and negative are always formed with *do*:

Do you ever have *nightmares?*
We did not have *an easy time getting here*

In the next pair of sentences, *have* is a verb of state, meaning 'possess'. When used in this sense, the interrogative and negative can be formed without *do*:

What have you *in common with the child of five whose photograph your mother keeps?* (George Orwell)
The truth was that he hadn't *the answer* (Joyce Cary)

In more informal language, the verb *got* is added, e.g. *What have you got, He hadn't got the answer*. This is not usually suitable for formal usage and is not usual in American English.

It was formerly usual to distinguish the sense 'experience' from the sense 'possess' by using *do* for the first but not for the second (but only in the present tense). Hence *I don't have indigestion* (as a rule) was kept distinct from *I haven't (got) indigestion* (at the moment). The use of the *do*-construction when the meaning was 'possess' was an Americanism, but it is now generally acceptable.

● However, the use of *do* as a substitute verb for *have*, common informally, is not acceptable in formal prose:

I had stronger feelings than she did (substitute *than she had*)

2. *Have* is often wrongly inserted after *I'd* in sentences like:

If I'd have *known she'd be here I don't suppose I'd have come* (Character in play by John Osborne)

This is common, and hardly noticed, in speech, but should not occur in formal writing. The correct construction is:

> *If* I'd known *she'd be here* . .

he who, she who

He who and *she who* are correctly used when *he* and *she* are the subject of the main clause, and *who* is the subject of the relative clause:

> He who *hesitates is lost*
> She who *was a star in the old play may find herself a super in the new* (C. S. Lewis)

In these examples *he* and *she* are the subjects of *is lost* and *may find* respectively; *who* is the subject of *hesitates* and *was*.

He who and *she who* should change to *him who* and *her who* if the personal pronouns are not the subject of the main clause:

> *The distinction between the man who gives with conviction and* him (not *he*) *who is simply buying a title*

Similarly *who* becomes *whom*—if it is not the subject of its clause:

> *I sought* him whom *my soul loveth* (Authorized Version)

See also *who* and *whom* (interrogative and relative pronouns).

-ics, nouns in

Nouns ending in *-ics* are sometimes treated as singular and sometimes as plural. Examples are:

> *economics*   *linguistics*   *physics*
> *electronics*   *mathematics*   *politics*
> *ethics*   *metaphysics*   *statistics*

When used strictly as the name of a discipline they are treated as singular:

> *Psychometrics* is *unable to investigate the nature of intelligence* (*Guardian*)
> *The quest for a hermeneutics* (TLS)

So also when the complement is singular:

> *Pure mathematics* is *a non-inductive* . . *science* (Gilbert Ryle)

When they mean a manifestation of qualities, often accompanied by a possessive, they are treated as plural:

> *His politics* were *a mixture of fear, greed and envy* (Joyce Cary)
> *The acoustics in this hall* are *dreadful*
> *Their tactics* were *cowardly*

So also when they denote activities or behaviour:

> *acrobatics*   *dramatics*   *heroics*
> *athletics*   *gymnastics*   *hysterics*

e.g. *The mental gymnastics required* are *beyond me.*

These words usually remain plural even with a singular complement:

> *The acrobatics* are *just the social side* (Tom Stoppard)

infinitive, present or perfect

The perfect infinitive is correctly used when it refers to an earlier time than that referred to by the verb on which it depends, e.g.

> *If it were real life and not a play, that is the part it would be best* to have acted (C. S. Lewis)
> *Someone seems* to have been making *a beast of himself here* (Evelyn Waugh)

In the above examples, the infinitives *to have acted* and *to have been making* relate to actions earlier in time than the verbs *would be best* and *seems*.

Only if both verbs refer to the past, and the infinitive to an earlier past, should a perfect infinitive follow a past or perfect verb, e.g.

> *When discussing sales with him yesterday, I should have liked to have seen the figures beforehand*

In this example *I should have liked* denotes the speaker's feelings during the discussion and *to have seen* denotes an action imagined as occurring before the discussion.

If the state or action denoted by the infinitive occurred at the same time as the other verb, then the present infinitive should be used:

> *She would have liked to see what was on the television* (Kingsley Amis)

The 'double past' is often accidentally used informally, e.g.

I should have liked to have gone *to the party*

A literary example is:

> *Mr. McGregor threw down the sack . . in a way that would have been extremely painful to the Flopsy Bunnies, if they* had happened to have been *inside it* (Beatrix Potter)

This should be avoided.

-ing (gerund and participle)

1. The *-ing* form of a verb can in some contexts be used in either of two constructions:

(i) as a gerund (verbal noun) with a possessive noun or pronoun, e.g.

> *In the event of* Randall's not going (Iris Murdoch)
>
> *She did not like* his being *High Church* (L. P. Hartley)

(ii) as a participle with a noun or objective pronoun, e.g.

> *What further need would there have been to speak of another* priest arising? (*New English Bible*)
>
> *Dixon did not like* him doing *that* (Kingsley Amis)

The choice arises only when the accompanying word is a proper or personal noun (e.g. *John, father, teacher*) or a personal pronoun.

In formal usage, prefer the possessive construction wherever it is possible and natural:

> *To whom, without* its being *ordered, the waiter immediately brought a plate of eggs and bacon* (Evelyn Waugh)
>
> *The danger of* Joyce's turning *them into epigrams* (Anthony Burgess)

But it is certainly not wrong to use the non-possessive construction if it sounds more natural, as in the *New English Bible* quotation above. Moreover, there is sometimes a nuance of meaning. *She did not like his being High Church* suggests merely that she did not like the fact that he was High Church, whereas *Dixon did not like him doing that* suggests an element of repugnance to the person as well as to his action.

When using most non-personal nouns (e.g. *luggage, permission*), groups of nouns (e.g. *father and mother*), non-personal pronouns (e.g. *something*), and groups of pronouns (e.g. *some of them*), the possessive would not sound idiomatic at all. Examples are:

> *Travellers in Italy could depend on their* luggage *not* being *stolen* (G. B. Shaw)
>
> *His lines were cited . . without his* permission having *been asked* (*The Times*)
>
> *Due to her* father and mother being *married* (Compton Mackenzie)
>
> *The air of* something *unusual* having *happened* (Arthur Conan Doyle)
>
> *He had no objection to* some of them listening (Arnold Bennett)

When the word preceding the *-ing* form is a regular plural noun ending in *-s*, there is no spoken distinction between the two forms. It is unnecessary to write an apostrophe:

> *If she knew about her* daughters *attending the party* (Anthony Powell)

2. There is also variation between the two uses of the *-ing* form after nouns like *difficulty, point, trouble,* and *use.*

Formal English requires the gerundial use, the gerund being introduced by *in* (or *of* after *use*):

> *There was . . no difficulty* in finding *parking space* (David Lodge)

Informal usage permits the placing of the *-ing* form immediately after the noun, forming a participial construction, e.g.

> *The chairman had difficulty* concealing *his irritation*

● This is not acceptable in formal usage.

I or *me, we* or *us*, etc.

There is often confusion about which case to use here.

1. When the personal pronoun stands alone, as when it forms the answer to a question, formal usage requires it to have the case it would have if the verb were supplied:

> *Who killed Cock Robin?*—I (in full, *I killed him*)

Which of you did he approach?—Me (in full, *he approached me*)

Informal usage permits the objective case in both kinds of sentence, but this is not acceptable in formal style. However, the subjective case often sounds stilted. It is then best to provide a verb, e.g.

Who likes cooking?—I do
Who can cook?—I can

2. When a personal pronoun follows *it is*, *it was*, *it may be*, etc., it should have the subjective case in formal usage:

We are given no clue as to what it must have felt like to be he (C. S. Lewis)

Informal usage favours the objective case:

I thought it might have been him *at the door*
Don't tell me it's them *again!*

● This is not acceptable in formal usage.

When *who* or *whom* follows, the subjective case is obligatory in formal usage and quite usual informally:

It was she *who winched up that infernal machine* (Joseph Conrad)

The informal use of the objective case often sounds substandard:

It was her *who would get the blood off* (Character in work by Patrick White)

(For agreement between the personal pronoun antecedent and the verb in *It is I who* etc., see *I who, you who*, etc.)

In constructions which have the form *I am* + noun or noun phrase + *who*, the verb following *who* is always in the third person (singular or plural):

I am the sort of person who likes *peace and quiet*

I should or I would

There is often uncertainty whether to use *should* or *would* with *I* and *we* before verbs such as *like* or *think* and before *rather* and *sooner*.

1. *Should* is correct before verbs of liking, e.g. *be glad*, *be inclined*, *care*, *like*, and *prefer*:

Would you like a beer?—I should prefer *a cup of coffee, if you don't mind*

The very occasions on which we should *most like to write a slashing review* (C. S. Lewis)

2. *Should* is correct with verbs such as *imagine, say*, and *think*:

I should imagine *that you are right*
I should say *so*
I shouldn't *have* thought *it was difficult*

3. *Would* is correct before the adverbs *rather* and *sooner*, e.g.

I would *truly* rather *be in the middle of this than sitting in that church in a tight collar* (Susan Hill)

Would is always correct with *you, he, she, it*, and *they*.

See also *should* and *would*.

I who, you who, etc.

The verb following *I, you, he*, etc. + *who* should agree with the pronoun:

I, who have *no savings to speak of, had to pay for the work*

This remains so even with *me, him*, etc.:

They made me, who have *no savings at all, pay for the work* (not *who has*)

When *it is* etc. precedes *I who* etc., the same rule applies:

It's I who have *done it*
It could have been we who were *mistaken*

Informal usage sometimes permits the third person to be used (especially when the verb *to be* follows *who*):

You who's *supposed to be so practical!*

● This is not acceptable in formal usage.

-lily adverbs

When the suffix *-ly* is added to an adjective which already ends in *-ly*, the resulting adverb tends to sound odd, e.g. *friendlily*.

Adverbs of this kind are divided into three groups:

(i) Those formed from adjectives in which the final *-ly* is not a suffix, e.g. *holily, jollily, sillily*. These are the least objectionable and are quite often used.

(ii) Those of three syllables formed from adjectives in which the final *-ly* is itself a suffix, e.g. *friendlily, ghastlily, lovelily, statelily, uglily*. These are occasionally found.

(iii) Those of four (or more) syllables formed from adjectives in which the final *-ly* is itself a suffix, e.g. *heavenlily, scholarlily*. Such words are deservedly rare.

The adverbs of groups (ii) and (iii) should be avoided if possible, by using the adjective with a noun like *manner* or *way*, e.g. *In a scholarly manner*.

A few adjectives in *-ly* can be used adverbially to qualify other adjectives, e.g. *beastly cold, ghastly pale*.

may or might

There is sometimes confusion about whether to write *He may have* or *He might have*.

1. If at the time of speaking or writing the truth of the event is still unknown, then either *may* or *might* is acceptable:

> As they all wore so many different clothes of identically the same kind . ., there may *have been several more or several less* (Evelyn Waugh)
> For all we knew we were both bastards, although of course there might *have been a ceremony* (Graham Greene)

2. If the event did not in fact occur, use *might*:

> If that had come ten days ago my whole life might *have been different* (Evelyn Waugh)
> It might *have been better if the Russian Revolution had never taken place* (*The Times*)

● It is a common error to use *may* instead of *might* here:

> If he (President Galtieri) *had not invaded, then eventually the islands* may *have fallen into their lap*
> Schoenberg may *never have gone atonal but for the break-up of his marriage*

(*Might* should be substituted for *may* in each of the above.)

measurement, nouns of

There is some uncertainty about when to use the singular form, and when the plural, of nouns of measurement.

1. These nouns remain singular when compounded with a numeral and used attributively before another noun:

> A *six*-foot *wall*   A *five*-pound *note*
> A *three*-mile *walk*   A *1,000*-megaton *bomb*
> A *ten*-hectare *field*   A *three*-litre *bottle*

2. *Foot* remains in the singular form in expressions such as:

> I am six foot   She is five foot two

But *feet* is used where an adjective, or the word *inches*, follows, e.g.

> I am six feet tall   She is five feet three inches

Stone and *hundredweight* remain singular, e.g.

> I weigh eleven stone   Three hundredweight of coal

Metric measurements always take the plural form when not used attributively:

> This measures three metres by two metres

Informally, some other nouns of measurement are used in the singular form in plural expressions, e.g.

> That will be two pound fifty, please

● This is non-standard.

See also **quantity, nouns of**.

need

The verb *to need*, when followed by an infinitive, can be used either like an ordinary verb or like an auxiliary.

1. *Need* is used like an ordinary verb, and followed by the *to*-infinitive, in the present tense when the sentence is neither negative nor interrogative, in the past tense always, and in all compound tenses (e.g. the future and perfect):

> One needs friends, one needs to be a friend (Susan Hill)

One did not need to *be a clairvoyant to
see that war . . was coming* (George
Orwell)

2. *Need* can be used like an auxiliary verb
in the present tense in negative and interrogative sentences. This means that:

(*a*) The third person singular does not
add *-s*:

He need not come

(*b*) For the interrogative, *need I* (*you* etc.)
replaces *do I need*:

Need I *add that she is my bitterest
enemy?* (G. B. Shaw)

(*c*) The bare infinitive follows instead of
the *to*-infinitive:

*Company that keeps them smaller than
they need* be (*Bookseller*) (This is
negative in sense, for it implies
They need not be as small as this)

This auxiliary verb use is optional, not
obligatory. The regular constructions are
equally correct:

*He does not need to . .
Do I need to add . .
Smaller than they need to be . .*

It is important, however, to avoid mixing
the two kinds of construction, as in the two
following examples:

One needs not be *told that* (etc.)
What proved vexing, it needs be *said,
was* (etc.)

neither . . nor

Two singular subjects linked by *neither . .
nor* can be constructed with either a singular or a plural verb. Strictly and logically a
singular verb is required:

Neither he nor his wife has *arrived
There* is *neither a book nor a picture in
the house*

Informal usage permits the plural:

Neither painting nor fighting feed *men*
(Ruskin)

When one subject is plural and the other
singular, the verb should be plural and the
plural subject placed nearer to it:

Neither the teacher nor the pupils understand *the problem*

When one subject is *I* or *you* and the other
is a third person pronoun or a noun, or
when one is *I* and the other *you*, the verb
can agree with the nearer subject. However, this may sound odd, e.g.

Neither my son nor I am *good at figures*

One can recast the sentence, but this can
spoil the effect. It is often better to use the
plural:

Neither Isabel nor I are *timid people*
(H. G. Wells)

This is not illogical if *neither . . nor* is
regarded as the negative of *both . . and*.

neither (pronoun)

Neither is singular, and strictly requires a
singular verb:

Neither of us likes *to be told what to do*

Informal usage permits a plural verb and
complement:

Neither of us are *good players*

Although this iş widely regarded as incorrect, it has been an established construction for three or four centuries:

Neither were *great inventors* (Dryden)

One should prefer the singular unless it
leads to awkwardness, as when neither *he*
nor *she* is appropriate:

*John and Mary will have to walk.
Neither of them* have *brought their
cars*

none (pronoun)

The pronoun *none* can be followed either
by singular verb and singular pronouns,
or by plural ones. Either is acceptable.

Singular: *None of them* was *allowed to
              forget for a moment*
              (Anthony Powell)
Plural: *None of the fountains ever
              play* (Evelyn Waugh)

ought

Oughtn't or *didn't ought?*

The standard negative of *ought* is *ought
not* or *oughtn't*:

A look from Claudia showed me I ought not *to have begun it* (V. S. Pritchett)

Being an auxiliary verb, *ought* does not require the verb *do*. It is non-standard to form the negative with *do* (*didn't ought*):

> *I hope that none here will say I did anything I* didn't ought. (Character in work by Michael Innes)

When the negative is used in a 'question tag', it should be formed according to the rule above:

> *You ought to be pleased*, oughtn't you? (not *didn't you?*)

In the same way *do* should not be substituted for *ought*, e.g.

> *Ought he to go?—Yes, he* ought (not *he did*)
> *You ought not to be pleased*, ought *you?* (not *did you?*)

participles

A participle used in place of a verb in a subordinate clause must have an explicit subject to qualify. If no subject precedes it, the participle is understood to qualify the subject of the main sentence. In the following sentences the participles *running* and *propped* qualify the subjects *she* and *we*:

> Running *to catch a bus, she just missed it* (Anthony Powell)
> *We both lay there*, propped *on our elbows* (Lynne Reid Banks)

It is a frequent error to begin a sentence with a participial clause, and to continue it with a subject to which the participle is not related:

> Driving *along the road*, the church *appeared on our left*
> (*We*, not *the church*, is the subject of *driving*)
> Having been relieved *of his portfolio in 1976*, the scheme *was left to his successor at the Ministry to complete*
> (*He*, or a proper name, is the subject of *having been relieved*)

Participles that appear to be attached to the wrong subject are sometimes known as dangling (or unattached or hanging) participles.

Such sentences must be recast:

> Driving *along the road*, we saw *the church* appear *on our left*
> As we were *driving along the road, the church appeared on our left*
> Jones *having been relieved of his portfolio in 1976, the scheme was left to his successor at the Ministry to complete*

When the participial clause includes a subject it should not be separated by a comma from the participle:

> Bernadette being her niece, *she feels responsible for the girl's moral welfare* (David Lodge) (Not: *Bernadette, being her niece, she . .*)

But if the participle qualifies the subject of the main sentence, its clause is either marked off by a pair of commas or not marked off at all:

> *The man*, hoping to escape, *jumped on to a bus*
> *A man* carrying a parcel *jumped on to the bus*

The rule that a participle must have an explicit subject does not apply to participial clauses whose subject is indefinite (= 'one' or 'people'). In these the clause comments on the content of the sentence:

> Judging *from his appearance, he has had a night out*
> Roughly speaking, *this is how it went*

The participial clauses here are equivalent to 'If one judges . .', 'If one speaks . .'. Expressions of this kind are entirely acceptable.

See also **unattached phrases**.

preposition at end

It is a natural feature of the English language that many sentences and clauses end with a preposition, and the alleged rule that forbids this should be disregarded.

The preposition *cannot* be moved to an earlier place in many sentences, e.g.

> *What did you do that* for?
> *What a mess this room is* in!
> *The bed had not been slept* in

Where there is a choice, it is very often a matter of style. The preposition has been placed before the relative pronoun in:

The present is the only time in which *any duty can be done* (C. S. Lewis)

But it stands near the end in:

Harold's Philistine outlook, which she had acquiesced in *for ten years* (L. P. Hartley)

But notice that some prepositions cannot come at the end:

An annual sum, in return for *which she agreed to give me house room* (William Trevor)

During *which week will the festival be held?*

One would not write *Which she agreed to give me house room* in return for, and *Which week will the festival be held* during?

One should be guided by what sounds natural. There is no need to alter the position of the preposition merely in deference to the alleged rule.

quantity, nouns of

The numerals *hundred, thousand, million, billion, trillion,* and the words *dozen* and *score* are sometimes used in the singular and sometimes in the plural.

1. They always have the singular form if they are qualified by a preceding word, whether it is singular (e.g. *a, one*) or plural (e.g. *many, several, two, three,* etc.), and whether or not they are used attributively before a noun or with nothing following:

A hundred days
Three hundred will be enough
I will take two dozen
Two dozen eggs

● The use of the plural form here is incorrect:

The population is now three millions (correctly *three million*)

Although they are singular, they always take plural verbs:

There were *about a dozen of them approaching* (Anthony Powell)

2. They take the plural form when they denote indefinite quantities. Usually they are followed by *of* or stand alone:

Are there any errors?—Yes, hundreds
He has dozens of friends

Many thousands of people are homeless

See also **measurement, nouns of**.

reflexive pronouns

These normally refer back to the subject of the clause or sentence in which they occur, e.g.

I *congratulated* myself *on outwitting everyone else*

Can't you *do anything for* yourself?

Sometimes it is permissible to use a reflexive pronoun to refer to someone who is not the subject, e.g.

It was their success, both with myself *and others, that confirmed* me *in what has since been my career* (Evelyn Waugh)

You *have the feeling that all their adventures have happened to* yourself (George Orwell)

To have written *me* and *you* respectively in these sentences would not have been grammatically incorrect.

A reflexive pronoun is often used after such words as

as	but	like
as for	except	than

e.g. *For those who*, like himself, *felt it indelicate to raise an umbrella in the presence of death* (Iris Murdoch)

It can be a very useful way to avoid the difficult choice between *I, he, she,* etc. (which often sound stilted) and *me, him, her,* etc. (which are grammatically incorrect) after the words *as, but,* and *than*, e.g.

None of them was more surprised than myself *that I'd spoken* (Lynne Reid Banks)

Here *than I* would be strictly correct, while *than me* would be informal.

Naturally a reflexive pronoun cannot be used in the ways outlined above if confusion would result. One would not write:

John was as surprised as himself *that he had been appointed*

but would substitute the person's name, or *he himself was*, for *himself*, or recast the sentence.

relative clauses

A relative clause is a clause introduced by a relative pronoun and used to qualify a preceding noun or pronoun (called its antecedent), e.g. *The visitor* (antecedent) *whom* (relative pronoun) *you were expecting* (remainder of relative clause) *has arrived*; *He* who hesitates *is lost*.

Exceptionally, there are nominal relative clauses in which the antecedent and relative pronoun are combined in one *wh*-pronoun, e.g. What you need *is a drink*: see *what* (relative pronoun).

Relative clauses can be either restrictive or non-restrictive. A restrictive relative clause identifies the antecedent, e.g. *A suitcase* which has lost its handle *is useless*. Here the antecedent *suitcase* is defined by the clause.

A non-restrictive relative clause merely adds further information, e.g. *He carried the suitcase*, which had lost its handle, *on one shoulder*.

Notice that no commas are used to mark off a restrictive relative clause, but when a non-restrictive relative clause comes in the middle of the sentence, it is marked off by a comma at each end.

There are two kinds of relative pronouns:

(i) The *wh*-type: *who*, *whom*, *whose*, *which*, and, in nominal relative clauses only, *what*.

(ii) The pronoun *that* (which can be omitted in some circumstances: see *that* (relative pronoun), omission of).

When one relative clause is followed by another, the second relative pronoun

(a) may or may not be preceded by a conjunction; and

(b) may or may not be omitted.

(a) A conjunction is not required if the second relative clause qualifies an antecedent inside the first relative clause:

I found a firm which had some components for which they had no use

Here *for which* .. *use* qualifies *components* which is part of the relative clause qualifying *firm*. *And* or *but* should not be inserted before *for which*.

But if both clauses qualify the same antecedent, a conjunction is required:

Help me with these shelves which I have to take home but which will not fit in my car

(b) The second relative pronoun can be omitted if (i) it qualifies the same antecedent as the first, and (ii) it plays the same part in its clause as the first (i.e. subject or object):

George, who *takes infinite pains and* (who) *never cuts corners, is our most dependable worker*

Here both *who*'s qualify *George*, and are the subjects of their clauses, so the second can be omitted.

But if the second relative pronoun plays a different part in its clause, it cannot be omitted:

George, whom *everybody likes but* who *rarely goes to a party, is shy*

Here *whom* is the object, *who* is the subject, in their clauses, so *who* must be kept.

See also **preposition at end**, *that* (relative pronoun), omission of, *what* (relative pronoun), *which* or *that* (relative pronouns), *who* and *whom* (interrogative and relative pronouns), *who* or *which* (relative pronouns), *whose* or *of which* in relative clauses, *who/whom* or *that* (relative pronouns).

shall and will

'The horror of that moment', the King went on, 'I shall never, never forget!' 'You will, though,' the Queen said, 'if you don't make a memorandum of it.' (Lewis Carroll)

The traditional rule in standard British English is:

1. In the first person, singular and plural.

(a) *I shall*, *we shall* express the simple future, e.g.

I am not a manual worker and please God I never shall be one (George Orwell)

In the following pages we shall see good words .. losing their edge (C. S. Lewis)

(b) *I will*, *we will* express intention or promises on the part of the speaker, e.g.

I will *take you to see her tomorrow morning* (P. G. Wodehouse)

I will *no longer accept responsibility for the fruitless loss of life* (Susan Hill)

2. For the second and third persons, singular and plural, the rule is exactly the converse.

(*a*) *You, he, she, it,* or *they will* express the simple future, e.g.

Will *it disturb you if I keep the lamp on for a bit?* (Susan Hill)

Seraphina will *last much longer than a car.* (Graham Greene)

(*b*) *You, he, she, it,* or *they shall* express intention or promises made by the speaker, e.g.

One day you shall *know my full story* (Evelyn Waugh)

The two uses of *will*, and one of those of *shall*, are well illustrated by:

'*I* will *follow you to the ends of the earth,*' *replied Susan, passionately.* '*It* will *not be necessary,*' *said George. 'I am only going down to the coal-cellar. I* shall *spend the next half-hour or so there.*' (P. G. Wodehouse)

In informal usage *I* will and *we* will are quite often used for the simple future, e.g.

I will *be a different person when I live in England* (Character in work by Jean Rhys)

More often the distinction is covered up by using '*ll*, e.g.

I don't quite know when I'll *get the time to write again* (Susan Hill)

● The use of *will* for *shall* in the first person, though common, is not regarded as fully acceptable in formal usage.

should **and** would

When used for (*a*) the future in the past or (*b*) the conditional,

should goes with *I* and *we*

would goes with *you, he, she, it,* and *they*

(*a*) The future in the past.

First person:

Julia and I, who had left . ., thinking we should *not return* (Evelyn Waugh)

The person's imagined statement or thought at the time was:

We shall *not return*

with *shall*, not *will* (see shall **and** will).

Second and third persons:

He was there. Later, he would not be *there* (Susan Hill)

The person's statement or thought at the time was

He will *not be there*

(*b*) The conditional.

First person:

I should *view with the strongest disapproval any proposal to abolish manhood suffrage* (C. S. Lewis)

Second and third persons:

If you took 3 ft off the average car, you would *have another six million feet of road space* (*The Times*)

In informal usage, *I would* and *we would* are very common in both kinds of sentence:

I wondered whether I would *have to wear a black suit*

I would *have been content, I would never have repeated it* (Both examples from Graham Greene)

The use of *would* with the first person is understandable, because *should* (in all persons) has a number of uses, including 'ought to'; sometimes the context does not make it clear whether I should do means 'it would be the case that I did' or 'I ought to do', e.g.

I wondered whether, when I was cross-examined, I should *admit that I knew the defendant*

● This use of *I would* and *we would* is not, however, regarded as fully acceptable in formal language.

See also I should **or** I would.

singular or plural

1. When subject and complement are different in number (i.e. one is singular, the other plural), the verb normally agrees with the subject, e.g.

(Plural subject)

Ships are *his chief interest*

Liqueur chocolates are *our speciality*
(Singular subject)

What we need is *customers*
Our speciality is *liqueur chocolates*

2. A plural subject used as a name counts as singular, e.g.

Sons and Lovers has *always been one of Lawrence's most popular novels*

3. A singular phrase that happens to end with a plural word should nevertheless be followed by a singular verb, e.g.

One in six has (not *have*) *this problem*

4. A problem often arises when such words as *average, maximum, minimum,* and *total* are used like this:

An average of 27,000 quotations has (or *have*) *been sent in each year*
A total of 335 British cases of AIDS has (or *have*) *been reported*

Strictly speaking the verb should agree with the singular noun, but in practice it is often made to agree with the nearest (and in the above examples, plural) noun. This often seems more natural.

5. If the subject of a relative clause is the same as the antecedent, the verb in the relative clause agrees in number with the antecedent, e.g.

It is the children *who* are *the first consideration* (E. M. Forster)

If the relative clause follows *one of the* + a plural noun, either *one* or the noun may be the antecedent. If *one* is the antecedent the verb should be singular, e.g.

One of the most dependable of the older girls, who was *made responsible* (Flora Thompson)

If the plural noun is the antecedent the verb should be plural, e.g.

He is one of the few businessmen who like *journalists* (i.e. 'one of the few journalist-liking businessmen')

● The singular is often used by mistake, e.g. in

The theory of black holes . . may perhaps be considered as one of the aspects of general-relativistic physics which is *better understood* (*Nature*)

where the sense must be 'one of the better-understood aspects'.

See also **collective nouns, compound subject, -ics, nouns in, quantity, nouns of, -s plural or singular,** *what* **(relative pronoun).**

split infinitive

This means the separation of *to* from the infinitive by one or more intervening words, e.g. *He used* to continually refer *to the subject.* In this *continually* splits *to refer* into two parts.

It is often said that an infinitive should never be split, but this is too rigid a rule; rather, avoid splitting unless the avoidance leads to clumsiness or ambiguity.

1. Good writers usually avoid splitting the infinitive by placing the adverb before the infinitive:

One meets people who have learned actually to prefer *the tinned fruit to the fresh* (C. S. Lewis)
He did not want positively to suggest *that she was dominant* (Iris Murdoch)

On the other hand, it is quite natural in speech, and permissible in writing, to say:

What could it be like to actually live *in France?*
To really let *the fact that these mothers were mothers sink in*
(Both examples from Kingsley Amis)

2. Avoidance of ambiguity.

When an adverb closely qualifies the infinitive verb it may often be better to split the infinitive. The following example is ambiguous in writing, though in speech stress would make the meaning clear:

It fails completely to carry conviction

Either it means 'It totally fails . .', in which case *completely* should precede *fails*, or it means 'It fails to carry complete conviction', in which case that should be written, or the infinitive should be split.

3. Avoidance of clumsiness.

It took more than an excited elderly man . . socially to discompose him . . (Anthony Powell)

In this example *socially* belongs closely with *discompose* : it is not 'to discompose in a social way' but 'to cause social discomposure'. In such cases, it may be better either to split the infinitive or to recast the sentence than to separate the adverb from the verb.

4. Unavoidable split infinitive.

There are certain adverbial constructions which must immediately precede the verb and therefore split the infinitive, e.g. *more than*:

> *Enough new ships are delivered* to more than make up *for the old ones being retired*

And a writer may have sound stylistic reasons for allowing a parenthetic expression to split an infinitive:

> *It would be an act of gratuitous folly* to, as he had put it to Mildred, make *trouble for himself* (Iris Murdoch)

-s plural or singular

Some nouns that end in *-s* are treated as singulars, taking singular verbs and pronouns.

1. *news*

2. Diseases:

diabetes	rabies
measles	rickets
mumps	shingles

Measles and *rickets* can also be treated as ordinary plurals.

3. Games:

billiards	dominoes	ninepins
bowls	draughts	skittles

4. Countries:

the Bahamas	the Philippines
the Netherlands	the United States

These are treated as singular when considered as a political unit, or when the complement is singular, e.g.

> The Philippines *is a predominantly agricultural country*
> The United States *has withdrawn its ambassador*

The Bahamas and *the Philippines* are also the geographical names of groups of islands, and in this use can be treated as plurals, e.g.

> *The Bahamas* were *settled by British subjects*

Flanders and *Wales* are always singular. So are the city names *Athens, Brussels, Naples*, etc.

See also *-ics*, **nouns in.**

subjects joined by (*either . .*) or

When two singular subjects are joined by *or* or *either .. or*, the strict rule is that they require a singular verb and singular pronouns:

> *Either Peter or John* has *had* his *breakfast already*
> *A traffic warden or a policeman* is *always on the watch*

However, 'at all times there has been a tendency to use the plural with two or more singular subjects when their mutual exclusion is not emphasized' (*OED*), e.g.

> *On which rage or wantonness vented themselves* (George Eliot)

When one subject is plural, it is best to put the verb in the plural, and place the plural subject nearer to the verb:

> *Either the child or the parents* are *to blame*

When personal pronouns are involved, the verb is usually made to agree with the nearer of the two subjects:

> *Either he or I* am *going to win*
> *Either he or you* have *got to give in*
> *Either you or your teacher* has *made a mistake*

This form of expression very often sounds awkward:

> Am *I or he going to win?*

It is usually best to recast the sentence by adding another verb:

> Am *I going to win, or is he?*
> *Either he has got to give in, or you have*

subjunctive

The present subjunctive form is identical with the indicative, except in the third person singular, which does not end in *-s*. The past subjunctive is indentical with the indicative throughout. In the verb *to be*, however, the present subjunctive is *be*, whereas the present tense is *am*, *are*, or *is*. For the past subjunctive of *to be* (*were*) see *were* or *was*.

The subjunctive is familiar in a number of fixed expressions which cause no problems:

Be *that as it may*	*Heaven* help *us*
Come *what may*	*Long* live *the Queen*
God bless *you*	*So* be *it*
God save *the Queen*	Suffice *it to say that*

There are two other uses of the subjunctive that may cause difficulty, but they are entirely optional apart from the past subjunctive *were*.

1. In *that*-clauses after words expressing command, hope, intention, wish, etc. Typical introducing words are

demand that	*proposal that*
insist that	*suggest that*
be insistent that	*suggestion that*

Typical examples are:

He had been insisting that they keep *the night of the twenty-second free* (C. P. Snow)

Joseph was insistent that his wishes be *carried out* (W. Somerset Maugham)

Your suggestion that I fly *out* (David Lodge)

Until recently this use of the subjunctive was restricted to very formal language, where it is still usual, e.g.

The Lord Chancellor put the motion that the House go *into Committee*

It is, however, a usual American idiom, and is now quite acceptable in British English, but *should* or *may* or (especially in informal use) the ordinary indicative, depending on the context, will do equally well:

Your demand that he should pay *the money back surprised him*

I insist that the boy goes *to school this minute*

● Beware of constructions in which the sense hangs on a fine distinction between subjunctive and indicative, e.g.

The most important thing for Argentina is that Britain recognize *her sovereignty over the Falklands*

The implication is that Britain does not recognize it. A change of *recognize* to *recognizes* would drastically reverse this implication. The use of *should recognize* would render the sense unmistakable.

2. In certain clauses introduced by *though* and *if*, the subjunctive can be used to express reserve about an action or state, e.g.

Though he be *the devil himself he shall do as I say*

The University is a place where a poor man, if he be *virtuous, may live a life of dignity and simplicity* (A. C. Benson)

This is very formal. It should not be used in ordinary prose, where sometimes the indicative and sometimes an auxiliary such as *may* are entirely acceptable, e.g.

Though he may be *an expert, he should listen to advice*

If this is *the case, then I am in error*

than, case following

In the following sentences, the pronoun is in the subjective case, because it would be the subject if a verb were supplied:

You are two stone heavier than I (G. B. Shaw) (= *than I am*)

We pay more rent than they (= *than they do*)

In the sentence below, the objective case is used, because the pronoun would be the object if there were a verb:

Jones treated his wife badly. I think that he liked his dog better than her (= *than he liked her*)

Informal English permits the objective case everywhere, e.g.

You do it very well. Much better than me

The preferred formal alternative, with the subjective, often sounds stilted. When this is so, it can be avoided by supplying the verb:

We pay more rent than they do

The pronoun *whom* is always used after *than*, rather than *who*:

Professor Smith, than whom *there is scarcely anyone better qualified to judge, believes it to be pre-Roman*

that (conjunction), omission of

1. The conjunction *that* introducing a noun clause and used after verbs of saying, thinking, knowing, etc., can often be omitted in informal usage:

I told him (that) *he was wrong*
Are you sure (that) *this is the place?*

Generally speaking, the omission of *that* is inappropriate in formal prose.

That should never be omitted if other parts of the sentence (apart from the indirect object) intervene:

I told him, as I have told everyone, that he was wrong
Are you sure in your own mind that this is the place?

The omission of *that* makes it difficult, in written prose, to follow the sense.

2. When *that* is part of the correlative pairs of conjunctions *so . . that* and *such . . that*, or of the compound conjunctions *so that, now that,* it can be omitted in informal usage.

● It should not be omitted in formal style:

He walked so fast (or *at such a speed*) *that I could not keep up*
I'll move my car so that you can park in the drive
Are you lonely now that your children have left home?

that (relative pronoun), omission of

The relative pronoun *that* can often be omitted, but in formal contexts the omission is best limited to short clauses which stand next to their antecedents:

None of the cars (that) *I saw had been damaged*
Nothing (that) *I could say made any difference*

That cannot be omitted when it is the subject of the relative clause, e.g.

Nothing that *occurred to me made any difference*

None of the cars that *were under cover had been damaged*

See also **adverbial relative clauses** and *way,* **relative clause following.**

there is or *there are*

In a sentence introduced by *there* + part of *to be,* the latter agrees in number with whatever follows:

There was *a great deal to be said for this scheme*
There are *many advantages in doing it this way*

In very informal language *there is* or *there was* is often heard before a plural:

There's two coloured-glass windows in the chapel (Character in work by Evelyn Waugh)

● This is non-standard.

to

The preposition *to* can stand at the end of a clause or sentence as a substitute for an omitted *to*-infinitive, e.g.

He had tried not to think about Emma . ., but of course it was impossible not to (Iris Murdoch)

This is standard usage.

unattached participles: see participles.

unattached phrases

An adjectival or adverbial phrase, introducing a sentence, must qualify the subject of the sentence, e.g.

While not entirely in agreement with the plan, *he had no serious objections to it*
After two days on a life-raft, *the survivors were rescued by helicopter*

It is a common error to begin a sentence with a phrase of this kind, and then to continue it with a quite different subject, e.g.

After six hours without food in a plane on the perimeter at Heathrow, *the flight was cancelled*

The phrase *After . . Heathrow* anticipates a subject like *the passengers.* Such a sentence should either have a new beginning, e.g.

> *After* the passengers had spent *six hours* . .

or a new main clause, e.g.

> *After six hours* . . *Heathrow*, the passengers learnt that *the flight had been cancelled*

used to

The negative and interrogative of *used to* can be formed in two ways:

(i) Negative: *used not to*
    Interrogative: *used X to?*

Examples:

> *Used you to beat your mother?* (G. B. Shaw)
> *You used not to have a moustache, used you?* (Evelyn Waugh)

(ii) Negative: *did not use to, didn't use to*
     Interrogative: *did X use to?*

Examples:

> *She didn't use to find sex revolting* (John Braine)
> *Did you use to be a flirt?* (Eleanor Farjeon)

□ Either form is acceptable. On the whole *used you to, used he to,* etc. tend to sound rather stilted and over-formal.

● The correct spellings of the negative forms are:

> *usedn't to* and *didn't use to*

way, relative clause following

(The) way can be followed by a relative clause with or without *that*. There is no need to include the preposition *in*:

> *It may have been* the way he smiled (Jean Rhys)
> *She couldn't give a dinner party* the way the young lad's mother could (William Trevor)

were or was

There is often confusion about whether to use *were* or *was* in the first or third person singular.

Formal usage requires *were*

1. In conditional sentences where the condition is 'unreal', e.g.

> *It would probably be more marked if the subject* were *more dangerous* (George Orwell)
> (The 'subject' is not very 'dangerous' in fact)
> *If anyone* were *to try to save me, I would refuse* (Jean Rhys)
> (The condition is regarded as unlikely)

2. Following *as if* and *as though*, e.g.

> *He wore it with an air of melancholy, as though it* were *court mourning* (Evelyn Waugh)
> (For a permissible exception see p. 51)

3. In *that*-clauses after *to wish*, e.g.

> *He wishes he* were *travelling with you* (Angus Wilson)

4. In the fixed expressions *As it were, If I were you*

Notice that in all these constructions the clause with *were* refers to something unreal.

Were may also be used in dependent questions, e.g.

> *Hilliard wondered whether Barton* were *not right after all* (Susan Hill)

□ This is not obligatory even in very formal prose. *Was* is acceptable instead.

we (with phrase following)

Expressions consisting of *we* or *us* followed by a qualifying word or phrase are often misused with the wrong case.

If the expression is the subject, *we* should be used:

| (Correct) | *Not always laughing as heartily as* we *English are supposed to do* (J. B. Priestley) |
| (Incorrect) | *We all make mistakes, even* us *anarchists* (Character in work by Alison Lurie) |

If the expression is the object or the complement of a preposition, *us* should be used:

(Correct)	*Had shut down all their Dutch ports against us English* (Kipling)
(Incorrect)	*The Manchester Guardian has said some nice things about we in the North-East*

what (relative pronoun)

What can be used as a relative pronoun only when introducing nominal relative clauses, e.g.

> *So much of* what you tell me *is strange, different from* what I was led to expect (Jean Rhys)

Here *what* is equivalent to *that which* or *the thing(s) which*.

● *What* qualifies an antecedent only in non-standard speech, e.g.

> *The young gentleman* what's *arranged everything* (Character in work by Evelyn Waugh)

A *what*-clause used as the subject of a sentence almost always takes a singular verb, even if there is a plural complement, e.g.

> *What interests him is less events .. than the reverberations they set up* (Frederic Raphael)

Very occasionally the form of the sentence may render the plural more natural, e.g.

> *What once were great houses* are *now petty offices*

which or *that* (relative pronouns)

There is a degree of uncertainty about whether to use *which* or *that* with a non-personal antecedent (for personal antecedents see *who/whom* or *that*). The general rule is that *which* is used in relative clauses to which the reader's attention is to be drawn, while *that* is used in clauses which do not need special emphasis.

Which is almost always used in non-restrictive clauses, i.e. those that add further information. Example:

> *The men are getting rum issue,* which *they deserve* (Susan Hill)

● The use of *that* in non-restrictive clauses should be avoided, although it is sometimes employed by good writers to suggest a tone of familiarity, e.g.

> *Getting out of Alec's battered old car* that *looked as if it had been in collision with many rocks, Harold had a feeling of relief* (L. P. Hartley)

It should not, however, be used in ordinary prose.

Both *which* and *that* can be used in restrictive (i.e. identifying) relative clauses. Some guidelines follow:

1. *Which* preferred.

(*a*) Clauses which add significant information often sound better with *which*, e.g.

> *Not nearly enough for the social position* which *they had to keep up* (D. H. Lawrence)

(*b*) Clauses which are separated from their antecedent, especially by another noun, sound better with *which*, e.g.

> *Larry told her the story of the young airman* which *I narrated at the beginning of this book* (W. Somerset Maugham)

(*c*) *Which* after a preposition is often a better choice than *that* with the preposition at the end of the sentence (see also **preposition at end**), e.g.

> *I'm telling you about a dream* in which *ordinary things are marvellous* (William Trevor)
>
> (*A dream that ordinary things are marvellous in* would not sound natural)

2. *That* preferred.

In clauses that do not fall into the above categories *that* can usually be used. There is no reason to reject *that* if

(*a*) the antecedent is impersonal,
(*b*) the clause is restrictive,
(*c*) preposition precedes the relative pronoun, and
(*d*) the sentence does not sound strained or excessively colloquial.

Example:

> *I read the letters, none of them very revealing,* that *littered his writing table* (Evelyn Waugh)

Here, *which* would be acceptable, but is not necessary.

When the antecedent is an indefinite pronoun (e.g. *anything, everything*) or contains a superlative adjective qualifying the impersonal antecedent (e.g. *the biggest car*) English idiom tends to prefer *that* to *which*:

> Is there nothing small that *the children could buy you for Christmas?*
> This is the most expensive hat that *you could have bought*

Note that *that* can sometimes be used when one is not sure whether to use *who* or *which*:

> This was the creature, neither child nor woman, that *drove me through the dusk that summer evening* (Evelyn Waugh)

who and *whom* (interrogative and relative pronouns)

1. Formal usage restricts the use of *who* to the subject of the clause only, e.g.

> I who'd *never read anything before but the newspaper* (W. Somerset Maugham)

When the pronoun is the object or the complement of a preposition, *whom* must be used:

> Why are we being served by a man whom *neither of us likes?* (William Trevor)
> The real question is food *(or freedom) for* whom (C. S. Lewis)

● The use of *who* as object or prepositional complement is acceptable only informally, e.g.

> Who *are you looking for?*
> The person who *I'm looking for is rather elusive*

See also **than, case following**.

2. *Whom* for *who.*

Whom is sometimes mistakenly used for *who* because the writer believes it to be the object, or the complement of a preposition.

(*a*) For the interrogative pronoun, the case of *who/whom* is determined by its role in the interrogative clause:

> He never had any doubt about who was *the real credit to the family* (J. I. M. Stewart)

Who here is the subject of *was*. One should not be confused by *about*, which governs the whole clause, not *who* alone.

The error is seen in:

> Whom *among our poets* .. *could be called one of the interior decorators of the 1950s?*
> (Read *Who* .. because it is the subject of *be called*)

Whom is correct in:

> He knew whom *it was from* (L. P. Hartley)
> (Here *whom* is governed by *from*)

(*b*) For the relative pronoun, when followed by a parenthetic clause such as *they say, he thinks*, etc., the case of the pronoun *who/whom* is determined by the part it plays in the relative clause if the parenthetic statement is omitted:

> Sheikh Yamani, who they say *is the richest man in the Middle East*
> (Not *whom they say* since *who* is the subject of *is*, not the object of *say*)

But *whom* is correct in:

> Sheikh Yamani, whom they believe to be *the richest man in the Middle East*

Here *they believe* could not be removed leaving the sentence intact. *Whom* is its object: the simple clause would be *They believe* him to be *the richest man.*

See also *I who, you who*, etc.

who or *which* (relative pronouns)

A *wh*-pronoun introducing a relative clause must be *who* (*whom*) if the antecedent is personal, e.g.

> Suzanne was a woman who *had no notion of reticence* (W. Somerset Maugham)

But it must be *which* if the antecedent is non-personal, e.g.

There was a suppressed tension about her which *made me nervous* (Lynne Reid Banks)

If the relative clause is non-restrictive, i.e. it adds new information, the *wh*-type of pronoun *must* be used (as above).

If the relative clause is restrictive, i.e. identifying, one can use either the appropriate *wh*-pronoun (as above), or the non-variable pronoun *that*. See *which* or *that* (**relative pronouns**) and *who/whom* or *that* (**relative pronouns**).

whose or *of which* in relative clauses

The relative pronoun *whose* can be used as the possessive of *which* as well as of *who*. The rule sometimes enunciated that *of which* must always be used after a non-personal antecedent should be ignored, as it is by good writers, e.g.

The little book whose *yellowish pages she knew* (Virginia Woolf)

In some sentences, *of which* would be almost impossible, e.g.

The lawns about whose *closeness of cut his father worried the gardener daily* (Susan Hill)

There is, of course, no rule prohibiting *of which* if it sounds natural, e.g.

A little town the name of which *I have forgotten* (W. Somerset Maugham)

Whose can only be used as the non-personal possessive in *relative* clauses. Interrogative *whose* refers only to persons, as in *Whose book is this?*

who/whom or *that* (relative pronouns)

In formal usage, *who/whom* is always acceptable as the relative pronoun referring to a person. (See *who* and *whom* (**interrogative and relative pronouns**).)

In non-restrictive relative clauses, i.e. those which add new information, *who/whom* is obligatory, e.g.

It was not like Coulter, who *was a cheerful man* (Susan Hill)

In restrictive (i.e. identifying) relative clauses, *who/whom* is usually quite acceptable:

The masters who *taught me Divinity told me that biblical texts were highly untrustworthy* (Evelyn Waugh)

It is generally felt that the relative pronoun *that* is slightly depreciatory if applied to a person. Hence it tends to be avoided in formal usage.

However, if

(i) the relative pronoun is the object, and
(ii) the personality of the antecedent is suppressed

that may well be appropriate, e.g.

They looked now just like the GIs that *one saw in Viet Nam* (David Lodge)

Informally *that* is acceptable with any personal antecedent, e.g.

Honey, it's me that *should apologize* (David Lodge)

● This should be avoided in formal style.

you and I or *you and me*

When a personal pronoun is linked by *and* or *or* to a noun or another pronoun, the rule is exactly as it would be for the pronoun standing alone.

1. If the two words linked by *and* or *or* constitute the subject, the pronoun should be in the subjective case, e.g.

Only she *and her mother cared for the old house*

Who could go?—Either you or he

The use of the objective case is quite common, but it is non-standard, e.g. (examples from the speech of characters in novels)

That's how we look at it, me *and Martha* (Kingsley Amis)

Either Mary had to leave or me (David Lodge)

2. If the two words linked by *and* or *or* constitute the object of the verb, or the complement of a preposition, the objective case must be used:

The afternoon would suit her *and John better*

● Although the use of the subjective case is very common informally, it remains non-standard, e.g.

It was this that set Charles and I *talking of old times*

Between you and I

This last expression is very commonly heard. *Between you and me* should always be substituted.

Appendix I
Principles of punctuation

apostrophe

1. Used to indicate the possessive case: see p. 19 f.

2. Used to mark an omission, e.g. *e'er*, *we'll*, *he's*, *'69*.

● Sometimes written, but unnecessary, in a number of curtailed words, e.g. *bus*, *cello* (not *'bus*, etc.). See also p. 19 f.

brackets

See: 1. **parentheses**.
    2. **square brackets**.

colon

1. Links two grammatically complete clauses, but marks a step forward to main theme, to effect, to conclusion, e.g. *To commit sin is to break God's law: sin, in fact, is lawlessness.*

2. Introduces a list of items (a dash should not be added), e.g. *The following were present: J. Smith, J. Brown, M. Jones.*

It is used after such expressions as *for example, namely, the following, to resume, to sum up.*

3. Introduces, formally and emphatically, speech or a quotation, e.g. *I told them: 'Do not in any circumstances open this door.'*

comma

1. Used between adjectives which each qualify a noun in the same way, e.g. *A cautious, eloquent man.*

But when adjectives qualify the noun in different ways, or when one adjective qualifies another, no comma is used, e.g. *A distinguished foreign author, a bright red tie.*

2. Separates items (including the last) in a list of more than two, e.g. *Potatoes, peas, and carrots; Potatoes, peas, or carrots; Potatoes, peas, etc.; He has shares in Guinness, Tate and Lyle, and Marks and Spencer.*

● But *A black and white TV set.*

3. Separates coordinated main clauses, e.g. *Cars will turn here, and coaches will go straight on.* But not when they are closely linked, e.g. *Do as I tell you and you'll never regret it.*

4. Marks the beginning and end of a parenthesis, e.g. *I am sure, however, that it will not happen; Fred, who is bald, complained of the cold.*

● Not with restrictive relative clauses, e.g. *Men who are bald should wear hats.*

5. Follows a participial or verbless clause, a salutation, or a vocative, e.g. *Having had breakfast, I went for a walk; The sermon over, the congregation filed out; Ladies and gentlemen, I give you a toast.*

● Not *The sermon, being over,* (etc.).

● No comma in expressions like *My son John.*

6. Separates a phrase or subordinate clause from the main clause so as to avoid misunderstanding, e.g. *He did not go to church, because he was playing golf; In 1982, 1918 seemed a long time ago.*

● A comma should not separate a phrasal subject from its predicate, or a verb from an object that is a clause: *A car with such a high-powered engine, should not let you down* and *They believed, that nothing could go wrong* are both incorrect.

7. Introduces direct speech, e.g. *They answered, 'Here we are.'*

8. Follows *Dear Sir, Dear John,* etc., in letters, and *Yours sincerely,* etc.

● No comma is needed between month and year in dates, e.g. *In December 1992* or between number and road in addresses, e.g. *12 Acacia Avenue.*

dash

1. The *en rule* is distinct (in print) from the **hyphen** (see p. 12 f.) and joins items wherever movement or opposition, rather than cooperation or unity, is felt; it resembles *to* or *versus*, e.g. *The 1914–18 war*; *current–voltage characteristic*; *The London–Horsham–Brighton route*; *The Fischer–Spassky match*; *The Marxist–Trotskyite split.*

● Note *The Marxist-Leninist position*; *The Franco-Prussian war* with hyphens.

It is also used for joint authors, e.g. *The Lloyd–Jones hypothesis* (two men), but *The Lloyd-Jones hypothesis* (one double-barrelled name).

2. The *em rule* (the familiar dash) marks an interruption in a sentence. A pair of them can enclose a parenthesis or a statement interrupted by an interlocutor; e.g. *He was not—you may disagree with me, Henry—much of an artist; 'I didn't—' 'Speak up, boy!' '—hear anything.'* It can be used informally to replace the colon (use 1).

exclamation mark

Used after an exclamatory word, phrase, or sentence. It usually counts as the concluding full stop. It may also be used within square brackets, after a quotation, to express the editor's amusement, dissent, or surprise.

full stop

1. Used at the end of all sentences which are not questions or exclamations. The next word should normally begin with a capital letter.

2. Used after **abbreviations**: see p. 7. If the abbreviation ends the sentence, the point serves as the closing full stop, e.g. *She kept dogs, cats, birds, etc.* but *She kept pets (dogs, cats, birds, etc.).*

3. When a sentence concludes with a quotation which itself ends with a full stop, question mark, or exclamation mark, no further full stop is needed, e.g. *He cried, 'Be off!'* But if the quotation is short, and the introducing sentence has much greater weight, the full stop follows the quotation mark, e.g. *Over the entrance to the temple at Delphi were written the words 'Know thyself'.*

4. A sequence of three full stops marks an omission; a fourth is added if this ends a sentence, e.g. *One critic wrote 'A guidebook ... that I would not want to be without. ... It has been my constant companion.'*

hyphen: see p. 12 f.

parentheses

Enclose:

1. Interpolations by the writer himself, e.g. *Mr. X (as I shall call him) now spoke.*
2. An authority, explanation, reference, or translation.
3. In the report of a speech, interruptions by the audience.
4. Reference letters or figures, e.g. (1), (*a*).
5. Optional words, e.g. *There are many (apparent) difficulties.*

period: see **full stop**.

question mark

1. Follows every question which expects a separate answer. The next word should begin with a capital letter.

● Not used after indirect questions, e.g. *He asked me why I was there.*

2. May be placed before a word, etc., whose accuracy is doubted, e.g. *T. Tallis ?1505–85.*

quotation marks

1. Single quotation marks are used for a first quotation; double for a quotation within this; single again for a further quotation inside that.

2. The closing quotation mark should come before all punctuation marks unless these form part of the quotation itself, e.g. *Did Nelson really say 'Kiss me, Hardy'?* but *Then she asked, 'What is your name?'* (see also **full stop,** 3).

The comma at the end of a quotation, when words such as *he said* follow, is kept inside the quotation, e.g. *'That is nonsense,' he said*. The commas on either side of *he said*, etc., when these words interrupt the quotation, should be outside the quotation marks, e.g. *'That', he said, 'is nonsense.'* But the first comma goes inside the quotation marks if it would be part of the utterance even if there were no interruption, e.g. *'That, my dear fellow,' he said, 'is nonsense'*.

3. Quotation marks are used when citing titles of articles in magazines, chapters of books, poems, and songs.

● Not for titles of books of the Bible; nor for any passage that is not a verbatim quotation.

Titles of books and magazines are usually printed in italic.

semicolon

Separates clauses of similar importance that are too closely linked to require a full stop, e.g. *To err is human; to forgive, divine.* It is often used as a stronger division in a sentence that already includes commas, e.g. *He came out of the house, which lay back from the road, and saw her at the end of the path; but instead of continuing towards her, he hid until she had gone.*

square brackets

Enclose comments, corrections, explanations, interpolations, notes, or translations, which have been added by subsequent editors, e.g. *My right honourable friend* [*John Brown*] *is mistaken.*

Appendix II
Clichés and modish and inflated diction

A cliché is an outworn phrase. One cannot avoid using some clichés: they are too common, and are often useful. In writing serious prose, however, one should choose one's own words if they express the idea more precisely. 'Modish and inflated diction' refers to currently fashionable words and phrases. Some of these are scientific or technical in origin, others may be the creation of the media; but what they have in common is their popularity. It would be difficult to ban them completely, but they should be used with restraint. Some examples follow, of both cliché and modish diction.

at the end of the day
at this moment (or *point*) *in time*
-awareness (e.g. *brand-awareness*)
back burner (*on the* ——)
ball game (*a different*, etc., ——)
basically (as a filler)
bottom line
by and large (sometimes used with no meaning)
-centred (e.g. *discovery-centred*)
conspicuous by one's absence
constructive (used tautologously, e.g. *A constructive suggestion*)
definitely
-deprivation (e.g. *status-deprivation*)
dialogue
dimension (= feature, factor)
-directed (e.g. *task-directed*)
-driven (e.g. *consumer-driven*)
environment
escalate (= increase, intensify)
-friendly (e.g. *consumer-friendly*)
grind to a halt (= end, stop)
if you like (explanatory tag)
integrate, integrated
in terms of
in the order of (= about)
in this day and age

-ize (suffix, forming vogue words, e.g. *normalize, permanentize, prioritize, respectabilize*)
leave severely alone
life-style
low profile (*keep*, or *maintain, a* ——)
massive (= huge)
matrix
methodology (= method)
name of the game, the
-oriented (e.g. *marketing-oriented*)
overkill
persona (= character)
proposition
quantum jump / leap
real (especially in *very real*)
-related (e.g. *church-related*)
simplistic (= oversimplified)
syndrome
take on board (= accept, grasp)
totality of, the
track-record (= record)
until such time as
utilize (= use)
valid
viability
vibrant
you know (as a filler)
you name it

See also the entries in Section III for:

antithetical	*exposure*
author	*feasible*
aware	*following*
character	*hopefully*
crucial	*impact*
decimate	*interface*
dichotomy	*ironic*
differential	*literally*
dilemma	*locate*
event (in the event that)	*maximize*
excess (in excess of)	*nature*
	neighbourhood (in the neighbourhood of)

no way	*overly*	*pre-empt*	*region of)*
obligate	*parameter*	*pristine*	*scenario*
obscene	*pivotal*	*proportion*	*situation*
ongoing	*predicate*	*region* (in the	*substantial*

Index

Words and phrases are entered in strict alphabetical order, ignoring spaces between two or more words forming a compound or phrase (hence *as for* follows *ascendant* and *court martial* follows *courtesy*).

An asterisk is placed in front of forms or spellings that are not recommended; reference to the page(s) indicated will show the reason for this ruling in each case.

Individual words, parts of words, and phrases discussed in this book are given in *italics*, to distinguish them from subjects, which are in roman type.

Dictionary

Features of the dictionary

Headwords

(words given their own entries) are in bold type:

abandon /ə'bænd(ə)n/ ● *verb* desert ...

or in bold italic type if they are borrowed from another language and are usually printed in italics:

autobahn

Variant spellings are shown:

almanac ... (also **almanack**)

Words that are different but are spelt the same way (homographs) are printed with raised numbers:

abode[1]
abode[2]

Variant American spellings are labelled *US*:

anaemia ... (*US* **anemia**)

Pronunciations

are given in the International Phonetic Alphabet. See p. 155 for an explanation.

Parts of speech

are shown in italic:

abhor ... *verb*
abhorrence ... *noun*

If a word is used as more than one part of speech, each comes after a ● :

abandon ... ● *noun* ... ● *verb* ...

For explanations of parts of speech, see the panels at the dictionary entries for *noun*, *verb*, etc.

Inflections

Irregular and difficult forms are given for:

nouns:

ability ... (*plural* **-ies**)
sheep ... (*plural* same)
tomato ... (*plural* **-es**)

(Irregular plurals are not given for compounds such as *footman* and *school-child*.)

verbs:

abate ... (**-ting**)
abut ... (**-tt-**) [indicating **abutted**, **abutting**]
ring ... (*past tense* **rang**; *past participle* **rung**)

adjectives:

good ... (**better**, **best**)
narrow ... (**-er**, **-est**)
able ... (**-r**, **-st**)

adverbs:

well ... (**better**, **best**)

Definitions

Round brackets are used for

a optional words, e.g. at

back ... *verb* (cause to) go backwards

(because *back* can mean either 'go backwards' or 'cause to go backwards')

b typical objects of verbs:

bank ... *verb* deposit (money) at bank

c typical subjects of verbs:

break ... *verb* (of waves) curl over and foam

d typical nouns qualified by an adjective:

catchy ... (of tune) easily remembered

Subject labels

are sometimes used to help define a word:

sharp ... *Music* above true pitch

Register labels

are used if a word is slang, colloquial, or formal:

ace ... *adjective slang* excellent

Coarse slang means that a word, although widely used, is still unacceptable to many people.

Offensive means that a word is offensive to members of a particular ethnic, religious, or other group.

Phrases

are entered under their main word:

company ... **in company with**

A comma in a phrase indicates alternatives:

in, to excess

means that *in excess* and *to excess* are both phrases.

Compounds

are entered under their main word or element (usually the first):

air ... **air speed** ... **airstrip**

unless they need entries of their own:

broad
broadcast
broadside

A comma in a compound indicates alternatives:

block capitals, letters

means that *block capitals* and *block letters* are both compounds.

Derivatives

are put at the end of the entry for the word they are derived from:

rob ... **robber** *noun*

unless they need defining:

drive ...
driver *noun* person who drives; golf club for driving from tee.

Cross-references

are printed in small capitals:

anatto = ANNATTO.
arose *past* of ARISE.

Definitions will be found at the entries referred to.

Note on proprietary terms

This dictionary includes some words which are, or are asserted to be, proprietary names or trade marks. Their inclusion does not imply that they have acquired for legal purposes a non-proprietary or general significance, nor is any other judgement implied concerning their legal status. In cases where the editor has some evidence that a word is used as a proprietary name or trade mark this is indicated by the label *proprietary term*, but no judgement concerning the legal status of such words is made or implied thereby.

Pronunciation symbols

Consonants		Vowels	
b	*b*ut	æ	*ca*t
d	*d*og	ɑː	*ar*m
f	*f*ew	e	b*e*d
g	*g*et	ɜː	h*er*
h	*h*e	ɪ	s*i*t
j	*y*es	iː	s*ee*
k	*c*at	ɒ	h*o*t
l	*l*eg	ɔː	s*aw*
m	*m*an	ʌ	r*u*n
n	*n*o	ʊ	p*u*t
p	*p*en	uː	t*oo*
r	*r*ed	ə	*a*go
s	*s*it	aɪ	m*y*
t	*t*op	aʊ	h*ow*
v	*v*oice	eɪ	d*ay*
w	*w*e	əʊ	n*o*
z	*z*oo	eə	h*air*
ʃ	*sh*e	ɪə	n*ear*
ʒ	vi*si*on	ɔɪ	b*oy*
θ	*th*in	ʊə	p*oor*
ð	*th*is	aɪə	f*ire*
ŋ	ri*ng*	aʊə	s*our*
x	lo*ch*		
tʃ	*ch*ip		
dʒ	*j*ar		

(ə) signifies the indeterminate sound in g*a*rden, carn*a*l, and rhyth*m*.

The mark ˜ indicates a nasalized sound, as in the following vowels that are not natural in English:

æ̃ (*in*génue)
ɑ̃ (él*an*)
ɔ̃ (b*on* voyage)

The main or primary stress of a word is shown by ' before the relevant syllable.

A *abbreviation* ampere(s). □ **A-bomb** atomic bomb; **A level** advanced level in GCE exam.

a /ə, eɪ/ *adjective* (called the indefinite article) (also **an** /æn, ən/ before vowel sound) one, some, any; per.

AA *abbreviation* Automobile Association; Alcoholics Anonymous; anti-aircraft.

aardvark /ˈɑːdvɑːk/ *noun* mammal with tubular snout and long tongue.

aback /əˈbæk/ *adverb* □ **taken aback** disconcerted, surprised.

abacus /ˈæbəkəs/ *noun* (*plural* **-es**) frame with wires along which beads are slid for calculating.

abaft /əˈbɑːft/ *Nautical* ● *adverb* in or towards stern of ship. ● *preposition* nearer stern than.

abandon /əˈbænd(ə)n/ ● *verb* desert; give up (hope etc.). ● *noun* freedom from inhibitions. □ **abandonment** *noun*.

abandoned *adjective* deserted; unrestrained.

abase /əˈbeɪs/ *verb* (**-sing**) humiliate; degrade. □ **abasement** *noun*.

abashed /əˈbæʃt/ *adjective* embarrassed; disconcerted.

abate /əˈbeɪt/ *verb* (**-ting**) make or become less strong etc. □ **abatement** *noun*.

abattoir /ˈæbətwɑː/ *noun* slaughterhouse.

abbess /ˈæbɪs/ *noun* female head of abbey of nuns.

abbey /ˈæbɪ/ *noun* (*plural* **-s**) (building occupied by) community of monks or nuns.

abbot /ˈæbət/ *noun* head of community of monks.

abbreviate /əˈbriːvɪeɪt/ *verb* shorten. □ **abbreviation** *noun*.

ABC /eɪbiːˈsiː/ *noun* alphabet; rudiments of subject; alphabetical guide.

abdicate /ˈæbdɪkeɪt/ *verb* renounce or resign from (throne etc.). □ **abdication** *noun*.

abdomen /ˈæbdəmən/ *noun* belly; rear part of insect etc. □ **abdominal** /æbˈdɒmɪn(ə)l/ *adjective*.

abduct /æbˈdʌkt/ *verb* carry off illegally, kidnap. □ **abduction** *noun*; **abductor** *noun*.

aberrant /æˈberənt/ *adjective* showing aberration.

aberration /æbəˈreɪʃ(ə)n/ *noun* deviation from normal type or accepted standard; distortion.

abet /əˈbet/ *verb* encourage (offender), assist (offence). □ **abetter**, *Law* **abettor** *noun*.

abeyance /əˈbeɪəns/ *noun* (usually after *in*, *into*) temporary disuse; suspension.

abhor /əbˈhɔː/ *verb* (**-rr-**) detest; regard with disgust.

abhorrence /əbˈhɒrəns/ *noun* disgust, detestation.

abhorrent *adjective* (often + *to*) disgusting.

abide /əˈbaɪd/ *verb* (**-ding**, *past & past participle* **abode** /əˈbəʊd/ or **abided**) tolerate; (+ *by*) act in accordance with (rule); keep (promise).

abiding /əˈbaɪdɪŋ/ *adjective* enduring, permanent.

ability /əˈbɪlɪtɪ/ *noun* (*plural* **-ies**) (often + *to do*) capacity, power; cleverness, talent.

abject /ˈæbdʒekt/ *adjective* miserable; degraded; despicable. □ **abjection** /-ˈdʒek-/ *noun*.

abjure /əbˈdʒʊə/ *verb* renounce on oath. □ **abjuration** /-dʒʊˈreɪ-/ *noun*.

ablaze /əˈbleɪz/ *adjective & adverb* on fire; glittering; excited.

able /ˈeɪb(ə)l/ *adjective* (**-r**, **-st**) (+ *to do*) having power; talented. □ **able-bodied** healthy, fit. □ **ably** *adverb*.

ablution /əˈbluːʃ(ə)n/ *noun* (usually in *plural*) ceremonial washing of hands etc.; *colloquial* washing onself.

abnegate /ˈæbnɪgeɪt/ *verb* (**-ting**) give up, renounce. □ **abnegation** *noun*.

abnormal /æbˈnɔːm(ə)l/ *adjective* exceptional; deviating from the norm. □ **abnormality** /-ˈmæl-/ *noun*; **abnormally** *adverb*.

aboard /əˈbɔːd/ *adverb & preposition* on or into (ship, aircraft, etc.).

abode¹ /əˈbəʊd/ *noun* dwelling place.

abode² *past & past participle* of ABIDE.

abolish /əˈbɒlɪʃ/ *verb* end existence of. □ **abolition** /æbəˈlɪʃ(ə)n/ *noun*; **abolitionist** /æbəˈlɪʃənɪst/ *noun*.

abominable /əˈbɒmɪnəb(ə)l/ *adjective* detestable, loathsome; *colloquial* very unpleasant. □ **Abominable Snowman** yeti. □ **abominably** *adverb*.

abominate /əˈbɒmɪneɪt/ *verb* (**-ting**) detest, loathe. □ **abomination** *noun*.

aboriginal /æbəˈrɪdʒɪn(ə)l/ ● *adjective* indigenous; (usually **Aboriginal**) of the Australian Aborigines. ● *noun* aboriginal inhabitant, esp. (usually **Aboriginal**) of Australia.

aborigines /æbəˈrɪdʒɪnɪz/ *plural noun* aboriginal inhabitants, esp. (usually **Aborigines**) of Australia.

■ **Usage** It is best to refer to one *Aboriginal* but several *Aborigines*, although *Aboriginals* is also acceptable.

abort /əˈbɔːt/ *verb* miscarry; effect abortion of; (cause to) end before completion.

abortion /əˈbɔːʃ(ə)n/ *noun* natural or (esp.) induced expulsion of foetus before it can survive; stunted or misshapen creature. □ **abortionist** *noun*.

abortive /əˈbɔːtɪv/ *adjective* fruitless, unsuccessful.

abound /əˈbaʊnd/ *verb* be plentiful; (+ *in*, *with*) be rich in, teem with.

about /əˈbaʊt/ ● *preposition* on subject of; relating to, in relation to; at a time near to; around (in); surrounding; here and there in. ● *adverb* approximately; nearby; in every direction; on the move, in action; all around. □ **about-face**, **-turn** turn made so as to face opposite direction, change of policy etc.; **be about to do** be on the point of doing.

above /əˈbʌv/ ● *preposition* over, on top of, higher than; more than; higher in rank, importance, etc. than; too great or good for; beyond reach of. ● *adverb* at or to higher point, overhead; earlier on page or in book. □ **above all** more than anything else; **above-board** without concealment.

abracadabra /æbrəkəˈdæbrə/ *interjection* supposedly magic word.

abrade /əˈbreɪd/ *verb* (**-ding**) scrape or wear away by rubbing.

abrasion /əˈbreɪʒ(ə)n/ *noun* rubbing or scraping away; resulting damaged area.

abrasive /əˈbreɪsɪv/ ● *adjective* capable of rubbing or grinding down; harsh or hurtful in manner. ● *noun* abrasive substance.

abreast /əˈbrest/ *adverb* side by side and facing same way; (+ *of*) up to date with.

abridge /əˈbrɪdʒ/ *verb* (**-ging**) shorten (a book etc.). □ **abridgement** *noun*.

abroad /əˈbrɔːd/ *adverb* in or to foreign country; widely; in circulation.

abrogate /'æbrəgeɪt/ verb (**-ting**) repeal, abolish (law etc.). □ **abrogation** noun.

abrupt /ə'brʌpt/ adjective sudden, hasty; curt; steep. □ **abruptly** adverb; **abruptness** noun.

abscess /'æbsɪs/ noun (plural **-es**) swelling containing pus.

abscond /əb'skɒnd/ verb flee, esp. to avoid arrest; escape.

abseil /'æbseɪl/ ● verb descend (building etc.) by using doubled rope fixed at higher point. ● noun such a descent.

absence /'æbsəns/ noun being away; duration of this; (+ of) lack. □ **absence of mind** inattentiveness.

absent ● adjective /'æbsənt/ not present or existing; lacking; inattentive. ● verb /əb'sent/ (**absent oneself**) go or stay away. □ **absently** adverb.

absentee /æbsən'ti:/ noun person not present.

absenteeism /æbsən'ti:ɪz(ə)m/ noun absenting oneself from work, school, etc.

absent-minded adjective forgetful, inattentive. □ **absent-mindedly** adverb; **absent-mindedness** noun.

absinthe /'æbsɪnθ/ noun wormwood-based, aniseed-flavoured liqueur.

absolute /'æbsəlu:t/ adjective complete, utter; unconditional; despotic; not relative; (of adjective or transitive verb) without expressed noun or object; (of decree etc.) final. □ **absolute majority** one over all rivals combined; **absolute temperature** one measured from absolute zero; **absolute zero** lowest possible temperature (−273.15°C or 0°K).

absolutely adverb completely; in an absolute sense; colloquial quite so, yes.

absolution /æbsə'lu:ʃ(ə)n/ noun formal forgiveness of sins.

absolutism /'æbsəlu:tɪz(ə)m/ noun absolute government. □ **absolutist** noun.

absolve /əb'zɒlv/ verb (**-ving**) (often + from, of) free from blame or obligation.

absorb /əb'sɔːb/ verb incorporate; assimilate; take in (heat etc.); deal with easily, reduce intensity of; (often as **absorbing** adjective) engross attention of; consume (resources).

absorbent /əb'sɔːbənt/ ● adjective tending to absorb. ● noun absorbent substance.

absorption /əb'sɔːpʃ(ə)n/ noun absorbing, being absorbed. □ **absorptive** adjective.

abstain /əb'stem/ verb (usually + from) refrain (from indulging); decline to vote.

abstemious /əb'sti:mɪəs/ adjective moderate or ascetic, esp. in eating and drinking. □ **abstemiously** adverb.

abstention /əb'stenʃ(ə)n/ noun abstaining, esp. from voting.

abstinence /'æbstɪnəns/ noun abstaining, esp. from food or alcohol. □ **abstinent** adjective.

abstract ● adjective /'æbstrækt/ of or existing in theory rather than practice, not concrete; (of art etc.) not representational. ● verb /əb'strækt/ (often + from) remove; summarize. ● noun /'æbstrækt/ summary; abstract idea, work of art, etc.

abstracted adjective inattentive. □ **abstractedly** adverb.

abstraction /əb'strækʃ(ə)n/ noun abstracting; abstract idea; abstract qualities in art; absent-mindedness.

abstruse /əb'stru:s/ adjective hard to understand; profound.

absurd /əb'sɜːd/ adjective wildly inappropriate; ridiculous. □ **absurdity** noun (plural **-ies**); **absurdly** adverb.

ABTA /'æbtə/ abbreviation Association of British Travel Agents.

abundance /ə'bʌnd(ə)ns/ noun plenty; more than enough; wealth.

abundant adjective plentiful; (+ in) rich. □ **abundantly** adverb.

abuse ● verb /ə'bju:z/ (**-sing**) use improperly; misuse; maltreat; insult verbally. ● noun /ə'bju:s/ misuse; insulting language; corrupt practice. □ **abuser** /ə'bju:zə/ noun.

abusive /ə'bju:sɪv/ adjective insulting, offensive. □ **abusively** adverb.

abut /ə'bʌt/ verb (**-tt-**) (+ on) border on; (+ on, against) touch or lean on.

abysmal /ə'bɪzm(ə)l/ adjective very bad; dire. □ **abysmally** adverb.

abyss /ə'bɪs/ noun deep chasm.

AC abbreviation alternating current.

a/c abbreviation account.

acacia /ə'keɪʃə/ noun tree with yellow or white flowers.

academia /ækə'di:mɪə/ noun the world of scholars.

academic /ækə'demɪk/ ● adjective scholarly; of learning; of no practical relevance. ● noun teacher or scholar in university etc. □ **academically** adverb.

academician /əkædə'mɪʃ(ə)n/ noun member of Academy.

academy /ə'kædəmɪ/ noun (plural **-ies**) place of specialized training; (**Academy**) society of distinguished scholars, artists, scientists, etc.; Scottish secondary school.

acanthus /ə'kænθəs/ noun (plural **-es**) spring herbaceous plant with spiny leaves.

ACAS /'eɪkæs/ abbreviation Advisory, Conciliation, and Arbitration Service.

accede /æk'si:d/ verb (**-ding**) (+ to) take office, esp. as monarch; assent to.

accelerate /æk'seləreɪt/ verb (**-ting**) increase speed (of); (cause to) happen earlier. □ **acceleration** noun.

accelerator noun device for increasing speed, esp. pedal in vehicle; Physics apparatus for imparting high speeds to charged particles.

accent ● noun /'æksənt/ style of pronunciation of region or social group (see panel); emphasis; prominence given to syllable by stress or pitch; mark on letter indicating pronunciation (see panel). ● verb /æk'sent/ emphasize; write or print accents on.

accentuate /æk'sentʃʊeɪt/ verb (**-ting**) emphasize, make prominent. □ **accentuation** noun.

accept /æk'sept/ verb willingly receive; answer (invitation etc.) affirmatively; regard favourably; receive as valid or suitable. □ **acceptance** noun.

acceptable adjective worth accepting; tolerable. □ **acceptability** noun; **acceptably** adverb.

access /'ækses/ ● noun way of approach or entry; right or opportunity to reach, use, or visit. ● verb gain access to (data) in computer.

accessible /æk'sesɪb(ə)l/ adjective reachable or obtainable; easy to understand. □ **accessibility** noun.

accession /æk'seʃ(ə)n/ noun taking office, esp. as monarch; thing added.

accessory /æk'sesərɪ/ noun (plural **-ies**) additional or extra thing; (usually in plural) small attachment or item of dress; (often + to) person who abets in or is privy to illegal act.

accident /'æksɪd(ə)nt/ noun unintentional unfortunate esp. harmful event; event without apparent cause; unexpected event. □ **accident-prone** clumsy; **by accident** unintentionally.

accidental /æksɪ'dent(ə)l/ ● adjective happening or done by chance or accident. ● noun Music sharp, flat, or natural indicating momentary departure of note from key signature. □ **accidentally** adverb.

acclaim /ə'kleɪm/ ● verb welcome or applaud enthusiastically. ● noun applause; welcome; public praise. □ **acclamation** /æklə-/ noun.

acclimatize /ə'klaɪmətaɪz/ verb (also **-ise**) (**-zing** or **-sing**) adapt to new climate or conditions. □ **acclimatization** noun.

accolade /'ækəleɪd/ noun praise given; touch made with sword at conferring of knighthood.

accommodate /ə'kɒmədeɪt/ verb (**-ting**) provide lodging or room for; adapt, harmonize, reconcile; do favour to; (+ with) supply.

■ **Usage** Accommodate, accommodation, etc. are spelt with two ms, not one.

accommodating adjective obliging.

accommodation noun lodgings; adjustment, adaptation; convenient arrangement. □ **accommodation address** postal address used instead of permanent one.

accompaniment /ə'kʌmpənɪmənt/ noun instrumental or orchestral support for solo instrument, voice, or group; accompanying thing.

accompany /ə'kʌmpənɪ/ verb (**-ies**, **-ied**) go with, attend; (usually in passive; + with, by) be done or found with; Music play accompaniment for. □ **accompanist** noun Music.

accomplice /ə'kʌmplɪs/ noun partner in crime.

accomplish /ə'kʌmplɪʃ/ verb succeed in doing; achieve, complete.

accomplished adjective clever, skilled.

accomplishment noun completion (of task etc.); acquired esp. social skill; thing achieved.

accord /ə'kɔːd/ ● verb (often + with) be consistent or in harmony; grant, give. ● noun agreement; consent. □ **of one's own accord** on one's own initiative.

accordance noun □ **in accordance with** in conformity to.

according adverb (+ to) as stated by; (+ to, as) in proportion to or as.

accordingly adverb as circumstances suggest or require; consequently.

accordion /ə'kɔːdɪən/ noun musical reed instrument with concertina-like bellows, keys, and buttons.

accost /ə'kɒst/ verb approach and speak boldly to.

account /ə'kaʊnt/ ● noun narration, description; arrangement at bank etc. for depositing and withdrawing money etc.; statement of financial transactions with balance; importance; behalf. ● verb consider as. □ **account for** explain, answer for, kill, destroy; **on account** to be paid for later, in part payment; **on account of** because of; **on no account** under no circumstances; **take account of, take into account** consider.

accountable adjective responsible, required to account for one's conduct; explicable. □ **accountability** noun.

accountant noun professional keeper or verifier of financial accounts. □ **accountancy** noun; **accounting** noun.

accoutrements /ə'kuːtrəmənts/ plural noun equipment, trappings.

accredit /ə'kredɪt/ verb (**-t-**) (+ to) attribute; (+ with) credit; (usually + to, at) send (ambassador etc.) with credentials.

accredited adjective officially recognized; generally accepted.

accretion /ə'kriːʃ(ə)n/ noun growth by accumulation or organic enlargement; the resulting whole; matter so added.

accrue /ə'kruː/ verb (**-ues**, **-ued**, **-uing**) (often + to) come as natural increase or advantage, esp. financial.

accumulate /ə'kjuːmjʊleɪt/ verb (**-ting**) acquire increasing number or quantity of; amass, collect; grow numerous; increase. □ **accumulation** noun; **accumulative** /-lətɪv/ adjective.

accumulator noun rechargeable electric cell; bet placed on sequence of events, with winnings and stake from each placed on next.

accurate /'ækjʊrət/ adjective precise; conforming exactly with truth etc. □ **accuracy** noun; **accurately** adverb.

accursed /ə'kɜːsɪd/ adjective under a curse; colloquial detestable, annoying.

accusative /ə'kjuːzətɪv/ Grammar ● noun case expressing object of action. ● adjective of or in accusative.

accuse /ə'kjuːz/ verb (**-sing**) (often + of) charge with fault or crime; blame. □ **accusation** /æk-/ noun; **accusatory** adjective.

accustom /ə'kʌstəm/ verb (+ to) make used to.

accustomed adjective (usually + to) used (to a thing); customary.

ace ● noun playing card with single spot; person who excels in some activity; Tennis unreturnable service.

Accent

1 A person's accent is the way he or she pronounces words, and people from different regions and different groups in society have different accents. For instance, most people in northern England say *path* with a 'short' *a*, while most people in southern England say it with a 'long' *a*, and in America and Canada the *r* in *far* and *port* is generally pronounced, while in south-eastern England, for example, it is not. Everyone speaks with an accent, although some accents may be regarded as having more prestige, such as 'Received Pronunciation' (RP) in the UK.

2 An accent on a letter is a mark added to it to alter the sound it stands for. In French, for example, there are

    ´ (acute), as in *état*   ¨ (diaeresis), as in *Noël*

    ` (grave), as in *mère*   , (cedilla), as in *français*

    ^ (circumflex), as in *guêpe*

and German has

    ¨ (umlaut), as in *München*.

There are no accents on native English words, but many words borrowed from other languages still have them, such as *blasé* and *façade*.

● *adjective slang* excellent. □ **within an ace of** on the verge of.

acerbic /ə'sɜːbɪk/ *adjective* harsh and sharp, esp. in speech or manner. □ **acerbity** *noun* (*plural* **-ies**).

acetate /'æsɪteɪt/ *noun* compound of acetic acid, esp. the cellulose ester; fabric made from this.

acetic /ə'siːtɪk/ *adjective* of or like vinegar. □ **acetic acid** clear liquid acid in vinegar.

acetone /'æsɪtəʊn/ *noun* colourless volatile solvent of organic compounds.

acetylene /ə'setɪliːn/ *noun* inflammable hydrocarbon gas, used esp. in welding.

ache /eɪk/ ● *noun* continuous dull pain; mental distress. ● *verb* (**aching**) suffer from or be the source of an ache.

achieve /ə'tʃiːv/ *verb* (**-ving**) reach or attain by effort; accomplish (task etc.); be successful. □ **achiever** *noun*; **achievement** *noun*.

Achilles /ə'kɪliːz/ *noun* □ **Achilles heel** vulnerable point; **Achilles tendon** tendon attaching calf muscles to heel.

achromatic /ækrəʊ'mætɪk/ *adjective* transmitting light without separating it into colours; free from colour. □ **achromatically** *adverb*.

achy /'eɪkɪ/ *adjective* (**-ier, -iest**) suffering from aches.

acid /'æsɪd/ ● *noun* Chemistry substance that neutralizes alkalis, turns litmus red, and usually contains hydrogen and is sour; *slang* drug LSD. ● *adjective* having properties of acid; sour; biting, sharp. □ **acid drop** sharp-tasting boiled sweet; **acid house** synthesized music with simple beat, associated with hallucinogenic drugs; **acid rain** rain containing acid formed from industrial waste in atmosphere; **acid test** severe or conclusive test. □ **acidic** /ə'sɪd-/ *adjective*; **acidify** /ə'sɪd-/ *verb* (**-ies, -ied**); **acidity** /-'sɪd-/ *noun*.

acidulous /ə'sɪdjʊləs/ *adjective* somewhat acid.

acknowledge /ək'nɒlɪdʒ/ *verb* (**-ging**) recognize, accept truth of; confirm receipt of (letter etc.); show that one has noticed; express gratitude for.

acknowledgement *noun* (also **acknowledgment**) acknowledging; thing given or done in gratitude; letter etc. confirming receipt; (usually in *plural*) author's thanks, prefacing book.

acme /'ækmɪ/ *noun* highest point.

acne /'æknɪ/ *noun* skin condition with red pimples.

acolyte /'ækəlaɪt/ *noun* assistant, esp. of priest.

aconite /'ækənaɪt/ *noun* any of various poisonous plants, esp. monkshood; drug made from these.

acorn /'eɪkɔːn/ *noun* fruit of oak.

acoustic /ə'kuːstɪk/ *adjective* of sound or sense of hearing; (of musical instrument etc.) without electrical amplification. □ **acoustically** *adverb*.

acoustics *plural noun* properties (of a room etc.) in transmitting sound; (treated as *singular*) science of sound.

acquaint /ə'kweɪnt/ *verb* (+ *with*) make aware of or familiar with. □ **be acquainted with** know.

acquaintance *noun* being acquainted; person one knows slightly. □ **acquaintanceship** *noun*.

acquiesce /ækwɪ'es/ *verb* (**-cing**) agree, esp. tacitly. □ **acquiescence** *noun*; **acquiescent** *adjective*.

acquire /ə'kwaɪə/ *verb* (**-ring**) gain possession of. □ **acquired immune deficiency syndrome** = Aids; **acquired taste** liking developed by experience.

acquirement *noun* thing acquired or attained.

acquisition /ækwɪ'zɪʃ(ə)n/ *noun* (esp. useful) thing acquired; acquiring, being acquired.

acquisitive /ə'kwɪzɪtɪv/ *adjective* keen to acquire things.

acquit /ə'kwɪt/ *verb* (**-tt-**) (often + *of*) declare not guilty; (**acquit oneself**) behave, perform, (+ *of*) discharge (duty etc.). □ **acquittal** *noun*.

acre /'eɪkə/ *noun* measure of land, 4840 sq. yards, 0.405 ha.

acreage /'eɪkərɪdʒ/ *noun* number of acres.

acrid /'ækrɪd/ *adjective* bitterly pungent. □ **acridity** /-'krɪd-/ *noun*.

acrimonious /ækrɪ'məʊnɪəs/ *adjective* bitter in manner or temper. □ **acrimony** /'ækrɪmənɪ/ *noun*.

acrobat /'ækrəbæt/ *noun* performer of acrobatics. □ **acrobatic** /-'bæt-/ *adjective*.

acrobatics /ækrə'bætɪks/ *plural noun* gymnastic feats.

acronym /'ækrənɪm/ *noun* word formed from initial letters of other words (e.g. *laser*, *NATO*).

acropolis /ə'krɒpəlɪs/ *noun* citadel of ancient Greek city.

across /ə'krɒs/ ● *preposition* to or on other side of; from one side to another side of. ● *adverb* to or on other side; from one side to another. □ **across the board** applying to all.

acrostic /ə'krɒstɪk/ *noun* poem etc. in which first (or first and last) letters of lines form word(s).

acrylic /ə'krɪlɪk/ ● *adjective* made from acrylic acid. ● *noun* acrylic fibre, fabric, or paint.

acrylic acid *noun* a pungent liquid organic acid.

act ● *noun* thing done, deed; process of doing; item of entertainment; pretence; main division of play; decree of legislative body. ● *verb* behave; perform actions or functions; (often + *on*) have effect; perform in play etc.; pretend; play part of. □ **act for** be (legal) representative of; **act up** *colloquial* misbehave, give trouble.

acting *adjective* serving temporarily as.

actinism /'æktɪnɪz(ə)m/ *noun* property of short-wave radiation that produces chemical changes, as in photography.

action /'ækʃ(ə)n/ *noun* process of doing or acting; forcefulness, energy; exertion of energy or influence; deed, act; (**the action**) series of events in story, play, etc., *slang* exciting activity; battle; mechanism of instrument; style of movement; lawsuit. □ **action-packed** full of action or excitement; **action replay** playback of part of television broadcast; **out of action** not functioning.

actionable *adjective* providing grounds for legal action.

activate /'æktɪveɪt/ *verb* (**-ting**) make active or radioactive. □ **activation** *noun*.

active /'æktɪv/ ● *adjective* marked by action; energetic, diligent; working, operative; Grammar (of verb) of which subject performs action (e.g. *saw* in *he saw a film*). ● *noun* Grammar active form or voice. □ **active service** military service in wartime. □ **actively** *adverb*.

activism *noun* policy of vigorous action, esp. for a political cause. □ **activist** *noun*.

activity /æk'tɪvɪtɪ/ *noun* (*plural* **-ies**) being active; busy or energetic action; (often in *plural*) occupation, pursuit.

actor /'æktə/ *noun* person who acts in play, film, etc.

actress /'æktrɪs/ *noun* female actor.

actual /'æktʃʊəl/ *adjective* existing, real; current. □ **actuality** /-'æl-/ *noun* (*plural* **-ies**).

actually *adverb* in fact, really.

actuary /'æktʃʊərɪ/ *noun* (*plural* **-ies**) statistician, esp. one calculating insurance risks and premiums. □ **actuarial** /-'eər-/ *adjective*.

actuate /'æktʃʊeɪt/ *verb* (**-ting**) cause to move, function, act.

acuity /ə'kjuːɪtɪ/ *noun* acuteness.

acumen /'ækjʊmen/ noun keen insight or discernment.

acupuncture /'ækjuːpʌŋktʃə/ noun medical treatment using needles in parts of the body. □ **acupuncturist** noun.

acute /ə'kjuːt/ adjective (**-r, -st**) keen, penetrating; shrewd; (of disease) coming quickly to crisis; (of angle) less than 90°. □ **acute** (**accent**) mark (´) over letter indicating pronunciation. □ **acutely** adverb.

AD abbreviation of the Christian era (Anno Domini).

ad noun colloquial advertisement.

adage /'ædɪdʒ/ noun proverb, maxim.

adagio /ə'dɑːʒɪəʊ/ Music ● adverb & adjective in slow time. ● noun (plural **-s**) adagio passage.

adamant /'ædəmənt/ adjective stubbornly resolute. □ **adamantly** adverb.

Adam's apple /'ædəmz/ noun cartilaginous projection at front of neck.

adapt /ə'dæpt/ verb (+ to) fit, adjust; (+ to, for) make suitable, modify; (usually + to) adjust to new conditions. □ **adaptable** adjective; **adaptation** /æd-/ noun.

adaptor noun device for making equipment compatible; Electricity device for connecting several electrical plugs to one socket.

add verb join as increase or supplement; unite (numbers) to get their total; say further. □ **add up** find total of; (+ to) amount to.

addendum /ə'dendəm/ noun (plural **-da**) thing to be added; material added at end of book.

adder /'ædə/ noun small venomous snake.

addict /'ædɪkt/ noun person addicted, esp. to drug; colloquial devotee.

addicted /ə'dɪktɪd/ adjective (usually + to) dependent on a drug as a habit; devoted to an interest. □ **addiction** noun.

addictive /ə'dɪktɪv/ adjective causing addiction.

addition /ə'dɪʃ(ə)n/ noun adding; person or thing added. □ **in addition** (often + to) also, as well.

additional adjective added, extra. □ **additionally** adverb.

additive /'ædɪtɪv/ noun substance added, esp. to colour, flavour, or preserve food.

addle /'æd(ə)l/ verb (**-ling**) muddle, confuse; (usually as **addled** adjective) (of egg) become rotten.

address /ə'dres/ ● noun place where person lives or organization is situated; particulars of this, esp. for postal purposes; speech delivered to an audience. ● verb write postal directions on; direct (remarks etc.); speak or write to; direct one's attention to.

addressee /ædre'siː/ noun person to whom letter etc. is addressed.

adduce /ə'djuːs/ verb (**-cing**) cite as proof or instance. □ **adducible** adjective.

adenoids /'ædɪnɔɪdz/ plural noun enlarged lymphatic tissue between nose and throat, often hindering breathing. □ **adenoidal** /-'nɔɪ-/ adjective.

adept ● adjective /ə'dept, 'ædept/ (+ at, in) skilful. ● noun /'ædept/ adept person.

adequate /'ædɪkwət/ adjective sufficient, satisfactory. □ **adequacy** noun; **adequately** adverb.

adhere /əd'hɪə/ verb (**-ring**) (usually + to) stick fast; behave according to (rule etc.); give allegiance.

adherent ● noun supporter. ● adjective adhering. □ **adherence** noun.

adhesion /əd'hiːʒ(ə)n/ noun adhering.

adhesive /əd'hiːsɪv/ ● adjective sticky, causing adhesion. ● noun adhesive substance.

ad hoc /æd 'hɒk/ adverb & adjective for one particular occasion or use.

adieu /ə'djuː/ interjection goodbye.

ad infinitum /æd ɪnfɪ'naɪtəm/ adverb without limit; for ever.

adipose /'ædɪpəʊz/ adjective of fat, fatty. □ **adiposity** /-'pɒs-/ noun.

adjacent /ə'dʒeɪs(ə)nt/ adjective lying near; adjoining. □ **adjacency** noun.

adjective /'ædʒɪktɪv/ noun word indicating quality of noun or pronoun (see panel). □ **adjectival** /-'taɪv-/ adjective.

adjoin /ə'dʒɔɪn/ verb be next to and joined with.

adjourn /ə'dʒɜːn/ verb postpone, break off; (+ to) transfer to (another place). □ **adjournment** noun.

adjudge /ə'dʒʌdʒ/ verb (**-ging**) pronounce judgement on; pronounce or award judicially. □ **adjudg(e)ment** noun.

adjudicate /ə'dʒuːdɪkeɪt/ verb (**-ting**) act as judge; adjudge. □ **adjudication** noun; **adjudicator** noun.

adjunct /'ædʒʌŋkt/ noun (+ to, of) subordinate or incidental thing.

adjure /ə'dʒʊə/ verb (**-ring**) (usually + to do) beg or command. □ **adjuration** noun.

Adjective

An adjective is a word that describes a noun or pronoun, e.g.

red, clever, German, depressed, battered, sticky, shining

Most can be used either before a noun, e.g.

the red house   *a clever woman*

or after a verb like *be, seem,* or *call,* e.g.

The house is red.   *I wouldn't call him lazy.*
She seems very clever.

Some can be used only before a noun, e.g.

the chief reason (one cannot say **the reason is chief*)

Some can be used only after a verb, e.g.

The ship is still afloat. (one cannot say **an afloat ship*)

A few can be used only immediately after a noun, e.g.

the president elect (one cannot say either **an elect president* or **The president is elect*)

adjust /əˈdʒʌst/ verb order, position; regulate; arrange; (usually + to) adapt; harmonize. □ **adjustable** adjective; **adjustment** noun.

adjutant /ˈædʒʊt(ə)nt/ noun army officer assisting superior in administrative duties.

ad lib /æd ˈlɪb/ ● verb (-**bb**-) improvise. ● adjective improvised. ● adverb to any desired extent.

Adm. abbreviation Admiral.

administer /ədˈmɪnɪstə/ verb manage (affairs); formally deliver, dispense.

administration /ədmɪnɪˈstreɪʃ(ə)n/ noun administering, esp. public affairs; government in power.

administrative /ədˈmɪnɪstrətɪv/ adjective of the management of affairs.

administrator /ədˈmɪnɪstreɪtə/ noun manager of business, public affairs, or person's estate.

admirable /ˈædmərəb(ə)l/ adjective deserving admiration; excellent. □ **admirably** adverb.

admiral /ˈædmər(ə)l/ noun commander-in-chief of navy; high-ranking naval officer, commander.

Admiralty noun (plural **-ies**) (in full **Admiralty Board**) historical committee superintending Royal Navy.

admire /ədˈmaɪə/ verb regard with approval, respect, or satisfaction; express admiration of. □ **admiration** /ædməˈreɪ-/ noun; **admirer** noun; **admiring** adjective; **admiringly** adverb.

admissible /ədˈmɪsɪb(ə)l/ adjective worth accepting or considering; allowable. □ **admissibility** noun.

admission /ədˈmɪʃ(ə)n/ noun acknowledgement (of error etc.); (right of) entering; entrance charge.

admit /ədˈmɪt/ verb (-**tt**-) (often + to be, that) acknowledge, recognize as true; (+ to) confess to; let in; accommodate; take (patient) into hospital; (+ of) allow as possible.

admittance noun admitting or being admitted, usually to a place.

admittedly adverb as must be admitted.

admixture /ædˈmɪkstʃə/ noun thing added, esp. minor ingredient; adding of this.

admonish /ədˈmɒnɪʃ/ verb reprove; urge; (+ of) warn. □ **admonishment** noun; **admonition** /ædməˈnɪ-/ noun; **admonitory** adjective.

ad nauseam /æd ˈnɔːzɪæm/ adverb to a sickening extent.

ado /əˈduː/ noun fuss; trouble.

adobe /əˈdəʊbɪ/ noun sun-dried brick.

adolescent /ædəˈlesənt/ ● adjective between childhood and adulthood. ● noun adolescent person. □ **adolescence** noun.

adopt /əˈdɒpt/ verb legally take (child) as one's own; take over (another's idea etc.); choose; accept responsibility for; approve (report etc.). □ **adoption** noun.

adoptive adjective because of adoption.

adorable /əˈdɔːrəb(ə)l/ adjective deserving adoration; colloquial delightful, charming.

adore /əˈdɔː/ verb (-**ring**) love intensely; worship; colloquial like very much. □ **adoration** /ædəˈreɪ-/ noun; **adorer** noun.

adorn /əˈdɔːn/ verb add beauty to, decorate. □ **adornment** noun.

adrenal /əˈdriːn(ə)l/ ● adjective of adrenal glands. ● noun (in full **adrenal gland**) either of two ductless glands above the kidneys.

adrenalin /əˈdrenəlɪn/ noun stimulative hormone secreted by adrenal glands.

adrift /əˈdrɪft/ adverb & adjective drifting; colloquial unfastened, out of order.

adroit /əˈdrɔɪt/ adjective dexterous, skilful.

adsorb /ədˈsɔːb/ verb attract and hold thin layer of (gas or liquid) on its surface. □ **adsorbent** adjective & noun; **adsorption** noun.

adulation /ædjʊˈleɪʃ(ə)n/ noun obsequious flattery.

adult /ˈædʌlt/ ● adjective grown-up, mature; of or for adults. ● noun adult person. □ **adulthood** noun.

adulterate /əˈdʌltəreɪt/ verb (-**ting**) debase (esp. food) by adding other substances. □ **adulteration** noun.

adultery /əˈdʌltərɪ/ noun voluntary sexual intercourse of married person other than with spouse. □ **adulterer**, **adulteress** noun; **adulterous** adjective.

adumbrate /ˈædʌmbreɪt/ verb (-**ting**) indicate faintly or in outline; foreshadow. □ **adumbration** noun.

advance /ədˈvɑːns/ ● verb (-**cing**) move or put forward; progress; pay or lend beforehand; promote; present (idea etc.). ● noun going forward; progress; prepayment, loan; payment beforehand; (in plural) amorous approaches; rise in price. ● adjective done etc. beforehand. □ **advance on** approach threateningly; **in advance** ahead, beforehand.

advanced adjective well ahead; socially progressive. □ **advanced level** high level GCE exam.

advancement noun promotion of person, cause, etc.

advantage /ədˈvɑːntɪdʒ/ ● noun beneficial feature; benefit, profit; (often + over) superiority; Tennis next point after deuce. ● verb (-**ging**) benefit, favour. □ **take advantage of** make good use of; exploit. □ **advantageous** /ædvənˈteɪdʒəs/ adjective.

Advent /ˈædvent/ noun season before Christmas; coming of Christ; (**advent**) arrival.

Adventist noun member of sect believing in imminent second coming of Christ.

adventure /ədˈventʃə/ ● noun unusual and exciting experience; enterprise. ● verb (-**ring**) dare, venture. □ **adventure playground** one with climbing frames etc.

adventurer noun (feminine **adventuress**) person who seeks adventure esp. for personal gain or pleasure; financial speculator.

adventurous adjective venturesome, enterprising.

adverb /ˈædvɜːb/ noun word indicating manner, degree, circumstance, etc. used to modify verb, adjective, or other adverb (see panel). □ **adverbial** /ədˈvɜː-/ adjective.

adversary /ˈædvəsərɪ/ noun (plural **-ies**) enemy; opponent. □ **adversarial** /-ˈseə-/ adjective.

adverse /ˈædvɜːs/ adjective unfavourable; harmful. □ **adversely** adverb.

adversity /ədˈvɜːsɪtɪ/ noun misfortune.

advert /ˈædvɜːt/ noun colloquial advertisement.

advertise /ˈædvətaɪz/ verb (-**sing**) promote publicly to increase sales; make generally known; seek to sell, fill (vacancy), or (+ for) buy or employ by notice in newspaper etc.

advertisement /ədˈvɜːtɪsmənt/ noun public announcement advertising something; advertising.

advice /ədˈvaɪs/ noun recommendation on how to act; information; notice of transaction.

advisable /ədˈvaɪzəb(ə)l/ adjective to be recommended; expedient. □ **advisability** noun.

advise /ədˈvaɪz/ verb (-**sing**) give advice (to); recommend; (usually + of, that) inform.

advisedly /ədˈvaɪzɪdlɪ/ adverb deliberately.

adviser noun person who advises, esp. officially.

advisory /ədˈvaɪzərɪ/ adjective giving advice.

advocaat /ˈædvəkɑːt/ noun liqueur of eggs, sugar, and brandy.

advocacy /ˈædvəkəsɪ/ noun support or argument for cause etc.

advocate ● noun /ˈædvəkət/ (+ of) person who speaks in favour; person who pleads for another, esp. in law court. ● *verb* /'ædvəkeɪt/ (**-ting**) recommend by argument.

adze /ædz/ *noun* (US **adz**) axe with arched blade at right angles to handle.

aegis /'iːdʒɪs/ *noun* protection; support.

aeolian harp /iː'əʊlɪən/ *noun* (US **eolian harp**) stringed instrument sounding when wind passes through it.

aeon /'iːɒn/ *noun* (also **eon**) long or indefinite period; an age.

aerate /'eəreɪt/ *verb* (**-ting**) charge with carbon dioxide; expose to air. □ **aeration** *noun*.

aerial /'eərɪəl/ ● *noun* device for transmitting or receiving radio signals. ● *adjective* from the air; existing in the air; like air.

aero- *combining form* air; aircraft.

aerobatics /eərə'bætɪks/ *plural noun* feats of spectacular flying of aircraft; (treated as *singular*) performance of these.

aerobics /eə'rəʊbɪks/ *plural noun* vigorous exercises designed to increase oxygen intake. □ **aerobic** *adjective*.

aerodrome /'eərədrəʊm/ *noun* small airport or airfield.

aerodynamics /eərəʊdaɪ'næmɪks/ *plural noun* (usually treated as *singular*) dynamics of solid bodies moving through air. □ **aerodynamic** *adjective*.

aerofoil /'eərəfɔɪl/ *noun* structure with curved surfaces (e.g. aircraft wing), designed to give lift in flight.

aeronautics /eərəʊ'nɔːtɪks/ *plural noun* (usually treated as *singular*) science or practice of motion in the air. □ **aeronautical** *adjective*.

aeroplane /'eərəpleɪn/ *noun* powered heavier-than-air aircraft with wings.

aerosol /'eərəsɒl/ *noun* pressurized container releasing substance as fine spray.

aerospace /'eərəʊspeɪs/ *noun* earth's atmosphere and outer space; aviation in this.

aesthete /'iːsθiːt/ *noun* person who appreciates beauty.

aesthetic /iːs'θetɪk/ *adjective* of or sensitive to beauty; tasteful. □ **aesthetically** *adverb*; **aestheticism** /-sɪz(ə)m/ *noun*.

aetiology /iːtɪ'ɒlədʒɪ/ *noun* (US **etiology**) study of causation or of causes of disease. □ **aetiological** /-ə'lɒdʒ-/ *adjective*.

afar /ə'fɑː/ *adverb* at or to a distance.

affable /'æfəb(ə)l/ *adjective* friendly; courteous. □ **affability** *noun*; **affably** *adverb*.

affair /ə'feə/ *noun* matter, concern; love affair; *colloquial* thing, event; (in *plural*) business.

affect /ə'fekt/ *verb* produce effect on; (of disease etc.) attack; move emotionally; use for effect; pretend to feel; (+ *to do*) pretend.

■ **Usage** *Affect* is often confused with *effect*, which means 'to bring about'.

affectation /æfek'teɪʃ(ə)n/ *noun* artificial manner; pretentious display.

affected *adjective* pretended; full of affectation.

affection /ə'fekʃ(ə)n/ *noun* goodwill, fond feeling; disease.

affectionate /ə'fekʃənət/ *adjective* loving. □ **affectionately** *adverb*.

affidavit /æfɪ'deɪvɪt/ *noun* written statement on oath.

affiliate /ə'fɪlɪeɪt/ *verb* (**-ting**) (+ *to, with*) attach to, connect to, or adopt as member or branch.

affiliation *noun* affiliating, being affiliated. □ **affiliation order** legal order compelling supposed father to support illegitimate child.

affinity /ə'fɪnɪtɪ/ *noun* (*plural* **-ies**) attraction; relationship; resemblance; *Chemistry* tendency of substances to combine with others.

affirm /ə'fɜːm/ *verb* state as fact; make solemn declaration in place of oath. □ **affirmation** /æfə'meɪʃ(ə)n/ *noun*.

affirmative /ə'fɜːmətɪv/ ● *adjective* affirming, expressing approval. ● *noun* affirmative statement.

affix ● *verb* /ə'fɪks/ attach, fasten; add in writing. ● *noun* /'æfɪks/ addition; prefix, suffix.

afflict /ə'flɪkt/ *verb* distress physically or mentally.

affliction *noun* distress, suffering; cause of this.

Adverb

An adverb is used:

1 with a verb, to say:
   a how something happens, e.g. *He walks* quickly.
   b where something happens, e.g. *I live* here.
   c when something happens, e.g. *They visited us* yesterday.
   d how often something happens, e.g. *We* usually *have coffee.*

2 to strengthen or weaken the meaning of:
   a a verb, e.g. *He* really *meant it. I* almost *fell asleep.*
   b an adjective, e.g. *She is* very *clever. This is a* slightly *better result.*
   c another adverb, e.g. *It comes off* terribly *easily. The boys* nearly *always get home late.*

3 to add to the meaning of a whole sentence, e.g.
   He is probably *our best player.* Luckily, *no one was hurt.*

In writing or in formal speech, it is **incorrect** to use an adjective instead of an adverb. For example, use
   Do it properly.   and not   **Do it* proper.
but note that many words are both an adjective and an adverb, e.g.

adjective	*adverb*
a fast horse	*He ran* fast.
a long time	*Have you been here* long?

affluent /ˈæflʊənt/ *adjective* rich. □ **affluence** *noun*.

afford /əˈfɔːd/ *verb* (after *can, be able to*) have enough money, time, etc., for; be able to spare (time etc.); (+ *to do*) be in a position; provide.

afforest /əˈfɒrɪst/ *verb* convert into forest; plant with trees. □ **afforestation** *noun*.

affray /əˈfreɪ/ *noun* breach of peace by fighting or rioting in public.

affront /əˈfrʌnt/ ● *noun* open insult. ● *verb* insult openly; embarrass.

Afghan /ˈæfɡæn/ ● *noun* native, national, or language of Afghanistan. ● *adjective* of Afghanistan. □ **Afghan hound** tall dog with long silky hair.

afield /əˈfiːld/ *adverb* to or at a distance.

aflame /əˈfleɪm/ *adverb & adjective* in flames; very excited.

afloat /əˈfləʊt/ *adverb & adjective* floating; at sea; out of debt.

afoot /əˈfʊt/ *adverb & adjective* in operation; progressing.

afore /əˈfɔː/ *preposition & adverb archaic* before.

afore- *combining form* previously.

aforethought *adjective* (after noun) premeditated.

a fortiori /eɪ fɔːtɪˈɔːraɪ/ *adverb & adjective* with stronger reason. [Latin]

afraid /əˈfreɪd/ *adjective* alarmed, frightened. □ **be afraid** *colloquial* politely regret.

afresh /əˈfreʃ/ *adverb* anew; with fresh start.

African /ˈæfrɪkən/ ● *noun* native of Africa; person of African descent. ● *adjective* of Africa.

Afrikaans /æfrɪˈkɑːns/ *noun* language derived from Dutch, used in S. Africa.

Afrikaner /æfrɪˈkɑːnə/ *noun* Afrikaans-speaking white person in S. Africa.

Afro /ˈæfrəʊ/ ● *adjective* (of hair) tightly-curled and bushy. ● *noun* (*plural* **-s**) Afro hairstyle.

Afro- *combining form* African.

aft /ɑːft/ *adverb* at or towards stern or tail.

after /ˈɑːftə/ ● *preposition* following in time; in view of; despite; behind; in pursuit or quest of; about, concerning; in allusion to or imitation of. ● *conjunction* later than. ● *adverb* later; behind. ● *adjective* later. □ **after all** in spite of everything; **afterbirth** placenta etc. discharged after childbirth; **aftercare** attention after leaving hospital etc.; **after-effect** delayed effect of accident etc.; **afterlife** life after death; **afters** *colloquial* sweet dessert; **aftershave** lotion applied to face after shaving; **afterthought** thing thought of or added later.

aftermath /ˈɑːftəmæθ/ *noun* consequences.

afternoon /ɑːftəˈnuːn/ *noun* time between midday and evening.

afterwards /ˈɑːftəwədz/ *adverb* later, subsequently.

again /əˈɡen/ *adverb* another time; as previously; in addition; on the other hand. □ **again and again** repeatedly.

against /əˈɡenst/ *preposition* in opposition to; into collision or in contact with; to the disadvantage of; in contrast to; in anticipation of; as compensating factor to; in return for.

agape /əˈɡeɪp/ *adjective* gaping.

agate /ˈæɡət/ *noun* usually hard streaked chalcedony.

agave /əˈɡeɪvɪ/ *noun* spiny-leaved plant.

age ● *noun* length of past life or existence; *colloquial* (often in *plural*) a long time; historical period; old age. ● *verb* (**ageing**) (cause to) show signs of age; grow old; mature. □ **come of age** reach legal adult status; **under age** not old enough.

aged *adjective* /eɪdʒd/ of the age of; /ˈeɪdʒɪd/ old.

ageism /ˈeɪdʒɪz(ə)m/ *noun* prejudice or discrimination on grounds of age.

ageless /ˈeɪdʒlɪs/ *adjective* never growing or appearing old.

agency /ˈeɪdʒənsɪ/ *noun* (*plural* **-ies**) business or premises of agent; action; intervention.

agenda /əˈdʒendə/ *noun* (*plural* **-s**) list of items to be considered at meeting; things to be done.

agent /ˈeɪdʒ(ə)nt/ *noun* person acting for another in business etc.; person or thing producing effect.

agent provocateur /ɑːʒ̃ prəvɒkəˈtɜː/ *noun* (*plural* **agents provocateurs** same pronunciation) person tempting suspected offenders to self-incriminating action. [French]

agglomerate /əˈɡlɒməreɪt/ *verb* (**-ting**) collect into mass. □ **agglomeration** *noun*.

agglutinate /əˈɡluːtɪneɪt/ *verb* (**-ting**) stick as with glue. □ **agglutination** *noun*; **agglutinative** /-nətɪv/ *adjective*.

aggrandize /əˈɡrændaɪz/ *verb* (also **-ise**) (**-zing** or **-sing**) increase power, rank, or wealth of; make seem greater. □ **aggrandizement** /-dɪz-/ *noun*.

aggravate /ˈæɡrəveɪt/ *verb* (**-ting**) increase seriousness of; *colloquial* annoy. □ **aggravation** *noun*.

■ **Usage** The use of *aggravate* to mean 'annoy' is considered incorrect by some people, but it is common in informal use.

aggregate ● *noun* /ˈæɡrɪɡət/ sum total; crushed stone etc. used in making concrete. ● *adjective* /ˈæɡrɪɡət/ collective, total. ● *verb* /ˈæɡrɪɡeɪt/ collect together, unite; *colloquial* amount to. □ **aggregation** *noun*.

aggression /əˈɡreʃ(ə)n/ *noun* unprovoked attack; hostile act or feeling. □ **aggressor** *noun*.

aggressive /əˈɡresɪv/ *adjective* given to aggression; forceful, self-assertive. □ **aggressively** *adverb*.

aggrieved /əˈɡriːvd/ *adjective* having grievance.

aggro /ˈæɡrəʊ/ *noun slang* aggression; difficulty.

aghast /əˈɡɑːst/ *adjective* amazed and horrified.

agile /ˈædʒaɪl/ *adjective* quick-moving; nimble. □ **agility** /əˈdʒɪlɪtɪ/ *noun*.

agitate /ˈædʒɪteɪt/ *verb* (**-ting**) disturb, excite; (often + *for, against*) campaign, esp. politically; shake briskly. □ **agitation** *noun*; **agitator** *noun*.

AGM *abbreviation* annual general meeting.

agnail /ˈæɡneɪl/ *noun* torn skin at root of fingernail; resulting soreness.

agnostic /æɡˈnɒstɪk/ ● *noun* person who believes that existence of God is not provable. ● *adjective* of agnosticism. □ **agnosticism** /-sɪz(ə)m/ *noun*.

ago /əˈɡəʊ/ *adverb* in the past.

agog /əˈɡɒɡ/ *adjective* eager, expectant.

agonize /ˈæɡənaɪz/ *verb* (also **-ise**) (**-zing** or **-sing**) undergo mental anguish; (cause to) suffer agony; (as **agonized** *adjective*) expressing agony.

agony /ˈæɡənɪ/ *noun* (*plural* **-ies**) extreme physical or mental suffering; severe struggle. □ **agony aunt** *colloquial* writer answering letters in **agony column** *colloquial*, section of magazine etc. offering personal advice.

agoraphobia /æɡərəˈfəʊbɪə/ *noun* extreme fear of open spaces. □ **agoraphobic** *adjective*.

agrarian /əˈɡreərɪən/ ● *adjective* of land or its cultivation. ● *noun* advocate of redistribution of land.

agree /əˈɡriː/ *verb* (**-ees**, **-eed**,) (often + *with*) hold similar opinion, be or become in harmony, suit, be compatible; (+ *to do*) consent; reach agreement about.

agreeable *adjective* pleasing; willing to agree. □ **agreeably** *adverb*.

agreement *noun* act or state of agreeing; arrangement, contract.

agriculture /'ægrɪkʌltʃə/ *noun* cultivation of the soil and rearing of animals. □ **agricultural** /-'kʌl-/ *adjective*; **agriculturalist** /-'kʌl-/ *noun*.

agronomy /ə'grɒnəmɪ/ *noun* science of soil management and crop production. □ **agronomist** *noun*.

aground /ə'graʊnd/ *adjective & adverb* on(to) bottom of shallow water.

ague /'eɪgju:/ *noun* shivering fit; *historical* malarial fever.

ah /ɑ:/ *interjection expressing surprise, pleasure, or realization.*

aha /ɑː'hɑ:/ *interjection expressing surprise, triumph, mockery, etc.*

ahead /ə'hed/ *adverb* in advance, in front; (often + *on*) in the lead (on points etc.).

ahoy /ə'hɔɪ/ *interjection Nautical* call used in hailing.

AI *abbreviation* artificial insemination; artificial intelligence.

aid ● *noun* help; person or thing that helps. ● *verb* help; promote (recovery etc.). □ **in aid of** in support of, *colloquial* for purpose of.

aide /eɪd/ *noun* aide-de-camp; assistant.

aide-de-camp /eɪd də 'kɑ̃/ *noun* (*plural* **aides-** same pronunciation) officer assisting senior officer.

Aids *noun* (also **AIDS**) acquired immune deficiency syndrome.

ail *verb* be ill or in poor condition.

aileron /'eɪlərɒn/ *noun* hinged flap on aircraft wing.

ailment *noun* illness, esp. minor one.

aim ● *verb* intend, try; (usually + *at*) direct, point; take aim. ● *noun* purpose, object; directing of weapon etc. at object. □ **take aim** direct weapon etc. at object.

aimless *adjective* purposeless. □ **aimlessly** *adverb*.

ain't /eɪnt/ *colloquial* am not, is not, are not; has not, have not.

■ **Usage** The use of *ain't* is incorrect in standard English.

air ● *noun* mixture chiefly of oxygen and nitrogen surrounding earth; open space; earth's atmosphere, often as place where aircraft operate; appearance, manner; (in *plural*) affected manner; tune. ● *verb* expose (room, clothes, etc.) to air, ventilate; express and discuss publicly. □ **airbase** base for military aircraft; **air-bed** inflatable mattress; **airborne** transported by air, (of aircraft) in the air; **airbrick** brick perforated for ventilation; **Air Commodore** RAF officer next above Group Captain; **air-conditioned** *adjective* equipped with **air-conditioning**, regulation of humidity and temperature in building, apparatus for this; **airfield** area with runway(s) for aircraft; **air force** branch of armed forces fighting in the air; **airgun** gun using compressed air to fire pellets; **air hostess** stewardess in aircraft; **air letter** sheet of paper forming airmail letter; **airlift** *noun* emergency transport of supplies etc. by air, *verb* transport thus; **airline** public air transport company; **airliner** large passenger aircraft; **airlock** stoppage of flow by air bubble in pipe etc., compartment giving access to pressurized chamber; **airmail** system of transporting mail by air, mail carried thus; **airman** pilot or member of aircraft crew; **Air (Chief, Vice-) Marshal** high ranks in RAF; **airplane** *US* aeroplane; **airport** airfield with facilities for passengers and cargo; **air raid** attack by aircraft; **air rifle** rifle using compressed air to fire pellets; **airs and graces** affected manner; **airship** powered aircraft lighter than air; **airsick** nauseous from air travel; **airspace** air above a country; **air speed** aircraft's speed relative to air; **airstrip** strip of ground for take-off and landing of aircraft; **air terminal** building with transport to and from airport;

air traffic controller official who controls air traffic by radio; **airway** recognized route of aircraft, passage for air into lungs; **airwoman** woman pilot or member of aircraft crew; **by air** by or in aircraft; **on the air** being broadcast.

aircraft *noun* (*plural* same) aeroplane, helicopter. □ **aircraft carrier** warship that carries and acts as base for aircraft; **aircraftman**, **aircraftwoman** lowest rank in RAF.

Airedale /'eədeɪl/ *noun* terrier of large rough-coated breed.

airless *adjective* stuffy; still, calm.

airtight *adjective* impermeable to air.

airworthy *adjective* (of aircraft) fit to fly. □ **airworthiness** *noun*.

airy *adjective* (**-ier, -iest**) well-ventilated; flippant; light as air. □ **airy-fairy** *colloquial* unrealistic, impractical.

aisle /aɪl/ *noun* side part of church divided by pillars from nave; passage between rows of pews, seats, etc.

aitchbone /'eɪtʃbəʊn/ *noun* rump bone of animal; cut of beef over this.

ajar /ə'dʒɑ:/ *adverb & adjective* (of door etc.) slightly open.

Akela /ɑː'keɪlə/ *noun* adult leader of Cub Scouts.

akimbo /ə'kɪmbəʊ/ *adverb* (of arms) with hands on hips and elbows out.

akin /ə'kɪn/ *adjective* related; similar.

alabaster /'æləbɑːstə/ ● *noun* translucent usually white form of gypsum. ● *adjective* of alabaster; white, smooth.

à la carte /æ lɑː 'kɑːt/ *adverb & adjective* with individually priced dishes.

alacrity /ə'lækrɪtɪ/ *noun* briskness; readiness.

à la mode /æ lɑː 'məʊd/ *adverb & adjective* in fashion; fashionable.

alarm /ə'lɑːm/ ● *noun* warning of danger etc.; warning sound or device; alarm clock; apprehension. ● *verb* frighten, disturb; warn. □ **alarm clock** clock that rings at set time. □ **alarming** *adjective*.

alarmist /ə'lɑːmɪst/ *noun* person spreading unnecessary alarm.

alas /ə'læs/ *interjection expressing grief or regret.*

alb *noun* long white vestment worn by Christian priests.

albatross /'ælbətrɒs/ *noun* long-winged seabird related to petrel; *Golf* score of 3 strokes under par for hole.

albeit /ɔːl'biːɪt/ *conjunction* although.

albino /æl'biːnəʊ/ *noun* (*plural* **-s**) person or animal lacking pigment in skin, hair, and eyes. □ **albinism** /'ælbɪnɪz(ə)m/ *noun*.

album /'ælbəm/ *noun* book for displaying photographs etc.; long-playing gramophone record; set of these.

albumen /'ælbjʊmɪn/ *noun* egg white.

albumin /'ælbjʊmɪn/ *noun* water-soluble protein found in egg white, milk, blood, etc.

alchemy /'ælkəmɪ/ *noun* medieval chemistry, esp. seeking to turn base metals into gold. □ **alchemist** *noun*.

alcohol /'ælkəhɒl/ *noun* colourless volatile liquid, esp. as intoxicant present in wine, beer, spirits, etc. and as a solvent, fuel, etc.; liquor containing this; other compound of this type.

alcoholic /ælkə'hɒlɪk/ ● *adjective* of, like, containing, or caused by alcohol. ● *noun* person suffering from alcoholism.

alcoholism /'ælkəhɒlɪz(ə)m/ *noun* condition resulting from addiction to alcohol.

alcove /'ælkəʊv/ *noun* recess in wall of room, garden, etc.

alder /'ɔːldə/ *noun* tree related to birch.

alderman /'ɔːldəmən/ *noun esp. historical* civic dignitary next in rank to mayor.

ale *noun* beer.

alert /ə'lɜːt/ ● *adjective* watchful. ● *noun* alarm; state or period of special vigilance. ● *verb* (often + *to*) warn.

alfalfa /æl'fælfə/ *noun* clover-like plant used for fodder.

alfresco /æl'freskəʊ/ *adjective & adverb* in the open air.

alga /'ælgə/ *noun* (*plural* **-gae** /-dʒiː/) (usually in *plural*) non-flowering stemless water plant.

algebra /'ældʒɪbrə/ *noun* branch of mathematics using letters to represent numbers. □ **algebraic** /-'breɪk/ *adjective*.

Algol /'ælgɒl/ *noun* high-level computer-programming language.

algorithm /'ælgərɪð(ə)m/ *noun* process or rules for (esp. computer) calculation etc.

alias /'eɪlɪəs/ ● *adverb* also known as. ● *noun* assumed name.

alibi /'ælɪbaɪ/ *noun* (*plural* **-s**) proof that one was elsewhere; excuse.

■ **Usage** The use of *alibi* to mean 'an excuse' is considered incorrect by some people.

alien /'eɪlɪən/ ● *adjective* (often + *to*) unfamiliar, repugnant; foreign; of beings from another world. ● *noun* non-naturalized foreigner; a being from another world.

alienate /'eɪlɪəneɪt/ *verb* (**-ting**) estrange; transfer ownership of. □ **alienation** *noun*.

alight[1] /ə'laɪt/ *adjective* on fire; lit up.

alight[2] /ə'laɪt/ *verb* (often + *from*) get down or off; come to earth, settle.

align /ə'laɪn/ *verb* place in or bring into line; (usually + *with*) ally (oneself etc.). □ **alignment** *noun*.

alike /ə'laɪk/ ● *adjective* similar, like. ● *adverb* in similar way.

alimentary /ælɪ'mentərɪ/ *adjective* concerning nutrition; nourishing. □ **alimentary canal** channel through which food passes during digestion.

alimony /'ælɪmənɪ/ *noun* money payable to a divorced or separated spouse.

alive /ə'laɪv/ *adjective* living; lively, active; (usually + *to*) alert to; (usually + *with*) swarming with.

alkali /'ælkəlaɪ/ *noun* (*plural* **-s**) substance that neutralizes acids, turns litmus blue, and forms caustic solutions in water. □ **alkaline** *adjective*; **alkalinity** /-'lɪn-/ *noun*.

alkaloid /'ælkəlɔɪd/ *noun* plant-based compound often used as drug, e.g. morphine, quinine.

all /ɔːl/ ● *adjective* whole amount, number, or extent of. ● *noun* all people or things concerned; (+ *of*) the whole of. ● *adverb* entirely, quite. □ **all along** from the beginning; **all but** very nearly; **all for** *colloquial* strongly in favour of; **all-clear** signal that danger or difficulty is over; **all fours** hands and knees; **all in** exhausted; **all-in** inclusive of all; **all in all** everything considered; **all out** (**all-out** before noun) involving all one's strength etc.; **all over** completely finished, in or on all parts of one's body; **all-purpose** having many uses; **all right** satisfactory, safe and sound, in good condition, satisfactorily, I consent; **all-right** (before noun) *colloquial* acceptable; **all round** in all respects, for each person; **all-round** (of person) versatile; **all-rounder** versatile person; **All Saints' Day** 1 Nov.; **all the same** nevertheless; **all there** *colloquial* mentally alert or normal; **all together** all at once, all in one place; **at all** (with negative or in questions) in any way, to any extent; **in all** in total, altogether.

■ **Usage** See note at ALTOGETHER.

Allah /'ælə/ *noun: Muslim name of* God.

allay /ə'leɪ/ *verb* lessen; alleviate.

allege /ə'ledʒ/ *verb* declare, esp. without proof. □ **allegation** /ælɪ'geɪʃ(ə)n/ *noun*; **allegedly** /ə'ledʒɪdlɪ/ *adverb*.

allegiance /ə'liːdʒ(ə)ns/ *noun* loyalty; duty of subject.

allegory /'ælɪgərɪ/ *noun* (*plural* **-ies**) story with moral represented symbolically. □ **allegorical** /-'gɒr-/ *adjective*; **allegorize** *verb* (also **-ise**) (**-zing** or **-sing**).

allegretto /ælɪ'gretəʊ/ *Music* ● *adverb & adjective* in fairly brisk tempo. ● *noun* (*plural* **-s**) allegretto movement or passage.

allegro /ə'legrəʊ/ *Music* ● *adverb & adjective* in lively tempo. ● *noun* (*plural* **-s**) allegro movement or passage.

alleluia /ælɪ'luːjə/ (also **hallelujah** /hæl-/) ● *interjection* God be praised. ● *noun* (*plural* **-s**) song of praise to God.

allergic /ə'lɜːdʒɪk/ *adjective* (+ *to*) having allergy to, *colloquial* having strong dislike for; caused by allergy.

allergy /'ælədʒɪ/ *noun* (*plural* **-ies**) reaction to certain substances.

alleviate /ə'liːvɪeɪt/ *verb* (**-ting**) make (pain etc.) less severe. □ **alleviation** *noun*.

alley /'ælɪ/ *noun* (*plural* **-s**) narrow street or passage; enclosure for skittles, bowling, etc.

alliance /ə'laɪəns/ *noun* formal union or association of states, political parties, etc. or of families by marriage.

allied /'ælaɪd/ *adjective* connected or related; (also **Allied**) associated in an alliance.

alligator /'ælɪgeɪtə/ *noun* large reptile of crocodile family.

alliteration /əlɪtə'reɪʃ(ə)n/ *noun* recurrence of same initial letter or sound in adjacent or nearby words, as in *The fair breeze blew, the white foam flew, the furrow followed free*. □ **alliterate** /-'lɪt-/ *verb*; **alliterative** /-'lɪtərətɪv/ *adjective*.

allocate /'æləkeɪt/ *verb* (**-ting**) (usually + *to*) assign. □ **allocation** *noun*.

allot /ə'lɒt/ *verb* (**-tt-**) apportion or distribute to (person).

allotment /ə'lɒtmənt/ *noun* small plot of land rented for cultivation; share; allotting.

allow /ə'laʊ/ *verb* (often + *to do*) permit; assign fixed sum to; (usually + *for*) provide or set aside for a purpose. □ **allow for** take into consideration.

allowance *noun* amount or sum allowed, esp. regularly; deduction, discount. □ **make allowances** (often + *for*) judge leniently.

alloy /'ælɔɪ/ ● *noun* mixture of metals; inferior metal mixed esp. with gold or silver. ● *verb* mix (metals); /ə'lɔɪ/ debase by admixture; spoil (pleasure).

allspice /'ɔːlspaɪs/ *noun* spice made from berry of pimento plant; this berry.

allude /ə'luːd/ *verb* (**-ding**) (+ *to*) make allusion to.

allure /ə'ljʊə/ ● *verb* (**-ring**) attract, charm, entice. ● *noun* attractiveness, charm. □ **allurement** *noun*.

allusion /ə'luːʒ(ə)n/ *noun* (often + *to*) passing or indirect reference. □ **allusive** /-sɪv/ *adjective*.

alluvium /ə'luːvɪəm/ *noun* (*plural* **-via**) deposit left by flood, esp. in river valley. □ **alluvial** *adjective*.

ally ● *noun* /'ælaɪ/ (*plural* **-ies**) state or person formally cooperating or united with another, esp. in war. ● *verb* (also /ə'laɪ/) (**-ies**, **-ied**) (often **ally oneself with**) combine in alliance (with).

Alma Mater /ælmə 'mɑːtə/ *noun* one's university, school, or college.

almanac /'ɔːlmənæk/ *noun* (also **almanack**) calendar, usually with astronomical data.

almighty /ɔːl'maɪtɪ/ ● adjective infinitely powerful; very great. ● noun (**the Almighty**) God.

almond /'ɑːmənd/ noun kernel of nutlike fruit related to plum; tree bearing this.

almoner /'ɑːmənə/ noun social worker attached to hospital.

almost /'ɔːlməʊst/ adverb all but, very nearly.

alms /ɑːmz/ plural noun historical donation of money or food to the poor. □ **almshouse** charitable institution for the poor.

aloe /'æləʊ/ noun plant with toothed fleshy leaves; (in plural) strong laxative from aloe juice. □ **aloe vera** /'vɪərə/ variety yielding substance used in cosmetics, this substance.

aloft /ə'lɒft/ adjective & adverb high up, overhead.

alone /ə'ləʊn/ ● adjective without company or help; lonely. ● adverb only, exclusively.

along /ə'lɒŋ/ ● preposition beside or through (part of) the length of. ● adverb onward, into more advanced state; with oneself or others; beside or through (part of) thing's length. □ **alongside** at or close to side (of); **along with** in addition to.

aloof /ə'luːf/ ● adjective unconcerned, unsympathetic. ● adverb away, apart.

aloud /ə'laʊd/ adverb audibly.

alp noun high mountain, esp. (**the Alps**) those in Switzerland and adjacent countries.

alpaca /æl'pækə/ noun S. American llama-like animal; its long wool; fabric made from this.

alpha /'ælfə/ noun first letter of Greek alphabet (A, α). □ **alpha and omega** beginning and end; **alpha particle** helium nucleus emitted by radioactive substance.

alphabet /'ælfəbet/ noun set of letters or signs used in a language. □ **alphabetical** /-'bet-/ adjective.

alphanumeric /ælfənjuː'merɪk/ adjective containing both letters and numbers.

alpine /'ælpaɪn/ ● adjective of high mountains or (**Alpine**) the Alps. ● noun plant suited to mountain regions; = rock plant.

already /ɔːl'redɪ/ adverb before the time in question; as early as this.

alright adverb = ALL RIGHT.

■ **Usage** Although *alright* is widely used, it is not correct in standard English.

Alsatian /æl'seɪʃ(ə)n/ noun large dog of a breed of wolfhound.

also /'ɔːlsəʊ/ adverb in addition, besides. □ **also-ran** loser in race, undistinguished person.

altar /'ɔːltə/ noun flat table or block for offerings to deity; Communion table.

alter /'ɔːltə/ verb change in character, shape, etc. □ **alteration** noun.

altercation /ɔːltə'keɪʃ(ə)n/ noun dispute, wrangle.

alternate ● adjective /ɔːl'tɜːnət/ (with noun in plural) every other; (of things of two kinds) alternating. ● verb /'ɔːltəneɪt/ (**-ting**) (often + *with*) arrange or occur by turns; (+ *between*) go repeatedly from one to another. □ **alternating current** electric current regularly reversing direction. □ **alternately** adverb; **alternation** noun.

■ **Usage** See note at ALTERNATIVE.

alternative /ɔːl'tɜːnətɪv/ ● adjective available as another choice; unconventional. ● noun any of two or more possibilities; choice. □ **alternatively** adverb.

■ **Usage** The adjective *alternative* is often confused with *alternate*, which is correctly used in 'there will be a dance on alternate Saturdays'.

alternator /'ɔːltəneɪtə/ noun dynamo generating alternating current.

although /ɔːl'ðəʊ/ conjunction though.

altimeter /'æltɪmiːtə/ noun instrument measuring altitude.

altitude /'æltɪtjuːd/ noun height, esp. of object above sea level or horizon.

alto /'æltəʊ/ ● noun (plural **-s**) = CONTRALTO; highest adult male singing voice; singer with this. ● adjective having range of alto.

altogether /ɔːltə'geðə/ adverb totally; on the whole; in total.

■ **Usage** Note that *altogether* means 'in total', as in *six rooms altogether*, whereas *all together* means 'all at once' or 'all in one place' as in *six rooms all together*.

altruism /'æltruːɪz(ə)m/ noun unselfishness as principle of action. □ **altruist** noun; **altruistic** /-'ɪs-/ adjective.

alumina /ə'luːmɪnə/ noun aluminium oxide; emery.

aluminium /æljʊ'mɪnɪəm/ noun (US **aluminum** /ə'luːmɪnəm/) a light silvery metallic element.

alumnus /ə'lʌmnəs/ noun (plural **-ni** /-naɪ/) former pupil or student.

always /'ɔːlweɪz/ adverb at all times; whatever the circumstances; repeatedly.

Alzheimer's disease /'æltshaɪməz/ noun brain disorder causing senility.

AM abbreviation amplitude modulation.

am 1st singular present of BE.

a.m. abbreviation before noon (*ante meridiem*).

amalgam /ə'mælgəm/ noun mixture, blend; alloy of any metal with mercury.

amalgamate /ə'mælgəmeɪt/ verb (**-ting**) mix; unite. □ **amalgamation** noun.

amanuensis /əmænjuː'ensɪs/ noun (plural **-enses** /-siːz/) assistant, esp. writing from dictation.

amaranth /'æmərænθ/ noun plant with green, red, or purple flowers; imaginary unfading flower. □ **amaranthine** /-'rænθaɪn/ adjective.

amaryllis /æmə'rɪlɪs/ noun plant with lily-like flowers.

amass /ə'mæs/ verb heap together, accumulate.

amateur /'æmətə/ noun person engaging in pursuit as pastime not profession; person with limited skill. □ **amateurish** adjective; **amateurism** noun.

amatory /'æmətərɪ/ adjective of sexual love.

amaze /ə'meɪz/ verb (**-zing**) fill with surprise or wonder. □ **amazement** noun; **amazing** adjective.

Amazon /'æməzən/ noun one of a mythical race of female warriors; (**amazon**) strong or athletic woman. □ **Amazonian** /-'zəʊ-/ adjective.

ambassador /æm'bæsədə/ noun diplomat living abroad as representative of his or her country; promoter. □ **ambassadorial** /-'dɔː-/ adjective.

amber /'æmbə/ ● noun yellow translucent fossil resin; colour of this. ● adjective of or like amber.

ambergris /'æmbəgriːs/ noun waxlike substance from sperm whale, used in perfumes.

ambidextrous /æmbɪ'dekstrəs/ adjective able to use either hand equally well.

ambience /'æmbɪəns/ noun surroundings, atmosphere.

ambient /'æmbɪənt/ adjective surrounding.

ambiguous /æm'bɪgjʊəs/ adjective having a double meaning; difficult to classify. □ **ambiguity** /-'gjuː-/ noun (plural **-ies**).

ambit /'æmbɪt/ noun scope, bounds.

ambition /æm'bɪʃ(ə)n/ noun determination to succeed; object of this.

ambitious *adjective* full of ambition.

ambivalent /æm'bɪvələnt/ *adjective* having mixed feelings towards person or thing. □ **ambivalence** *noun*.

amble /'æmb(ə)l/ ● *verb* (**-ling**) walk at leisurely pace. ● *noun* leisurely pace.

ambrosia /æm'brəʊzɪə/ *noun* food of the gods in classical mythology; delicious food etc.

ambulance /'æmbjʊləns/ *noun* vehicle for taking patients to hospital; mobile army hospital.

ambulatory /'æmbjʊlətərɪ/ *adjective* of or for walking.

ambuscade /æmbəs'keɪd/ *noun & verb* (**-ding**) ambush.

ambush /'æmbʊʃ/ ● *noun* surprise attack by people hiding; hiding place for this. ● *verb* attack from ambush; waylay.

ameliorate /ə'miːlɪəreɪt/ *verb* (**-ting**) make or become better. □ **amelioration** *noun*; **ameliorative** /-rətɪv/ *adjective*.

amen /ɑː'men/ *interjection* (esp. at end of prayer) so be it.

amenable /ə'miːnəb(ə)l/ *adjective* responsive, docile; (often + *to*) answerable (to law etc.).

amend /ə'mend/ *verb* correct error in; make minor alterations in.

amendment *noun* minor alteration or addition in document etc.

amends *noun* □ **make amends** (often + *for*) give compensation.

amenity /ə'miːnɪtɪ/ *noun* (*plural* **-ies**) pleasant or useful feature or facility; pleasantness (of a place etc.).

American /ə'merɪkən/ ● *adjective* of America, esp. the US. ● *noun* native, citizen, or inhabitant of America, esp. the US; English as spoken in the US. □ **Americanize** *verb* (also **-ise**) (**-zing** or **-sing**).

Americanism *noun* word etc. of US origin or usage.

amethyst /'æməθɪst/ *noun* purple or violet semiprecious stone.

amiable /'eɪmɪəb(ə)l/ *adjective* friendly and pleasant, likeable. □ **amiability** *noun*; **amiably** *adverb*.

amicable /'æmɪkəb(ə)l/ *adjective* friendly. □ **amicably** *adverb*.

amid /ə'mɪd/ *preposition* in the middle of.

amidships /ə'mɪdʃɪps/ *adverb* in(to) the middle of a ship.

amidst /ə'mɪdst/ = AMID.

amino acid /ə'miːnəʊ/ *noun* organic acid found in proteins.

amir = EMIR.

amiss /ə'mɪs/ ● *adjective* out of order, wrong. ● *adverb* wrong(ly), inappropriately. □ **take amiss** be offended by.

amity /'æmɪtɪ/ *noun* friendship.

ammeter /'æmɪtə/ *noun* instrument for measuring electric current.

ammo /'æməʊ/ *noun slang* ammunition.

ammonia /ə'məʊnɪə/ *noun* pungent strongly alkaline gas; solution of this in water.

ammonite /'æmənaɪt/ *noun* coil-shaped fossil shell.

ammunition /æmjʊ'nɪʃ(ə)n/ *noun* bullets, shells, grenades, etc.; information usable in argument.

amnesia /æm'niːzɪə/ *noun* loss of memory. □ **amnesiac** *adjective* & *noun*.

amnesty /'æmnɪstɪ/ *noun* (*plural* **-ies**) general pardon, esp. for political offences.

amniocentesis /æmnɪəʊsen'tiːsɪs/ *noun* (*plural* **-teses** /-siːz/) sampling of amniotic fluid to detect foetal abnormality.

amniotic fluid /æmnɪ'ɒtɪk/ *noun* fluid surrounding embryo.

amoeba /ə'miːbə/ *noun* (*plural* **-s**) microscopic single-celled organism living in water.

amok /ə'mɒk/ *adverb* □ **run amok, amuck** /ə'mʌk/ run wild.

among /ə'mʌŋ/ *preposition* (also **amongst**) surrounded by; included in or in the category of; from the joint resources of; between.

amoral /eɪ'mɒr(ə)l/ *adjective* beyond morality; without moral principles.

amorous /'æmərəs/ *adjective* showing or feeling sexual love.

amorphous /ə'mɔːfəs/ *adjective* of no definite shape; vague; non-crystalline.

amount /ə'maʊnt/ ● *noun* total number, size, value, extent, etc. ● *verb* (+ *to*) be equivalent in number, size, etc. to.

amour /ə'mʊə/ *noun* (esp. secret) love affair.

amp *noun* ampere; *colloquial* amplifier.

ampere /'æmpeə/ *noun* SI unit of electric current.

ampersand /'æmpəsænd/ *noun* the sign '&' (= *and*).

amphetamine /æm'fetəmiːn/ *noun* synthetic stimulant drug.

amphibian /æm'fɪbɪən/ *noun* amphibious animal or vehicle.

amphibious /æm'fɪbɪəs/ *adjective* living or operating on land and in water; involving military forces landed from the sea.

amphitheatre /'æmfɪθɪətə/ *noun* round open building with tiers of seats surrounding central space.

amphora /'æmfərə/ *noun* (*plural* **-rae** /-riː/) Greek or Roman two-handled jar.

ample /'æmp(ə)l/ *adjective* (**-r**, **-st**) plentiful, extensive; more than enough. □ **amply** *adverb*.

amplifier /'æmplɪfaɪə/ *noun* device for amplifying sounds or electrical signals.

amplify /'æmplɪfaɪ/ *verb* (**-ies**, **-ied**) increase strength of (sound or electrical signal); add details to (story etc.). □ **amplification** *noun*.

amplitude /'æmplɪtjuːd/ *noun* spaciousness; maximum departure from average of oscillation, alternating current, etc. □ **amplitude modulation** modulation of a wave by variation of its amplitude.

ampoule /'æmpuːl/ *noun* small sealed capsule holding solution for injection.

amputate /'æmpjʊteɪt/ *verb* (**-ting**) cut off surgically (limb etc.). □ **amputation** *noun*; **amputee** /-'tiː/ *noun*.

amuck = AMOK.

amulet /'æmjʊlɪt/ *noun* charm worn against evil.

amuse /ə'mjuːz/ *verb* (**-sing**) cause to laugh or smile; interest, occupy. □ **amusing** *adjective*.

amusement *noun* being amused; thing that amuses, esp. device for entertainment at fairground etc. □ **amusement arcade** indoor area with slot machines etc.

an see A.

anabolic steroid /ænə'bɒlɪk/ *noun* synthetic steroid hormone used to build muscle.

anachronism /ə'nækrənɪz(ə)m/ *noun* attribution of custom, event, etc. to wrong period; thing thus attributed; out-of-date person or thing. □ **anachronistic** /-'nɪs-/ *adjective*.

anaconda /ænə'kɒndə/ *noun* large S. American constrictor.

anaemia /ə'niːmɪə/ *noun* (US **anemia**) deficiency of red blood cells or their haemoglobin, causing pallor and listlessness. □ **anaemic** *adjective*.

anaesthesia /ænɪs'θiːzɪə/ *noun* (US **anes-**) artificially induced insensibility to pain.

anaesthetic /ænɪs'θetɪk/ (US **anes-**) ● *noun* drug, gas, etc., producing anaesthesia. ● *adjective* producing anaesthesia.

anaesthetist /əˈniːsθətɪst/ *noun* (*US* **anes-**) person who administers anaesthetics.

anaesthetize /əˈniːsθətaɪz/ *verb* (also **-ise**; *US* also **anes-**) (**-zing** or **-sing**) administer anaesthetic to.

anagram /ˈænəɡræm/ *noun* word or phrase formed by transposing letters of another.

anal /ˈeɪn(ə)l/ *adjective* of the anus.

analgesia /ænəlˈdʒiːziə/ *noun* absence or relief of pain.

analgesic /ænəlˈdʒiːsɪk/ ● *noun* pain-killing drug. ● *adjective* pain-killing.

analogous /əˈnæləɡəs/ *adjective* (usually + *to*) partially similar or parallel.

analogue /ˈænəlɒɡ/ (*US* **analog**) ● *noun* analogous thing. ● *adjective* (of computer (usually **analog**), watch, etc.) using physical variables (e.g. voltage, position of hands) to represent numbers.

analogy /əˈnælədʒɪ/ *noun* (*plural* **-ies**) correspondence, similarity; reasoning from parallel cases.

analyse /ˈænəlaɪz/ *verb* (**-sing**) (*US* **analyze**; **-zing**) perform analysis on.

analysis /əˈnælɪsɪs/ *noun* (*plural* **-lyses** /-siːz/) detailed examination; *Chemistry* determination of constituent parts; psychoanalysis.

analyst /ˈænəlɪst/ *noun* person who analyses.

analytical /ænəˈlɪtɪkəl/ *adjective* (also **analytic**) of or using analysis.

analyze *US* = ANALYSE.

anarchism /ˈænəkɪz(ə)m/ *noun* belief that government and law should be abolished. □ **anarchist** *noun*; **anarchistic** /-ˈkɪstɪk/ *adjective*.

anarchy /ˈænəkɪ/ *noun* disorder, esp. political. □ **anarchic** /əˈnɑːkɪk/ *adjective*.

anathema /əˈnæθəmə/ *noun* (*plural* **-s**) detested thing; Church's curse.

anatomy /əˈnætəmɪ/ *noun* (*plural* **-ies**) (science of) animal or plant structure. □ **anatomical** /ænəˈtɒmɪk(ə)l/ *adjective*; **anatomist** *noun*.

anatto = ANNATTO.

ANC *abbreviation* African National Congress.

ancestor /ˈænsestə/ *noun* person, animal, or plant from which another has descended or evolved; prototype.

ancestral /ænˈsestr(ə)l/ *adjective* inherited from ancestors.

ancestry /ˈænsestrɪ/ *noun* (*plural* **-ies**) lineage; ancestors collectively.

anchor /ˈæŋkə/ ● *noun* metal device used to moor ship to sea-bottom. ● *verb* secure with anchor; fix firmly; cast anchor. □ **anchorman** coordinator, esp. compère in broadcast.

anchorage /ˈæŋkərɪdʒ/ *noun* place for anchoring; lying at anchor.

anchorite /ˈæŋkəraɪt/ *noun* hermit, recluse.

anchovy /ˈæntʃəvɪ/ *noun* (*plural* **-ies**) small strong-flavoured fish of herring family.

ancien régime /ãsjæ reˈʒiːm/ *noun* superseded regime, esp. that of pre-Revolutionary France. [French]

ancient /ˈeɪnʃ(ə)nt/ *adjective* of times long past; very old.

ancillary /ænˈsɪlərɪ/ ● *adjective* subsidiary, auxiliary; (esp. of health workers) providing essential support. ● *noun* (*plural* **-ies**) auxiliary; ancillary worker.

and *conjunction connecting words, clauses, or sentences.*

andante /ænˈdæntɪ/ *Music* ● *adverb* & *adjective* in moderately slow time. ● *noun* andante movement or passage.

androgynous /ænˈdrɒdʒɪnəs/ *adjective* hermaphrodite.

android /ˈændrɔɪd/ *noun* robot with human appearance.

anecdote /ˈænɪkdəʊt/ *noun* short, esp. true, story. □ **anecdotal** /-ˈdəʊt(ə)l/ *adjective*.

anemia *US* = ANAEMIA.

anemic *US* = ANAEMIC.

anemometer /ænɪˈmɒmɪtə/ *noun* instrument for measuring wind force.

anemone /əˈnemənɪ/ *noun* plant related to buttercup.

aneroid barometer /ˈænərɔɪd/ *noun* barometer that measures air pressure by registering its action on lid of box containing vacuum.

anesthesia etc. *US* = ANAESTHESIA etc.

aneurysm /ˈænjʊrɪz(ə)m/ *noun* (also **aneurism**) excessive enlargement of artery.

anew /əˈnjuː/ *adverb* again; in different way.

angel /ˈeɪndʒ(ə)l/ *noun* attendant or messenger of God usually represented as human with wings; kind or virtuous person. □ **angel cake** light sponge cake; **angelfish** small fish with winglike fins. □ **angelic** /ænˈdʒelɪk/ *adjective*; **angelically** *adverb*.

angelica /ænˈdʒelɪkə/ *noun* aromatic plant; its candied stalks.

angelus /ˈændʒɪləs/ *noun* RC prayers said at morning, noon, and sunset; bell rung for this.

anger /ˈæŋɡə/ ● *noun* extreme displeasure. ● *verb* make angry.

angina /ænˈdʒaɪnə/ *noun* (in full **angina pectoris**) chest pain brought on by exertion, owing to poor blood supply to heart.

angle[1] /ˈæŋɡ(ə)l/ ● *noun* space between two meeting lines or surfaces, esp. as measured in degrees; corner; point of view. ● *verb* (**-ling**) move or place obliquely; present (information) in biased way.

angle[2] /ˈæŋɡ(ə)l/ *verb* (**-ling**) fish with line and hook; (+ *for*) seek objective indirectly. □ **angler** *noun*.

Anglican /ˈæŋɡlɪkən/ ● *adjective* of Church of England. ● *noun* member of Anglican Church. □ **Anglicanism** *noun*.

Anglicism /ˈæŋɡlɪsɪz(ə)m/ *noun* English expression or custom.

Anglicize /ˈæŋɡlɪsaɪz/ *verb* (also **-ise**) (**-zing** or **-sing**) make English in character etc.

Anglo- *combining form* English or British (and).

Anglo-Catholic /æŋɡləʊˈkæθəlɪk/ ● *adjective* of High Church Anglican group emphasizing its Catholic tradition. ● *noun* member of this group.

Anglo-Indian /æŋɡləʊˈɪndɪən/ ● *adjective* of England and India; (of British descent but Indian residence. ● *noun* Anglo-Indian person.

Anglophile /ˈæŋɡləʊfaɪl/ *noun* admirer of England or the English.

Anglo-Saxon /æŋɡləʊˈsæks(ə)n/ ● *adjective* of English Saxons before Norman Conquest; of English descent. ● *noun* Anglo-Saxon person or language; *colloquial* plain (esp. crude) English.

angora /æŋˈɡɔːrə/ *noun* fabric made from hair of angora goat or rabbit. □ **angora cat, goat, rabbit** long-haired varieties.

angostura /æŋɡəˈstjʊərə/ *noun* aromatic bitter bark of S. American tree.

angry /ˈæŋɡrɪ/ *adjective* (**-ier, -iest**) feeling or showing anger; (of wound etc.) inflamed, painful. □ **angrily** *adverb*.

angst /æŋst/ *noun* anxiety, neurotic fear; guilt.

angstrom /ˈæŋstrəm/ *noun* unit of wavelength measurement.

anguish /ˈæŋɡwɪʃ/ *noun* severe mental or physical pain. □ **anguished** *adjective*.

angular /ˈæŋɡjʊlə/ *adjective* having sharp corners or (of person) features; (of distance) measured by angle. □ **angularity** /-ˈlær-/ *noun*.

aniline /ˈænɪliːn/ *noun* colourless oily liquid used in dyes, drugs, and plastics.

animadvert /ˌænɪmædˈvɜːt/ *verb* (+ *on*) *literary* criticize, censure. □ **animadversion** *noun*.

animal /ˈænɪm(ə)l/ ● *noun* living organism, esp. other than man, having sensation and usually ability to move; brutish person. ● *adjective* of or like animal; carnal.

animality /ˌænɪˈmælɪtɪ/ *noun* the animal world; animal behaviour.

animate *adjective* /ˈænɪmət/ having life; lively. ● *verb* /ˈænɪmeɪt/ (**-ting**) enliven; give life to.

animated /ˈænɪmeɪtɪd/ *adjective* lively; living; (of film) using animation.

animation /ˌænɪˈmeɪʃ(ə)n/ *noun* liveliness; being alive; technique of film-making by photographing sequence of drawings or positions of puppets etc. to create illusion of movement.

animator /ˈænɪmeɪtə/ *noun* artist who prepares animated films.

animism /ˈænɪmɪz(ə)m/ *noun* belief that inanimate objects and natural phenomena have souls. □ **animist** *noun*; **animistic** /-ˈmɪs-/ *adjective*.

animosity /ˌænɪˈmɒsɪtɪ/ *noun* (*plural* **-ies**) hostility.

animus /ˈænɪməs/ *noun* hostility, ill feeling.

anion /ˈænaɪən/ *noun* negatively charged ion.

anise /ˈænɪs/ *noun* plant with aromatic seeds.

aniseed /ˈænɪsiːd/ *noun* seed of anise.

ankle /ˈæŋk(ə)l/ *noun* joint connecting foot with leg.

anklet /ˈæŋklɪt/ *noun* ornament worn round ankle.

ankylosis /ˌæŋkɪˈləʊsɪs/ *noun* stiffening of joint by fusing of bones.

annals /ˈæn(ə)lz/ *plural noun* narrative of events year by year; historical records. □ **annalist** *noun*.

annatto /əˈnætəʊ/ *noun* (also **anatto**) orange-red food colouring made from tropical fruit.

anneal /əˈniːl/ *verb* heat (metal, glass) and cool slowly, esp. to toughen.

annelid /ˈænəlɪd/ *noun* segmented worm, e.g. earthworm.

annex /æˈneks/ *verb* (often + *to*) add as subordinate part; take possession of. □ **annexation** *noun*.

annexe /ˈæneks/ *noun* supplementary building.

annihilate /əˈnaɪəleɪt/ *verb* (**-ting**) destroy utterly. □ **annihilation** *noun*.

anniversary /ˌænɪˈvɜːsərɪ/ *noun* (*plural* **-ies**) yearly return of date of event; celebration of this.

Anno Domini /ˌænəʊ ˈdɒmɪnaɪ/ see AD.

annotate /ˈænəteɪt/ *verb* (**-ting**) add explanatory notes to. □ **annotation** *noun*.

announce /əˈnaʊns/ *verb* (**-cing**) make publicly known; make known the approach of. □ **announcement** *noun*.

announcer *noun* person who announces, esp. in broadcasting.

annoy /əˈnɔɪ/ *verb* (often in *passive* + *at*, *with*) anger or distress slightly; harass. □ **annoyance** *noun*.

annual /ˈænjʊəl/ ● *adjective* reckoned by the year; recurring yearly. ● *noun* book etc. published yearly; plant living only one year. □ **annually** *adverb*.

annuity /əˈnjuːɪtɪ/ *noun* (*plural* **-ies**) yearly grant or allowance; investment yielding fixed annual sum for stated period.

annul /əˈnʌl/ *verb* (**-ll-**) declare invalid; cancel, abolish. □ **annulment** *noun*.

annular /ˈænjʊlə/ *adjective* ring-shaped.

annulate /ˈænjʊlət/ *adjective* marked with or formed of rings.

annunciation /əˌnʌnsɪˈeɪʃ(ə)n/ *noun* announcement, esp. (**Annunciation**) that made by the angel Gabriel to Mary.

anode /ˈænəʊd/ *noun* positive electrode.

anodize /ˈænədaɪz/ *verb* (also **-ise**) (**-zing** or **-sing**) coat (metal) with protective layer by electrolysis.

anodyne /ˈænədaɪn/ ● *adjective* pain-relieving; soothing. ● *noun* anodyne drug etc.

anoint /əˈnɔɪnt/ *verb* apply oil or ointment to, esp. ritually.

anomalous /əˈnɒmələs/ *adjective* irregular, abnormal.

anomaly /əˈnɒməlɪ/ *noun* (*plural* **-ies**) anomalous thing.

anon /əˈnɒn/ *adverb archaic* soon.

anon. *abbreviation* anonymous.

anonymous /əˈnɒnɪməs/ *adjective* of unknown name or authorship; featureless. □ **anonymity** /ˌænəˈnɪm-/ *noun*.

anorak /ˈænəræk/ *noun* waterproof usually hooded jacket.

anorexia /ˌænəˈreksɪə/ *noun* lack of appetite, esp. (in full **anorexia nervosa** /nɜːˈvəʊsə/) obsessive desire to lose weight by refusing to eat. □ **anorexic** *adjective & noun*.

another /əˈnʌðə/ ● *adjective* an additional or different. ● *pronoun* an additional or different person or thing.

answer /ˈɑːnsə/ ● *noun* something said or done in reaction to a question, statement, or circumstance; solution to problem. ● *verb* make an answer or response (to); suit; (+ *to*, *for*) be responsible to or for; (+ *to*) correspond to (esp. description). □ **answer back** answer insolently; **answering machine**, **answerphone** tape recorder which answers telephone calls and takes messages.

answerable *adjective* (usually + *to*, *for*) responsible; that can be answered.

ant *noun* small usually wingless insect living in complex social group. **anteater** mammal feeding on ants; **anthill** moundlike ants' nest.

antacid /ænˈtæsɪd/ *noun & adjective* preventive or corrective of acidity.

antagonism /ænˈtæɡənɪz(ə)m/ *noun* active hostility.

antagonist /ænˈtæɡənɪst/ *noun* opponent. □ **antagonistic** /-ˈnɪs-/ *adjective*.

antagonize /ænˈtæɡənaɪz/ *verb* (also **-ise**) (**-zing** or **-sing**) provoke.

Antarctic /ænˈtɑːktɪk/ ● *adjective* of south polar region. ● *noun* this region.

ante /ˈæntɪ/ *noun* stake put up by poker player before receiving cards; amount payable in advance.

ante- /ˈæntɪ/ *prefix* before.

antecedent /ˌæntɪˈsiːd(ə)nt/ ● *noun* preceding thing or circumstance; *Grammar* word, phrase, etc., to which another word refers; (in *plural*) person's ancestors. ● *adjective* previous.

antechamber /ˈæntɪtʃeɪmbə/ *noun* ante-room.

antedate /ˌæntɪˈdeɪt/ *verb* (**-ting**) precede in time; give earlier than true date to.

antediluvian /ˌæntɪdɪˈluːvɪən/ *adjective* before the Flood; *colloquial* very old.

antelope /ˈæntɪləʊp/ *noun* (*plural* same or **-s**) swift deerlike animal.

antenatal /ˌæntɪˈneɪtl/ *adjective* before birth; of pregnancy.

antenna /ænˈtenə/ *noun* (*plural* **-tennae** /-niː/) each of pair of feelers on head of insect or crustacean; (*plural* **-s**) aerial.

anterior /ænˈtɪərɪə/ *adjective* nearer the front; (often + *to*) prior.

ante-room /ˈæntɪruːm/ *noun* small room leading to main one.

anthem /'ænθəm/ *noun* choral composition for church use; song of praise, esp. for nation.

anther /'ænθə/ *noun* part of stamen containing pollen.

anthology /æn'θɒlədʒɪ/ *noun* (*plural* **-ies**) collection of poems, essays, stories, etc.

anthracite /'ænθrəsaɪt/ *noun* hard kind of coal.

anthrax /'ænθræks/ *noun* disease of sheep and cattle transmissible to humans.

anthropocentric /ænθrəpəʊ'sentrɪk/ *adjective* regarding humankind as centre of existence.

anthropoid /'ænθrəpɔɪd/ ● *adjective* human in form. ● *noun* anthropoid ape.

anthropology /ænθrə'pɒlədʒɪ/ *noun* study of humankind, esp. societies and customs. □ **anthropological** /-pə'lɒdʒ-/ *adjective*; **anthropologist** *noun*.

anthropomorphism /ænθrəpə'mɔːfɪz(ə)m/ *noun* attributing of human characteristics to god, animal, or thing. □ **anthropomorphic** *adjective*; **anthropomorphize** *verb* (also **-ise**) (**-zing** or **-sing**).

anti- /'æntɪ/ *prefix* opposed to; preventing; opposite of; unconventional.

anti-abortion /-ə'bɔː(ə)n/ *adjective* opposing abortion. □ **anti-abortionist** *noun*.

anti-aircraft /-'eəkrɑːft/ *adjective* for defence against enemy aircraft.

antibiotic /-baɪ'ɒtɪk/ ● *noun* substance that can inhibit or destroy bacteria etc. ● *adjective* functioning as antibiotic.

antibody /'æntɪbɒdɪ/ *noun* (*plural* **-ies**) blood protein produced in reaction to antigens.

antic /'æntɪk/ *noun* (usually in *plural*) foolish behaviour.

anticipate /æn'tɪsɪpeɪt/ *verb* (**-ting**) deal with or use before normal time; expect; forestall. □ **anticipation** *noun*; **anticipatory** *adjective*.

anticlimax /-'klaɪmæks/ *noun* disappointing conclusion to something significant.

anticlockwise /-'klɒkwaɪz/ ● *adverb* in opposite direction to hands of clock. ● *adjective* moving anticlockwise.

anticyclone /-'saɪkləʊn/ *noun* system of winds rotating outwards from area of high pressure, producing fine weather.

antidepressant /-dɪ'pres(ə)nt/ ● *noun* drug etc. alleviating depression. ● *adjective* alleviating depression.

antidote /'æntɪdəʊt/ *noun* medicine used to counteract poison.

antifreeze /'æntɪfriːz/ *noun* substance added to water (esp. in vehicle's radiator) to lower its freezing point.

antigen /'æntɪdʒ(ə)n/ *noun* foreign substance causing body to produce antibodies.

anti-hero /'æntɪhɪərəʊ/ *noun* (*plural* **-es**) central character in story, lacking conventional heroic qualities.

antihistamine /-'hɪstəmiːn/ *noun* drug that counteracts effect of histamine, used esp. to treat allergies.

antiknock /'æntɪnɒk/ *noun* substance added to motor fuel to prevent premature combustion.

anti-lock /'æntɪlɒk/ *adjective* (of brakes) not locking when applied suddenly.

antimony /'æntɪmənɪ/ *noun* brittle silvery metallic element.

anti-nuclear /-'njuːklɪə/ *adjective* opposed to development of nuclear weapons or power.

antipathy /æn'tɪpəθɪ/ *noun* (*plural* **-ies**) (often + *to, for, between*) strong aversion or dislike. □ **antipathetic** /-'θet-/ *adjective*.

antiperspirant /-'pɜːspərənt/ *noun* substance inhibiting perspiration.

antiphon /'æntɪf(ə)n/ *noun* hymn sung alternately by two groups. □ **antiphonal** /-'tɪf-/ *adjective*.

antipodes /æn'tɪpədiːz/ *plural noun* places diametrically opposite each other on the earth, esp. (also **Antipodes**) Australasia in relation to Europe. □ **antipodean** /-'diːən/ *adjective & noun*.

antiquarian /æntɪ'kweərɪən/ ● *adjective* of or dealing in rare books. ● *noun* antiquary.

antiquary /'æntɪkwərɪ/ *noun* (*plural* **-ies**) student or collector of antiques etc.

antiquated /'æntɪkweɪtɪd/ *adjective* old-fashioned.

antique /æn'tiːk/ ● *noun* old valuable object, esp. piece of furniture etc. ● *adjective* of or existing since old times; old-fashioned.

antiquity /æn'tɪkwətɪ/ *noun* (*plural* **-ies**) ancient times, esp. before Middle Ages; (in *plural*) great age; remains from ancient times.

antirrhinum /æntɪ'raɪnəm/ *noun* snapdragon.

anti-Semitic /-sɪ'mɪtɪk/ *adjective* prejudiced against Jews. □ **anti-Semite** /-'siːmaɪt/ *noun*; **anti-Semitism** /-'sem-/ *noun*.

antiseptic /-'septɪk/ ● *adjective* counteracting sepsis by destroying germs. ● *noun* antiseptic substance.

antisocial /-'səʊʃ(ə)l/ *adjective* not sociable; opposed or harmful to society.

■ **Usage** It is a mistake to use *antisocial* instead of *unsocial* in the phrase *unsocial hours*.

antistatic /-'stætɪk/ *adjective* counteracting effect of static electricity.

antithesis /æn'tɪθəsɪs/ *noun* (*plural* **-theses** /-siːz/) (often + *of, to*) direct opposite; contrast; rhetorical use of strongly contrasted words. □ **antithetical** /-'θet-/ *adjective*.

antitoxin /-'tɒksɪn/ *noun* antibody counteracting toxin. □ **antitoxic** *adjective*.

antitrades /-'treɪdz/ *plural noun* winds blowing above and in opposite direction to trade winds.

antiviral /-'vaɪər(ə)l/ *adjective* effective against viruses.

antler /'æntlə/ *noun* branched horn of deer.

antonym /'æntənɪm/ *noun* word opposite in meaning to another, e.g. *wet* is an antonym of *dry*.

anus /'eɪnəs/ *noun* (*plural* **-es**) excretory opening at end of alimentary canal.

anvil /'ænvɪl/ *noun* iron block on which metals are worked.

anxiety /æŋ'zaɪətɪ/ *noun* (*plural* **-ies**) troubled state of mind; worry; eagerness.

anxious /'æŋkʃəs/ *adjective* mentally troubled; marked by anxiety; (+ *to do*) uneasily wanting. □ **anxiously** *adverb*.

any /'enɪ/ ● *adjective* one or some, no matter which. ● *pronoun* any one; any number or amount. ● *adverb* at all. □ **anybody** *pronoun* any person, *noun* an important person; **anyhow** anyway, at random; **anyone** anybody; **anything** any thing, a thing of any kind; **anyway** in any way, in any case; **anywhere** (in or to) any place.

AOB *abbreviation* any other business.

aorta /eɪ'ɔːtə/ *noun* (*plural* **-s**) main artery carrying blood from heart.

apace /ə'peɪs/ *adverb literary* swiftly.

apart /ə'pɑːt/ *adverb* separately; into pieces; at or to a distance.

apartheid /ə'pɑːteɪt/ *noun* racial segregation, esp. in S. Africa.

apartment /ə'pɑːtmənt/ *noun* (*US* or esp. for holidays) flat; (usually in *plural*) room.

apathy /'æpəθɪ/ *noun* lack of interest, indifference. □ **apathetic** /-'θet-/ *adjective*.

apatosaurus /əpætə'sɔːrəs/ noun (plural **-ruses**) large long-necked plant-eating dinosaur.

ape ● noun tailless monkey; imitator. ● verb (**-ping**) imitate.

aperient /ə'perɪənt/ adjective & noun laxative.

aperitif /əperɪ'tiːf/ noun alcoholic drink before meal.

aperture /'æpətʃə/ noun opening or gap, esp. variable one letting light into camera.

apex /'eɪpeks/ noun (plural **-es**) highest point; tip.

aphasia /ə'feɪzɪə/ noun loss of verbal understanding or expression.

aphelion /ə'fiːlɪən/ noun (plural **-lia**) point of orbit farthest from sun.

aphid /'eɪfɪd/ noun insect infesting plants.

aphis /'eɪfɪs/ noun (plural **aphides** /-diːz/) aphid.

aphorism /'æfərɪz(ə)m/ noun short wise saying. □ **aphoristic** /-'rɪs-/ adjective.

aphrodisiac /æfrə'dɪzɪæk/ ● adjective arousing sexual desire. ● noun aphrodisiac substance.

apiary /'eɪpɪərɪ/ noun (plural **-ies**) place where bees are kept. □ **apiarist** noun.

apiculture /'eɪpɪkʌltʃə/ noun bee-keeping.

apiece /ə'piːs/ adverb for each one.

aplomb /ə'plɒm/ noun self-assurance.

apocalypse /ə'pɒkəlɪps/ noun destructive event; revelation, esp. about the end of the world. □ **apocalyptic** /-'lɪp-/ adjective.

Apocrypha /ə'pɒkrɪfə/ plural noun Old Testament books not in Hebrew Bible; (**apocrypha**) writings etc. not considered genuine. □ **apocryphal** adjective.

apogee /'æpədʒiː/ noun highest point; point farthest from earth in orbit of moon etc.

apolitical /eɪpə'lɪtɪk(ə)l/ adjective not interested or involved in politics.

apologetic /əpɒlə'dʒetɪk/ adjective expressing regret. □ **apologetically** adverb.

apologia /æpə'ləʊdʒə/ noun formal defence of conduct or opinions.

apologist /ə'pɒlədʒɪst/ noun person who defends by argument.

apologize /ə'pɒlədʒaɪz/ verb (also **-ise**) (**-zing** or **-sing**) make apology.

apology /ə'pɒlədʒɪ/ noun (plural **-ies**) regretful acknowledgement of offence or failure; explanation.

apophthegm /'æpəθem/ noun short wise saying.

apoplexy /'æpəpleksɪ/ noun sudden paralysis caused by blockage or rupture of brain artery. □ **apoplectic** /-'plek-/ adjective.

apostasy /ə'pɒstəsɪ/ noun (plural **-ies**) abandonment of belief, faith, etc.

apostate /ə'pɒsteɪt/ noun person who renounces belief. □ **apostatize** /-tət-/ verb (also **-ise**) (**-zing** or **-sing**).

a posteriori /eɪ pɒsterɪ'ɔːraɪ/ adjective & adverb from effects to causes.

Apostle /ə'pɒs(ə)l/ noun any of twelve men sent by Christ to preach gospel; (**apostle**) leader of reform.

apostolic /æpəs'tɒlɪk/ adjective of Apostles; of the Pope.

apostrophe /ə'pɒstrəfɪ/ noun punctuation mark (') indicating possession or marking omission of letter(s) or number(s) (see panel).

apostrophize verb (also **-ise**) (**-zing** or **-sing**) address (esp. absent person or thing).

apothecary /ə'pɒθəkərɪ/ noun (plural **-ies**) archaic pharmacist.

Apostrophe '

This is used:

1 to indicate possession:

with a singular noun:

a boy's book; a week's work; the boss's salary.

with a plural already ending with *s*:

a girls' school; two weeks' newspapers; the bosses' salaries.

with a plural not already ending with *s*:

the children's books; women's liberation.

with a singular name:

Bill's book; John's coat; Barnabas' (or *Barnabas's*) *book; Nicholas'* (or *Nicholas's*) *coat.*

with a name ending in *-es* that is pronounced /-ɪz/:

Bridges' poems; Moses' mother

and before the word *sake*:

for God's sake; for goodness' sake; for Nicholas' sake

but it is often omitted in a business name:

Barclays Bank.

2 to mark an omission of one or more letters or numbers:

he's (he is or he has)   haven't (have not)
can't (cannot)   we'll (we shall)
won't (will not)   o'clock (of the clock)
the summer of '68 (1968)

3 when letters or numbers are referred to in plural form:

mind your p's and q's; find all the number 7's.

but it is unnecessary in, e.g.

MPs; the 1940s.

apotheosis /əpɒθɪˈəʊsɪs/ noun (plural **-oses** /-siːz/) deification; glorification or sublime example (of thing).

appal /əˈpɔːl/ verb (**-ll-**) dismay; horrify.

apparatus /æpəˈreɪtəs/ noun equipment for scientific or other work.

apparel /əˈpær(ə)l/ noun formal clothing. □ **apparelled** adjective.

apparent /əˈpærənt/ adjective obvious; seeming. □ **apparently** adverb.

apparition /æpəˈrɪʃ(ə)n/ noun thing that appears, esp. of startling kind; ghost.

appeal /əˈpiːl/ ● verb make earnest or formal request; (usually + to) be attractive; (+ to) resort to for support; (often + to) apply to higher court for revision of judicial decision; Cricket ask umpire to declare batsman out. ● noun appealing; request for aid; attractiveness.

appear /əˈpɪə/ verb become or be visible; seem; present oneself; be published.

appearance noun appearing; outward form; (in plural) outward show of prosperity, virtue, etc.

appease /əˈpiːz/ verb (**-sing**) make calm or quiet, esp. conciliate (aggressor) with concessions; satisfy (appetite etc.). □ **appeasement** noun.

appellant /əˈpelənt/ noun person who appeals to higher court.

appellation /æpəˈleɪʃ(ə)n/ noun formal name, title.

append /əˈpend/ verb (usually + to) attach, affix; add.

appendage /əˈpendɪdʒ/ noun thing attached; addition.

appendectomy /æpenˈdektəmɪ/ noun (also **appendicectomy** /əpendɪˈsektəmɪ/) (plural **-ies**) surgical removal of appendix.

appendicitis /əpendɪˈsaɪtɪs/ noun inflammation of appendix.

appendix /əˈpendɪks/ noun (plural **-dices** /-siːz/) tubular sac attached to large intestine; addition to book etc.

appertain /æpəˈteɪn/ verb (+ to) belong, relate to.

appetite /ˈæpɪtaɪt/ noun (usually + for) desire (esp. for food); inclination, desire.

appetizer /ˈæpɪtaɪzə/ noun (also **-iser**) thing eaten or drunk to stimulate appetite.

appetizing /ˈæpɪtaɪzɪŋ/ adjective (also **-ising**) (esp. of food) stimulating appetite.

applaud /əˈplɔːd/ verb express approval (of), esp. by clapping; commend.

applause /əˈplɔːz/ noun warm approval, esp. clapping.

apple /ˈæp(ə)l/ noun roundish firm fruit. □ **apple of one's eye** cherished person or thing; **apple-pie bed** bed with sheets folded so that one cannot stretch out one's legs; **apple-pie order** extreme neatness.

appliance /əˈplaɪəns/ noun device etc. for specific task.

applicable /ˈæplɪkəb(ə)l/ adjective (often + to) that may be applied. □ **applicability** noun.

applicant /ˈæplɪkənt/ noun person who applies for job etc.

application /æplɪˈkeɪʃ(ə)n/ noun formal request; applying; thing applied; diligence; relevance; use.

applicator /ˈæplɪkeɪtə/ noun device for applying ointment etc.

appliqué /æˈpliːkeɪ/ ● noun work in which cut-out fabric is fixed on to other fabric. ● verb (**-qués**, **-quéd**, **-quéing**) decorate with appliqué.

apply /əˈplaɪ/ verb (**-ies**, **-ied**) (often + for, to, to do) make formal request; (often + to) be relevant; make

use of; (often + to) put or spread (on); (**apply oneself**; often + to) devote oneself.

appoint /əˈpɔɪnt/ verb assign job or office to; (often + for) fix (time etc.); (as **appointed** adjective) equipped, furnished.

appointment noun appointing, being appointed; arrangement for meeting; job available; (in plural) equipment, fittings.

apportion /əˈpɔːʃ(ə)n/ verb (often + to) share out. □ **apportionment** noun.

apposite /ˈæpəzɪt/ adjective (often + to) well expressed, appropriate.

apposition /æpəˈzɪʃ(ə)n/ noun juxtaposition, esp. of syntactically parallel words etc. (e.g. my friend Sue).

appraise /əˈpreɪz/ verb (**-sing**) estimate value or quality of. □ **appraisal** noun.

appreciable /əˈpriːʃəb(ə)l/ adjective significant; considerable.

appreciate /əˈpriːʃɪeɪt/ verb (**-ting**) (highly) value; be grateful for; understand, recognize; rise in value. □ **appreciation** noun; **appreciative** /-ʃətɪv/ adjective.

apprehend /æprɪˈhend/ verb arrest; understand.

apprehension /æprɪˈhenʃ(ə)n/ noun fearful anticipation; arrest; understanding.

apprehensive /æprɪˈhensɪv/ adjective uneasy, fearful. □ **apprehensively** adverb.

apprentice /əˈprentɪs/ ● noun person learning trade by working for agreed period. ● verb (usually + to) engage as apprentice. □ **apprenticeship** noun.

apprise /əˈpraɪz/ verb (**-sing**) (usually + of) inform.

approach /əˈprəʊtʃ/ ● verb come nearer (to) in space or time; be similar to; approximate to; set about; make tentative proposal to. ● noun act or means of approaching; approximation; technique; part of aircraft's flight before landing.

approachable /əˈprəʊtʃəb(ə)l/ adjective friendly; able to be approached.

approbation /æprəˈbeɪʃ(ə)n/ noun approval, consent.

appropriate ● adjective /əˈprəʊprɪət/ suitable, proper. ● verb (**-ting**) /əˈprəʊprɪeɪt/ take possession of; devote (money etc.) to special purpose. □ **appropriately** adverb; **appropriation** noun.

approval /əˈpruːv(ə)l/ noun approving; consent. □ **on approval** returnable if not satisfactory.

approve /əˈpruːv/ verb (**-ving**) sanction; (often + of) regard with favour.

approx. abbreviation approximate(ly).

approximate ● adjective /əˈprɒksɪmət/ fairly correct; near to the actual. ● verb /əˈprɒksɪmeɪt/ (**-ting**) (often + to) be or make near. □ **approximately** adverb; **approximation** noun.

appurtenances /əˈpɜːtɪnənsɪz/ plural noun accessories; belongings.

APR abbreviation annual(ized) percentage rate.

Apr. abbreviation April.

après-ski /æpreɪˈskiː/ ● noun activities after a day's skiing. ● adjective suitable for these. [French]

apricot /ˈeɪprɪkɒt/ ● noun small orange-yellow peach-like fruit; its colour. ● adjective orange-yellow.

April /ˈeɪpr(ə)l/ noun fourth month of year. □ **April Fool** victim of hoax on 1 Apr.

a priori /eɪ praɪˈɔːraɪ/ ● adjective from cause to effect; not derived from experience; assumed without investigation. ● adverb deductively; as far as one knows.

apron /ˈeɪprən/ noun garment protecting front of clothes; area on airfield for manoeuvring or loading; part of stage in front of curtain.

apropos /æprəˈpəʊ/ ● adjective appropriate; colloquial (often + of) in respect of. ● adverb appropriately; incidentally.

apse /æps/ *noun* arched or domed recess esp. at end of church.

apsis /'æpsis/ *noun* (*plural* **apsides** /-di:z/) aphelion or perihelion of planet, apogee or perigee of moon.

apt *adjective* suitable, appropriate; (+ *to do*) having a tendency; quick to learn.

aptitude /'æptɪtjuːd/ *noun* talent; ability, esp. specified.

aqualung /'ækwəlʌŋ/ *noun* portable underwater breathing-apparatus.

aquamarine /ækwəmə'riːn/ ● *noun* bluish-green beryl; its colour. ● *adjective* bluish-green.

aquaplane /'ækwəpleɪn/ ● *noun* board for riding on water, pulled by speedboat. ● *verb* (**-ning**) ride on this; (of vehicle) glide uncontrollably on wet surface.

aquarelle /ækwə'rel/ *noun* painting in transparent water-colours.

aquarium /ə'kweərɪəm/ *noun* (*plural* **-s**) tank for keeping fish etc.

Aquarius /ə'kweərɪəs/ *noun* eleventh sign of zodiac.

aquatic /ə'kwætɪk/ *adjective* growing or living in water; done in or on water.

aquatint /'ækwətɪnt/ *noun* etched print like water-colour.

aqueduct /'ækwɪdʌkt/ *noun* water channel, esp. raised structure across valley.

aqueous /'eɪkwɪəs/ *adjective* of or like water.

aquiline /'ækwɪlaɪn/ *adjective* of or like an eagle; (of nose) curved.

Arab /'ærəb/ ● *noun* member of Semitic people inhabiting originally Saudi Arabia, now Middle East generally; horse of breed originally native to Arabia. ● *adjective* of Arabia or Arabs.

arabesque /ærə'besk/ *noun* decoration with intertwined leaves, scrollwork, etc.; ballet posture with one leg extended horizontally backwards.

Arabian /ə'reɪbɪən/ ● *adjective* of Arabia. ● *noun* Arab.

Arabic /'ærəbɪk/ ● *noun* language of Arabs. ● *adjective* of Arabs or their language. □ **arabic numerals** 1, 2, 3, etc.

arable /'ærəb(ə)l/ *adjective* fit for growing crops.

arachnid /ə'ræknɪd/ *noun* creature of class comprising spiders, scorpions, etc.

Aramaic /ærə'meɪk/ ● *noun* language of Syria at time of Christ. ● *adjective* of or in Aramaic.

arbiter /'ɑːbɪtə/ *noun* arbitrator; person influential in specific field.

arbitrary /'ɑːbɪtrərɪ/ *adjective* random; capricious, despotic. □ **arbitrarily** *adverb*.

arbitrate /'ɑːbɪtreɪt/ *verb* (**-ting**) settle dispute between others. □ **arbitration** *noun*; **arbitrator** *noun*.

arboreal /ɑː'bɔːrɪəl/ *adjective* of or living in trees.

arboretum /ɑːbə'riːtəm/ *noun* (*plural* **-ta**) tree-garden.

arboriculture /'ɑːbərɪkʌltʃə/ *noun* cultivation of trees and shrubs.

arbour /'ɑːbə/ *noun* (US **arbor**) shady garden alcove enclosed by trees etc.

arc *noun* part of circumference of circle or other curve; luminous discharge between two electrodes. □ **arc lamp** one using electric arc; **arc welding** using electric arc to melt metals to be welded.

arcade /ɑː'keɪd/ *noun* covered walk, esp. lined with shops; series of arches supporting or along wall.

Arcadian /ɑː'keɪdɪən/ *adjective* ideally rustic.

arcane /ɑː'keɪn/ *adjective* mysterious, secret.

arch[1] ● *noun* curved structure supporting bridge, floor, etc. as opening or ornament. ● *verb* form arch; provide with or form into arch.

arch[2] *adjective* self-consciously or affectedly playful.

archaeology /ɑːkɪ'ɒlədʒɪ/ *noun* (US **archeology**) study of ancient cultures, esp. by excavation of physical remains. □ **archaeological** /-ə'lɒdʒ-/ *adjective*; **archaeologist** *noun*.

archaic /ɑː'keɪɪk/ *adjective* antiquated; (of word) no longer in ordinary use; of early period in culture.

archaism /'ɑːkeɪɪz(ə)m/ *noun* archaic word etc.; use of the archaic. **archaistic** /-'ɪst-/ *adjective*.

archangel /'ɑːkeɪndʒ(ə)l/ *noun* angel of highest rank.

archbishop /ɑːtʃ'bɪʃəp/ *noun* chief bishop.

archbishopric *noun* office or diocese of archbishop.

archdeacon /ɑːtʃ'diːkən/ *noun* church dignitary next below bishop. □ **archdeaconry** *noun* (*plural* **-ies**).

archdiocese /ɑːtʃ'daɪəsɪs/ *noun* archbishop's diocese. □ **archdiocesan** /-daɪ'ɒsɪs(ə)n/ *adjective*.

arch-enemy /ɑːtʃ'enəmɪ/ *noun* (*plural* **-ies**) chief enemy.

archeology *US* = ARCHAEOLOGY.

archer /'ɑːtʃə/ *noun* person who shoots with bow and arrows.

archery /'ɑːtʃərɪ/ *noun* shooting with bow and arrows.

archetype /'ɑːkɪtaɪp/ *noun* original model, typical specimen. □ **archetypal** /-'taɪp-/ *adjective*.

archipelago /ɑːkɪ'peləgəʊ/ *noun* (*plural* **-s**) group of islands; sea with many islands.

architect /'ɑːkɪtekt/ *noun* designer of buildings etc.; (+ *of*) person who brings about specified thing.

architectonic /ɑːkɪtek'tɒnɪk/ *adjective* of architecture.

architecture /'ɑːkɪtektʃə/ *noun* design and construction of buildings; style of building. □ **architectural** /-'tek-/ *adjective*.

architrave /'ɑːkɪtreɪv/ *noun* moulded frame round doorway or window; main beam laid across tops of classical columns.

archive /'ɑːkaɪv/ *noun* (usually in *plural*) collection of documents or records; place where these are kept.

archivist /'ɑːkɪvɪst/ *noun* keeper of archives.

archway /'ɑːtʃweɪ/ *noun* arched entrance or passage.

Arctic /'ɑːktɪk/ ● *adjective* of north polar region; (**arctic**) very cold. ● *noun* Arctic region.

ardent /'ɑːd(ə)nt/ *adjective* eager, fervent, passionate; burning. □ **ardently** *adverb*.

ardour /'ɑːdə/ *noun* zeal, enthusiasm.

arduous /'ɑːdjʊəs/ *adjective* hard to accomplish; strenuous.

are see BE.

area /'eərɪə/ *noun* extent or measure of surface; region; space set aside for a purpose; scope, range; space in front of house basement.

arena /ə'riːnə/ *noun* centre of amphitheatre; scene of conflict; sphere of action.

aren't /ɑːnt/ are not; (in questions) am not.

arête /æ'reɪt/ *noun* sharp mountain ridge.

argon /'ɑːgɒn/ *noun* inert gaseous element.

argot /'ɑːgəʊ/ *noun* jargon of group or class.

argue /'ɑːgjuː/ *verb* (**-ues, -ued, -uing**) exchange views, esp. heatedly; (often + *that*) maintain by reasoning; (+ *for, against*) reason. □ **arguable** *adjective*; **arguably** *adverb*.

argument /'ɑːgjʊmənt/ *noun* (esp. heated) exchange of views; reason given; reasoning; summary of book etc. □ **argumentation** /-men-/ *noun*.

argumentative /ɑːgjʊ'mentətɪv/ *adjective* fond of arguing.

argy-bargy /ɑːdʒɪ'bɑːdʒɪ/ *noun jocular* dispute, wrangle.

aria /'ɑːrɪə/ *noun* song for one voice in opera, oratorio, etc.

arid /'ærɪd/ *noun* dry, parched. □ **aridity** /ə'rɪd-/ *noun*.

Aries /'eəriːz/ *noun* first sign of zodiac.

aright /əˈraɪt/ *adverb* rightly.

arise /əˈraɪz/ *verb* (**-sing**; *past* **arose** /əˈrəʊz/; *past participle* **arisen** /əˈrɪz(ə)n/) originate; (usually + *from, out of*) result; emerge; rise.

aristocracy /ˌærɪsˈtɒkrəsi/ *noun* (*plural* **-ies**) ruling class, nobility.

aristocrat /ˈærɪstəkræt/ *noun* member of aristocracy.

aristocratic /ˌærɪstəˈkrætɪk/ *adjective* of the aristocracy; grand, distinguished.

arithmetic ● *noun* /əˈrɪθmətɪk/ science of numbers; computation, use of numbers. ● *adjective* /ˌærɪθˈmetɪk/ (also **arithmetical**) of arithmetic.

ark *noun* ship in which Noah escaped the Flood. □ **Ark of the Covenant** wooden chest containing tables of Jewish law.

arm¹ *noun* upper limb of human body; sleeve; raised side part of chair; branch; armlike thing. □ **armchair** chair with arms, theoretical rather than active; **arm in arm** with arms linked; **armpit** hollow under arm at shoulder; **at arm's length** at a distance; **with open arms** cordially. □ **armful** *noun*.

arm² ● *noun* (usually in *plural*) weapon; branch of military forces; (in *plural*) heraldic devices. ● *verb* equip with arms; equip oneself with arms; make (bomb) ready. □ **up in arms** (usually + *against, about*) actively resisting.

armada /ɑːˈmɑːdə/ *noun* fleet of warships.

armadillo /ˌɑːməˈdɪləʊ/ *noun* (*plural* **-s**) S. American burrowing mammal with plated body.

Armageddon /ˌɑːməˈged(ə)n/ *noun* huge battle at end of world.

armament /ˈɑːməmənt/ *noun* military weapon etc.; equipping for war.

armature /ˈɑːmətʃə/ *noun* rotating coil or coils of dynamo or electric motor; iron bar placed across poles of magnet; framework on which sculpture is moulded.

armistice /ˈɑːmɪstɪs/ *noun* truce.

armlet /ˈɑːmlɪt/ *noun* band worn round arm.

armorial /ɑːˈmɔːrɪəl/ *adjective* of heraldic arms.

armour /ˈɑːmə/ *noun* protective covering formerly worn in fighting; metal plates etc. protecting ship, car, tank, etc.; armoured vehicles. □ **armoured** *adjective*.

armourer *noun* maker of arms or armour; official in charge of arms.

armoury /ˈɑːməri/ *noun* (*plural* **-ies**) arsenal.

army /ˈɑːmi/ *noun* (*plural* **-ies**) organized armed land force; vast number; organized body.

arnica /ˈɑːnɪkə/ *noun* plant with yellow flowers; medicine made from it.

aroma /əˈrəʊmə/ *noun* pleasing smell; subtle quality. □ **aromatic** /ˌærəˈmætɪk/ *adjective*.

aromatherapy *noun* use of plant extracts and oils in massage. □ **aromatherapist** *noun*.

arose *past* of ARISE.

around /əˈraʊnd/ ● *adverb* on every side; all round; *colloquial* in existence, near at hand. ● *preposition* on or along the circuit of; on every side of; here and there in or near; about.

arouse /əˈraʊz/ *verb* (**-sing**) induce (esp. emotion); awake from sleep; stir into activity; stimulate sexually. □ **arousal** *noun*.

arpeggio /ɑːˈpedʒɪəʊ/ *noun* (*plural* **-s**) notes of chord played in rapid succession.

arrack /ˈærak/ *noun* alcoholic spirit made esp. from rice.

arraign /əˈreɪn/ *verb* indict, accuse; find fault with. □ **arraignment** *noun*.

arrange /əˈreɪndʒ/ *verb* (**-ging**) put in order; plan or provide for; (+ *to do, for*) take measures; (+ *with*

person) agree about procedure for; *Music* adapt (piece). □ **arrangement** *noun*.

arrant /ˈærənt/ *adjective* downright, utter.

arras /ˈærəs/ *noun* tapestry wall-hanging.

array /əˈreɪ/ ● *noun* imposing series; ordered arrangement, esp. of troops. ● *verb* deck, adorn; set in order; marshal (forces).

arrears /əˈrɪəz/ *plural noun* outstanding debt; what remains undone. □ **in arrears** behindhand, esp. in payment.

arrest /əˈrest/ ● *verb* lawfully seize; stop; catch attention of. ● *noun* arresting, being arrested; stoppage.

arrival /əˈraɪv(ə)l/ *noun* arriving; person or thing arriving.

arrive /əˈraɪv/ *verb* (**-ving**) come to destination; (+ *at*) reach (conclusion); *colloquial* become successful, be born.

arrogant /ˈærəgənt/ *adjective* aggressively assertive or presumptuous. □ **arrogance** *noun*; **arrogantly** *adverb*.

arrogate /ˈærəgeɪt/ *verb* (**-ting**) claim without right. □ **arrogation** *noun*.

arrow /ˈærəʊ/ *noun* pointed missile shot from bow; representation of this, esp. to show direction. □ **arrowhead** pointed tip of arrow.

arrowroot /ˈærəʊruːt/ *noun* nutritious starch.

arsenal /ˈɑːsən(ə)l/ *noun* place where weapons and ammunition are made or stored.

arsenic /ˈɑːsənɪk/ *noun* brittle semi-metallic element; its highly poisonous trioxide.

arson /ˈɑːsən/ *noun* crime of deliberately setting property on fire. □ **arsonist** *noun*.

art *noun* human creative skill, its application; branch of creative activity concerned with imitative and imaginative designs, sounds, or ideas, e.g. painting, music, writing; creative activity resulting in visual representation; thing in which skill can be exercised; (in *plural*) certain branches of learning (esp. languages, literature, history, etc.) as distinct from sciences; knack; cunning. □ **art nouveau** /ɑː nuːˈvəʊ/ art style of late 19th c., with flowing lines.

artefact /ˈɑːtɪfækt/ *noun* (also **artifact**) man-made object.

arterial /ɑːˈtɪərɪəl/ *adjective* of or like artery. □ **arterial road** important main road.

arteriosclerosis /ɑːˌtɪərɪəʊsklɪəˈrəʊsɪs/ *noun* hardening and thickening of artery walls.

artery /ˈɑːtəri/ *noun* (*plural* **-ies**) blood vessel carrying blood from heart; main road or railway line.

artesian well /ɑːˈtiːzɪən/ well in which water rises by natural pressure through vertically drilled hole.

artful /ˈɑːtfʊl/ *adjective* sly, crafty. □ **artfully** *adverb*.

arthritis /ɑːˈθraɪtɪs/ *noun* inflammation of joint. □ **arthritic** /-ˈθrɪt-/ *adjective & noun*.

arthropod /ˈɑːθrəpɒd/ *noun* animal with segmented body and jointed limbs, e.g. insect, spider, crustacean.

artichoke /ˈɑːtɪtʃəʊk/ *noun* plant allied to thistle; its partly edible flower; Jerusalem artichoke.

article /ˈɑːtɪk(ə)l/ ● *noun* item or thing; short piece of non-fiction in newspaper etc.; clause of agreement etc.; = DEFINITE ARTICLE, INDEFINITE ARTICLE. ● *verb* employ under contract as trainee.

articular /ɑːˈtɪkjʊlə/ *adjective* of joints.

articulate ● *adjective* /ɑːˈtɪkjʊlət/ fluent and clear in speech; (of speech) in which separate sounds and words are clear; having joints. ● *verb* /ɑːˈtɪkjʊleɪt/ (**-ting**) speak distinctly; express clearly; connect with joints. □ **articulated lorry** one with sections connected by flexible joint. □ **articulately** *adverb*; **articulation** *noun*.

artifact = ARTEFACT.

artifice /'ɑːtɪfɪs/ noun trick; cunning; skill.

artificer /ɑːtɪfɪsə/ noun craftsman.

artificial /ɑːtɪ'fɪʃ(ə)l/ adjective not natural; imitating nature; insincere. □ **artificial insemination** nonsexual injection of semen into uterus; **artificial intelligence** (use of) computers replacing human intelligence; **artificial respiration** manual or mechanical stimulation of breathing. □ **artificiality** /-ʃɪ'æl-/ noun; **artificially** adverb.

artillery /ɑː'tɪlərɪ/ noun large guns used in fighting on land; branch of army using these. □ **artilleryman** noun.

artisan /ɑːtɪ'zæn/ noun skilled worker or craftsman.

artist /'ɑːtɪst/ noun person who practises any art, esp. painting; artiste. □ **artistic** adjective; **artistically** adverb; **artistry** noun.

artiste /ɑː'tiːst/ noun professional singer, dancer, etc.

artless adjective guileless, ingenuous; natural; clumsy. □ **artlessly** adverb.

arty adjective (**-ier**, **-iest**) pretentiously or affectedly artistic.

arum /'eərəm/ noun plant with arrow-shaped leaves.

Aryan /'eərɪən/ ● noun speaker of any Indo-European language. ● adjective of Aryans.

as /æz, əz/ ● adverb to the same extent. ● conjunction in the same way that; while, when; since, seeing that; although. ● preposition in the capacity or form of. □ **as ... as ...** to the same extent that ... is, does, etc.

asafoetida /æsə'fetɪdə/ noun (US **asafetida**) resinous pungent gum.

asbestos /æs'bestɒs/ noun fibrous silicate mineral; heat-resistant or insulating substance made from this.

ascend /ə'send/ verb slope upwards; go or come up, climb.

ascendancy noun (often + over) dominant control.

ascendant adjective rising. □ **in the ascendant** gaining or having power or authority.

ascension /ə'senʃ(ə)n/ noun ascent, esp. (**Ascension**) of Christ into heaven.

ascent /ə'sent/ noun ascending, rising; upward path or slope.

ascertain /æsə'teɪn/ verb find out for certain. □ **ascertainment** noun.

ascetic /ə'setɪk/ ● adjective severely abstinent; self-denying. ● noun ascetic person. □ **asceticism** /-tɪs-/ noun.

ascorbic acid /ə'skɔːbɪk/ noun vitamin C.

ascribe /ə'skraɪb/ verb (**-bing**) (usually + to) attribute; regard as belonging. □ **ascription** /-'skrɪp-/ noun.

asepsis /eɪ'sepsɪs/ noun absence of sepsis or harmful bacteria; aseptic method in surgery. □ **aseptic** adjective.

asexual /eɪ'seksjʊəl/ adjective without sex or sexuality; (of reproduction) not involving fusion of gametes. □ **asexually** adverb.

ash[1] noun (often in plural) powdery residue left after burning; (in plural) human remains after cremation; (**the Ashes**) trophy in cricket between England and Australia. □ **ashcan** US dustbin; **ashtray** receptacle for tobacco ash; **Ash Wednesday** first day of Lent.

ash[2] noun tree with silver-grey bark; its wood.

ashamed /ə'ʃeɪmd/ adjective embarrassed by shame; (+ to do) reluctant owing to shame.

ashen /'æʃ(ə)n/ adjective grey, pale.

ashore /ə'ʃɔː/ adverb to or on shore.

ashram /'æʃræm/ noun religious retreat for Hindus.

Asian /'eɪʃ(ə)n/ ● adjective of Asia. ● noun native of Asia; person of Asian descent.

aside /ə'saɪd/ ● adverb to or on one side; away, apart. ● noun words spoken aside, esp. by actor to audience.

asinine /'æsɪnaɪn/ adjective asslike; stupid.

ask /ɑːsk/ verb call for answer to or about; seek to obtain from another person; invite; (+ for) seek to obtain or meet. □ **ask after** inquire about (esp. person).

askance /ə'skæns/ adverb sideways. □ **look askance at** regard suspiciously.

askew /ə'skjuː/ ● adverb crookedly. ● adjective oblique; awry.

aslant /ə'slɑːnt/ ● adverb at a slant. ● preposition obliquely across.

asleep /ə'sliːp/ ● adjective sleeping; colloquial inattentive; (of limb) numb. ● adverb into state of sleep.

asp noun small venomous snake.

asparagus /əs'pærəgəs/ noun plant of lily family; its edible shoots.

aspect /'æspekt/ noun feature, viewpoint, etc. to be considered; appearance, look; side facing specified direction.

aspen /'æspən/ noun poplar with fluttering leaves.

asperity /æs'perɪtɪ/ noun sharpness of temper or tone; roughness.

aspersion /əs'pɜːʃ(ə)n/ noun □ **cast aspersions on** defame.

asphalt /'æsfælt/ ● noun bituminous pitch; mixture of this with gravel etc. for surfacing roads etc. ● verb surface with asphalt.

asphodel /'æsfədel/ noun kind of lily.

asphyxia /æs'fɪksɪə/ noun lack of oxygen in blood; suffocation.

asphyxiate /əs'fɪksɪeɪt/ verb (**-ting**) suffocate. □ **asphyxiation** noun.

aspic /'æspɪk/ noun clear savoury jelly.

aspidistra /æspɪ'dɪstrə/ noun house plant with broad tapering leaves.

aspirant /'æspɪrənt/ ● adjective aspiring. ● noun person who aspires.

aspirate ● noun /'æspərət/ sound of h; consonant blended with this. ● verb /'æspəreɪt/ (**-ting**) pronounce with h; draw (fluid) by suction from cavity.

aspiration /æspə'reɪʃ(ə)n/ noun ambition, desire; aspirating.

aspire /ə'spaɪə/ verb (**-ring**) (usually + to, after, to do) have ambition or strong desire.

aspirin /'æsprɪn/ noun (plural same or **-s**) white powder used to reduce pain and fever; tablet of this.

ass noun 4-legged animal with long ears, related to horse; donkey; stupid person.

assail /ə'seɪl/ verb attack physically or verbally. □ **assailant** noun.

assassin /ə'sæsɪn/ noun killer, esp. of political or religious leader.

assassinate /ə'sæsɪneɪt/ verb (**-ting**) kill for political or religious motives. □ **assassination** noun.

assault /ə'sɔːlt/ ● noun violent physical or verbal attack; Law threat or display of violence against person. ● verb make assault on. □ **assault and battery** Law threatening act resulting in physical harm to person.

assay /ə'seɪ/ ● noun test of metal or ore for ingredients and quality. ● verb make assay of.

assegai /'æsɪgaɪ/ noun light iron-tipped S. African spear.

assemblage /ə'semblɪdʒ/ noun assembled group.

assemble /ə'semb(ə)l/ verb (**-ling**) fit together parts of; fit (parts) together; bring or come together.

assembly /ə'semblɪ/ *noun* (*plural* **-ies**) assembling; assembled group, esp. as parliament etc.; fitting together of parts. □ **assembly line** machinery arranged so that product can be progressively assembled.

assent /ə'sent/ ● *noun* consent, approval. ● *verb* (usually + *to*) agree, consent.

assert /ə'sɜːt/ *verb* declare; enforce claim to; (**assert oneself**) insist on one's rights.

assertion /ə'sɜːʃ(ə)n/ *noun* declaration; forthright statement.

assertive *adjective* asserting oneself; forthright, positive. □ **assertively** *adverb*; **assertiveness** *noun*.

assess /ə'ses/ *verb* estimate size or quality of; estimate value of (property etc.) for taxation. □ **assessment** *noun*.

assessor *noun* person who assesses taxes etc.; judge's technical adviser in court.

asset /'æset/ *noun* useful or valuable person or thing; (usually in *plural*) property and possessions.

assiduous /ə'sɪdjʊəs/ *adjective* persevering, hardworking. □ **assiduity** /æsɪ'djuːɪtɪ/ *noun*; **assiduously** *adverb*.

assign /ə'saɪn/ *verb* allot; appoint; fix (time, place, etc.); (+ *to*) ascribe to, *Law* transfer formally to.

assignation /æsɪg'neɪʃ(ə)n/ *noun* appointment, esp. made by lovers; assigning, being assigned.

assignee /əsaɪ'niː/ *noun Law* person to whom property or right is assigned.

assignment /ə'saɪnmənt/ *noun* task or mission; assigning, being assigned.

assimilate /ə'sɪmɪleɪt/ *verb* (**-ting**) absorb or be absorbed into system; (usually + *to*) make like. □ **assimilable** *adjective*; **assimilation** *noun*; **assimilative** /-lətɪv/ *adjective*.

assist /ə'sɪst/ *verb* (often + *in*) help. □ **assistance** *noun*.

assistant *noun* helper; subordinate worker; = SHOP ASSISTANT.

assizes /ə'saɪzɪz/ *plural noun historical* court periodically administering civil and criminal law.

Assoc. *abbreviation* Association.

associate ● *verb* /ə'səʊʃɪeɪt/ (**-ting**) connect mentally; join, combine; (usually + *with*) have frequent dealings. ● *noun* /ə'səʊʃɪət/ partner, colleague; friend, companion. ● *adjective* /ə'səʊʃɪət/ joined, allied.

association /əsəʊsɪ'eɪʃ(ə)n/ *noun* group organized for joint purpose; associating, being associated; connection of ideas. □ **association football** kind played with round ball which may be handled only by goalkeeper.

assonance /'æsənəns/ *noun* partial resemblance of sound between syllables, as in *run-up*, or *wary* and *barely*. □ **assonant** *adjective*.

assorted /ə'sɔːtɪd/ *adjective* of various sorts, mixed.

assortment /ə'sɔːtmənt/ *noun* diverse group or mixture.

assuage /ə'sweɪdʒ/ *verb* (**-ging**) soothe; appease.

assume /ə'sjuːm/ *verb* (**-ming**) take to be true; undertake; simulate; take on (aspect, attribute, etc.).

assumption /ə'sʌmpʃ(ə)n/ *noun* assuming; thing assumed; (**Assumption**) reception of Virgin Mary bodily into heaven.

assurance *noun* declaration; insurance, esp. of life; certainty; self-confidence.

assure /ə'ʃʊə/ *verb* (**-ring**) (often + *of*) convince; tell (person) confidently; ensure, guarantee (result etc.); insure (esp. life).

assuredly /ə'ʃʊərɪdlɪ/ *adverb* certainly.

aster /'æstə/ *noun* plant with bright daisy-like flowers.

asterisk /'æstərɪsk/ *noun* symbol (*) used to indicate omission etc.

astern /ə'stɜːn/ *adverb* in or to rear of ship or aircraft; backwards.

asteroid /'æstərɔɪd/ *noun* any of numerous small planets between orbits of Mars and Jupiter.

asthma /'æsmə/ *noun* condition marked by difficulty in breathing. □ **asthmatic** /-'mæt-/ *adjective & noun*.

astigmatism /ə'stɪgmətɪz(ə)m/ *noun* eye or lens defect resulting in distorted images. □ **astigmatic** /æstɪg'mætɪk/ *adjective*.

astir /ə'stɜː/ *adverb & adjective* in motion; out of bed.

astonish /ə'stɒnɪʃ/ *verb* amaze, surprise. □ **astonishment** *noun*.

astound /ə'staʊnd/ *verb* astonish greatly.

astrakhan /æstrə'kæn/ *noun* dark curly fleece of Astrakhan lamb; cloth imitating this.

astral /'æstr(ə)l/ *adjective* of stars; starry.

astray /ə'streɪ/ *adverb & adjective* away from right way. □ **go astray** be lost.

astride /ə'straɪd/ ● *adverb* (often + *of*) with one leg on each side. ● *preposition* astride of.

astringent /ə'strɪndʒənt/ ● *adjective* contracting body tissue, esp. to check bleeding; austere, severe. ● *noun* astringent substance. □ **astringency** *noun*.

astrolabe /'æstrəleɪb/ *noun* instrument for measuring altitude of stars etc.

astrology /ə'strɒlədʒɪ/ *noun* study of supposed planetary influence on human affairs. □ **astrologer** *noun*; **astrological** /æstrə'lɒdʒ-/ *adjective*.

astronaut /'æstrənɔːt/ *noun* space traveller.

astronautics /æstrə'nɔːtɪks/ *plural noun* (treated as *singular*) science of space travel. □ **astronautical** *adjective*.

astronomical /æstrə'nɒmɪk(ə)l/ *adjective* (also **astronomic**) of astronomy; vast. □ **astronomically** *adverb*.

astronomy /ə'strɒnəmɪ/ *noun* science of celestial bodies. □ **astronomer** *noun*.

astrophysics /æstrəʊ'fɪzɪks/ *plural noun* (treated as *singular*) study of physics and chemistry of celestial bodies. □ **astrophysical** *adjective*; **astrophysicist** *noun*.

astute /ə'stjuːt/ *adjective* shrewd. □ **astutely** *adverb*; **astuteness** *noun*.

asunder /ə'sʌndə/ *adverb literary* apart.

asylum /ə'saɪləm/ *noun* sanctuary; = POLITICAL ASYLUM; *historical* mental institution.

asymmetry /eɪ'sɪmɪtrɪ/ *noun* lack of symmetry. □ **asymmetric(al)** /-'met-/ *adjective*.

at /æt, ət/ *preposition expressing position, point in time or on scale, engagement in activity, value or rate, or motion or aim towards.*

atavism /'ætəvɪz(ə)m/ *noun* resemblance to remote ancestors; reversion to earlier type. □ **atavistic** /-'vɪs-/ *adjective*.

ate *past of* EAT.

atelier /ə'telɪeɪ/ *noun* workshop; artist's studio.

atheism /'eɪθɪɪz(ə)m/ *noun* belief that no God exists. □ **atheist** *noun*; **atheistic** /-'ɪst-/ *adjective*.

atherosclerosis /æθərəʊsklɪə'rəʊsɪs/ *noun* formation of fatty deposits in the arteries.

athlete /'æθliːt/ *noun* person who engages in athletics, exercises, etc. □ **athlete's foot** fungal foot disease.

athletic /æθ'letɪk/ *adjective* of athletes or athletics; physically strong or agile. □ **athletically** *adverb*; **athleticism** *noun*.

athletics *plural noun* (usually treated as *singular*) physical exercises, esp. track and field events.

atlas /'ætləs/ *noun* book of maps.

atmosphere /ˈætməsfɪə/ noun gases enveloping earth, other planet, etc.; tone, mood, etc., of place, book, etc.; unit of pressure. □ **atmospheric** /-ˈfer-/ adjective.

atmospherics /ætməsˈferɪks/ plural noun electrical disturbance in atmosphere; interference with telecommunications caused by this.

atoll /ˈætɒl/ noun ring-shaped coral reef enclosing lagoon.

atom /ˈætəm/ noun smallest particle of chemical element that can take part in chemical reaction; this as source of nuclear energy; minute portion or thing. □ **atom bomb** bomb in which energy is released by nuclear fission.

atomic /əˈtɒmɪk/ adjective of atoms; of or using atomic energy or atom bombs. □ **atomic bomb** atom bomb; **atomic energy** nuclear energy; **atomic number** number of protons in nucleus of atom; **atomic weight** ratio of mass of one atom of element to 1/12 mass of atom of carbon-12.

atomize /ˈætəmaɪz/ verb (also **-ise**) (**-zing** or **-sing**) reduce to atoms or fine spray.

atomizer noun (also **-iser**) aerosol.

atonal /eɪˈtəʊn(ə)l/ adjective Music not written in any key. □ **atonality** /-ˈnæl-/ noun.

atone /əˈtəʊn/ verb (**-ning**) (usually + for) make amends. □ **atonement** noun.

atrium /ˈeɪtrɪəm/ noun (plural **-s** or **atria**) either of upper cavities of heart.

atrocious /əˈtrəʊʃəs/ adjective very bad; wicked. □ **atrociously** adverb.

atrocity /əˈtrɒsɪtɪ/ noun (plural **-ies**) wicked or cruel act.

atrophy /ˈætrəfɪ/ ● noun wasting away, esp. through disuse. ● verb (**-ies**, **-ied**) suffer atrophy; cause atrophy in.

atropine /ˈætrəpiːn/ noun poisonous alkaloid in deadly nightshade.

attach /əˈtætʃ/ verb fasten, affix, join; (in passive; + to) be very fond of; (+ to) attribute or be attributable to.

attaché /əˈtæʃeɪ/ noun specialist member of ambassador's staff. □ **attaché case** small rectangular document case.

attachment noun thing attached, esp. for particular purpose; affection, devotion; attaching, being attached.

attack /əˈtæk/ ● verb try to hurt or deflect using force; criticize adversely; act harmfully on; Sport try to score against; vigorously apply oneself to. ● noun act of attacking; sudden onset of illness. □ **attacker** noun.

attain /əˈteɪn/ verb gain, accomplish; reach; (+ to) arrive at (goal etc.).

attainment noun attaining; (often in plural) skill, achievement.

attar /ˈætɑː/ noun perfume made from rose-petals.

attempt /əˈtempt/ ● verb try; try to accomplish or conquer. ● noun (often + at, on) attempting; endeavour.

attend /əˈtend/ verb be present at; go regularly to; (often + to) apply mind or oneself; (+ to) deal with; accompany, wait on. □ **attender** noun.

attendance noun attending; number of people present.

attendant ● noun person attending, esp. to provide service. ● adjective accompanying; (often + on) waiting.

attention /əˈtenʃ(ə)n/ noun act or faculty of applying one's mind; notice; consideration, care; Military erect attitude of readiness; (in plural) courtesies.

attentive /əˈtentɪv/ adjective (+ to) paying attention. □ **attentively** adverb.

attenuate /əˈtenjʊeɪt/ verb (**-ting**) make thin; reduce in force or value. □ **attenuation** noun.

attest /əˈtest/ verb certify validity of; (+ to) bear witness to. □ **attestation** /æt-/ noun.

attic /ˈætɪk/ noun room or space immediately under roof of house.

attire /əˈtaɪə/ noun clothes, esp. formal.

attired adjective dressed, esp. formally.

attitude /ˈætɪtjuːd/ noun opinion, way of thinking; (often + to) behaviour reflecting this; bodily posture.

attitudinize /ætɪˈtjuːdɪnaɪz/ verb (also **-ise**) (**-zing** or **-sing**) adopt attitudes.

attorney /əˈtɜːnɪ/ noun person, esp. lawyer, appointed to act for another in business or legal matters; US qualified lawyer. □ **Attorney-General** chief legal officer of government.

attract /əˈtrækt/ verb (of magnet etc.) draw to itself or oneself; arouse interest or admiration in.

attraction /əˈtrækʃ(ə)n/ noun attracting, being attracted; attractive quality; person or thing that attracts.

attractive /əˈtræktɪv/ adjective attracting esp. interest or admiration; pleasing. □ **attractively** noun.

attribute ● verb /əˈtrɪbjuːt/ (**-ting**) (usually + to) regard as belonging to or as written, said, or caused by, etc. ● noun /ˈætrɪbjuːt/ quality ascribed to person or thing; characteristic quality; object frequently associated with person, office, or status. □ **attributable** /əˈtrɪbjʊtəb(ə)l/ adjective; **attribution** /ætrɪˈbjuːʃ(ə)n/ noun.

attributive /əˈtrɪbjʊtɪv/ adjective expressing an attribute; (of adjective or noun) preceding word it describes.

attrition /əˈtrɪʃ(ə)n/ noun gradual wearing down; friction, abrasion.

attune /əˈtjuːn/ verb (**-ning**) (usually + to) adjust; Music tune.

atypical /eɪˈtɪpɪk(ə)l/ adjective not typical. □ **atypically** adverb.

aubergine /ˈəʊbəʒiːn/ noun (plant with) oval usually purple fruit used as vegetable.

aubrietia /ɔːˈbriːʃə/ noun (also **aubretia**) dwarf perennial rock plant.

auburn /ˈɔːbən/ adjective (usually of hair) reddish-brown.

auction /ˈɔːkʃ(ə)n/ ● noun sale in which each article is sold to highest bidder. ● verb sell by auction.

auctioneer /ɔːkʃəˈnɪə/ noun person who conducts auctions.

audacious /ɔːˈdeɪʃəs/ adjective daring, bold; impudent. □ **audacity** /-ˈdæs-/ noun.

audible /ˈɔːdɪb(ə)l/ adjective that can be heard. □ **audibility** noun; **audibly** adverb.

audience /ˈɔːdɪəns/ noun group of listeners or spectators; group of people reached by any spoken or written message; formal interview.

audio /ˈɔːdɪəʊ/ noun (reproduction of) sound. □ **audiotape** magnetic tape for recording sound; **audio typist** person who types from tape recording; **audio-visual** using both sight and sound.

audit /ˈɔːdɪt/ ● noun official scrutiny of accounts. ● verb (**-t-**) conduct audit of. □ **auditor** noun.

audition /ɔːˈdɪʃ(ə)n/ ● noun test of performer's ability. ● verb assess or be assessed at audition.

auditorium /ɔːdɪˈtɔːrɪəm/ noun (plural **-s**) part of theatre etc. for audience.

auditory /ˈɔːdɪtərɪ/ adjective of hearing.

au fait /əʊ ˈfeɪ/ adjective (usually + with) conversant.

Aug. abbreviation August.

auger /'ɔ:gə/ noun tool with screw point for boring holes in wood.

aught /ɔ:t/ noun archaic anything.

augment /ɔ:g'ment/ verb make greater, increase. □ **augmentation** noun.

augur /'ɔ:gə/ verb portend; serve as omen.

augury /'ɔ:gjʊrɪ/ noun (plural **-ies**) omen; interpretation of omens.

August /'ɔ:gəst/ noun eighth month of year.

august /ɔ:'gʌst/ adjective venerable, imposing.

auk /ɔ:k/ noun black and white seabird with small wings.

aunt /ɑ:nt/ noun parent's sister; uncle's wife. □ **Aunt Sally** game in which sticks or balls are thrown at dummy, target of general abuse.

aunty /'ɑ:ntɪ/ noun (also **auntie**) (plural **-ies**) colloquial aunt.

au pair /əʊ 'peə/ noun young foreign woman who helps with housework in return for room and board.

aura /'ɔ:rə/ noun distinctive atmosphere; subtle emanation.

aural /'ɔ:r(ə)l/ adjective of ear or hearing. □ **aurally** adverb.

aureole /'ɔ:rɪəʊl/ noun (also **aureola** /ɔ:'ri:ələ/) halo.

au revoir /əʊ rə'vwɑ:/ interjection & noun goodbye (until we meet again). [French]

auricle /'ɔ:rɪk(ə)l/ noun external ear of animal; atrium of heart.

auriferous /ɔ:'rɪfərəs/ adjective yielding gold.

aurora /ɔ:'rɔ:rə/ noun (plural **-s** or **-rae** /-ri:/) streamers of light above northern (**aurora borealis** /bɒrɪ'eɪlɪs/) or southern (**aurora australis** /ɔ:'streɪlɪs/) polar region.

auscultation /ɔ:skəl'teɪʃ(ə)n/ noun listening to sound of heart etc. to help diagnosis.

auspice /'ɔ:spɪs/ noun omen; (in plural) patronage.

auspicious /ɔ:'spɪʃəs/ adjective promising; favourable.

Aussie /'ɒzɪ/ noun & adjective slang Australian.

austere /ɔ:'stɪə/ adjective (**-r**, **-st**) severely simple; stern; morally strict. □ **austerity** /-'ter-/ noun.

austral /ɔ:'str(ə)l/ adjective southern.

Australasian /ɒstrə'leɪʒ(ə)n/ adjective of Australia and SW Pacific islands.

Australian /ɒ'streɪlɪən/ ● adjective of Australia. ● noun native or national of Australia.

autarchy /'ɔ:tɑ:kɪ/ noun absolute rule.

autarky /'ɔ:tɑ:kɪ/ noun self-sufficiency.

authentic /ɔ:'θentɪk/ adjective of undisputed origin, genuine; trustworthy. □ **authentically** adverb; **authenticity** /-'tɪs-/ noun.

authenticate /ɔ:'θentɪkeɪt/ verb (**-ting**) establish as true, genuine, or valid. □ **authentication** noun.

author /'ɔ:θə/ noun (feminine **authoress** /'ɔ:rɪs/) writer of book etc.; originator. □ **authorship** noun.

authoritarian /ɔ:θɒrɪ'teərɪən/ ● adjective favouring strict obedience to authority. ● noun authoritarian person.

authoritative /ɔ:'θɒrɪtətɪv/ adjective reliable, esp. having authority.

authority /ɔ:'θɒrɪtɪ/ noun (plural **-ies**) power or right to enforce obedience; (esp. in plural) body having this; delegated power; influence based on recognized knowledge or expertise; expert.

authorize /'ɔ:θəraɪz/ verb (also **-ise**) (**-zing** or **-sing**) (+ to do) give authority to (person); sanction officially. □ **Authorized Version** English translation (1611) of Bible. □ **authorization** noun.

autism /'ɔ:tɪz(ə)m/ noun condition characterized by self-absorption and withdrawal. □ **autistic** /-'tɪs-/ adjective.

auto- combining form self; one's own; of or by oneself or itself.

autobahn /'ɔ:təʊbɑ:n/ noun German, Austrian, or Swiss motorway. [German]

autobiography /ɔ:təʊbaɪ'ɒgrəfɪ/ noun (plural **-ies**) story of one's own life. □ **autobiographer** noun; **autobiographical** /-ə'græf-/ adjective.

autocracy /ɔ:'tɒkrəsɪ/ noun (plural **-ies**) absolute rule by one person.

autocrat /'ɔ:təkræt/ noun absolute ruler. □ **autocratic** /-'kræt-/ adjective; **autocratically** /-'kræt-/ adverb.

autocross /'ɔ:təʊkrɒs/ noun motor racing across country or on unmade roads.

autograph /'ɔ:təgrɑ:f/ ● noun signature, esp. of celebrity. ● verb write on or sign in one's own handwriting.

automate /'ɔ:təmeɪt/ verb (**-ting**) convert to or operate by automation.

automatic /ɔ:tə'mætɪk/ ● adjective working by itself, without direct human involvement; done spontaneously; following inevitably; (of firearm) that can be loaded and fired continuously; (of vehicle or its transmission) using gears that change automatically. ● noun automatic firearm, vehicle, etc. □ **automatically** adverb.

automation noun use of automatic equipment in place of manual labour.

automaton /ɔ:'tɒmət(ə)n/ noun (plural **-mata** or **-s**) machine controlled automatically.

automobile /'ɔ:təməbi:l/ noun US motor car.

automotive /ɔ:tə'məʊtɪv/ adjective of motor vehicles.

autonomous /ɔ:'tɒnəməs/ adjective self-governing; free to act independently. □ **autonomy** noun.

autopsy /'ɔ:tɒpsɪ/ noun (plural **-ies**) post-mortem.

auto-suggestion /ɔ:təʊsə'dʒestʃ(ə)n/ noun hypnotic or subconscious suggestion made to oneself.

autumn /'ɔ:təm/ noun season between summer and winter. □ **autumnal** /ɔ:'tʌmn(ə)l/ adjective.

auxiliary /ɔ:g'zɪljərɪ/ ● adjective giving help; additional, subsidiary. ● noun (plural **-ies**) auxiliary person or thing; (in plural) foreign or allied troops in service of nation at war; auxiliary verb. □ **auxiliary verb** one used with another verb to form tenses etc. (see panel).

avail /ə'veɪl/ ● verb (often + to) be of use; help; (**avail oneself of**) use, profit by. ● noun use, profit by.

available adjective at one's disposal; (of person) free, able to be contacted. □ **availability** noun.

avalanche /'ævəlɑ:ntʃ/ noun mass of snow and ice rapidly sliding down mountain; sudden abundance.

avant-garde /ævã'gɑ:d/ ● noun innovators, esp. in the arts. ● adjective new, pioneering.

avarice /'ævərɪs/ noun greed for wealth. □ **avaricious** /-'rɪʃ-/ adjective.

avatar /'ævətɑ:/ noun Hindu Mythology descent of god to earth in bodily form.

avenge /ə'vendʒ/ verb (**-ging**) inflict retribution on behalf of; exact retribution for.

avenue /'ævənju:/ noun road or path, usually tree-lined; way of approach.

aver /ə'vɜ:/ verb (**-rr-**) formal assert, affirm.

average /'ævərɪdʒ/ ● noun usual amount, extent, or rate; number obtained by dividing sum of given numbers by how many there are. ● adjective usual, ordinary; mediocre; constituting average. ● verb (**-ging**) amount on average to; do on average; estimate average of. □ **average out (at)** result in average (of); **on average** as an average rate etc.

averse /ə'vɜ:s/ adjective (usually + to) opposed, disinclined.

aversion /ə'vɜːʃ(ə)n/ *noun* (usually + *to, for*) dislike, unwillingness; object of this.

avert /ə'vɜːt/ *verb* prevent; (often + *from*) turn away.

aviary /'eɪvɪərɪ/ *noun* (*plural* **-ies**) large cage or building for keeping birds.

aviation /eɪvɪ'eɪʃ(ə)n/ *noun* the flying of aircraft.

aviator /'eɪvɪeɪtə/ *noun* person who flies aircraft.

avid /'ævɪd/ *adjective* eager; greedy. □ **avidity** /-'vɪd-/ *noun*; **avidly** *adverb*.

avocado /ævə'kɑːdəʊ/ *noun* (*plural* **-s**) (in full **avocado pear**) dark green pear-shaped fruit with creamy flesh.

avocet /'ævəset/ *noun* wading bird with long upturned bill.

avoid /ə'vɔɪd/ *verb* keep away or refrain from; escape; evade. □ **avoidable** *adjective*; **avoidance** *noun*.

avoirdupois /ævədə'pɔɪz/ *noun* system of weights based on pound of 16 ounces.

avow /ə'vaʊ/ *verb formal* declare; confess. □ **avowal** *noun*; **avowedly** /ə'vaʊɪdlɪ/ *adverb*.

avuncular /ə'vʌŋkjʊlə/ *adjective* of or like an uncle.

await /ə'weɪt/ *verb* wait for; be in store for.

awake /ə'weɪk/ ● *verb* (**-king**; *past* **awoke**; *past participle* **awoken**) (also **awaken**) rouse from sleep; cease to sleep; (often + *to*) become alert, aware, or active. ● *adjective* not asleep; alert.

award /ə'wɔːd/ ● *verb* give or order to be given as payment, penalty, or prize. ● *noun* thing awarded; judicial decision.

aware /ə'weə/ *adjective* (often + *of, that*) conscious, having knowledge. □ **awareness** *noun*.

awash /ə'wɒʃ/ *adjective* at surface of and just covered by water; (+ *with*) abounding.

away /ə'weɪ/ ● *adverb* to or at distance; into non-existence; constantly, persistently. ● *adjective* (of match etc.) played on opponent's ground.

awe /ɔː/ ● *noun* reverential fear or wonder. ● *verb* (**awing**) inspire with awe. □ **awe-inspiring** awesome, magnificent.

aweigh /ə'weɪ/ *adjective* (of anchor) just lifted from sea bottom.

awesome *adjective* inspiring awe.

awful /'ɔːfʊl/ *adjective colloquial* very bad; very great; *poetical* inspiring awe.

awfully *adverb colloquial* badly; very.

awhile /ə'waɪl/ *adverb* for a short time.

awkward /'ɔːkwəd/ *adjective* difficult to use; clumsy; embarrassing, embarrassed; hard to deal with.

awl /ɔːl/ *noun* small tool for pricking holes, esp. in leather.

awning /'ɔːnɪŋ/ *noun* fabric roof, shelter.

awoke *past* of AWAKE.

awoken *past participle* of AWAKE.

AWOL /'eɪwɒl/ *abbreviation colloquial* absent without leave.

awry /ə'raɪ/ ● *adverb* crookedly; amiss. ● *adjective* crooked; unsound.

axe /æks/ ● *noun* (*US* **ax**) chopping-tool with heavy blade; (**the axe**) dismissal (of employees), abandonment of project etc. ● *verb* (**axing**) cut (staff, services, etc.); abandon (project).

axial /'æksɪəl/ *adjective* of, forming, or placed round axis.

axiom /'æksɪəm/ *noun* established principle; self-evident truth. □ **axiomatic** /-'mæt-/ *adjective*.

axis /'æksɪs/ *noun* (*plural* **axes** /-siːz/) imaginary line about which object rotates; line dividing regular figure symmetrically; reference line for measurement of coordinates etc.

axle /'æks(ə)l/ *noun* spindle on which wheel turns or is fixed.

ayatollah /aɪə'tɒlə/ *noun* religious leader in Iran.

aye /aɪ/ ● *adverb archaic or dialect* yes. ● *noun* affirmative answer or vote.

azalea /ə'zeɪlɪə/ *noun* kind of rhododendron.

azimuth /'æzɪməθ/ *noun* angular distance between point below star etc. and north or south. □ **azimuthal** *adjective*.

azure /'æʒə/ *adjective & noun* sky-blue.

Auxiliary verb

An auxiliary verb is used in front of another verb to alter its meaning. Mainly, it expresses:

1 when something happens, by forming a tense of the main verb, e.g. *I* shall *go. He* was *going.*

2 permission, obligation, or ability to do something, e.g. *They* may *go. You* must *go. I* can't *go.*

3 the likelihood of something happening, e.g. *I* might *go. She* would *go if she could.*

The principal auxiliary verbs are:

be	*have*	*must*	*will*
can	*let*	*ought*	*would*
could	*may*	*shall*	
do	*might*	*should*	

Bb

B *abbreviation* black (pencil lead).

b. *abbreviation* born.

BA *abbreviation* Bachelor of Arts.

baa /bɑː/ *noun & verb* (**baas, baaed** or **baa'd**) bleat.

babble /'bæb(ə)l/ ● *verb* (**-ling**) talk, chatter, or say incoherently or excessively; (of stream) murmur; repeat foolishly. ● *noun* babbling; murmur of water etc.

babe *noun* baby.

babel /'beɪb(ə)l/ *noun* confused noise, esp. of voices.

baboon /bə'buːn/ *noun* large kind of monkey.

baby /'beɪbɪ/ *noun* (*plural* **-ies**) very young child; childish person; youngest member of family etc.; very young animal; small specimen. □ **baby boom** *colloquial* temporary increase in birth rate; **baby grand** small grand piano.

babysit *verb* (**-tt-**; *past & past participle* **-sat**) look after child while parents are out. □ **babysitter** *noun*.

baccarat /'bækərɑː/ *noun* gambling card game.

bachelor /'bætʃələ/ *noun* unmarried man; person with a university first degree.

bacillus /bə'sɪləs/ *noun* (*plural* **bacilli** /-laɪ/) rod-shaped bacterium. □ **bacillary** *adjective*.

back ● *noun* rear surface of human body from shoulders to hips; upper surface of animal's body; spine; reverse or more distant part; part of garment covering back; defensive player in football etc. ● *adverb* to rear; away from front; in(to) the past or an earlier or normal position or condition; in return; at a distance. ● *verb* help with money or moral support; (often + *up*) (cause to) go backwards; bet on; provide with or serve as back, support, or backing to; *Music* accompany. ● *adjective* situated to rear; past, not current; reversed. □ **backache** ache in back; **back-bencher** MP without senior office; **backbiting** malicious talk; **back boiler** one behind domestic fire etc.; **backbone** spine, main support, firmness of character; **backchat** *colloquial* verbal insolence; **backcloth** painted cloth at back of stage; **backdate** make retrospectively valid, put earlier date to; **back door** secret or ingenious means; **back down** withdraw from confrontation; **backdrop** backcloth; **backfire** (of engine or vehicle) undergo premature explosion in cylinder or exhaust pipe, (of plan etc.) have opposite of intended effect; **backhand** *Tennis etc.* (stroke) made with hand across body; **backhanded** indirect, ambiguous; **backhander** *slang* bribe; **backlash** violent, usually hostile, reaction; **backlog** arrears (of work etc.); **back number** old issue of magazine etc.; **back out** (often + *of*) withdraw; **backpack** rucksack; **back-pedal** reverse previous action or opinion; **back room** place where (esp. secret) work goes on; **back seat** less prominent or important position; **backside** *colloquial* buttocks; **backslide** return to bad ways; **backstage** behind the scenes; **backstreet** *noun* side-street, alley, *adjective* illicit, illegal; **backstroke** stroke made by swimmer lying on back; **back to front** with back and front reversed; **backtrack** retrace one's steps, reverse one's policy or opinion; **back up** give (esp. moral) support to, *Computing* make backup of; **backup** support, *Computing* (making of) spare copy of data; **backwash** receding waves, repercussions; **backwater** peaceful, secluded, or dull place, stagnant water fed from stream; **backwoods** remote uncleared forest land.

backgammon /'bækgæmən/ *noun* board game with pieces moved according to throw of dice.

background /'bækgraʊnd/ *noun* back part of scene etc.; inconspicuous position; person's education, social circumstances, etc.; explanatory information etc.

backing *noun* help or support; material used for thing's back or support; musical accompaniment.

backward *adjective* directed backwards; slow in learning; shy.

backwards *adverb* away from one's front; back foremost; in reverse of usual way; into worse state; into past; back towards starting point □ **bend over backwards** *colloquial* make every effort.

bacon /'beɪkən/ *noun* cured meat from back and sides of pig.

bacteriology /bæktɪərɪ'ɒlədʒɪ/ *noun* study of bacteria.

bacterium /bæk'tɪərɪəm/ *noun* (*plural* **-ria**) single-celled micro-organism. □ **bacterial** *adjective*.

■ **Usage** It is a mistake to use the plural form *bacteria* when only one bacterium is meant.

bad *adjective* (**worse, worst**) inadequate, defective; unpleasant; harmful; decayed; ill, injured; regretful, guilty; serious, severe; wicked; naughty; incorrect, not valid. □ **bad debt** debt that is not recoverable; **bad-tempered** irritable.

bade *archaic past of* BID.

badge *noun* small flat emblem worn as sign of office, membership, etc. or bearing slogan etc.

badger /'bædʒə/ ● *noun* nocturnal burrowing mammal with black and white striped head. ● *verb* pester.

badinage /'bædmɑːʒ/ *noun* banter. [French]

badly *adverb* (**worse, worst**) in bad manner; severely; very much.

badminton /'bædmɪnt(ə)n/ *noun* game played with rackets and shuttlecock.

baffle /'bæf(ə)l/ ● *verb* perplex; frustrate. ● *noun* device that hinders flow of fluid or sound. □ **bafflement** *noun*.

bag ● *noun* soft open-topped receptacle; piece of luggage; (in *plural*; usually + *of*) *colloquial* large amount; animal's sac; amount of game shot by one person. ● *verb* secure, take possession of; bulge, hang loosely; put in bag; shoot (game).

bagatelle /bægə'tel/ *noun* game in which small balls are struck into holes on inclined board; mere trifle.

bagel /'beɪg(ə)l/ *noun* ring-shaped bread roll.

baggage /'bægɪdʒ/ *noun* luggage; portable equipment of army.

baggy *adjective* (**-ier, -iest**) hanging loosely.

bagpipes /'bægpaɪps/ *plural noun* musical instrument with windbag for pumping air through reeded pipes.

baguette /bæ'get/ *noun* long thin French loaf.

bail¹ ● *noun* security given for released prisoner's return for trial; person(s) pledging this. ● *verb* (usually + *out*) give bail for and secure release of (prisoner).

bail² *noun Cricket* either of two crosspieces resting on stumps.

bail³ *verb* (also **bale**) (usually + *out*) scoop (water) out of (boat etc.). □ **bail out** = BALE OUT.

bailey /'beɪlɪ/ *noun* (*plural* **-s**) outer wall of castle; court enclosed by this.

bailiff /'beɪlɪf/ *noun* sheriff's officer who executes writs, performs distraints, etc.; landlord's agent or steward.

bailiwick /'beɪlɪwɪk/ *noun* district of bailiff.

bairn /beən/ *noun* *Scottish & Northern English* child.

bait ● *noun* food to entice prey; allurement. ● *verb* torment (chained animal); harass (person); put bait on or in (fish-hook, trap, etc.).

baize /beɪz/ *noun* usually green felted woollen fabric used for coverings etc.

bake *verb* (**-king**) cook or become cooked by dry heat esp. in oven; *colloquial* be very hot; harden by heat. □ **baking powder** mixture used as raising agent.

Bakelite /'beɪkəlaɪt/ *noun proprietary term* kind of plastic.

baker /'beɪkə/ *noun* professional bread-maker. □ **baker's dozen** thirteen.

bakery /'beɪkərɪ/ *noun* (*plural* **-ies**) place where bread is made or sold.

baksheesh /'bækʃiːʃ/ *noun* gratuity, tip.

Balaclava /bælə'klɑːvə/ *noun* (in full **Balaclava helmet**) woollen covering for head and neck.

balalaika /bælə'laɪkə/ *noun* Russian triangular-bodied guitar-like musical instrument.

balance /'bæləns/ ● *noun* even distribution of weight or amount; stability of body or mind; weighing apparatus; counteracting weight or force; regulating device in clock etc.; decisive weight or amount; difference between credits and debits; remainder. ● *verb* (**-cing**) bring or come into or keep in equilibrium; offset, compare; equal, neutralize; (usually as **balanced** *adjective*) make well-proportioned and harmonious; equalize debits and credits of account, have debits and credits equal. □ **balance of payments** difference between payments into and out of a country; **balance of power** position in which no country etc. predominates, power held by small group when larger groups are of (almost) equal strength; **balance of trade** difference between exports and imports; **balance sheet** statement giving balance of account; **on balance** all things considered.

balcony /'bælkənɪ/ *noun* (*plural* **-ies**) outside balustraded or railed platform with access from upper floor; upper tier of seats in theatre etc.

bald /bɔːld/ *adjective* lacking some or all hair on scalp; without fur, feathers, etc.; with surface worn away; direct. □ **baldly** *adverb*; **baldness** *noun*.

balderdash /'bɔːldədæʃ/ *noun* nonsense.

balding /'bɔːldɪŋ/ *adjective* becoming bald.

bale¹ ● *noun* bundle of merchandise or hay. ● *verb* (**-ling**) make up into bales. □ **bale out** (also **bail out**) make emergency parachute jump from aircraft.

bale² = BAIL³.

baleful /'beɪlfʊl/ *adjective* menacing; destructive; malignant.

balk = BAULK.

ball¹ /bɔːl/ *noun* spherical object or mass; usually spherical object used in game; rounded part of foot or hand at base of big toe or thumb; cannon ball; delivery or pass of ball in game. □ **ball-bearing** bearing using ring of small balls between its two parts, one such ball; **ballcock** valve operated by floating ball that controls level of water in cistern; **ball game** *US* baseball game, *colloquial* affair or matter; **ballpoint (pen)** pen with tiny ball as writing point.

ball² /bɔːl/ *noun* formal social gathering for dancing; *slang* enjoyable time.

ballad /'bæləd/ *noun* poem or song narrating popular story; slow sentimental song. □ **balladry** *noun*.

ballast /'bæləst/ ● *noun* heavy material stabilizing ship, controlling height of balloon, etc.; coarse stone etc. as bed of road or railway. ● *verb* provide with ballast.

ballerina /bælə'riːnə/ *noun* female ballet dancer.

ballet /'bæleɪ/ *noun* dramatic or representational style of dancing to music; piece or performance of ballet. □ **ballet dancer** dancer of ballet. □ **balletic** /bə'letɪk/ *adjective*.

ballistic /bə'lɪstɪk/ *adjective* of projectiles. □ **ballistic missile** one that is powered and guided but falls by gravity.

ballistics *plural noun* (usually treated as *singular*) science of projectiles and firearms.

balloon /bə'luːn/ ● *noun* small inflatable rubber toy or decoration; large inflatable flying bag, esp. one with basket below for passengers; outline containing words or thoughts in strip cartoon. ● *verb* (cause to) swell out like balloon. □ **balloonist** *noun*.

ballot /'bælət/ ● *noun* voting in writing and usually secret; votes recorded in ballot. ● *verb* (**-t-**) hold ballot; vote by ballot; take ballot of (voters). □ **ballot box** container for **ballot papers**, slips for marking votes.

ballroom /'bɔːlrʊm/ *noun* large room for dancing. □ **ballroom dancing** formal social dancing for couples.

bally /'bælɪ/ *adjective & adverb* slang *mild form of* BLOODY.

ballyhoo /bælɪ'huː/ *noun* loud noise, fuss; noisy publicity.

balm /bɑːm/ *noun* aromatic ointment; fragrant oil or resin exuded from some trees; thing that heals or soothes; aromatic herb.

balmy /'bɑːmɪ/ *adjective* (**-ier, -iest**) fragrant, mild, soothing; slang crazy.

balsa /'bɔːlsə/ *noun* lightweight tropical American wood used for making models.

balsam /'bɔːlsəm/ *noun* balm from trees; ointment; tree yielding balsam; any of several flowering plants.

baluster /'bæləstə/ *noun* short pillar supporting rail.

balustrade /bælə'streɪd/ *noun* railing supported by balusters, esp. on balcony.

bamboo /bæm'buː/ *noun* tropical giant woody grass; its hollow stem.

bamboozle /bæm'buːz(ə)l/ *verb* (**-ling**) *colloquial* cheat; mystify.

ban ● *verb* (**-nn-**) prohibit, esp. formally. ● *noun* formal prohibition.

banal /bə'nɑːl/ *adjective* commonplace, trite. □ **banality** /-'næl-/ *noun* (*plural* **-ies**).

banana /bə'nɑːnə/ *noun* long curved yellow tropical fruit; treelike plant bearing it.

band ● *noun* flat strip or loop of thin material; stripe; group of musicians; organized group of criminals etc.; range of values, esp. frequencies or wavelengths. ● *verb* (usually + *together*) unite; put band on; mark with stripes. □ **bandbox** hatbox; **bandmaster** conductor of band; **bandsman** player in band; **bandstand** outdoor platform for musicians.

bandage /'bændɪdʒ/ ● *noun* strip of material for binding wound etc. ● *verb* (**-ging**) bind with bandage.

bandanna /bæn'dænə/ *noun* large patterned handkerchief.

bandeau /'bændəʊ/ *noun* (*plural* **-x** /-z/) narrow headband.

bandit /'bændɪt/ *noun* robber, esp. of travellers. □ **banditry** *noun*.

bandolier /bændə'lɪə/ *noun* (also **bandoleer**) shoulder belt with loops or pockets for cartridges.

bandwagon *noun* □ **climb, jump on the bandwagon** join popular or successful cause.

bandy¹ /'bændɪ/ *adjective* (**-ier, -iest**) (of legs) curved wide apart at knees. □ **bandy-legged** *adjective*.

bandy² /'bændɪ/ verb (-ies, -ied) (often + about) pass (story etc.) to and fro, discuss disparagingly; (often + with) exchange (blows, insults, etc.).

bane noun cause of ruin or trouble.

bang ● noun loud short sound; sharp blow. ● verb strike or shut noisily; (cause to) make bang. ● adverb with bang; colloquial exactly. □ **bang on** colloquial exactly right.

banger noun firework making bang; slang sausage, noisy old car.

bangle /'bæŋg(ə)l/ noun rigid bracelet or anklet.

banian = BANYAN.

banish /'bænɪʃ/ verb condemn to exile; dismiss from one's mind. □ **banishment** noun.

banister /'bænɪstə/ noun (also **bannister**) (usually in plural) uprights and handrail beside staircase.

banjo /'bændʒəʊ/ noun (plural **-s** or **-es**) round-bodied guitar-like musical instrument. □ **banjoist** noun.

bank¹ ● noun sloping ground on each side of river; raised shelf of ground, esp. in sea; mass of cloud etc. ● verb (often + up) heap or rise into banks; pack (fire) tightly for slow burning; (cause to) travel round curve with one side higher than the other.

bank² ● noun establishment, usually a public company, where money is deposited, withdrawn, and borrowed; pool of money in gambling game; storage place. ● verb deposit (money) at bank; (often + at, with) keep money (at bank). □ **bank card** cheque card; **bank holiday** public holiday when banks are closed; **banknote** piece of paper money; **bank on** colloquial rely on.

bank³ noun row (of lights, switches, organ keys, etc.).

banker noun owner or manager of bank; keeper of bank in gambling game. □ **banker's card** cheque card.

bankrupt /'bæŋkrʌpt/ ● adjective insolvent; (often + of) drained (of emotion etc.). ● noun insolvent person. ● verb make bankrupt. □ **bankruptcy** noun (plural **-ies**).

banner /'bænə/ noun large portable cloth sign bearing slogan or design; flag.

bannister = BANISTER.

bannock /'bænək/ noun Scottish & Northern English round flat loaf, usually unleavened.

banns plural noun announcement of intended marriage read in church.

banquet /'bæŋkwɪt/ ● noun sumptuous esp. formal dinner. ● verb (**-t-**) give banquet for; attend banquet.

banquette /bæŋ'ket/ noun upholstered bench along wall.

banshee /bæn'ʃiː/ noun female spirit whose wail warns of death in a house.

bantam /'bæntəm/ noun kind of small domestic fowl; small but aggressive person. □ **bantamweight** boxing weight (51–54 kg).

banter /'bæntə/ ● noun good-humoured teasing. ● verb tease; exchange banter.

banyan /'bænjən/ noun (also **banian**) Indian fig tree with self-rooting branches.

baobab /'beɪəʊbæb/ noun African tree with massive trunk and edible fruit.

bap noun soft flattish bread roll.

baptism /'bæptɪz(ə)m/ noun symbolic admission to Christian Church, with immersing in or sprinkling with water and usually name-giving. □ **baptismal** /-'tɪz-/ adjective.

Baptist /'bæptɪst/ noun member of Church practising adult baptism by immersion.

baptize /bæp'taɪz/ verb (also **-ise**) (**-zing** or **-sing**) administer baptism to; give name to.

bar¹ ● noun long piece of rigid material, esp. used to confine or obstruct; (often + of) oblong piece (of chocolate, soap, etc.); band of colour or light; counter for serving alcoholic drinks etc., room or building containing it; counter for particular service; barrier; prisoner's enclosure in law court; section of music between vertical lines; heating element of electric fire; strip below clasp of medal as extra distinction; (**the Bar**) barristers, their profession. ● verb (**-rr-**) fasten with bar; (usually + in, out) keep in or out; obstruct, prevent; (usually + from) exclude. ● preposition except. □ **bar code** machine-readable striped code on packaging etc.; **barmaid, barman, bartender** woman, man, person serving in pub etc.

bar² noun unit of atmospheric pressure.

barathea /bærə'θiːə/ noun fine wool cloth.

barb ● noun backward-facing point on arrow, fish-hook, etc.; hurtful remark. ● verb fit with barb. □ **barbed wire** wire with spikes, used for fences.

barbarian /bɑː'beərɪən/ ● noun uncultured or primitive person. ● adjective uncultured; primitive.

barbaric /bɑː'bærɪk/ adjective uncultured; cruel; primitive.

barbarism /'bɑːbərɪz(ə)m/ noun barbaric state or act; non-standard word or expression.

barbarity /bɑː'bærɪtɪ/ noun (plural **-ies**) savage cruelty; barbaric act.

barbarous /'bɑːbərəs/ adjective uncultured; cruel.

barbecue /'bɑːbɪkjuː/ ● noun meal cooked over charcoal etc. out of doors; party for this; grill etc. used for this. ● verb (**-cues, -cued, -cuing**) cook on barbecue.

barber /'bɑːbə/ noun person who cuts men's hair.

barbican /'bɑːbɪkən/ noun outer defence, esp. double tower over gate or bridge.

barbiturate /bɑː'bɪtjʊrət/ noun sedative derived from **barbituric acid** /bɑːbɪ'tjʊərɪk/, an organic acid.

bard noun poet; historical Celtic minstrel; prizewinner at Eisteddfod. □ **bardic** adjective.

bare /beə/ ● adjective unclothed, uncovered; leafless; unadorned, plain; scanty, just sufficient. ● verb (**-ring**) uncover, reveal. □ **bareback** without saddle; **barefaced** shameless, impudent; **barefoot** with bare feet; **bareheaded** without hat.

barely adverb scarcely; scantily.

bargain /'bɑːgɪn/ ● noun agreement on terms of sale etc.; cheap thing. ● verb discuss terms of sale etc. □ **bargain for** be prepared for; **into the bargain** moreover.

barge /bɑːdʒ/ ● noun large flat-bottomed cargo boat on canal or river; long ornamental pleasure boat. ● verb (**-ging**) (+ into) collide with. □ **barge in** interrupt.

bargee /bɑː'dʒiː/ noun person in charge of barge.

baritone /'bærɪtəʊn/ noun adult male singing voice between tenor and bass; singer with this.

barium /'beərɪəm/ noun white metallic element. □ **barium meal** mixture swallowed to reveal digestive tract on X-ray.

bark¹ ● noun sharp explosive cry of dog etc. ● verb give a bark; speak or utter sharply or brusquely.

bark² ● noun tough outer layer of tree. ● verb graze (shin etc.); strip bark from.

barker noun tout at auction or sideshow.

barley /'bɑːlɪ/ noun cereal used as food and in spirits; (also **barleycorn**) its grain. □ **barley sugar** hard sweet made from sugar; **barley water** drink made from boiled barley.

barm noun froth on fermenting malt liquor.

bar mitzvah /bɑː 'mɪtsvə/ noun religious initiation of Jewish boy at 13.

barmy /'bɑːmɪ/ adjective (**-ier, -iest**) slang crazy.

barn noun building for storing grain etc. □ **barn dance** social gathering for country dancing; **barn owl** kind of owl frequenting barns.

barnacle /'bɑːnək(ə)l/ *noun* small shellfish clinging to rocks, ships' bottoms, etc. □ **barnacle goose** kind of Arctic goose.

barney /'bɑːnɪ/ *noun (plural -s) colloquial* noisy quarrel.

barometer /bə'rɒmɪtə/ *noun* instrument measuring atmospheric pressure. □ **barometric** /bærə'met-rɪk/ *adjective*.

baron /'bærən/ *noun* member of lowest order of British or foreign nobility; powerful businessman etc. □ **baronial** /bə'rəʊnɪəl/ *adjective*.

baroness /'bærənɪs/ *noun* woman holding rank of baron; baron's wife or widow.

baronet /'bærənɪt/ *noun* member of lowest British hereditary titled order. □ **baronetcy** *noun (plural -ies)*.

barony /'bærənɪ/ *noun (plural -ies)* rank or domain of baron.

baroque /bə'rɒk/ ● *adjective* (esp. of 17th- & 18th-c. European architecture and music) ornate and extravagant in style. ● *noun* baroque style.

barque /bɑːk/ *noun* kind of sailing ship.

barrack[1] /'bærək/ *noun* (usually in *plural*, often treated as *singular*) housing for soldiers; large bleak building.

barrack[2] /'bærək/ *verb* shout or jeer (at).

barracuda /bærə'kuːdə/ *noun (plural same or -s)* large voracious tropical sea fish.

barrage /'bærɑːʒ/ *noun* concentrated artillery bombardment; rapid succession of questions etc.; artificial barrier in river etc.

barrel /'bær(ə)l/ ● *noun* cylindrical usually convex container; contents or capacity of this; tube forming part of thing, esp. gun or pen. ● *verb* (-**ll-**; *US* -**l-**) put in barrels. □ **barrel organ** musical instrument with rotating pin-studded cylinder.

barren /'bærən/ *adjective* (-**er**, -**est**) unable to bear young; unable to produce fruit or vegetation; unprofitable; dull. □ **barrenness** *noun*.

barricade /bærɪ'keɪd/ ● *noun* barrier, esp. improvised. ● *verb* (-**ding**) block or defend with this.

barrier /'bærɪə/ *noun* fence etc. barring advance or access; obstacle to communication etc. □ **barrier cream** protective skin cream; **barrier reef** coral reef separated from land by channel.

barrister /'bærɪstə/ *noun* advocate practising in higher courts.

barrow[1] /'bærəʊ/ *noun* two-wheeled handcart; wheelbarrow.

barrow[2] /'bærəʊ/ *noun* ancient grave mound.

Bart. *abbreviation* Baronet.

barter /'bɑːtə/ ● *verb* exchange goods, rights, etc., without using money. ● *noun* trade by bartering.

basal /'beɪs(ə)l/ *adjective* of, at, or forming base.

basalt /'bæsɔːlt/ *noun* dark volcanic rock. □ **basaltic** /bə'sɔːltɪk/ *adjective*.

base[1] /beɪs/ ● *noun* what a thing rests or depends on, foundation; principle; starting point; headquarters; main ingredient; number in terms of which other numbers are expressed; substance combining with acid to form salt. ● *verb* (-**sing**) (usually + *on, upon*) found, establish; station. □ **base rate** interest rate set by Bank of England and used as basis for other banks' rates.

base[2] *adjective* cowardly; despicable; menial; (of coin) alloyed; (of metal) low in value.

baseball *noun* game played esp. in US with bat and ball and circuit of 4 bases.

baseless *adjective* unfounded, groundless.

basement /'beɪsmənt/ *noun* floor below ground level.

bases *plural* of BASE[1], BASIS.

bash ● *verb* strike bluntly or heavily; (often + *up*) *colloquial* attack violently. ● *noun* heavy blow; *slang* attempt, party.

bashful /'bæʃfʊl/ *adjective* shy; diffident.

BASIC /'beɪsɪk/ *noun* computer programming language using familiar English words.

basic /'beɪsɪk/ ● *adjective* serving as base; fundamental; simplest, lowest in level. ● *noun* (usually in *plural*) fundamental fact or principle. □ **basically** *adverb*.

basil /'bæz(ə)l/ *noun* aromatic herb.

basilica /bə'zɪlɪkə/ *noun* ancient Roman hall with apse and colonnades; similar church.

basilisk /'bæzɪlɪsk/ *noun* mythical reptile with lethal breath and look; American crested lizard.

basin /'beɪs(ə)n/ *noun* round vessel for liquids or preparing food in; washbasin; hollow depression; sheltered mooring area; round valley; area drained by river.

basis /'beɪsɪs/ *noun (plural **bases** /-siːz/)* foundation; main ingredient or principle; starting point for discussion etc.

bask /bɑːsk/ *verb* relax in warmth and light; (+ *in*) revel in.

basket /'bɑːskɪt/ *noun* container made of woven canes, wire, etc.; amount held by this. □ **basketball** team game in which goals are scored by putting ball through high nets; **basketry, basketwork** art of weaving cane etc., work so produced.

bas-relief /'bæsrɪliːf/ *noun* carving or sculpture projecting slightly from background.

bass[1] /beɪs/ ● *noun* lowest adult male voice; singer with this; *colloquial* double bass, bass guitar; low-frequency sound of radio, record player, etc. ● *adjective* lowest in pitch; deep-sounding. □ **bass guitar** electric guitar playing low notes. □ **bassist** *noun*.

bass[2] /bæs/ *noun (plural same or -es)* common perch; other fish of perch family.

basset /'bæsɪt/ *noun* (in full **basset-hound**) short-legged hunting dog.

bassoon /bə'suːn/ *noun* bass instrument of oboe family. □ **bassoonist** *noun*.

bast /bæst/ *noun* fibre from inner bark of tree, esp. lime.

bastard /'bɑːstəd/ *often offensive* ● *noun* person born of parents not married to each other; *slang* person regarded with dislike or pity, difficult or awkward thing. ● *adjective* illegitimate by birth; hybrid. □ **bastardy** *noun*.

bastardize /'bɑːstədaɪz/ *verb* (also -**ise**) (-**zing** or -**sing**) corrupt, debase; declare illegitimate.

baste[1] /beɪst/ *verb* (-**ting**) moisten (roasting meat etc.) with fat etc.; beat, thrash.

baste[2] /beɪst/ *verb* (-**ting**) sew with long loose stitches, tack.

bastinado /bæstɪ'neɪdəʊ/ ● *noun* caning on soles of feet. ● *verb* (-**es**, -**ed**) punish with this.

bastion /'bæstɪən/ *noun* projecting part of fortification; thing regarded as protection.

bat[1] /bæt/ ● *noun* implement with handle for hitting ball in games; turn at using this; batsman. ● *verb* (-**tt-**) use bat; hit (as) with bat; take one's turn at batting. □ **batsman** person who bats, esp. at cricket.

bat[2] *noun* mouselike nocturnal flying mammal. □ **bats** *slang* crazy.

bat[3] *verb* (-**tt-**) □ **not bat an eyelid** *colloquial* show no reaction.

batch ● *noun* group, collection, set; loaves baked at one time. ● *verb* arrange in batches.

bated /'beɪtɪd/ *adjective* □ **with bated breath** anxiously.

Bath /bɑːθ/ *noun* □ **Bath bun** round spiced bun with currants; **Bath chair** invalid's wheelchair.

bath /bɑːθ/ ● *noun* (plural -**s** /bɑːðz/) container for sitting in and washing the body; its contents; act of washing in it; (usually in *plural*) building for swimming or bathing. ● *verb* wash in bath. □ **bath cube** cube of **bath salts**, substance for scenting and softening bath water; **bathroom** room with bath, *US* room with lavatory.

bathe /beɪð/ ● *verb* (**-thing**) immerse oneself in water etc., esp. to swim or wash; immerse in or treat with liquid; (of sunlight etc.) envelop. ● *noun* swim. □ **bathing costume** garment worn for swimming.

bathos /'beɪθɒs/ *noun* lapse from sublime to trivial; anticlimax. □ **bathetic** /bə'θetɪk/ *adjective.*

bathyscaphe /'bæθɪskæf/, **bathysphere** /-sfɪə/ *nouns* vessel for deep-sea diving.

batik /bə'tiːk/ *noun* method of dyeing textiles by waxing parts to be left uncoloured.

batiste /bæ'tiːst/ *noun* fine cotton or linen fabric.

batman /'bætmən/ *noun* army officer's servant.

baton /'bæt(ə)n/ *noun* thin stick for conducting orchestra etc.; short stick carried in relay race; stick carried by drum major; staff of office.

batrachian /bə'treɪkɪən/ ● *noun* amphibian that discards gills and tail, esp. frog or toad. ● *adjective* of batrachians.

battalion /bə'tæljən/ *noun* army unit usually of 300–1000 men.

batten[1] /'bæt(ə)n/ ● *noun* long narrow piece of squared timber; strip for securing tarpaulin over ship's hatchway. ● *verb* strengthen or (often + *down*) fasten with battens.

batten[2] /'bæt(ə)n/ *verb* (often + *on*) thrive at the expense of.

batter /'bætə/ ● *verb* strike hard and repeatedly; (esp. as **battered** *adjective*) subject to long-term violence. ● *noun* mixture of flour and eggs beaten up with liquid for cooking. □ **battering ram** *historical* swinging beam for breaching walls.

battery /'bætərɪ/ *noun* (*plural* **-ies**) portable container of cell or cells for supplying electricity; series of cages etc. for poultry or cattle; set of connected or similar instruments etc.; emplacement for heavy guns; *Law* physical violence inflicted on person.

battle /'bæt(ə)l/ ● *noun* prolonged fight, esp. between armed forces; contest. ● *verb* (**-ling**) (often + *with*, *for*) struggle. □ **battleaxe** medieval weapon, *colloquial* domineering middle-aged woman; **battle-cruiser** *historical* heavy-gunned ship of higher speed and lighter armour than battleship; **battledress** soldier's everyday uniform; **battlefield** scene of battle; **battleship** most heavily armed and armoured warship.

battlement /'bæt(ə)lmənt/ *noun* (usually in *plural*) parapet with gaps at intervals at top of wall.

batty /'bætɪ/ *adjective* (**-ier, -iest**) *slang* crazy.

batwing *adjective* (esp. of sleeve) shaped like a bat's wing.

bauble /'bɔːb(ə)l/ *noun* showy trinket.

baulk /bɔːlk/ (also **balk**) ● *verb* (often + *at*) jib, hesitate; thwart, hinder, disappoint. ● *noun* hindrance; stumbling block.

bauxite /'bɔːksaɪt/ *noun* claylike mineral, chief source of aluminium.

bawdy /'bɔːdɪ/ ● *adjective* (**-ier, -iest**) humorously indecent. ● *noun* bawdy talk or writing. □ **bawdy house** brothel.

bawl *verb* shout or weep noisily. □ **bawl out** *colloquial* reprimand severely.

bay[1] *noun* broad curving inlet of sea.

bay[2] *noun* laurel with deep green leaves; (in *plural*) victor's or poet's bay wreath, fame. □ **bay leaf** leaf of bay tree, used for flavouring.

bay[3] *noun* recess; alcove in wall; compartment; allotted area. □ **bay window** window projecting from line of wall.

bay[4] ● *adjective* reddish-brown (esp. of horse). ● *noun* bay horse.

bay[5] ● *verb* bark loudly. ● *noun* bark of large dog, esp. chorus of pursuing hounds. □ **at bay** unable to escape; **keep at bay** ward off.

bayonet /'beɪənət/ ● *noun* stabbing-blade attachable to rifle. ● *verb* (**-t-**) stab with bayonet. □ **bayonet fitting** connecting-part engaged by pushing and twisting.

bazaar /bə'zɑː/ *noun* oriental market; sale of goods, esp. for charity.

bazooka /bə'zuːkə/ *noun* anti-tank rocket launcher.

BBC *abbreviation* British Broadcasting Corporation.

BC *abbreviation* before Christ; British Columbia.

BCG *abbreviation* Bacillus Calmette-Guérin, an anti-tuberculosis vaccine.

be /biː/ ● *verb* (*present singular 1st* **am**, *2nd* **are** /ɑː/, *3rd* **is** /ɪz/, *plural* **are** /ɑː/; *past singular 1st* **was** /wɒz/, *2nd* **were** /wɜː/, *3rd* **was** /wɒz/, *plural* **were** /wɜː/; *present participle* **being**; *past participle* **been**) exist, live; occur; remain, continue; have specified identity, state, or quality. ● *auxiliary verb with past participle to form passive, with present participle to form continuous tenses, with infinitive to express duty, intention, possibility, etc.* □ **be-all and end-all** *colloquial* whole being, essence.

beach ● *noun* sandy or pebbly shore of sea, lake, etc. ● *verb* run or haul (boat etc.) on shore. □ **beachcomber** person who searches beaches for articles of value; **beachhead** fortified position set up on beach by landing forces.

beacon /'biːkən/ *noun* signal-fire on hill or pole; signal; signal-station; Belisha beacon.

bead ● *noun* small ball of glass, stone, etc. pierced for threading with others; drop of liquid; small knob in front sight of gun. ● *verb* adorn with bead(s) or beading.

beading *noun* moulding like series of beads.

beadle /'biːd(ə)l/ *noun* ceremonial officer of church, college, etc.

beady *adjective* (**-ier, -iest**) (of eyes) small and bright. □ **beady-eyed** with beady eyes, observant.

beagle /'biːg(ə)l/ *noun* small hound used for hunting hares.

beak *noun* bird's horny projecting jaws; *slang* hooked nose; *historical* prow of warship; spout.

beaker /'biːkə/ *noun* tall cup for drinking; lipped glass vessel for scientific experiments.

beam ● *noun* long piece of squared timber or metal used in house-building etc.; ray of light or radiation; bright smile; series of radio or radar signals as guide to ship or aircraft; crossbar of balance; (in *plural*) horizontal cross-timbers of ship. ● *verb* emit (light, radio waves, etc.); shine; smile radiantly. □ **off beam** *colloquial* mistaken.

bean *noun* climbing plant with kidney-shaped seeds in long pods; seed of this or of coffee or other plant. □ **beanbag** small bag filled with dried beans and used as ball, large bag filled with polystyrene pieces and used as seat; **bean sprout** sprout of bean seed as food; **full of beans** *colloquial* lively, exuberant; **not a bean** *slang* no money.

beano /'biːnəʊ/ *noun* (*plural* **-s**) *slang* party, celebration.

bear[1] /beə/ *verb* (*past* **bore**; *past participle* **borne** or **born**) carry; show; produce, yield (fruit); give birth to; sustain; endure, tolerate.

bear[2] /beə/ *noun* heavy thick-furred mammal; rough surly person; person who sells shares for future delivery in hope of buying them more cheaply before then. □ **beargarden** noisy or rowdy scene; **bear-hug** powerful embrace; **bearskin** guardsman's tall furry cap.

bearable adjective endurable.

beard /bɪəd/ ● noun facial hair on chin etc.; part on animal (esp. goat) resembling beard. ● verb oppose, defy. □ **bearded** adjective.

bearer noun carrier of message, cheque, etc.; carrier of coffin, equipment, etc.

bearing noun outward behaviour, posture; (usually + on, upon) relation, relevance; part of machine supporting rotating part; direction relative to fixed point; (in plural) relative position; heraldic device or design.

beast noun animal, esp. wild mammal; brutal person; colloquial disliked person or thing.

beastly adjective (**-ier**, **-iest**) like a beast; colloquial unpleasant.

beat ● verb (past **beat**; past participle **beaten**) strike repeatedly or persistently; inflict blows on; overcome, surpass; exhaust, perplex; (often + up) whisk (eggs etc.) vigorously; (often + out) shape (metal etc.) by blows; pulsate; mark (time of music) with baton, foot, etc.; move or cause (wings) to move up and down. ● noun main accent in music or verse; strongly marked rhythm of popular music etc.; stroke on drum; movement of conductor's baton; throbbing; police officer's appointed course; one's habitual round. ● adjective slang exhausted, tired out. □ **beat about the bush** not come to the point; **beat down** cause (seller) to lower price by bargaining, (of sun, rain, etc.) shine or fall relentlessly; **beat it** slang go away; **beat up** beat with punches and kicks; **beat-up** colloquial dilapidated.

beater noun whisk; implement for beating carpet; person who rouses game at a shoot.

beatific /biːəˈtɪfɪk/ adjective making blessed; colloquial blissful.

beatify /biːˈætɪfaɪ/ verb (**-ies**, **-ied**) RC Church declare to be blessed as first step to canonization; make happy. □ **beatification** noun.

beatitude /biːˈætɪtjuːd/ noun blessedness; (in plural) blessings in Matthew 5: 3–11.

beau /bəʊ/ noun (plural **-x** /-z/) boyfriend; dandy.

Beaufort scale /ˈbəʊfət/ noun scale of wind speeds.

Beaujolais /ˈbəʊʒəleɪ/ noun red or white wine from Beaujolais district of France.

beauteous /ˈbjuːtɪəs/ adjective poetical beautiful.

beautician /bjuːˈtɪʃ(ə)n/ noun specialist in beauty treatment.

beautiful /ˈbjuːtɪfʊl/ adjective having beauty; colloquial excellent. □ **beautifully** adverb.

beautify /ˈbjuːtɪfaɪ/ verb (**-ies**, **-ied**) make beautiful, adorn. □ **beautification** noun.

beauty /ˈbjuːtɪ/ noun (plural **-ies**) combination of qualities that delights the sight or other senses or the mind; person or thing having this. □ **beauty queen** woman judged most beautiful in contest; **beauty parlour**, **salon** establishment for cosmetic treatment; **beauty spot** beautiful locality.

beaver ● noun large amphibious broad-tailed rodent; its fur; hat of this; (**Beaver**) member of most junior branch of Scout Association. ● verb colloquial (usually + away) work hard.

becalm /bɪˈkɑːm/ verb deprive (ship etc.) of wind.

became past of BECOME.

because /bɪˈkɒz/ conjunction for the reason that. □ **because of** by reason of.

beck¹ noun brook, mountain stream.

beck² noun □ **at (person's) beck and call** subject to his or her constant orders.

beckon /ˈbekən/ verb (often + to) summon by gesture; entice.

become /bɪˈkʌm/ verb (**-ming**; past **became**; past participle **become**) come to be, begin to be; suit, look well on. □ **become of** happen to.

becquerel /ˈbekərel/ noun SI unit of radioactivity.

bed ● noun place to sleep or rest, esp. piece of furniture for sleeping on; garden plot for plants; bottom of sea, river, etc.; flat base on which thing rests; stratum. ● verb (**-dd-**) (usually + down) put or go to bed; plant in bed; fix firmly; colloquial have sexual intercourse with. □ **bedclothes** sheets, blankets, etc.; **bedpan** pan for use as toilet by invalid in bed; **bedridden** confined to bed by infirmity; **bedrock** solid rock under alluvial deposits etc., basic principles; **bedroom** room for sleeping in; **bedsitting room**, **bedsitter** combined bedroom and sitting-room; **bedsore** sore developed by lying in bed; **bedspread** cloth for covering bed; **bedstead** framework of bed; **bedtime** hour for going to bed.

bedaub /bɪˈdɔːb/ verb smear with paint etc.

bedding noun mattress and bedclothes; litter for cattle etc. □ **bedding plant** annual flowering plant put in garden bed.

bedeck /bɪˈdek/ verb adorn, decorate.

bedevil /bɪˈdev(ə)l/ verb (**-ll-**; US **-l-**) torment, confuse, trouble. □ **bedevilment** noun.

bedlam /ˈbedləm/ noun scene of confusion or uproar.

Bedouin /ˈbeduɪn/ noun (plural same) nomadic Arab of the desert.

bedraggled /bɪˈdræg(ə)ld/ adjective dishevelled, untidy.

bee noun 4-winged stinging insect, collecting nectar and pollen and producing wax and honey; busy worker; meeting for combined work or amusement. □ **beehive** hive; **beeline** straight line between two places; **beeswax** wax secreted by bees for honeycomb.

Beeb noun (**the Beeb**) colloquial the BBC.

beech noun smooth-barked glossy-leaved tree; its wood. □ **beechmast** fruit of beech.

beef ● noun meat of ox, bull, or cow; (plural **beeves** or US **-s**) beef animal; (plural **-s**) slang protest. ● verb slang complain. □ **beefburger** hamburger; **beefeater** warder in Tower of London; **beefsteak** thick slice of beef for grilling or frying; **beef tea** stewed beef extract for invalids; **beef tomato** large tomato.

beefy adjective (**-ier**, **-iest**) like beef; solid, muscular.

been past participle of BE.

beep ● noun short high-pitched sound. ● verb emit beep.

beer /bɪə/ noun alcoholic liquor made from fermented malt etc. flavoured esp. with hops. □ **beer garden** garden where beer is sold and drunk; **beer mat** small mat for beer glass.

beery adjective (**-ier**, **-iest**) showing influence of beer; like beer.

beeswing /ˈbiːzwɪŋ/ noun filmy crust on old port wine etc.

beet noun plant with succulent root used for salads etc. and sugar-making (see BEETROOT, SUGAR BEET).

beetle¹ /ˈbiːt(ə)l/ ● noun insect with hard protective outer wings. ● verb (**-ling**) colloquial (+ about, off, etc.) hurry, scurry.

beetle² /ˈbiːt(ə)l/ ● adjective projecting, shaggy, scowling. ● verb (usually as **beetling** adjective) overhang.

beetle³ /ˈbiːt(ə)l/ noun heavy-headed tool for ramming, crushing, etc.

beetroot noun beet with dark red root used as vegetable.

befall /bɪˈfɔːl/ verb (past **befell**; past participle **befallen**) poetical happen; happen to.

befit /bɪˈfɪt/ *verb* (**-tt-**) be appropriate for.

befog /bɪˈfɒɡ/ *verb* (**-gg-**) obscure; envelop in fog.

before /bɪˈfɔː/ ● *conjunction* sooner than; rather than. ● *preposition* earlier than; in front of, ahead of; in presence of. ● *adverb* ahead, in front; previously, already; in the past.

beforehand *adverb* in anticipation, in readiness, before time.

befriend /bɪˈfrend/ *verb* act as friend to; help.

befuddle /bɪˈfʌd(ə)l/ *verb* (**-ling**) make drunk; confuse.

beg *verb* (**-gg-**) ask for as gift; ask earnestly, entreat; live by begging; ask formally. □ **beg the question** assume truth of thing to be proved; **go begging** be unwanted.

■ **Usage** The expression *beg the question* is often used incorrectly to mean 'to invite the obvious question (that …)'.

began *past* of BEGIN.

begat *archaic past* of BEGET.

beget /bɪˈɡet/ *verb* (**-tt-**; *past* **begot**, *archaic* **begat**; *past participle* **begotten**) *literary* be the father of; give rise to.

beggar /ˈbeɡə/ ● *noun* person who begs or lives by begging; *colloquial* person. ● *verb* make poor; be too extraordinary for (belief, description, etc.).

beggarly *adjective* mean; poor, needy.

begin /bɪˈɡɪn/ *verb* (**-nn-**; *past* **began**; *past participle* **begun**) perform first part of; come into being; (often + *to do*) start, take first step, (usually in negative) *colloquial* show any likelihood, be sufficient.

beginner *noun* learner.

beginning *noun* time at which thing begins; source, origin; first part.

begone /bɪˈɡɒn/ *interjection poetical* go away at once!

begonia /bɪˈɡəʊnɪə/ *noun* plant with ornamental foliage and bright flowers.

begot *past* of BEGET.

begotten *past participle* of BEGET.

begrudge /bɪˈɡrʌdʒ/ *verb* (**-ging**) grudge; feel or show resentment at or envy of; be dissatisfied at.

beguile /bɪˈɡaɪl/ *verb* (**-ling**) charm, divert; delude, cheat. □ **beguilement** *noun*.

beguine /bɪˈɡiːn/ *noun* W. Indian dance.

begum /ˈbeɪɡəm/ *noun* (in India, Pakistan, and Bangladesh) Muslim woman of high rank; (**Begum**) *title of married Muslim woman*.

begun *past participle* of BEGIN.

behalf /bɪˈhɑːf/ *noun* □ **on behalf of, on (person's) behalf** in the interests of, as representative of.

behave /bɪˈheɪv/ *verb* (**-ving**) react or act in specified way; (often **behave oneself**) conduct oneself properly; work well (or in specified way).

behaviour /bɪˈheɪvjə/ *noun* (US **behavior**) manners, conduct, way of behaving. □ **behavioural** *adjective*.

behaviourism *noun* (US **behaviorism**) study of human actions by analysis of stimulus and response. □ **behaviourist** *noun*.

behead /bɪˈhed/ *verb* cut head from (person); execute thus.

beheld *past & past participle* of BEHOLD.

behest /bɪˈhest/ *noun literary* command, request.

behind /bɪˈhaɪnd/ ● *preposition* in or to rear of; hidden by, on farther side of; in past in relation to; inferior to; in support of. ● *adverb* in or to rear; on far side; remaining after others' departure; (usually + *with*) in arrears. ● *noun colloquial* buttocks. □ **behindhand** in arrears, behind time, too late; **behind time** unpunctual; **behind the times** old-fashioned, antiquated.

behold /bɪˈhəʊld/ *verb* (*past & past participle* **beheld**) *literary* look at; take notice, observe.

beholden /bɪˈhəʊld(ə)n/ *adjective* (usually + *to*) under obligation.

behove /bɪˈhəʊv/ *verb* (**-ving**) *formal* be incumbent on; befit.

beige /beɪʒ/ ● *noun* pale sandy fawn colour. ● *adjective* of this colour.

being /ˈbiːɪŋ/ *noun* existence; constitution, nature; existing person etc.

belabour /bɪˈleɪbə/ *verb* (US **belabor**) attack physically or verbally.

belated /bɪˈleɪtɪd/ *adjective* coming (too) late. □ **belatedly** *adverb*.

bel canto /bel ˈkæntəʊ/ *noun* singing marked by full rich tone.

belch ● *verb* emit wind from stomach through mouth; (of volcano, gun, etc.) emit (fire, smoke, etc.). ● *noun* act of belching.

beleaguer /bɪˈliːɡə/ *verb* besiege; vex; harass.

belfry /ˈbelfrɪ/ *noun* (*plural* **-ies**) bell tower; space for bells in church tower.

belie /bɪˈlaɪ/ *verb* (**belying**) give false impression of; fail to confirm, fulfil, or justify.

belief /bɪˈliːf/ *noun* act of believing; what one believes; trust, confidence; acceptance as true.

believe /bɪˈliːv/ *verb* (**-ving**) accept as true; think; (+ *in*) have faith or confidence in; trust word of; have religious faith. □ **believable** *adjective*; **believer** *noun*.

Belisha beacon /bəˈliːʃə/ *noun* flashing orange ball on striped post, marking pedestrian crossing.

belittle /bɪˈlɪt(ə)l/ *verb* (**-ling**) disparage. □ **belittlement** *noun*.

bell *noun* hollow esp. cup-shaped metal body emitting musical sound when struck; sound of bell; bell-shaped thing. □ **bell-bottomed** (of trousers) widening below knee; **bell pull** cord pulled to sound bell; **bell push** button pressed to ring electric bell; **give (person) a bell** *colloquial* telephone him or her.

belladonna /beləˈdɒnə/ *noun* deadly nightshade; drug obtained from this.

belle /bel/ *noun* handsome woman; reigning beauty.

belles-lettres /bel ˈletr/ *plural noun* (also treated as *singular*) writings or studies of purely literary kind.

bellicose /ˈbelɪkəʊs/ *adjective* eager to fight.

belligerent /bɪˈlɪdʒərənt/ ● *adjective* engaged in war; given to constant fighting; pugnacious. ● *noun* belligerent person or nation. □ **belligerence** *noun*.

bellow /ˈbeləʊ/ ● *verb* emit deep loud roar. ● *noun* bellowing sound.

bellows /ˈbeləʊz/ *plural noun* (also treated as *singular*) device for driving air into fire, organ, etc.; expandable part of camera etc.

belly /ˈbelɪ/ ● *noun* (*plural* **-ies**) cavity of body containing stomach, bowels, etc.; stomach; front of body from waist to groin; underside of animal; cavity or bulging part of anything. ● *verb* (**-ies, -ied**) swell out. □ **bellyache** *noun colloquial* stomach pain, *verb slang* complain noisily or persistently; **belly button** *colloquial* navel; **belly dance** dance by woman (**belly dancer**) with voluptuous movements of belly; **belly laugh** loud unrestrained laugh.

bellyful *noun* enough to eat; *colloquial* more than one can tolerate.

belong /bɪˈlɒŋ/ *verb* (+ *to*) be property of, assigned to, or member of; fit socially; be rightly placed or classified.

belongings *plural noun* possessions, luggage.

beloved /bɪˈlʌvɪd/ ● *adjective* loved. ● *noun* beloved person.

below /bɪˈləʊ/ ● *preposition* under; lower than; less than; of lower rank or importance etc. than; unworthy of. ● *adverb* at or to lower point or level; further on in book etc.

belt ● *noun* strip of leather etc. worn round waist or across chest; continuous band in machinery; distinct strip of colour etc.; zone, district. ● *verb* put belt round; *slang* thrash; *slang* move rapidly. □ **below the belt** unfair(ly); **belt out** *slang* sing or play (music) loudly; **belt up** *slang* be quiet, *colloquial* put on seat belt; **tighten one's belt** economize; **under one's belt** securely acquired.

bemoan /bɪˈməʊn/ *verb* lament, complain about.

bemuse /bɪˈmjuːz/ *verb* (**-sing**) make (person) confused.

bench *noun* long seat of wood or stone; carpenter's or laboratory table; magistrate's or judge's seat; lawcourt. □ **benchmark** surveyor's mark at point in line of levels; standard, point of reference.

bend ● *verb* (*past & past participle* **bent** except in *bended knee*) force into curve or angle; be altered in this way; incline from vertical; bow, stoop; interpret or modify (rule) to suit oneself; (force to) submit. ● *noun* bending, curve; bent part of thing; **(the bends)** *colloquial* symptoms due to too rapid decompression under water. □ **round the bend** *colloquial* crazy, insane.

bender *noun slang* wild drinking spree.

beneath /bɪˈniːθ/ ● *preposition* below, under; unworthy of. ● *adverb* below, underneath.

Benedictine /benɪˈdɪktɪn/ ● *noun* monk or nun of Order of St Benedict; /-tiːn/ *proprietary term* kind of liqueur. ● *adjective* of St Benedict or his order.

benediction /benɪˈdɪkʃ(ə)n/ *noun* utterance of blessing. □ **benedictory** *adjective*.

benefaction /benɪˈfækʃ(ə)n/ *noun* charitable gift; doing good.

benefactor /ˈbenɪfæktə/ *noun* (*feminine* **benefactress**) person who has given financial or other help.

benefice /ˈbenɪfɪs/ *noun* living from a church office.

beneficent /bɪˈnefɪsənt/ *adjective* doing good; actively kind. □ **beneficence** *noun*.

beneficial /benɪˈfɪʃ(ə)l/ *adjective* advantageous. □ **beneficially** *adverb*.

beneficiary /benɪˈfɪʃərɪ/ *noun* (*plural* **-ies**) receiver of benefits; holder of church living.

benefit /ˈbenɪfɪt/ ● *noun* advantage, profit; payment made under insurance or social security; performance or game etc. of which proceeds go to particular player or charity. ● *verb* (**-t-**; *US* **-tt-**) do good to; receive benefit. □ **benefit of the doubt** assumption of innocence rather than guilt.

benevolent /bɪˈnevələnt/ *adjective* wishing to do good; charitable; kind and helpful. □ **benevolence** *noun*.

Bengali /beŋˈɡɔːlɪ/ ● *noun* (*plural* **-s**) native or language of Bengal. ● *adjective* of Bengal.

benighted /bɪˈnaɪtɪd/ *adjective* intellectually or morally ignorant.

benign /bɪˈnaɪn/ *adjective* kindly, gentle; favourable; salutary; *Medicine* mild, not malignant. □ **benignity** /bɪˈnɪɡnɪtɪ/ *noun*.

benignant /bɪˈnɪɡnənt/ *adjective* kindly; beneficial. □ **benignancy** *noun*.

bent ● *past & past participle* of BEND. ● *adjective* curved or having angle; *slang* dishonest, illicit; (+ *on*) set on doing or having. ● *noun* inclination, bias; (+ *for*) talent for.

benumb /bɪˈnʌm/ *verb* make numb; deaden; paralyse.

benzene /ˈbenziːn/ *noun* chemical got from coal tar and used as solvent.

benzine /ˈbenziːn/ *noun* spirit obtained from petroleum and used as cleaning agent.

benzoin /ˈbenzəʊɪn/ *noun* fragrant resin of E. Asian tree. □ **benzoic** /-ˈzəʊɪk/ *adjective*.

bequeath /bɪˈkwiːð/ *verb* leave by will; transmit to posterity.

bequest /bɪˈkwest/ *noun* bequeathing; thing bequeathed.

berate /bɪˈreɪt/ *verb* (**-ting**) scold.

bereave /bɪˈriːv/ *verb* (**-ving**) (esp. as **bereaved** *adjective*) (often + *of*) deprive of relative, friend, etc., esp. by death. □ **bereavement** *noun*.

bereft /bɪˈreft/ *adjective* (+ *of*) deprived of.

beret /ˈbereɪ/ *noun* round flat brimless cap of felt etc.

berg *noun* iceberg.

bergamot /ˈbɜːɡəmɒt/ *noun* perfume from fruit of a dwarf orange tree; an aromatic herb.

beriberi /berɪˈberɪ/ *noun* nervous disease caused by deficiency of vitamin B'.

Bermuda shorts /bəˈmjuːdə/ *plural noun* close-fitting knee-length shorts.

berry /ˈberɪ/ *noun* (*plural* **-ies**) any small round juicy stoneless fruit.

berserk /bəˈzɜːk/ *adjective* (esp. after *go*) wild, frenzied.

berth ● *noun* sleeping place; ship's place at wharf; searoom; *colloquial* situation, appointment. ● *verb* moor (ship) in berth; provide sleeping berth for.

beryl /ˈberɪl/ *noun* transparent (esp. green) precious stone; mineral species including this and emerald.

beryllium /bəˈrɪlɪəm/ *noun* hard white metallic element.

beseech /bɪˈsiːtʃ/ *verb* (*past & past participle* **besought** /-ˈsɔːt/ or **beseeched**) entreat; ask earnestly for.

beset /bɪˈset/ *verb* (**-tt-**; *past & past participle* **beset**) attack or harass persistently.

beside /bɪˈsaɪd/ *preposition* at side of, close to; compared with; irrelevant to. □ **beside oneself** frantic with anger or worry etc.

besides ● *preposition* in addition to; apart from. ● *adverb* also, as well.

besiege /bɪˈsiːdʒ/ *verb* (**-ging**) lay siege to; crowd round eagerly; assail with requests.

besmirch /bɪˈsmɜːtʃ/ *verb* soil, dishonour.

besom /ˈbiːz(ə)m/ *noun* broom made of twigs.

besotted /bɪˈsɒtɪd/ *adjective* infatuated; stupefied.

besought *past & past participle* of BESEECH.

bespatter /bɪˈspætə/ *verb* spatter all over; defame.

bespeak /bɪˈspiːk/ *verb* (*past* **bespoke**; *past participle* **bespoken**) engage beforehand; order (goods); be evidence of.

bespectacled /bɪˈspektək(ə)ld/ *adjective* wearing spectacles.

bespoke /bɪˈspəʊk/ *adjective* made to order.

best ● *adjective* (*superlative* of GOOD) most excellent. ● *adverb* (*superlative* of WELL¹) in the best way; to greatest degree. ● *noun* that which is best. ● *verb colloquial* defeat, outwit. □ **best man** bridegroom's chief attendant at wedding; **best-seller** book with large sale, author of such book; **do one's best** do all one can.

bestial /ˈbestɪəl/ *adjective* brutish; of or like beasts. □ **bestiality** /-ˈæl-/ *noun*.

bestiary /ˈbestɪərɪ/ *noun* (*plural* **-ies**) medieval treatise on beasts.

bestir /bɪˈstɜː/ *verb* (**-rr-**) (**bestir oneself**) exert or rouse oneself.

bestow /bɪˈstəʊ/ *verb* (+ *on*, *upon*) confer as gift. □ **bestowal** *noun*.

bestrew /bɪˈstruː/ *verb* (*past participle* **bestrewed** or **bestrewn**) strew; lie scattered over.

bestride /bɪ'straɪd/ verb (**-ding**; past **bestrode**; past participle **bestridden**) sit astride on; stand astride over.

bet ● verb (**-tt-**; past & past participle **bet** or **betted**) risk one's money etc. against another's on result of event. ● noun such arrangement; sum of money bet.

beta /'biːtə/ noun second letter of Greek alphabet (Β, β). □ **beta-blocker** drug used to prevent unwanted stimulation of the heart in angina etc.; **beta particle** fast-moving electron emitted by radioactive substance.

betake /bɪ'teɪk/ verb (**-king**; past **betook**; past participle **betaken**) (**betake oneself**) go.

betatron /'biːtətrɒn/ noun apparatus for accelerating electrons.

betel /'biːt(ə)l/ noun leaf chewed with betel-nut. □ **betel-nut** seed of tropical palm.

bête noire /beɪt 'nwɑː/ noun (plural **bêtes noires** same pronunciation) particularly disliked person or thing. [French]

bethink /bɪ'θɪŋk/ verb (past & past participle **bethought** /-'θɔːt/) (**bethink oneself**) formal reflect, stop to think; be reminded.

betide /bɪ'taɪd/ verb □ **woe betide (person)** misfortune will befall him or her.

betimes /bɪ'taɪmz/ adverb literary in good time, early.

betoken /bɪ'təʊkən/ verb be sign of.

betook past of BETAKE.

betray /bɪ'treɪ/ verb be disloyal to (a person, one's country, etc.); give up or reveal treacherously; reveal involuntarily; be evidence of. □ **betrayal** noun.

betroth /bɪ'trəʊð/ verb (usually as **betrothed** adjective) bind with promise to marry. □ **betrothal** noun.

better /'betə/ ● adjective (comparative of GOOD) more excellent; partly or fully recovered from illness. ● adverb (comparative of WELL[1]) in better manner; to greater degree. ● noun better thing or person. ● verb improve (upon); surpass. □ **better off** in better (esp. financial) situation; **get the better of** defeat, outwit.

betterment noun improvement.

between /bɪ'twiːn/ ● preposition in or into space or interval; separating; shared by; to and from; taking one or other of. ● adverb (also **in between**) between two or more points, between two extremes.

bevel /'bev(ə)l/ ● noun slope from horizontal or vertical in carpentry etc.; sloping edge or surface; tool for marking angles. ● verb (**-ll-**; US **-l-**) impart bevel to, slant.

beverage /'bevərɪdʒ/ noun formal drink.

bevvy /'bevɪ/ slang ● noun (plural **-ies**) ● verb (**-ies**, **-ied**) drink.

bevy /'bevɪ/ noun (plural **-ies**) company, flock.

bewail /bɪ'weɪl/ verb wail over; mourn for.

beware /bɪ'weə/ verb (only in imperative or infinitive) take heed; (+ of) be cautious of.

bewilder /bɪ'wɪldə/ verb perplex, confuse. □ **bewilderment** noun.

bewitch /bɪ'wɪtʃ/ verb enchant, greatly delight; cast spell on.

beyond /bɪ'jɒnd/ ● preposition at or to further side of; outside the range or understanding of; more than. ● adverb at or to further side, further on. ● noun (**the beyond**) life after death. □ **back of beyond** very remote place.

bezel /'bez(ə)l/ noun sloped edge of chisel etc.; oblique face of cut gem; groove holding watch-glass or gem.

bezique /bɪ'ziːk/ noun card game for two.

biannual /baɪ'ænjʊəl/ adjective occurring etc. twice a year.

bias /'baɪəs/ ● noun predisposition, prejudice; distortion of statistical results; edge cut obliquely across weave of fabric; Sport bowl's curved course

due to its lopsided form. ● verb (**-s-** or **-ss-**) give bias to; prejudice; (as **biased** adjective) influenced (usually unfairly). □ **bias binding** strip of fabric cut obliquely and used to bind edges.

biathlon /baɪ'æθlən/ noun athletic contest in skiing and shooting. □ **biathlete** noun.

bib noun cloth put under child's chin while eating; upper part of apron etc.

Bible /'baɪb(ə)l/ noun Christian scriptures; (**bible**) copy of these; (**bible**) colloquial any authoritative book. □ **biblical** /'bɪb-/ adjective.

bibliography /bɪblɪ'ɒgrəfɪ/ noun (plural **-ies**) list of books of any author, subject, etc.; history of books, their editions, etc. □ **bibliographer** noun; **bibliographical** /-ə'græf-/ adjective.

bibliophile /'bɪblɪəfaɪl/ noun collector of books, booklover.

bibulous /'bɪbjʊləs/ adjective fond of or addicted to alcoholic drink.

bicameral /baɪ'kæmər(ə)l/ adjective having two legislative chambers.

bicarb /'baɪkɑːb/ noun colloquial bicarbonate of soda.

bicarbonate /baɪ'kɑːbənɪt/ noun any acid salt of carbonic acid; (in full **bicarbonate of soda**) compound used in cooking and as antacid.

bicentenary /baɪsen'tiːnərɪ/ noun (plural **-ies**) 200th anniversary.

bicentennial /baɪsen'tenɪəl/ ● noun bicentenary. ● adjective recurring every 200 years.

biceps /'baɪseps/ noun (plural same) muscle with double head or attachment, esp. that at front of upper arm.

bicker /'bɪkə/ verb quarrel, wrangle pettily.

bicuspid /baɪ'kʌspɪd/ ● adjective having two cusps. ● noun bicuspid premolar tooth.

bicycle /'baɪsɪk(ə)l/ ● noun two-wheeled pedal-driven vehicle. ● verb (**-ling**) ride bicycle.

bid ● verb (**-dd-**; past **bid**, archaic **bade** /bæd, beɪd/; past participle **bid**, archaic **bidden**) make offer; make bid; command, invite; literary utter (greeting, farewell) to; Cards state before play number of tricks intended. ● noun act of bidding; amount bid; colloquial attempt, effort.

biddable adjective obedient, docile.

bidding noun command, invitation.

bide verb (**-ding**) archaic or dialect stay, remain. □ **bide one's time** wait for good opportunity.

bidet /'biːdeɪ/ noun low basin that one can sit astride to wash crotch area.

biennial /baɪ'enɪəl/ ● adjective lasting 2 years; recurring every 2 years. ● noun plant that flowers, fruits, and dies in second year.

bier /bɪə/ noun movable stand on which coffin or corpse rests.

biff slang ● noun smart blow. ● verb strike.

bifid /'baɪfɪd/ adjective divided by cleft into two parts.

bifocal /baɪ'fəʊk(ə)l/ ● adjective (of spectacle lenses) with two parts of different focal lengths. ● noun (in plural) bifocal spectacles.

bifurcate /'baɪfəkeɪt/ verb (**-ting**) divide into two branches; fork. □ **bifurcation** noun.

big ● adjective (**-gg-**) large; important; grown-up; boastful; colloquial ambitious, generous; (usually + with) advanced in pregnancy. ● adverb colloquial in big manner; with great effect, impressively. □ **Big Apple** US slang New York City; **Big Brother** seemingly benevolent dictator; **big business** large-scale commerce; **big end** end of connecting rod in engine, encircling crank-pin; **big-head** colloquial conceited person; **big-headed** conceited; **big-hearted** generous; **big shot** colloquial important person; **big time** slang highest rank among entertainers; **big top** main tent at circus;

bigwig *colloquial* important person; **in a big way** *colloquial* with great enthusiasm. □ **biggish** *adjective*.

bigamy /'bɪgəmɪ/ *noun* (*plural* **-ies**) crime of making second marriage while first is still valid. □ **bigamist** *noun*; **bigamous** *adjective*.

bight /baɪt/ *noun* recess of coast, bay; loop of rope.

bigot /'bɪgət/ *noun* obstinate and intolerant adherent of creed or view. □ **bigoted** *adjective*; **bigotry** *noun*.

bijou /'biːʒuː/ ● *noun* (*plural* **-x** same pronunciation) jewel, trinket. ● *adjective* (**bijou**) small and elegant. [French]

bike *colloquial* ● *noun* bicycle; motorcycle. ● *verb* (**-king**) ride a bike. □ **biker** *noun*.

bikini /bɪ'kiːnɪ/ *noun* (*plural* **-s**) woman's brief two-piece bathing suit.

bilateral /baɪ'lætər(ə)l/ *adjective* of, on, or with two sides; between two parties. □ **bilaterally** *adverb*.

bilberry /'bɪlbərɪ/ *noun* (*plural* **-ies**) N. European heath-land shrub; its small dark blue edible berry.

bile *noun* bitter fluid secreted by liver to aid digestion; bad temper, peevishness.

bilge /bɪldʒ/ *noun* nearly flat part of ship's bottom; (in full **bilge-water**) foul water in bilge; *slang* nonsense, rubbish.

bilharzia /bɪl'hɑːtsɪə/ *noun* disease caused by tropical parasitic flatworm.

biliary /'bɪlɪərɪ/ *adjective* of bile.

bilingual /baɪ'lɪŋgw(ə)l/ *adjective* of, in, or speaking two languages.

bilious /'bɪlɪəs/ *adjective* affected by disorder of the bile; bad-tempered.

bilk *verb slang* evade payment of, cheat.

bill¹ ● *noun* statement of charges for goods, work done, etc.; draft of proposed law; poster; programme of entertainment; *US* banknote. ● *verb* send statement of charges to; announce; put in programme; (+ *as*) advertise as. □ **bill of exchange** written order to pay sum on given date; **bill of fare** menu; **billposter**, **billsticker** person who pastes up advertisements on hoardings etc.

bill² ● *noun* beak of bird; narrow promontory. ● *verb* (of doves etc.) stroke bill with bill. □ **bill and coo** exchange caresses.

bill³ *noun historical* weapon with hook-shaped blade.

billabong /'bɪləbɒŋ/ *noun Australian* branch of river forming backwater.

billboard *noun* large outdoor board for advertisements.

billet¹ /'bɪlɪt/ ● *noun* place where soldier etc. is lodged; *colloquial* appointment, job. ● *verb* (**-t-**) quarter (soldiers etc.).

billet² /'bɪlɪt/ *noun* thick piece of firewood; small metal bar.

billet-doux /bɪlɪ'duː/ *noun* (*plural* **billets-doux** /-'duːz/) love letter.

billhook *noun* concave-edged pruning-instrument.

billiards /'bɪljədz/ *noun* game played with cues and 3 balls on cloth-covered table. □ **billiard ball, room, table**, etc., ones used for billiards.

billion /'bɪljən/ *noun* (*plural* same) thousand million; million million; (**billions**) *colloquial* very large number. □ **billionth** *adjective & noun*.

billow /'bɪləʊ/ ● *noun* wave; any large mass. ● *verb* rise or move in billows. □ **billowy** *adjective*.

billy¹ /'bɪlɪ/ *noun* (*plural* **-ies**) (in full **billycan**) *Australian* tin or enamel outdoor cooking pot.

billy² /'bɪlɪ/ *noun* (*plural* **-ies**) (in full **billy goat**) male goat.

bin *noun* large receptacle for rubbish or storage. □ **bin-liner** bag for lining rubbish bin; **binman** *colloquial* dustman.

binary /'baɪnərɪ/ *adjective* of two parts, dual; of system using digits 0 and 1 to code information.

bind /baɪnd/ ● *verb* (*past & past participle* **bound** /baʊnd/) tie or fasten tightly; restrain; (cause to) cohere; compel, impose duty on; edge with braid etc.; fasten (pages of book) into cover. ● *noun colloquial* nuisance; restriction.

binder *noun* cover for loose papers; substance that binds things together; *historical* sheaf-binding machine; bookbinder.

bindery *noun* (*plural* **-ies**) bookbinder's workshop.

binding ● *noun* book cover; braid etc. for edging. ● *adjective* obligatory.

bindweed *noun* convolvulus.

binge /bɪndʒ/ *slang* ● *noun* bout of excessive eating, drinking, etc.; spree. ● *verb* (**-ging**) indulge in binge.

bingo /'bɪŋgəʊ/ *noun* gambling game in which each player marks off numbers on card as they are called.

binnacle /'bɪnæk(ə)l/ *noun* case for ship's compass.

binocular /baɪ'nɒkjʊlə/ *adjective* for both eyes.

binoculars /bɪ'nɒkjʊləz/ *plural noun* instrument with lens for each eye, for viewing distant objects.

binomial /baɪ'nəʊmɪəl/ ● *noun* algebraic expression of sum or difference of two terms. ● *adjective* consisting of two terms.

bio- *combining form* biological; life.

biochemistry /baɪəʊ'kemɪstrɪ/ *noun* chemistry of living organisms. □ **biochemical** *adjective*; **biochemist** *noun*.

biodegradable /baɪəʊdɪ'greɪdəb(ə)l/ *adjective* able to be decomposed by bacteria or other living organisms.

biography /baɪ'ɒgrəfɪ/ *noun* (*plural* **-ies**) written life of person. □ **biographer** *noun*; **biographical** /-ə'græf-/ *adjective*.

biological /baɪə'lɒdʒɪk(ə)l/ *adjective* of biology; of living organisms. □ **biological warfare** use of bacteria etc. to spread disease among enemy. □ **biologically** *adverb*.

biology /baɪ'ɒlədʒɪ/ *noun* study of living organisms. □ **biologist** *noun*.

bionic /baɪ'ɒnɪk/ *adjective* having electronically operated body parts.

biorhythm /'baɪəʊrɪð(ə)m/ *noun* biological cycle thought to affect person's physical or mental state.

biosphere /'baɪəʊsfɪə/ *noun* earth's crust and atmosphere containing life.

bipartite /baɪ'pɑːtaɪt/ *adjective* of two parts; involving two parties.

biped /'baɪped/ ● *noun* two-footed animal. ● *adjective* two-footed.

biplane /'baɪpleɪn/ *noun* aeroplane with two pairs of wings, one above the other.

birch ● *noun* tree with thin peeling bark; bundle of birch twigs used for flogging. ● *verb* flog with birch.

bird *noun* feathered vertebrate with two wings and two feet; *slang* young woman. □ **a bird in the hand** something secured or certain; **birdlime** sticky stuff spread to catch birds; **bird of passage** migratory bird, person who travels habitually; **bird of prey** one hunting animals for food; **birdseed** seeds as food for caged birds; **bird's-eye view** general view from above; **birds of a feather** similar people; **bird table** platform on which food for wild birds is placed.

birdie /'bɜːdɪ/ *noun colloquial* little bird; *Golf* hole played in one under par.

biretta /bɪ'retə/ *noun* square cap of RC priest.

Biro /'baɪərəʊ/ *noun* (*plural* **-s**) *proprietary term* kind of ballpoint pen.

birth *noun* emergence of young from mother's body; origin, beginning; ancestry; inherited position. □ **birth control** prevention of undesired pregnancy;

birthday anniversary of birth; **birthmark** unusual mark on body from birth; **birth rate** number of live births per thousand of population per year; **birthright** rights belonging to one by birth; **give birth to** produce (young).

biscuit /'bɪskɪt/ noun thin unleavened cake, usually crisp and sweet; fired unglazed pottery; light brown colour.

bisect /bar'sekt/ verb divide into two (usually equal) parts. □ **bisection** noun; **bisector** noun.

bisexual /bar'sekʃʊəl/ ● adjective feeling or involving sexual attraction to members of both sexes; hermaphrodite. ● noun bisexual person. □ **bisexuality** /-'æl-/ noun.

bishop /'bɪʃəp/ noun senior clergyman usually in charge of diocese; mitre-shaped chess piece.

bishopric /'bɪʃəprɪk/ noun office or diocese of bishop.

bismuth /'bɪzməθ/ noun reddish-white metallic element; compound of it used medicinally.

bison /'baɪs(ə)n/ noun (plural same) wild ox.

bisque¹ /bi:sk/ noun rich soup.

bisque² /bɪsk/ noun advantage of one free point or stroke in certain games.

bisque³ /bɪsk/ noun fired unglazed pottery.

bistre /'bɪstə/ noun brown pigment made from soot.

bistro /'bi:strəʊ/ noun (plural **-s**) small informal restaurant.

bit¹ noun small piece or amount; short time or distance; mouthpiece of bridle; cutting part of tool etc. ● **bit by bit** gradually.

bit² past of BITE.

bit³ noun Computing unit of information expressed as choice between two possibilities.

bitch /bɪtʃ/ ● noun female dog, fox, or wolf; offensive slang spiteful woman. ● verb colloquial speak spitefully; grumble.

bitchy adjective slang spiteful. □ **bitchily** adverb; **bitchiness** noun.

bite ● verb (**-ting**; past **bit**; past participle **bitten**) nip or cut into or off with teeth; sting; penetrate, grip; accept bait; be harsh in effect, esp. intentionally. ● noun act of biting; wound so made; small amount to eat; pungency; incisiveness.

bitter /'bɪtə/ ● adjective having sharp pungent taste, not sweet; showing or feeling resentment; harsh, virulent; piercingly cold. ● noun bitter beer, strongly flavoured with hops; (in plural) liquor with bitter flavour, esp. of wormwood. □ **bitterly** adverb; **bitterness** noun.

bittern /'bɪt(ə)n/ noun wading bird of heron family.

bitty adjective (**-ier, -iest**) made up of bits.

bitumen /'bɪtjʊmɪn/ noun tarlike mixture of hydrocarbons derived from petroleum. □ **bituminous** /bɪ'tju:mɪnəs/ adjective.

bivalve /'baɪvælv/ ● noun aquatic mollusc with hinged double shell. ● adjective with such a shell.

bivouac /'bɪvʊæk/ ● noun temporary encampment without tents. ● verb (**-ck-**) make, or camp in, bivouac.

bizarre /bɪ'zɑ:/ adjective strange in appearance or effect; grotesque.

blab verb (**-bb-**) talk or tell foolishly or indiscreetly.

black ● adjective colourless from absence or complete absorption of light; very dark-coloured; (of human group with dark skin, as African; heavily overcast; angry, gloomy; sinister, wicked; declared untouchable by workers in dispute. ● noun black colour, paint, clothes, etc.; (player using) darker pieces in chess etc.; (of tea or coffee) without milk; member of dark-skinned race, esp. African. ● verb make black; declare (goods etc.) 'black'. □ **black and blue** badly bruised; **black and white** not in colour, comprising

only opposite extremes, (after in) in print; **black art** black magic; **blackball** exclude from club, society, etc.; **black beetle** common cockroach; **black belt** (holder of) highest grade of proficiency in judo, karate, etc.; **black box** flight recorder; **black comedy** comedy presenting tragedy in comic terms; **black eye** bruised skin round eye; **blackfly** kind of aphid; **Black Forest gateau** chocolate sponge with cherries and whipped cream; **blackhead** black-topped pimple; **black hole** region of space from which matter and radiation cannot escape; **black ice** thin hard transparent ice; **blacklead** graphite; **blackleg** derogatory person refusing to join strike etc.; **black magic** magic supposed to invoke evil spirits; **Black Maria** slang police van; **black market** illicit traffic in rationed, prohibited, or scarce commodities; **Black Mass** travesty of Mass in worship of Satan; **black out** effect blackout on, undergo blackout; **blackout** temporary loss of consciousness or memory; loss of electric power, radio reception, etc.; compulsory darkness as precaution against air raids; **black pudding** sausage of blood, suet, etc.; **Black Rod** chief usher of House of Lords; **black sheep** disreputable member; **blackshirt** historical Fascist; **black spot** place of danger or trouble; **blackthorn** thorny shrub bearing white flowers and sloes; **black tie** man's formal evening dress; **black velvet** mixture of stout and champagne; **black widow** venomous spider of which female devours male; **in the black** in credit or surplus.

blackberry noun (plural **-ies**) dark edible fruit of bramble.

blackbird noun European songbird.

blackboard noun board for chalking on in classroom etc.

blackcurrant noun small black fruit; shrub on which it grows.

blacken verb make or become black; slander.

blackguard /'blægɑ:d/ noun villain, scoundrel. □ **blackguardly** adjective.

blacking noun black polish for boots and shoes.

blacklist ● noun list of people etc. in disfavour. ● verb put on blacklist.

blackmail ● noun extortion of payment in return for silence; use of threats or pressure. ● verb extort money from (person) thus. □ **blackmailer** noun.

blacksmith noun smith working in iron.

bladder /'blædə/ noun sac in humans and other animals, esp. that holding urine.

blade noun cutting part of knife etc.; flat part of oar, spade, propeller, etc.; flat narrow leaf of grass and cereals; flat bone in shoulder.

blame ● verb (**-ming**) assign fault or responsibility to; (+ on) assign responsibility for (error etc.) to. ● noun responsibility for bad result; blaming, attributing of responsibility. □ **blameworthy** deserving blame. □ **blameless** adjective.

blanch /blɑ:ntʃ/ verb make or grow pale; peel (almonds etc.) by scalding; immerse briefly in boiling water; whiten (plant) by depriving it of light.

blancmange /blə'mɒndʒ/ noun sweet opaque jelly of flavoured cornflour and milk.

bland adjective mild; insipid, tasteless; gentle, suave. □ **blandly** adverb.

blandishment /'blændɪʃmənt/ noun (usually in plural) flattering attention; cajolery.

blank ● adjective not written or printed on; (of form etc.) not filled in; (of space) empty; without interest, result, or expression. ● noun space to be filled up in form etc.; blank cartridge; empty surface; dash written in place of word. □ **blank cartridge** one without bullet; **blank cheque** one with amount left

for payee to fill in; **blank verse** unrhymed verse,
esp. iambic pentameters. □ **blankly** adverb.

blanket /'blæŋkɪt/ ● noun large esp. woollen sheet
as bed-covering etc.; thick covering layer. ● adjective
general, covering all cases or classes. ● verb (**-t-**)
cover (as) with blanket. □ **blanket stitch** stitch
used to finish edges of blanket etc.

blare ● verb (**-ring**) sound or utter loudly; make sound
of trumpet. ● noun blaring sound.

blarney /'blɑːnɪ/ ● noun cajoling talk, flattery. ● verb
(**-eys, -eyed**) flatter, use blarney.

blasé /'blɑːzeɪ/ adjective bored or indifferent, esp.
through familiarity.

blaspheme /blæs'fiːm/ verb (**-ming**) treat religious
name or subject irreverently; talk irreverently
about.

blasphemy /'blæsfəmɪ/ noun (plural **-ies**) (instance of)
blaspheming. □ **blasphemous** adjective.

blast /blɑːst/ ● noun strong gust; explosion; destructive wave of air from this; loud note from wind
instrument, car horn, whistle, etc.; colloquial severe
reprimand. ● verb blow up with explosive; blight;
(cause to) make explosive sound. ● interjection damn.
□ **blast furnace** one for smelting with compressed
hot air driven in; **blast off** (of rocket) take off from
launching site; **blast-off** noun.

blasted colloquial ● adjective annoying. ● adverb extremely.

blatant /'bleɪt(ə)nt/ adjective flagrant, unashamed.
□ **blatantly** adverb.

blather /'blæðə/ ● noun (also **blether** /'bleðə/) foolish talk. ● verb talk foolishly.

blaze[1] ● noun bright flame or fire; violent outburst
of passion; bright display or light. ● verb (**-zing**) burn
or shine brightly or fiercely; burn with excitement
etc. □ **blaze away** shoot continuously.

blaze[2] ● noun white mark on face of horse or chipped
in bark of tree. ● verb (**-zing**) mark (tree, path) with
blaze(s).

blazer noun jacket without matching trousers, esp.
lightweight and part of uniform.

blazon /'bleɪz(ə)n/ verb proclaim; describe or paint
(coat of arms). □ **blazonry** noun.

bleach ● verb whiten in sunlight or by chemical
process. ● noun bleaching substance or process.

bleak adjective exposed, windswept; dreary, grim.

bleary /'blɪərɪ/ adjective (**-ier, -iest**) dim-sighted,
blurred. □ **bleary-eyed** having dim sight.

bleat ● verb utter cry of sheep, goat, etc.; speak plaintively. ● noun bleating cry.

bleed verb (past & past participle **bled**) emit blood; draw
blood from; colloquial extort money from.

bleep ● noun intermittent high-pitched sound. ● verb
make bleep; summon by bleep.

bleeper noun small electronic device alerting person
to message by bleeping.

blemish /'blemɪʃ/ ● noun flaw, defect, stain. ● verb
spoil, mark, stain.

blench verb flinch, quail.

blend ● verb mix (various sorts) into required sort;
become one; mingle intimately. ● noun mixture.

blender noun machine for liquidizing or chopping
food.

blenny /'blenɪ/ noun (plural **-ies**) spiny-finned sea fish.

bless verb ask God to look favourably on; consecrate;
glorify (God); thank; make happy.

blessed /'blesɪd/ adjective holy; euphemistic cursed; RC
Church beatified.

blessing noun invocation of divine favour; grace said
at meals; benefit, advantage.

blether = BLATHER.

blew past of BLOW[1].

blight /blaɪt/ ● noun disease of plants caused esp. by
insects; such insect; harmful or destructive force.
● verb affect with blight; destroy; spoil.

blighter noun colloquial annoying person.

blimey /'blaɪmɪ/ interjection slang: expressing surprise.

blimp noun small non-rigid airship; (also (**Colonel**)
Blimp) reactionary person.

blind /blaɪnd/ ● adjective without sight; without adequate foresight, discernment, or information; (often
+ **to**) unwilling or unable to appreciate (a factor);
not governed by purpose; reckless; concealed; closed
at one end. ● verb deprive of sight or judgement;
deceive. ● noun screen for window; thing used to
hide truth; obstruction to sight or light. ● adverb
blindly. □ **blind date** colloquial date between two
people who have not met before; **blind man's buff**
game in which blindfold player tries to catch others;
blind spot spot on retina insensitive to light, area
where vision or judgement fails; **blindworm** slow-
worm. □ **blindly** adverb; **blindness** noun.

blindfold ● verb cover eyes of (person) with tied cloth
etc. ● noun cloth etc. so used. ● adjective & adverb with
eyes covered; without due care.

blink ● verb shut and open eyes quickly; (often +
back) prevent (tears) by blinking; shine unsteadily,
flicker. ● noun act of blinking; momentary gleam.
□ **blink at** ignore, shirk; **on the blink** slang (of
machine etc.) out of order.

blinker ● noun (usually in plural) either of screens on
bridle preventing horse from seeing sideways. ● verb
obscure with blinkers; (as **blinkered** adjective) prejudiced, narrow-minded.

blinking adjective & adverb slang: expressing mild annoyance.

blip noun minor deviation or error; quick popping
sound; small image on radar screen.

bliss noun perfect joy; being in heaven. □ **blissful**
adjective; **blissfully** adverb.

blister /'blɪstə/ ● noun small bubble on skin filled
with watery fluid; any swelling resembling this.
● verb become covered with blisters; raise blister
on.

blithe /blaɪð/ adjective cheerful, happy; carefree,
casual. □ **blithely** adverb.

blithering /'blɪðərɪŋ/ adjective colloquial utter, hopeless;
contemptible.

blitz /blɪts/ colloquial ● noun intensive (esp. aerial) attack. ● verb inflict blitz on.

blizzard /'blɪzəd/ noun severe snowstorm.

bloat verb inflate, swell.

bloater noun herring cured by salting and smoking.

blob noun small drop or spot.

bloc noun group of governments etc. sharing some
common purpose.

block ● noun solid piece of hard material; large building, esp. when subdivided; group of buildings surrounded by streets; obstruction; large quantity as a
unit; piece of wood or metal engraved for printing.
● verb obstruct; restrict use of; stop (cricket ball)
with bat. □ **blockbuster** slang very successful film,
book, etc.; **blockhead** stupid person; **block capitals, letters** separate capital letters; **block out**
shut out (light, noise, view, etc.); **block up** shut in,
fill (window etc.) in; **block vote** vote proportional
in size to number of people voter represents; **mental
block** mental inability due to subconscious factors.

blockade /blɒ'keɪd/ ● noun surrounding or blocking
of place by enemy. ● verb (**-ding**) subject to blockade.

blockage noun obstruction.

bloke noun slang man, fellow.

blond (of woman, usually **blonde**) ● adjective light-coloured, fair-haired. ● noun blond person.

blood /blʌd/ ● noun fluid, usually red, circulating in arteries and veins of animals; killing; bloodshed; passion, temperament; race, descent; relationship. ● verb give first taste of blood to (hound); initiate (person). □ **blood bank** store of blood for transfusion; **bloodbath** massacre; **blood count** number of corpuscles in blood; **blood-curdling** horrifying; **blood donor** giver of blood for transfusion; **blood group** any of types of human blood; **bloodhound** large keen-scented dog used for tracking; **blood-letting** surgical removal of blood; **blood orange** red-fleshed orange; **blood poisoning** diseased condition due to bacteria in blood; **blood pressure** pressure of blood in arteries; **blood relation** one related by birth; **bloodshed** killing; **bloodshot** (of eyeball) inflamed; **blood sport** one involving killing of animals; **bloodstream** circulating blood; **bloodsucker** leech, extortioner; **bloodthirsty** eager for bloodshed; **blood vessel** vein, artery, or capillary carrying blood.

bloodless adjective without blood or bloodshed; unemotional; pale.

bloody ● adjective (**-ier**, **-iest**) of or like blood; running or stained with blood; involving bloodshed, cruel; coarse slang annoying, very great. ● verb (**-ies**, **-ied**) stain with blood. ● adverb coarse slang extremely. □ **bloody-minded** colloquial deliberately uncooperative.

bloom /bluːm/ ● noun flower; flowering state; prime; freshness; fine powder on fruit etc. ● verb bear flowers; be in flower; flourish.

bloomer[1] noun slang blunder.

bloomer[2] noun long loaf with diagonal marks.

bloomers plural noun colloquial woman's long loose knickers.

blooming ● adjective flourishing, healthy; slang annoying, very great. ● adverb slang extremely.

blossom /ˈblɒsəm/ ● noun flower; mass of flowers on tree. ● verb open into flower; flourish.

blot ● noun spot of ink etc.; disgraceful act; blemish. ● verb (**-tt-**) make blot on; stain; dry with blotting paper. □ **blot out** obliterate, obscure; **blotting paper** absorbent paper for drying wet ink.

blotch noun inflamed patch on skin; irregular patch of colour. □ **blotchy** adjective (**-ier**, **-iest**).

blotter noun device holding blotting paper.

blouse /blaʊz/ noun woman's shirtlike garment; type of military jacket.

blow[1] /bləʊ/ ● verb (past **blew** /bluː/; past participle **blown**) send directed air-current esp. from mouth; drive or be driven by blowing; move as wind does; sound (wind instrument); (past participle **blowed**) slang curse, confound; clear (nose) by forceful breath; pant; make or shape by blowing; break or burst suddenly; (cause to) break electric circuit; slang squander. ● noun blowing; short spell in fresh air. □ **blow-dry** arrange (hair) while using hand-held dryer; **blowfly** bluebottle; **blow in** send inwards by explosion, colloquial arrive unexpectedly; **blowlamp** device with flame for plumbing, burning off paint, etc.; **blow out** extinguish by blowing, send outwards by explosion; **blow-out** colloquial burst tyre, slang large meal; **blow over** fade away; **blowpipe** tube for blowing through, esp. one from which dart or arrow is projected; **blowtorch** US blowlamp; **blow up** explode, colloquial rebuke strongly, inflate, colloquial enlarge (photograph); **blow-up** colloquial enlargement of photograph.

blow[2] /bləʊ/ noun hard stroke with hand or weapon; disaster, shock.

blower /ˈbləʊə/ noun device for blowing; colloquial telephone.

blowy /ˈbləʊɪ/ adjective (**-ier**, **-iest**) windy.

blowzy /ˈblaʊzɪ/ adjective (**-ier**, **-iest**) coarse-looking, red-faced; dishevelled.

blub verb (**-bb-**) slang sob.

blubber /ˈblʌbə/ ● noun whale fat. ● verb sob noisily. □ **blubbery** adjective.

bludgeon /ˈblʌdʒ(ə)n/ ● noun heavy club. ● verb beat with bludgeon; coerce.

blue /bluː/ ● adjective (**-r**, **-st**) coloured like clear sky; sad, depressed; pornographic. ● noun blue colour, paint, clothes, etc.; person who represents Oxford or Cambridge University at sport; (in plural) type of melancholy music of American black origin, (**the blues**) depression. ● verb (**blues**, **blued**, **bluing** or **blueing**) slang squander. □ **blue baby** one with congenital heart defect; **bluebell** woodland plant with bell-shaped blue flowers; **blueberry** small edible blue or blackish fruit of various plants; **blue blood** noble birth; **bluebottle** large buzzing fly; **blue cheese** cheese with veins of blue mould; **blue-collar** manual, industrial; **blue-eyed boy** colloquial favourite; **bluegrass** type of country and western music; **Blue Peter** blue flag with central white square hoisted before sailing; **blueprint** photographic print of building plans etc. in white on blue paper, detailed plan; **bluestocking** usually derogatory intellectual woman; **blue tit** small blue and yellow bird; **blue whale** rorqual (largest known living mammal).

bluff[1] ● verb pretend to have strength, knowledge, etc. ● noun bluffing.

bluff[2] ● adjective blunt, frank, hearty; with steep or vertical broad front. ● noun bluff headland.

blunder /ˈblʌndə/ ● noun serious or foolish mistake. ● verb make blunder; move about clumsily.

blunderbuss /ˈblʌndəbʌs/ noun historical short large-bored gun.

blunt ● adjective without sharp edge or point; plain-spoken. ● verb make blunt. □ **bluntly** adverb; **bluntness** noun.

blur ● verb (**-rr-**) make or become less distinct; smear. ● noun indistinct object, sound, memory, etc.

blurb noun promotional description, esp. of book.

blurt verb (usually + out) utter abruptly or tactlessly.

blush ● verb be or become red (as) with shame or embarrassment; be ashamed. ● noun blushing; pink tinge.

blusher noun coloured cosmetic for cheeks.

bluster /ˈblʌstə/ ● verb behave pompously; storm boisterously. ● noun noisy pompous talk, empty threats. □ **blustery** adjective.

BMA abbreviation British Medical Association.

BMX noun organized bicycle racing on dirt track; bicycle used for this.

BO abbreviation colloquial body odour.

boa /ˈbəʊə/ noun large snake that kills its prey by crushing it; long stole of fur or feathers. □ **boa constrictor** species of boa.

boar noun male wild pig; uncastrated male pig.

board ● noun thin piece of sawn timber; material resembling this; slab of wood etc., e.g. ironing board, notice board; thick stiff card; provision of meals; directors of company; committee; (**the boards**) stage. ● verb go on board (ship etc.); receive, or provide with, meals and usually lodging; (usually + up) cover with boards. □ **board game** game played on a board; **boarding house** unlicensed house providing board and lodging; **boarding school** one in which pupils live in term-time; **boardroom** room where board of directors meets; **on board** on or into ship, train, aircraft, etc.

boarder *noun* person who boards, esp. at boarding school.

boast ● *verb* declare one's achievements etc. with excessive pride; have (desirable thing). ● *noun* boasting; thing one is proud of. □ **boastful** *adjective*.

boat ● *noun* small vessel propelled by oars, sails, or engine; ship; long low jug for sauce etc. ● *verb* go in boat, esp. for pleasure. □ **boat-hook** long pole with hook for moving boats; **boathouse** shed at water's edge for boats; **boatman** person who hires out or provides transport by boats; **boat people** refugees travelling by sea; **boat-train** train scheduled to connect with ship.

boater *noun* flat straw hat with straight brim.

boatswain /ˈbəʊs(ə)n/ *noun* (also **bosun**) ship's officer in charge of equipment and crew.

bob¹ ● *verb* (**-bb-**) move up and down; rebound; cut (hair) in bob; curtsy. ● *noun* bobbing movement; curtsy; hairstyle with hair hanging evenly above shoulders; weight on pendulum etc. □ **bobtail** docked tail, horse or dog with this.

bob² *noun* (*plural* same) *historical slang* shilling (= 5p).

bobbin /ˈbɒbɪn/ *noun* spool or reel for thread etc.

bobble /ˈbɒb(ə)l/ *noun* small woolly ball on hat etc.

bobby /ˈbɒbɪ/ *noun* (*plural* **-ies**) *colloquial* police officer.

bobsled *noun US* bobsleigh.

bobsleigh *noun* racing sledge steered and braked mechanically.

bod *noun colloquial* person.

bode *verb* (**-ding**) □ **bode well, ill** be good or bad sign.

bodge /bɒdʒ/ = ˈBOTCH.

bodice /ˈbɒdɪs/ *noun* part of woman's dress above waist.

bodily /ˈbɒdɪlɪ/ ● *adjective* of the body. ● *adverb* as a whole (body); in person.

bodkin /ˈbɒdkɪn/ *noun* blunt thick needle for drawing tape etc. through hem.

body /ˈbɒdɪ/ *noun* (*plural* **-ies**) physical structure of person or animal, alive or dead; person's or animal's trunk; main part; group of people regarded as unit; quantity, mass; piece of matter; *colloquial* person; full or substantial quality of flavour etc.; body stocking. □ **body-building** exercises to enlarge and strengthen muscles; **bodyguard** escort or personal guard; **body politic** state, nation; **body shop** workshop where bodywork is repaired; **body stocking** woman's undergarment covering trunk; **bodywork** outer shell of vehicle.

Boer /ˈbɔː/ *noun* S. African of Dutch descent.

boffin /ˈbɒfɪn/ *noun colloquial* research scientist.

bog *noun* (area of) wet spongy ground; *slang* lavatory. □ **bogged down** unable to move or make progress. □ **boggy** *adjective* (**-ier, -iest**).

bogey¹ /ˈbəʊgɪ/ *noun* (*plural* **-s**) *Golf* score of one more than par for hole; (formerly) par.

bogey² /ˈbəʊgɪ/ *noun* (also **bogy**) (*plural* **-eys** or **-ies**) evil or mischievous spirit; awkward thing.

boggle /ˈbɒg(ə)l/ *verb* (**-ling**) *colloquial* be startled or baffled.

bogie /ˈbəʊgɪ/ *noun* wheeled undercarriage below locomotive etc.

bogus /ˈbəʊgəs/ *adjective* sham, spurious.

bogy = BOGEY².

Bohemian /bəʊˈhiːmɪən/ ● *noun* native of Bohemia; (also **bohemian**) socially unconventional person, esp. artist or writer. ● *adjective* of Bohemia; (also **bohemian**) socially unconventional. □ **bohemianism** *noun*.

boil¹ ● *verb* (of liquid or its vessel) bubble up with heat, reach temperature at which liquid turns to vapour; bring to boiling point; subject to heat of boiling water, cook thus; be agitated like boiling water. ● *noun* boiling; boiling point. □ **boiling (hot)** *colloquial* very hot; **boiling point** temperature at which a liquid boils; **boil over** spill over in boiling.

boil² *noun* inflamed pus-filled swelling under skin.

boiler *noun* apparatus for heating hot-water supply; tank for heating water or turning it into steam; vessel for boiling things in. □ **boiler suit** protective garment combining trousers and shirt.

boisterous /ˈbɔɪstərəs/ *adjective* noisily cheerful; violent, rough.

bold /bəʊld/ *adjective* confident; adventurous; courageous; impudent; distinct, vivid. □ **boldly** *adverb*; **boldness** *noun*.

bole *noun* trunk of tree.

bolero *noun* (*plural* **-s**) /bəˈleərəʊ/ Spanish dance; /ˈbɒlərəʊ/ woman's short jacket without fastenings.

boll /bəʊl/ *noun* round seed vessel of cotton, flax, etc.

bollard /ˈbɒlɑːd/ *noun* short thick post in street etc.; post on ship or quay for securing ropes to.

boloney /bəˈləʊnɪ/ *noun slang* nonsense.

bolshie /ˈbɒlʃɪ/ *adjective* (**-r, -st**) (also **Bolshie**) *slang* rebellious, uncooperative.

bolster /ˈbəʊlstə/ ● *noun* long cylindrical pillow. ● *verb* (usually + *up*) encourage, support, prop up.

bolt¹ ● *noun* door-fastening of metal bar and socket; headed metal pin secured with rivet or nut; discharge of lightning; bolting. ● *verb* fasten with bolt; (+ *in, out*) keep in or out by bolting door; dart off, run away; (of horse) escape from control; gulp down unchewed; run to seed. □ **bolt-hole** means of escape; **bolt upright** erect.

bolt² /bəʊlt/ *verb* (also **boult**) sift.

bomb /bɒm/ ● *noun* container filled with explosive, incendiary material, etc., designed to explode and cause damage; **(the bomb)** the atomic bomb; *slang* large amount of money. ● *verb* attack with bombs; drop bombs on; *colloquial* travel fast. □ **bombshell** great surprise or disappointment.

bombard /bɒmˈbɑːd/ *verb* attack with heavy guns etc.; question or abuse persistently; subject to stream of high-speed particles. □ **bombardment** *noun*.

bombardier /bɒmbəˈdɪə/ *noun* artillery NCO below sergeant; *US* airman who releases bombs from aircraft.

bombast /ˈbɒmbæst/ *noun* pompous or extravagant language. □ **bombastic** /-ˈbæs-/ *adjective*.

Bombay duck /ˈbɒmbeɪ/ *noun* dried fish eaten as relish, esp. with curry.

bomber *noun* aircraft equipped for bombing; person who throws or plants bomb. □ **bomber jacket** one gathered at waist and cuffs.

bona fide /bəʊnə ˈfaɪdɪ/ *adjective & adverb* in good faith, genuine(ly).

bonanza /bəˈnænzə/ *noun* source of great wealth; large output, esp. from mine.

bon-bon *noun* sweet.

bond ● *noun* thing or force that unites or (usually in *plural*) restrains; binding agreement; certificate issued by government or company promising to repay money at fixed rate of interest; adhesiveness; document binding person to pay or repay money; linkage of atoms in molecule. ● *verb* bind or connect together; put in bond. □ **bond paper** high-quality writing paper; **in bond** stored by Customs until duty is paid.

bondage /ˈbɒndɪdʒ/ *noun* slavery; subjection to constraint.

bondsman /ˈbɒndzmən/ *noun* serf, slave.

bone ● *noun* any of separate parts of vertebrate skeleton; (in *plural*) skeleton, esp. as remains; substance of which bones consist. ● *verb* (**-ning**) remove bones from. □ **bone china** fine semi-translucent earthenware; **bone dry** completely dry; **bone idle** completely idle; **bone marrow** fatty substance in cavity of bones; **bonemeal** crushed bone as fertilizer; **boneshaker** jolting vehicle.

bonfire *noun* open-air fire.

bongo /ˈbɒŋgəʊ/ *noun* (*plural* **-s** or **-es**) either of pair of small drums played with fingers.

bonhomie /ˈbɒnɒˈmiː/ *noun* geniality.

bonkers /ˈbɒŋkəz/ *adjective slang* crazy.

bonnet /ˈbɒnɪt/ *noun* woman's or child's hat tied under chin; Scotsman's floppy beret; hinged cover over engine of vehicle.

bonny /ˈbɒnɪ/ *adjective* (**-ier, -iest**) *esp. Scottish & Northern English* healthy-looking, attractive.

bonsai /ˈbɒnsaɪ/ *noun* (*plural* same) dwarfed tree or shrub; art of growing these.

bonus /ˈbəʊnəs/ *noun* extra benefit or payment.

bon voyage /bɔ̃ vwaːˈjɑːʒ/ *interjection* have a good trip. [French]

bony /ˈbəʊnɪ/ *adjective* (**-ier, -iest**) thin with prominent bones; having many bones; of or like bone.

boo ● *interjection expressing disapproval or contempt; sound intended to surprise.* ● *noun* utterance of 'boo'. ● *verb* (**boos, booed**) utter boos (at).

boob ● *noun colloquial* silly mistake; *slang* woman's breast. ● *verb colloquial* make mistake.

booby /ˈbuːbɪ/ *noun* (*plural* **-ies**) silly or awkward person. □ **booby prize** prize for coming last; **booby trap** practical joke in form of trap, disguised bomb etc. triggered by unknowing victim.

book /bʊk/ ● *noun* written or printed work with pages bound along one side; work intended for publication; bound set of tickets, stamps, matches, cheques, etc.; (in *plural*) set of records or accounts; main division of literary work or Bible; telephone directory; *colloquial* magazine; libretto; record of bets made. ● *verb* reserve (seat etc.) in advance; engage (entertainer etc.); take personal details of (offender); enter in book or list. □ **bookcase** cabinet of shelves for books; **bookend** prop to keep books upright; **bookkeeper** person who keeps accounts; **bookmaker** professional taker of bets; **bookmark** thing for marking place in book; **bookplate** decorative personalized label in book; **book token** voucher exchangeable for books; **bookworm** *colloquial* devoted reader, larva that eats through books.

bookie /ˈbʊkɪ/ *noun colloquial* bookmaker.

bookish *adjective* fond of reading; getting knowledge mainly from books.

booklet /ˈbʊklɪt/ *noun* small usually paper-covered book.

boom[1] /buːm/ ● *noun* deep resonant sound. ● *verb* make or speak with boom.

boom[2] /buːm/ ● *noun* period of economic prosperity or activity. ● *verb* be suddenly prosperous.

boom[3] /buːm/ *noun* pivoted spar to which sail is attached; long pole carrying camera, microphone, etc.; barrier across harbour etc.

boomerang /ˈbuːməræŋ/ ● *noun* flat V-shaped Australian hardwood missile returning to thrower. ● *verb* (of plan) backfire.

boon[1] /buːn/ *noun* advantage; blessing.

boon[2] /buːn/ *adjective* intimate, favourite.

boor /bʊə/ *noun* ill-mannered person. □ **boorish** *adjective*.

boost /buːst/ *colloquial* ● *verb* promote, encourage; increase, assist; push from below. ● *noun* boosting.

booster *noun* device for increasing power or voltage; auxiliary engine or rocket for initial speed; dose renewing effect of earlier one.

boot /buːt/ ● *noun* outer foot-covering reaching above ankle; luggage compartment of car; *colloquial* firm kick, dismissal. ● *verb* kick; (often + *out*) eject forcefully; (usually + *up*) make (computer) ready.

bootee /buːˈtiː/ *noun* baby's soft shoe.

booth /buːð/ *noun* temporary structure used esp. as market stall; enclosure for telephoning, voting, etc.

bootleg /ˈbuːtleg/ ● *adjective* smuggled, illicit. ● *verb* (**-gg-**) illicitly make or deal in. □ **bootlegger** *noun*.

bootstrap /ˈbuːtstræp/ *noun* □ **pull oneself up by one's bootstraps** better oneself by one's unaided effort.

booty /ˈbuːtɪ/ *noun* loot, spoils; *colloquial* prize.

booze *colloquial* ● *noun* alcoholic drink. ● *verb* (**-zing**) drink alcohol, esp. excessively. □ **boozy** *adjective* (**-ier, -iest**).

boozer *noun colloquial* habitual drinker; public house.

bop *colloquial* ● *noun* spell of dancing, esp. to pop music; *colloquial* hit, blow. ● *verb* (**-pp-**) dance, esp. to pop music; *colloquial* hit.

boracic /bəˈræsɪk/ *adjective* of borax. □ **boracic acid** boric acid.

borage /ˈbɒrɪdʒ/ *noun* plant with leaves used as flavouring.

borax /ˈbɔːræks/ *noun* salt of boric acid used as antiseptic.

border /ˈbɔːdə/ ● *noun* edge, boundary, or part near it; line or region separating countries; distinct edging, esp. ornamental strip; long narrow flower-bed. ● *verb* put or be border to; adjoin. □ **borderline** *noun* line marking boundary or dividing two conditions, *adjective* on borderline.

bore[1] ● *verb* (**-ring**) make (hole), esp. with revolving tool; make hole in. ● *noun* hollow of firearm barrel or cylinder; diameter of this; deep hole made to find water etc.

bore[2] ● *noun* tiresome or dull person or thing. ● *verb* (**-ring**) weary by tedious talk or dullness. □ **bored** *adjective*; **boring** *adjective*.

bore[3] *noun* very high tidal wave rushing up estuary.

bore[4] *past of* BEAR[1].

boredom *noun* being bored (BORE[2]).

boric acid /ˈbɔːrɪk/ *noun* acid used as antiseptic.

born *adjective* existing as a result of birth; being (specified thing) by nature; (usually + *to do*) destined.

borne *past participle of* BEAR[1].

boron /ˈbɔːrɒn/ *noun* non-metallic element.

borough /ˈbʌrə/ *noun* administrative area, esp. of Greater London; *historical* town with municipal corporation.

borrow /ˈbɒrəʊ/ *verb* get temporary use of (something to be returned); use another's (invention, idea, etc.). □ **borrower** *noun*.

Borstal /ˈbɔːst(ə)l/ *noun historical* residential institution for youth custody.

bosom /ˈbʊz(ə)m/ *noun* person's breasts; *colloquial* each of woman's breasts; enclosure formed by breast and arms; emotional centre. □ **bosom friend** intimate friend.

boss[1] *colloquial* ● *noun* employer, manager, or supervisor. ● *verb* (usually + *about, around*) give orders to.

boss[2] *noun* round knob or stud.

boss-eyed *adjective colloquial* cross-eyed; crooked.

bossy *adjective* (**-ier, -iest**) *colloquial* domineering. □ **bossiness** *noun*.

bosun = BOATSWAIN.

botany /'bɒtənɪ/ *noun* study of plants. □ **botanic(al)** /bə'tæn-/ *adjective*; **botanist** *noun*.

botch ● *verb* bungle; patch clumsily. ● *noun* bungled or spoilt work.

both /bəʊθ/ ● *adjective & pronoun* the two (not only one). ● *adverb* with equal truth in two cases.

bother /'bɒðə/ ● *verb* trouble, worry; take trouble. ● *noun* person or thing that bothers; nuisance; trouble, worry. ● *interjection of irritation*. □ **bothersome** /-səm/ *adjective*.

bottle /'bɒt(ə)l/ ● *noun* container, esp. glass or plastic, for storing liquid; liquid in bottle; *slang* courage. ● *verb* (**-ling**) put into bottles; preserve (fruit etc.) in jars; (+ *up*) restrain (feelings etc.). □ **bottle bank** place for depositing bottles for recycling; **bottle green** dark green; **bottleneck** narrow congested area esp. on road etc., thing that impedes; **bottle party** one to which guests bring bottles of drink.

bottom /'bɒtəm/ ● *noun* lowest point or part; buttocks; less honourable end of table, class, etc.; ground under water; basis; essential character. ● *adjective* lowest, last. ● *verb* find extent of; touch bottom (of); (usually + *out*) reach its lowest level. □ **bottom line** *colloquial* underlying truth, ultimate criterion.

bottomless *adjective* without bottom; inexhaustible.

botulism /'bɒtjʊlɪz(ə)m/ *noun* poisoning caused by bacillus in badly preserved food.

boudoir /'bu:dwɑ:/ *noun* woman's private room.

bougainvillaea /bu:gən'vɪlɪə/ *noun* tropical plant with large coloured bracts.

bough /baʊ/ *noun* branch of tree.

bought *past & past participle of* BUY.

bouillon /'bu:jɒn/ *noun* clear broth.

boulder /'bəʊldə/ *noun* large smooth rock.

boulevard /'bu:ləvɑ:d/ *noun* broad tree-lined street.

boult = BOLT².

bounce /baʊns/ ● *verb* (**-cing**) (cause to) rebound; *slang* (of cheque) be returned to payee by bank when there are no funds to meet it; rush boisterously. ● *noun* rebound; *colloquial* swagger, self-confidence; *colloquial* liveliness. □ **bouncy** *adjective* (**-ier, -iest**).

bouncer *noun slang* doorman ejecting troublemakers from nightclub etc.

bouncing *adjective* big and healthy.

bound¹ /baʊnd/ ● *verb* spring, leap; (of ball etc.) bounce. ● *noun* springy leap; bounce.

bound² /baʊnd/ ● *noun* (usually in *plural*) limitation, restriction; border, boundary. ● *verb* limit; be boundary of. □ **out of bounds** outside permitted area.

bound³ /baʊnd/ *adjective* (usually + *for*) starting or having started.

bound⁴ /baʊnd/ *past & past participle of* BIND. □ **bound to** certain to; **bound up with** closely associated with.

boundary /'baʊndərɪ/ *noun* (*plural* **-ies**) line marking limits; *Cricket* hit crossing limit of field, runs scored for this.

boundless *adjective* unlimited.

bounteous /'baʊntɪəs/ *adjective poetical* bountiful.

bountiful /'baʊntɪfʊl/ *adjective* generous; ample.

bounty /'baʊntɪ/ *noun* (*plural* **-ies**) generosity; official reward; gift.

bouquet /bu:'keɪ/ *noun* bunch of flowers; scent of wine; compliment. □ **bouquet garni** (/'gɑ:nɪ/) bunch or bag of herbs for flavouring.

bourbon /'bɜ:bən/ *noun US* whisky from maize and rye.

bourgeois /'bʊəʒwɑ:/ *often derogatory* ● *adjective* conventionally middle-class; materialist; capitalist. ● *noun* (*plural* same) bourgeois person.

bourgeoisie /bʊəʒwɑ:'zi:/ *noun* bourgeois class.

bourn /bɔ:n/ *noun* stream.

bourse /bʊəs/ *noun* money market, esp. (**Bourse**) Stock Exchange in Paris.

bout /baʊt/ *noun* spell of work etc.; fit of illness; wrestling or boxing match.

boutique /bu:'ti:k/ *noun* small shop selling fashionable clothes etc.

bouzouki /bu:'zu:kɪ/ *noun* (*plural* **-s**) form of Greek mandolin.

bovine /'bəʊvaɪn/ *adjective* of cattle; dull, stupid.

bow¹ /bəʊ/ ● *noun* weapon for shooting arrows; rod with horsehair stretched from end to end for playing violin etc.; knot with two loops, ribbon etc. so tied; shallow curve or bend. ● *verb* use bow on (violin etc.). □ **bow-legged** having bandy legs; **bow tie** necktie in form of bow; **bow window** curved bay window.

bow² /baʊ/ ● *verb* incline head or body, esp. in greeting or acknowledgement; submit; incline (head etc.). ● *noun* bowing.

bow³ /baʊ/ *noun* (often in *plural*) front end of boat or ship; rower nearest bow.

bowdlerize /'baʊdləraɪz/ *verb* (also **-ise**) (**-zing** or **-sing**) expurgate. □ **bowdlerization** *noun*.

bowel /'baʊəl/ *noun* (often in *plural*) intestine; (in *plural*) innermost parts.

bower /'baʊə/ *noun* arbour; summer house. □ **bowerbird** Australasian bird, the male of which constructs elaborate runs.

bowie knife /'bəʊɪ/ *noun* long hunting knife.

bowl¹ /bəʊl/ *noun* dish, esp. for food or liquid; hollow part of tobacco pipe, spoon, etc.

bowl² /bəʊl/ ● *noun* hard heavy ball made with bias to run in curve; (in *plural*; usually treated as *singular*) game with these on grass. ● *verb* roll (ball etc.); play bowls; *Cricket* deliver ball, (often + *out*) put (batsman) out by knocking off bails with bowled ball; (often + *along*) go along rapidly. □ **bowling alley** long enclosure for skittles or tenpin bowling; **bowling green** lawn for playing bowls.

bowler¹ /'bəʊlə/ *noun Cricket etc.* player who bowls.

bowler² /'bəʊlə/ *noun* hard round felt hat.

bowsprit /'bəʊsprɪt/ *noun* spar running forward from ship's bow.

box¹ ● *noun* container, usually flat-sided and firm; amount contained in this; compartment in theatre, law court, etc.; telephone box; facility at newspaper office for replies to advertisement; (**the box**) *colloquial* television; enclosed area or space. ● *verb* put in or provide with box. □ **box girder** hollow girder with square cross-section; **box junction** yellow-striped road area which vehicle may enter only if exit is clear; **box office** ticket office at theatre etc.; **box pleat** two parallel pleats forming raised band.

box² ● *verb* fight with fists as sport; slap (person's ears). ● *noun* slap on ear.

box³ *noun* evergreen shrub with small dark green leaves; its wood.

boxer *noun* person who boxes; short-haired dog with puglike face. □ **boxer shorts** man's loose underpants.

boxing *noun* fighting with fists, esp. as sport. □ **boxing glove** padded glove worn in this.

Boxing Day *noun* first weekday after Christmas Day.

boy ● *noun* male child, young man; son; male servant. ● *interjection expressing pleasure, surprise, etc.* □ **boyfriend** person's regular male companion; **boy scout** Scout. □ **boyhood** *noun*; **boyish** *adjective*.

boycott /'bɔɪkɒt/ ● *verb* refuse social or commercial relations with; refuse to handle (goods). ● *noun* such refusal.

bra /brɑː/ *noun* woman's undergarment supporting breasts.

brace ● *noun* device that clamps or fastens tightly; timber etc. strengthening framework; (in *plural*) straps supporting trousers from shoulders; wire device for straightening teeth; (*plural* same) pair. ● *verb* (**-cing**) make steady by supporting; fasten tightly; (esp. as **bracing** *adjective*) invigorate; (often **brace oneself**) prepare for difficulty, shock, etc.

bracelet /'breislit/ *noun* ornamental band or chain worn on wrist or arm; *slang* handcuff.

brachiosaurus /ˌbrækɪə'sɔːrəs/ *noun* (*plural* **-ruses**) huge long-necked plant-eating dinosaur.

bracken /'brækən/ *noun* large coarse fern; mass of these.

bracket /'brækɪt/ ● *noun* support projecting from vertical surface; shelf fixed to wall with this; punctuation mark used in pairs—( ), [ ]—enclosing words or figures (see panel); group classified as similar or falling between limits. ● *verb* (**-t-**) enclose in brackets; group in same category.

brackish /'brækɪʃ/ *adjective* (of water) slightly salty.

bract *noun* leaflike part of plant growing before flower.

brad *noun* thin flat nail.

bradawl /'brædɔːl/ *noun* small boring-tool.

brae /brei/ *noun* Scottish hillside.

brag ● *verb* (**-gg-**) talk boastfully. ● *noun* card game like poker; boastful statement or talk.

braggart /'brægət/ *noun* boastful person.

Brahma /'brɑːmə/ *noun* Hindu Creator; supreme Hindu reality.

Brahman /'brɑːmən/ *noun* (*plural* **-s**) (also **Brahmin**) member of Hindu priestly caste.

braid ● *noun* woven band as edging or trimming; *US* plait of hair. ● *verb US* plait; trim with braid.

Braille /breil/ *noun* system of writing and printing for the blind, with patterns of raised dots.

brain ● *noun* organ of soft nervous tissue in vertebrate's skull; centre of sensation or thought; (often in *plural*) intelligence, *colloquial* intelligent person. ● *verb* dash out brains of. □ **brainchild** *colloquial* person's clever idea or invention; **brain drain** *colloquial* emigration of skilled people; **brainstorm** mental disturbance; **brainstorming** pooling of spontaneous ideas about problem etc.; **brains trust** group of experts answering questions, usually impromptu;

brainwash implant ideas or esp. ideology into (person) by repetition etc.; **brainwave** *colloquial* bright idea.

brainy *adjective* (**-ier, -iest**) intellectually clever.

braise /breiz/ *verb* (**-sing**) stew slowly in closed container with little liquid.

brake ● *noun* device for stopping or slowing wheel or vehicle; thing that impedes. ● *verb* (**-king**) apply brake; slow or stop with brake.

bramble /'bræmb(ə)l/ *noun* wild thorny shrub, esp. blackberry.

bran *noun* husks separated from flour.

branch /brɑːntʃ/ ● *noun* limb or bough of tree; lateral extension or subdivision of river, railway, family, etc.; local office of business. ● *verb* (often + *off*) divide, diverge. □ **branch out** extend one's field of interest.

brand ● *noun* particular make of goods; trade mark, label, etc.; (usually + *of*) characteristic kind; identifying mark made with hot iron, iron stamp for this; piece of burning or charred wood; stigma; *poetical* torch. ● *verb* mark with hot iron; stigmatize; assign trade mark etc. to; impress unforgettably. □ **brand new** completely new.

brandish /'brændɪʃ/ *verb* wave or flourish.

brandy /'brændɪ/ *noun* (*plural* **-ies**) strong spirit distilled from wine or fermented fruit juice. □ **brandy snap** crisp rolled gingerbread wafer.

brash *adjective* vulgarly assertive; impudent. □ **brashly** *adverb*; **brashness** *noun*.

brass /brɑːs/ ● *noun* yellow alloy of copper and zinc; brass objects; brass wind instruments; *slang* money; brass memorial tablet; *colloquial* effrontery. ● *adjective* made of brass. □ **brass band** band of brass instruments; **brass rubbing** reproducing of design from engraved brass on paper by rubbing with heel-ball, impression obtained thus; **brass tacks** *slang* essential details.

brasserie /'bræsərɪ/ *noun* restaurant, originally one serving beer with food.

brassica /'bræsɪkə/ *noun* plant of cabbage family.

brassière /'bræzɪə/ *noun* bra.

brassy /'brɑːsɪ/ *adjective* (**-ier, -iest**) of or like brass; impudent; vulgarly showy; loud and blaring.

brat *noun* usually derogatory child.

bravado /brə'vɑːdəʊ/ *noun* show of boldness.

Brackets ( ) [ ]

Round brackets, also called parentheses, are used mainly to enclose:

1 explanations and extra information or comment, e.g.

> *Zimbabwe (formerly Rhodesia)*
> *He is (as he always was) a rebel.*
> *This is done using integrated circuits (see page 38).*

2 in this dictionary, optional words or parts of words, e.g.

> **crossword (puzzle)**   **king-size(d)**

and the type of word which can be used with the word being defined, e.g.

> **low** . . . (of opinion) unfavourable
> **can** . . . preserve (food etc.) in can

Square brackets are used mainly to enclose:

1 words added by someone other than the original writer or speaker, e.g.

> *Then the man said, 'He [the police officer] can't prove I did it.'*

2 various special types of information, such as stage directions, e.g.

> HEDLEY: Goodbye! [Exit].

brave ● *adjective* (**-r, -st**) able to face and endure danger or pain; *formal* splendid, spectacular. ● *verb* (**-ving**) face bravely or defiantly. ● *noun* N. American Indian warrior. □ **bravely** *adverb*; **bravery** *noun*.

bravo /brɑːˈvəʊ/ *interjection & noun* (*plural* **-s**) cry of approval.

bravura /brəˈvjʊərə/ *noun* brilliance of execution; music requiring brilliant technique.

brawl ● *noun* noisy quarrel or fight. ● *verb* engage in brawl; (of stream) flow noisily.

brawn *noun* muscular strength; muscle, lean flesh; jellied meat made esp. from pig's head. □ **brawny** *adjective* (**-ier, -iest**).

bray ● *noun* cry of donkey; harsh sound. ● *verb* make a bray; utter harshly.

braze *verb* (**-zing**) solder with alloy of brass.

brazen /ˈbreɪz(ə)n/ ● *adjective* shameless; of or like brass. ● *verb* (+ *out*) face or undergo defiantly. □ **brazenly** *adverb*.

brazier /ˈbreɪzɪə/ *noun* pan or stand for holding burning coals.

Brazil nut /brəˈzɪl/ *noun* large 3-sided S. American nut.

breach /briːtʃ/ ● *noun* breaking or neglect of rule, duty, promise, etc.; breaking off of relations, quarrel; gap. ● *verb* break through; make gap in; break (law etc.).

bread /bred/ *noun* baked dough of flour usually leavened with yeast; necessary food; *slang* money. □ **breadcrumb** small fragment of bread, esp. (in *plural*) for use in cooking; **breadline** subsistence level; **breadwinner** person whose work supports a family.

breadth /bredθ/ *noun* broadness, distance from side to side; freedom from mental limitations or prejudices.

break /breɪk/ ● *verb* (*past* **broke**; *past participle* **broken** /ˈbrəʊk(ə)n/) separate into pieces under blow or strain; shatter; make or become inoperative; break bone in (limb etc.); interrupt, pause; fail to observe or keep; make or become weak, destroy; weaken effect of (fall, blow, etc.); tame, subdue; surpass (record); reveal or be revealed; come, produce, change, etc., with suddenness or violence; (of waves) curl over and foam; (of voice) change in quality at manhood or with emotion; escape, emerge from. ● *noun* breaking; point where thing is broken; gap; pause in work etc.; sudden dash; a chance; *Cricket* deflection of ball on bouncing; points scored in one sequence at billiards etc. □ **break away** make or become free or separate; **break down** fail or collapse, demolish, analyse; **breakdown** mechanical failure, loss of (esp. mental) health, collapse, analysis; **break even** make neither profit nor loss; **break in** intrude forcibly esp. as thief, interrupt, accustom to habit; **breakneck** (of speed) dangerously fast; **break off** detach by breaking, bring to an end, cease talking etc.; **break open** open forcibly; **break out** escape by force, begin suddenly, (+ *in*) become covered in (rash etc.); **breakthrough** major advance in knowledge etc.; **break up** break into pieces, disband, part; **breakup** disintegration, collapse; **breakwater** barrier breaking force of waves; **break wind** release gas from anus.

breakable *adjective* easily broken.

breakage *noun* broken thing; breaking.

breaker *noun* heavy breaking wave.

breakfast /ˈbrekfəst/ ● *noun* first meal of day. ● *verb* have breakfast.

bream *noun* (*plural* same) yellowish freshwater fish; similar sea fish.

breast /brest/ ● *noun* either of two milk-secreting organs on woman's chest; chest; part of garment covering this; seat of emotions. ● *verb* contend with; reach top of (hill). □ **breastbone** bone connecting ribs in front; **breastfeed** feed (baby) from breast; **breastplate** armour covering chest; **breaststroke** stroke made while swimming on breast by extending arms forward and sweeping them back.

breath /breθ/ *noun* air drawn into or expelled from lungs; one respiration; breath as perceived by senses; slight movement of air. □ **breathtaking** astounding, awe-inspiring; **breath test** test with Breathalyser.

breathalyse *verb* give breath test to.

Breathalyser /ˈbreθəlaɪzə/ *noun* proprietary term instrument for measuring alcohol in breath.

breathe /briːð/ *verb* (**-thing**) take air into lungs and send it out again; live; utter or sound, esp. quietly; pause; send out or take in (as) with breathed air. □ **breathing-space** time to recover, pause.

breather /ˈbriːðə/ *noun* short rest period.

breathless /ˈbreθlɪs/ *adjective* panting, out of breath; still, windless. □ **breathlessly** *adverb*.

bred *past & past participle* of BREED.

breech /briːtʃ/ *noun* back part of gun or gun barrel; (in *plural*) short trousers fastened below knee. □ **breech birth** birth in which buttocks emerge first.

breed ● *verb* (*past & past participle* **bred**) produce offspring; propagate; raise (animals); yield, result in; arise, spread; train, bring up; create (fissile material) by nuclear reaction. ● *noun* stock of animals within species; race, lineage; sort, kind. □ **breeder reactor** nuclear reactor creating surplus fissile material. □ **breeder** *noun*.

breeding *noun* raising of offspring; social behaviour; ancestry.

breeze[1] ● *noun* gentle wind. ● *verb* (**-zing**) (+ *in, out, along*, etc.) *colloquial* saunter casually.

breeze[2] *noun* small cinders. **breeze-block** lightweight building block made from breeze.

breezy *adjective* (**-ier, -iest**) slightly windy.

Bren *noun* lightweight quick-firing machine-gun.

brent *noun* small migratory goose.

brethren *see* BROTHER.

Breton /ˈbret(ə)n/ ● *noun* native or language of Brittany. ● *adjective* of Brittany.

breve /briːv/ *noun Music* note equal to two semibreves; mark (˘) indicating short or unstressed vowel.

breviary /ˈbriːvɪərɪ/ *noun* (*plural* **-ies**) book containing RC daily office.

brevity /ˈbrevɪtɪ/ *noun* conciseness, shortness.

brew ● *verb* make (beer etc.) by infusion, boiling, and fermenting; make (tea etc.) by infusion; undergo these processes; be forming. ● *noun* amount brewed; liquor brewed. □ **brewer** *noun*.

brewery /ˈbruːərɪ/ *noun* (*plural* **-ies**) factory for brewing beer etc.

briar[1,2] = BRIER[1,2].

bribe ● *verb* (**-bing**) persuade to act improperly by gift of money etc. ● *noun* money or services offered in bribing. □ **bribery** *noun*.

bric-a-brac /ˈbrɪkəbræk/ *noun* cheap ornaments, trinkets, etc.

brick ● *noun* small rectangular block of baked clay, used in building; toy building block; brick-shaped thing; *slang* generous or loyal person. ● *verb* (+ *in, up*) close or block with brickwork. ● *adjective* made of bricks. □ **brickbat** piece of brick, esp. as missile, insult; **bricklayer** person who builds with bricks; **brickwork** building or work in brick.

bridal /ˈbraɪd(ə)l/ *adjective* of bride or wedding.

bride *noun* woman on her wedding day and shortly before and after it. **bridegroom** man on his wedding day and shortly before and after it; **bridesmaid** woman or girl attending bride at wedding.

bridge¹ ● *noun* structure providing way over road, railway, river, etc.; thing joining or connecting; superstructure from which ship is directed; upper bony part of nose; prop under strings of violin etc.; bridgework. ● *verb* (**-ging**) be or make bridge over. □ **bridgehead** position held on enemy's side of river etc.; **bridgework** dental structure covering gap and joined to teeth on either side; **bridging loan** loan to cover interval between buying one house and selling another.

bridge² *noun* card game derived from whist.

bridle /ˈbraɪd(ə)l/ ● *noun* headgear for controlling horse etc.; restraining thing. ● *verb* (**-ling**) put bridle on, control, curb; express resentment, esp. by throwing up head and drawing in chin. □ **bridle path** rough path for riders or walkers.

Brie /briː/ *noun* flat round soft creamy French cheese.

brief /briːf/ ● *adjective* of short duration; concise; scanty. ● *noun* (in *plural*) short pants; summary of case for guidance of barrister; instructions for a task. ● *verb* instruct (barrister) by brief; inform or instruct in advance. □ **in brief** to sum up. □ **briefly** *adverb*.

briefcase /ˈbriːfkeɪs/ *noun* flat document case.

brier¹ /braɪə/ *noun* (also **briar**) wild-rose bush.

brier² /braɪə/ *noun* (also **briar**) white heath of S. Europe; tobacco pipe made from its root.

brig¹ *noun* two-masted square-rigged ship.

brig² *noun Scottish & Northern English* bridge.

brigade /brɪˈɡeɪd/ *noun* military unit forming part of division; organized band of workers etc.

brigadier /brɪɡəˈdɪə/ *noun* army officer next below major-general.

brigand /ˈbrɪɡənd/ *noun* member of robber gang.

bright /braɪt/ *adjective* emitting or reflecting much light, shining; vivid; clever; cheerful. □ **brighten** *verb*; **brightly** *adverb*; **brightness** *noun*.

brill¹ *noun* (*plural* same) flatfish resembling turbot.

brill² *adjective colloquial* excellent.

brilliant /ˈbrɪlɪənt/ ● *adjective* bright, sparkling; highly talented; showy; *colloquial* excellent. ● *noun* diamond of finest quality. □ **brilliance** *noun*; **brilliantly** *adverb*.

brilliantine /ˈbrɪljəntiːn/ *noun* cosmetic for making hair glossy.

brim ● *noun* edge of vessel; projecting edge of hat. ● *verb* (**-mm-**) fill or be full to brim.

brimstone /ˈbrɪmstəʊn/ *noun archaic* sulphur.

brindled /ˈbrɪnd(ə)ld/ *adjective* brown with streaks of other colour.

brine *noun* salt water; sea water.

bring *verb* (*past & past participle* **brought** /brɔːt/) come with, carry, convey; cause, result in; be sold for; submit (criminal charge); initiate (legal action). □ **bring about** cause to happen; **bring down** cause to fall; **bring forward** move to earlier time, transfer from previous page or account, draw attention to; **bring in** introduce, produce as profit; **bring off** succeed in; **bring on** cause to happen, appear or progress; **bring out** emphasize, publish; **bring round** restore to consciousness, win over; **bring up** raise and educate, vomit, draw attention to.

brink *noun* edge of precipice etc.; furthest point before danger, discovery, etc. □ **brinkmanship** policy of pursuing dangerous course to brink of catastrophe.

briny /ˈbraɪnɪ/ ● *adjective* (**-ier, -iest**) of brine or sea, salt. ● *noun* (**the briny**) *slang* the sea.

briquette /brɪˈket/ *noun* block of compressed coal dust as fuel.

brisk *adjective* active, lively, quick. □ **briskly** *adverb*.

brisket /ˈbrɪskɪt/ *noun* animal's breast, esp. as joint of meat.

brisling /ˈbrɪzlɪŋ/ *noun* (*plural* same or **-s**) small herring or sprat.

bristle /ˈbrɪs(ə)l/ ● *noun* short stiff hair, esp. one used in brushes etc. ● *verb* (**-ling**) (of hair etc.) stand up; cause to bristle; show irritation; (usually + *with*) be covered (with) or abundant (in). □ **bristly** *adjective*.

British /ˈbrɪtɪʃ/ ● *adjective* of Britain. ● *plural noun* (**the British**) the British people. □ **British Summer Time** = SUMMER TIME.

Briton /ˈbrɪt(ə)n/ *noun* inhabitant of S. Britain before Roman conquest; native of Great Britain.

brittle /ˈbrɪt(ə)l/ *adjective* apt to break, fragile.

broach /brəʊtʃ/ *verb* raise for discussion; pierce (cask) to draw liquor; open and start using.

broad /brɔːd/ ● *adjective* large across, extensive; of specified breadth; full, clear; explicit; general; tolerant; coarse; (of accent) marked, strong. ● *noun* broad part; *US slang* woman; (**the Broads**) large areas of water in E. Anglia. □ **broad bean** bean with large flat seeds, one such seed; **broadloom** (carpet) woven in broad width; **broad-minded** tolerant, liberal; **broadsheet** large-sized newspaper. □ **broaden** *verb*; **broadly** *adverb*.

broadcast ● *verb* (*past & past participle* **-cast**) transmit by radio or television; take part in such transmission; scatter (seed) etc.; disseminate widely. ● *noun* radio or television programme or transmission. □ **broadcaster** *noun*; **broadcasting** *noun*.

broadside *noun* vigorous verbal attack; firing of all guns on one side of ship. □ **broadside on** sideways on.

brocade /brəˈkeɪd/ *noun* fabric woven with raised pattern.

broccoli /ˈbrɒkəlɪ/ *noun* brassica with greenish flower heads.

brochure /ˈbrəʊʃə/ *noun* booklet, pamphlet, esp. containing descriptive information.

broderie anglaise /brəʊdəri ɑ̃ˈɡleɪz/ *noun* open embroidery on usually white cotton or linen.

brogue /brəʊɡ/ *noun* strong shoe with ornamental perforations; rough shoe of untanned leather; marked local, esp. Irish, accent.

broil *verb* grill (meat); make or be very hot.

broiler *noun* young chicken for broiling.

broke ● *past* of BREAK. ● *adjective colloquial* having no money, bankrupt.

broken /ˈbrəʊkən/ ● *past participle* of BREAK. ● *adjective* that has been broken; reduced to despair; (of language) spoken imperfectly; interrupted. □ **broken-hearted** crushed by grief; **broken home** family disrupted by divorce or separation.

broker *noun* middleman, agent; stockbroker. □ **broking** *noun*.

brokerage *noun* broker's fee or commission.

brolly /ˈbrɒlɪ/ *noun* (*plural* **-ies**) *colloquial* umbrella.

bromide /ˈbrəʊmaɪd/ *noun* binary compound of bromine, esp. one used as sedative; trite remark.

bromine /ˈbrəʊmiːn/ *noun* poisonous liquid nonmetallic element with choking smell.

bronchial /ˈbrɒŋkɪəl/ *adjective* of two main divisions of windpipe or smaller tubes into which they divide.

bronchitis /brɒŋˈkaɪtɪs/ *noun* inflammation of bronchial mucous membrane.

bronco /ˈbrɒŋkəʊ/ *noun* (*plural* **-s**) wild or half-tamed horse of western US.

brontosaurus /brɒntəˈsɔːrəs/ *noun* (*plural* **-ruses**) = APATOSAURUS.

bronze /brɒnz/ ● *noun* brown alloy of copper and tin; its colour; work of art or medal in it. ● *adjective* made of or coloured like bronze. ● *verb* (**-zing**) make or grow brown; tan. □ **Bronze Age** period when tools were of bronze; **bronze medal** medal given usually as third prize.

brooch /brəʊtʃ/ noun ornamental hinged pin.

brood /bruːd/ ● noun bird's or other animal's young produced at one hatch or birth; colloquial children of a family. ● verb worry or ponder, esp. resentfully; (of hen) sit on eggs.

broody adjective (**-ier, -iest**) (of hen) wanting to brood; sullenly thoughtful; colloquial (of woman) wanting pregnancy.

brook[1] /brʊk/ noun small stream.

brook[2] /brʊk/ verb tolerate; allow.

broom /bruːm/ noun long-handled brush for sweeping; chiefly yellow-flowered shrub. □ **broomstick** broom-handle.

Bros. abbreviation Brothers.

broth /brɒθ/ noun thin meat or fish soup.

brothel /ˈbrɒθ(ə)l/ noun premises for prostitution.

brother /ˈbrʌðə/ noun man or boy in relation to his siblings; close man friend; (plural also **brethren** /ˈbreðrɪn/) member of male religious order; (plural also **brethren**) fellow Christian etc.; fellow human being. □ **brother-in-law** (plural **brothers-in-law**) wife's or husband's brother, sister's husband. □ **brotherly** adjective.

brotherhood noun relationship (as) between brothers; (members of) association for mutual help etc.

brought past & past participle of BRING.

brow /braʊ/ noun forehead; (usually in plural) eyebrow; summit of hill; edge of cliff etc.

browbeat verb (past **-beat**, past participle **-beaten**) intimidate, bully.

brown /braʊn/ ● adjective of colour of dark wood or rich soil; dark-skinned; tanned. ● noun brown colour, paint, clothes, etc. ● verb make or become brown. □ **brown bread** bread made of wholemeal or wheatmeal flour; **browned off** colloquial bored, fed up; **Brown Owl** adult leader of Brownies; **brown rice** unpolished rice; **brown sugar** partially refined sugar. **brownish** adjective.

Brownie /ˈbraʊnɪ/ noun junior Guide; (**brownie**) small square of chocolate cake with nuts; (**brownie**) benevolent elf.

browse /braʊz/ ● verb (**-sing**) read or look around desultorily; feed on leaves and young shoots. ● noun browsing; twigs, shoots, etc. as fodder.

bruise /bruːz/ ● noun discoloration of skin caused by blow or pressure; similar damage on fruit etc. ● verb (**-sing**) inflict bruise on; be susceptible to bruises.

bruiser noun colloquial tough brutal person.

bruit /bruːt/ verb (often + abroad, about) spread (report or rumour).

brunch noun combination of breakfast and lunch.

brunette /bruːˈnet/ noun woman with dark hair.

brunt noun chief impact of attack etc.

brush ● noun cleaning or hairdressing or painting implement of bristles etc. set in holder; application of brush; short esp. unpleasant encounter; fox's tail; carbon or metal piece serving as electrical contact. ● verb use brush on; touch lightly, graze in passing. □ **brush off** dismiss abruptly; **brush-off** dismissal, rebuff; **brush up** clean up or smarten, revise (subject, skill); **brushwood** undergrowth, thicket, cut or broken twigs etc.; **brushwork** painter's way of using brush.

brusque /brʊsk/ adjective abrupt, offhand. □ **brusquely** adverb; **brusqueness** noun.

Brussels sprout /ˈbrʌs(ə)lz/ noun brassica with small cabbage-like buds on stem; such bud.

brutal /ˈbruːt(ə)l/ adjective savagely cruel; mercilessly frank. □ **brutality** /-ˈtæl-/ noun (plural **-ies**); **brutalize** verb (also **-ise**) (**-zing, -sing**).

brute /bruːt/ ● noun cruel person; colloquial unpleasant person; animal other than man. ● adjective unthinking; cruel, stupid. □ **brutish** adjective.

bryony /ˈbraɪənɪ/ noun (plural **-ies**) climbing hedge plant.

B.Sc. abbreviation Bachelor of Science.

BST abbreviation British Summer Time.

Bt. abbreviation Baronet.

bubble /ˈbʌb(ə)l/ ● noun thin sphere of liquid enclosing air or gas; air-filled cavity in glass etc.; transparent domed cavity. ● verb (**-ling**) send up or rise in bubbles; make sound of boiling. □ **bubble and squeak** cooked potatoes and cabbage fried together; **bubble bath** additive to make bathwater bubbly; **bubblegum** chewing gum that can be blown into bubbles.

bubbly ● adjective (**-ier, -iest**) full of bubbles; exuberant. ● noun colloquial champagne.

bubonic /bjuːˈbɒnɪk/ adjective (of plague) marked by swellings esp. in groin and armpits.

buccaneer /bʌkəˈnɪə/ noun pirate; adventurer. □ **buccaneering** adjective & noun.

buck[1] ● noun male deer, hare, or rabbit. ● verb (of horse) jump vertically with back arched, throw (rider) thus; (usually + up) colloquial cheer up, hurry up. □ **buckshot** coarse shot for gun; **buck-tooth** projecting upper tooth.

buck[2] noun US & Australian slang dollar.

buck[3] noun slang small object placed before dealer at poker. □ **pass the buck** colloquial shift responsibility.

bucket /ˈbʌkɪt/ ● noun usually round open container with handle, for carrying or holding water etc.; amount contained in this; (in plural) colloquial large quantities; compartment or scoop in waterwheel, dredger, or grain elevator. ● verb (**-t-**) colloquial (often + down) (esp. of rain) pour heavily; (often + along) move jerkily or bumpily. □ **bucket seat** one with rounded back, to fit one person; **bucket shop** agency dealing in cheap airline tickets, unregistered broking agency.

buckle /ˈbʌk(ə)l/ ● noun clasp with usually hinged pin for securing strap or belt etc. ● verb (**-ling**) fasten with buckle; (cause to) crumple under pressure. □ **buckle down** make determined effort.

buckram /ˈbʌkrəm/ noun coarse linen etc. stiffened with paste etc.

buckshee /bʌkˈʃiː/ adjective & adverb slang free of charge.

buckwheat noun seed of plant related to rhubarb.

bucolic /bjuːˈkɒlɪk/ adjective of shepherds, rustic, pastoral.

bud ● noun projection from which branch, leaf, or flower develops; flower or leaf not fully open; asexual growth separating from organism as new animal. ● verb (**-dd-**) form buds; begin to grow or develop; graft bud of (plant) on another plant.

Buddhism /ˈbʊdɪz(ə)m/ noun Asian religion founded by Gautama Buddha. □ **Buddhist** adjective & noun.

buddleia /ˈbʌdlɪə/ noun shrub with flowers attractive to butterflies.

buddy /ˈbʌdɪ/ noun (plural **-ies**) colloquial friend; mate.

budge verb (**-ging**) move in slightest degree; (+ up) move to make room for another person.

budgerigar /ˈbʌdʒərɪgɑː/ noun small parrot often kept as pet.

budget /ˈbʌdʒɪt/ ● noun amount of money needed or available; (**the Budget**) annual estimate of country's revenue and expenditure; similar estimate for person or group. ● *verb* (**-t-**) (often + *for*) allow or arrange for in budget. □ **budgetary** *adjective*.

budgie /'bʌdʒɪ/ *noun colloquial* budgerigar.

buff ● *adjective* of yellowish beige colour. ● *noun* this colour; *colloquial* enthusiast; velvety dull yellow leather. ● *verb* polish; make (leather) velvety. □ **in the buff** *colloquial* naked.

buffalo /'bʌfələʊ/ *noun* (*plural* same or **-es**) any of various kinds of ox; American bison.

buffer¹ *noun* apparatus for deadening impact esp. of railway vehicles. □ **buffer state** minor one between two larger ones, regarded as reducing friction.

buffer² *noun slang* old or incompetent fellow.

buffet¹ /'bʊfeɪ/ *noun* room or counter where refreshments are sold; self-service meal of several dishes set out at once; (also /'bʌfɪt/) sideboard. □ **buffet car** railway coach in which refreshments are served.

buffet² /'bʌfɪt/ ● *verb* (**-t-**) strike repeatedly. ● *noun* blow with hand; shock.

buffoon /bə'fuːn/ *noun* silly or ludicrous person; jester. □ **buffoonery** *noun*.

bug ● *noun* small insect; concealed microphone; *colloquial* error in computer program etc.; *slang* virus, infection; *slang* enthusiasm, obsession. ● *verb* (**-gg-**) conceal microphone in; *slang* annoy.

bugbear *noun* cause of annoyance; object of baseless fear.

buggy /'bʌgɪ/ *noun* (*plural* **-ies**) small sturdy motor vehicle; lightweight pushchair; light horse-drawn vehicle for one or two people.

bugle /'bjuːg(ə)l/ *noun* brass instrument like small trumpet. ● *verb* (**-ling**) sound bugle. □ **bugler** *noun*.

build /bɪld/ ● *verb* (*past & past participle* **built** /bɪlt/) construct or cause to be constructed; develop or establish. ● *noun* physical proportions; style of construction. □ **build in** incorporate; **build up** increase in size or strength, praise, gradually establish or be established; **build-up** favourable description in advance, gradual approach to climax, accumulation.

builder *noun* contractor who builds houses etc.

building *noun* house or other structure with roof and walls. □ **building society** financial organization (not public company) that pays interest on savings accounts, lends money esp. for mortgages, etc.

built /bɪlt/ *past & past participle* of BUILD. □ **built-in** integral; **built-up** covered with buildings.

bulb *noun* rounded base of stem of some plants; light bulb; bulb-shaped thing or part.

bulbous /'bʌlbəs/ *adjective* bulb-shaped; bulging.

bulge ● *noun* irregular swelling; *colloquial* temporary increase. ● *verb* (**-ging**) swell outwards. □ **bulgy** *adjective*.

bulimia /bjʊ'lɪmɪə/ *noun* (in full **bulimia nervosa** /nɜː'vəʊsə/) disorder in which overeating alternates with self-induced vomiting, fasting, etc.

bulk ● *noun* size, magnitude, esp. when great; (**the bulk**) the greater part; large quantity. ● *verb* seem (in size or importance); make thicker. □ **bulk buying** buying in quantity at discount; **bulkhead** upright partition in ship, aircraft, etc.

bulky /'bʌlkɪ/ *adjective* (**-ier**, **-iest**) large, unwieldy.

bull¹ /bʊl/ *noun* uncastrated male ox; male whale or elephant etc.; bull's-eye of target; person who buys shares in hope of selling at higher price later. □ **bulldog** short-haired heavy-jowled sturdy dog, tenacious and courageous person; **Bulldog clip** strong sprung clip for papers etc.; **bulldoze** clear with bulldozer, *colloquial* intimidate, *colloquial* make (one's way) forcibly; **bulldozer** powerful tractor

with broad upright blade for clearing ground; **bullfight** public baiting, and usually killing, of bulls; **bullfinch** pink and black finch; **bullfrog** large American frog with booming croak; **bullring** arena for bullfight; **bull's-eye** centre of target, hard minty sweet; **bull terrier** cross between bulldog and terrier. □ **bullish** *adjective*.

bull² /bʊl/ *noun* papal edict.

bull³ /bʊl/ *noun slang* nonsense; *slang* unnecessary routine tasks; absurdly illogical statement.

bullet /'bʊlɪt/ *noun* small pointed missile fired from revolver etc. □ **bulletproof** resistant to bullets.

bulletin /'bʊlɪtɪn/ *noun* short official statement; short broadcast news report.

bullion /'bʊlɪən/ *noun* gold or silver in lump or valued by weight.

bullock /'bʊlək/ *noun* castrated bull.

bully¹ /'bʊlɪ/ ● *noun* (*plural* **-ies**) person coercing others by fear. ● *verb* (**-ies**, **-ied**) persecute or oppress by force or threats. ● *interjection* (+ *for*) very good.

bully² /'bʊlɪ/ (in full **bully off**) ● *noun* (*plural* **-ies**) putting ball into play in hockey. ● *verb* (**-ies**, **-ied**) start play thus.

bully³ /'bʊlɪ/ *noun* (in full **bully beef**) corned beef.

bulrush /'bʊlrʌʃ/ *noun* tall rush; *Biblical* papyrus.

bulwark /'bʊlwək/ *noun* defensive wall, esp. of earth; person or principle that protects; (usually in *plural*) ship's side above deck.

bum¹ *noun slang* buttocks. □ **bumbag** small pouch worn round waist.

bum² *US slang* ● *noun* loafer, dissolute person. ● *verb* (**-mm-**) (often + *around*) loaf, wander around; cadge. ● *adjective* of poor quality.

bumble /'bʌmb(ə)l/ *verb* (**-ling**) (+ *on*) speak ramblingly; be inept; blunder. □ **bumble-bee** large bee with loud hum.

bump ● *noun* dull-sounding blow or collision; swelling caused by it; uneven patch on road etc.; prominence on skull, thought to indicate mental faculty. ● *verb* come or strike with bump against; hurt thus; (usually + *along*) move along with jolts. □ **bump into** *colloquial* meet by chance; **bump off** *slang* murder; **bump up** *colloquial* increase. □ **bumpy** *adjective* (**-ier**, **-iest**).

bumper ● *noun* horizontal bar on motor vehicle to reduce damage in collisions; *Cricket* ball rising high after pitching; brim-full glass. ● *adjective* unusually large or abundant.

bumpkin /'bʌmpkɪn/ *noun* rustic or awkward person.

bumptious /'bʌmpʃəs/ *adjective* self-assertive, conceited.

bun *noun* small sweet cake or bread roll often with dried fruit; small coil of hair at back of head.

bunch ● *noun* cluster of things growing or fastened together; lot; *colloquial* gang, group. ● *verb* arrange in bunch(es); gather in folds; come, cling, or crowd together.

bundle /'bʌnd(ə)l/ ● *noun* collection of things tied or fastened together; set of nerve fibres etc.; *slang* large amount of money. ● *verb* (**-ling**) (usually + *up*) tie in bundle; (usually + *into*) throw or move carelessly; (usually + *out*, *off*, *away*, etc.) send away hurriedly.

bung ● *noun* stopper, esp. for cask. ● *verb* stop with bung; *slang* throw. □ **bunged up** blocked up.

bungalow /'bʌŋgələʊ/ *noun* one-storeyed house.

bungee /'bʌndʒɪ/ *noun* elasticated cord. □ **bungee jumping** sport of jumping from great height while secured by bungee.

bungle /'bʌŋg(ə)l/ ● *verb* (**-ling**) mismanage, fail to accomplish; work awkwardly. ● *noun* bungled work or attempt.

bunion /ˈbʌnjən/ *noun* swelling on foot, esp. on side of big toe.

bunk[1] *noun* shelflike bed against wall. □ **bunk bed** each of two or more bunks one above the other.

bunk[2] *slang* □ **do a bunk** run away.

bunk[3] *noun slang* nonsense, humbug.

bunker *noun* container for fuel; reinforced underground shelter; sandy hollow in golf course.

bunkum /ˈbʌŋkəm/ *noun* nonsense, humbug.

bunny /ˈbʌnɪ/ *noun* (*plural* **-ies**) *childish name for* rabbit.

Bunsen burner /ˈbʌns(ə)n/ *noun* small adjustable gas burner used in laboratory.

bunting[1] /ˈbʌntɪŋ/ *noun* small bird related to finches.

bunting[2] /ˈbʌntɪŋ/ *noun* flags and other decorations; loosely woven fabric for these.

buoy /bɔɪ/ ● *noun* anchored float as navigational mark etc.; lifebuoy. ● *verb* (usually + *up*) keep afloat, encourage; (often + *out*) mark with buoy(s).

buoyant /ˈbɔɪənt/ *adjective* apt to float; resilient; exuberant. □ **buoyancy** *noun*.

bur *noun* (also **burr**) clinging seed vessel or flower head, plant producing burs; clinging person.

burble /ˈbɜːb(ə)l/ *verb* (**-ling**) talk ramblingly; make bubbling sound.

burden /ˈbɜːd(ə)n/ ● *noun* thing carried, load; oppressive duty, expense, emotion, etc.; refrain of song; theme. ● *verb* load, encumber, oppress. □ **burden of proof** obligation to prove one's case. □ **burdensome** *adjective*.

burdock /ˈbɜːdɒk/ *noun* plant with prickly flowers and docklike leaves.

bureau /ˈbjʊərəʊ/ *noun* (*plural* **-s** or **-x** /-z/) writing desk with drawers; *US* chest of drawers; office or department for specific business; government department.

bureaucracy /bjʊəˈrɒkrəsɪ/ *noun* (*plural* **-ies**) government by central administration; government officials esp. regarded as oppressive and inflexible; conduct typical of these.

bureaucrat /ˈbjʊərəkræt/ *noun* official in bureaucracy. □ **bureaucratic** /-ˈkrætɪk/ *adjective*.

burgeon /ˈbɜːdʒ(ə)n/ *verb* grow rapidly, flourish.

burger /ˈbɜːgə/ *noun colloquial* hamburger.

burgher /ˈbɜːgə/ *noun* citizen, esp. of foreign town.

burglar /ˈbɜːglə/ *noun* person who commits burglary.

burglary *noun* (*plural* **-ies**) illegal entry into building to commit theft or other crime.

burgle /ˈbɜːg(ə)l/ *verb* (**-ling**) commit burglary (on).

burgundy /ˈbɜːgəndɪ/ *noun* (*plural* **-ies**) red or white wine produced in Burgundy; dark red colour.

burial /ˈberɪəl/ *noun* burying, esp. of corpse; funeral.

burlesque /bɜːˈlesk/ ● *noun* comic imitation, parody; *US* variety show, esp. with striptease. ● *adjective* of or using burlesque. ● *verb* (**-ques, -qued, -quing**) parody.

burly /ˈbɜːlɪ/ *adjective* (**-ier, -iest**) large and sturdy.

burn[1] ● *verb* (*past & past participle* **burnt** or **burned**) (cause to) be consumed by fire; blaze or glow with fire; (cause to) be injured or damaged by fire, sun, or great heat; use or be used as fuel; produce (hole etc.) by fire or heat; char in working; brand; give or feel sensation or pain (as) of heat. ● *noun* sore or mark made by burning. □ **burn out** be reduced to nothing by burning, (cause to) fail by burning, (usually **burn oneself out**) suffer exhaustion; **burnt offering** sacrifice offered by burning.

burn[2] *noun* Scottish brook.

burner *noun* part of lamp or cooker etc. that emits flame.

burnish /ˈbɜːnɪʃ/ *verb* polish by rubbing.

burnt *past & past participle of* BURN[1].

burp *verb & noun colloquial* belch.

burr[1] *noun* whirring sound; rough sounding of *r*; rough edge on metal etc.

burr[2] = BUR.

burrow /ˈbʌrəʊ/ ● *noun* hole dug by animal as dwelling. ● *verb* make burrow; make by digging; (+ *into*) investigate or search.

bursar /ˈbɜːsə/ *noun* treasurer of college etc.; holder of bursary.

bursary /ˈbɜːsərɪ/ *noun* (*plural* **-ies**) grant, esp. scholarship.

burst ● *verb* (*past & past participle* **burst**) fly violently apart or give way suddenly, explode; rush, move, speak, be spoken, etc. suddenly or violently. ● *noun* bursting, explosion, outbreak; spurt.

burton /ˈbɜːt(ə)n/ *noun* □ **go for a burton** *slang* be lost, destroyed, or killed.

bury /ˈberɪ/ *verb* (**-ies, -ied**) place (corpse) in ground, tomb, or sea; put underground, hide in earth; consign to obscurity; (**bury oneself** or in *passive*) involve (oneself) deeply. □ **bury the hatchet** cease to quarrel.

bus ● *noun* (*plural* **buses**, *US* **busses**) large public passenger vehicle usually plying on fixed route. ● *verb* (**buses** or **busses**, **bussed**, **bussing**) go by bus; *US* transport by bus (esp. to aid racial integration). □ **busman's holiday** leisure spent in same occupation as working hours; **bus shelter** shelter for people waiting for bus; **bus station** centre where buses depart and arrive; **bus stop** regular stopping place of bus.

busby /ˈbʌzbɪ/ *noun* (*plural* **-ies**) tall fur cap worn by hussars etc.

bush[1] /bʊʃ/ *noun* shrub, clump of shrubs; clump of hair or fur; *Australian etc.* uncultivated land, woodland. □ **bush-baby** small African lemur; **Bushman** member or language of a S. African aboriginal people; **bushman** dweller or traveller in Australian bush; **bush telegraph** rapid informal spreading of information etc.

bush[2] /bʊʃ/ *noun* metal lining of axle-hole etc.; electrically insulating sleeve.

bushel /ˈbʊʃ(ə)l/ *noun* measure of capacity for corn, fruit, etc. (8 gallons, 36.4 litres).

bushy *adjective* (**-ier, -iest**) growing thickly or like bush; having many bushes.

business /ˈbɪznɪs/ *noun* one's occupation or profession; one's own concern, task, duty; serious work; (difficult or unpleasant) matter or affair; thing(s) needing dealing with; buying and selling, trade; commercial firm. □ **businesslike** practical, systematic; **businessman**, **businesswoman** person engaged in trade or commerce.

busk *verb* perform esp. music in street etc. for tips. □ **busker** *noun*.

bust[1] *noun* human chest, esp. of woman; sculpture of head, shoulders, and chest.

bust[2] *colloquial* ● *verb* (*past & past participle* **bust** or **busted**) burst, break; raid, search; arrest. ● *adjective* burst, broken; bankrupt. □ **bust-up** quarrel, violent split or separation.

bustard /ˈbʌstəd/ *noun* large swift-running bird.

bustle[1] /ˈbʌs(ə)l/ ● *verb* (**-ling**) (often + *about*) move busily and energetically; make (person) hurry; (as **bustling** *adjective*) active, lively. ● *noun* excited activity.

bustle[2] /ˈbʌs(ə)l/ *noun historical* padding worn under skirt to puff it out behind.

busy /ˈbɪzɪ/ ● *adjective* (**-ier, -iest**) occupied or engaged in work etc.; full of activity; fussy. ● *verb* (**-ies, -ied**) occupy, keep busy. □ **busybody** meddlesome person; **busy Lizzie** house plant with usually red, pink, or white flowers. □ **busily** adverb.

but ● conjunction however; on the other hand; otherwise than. ● preposition except, apart from. ● adverb only. □ **but for** without the help or hindrance etc. of; **but then** however.

butane /ˈbjuːteɪn/ noun hydrocarbon used in liquefied form as fuel.

butch /bʊtʃ/ adjective slang masculine, tough-looking.

butcher /ˈbʊtʃə/ ● noun person who sells meat; slaughterer of animals for food; brutal murderer. ● verb slaughter or cut up (animal); kill wantonly or cruelly; colloquial ruin through incompetence. □ **butchery** noun (plural **-ies**).

butler /ˈbʌtlə/ noun chief manservant of household.

butt[1] ● verb push with head; (cause to) meet end to end. ● noun push or blow with head or horns. □ **butt in** interrupt, meddle.

butt[2] noun (often + of) object of ridicule etc.; mound behind target; (in plural) shooting range.

butt[3] noun thicker end, esp. of tool or weapon; stub of cigarette etc.

butt[4] noun cask.

butter /ˈbʌtə/ ● noun yellow fatty substance made from cream, used as spread and in cooking; substance of similar texture. ● verb spread, cook, etc., with butter. □ **butter-bean** dried large flat white kind; **buttercup** plant with yellow flowers; **butterfingers** colloquial person likely to drop things; **buttermilk** liquid left after butter-making; **butter muslin** thin loosely woven cloth; **butterscotch** sweet made of butter and sugar; **butter up** colloquial flatter.

butterfly /ˈbʌtəflaɪ/ noun (plural **-ies**) insect with 4 often showy wings; (in plural) nervous sensation in stomach. □ **butterfly nut** kind of wing-nut; **butterfly stroke** method of swimming with both arms lifted at same time.

buttery[1] adjective like or containing butter.

buttery[2] noun (plural **-ies**) food store or snack-bar, esp. in college.

buttock /ˈbʌtək/ noun either protuberance on lower rear part of human trunk; corresponding part of animal.

button /ˈbʌt(ə)n/ ● noun disc or knob sewn to garment etc. as fastening or for ornament; knob etc. pressed to operate electronic equipment. ● verb (often + up) fasten with buttons. □ **button mushroom** small unopened mushroom.

buttonhole ● noun slit in cloth for button; flower(s) worn in lapel buttonhole. ● verb (-**ling**) colloquial accost and detain (reluctant listener).

buttress /ˈbʌtrɪs/ ● noun support built against wall etc. ● verb support or strengthen.

buxom /ˈbʌksəm/ adjective plump and rosy, large and shapely.

buy /baɪ/ ● verb (**buys**, **buying**; past & past participle **bought** /bɔːt/) obtain in exchange for money etc.; procure by bribery, bribe; get by sacrifice etc.; slang accept, believe. ● noun colloquial purchase. □ **buy out** pay (a person) for ownership, an interest, etc.; **buyout** purchase of controlling share in company; **buy up** buy as much as possible of.

buyer noun person who buys, esp. stock for large shop. □ **buyer's market** time when goods are plentiful and cheap.

buzz ● noun hum of bee etc.; sound of buzzer; low murmur; hurried activity; slang telephone call; slang thrill. ● verb hum; summon with buzzer; (often + about) move busily; be filled with activity or excitement. □ **buzzword** colloquial fashionable technical word, catchword.

buzzard /ˈbʌzəd/ noun large bird of hawk family.

buzzer noun electrical buzzing device as signal.

by /baɪ/ ● preposition near, beside, along; through action, agency, or means of; not later than; past; via; during; to extent of; according to. ● adverb near; aside, in reserve; past. □ **by and by** before long; **by-election** parliamentary election between general elections; **by-product** substance etc. produced incidentally in making of something else; **byroad** minor road; **by the by, by the way** incidentally; **byway** byroad or secluded path; **byword** person or thing as notable example, proverb.

bye[1] /baɪ/ noun Cricket run made from ball that passes batsman without being hit; (in tournament) position of competitor left without opponent in round.

bye[2] /baɪ/ interjection (also **bye-bye**) colloquial goodbye.

bygone adjective past, departed. □ **let bygones be bygones** forgive and forget past quarrels.

by-law noun regulation made by local authority etc.

byline noun line in newspaper etc. naming writer of article etc.

bypass ● noun main road round town or its centre. ● verb avoid.

byre /baɪə/ noun cowshed.

bystander noun person present but not taking part.

byte /baɪt/ noun Computing group of 8 binary digits, often representing one character.

Byzantine /bɪˈzæntaɪn/ adjective of Byzantium or E. Roman Empire; of architectural etc. style developed in Eastern Empire; complicated, underhand.

Cc

C¹ *noun* (also **c**) (Roman numeral) 100.

C² *abbreviation* Celsius; centigrade.

c.¹ *abbreviation* century; cent(s).

c.² *abbreviation* circa.

ca. *abbreviation* circa.

CAA *abbreviation* Civil Aviation Authority.

cab *noun* taxi; driver's compartment in lorry, train, crane, etc.

cabal /kə'bæl/ *noun* secret intrigue; political clique.

cabaret /'kæbəreɪ/ *noun* entertainment in restaurant etc.

cabbage /'kæbɪdʒ/ *noun* vegetable with green or purple leaves forming a round head; *colloquial* dull or inactive person. □ **cabbage white** kind of white butterfly.

cabby /'kæbɪ/ *noun* (*plural* **-ies**) *colloquial* taxi driver.

caber /'keɪbə/ *noun* tree trunk tossed as sport in Scotland.

cabin /'kæbɪn/ *noun* small shelter or house, esp. of wood; room or compartment in aircraft, ship, etc. □ **cabin boy** boy steward on ship; **cabin cruiser** large motor boat with accommodation.

cabinet /'kæbɪnɪt/ *noun* cupboard or case for storing or displaying things; casing of radio, television, etc.; (**Cabinet**) group of senior ministers in government. □ **cabinetmaker** skilled joiner.

cable /'keɪb(ə)l/ ● *noun* encased group of insulated wires for transmitting electricity etc.; thick rope of wire or hemp; cablegram. ● *verb* (**-ling**) send (message) or inform (person) by cable. □ **cable car** small cabin on loop of cable for carrying passengers up and down mountain etc.; **cablegram** message sent by undersea cable etc.; **cable stitch** knitting stitch resembling twisted rope; **cable television** transmission of television programmes by cable to subscribers.

caboodle /kə'bu:d(ə)l/ *noun*. □ **the whole caboodle** *slang* the whole lot.

caboose /kə'bu:s/ *noun* kitchen on ship's deck; *US* guard's van on train.

cabriolet /kæbrɪəʊ'leɪ/ *noun* car with folding top.

cacao /kə'kaʊ/ *noun* (*plural* **-s**) seed from which cocoa and chocolate are made; tree bearing it.

cache /kæʃ/ ● *noun* hiding place for treasure, supplies, etc.; things so hidden. ● *verb* (**-ching**) place in cache.

cachet /'kæʃeɪ/ *noun* prestige; distinguishing mark or seal; flat capsule for medicine.

cack-handed /kæk'hændɪd/ *adjective colloquial* clumsy, left-handed.

cackle /'kæk(ə)l/ ● *noun* clucking of hen; raucous laugh; noisy chatter. ● *verb* (**-ling**) emit cackle; chatter noisily.

cacophony /kə'kɒfənɪ/ *noun* (*plural* **-ies**) harsh discordant sound. □ **cacophonous** *adjective*.

cactus /'kæktəs/ *noun* (*plural* **-ti** /-taɪ/ or **-tuses**) plant with thick fleshy stem and usually spines but no leaves.

CAD *abbreviation* computer-aided design.

cad *noun* man who behaves dishonourably. □ **caddish** *adjective*.

cadaver /kə'dævə/ *noun* corpse. □ **cadaverous** *adjective*.

caddie /'kædɪ/ (also **caddy**) ● *noun* (*plural* **-ies**) golfer's attendant carrying clubs etc. ● *verb* (**caddying**) act as caddie.

caddis /'kædɪs/ *noun* □ **caddis-fly** small nocturnal insect living near water; **caddis-worm** larva of caddis-fly.

caddy¹ /'kædɪ/ *noun* (*plural* **-ies**) small container for tea.

caddy² = CADDIE.

cadence /'keɪd(ə)ns/ *noun* rhythm; fall in pitch of voice; tonal inflection; close of musical phrase.

cadenza /kə'denzə/ *noun Music* virtuoso passage for soloist during concerto.

cadet /kə'det/ *noun* young trainee in armed services or police force.

cadge *verb* (**-ging**) *colloquial* get or seek by begging.

cadi /'kɑːdɪ/ *noun* (*plural* **-s**) judge in Muslim country.

cadmium /'kædmɪəm/ *noun* soft bluish-white metallic element.

cadre /'kɑːdə/ *noun* basic unit, esp. of servicemen; group of esp. Communist activists.

caecum /'siːkəm/ *noun* (*US* **cecum**) (*plural* **-ca**) pouch between small and large intestines.

Caerphilly /keə'fɪlɪ/ *noun* kind of mild pale cheese.

Caesarean /sɪ'zeərɪən/ (*US* **Cesarean, Cesarian**) ● *adjective* (of birth) effected by Caesarean section. ● *noun* (in full **Caesarean section**) delivery of child by cutting into mother's abdomen.

caesura /sɪ'zjʊərə/ *noun* (*plural* **-s**) pause in line of verse.

café /'kæfeɪ/ *noun* coffee house, restaurant.

cafeteria /kæfɪ'tɪərɪə/ *noun* self-service restaurant.

cafetière /kæfə'tjeə/ *noun* coffee pot with plunger for pressing grounds to bottom.

caffeine /'kæfiːn/ *noun* alkaloid stimulant in tea leaves and coffee beans.

caftan /'kæftæn/ *noun* (also **kaftan**) long tunic worn by men in Near East; long loose dress.

cage ● *noun* structure of bars or wires, esp. for confining animals; open framework, esp. lift in mine etc. ● *verb* (**-ging**) confine in cage.

cagey /'keɪdʒɪ/ *adjective* (**-ier, -iest**) *colloquial* cautious and non-committal. □ **cagily** *adverb*.

cagoule /kə'guːl/ *noun* light hooded windproof jacket.

cahoots /kə'huːts/ *plural noun* □ **in cahoots** *slang* in collusion.

caiman = CAYMAN.

cairn /keən/ *noun* mound of stones. □ **cairn terrier** small shaggy short-legged terrier.

cairngorm /'keəngɔːm/ *noun* yellow or wine-coloured semiprecious stone.

caisson /'keɪs(ə)n/ *noun* watertight chamber for underwater construction work.

cajole /kə'dʒəʊl/ *verb* (**-ling**) persuade by flattery, deceit, etc. □ **cajolery** *noun*.

cake ● *noun* mixture of flour, butter, eggs, sugar, etc. baked in oven; flattish compact mass. ● *verb* (**-king**) form into compact mass; (usually + *with*) cover (with sticky mass).

calabash /'kæləbæʃ/ *noun* tropical American tree bearing gourds; bowl or pipe made from gourd.

calabrese /'kæləbriːs, kælə'breɪsɪ/ *noun* variety of broccoli.

calamine /'kæləmaɪn/ *noun* powdered zinc carbonate and ferric oxide used in skin lotion.

calamity /kə'læmɪtɪ/ *noun* (*plural* **-ies**) disaster. □ **calamitous** *adjective*.

calcareous /kæl'keərɪəs/ *adjective* of or containing calcium carbonate.

calceolaria /kælsɪə'leərɪə/ *noun* plant with slipper-shaped flowers.

calcify /'kælsɪfaɪ/ *verb* (**-ies**, **-ied**) harden by deposit of calcium salts. □ **calcification** *noun*.

calcine /'kælsaɪn/ *verb* (**-ning**) decompose or be decomposed by roasting or burning. □ **calcination** /-sɪn-/ *noun*.

calcium /'kælsɪəm/ *noun* soft grey metallic element.

calculate /'kælkjʊleɪt/ *verb* (**-ting**) ascertain or forecast by exact reckoning; plan deliberately. □ **calculable** *adjective*; **calculation** *noun*.

calculated *adjective* done with awareness of likely consequences; (+ *to do*) designed.

calculating *adjective* scheming, mercenary.

calculator *noun* device (esp. small electronic one) used for making calculations.

calculus /'kælkjʊləs/ *noun* (*plural* **-luses** or **-li** /-laɪ/) *Mathematics* particular method of calculation; stone in body.

Caledonian /kælɪ'dəʊnɪən/ *literary* ● *adjective* of Scotland. ● *noun* Scot.

calendar /'kælɪndə/ *noun* system fixing year's beginning, length, and subdivision; chart etc. showing such subdivisions; list of special dates or events. □ **calendar year** period from 1 Jan. to 31 Dec. inclusive.

calends /'kælendz/ *plural noun* (also **kalends**) first of month in ancient Roman calendar.

calf[1] /kɑːf/ *noun* (*plural* **calves** /kɑːvz/) young cow, bull, elephant, whale, etc.; calf leather. □ **calf-love** romantic adolescent love.

calf[2] /kɑːf/ *noun* (*plural* **calves** /kɑːvz/) fleshy hind part of human leg below knee.

calibrate /'kælɪbreɪt/ *verb* (**-ting**) mark (gauge) with scale of readings; correlate readings of (instrument) with standard; find calibre of (gun). □ **calibration** *noun*.

calibre /'kælɪbə/ *noun* (*US* **caliber**) internal diameter of gun or tube; diameter of bullet or shell; strength or quality of character; ability; importance.

calico /'kælɪkəʊ/ ● *noun* (*plural* **-es** or *US* **-s**) cotton cloth, esp. white or unbleached; *US* printed cotton cloth. ● *adjective* of calico; *US* multicoloured.

caliper = CALLIPER.

caliph /'keɪlɪf/ *noun historical* chief Muslim civil and religious ruler.

calk *US* = CAULK.

call /kɔːl/ ● *verb* (often + *out*) cry, shout, speak loudly; emit characteristic sound; communicate with by radio or telephone; summon; make brief visit; order to take place; name, describe, or regard as; rouse from sleep; (+ *for*) demand. ● *noun* shout; bird's cry; brief visit; telephone conversation; summons; need, demand. □ **call box** telephone box; **call-girl** prostitute accepting appointments by telephone; **call in** withdraw from circulation, seek advice or services of; **call off** cancel, order (pursuer) to desist; **call the shots**, **tune** *colloquial* be in control; **call up** *verb* telephone, recall, summon (esp. to do military service); **call-up** *noun* summons to do military service. □ **caller** *noun*.

calligraphy /kə'lɪgrəfɪ/ *noun* beautiful handwriting; art of this. □ **calligrapher** *noun*; **calligraphic** /kælɪ'græfɪk/ *adjective*.

calling *noun* profession, occupation; vocation.

calliper /'kælɪpə/ *noun* (also **caliper**) metal splint to support leg; (in *plural*) compasses for measuring diameters.

callisthenics /kælɪs'θenɪks/ *plural noun* exercises for fitness and grace. □ **callisthenic** *adjective*.

callosity /kə'lɒsɪtɪ/ *noun* (*plural* **-ies**) callus.

callous /'kæləs/ *adjective* unfeeling, unsympathetic; (also **calloused**) (of skin) hardened. □ **callously** *adverb*; **callousness** *noun*.

callow /'kæləʊ/ *adjective* inexperienced, immature.

callus /'kæləs/ *noun* (*plural* **calluses**) area of hard thick skin.

calm /kɑːm/ ● *adjective* tranquil, windless; not agitated. ● *noun* calm condition or period. ● *verb* (often + *down*) make or become calm. □ **calmly** *adverb*; **calmness** *noun*.

calomel /'kæləmel/ *noun* compound of mercury used as laxative.

Calor gas /'kælə/ *noun proprietary term* liquefied butane under pressure in containers for domestic use.

calorie /'kælərɪ/ *noun* unit of heat, amount required to raise temperature of one gram (**small calorie**) or one kilogram (**large calorie**) of water by 1°C.

calorific /kælə'rɪfɪk/ *adjective* producing heat.

calumny /'kæləmnɪ/ *noun* (*plural* **-ies**) slander; malicious misrepresentation. □ **calumnious** /kə'lʌm-/ *adjective*.

calvados /'kælvədɒs/ *noun* apple brandy.

calve /kɑːv/ *verb* (**-ving**) give birth to (calf).

calves *plural of* CALF[1,2].

Calvinism /'kælvɪnɪz(ə)m/ *noun* Calvin's theology, stressing predestination. □ **Calvinist** *noun & adjective*; **Calvinistic** /-'nɪs-/ *adjective*.

calx *noun* (*plural* **calces** /'kælsiːz/) powdery residue left after heating of ore or mineral.

calypso /kə'lɪpsəʊ/ *noun* (*plural* **-s**) W. Indian song with improvised usually topical words.

calyx /'keɪlɪks/ *noun* (*plural* **calyces** /-lɪsiːz/ or **-es**) leaves forming protective case of flower in bud.

cam *noun* projection on wheel etc., shaped to convert circular into reciprocal or variable motion.

camaraderie /kæmə'rɑːdərɪ/ *noun* friendly comradeship.

camber /'kæmbə/ ● *noun* convex surface of road, deck, etc. ● *verb* construct with camber.

cambric /'kæmbrɪk/ *noun* fine linen or cotton cloth.

camcorder /'kæmkɔːdə/ *noun* combined portable video camera and recorder.

came *past of* COME.

camel /'kæm(ə)l/ *noun* long-legged ruminant with one hump (**Arabian camel**) or two humps (**Bactrian camel**); fawn colour.

camellia /kə'miːlɪə/ *noun* evergreen flowering shrub.

Camembert /'kæməmbeə/ *noun* kind of soft creamy cheese.

cameo /'kæmɪəʊ/ *noun* (*plural* **-s**) small piece of hard stone carved in relief; short literary sketch or acted scene; small part in play or film.

camera /'kæmrə/ *noun* apparatus for taking photographs or for making motion film or television pictures. □ **cameraman** operator of film or television camera; **in camera** in private.

camiknickers /'kæmɪnɪkəz/ *plural noun* woman's knickers and vest combined.

camisole /'kæmɪsəʊl/ *noun* woman's under-bodice.

camomile /'kæməmaɪl/ *noun* (also **chamomile**) aromatic herb with flowers used to make tea.

camouflage /'kæməflɑːʒ/ ● *noun* disguising of soldiers, tanks, etc., so that they blend into background; such disguise; animal's natural blending colouring. ● *verb* (**-ging**) hide by camouflage.

camp¹ ● *noun* place where troops are lodged or trained; temporary accommodation of tents, huts, etc., for detainees, holiday-makers, etc.; fortified site; party supporters regarded collectively. ● *verb* set up or live in camp. □ **camp bed** portable folding bed; **camp follower** civilian worker in military camp, disciple; **campsite** place for camping.

camp² *colloquial* ● *adjective* affected, theatrically exaggerated; effeminate; homosexual. ● *noun* camp manner. ● *verb* behave or do in camp way.

campaign /kæm'peɪn/ ● *noun* organized course of action, esp. to gain publicity; series of military operations. ● *verb* take part in campaign. □ **campaigner** *noun*.

campanile /kæmpə'niːlɪ/ *noun* bell tower, usually free-standing.

campanology /kæmpə'nɒlədʒɪ/ *noun* study of bells; bell-ringing. □ **campanologist** *noun*.

campanula /kæm'pænjʊlə/ *noun* plant with bell-shaped flowers.

camper *noun* person who camps; motor vehicle with beds.

camphor /'kæmfə/ *noun* pungent crystalline substance used in medicine and formerly mothballs.

camphorate *verb* (**-ting**) impregnate with camphor.

campion /'kæmpɪən/ *noun* wild plant with usually pink or white notched flowers.

campus /'kæmpəs/ *noun* (*plural* **-es**) grounds of university or college.

camshaft *noun* shaft carrying cam(s).

can¹ *auxiliary verb* (*3rd singular present* **can**; *past* **could** /kʊd/) be able to; have the potential to; be permitted to.

can² ● *noun* metal vessel for liquid; sealed tin container for preservation of food or drink; (*in plural*) *slang* headphones; (**the can**) *slang* prison, *US* lavatory. ● *verb* (**-nn-**) preserve (food etc.) in can. □ **canned music** pre-recorded music; **carry the can** bear responsibility; **in the can** *colloquial* completed.

canal /kə'næl/ *noun* artificial inland waterway; tubular duct in plant or animal.

canalize /'kænəlaɪz/ *verb* (also **-ise**) (**-zing** or **-sing**) convert (river) into canal; provide (area) with canal(s); channel. □ **canalization** *noun*.

canapé /'kænəpeɪ/ *noun* small piece of bread or pastry with savoury topping.

canard /'kænɑːd/ *noun* unfounded rumour.

canary /kə'neərɪ/ *noun* (*plural* **-ies**) small songbird with yellow feathers.

canasta /kə'næstə/ *noun* card game resembling rummy.

cancan /'kænkæn/ *noun* high-kicking dance.

cancel /'kæns(ə)l/ *verb* (**-ll-**; *US* **-l-**) revoke, discontinue (arrangement); delete; mark (ticket, stamp, etc.) to invalidate it; annul; (often + *out*) neutralize, counterbalance; *Mathematics* strike out (equal factor) on each side of equation etc. □ **cancellation** *noun*.

cancer /'kænsə/ *noun* malignant tumour, disease caused by this; corruption; (**Cancer**) fourth sign of zodiac. □ **cancerous** *adjective*.

candela /kæn'diːlə/ *noun* SI unit of luminous intensity.

candelabrum /kændɪ'lɑːbrəm/ *noun* (also **-bra**) (*plural* **-bra**, *US* **-brums**, **-bras**) large branched candlestick or lampholder.

candid /'kændɪd/ *adjective* frank; (of photograph) taken informally, usually without subject's knowledge. □ **candidly** *adverb*.

candidate /'kændɪdət/ *noun* person nominated for, seeking, or likely to gain, office, position, award, etc.; person entered for exam. □ **candidacy** *noun*; **candidature** *noun*.

candle /'kænd(ə)l/ *noun* (usually cylindrical) block of wax or tallow enclosing wick which gives light when burning. □ **candlelight** light from candle(s); **candlelit** lit by candle(s); **candlestick** holder for candle(s); **candlewick** thick soft yarn, tufted material made from this.

candour /'kændə/ *noun* (*US* **candor**) frankness.

candy /'kændɪ/ ● *noun* (*plural* **-ies**) (in full **sugar-candy**) sugar crystallized by repeated boiling and evaporation; *US* sweets, a sweet. ● *verb* (**-ies**, **-ied**) (usually as **candied** *adjective*) preserve (fruit etc.) in candy. □ **candyfloss** fluffy mass of spun sugar; **candy stripe** alternate white and esp. pink stripes.

candytuft /'kændɪtʌft/ *noun* plant with white, pink, or purple flowers in tufts.

cane ● *noun* hollow jointed stem of giant reed or grass, or solid stem of slender palm, used for wickerwork or as walking stick, plant support, instrument of punishment, etc.; sugar cane. ● *verb* (**-ning**) beat with cane; weave cane into (chair etc.).

canine /'keɪnaɪn/ ● *adjective* of a dog or dogs. ● *noun* dog; (in full **canine tooth**) tooth between incisors and molars.

canister /'kænɪstə/ *noun* small usually metal box for tea etc.; cylinder of shot, tear gas, etc.

canker /'kæŋkə/ ● *noun* disease of trees and plants; ulcerous ear disease of animals; corrupting influence. ● *verb* infect with canker; corrupt. □ **cankerous** *adjective*.

cannabis /'kænəbɪs/ *noun* hemp plant; parts of it used as narcotic.

cannelloni /kænə'ləʊnɪ/ *plural noun* tubes of pasta stuffed with savoury mixture.

cannibal /'kænɪb(ə)l/ *noun* person or animal that eats its own species. □ **cannibalism** *noun*; **cannibalistic** /-'lɪs-/ *adjective*.

cannibalize /'kænɪbəlaɪz/ *verb* (also **-ise**) (**-zing** or **-sing**) use (machine etc.) as source of spare parts.

cannon /'kænən/ ● *noun* automatic aircraft gun firing shells; *historical* (*plural* usually same) large gun; hitting of two balls successively by player's ball in billiards. ● *verb* (usually + *against*, *into*) collide. □ **cannon ball** *historical* large ball fired by cannon.

cannot /'kænɒt/ can not.

canny /'kænɪ/ *adjective* (**-ier**, **-iest**) shrewd; thrifty.

canoe /kə'nuː/ ● *noun* light narrow boat, usually paddled. ● *verb* (**-noes**, **-noed**, **-noeing**) travel in canoe. □ **canoeist** *noun*.

canon /'kænən/ *noun* general law, rule, principle, or criterion; church decree; member of cathedral chapter; set of (esp. sacred) writings accepted as genuine; part of RC Mass containing words of consecration; *Music* piece with different parts taking up same theme successively. □ **canon law** ecclesiastical law.

canonical /kə'nɒnɪk(ə)l/ ● *adjective* according to canon law; included in canon of Scripture; authoritative, accepted; of (member of) cathedral chapter. ● *noun* (*in plural*) canonical dress of clergy.

canonize /'kænənaɪz/ *verb* (also **-ise**) (**-zing** or **-sing**) declare officially to be saint. □ **canonization** *noun*.

canopy /'kænəpɪ/ ● *noun* (*plural* **-ies**) suspended covering over throne, bed, etc.; sky; overhanging shelter; rooflike projection. ● *verb* (**-ies**, **-ied**) supply or be canopy to.

cant¹ ● *noun* insincere pious or moral talk; language peculiar to class, profession, etc.; jargon. ● *verb* use cant.

cant² ● *noun* slanting surface, bevel; oblique push or jerk; tilted position. ● *verb* push or pitch out of level.

can't /kɑːnt/ can not.

cantabile /kæn'tɑːbɪleɪ/ *Music* ● *adverb & adjective* in smooth flowing style. ● *noun* cantabile passage or movement.

cantaloupe /'kæntəluːp/ *noun* (also **cantaloup**) small round ribbed melon.

cantankerous /kæn'tæŋkərəs/ *adjective* bad-tempered, quarrelsome. □ **cantankerously** *adverb*; **cantankerousness** *noun*.

cantata /kæn'tɑːtə/ *noun* composition for vocal soloists and usually chorus and orchestra.

canteen /kæn'tiːn/ *noun* restaurant for employees in office, factory, etc.; shop for provisions in barracks or camp; case of cutlery; soldier's or camper's water-flask.

canter /'kæntə/ ● *noun* horse's pace between trot and gallop. ● *verb* (cause to) go at a canter.

canticle /'kæntɪk(ə)l/ *noun* song or chant with biblical text.

cantilever /'kæntiliːvə/ *noun* bracket, beam, etc. projecting from wall to support balcony etc.; beam or girder fixed at one end only. □ **cantilever bridge** bridge made of cantilevers projecting from piers and connected by girders. □ **cantilevered** *adjective*.

canto /'kæntəʊ/ *noun* (*plural* **-s**) division of long poem.

canton ● *noun* /'kæntɒn/ subdivision of country, esp. Switzerland. ● *verb* /kæn'tuːn/ put (troops) into quarters.

cantonment /kæn'tuːnmənt/ *noun* lodgings of troops.

cantor /'kæntɔː/ *noun* church choir leader; precentor in synagogue.

canvas /'kænvəs/ *noun* strong coarse cloth used for sails and tents etc. and for oil painting; a painting on canvas.

canvass /'kænvəs/ ● *verb* solicit votes (from), ascertain opinions of; seek custom from; propose (idea etc.). ● *noun* canvassing. □ **canvasser** *noun*.

canyon /'kænjən/ *noun* deep gorge.

CAP *abbreviation* Common Agricultural Policy (of EC).

cap ● *noun* soft brimless hat, often with peak; head-covering of nurse etc.; cap as sign of membership of sports team; academic mortarboard; cover resembling cap, or designed to close, seal, or protect something; contraceptive diaphragm; percussion cap; dental crown. ● *verb* (**-pp-**) put cap on; cover top or end of; limit; award sports cap to; form top of; surpass.

capable /'keɪpəb(ə)l/ *adjective* competent, able; (+ *of*) having ability, fitness, etc. for. □ **capability** *noun* (*plural* **-ies**); **capably** *adverb*.

capacious /kə'peɪʃəs/ *adjective* roomy. □ **capaciousness** *noun*.

capacitance /kə'pæsɪt(ə)ns/ *noun* ability to store electric charge.

capacitor /kə'pæsɪtə/ *noun* type of device for storing electric charge.

capacity /kə'pæsɪtɪ/ ● *noun* (*plural* **-ies**) power to contain, receive, experience, or produce; maximum amount that can be contained etc.; mental power; position or function. ● *adjective* fully occupying available space etc.

caparison /kə'pærɪs(ə)n/ *literary* ● *noun* horse's trappings; finery. ● *verb* adorn.

cape¹ *noun* short cloak.

cape² *noun* headland, promontory; (**the Cape**) Cape of Good Hope.

caper¹ /'keɪpə/ ● *verb* jump playfully. ● *noun* playful leap; prank; *slang* illicit activity.

caper² /'keɪpə/ *noun* bramble-like shrub; (in *plural*) its pickled buds.

capercaillie /kæpə'keɪlɪ/ *noun* (also **capercailzie** /-'keɪlzɪ/) large European grouse.

capillarity /kæpɪ'lærɪtɪ/ *noun* rise or depression of liquid in narrow tube.

capillary /kə'pɪlərɪ/ ● *adjective* of hair; of narrow diameter. ● *noun* (*plural* **-ies**) capillary tube or blood vessel. □ **capillary action** capillarity.

capital /'kæpɪt(ə)l/ ● *noun* chief town or city of a country or region; money etc. with which company starts in business; accumulated wealth; capital letter; head of column or pillar. ● *adjective* involving punishment by death; most important; *colloquial* excellent. □ **capital gain** profit from sale of investments or property; **capital goods** machinery, plant, etc.; **capital letter** large kind, used to begin sentence or name; **capital transfer tax** *historical* tax levied on transfer of capital by gift or bequest etc.

capitalism *noun* economic and political system dependent on private capital and profit-making.

capitalist ● *noun* person using or possessing capital; advocate of capitalism. ● *adjective* of or favouring capitalism. □ **capitalistic** /-'lɪs-/ *adjective*.

capitalize *verb* (also **-ise**) (**-zing** or **-sing**) convert into or provide with capital; write (letter of alphabet) as capital, begin (word) with capital letter; (+ *on*) use to one's advantage. □ **capitalization** *noun*.

capitulate /kə'pɪtjʊleɪt/ *verb* (**-ting**) surrender. □ **capitulation** *noun*.

capon /'keɪpən/ *noun* castrated cock.

cappuccino /kæpʊ'tʃiːnəʊ/ *noun* (*plural* **-s**) frothy milky coffee.

caprice /kə'priːs/ *noun* whim; lively or fanciful work of music etc.

capricious /kə'prɪʃəs/ *adjective* subject to whims, unpredictable. □ **capriciously** *adverb*; **capriciousness** *noun*.

Capricorn /'kæprɪkɔːn/ *noun* tenth sign of zodiac.

capsicum /'kæpsɪkəm/ *noun* plant with edible fruits; red, green, or yellow fruit of this.

capsize /kæp'saɪz/ *verb* (**-zing**) (of boat) be overturned; overturn (boat).

capstan /'kæpst(ə)n/ *noun* thick revolving cylinder for winding cable etc.; revolving spindle controlling speed of tape on tape recorder. □ **capstan lathe** lathe with revolving tool holder.

capsule /'kæpsjuːl/ *noun* small soluble case enclosing medicine; detachable compartment of spacecraft or nose-cone of rocket; enclosing membrane; dry fruit releasing seeds when ripe.

Capt. *abbreviation* Captain.

captain /'kæptɪn/ ● *noun* chief, leader; leader of team; commander of ship; pilot of civil aircraft; army officer next above lieutenant. ● *verb* be captain of. □ **captaincy** *noun* (*plural* **-ies**).

caption /'kæpʃ(ə)n/ ● *noun* wording appended to illustration or cartoon; wording on cinema or television screen; heading of chapter, article etc. ● *verb* provide with caption.

captious /'kæpʃəs/ *adjective* fault-finding.

captivate /'kæptɪveɪt/ *verb* (**-ting**) fascinate, charm. □ **captivation** *noun*.

captive /'kæptɪv/ ● *noun* confined or imprisoned person or animal. ● *adjective* taken prisoner; confined; unable to escape. □ **captivity** /-'tɪv-/ *noun*.

captor /'kæptə/ *noun* person who captures.

capture /'kæptʃə/ ● *verb* (**-ring**) take prisoner; seize; portray in permanent form; record on film or for use in computer. ● *noun* act of capturing; thing or person captured.

Capuchin /'kæpjʊtʃɪn/ *noun* friar of branch of Franciscans; (**capuchin**) monkey with hair like black hood.

car *noun* motor vehicle for driver and small number of passengers; railway carriage of specified type; *US* any railway carriage or van. □ **car bomb** terrorist bomb placed in or under parked car; **car boot sale** sale of goods from (tables stocked from) boots of cars; **car park** area for parking cars; **car phone** radio-telephone for use in car etc.; **carport** roofed open-sided shelter for car; **carsick** nauseous through car travel.

caracul = KARAKUL.

carafe /kə'ræf/ noun glass container for water or wine.

caramel /'kærəmel/ noun burnt sugar or syrup; kind of soft toffee. □ **caramelize** verb.

carapace /'kærəpeɪs/ noun upper shell of tortoise or crustacean.

carat /'kærət/ noun unit of weight for precious stones; measure of purity of gold.

caravan /'kærəvæn/ noun vehicle equipped for living in and usually towed by car; people travelling together, esp. across desert. □ **caravanner** noun.

caravanserai /kærə'vænsəraɪ/ noun Eastern inn with central courtyard.

caravel /'kærəvel/ noun historical small light fast ship.

caraway /'kærəweɪ/ noun plant with small aromatic fruit (**caraway seed**) used in cakes etc.

carbide /'kɑːbaɪd/ noun binary compound of carbon.

carbine /'kɑːbaɪn/ noun kind of short rifle.

carbohydrate /kɑːbə'haɪdreɪt/ noun energy-producing compound of carbon, hydrogen, and oxygen.

carbolic /kɑː'bɒlɪk/ noun (in full **carbolic acid**) kind of disinfectant and antiseptic. □ **carbolic soap** soap containing this.

carbon /'kɑːbən/ noun non-metallic element occurring as diamond, graphite, and charcoal, and in all organic compounds; carbon copy, carbon paper. □ **carbon copy** copy made with carbon paper; **carbon dating** determination of age of object from decay of carbon-14; **carbon dioxide** gas found in atmosphere and formed by respiration; **carbon fibre** thin filament of carbon used as strengthening material; **carbon-14** radioactive carbon isotope of mass 14; **carbon monoxide** poisonous gas formed by burning carbon incompletely; **carbon paper** thin carbon-coated paper for making copies; **carbon tax** tax on fuels producing greenhouse gases; **carbon-12** stable isotope of carbon used as a standard.

carbonate /'kɑːbəneɪt/ ● noun salt of carbonic acid. ● verb (**-ting**) fill with carbon dioxide.

carbonic /kɑː'bɒnɪk/ adjective containing carbon. □ **carbonic acid** weak acid formed from carbon dioxide in water.

carboniferous /kɑːbə'nɪfərəs/ adjective producing coal.

carbonize /'kɑːbənaɪz/ verb (also **-ise**) (**-zing** or **-sing**) reduce to charcoal or coke; convert to carbon; coat with carbon. □ **carbonization** noun.

carborundum /kɑːbə'rʌndəm/ noun compound of carbon and silicon used esp. as abrasive.

carboy /'kɑːbɔɪ/ noun large globular glass bottle.

carbuncle /'kɑːbʌŋk(ə)l/ noun severe skin abscess; bright red jewel.

carburettor /kɑːbə'retə/ noun apparatus mixing air with petrol vapour in internal-combustion engine.

carcass /'kɑːkəs/ noun (also **carcase**) dead body of animal or bird or (colloquial) person; framework; worthless remains.

carcinogen /kɑː'sɪnədʒ(ə)n/ noun substance producing cancer. □ **carcinogenic** /-'dʒen-/ adjective.

card¹ noun thick stiff paper or thin pasteboard; piece of this for writing or printing on, esp. to send greetings, to identify person, or to record information; small rectangular piece of plastic used to obtain credit etc.; playing card; (in plural) card-playing; (in

plural) colloquial employee's tax etc. documents; programme of events at race meeting etc.; colloquial eccentric person. □ **cardcarrying** registered as member (esp. of political party); **card index** index with separate card for each item; **cardphone** public telephone operated by card instead of money; **cardsharp** swindler at card games; **card vote** block vote.

card² ● noun wire brush etc. for raising nap on cloth etc. ● verb brush with card.

cardamom /'kɑːdəməm/ noun seeds of SE Asian aromatic plant used as spice.

cardboard noun pasteboard or stiff paper.

cardiac /'kɑːdɪæk/ adjective of the heart.

cardigan /'kɑːdɪgən/ noun knitted jacket.

cardinal /'kɑːdɪn(ə)l/ ● adjective chief, fundamental; deep scarlet. ● noun one of leading RC dignitaries who elect Pope. □ **cardinal number** number representing quantity (1, 2, 3, etc.); compare ORDINAL.

cardiogram /'kɑːdɪəʊgræm/ noun record of heart movements.

cardiograph /'kɑːdɪəʊgrɑːf/ noun instrument recording heart movements. □ **cardiographer** /-'ɒgrəfə/ noun; **cardiography** /-'ɒgrəfɪ/ noun.

cardiology /kɑːdɪ'ɒlədʒɪ/ noun branch of medicine concerned with heart. □ **cardiologist** noun.

cardiovascular /kɑːdɪəʊ'væskjʊlə/ adjective of heart and blood vessels.

care /keə/ ● noun (cause of) anxiety or concern; serious attention; caution; protection, charge; task. ● verb (**-ring**) (usually + about, for, whether) feel concern or interest or affection. □ **in care** (of child) under local authority supervision; **take care** be careful, (+ to do) not fail or neglect; **take care of** look after, deal with, dispose of.

careen /kə'riːn/ verb turn (ship) on side for repair; move or swerve wildly.

career /kə'rɪə/ ● noun professional etc. course through life; profession or occupation; swift course. ● adjective pursuing or wishing to pursue a career; working permanently in specified profession. ● verb move or swerve wildly.

careerist noun person predominantly concerned with personal advancement.

carefree adjective light-hearted, joyous.

careful adjective painstaking; cautious; taking care, not neglecting. □ **carefully** adverb; **carefulness** noun.

careless adjective lacking care or attention; unthinking, insensitive; light-hearted. □ **carelessly** adverb; **carelessness** noun.

carer noun person who cares for sick or elderly person, esp. at home.

caress /kə'res/ ● verb touch lovingly. ● noun loving touch.

caret /'kærət/ noun mark indicating insertion in text.

caretaker ● noun person in charge of maintenance of building. ● adjective taking temporary control.

careworn adjective showing effects of prolonged anxiety.

cargo /'kɑːgəʊ/ noun (plural **-es** or **-s**) goods carried by ship or aircraft.

Caribbean /kærə'biːən/ adjective of the West Indies.

caribou /'kærɪbuː/ noun (plural same) N. American reindeer.

caricature /'kærɪkətʃʊə/ ● noun grotesque usually comically exaggerated representation. ● verb (**-ring**) make or give caricature of. □ **caricaturist** noun.

caries /'keəriːz/ noun (plural same) decay of tooth or bone.

carillon /kə'rɪljən/ noun set of bells sounded from keyboard or mechanically; tune played on this.

Carmelite /'kɑːməlaɪt/ ● *noun* friar of Order of Our Lady of Mount Carmel; nun of similar order. ● *adjective* of Carmelites.

carminative /'kɑːmɪnətɪv/ ● *adjective* relieving flatulence. ● *noun* carminative drug.

carmine /'kɑːmaɪn/ ● *adjective* of vivid crimson colour. ● *noun* this colour; pigment from cochineal.

carnage /'kɑːnɪdʒ/ *noun* great slaughter.

carnal /'kɑːn(ə)l/ *adjective* worldly; sensual; sexual. □ **carnality** *noun*.

carnation /kɑː'neɪʃ(ə)n/ ● *noun* clove-scented pink; rosy-pink colour. ● *adjective* rosy-pink.

carnelian = CORNELIAN.

carnival /'kɑːnɪv(ə)l/ *noun* festivities or festival, esp. preceding Lent; merrymaking.

carnivore /'kɑːnɪvɔː/ *noun* animal or plant that feeds on flesh. □ **carnivorous** /-'nɪvərəs-/ *adjective*.

carob /'kærəb/ *noun* seed pod of Mediterranean tree used as chocolate substitute.

carol /'kær(ə)l/ ● *noun* joyous song, esp. Christmas hymn. ● *verb* (**-ll-**; *US* **-l-**) sing carols; sing joyfully.

carotene /'kærətiːn/ *noun* orange-coloured pigment in carrots etc.

carotid /kə'rɒtɪd/ ● *noun* each of two main arteries carrying blood to head. ● *adjective* of these arteries.

carouse /kə'raʊz/ ● *verb* (**-sing**) have lively drinking party. ● *noun* such party. □ **carousal** *noun*; **carouser** *noun*.

carp[1] *noun* (*plural* same) freshwater fish often bred for food.

carp[2] *verb* find fault, complain. □ **carper** *noun*.

carpal /'kɑːp(ə)l/ ● *adjective* of the wrist-bones. ● *noun* wrist-bone.

carpel /'kɑːp(ə)l/ *noun* female reproductive organ of flower.

carpenter /'kɑːpɪntə/ ● *noun* person skilled in woodwork. ● *verb* do woodwork; make by woodwork. □ **carpentry** *noun*.

carpet /'kɑːpɪt/ ● *noun* thick fabric for covering floors etc.; piece of this; thing resembling this. ● *verb* (**-t-**) cover (as) with carpet; *colloquial* rebuke. □ **carpet-bag** travelling bag originally made of carpet-like material; **carpet-bagger** *colloquial* political candidate etc. without local connections; **carpet slipper** soft slipper; **carpet sweeper** implement for sweeping carpets.

carpeting *noun* material for carpets; carpets collectively.

carpus /'kɑːpəs/ *noun* (*plural* **-pi** /-paɪ/) group of small bones forming wrist.

carrageen /'kærəgiːn/ *noun* edible red seaweed.

carriage /'kærɪdʒ/ *noun* railway passenger vehicle; wheeled horse-drawn passenger vehicle; conveying of goods; cost of this; bearing, deportment; part of machine that carries other parts; gun carriage. □ **carriage clock** portable clock with handle; **carriageway** part of road used by vehicles.

carrier /'kærɪə/ *noun* person or thing that carries; transport or freight company; carrier bag; framework on bicycle for carrying luggage or passenger; person or animal that may transmit disease without suffering from it; aircraft carrier. □ **carrier bag** plastic or paper bag with handles; **carrier pigeon** pigeon trained to carry messages; **carrier wave** high-frequency electromagnetic wave used to convey signal.

carrion /'kærɪən/ *noun* dead flesh; filth. □ **carrion crow** crow feeding on carrion.

carrot /'kærət/ *noun* plant with edible tapering orange root; this root; incentive. □ **carroty** *adjective*.

carry /'kærɪ/ *verb* (**-ies, -ied**) support or hold up, esp. while moving; have with one; convey; (often + *to*) take (process etc.) to specified point; involve; transfer (figure) to column of higher value; hold in specified way; (of newspaper etc.) publish; (of radio or television station) broadcast; keep (goods) in stock; (of sound) be audible at a distance; win victory or acceptance for; win acceptance from; capture. □ **carry away** remove, inspire, deprive of self-control; **carrycot** portable cot for baby; **carry forward** transfer (figure) to new page or account; **carry it off** do well under difficulties; **carry off** remove (esp. by force), win, (esp. of disease) kill; **carry on** continue, *colloquial* behave excitedly, (often + *with*) *colloquial* flirt; **carry-on** *colloquial* fuss; **carry out** put into practice; **carry-out** take-away; **carry over** carry forward, postpone; **carry through** complete, bring safely out of difficulties.

cart ● *noun* open usually horse-drawn vehicle for carrying loads; light vehicle for pulling by hand. ● *verb* carry in cart; *slang* carry with difficulty. □ **cart horse** horse of heavy build; **cartwheel** wheel of cart, sideways somersault with arms and legs extended.

carte blanche /kɑːt 'blɑːʃ/ *noun* full discretionary power.

cartel /kɑː'tel/ *noun* union of suppliers etc. set up to control prices.

Cartesian coordinates /kɑː'tiːzɪən/ *plural noun* system of locating point by its distance from two perpendicular axes.

Carthusian /kɑː'θjuːzɪən/ ● *noun* monk of contemplative order founded by St Bruno. ● *adjective* of this order.

cartilage /'kɑːtɪlɪdʒ/ *noun* firm flexible connective tissue in vertebrates. □ **cartilaginous** /-'lædʒ-/ *adjective*.

cartography /kɑː'tɒɡrəfɪ/ *noun* map-drawing. □ **cartographer** *noun*; **cartographic** /-tə'ɡræf-/ *adjective*.

carton /'kɑːt(ə)n/ *noun* light esp. cardboard container.

cartoon /kɑː'tuːn/ *noun* humorous esp. topical drawing in newspaper etc.; sequence of drawings telling story; such sequence animated on film; full-size preliminary design for work of art. □ **cartoonist** *noun*.

cartouche /kɑː'tuːʃ/ *noun* scroll-like ornament; oval enclosing name and title of pharaoh.

cartridge /'kɑːtrɪdʒ/ *noun* case containing explosive charge or bullet; sealed container of film etc.; component carrying stylus on record player; ink-container for insertion in pen. □ **cartridge-belt** belt with pockets or loops for cartridges; **cartridge paper** thick paper for drawing etc.

carve *verb* (**-ving**) make or shape by cutting; cut pattern etc. in; (+ *into*) form pattern etc. from; cut (meat) into slices. □ **carve out** take from larger whole; **carve up** subdivide, drive aggressively into path of (another vehicle). □ **carver** *noun*.

carvery *noun* (*plural* **-ies**) restaurant etc. with joints displayed for carving.

carving *noun* carved object, esp. as work of art. □ **carving knife** knife for carving meat.

cascade /kæs'keɪd/ ● *noun* waterfall, esp. one in series. ● *verb* (**-ding**) fall in or like cascade.

case[1] /keɪs/ *noun* instance of something occurring; hypothetical or actual situation; person's illness, circumstances, etc. as regarded by doctor, social worker, etc.; such a person; crime etc. investigated by detective or police; suit at law; sum of arguments on one side; (valid) set of arguments; *Grammar* relation of word to others in sentence, form of word expressing this. □ **case law** law as established by decided cases; **casework** social work concerned with individual's background; **in any case** whatever the truth or possible outcome is; **in case** in the event that, lest, in provision against a possibility; **in case of** in the event of; **is (not) the case** is (not) so.

case² /keɪs/ ● noun container or cover enclosing something. ● verb (**-sing**) enclose in case; (+ with) surround with; slang inspect closely, esp. for criminal purpose. □ **case-harden** harden surface of (esp. steel), make callous.

casein /'keɪsɪn/ noun main protein in milk and cheese.

casement /'keɪsmənt/ noun (part of) window hinged to open like door.

cash ● noun money in coins or notes; full payment at time of purchase. ● verb give or obtain cash for. □ **cash and carry** (esp. wholesaling) system of cash payment for goods removed by buyer, store where this operates; **cashcard** plastic card for use in cash dispenser; **cash crop** crop produced for sale; **cash desk** counter etc. where goods are paid for; **cash dispenser** automatic machine for withdrawal of cash; **cash flow** movement of money into and out of a business; **cash in** obtain cash for, (usually + on) colloquial profit (from); **cash register** till recording sales, totalling receipts, etc.; **cash up** count day's takings.

cashew /'kæʃuː/ noun evergreen tree bearing kidney-shaped edible nut; this nut.

cashier¹ /kæ'ʃɪə/ noun person dealing with cash transactions in bank etc.

cashier² /kæ'ʃɪə/ verb dismiss from service.

cashmere /kæʃ'mɪə/ noun fine soft (material of) wool, esp. of Kashmir goat.

casing noun enclosing material or cover.

casino /kə'siːnəʊ/ noun (plural **-s**) public room etc. for gambling.

cask /kɑːsk/ noun barrel, esp. for alcoholic liquor.

casket /'kɑːskɪt/ noun small box for holding valuables; US coffin.

cassava /kə'sɑːvə/ noun plant with starchy roots; starch or flour from these.

casserole /'kæsərəʊl/ ● noun covered dish for cooking food in oven; food cooked in this. ● verb (**-ling**) cook in casserole.

cassette /kə'set/ noun sealed case containing magnetic tape, film, etc., ready for insertion in tape recorder, camera, etc.

cassia /'kæsɪə/ noun tree whose leaves and pod yield senna.

cassis /kæ'siːs/ noun blackcurrant flavouring for drinks etc.

cassock /'kæsək/ noun long usually black or red clerical garment.

cassowary /'kæsəweərɪ/ noun (plural **-ies**) large flightless Australian bird.

cast /kɑːst/ ● verb (past & past participle **cast**) throw; direct, cause to fall; express (doubts etc.); let down (anchor etc.); shed or lose; register (vote); shape (molten metal etc.) in mould; make (product) thus; (usually + as) assign (actor) to role; allocate roles in (play, film, etc.); (+ in, into) arrange (facts etc.) in specified form. ● noun throwing of missile, dice, fishing line, etc.; thing made in mould; moulded mass of solidified material; actors in play etc.; form, type, or quality; tinge of colour; slight squint; wormcast. □ **cast about, around** search; **cast aside** abandon; **casting vote** deciding vote when votes on two sides are equal; **cast iron** hard but brittle iron alloy; **cast-iron** of cast iron, very strong, unchallengeable; **cast off** abandon, finish piece of knitting; **cast-off** abandoned or discarded (thing, esp. garment); **cast on** make first row of piece of knitting.

castanet /kæstə'net/ noun (usually in plural) each of pair of hand-held wooden or ivory shells clicked together in time with esp. Spanish dancing.

castaway /'kɑːstəweɪ/ ● noun shipwrecked person. ● adjective shipwrecked.

caste /kɑːst/ noun any of Hindu hereditary classes whose members have no social contact with other classes; exclusive social class.

castellated /'kæstəleɪtɪd/ adjective built with battlements. □ **castellation** noun.

caster = CASTOR.

castigate /'kæstɪgeɪt/ verb (**-ting**) rebuke; punish. □ **castigation** noun.

castle /'kɑːs(ə)l/ ● noun large fortified residential building; Chess rook. ● verb (**-ling**) Chess make combined move of king and rook.

castor /'kɑːstə/ noun (also **caster**) small swivelled wheel enabling heavy furniture to be moved; container perforated for sprinkling sugar etc. □ **castor sugar** finely granulated white sugar.

castor oil noun vegetable oil used as laxative and lubricant.

castrate /kæs'treɪt/ verb (**-ting**) remove testicles of. □ **castration** noun.

casual /'kæʒʊəl/ ● adjective chance; not regular or permanent; unconcerned, careless; (of clothes etc.) informal. ● noun casual worker; (usually in plural) casual clothes or shoes. □ **casually** adverb.

casualty /'kæʒʊəltɪ/ noun (plural **-ies**) person killed or injured in war or accident; thing lost or destroyed; casualty department; accident. □ **casualty department** part of hospital for treatment of casualties.

casuist /'kæʒʊɪst/ noun person who resolves cases of conscience etc., esp. cleverly but falsely; sophist, quibbler. □ **casuistic** adjective; **casuistry** /-'ɪs-/ noun.

cat noun small furry domestic quadruped; wild animal of same family; colloquial malicious or spiteful woman; cat-o'-nine-tails. □ **cat burglar** burglar who enters by climbing to upper storey; **catcall** (make) shrill whistle of disapproval; **catfish** fish with whisker-like filaments round mouth; **cat flap** small flap allowing cat passage through outer door; **catnap** (have) short sleep; **cat-o'-nine-tails** historical whip with nine knotted cords; **cat's cradle** child's game with string; **cat's-eye** proprietary term reflector stud set into road; **cat's-paw** person used as tool by another; **catsuit** close-fitting garment with trouser legs, covering whole body; **catwalk** narrow walkway; **rain cats and dogs** rain hard.

catachresis /kætə'kriːsɪs/ noun (plural **-chreses** /-iːsiːz/) incorrect use of words. □ **catachrestic** /-'kres-/ adjective.

cataclysm /'kætəklɪz(ə)m/ noun violent upheaval. □ **cataclysmic** /-'klɪz-/ adjective.

catacomb /'kætəkuːm/ noun (often in plural) underground cemetery.

catafalque /'kætəfælk/ noun decorated bier, esp. for state funeral etc.

Catalan /'kætəlæn/ ● noun native or language of Catalonia in Spain. ● adjective of Catalonia.

catalepsy /'kætəlepsɪ/ noun trance or seizure with rigidity of body. □ **cataleptic** /-'lep-/ adjective & noun.

catalogue /'kætəlɒg/ (US **catalog**) ● noun complete or extensive list, usually in alphabetical or other systematic order. ● verb (**-logues**, **-logued**, **-loguing**; US **-logs**, **-loged**, **-loging**) make catalogue of; enter in catalogue.

catalysis /kə'tælɪsɪs/ noun (plural **-lyses** /-siːz/) acceleration of chemical reaction by catalyst. □ **catalyse** verb (**-sing**) (US **-lyze**; **-zing**).

catalyst /'kætəlɪst/ *noun* substance speeding chemical reaction without itself permanently changing; person or thing that precipitates change.

catalytic /kætə'lɪtɪk/ *adjective* involving or causing catalysis. □ **catalytic converter** device in vehicle for converting pollutant gases into less harmful ones.

catamaran /kætəmə'ræn/ *noun* boat or raft with two parallel hulls.

catapult /'kætəpʌlt/ ● *noun* forked stick with elastic for shooting stones; *historical* military machine for hurling stones etc.; device for launching glider etc. ● *verb* launch with catapult; fling forcibly; leap or be hurled forcibly.

cataract /'kætərækt/ *noun* waterfall, downpour; progressive opacity of eye lens.

catarrh /kə'taː/ *noun* inflammation of mucous membrane, air-passages, etc.; mucus in nose caused by this. □ **catarrhal** *adjective*.

catastrophe /kə'tæstrəfɪ/ *noun* great usually sudden disaster; denouement of drama. □ **catastrophic** /kætə'strɒf-/ *adjective*; **catastrophically** /kætə'strɒf-/ *adverb*.

catch /kætʃ/ ● *verb* (*past & past participle* **caught** /kɔːt/) capture in trap, hands, etc.; detect or surprise; intercept and hold (moving thing) in hand etc.; *Cricket* dismiss (batsman) by catching ball before it hits ground; contract (disease) by infection etc.; reach in time and board (train etc.); apprehend; check or be checked; become entangled; (of artist etc.) reproduce faithfully; reach or overtake. ● *noun* act of catching; *Cricket* chance or act of catching ball; amount of thing caught; thing or person caught or worth catching; question etc. intended to deceive etc.; unexpected difficulty or disadvantage; device for fastening door etc.; musical round. □ **catch fire** begin to burn; **catch on** *colloquial* become popular, understand what is meant; **catch out** detect in mistake etc., *Cricket* catch; **catchpenny** intended merely to sell quickly; **catchphrase** phrase in frequent use; **catch up** (often + *with*) reach (person etc. ahead), make up arrears, involve, fasten; **catchword** phrase or word in frequent use, word so placed as to draw attention.

catching *adjective* infectious.

catchment area *noun* area served by school, hospital, etc.; area from which rainfall flows into river etc.

catchy *adjective* (**-ier**, **-iest**) (of tune) easily remembered, attractive.

catechism /'kætɪkɪz(ə)m/ *noun* (book containing) principles of a religion in form of questions and answers; series of questions.

catechize /'kætɪkaɪz/ *verb* (also **-ise**) (**-zing** or **-sing**) instruct by question and answer. □ **catechist** *noun*.

catechumen /kætɪ'kjuːmən/ *noun* person being instructed before baptism.

categorical /kætɪ'gɒrɪk(ə)l/ *adjective* unconditional, absolute, explicit. □ **categorically** *adverb*.

categorize /'kætɪgəraɪz/ *verb* (also **-ise**) (**-zing** or **-sing**) place in category. □ **categorization** *noun*.

category /'kætɪgərɪ/ *noun* (*plural* **-ies**) class or division (of things, ideas, etc.).

cater /'keɪtə/ *verb* supply food; (+ *for*) provide what is required for. □ **caterer** *noun*.

caterpillar /'kætəpɪlə/ *noun* larva of butterfly or moth; (**Caterpillar**) (in full **Caterpillar track**) *proprietary term* articulated steel band passing round wheels of vehicle for travel on rough ground.

caterwaul /'kætəwɔːl/ *verb* howl like cat.

catgut *noun* thread made from intestines of sheep etc. used for strings of musical instruments etc.

catharsis /kə'θaːsɪs/ *noun* (*plural* **catharses** /-siːz/) emotional release; emptying of bowels.

cathartic /kə'θaːtɪk/ ● *adjective* effecting catharsis. ● *noun* laxative.

cathedral /kə'θiːdr(ə)l/ *noun* principal church of diocese.

Catherine wheel /'kæθrɪn/ *noun* rotating firework.

catheter /'kæθɪtə/ *noun* tube inserted into body cavity to introduce or drain fluid.

cathode /'kæθəʊd/ *noun* negative electrode of cell; positive terminal of battery. □ **cathode ray** beam of electrons from cathode of vacuum tube; **cathode ray tube** vacuum tube in which cathode rays produce luminous image on fluorescent screen.

catholic /'kæθlɪk/ ● *adjective* universal; broadminded; all-embracing; (**Catholic**) Roman Catholic; (**Catholic**) including all Christians or all of Western Church. ● *noun* (**Catholic**) Roman Catholic. □ **Catholicism** /kə'θɒlɪs-/ *noun*; **catholicity** /-ə'lɪs-/ *noun*.

cation /'kætaɪən/ *noun* positively charged ion. □ **cationic** /-'ɒnɪk/ *adjective*.

catkin /'kætkɪn/ *noun* spike of usually hanging flowers of willow, hazel, etc.

catmint *noun* pungent plant attractive to cats.

catnip *noun* catmint.

cattery *noun* (*plural* **-ies**) place where cats are boarded.

cattle /'kæt(ə)l/ *plural noun* large ruminants, bred esp. for milk or meat. □ **cattle grid** grid over ditch, allowing vehicles to pass over but not livestock.

catty *adjective* (**-ier**, **-iest**) spiteful. □ **cattily** *adverb*; **cattiness** *noun*.

Caucasian /kɔː'keɪʒ(ə)n/ ● *adjective* of the white or light-skinned race. ● *noun* Caucasian person.

caucus /'kɔːkəs/ *noun* (*plural* **-es**) US meeting of party members to decide policy; *often derogatory* (meeting of) group within larger organization.

caudal /'kɔːd(ə)l/ *adjective* of, like, or at tail.

caudate /'kɔːdeɪt/ *adjective* tailed.

caught *past & past participle* of CATCH.

caul /kɔːl/ *noun* membrane enclosing foetus; part of this sometimes found on child's head at birth.

cauldron /'kɔːldrən/ *noun* large vessel for boiling things in.

cauliflower /'kɒlɪflaʊə/ *noun* cabbage with large white flower head.

caulk /kɔːk/ *verb* (US **calk**) stop up (ship's seams); make watertight.

causal /'kɔːz(ə)l/ *adjective* relating to cause (and effect). □ **causality** /-'zæl-/ *noun*.

causation /kɔː'zeɪʃ(ə)n/ *noun* causing, causality.

cause /kɔːz/ ● *noun* thing producing effect; reason or motive; justification; principle, belief, or purpose; matter to be settled, or case offered, at law. ● *verb* (**-sing**) be cause of; produce; (+ *to do*) make.

cause célèbre /kɔːz se'lebr/ *noun* (*plural* **causes célèbres** same pronunciation) lawsuit that excites much interest. [French]

causeway /'kɔːzweɪ/ *noun* raised road across low ground or water; raised path by road.

caustic /'kɔːstɪk/ ● *adjective* corrosive, burning; sarcastic, biting. ● *noun* caustic substance. □ **caustic soda** sodium hydroxide. □ **causticity** /-'tɪs-/ *noun*.

cauterize /'kɔːtəraɪz/ *verb* (also **-ise**) (**-zing** or **-sing**) burn (tissue), esp. to stop bleeding.

caution /'kɔːʃ(ə)n/ ● *noun* attention to safety; warning; *colloquial* amusing or surprising person or thing. ● *verb* warn, admonish.

cautionary *adjective* warning.

cautious /'kɔːʃəs/ *adjective* having or showing caution. □ **cautiously** *adverb*; **cautiousness** *noun*.

cavalcade /kævəl'keɪd/ *noun* procession of riders, cars, etc.

cavalier /ˌkævəˈlɪə/ ● noun courtly gentleman; archaic horseman; (**Cavalier**) historical supporter of Charles I in English Civil War. ● adjective offhand, supercilious, curt.

cavalry /ˈkævəlrɪ/ noun (plural **-ies**) (usually treated as plural) soldiers on horseback or in armoured vehicles.

cave ● noun large hollow in side of cliff, hill, etc., or underground. ● verb (**-ving**) explore caves. □ **cave in** (cause to) subside or collapse, yield, submit.

caveat /ˈkævɪæt/ noun warning, proviso.

cavern /ˈkæv(ə)n/ noun cave, esp. large or dark one.

cavernous adjective full of caverns; huge or deep as cavern.

caviar /ˈkævɪɑː/ noun (also **caviare**) pickled sturgeon-roe.

cavil /ˈkævɪl/ ● verb (**-ll-**; US **-l-**) (usually + at, about) make petty objections. ● noun petty objection.

cavity /ˈkævɪtɪ/ noun (plural **-ies**) hollow within solid body; decayed part of tooth. □ **cavity wall** two walls separated by narrow space.

cavort /kəˈvɔːt/ verb caper.

caw ● noun cry of rook etc. ● verb utter this cry.

cayenne /keɪˈen/ noun (in full **cayenne pepper**) powdered red pepper.

cayman /ˈkeɪmən/ noun (also **caiman**) (plural **-s**) S. American alligator-like reptile.

CB abbreviation citizens' band; Commander of the Order of the Bath.

CBE abbreviation Commander of the Order of the British Empire.

CBI abbreviation Confederation of British Industry.

cc abbreviation cubic centimetre(s).

CD abbreviation compact disc; Corps Diplomatique.

CD-ROM abbreviation compact disc read-only memory.

cease /siːs/ formal verb (**-sing**) stop; bring or come to an end. □ **cease-fire** (order for) truce; **without cease** unending.

ceaseless adjective without end. □ **ceaselessly** adverb.

cedar /ˈsiːdə/ noun evergreen conifer; its durable fragrant wood.

cede /siːd/ verb (**-ding**) formal give up one's rights to or possession of.

cedilla /sɪˈdɪlə/ noun mark ( ) under c (in French, to show it is pronounced /s/, not /k/).

ceilidh /ˈkeɪlɪ/ noun informal gathering for music, dancing, etc.

ceiling /ˈsiːlɪŋ/ noun upper interior surface of room; upper limit; maximum altitude of aircraft.

celandine /ˈseləndaɪn/ noun yellow-flowered plant.

celebrant /ˈselɪbrənt/ noun person performing rite, esp. priest at Eucharist.

celebrate /ˈselɪbreɪt/ verb (**-ting**) mark with or engage in festivities; perform (rite or ceremony); praise publicly. □ **celebration** noun; **celebratory** /-ˈbreɪt-/ adjective.

celebrity /sɪˈlebrɪtɪ/ noun (plural **-ies**) well-known person; fame.

celeriac /sɪˈlerɪæk/ noun variety of celery.

celery /ˈselərɪ/ noun plant of which stalks are used as vegetable.

celesta /sɪˈlestə/ noun keyboard instrument with steel plates struck with hammers.

celestial /sɪˈlestɪəl/ adjective of sky or heavenly bodies; heavenly, divinely good.

celibate /ˈselɪbət/ ● adjective unmarried, or abstaining from sexual relations, often for religious reasons. ● noun celibate person. □ **celibacy** noun.

cell /sel/ noun small room, esp. in prison or monastery; small compartment, e.g. in honeycomb; small active political group; unit of structure of organic matter; enclosed cavity in organism etc.; vessel containing electrodes for current-generation or electrolysis. □ **cellphone** portable radio-telephone.

cellar /ˈselə/ noun underground storage room; stock of wine in cellar.

cello /ˈtʃeləʊ/ noun (plural **-s**) bass instrument of violin family, held between legs of seated player. □ **cellist** noun.

Cellophane /ˈseləfeɪn/ noun proprietary term thin transparent wrapping material.

cellular /ˈseljʊlə/ adjective consisting of cells; of open texture, porous. □ **cellularity** /-ˈlær-/ noun.

cellulite /ˈseljʊlaɪt/ noun lumpy fat, esp. on women's hips and thighs.

celluloid /ˈseljʊlɔɪd/ noun plastic made from camphor and cellulose nitrate; cinema film.

cellulose /ˈseljʊləʊs/ noun carbohydrate forming plant-cell walls; paint or lacquer consisting of cellulose acetate or nitrate in solution.

Celsius /ˈselsɪəs/ adjective of scale of temperature on which water freezes at 0° and boils at 100°.

Celt /kelt/ noun (also **Kelt**) member of an ethnic group including inhabitants of Ireland, Wales, Scotland, Cornwall, and Brittany.

Celtic /ˈkeltɪk/ ● adjective of the Celts. ● noun group of Celtic languages.

cement /sɪˈment/ ● noun substance made from lime and clay, mixed with water, sand, etc. to form mortar or concrete; adhesive. ● verb unite firmly, strengthen; apply cement to.

cemetery /ˈsemɪtrɪ/ noun (plural **-ies**) burial ground, esp. one not in churchyard.

cenotaph /ˈsenətɑːf/ noun tomblike monument to person(s) whose remains are elsewhere.

Cenozoic /ˌsiːnəˈzəʊɪk/ ● adjective of most recent geological era, marked by evolution of mammals etc. ● noun this era.

censer /ˈsensə/ noun incense-burning vessel.

censor /ˈsensə/ ● noun official with power to suppress or expurgate books, films, news, etc., on grounds of obscenity, threat to security, etc. ● verb act as censor of; make deletions or changes in. □ **censorial** /-ˈsɔːr-/ adjective; **censorship** noun.

■ **Usage** As a verb, censor is often confused with censure, which means 'to criticize harshly'.

censorious /senˈsɔːrɪəs/ adjective severely critical.

censure /ˈsenʃə/ ● verb (**-ring**) criticize harshly; reprove. ● noun hostile criticism; disapproval.

census /ˈsensəs/ noun (plural **-suses**) official count of population etc.

cent /sent/ noun one-hundredth of dollar or other decimal unit of currency.

cent. abbreviation century.

centaur /ˈsentɔː/ noun creature in Greek mythology with head, arms, and trunk of man joined to body and legs of horse.

centenarian /ˌsentɪˈneərɪən/ ● noun person 100 or more years old. ● adjective 100 or more years old.

centenary /senˈtiːnərɪ/ ● noun (plural **-ies**) (celebration of) 100th anniversary. ● adjective of a centenary; recurring every 100 years.

centennial /senˈtenɪəl/ ● adjective lasting 100 years; recurring every 100 years. ● noun US centenary.

centi- combining form one-hundredth.

centigrade /ˈsentɪgreɪd/ adjective Celsius.

■ **Usage** Celsius is the better term to use in technical contexts.

centilitre /ˈsentɪliːtə/ noun (US **centiliter**) one-hundredth of litre (0.018 pint).

centime /ˈsɑ̃tiːm/ noun one-hundredth of franc.

centimetre /'sentimi:tə/ *noun* (*US* **centimeter**) one-hundredth of metre (0.394 in.).

centipede /'sentɪpi:d/ *noun* arthropod with wormlike body and many legs.

central /'sentr(ə)l/ *adjective* of, forming, at, or from centre; essential, principal. □ **central bank** national bank issuing currency etc.; **central heating** heating of building from central source; **central processor**, **central processing unit** computer's main operating part. □ **centrality** *noun*; **centrally** *adverb*.

centralize *verb* (also **-ise**) (**-zing** or **-sing**) concentrate (administration etc.) at single centre; subject (state etc.) to this system. □ **centralization** *noun*.

centre /'sentə/ (*US* **center**) ● *noun* middle point; pivot; place or buildings forming a central point or main area for an activity; point of concentration or dispersion; political party holding moderate opinions; filling in chocolate etc. ● *verb* (**-ring**) (+ *in*, *on*, *round*) have as main centre; place in centre. □ **centrefold** centre spread that folds out, esp. with nude photographs; **centre forward**, **back** *Football etc.* middle player in forward or half-back line; **centre of gravity** point at which the mass of an object effectively acts; **centrepiece** ornament for middle of table, main item; **centre spread** two facing middle pages of magazine etc.

centrifugal /sentrɪ'fju:g(ə)l/ *adjective* moving or tending to move from centre. □ **centrifugal force** apparent force acting outwards on body revolving round centre. □ **centrifugally** *adverb*.

centrifuge /'sentrɪfju:dʒ/ *noun* rapidly rotating machine for separating e.g. cream from milk.

centripetal /sen'trɪpɪt(ə)l/ *adjective* moving or tending to move towards centre. □ **centripetally** *adverb*.

centrist /'sentrɪst/ *noun* (often derogatory) person holding moderate views. □ **centrism** *noun*.

cents. *abbreviation* centuries.

centurion /sen'tjʊərɪən/ *noun* commander of century in ancient Roman army.

century /'sentʃərɪ/ *noun* (*plural* **-ies**) 100 years; *Cricket* score of 100 runs by one batsman; company in ancient Roman army.

■ **Usage** Strictly speaking, because the 1st century ran from the year 1 to the year 100, the first year of a century ends in 1. However, a century is commonly regarded as starting with a year ending in 00, the 20th century thus running from 1900 to 1999.

cephalic /sə'fælɪk/ *adjective* of or in head.

cephalopod /'sefələpɒd/ *noun* mollusc with tentacles on head, e.g. octopus.

ceramic /sɪ'ræmɪk/ ● *adjective* made of esp. baked clay; of ceramics. ● *noun* ceramic article.

ceramics *plural noun* ceramic products collectively; (usually treated as *singular*) ceramic art.

cereal /'sɪərɪəl/ ● *noun* edible grain; breakfast food made from cereal. ● *adjective* of edible grain.

cerebellum /serɪ'beləm/ *noun* (*plural* **-s** or **-bella**) part of brain at back of skull.

cerebral /'serɪbr(ə)l/ *adjective* of brain; intellectual. □ **cerebral palsy** paralysis resulting from brain damage before or at birth.

cerebration /serɪ'breɪʃ(ə)n/ *noun* working of brain.

cerebrospinal /serɪbrəʊ'spaɪn(ə)l/ *adjective* of brain and spine.

cerebrum /'serɪbrəm/ *noun* (*plural* **-bra**) principal part of brain, at front of skull.

ceremonial /serɪ'məʊnɪəl/ ● *adjective* of or with ceremony, formal. ● *noun* system of rites or ceremonies.

ceremonious /serɪ'məʊnɪəs/ *adjective* fond of or characterized by ceremony, formal. □ **ceremoniously** *adverb*.

ceremony /'serɪmənɪ/ *noun* (*plural* **-ies**) formal procedure; formalities, esp. ritualistic; excessively polite behaviour. □ **stand on ceremony** insist on formality.

cerise /sə'ri:z/ *noun* & *adjective* light clear red.

cert /sɜ:t/ *noun* (esp. **dead cert**) *slang* a certainty.

certain /'sɜ:t(ə)n/ *adjective* convinced; indisputable; (often + *to do*) sure, destined; reliable; particular but not specified; some.

certainly *adverb* undoubtedly; (in answer) yes.

certainty *noun* (*plural* **-ies**) undoubted fact; absolute conviction; reliable thing or person.

certificate ● *noun* /sə'tɪfɪkət/ document formally attesting fact. ● *verb* /sə'tɪfɪkeɪt/ (**-ting**) (esp. as **certificated** *adjective*) provide with certificate; license or attest by certificate. □ **certification** /sɜ:-/ *noun*.

certify /'sɜ:tɪfaɪ/ *verb* (**-ies**, **-ied**) attest (to); declare by certificate; officially declare insane. □ **certifiable** *adjective*.

certitude /'sɜ:tɪtju:d/ *noun* feeling certain.

cerulean /sə'ru:lɪən/ *adjective* sky-blue.

cervical /sə'vaɪk(ə)l/ *adjective* of cervix or neck. □ **cervical smear** specimen from neck of womb for examination.

cervix /'sɜ:vɪks/ *noun* (*plural* **cervices** /-si:z/) necklike structure, esp. neck of womb; neck.

Cesarean (also **Cesarian**) *US* = CAESAREAN.

cessation /se'seɪʃ(ə)n/ *noun* ceasing.

cession /'seʃ(ə)n/ *noun* ceding; territory ceded.

cesspit /'sespɪt/ *noun* pit for liquid waste or sewage.

cesspool /'sespu:l/ *noun* cesspit.

cetacean /sɪ'teɪʃ(ə)n/ ● *noun* member of order of marine mammals including whales. ● *adjective* of cetaceans.

cf. *abbreviation* compare (Latin *confer*).

CFC *abbreviation* chlorofluorocarbon (compound used as refrigerant, aerosol propellant, etc.).

cg *abbreviation* centigram(s).

CH *abbreviation* Companion of Honour.

Chablis /'ʃæbli:/ *noun* (*plural* same /-li:z/) dry white wine from Chablis in France.

chaconne /ʃə'kɒn/ *noun* musical variations over ground bass; dance to this.

chafe /tʃeɪf/ ● *verb* (**-fing**) make or become sore or damaged by rubbing; irritate; show irritation, fret; rub (esp. skin) to warm. ● *noun* sore caused by rubbing.

chaff /tʃɑ:f/ ● *noun* separated grain-husks; chopped hay or straw; good-humoured teasing; worthless stuff. ● *verb* tease, banter.

chaffinch /'tʃæfɪntʃ/ *noun* a common European finch.

chafing dish /'tʃeɪfɪŋ/ *noun* vessel in which food is cooked or kept warm at table.

chagrin /'ʃægrɪn/ ● *noun* acute vexation or disappointment. ● *verb* affect with this.

chain ● *noun* connected series of links, thing resembling this; (in *plural*) fetters, restraining force; sequence, series, or set; unit of length (66 ft). ● *verb* (often + *up*) secure with chain. □ **chain gang** *historical* convicts chained together at work etc.; **chain mail** armour made from interlaced rings; **chain reaction** reaction forming products which themselves cause further reactions, series of events each due to previous one; **chainsaw** motor-driven saw with teeth on loop of chain; **chain-smoke** smoke continuously, esp. by lighting next cigarette etc. from previous one; **chain store** one of series of shops owned by one firm.

chair ● *noun* seat usually with back for one person; (office of) chairperson; professorship; *US* electric chair. ● *verb* be chairperson of (meeting); carry aloft in triumph. □ **chairlift** series of chairs on loop of cable for carrying passengers up and down mountain etc.; **chairman, chairperson, chairwoman** person who presides over meeting, board, or committee.

chaise /ʃeɪz/ *noun* horse-drawn usually open carriage for one or two people.

chaise longue /ʃeɪz 'lɒŋg/ *noun* (*plural* **chaise longues** or **chaises longues** /'lɒŋg(z)/) sofa with one arm rest.

chalcedony /kæl'sedənɪ/ *noun* (*plural* **-ies**) type of quartz.

chalet /'ʃæleɪ/ *noun* Swiss hut or cottage; similar house; small cabin in holiday camp etc.

chalice /'tʃælɪs/ *noun* goblet; Eucharistic cup.

chalk /tʃɔːk/ ● *noun* white soft limestone; (piece of) similar, sometimes coloured, substance for writing or drawing. ● *verb* rub, mark, draw, or write with chalk. □ **chalky** *adjective* (**-ier, -iest**).

challenge /'tʃælɪndʒ/ ● *noun* call to take part in contest etc. or to prove or justify something; demanding or difficult task; call to respond. ● *verb* (**-ging**) issue challenge to; dispute; (as **challenging** *adjective*) stimulatingly difficult. □ **challenger** *noun*.

chamber /'tʃeɪmbə/ *noun* hall used by legislative or judicial body; body that meets in it, esp. a house of a parliament; (in *plural*) set of rooms for barrister(s), esp. in Inns of Court; (in *plural*) judge's room for hearing cases not needing to be taken in court; *archaic* room, esp. bedroom; cavity or compartment in body, machinery, etc. (esp. part of gun that contains charge). □ **chambermaid** woman who cleans hotel bedrooms; **chamber music** music for small group of instruments; **Chamber of Commerce** association to promote local commercial interests; **chamber pot** vessel for urine etc., used in bedroom.

chamberlain /'tʃeɪmbəlɪn/ *noun* officer managing royal or noble household; treasurer of corporation etc.

chameleon /kə'miːliən/ *noun* lizard able to change colour for camouflage.

chamfer /'tʃæmfə/ ● *verb* bevel symmetrically. ● *noun* bevelled surface.

chamois /'ʃæmwɑː/ *noun* (*plural* same /-wɑːz/) small mountain antelope; /'ʃæmɪ/ (piece of) soft leather from sheep, goats, etc.

chamomile = CAMOMILE.

champ[1] ● *verb* munch or bite noisily. ● *noun* chewing noise. □ **champ at the bit** show impatience.

champ[2] *noun slang* champion.

champagne /ʃæm'peɪn/ *noun* white sparkling wine from Champagne in France.

champion /'tʃæmpɪən/ ● *noun* person or thing that has defeated all rivals; person who fights for cause or another person. ● *verb* support cause of, defend. ● *adjective colloquial* splendid.

championship *noun* (often in *plural*) contest to decide champion in sport etc.; position of champion.

chance /tʃɑːns/ ● *noun* possibility; (often in *plural*) probability; unplanned occurrence; fate. ● *adjective* fortuitous. ● *verb* (**-cing**) *colloquial* risk; happen. □ **chance on** happen to find.

chancel /'tʃɑːns(ə)l/ *noun* part of church near altar.

chancellery /'tʃɑːnsələrɪ/ *noun* (*plural* **-ies**) chancellor's department, staff, or residence; *US* office attached to embassy.

chancellor /'tʃɑːnsələ/ *noun* state or legal official; head of government in some European countries; nonresident honorary head of university; (in full **Lord Chancellor**) highest officer of the Crown, presiding in House of Lords; (in full **Chancellor of the Exchequer**) UK finance minister.

Chancery /'tʃɑːnsərɪ/ *noun* Lord Chancellor's division of High Court of Justice.

chancy /'tʃɑːnsɪ/ *adjective* (**-ier, -iest**) uncertain; risky.

chandelier /ʃændə'lɪə/ *noun* branched hanging support for lights.

chandler /'tʃɑːndlə/ *noun* dealer in oil, candles, soap, paint, etc.

change /tʃeɪndʒ/ ● *noun* making or becoming different; low-value money in small coins; money returned as balance of that given in payment; new experience; substitution of one thing or person for another; one of different orders in which bells can be rung. ● *verb* (**-ging**) undergo, show, or subject to change; take or use another instead of; interchange; give or get money in exchange for; put fresh clothes or coverings on; (often + *with*) exchange. □ **change hands** be passed to different owner. □ **changeful** *adjective*; **changeless** *adjective*.

changeable *adjective* inconstant; able to change or be changed.

changeling *noun* child believed to be substitute for another.

channel /'tʃæn(ə)l/ ● *noun* piece of water connecting two seas; (**the Channel**) the English Channel; medium of communication, agency; band of frequencies used for radio and television transmission; course in which thing moves; hollow bed of water; navigable part of waterway; passage for liquid; lengthwise strip on recording tape etc. ● *verb* (**-ll-**; *US* **-l-**) guide, direct; form channel(s) in.

chant /tʃɑːnt/ ● *noun* spoken singsong phrase; melody for reciting unmetrical texts; song. ● *verb* talk or repeat monotonously; sing or intone (psalm etc.).

chanter *noun* melody-pipe of bagpipes.

chantry /'tʃɑːntrɪ/ *noun* (*plural* **-ies**) endowment for singing of masses; priests, chapel, etc., so endowed.

chaos /'keɪɒs/ *noun* utter confusion; formless matter supposed to have existed before universe's creation. □ **chaotic** /keɪ'ɒtɪk/ *adjective*.

chap[1] *noun colloquial* man, boy.

chap[2] ● *verb* (**-pp-**) (esp. of skin) develop cracks or soreness; (of wind etc.) cause this. ● *noun* (usually in *plural*) crack in skin etc.

chaparral /ʃæpə'ræl/ *noun US* dense tangled brushwood.

chapatti /tʃə'pɑːtɪ/ *noun* (also **chupatty**) (*plural* **chapattis** or **chupatties**) flat thin cake of unleavened bread.

chapel /'tʃæp(ə)l/ *noun* place for private worship in cathedral or church, with its own altar; place of worship attached to private house, institution, etc.; place or service of worship for Nonconformists; branch of printers' or journalists' trade union at a workplace.

chaperon /'ʃæpərəʊn/ ● *noun* person, esp. older woman, in charge of young unmarried woman on certain social occasions. ● *verb* act as chaperon to.

chaplain /'tʃæplɪn/ *noun* member of clergy attached to private chapel, institution, ship, regiment, etc. □ **chaplaincy** *noun* (*plural* **-ies**).

chaplet /'tʃæplɪt/ *noun* wreath or circlet for head; string of beads, short rosary.

chapter /'tʃæptə/ *noun* division of book; period of time; canons of cathedral etc.; meeting of these.

char[1] *verb* (**-rr-**) blacken with fire, scorch; burn to charcoal.

char[2] *colloquial* ● *noun* charwoman. ● *verb* (**-rr-**) work as charwoman. □ **charlady, charwoman** one employed to do housework.

char[3] *noun slang* tea.

char[4] *noun* (*plural* same) a kind of trout.

charabanc /'ʃærəbæn/ noun early form of motor coach.

character /'kærɪktə/ noun distinguishing qualities or characteristics; moral strength; reputation; person in novel, play, etc.; colloquial (esp. eccentric) person; letter, symbol; testimonial.

characteristic /kærɪktə'rɪstɪk/ ● adjective typical, distinctive. ● noun characteristic feature or quality. □ **characteristically** adverb.

characterize verb (also **-ise**) (**-zing** or **-sing**) describe character of; (+ as) describe as; be characteristic of. □ **characterization** noun.

charade /ʃə'rɑːd/ noun (usually in plural, treated as singular) game of guessing word(s) from acted clues; absurd pretence.

charcoal noun black residue of partly burnt wood etc.

charge ● verb (**-ging**) ask (amount) as price; ask (person) for amount as price; (+ to, up to) debit cost of to; (often + with) accuse (of offence); (+ to do) instruct or urge to do; (+ with) entrust with; make rushing attack (on); (often + up) give electric charge to, store energy in; (often + with) load, fill. ● noun price, financial liability; accusation; task; custody; person or thing entrusted; (signal for) impetuous attack, esp. in battle; appropriate amount of material to be put in mechanism at one time, esp. explosive in gun; cause of electrical phenomena in matter. □ **charge card** credit card, esp. used at particular shop; **in charge** having command. □ **chargeable** adjective.

chargé d'affaires /ʃɑːʒeɪ dæ'feə/ noun (plural **chargés d'affaires** same pronunciation) ambassador's deputy; envoy to minor country.

charger noun cavalry horse; apparatus for charging battery.

chariot /'tʃærɪət/ noun historical two-wheeled horse-drawn vehicle used in ancient warfare and racing.

charioteer /tʃærɪə'tɪə/ noun chariot driver.

charisma /kə'rɪzmə/ noun power to inspire or attract others; divinely conferred power or talent. □ **charismatic** /kærɪz'mætɪk/ adjective.

charitable /'tʃærɪtəb(ə)l/ adjective generous to those in need; of or connected with a charity; lenient in judging others. □ **charitably** adverb.

charity /'tʃærɪtɪ/ noun (plural **-ies**) giving voluntarily to those in need; organization for helping those in need; love of fellow men; lenience in judging others.

charlatan /'ʃɑːlət(ə)n/ noun person falsely claiming knowledge or skill. □ **charlatanism** noun.

charlotte /'ʃɑːlɒt/ noun pudding of stewed fruit under bread etc.

charm ● noun power of delighting, attracting, or influencing; trinket on bracelet etc.; object, act, or word(s) supposedly having magic power. ● verb delight, captivate; influence or protect (as) by magic; obtain or gain by charm. □ **charmer** noun.

charming adjective delightful. □ **charmingly** adverb.

charnel house /'tʃɑːn(ə)l/ noun place containing corpses or bones.

chart ● noun map esp. for sea or air navigation or showing weather conditions etc.; sheet of information in form of tables or diagrams; (usually in plural) colloquial list of currently best-selling pop records. ● verb make chart of.

charter ● noun written grant of rights, esp. by sovereign or legislature; written description of organization's functions etc. ● verb grant charter to; hire (aircraft etc.). □ **charter flight** flight by chartered aircraft.

chartered adjective qualified as member of professional body that has royal charter.

Chartism noun working-class reform movement of 1837–48. □ **Chartist** noun.

chartreuse /ʃɑː'trɜːz/ noun green or yellow brandy liqueur.

chary /'tʃeərɪ/ adjective (**-ier, -iest**) cautious; sparing.

chase¹ /tʃeɪs/ ● verb (**-sing**) pursue; (+ from, out of, to, etc.) drive; hurry; (usually + up) colloquial pursue (thing overdue); colloquial try to attain; court persistently. ● noun pursuit; unenclosed hunting-land.

chase² /tʃeɪs/ verb (**-sing**) emboss or engrave (metal).

chaser noun horse for steeplechasing; colloquial drink taken after another of different kind.

chasm /'kæz(ə)m/ noun deep cleft in earth, rock, etc.; wide difference in opinion etc.

chassis /'ʃæsɪ/ noun (plural same -sɪz/) base frame of vehicle; frame for (radio etc.) components.

chaste /tʃeɪst/ adjective abstaining from extramarital or from all sexual intercourse; pure, virtuous; unadorned. □ **chastely** adverb; **chasteness** noun.

chasten /'tʃeɪs(ə)n/ verb (esp. as **chastening**, **chastened** adjectives) restrain; punish.

chastise /tʃæs'taɪz/ verb (**-sing**) rebuke severely; punish, beat. □ **chastisement** noun.

chastity /'tʃæstɪtɪ/ noun being chaste.

chasuble /'tʃæzjʊb(ə)l/ noun sleeveless outer vestment worn by celebrant of Eucharist.

chat ● verb (**-tt-**) talk in light familiar way. ● noun informal talk. □ **chatline** telephone service setting up conversations between groups of people on separate lines; **chat show** television or radio broadcast with informal celebrity interviews; **chat up** colloquial chat to, esp. flirtatiously.

chateau /'ʃætəʊ/ noun (plural **-x** /-z/) large French country house.

chatelaine /'ʃætəleɪn/ noun mistress of large house; historical appendage to woman's belt for carrying keys etc.

chattel /'tʃæt(ə)l/ noun (usually in plural) movable possession.

chatter /'tʃætə/ ● verb talk fast, incessantly, or foolishly. ● noun such talk.

chatty adjective (**-ier, -iest**) fond of or resembling chat.

chauffeur /'ʃəʊfə/ noun person employed to drive car. ● verb drive (car or person).

chauvinism /'ʃəʊvɪnɪz(ə)m/ noun exaggerated or aggressive patriotism; excessive or prejudiced support or loyalty for something. □ **chauvinist** noun; **chauvinistic** /-'nɪs-/ adjective.

cheap adjective low in price; charging low prices; of low quality or worth; easily got. □ **cheaply** adverb; **cheapness** noun.

cheapen verb make or become cheap; degrade.

cheapskate noun esp. US colloquial stingy person.

cheat ● verb (often + into, out of) deceive; (+ of) deprive of; gain unfair advantage. ● noun person who cheats; deception. □ **cheat on** colloquial be sexually unfaithful to.

check ● verb test, examine, verify; stop or slow motion of; colloquial rebuke; threaten opponent's king at chess; US agree on comparison; US deposit (luggage etc.). ● noun test for accuracy, quality, etc.; stopping or slowing of motion; rebuff; restraint; pattern of small squares; fabric so patterned; (also as interjection) exposure of chess king to attack; US restaurant bill; US cheque; US token of identification for left luggage etc.; US counter used in card games. □ **check in** register at hotel, airport, etc.; **check-in** act or place of checking in; **check out** leave hotel etc. with due formalities; **checkout** act of checking out, pay-desk in supermarket etc.; **check-up** thorough (esp. medical) examination.

checked adjective having a check pattern.

checker = CHEQUER.

checkmate ● noun (also as interjection) check at chess from which king cannot escape. ● verb (**-ting**) put into checkmate; frustrate.

Cheddar /'tʃedə/ noun kind of firm smooth cheese.

cheek ● noun side of face below eye; impertinence, impertinent speech; slang buttock. ● verb be impertinent to.

cheeky adjective (**-ier, -iest**) impertinent. □ **cheekily** adverb; **cheekiness** noun.

cheep ● noun shrill feeble note of young bird. ● verb make such cry.

cheer ● noun shout of encouragement or applause; mood, disposition; (as **cheers** interjection) colloquial: expressing good wishes or thanks. ● verb applaud; (usually + on) urge with shouts; shout for joy; gladden, comfort. □ **cheer up** make or become less sad.

cheerful adjective in good spirits; bright, pleasant. □ **cheerfully** adverb; **cheerfulness** noun.

cheerless adjective gloomy, dreary.

cheery adjective (**-ier, -iest**) cheerful. □ **cheerily** adverb.

cheese /tʃiːz/ noun food made from milk curds; cake of this with rind; thick conserve of fruit. □ **cheeseburger** hamburger with cheese in or on it; **cheesecake** tart filled with sweetened curds, slang sexually stimulating display of women; **cheesecloth** thin loosely woven cloth; **cheesed** slang (often + off) bored, fed up; **cheese-paring** stingy; **cheese plant** climbing plant with holey leaves. □ **cheesy** adjective.

cheetah /'tʃiːtə/ noun swift-running spotted feline resembling leopard.

chef /ʃef/ noun (esp. chief) cook in restaurant etc.

Chelsea /'tʃelsɪ/ noun □ **Chelsea bun** kind of spiral-shaped currant bun; **Chelsea pensioner** inmate of Chelsea Royal Hospital for old or disabled soldiers.

chemical /'kemɪk(ə)l/ ● adjective of, made by, or employing chemistry. ● noun substance obtained or used in chemistry. □ **chemical warfare** warfare using poison gas and other chemicals. □ **chemically** adverb.

chemise /ʃə'miːz/ noun historical woman's loose-fitting undergarment or dress.

chemist /'kemɪst/ noun dealer in medicinal drugs etc.; expert in chemistry.

chemistry /'kemɪstrɪ/ noun (plural **-ies**) science of elements and their laws of combination and change; colloquial sexual attraction.

chenille /ʃə'niːl/ noun tufted velvety yarn; fabric made of this.

cheque /tʃek/ noun written order to bank to pay sum of money; printed form for this. □ **chequebook** book of forms for writing cheques; **cheque card** card issued by bank to guarantee honouring of cheques up to stated amount.

chequer /'tʃekə/ (also **checker**) ● noun (often in plural) pattern of squares often alternately coloured; (in plural; usually **checkers**) US game of draughts. ● verb mark with chequers; variegate, break uniformity of; (as **chequered** adjective) with varied fortunes.

cherish /'tʃerɪʃ/ verb tend lovingly; hold dear; cling to.

cheroot /ʃə'ruːt/ noun cigar with both ends open.

cherry /'tʃerɪ/ ● noun (plural **-ies**) small stone fruit, tree bearing it, wood of this; light red. ● adjective of light red colour.

cherub /'tʃerəb/ noun representation of winged child; beautiful child; (plural **-im**) angelic being. □ **cherubic** /tʃɪ'ruːbɪk/ adjective.

chervil /'tʃɜːvɪl/ noun herb with aniseed flavour.

chess noun game for two players with 16 **chessmen** each, on chequered **chessboard** of 64 squares.

chest noun large strong box; part of body enclosed by ribs, front surface of body from neck to bottom of ribs; small cabinet for medicines etc. □ **chest of drawers** piece of furniture with set of drawers in frame.

chesterfield /'tʃestəfiːld/ noun sofa with arms and back of same height.

chestnut /'tʃesnʌt/ ● noun glossy hard brown edible nut; tree bearing it; horse chestnut; reddish-brown horse; colloquial stale joke etc.; reddish-brown. ● adjective reddish-brown.

chesty adjective (**-ier, -iest**) colloquial inclined to or symptomatic of chest disease. □ **chestily** adverb; **chestiness** noun.

cheval glass /ʃə'væl/ noun tall mirror pivoting in upright frame.

chevalier /ʃevə'lɪə/ noun member of certain orders of knighthood etc.

chevron /'ʃevrən/ noun V-shaped line or stripe.

chew ● verb work (food etc.) between teeth. ● noun act of chewing; chewy sweet. □ **chewing gum** flavoured gum for chewing; **chew on** work continuously between teeth, think about; **chew over** discuss, think about.

chewy adjective (**-ier, -iest**) requiring or suitable for chewing.

chez /ʃeɪ/ preposition at the home of. [French]

Chianti /kɪ'æntɪ/ noun (plural **-s**) red wine from Chianti in Italy.

chiaroscuro /kɪɑːrə'skʊərəʊ/ noun treatment of light and shade in painting; use of contrast in literature etc.

chic /ʃiːk/ ● adjective (**chic-er, chic-est**) stylish, elegant. ● noun stylishness, elegance.

chicane /ʃɪ'keɪn/ ● noun artificial barrier or obstacle on motor-racing course; chicanery. ● verb (**-ning**) archaic use chicanery; (usually + into, out of, etc.) cheat (person).

chicanery /ʃɪ'keɪnərɪ/ noun (plural **-ies**) clever but misleading talk; trickery, deception.

chick noun young bird; slang young woman.

chicken /'tʃɪkɪn/ ● noun domestic fowl; its flesh as food; young domestic fowl; youthful person. ● adjective colloquial cowardly. ● verb (+ out) colloquial withdraw through cowardice. □ **chicken feed** food for poultry, colloquial insignificant amount esp. of money; **chickenpox** infectious disease with rash of small blisters; **chicken wire** light wire netting.

chickpea noun pealike seed used as vegetable.

chickweed noun a small weed.

chicle /'tʃɪk(ə)l/ noun juice of tropical tree, used in chewing gum.

chicory /'tʃɪkərɪ/ noun (plural **-ies**) salad plant; its root, roasted and ground and used with or instead of coffee; endive.

chide verb (**-ding**; past chided or chid; past participle **chided** or **chidden**) archaic scold, rebuke.

chief /tʃiːf/ ● noun leader, ruler; head of tribe, clan, etc.; head of department etc. ● adjective first in position, importance, or influence; prominent, leading.

chiefly adverb above all; mainly but not exclusively.

chieftain /'tʃiːft(ə)n/ noun leader of tribe, clan, etc. □ **chieftaincy** noun (plural **-ies**).

chiffchaff /'tʃɪftʃæf/ noun small European warbler.

chiffon /'ʃɪfɒn/ noun diaphanous silky fabric.

chignon /'ʃiːnjɒ/ noun coil of hair at back of head.

chihuahua /tʃɪ'wɑːwə/ noun tiny smooth-coated dog.

chilblain /'tʃɪlbleɪn/ noun itching swelling on hand, foot, etc., caused by exposure to cold.

child /tʃaɪld/ noun (plural **children** /'tʃɪldrən/) young human being; one's son or daughter; (+ of) descendant, follower, or product of. □ **child benefit** regular state payment to parents of child up to certain age; **childbirth** giving birth to child; **child's play** easy task. □ **childless** adjective.

childhood noun state or period of being a child.

childish adjective of or like child; immature, silly. □ **childishly** adverb; **childishness** noun.

childlike adjective innocent, frank, etc., like child.

chili = CHILLI.

chill ● noun cold sensation; feverish cold; unpleasant coldness (of air etc.); depressing influence. ● verb make or become cold; depress, horrify; preserve (food or drink) by cooling. ● adjective literary chilly.

chilli /'tʃɪli/ noun (also **chili**) (plural **-es**) hot-tasting dried red capsicum pod. □ **chilli con carne** /kɒn 'kɑːni/ chilli-flavoured mince and beans.

chilly adjective (**-ier**, **-iest**) rather cold; sensitive to cold; unfriendly, unemotional.

chime ● noun set of attuned bells; sounds made by this. ● verb (**-ming**) (of bells) ring; show (time) by chiming; (usually + *together*, *with*) be in agreement. □ **chime in** interject remark, join in harmoniously.

chimera /kaɪ'mɪərə/ noun monster in Greek mythology with lion's head, goat's body, and serpent's tail; bogey; wild impossible scheme or fancy. □ **chimerical** /-'merɪk(ə)l/ adjective.

chimney /'tʃɪmnɪ/ noun (plural **-s**) channel conducting smoke etc. away from fire etc.; part of this above roof; glass tube protecting lamp-flame. □ **chimney breast** projecting wall round chimney; **chimney pot** pipe at top of chimney; **chimney sweep** person who clears chimneys of soot.

chimp noun colloquial chimpanzee.

chimpanzee /tʃɪmpən'ziː/ noun manlike African ape.

chin noun front of lower jaw. □ **chinless wonder** ineffectual person; **chinwag** noun & verb slang chat.

china /'tʃaɪnə/ ● noun fine white or translucent ceramic ware; things made of this. ● adjective made of china. □ **china clay** kaolin.

chinchilla /tʃɪn'tʃɪlə/ noun S. American rodent; its soft grey fur; breed of cat or rabbit.

chine ● noun backbone; joint of meat containing this; ridge. ● verb (**-ning**) cut (meat) through backbone.

Chinese /tʃaɪ'niːz/ ● adjective of China. ● noun Chinese language; (plural same) native or national of China, person of Chinese descent. □ **Chinese lantern** collapsible paper lantern, plant with inflated orange-red calyx; **Chinese leaf** lettuce-like cabbage.

chink¹ noun narrow opening.

chink² ● verb (cause to) make sound of glasses or coins striking together. ● noun this sound.

chintz noun printed multicoloured usually glazed cotton cloth.

chip ● noun small piece cut or broken off; place where piece has been broken off; strip of potato usually fried; US potato crisp; counter used as money in some games; microchip. ● verb (**-pp-**) (often + off) cut or break (piece) from hard material; (often + at, away at) cut pieces off (hard material); be apt to break at edge; (usually as **chipped** adjective) make (potato) into chips. □ **chipboard** board made of compressed wood chips.

chipmunk /'tʃɪpmʌŋk/ noun N. American striped ground squirrel.

chipolata /tʃɪpə'lɑːtə/ noun small thin sausage.

Chippendale /'tʃɪpəndeɪl/ adjective of an 18th-c. elegant style of furniture.

chiropody /kɪ'rɒpədɪ/ noun treatment of feet and their ailments. □ **chiropodist** noun.

chiropractic /kaɪərəʊ'præktɪk/ noun treatment of disease by manipulation of spinal column. □ **chiropractor** /'kaɪə-/ noun.

chirp ● verb (of small bird etc.) utter short thin sharp note; speak merrily. ● noun chirping sound.

chirpy adjective (**-ier**, **-iest**) colloquial cheerful. □ **chirpily** adverb.

chirrup /'tʃɪrəp/ ● verb (**-p-**) chirp, esp. repeatedly. ● noun chirruping sound.

chisel /'tʃɪz(ə)l/ ● noun tool with bevelled blade for shaping wood, stone, or metal. ● verb (**-ll-**; US **-l-**) cut or shape with chisel; (as **chiselled** adjective) (of features) clear-cut; slang defraud.

chit¹ noun derogatory or jocular young small woman; young child.

chit² noun written note.

chit-chat noun colloquial light conversation, gossip.

chivalry /'ʃɪvəlrɪ/ noun medieval knightly system; honour and courtesy, esp. to the weak. □ **chivalrous** adjective; **chivalrously** adverb.

chive noun herb related to onion.

chivvy /'tʃɪvɪ/ verb (**-ies**, **-ied**) urge persistently, nag.

chloral /'klɔːr(ə)l/ noun compound used in making DDT, sedatives, etc.

chloride /'klɔːraɪd/ noun compound of chlorine and another element or group.

chlorinate /'klɔːrɪneɪt/ verb (**-ting**) impregnate or treat with chlorine. □ **chlorination** noun.

chlorine /'klɔːriːn/ noun poisonous gas used for bleaching and disinfecting.

chlorofluorocarbon see CFC.

chloroform /'klɒrəfɔːm/ ● noun colourless volatile liquid formerly used as general anaesthetic. ● verb render unconscious with this.

chlorophyll /'klɒrəfɪl/ noun green pigment in most plants.

choc noun colloquial chocolate. □ **choc ice** bar of ice cream covered with chocolate.

chock ● noun block of wood, wedge. ● verb make fast with chock(s). □ **chock-a-block** (often + with) crammed together, full; **chock-full** (often + of) crammed full.

chocolate /'tʃɒklət/ ● noun food made as paste, powder, or solid block from ground cacao seeds; sweet made of or covered with this; drink containing chocolate; dark brown. ● adjective made from chocolate; dark brown.

choice ● noun act of choosing; thing or person chosen; range to choose from; power to choose. ● adjective of superior quality.

choir /kwaɪə/ noun regular group of singers; chancel in large church. □ **choirboy**, **choirgirl** boy or girl singer in church choir.

choke ● verb (**-king**) stop breathing of (person or animal); suffer such stoppage; block up; (as **choked** adjective) speechless from emotion, disgusted, disappointed. ● noun valve in carburettor controlling inflow of air; device for smoothing variations of alternating electric current.

choker noun close-fitting necklace.

choler /'kɒlə/ noun historical bile; archaic anger, irascibility.

cholera /'kɒlərə/ noun infectious often fatal bacterial disease of small intestine.

choleric /'kɒlərɪk/ adjective easily angered.

cholesterol /kə'lestərɒl/ noun sterol present in human tissues including the blood.

choose /tʃuːz/ verb (**-sing**; past **chose** /tʃəʊz/; past participle **chosen**) select out of greater number; (usually + between, from) take one or another; (usually + to do) decide.

choosy /ˈtʃuːzɪ/ adjective (**-ier, -iest**) colloquial fussy; hard to please.

chop[1] ● verb (**-pp-**) (usually + off, down, etc.) cut with axe etc.; (often + up) cut into small pieces; strike (ball) with heavy edgewise blow. ● noun cutting blow; thick slice of meat usually including rib; (**the chop**) slang dismissal from job, killing, being killed.

chop[2] noun (usually in plural) jaw.

chop[3] verb (**-pp-**) □ **chop and change** vacillate.

chopper noun large-bladed short axe; cleaver; colloquial helicopter.

choppy adjective (**-ier, -iest**) (of sea etc.) fairly rough.

chopstick /ˈtʃɒpstɪk/ noun each of pair of sticks held in one hand as eating utensils by Chinese, Japanese, etc.

chop suey /tʃɒpˈsuːɪ/ noun (plural **-s**) Chinese-style dish of meat fried with vegetables.

choral /ˈkɔːr(ə)l/ adjective of, for, or sung by choir or chorus.

chorale /kəˈrɑːl/ noun simple stately hymn tune; choir.

chord[1] /kɔːd/ noun combination of notes sounded together.

chord[2] /kɔːd/ noun straight line joining ends of arc; string of harp etc.

chore noun tedious or routine task, esp. domestic.

choreography /kɒrɪˈɒɡrəfɪ/ noun design or arrangement of ballet etc. □ **choreograph** /ˈkɒrɪəɡrɑːf/ verb; **choreographer** noun; **choreographic** /-əˈɡræf-/ adjective.

chorister /ˈkɒrɪstə/ noun member of choir, esp. choirboy.

chortle /ˈtʃɔːt(ə)l/ ● noun gleeful chuckle. ● verb (**-ling**) chuckle gleefully.

chorus /ˈkɔːrəs/ ● noun (plural **-es**) group of singers, choir; music for choir; refrain of song; simultaneous utterance; group of singers and dancers performing together; group of performers commenting on action in ancient Greek play, any of its utterances. ● verb (**-s-**) utter simultaneously.

chose past of CHOOSE.

chosen past participle of CHOOSE.

chough /tʃʌf/ noun red-legged crow.

choux pastry /ʃuː/ noun very light pastry made with eggs.

chow noun slang food; Chinese breed of dog.

chow mein /tʃaʊ ˈmeɪn/ noun Chinese-style dish of fried noodles usually with shredded meat and vegetables.

christen /ˈkrɪs(ə)n/ verb baptize; name. □ **christening** noun.

Christendom /ˈkrɪsəndəm/ noun Christians worldwide.

Christian /ˈkrɪstʃ(ə)n/ ● adjective of Christ's teaching; believing in or following Christian religion; charitable, kind. ● noun adherent of Christianity. □ **Christian era** era counted from Christ's birth; **Christian name** forename, esp. given at christening; **Christian Science** system of belief including power of healing by prayer alone; **Christian Scientist** adherent of this.

Christianity /krɪstɪˈænɪtɪ/ noun Christian religion, quality, or character.

Christmas /ˈkrɪsməs/ noun (period around) festival of Christ's birth celebrated on 25 Dec. □ **Christmas box** present or tip given at Christmas; **Christmas Day** 25 Dec.; **Christmas Eve** 24 Dec.; **Christmas pudding** rich boiled pudding with dried fruit; **Christmas rose** white-flowered hellebore flowering in winter; **Christmas tree** evergreen tree decorated at Christmas. □ **Christmassy** adjective.

chromatic /krəˈmætɪk/ adjective of colour, in colours; Music of or having notes not belonging to prevailing key. □ **chromatic scale** scale that proceeds by semitones. □ **chromatically** adverb.

chrome /krəʊm/ noun chromium; yellow pigment got from a compound of chromium.

chromium /ˈkrəʊmɪəm/ noun metallic element used as shiny decorative or protective coating.

chromosome /ˈkrəʊməsəʊm/ noun Biology threadlike structure occurring in pairs in cell nucleus, carrying genes.

chronic /ˈkrɒnɪk/ adjective (of disease) long-lasting; (of patient) having chronic illness; colloquial bad, intense, severe. □ **chronically** adverb.

chronicle /ˈkrɒnɪk(ə)l/ ● noun record of events in order of occurrence. ● verb (**-ling**) record (events) thus.

chronological /krɒnəˈlɒdʒɪk(ə)l/ adjective according to order of occurrence. □ **chronologically** adverb.

chronology /krəˈnɒlədʒɪ/ noun (plural **-ies**) science of computing dates; (document displaying) arrangement of events etc. according to date.

chronometer /krəˈnɒmɪtə/ noun time-measuring instrument, esp. one used in navigation.

chrysalis /ˈkrɪsəlɪs/ noun (plural **-lises**) pupa of butterfly or moth; case enclosing it.

chrysanthemum /krɪˈsænθəməm/ noun garden plant flowering in autumn.

chub noun (plural same) thick-bodied river fish.

chubby adjective (**-ier, -iest**) plump, round.

chuck[1] ● verb colloquial fling or throw carelessly; (often + in, up) give up; touch playfully, esp. under chin. ● noun act of chucking; (**the chuck**) slang dismissal. □ **chuck out** colloquial expel, discard.

chuck[2] ● noun cut of beef from neck to ribs; device for holding workpiece or bit. ● verb fix in chuck.

chuckle /ˈtʃʌk(ə)l/ ● verb (**-ling**) laugh quietly or inwardly. ● noun quiet or suppressed laugh.

chuff verb (of engine etc.) work with regular sharp puffing sound.

chuffed adjective slang delighted.

chug verb (**-gg-**) make intermittent explosive sound; move with this.

chukker /ˈtʃʌkə/ noun period of play in polo.

chum noun colloquial close friend. □ **chum up (-mm-)** (often + with) become close friend (of). □ **chummy** adjective (**-ier, -iest**).

chump noun colloquial foolish person; thick end of loin of lamb or mutton; lump of wood.

chunk noun lump cut or broken off.

chunky adjective (**-ier, -iest**) consisting of or resembling chunks; small and sturdy.

chunter /ˈtʃʌntə/ verb colloquial mutter, grumble.

chupatty = CHAPATTI.

church noun building for public Christian worship; public worship; (**Church**) Christians collectively, clerical profession, organized Christian society. □ **churchgoer** person attending church regularly; **churchman** member of clergy or Church; **churchwarden** elected lay representative of Anglican parish; **churchyard** enclosed ground round church, esp. used for burials.

churl noun bad-mannered, surly, or stingy person. □ **churlish** adjective.

churn ● noun large milk can; butter-making machine. ● verb agitate (milk etc.) in churn; make (butter) in churn; (usually + up) upset, agitate. □ **churn out** produce in large quantities.

chute[1] /ʃuːt/ noun slide for taking things to lower level.

chute[2] /ʃuːt/ noun colloquial parachute.

chutney /ˈtʃʌtnɪ/ noun (plural **-s**) relish made of fruits, vinegar, spices, etc.

chyle /kaɪl/ noun milky fluid into which chyme is converted.

chyme /kaɪm/ noun pulp formed from partly-digested food.

CIA abbreviation (in US) Central Intelligence Agency.

ciabatta /tʃəˈbɑːtə/ noun Italian bread made with olive oil.

ciao /tʃaʊ/ interjection colloquial goodbye; hello.

cicada /sɪˈkɑːdə/ noun winged chirping insect.

cicatrice /ˈsɪkətrɪs/ noun scar of healed wound.

cicely /ˈsɪsəlɪ/ noun (plural **-ies**) flowering plant related to parsley and chervil.

CID abbreviation Criminal Investigation Department.

cider /ˈsaɪdə/ noun drink of fermented apple juice.

cigar /sɪˈgɑː/ noun roll of tobacco leaves for smoking.

cigarette /sɪgəˈret/ noun finely-cut tobacco rolled in paper for smoking.

cilium /ˈsɪlɪəm/ noun (plural **cilia**) hairlike structure on animal cells; eyelash. □ **ciliary** adjective.

cinch /sɪntʃ/ noun colloquial certainty; easy task.

cinchona /sɪŋˈkəʊnə/ noun S. American evergreen tree; (drug from) its bark which contains quinine.

cincture /ˈsɪŋktʃə/ noun literary girdle, belt, or border.

cinder /ˈsɪndə/ noun residue of coal etc. after burning.

Cinderella /sɪndəˈrelə/ noun person or thing of unrecognized merit.

cine- /sɪnɪ/ combining form cinematographic.

cinema /ˈsɪnɪmɑː/ noun theatre where films are shown; films collectively; art or industry of producing films. □ **cinematic** /-ˈmæt-/ adjective.

cinematography /sɪnɪməˈtɒgrəfɪ/ noun art of making films. □ **cinematographer** noun; **cinematographic** /-mætəˈgræfɪk/ adjective.

cineraria /sɪnəˈreərɪə/ noun plant with bright flowers and downy leaves.

cinnabar /ˈsɪnəbɑː/ noun red mercuric sulphide; vermilion.

cinnamon /ˈsɪnəmən/ noun aromatic spice from bark of SE Asian tree; this tree; yellowish-brown.

cinquefoil /ˈsɪŋkfɔɪl/ noun plant with compound leaf of 5 leaflets.

Cinque Port /sɪŋk/ noun any of (originally 5) ports in SE England with ancient privileges.

cipher /ˈsaɪfə/ (also **cypher**) ● noun secret or disguised writing, key to this; arithmetical symbol 0; person or thing of no importance. ● verb write in cipher.

circa /ˈsɜːkə/ preposition (usually before date) about. [Latin]

circle /ˈsɜːk(ə)l/ ● noun perfectly round plane figure; roundish enclosure or structure; curved upper tier of seats in theatre etc.; circular route; set or restricted group; people grouped round centre of interest. ● verb (**-ling**) (often + round, about) move in or form circle.

circlet /ˈsɜːklɪt/ noun small circle; circular band, esp. as ornament.

circuit /ˈsɜːkɪt/ noun line, course, or distance enclosing an area; path of electric current, apparatus through which current passes; judge's itinerary through district, such a district; chain of theatres, cinemas, etc. under single management; motor-racing track; sphere of operation; sequence of sporting events.

circuitous /sɜːˈkjuːɪtəs/ adjective indirect, roundabout.

circuitry /ˈsɜːkɪtrɪ/ noun (plural **-ies**) system of electric circuits.

circular /ˈsɜːkjʊlə/ ● adjective having form of or moving in circle; (of reasoning) using point to be proved as argument for its own truth; (of letter etc.) distributed to several people. ● noun circular letter etc. □ **circular saw** power saw with rotating toothed disc. □ **circularity** /-ˈlærɪtɪ/ noun.

circularize verb (also **-ise**) (**-zing** or **-sing**) send circular to.

circulate /ˈsɜːkjʊleɪt/ verb (**-ting**) be or put in circulation; send circulars to; mingle among guests etc.

circulation noun movement from and back to starting point, esp. that of blood from and to heart; transmission, distribution; number of copies sold. □ **circulatory** adjective.

circumcise /ˈsɜːkəmsaɪz/ verb (**-sing**) cut off foreskin or clitoris of. □ **circumcision** /-ˈsɪʒ(ə)n/ noun.

circumference /səˈkʌmfərəns/ noun line enclosing circle; distance round.

circumflex /ˈsɜːkəmfleks/ noun (in full **circumflex accent**) mark (ˆ) over vowel indicating pronunciation.

circumlocution /sɜːkəmləˈkjuːʃ(ə)n/ noun roundabout expression; evasive speech; verbosity. □ **circumlocutory** /-ˈlɒkjʊt-/ adjective.

circumnavigate /sɜːkəmˈnævɪgeɪt/ verb (**-ting**) sail round. □ **circumnavigation** noun.

circumscribe /ˈsɜːkəmskraɪb/ verb (**-bing**) enclose or outline; lay down limits of; confine, restrict. □ **circumscription** /-ˈskrɪpʃ(ə)n/ noun.

circumspect /ˈsɜːkəmspekt/ adjective cautious, taking everything into account. □ **circumspection** /-ˈspekʃ(ə)n/ noun; **circumspectly** adverb.

circumstance /ˈsɜːkəmst(ə)ns/ noun fact, occurrence, or condition, esp. (in plural) connected with or affecting an event etc.; (in plural) financial condition; ceremony, fuss.

circumstantial /sɜːkəmˈstænʃ(ə)l/ adjective (of account, story) detailed; (of evidence) tending to establish a conclusion by reasonable inference.

circumvent /sɜːkəmˈvent/ verb evade, outwit.

circus /ˈsɜːkəs/ noun (plural **-es**) travelling show of performing acrobats, clowns, animals, etc.; colloquial scene of lively action, group of people in common activity; open space in town, where several streets converge; historical arena for sports and games.

cirrhosis /sɪˈrəʊsɪs/ noun chronic liver disease.

cirrus /ˈsɪrəs/ noun (plural **cirri** /-raɪ/) white wispy cloud.

cissy = SISSY.

Cistercian /sɪsˈtɜːʃ(ə)n/ ● noun monk or nun of strict Benedictine order. ● adjective of the Cistercians.

cistern /ˈsɪst(ə)n/ noun tank for storing water; underground reservoir.

citadel /ˈsɪtəd(ə)l/ noun fortress protecting or dominating city.

citation /saɪˈteɪʃ(ə)n/ noun citing or passage cited; description of reasons for award.

cite verb (**-ting**) mention as example; quote (book etc.) in support; mention in military dispatches; summon to law court.

citizen /ˈsɪtɪz(ə)n/ noun native or national of state; inhabitant of a city. □ **citizen's band** system of local intercommunication by radio. □ **citizenship** noun.

citrate /ˈsɪtreɪt/ noun salt of citric acid.

citric /ˈsɪtrɪk/ adjective □ **citric acid** sharp-tasting acid in citrus fruits.

citron /ˈsɪtrən/ noun tree bearing large lemon-like fruits; this fruit.

citronella /sɪtrəˈnelə/ noun a fragrant oil; grass from S. Asia yielding it.

citrus /'sɪtrəs/ *noun* (*plural* **-es**) tree of group including orange, lemon, and grapefruit; (in full **citrus fruit**) fruit of such tree.

city /'sɪtɪ/ *noun* (*plural* **-ies**) large town; town created city by charter and containing cathedral; (**the City**) part of London governed by Lord Mayor and Corporation, business quarter of this, commercial circles.

civet /'sɪvɪt/ *noun* (in full **civet cat**) catlike animal of Central Africa; strong musky perfume got from this.

civic /'sɪvɪk/ *adjective* of city or citizenship.

civics *plural noun* (usually treated as *singular*) study of civic rights and duties.

civil /'sɪv(ə)l/ *adjective* of or belonging to citizens; non-military; polite, obliging; *Law* concerning private rights and not criminal offences. □ **civil defence** organization for protecting civilians in wartime; **civil engineer** person who designs or maintains roads, bridges, etc.; **civil list** annual allowance by Parliament for royal family's household expenses; **civil marriage** one solemnized without religious ceremony; **civil servant** member of civil service; **civil service** all non-military and non-judicial branches of state administration; **civil war** one between citizens of same country.

civilian /sɪ'vɪlɪən/ ● *noun* person not in armed forces. ● *adjective* of or for civilians.

civility /sɪ'vɪlɪtɪ/ *noun* (*plural* **-ies**) politeness; act of politeness.

civilization *noun* (also **-sation**) advanced stage of social development; peoples regarded as having achieved, or been instrumental in evolving, this.

civilize /'sɪvɪlaɪz/ *verb* (also **-ise**) (**-zing** or **-sing**) bring out of barbarism; enlighten, refine.

cl *abbreviation* centilitre(s).

clack ● *verb* make sharp sound as of boards struck together. ● *noun* such sound.

clad *adjective* clothed; provided with cladding.

cladding *noun* protective covering or coating.

claim ● *verb* assert; demand as one's due; represent oneself as having; (+ *to do*) profess. ● *noun* demand; (+ *to*, *on*) right or title; assertion; thing claimed.

claimant *noun* person making claim, esp. in lawsuit or for state benefit.

clairvoyance /kleə'vɔɪəns/ *noun* supposed faculty of perceiving the future or the unseen. □ **clairvoyant** *noun* & *adjective*.

clam ● *noun* edible bivalve mollusc. ● *verb* (**-mm-**) (+ *up*) *colloquial* refuse to talk.

clamber /'klæmbə/ *verb* climb using hands or with difficulty.

clammy /'klæmɪ/ *adjective* (**-ier**, **-iest**) damp and sticky.

clamour /'klæmə/ (*US* **clamor**) ● *noun* shouting, confused noise; protest, demand. ● *verb* make clamour, shout. □ **clamorous** *adjective*.

clamp¹ ● *noun* device, esp. brace or band of iron etc., for strengthening or holding things together; device for immobilizing illegally parked vehicles. ● *verb* strengthen or fasten with clamp; immobilize with clamp. □ **clamp down** (usually + *on*) become stricter (about).

clamp² *noun* heap of earth and straw over harvested potatoes etc.

clan *noun* group of families with common ancestor, esp. in Scotland; family holding together; group with common interest. □ **clannish** *adjective*; **clansman**, **clanswoman** *noun*.

clandestine /klæn'destɪn/ *adjective* surreptitious, secret.

clang ● *noun* loud resonant metallic sound. ● *verb* (cause to) make clang.

clangour /'klæŋgə/ *noun* (*US* **clangor**) continued clanging. □ **clangorous** *adjective*.

clank ● *noun* sound as of metal on metal. ● *verb* (cause to) make clank.

clap ● *verb* (**-pp-**) strike palms of hands together, esp. as applause; put or place quickly or with determination; (+ *on*) give friendly slap on. ● *noun* act of clapping; explosive noise, esp. of thunder; slap. □ **clap eyes on** *colloquial* see.

clapper *noun* tongue or striker of bell. □ **clapperboard** device in film-making for making sharp noise to synchronize picture and sound.

claptrap *noun* insincere or pretentious talk; nonsense.

claque /klæk/ *noun* people hired to applaud.

claret /'klærət/ *noun* red Bordeaux wine.

clarify /'klærɪfaɪ/ *verb* (**-ies**, **-ied**) make or become clear; free from impurities; make transparent. □ **clarification** *noun*.

clarinet /klærɪ'net/ *noun* woodwind instrument with single reed. □ **clarinettist** *noun*.

clarion /'klærɪən/ *noun* rousing sound; *historical* war-trumpet.

clarity /'klærɪtɪ/ *noun* clearness.

clash ● *noun* loud jarring sound as of metal objects struck together; collision; conflict; discord of colours etc. ● *verb* (cause to) make clash; coincide awkwardly; (often + *with*) be discordant or at variance.

clasp /klɑːsp/ ● *noun* device with interlocking parts for fastening; embrace, handshake; bar on medal-ribbon. ● *verb* fasten (as) with clasp; grasp, embrace. □ **clasp-knife** large folding knife.

class /klɑːs/ ● *noun* any set of people or things grouped together or differentiated from others; division or order of society; *colloquial* high quality; set of students taught together; their time of meeting; their course of instruction. ● *verb* place in a class. □ **classmate** person in same class at school; **classroom** room where class of students is taught. □ **classless** *adjective*.

classic /'klæsɪk/ ● *adjective* first-class; of lasting importance; typical; of ancient Greek or Latin culture etc.; (of style) simple and harmonious; famous because long-established. ● *noun* classic writer, artist, work, or example; (in *plural*) study of ancient Greek and Latin.

classical *adjective* of ancient Greek or Latin literature etc.; (of language) having form used by standard authors; (of music) serious or conventional.

classicism /'klæsɪsɪz(ə)m/ *noun* following of classic style; classical scholarship. □ **classicist** *noun*.

classify /'klæsɪfaɪ/ *verb* (**-ies**, **-ied**) arrange in classes; class; designate as officially secret. □ **classification** *noun*.

classy /'klɑːsɪ/ *adjective* (**-ier**, **-iest**) *colloquial* superior. □ **classiness** *noun*.

clatter /'klætə/ ● *noun* sound as of hard objects struck together. ● *verb* (cause to) make clatter.

clause /klɔːz/ *noun* group of words including finite verb (see panel); single statement in treaty, law, contract, etc.

claustrophobia /klɔːstrə'fəʊbɪə/ *noun* abnormal fear of confined places. □ **claustrophobic** *adjective*.

clavichord /'klævɪkɔːd/ *noun* small keyboard instrument with very soft tone.

clavicle /'klævɪk(ə)l/ *noun* collar-bone.

claw ● *noun* pointed nail on animal's foot; foot armed with claws; pincers of shellfish; device for grappling, holding, etc. ● *verb* scratch, maul, or pull with claws or fingernails.

clay *noun* stiff sticky earth, used for bricks, pottery, etc. □ **clay pigeon** breakable disc thrown into air as target for shooting. □ **clayey** *adjective*.

claymore /'kleɪmɔː/ *noun historical* Scottish two-edged broad-bladed sword.

clean ● *adjective* free from dirt; clear; pristine; not obscene or indecent; attentive to cleanliness; clear-cut; without record of crime etc.; fair. ● *adverb* completely; simply; in a clean way. ● *verb* make or become clean. ● *noun* process of cleaning. □ **clean-cut** sharply outlined, (of person) clean and tidy; **clean out** clean thoroughly, *slang* empty or deprive (esp. of money); **clean-shaven** without beard or moustache; **clean up** make tidy or clean, *slang* acquire as or make profit. □ **cleaner** *noun*; **cleanness** *noun*.

cleanly[1] *adverb* in a clean way.

cleanly[2] /'klenlɪ/ *adjective* (**-ier**, **-iest**) habitually clean; attentive to cleanness and hygiene. □ **cleanliness** *noun*.

cleanse /klenz/ *verb* (**-sing**) make clean or pure. □ **cleanser** *noun*.

clear ● *adjective* free from dirt or contamination; not clouded; transparent; readily perceived or understood; able to discern readily; convinced; (of conscience) guiltless; unobstructed; net; complete; (often + *of*) free, unhampered. ● *adverb* clearly; completely; apart. ● *verb* make or become clear; (often + *of*) free from obstruction etc.; (often + *of*) show (person) to be innocent; approve (person etc.) for special duty, access, etc.; pass through (customs); pass over or by without touching; make (sum) as net gain; pass (cheque) through clearing house. □ **clear-cut** sharply defined; **clear off** *colloquial* go away; **clear out** empty, remove, *colloquial* go away; **clear-out** tidying by emptying and sorting; **clear up** tidy, solve; **clearway** road where vehicles may not stop. □ **clearly** *adverb*; **clearness** *noun*.

clearance *noun* removal of obstructions etc.; space allowed for passing of two objects; special authorization; clearing for special duty, of cheque, etc.; clearing out.

clearing *noun* treeless area in forest. □ **clearing bank** member of clearing house; **clearing house** bankers' institution where cheques etc. are exchanged, agency for collecting and distributing information etc.

cleat *noun* device for fastening ropes to projection on gangway, sole, etc. to provide grip.

cleavage *noun* hollow between woman's breasts; division; line along which rocks etc. split.

cleave[1] *verb* (**-ving**; *past* **clove** /kləʊv/, **cleft**, or **cleaved**; *past participle* **cloven**, **cleft**, or **cleaved**) *literary* break or come apart; make one's way through.

cleave[2] *verb* (**-ving**) (+ *to*) *literary* adhere.

cleaver *noun* butcher's heavy chopping tool.

clef *noun Music* symbol at start of staff showing pitch of notes on it.

cleft[1] *adjective* split, partly divided. □ **cleft palate** congenital split in roof of mouth.

cleft[2] *noun* split, fissure.

clematis /'klemətɪs/ *noun* climbing flowering plant.

clement /'klemənt/ *adjective* mild; merciful. □ **clemency** *noun*.

clementine /'klemənti:n/ *noun* small tangerine-like fruit.

clench ● *verb* close tightly; grasp firmly. ● *noun* clenching action; clenched state.

clergy /'klɜːdʒɪ/ *noun* (*plural* **-ies**) (usually treated as *plural*) those ordained for religious duties.

clergyman /'klɜːdʒɪmən/ *noun* member of clergy.

cleric /'klerɪk/ *noun* member of clergy.

clerical *adjective* of clergy or clergymen; of or done by clerks.

clerihew /'klerɪhjuː/ *noun* witty or comic 4-line biographical verse.

clerk /klɑːk/ ● *noun* person employed to keep records, accounts, etc.; secretary or agent of local council, court, etc.; lay officer of church. ● *verb* work as clerk.

clever /'klevə/ *adjective* (**-er**, **-est**) skilful, talented, quick to understand and learn; adroit; ingenious. □ **cleverly** *adverb*; **cleverness** *noun*.

cliché /'kliːʃeɪ/ *noun* hackneyed phrase or opinion.

clichéd *adjective* hackneyed, full of clichés.

click ● *noun* slight sharp sound. ● *verb* (cause to) make click; *colloquial* become clear, understood, or popular; (+ *with*) become friendly with.

client /'klaɪənt/ *noun* person using services of lawyer or other professional person; customer.

clientele /kliːɒn'tel/ *noun* clients collectively; customers.

cliff *noun* steep rock face, esp. on coast. □ **cliff-hanger** story etc. with strong element of suspense.

climacteric /klaɪˈmæktərɪk/ *noun* period of life when fertility and sexual activity are in decline.

climate /'klaɪmɪt/ *noun* prevailing weather conditions of an area; region with particular weather conditions; prevailing trend of opinion etc. □ **climatic** /-'mæt-/ *adjective*; **climatically** /-'mæt-/ *adverb*.

climax /'klaɪmæks/ ● *noun* event or point of greatest intensity or interest, culmination. ● *verb colloquial* reach or bring to a climax. □ **climactic** *adjective*.

climb /klaɪm/ ● *verb* (often + *up*) ascend, mount, go up; (of plant) grow up wall etc. by clinging etc.; rise, esp. in social rank. ● *noun* action of climbing; hill etc. (to be) climbed. □ **climber** *noun*.

clime *noun literary* region; climate.

clinch ● *verb* confirm or settle conclusively; (of boxers) become too closely engaged; secure (nail or rivet) by driving point sideways when through. ● *noun* clinching, resulting state; *colloquial* embrace.

cling *verb* (*past & past participle* **clung**) (often + *to*) adhere; (+ *to*) be emotionally dependent on or unwilling to give up; (often + *to*) maintain grasp. □ **cling film** thin transparent plastic covering for food. □ **clingy** *adjective* (**-ier**, **-iest**).

Clause

A clause is a group of words that includes a finite verb. If it makes complete sense by itself, it is known as a main clause, e.g.

The sun came out.

Otherwise, although it makes some sense, it must be attached to a main clause; this is known as a subordinate clause, e.g.

when the sun came out
(as in *When the sun came out, we went outside.*)

clinic /'klɪnɪk/ *noun* private or specialized hospital; place or occasion for giving medical treatment or specialist advice; teaching of medicine at hospital bedside.

clinical *adjective* of or for the treatment of patients; objective, coldly detached; (of room etc.) bare, functional. □ **clinically** *adverb.*

clink¹ ● *noun* sharp ringing sound. ● *verb* (cause to) make clink.

clink² *noun slang* prison.

clinker /'klɪŋkə/ *noun* mass of slag or lava; stony residue from burnt coal.

clinker-built *adjective* (of boat) with external planks overlapping downwards.

clip¹ ● *noun* device for holding things together; piece of jewellery fastened by clip; set of attached cartridges for firearm. ● *verb* (**-pp-**) fix with clip. □ **clipboard** board with spring clip for holding papers etc.

clip² ● *verb* (**-pp-**) cut with shears or scissors; cut hair or wool of; *colloquial* hit sharply; omit (letter) from word; omit parts of (words uttered); punch hole in (ticket) to show it has been used; cut from newspaper etc. ● *noun* clipping; *colloquial* sharp blow; extract from motion picture; yield of wool.

clipper *noun* (usually in *plural*) instrument for clipping; *historical* fast sailing ship.

clipping *noun* piece clipped, esp. from newspaper.

clique /kliːk/ *noun* exclusive group of people. □ **cliquey** *adjective* (**cliquier, cliquiest**); **cliquish** *adjective.*

clitoris /'klɪtərɪs/ *noun* small erectile part of female genitals.

Cllr. *abbreviation* Councillor.

cloak ● *noun* loose usually sleeveless outdoor garment; covering. ● *verb* cover with cloak; conceal, disguise. □ **cloakroom** room for outdoor clothes or luggage, *euphemistic* lavatory.

clobber¹ /'klɒbə/ *verb slang* hit (repeatedly); defeat; criticize severely.

clobber² /'klɒbə/ *noun slang* clothing, belongings.

cloche /klɒʃ/ *noun* small translucent cover for outdoor plants; woman's close-fitting bell-shaped hat.

clock¹ ● *noun* instrument measuring and showing time; measuring device resembling this; *colloquial* speedometer, taximeter, or stopwatch; seed-head of dandelion. ● *verb colloquial* (often + *up*) attain or register (distance etc.); time (race etc.) by stopwatch. □ **clock in** (or **on**), or **out** (or **off**) register time of arrival, or departure, by automatic clock; **clockwise** (moving) in same direction as hands of clock; **clockwork** mechanism with coiled springs etc. on clock principle; **like clockwork** with mechanical precision.

clock² *noun* ornamental pattern on side of stocking or sock.

clod *noun* lump of earth or clay.

clog ● *noun* wooden-soled shoe. ● *verb* (**-gg-**) (often + *up*) (cause to) become obstructed, choke; impede.

cloister /'klɔɪstə/ ● *noun* covered walk esp. in college or ecclesiastical building; monastic life; seclusion. ● *verb* seclude.

clone ● *noun* group of organisms produced asexually from one ancestor; one such organism; *colloquial* person or thing regarded as identical to another. ● *verb* (**-ning**) propagate as clone.

close¹ /kləʊs/ ● *adjective* (often + *to*) at short distance or interval; having strong or immediate relation; (almost) in contact; dense, compact; nearly equal; rigorous; concentrated; stifling; shut; secret; niggardly. ● *adverb* at short distance or interval. ● *noun* street closed at one end; precinct of cathedral.

□ **close harmony** singing of parts within an octave; **close-knit** tightly interlocked, closely united; **close season** season when killing of game etc. is illegal; **close shave** *colloquial* narrow escape; **close-up** photograph etc. taken at short range. □ **closely** *adverb*; **closeness** *noun.*

close² /kləʊz/ ● *verb* (**-sing**) shut; block up; bring or come to an end; end day's business; bring or come closer or into contact; make (electric circuit) continuous. ● *noun* conclusion, end. □ **closed-circuit** (of television) transmitted by wires to restricted number of receivers; **closed shop** business etc. where employees must belong to specified trade union.

closet /'klɒzɪt/ ● *noun* small room; cupboard; water-closet. ● *adjective* secret. ● *verb* (**-t-**) shut away, esp. in private consultation etc.

closure /'kləʊʒə/ *noun* closing, closed state; procedure for ending debate.

clot ● *noun* thick lump formed from liquid, esp. blood; *colloquial* foolish person. ● *verb* (**-tt-**) form into clots.

cloth /klɒθ/ *noun* woven or felted material; piece of this; (**the cloth**) the clergy.

clothe /kləʊð/ *verb* (**-thing**; *past & past participle* **clothed** or **clad**) put clothes on; provide with clothes; cover as with clothes.

clothes /kləʊðz/ *plural noun* things worn to cover body and limbs; bedclothes. □ **clothes-horse** frame for airing washed clothes.

clothier /'kləʊðɪə/ *noun* dealer in men's clothes.

clothing /'kləʊðɪŋ/ *noun* clothes.

cloud /klaʊd/ ● *noun* visible mass of condensed watery vapour floating in air; mass of smoke or dust; (+ *of*) great number of (birds, insects, etc.) moving together; state of gloom, trouble, or suspicion. ● *verb* cover or darken with cloud(s); (often + *over*, *up*) become overcast or gloomy; make unclear. □ **cloudburst** sudden violent rainstorm. □ **cloudless** *adjective.*

cloudy *adjective* (**-ier, -iest**) covered with clouds; not transparent, unclear. □ **cloudiness** *noun.*

clout ● *noun* heavy blow; *colloquial* influence, power of effective action; piece of cloth or clothing. ● *verb* hit hard.

clove¹ /kləʊv/ *noun* dried bud of tropical tree, used as spice.

clove² /kləʊv/ *noun* segment of compound bulb, esp. of garlic.

clove³ *past* of CLEAVE¹.

clove hitch *noun* knot for fastening rope round pole etc.

cloven /'kləʊv(ə)n/ *adjective* split. □ **cloven hoof, foot** divided hoof, as of oxen, sheep, etc., or the Devil.

clover /'kləʊvə/ *noun* kind of trefoil used as fodder. □ **in clover** in ease and luxury.

clown /klaʊn/ ● *noun* comic entertainer, esp. in circus; foolish or playful person. ● *verb* (often + *about, around*) behave like clown.

cloy *verb* satiate or sicken by sweetness, richness, etc.

club ● *noun* heavy stick used as weapon; stick with head, used in golf; association of people for social, sporting, etc. purposes; premises of this; playing card of suit marked with black trefoils; (in *plural*) this suit. ● *verb* (**-bb-**) strike (as) with club; (+ *together*) combine, esp. to make up sum of money. □ **club foot** congenitally deformed foot; **clubhouse** premises of club; **clubland** area with many nightclubs; **club-root** disease of cabbages etc.; **club sandwich** sandwich with 2 layers of filling and 3 slices of bread or toast.

cluck ● *noun* chattering cry of hen. ● *verb* emit cluck(s).

clue ● *noun* guiding or suggestive fact; piece of evidence used in detection of crime; word(s) used to indicate word(s) for insertion in crossword. ● *verb* (**clues, clued, cluing** or **clueing**) provide clue to. □ **clue in, up** *slang* inform.

clump ● *noun* (+ *of*) cluster, esp. of trees. ● *verb* form clump; heap or plant together; tread heavily.

clumsy /'klʌmzɪ/ *adjective* (**-ier, -iest**) awkward in movement or shape; difficult to handle or use; tactless. □ **clumsily** *adverb*; **clumsiness** *noun*.

clung *past & past participle of* CLING.

cluster /'klʌstə/ ● *noun* close group or bunch of similar people or things. ● *verb* be in or form into cluster(s); (+ *round, around*) gather round.

clutch[1] ● *verb* seize eagerly; grasp tightly; (+ *at*) snatch at. ● *noun* tight or (in *plural*) cruel grasp; (in vehicle) device for connecting engine to transmission, pedal operating this. □ **clutch bag** handbag without handles.

clutch[2] *noun* set of eggs; brood of chickens.

clutter /'klʌtə/ ● *noun* crowded untidy collection of things. ● *verb* (often + *up, with*) crowd untidily, fill with clutter.

cm *abbreviation* centimetre(s).

Cmdr. *abbreviation* Commander.

CND *abbreviation* Campaign for Nuclear Disarmament.

CO *abbreviation* Commanding Officer.

Co. *abbreviation* company; county.

c/o *abbreviation* care of.

coach ● *noun* single-decker bus usually for longer journeys; railway carriage; closed horse-drawn carriage; sports trainer or private tutor. ● *verb* train or teach. □ **coachload** group of tourists etc. travelling by coach; **coachman** driver of horse-drawn carriage; **coachwork** bodywork of road or rail vehicle.

coagulate /kəʊ'ægjʊleɪt/ *verb* (**-ting**) change from liquid to semi-solid; clot, curdle. □ **coagulant** *noun*; **coagulation** *noun*.

coal *noun* hard black mineral used as fuel etc.; piece of this. □ **coalface** exposed surface of coal in mine; **coalfield** area yielding coal; **coal gas** mixed gases formerly extracted from coal and used for heating, cooking, etc.; **coal mine** place where coal is dug; **coal miner** worker in coal mine; **coal scuttle** container for coal for domestic fire; **coal tar** tar extracted from coal; **coal tit** small bird with greyish plumage.

coalesce /kəʊə'les/ *verb* (**-cing**) come together and form a whole. □ **coalescence** *noun*; **coalescent** *adjective*.

coalition /kəʊə'lɪʃ(ə)n/ *noun* temporary alliance, esp. of political parties; fusion into one whole.

coaming /'kəʊmɪŋ/ *noun* raised border round ship's hatches etc.

coarse /kɔːs/ *adjective* rough or loose in texture; of large particles; lacking refinement; crude, obscene. □ **coarse fish** freshwater fish other than salmon and trout. □ **coarsely** *adverb*; **coarsen** *verb*; **coarseness** *noun*.

coast ● *noun* border of land near sea; seashore. ● *verb* ride or move (usually downhill) without use of power; make progress without exertion; sail along coast. □ **coastguard** (member of) group of people employed to keep watch on coasts, prevent smuggling, etc.; **coastline** line of seashore, esp. with regard to its shape. □ **coastal** *adjective*.

coaster *noun* ship that sails along coast; tray or mat for bottle or glass.

coat ● *noun* sleeved outer garment, overcoat, jacket; animal's fur or hair; layer of paint etc. ● *verb* (usually + *with, in*) cover with coat or layer; form covering on. □ **coat of arms** heraldic bearings or shield; **coat-hanger** shaped piece of wood etc. for hanging clothes on.

coating *noun* layer of paint etc.; cloth for coats.

coax *verb* persuade gradually or by flattery; (+ *out of*) obtain (thing) from (person) thus; manipulate gently.

coaxial /kəʊ'æksɪəl/ *adjective* having common axis; (of electric cable etc.) transmitting by means of two concentric conductors separated by insulator.

cob *noun* roundish lump; domed loaf; corn cob; large hazelnut; sturdy short-legged riding-horse; male swan.

cobalt /'kəʊbɔːlt/ *noun* silvery-white metallic element; (colour of) deep blue pigment made from it.

cobber /'kɒbə/ *noun* Australian & NZ *colloquial* companion, friend.

cobble[1] /'kɒb(ə)l/ ● *noun* (in full **cobblestone**) rounded stone used for paving. ● *verb* (**-ling**) pave with cobbles.

cobble[2] /'kɒb(ə)l/ *verb* (**-ling**) mend or patch (esp. shoes); (often + *together*) assemble roughly.

cobbler *noun* mender of shoes; (in *plural*) *slang* nonsense.

COBOL /'kəʊbɒl/ *noun* computer language for use in business operations.

cobra /'kəʊbrə/ *noun* venomous hooded snake.

cobweb /'kɒbweb/ *noun* spider's network or thread. □ **cobwebby** *adjective*.

coca /'kəʊkə/ *noun* S. American shrub; its leaves chewed as stimulant.

cocaine /kəʊ'keɪn/ *noun* drug from coca, used as local anaesthetic and as stimulant.

coccyx /'kɒksɪks/ *noun* (*plural* **coccyges** /-dʒiːz/) bone at base of spinal column.

cochineal /kɒtʃɪ'niːl/ *noun* scarlet dye; insects whose dried bodies yield this.

cock[1] ● *noun* male bird, esp. domestic fowl; *slang* (as form of address) friend, fellow; *slang* nonsense; firing lever in gun released by trigger; tap or valve controlling flow. ● *verb* raise or make upright; turn or move (eye or ear) attentively or knowingly; set (hat etc.) aslant; raise cock of (gun). □ **cock-a-hoop** exultant; **cock-a-leekie** Scottish soup of boiled fowl with leeks; **cockcrow** dawn; **cock-eyed** *colloquial* crooked, askew, absurd.

cock[2] *noun* conical heap of hay or straw.

cockade /kɒ'keɪd/ *noun* rosette etc. worn in hat.

cockatoo /kɒkə'tuː/ *noun* crested parrot.

cockchafer /'kɒktʃeɪfə/ *noun* large pale brown beetle.

cocker /'kɒkə/ *noun* (in full **cocker spaniel**) small spaniel.

cockerel /'kɒkər(ə)l/ *noun* young cock.

cockle /'kɒk(ə)l/ *noun* edible bivalve shellfish; its shell; (in full **cockleshell**) small shallow boat; pucker or wrinkle. □ **cockles of the heart** innermost feelings.

cockney /'kɒknɪ/ ● *noun* (*plural* **-s**) native of London, esp. East End; cockney dialect. ● *adjective* of cockneys.

cockpit *noun* place for pilot etc. in aircraft or spacecraft or for driver in racing car; arena of war etc.

cockroach /'kɒkrəʊtʃ/ *noun* dark brown insect infesting esp. kitchens.

cockscomb /'kɒkskəʊm/ *noun* cock's crest.

cocksure /kɒk'ʃɔː/ *adjective* arrogantly confident.

cocktail /'kɒkteɪl/ *noun* drink of spirits, fruit juices, etc.; appetizer containing shellfish etc.; any hybrid mixture. □ **cocktail stick** small pointed stick.

cocky *adjective* (**-ier, -iest**) *colloquial* conceited, arrogant. □ **cockiness** *noun*.

coco /'kəʊkəʊ/ *noun* (*plural* **-s**) coconut palm.

cocoa /'kəʊkəʊ/ *noun* powder of crushed cacao seeds; drink made from this.

coconut /'kəʊkənʌt/ *noun* large brown seed of coco, with edible white lining enclosing milky juice. □ **coconut matting** matting made from fibre of coconut husks; **coconut shy** fairground sideshow where balls are thrown to dislodge coconuts.

cocoon /kə'ku:n/ ● *noun* silky case spun by larva to protect it as pupa; protective covering. ● *verb* wrap (as) in cocoon.

cocotte /kə'kɒt/ *noun* small fireproof dish for cooking and serving food.

COD *abbreviation* cash (*US* collect) on delivery.

cod[1] *noun* (also **codfish**) (*plural* same) large sea fish. □ **cod liver oil** medicinal oil rich in vitamins.

cod[2] *noun* & *verb* (**-dd-**) *slang* hoax, parody.

coda /'kəʊdə/ *noun* final passage of piece of music.

coddle /'kɒd(ə)l/ *verb* (**-ling**) treat as an invalid, pamper; cook in water just below boiling point. □ **coddler** *noun*.

code ● *noun* system of signals or of symbols etc. used for secrecy, brevity, or computer processing of information; systematic set of laws etc.; standard of moral behaviour. ● *verb* (**-ding**) put into code.

codeine /'kəʊdi:n/ *noun* alkaloid derived from morphine, used as pain-killer.

codex /'kəʊdeks/ *noun* (*plural* **codices** /'kəʊdɪsi:z/) manuscript volume esp. of ancient texts.

codger /'kɒdʒə/ *noun* (usually in **old codger**) *colloquial* (strange) person.

codicil /'kəʊdɪsɪl/ *noun* addition to will.

codify /'kəʊdɪfaɪ/ *verb* (**-ies**, **-ied**) arrange (laws etc.) into code. □ **codification** *noun*.

codling[1] /'kɒdlɪŋ/ *noun* (also **codlin**) variety of apple; moth whose larva feeds on apples.

codling[2] *noun* (*plural* same) small cod.

co-education /kəʊedju:'keɪʃ(ə)n/ *noun* education of both sexes together. □ **co-educational** *adjective*.

coefficient /kəʊɪ'fɪʃ(ə)nt/ *noun* *Mathematics* quantity or expression placed before and multiplying another; *Physics* multiplier or factor by which a property is measured.

coeliac disease /'si:lɪæk/ *noun* intestinal disease whose symptoms include adverse reaction to gluten.

coequal /kəʊ'i:kw(ə)l/ *adjective* & *noun* equal.

coerce /kəʊ'ɜːs/ *verb* (**-cing**) persuade or restrain by force. □ **coercion** /-'ɜːʃ(ə)n/ *noun*; **coercive** *adjective*.

coeval /kəʊ'i:v(ə)l/ *formal* ● *adjective* of the same age; contemporary. ● *noun* coeval person or thing.

coexist /kəʊɪg'zɪst/ *verb* (often + *with*) exist together, esp. in mutual tolerance. □ **coexistence** *noun*; **coexistent** *adjective*.

coextensive /kəʊɪk'stensɪv/ *adjective* extending over same space or time.

C. of E. *abbreviation* Church of England.

coffee /'kɒfɪ/ *noun* drink made from roasted and ground seeds of tropical shrub; cup of this; the shrub; the seeds; pale brown. □ **coffee bar** café selling coffee and light refreshments from bar; **coffee bean** seed of coffee; **coffee mill** small machine for grinding coffee beans; **coffee morning** morning gathering, esp. for charity, at which coffee is served; **coffee shop** small restaurant, esp. in hotel or store; **coffee table** small low table; **coffee-table book** large illustrated book.

coffer /'kɒfə/ *noun* large box for valuables; (in *plural*) funds, treasury; sunken panel in ceiling etc.

coffin /'kɒfɪn/ *noun* box in which corpse is buried or cremated.

cog *noun* each of series of projections on wheel etc. transferring motion by engaging with another series.

cogent /'kəʊdʒ(ə)nt/ *adjective* (of argument etc.) convincing, compelling. □ **cogency** *noun*; **cogently** *adverb*.

cogitate /'kɒdʒɪteɪt/ *verb* (**-ting**) ponder, meditate. □ **cogitation** *noun*.

cognac /'kɒnjæk/ *noun* French brandy.

cognate /'kɒgneɪt/ ● *adjective* descended from same ancestor or root. ● *noun* cognate person or word.

cognition /kɒg'nɪʃ(ə)n/ *noun* knowing, perceiving, or conceiving, as distinct from emotion and volition. □ **cognitive** /'kɒg-/ *adjective*.

cognizance /'kɒgnɪz(ə)ns/ *noun* *formal* knowledge or awareness.

cognizant /'kɒgnɪz(ə)nt/ *adjective* *formal* (+ *of*) having knowledge or being aware of.

cognomen /kɒg'nəʊmen/ *noun* nickname; *Roman History* surname.

cohabit /kəʊ'hæbɪt/ *verb* (**-t-**) live together as husband and wife. □ **cohabitation** *noun*.

cohere /kəʊ'hɪə/ *verb* (**-ring**) stick together; (of reasoning) be logical or consistent.

coherent *adjective* intelligible; consistent, easily understood. □ **coherence** *noun*; **coherently** *adverb*.

cohesion /kəʊ'hi:ʒ(ə)n/ *noun* sticking together; tendency to cohere. □ **cohesive** /-sɪv/ *adjective*.

cohort /'kəʊhɔːt/ *noun* one-tenth of Roman legion; people banded together.

coif /kɔɪf/ *noun* *historical* close-fitting cap.

coiffeur /kwa:'fɜː/ *noun* (*feminine* **coiffeuse** /-'fɜːz/) hairdresser.

coiffure /kwa:'fjʊə/ *noun* hairstyle.

coil ● *verb* arrange or be arranged in concentric rings; move sinuously. ● *noun* coiled arrangement (of rope, electrical conductor, etc.); single turn of something coiled; flexible contraceptive device in womb.

coin ● *noun* stamped disc of metal as official money; metal money. ● *verb* make (coins) by stamping; invent (word, phrase). □ **coin box** telephone operated by coins.

coinage *noun* coining; system of coins in use; invention of word, invented word.

coincide /kəʊɪn'saɪd/ *verb* (**-ding**) occur at same time; (often + *with*) agree or be identical.

coincidence /kəʊ'ɪnsɪd(ə)ns/ *noun* remarkable concurrence of events etc., apparently by chance. □ **coincident** *adjective*.

coincidental /kəʊɪnsɪ'dent(ə)l/ *adjective* in the nature of or resulting from coincidence. □ **coincidentally** *adverb*.

coir /'kɔɪə/ *noun* coconut fibre used for ropes, matting, etc.

coition /kəʊ'ɪʃ(ə)n/ *noun* coitus.

coitus /'kəʊɪtəs/ *noun* sexual intercourse. □ **coital** *adjective*.

coke[1] ● *noun* solid left after gases have been extracted from coal. ● *verb* (**-king**) convert (coal) into coke.

coke[2] *noun* *slang* cocaine.

Col. *abbreviation* Colonel.

col *noun* depression in summit-line of mountain chain.

cola /'kəʊlə/ *noun* W. African tree with seeds containing caffeine; carbonated drink flavoured with these.

colander /'kʌləndə/ *noun* perforated vessel used as strainer in cookery.

cold /kəʊld/ ● *adjective* of or at low temperature; not heated; having lost heat; feeling cold; (of colour) suggesting cold; *colloquial* unconscious; lacking ardour or friendliness; dispiriting; (of hunting-scent) grown faint. ● *noun* prevalence of low temperature; cold weather; infection of nose or throat. ● *adverb* unrehearsed. □ **cold-blooded** having body temperature varying with that of environment, callous; **cold call** marketing call on person not previously interested in product; **cold cream** cleansing ointment; **cold feet** fear, reluctance; **cold fusion** nuclear fusion at room temperature; **cold shoulder** unfriendly treatment; **cold turkey** *slang* abrupt withdrawal from addictive drugs; **cold war** hostility between nations without actual fighting; **in cold blood** without emotion; **throw cold water on** discourage. □ **coldly** *adverb*; **coldness** *noun*.

coleslaw /ˈkəʊlslɔː/ *noun* salad of sliced raw cabbage etc.

coley /ˈkəʊlɪ/ *noun* (*plural* **-s**) any of several edible fish, esp. rock-salmon.

colic /ˈkɒlɪk/ *noun* spasmodic abdominal pain. □ **colicky** *adjective*.

colitis /kəˈlaɪtɪs/ *noun* inflammation of colon.

collaborate /kəˈlæbəreɪt/ *verb* (**-ting**) (often + *with*) work jointly. □ **collaboration** *noun*; **collaborative** /-rətɪv/ *adjective*; **collaborator** *noun*.

collage /ˈkɒlɑːʒ/ *noun* picture made by gluing pieces of paper etc. on to backing.

collapse /kəˈlæps/ ● *noun* falling down of structure; sudden failure of plan etc.; physical or mental breakdown. ● *verb* (**-sing**) (cause to) undergo collapse; *colloquial* relax completely after effort. □ **collapsible** *adjective*.

collar /ˈkɒlə/ ● *noun* neckband, upright or turned over, of coat, shirt, dress, etc.; leather band round animal's neck; band, ring, or pipe in machinery. ● *verb* capture, seize, appropriate; *colloquial* accost. □ **collar-bone** bone joining breastbone and shoulder blade.

collate /kəˈleɪt/ *verb* (**-ting**) collect and put in order. □ **collator** *noun*.

collateral /kəˈlætər(ə)l/ ● *noun* security pledged as guarantee for repayment of loan. ● *adjective* side by side; additional but subordinate; descended from same ancestor but by different line. □ **collaterally** *adverb*.

collation *noun* collating; light meal.

colleague /ˈkɒliːg/ *noun* fellow worker, esp. in profession or business.

collect[1] /kəˈlekt/ ● *verb* bring or come together; assemble, accumulate; seek and acquire (books, stamps, etc.); obtain (contributions, taxes, etc.) from people; call for, fetch; concentrate (one's thoughts etc.); (as **collected** *adjective*) not perturbed or distracted. ● *adjective & adverb US* (of telephone call, parcel, etc.) to be paid for by recipient.

collect[2] /ˈkɒlekt/ *noun* short prayer of Anglican or RC Church.

collectable /kəˈlektəb(ə)l/ *adjective* worth collecting.

collection /kəˈlekʃ(ə)n/ *noun* collecting, being collected; things collected; money collected, esp. at church service etc.

collective /kəˈlektɪv/ ● *adjective* of or relating to group or society as a whole; joint; shared. ● *noun* cooperative enterprise; its members. □ **collective bargaining** negotiation of wages etc. by organized group of employees; **collective noun** singular noun denoting group of individuals. □ **collectively** *adverb*; **collectivize** *verb* (also **-ise**) (**-zing** or **-sing**).

collectivism *noun* theory or practice of collective ownership of land and means of production. □ **collectivist** *noun & adjective*.

collector *noun* person collecting things of interest; person collecting taxes, rents, etc.

colleen /ˈkɒliːn/ *noun Irish* girl.

college /ˈkɒlɪdʒ/ *noun* establishment for further, higher, or professional education; teachers and students in a college; school; organized group of people with shared functions and privileges.

collegiate /kəˈliːdʒɪət/ *adjective* of or constituted as college, corporate; (of university) consisting of different colleges.

collide /kəˈlaɪd/ *verb* (**-ding**) (often + *with*) come into collision or conflict.

collie /ˈkɒlɪ/ *noun* sheepdog originally of Scottish breed.

collier /ˈkɒlɪə/ *noun* coal miner; coal ship, member of its crew.

colliery /ˈkɒlɪərɪ/ *noun* (*plural* **-ies**) coal mine and its buildings.

collision /kəˈlɪʒ(ə)n/ *noun* violent impact of moving body against another or fixed object; clashing of interests etc.

collocate /ˈkɒləkeɪt/ *verb* (**-ting**) place (word etc.) next to another. □ **collocation** *noun*.

colloid /ˈkɒlɔɪd/ *noun* substance consisting of minute particles; mixture, esp. viscous solution, of this and another substance. □ **colloidal** *adjective*.

colloquial /kəˈləʊkwɪəl/ *adjective* of ordinary or familiar conversation, informal. □ **colloquially** *adverb*.

colloquialism /kəˈləʊkwɪəlɪz(ə)m/ *noun* colloquial word or phrase.

colloquy /ˈkɒləkwɪ/ *noun* (*plural* **-quies**) *literary* talk, dialogue.

collude /kəˈluːd/ *verb* (**-ding**) conspire. □ **collusion** /-ʒ(ə)n/ *noun*; **collusive** /-sɪv/ *adjective*.

collywobbles /ˈkɒlɪwɒb(ə)lz/ *plural noun colloquial* ache or rumbling in stomach; apprehensive feeling.

cologne /kəˈləʊn/ *noun* eau-de-Cologne or similar toilet water.

colon[1] /ˈkəʊlən/ *noun* punctuation mark (:) used between main clauses or before list or quotation (see panel).

colon[2] /ˈkəʊlən/ *noun* lower and greater part of large intestine.

colonel /ˈkɜːn(ə)l/ *noun* army officer commanding regiment, next in rank below brigadier. □ **colonelcy** *noun* (*plural* **-ies**).

colonial /kəˈləʊnɪəl/ ● *adjective* of a colony or colonies; of colonialism. ● *noun* inhabitant of colony.

colonialism *noun* policy of having colonies.

colonist /ˈkɒlənɪst/ *noun* settler in or inhabitant of colony.

colonize /ˈkɒlənaɪz/ *verb* (also **-ise**) (**-zing** or **-sing**) establish colony in; join colony. □ **colonization** *noun*.

colonnade /kɒləˈneɪd/ *noun* row of columns, esp. supporting roof. □ **colonnaded** *adjective*.

colony /ˈkɒlənɪ/ *noun* (*plural* **-ies**) settlement or settlers in new territory remaining subject to mother country; people of one nationality, occupation, etc. forming community in town etc.; group of animals that live close together.

colophon /ˈkɒləf(ə)n/ *noun* tailpiece in book.

color etc. *US* = COLOUR etc.

Colorado beetle /kɒləˈrɑːdəʊ/ *noun* small beetle destructive to potato.

coloration /kʌləˈreɪʃ(ə)n/ *noun* (also **colouration**) colouring, arrangement of colours.

coloratura /kɒlərəˈtʊərə/ *noun* elaborate passages in vocal music; singer of these, esp. soprano.

colossal /kəˈlɒs(ə)l/ *adjective* huge; *colloquial* splendid. □ **colossally** *adverb*.

colossus /kəˈlɒsəs/ *noun* (*plural* **-ssi** /-saɪ/ or **-ssuses**) statue much bigger than life size; gigantic or remarkable person etc.

colour /'kʌlə/ (*US* **color**) ● *noun* one, or any mixture, of the constituents into which light is separated in rainbow etc.; use of all colours as in photography; colouring substance; esp. paint; skin pigmentation, esp. when dark; ruddiness of face; appearance or aspect; (in *plural*) flag of regiment or ship etc.; coloured ribbon, rosette, etc. worn as symbol of school, club, political party, etc. ● *verb* give colour to; paint, stain, dye; blush; influence. □ **colour-blind** unable to distinguish certain colours; **colour-blindness** *noun*; **colour scheme** arrangement of colours; **colour supplement** magazine with colour printing, sold with newspaper.

coloured (*US* **colored**) ● *adjective* having colour; wholly or partly of non-white descent; *South African* of mixed white and non-white descent. ● *noun* coloured person.

colourful *adjective* (*US* **colorful**) full of colour or interest. □ **colourfully** *adverb*.

colouring *noun* (*US* **coloring**) appearance as regards colour, esp. facial complexion; application of colour; substance giving colour.

colourless *adjective* (*US* **colorless**) without colour, lacking interest.

colt /kəʊlt/ *noun* young male horse; *Sport* inexperienced player.

colter *US* = COULTER.

coltsfoot *noun* (*plural* **-s**) yellow wild flower with large leaves.

columbine /'kɒləmbaɪn/ *noun* garden plant with purple-blue flowers.

column /'kɒləm/ *noun* pillar, usually round, with base and capital; column-shaped thing; series of numbers, one under the other; vertical division of printed page; part of newspaper regularly devoted to particular subject or written by one writer; long, narrow arrangement of advancing troops, vehicles, etc.

columnist /'kɒləmnɪst/ *noun* journalist contributing regularly to newspaper etc.

coma /'kəʊmə/ *noun* (*plural* **-s**) prolonged deep unconsciousness.

comatose /'kəʊmətəʊs/ *adjective* in coma; sleepy.

comb /kəʊm/ ● *noun* toothed strip of rigid material for arranging hair; thing like comb, esp. for dressing wool etc.; red fleshy crest of fowl, esp. cock etc.; honeycomb. ● *verb* draw comb through (hair), dress (wool etc.) with comb; *colloquial* search (place) thoroughly.

combat /'kɒmbæt/ ● *noun* struggle, fight. ● *verb* (**-t-**) do battle (with); strive against, oppose.

combatant /'kɒmbət(ə)nt/ ● *noun* fighter. ● *adjective* fighting.

combative /'kɒmbətɪv/ *adjective* pugnacious.

combe = COOMB.

combination /kɒmbɪ'neɪʃ(ə)n/ *noun* combining, being combined; combined state; combined set of things or people; motorcycle with side-car; sequence of numbers etc. used to open **combination lock**.

combine ● *verb* /kəm'baɪn/ (**-ning**) join together; unite; form into chemical compound. ● *noun* /'kɒmbaɪn/ combination of esp. businesses. □ **combine harvester** /'kɒmbaɪn/ combined reaping and threshing machine.

combustible /kəm'bʌstɪb(ə)l/ ● *adjective* capable of or used for burning. ● *noun* combustible substance. □ **combustibility** *noun*.

combustion /kəm'bʌstʃ(ə)n/ *noun* burning; development of light and heat from combination of substance with oxygen.

come /kʌm/ *verb* (**-ming**; *past* **came**; *past participle* **come**) move or be brought towards or reach a place, time, situation, or result; be available; become; traverse; *colloquial* behave like. □ **come about** happen; **come across** meet or find by chance, give specified impression, *colloquial* be effective or understood; **come again** *colloquial* what did you say?; **come along** make progress, hurry up; **come apart** disintegrate; **come at** attack; **comeback** return to success, *slang* retort or retaliation; **come back (to)** recur to memory (of); **come by** obtain; **come clean** *colloquial* confess; **comedown** loss of status; **come down** lose position, be handed down, be reduced; **come forward** offer oneself for task etc.; **come in** become fashionable or seasonable, prove to be; **come in for** receive; **come into** inherit; **come off** succeed, occur, fare; **come off it** *colloquial expression of disbelief*; **come on** make progress; **come out** emerge, become known, be published, go on strike, (of photograph or its subject) be (re)produced clearly, (of stain) be removed; **come out with** declare, disclose; **come over** come some distance to visit, (of feeling) affect, appear or sound in specifed way; **come round** pay informal visit, recover consciousness, be converted to another's opinion; **come through** survive; **come to** recover consciousness, amount to; **come up** arise, be mentioned or discussed, attain position; **come up with** produce (idea etc.); **come up against** be faced with; **come upon** meet or find by chance.

comedian /kə'miːdɪən/ *noun* humorous performer; actor in comedy; *slang* buffoon.

comedienne /kəmiːdɪ'en/ *noun* female comedian.

comedy /'kɒmədɪ/ *noun* (*plural* **-ies**) play or film of amusing character; humorous kind of drama etc.; humour; amusing aspects. □ **comedic** /kə'miːdɪk/ *adjective*.

comely /'kʌmlɪ/ *adjective* (**-ier, -iest**) *literary* handsome, good-looking. □ **comeliness** *noun*.

comestibles /kə'mestɪb(ə)lz/ *plural noun formal* things to eat.

Colon :

This is used:

1 between two main clauses of which the second explains, enlarges on, or follows from the first, e.g.

It was not easy: to begin with I had to find the right house.

2 to introduce a list of items (a dash should not be added), and after expressions such as *namely, for example, to resume, to sum up,* and *the following,* e.g.

You will need: a tent, a sleeping bag, cooking equipment, and a rucksack.

3 before a quotation, e.g.

The poem begins: 'Earth has not anything to show more fair'.

comet /'kɒmɪt/ *noun* hazy object with 'tail' moving in path round sun.

comeuppance /kʌm'ʌpəns/ *noun colloquial* deserved punishment.

comfort /'kʌmf(ə)t/ ● *noun* physical or mental well-being; consolation; person or thing bringing consolation; (usually in *plural*) things that make life comfortable. ● *verb* console. □ **comfortless** *adjective*.

comfortable /'kʌmfətəb(ə)l/ *adjective* giving ease; at ease; having adequate standard of living; appreciable. □ **comfortably** *adverb*.

comforter /'kʌmfətə/ *noun* person who comforts; baby's dummy; *archaic* woollen scarf.

comfrey /'kʌmfrɪ/ *noun* tall plant with bell-like flowers.

comfy /'kʌmfɪ/ *adjective* (**-ier**, **-iest**) *colloquial* comfortable.

comic /'kɒmɪk/ ● *adjective* of or like comedy; funny. ● *noun* comedian; periodical in form of comic strips.

□ **comic strip** sequence of drawings telling comic story. □ **comical** *adjective*; **comically** *adverb*.

comma /'kɒmə/ *noun* punctuation mark (,) indicating pause or break between parts of sentence (see panel).

command /kə'mɑːnd/ ● *verb* give formal order to; have authority or control over; have at one's disposal; deserve and get; look down over, dominate. ● *noun* order, instruction; holding of authority, esp. in armed forces; mastery; troops or district under commander. □ **command module** control compartment in spacecraft; **command performance** one given at royal request.

commandant /'kɒməndænt/ *noun* commanding officer, esp. of military academy.

commandeer /kɒmən'dɪə/ *verb* seize (esp. goods) for military use; take possession of without permission.

commander *noun* person who commands, esp. naval officer next below captain. □ **commander-in-chief** (*plural* **commanders-in-chief**) supreme commander, esp. of nation's forces.

Comma ,

The comma marks a slight break between words, phrases, etc. In particular, it is used:

1 to separate items in a list, e.g.

> *red, white, and blue* or *red, white and blue*
> *We bought some shoes, socks, gloves, and handkerchiefs.*
> *potatoes, peas, or carrots* or *potatoes, peas or carrots*

2 to separate adjectives that describe something in the same way, e.g.

> *It is a hot, dry, dusty place.*

but not if they describe it in different ways, e.g.

> *a distinguished foreign author*

or if one adjective adds to or alters the meaning of another, e.g.

> *a bright red tie.*

3 to separate main clauses, e.g.

> *Cars will park here, and coaches will turn left.*

4 to separate a name or word used to address someone, e.g.

> *David, I'm here.*
> *Well, Mr Jones, we meet again.*
> *Have you seen this, my friend?*

5 to separate a phrase, e.g.

> *Having had lunch, we went back to work.*

especially in order to clarify meaning, e.g.

> *In the valley below, the village looked very small.*

6 after words that introduce direct speech, or after direct speech where there is no question mark or exclamation mark, e.g.

> *They answered, 'Here we are.'*
> *'Here we are,' they answered.*

7 after *Dear Sir, Dear Sarah*, etc., and *Yours faithfully, Yours sincerely*, etc. in letters.

8 to separate a word, phrase, or clause that is secondary or adds information or a comment, e.g.

> *I am sure, however, that it will not happen.*
> *Fred, who is bald, complained of the cold.*

but not with a relative clause (one usually beginning with *who, which*, or *that*) that restricts the meaning of the noun it follows, e.g.

> *Men who are bald should wear hats.*

No comma is needed between a month and a year in dates, e.g.

> *in December 1993*

or between a number and a road in addresses, e.g.

> *17 Devonshire Avenue*

commanding *adjective* impressive; giving wide view; substantial.

commandment *noun* divine command.

commando /kə'mɑ:ndəʊ/ *noun* (*plural* **-s**) unit of shock troops; member of this.

commemorate /kə'meməreɪt/ *verb* (**-ting**) preserve in memory by celebration or ceremony; be memorial of. □ **commemoration** *noun*; **commemorative** /-rətɪv/ *adjective*.

commence /kə'mens/ *verb* (**-cing**) *formal* begin. □ **commencement** *noun*.

commend /kə'mend/ *verb* praise; recommend; entrust. □ **commendation** /kɒm-/ *noun*.

commendable *adjective* praiseworthy. □ **commendably** *adverb*.

commensurable /kə'menʃərəb(ə)l/ *adjective* (often + **with**, **to**) measurable by same standard; (+ **to**) proportionate to. □ **commensurability** *noun*.

commensurate /kə'menʃərət/ *adjective* (usually + **with**) extending over same space or time; (often + **to**, **with**) proportionate.

comment /'kɒment/ ● *noun* brief critical or explanatory note or remark; opinion; commenting. ● *verb* (often + **on**, **that**) make comment(s). □ **no comment** *colloquial* I decline to answer your question.

commentary /'kɒməntərɪ/ *noun* (*plural* **-ies**) broadcast description of event happening; series of comments on book or performance etc.

commentate /'kɒmənteɪt/ *verb* (**-ting**) act as commentator.

commentator *noun* writer or speaker of commentary.

commerce /'kɒmɜːs/ *noun* buying and selling; trading.

commercial /kə'mɜːʃ(ə)l/ ● *adjective* of, in, or for commerce; done or run primarily for financial profit; (of broadcasting) financed by advertising. ● *noun* television or radio advertisement. □ **commercial broadcasting** broadcasting financed by advertising; **commercial traveller** firm's representative visiting shops etc. to get orders. □ **commercially** *adverb*.

commercialize *verb* (also **-ise**) (**-zing** or **-sing**) exploit or spoil for profit; make commercial. □ **commercialization** *noun*.

Commie /'kɒmɪ/ *noun slang derogatory* Communist.

commingle /kə'mɪŋɡ(ə)l/ *verb* (**-ling**) *literary* mix, unite.

commiserate /kə'mɪzəreɪt/ *verb* (**-ting**) (usually + **with**) have or express sympathy. □ **commiseration** *noun*.

commissar /'kɒmɪsɑː/ *noun historical* head of government department in USSR.

commissariat /kɒmɪ'seərɪət/ *noun* department responsible for supply of food etc. for army; food supplied.

commissary /'kɒmɪsərɪ/ *noun* (*plural* **-ies**) deputy, delegate.

commission /kə'mɪʃ(ə)n/ ● *noun* authority to perform task; person(s) given such authority; order for specially produced thing; warrant conferring officer rank in armed forces; rank so conferred; pay or percentage received by agent; committing. ● *verb* empower; give authority to; give (artist etc.) order for work; order (work) to be written etc.; give (officer) command of ship; prepare (ship) for active service; bring (machine etc.) into operation. □ **in** or **out of commission** ready or not ready for active service.

commissionaire /kəmɪʃə'neə/ *noun* uniformed door attendant.

commissioner *noun* person commissioned to perform specific task; member of government commission; representative of government in district etc.

commit /kə'mɪt/ *verb* (**-tt-**) do or make (crime, blunder, etc.); (usually + **to**) entrust, consign; send (person) to prison; pledge or bind (esp. oneself) to policy or course of action; (as **committed** *adjective*) (often + **to**) dedicated, obliged.

commitment *noun* engagement, obligation; committing, being committed; dedication, committing oneself.

committal *noun* act of committing esp. to prison, grave, etc.

committee /kə'mɪtɪ/ *noun* group of people appointed for special function by (and usually out of) larger body.

commode /kə'məʊd/ *noun* chamber pot in chair or box with cover; chest of drawers.

commodious /kə'məʊdɪəs/ *adjective* roomy.

commodity /kə'mɒdɪtɪ/ *noun* (*plural* **-ies**) article of trade.

commodore /'kɒmədɔː/ *noun* naval officer next above captain; commander of squadron or other division of fleet; president of yacht club.

common /'kɒmən/ ● *adjective* (**-er**, **-est**) occurring often; ordinary, of the most familiar kind; shared by all; belonging to the whole community; *derogatory* inferior, vulgar; *Grammar* (of gender) referring to individuals of either sex. ● *noun* piece of open public land. □ **common ground** point or argument accepted by both sides; **common law** unwritten law based on custom and precedent; **common-law husband**, **wife** partner recognized by common law without formal marriage; **Common Market** European Community; **common or garden** *colloquial* ordinary; **common room** room for social use of students or teachers at college etc.; **common sense** good practical sense; **common time** *Music* 4 crotchets in a bar; **in common** shared, in joint use.

commonalty /'kɒmənltɪ/ *noun* (*plural* **-ies**) general community, common people.

commoner *noun* person below rank of peer.

commonly *adverb* usually, frequently.

commonplace /'kɒmənpleɪs/ ● *adjective* lacking originality; ordinary. ● *noun* event, topic, etc. that is ordinary or usual; trite remark.

commons /'kɒmənz/ *plural noun* the common people; **(the Commons)** House of Commons.

commonwealth /'kɒmənwelθ/ *noun* independent state or community; **(the Commonwealth)** association of UK with states previously part of British Empire; republican government of Britain 1649–60.

commotion /kə'məʊʃ(ə)n/ *noun* noisy disturbance.

communal /'kɒmjʊn(ə)l/ *adjective* shared between members of group or community; (of conflict etc.) between communities. □ **communally** *adverb*.

commune[1] /'kɒmjuːn/ *noun* group of people sharing accommodation and goods; small administrative district in France etc.

commune[2] /kə'mjuːn/ *verb* (**-ning**) (usually + **with**) speak intimately; feel in close touch.

communicant /kə'mjuːnɪkənt/ *noun* receiver of Holy Communion.

communicate /kə'mjuːnɪkeɪt/ *verb* (**-ting**) impart, transmit (news, feelings, disease, ideas, etc.); (often + **with**) have social dealings. □ **communicator** *noun*.

communication *noun* communicating, being communicated; letter, message, etc.; connection or means of access; social dealings; (in *plural*) science and practice of transmitting information.

□ **communication cord** cord or chain pulled to stop train in emergency; **communication(s) satellite** artificial satellite used to relay telephone calls, TV, radio, etc.

communicative /kə'mjuːnɪkətɪv/ adjective ready to talk and impart information.

communion /kə'mjuːnɪən/ noun sharing, esp. of thoughts, interests, etc.; fellowship; group of Christians of same denomination; (**Holy Communion**) Eucharist.

communiqué /kə'mjuːnɪkeɪ/ noun official communication, esp. news report.

communism /'kɒmjʊnɪz(ə)m/ noun social system based on public ownership of most property; political theory advocating this; (usually **Communism**) form of socialist society in Cuba, China, etc. □ **communist, Communist** noun & adjective; **communistic** /-'nɪstɪk/ adjective.

community /kə'mjuːnɪtɪ/ (plural **-ies**) noun group of people living in one place or having same religion, ethnic origin, profession, etc.; commune; joint ownership. □ **community centre** place providing social facilities for neighbourhood; **community charge** historical tax levied locally on every adult; **community home** institution housing young offenders; **community singing** singing by large group; **community spirit** feeling of belonging to community.

commute /kə'mjuːt/ verb (**-ting**) travel some distance to and from work; (usually + to) change (punishment) to one less severe.

commuter noun person who commutes to and from work.

compact¹ ● adjective /kəm'pækt/ closely packed together; economically designed; concise; (of person) small but well-proportioned. ● verb /kəm'pækt/ make compact. ● noun /'kɒmpækt/ small flat case for face powder etc. □ **compact disc** disc from which digital information or sound is reproduced by reflection of laser light. □ **compactly** adverb; **compactness** noun.

compact² /'kɒmpækt/ noun agreement, contract.

companion /kəm'pænjən/ noun person who accompanies or associates with another; person paid to live with another; handbook, reference book; thing that matches another; (**Companion**) member of some orders of knighthood. ● **companionway** staircase from ship's deck to cabins etc.

companionable adjective sociable, friendly. □ **companionably** adverb.

companionship noun friendship; being together.

company /'kʌmpənɪ/ noun (plural **-ies**) number of people assembled; guest(s); commercial business; actors etc. working together; subdivision of infantry battalion. □ **in company with** together with; **part company** (often + with) separate; **ship's company** entire crew.

comparable /'kɒmpərəb(ə)l/ adjective (often + with, to) able to be compared. □ **comparability** noun; **comparably** adverb.

■ **Usage** Comparable is often pronounced /kəm'pærəb(ə)l/ (with the stress on the -par-), but this is considered incorrect by some people.

comparative /kəm'pærətɪv/ ● adjective perceptible or estimated by comparison; relative; of or involving comparison; Grammar (of adjective or adverb) expressing higher degree of a quality. ● noun Grammar comparative expression or word. □ **comparatively** adverb.

compare /kəm'peə/ ● verb (**-ring**) (usually + to) express similarities in; (often + to, with) estimate similarity of; (often + with) bear comparison. ● noun

comparison. □ **compare notes** exchange ideas or opinions.

comparison /kəm'pærɪs(ə)n/ noun comparing; example of similarity; (in full **degrees of comparison**) Grammar positive, comparative, and superlative forms of adjectives and adverbs. □ **bear comparison** (often + with) be able to be compared favourably.

compartment /kəm'pɑːtmənt/ noun space partitioned off within larger space.

compass /'kʌmpəs/ noun instrument showing direction of magnetic north and bearings from it; (usually in plural) V-shaped hinged instrument for drawing circles and taking measurements; scope, range.

compassion /kəm'pæʃ(ə)n/ noun pity.

compassionate /kəm'pæʃənət/ adjective showing compassion; sympathetic. □ **compassionate leave** leave granted on grounds of bereavement etc. □ **compassionately** adverb.

compatible /kəm'pætɪb(ə)l/ adjective (often + with) able to coexist; (of equipment) able to be used in combination. □ **compatibility** noun.

compatriot /kəm'pætrɪət/ noun person from one's own country.

compel /kəm'pel/ verb (**-ll-**) force, constrain; arouse irresistibly; (as **compelling** adjective) arousing strong interest.

compendious /kəm'pendɪəs/ adjective comprehensive but brief.

compendium /kəm'pendɪəm/ noun (plural **-s** or **-dia**) abridgement, summary; collection of table games etc.

compensate /'kɒmpenseɪt/ verb (**-ting**) recompense, make amends; counterbalance.

compensation noun compensating, being compensated; money etc. given as recompense. □ **compensatory** /-'seɪt-/ adjective.

compère /'kɒmpeə/ ● noun person introducing variety show. ● verb (**-ring**) act as compère (to).

compete /kəm'piːt/ verb (**-ting**) take part in contest etc.; (often + with or against person, for thing) strive.

competence /'kɒmpɪt(ə)ns/ noun being competent; ability.

competent adjective adequately qualified or capable; effective. □ **competently** adverb.

competition /kɒmpə'tɪʃ(ə)n/ noun (often + for) competing; event in which people compete; other people competing; opposition.

competitive /kəm'petɪtɪv/ adjective of or involving competition; (of prices etc.) comparing well with those of rivals; having strong urge to win. □ **competitiveness** noun.

competitor /kəm'petɪtə/ noun person who competes; rival, esp. in business.

compile /kəm'paɪl/ verb (**-ling**) collect and arrange (material) into list, book, etc. □ **compilation** /kɒmpɪ'leɪʃ(ə)n/ noun.

complacent /kəm'pleɪs(ə)nt/ adjective smugly self-satisfied or contented. □ **complacency** noun.

complain /kəm'pleɪn/ verb express dissatisfaction; (+ of) say that one is suffering from (an ailment), state grievance concerning. □ **complainant** noun.

complaint noun complaining; grievance, cause of dissatisfaction; formal protest; ailment.

complaisant /kəm'pleɪz(ə)nt/ adjective formal deferential; willing to please; acquiescent. □ **complaisance** noun.

complement ● noun /'kɒmplɪmənt/ thing that completes; full number; word(s) added to verb to complete predicate of sentence; amount by which angle is less than 90°. ● verb /-ment/ complete; form complement to. □ **complementary** /-'men-/ adjective.

complete /kəm'pli:t/ ● adjective having all its parts; finished, total. ● verb (**-ting**) finish; make complete; fill in (form etc.). □ **completely** adverb; **completeness** noun; **completion** noun.

complex /'kɒmpleks/ ● noun buildings, rooms, etc. made up of related parts; group of usually repressed feelings or thoughts causing abnormal behaviour or mental state. ● adjective complicated; consisting of related parts. □ **complexity** /kəm'pleks-/ noun (plural **-ies**).

complexion /kəm'plekʃ(ə)n/ noun natural colour, texture, and appearance of skin, esp. of face; aspect.

compliance /kəm'plaɪəns/ noun obedience to request, command, etc.; capacity to yield.

compliant adjective obedient; yielding. □ **compliantly** adverb.

complicate /'kɒmplɪkeɪt/ verb (**-ting**) make difficult or complex; (as **complicated** adjective) complex, intricate.

complication noun involved or confused condition; complicating circumstance; difficulty; (often in plural) disease or condition arising out of another.

complicity /kəm'plɪsɪtɪ/ noun partnership in wrongdoing.

compliment ● noun /'kɒmplɪmənt/ polite expression of praise; (in plural) formal greetings accompanying gift etc. ● verb /-ment/ (often + on) congratulate; praise.

complimentary /kɒmplɪ'mentərɪ/ adjective expressing compliment; given free of charge.

comply /kəm'plaɪ/ verb (**-ies, -ied**) (often + with) act in accordance (with request or command).

component /kəm'pəʊnənt/ ● adjective being part of larger whole. ● noun component part.

comport /kəm'pɔːt/ verb (**comport oneself**) literary conduct oneself; behave. □ **comportment** noun.

compose /kəm'pəʊz/ verb (**-sing**) create in music or writing; make up, constitute; arrange artistically; set up (type); arrange in type; (as **composed** adjective) calm, self-possessed.

composer noun person who composes esp. music.

composite /'kɒmpəzɪt/ ● adjective made up of parts; (of plant) having head of many flowers forming one bloom. ● noun composite thing or plant.

composition /kɒmpə'zɪʃ(ə)n/ noun act of putting together; thing composed; school essay; arrangement of parts of picture etc.; constitution of substance; compound artificial substance.

compositor /kəm'pɒzɪtə/ noun person who sets up type for printing.

compost /'kɒmpɒst/ noun mixture of decayed organic matter used as fertilizer.

composure /kəm'pəʊʒə/ noun calm manner.

compote /'kɒmpəʊt/ noun fruit in syrup.

compound¹ /'kɒmpaʊnd/ ● noun mixture of two or more things; word made up of two or more existing words; substance formed from two or more elements chemically united. ● adjective made up of two or more ingredients or parts; combined, collective. ● verb /kəm'paʊnd/ mix or combine; increase (difficulties etc.); make up (whole); settle (matter) by mutual agreement. □ **compound fracture** one complicated by wound; **compound interest** interest paid on capital and accumulated interest.

compound² /'kɒmpaʊnd/ noun enclosure, fenced-in space.

comprehend /kɒmprɪ'hend/ verb understand; include.

comprehensible adjective that can be understood.

comprehension noun understanding; text set as test of understanding; inclusion.

comprehensive ● adjective including all or nearly all; (of motor insurance) providing protection against most risks. ● noun (in full **comprehensive school**) secondary school for children of all abilities. □ **comprehensively** adverb.

compress ● verb /kəm'pres/ squeeze together, bring into smaller space or shorter time. ● noun /'kɒmpres/ pad pressed on part of body to relieve inflammation, stop bleeding, etc. □ **compressible** adjective.

compression /kəm'preʃ(ə)n/ noun compressing; reduction in volume of fuel mixture in internal-combustion engine before ignition.

compressor noun machine for compressing air or other gas.

comprise /kəm'praɪz/ verb (**-sing**) include; consist of.

■ **Usage** It is a mistake to use comprise to mean 'to compose or make up'.

compromise /'kɒmprəmaɪz/ ● noun agreement reached by mutual concession; (often + between) intermediate state between conflicting opinions etc. ● verb (**-sing**) settle dispute by compromise; modify one's opinions, demands, etc.; bring into disrepute or danger by indiscretion.

comptroller /kən'trəʊlə/ noun controller.

compulsion /kəm'pʌlʃ(ə)n/ noun compelling, being compelled; irresistible urge.

compulsive adjective compelling; resulting or acting (as if) from compulsion; irresistible. □ **compulsively** adverb.

compulsory adjective required by law or rule. □ **compulsorily** adverb.

compunction /kəm'pʌŋkʃ(ə)n/ noun guilty feeling; slight regret.

compute /kəm'pju:t/ verb (**-ting**) calculate; use computer. □ **computation** /kɒm-/ noun.

computer noun electronic device for storing and processing data, making calculations, or controlling machinery. □ **computer-literate** able to use computers; **computer science** study of computers; **computer virus** code maliciously introduced into program to destroy data etc.

computerize /kəm'pju:təraɪz/ verb (also **-ise**) (**-zing** or **-sing**) equip with or store, perform, or produce by computer. □ **computerization** noun.

comrade /'kɒmreɪd/ noun companion in some activity; fellow socialist or Communist. □ **comradeship** noun.

con¹ slang ● noun confidence trick. ● verb (**-nn-**) swindle, deceive.

con² noun (usually in plural) reason against.

con³ verb (US **conn**) (**-nn-**) direct steering of (ship).

concatenation /kɒnkætɪ'neɪʃ(ə)n/ noun series of linked things or events.

concave /kɒn'keɪv/ adjective curved like interior of circle or sphere. □ **concavity** /-'kæv-/ noun.

conceal /kən'si:l/ verb hide; keep secret. □ **concealment** noun.

concede /kən'si:d/ verb (**-ding**) admit to be true; admit defeat in; grant.

conceit /kən'si:t/ noun personal vanity; literary far-fetched comparison.

conceited adjective vain. □ **conceitedly** adverb.

conceive /kən'si:v/ verb (**-ving**) become pregnant (with); (often + of) imagine; (usually in passive) formulate (plan etc.). □ **conceivable** adjective; **conceivably** adverb.

concentrate /'kɒnsəntreɪt/ ● verb (**-ting**) (often + on) focus one's attention; bring together to one point;

increase strength of (liquid etc.) by removing water etc.; (as **concentrated** *adjective*) strong. ● *noun* concentrated solution.

concentration *noun* concentrating, being concentrated; weight of substance in given amount of mixture; mental attention. □ **concentration camp** place for detention of political prisoners etc.

concentric /kən'sɛntrɪk/ *adjective* having common centre. □ **concentrically** *adverb*.

concept /'kɒnsept/ *noun* general notion; abstract idea.

conception /kən'sepʃ(ə)n/ *noun* conceiving, being conceived; idea; understanding.

conceptual /kən'septjʊəl/ *adjective* of mental concepts. □ **conceptually** *adverb*.

conceptualize *verb* (also **-ise**) **(-zing** or **-sing)** form concept or idea of. □ **conceptualization** *noun*.

concern /kən'sɜːn/ ● *verb* be relevant or important to; relate to, be about; worry, affect; (**concern oneself**; often + *with*, *about*, *in*) interest or involve oneself. ● *noun* anxiety, worry; matter of interest or importance to one; firm, business.

concerned *adjective* involved, interested; anxious, troubled.

concerning *preposition* about, regarding.

concert /'kɒnsət/ *noun* musical performance; agreement.

concerted /kən'sɜːtɪd/ *adjective* jointly planned.

concertina /kɒnsə'tiːnə/ ● *noun* portable musical instrument like accordion but smaller. ● *verb* (**-nas, -naed** /-nəd/ or **-na'd, -naing**) compress or collapse in folds like those of concertina.

concerto /kən'tʃeətəʊ/ *noun* (*plural* **-tos** or **-ti** /-tɪ/) composition for solo instrument(s) and orchestra.

concession /kən'seʃ(ə)n/ *noun* conceding, thing conceded; reduction in price for certain category of people; right to use land, sell goods, etc. □ **concessionary** *adjective*.

conch /kɒntʃ/ *noun* large spiral shell of various marine gastropod molluscs; such gastropod.

conchology /kɒŋ'kɒlədʒɪ/ *noun* study of shells.

conciliate /kən'sɪlɪeɪt/ *verb* (**-ting**) make calm; pacify; reconcile. □ **conciliation** *noun*; **conciliator** *noun*; **conciliatory** *adjective*.

concise /kən'saɪs/ *adjective* brief but comprehensive. □ **concisely** *adverb*; **conciseness** *noun*; **concision** *noun*.

conclave /'kɒnkleɪv/ *noun* private meeting; assembly or meeting-place of cardinals for election of pope.

conclude /kən'kluːd/ *verb* (**-ding**) bring or come to end; (often + *from*, *that*) infer; settle (treaty etc.).

conclusion /kən'kluːʒ(ə)n/ *noun* ending; judgement reached by reasoning; summing-up; settling of peace etc. □ **in conclusion** lastly.

conclusive /kən'kluːsɪv/ *adjective* decisive, convincing. □ **conclusively** *adverb*.

concoct /kən'kɒkt/ *verb* make by mixing ingredients; invent (story, lie, etc.). □ **concoction** *noun*.

concomitant /kən'kɒmɪt(ə)nt/ ● *adjective* (often + *with*) accompanying. ● *noun* accompanying thing. □ **concomitance** *noun*.

concord /'kɒŋkɔːd/ *noun* agreement, harmony. □ **concordant** /kən'kɔːd(ə)nt/ *adjective*.

concordance /kən'kɔːd(ə)ns/ *noun* agreement; index of words used in book or by author.

concordat /kən'kɔːdæt/ *noun* agreement, esp. between Church and state.

concourse /'kɒŋkɔːs/ *noun* crowd; large open area in railway station etc.

concrete /'kɒŋkriːt/ ● *adjective* existing in material form, real; definite. ● *noun* mixture of gravel, sand,

cement, and water used for building. ● *verb* (**-ting**) cover with or embed in concrete.

concretion /kən'kriːʃ(ə)n/ *noun* hard solid mass; forming of this by coalescence.

concubine /'kɒŋkjʊbaɪn/ *noun* *literary* mistress; (among polygamous peoples) secondary wife.

concupiscence /kən'kjuːpɪs(ə)ns/ *noun* *formal* lust. □ **concupiscent** *adjective*.

concur /kən'kɜː/ *verb* (**-rr-**) (often + *with*) agree; coincide.

concurrent /kən'kʌrənt/ *adjective* (often + *with*) existing or in operation at the same time. □ **concurrence** *noun*; **concurrently** *adverb*.

concuss /kən'kʌs/ *verb* subject to concussion.

concussion /kən'kʌʃ(ə)n/ *noun* temporary unconsciousness or incapacity due to head injury; violent shaking.

condemn /kən'dem/ *verb* express strong disapproval of; (usually + *to*) sentence (to punishment), doom (to something unpleasant); pronounce unfit for use. □ **condemnation** /kɒndem'neɪʃ(ə)n/ *noun*.

condensation /kɒnden'seɪʃ(ə)n/ *noun* condensing, being condensed; condensed liquid; abridgement.

condense /kən'dens/ *verb* (**-sing**) make denser or more concise; reduce or be reduced from gas to liquid.

condescend /kɒndɪ'send/ *verb* (+ *to do*) graciously consent to do a thing while showing one's superiority; (+ *to*) pretend to be on equal terms with (inferior); (as **condescending** *adjective*) patronizing. □ **condescendingly** *adverb*; **condescension** *noun*.

condiment /'kɒndɪmənt/ *noun* seasoning or relish for food.

condition /kən'dɪʃ(ə)n/ ● *noun* stipulation; thing on fulfilment of which something else depends; state of being or fitness of person or thing; ailment; (in *plural*) circumstances. ● *verb* bring into desired state; accustom; determine; be essential to.

conditional *adjective* (often + *on*) dependent, not absolute; *Grammar* (of clause, mood, etc.) expressing condition. □ **conditionally** *adverb*.

condole /kən'dəʊl/ *verb* (**-ling**) (+ *with*) express sympathy with (person) over loss etc.

■ **Usage** Condole is commonly confused with *console*, which means 'to comfort'.

---

condolence *noun* (often in *plural*) expression of sympathy.

condom /'kɒndɒm/ *noun* contraceptive sheath.

condominium /kɒndə'mɪnɪəm/ *noun* joint rule or sovereignty; *US* building containing individually owned flats.

condone /kən'dəʊn/ *verb* (**-ning**) forgive, overlook.

condor /'kɒndɔː/ *noun* large S. American vulture.

conducive /kən'djuːsɪv/ *adjective* (often + *to*) contributing or helping (towards something).

conduct ● *noun* /'kɒndʌkt/ behaviour; manner of conducting business, war, etc. ● *verb* /kən'dʌkt/ lead, guide; control, manage; be conductor of (orchestra etc.); transmit by conduction; (**conduct oneself**) behave.

conduction /kən'dʌkʃ(ə)n/ *noun* transmission of heat, electricity, etc.

conductive /kən'dʌktɪv/ *adjective* transmitting heat, electricity, etc. □ **conductivity** /kɒndʌk'tɪv-/ *noun*.

conductor *noun* director of orchestra etc.; (*feminine* **conductress**) person who collects fares on bus etc.; conductive thing.

conduit /'kɒndɪt/ *noun* channel or pipe for conveying liquid or protecting insulated cable.

cone *noun* solid figure with usually circular base and tapering to a point; cone-shaped object; dry fruit of pine or fir; ice cream cornet.

coney = CONY.

confab /ˈkɒnfæb/ *noun colloquial* confabulation.

confabulate /kənˈfæbjʊleɪt/ *verb* (**-ting**) talk together. □ **confabulation** *noun*.

confection /kənˈfekʃ(ə)n/ *noun* sweet dish or delicacy.

confectioner *noun* dealer in sweets or pastries etc. □ **confectionery** *noun*.

confederacy /kənˈfedərəsɪ/ *noun* (*plural* **-ies**) alliance or league, esp. of confederate states.

confederate /kənˈfedərət/ ● *adjective* esp. *Politics* allied. ● *noun* ally; accomplice. ● *verb* /-reɪt/ (**-ting**) (often + *with*) bring or come into alliance. □ **Confederate States** those which seceded from US in 1860–1.

confederation /kənfedəˈreɪʃ(ə)n/ *noun* union or alliance, esp. of states.

confer /kənˈfɜː/ *verb* (**-rr-**) (often + *on*, *upon*) grant, bestow; (often + *with*) meet for discussion.

conference /ˈkɒnfər(ə)ns/ *noun* consultation; meeting for discussion.

conferment /kənˈfɜːmənt/ *noun* conferring (of honour etc.).

confess /kənˈfes/ *verb* acknowledge, admit; declare one's sins, esp. to priest; (of priest) hear confession of.

confessedly /kənˈfesɪdlɪ/ *adverb* by one's own or general admission.

confession /kənˈfeʃ(ə)n/ *noun* act of confessing; thing confessed; statement of principles etc.

confessional ● *noun* enclosed place where priest hears confession. ● *adjective* of confession.

confessor *noun* priest who hears confession.

confetti /kənˈfetɪ/ *noun* small bits of coloured paper thrown by wedding guests at bride and groom.

confidant /ˈkɒnfɪdænt/ *noun* (*feminine* **confidante** same pronunciation) person trusted with knowledge of one's private affairs.

confide /kənˈfaɪd/ *verb* (**-ding**) (usually + *to*) tell (secret) or entrust (task). □ **confide in** talk confidentially to.

confidence /ˈkɒnfɪd(ə)ns/ *noun* firm trust; feeling of certainty; self-reliance; boldness; something told as a secret. □ **confidence trick** swindle in which victim is persuaded to trust swindler; **confidence trickster** person using confidence tricks; **in confidence** as a secret; **in (person's) confidence** trusted with his or her secrets.

confident *adjective* feeling or showing confidence. □ **confidently** *adverb*.

confidential /kɒnfɪˈdenʃ(ə)l/ *adjective* spoken or written in confidence; entrusted with secrets; confiding. □ **confidentiality** /-ʃɪˈæl-/ *noun*; **confidentially** *adjective*.

configuration /kənfɪgjʊˈreɪʃ(ə)n/ *noun* manner of arrangement; shape; outline. □ **configure** /-ˈfɪgə/ *verb*.

confine ● *verb* /kənˈfaɪn/ (**-ning**) keep or restrict within certain limits; imprison. ● *noun* /ˈkɒnfaɪn/ (usually in *plural*) boundary. □ **be confined** be in childbirth.

confinement /kənˈfaɪnmənt/ *noun* confining, being confined; childbirth.

confirm /kənˈfɜːm/ *verb* provide support for truth or correctness of; establish more firmly; formally make definite; administer confirmation to.

confirmation /kɒnfəˈmeɪʃ(ə)n/ *noun* confirming circumstance or statement; rite confirming baptized person as member of Christian Church.

confirmed *adjective* firmly settled in habit or condition.

confiscate /ˈkɒnfɪskeɪt/ *verb* (**-ting**) take or seize by authority. □ **confiscation** *noun*.

conflagration /kɒnfləˈgreɪʃ(ə)n/ *noun* large destructive fire.

conflate /kənˈfleɪt/ *verb* (**-ting**) fuse together, blend. □ **conflation** *noun*.

conflict ● *noun* /ˈkɒnflɪkt/ struggle, fight; opposition; (often + *of*) clashing of opposed interests etc. ● *verb* /kənˈflɪkt/ clash, be incompatible.

confluent ● *adjective* merging into one. ● *noun* stream joining another. □ **confluence** *noun*.

conform /kənˈfɔːm/ *verb* comply with rules or general custom; (+ *to*, *with*) be in accordance with.

conformable *adjective* (often + *to*) similar; (often + *with*) consistent.

conformation /kɒnfɔːˈmeɪʃ(ə)n/ *noun* thing's structure or shape.

conformist ● *noun* person who conforms to established practice. ● *adjective* conventional. □ **conformism** *noun*.

conformity *noun* conforming with established practice; suitability.

confound /kənˈfaʊnd/ ● *verb* baffle; confuse; *archaic* defeat. □ **confound (person, thing)!** *interjection* expressing annoyance.

confounded *adjective colloquial* damned.

confront /kənˈfrʌnt/ *verb* meet or stand facing, esp. in hostility or defiance; (of problem etc.) present itself to; (+ *with*) bring face to face with. □ **confrontation** /kɒn-/ *noun*; **confrontational** /kɒn-/ *adjective*.

confuse /kənˈfjuːz/ *verb* (**-sing**) bewilder; mix up; make obscure; (often as **confused** *adjective*) throw into disorder. □ **confusing** *adjective*; **confusion** *noun*.

confute /kənˈfjuːt/ *verb* (**-ting**) prove to be false or wrong. □ **confutation** /kɒn-/ *noun*.

conga /ˈkɒŋgə/ *noun* Latin American dance, usually performed in single file; tall narrow drum beaten with hands.

congeal /kənˈdʒiːl/ *verb* make or become semi-solid by cooling; (of blood) coagulate.

congenial /kənˈdʒiːnɪəl/ *adjective* having sympathetic nature, similar interests, etc.; (often + *to*) suited or agreeable. □ **congeniality** /-ˈæl-/ *noun*; **congenially** *adverb*.

congenital /kənˈdʒenɪt(ə)l/ *adjective* existing or as such from birth. □ **congenitally** *adverb*.

conger /ˈkɒŋgə/ *noun* large sea eel.

congest /kənˈdʒest/ *verb* (esp. as **congested** *adjective*) affect with congestion.

congestion *noun* abnormal accumulation or obstruction, esp. of traffic etc. or of mucus in nose etc.

conglomerate /kənˈglɒmərət/ ● *adjective* gathered into rounded mass. ● *noun* heterogeneous mass; business etc. corporation of merged firms. ● *verb* /-reɪt/ (**-ting**) collect into coherent mass. □ **conglomeration** *noun*.

congratulate /kənˈgrætʃʊleɪt/ *verb* (**-ting**) (often + *on*) express pleasure at happiness, excellence, or good fortune of (person). □ **congratulatory** /-lətərɪ/ *adjective*.

congratulation *noun* congratulating, (usually in *plural*) expression of this.

congregate /ˈkɒŋgrɪgeɪt/ *verb* (**-ting**) collect or gather in crowd.

congregation *noun* assembly of people, esp. for religious worship; group of people regularly attending particular church etc.

congregational *adjective* of a congregation; (**Congregational**) of or adhering to Congregationalism. **Congregationalism** *noun* system in which individual churches are self-governing. □ **Congregationalist** *noun*.

congress /'kɒŋgres/ *noun* formal meeting of delegates for discussion; (**Congress**) national legislative body of US etc. □ **congressman, congresswoman** member of US Congress. □ **congressional** /kən'greʃ-/ *adjective*.

congruent /'kɒŋgrʊənt/ *adjective* (often + *with*) suitable, agreeing; *Geometry* (of figures) coinciding exactly when superimposed. □ **congruence** *noun*.

conic /'kɒnɪk/ *adjective* of a cone.

conical *adjective* cone-shaped.

conifer /'kɒnɪfə/ *noun* cone-bearing tree. □ **coniferous** /kə'nɪfərəs/ *adjective*.

conjectural /kən'dʒektʃər(ə)l/ *adjective* involving conjecture.

conjecture /kən'dʒektʃə/ ● *noun* formation of opinion on incomplete information, guess. ● *verb* (**-ring**) guess.

conjoin /kən'dʒɔɪn/ *verb formal* join, combine.

conjoint /kən'dʒɔɪnt/ *adjective formal* associated, conjoined.

conjugal /'kɒndʒʊg(ə)l/ *adjective* of marriage; between husband and wife.

conjugate ● *verb* /'kɒndʒʊgeɪt/ (**-ting**) give the different forms of (verb); unite, become fused. ● *adjective* /-gət/ joined together.

conjugation *noun Grammar* system of verbal inflection.

conjunct /kən'dʒʌŋkt/ *adjective* joined; combined; associated.

conjunction *noun* joining, connection; word used to connect sentences, clauses, or words (see panel); combination of events or circumstances. □ **conjunctive** *adjective*.

conjunctiva /kɒndʒʌŋk'taɪvə/ *noun* (*plural* **-s**) mucous membrane covering front of eye and inside of eyelid.

conjunctivitis /kəndʒʌŋktɪ'vaɪtɪs/ *noun* inflammation of conjunctiva.

conjure /'kʌndʒə/ *verb* (**-ring**) perform seemingly magical tricks, esp. by movement of hands. □ **conjure up** produce as if by magic, evoke.

conjuror *noun* (also **conjurer**) performer of conjuring tricks.

conk[1] *verb colloquial* (usually + *out*) break down; become exhausted; faint; fall asleep.

conk[2] *slang* ● *noun* (punch on) nose or head. ● *verb* hit on nose or head.

conker /'kɒŋkə/ *noun* horse chestnut fruit; (in *plural*) children's game played with conkers on strings.

con man *noun* confidence trickster.

connect /kə'nekt/ *verb* (often + *to*, *with*) join, be joined; associate mentally or practically; (+ *with*) (of train etc.) arrive in time for passengers to transfer to another; put into communication by telephone; (usually in *passive*; + *with*) unite or associate with (others) in relationship etc. □ **connecting rod** rod between piston and crankpin etc. in engine. □ **connector** *noun*.

connection *noun* (also **connexion**) connecting, being connected; point at which things are connected; association of ideas; link, esp. by telephone; (often in *plural*) (esp. influential) relative or associate; connecting train etc.

connective *adjective* connecting. □ **connective tissue** body tissue forming tendons and ligaments, supporting organs, etc.

conning tower /'kɒnɪŋ/ *noun* raised structure of submarine containing periscope; wheelhouse of warship.

connive /kə'naɪv/ *verb* (**-ving**) (+ *at*) tacitly consent to (wrongdoing); conspire. □ **connivance** *noun*.

connoisseur /kɒnə'sɜː/ *noun* (often + *of*, *in*) person with good taste and judgement.

connote /kə'nəʊt/ *verb* (**-ting**) imply in addition to literal meaning; mean. □ **connotation** /kɒnə-/ *noun*; **connotative** /'kɒnəteɪtɪv/ *adjective*.

connubial /kə'njuːbɪəl/ *adjective* conjugal.

conquer /'kɒŋkə/ *verb* overcome, defeat; be victorious; subjugate. □ **conqueror** *noun*.

conquest /'kɒŋkwest/ *noun* conquering; something won; person whose affections have been won.

consanguineous /kɒnsæŋ'gwɪnɪəs/ *adjective* descended from same ancestor; akin. □ **consanguinity** *noun*.

conscience /'kɒnʃ(ə)ns/ *noun* moral sense of right and wrong, esp. as affecting behaviour. □ **conscience money** money paid to relieve conscience, esp. in respect of evaded payment etc.; **conscience-stricken** made uneasy by bad conscience.

conscientious /kɒnʃɪ'enʃəs/ *adjective* diligent and scrupulous. □ **conscientious objector** person who refuses to do military service on grounds of conscience. □ **conscientiously** *adverb*; **conscientiousness** *noun*.

conscious /'kɒnʃəs/ *adjective* awake and aware of one's surroundings etc.; (usually + *of*, *that*) aware, knowing; intentional. □ **consciously** *adverb*; **consciousness** *noun*.

conscript ● *verb* /kən'skrɪpt/ summon for compulsory state (esp. military) service. ● *noun* /'kɒnskrɪpt/ conscripted person. □ **conscription** *noun*.

Conjunction

A conjunction is used to join parts of sentences which usually, but not always, contain their own verbs, e.g.

He found it difficult but *I helped him.*
They made lunch for Alice and *Mary.*
I waited until *you came.*

The most common conjunctions are:

after	*for*	*since*	*unless*
although	*if*	*so*	*until*
and	*in order that*	*so that*	*when*
as	*like*	*than*	*where*
because	*now*	*that*	*whether*
before	*once*	*though*	*while*
but	*or*	*till*	

consecrate /'kɒnsɪkreɪt/ verb (-ting) make or declare sacred; dedicate formally to religious purpose; (+ to) devote to (a purpose). □ **consecration** noun.

consecutive /kən'sekjʊtɪv/ adjective following continuously; in unbroken or logical order. □ **consecutively** adverb.

consensus /kən'sensəs/ noun (often + of) general agreement or opinion.

consent /kən'sent/ ● verb (often + to) express willingness, give permission; agree. ● noun agreement; permission.

consequence /'kɒnsɪkwəns/ noun result of what has gone before; importance.

consequent /'kɒnsɪkwənt/ adjective that results; (often + on, upon) following as consequence. □ **consequently** adverb.

consequential /kɒnsɪ'kwenʃ(ə)l/ adjective resulting, esp. indirectly; important.

conservancy /kən'sɜːvənsɪ/ noun (plural -ies) body controlling river, port, etc. or concerned with conservation; official environmental conservation.

conservation /kɒnsə'veɪʃ(ə)n/ noun preservation, esp. of natural environment. □ **conservationist** noun.

conservative /kən'sɜːvətɪv/ ● adjective averse to rapid change; (of estimate) purposely low; (usually **Conservative**) of Conservative Party. ● noun conservative person; (usually **Conservative**) member or supporter of Conservative Party. □ **Conservative Party** political party promoting free enterprise. □ **conservatism** noun.

conservatoire /kən'sɜːvətwɑː/ noun (usually European) school of music or other arts.

conservatory /kən'sɜːvətrɪ/ noun (plural -ies) greenhouse for tender plants; esp. US conservatoire.

conserve ● verb /kən'sɜːv/ (-ving) preserve, keep from harm or damage. ● noun /'kɒnsɜːv/ fruit etc. preserved in sugar; fruit jam, esp. fresh.

consider /kən'sɪdə/ verb contemplate; deliberate thoughtfully; make allowance for, take into account; (+ that) have the opinion that; show consideration for; regard as; (as **considered** adjective) (esp. of an opinion) formed after careful thought.

considerable adjective a lot of; notable, important. □ **considerably** adverb.

considerate /kən'sɪdərət/ adjective giving thought to feelings or rights of others. □ **considerately** adverb.

consideration /kənsɪdə'reɪʃ(ə)n/ noun careful thought; being considerate; fact or thing taken into account; compensation, payment. □ **take into consideration** make allowance for.

considering preposition in view of.

consign /kən'saɪn/ verb (often + to) commit, deliver; send (goods etc.). □ **consignee** /kənsaɪ'niː/ noun; **consignor** noun.

consignment noun consigning, goods consigned.

consist /kən'sɪst/ verb (+ of) be composed of; (+ in, of) have its essential features in.

consistency noun (plural -ies) degree of density or firmness, esp. of thick liquids; being consistent.

consistent adjective constant to same principles; (usually + with) compatible. □ **consistently** adverb.

consistory noun (plural -ies) RC Church council of cardinals.

consolation /kɒnsə'leɪʃ(ə)n/ noun alleviation of grief or disappointment; consoling person or thing. □ **consolation prize** one given to competitor just failing to win main prize. □ **consolatory** /kən'sɒl-/ adjective.

console¹ /kən'səʊl/ verb (-ling) bring consolation to.

■ **Usage** Console is often confused with condole. To condole with someone is to express sympathy with them.

console² /'kɒnsəʊl/ noun panel for switches, controls, etc.; cabinet for television etc.; cabinet with keys and stops of organ; bracket supporting shelf etc.

consolidate /kən'sɒlɪdeɪt/ verb (-ting) make or become strong or secure; combine (territories, companies, debts, etc.) into one whole. □ **consolidation** noun.

consommé /kən'sɒmeɪ/ noun clear meat soup.

consonance /'kɒnsənəns/ noun agreement, harmony.

consonant ● noun speech sound that forms syllable only in combination with vowel; letter(s) representing this. ● adjective (+ with, to) consistent with; in agreement or harmony. □ **consonantal** /-'næn-/ adjective.

consort¹ ● noun /'kɒnsɔːt/ wife or husband, esp. of royalty. ● verb /kən'sɔːt/ (usually + with, together) keep company; harmonize.

consort² /'kɒnsɔːt/ noun Music group of players or instruments.

consortium /kən'sɔːtɪəm/ noun (plural -tia or -s) association, esp. of several business companies.

conspicuous /kən'spɪkjʊəs/ adjective clearly visible; attracting attention. □ **conspicuously** adverb.

conspiracy /kən'spɪrəsɪ/ noun (plural -ies) act of conspiring; plot.

conspirator /kən'spɪrətə/ noun person who takes part in conspiracy. □ **conspiratorial** /-'tɔː-/ adjective.

conspire /kən'spaɪə/ verb (-ring) combine secretly for unlawful or harmful purpose; (of events) seemingly work together.

constable /'kʌnstəb(ə)l/ noun (also **police constable**) police officer of lowest rank; governor of royal castle. □ **Chief Constable** head of police force of county etc.

constabulary /kən'stæbjʊlərɪ/ noun (plural -ies) police force.

constancy /'kɒnstənsɪ/ noun dependability; faithfulness.

constant ● adjective continuous; frequently occurring; having constancy. ● noun Mathematics & Physics unvarying quantity. □ **constantly** adverb.

constellation /kɒnstə'leɪʃ(ə)n/ noun group of fixed stars.

consternation /kɒnstə'neɪʃ(ə)n/ noun amazement, dismay.

constipate /'kɒnstɪpeɪt/ verb (-ting) (esp. as **constipated** adjective) affect with constipation.

constipation noun difficulty in emptying bowels.

constituency /kən'stɪtjʊənsɪ/ noun (plural -ies) body electing representative; area represented.

constituent /kən'stɪtjʊənt/ ● adjective making part of whole; appointing, electing. ● noun member of constituency; component part.

constitute /'kɒnstɪtjuːt/ verb (-ting) be essence or components of; amount to; establish.

constitution /kɒnstɪ'tjuːʃ(ə)n/ noun composition; set of principles by which state etc. is governed; person's inherent state of health, strength, etc.

constitutional ● adjective of or in line with the constitution; inherent. ● noun walk taken as exercise. □ **constitutionally** adverb.

constitutive /'kɒnstɪtjuːtɪv/ adjective able to form or appoint; constituent.

constrain /kən'streɪn/ verb compel; confine; (as **constrained** adjective) forced, embarrassed.

constraint noun compulsion; restriction; self-control.

constrict /kən'strɪkt/ verb make narrow or tight; compress. □ **constriction** noun; **constrictive** adjective.

constrictor noun snake that kills by compressing; muscle that contracts a part.

construct ● verb /kən'strʌkt/ fit together, build; Geometry draw. ● noun /'kɒnstrʌkt/ thing constructed, esp. by the mind. □ **constructor** /kən'strʌktə/ noun.

construction /kən'strʌkʃ(ə)n/ noun constructing; thing constructed; syntactical arrangement; interpretation. □ **constructional** adjective.

constructive /kən'strʌktɪv/ adjective positive, helpful. □ **constructively** adverb.

construe /kən'struː/ verb (**-strues**, **-strued**, **struing**) interpret; (often + with) combine (words) grammatically; translate literally.

consubstantiation /kɒnsəbstænʃɪ'eɪʃ(ə)n/ noun presence of Christ's body and blood together with bread and wine in Eucharist.

consul /'kɒns(ə)l/ noun official appointed by state to protect its interests and citizens in foreign city; historical either of two annually-elected magistrates in ancient Rome. □ **consular** -sjulə/ adjective.

consulate /'kɒnsjulət/ noun offices or position of consul.

consult /kən'sʌlt/ verb seek information or advice from; (often + with) refer to; take into consideration.

consultant /kən'sʌlt(ə)nt/ noun person who gives professional advice; senior medical specialist. □ **consultancy** noun.

consultation /kɒnsəl'teɪʃ(ə)n/ noun (meeting for) consulting.

consultative /kən'sʌltətɪv/ adjective of or for consultation.

consume /kən'sjuːm/ verb (**-ming**) eat or drink; use up; destroy. □ **consumable** adjective.

consumer noun user of product or service. □ **consumer goods** goods for consumers, not for producing other goods.

consumerism noun protection or promotion of consumers' interests; often derogatory continual increase in consumption. □ **consumerist** adjective.

consummate ● verb /'kɒnsəmeɪt/ (**-ting**) complete (esp. marriage by sexual intercourse). ● adjective /kən'sʌmɪt/ complete, perfect; fully skilled. □ **consummation** /kɒnsə-/ noun.

consumption /kən'sʌmpʃ(ə)n/ noun consuming, being consumed; purchase and use of goods etc.; archaic tuberculosis of lungs.

consumptive /kən'sʌmptɪv/ archaic ● adjective suffering or tending to suffer from tuberculosis. ● noun consumptive person.

cont. abbreviation continued.

contact /'kɒntækt/ ● noun condition or state of touching, meeting, or communicating; person who is, or may be, contacted for information etc.; person likely to carry contagious disease through being near infected person; connection for passage of electric current. ● verb get in touch with. □ **contact lens** small lens placed on eyeball to correct vision.

contagion /kən'teɪdʒ(ə)n/ noun spreading of disease by contact; moral corruption. □ **contagious** adjective.

contain /kən'teɪn/ verb hold or be capable of holding within itself; include; comprise; prevent from moving or extending; control, restrain.

container noun box etc. for holding things; large metal box for transporting goods.

containment /kən'teɪnmənt/ noun action or policy of preventing expansion of hostile country or influence.

contaminate /kən'tæmɪneɪt/ verb (**-ting**) pollute; infect. □ **contaminant** noun; **contamination** noun.

contemplate /'kɒntəmpleɪt/ verb (**-ting**) survey with eyes or mind; regard as possible; intend. □ **contemplation** noun.

contemplative /kən'templətɪv/ adjective of or given to (esp. religious) contemplation.

contemporaneous /kəntempə'reɪnɪəs/ adjective (usually + with) existing or occurring at same time.

contemporary /kən'tempərəri/ ● adjective belonging to same time; of same age; modern in style or design. ● noun (plural **-ies**) contemporary person or thing.

contempt /kən'tempt/ noun feeling that person or thing deserves scorn or reproach; condition of being held in contempt; (in full **contempt of court**) disobedience to or disrespect for court of law. □ **contemptible** adjective.

contemptuous adjective feeling or showing contempt. □ **contemptuously** adverb.

contend /kən'tend/ verb compete; (usually + with) argue; (+ that) maintain that. □ **contender** noun.

content[1] /kən'tent/ ● adjective satisfied; (+ to do) willing. ● verb make content; satisfy. ● noun contented state; satisfaction. □ **contented** adjective; **contentment** noun.

content[2] /'kɒntent/ noun (usually in plural) what is contained, esp. in vessel, house, or book; amount contained; substance of book etc. as opposed to form; capacity, volume.

contention /kən'tenʃ(ə)n/ noun dispute, rivalry; point contended for in argument.

contentious /kən'tenʃəs/ adjective quarrelsome; likely to cause argument.

contest ● noun /'kɒntest/ contending; a competition. ● verb /kən'test/ dispute; contend or compete for; compete in.

contestant /kən'test(ə)nt/ noun person taking part in contest.

context /'kɒntekst/ noun what precedes and follows word or passage; relevant circumstances. □ **contextual** /kən'tekstjʊəl/ adjective.

contiguous /kən'tɪgjʊəs/ adjective (usually + with, to) touching, in contact.

continent[1] /'kɒntɪnənt/ noun any of the earth's main continuous bodies of land; (**the Continent**) the mainland of Europe.

continent[2] /'kɒntɪnənt/ adjective able to control bowels and bladder; exercising esp. sexual self-restraint. □ **continence** noun.

continental /kɒntɪ'nent(ə)l/ adjective of or characteristic of a continent or (**Continental**) the Continent. □ **continental breakfast** light breakfast of coffee, rolls, etc.; **continental quilt** duvet; **continental shelf** shallow seabed bordering continent.

contingency /kən'tɪndʒənsɪ/ noun (plural **-ies**) event that may or may not occur; something dependent on another uncertain event.

contingent ● adjective (usually + on, upon) conditional, dependent; that may or may not occur; fortuitous. ● noun group (of troops, ships, etc.) forming part of larger group; people sharing interest, origin, etc.

continual /kən'tɪnjʊəl/ adjective frequently recurring; always happening. □ **continually** adverb.

continuance /kən'tɪnjʊəns/ noun continuing in existence or operation; duration.

continuation /kəntɪnjuˈeɪʃ(ə)n/ noun continuing, being continued; thing that continues something else.

continue /kən'tɪnjuː/ verb (**-ues**, **-ued**, **-uing**) maintain; resume; prolong; remain.

continuity /kɒntɪ'njuːɪtɪ/ noun (plural **-ies**) being continuous; logical sequence; detailed scenario of film; linkage of broadcast items.

continuo /kən'tɪnjʊəʊ/ noun (plural **-s**) Music bass accompaniment played usually on keyboard instrument.

continuous /kən'tɪnjʊəs/ adjective connected without break; uninterrupted. □ **continuously** adverb.

continuum /kən'tɪnjʊəm/ noun (plural **-nua**) thing with continuous structure.

contort /kən'tɔːt/ verb twist or force out of normal shape. □ **contortion** noun.

contortionist noun entertainer who adopts contorted postures.

contour /'kɒntʊə/ noun outline; (in full **contour line**) line on map joining points at same altitude.

contraband /'kɒntrəbænd/ ● noun smuggled goods. ● adjective forbidden to be imported or exported.

contraception /kɒntrə'sepʃ(ə)n/ noun use of contraceptives.

contraceptive /kɒntrə'septɪv/ ● adjective preventing pregnancy. ● noun contraceptive device or drug.

contract ● noun /'kɒntrækt/ written or spoken agreement, esp. one enforceable by law; document recording it. ● verb /kən'trækt/ make or become smaller; (usually + *with*) make contract; (often + *out*) arrange (work) to be done by contract; become affected by (a disease); incur (debt); draw together; shorten. □ **contract bridge** type of bridge in which only tricks bid and won count towards game; **contract in** (or **out**) elect (not) to enter scheme etc.

contraction /kən'trækʃ(ə)n/ noun contracting; shortening of uterine muscles during childbirth; shrinking; diminution; shortened word.

contractor /kən'træktə/ noun person who undertakes contract, esp. in building, engineering, etc.

contractual /kən'træktjʊəl/ adjective of or in the nature of a contract.

contradict /kɒntrə'dɪkt/ verb deny; oppose verbally; be at variance with. □ **contradiction** noun; **contradictory** adjective.

contradistinction /kɒntrədɪs'tɪŋkʃ(ə)n/ noun distinction made by contrasting.

contraflow /'kɒntrəfləʊ/ noun transfer of traffic from usual half of road to lane(s) of other half.

contralto /kən'træltəʊ/ noun (plural **-s**) lowest female singing voice; singer with this voice.

contraption /kən'træpʃ(ə)n/ noun machine or device, esp. strange one.

contrapuntal /kɒntrə'pʌnt(ə)l/ adjective Music of or in counterpoint.

contrariwise /kən'treərɪwaɪz/ adverb on the other hand; in the opposite way.

contrary /'kɒntrərɪ/ ● adjective (usually + *to*) opposed in nature, tendency, or direction; /kən'treərɪ/ perverse, self-willed. ● noun (**the contrary**) the opposite. ● adverb (+ *to*) in opposition. □ **on the contrary** the opposite is true.

contrast ● noun /'kɒntrɑːst/ comparison showing differences; difference so revealed; (often + *to*) thing or person having different qualities; degree of difference between tones in photograph or television picture. ● verb /kən'trɑːst/ (often + *with*) compare to reveal contrast; show contrast.

contravene /kɒntrə'viːn/ verb (**-ning**) infringe; conflict with. □ **contravention** /-'ven-/ noun.

contretemps /'kɒntrətã/ noun (plural same /-tãz/) unlucky accident; unfortunate occurrence.

contribute /kən'trɪbjuːt/ verb (**-ting**) (often + *to*) give jointly with others to common purpose; supply (article etc.) for publication with others; (+ *to*) help to bring about. □ **contribution** /kɒntrɪ'bjuːʃ(ə)n/ noun; **contributor** noun; **contributory** adjective.

■ **Usage** *Contribute* is often pronounced /'kɒntrɪbjuːt/ (with the stress on the *con-*), but this is considered incorrect by some people.

contrite /kən'traɪt/ adjective penitent, feeling guilt. □ **contrition** /-'trɪʃ-/ noun.

contrivance noun something contrived, esp. device or plan; act of contriving.

contrive /kən'traɪv/ verb (**-ving**) devise, plan; (often + *to do*) manage.

contrived adjective artificial, forced.

control /kən'trəʊl/ ● noun power of directing or restraining; self-restraint; means of restraining or regulating; (usually in *plural*) device to operate machine, vehicle, etc.; place where something is controlled or verified; standard of comparison for checking results of experiment. ● verb (**-ll-**) have control of; regulate; hold in check; verify. ■ **in control** (often + *of*) in charge; **out of control** no longer manageable.

controller noun person or thing that controls; person controlling expenditure.

controversial /kɒntrə'vɜːʃ(ə)l/ adjective causing or subject to controversy.

controversy /'kɒntrəvɜːsɪ/ noun (plural **-ies**) dispute, argument.

■ **Usage** *Controversy* is often pronounced /kən'trɒvəsɪ/ (with the stress on the *-trov-*), but this is considered incorrect by some people.

controvert /kɒntrə'vɜːt/ verb dispute, deny.

contuse /kən'tjuːz/ verb (**-sing**) bruise. □ **contusion** noun.

conundrum /kə'nʌndrəm/ noun riddle; hard question.

conurbation /kɒnɜː'beɪʃ(ə)n/ noun group of towns united by expansion.

convalesce /kɒnvə'les/ verb (**-cing**) recover health after illness.

convalescent /kɒnvə'les(ə)nt/ ● adjective recovering from illness. ● noun convalescent person. □ **convalescence** noun.

convection /kən'vekʃ(ə)n/ noun heat transfer by upward movement of heated medium.

convector /kən'vektə/ noun heating appliance that circulates warm air by convection.

convene /kən'viːn/ verb (**-ning**) summon; assemble. □ **convener, convenor** noun.

convenience /kən'viːnɪəns/ noun state of being convenient; suitability; advantage; useful thing; public lavatory. □ **convenience food** food needing little preparation.

convenient adjective serving one's comfort or interests; suitable; available or occurring at suitable time or place; well situated. □ **conveniently** adverb.

convent /'kɒnv(ə)nt/ noun religious community, esp. of nuns; its house.

convention /kən'venʃ(ə)n/ noun general agreement on social behaviour etc. by implicit consent of majority; customary practice; assembly, conference; agreement, treaty.

conventional adjective depending on or according with convention; bound by social conventions; not spontaneous or sincere; (of weapons etc.) non-nuclear. □ **conventionally** adverb.

converge /kən'vɜːdʒ/ verb (**-ging**) come together or towards same point; (+ *on, upon*) approach from different directions. □ **convergence** noun; **convergent** adjective.

conversant /kən'vɜːs(ə)nt/ adjective (+ *with*) well acquainted with.

conversation /kɒnvə'seɪʃ(ə)n/ noun informal spoken communication; instance of this.

conversational *adjective* of or in conversation; colloquial. □ **conversationally** *adverb*.

conversationalist *noun* person fond of or good at conversation.

converse¹ /kən'vɜːs/ *verb* (**-sing**) (often + *with*) talk.

converse² /'kɒnvɜːs/ ● *adjective* opposite, contrary, reversed. ● *noun* converse statement or proposition. □ **conversely** *adverb*.

conversion /kən'vɜːʃ(ə)n/ *noun* converting, being converted; converted (part of) building.

convert ● *verb* /kən'vɜːt/ (usually + *into*) change; cause (person) to change belief etc.; change (money etc.) into different form or currency etc.; alter (building) for new purpose; *Rugby* kick goal after (try). ● *noun* /'kɒnvɜːt/ person converted, esp. to religious faith.

convertible /kən'vɜːtɪb(ə)l/ ● *adjective* able to be converted. ● *noun* car with folding or detachable roof.

convex /'kɒnveks/ *adjective* curved like outside of sphere or circle.

convey /kən'veɪ/ *verb* transport, carry; communicate (meaning etc.); transfer by legal process; transmit (sound etc.).

conveyance *noun* conveying, being conveyed; vehicle; legal transfer of property, document effecting this.

conveyancing *noun* branch of law dealing with transfer of property. □ **conveyancer** *noun*.

conveyor *noun* person or thing that conveys. □ **conveyor belt** endless moving belt conveying articles in factory etc.

convict ● *verb* /kən'vɪkt/ (often + *of*) prove or declare guilty. ● *noun* /'kɒnvɪkt/ *esp. historical* sentenced criminal.

conviction /kən'vɪkʃ(ə)n/ *noun* convicting, being convicted; being convinced; firm belief.

convince /kən'vɪns/ *verb* (**-cing**) firmly persuade. □ **convincing** *adjective*; **convincingly** *adverb*.

convivial /kən'vɪvɪəl/ *adjective* fond of company; sociable, lively. □ **conviviality** /-'æl-/ *noun*.

convocation /kɒnvə'keɪʃ(ə)n/ *noun* convoking; large formal gathering.

convoke /kən'vəʊk/ *verb* (**-king**) call together; summon to assemble.

convoluted /kɒnvə'luːtɪd/ *adjective* coiled, twisted; complex.

convolution /kɒnvə'luːʃ(ə)n/ *noun* coiling; coil, twist; complexity.

convolvulus /kən'vɒlvjʊləs/ *noun* (*plural* **-es**) twining plant, esp. bindweed.

convoy /'kɒnvɔɪ/ *noun* group of ships, vehicles, etc. travelling together. □ **in convoy** as a group.

convulse /kən'vʌls/ *verb* (**-sing**) affect with convulsions.

convulsion *noun* (usually in *plural*) violent irregular motion of limbs or body caused by involuntary contraction of muscles; violent disturbance; (in *plural*) uncontrollable laughter. □ **convulsive** *adjective*; **convulsively** *adverb*.

cony /'kəʊnɪ/ *noun* (*plural* **-ies**) (also **coney**) rabbit; its fur.

coo ● *noun* soft murmuring sound as of doves. ● *verb* (**coos, cooed**) emit coo.

cooee /'kuːiː/ *interjection used to attract attention*.

cook /kʊk/ ● *verb* prepare (food) by heating; undergo cooking; *colloquial* falsify (accounts etc.). ● *noun* person who cooks. □ **cookbook** *US* cookery book; **cooking apple** one suitable for eating cooked.

cooker *noun* appliance or vessel for cooking food; fruit (esp. apple) suitable for cooking.

cookery *noun* art of cooking. □ **cookery book** book containing recipes.

cookie /'kʊkɪ/ *noun US* sweet biscuit.

cool /kuːl/ ● *adjective* of or at fairly low temperature; suggesting or achieving coolness; calm; lacking enthusiasm; unfriendly; *slang esp. US* marvellous. ● *noun* coolness; cool place; *slang* composure. ● *verb* (often + *down, off*) make or become cool. □ **coolly** /'kuːllɪ/ *adverb*; **coolness** *noun*.

coolant *noun* cooling agent, esp. fluid.

cooler *noun* vessel in which thing is cooled; *slang* prison cell.

coomb /kuːm/ *noun* (also **combe**) valley on side of hill; short valley running up from coast.

coon /kuːn/ *noun US* racoon.

coop /kuːp/ ● *noun* cage for keeping poultry. ● *verb* (often + *up, in*) confine.

co-op /'kəʊɒp/ *noun colloquial* cooperative society or shop.

cooper *noun* maker or repairer of casks and barrels.

cooperate /kəʊ'ɒpəreɪt/ *verb* (also **co-operate**) (**-ting**) (often + *with*) work or act together. □ **cooperation** *noun*.

cooperative /kəʊ'ɒpərətɪv/ (also **co-operative**) ● *adjective* willing to cooperate; (of business etc.) jointly owned and run by members, with profits shared. ● *noun* cooperative society or enterprise.

co-opt /kəʊ'ɒpt/ *verb* appoint to committee etc. by invitation of existing members. □ **co-option** *noun*; **co-optive** *adjective*.

coordinate (also **co-ordinate**) ● *verb* /kəʊ'ɔːdɪneɪt/ (**-ting**) cause to work together efficiently; work or act together effectively. ● *adjective* /-nət/ equal in status. ● *noun* /-nət/ *Mathematics* each of set of quantities used to fix position of point, line, or plane; (in *plural*) matching items of clothing. □ **coordination** *noun*; **coordinator** *noun*.

coot /kuːt/ *noun* black waterfowl with white horny plate on head; *colloquial* stupid person.

cop *slang* ● *noun* police officer; capture. ● *verb* (**-pp-**) catch. □ **cop-out** cowardly evasion; **not much cop** of little value or use.

copal /'kəʊp(ə)l/ *noun* kind of resin used for varnish.

copartner /kəʊ'pɑːtnə/ *noun* partner, associate. □ **copartnership** *noun*.

cope¹ *verb* (**-ping**) deal effectively or contend; (often + *with*) manage.

cope² *noun* priest's long cloaklike vestment.

copeck /'kəʊpek/ *noun* (also **kopek, kopeck**) hundredth of rouble.

copier /'kɒpɪə/ *noun* machine that copies (esp. documents).

copilot /'kəʊpaɪlət/ *noun* second pilot in aircraft.

coping /'kəʊpɪŋ/ *noun* top (usually sloping) course of masonry in wall. □ **coping stone** stone used in coping.

copious /'kəʊpɪəs/ *adjective* abundant; producing much. □ **copiously** *adverb*.

copper¹ /'kɒpə/ ● *noun* red-brown metal; bronze coin; large metal vessel for boiling laundry. ● *adjective* made of or coloured like copper. □ **copperplate** copper plate for engraving or etching, print taken from it, ornate sloping handwriting.

copper² /'kɒpə/ *noun slang* police officer.

coppice /'kɒpɪs/ *noun* area of undergrowth and small trees.

copulate /'kɒpjʊleɪt/ *verb* (**-ting**) (often + *with*) (esp. of animals) have sexual intercourse. □ **copulation** *noun*.

copy /'kɒpɪ/ ● *noun* (*plural* **-ies**) thing made to look like another; specimen of book etc.; material to be printed, esp. regarded as good etc. reading matter.

● *verb* (**-ies**, **-ied**) make copy of; imitate. □ **copy-typist** typist working from document or recording; **copywriter** writer of copy, esp. for advertisements.

copyist /ˈkɒpɪɪst/ *noun* person who makes copies.

copyright ● *noun* exclusive right to print, publish, perform, etc., material. ● *adjective* protected by copyright. ● *verb* secure copyright for (material).

coquette /kəˈket/ *noun* woman who flirts. □ **coquettish** *adjective*; **coquetry** /ˈkɒkɪtrɪ/ *noun* (*plural* **-ies**).

coracle /ˈkɒrək(ə)l/ *noun* small boat of wickerwork covered with waterproof material.

coral /ˈkɒr(ə)l/ ● *noun* hard substance built up by marine polyps. ● *adjective* of (red or pink colour of) coral. □ **coral island, reef** one formed by growth of coral.

cor anglais /kɔːr ˈɒŋgleɪ/ *noun* (*plural* **cors anglais** /kɔːz/) woodwind instrument like oboe but lower in pitch.

corbel /ˈkɔːb(ə)l/ *noun* stone or timber projection from wall, acting as supporting bracket.

cord ● *noun* thick string; piece of this; similar structure in body; ribbed cloth, esp. corduroy; (in *plural*) corduroy trousers; electric flex. ● *verb* secure with cords.

cordial /ˈkɔːdɪəl/ ● *adjective* heartfelt; friendly. ● *noun* fruit-flavoured drink. □ **cordiality** /-ˈæl-/ *noun*; **cordially** *adverb*.

cordite /ˈkɔːdaɪt/ *noun* smokeless explosive.

cordless *adjective* (of handheld electric device) battery-powered.

cordon /ˈkɔːd(ə)n/ ● *noun* line or circle of police etc.; ornamental cord or braid; fruit tree trained to grow as single stem. ● *verb* (often + *off*) enclose or separate with cordon of police etc.

cordon bleu /kɔːdɒn ˈblɜː/ *adjective* (of cooking) first-class.

corduroy /ˈkɔːdərɔɪ/ *noun* fabric with velvety ribs.

core ● *noun* horny central part of certain fruits, containing seeds; centre or most important part; part of nuclear reactor containing fissile material; inner strand of electric cable; piece of soft iron forming centre of magnet etc. ● *verb* (**-ring**) remove core from.

co-respondent /kəʊrɪˈspɒnd(ə)nt/ *noun* person cited in divorce case as having committed adultery with respondent.

corgi /ˈkɔːgɪ/ *noun* (*plural* **-s**) short-legged breed of dog.

coriander /kɒrɪˈændə/ *noun* aromatic plant; its seed, used as flavouring.

cork ● *noun* thick light bark of S. European oak; bottle-stopper made of cork etc. ● *verb* (often + *up*) stop, confine; restrain (feelings etc.).

corkage *noun* charge made by restaurant etc. for serving customer's own wine etc.

corked *adjective* (of wine) spoilt by defective cork.

corkscrew ● *noun* spiral steel device for extracting corks from bottles. ● *verb* move spirally.

corm *noun* swollen underground stem in certain plants, e.g. crocus.

cormorant /ˈkɔːmərənt/ *noun* diving seabird with black plumage.

corn[1] *noun* cereal before or after harvesting, esp. chief crop of a region; grain or seed of cereal plant; *colloquial* something corny. □ **corn cob** cylindrical centre of maize ear; **corncrake** ground-nesting bird with harsh cry; **corn dolly** plaited straw figure; **cornflakes** breakfast cereal of toasted maize flakes; **cornflour** fine-ground maize flour; **cornflower** blue-flowered plant originally growing in cornfields; **corn on the cob** maize eaten from the corn cob.

corn[2] *noun* small tender hard area of skin, esp. on toe.

cornea /ˈkɔːnɪə/ *noun* transparent circular part of front of eyeball.

corned *adjective* preserved in salt or brine.

cornelian /kɔːˈniːlɪən/ *noun* (also **carnelian** /kɑː-/) dull red variety of chalcedony.

corner /ˈkɔːnə/ ● *noun* place where converging sides, edges, streets, etc. meet; recess formed by meeting of two internal sides of room, box, etc.; difficult or inescapable position; remote or secluded place; action or result of buying whole available stock of a commodity; *Football & Hockey* free kick or hit from corner of pitch. ● *verb* force into difficult or inescapable position; buy whole available stock of (commodity); dominate (market) in this way; go round corner. □ **cornerstone** stone in projecting angle of wall, indispensable part or basis.

cornet /ˈkɔːnɪt/ *noun* brass instrument resembling trumpet; conical wafer for holding ice cream.

cornice /ˈkɔːnɪs/ *noun* ornamental moulding, esp. along top of internal wall.

Cornish /ˈkɔːnɪʃ/ ● *adjective* of Cornwall. ● *noun* Celtic language of Cornwall. □ **Cornish pasty** pastry envelope containing meat and vegetables.

cornucopia /kɔːnjʊˈkəʊpɪə/ *noun* horn overflowing with flowers, fruit, etc., as symbol of plenty.

corny *adjective* (**-ier**, **-iest**) *colloquial* banal; feebly humorous; sentimental.

corolla /kəˈrɒlə/ *noun* whorl of petals forming inner envelope of flower.

corollary /kəˈrɒlərɪ/ *noun* (*plural* **-ies**) proposition that follows from one proved; (often + *of*) natural consequence.

corona /kəˈrəʊnə/ *noun* (*plural* **-nae** /-niː/) halo round sun or moon, esp. that seen in total eclipse of sun.

coronary /ˈkɒrənərɪ/ *noun* (*plural* **-ies**) coronary thrombosis. □ **coronary artery** artery supplying blood to heart; **coronary thrombosis** blockage of coronary artery by blood clot.

coronation /kɒrəˈneɪʃ(ə)n/ *noun* ceremony of crowning sovereign.

coroner /ˈkɒrənə/ *noun* official holding inquest on deaths thought to be violent or accidental.

coronet /ˈkɒrənɪt/ *noun* small crown.

corpora *plural* of CORPUS.

corporal[1] /ˈkɔːpr(ə)l/ *noun* army or air-force NCO next below sergeant.

corporal[2] /ˈkɔːpər(ə)l/ *adjective* of human body. □ **corporal punishment** physical punishment.

corporate /ˈkɔːpərət/ *adjective* of, being, or belonging to a corporation or group.

corporation /kɔːpəˈreɪʃ(ə)n/ *noun* group of people authorized to act as individual, esp. in business; civic authorities.

corporative /ˈkɔːpərətɪv/ *adjective* governed by or organized in corporations.

corporeal /kɔːˈpɔːrɪəl/ *adjective* bodily, physical, material.

corps /kɔː/ *noun* (*plural* same /kɔːz/) military unit with particular function; organized group of people.

corpse /kɔːps/ *noun* dead body.

corpulent /ˈkɔːpjʊlənt/ *adjective* fleshy, bulky. □ **corpulence** *noun*.

corpus /ˈkɔːpəs/ *noun* (*plural* **-pora** /-pərə/) body or collection of writings, texts, etc.

corpuscle /ˈkɔːpʌs(ə)l/ *noun* minute body or cell in organism, esp. (in *plural*) red or white cells in blood of vertebrates. □ **corpuscular** /-ˈpʌskjʊlə/ *adjective*.

corral /kəˈrɑːl/ ● *noun* *US* pen for horses, cattle, etc.; enclosure for capturing wild animals. ● *verb* (**-ll-**) put or keep in corral.

correct /kəˈrekt/ ● *adjective* true, accurate; proper, in accordance with taste, standards, etc. ● *verb* set right; mark errors in; admonish; counteract. □ **correctly** *adverb*; **correctness** *noun*.

correction *noun* correcting, being corrected; thing substituted for what is wrong.

correctitude /kə'rektɪtjuːd/ *noun* consciously correct behaviour.

corrective ● *adjective* serving to correct or counteract. ● *noun* corrective measure or thing.

correlate /'kɒrəleɪt/ *verb* (**-ting**) (usually + *with*, *to*) have or bring into mutual relation. ● *noun* either of two related or complementary things. □ **correlation** *noun*.

correlative /kə'relətɪv/ ● *adjective* (often + *with*, *to*) having a mutual relation; (of words) corresponding and regularly used together. ● *noun* correlative thing or word.

correspond /kɒrɪ'spɒnd/ *verb* (usually + *to*) be similar or equivalent; (usually + *to*, *with*) agree; (usually + *with*) exchange letters.

correspondence *noun* agreement or similarity; (exchange of) letters. □ **correspondence course** course of study conducted by post.

correspondent *noun* person who writes letter(s); person employed to write or report for newspaper or broadcasting.

corridor /'kɒrɪdɔː/ *noun* passage giving access into rooms; passage in train giving access into compartments; strip of territory of one state running through that of another; route for aircraft over foreign country.

corrigendum /kɒrɪ'dʒendəm/ *noun* (*plural* **-da**) error to be corrected.

corrigible /'kɒrɪdʒɪb(ə)l/ *adjective* able to be corrected.

corroborate /kə'rɒbəreɪt/ *verb* (**-ting**) give support to, confirm. □ **corroboration** *noun*; **corroborative** /-rətɪv/ *adjective*; **corroboratory** /-rət(ə)rɪ/ *adjective*.

corrode /kə'rəʊd/ *verb* (**-ding**) wear away, esp. by chemical action; destroy gradually; decay.

corrosion /kə'rəʊʒ(ə)n/ *noun* corroding, being corroded; corroded area. □ **corrosive** /-sɪv/ *adjective & noun*.

corrugate /'kɒrəgeɪt/ *verb* (**-ting**) (esp. as **corrugated** *adjective*) bend into wavy ridges. □ **corrugation** *noun*.

corrupt /kə'rʌpt/ ● *adjective* influenced by or using bribery; immoral, wicked. ● *verb* make or become corrupt. □ **corruptible** *adjective*; **corruption** *noun*; **corruptly** *adverb*.

corsage /kɔː'sɑːʒ/ *noun* small bouquet worn by woman.

corsair /kɔː'seə/ *noun* pirate ship; pirate.

corset /'kɔːsɪt/ *noun* tight-fitting supporting undergarment worn esp. by women. □ **corsetry** *noun*.

cortège /kɔː'teɪʒ/ *noun* procession, esp. for funeral.

cortex /'kɔːteks/ *noun* (*plural* **-tices** /-tɪsiːz/) outer part of organ, esp. brain. □ **cortical** *adjective*.

cortisone /'kɔːtɪzəʊn/ *noun* hormone used in treating inflammation and allergy.

corvette /kɔː'vet/ *noun* small naval escort-vessel.

cos¹ /kɒs/ *noun* crisp long-leaved lettuce.

cos² /kɒz/ *abbreviation* cosine.

cosh *colloquial* ● *noun* heavy blunt weapon. ● *verb* hit with cosh.

cosine /'kəʊsaɪn/ *noun* ratio of side adjacent to acute angle (in right-angled triangle) to hypotenuse.

cosmetic /kɒz'metɪk/ ● *adjective* beautifying, enhancing; superficially improving; (of surgery etc.) restoring or enhancing normal appearance. ● *noun* cosmetic preparation. □ **cosmetically** *adverb*.

cosmic /'kɒzmɪk/ *adjective* of the cosmos; of or for space travel. □ **cosmic rays** high-energy radiations from outer space.

cosmogony /kɒz'mɒgənɪ/ *noun* (*plural* **-ies**) (theory about) origin of universe.

cosmology /kɒz'mɒlədʒɪ/ *noun* science or theory of universe. □ **cosmological** /-mə'lɒdʒ-/ *adjective*; **cosmologist** *noun*.

cosmonaut /'kɒzmənɔːt/ *noun* Russian astronaut.

cosmopolitan /kɒzmə'pɒlɪt(ə)n/ ● *adjective* of or knowing all parts of world; free from national limitations. ● *noun* cosmopolitan person. □ **cosmopolitanism** *noun*.

cosmos /'kɒzmɒs/ *noun* universe as a well-ordered whole.

Cossack /'kɒsæk/ *noun* member of S. Russian people famous as horsemen.

cosset /'kɒsɪt/ *verb* (**-t-**) pamper.

cost ● *verb* (*past & past participle* **cost**) have as price; involve as loss or sacrifice; (*past & past participle* **costed**) fix or estimate cost of. ● *noun* price; loss, sacrifice; (in *plural*) legal expenses. □ **cost-effective** effective in relation to cost; **cost of living** cost of basic necessities of life; **cost price** price paid for thing by person who later sells it.

costal /'kɒst(ə)l/ *adjective* of ribs.

costermonger /'kɒstəmʌŋgə/ *noun* person who sells fruit etc. from barrow.

costive /'kɒstɪv/ *adjective* constipated.

costly *adjective* (**-ier**, **-iest**) costing much, expensive. □ **costliness** *noun*.

costume /'kɒstjuːm/ ● *noun* style of dress, esp. of particular place or period; set of clothes; clothing for particular activity; actor's clothes for part. ● *verb* provide with costume. □ **costume jewellery** artificial jewellery.

costumier /kɒs'tjuːmɪə/ *noun* person who deals in or makes costumes.

cosy /'kəʊzɪ/ (*US* **cozy**) ● *adjective* (**-ier**, **-iest**) snug, comfortable. ● *noun* (*plural* **-ies**) cover to keep teapot etc. hot. □ **cosily** *adverb*; **cosiness** *noun*.

cot *noun* small high-sided bed for child etc.; small light bed. □ **cot death** unexplained death of sleeping baby.

cote *noun* shelter for birds or animals.

coterie /'kəʊtərɪ/ *noun* exclusive group of people sharing interests.

cotoneaster /kətəʊnɪ'æstə/ *noun* shrub bearing red or orange berries.

cottage /'kɒtɪdʒ/ *noun* small house, esp. in the country. □ **cottage cheese** soft white lumpy cheese; **cottage industry** small business carried on at home; **cottage pie** shepherd's pie.

cottager *noun* person who lives in cottage.

cotter /'kɒtə/ *noun* (also **cotter pin**) wedge or pin for securing machine part such as bicycle pedal crank.

cotton /'kɒt(ə)n/ *noun* soft white fibrous substance covering seeds of certain plants; such a plant; thread or cloth from this. □ **cotton on** (often + *to*) *colloquial* begin to understand; **cotton wool** wadding originally made from raw cotton.

cotyledon /kɒtɪ'liːd(ə)n/ *noun* first leaf produced by plant embryo.

couch¹ /kaʊtʃ/ ● *noun* upholstered piece of furniture for several people; sofa. ● *verb* (+ *in*) express in (language of specified kind). □ **couch potato** *US slang* person who likes lazing at home.

couch² /kuːtʃ/ *noun* (in full **couch grass**) kind of grass with long creeping roots.

couchette /kuː'ʃet/ *noun* railway carriage with seats convertible into sleeping berths; berth in this.

cougar /'kuːgə/ *noun* *US* puma.

cough /kɒf/ ● *verb* expel air from lungs with sudden sharp sound. ● *noun* (sound of) coughing; condition of respiratory organs causing coughing. □ **cough mixture** medicine to relieve cough; **cough up** eject with coughs, *slang* give (money, information, etc.) reluctantly.

could *past of* CAN¹.

couldn't /'kʊd(ə)nt/ could not.

coulomb /'kuːlɒm/ *noun* SI unit of electrical charge.

coulter /'kəʊltə/ *noun* (*US* **colter**) vertical blade in front of ploughshare.

council /'kaʊns(ə)l/ *noun* (meeting of) advisory, deliberative, or administrative body; local administrative body of county, city, town, etc. □ **council flat, house** one owned and let by local council; **council tax** local tax based on value of property and number of residents.

councillor *noun* member of (esp. local) council.

counsel /'kaʊns(ə)l/ ● *noun* advice, esp. formal; consultation; (*plural same*) legal adviser, esp. barrister; group of these. ● *verb* (**-ll-**; *US* **-l-**) advise, esp. on personal problems. □ **counsellor** (*US* **counselor**) *noun*.

count¹ ● *verb* find number of, esp. by assigning successive numerals; repeat numbers in order; (+ *in*) include or be included in reckoning; consider to be. ● *noun* counting, reckoning; total; *Law* each charge in an indictment. □ **countdown** counting numbers backwards to zero, esp. before launching rocket etc.; **count on** rely on; **count out** exclude, disregard.

count² *noun* foreign noble corresponding to earl.

countenance /'kaʊntɪnəns/ ● *noun* face or its expression; composure; moral support. ● *verb* (**-cing**) support, approve.

counter¹ *noun* flat-topped fitment in shop etc. across which business is conducted; small disc used for playing or scoring in board games, cards, etc.; device for counting things.

counter² ● *verb* oppose, contradict; meet by countermove. ● *adverb* in opposite direction. ● *adjective* opposite. ● *noun* parry, countermove.

counteract /kaʊntə'rækt/ *verb* neutralize or hinder by contrary action. □ **counteraction** *noun*.

counter-attack *verb & noun* attack in reply to enemy's attack.

counterbalance ● *noun* weight or influence balancing another. ● *verb* (**-cing**) act as counterbalance to.

counter-clockwise *adverb & adjective US* anticlockwise.

counter-espionage *noun* action taken against enemy spying.

counterfeit /'kaʊntəfɪt/ ● *adjective* imitation; forged; not genuine. ● *noun* forgery, imitation. ● *verb* imitate fraudulently; forge.

counterfoil *noun* part of cheque, receipt, etc. retained as record.

counter-intelligence *noun* counter-espionage.

countermand /kaʊntə'mɑːnd/ *verb* revoke, recall by contrary order.

countermeasure *noun* action taken to counteract danger, threat, etc.

countermove *noun* move or action in opposition to another.

counterpane *noun* bedspread.

counterpart *noun* person or thing equivalent or complementary to another; duplicate.

counterpoint *noun* harmonious combination of melodies in music; melody combined with another; contrasting argument, plot, literary theme, etc.

counterpoise ● *noun* counterbalance; state of equilibrium. ● *verb* (**-sing**) counterbalance.

counter-productive *adjective* having opposite of desired effect.

counter-revolution *noun* revolution opposing former one or reversing its results.

countersign ● *verb* add confirming signature to. ● *noun* password spoken to person on guard.

countersink *verb* (*past & past participle* **-sunk**) shape (screw-hole) so that screw-head lies level with surface; provide (screw) with countersink hole.

counter-tenor *noun* male alto singing voice; singer with this.

countervailing /'kaʊntəveɪlɪŋ/ *adjective* (of influence etc.) counterbalancing.

counterweight *noun* counterbalancing weight.

countess /'kaʊntɪs/ *noun* earl's or count's wife or widow; woman with rank of earl or count.

countless *adjective* too many to count.

countrified /'kʌntrɪfaɪd/ *adjective* rustic.

country /'kʌntrɪ/ *noun* (*plural* **-ies**) nation's territory, state; land of person's birth or citizenship; rural districts, as opposed to towns; region with regard to its aspect, associations, etc.; national population, esp. as voters. □ **country and western** type of folk music originated by southern US whites; **country dance** traditional dance; **countryman, countrywoman** person of one's own country or district; person living in rural area; **countryside** rural areas.

county /'kaʊntɪ/ *noun* (*plural* **-ies**) territorial division of country, forming chief unit of local administration; *US* political and administrative division of State; people, esp. gentry, of county. □ **county council** elected governing body of county; **county court** law court for civil cases; **county town** administrative capital of county.

coup /kuː/ *noun* (*plural* **-s** /kuːz/) successful stroke or move; *coup d'état*.

coup de grâce /kuː də ˈɡrɑːs/ *noun* finishing stroke. [French]

coup d'état /kuː deɪˈtɑː/ *noun* (*plural* **coups d'état** same pronunciation) sudden overthrow of government, esp. by force. [French]

coupé /'kuːpeɪ/ *noun* (*US* **coupe** /kuːp/) two-door car with hard roof and sloping back.

couple /'kʌp(ə)l/ ● *noun* (about) two; two people who are married or in a sexual relationship; pair of partners in a dance etc. ● *verb* (**-ling**) link, fasten, or associate together; copulate.

couplet /'kʌplɪt/ *noun* two successive lines of rhyming verse.

coupling /'kʌplɪŋ/ *noun* link connecting railway carriages or parts of machinery.

coupon /'kuːpɒn/ *noun* ticket or form entitling holder to something.

courage /'kʌrɪdʒ/ *noun* ability to disregard fear; bravery. □ **courageous** /kəˈreɪdʒəs/ *adjective*; **courageously** *adverb*.

courgette /kʊəˈʒet/ *noun* small vegetable marrow.

courier /'kʊrɪə/ *noun* person employed to guide and assist group of tourists; special messenger.

course /kɔːs/ ● *noun* onward movement or progression; direction taken; line of conduct; series of lectures, lessons, etc.; each successive part of meal; golf course, race-course, etc.; sequence of medical treatment etc.; continuous line of masonry or bricks at one level of building; channel in which water flows. ● *verb* (**-sing**) use hounds to hunt (esp. hares); move or flow freely. □ **in the course of** during; **of course** naturally, as expected, admittedly.

court /kɔːt/ ● *noun* number of houses enclosing a yard; courtyard; rectangular area for a game; (in full **court of law**) judicial body hearing legal cases; courtroom; sovereign's establishment and retinue. ● *verb* pay amorous attention to, seek to win favour of; try to win (fame etc.); unwisely invite. □ **court card** playing card that is king, queen, or jack; **court house** building in which judicial court is held, *US* county administrative offices; **court martial** (*plural* **courts martial**) judicial court of military officers; **court-martial** (**-ll-**; *US* **-l-**) try by court martial; **courtroom** room in which court of law sits; **court shoe** woman's light shoe with low cut upper; **courtyard** space enclosed by walls or buildings.

courteous /'kɜːtɪəs/ *adjective* polite, considerate. □ **courteously** *adverb*; **courteousness** *noun*.

courtesan /kɔːtɪ'zæn/ *noun* prostitute, esp. one with wealthy or upper-class clients.

courtesy /'kɜːtəsɪ/ *noun* (*plural* **-ies**) courteous behaviour or act. □ **by courtesy of** with formal permission of; **courtesy light** light in car switched on when door is opened.

courtier /'kɔːtɪə/ *noun* person who attends sovereign's court.

courtly *adjective* (**-ier**, **-iest**) dignified; refined in manners. □ **courtliness** *noun*.

courtship *noun* courting, wooing.

couscous /'kuːskuːs/ *noun* N. African dish of cracked wheat steamed over broth.

cousin /'kʌz(ə)n/ *noun* (also **first cousin**) child of one's uncle or aunt.

couture /kuː'tjʊə/ *noun* design and making of fashionable garments.

couturier /kuː'tjʊərɪeɪ/ *noun* fashion designer.

cove /kəʊv/ *noun* small bay or inlet; sheltered recess.

coven /'kʌv(ə)n/ *noun* assembly of witches.

covenant /'kʌvənənt/ ● *noun* agreement; *Law* sealed contract. ● *verb* agree, esp. by legal covenant.

Coventry /'kɒvəntrɪ/ *noun* □ **send to Coventry** refuse to associate with or speak to.

cover /'kʌvə/ ● *verb* (often + *with*) protect or conceal with cloth, lid, etc.; extend over; protect, clothe; include; (of sum) be large enough to meet (expense); protect by insurance; report on for newspaper, television, etc.; travel (specified distance); aim gun etc. at; protect by aiming gun. ● *noun* thing that covers, esp. lid, wrapper, etc.; shelter, protection; funds to meet liability or contingent loss; place-setting at table. □ **cover charge** service charge per person in restaurant; **cover note** temporary certificate of insurance; **cover up** *verb* cover completely, conceal; **cover-up** *noun* concealing of facts; **take cover** find shelter.

coverage *noun* area or amount covered; reporting of events in newspaper etc.

covering letter *noun* explanatory letter with other documents.

coverlet /'kʌvəlɪt/ *noun* bedspread.

covert /'kʌvət/ ● *adjective* secret, disguised. ● *noun* shelter, esp. thicket hiding game. □ **covertly** *adverb*.

covet /'kʌvɪt/ *verb* (**-t-**) desire greatly (esp. thing belonging to another person). □ **covetous** *adjective*.

covey /'kʌvɪ/ *noun* (*plural* **-s**) brood of partridges; family, set.

coving /'kəʊvɪŋ/ *noun* curved surface at junction of wall and ceiling.

cow¹ /kaʊ/ *noun* fully-grown female of esp. domestic bovine animal; female of elephant, rhinoceros, whale, seal, etc. □ **cowboy**, **cowgirl** person who tends cattle, esp. in western US, *colloquial* unscrupulous or incompetent business person; **cowherd** person who tends cattle; **cowhide** (leather made from) cow's hide; **cow-pat** round flat piece of cow-dung; **cowpox** disease of cows, source of smallpox vaccine.

cow² /kaʊ/ *verb* intimidate.

coward /'kaʊəd/ *noun* person easily frightened. □ **cowardly** *adjective*.

cowardice /'kaʊədɪs/ *noun* lack of bravery.

cower /'kaʊə/ *verb* crouch or shrink back in fear.

cowl /kaʊl/ *noun* (hood of) monk's cloak; (also **cowling**) hood-shaped covering of chimney or shaft. □ **cowl neck** wide loose roll neck on garment.

cowrie /'kaʊrɪ/ *noun* tropical mollusc with bright shell; its shell as money in parts of Asia etc.

cowslip /'kaʊslɪp/ *noun* yellow-flowered primula growing in pastures etc.

cox ● *noun* coxswain. ● *verb* act as cox (of).

coxcomb /'kɒkskəʊm/ *noun* conceited showy person.

coxswain /'kɒks(ə)n/ *noun* person who steers esp. rowing boat.

coy *adjective* affectedly shy; irritatingly reticent. □ **coyly** *adverb*.

coyote /kɔɪ'əʊtɪ/ *noun* (*plural* same or **-s**) N. American wild dog.

coypu /'kɔɪpuː/ *noun* (*plural* **-s**) amphibious rodent like small beaver, originally from S. America.

cozen /'kʌz(ə)n/ *verb literary* cheat, defraud; beguile.

cozy *US* = COSY.

crab ● *noun* shellfish with 10 legs; this as food; (in full **crab-louse**) (often in *plural*) parasite infesting human body. ● *verb* (**-bb-**) *colloquial* criticize, grumble; spoil. □ **catch a crab** (in rowing) get oar jammed under water, miss water; **crab-apple** wild apple tree, its sour fruit.

crabbed /'kræbɪd/ *adjective* crabby; (of handwriting) ill-formed, illegible.

crabby *adjective* (**-ier**, **-iest**) morose, irritable. □ **crabbily** *adverb*.

crack ● *noun* sudden sharp noise; sharp blow; narrow opening; break or split; *colloquial* joke, malicious remark; sudden change in vocal pitch; *slang* crystalline cocaine. ● *verb* (cause to) make crack; suffer crack or partial break; (of voice) change pitch sharply; tell (joke); open (bottle of wine etc.); break into (safe); find solution to (problem); give way, yield; hit sharply; (as **cracked** *adjective*) crazy, (of wheat) coarsely broken. □ **crack-brained** crazy; **crackdown** *colloquial* severe measures (esp. against lawbreakers); **crack down on** *colloquial* take severe measures against; **crack of dawn** daybreak; **crackpot** *colloquial* eccentric or impractical person; **crack up** *colloquial* collapse under strain.

cracker *noun* small paper cylinder containing paper hat, joke, etc., exploding with crack when ends are pulled; explosive firework; thin crisp savoury biscuit.

crackers *adjective slang* crazy.

crackle /'kræk(ə)l/ ● *verb* (**-ling**) make repeated light cracking sound. ● *noun* such a sound. □ **crackly** *adjective*.

crackling *noun* crisp skin of roast pork.

cracknel /'kræknəl/ *noun* light crisp biscuit.

cradle /'kreɪd(ə)l/ ● *noun* baby's bed, esp. on rockers; place regarded as origin of something; supporting framework or structure. ● *verb* (**-ling**) contain or shelter as in cradle.

craft /krɑːft/ *noun* special skill or technique; occupation needing this; (*plural* same) boat, vessel, aircraft, or spacecraft; cunning.

craftsman /'krɑːftsmən/ *noun* (*feminine* **-woman**) person who practises a craft. □ **craftsmanship** *noun*.

crafty *adjective* (**-ier**, **-iest**) cunning, artful. □ **craftily** *adverb*.

crag *noun* steep rugged rock.

craggy *adjective* (**-ier**, **-iest**) rugged; rough-textured.

cram *verb* (**-mm-**) fill to bursting; (often + *in*, *into*) force; study or teach intensively for exam.

crammer *noun* institution that crams pupils for exam.

cramp ● *noun* painful involuntary contraction of muscles. ● *verb* affect with cramp; restrict, confine.

cramped *adjective* (of space) small; (of handwriting) small and with the letters close together.

crampon /'kræmpɒn/ *noun* spiked iron plate fixed to boot for climbing on ice.

cranberry /'krænbərɪ/ *noun* (*plural* **-ies**) (shrub bearing) small red acid berry.

crane ● *noun* machine with projecting arm for moving heavy weights; large long-legged wading bird. ● *verb* (**-ning**) stretch (one's neck) in order to see something. □ **crane-fly** two-winged long-legged fly; **cranesbill** kind of wild geranium.

cranium /'kreɪnɪəm/ *noun* (*plural* **-s** or **-nia**) bones enclosing brain, skull. □ **cranial** *adjective*.

crank ● *noun* part of axle or shaft bent at right angles for converting rotary into reciprocal motion or vice versa; eccentric person. ● *verb* turn with crank. □ **crankpin** pin attaching connecting rod to crank; **crankshaft** shaft driven by crank; **crank up** start (engine) by turning crank.

cranky *adjective* (**-ier**, **-iest**) eccentric; shaky; *esp. US* crotchety.

cranny /'krænɪ/ *noun* (*plural* **-ies**) chink, crevice.

crape *noun* crêpe, usually of black silk, formerly used for mourning.

craps *plural noun* (also **crap game**) *US* gambling game played with dice.

crapulent /'kræpjʊlənt/ *adjective* suffering the effects of drunkenness. □ **crapulence** *noun*; **crapulous** *adjective*.

crash ● *verb* (cause to) make loud smashing noise; (often + *into*) (cause to) collide or fall violently; fail, esp. financially; *colloquial* gatecrash; (of computer, system, etc.) fail suddenly; (often + *out*) *slang* fall asleep, sleep. ● *noun* sudden violent noise; violent fall or impact, esp. of vehicle; ruin, esp. financial; sudden collapse, esp. of computer, system, etc. ● *adjective* done rapidly or urgently. □ **crash barrier** barrier to prevent car leaving road; **crash-dive** *verb* (of submarine) dive hastily and steeply, (of aircraft) dive and crash, *noun* such a dive; **crash-helmet** helmet worn to protect head; **crash-land** land or cause (aircraft etc.) to land with crash; **crash landing** instance of crash-landing.

crass *adjective* grossly stupid; insensitive. □ **crassly** *adverb*; **crassness** *noun*.

crate ● *noun* slatted wooden case; *slang* old aircraft, car, etc. ● *verb* (**-ting**) pack in crate.

crater /'kreɪtə/ *noun* mouth of volcano; bowl-shaped cavity, esp. hollow on surface of moon etc.

cravat /krə'væt/ *noun* man's scarf worn inside open-necked shirt.

crave *verb* (**-ving**) (often + *for*) long or beg for.

craven /'kreɪv(ə)n/ *adjective* cowardly, abject.

craving *noun* strong desire, longing.

craw *noun* crop of bird or insect.

crawfish *noun* (*plural* same) large spiny sea-lobster.

crawl ● *verb* move slowly, esp. on hands and knees or with body close to ground; *colloquial* behave obsequiously; (often + *with*) be filled with moving people or things; (esp. of skin) creep. ● *noun* crawling motion; slow rate of motion; fast swimming stroke.

crayfish /'kreɪfɪʃ/ *noun* (*plural* same) lobster-like freshwater crustacean; crawfish.

crayon /'kreɪən/ ● *noun* stick or pencil of coloured wax, chalk, etc. ● *verb* draw or colour with crayons.

craze ● *verb* (**-zing**) (usually as **crazed** *adjective*) make insane; produce fine surface cracks on, develop such cracks. ● *noun* usually temporary enthusiasm; object of this.

crazy *adjective* (**-ier**, **-iest**) insane, mad; foolish; (usually + *about*) *colloquial* extremely enthusiastic. □ **crazy paving** paving made of irregular pieces. □ **crazily** *adverb*.

creak ● *noun* harsh scraping or squeaking sound. ● *verb* emit creak; move stiffly. □ **creaky** *adjective* (**-ier**, **-iest**).

cream ● *noun* fatty part of milk; its yellowish-white colour; food or drink like or made with cream; cream-like cosmetic etc.; (usually + *the*) best part or pick of something. ● *verb* take cream from; make creamy; form cream or scum. ● *adjective* yellowish-white. □ **cream cheese** soft rich cheese made of cream and unskimmed milk; **cream cracker** crisp unsweetened biscuit; **cream off** remove best part of; **cream of tartar** purified tartar, used in medicine, baking powder, etc.; **cream tea** afternoon tea with scones, jam, and cream. □ **creamy** *adjective* (**-ier**, **-iest**).

creamer *noun* cream substitute for coffee; jug for cream.

creamery *noun* (*plural* **-ies**) factory producing dairy products; dairy.

crease /kriːs/ ● *noun* line made by folding or crushing; *Cricket* line defining position of bowler or batsman. ● *verb* (**-sing**) make creases in, develop creases.

create /kriː'eɪt/ *verb* (**-ting**) bring into existence; originate; invest with rank; *slang* make fuss.

creation /kriː'eɪʃ(ə)n/ *noun* creating, being created; (usually **the Creation**) God's creating of the universe; (usually **Creation**) all created things; product of imaginative work.

creative /kriː'eɪtɪv/ *adjective* inventive, imaginative. □ **creatively** *adverb*; **creativity** /-'tɪv-/ *noun*.

creator /kriː'eɪtə/ *noun* person who creates; (**the Creator**) God.

creature /'kriːtʃə/ *noun* living being, esp. animal; person, esp. one in subservient position; anything created.

crèche /kreʃ/ *noun* day nursery.

credence /'kriːd(ə)ns/ *noun* belief.

credentials /krɪ'denʃ(ə)lz/ *plural noun* documents attesting to person's education, character, etc.

credible /'kredɪb(ə)l/ *adjective* believable; worthy of belief. □ **credibility** *noun*.

■ **Usage** *Credible* is sometimes confused with *credulous*, which means 'gullible'.

credit /'kredɪt/ ● *noun* belief, trust; good reputation; person's financial standing; power to obtain goods before payment; acknowledgement of payment by entry in account, sum entered; acknowledgement of merit or (usually in *plural*) of contributor's services to film, book, etc.; grade above pass in exam; educational course counting towards degree. ● *verb* (**-t-**) believe; (usually + *to*, *with*) enter on credit side of account. □ **credit card** card authorizing purchase of goods on credit; **credit (person) with** ascribe to him or her; **credit rating** estimate of person's suitability for commercial credit; **creditworthy** suitable to receive credit; **on credit** with arrangement to pay later; **to one's credit** in one's favour.

creditable *adjective* praiseworthy. □ **creditably** *adverb*.

creditor *noun* person to whom debt is owing.

credo /'kriːdəʊ/ *noun* (*plural* **-s**) creed.

credulous /'kredjʊləs/ *adjective* too ready to believe; gullible. □ **credulity** /krɪ'djuː-/ *noun*.

■ **Usage** *Credulous* is sometimes confused with *credible*, which means 'believable'.

creed noun set of beliefs; system of beliefs; (often **the Creed**) formal summary of Christian doctrine.

creek noun inlet on sea-coast; arm of river; stream.

creel noun fisherman's wicker basket.

creep ● verb (past & past participle **crept**) crawl; move stealthily, timidly, or slowly; (of plant) grow along ground or up wall etc.; advance or develop gradually; (of flesh) shudder with horror etc. ● noun act of creeping; (**the creeps**) colloquial feeling of revulsion or fear; slang unpleasant person; gradual change in shape of metal under stress.

creeper noun creeping or climbing plant.

creepy adjective (**-ier, -iest**) colloquial feeling or causing horror or fear. □ **creepy-crawly** (plural **-crawlies**) small crawling insect etc. □ **creepily** adverb.

cremate /krɪˈmeɪt/ verb (**-ting**) burn (corpse) to ashes. □ **cremation** noun.

crematorium /kremaˈtɔːrɪəm/ noun (plural **-ria** or **-s**) place where corpses are cremated.

crenellated /ˈkrenəleɪtɪd/ adjective having battlements. □ **crenellation** noun.

Creole /ˈkriːəʊl/ ● noun descendant of European settlers in W. Indies or Central or S. America, or of French settlers in southern US; person of mixed European and black descent; language formed from a European and African language. ● adjective of Creoles; (usually **creole**) of Creole origin etc.

creosote /ˈkriːəsəʊt/ ● noun oily wood-preservative distilled from coal tar. ● verb (**-ting**) treat with creosote.

crêpe /kreɪp/ noun fine crinkled fabric; thin pancake with savoury or sweet filling; wrinkled sheet rubber used for shoe-soles etc. □ **crêpe de Chine** /də ˈʃiːn/ fine silk crêpe; **crêpe paper** thin crinkled paper.

crept past & past participle of CREEP.

crepuscular /krɪˈpʌskjʊlə/ adjective of twilight; (of animal) active etc. at twilight.

crescendo /krɪˈʃendəʊ/ Music ● noun (plural **-s**) gradual increase in loudness. ● adjective & adverb increasing in loudness.

■ **Usage** Crescendo is sometimes wrongly used to mean a climax rather than the progress towards it.

crescent /ˈkres(ə)nt/ ● noun sickle shape, as of waxing or waning moon; thing with this shape, esp. curved street. ● adjective crescent-shaped.

cress noun plant with pungent edible leaves.

crest ● noun comb or tuft on animal's head; plume of helmet; top of mountain, wave, etc.; Heraldry device above shield or on writing paper etc. ● verb reach crest of; crown; serve as crest to; form crest. □ **crestfallen** dejected. □ **crested** adjective.

cretaceous /krɪˈteɪʃəs/ adjective chalky.

cretin /ˈkretɪn/ noun person with deformity and mental retardation caused by thyroid deficiency; colloquial stupid person. □ **cretinism** noun; **cretinous** adjective.

cretonne /ˈkretɒn/ noun heavy cotton usually floral upholstery fabric.

crevasse /krəˈvæs/ noun deep open crack in glacier.

crevice /ˈkrevɪs/ noun narrow opening or fissure, esp. in rock.

crew¹ /kruː/ ● noun group of people working together, esp. manning ship, aircraft, spacecraft, etc.; these, other than the officers. ● verb supply or act as crew (member) for; act as crew. □ **crew cut** close-cropped hairstyle; **crew neck** round close-fitting neckline.

crew² archaic past of CROW.

crewel /ˈkruːəl/ noun thin worsted yarn for embroidery.

crib ● noun baby's small bed or cot; model of Nativity with manger; colloquial plagiarism; translation; colloquial cribbage. ● verb (**-bb-**) copy unfairly; confine in small space.

cribbage /ˈkrɪbɪdʒ/ noun a card game.

crick ● noun sudden painful stiffness, esp. in neck. ● verb cause crick in.

cricket¹ /ˈkrɪkɪt/ noun team game, played on grass pitch, in which ball is bowled at wicket defended with bat by player of other team. □ **not cricket** colloquial unfair behaviour. □ **cricketer** noun.

cricket² /ˈkrɪkɪt/ noun jumping chirping insect.

cried past & past participle of CRY.

crier /ˈkraɪə/ noun (also **cryer**) official making public announcements in law court or street.

crikey /ˈkraɪkɪ/ interjection slang: expressing astonishment.

crime noun act punishable by law; such acts collectively; evil act; colloquial shameful act.

criminal /ˈkrɪmɪn(ə)l/ ● noun person guilty of crime. ● adjective of, involving, or concerning crime; colloquial deplorable. □ **criminality** /-ˈnæl-/ noun; **criminally** adverb.

criminology /krɪmɪˈnɒlədʒɪ/ noun study of crime. □ **criminologist** noun.

crimp verb press into small folds or waves; corrugate.

Crimplene /ˈkrɪmpliːn/ noun proprietary term synthetic crease-resistant fabric.

crimson /ˈkrɪmz(ə)n/ adjective & noun rich deep red.

cringe verb (**-ging**) cower; (often + to) behave obsequiously.

crinkle /ˈkrɪŋk(ə)l/ ● noun wrinkle, crease. ● verb (**-ling**) form crinkles (in). □ **crinkly** adjective.

crinoline /ˈkrɪnəlɪn/ noun hooped petticoat.

cripple /ˈkrɪp(ə)l/ ● noun lame person. ● verb (**-ling**) lame, disable; damage seriously.

crisis /ˈkraɪsɪs/ noun (plural **crises** /-siːz/) time of acute danger or difficulty; decisive moment.

crisp ● adjective hard but brittle; bracing; brisk, decisive; clear-cut; crackling; curly. ● noun (in full **potato crisp**) very thin fried slice of potato. ● verb make or become crisp. □ **crispbread** thin crisp biscuit. □ **crisply** adverb; **crispness** noun.

crispy adjective (**-ier, -iest**) crisp.

criss-cross ● noun pattern of crossing lines. ● adjective crossing; in crossing lines. ● adverb crosswise. ● verb intersect repeatedly; mark with criss-cross lines.

criterion /kraɪˈtɪərɪən/ noun (plural **-ria**) principle or standard of judgement.

■ **Usage** It is a mistake to use the plural form criteria when only one criterion is meant.

critic /ˈkrɪtɪk/ noun person who criticizes; reviewer of literary, artistic, etc. works.

critical adjective fault-finding; expressing criticism; providing textual criticism; of the nature of a crisis, decisive; marking transition from one state to another. □ **critically** adverb.

criticism /ˈkrɪtɪsɪz(ə)m/ noun finding fault, censure; work of critic; critical article, remark, etc.

criticize /ˈkrɪtɪsaɪz/ verb (also **-ise**) (**-zing** or **-sing**) find fault with; discuss critically.

critique /krɪˈtiːk/ noun critical analysis.

croak ● noun deep hoarse sound, esp. of frog. ● verb utter or speak with croak; slang die. □ **croaky** adjective (**-ier, -iest**); **croakily** adverb.

Croat /ˈkrəʊæt/ (also **Croatian** /krəʊˈeɪʃ(ə)n/) ● noun native of Croatia; person of Croatian descent; Slavonic dialect of Croats. ● adjective of Croats or their dialect.

crochet /'krəʊʃeɪ/ ● noun needlework of hooked yarn producing lacy patterned fabric. ● verb (**crocheted** /-ʃeɪd/; **crocheting** /-ʃeɪɪŋ/) make by crochet.

crock[1] noun colloquial old or worn-out person or vehicle.

crock[2] noun earthenware jar; broken piece of this.

crockery noun earthenware or china dishes, plates, etc.

crocodile /'krɒkədaɪl/ noun large amphibious reptile; colloquial line of school children etc. walking in pairs. □ **crocodile tears** insincere grief.

crocus /'krəʊkəs/ noun (plural **-es**) small plant with corm and yellow, purple, or white flowers.

croft ● noun small piece of arable land; small rented farm in Scotland or N. England. ● verb farm croft.

crofter noun person who farms croft.

Crohn's disease /krəʊnz/ noun inflammatory disease of alimentary tract.

croissant /'krwʌsɑ̃/ noun rich crescent-shaped roll.

cromlech /'krɒmlek/ noun dolmen; prehistoric stone circle.

crone noun withered old woman.

crony /'krəʊnɪ/ noun (plural **-ies**) friend; companion.

crook /krʊk/ ● noun hooked staff of shepherd or bishop; bend, curve; colloquial swindler, criminal. ● verb bend, curve.

crooked /'krʊkɪd/ adjective (**-er, -est**) not straight, bent; colloquial dishonest. □ **crookedly** adverb; **crookedness** noun.

croon /kruːn/ ● verb hum or sing in low voice. ● noun such singing. □ **crooner** noun.

crop ● noun produce of any cultivated plant or of land; group or amount produced at one time; handle of whip; very short haircut; pouch in bird's gullet where food is prepared for digestion. ● verb (**-pp-**) cut off; bite off, eat down; cut (hair) short; raise crop on (land); bear crop. □ **crop circle** circle of crops inexplicably flattened; **crop up** occur unexpectedly.

cropper noun slang □ **come a cropper** fall heavily, fail badly.

croquet /'krəʊkeɪ/ ● noun lawn game with hoops, wooden balls, and mallets; croqueting. ● verb (**croqueted** /-keɪd/; **croqueting** /-keɪɪŋ/) drive away (opponent's ball) by striking one's own ball placed in contact with it.

croquette /krə'ket/ noun fried breaded ball of meat, potato, etc.

crosier /'krəʊzɪə/ noun (also **crozier**) bishop's ceremonial hooked staff.

cross ● noun upright stake with transverse bar, used in antiquity for crucifixion; representation of this as emblem of Christianity; cross-shaped thing or mark, esp. two short intersecting lines (+ or ×); cross-shaped military etc. decoration; intermixture of breeds, hybrid; (+ *between*) mixture of two things; trial, affliction. ● verb (often + *over*) go across; place crosswise; draw line(s) across; make sign of cross on or over; meet and pass; thwart; (cause to) interbreed; cross-fertilize (plants). ● adjective (often + *with*) peevish, angry; transverse; reaching from side to side; intersecting; reciprocal. □ **at cross purposes** misunderstanding each other; **crossbar** horizontal bar, esp. between uprights; **cross-bench** bench in House of Lords for non-party members; **crossbones** see SKULL AND CROSSBONES; **crossbow** bow fixed across wooden stock with mechanism working string; **cross-breed** (produce) hybrid animal or plant; **cross-check** check by alternative method; **cross-country** across fields etc., not following roads, noun such a race; **cross-examine** question (esp. opposing witness in law court); **cross-examination** such questioning; **cross-eyed** having one or both eyes turned inwards; **cross-fertilize** fertilize (animal or plant) from another of same species; **crossfire** firing of guns in two crossing directions; **cross-grained** (of wood) with grain running irregularly, (of person) perverse or intractable; **cross-hatch** shade with crossing parallel lines; **cross-legged** (sitting) with legs folded across each other; **cross off, out** cancel, expunge; **crossover** point or process of crossing; **crosspatch** colloquial bad-tempered person; **cross-ply** (of tyre) having crosswise layers of cords; **cross-question** cross-examine, quiz; **cross-reference** reference to another passage in same book; **cross-road** (usually in plural) intersection of roads; **cross-section** drawing etc. of thing as if cut through, representative sample; **cross stitch** cross-shaped stitch; **crosswise** intersecting, diagonally; **cross-word (puzzle)** puzzle in which words crossing each other vertically and horizontally have to be filled in from clues; **on the cross** diagonally. □ **crossly** adverb; **crossness** noun.

crossing noun place where things (esp. roads) meet; place for crossing street; journey across water.

crotch noun fork, esp. between legs (of person, trousers, etc.).

crotchet /'krɒtʃɪt/ noun Music black-headed note with stem, equal to quarter of semibreve and usually one beat.

crotchety adjective peevish.

crouch ● verb stand, squat, etc. with legs bent close to body. ● noun this position.

croup[1] /kruːp/ noun laryngitis in children, with sharp cough.

croup[2] /kruːp/ noun rump, esp. of horse.

croupier /'kruːpɪə/ noun person in charge of gaming table.

croûton /'kruːtɒn/ noun small piece of fried or toasted bread served esp. with soup.

crow /krəʊ/ ● noun any of various kinds of large black-plumaged bird; cry of cock or baby. ● verb (past **crowed** or archaic **crew** /kruː/) (of cock) utter loud cry; (of baby) utter happy sounds; exult. □ **crow's-foot** wrinkle at outer corner of eye; **crow's-nest** shelter for look-out man at ship's masthead.

crowbar noun iron bar used as lever.

crowd /kraʊd/ ● noun large gathering of people; colloquial particular set of people. ● verb (cause to) collect in crowd; (+ *with*) cram with; (+ *into, through*, etc.) force way into, through, etc.; colloquial come aggressively close to. □ **crowd out** exclude by crowding.

crown /kraʊn/ ● noun monarch's jewelled headdress; (**the Crown**) monarch as head of state, his or her authority; wreath for head as emblem of victory; top part of head, hat, etc.; visible part of tooth, artificial replacement for this; coin worth 5 shillings or 25 pence. ● verb put crown on; make king or queen; (often as **crowning** adjective) be consummation, reward, or finishing touch to; slang hit on head. □ **Crown colony** British colony controlled by the Crown; **Crown Court** court of criminal jurisdiction in England and Wales; **crown jewels** sovereign's regalia; **crown prince** male heir to throne; **crown princess** wife of crown prince, female heir to throne.

crozier = CROSIER.

CRT abbreviation cathode ray tube.

cruces plural of CRUX.

crucial /'kruːʃ(ə)l/ adjective decisive, critical; very important; slang excellent. □ **crucially** adverb.

crucible /'kruːsɪb(ə)l/ noun melting pot for metals.

cruciferous /kruː'sɪfərəs/ adjective with 4 equal petals arranged crosswise.

crucifix /'kruːsɪfɪks/ noun image of Christ on Cross.

crucifixion /kruːsɪˈfɪkʃ(ə)n/ *noun* crucifying, esp. of Christ.

cruciform /ˈkruːsɪfɔːm/ *adjective* cross-shaped.

crucify /ˈkruːsɪfaɪ/ *verb* (**-ies**, **-ied**) put to death by fastening to cross; persecute, torment.

crude ● *adjective* in natural or raw state; lacking finish, unpolished; rude, blunt; indecent. ● *noun* natural mineral oil. □ **crudely** *adverb*; **crudeness** *noun*; **crudity** *noun*.

crudités /kruːdɪˈteɪ/ *plural noun* hors d'oeuvre of mixed raw vegetables. [French]

cruel /ˈkruːəl/ *adjective* (**-ll-** or **-l-**) causing pain or suffering, esp. deliberately; harsh, severe. □ **cruelly** *adverb*; **cruelty** *noun* (*plural* **-ies**).

cruet /ˈkruːɪt/ *noun* set of small salt, pepper, etc. containers for use at table.

cruise /kruːz/ ● *verb* (**-sing**) sail about, esp. travel by sea for pleasure, calling at ports; travel at relaxed or economical speed; achieve objective with ease. ● *noun* cruising voyage. □ **cruise missile** one able to fly low and guide itself.

cruiser *noun* high-speed warship; cabin cruiser. □ **cruiserweight** light heavyweight.

crumb /krʌm/ ● *noun* small fragment esp. of bread; soft inner part of loaf; (**crumbs** *interjection*) *slang*: expressing dismay. ● *verb* coat with breadcrumbs; crumble (bread). □ **crumby** *adjective*.

crumble /ˈkrʌmb(ə)l/ ● *verb* (**-ling**) break or fall into fragments, disintegrate. ● *noun* dish of cooked fruit with crumbly topping. □ **crumbly** *adjective* (**-ier**, **-iest**).

crumhorn = KRUMMHORN.

crummy /ˈkrʌmɪ/ *adjective* (**-ier**, **-iest**) *slang* squalid, inferior.

crumpet /ˈkrʌmpɪt/ *noun* flat soft yeasty cake eaten toasted.

crumple /ˈkrʌmp(ə)l/ *verb* (**-ling**) (often + *up*) crush or become crushed into creases; give way, collapse.

crunch ● *verb* crush noisily with teeth; make or emit crunch. ● *noun* crunching sound; *colloquial* decisive event. □ **crunchy** *adjective* (**-ier**, **-iest**).

crupper /ˈkrʌpə/ *noun* strap looped under horse's tail to hold harness back.

crusade /kruːˈseɪd/ ● *noun historical* medieval Christian military expedition to recover Holy Land from Muslims; vigorous campaign for cause. ● *verb* (**-ding**) take part in crusade. □ **crusader** *noun*.

cruse /kruːz/ *noun archaic* earthenware jar.

crush ● *verb* compress violently so as to break, bruise, etc.; crease, crumple; defeat or subdue completely. ● *noun* act of crushing; crowded mass of people; drink made from juice of crushed fruit; (usually + *on*) *colloquial* infatuation.

crust ● *noun* hard outer part of bread etc.; pastry covering pie; rocky outer part of the earth; deposit, esp. on sides of wine bottle. ● *verb* cover with, form into, or become covered with crust.

crustacean /krʌˈsteɪʃ(ə)n/ ● *noun* hard-shelled usually aquatic animals, e.g. crab or lobster. ● *adjective* of crustaceans.

crusty *adjective* (**-ier**, **-iest**) having a crisp crust; irritable, curt.

crutch *noun* support for lame person, usually with cross-piece fitting under armpit; support; crotch.

crux *noun* (*plural* **-es** or **cruces** /ˈkruːsiːz/) decisive point at issue.

cry /kraɪ/ ● *verb* (**cries**, **cried**) (often + *out*) make loud or shrill sound, esp. to express pain, grief, joy, etc.; weep; (often + *out*) utter loudly, exclaim; (+ *for*) appeal for. ● *noun* (*plural* **cries**) loud shout of grief, fear, joy, etc.; loud excited utterance; urgent appeal; fit of weeping; call of animal. □ **cry-baby**

person who weeps frequently; **cry down** disparage; **cry off** withdraw from undertaking; **cry out for** need badly; **cry wolf** see WOLF; **a far cry** a long way.

cryer = CRIER.

crying *adjective* (of injustice etc.) flagrant, demanding redress.

cryogenics /kraɪəʊˈdʒɛnɪks/ *noun* branch of physics dealing with very low temperatures. □ **cryogenic** *adjective*.

crypt /krɪpt/ *noun* vault, esp. below church, usually used as burial place.

cryptic *adjective* obscure in meaning; secret, mysterious. □ **cryptically** *adverb*.

cryptogam /ˈkrɪptəgæm/ *noun* plant with no true flowers or seeds, e.g. fern or fungus. □ **cryptogamic** /-ˈgæm-/ *adjective*.

cryptogram /ˈkrɪptəgræm/ *noun* text written in cipher.

crystal /ˈkrɪst(ə)l/ ● *noun* (piece of) transparent colourless mineral; (articles of) highly transparent glass; substance solidified in definite geometrical form. ● *adjective* of or as clear as crystal. □ **crystal ball** glass globe supposedly used in foretelling the future.

crystalline /ˈkrɪstəlaɪn/ *adjective* of or as clear as crystal.

crystallize /ˈkrɪstəlaɪz/ *verb* (also **-ise**) (**-zing** or **-sing**) form into crystals; make or become definite; preserve or be preserved in sugar. □ **crystallization** *noun*.

CS gas *noun* tear gas used to control riots.

cu. *abbreviation* cubic.

cub ● *noun* young of fox, bear, lion, etc.; **Cub** (**Scout**) junior Scout; *colloquial* young newspaper reporter. ● *verb* give birth to (cubs).

cubby-hole /ˈkʌbɪhəʊl/ *noun* very small room; snug space.

cube /kjuːb/ ● *noun* solid contained by 6 equal squares; cube-shaped block; product of a number multiplied by its square. ● *verb* (**-bing**) find cube of; cut into small cubes. □ **cube root** number which produces given number when cubed.

cubic /ˈkjuːbɪk/ *adjective* of 3 dimensions; involving cube of a quantity. □ **cubic metre** etc., volume of cube whose edge is one metre etc. □ **cubical** *adjective*.

cubicle /ˈkjuːbɪk(ə)l/ *noun* small screened space, esp. sleeping compartment.

cubism /ˈkjuːbɪz(ə)m/ *noun* art style in which objects are represented geometrically. □ **cubist** *adjective & noun*.

cubit /ˈkjuːbɪt/ *noun* ancient measure of length, approximately length of forearm.

cuboid /ˈkjuːbɔɪd/ ● *adjective* like a cube; cube-shaped. ● *noun* solid with 6 rectangular faces.

cuckold /ˈkʌkəʊld/ ● *noun* husband of adulteress. ● *verb* make cuckold of.

cuckoo /ˈkʊkuː/ ● *noun* bird with characteristic cry and laying eggs in nests of small birds. ● *adjective slang* crazy. □ **cuckoo clock** clock with figure of cuckoo emerging to make call on the hour; **cuckoo-pint** wild arum; **cuckoo-spit** froth exuded by larvae of certain insects.

cucumber /ˈkjuːkʌmbə/ *noun* long green fleshy fruit used in salads.

cud *noun* half-digested food chewed by ruminant.

cuddle /ˈkʌd(ə)l/ ● *verb* (**-ling**) hug; lie close and snug; nestle. ● *noun* prolonged hug.

cuddly *adjective* (**-ier**, **-iest**) soft and yielding.

cudgel /ˈkʌdʒ(ə)l/ ● *noun* thick stick used as weapon. ● *verb* (**-ll-**; *US* **-l-**) beat with cudgel.

cue[1] /kjuː/ ● *noun* last words of actor's speech as signal for another to begin; signal, hint. ● *verb* (**cues**,

cued, cueing or **cuing**) give cue to. □ **cue in** insert cue for; **on cue** at correct moment.

cue² /kjuː/ ● noun long rod for striking ball in billiards etc. ● verb (**cues, cued, cueing** or **cuing**) strike with cue. □ **cue ball** ball to be struck with cue.

cuff¹ noun end part of sleeve; trouser turn-up; (in plural) colloquial handcuffs. □ **cuff link** either of pair of fasteners for shirt cuffs; **off the cuff** extempore, without preparation.

cuff² ● verb strike with open hand. ● noun such a blow.

cuisine /kwɪˈziːn/ noun style of cooking.

cul-de-sac /ˈkʌldəsæk/ noun (plural **culs-de-sac** same pronunciation, or **cul-de-sacs** /-sæks/) road etc. closed at one end.

culinary /ˈkʌlɪnərɪ/ adjective of or for cooking.

cull ● verb select, gather; pick (flowers); select and kill (surplus animals). ● noun culling; animal(s) culled.

culminate /ˈkʌlmɪneɪt/ verb (**-ting**) (usually + in) reach highest or final point. □ **culmination** noun.

culottes /kjuːˈlɒts/ plural noun woman's trousers cut like skirt.

culpable /ˈkʌlpəb(ə)l/ adjective deserving blame. □ **culpability** noun.

culprit /ˈkʌlprɪt/ noun guilty person.

cult noun religious system, sect, etc.; devotion or homage to person or thing.

cultivar /ˈkʌltɪvɑː/ noun plant variety produced by cultivation.

cultivate /ˈkʌltɪveɪt/ verb (**-ting**) prepare and use (soil) for crops; raise (plant etc.); (often as **cultivated** adjective) improve (manners etc.); nurture (friendship etc.). □ **cultivation** noun.

cultivator noun agricultural implement for breaking up ground etc.

culture /ˈkʌltʃə/ ● noun intellectual and artistic achievement or expression; refined appreciation of arts etc.; customs and civilization of a particular time or people; improvement by mental or physical training; cultivation of plants, rearing of bees etc.; quantity of bacteria grown for study. ● verb (**-ring**) grow (bacteria) for study. □ **culture shock** disorientation felt by person subjected to unfamiliar way of life. □ **cultural** adjective.

cultured adjective having refined tastes etc. □ **cultured pearl** one formed by oyster after insertion of foreign body into its shell.

culvert /ˈkʌlvət/ noun underground channel carrying water under road etc.

cumbersome /ˈkʌmbəsəm/ adjective (also **cumbrous** /ˈkʌmbrəs/) inconveniently bulky, unwieldy.

cumin /ˈkʌmɪn/ noun (also **cummin**) plant with aromatic seeds; these as flavouring.

cummerbund /ˈkʌməbʌnd/ noun waist sash.

cumulative /ˈkjuːmjʊlətɪv/ adjective increasing in force etc. by successive additions. □ **cumulatively** adverb.

cumulus /ˈkjuːmjʊləs/ noun (plural **-li** /-laɪ/) cloud formation of heaped-up rounded masses.

cuneiform /ˈkjuːnɪfɔːm/ ● noun writing made up of wedge shapes. ● adjective of or using cuneiform.

cunning /ˈkʌnɪŋ/ ● adjective (**-er, -est**) deceitful, crafty; ingenious. ● noun ingenuity; craft. □ **cunningly** adverb.

cup ● noun small bowl-shaped drinking vessel; cupful; cup-shaped thing; flavoured usually chilled wine, cider, etc.; cup-shaped trophy as prize. ● verb (**-pp-**) make cup-shaped; hold as in cup. □ **Cup Final** final match in (esp. football) competition; **cup-tie** match in such competition. □ **cupful** noun.

■ **Usage** A *cupful* is a measure, and so *three cupfuls* is a quantity of something; *three cups full* means the actual cups and their contents, as in *He brought us three cups full of water.*

---

cupboard /ˈkʌbəd/ noun recess or piece of furniture with door and usually shelves.

Cupid /ˈkjuːpɪd/ noun Roman god of love, pictured as winged boy with bow.

cupidity /kjuːˈpɪdɪtɪ/ noun greed, avarice.

cupola /ˈkjuːpələ/ noun small dome; revolving gun-turret on ship or in fort.

cuppa /ˈkʌpə/ noun colloquial cup of (tea).

cur noun mangy bad-tempered dog; contemptible person.

curable /ˈkjʊərəb(ə)l/ adjective able to be cured.

curaçao /ˈkjʊərəsəʊ/ noun (plural **-s**) orange-flavoured liqueur.

curacy /ˈkjʊərəsɪ/ noun (plural **-ies**) curate's office or position.

curare /kjʊəˈrɑːrɪ/ noun vegetable poison used on arrows by S. American Indians.

curate /ˈkjʊərət/ noun assistant to parish priest. □ **curate's egg** thing good in parts.

curative /ˈkjʊərətɪv/ ● adjective tending to cure. ● noun curative agent.

curator /kjʊəˈreɪtə/ noun custodian of museum etc.

curb ● noun check, restraint; (bit with) chain etc. passing under horse's lower jaw; kerb. ● verb restrain; put curb on.

curd noun (often in plural) coagulated acidic milk product, made into cheese or eaten as food.

curdle /ˈkɜːd(ə)l/ verb (**-ling**) coagulate. □ **make one's blood curdle** horrify one.

cure /kjʊə/ ● verb (often + of) restore to health, relieve; eliminate (evil etc.); preserve (meat etc.) by salting etc. ● noun restoration to health; thing that cures; course of treatment.

curé /ˈkjʊəreɪ/ noun parish priest in France etc. [French]

curette /kjʊəˈret/ ● noun surgeon's scraping-instrument. ● verb (**-tting**) scrape with this. □ **curettage** noun.

curfew /ˈkɜːfjuː/ noun signal or time after which people must remain indoors.

curie /ˈkjʊərɪ/ noun unit of radioactivity.

curio /ˈkjʊərɪəʊ/ noun (plural **-s**) rare or unusual object.

curiosity /kjʊərɪˈɒsɪtɪ/ noun (plural **-ies**) desire to know; inquisitiveness; rare or strange thing.

curious /ˈkjʊərɪəs/ adjective eager to learn; inquisitive; strange, surprising. □ **curiously** adverb.

curl ● verb (often + up) bend or coil into spiral; move in curve; (of upper lip) be raised in contempt; play curling. ● noun curled lock of hair; anything spiral or curved inwards. □ **curly** adjective (**-ier, -iest**).

curler noun pin, roller, etc. for curling hair.

curlew /ˈkɜːljuː/ noun long-billed wading bird with musical cry.

curling noun game like bowls played on ice with round flat stones.

curmudgeon /kəˈmʌdʒ(ə)n/ noun bad-tempered or miserly person. □ **curmudgeonly** adjective.

currant /ˈkʌrənt/ noun small seedless dried grape; (fruit of) any of various shrubs producing red, black, or white berries.

currency /ˈkʌrənsɪ/ noun (plural **-ies**) money in use in a country; being current; prevalence (of ideas etc.).

current ● adjective belonging to present time; happening now; in general circulation or use. ● noun body of moving water, air, etc., passing through still water etc.; movement of electrically charged particles; general tendency or course. □ **current account** bank account that may be drawn on by cheque without notice. □ **currently** adverb.

curriculum /kə'rɪkjʊləm/ noun (plural **-la**) course of study. □ **curriculum vitae** /'vi:taɪ/ brief account of one's education, career, etc.

curry¹ /'kʌrɪ/ ● noun (plural **-ies**) meat, vegetables, etc. cooked in spicy sauce, usually served with rice. ● verb (**-ies, -ied**) make into or flavour like curry. □ **curry powder** mixture of spices for making curry.

curry² /'kʌrɪ/ verb (**-ies, -ied**) groom (horse etc.) with curry-comb; dress (leather). □ **curry-comb** metal device for grooming horses etc.; **curry favour** ingratiate oneself.

curse /kɜːs/ ● noun invocation of destruction or punishment; violent or profane exclamation; thing causing evil. ● verb (**-sing**) utter curse against; (usually in passive; + with) afflict with; swear. □ **cursed** /'kɜːsɪd/ adjective.

cursive /'kɜːsɪv/ ● adjective (of writing) having joined characters. ● noun cursive writing.

cursor /'kɜːsə/ noun indicator on VDU screen showing particular position in displayed matter.

cursory /'kɜːsərɪ/ adjective hasty, hurried. □ **cursorily** adverb.

curt adjective noticeably or rudely brief. □ **curtly** adverb; **curtness** noun.

curtail /kɜː'teɪl/ verb cut short, reduce. □ **curtailment** noun.

curtain /'kɜːt(ə)n/ ● noun piece of cloth etc. hung up as screen, esp. at window; rise or fall of stage curtain; curtain-call; (in plural) slang the end. ● verb provide or (+ off) shut off with curtains. □ **curtain-call** audience's applause summoning actors to take bow; **curtain-raiser** short opening play etc., preliminary event.

curtsy /'kɜːtsɪ/ (also **curtsey**) ● noun (plural **-ies** or **-eys**) woman's or girl's acknowledgement or greeting made by bending knees. ● verb (**-ies, -ied** or **-eys, -eyed**) make curtsy.

curvaceous /kɜː'veɪʃəs/ adjective colloquial (esp. of woman) shapely.

curvature /'kɜːvətʃə/ noun curving; curved form; deviation of curve from plane.

curve ● noun line or surface of which no part is straight; curved line on graph. ● verb (**-ving**) bend or shape so as to form curve. □ **curvy** adjective (**-ier, -iest**).

curvet /kɜː'vet/ ● noun horse's frisky leap. ● verb (**-tt-** or **-t-**) perform curvet.

curvilinear /kɜːvɪ'lɪnɪə/ adjective contained by or consisting of curved lines.

cushion /'kʊʃ(ə)n/ ● noun bag stuffed with soft material for sitting on etc.; protection against shock; padded rim of billiard table; air supporting hovercraft. ● verb provide or protect with cushions; mitigate effects of.

cushy /'kʊʃɪ/ adjective (**-ier, -iest**) colloquial (of job etc.) easy, pleasant.

cusp noun point at which two curves meet, e.g. horn of crescent moon.

cuss colloquial ● noun curse; awkward person. ● verb curse.

cussed /'kʌsɪd/ adjective colloquial awkward, stubborn.

custard /'kʌstəd/ noun pudding or sweet sauce of eggs or flavoured cornflour and milk.

custodian /kʌs'təʊdɪən/ noun guardian, keeper.

custody /'kʌstədɪ/ noun guardianship; imprisonment. □ **custodial** /-'stəʊ-/ adjective.

custom /'kʌstəm/ noun usual behaviour; established usage; business dealings, customers; (in plural; also

treated as singular) duty on imports, government department or (part of) building at port etc. dealing with this. □ **custom house** customs office at frontier etc.; **custom-built, -made** made to customer's order.

customary /'kʌstəmərɪ/ adjective in accordance with custom; usual. □ **customarily** adverb.

customer noun person who buys goods or services; colloquial person of specified (esp. awkward) kind.

customize verb (also **-ise**) (**-zing** or **-sing**) make or modify to order; personalize.

cut ● verb (**-tt-**; past & past participle **cut**) divide, wound, or penetrate with edged instrument; detach, trim, etc. by cutting; (+ loose, open, etc.) loosen by cutting; (esp. as **cutting** adjective) cause pain to; reduce (prices, wages, services, etc.); make by cutting or removing material; cross, intersect; divide (pack of cards); edit (film), stop cameras; end acquaintance or ignore presence of; US deliberately miss (class etc.); chop (ball); switch off (engine etc.); (+ across, through, etc.) pass through as shorter route. ● noun act of cutting; division or wound made by cutting; stroke with knife, sword, whip, etc.; reduction (in price, wages, services, etc.); cessation (of power supply etc.); removal of part of play, film, etc.; slang commission, share of profits, etc.; style in which hair, clothing, etc. is cut; particular piece of meat; cutting of ball; deliberate ignoring of person. □ **a cut above** noticeably superior to; **cut and dried** completely decided, inflexible; **cut back** reduce (expenditure), prune; **cut-back** reduction in expenditure; **cut both ways** serve both sides; **cut corners** do task perfunctorily; **cut glass** glass with patterns cut on it; **cut in** interrupt, pull in too closely in front of another vehicle; **cut one's losses** abandon an unprofitable scheme; **cut no ice** slang have no influence; **cut off** verb remove by cutting, bring to abrupt end, interrupt, disconnect, adjective isolated; **cut out** shape by cutting, (cause to) cease functioning, stop doing or using; **cut-out** device for automatic disconnection; **cutthroat** noun murderer, adjective murderous, (of competition) intense and merciless; **cutthroat razor** one with long unguarded blade set in handle; **cut a tooth** have it appear through gum; **cut up** cut in pieces, (usually in passive) greatly distress; **cut up rough** show resentment.

cutaneous /kju:'teɪnɪəs/ adjective of the skin.

cute /kju:t/ adjective colloquial esp. US attractive, sweet; clever, ingenious. □ **cutely** adverb; **cuteness** noun.

cuticle /'kju:tɪk(ə)l/ noun skin at base of fingernail or toenail.

cutlass /'kʌtləs/ noun historical short broad-bladed curved sword.

cutlery /'kʌtlərɪ/ noun knives, forks, and spoons for use at table.

cutlet /'kʌtlɪt/ noun neck-chop of mutton or lamb; small piece of veal etc. for frying; flat cake of minced meat etc.

cutter noun person or thing that cuts; (in plural) cutting tool; small fast sailing ship; small boat carried by large ship.

cutting ● noun piece cut from newspaper etc.; piece cut from plant for replanting; excavated channel in hillside etc. for railway or road. ● adjective that cuts; hurtful. □ **cuttingly** adverb.

cuttlefish /'kʌt(ə)lfɪʃ/ noun (plural same or **-es**) 10-armed sea mollusc ejecting black fluid when pursued.

cutwater noun forward edge of ship's prow; wedge-shaped projection from pier of bridge.

C.V. abbreviation (also **CV**) curriculum vitae.

cwm /ku:m/ noun (in Wales) coomb.

cwt abbreviation hundredweight.

cyanide /'saɪənaɪd/ *noun* highly poisonous substance used in extraction of gold and silver.

cyanosis /saɪə'nəʊsɪs/ *noun* bluish skin due to oxygen-deficient blood.

cybernetics /saɪbə'netɪks/ *plural noun* (usually treated as *singular*) science of control systems and communications in animals and machines. □ **cybernetic** *adjective*.

cyclamen /'sɪkləmən/ *noun* plant with pink, red, or white flowers with backward-turned petals.

cycle /'saɪk(ə)l/ ● *noun* recurrent round or period (of events, phenomena, etc.); series of related poems etc.; bicycle, tricycle, etc. ● *verb* (**-ling**) ride bicycle etc.; move in cycles. □ **cycle lane** part of road reserved for bicycles; **cycle track**, **cycleway** path for bicycles.

cyclic /'saɪklɪk/ *adjective* (also **cyclical** /'sɪklɪk(ə)l/) recurring in cycles; belonging to chronological cycle. □ **cyclically** *adverb*.

cyclist /'saɪklɪst/ *noun* rider of bicycle.

cyclone /'saɪkləʊn/ *noun* winds rotating around low-pressure region; violent destructive form of this. □ **cyclonic** /-'klɒn-/ *adjective*.

cyclotron /'saɪklətrɒn/ *noun* apparatus for acceleration of charged atomic particles revolving in magnetic field.

cygnet /'sɪgnɪt/ *noun* young swan.

cylinder /'sɪlɪndə/ *noun* solid or hollow roller-shaped body; container for liquefied gas etc.; piston-chamber in engine. □ **cylindrical** /-'lɪn-/ *adjective*.

cymbal /'sɪmb(ə)l/ *noun* concave disc struck usually with another to make ringing sound.

cynic /'sɪnɪk/ *noun* person with pessimistic view of human nature. □ **cynical** *adjective*; **cynically** *adverb*; **cynicism** /-sɪz(ə)m/ *noun*.

cynosure /'saɪnəzjʊə/ *noun* centre of attention or admiration.

cypher = CIPHER.

cypress /'saɪprəs/ *noun* conifer with dark foliage.

Cypriot /'sɪprɪət/ (also **Cypriote** /-əʊt/) ● *noun* native or national of Cyprus. ● *adjective* of Cyprus.

Cyrillic /sɪ'rɪlɪk/ ● *adjective* of alphabet used esp. for Russian and Bulgarian. ● *noun* this alphabet.

cyst /sɪst/ *noun* sac formed in body, containing liquid matter.

cystic *adjective* of the bladder; like a cyst. □ **cystic fibrosis** hereditary disease usually with respiratory infections.

cystitis /sɪ'staɪtɪs/ *noun* inflammation of the bladder.

czar = TSAR.

czarina = TSARINA.

Czech /tʃek/ ● *noun* native or national of Czech Republic, or *historical* Czechoslovakia; language of Czech people. ● *adjective* of Czechs or their language; of Czech Republic.

Czechoslovak /tʃekə'sləʊvæk/ (also **Czechoslovakian** /-slə'vækɪən/) *historical* ● *noun* native or national of Czechoslovakia. ● *adjective* of Czechoslovaks or Czechoslovakia.

Dd

D *noun* (also **d**) (Roman numeral) 500. □ **D-Day** day of Allied invasion of France (6 June 1944), important or decisive day.

d. *abbreviation* died; (pre-decimal) penny.

dab¹ ● *verb* (**-bb-**) (often + *at*) press briefly and repeatedly with cloth etc.; (+ *on*) apply by dabbing; (often + *at*) aim feeble blow; strike lightly. ● *noun* dabbing; small amount (of paint etc.) dabbed on; light blow.

dab² *noun* (*plural* same) kind of marine flatfish.

dabble /'dæb(ə)l/ *verb* (**-ling**) (usually + *in, at*) engage (in an activity etc.) superficially; move about in shallow water etc. □ **dabbler** *noun*.

dabchick *noun* little grebe.

dab hand *noun* (usually + *at*) expert.

da capo /dɑː ˈkɑːpəʊ/ *adverb Music* repeat from beginning.

dace *noun* (*plural* same) small freshwater fish.

dacha /'dætʃə/ *noun* Russian country cottage.

dachshund /'dækshʊnd/ *noun* short-legged long-bodied dog.

dactyl /'dæktɪl/ *noun* metrical foot of one long followed by two short syllables. □ **dactylic** /-'tɪl-/ *adjective*.

dad *noun colloquial* father.

daddy /'dædɪ/ *noun* (*plural* **-ies**) *colloquial* father. □ **daddy-long-legs** crane-fly.

dado /'deɪdəʊ/ *noun* (*plural* **-s**) lower, differently decorated, part of interior wall.

daffodil /'dæfədɪl/ *noun* spring bulb with trumpet-shaped yellow flowers.

daft /dɑːft/ *adjective* (**-er, -est**) foolish, silly, crazy.

dagger /'dægə/ *noun* short knifelike weapon; obelus.

daguerreotype /də'gerəʊtaɪp/ *noun* early photograph using silvered plate.

dahlia /'deɪlɪə/ *noun* garden plant with large showy flowers.

Dáil (Eireann) /dɔɪl 'eɪrən/ *noun* lower house of Parliament in Republic of Ireland.

daily /'deɪlɪ/ ● *adjective* done, produced, or occurring every (week)day. ● *adverb* every day; constantly. ● *noun* (*plural* **-ies**) *colloquial* daily newspaper; cleaning woman.

dainty /'deɪntɪ/ ● *adjective* (**-ier, -iest**) delicately pretty or small; choice; fastidious. ● *noun* (*plural* **-ies**) delicacy. □ **daintily** *adverb*; **daintiness** *noun*.

daiquiri /'dækərɪ/ *noun* (*plural* **-s**) cocktail of rum, lime juice, etc.

dairy /'deərɪ/ ● *noun* (*plural* **-ies**) place for processing, distributing, or selling milk and milk products. ● *adjective* of, containing, or used for milk and milk products. □ **dairymaid** woman employed in dairy; **dairyman** man looking after cows.

dais /'deɪɪs/ *noun* low platform, esp. at upper end of hall.

daisy /'deɪzɪ/ *noun* (*plural* **-ies**) flowering plant with white radiating petals. □ **daisy chain** string of field daisies threaded together; **daisy wheel** spoked disc bearing printing characters, used in word processors and typewriters.

dale *noun* valley.

dally /'dælɪ/ *verb* (**-ies, -ied**) delay; waste time; (often + *with*) flirt. □ **dalliance** *noun*.

Dalmatian /dæl'meɪʃ(ə)n/ *noun* large white dog with dark spots.

dam¹ ● *noun* barrier across river etc., usually forming reservoir or preventing flooding. ● *verb* (**-mm-**) provide or confine with dam; (often + *up*) block up, obstruct.

dam² *noun* mother (of animal).

damage /'dæmɪdʒ/ ● *noun* harm; injury; (in *plural*) financial compensation for loss or injury; (**the damage**) *slang* cost. ● *verb* (**-ging**) inflict damage on.

damask /'dæməsk/ ● *noun* fabric with woven design made visible by reflection of light. ● *adjective* made of damask; velvety pink. □ **damask rose** old sweet-scented rose.

dame *noun* (**Dame**) (title of) woman who has been knighted; comic female pantomime character played by man; *US slang* woman.

damn /dæm/ ● *verb* (often as *interjection*) curse; censure; condemn to hell; (often as **damning** *adjective*) show or prove to be guilty. ● *noun* uttered curse. ● *adjective & adverb* damned. □ **damn all** *slang* nothing.

damnable /'dæmnəb(ə)l/ *adjective* hateful; annoying.

damnation /dæm'neɪʃ(ə)n/ ● *noun* eternal punishment in hell. ● *interjection* expressing anger.

damned /dæmd/ ● *adjective* damnable. ● *adverb* extremely.

damp ● *adjective* slightly wet. ● *noun* slight diffused or condensed moisture. ● *verb* make damp; (often + *down*) discourage, make burn less strongly; *Music* stop vibration of (string etc.). □ **damp course** layer of damp-proof material in wall to keep damp from rising. □ **dampness** *noun*.

dampen *verb* make or become damp; discourage.

damper *noun* device that reduces shock, vibration, or noise; discouraging person or thing; metal plate in flue to control draught.

damsel /'dæmz(ə)l/ *noun archaic* young unmarried woman.

damson /'dæmz(ə)n/ *noun* small dark purple plum.

dance /dɑːns/ ● *verb* (**-cing**) move rhythmically, usually to music; perform (dance role etc.); jump or bob about. ● *noun* dancing as art; style or form of this; social gathering for dancing; lively motion. □ **dance attendance** (**on**) serve obsequiously. □ **dancer** *noun*.

dandelion /'dændɪlaɪən/ *noun* yellow-flowered wild plant.

dander *noun* □ **get one's dander up** *colloquial* become angry.

dandle /'dænd(ə)l/ *verb* (**-ling**) bounce (child) on one's knees etc.

dandruff /'dændrʌf/ *noun* flakes of dead skin in hair.

dandy /'dændɪ/ ● *noun* (*plural* **-ies**) man excessively devoted to style and fashion. ● *adjective* (**-ier, -iest**) *colloquial* splendid. □ **dandy-brush** stiff brush for grooming horses.

Dane *noun* native or national of Denmark; *historical* Viking invader of England.

danger /'deɪndʒə/ *noun* liability or exposure to harm; thing causing harm. □ **danger list** list of those dangerously ill; **danger money** extra payment for dangerous work.

dangerous *adjective* involving or causing danger. □ **dangerously** *adverb*.

dangle /'dæŋg(ə)l/ *verb* (**-ling**) hang loosely; hold or carry swaying loosely; hold out (temptation etc.).

Danish /'deɪnɪʃ/ ● *adjective* of Denmark. ● *noun* Danish language; (**the Danish**) the Danish people. ▫ **Danish blue** white blue-veined cheese; **Danish pastry** yeast cake with icing, nuts, fruit, etc.

dank *adjective* damp and cold.

daphne /'dæfnɪ/ *noun* a flowering shrub.

dapper *adjective* neat and precise, esp. in dress; sprightly.

dapple /'dæp(ə)l/ *verb* (**-ling**) mark with spots of colour or shade; mottle. ● *adjective* ▫ **dapple-grey** (of horse) grey with darker spots; **dapple grey** such a horse.

Darby and Joan *noun* devoted old married couple. ▫ **Darby and Joan club** social club for pensioners.

dare /deə/ ● *verb* (**-ring**; *3rd singular present* often **dare**) (+ *(to) do*) have the courage or impudence (to); (usually + *to do*) defy, challenge. ● *noun* challenge. ▫ **daredevil** reckless (person); **I dare say** very likely, I grant that.

daring ● *noun* adventurous courage. ● *adjective* bold, prepared to take risks. ▫ **daringly** *adverb*.

dariole /'dærɪəʊl/ *noun* dish cooked and served in a small mould.

dark ● *adjective* with little or no light; of deep or sombre colour; (of a person) with dark colouring; gloomy; sinister; angry; secret, mysterious. ● *noun* absence of light or knowledge; unlit place. ▫ **after dark** after nightfall; **Dark Ages** 5th–10th-c., unenlightened period; **dark horse** little-known person who is unexpectedly successful; **darkroom** darkened room for photographic work; **in the dark** without information or light. ▫ **darken** *verb*; **darkly** *adverb*; **darkness** *noun*.

darling /'dɑːlɪŋ/ ● *noun* beloved or endearing person or animal. ● *adjective* beloved, lovable; *colloquial* charming.

darn¹ ● *verb* mend by interweaving wool etc. across hole. ● *noun* darned area.

darn² *verb, interjection, adjective, & adverb colloquial mild form of* DAMN.

darnel /'dɑːn(ə)l/ *noun* grass growing in cereal crops.

dart ● *noun* small pointed missile; (in *plural* treated as *singular*) indoor game of throwing darts at a dartboard; sudden rapid movement; tapering tuck in garment. ● *verb* (often + *out, in, past,* etc.) move, send, or go suddenly or rapidly. ▫ **dartboard** circular target in game of darts.

Darwinian /dɑː'wɪnɪən/ ● *adjective* of Darwin's theory of evolution. ● *noun* adherent of this. ▫ **Darwinism** /'dɑː-/ *noun*; **Darwinist** /'dɑː-/ *noun*.

dash ● *verb* rush; strike or fling forcefully so as to shatter; frustrate, dispirit; *colloquial* (as *interjection*)

damn. ● *noun* rush, onset; punctuation mark (—) used to indicate break in sense (see panel); longer signal of two in Morse code; slight admixture; (capacity for) impetuous vigour. ▫ **dashboard** instrument panel of vehicle or aircraft; **dash off** write hurriedly.

dashing *adjective* spirited; showy.

dastardly /'dæstədlɪ/ *adjective* cowardly, despicable.

data /'deɪtə/ *plural noun* (also treated as *singular*) known facts used for inference or reckoning; quantities or characters operated on by computer. ▫ **data bank** store or source of data; **database** structured set of data held in computer; **data processing** series of operations on data by computer.

■ **Usage** In scientific, philosophical, and general use, *data* is usually considered to mean a number of items and is treated as plural, with *datum* as its singular. In computing and allied subjects (and sometimes in general use), it is treated as singular, as in *Much useful data has been collected*. However, *data* is not singular, and it is wrong to say *a data* or *every data* or to make the plural form *datas*.

---

date¹ ● *noun* day of month; historical day or year; day, month, and year of writing etc. at head of document etc.; period to which work of art etc. belongs; time when an event takes place; *colloquial* social appointment, esp. with person of opposite sex; *US colloquial* person to be met at this. ● *verb* (**-ting**) mark with date; assign date to; (+ *to*) assign to a particular time, period, etc.; (often + *from, back to,* etc.) have origin at a particular time; expose as or appear old-fashioned; *US colloquial* make date with, go out together as sexual partners. ▫ **date line** line partly along meridian 180° from Greenwich, to the east of which date is a day earlier than to the west; date and place of writing at head of newspaper article etc.; **out of date** (**out-of-date** before noun) old-fashioned, obsolete; **to date** until now; **up to date** (**up-to-date** before noun) fashionable, current.

date² *noun* oval stone fruit; (in full **date-palm**) tree bearing this.

dative /'deɪtɪv/ *Grammar* ● *noun* case expressing indirect object or recipient. ● *adjective* of or in the dative.

datum /'deɪtəm/ *singular of* DATA.

daub /dɔːb/ ● *verb* paint or spread (paint etc.) crudely or unskilfully; smear (surface) with paint etc. ● *noun* paint etc. daubed on a surface; crude painting; clay etc. coating wattles to form wall.

daughter /'dɔːtə/ *noun* female child in relation to her parents; female descendant or member of family etc. ▫ **daughter-in-law** (*plural* **daughters-in-law**) son's wife.

Dash –

This is used:

1 to mark the beginning and end of an interruption in the structure of a sentence:

> *My son—where has he gone?—would like to meet you.*

2 to show faltering speech in conversation:

> *Yes—well—I would—only you see—it's not easy.*

3 to show other kinds of break in a sentence, where a comma, semicolon, or colon would traditionally be used, e.g.

> *Come tomorrow—if you can.*
> *The most important thing is this—don't rush the work.*

A dash is not used in this way in formal writing.

daunt /dɔ:nt/ verb discourage, intimidate. □ **daunting** adjective.

dauntless adjective intrepid, persevering.

dauphin /'dɔ:fɪn/ noun historical eldest son of King of France.

Davenport /'dævənpɔ:t/ noun kind of writing desk; US large sofa.

davit /'dævɪt/ noun small crane on ship for holding lifeboat.

daw noun jackdaw.

dawdle /'dɔ:d(ə)l/ verb (**-ling**) walk slowly and idly; waste time, procrastinate.

dawn ● noun daybreak; beginning. ● verb (of day) begin, grow light; (often + on, upon) become evident (to). □ **dawn chorus** birdsong at daybreak.

day noun time between sunrise and sunset; 24 hours as a unit of time; daylight; time during which work is normally done; (also plural) historical period; (**the day**) present time; period of prosperity. □ **daybreak** first light in morning; **day centre** place for care of elderly or handicapped during day; **daydream** (indulge in) fantasy etc. while awake; **day off** day's holiday; **day release** part-time education for employees; **day return** reduced fare or ticket for a return journey in one day; **day school** school for pupils living at home; **daytime** part of day when there is natural light; **day-to-day** mundane, routine; **day-trip** trip completed in one day.

daylight noun light of day; dawn; visible gap between things; (usually in plural) slang life. □ **daylight robbery** blatantly excessive charge; **daylight saving** longer summer evening daylight, achieved by putting clocks forward.

daze ● verb (**-zing**) stupefy, bewilder. ● noun dazed state.

dazzle /'dæz(ə)l/ ● verb (**-ling**) blind or confuse temporarily with sudden bright light; impress or overpower with knowledge, ability, etc. ● noun bright confusing light. □ **dazzling** adjective.

dB abbreviation decibel(s).

DC abbreviation direct current; District of Columbia; da capo.

DDT abbreviation colourless chlorinated hydrocarbon used as insecticide.

deacon /'di:kən/ noun (in episcopal churches) minister below priest; (feminine **deaconess** /-'nes/) (in Nonconformist churches) lay officer.

deactivate /di'æktɪveɪt/ verb (**-ting**) make inactive or less reactive.

dead /ded/ ● adjective no longer alive; numb; colloquial extremely tired or unwell; (+ to) insensitive to; not effective; extinct; extinguished; inanimate; lacking vigour; not resonant; quiet; not transmitting sounds; out of play; abrupt; complete. ● adverb absolutely, completely; colloquial very. ● noun time of silence or inactivity. □ **dead beat** utterly exhausted; **deadbeat** tramp; **dead duck** useless person or thing; **dead end** closed end of road etc.; **dead-end** having no prospects; **dead heat** race in which competitors tie; **dead letter** law etc. no longer observed; **deadline** time limit; **deadlock** noun state of unresolved conflict, verb bring or come to a standstill; **dead loss** useless person or thing; **dead man's handle** handle on electric train etc. disconnecting power supply if released; **dead march** funeral march; **dead on** exactly right; **deadpan** lacking expression or emotion; **dead reckoning** estimation of ship's position from log, compass, etc., when visibility is bad; **dead shot** unerring marksman; **dead weight** inert mass, heavy burden; **dead wood** colloquial useless person(s) or thing(s).

deaden verb deprive of or lose vitality, force, etc.; (+ to) make insensitive.

deadly ● adjective (**-ier, -iest**) causing fatal injury or serious damage; intense; accurate; deathlike; dreary. ● adverb as if dead; extremely. □ **deadly nightshade** plant with poisonous black berries.

deaf /def/ adjective wholly or partly unable to hear; (+ to) refusing to listen or comply. □ **deaf-aid** hearing aid; **deaf-and-dumb alphabet, language** sign language; **deaf mute** deaf and dumb person. □ **deafness** noun.

deafen verb (often as **deafening** adjective) overpower or make deaf with noise, esp. temporarily. □ **deafeningly** adverb.

deal[1] ● verb (past & past participle **dealt** /delt/) (+ with) take measures to resolve, placate, etc., do business or associate with, treat (subject); (often + by, with) behave in specified way; (+ in) sell; (often + out, round) distribute; administer. ● noun (usually **a good** or **great deal**) large amount, considerably; business arrangement etc.; specified treatment; dealing of cards, player's turn to deal.

deal[2] noun fir or pine timber, esp. as boards.

dealer noun trader; player dealing at cards.

dealings plural noun conduct or transactions.

dean noun head of ecclesiastical chapter; (usually **rural dean**) clergyman supervising parochial clergy; college or university official with disciplinary functions; head of university faculty.

deanery noun (plural **-ies**) dean's house or position; parishes presided over by rural dean.

dear ● adjective beloved; used before person's name, esp. at beginning of letter; (+ to) precious; expensive. ● noun dear person. ● adverb at great cost. ● interjection (usually **oh dear!** or **dear me!**) expressing surprise, dismay, etc. □ **dearly** adverb.

dearth /dɜ:θ/ noun scarcity, lack.

death /deθ/ noun dying, end of life; being dead; cause of death; destruction. □ **deathblow** blow etc. causing death, or action, event, etc. ending something; **death-mask** cast of dead person's face; **death penalty** capital punishment; **death rate** yearly deaths per 1000 of population; **death-rattle** gurgling in throat at death; **death row** part of prison for those sentenced to death; **death squad** paramilitary group; **death-trap** unsafe place, vehicle, etc.; **death-warrant** order of execution; **death-watch beetle** beetle that bores into wood and makes ticking sound. □ **deathlike** adjective.

deathly ● adjective (**-ier, -iest**) like death. ● adverb in deathly manner.

deb noun colloquial débutante.

débâcle /deɪ'bɑ:k(ə)l/ noun utter collapse; confused rush.

debar /dɪ'bɑ:/ verb (**-rr-**) (+ from) exclude. □ **debarment** noun.

debase /dɪ'beɪs/ verb (**-sing**) lower in character, quality, or value; depreciate (coin) by alloying etc. □ **debasement** noun.

debatable /dɪ'beɪtəb(ə)l/ adjective questionable.

debate /dɪ'beɪt/ ● verb (**-ting**) discuss or dispute, esp. formally; consider, ponder. ● noun discussion, esp. formal.

debauch /dɪ'bɔ:tʃ/ ● verb corrupt, deprave, debase; (as **debauched** adjective) dissolute. ● noun bout of debauchery.

debauchee /dɪbɔ:'tʃi:/ noun debauched person.

debauchery noun excessive sensual indulgence.

debenture /dɪ'bentʃə/ noun company bond providing for payment of interest.

debilitate /dɪ'bɪlɪteɪt/ verb (**-ting**) enfeeble. □ **debilitation** noun.

debility noun feebleness, esp. of health.

debit /'debɪt/ ● *noun* entry in account recording sum owed. ● *verb* (**-t-**) (+ *against, to*) enter on debit side of account.

debonair /debə'neə/ *adjective* self-assured; pleasant.

debouch /dɪ'baʊtʃ/ *verb* come out into open ground; (often + *into*) (of river etc.) merge. □ **debouchment** *noun.*

debrief /diː'briːf/ *verb* question (diplomat etc.) about completed mission. □ **debriefing** *noun.*

debris /'debriː/ *noun* scattered fragments; wreckage.

debt /det/ *noun* money etc. owing; obligation; state of owing.

debtor *noun* person owing money etc.

debug /diː'bʌg/ *verb* (**-gg-**) remove hidden microphones from; remove defects from.

debunk /diː'bʌŋk/ *verb colloquial* expose as spurious or false.

début /'deɪbjuː/ *noun* first public appearance.

débutante /'debjuːtɑːnt/ *noun* young woman making her social début.

Dec. *abbreviation* December.

deca- *combining form* ten.

decade /'dekeɪd/ *noun* 10 years; set or series of 10.

decadence /'dekəd(ə)ns/ *noun* moral or cultural decline; immoral behaviour. □ **decadent** *adjective.*

decaffeinated /diː'kæfɪneɪtɪd/ *adjective* with caffeine removed.

decagon /'dekəgən/ *noun* plane figure with 10 sides and angles. □ **decagonal** /-'kæg-/ *adjective.*

decahedron /dekə'hiːdrən/ *noun* solid figure with 10 faces. □ **decahedral** *adjective.*

decamp /diː'kæmp/ *verb* depart suddenly; break up or leave camp.

decant /dɪ'kænt/ *verb* pour off (wine etc.) leaving sediment behind.

decanter *noun* stoppered glass container for decanted wine or spirit.

decapitate /dɪ'kæpɪteɪt/ *verb* (**-ting**) behead. □ **decapitation** *noun.*

decarbonize /diː'kɑːbənaɪz/ *verb* (also **-ise**) (**-zing** or **-sing**) remove carbon etc. from (engine of car etc.). □ **decarbonization** *noun.*

decathlon /dɪ'kæθlən/ *noun* athletic contest of 10 events. □ **decathlete** *noun.*

decay /dɪ'keɪ/ ● *verb* (cause to) rot or decompose; decline in quality, power, etc. ● *noun* rotten state; decline.

decease /dɪ'siːs/ *noun formal esp. Law* death.

deceased *formal* ● *adjective* dead. ● *noun* (**the deceased**) person who has died.

deceit /dɪ'siːt/ *noun* deception; trick. □ **deceitful** *adjective.*

deceive /dɪ'siːv/ *verb* (**-ving**) make (person) believe what is false; (**deceive oneself**) persist in mistaken belief; mislead; be unfaithful to.

decelerate /diː'seləreɪt/ *verb* (**-ting**) (cause to) reduce speed. □ **deceleration** *noun.*

December /dɪ'sembə/ *noun* twelfth month of year.

decency /'diːsənsɪ/ *noun* (*plural* **-ies**) correct, honourable, or modest behaviour; (in *plural*) proprieties, manners.

decennial /dɪ'senɪəl/ *adjective* lasting 10 years; recurring every 10 years.

decent /'diːs(ə)nt/ *adjective* conforming with standards of decency; not obscene; respectable; acceptable; kind. □ **decently** *adverb.*

decentralize /diː'sentrəlaɪz/ *verb* (also **-ise**) (**-zing** or **-sing**) transfer (power etc.) from central to local authority. □ **decentralization** *noun.*

deception /dɪ'sepʃ(ə)n/ *noun* deceiving, being deceived; thing that deceives.

deceptive /dɪ'septɪv/ *adjective* likely to mislead.

deci- *combining form* one-tenth.

decibel /'desɪbel/ *noun* unit used in comparison of sound etc. levels.

decide /dɪ'saɪd/ *verb* (**-ding**) (usually + *to do, that, on, about*) resolve after consideration; settle (issue etc.); (usually + *between, for, against, in favour of, that*) give judgement.

decided *adjective* definite, unquestionable; positive, resolute. □ **decidedly** *adverb.*

deciduous /dɪ'sɪdjʊəs/ *adjective* (of tree) shedding leaves annually; (of leaves etc.) shed periodically.

decimal /'desɪm(ə)l/ ● *adjective* (of system of numbers, weights, measures, etc.) based on 10; of tenths or 10; proceeding by tens. ● *noun* decimal fraction. □ **decimal fraction** fraction expressed in tenths, hundredths, etc., esp. by units to right of decimal point; **decimal point** dot placed before fraction in decimal fraction.

decimalize *verb* (also **-ise**) (**-zing** or **-sing**) express as decimal; convert to decimal system. □ **decimalization** *noun.*

decimate /'desɪmeɪt/ *verb* (**-ting**) destroy large proportion of. □ **decimation** *noun.*

■ **Usage** *Decimate* should not be used to mean 'defeat utterly'.

decipher /dɪ'saɪfə/ *verb* convert (coded information) into intelligible language; determine the meaning of. □ **decipherable** *adjective.*

decision /dɪ'sɪʒ(ə)n/ *noun* deciding; resolution after consideration; settlement; resoluteness.

decisive /dɪ'saɪsɪv/ *adjective* conclusive, settling an issue; quick to decide. □ **decisively** *adverb*; **decisiveness** *noun.*

deck ● *noun* platform in a ship serving as a floor; floor of bus etc.; section for playing discs or tapes etc. in sound system; *US* pack of cards. ● *verb* (often + *out*) decorate. □ **deck-chair** outdoor folding chair.

declaim /dɪ'kleɪm/ *verb* speak, recite, etc. as if addressing audience. □ **declamation** *noun*; **declamatory** /-'klæm-/ *adjective.*

declaration /deklə'reɪʃ(ə)n/ *noun* declaring; emphatic, deliberate, or formal statement.

declare /dɪ'kleə/ *verb* (**-ring**) announce openly or formally; pronounce; (usually + *that*) assert emphatically; acknowledge possession of (dutiable goods, income, etc.); *Cricket* close (innings) voluntarily before team is out; *Cards* name trump suit. □ **declaratory** /-'klær-/ *adjective.*

declassify /diː'klæsɪfaɪ/ *verb* (**-ies, -ied**) declare (information etc.) to be no longer secret. □ **declassification** *noun.*

declension /dɪ'klenʃ(ə)n/ *noun Grammar* variation of form of noun etc., to show grammatical case; class of nouns with same inflections; deterioration.

declination /deklɪ'neɪʃ(ə)n/ *noun* downward bend; angular distance north or south of celestial equator; deviation of compass needle from true north.

decline /dɪ'klaɪn/ ● *verb* (**-ning**) deteriorate, lose strength or vigour; decrease; refuse; slope or bend downwards; *Grammar* state case forms of (noun etc.). ● *noun* deterioration.

declivity /dɪ'klɪvɪtɪ/ *noun* (*plural* **-ies**) downward slope.

declutch /diː'klʌtʃ/ *verb* disengage clutch of motor vehicle.

decode /diː'kəʊd/ *verb* (**-ding**) decipher. □ **decoder** *noun.*

decoke /diː'kəʊk/ *verb* (**-king**) *colloquial* decarbonize.

décolletage /deɪkɒl'tɑːʒ/ *noun* low neckline of woman's dress. [French]

décolleté /deɪˈkɒlteɪ/ adjective (also **décolletée**) having low neckline. [French]

decompose /diːkəmˈpəʊz/ verb (**-sing**) rot; separate into elements. □ **decomposition** /diːkɒmpəˈzɪʃ(ə)n/ noun.

decompress /diːkəmˈpres/ verb subject to decompression.

decompression /diːkəmˈpreʃ(ə)n/ noun release from compression; reduction of pressure on deep-sea diver etc. □ **decompression chamber** enclosed space for decompression.

decongestant /diːkənˈdʒest(ə)nt/ noun medicine etc. that relieves nasal congestion.

decontaminate /diːkənˈtæmɪneɪt/ verb (**-ting**) remove contamination from. □ **decontamination** noun.

décor /ˈdeɪkɔː/ noun furnishings and decoration of room, stage, etc.

decorate /ˈdekəreɪt/ verb (**-ting**) adorn; paint, wallpaper, etc. (room etc.); give medal or award to.

decoration noun decorating; thing that decorates; medal etc.; (in plural) flags etc. put up on festive occasion.

decorative /ˈdekərətɪv/ adjective pleasing in appearance. □ **decoratively** adverb.

decorator noun person who decorates for a living.

decorous /ˈdekərəs/ adjective having or showing decorum. □ **decorously** adverb.

decorum /dɪˈkɔːrəm/ noun polite dignified behaviour.

decoy ● noun /ˈdiːkɔɪ/ thing or person used as lure; bait, enticement. ● verb /dɪˈkɔɪ/ lure by decoy.

decrease ● verb /dɪˈkriːs/ (**-sing**) make or become smaller or fewer. ● noun /ˈdiːkriːs/ decreasing; amount of this.

decree /dɪˈkriː/ ● noun official legal order; legal decision. ● verb (**-ees**, **-eed**) ordain by decree. □ **decree absolute** final order for completion of divorce; **decree nisi** /ˈnaɪsaɪ/ provisional order for divorce.

decrepit /dɪˈkrepɪt/ adjective weakened by age or infirmity; dilapidated. □ **decrepitude** noun.

decry /dɪˈkraɪ/ verb (**-ies**, **-ied**) disparage.

dedicate /ˈdedɪkeɪt/ verb (**-ting**) (often + *to*) devote (oneself) to a purpose etc.; address (book etc.) to friend or patron etc.; devote (building etc.) to saint etc.; (as **dedicated** adjective) having single-minded loyalty. □ **dedicatory** adjective.

dedication noun dedicating; words with which book is dedicated.

deduce /dɪˈdjuːs/ verb (**-cing**) (often + *from*) infer logically. □ **deducible** adjective.

deduct /dɪˈdʌkt/ verb (often + *from*) subtract; take away; withhold.

deductible adjective that may be deducted esp. from tax or taxable income.

deduction /dɪˈdʌkʃ(ə)n/ noun deducting; amount deducted; inference from general to particular.

deductive adjective of or reasoning by deduction.

deed noun thing done; action; legal document. □ **deed of covenant** agreement to pay regular sum, esp. to charity; **deed poll** deed made by one party only, esp. to change one's name.

deem verb formal consider, judge.

deep ● adjective extending far down or in; to or at specified depth; low-pitched; intense; profound; (+ *in*) fully absorbed, overwhelmed. ● adverb deeply; far down or in. ● noun deep state; (**the deep**) poetical the sea. □ **deep-freeze** noun freezer, verb freeze or store in freezer; **deep-fry** fry with fat covering food. □ **deepen** verb; **deeply** adverb.

deer noun (plural same) 4-hoofed grazing animal, male usually with antlers. □ **deerstalker** cloth peaked cap with ear-flaps.

deface /dɪˈfeɪs/ verb (**-cing**) disfigure. □ **defacement** noun.

de facto /deɪ ˈfæktəʊ/ ● adjective existing in fact, whether by right or not. ● adverb in fact.

defame /dɪˈfeɪm/ verb (**-ming**) attack good name of. □ **defamation** /defəˈmeɪʃ(ə)n/ noun; **defamatory** /-ˈfæm-/ adjective.

default /dɪˈfɔːlt/ ● noun failure to act, appear, or pay; option selected by computer program etc. unless given alternative instruction. ● verb fail to fulfil obligations. □ **by default** because of lack of an alternative etc. □ **defaulter** noun.

defeat /dɪˈfiːt/ ● verb overcome in battle, contest, etc.; frustrate, baffle. ● noun defeating, being defeated.

defeatism noun readiness to accept defeat. □ **defeatist** noun & adjective.

defecate /ˈdiːfɪkeɪt/ verb (**-ting**) evacuate the bowels. □ **defecation** noun.

defect ● noun /ˈdiːfekt/ shortcoming; fault. ● verb /dɪˈfekt/ desert one's country, cause, etc., for another. □ **defection** noun; **defector** noun.

defective /dɪˈfektɪv/ adjective faulty; imperfect. □ **defectiveness** noun.

defence /dɪˈfens/ noun (US **defense**) (means of) defending; justification; defendant's case or counsel; players in defending position; (in plural) fortifications. □ **defenceless** adjective.

defend /dɪˈfend/ verb (often + *against*, *from*) resist attack made on; protect; uphold by argument; Law conduct defence (of); compete to retain (title). □ **defender** noun.

defendant noun person accused or sued in court of law.

defense US = DEFENCE.

defensible /dɪˈfensɪb(ə)l/ adjective able to be defended or justified.

defensive /dɪˈfensɪv/ adjective done or intended for defence; over-reacting to criticism. □ **on the defensive** expecting criticism, ready to defend. □ **defensively** adverb; **defensiveness** noun.

defer[1] /dɪˈfɜː/ verb (**-rr-**) postpone. □ **deferment** noun.

defer[2] /dɪˈfɜː/ verb (**-rr-**) (+ *to*) yield or make concessions.

deference /ˈdefərəns/ noun respectful conduct; compliance with another's wishes. □ **in deference to** out of respect for.

deferential /defəˈrenʃ(ə)l/ adjective respectful. □ **deferentially** adverb.

defiance /dɪˈfaɪəns/ noun open disobedience; bold resistance. □ **defiant** adjective; **defiantly** adverb.

deficiency /dɪˈfɪʃənsɪ/ noun (plural **-ies**) being deficient; (usually + *of*) lack or shortage; thing lacking; deficit. □ **deficiency disease** disease caused by lack of essential element in diet.

deficient /dɪˈfɪʃ(ə)nt/ adjective (often + *in*) incomplete or insufficient.

deficit /ˈdefɪsɪt/ noun amount by which total falls short; excess of liabilities over assets.

defile[1] /dɪˈfaɪl/ verb (**-ling**) make dirty; pollute; profane. □ **defilement** noun.

defile[2] /dɪˈfaɪl/ ● noun narrow gorge or pass. ● verb (**-ling**) march in file.

define /dɪˈfaɪn/ verb (**-ning**) give meaning of; describe scope of; outline; mark out the boundary of. □ **definable** adjective.

definite /ˈdefɪnɪt/ adjective certain; clearly defined; precise. □ **definite article** the word (*the* in English) placed before a noun and implying a specific object, person, or idea. □ **definitely** adverb.

definition /defɪ'nɪʃ(ə)n/ *noun* defining; statement of meaning of word etc.; distinctness in outline.

definitive /dɪ'fɪnɪtɪv/ *adjective* decisive, unconditional, final; most authoritative.

deflate /dɪ'fleɪt/ *verb* (**-ting**) let air out of (tyre etc.); (cause to) lose confidence; subject (economy) to deflation.

deflation *noun* deflating; reduction of money in circulation to combat inflation. □ **deflationary** *adjective*.

deflect /dɪ'flekt/ *verb* bend or turn aside from purpose or course; (often + *from*) (cause to) deviate. □ **deflection** *noun*.

deflower /di:'flaʊə/ *verb* deprive of virginity; ravage.

defoliate /di:'fəʊlɪeɪt/ *verb* (**-ting**) destroy leaves of. □ **defoliant** *noun*; **defoliation** *noun*.

deforest /di:'fɒrɪst/ *verb* clear of forests. □ **deforestation** *noun*.

deform /dɪ'fɔːm/ *verb* (often as **deformed** *adjective*) make ugly or misshapen, disfigure. □ **deformation** /di:-/ *noun*.

deformity /dɪ'fɔːmɪtɪ/ *noun* (*plural* **-ies**) being deformed; malformation.

defraud /dɪ'frɔːd/ *verb* (often + *of*) cheat by fraud.

defray /dɪ'freɪ/ *verb* provide money for (cost). □ **defrayal** *noun*.

defrock /di:'frɒk/ *verb* deprive (esp. priest) of office.

defrost /di:'frɒst/ *verb* remove frost or ice from; unfreeze; become unfrozen.

deft *adjective* dexterous, skilful. □ **deftly** *adverb*; **deftness** *noun*.

defunct /dɪ'fʌŋkt/ *adjective* no longer existing or in use; dead.

defuse /di:'fjuːz/ *verb* (**-sing**) remove fuse from (bomb etc.); reduce tension in (crisis etc.).

defy /dɪ'faɪ/ *verb* (**-ies**, **-ied**) resist openly; present insuperable obstacles to; (+ *to do*) challenge to do or prove something.

degenerate /dɪ'dʒenərət/ ● *adjective* having lost usual or good qualities; immoral. ● *noun* degenerate person etc. ● *verb* /-reɪt/ (**-ting**) become degenerate; get worse. □ **degeneracy** *noun*; **degeneration** *noun*.

degrade /dɪ'greɪd/ *verb* (**-ding**) (often as **degrading** *adjective*) humiliate; dishonour; reduce to lower rank. □ **degradation** /degrə'deɪʃ(ə)n/ *noun*.

degree /dɪ'griː/ *noun* stage in scale, series, or process; unit of measurement of angle or temperature; extent of burns; academic rank conferred by university etc.

dehumanize /di:'hjuːmənaɪz/ *verb* (also **-ise**) (**-zing** or **-sing**) remove human qualities from; make impersonal. □ **dehumanization** *noun*.

dehydrate /di:har'dreɪt/ *verb* (**-ting**) remove water from; make dry; (often as **dehydrated** *adjective*) deprive of fluids, make very thirsty. □ **dehydration** *noun*.

de-ice /di:'aɪs/ *verb* (**-cing**) remove ice from; prevent formation of ice on. □ **de-icer** *noun*.

deify /'di:ɪfaɪ/ *verb* (**-ies**, **-ied**) make god or idol of. □ **deification** *noun*.

deign /deɪn/ *verb* (+ *to do*) condescend.

deism /'di:ɪz(ə)m/ *noun* reasoned belief in existence of a god. □ **deist** *noun*; **deistic** /-'ɪstɪk/ *adjective*.

deity /'deɪɪtɪ/ *noun* (*plural* **-ies**) god or goddess; divine status or nature.

déjà vu /deɪʒɑː 'vuː/ *noun* illusion of having already experienced present situation. [French]

dejected /dɪ'dʒektɪd/ *adjective* sad, depressed. □ **dejectedly** *adverb*; **dejection** *noun*.

delay /dɪ'leɪ/ ● *verb* postpone; make or be late. ● *noun* delaying, being delayed; time lost by this.

delectable /dɪ'lektəb(ə)l/ *adjective* delightful.

delectation /di:lek'teɪʃ(ə)n/ *noun* enjoyment.

delegate ● *noun* /'delɪgət/ elected representative sent to conference; member of delegation etc. ● *verb* /'delɪgeɪt/ (**-ting**) (often + *to*) commit (power etc.) to deputy etc.; entrust (task) to another; send or authorize as representative.

delegation /delɪ'geɪʃ(ə)n/ *noun* group representing others; delegating, being delegated.

delete /dɪ'liːt/ *verb* (**-ting**) strike out (word etc.). □ **deletion** *noun*.

deleterious /delɪ'tɪərɪəs/ *adjective* harmful.

delft *noun* (also **delftware**) type of glazed earthenware.

deli /'delɪ/ *noun* (*plural* **-s**) *colloquial* delicatessen.

deliberate ● *adjective* /dɪ'lɪbərət/ intentional, considered; unhurried. ● *verb* /dɪ'lɪbəreɪt/ (**-ting**) think carefully; discuss. □ **deliberately** *adverb*.

deliberation /dɪlɪbə'reɪʃ(ə)n/ *noun* careful consideration or slowness.

deliberative /dɪ'lɪbərətɪv/ *adjective* (esp. of assembly etc.) of or for deliberation.

delicacy /'delɪkəsɪ/ *noun* (*plural* **-ies**) being delicate; choice food.

delicate /'delɪkət/ *adjective* fine in texture, quality, etc.; subtle, hard to discern; susceptible, tender; requiring tact. □ **delicately** *adverb*.

delicatessen /delɪkə'tes(ə)n/ *noun* shop selling esp. exotic cooked meats, cheeses, etc.

delicious /dɪ'lɪʃəs/ *adjective* highly enjoyable esp. to taste or smell. □ **deliciously** *adverb*.

delight /dɪ'laɪt/ ● *verb* (often as **delighted** *adjective*) please greatly; (+ *in*) take great pleasure in. ● *noun* great pleasure; thing that delights. □ **delightful** *adjective*; **delightfully** *adverb*.

delimit /dɪ'lɪmɪt/ *verb* (**-t-**) fix limits or boundary of. □ **delimitation** *noun*.

delineate /dɪ'lɪnɪeɪt/ *verb* (**-ting**) portray by drawing or in words. □ **delineation** *noun*.

delinquent /dɪ'lɪŋkwənt/ ● *noun* offender. ● *adjective* guilty of misdeed; failing in a duty. □ **delinquency** *noun*.

deliquesce /delɪ'kwes/ *verb* (**-cing**) become liquid; dissolve in moisture from the air. □ **deliquescence** *noun*; **deliquescent** *adjective*.

delirious /dɪ'lɪrɪəs/ *adjective* affected with delirium; wildly excited. □ **deliriously** *adverb*.

delirium /dɪ'lɪrɪəm/ *noun* disordered state of mind, with incoherent speech etc.; wildly excited mood. □ **delirium tremens** /'triːmenz/ psychosis of chronic alcoholism with tremors and hallucinations.

deliver /dɪ'lɪvə/ *verb* convey (letters, goods) to destination; (often + *to*) hand over; (often + *from*) save, rescue; set free; assist in giving birth or at birth of; utter (speech); launch or aim (blow etc.); (in full **deliver the goods**) *colloquial* provide or carry out what is required.

deliverance *noun* rescuing.

delivery /dɪ'lɪvərɪ/ *noun* (*plural* **-ies**) delivering; distribution of letters etc.; thing delivered; childbirth; manner of delivering.

dell *noun* small wooded valley.

delouse /di:'laʊs/ *verb* (**-sing**) rid of lice.

delphinium /del'fɪnɪəm/ *noun* (*plural* **-s**) garden plant with spikes of usually blue flowers.

delta /'deltə/ *noun* triangular alluvial tract at mouth of river; fourth letter of Greek alphabet (Δ, δ); fourth-class mark for work etc. □ **delta wing** triangular swept-back wing of aircraft.

delude /dɪ'luːd/ *verb* (**-ding**) deceive, mislead.

deluge /'deljuːdʒ/ ● *noun* flood; downpour of rain; overwhelming rush. ● *verb* (**-ging**) flood, inundate.

delusion /dɪ'luːʒ(ə)n/ *noun* false belief or hope. □ **delusive** *adjective*; **delusory** *adjective*.

de luxe /də 'lʌks/ *adjective* luxurious; superior; sumptuous.

delve *verb* (**-ving**) (often + *in, into*) research, search deeply; refute; *poetical* dig.

demagogue /'deməgɒg/ *noun* political agitator appealing to emotion. □ **demagogic** /-'gɒgɪk/ *adjective*; **demagogy** /-gɒgɪ/) *noun*.

demand /dɪ'mɑːnd/ ● *noun* insistent and peremptory request; desire for commodity; urgent claim. ● *verb* (often + *of, from, to do, that*) ask for insistently; require; (as **demanding** *adjective*) requiring effort, attention, etc. □ **demand feeding** feeding baby whenever it cries.

demarcation /diːmɑː'keɪʃ(ə)n/ *noun* marking of boundary or limits; trade union practice of restricting job to one union. □ **demarcate** /'diː-/ *verb* (**-ting**).

demean /dɪ'miːn/ *verb* (usually **demean oneself**) lower dignity of.

demeanour /dɪ'miːnə/ *noun* (*US* **demeanor**) bearing; outward behaviour.

demented /dɪ'mentɪd/ *adjective* mad.

dementia /dɪ'menʃə/ *noun* chronic insanity. □ **dementia praecox** /'priːkɒks/ schizophrenia.

demerara /demə'reərə/ *noun* light brown cane sugar.

demerit /diː'merɪt/ *noun* fault, defect.

demesne /dɪ'miːn/ *noun* landed property, estate; possession (of land) as one's own.

demigod /'demɪgɒd/ *noun* partly divine being; *colloquial* godlike person.

demijohn /'demɪdʒɒn/ *noun* large wicker-cased bottle.

demilitarize /diː'mɪlɪtəraɪz/ *verb* (also **-ise**) (**-zing** or **-sing**) remove army etc. from (zone etc.).

demi-monde /'demɪmɒnd/ *noun* class of women of doubtful morality; semi-respectable group. [French]

demise /dɪ'maɪz/ *noun* death; termination.

demisemiquaver /demɪ'semɪkweɪvə/ *noun* *Music* note equal to half semiquaver.

demist /diː'mɪst/ *verb* clear mist from (windscreen etc.). □ **demister** *noun*.

demo /'deməʊ/ *noun* (*plural* **-s**) *colloquial* demonstration, esp. political.

demobilize /diː'məʊbɪlaɪz/ *verb* (also **-ise**) (**-zing** or **-sing**) disband (troops etc.). □ **demobilization** *noun*.

democracy /dɪ'mɒkrəsɪ/ *noun* (*plural* **-ies**) government by the whole population, usually through elected representatives; state so governed.

democrat /'deməkræt/ *noun* advocate of democracy; (**Democrat**) member of US Democratic Party.

democratic /demə'krætɪk/ *adjective* of, like, or practising democracy; favouring social equality. □ **democratically** *adverb*; **democratize** /dɪ'mɒkrətaɪz/ *verb* (also **-ise**) (**-zing** or **-sing**); **democratization** *noun*.

demography /dɪ'mɒgrəfɪ/ *noun* study of statistics of birth, deaths, disease, etc. □ **demographic** /demə'græfɪk/ *adjective*.

demolish /dɪ'mɒlɪʃ/ *verb* pull down (building); destroy; refute; eat up voraciously. □ **demolition** /demə'lɪʃ(ə)n/ *noun*.

demon /'diːmən/ *noun* devil; evil spirit; forceful or skilful performer. □ **demonic** /dɪ'mɒnɪk/ *adjective*.

demoniac /dɪ'məʊnɪæk/ ● *adjective* frenzied; supposedly possessed by evil spirit; of or like demons. ● *noun* demoniac person. □ **demoniacal** /diːmə'naɪək(ə)l/ *adjective*.

demonology /diːmə'nɒlədʒɪ/ *noun* study of demons.

demonstrable /'demənstrəb(ə)l/ *adjective* able to be shown or proved. □ **demonstrably** *adverb*.

demonstrate /'demənstreɪt/ *verb* (**-ting**) show (feelings etc.); describe and explain by experiment etc.; prove truth or existence of; take part in public demonstration.

demonstration *noun* demonstrating; (+ *of*) show of feeling etc.; political public march, meeting, etc.; proof by logic, argument, etc.

demonstrative /dɪ'mɒnstrətɪv/ *adjective* showing feelings readily; affectionate; *Grammar* indicating person or thing referred to. □ **demonstratively** *adverb*; **demonstrativeness** *noun*.

demonstrator /'demənstreɪtə/ *noun* person making or taking part in demonstration.

demoralize /dɪ'mɒrəlaɪz/ *verb* (also **-ise**) (**-zing** or **-sing**) destroy morale of. □ **demoralization** *noun*.

demote /diː'məʊt/ *verb* (**-ting**) reduce to lower rank or class. □ **demotion** /-'məʊʃ(ə)n/ *noun*.

demotic /dɪ'mɒtɪk/ ● *noun* colloquial form of a language. ● *adjective* colloquial, vulgar.

demotivate /diː'məʊtɪveɪt/ *verb* (**-ting**) cause to lose motivation. □ **demotivation** *noun*.

demur /dɪ'mɜː/ ● *verb* (**-rr-**) (often + *to, at*) raise objections. ● *noun* (usually in negative) objection, objecting.

demure /dɪ'mjʊə/ *adjective* (**-r, -st**) quiet, modest; coy. □ **demurely** *adverb*.

demystify /diː'mɪstɪfaɪ/ *verb* (**-ies, -ied**) remove mystery from.

den *noun* wild animal's lair; place of crime or vice; small private room.

denarius /dɪ'neərɪəs/ *noun* (*plural* **-rii** /-rɪaɪ/) ancient Roman silver coin.

denationalize /diː'næʃənəlaɪz/ *verb* (also **-ise**) (**-zing** or **-sing**) transfer (industry etc.) from national to private ownership. □ **denationalization** *noun*.

denature /diː'neɪtʃə/ *verb* (**-ring**) change properties of; make (alcohol) unfit for drinking.

dendrology /den'drɒlədʒɪ/ *noun* study of trees. □ **dendrologist** *noun*.

denial /dɪ'naɪəl/ *noun* denying or refusing.

denier /'denjə/ *noun* unit of weight measuring fineness of silk, nylon, etc.

denigrate /'denɪgreɪt/ *verb* (**-ting**) sully reputation of. □ **denigration** *noun*; **denigratory** /-'greɪt-/ *adjective*.

denim /'denɪm/ *noun* twilled cotton fabric; (in *plural*) jeans etc. made of this.

denizen /'denɪz(ə)n/ *noun* (usually + *of*) inhabitant or occupant.

denominate /dɪ'nɒmɪneɪt/ *verb* (**-ting**) give name to, describe as, call.

denomination *noun* Church or religious sect; class of measurement or money; name, esp. for classification. □ **denominational** *adjective*.

denominator *noun* number below line in vulgar fraction; divisor.

denote /dɪ'nəʊt/ *verb* (**-ting**) (often + *that*) be sign of; indicate; be name for, signify. □ **denotation** /diːnə'teɪʃ(ə)n/ *noun*.

denouement /deɪ'nuːmɑ̃/ *noun* final resolution in play, novel, etc.

denounce /dɪ'naʊns/ *verb* (**-cing**) accuse publicly; inform against.

dense /dens/ *adjective* closely compacted; crowded together; stupid. □ **densely** *adverb*; **denseness** *noun*.

density /'densɪtɪ/ *noun* (*plural* **-ies**) denseness; quantity of mass per unit volume; opacity of photographic image.

dent ● *noun* depression in surface; noticeable adverse effect. ● *verb* make dent in.

dental /'dent(ə)l/ *adjective* of teeth or dentistry; (of sound) made with tongue-tip against front teeth. □ **dental floss** thread used to clean between teeth; **dental surgeon** dentist.

dentate /'denteɪt/ adjective toothed, notched.

dentifrice /'dentɪfrɪs/ noun tooth powder or tooth-paste.

dentine /'dentiːn/ noun hard dense tissue forming most of tooth.

dentist /'dentɪst/ noun person qualified to treat, extract, etc., teeth. □ **dentistry** noun.

denture /'dentʃə/ noun (usually in plural) removable artificial teeth.

denude /dɪ'njuːd/ verb (**-ding**) make naked or bare; (+ of) strip of (covering etc.). □ **denudation** /diː-/ noun.

denunciation /dɪnʌnsɪ'eɪʃ(ə)n/ noun denouncing.

deny /dɪ'naɪ/ verb (**-ies**, **-ied**) declare untrue or non-existent; repudiate; (often + to) withhold from; (**deny oneself**) be abstinent.

deodorant /diː'əʊdərənt/ noun substance applied to body or sprayed into air to conceal smells.

deodorize /diː'əʊdəraɪz/ verb (also **-ise**) (**-zing** or **-sing**) remove smell of. □ **deodorization** noun.

deoxyribonucleic acid /diːɒksɪraɪbəʊnjuː'kleɪk/ see DNA.

dep. abbreviation departs; deputy.

depart /dɪ'pɑːt/ verb (often + from) go away, leave; (usually + for) set out; (usually + from) deviate. □ **depart this life** formal die.

departed ● adjective bygone. ● noun (**the departed**) euphemistic dead person or people.

department noun separate part of complex whole, esp. branch of administration; division of school etc.; section of large store; area of expertise; French administrative district. □ **department store** shop with many departments. □ **departmental** /diːpɑːt'ment(ə)l/ adjective.

departure /dɪ'pɑːtʃə/ noun departing; new course of action etc.

depend /dɪ'pend/ verb (often + on, upon) be controlled or determined by; (+ on, upon) need, rely on.

dependable adjective reliable. □ **dependability** noun.

dependant noun person supported, esp. financially, by another.

dependence noun depending, being dependent; reliance.

dependency noun (plural **-ies**) country etc. controlled by another; dependence (on drugs etc.).

dependent adjective (usually + on) depending; unable to do without (esp. drug); maintained at another's cost; (of clause etc.) subordinate to word etc.

depict /dɪ'pɪkt/ verb represent in painting etc.; describe. □ **depiction** noun.

depilate /'depɪleɪt/ verb (**-ting**) remove hair from. □ **depilation** noun; **depilator** noun.

depilatory /dɪ'pɪlətərɪ/ ● adjective that removes unwanted hair. ● noun (plural **-ies**) depilatory substance.

deplete /dɪ'pliːt/ verb (**-ting**) (esp. as **depleted** adjective) reduce in numbers, quantity, etc.; exhaust. □ **depletion** noun.

deplorable /dɪ'plɔːrəb(ə)l/ adjective exceedingly bad. □ **deplorably** adverb.

deplore /dɪ'plɔː/ verb (**-ring**) find deplorable; regret.

deploy /dɪ'plɔɪ/ verb spread out (troops) into line for action; use (arguments etc.) effectively. □ **deployment** noun.

deponent /dɪ'pəʊnənt/ noun person making deposition under oath.

depopulate /diː'pɒpjʊleɪt/ verb (**-ting**) reduce population of. □ **depopulation** noun.

deport /dɪ'pɔːt/ verb remove forcibly or exile to another country; (**deport oneself**) behave (well, badly, etc.). □ **deportation** /diː-/ noun.

deportee /diːpɔː'tiː/ noun deported person.

deportment noun bearing, demeanour.

depose /dɪ'pəʊz/ verb (**-sing**) remove from office; dethrone; (usually + to, that) testify on oath.

deposit /dɪ'pɒzɪt/ ● noun money in bank account; thing stored for safe keeping; payment as pledge or first instalment; returnable sum paid on hire of item; layer of accumulated matter. ● verb (**-t-**) entrust for keeping; pay or leave as deposit; put or lay down. □ **deposit account** bank account that pays interest but is not usually immediately accessible.

depositary /dɪ'pɒzɪtərɪ/ noun (plural **-ies**) person to whom thing is entrusted.

deposition /depə'zɪʃ(ə)n/ noun deposing; sworn evidence; giving of this; depositing.

depositor noun person who deposits money, property, etc.

depository /dɪ'pɒzɪtərɪ/ noun (plural **-ies**) storehouse; store (of wisdom etc.); depositary.

depot /'depəʊ/ noun military storehouse or headquarters; place where vehicles, e.g. buses, are kept; goods yard.

deprave /dɪ'preɪv/ verb (**-ving**) corrupt morally.

depravity /dɪ'prævɪtɪ/ noun (plural **-ies**) moral corruption; wickedness.

deprecate /'deprɪkeɪt/ verb (**-ting**) express disapproval of. □ **deprecation** noun; **deprecatory** /-'keɪtərɪ/ adjective.

■ **Usage** Deprecate is often confused with depreciate.

depreciate /dɪ'priːʃɪeɪt/ verb (**-ting**) diminish in value; belittle. □ **depreciatory** /-ʃətərɪ/ adjective.

■ **Usage** Depreciate is often confused with deprecate.

depreciation noun depreciating; decline in value.

depredation /deprɪ'deɪʃ(ə)n/ noun (usually in plural) despoiling, ravaging.

depress /dɪ'pres/ verb make dispirited; lower; push down; reduce activity of (esp. trade); (as **depressed** adjective) suffering from depression. □ **depressing** adjective; **depressingly** adverb.

depressant ● adjective reducing activity, esp. of body function. ● noun depressant substance.

depression /dɪ'preʃ(ə)n/ noun extreme dejection; long slump; lowering of atmospheric pressure; hollow on a surface.

depressive /dɪ'presɪv/ ● adjective tending towards depression; tending to depress. ● noun chronically depressed person.

deprivation /deprɪ'veɪʃ(ə)n/ noun depriving, being deprived.

deprive /dɪ'praɪv/ verb (**-ving**) (usually + of) prevent from having or enjoying; (as **deprived** adjective) lacking what is needed, underprivileged.

Dept. abbreviation Department.

depth noun deepness; measure of this; wisdom; intensity; (usually in plural) deep, lowest, or inmost part, middle (of winter etc.), abyss, depressed state. □ **depth-charge** bomb exploding under water; **in depth** thoroughly.

deputation /depjʊ'teɪʃ(ə)n/ noun delegation.

depute /dɪ'pjuːt/ verb (**-ting**) (often + to) delegate (task, authority); authorize as representative.

deputize /'depjʊtaɪz/ verb (also **-ise**) (**-zing** or **-sing**) (usually + for) act as deputy.

deputy /'depjʊtɪ/ noun (plural **-ies**) person appointed to act for another; parliamentary representative in some countries.

derail /diː'reɪl/ verb cause (train etc.) to leave rails. □ **derailment** noun.

derange /dɪ'reɪndʒ/ verb (**-ging**) (usually as **deranged** adjective) make insane. □ **derangement** noun.

Derby /'dɑːbɪ/ noun (plural **-ies**) annual horse race at Epsom; similar race or sporting event.

derelict /'derɪlɪkt/ ● adjective dilapidated; abandoned. ● noun vagrant; abandoned property.

dereliction /derɪ'lɪkʃ(ə)n/ noun (usually + of) neglect (of duty etc.).

deride /dɪ'raɪd/ verb (**-ding**) mock. □ **derision** /-'rɪʒ-/ noun.

de rigueur /də rɪ'gɜː/ adjective required by fashion or etiquette.

derisive /dɪ'raɪsɪv/ adjective scoffing, ironical. □ **derisively** adverb.

derisory /dɪ'raɪsərɪ/ adjective (of sum offered etc.) ridiculously small; derisive.

derivation /derɪ'veɪʃ(ə)n/ noun deriving, being derived; origin or formation of word; tracing of this.

derivative /dɪ'rɪvətɪv/ ● adjective derived, not original. ● noun derived word or thing.

derive /dɪ'raɪv/ verb (**-ving**) (usually + from) get or trace from a source; (+ from) arise from; (usually + from) assert origin and formation of (word etc.).

dermatitis /dɜːmə'taɪtɪs/ noun inflammation of skin.

dermatology /dɜːmə'tɒlədʒɪ/ noun study of skin diseases. □ **dermatological** /-tə'lɒdʒ-/ adjective; **dermatologist** noun.

derogatory /dɪ'rɒgətərɪ/ adjective disparaging; insulting.

derrick /'derɪk/ noun crane; framework over oil well etc. for drilling machinery.

derris /'derɪs/ noun insecticide made from powdered root of tropical plant.

derv noun diesel fuel for road vehicles.

dervish /'dɜːvɪʃ/ noun member of Muslim fraternity vowed to poverty and austerity.

DES abbreviation historical Department of Education and Science.

descale /diː'skeɪl/ verb (**-ling**) remove scale from.

descant /'deskænt/ noun harmonizing treble melody above basic hymn tune etc.

descend /dɪ'send/ verb come, go, or slope down; sink; (usually + on) make sudden attack or visit; (+ to) stoop (to unworthy act); be passed on by inheritance. □ **be descended from** have as an ancestor.

descendant /dɪ'send(ə)nt/ noun person etc. descended from another.

descent /dɪ'sent/ noun act or way of descending; downward slope; lineage; decline, fall; sudden attack.

describe /dɪ'skraɪb/ verb (**-bing**) state appearance, characteristics, etc. of; (+ as) assert to be; draw or move in (curve etc.).

description /dɪ'skrɪpʃ(ə)n/ noun describing, being described; sort, kind.

descriptive /dɪ'skrɪptɪv/ adjective describing, esp. vividly.

descry /dɪ'skraɪ/ verb (**-ies, -ied**) catch sight of; discern.

desecrate /'desɪkreɪt/ verb (**-ting**) violate sanctity of. □ **desecration** noun; **desecrator** noun.

desegregate /diː'segrɪgeɪt/ verb (**-ting**) abolish racial segregation in. □ **desegregation** noun.

deselect /diː'sɪ'lekt/ verb reject (esp. sitting MP) in favour of another. □ **deselection** noun.

desensitize /diː'sensɪtaɪz/ verb (also **-ise**) (**-zing** or **-sing**) reduce or destroy sensitivity of. □ **desensitization** noun.

desert[1] /dɪ'zɜːt/ verb leave without intending to return; (esp. as **deserted** adjective) forsake, abandon; run away from military service. □ **deserter** noun Military; **desertion** noun.

desert[2] /'dezət/ noun dry barren, esp. sandy, tract. □ **desert island** (usually tropical) uninhabited island.

desertification /dɪzɜːtɪfɪ'keɪʃ(ə)n/ noun making or becoming a desert.

deserts /dɪ'zɜːts/ plural noun deserved reward or punishment.

deserve /dɪ'zɜːv/ verb (**-ving**) (often + to do) be worthy of (reward, punishment); (as **deserving** adjective) (often + of) worthy (esp. of help, praise, etc.). □ **deservedly** /-vɪdlɪ/ adverb.

desiccate /'desɪkeɪt/ verb (**-ting**) remove moisture from, dry out. □ **desiccation** noun.

desideratum /dɪzɪdə'rɑːtəm/ noun (plural **-ta**) something lacking but desirable.

design /dɪ'zaɪn/ ● noun (art of producing) sketch or plan for product; lines or shapes as decoration; layout; established form of product; mental plan; purpose. ● verb produce design for; be designer; intend; (as **designing** adjective) crafty, scheming. □ **have designs on** plan to take, seduce, etc.

designate ● verb /'dezɪgneɪt/ (**-ting**) (often + as) appoint to office or function; specify; (often + as) describe as. ● adjective /'dezɪgnət/ (after noun) appointed but not yet installed.

designation /dezɪg'neɪʃ(ə)n/ noun name or title; designating.

designedly /dɪ'zaɪnɪdlɪ/ adverb intentionally.

designer ● noun person who designs e.g. clothing, machines, theatre sets; draughtsman. ● adjective bearing label of famous fashion designer; prestigious. □ **designer drug** synthetic equivalent of illegal drug.

desirable /dɪ'zaɪərəb(ə)l/ adjective worth having or doing; sexually attractive. □ **desirability** noun.

desire /dɪ'zaɪə/ ● noun unsatisfied longing; expression of this; request; thing desired; sexual appetite. ● verb (**-ring**) (often + to do, that) long for; request.

desirous adjective (usually + of) desiring, wanting; hoping.

desist /dɪ'zɪst/ verb (often + from) cease.

desk noun piece of furniture with writing surface, and often drawers; counter in hotel, bank, etc.; section of newspaper office.

desktop noun working surface of desk; computer for use on ordinary desk. □ **desktop publishing** printing with desktop computer and high-quality printer.

desolate ● adjective /'desələt/ left alone; uninhabited; dreary, forlorn. ● verb /'desəleɪt/ (**-ting**) depopulate; devastate; (esp. as **desolated** adjective) make wretched. □ **desolately** /-lətlɪ/ adverb; **desolation** noun.

despair /dɪ'speə/ ● noun loss or absence of hope; cause of this. ● verb (often + of) lose all hope.

despatch = DISPATCH.

desperado /despə'rɑːdəʊ/ noun (plural **-es** or US **-s**) desperate or reckless criminal etc.

desperate /'despərət/ adjective reckless from despair; violent and lawless; extremely dangerous or serious; (usually + for) needing or desiring very much. □ **desperately** adverb; **desperation** noun.

despicable /'despɪkəb(ə)l, dɪ'spɪk-/ adjective contemptible. □ **despicably** adverb.

despise /dɪ'spaɪz/ verb (**-sing**) regard as inferior or contemptible.

despite /dɪ'spaɪt/ preposition in spite of.

despoil /dɪ'spɔɪl/ verb (often + of) plunder, rob. □ **despoliation** /-spəʊlɪ-/ noun.

despondent /dɪˈspɒnd(ə)nt/ *adjective* in low spirits, dejected. □ **despondence** *noun*; **despondency** *noun*; **despondently** *adverb*.

despot /ˈdespɒt/ *noun* absolute ruler; tyrant. □ **despotic** /-ˈspɒt-/ *adjective*.

despotism /ˈdespətɪz(ə)m/ *noun* rule by despot.

dessert /dɪˈzɜːt/ *noun* sweet course of a meal. □ **dessertspoon** medium-sized spoon for dessert, (also **dessertspoonful**) amount held by this.

destabilize /diːˈsteɪbɪlaɪz/ *verb* (also **-ise**) (**-zing** or **-sing**) make unstable; subvert (esp. foreign government). □ **destabilization** *noun*.

destination /destɪˈneɪʃ(ə)n/ *noun* place to which person or thing is going.

destine /ˈdestɪn/ *verb* (**-ning**) (often + *to, for, to do*) appoint; preordain; intend. □ **be destined to** be fated to.

destiny /ˈdestɪnɪ/ *noun* (*plural* **-ies**) fate; this as power.

destitute /ˈdestɪtjuːt/ *adjective* without food or shelter etc.; (usually + *of*) lacking. □ **destitution** /-ˈtjuː-/ *noun*.

destroy /dɪˈstrɔɪ/ *verb* pull or break down; kill; make useless; ruin financially; defeat.

destroyer /dɪˈstrɔɪə/ *noun* fast medium-sized warship; person or thing that destroys.

destruct /dɪˈstrʌkt/ *verb* destroy or be destroyed deliberately. □ **destructible** *adjective*.

destruction *noun* destroying, being destroyed.

destructive *adjective* destroying or tending to destroy; negatively critical.

desuetude /dɪˈsjuːɪtjuːd/ *noun formal* state of disuse.

desultory /ˈdezəltərɪ/ *adjective* constantly turning from one subject to another; unmethodical.

detach /dɪˈtætʃ/ *verb* (often + *from*) unfasten and remove; send (troops) on separate mission; (as **detached** *adjective*) impartial, unemotional, (of house) standing separate. □ **detachable** *adjective*.

detachment *noun* indifference; impartiality; detaching, being detached; troops etc. detached for special duty.

detail /ˈdiːteɪl/ ● *noun* small separate item or particular; these collectively; minor or intricate decoration; small part of picture etc. shown alone; small military detachment. ● *verb* give particulars of, relate in detail; (as **detailed** *adjective*) containing many details, itemized; assign for special duty. □ **in detail** item by item, minutely.

detain /dɪˈteɪn/ *verb* keep waiting, delay; keep in custody. □ **detainment** *noun*.

detainee /diːteɪˈniː/ *noun* person kept in custody, esp. for political reasons.

detect /dɪˈtekt/ *verb* discover; perceive. □ **detectable** *adjective*; **detection** *noun*; **detector** *noun*.

detective /dɪˈtektɪv/ *noun* person, usually police officer, investigating crime etc.

détente /deɪˈtɑ̃t/ *noun* relaxing of strained international relations. [French]

detention /dɪˈtenʃ(ə)n/ *noun* detaining, being detained. □ **detention centre** short-term prison for young offenders.

deter /dɪˈtɜː/ *verb* (**-rr-**) (often + *from*) discourage or prevent, esp. through fear.

detergent /dɪˈtɜːdʒ(ə)nt/ ● *noun* synthetic cleansing agent used with water. ● *adjective* cleansing.

deteriorate /dɪˈtɪərɪəreɪt/ *verb* (**-ting**) become worse. □ **deterioration** *noun*.

determinant /dɪˈtɜːmɪnənt/ *noun* decisive factor.

determinate /dɪˈtɜːmɪnət/ *adjective* limited; of definite scope or nature.

determination /dɪtɜːmɪˈneɪʃ(ə)n/ *noun* resolute purpose; deciding, determining.

determine /dɪˈtɜːmɪn/ *verb* (**-ning**) find out precisely; settle, decide; (+ *to do*) resolve; be decisive factor in.

determined *adjective* resolute. □ **be determined** (usually + *to do*) be resolved. □ **determinedly** *adverb*.

determinism /dɪˈtɜːmɪnɪz(ə)m/ *noun* theory that action is determined by forces independent of will. □ **determinist** *noun & adjective*; **deterministic** /-ˈnɪs-/ *adjective*.

deterrent /dɪˈterənt/ ● *adjective* deterring. ● *noun* thing that deters (esp. nuclear weapon).

detest /dɪˈtest/ *verb* hate, loathe. □ **detestation** /diːtesˈteɪʃ(ə)n/ *noun*.

detestable /dɪˈtestəb(ə)l/ *adjective* hated, loathed.

dethrone /diːˈθrəʊn/ *verb* (**-ning**) remove from throne or high regard. □ **dethronement** *noun*.

detonate /ˈdetəneɪt/ *verb* (**-ting**) set off (explosive charge); be set off. □ **detonation** *noun*.

detonator *noun* device for detonating.

detour /ˈdiːtʊə/ *noun* divergence from usual route; roundabout course.

detoxify /diːˈtɒksɪfaɪ/ *verb* (**-ies, -ied**) remove poison or harmful substances from. □ **detoxification** *noun*.

detract /dɪˈtrækt/ *verb* (+ *from*) diminish. □ **detraction** *noun*.

detractor *noun* person who criticizes unfairly.

detriment /ˈdetrɪmənt/ *noun* damage, harm; cause of this. □ **detrimental** /-ˈmen-/ *adjective*.

detritus /dɪˈtraɪtəs/ *noun* gravel, rock, etc. produced by erosion; debris.

de trop /də ˈtrəʊ/ *adjective* superfluous; in the way. [French]

deuce[1] /djuːs/ *noun* two on dice or cards; *Tennis* score of 40 all.

deuce[2] /djuːs/ *noun* (**the deuce**) (in exclamations) the Devil.

deuterium /djuːˈtɪərɪəm/ *noun* stable isotope of hydrogen with mass about twice that of the usual isotope.

Deutschmark /ˈdɔɪtʃmɑːk/ *noun* chief monetary unit of Germany.

devalue /diːˈvæljuː/ *verb* (**-ues, -ued, -uing**) reduce value of, esp. currency relative to others or to gold. □ **devaluation** *noun*.

devastate /ˈdevəsteɪt/ *verb* (**-ting**) lay waste; cause great destruction to; (often as **devastated** *adjective*) overwhelm with shock or grief. □ **devastation** *noun*.

devastating *adjective* crushingly effective; overwhelming; *colloquial* stunningly beautiful. □ **devastatingly** *adverb*.

develop /dɪˈveləp/ *verb* (**-p-**) make or become fuller, bigger, or more elaborate, etc.; bring or come to active, visible, or mature state; begin to exhibit or suffer from; build on (land); convert (land) to new use; treat (photographic film) to make image visible. □ **developing country** poor or primitive country. □ **developer** *noun*.

development *noun* developing, being developed; stage of growth or advancement; newly developed thing, event, etc.; area of developed land, esp. with buildings. □ **developmental** /-ˈment(ə)l/ *adjective*.

deviant /ˈdiːvɪənt/ ● *adjective* deviating from normal, esp. sexual, behaviour. ● *noun* deviant person or thing. □ **deviance** *noun*; **deviancy** *noun* (*plural* **-ies**).

deviate /ˈdiːvɪeɪt/ *verb* (**-ting**) (often + *from*) turn aside; diverge. □ **deviation** *noun*.

device /dɪˈvaɪs/ *noun* thing made or adapted for particular purpose; scheme, trick; heraldic design. □ **leave** (**person**) **to his** or **her own devices** leave (person) to do as he or she wishes.

devil /'dev(ə)l/ ● noun (usually **the Devil**) Satan; supreme spirit of evil; personified evil; mischievously clever person. ● verb (**-ll-**; US **-l-**) (usually as **devilled** adjective) cook with hot spices. □ **devil-may-care** cheerful and reckless; **devil's advocate** person who tests proposition by arguing against it.

devilish ● adjective of or like a devil; mischievous. ● adverb colloquial very. □ **devilishly** adverb.

devilment noun mischief; wild spirits.

devilry /'devəlrɪ/ noun (plural **-ies**) wickedness; reckless mischief; black magic.

devious /'diːvɪəs/ adjective not straightforward, underhand; winding, circuitous. □ **deviously** adverb; **deviousness** noun.

devise /dɪ'vaɪz/ verb (**-sing**) plan or invent; Law leave (real estate) by will.

devoid /dɪ'vɔɪd/ adjective (+ of) lacking, free from.

devolution /diːvə'luːʃ(ə)n/ noun delegation of power esp. to local or regional administration. □ **devolutionist** noun & adjective.

devolve /dɪ'vɒlv/ verb (**-ving**) (+ on, upon, etc.) (of duties etc.) pass or be passed to another; (+ on, to, upon) (of property) descend to.

devote /dɪ'vəʊt/ verb (**-ting**) (+ to) apply or give over to (particular activity etc.).

devoted adjective loving, loyal. □ **devotedly** adverb.

devotee /devəʊ'tiː/ noun (usually + of) enthusiast, supporter; pious person.

devotion /dɪ'vəʊʃ(ə)n/ noun (usually + to) great love or loyalty; worship; (in plural) prayers. □ **devotional** adjective.

devour /dɪ'vaʊə/ verb eat voraciously; (of fire etc.) engulf, destroy; take in greedily (with eyes or ears).

devout /dɪ'vaʊt/ adjective earnestly religious or sincere. □ **devoutly** adverb; **devoutness** noun.

dew noun condensed water vapour forming on cool surfaces at night; similar glistening moisture. □ **dewberry** fruit like blackberry; **dew-claw** rudimentary inner toe on some dogs; **dewdrop** drop of dew; **dew point** temperature at which dew forms. □ **dewy** adjective (**-ier, -iest**).

Dewey Decimal system /'djuːɪ/ noun system of library classification.

dewlap noun fold of loose skin hanging from throat esp. in cattle.

dexter /'dekstə/ adjective on or of the right-hand side (observer's left) of a heraldic shield etc.

dexterous /'dekstrəs/ adjective (also **dextrous**) skilful at handling. □ **dexterity** /-'ter-/ noun; **dexterously** adverb.

dhal /dɑːl/ noun (also **dal**) kind of split pulse from India; dish made with this.

dharma /'dɑːmə/ noun right behaviour; Buddhist truth; Hindu moral law.

dhoti /'dəʊtɪ/ noun (plural **-s**) loincloth worn by male Hindus.

dia. abbreviation diameter.

diabetes /daɪə'biːtiːz/ noun disease in which sugar and starch are not properly absorbed by the body.

diabetic /daɪə'betɪk/ ● adjective of or having diabetes; for diabetics. ● noun diabetic person.

diabolical /daɪə'bɒlɪk(ə)l/ adjective (also **diabolic**) of the Devil; inhumanly cruel or wicked; extremely bad. □ **diabolically** adverb.

diabolism /daɪ'æbəlɪz(ə)m/ noun worship of the Devil; sorcery.

diaconate /daɪ'ækənət/ noun office of deacon; deacons collectively.

diacritic /daɪə'krɪtɪk/ noun sign (e.g. accent) indicating sound or value of letter.

diacritical adjective distinguishing.

diadem /'daɪədem/ noun crown.

diaeresis /daɪ'ɪərəsɪs/ noun (plural **-reses** /-siːz/) (US **dieresis**) mark ('') over vowel to show it is sounded separately.

diagnose /daɪəg'nəʊz/ verb (**-sing**) make diagnosis of.

diagnosis /daɪəg'nəʊsɪs/ noun (plural **-noses** /-siːz/) identification of disease or fault from symptoms etc.

diagnostic /daɪəg'nɒstɪk/ ● adjective of or assisting diagnosis. ● noun symptom.

diagnostics noun (treated as plural) programs etc. used to identify faults in computing; (treated as singular) science of diagnosing disease.

diagonal /daɪ'ægən(ə)l/ ● adjective crossing a straight-sided figure from corner to corner, oblique. ● noun straight line joining two opposite corners. □ **diagonally** adverb.

diagram /'daɪəgræm/ noun outline drawing, plan, etc. of thing or process. □ **diagrammatic** /-grə'mætɪk/ adjective.

dial /'daɪəl/ ● noun plate with scale and pointer for measuring; numbered disc on telephone for making connection; face of clock or watch; disc on television etc. for selecting channel etc. ● verb (**-ll-**; US **-l-**) select (telephone number) with dial. □ **dialling tone** sound indicating that telephone caller may dial.

dialect /'daɪəlekt/ noun regional form of language (see panel).

dialectic /daɪə'lektɪk/ noun process or situation involving contradictions or conflict of opposites and their resolution; = DIALECTICS.

dialectical adjective of dialectic. □ **dialectical materialism** Marxist theory that historical events arise from conflicting economic (and therefore social) conditions. □ **dialectically** adverb.

dialectics noun (treated as singular or plural) art of investigating truth by discussion and logic.

dialogue /'daɪəlɒg/ noun (US **dialog**) conversation, esp. in a play, novel, etc.; discussion between people of different opinions.

dialysis /daɪ'æləsɪs/ noun (plural **-lyses** /-siːz/) separation of particles in liquid by differences in their ability to pass through membrane; purification of blood by this technique.

diamanté /dɪə'mɑnteɪ/ adjective decorated with synthetic diamonds etc.

Dialect

Everyone speaks a particular dialect: that is, a particular type of English distinguished by its vocabulary and its grammar. Different parts of the world and different groups of people speak different dialects: for example, Australians may say *arvo* while others say *afternoon*, and a London Cockney may say *I done it* while most other people say *I did it*. A dialect is not the same thing as an accent, which is the way a person pronounces words.

See also the panel at STANDARD ENGLISH.

diameter /daɪˈæmɪtə/ noun straight line passing through centre of circle or sphere to its edges; transverse measurement.

diametrical /daɪəˈmetrɪk(ə)l/ adjective (also **diametric**) of or along diameter; (of opposites) absolute. □ **diametrically** adverb.

diamond /ˈdaɪəmənd/ noun transparent very hard precious stone; rhombus; playing card of suit marked with red rhombuses. □ **diamond jubilee, wedding** 60th (or 75th) anniversary of reign or wedding.

diapason /daɪəˈpeɪz(ə)n/ noun compass of musical instrument or voice; either of two main organ stops.

diaper /ˈdaɪəpə/ noun US baby's nappy.

diaphanous /daɪˈæfənəs/ adjective (of fabric etc.) light and almost transparent.

diaphragm /ˈdaɪəfræm/ noun muscular partititon between thorax and abdomen in mammals; = DUTCH CAP; vibrating disc in microphone, telephone, loudspeaker, etc.; device for varying aperture of camera lens.

diapositive /daɪəˈpɒsɪtɪv/ noun positive photographic transparency.

diarist /ˈdaɪərɪst/ noun person famous for keeping diary.

diarrhoea /daɪəˈriːə/ noun (US **diarrhea**) condition of excessively loose and frequent bowel movements.

diary /ˈdaɪərɪ/ noun (plural **-ies**) daily record of events etc.; book for this or for noting future engagements.

Diaspora /daɪˈæspərə/ noun dispersion of the Jews; the dispersed Jews.

diatonic /daɪəˈtɒnɪk/ adjective Music (of scale etc.) involving only notes of prevailing key.

diatribe /ˈdaɪətraɪb/ noun forceful verbal criticism.

diazepam /daɪˈæzɪpæm/ noun tranquillizing drug.

dibble /ˈdɪb(ə)l/ ● noun (also **dibber** /ˈdɪbə/) tool for making small holes for planting. ● verb (**-ling**) plant with dibble.

dice ● noun (plural same) small cube marked on each face with 1–6 spots, used in games or gambling; game played with dice. ● verb (**-cing**) gamble, take risks; cut into small cubes.

dicey /ˈdaɪsɪ/ adjective (**dicier, diciest**) slang risky, unreliable.

dichotomy /daɪˈkɒtəmɪ/ noun (plural **-ies**) division into two.

dichromatic /daɪkrəʊˈmætɪk/ adjective of two colours.

dick[1] noun colloquial (esp. in **clever dick**) person.

dick[2] noun slang detective.

dickens /ˈdɪkɪnz/ noun (**the dickens**) (usually after how, what, why, etc.) colloquial the Devil.

dicky /ˈdɪkɪ/ ● noun (plural **-ies**) colloquial false shirt-front. ● adjective (**-ier, -iest**) slang unsound. □ **dicky bow** colloquial bow tie.

dicotyledon /daɪkɒtɪˈliːd(ə)n/ noun flowering plant with two cotyledons. □ **dicotyledonous** adjective.

Dictaphone /ˈdɪktəfəʊn/ noun proprietary term machine for recording and playing back dictation for typing.

dictate ● verb /dɪkˈteɪt/ (**-ting**) say or read aloud (material to be recorded etc.); state authoritatively; order peremptorily. ● noun /ˈdɪkt-/ (usually in plural) authoritative requirement of conscience etc. □ **dictation** noun.

dictator noun usually unelected absolute ruler; omnipotent or domineering person. □ **dictatorship** noun.

dictatorial /dɪktəˈtɔːrɪəl/ adjective of or like a dictator; overbearing. □ **dictatorially** adverb.

diction /ˈdɪkʃ(ə)n/ noun manner of enunciation.

dictionary /ˈdɪkʃənərɪ/ noun (plural **-ies**) book listing (usually alphabetically) and explaining words of a language, or giving corresponding words in another language; similar book of terms for reference.

dictum /ˈdɪktəm/ noun (plural **dicta** or **-s**) formal expression of opinion; a saying.

did past of DO[1].

didactic /dɪˈdæktɪk/ adjective meant to instruct; (of person) tediously pedantic. □ **didactically** adverb; **didacticism** /-sɪz(ə)m/ noun.

diddle /ˈdɪd(ə)l/ verb (**-ling**) colloquial swindle.

didgeridoo /dɪdʒərɪˈduː/ noun long tubular Australian Aboriginal musical instrument.

didn't /ˈdɪd(ə)nt/ did not.

die[1] /daɪ/ verb (**dying** /ˈdaɪɪŋ/) cease to live or exist; fade away; (of fire) go out; (+ on) cease to live or function while in the presence or charge of (person); (+ of, from, with) be exhausted or tormented. □ **be dying for, to** desire greatly; **die down** become less loud or strong; **die hard** (of habits etc.) die reluctantly; **die-hard** conservative or stubborn person; **die off** die one after another; **die out** become extinct, cease to exist.

die[2] /daɪ/ noun engraved device for stamping coins etc.; (plural **dice**) a dice. □ **die-casting** process or product of casting from metal moulds.

dielectric /daɪɪˈlektrɪk/ ● adjective not conducting electricity. ● noun dielectric substance.

dieresis US = DIAERESIS.

diesel /ˈdiːz(ə)l/ noun (in full **diesel engine**) internal-combustion engine in which heat produced by compression of air in the cylinder ignites the fuel; vehicle driven by or fuel for diesel engine. □ **diesel-electric** driven by electric current from diesel-engined generator; **diesel oil** petroleum fraction used in diesel engines.

diet[1] /ˈdaɪət/ ● noun habitual food; prescribed food. ● verb (**-t-**) keep to special diet, esp. to slim. □ **dietary** adjective; **dieter** noun.

diet[2] /ˈdaɪət/ noun legislative assembly; historical congress.

dietetic /daɪəˈtetɪk/ adjective of diet and nutrition.

dietetics plural noun (usually treated as singular) study of diet and nutrition.

dietitian /daɪəˈtɪʃ(ə)n/ noun (also **dietician**) expert in dietetics.

differ /ˈdɪfə/ verb (often + from) be unlike or distinguishable; (often + with) disagree.

difference /ˈdɪfrəns/ noun being different or unlike; degree of this; way in which things differ; remainder after subtraction; disagreement. □ **make a** (or **all the, no**, etc.) **difference** have significant (or very significant, no, etc.) effect; **with a difference** having new or unusual feature.

different /ˈdɪfrənt/ adjective (often + from, to) unlike, of another kind; separate, unusual. □ **differently** adverb.

■ **Usage** It is safer to use different from, but different to is common in informal use.

differential /dɪfəˈrenʃ(ə)l/ ● adjective constituting or relating to specific difference; of, exhibiting, or depending on a difference; Mathematics relating to infinitesimal differences. ● noun difference, esp. between rates of interest or wage-rates. □ **differential calculus** method of calculating rates of change, maximum or minimum values, etc.; **differential gear** gear enabling wheels to revolve at different speeds on corners.

differentiate /dɪfəˈrenʃɪeɪt/ verb (**-ting**) constitute difference between or in; distinguish; become different. □ **differentiation** noun.

difficult /ˈdɪfɪk(ə)lt/ adjective hard to do, deal with, or understand; troublesome.

difficulty /'dɪfɪkəltɪ/ *noun* (*plural* **-ies**) being difficult; difficult thing; hindrance; (often in *plural*) distress, esp. financial.

diffident /'dɪfɪd(ə)nt/ *adjective* lacking self-confidence. □ **diffidence** *noun*; **diffidently** *adverb*.

diffract /dɪ'frækt/ *verb* break up (beam of light) into series of dark and light bands or coloured spectra. □ **diffraction** *noun*; **diffractive** *adjective*.

diffuse ● *verb* /dɪ'fjuːz/ (**-sing**) spread widely or thinly; intermingle. ● *adjective* /dɪ'fjuːs/ spread out; not concentrated; not concise. □ **diffusible** *adjective*; **diffusive** *adjective*; **diffusion** *noun*.

dig ● *verb* (**-gg-**; *past & past participle* **dug**) (often + *up*) break up and turn over (ground etc.); make (hole etc.) by digging; (+ *up, out*) obtain by digging, find, discover; excavate; *slang* like, understand; (+ *in, into*) thrust, prod. ● *noun* piece of digging; thrust, poke; *colloquial* pointed remark; archaeological excavation; (in *plural*) lodgings. □ **dig in** *colloquial* begin eating; **dig oneself in** prepare defensive position.

digest ● *verb* /daɪ'dʒest/ assimilate (food, information, etc.). ● *noun* /'daɪdʒest/ periodical synopsis of current news etc.; summary, esp. of laws. □ **digestible** *adjective*.

digestion *noun* digesting; capacity to digest food.

digestive ● *adjective* of or aiding digestion. ● *noun* (in full **digestive biscuit**) wholemeal biscuit.

digger /'dɪgə/ *noun* person or machine that digs; *colloquial* Australian, New Zealander.

digit /'dɪdʒɪt/ *noun* any numeral from 0 to 9; finger or toe.

digital /'dɪdʒɪt(ə)l/ *adjective* of digits; (of clock, etc.) giving a reading by displayed digits; (of computer) operating on data represented by digits; (of recording) sound-information represented by digits for more reliable transmission. □ **digitally** *adverb*.

digitalis /dɪdʒɪ'teɪlɪs/ *noun* heart stimulant made from foxgloves.

digitize *verb* (also **ise**) (**-zing** or **-sing**) convert (computer data etc.) into digital form.

dignified /'dɪgnɪfaɪd/ *adjective* having or showing dignity.

dignify /'dɪgnɪfaɪ/ *verb* (**ies, -ied**) give dignity to.

dignitary /'dɪgnɪtərɪ/ *noun* (*plural* **-ies**) person of high rank or office.

dignity /'dɪgnɪtɪ/ *noun* (*plural* **-ies**) composed and serious manner; being worthy of respect; high rank or position.

digraph /'daɪgrɑːf/ *noun* two letters representing one sound, e.g. *sh* in *show*, or *ey* in *key*.

■ **Usage** *Digraph* is sometimes confused with *ligature*, which means 'two or more letters joined'.

digress /daɪ'gres/ *verb* depart from main subject. □ **digression** *noun*.

dike = DYKE.

dilapidated /dɪ'læpɪdeɪtɪd/ *adjective* in disrepair. □ **dilapidation** *noun*.

dilate /daɪ'leɪt/ *verb* (**-ting**) widen or expand; speak or write at length. □ **dilatation** *noun*; **dilation** *noun*.

dilatory /'dɪlətərɪ/ *adjective* given to or causing delay.

dilemma /daɪ'lemə/ *noun* situation in which difficult choice has to be made.

■ **Usage** *Dilemma* is sometimes also used to mean 'a difficult situation or predicament', but this is considered incorrect by some people.

dilettante /dɪlɪ'tæntɪ/ *noun* (*plural* **dilettanti** /-tɪ/ or **-s**) dabbler in a subject. □ **dilettantism** *noun*.

diligent /'dɪlɪdʒ(ə)nt/ *adjective* hard-working; showing care and effort. □ **diligence** *noun*; **diligently** *adverb*.

dill *noun* herb with aromatic leaves and seeds.

dilly-dally /dɪlɪ'dælɪ/ *verb* (**-ies, -ied**) *colloquial* dawdle, vacillate.

dilute /daɪ'ljuːt/ ● *verb* (**-ting**) reduce strength (of fluid) by adding water etc.; weaken in effect. ● *adjective* diluted. □ **dilution** *noun*.

diluvial /daɪ'luːvɪəl/ *adjective* of flood, esp. Flood in Genesis.

dim ● *adjective* (**-mm-**) not bright; faintly luminous or visible; indistinctly perceived or remembered; (of eyes) not seeing clearly; *colloquial* stupid. ● *verb* (**-mm-**) make or become dim. □ **dimly** *adverb*; **dimness** *noun*.

dime *noun* *US* 10-cent coin.

dimension /daɪ'menʃ(ə)n/ *noun* any measurable extent; (in *plural*) size; aspect. □ **dimensional** *adjective*.

diminish /dɪ'mɪnɪʃ/ *verb* make or become smaller or less; (often as **diminished** *adjective*) lessen reputation of (person), humiliate.

diminuendo /dɪmɪnjʊ'endəʊ/ *Music* ● *noun* (*plural* **-s**) gradual decrease in loudness. ● *adverb & adjective* decreasing in loudness.

diminution /dɪmɪ'njuːʃ(ə)n/ *noun* diminishing.

diminutive /dɪ'mɪnjʊtɪv/ ● *adjective* tiny; (of word or suffix) implying smallness or affection. ● *noun* diminutive word or suffix.

dimmer *noun* (in full **dimmer switch**) device for varying brightness of electric light.

dimple /'dɪmp(ə)l/ ● *noun* small hollow, esp. in cheek or chin. ● *verb* (**-ling**) produce dimples (in).

din ● *noun* prolonged loud confused noise. ● *verb* (**-nn-**) (+ *into*) force (information) into person by repetition; make din.

dinar /'diːnɑː/ *noun* chief monetary unit of (former) Yugoslavia and several Middle Eastern and N. African countries.

dine *verb* (**-ning**) eat dinner; (+ *on, upon*) eat for dinner; (esp. in **wine and dine**) entertain with food. □ **dining-car** restaurant on train; **dining-room** room in which meals are eaten.

diner *noun* person who dines; small dining-room; dining-car; *US* restaurant.

ding-dong /'dɪŋdɒŋ/ *noun* sound of chimes; *colloquial* heated argument.

dinghy /'dɪŋgɪ/ *noun* (*plural* **-ies**) small, often inflatable, boat.

dingle /'dɪŋg(ə)l/ *noun* deep wooded valley.

dingo /'dɪŋgəʊ/ *noun* (*plural* **-es**) wild Australian dog.

dingy /'dɪndʒɪ/ *adjective* (**-ier, -iest**) drab; dirty-looking. □ **dinginess** *noun*.

dinkum /'dɪŋkəm/ *adjective & adverb* (in full **fair dinkum**) *Australian & NZ colloquial* genuine(ly), honest(ly).

dinky /'dɪŋkɪ/ *adjective* (**-ier, -iest**) *colloquial* pretty, small and neat.

dinner /'dɪnə/ *noun* main meal, at midday or in the evening. □ **dinner-dance** formal dinner followed by dancing; **dinner jacket** man's formal evening jacket; **dinner lady** woman who supervises school dinners; **dinner service** set of matching crockery for dinner.

dinosaur /'daɪnəsɔː/ *noun* extinct usually large reptile.

dint ● *noun* dent. ● *verb* mark with dints. □ **by dint of** by force or means of.

diocese /'daɪəsɪs/ *noun* district under bishop's pastoral care. □ **diocesan** /daɪ'ɒsɪs(ə)n/ *adjective*.

diode /'daɪəʊd/ *noun* semiconductor allowing current in one direction and having two terminals; thermionic valve with two electrodes.

dioxide /daɪ'ɒksaɪd/ *noun* oxide with two atoms of oxygen.

Dip. *abbreviation* Diploma.

dip ● *verb* (**-pp-**) put or lower briefly into liquid etc.; immerse; go below a surface or level; decline slightly or briefly; slope or extend downwards; go briefly under water; (+ *into*) look cursorily into (book, subject, etc.); (+ *into*) put (hand etc.) into (container) to take something out, use part of (resources); lower or be lowered, esp. in salute; lower beam of (headlights). ● *noun* dipping, being dipped; liquid for dipping; brief bathe in sea etc.; downward slope or hollow; sauce into which food is dipped. □ **dipswitch** switch for dipping vehicle's headlights.

diphtheria /dɪf'θɪərɪə/ *noun* infectious disease with inflammation of mucous membrane esp. of throat.

diphthong /'dɪfθɒŋ/ *noun* union of two vowels in one syllable.

diplodocus /dɪ'plɒdəkəs/ *noun* (*plural* **-cuses**) huge long-necked plant-eating dinosaur.

diploma /dɪ'pləʊmə/ *noun* certificate of educational qualification; document conferring honour, privilege, etc.

diplomacy /dɪ'pləʊməsɪ/ *noun* management of international relations; tact.

diplomat /'dɪpləmæt/ *noun* member of diplomatic service; tactful person.

diplomatic /dɪplə'mætɪk/ *adjective* of or involved in diplomacy; tactful. □ **diplomatic bag** container for dispatching embassy mail; **diplomatic immunity** exemption of foreign diplomatic staff from arrest, taxation, etc.; **diplomatic service** branch of civil service concerned with representing a country abroad. □ **diplomatically** *adverb*.

diplomatist /dɪ'pləʊmətɪst/ *noun* diplomat.

dipper /'dɪpə/ *noun* diving bird; ladle.

dippy /'dɪpɪ/ *adjective* (**-ier, -iest**) *slang* crazy, silly.

dipsomania /dɪpsə'meɪnɪə/ *noun* alcoholism. □ **dipsomaniac** *noun*.

dipstick *noun* rod for measuring depth, esp. of oil in vehicle's engine.

dipterous /'dɪptərəs/ *adjective* two-winged.

diptych /'dɪptɪk/ *noun* painted altarpiece on two hinged panels.

dire *adjective* dreadful; ominous; *colloquial* very bad; urgent.

direct /daɪ'rekt/ ● *adjective* extending or moving in straight line or by shortest route, not crooked or circuitous; straightforward, frank; without intermediaries; complete, greatest possible. ● *adverb* in a direct way; by direct route. ● *verb* control; guide; (+ *to do, that*) order; (+ *to*) tell way to (place); address (letter etc.); (+ *at, to, towards*) point, aim, or turn; supervise acting etc. of (film, play, etc.). □ **direct current** electric current flowing in one direction only; **direct debit** regular debiting of bank account at request of payee; **direct-grant school** school funded by government, not local authority; **direct object** primary object of verbal action (see panel at OBJECT); **direct speech** words actually spoken, not reported (see panel); **direct tax** tax on income, paid directly to government. □ **directness** *noun*.

direction /daɪ'rekʃ(ə)n/ *noun* directing; (usually in *plural*) orders, instructions; point to, from, or along which person or thing moves or looks.

directional *adjective* of or indicating direction; sending or receiving radio or sound waves in one direction only.

directive /daɪ'rektɪv/ *noun* order from an authority.

directly ● *adverb* at once, without delay; presently, shortly; exactly; in a direct way. ● *conjunction colloquial* as soon as.

director *noun* person who directs, esp. for stage etc. or as member of board of company. □ **director-general** chief executive. □ **directorial** /-'tɔː-/ *adjective*; **directorship** *noun*.

directorate /daɪ'rektərət/ *noun* board of directors; office of director.

directory /daɪ'rektərɪ/ *noun* (*plural* **-ies**) book with list of telephone subscribers, inhabitants of town etc., members of profession, etc. □ **directory enquiries** telephone service providing subscriber's number on request.

dirge *noun* lament for the dead; dreary piece of music.

dirham /'dɪrəm/ *noun* monetary unit of Morocco and United Arab Emirates.

dirigible /'dɪrɪdʒɪb(ə)l/ ● *adjective* that can be steered. ● *noun* dirigible balloon or airship.

dirk *noun* short dagger.

dirndl /'dɜːnd(ə)l/ *noun* dress with close-fitting bodice and full skirt; gathered full skirt with tight waistband.

dirt *noun* unclean matter that soils; earth; foul or malicious talk; excrement. □ **dirt cheap** *colloquial* extremely cheap; **dirt track** racing track with surface of earth or cinders etc.

dirty /'dɜːtɪ/ ● *adjective* (**-ier, -iest**) soiled, unclean; sordid, obscene; unfair; (of weather) rough; muddy-looking. ● *adverb slang* very; in a dirty or obscene way. ● *verb* (**-ies, -ied**) make or become dirty. □ **dirty look** *colloquial* look of disapproval or disgust. □ **dirtiness** *noun*.

Direct Speech

Direct speech is the actual words of a speaker quoted in writing.

1 In a novel etc., speech punctuation is used for direct speech:

  a The words spoken are usually put in quotation marks.
  b Each new piece of speech begins with a capital letter.
  c Each paragraph within one person's piece of speech begins with quotation marks, but only the last paragraph ends with them.

2 In a script (the written words of a play, a film, or a radio or television programme):

  a The names of speakers are written in the margin in capital letters.
  b Each name is followed by a colon.
  c Quotation marks are not needed.
  d Any instructions about the way the words are spoken or about the scenery or the actions of the speakers (stage directions) are written in the present tense in brackets or italics.

For example:

  CHRISTOPHER: [Looks into box.] There's nothing in here.

disability /dɪsəˈbɪlɪtɪ/ noun (plural **-ies**) permanent physical or mental incapacity; lack of some capacity, preventing action.

disable /dɪˈseɪb(ə)l/ verb (**-ling**) deprive of an ability; (often as **disabled** adjective) physically incapacitate. □ **disablement** noun.

disabuse /dɪsəˈbjuːz/ verb (**-sing**) (usually + of) free from mistaken idea; disillusion.

disadvantage /dɪsədˈvɑːntɪdʒ/ ● noun unfavourable condition or circumstance; loss; damage. ● verb (**-ging**) cause disadvantage to. □ **at a disadvantage** in an unfavourable position. □ **disadvantageous** /dɪsædvənˈteɪdʒəs/ adjective.

disadvantaged adjective lacking normal opportunities through poverty, disability, etc.

disaffected /dɪsəˈfektɪd/ adjective discontented, alienated (esp. politically). □ **disaffection** noun.

disagree /dɪsəˈɡriː/ verb (**-ees**, **-eed**) (often + with) hold different opinion; not correspond; upset. □ **disagreement** noun.

disagreeable adjective unpleasant; bad-tempered. □ **disagreeably** adverb.

disallow /dɪsəˈlaʊ/ verb refuse to allow or accept; prohibit.

disappear /dɪsəˈpɪə/ verb cease to be visible or in existence or circulation etc.; go missing. □ **disappearance** noun.

disappoint /dɪsəˈpɔɪnt/ verb fail to fulfil desire or expectation of; frustrate. □ **disappointing** adjective; **disappointment** noun.

disapprobation /dɪsæprəˈbeɪʃ(ə)n/ noun disapproval.

disapprove /dɪsəˈpruːv/ verb (**-ving**) (usually + of) have or express unfavourable opinion. □ **disapproval** noun.

disarm /dɪˈsɑːm/ verb deprive of weapons; abandon or reduce one's own weapons; (often as **disarming** adjective) make less hostile, charm, win over. □ **disarmament** noun; **disarmingly** adverb.

disarrange /dɪsəˈreɪndʒ/ verb (**-ging**) put into disorder.

disarray /dɪsəˈreɪ/ noun disorder.

disassociate /dɪsəˈsəʊʃɪeɪt/ verb (**-ting**) dissociate. □ **disassociation** noun.

disaster /dɪˈzɑːstə/ noun sudden or great misfortune; colloquial complete failure. □ **disastrous** adjective; **disastrously** adverb.

disavow /dɪsəˈvaʊ/ verb disclaim knowledge or approval of or responsibility for. □ **disavowal** noun.

disband /dɪsˈbænd/ verb break up, disperse.

disbar /dɪsˈbɑː/ verb (**-rr-**) deprive of status of barrister. □ **disbarment** noun.

disbelieve /dɪsbɪˈliːv/ verb (**-ving**) refuse to believe; not believe; be sceptical. □ **disbelief** noun; **disbelievingly** adverb.

disburse /dɪsˈbɜːs/ verb (**-sing**) pay out (money). □ **disbursement** noun.

disc noun flat thinnish circular object; round flat or apparently flat surface or mark; layer of cartilage between vertebrae; gramophone record; Computing = DISK. □ **disc brake** one using friction of pads against a disc; **disc jockey** presenter of recorded popular music.

discard /dɪsˈkɑːd/ verb reject as unwanted; remove or put aside.

discern /dɪˈsɜːn/ verb perceive clearly with mind or senses; make out. □ **discernible** adjective.

discerning adjective having good judgement or insight. □ **discernment** noun.

discharge ● verb /dɪsˈtʃɑːdʒ/ (**-ging**) release, let go; dismiss from office or employment; fire (gun etc.); throw; eject; emit, pour out; pay or perform (debt, duty); relieve (bankrupt) of residual liability; release an electrical charge from; relieve of cargo; unload. ● noun /ˈdɪstʃɑːdʒ/ discharging, being discharged; matter or thing discharged; release of electric charge, esp. with spark.

disciple /dɪˈsaɪp(ə)l/ noun follower of a teacher or leader, esp. of Christ.

disciplinarian /dɪsɪplɪˈneərɪən/ noun enforcer of or believer in strict discipline.

disciplinary /dɪsɪˈplɪnərɪ/ adjective of or enforcing discipline.

discipline /ˈdɪsɪplɪn/ ● noun control or order exercised over people or animals; system of rules for this; training or way of life aimed at self-control or conformity; branch of learning; punishment. ● verb (**-ning**) punish; control by training in obedience.

disclaim /dɪsˈkleɪm/ verb disown, deny; renounce legal claim to.

disclaimer noun statement disclaiming something.

disclose /dɪsˈkləʊz/ verb (**-sing**) expose, make known, reveal. □ **disclosure** noun.

disco /ˈdɪskəʊ/ noun (plural **-s**) colloquial discothèque.

discolour /dɪsˈkʌlə/ verb (US **discolor**) cause to change from its usual colour; stain or become stained. □ **discoloration** noun.

discomfit /dɪsˈkʌmfɪt/ verb (**-t-**) disconcert; baffle; frustrate. □ **discomfiture** noun.

■ **Usage** Discomfit is sometimes confused with discomfort.

discomfort /dɪsˈkʌmfət/ noun lack of comfort; uneasiness of body or mind.

■ **Usage** As a verb, discomfort is sometimes confused with discomfit.

discompose /dɪskəmˈpəʊz/ verb (**-sing**) disturb composure of. □ **discomposure** noun.

disconcert /dɪskənˈsɜːt/ verb disturb composure of; fluster.

disconnect /dɪskəˈnekt/ verb break connection of or between; put (apparatus) out of action by disconnecting parts. □ **disconnection** noun.

disconnected adjective incoherent and illogical.

disconsolate /dɪsˈkɒnsələt/ adjective forlorn, unhappy; disappointed. □ **disconsolately** adverb.

discontent /dɪskənˈtent/ ● noun dissatisfaction; lack of contentment. ● verb (esp. as **discontented** adjective) make dissatisfied.

discontinue /dɪskənˈtɪnjuː/ verb (**-ues**, **-ued**, **-uing**) (cause to) cease; not go on with (activity).

discontinuous /dɪskənˈtɪnjʊəs/ adjective lacking continuity; intermittent. □ **discontinuity** /-kɒntɪˈnjuːɪtɪ/ noun.

discord /ˈdɪskɔːd/ noun disagreement, strife; harsh noise, clashing sounds; lack of harmony. □ **discordant** /-ˈkɔːdənt/ adjective.

discothèque /ˈdɪskətek/ noun nightclub etc. where pop records are played for dancing.

discount ● noun /ˈdɪskaʊnt/ amount deducted from normal price. ● verb /dɪsˈkaʊnt/ disregard as unreliable or unimportant; deduct amount from (price etc.); give or get present value of (investment certificate which has yet to mature). □ **at a discount** below nominal or usual price.

discountenance /dɪsˈkaʊntɪnəns/ verb (**-cing**) disconcert; refuse to approve of.

discourage /dɪsˈkʌrɪdʒ/ verb (**-ging**) reduce confidence or spirits of; dissuade, deter; show disapproval of. □ **discouragement** noun.

discourse ● noun /'dɪskɔːs/ conversation; lengthy treatment of theme; lecture, speech. ● verb /dɪs'kɔːs/ (**-sing**) converse; speak or write at length.

discourteous /dɪs'kɜːtɪəs/ adjective rude, uncivil. □ **discourteously** adverb; **discourtesy** noun (plural **-ies**).

discover /dɪs'kʌvə/ verb find or find out, by effort or chance; be first to find or find out in particular case; find and promote (little-known performer).

discovery noun (plural **-ies**) discovering, being discovered; person or thing discovered.

discredit /dɪs'kredɪt/ ● verb (**-t-**) cause to be disbelieved; harm good reputation of; refuse to believe. ● noun harm to reputation; cause of this; lack of credibility.

discreditable adjective bringing discredit, shameful.

discreet /dɪs'kriːt/ adjective (**-er**, **-est**) tactful, prudent; cautious in speech or action; unobtrusive. □ **discreetly** adverb; **discreetness** noun.

discrepancy /dɪs'krepənsɪ/ noun (plural **-ies**) difference; inconsistency.

discrete /dɪs'kriːt/ adjective separate; distinct.

discretion /dɪs'kreʃ(ə)n/ noun being discreet; prudence, judgement; freedom or authority to act as one thinks fit. □ **discretionary** adjective.

discriminate /dɪs'krɪmɪneɪt/ verb (**-ting**) (often + between) make or see a distinction; (usually + against, in favour of) treat badly or well, esp. on the basis of race, gender, etc. □ **discriminating** adjective; **discrimination** noun; **discriminatory** /-nətərɪ/ adjective.

discursive /dɪs'kɜːsɪv/ adjective rambling, tending to digress.

discus /'dɪskəs/ noun (plural **-cuses**) heavy disc thrown in athletic events.

discuss /dɪs'kʌs/ verb talk about; talk or write about (subject) in detail. □ **discussion** noun.

disdain /dɪs'deɪn/ ● noun scorn, contempt. ● verb regard with disdain; refrain or refuse out of disdain. □ **disdainful** adjective.

disease /dɪ'ziːz/ noun unhealthy condition of organism or part of organism; (specific) disorder or illness. □ **diseased** adjective.

disembark /dɪsɪm'bɑːk/ verb put or go ashore; get off aircraft, bus, etc. □ **disembarkation** /-embɑː-/ noun.

disembarrass /dɪsɪm'bærəs/ verb (usually + of) rid or relieve (of a load etc.); free from embarrassment. □ **disembarrassment** noun.

disembodied /dɪsɪm'bɒdɪd/ adjective (of soul etc.) separated from body or concrete form; without a body.

disembowel /dɪsɪm'baʊəl/ verb (**-ll-**; US **-l-**) remove entrails of. □ **disembowelment** noun.

disenchant /dɪsɪn'tʃɑːnt/ verb disillusion. □ **disenchantment** noun.

disencumber /dɪsɪn'kʌmbə/ verb free from encumbrance.

disenfranchise /dɪsɪn'fræntʃaɪz/ verb (**-sing**) deprive of right to vote, of citizen's rights, or of franchise held. □ **disenfranchisement** noun.

disengage /dɪsɪn'geɪdʒ/ verb (**-ging**) detach; loosen; release; remove (troops) from battle etc.; become detached; (as **disengaged** adjective) at leisure, uncommitted. □ **disengagement** noun.

disentangle /dɪsɪn'tæŋg(ə)l/ verb (**-ling**) free or become free of tangles or complications. □ **disentanglement** noun.

disestablish /dɪsɪ'stæblɪʃ/ verb deprive (Church) of state support; end the establishment of. □ **disestablishment** noun.

disfavour /dɪs'feɪvə/ noun (US **disfavor**) dislike; disapproval; being disliked.

disfigure /dɪs'fɪgə/ verb (**-ring**) spoil appearance of. □ **disfigurement** noun.

disgorge /dɪs'gɔːdʒ/ verb (**-ging**) eject from throat; pour forth (food, fluid, etc.).

disgrace /dɪs'greɪs/ ● noun shame, ignominy; shameful or very bad person or thing. ● verb (**-cing**) bring shame or discredit on; dismiss from position of honour or favour.

disgraceful adjective causing disgrace; shameful. □ **disgracefully** adverb.

disgruntled /dɪs'grʌnt(ə)ld/ adjective discontented; sulky.

disguise /dɪs'gaɪz/ ● verb (**-sing**) conceal identity of, make unrecognizable; conceal. ● noun costume, make-up, etc. used to disguise; action, manner, etc. used to deceive; disguised condition.

disgust /dɪs'gʌst/ ● noun strong aversion; repugnance. ● verb cause disgust in. □ **disgusting** adjective; **disgustingly** adverb.

dish ● noun shallow flat-bottomed container for food; food served in dish; particular kind of food; (in plural) crockery etc. to be washed etc. after a meal; dish-shaped object or cavity; colloquial sexually attractive person. ● verb make dish-shaped; colloquial outmanoeuvre, frustrate. □ **dish out** colloquial distribute, allocate; **dish up** (prepare to) serve meal.

disharmony /dɪs'hɑːmənɪ/ noun lack of harmony, discord.

dishearten /dɪs'hɑːt(ə)n/ verb cause to lose courage or confidence.

dishevelled /dɪ'ʃev(ə)ld/ adjective (US **disheveled**) ruffled, untidy.

dishonest /dɪs'ɒnɪst/ adjective fraudulent; insincere. □ **dishonestly** adverb; **dishonesty** noun.

dishonour /dɪs'ɒnə/ (US **dishonor**) ● noun loss of honour, disgrace; cause of this. ● verb disgrace (person, family, etc.); refuse to pay (cheque etc.).

dishonourable adjective (US **dishonorable**) causing disgrace; ignominious; unprincipled. □ **dishonourably** adverb.

dishy adjective (**-ier**, **-iest**) colloquial sexually attractive.

disillusion /dɪsɪ'luːʒ(ə)n/ ● verb free from illusion or mistaken belief, esp. disappointingly. ● noun disillusioned state. □ **disillusionment** noun.

disincentive /dɪsɪn'sentɪv/ noun thing that discourages, esp. from a particular line of action.

disincline /dɪsɪn'klaɪn/ verb (**-ning**) (usually as **disinclined** adjective) make unwilling. □ **disinclination** /-klɪ'neɪ-/ noun.

disinfect /dɪsɪn'fekt/ verb cleanse of infection. □ **disinfection** noun.

disinfectant ● noun substance that destroys germs etc. ● adjective disinfecting.

disinformation /dɪsɪnfə'meɪʃ(ə)n/ noun false information, propaganda.

disingenuous /dɪsɪn'dʒenjʊəs/ adjective insincere; not candid. □ **disingenuously** adverb; **disingenuousness** noun.

disinherit /dɪsɪn'herɪt/ verb (**-t-**) deprive of right to inherit; reject as one's heir. □ **disinheritance** noun.

disintegrate /dɪs'ɪntɪgreɪt/ verb (**-ting**) separate into component parts; break up; colloquial break down, esp. mentally. □ **disintegration** noun.

disinter /dɪsɪn'tɜː/ verb (**-rr-**) dig up (esp. corpse). □ **disinterment** noun.

disinterested /dɪs'ɪntrɪstɪd/ adjective impartial; uninterested. □ **disinterest** noun; **disinterestedly** adverb.

■ **Usage** The use of disinterested to mean 'uninterested' is common in informal use but is widely considered incorrect. The use of the noun disinterest to mean 'lack of interest' is also objected to, but it is rarely used in any other sense and the alternative *uninterest* is rare.

disjointed /dɪs'dʒɔɪntɪd/ *adjective* disconnected, incoherent.

disjunction /dɪs'dʒʌŋkʃ(ə)n/ *noun* separation.

disjunctive /dɪs'dʒʌŋktɪv/ *adjective* involving separation; (of a conjunction) expressing alternative.

disk *noun* flat circular computer storage device. □ **disk drive** mechanism for rotating disk and reading or writing data from or to it.

dislike /dɪs'laɪk/ ● *verb* (**-king**) have aversion to, not like. ● *noun* feeling of repugnance or not liking; object of this.

dislocate /'dɪsləkeɪt/ *verb* (**-ting**) disturb normal connection of (esp. a joint in the body); disrupt. □ **dislocation** *noun*.

dislodge /dɪs'lɒdʒ/ *verb* (**-ging**) disturb or move. □ **dislodgement** *noun*.

disloyal /dɪs'lɔɪəl/ *adjective* unfaithful; lacking loyalty. □ **disloyalty** *noun*.

dismal /'dɪzm(ə)l/ *adjective* gloomy; miserable; dreary; *colloquial* feeble, inept. □ **dismally** *adverb*.

dismantle /dɪs'mænt(ə)l/ *verb* (**-ling**) pull down, take to pieces; deprive of defences, equipment, etc.

dismay /dɪs'meɪ/ ● *noun* feeling of intense disappointment and discouragement. ● *verb* affect with dismay.

dismember /dɪs'membə/ *verb* remove limbs from; partition (country etc.). □ **dismemberment** *noun*.

dismiss /dɪs'mɪs/ *verb* send away; disband; allow to go; terminate employment of, esp. dishonourably; put out of one's thoughts; *Law* refuse further hearing to; *Cricket* put (batsman, side) out. □ **dismissal** *noun*.

dismissive *adjective* dismissing rudely or casually; disdainful. □ **dismissively** *adverb*.

dismount /dɪs'maʊnt/ *verb* get off or down from cycle or horseback etc.; remove (thing) from mounting.

disobedient /dɪsə'biːdɪənt/ *adjective* disobeying; rebellious. □ **disobedience** *noun*; **disobediently** *adverb*.

disobey /dɪsə'beɪ/ *verb* fail or refuse to obey.

disoblige /dɪsə'blaɪdʒ/ *verb* (**-ging**) refuse to help or cooperate with (person).

disorder /dɪs'ɔːdə/ *noun* confusion; tumult, riot; bodily or mental ailment. □ **disordered** *adjective*.

disorderly *adjective* untidy; confused; riotous.

disorganize /dɪs'ɔːɡənaɪz/ *verb* (also **-ise**) (**-zing** or **-sing**) throw into confusion or disorder; (as **disorganized** *adjective*) badly organized, untidy. □ **disorganization** *noun*.

disorientate /dɪs'ɔːrɪənteɪt/ *verb* (also **disorient**) (**-ting**) confuse (person) as to his or her bearings. □ **disorientation** *noun*.

disown /dɪs'əʊn/ *verb* deny or give up any connection with; repudiate.

disparage /dɪ'spærɪdʒ/ *verb* (**-ging**) criticize; belittle. □ **disparagement** *noun*.

disparate /'dɪspərət/ *adjective* essentially different, unrelated.

disparity /dɪ'spærɪtɪ/ *noun* (*plural* **-ies**) inequality, difference; incongruity.

dispassionate /dɪ'spæʃənət/ *adjective* free from emotion; impartial. □ **dispassionately** *adverb*.

dispatch /dɪ'spætʃ/ (also **despatch**) ● *verb* send off; perform (task etc.) promptly; kill; *colloquial* eat (food) quickly. ● *noun* dispatching, being dispatched; official written message, esp. military or political; promptness, efficiency. □ **dispatch box** case for esp. parliamentary documents; **dispatch rider** motorcyclist etc. carrying messages.

dispel /dɪ'spel/ *verb* (**-ll-**) drive away (esp. unwanted ideas or feelings); scatter.

dispensable /dɪ'spensəb(ə)l/ *adjective* that can be dispensed with.

dispensary /dɪ'spensərɪ/ *noun* (*plural* **-ies**) place where medicines etc. are dispensed.

dispensation /dɪspen'seɪʃ(ə)n/ *noun* distributing, dispensing; exemption from penalty, rule, etc.; ordering or management, esp. of world by Providence.

dispense /dɪ'spens/ *verb* (**-sing**) distribute; administer; make up and give out (medicine); (+ *with*) do without, make unnecessary.

dispenser *noun* person who dispenses something; device that dispenses selected amount at a time.

disperse /dɪ'spɜːs/ *verb* (**-sing**) go or send widely or in different directions, scatter; station at different points; disseminate; separate (light) into coloured constituents. □ **dispersal** *noun*; **dispersion** *noun*.

dispirit /dɪ'spɪrɪt/ *verb* (esp. as **dispiriting**, **dispirited** *adjectives*) make despondent.

displace /dɪs'pleɪs/ *verb* (**-cing**) move from its place; remove from office; oust, take the place of. □ **displaced person** refugee in war etc. or from persecution.

displacement *noun* displacing, being displaced; amount of fluid displaced by object floating or immersed in it.

display /dɪ'spleɪ/ ● *verb* show; exhibit. ● *noun* displaying; exhibition; ostentation; image shown on a visual display unit etc.

displease /dɪs'pliːz/ *verb* (**-sing**) offend; make angry or upset. □ **displeasure** /-'pleʒə/ *noun*.

disport /dɪ'spɔːt/ *verb* (also **disport oneself**) frolic, enjoy oneself.

disposable *adjective* that can be disposed of; designed to be discarded after one use.

disposal *noun* disposing of. □ **at one's disposal** available.

dispose /dɪ'spəʊz/ *verb* (**-sing**) (usually + *to*, *to do*) (usually in *passive*) incline, make willing; (in *passive*) tend; arrange suitably; (as **disposed** *adjective*) having a specified inclination; determine events. □ **dispose of** get rid of, deal with, finish.

disposition /dɪspə'zɪʃ(ə)n/ *noun* natural tendency; temperament; arrangement (of parts etc.).

dispossess /dɪspə'zes/ *verb* (usually + *of*) (esp. as **dispossessed** *adjective*) deprive; oust, dislodge. □ **dispossession** *noun*.

disproof /dɪs'pruːf/ *noun* refutation.

disproportion /dɪsprə'pɔːʃ(ə)n/ *noun* lack of proportion.

disproportionate *adjective* out of proportion; relatively too large or too small. □ **disproportionately** *adverb*.

disprove /dɪs'pruːv/ *verb* (**-ving**) prove (theory etc.) false.

disputable *adjective* open to question.

disputant *noun* person in dispute.

disputation /dɪspjuː'teɪʃ(ə)n/ *noun* debate, esp. formal; argument, controversy.

disputatious /dɪspjuː'teɪʃəs/ *adjective* argumentative.

dispute /dɪ'spjuːt/ ● *verb* (**-ting**) hold debate; quarrel; question truth or validity of; contend for; resist. ● *noun* controversy, debate; quarrel; disagreement leading to industrial action.

disqualify /dɪs'kwɒlɪfaɪ/ *verb* (**-ies**, **-ied**) make or pronounce (competitor, applicant, etc.) unfit or ineligible. □ **disqualification** *noun*.

disquiet /dɪs'kwaɪət/ ● *verb* make anxious. ● *noun* uneasiness, anxiety. □ **disquietude** *noun*.

disquisition /dɪskwɪ'zɪʃ(ə)n/ *noun* discursive treatise or discourse.

disregard /dɪsrɪˈgɑːd/ ● *verb* ignore, treat as unimportant. ● *noun* indifference, neglect.

disrepair /dɪsrɪˈpeə/ *noun* bad condition due to lack of repairs.

disreputable /dɪsˈrepjʊtəb(ə)l/ *adjective* having a bad reputation; not respectable. □ **disreputably** *adverb*.

disrepute /dɪsrɪˈpjuːt/ *noun* lack of good reputation; discredit.

disrespect /dɪsrɪˈspekt/ *noun* lack of respect. □ **disrespectful** *adjective*.

disrobe /dɪsˈrəʊb/ *verb* (**-bing**) *literary* undress.

disrupt /dɪsˈrʌpt/ *verb* interrupt continuity of; bring disorder to; break (thing) apart. □ **disruption** *noun*; **disruptive** *adjective*.

dissatisfy /dɪˈsætɪsfaɪ/ *verb* (**-ies**, **-ied**) (usually as **dissatisfied** *adjective*; often + *with*) fail to satisfy; make discontented. □ **dissatisfaction** /-ˈfæk-/ *noun*.

dissect /dɪˈsekt/ *verb* cut in pieces, esp. for examination or post-mortem; analyse or criticize in detail. □ **dissection** *noun*.

■ **Usage** *Dissect* is often wrongly pronounced /daɪˈsekt/ (and sometimes written with only one *s*) because of confusion with *bisect*.

dissemble /dɪˈsemb(ə)l/ *verb* (**-ling**) be hypocritical or insincere; conceal or disguise (a feeling, intention, etc.).

disseminate /dɪˈsemɪneɪt/ *verb* (**-ting**) scatter about, spread (esp. ideas) widely. □ **dissemination** *noun*.

dissension /dɪˈsenʃ(ə)n/ *noun* angry disagreement.

dissent /dɪˈsent/ ● *verb* (often + *from*) disagree, esp. openly; differ, esp. from established or official opinion. ● *noun* such difference; expression of this.

dissenter *noun* person who dissents; (**Dissenter**) Protestant dissenting from Church of England.

dissentient /dɪˈsenʃ(ə)nt/ ● *adjective* disagreeing with the established or official view. ● *noun* person who dissents.

dissertation /dɪsəˈteɪʃ(ə)n/ *noun* detailed discourse, esp. as submitted for academic degree.

disservice /dɪsˈsɜːvɪs/ *noun* harmful action.

dissident /ˈdɪsɪd(ə)nt/ ● *adjective* disagreeing, esp. with established government. ● *noun* dissident person.

dissimilar /dɪˈsɪmɪlə/ *adjective* not similar. □ **dissimilarity** /-ˈlærɪtɪ/ *noun* (*plural* **-ies**).

dissimulate /dɪˈsɪmjʊleɪt/ *verb* (**-ting**) dissemble. □ **dissimulation** *noun*.

dissipate /ˈdɪsɪpeɪt/ *verb* (**-ting**) dispel, disperse; squander; (as **dissipated** *adjective*) dissolute.

dissipation *noun* dissolute way of life; dissipating, being dissipated.

dissociate /dɪˈsəʊʃɪeɪt/ *verb* (**-ting**) disconnect or separate; become disconnected; (**dissociate oneself from**) declare oneself unconnected with. □ **dissociation** *noun*.

dissolute /ˈdɪsəluːt/ *adjective* lax in morals, licentious.

dissolution /dɪsəˈluːʃ(ə)n/ *noun* dissolving, being dissolved; dismissal or dispersal of assembly, esp. parliament; breaking up, abolition (of institution); death.

dissolve /dɪˈzɒlv/ *verb* (**-ving**) make or become liquid, esp. by immersion or dispersion in liquid; (cause to) disappear gradually; dismiss (assembly); put an end to, annul; (often + *in*, *into*) be overcome (by tears, laughter, etc.).

dissonant /ˈdɪsənənt/ *adjective* discordant, harsh-toned; incongruous. □ **dissonance** *noun*.

dissuade /dɪˈsweɪd/ *verb* (**-ding**) (often + *from*) discourage, persuade against. □ **dissuasion** /-ˈsweɪʒ(ə)n/ *noun*.

distaff /ˈdɪstɑːf/ *noun* cleft stick holding wool etc. for spinning by hand. □ **distaff side** female branch of family.

distance /ˈdɪst(ə)ns/ ● *noun* being far off; remoteness; space between two points; distant point; aloofness, reserve; remoter field of vision. ● *verb* (**-cing**) place or cause to seem far off; leave behind in race etc. □ **at a distance** far off; **keep one's distance** remain aloof.

distant *adjective* at specified distance; remote in space, time, relationship, etc.; aloof; abstracted; faint. □ **distantly** *adverb*.

distaste /dɪsˈteɪst/ *noun* (usually + *for*) dislike; aversion. □ **distasteful** *adjective*.

distemper[1] /dɪˈstempə/ ● *noun* paint for walls, using glue etc. as base. ● *verb* paint with distemper.

distemper[2] /dɪˈstempə/ *noun* catarrhal disease of dogs etc.

distend /dɪˈstend/ *verb* swell out by pressure from within. □ **distension** /-ˈsten-/ *noun*.

distich /ˈdɪstɪk/ *noun* verse couplet.

distil /dɪˈstɪl/ *verb* (US **distill**) (**-ll-**) purify or extract essence from (substance) by vaporizing and condensing it and collecting remaining liquid; extract gist of (idea etc.); make (whisky, essence, etc.) by distilling. □ **distillation** *noun*.

distiller *noun* person who distils, esp. alcoholic liquor.

distillery *noun* (*plural* **-ies**) factory etc. for distilling alcoholic liquor.

distinct /dɪˈstɪŋkt/ *adjective* (often + *from*) separate, different in quality or kind; clearly perceptible; definite, decided. □ **distinctly** *adverb*.

distinction /dɪˈstɪŋkʃ(ə)n/ *noun* discriminating, distinguishing; difference between things; thing that differentiates; special consideration or honour; excellence; mark of honour.

distinctive *adjective* distinguishing, characteristic. □ **distinctively** *adverb*; **distinctiveness** *noun*.

distingué /dɪˈstæŋgeɪ/ *adjective* having distinguished air, manners, etc. [French]

distinguish /dɪˈstɪŋgwɪʃ/ *verb* (often + *from*, *between*) see or draw distinctions; characterize; make out by listening or looking etc.; (usually **distinguish oneself**; often + *by*) make prominent. □ **distinguishable** *adjective*.

distinguished *adjective* eminent, famous; dignified.

distort /dɪˈstɔːt/ *verb* pull or twist out of shape; misrepresent (facts etc.); transmit (sound) inaccurately. □ **distortion** *noun*.

distract /dɪˈstrækt/ *verb* (often + *from*) draw away attention of; bewilder; (as **distracted** *adjective*) confused, mad, or angry; amuse, esp. to divert from pain etc.

distraction /dɪˈstrækʃ(ə)n/ *noun* distracting, being distracted; thing which distracts; amusement, relaxation; mental confusion; frenzy, madness.

distrain /dɪˈstreɪn/ *verb* (usually + *upon*) impose distraint (on person, goods, etc.).

distraint /dɪˈstreɪnt/ *noun* seizure of goods to enforce payment.

distrait /dɪˈstreɪ/ *adjective* inattentive; distraught. [French]

distraught /dɪˈstrɔːt/ *adjective* distracted with worry, fear, etc.; very agitated.

distress /dɪˈstres/ ● *noun* suffering caused by pain, grief, anxiety, etc.; poverty; *Law* distraint. ● *verb* cause distress to; make unhappy. □ **distressed** *adjective*; **distressing** *adjective*.

distribute /dɪˈstrɪbjuːt/ *verb* (**-ting**) give shares of; deal out; spread about; put at different points; arrange, classify. □ **distribution** /-ˈbjuː-/ *noun*; **distributive** *adjective*.

■ **Usage** *Distribute* is often pronounced /'dɪs-trɪbjuːt/ (with the stress on the *dis-*), but this is considered incorrect by some people.

distributor *noun* agent who supplies goods; device in internal-combustion engine for passing current to each spark plug in turn.

district /'dɪstrɪkt/ *noun* region; administrative division. □ **district attorney** (in the US) public prosecutor of district; **district nurse** nurse who makes home visits in an area.

distrust /dɪs'trʌst/ ● *noun* lack of trust; suspicion. ● *verb* have no confidence in. □ **distrustful** *adjective*.

disturb /dɪ'stɜːb/ *verb* break rest or quiet of; worry; disorganize; (as **disturbed** *adjective*) emotionally or mentally unstable.

disturbance *noun* disturbing, being disturbed; tumult, disorder, agitation.

disunion /dɪs'juːnɪən/ *noun* separation; lack of union.

disunite /dɪsjuː'naɪt/ *verb* (**-ting**) separate; divide. □ **disunity** /-'juː-/ *noun*.

disuse /dɪs'juːs/ *noun* state of no longer being used.

disused /dɪs'juːzd/ *adjective* no longer in use.

disyllable /daɪ'sɪləb(ə)l/ *noun* word or metrical foot of two syllables. □ **disyllabic** /-'læb-/ *adjective*.

ditch ● *noun* long narrow excavation esp. for drainage or as boundary. ● *verb* make or repair ditches; *slang* abandon, discard.

dither /'dɪðə/ ● *verb* hesitate; be indecisive; tremble, quiver. ● *noun* colloquial state of agitation or hesitation. □ **ditherer** *noun*; **dithery** *adjective*.

dithyramb /'dɪθɪræm/ *noun* ancient Greek wild choral hymn; passionate or inflated poem etc. □ **dithyrambic** /-'ræmbɪk/ *adjective*.

ditto /'dɪtəʊ/ *noun* (*plural* **-s**) the aforesaid, the same (in accounts, lists, etc., or *colloquial* in speech).

ditty /'dɪtɪ/ *noun* (*plural* **-ies**) short simple song.

diuretic /daɪjʊ'retɪk/ ● *adjective* causing increased output of urine. ● *noun* diuretic drug.

diurnal /daɪ'ɜːn(ə)l/ *adjective* in or of day; daily; occupying one day.

diva /'diːvə/ *noun* (*plural* **-s**) great woman opera singer.

divan /dɪ'væn/ *noun* low couch or bed without back or ends.

dive ● *verb* (**-ving**) plunge head foremost into water; (of aircraft) descend fast and steeply; (of submarine or diver) submerge; go deeper; (+ *into*) colloquial put one's hand into. ● *noun* act of diving; plunge; colloquial disreputable nightclub, bar, etc. □ **dive-bomb** bomb (target) from diving aircraft; **diving board** elevated board for diving from.

diver *noun* person who dives, esp. one who works under water; diving bird.

diverge /daɪ'vɜːdʒ/ *verb* (**-ging**) (often + *from*) depart from set course; (of opinions etc.) differ; take different courses; spread outward from central point. □ **divergence** *noun*; **divergent** *adjective*.

divers /'daɪvɜːz/ *adjective* archaic various, several.

diverse /daɪ'vɜːs/ *adjective* varied.

diversify /daɪ'vɜːsɪfaɪ/ *verb* (**-ies**, **-ied**) make diverse; vary; spread (investment) over several enterprises; (often + *into*) expand range of products. □ **diversification** *noun*.

diversion /daɪ'vɜːʃ(ə)n/ *noun* diverting, being diverted; recreation, pastime; alternative route when road is temporarily closed; stratagem for diverting attention. □ **diversionary** *adjective*.

diversity /daɪ'vɜːsɪtɪ/ *noun* variety.

divert /daɪ'vɜːt/ *verb* turn aside; deflect; distract (attention); (often as **diverting** *adjective*) entertain, amuse.

divest /daɪ'vest/ *verb* (usually + *of*) unclothe, strip; deprive, rid.

divide /dɪ'vaɪd/ ● *verb* (**-ding**) (often + *in, into*) separate into parts; split or break up; (often + *out*) distribute, deal, share; separate (one thing) from another; classify into parts or groups; cause to disagree; (+ *by*) find how many times number contains another; (+ *into*) be contained exact number of times; (of parliament) vote (by members entering either of two lobbies). ● *noun* dividing line; watershed.

dividend /'dɪvɪdend/ *noun* share of profits paid to shareholders, football pools winners, etc.; number to be divided.

divider *noun* screen etc. dividing room; (in *plural*) measuring compasses.

divination /dɪvɪ'neɪʃ(ə)n/ *noun* supposed foreseeing of the future, using special technique.

divine /dɪ'vaɪn/ ● *adjective* (**-r**, **-st**) of, from, or like God or a god; sacred; colloquial excellent. ● *verb* (**-ning**) discover by intuition or guessing; foresee; practise divination. ● *noun* theologian. □ **divining-rod** dowser's forked twig. □ **divinely** *adverb*.

diviner *noun* practitioner of divination; dowser.

divinity /dɪ'vɪnɪtɪ/ *noun* (*plural* **-ies**) being divine; god; theology.

divisible /dɪ'vɪzɪb(ə)l/ *adjective* capable of being divided. □ **divisibility** *noun*.

division /dɪ'vɪʒ(ə)n/ *noun* dividing, being divided; dividing one number by another; disagreement; one of parts into which thing is divided; administrative unit, esp. group of army units or of teams in sporting league. □ **divisional** *adjective*.

divisive /dɪ'vaɪsɪv/ *adjective* causing disagreement. □ **divisively** *adverb*; **divisiveness** *noun*.

divisor /dɪ'vaɪzə/ *noun* number by which another is to be divided.

divorce /dɪ'vɔːs/ ● *noun* legal dissolution of marriage; separation. ● *verb* (**-cing**) (usually as **divorced** *adjective*) (often + *from*) legally dissolve marriage of; separate by divorce; end marriage with by divorce; separate.

divorcee /dɪvɔː'siː/ *noun* divorced person.

divot /'dɪvət/ *noun* piece of turf dislodged by head of golf club.

divulge /daɪ'vʌldʒ/ *verb* (**-ging**) disclose (secret).

divvy /'dɪvɪ/ colloquial ● *noun* (*plural* **-ies**) dividend. ● *verb* (**-ies**, **-ied**) (often + *up*) share out.

Dixie /'dɪksɪ/ *noun* Southern States of US. □ **Dixieland** Dixie, kind of jazz.

dixie /'dɪksɪ/ *noun* large iron cooking pot.

DIY *abbreviation* do-it-yourself.

dizzy /'dɪzɪ/ ● *adjective* (**-ier**, **-iest**) giddy; dazed; causing dizziness. ● *verb* (**-ies**, **-ied**) make dizzy; bewilder. □ **dizzily** *adverb*; **dizziness** *noun*.

DJ *abbreviation* disc jockey; dinner jacket.

dl *abbreviation* decilitre(s).

D.Litt. *abbreviation* Doctor of Letters.

DM *abbreviation* Deutschmark.

dm *abbreviation* decimetre(s).

DNA *abbreviation* deoxyribonucleic acid (substance carrying genetic information in chromosomes).

do[1] /duː/ ● *verb* (3rd *singular present* **does** /dʌz/; *past* **did**; *past participle* **done** /dʌn/; *present participle* **doing**) perform, carry out; produce, make; impart; act, proceed; work at; be suitable, satisfy; attend to, deal with; fare; solve; colloquial finish; (as **done** *adjective*) finished, completely cooked; colloquial exhaust, defeat, kill; colloquial cater for; *slang* rob, swindle, prosecute, convict. ● *auxiliary verb used in questions and negative or emphatic statements and commands; as verbal substitute to avoid repetition*. ● *noun* (*plural* **dos** or

do's) *colloquial* elaborate party or other undertaking. □ **do away with** *colloquial* abolish, kill; **do down** *colloquial* swindle, overcome; **do for** be sufficient for, *colloquial* (esp. as **done for** *adjective*) destroy or ruin or kill, *colloquial* do housework for; **do in** *slang* kill, *colloquial* exhaust; **do-it-yourself** (to be) done or made by householder etc.; **do up** fasten, *colloquial* restore, repair, dress up; **do with** (after *could*) would appreciate, would profit by; **do without** forgo, manage without.

do² = DOH.

do. *abbreviation* ditto.

docile /'dəʊsaɪl/ *adjective* submissive, easily managed. □ **docility** /-'sɪl-/ *noun*.

dock¹ ● *noun* enclosed harbour for loading, unloading, and repair of ships; (usually in *plural*) range of docks with wharves, warehouses, etc. ● *verb* bring or come into dock; join (spacecraft) together in space, be thus joined. □ **dockyard** area with docks and equipment for building and repairing ships.

dock² *noun* enclosure in criminal court for accused.

dock³ *noun* weed with broad leaves.

dock⁴ *verb* cut short (tail); reduce or deduct (money, etc.).

docker *noun* person employed to load and unload ships.

docket /'dɒkɪt/ ● *noun* document listing goods delivered, jobs done, contents of package, etc. ● *verb* (**-t-**) label with or enter on docket.

doctor /'dɒktə/ ● *noun* qualified medical practitioner; holder of doctorate. ● *verb colloquial* tamper with, adulterate; castrate, spay.

doctoral *adjective* of the degree of doctor.

doctorate /'dɒktərət/ *noun* highest university degree in any faculty.

doctrinaire /dɒktrɪ'neə/ *adjective* applying theory or doctrine dogmatically.

doctrine /'dɒktrɪn/ *noun* what is taught; principle or set of principles of religious or political etc. belief. □ **doctrinal** /-'traɪn(ə)l/ *adjective*.

document ● *noun* /'dɒkjʊmənt/ something written etc. that provides record or evidence of events, circumstances, etc. ● *verb* /'dɒkjʊment/ prove by or support with documents. □ **documentation** *noun*.

documentary /dɒkjʊ'mentərɪ/ ● *adjective* consisting of documents; factual, based on real events. ● *noun* (*plural* **-ies**) documentary film etc.

dodder /'dɒdə/ *verb* tremble, totter, be feeble. □ **dodderer** *noun*; **doddery** *adjective*.

doddle /'dɒd(ə)l/ *noun colloquial* easy task.

dodecagon /dəʊ'dekəgən/ *noun* plane figure with 12 sides.

dodecahedron /dəʊdəkə'hi:drən/ *noun* solid figure with 12 faces.

dodge ● *verb* (**-ging**) move quickly to elude pursuer, blow, etc.; evade by cunning or trickery. ● *noun* quick evasive movement; trick, clever expedient.

dodgem /'dɒdʒəm/ *noun* small electrically powered car at funfair, bumped into others in enclosure.

dodgy *adjective* (**-ier, -iest**) *colloquial* unreliable, risky.

dodo /'dəʊdəʊ/ *noun* (*plural* **-s**) large extinct flightless bird.

DoE *abbreviation* Department of the Environment.

doe *noun* (*plural* same or **-s**) female fallow deer, reindeer, hare, or rabbit.

does 3rd singular present of DO¹.

doesn't /'dʌz(ə)nt/ does not.

doff *verb* take off (hat etc.).

dog ● *noun* 4-legged flesh-eating animal of many breeds akin to wolf etc.; male of this or of fox or wolf; *colloquial* despicable person; **(the dogs)** *colloquial* greyhound racing; mechanical device for gripping. ● *verb* (**-gg-**) follow closely; pursue, track. □ **dogcart** two-wheeled driving-cart with cross seats back to back; **dog-collar** *colloquial* clergyman's stiff collar; **dog days** hottest period of year; **dog-eared** (of book-page etc.) with worn corners; **dog-end** *slang* cigarette-end; **dogfight** fight between aircraft, rough fight; **dogfish** small shark; **doghouse** *US & Australian* kennel (**in the doghouse** *slang* in disgrace); **dog rose** wild hedge-rose; **dogsbody** *colloquial* drudge; **dog-star** Sirius; **dog-tired** tired out.

doge /dəʊdʒ/ *noun historical* chief magistrate of Venice or Genoa.

dogged /'dɒgɪd/ *adjective* tenacious. □ **doggedly** *adverb*.

doggerel /'dɒgər(ə)l/ *noun* poor or trivial verse.

doggo /'dɒgəʊ/ *adverb slang* □ **lie doggo** wait motionless or hidden.

doggy *adjective* of or like dogs; devoted to dogs. □ **doggy bag** bag for restaurant customer to take home leftovers; **doggy-paddle** elementary swimming stroke.

dogma /'dɒgmə/ *noun* principle, tenet; doctrinal system.

dogmatic /dɒg'mætɪk/ *adjective* imposing personal opinions; authoritative, arrogant. □ **dogmatically** *adverb*; **dogmatism** /'dɒgmətɪz(ə)m/ *noun*.

doh /dəʊ/ *noun* (also **do**) *Music* first note of scale in tonic sol-fa.

doily /'dɔɪlɪ/ *noun* (*plural* **-ies**) small lacy paper mat placed on plate for cakes etc.

doings /'du:ɪŋz/ *plural noun* actions, exploits; *slang* thing(s) needed.

Dolby /'dɒlbɪ/ *noun proprietary term* system used esp. in tape-recording to reduce hiss.

doldrums /'dɒldrəmz/ *plural noun* (usually **the doldrums**) low spirits; period of inactivity; equatorial ocean region of calms.

dole ● *noun* unemployment benefit; charitable (esp. niggardly) gift or distribution. ● *verb* (**-ling**) (usually + *out*) distribute sparingly. □ **on the dole** *colloquial* receiving unemployment benefit.

doleful /'dəʊlfʊl/ *adjective* mournful; dreary, dismal. □ **dolefully** *adverb*.

doll ● *noun* model of esp. infant human figure as child's toy; *colloquial* attractive young woman; ventriloquist's dummy. ● *verb* (+ *up*) *colloquial* dress smartly.

dollar /'dɒlə/ *noun* chief monetary unit in US, Australia, etc.

dollop /'dɒləp/ *noun* shapeless lump of food etc.

dolly *noun* (*plural* **-ies**) *child's word for* doll; movable platform for cine-camera etc.

dolman sleeve /'dɒlmən/ *noun* loose sleeve cut in one piece with bodice.

dolmen /'dɒlmən/ *noun* megalithic tomb with large flat stone laid on upright ones.

dolomite /'dɒləmaɪt/ *noun* mineral or rock of calcium magnesium carbonate.

dolphin /'dɒlfɪn/ *noun* large porpoise-like sea mammal.

dolt /dəʊlt/ *noun* stupid person. □ **doltish** *adjective*.

Dom *noun*: *title prefixed to names of some RC dignitaries and Carthusian and Benedictine monks.*

domain /də'meɪn/ *noun* area ruled over; realm; estate etc. under one's control; sphere of authority.

dome ● *noun* rounded vault as roof; dome-shaped thing. ● *verb* (**-ming**) (usually as **domed** *adjective*) cover with or shape as dome.

domestic /də'mestɪk/ ● *adjective* of home, household, or family affairs; of one's own country; (of animal) tamed; fond of home life. ● *noun* household servant.

domesticate /də'mestɪkeɪt/ *verb* (**-ting**) tame (animal) to live with humans; accustom to housework etc. □ **domestication** *noun*.

domesticity /dɒmə'stɪsɪtɪ/ *noun* being domestic; home life.

domicile /'dɒmɪsaɪl/ ● *noun* dwelling place; place of permanent residence. ● *verb* (**-ling**) (usually as **domiciled** *adjective*) (usually + *at*, *in*) settle in a place.

domiciliary /dɒmɪ'sɪlɪərɪ/ *adjective formal* (esp. of doctor's etc. visit) to or at person's home.

dominant /'dɒmɪnənt/ ● *adjective* dominating, prevailing. ● *noun Music* 5th note of diatonic scale. □ **dominance** *noun*.

dominate /'dɒmɪneɪt/ *verb* (**-ting**) command, control; be most influential or obvious; (of place) overlook. □ **domination** *noun*.

domineer /dɒmɪ'nɪə/ *verb* (often as **domineering** *adjective*) behave overbearingly.

Dominican /də'mɪnɪkən/ ● *noun* friar or nun of order founded by St Dominic. ● *adjective* of this order.

dominion /də'mɪnjən/ *noun* sovereignty; realm; domain; *historical* self-governing territory of British Commonwealth.

domino /'dɒmɪnəʊ/ *noun* (*plural* **-es**) any of 28 small oblong pieces marked with 0–6 pips in each half; (in *plural*) game played with these; loose cloak worn with half-mask.

don[1] *noun* university teacher, esp. senior member of college at Oxford or Cambridge; (**Don**) *Spanish title prefixed to man's name*.

don[2] *verb* (**-nn-**) put on (garment).

donate /dəʊ'neɪt/ *verb* (**-ting**) give (money etc.), esp. to charity.

donation *noun* donating, being donated; thing (esp. money) donated.

done /dʌn/ ● *past participle* of DO[1]. ● *adjective* completed; cooked; *colloquial* socially acceptable; (often + *in*) *colloquial* tired out; (esp. as *interjection* in response to offer etc.) accepted. □ **be done with** have or be finished with; **done for** *colloquial* in serious trouble.

doner kebab /'dɒnə kɪ'bæb/ *noun* spiced lamb cooked on spit and served in slices, often with pitta bread.

donkey /'dɒŋkɪ/ *noun* (*plural* **-s**) domestic ass; *colloquial* stupid person. □ **donkey jacket** thick weatherproof jacket; **donkey's years** *colloquial* very long time; **donkey-work** drudgery.

Donna /'dɒnə/ *noun: title of Italian, Spanish, or Portuguese lady*.

donnish *adjective* like a college don; pedantic.

donor /'dəʊnə/ *noun* person who donates; person who provides blood for transfusion, organ for transplantation, etc.

don't /dəʊnt/ ● *verb* do not. ● *noun* prohibition.

doodle /'du:d(ə)l/ ● *verb* (**-ling**) scribble or draw absent-mindedly. ● *noun* such scribble or drawing.

doom /du:m/ ● *noun* terrible fate or destiny; ruin, death. ● *verb* (usually + *to*) condemn or destine; (esp. as **doomed** *adjective*) consign to ruin, destruction, etc. □ **doomsday** day of Last Judgement.

door /dɔ:/ *noun* hinged or sliding barrier closing entrance to building, room, cupboard, etc.; doorway. □ **doormat** mat for wiping shoes on, *colloquial* subservient person; **doorstep** step or area immediately outside esp. outer door, *slang* thick slice of bread; **doorstop** device for keeping door open or to keep it from striking wall; **door-to-door** (of selling etc.) done at each house in turn; **doorway** opening filled by door; **out of doors** in(to) open air.

dope ● *noun slang* drug, esp. narcotic; thick liquid used as lubricant etc.; varnish; *slang* stupid person;

slang information. ● *verb* (**-ping**) give or add drug to; apply dope to.

dopey *adjective* (also **dopy**) (**dopier, dopiest**) *colloquial* half asleep, stupefied; stupid.

doppelganger /'dɒp(ə)lgæŋə/ *noun* (also **doppelgänger** /-geŋə/) apparition or double of living person.

Doppler effect /'dɒplə/ *noun* change in frequency of esp. sound waves when source and observer are moving closer or apart.

dormant /'dɔ:mənt/ *adjective* lying inactive; sleeping; inactive. □ **dormancy** *noun*.

dormer /'dɔ:mə/ *noun* (in full **dormer window**) upright window in sloping roof.

dormitory /'dɔ:mɪtərɪ/ *noun* (*plural* **-ies**) sleeping-room with several beds; (in full **dormitory town** etc.) commuter town or suburb.

dormouse /'dɔ:maʊs/ *noun* (*plural* **-mice**) small mouse-like hibernating rodent.

dorsal /'dɔ:s(ə)l/ *adjective* of or on back.

dory /'dɔ:rɪ/ *noun* (*plural* same or **-ies**) edible sea fish.

dosage *noun* size of dose; giving of dose.

dose /dəʊs/ ● *noun* single portion of medicine; amount of radiation received. ● *verb* (**-sing**) give medicine to; (+ *with*) treat with.

doss *verb* (often + *down*) *slang* sleep on makeshift bed or in doss-house. □ **doss-house** cheap lodging house. □ **dosser** *noun*.

dossier /'dɒsɪeɪ/ *noun* file containing information about person, event, etc.

dot *noun* small spot, esp. as decimal point, part of *i* or *j* etc.; shorter signal of the two in Morse code. ● *verb* (**-tt-**) mark or scatter with dot(s); (often + *about*) scatter like dots; place dot over (letter); partly cover as with dots; *slang* hit. □ **dotted line** line of dots for signature etc. on document; **on the dot** exactly on time.

dotage /'dəʊtɪdʒ/ *noun* feeble-minded senility.

dote *verb* (**-ting**) (usually + *on* or as **doting** *adjective*) be excessively fond of.

dotterel /'dɒtər(ə)l/ *noun* small plover.

dotty *adjective* (**-ier, -iest**) *colloquial* eccentric, silly, crazy; (+ *about*) infatuated with.

double /'dʌb(ə)l/ ● *adjective* consisting of two things; multiplied by two; twice as much or many or large etc.; having twice the usual size, quantity, strength, etc.; having some part double; (of flower) with two or more circles of petals; ambiguous; deceitful. ● *adverb* at or to twice the amount; two together. ● *noun* double quantity (of spirits etc.) or thing; twice the amount or quantity; person or thing looking exactly like another; (in *plural*) game between two pairs of players; pair of victories; bet in which winnings and stake from first bet are transferred to second. ● *verb* (**-ling**) make or become double; increase twofold; amount to twice as much as; fold over upon itself; become folded; play (two parts) in same play etc.; (usually + *as*) play twofold role; turn sharply; *Nautical* get round (headland). □ **at the double** running; **double agent** spy working for two rival countries etc.; **double-barrelled** (of gun) having two barrels, (of surname) hyphenated; **double-bass** largest instrument of violin family; **double-book** mistakenly reserve (seat, room, etc.) for two people at once; **double-breasted** (of garment) overlapping across body; **double chin** chin with fold of flesh below it; **double cream** thick cream with high fat-content; **double-cross** deceive or betray; **double-dealing** (practising) deceit, esp. in business; **double-decker** bus etc. with two decks, *colloquial* sandwich with two layers of filling; **double Dutch** *colloquial* gibberish; **double eagle** figure of eagle with two heads; **double-edged** presenting both a danger and an advantage; **double figures** numbers from 10 to 99; **double glazing** two layers of glass in window; **double negative** *Grammar* negative statement (incorrectly) containing two negative elements (see note below); **double pneumonia** pneumonia of both lungs; **double standard** rule or principle not impartially applied; **double take** delayed reaction to unexpected element of situation; **double-talk** (usually deliberately) ambiguous or misleading speech.

■ **Usage** Double negatives like *He didn't do nothing* and *I'm never going nowhere like that* are mistakes in standard English because one negative element is redundant. However, two negatives are perfectly acceptable in, for instance, *a not ungenerous sum* (meaning 'quite a generous sum').

double entendre /duːb(ə)l ɑːnˈtɑːndrə/ *noun* phrase capable of two meanings, one usually indecent. [French]

doublet /ˈdʌblɪt/ *noun* *historical* man's close-fitting jacket; one of pair of similar things.

doubloon /dʌˈbluːn/ *noun* *historical* Spanish gold coin.

doubt /daʊt/ ● *noun* uncertainty; undecided state of mind; cynicism; uncertain state. ● *verb* feel uncertain or undecided about; hesitate to believe; call in question. □ **in doubt** open to question; **no doubt** certainly, admittedly.

doubtful *adjective* feeling or causing doubt; unreliable. □ **doubtfully** *adverb*.

doubtless *adverb* certainly; probably.

douche /duːʃ/ ● *noun* jet of liquid applied to part of body for cleansing or medicinal purposes; device for producing this. ● *verb* (**-ching**) treat with douche; use douche.

dough /dəʊ/ *noun* thick paste of flour mixed with liquid for baking; *slang* money. □ **doughnut** (*US* **donut**) small fried cake of sweetened dough. □ **doughy** *adjective* (**-ier**, **-iest**).

doughty /ˈdaʊtɪ/ *adjective* (**-ier**, **-iest**) *archaic* valiant. □ **doughtily** *adverb*.

dour /dʊə/ *adjective* stern, grim, obstinate.

douse /daʊs/ *verb* (also **dowse**) (**-sing**) throw water over; plunge into water; extinguish (light).

dove /dʌv/ *noun* bird with short legs and full breast; advocate of peaceful policies; gentle or innocent person. □ **dovecot(e)** pigeon house.

dovetail ● *noun* mortise-and-tenon joint shaped like dove's spread tail. ● *verb* fit together, combine neatly; join with dovetails.

dowager /ˈdaʊədʒə/ *noun* woman with title or property from her late husband.

dowdy /ˈdaʊdɪ/ *adjective* (**-ier**, **-iest**) (of clothes) unattractively dull; dressed dowdily. □ **dowdily** *adverb*; **dowdiness** *noun*.

dowel /ˈdaʊəl/ *noun* cylindrical peg for holding parts of structure together.

dowelling *noun* rods for cutting into dowels.

dower /ˈdaʊə/ *noun* widow's share for life of husband's estate.

down[1] /daʊn/ ● *adverb* towards or into lower place, esp. to ground; in lower place or position; to or in place regarded as lower, esp. southwards or away from major city or university; in or into low or weaker position or condition; losing by; (of a computer system) out of action; from earlier to later time; in written or recorded form. ● *preposition* downwards along, through, or into; from top to bottom of; along; at lower part of. ● *adjective* directed downwards. ● *verb* *colloquial* knock or bring etc. down; swallow. ● *noun* reverse of fortune; *colloquial* period of depression. □ **be down to** be the responsibility of, have nothing left but; **down and out** destitute;

down-and-out destitute person; **downcast** dejected, (of eyes) looking down; **downfall** fall from prosperity or power, cause of this; **downgrade** reduce in rank etc.; **downhearted** despondent; **downhill** *adverb* in descending direction, on a decline, *adjective* sloping down, declining; **down in the mouth** looking unhappy; **down-market** of or to cheaper sector of market; **downpour** heavy fall of rain; **downside** negative aspect, drawback; **downstairs** *adverb* down the stairs, to or on lower floor, *adjective* situated downstairs; **downstream** in direction of flow of stream etc.; **down-to-earth** practical, realistic; **downtown** *US* (of) lower or central part of town or city; **downtrodden** oppressed; **downturn** decline, esp. in economic activity; **down under** *colloquial* in Australia or NZ; **downwind** in direction in which wind is blowing; **down with** *expressing rejection of person or thing*; **have a down on** *colloquial* be hostile to. □ **downward** *adjective* & *adverb*; **downwards** *adverb*.

down[2] /daʊn/ *noun* baby birds' fluffy covering; bird's under-plumage; fine soft feathers or hairs.

down[3] /daʊn/ *noun* open rolling land; (in *plural*) chalk uplands of S. England etc.

downright ● *adjective* plain, straightforward; utter. ● *adverb* thoroughly.

Down's syndrome *noun* congenital disorder with mental retardation and physical abnormalities.

downy *adjective* (**-ier**, **-iest**) of, like, or covered with down.

dowry /ˈdaʊərɪ/ *noun* (*plural* **-ies**) property brought by bride to her husband.

dowse[1] /daʊz/ *verb* (**-sing**) search for underground water or minerals by holding stick or rod which dips abruptly when over right spot. □ **dowser** *noun*.

dowse[2] = DOUSE.

doxology /dɒkˈsɒlədʒɪ/ *noun* (*plural* **-ies**) liturgical hymn etc. of praise to God.

doyen /ˈdɔɪən/ *noun* (*feminine* **doyenne** /dɔɪˈen/) senior member of group.

doz. *abbreviation* dozen.

doze ● *verb* (**-zing**) sleep lightly, be half asleep. ● *noun* short light sleep. □ **doze off** fall lightly asleep.

dozen /ˈdʌz(ə)n/ *noun* (*plural* same (after numeral) or **-s**) set of twelve; (**dozens**, usually + *of*) *colloquial* very many.

D.Phil. *abbreviation* Doctor of Philosophy.

Dr *abbreviation* Doctor.

drab *adjective* (**-bb-**) dull, uninteresting; of dull brownish colour. □ **drabness** *noun*.

drachm /dræm/ *noun* weight formerly used by apothecaries, = 1/8 ounce.

drachma /ˈdrækmə/ *noun* (*plural* **-s**) chief monetary unit of Greece.

Draconian /drəˈkəʊnɪən/ *adjective* (of laws) harsh, cruel.

draft /drɑːft/ ● *noun* preliminary written outline of scheme or version of speech, document, etc.; written order for payment of money by bank; drawing of money on this; detachment from larger group; selection of this; *US* conscription; *US* draught. ● *verb* prepare draft of; select for special duty or purpose; *US* conscript.

draftsman /ˈdrɑːftsmən/ *noun* person who drafts documents; person who makes drawings.

drafty *US* = DRAUGHTY.

drag ● *verb* (**-gg-**) pull along with effort; (allow to) trail; (of time etc.) pass tediously or slowly; search bottom of (river etc.) with grapnels, nets, etc. ● *noun* obstruction to progress, retarding force; *colloquial* boring or tiresome task, person, etc.; lure before hounds as substitute for fox; apparatus for dredging; *colloquial* pull at cigarette; *slang* women's clothes worn by men. □ **drag out** protract.

draggle /'dræg(ə)l/ *verb* (**-ling**) make dirty and wet by trailing; hang trailing.

dragon /'drægən/ *noun* mythical monster like reptile, usually with wings and able to breathe fire; fierce woman.

dragonfly *noun* (*plural* **-ies**) large long-bodied gauzy-winged insect.

dragoon /drə'gu:n/ ● *noun* cavalryman; fierce fellow. ● *verb* (+ *into*) coerce or bully into.

drain ● *verb* draw off liquid from; draw off (liquid); flow or trickle away; dry or become dry; exhaust; drink to the dregs; empty (glass etc.) by drinking. ● *noun* channel or pipe carrying off liquid, sewage, etc.; constant outflow or expenditure. □ **draining board** sloping grooved surface beside sink for draining dishes; **drainpipe** pipe for carrying off water etc.

drainage *noun* draining; system of drains; what is drained off.

drake *noun* male duck.

dram *noun* small drink of spirits etc.; drachm.

drama /'drɑːmə/ *noun* play for stage or broadcasting; art of writing, acting, or presenting plays; dramatic event or quality.

dramatic /drə'mætɪk/ *adjective* of drama; unexpected and exciting; striking; theatrical. □ **dramatically** *adverb*.

dramatics *plural noun* (often treated as *singular*) performance of plays; exaggerated behaviour.

dramatis personae /'dræmətɪs pɜː'səʊnaɪ/ *plural noun* characters in a play.

dramatist /'dræmətɪst/ *noun* writer of plays.

dramatize /'dræmətaɪz/ *verb* (also **-ise**) (**-zing** or **-sing**) convert into play; make dramatic; behave dramatically. □ **dramatization** *noun*.

drank *past* of DRINK.

drape ● *verb* (**-ping**) cover or hang or adorn with cloth etc.; arrange in graceful folds. ● *noun* (in *plural*) US curtains.

draper *noun* retailer of textile fabrics.

drapery *noun* (*plural* **-ies**) clothing or hangings arranged in folds; draper's trade or fabrics.

drastic /'dræstɪk/ *adjective* far-reaching in effect; severe. □ **drastically** *adverb*.

drat *colloquial* ● *verb* (**-tt-**) (usually as *interjection*) curse. ● *interjection* expressing annoyance.

draught /drɑːft/ *noun* (US **draft**) current of air indoors; traction; depth of water needed to float ship; drawing of liquor from cask etc.; single act of drinking or inhaling; amount so drunk; (in *plural*) game for two with 12 pieces each, on **draughtboard** (like chessboard). □ **draught beer** beer drawn from cask, not bottled.

draughtsman /'drɑːftsmən/ *noun* person who makes drawings; piece in game of draughts.

draughty *adjective* (US **drafty**) (**-ier**, **-iest**) (of a room etc.) letting in sharp currents of air.

draw ● *verb* (*past* **drew** /dru:/; *past participle* **drawn**) pull or cause to move towards or after one; pull (thing) up, over, or across; attract; pull (curtains) open or shut; take in; (+ *at, on*) inhale from; extract; take from or out; make (line, mark, or outline); make (picture) in this way; represent (thing) in this way; finish (game etc.) with equal scores; proceed to specified position; infer; elicit, evoke; induce; haul up (water) from well; bring out (liquid from tap, wound, etc.); draw lots; obtain by lot; (of tea) infuse; (of chimney, pipe, etc.) promote or allow draught; write out (bill, cheque); search (cover) for game etc.; (as **drawn** *adjective*) looking strained and tense. ● *noun*

act of drawing; person or thing that draws custom or attention; drawing of lots, raffle; drawn game etc. □ **draw back** withdraw; **drawback** disadvantage; **drawbridge** hinged retractable bridge; **draw in** (of days etc.) become shorter, (of train etc.) arrive at station; **draw out** prolong, induce to talk, (of days etc.) become longer; **drawstring** string or cord threaded through waistband, bag opening, etc.; **draw up** draft (document etc.), bring into order, come to a halt, (**draw oneself up**) make oneself erect.

drawer /'drɔːə/ *noun* person who draws; (also /drɔː/) receptacle sliding in and out of frame (**chest of drawers**) or of table etc.; (in *plural*) knickers, underpants.

drawing *noun* art of representing by line with pencil etc.; picture etc. made thus. □ **drawing-board** board on which paper is fixed for drawing on; **drawing-pin** flat-headed pin for fastening paper to a surface.

drawing-room *noun* room in private house for sitting or entertaining in.

drawl ● *verb* speak with drawn-out vowel sounds. ● *noun* drawling utterance or way of speaking.

dray *noun* low cart without sides for heavy loads, esp. beer barrels.

dread /dred/ ● *verb* fear greatly, esp. in advance. ● *noun* great fear or apprehension. ● *adjective* dreaded; *archaic* awe-inspiring.

dreadful *adjective* terrible; *colloquial* very annoying, very bad. □ **dreadfully** *adverb*.

dream ● *noun* series of scenes in mind of sleeping person; daydream or fantasy; ideal; aspiration. ● *verb* (*past & past participle* **dreamt** /dremt/ or **dreamed**) experience dream; imagine as in dream; (esp. in negative; + *of, that*) consider possible or acceptable; be inactive or unrealistic. □ **dreamer** *noun*.

dreamy *adjective* (**-ier**, **-iest**) given to daydreaming; dreamlike; vague; *colloquial* delightful. □ **dreamily** *adverb*.

dreary /'drɪərɪ/ *adjective* (**-ier**, **-iest**) dismal, gloomy, dull. □ **drearily** *adverb*; **dreariness** *noun*.

dredge[1] ● *noun* apparatus used to collect oysters etc., or to clear mud etc., from bottom of sea etc. ● *verb* (**-ging**) bring up or clear (mud etc.) with dredge; (+ *up*) bring up (something forgotten); clean with or use dredge.

dredge[2] *verb* (**-ging**) sprinkle with flour etc.

dredger[1] *noun* boat with dredge; dredge.

dredger[2] *noun* container with perforated lid for sprinkling flour etc.

dregs *plural noun* sediment, grounds; worst part.

drench ● *verb* wet thoroughly; force (animal) to take medicine. ● *noun* dose of medicine for animal.

dress ● *verb* put clothes on; have and wear clothes; put on evening dress; arrange or adorn; put dressing on (wound etc.); prepare (poultry, crab, etc.) for cooking or eating; apply manure to. ● *noun* woman's one-piece garment of bodice and skirt; clothing, esp. whole outfit. □ **dress circle** first gallery in theatre; **dressmaker** person who makes women's clothes, esp. for a living; **dress rehearsal** (esp. final) rehearsal in costume; **dress up** put on special clothes, make (person, thing) more attractive or interesting.

dressage /'dresɑːʒ/ *noun* training of horse in obedience and deportment.

dresser[1] /'dresə/ *noun* tall kitchen sideboard with shelves.

dresser[2] *noun* person who helps actors or actresses to dress for stage.

dressing *noun* putting one's clothes on; sauce, esp. of oil, vinegar, etc., for salads; bandage, ointment, etc. for wound; compost etc. spread over land.

□ **dressing down** colloquial scolding; **dressing gown** loose robe worn while one is not fully dressed; **dressing table** table with mirror etc. for use while dressing, applying make-up, etc.

dressy adjective (**-ier, -iest**) colloquial (of clothes or person) smart, elegant.

drew past of DRAW.

drey /dreɪ/ noun squirrel's nest.

dribble /'drɪb(ə)l/ ● verb (**-ling**) allow saliva to flow from the mouth; flow or allow to flow in drops; Football etc. move (ball) forward with slight touches of feet etc. ● noun act of dribbling; dribbling flow.

driblet /'drɪblɪt/ noun small quantity (of liquid etc.).

dribs and drabs plural noun colloquial small scattered amounts.

dried past & past participle of DRY.

drier[1] comparative of DRY.

drier[2] /'draɪə/ noun (also **dryer**) machine for drying hair, laundry, etc.

driest superlative of DRY.

drift ● noun slow movement or variation; this caused by current; intention, meaning, etc. of what is said etc.; mass of snow etc. heaped up by wind; state of inaction; deviation of craft etc. due to current, wind, etc. ● verb be carried by or as if by current of air or water; progress casually or aimlessly; (of current) carry; heap or be heaped into drifts. □ **drift-net** net for sea fishing, which is allowed to drift; **driftwood** wood floating on moving water or washed ashore.

drifter noun aimless person; fishing boat with drift-net.

drill[1] ● noun tool or machine for boring holes; instruction in military exercises; routine procedure in emergency; thorough training, esp. by repetition; colloquial recognized procedure. ● verb make hole in or through with drill; make (hole) with drill; train or be trained by drill.

drill[2] ● noun machine for making furrows, sowing, and covering seed; small furrow for sowing seed in; row of seeds sown by drill. ● verb plant in drills.

drill[3] noun coarse twilled cotton or linen fabric.

drill[4] noun W. African baboon related to mandrill.

drily adverb (also **dryly**) in a dry way.

drink ● verb (past **drank**; past participle **drunk**) swallow (liquid); take alcohol, esp. to excess; (of plant etc.) absorb (moisture). ● noun liquid for drinking; draught or specified amount of this; alcoholic liquor; glass, portion, etc., of this; (**the drink**) colloquial the sea. □ **drink-driver** colloquial person driving with excess alcohol in the blood; **drink in** listen eagerly to; **drink to** toast, wish success to; **drink up** drink all or remainder of. □ **drinker** noun.

drip ● verb (**-pp-**) fall or let fall in drops; (often + with) be so wet as to shed drops. ● noun liquid falling in drops; drop of liquid; sound of dripping; colloquial dull or ineffectual person.

drip-dry ● verb dry or leave to dry crease-free when hung up. ● adjective able to be drip-dried.

drip-feed ● verb feed intravenously in drops. ● noun feeding thus; apparatus for doing this.

dripping noun fat melted from roasting meat.

drive ● verb (**-ving**; past **drove** /drəʊv/; past participle **driven** /'drɪv(ə)n/) urge forward, esp. forcibly; compel; force into specified state; operate and direct (vehicle etc.); carry or be carried in vehicle; strike golf ball from tee; (of wind etc.) carry along, propel. ● noun excursion in vehicle; driveway; street, road; motivation and energy; inner urge; forcible stroke of bat etc.; organized group effort; transmission of power to machinery or wheels of motor vehicle etc.; organized whist, bingo, etc. competition. □ **drive at** seek, intend, mean; **drive-in** (bank, cinema, etc.)

used while one sits in one's car; **driveway** private road through garden to house; **driving licence** licence permitting person to drive vehicle; **driving test** official test of competence to drive; **driving wheel** wheel transmitting power of vehicle to ground.

drivel /'drɪv(ə)l/ ● noun silly nonsense. ● verb (**-ll-**; US **-l-**) talk drivel; run at mouth or nose.

driver noun person who drives; golf club for driving from tee.

drizzle /'drɪz(ə)l/ ● noun very fine rain. ● verb (**-ling**) fall in very fine drops.

droll /drəʊl/ adjective quaintly amusing, strange, odd. □ **drollery** noun (plural **-ies**).

dromedary /'drɒmɪdərɪ/ noun (plural **-ies**) one-humped (esp. Arabian) camel bred for riding.

drone ● noun non-working male of honey-bee; idler; deep humming sound; monotonous speaking tone; bass-pipe of bagpipes or its continuous note. ● verb (**-ning**) make deep humming sound; speak or utter monotonously.

drool verb slobber, dribble; (often + over) admire extravagantly.

droop /druːp/ ● verb bend or hang down, esp. from fatigue or lack of food, drink, etc.; flag. ● noun drooping position; loss of spirit. □ **droopy** adjective.

drop ● noun globule of liquid that falls, hangs, or adheres to surface; very small amount of liquid; abrupt fall or slope; amount of this; act of dropping; fall in prices, temperature, etc.; drop-shaped thing, esp. pendant or sweet; (in plural) liquid medicine swallowed in drops. ● verb (**-pp-**) fall, allow to fall; let go; fall, let fall, or shed in drops; sink down from exhaustion or injury; cease, lapse, abandon; colloquial cease to associate with or discuss; set down (passenger etc.); utter or be uttered casually; fall or let fall in direction, amount, degree, pitch, etc.; (of person) jump down lightly; let oneself fall; omit; give birth to (lamb); deliver from the air by parachute etc.; Football send (ball) or score (goal) by drop-kick. □ **drop back, behind** fall back, get left behind; **drop in, by** colloquial visit casually; **drop-kick** kick at football made by dropping ball and kicking it as it touches ground; **drop off** fall asleep, drop (passenger); **drop out** (often + of) colloquial cease to participate (in); **drop-out** colloquial person who has dropped out of esp. course of study or conventional society; **drop scone** scone made by dropping spoonful of mixture into pan etc.; **drop-shot** tennis shot dropping abruptly after clearing net. □ **droplet** noun.

dropper noun device for releasing liquid in drops.

droppings plural noun dung; thing that falls or has fallen in drops.

dropsy /'drɒpsɪ/ noun oedema. □ **dropsical** adjective.

dross noun rubbish; scum of molten metal; impurities.

drought /draʊt/ noun prolonged absence of rain.

drove[1] past of DRIVE.

drove[2] /drəʊv/ noun moving crowd; (in plural) colloquial great number; herd or flock moving together.

drover noun herder of cattle.

drown /draʊn/ verb kill or die by submersion; submerge; flood; drench; deaden (grief etc.) by drinking; (often + out) overpower (sound) with louder sound.

drowse /draʊz/ verb (**-sing**) be lightly asleep.

drowsy /'draʊzɪ/ adjective (**-ier, -iest**) very sleepy, almost asleep. □ **drowsily** adverb; **drowsiness** noun.

drub verb (**-bb-**) thrash, beat; defeat thoroughly. □ **drubbing** noun.

drudge ● noun person who does dull, laborious, or menial work. ● verb (**-ging**) work hard or laboriously. □ **drudgery** noun.

drug ● *noun* medicinal substance; (esp. addictive) hallucinogen, stimulant, narcotic, etc. ● *verb* (**-gg-**) add drug to (drink, food, etc.); administer drug to; stupefy. □ **drugstore** *US* combined chemist's shop and café.

drugget /'drʌgɪt/ *noun* coarse woven fabric used for floor coverings etc.

druggist *noun* pharmacist.

Druid /'druːɪd/ *noun* ancient Celtic priest; member of a modern Druidic order, esp. the Gorsedd. □ **Druidic** /-'ɪdɪk/ *adjective*; **Druidism** *noun*.

drum ● *noun* hollow esp. cylindrical percussion instrument covered at one or both ends with plastic, skin, etc.; sound of this; cylindrical structure or object; cylinder used for storage etc.; eardrum. ● *verb* (**-mm-**) play drum; beat or tap continuously with fingers etc.; (of bird etc.) make loud noise with wings. □ **drumbeat** stroke or sound of stroke on drum; **drum brake** kind in which shoes on vehicle press against drum on wheel; **drum into** drive (facts etc.) into (person) by persistence; **drum machine** electronic device that simulates percussion; **drum major** leader of marching band; **drum majorette** female baton-twirling member of parading group; **drum out** dismiss with ignominy; **drumstick** stick for beating drum, lower leg of fowl for eating; **drum up** summon or get by vigorous effort.

drummer *noun* player of drum.

drunk /drʌŋk/ ● *past participle* of DRINK. ● *adjective* lacking control from drinking alcohol; (often + *with*) overcome with joy, success, power, etc. ● *noun* person who is drunk, esp. habitually.

drunkard /'drʌŋkəd/ *noun* person habitually drunk.

drunken /'drʌŋkən/ *adjective* drunk; caused by or involving drunkenness; often drunk. □ **drunkenly** *adverb*; **drunkenness** *noun*.

drupe /druːp/ *noun* fleshy stone fruit.

dry ● *adjective* (**drier, driest**) free from moisture, esp. with moisture having evaporated, drained away, etc; (of eyes) free from tears; (of climate) not rainy; (of river, well, etc.) dried up; (of wine etc.) not sweet; plain, unelaborated; uninteresting; (of sense of humour) ironic, understated; prohibiting sale of alcohol; (of bread) without butter etc.; (of provisions etc.) solid, not liquid; *colloquial* thirsty. ● *verb* (**dries, dried**) make or become dry; (usually as **dried** *adjective*) preserve (food) by removing moisture. □ **dry-clean** clean (clothes etc.) with solvents without water; **dry-fly** (of fishing) with floating artificial fly; **dry ice** solid carbon dioxide; **dry out** make or become fully dry, treat or be treated for alcoholism; **dry rot** decay in wood not exposed to air, fungi causing this; **dry run** *colloquial* rehearsal; **dry-shod** without wetting one's shoes; **dry up** make or become completely dry, dry dishes. □ **dryness** *noun*.

dryad /'draɪæd/ *noun* wood nymph.

dryer = DRIER[2].

dryly = DRILY.

D.Sc. *abbreviation* Doctor of Science.

DSC, DSM, DSO *abbreviations* Distinguished Service Cross, Medal, Order.

DSS *abbreviation* Department of Social Security (formerly DHSS).

DT *abbreviation* (also **DT's** /diː'tiːz/) delirium tremens.

DTI *abbreviation* Department of Trade and Industry.

dual /'djuːəl/ ● *adjective* in two parts; twofold; double. ● *noun Grammar* dual number or form. □ **dual carriageway** road with dividing strip between traffic flowing in opposite directions; **dual control** two linked sets of controls, esp. of vehicle used for teaching driving etc., enabling operation by either of two people. □ **duality** /-'æl-/ *noun*.

dub[1] *verb* (**-bb-**) make (person) into knight; give name or nickname to.

dub[2] *verb* (**-bb-**) provide (film etc.) with alternative, esp. translated, soundtrack; add (sound effects, music) to film or broadcast.

dubbin /'dʌbɪn/ *noun* (also **dubbing**) grease for softening and waterproofing leather.

dubiety /djuː'baɪətɪ/ *noun literary* doubt.

dubious /'djuːbɪəs/ *adjective* doubtful; questionable; unreliable. □ **dubiously** *adverb*; **dubiousness** *noun*.

ducal /'djuːk(ə)l/ *adjective* of or like duke.

ducat /'dʌkət/ *noun* gold coin formerly current in most European countries.

duchess /'dʌtʃɪs/ *noun* duke's wife or widow; woman holding rank of duke.

duchy /'dʌtʃɪ/ *noun* (*plural* **-ies**) duke's or duchess's territory.

duck ● *noun* (*plural* same or **-s**) swimming bird, esp. domesticated form of mallard or wild duck; female of this; its flesh as food; *Cricket* batsman's score of 0; (also **ducks**) *colloquial* (esp. as form of address) darling. ● *verb* bob down, esp. to avoid being seen or hit; dip head briefly under water; plunge (person) briefly in water. □ **duckweed** any of various plants that grow on surface of still water.

duckling *noun* young duck.

duct *noun* channel; tube; tube in body carrying secretions etc.

ductile /'dʌktaɪl/ *adjective* (of metal) capable of being drawn into wire; pliable; easily moulded; docile. □ **ductility** /-'tɪl-/ *noun*.

ductless *adjective* (of gland) secreting directly into bloodstream.

dud *slang* ● *noun* useless or broken thing; counterfeit article; (in *plural*) clothes, rags. ● *adjective* defective, useless.

dude /duːd/ *noun slang* fellow; *US* dandy; *US* city man staying on ranch.

dudgeon /'dʌdʒ(ə)n/ *noun* resentment; indignation.

due ● *adjective* owing, payable; merited, appropriate; (often + *to do*) expected or under obligation to do something or arrive at certain time. ● *noun* what one owes or is owed; (usually in *plural*) fee or amount payable. ● *adverb* (of compass point) exactly, directly. □ **due to** because of, caused by.

■ **Usage** Many people believe that *due to*, meaning 'because of', should only be used after the verb *to be*, as in *The mistake was due to ignorance*, and not as in *All trains may be delayed due to a signal failure*. Instead, *owing to a signal failure* could be used.

duel /'djuːəl/ ● *noun* armed contest between two people, usually to the death; two-sided contest. ● *verb* (**-ll-**; *US* **-l-**) fight duel. □ **duellist** *noun*.

duenna /djuː'enə/ *noun* older woman acting as chaperon to girls, esp. in Spain.

duet /djuː'et/ *noun* musical composition for two performers.

duff ● *noun* boiled pudding. ● *adjective slang* worthless, useless, counterfeit.

duffer /'dʌfə/ *noun colloquial* inefficient or stupid person.

duffle /'dʌf(ə)l/ *noun* (also **duffel**) coarse woollen cloth. □ **duffle bag** cylindrical canvas bag closed by drawstring; **duffle-coat** hooded overcoat of duffle with toggle fastenings.

dug[1] *past & past participle* of DIG.

dug[2] *noun* udder, teat.

dugong /'duːgɒŋ/ *noun* (*plural* same or **-s**) Asian sea mammal.

dugout *noun* roofed shelter, esp. for troops in trenches; underground shelter; canoe made from tree trunk.

duke /dju:k/ *noun* person holding highest hereditary title of the nobility; sovereign prince ruling duchy or small state. □ **dukedom** *noun*.

dulcet /'dʌlsɪt/ *adjective* sweet-sounding.

dulcimer /'dʌlsɪmə/ *noun* metal-stringed instrument struck with two hand-held hammers.

dull ● *adjective* tedious; not interesting; (of weather) overcast; (of colour, light, sound, etc.) not bright, vivid, or clear; slow-witted; stupid; (of knife-edge etc.) blunt; listless, depressed. ● *verb* make or become dull. □ **dullard** *noun*; **dullness** *noun*; **dully** /'dʌllɪ/ *adverb*.

duly /'dju:lɪ/ *adverb* in due time or manner; rightly, properly.

dumb /dʌm/ *adjective* unable to speak; silent, taciturn; *colloquial* stupid, ignorant. □ **dumb-bell** short bar with weight at each end, for muscle-building etc.; **dumbstruck** speechless with surprise.

dumbfound /dʌm'faʊnd/ *verb* nonplus; make speechless with surprise.

dumdum /'dʌmdʌm/ *noun* (in full **dumdum bullet**) soft-nosed bullet that expands on impact.

dummy /'dʌmɪ/ ● *noun* (*plural* **-ies**) model of human figure, esp. as used to display clothes or by ventriloquist or as target; imitation object used to replace real or normal one; baby's rubber teat; *colloquial* stupid person; imaginary player in bridge etc., whose cards are exposed and played by partner. ● *adjective* sham, imitation. ● *verb* (**-ies, -ied**) make pretended pass etc. in football. □ **dummy run** trial attempt.

dump ● *noun* place for depositing rubbish; *colloquial* unpleasant or dreary place; temporary store of ammunition etc. ● *verb* put down firmly or clumsily; deposit as rubbish; *colloquial* abandon; sell (surplus goods) to foreign market at low price; copy (contents of computer memory etc.) as diagnostic aid or for security.

dumpling /'dʌmplɪŋ/ *noun* ball of dough boiled in stew or containing apple etc.

dumps *plural noun* (usually in **down in the dumps**) *colloquial* low spirits.

dumpy /'dʌmpɪ/ *adjective* (**-ier, -iest**) short and stout.

dun ● *adjective* greyish-brown. ● *noun* dun colour; dun horse.

dunce *noun* person slow at learning.

dunderhead /'dʌndəhed/ *noun* stupid person.

dune /dju:n/ *noun* drift of sand etc. formed by wind.

dung ● *noun* excrement of animals; manure. ● *verb* apply dung to (land). □ **dunghill** heap of dung or refuse.

dungarees /dʌŋgə'ri:z/ *plural noun* trousers with bib attached.

dungeon /'dʌndʒ(ə)n/ *noun* underground prison cell.

dunk *verb* dip food into liquid before eating it.

dunlin /'dʌnlɪn/ *noun* red-backed sandpiper.

dunnock /'dʌnək/ *noun* hedge sparrow.

duo /'dju:əʊ/ *noun* (*plural* **-s**) pair of performers; duet.

duodecimal /dju:əʊ'desɪm(ə)l/ *adjective* of twelfths or 12; proceeding by twelves.

duodenum /dju:əʊ'di:nəm/ *noun* (*plural* **-s**) part of small intestine next to stomach. □ **duodenal** *adjective*.

duologue /'dju:əlɒg/ *noun* dialogue between two people.

dupe /dju:p/ ● *noun* victim of deception. ● *verb* (**-ping**) deceive, trick.

duple /'dju:p(ə)l/ *adjective* of two parts. □ **duple time** *Music* rhythm with two beats to bar.

duplex /'dju:pleks/ ● *noun US* flat on two floors, house subdivided for two families. ● *adjective* having two elements; twofold.

duplicate ● *adjective* /'dju:plɪkət/ identical; doubled. ● *noun* /-kət/ identical thing, esp. copy. ● *verb* /-keɪt/

(**-ting**) double; make or be exact copy of; repeat (an action etc.), esp. unnecessarily. □ **in duplicate** in two exact copies. □ **duplication** *noun*.

duplicator *noun* machine for producing multiple copies of texts.

duplicity /dju:'plɪsɪtɪ/ *noun* doubledealing; deceitfulness. □ **duplicitous** *adjective*.

durable /'djʊərəb(ə)l/ *adjective* lasting; hard-wearing. □ **durability** *noun*.

duration /djʊə'reɪʃ(ə)n/ *noun* time taken by event. □ **for the duration** until end of event, for very long time.

duress /djʊə'res/ *noun* compulsion, esp. illegal use of force or threats.

Durex /'djʊəreks/ *noun* proprietary term condom.

during /'djʊərɪŋ/ *preposition* throughout; at some point in.

dusk *noun* darker stage of twilight.

dusky *adjective* (**-ier, -iest**) shadowy, dim; dark-coloured.

dust ● *noun* finely powdered earth or other material etc.; dead person's remains. ● *verb* wipe the dust from (furniture etc.); sprinkle with powder, sugar, etc. □ **dustbin** container for household refuse; **dust bowl** desert made by drought or erosion; **dustcover** dust-sheet, dust-jacket; **dust-jacket** paper cover on hardback book; **dustman** man employed to collect household refuse; **dustpan** pan into which dust is brushed from floor etc.; **dust-sheet** protective cloth over furniture; **dust-up** *colloquial* fight, disturbance.

duster *noun* cloth etc. for dusting furniture etc.

dusty *adjective* (**-ier, -iest**) covered with or full of or like dust.

Dutch ● *adjective* of the Netherlands or its people or language. ● *noun* Dutch language; (**the Dutch**) (treated as *plural*) the people of the Netherlands. □ **Dutch auction** one in which price is progressively reduced; **Dutch barn** roof on poles over hay etc.; **Dutch cap** dome-shaped contraceptive device fitting over cervix; **Dutch courage** courage induced by alcohol; **Dutchman, Dutchwoman** native or national of the Netherlands; **Dutch treat** party, outing, etc. at which people pay for themselves; **go Dutch** share expenses on outing.

dutiable /'dju:tɪəb(ə)l/ *adjective* requiring payment of duty.

dutiful /'dju:tɪfʊl/ *adjective* doing one's duty; obedient. □ **dutifully** *adverb*.

duty /'dju:tɪ/ *noun* (*plural* **-ies**) moral or legal obligation; responsibility; tax on certain goods, imports, etc.; job or function arising from a business or office. □ **duty-free** (of goods) on which duty is not payable; **on, off duty** working or not working.

duvet /'du:veɪ/ *noun* thick soft quilt used instead of sheets and blankets.

dwarf /dwɔ:f/ ● *noun* (*plural* **-s** or **dwarves** /dwɔ:vz/) person, animal, or plant much below normal size, esp. with normal-sized head and body but short limbs; small mythological being with magical powers. ● *verb* stunt in growth; make look small by contrast.

dwell *verb* (*past & past participle* **dwelt** or **dwelled**) reside, live. □ **dwell on** think, write, or speak at length on. □ **dweller** *noun*.

dwelling *noun* house, residence.

dwindle /'dwɪnd(ə)l/ *verb* (**-ling**) become gradually less or smaller; lose importance.

dye /daɪ/ ● *noun* substance used to change colour of fabric, wood, hair, etc.; colour produced by this. ● *verb* (**dyeing, dyed**) colour with dye; dye a specified colour. □ **dyer** *noun*.

dying /ˈdaɪɪŋ/ ● *present participle of* DIE[1]. ● *adjective* of, or at the time of, death.

dyke /daɪk/ (also **dike**) ● *noun* embankment built to prevent flooding; low wall. ● *verb* (**-king**) provide or protect with dyke(s).

dynamic /daɪˈnæmɪk/ *adjective* energetic, active; of motive force; of force in operation; of dynamics. □ **dynamically** *adverb*.

dynamics *plural noun* (usually treated as *singular*) mathematical study of motion and forces causing it.

dynamism /ˈdaɪnəmɪz(ə)m/ *noun* energy; dynamic power.

dynamite /ˈdaɪnəmaɪt/ ● *noun* highly explosive mixture containing nitroglycerine. ● *verb* (**-ting**) charge or blow up with this.

dynamo /ˈdaɪnəməʊ/ *noun* (*plural* **-s**) machine converting mechanical into electrical energy; *colloquial* energetic person.

dynast /ˈdɪnəst/ *noun* ruler; member of dynasty.

dynasty /ˈdɪnəstɪ/ *noun* (*plural* **-ies**) line of hereditary rulers. □ **dynastic** /-ˈnæs-/ *adjective*.

dyne *noun* Physics force required to give a mass of one gram an acceleration of one centimetre per second per second.

dysentery /ˈdɪsəntrɪ/ *noun* inflammation of bowels, causing severe diarrhoea.

dysfunction /dɪsˈfʌŋkʃ(ə)n/ *noun* abnormality or impairment of functioning.

dyslexia /dɪsˈleksɪə/ *noun* abnormal difficulty in reading and spelling. □ **dyslectic** /-ˈlektɪk/ *adjective & noun*; **dyslexic** *adjective & noun*.

dyspepsia /dɪsˈpepsɪə/ *noun* indigestion. □ **dyspeptic** *adjective & noun*.

dystrophy /ˈdɪstrəfɪ/ *noun* defective nutrition.

Ee

E abbreviation (also **E.**) east(ern). □ **E-number** number prefixed by letter E identifying food additive.

each ● adjective every one of two or more, regarded separately. ● pronoun each person or thing. □ **each way** (of bet) backing horse etc. to win or come second or third.

eager /ˈiːgə/ adjective keen, enthusiastic. □ **eagerly** adverb; **eagerness** noun.

eagle /ˈiːg(ə)l/ noun large bird of prey; Golf score of two under par for hole. □ **eagle eye** keen sight, watchfulness; **eagle-eyed** adjective.

eaglet /ˈiːglɪt/ noun young eagle.

ear¹ /ɪə/ noun organ of hearing, esp. external part; faculty of discriminating sound; attention. □ **all ears** listening attentively; **earache** pain in inner ear; **eardrum** membrane of middle ear; **earphone** (usually in plural) device worn on ear to listen to recording, radio, etc.; **earplug** device worn in ear as protection from water, noise, etc.; **earring** jewellery worn on ear; **earshot** hearing-range; **ear-trumpet** trumpet-shaped tube formerly used as hearing aid.

ear² /ɪə/ noun seed-bearing head of cereal plant.

earl /ɜːl/ noun British nobleman ranking between marquess and viscount. □ **earldom** noun.

early /ˈɜːlɪ/ adjective & adverb (**-ier, -iest**) before due, usual, or expected time; not far on in day or night or in development etc. □ **early bird** colloquial person who arrives, gets up, etc. early; **early days** too soon to expect results etc.

earmark verb set aside for special purpose.

earn /ɜːn/ verb obtain as reward for work or merit; bring as income or interest. □ **earner** noun.

earnest /ˈɜːnɪst/ adjective intensely serious. □ **in earnest** serious(ly). □ **earnestly** adverb; **earnestness** noun.

earnings /ˈɜːnɪŋz/ plural noun money earned.

earth /ɜːθ/ ● noun planet we live on (also **Earth**); land and sea as opposed to sky; ground; soil, mould; this world as opposed to heaven or hell; Electricity connection to earth as completion of circuit; hole of fox etc. ● verb Electricity connect to earth; cover (roots) with earth. □ **earthwork** bank of earth in fortification; **earthworm** worm living in earth; **run to earth** find after long search.

earthen adjective made of earth or baked clay. □ **earthenware** pottery made of fired clay.

earthly adjective of earth, terrestrial; colloquial (usually with negative) remotely possible. □ **not an earthly** colloquial no chance or idea whatever.

earthquake noun violent shaking of earth's surface.

earthy adjective (**-ier, -iest**) of or like earth or soil; coarse, crude.

earwig noun insect with pincers at rear end.

ease /iːz/ ● noun facility, effortlessness; freedom from pain, trouble, or constraint. ● verb (**-sing**) relieve from pain etc.; (often + off, up) become less burdensome or severe; relax, slacken; move or be moved by gentle force.

easel /ˈiːz(ə)l/ noun stand for painting, blackboard, etc.

easement noun Law right of way over another's property.

easily /ˈiːzɪlɪ/ adverb without difficulty; by far; very probably.

east ● noun point of horizon where sun rises at equinoxes; corresponding compass point; (usually **the East**) eastern part of world, country, town, etc. ● adjective towards, at, near, or facing east; (of wind) from east. ● adverb towards, at, or near east; (+ of) further east than. □ **eastbound** travelling or leading east; **East End** part of London east of City; **east-north-east, east-south-east** point midway between east and north-east or south-east. □ **eastward** adjective, adverb, & noun; **eastwards** adverb.

Easter /ˈiːstə/ noun festival of Christ's resurrection. □ **Easter egg** artificial usually chocolate egg given at Easter; **Easter Saturday** day before Easter, (properly) Saturday after Easter.

easterly /ˈiːstəlɪ/ adjective & adverb in eastern position or direction; (of wind) from east.

eastern /ˈiːst(ə)n/ adjective of or in east. □ **Eastern Church** Orthodox Church. □ **easternmost** adjective.

easterner noun native or inhabitant of east.

easy /ˈiːzɪ/ ● adjective (**-ier, -iest**) not difficult; free from pain, trouble, or anxiety; relaxed and pleasant; compliant. ● adverb towards, at, or near east; in an effortless or relaxed way. □ **easy chair** large comfortable armchair; **easygoing** placid and tolerant; **go easy** (usually + on, with) be sparing or cautious; **take it easy** proceed gently, relax.

eat verb (past **ate** /et, eɪt/; past participle **eaten**) chew and swallow (food); consume food, have meal; destroy, consume. □ **eating apple** one suitable for eating raw; **eat out** have meal away from home, esp. in restaurant; **eat up** eat completely.

eatable ● adjective fit to be eaten. ● noun (usually in plural) food.

eater noun person who eats; eating apple.

eau-de-Cologne /əʊdəkəˈləʊn/ noun toilet water originally from Cologne.

eaves /iːvz/ plural noun underside of projecting roof.

eavesdrop verb (**-pp-**) listen to private conversation. □ **eavesdropper** noun.

ebb ● noun outflow of tide. ● verb flow back; decline.

ebony /ˈebənɪ/ ● noun hard heavy black tropical wood. ● adjective made of or black as ebony.

ebullient /ɪˈbʌlɪənt/ adjective exuberant. □ **ebullience** noun; **ebulliently** adverb.

EC abbreviation European Community; East Central.

eccentric /ɪkˈsentrɪk/ ● adjective odd or capricious in behaviour or appearance; not placed centrally, not having axis etc. placed centrally; not concentric; not circular. ● noun eccentric person. □ **eccentrically** adverb; **eccentricity** /eksenˈtrɪs-/ noun (plural **-ies**).

ecclesiastic /ɪkliːzɪˈæstɪk/ noun clergyman.

ecclesiastical adjective of the Church or clergy.

ECG abbreviation electrocardiogram.

echelon /ˈeʃəlɒn/ noun level in organization, society, etc.; wedge-shaped formation of troops, aircraft, etc.

echidna /ɪˈkɪdnə/ noun Australian egg-laying spiny mammal.

echo /ˈekəʊ/ ● noun (plural **-es**) repetition of sound by reflection of sound waves; reflected radio or radar beam; close imitation; circumstance or event reminiscent of earlier one. ● verb (**-es, -ed**) resound with echo; repeat, imitate; be repeated.

éclair /eɪˈkleə/ noun finger-shaped iced cake of choux pastry filled with cream.

éclat /eɪˈklɑː/ *noun* brilliant display; conspicuous success; prestige.

eclectic /ɪˈklektɪk/ ● *adjective* selecting ideas, style, etc. from various sources. ● *noun* eclectic person. □ **eclecticism** /-tɪs-/ *noun*.

eclipse /ɪˈklɪps/ ● *noun* obscuring of light of sun by moon (**solar eclipse**) or of moon by earth (**lunar eclipse**); loss of light or importance. ● *verb* (**-sing**) cause eclipse of; intercept (light); outshine, surpass.

eclogue /ˈeklɒg/ *noun* short pastoral poem.

ecology /ɪˈkɒlədʒɪ/ *noun* study of relations of organisms to one another and their surroundings. □ **ecological** /iːkəˈlɒdʒ-/ *adjective*; **ecologically** /iːkəˈlɒdʒ-/ *adverb*; **ecologist** *noun*.

economic /iːkəˈnɒmɪk/ *adjective* of economics; profitable; connected with trade and industry. □ **economically** *adverb*.

economical /iːkəˈnɒmɪk(ə)l/ *adjective* sparing; avoiding waste. □ **economically** *adverb*.

economics /iːkəˈnɒmɪks/ *plural noun* (treated as *singular*) science of production and distribution of wealth; application of this to particular subject. □ **economist** /ɪˈkɒnəmɪst/ *noun*.

economize /ɪˈkɒnəmaɪz/ *verb* (also **-ise**) (**-zing** or **-sing**) make economies; reduce expenditure.

economy /ɪˈkɒnəmɪ/ *noun* (*plural* **-ies**) community's system of wealth creation; frugality, instance of this; sparing use.

ecosystem /ˈiːkəʊsɪstəm/ *noun* biological community of interacting organisms and their physical environment.

ecru /ˈeɪkruː/ *noun* light fawn colour.

ecstasy /ˈekstəsɪ/ *noun* (*plural* **-ies**) overwhelming joy or rapture; *slang* type of hallucinogenic drug. □ **ecstatic** /ɪkˈstætɪk/ *adjective*.

ECT *abbreviation* electroconvulsive therapy.

ectoplasm /ˈektəʊplæz(ə)m/ *noun* supposed substance exuding from body of spiritualistic medium during trance.

ecu /ˈekjuː/ *noun* (also **Ecu**) (*plural* **-s**) European Currency Unit.

ecumenical /iːkjuːˈmenɪk(ə)l/ *adjective* of or representing whole Christian world; seeking worldwide Christian unity. □ **ecumenism** /iːˈkjuːmən-/ *noun*.

eczema /ˈeksɪmə/ *noun* kind of inflammation of skin.

ed. *abbreviation* edited by; edition; editor.

Edam /ˈiːdæm/ *noun* round Dutch cheese with red rind.

eddy /ˈedɪ/ ● *noun* (*plural* **-ies**) circular movement of water, smoke, etc. ● *verb* (**-ies, -ied**) move in eddies.

edelweiss /ˈeɪd(ə)lvaɪs/ *noun* Alpine plant with woolly white bracts.

edema *US* = OEDEMA.

Eden /ˈiːd(ə)n/ *noun* (in full **Garden of Eden**) home of Adam and Eve; delightful place or state.

edge ● *noun* boundary-line or margin of area or surface; narrow surface of thin object; meeting-line of surfaces; sharpness; sharpened side of blade; brink of precipice; crest of ridge; effectiveness. ● *verb* (**-ging**) advance gradually or furtively; give or form border to; sharpen. □ **edgeways, edgewise** with edge foremost or uppermost; **have the edge on, over** have slight advantage over; **on edge** excited or irritable; **set (person's) teeth on edge** cause unpleasant nervous sensation in.

edging *noun* thing forming edge.

edgy *adjective* (**-ier, -iest**) irritable; anxious.

edible /ˈedɪb(ə)l/ *adjective* fit to be eaten.

edict /ˈiːdɪkt/ *noun* order proclaimed by authority.

edifice /ˈedɪfɪs/ *noun* building, esp. imposing one.

edify /ˈedɪfaɪ/ *verb* (**-ies, -ied**) improve morally. □ **edification** *noun*.

edit /ˈedɪt/ *verb* (**-t-**) prepare for publication or broadcast; be editor of; cut and collate (films etc.) to make unified sequence; reword, modify; (+ *out*) remove (part) from text, recording, etc.

edition /ɪˈdɪʃ(ə)n/ *noun* edited or published form of book etc.; copies of book or newspaper etc. issued at one time; instance of regular broadcast.

editor /ˈedɪtə/ *noun* person who edits; person who directs writing of newspaper or news programme or section of one; person who selects material for publication. □ **editorship** *noun*.

editorial /edɪˈtɔːrɪəl/ ● *adjective* of editing or an editor. ● *noun* article giving newspaper's views on current topic.

educate /ˈedjʊkeɪt/ *verb* (**-ting**) train or instruct mentally and morally; provide systematic instruction for. □ **educable** *adjective*; **education** *noun*; **educational** *adjective*; **educator** *noun*.

educationist *noun* (also **educationalist**) expert in educational methods.

Edwardian /edˈwɔːdɪən/ ● *adjective* of or characteristic of reign (1901–10) of Edward VII. ● *noun* person of this period.

EEC *abbreviation* European Economic Community.

EEG *abbreviation* electroencephalogram.

eel *noun* snakelike fish.

eerie /ˈɪərɪ/ *adjective* (**-r, -st**) strange; weird. □ **eerily** *adverb*.

efface /ɪˈfeɪs/ *verb* (**-cing**) rub or wipe out; surpass, eclipse; (**efface oneself**) treat oneself as unimportant. □ **effacement** *noun*.

effect /ɪˈfekt/ ● *noun* result, consequence; efficacy; impression; (in *plural*) possessions; (in *plural*) lighting, sound, etc. giving realism to play etc.; physical phenomenon. ● *verb* bring about.

▪ **Usage** As a verb, *effect* should not be confused with *affect*. *He effected an entrance* means 'He got in (somehow)', but *This won't affect me* means 'My life won't be changed by this'.

effective *adjective* operative; impressive; actual; producing intended result. □ **effectively** *adverb*; **effectiveness** *noun*.

effectual /ɪˈfektʃʊəl/ *adjective* producing required effect; valid.

effeminate /ɪˈfemɪnət/ *adjective* (of a man) unmanly, womanish. □ **effeminacy** *noun*.

effervesce /efəˈves/ *verb* (**-cing**) give off bubbles of gas. □ **effervescence** *noun*; **effervescent** *adjective*.

effete /ɪˈfiːt/ *adjective* feeble; effeminate.

efficacious /efɪˈkeɪʃəs/ *adjective* producing desired effect. □ **efficacy** /ˈefɪkəsɪ/ *noun*.

efficient /ɪˈfɪʃ(ə)nt/ *adjective* productive with minimum waste of effort; competent, capable. □ **efficiency** *noun*; **efficiently** *adverb*.

effigy /ˈefɪdʒɪ/ *noun* (*plural* **-ies**) sculpture or model of person.

effloresce /eflɔːˈres/ *verb* (**-cing**) burst into flower. □ **efflorescence** *noun*.

effluence /ˈeflʊəns/ *noun* flowing out (of light, electricity, etc.); what flows out.

effluent /ˈefluənt/ ● *adjective* flowing out. ● *noun* sewage or industrial waste discharged into river etc.; stream flowing from lake etc.

effluvium /ɪˈfluːvɪəm/ *noun* (*plural* **-via**) unpleasant or harmful outflow.

effort /ˈefət/ *noun* exertion; determined attempt; force exerted; *colloquial* something accomplished. □ **effortless** *adjective*; **effortlessly** *adverb*.

effrontery /ɪˈfrʌntərɪ/ *noun* impudence.

effuse /ɪˈfjuːz/ *verb* (**-sing**) pour forth.

effusion /ɪˈfjuːʒ(ə)n/ *noun* outpouring.

effusive /ɪˈfjuːsɪv/ adjective demonstrative; gushing. □ **effusively** adverb; **effusiveness** noun.

EFL abbreviation English as a foreign language.

Efta /ˈeftə/ noun (also **EFTA**) European Free Trade Association.

e.g. abbreviation for example.

egalitarian /ɪɡælɪˈteərɪən/ ● adjective of or advocating equal rights for all. ● noun egalitarian person. □ **egalitarianism** noun.

egg¹ noun body produced by female of birds, insects, etc., capable of developing into new individual; edible egg of domestic hen; ovum. □ **eggcup** cup for holding boiled egg; **egghead** colloquial intellectual; **eggplant** aubergine; **egg white** white or clear part round yolk of egg.

egg² verb (+ on) urge.

eglantine /ˈeɡləntaɪn/ noun sweet-brier.

ego /ˈiːɡəʊ/ noun (plural -s) the self; part of mind that has sense of individuality; self-esteem.

egocentric /iːɡəʊˈsentrɪk/ adjective self-centred.

egoism /ˈiːɡəʊɪz(ə)m/ noun self-interest as moral basis of behaviour; systematic selfishness; egotism. □ **egoist** noun; **egoistic** /-ˈɪs-/ adjective.

egotism /ˈiːɡətɪz(ə)m/ noun self-conceit; selfishness. □ **egotist** noun; **egotistic(al)** /-ˈtɪs-/ adjective.

egregious /ɪˈɡriːdʒəs/ adjective extremely bad; archaic remarkable.

egress /ˈiːɡres/ noun going out; way out.

egret /ˈiːɡrɪt/ noun kind of white heron.

Egyptian /ɪˈdʒɪpʃ(ə)n/ ● adjective of Egypt. ● noun native or national of Egypt; language of ancient Egyptians.

Egyptology /iːdʒɪpˈtɒlədʒɪ/ noun study of ancient Egypt. □ **Egyptologist** noun.

eh /eɪ/ interjection colloquial: expressing inquiry, surprise, etc.

eider /ˈaɪdə/ noun northern species of duck. □ **eiderdown** quilt stuffed with soft material, esp. down.

eight /eɪt/ adjective & noun one more than seven; 8-oared boat, its crew. □ **eightsome reel** lively Scottish dance for 8 people. □ **eighth** /eɪtθ/ adjective & noun.

eighteen /eɪˈtiːn/ adjective & noun one more than seventeen. □ **eighteenth** adjective & noun.

eighty /ˈeɪtɪ/ adjective & noun (plural -ies) eight times ten. □ **eightieth** adjective & noun.

eisteddfod /aɪˈstedfəd/ noun congress of Welsh poets and musicians gathering for musical and literary competition.

either /ˈaɪðə, ˈiːðə/ ● adjective & pronoun one or other of two; each of two. ● adverb (with negative) any more than the other. □ **either ... or ...** as one possibility ... and as the other ...

ejaculate /ɪˈdʒækjʊleɪt/ verb (-ting) emit (semen) in orgasm; exclaim. □ **ejaculation** noun.

eject /ɪˈdʒekt/ verb throw out, expel; (of pilot etc.) cause oneself to be propelled from aircraft in emergency; emit. □ **ejection** noun.

ejector seat noun device in aircraft for emergency ejection of pilot etc.

eke verb (**eking**) □ **eke out** supplement (income etc.), make (living) or support (existence) with difficulty.

elaborate ● adjective /ɪˈlæbərət/ minutely worked out; complicated. ● verb /ɪˈlæbəreɪt/ (**-ting**) work out or explain in detail. □ **elaborately** adverb; **elaboration** noun.

élan /eɪˈlɑ̃/ noun vivacity, dash. [French]

eland /ˈiːlənd/ noun (plural same or **-s**) large African antelope.

elapse /ɪˈlæps/ verb (**-sing**) (of time) pass by.

elastic /ɪˈlæstɪk/ ● adjective able to resume normal bulk or shape after being stretched or squeezed; springy; flexible. ● noun elastic cord or fabric, usually woven with strips of rubber. □ **elastic band** rubber band. □ **elasticity** /iːlæˈstɪs-/ noun.

elasticated /ɪˈlæstɪkeɪtɪd/ adjective (of fabric) made elastic by weaving with rubber thread.

elate /ɪˈleɪt/ verb (**-ting**) (esp. as **elated** adjective) make delighted or proud. □ **elation** noun.

elbow /ˈelbəʊ/ ● noun joint between forearm and upper arm; part of sleeve covering elbow; elbow-shaped thing. ● verb thrust or jostle (person); make (one's way) thus. □ **elbow-grease** jocular vigorous polishing, hard work; **elbow-room** sufficient space to move or work in.

elder¹ /ˈeldə/ ● adjective older; senior. ● noun older person; official in early Christian and some modern Churches.

elder² /ˈeldə/ noun tree with white flowers and black **elderberries**.

elderly /ˈeldəlɪ/ adjective rather old.

eldest /ˈeldɪst/ adjective first-born; oldest surviving.

eldorado /eldəˈrɑːdəʊ/ noun (plural **-s**) imaginary land of great wealth.

elect /ɪˈlekt/ ● verb choose by voting; choose, decide. ● adjective chosen; select, choice; (after noun) chosen but not yet in office.

election /ɪˈlekʃ(ə)n/ noun electing, being elected; occasion for this.

electioneer /ɪlekʃəˈnɪə/ verb take part in election campaign.

elective /ɪˈlektɪv/ adjective chosen by or derived from election; entitled to elect; optional.

elector /ɪˈlektə/ noun person entitled to vote in election. □ **electoral** adjective.

electorate /ɪˈlektərət/ noun group of electors.

electric /ɪˈlektrɪk/ adjective of, worked by, or charged with electricity; causing or charged with excitement. □ **electric blanket** one heated by internal wires; **electric chair** chair used for electrocution of criminals; **electric eel** eel-like fish able to give electric shock; **electric fire** portable electric heater; **electric shock** effect of sudden discharge of electricity through body of person etc. □ **electrically** adverb.

electrical adjective of or worked by electricity. □ **electrically** adverb.

electrician /ɪlekˈtrɪʃ(ə)n/ noun person who installs or maintains electrical equipment.

electricity /ɪlekˈtrɪsɪtɪ/ noun form of energy present in protons and electrons; science of electricity; supply of electricity.

electrify /ɪˈlektrɪfaɪ/ verb (**-ies, -ied**) charge with electricity; convert to electric working; startle, excite. □ **electrification** noun.

electro- combining form of or caused by electricity.

electrocardiogram /ɪlektrəʊˈkɑːdɪəɡræm/ noun record of electric currents generated by heartbeat. □ **electrocardiograph** instrument for recording such currents.

electroconvulsive /ɪlektrəʊkənˈvʌlsɪv/ adjective (of therapy) using convulsive response to electric shocks.

electrocute /ɪˈlektrəkjuːt/ verb (**-ting**) kill by electric shock. □ **electrocution** /-ˈkjuːʃ(ə)n/ noun.

electrode /ɪˈlektrəʊd/ noun conductor through which electricity enters or leaves electrolyte, gas, vacuum, etc.

electroencephalogram /ɪlektrəʊɪnˈsefələɡræm/ noun record of electrical activity of brain. □ **electroencephalograph** instrument for recording such activity.

electrolysis /ɪlek'trɒlɪsɪs/ noun chemical decomposition by electric action; breaking up of tumours, hair-roots, etc. thus.

electrolyte /ɪ'lektrəlaɪt/ noun solution that can conduct electricity; substance that can dissolve to produce this. □ **electrolytic** /-trəʊ'lɪt-/ adjective.

electromagnet /ɪlektrəʊ'mægnɪt/ noun soft metal core made into magnet by electric current through coil surrounding it.

electromagnetism /ɪlektrəʊ'mægnɪtɪz(ə)m/ noun magnetic forces produced by electricity; study of these.

electron /ɪ'lektrɒn/ noun stable elementary particle with charge of negative electricity, found in all atoms and acting as primary carrier of electricity in solids. □ **electron microscope** one with high magnification, using electron beam instead of light.

electronic /ɪlek'trɒnɪk/ adjective of electrons or electronics; (of music) produced electronically. □ **electronic mail** messages distributed by a computer system. □ **electronically** adverb.

electronics plural noun (treated as singular) science of movement of electrons in vacuum, gas, semiconductor, etc.

electroplate /ɪ'lektrəʊpleɪt/ ● verb (**-ting**) coat with chromium, silver, etc. by electrolysis. ● noun electroplated articles.

elegant /'elɪgənt/ adjective graceful, tasteful, refined; ingeniously simple. □ **elegance** noun; **elegantly** adverb.

elegy /'elɪdʒɪ/ noun (plural **-ies**) sorrowful song or poem, esp. for the dead. □ **elegiac** /-'dʒaɪək/ adjective.

element /'elɪmənt/ noun component part; substance which cannot be resolved by chemical means into simpler substances; any of **the four elements** (earth, water, air, fire) formerly supposed to make up all matter; wire that gives out heat in electric heater, cooker, etc.; (in plural) atmospheric agencies; (in plural) rudiments, first principles; (in plural) bread and wine of Eucharist. □ **in one's element** in one's preferred situation.

elemental /elɪ'ment(ə)l/ adjective of or like the elements or the forces of nature; basic, essential.

elementary /elɪ'mentərɪ/ adjective dealing with simplest facts of subject; unanalysable. □ **elementary particle** Physics subatomic particle, esp. one not known to consist of simpler ones.

elephant /'elɪf(ə)nt/ noun (plural same or **-s**) largest living land animal, with trunk and ivory tusks.

elephantiasis /elɪfən'taɪəsɪs/ noun skin disease causing gross enlargement of limbs etc.

elephantine /elɪ'fæntaɪn/ adjective of elephants; huge; clumsy.

elevate /'elɪveɪt/ verb (**-ting**) lift up, raise; exalt in rank etc.; (usually as **elevated** adjective) raise morally or intellectually.

elevation noun elevating, being elevated; angle above horizontal; height above given level; drawing showing one side of building.

elevator noun US lift; movable part of tailplane for changing aircraft's altitude; hoisting machine.

eleven /ɪ'lev(ə)n/ adjective & noun one more than ten; team of 11 people in cricket etc. □ **eleventh hour** last possible moment. □ **eleventh** adjective & noun.

elevenses /ɪ'levənzɪz/ noun colloquial light mid-morning refreshment.

elf noun (plural **elves** /elvz/) mythological being, esp. small and mischievous one. □ **elfish** adjective.

elfin /'elfɪn/ adjective of elves; elflike.

elicit /ɪ'lɪsɪt/ verb (**-t-**) draw out (facts, response, etc.).

elide /ɪ'laɪd/ verb (**-ding**) omit in pronunciation.

eligible /'elɪdʒɪb(ə)l/ adjective (often + for) fit or entitled to be chosen; desirable or suitable, esp. for marriage. □ **eligibility** noun.

eliminate /ɪ'lɪmɪneɪt/ verb (**-ting**) remove, get rid of; exclude. □ **elimination** noun; **eliminator** noun.

elision /ɪ'lɪʒ(ə)n/ noun omission of vowel or syllable in pronunciation.

élite /ɪ'liːt/ noun select group or class; (**the élite**) the best (of a group).

élitism noun advocacy of or reliance on dominance by select group. □ **élitist** noun & adjective.

elixir /ɪ'lɪksɪə/ noun alchemist's preparation supposedly able to change metal into gold or prolong life indefinitely; aromatic medicine.

Elizabethan /ɪlɪzə'biːθ(ə)n/ ● adjective of time of Elizabeth I or II. ● noun person of this time.

elk noun (plural same or **-s**) large type of deer.

ellipse /ɪ'lɪps/ noun regular oval.

ellipsis /ɪ'lɪpsɪs/ noun (plural **ellipses** /-siːz/) omission of words needed to complete construction or sense.

elliptical /ɪ'lɪptɪk(ə)l/ adjective of or like an ellipse; (of language) confusingly concise.

elm noun tree with rough serrated leaves; its wood.

elocution /elə'kjuːʃ(ə)n/ noun art of clear and expressive speaking.

elongate /'iːlɒŋgeɪt/ verb (**-ting**) extend, lengthen. □ **elongation** noun.

elope /ɪ'ləʊp/ verb (**-ping**) run away to marry secretly. □ **elopement** noun.

eloquence /'eləkwəns/ noun fluent and effective use of language. □ **eloquent** adjective; **eloquently** adverb.

else /els/ adverb besides; instead; otherwise, if not. □ **elsewhere** in or to some other place.

elucidate /ɪ'luːsɪdeɪt/ verb (**-ting**) throw light on, explain. □ **elucidation** noun.

elude /ɪ'luːd/ verb (**-ding**) escape adroitly from; avoid; baffle.

elusive /ɪ'luːsɪv/ adjective difficult to find, catch, or remember; avoiding the point raised. □ **elusiveness** noun.

elver /'elvə/ noun young eel.

elves plural of ELF.

Elysium /ɪ'lɪzɪəm/ noun Greek Mythology home of the blessed after death; place of ideal happiness. □ **Elysian** adjective.

em noun Printing unit of measurement approximately equal to width of M.

emaciate /ɪ'meɪsɪeɪt/ verb (**-ting**) (esp. as **emaciated** adjective) make thin or feeble. □ **emaciation** noun.

emanate /'eməneɪt/ verb (**-ting**) (usually + from) issue or originate (from source). □ **emanation** noun.

emancipate /ɪ'mænsɪpeɪt/ verb (**-ting**) free from social, political, or moral restraint. □ **emancipation** noun.

emasculate ● verb /ɪ'mæskjʊleɪt/ (**-ting**) enfeeble; castrate. ● adjective /ɪ'mæskjʊlət/ enfeebled; castrated; effeminate. □ **emasculation** noun.

embalm /ɪm'bɑːm/ verb preserve (corpse) from decay; preserve from oblivion; make fragrant.

embankment /ɪm'bæŋkmənt/ noun bank constructed to confine water or carry road or railway.

embargo /ɪm'bɑːgəʊ/ ● noun (plural **-es**) order forbidding ships to enter or leave port; suspension of commerce or other activity. ● verb (**-es**, **-ed**) place under embargo.

embark /ɪm'bɑːk/ verb put or go on board ship; (+ on, in) begin (enterprise).

embarkation /embɑː'keɪʃ(ə)n/ noun embarking on ship.

embarrass /ɪm'barəs/ verb make (person) feel awkward or ashamed; encumber; (as **embarrassed** adjective) encumbered with debts. □ **embarrassment** noun.

embassy /'embəsɪ/ noun (plural **-ies**) ambassador's residence or offices; deputation to foreign government.

embattled /ɪm'bæt(ə)ld/ adjective prepared or arrayed for battle; fortified with battlements; under heavy attack, in trying circumstances.

embed /ɪm'bed/ verb (also **imbed**) (**-dd-**) (esp. as **embedded** adjective) fix in surrounding mass.

embellish /ɪm'belɪʃ/ verb beautify, adorn; make fictitious additions to. □ **embellishment** noun.

ember /'embə/ noun (usually in plural) small piece of glowing coal etc. in dying fire. □ **ember days** days of fasting and prayer in Christian Church, associated with ordinations.

embezzle /ɪm'bez(ə)l/ verb (**-ling**) divert (money) fraudulently to own use. □ **embezzlement** noun; **embezzler** noun.

embitter /ɪm'bɪtə/ verb arouse bitter feelings in. □ **embitterment** noun.

emblazon /ɪm'bleɪz(ə)n/ verb portray or adorn conspicuously.

emblem /'embləm/ noun symbol; (+ of) type, embodiment; distinctive badge. □ **emblematic** /-'mæt-/ adjective.

embody /ɪm'bɒdɪ/ verb (**-ies**, **-ied**) give concrete form to; be expression of; include, comprise. □ **embodiment** noun.

embolden /ɪm'bəʊld(ə)n/ verb encourage.

embolism /'embəlɪz(ə)m/ noun obstruction of artery by blood clot etc.

emboss /ɪm'bɒs/ verb carve or decorate with design in relief.

embrace /ɪm'breɪs/ ● verb (**-cing**) hold closely in arms; enclose; accept, adopt; include. ● noun act of embracing, clasp.

embrasure /ɪm'breɪʒə/ noun bevelling of wall at sides of window etc.; opening in parapet for gun.

embrocation /embrə'keɪʃ(ə)n/ noun liquid for rubbing on body to relieve muscular pain.

embroider /ɪm'brɔɪdə/ verb decorate with needlework; embellish. □ **embroidery** noun.

embroil /ɪm'brɔɪl/ verb (often + in) involve (in conflict or difficulties).

embryo /'embrɪəʊ/ noun (plural **-s**) unborn or unhatched offspring; thing in rudimentary stage. □ **embryonic** /-'ɒn-/ adjective.

emend /ɪ'mend/ verb correct, remove errors from (text etc.). □ **emendation** /iː-/ noun.

emerald /'emər(ə)ld/ ● noun bright green gem; colour of this. ● adjective bright green.

emerge /ɪ'mɜːdʒ/ verb (**-ging**) come up or out into view or notice. □ **emergence** noun; **emergent** adjective.

emergency /ɪ'mɜːdʒənsɪ/ noun (plural **-ies**) sudden state of danger etc., requiring immediate action.

emeritus /ɪ'merɪtəs/ adjective retired and holding honorary title.

emery /'emərɪ/ noun coarse corundum for polishing metal etc. □ **emery board** emery-coated nail-file.

emetic /ɪ'metɪk/ ● adjective that causes vomiting. ● noun emetic medicine.

emigrate /'emɪgreɪt/ verb (**-ting**) leave own country to settle in another. □ **emigrant** noun & adjective; **emigration** noun.

émigré /'emɪgreɪ/ noun emigrant, esp. political exile.

eminence /'emɪnəns/ noun recognized superiority; high ground; (**His, Your Eminence**) title used of or to cardinal.

eminent /'emɪnənt/ adjective distinguished, notable. □ **eminently** adverb.

emir /e'mɪə/ noun (also **amir** /ə'mɪə/) title of various Muslim rulers.

emirate /'emɪrət/ noun position, reign, or domain of emir.

emissary /'emɪsərɪ/ noun (plural **-ies**) person sent on diplomatic mission.

emit /ɪ'mɪt/ verb (**-tt-**) give or send out; discharge. □ **emission** /ɪ'mɪʃ(ə)n/ noun.

emollient /ɪ'mɒlɪənt/ ● adjective softening; soothing. ● noun emollient substance.

emolument /ɪ'mɒljʊmənt/ noun fee from employment, salary.

emotion /ɪ'məʊʃ(ə)n/ noun strong instinctive feeling such as love or fear; emotional intensity or sensibility.

emotional adjective of or expressing emotion(s); especially liable to emotion; arousing emotion. □ **emotionalism** noun; **emotionally** adverb.

■ **Usage** See note at EMOTIVE.

emotive /ɪ'məʊtɪv/ adjective of or arousing emotion.

■ **Usage** Although the senses of *emotive* and *emotional* overlap, *emotive* is more common in the sense 'arousing emotion', as in *an emotive issue*, and only *emotional* can mean 'especially liable to emotion', as in *a highly emotional person*.

empanel /ɪm'pæn(ə)l/ verb (also **impanel**) (**-ll-**; US **-l-**) enter (jury) on panel.

empathize /'empəθaɪz/ verb (also **-ise**) (**-zing** or **-sing**) (usually + with) exercise empathy.

empathy /'empəθɪ/ noun ability to identify with person or object.

emperor /'empərə/ noun ruler of empire.

emphasis /'emfəsɪs/ noun (plural **emphases** /-siːz/) importance attached to something; significant stress on word(s); vigour of expression etc.

emphasize /'emfəsaɪz/ verb (also **-ise**) (**-zing** or **-sing**) lay stress on.

emphatic /ɪm'fætɪk/ adjective forcibly expressive; (of word) bearing emphasis (e.g. *myself* in *I did it myself*). □ **emphatically** adverb.

emphysema /emfɪ'siːmə/ noun disease of lungs causing breathlessness.

empire /'empaɪə/ noun large group of states under single authority; supreme dominion; large commercial organization etc. owned or directed by one person.

empirical /ɪm'pɪrɪk(ə)l/ adjective based on observation or experiment, not on theory. □ **empiricism** /-rɪs-/ noun; **empiricist** /-rɪs-/ noun.

emplacement /ɪm'pleɪsmənt/ noun platform for gun(s); putting in position.

employ /ɪm'plɔɪ/ verb use services of (person) in return for payment; use (thing, time, energy, etc.); keep (person) occupied. □ **in the employ of** employed by. □ **employer** noun.

employee /emplɔɪ'iː/ noun person employed for wages.

employment noun employing, being employed; person's trade or profession. □ **employment office** government office finding work for the unemployed.

emporium /em'pɔːrɪəm/ noun large shop; centre of commerce.

empower /ɪm'paʊə/ verb give power to.

empress /'emprɪs/ noun wife or widow of emperor; woman emperor.

empty /'emptɪ/ ● adjective (**-ier**, **-iest**) containing nothing; vacant, unoccupied; hollow, insincere; without purpose; colloquial hungry; vacuous, foolish.

● *verb* (**-ies, -ied**) remove contents of; transfer (contents); become empty; (of river) discharge itself. ● *noun* (*plural* **-ies**) *colloquial* emptied bottle etc. □ **empty-handed** bringing or taking nothing. □ **emptiness** *noun*.

EMS *abbreviation* European Monetary System.

emu /ˈiːmjuː/ *noun* (*plural* **-s**) large flightless Australian bird.

emulate /ˈemjʊleɪt/ *verb* (**-ting**) try to equal or excel; imitate. □ **emulation** *noun*; **emulator** *noun*.

emulsify /ɪˈmʌlsɪfaɪ/ *verb* (**-ies, -ied**) make emulsion of. □ **emulsifier** *noun*.

emulsion /ɪˈmʌlʃ(ə)n/ *noun* fine dispersion of one liquid in another, esp. as paint, medicine, etc.

en *noun* *Printing* unit of measurement equal to half em.

enable /ɪˈneɪb(ə)l/ *verb* (**-ling**) (+ *to do*) supply with means or authority; make possible.

enact /ɪˈnækt/ *verb* ordain, decree; make (bill etc.) law; play (part). □ **enactment** *noun*.

enamel /ɪˈnæm(ə)l/ ● *noun* glasslike opaque coating on metal; any hard smooth coating; kind of hard gloss paint; hard coating of teeth. ● *verb* (**-ll-**; *US* **-l-**) coat with enamel.

enamour /ɪˈnæmə/ *verb* (*US* **enamor**) (usually in *passive*; + *of*) inspire with love or delight.

en bloc /ɑ̃ ˈblɒk/ *adverb* in a block, all at same time. [French]

encamp /ɪnˈkæmp/ *verb* settle in (esp. military) camp. □ **encampment** *noun*.

encapsulate /ɪnˈkæpsjʊleɪt/ *verb* (**-ting**) enclose (as) in capsule; summarize.

encase /ɪnˈkeɪs/ *verb* (**-sing**) confine (as) in a case.

encash /ɪnˈkæʃ/ *verb* convert into cash. □ **encashment** *noun*.

encephalitis /ensefəˈlaɪtɪs/ *noun* inflammation of brain.

enchant /ɪnˈtʃɑːnt/ *verb* delight; bewitch. □ **enchanting** *adjective*; **enchantment** *noun*.

enchanter *noun* (*feminine* **enchantress**) person who enchants, esp. by magic.

encircle /ɪnˈsɜːk(ə)l/ *verb* (**-ling**) surround. □ **encirclement** *noun*.

enclave /ˈenkleɪv/ *noun* part of territory of one state surrounded by that of another; group of people distinct from those surrounding them, esp. ethnically.

enclose /ɪnˈkləʊz/ *verb* (**-sing**) surround with wall, fence, etc.; shut in; put in receptacle (esp. in envelope besides letter); (as **enclosed** *adjective*) (of religious community) secluded from outside world.

enclosure /ɪnˈkləʊʒə/ *noun* enclosing; enclosed space or area; thing enclosed.

encode /ɪnˈkəʊd/ *verb* (**-ding**) put into code.

encomium /ɪnˈkəʊmɪəm/ *noun* (*plural* **-s**) formal praise.

encompass /ɪnˈkʌmpəs/ *verb* contain, include; surround.

encore /ˈɒŋkɔː/ ● *noun* audience's call for repetition of item, or for further item; such item. ● *verb* (**-ring**) call for repetition of or by. ● *interjection* again.

encounter /ɪnˈkaʊntə/ ● *verb* meet by chance; meet as adversary. ● *noun* meeting by chance or in conflict.

encourage /ɪnˈkʌrɪdʒ/ *verb* (**-ging**) give courage to; urge; promote. □ **encouragement** *noun*.

encroach /ɪnˈkrəʊtʃ/ *verb* (usually + *on, upon*) intrude on other's territory etc. □ **encroachment** *noun*.

encrust /ɪnˈkrʌst/ *verb* cover with or form crust; coat with hard casing or deposit.

encumber /ɪnˈkʌmbə/ *verb* be burden to; hamper.

encumbrance /ɪnˈkʌmbrəns/ *noun* burden; impediment.

encyclical /ɪnˈsɪklɪk(ə)l/ *noun* papal letter to all RC bishops.

encyclopedia /ɪnsaɪkləˈpiːdɪə/ *noun* (also **-paedia**) book of information on many subjects or on many aspects of one subject.

encyclopedic *adjective* (also **-paedic**) (of knowledge or information) comprehensive.

end ● *noun* limit; farthest point; extreme point or part; conclusion; latter part; destruction; death; result; goal, object; remnant. ● *verb* bring or come to end. □ **endpaper** blank leaf of paper at beginning or end of book; **end-product** final product of manufacture etc.; **end up** be or become eventually, arrive; **in the end** finally; **make ends meet** live within one's income; **no end** *colloquial* to a great extent.

endanger /ɪnˈdeɪndʒə/ *verb* place in danger. □ **endangered species** one in danger of extinction.

endear /ɪnˈdɪə/ *verb* (usually + *to*) make dear. □ **endearing** *adjective*.

endearment *noun* expression of affection.

endeavour /ɪnˈdevə/ (*US* **endeavor**) ● *verb* try, strive. ● *noun* attempt, effort.

endemic /enˈdemɪk/ *adjective* (often + *to*) regularly found among particular people or in particular area. □ **endemically** *adverb*.

ending *noun* end of word or story.

endive /ˈendaɪv/ *noun* curly-leaved plant used in salads.

endless *adjective* infinite; continual. □ **endlessly** *adverb*.

endocrine /ˈendəʊkraɪn/ *adjective* (of gland) secreting directly into blood.

endogenous /enˈdɒdʒɪnəs/ *adjective* growing or originating from within.

endorse /ɪnˈdɔːs/ *verb* (**-sing**) approve; write on (document), esp. sign (cheque); enter details of offence on (driving licence). □ **endorsement** *noun*.

endoskeleton /ˈendəʊskelɪtən/ *noun* internal skeleton.

endow /ɪnˈdaʊ/ *verb* give permanent income to; (esp. as **endowed** *adjective*) provide with talent or ability.

endowment *noun* endowing; money with which person or thing is endowed. □ **endowment mortgage** one in which borrower pays only premiums until policy repays mortgage capital; **endowment policy** life insurance policy paying out on set date or earlier death.

endue /ɪnˈdjuː/ *verb* (**-dues, -dued, -duing**) (+ *with*) provide (person) with (quality etc.).

endurance *noun* power of enduring.

endure /ɪnˈdjʊə/ *verb* (**-ring**) undergo; bear; last.

endways *adverb* with an end facing forwards.

ENE *abbreviation* east-north-east.

enema /ˈenɪmə/ *noun* injection of liquid etc. into rectum, esp. to expel its contents; liquid used for this.

enemy /ˈenəmɪ/ ● *noun* (*plural* **-ies**) person actively hostile to another; hostile army or nation; member of this; adversary, opponent. ● *adjective* of or belonging to enemy.

energetic /enəˈdʒetɪk/ *adjective* full of energy. □ **energetically** *adverb*.

energize /ˈenədʒaɪz/ *verb* (also **-ise**) (**-zing** or **-sing**) give energy to.

energy /ˈenədʒɪ/ *noun* (*plural* **-ies**) force, vigour, activity; ability of matter or radiation to do work.

enervate /ˈenəveɪt/ *verb* (**-ting**) deprive of vigour. □ **enervation** *noun*.

en famille /ɑ̃ fæˈmiː/ *adverb* in or with one's family. [French]

enfant terrible /ãfã teˈriːbl/ *noun* (*plural* **enfants terribles** same pronunciation) indiscreet or unruly person. [French]

enfeeble /ɪnˈfiːb(ə)l/ *verb* (**-ling**) make feeble. □ **enfeeblement** *noun*.

enfilade /enfɪˈleɪd/ ● *noun* gunfire directed down length of enemy position. ● *verb* (**-ding**) direct enfilade at.

enfold /ɪnˈfəʊld/ *verb* wrap; embrace.

enforce /ɪnˈfɔːs/ *verb* (**-cing**) compel observance of; impose. □ **enforceable** *adjective*; **enforcement** *noun*.

enfranchise /ɪnˈfræntʃaɪz/ *verb* (**-sing**) give (person) right to vote. □ **enfranchisement** /-tʃɪz-/ *noun*.

engage /ɪnˈɡeɪdʒ/ *verb* (**-ging**) employ, hire; (as **engaged** *adjective*) occupied, busy, having promised to marry; hold (person's attention); cause parts of (gear) to interlock; fit, interlock; bring into battle; come into battle with (enemy); (usually + *in*) take part; (+ *that, to do*) undertake. □ **engagement** *noun*.

engender /ɪnˈdʒendə/ *verb* give rise to.

engine /ˈendʒɪn/ *noun* mechanical contrivance of parts working together, esp. as source of power; railway locomotive.

engineer /endʒɪˈnɪə/ ● *noun* person skilled in a branch of engineering; person who makes or is in charge of engines etc.; person who designs and constructs military works; mechanic, technician. ● *verb* contrive, bring about; act as engineer; construct or manage as engineer.

engineering *noun* application of science to design, building, and use of machines etc.

English /ˈɪŋɡlɪʃ/ ● *adjective* of England. ● *noun* language of England, now used in UK, US, and most Commonwealth countries; (**the English**) (treated as *plural*) the people of England. □ **Englishman, Englishwoman** native of England.

engraft /ɪnˈɡrɑːft/ *verb* (usually + *into, on*) graft, implant, incorporate.

engrave /ɪnˈɡreɪv/ *verb* (**-ving**) inscribe or cut (design) on hard surface; inscribe (surface) thus; (often + *on*) impress deeply (on memory etc.). □ **engraver** *noun*.

engraving *noun* print made from engraved plate.

engross /ɪnˈɡrəʊs/ *verb* (usually as **engrossed** *adjective* + *in*) fully occupy.

engulf /ɪnˈɡʌlf/ *verb* flow over and swamp, overwhelm.

enhance /ɪnˈhɑːns/ *verb* (**-cing**) intensify; improve. □ **enhancement** *noun*.

enigma /ɪˈnɪɡmə/ *noun* puzzling person or thing; riddle. □ **enigmatic** /enɪɡˈmætɪk/ *adjective*.

enjoin /ɪnˈdʒɔɪn/ *verb* command, order.

enjoy /ɪnˈdʒɔɪ/ *verb* find pleasure in; (**enjoy oneself**) find pleasure; have use or benefit of; experience. □ **enjoyable** *adjective*; **enjoyably** *adverb*; **enjoyment** *noun*.

enlarge /ɪnˈlɑːdʒ/ *verb* (**-ging**) make or become larger; (often + *on, upon*) describe in greater detail; reproduce on larger scale. □ **enlargement** *noun*.

enlarger *noun* apparatus for enlarging photographs.

enlighten /ɪnˈlaɪt(ə)n/ *verb* inform; (as **enlightened** *adjective*) progressive. □ **enlightenment** *noun*.

enlist /ɪnˈlɪst/ *verb* enrol in armed services; secure as means of help or support. □ **enlistment** *noun*.

enliven /ɪnˈlaɪv(ə)n/ *verb* make lively or cheerful. □ **enlivenment** *noun*.

en masse /ã ˈmæs/ *adverb* all together. [French]

enmesh /ɪnˈmeʃ/ *verb* entangle (as) in net.

enmity /ˈenmɪtɪ/ *noun* (*plural* **-ies**) hostility; state of being an enemy.

ennoble /ɪˈnəʊb(ə)l/ *verb* (**-ling**) make noble. □ **ennoblement** *noun*.

ennui /ɒnˈwiː/ *noun* boredom.

enormity /ɪˈnɔːmɪtɪ/ *noun* (*plural* **-ies**) great wickedness; monstrous crime; great size.

■ **Usage** Many people believe it is wrong to use *enormity* to mean 'great size'.

enormous /ɪˈnɔːməs/ *adjective* huge. □ **enormously** *adverb*.

enough /ɪˈnʌf/ ● *adjective* as much or as many as required. ● *noun* sufficient amount or quantity. ● *adverb* to required degree; fairly; very, quite.

enquire /ɪnˈkwaɪə/ *verb* (**-ring**) seek information; ask question; inquire.

enquiry *noun* (*plural* **-ies**) asking; inquiry.

enrage /ɪnˈreɪdʒ/ *verb* (**-ging**) make furious.

enrapture /ɪnˈræptʃə/ *verb* (**-ring**) delight intensely.

enrich /ɪnˈrɪtʃ/ *verb* make rich(er). □ **enrichment** *noun*.

enrol /ɪnˈrəʊl/ *verb* (*US* **enroll**) (**-ll-**) (cause to) join society, course, etc.; write name of (person) on list. □ **enrolment** *noun*.

en route /ã ˈruːt/ *adverb* on the way. [French]

ensconce /ɪnˈskɒns/ *verb* (**-cing**) (usually **ensconce oneself** or in *passive*) settle comfortably.

ensemble /ɒnˈsɒmb(ə)l/ *noun* thing viewed as whole; set of clothes worn together; group of performers working together; *Music* passage for ensemble.

enshrine /ɪnˈʃraɪm/ *verb* (**-ning**) enclose in shrine; protect, make inviolable.

ensign /ˈensaɪn/ *noun* banner, flag, esp. military or naval flag of nation; standard-bearer; *historical* lowest commissioned infantry officer; *US* lowest commissioned naval officer.

enslave /ɪnˈsleɪv/ *verb* (**-ving**) make slave of. □ **enslavement** *noun*.

ensnare /ɪnˈsneə/ *verb* (**-ring**) entrap.

ensue /ɪnˈsjuː/ *verb* (**-sues, -sued, -suing**) happen later or as a result.

en suite /ã ˈswiːt/ ● *adverb* forming single unit. ● *adjective* (of bathroom) attached to bedroom; (of bedroom) with bathroom attached.

ensure /ɪnˈʃʊə/ *verb* (**-ring**) make certain or safe.

ENT *abbreviation* ear, nose, and throat.

entail /ɪnˈteɪl/ ● *verb* necessitate or involve unavoidably; *Law* bequeath (estate) to specified line of beneficiaries. ● *noun* entailed estate.

entangle /ɪnˈtæŋɡ(ə)l/ *verb* (**-ling**) catch or hold fast in snare etc.; involve in difficulties; complicate. □ **entanglement** *noun*.

entente /ɒnˈtɒnt/ *noun* friendly understanding between states. □ **entente cordiale** entente, esp. between Britain and France since 1904.

enter /ˈentə/ *verb* go or come in or into; come on stage; penetrate; put (name, fact, etc.) into list or record etc.; (usually + *for*) name, or name oneself, as competitor; become member of. □ **enter into** engage in, bind oneself by, form part of, sympathize with; **enter (up)on** begin, begin to deal with, assume possession of.

enteric /enˈterɪk/ *adjective* of intestines.

enteritis /entəˈraɪtɪs/ *noun* inflammation of intestines.

enterprise /ˈentəpraɪz/ *noun* bold undertaking; readiness to engage in this; business firm or venture.

enterprising *adjective* showing enterprise.

entertain /entəˈteɪn/ *verb* amuse; receive as guest; harbour (feelings); consider (idea). □ **entertainer** *noun*; **entertaining** *adjective*.

entertainment *noun* entertaining; thing that entertains, performance.

enthral /ɪnˈθrɔːl/ *verb* (*US* **enthrall**) (**-ll-**) captivate; please greatly. □ **enthralment** *noun*.

enthrone /ɪn'θrəʊn/ *verb* (**-ning**) place on throne. □ **enthronement** *noun*.

enthuse /ɪn'θjuːz/ *verb* (**-sing**) *colloquial* be or make enthusiastic.

enthusiasm /ɪn'θjuːzɪæz(ə)m/ *noun* great eagerness or admiration; object of this. □ **enthusiast** *noun*; **enthusiastic** /-'æst-/ *adjective*; **enthusiastically** *adverb*.

entice /ɪn'taɪs/ *verb* (**-cing**) attract by offer of pleasure or reward. □ **enticement** *noun*; **enticing** *adjective*; **enticingly** *adverb*.

entire /ɪn'taɪə/ *adjective* complete; unbroken; absolute; in one piece.

entirely *adverb* wholly.

entirety /ɪn'taɪərətɪ/ *noun* (*plural* **-ies**) completeness; sum total. □ **in its entirety** in its complete form.

entitle /ɪn'taɪt(ə)l/ *verb* (**-ling**) (usually + *to*) give (person) right or claim; give title to. □ **entitlement** *noun*.

entity /'entɪtɪ/ *noun* (*plural* **-ies**) thing with distinct existence; thing's existence.

entomb /ɪn'tuːm/ *verb* place in tomb; serve as tomb for. □ **entombment** *noun*.

entomology /entə'mɒlədʒɪ/ *noun* study of insects. □ **entomological** /-mə'lɒdʒ-/ *adjective*; **entomologist** *noun*.

entourage /'ɒntʊərɑːʒ/ *noun* people attending important person.

entr'acte /'ɒntrækt/ *noun* (music or dance performed in) interval in play.

entrails /'entreɪlz/ *plural noun* intestines; inner parts.

entrance¹ /'entrəns/ *noun* place for entering; coming or going in; right of admission.

entrance² /ɪn'trɑːns/ *verb* (**-cing**) enchant, delight; put into trance.

entrant /'entrənt/ *noun* person who enters exam, profession, etc.

entrap /ɪn'træp/ *verb* (**-pp-**) catch (as) in trap.

entreat /ɪn'triːt/ *verb* ask earnestly, beg.

entreaty *noun* (*plural* **-ies**) earnest request.

entrecôte /'ɒntrəkəʊt/ *noun* boned steak cut off sirloin.

entrée /'ɒntreɪ/ *noun* main dish of meal; dish served between fish and meat courses; right of admission.

entrench /ɪn'trentʃ/ *verb* establish firmly; (as **entrenched** *adjective*) (of attitude etc.) not easily modified; surround or fortify with trench. □ **entrenchment** *noun*.

entrepreneur /ɒntrəprə'nɜː/ *noun* person who undertakes commercial venture. □ **entrepreneurial** *adjective*.

entropy /'entrəpɪ/ *noun* measure of disorganization of universe; measure of unavailability of system's thermal energy for conversion into mechanical work.

entrust /ɪn'trʌst/ *verb* (+ *to*) give (person, thing) into care of; (+ *with*) assign responsibility for (person, thing) to.

entry /'entrɪ/ *noun* (*plural* **-ies**) coming or going in; entering, item entered; place of entrance; alley.

entwine /ɪn'twaɪn/ *verb* (**-ning**) twine round, interweave.

enumerate /ɪ'njuːməreɪt/ *verb* (**-ting**) specify (items); count. □ **enumeration** *noun*.

enunciate /ɪ'nʌnsɪeɪt/ *verb* (**-ting**) pronounce (words) clearly; state definitely. □ **enunciation** *noun*.

envelop /ɪn'veləp/ *verb* (**-p-**) wrap up, cover; surround. □ **envelopment** *noun*.

envelope /'envələʊp/ *noun* folded paper cover for letter etc.; wrapper, covering.

enviable /'envɪəb(ə)l/ *adjective* likely to excite envy. □ **enviably** *adverb*.

envious /'envɪəs/ *adjective* feeling or showing envy.

environment /ɪn'vaɪərənmənt/ *noun* surroundings; circumstances affecting person's life. □ **environmental** /-'men-/ *adjective*; **environmentally** /-'men-/ *adverb*.

environmentalist /ɪnvaɪərən'mentəlɪst/ *noun* person concerned with protection of natural environment.

environs /ɪn'vaɪərəns/ *plural noun* district round town etc.

envisage /ɪn'vɪzɪdʒ/ *verb* (**-ging**) visualize, imagine, contemplate.

envoy /'envɔɪ/ *noun* messenger, representative; diplomat ranking below ambassador.

envy /'envɪ/ ● *noun* (*plural* **-ies**) discontent aroused by another's better fortune etc.; object or cause of this. ● *verb* (**-ies, -ied**) feel envy of.

enzyme /'enzaɪm/ *noun* protein catalyst of specific biochemical reaction.

eolian harp *US* = AEOLIAN HARP.

eon = AEON.

EP *abbreviation* extended-play (record).

epaulette /'epəlet/ *noun* (*US* **epaulet**) ornamental shoulder-piece, esp. on uniform.

ephedrine /'efədrɪn/ *noun* alkaloid drug used to relieve asthma etc.

ephemera /ɪ'femərə/ *plural noun* things of only short-lived relevance.

ephemeral *adjective* short-lived, transitory.

epic /'epɪk/ ● *noun* long poem narrating adventures of heroic figure etc.; book or film based on this. ● *adjective* like an epic; grand, heroic.

epicene /'episiːn/ *adjective* of or for both sexes; having characteristics of both sexes or of neither sex.

epicentre /'episentə/ *noun* (*US* **epicenter**) point at which earthquake reaches earth's surface.

epicure /'epɪkjʊə/ *noun* person with refined taste in food and drink. □ **epicurism** *noun*.

epicurean /epɪkjʊə'riːən/ ● *noun* person fond of pleasure and luxury. ● *adjective* characteristics of an epicurean. □ **epicureanism** *noun*.

epidemic /epɪ'demɪk/ ● *noun* widespread occurrence of particular disease in community at particular time. ● *adjective* in the nature of an epidemic.

epidemiology /epɪdiːmɪ'ɒlədʒɪ/ *noun* study of epidemics and their control.

epidermis /epɪ'dɜːmɪs/ *noun* outer layer of skin.

epidiascope /epɪ'daɪəskəʊp/ *noun* optical projector giving images of both opaque and transparent objects.

epidural /epɪ'djʊər(ə)l/ ● *adjective* (of anaesthetic) injected close to spinal cord. ● *noun* epidural injection.

epiglottis /epɪ'glɒtɪs/ *noun* flap of cartilage at root of tongue that covers windpipe during swallowing. □ **epiglottal** *adjective*.

epigram /'epɪgræm/ *noun* short poem with witty ending; pointed saying. □ **epigrammatic** /-grə'mæt-/ *adjective*.

epigraph /'epɪgrɑːf/ *noun* inscription.

epilepsy /'epɪlepsɪ/ *noun* nervous disorder with convulsions and often loss of consciousness. □ **epileptic** /-'lep-/ *adjective* & *noun*.

epilogue /'epɪlɒg/ *noun* short piece ending literary work; short speech at end of play etc.

Epiphany /ɪ'pɪfənɪ/ *noun* (festival on 6 Jan. commemorating) visit of Magi to Christ.

episcopacy /ɪ'pɪskəpəsɪ/ *noun* (*plural* **-ies**) government by bishops; bishops collectively.

episcopal /ɪ'pɪskəp(ə)l/ *adjective* of bishop or bishops; (of church) governed by bishops. □ **Episcopal Church** Anglican Church in Scotland and US.

Episcopalian /ɪpɪskə'peɪlɪən/ ● *adjective* of the Episcopal Church or (**episcopalian**) an episcopal church. ● *noun* member of the Episcopal Church.

episcopate /ɪ'pɪskəpət/ *noun* office or tenure of bishop; bishops collectively.

episode /'epɪsəʊd/ *noun* event as part of sequence; part of serial story; incident in narrative. □ **episodic** /-'sɒd-/ *adjective*.

epistemology /ɪpɪstɪ'mɒlədʒɪ/ *noun* philosophy of knowledge. □ **epistemological** /-ə'lɒdʒ-/ *adjective*.

epistle /ɪ'pɪs(ə)l/ *noun* letter; poem etc. in form of letter.

epistolary /ɪ'pɪstələrɪ/ *adjective* of or in form of letters.

epitaph /'epɪtɑːf/ *noun* words in memory of dead person, esp. on tomb.

epithelium /epɪ'θiːlɪəm/ *noun* (*plural* **-s** or **-lia**) *Biology* tissue forming outer layer of body and lining many hollow structures. □ **epithelial** *adjective*.

epithet /'epɪθet/ *noun* adjective etc. expressing quality or attribute.

epitome /ɪ'pɪtəmɪ/ *noun* person or thing embodying a quality etc.

epitomize *verb* (also **-ise**) (**-zing** or **-sing**) make or be perfect example of (a quality etc.).

EPNS *abbreviation* electroplated nickel silver.

epoch /'iːpɒk/ *noun* period marked by special events; beginning of era. □ **epoch-making** notable, significant.

eponym /'epənɪm/ *noun* word derived from person's name; person whose name is used in this way. □ **eponymous** /ɪ'pɒnɪməs/ *adjective*.

epoxy resin /ɪ'pɒksɪ/ *noun* synthetic thermosetting resin, used esp. as glue.

Epsom salts /'epsəm/ *noun* magnesium sulphate used as purgative.

equable /'ekwəb(ə)l/ *adjective* not varying; moderate; not easily disturbed. □ **equably** *adverb*.

equal /'iːkw(ə)l/ ● *adjective* same in number, size, merit, etc.; evenly matched; having same rights or status. ● *noun* person etc. equal to another. ● *verb* (**-ll-**; *US* **-l-**) be equal to; achieve something equal to. □ **equal opportunity** (often in *plural*) opportunity to compete equally for jobs regardless of race, sex, etc. □ **equally** *adverb*.

■ *Usage* It is a mistake to say *equally as*, as in *She was equally as guilty*. The correct version is *She was equally guilty* or possibly, for example, *She was as guilty as he was*.

equality /ɪ'kwɒlɪtɪ/ *noun* being equal.

equalize *verb* (also **-ise**) (**-zing** or **-sing**) make or become equal; (in games) reach opponent's score. □ **equalization** *noun*.

equalizer *noun* (also **-iser**) equalizing goal etc.

equanimity /ekwə'nɪmɪtɪ/ *noun* composure, calm.

equate /ɪ'kweɪt/ *verb* (**-ting**) (usually + *to, with*) regard as equal or equivalent; (+ *with*) be equal or equivalent to.

equation /ɪ'kweɪʒ(ə)n/ *noun* making or being equal; *Mathematics* statement that two expressions are equal; *Chemistry* symbolic representation of reaction.

equator /ɪ'kweɪtə/ *noun* imaginary line round the earth or other body, equidistant from poles.

equatorial /ekwə'tɔːrɪəl/ *adjective* of or near equator.

equerry /'ekwərɪ/ *noun* (*plural* **-ies**) officer attending British royal family.

equestrian /ɪ'kwestrɪən/ *adjective* of horse-riding; on horseback. □ **equestrianism** *noun*.

equiangular /iːkwɪ'æŋgjʊlə/ *adjective* having equal angles.

equidistant /iːkwɪ'dɪst(ə)nt/ *adjective* at equal distances.

equilateral /iːkwɪ'lætər(ə)l/ *adjective* having all sides equal.

equilibrium /iːkwɪ'lɪbrɪəm/ *noun* state of balance; composure.

equine /'ekwaɪn/ *adjective* of or like horse.

equinox /'iːkwɪnɒks/ *noun* time or date at which sun crosses equator and day and night are of equal length.

equip /ɪ'kwɪp/ *verb* (**-pp-**) supply with what is needed.

equipment *noun* necessary tools, clothing, etc.; equipping, being equipped.

equipoise /'ekwɪpɔɪz/ *noun* equilibrium; counterbalancing thing.

equitable /'ekwɪtəb(ə)l/ *adjective* fair, just; *Law* valid in equity. □ **equitably** *adverb*.

equitation /ekwɪ'teɪʃ(ə)n/ *noun* horsemanship; horse-riding.

equity /'ekwɪtɪ/ *noun* (*plural* **-ies**) fairness; principles of justice supplementing law; value of shares issued by company; (in *plural*) stocks and shares not bearing fixed interest.

equivalent /ɪ'kwɪvələnt/ ● *adjective* (often + *to*) equal in value, meaning, etc.; corresponding. ● *noun* equivalent amount etc. □ **equivalence** *noun*.

equivocal /ɪ'kwɪvək(ə)l/ *adjective* of double or doubtful meaning; of uncertain nature; (of person etc.) questionable. □ **equivocally** *adverb*.

equivocate /ɪ'kwɪvəkeɪt/ *verb* (**-ting**) use words ambiguously to conceal truth. □ **equivocation** *noun*.

ER *abbreviation* Queen Elizabeth (*Elizabetha Regina*).

era /'ɪərə/ *noun* system of chronology starting from particular point; historical or other period.

eradicate /ɪ'rædɪkeɪt/ *verb* (**-ting**) root out, destroy. □ **eradication** *noun*.

erase /ɪ'reɪz/ *verb* (**-sing**) rub out; obliterate; remove recording from (magnetic tape etc.).

eraser *noun* piece of rubber etc. for removing esp. pencil marks.

erasure /ɪ'reɪʒə/ *noun* erasing; erased word etc.

ere /eə/ *preposition & conjunction* *poetical or archaic* before.

erect /ɪ'rekt/ ● *adjective* upright, vertical; (of part of body) enlarged and rigid, esp. from sexual excitement. ● *verb* raise, set upright; build; establish. □ **erection** *noun*.

erectile /ɪ'rektaɪl/ *adjective* that can become erect.

erg *noun* unit of work or energy.

ergo /'ɜːgəʊ/ *adverb* therefore. [Latin]

ergonomics /ɜːgə'nɒmɪks/ *plural noun* (treated as *singular*) study of relationship between people and their working environment. □ **ergonomic** *adjective*.

ergot /'ɜːgət/ *noun* disease of rye etc. caused by fungus.

ERM *abbreviation* Exchange Rate Mechanism.

ermine /'ɜːmɪn/ *noun* (*plural* same or **-s**) stoat, esp. in its white winter fur; this fur.

Ernie /'ɜːnɪ/ *noun* device for drawing prize-winning numbers of Premium Bonds.

erode /ɪ'rəʊd/ *verb* (**-ding**) wear away, gradually destroy. □ **erosion** *noun*; **erosive** *adjective*.

erogenous /ɪ'rɒdʒɪnəs/ *adjective* (of part of body) sexually sensitive.

erotic /ɪ'rɒtɪk/ *adjective* arousing sexual desire or excitement. □ **erotically** *adverb*; **eroticism** /-sɪz-/ *noun*.

erotica /ɪ'rɒtɪkə/ *plural noun* erotic literature or art.

err /ɜː/ *verb* be mistaken or incorrect; sin.

errand /'erənd/ *noun* short journey, esp. on another's behalf, to take message etc.; object of journey.

errant /'erənt/ *adjective* erring; *literary* travelling in search of adventure.

erratic /ɪ'rætɪk/ *adjective* inconsistent or uncertain in movement or conduct etc. □ **erratically** *adverb*.

erratum /ɪ'rɑːtəm/ *noun* (*plural* **-ta**) error in printing etc.

erroneous /ɪ'rəʊnɪəs/ *adjective* incorrect. □ **erroneously** *adverb*.

error /'erə/ *noun* mistake; condition of being morally wrong; degree of inaccuracy in calculation or measurement.

ersatz /'eəzæts/ *adjective & noun* substitute; imitation.

erstwhile /'ɜːstwaɪl/ *adjective* former.

eructation /iːrʌk'teɪʃ(ə)n/ *noun formal* belching.

erudite /'eruːdaɪt/ *adjective* learned. □ **erudition** /-'dɪʃ-/ *noun*.

erupt /ɪ'rʌpt/ *verb* break out; (of volcano) shoot out lava etc.; (of rash) appear on skin. □ **eruption** *noun*.

erysipelas /erɪ'sɪpɪləs/ *noun* disease causing deep red inflammation of skin.

escalate /'eskəleɪt/ *verb* (**-ting**) increase or develop by stages. □ **escalation** *noun*.

escalator *noun* moving staircase.

escalope /'eskəlɒp/ *noun* thin slice of meat, esp. veal.

escapade /'eskəpeɪd/ *noun* piece of reckless behaviour.

escape /ɪs'keɪp/ ● *verb* (**-ping**) get free; leak; avoid punishment etc.; get free of; elude, avoid. ● *noun* escaping; means of escaping; leakage. □ **escape clause** clause releasing contracting party from obligation in specified circumstances.

escapee /ɪskeɪ'piː/ *noun* person who has escaped.

escapism *noun* pursuit of distraction and relief from reality. □ **escapist** *adjective & noun*.

escapology /eskə'pɒlədʒɪ/ *noun* techniques of escaping from confinement, esp. as entertainment. □ **escapologist** *noun*.

escarpment /ɪs'kɑːpmənt/ *noun* long steep slope at edge of plateau etc.

eschatology /eskə'tɒlədʒɪ/ *noun* doctrine of death and final destiny. □ **eschatological** /-tə'lɒdʒ-/ *adjective*.

escheat /ɪs'tʃiːt/ ● *noun* lapse of property to the state etc.; property so lapsing. ● *verb* hand over as escheat, confiscate; revert by escheat.

eschew /ɪs'tʃuː/ *verb formal* abstain from.

escort ● *noun* /'eskɔːt/ person(s) etc. accompanying another for protection or as courtesy; person accompanying another of opposite sex socially. ● *verb* /ɪ'skɔːt/ act as escort to.

escritoire /eskrɪ'twɑː/ *noun* writing desk with drawers etc.

escutcheon /ɪ'skʌtʃ(ə)n/ *noun* shield bearing coat of arms.

ESE *abbreviation* east-south-east.

Eskimo /'eskɪməʊ/ ● *noun* (*plural* same or **-s**) member of people inhabiting N. Canada, Alaska, Greenland, and E. Siberia; their language. ● *adjective* of Eskimos or their language.

■ **Usage** The Eskimos of N. America prefer the name *Inuit*.

ESN *abbreviation* educationally subnormal.

esophagus *US* = OESOPHAGUS.

esoteric /esə'terɪk, iːsə'terɪk/ *adjective* intelligible only to those with special knowledge.

ESP *abbreviation* extrasensory perception.

esp. *abbreviation* especially.

espadrille /espə'drɪl/ *noun* light canvas shoe with plaited fibre sole.

espalier /ɪ'spælɪə/ *noun* framework for training tree etc.; tree trained on this.

esparto /e'spɑːtəʊ/ *noun* kind of grass used to make paper.

especial /ɪ'speʃ(ə)l/ *adjective* special, notable.

especially *adverb* in particular; more than in other cases; particularly.

Esperanto /espə'ræntəʊ/ *noun* artificial universal language.

espionage /'espɪənɑːʒ/ *noun* spying or using spies.

esplanade /esplə'neɪd/ *noun* level space, esp. used as public promenade.

espousal /ɪ'spaʊz(ə)l/ *noun* espousing; *archaic* marriage, betrothal.

espouse /ɪ'spaʊz/ *verb* (**-sing**) support (cause); *archaic* marry.

espresso /e'spresəʊ/ *noun* (*plural* **-s**) coffee made under steam pressure.

esprit de corps /espri: də 'kɔː/ *noun* devotion to and pride in one's group. [French]

espy /ɪ'spaɪ/ *verb* (**-ies, -ied**) catch sight of.

Esq. *abbreviation* Esquire.

esquire /ɪ'skwaɪə/ *noun: title placed after man's name in writing*.

essay ● *noun* /'eseɪ/ short piece of writing, esp. on given subject; *formal* attempt. ● *verb* /e'seɪ/ attempt.

essayist *noun* writer of essays.

essence /'es(ə)ns/ *noun* fundamental nature, inherent characteristics; extract obtained by distillation etc.; perfume. □ **in essence** fundamentally.

essential /ɪ'sen∫(ə)l/ ● *adjective* necessary, indispensable; of or constituting a thing's essence. ● *noun* (esp. in *plural*) indispensable element or thing. □ **essential oil** volatile oil with characteristic odour. □ **essentially** *adverb*.

establish /ɪ'stæblɪʃ/ *verb* set up; settle; (esp. as **established** *adjective*) achieve permanent acceptance for; place beyond dispute. □ **Established Church** Church recognized by state.

establishment *noun* establishing, being established; public institution; place of business; staff, household, etc.; Church system established by law; (**the Establishment**) social group with authority or influence and resisting change.

estate /ɪ'steɪt/ *noun* landed property; area of homes or businesses planned as a whole; dead person's collective assets and liabilities. □ **estate agent** person whose business is sale and lease of buildings and land on behalf of others; **estate car** car with continuous area for rear passengers and luggage.

esteem /ɪ'stiːm/ ● *verb* (usually in *passive*) think highly of; *formal* consider. ● *noun* high regard.

ester /estə/ *noun* compound formed by replacing the hydrogen of an acid by an organic radical.

estimable /'estɪməb(ə)l/ *adjective* worthy of esteem.

estimate ● *noun* /'estɪmət/ approximate judgement of cost, value, etc.; approximate price stated in advance for work. ● *verb* /'estɪmeɪt/ (**-ting**) form estimate of; (+ *that*) make rough calculation; (+ *at*) put (sum etc.) at by estimating.

estimation /estɪ'meɪʃ(ə)n/ *noun* estimating; judgement of worth.

estrange /ɪ'streɪndʒ/ *verb* (**-ging**) (usually in *passive*; often + *from*) alienate, make hostile or indifferent; (as **estranged** *adjective*) no longer living with spouse. □ **estrangement** *noun*.

estrogen *US* = OESTROGEN.

estuary /'estjʊərɪ/ *noun* (*plural* **-ies**) tidal mouth of river.

ETA *abbreviation* estimated time of arrival.

et al. *abbreviation* and others (*et alii*).

etc. *abbreviation* et cetera.

et cetera /et 'setrə/ *adverb* (also **etcetera**) and the rest; and so on. **etceteras** *plural noun* the usual extras.

etch *verb* reproduce (picture etc.) by engraving metal plate with acid, esp. to print copies; engrave (plate) thus; practise this craft; (usually + *on*, *upon*) impress deeply.

etching *noun* print made from etched plate.

eternal /ɪ'tɜ:n(ə)l/ *adjective* existing always; without end or beginning; unchanging; *colloquial* constant, too frequent. □ **eternally** *adverb*.

eternity /ɪ'tɜ:nɪtɪ/ *noun* infinite time; endless life after death; (**an eternity**) *colloquial* a very long time.

ethane /'i:θeɪn/ *noun* hydrocarbon gas present in petroleum and natural gas.

ethanol /'eθənɒl/ *noun* alcohol.

ether /'i:θə/ *noun* volatile liquid used as anaesthetic or solvent; clear sky, upper air.

ethereal /ɪ'θɪərɪəl/ *adjective* light, airy; delicate, esp. in appearance; heavenly.

ethic /'eθɪk/ *noun* set of moral principles.

ethical *adjective* relating to morals or ethics; morally correct; (of drug etc.) available only on prescription. □ **ethically** *adverb*.

ethics *plural noun* (also treated as *singular*) moral philosophy; (set of) moral principles.

Ethiopian /i:θɪ'əʊpɪən/ ● *noun* native or national of Ethiopia. ● *adjective* of Ethiopia.

ethnic /'eθnɪk/ *adjective* (of social) group having common national or cultural tradition; (of clothes etc.) resembling those of an exotic people; (of person) having specified origin by birth or descent rather than nationality. □ **ethnic cleansing** *euphemistic* expulsion or murder of people of ethnic or religious group in certain area. □ **ethnically** *adverb*.

ethnology /eθ'nɒlədʒɪ/ *noun* comparative study of peoples. □ **ethnological** /-nə'lɒdʒ-/ *adjective*.

ethos /'i:θɒs/ *noun* characteristic spirit of community, people, or system.

ethylene /'eθɪli:n/ *noun* flammable hydrocarbon gas.

etiolate /'i:tɪəleɪt/ *verb* (**-ting**) make pale by excluding light; give sickly colour to. □ **etiolation** *noun*.

etiology *US* = AETIOLOGY.

etiquette /'etɪket/ *noun* conventional rules of social behaviour or professional conduct.

étude /eɪ'tju:d/ *noun* musical composition designed to develop player's skill.

etymology /etɪ'mɒlədʒɪ/ *noun* (*plural* **-ies**) origin and sense-development of word; account of these. □ **etymological** /-mə'lɒdʒ-/ *adjective*.

eucalyptus /ju:kə'lɪptəs/ *noun* (*plural* **-tuses** or **-ti** /-taɪ/) tall evergreen tree; its oil, used as antiseptic etc.

Eucharist /'ju:kərɪst/ *noun* Christian sacrament in which bread and wine are consecrated and consumed; consecrated elements, esp. bread. □ **Eucharistic** /-'rɪs-/ *adjective*.

eugenics /ju:'dʒenɪks/ *plural noun* (also treated as *singular*) improvement of qualities of race by control of inherited characteristics. □ **eugenic** *adjective*; **eugenically** *adverb*.

eulogize /'ju:lədʒaɪz/ *verb* (also **-ise**) (**-zing** or **-sing**) extol; praise.

eulogy /'ju:lədʒɪ/ *noun* (*plural* **-ies**) speech or writing in praise or commendation. □ **eulogistic** /-'dʒɪs-/ *adjective*.

eunuch /'ju:nək/ *noun* castrated man.

euphemism /'ju:fɪmɪz(ə)m/ *noun* mild expression substituted for blunt one. □ **euphemistic** /-'mɪs-/ *adjective*; **euphemistically** /-'mɪs-/ *adverb*.

euphonium /ju:'fəʊnɪəm/ *noun* brass instrument of tuba family.

euphony /'ju:fənɪ/ *noun* pleasantness of sound, esp. in words. □ **euphonious** /-'fəʊ-/ *adjective*.

euphoria /ju:'fɔ:rɪə/ *noun* intense sense of well-being and excitement. □ **euphoric** /-'fɒr-/ *adjective*.

Eurasian /jʊə'reɪʒ(ə)n/ ● *adjective* of mixed European and Asian parentage; of Europe and Asia. ● *noun* Eurasian person.

eureka /jʊə'ri:kə/ *interjection* I have found it!

Eurodollar /'jʊərəʊdɒlə/ *noun* dollar held in bank in Europe etc.

European /jʊərə'pɪən/ ● *adjective* of, in, or extending over Europe. ● *noun* native or inhabitant of Europe; descendant of one.

Eustachian tube /ju:'steɪʃ(ə)n/ *noun* passage between middle ear and back of throat.

euthanasia /ju:θə'neɪzɪə/ *noun* killing person painlessly, esp. one who has incurable painful disease.

evacuate /ɪ'vækjʊeɪt/ *verb* (**-ting**) remove (people) from place of danger; make empty, clear; withdraw from (place); empty (bowels). □ **evacuation** *noun*.

evacuee /ɪvækju:'i:/ *noun* person evacuated.

evade /ɪ'veɪd/ *verb* (**-ding**) escape from, avoid; avoid doing or answering directly; avoid paying (tax) illegally.

evaluate /ɪ'væljʊeɪt/ *verb* (**-ting**) assess, appraise; find or state number or amount of. □ **evaluation** *noun*.

evanesce /evə'nes/ *verb* (**-cing**) *literary* fade from sight. □ **evanescence** *noun*; **evanescent** *adjective*.

evangelical /i:væn'dʒelɪk(ə)l/ ● *adjective* of or according to gospel teaching; of Protestant groups maintaining doctrine of salvation by faith. ● *noun* member of evangelical group. □ **evangelicalism** *noun*.

evangelist /ɪ'vændʒəlɪst/ *noun* writer of one of the 4 Gospels; preacher of gospel. □ **evangelism** *noun*; **evangelistic** /-'lɪs-/ *adjective*.

evangelize *verb* (also **-ise**) (**-zing** or **-sing**) preach gospel to. □ **evangelization** *noun*.

evaporate /ɪ'væpəreɪt/ *verb* (**-ting**) turn into vapour; (cause to) lose moisture as vapour; (cause to) disappear. □ **evaporation** *noun*.

evasion /ɪ'veɪʒ(ə)n/ *noun* evading; evasive answer.

evasive /ɪ'veɪsɪv/ *adjective* seeking to evade.

eve *noun* evening or day before festival etc.; time just before event; *archaic* evening.

even /'i:v(ə)n/ ● *adjective* (**-er**, **-est**) level, smooth; uniform; equal; equable, calm; divisible by two. ● *adverb* still, yet; (with negative) so much as. ● *verb* (often + *up*) make or become even. □ **even if** in spite of the fact that, no matter whether; **even out** become level or regular, spread (thing) over period or among group. □ **evenly** *adverb*.

evening /'i:vnɪŋ/ *noun* end part of day, esp. from about 6 p.m. to bedtime. □ **evening class** adult education class held in evening; **evening dress** formal clothes for evening wear; **evening star** planet, esp. Venus, conspicuous in west after sunset.

evensong *noun* evening service in Church of England.

event /ɪ'vent/ *noun* thing that happens; fact of thing occurring; item in (esp. sports) programme. □ **in any event**, **at all events** whatever happens; **in the event** as it turns or turned out; **in the event of** if (thing) happens.

eventful *adjective* marked by noteworthy events.

eventual /ɪ'ventʃʊəl/ *adjective* occurring in due course. □ **eventually** *adverb*.

eventuality /ɪventʃʊ'ælɪtɪ/ *noun* (*plural* **-ies**) possible event.

ever /'evə/ adverb at all times; always; at any time. □ **ever since** throughout period since (then); **ever so** colloquial very; **ever such a(n)** colloquial a very.

evergreen ● adjective retaining green leaves throughout year. ● noun evergreen plant.

everlasting adjective lasting for ever or a long time; (of flower) retaining shape and colour when dried.

evermore adverb for ever; always.

every /'evrɪ/ adjective each; all. □ **everybody** every person; **everyday** occurring every day, ordinary; **Everyman** ordinary or typical human being; **every now and again** or **then** occasionally; **everyone** everybody; **every other** each alternate; **everything** all things, the most important thing; **everywhere** in every place.

evict /ɪ'vɪkt/ verb expel (tenant) by legal process. □ **eviction** noun.

evidence /'evɪd(ə)ns/ ● noun (often + for, of) indication, sign; information given to establish fact etc.; statement etc. admissible in court of law. ● verb (-cing) be evidence of.

evident adjective obvious, manifest.

evidential /evɪ'denʃ(ə)l/ adjective of or providing evidence.

evidently adverb seemingly; as shown by evidence.

evil /'iːv(ə)l/ ● adjective wicked; harmful. ● noun evil thing; wickedness. □ **evil eye** gaze believed to cause harm. □ **evilly** adverb.

evince /ɪ'vɪns/ verb (-cing) show, indicate.

eviscerate /ɪ'vɪsəreɪt/ verb (-ting) disembowel. □ **evisceration** noun.

evocative /ɪ'vɒkətɪv/ adjective evoking (feelings etc.).

evoke /ɪ'vəʊk/ verb (-king) call up (feeling etc.). □ **evocation** /evə-/ noun.

evolution /iːvə'luːʃ(ə)n/ noun evolving; development of species from earlier forms; unfolding of events etc.; change in disposition of troops or ships. □ **evolutionary** adjective.

evolutionist noun person who regards evolution as explaining origin of species.

evolve /ɪ'vɒlv/ verb (-ving) develop gradually and naturally; devise; unfold, open out.

ewe /juː/ noun female sheep.

ewer /'juːə/ noun water-jug with wide mouth.

ex¹ preposition (of goods) sold from (warehouse etc.).

ex² noun colloquial former husband or wife.

ex- prefix formerly.

exacerbate /ek'sæsəbeɪt/ verb (-ting) make worse; irritate. □ **exacerbation** noun.

exact /ɪg'zækt/ ● adjective accurate; correct in all details. ● verb demand and enforce payment of (fees etc.); demand, insist on. □ **exactness** noun.

exaction noun exacting, being exacted; illegal or exorbitant demand.

exactitude noun exactness.

exactly adverb precisely; I agree.

exaggerate /ɪg'zædʒəreɪt/ verb (-ting) make seem larger or greater than it really is; increase beyond normal or due proportions. □ **exaggeration** noun.

exalt /ɪg'zɔːlt/ verb raise in rank, power, etc.; praise; extol; (usually as **exalted** adjective) make lofty or noble. □ **exaltation** /eg-/ noun.

exam /ɪg'zæm/ noun examination, test.

examination /ɪgzæmɪ'neɪʃ(ə)n/ noun examining, being examined; detailed inspection; testing of knowledge or ability by questions; formal questioning of witness etc. in court.

examine /ɪg'zæmɪn/ verb (-ning) inquire into; look closely at; test knowledge or ability of; check health of; question formally. □ **examinee** /-'niː/ noun; **examiner** noun.

example /ɪg'zɑːmp(ə)l/ noun thing illustrating general rule; model, pattern; specimen; precedent; warning to others. □ **for example** by way of illustration.

exasperate /ɪg'zɑːspəreɪt/ verb (-ting) irritate intensely. □ **exasperation** noun.

ex cathedra /eks kə'θiːdrə/ adjective & adverb with full authority (esp. of papal pronouncement). [Latin]

excavate /'ekskəveɪt/ verb (-ting) make (hole etc.) by digging; dig out material from (ground); reveal or extract by digging; dig systematically to explore (archaeological site). □ **excavation** noun; **excavator** noun.

exceed /ɪk'siːd/ verb be more or greater than; go beyond, do more than is warranted by; surpass.

exceedingly adverb very.

excel /ɪk'sel/ verb (-ll-) surpass; be pre-eminent.

excellence /'eksələns/ noun great merit.

Excellency noun (plural **-ies**) (**His, Her, Your Excellency**) title used of or to ambassador, governor, etc.

excellent adjective extremely good.

except /ɪk'sept/ ● verb exclude from general statement etc. ● preposition (often + for) not including, other than.

excepting preposition except.

exception /ɪk'sepʃ(ə)n/ noun excepting; thing or case excepted. □ **take exception** (often + to) object.

exceptionable adjective open to objection.

■ **Usage** Exceptionable is sometimes confused with exceptional.

---

exceptional adjective forming exception; unusual. □ **exceptionally** adverb.

■ **Usage** Exceptional is sometimes confused with exceptionable.

---

excerpt ● noun /'eksɜːpt/ short extract from book, film, etc. ● verb /ɪk'sɜːpt/ take excerpts from. □ **excerption** /ɪk'sɜːpʃ(ə)n/ noun.

excess ● noun /ɪk'ses/ exceeding; amount by which thing exceeds; intemperance in eating or drinking. ● adjective /'ekses/ that exceeds limit or given amount. □ **in, to excess** exceeding proper amount or degree; **in excess of** more than.

excessive /ɪk'sesɪv/ adjective too much; too great. □ **excessively** adverb.

exchange /ɪks'tʃeɪndʒ/ ● noun giving one thing and receiving another in its place; exchanging of money for equivalent, esp. in other currency; centre where telephone connections are made; place where merchants, stockbrokers, etc. transact business; employment office; short conversation. ● verb (-ging) give or receive in exchange; interchange. □ **exchange rate** price of one currency expressed in another. □ **exchangeable** adjective.

exchequer /ɪks'tʃekə/ noun former government department in charge of national revenue; royal or national treasury.

excise¹ /'eksaɪz/ noun tax levied on goods produced or sold within the country; tax on certain licences.

excise² /ɪk'saɪz/ verb (-sing) cut out or away. □ **excision** /-'sɪʒ-/ noun.

excitable adjective easily excited. □ **excitability** noun.

excite /ɪk'saɪt/ verb (-ting) move to strong emotion; arouse (feelings etc.); provoke (action etc.); stimulate to activity. □ **excitement** noun; **exciting** adjective.

exclaim /ɪk'skleɪm/ verb cry out suddenly; utter or say thus.

exclamation /eksklə'meɪʃ(ə)n/ noun exclaiming; word(s) etc. exclaimed. □ **exclamation mark** punctuation mark (!) indicating exclamation (see panel). □ **exclamatory** /ɪk'sklæmətərɪ/ adjective.

exclude /ɪk'sklu:d/ verb (**-ding**) shut out, leave out; make impossible, preclude. □ **exclusion** noun.

exclusive /ɪk'sklu:sɪv/ ● adjective excluding other things; (+ of) not including; (of society etc.) tending to exclude outsiders; high-class; not obtainable or published elsewhere. ● noun exclusive item of news, film, etc. □ **exclusively** adverb; **exclusiveness** noun; **exclusivity** /ɛksklu:'sɪvɪtɪ/ noun.

excommunicate /ɛkskə'mju:nɪkeɪt/ verb (**-ting**) deprive (person) of membership and sacraments of Church. □ **excommunication** noun.

excoriate /ɛks'kɔːrɪeɪt/ verb (**-ting**) remove part of skin of by abrasion; remove (skin); censure severely. □ **excoriation** noun.

excrement /'ɛkskrɪmənt/ noun faeces.

excrescence /ɪk'skrɛs(ə)ns/ noun abnormal or morbid outgrowth. □ **excrescent** adjective.

excreta /ɪk'skri:tə/ plural noun faeces and urine.

excrete /ɪk'skri:t/ verb (**-ting**) (of animal or plant) expel (waste). □ **excretion** noun; **excretory** adjective.

excruciating /ɪk'skru:ʃɪeɪtɪŋ/ adjective acutely painful. □ **excruciatingly** adverb.

exculpate /'ɛkskʌlpeɪt/ verb (**-ting**) formal free from blame. □ **exculpation** noun.

excursion /ɪk'skɜːʃ(ə)n/ noun journey to place and back, made for pleasure.

excursive /ɪk'skɜːsɪv/ adjective literary digressive.

excuse ● verb /ɪk'skju:z/ (**-sing**) try to lessen blame attaching to; serve as reason to judge (person, act) less severely; (often + from) grant exemption to; forgive. ● noun /ɪk'skju:s/ reason put forward to mitigate or justify offence; apology. □ **be excused** be allowed not to do something or to leave or be absent; **excuse me** polite request to be allowed to pass, polite apology for interrupting or disagreeing. □ **excusable** /-'sku:z-/ adjective.

ex-directory adjective not listed in telephone directory, at subscriber's wish.

execrable /'ɛksɪkrəb(ə)l/ adjective abominable.

execrate /'ɛksɪkreɪt/ verb (**-ting**) express or feel abhorrence for; curse. □ **execration** noun.

execute /'ɛksɪkju:t/ verb (**-ting**) carry out, perform; put to death.

execution /ɛksɪ'kju:ʃ(ə)n/ noun carrying out, performance; capital punishment.

executioner noun person carrying out death sentence.

executive /ɪg'zɛkjʊtɪv/ noun person or body with managerial or administrative responsibility; branch of government etc. concerned with executing laws, agreements, etc. ● adjective concerned with executing laws, agreements, etc. or with administration etc.

executor /ɪg'zɛkjʊtə/ noun (feminine **executrix** /-trɪks/) person appointed by testator to carry out terms of will. □ **executorial** /-'tɔːrɪəl/ adjective.

exegesis /ɛksɪ'dʒi:sɪs/ noun explanation, esp. of Scripture. □ **exegetic** /-'dʒɛtɪk/ adjective.

exemplar /ɪg'zɛmplə/ noun model; typical instance.

exemplary adjective outstandingly good; serving as example or warning.

exemplify /ɪg'zɛmplɪfaɪ/ verb (**-ies**, **-ied**) give or be example of. □ **exemplification** noun.

exempt /ɪg'zɛmpt/ ● adjective (often + from) free from obligation or liability imposed on others. ● verb (+ from) make exempt from. □ **exemption** noun.

exercise /'ɛksəsaɪz/ ● noun use of muscles etc., esp. for health; task set for physical or other training; use or application of faculties etc.; practice; (often in plural) military drill or manoeuvres. ● verb (**-sing**) use; perform (function); take exercise; give exercise to; tax powers of; perplex, worry.

exert /ɪg'zɜːt/ verb use; bring to bear; (**exert oneself**) make effort. □ **exertion** noun.

exfoliate /ɛks'fəʊlɪeɪt/ verb (**-ting**) come off in scales or layers. □ **exfoliation** noun.

ex gratia /ɛks 'ɡreɪʃə/ ● adverb as favour and not under (esp. legal) compulsion. ● adjective granted on this basis. [Latin]

exhale /ɛks'heɪl/ verb (**-ling**) breathe out; give off or be given off in vapour. □ **exhalation** /-hə-/ noun.

exhaust /ɪg'zɔːst/ ● verb (often as **exhausted** adjective or **exhausting** adjective) consume, use up; tire out; study or expound completely; empty of contents. ● noun waste gases etc. expelled from engine after combustion; pipe or system through which they are expelled. □ **exhaustible** adjective; **exhaustion** noun.

exhaustive adjective complete, comprehensive. □ **exhaustively** adverb.

exhibit /ɪg'zɪbɪt/ ● verb (**-t-**) show, esp. publicly; display. ● noun thing exhibited. □ **exhibitor** noun.

exhibition /ɛksɪ'bɪʃ(ə)n/ noun display, public show; exhibiting, being exhibited; scholarship, esp. from funds of college etc.

exhibitioner noun student receiving exhibition.

exhibitionism noun tendency towards attention-seeking behaviour; compulsion to expose genitals in public. □ **exhibitionist** noun.

exhilarate /ɪg'zɪləreɪt/ verb (**-ting**) (often as **exhilarating** adjective or **exhilarated** adjective) enliven, gladden. □ **exhilaration** noun.

exhort /ɪg'zɔːt/ verb (often + to do) urge strongly or earnestly. □ **exhortation** /eg-/ noun; **exhortative** adjective; **exhortatory** adjective.

exhume /ɛks'hju:m/ verb (**-ming**) dig up. □ **exhumation** noun.

exigency /'ɛksɪdʒənsɪ/ noun (plural **-ies**) (also **exigence**) urgent need; emergency. □ **exigent** adjective.

exiguous /eg'zɪgjʊəs/ adjective scanty, small. □ **exiguity** /-'gju:ɪtɪ/ noun.

exile /'ɛksaɪl/ ● noun expulsion or long absence from one's country etc.; person in exile. ● verb (**-ling**) send into or condemn to exile.

exist /ɪg'zɪst/ verb be, have being; occur, be found; live with no pleasure; live.

existence noun fact or manner of existing; all that exists. □ **existent** adjective.

existential /ɛgzɪ'stɛnʃ(ə)l/ adjective of or relating to existence.

existentialism noun philosophical theory emphasizing existence of individual as free and self-determining agent. □ **existentialist** adjective & noun.

Exclamation mark !

This is used instead of a full stop at the end of a sentence to show that the speaker or writer is very angry, enthusiastic, insistent, disappointed, hurt, surprised, etc., e.g.

> *I am not pleased at all!*
> *I just love sweets!*
> *Go away!*

> *I wish I could have gone!*
> *Ow!*
> *He didn't even say goodbye!*

exit /'eksɪt/ ● *noun* way out; going out; place where vehicles leave motorway etc.; departure. ● *verb* (**-t-**) make one's exit.

exodus /'eksədəs/ *noun* mass departure; (**Exodus**) that of Israelites from Egypt.

ex officio /eks ə'fɪʃɪəʊ/ *adverb & adjective* by virtue of one's office.

exonerate /ɪg'zɒnəreɪt/ *verb* (**-ting**) free or declare free from blame. □ **exoneration** *noun*.

exorbitant /ɪg'zɔːbɪt(ə)nt/ *adjective* grossly excessive.

exorcize /'eksɔːsaɪz/ *verb* (also **-ise**) (**-zing** or **-sing**) drive out (evil spirit) by prayers etc.; free (person, place) thus. □ **exorcism** *noun*; **exorcist** *noun*.

exoskeleton /'eksəʊskelɪtən/ *noun* external skeleton.

exotic /ɪg'zɒtɪk/ ● *adjective* introduced from abroad; strange, unusual. ● *noun* exotic plant etc. □ **exotically** *adverb*.

expand /ɪk'spænd/ *verb* increase in size or importance; (often + *on*) give fuller account; become more genial; write out in full; spread out flat. □ **expandable** *adjective*; **expansion** *noun*.

expanse /ɪk'spæns/ *noun* wide area or extent of land, space, etc.

expansionism *noun* advocacy of expansion, esp. of state's territory. □ **expansionist** *noun & adjective*.

expansive *adjective* able or tending to expand; extensive; genial.

expatiate /ɪk'speɪʃɪeɪt/ *verb* (**-ting**) (usually + *on, upon*) speak or write at length. □ **expatiation** *noun*.

expatriate ● *adjective* /eks'pætrɪət/ living abroad; exiled. ● *noun* /eks'pætrɪət/ expatriate person. ● *verb* /eks'pætrɪeɪt/ (**-ting**) expel from native country.

expect /ɪk'spekt/ *verb* regard as likely; look for as one's due; *colloquial* suppose. □ **be expecting** *colloquial* be pregnant.

expectant *adjective* expecting; expecting to become; pregnant. □ **expectancy** *noun*; **expectantly** *adverb*.

expectation /ekspek'teɪʃ(ə)n/ *noun* expecting, anticipation; what one expects; probability; (in *plural*) prospects of inheritance.

expectorant /ek'spektərənt/ ● *adjective* causing expectoration. ● *noun* expectorant medicine.

expectorate /ek'spektəreɪt/ *verb* (**-ting**) cough or spit out from chest or lungs; spit. □ **expectoration** *noun*.

expedient /ɪk'spiːdɪənt/ ● *adjective* advantageous; advisable on practical rather than moral grounds. ● *noun* means of achieving an end; resource. □ **expediency** *noun*.

expedite /'ekspɪdaɪt/ *verb* (**-ting**) assist progress of; accomplish quickly.

expedition /ekspɪ'dɪʃ(ə)n/ *noun* journey or voyage for particular purpose; people etc. undertaking this; speed.

expeditionary *adjective* of or used on expedition.

expeditious /ekspɪ'dɪʃəs/ *adjective* acting or done with speed and efficiency.

expel /ɪk'spel/ *verb* (**-ll-**) deprive of membership; force out; eject.

expend /ɪk'spend/ *verb* spend (money, time, etc.); use up.

expendable *adjective* that may be sacrificed or dispensed with.

expenditure /ɪk'spendɪtʃə/ *noun* expending; amount expended.

expense /ɪk'spens/ *noun* cost, charge; (in *plural*) costs incurred in doing job etc., reimbursement of this.

expensive *adjective* costing or charging much. □ **expensively** *adverb*.

experience /ɪk'spɪərɪəns/ ● *noun* personal observation or contact; knowledge or skill based on

this; event that affects one. ● *verb* (**-cing**) have experience of; undergo; feel. □ **experiential** /-'en-/ *adjective*.

experienced *adjective* having had much experience; skilful through experience.

experiment /ɪk'sperɪmənt/ ● *noun* procedure adopted to test hypothesis or demonstrate known fact. ● *verb* (also /-mənt/) make experiment(s). □ **experimentation** /-men-/ *noun*; **experimenter** *noun*.

experimental /ɪksperɪ'ment(ə)l/ *adjective* based on or done by way of experiment. □ **experimentally** *adverb*.

expert /'ekspɜːt/ (often + *at, in*) ● *adjective* well informed or skilful in a subject. ● *noun* expert person. □ **expertly** *adverb*.

expertise /ekspɜː'tiːz/ *noun* special skill or knowledge.

expiate /'ekspɪeɪt/ *verb* (**-ting**) pay penalty or make amends for (wrong). □ **expiation** *noun*.

expire /ɪk'spaɪə/ *verb* (**-ring**) come to an end; cease to be valid; die; breathe out. □ **expiration** /ekspɪ-/ *noun*.

expiry *noun* end of validity or duration.

explain /ɪks'pleɪn/ *verb* make intelligible; make known; say by way of explanation; account for. □ **explanation** /eksplə-/ *noun*.

explanatory /ɪk'splænətərɪ/ *adjective* serving to explain.

expletive /ɪk'spliːtɪv/ *noun* swear-word or exclamation.

explicable /ɪk'splɪkəb(ə)l/ *adjective* explainable.

explicit /ɪk'splɪsɪt/ *adjective* expressly stated; stated in detail; definite; outspoken. □ **explicitly** *adverb*; **explicitness** *noun*.

explode /ɪk'spləʊd/ (**-ding**) *verb* expand violently with loud noise; cause (bomb etc.) to do this; give vent suddenly to emotion, esp. anger; (of population etc.) increase suddenly; discredit.

exploit ● *noun* /'eksplɔɪt/ daring feat. ● *verb* /ɪk'splɔɪt/ use or develop for one's own ends; take advantage of (esp. person). □ **exploitation** /eksplɔɪ-/ *noun*; **exploitative** /ɪk'splɔɪt-/ *adjective*.

explore /ɪk'splɔː/ *verb* (**-ring**) travel through (country etc.) to learn about it; inquire into; examine (part of body), probe (wound). □ **exploration** /eksplə-/ *noun*; **exploratory** /-'splɒr-/ *adjective*; **explorer** *noun*.

explosion /ɪk'spləʊʒ(ə)n/ *noun* exploding; loud noise caused by this; outbreak; sudden increase.

explosive /ɪk'spləʊsɪv/ ● *adjective* tending to explode; likely to cause violent outburst etc. ● *noun* explosive substance.

exponent /ɪk'spəʊnənt/ *noun* person promoting idea etc.; practitioner of activity, profession, etc.; person who explains or interprets; type, representative; *Mathematics* raised number or symbol showing how many of a number are to be multiplied together, e.g. ^{3} in $2^3 = 2 \times 2 \times 2$.

exponential /ekspə'nenʃ(ə)l/ *adjective* (of increase) more and more rapid. □ **exponentially** *adverb*.

export /ɪk'spɔːt/ ● *verb* sell or send (goods or services) to another country. ● *noun* /'ekspɔːt/ exporting; exported article or service; (in *plural*) amount exported. □ **exportation** *noun*; **exporter** /ɪk'spɔːtə/ *noun*.

expose /ɪk'spəʊz/ *verb* (**-sing**) leave unprotected, esp. from weather; (+ *to*) put at risk of, subject to (influence etc.); *Photography* subject (film etc.) to light; reveal, disclose; exhibit, display; (**expose oneself**) display one's genitals indecently in public.

exposé /ek'spəʊzeɪ/ *noun* orderly statement of facts; disclosure of discreditable thing.

exposition /ɛkspəˈzɪʃ(ə)n/ *noun* expounding, explanation; *Music* part of movement in which principal themes are presented; exhibition.

ex post facto /eks pəʊst ˈfæktəʊ/ *adjective & adverb* retrospective(ly). [Latin]

expostulate /ɪkˈspɒstjʊleɪt/ *verb* (**-ting**) make protest, remonstrate. ☐ **expostulation** *noun*.

exposure /ɪkˈspəʊʒə/ *noun* exposing, being exposed; physical condition resulting from being exposed to elements; *Photography* length of time film etc. is exposed, section of film etc. exposed at one time.

expound /ɪkˈspaʊnd/ *verb* set out in detail; explain, interpret.

express /ɪkˈspres/ ● *verb* represent by symbols etc. or in language; put into words; squeeze out (juice, milk, etc.); (**express oneself**) communicate what one thinks, feels, or means. ● *adjective* operating at high speed; definitely stated; delivered by specially fast service. ● *adverb* with speed; by express messenger or train. ● *noun* express train etc. ☐ **expressible** *adjective*.

expression /ɪkˈspreʃ(ə)n/ *noun* expressing, being expressed; wording, word, phrase; conveying or depiction of feeling; appearance (of face), intonation (of voice); *Mathematics* collection of symbols expressing quantity. ☐ **expressionless** *adjective*.

expressionism *noun* style of painting etc. seeking to express emotion rather than depict external world. ☐ **expressionist** *noun & adjective*.

expressive *adjective* full of expression; (+ *of*) serving to express. ☐ **expressiveness** *noun*.

expressly *adverb* explicitly.

expropriate /ɪksˈprəʊprɪeɪt/ *verb* (**-ting**) take away (property); dispossess. ☐ **expropriation** *noun*; **expropriator** *noun*.

expulsion /ɪkˈspʌlʃ(ə)n/ *noun* expelling, being expelled.

expunge /ɪkˈspʌndʒ/ *verb* (**-ging**) erase, remove.

expurgate /ˈekspəgeɪt/ *verb* (**-ting**) remove matter considered objectionable from (book etc.); clear away (such matter). ☐ **expurgation** *noun*; **expurgator** *noun*.

exquisite /ˈekskwɪzɪt, ekˈskwɪzɪt/ *adjective* extremely beautiful or delicate; acute, keen. ☐ **exquisitely** *adverb*.

ex-serviceman /eksˈsɜːvɪsmən/ *noun* man formerly member of armed forces.

extant /ekˈstænt/ *adjective* still existing.

extempore /ɪkˈstempərɪ/ *adverb & adjective* without preparation.

extemporize /ɪkˈstempəraɪz/ *verb* (also **-ise**) (**-zing** or **-sing**) improvise. ☐ **extemporization** *noun*.

extend /ɪkˈstend/ *verb* lengthen in space or time; lay out at full length; reach or be or make continuous over certain area; (+ *to*) have certain scope; offer or accord (feeling, invitation, etc.); tax powers of. ☐ **extendible** *adjective*; **extensible** *adjective*.

extension /ɪkˈstenʃ(ə)n/ *noun* extending; enlargement, additional part; subsidiary telephone on same line as main one; additional period of time.

extensive /ɪkˈstensɪv/ *adjective* large, far-reaching. ☐ **extensively** *adverb*.

extent /ɪkˈstent/ *noun* space covered; width of application, scope.

extenuate /ɪkˈstenjʊeɪt/ *verb* (**-ting**) (often as **extenuating** *adjective*) make (guilt etc.) seem less serious by partial excuse. ☐ **extenuation** *noun*.

exterior /ɪkˈstɪərɪə/ ● *adjective* outer; coming from outside. ● *noun* exterior aspect or surface; outward demeanour.

exterminate /ɪkˈstɜːmɪneɪt/ *verb* (**-ting**) destroy utterly. ☐ **extermination** *noun*; **exterminator** *noun*.

external /ɪkˈstɜːn(ə)l/ ● *adjective* of or on the outside; coming from outside; relating to a country's foreign affairs; (of medicine) for use on outside of body. ● *noun* (in *plural*) external features or circumstances. ☐ **externality** /ekstɜːˈnælɪtɪ/ *noun*; **externally** *adverb*.

externalize *verb* (also **-ise**) (**-zing** or **-sing**) give or attribute external existence to.

extinct /ɪkˈstɪŋkt/ *adjective* no longer existing; no longer burning; (of volcano) that no longer erupts; obsolete.

extinction *noun* making or becoming extinct; extinguishing, being extinguished.

extinguish /ɪkˈstɪŋgwɪʃ/ *verb* put out (flame, light, etc.); terminate, destroy; wipe out (debt).

extinguisher *noun* = FIRE EXTINGUISHER.

extirpate /ˈekstəpeɪt/ *verb* (**-ting**) destroy; root out. ☐ **extirpation** *noun*.

extol /ɪkˈstəʊl/ *verb* (**-ll-**) praise enthusiastically.

extort /ɪkˈstɔːt/ *verb* get by coercion.

extortion *noun* extorting, esp. of money; illegal exaction.

extortionate /ɪkˈstɔːʃənət/ *adjective* exorbitant.

extra /ˈekstrə/ ● *adjective* additional; more than usual or necessary. ● *adverb* more than usually; additionally. ● *noun* extra thing; thing for which one is charged extra; person playing one of crowd etc. in film; special edition of newspaper; *Cricket* run not scored from hit with bat.

extra- *combining form* outside, beyond scope of.

extract ● *verb* /ɪkˈstrækt/ take out; obtain against person's will; obtain from earth; copy out, quote; obtain (juice etc.) by pressure, distillation, etc.; derive (pleasure etc.); *Mathematics* find (root of number). ● *noun* /ˈekstrækt/ passage from book etc.; preparation containing concentrated constituent of substance.

extraction /ɪkˈstrækʃ(ə)n/ *noun* extracting; removal of tooth; lineage.

extractor /ɪkˈstræktə/ *noun* machine that extracts. ☐ **extractor fan** one that extracts bad air etc.

extracurricular /ekstrəkəˈrɪkjʊlə/ *adjective* outside normal curriculum.

extraditable *adjective* liable to extradition; (of crime) warranting extradition.

extradite /ˈekstrədaɪt/ *verb* (**-ting**) hand over (person accused of crime) to state where crime was committed. ☐ **extradition** /-ˈdɪʃ-/ *noun*.

extramarital /ekstrəˈmærɪt(ə)l/ *adjective* (of sexual relationship) outside marriage.

extramural /ekstrəˈmjʊər(ə)l/ *adjective* additional to ordinary teaching or studies.

extraneous /ɪkˈstreɪnɪəs/ *adjective* of external origin; (often + *to*) separate, irrelevant, unrelated.

extraordinary /ɪkˈstrɔːdɪnərɪ/ *adjective* unusual, remarkable; unusually great; (of meeting etc.) additional. ☐ **extraordinarily** *adverb*.

extrapolate /ɪkˈstræpəleɪt/ *verb* (**-ting**) estimate (unknown facts or values) from known data. ☐ **extrapolation** *noun*.

extrasensory /ekstrəˈsensərɪ/ *adjective* derived by means other than known senses.

extraterrestrial /ekstrətɪˈrestrɪəl/ ● *adjective* outside the earth or its atmosphere. ● *noun* fictional being from outer space.

extravagant /ɪkˈstrævəgənt/ *adjective* spending (esp. money) excessively; excessive; absurd; costing much. ☐ **extravagance** *noun*; **extravagantly** *adverb*.

extravaganza /ɪkstrævəˈgænzə/ *noun* spectacular theatrical or television production; fanciful composition.

extreme /ɪkˈstriːm/ ● *adjective* reaching high or highest degree; severe, not moderate; outermost; utmost.

● *noun* either of two things as remote or different as possible; thing at either end; highest degree. □ **extreme unction** anointing by priest of dying person. □ **extremely** *adverb*.

extremis see IN EXTREMIS.

extremism *noun* advocacy of extreme measures. □ **extremist** *adjective & noun*.

extremity /ɪkˈstrɛmɪtɪ/ *noun* (*plural* **-ies**) extreme point, end; (in *plural*) hands and feet; condition of extreme adversity.

extricate /ˈekstrɪkeɪt/ *verb* (**-ting**) disentangle, release. □ **extrication** *noun*.

extrinsic /ekˈstrɪnsɪk/ *adjective* not inherent or intrinsic; (often + *to*) extraneous. □ **extrinsically** *adverb*.

extrovert /ˈekstrəvɜːt/ ● *noun* sociable or unreserved person; person mainly concerned with external things. ● *adjective* typical or having nature of extrovert. □ **extroversion** /-ˈvɜː-/ *noun*.

extrude /ɪkˈstruːd/ *verb* (**-ding**) thrust or squeeze out; shape by forcing through nozzle. □ **extrusion** *noun*.

exuberant /ɪgˈzjuːbərənt/ *adjective* high-spirited, lively; luxuriant, prolific; (of feelings etc.) abounding. □ **exuberance** *noun*.

exude /ɪgˈzjuːd/ *verb* (**-ding**) ooze out; give off; display (emotion) freely. □ **exudation** *noun*.

exult /ɪgˈzʌlt/ *verb* rejoice. □ **exultant** *adjective*; **exultation** /eg-/ *noun*.

eye /aɪ/ ● *noun* organ or faculty of sight; iris of eye; region round eye; gaze; perception; eyelike thing; leaf bud of potato; centre of hurricane; spot, hole, loop. ● *verb* (**eyes, eyed, eyeing** or **eying**) (often + *up*) observe, watch suspiciously or closely. □ **all eyes** watching intently; **eyeball** ball of eye within lids and socket; **eyebath** vessel for applying lotion to eye; **eye-brow** hair growing on ridge over eye; **eye-catching** *colloquial* striking; **eyeglass** lens for defective eye; **eyehole** hole to look through; **eyelash** any of hairs on edge of eyelid; **eyelid** fold of skin that can cover eye; **eyeliner** cosmetic applied as line round eye; **eye-opener** *colloquial* enlightening experience, unexpected revelation; **eyepiece** lens(es) to which eye is applied at end of optical instrument; **eye-shade** device to protect eyes from strong light; **eye-shadow** cosmetic for eyelids; **eyesight** faculty or power of sight; **eyesore** ugly thing; **eye-tooth** canine tooth in upper jaw; **eyewash** lotion for eyes, *slang* nonsense; **eyewitness** person who saw thing happen and can tell of it; **have one's eye on** wish or plan to obtain; **keep an eye on** watch, look after; **see eye to eye** (often + *with*) agree; **set eyes on** see.

eyeful *noun* (*plural* **-s**) *colloquial* good look, visually striking person or thing.

eyelet /ˈaɪlɪt/ *noun* small hole for passing cord etc. through.

eyrie /ˈɪərɪ/ *noun* nest of bird of prey, esp. eagle, built high up.

Ff

F *abbreviation* Fahrenheit.

f *abbreviation* (also **f.**) female; feminine; *Music* forte.

FA *abbreviation* Football Association.

fa = FAH.

fable /ˈfeɪb(ə)l/ *noun* fictional tale, esp. legendary, or moral tale, often with animal characters.

fabled *adjective* celebrated; legendary.

fabric /ˈfæbrɪk/ *noun* woven material; walls, floor, and roof of building; structure.

fabricate /ˈfæbrɪkeɪt/ *verb* (**-ting**) construct, esp. from components; invent (fact), forge (document). □ **fabrication** *noun*.

fabulous /ˈfæbjʊləs/ *adjective colloquial* marvellous; legendary. □ **fabulously** *adverb*.

façade /fəˈsɑːd/ *noun* face or front of building; outward, esp. deceptive, appearance.

face ● *noun* front of head; facial expression; surface; façade of building; side of mountain; dial of clock etc.; functional side of tool, bat, etc.; effrontery; aspect, feature. ● *verb* (**-cing**) look or be positioned towards; be opposite; meet resolutely, confront; put facing on (garment, wall, etc.). □ **face-lift** cosmetic surgery to remove wrinkles etc., improvement in appearance; **face up to** accept bravely; **face value** nominal value, superficial appearance; **lose face** be humiliated; **on the face of it** apparently; **pull a face** distort features; **save face** avoid humiliation.

faceless *adjective* without identity; not identifiable.

facet /ˈfæsɪt/ *noun* aspect; side of cut gem etc.

facetious /fəˈsiːʃəs/ *adjective* intended to be amusing, esp. inappropriately. □ **facetiously** *adverb*; **facetiousness** *noun*.

facia = FASCIA.

facial /ˈfeɪʃ(ə)l/ ● *adjective* of or for the face. ● *noun* beauty treatment for the face. □ **facially** *adverb*.

facile /ˈfæsaɪl/ *adjective* easily achieved but of little value; glib.

facilitate /fəˈsɪlɪteɪt/ *verb* (**-ting**) ease (process etc.). □ **facilitation** *noun*.

facility /fəˈsɪlɪtɪ/ *noun* (*plural* **-ies**) ease, absence of difficulty; dexterity; (esp. in *plural*) opportunity or equipment for doing something.

facing *noun* material over part of garment etc. for contrast or strength; outer covering on wall etc.

facsimile /fækˈsɪmɪlɪ/ *noun* exact copy of writing, picture, etc.

fact *noun* thing known to exist or be true; reality. □ **factsheet** information leaflet; **in fact** in reality, in short; **the facts of life** information on sexual functions etc.

faction /ˈfækʃ(ə)n/ *noun* small dissenting group within larger one, esp. in politics; such dissension. □ **factional** *adjective*.

factious /ˈfækʃəs/ *adjective* of or inclined to faction.

factitious /fækˈtɪʃəs/ *adjective* specially contrived; artificial.

factor /ˈfæktə/ *noun* thing contributing to result; whole number etc. that when multiplied produces given number (e.g. 2, 3, 4, and 6 are the factors of 12).

factorial /fækˈtɔːrɪəl/ *noun* the product of a number and all whole numbers below it.

factory /ˈfæktərɪ/ *noun* (*plural* **-ies**) building(s) for manufacture of goods. □ **factory farming** using intensive or industrial methods of rearing livestock.

factotum /fækˈtəʊtəm/ *noun* (*plural* **-s**) employee doing all kinds of work.

factual /ˈfæktjʊəl/ *adjective* based on or concerned with fact. □ **factually** *adverb*.

faculty /ˈfækəltɪ/ *noun* (*plural* **-ies**) aptitude for particular activity; physical or mental power; group of related university departments; *US* teaching staff of university etc.

fad *noun* craze; peculiar notion.

faddy *adjective* (**-ier**, **-iest**) having petty likes and dislikes.

fade ● *verb* (**-ding**) (cause to) lose colour, light, or sound; slowly diminish; lose freshness or strength. ● *noun* action of fading. □ **fade away** die away, disappear, *colloquial* languish, grow thin.

faeces /ˈfiːsiːz/ *plural noun* (*US* **feces**) waste matter from bowels. □ **faecal** /-k(ə)l/ *adjective*.

fag ● *noun colloquial* tedious task; *slang* cigarette; (at public schools) junior boy who runs errands for a senior. ● *verb* (**-gg-**) (often + *out*) *colloquial* exhaust; act as fag. □ **fag-end** *slang* cigarette-end.

faggot /ˈfægət/ *noun* (*US* **fagot**) baked or fried ball of seasoned chopped liver etc.; bundle of sticks etc.

fah /fɑː/ *noun* (also **fa**) *Music* fourth note of scale in tonic sol-fa.

Fahrenheit /ˈfærənhaɪt/ *adjective* of scale of temperature on which water freezes at 32° and boils at 212°.

faience /faɪˈɑ̃s/ *noun* decorated and glazed earthenware and porcelain.

fail ● *verb* not succeed; be or judge to be unsuccessful in (exam etc.); (+ *to do*) be unable, neglect; disappoint; be absent or insufficient; become weaker; cease functioning. ● *noun* failure in exam. □ **fail-safe** reverting to safe condition when faulty; **without fail** for certain, whatever happens.

failed *adjective* unsuccessful; bankrupt.

failing ● *noun* fault; weakness. ● *preposition* in default of.

failure /ˈfeɪljə/ *noun* lack of success; unsuccessful person or thing; non-performance; breaking down, ceasing to function; running short of supply etc.

fain *archaic* ● *adjective* (+ *to do*) willing, obliged. ● *adverb* gladly.

faint ● *adjective* dim, pale; weak, giddy; slight; timid. ● *verb* lose consciousness; become faint. ● *noun* act or state of fainting. □ **faint-hearted** cowardly, timid. □ **faintly** *adverb*; **faintness** *noun*.

fair[1] ● *adjective* just, equitable; blond, not dark; moderate in quality or amount; (of weather) fine; (of wind) favourable; *archaic* beautiful. ● *adverb* in a fair or just manner; exactly, completely. □ **fair and square** exactly, straightforwardly; **fair copy** transcript free from corrections; **fair game** legitimate target or object; **fair play** just treatment or behaviour; **fair-weather friend** friend or ally who deserts in crisis. □ **fairness** *noun*.

fair[2] *noun* stalls, amusements, etc. for public entertainment; periodic market, often with entertainments; trade exhibition. □ **fairground** outdoor site for fair.

Fair Isle *noun* multicoloured knitwear design characteristic of Fair Isle in the Shetlands.

fairly *adverb* in a fair way; moderately; to a noticeable degree.

fairway *noun* navigable channel; mown grass between golf tee and green.

fairy /ˈfeərɪ/ *noun* (*plural* **-ies**) small winged legendary being. ● **fairy cake** small iced sponge cake; **fairy godmother** benefactress; **fairyland** home of fairies, enchanted region; **fairy lights** small coloured lights for decoration; **fairy ring** ring of darker grass caused by fungi, **fairy story, tale** tale about fairies, unbelievable story, lie.

fait accompli /feɪt əˈkɒmpliː/ *noun* thing done and past arguing about. [French]

faith /feɪθ/ *noun* trust; religious belief; creed; loyalty, trustworthiness. □ **faith-healer** person who practises **faith-healing**, healing dependent on faith rather than treatment.

faithful *adjective* showing faith; (often + *to*) loyal, trustworthy; accurate.

faithfully *adverb* in a faithful way. □ **Yours faithfully** *written before signature at end of business letter*.

faithless *adjective* disloyal; without religious faith.

fake ● *noun* thing or person that is not genuine. ● *adjective* counterfeit, not genuine. ● *verb* (**-king**) make fake or imitation of; feign.

fakir /ˈfeɪkɪə/ *noun* Muslim or Hindu religious beggar or ascetic.

falcon /ˈfɔːlkən/ *noun* small hawk trained to hunt.

falconry *noun* breeding and training of hawks.

fall /fɔːl/ ● *verb* (*past* **fell**; *past participle* **fallen**) go or come down freely; descend; (often + *over*) lose balance and come suddenly to ground; slope or hang down; sink lower, decline in power, status, etc.; subside; occur; become; (of face) show dismay etc.; be defeated; die. ● *noun* falling; amount or thing that falls; overthrow; (esp. in *plural*) waterfall; *US* autumn. □ **fall back on** have recourse to; **fall behind** be outstripped, be in arrears; **fall down (on)** *colloquial* fail (in); **fall for** be captivated or deceived by; **fall foul of** come into conflict with; **fall guy** *slang* easy victim, scapegoat; **fall in** *Military* take place in parade; **fall in with** meet by chance, agree or coincide with; **falling star** meteor; **fall off** decrease, deteriorate; **fall out** *verb* quarrel, (of hair, teeth, etc.) become detached, result, occur, *Military* come out of formation; **fallout** *noun* radioactive nuclear debris; **fall short of** fail to reach or obtain; **fall through** fail; **fall to** start eating, working, etc.

fallacy /ˈfæləsɪ/ *noun* (*plural* **-ies**) mistaken belief; faulty reasoning; misleading argument. □ **fallacious** /fəˈleɪʃəs/ *adjective*.

fallible /ˈfælɪb(ə)l/ *adjective* capable of making mistakes. □ **fallibility** *noun*.

Fallopian tube /fəˈləʊpɪən/ *noun* either of two tubes along which ova travel from ovaries to womb.

fallow /ˈfæləʊ/ ● *adjective* (of land) ploughed but left unsown; uncultivated. ● *noun* fallow land.

fallow deer *noun* small deer with white-spotted reddish-brown summer coat.

false /fɔːls/ *adjective* wrong, incorrect; sham, artificial; (+ *to*) deceitful, treacherous, unfaithful; deceptive. □ **false alarm** alarm given needlessly; **false pretences** misrepresentations meant to deceive. □ **falsely** *adverb*; **falsity** *noun*; **faiseness** *noun*.

falsehood /ˈfɔːlshʊd/ *noun* untrue thing; lying, lie.

falsetto /fɔːlˈsetəʊ/ *noun* male voice above normal range.

falsify /ˈfɔːlsɪfaɪ/ *verb* (**-ies, -ied**) fraudulently alter; misrepresent. □ **falsification** *noun*.

falter /ˈfɔːltə/ *verb* stumble; go unsteadily; lose courage; speak hesitatingly.

fame *noun* renown, being famous; *archaic* reputation.

famed *adjective* (+ *for*) much spoken of or famous because of.

familial /fəˈmɪlɪəl/ *adjective* of a family or its members.

familiar /fəˈmɪlɪə/ ● *adjective* (often + *to*) well known, often encountered; (+ *with*) knowing (a thing) well; (excessively) informal. ● *noun* intimate friend; supposed attendant of witch etc. □ **familiarity** /-ˈær-/ *noun* (*plural* **-ies**); **familiarly** *adverb*.

familiarize /fəˈmɪlɪəraɪz/ *verb* (also **-ise**) (**-zing** or **-sing**) (usually + *with*) make (person etc.) conversant. □ **familiarization** *noun*.

family /ˈfæmɪlɪ/ *noun* (*plural* **-ies**) set of relations, esp. parents and children; person's children; household; all the descendants of common ancestor; group of similar things, people, etc.; group of related genera of animals or plants. □ **family credit** regular state payment to low-income family; **family planning** birth control; **family tree** genealogical chart.

famine /ˈfæmɪn/ *noun* extreme scarcity, esp. of food.

famish /ˈfæmɪʃ/ *verb* (usually as **famished** *adjective colloquial*) make or become extremely hungry.

famous /ˈfeɪməs/ *adjective* (often + *for*) well-known; celebrated; *colloquial* excellent. □ **famously** *adverb*.

fan[1] ● *noun* apparatus, usually with rotating blades, for ventilation etc.; device, semicircular and folding, waved to cool oneself; fan-shaped thing. ● *verb* (**-nn-**) blow air on, (as) with fan; (usually + *out*) spread out like fan. □ **fan belt** belt driving fan to cool radiator in vehicle; **fanlight** small, originally semicircular, window over door etc.; **fantail** pigeon with broad tail.

fan[2] *noun* devotee. □ **fan club** (club of) devotees; **fan mail** letters from fans.

fanatic /fəˈnætɪk/ ● *noun* person obsessively devoted to a belief, activity, etc. ● *adjective* excessively enthusiastic. □ **fanatical** *adjective*; **fanatically** *adverb*; **fanaticism** /-tɪsɪz(ə)m/ *noun*.

fancier /ˈfænsɪə/ *noun* connoisseur, enthusiast; breeder, esp. of pigeons.

fanciful /ˈfænsɪfʊl/ *adjective* imaginary; indulging in fancies. □ **fancifully** *adverb*.

fancy /ˈfænsɪ/ ● *noun* (*plural* **-ies**) inclination, whim; supposition; imagination. ● *adjective* (**-ier, -iest**) extravagant; ornamental. ● *verb* (**-ies, -ied**) (+ *that*) imagine; suppose; *colloquial* find attractive, desire; have unduly high opinion of. □ **fancy dress** costume for masquerading; **fancy-free** without (emotional) commitments; **fancy man, woman** woman's or man's lover. □ **fancily** *adverb*.

fandango /fænˈdæŋgəʊ/ *noun* (*plural* **-es** or **-s**) lively Spanish dance.

fanfare /ˈfænfeə/ *noun* short showy sounding of trumpets etc.

fang *noun* canine tooth, esp. of dog or wolf; tooth of venomous snake; (prong of) root of tooth.

fantasia /fænˈteɪzɪə/ *noun* free or improvisatory musical etc. composition.

fantasize /ˈfæntəsaɪz/ *verb* (also **-ise**) (**-zing** or **-sing**) daydream; imagine; create fantasy about.

fantastic /fænˈtæstɪk/ *adjective* extravagantly fanciful; grotesque, quaint; *colloquial* excellent, extraordinary. □ **fantastically** *adverb*.

fantasy /ˈfæntəsɪ/ *noun* (*plural* **-ies**) imagination, esp. when unrelated to reality; mental image, daydream; fantastic invention or composition.

fanzine /ˈfænziːn/ *noun* magazine for fans of science fiction, a football team, etc.

far (**further, furthest** or **farther, farthest**) ● *adverb* at, to, or by a great distance in space or time; by much. ● *adjective* distant; remote; extreme. □ **far and wide** over large area; **far-away** remote, dreamy, distant; **the Far East** countries of E. Asia; **far-fetched** unconvincing, exaggerated, fanciful; **far-flung** widely scattered, remote; **far from** almost the opposite of; **far gone** very ill, drunk, etc.; **far-off** remote; **far-out** *slang* unconventional, excellent; **far-reaching** widely influential or applicable; **far-seeing** showing foresight; **far-sighted** having foresight, *esp. US* long-sighted.

farad /'færəd/ *noun* SI unit of electrical capacitance.

farce /fɑːs/ *noun* comedy with ludicrously improbable plot; absurdly futile proceedings; pretence. □ **farcical** *adjective.*

fare ● *noun* price of journey on public transport; passenger; food. ● *verb* (**-ring**) progress; get on. □ **fare-stage** section of bus route for which fixed fare is charged; stop marking this.

farewell /feə'wel/ ● *interjection* goodbye. ● *noun* leave-taking.

farina /fə'riːnə/ *noun* flour of corn, nuts, or starchy roots. □ **farinaceous** /færɪ'neɪʃəs/ *adjective.*

farm ● *noun* land and its buildings used for growing crops, rearing animals, etc.; farmhouse. ● *verb* use (land) thus; be farmer; breed (fish etc.) commercially; (+ *out*) delegate or subcontract (work). □ **farmhand** worker on farm; **farmhouse** house attached to farm; **farmyard** yard adjacent to farmhouse. □ **farming** *noun.*

farmer *noun* owner or manager of farm.

faro /'feərəʊ/ *noun* gambling card game.

farrago /fə'rɑːgəʊ/ *noun* (*plural* **-s** or *US* **-es**) medley, hotchpotch.

farrier /'færɪə/ *noun* smith who shoes horses.

farrow /'færəʊ/ ● *verb* give birth to (piglets). ● *noun* litter of pigs.

Farsi /'fɑːsɪ/ *noun* modern Persian language.

farther = FURTHER.

farthest = FURTHEST.

farthing /'fɑːðɪŋ/ *noun historical* coin worth quarter of old penny.

farthingale /'fɑːðɪŋgeɪl/ *noun historical* hooped petticoat.

fascia /'feɪʃə/ *noun* (also **facia**) (*plural* **-s**) instrument panel of vehicle; similar panel etc. for operating machinery; long flat surface of wood or stone.

fascicle /'fæsɪk(ə)l/ *noun* instalment of book.

fascinate /'fæsɪneɪt/ *verb* (**-ting**) (often as **fascinating** *adjective*) capture interest of; attract. □ **fascination** *noun.*

Fascism /'fæʃɪz(ə)m/ *noun* extreme right-wing totalitarian nationalist movement in Italy (1922–43); (also **fascism**) any similar movement. □ **Fascist, fascist** *noun & adjective;* **Fascistic, fascistic** /-'ʃɪs-/ *adjective.*

fashion /'fæʃ(ə)n/ ● *noun* current popular custom or style, esp. in dress; manner of doing something. ● *verb* (often + *into*) form, make. □ **in fashion** fashionable; **out of fashion** not fashionable.

fashionable *adjective* of or conforming to current fashion; of or favoured by high society. □ **fashionably** *adverb.*

fast¹ /fɑːst/ ● *adjective* rapid; capable of or intended for high speed; (of clock) ahead of correct time; firm, fixed, (of colour) not fading; pleasure-seeking. ● *adverb* quickly; firmly; soundly, completely. □ **fastback** car with sloping rear; **fast breeder (reactor)** reactor using neutrons with high kinetic energy; **fast food** restaurant food that is produced quickly; **pull a fast one** *colloquial* try to deceive someone.

fast² /fɑːst/ ● *verb* abstain from food. ● *noun* act or period of fasting.

fasten /'fɑːs(ə)n/ *verb* make or become fixed or secure; (+ *in, up*) shut in, lock securely; (+ *on*) direct (attention) towards; (+ *off*) fix with knot or stitches.

fastener *noun* (also **fastening**) device that fastens.

fastidious /fæ'stɪdɪəs/ *adjective* fussy; easily disgusted, squeamish.

fastness /'fɑːstnɪs/ *noun* stronghold.

fat ● *noun* oily substance, esp. in animal bodies; part of meat etc. containing this. ● *adjective* (**-tt-**) plump; containing much fat; thick, substantial. ● *verb* (**-tt-**) (esp. as **fatted** *adjective*) make or become fat. □ **fathead** *colloquial* stupid person; **fat-headed** stupid; **a fat lot** *colloquial* very little. □ **fatless** *adjective;* **fatten** *verb.*

fatal /'feɪt(ə)l/ *adjective* causing or ending in death or ruin. □ **fatally** *adverb.*

fatalism *noun* belief in predetermination; submissive acceptance. □ **fatalist** *noun;* **fatalistic** /-'lɪs-/ *adjective.*

fatality /fə'tælɪtɪ/ *noun* (*plural* **-ies**) death by accident, in war, etc.

fate ● *noun* supposed power predetermining events; destiny; death, destruction. ● *verb* (**-ting**) preordain; (as **fated** *adjective*) doomed, (+ *to do*) preordained.

fateful *adjective* decisive; important; controlled by fate.

father /'fɑːðə/ ● *noun* male parent; (usually in *plural*) forefather; originator; early leader; (also **Father**) priest; (**the Father**) God; (in *plural*) elders. ● *verb* be father of; originate. □ **father-in-law** (*plural* **fathers-in-law**) wife's or husband's father; **fatherland** native country. □ **fatherhood** *noun;* **fatherless** *adjective.*

fatherly *adjective* of or like a father.

fathom /'fæð(ə)m/ ● *noun* measure of 6ft, esp. in soundings. ● *verb* comprehend; measure depth of (water). □ **fathomable** *adjective.*

fathomless *adjective* too deep to fathom.

fatigue /fə'tiːg/ ● *noun* extreme tiredness; weakness in metals etc. from repeated stress; non-military army duty, (in *plural*) clothing for this. ● *verb* (**-gues, -gued, -guing**) cause fatigue in.

fatty ● *adjective* (**-ier, -iest**) like or containing fat. ● *noun* (*plural* **-ies**) *colloquial* fat person. □ **fatty acid** type of organic compound.

fatuous /'fætjʊəs/ *adjective* vacantly silly; purposeless. □ **fatuity** /fə'tjuːɪtɪ/ *noun* (*plural* **-ies**); **fatuously** *adverb;* **fatuousness** *noun.*

fatwa /'fætwɑː/ *noun* legal ruling by Islamic religious leader.

faucet /'fɔːsɪt/ *noun esp. US* tap.

fault /fɔːlt/ ● *noun* defect, imperfection; responsibility for wrongdoing, error, etc.; break in electric circuit; *Tennis* etc. incorrect service; break in rock strata. ● *verb* find fault with. □ **find fault** (often + *with*) criticize or complain (about); **to a fault** excessively. □ **faultless** *adjective;* **faultlessly** *adverb.*

faulty *adjective* (**-ier, -iest**) having faults. □ **faultily** *adverb.*

faun /fɔːn/ *noun* Latin rural deity with goat's horns, legs, and tail.

fauna /'fɔːnə/ *noun* (*plural* **-s**) animal life of a region or period.

faux pas /fəʊ 'pɑː/ *noun* (*plural* same /'pɑːz/) tactless mistake. [French]

favour /'feɪvə/ (*US* **favor**) ● *noun* kind act; approval, goodwill; partiality; badge, ribbon, etc. as emblem of support. ● *verb* regard or treat with favour; support, facilitate; tend to confirm (idea etc.); (+ *with*) oblige; (as **favoured** *adjective*) having special advantages. □ **in favour** approved of, (+ *of*) in support of or to the advantage of; **out of favour** disapproved of.

favourable *adjective* (*US* **favorable**) well-disposed; approving; promising; helpful, suitable. □ **favourably** *adverb.*

favourite /'feɪvərɪt/ (*US* **favorite**) ● *adjective* preferred to all others. ● *noun* favourite person or thing; competitor thought most likely to win.

favouritism noun (US **favoritism**) unfair favouring of one person etc.

fawn[1] ● noun deer in first year; light yellowish brown. ● adjective fawncoloured. ● verb give birth to fawn.

fawn[2] verb (often + on, upon) behave servilely; (of dog) show extreme affection.

fax ● noun electronic transmission of exact copy of document etc.; such copy; (in full **fax machine**) apparatus used for this. ● verb transmit in this way.

faze verb (**-zing**) (often as **fazed** adjective) colloquial disconcert.

FBI abbreviation Federal Bureau of Investigation.

FC abbreviation Football Club.

FCO abbreviation Foreign and Commonwealth Office.

FE abbreviation further education.

fealty /ˈfiːəltɪ/ noun (plural **-ies**) fidelity to feudal lord; allegiance.

fear ● noun panic etc. caused by impending danger, pain, etc.; cause of this; alarm, dread. ● verb be afraid of; (+ for) feel anxiety about; dread; shrink from; revere (God).

fearful adjective afraid; terrible, awful; extremely unpleasant. □ **fearfully** adverb; **fearfulness** noun.

fearless adjective not afraid; brave. □ **fearlessly** adverb; **fearlessness** noun.

fearsome adjective frightening. □ **fearsomely** adverb.

feasible /ˈfiːzɪb(ə)l/ adjective practicable, possible. □ **feasibility** noun; **feasibly** adverb.

■ **Usage** Feasible should not be used to mean 'likely'. Possible or probable should be used instead.

feast ● noun sumptuous meal; religious festival; sensual or mental pleasure. ● verb (often + on) have feast, eat and drink sumptuously; regale.

feat noun remarkable act or achievement.

feather /ˈfeðə/ ● noun one of structures forming bird's plumage, with fringed horny shaft; these as material. ● verb cover or line with feathers; turn (oar) through air edgeways. □ **feather bed** noun bed with feather-stuffed mattress; **feather-bed** verb cushion, esp. financially; **feather-brained**, **-headed** silly; **featherweight** amateur boxing weight (54–57 kg). □ **feathery** adjective.

feature /ˈfiːtʃə/ ● noun characteristic or distinctive part; (usually in plural) part of face; specialized article in newspaper etc.; (in full **feature film**) main film in cinema programme. ● verb (**-ring**) make or be special feature of; emphasize; take part in. □ **featureless** adjective.

Feb. abbreviation February.

febrile /ˈfiːbraɪl/ adjective of fever.

February /ˈfebrʊərɪ/ noun (plural **-ies**) second month of year.

fecal US = FAECAL.

feces US = FAECES.

feckless /ˈfeklɪs/ adjective feeble, ineffectual; irresponsible.

fecund /ˈfekənd/ adjective fertile. □ **fecundity** /fɪˈkʌndɪtɪ/ noun.

fecundate /ˈfekəndeɪt/ verb (**-ting**) make fruitful; fertilize. □ **fecundation** noun.

fed past & past participle of FEED. □ **fed up** (often + with) discontented, bored.

federal /ˈfedər(ə)l/ adjective of system of government in which self-governing states unite for certain functions; of such a federation; (**Federal**) US of Northern States in Civil War. □ **federalism** noun; **federalist** noun; **federalize** verb (also **-ise**) (**-zing** or **-sing**); **federalization** noun; **federally** adverb.

federate ● verb /ˈfedəreɪt/ (**-ting**) unite on federal basis. ● adjective /ˈfedərət/ federally organized. □ **federative** /-rətɪv/ adjective.

federation /fedəˈreɪʃ(ə)n/ noun federal group; act of federating.

fee noun payment for professional advice or services; (often in plural) payment for admission, membership, licence, education, exam, etc.; money paid for transfer of footballer etc. □ **fee-paying** paying fee(s), (of school) charging fees.

feeble /ˈfiːb(ə)l/ adjective (**-r**, **-st**) weak; lacking energy, strength, or effectiveness. □ **feebly** adverb.

feed ● verb (past & past participle **fed**) supply with food; put food in mouth of; eat; graze; keep supplied with; (+ into) supply (material) to machine etc.; (often + on) nourish, be nourished by. ● noun food, esp. for animals or infants; feeding; colloquial meal. □ **feedback** information about result of experiment, response, Electronics return of part of output signal to input.

feeder noun person or thing that feeds in specified way; baby's feeding bottle; bib; tributary; branch road or railway line; electricity main supplying distribution point; feeding apparatus in machine.

feel ● verb (past & past participle **felt**) examine, search, or perceive by touch; experience; be affected by; (+ that) have impression; consider, think; seem; be consciously; (+ for, with) have sympathy or pity for. ● noun feeling; sense of touch; sensation characterizing something. □ **feel like** have wish or inclination for; **feel up to** be ready to face or deal with.

feeler noun organ in certain animals for touching, foraging, etc. □ **put out feelers** make tentative proposal.

feeling ● noun capacity to feel; sense of touch; physical sensation; emotion; (in plural) susceptibilities; sensitivity; notion, opinion. ● adjective sensitive; sympathetic. □ **feelingly** adverb.

feet plural of FOOT.

feign /feɪn/ verb simulate; pretend.

feint /feɪnt/ ● noun sham attack or diversionary blow; pretence. ● verb make a feint. ● adjective (of paper etc.) having faintly ruled lines.

feldspar /ˈfeldspɑː/ noun (also **felspar** /ˈfelspɑː/) common aluminium silicate.

felicitation /fəlɪsɪˈteɪʃ(ə)n/ noun (usually in plural) congratulation.

felicitous /fəˈlɪsɪtəs/ adjective apt; well-chosen.

felicity /fəˈlɪsɪtɪ/ noun (plural **-ies**) formal great happiness; capacity for apt expression.

feline /ˈfiːlaɪn/ ● adjective of cat family; catlike. ● noun animal of cat family.

fell[1] past of FALL.

fell[2] verb cut down (tree); strike down.

fell[3] noun hill or stretch of hills in N. England.

fell[4] adjective □ **at**, **in one fell swoop** in a single (originally deadly) action.

fell[5] noun animal's hide or skin with hair.

fellow /ˈfeləʊ/ ● noun comrade, associate; counterpart, equal; colloquial man, boy; incorporated senior member of college; member of learned society. ● adjective of same group etc. □ **fellow-feeling** sympathy; **fellow-traveller** person who travels with another, sympathizer with Communist party.

fellowship /ˈfeləʊʃɪp/ noun friendly association, companionship; group of associates; position or income of college fellow.

felon /ˈfelən/ noun person who has committed felony.

felony /ˈfelənɪ/ noun (plural **-ies**) serious usually violent crime. □ **felonious** /frˈləʊ-/ adjective.

felspar = FELDSPAR.

felt[1] ● noun fabric of matted and pressed fibres of wool etc. ● verb make into or cover with felt; become matted. □ **felt tip** or **pen**, **felt-tip(ped) pen** pen with fibre point.

felt² *past & past participle of* FEEL.

female /'fiːmeɪl/ ● *adjective* of the sex that can give birth or produce eggs; (of plants) fruit-bearing; of female people, animals, or plants; (of screw, socket, etc.) hollow to receive inserted part. ● *noun* female person, animal, or plant.

feminine /'femɪnɪn/ *adjective* of women; womanly; *Grammar* (of noun) belonging to gender including words for most female people and animals. □ **femininity** /-'nɪn-/ *noun*.

feminism /'femɪnɪz(ə)m/ *noun* advocacy of women's rights and sexual equality. □ **feminist** *noun & adjective*.

femme fatale /fæm fæ'tɑːl/ *noun* (*plural* **femmes fatales** same pronunciation) dangerously seductive woman. [French]

femur /'fiːmə/ *noun* (*plural* **-s** or **femora** /'femərə/) thigh-bone. □ **femoral** /'femər(ə)l/ *adjective*.

fen *noun* low marshy land.

fence ● *noun* barrier or railing enclosing field, garden, etc.; jump for horses; *slang* receiver of stolen goods. ● *verb* (**-cing**) surround (as) with fence; practise sword play; be evasive; deal in (stolen goods). □ **fencer** *noun*.

fencing *noun* fences, material for fences; sword-fighting, esp. as sport.

fend *verb* (+ *off*) ward off; (+ *for*) look after (esp. oneself).

fender *noun* low frame round fireplace; matting etc. to protect side of ship; *US* bumper of vehicle.

fennel /'fen(ə)l/ *noun* fragrant plant with edible leafstalks and seeds.

fenugreek /'fenjuːgriːk/ *noun* leguminous plant with aromatic seeds used for flavouring.

feral /'fer(ə)l/ *adjective* wild; (of animal) escaped and living wild.

ferial /'fɪərɪəl/ *adjective* (of day) not a church festival or fast.

ferment ● *noun* /'fɜːment/ excitement; fermentation; fermenting agent. ● *verb* /fə'ment/ undergo or subject to fermentation; excite.

fermentation /fɜːmen'teɪʃ(ə)n/ *noun* breakdown of substance by yeasts, bacteria, etc.; excitement.

fern *noun* flowerless plant usually with feathery fronds.

ferocious /fə'rəʊʃəs/ *adjective* fierce. □ **ferociously** *adverb*; **ferocity** /-'rɒs-/ *noun*.

ferret /'ferɪt/ ● *noun* small polecat used in catching rabbits, rats, etc. ● *verb* (**-t-**) hunt with ferrets; (often + *out*, *about*, etc.) rummage; (+ *out*) search out.

ferric /'ferɪk/ *adjective* of iron; containing iron in trivalent form.

Ferris wheel /'ferɪs/ *noun* tall revolving vertical wheel with passenger cars in fairgrounds etc.

ferroconcrete /ferəʊ'kɒŋkriːt/ *noun* reinforced concrete.

ferrous /'ferəs/ *adjective* containing iron, esp. in divalent form.

ferrule /'feruːl/ *noun* ring or cap on end of stick etc.

ferry ● *noun* (*plural* **-ies**) boat etc. for esp. regular transport across water; ferrying place or service. ● *verb* (**-ies**, **-ied**) take or go in ferry; transport from place to place, esp. regularly. □ **ferryman** *noun*.

fertile /'fɜːtaɪl/ *adjective* (of soil) abundantly productive; fruitful; (of seed, egg, etc.) capable of growth; inventive; (of animal or plant) able to reproduce. □ **fertility** /-'tɪl-/ *noun*.

fertilize /'fɜːtɪlaɪz/ *verb* (also **-ise**) (**-zing** or **-sing**) make fertile; cause (egg, female animal, etc.) to develop new individual. □ **fertilization** *noun*.

fertilizer *noun* (also **-iser**) substance added to soil to make it more fertile.

fervent /'fɜːv(ə)nt/ *adjective* ardent, intense. □ **fervency** *noun*; **fervently** *adverb*.

fervid /'fɜːvɪd/ *adjective* fervent. □ **fervidly** *adverb*.

fervour /'fɜːvə/ *noun* (*US* **fervor**) passion, zeal.

fescue /'feskjuː/ *noun* pasture and fodder grass.

fester /'festə/ *verb* make or become septic; cause continuing bitterness; rot; stagnate.

festival /'festɪv(ə)l/ *noun* day or period of celebration; series of cultural events in town etc.

festive /'festɪv/ *adjective* of or characteristic of festival; joyous.

festivity /fe'stɪvɪtɪ/ *noun* (*plural* **-ies**) gaiety, (in *plural*) celebration; party.

festoon /fe'stuːn/ ● *noun* curved hanging chain of flowers, ribbons, etc. ● *verb* (often + *with*) adorn with or form into festoons.

feta /'fetə/ *noun* salty white Greek cheese made from ewe's or goat's milk.

fetal *US* = FOETAL.

fetch *verb* go for and bring back; be sold for; draw forth; deal (blow). □ **fetch up** *colloquial* arrive, come to rest.

fetching *adjective* attractive. □ **fetchingly** *adverb*.

fête /feɪt/ ● *noun* outdoor fund-raising event. ● *verb* (**-ting**) honour or entertain lavishly.

fetid /'fetɪd/ *adjective* (also **foetid**) stinking.

fetish /'fetɪʃ/ *noun* abnormal object of sexual desire; object worshipped by primitive peoples; object of obsessive concern. □ **fetishism** *noun*; **fetishist** *noun*; **fetishistic** /-'ʃɪs-/ *adjective*.

fetlock /'fetlɒk/ *noun* back of horse's leg where tuft of hair grows above hoof.

fetter /'fetə/ ● *noun* shackle for ankles; (in *plural*) captivity; restraint. ● *verb* put into fetters, restrict.

fettle /'fet(ə)l/ *noun* condition, trim.

fetus *US* = FOETUS.

feud /fjuːd/ ● *noun* prolonged hostility, esp. between families, tribes, etc. ● *verb* conduct feud.

feudal /'fjuːd(ə)l/ *adjective* of, like, or according to feudal system; reactionary. □ **feudal system** medieval system in which vassal held land in exchange for allegiance and service to landowner. □ **feudalism** *noun*; **feudalistic** /-'lɪs-/ *adjective*.

fever /'fiːvə/ ● *noun* abnormally high body temperature; disease characterized by this; nervous agitation. ● *verb* (esp. as **fevered** *adjective*) affect with fever or excitement. □ **fever pitch** state of extreme excitement.

feverfew /'fiːvəfjuː/ *noun* aromatic plant, used formerly to reduce fever, now to treat migraine.

feverish *adjective* having symptoms of fever; excited, restless. □ **feverishly** *adverb*.

few ● *adjective* not many. ● *noun* (treated as *plural*) not many; (**a few**) some but not many. □ **a good few** a considerable number (of); **quite a few** *colloquial* a fairly large number (of); **very few** a very small number (of).

fey /feɪ/ *adjective* strange, other-worldly; whimsical.

fez *noun* (*plural* **fezzes**) man's flat-topped conical red cap, worn by some Muslims.

ff *abbreviation Music* fortissimo.

ff. *abbreviation* following pages etc.

fiancé /fɪ'ɒnseɪ/ *noun* (feminine **-cée** same pronunciation) person one is engaged to.

fiasco /fɪ'æskəʊ/ *noun* (*plural* **-s**) ludicrous or humiliating failure.

fiat /'faɪæt/ *noun* authorization; decree.

fib ● *noun* trivial lie. ● *verb* (**-bb-**) tell fib. □ **fibber** *noun*.

fibre /'faɪbə/ noun (US **fiber**) thread or filament forming tissue or textile; piece of threadlike glass; substance formed of fibres; moral character; roughage. □ **fibreboard** board made of compressed wood etc. fibres; **fibreglass** fabric made from woven glass fibres, plastic reinforced with glass fibres; **fibre optics** optics using glass fibres, usually to carry signals. □ **fibrous** adjective.

fibril /'faɪbrɪl/ noun small fibre.

fibroid /'faɪbrɔɪd/ ● adjective of, like, or containing fibrous tissue or fibres. ● noun benign fibrous tumour, esp. in womb.

fibrosis /faɪˈbrəʊsɪs/ noun thickening and scarring of connective tissue.

fibrositis /faɪbrəˈsaɪtɪs/ noun rheumatic inflammation of fibrous tissue.

fibula /'fɪbjʊlə/ noun (plural **-lae** /-liː/ or **-s**) bone on outer side of lower leg.

fiche /fiːʃ/ noun microfiche.

fickle /'fɪk(ə)l/ adjective inconstant, changeable. □ **fickleness** noun.

fiction /'fɪkʃ(ə)n/ noun non-factual literature, esp. novels; invented idea, thing, etc.; generally accepted falsehood. □ **fictional** adjective.

fictitious /fɪkˈtɪʃəs/ adjective imaginary, unreal; not genuine.

fiddle /'fɪd(ə)l/ ● noun colloquial violin; colloquial cheat, fraud; fiddly task. ● verb (**-ling**) (often + with, at) play restlessly; (often + about) move aimlessly; (usually + with) tamper, tinker; slang falsify, swindle, get by cheating; play fiddle. □ **fiddler** noun.

fiddling adjective petty, trivial; colloquial fiddly.

fiddly adjective (**-ier**, **-iest**) colloquial awkward to do or use.

fidelity /fɪˈdelɪtɪ/ noun faithfulness, loyalty; accuracy, precision in sound reproduction.

fidget /'fɪdʒɪt/ ● verb (**-t-**) move restlessly; be or make uneasy. ● noun person who fidgets; (**the fidgets**) restless state or mood. □ **fidgety** adjective.

fiduciary /fɪˈdjuːʃərɪ/ ● adjective of a trust, trustee, etc.; held or given in trust; (of currency) dependent on public confidence. ● noun (plural **-ies**) trustee.

fief /fiːf/ noun land held under feudal system.

field /fiːld/ ● noun area of esp. cultivated enclosed land; area rich in some natural product; competitors; expanse of sea, snow, etc.; battlefield; area of activity or study; Computing part of record, representing item of data. ● verb Cricket etc. act as fielder(s), stop and return (ball); select (player, candidate, etc.); deal with (questions etc.). □ **field-day** exciting or successful time, military exercise or review; **field events** athletic events other than races; **field glasses** outdoor binoculars; **Field Marshal** army officer of highest rank; **fieldmouse** small long-tailed rodent; **fieldsman** = FIELDER; **field sports** outdoor sports, esp. hunting, shooting, and fishing; **fieldwork** practical surveying, science, sociology, etc. conducted in natural environment; **fieldworker** person doing fieldwork.

fielder noun Cricket etc. member (other than bowler) of fielding side.

fieldfare noun grey thrush.

fiend /fiːnd/ noun evil spirit; wicked or cruel person; mischievous or annoying person; slang devotee; difficult or unpleasant thing. □ **fiendish** adjective; **fiendishly** adverb.

fierce adjective (**-r**, **-st**) violently aggressive or frightening; eager; intense. □ **fiercely** adverb; **fierceness** noun.

fiery /'faɪərɪ/ adjective (**-ier**, **-iest**) consisting of or flaming with fire; bright red; burning hot; spirited.

fiesta /fɪˈestə/ noun festival, holiday.

FIFA /'fiːfə/ abbreviation International Football Federation (Fédération Internationale de Football Association).

fife /faɪf/ noun small shrill flute.

fifteen /fɪfˈtiːn/ adjective & noun one more than fourteen; Rugby team of fifteen players. □ **fifteenth** adjective & noun.

fifth ● adjective & noun next after fourth; any of 5 equal parts of thing. □ **fifth column** group working for enemy within country at war.

fifty /'fɪftɪ/ adjective & noun (plural **-ies**) five times ten. □ **fifty-fifty** half and half, equal(ly). □ **fiftieth** adjective & noun.

fig noun soft fruit with many seeds; tree bearing it. □ **fig leaf** device concealing genitals.

fig. abbreviation figure.

fight /faɪt/ ● verb (past & past participle **fought** /fɔːt/) (often + against, with) contend with in war, combat, etc.; engage in (battle etc.); (+ for) strive to secure or on behalf of; contest (election); strive to overcome; (as **fighting** adjective) able and eager or trained to fight. ● noun combat; boxing match; battle; struggle; power or inclination to fight. □ **fight back** counter-attack, suppress (tears etc.); **fighting chance** chance of success if effort is made; **fighting fit** extremely fit; **fight off** repel with effort; **fight shy of** avoid; **put up a fight** offer resistance.

fighter noun person who fights; aircraft designed for attacking other aircraft.

figment /'fɪgmənt/ noun imaginary thing.

figurative /'fɪgərətɪv/ adjective metaphorical; (of art) not abstract, representational. □ **figuratively** adverb.

figure /'fɪgə/ ● noun external form, bodily shape; person of specified kind; representation of human form; image; numerical symbol or number, esp. 0–9; value, amount; (in plural) arithmetical calculations; diagram, illustration; dance etc. movement or sequence; (in full **figure of speech**) metaphor, hyperbole, etc. ● verb (**-ring**) appear, be mentioned; (usually as **figured** adjective) embellish with pattern; calculate; esp. US colloquial understand, consider, make sense. □ **figurehead** nominal leader, carved image etc. over ship's prow; **figure on** esp. US colloquial count on, expect; **figure out** work out by arithmetic or logic; **figure-skating** skating in prescribed patterns.

figurine /fɪgəˈriːn/ noun statuette.

filament /'fɪləmənt/ noun threadlike strand or fibre; conducting wire or thread in electric bulb.

filbert /'fɪlbət/ noun (nut of) cultivated hazel.

filch verb steal, pilfer.

file¹ ● noun folder, box, etc. for holding loose papers; paper kept in this; collection of related computer data; row of people or things one behind another. ● verb (**-ling**) place in file or among records; submit (petition for divorce etc.); walk in line. □ **filing cabinet** cabinet with drawers for storing files.

file² ● noun tool with rough surface for smoothing wood, fingernails, etc. ● verb (**-ling**) smooth or shape with file.

filial /'fɪlɪəl/ adjective of or due from son or daughter.

filibuster /'fɪlɪbʌstə/ ● noun obstruction of progress in legislative assembly; esp. US person who engages in this. ● verb act as filibuster.

filigree /'fɪlɪgriː/ noun fine ornamental work in gold etc. wire; similar delicate work.

filings plural noun particles rubbed off by file.

Filipino /fɪlɪˈpiːnəʊ/ ● noun (plural **-s**) native or national of Philippines. ● adjective of Philippines or Filipinos.

fill ● verb (often + with) make or become full; occupy completely; spread over or through; block up (hole, tooth, etc.); appoint to or hold (office etc.); (as **filling**

adjective) (of food) satisfying. ● *noun* enough to satisfy or fill. □ **fill in** complete (form etc.), fill completely, (often + *for*) act as substitute, *colloquial* inform more fully; **fill out** enlarge or become enlarged, esp. to proper size, fill in (form etc.); **fill up** fill completely, fill petrol tank (of).

filler *noun* material used to fill cavity or increase bulk.

fillet /'fɪlɪt/ ● *noun* boneless piece of fish or meat; (in full **fillet steak**) undercut of sirloin; ribbon etc. binding hair; narrow flat band between mouldings. ● *verb* (**-t-**) remove bones from (fish etc.) or divide into fillets; bind or provide with fillet(s).

filling *noun* material used to fill tooth, sandwich, pie, etc. □ **filling-station** garage selling petrol etc.

fillip /'fɪlɪp/ *noun* stimulus, incentive.

filly /'fɪlɪ/ *noun* (*plural* **-ies**) young female horse.

film ● *noun* thin coating or layer; strip or sheet of plastic etc. coated with light-sensitive emulsion for exposure in camera; story etc. on film; (in *plural*) cinema industry; slight veil, haze, etc. ● *verb* make photographic film of; (often + *over*) cover or become covered (as) with film. □ **film star** well-known film actor or actress. □ **filmy** *adjective* (**-ier, -iest**).

filmsetting *noun* typesetting by projecting characters on to photographic film. □ **filmset** *verb*; **filmsetter** *noun*.

Filofax /'faɪləʊfæks/ *noun* *proprietary term* personal organizer.

filo pastry /'fiːləʊ/ *noun* pastry in very thin sheets.

filter /'fɪltə/ ● *noun* porous esp. paper device for removing impurities from liquid or gas or making coffee; screen for absorbing or modifying light; device for suppressing unwanted electrical or sound waves; arrangement for filtering traffic. ● *verb* pass through filter; (usually as **filtered** *adjective*) make (coffee) by dripping hot water through ground beans; (+ *through, into, etc.*) make way gradually through, into, etc.; (of traffic) be allowed to turn left or right at junction when other traffic is held up. □ **filter tip** (cigarette with) filter for removing some impurities.

filth *noun* disgusting dirt; obscenity.

filthy ● *adjective* (**-ier, -iest**) disgustingly dirty; obscene; (of weather) very unpleasant. ● *adverb* *colloquial* extremely. □ **filthy lucre** dishonourable gain; money.

filtrate /'fɪltreɪt/ ● *verb* (**-ting**) filter. ● *noun* filtered liquid. □ **filtration** *noun*.

fin *noun* organ, esp. of fish, for propelling and steering; similar projection for stabilizing aircraft etc.

finagle /fɪ'neɪg(ə)l/ *verb* (**-ling**) *colloquial* act or obtain dishonestly.

final /'faɪn(ə)l/ ● *adjective* at the end, coming last; conclusive, decisive. ● *noun* last or deciding heat or game; last edition of day's newspaper; (usually in *plural*) exams at end of degree course. □ **finality** /-'næl-/ *noun*; **finally** *adverb*.

finale /fɪ'nɑːlɪ/ *noun* last movement or section of drama, piece of music, etc.

finalist *noun* competitor in final.

finalize *verb* (also **-ise**) (**-zing** or **-sing**) put in final form; complete. □ **finalization** *noun*.

finance /'faɪnæns/ ● *noun* management of money; monetary support for enterprise; (in *plural*) money resources. ● *verb* (**-cing**) provide capital for. □ **financial** /-'næn-/ *adjective*; **financially** /-'næn-/ *adverb*.

financier /faɪ'nænsɪə/ *noun* capitalist; entrepreneur.

finch *noun* small seed-eating bird.

find /faɪnd/ ● *verb* (*past & past participle* **found**) discover, get by chance or after search; become aware of; obtain, provide; summon up; perceive, experience; consider to be; (often in *passive*) discover to be present;

reach; *Law* judge and declare. ● *noun* discovery of treasure etc.; valued thing or person newly discovered. □ **all found** (of wages) with board and lodging provided free; **find out** (often + *about*) discover, detect. □ **finder** *noun*.

finding *noun* (often in *plural*) conclusion reached by inquiry.

fine¹ ● *adjective* of high quality; excellent; good, satisfactory; pure, refined; imposing; bright and clear; small or thin, in small particles; smart, showy; flattering. ● *adverb* finely; very well. □ **fine arts** poetry, music, painting, sculpture, architecture, etc.; **fine-spun** delicate, too subtle; **fine-tune** make small adjustments to. □ **finely** *adverb*.

fine² ● *noun* money paid as penalty. ● *verb* (**-ning**) punish by fine.

finery /'faɪnərɪ/ *noun* showy dress or decoration.

finesse /fɪ'nes/ ● *noun* refinement; subtlety; artfulness; *Cards* attempt to win trick with card that is not the highest held. ● *verb* (**-ssing**) use or manage by finesse; *Cards* make finesse.

finger /'fɪŋgə/ ● *noun* any of terminal projections of hand (usually excluding thumb); part of glove for finger; finger-like object. ● *verb* touch, turn about, or play with fingers. □ **finger-bowl** bowl for rinsing fingers during meal; **finger-dry** dry and style hair by running fingers through it; **fingernail** nail on each finger; **fingerprint** impression made on surface by fingers, used in detecting crime; **finger-stall** protective cover for injured finger; **fingertip** tip of finger.

fingering *noun* manner of using fingers in music; indication of this in score.

finial /'fɪnɪəl/ *noun* ornamental top to gable, canopy, etc.

finicky /'fɪnɪkɪ/ *adjective* (also **finical, finicking**) overparticular; fastidious; detailed; fiddly.

finis /'fɪnɪs/ *noun* end, esp. of book.

finish /'fɪnɪʃ/ ● *verb* (often + *off*) bring or come to end or end of; complete; (often + *off, up*) complete consuming; treat surface of. ● *noun* last stage, completion; end of race etc.; method etc. of surface treatment.

finite /'faɪnaɪt/ *adjective* limited, not infinite; (of verb) having specific number and person.

Finn *noun* native or national of Finland.

finnan /'fɪnən/ *noun* (in full **finnan haddock**) smoke-cured haddock.

Finnish ● *adjective* of Finland. ● *noun* language of Finland.

fiord /fjɔːd/ *noun* (also **fjord**) narrow inlet of sea as in Norway.

fir *noun* evergreen conifer with needles growing singly on the stems; its wood. □ **fir-cone** its fruit.

fire ● *noun* state of combustion of substance with oxygen, giving out light and heat; flame, glow; destructive burning; burning fuel in grate etc.; electric or gas heater; firing of guns; fervour, spirit; burning heat. ● *verb* (**-ring**) shoot (gun etc. or missile from it); shoot gun or missile; produce (salute etc.) by shooting; (of gun) be discharged; deliver or utter rapidly; detonate; dismiss (employee); set fire to; supply with fuel; stimulate, enthuse; undergo ignition; bake or dry (pottery, bricks, etc.). □ **fire-alarm** bell etc. warning of fire; **firearm** gun, esp. pistol or rifle; **fire-ball** large meteor, ball of flame; **fire-bomb** incendiary bomb; **firebrand** piece of burning wood, trouble-maker; **fire-break** obstacle preventing spread of fire in forest etc.; **fire-brick** fireproof brick in grate; **fire brigade** group of firefighters; **firedog** support for logs in hearth; **fire door** fire-resistant door; **fire-drill** rehearsal of procedure in case of fire; **fire-engine** vehicle carrying hoses, firefighters, etc.; **fire-escape** emergency staircase etc. for use in fire; **fire extinguisher** apparatus discharging water, foam, etc. to extinguish fire; **firefighter** person who extinguishes fires; **firefly** insect emitting phosphorescent light, e.g. glow-worm; **fire-irons** tongs, poker, and shovel for domestic fire; **fireman** male firefighter, person who tends steam engine or steamship furnace; **fireplace** place in wall for domestic fire; **fire-power** destructive capacity of guns etc.; **fire-practice** fire-drill; **fire-raiser** arsonist; **fireside** area round fireplace; **fire-screen** ornamental screen for fireplace, screen against direct heat of fire; **fire station** headquarters of local fire brigade; **fire-trap** building without fire-escapes etc.; **firework** device producing flashes, bangs, etc. from burning chemicals, (in *plural*) outburst of anger etc.; **on fire** burning, excited; **under fire** being shot at or criticized.

firing *noun* discharge of guns. □ **firing line** front line in battle, centre of criticism etc.; **firing squad** soldiers ordered to shoot condemned person.

firm[1] *adjective* solid; fixed, steady; resolute; steadfast; (of offer etc.) definite. ● *verb* (often + *up*) make or become firm or secure. □ **firmly** *adverb*; **firmness** *noun*.

firm[2] *noun* business concern, its members.

firmament /'fɜːməmənt/ *noun* sky regarded as vault.

first ● *adjective* foremost in time, order, or importance. ● *noun* (**the first**) first person or thing; beginning; first occurrence of something notable; first-class degree; first gear; first place in race. ● *adverb* before all or something else; for the first time. □ **at first hand** directly from original source; **first aid** emergency medical treatment; **first class** *noun* best category or accommodation, mail given priority, highest division in exam; **first-class** *adjective & adverb* of or by first class, excellent(ly); **first floor** (*US* **second floor**) floor above ground floor; **first-footing** first crossing of threshold in New Year; **firsthand** direct, original; **first mate** (on merchant ship) second in command; **first name** personal or Christian name; **first night** first public performance of play etc.; **first-rate** excellent; **first thing** before anything else, very early. □ **firstly** *adverb*.

firth /fɜːθ/ *noun* inlet, estuary.

fiscal /'fɪsk(ə)l/ ● *adjective* of public revenue. ● *noun* *Scottish* procurator fiscal. □ **fiscal year** financial year.

fish[1] ● *noun* (*plural* same or **-es**) vertebrate cold-blooded animal living in water; its flesh as food; person of specified kind. ● *verb* try to catch fish (in); (+ *for*) search for; seek indirectly; (+ *up*, *out*) retrieve with effort. □ **fish cake** fried cake of fish and mashed potato; **fish-eye lens** wide-angled lens; **fish farm** place where fish are bred for food; **fish finger** small oblong piece of fish in breadcrumbs; **fish-hook** barbed hook for catching fish; **fish-kettle** oval pan for boiling fish; **fish-knife** knife for eating or serving fish; **fish-meal** ground dried fish as fertilizer etc.; **fishmonger** dealer in fish; **fishnet** open-meshed fabric; **fish-slice** slotted cooking utensil; **fishwife** coarse or noisy woman, woman selling fish.

fish[2] *noun* piece of wood or iron for strengthening mast etc. □ **fish-plate** flat plate of iron etc. holding rails together.

fisherman /'fɪʃəmən/ *noun* man who catches fish as occupation or sport.

fishery *noun* (*plural* **-ies**) place where fish are caught or reared; industry of fishing or breeding fish.

fishing *noun* occupation or sport of trying to catch fish. □ **fishing-rod** tapering rod for fishing.

fishy *adjective* (**-ier**, **-iest**) of or like fish; *slang* dubious, suspect.

fissile /'fɪsaɪl/ *adjective* capable of undergoing nuclear fission; tending to split.

fission /'fɪʃ(ə)n/ ● *noun* splitting of atomic nucleus; division of cell as mode of reproduction. ● *verb* (cause to) undergo fission.

fissure /'fɪʃə/ ● *noun* narrow crack or split. ● *verb* (**-ring**) split.

fist *noun* clenched hand. □ **fisticuffs** fighting with the fists. □ **fistful** *noun* (*plural* **-s**).

fistula /'fɪstjʊlə/ *noun* (*plural* **-s** or **fistulae** /-liː/) abnormal or artificial passage in body. □ **fistular** *adjective*; **fistulous** *adjective*.

fit[1] ● *adjective* (**-tt-**) well suited; qualified, competent; in good health or condition; (+ *for*) good enough, right; ready. ● *verb* (**-tt-**) be of right size and shape; find room for; (often + *in*, *into*) be correctly positioned; (+ *on*, *together*) fix in place; (+ *with*) supply; befit. ● *noun* way thing fits. □ **fit in** (often + *with*) be compatible, accommodate, make room or time for; **fit out**, **up** equip. □ **fitness** *noun*.

fit[2] *noun* sudden esp. epileptic seizure; sudden brief bout or burst.

fitful *adjective* spasmodic, intermittent. □ **fitfully** *adverb*.

fitment *noun* (usually in *plural*) fixed item of furniture.

fitted *adjective* made to fit closely; with built-in fittings; built-in.

fitter *noun* mechanic who fits together and adjusts machinery etc.; supervisor of cutting, fitting, etc. of garments.

fitting ● *noun* action of fitting on a garment; (usually in *plural*) fixture, fitment. ● *adjective* proper, befitting. □ **fittingly** *adverb*.

five *adjective & noun* one more than four. □ **five o'clock shadow** beard growth visible in latter part of day; **five-star** of highest class; **fivestones** jacks played with five pieces of metal etc. and usually no ball.

fiver *noun* *colloquial* five-pound note.

fives *noun* game in which ball is struck with gloved hand or bat against walls of court.

fix ● *verb* make firm, stable, or permanent; fasten, secure; settle, specify; mend, repair; (+ *on*, *upon*) direct (eyes etc.) steadily on; attract and hold (attention etc.); identify, locate; *US* *colloquial* prepare (food, drink); *colloquial* kill, deal with (person); arrange result fraudulently. ● *noun* dilemma, predicament; position determined by bearings etc.; *slang* dose of addictive drug; *colloquial* fraudulently arranged result. □ **fix up** arrange, (often + *with*) provide (person). □ **fixer** *noun*.

fixate /fɪk'seɪt/ *verb* (**-ting**) *Psychology* (usually in *passive*, often + *on*, *upon*) cause to become abnormally attached to person or thing.

fixation /fɪk'seɪʃ(ə)n/ *noun* fixating, being fixated; obsession.

fixative /'fɪksətɪv/ ● *adjective* tending to fix (colours etc.). ● *noun* fixative substance.

fixedly /'fɪksɪdlɪ/ *adverb* intently.

fixity *noun* fixed state; stability, permanence.

fixture /'fɪkstʃə/ *noun* thing fixed in position; (date fixed for) sporting event; (in *plural*) articles belonging to land or house.

fizz ● *verb* make hissing or spluttering sound; effervesce. ● *noun* fizzing sound; effervescence; *colloquial* effervescent drink. □ **fizzy** *adjective* (**-ier**, **-iest**).

fizzle /'fɪz(ə)l/ ● *verb* (**-ling**) hiss or splutter feebly. ● *noun* fizzling sound. □ **fizzle out** end feebly.

fjord = FIORD.

fl. *abbreviation* fluid; floruit.

flab *noun* *colloquial* fat, flabbiness.

flabbergast /'flæbəɡɑːst/ *verb* (esp. as **flabbergasted** *adjective*) *colloquial* astonish; dumbfound.

flabby /'flæbɪ/ adjective (**-ier**, **-iest**) (of flesh) limp, not firm; feeble. □ **flabbiness** noun.

flaccid /'flæksɪd/ adjective flabby. □ **flaccidity** /-'sɪd-/ noun.

flag¹ ● noun piece of cloth attached by one edge to pole or rope as country's emblem, standard, or signal. ● verb (**-gg-**) grow tired; lag; droop; mark out with flags. □ **flag-day** day when charity collects money and gives stickers to contributors; **flag down** signal to stop; **flag-officer** admiral or vice or rear admiral; **flag-pole** flagstaff; **flagship** ship with admiral on board, leading example of thing; **flagstaff** pole on which flag is hung; **flag-waving** noun populist agitation, chauvinism, adjective chauvinistic.

flag² ● noun (also **flagstone**) flat paving stone. ● verb (**-gg-**) pave with flags.

flag³ noun plant with bladed leaf, esp. iris.

flagellant /'flædʒələnt/ ● noun person who flagellates himself, herself, or others. ● adjective of flagellation.

flagellate /'flædʒəleɪt/ verb (**-ting**) whip or flog, esp. as religious discipline or sexual stimulus. □ **flagellation** noun.

flageolet /flædʒə'let/ noun small flute blown at end.

flagon /'flægən/ noun quart bottle or other vessel for wine etc.

flagrant /'fleɪgrənt/ adjective blatant; scandalous. □ **flagrancy** noun; **flagrantly** adverb.

flagrante see IN FLAGRANTE DELICTO.

flail ● verb (often + about) wave or swing wildly; beat (as) with flail. ● noun staff with heavy stick swinging from it, used for threshing.

flair noun natural talent; style, finesse.

flak noun anti-aircraft fire; criticism; abuse.

flake ● noun thin light piece of snow etc.; thin broad piece peeled or split off. ● verb (**-king**) (often + away, off) take or come away in flakes; fall in or sprinkle with flakes. □ **flake out** fall asleep or drop from exhaustion, faint.

flaky adjective (**-ier**, **-iest**) of, like, or in flakes. □ **flaky pastry** lighter version of puff pastry.

flambé /'flɒmbeɪ/ adjective (of food) covered with alcohol and set alight briefly.

flamboyant /flæm'bɔɪənt/ adjective ostentatious, showy; florid. □ **flamboyance** noun; **flamboyantly** adverb.

flame ● noun ignited gas; portion of this; bright light; brilliant orange colour; passion, esp. love; colloquial sweetheart. ● verb (**-ming**) (often + out, up) burn; blaze; (of passion) break out; become angry; shine or glow like flame.

flamenco /flə'meŋkəʊ/ noun (plural **-s**) Spanish Gypsy guitar music with singing and dancing.

flaming adjective emitting flames; very hot; passionate; brightly coloured; colloquial expressing annoyance.

flamingo /flə'mɪŋgəʊ/ noun (plural **-s** or **-es**) tall long-necked wading bird with usually pink plumage.

flammable /'flæməb(ə)l/ adjective inflammable.

■ **Usage** Flammable is often used because inflammable could be taken to mean 'not flammable'. The negative of flammable is non-flammable.

flan noun pastry case with savoury or sweet filling; sponge base with sweet topping.

flange /flændʒ/ noun projecting flat rim, for strengthening etc.

flank ● noun side of body between ribs and hip; side of mountain, army, etc. ● verb (often as **flanked** adjective) be at or move along side of.

flannel /'flæn(ə)l/ ● noun woven woollen usually napless fabric; (in plural) flannel trousers; face-cloth; slang nonsense, flattery. ● verb (**-ll-**; US **-l-**) slang flatter; wash with flannel.

flannelette /flænə'let/ noun napped cotton fabric like flannel.

flap ● verb (**-pp-**) move or be moved loosely up and down; beat; flutter; colloquial be agitated or panicky; colloquial (of ears) listen intently. ● noun piece of cloth, wood, etc. attached by one side, esp. to cover gap; flapping; colloquial agitation; aileron. □ **flapjack** sweet oatcake, esp. US small pancake.

flapper noun person apt to panic; slang (in 1920s) young unconventional woman.

flare ● verb (**-ring**) blaze with bright unsteady flame; (usually as **flared** adjective) widen gradually; burst out, esp. angrily. ● noun bright unsteady flame, outburst of this; flame or bright light as signal etc.; gradual widening; (in plural) wide-bottomed trousers. □ **flare-path** line of lights on runway to guide aircraft; **flare up** verb burst into blaze, anger, activity, etc.; **flare-up** noun outburst.

flash ● verb (cause to) emit brief or sudden light; gleam; send or reflect like sudden flame; burst suddenly into view etc.; move swiftly; send (news etc.) by radio etc.; signal (to) with vehicle lights; show ostentatiously; slang indecently expose oneself. ● noun sudden bright light or flame; an instant; sudden brief feeling or display; newsflash; Photography flashlight. ● adjective colloquial gaudy, showy; vulgar. □ **flashback** scene set in earlier time than main action; **flash bulb** Photography bulb for flashlight; **flash-gun** device operating camera flashlight; **flash in the pan** promising start followed by failure; **flash-lamp** portable flashing electric lamp; **flashlight** Photography light giving intense flash, US electric torch; **flashpoint** temperature at which vapour from oil etc. will ignite in air, point at which anger is expressed.

flasher noun slang man who indecently exposes himself; automatic device for switching lights rapidly on and off.

flashing noun (usually metal) strip to prevent water penetration at roof joint etc.

flashy adjective (**-ier**, **-iest**) showy; cheaply attractive. □ **flashily** adverb.

flask /flɑːsk/ noun narrow-necked bulbous bottle; hip-flask; vacuum flask.

flat¹ ● adjective (**-tt-**) horizontally level; smooth, even; level and shallow; downright; dull; dejected; having lost its effervescence; (of battery) having exhausted its charge; (of tyre etc.) deflated; Music below correct or normal pitch, having flats in key signature. ● adverb spread out; completely, exactly; flatly. ● noun flat part; level esp. marshy ground; Music note lowered by semitone, sign (♭) indicating this; flat theatre scenery on frame; punctured tyre; (**the flat**) flat racing, its season. □ **flatfish** fish with flattened body, e.g. sole, plaice; **flat foot** foot with flattened arch; **flat-footed** having flat feet, colloquial uninspired; **flat out** at top speed, using all one's strength etc.; **flat race** horse race over level ground without jumps; **flat rate** unvarying rate or charge; **flat spin** aircraft's nearly horizontal spin, colloquial state of panic; **flatworm** worm with flattened body, e.g. fluke. □ **flatly** adverb; **flatness** noun; **flattish** adjective.

flat² noun set of rooms, usually on one floor, as residence. □ **flatmate** person sharing flat. □ **flatlet** noun.

flatten verb make or become flat; colloquial humiliate; knock down.

flatter /'flætə/ verb compliment unduly; enhance appearance of; (usually **flatter oneself**; usually + that) congratulate or delude (oneself etc.).

□ **flatterer** *noun*; **flattering** *adjective*; **flatteringly** *adverb*; **flattery** *noun*.

flatulent /'flætjʊlənt/ *adjective* causing, caused by, or troubled with, intestinal wind; inflated, pretentious. □ **flatulence** *noun*.

flaunt /flɔ:nt/ *verb* display proudly; show off, parade.

■ **Usage** *Flaunt* is often confused with *flout*, which means 'to disobey contemptuously'.

flautist /'flɔ:tɪst/ *noun* flute-player.

flavour /'fleɪvə/ (*US* **flavor**) ● *noun* mixed sensation of smell and taste; distinctive taste, characteristic quality. ● *verb* give flavour to, season. □ **flavour of the month** temporary trend or fashion. □ **flavourless** *adjective*; **flavoursome** *adjective*.

flavouring *noun* (*US* **flavoring**) substance used to flavour food or drink.

flaw ● *noun* imperfection; blemish; crack; invalidating defect. ● *verb* damage; spoil; (as **flawed** *adjective*) morally etc. defective. □ **flawless** *adjective*.

flax *noun* blue-flowered plant grown for its oily seeds (linseed) and for making into linen.

flaxen *adjective* of flax; (of hair) pale yellow.

flay *verb* strip skin or hide off; criticize severely; peel off.

flea *noun* small wingless jumping parasitic insect. □ **flea market** street market selling second-hand goods etc.

fleck ● *noun* small patch of colour or light; speck. ● *verb* mark with flecks.

flection *US* = FLEXION.

fled past & past participle of FLEE.

fledgling /'fledʒlɪŋ/ (also **fledgeling**) ● *noun* young bird. ● *adjective* new, inexperienced.

flee *verb* (**flees**; *past & past participle* **fled**) run away (from); leave hurriedly.

fleece ● *noun* woolly coat of sheep etc.; this shorn from sheep; fleecy lining etc. ● *verb* (**-cing**) (often + *of*) strip of money etc., swindle; shear; (as **fleeced** *adjective*) cover as with fleece. □ **fleecy** *adjective* (**-ier, -iest**).

fleet ● *noun* warships under one commander-in-chief; (**the fleet**) navy; vehicles in one company etc. ● *adjective* swift, nimble.

fleeting *adjective* transitory; brief. □ **fleetingly** *adverb*.

Fleming /'flemɪŋ/ *noun* native of medieval Flanders; member of Flemish-speaking people of N. and W. Belgium.

Flemish /'flemɪʃ/ ● *adjective* of Flanders. ● *noun* language of the Flemings.

flesh *noun* soft substance between skin and bones; plumpness, fat; body, esp. as sinful; pulpy substance of fruit etc.; (also **flesh-colour**) yellowish pink colour. □ **flesh and blood** human body, human nature, esp. as fallible, humankind, near relations; **flesh out** make or become substantial; **fleshpots** luxurious living; **flesh-wound** superficial wound; **in the flesh** in person. □ **fleshy** *adjective* (**-ier, -iest**).

fleshly /'fleʃlɪ/ *adjective* worldly; carnal.

fleur-de-lis /flɜ:də'li:/ *noun* (also **fleur-de-lys**) (*plural* **fleurs-** same pronunciation) iris flower; *Heraldry* lily of 3 petals; former royal arms of France.

flew past of FLY[1].

flews *plural noun* hanging lips of bloodhound etc.

flex[1] *verb* bend (joint, limb); move (muscle) to bend joint.

flex[2] *noun* flexible insulated cable.

flexible /'fleksɪb(ə)l/ *adjective* able to bend without breaking; pliable; adaptable. □ **flexibility** *noun*; **flexibly** *adverb*.

flexion /'flekʃ(ə)n/ *noun* (*US* **flection**) bending; bent part.

flexitime /'fleksɪtaɪm/ *noun* system of flexible working hours.

flibbertigibbet /'flɪbətɪ'dʒɪbɪt/ *noun* gossiping, frivolous, or restless person.

flick ● *noun* light sharp blow; sudden release of bent finger etc. to propel thing; jerk; *colloquial* cinema film; (**the flicks**) the cinema. ● *verb* (often + *away, off*) strike or move with flick. □ **flick-knife** knife with blade that springs out; **flick through** glance at or through by turning over (pages etc.) rapidly.

flicker /'flɪkə/ ● *verb* shine or burn unsteadily; flutter; waver. ● *noun* flickering light or motion; brief feeling (of hope etc.); slightest reaction or degree. □ **flicker out** die away.

flier = FLYER.

flight[1] /flaɪt/ *noun* act or manner of flying; movement, passage, or journey through air or space; timetabled airline journey; flock of birds etc.; (usually + *of*) series of stairs etc.; imaginative excursion; volley; tail of dart. □ **flight bag** small zipped shoulder bag for air travel; **flight-deck** cockpit of large aircraft, deck of aircraft carrier; **flight lieutenant** RAF officer next below squadron leader; **flight path** planned course of aircraft etc.; **flight recorder** device in aircraft recording technical details of flight; **flight sergeant** RAF rank next above sergeant.

flight[2] /flaɪt/ *noun* fleeing; hasty retreat.

flightless *adjective* (of bird etc.) unable to fly.

flighty *adjective* (**-ier, -iest**) frivolous; fickle.

flimsy /'flɪmzɪ/ *adjective* (**-ier, -iest**) insubstantial, rickety; unconvincing; (of clothing) thin. □ **flimsily** *adverb*.

flinch *verb* draw back in fear etc.; shrink; wince.

fling ● *verb* (*past & past participle* **flung**) throw, hurl; rush, esp. angrily; discard rashly. ● *noun* flinging; throw; bout of wild behaviour; whirling Scottish dance.

flint *noun* hard grey stone; piece of this, esp. as tool or weapon; piece of hard alloy used to produce spark. □ **flintlock** old type of gun fired by spark from flint. □ **flinty** *adjective* (**-ier, -iest**).

flip ● *verb* (**-pp-**) toss (coin etc.) so that it spins in air; turn or flick (small object) over; *slang* flip one's lid. ● *noun* act of flipping. ● *adjective* glib; flippant. □ **flip chart** large pad of paper on stand; **flip-flop** sandal with thong between toes; **flip one's lid** *slang* lose selfcontrol, go mad; **flip side** reverse side of gramophone record etc.; **flip through** flick through.

flippant /'flɪpənt/ *adjective* frivolous; disrespectful. □ **flippancy** *noun*; **flippantly** *adverb*.

flipper *noun* limb of turtle, penguin, etc., used in swimming; rubber attachment to foot for underwater swimming.

flirt ● *verb* try to attract sexually but without serious intent; (usually + *with*) superficially engage in, trifle. ● *noun* person who flirts. □ **flirtation** *noun*; **flirtatious** *adjective*; **flirtatiously** *adverb*; **flirtatiousness** *noun*.

flit ● *verb* (**-tt-**) pass lightly or rapidly; make short flights; disappear secretly, esp. to escape creditors. ● *noun* act of flitting.

flitch *noun* side of bacon.

flitter *verb* flit about.

float ● *verb* (cause to) rest or drift on surface of liquid; move or be suspended freely in liquid or gas; launch (company, scheme); offer (stocks, shares, etc.) on stock market; (cause or allow to) have fluctuating exchange rate; circulate or cause (rumour, idea) to circulate. ● *noun* device or structure that floats; electrically powered vehicle or cart; decorated platform or tableau on lorry in procession etc.; supply of loose change, petty cash.

floating *adjective* not settled; variable; not committed. □ **floating rib** lower rib not attached to breastbone.

floaty *adjective* (**-ier**, **-iest**) (of fabric) light and airy.

flocculent /'flɒkjʊlənt/ *adjective* like tufts of wool.

flock[1] ● *noun* animals, esp. birds or sheep, as group or unit; large crowd of people; people in care of priest, teacher, etc. ● *verb* (often + *to*, *in*, *out*, *together*) congregate; mass; troop.

flock[2] *noun* shredded wool, cotton, etc. used as stuffing; powdered wool used to make pattern on wallpaper.

floe *noun* sheet of floating ice.

flog *verb* (**-gg-**) beat with whip, stick, etc.; (often + *off*) *slang* sell.

flood /flʌd/ ● *noun* overflowing or influx of water, esp. over land; outburst, outpouring; inflow of tide; (**the Flood**) the flood described in Genesis. ● *verb* overflow; cover or be covered with flood; irrigate; deluge; come in great quantities; overfill (carburettor) with petrol. □ **floodgate** gate for admitting or excluding water, (usually in *plural*) last restraint against fear, anger, etc.; **floodlight** (illuminate with) large powerful light; **floodlit** lit thus.

floor /flɔː/ ● *noun* lower surface of room; bottom of sea, cave, etc.; storey; part of legislative chamber where members sit and speak; right to speak in debate; minimum of prices, wages, etc. ● *verb* provide with floor; knock down; baffle; overcome. □ **floor manager** stage manager of television production; **floor plan** diagram of rooms etc. on one storey; **floor show** cabaret.

flop ● *verb* (**-pp-**) sway about heavily or loosely; (often + *down*, *on*, *into*) move, fall, sit, etc. awkwardly or suddenly; *slang* collapse, fail; make dull soft thud or splash. ● *noun* flopping motion or sound; *slang* failure. ● *adverb* with a flop.

floppy ● *adjective* (**-ier**, **-iest**) tending to flop; flaccid. ● *noun* (*plural* **-ies**) (in full **floppy disk**) flexible disc for storage of computer data.

flora /'flɔːrə/ *noun* (*plural* **-s** or **-rae** /-riː/) plant life of region or period.

floral *adjective* of or decorated with flowers.

floret /'flɒrɪt/ *noun* each of small flowers of composite flower head; each stem of head of cauliflower, broccoli, etc.

florid /'flɒrɪd/ *adjective* ruddy; ornate; showy.

florin /'flɒrɪn/ *noun historical* gold or silver coin, esp. British two-shilling coin.

florist /'flɒrɪst/ *noun* person who deals in or grows flowers.

floruit /'flɒruːɪt/ *verb* (of painter, writer, etc.) lived and worked.

floss ● *noun* rough silk of silkworm's cocoon; dental floss. ● *verb* clean (teeth) with dental floss. □ **flossy** *adjective* (**-ier**, **-iest**).

flotation /fləʊ'teɪʃ(ə)n/ *noun* launching of commercial enterprise etc.

flotilla /flə'tɪlə/ *noun* small fleet; fleet of small ships.

flotsam /'flɒtsəm/ *noun* floating wreckage. □ **flotsam and jetsam** odds and ends, vagrants.

flounce[1] /flaʊns/ ● *verb* (**-cing**) (often + *off*, *out*, etc.) go or move angrily or impatiently. ● *noun* flouncing movement.

flounce[2] /flaʊns/ ● *noun* frill on dress, skirt, etc. ● *verb* (**-cing**) (usually as **flounced** *adjective*) trim with flounces.

flounder[1] /'flaʊndə/ *verb* struggle helplessly; do task clumsily.

flounder[2] /'flaʊndə/ *noun* (*plural* same) small flatfish.

flour /flaʊə/ ● *noun* meal or powder from ground wheat etc. ● *verb* sprinkle with flour. □ **floury** *adjective* (**-ier**, **-iest**).

flourish /'flʌrɪʃ/ ● *verb* grow vigorously; thrive, prosper; wave, brandish. ● *noun* showy gesture; ornamental curve in writing; *Music* ornate passage; fanfare.

flout *verb* disobey (law etc.) contemptuously.

■ *Usage Flout* is often confused with *flaunt*, which means 'to display proudly or show off'.

flow /fləʊ/ ● *verb* glide along, move smoothly; gush out; circulate; be plentiful or in flood; (often + *from*) result. ● *noun* flowing movement or liquid; stream; rise of tide. □ **flow chart**, **diagram**, **sheet** diagram of movement or action in complex activity.

flower /'flaʊə/ ● *noun* part of plant from which seed or fruit develops; plant bearing blossom. ● *verb* bloom; reach peak. □ **flower-bed** garden bed for flowers; **the flower of** the best of; **flowerpot** pot for growing plant in; **in flower** blooming. □ **flowered** *adjective*.

flowery *adjective* florally decorated; (of speech etc.) high-flown; full of flowers.

flowing *adjective* fluent; smoothly continuous; (of hair etc.) unconfined.

flown *past participle* of FLY[1].

flu *noun colloquial* influenza.

fluctuate /'flʌktʃʊeɪt/ *verb* (**-ting**) vary, rise and fall. □ **fluctuation** *noun*.

flue *noun* smoke duct in chimney; channel for conveying heat.

fluent /'fluːənt/ *adjective* expressing oneself easily and naturally, esp. in foreign language. □ **fluency** *noun*; **fluently** *adverb*.

fluff ● *noun* soft fur, feathers, fabric particles, etc.; *slang* mistake in performance etc. ● *verb* (often + *up*) shake into or become soft mass; *slang* make mistake in performance etc. □ **fluffy** *adjective* (**-ier**, **-iest**).

flugelhorn /'fluːg(ə)lhɔːn/ *noun* brass instrument like cornet.

fluid /'fluːɪd/ ● *noun* substance, esp. gas or liquid, capable of flowing freely; liquid secretion. ● *adjective* able to flow freely; constantly changing. ● **fluid ounce** twentieth or *US* sixteenth of pint. □ **fluidity** /-'ɪdɪtɪ/ *noun*.

fluke[1] /fluːk/ *noun* lucky accident. □ **fluky** *adjective* (**-ier**, **-iest**).

fluke[2] /fluːk/ *noun* parasitic flatworm.

flummery /'flʌmərɪ/ *noun* (*plural* **-ies**) nonsense; flattery; sweet milk dish.

flummox /'flʌməks/ *verb colloquial* bewilder.

flung *past & past participle* of FLING.

flunk *verb US colloquial* fail (esp. exam).

flunkey /'flʌŋkɪ/ *noun* (also **flunky**) (*plural* **-eys** or **-ies**) *usually derogatory* footman.

fluorescence /flʊə'res(ə)ns/ *noun* light radiation from certain substances; property of absorbing invisible light and emitting visible light. □ **fluoresce** *verb* (**-scing**); **fluorescent** *adjective*.

fluoridate /'flʊərɪdeɪt/ *verb* (**-ting**) add fluoride to (water). □ **fluoridation** *noun*.

fluoride /'flʊəraɪd/ *noun* compound of fluorine with metal, esp. used to prevent tooth decay.

fluorinate /'flʊərɪneɪt/ *verb* (**-ting**) fluoridate; introduce fluorine into (compound). □ **fluorination** *noun*.

fluorine /'flʊəriːn/ *noun* poisonous pale yellow gaseous element.

flurry /'flʌrɪ/ ● *noun* (*plural* **-ies**) gust, squall; burst of activity, excitement, etc. ● *verb* (**-ies**, **-ied**) agitate, confuse.

flush[1] ● *verb* (often as **flushed** *adjective* + *with*) (cause to) glow or blush (with pride etc.); cleanse (drain, lavatory, etc.) by flow of water; (often + *away*, *down*) dispose of thus. ● *noun* glow, blush; rush of water;

cleansing (of lavatory etc.) thus; rush of esp. elation or triumph; freshness, vigour; (also **hot flush**) sudden hot feeling during menopause; feverish redness or temperature etc. ● *adjective* level, in same plane; *colloquial* having plenty of money.

flush² *noun* hand of cards all of one suit.

flush³ *verb* (cause to) fly up suddenly. □ **flush out** reveal, drive out.

fluster /ˈflʌstə/ ● *verb* confuse, make nervous. ● *noun* confused or agitated state.

flute /fluːt/ ● *noun* high-pitched woodwind instrument held sideways; vertical groove in pillar etc. ● *verb* (**-ting**) (often as **fluted** *adjective*) make grooves in; play on flute. □ **fluting** *noun*.

flutter /ˈflʌtə/ ● *verb* flap (wings) in flying or trying to fly; fall quiveringly; wave or flap quickly; move about restlessly; (of pulse etc.) beat feebly or irregularly. ● *noun* fluttering; tremulous excitement; *slang* small bet on horse etc.; abnormally rapid heartbeat; rapid variation of pitch, esp. of recorded sound.

fluvial /ˈfluːvɪəl/ *adjective* of or found in rivers.

flux *noun* flowing, flowing out; discharge; continuous change; substance mixed with metal etc. to assist fusion.

fly¹ /flaɪ/ ● *verb* (**flies**; *past* **flew** /fluː/; *past participle* **flown** /fləʊn/) move or travel through air with wings or in aircraft; control flight of (aircraft); cause to fly or remain aloft; wave; move swiftly; be driven forcefully; flee (from); (+ *at, upon*) attack or criticize fiercely. ● *noun* (*plural* **-ies**) (usually in *plural*) flap to cover front fastening on trousers, this fastening; flap at entrance of tent; (in *plural*) space over stage, for scenery and lighting; act of flying. □ **fly-by-night** unreliable; **fly-half** *Rugby* stand-off half; **flyleaf** blank leaf at beginning or end of book; **flyover** bridge carrying road etc. over another; **fly-past** ceremonial flight of aircraft; **fly-post** fix (posters etc.) illegally; **flysheet** canvas cover over tent for extra protection, short tract or circular; **fly-tip** illegally dump (waste); **flywheel** heavy wheel regulating machinery or accumulating power.

fly² /flaɪ/ (*plural* **flies**) *noun* two-winged insect; disease caused by flies; (esp. artificial) fly used as bait in fishing. □ **fly-blown** tainted by flies; **flycatcher** bird that catches flies in flight; **fly-fish** *verb* fish with fly; **fly in the ointment** minor irritation or setback; **fly on the wall** unnoticed observer; **fly-paper** sticky treated paper for catching flies; **fly-trap** plant that catches flies; **flyweight** amateur boxing weight (48–51 kg).

fly³ /flaɪ/ *adjective slang* knowing, clever.

flyer *noun* (also **flier**) airman, airwoman; thing or person that flies in specified way; small handbill.

flying ● *adjective* that flies; hasty. ● *noun* flight. □ **flying boat** boatlike seaplane; **flying buttress** (usually arched) buttress running from upper part of wall to outer support; **flying doctor** doctor who uses aircraft to visit patients; **flying fish** fish gliding through air with winglike fins; **flying fox** fruit-eating bat; **flying officer** RAF officer next below flight lieutenant; **flying saucer** supposed alien spaceship; **flying squad** rapidly mobile police detachment, midwifery unit, etc.; **flying start** start (of race) at full speed, vigorous start.

FM *abbreviation* Field Marshal; frequency modulation.

FO *abbreviation* Flying Officer.

foal ● *noun* young of horse or related animal. ● *verb* give birth to (foal).

foam ● *noun* froth formed in liquid; froth of saliva or sweat; spongy rubber or plastic. ● *verb* emit foam; froth. □ **foam at the mouth** be very angry. □ **foamy** *adjective* (**-ier, -iest**).

fob¹ *noun* (attachment to) watch-chain; small pocket for watch etc.

fob² *verb* (**-bb-**) □ **fob off** (often + *with*) deceive into accepting something inferior, (often + *on, on to*) offload (unwanted thing on person).

focal /ˈfəʊk(ə)l/ *adjective* of or at a focus. □ **focal distance, length** distance between centre of lens etc. and its focus; **focal point** focus, centre of interest or activity.

fo'c's'le = FORECASTLE.

focus /ˈfəʊkəs/ ● *noun* (*plural* **focuses** or **foci** /ˈfəʊsaɪ/) point at which rays etc. meet after reflection or refraction or from which rays etc. seem to come; point at which object must be situated to give clearly defined image; adjustment of eye or lens to produce clear image; state of clear definition; centre of interest or activity. ● *verb* (**-s-** or **-ss-**) bring into focus; adjust focus of (lens, eye); concentrate or be concentrated on; (cause to) converge to focus.

fodder /ˈfɒdə/ *noun* hay, straw, etc. as animal food.

foe *noun* enemy.

foetid = FETID.

foetus /ˈfiːtəs/ *noun* (US **fetus**) (*plural* **-tuses**) unborn mammalian offspring, esp. human embryo of 8 weeks or more. □ **foetal** *adjective*.

fog ● *noun* thick cloud of water droplets or smoke suspended at or near earth's surface; thick mist; cloudiness on photographic negative; confused state. ● *verb* (**-gg-**) envelop (as) in fog; perplex. □ **fog-bank** mass of fog at sea; **foghorn** horn warning ships in fog, *colloquial* penetrating voice.

fogey /ˈfəʊgɪ/ *noun* (also **fogy**) (*plural* **-ies** or **-eys**) (esp. **old fogey**) dull old-fashioned person.

foggy *adjective* (**-ier, -iest**) full of fog; of or like fog; vague. □ **not the foggiest** *colloquial* no idea.

foible /ˈfɔɪb(ə)l/ *noun* minor weakness or idiosyncrasy.

foil¹ *verb* frustrate, defeat.

foil² *noun* thin sheet of metal; person or thing setting off another to advantage.

foil³ *noun* blunt fencing sword.

foist *verb* (+ *on*) force (thing, oneself) on to (unwilling person).

fold¹ /fəʊld/ ● *verb* double (flexible thing) over on itself; bend portion of; become or be able to be folded; (+ *away, up*) make compact by folding; (often + *up*) *colloquial* collapse, cease to function; enfold; clasp; (+ *in*) mix in gently. ● *noun* folding; line made by folding; hollow among hills.

fold² /fəʊld/ *noun* sheepfold; religious group or congregation.

folder *noun* folding cover or holder for loose papers.

foliaceous /ˌfəʊlɪˈeɪʃəs/ *adjective* of or like leaves; laminated.

foliage /ˈfəʊlɪdʒ/ *noun* leaves, leafage.

foliar /ˈfəʊlɪə/ *adjective* of leaves. □ **foliar feed** fertilizer supplied to leaves.

foliate ● *adjective* /ˈfəʊlɪət/ leaflike; having leaves. ● *verb* /ˈfəʊlɪeɪt/ (**-ting**) split into thin layers. □ **foliation** *noun*.

folio /ˈfəʊlɪəʊ/ ● *noun* (*plural* **-s**) leaf of paper etc. numbered only on front; sheet of paper folded once; book of such sheets. ● *adjective* (of book) made of folios.

folk /fəʊk/ ● *noun* (*plural* same or **-s**) (treated as *plural*) people in general or of specified class; (in *plural*, usually **folks**) one's relatives; (treated as *singular*) a people or nation; (in full **folk-music**) (treated as *singular*) traditional, esp. working-class, music, or music in style of this. ● *adjective* of popular origin. □ **folklore** traditional beliefs etc., study of these; **folkweave** rough loosely woven fabric.

folksy /'fəʊksɪ/ *adjective* (**-ier, -iest**) of or like folk art; in deliberately popular style.

follicle /'fɒlɪk(ə)l/ *noun* small sac or vesicle, esp. for hair-root. □ **follicular** /fə'lɪkjʊlə/ *adjective*.

follow /'fɒləʊ/ *verb* go or come after; go along; come next in order or time; practise; understand; take as guide; take interest in; (+ *with*) provide with (sequel etc.); (+ *from*) result from; be necessary inference. □ **follow on** *verb* continue, (of cricket team) bat twice in succession; **follow-on** *noun* instance of this; **follow suit** play card of suit led, conform to another's actions; **follow through** *verb* continue to conclusion, continue movement of stroke after hitting the ball; **follow-through** *noun* instance of this; **follow up** *verb* act or investigate further; **follow-up** *noun* subsequent action.

follower *noun* supporter, devotee; person who follows.

following ● *preposition* after in time; as sequel to. ● *noun* group of supporters. ● *adjective* that follows. □ **the following** what follows, now to be mentioned.

folly /'fɒlɪ/ *noun* (*plural* **-ies**) foolishness; foolish act, idea, etc.; building for display only.

foment /fə'ment/ *verb* instigate, stir up (trouble etc.). □ **fomentation** /fəʊmen'teɪʃ(ə)n/ *noun*.

fond *adjective* (+ *of*) liking; affectionate; doting; foolishly optimistic. □ **fondly** *adverb*; **fondness** *noun*.

fondant /'fɒnd(ə)nt/ *noun* soft sugary sweet.

fondle /'fɒnd(ə)l/ *verb* (**-ling**) caress.

fondue /'fɒndjuː/ *noun* dish of melted cheese.

font¹ *noun* receptacle for baptismal water.

font² = FOUNT².

fontanelle /fɒntə'nel/ *noun* (*US* **fontanel**) space in infant's skull, which later closes up.

food /fuːd/ *noun* substance taken in to maintain life and growth; solid food; mental stimulus. □ **food-chain** series of organisms each dependent on next for food; **food poisoning** illness due to bacteria etc. in food; **food processor** machine for chopping and mixing food; **foodstuff** substance used as food.

foodie /'fuːdɪ/ *noun colloquial* person who makes a cult of food.

fool¹ ● *noun* unwise or stupid person; *historical* jester, clown. ● *verb* deceive; trick; cheat; joke; tease; (+ *around, about*) play, trifle. □ **act, play the fool** behave in silly way; **foolproof** incapable of misuse or mistake; **fool's paradise** illusory happiness; **make a fool of** make (a person) look foolish, trick.

fool² *noun* dessert of fruit purée with cream or custard.

foolery *noun* foolish behaviour.

foolhardy *adjective* (**-ier, -iest**) foolishly bold; reckless. □ **foolhardily** *adverb*; **foolhardiness** *noun*.

foolish *adjective* lacking good sense or judgement. □ **foolishly** *adverb*; **foolishness** *noun*.

foolscap /'fuːlskæp/ *noun* large size of paper, about 330 mm x 200 (or 400) mm.

foot /fʊt/ ● *noun* (*plural* **feet**) part of leg below ankle; lower part or end; (*plural* same or **feet**) linear measure of 12 in. (30.48 cm); metrical unit of verse forming part of line; *historical* infantry. ● *verb* pay (bill); (usually as **foot it**) go on foot. □ **foot-and-mouth (disease)** contagious viral disease of cattle etc.; **footfall** sound of footstep; **foot-fault** (in tennis) serving with foot over baseline; **foothill** low hill lying at base of mountain or range; **foothold** secure place for feet in climbing, secure initial position; **footlights** row of floor-level lights along front of stage; **footloose** free to act as one pleases; **footman** liveried servant; **footmark** footprint; **footnote** note at foot of page; **footpath** path for pedestrians only; **footplate** platform for crew in locomotive; **footprint** impression left by foot or shoe; **footsore** having sore feet, esp. from walking; **footstep** (sound of) step taken in walking; **footstool** stool for resting feet on when sitting; **on foot** walking. □ **footless** *adjective*.

footage *noun* a length of TV or cinema film etc.; length in feet.

football *noun* large inflated usually leather ball; team game played with this. □ **football pool(s)** organized gambling on results of football matches. □ **footballer** *noun*.

footing *noun* foothold; secure position; operational basis; relative position or status; (often in *plural*) foundations of wall.

footling /'fuːtlɪŋ/ *adjective colloquial* trivial, silly.

Footsie /'fʊtsɪ/ *noun* FT-SE.

footsie /'fʊtsɪ/ *noun colloquial* amorous play with feet.

fop *noun* dandy. □ **foppery** *noun*; **foppish** *adjective*.

for /fə, fɔː/ ● *preposition* in interest, defence, or favour of; appropriate to; regarding; representing; at the price of; as consequence or on account of; in order to get or reach; so as to start promptly at; notwithstanding. ● *conjunction* because, since. □ **be for it** be liable or about to be punished.

forage /'fɒrɪdʒ/ ● *noun* food for horses and cattle; searching for food. ● *verb* (**-ging**) (often + *for*) search for food; rummage; collect food from. □ **forage cap** infantry undress cap.

foray /'fɒreɪ/ ● *noun* sudden attack, raid. ● *verb* make foray.

forbade (also **forbad**) past of FORBID.

forbear¹ /fɔː'beə/ *verb* (past **forbore**; past participle **forborne**) *formal* abstain or refrain from.

forbear² = FOREBEAR.

forbearance *noun* patient self-control; tolerance.

forbid /fə'bɪd/ *verb* (**forbidding**; past **forbade** /-bæd/ or **forbad**; past participle **forbidden**) (+ *to do*) order not; not allow; refuse entry to. □ **forbidden fruit** thing desired esp. because not allowed.

forbidding *adjective* stern, threatening. □ **forbiddingly** *adverb*.

forbore past of FORBEAR¹.

forborne past participle of FORBEAR¹.

force ● *noun* strength, power, intense effort; group of soldiers, police, etc.; coercion, compulsion; influence (person etc.) with moral power. ● *verb* (**-cing**) compel, coerce; make way, break into or open by force; drive, propel; (+ *on, upon*) impose or press on (person); cause or produce by effort; strain; artificially hasten maturity of; accelerate. □ **forced landing** emergency landing of aircraft; **forced march** lengthy and vigorous march, esp. by troops; **force-feed** feed (prisoner etc.) against his or her will; **force (person's) hand** make him or her act prematurely or unwillingly.

forceful *adjective* powerful; impressive. □ **forcefully** *adverb*; **forcefulness** *noun*.

force majeure /fɔːs mæ'ʒɜː/ *noun* irresistible force; unforeseeable circumstances. [French]

forcemeat /'fɔːsmiːt/ *noun* minced seasoned meat for stuffing etc.

forceps /'fɔːseps/ *noun* (*plural* same) surgical pincers.

forcible /'fɔːsɪb(ə)l/ *adjective* done by or involving force; forceful. □ **forcibly** *adverb*.

ford ● *noun* shallow place where river etc. may be crossed. ● *verb* cross (water) at ford. □ **fordable** *adjective*.

fore ● *adjective* situated in front. ● *noun* front part; bow of ship. ● *interjection* (in *golf*) *warning to person in path of ball*. □ **fore-and-aft** (of sails or rigging) lengthwise, at bow and stern; **to the fore** conspicuous.

forearm¹ /'fɔːrɑːm/ *noun* arm from elbow to wrist or fingertips.

forearm² /fɔː'rɑːm/ *verb* arm beforehand, prepare.

forebear /ˈfɔːbeə/ noun (also **forbear**) (usually in plural) ancestor.

forebode /fɔːˈbəʊd/ verb (**-ding**) be advance sign of; portend.

foreboding noun expectation of trouble.

forecast ● verb (past & past participle **-cast** or **-casted**) predict; estimate beforehand ● noun prediction, esp. of weather. □ **forecaster** noun.

forecastle /ˈfəʊks(ə)l/ noun (also **fo'c's'le**) forward part of ship, formerly living quarters.

foreclose /fɔːˈkləʊz/ verb (**-sing**) stop (mortgage) from being redeemable; repossess mortgaged property of (person) when loan is not duly repaid; exclude, prevent. □ **foreclosure** noun.

forecourt noun part of filling-station with petrol pumps; enclosed space in front of building.

forefather noun (usually in plural) ancestor.

forefinger noun finger next to thumb.

forefoot noun front foot of animal.

forefront noun leading position; foremost part.

forego = FORGO.

foregoing /fɔːˈgəʊɪŋ/ adjective preceding; previously mentioned.

foregone conclusion /ˈfɔːgɒn/ noun easily foreseeable result.

foreground noun part of view nearest observer.

forehand Tennis etc. ● adjective (of stroke) played with palm of hand facing forward. ● noun forehand stroke.

forehead /ˈfɒrɪd, ˈfɔːhed/ noun part of face above eyebrows.

foreign /ˈfɒrən/ adjective of, from, in, or characteristic of country or language other than one's own; dealing with other countries; of another district, society, etc.; (often + to) unfamiliar, alien; coming from outside. □ **foreign legion** group of foreign volunteers in (esp. French) army. □ **foreignness** noun.

foreigner noun person born in or coming from another country.

foreknowledge /fɔːˈnɒlɪdʒ/ noun knowledge in advance of (an event etc.).

foreleg noun animal's front leg.

forelock noun lock of hair just above forehead. □ **touch one's forelock** defer to person of higher social rank.

foreman /ˈfɔːmən/ noun (feminine **forewoman**) worker supervising others; spokesman of jury.

foremast noun mast nearest bow of ship.

foremost ● adjective most notable, best; first, front. ● adverb most importantly.

forename noun first or Christian name.

forensic /fəˈrensɪk/ adjective of or used in courts of law; of or involving application of science to legal problems.

foreplay noun stimulation preceding sexual intercourse.

forerunner noun predecessor.

foresail noun principal sail on foremast.

foresee /fɔːˈsiː/ verb (past **-saw**; past participle **-seen**) see or be aware of beforehand. □ **foreseeable** adjective.

foreshadow /fɔːˈʃædəʊ/ verb be warning or indication of (future event).

foreshore noun shore between high and low water marks.

foreshorten /fɔːˈʃɔːt(ə)n/ verb portray (object) with apparent shortening due to perspective.

foresight noun care or provision for future; foreseeing.

foreskin noun fold of skin covering end of penis.

forest /ˈfɒrɪst/ ● noun large area of trees; large number, dense mass. ● verb plant with trees; convert into forest.

forestall /fɔːˈstɔːl/ verb prevent by advance action; deal with beforehand.

forester noun manager of forest; expert in forestry; dweller in forest.

forestry noun science or management of forests.

foretaste noun small preliminary experience of something.

foretell /fɔːˈtel/ verb (past & past participle **-told**) predict, prophesy; indicate approach of.

forethought noun care or provision for future; deliberate intention.

forever /fəˈrevə/ adverb always, constantly.

forewarn /fɔːˈwɔːn/ verb warn beforehand.

foreword noun introductory remarks in book, often not by author.

forfeit /ˈfɔːfɪt/ ● noun (thing surrendered as) penalty. ● adjective lost or surrendered as penalty. ● verb (**-t-**) lose right to, surrender as penalty. □ **forfeiture** noun.

forgather /fɔːˈgæðə/ verb assemble; associate.

forgave past of FORGIVE.

forge[1] ● verb (**-ging**) make or write in fraudulent imitation; shape by heating and hammering. ● noun furnace etc. for melting or refining metal; blacksmith's workshop. □ **forger** noun.

forge[2] verb (**-ging**) advance gradually. □ **forge ahead** take lead, progress rapidly.

forgery /ˈfɔːdʒərɪ/ noun (plural **-ies**) (making of) forged document etc.

forget /fəˈget/ verb (**forgetting**; past **forgot**; past participle **forgotten** or US **forgot**) lose remembrance of; neglect, overlook; cease to think of; (**forget oneself**) act without dignity. □ **forget-me-not** plant with small blue flowers. □ **forgettable** adjective.

forgetful adjective apt to forget; (often + of) neglectful. □ **forgetfully** adverb; **forgetfulness** noun.

forgive /fəˈgɪv/ verb (**-ving**; past **forgave**; past participle **forgiven**) cease to resent; pardon; remit (debt). □ **forgivable** adjective; **forgiveness** noun; **forgiving** adjective.

forgo /fɔːˈgəʊ/ verb (also **forego**) (**-goes**; past **-went**; past participle **-gone**) go without, relinquish.

forgot past of FORGET.

forgotten past participle of FORGET.

fork ● noun pronged item of cutlery; similar large tool for digging etc.; forked part, esp. of bicycle frame; (place of) divergence of road etc. ● verb form fork or branch; take one road at fork; dig with fork. □ **forklift truck** vehicle with fork for lifting and carrying; **fork out** slang pay, esp. reluctantly.

forlorn /fəˈlɔːn/ adjective sad and abandoned; pitiful. □ **forlorn hope** faint remaining hope or chance. □ **forlornly** adverb.

form ● noun shape, arrangement of parts, visible aspect; person or animal as visible or tangible; mode in which thing exists or manifests itself; kind, variety; document with blanks to be filled in; class in school; (often as **the form**) customary or correct behaviour or method; set order of words; (of athlete, horse, etc.) condition of health and training; disposition; bench. ● verb make, be made; constitute; develop or establish as concept, practice, etc.; (+ into) organize; (of troops etc.) bring or move into formation; mould, fashion.

formal /ˈfɔːm(ə)l/ adjective in accordance with rules, convention, or ceremony; (of garden etc.) symmetrical; prim, stiff; perfunctory; drawn up correctly; concerned with outward form. □ **formally** adverb.

formaldehyde /fɔːˈmældɪhaɪd/ noun colourless gas used as preservative and disinfectant.

formalin /ˈfɔːməlɪn/ noun solution of formaldehyde in water.

formalism *noun* strict adherence to external form, esp. in art. □ **formalist** *noun*.

formality /fɔːˈmælɪtɪ/ *noun* (*plural* **-ies**) formal, esp. meaningless, regulation or act; rigid observance of rules or convention.

formalize *verb* (also **-ise**) (**-zing** or **-sing**) give definite (esp. legal) form to; make formal. □ **formalization** *noun*.

format /ˈfɔːmæt/ ● *noun* shape and size (of book etc.); style or manner of procedure etc.; arrangement of computer data etc. ● *verb* (**-tt-**) arrange in format; prepare (storage medium) to receive computer data.

formation /fɔːˈmeɪʃ(ə)n/ *noun* forming; thing formed; particular arrangement (e.g. of troops); rocks or strata with common characteristic.

formative /ˈfɔːmətɪv/ *adjective* serving to form; of formation.

former /ˈfɔːmə/ *adjective* of the past, earlier, previous; (**the former**) the first or first-named of two.

formerly *adverb* in former times; previously.

Formica /fɔːˈmaɪkə/ *noun proprietary term* hard plastic laminate for surfaces.

formic acid /ˈfɔːmɪk/ *noun* colourless irritant volatile acid contained in fluid emitted by ants.

formidable /ˈfɔːmɪdəb(ə)l/ *adjective* inspiring awe, respect, or dread; difficult to deal with. □ **formidably** *adverb*.

■ **Usage** *Formidable* is also pronounced /fəˈmɪdəb(ə)l/ (with the stress on the -*mid*-), but this is considered incorrect by some people.

formless *adjective* without definite or regular form. □ **formlessness** *noun*.

formula /ˈfɔːmjʊlə/ *noun* (*plural* **-s** or **-lae** /-liː/) chemical symbols showing constituents of substance; mathematical rule expressed in symbols; fixed form of words; list of ingredients; classification of racing car, esp. by engine capacity. □ **formulaic** /-ˈleɪɪk/ *adjective*.

formulate /ˈfɔːmjʊleɪt/ *verb* express in formula; express clearly and precisely. □ **formulation** *noun*.

fornicate /ˈfɔːnɪkeɪt/ *verb* (**-ting**) *usually jocular* have extramarital sexual intercourse. □ **fornication** *noun*; **fornicator** *noun*.

forsake /fəˈseɪk/ *verb* (**-king**; *past* **forsook** /-ˈsʊk/; *past participle* **forsaken**) *literary* give up, renounce; desert, abandon.

forswear /fɔːˈsweə/ *verb* (*past* **forswore**; *past participle* **forsworn**) abjure, renounce; (**forswear oneself**) perjure oneself; (as **forsworn** *adjective*) perjured.

forsythia /fɔːˈsaɪθɪə/ *noun* shrub with bright yellow flowers.

fort *noun* fortified building or position. □ **hold the fort** act as temporary substitute.

forte[1] /ˈfɔːteɪ/ *noun* thing in which one excels or specializes.

forte[2] /ˈfɔːteɪ/ *Music* ● *adjective* loud. ● *adverb* loudly. ● *noun* loud playing, singing, or passage.

forth /fɔːθ/ *adverb* forward(s); out; onwards in time. □ **forthcoming** /fɔːθˈkʌmɪŋ/ coming or available soon, produced when wanted, informative, responsive.

forthright *adjective* straightforward, outspoken, decisive.

forthwith /fɔːθˈwɪθ/ *adverb* immediately, without delay.

fortification /fɔːtɪfɪˈkeɪʃ(ə)n/ *noun* fortifying; (usually in *plural*) defensive works.

fortify /ˈfɔːtɪfaɪ/ *verb* (**-ies**, **-ied**) provide with fortifications; strengthen; (usually as **fortified** *adjective*) strengthen (wine etc.) with alcohol, increase nutritive value of (food, esp. with vitamins).

fortissimo /fɔːˈtɪsɪməʊ/ *Music* ● *adjective* very loud. ● *adverb* very loudly. ● *noun* (*plural* **-mos** or **-mi** /-miː/) very loud playing, singing, or passage.

fortitude /ˈfɔːtɪtjuːd/ *noun* courage in pain or adversity.

fortnight /ˈfɔːtnaɪt/ *noun* two weeks.

fortnightly ● *adjective* done, produced, or occurring once a fortnight. ● *adverb* every fortnight. ● *noun* (*plural* **-ies**) fortnightly magazine etc.

Fortran /ˈfɔːtræn/ *noun* (also **FORTRAN**) computer language used esp. for scientific calculations.

fortress /ˈfɔːtrɪs/ *noun* fortified building or town.

fortuitous /fɔːˈtjuːɪtəs/ *adjective* happening by chance. □ **fortuitously** *adverb*; **fortuitousness** *noun*; **fortuity** *noun* (*plural* **-ies**).

fortunate /ˈfɔːtʃənət/ *adjective* lucky, auspicious. □ **fortunately** *adverb*.

fortune /ˈfɔːtʃ(ə)n/ *noun* chance or luck in human affairs; person's destiny; prosperity, wealth; *colloquial* large sum of money. □ **fortune-teller** person claiming to foretell one's destiny.

forty /ˈfɔːtɪ/ *adjective & noun* (*plural* **-ies**) four times ten. □ **forty winks** *colloquial* short sleep. □ **fortieth** *adjective & noun*.

forum /ˈfɔːrəm/ *noun* place of or meeting for public discussion; court, tribunal.

forward /ˈfɔːwəd/ ● *adjective* onward, towards front; bold, precocious, presumptuous; relating to the future; well-advanced. ● *noun* attacking player in football etc. ● *adverb* to front; into prominence; so as to make progress; towards future; forwards. ● *verb* send (letter etc.) on; dispatch; help to advance, promote.

forwards *adverb* in direction one is facing.

forwent *past* of FORGO.

fossil /ˈfɒs(ə)l/ ● *noun* remains or impression of (usually prehistoric) plant or animal hardened in rock; *colloquial* antiquated or unchanging person or thing. ● *adjective* of or like fossil. □ **fossil fuel** natural fuel extracted from ground. □ **fossilize** *verb* (also **-ise**) (**-zing** or **-sing**); **fossilization** *noun*.

foster /ˈfɒstə/ *verb* promote growth of; encourage or harbour (feeling); bring up (another's child); assign as foster-child. ● *adjective* related by or concerned with fostering.

fought *past & past participle* of FIGHT.

foul /faʊl/ ● *adjective* offensive, loathsome, stinking; dirty, soiled; *colloquial* awful; noxious; obscene; unfair, against rules; (of weather) rough; entangled. ● *noun* foul blow or play; entanglement. ● *adverb* unfairly. ● *verb* make or become foul; commit foul on (player); (often + *up*) (cause to) become entangled or blocked. □ **foul-mouthed** using obscene or offensive language; **foul play** unfair play, treacherous or violent act, esp. murder. □ **foully** /ˈfaʊllɪ/ *adverb*; **foulness** *noun*.

found[1] *past & past participle* of FIND.

found[2] /faʊnd/ *verb* establish, originate; lay base of; base. □ **founder** *noun*.

found[3] /faʊnd/ *verb* melt and mould (metal), fuse (materials for glass); make thus. □ **founder** *noun*.

foundation /faʊnˈdeɪʃ(ə)n/ *noun* solid ground or base under building; (usually in *plural*) lowest part of building, usually below ground; basis; underlying principle; establishing (esp. endowed institution); base for cosmetics; (in full **foundation garment**) woman's supporting undergarment. □ **foundation-stone** one laid ceremonially at founding of building, basis.

founder /ˈfaʊndə/ *verb* (of ship) fill with water and sink; (of plan) fail; (of horse) stumble, fall lame.

foundling /ˈfaʊndlɪŋ/ *noun* abandoned infant of unknown parentage.

foundry /'faʊndrɪ/ noun (plural **-ies**) workshop for casting metal.

fount¹ /faʊnt/ noun poetical source, spring, fountain.

fount² /fɒnt/ noun (also **font**) set of printing type of same size and face.

fountain /'faʊntɪn/ noun jet(s) of water as ornament or for drinking; spring; (often + of) source. □ **fountain-head** source; **fountain pen** pen with reservoir or cartridge for ink.

four /fɔː/ adjective & noun one more than three; 4-oared boat, its crew. □ **four-letter word** short obscene word; **four-poster** bed with 4 posts supporting canopy; **four-square** adjective solidly based, steady, adverb resolutely; **four-stroke** (of internal-combustion engine) having power cycle completed in two up-and-down movements of piston; **four-wheel drive** drive acting on all 4 wheels of vehicle.

fourfold adjective & adverb four times as much or many.

foursome noun group of 4 people; golf match between two pairs.

fourteen /fɔːˈtiːn/ adjective & noun one more than thirteen. □ **fourteenth** adjective & noun.

fourth /fɔːθ/ adjective & noun next after third; any of four equal parts of thing. □ **fourthly** adverb.

fowl /faʊl/ noun (plural same or **-s**) chicken kept for eggs and meat; poultry as food.

fox ● noun wild canine animal with red or grey fur and bushy tail; its fur; crafty person. ● verb deceive; puzzle. □ **foxglove** tall plant with purple or white flowers; **foxhole** hole in ground as shelter etc. in battle; **foxhound** hound bred to hunt foxes; **foxhunting** hunting foxes with hounds; **fox-terrier** small short-haired terrier; **foxtrot** ballroom dance with slow and quick steps. □ **foxlike** adjective.

foxy adjective (**-ier**, **-iest**) foxlike; sly, cunning; reddish-brown. □ **foxily** adverb.

foyer /'fɔɪeɪ/ noun entrance hall in hotel, theatre, etc.

FPA abbreviation Family Planning Association.

Fr. abbreviation Father; French.

fr. abbreviation franc(s).

fracas /'frækɑː/ noun (plural same /-kɑːz/) noisy quarrel.

fraction /'frækʃ(ə)n/ noun part of whole number; small part, amount, etc.; portion of mixture obtainable by distillation etc. □ **fractional** adjective; **fractionally** adverb.

fractious /'frækʃəs/ adjective irritable, peevish.

fracture /'fræktʃə/ ● noun breakage, esp. of bone. ● verb (**-ring**) cause fracture in, suffer fracture.

fragile /'frædʒaɪl/ adjective easily broken; delicate. □ **fragility** /frə'dʒɪl-/ noun.

fragment ● noun /'frægmənt/ part broken off; remains or unfinished portion of book etc. ● verb /fræg'ment/ break into fragments. □ **fragmental** /-'men-/ adjective; **fragmentary** adjective; **fragmentation** noun.

fragrance /'freɪɡrəns/ noun sweetness of smell; sweet scent.

fragrant adjective sweet-smelling.

frail adjective fragile, delicate; morally weak. □ **frailly** /'freɪllɪ/ adverb; **frailness** noun.

frailty noun (plural **-ies**) frail quality; weakness, foible.

frame ● noun case or border enclosing picture etc.; supporting structure; (in plural) structure of spectacles holding lenses; build of person or animal; framework; construction; (in full **frame of mind**) temporary state; single picture on photographic film; (in snooker etc.) triangular structure for positioning balls, round of play; glazed structure to protect plants. ● verb (**-ming**) set in frame; serve as frame for; construct, devise; (+ to, into) adapt, fit; slang concoct false charge etc. against; articulate (words).

□ **frame-up** slang conspiracy to convict innocent person; **framework** essential supporting structure, basic system.

franc noun French, Belgian, Swiss, etc. unit of currency.

franchise /'fræntʃaɪz/ ● noun right to vote; citizenship; authorization to sell company's goods etc. in particular area; right granted to person or corporation. ● verb (**-sing**) grant franchise to.

Franciscan /fræn'sɪskən/ ● adjective of (order of) St Francis. ● noun Franciscan friar or nun.

franglais /'frɑːɡleɪ/ noun French with many English words and idioms. [French]

Frank noun member of Germanic people that conquered Gaul in 6th c. □ **Frankish** adjective.

frank ● adjective candid, outspoken; undisguised; open. ● verb mark (letter etc.) to record payment of postage. ● noun franking signature or mark. □ **frankly** adverb; **frankness** noun.

frankfurter /'fræŋkfɜːtə/ noun seasoned smoked sausage.

frankincense /'fræŋkɪnsens/ noun aromatic gum resin burnt as incense.

frantic /'fræntɪk/ adjective wildly excited; frenzied; hurried, anxious; desperate, violent; colloquial extreme. □ **frantically** adverb.

fraternal /frə'tɜːn(ə)l/ adjective of brothers, brotherly; comradely. □ **fraternally** adverb.

fraternity /frə'tɜːnɪtɪ/ noun (plural **-ies**) religious brotherhood; group with common interests or of same professional class; US male students' society; brotherliness.

fraternize /'frætənaɪz/ verb (also **-ise**) (**-zing** or **-sing**) (often + with) associate, make friends, esp. with enemy etc. □ **fraternization** noun.

fratricide /'frætrɪsaɪd/ noun killing of one's brother or sister; person who does this. □ **fratricidal** /-'saɪd(ə)l/ adjective.

Frau /fraʊ/ noun (plural **Frauen** /'fraʊən/) title used of or to married or widowed German-speaking woman.

fraud /frɔːd/ noun criminal deception; dishonest trick; impostor.

fraudulent /'frɔːdjʊlənt/ adjective of, involving, or guilty of fraud. □ **fraudulence** noun; **fraudulently** adverb.

fraught /frɔːt/ adjective (+ with) filled or attended with (danger etc.); colloquial distressing; tense.

Fräulein /'frɔɪlaɪn/ noun: title used of or to unmarried German-speaking woman.

fray¹ verb wear or become worn; unravel at edge; (esp. as **frayed** adjective) (of nerves) become strained.

fray² noun fight, conflict; brawl.

frazzle /'fræz(ə)l/ colloquial ● noun worn, exhausted, or shrivelled state. ● verb (**-ling**) (usually as **frazzled** adjective) wear out; exhaust.

freak ● noun monstrosity; abnormal person or thing; colloquial unconventional person, fanatic of specified kind. ● verb (often + out) colloquial make or become very angry; (cause to) undergo esp. drug-induced etc. hallucinations or strong emotional experience. □ **freakish** adjective; **freaky** adjective (**-ier**, **-iest**).

freckle /'frek(ə)l/ ● noun light brown spot on skin. ● verb (**-ling**) (usually as **freckled** adjective) spot or be spotted with freckles. □ **freckly** adjective (**-ier**, **-iest**).

free ● adjective (**freer** /'friːə/, **freest** /'friːɪst/) not a slave; having personal rights and social and political liberty; autonomous; democratic; unrestricted, not confined; (+ of, from or in combination) exempt from, not containing or subject to; (+ to do) permitted, at liberty; costing nothing; available; spontaneous; lavish, unreserved; (of translation) not literal.

● *adverb* freely; without cost. ● *verb* (**frees, freed**) make free, liberate; disentangle. ☐ **for free** *colloquial* gratis; **freebooter** pirate; **freeboard** part of ship's side between waterline and deck; **Free Church** Nonconformist Church; **free enterprise** freedom of private business from state control; **free fall** movement under force of gravity only; **free hand** *noun* liberty to act at one's own discretion; **freehand** *adjective* (of drawing) done without ruler, compasses, etc., *adverb* in a freehand way; **free house** pub not controlled by brewery; **freeloader** *slang* sponger; **freeman** holder of freedom of city etc.; **free port** port without customs duties, or open to all traders; **free-range** (of hens etc.) roaming freely, (of eggs) produced by such hens; **free spirit** independent or uninhibited person; **free-standing** not supported by another structure; **freestyle** swimming race in which any stroke may be used, wrestling allowing almost any hold; **freethinker** /-'θɪŋkə/ person who rejects dogma, esp. in religious belief; **free trade** trade without import restrictions etc.; **freeway** US motorway; **freewheel** ride bicycle with pedals at rest, act without constraint; **free will** power of acting independently of fate or without coercion.

freebie /'fri:bɪ/ *noun* *colloquial* thing given free of charge.

freedom *noun* being free; personal or civil liberty; liberty of action; (+ *from*) exemption from; (+ *of*) honorary membership or citizenship of, unrestricted use of (house etc.).

freehold *noun* complete ownership of property for unlimited period; such property. ☐ **freeholder** *noun*.

freelance ● *noun* person working for no fixed employer. ● *verb* work as freelance. ● *adverb* as freelance.

Freemason /'fri:meɪs(ə)n/ *noun* member of fraternity for mutual help with secret rituals. ☐ **Freemasonry** *noun*.

freesia /'fri:zjə/ *noun* fragrant flowering African bulb.

freeze ● *verb* (**-zing**; *past* **froze**; *past participle* **frozen** /'frəʊz(ə)n/) turn into ice or other solid by cold; make or become rigid from cold; be or feel very cold; cover or be covered with ice; refrigerate below freezing point; make or become motionless; (as **frozen** *adjective*) devoid of emotion; make (assets etc.) unrealizable; fix (prices etc.) at certain level; stop (movement in film). ● *noun* period or state of frost; price-fixing etc.; (in full **freeze-frame**) still filmshot. ☐ **freeze-dry** preserve (food) by freezing and then drying in vacuum; **freeze up** *verb* obstruct or be obstructed by ice; **freeze-up** *noun* period of extreme cold; **freezing point** temperature at which liquid freezes.

freezer *noun* refrigerated cabinet for preserving food in frozen state.

freight /freɪt/ *noun* transport of goods; goods transported; charge for transport of goods.

freighter *noun* ship or aircraft for carrying freight.

French ● *adjective* of France or its people or language. ● *noun* French language; (**the French**) (*plural*) the French people. ☐ **French bean** kidney or haricot bean as unripe pods or as ripe seeds; **French bread** long crisp loaf; **French dressing** salad dressing of oil and vinegar; **French fried potatoes, French fries** chips; **French horn** coiled brass wind instrument; **French letter** *colloquial* condom; **Frenchman, Frenchwoman** native or national of France; **French polish** *noun* shellac polish for wood; **Frenchpolish** *verb*; **French window** glazed door in outside wall.

frenetic /frə'netɪk/ *adjective* frantic, frenzied. ☐ **frenetically** *adverb*.

frenzy /'frenzɪ/ ● *noun* (*plural* **-ies**) wild excitement or fury. ● *verb* (**-ies, -ied**) (usually as **frenzied** *adjective*) drive to frenzy. ☐ **frenziedly** *adverb*.

frequency /'fri:kwənsɪ/ *noun* (*plural* **-ies**) commonness of occurrence; frequent occurrence; rate of recurrence (of vibration etc.). ☐ **frequency modulation** *Electronics* modulation by varying carrier-wave frequency.

frequent ● *adjective* /'fri:kwənt/ occurring often or in close succession; habitual. ● *verb* /frɪ'kwent/ go to habitually. ☐ **frequently** /'fri:kwəntlɪ/ *adverb*.

fresco /'freskəʊ/ *noun* (*plural* **-s**) painting in water-colour on fresh plaster.

fresh ● *adjective* newly made or obtained; other, different; new; additional; (+ *from*) lately arrived from; not stale or faded; (of food) not preserved; (of water) not salty; pure; refreshing; (of wind) brisk; *colloquial* cheeky, amorously impudent; inexperienced. ● *adverb* newly, recently. ☐ **freshwater** (of fish etc.) not of the sea. ☐ **freshly** *adverb*; **freshness** *noun*.

freshen *verb* make or become fresh; (+ *up*) wash, tidy oneself, etc.; revive.

fresher *noun* *colloquial* first-year student at university or (US) high school.

freshet /'freʃɪt/ *noun* rush of fresh water into sea; river flood.

freshman /'freʃmən/ *noun* fresher.

fret[1] ● *verb* (**-tt-**) be worried or distressed. ● *noun* worry, vexation. ☐ **fretful** *adjective*; **fretfully** *adverb*.

fret[2] ● *noun* ornamental pattern of straight lines joined usually at right angles. ● *verb* (**-tt-**) adorn with fret etc. ☐ **fretsaw** narrow saw on frame for cutting thin wood in patterns; **fretwork** work done with fretsaw.

fret[3] *noun* bar or ridge on finger-board of guitar etc.

Freudian /'frɔɪdɪən/ ● *adjective* of Freud's theories or method of psychoanalysis. ● *noun* follower of Freud. ☐ **Freudian slip** unintentional verbal error revealing subconscious feelings.

Fri. *abbreviation* Friday.

friable /'fraɪəb(ə)l/ *adjective* easily crumbled. ☐ **friability** *noun*.

friar /'fraɪə/ *noun* member of male non-enclosed religious order. ☐ **friar's balsam** type of inhalant.

friary /'fraɪərɪ/ *noun* (*plural* **-ies**) monastery for friars.

fricassee /'frɪkəseɪ/ ● *noun* pieces of meat in thick sauce. ● *verb* (**fricassees, fricasseed**) make fricassee of.

fricative /'frɪkətɪv/ ● *adjective* sounded by friction of breath in narrow opening. ● *noun* such consonant (e.g. *f*, *th*).

friction /'frɪkʃ(ə)n/ *noun* rubbing of one object against another; resistance so encountered; clash of wills, opinions, etc. ☐ **frictional** *adjective*.

Friday /'fraɪdeɪ/ *noun* day of week following Thursday.

fridge *noun* *colloquial* refrigerator. ☐ **fridge-freezer** combined refrigerator and freezer.

friend /frend/ *noun* supportive and respected associate, esp. one for whom affection is felt; ally; kind person; person already mentioned; (**Friend**) Quaker.

friendly ● *adjective* (**-ier, -iest**) outgoing, kindly; (often + *with*) on amicable terms; not hostile; user-friendly. ● *noun* (*plural* **-ies**) friendly match. ☐ **-friendly** not harming, helping; **friendly match** match played for enjoyment rather than competition; **Friendly Society** society for insurance against sickness etc. ☐ **friendliness** *noun*.

friendship *noun* friendly relationship or feeling.

frier = FRYER.

Friesian /'fri:zɪən/ ● *noun* one of breed of black and white dairy cattle. ● *adjective* of Friesians.

frieze /friːz/ *noun* part of entablature, often filled with sculpture, between architrave and cornice; band of decoration, esp. at top of wall.

frigate /ˈfrɪgɪt/ *noun* naval escort-vessel.

fright /fraɪt/ *noun* (instance of) sudden or extreme fear; grotesque-looking person or thing. □ **take fright** become frightened.

frighten *verb* fill with fright; (+ *away, off, out of, into*) drive by fright. □ **frightening** *adjective*; **frighteningly** *adverb*.

frightful *adjective* dreadful, shocking; ugly; *colloquial* extremely bad; *colloquial* extreme. □ **frightfully** *adverb*.

frigid /ˈfrɪdʒɪd/ *adjective* unfriendly, cold; (of woman) sexually unresponsive; cold. □ **frigidity** /-ˈdʒɪd-/ *noun*.

frill ● *noun* ornamental edging of gathered or pleated material; (in *plural*) unnecessary embellishments. ● *verb* (usually as **frilled** *adjective*) decorate with frill. □ **frilly** *adjective* (**-ier, -iest**).

fringe ● *noun* border of tassels or loose threads; front hair cut to hang over forehead; outer limit; unimportant area or part. ● *verb* (**-ging**) adorn with fringe; serve as fringe to. □ **fringe benefit** employee's benefit additional to salary.

frippery /ˈfrɪpərɪ/ *noun* (*plural* **-ies**) showy finery; empty display; (usually in *plural*) knick-knacks.

frisk ● *verb* leap or skip playfully; *slang* search (person). ● *noun* playful leap or skip.

frisky *adjective* (**-ier, -iest**) lively, playful.

frisson /ˈfriːsɒn/ *noun* emotional thrill. [French]

fritillary /frɪˈtɪlərɪ/ *noun* (*plural* **-ies**) plant with bell-like flowers; butterfly with red and black chequered wings.

fritter[1] /ˈfrɪtə/ *verb* (usually + *away*) waste triflingly.

fritter[2] /ˈfrɪtə/ *noun* fruit, meat, etc. coated in batter and fried.

frivolous /ˈfrɪvələs/ *adjective* not serious, shallow, silly; trifling. □ **frivolity** /-ˈvɒl-/ *noun* (*plural* **-ies**).

frizz ● *verb* form (hair) into tight curls. ● *noun* frizzed hair or state. □ **frizzy** *adjective* (**-ier, -iest**).

frizzle[1] /ˈfrɪz(ə)l/ *verb* (**-ling**) fry or cook with sizzling noise; (often + *up*) burn, shrivel.

frizzle[2] /ˈfrɪz(ə)l/ *verb* (**-ling**) & *noun* frizz.

frock *noun* woman's or girl's dress; monk's or priest's gown. □ **frock-coat** man's long-skirted coat.

frog *noun* tailless leaping amphibian. □ **frog in one's throat** *colloquial* phlegm in throat that hinders speech; **frogman** underwater swimmer equipped with rubber suit and flippers; **frogmarch** hustle forward with arms pinned behind; **frog-spawn** frog's eggs.

frolic /ˈfrɒlɪk/ ● *verb* (**-ck-**) play about merrily. ● *noun* merrymaking.

frolicsome *adjective* playful.

from /frəm/ *preposition expressing separation or origin.*

fromage frais /frɒmɑːʒ ˈfreɪ/ *noun* type of soft cheese.

frond *noun* leaflike part of fern or palm.

front /frʌnt/ ● *noun* side or part most prominent or important, or nearer spectator or direction of motion; line of battle; scene of actual fighting; organized political group; demeanour; pretext, bluff; person etc. as cover for subversive or illegal activities; land along edge of sea or lake, esp. in town; forward edge of advancing cold or warm air; auditorium; breast of garment. ● *adjective* of or at front. ● *verb* (+ *on, to, towards*, etc.) have front facing or directed towards; (+ *for*) *slang* act as front for; (usually as **fronted** *adjective* + *with*) provide with or have front; lead (band, organization, etc.). □ **front bench** seats in Parliament for leading members of government and opposition; **front line** foremost part of army or group under attack; **front runner** favourite in race etc.

frontage *noun* front of building; land next to street, water, etc.; extent of front.

frontal *adjective* of or on front; of forehead.

frontier /ˈfrʌntɪə/ *noun* border between countries, district on each side of this; limits of attainment or knowledge in subject; *esp. US historical* border between settled and unsettled country. □ **frontiersman** *noun*.

frontispiece /ˈfrʌntɪspiːs/ *noun* illustration facing title-page of book.

frost ● *noun* frozen dew or vapour; temperature below freezing point. ● *verb* (usually + *over, up*) become covered with frost; cover (as) with frost; (usually as **frosted** *adjective*) roughen surface of (glass) to make opaque. □ **frostbite** injury to body tissue due to freezing; **frostbitten** *adjective*.

frosting *noun* icing for cakes.

frosty *adjective* (**-ier, -iest**) cold or covered with frost; unfriendly.

froth ● *noun* foam; idle talk. ● *verb* emit or gather froth. □ **frothy** *adjective* (**-ier, -iest**).

frown ● *verb* wrinkle brows, esp. in displeasure or concentration; (+ *at, on*) disapprove of. ● *noun* act of frowning, frowning look.

frowsty /ˈfraʊstɪ/ *adjective* (**-ier, -iest**) fusty, stuffy.

frowzy /ˈfraʊzɪ/ *adjective* (also **frowsy**) (**-ier, -iest**) fusty; slatternly, dingy.

froze *past* of FREEZE.

frozen *past participle* of FREEZE.

FRS *abbreviation* Fellow of the Royal Society.

fructify /ˈfrʌktɪfaɪ/ *verb* (**-ies, -ied**) bear fruit; make fruitful.

fructose /ˈfrʌktəʊz/ *noun* sugar in fruits, honey, etc.

frugal /ˈfruːg(ə)l/ *adjective* sparing; meagre. □ **frugality** /-ˈgæl-/ *noun*; **frugally** *adverb*.

fruit /fruːt/ ● *noun* seed-bearing part of plant or tree; this as food; (usually in *plural*) products, profits, rewards. ● *verb* bear fruit. □ **fruit cake** cake containing dried fruit; **fruit cocktail** diced fruit salad; **fruit machine** gambling machine operated by coins; **fruit salad** dessert of mixed fruit; **fruit sugar** fructose.

fruiterer /ˈfruːtərə/ *noun* dealer in fruit.

fruitful *adjective* productive; successful. □ **fruitfully** *adverb*.

fruition /fruːˈɪʃ(ə)n/ *noun* realization of aims or hopes.

fruitless *adjective* not bearing fruit; useless, unsuccessful. □ **fruitlessly** *adverb*.

fruity *adjective* (**-ier, -iest**) of or resembling fruit; (of voice) deep and rich; *colloquial* slightly indecent.

frump *noun* dowdy woman. □ **frumpish** *adjective*; **frumpy** *adjective* (**-ier, -iest**).

frustrate /frʌsˈtreɪt/ *verb* (**-ting**) make (efforts) ineffective; prevent from achieving purpose; (as **frustrated** *adjective*) discontented, unfulfilled. □ **frustrating** *adjective*; **frustratingly** *adverb*; **frustration** *noun*.

fry[1] ● *verb* (**fries, fried**) cook in hot fat. ● *noun* fried food, esp. (usually **fries**) chips. □ **frying-pan** shallow long-handled pan for frying; **fry-up** *colloquial* fried bacon, eggs, etc.

fry[2] *plural noun* young or freshly hatched fishes.

fryer *noun* (also **frier**) person who fries; vessel for frying esp. fish.

ft *abbreviation* foot, feet.

FT-SE *abbreviation* Financial Times Stock Exchange (100 share index).

fuchsia /ˈfjuːʃə/ *noun* shrub with drooping flowers.

fuddle /ˈfʌd(ə)l/ ● *verb* (**-ling**) confuse, esp. with alcohol. ● *noun* confusion; intoxication.

fuddy-duddy /ˈfʌdɪdʌdɪ/ *slang* ● *adjective* fussy, old-fashioned. ● *noun* (*plural* **-ies**) such person.

fudge ● *noun* soft toffee-like sweet; faking. ● *verb* (**-ging**) make or do clumsily or dishonestly; fake.

fuel /'fjuːəl/ ● *noun* material for burning or as source of heat, power, or nuclear energy; thing that sustains or inflames passion etc. ● *verb* (**-ll-**; *US* **-l-**) supply with fuel; inflame (feeling).

fug *noun colloquial* stuffy atmosphere. □ **fuggy** *adjective* (**-ier, -iest**).

fugitive /'fjuːdʒɪtɪv/ ● *noun* (often + *from*) person who flees. ● *adjective* fleeing; transient, fleeting.

fugue /fjuːg/ *noun* piece of music in which short melody or phrase is introduced by one part and developed by others. □ **fugal** *adjective*.

fulcrum /'fʌlkrəm/ *noun* (*plural* **-s** or **-cra**) point on which lever is supported.

fulfil /fʊl'fɪl/ *verb* (*US* **fulfill**) (**-ll-**) carry out; satisfy; (as **fulfilled** *adjective*) completely happy; (**fulfil oneself**) realize one's potential. □ **fulfilment** *noun*.

full /fʊl/ ● *adjective* holding all it can; replete; abundant; satisfying; (+ *of*) having abundance of, engrossed in; complete, perfect; resonant; plump; ample. ● *adverb* quite, exactly. ● **full back** defensive player near goal in football etc.; **full-blooded** vigorous, sensual, not hybrid; **full-blown** fully developed; **full board** provision of bed and all meals; **full-bodied** rich in quality, tone, etc.; **full frontal** (of nude) fully exposed at front, explicit; **full house** maximum attendance at theatre etc., hand in poker with 3 of a kind and a pair; **full-length** of normal length, not shortened, (of portrait) showing whole figure; **full moon** moon with whole disc illuminated; **full stop** punctuation mark (.) at end of sentence etc. (see panel), complete cessation; **full term** completion of normal pregnancy; **full-time** *adjective* for or during whole of working week, *adverb* on full-time basis. □ **fullness** *noun*.

fully *adverb* completely; at least.

fulmar /'fʊlmə/ *noun* kind of petrel.

fulminate /'fʊlmɪneɪt/ *verb* (**-ting**) criticize loudly and forcibly; explode, flash. □ **fulmination** *noun*.

fulsome /'fʊlsəm/ *adjective* excessive, cloying; insincere. □ **fulsomely** *adverb*.

■ **Usage** *Fulsome* is sometimes wrongly used to mean 'generous', as in *fulsome praise*, or 'generous with praise', as in *a fulsome tribute*.

fumble /'fʌmb(ə)l/ ● *verb* (**-ling**) grope about; handle clumsily or nervously. ● *noun* act of fumbling.

fume ● *noun* (usually in *plural*) exuded smoke, gas, or vapour. ● *verb* (**-ming**) emit fumes; be very angry; subject (oak etc.) to fumes to darken.

fumigate /'fjuːmɪgeɪt/ *verb* (**-ting**) disinfect or purify with fumes. □ **fumigation** *noun*; **fumigator** *noun*.

fun *noun* playful amusement; source of this; mockery. □ **funfair** fair consisting of amusements and sideshows; **fun run** *colloquial* sponsored run for charity; **make fun of, poke fun at** ridicule.

function /'fʌŋkʃ(ə)n/ ● *noun* proper role etc.; official duty; public or social occasion; *Mathematics* quantity whose value depends on varying values of others. ● *verb* fulfil function; operate.

functional *adjective* of or serving a function; practical rather than attractive. □ **functionally** *adverb*.

functionalism *noun* belief that function should determine design. □ **functionalist** *noun & adjective*.

functionary *noun* (*plural* **-ies**) official.

fund ● *noun* permanently available stock; money set apart for purpose; (in *plural*) money resources. ● *verb* provide with money; make (debt) permanent at fixed interest. □ **fund-raising** raising money for charity etc.; **fund-raiser** *noun*.

fundamental /fʌndə'ment(ə)l/ ● *adjective* of or serving as base or foundation; essential, primary. ● *noun* fundamental principle. □ **fundamentally** *adverb*.

fundamentalism *noun* strict adherence to traditional religious beliefs. □ **fundamentalist** *noun & adjective*.

funeral /'fjuːnər(ə)l/ ● *noun* ceremonial burial or cremation of dead. ● *adjective* of or used at funerals. □ **funeral director** undertaker; **funeral parlour** establishment where corpses are prepared for funerals.

funerary /'fjuːnərərɪ/ *adjective* of or used at funerals.

funereal /fjuː'nɪərɪəl/ *adjective* of or appropriate to funeral; dismal, dark.

Full stop .

This is used:

1 at the end of a sentence, e.g.

> *I am going to the cinema tonight.*
> *The film begins at seven.*

The full stop is replaced by a question mark at the end of a question, and by an exclamation mark at the end of an exclamation.

2 after an abbreviation, e.g.

> *H. G. Wells*   *p. 19* (= *page 19*)   *Sun.* (= *Sunday*)
> *Ex. 6* (= *Exercise 6*).

Full stops are **not** used with:

- **a** numerical abbreviations, e.g. *1st, 2nd, 15th, 23rd*
- **b** acronyms, e.g. *FIFA, NATO*
- **c** abbreviations that are used as ordinary words, e.g. *con, demo, recap*
- **d** chemical symbols, e.g. Fe, K, H_2O

Full stops are not essential for:

- **a** abbreviations consisting entirely of capitals, e.g. *BBC, AD, BC, PLC*
- **b** *C* (= *Celsius*), *F* (= *Fahrenheit*)
- **c** measures of length, weight, time, etc., except for *in.* (= *inch*), *st.* (= *stone*)
- **d** *Dr, Revd* (but note *Rev.*), *Mr, Mrs, Ms, Mme, Mlle, St* (= *Saint*), *Hants, Northants, p* (= *penny* or *pence*).

fungicide /ˈfʌndʒɪsaɪd/ *noun* substance that kills fungus. □ **fungicidal** /-ˈsaɪd(ə)l/ *adjective*.

fungus /ˈfʌŋgəs/ *noun* (*plural* **-gi** /-gaɪ/ or **-guses**) mushroom, toadstool, or allied plant; spongy morbid growth. □ **fungal** *adjective*; **fungoid** *adjective*; **fungous** *adjective*.

funicular /fjuːˈnɪkjʊlə/ *noun* (in full **funicular railway**) cable railway with ascending and descending cars counterbalanced.

funk *slang* ● *noun* fear, panic. ● *verb* evade through fear.

funky *adjective* (**-ier**, **-iest**) *slang* (esp. of jazz etc.) with heavy rhythm.

funnel /ˈfʌn(ə)l/ ● *noun* tube widening at top, for pouring liquid etc. into small opening; chimney of steam engine or ship. ● *verb* (**-ll-**; *US* **-l-**) (cause to) move (as) through funnel.

funny /ˈfʌnɪ/ *adjective* (**-ier**, **-iest**) amusing, comical; strange. □ **funny bone** part of elbow over which very sensitive nerve passes. □ **funnily** *adverb*.

fur ● *noun* short fine animal hair; hide with fur on it; garment of or lined with this; coating inside kettle etc. ● *verb* (**-rr-**) (esp. as **furred** *adjective*) line or trim with fur; (often + *up*) (of kettle etc.) become coated with fur.

furbelow /ˈfɜːbɪləʊ/ *noun* (in *plural*) showy ornaments.

furbish /ˈfɜːbɪʃ/ *verb* (often + *up*) refurbish.

furcate /ˈfɜːkeɪt/ ● *adjective* forked, branched. ● *verb* (**-ting**) fork, divide. □ **furcation** *noun*.

furious /ˈfjʊərɪəs/ *adjective* very angry, raging, frantic. □ **furiously** *adverb*.

furl *verb* roll up (sail, umbrella); become furled.

furlong /ˈfɜːlɒŋ/ *noun* eighth of mile.

furlough /ˈfɜːləʊ/ *noun* leave of absence.

furnace /ˈfɜːnɪs/ *noun* chamber for intense heating by fire; very hot place.

furnish /ˈfɜːnɪʃ/ *verb* provide with furniture; (often + *with*) supply; (as **furnished** *adjective*) let with furniture. □ **furnishings** *plural noun*.

furniture /ˈfɜːnɪtʃə/ *noun* movable contents of building or room; ship's equipment; accessories, e.g. handles and locks.

furore /fjʊəˈrɔːrɪ/ *noun* (*US* **furor** /ˈfjʊərɔː/) uproar; enthusiasm.

furrier /ˈfʌrɪə/ *noun* dealer in or dresser of furs.

furrow /ˈfʌrəʊ/ ● *noun* narrow trench made by plough; rut; wrinkle. ● *verb* plough; make furrows in.

furry /ˈfɜːrɪ/ *adjective* (**-ier**, **-iest**) like or covered with fur.

further /ˈfɜːðə/ ● *adverb* (also **farther** /ˈfɑːðə/) more distant in space or time; more, to greater extent; in addition. ● *adjective* (also **farther** /ˈfɑːθə/) more distant or advanced; more, additional. ● *verb* promote, favour. □ **further education** education for people above school age; **furthermore** in addition, besides.

furtherance *noun* furthering of scheme etc.

furthest /ˈfɜːðɪst/ (also **farthest** /ˈfɑːðɪst/) ● *adjective* most distant. ● *adverb* to or at the greatest distance.

furtive /ˈfɜːtɪv/ *adjective* sly, stealthy. □ **furtively** *adverb*.

fury /ˈfjʊərɪ/ *noun* (*plural* **-ies**) wild and passionate anger; violence (of storm etc.); (**Fury**) (usually in *plural*) avenging goddess; angry woman.

furze *noun* gorse. □ **furzy** *adjective* (**-ier**, **-iest**).

fuse[1] /fjuːz/ ● *verb* (**-sing**) melt with intense heat; blend by melting; supply with fuse; fail due to melting of fuse; cause fuse(s) of to melt. ● *noun* easily melted wire in circuit, designed to melt when circuit is overloaded.

fuse[2] /fjuːz/ ● *noun* combustible device for igniting bomb etc. ● *verb* (**-sing**) fit fuse to.

fuselage /ˈfjuːzəlɑːʒ/ *noun* body of aircraft.

fusible /ˈfjuːzɪb(ə)l/ *adjective* that can be melted. □ **fusibility** *noun*.

fusilier /fjuːzɪˈlɪə/ *noun* soldier of any of several regiments formerly armed with light muskets.

fusillade /fjuːzɪˈleɪd/ *noun* continuous discharge of firearms or outburst of criticism etc.

fusion /ˈfjuːʒ(ə)n/ *noun* fusing; blending, coalition; nuclear fusion.

fuss ● *noun* excited commotion; bustle; excessive concern about trivial thing; sustained protest. ● *verb* behave with nervous concern; agitate, worry. □ **fusspot** *colloquial* person given to fussing; **make a fuss** complain vigorously; **make a fuss of**, **over** treat affectionately.

fussy *adjective* (**-ier**, **-iest**) inclined to fuss; over-elaborate; fastidious.

fustian /ˈfʌstɪən/ *noun* thick usually dark twilled cotton cloth; bombast.

fusty /ˈfʌstɪ/ *adjective* (**-ier**, **-iest**) musty, stuffy; antiquated.

futile /ˈfjuːtaɪl/ *adjective* useless, ineffectual. □ **futility** /-ˈtɪl-/ *noun*.

futon /ˈfuːtɒn/ *noun* Japanese mattress used as bed; this with frame, convertible into couch.

future /ˈfjuːtʃə/ ● *adjective* about to happen, be, or become; of time to come; *Grammar* (of tense) describing event yet to happen. ● *noun* time to come; future condition or events etc.; prospect of success etc.; *Grammar* future tense; (in *plural*) (on stock exchange) goods etc. sold for future delivery. □ **future perfect** *Grammar* tense giving sense 'will have done'.

futurism *noun* 20th-c. artistic movement celebrating technology etc. □ **futurist** *adjective & noun*.

futuristic /fjuːtʃəˈrɪstɪk/ *adjective* suitable for the future; ultra-modern; of futurism.

futurity /fjuːˈtjʊərɪtɪ/ *noun* (*plural* **-ies**) *literary* future time, events, etc.

fuzz *noun* fluff; fluffy or frizzy hair; (**the fuzz**) *slang* police (officer).

fuzzy /ˈfʌzɪ/ *adjective* (**-ier**, **-iest**) fluffy; blurred, indistinct.

Gg

G □ **G-man** *US colloquial* FBI special agent; **G-string** narrow strip of cloth etc. attached to string round waist for covering genitals.

g *abbreviation* (also **g.**) gram(s).

gab *noun colloquial* talk, chatter.

gabardine /ˈɡæbəˈdiːn/ *noun* a strong twilled cloth; raincoat etc. of this.

gabble /ˈɡæb(ə)l/ ● *verb* (**-ling**) talk or utter unintelligibly or too fast. ● *noun* rapid talk.

gaberdine = GABARDINE.

gable /ˈɡeɪb(ə)l/ *noun* triangular part of wall at end of ridged roof. □ **gabled** *adjective*.

gad *verb* (**-dd-**) (+ *about*) go about idly or in search of pleasure. □ **gadabout** person who gads about.

gadfly /ˈɡædflaɪ/ *noun* (*plural* **-ies**) fly that bites cattle.

gadget /ˈɡædʒɪt/ *noun* small mechanical device or tool. □ **gadgetry** *noun*.

Gael /ɡeɪl/ *noun* Scottish or Gaelic-speaking Celt.

Gaelic /ˈɡeɪlɪk/ ● *noun* Celtic language of Scots (also /ˈɡælɪk/) or Irish. ● *adjective* of Gaelic or Gaelic-speaking people.

gaff¹ ● *noun* stick with hook for landing fish; barbed fishing-spear. ● *verb* seize (fish) with gaff.

gaff² *noun slang* □ **blow the gaff** let out secret.

gaffe /ɡæf/ *noun* blunder, tactless mistake.

gaffer /ˈɡæfə/ *noun* old man; *colloquial* foreman, boss; chief electrician in film unit.

gag ● *noun* thing thrust into or tied across mouth to prevent speech etc.; joke or comic scene. ● *verb* (**-gg-**) apply gag to; silence; choke, retch; make jokes.

gaga /ˈɡɑːɡɑː/ *adjective slang* senile; crazy.

gage¹ *noun* pledge, security; challenge.

gage² *US* = GAUGE.

gaggle /ˈɡæɡ(ə)l/ *noun* flock (of geese); *colloquial* disorganized group.

gaiety /ˈɡeɪətɪ/ *noun* (*US* **gayety**) being gay, mirth; merrymaking; bright appearance.

gaily /ˈɡeɪlɪ/ *adverb* in a gay way.

gain ● *verb* obtain, win; acquire, earn; (often + *in*) increase, improve; benefit; (of clock etc.) become fast (by); reach; (often + *on, upon*) get closer to (person or thing one is following). ● *noun* increase (of wealth), profit; (in *plural*) money made in trade etc.

gainful /ˈɡeɪnfʊl/ *adjective* paid, lucrative. □ **gainfully** *adverb*.

gainsay /ɡeɪnˈseɪ/ *verb* deny, contradict.

gait *noun* manner of walking or proceeding.

gaiter /ˈɡeɪtə/ *noun* covering of leather etc. for lower leg.

gal. *abbreviation* gallon(s).

gala /ˈɡɑːlə/ *noun* festive occasion or gathering.

galactic /ɡəˈlæktɪk/ *adjective* of galaxy.

galantine /ˈɡæləntiːn/ *noun* cold dish of meat boned, spiced, and covered in jelly.

galaxy /ˈɡæləksɪ/ *noun* (*plural* **-ies**) independent system of stars etc. in space; (**the Galaxy**) Milky Way; (+ *of*) gathering of beautiful or famous people.

gale *noun* strong wind; outburst, esp. of laughter.

gall¹ /ɡɔːl/ *noun colloquial* impudence; rancour; bile. □ **gall bladder** bodily organ containing bile; **gallstone** small hard mass that forms in gall bladder.

gall² /ɡɔːl/ ● *noun* sore made by chafing; (cause of) vexation; place rubbed bare. ● *verb* rub sore; vex, humiliate.

gall³ /ɡɔːl/ *noun* growth produced on tree etc. by insect etc.

gallant /ˈɡælənt/ ● *adjective* brave; fine, stately; (/ɡəˈlænt/) attentive to women. ● *noun* (/ɡəˈlænt/) ladies' man. □ **gallantly** *adverb*.

gallantry /ˈɡæləntrɪ/ *noun* (*plural* **-ies**) bravery; courteousness to women; polite act or speech.

galleon /ˈɡælɪən/ *noun historical* (usually Spanish) warship.

galleria /ɡæləˈriːə/ *noun* group of small shops, cafés, etc. under one roof.

gallery /ˈɡælərɪ/ *noun* (*plural* **-ies**) room etc. for showing works of art; balcony, esp. in church, hall, etc.; highest balcony in theatre; covered walk, colonnade; passage, corridor.

galley /ˈɡælɪ/ *noun* (*plural* **-s**) *historical* long flat one-decked vessel usually rowed by slaves or criminals; ship's or aircraft's kitchen; (in full **galley proof**) printer's proof before division into pages.

Gallic /ˈɡælɪk/ *adjective* (typically) French; of Gaul or Gauls.

Gallicism /ˈɡælɪsɪz(ə)m/ *noun* French idiom.

gallimimus /ɡælɪˈmaɪməs/ *noun* (*plural* **-muses**) medium-sized dinosaur that ran fast on two legs.

gallinaceous /ɡælɪˈneɪʃəs/ *adjective* of order of birds including domestic poultry.

gallivant /ˈɡælɪvænt/ *verb colloquial* gad about.

gallon /ˈɡælən/ *noun* measure of capacity (4.546 litres).

gallop /ˈɡæləp/ ● *noun* horse's fastest pace; ride at this pace. ● *verb* (**-p-**) (cause to) go at gallop; talk etc. fast; progress rapidly.

gallows /ˈɡæləʊz/ *plural noun* (usually treated as *singular*) structure for hanging criminals.

Gallup poll /ˈɡæləp/ *noun* kind of opinion poll.

galore /ɡəˈlɔː/ *adverb* in plenty.

galosh /ɡəˈlɒʃ/ *noun* waterproof overshoe.

galumph /ɡəˈlʌmf/ *verb colloquial* (esp. as **galumphing** *adjective*) move noisily or clumsily.

galvanic /ɡælˈvænɪk/ *adjective* producing an electric current by chemical action; (of electric current) produced thus; stimulating, full of energy.

galvanize /ˈɡælvənaɪz/ *verb* (also **-ise**) (**-zing** or **-sing**) (often + *into*) rouse by shock; stimulate (as) by electricity; coat (iron, steel) with zinc to protect from rust.

galvanometer /ɡælvəˈnɒmɪtə/ *noun* instrument for measuring electric currents.

gambit /ˈɡæmbɪt/ *noun Chess* opening with sacrifice of pawn etc.; trick, device.

gamble /ˈɡæmb(ə)l/ ● *verb* (**-ling**) play games of chance for money; bet (sum of money); (often + *away*) lose by gambling. ● *noun* risky undertaking; spell of gambling. □ **gambler** *noun*.

gambol /ˈɡæmb(ə)l/ ● *verb* (**-ll-**; *US* **-l-**) jump about playfully. ● *noun* caper.

game¹ ● *noun* form or period of play or sport, esp. competitive one organized with rules; portion of play forming scoring unit; (in *plural*) athletic contests; piece of fun, (in *plural*) tricks; *colloquial* scheme, activity; wild animals or birds etc. hunted for sport or food; their flesh as food. ● *adjective* spirited, eager. ● *verb* (**-ming**) gamble for money. □ **gamekeeper** person employed to breed and protect game; **gamesmanship** art of winning games by psychological means. □ **gamely** *adverb*.

game² *adjective colloquial* (of leg etc.) crippled.

gamete /'gæmiːt/ *noun* mature germ cell uniting with another in sexual reproduction.

gamin /'gæmɪn/ *noun* street urchin; impudent child.

gamine /gæˈmiːn/ *noun* girl gamin; attractively mischievous or boyish girl.

gamma /'gæmə/ *noun* third letter of Greek alphabet (Γ, γ). □ **gamma rays** very short X-rays emitted by radioactive substances.

gammon /'gæmən/ *noun* back end of side of bacon, including leg.

gammy /'gæmɪ/ *adjective* (**-ier, -iest**) *slang* (of leg etc.) crippled.

gamut /'gæmət/ *noun* entire range or scope. □ **run the gamut of** experience or perform complete range of.

gamy /'geɪmɪ/ *adjective* (**-ier, -iest**) smelling or tasting like high game.

gander /'gændə/ *noun* male goose.

gang ● *noun* set of associates, esp. for criminal purposes; set of workers, slaves, or prisoners. ● *verb colloquial* (+ *up with*) act together with; (+ *up on*) combine against.

ganger /'gæŋə/ *noun* foreman of gang of workers.

gangling /'gæŋglɪŋ/ *adjective* (of person) tall and thin, lanky.

ganglion /'gæŋglɪən/ *noun* (*plural* **ganglia** or **-s**) knot on nerve containing assemblage of nerve cells.

gangly *adjective* (**-ier, -iest**) gangling.

gangplank /'gæŋplæŋk/ *noun* plank for walking on to or off boat etc.

gangrene /'gæŋɡriːn/ *noun* death of body tissue, usually caused by obstruction of circulation. □ **gangrenous** *adjective*.

gangster /'gæŋstə/ *noun* member of gang of violent criminals.

gangue /gæŋ/ *noun* valueless part of ore deposit.

gangway *noun* passage, esp. between rows of seats; opening in ship's bulwarks; bridge.

gannet /'gænɪt/ *noun* large seabird; *slang* greedy person.

gantry /'gæntrɪ/ *noun* (*plural* **-ies**) structure supporting travelling crane, railway or road signals, rocket-launching equipment, etc.

gaol etc. = JAIL etc.

gap *noun* empty space, interval; deficiency; breach in hedge, wall, etc.; wide divergence.

gape ● *verb* (**-ping**) open mouth wide; be or become wide open; (+ *at*) stare at. ● *noun* open-mouthed stare; opening.

garage /'gærɑːdʒ/ ● *noun* building for keeping vehicle(s) in; establishment selling petrol etc. or repairing and selling vehicles. ● *verb* (**-ging**) put or keep in garage.

garb ● *noun* clothing, esp. of distinctive kind. ● *verb* dress.

garbage /'gɑːbɪdʒ/ *noun US* refuse; *colloquial* nonsense.

garble /'gɑːb(ə)l/ *verb* (**-ling**) (esp. as **garbled** *adjective*) distort or confuse (facts, statements, etc.).

garden /'gɑːd(ə)n/ ● *noun* piece of ground for growing flowers, fruit, or vegetables, or for recreation; (esp. in *plural*) public pleasure-grounds. ● *verb* cultivate or tend garden. □ **garden centre** place selling plants and garden equipment. □ **gardener** *noun*; **gardening** *noun*.

gardenia /gɑːˈdiːnɪə/ *noun* tree or shrub with fragrant flowers.

gargantuan /gɑːˈgæntjʊən/ *adjective* gigantic.

gargle /'gɑːg(ə)l/ ● *verb* (**-ling**) rinse (throat) with liquid kept in motion by breath. ● *noun* liquid so used.

gargoyle /'gɑːgɔɪl/ *noun* grotesque carved spout projecting from gutter of building.

garish /'geərɪʃ/ *adjective* obtrusively bright, gaudy. □ **garishly** *adverb*; **garishness** *noun*.

garland /'gɑːlənd/ ● *noun* wreath of flowers etc. as decoration. ● *verb* adorn or crown with garland(s).

garlic /'gɑːlɪk/ *noun* plant with pungent bulb used in cookery. □ **garlicky** *adjective colloquial*.

garment /'gɑːmənt/ *noun* article of dress.

garner /'gɑːnə/ ● *verb* collect, store. ● *noun* storehouse for corn etc.

garnet /'gɑːnɪt/ *noun* glassy mineral, esp. red kind used as gem.

garnish /'gɑːnɪʃ/ ● *verb* decorate (esp. food). ● *noun* decoration, esp. to food.

garret /'gærɪt/ *noun* room, esp. small, cold, etc. immediately under roof.

garrison /'gærɪs(ə)n/ ● *noun* troops stationed in town. ● *verb* (**-n-**) provide with or occupy as garrison.

garrotte /gəˈrɒt/ (also **garotte**, *US* **garrote**) ● *verb* (**garrotting**, *US* **garroting**) execute by strangulation, esp. with wire collar. ● *noun* device for this.

garrulous /'gærələs/ *adjective* talkative. □ **garrulity** /gəˈruːlɪtɪ/ *noun*; **garrulousness** *noun*.

garter /'gɑːtə/ *noun* band to keep sock or stocking up; **(the Garter)** (badge of) highest order of English knighthood. □ **garter stitch** plain knitting stitch.

gas /gæs/ ● *noun* (*plural* **-es**) any airlike substance (i.e. not liquid or solid); such substance (esp. coal gas or natural gas) used as fuel; gas used as anaesthetic; poisonous gas used in war; *US colloquial* petrol; *slang* empty talk, boasting; *slang* amusing thing or person. ● *verb* (**gases, gassed, gassing**) expose to gas, esp. to kill; *colloquial* talk emptily or boastfully. □ **gasbag** *slang* empty talker; **gas chamber** room filled with poisonous gas to kill people or animals; **gasholder** gasometer; **gas mask** respirator for protection against harmful gases; **gas ring** ring pierced with gas jet(s) for cooking etc.; **gasworks** place where gas is manufactured.

gaseous /'gæsɪəs/ *adjective* of or as gas.

gash ● *noun* long deep cut or wound. ● *verb* make gash in.

gasify /'gæsɪfaɪ/ *verb* (**-ies, -ied**) convert into gas. □ **gasification** *noun*.

gasket /'gæskɪt/ *noun* sheet or ring of rubber etc. to seal joint between metal surfaces.

gasoline /'gæsəliːn/ *noun* (also **gasolene**) *US* petrol.

gasometer /gæˈsɒmɪtə/ *noun* large tank from which gas is distributed.

gasp /gɑːsp/ ● *verb* catch breath with open mouth; utter with gasps. ● *noun* convulsive catching of breath.

gassy /'gæsɪ/ *adjective* (**-ier, -iest**) of, like, or full of gas; *colloquial* verbose.

gastric /'gæstrɪk/ *adjective* of stomach. □ **gastric flu** *colloquial* intestinal disorder of unknown cause; **gastric juice** digestive fluid secreted by stomach glands.

gastritis /gæˈstraɪtɪs/ *noun* inflammation of stomach.

gastroenteritis /ˌgæstrəʊentəˈraɪtɪs/ *noun* inflammation of stomach and intestines.

gastronome /'gæstrənəʊm/ *noun* gourmet. □ **gastronomic** /-'nɒm-/ *adjective*; **gastronomical** /-'nɒm-/ *adjective*; **gastronomically** /-'nɒm-/ *adverb*; **gastronomy** /-'strɒn-/ *noun*.

gastropod /'gæstrəpɒd/ *noun* mollusc that moves using underside of abdomen, e.g. snail.

gate *noun* barrier, usually hinged, used to close opening in wall, fence, etc.; such opening; means of entrance or exit; numbered place of access to aircraft at airport; device regulating passage of water in lock etc.; number of people paying to enter stadium etc., money thus taken. □ **gateleg** (**table**) table with legs in gatelike frame for supporting folding flaps; **gatepost** post at either side of gate; **gateway** opening closed by gate, means of access.

gateau /ˈgætəʊ/ *noun* (*plural* **-s** or **-x** /-z/) large rich elaborate cake.

gatecrash *verb* attend (party etc.) uninvited. □ **gatecrasher** *noun*.

gather /ˈgæðə/ ● *verb* bring or come together; collect (harvest, dust, etc.); infer, deduce; increase (speed); summon up (energy etc.); draw together in folds or wrinkles; (of boil etc.) come to a head. ● *noun* fold or pleat.

gathering *noun* assembly; pus-filled swelling.

GATT /gæt/ *abbreviation* General Agreement on Tariffs and Trade.

gauche /gəʊʃ/ *adjective* socially awkward, tactless. □ **gauchely** *adverb*; **gaucheness** *noun*.

gaucho /ˈgautʃəʊ/ *noun* (*plural* **-s**) cowboy in S. American pampas.

gaudy /ˈgɔːdɪ/ *adjective* (**-ier**, **-iest**) tastelessly showy. □ **gaudily** *adverb*; **gaudiness** *noun*.

gauge /geɪdʒ/ (*US* **gage**) ● *noun* standard measure; instrument for measuring; distance between rails or opposite wheels; capacity, extent; criterion, test. ● *verb* (**-ging**) measure exactly; measure contents of; estimate.

Gaul /gɔːl/ *noun* inhabitant of ancient Gaul. □ **Gaulish** *adjective & noun*.

gaunt /gɔːnt/ *adjective* lean, haggard; grim. □ **gauntness** *noun*.

gauntlet¹ /ˈgɔːntlɪt/ *noun* glove with long loose wrist; *historical* armoured glove.

gauntlet² /ˈgɔːntlɪt/ *noun* □ **run the gauntlet** undergo criticism, pass between two rows of people wielding sticks etc., as punishment.

gauze /gɔːz/ *noun* thin transparent fabric; fine mesh of wire etc. □ **gauzy** *adjective* (**-ier**, **-iest**).

gave *past of* GIVE.

gavel /ˈgæv(ə)l/ *noun* auctioneer's, chairman's, or judge's hammer.

gavotte /gəˈvɒt/ *noun* 18th-c. French dance; music for this.

gawk ● *verb colloquial* gawp. ● *noun* awkward or bashful person. □ **gawky** *adjective* (**-ier**, **-iest**).

gawp *verb colloquial* stare stupidly.

gay ● *adjective* light-hearted, cheerful; showy; homosexual; *colloquial* carefree. ● *noun* (esp. male) homosexual.

gayety *US* = GAIETY.

gaze ● *verb* (**-zing**) (+ *at*, *into*, *on*, etc.) look fixedly. ● *noun* intent look.

gazebo /gəˈziːbəʊ/ *noun* (*plural* **-s**) summer house etc. giving view.

gazelle /gəˈzel/ *noun* (*plural* same or **-s**) small graceful antelope.

gazette /gəˈzet/ ● *noun* newspaper; official publication. ● *verb* (**-tting**) publish in official gazette.

gazetteer /gæzɪˈtɪə/ *noun* geographical index.

gazump /gəˈzʌmp/ *verb colloquial* raise price after accepting offer from (buyer); swindle.

gazunder /gəˈzʌndə/ *verb colloquial* lower an offer made to (seller) just before exchange of contracts.

GB *abbreviation* Great Britain.

GBH *abbreviation* grievous bodily harm.

GC *abbreviation* George Cross.

GCE *abbreviation* General Certificate of Education.

GCSE *abbreviation* General Certificate of Secondary Education.

GDR *abbreviation historical* German Democratic Republic.

gear /gɪə/ ● *noun* (often in *plural*) set of toothed wheels working together, esp. those connecting engine to road wheels; particular setting of these; equipment; *colloquial* clothing. ● *verb* (+ *to*) adjust or adapt to; (often + *up*) equip with gears; (+ *up*) make ready. □ **gearbox** (case enclosing) gears of machine or vehicle; **gear lever** lever moved to engage or change gear; **in gear** with gear engaged.

gecko /ˈgekəʊ/ *noun* (*plural* **-s**) tropical house-lizard.

gee /dʒiː/ *interjection expressing surprise etc.*

geese *plural of* GOOSE.

geezer /ˈgiːzə/ *noun slang* man, esp. old one.

Geiger counter /ˈgaɪgə/ *noun* instrument for measuring radioactivity.

geisha /ˈgeɪʃə/ *noun* (*plural* same or **-s**) Japanese professional hostess and entertainer.

gel /dʒel/ ● *noun* semi-solid jelly-like colloid; jelly-like substance for hair. ● *verb* (**-ll-**) form gel; jell.

gelatin /ˈdʒelətɪn/ *noun* (also **gelatine** /-tiːn/) transparent tasteless substance used in cookery, photography, etc. □ **gelatinous** /dʒɪˈlæt-/ *adjective*.

geld /geld/ *verb* castrate.

gelding /ˈgeldɪŋ/ *noun* castrated horse etc.

gelignite /ˈdʒelɪgnaɪt/ *noun* nitroglycerine explosive.

gem /dʒem/ ● *noun* precious stone; thing or person of great beauty or worth. ● *verb* (**-mm-**) adorn with gems.

Gemini /ˈdʒemɪnaɪ/ *noun* third sign of zodiac.

Gen. *abbreviation* General.

gen /dʒen/ *slang* ● *noun* information. ● *verb* (**-nn-**) (+ *up*) gain or give information.

gendarme /ˈʒɒndɑːm/ *noun* police officer in France etc.

gender /ˈdʒendə/ *noun* (grammatical) classification roughly corresponding to the two sexes and sexlessness; one of these classes; person's sex.

gene /dʒiːn/ *noun* unit in chromosome, controlling particular inherited characteristic.

genealogy /dʒiːnɪˈælədʒɪ/ *noun* (*plural* **-ies**) descent traced continuously from ancestor, pedigree; study of pedigrees. □ **genealogical** /-əˈlɒdʒ-/ *adjective*; **genealogically** /-əˈlɒdʒ-/ *adverb*; **genealogist** *noun*.

genera *plural of* GENUS.

general /ˈdʒenər(ə)l/ ● *adjective* including, affecting, or applicable to (nearly) all; prevalent, usual; vague; not partial or particular; lacking detail; chief, head. ● *noun* army officer next below Field Marshal; commander of army. □ **general anaesthetic** one affecting whole body; **general election** national election of representatives to parliament; **general practice** work of **general practitioner**, doctor treating cases of all kinds; **general strike** simultaneous strike of workers in all or most trades; **in general** as a rule, usually.

generalissimo /dʒenərəˈlɪsɪməʊ/ *noun* (*plural* **-s**) commander of combined forces.

generality /dʒenəˈrælɪtɪ/ *noun* (*plural* **-ies**) general statement; general applicability; indefiniteness; (+ *of*) majority of.

generalize /ˈdʒenərəlaɪz/ *verb* (also **-ise**) (**-zing** or **-sing**) speak in general or indefinite terms, form general notion(s); reduce to general statement; infer (rule etc.) from particular cases; bring into general use. □ **generalization** *noun*.

generally /ˈdʒenərəlɪ/ *adverb* usually; in most respects; in general sense; in most cases.

generate /ˈdʒenəreɪt/ *verb* (**-ting**) bring into existence, produce.

generation *noun* all people born about same time; stage in family history or in (esp. technological) development; period of about 30 years; production, esp. of electricity; procreation.

generative /'dʒenərətɪv/ *adjective* of procreation; productive.

generator *noun* dynamo; apparatus for producing gas, steam, etc.

generic /dʒɪ'nerɪk/ *adjective* characteristic of or relating to class or genus; not specific or special; (of esp. drug) with no brand name. □ **generically** *adverb*.

generous /'dʒenərəs/ *adjective* giving or given freely; magnanimous; abundant. □ **generosity** /-'rɒs-/ *noun*; **generously** *adverb*.

genesis /'dʒenɪsɪs/ *noun* origin, mode of formation; **(Genesis)** first book of Old Testament.

genetic /dʒɪ'netɪk/ *adjective* of genetics; of or in origin. □ **genetic engineering** manipulation of DNA to modify hereditary features; **genetic fingerprinting** identification of individuals by DNA patterns. □ **genetically** *adverb*.

genetics *plural noun* (treated as *singular*) study of heredity and variation among animals and plants. □ **geneticist** /-sɪst/ *noun*.

genial /'dʒiːnɪəl/ *adjective* sociable, kindly; mild, warm; cheering. □ **geniality** /-'æl-/ *noun*; **genially** *adverb*.

genie /'dʒiːnɪ/ *noun* (*plural* **genii** /-nɪaɪ/) sprite or goblin of Arabian tales.

genital /'dʒenɪt(ə)l/ ● *adjective* of animal reproduction or reproductive organs. ● *noun* (in *plural*; also **genitalia**) external reproductive organs.

genitive /'dʒenɪtɪv/ *Grammar* ● *noun* case expressing possession, origin, etc., corresponding to *of, from,* etc. ● *adjective* of or in this case.

genius /'dʒiːnɪəs/ *noun* (*plural* **-es**) exceptional natural ability; person having this; guardian spirit.

genocide /'dʒenəsaɪd/ *noun* mass murder, esp. among particular race or nation.

genre /'ʒɑ̃rə/ *noun* kind or style of art etc.; portrayal of scenes from ordinary life.

gent /dʒent/ *noun colloquial* gentleman; **(the Gents)** *colloquial* men's public lavatory.

genteel /dʒen'tiːl/ *adjective* affectedly refined; upperclass.

gentian /'dʒenʃ(ə)n/ *noun* mountain plant with usually blue flowers. □ **gentian violet** violet dye used as antiseptic.

Gentile /'dʒentaɪl/ ● *adjective* not Jewish; heathen. ● *noun* non-Jewish person.

gentility /dʒen'tɪlɪtɪ/ *noun* social superiority; genteel habits.

gentle /'dʒent(ə)l/ *adjective* **(-r, -st)** not rough or severe; mild, kind; well-born; quiet. □ **gentleness** *noun*; **gently** *adverb*.

gentlefolk /'dʒentəlfəʊk/ *noun* people of good family.

gentleman /'dʒentəlmən/ *noun* man; chivalrous well-bred man; man of good social position. □ **gentlemanly** *adjective*.

gentlewoman *noun archaic* woman of good birth or breeding.

gentrification /dʒentrɪfɪ'keɪʃ(ə)n/ *noun* upgrading of working-class urban area by arrival of affluent residents. □ **gentrify** *verb* **(-ies, -ied)**.

gentry /'dʒentrɪ/ *plural noun* people next below nobility; *derogatory* people.

genuflect /'dʒenjuːflekt/ *verb* bend knee, esp. in worship. □ **genuflection, genuflexion** /-'flekʃ(ə)n/ *noun*.

genuine /'dʒenjuːɪn/ *adjective* really coming from its reputed source; properly so called; not sham. □ **genuinely** *adverb*; **genuineness** *noun*.

genus /'dʒiːnəs/ *noun* (*plural* **genera** /'dʒenərə/) group of animals or plants with common structural characteristics, usually containing several species; kind, class.

geocentric /dʒiːə'sentrɪk/ *adjective* considered as viewed from earth's centre; having earth as centre.

geode /'dʒiːəʊd/ *noun* cavity lined with crystals; rock containing this.

geodesic /dʒiːəʊ'diːzɪk/ *adjective* (also **geodetic** /-'det-/) of geodesy. □ **geodesic line** shortest possible line on surface between two points.

geodesy /dʒiː'ɒdɪsɪ/ *noun* study of shape and area of the earth.

geography /dʒiː'ɒɡrəfɪ/ *noun* science of earth's physical features, resources, etc.; features of place. □ **geographer** *noun*; **geographic(al)** /-ə'ɡræf-/ *adjective*; **geographically** /-ə'ɡræf-/ *adverb*.

geology /dʒiː'ɒlədʒɪ/ *noun* science of earth's crust, strata, etc. □ **geological** /-ə'lɒdʒ-/ *adjective*; **geologist** *noun*.

geometry /dʒɪ'ɒmətrɪ/ *noun* science of properties and relations of lines, surfaces, and solids. □ **geometric(al)** /-ə'met-/ *adjective*; **geometrician** /-'trɪʃ(ə)n/ *noun*.

Geordie /'dʒɔːdɪ/ *noun* native of Tyneside.

georgette /dʒɔː'dʒet/ *noun* kind of fine dress material.

Georgian /'dʒɔːdʒ(ə)n/ *adjective* of time of George I–IV or George V and VI.

geranium /dʒə'reɪnɪəm/ *noun* (*plural* **-s**) cultivated pelargonium; herb or shrub with fruit shaped like crane's bill.

gerbil /'dʒɜːbɪl/ *noun* mouselike desert rodent with long hind legs.

geriatric /dʒerɪ'ætrɪk/ ● *adjective* of geriatrics or old people; *derogatory* old. ● *noun often derogatory* old person.

geriatrics /dʒerɪ'ætrɪks/ *plural noun* (usually treated as *singular*) branch of medicine dealing with health and care of old people. □ **geriatrician** /-ə'trɪʃ(ə)n/ *noun*.

germ /dʒɜːm/ *noun* microbe; portion of organism capable of developing into new one; thing that may develop; rudiment, elementary principle.

German /'dʒɜːmən/ ● *noun* (*plural* **-s**) native, national, or language of Germany. ● *adjective* of Germany. □ **German measles** disease like mild measles; **German shepherd (dog)** Alsatian.

german /'dʒɜːmən/ *adjective* (placed after *brother, sister,* or *cousin*) having same two parents or grandparents.

germander /dʒɜː'mændə/ *noun* plant of mint family.

germane /dʒɜː'meɪn/ *adjective* (usually + *to*) relevant.

Germanic /dʒɜː'mænɪk/ ● *adjective* having German characteristics. ● *noun* group of languages including English, German, Dutch, and Scandinavian languages.

germicide /'dʒɜːmɪsaɪd/ *noun* substance that destroys germs. □ **germicidal** /-'saɪd(ə)l/ *adjective*.

germinal /'dʒɜːmɪn(ə)l/ *adjective* of germs; in earliest stage of development.

germinate /'dʒɜːmɪneɪt/ *verb* **(-ting)** (cause to) sprout or bud. □ **germination** *noun*.

gerontology /dʒerɒn'tɒlədʒɪ/ *noun* study of old age and ageing.

gerrymander /dʒerɪ'mændə/ *verb* manipulate boundaries of (constituency etc.) to gain unfair electoral advantage.

gerund /'dʒerənd/ *noun* verbal noun, in English ending in *-ing*.

Gestapo /ɡe'stɑːpəʊ/ *noun historical* Nazi secret police.

gestation /dʒe'steɪʃ(ə)n/ *noun* carrying or being carried in womb between conception and birth; this period; development of plan etc. □ **gestate** *verb* **(-ting)**.

gesticulate /dʒe'stɪkjʊleɪt/ *verb* **(-ting)** use gestures instead of or with speech. ● **gesticulation** *noun*.

gesture /ˈdʒestʃə/ ● noun meaningful movement of limb or body; action performed as courtesy or to indicate intention. ● verb (**-ring**) gesticulate.

get /get/ verb (**getting**; past **got**; past participle **got** or US **gotten**) obtain, earn; fetch, procure; go to reach or catch; prepare (meal); (cause to) reach some state or become; obtain from calculation; contract (disease); contact; have (punishment) inflicted on one; succeed in bringing, placing, etc.; (cause to) succeed in coming or going; colloquial understand, annoy, harm, attract; archaic beget. □ **get about** go from place to place; **get across** communicate; **get along** (often + with) live harmoniously; **get around** = GET ABOUT; **get at** reach, get hold of, colloquial imply, colloquial nag; **get away** escape; **getaway** noun; **get by** colloquial cope; **get in** obtain place at college etc., win election; **get off** alight (from), colloquial escape with little or no punishment, start, depart, (+ with) colloquial start sexual relationship with; **get on** make progress, manage, advance, enter (bus etc.), (often + with) live harmoniously, (usually as **be getting on**) age; **get out of** avoid, escape; **get over** recover from, surmount; **get round** coax or cajole (person), evade (law etc.), (+ to) deal with (task) in due course; **get through** pass (exam etc.), use up (resources), make contact by telephone, (+ to) succeed in making (person) understand; **get-together** colloquial social assembly; **get up** rise esp. from bed, (of wind etc.) strengthen, organize, stimulate, arrange appearance of; **get-up** colloquial style of dress etc.; **have got** possess, (+ to do) must.

geyser /ˈgiːzə/ noun hot spring; apparatus for heating water.

ghastly /ˈgɑːstlɪ/ adjective (**-ier, -iest**) horrible, frightful; deathlike, pallid.

ghee /giː/ noun Indian clarified butter.

gherkin /ˈgɜːkɪn/ noun small cucumber for pickling.

ghetto /ˈgetəʊ/ noun (plural **-s**) part of city occupied by minority group; historical Jews' quarter in city; segregated group or area. □ **ghetto-blaster** large portable radio or cassette player.

ghost /ɡəʊst/ ● noun apparition of dead person etc., disembodied spirit; (+ of) semblance; secondary image in defective telescope or television picture. ● verb (often + for) act as ghost-writer of (book etc.). □ **ghost-writer** writer doing work for which another takes credit. □ **ghostly** adjective (**-ier, -iest**).

ghoul /ɡuːl/ noun person morbidly interested in death etc.; evil spirit; (in Arabic mythology) spirit preying on corpses. □ **ghoulish** adjective.

GHQ abbreviation General Headquarters.

ghyll /gɪl/ = GILL[3].

GI /dʒiːˈaɪ/ noun soldier in US army.

giant /ˈdʒaɪənt/ ● noun mythical being of human form but superhuman size; person, animal, or thing of extraordinary size, ability, etc. ● adjective gigantic.

gibber /ˈdʒɪbə/ verb chatter inarticulately.

gibberish /ˈdʒɪbərɪʃ/ noun unintelligible or meaningless speech or sounds.

gibbet /ˈdʒɪbɪt/ noun historical gallows; post with arm from which executed criminal was hung after execution.

gibbon /ˈgɪbən/ noun long-armed ape.

gibbous /ˈgɪbəs/ adjective convex; (of moon etc.) with bright part greater than semicircle.

gibe /dʒaɪb/ (also **jibe**) ● verb (**-bing**) (often + at) jeer, mock. ● noun jeering remark, taunt.

giblets /ˈdʒɪblɪts/ plural noun liver, gizzard, etc. of bird removed and usually cooked separately.

giddy /ˈgɪdɪ/ adjective (**-ier, -iest**) dizzy, tending to fall or stagger; mentally intoxicated; excitable, flighty; making dizzy. □ **giddiness** noun.

gift /gɪft/ noun thing given, present; talent; colloquial easy task.

gifted adjective talented.

gig[1] /gɪg/ noun light two-wheeled one-horse carriage; light boat on ship; rowing boat, esp. for racing.

gig[2] /gɪg/ colloquial ● noun engagement to play music, usually on one occasion. ● verb (**-gg-**) perform gig.

giga- /ˈgɪgə/ combining form one thousand million.

gigantic /dʒaɪˈgæntɪk/ adjective huge, giant-like.

giggle /ˈgɪg(ə)l/ ● verb (**-ling**) laugh in half-suppressed spasms. ● noun such laugh; colloquial amusing person or thing. □ **giggly** adjective (**-ier, -iest**).

gigolo /ˈdʒɪgələʊ/ noun (plural **-s**) young man paid by older woman to be escort or lover.

gild[1] /gɪld/ verb (past participle **gilded** or as adjective **gilt**) cover thinly with gold; tinge with golden colour.

gild[2] = GUILD.

gill[1] /gɪl/ noun (usually in plural) respiratory organ of fish etc.; vertical radial plate on underside of mushroom etc.; flesh below person's jaws and ears.

gill[2] /dʒɪl/ noun quarter-pint measure.

gill[3] /gɪl/ noun (also **ghyll**) deep wooded ravine; narrow mountain torrent.

gillie /ˈgɪlɪ/ noun Scottish man or boy attending hunter or angler.

gillyflower /ˈdʒɪlɪflaʊə/ noun clove-scented flower, e.g. wallflower.

gilt[1] /gɪlt/ ● adjective overlaid (as) with gold. ● noun gilding. □ **gilt-edged** (of securities etc.) having high degree of reliability.

gilt[2] /gɪlt/ noun young sow.

gimbals /ˈdʒɪmb(ə)lz/ plural noun contrivance of rings etc. for keeping things horizontal in ship, aircraft, etc.

gimcrack /ˈdʒɪmkræk/ ● adjective flimsy, tawdry. ● noun showy ornament etc.

gimlet /ˈgɪmlɪt/ noun small boring-tool.

gimmick /ˈgɪmɪk/ noun trick or device, esp. to attract attention. □ **gimmickry** noun; **gimmicky** adjective.

gimp /ˈgɪmp/ noun twist of silk etc. with cord or wire running through.

gin[1] /dʒɪn/ noun spirit distilled from grain or malt and flavoured with juniper berries.

gin[2] /dʒɪn/ ● noun snare, trap; machine separating cotton from seeds; kind of crane or windlass. ● verb (**-nn-**) treat (cotton) in gin; trap.

ginger /ˈdʒɪndʒə/ ● noun hot spicy root used in cooking; plant having this root; light reddish-yellow. ● adjective of ginger colour. ● verb flavour with ginger; (+ up) enliven. □ **ginger ale**, **beer** ginger-flavoured fizzy drinks; **gingerbread** ginger-flavoured treacle cake; **ginger group** group urging party or movement to stronger action; **ginger-nut** kind of ginger-flavoured biscuit. □ **gingery** adjective.

gingerly /ˈdʒɪndʒəlɪ/ ● adverb in a careful or cautious way. ● adjective showing extreme care or caution.

gingham /ˈgɪŋəm/ noun plain-woven usually checked cotton cloth.

gingivitis /dʒɪndʒɪˈvaɪtɪs/ noun inflammation of the gums.

ginkgo /ˈgɪŋkəʊ/ noun (plural **-s**) tree with fan-shaped leaves and yellow flowers.

ginseng /ˈdʒɪnseŋ/ noun plant found in E. Asia and N. America; medicinal root of this.

Gipsy = GYPSY.

giraffe /dʒɪˈrɑːf/ noun (plural same or **-s**) tall 4-legged African animal with long neck.

gird /gɜːd/ (past & past participle **girded** or **girt**) encircle or fasten (on) with waistbelt etc. □ **gird (up) one's loins** prepare for action.

girder /'gɜːdə/ *noun* iron or steel beam or compound structure used for bridges etc.

girdle¹ /'gɜːd(ə)l/ ● *noun* belt or cord worn round waist; corset; thing that surrounds; bony support for limbs. ● *verb* (**-ling**) surround with girdle.

girdle² /'gɜːd(ə)l/ *noun Scottish & Northern English* = GRIDDLE.

girl /gɜːl/ *noun* female child; *colloquial* young woman; *colloquial* girlfriend; female servant. □ **girlfriend** person's regular female companion; **girl guide** Guide; **girl scout** female Scout. □ **girlhood** *noun*; **girlish** *adjective*; **girly** *adjective*.

giro /'dʒaɪrəʊ/ ● *noun* (*plural* **-s**) system of credit transfer between banks, Post Offices, etc.; cheque or payment by giro. ● *verb* (**-es**, **-ed**) pay by giro.

girt *past & past participle of* GIRD.

girth /gɜːθ/ *noun* distance round a thing; band round body of horse securing saddle.

gist /dʒɪst/ *noun* substance or essence of a matter.

gîte /ʒiːt/ *noun* furnished holiday house in French countryside. [French]

give /gɪv/ ● *verb* (**-ving**; *past* **gave**; *past participle* **given**) transfer possession of freely; provide with; administer; deliver; (often + *for*) make over in exchange or payment; confer; accord; pledge; perform (action etc.); utter, declare; yield to pressure; collapse; yield as product; consign; devote; present, offer (one's hand, arm, etc.); impart, be source of; concede; assume, grant, specify. ● *noun* capacity to comply; elasticity. □ **give and take** exchange of talk or ideas, ability to compromise; **give away** transfer as gift, hand over (bride) to bridegroom, betray or expose; **give-away** *colloquial* unintentional disclosure, free or inexpensive thing; **give in** yield, hand in; **give off** emit; **give out** announce, emit, distribute, be exhausted, run short; **give over** *colloquial* desist, hand over, devote; **give up** resign, surrender, part with, renounce hope (of), cease (activity). □ **giver** *noun*.

given ● *past participle of* GIVE. ● *adjective* (+ *to*) disposed or prone to; assumed as basis of reasoning etc.; fixed, specified.

gizmo /'ɡɪzməʊ/ *noun* (*plural* **-s**) gadget.

gizzard /'ɡɪzəd/ *noun* bird's second stomach, for grinding food.

glacé /'ɡlæseɪ/ *adjective* (of fruit) preserved in sugar; (of cloth etc.) smooth, polished.

glacial /'ɡleɪʃ(ə)l/ *adjective* of ice or glaciers.

glaciated /'ɡleɪsɪeɪtɪd/ *adjective* marked or polished by moving ice; covered with glaciers. □ **glaciation** *noun*.

glacier /'ɡlæsɪə/ *noun* slowly moving mass of ice on land.

glad *adjective* (**-dd-**) pleased; joyful, cheerful. □ **glad rags** *colloquial* best clothes. □ **gladden** *verb*; **gladly** *adverb*; **gladness** *noun*.

glade *noun* clear space in forest.

gladiator /'ɡlædɪeɪtə/ *noun historical* trained fighter in ancient Roman shows. □ **gladiatorial** /-ə'tɔːrɪəl/ *adjective*.

gladiolus /ɡlædɪ'əʊləs/ *noun* (*plural* **-li** /-laɪ/) plant of lily family with bright flower-spikes.

gladsome *adjective poetical* cheerful, joyful.

Gladstone bag /'ɡlædst(ə)n/ *noun* kind of light portmanteau.

glair *noun* white of egg; similar or derivative viscous substance.

glamour /'ɡlæmə/ *noun* (*US* **glamor**) physical, esp. cosmetic, attractiveness; alluring or exciting beauty or charm. □ **glamorize** *verb* (also **-ise**) (**-zing** or **-sing**); **glamorous** *adjective*; **glamorously** *adverb*.

glance /ɡlɑːns/ ● *verb* (**-cing**) (often + *down*, *up*, *over*, etc.) look or refer briefly; (often + *off*) hit at fine angle and bounce off. ● *noun* brief look; flash, gleam; swift oblique stroke in cricket. □ **at a glance** immediately on looking.

gland *noun* organ etc. secreting substances for use in body; similar organ in plant.

glanders /'ɡlændəz/ *plural noun* contagious horse disease.

glandular /'ɡlændjʊlə/ *adjective* of gland(s). □ **glandular fever** infectious disease with swelling of lymph glands.

glare /ɡleə/ ● *verb* (**-ring**) look fiercely; shine oppressively; (esp. as **glaring** *adjective*) be very evident. ● *noun* oppressive light or public attention; fierce look; tawdry brilliance. □ **glaringly** *adverb*.

glasnost /'ɡlæznɒst/ *noun* (in former USSR) policy of more open government.

glass /ɡlɑːs/ ● *noun* hard, brittle, usually transparent substance made by fusing sand with soda and lime etc.; glass objects collectively; glass drinking vessel, its contents; glazed frame for plants; barometer; covering of watch-face; lens; (in *plural*) spectacles, binoculars; mirror. ● *verb* (usually as **glassed** *adjective*) fit with glass. □ **glass-blowing** blowing of semi-molten glass to make glass objects; **glass fibre** glass filaments made into fabric or reinforcing plastic; **glasshouse** greenhouse, *slang* military prison; **glass-paper** paper covered with powdered glass, for smoothing etc.; **glass wool** fine glass fibres for packing and insulation. □ **glassful** *noun* (*plural* **-s**).

glassy /'ɡlɑːsɪ/ *adjective* (**-ier**, **-iest**) like glass; (of eye etc.) dull, fixed.

glaucoma /ɡlɔː'kəʊmə/ *noun* eye disease with pressure in eyeball and gradual loss of sight.

glaze ● *verb* (**-zing**) fit with glass or windows; cover (pottery etc.) with vitreous substance or (surface) with smooth shiny coating; (often + *over*) (of eyes) become glassy. ● *noun* substance used for or surface produced by glazing.

glazier /'ɡleɪzɪə/ *noun* person who glazes windows etc.

gleam ● *noun* faint or brief light or show. ● *verb* emit gleam(s).

glean *verb* gather (facts etc.); gather (corn left by reapers). □ **gleanings** *plural noun*.

glebe *noun* piece of land yielding revenue to benefice.

glee *noun* mirth, delight; musical composition for several voices. □ **gleeful** *adjective*; **gleefully** *adverb*.

glen *noun* narrow valley.

glengarry /ɡlen'ɡærɪ/ *noun* (*plural* **-ies**) kind of Highland cap.

glib *adjective* (**-bb-**) speaking or spoken fluently but insincerely. □ **glibly** *adverb*; **glibness** *noun*.

glide ● *verb* (**-ding**) move smoothly or continuously; (of aircraft) fly without engine-power; go stealthily. ● *noun* gliding motion.

glider /'ɡlaɪdə/ *noun* light aircraft without engine.

glimmer /'ɡlɪmə/ ● *verb* shine faintly or intermittently. ● *noun* faint or wavering light; (also **glimmering**) (usually + *of*) small sign.

glimpse /ɡlɪmps/ ● *noun* (often + *of*, *at*) brief view; faint transient appearance. ● *verb* (**-sing**) have brief view of.

glint *verb & noun* flash, glitter.

glissade /ɡlɪ'sɑːd/ ● *noun* controlled slide down snow slope; gliding. ● *verb* (**-ding**) perform glissade.

glissando /ɡlɪ'sændəʊ/ *noun* (*plural* **-di** /-dɪ/ or **-s**) *Music* continuous slide of adjacent notes.

glisten /'ɡlɪs(ə)n/ ● *verb* shine like wet or polished surface. ● *noun* glitter.

glitch *noun colloquial* irregularity, malfunction.

glitter /'glɪtə/ ● *verb* shine with brilliant reflected light, sparkle; (often + *with*) be showy. ● *noun* sparkle; showiness; tiny pieces of glittering material.

glitz *noun slang* showy glamour. □ **glitzy** *adjective* (**-ier, -iest**).

gloaming /'gləʊmɪŋ/ *noun* twilight.

gloat *verb* (often + *over* etc.) look or ponder with greedy or malicious pleasure.

global /'gləʊb(ə)l/ *adjective* worldwide; all-embracing. □ **global warming** increase in temperature of earth's atmosphere. □ **globally** *adverb*.

globe *noun* spherical object; spherical map of earth; (**the globe**) the earth. □ **globe artichoke** partly edible head of artichoke plant; **globe-trotter** person travelling widely.

globular /'glɒbjʊlə/ *adjective* globe-shaped; composed of globules.

globule /'glɒbjuːl/ *noun* small globe, round particle, or drop.

glockenspiel /'glɒkənspiːl/ *noun* musical instrument of bells or metal bars played with hammers.

gloom /gluːm/ *noun* darkness; melancholy, depression.

gloomy /'gluːmɪ/ *adjective* (**-ier, -iest**) dark; depressed, depressing.

glorify /'glɔːrɪfaɪ/ *verb* (**-ies, -ied**) make glorious; make seem more splendid than is the case; (as **glorified** *adjective*) treated as more important etc. than it is; extol. □ **glorification** *noun*.

glorious /'glɔːrɪəs/ *adjective* possessing or conferring glory; *colloquial* splendid, excellent. □ **gloriously** *adverb*.

glory /'glɔːrɪ/ ● *noun* (*plural* **-ies**) (thing bringing) renown, honourable fame, etc.; adoring praise; resplendent majesty, beauty, etc.; halo of saint. ● *verb* (**-ies, -ied**) (often + *in*) take pride.

gloss[1] ● *noun* surface lustre; deceptively attractive appearance; (in full *gloss paint*) paint giving glossy finish. ● *verb* make glossy. □ **gloss over** seek to conceal.

gloss[2] ● *noun* explanatory comment added to text; interpretation. ● *verb* add gloss to.

glossary /'glɒsərɪ/ *noun* (*plural* **-ies**) dictionary of technical or special words, esp. as appendix.

glossy ● *adjective* (**-ier, -iest**) smooth and shiny; printed on such paper. ● *noun* (*plural* **-ies**) *colloquial* glossy magazine or photograph.

glottal /'glɒt(ə)l/ *adjective* of the glottis. □ **glottal stop** sound produced by sudden opening or shutting of glottis.

glottis /'glɒtɪs/ *noun* opening at upper end of windpipe between vocal cords.

glove /glʌv/ ● *noun* hand-covering for protection, warmth, etc.; boxing glove. ● *verb* (**-ving**) cover or provide with gloves. □ **glove compartment** recess for small articles in car dashboard; **glove puppet** small puppet fitted on hand.

glow /gləʊ/ ● *verb* emit flameless light and heat; (often + *with*) feel bodily heat or strong emotion; show warm colour; (as **glowing** *adjective*) expressing pride or satisfaction. ● *noun* glowing state, appearance, or feeling. □ **glow-worm** beetle that emits green light.

glower /'glaʊə/ *verb* (often + *at*) scowl.

glucose /'gluːkəʊs/ *noun* kind of sugar found in blood, fruits, etc.

glue ● *noun* substance used as adhesive. ● *verb* (**glues, glued, gluing** or **glueing**) attach (as) with glue; hold closely. □ **glue ear** blocking of (esp. child's) Eustachian tube; **glue-sniffing** inhalation of fumes

from adhesives as intoxicant. □ **gluey** *adjective* (**gluier, gluiest**).

glum *adjective* (**-mm-**) dejected, sullen. □ **glumly** *adverb*; **glumness** *noun*.

glut ● *verb* (**-tt-**) feed or indulge to the full, satiate; overstock. ● *noun* excessive supply; surfeit.

gluten /'gluːt(ə)n/ *noun* sticky part of wheat flour.

glutinous /'gluːtɪnəs/ *adjective* sticky, gluelike.

glutton /'glʌt(ə)n/ *noun* excessive eater; (often + *for*) *colloquial* insatiably eager person; voracious animal of weasel family. □ **gluttonous** *adjective*; **gluttonously** *adverb*; **gluttony** *noun*.

glycerine /'glɪsəriːn/ *noun* (also **glycerol**, US **glycerin**) colourless sweet viscous liquid used in medicines, explosives, etc.

gm *abbreviation* gram(s).

GMT *abbreviation* Greenwich Mean Time.

gnarled /nɑːld/ *adjective* knobbly, twisted, rugged.

gnash /næʃ/ *verb* grind (one's teeth); (of teeth) strike together.

gnat /næt/ *noun* small biting fly.

gnaw /nɔː/ *verb* (usually + *away* etc.) wear away by biting; (often + *at, into*) bite persistently; corrode; torment.

gneiss /naɪs/ *noun* coarse-grained rock of feldspar, quartz, and mica.

gnome /nəʊm/ *noun* dwarf, goblin; (esp. in *plural*) *colloquial* person with sinister influence, esp. financial.

gnomic /'nəʊmɪk/ *adjective* of aphorisms; sententious.

gnomon /'nəʊmɒn/ *noun* rod etc. on sundial, showing time by its shadow.

gnostic /'nɒstɪk/ ● *adjective* of knowledge; having special mystic knowledge. ● *noun* (**Gnostic**) early Christian heretic claiming mystical knowledge. □ **Gnosticism** *-sɪz(ə)m/ noun*.

GNP *abbreviation* gross national product.

gnu /nuː/ *noun* (*plural* same or **-s**) oxlike antelope.

go[1] ● *verb* (3rd singular present **goes** /gəʊz/; past **went**; past participle **gone** /gɒn/) walk, travel, proceed; participate in (doing something); extend in a certain direction; depart; move, function; make specified movement or sound, *colloquial* say; be, become; elapse, be traversed; (of song etc.) have specified wording etc.; match; be regularly kept, fit; be successful; be sold, (of money) be spent; be relinquished, fail, decline, collapse; be acceptable or accepted; (often + *by, with, on, upon*) be guided by; attend regularly; (+ *to, towards*) contribute to; (+ *for*) apply to. ● *noun* (*plural* **goes**) animation; vigorous activity; success; turn, attempt. □ **go-ahead** *adjective* enterprising, *noun* permission to proceed; **go-between** intermediary; **go down** descend, become less, decrease (in price), subside, sink, (of sun) set, deteriorate, cease to function, be recorded, be swallowed, (+ *with*) find acceptance with, *colloquial* leave university, *colloquial* be sent to prison, (+ *with*) become ill with; **go for** go to fetch, prefer, choose, pass or be accounted as, *colloquial* attack, *colloquial* strive to attain; **go-getter** *colloquial* pushily enterprising person; **go in for** compete or engage in; **go-kart, -cart** miniature racing car with skeleton body; **go off** explode, deteriorate, fall asleep, begin to dislike; **go off well, badly** succeed, fail; **go on** continue, proceed, *colloquial* talk at great length, (+ *at*) *colloquial* nag, use as evidence; **go out** leave room or house, be extinguished, be broadcast, cease to be fashionable, (often + *with*) have romantic or sexual relationship, (usually + *to*) sympathize; **go over** inspect details of, rehearse; **go round** spin, revolve, suffice for all; **go slow** work slowly as industrial protest; **go under** sink, succumb, fail; **go up** rise, increase (in price), be consumed (in flames etc.), explode, *colloquial* enter university; **go without** manage without or forgo (something); **have a go at** attack, attempt; **on the go** *colloquial* active.

go² *noun* Japanese board game.

goad ● *verb* urge with goad; (usually + *on*, *into*) irritate, stimulate. ● *noun* spiked stick for urging cattle; thing that torments or incites.

goal *noun* object of effort; destination; structure into or through which ball is to be driven in certain games; point(s) so won; point where race ends. □ **goalkeeper** player protecting goal; **goalpost** either post supporting crossbar of goal.

goalie *noun* *colloquial* goalkeeper.

goat *noun* small domesticated mammal with horns and (in male) beard; licentious man; *colloquial* fool. □ **get (person's) goat** *colloquial* irritate him or her.

goatee /gəʊˈtiː/ *noun* small pointed beard.

gob¹ *noun* *slang* mouth. □ **gobsmacked** *slang* flabbergasted; **gob-stopper** large hard sweet.

gob² *slang* ● *noun* clot of slimy matter. ● *verb* (**-bb-**) spit.

gobbet /ˈgɒbɪt/ *noun* lump of flesh, food, etc.; extract from text set for translation or comment.

gobble¹ /ˈgɒb(ə)l/ *verb* (**-ling**) eat hurriedly and noisily.

gobble² /ˈgɒb(ə)l/ *verb* (**-ling**) (of turkeycock) make guttural sound; speak thus.

gobbledegook /ˈgɒbəldɪguːk/ *noun* (also **gobbledeygook**) *colloquial* pompous or unintelligible jargon.

goblet /ˈgɒblɪt/ *noun* drinking vessel with foot and stem.

goblin /ˈgɒblɪn/ *noun* mischievous demon.

goby /ˈgəʊbɪ/ *noun* (*plural* **-ies**) small fish with sucker on underside.

god *noun* superhuman being worshipped as possessing power over nature, human fortunes, etc.; (**God**) creator and ruler of universe; idol; adored person; (**the gods**) (occupants of) gallery in theatre. □ **godchild** person in relation to godparent; **god-daughter** female godchild; **godfather** male godparent; **God-fearing** religious; **God-forsaken** dismal; **godmother** female godparent; **godparent** person who responds on behalf of candidate at baptism; **godsend** unexpected welcome event or acquisition; **godson** male godchild. □ **godlike** *adjective*.

goddess /ˈgɒdɪs/ *noun* female deity; adored woman.

godhead *noun* divine nature; deity.

godless *adjective* impious, wicked; not believing in God. □ **godlessness** *noun*.

godly /ˈgɒdlɪ/ *adjective* (**-ier**, **-iest**) pious, devout. □ **godliness** *noun*.

goer /ˈgəʊə/ *noun* person or thing that goes; *colloquial* lively or sexually promiscuous person. □ **-goer** regular attender.

goggle /ˈgɒg(ə)l/ ● *verb* (**-ling**) (often + *at*) look with wide-open eyes; (of eyes) be rolled, project; roll (eyes). ● *adjective* (of eyes) protuberant, rolling. ● *noun* (in *plural*) spectacles for protecting eyes. □ **goggle-box** *colloquial* television set.

going /ˈgəʊɪŋ/ ● *noun* condition of ground as affecting riding etc. ● *adjective* in action; existing, available; current, prevalent. □ **going concern** thriving business; **going-over** (*plural* **goings-over**) *colloquial* inspection or overhaul; *slang* thrashing; **goings-on** strange conduct.

goitre /ˈgɔɪtə/ *noun* (*US* **goiter**) abnormal enlargement of thyroid gland.

gold /gəʊld/ ● *noun* precious yellow metal; colour of this; coins or articles of gold. ● *adjective* of or coloured like gold. □ **gold-digger** *slang* woman who goes after men for their money; **gold field** area with naturally

occurring gold; **goldfinch** brightly coloured songbird; **goldfish** small golden-red Chinese carp; **gold leaf** gold beaten into thin sheet; **gold medal** medal given usually as first prize; **gold plate** vessels of gold, material plated with gold; **gold-plate** plate with gold; **gold-rush** rush to newly discovered gold field; **goldsmith** worker in gold; **gold standard** financial system in which value of money is based on gold.

golden /ˈgəʊld(ə)n/ *adjective* of gold; coloured or shining like gold; precious, excellent. □ **golden handshake** *colloquial* gratuity as compensation for redundancy or compulsory retirement; **golden jubilee** 50th anniversary of reign; **golden mean** principle of moderation; **golden retriever** retriever with gold-coloured coat; **golden wedding** 50th anniversary of wedding.

golf ● *noun* game in which small hard ball is struck with clubs over ground into series of small holes. ● *verb* play golf. □ **golf ball** ball used in golf, spherical unit carrying type in some electric typewriters; **golf course** area of land on which golf is played; **golf club** club used in golf, (premises of) association for playing golf. □ **golfer** *noun*.

golliwog /ˈgɒlɪwɒg/ *noun* black-faced soft doll with fuzzy hair.

gonad /ˈgəʊnæd/ *noun* animal organ producing gametes, e.g. testis or ovary.

gondola /ˈgɒndələ/ *noun* light Venetian canal-boat; car suspended from airship.

gondolier /gɒndəˈlɪə/ *noun* oarsman of gondola.

gone /gɒn/ ● *past participle* of GO¹. ● *adjective* (of time) past; lost, hopeless, dead; *colloquial* pregnant for specified time.

goner /ˈgɒnə/ *noun* *slang* person or thing that is doomed or irrevocably lost.

gong *noun* metal disc giving resonant note when struck; saucer-shaped bell; *slang* medal.

gonorrhoea /gɒnəˈrɪə/ *noun* (*US* **gonorrhea**) a venereal disease.

goo *noun* *colloquial* sticky or slimy substance; sickly sentiment. □ **gooey** *adjective* (**gooier**, **gooiest**).

good /gʊd/ ● *adjective* (**better**, **best**) having right qualities, adequate; competent, effective; kind, morally excellent, virtuous; well-behaved; agreeable; considerable; not less than; beneficial; valid. ● *noun* (only in *singular*) good quality or circumstance; (in *plural*) movable property, merchandise. □ **good-for-nothing** worthless (person); **good humour** genial mood; **good-looking** handsome; **good nature** kindly disposition; **goodwill** kindly feeling, established value-enhancing reputation of a business.

goodbye /gʊdˈbaɪ/ (*US* **goodby**) ● *interjection* expressing good wishes at parting. ● *noun* (*plural* **-byes** or *US* **-bys**) parting, farewell.

goodly /ˈgʊdlɪ/ *adjective* (**-ier**, **-iest**) handsome; of imposing size etc.

goodness /ˈgʊdnɪs/ *noun* virtue; excellence; kindness; nutriment.

goody /ˈgʊdɪ/ ● *noun* (*plural* **-ies**) *colloquial* good person; (usually in *plural*) something good or attractive, esp. to eat. ● *interjection* expressing childish delight. □ **goody-goody** *colloquial* (person who is) smugly or obtrusively virtuous.

goof /guːf/ *slang* ● *noun* foolish or stupid person or mistake. ● *verb* bungle, blunder. □ **goofy** *adjective* (**-ier**, **-iest**).

googly /ˈguːglɪ/ *noun* (*plural* **-ies**) *Cricket* ball bowled so as to bounce in unexpected direction.

goon /guːn/ *noun* *slang* stupid person; *esp.* *US* hired ruffian.

goose /guːs/ *noun* (*plural* **geese** /giːs/) large web-footed bird; female of this; *colloquial* simpleton.

□ **goose-flesh, -pimples** (*US* **-bumps**) bristling state of skin due to cold or fright; **goose-step** stiff-legged marching step.

gooseberry /ˈgʊzbərɪ/ *noun* (*plural* **-ies**) small green usually sour berry; thorny shrub bearing this.

gopher /ˈgəʊfə/ *noun* American burrowing rodent.

gore¹ *noun* clotted blood.

gore² *verb* (**-ring**) pierce with horn, tusk, etc.

gore³ ● *noun* wedge-shaped piece in garment; triangular or tapering piece in umbrella etc. ● *verb* (**-ring**) shape with gore.

gorge ● *noun* narrow opening between hills; surfeit; contents of stomach. ● *verb* (**-ging**) feed greedily; satiate.

gorgeous /ˈgɔːdʒəs/ *adjective* richly coloured; *colloquial* splendid; *colloquial* strikingly beautiful. □ **gorgeously** *adverb*.

gorgon /ˈgɔːgən/ *noun* (in Greek mythology) any of 3 snake-haired sisters able to turn people to stone; frightening or repulsive woman.

Gorgonzola /ɡɔːgənˈzəʊlə/ *noun* rich blue-veined Italian cheese.

gorilla /ɡəˈrɪlə/ *noun* largest anthropoid ape.

gormless /ˈgɔːmlɪs/ *adjective* *colloquial* foolish, lacking sense. □ **gormlessly** *adverb*.

gorse /gɔːs/ *noun* prickly shrub with yellow flowers.

Gorsedd /ˈgɔːseð/ *noun* Druidic order meeting before eisteddfod.

gory /ˈgɔːrɪ/ *adjective* (**-ier, -iest**) involving bloodshed; bloodstained.

gosh *interjection* *expressing surprise*.

goshawk /ˈgɒshɔːk/ *noun* large short-winged hawk.

gosling /ˈgɒzlɪŋ/ *noun* young goose.

gospel /ˈgɒsp(ə)l/ *noun* teaching or revelation of Christ; (**Gospel**) (each of 4 books giving) account of Christ's life in New Testament; portion of this read at church service; thing regarded as absolutely true. □ **gospel music** black American religious singing.

gossamer /ˈgɒsəmə/ ● *noun* filmy substance of small spiders' webs; delicate filmy material. ● *adjective* light and flimsy as gossamer.

gossip /ˈgɒsɪp/ ● *noun* unconstrained talk or writing, esp. about people; idle talk; person indulging in gossip. ● *verb* (**-p-**) talk or write gossip. □ **gossip column** regular newspaper column of gossip. □ **gossipy** *adjective*.

got *past & past participle of* GET.

Goth *noun* member of Germanic tribe that invaded Roman Empire in 3rd– 5th c.

Gothic *adjective* of Goths; *Architecture* in the pointed-arch style prevalent in W. Europe in 12th–16th c.; (of novel etc.) in a style popular in 18th & 19th c., with supernatural or horrifying events.

gotten *US past participle of* GET.

gouache /guːˈɑːʃ/ *noun* painting with opaque water-colour; pigments used for this.

Gouda /ˈgaʊdə/ *noun* flat round Dutch cheese.

gouge /gaʊdʒ/ ● *noun* concave-bladed chisel. ● *verb* (**-ging**) cut or (+ *out*) force out (as) with gouge.

goulash /ˈguːlæʃ/ *noun* stew of meat and vegetables seasoned with paprika.

gourd /gʊəd/ *noun* fleshy fruit of trailing or climbing cucumber-like plant; this plant; dried rind of this fruit used as bottle etc.

gourmand /ˈgʊəmənd/ *noun* glutton; gourmet.

■ **Usage** The use of *gourmand* to mean a 'gourmet' is considered incorrect by some people.

gourmet /ˈgʊəmeɪ/ *noun* connoisseur of good food.

gout /gaʊt/ *noun* disease with inflammation of small joints. □ **gouty** *adjective*.

govern /ˈgʌv(ə)n/ *verb* rule with authority; conduct policy and affairs of; influence or determine; curb, control.

governance *noun* act, manner, or function of governing.

governess /ˈgʌvənɪs/ *noun* woman employed to teach children in private household.

government *noun* manner or system of governing; group of people governing state. □ **governmental** /-ˈmen-/ *adjective*.

governor *noun* ruler; official governing a province, town, etc.; executive head of each State of US; member of governing body of institution; *slang* one's employer or father; automatic regulator controlling speed of engine etc. □ **Governor-General** representative of Crown in Commonwealth country regarding Queen as head of state. □ **governorship** *noun*.

gown /gaʊn/ *noun* woman's, esp. formal or elegant, long dress; official robe of alderman, judge, cleric, academic, etc.; surgeon's overall.

goy *noun* (*plural* **-im** or **-s**) *Jewish name for* non-Jew.

GP *abbreviation* general practitioner.

GPO *abbreviation* General Post Office.

gr *abbreviation* (also **gr.**) gram(s); grain(s); gross.

grab ● *verb* (**-bb-**) seize suddenly; take greedily; *slang* impress; (+ *at*) snatch at. ● *noun* sudden clutch or attempt to seize; device for clutching.

grace ● *noun* elegance of proportions, manner, or movement; courteous good will; attractive feature; unmerited favour of God; goodwill; delay granted; thanksgiving at meals; (**His, Her, Your Grace**) *title used of or* to duke, duchess, *or archbishop*. ● *verb* (**-cing**) (often + *with*) add grace to; bestow honour on. □ **grace note** *Music* note embellishing melody.

graceful *adjective* full of grace or elegance. □ **gracefully** *adverb*.

graceless *adjective* lacking grace or charm.

gracious /ˈgreɪʃəs/ *adjective* kindly, esp. to inferiors; merciful. □ **gracious living** elegant way of life. □ **graciously** *adverb*; **graciousness** *noun*.

gradate /grəˈdeɪt/ *verb* (**-ting**) (cause to) pass gradually from one shade to another; arrange in steps or grades.

gradation *noun* (usually in *plural*) stage of transition or advance; degree in rank, intensity, etc.; arrangement in grades. □ **gradational** *adjective*.

grade ● *noun* degree in rank, merit, etc.; mark indicating quality of student's work; slope; *US* class in school. ● *verb* (**-ding**) arrange in grades; (+ *up, down, off, into*, etc.) pass between grades; give grade to; reduce to easy gradients. □ **make the grade** succeed.

gradient /ˈgreɪdɪənt/ *noun* sloping road etc.; amount of such slope.

gradual /ˈgrædjʊəl/ *adjective* happening by degrees; not steep or abrupt. □ **gradually** *adverb*.

graduate ● *noun* /ˈgrædjʊət/ holder of academic degree. ● *verb* /-eɪt/ (**-ting**) obtain academic degree; (+ *to*) move up to; mark in degrees or portions; arrange in gradations; apportion (tax etc.) according to scale. □ **graduation** *noun*.

graffiti /grəˈfiːtɪ/ *plural noun* (*singular* **graffito**) writing or drawing on wall etc.

■ **Usage** *Graffiti* should be used with plural verbs, as in *Graffiti have appeared everywhere*.

graft¹ /grɑːft/ ● *noun* shoot or scion planted in slit in another stock; piece of transplanted living tissue; *slang* hard work. ● *verb* (often + *in, on, together*, etc.) insert (graft); transplant (living tissue); (+ *in, on*) insert or fix (thing) permanently to another; *slang* work hard.

graft² /grɑːft/ *colloquial* ● *noun* practices for securing illicit gains in politics or business; such gains. ● *verb* seek or make graft.

Grail *noun* (in full **Holy Grail**) legendary cup or platter used by Christ at Last Supper.

grain ● *noun* fruit or seed of cereal; wheat or allied food-grass; corn; particle of sand, salt, etc.; unit of weight (0.065 g); least possible amount; texture in skin, wood, stone, etc.; arrangement of lines of fibre in wood. ● *verb* paint in imitation of grain of wood; form into grains.

gram *noun* (also **gramme**) metric unit of weight.

grammar /'græmə/ *noun* study or rules of relations between words in (a) language; application of such rules; book on grammar. □ **grammar school** *esp. historical* secondary school with academic curriculum.

grammarian /grə'meərɪən/ *noun* expert in grammar.

grammatical /grə'mætɪk(ə)l/ *adjective* of or according to grammar.

gramophone /'græməfəʊn/ *noun* record player.

grampus /'græmpəs/ *noun* (*plural* **-es**) sea mammal of dolphin family.

gran *noun colloquial* grandmother.

granary /'grænərɪ/ *noun* (*plural* **-ies**) storehouse for grain; region producing much corn.

grand ● *adjective* splendid, imposing; chief, of chief importance; (**Grand**) of highest rank; *colloquial* excellent. ● *noun* grand piano; (*plural* same) (usually in *plural*) *slang* 1,000 dollars or pounds. □ **grand jury** jury to examine validity of accusation before trial; **grand piano** piano with horizontal strings; **grand slam** winning of all kinds of matches; **grand total** sum of other totals. □ **grandly** *adverb*; **grandness** *noun*.

grandad *noun* (also **grand-dad**) *colloquial* grandfather.

grandchild *noun* child of one's son or daughter.

granddaughter *noun* one's child's daughter.

grandee /græn'diː/ *noun* Spanish or Portuguese noble of highest rank; great personage.

grandeur /'grændʒə/ *noun* majesty, splendour, dignity; high rank, eminence.

grandfather *noun* one's parent's father. □ **grandfather clock** clock in tall wooden case.

grandiloquent /græn'dɪləkwənt/ *adjective* pompous or inflated in language. □ **grandiloquence** *noun*.

grandiose /'grændɪəʊs/ *adjective* imposing; planned on large scale. □ **grandiosity** /-'ɒsɪtɪ/ *noun*.

grandma *noun colloquial* grandmother.

grandmother *noun* one's parent's mother.

grandparent *noun* one's parent's parent.

Grand Prix /grɑ̃ 'priː/ *noun* any of several international motor-racing events.

grandson *noun* one's child's son.

grandstand *noun* main stand for spectators at racecourse etc.

grange /greɪndʒ/ *noun* country house with farm buildings.

granite /'grænɪt/ *noun* granular crystalline rock of quartz, mica, etc.

granny /'grænɪ/ *noun* (also **grannie**) (*plural* **-ies**) *colloquial* grandmother; (in full **granny knot**) reef-knot crossed wrong way.

grant /grɑːnt/ ● *verb* consent to fulfil; allow to have; give formally, transfer legally; (often + *that*) admit, concede. ● *noun* granting; thing, esp. money, granted. □ **take for granted** assume to be true, cease to appreciate through familiarity. □ **grantor** /grɑːn'tɔː/ *noun*.

granular /'grænjʊlə/ *adjective* of or like grains or granules.

granulate /'grænjʊleɪt/ *verb* (**-ting**) form into grains; roughen surface of. □ **granulation** *noun*.

granule /'grænjuːl/ *noun* small grain.

grape *noun* usually green or purple berry growing in clusters on vine. □ **grapeshot** *historical* small balls as scattering charge for cannon etc.; **grapevine** vine, means of transmission of rumour.

grapefruit /'greɪpfruːt/ *noun* (*plural* same) large round usually yellow citrus fruit.

graph /grɑːf/ ● *noun* symbolic diagram representing relation between two or more variables. ● *verb* plot on graph.

graphic /'græfɪk/ *adjective* of writing, drawing, etc.; vividly descriptive. □ **graphic arts** visual and technical arts involving design or lettering. □ **graphically** *adverb*.

graphics *plural noun* (usually treated as *singular*) products of graphic arts; use of diagrams in calculation and design.

graphite /'græfaɪt/ *noun* crystalline form of carbon used as lubricant, in pencils, etc.

graphology /grə'fɒlədʒɪ/ *noun* study of handwriting. □ **graphologist** *noun*.

grapnel /'græpn(ə)l/ *noun* iron-clawed instrument for dragging or grasping; small many-fluked anchor.

grapple /'græp(ə)l/ ● *verb* (**-ling**) (often + *with*) fight at close quarters; (+ *with*) try to manage (problem etc.); grip with hands, come to close quarters with; seize. ● *noun* hold (as) of wrestler; contest at close quarters; clutching-instrument. □ **grappling-iron, -hook** grapnel.

grasp /grɑːsp/ ● *verb* clutch at, seize greedily; hold firmly; understand, realize. ● *noun* firm hold, grip; (+ *of*) mastery, mental hold.

grasping *adjective* avaricious.

grass /grɑːs/ ● *noun* (any of several) plants with bladelike leaves eaten by ruminants; pasture land; grass-covered ground; grazing; *slang* marijuana; *slang* informer. ● *verb* cover with turf; *US* pasture; *slang* betray, inform police. □ **grass roots** fundamental level or source, rank and file; **grass snake** small non-poisonous snake; **grass widow, widower** person whose husband or wife is temporarily absent. □ **grassy** *adjective* (**-ier, -iest**).

grasshopper /'grɑːshɒpə/ *noun* jumping and chirping insect.

grate¹ *verb* (**-ting**) reduce to small particles by rubbing on rough surface; (often + *against, on*) rub with, utter with, or make harsh sound, have irritating effect; grind, creak. □ **grater** *noun*.

grate² *noun* (metal) frame holding fuel in fireplace etc.

grateful /'greɪtfʊl/ *adjective* thankful; feeling or showing gratitude. □ **gratefully** *adverb*.

gratify /'grætɪfaɪ/ *verb* (**-ies, -ied**) please, delight; indulge. □ **gratification** *noun*.

grating /'greɪtɪŋ/ *noun* framework of parallel or crossed metal bars.

gratis /'grɑːtɪs/ *adverb & adjective* free, without charge.

gratitude /'grætɪtjuːd/ *noun* being thankful.

gratuitous /grə'tjuːɪtəs/ *adjective* given or done gratis; uncalled-for, motiveless. □ **gratuitously** *adverb*; **gratuitousness** *noun*.

gratuity /grə'tjuːɪtɪ/ *noun* (*plural* **-ies**) money given for good service.

grave¹ /greɪv/ *noun* hole dug for burial of corpse; mound or monument over this; (**the grave**) death. □ **gravestone** (usually inscribed) stone over grave; **graveyard** burial ground.

grave² /greɪv/ *adjective* weighty, serious; dignified, solemn; threatening. □ **gravely** *adverb*.

grave³ /greɪv/ *verb* (**-ving**; *past participle* **graven** or **graved**) (+ *in, on*) fix indelibly on (memory etc.); *archaic* engrave, carve. □ **graven image** idol.

grave⁴ /grɑːv/ *noun* (in full **grave accent**) mark (`) over letter indicating pronunciation.

gravel /ˈgræv(ə)l/ ● *noun* coarse sand and small stones; formation of crystals in bladder. ● *verb* (**-ll-**; *US* **-l-**) lay with gravel.

gravelly /ˈgrævəlɪ/ *adjective* of or like gravel; (of voice) deep and rough-sounding.

gravid /ˈgrævɪd/ *adjective* pregnant.

gravitate /ˈgrævɪteɪt/ *verb* (**-ting**) (+ *to, towards*) move, be attracted, or tend by force of gravity to(wards); sink or drop by gravity.

gravitation *noun* attraction between each particle of matter and every other; effect of this, esp. falling of bodies to earth. □ **gravitational** *adjective*.

gravity /ˈgrævɪtɪ/ *noun* force that attracts body to centre of earth etc.; intensity of this; weight; importance, seriousness; solemnity.

gravy /ˈgreɪvɪ/ *noun* (*plural* **-ies**) (sauce made from) juices exuding from meat in and after cooking. □ **gravy-boat** long shallow jug for gravy; **gravy train** *slang* source of easy financial benefit.

gray *US* = GREY.

grayling *noun* (*plural* same) silver-grey freshwater fish.

graze¹ *verb* (**-zing**) feed on growing grass; pasture cattle.

graze² ● *verb* (**-zing**) rub or scrape (part of body); (+ *against, along*, etc.) touch lightly in passing, move with such contact. ● *noun* abrasion.

grazier /ˈgreɪzɪə/ *noun* person who feeds cattle for market.

grazing *noun* grassland suitable for pasturage.

grease /griːs/ ● *noun* oily or fatty matter, esp. as lubricant; melted fat of dead animal. ● *verb* (**-sing**) smear or lubricate with grease. □ **greasepaint** actor's make-up; **greaseproof** impervious to grease.

greasy /ˈgriːsɪ/ *adjective* (**-ier, -iest**) of, like, smeared with, or having too much grease; (of person, manner) unctuous. □ **greasiness** *noun*.

great /greɪt/ ● *adjective* above average in bulk, number, extent, or intensity; important, pre-eminent; imposing, distinguished; of remarkable ability etc.; (+ *at, on*) competent, well-informed; *colloquial* very satisfactory. ● *noun* great person or thing. □ **greatcoat** heavy overcoat; **Great Dane** dog of large short-haired breed. □ **greatness** *noun*.

great- /greɪt/ *combining form* (of family relationships) one degree more remote (*great-grandfather, great-niece*, etc.).

greatly *adverb* much.

grebe *noun* a diving bird.

Grecian /ˈgriːʃ(ə)n/ *adjective* Greek.

greed *noun* excessive desire, esp. for food or wealth.

greedy /ˈgriːdɪ/ *adjective* (**-ier, -iest**) showing greed; (+ *for, to do*) eager. □ **greedily** *adverb*.

Greek ● *noun* native, national, or language of Greece. ● *adjective* of Greece.

green ● *adjective* coloured like grass; unripe, unseasoned; not dried, smoked, or tanned; inexperienced; jealous; (also **Green**) concerned with protection of environment, not harmful to environment. ● *noun* green colour, paint, clothes, etc.; piece of grassy public land; grassy area for special purpose; (in *plural*) green vegetables; (also **Green**) supporter of protection of environment. □ **green belt** area of open land for preservation round city; **green card** motorist's international insurance document; **greenfinch** bird with greenish plumage; **green fingers** *colloquial* skill in gardening; **greenfly**

green aphid; **greengage** round green plum; **greenhorn** novice; **green light** signal or permission to proceed; **green pound** the agreed value of the pound for payments to agricultural producers in EC; **green-room** room in theatre for actors when off stage; **greensward** grassy turf.

greenery *noun* green foliage.

greengrocer /ˈgriːnɡrəʊsə/ *noun* retailer of fruit and vegetables. □ **greengrocery** *noun* (*plural* **-ies**).

greenhouse *noun* structure with sides and roof mainly of glass, for rearing plants. □ **greenhouse effect** trapping of sun's warmth in earth's lower atmosphere; **greenhouse gas** gas contributing to greenhouse effect, esp. carbon dioxide.

greet *verb* address on meeting or arrival; receive or acknowledge in specified way; become apparent to (eye, ear, etc.).

greeting *noun* act or words used to greet. □ **greetings card** decorative card carrying goodwill message etc.

gregarious /grɪˈɡeərɪəs/ *adjective* fond of company; living in flocks etc. □ **gregariousness** *noun*.

Gregorian calendar /grɪˈɡɔːrɪən/ *noun* calendar introduced in 1582 by Pope Gregory XIII.

Gregorian chant /grɪˈɡɔːrɪən/ *noun* form of plainsong named after Pope Gregory I.

gremlin /ˈɡremlɪn/ *noun* *colloquial* mischievous sprite said to cause mechanical faults etc.

grenade /grɪˈneɪd/ *noun* small bomb thrown by hand or shot from rifle.

grenadier /grenəˈdɪə/ *noun* (**Grenadier**) member of first regiment of royal household infantry; *historical* soldier armed with grenades.

grew *past of* GROW.

grey /greɪ/ (*US* **gray**) ● *adjective* of colour between black and white; clouded, dull; (of hair) turning white, (of person) having grey hair; anonymous, unidentifiable; undistinguished, boring. ● *noun* grey colour, paint, clothes, etc.; grey horse. ● *verb* make or become grey. □ **grey area** indefinite situation or topic; **Grey Friar** Franciscan friar; **grey matter** darker tissues of brain, *colloquial* intelligence.

greyhound *noun* slender swift dog used in racing.

greylag *noun* European wild goose.

grid *noun* grating; system of numbered squares for map references; network of lines, electric power connections, etc.; pattern of lines marking starting-place on motor-racing track.

griddle /ˈɡrɪd(ə)l/ *noun* iron plate placed over heat for baking etc.

gridiron /ˈɡrɪdaɪən/ *noun* barred metal frame for broiling or grilling; American football field.

grief /griːf/ *noun* (cause of) intense sorrow. □ **come to grief** meet with disaster.

grievance *noun* real or imagined cause for complaint.

grieve /griːv/ *verb* (**-ving**) (cause to) feel grief.

grievous /ˈɡriːvəs/ *adjective* severe; causing grief; injurious; flagrant, heinous. □ **grievously** *adverb*.

griffin /ˈɡrɪfɪn/ *noun* (also **gryphon** /-f(ə)n/) mythical creature with eagle's head and wings and lion's body.

griffon /ˈɡrɪf(ə)n/ *noun* small coarse-haired terrier-like dog; large vulture; griffin.

grill ● *noun* device on cooker for radiating heat downwards; gridiron; grilled food; (in full **grill room**) restaurant specializing in grills. ● *verb* cook under grill or on gridiron; subject to or experience extreme heat; subject to severe questioning.

grille /grɪl/ *noun* (also **grill**) grating, latticed screen; metal grid protecting vehicle radiator.

grilse /grɪls/ *noun* (*plural* same or **-s**) young salmon that has been to the sea only once.

grim *adjective* (**-mm-**) of stern appearance; harsh, merciless; ghastly, joyless; unpleasant. □ **grimly** *adverb*; **grimness** *noun*.

grimace /'grɪməs/ ● *noun* distortion of face made in disgust etc. or to amuse. ● *verb* (**-cing**) make grimace.

grime ● *noun* deeply ingrained dirt. ● *verb* (**-ming**) blacken, befoul. □ **grimy** *adjective* (**-ier, -iest**).

grin ● *verb* (**-nn-**) smile broadly. ● *noun* broad smile.

grind /graɪnd/ ● *verb* (*past & past participle* **ground** /graʊnd/) crush to small particles; sharpen; rub gratingly; (often + *down*) oppress; (often + *away*) work or study hard. ● *noun* grinding; *colloquial* hard dull work. □ **grindstone** thick revolving abrasive disc for grinding, sharpening, etc. □ **grinder** *noun*.

grip ● *verb* (**-pp-**) grasp tightly; take firm hold; compel attention of. ● *noun* firm hold, grasp; way of holding; power of holding attention; intellectual mastery; control of one's behaviour; part of machine that grips; part of weapon etc. that is gripped; hairgrip; travelling bag.

gripe ● *verb* (**-ping**) *colloquial* complain; affect with colic. ● *noun* (usually in *plural*) colic; *colloquial* complaint. □ **Gripe Water** *proprietary term* medicine to relieve colic in babies.

grisly /'grɪzlɪ/ *adjective* (**-ier, -iest**) causing horror, disgust, or fear.

grist *noun* corn for grinding. □ **grist to the mill** source of profit or advantage.

gristle /'grɪs(ə)l/ *noun* tough flexible tissue; cartilage. □ **gristly** *adjective*.

grit ● *noun* small particles of sand etc.; coarse sandstone; *colloquial* pluck, endurance. ● *verb* (**-tt-**) spread grit on (icy roads etc.); clench (teeth); make grating sound. □ **gritty** *adjective* (**-ier, -iest**).

grits *plural noun* coarse oatmeal; unground husked oats.

grizzle /'grɪz(ə)l/ *verb* (**-ling**) *colloquial* cry fretfully. □ **grizzly** *adjective* (**-ier, -iest**).

grizzled *adjective* grey-haired.

grizzly /'grɪzlɪ/ *adjective* (**-ier, -iest**) grey-haired. ● *noun* (*plural* **-ies**) (in full **grizzly bear**) large fierce N. American bear.

groan ● *verb* make deep sound expressing pain, grief, or disapproval; (usually + *under, beneath, with*) be loaded or oppressed. ● *noun* sound made in groaning.

groat *noun historical* silver coin worth 4 old pence.

groats *plural noun* hulled or crushed grain, esp. oats.

grocer /'grəʊsə/ *noun* dealer in food and household provisions.

grocery /'grəʊsərɪ/ *noun* (*plural* **-ies**) grocer's trade, shop, or (in *plural*) goods.

grog *noun* drink of spirit (originally rum) and water.

groggy /'grɒgɪ/ *adjective* (**-ier, -iest**) incapable, unsteady. □ **groggily** *adverb*.

groin¹ ● *noun* depression between belly and thigh; edge formed by intersecting vaults. ● *verb* build with groins.

groin² *US* = GROYNE.

grommet /'grɒmɪt/ *noun* eyelet placed in hole to protect or insulate rope or cable passed through it; tube passed through eardrum to middle ear.

groom /gruːm/ ● *noun* person employed to tend horses; bridegroom. ● *verb* tend (horse); give neat or attractive appearance to; prepare (person) for office or occasion etc.

groove ● *noun* channel, elongated hollow; spiral cut in gramophone record for needle. ● *verb* (**-ving**) make groove(s) in.

groovy /'gruːvɪ/ *adjective* (**-ier, -iest**) *slang* excellent; of or like a groove.

grope ● *verb* (**-ping**) (usually + *for*) feel about or search blindly; (+ *for, after*) search mentally; fondle

clumsily for sexual pleasure; feel (one's way). ● *noun* act of groping.

grosgrain /'grəʊɡreɪn/ *noun* corded fabric of silk etc.

gross /grəʊs/ ● *adjective* overfed, bloated; coarse, indecent; flagrant; total, not net. ● *verb* produce as gross profit. ● *noun* (*plural* same) 12 dozen. □ **grossly** *adverb*.

grotesque /grəʊ'tesk/ ● *adjective* comically or repulsively distorted; incongruous, absurd. ● *noun* decoration interweaving human and animal features; comically distorted figure or design. □ **grotesquely** *adverb*.

grotto /'grɒtəʊ/ *noun* (*plural* **-es** or **-s**) picturesque cave; structure imitating cave.

grotty /'grɒtɪ/ *adjective* (**-ier, -iest**) *slang* unpleasant, dirty, ugly.

grouch /graʊtʃ/ *colloquial* ● *verb* grumble. ● *noun* grumbler; complaint; sulky grumbling mood. □ **grouchy** *adjective* (**-ier, -iest**).

ground¹ /graʊnd/ ● *noun* surface of earth; extent of subject; (often in *plural*) foundation, motive; area of special kind; (in *plural*) enclosed land attached to house etc.; area or basis for agreement etc.; surface worked on in painting; (in *plural*) dregs; bottom of sea; floor of room etc. ● *verb* prevent from taking off or flying; run aground, strand; (+ *in*) instruct thoroughly; (often as **grounded** *adjective*) (+ *on*) base cause or principle on. □ **ground control** personnel directing landing etc. of aircraft etc.; **ground cover** low-growing plants; **ground floor** storey at ground level; **ground frost** frost on surface of ground; **groundnut** peanut; **ground-rent** rent for land leased for building; **groundsman** person who maintains sports ground; **ground speed** aircraft's speed relative to ground; **ground swell** heavy sea due to distant or past storm etc.; **groundwork** preliminary or basic work.

ground² *past & past participle* of GRIND.

grounding *noun* basic instruction.

groundless *adjective* without motive or foundation.

groundsel /'graʊnds(ə)l/ *noun* yellow-flowered weed.

group /gruːp/ ● *noun* number of people or things near, classed, or working together; number of companies under common ownership; pop group; division of air force. ● *verb* form into group; place in group(s). □ **group captain** RAF officer next below air commodore.

groupie *noun slang* ardent follower of touring pop group(s).

grouse¹ /graʊs/ *noun* (*plural* same) game bird with feathered feet.

grouse² /graʊs/ *verb* (**-sing**) & *noun colloquial* grumble.

grout /graʊt/ ● *noun* thin fluid mortar. ● *verb* apply grout to.

grove /grəʊv/ *noun* small wood; group of trees.

grovel /'grɒv(ə)l/ *verb* (**-ll-**; *US* **-l-**) behave obsequiously; lie prone.

grow /grəʊ/ *verb* (*past* **grew**; *past participle* **grown**) increase in size, height, amount, etc.; develop or exist as living plant or natural product; produce by cultivation; become gradually; (+ *on*) become more favoured by; (in *passive*; + *over*) be covered with growth. □ **grown-up** adult; **grow up** mature. □ **grower** *noun*.

growl /graʊl/ ● *verb* (often + *at*) make low guttural sound, usually of anger; rumble. ● *noun* growling sound; angry murmur.

grown *past participle* of GROW.

growth /grəʊθ/ *noun* process of growing; increase; what has grown or is growing; tumour. □ **growth industry** one that is developing rapidly.

groyne /grɔɪn/ *noun* (*US* **groin**) wall built out into sea to stop beach erosion.

grub ● *noun* larva of insect; *colloquial* food. ● *verb* (**-bb-**) dig superficially; (+ *up*, *out*) extract by digging.

grubby /'grʌbɪ/ *adjective* (**-ier, -iest**) dirty.

grudge ● *noun* persistent resentment or ill will. ● *verb* (**-ging**) be unwilling to give or allow, feel resentful about (doing something).

gruel /'gruəl/ *noun* liquid food of oatmeal etc. boiled in milk or water.

gruelling (*US* **grueling**) *adjective* exhausting, punishing.

gruesome /'gru:səm/ *adjective* grisly, disgusting.

gruff *adjective* rough-voiced; surly. □ **gruffly** *adverb*.

grumble /'grʌmb(ə)l/ ● *verb* (**-ling**) complain peevishly; rumble. ● *noun* complaint; rumble. □ **grumbler** *noun*.

grumpy /'grʌmpɪ/ *adjective* (**-ier, -iest**) ill-tempered.

grunt ● *noun* low guttural sound characteristic of pig. ● *verb* utter (with) grunt.

Gruyère /'gru:jeə/ *noun* kind of Swiss cheese with holes in.

gryphon = GRIFFIN.

guano /'gwɑːnəʊ/ *noun* (*plural* **-s**) excrement of seabirds, used as manure.

guarantee /gærən'tiː/ ● *noun* formal promise or assurance; guaranty; giver of guaranty or security. ● *verb* (**-tees, -teed**) give or serve as guarantee for; promise; secure. □ **guarantor** *noun*.

guaranty /'gærəntɪ/ *noun* (*plural* **-ies**) written or other undertaking to answer for performance of obligation; thing serving as security.

guard /gɑːd/ ● *verb* (often + *from*, *against*) defend, protect; keep watch, prevent from escaping; keep in check; (+ *against*) take precautions against. ● *noun* vigilant state; protector; soldiers etc. protecting place or person; official in charge of train; (in *plural*) (usually **Guards**) household troops of monarch; device to prevent injury or accident; defensive posture. □ **guardhouse, guardroom** building or room for accommodating military guard or for detaining prisoners; **guardsman** soldier in guards or Guards.

guarded *adjective* (of remark etc.) cautious. □ **guardedly** *adverb*.

guardian /'gɑːdɪən/ *noun* protector, keeper; person having custody of another, esp. minor. □ **guardianship** *noun*.

guava /'gwɑːvə/ *noun* edible orange acid fruit; tropical tree bearing this.

gubernatorial /gjuːbənə'tɔːrɪəl/ *adjective US* of governor.

gudgeon[1] /'gʌdʒ(ə)n/ *noun* small freshwater fish.

gudgeon[2] /'gʌdʒ(ə)n/ *noun* kind of pivot or pin; tubular part of hinge; socket for rudder.

guelder rose /'geldə/ *noun* shrub with round bunches of white flowers.

Guernsey /'gɜːnzɪ/ *noun* (*plural* **-s**) one of breed of cattle from Guernsey; (**guernsey**) type of thick knitted woollen jersey.

guerrilla /gə'rɪlə/ *noun* (also **guerilla**) member of one of several independent groups fighting against regular forces.

guess /ges/ ● *verb* estimate without calculation or measurement; conjecture, think likely; conjecture rightly. ● *noun* estimate, conjecture. □ **guesswork** guessing.

guest /gest/ *noun* person invited to visit another's house or have meal etc. at another's expense, or lodging at hotel etc. □ **guest house** superior boarding house.

guestimate /'gestɪmət/ *noun* (also **guesstimate**) estimate based on guesswork and calculation.

guffaw /gʌ'fɔː/ ● *noun* boisterous laugh. ● *verb* utter guffaw.

guidance /'gaɪd(ə)ns/ *noun* advice; guiding.

guide /gaɪd/ ● *noun* person who shows the way; conductor of tours; adviser; directing principle; guidebook; (**Guide**) member of girls' organization similar to Scouts. ● *verb* (**-ding**) act as guide to; lead, direct. □ **guidebook** book of information about place etc.; **guided missile** missile under remote control or directed by equipment within itself; **guide-dog** dog trained to lead blind person; **guideline** principle directing action.

Guider /'gaɪdə/ *noun* adult leader of Guides.

guild /gɪld/ *noun* (also **gild**) society for mutual aid or with common object; medieval association of craftsmen. □ **guildhall** meeting-place of medieval guild, town hall.

guilder /'gɪldə/ *noun* monetary unit of Netherlands.

guile /gaɪl/ *noun* sly behaviour; treachery, deceit. □ **guileless** *adjective*.

guillemot /'gɪlɪmɒt/ *noun* kind of auk.

guillotine /'gɪləti:n/ ● *noun* beheading machine; machine for cutting paper; method of shortening debate in parliament by fixing time of vote. ● *verb* (**-ning**) use guillotine on.

guilt /gɪlt/ *noun* fact of having committed offence; (feeling of) culpability.

guiltless *adjective* (often + *of*) innocent.

guilty *adjective* (**-ier, -iest**) having, feeling, or causing feeling of guilt. □ **guiltily** *adverb*.

guinea /'gɪnɪ/ *noun* (*historical*) coin worth? £1.05. □ **guinea fowl** domestic fowl with white-spotted grey plumage; **guinea pig** domesticated S. American rodent, person used in experiment.

guipure /'giːpjʊə/ *noun* heavy lace of patterned pieces joined by stitches.

guise /gaɪz/ *noun* external, esp. assumed, appearance; pretence.

guitar /gɪ'tɑː/ *noun* usually 6-stringed musical instrument played with fingers or plectrum. □ **guitarist** *noun*.

gulch *noun US* ravine, gully.

gulf *noun* large area of sea with narrow-mouthed inlet; deep hollow, chasm; wide difference of opinion etc. □ **Gulf Stream** warm current from Gulf of Mexico to Europe.

gull[1] *noun* long-winged web-footed seabird.

gull[2] *verb* dupe, fool.

gullet /'gʌlɪt/ *noun* food-passage from mouth to stomach.

gullible /'gʌlɪb(ə)l/ *adjective* easily persuaded or deceived. □ **gullibility** *noun*.

gully /'gʌlɪ/ *noun* (*plural* **-ies**) water-worn ravine; gutter, drain; *Cricket* fielding position between point and slips.

gulp ● *verb* (often + *down*) swallow hastily or with effort; choke; (+ *down*, *back*) suppress. ● *noun* act of gulping; large mouthful.

gum[1] ● *noun* sticky secretion of some trees and shrubs, used as glue etc.; chewing gum; (also **gum-drop**) hard jelly sweet. ● *verb* (**-mm-**) (usually + *down*, *together*, etc.) fasten with gum; apply gum to. □ **gum arabic** gum exuded by some kinds of acacia; **gumboot** rubber boot; **gum tree** tree exuding gum, esp. eucalyptus; **gum up** *colloquial* interfere with, spoil.

gum[2] *noun* (usually in *plural*) firm flesh around roots of teeth. □ **gumboil** small abscess on gum.

gummy[1] /'gʌmɪ/ *adjective* (**-ier, -iest**) sticky; exuding gum.

gummy[2] /'gʌmɪ/ *adjective* (**-ier, -iest**) toothless.

gumption /'gʌmpʃ(ə)n/ *noun colloquial* resourcefulness, enterprise; common sense.

gun ● *noun* metal tube for throwing missiles with explosive propellant; device for discharging grease, electrons, etc., in desired direction; member of shooting party. ● *verb* (**-nn-**) (usually + *down*) shoot with gun; (+ *for*) seek out determinedly to attack or rebuke. □ **gunboat** small warship with heavy guns; **gun carriage** wheeled support for gun; **gun cotton** cotton steeped in acids, used as explosive; **gun dog** dog trained to retrieve game; **gunfire** firing of guns; **gunman** armed lawbreaker; **gun metal** bluish-grey colour, alloy of copper, tin, and usually zinc; **gunpowder** explosive of saltpetre, sulphur, and charcoal; **gunrunner** person selling or bringing guns into country illegally; **gunshot** shot from gun, the range of a gun; **gunslinger** *esp. US* gunman; **gunsmith** maker and repairer of small firearms.

gunge /gʌndz/ *colloquial* ● *noun* sticky substance. ● *verb* (**-ging**) (usually + *up*) clog with gunge. □ **gungy** *adjective*.

gung-ho /gʌŋ'həʊ/ *adjective* (arrogantly) eager.

gunner /'gʌnə/ *noun* artillery soldier; *Nautical* warrant officer in charge of battery, magazine, etc.; airman who operates gun.

gunnery /'gʌnərɪ/ *noun* construction and management, or firing, of large guns.

gunny /'gʌnɪ/ *noun* (*plural* **-ies**) coarse sacking usually of jute fibre; sack made of this.

gunwale /'gʌn(ə)l/ *noun* upper edge of ship's or boat's side.

guppy /'gʌpɪ/ *noun* (*plural* **-ies**) very small brightly coloured tropical freshwater fish.

gurgle /'gɜːg(ə)l/ ● *verb* (**-ling**) make bubbling sound as of water; utter with such sound. ● *noun* bubbling sound.

gurnard /'gɜːnəd/ *noun* (*plural* same or **-s**) sea fish with large spiny head.

guru /'gʊruː/ *noun* (*plural* **-s**) Hindu spiritual teacher; influential or revered teacher.

gush ● *verb* flow in sudden or copious stream; speak or behave effusively. ● *noun* sudden or copious stream; effusiveness.

gusher /'gʌʃə/ *noun* oil well emitting unpumped oil; effusive person.

gusset /'gʌsɪt/ *noun* piece let into garment etc. to strengthen or enlarge it.

gust ● *noun* sudden violent rush of wind; burst of rain, smoke, anger, etc. ● *verb* blow in gusts. □ **gusty** *adjective* (**-ier, -iest**).

gusto /'gʌstəʊ/ *noun* zest, enjoyment.

gut ● *noun* intestine; (in *plural*) bowels, entrails; (in *plural*) *colloquial* courage and determination; *slang* stomach; (in *plural*) contents, essence; material for violin etc. strings or for fishing line; instinctive, fundamental. ● *verb* (**-tt-**) remove or destroy internal fittings of (buildings); remove guts of. □ **gutless** *adjective*.

gutsy /'gʌtsɪ/ *adjective* (**-ier, iest**) *colloquial* courageous; greedy.

gutta-percha /gʌtə'pɜːtʃə/ *noun* tough plastic substance made from latex.

gutted *adjective* *slang* bitterly disappointed.

gutter /'gʌtə/ ● *noun* shallow trough below eaves, or channel at side of street, for carrying off rainwater; **(the gutter)** poor or degraded environment; channel, groove. ● *verb* (of candle) burn unsteadily and melt away.

guttering *noun* (material for) gutters.

guttersnipe *noun* street urchin.

guttural /'gʌtər(ə)l/ ● *adjective* throaty, harsh-sounding; (of sound) produced in throat. ● *noun* guttural consonant.

guy[1] /gaɪ/ ● *noun* *colloquial* man; effigy of Guy Fawkes burnt on 5 Nov. ● *verb* ridicule.

guy[2] /gaɪ/ ● *noun* rope or chain to secure tent or steady crane-load etc. ● *verb* secure with guy(s).

guzzle /'gʌz(ə)l/ *verb* (**-ling**) eat or drink greedily.

gybe /dʒaɪb/ *verb* (*US* **jibe**) (of fore-and-aft sail or boom) swing across boat, momentarily pointing into wind; cause (sail) to do this; (of boat etc.) change course thus.

gym /dʒɪm/ *noun* *colloquial* gymnasium; gymnastics. □ **gymslip, gym tunic** schoolgirl's sleeveless dress.

gymkhana /dʒɪm'kɑːnə/ *noun* horse-riding competition.

gymnasium /dʒɪm'neɪzɪəm/ *noun* (*plural* **-siums** or **-sia**) room etc. equipped for gymnastics.

gymnast /'dʒɪmnæst/ *noun* expert in gymnastics.

gymnastic /dʒɪm'næstɪk/ *adjective* of gymnastics. □ **gymnastically** *adverb*.

gymnastics *plural noun* (also treated as *singular*) exercises to develop or demonstrate physical (or mental) agility.

gynaecology /gaɪnɪ'kɒlədʒɪ/ *noun* (*US* **gynecology**) science of physiological functions and diseases of women. □ **gynaecological** /-kə'lɒdʒ-/ *adjective*; **gynaecologist** *noun*.

gypsum /'dʒɪpsəm/ *noun* mineral used esp. to make plaster of Paris.

Gypsy /'dʒɪpsɪ/ *noun* (also **Gipsy**) (*plural* **-ies**) member of nomadic dark-skinned people of Europe.

gyrate /dʒaɪə'reɪt/ *verb* (**-ting**) move in circle or spiral. □ **gyration** *noun*; **gyratory** *adjective*.

gyro /'dʒaɪərəʊ/ *noun* (*plural* **-s**) *colloquial* gyroscope.

gyroscope /'dʒaɪərəskəʊp/ *noun* rotating wheel whose axis is free to turn but maintains fixed direction unless perturbed, esp. used for stabilization.

Hh

H *abbreviation* hard (pencil lead); (water) hydrant; *slang* heroin. □ **H-bomb** hydrogen bomb.

h. *abbreviation* (also **h**) hour(s); (also *h*) height; hot. □ **h. & c.** hot and cold (water).

ha¹ /hɑː/ (also **hah**) *interjection expressing surprise, triumph, etc.*

ha² *abbreviation* hectare(s).

habeas corpus /ˌheɪbɪəs ˈkɔːpəs/ *noun* writ requiring person to be brought before judge etc., esp. to investigate lawfulness of his or her detention.

haberdasher /ˈhæbədæʃə/ *noun* dealer in dress accessories and sewing goods. □ **haberdashery** *noun* (*plural* **-ies**).

habit /ˈhæbɪt/ *noun* settled tendency or practice; practice that is hard to give up; mental constitution or attitude; clothes, esp. of religious order.

habitable /ˈhæbɪtəb(ə)l/ *adjective* suitable for living in. □ **habitability** *noun*.

habitat /ˈhæbɪtæt/ *noun* natural home of plant or animal.

habitation /hæbɪˈteɪʃ(ə)n/ *noun* inhabiting; house, home.

habitual /həˈbɪtʃʊəl/ *adjective* done as a habit; usual; given to a habit. □ **habitually** *adverb*.

habituate /həˈbɪtʃʊeɪt/ *verb* (**-ting**) (often + *to*) accustom. □ **habituation** *noun*.

habitué /həˈbɪtʃʊeɪ/ *noun* (often + *of*) frequent visitor or resident. [French]

háček /ˈhætʃek/ *noun* mark used (ˇ) over letter to modify its sound in some languages. [Czech]

hacienda /hæsɪˈendə/ *noun* (in Spanish-speaking countries) plantation etc. with dwelling house.

hack¹ ● *verb* cut or chop roughly; kick shin of; (often + *at*) deal cutting blows; cut (one's way) through; *colloquial* gain unauthorized access to (computer data); *slang* manage, tolerate. ● *noun* kick with toe of boot, wound from this. □ **hacksaw** saw for cutting metal.

hack² ● *noun* horse for ordinary riding; hired horse; person hired to do dull routine work, esp. as writer. ● *adjective* used as hack; commonplace. ● *verb* ride on horseback on road at ordinary pace.

hacker *noun colloquial* computer enthusiast; person who gains unauthorized access to computer network.

hacking *adjective* (of cough) short, dry, and frequent.

hackle /ˈhæk(ə)l/ *noun* (in *plural*) hairs on animal's neck which rise when it is angry or alarmed; long feather(s) on neck of domestic cock etc.; steel flax-comb. □ **make (person's) hackles rise** arouse anger or indignation.

hackney /ˈhæknɪ/ *noun* (*plural* **-s**) horse for ordinary riding. □ **hackney carriage** taxi.

hackneyed /ˈhæknɪd/ *adjective* overused, trite.

had *past & past participle* of HAVE.

haddock /ˈhædək/ *noun* (*plural* same) common edible sea fish.

Hades /ˈheɪdiːz/ *noun* (in Greek mythology) the underworld.

hadj = HAJJ.

hadji = HAJJI.

hadn't /ˈhæd(ə)nt/ had not.

haematite /ˈhiːmətaɪt/ *noun* (US **hem-**) red or brown iron ore.

haematology /hiːməˈtɒlədʒɪ/ *noun* (US **hem-**) study of the blood. □ **haematologist** *noun*.

haemoglobin /hiːməˈɡləʊbɪn/ *noun* (US **hem-**) oxygen-carrying substance in red blood cells.

haemophilia /hiːməˈfɪlɪə/ *noun* (US **hem-**) hereditary tendency to severe bleeding from even a slight injury through failure of blood to clot. □ **haemophiliac** *noun*.

haemorrhage /ˈhemərɪdʒ/ (US **hem-**) ● *noun* profuse bleeding. ● *verb* (**-ging**) suffer haemorrhage.

haemorrhoids /ˈhemərɔɪdz/ *plural noun* (US **hem-**) swollen veins near anus, piles.

haft /hɑːft/ *noun* handle of knife etc.

hag *noun* ugly old woman; witch. □ **hagridden** afflicted by nightmares or fears.

haggard /ˈhægəd/ *adjective* looking exhausted and distraught.

haggis /ˈhæɡɪs/ *noun* Scottish dish of offal boiled in bag with oatmeal etc.

haggle /ˈhæɡ(ə)l/ ● *verb* (**-ling**) (often + *over, about*) bargain persistently. ● *noun* haggling.

hagiography /hæɡɪˈɒɡrəfɪ/ *noun* writing about saints' lives. □ **hagiographer** *noun*.

hah = HA¹.

ha ha /hɑːˈhɑː/ *interjection representing laughter.*

ha-ha /ˈhɑːhɑː/ *noun* ditch with wall in it bounding park or garden.

haiku /ˈhaɪkuː/ *noun* (*plural* same) Japanese 3-line poem of usually 17 syllables.

hail¹ ● *noun* pellets of frozen rain; (+ *of*) barrage, onslaught. ● *verb* (after *it*) hail falls; pour down as or like hail. □ **hailstone** pellet of hail; **hailstorm** period of heavy hail.

hail² ● *verb* signal (taxi etc.) to stop; greet enthusiastically; (+ *from*) originate. ● *interjection archaic or jocular: expressing greeting.* ● *noun* act of hailing.

hair *noun* any or all of fine filaments growing from skin of mammals, esp. of human head; hairlike thing. □ **haircut** (style of) cutting hair; **hairdo** style of or act of styling hair; **hairdresser** person who cuts and styles hair; **hairdressing** *noun*; **hair-drier, -dryer** device for drying hair with warm air; **hairgrip** flat hairpin with ends close together; **hairline** edge of person's hair on forehead, very narrow crack or line; **hairnet** piece of netting for confining hair; **hair of the dog** further alcoholic drink taken to cure effects of previous drinking; **hairpiece** false hair augmenting person's natural hair; **hairpin** U-shaped pin for fastening the hair; **hairpin bend** U-shaped bend in road; **hair-raising** terrifying; **hair's breadth** minute distance; **hair shirt** ascetic's or penitent's shirt made of hair; **hair-slide** clip for keeping hair in position; **hair-splitting** quibbling; **hairspray** liquid sprayed on hair to keep it in place; **hairspring** fine spring regulating balance-wheel of watch; **hairstyle** particular way of arranging hair; **hairstylist** *noun*; **hair-trigger** trigger acting on very slight pressure. □ **hairless** *adjective*; **hairy** *adjective* (**-ier, -iest**).

hajj /hædʒ/ *noun* (also **hadj**) Islamic pilgrimage to Mecca.

hajji /ˈhædʒɪ/ *noun* (also **hadji**) (*plural* **-s**) Muslim who has made pilgrimage to Mecca.

haka /ˈhɑːkə/ *noun NZ* Maori ceremonial war dance; similar dance by sports team before match.

hake *noun* (*plural* same) codlike sea fish.

halal /haː'laːl/ noun (also **hallal**) meat from animal killed according to Muslim law.

halberd /'hælbəd/ noun historical combined spear and battleaxe.

halcyon /'hælsɪən/ adjective calm, peaceful, happy.

hale adjective strong and healthy (esp. in **hale and hearty**).

half /haːf/ ● noun (plural **halves** /haːvz/) either of two (esp. equal) parts into which a thing is divided; colloquial half pint, esp. of beer; Sport either of two equal periods of play, half-back; half-price (esp. child's) ticket. ● adjective forming a half. ● adverb partly. □ **half and half** being half one thing and half another; **half-back** player between forwards and full back(s) in football etc.; **half-baked** not thoroughly thought out; **half board** provision of bed, breakfast, and one main meal; **half-brother, -sister** one having only one parent in common; **half-crown** historical coin worth 2 shillings and 6 pence (= 12½p); **half-dozen** (about) six; **half-hearted** lacking courage or zeal; **half-heartedly** adverb; **half holiday** half day as holiday; **half-hour, half an hour** 30 minutes, point of time 30 minutes after any hour o'clock; **half-hourly** adjective & adverb; **half-life** time after which radioactivity etc. is half its original value; **half-mast** position of flag halfway down mast as symbol of mourning; **half measures** unsatisfactory compromise etc.; **half-moon** (shape of) moon with disc half illuminated; **half nelson** see NELSON; **half-term** short holiday halfway through school term; **half-timbered** having walls with timber frame and brick or plaster filling; **half-time** (short break at) midpoint of game or contest; **halftone** photograph representing tones by large or small dots; **half-truth** statement that conveys only part of truth; **half-volley** playing of ball as soon as it bounces off ground; **halfwit** stupid person; **halfwitted** adjective.

halfpenny /'heɪpnɪ/ noun (plural **-pennies** or **-pence** /'heɪpəns/) historical coin worth half penny (withdrawn in 1984).

halfway ● adverb at a point midway between two others; to some extent. ● adjective situated halfway. □ **halfway house** compromise, halfway point, rehabilitation centre, inn etc. between two towns.

halibut /'hælɪbət/ noun (plural same) large flatfish.

halitosis /hælɪ'təʊsɪs/ noun bad breath.

hall /hɔːl/ noun entrance area of house; large room or building for meetings, concerts, etc.; large country house or estate; (in full **hall of residence**) residence for students; college dining-room; large public room; esp. US corridor. □ **hallmark** mark used to show standard of gold, silver, and platinum, distinctive feature; **hallway** entrance hall or corridor.

hallal = HALAL.

hallelujah = ALLELUIA.

hallo = HELLO.

hallow /'hæləʊ/ verb (usually as **hallowed** adjective) make or honour as holy.

Hallowe'en /hæləʊ'iːn/ noun eve of All Saints' Day, 31 Oct.

hallucinate /hə'luːsɪneɪt/ verb (**-ting**) experience hallucinations.

hallucination noun illusion of seeing or hearing something not actually present. □ **hallucinatory** /hə'luːsɪnətərɪ/ adjective.

hallucinogen /hə'luːsɪnədʒ(ə)n/ noun drug causing hallucinations. □ **hallucinogenic** /-'dʒen-/ adjective.

halm = HAULM.

halo /'heɪləʊ/ ● noun (plural **-es**) disc of light shown round head of sacred person; glory associated with idealized person; circle of light round sun or moon etc. ● verb (**-es, -ed**) surround with halo.

halogen /'hælədʒ(ə)n/ noun any of the non-metallic elements (fluorine, chlorine, etc.) which form a salt when combined with a metal.

halon /'heɪlɒn/ noun gaseous halogen compound used to extinguish fires.

halt¹ /hɔːlt/ ● noun stop (usually temporary); minor stopping place on local railway line. ● verb (cause to) make a halt.

halt² /hɔːlt/ ● verb (esp. as **halting** adjective) proceed hesitantly. □ **haltingly** adverb.

halter /'hɔːltə/ noun rope with headstall for leading or tying up horses etc.; strap passing round back of neck holding dress etc. up, (also **halterneck**) dress etc. held by this.

halva /'hælvə/ noun confection of sesame flour, honey, etc.

halve /haːv/ verb (**-ving**) divide into halves; reduce to half.

halves plural of HALF.

halyard /'hæljəd/ noun rope or tackle for raising and lowering sail etc.

ham ● noun upper part of pig's leg cured for food; back of thigh; thigh and buttock; colloquial inexpert or unsubtle performer or actor; colloquial operator of amateur radio station. ● verb (**-mm-**) (usually in **ham it up**) colloquial overact. □ **ham-fisted, -handed** colloquial clumsy.

hamburger /'hæmbɜːgə/ noun cake of minced beef, usually eaten in soft bread roll.

hamlet /'hæmlɪt/ noun small village, esp. without church.

hammer /'hæmə/ ● noun tool with heavy metal head at right angles to handle, used for driving nails etc.; similar device, as for exploding charge in gun, striking strings of piano, etc.; auctioneer's mallet; metal ball attached to a wire for throwing as athletic contest. ● verb strike or drive (as) with hammer; colloquial defeat utterly. □ **hammer and tongs** colloquial with great energy; **hammerhead** shark with flattened hammer-shaped head; **hammerlock** wrestling hold in which twisted arm is bent behind back; **hammer-toe** toe bent permanently downwards. □ **hammering** noun.

hammock /'hæmək/ noun bed of canvas or netting suspended by cords at ends.

hamper¹ /'hæmpə/ noun large basket, usually with hinged lid and containing food.

hamper² /'hæmpə/ verb obstruct movement of; hinder.

hamster /'hæmstə/ noun short-tailed mouselike rodent often kept as pet.

hamstring ● noun any of 5 tendons at back of human knee; (in quadruped) tendon at back of hock. ● verb (past & past participle **-strung** or **-stringed**) cripple by cutting hamstrings; impair efficiency of.

hand ● noun end part of human arm beyond wrist; similar member of monkey; (often in plural) control, disposal, agency; share in action, active support; handlike thing, esp. pointer of clock etc.; right or left side, direction, etc.; skill or style, esp. of writing; person who does or makes something; person etc. as source; manual worker in factory etc.; pledge of marriage; playing cards dealt to player, round or game of cards; colloquial round of applause; measure of horse's height, = 4 in. (10.16 cm). ● verb (+ in, to, over, round, etc.) deliver or transfer (as) with hand. □ **at hand** close by; **by hand** by person not machine, not by post; **handbag** small bag carried esp. by woman; **handball** game with ball thrown by hand, Football foul touching of ball; **handbell** small bell for ringing by hand; **handbook** short manual or guidebook; **handbrake** brake operated by hand; **handcuff** secure (prisoner) with **handcuffs**, pair of lockable metal rings joined by short chain; **handgun** small firearm held in one hand; **handhold** something for hand to grip; **hand in glove** in collusion; **handmade** made by hand (rather than machine); **hand-me-down** article passed on from another person; **handout** thing given to needy person, information etc. distributed to press etc., notes given out in class; **handover** act of handing over; **hand-over-fist** colloquial with rapid progress; **hand-picked** carefully chosen; **handrail** rail along edge of stairs etc.; **hands down** without effort; **handset** part of telephone held in hand; **handshake** clasping of person's hand, esp. as greeting etc.; **hands-on** practical rather than theoretical; **handstand** act of supporting oneself vertically on one's hands; **hand-to-hand** (of fighting) at close quarters; **handwriting** (style of) writing by hand; **take in hand** start doing or dealing with, undertake control or reform of; **to hand** within reach.

handful noun (plural **-s**) enough to fill the hand; small number or quantity; colloquial troublesome person or task.

handicap /ˈhændɪkæp/ ● noun physical or mental disability; thing that makes progress difficult; disadvantage imposed on superior competitor to equalize chances; race etc. in which this is imposed. ● verb (**-pp-**) impose handicap on; place at disadvantage.

handicapped adjective suffering from physical or mental disability.

handicraft /ˈhændɪkrɑːft/ noun work requiring manual and artistic skill.

handiwork /ˈhændɪwɜːk/ noun work done or thing made by hand, or by particular person.

handkerchief /ˈhæŋkətʃɪf/ noun (plural **-s** or **-chieves** /-tʃiːvz/) square of cloth used to wipe nose etc.

handle /ˈhænd(ə)l/ ● noun part by which thing is held. ● verb (**-ling**) touch, feel, operate, etc. with hands; manage, deal with; deal in (goods etc.). □ **handlebar** (usually in plural) steering-bar of bicycle etc.

handler noun person in charge of trained dog etc.

handsome /ˈhænsəm/ adjective (**-r**, **-st**) good-looking; imposing; generous; considerable. □ **handsomely** adverb.

handy adjective (**-ier**, **-iest**) convenient to handle; ready to hand; clever with hands. □ **handyman** person able to do odd jobs.

hang ● verb (past & past participle **hung** except as below) (cause to) be supported from above, attach by suspending from top; set up on hinges etc.; place (picture) on wall or in exhibition; attach (wallpaper); (past & past participle **hanged**) suspend or be suspended by neck, esp. as capital punishment; let droop; remain or be hung. ● noun way thing hangs. □ **get the hang of** colloquial get knack of, understand; **hang about**, **around** loiter, not move away; **hangdog** shamefaced; **hang fire** delay acting; **hang-glider** fabric wing on light frame from which pilot is suspended; **hang-gliding** noun; **hangman** executioner by hanging; **hangnail** agnail; **hang on** (often + to) continue to hold, retain, wait for short time; not ring off during pause in telephoning; **hangover** after-effects of excess of alcohol; **hang up** verb hang from hook etc., end telephone conversation; **hang-up** noun slang emotional inhibition.

hangar /ˈhæŋə/ noun building for housing aircraft etc.

hanger noun person or thing that hangs; (in full **coat-hanger**) shaped piece of wood etc. for hanging clothes on. □ **hanger-on** (plural **hangers-on**) follower, dependant.

hanging noun execution by suspending by neck; (usually in plural) drapery for walls etc.

hank noun coil of yarn etc.

hanker /ˈhæŋkə/ verb (+ for, after, to do) crave, long for. □ **hankering** noun.

hanky /ˈhæŋkɪ/ noun (also **hankie**) (plural **-ies**) colloquial handkerchief.

hanky-panky /ˌhæŋkɪˈpæŋkɪ/ noun slang misbehaviour; trickery.

Hansard /ˈhænsɑːd/ noun verbatim record of parliamentary debates.

hansom /ˈhænsəm/ noun (in full **hansom cab**) historical two-wheeled horse-drawn cab.

haphazard /hæpˈhæzəd/ adjective casual, random. □ **haphazardly** adverb.

hapless /ˈhæplɪs/ adjective unlucky.

happen /ˈhæpən/ verb occur; (+ to do) have the (good or bad) fortune; (+ to) be fate or experience of; (+ on) come by chance on. □ **happening** noun.

happy /ˈhæpɪ/ adjective (**-ier**, **-iest**) feeling or showing pleasure or contentment; fortunate; apt, pleasing. □ **happy-go-lucky** taking things cheerfully as they happen; **happy hour** time of day when drinks are sold at reduced prices; **happy medium** compromise. □ **happily** adverb; **happiness** noun.

hara-kiri /ˌhærəˈkɪrɪ/ noun historical Japanese suicide by ritual disembowelling.

harangue /həˈræŋ/ ● noun lengthy and earnest speech. ● verb (**-guing**) make harangue to.

harass /ˈhærəs/ verb trouble, annoy; attack repeatedly. □ **harassment** noun.

■ **Usage** Harass is often pronounced /həˈræs/ (with the stress on the -rass), but this is considered incorrect by some people.

harbinger /ˈhɑːbɪndʒə/ noun person or thing announcing another's approach, forerunner.

harbour /ˈhɑːbə/ (US **harbor**) ● noun place of shelter for ships; shelter. ● verb give shelter to; entertain (thoughts etc.).

hard ● adjective firm, solid; difficult to bear, do, or understand; unfeeling, harsh, severe; strenuous, enthusiastic; Politics extreme, radical; (of drinks) strongly alcoholic; (of drug) potent and addictive; (of water) difficult to lather; (of currency etc.) not likely to fall in value; not disputable. ● adverb strenuously, severely, intensely. □ **hard and fast** (of rule etc.) strict; **hardback** (book) bound in stiff covers; **hardbitten** colloquial tough, cynical; **hardboard** stiff board of compressed wood pulp; **hard-boiled** (of eggs) boiled until yolk and white are solid, (of person) tough, shrewd; **hard cash** coins and banknotes, not cheques etc.; **hard copy** printed material produced by computer; **hardcore** stones, rubble, etc. as foundation; **hard core** central or most enduring part; **hard disk** Computing rigid storage disk, esp. fixed in computer; **hard-done-by** unfairly treated; **hard-headed** practical, not sentimental; **hard-hearted** unfeeling; **hard line** firm adherence to policy; **hardliner** noun; **hard-nosed** colloquial realistic, uncompromising; **hard of hearing** somewhat deaf; **hard-pressed** closely pursued, burdened with urgent business; **hard sell** aggressive salesmanship; **hard shoulder** strip at side of motorway for emergency stops; **hard up** short of money; **hardware** tools, weapons, machinery, etc., mechanical and electronic components of computer; **hardwood** wood of deciduous tree. □ **hardness** noun.

harden verb make or become hard or unyielding.

hardihood /ˈhɑːdɪhʊd/ noun boldness.

hardly adverb scarcely; with difficulty.

hardship noun severe suffering or privation.

hardy /ˈhɑːdɪ/ adjective (**-ier**, **-iest**) robust; capable of endurance; (of plant) able to grow in the open all year. □ **hardiness** noun.

hare /heə/ ● *noun* mammal like large rabbit, with long ears, short tail, and long hind legs. ● *verb* (**-ring**) run rapidly. □ **hare-brained** rash, wild.

harebell *noun* plant with pale blue bell-shaped flowers.

harem /'hɑːriːm/ *noun* women of Muslim household; their quarters.

haricot /'hærɪkəʊ/ *noun* (in full **haricot bean**) French bean with small white seeds; these as vegetable.

hark *verb* (usually in *imperative*) *archaic* listen. □ **hark back** revert to earlier topic.

Harlequin /'hɑːlɪkwɪn/ ● *noun* masked pantomime character in diamond-patterned costume. ● *adjective* (**harlequin**) in varied colours.

harlot /'hɑːlət/ *noun archaic* prostitute.

harm *noun & verb* damage, hurt.

harmful *adjective* causing or likely to cause harm. □ **harmfully** *adverb*.

harmless *adjective* not able or likely to harm. □ **harmlessly** *adverb*.

harmonic /hɑː'mɒnɪk/ ● *adjective* of or relating to harmony; harmonious. ● *noun Music* overtone accompanying (and forming a note with) a fundamental at a fixed interval.

harmonica /hɑː'mɒnɪkə/ *noun* small rectangular instrument played by blowing and sucking air through it.

harmonious /hɑː'məʊnɪəs/ *adjective* sweet-sounding, tuneful; forming a pleasant or consistent whole; free from dissent. □ **harmoniously** *adverb*.

harmonium /hɑː'məʊnɪəm/ *noun* keyboard instrument with bellows and metal reeds.

harmonize /'hɑːmənaɪz/ *verb* (also **-ise**) (**-zing** or **-sing**) add notes to (melody) to produce harmony; bring into or be in harmony. □ **harmonization** *noun*.

harmony /'hɑːmənɪ/ *noun* (*plural* **-ies**) combination of notes to form chords; melodious sound; agreement, concord.

harness /'hɑːnɪs/ ● *noun* straps etc. by which horse is fastened to cart etc. and controlled; similar arrangement for fastening thing to person. ● *verb* put harness on; utilize (natural forces), esp. to produce energy.

harp ● *noun* large upright stringed instrument plucked with fingers. ● *verb* (+ *on*, *on about*) dwell on tediously. □ **harpist** *noun*.

harpoon /hɑː'puːn/ ● *noun* spearlike missile for shooting whales etc. ● *verb* spear with harpoon.

harpsichord /'hɑːpsɪkɔːd/ *noun* keyboard instrument with strings plucked mechanically. □ **harpsichordist** *noun*.

harpy /'hɑːpɪ/ *noun* (*plural* **-ies**) mythological monster with woman's face and bird's wings and claws; grasping unscrupulous person.

harridan /'hærɪd(ə)n/ *noun* bad-tempered old woman.

harrier /'hærɪə/ *noun* hound used in hunting hares; kind of falcon.

harrow /'hærəʊ/ ● *noun* frame with metal teeth or discs for breaking clods of earth. ● *verb* draw harrow over; (usually as **harrowing** *adjective*) distress greatly.

harry /'hærɪ/ *verb* (**-ies**, **-ied**) ravage, despoil; harass.

harsh *adjective* rough to hear, taste, etc.; severe, cruel. □ **harshly** *adverb*; **harshness** *noun*.

hart *noun* (*plural* same or **-s**) male of (esp. red) deer.

hartebeest /'hɑːtɪbiːst/ *noun* large African antelope with curved horns.

harum-scarum /heərəm'skeərəm/ *adjective colloquial* reckless, wild.

harvest /'hɑːvɪst/ ● *noun* gathering in of crops etc.; season for this; season's yield; product of any action. ● *verb* reap and gather in.

harvester *noun* reaper, reaping machine.

has *3rd singular present of* HAVE.

hash[1] ● *noun* dish of reheated pieces of cooked meat; mixture, jumble; recycled material. ● *verb* (often + *up*) recycle (old material). □ **make a hash of** *colloquial* make a mess of, bungle.

hash[2] *noun colloquial* hashish.

hashish /'hæʃɪʃ/ *noun* narcotic drug got from hemp.

hasn't /'hæz(ə)nt/ has not.

hasp /hɑːsp/ *noun* hinged metal clasp passing over staple and secured by padlock.

hassle /'hæs(ə)l/ *colloquial* ● *noun* trouble, problem; argument. ● *verb* (**-ling**) harass.

hassock /'hæsək/ *noun* kneeling-cushion.

haste /heɪst/ *noun* urgency of movement; hurry. □ **make haste** be quick.

hasten /'heɪs(ə)n/ *verb* (cause to) proceed or go quickly.

hasty /'heɪstɪ/ *adjective* (**-ier**, **-iest**) hurried; said, made, or done too quickly. □ **hastily** *adverb*; **hastiness** *noun*.

hat *noun* (esp. outdoor) head-covering. □ **hat trick** *Cricket* taking 3 wickets with successive balls, *Football* scoring of 3 goals in one match by same player, 3 consecutive successes.

hatch[1] *noun* opening in wall between kitchen and dining-room for serving food; opening or door in aircraft etc.; (cover for) hatchway. □ **hatchback** car with rear door hinged at top; **hatchway** opening in ship's deck for lowering cargo.

hatch[2] ● *verb* (often + *out*) emerge from egg; (of egg) produce young animal; incubate; (also + *up*) devise (plot). ● *noun* hatching; brood hatched.

hatch[3] *verb* mark with parallel lines. □ **hatching** *noun*.

hatchet /'hætʃɪt/ *noun* light short axe.

hate ● *verb* (**-ting**) dislike intensely. ● *noun* hatred.

hateful *adjective* arousing hatred.

hatred /'heɪtrɪd/ *noun* intense dislike; ill will.

hatter *noun* maker or seller of hats.

haughty /'hɔːtɪ/ *adjective* (**-ier**, **-iest**) proud, arrogant. □ **haughtily** *adverb*; **haughtiness** *noun*.

haul /hɔːl/ ● *verb* pull or drag forcibly; transport by lorry, cart, etc. ● *noun* hauling; amount gained or acquired; distance to be traversed.

haulage *noun* (charge for) commercial transport of goods.

haulier /'hɔːlɪə/ *noun* person or firm engaged in transport of goods.

haulm /hɔːm/ *noun* (also **halm**) stalk or stem; stalks of beans, peas, potatoes, etc. collectively.

haunch /hɔːntʃ/ *noun* fleshy part of buttock and thigh; leg and loin of deer etc. as food.

haunt /hɔːnt/ ● *verb* (of ghost etc.) visit regularly; frequent (place); linger in mind of. ● *noun* place frequented by person.

haunting *adjective* (of memory, melody, etc.) lingering; poignant, evocative.

haute couture /əʊt kuːˈtjʊə/ *noun* (world of) high fashion.

hauteur /əʊ'tɜː/ *noun* haughtiness.

have /hæv/ ● *verb* (**having**; *3rd singular present* **has** /hæz/; *past & past participle* **had**) *used as auxiliary verb with past participle to form past tenses*; hold in possession or relationship; be provided with; contain as part or quality; experience; (come to) be subjected to a specified state; engage in; tolerate, permit to; give birth to; receive; obtain or know (qualification, language, etc.); *colloquial* get the better of, (usually in *passive*) cheat. ● *noun* (usually in *plural*) *colloquial* wealthy person; *slang* swindle. □ **have on** wear (clothes),

have (engagement), *colloquial* hoax; **have-not** (usually in *plural*) person lacking wealth; **have to** be obliged to, must.

haven /ˈheɪv(ə)n/ *noun* refuge; harbour.

haven't /ˈhæv(ə)nt/ have not.

haver /ˈheɪvə/ *verb* hesitate; talk foolishly.

haversack /ˈhævəsæk/ *noun* canvas bag carried on back or over shoulder.

havoc /ˈhævək/ *noun* devastation, confusion.

haw *noun* hawthorn berry.

hawk¹ ● *noun* bird of prey with rounded wings; *Politics* person who advocates aggressive policy. ● *verb* hunt with hawk.

hawk² *verb* carry (goods) about for sale.

hawk³ *verb* clear throat noisily; (+ *up*) bring (phlegm etc.) up thus.

hawker *noun* person who hawks goods.

hawser /ˈhɔːzə/ *noun* thick rope or cable for mooring ship.

hawthorn *noun* thorny shrub with red berries.

hay *noun* grass mown and dried for fodder. □ **haycock** conical heap of hay; **hay fever** allergic irritation of nose, throat, etc. caused by pollen, dust, etc.; **haymaking** mowing grass and spreading it to dry; **hayrick**, **haystack** packed pile of hay; **haywire** *colloquial* badly disorganized, out of control.

hazard /ˈhæzəd/ ● *noun* danger, risk; obstacle on golf course. ● *verb* venture on (guess etc.); risk.

hazardous *adjective* risky.

haze *noun* slight mist; mental obscurity, confusion.

hazel /ˈheɪz(ə)l/ *noun* nut-bearing hedgerow shrub; greenish-brown. □ **hazelnut** nut of hazel.

hazy *adjective* (**-ier**, **-iest**) misty; vague; confused. □ **hazily** *adverb*; **haziness** *noun*.

HB *abbreviation* hard black (pencil lead).

HE *abbreviation* His or Her Excellency; high explosive.

he /hiː/ *pronoun* (as subject of verb) the male person or animal in question; person of unspecified sex. □ **he-man** masterful or virile man.

head /hed/ ● *noun* uppermost part of human body, or foremost part of body of animal, containing brain, sense organs, etc.; seat of intellect; thing like head in form or position; top, front, or upper end; person in charge, esp. of school; position of command; individual as unit; side of coin bearing image of head, (in *plural*) this as call when tossing coin; signal-converting device on tape recorder etc.; foam on top of beer etc.; confined body of water or steam, pressure exerted by this; (usually in **come to a head**) climax, crisis. ● *verb* be at front or in charge of; (often + *for*) move or send in specified direction; provide with heading; *Football* strike (ball) with head. □ **headache** continuous pain in head, *colloquial* troublesome problem; **headachy** *adjective*; **headband** band worn round head as decoration or to confine hair; **headboard** upright panel at head of bed; **headcount** (counting of) total number of people; **headdress** (esp. ornamental) covering for head; **head-hunting** collecting of enemies' heads as trophies, seeking of staff by approaching people employed elsewhere; **headlamp**, **headlight** (main) light at front of vehicle; **headland** promontory; **headline** heading at top of page, newspaper article, etc., (in *plural*) summary of broadcast news; **headlock** wrestling hold round opponent's head; **headlong** with head foremost, in a rush; **headman** tribal chief; **headmaster**, **headmistress** head teacher; **head-on** (of collision etc.) with front foremost; **headphones** pair of earphones fitting over head; **headquarters** (treated as *singular* or *plural*) organization's administrative centre; **headroom** overhead space;

headset headphones, often with microphone; **headshrinker** *slang* psychiatrist; **headstall** part of bridle or halter fitting round horse's head; **head start** advantage granted or gained at early stage; **headstone** stone set up at head of grave; **headstrong** self-willed; **head teacher** teacher in charge of school; **headway** progress; **head wind** one blowing from directly in front.

header *noun* *Football* act of heading ball; *colloquial* headlong dive or plunge.

heading *noun* title at head of page etc.

heady *adjective* (**-ier**, **-iest**) (of liquor etc.) potent; exciting, intoxicating; impetuous; headachy.

heal *verb* (often + *up*) become healthy again; cure; put right (differences). □ **healer** *noun*.

health /helθ/ *noun* state of being well in body or mind; mental or physical condition. □ **health centre** building containing local medical services; **health food** natural food, thought to promote good health; **health service** public medical service; **health visitor** nurse who visits mothers and babies, the elderly, etc. at home.

healthy *adjective* (**-ier**, **-iest**) having, conducive to, or indicative of, good health. □ **healthily** *adverb*; **healthiness** *noun*.

heap ● *noun* disorderly pile; (esp. in *plural*) *colloquial* large number or amount; *slang* dilapidated vehicle. ● *verb* (+ *up*, *together*, etc.) pile or collect in heap; (+ *with*) load copiously with; (+ *on*, *upon*) offer copiously.

hear *verb* (*past & past participle* **heard** /hɜːd/) perceive with ear; listen to; listen judicially to; be informed; (+ *from*) receive message etc. from. □ **hearsay** rumour, gossip. □ **hearer** *noun*.

hearing *noun* faculty of perceiving sounds; range within which sounds may be heard; opportunity to state one's case; trial of case before court. □ **hearing-aid** small sound-amplifier worn by partially deaf person.

hearse /hɜːs/ *noun* vehicle for carrying coffin.

heart /hɑːt/ *noun* organ in body keeping up circulation of blood by contraction and dilation; region of heart, breast; seat of thought, feeling, or emotion (esp. love); courage; mood; central or innermost part, essence; tender inner part of vegetable etc.; (conventionally) heart-shaped thing; playing card of suit marked with red hearts. □ **at heart** in inmost feelings; **by heart** from memory; **have the heart** (usually in negative, + *to do*) be hard-hearted enough; **heartache** mental anguish; **heart attack** sudden heart failure; **heartbeat** pulsation of heart; **heartbreak** overwhelming distress; **heartbreaking** *adjective*; **heartbroken** *adjective*; **heartburn** burning sensation in chest from indigestion; **heartfelt** sincere; **heart-rending** very distressing; **heartsick** despondent; **heartstrings** deepest affections or pity; **heartthrob** *colloquial* object of (esp. immature) romantic feelings; **heart-to-heart** frank (talk); **heart-warming** emotionally moving and encouraging; **take to heart** be much affected by.

hearten *verb* make or become more cheerful. □ **heartening** *adjective*.

hearth /hɑːθ/ *noun* floor of fireplace. □ **hearthrug** rug laid before fireplace.

heartless *adjective* unfeeling, pitiless. □ **heartlessly** *adverb*.

hearty *adjective* (**-ier**, **-iest**) strong, vigorous; (of meal or appetite) large; warm, friendly. □ **heartily** *adverb*; **heartiness** *noun*.

heat ● *noun* condition or sensation of being hot; energy arising from motion of molecules; hot weather; warmth of feeling; anger; most intense part or period of activity; preliminary contest, winner(s) of which compete in final. ● *verb* make or become hot; inflame. □ **heatproof** able to resist great heat; **heatwave** period of very hot weather; **on heat** (of female animals) sexually receptive.

heated *adjective* angry, impassioned. □ **heatedly** *adverb*.

heater *noun* device for heating room, water, etc.

heath /hiːθ/ *noun* flattish tract of uncultivated land with low shrubs; plant growing on heath, esp. heather.

heathen /'hiːð(ə)n/ ● *noun* person not belonging to predominant religion. ● *adjective* of heathens; having no religion.

heather /'heðə/ *noun* purple-flowered plant of moors and heaths.

heating *noun* equipment used to heat building.

heave ● *verb* (**-ving**; *past & past participle* **heaved** or esp. Nautical **hove** /həʊv/) lift, haul, or utter with effort; *colloquial* throw; rise and fall periodically; *Nautical* haul by rope; retch. ● *noun* heaving. □ **heave in sight** come into view; **heave to** bring vessel to standstill.

heaven /'hev(ə)n/ *noun* home of God and of blessed after death; place or state of bliss, delightful thing; **(the heavens)** sky as seen from earth. □ **heavenly** *adjective*.

heavy /'hevɪ/ ● *adjective* (**-ier, -iest**) of great weight, difficult to lift; of great density; abundant; severe, extensive; striking or falling with force; (of machinery etc.) very large of its kind; needing much physical effort; hard to digest; hard to read or understand; (of ground) difficult to travel over; dull, tedious, oppressive; coarse, ungraceful. ● *noun* (*plural* **-ies**) *colloquial* thug (esp. hired); villain. □ **heavy-duty** designed to withstand hard use; **heavy-handed** clumsy, oppressive; **heavy hydrogen** deuterium; **heavy industry** that concerned with production of metal and machines etc.; **heavy metal** *colloquial* loud rock music with pounding rhythm; **heavy water** water composed of deuterium and oxygen; **heavyweight** amateur boxing weight (over 81 kg). □ **heavily** *adverb*; **heaviness** *noun*.

Hebraic /hiː'breɪɪk/ *adjective* of Hebrew or the Hebrews.

Hebrew /'hiːbruː/ ● *noun* member of a Semitic people in ancient Palestine; their language; modern form of this, used esp. in Israel. ● *adjective* of or in Hebrew; of the Jews.

heckle /'hek(ə)l/ ● *verb* (**-ling**) interrupt or harass (speaker). ● *noun* act of heckling. □ **heckler** *noun*.

hectare /'hekteə/ *noun* metric unit of square measure (2.471 acres).

hectic /'hektɪk/ *adjective* busy and confused; excited, feverish. □ **hectically** *adverb*.

hecto- /'hektəʊ/ *combining form* one hundred.

hector /'hektə/ *verb* bluster, bully. □ **hectoring** *adjective*.

he'd /hiːd/ he had; he would.

hedge ● *noun* fence of bushes or low trees; protection against possible loss. ● *verb* (**-ging**) surround with hedge; (+ *in*) enclose; secure oneself against loss on (bet etc.); avoid committing oneself. □ **hedgehog** small spiny insect-eating mammal; **hedge-hop** fly at low altitude; **hedgerow** row of bushes forming hedge; **hedge sparrow** common brown-backed bird.

hedonism /'hiːdənɪz(ə)m/ *noun* (behaviour based on) belief in pleasure as humankind's proper aim. □ **hedonist** *noun*; **hedonistic** /-'nɪs-/ *adjective*.

heed ● *verb* attend to; take notice of. ● *noun* care, attention. □ **heedless** *adjective*; **heedlessly** *adverb*.

hee-haw /'hiːhɔː/ *noun & verb* bray.

heel¹ ● *noun* back of foot below ankle; part of sock etc. covering this, or of shoe etc. supporting it; crust end of loaf; *colloquial* scoundrel; (as *interjection*) *command to dog to walk near owner's heel.* ● *verb* fit or renew heel on (shoe); touch ground with heel; (+ *out*) Rugby pass ball with heel. □ **cool, kick one's heels** be kept waiting; **heelball** shoemaker's polishing mixture of wax etc., esp. used in brass rubbing.

heel² ● *verb* (often + *over*) (of ship etc.) lean over; cause (ship) to do this. ● *noun* heeling.

hefty /'heftɪ/ *adjective* (**-ier, -iest**) (of person) big, strong; (of thing) heavy, powerful.

hegemony /hɪ'ɡemənɪ/ *noun* leadership.

heifer /'hefə/ *noun* young cow, esp. one that has not had more than one calf.

height /haɪt/ *noun* measurement from base to top; elevation above ground or other level; high point; top; extreme example.

heighten *verb* make or become higher or more intense.

heinous /'heɪnəs/ *adjective* atrocious.

heir /eə/ *noun* (*feminine* **heiress**) person entitled to property or rank as legal successor of former holder. □ **heir apparent** one whose claim cannot be superseded by birth of nearer heir; **heirloom** piece of property that has been in family for generations; **heir presumptive** one whose claim may be superseded by birth of nearer heir.

held *past & past participle* of HOLD¹.

helical /'helɪk(ə)l/ *adjective* spiral.

helices *plural* of HELIX.

helicopter /'helɪkɒptə/ *noun* wingless aircraft lifted and propelled by overhead blades revolving horizontally.

heliograph /'hiːlɪəɡrɑːf/ ● *noun* signalling apparatus reflecting flashes of sunlight. ● *verb* send (message) thus.

heliotrope /'hiːlɪətrəʊp/ *noun* plant with fragrant purple flowers.

heliport /'helɪpɔːt/ *noun* place where helicopters take off and land.

helium /'hiːlɪəm/ *noun* light nonflammable gaseous element.

helix /'hiːlɪks/ *noun* (*plural* **helices** /'hiːlɪsiːz/) spiral or coiled curve.

hell *noun* home of the damned after death; place or state of misery. □ **hellish** *adjective*; **hellishly** *adverb*.

he'll /hiːl/ he will; he shall.

hellebore /'helɪbɔː/ *noun* evergreen plant of kind including Christmas rose.

Hellene /'heliːn/ *noun* Greek. □ **Hellenic** /-'len-/ *adjective*; **Hellenism** /-lɪn-/ *noun*; **Hellenist** /-lɪn-/ *noun*.

Hellenistic /helɪ'nɪstɪk/ *adjective* of Greek history, language, and culture of late 4th to late 1st c. BC.

hello /hə'ləʊ/ (also **hallo, hullo**) ● *interjection* expressing informal greeting or surprise, or calling attention. ● *noun* (*plural* **-s**) cry of 'hello'.

helm *noun* tiller or wheel for managing rudder. □ **at the helm** in control; **helmsman** person who steers ship.

helmet /'helmɪt/ *noun* protective headcover of policeman, motorcyclist, etc.

help ● *verb* provide with means to what is needed or sought, be useful to; (usually in negative) prevent, refrain from; (**help oneself**) (often + *to*) serve oneself, take without permission. ● *noun* act of helping; person or thing that helps; *colloquial* domestic assistant or assistance; remedy etc. □ **helpline** telephone service providing help with problems. □ **helper** *noun*.

helpful *adjective* giving help, useful. □ **helpfully** *adverb*; **helpfulness** *noun*.

helping *noun* portion of food.

helpless adjective lacking help, defenceless; unable to act without help. ◻ **helplessly** adverb; **helplessness** noun.

helter-skelter /ˈheltəˈskeltə/ ● adverb & adjective in disorderly haste. ● noun spiral slide at funfair.

hem¹ ● noun border of cloth where edge is turned under and sewn down. ● verb (**-mm-**) sew edge thus. ◻ **hem in** confine, restrict; **hemline** lower edge of skirt etc.; **hemstitch** (make hem with) ornamental stitch.

hem² interjection expressing hesitation or calling attention by slight cough.

hemisphere /ˈhemɪsfɪə/ noun half sphere; half earth, esp. as divided by equator or by line passing through poles; each half of brain. ◻ **hemispherical** /-ˈsfer-/ adjective.

hemlock /ˈhemlɒk/ noun poisonous plant with small white flowers; poison made from it.

hemp (in full **Indian hemp**) Asian herbaceous plant; its fibre used for rope etc.; narcotic drug made from it.

hempen adjective made of hemp.

hen noun female bird, esp. of domestic fowl. ◻ **henbane** poisonous hairy plant; **hen-party** colloquial party of women only; **henpecked** (of husband) domineered over by his wife.

hence adverb from now; for this reason. ◻ **henceforth**, **henceforward** from this time onwards.

henchman /ˈhentʃmən/ noun usually derogatory trusted supporter.

henge noun prehistoric circle of wood or stone uprights, as at Stonehenge.

henna /ˈhenə/ ● noun tropical shrub; reddish dye made from it and used esp. to colour hair. ● verb (**hennaed**, **hennaing**) dye with henna.

henry /ˈhenrɪ/ noun (plural **-s**, **-ies**) SI unit of inductance.

hep = HIP⁴.

hepatitis /hepəˈtaɪtɪs/ noun inflammation of the liver.

hepta- combining form seven.

heptagon /ˈheptəgən/ noun plane figure with 7 sides and angles. ◻ **heptagonal** /-ˈtæg-/ adjective.

her ● pronoun (as object of verb) the female person or thing in question; colloquial she. ● adjective of or belonging to her.

herald /ˈher(ə)ld/ ● noun messenger; forerunner; official. ● verb proclaim approach of; usher in. ◻ **heraldic** /-ˈræld-/ adjective.

heraldry /ˈherəldrɪ/ noun (science or art of) armorial bearings.

herb noun non-woody seed-bearing plant; plant with leaves, seeds, or flowers used for flavouring, medicine, etc.

herbaceous /hɜːˈbeɪʃəs/ adjective of or like herbs. ◻ **herbaceous border** border in garden etc. containing flowering plants.

herbage noun vegetation collectively, esp. pasturage.

herbal ● adjective of herbs. ● noun book about herbs.

herbalist noun dealer in medicinal herbs; writer on herbs.

herbarium /hɜːˈbeərɪəm/ noun (plural **-ria**) collection of dried plants.

herbicide /ˈhɜːbɪsaɪd/ noun poison used to destroy unwanted vegetation.

herbivore /ˈhɜːbɪvɔː/ noun plant-eating animal. ◻ **herbivorous** /-ˈbɪvərəs/ adjective.

Herculean /hɜːkjʊˈliːən/ adjective having or requiring great strength or effort.

herd ● noun number of cattle etc. feeding or travelling together; (**the herd**) derogatory large number of people.

● verb (cause to) go in herd; tend. ◻ **herdsman** keeper of herds.

here ● adverb in or to this place; indicating a person or thing; at this point. ● noun this place. ◻ **hereabout(s)** somewhere near here; **hereafter** (in) future, (in) next world; **hereby** by this means; **herein** formal in this place, book, etc.; **hereinafter** formal from this point on, below (in document); **hereof** formal of this; **hereto** formal to this; **heretofore** formal formerly; **hereupon** after or in consequence of this; **herewith** with this.

hereditary /hɪˈredɪtərɪ/ adjective transmitted genetically from one generation to another; descending by inheritance; holding position by inheritance.

heredity /hɪˈredɪtɪ/ noun genetic transmission of physical or mental characteristics; these characteristics; genetic constitution.

heresy /ˈherəsɪ/ noun (plural **-ies**) esp. RC Church religious belief contrary to orthodox doctrine; opinion contrary to what is normally accepted.

heretic /ˈherətɪk/ noun believer in heresy. ◻ **heretical** /hɪˈret-/ adjective.

heritable /ˈherɪtəb(ə)l/ adjective that can be inherited.

heritage /ˈherɪtɪdʒ/ noun what is or may be inherited; inherited circumstances, benefits, etc.; nation's historic buildings, countryside, etc.

hermaphrodite /hɜːˈmæfrədaɪt/ ● noun person, animal, or plant with organs of both sexes. ● adjective combining both sexes. ◻ **hermaphroditic** /-ˈdɪt-/ adjective.

hermetic /hɜːˈmetɪk/ adjective with an airtight seal. ◻ **hermetically** adverb.

hermit /ˈhɜːmɪt/ noun person living in solitude. ◻ **hermit-crab** crab which lives in mollusc's cast-off shell.

hermitage noun hermit's dwelling; secluded residence.

hernia /ˈhɜːnɪə/ noun protrusion of part of organ through wall of cavity containing it.

hero /ˈhɪərəʊ/ noun (plural **-es**) person admired for courage, outstanding achievements, etc.; chief male character in play, story, etc. ◻ **hero-worship** idealization of admired person.

heroic /hɪˈrəʊɪk/ ● adjective fit for, or like, a hero; very brave. ● noun (in plural) over-dramatic talk or behaviour. ◻ **heroically** adverb.

heroin /ˈherəʊɪn/ noun sedative addictive drug prepared from morphine.

heroine /ˈherəʊɪn/ noun female hero; chief female character in play, story, etc.

heroism /ˈherəʊɪz(ə)m/ noun heroic conduct.

heron /ˈherən/ noun long-necked long-legged wading bird.

herpes /ˈhɜːpiːz/ noun virus disease causing blisters.

Herr /heə/ noun (plural **Herren** /ˈherən/) title of German man.

herring /ˈherɪŋ/ noun (plural same or **-s**) N. Atlantic edible fish. ◻ **herring-bone** stitch or weave of small 'V' shapes making zigzag pattern.

hers /hɜːz/ pronoun the one(s) belonging to her.

herself /həˈself/ pronoun: emphatic form of SHE or HER; reflexive form of HER.

hertz noun (plural same) SI unit of frequency (one cycle per second).

he's /hiːz/ he is; he has.

hesitant /ˈhezɪt(ə)nt/ adjective hesitating. ◻ **hesitance** noun; **hesitancy** noun; **hesitantly** adverb.

hesitate /ˈhezɪteɪt/ verb (**-ting**) feel or show indecision; pause; (often + to do) be reluctant. ◻ **hesitation** noun.

hessian /'hesɪən/ noun strong coarse hemp or jute sacking.

heterodox /'hetərəʊdɒks/ adjective not orthodox. □ **heterodoxy** noun.

heterogeneous /hetərəʊ'dʒiːnɪəs/ adjective diverse; varied in content. □ **heterogeneity** /-dʒɪ'niːɪtɪ/ noun.

heteromorphic /hetərəʊ'mɔːfɪk/ adjective (also **heteromorphous** /-'mɔːfəs/) Biology of dissimilar forms.

heterosexual /hetərəʊ'sekʃʊəl/ ● adjective feeling or involving sexual attraction to opposite sex. ● noun heterosexual person. □ **heterosexuality** /-'æl-/ noun.

het up adjective colloquial overwrought.

heuristic /hjʊə'rɪstɪk/ adjective serving to discover; using trial and error.

hew verb (past participle **hewn** /hjuːn/ or **hewed**) chop or cut with axe, sword, etc.; cut into shape.

hex ● verb practise witchcraft; bewitch. ● noun magic spell.

hexa- combining form six.

hexagon /'heksəgən/ noun plane figure with 6 sides and angles. □ **hexagonal** /-'sæg-/ adjective.

hexagram /'heksəgræm/ noun 6-pointed star formed by two intersecting equilateral triangles.

hexameter /hek'sæmɪtə/ noun verse line of 6 metrical feet.

hey /heɪ/ interjection calling attention or expressing surprise, inquiry, etc. □ **hey presto!** conjuror's phrase on completing trick.

heyday /'heɪdeɪ/ noun time of greatest success, prime.

HF abbreviation high frequency.

HGV abbreviation heavy goods vehicle.

HH abbreviation Her or His Highness; His Holiness; double-hard (pencil lead).

hi /haɪ/ interjection calling attention or as greeting.

hiatus /haɪ'eɪtəs/ noun (plural **-tuses**) gap in series etc.; break between two vowels coming together but not in same syllable.

hibernate /'haɪbəneɪt/ verb (**-ting**) (of animal) spend winter in dormant state. □ **hibernation** noun.

Hibernian /haɪ'bɜːnɪən/ archaic poetical ● adjective of Ireland. ● noun native of Ireland.

hibiscus /hɪ'bɪskəs/ noun (plural **-cuses**) cultivated shrub with large brightly coloured flowers.

hiccup /'hɪkʌp/ (also **hiccough**) ● noun involuntary audible spasm of respiratory organs; temporary or minor stoppage or difficulty. ● verb (**-p-**) make hiccup.

hick noun esp. US colloquial yokel.

hickory /'hɪkərɪ/ noun (plural **-ies**) N. American tree related to walnut; its wood.

hid past of HIDE[1].

hidden past participle of HIDE[1]. □ **hidden agenda** secret motivation behind policy etc., ulterior motive.

hide[1] ● verb (**-ding**; past **hid**; past participle **hidden** /'hɪd(ə)n/) put or keep out of sight; conceal oneself; (usually + from) conceal (fact). ● noun camouflaged shelter for observing wildlife. □ **hide-and-seek** game in which players hide and another searches for them; **hideaway** hiding place, retreat; **hide-out** colloquial hiding place.

hide[2] noun animal's skin, esp. tanned; colloquial human skin. □ **hidebound** rigidly conventional.

hideous /'hɪdɪəs/ adjective repulsive, revolting. □ **hideously** adverb.

hiding noun colloquial thrashing.

hierarchy /'haɪərɑːkɪ/ noun (plural **-ies**) system of grades of authority ranked one above another. □ **hierarchical** /-'rɑːk-/ adjective.

hieroglyph /'haɪərəglɪf/ noun picture representing word or syllable, esp. in ancient Egyptian.

hieroglyphic /-'glɪf-/ adjective; **hieroglyphics** /-'glɪf-/ plural noun.

hi-fi /'haɪfaɪ/ colloquial ● adjective of high fidelity. ● noun (plural **-s**) equipment for such sound reproduction.

higgledy-piggledy /hɪgəldɪ'pɪgəldɪ/ adverb & adjective in disorder.

high /haɪ/ ● adjective of great or specified upward extent; far above ground or sea level; coming above normal level; of exalted rank or position, of superior quality; extreme, intense; (often + on) colloquial intoxicated by alcohol or drugs; (of sound) shrill; (of period etc.) at its peak; (of meat etc.) beginning to go bad. ● noun high or highest level or number; area of high barometric pressure; slang euphoric state, esp. drug-induced. ● adverb far up, aloft; in or to high degree; at high price; (of sound) at high pitch. □ **high altar** chief altar in church; **highball** US drink of spirits and soda etc.; **highbrow** colloquial (person) of superior intellect or culture; **high chair** child's chair with long legs and meal-tray; **High Church** section of Church of England emphasizing ritual, priestly authority, and sacraments; **high command** army commander-in-chief and associated staff; **High Commission** embassy from one Commonwealth country to another; **High Court** supreme court of justice for civil cases; **highfalutin(g)** colloquial pompous, pretentious; **high fidelity** high-quality sound reproduction; **high-flown** extravagant, bombastic; **high-flyer, -flier** person of great potential or ambition; **high frequency** Radio 3–30 megahertz; **high-handed** overbearing; **high-handedly** adverb; **high-handedness** noun; **high heels** woman's shoes with high heels; **high jump** athletic event consisting of jumping over high bar, colloquial drastic punishment; **high-level** conducted by people of high rank, (of computer language) close to ordinary language; **high-minded** of firm moral principles; **high-mindedness** noun; **high pressure** high degree of activity, atmospheric condition with pressure above average; **high priest** chief priest, head of cult; **high-rise** (of building) having many storeys; **high road** main road; **high school** secondary school; **high sea(s)** seas outside territorial waters; **high-spirited** cheerful; **high street** principal shopping street of town; **high tea** early evening meal of tea and cooked food; **high-tech** employing, requiring, or involved in high technology, imitating its style; **high technology** advanced (esp. electronic) technology; **high tension, voltage** electrical potential large enough to injure or damage; **high tide, water** time or level of tide at its peak; **high water mark** level reached at high water.

highland /'haɪlənd/ ● noun (usually in plural) mountainous country, esp. (**the Highlands**) of N. Scotland. ● adjective of highland or Highlands. □ **highlander, Highlander** noun.

highlight ● noun moment or detail of vivid interest; bright part of picture; bleached streak in hair. ● verb bring into prominence; mark with highlighter.

highlighter noun coloured marker pen for emphasizing printed word.

highly adverb in high degree, favourably. □ **highlystrung** sensitive, nervous.

highness noun state of being high; (**His, Her, Your Highness**) title of prince, princess, etc.

highway noun public road, main route. □ **Highway Code** official handbook for road-users; **highwayman** historical (usually mounted) robber of stagecoaches.

hijack /'haɪdʒæk/ ● verb seize control of (vehicle, aircraft, etc.), esp. to force it to different destination; steal (goods) in transit. ● noun hijacking. □ **hijacker** noun.

hike ● *noun* long walk, esp. in country for pleasure; rise in prices etc. ● *verb* (**-king**) go on hike. □ **hiker** *noun*.

hilarious /hɪ'leərɪəs/ *adjective* extremely funny; boisterously merry. □ **hilariously** *adverb*; **hilarity** /-'lær-/ *noun*.

hill *noun* natural elevation of ground, lower than mountain; heap, mound. □ **hill-billy** *US colloquial often derogatory* person from remote rural area. □ **hilly** *adjective* (**-ier, -iest**).

hillock /'hɪlək/ *noun* small hill, mound.

hilt *noun* handle of sword, dagger, etc.

him *pronoun* (as object of verb) the male person or animal in question, person of unspecified sex; *colloquial* he.

himself /hɪm'self/ *pronoun: emphatic form of* HE *or* HIM; *reflexive form of* HIM.

hind[1] /haɪnd/ *adjective* at back. □ **hindquarters** rump and hind legs of quadruped; **hindsight** wisdom after event. □ **hindmost** *adjective*.

hind[2] /haɪnd/ *noun* female (esp. red) deer.

hinder[1] /'hɪndə/ *verb* impede; delay.

hinder[2] /'haɪndə/ *adjective* rear, hind.

Hindi /'hɪndɪ/ *noun* group of spoken languages in N. India; one of official languages of India, literary form of Hindustani.

hindrance /'hɪndrəns/ *noun* obstruction.

Hindu /'hɪndu:/ ● *noun* (*plural* **-s**) follower of Hinduism. ● *adjective* of Hindus or Hinduism.

Hinduism /'hɪndu:ɪz(ə)m/ *noun* main religious and social system of India, including belief in reincarnation and worship of several gods.

Hindustani /hɪndʊ'stɑːnɪ/ *noun* language based on Hindi, used in much of India.

hinge ● *noun* movable joint on which door, lid, etc. swings; principle on which all depends. ● *verb* (**-ging**) (+ *on*) depend on (event etc.); attach or be attached with hinge.

hinny /'hɪnɪ/ *noun* (*plural* **-ies**) offspring of female donkey and male horse.

hint ● *noun* indirect suggestion; slight indication; small piece of practical information; faint trace. ● *verb* suggest indirectly. □ **hint at** refer indirectly to.

hinterland /'hɪntəlænd/ *noun* district behind that lying along coast etc.

hip[1] *noun* projection of pelvis and upper part of thigh-bone. □ **hip-flask** small flask for spirits.

hip[2] *noun* fruit of rose.

hip[3] *interjection used to introduce cheer.*

hip[4] *adjective* (also **hep**) (**-pp-**) *slang* trendy, stylish. □ **hip hop, hip-hop** subculture combining rap music, graffiti art, and break-dancing.

hippie /'hɪpɪ/ *noun* (also **hippy**) (*plural* **-ies**) *colloquial* person (esp. in 1960s) rejecting convention, typically with long hair, jeans, etc.

hippo /'hɪpəʊ/ *noun* (*plural* **-s**) *colloquial* hippopotamus.

Hippocratic oath /hɪpə'krætɪk/ *noun* statement of ethics of medical profession.

hippodrome /'hɪpədrəʊm/ *noun* music-hall, dance hall, etc.; *historical* course for chariot races etc.

hippopotamus /hɪpə'pɒtəməs/ *noun* (*plural* **-muses** or **-mi** /-maɪ/) large African mammal with short legs and thick skin, living by rivers etc.

hippy = HIPPIE.

hipster[1] /'hɪpstə/ ● *adjective* (of garment) hanging from hips rather than waist. ● *noun* (in *plural*) such trousers.

hipster[2] /'hɪpstə/ *noun slang* hip person.

hire ● *verb* (**-ring**) obtain use of (thing) or services of (person) for payment. ● *noun* hiring, being hired; payment for this. □ **hire out** grant temporary use of (thing) for payment; **hire purchase** system of purchase by paying in instalments. □ **hirer** *noun*.

hireling /'haɪəlɪŋ/ *noun usually derogatory* person who works for hire.

hirsute /'hɜːsjuːt/ *adjective* hairy.

his /hɪz/ ● *adjective* of or belonging to him. ● *pronoun* the one(s) belonging to him.

Hispanic /hɪ'spænɪk/ ● *adjective* of Spain or Spain and Portugal; of Spanish and other Spanish-speaking countries. ● *noun* Spanish-speaking person living in US.

hiss /hɪs/ ● *verb* make sharp sibilant sound, as of letter *s*; express disapproval of thus; whisper urgently or angrily. ● *noun* sharp sibilant sound.

histamine /'hɪstəmiːn/ *noun* chemical compound in body tissues associated with allergic reactions.

histology /hɪ'stɒlədʒɪ/ *noun* study of tissue structure.

historian /hɪ'stɔːrɪən/ *noun* writer of history; person learned in history.

historic /hɪ'stɒrɪk/ *adjective* famous in history or potentially so; *Grammar* (of tense) used to narrate past events.

historical *adjective* of history; belonging to or dealing with the past; not legendary; studying development over period of time. □ **historically** *adverb*.

historicity /hɪstə'rɪsɪtɪ/ *noun* historical genuineness or accuracy.

historiography /hɪstɔːrɪ'ɒɡrəfɪ/ *noun* writing of history; study of this. □ **historiographer** *noun*.

history /'hɪstərɪ/ *noun* (*plural* **-ies**) continuous record of (esp. public) events; study of past events; total accumulation of these; (esp. eventful) past or record.

histrionic /hɪstrɪ'ɒnɪk/ ● *adjective* (of behaviour) theatrical, dramatic. ● *noun* (in *plural*) insincere and dramatic behaviour designed to impress.

hit ● *verb* (**-tt-**; *past & past participle* **hit**) strike with blow or missile; (of moving body) strike with force; affect adversely; (often + *at*) aim blow; propel (ball etc.) with bat etc.; achieve, reach; *colloquial* encounter, arrive at. ● *noun* blow; shot that hits target; *colloquial* popular success. □ **hit it off** (often + *with, together*) get on well; **hit-and-run** (of person) causing damage or injury and leaving immediately, (of accident etc.) caused by such person(s); **hit-or-miss** random.

hitch ● *verb* fasten with loop etc.; move (thing) with jerk; *colloquial* hitchhike; obtain (lift). ● *noun* temporary difficulty; snag; jerk; kind of noose or knot; *colloquial* free ride in vehicle. □ **hitchhike** travel by means of free lifts in passing vehicles; **hitchhiker** *noun*.

hi-tech /'haɪtek/ *adjective* high-tech.

hither /'hɪðə/ *adverb formal* to this place. □ **hitherto** up to now.

HIV *abbreviation* human immunodeficiency virus, either of two viruses causing Aids.

hive *noun* beehive. □ **hive off** (**-ving**) separate from larger group.

hives /haɪvz/ *plural noun* skin eruption, esp. nettle-rash.

HM *abbreviation* Her or His Majesty('s).

HMG *abbreviation* Her or His Majesty's Government.

HMI *abbreviation* Her or His Majesty's Inspector (of Schools).

HMS *abbreviation* Her or His Majesty's Ship.

HMSO *abbreviation* Her or His Majesty's Stationery Office.

HNC, HND *abbreviations* Higher National Certificate, Diploma.

ho /həʊ/ *interjection expressing triumph, derision, etc., or calling attention etc.*

hoard /hɔːd/ ● noun store (esp. of money or food). ● verb amass and store. □ **hoarder** noun.

hoarding /'hɔːdɪŋ/ noun structure erected to carry advertisements; temporary fence round building site etc.

hoar-frost /'hɔːfrɒst/ noun frozen water vapour on lawns.

hoarse /hɔːs/ adjective (of voice) rough, husky; having hoarse voice. □ **hoarsely** adverb; **hoarseness** noun.

hoary /'hɔːrɪ/ adjective (**-ier**, **-iest**) white or grey with age; aged; old and trite.

hoax ● noun humorous or malicious deception. ● verb deceive with hoax.

hob noun hotplates etc. on cooker or as separate unit; flat metal shelf at side of fire for heating pans etc. □ **hobnail** heavy-headed nail for boot-sole.

hobble /'hɒb(ə)l/ ● verb (**-ling**) walk lamely, limp; tie together legs (of horse etc.) to keep it from straying. ● noun limping gait; rope etc. used to hobble horse.

hobby /'hɒbɪ/ noun (plural **-ies**) leisure-time activity pursued for pleasure. □ **hobby-horse** stick with horse's head, used as toy, favourite subject or idea.

hobgoblin /'hɒbgɒblɪn/ noun mischievous imp; bogy.

hobnob /'hɒbnɒb/ verb (**-bb-**) (usually + *with*) mix socially or informally.

hobo /'həʊbəʊ/ noun (plural **-es** or **-s**) US wandering worker; tramp.

hock[1] noun joint of quadruped's hind leg between knee and fetlock.

hock[2] noun German white wine.

hock[3] verb esp. US colloquial pawn. □ **in hock** in pawn, in debt, in prison.

hockey /'hɒkɪ/ noun team game played with ball and hooked sticks.

hocus-pocus /həʊkəs'pəʊkəs/ noun trickery.

hod noun trough on pole for carrying bricks etc.; portable container for coal.

hodgepodge = HOTCHPOTCH.

hoe ● noun long-handled tool for weeding etc. ● verb (**hoes**, **hoed**, **hoeing**) weed (crops), loosen (soil), or dig up etc. with hoe.

hog ● noun castrated male pig; colloquial greedy person. ● verb (**-gg-**) colloquial take greedily; monopolize. □ **go the whole hog** colloquial do thing thoroughly; **hogwash** colloquial nonsense.

hogmanay /'hɒgməneɪ/ noun Scottish New Year's Eve.

hogshead /'hɒgzhed/ noun large cask; liquid or dry measure (about 50 gals.).

ho-ho /həʊ'həʊ/ interjection representing deep jolly laugh or expressing surprise, triumph, or derision.

hoick verb colloquial (often + *out*) lift or jerk.

hoi polloi /hɔɪ pə'lɔɪ/ noun the masses; ordinary people. [Greek]

hoist ● verb raise or haul up; raise with ropes and pulleys etc. ● noun act of hoisting; apparatus for hoisting. □ **hoist with one's own petard** caught by one's own trick etc.

hoity-toity /hɔɪtɪ'tɔɪtɪ/ adjective haughty.

hokum /'həʊkəm/ noun esp. US slang sentimental or unreal material in film etc.; bunkum, rubbish.

hold[1] /həʊld/ ● verb (past & past participle **held**) keep fast; grasp; keep in particular position; contain, have capacity for; possess, have (property, qualifications, job, etc.); conduct, celebrate; detain; think, believe; not give way; reserve. ● noun (+ *on*, *over*) power over; grasp; manner or means of holding. □ **holdall** large soft travelling bag; **hold back** impede, keep for oneself, (often + *from*) refrain; **hold down** repress, colloquially be competent enough to keep (job); **hold forth** speak at length or tediously; **hold on** maintain grasp, wait, not ring off; **hold one's tongue** colloquial remain silent; **hold out** stretch forth (hand etc.),

offer (inducement etc.), maintain resistance, (+ *for*) continue to demand; **hold over** postpone; **hold up** verb sustain, display, obstruct, stop and rob by force; **hold-up** noun stoppage, delay, robbery by force; **hold with** (usually in negative) colloquial approve of.

hold[2] /həʊld/ noun cavity in lower part of ship or aircraft for cargo.

holder noun device for holding something; possessor of title, shares, etc.; occupant of office etc.

holding noun tenure of land; stocks, property, etc. held. □ **holding company** one formed to hold shares of other companies.

hole noun empty space in solid body; opening in or through something; burrow; colloquial small or gloomy place; colloquial awkward situation; (in games) cavity or receptacle for ball, Golf section of course from tee to hole. □ **hole up** (**-ling**) US colloquial hide oneself. □ **holey** adjective.

holiday /'hɒlɪdeɪ/ ● noun (often in plural) extended period of recreation, esp. spent away from home; break from work or school. ● verb spend holiday.

holiness /'həʊlɪnɪs/ noun being holy or sacred; (**His, Your Holiness**) title of Pope.

holism /'həʊlɪz(ə)m/ noun (also **wholism**) theory that certain wholes are greater than sum of their parts; Medicine treating of whole person rather than symptoms of disease. □ **holistic** /-'lɪst-/ adjective.

hollandaise sauce /hɒlən'deɪz/ noun creamy sauce of butter, egg yolks, vinegar, etc.

holler /'hɒlə/ verb & noun US colloquial shout.

hollow /'hɒləʊ/ ● adjective having cavity; not solid; sunken; echoing; empty; hungry; meaningless; insincere. ● noun hollow place; hole; valley. ● verb (often + *out*) make hollow, excavate. ● adverb colloquial completely.

holly /'hɒlɪ/ noun (plural **-ies**) evergreen prickly-leaved shrub with red berries.

hollyhock /'hɒlɪhɒk/ noun tall plant with showy flowers.

holm /həʊm/ noun (in full **holm-oak**) evergreen oak.

holocaust /'hɒləkɔːst/ noun wholesale destruction; (**the Holocaust**) mass murder of Jews by Nazis 1939–45.

hologram /'hɒləgræm/ noun photographic pattern having 3-dimensional effect.

holograph /'hɒləgrɑːf/ ● adjective wholly in handwriting of person named as author. ● noun such document.

holography /hə'lɒgrəfɪ/ noun study or production of holograms.

holster /'həʊlstə/ noun leather case for pistol or revolver on belt etc.

holy /'həʊlɪ/ adjective (**-ier**, **-iest**) morally and spiritually excellent; belonging or devoted to God. □ **Holy Ghost** Holy Spirit; **Holy Land** area between River Jordan and Mediterranean; **holy of holies** inner chamber of Jewish temple, thing regarded as most sacred; **holy orders** those of bishop, priest, and deacon; **Holy Saturday** day before Easter; **Holy See** papacy, papal court; **Holy Spirit** Third Person of Trinity; **Holy Week** week before Easter; **Holy Writ** Bible.

homage /'hɒmɪdʒ/ noun tribute, expression of reverence.

Homburg /'hɒmbɜːg/ noun man's felt hat with narrow curled brim and lengthwise dent in crown.

home ● noun place where one lives; residence; (esp. good or bad) family circumstances; native land; institution caring for people or animals; place where thing originates, is kept, is most common, etc.; (in games) finishing line in race, goal, home match or win etc. ● adjective of or connected with home; carried on or done at home; not foreign; played etc. on team's own ground. ● *adverb* to or at home; to point aimed at. ● *verb* (**-ming**) (of pigeon) return home; (often + *on*, *in on*) (of missile etc.) be guided to destination. □ **at home** *adjective* in one's house or native land, at ease, well-informed, available to callers; **at-home** *noun* social reception in person's home; **home-brew** beer etc. brewed at home; **Home Counties** those lying round London; **home economics** study of household management; **homeland** native land, any of several areas reserved for black South Africans; **Home Office** British government department concerned with immigration, law and order, etc.; **home rule** self-government; **Home Secretary** minister in charge of Home Office; **homesick** depressed by absence from home; **homesickness** such depression; **homestead** house with outbuildings, farm; **homework** lessons to be done by schoolchild at home. □ **homeless** *adjective*; **homeward** *adjective & adverb*; **homewards** *adverb*.

homely *adjective* (**-ier**, **-iest**) plain; unpretentious; *US* unattractive; cosy. □ **homeliness** *noun*.

homeopathy etc. *US* = HOMOEOPATHY etc.

Homeric /həʊˈmerɪk/ *adjective* of or in style of the ancient Greek poet Homer; of Bronze Age Greece.

homey *adjective* (**-mier**, **-miest**) suggesting home; cosy.

homicide /ˈhɒmɪsaɪd/ *noun* killing of person by another; person who kills another. □ **homicidal** /-ˈsaɪd-/ *adjective*.

homily /ˈhɒmɪlɪ/ *noun* (*plural* **-ies**) short sermon; moralizing lecture. □ **homiletic** /-ˈlet-/ *adjective*.

homing *adjective* (of pigeon) trained to fly home; (of device) for guiding to target etc.

hominid /ˈhɒmɪnɪd/ ● *adjective* of mammal family of existing and fossil man. ● *noun* member of this.

hominoid /ˈhɒmɪnɔɪd/ ● *adjective* like a human. ● *noun* animal resembling human.

homoeopathy /ˌhəʊmɪˈɒpəθɪ/ *noun* (*US* **homeopathy**) treatment of disease by drugs that in healthy person would produce symptoms of the disease. □ **homoeopath** /ˈhəʊmɪəʊpæθ/ *noun*; **homoeopathic** /-ˈpæθ-/ *adjective*.

homogeneous /ˌhɒməˈdʒiːnɪəs/ *adjective* (having parts) of same kind or nature; uniform. □ **homogeneity** /-dʒɪˈniːɪtɪ/ *noun*; **homogeneously** *adverb*.

■ **Usage** *Homogeneous* is often confused with *homogenous* (and pronounced /həˈmɒdʒənəs/, with the stress on the *-mog-*), but that is a term in biology meaning 'similar owing to common descent'.

homogenize /həˈmɒdʒɪnaɪz/ *verb* (also **-ise**) (**-zing** or **-sing**) make homogeneous; treat (milk) so that cream does not separate.

homologous /həˈmɒləgəs/ *adjective* having same relation, relative position, etc.; corresponding.

homology /həˈmɒlədʒɪ/ *noun* homologous relation, correspondence.

homonym /ˈhɒmənɪm/ *noun* word spelt or pronounced like another but of different meaning.

homophobia /ˌhəʊmɪˈfəʊbɪə/ *noun* hatred or fear of homosexuals. □ **homophobe** /ˈhɒm-/ *noun*; **homophobic** *adjective*.

homophone /ˈhɒməfəʊn/ *noun* word pronounced like another but having different meaning, e.g. *beach*, *beech*.

Homo sapiens /ˌhəʊməʊ ˈsæpɪenz/ *noun* modern humans regarded as a species. [Latin]

homosexual /ˌhɒməˈsekʃʊəl/ ● *adjective* feeling or involving sexual attraction to people of same sex. ● *noun* homosexual person. □ **homosexuality** /-ˈæl-/ *noun*.

Hon. *abbreviation* Honorary; Honourable.

hone ● *noun* whetstone, esp. for razors. ● *verb* (**-ning**) sharpen (as) on hone.

honest /ˈɒnɪst/ ● *adjective* not lying, cheating, or stealing; sincere; fairly earned. ● *adverb colloquial* genuinely, really. □ **honestly** *adverb*.

honesty /ˈɒnɪstɪ/ *noun* being honest, truthfulness; plant with purple or white flowers and flat round pods.

honey /ˈhʌnɪ/ *noun* (*plural* **-s**) sweet sticky yellowish fluid made by bees from nectar; colour of this; sweetness; darling.

honeycomb ● *noun* beeswax structure of hexagonal cells for honey and eggs; pattern arranged hexagonally. ● *verb* fill with cavities; mark with honeycomb pattern.

honeydew *noun* sweet substance excreted by aphids; variety of melon.

honeyed *adjective* sweet, sweet-sounding.

honeymoon ● *noun* holiday of newly married couple; initial period of enthusiasm or goodwill. ● *verb* spend honeymoon.

honeysuckle *noun* climbing shrub with fragrant flowers.

honk ● *noun* sound of car horn; cry of wild goose. ● *verb* (cause to) make honk.

honky-tonk /ˈhɒŋkɪtɒŋk/ *noun colloquial* ragtime piano music.

honor *US* = HONOUR.

honorable *US* = HONOURABLE.

honorarium /ˌɒnəˈreərɪəm/ *noun* (*plural* **-s** or **-ria**) voluntary payment for professional services.

honorary /ˈɒnərərɪ/ *adjective* conferred as honour; unpaid.

honorific /ˌɒnəˈrɪfɪk/ *adjective* conferring honour; implying respect.

honour /ˈɒnə/ (*US* **honor**) ● *noun* high respect, public regard; adherence to what is right; nobleness of mind; thing conferred as distinction (esp. official award for bravery or achievement); privilege; (**His**, **Her**, **Your Honour**) *title of judge etc.*; person or thing that brings honour; chastity, reputation for this; (in *plural*) specialized degree course or special distinction in exam; (in *plural*) (in card games) 4 or 5 highest-ranking cards; *Golf* right of driving off first. ● *verb* respect highly; confer honour on; accept or pay (bill, cheque) when due. □ **do the honours** perform duties of host etc.

honourable *adjective* (*US* **honorable**) deserving, bringing, or showing honour; (**Honourable**) *courtesy title of MPs, certain officials, and children of certain ranks of the nobility*. □ **honourably** *adverb*.

hooch /huːtʃ/ *noun US colloquial* alcoholic spirits, esp. inferior or illicit.

hood[1] /hʊd/ ● *noun* covering for head and neck, esp. as part of garment; separate hoodlike garment; folding top of car etc.; *US* bonnet of car etc.; protective cover. ● *verb* cover with hood. □ **hooded** *adjective*.

hood[2] /hʊd/ *noun US slang* gangster; gunman.

hoodlum /ˈhuːdləm/ *noun* hooligan; gangster.

hoodoo /ˈhuːduː/ *noun US* bad luck; thing or person that brings this.

hoodwink *verb* deceive, delude.

hoof /huːf/ *noun* (*plural* **-s** or **hooves** /huːvz/) horny part of foot of horse etc. □ **hoof it** *slang* go on foot.

hook /hʊk/ ● *noun* bent piece of metal etc. for catching hold or for hanging things on; curved cutting instrument; hook-shaped thing; hooking stroke; *Boxing* short swinging blow. ● *verb* grasp, secure, fasten, or catch with hook; (in sports) send (ball) in curving or deviating path; *Rugby* secure (ball) in scrum with foot. □ **hook and eye** small hook and loop as fastener; **hook, line, and sinker** completely; **hook-up**

connection, esp. of broadcasting equipment; **hook-worm** worm infesting intestines of humans and animals.

hookah /ˈhʊkə/ noun tobacco pipe with long tube passing through water to cool smoke.

hooked adjective hook-shaped; (often + *on*) slang addicted or captivated.

hooker noun Rugby player in front row of scrum who tries to hook ball; slang prostitute.

hooligan /ˈhuːlɪgən/ noun young ruffian. □ **hooliganism** noun.

hoop /huːp/ ● noun circular band of metal, wood, etc., esp. as part of framework; wooden etc. circle bowled by child or used by circus performer etc.; arch through which balls are hit in croquet. ● verb bind with hoop(s). □ **hoop-la** game with rings thrown to encircle prizes.

hoopoe /ˈhuːpuː/ noun bird with variegated plumage and fanlike crest.

hooray = HURRAH.

hoot /huːt/ ● noun owl's cry; sound of car's horn etc.; shout of derision etc.; colloquial (cause of) laughter; (also **two hoots**) slang anything, in the slightest. ● verb utter hoot(s); greet or drive away with hoots; sound (horn).

hooter noun thing that hoots, esp. car's horn or siren; slang nose.

Hoover /ˈhuːvə/ ● noun proprietary term vacuum cleaner. ● verb (**hoover**) clean or (+ *up*) suck up with vacuum cleaner.

hooves plural of HOOF.

hop¹ ● verb (**-pp-**) (of bird, frog, etc.) spring with all feet at once; (of person) jump on one foot; move or go quickly, leap. ● noun hopping movement; colloquial dance; short journey, esp. flight. □ **hop in**, **out** colloquial get into or out of car etc.; **hopscotch** child's game of hopping over squares marked on ground.

hop² noun climbing plant with bitter cones used to flavour beer etc.; (in plural) these cones.

hope ● noun expectation and desire; person or thing giving cause for hope; what is hoped for. ● verb (**-ping**) feel hope; expect and desire.

hopeful adjective feeling or inspiring hope, promising.

hopefully adverb in a hopeful way; it is to be hoped.

■ **Usage** The use of *hopefully* to mean 'it is to be hoped' is common, but it is considered incorrect by some people.

hopeless adjective feeling or admitting no hope; inadequate, incompetent. □ **hopelessly** adverb; **hopelessness** noun.

hopper noun funnel-like device for feeding grain into mill etc.; hopping insect.

horde noun usually derogatory large group, gang.

horehound /ˈhɔːhaʊnd/ noun herb with aromatic bitter juice.

horizon /həˈraɪz(ə)n/ noun line at which earth and sky appear to meet; limit of mental perception, interest, etc.

horizontal /hɒrɪˈzɒnt(ə)l/ ● adjective parallel to plane of horizon; level, flat. ● noun horizontal line, plane, etc. □ **horizontally** adverb.

hormone /ˈhɔːməʊn/ noun substance produced by body and transported in tissue fluids to stimulate cells or tissues to growth etc.; similar synthetic substance. □ **hormone replacement therapy** treatment with hormones to relieve menopausal symptoms. □ **hormonal** /-ˈməʊn-/ adjective.

horn noun hard outgrowth, often curved and pointed, on head of animal; hornlike projection; substance of horns; brass wind instrument; instrument giving warning. □ **hornbeam** tough-wooded hedgerow

tree; **hornbill** bird with hornlike excrescence on bill; **horn of plenty** cornucopia; **horn-rimmed** (of spectacles) having rims of horn or similar substance. □ **horned** adjective.

hornblende /ˈhɔːnblend/ noun dark brown etc. mineral constituent of granite etc.

hornet /ˈhɔːnɪt/ noun large species of wasp.

hornpipe noun (music for) lively dance associated esp. with sailors.

horny adjective (**-ier**, **-iest**) of or like horn; hard; slang sexually excited. □ **horniness** noun.

horology /həˈrɒlədʒɪ/ noun clockmaking. □ **horological** /hɒrəˈlɒdʒ-/ adjective.

horoscope /ˈhɒrəskəʊp/ noun prediction of person's future based on position of planets at his or her birth.

horrendous /həˈrendəs/ adjective horrifying. □ **horrendously** adverb.

horrible /ˈhɒrɪb(ə)l/ adjective causing horror; colloquial unpleasant. □ **horribly** adverb.

horrid /ˈhɒrɪd/ adjective horrible; colloquial unpleasant.

horrific /həˈrɪfɪk/ adjective horrifying. □ **horrifically** adverb.

horrify /ˈhɒrɪfaɪ/ verb (**-ies**, **-ied**) arouse horror in; shock. □ **horrifying** adjective.

horror /ˈhɒrə/ ● noun intense loathing or fear; (often + *of*) deep dislike; colloquial intense dismay; horrifying thing. ● adjective (of films etc.) designed to arouse feelings of horror.

hors d'oeuvre /ɔːˈdɜːvr/ noun appetizer served at start of meal.

horse ● noun large 4-legged hoofed mammal with mane, used for riding etc.; adult male horse; vaulting-block; supporting frame. ● verb (often + *around*) fool about. □ **horsebox** closed vehicle for transporting horse(s); **horse brass** brass ornament originally for horse's harness; **horse chestnut** tree with conical clusters of flowers, its dark brown fruit; **horse-drawn** pulled by horse(s); **horsefly** biting insect troublesome to horses; **Horse Guards** cavalry brigade of British household troops; **horsehair** (padding etc. of) hair from mane or tail of horse; **horseman** (skilled) rider on horseback; **horsemanship** skill in riding; **horseplay** boisterous play; **horsepower** (plural same) unit of rate of doing work; **horse race** race between horses with riders; **horse racing** sport of racing horses; **horseradish** plant with pungent root used to make sauce; **horse sense** colloquial plain common sense; **horseshoe** U-shaped iron shoe for horse, thing of this shape; **horsetail** (plant resembling) horse's tail; **horsewhip** noun whip for horse, verb beat (person) with this; **horsewoman** (skilled) woman rider on horseback.

horsy adjective (**-ier**, **-iest**) of or like horse; concerned with horses.

horticulture /ˈhɔːtɪkʌltʃə/ noun art of gardening. □ **horticultural** /-ˈkʌlt-/ adjective; **horticulturist** /-ˈkʌlt-/ noun.

hosanna /həʊˈzænə/ noun & interjection cry of adoration.

hose /həʊz/ ● noun (also **hose-pipe**) flexible tube for conveying liquids; (treated as plural) stockings and socks collectively; historical breeches. ● verb (**-sing**) (often + *down*) water, spray, or drench with hose.

hosier /ˈhəʊzɪə/ noun dealer in stockings and socks. □ **hosiery** noun.

hospice /ˈhɒspɪs/ noun home for (esp. terminally) ill or destitute people; travellers' lodging kept by religious order etc.

hospitable /hɒsˈpɪtəb(ə)l/ adjective giving hospitality. □ **hospitably** adverb.

hospital /ˈhɒspɪt(ə)l/ noun institution providing medical and surgical treatment and nursing for ill and injured people; historical hospice.

hospitality /ˌhɒspɪˈtælɪtɪ/ noun friendly and generous reception of guests or strangers.

hospitalize /ˈhɒspɪtəlaɪz/ verb (also **-ise**) (**-zing** or **-sing**) send or admit to hospital. ◻ **hospitalization** noun.

host¹ /həʊst/ noun (usually + of) large number of people or things.

host² /həʊst/ ● noun person who entertains another as guest; compère; animal or plant having parasite; recipient of transplanted organ; landlord of inn. ● verb be host to (person) or of (event).

host³ /həʊst/ noun (usually **the Host**) bread consecrated in Eucharist.

hostage /ˈhɒstɪdʒ/ noun person seized or held as security for fulfilment of a condition.

hostel /ˈhɒst(ə)l/ noun house of residence for students etc.; youth hostel.

hostelling noun (US **hosteling**) practice of staying in youth hostels. ◻ **hosteller** noun.

hostelry noun (plural **-ies**) archaic inn.

hostess /ˈhəʊstɪs/ noun woman who entertains guests, or customers at nightclub.

hostile /ˈhɒstaɪl/ adjective of enemy; (often + to) unfriendly, opposed.

hostility /hɒˈstɪlɪtɪ/ noun (plural **-ies**) being hostile; enmity; warfare; (in plural) acts of war.

hot ● adjective (**-tt-**) having high temperature, very warm; causing sensation of or feeling heat; pungent; excited; (often + on, for) eager; (of news) fresh; skilful, formidable; (+ on) knowledgeable about; slang (of stolen goods) difficult to dispose of. ● verb (**-tt-**) (usually + up) colloquial make or become hot; become more active, exciting, or dangerous. ◻ **hot air** empty or boastful talk; **hot-air balloon** balloon containing air heated by burners, causing it to rise; **hotbed** (+ of) environment conducive to (vice etc.), bed of earth heated by fermenting manure; **hot cross bun** bun marked with cross, eaten on Good Friday; **hot dog** colloquial hot sausage in bread roll; **hotfoot** in eager haste; **hothead** impetuous person; **hotheaded** impetuous; **hothouse** heated (mainly glass) building for growing plants, environment conducive to rapid growth; **hotline** direct telephone line; **hotplate** heated metal plate for cooking food or keeping it hot; **hotpot** dish of stewed meat and vegetables; **hot rod** vehicle modified for extra power and speed; **hot seat** slang awkward or responsible position, electric chair; **hot water** colloquial difficulty, trouble; **hot-water bottle** container filled with hot water to warm bed etc. ◻ **hotly** adverb.

hotchpotch /ˈhɒtʃpɒtʃ/ noun (also **hodgepodge** /ˈhɒdʒpɒdʒ/) confused mixture, jumble, esp. of ideas.

hotel /həʊˈtel/ noun (usually licensed) place providing meals and accommodation for payment.

hotelier /həʊˈtelɪə/ noun hotel-keeper.

houmous = HUMMUS.

hound /haʊnd/ ● noun dog used in hunting; colloquial despicable man. ● verb harass or pursue.

hour /aʊə/ noun twenty-fourth part of day and night, 60 minutes; time of day, point in time; (in plural after numerals in form 18.00, 20.30, etc.) this number of hours and minutes past midnight on the 24-hour clock; period set aside for some purpose; (in plural) working or open period; short time; time for action etc.; (**the hour**) each time o'clock of a whole number of hours. ◻ **hourglass** two connected glass bulbs containing sand that takes an hour to pass from upper to lower bulb. ● **hourly** adjective & adverb.

houri /ˈhʊərɪ/ noun (plural **-s**) beautiful young woman in Muslim paradise.

house ● noun /haʊs/ (plural /ˈhaʊzɪz/) building for human habitation; building for special purpose or for keeping animals or goods; (buildings of) religious community; section of boarding school etc.; division of school for games etc.; royal family, dynasty; (premises of) firm or institution; (building for) legislative etc. assembly; audience or performance in theatre etc. ● verb /haʊz/ (**-sing**) provide house for; store; enclose or encase (part etc.); fix in socket etc. ◻ **house arrest** detention in one's own house; **houseboat** boat equipped for living in; **housebound** confined to one's house through illness etc.; **housebreaker** burglar; **housebreaking** burglary; **housefly** common fly; **house-husband** man who does wife's traditional duties; **housekeeper** woman managing affairs of house; **housekeeping** management of house, money for this, record-keeping etc.; **houseman** resident junior doctor of hospital; **house-martin** bird which builds nests on house walls etc.; **housemaster**, **housemistress** teacher in charge of house in boarding school; **house music** pop music with synthesized drums and bass and fast beat; **House of Commons** elected chamber of Parliament; **House of Lords** chamber of Parliament that is mainly hereditary; **house plant** one grown indoors; **house-proud** attentive to care etc. of home; **house-trained** (of domestic animal) trained to be clean in house; **house-warming** party celebrating move to new house; **housewife** woman whose chief occupation is managing household; **housewifely** adjective; **housework** regular cleaning and cooking etc. in home.

household noun occupants of house; house and its affairs. ◻ **household name** well-known name; **household troops** those nominally guarding sovereign; **household word** well-known saying or name.

householder noun person who owns or rents house; head of household.

housing /ˈhaʊzɪŋ/ noun (provision of) houses; protective casing. ◻ **housing estate** residential area planned as a unit.

hove past of HEAVE.

hovel /ˈhɒv(ə)l/ noun small miserable dwelling.

hover /ˈhɒvə/ verb (of bird etc.) remain in one place in air; (often + about, round) linger.

hovercraft noun (plural same) vehicle moving on air-cushion provided by downward blast.

hoverport noun terminal for hovercraft.

how /haʊ/ interrogative & relative adverb by what means, in what way; in what condition; to what extent. ◻ **however** nevertheless, in whatever way, to whatever extent.

howdah /ˈhaʊdə/ noun (usually canopied) seat for riding elephant or camel.

howitzer /ˈhaʊɪtsə/ noun short gun firing shells at high elevation.

howl /haʊl/ ● noun long doleful cry of dog etc.; prolonged wailing noise; loud cry of pain, rage, derision, or laughter. ● verb make howl; weep loudly; utter with howl.

howler noun colloquial glaring mistake.

hey interjection used to call attention.

hoyden /ˈhɔɪd(ə)n/ noun boisterous girl.

HP abbreviation hire purchase; (also **hp**) horsepower.

HQ abbreviation headquarters.

hr. abbreviation hour.

HRH abbreviation Her or His Royal Highness.

HRT abbreviation hormone replacement therapy.

HT abbreviation high tension.

hub noun central part of wheel, rotating on or with axle; centre of interest, activity, etc.

hubble-bubble /ˈhʌb(ə)lbʌb(ə)l/ noun simple hookah; confused sound or talk.

hubbub /'hʌbʌb/ *noun* confused noise of talking; disturbance.

hubby /'hʌbɪ/ *noun* (*plural* **-ies**) *colloquial* husband.

hubris /'hjuːbrɪs/ *noun* arrogant pride, presumption.

huckleberry /'hʌkəlbərɪ/ *noun* (*plural* **-ies**) low N. American shrub; its fruit.

huckster /'hʌkstə/ ● *noun* hawker; aggressive salesman. ● *verb* haggle; hawk (goods).

huddle /'hʌd(ə)l/ ● *verb* (**-ling**) (often + *up*) crowd together; nestle closely; (often + *up*) curl one's body up. ● *noun* confused mass; *colloquial* secret conference.

hue *noun* colour, tint.

hue and cry *noun* loud outcry.

huff ● *noun* *colloquial* fit of petulance. ● *verb* blow air, steam, etc.; (esp. **huff and puff**) bluster; remove (opponent's man) as forfeit in draughts. □ **huffy** *adjective* (**-ier, -iest**).

hug ● *verb* (**-gg-**) squeeze tightly in one's arms, esp. with affection; keep close to, fit tightly around. ● *noun* close clasp.

huge /hjuːdʒ/ *adjective* very large or great.

hugely *adverb* extremely, very much.

hugger-mugger /'hʌgəmʌgə/ *adjective & adverb* in secret; in confusion.

Huguenot /'hjuːgənəʊ/ *noun* *historical* French Protestant.

hula /'huːlə/ *noun* (also **hula-hula**) Polynesian women's dance. □ **hula hoop** large hoop spun round the body.

hulk *noun* body of dismantled ship; *colloquial* large clumsy-looking person or thing.

hulking *adjective colloquial* bulky, clumsy.

hull[1] *noun* body of ship etc.

hull[2] ● *noun* outer covering of fruit. ● *verb* remove hulls of.

hullabaloo /hʌləbə'luː/ *noun* uproar.

hullo = HELLO.

hum ● *verb* (**-mm-**) make low continuous sound like bee; sing with closed lips; make slight inarticulate sound; *colloquial* be active; *colloquial* smell unpleasantly. ● *noun* humming sound. □ **hummingbird** small tropical bird whose wings hum.

human /'hjuːmən/ ● *adjective* of or belonging to species *Homo sapiens*; consisting of human beings; having characteristics of humankind, as being weak, fallible, sympathetic, etc. ● *noun* (*plural* **-s**) human being. □ **human being** man, woman, or child; **human chain** line of people for passing things along etc.; **humankind** human beings collectively; **human rights** those held to belong to all people; **human shield** person(s) placed in line of fire to discourage attack.

humane /hjuː'meɪn/ *adjective* benevolent, compassionate; inflicting minimum pain; (of studies) tending to civilize. □ **humanely** *adverb*.

humanism /'hjuːmənɪz(ə)m/ *noun* non-religious philosophy based on liberal human values; (often **Humanism**) literary culture, esp. in Renaissance. □ **humanist** *noun*; **humanistic** /-'nɪst-/ *adjective*.

humanitarian /hjuːmænɪ'teərɪən/ ● *noun* person who seeks to promote human welfare. ● *adjective* of humanitarians. □ **humanitarianism** *noun*.

humanity /hjuː'mænɪtɪ/ *noun* (*plural* **-ies**) human race; human nature; humaneness, benevolence; (usually in *plural*) subjects concerned with human culture.

humanize *verb* (also **-ise**) (**-zing** or **-sing**) make human or humane. □ **humanization** *noun*.

humanly *adverb* within human capabilities; in a human way.

humble /'hʌmb(ə)l/ ● *adjective* (**-r, -st**) having or showing low self-esteem; lowly, modest. ● *verb* (**-ling**) make humble; lower rank of. □ **eat humble pie**

apologize humbly, accept humiliation. □ **humbly** *adverb*.

humbug /'hʌmbʌg/ ● *noun* deception, hypocrisy; impostor; striped peppermint-flavoured boiled sweet. ● *verb* (**-gg-**) be impostor; hoax.

humdinger /'hʌmdɪŋə/ *noun slang* remarkable person or thing.

humdrum /'hʌmdrʌm/ *adjective* dull, commonplace.

humerus /'hjuːmərəs/ *noun* (*plural* **-ri** /-raɪ/) bone of upper arm.

humid /'hjuːmɪd/ *adjective* warm and damp.

humidifier /hjuː'mɪdɪfaɪə/ *noun* device for keeping atmosphere moist.

humidify /hjuː'mɪdɪfaɪ/ *verb* (**-ies, -ied**) make (air etc.) humid.

humidity /hjuː'mɪdɪtɪ/ *noun* (*plural* **-ies**) dampness; degree of moisture, esp. in atmosphere.

humiliate /hjuː'mɪlɪeɪt/ *verb* (**-ting**) injure dignity or self-respect of. □ **humiliating** *adjective*; **humiliation** *noun*.

humility /hjuː'mɪlɪtɪ/ *noun* humbleness; meekness.

hummock /'hʌmək/ *noun* hillock, hump.

hummus /'hʊmʊs/ *noun* (also **houmous**) dip of chickpeas, sesame paste, lemon juice, and garlic.

humor *US* = HUMOUR.

humorist /'hjuːmərɪst/ *noun* humorous writer, talker, or actor.

humorous /'hjuːmərəs/ *adjective* showing humour, comic. □ **humorously** *adverb*.

humour /'hjuːmə/ (*US* **humor**) ● *noun* quality of being amusing; expression of humour in literature etc.; (in full **sense of humour**) ability to perceive or express humour; state of mind, mood; each of 4 fluids formerly held to determine physical and mental qualities. ● *verb* gratify or indulge (person, taste, etc.). □ **humourless** *adjective*.

hump ● *noun* rounded lump, esp. on back; rounded raised mass of earth etc.; (**the hump**) *slang* fit of depression or annoyance. ● *verb* (often + *about*) *colloquial* lift or carry with difficulty; make humpshaped. □ **humpback (whale)** whale with dorsal fin; **humpback bridge** one with steep approach to top; **over the hump** past the most difficult stage.

humph /həmf/ *interjection & noun* inarticulate sound of dissatisfaction etc.

humus /'hjuːməs/ *noun* organic constituent of soil formed by decomposition of plants.

hunch ● *verb* bend or arch into a hump. ● *noun* intuitive feeling; hump.

hundred /'hʌndrəd/ *adjective & noun* (*plural* same in first sense) ten times ten; *historical* subdivision of county; (**hundreds**) *colloquial* large number. □ **hundreds and thousands** tiny coloured sweets; **hundredweight** (*plural* same or **-s**) 112 lb (50.80 kg), *US* 100 lb. (45.4 kg) □ **hundredth** *adjective & noun*.

hundredfold *adjective & adverb* a hundred times as much or many.

hung *past & past participle* of HANG. □ **hung-over** suffering from hangover; **hung parliament** parliament in which no party has clear majority.

Hungarian /hʌŋ'geərɪən/ ● *noun* native, national, or language of Hungary. ● *adjective* of Hungary or its people or language.

hunger /'hʌŋgə/ ● *noun* lack of food; discomfort or exhaustion caused by this; (often + *for, after*) strong desire. ● *verb* (often + *for, after*) crave, desire; feel hunger. □ **hunger strike** refusal of food as protest.

hungry /'hʌŋgrɪ/ *adjective* (**-ier, -iest**) feeling, showing, or inducing hunger; craving. □ **hungrily** *adverb*.

hunk *noun* large piece cut off; *colloquial* sexually attractive man.

hunt ● *verb* pursue wild animals for food or sport; (of animal) pursue prey; (+ *after, for*) search; (as **hunted** *adjective*) (of look) frightened. ● *noun* hunting; hunting area or society. □ **huntsman** hunter, person in charge of hounds. □ **hunting** *noun*.

hunter *noun* (*feminine* **huntress**) person who hunts; horse ridden for hunting.

hurdle /'hɜːd(ə)l/ ● *noun* frame to be jumped over by athlete in race; (in *plural*) hurdle race; obstacle; portable rectangular frame used as temporary fence. ● *verb* (**-ling**) run in hurdle race. □ **hurdler** *noun*.

hurdy-gurdy /hɜːdɪ'gɜːdɪ/ *noun* (*plural* **-ies**) droning musical instrument played by turning handle; *colloquial* barrel organ.

hurl ● *verb* throw violently. ● *noun* violent throw.

hurley /'hɜːlɪ/ *noun* (also **hurling**) (stick used in) Irish game resembling hockey.

hurly-burly /hɜːlɪ'bɜːlɪ/ *noun* boisterous activity; commotion.

hurrah /hʊ'rɑː/ (also **hurray** /hʊ'reɪ/) ● *interjection* expressing joy or approval. ● *noun* utterance of 'hurrah'.

hurricane /'hʌrɪkən/ *noun* storm with violent wind, esp. W. Indian cyclone. □ **hurricane lamp** lamp with flame protected from wind.

hurry /'hʌrɪ/ ● *noun* great haste; eagerness; (with negative or in questions) need for haste. ● *verb* (**-ies**, **-ied**) (cause to) move or act hastily; (as **hurried** *adjective*) hasty, done rapidly. □ **hurriedly** *adverb*.

hurt ● *verb* (*past & past participle* **hurt**) cause pain, injury, or distress to; suffer pain. ● *noun* injury; harm. □ **hurtful** *adjective*; **hurtfully** *adverb*.

hurtle /'hɜːt(ə)l/ *verb* (**-ling**) move or hurl rapidly or noisily, come with crash.

husband /'hʌzbənd/ ● *noun* married man in relation to his wife. ● *verb* use (resources) economically.

husbandry *noun* farming; management of resources.

hush ● *verb* make, become, or be silent. ● *interjection* calling for silence. ● *noun* silence. □ **hush-hush** *colloquial* highly secret; **hush money** *slang* sum paid to ensure discretion; **hush up** suppress (fact).

husk ● *noun* dry outer covering of fruit or seed. ● *verb* remove husk from.

husky[1] /'hʌskɪ/ *adjective* (**-ier**, **-iest**) dry in the throat, hoarse; strong, hefty. □ **huskily** *adverb*.

husky[2] /'hʌskɪ/ *noun* (*plural* **-ies**) powerful dog used for pulling sledges.

hussar /hʊ'zɑː/ *noun* light-cavalry soldier.

hussy /'hʌsɪ/ *noun* (*plural* **-ies**) pert girl; promiscuous woman.

hustings /'hʌstɪŋz/ *noun* election proceedings.

hustle /'hʌs(ə)l/ ● *verb* (**-ling**) jostle; (+ *into, out of,* etc.) force, hurry; *slang* solicit business. ● *noun* act or instance of hustling. □ **hustler** *noun*.

hut *noun* small simple or crude house or shelter.

hutch *noun* box or cage for rabbits etc.

hyacinth /'haɪəsɪnθ/ *noun* bulbous plant with bell-shaped flowers.

hybrid /'haɪbrɪd/ ● *noun* offspring of two animals or plants of different species etc.; thing of mixed origins. ● *adjective* bred as hybrid; heterogeneous. □ **hybridism** *noun*; **hybridization** *noun*; **hybridize** *verb* (also **-ise**) (**-zing** or **-sing**).

hydra /'haɪdrə/ *noun* freshwater polyp; something hard to destroy.

hydrangea /haɪ'dreɪndʒə/ *noun* shrub with globular clusters of white, blue, or pink flowers.

hydrant /'haɪdrənt/ *noun* outlet for drawing water from main.

hydrate /'haɪdreɪt/ ● *noun* chemical compound of water with another compound etc. ● *verb* (**-ting**) (cause to) combine with water. □ **hydration** *noun*.

hydraulic /haɪ'drɔːlɪk/ *adjective* (of water etc.) conveyed through pipes etc.; operated by movement of liquid. □ **hydraulically** *adverb*.

hydraulics *plural noun* (usually treated as *singular*) science of conveyance of liquids through pipes etc., esp. as motive power.

hydro /'haɪdrəʊ/ *noun* (*plural* **-s**) *colloquial* hotel etc. originally providing hydropathic treatment; hydroelectric powerplant.

hydro- *combining form* water; combined with hydrogen.

hydrocarbon /haɪdrəʊ'kɑːbən/ *noun* compound of hydrogen and carbon.

hydrocephalus /haɪdrə'sefələs/ *noun* accumulated fluid in brain, esp. in young children. □ **hydrocephalic** /-sɪ'fælɪk/ *adjective*.

hydrochloric acid /haɪdrə'klɒrɪk/ *noun* solution of hydrogen chloride in water.

hydrodynamics /haɪdrəʊdaɪ'næmɪks/ *plural noun* (usually treated as *singular*) science of forces acting on or exerted by liquids.

hydroelectric /haɪdrəʊɪ'lektrɪk/ *adjective* generating electricity by water-power; (of electricity) so generated. □ **hydroelectricity** /-'trɪs-/ *noun*.

hydrofoil /'haɪdrəfɔɪl/ *noun* boat fitted with planes for raising hull out of water at speed; such a plane.

hydrogen /'haɪdrədʒ(ə)n/ *noun* light colourless odourless gas combining with oxygen to form water. □ **hydrogen bomb** immensely powerful bomb utilizing explosive fusion of hydrogen nuclei; **hydrogen peroxide** see PEROXIDE.

hydrogenate /haɪ'drɒdʒɪneɪt/ *verb* (**-ting**) charge with or cause to combine with hydrogen. □ **hydrogenation** *noun*.

hydrography /haɪ'drɒgrəfɪ/ *noun* science of surveying and charting seas, lakes, rivers, etc. □ **hydrographer** *noun*; **hydrographic** /-drə'græf-/ *adjective*.

hydrology /haɪ'drɒlədʒɪ/ *noun* science of relationship between water and land.

hydrolyse /'haɪdrəlaɪz/ *verb* (**-sing**) (*US* **-lyze**; **-zing**) decompose by hydrolysis.

hydrolysis /haɪ'drɒlɪsɪs/ *noun* decomposition by chemical reaction with water.

hydrometer /haɪ'drɒmɪtə/ *noun* instrument for measuring density of liquids.

hydropathy /haɪ'drɒpəθɪ/ *noun* (medically unorthodox) treatment of disease by water. □ **hydropathic** /-drə'pæθ-/ *adjective*.

hydrophobia /haɪdrə'fəʊbɪə/ *noun* aversion to water, esp. as symptom of rabies in humans; rabies. □ **hydrophobic** *adjective*.

hydroplane /'haɪdrəpleɪn/ *noun* light fast motor boat; finlike device enabling submarine to rise or fall.

hydroponics /haɪdrə'pɒnɪks/ *noun* growing plants without soil, in sand, water, etc. with added nutrients.

hydrostatic /haɪdrə'stætɪk/ *adjective* of the equilibrium of liquids and the pressure exerted by liquids at rest.

hydrostatics *plural noun* (usually treated as *singular*) study of hydrostatic properties of liquids.

hydrotherapy /haɪdrə'θerəpɪ/ *noun* use of water, esp. swimming, in treatment of disease.

hydrous /'haɪdrəs/ *adjective* containing water.

hyena /haɪ'iːnə/ *noun* doglike flesh-eating mammal.

hygiene /'haɪdʒiːn/ *noun* conditions or practices conducive to maintaining health; cleanliness; sanitary science. □ **hygienic** /-'dʒiːn-/ *adjective*; **hygienically** /-'dʒiːn-/ *adverb*; **hygienist** *noun*.

hygrometer /haɪ'grɒmɪtə/ *noun* instrument for measuring humidity of air etc.

hygroscopic /haɪgrəˈskɒpɪk/ *adjective* tending to absorb moisture from air.

hymen /ˈhaɪmen/ *noun* membrane at opening of vagina, usually broken at first sexual intercourse.

hymenopterous /haɪməˈnɒptərəs/ *adjective* of order of insects with 4 membranous wings, including bees and wasps.

hymn /hɪm/ ● *noun* song of esp. Christian praise. ● *verb* praise or celebrate in hymns.

hymnal /ˈhɪmn(ə)l/ *noun* book of hymns.

hymnology /hɪmˈnɒlədʒɪ/ *noun* composition or study of hymns. □ **hymnologist** *noun*.

hyoscine /ˈhaɪəsiːn/ *noun* alkaloid used to prevent motion sickness etc.

hype /haɪp/ *slang* ● *noun* intensive promotion of product etc. ● *verb* (**-ping**) promote with hype. □ **hyped up** excited.

hyper /ˈhaɪpə/ *adjective slang* hyperactive.

hyper- /ˈhaɪpə/ *prefix* over, above; too.

hyperbola /haɪˈpɜːbələ/ *noun* (*plural* **-s** or **-lae** /-liː/) curve produced when cone is cut by plane making larger angle with base than side of cone makes. □ **hyperbolic** /-pəˈbɒl-/ *adjective*.

hyperbole /haɪˈpɜːbəlɪ/ *noun* exaggeration, esp. for effect. □ **hyperbolical** /-ˈbɒl-/ *adjective*.

hyperglycaemia /haɪpəglarˈsiːmɪə/ *noun* (US **hyperglycemia**) excess of glucose in bloodstream.

hypermarket /ˈhaɪpəmɑːkɪt/ *noun* very large supermarket.

hypermedia /ˈhaɪpəmiːdɪə/ *noun* provision of several media (audio, video, etc.) on one computer system.

hypersensitive /haɪpəˈsensɪtɪv/ *adjective* excessively sensitive. □ **hypersensitivity** /-ˈtɪv-/ *noun*.

hypersonic /haɪpəˈsɒnɪk/ *adjective* of speeds more than 5 times that of sound.

hypertension /haɪpəˈtenʃ(ə)n/ *noun* abnormally high blood pressure; extreme tension.

hypertext /ˈhaɪpətekst/ *noun* provision of several texts on one computer system.

hyperthermia /haɪpəˈθɜːmɪə/ *noun* abnormally high body-temperature.

hyperthyroidism /haɪpəˈθaɪrɔɪdɪz(ə)m/ *noun* overactivity of thyroid gland.

hyperventilation /haɪpəventɪˈleɪʃ(ə)n/ *noun* abnormally rapid breathing. □ **hyperventilate** *verb* (**-ting**).

hyphen /ˈhaɪf(ə)n/ ● *noun* punctuation mark (-) used to join or divide words (see panel). ● *verb* hyphenate.

hyphenate /ˈhaɪfəneɪt/ *verb* (**-ting**) join or divide with hyphen. □ **hyphenation** *noun*.

hypnosis /hɪpˈnəʊsɪs/ *noun* state like sleep in which subject acts only on external suggestion; artificially induced sleep.

hypnotherapy /hɪpnəʊˈθerəpɪ/ *noun* treatment of mental disorders by hypnosis.

hypnotic /hɪpˈnɒtɪk/ ● *adjective* of or causing hypnosis; sleep-inducing. ● *noun* hypnotic drug or influence. □ **hypnotically** *adverb*.

hypnotism /ˈhɪpnətɪz(ə)m/ *noun* study or practice of hypnosis. □ **hypnotist** *noun*.

hypnotize /ˈhɪpnətaɪz/ *verb* (also **-ise**) (**-zing** or **-sing**) produce hypnosis in; fascinate.

hypo /ˈhaɪpəʊ/ *noun* sodium thiosulphate, used as photographic fixer.

hypo- /ˈhaɪpəʊ/ *prefix* under; below normal; slightly.

hypochondria /haɪpəˈkɒndrɪə/ *noun* abnormal anxiety about one's health.

Hyphen -

This is used:

1 to join two or more words so as to form a compound or single expression, e.g.
   mother-in-law, non-stick, dressing-table

This use is growing less common; often you can do without such hyphens:
   nonstick, treelike, dressing table

2 to join words in an attributive compound (one put before a noun, like an adjective), e.g.
   a well-known man (but *the man is well known*)
   an out-of-date list (but *the list is out of date*)

3 to join a prefix etc. to a proper name, e.g.
   anti-Darwinian; half-Italian; non-British

4 to make a meaning clear by linking words, e.g.
   twenty-odd people/twenty odd people
or by separating a prefix, e.g.
   re-cover/recover; re-present/represent; re-sign/resign

5 to separate two identical letters in adjacent parts of a word, e.g.
   pre-exist, Ross-shire

6 to represent a common second element in the items of a list, e.g.
   two-, three-, or fourfold.

7 to divide a word if there is no room to complete it at the end of the line, e.g.
   . . . diction-
   ary . . .

The hyphen comes at the end of the line, not at the beginning of the next line. In general, words should be divided at the end of a syllable: *dicti-onary* would be quite wrong. In handwriting, typing, and word-processing, it is safest (and often neatest) not to divide words at all.

hypochondriac /haɪpə'kɒndrɪæk/ ● *noun* person given to hypochondria. ● *adjective* of hypochondria.

hypocrisy /hɪ'pəkrɪsɪ/ *noun* (*plural* **-ies**) simulation of virtue; insincerity.

hypocrite /'hɪpəkrɪt/ *noun* person guilty of hypocrisy. □ **hypocritical** /-'krɪt-/ *adjective*; **hypocritically** /-'krɪt-/ *adverb*.

hypodermic /haɪpə'dɜːmɪk/ ● *adjective* (of drug, syringe, etc.) introduced under the skin. ● *noun* hypodermic injection or syringe.

hypotension /haɪpəʊ'tenʃ(ə)n/ *noun* abnormally low blood pressure.

hypotenuse /haɪ'pɒtənjuːz/ *noun* side opposite right angle of right-angled triangle.

hypothalamus /haɪpə'θæləməs/ *noun* (*plural* **-mi** /-maɪ/) region of brain controlling body temperature, thirst, hunger, etc.

hypothermia /haɪpəʊ'θɜːmɪə/ *noun* abnormally low body-temperature.

hypothesis /haɪ'pɒθɪsɪs/ *noun* (*plural* **-theses** /-siːz/) supposition made as basis for reasoning etc. □ **hypothesize** *verb* (also **-ise**) (**-zing** or **-sing**).

hypothetical /haɪpə'θetɪk(ə)l/ *adjective* of or resting on hypothesis. □ **hypothetically** *adverb*.

hypothyroidism /haɪpəʊ'θaɪrɔɪdɪz(ə)m/ *noun* subnormal activity of the thyroid gland.

hypoventilation /haɪpəʊventɪ'leɪʃ(ə)n/ *noun* abnormally slow breathing.

hyssop /'hɪsəp/ *noun* small bushy aromatic herb.

hysterectomy /hɪstə'rektəmɪ/ *noun* (*plural* **-ies**) surgical removal of womb.

hysteria /hɪ'stɪərɪə/ *noun* uncontrollable emotion or excitement; functional disturbance of nervous system.

hysteric /hɪ'sterɪk/ *noun* (in *plural*) fit of hysteria, *colloquial* overwhelming laughter; hysterical person. □ **hysterical** *adjective*; **hysterically** *adverb*.

Hz *abbreviation* hertz.

I¹ *noun* (also **i**) (Roman numeral) 1.
I² /aɪ/ *pronoun used by speaker or writer to refer to himself or herself as subject of verb.*
I³ *abbreviation* (also **I.**) Island(s); Isle(s).
iambic /aɪˈæmbɪk/ ● *adjective* of or using iambuses. ● *noun* (usually in *plural*) iambic verse.
iambus /aɪˈæmbəs/ *noun* (*plural* **-buses** or **-bi** /-baɪ/) metrical foot of one short followed by one long syllable.
IBA *abbreviation* Independent Broadcasting Authority.
ibex /ˈaɪbeks/ *noun* (*plural* **-es**) wild mountain goat with large backward-curving ridged horns.
ibid. /ˈɪbɪd/ *abbreviation* in same book or passage etc. (*ibidem*).
ibis /ˈaɪbɪs/ *noun* (*plural* **-es**) stork-like bird with long curved bill.
ice ● *noun* frozen water; portion of ice cream etc. ● *verb* (**icing**) mix with or cool in ice; (often + *over, up*) cover or become covered (as) with ice; freeze; cover (a cake etc.) with icing. □ **ice age** glacial period; **icebox** compartment in refrigerator for making or storing ice, *US* refrigerator; **ice-breaker** boat designed to break through ice; **icecap** mass of thick ice permanently covering polar region etc.; **ice cream** sweet creamy frozen food; **ice field** extensive sheet of floating ice; **ice hockey** form of hockey played on ice with flat disc instead of ball; **ice lolly** flavoured ice on stick; **ice rink** area of ice for skating etc.; **ice-skate** *noun* boot with blade attached for gliding over ice, *verb* move on ice-skates; **on ice** performed by ice-skaters, *colloquial* in reserve.
iceberg /ˈaɪsbɜːɡ/ *noun* mass of floating ice at sea. □ **tip of the iceberg** small perceptible part of something very large or complex.
Icelander /ˈaɪsləndə/ *noun* native of Iceland.
Icelandic /aɪsˈlændɪk/ ● *adjective* of Iceland. ● *noun* language of Iceland.
ichneumon /ɪkˈnjuːmən/ *noun* (in full **ichneumon fly**) wasplike insect parasitic on other insects; mongoose of N. Africa etc.
ichthyology /ɪkθɪˈɒlədʒɪ/ *noun* study of fishes. □ **ichthyological** /-əˈlɒdʒɪk(ə)l/ *adjective*; **ichthyologist** *noun*.
ichthyosaur /ˈɪkθɪəsɔː/ *noun* large extinct reptile like dolphin.
icicle /ˈaɪsɪk(ə)l/ *noun* tapering hanging spike of ice, formed from dripping water.
icing *noun* sugar etc. coating for cake etc.; formation of ice on ship or aircraft. □ **icing sugar** finely powdered sugar.
icon /ˈaɪkɒn/ *noun* (also **ikon**) sacred painting, mosaic, etc.; image, statue. □ **iconic** /-ˈkɒn-/ *adjective*.
iconoclast /aɪˈkɒnəklæst/ *noun* person who attacks cherished beliefs; *historical* breaker of religious images. □ **iconoclasm** *noun*; **iconoclastic** /-ˈklæstɪk/ *adjective*.
iconography /aɪkəˈnɒɡrəfɪ/ *noun* illustration of subject by drawings etc.; study of portraits, esp. of one person, or of artistic images or symbols.
icy /ˈaɪsɪ/ *adjective* (**-ier, -iest**) very cold; covered with or abounding in ice; (of manner) unfriendly.
ID *abbreviation* identification, identity.
I'd /aɪd/ I had; I should; I would.
id *noun Psychology* part of mind comprising instinctive impulses of individual etc.

idea /aɪˈdɪə/ *noun* plan etc. formed by mental effort; mental impression or concept; vague belief or fancy; purpose, intention. □ **have no idea** *colloquial* not know at all, be completely incompetent.
ideal /aɪˈdiːəl/ ● *adjective* perfect; existing only in idea; visionary. ● *noun* perfect type, thing, principle, etc. as standard for imitation.
idealism *noun* forming or pursuing ideals; representation of things in ideal form; philosophy in which objects are held to be dependent on mind. □ **idealist** *noun*; **idealistic** /-ˈlɪst-/ *adjective*.
idealize *verb* (also **-ise**) (**-zing** or **-sing**) regard or represent as ideal. □ **idealization** *noun*.
identical /aɪˈdentɪk(ə)l/ *adjective* (often + *with*) absolutely alike; same; (of twins) developed from single ovum and very similar in appearance. □ **identically** *adverb*.
identify /aɪˈdentɪfaɪ/ *verb* (**-ies, -ied**) establish identity of; select, discover; (+ *with*) closely associate with; (+ *with*) regard oneself as sharing basic characteristics with; (often + *with*) treat as identical. □ **identification** *noun*.
identity /aɪˈdentɪtɪ/ *noun* (*plural* **-ies**) being specified person or thing; individuality; identification or the result of it; absolute sameness.
ideogram /ˈɪdɪəɡræm/ *noun* (also **ideograph** /-ɡrɑːf/) symbol representing thing or idea without indicating sounds in its name (e.g. Chinese character, or ' = ' for 'equals').
ideology /aɪdɪˈɒlədʒɪ/ *noun* (*plural* **-ies**) scheme of ideas at basis of political etc. theory or system; characteristic thinking of class etc. □ **ideological** /-əˈlɒdʒ-/ *adjective*.
idiocy /ˈɪdɪəsɪ/ *noun* (*plural* **-ies**) utter foolishness; foolish act; mental condition of idiot.
idiom /ˈɪdɪəm/ *noun* phrase etc. established by usage and not immediately comprehensible from the words used; form of expression peculiar to a language; language; characteristic mode of expression. □ **idiomatic** /-ˈmæt-/ *adjective*.
idiosyncrasy /ɪdɪəʊˈsɪŋkrəsɪ/ *noun* (*plural* **-ies**) attitude or form of behaviour peculiar to person. □ **idiosyncratic** /-ˈkræt-/ *adjective*.
idiot /ˈɪdɪət/ *noun* stupid person; person too deficient in mind to be capable of rational conduct. □ **idiotic** /-ˈɒt-/ *adjective*.
idle /ˈaɪd(ə)l/ ● *adjective* (**-r, -st**) lazy, indolent; not in use; unoccupied; useless, purposeless. ● *verb* (**-ling**) be idle; (of engine) run slowly without doing any work; pass (time) in idleness. □ **idleness** *noun*; **idler** *noun*; **idly** *adverb*.
idol /ˈaɪd(ə)l/ *noun* image as object of worship; object of devotion.
idolater /aɪˈdɒlətə/ *noun* worshipper of idols; devout admirer. □ **idolatrous** *adjective*; **idolatry** *noun*.
idolize *verb* (also **-ise**) (**-zing** or **-sing**) venerate or love to excess; treat as idol. □ **idolization** *noun*.
idyll /ˈɪdɪl/ *noun* account of picturesque scene or incident etc.; such scene etc. □ **idyllic** /ɪˈdɪlɪk/ *adjective*.
i.e. *abbreviation* that is to say (*id est*).
if *conjunction* on condition or supposition that; (*with past tense*) *implying that the condition is not fulfilled*; even though; whenever; whether; *expressing wish, request, or (with negative) surprise*. □ **if only** even if for no other reason than, I wish that.

igloo /'ɪgluː/ *noun* dome-shaped snow house.

igneous /'ɪgnɪəs/ *adjective* of fire; (esp. of rocks) produced by volcanic action.

ignite /ɪg'naɪt/ *verb* (**-ting**) set fire to; catch fire; provoke or excite (feelings etc.).

ignition /ɪg'nɪʃ(ə)n/ *noun* mechanism for starting combustion in cylinder of motor engine; igniting.

ignoble /ɪg'nəʊb(ə)l/ *adjective* (**-r, -st**) dishonourable; of low birth or position.

ignominious /ɪgnə'mɪnɪəs/ *adjective* humiliating. □ **ignominiously** *adverb*.

ignominy /'ɪgnəmɪnɪ/ *noun* dishonour, infamy.

ignoramus /ɪgnə'reɪməs/ *noun* (*plural* **-muses**) ignorant person.

ignorant /'ɪgnərənt/ *adjective* lacking knowledge; (+ *of*) uninformed; *colloquial* uncouth. □ **ignorance** *noun*.

ignore /ɪg'nɔː/ *verb* (**-ring**) refuse to take notice of.

iguana /ɪg'wɑːnə/ *noun* large Central and S. American tree lizard.

iguanodon /ɪg'wɑːnədɒn/ *noun* large plant-eating dinosaur.

ikebana /ɪkɪ'bɑːnə/ *noun* Japanese art of flower arrangement.

ikon = ICON.

ilex /'aɪleks/ *noun* (*plural* **-es**) plant of genus including holly; holm-oak.

iliac /'ɪlɪæk/ *adjective* of flank or hip-bone.

ilk *noun colloquial* sort, kind. □ **of that ilk** *Scottish* of ancestral estate of same name as family.

I'll /aɪl/ I shall; I will.

ill ● *adjective* in bad health; sick; harmful, unfavourable; hostile, unkind; faulty, deficient. ● *adverb* badly, unfavourably; scarcely. ● *noun* harm; evil. □ **ill-advised** unwise; **ill-bred** rude; **ill-favoured** unattractive; **ill-gotten** gained unlawfully or wickedly; **ill health** poor physical condition; **ill-mannered** rude; **ill-natured** churlish; **ill-tempered** morose, irritable; **ill-timed** done or occurring at unsuitable time; **ill-treat, -use** treat badly.

illegal /ɪ'liːg(ə)l/ *adjective* contrary to law. □ **illegality** /-'gæl-/ *noun* (*plural* **-ies**); **illegally** *adverb*.

illegible /ɪ'ledʒɪb(ə)l/ *adjective* not legible, unreadable. □ **illegibility** *noun*; **illegibly** *adverb*.

illegitimate /ɪlɪ'dʒɪtɪmət/ *adjective* born of parents not married to each other; unlawful; improper; wrongly inferred. □ **illegitimacy** *noun*.

illiberal /ɪ'lɪbər(ə)l/ *adjective* narrow-minded; stingy. □ **illiberality** /-'ræl-/ *noun*.

illicit /ɪ'lɪsɪt/ *adjective* unlawful; forbidden. □ **illicitly** *adverb*.

illiterate /ɪ'lɪtərət/ ● *adjective* unable to read; uneducated. ● *noun* illiterate person. □ **illiteracy** *noun*.

illness *noun* disease; ill health.

illogical /ɪ'lɒdʒɪk(ə)l/ *adjective* devoid of or contrary to logic. □ **illogicality** /-'kæl-/ *noun* (*plural* **-ies**); **illogically** *adverb*.

illuminate /ɪ'luːmɪneɪt/ *verb* (**-ting**) light up; decorate with lights; decorate (manuscript etc.) with gold, colour, etc.; help to explain (subject etc.); enlighten spiritually or intellectually. □ **illuminating** *adjective*; **illumination** *noun*.

illumine /ɪ'ljuːmɪn/ *verb* (**-ning**) *literary* light up; enlighten.

illusion /ɪ'luːʒ(ə)n/ *noun* false belief; deceptive appearance. □ **be under the illusion** (+ *that*) believe mistakenly. □ **illusive** *adjective*; **illusory** *adjective*.

illusionist *noun* conjuror.

illustrate /'ɪləstreɪt/ *verb* (**-ting**) provide with pictures; make clear, esp. by examples or drawings; serve as example of. □ **illustrator** *noun*.

illustration *noun* drawing etc. in book; explanatory example; illustrating.

illustrative /'ɪləstrətɪv/ *adjective* (often + *of*) explanatory.

illustrious /ɪ'lʌstrɪəs/ *adjective* distinguished, renowned.

I'm /aɪm/ I am.

image /'ɪmɪdʒ/ ● *noun* representation of object, esp. figure of saint or divinity; reputation or persona of person, company, etc.; appearance as seen in mirror or through lens; idea, conception; simile, metaphor. ● *verb* (**-ging**) make image of; mirror; picture.

imagery /'ɪmɪdʒərɪ/ *noun* figurative illustration; use of images in literature etc.; images, statuary; mental images collectively.

imaginary /ɪ'mædʒɪnərɪ/ *adjective* existing only in imagination.

imagination /ɪmædʒɪ'neɪʃ(ə)n/ *noun* mental faculty of forming images of objects not present to senses; creative faculty of mind.

imaginative /ɪ'mædʒɪnətɪv/ *adjective* having or showing high degree of imagination. □ **imaginatively** *adverb*.

imagine /ɪ'mædʒɪn/ *verb* (**-ning**) form mental image of, conceive; suppose, think.

imago /ɪ'meɪgəʊ/ *noun* (*plural* **-s** or **imagines** /ɪ'mædʒɪniːz/) fully developed stage of insect.

imam /ɪ'mɑːm/ *noun* prayer-leader of mosque; *title of some Muslim leaders.*

imbalance /ɪm'bæləns/ *noun* lack of balance; disproportion.

imbecile /'ɪmbɪsiːl/ ● *noun colloquial* stupid person; adult with mental age of about 5. ● *adjective* mentally weak, stupid. □ **imbecilic** /-'sɪlɪk/ *adjective*; **imbecility** /-'sɪlɪtɪ/ *noun* (*plural* **-ies**).

imbed = EMBED.

imbibe /ɪm'baɪb/ *verb* (**-bing**) drink; drink in; absorb; inhale.

imbroglio /ɪm'brəʊlɪəʊ/ *noun* (*plural* **-s**) confused or complicated situation.

imbue /ɪm'bjuː/ *verb* (**-bues, -bued, -buing**) (often + *with*) inspire; saturate, dye.

imitate /'ɪmɪteɪt/ *verb* (**-ting**) follow example of; mimic; make copy of; be like. □ **imitable** *adjective*; **imitative** /-tətɪv/ *adjective*; **imitator** *noun*.

imitation *noun* imitating, being imitated; copy; counterfeit.

immaculate /ɪ'mækjʊlət/ *adjective* perfectly clean, spotless; faultless; innocent, sinless. □ **immaculately** *adverb*; **immaculateness** *noun*.

immanent /'ɪmənənt/ *adjective* inherent; (of God) omnipresent. □ **immanence** *noun*.

immaterial /ɪmə'tɪərɪəl/ *adjective* unimportant; irrelevant; not material. □ **immateriality** /-'æl-/ *noun*.

immature /ɪmə'tjʊə/ *adjective* not mature; undeveloped, esp. emotionally. □ **immaturity** *noun*.

immeasurable /ɪ'meʒərəb(ə)l/ *adjective* not measurable, immense. □ **immeasurably** *adverb*.

immediate /ɪ'miːdɪət/ *adjective* occurring at once; direct; nearest; having priority. □ **immediacy** *noun*; **immediately** *adverb*.

immemorial /ɪmɪ'mɔːrɪəl/ *adjective* ancient beyond memory.

immense /ɪ'mens/ *adjective* vast, huge. □ **immensity** *noun*.

immensely *adverb colloquial* vastly, very much.

immerse /ɪ'mɜːs/ *verb* (**-sing**) (often + *in*) dip, plunge; put under water; (often **immerse oneself** or in *passive*; often + *in*) involve deeply, embed.

immersion /ɪ'mɜːʃ(ə)n/ *noun* immersing, being immersed. □ **immersion heater** electric heater designed to be immersed in liquid to be heated.

immigrant /ˈɪmɪgrənt/ ● *noun* person who immigrates. ● *adjective* immigrating; of immigrants.

immigrate /ˈɪmɪgreɪt/ *verb* (**-ting**) enter a country to settle permanently. □ **immigration** *noun*.

imminent /ˈɪmɪnənt/ *adjective* soon to happen. □ **imminence** *noun*; **imminently** *adverb*.

immobile /ɪˈməʊbaɪl/ *adjective* motionless; immovable. □ **immobility** *noun*.

immobilize /ɪˈməʊbɪlaɪz/ *verb* (also **-ise**) (**-zing** or **-sing**) prevent from being moved. □ **immobilization** *noun*.

immoderate /ɪˈmɒdərət/ *adjective* excessive. □ **immoderately** *adverb*.

immodest /ɪˈmɒdɪst/ *adjective* conceited; indecent. □ **immodesty** *noun*.

immolate /ˈɪməleɪt/ *verb* (**-ting**) kill as sacrifice. □ **immolation** *noun*.

immoral /ɪˈmɒr(ə)l/ *adjective* opposed to, or not conforming to, (esp. sexual) morality; dissolute. □ **immorality** /ɪˈmɒrælɪtɪ/ *noun*.

immortal /ɪˈmɔːt(ə)l/ ● *adjective* living for ever; unfading; divine; famous for all time. ● *noun* immortal being, esp. (in *plural*) gods of antiquity. □ **immortality** /-ˈtæl-/ *noun*; **immortalize** *verb* (also **-ise**) (**-zing** or **-sing**).

immovable /ɪˈmuːvəb(ə)l/ *adjective* not movable; unyielding. □ **immovability** *noun*.

immune /ɪˈmjuːn/ *adjective* having immunity; relating to immunity; exempt.

immunity *noun* (*plural* **-ies**) living organism's power of resisting and overcoming infection; (often + *from*) freedom, exemption.

immunize /ˈɪmjuːnaɪz/ *verb* (also **-ise**) (**-zing** or **-sing**) make immune. □ **immunization** *noun*.

immure /ɪˈmjʊə/ *verb* (**-ring**) imprison.

immutable /ɪˈmjuːtəb(ə)l/ *adjective* unchangeable. □ **immutability** *noun*.

imp *noun* mischievous child; little devil.

impact ● *noun* /ˈɪmpækt/ collision, striking; (immediate) effect or influence. ● *verb* /ɪmˈpækt/ drive or wedge together; (as **impacted** *adjective*) (of tooth) wedged between another tooth and jaw. □ **impaction** /ɪmˈpækʃ(ə)n/ *noun*.

impair /ɪmˈpeə/ *verb* damage, weaken. □ **impairment** *noun*.

impala /ɪmˈpɑːlə/ *noun* (*plural* same or **-s**) small African antelope.

impale /ɪmˈpeɪl/ *verb* (**-ling**) transfix on stake. □ **impalement** *noun*.

impalpable /ɪmˈpælpəb(ə)l/ *adjective* not easily grasped; imperceptible to touch.

impart /ɪmˈpɑːt/ *verb* communicate (news etc.); give share of.

impartial /ɪmˈpɑːʃ(ə)l/ *adjective* fair, not partial. □ **impartiality** /-ʃɪˈæl-/ *noun*; **impartially** *adverb*.

impassable /ɪmˈpɑːsəb(ə)l/ *adjective* that cannot be traversed. □ **impassability** *noun*.

impasse /ˈæmpæs/ *noun* deadlock.

impassioned /ɪmˈpæʃ(ə)nd/ *adjective* filled with passion, ardent.

impassive /ɪmˈpæsɪv/ *adjective* not feeling or showing emotion. □ **impassively** *adverb*; **impassivity** /-ˈsɪv-/ *noun*.

impasto /ɪmˈpæstəʊ/ *noun* technique of laying on paint thickly.

impatiens /ɪmˈpeɪʃɪenz/ *noun* any of several plants including busy Lizzie.

impatient /ɪmˈpeɪʃ(ə)nt/ *adjective* not patient; intolerant; restlessly eager. □ **impatience** *noun*; **impatiently** *adverb*.

impeach /ɪmˈpiːtʃ/ *verb* accuse, esp. of treason etc.; call in question; disparage. □ **impeachment** *noun*.

impeccable /ɪmˈpekəb(ə)l/ *adjective* faultless; exemplary. □ **impeccability** *noun*; **impeccably** *adverb*.

impecunious /ɪmpɪˈkjuːnɪəs/ *adjective* having little or no money.

impedance /ɪmˈpiːd(ə)ns/ *noun* total effective resistance of electric circuit etc. to alternating current.

impede /ɪmˈpiːd/ *verb* (**-ding**) obstruct; hinder.

impediment /ɪmˈpedɪmənt/ *noun* hindrance; defect in speech, esp. lisp or stammer.

impedimenta /ɪmpedɪˈmentə/ *plural noun* encumbrances; baggage, esp. of army.

impel /ɪmˈpel/ *verb* (**-ll-**) drive, force; propel.

impend /ɪmˈpend/ *verb* be imminent; hang. □ **impending** *adjective*.

impenetrable /ɪmˈpenɪtrəb(ə)l/ *adjective* not penetrable; inscrutable; inaccessible to influences etc. □ **impenetrability** *noun*.

impenitent /ɪmˈpenɪt(ə)nt/ *adjective* not penitent. □ **impenitence** *noun*.

imperative /ɪmˈperətɪv/ ● *adjective* urgent, obligatory; peremptory; *Grammar* (of mood) expressing command. ● *noun Grammar* imperative mood; command; essential or urgent thing.

imperceptible /ɪmpəˈseptɪb(ə)l/ *adjective* not perceptible; very slight or gradual. □ **imperceptibility** *noun*; **imperceptibly** *adverb*.

imperfect /ɪmˈpɜːfɪkt/ ● *adjective* not perfect; incomplete; faulty; *Grammar* (of past tense) implying action going on but not completed. ● *noun* imperfect tense. □ **imperfectly** *adverb*.

imperfection /ɪmpəˈfekʃ(ə)n/ *noun* imperfectness; fault, blemish.

imperial /ɪmˈpɪərɪəl/ *adjective* of empire or sovereign state ranking with this; of emperor; majestic; (of non-metric weights and measures) used by statute in UK.

imperialism *noun* imperial system of government etc.; *usually derogatory* policy of dominating other nations by acquisition of dependencies or through trade etc. □ **imperialist** *noun & adjective*.

imperil /ɪmˈperɪl/ *verb* (**-ll-**; *US* **-l-**) endanger.

imperious /ɪmˈpɪərɪəs/ *adjective* overbearing, domineering. □ **imperiously** *adverb*.

imperishable /ɪmˈperɪʃəb(ə)l/ *adjective* that cannot perish.

impermanent /ɪmˈpɜːmənənt/ *adjective* not permanent. □ **impermanence** *noun*.

impermeable /ɪmˈpɜːmɪəb(ə)l/ *adjective* not permeable. □ **impermeability** *noun*.

impersonal /ɪmˈpɜːsən(ə)l/ *adjective* having no personality or personal feeling or reference; impartial; unfeeling; *Grammar* (of verb) used esp. with *it* as subject. □ **impersonality** /-ˈnæl-/ *noun*.

impersonate /ɪmˈpɜːsəneɪt/ *verb* (**-ting**) pretend to be, play part of. □ **impersonation** *noun*; **impersonator** *noun*.

impertinent /ɪmˈpɜːtɪnənt/ *adjective* insolent, saucy; irrelevant. □ **impertinence** *noun*; **impertinently** *adverb*.

imperturbable /ɪmpəˈtɜːbəb(ə)l/ *adjective* not excitable; calm. □ **imperturbability** *noun*; **imperturbably** *adverb*.

impervious /ɪmˈpɜːvɪəs/ *adjective* (usually + *to*) impermeable; not responsive.

impetigo /ɪmpɪˈtaɪgəʊ/ *noun* contagious skin disease.

impetuous /ɪmˈpetjʊəs/ *adjective* acting or done rashly or suddenly; moving violently or fast. □ **impetuosity** /-ˈɒs-/ *noun*; **impetuously** *adverb*.

impetus /ˈɪmpɪtəs/ *noun* moving force; momentum; impulse.

impiety /ɪmˈpaɪətɪ/ *noun* (*plural* **-ies**) lack of piety; act showing this.

impinge /ɪmˈpɪndʒ/ *verb* (**-ging**) (usually + *on*) make impact; (usually + *upon*) encroach.

impious /ˈɪmpɪəs/ *adjective* not pious; wicked.

impish *adjective* of or like imp, mischievous. □ **impishly** *adverb*.

implacable /ɪmˈplækəb(ə)l/ *adjective* not appeasable. □ **implacability** *noun*; **implacably** *adverb*.

implant ● *verb* /ɪmˈplɑːnt/ insert, fix; instil; plant; (in *passive*) (of fertilized ovum) become attached to wall of womb. ● *noun* /ˈɪmplɑːnt/ thing implanted. □ **implantation** *noun*.

implausible /ɪmˈplɔːzɪb(ə)l/ *adjective* not plausible. □ **implausibly** *adverb*.

implement ● *noun* /ˈɪmplɪmənt/ tool, utensil. ● *verb* /ˈɪmplɪment/ carry into effect. □ **implementation** *noun*.

implicate /ˈɪmplɪkeɪt/ *verb* (**-ting**) (often + *in*) show (person) to be involved (in crime etc.); imply.

implication *noun* thing implied; implying; implicating.

implicit /ɪmˈplɪsɪt/ *adjective* implied though not expressed; unquestioning. □ **implicitly** *adverb*.

implode /ɪmˈpləʊd/ *verb* (**-ding**) (cause to) burst inwards. □ **implosion** /ɪmˈpləʊʒ(ə)n/ *noun*.

implore /ɪmˈplɔː/ *verb* (**-ring**) beg earnestly.

imply /ɪmˈplaɪ/ *verb* (**-ies**, **-ied**) (often + *that*) insinuate, hint; mean.

impolite /ɪmpəˈlaɪt/ *adjective* uncivil, rude. □ **impolitely** *adverb*; **impoliteness** *noun*.

impolitic /ɪmˈpɒlɪtɪk/ *adjective* inexpedient, not advisable. □ **impoliticly** *adverb*.

imponderable /ɪmˈpɒndərəb(ə)l/ ● *adjective* that cannot be estimated; very light. ● *noun* (usually in *plural*) imponderable thing. □ **imponderability** *noun*; **imponderably** *adverb*.

import ● *verb* /ɪmˈpɔːt/ bring in (esp. foreign goods) from abroad; imply, mean. ● *noun* /ˈɪmpɔːt/ article or (in *plural*) amount imported; importing; meaning, implication; importance. □ **importation** *noun*; **importer** /-ˈpɔːtə/ *noun*.

important /ɪmˈpɔːt(ə)nt/ *adjective* (often + *to*) of great consequence; momentous; (of person) having position of authority or rank; pompous. □ **importance** *noun*; **importantly** *adverb*.

importunate /ɪmˈpɔːtjʊnət/ *adjective* making persistent or pressing requests. □ **importunity** /-ˈtjuːn-/ *noun*.

importune /ɪmpəˈtjuːn/ *verb* (**-ning**) pester (person) with requests; solicit as prostitute.

impose /ɪmˈpəʊz/ *verb* (**-sing**) enforce compliance with; (often + *on*) inflict, lay (tax etc.); (+ *on*, *upon*) take advantage of.

imposing *adjective* impressive, esp. in appearance.

imposition /ɪmpəˈzɪʃ(ə)n/ *noun* imposing, being imposed; unfair demand or burden; tax, duty.

impossible /ɪmˈpɒsɪb(ə)l/ *adjective* not possible; not easy or convenient; *colloquial* outrageous, intolerable. □ **impossibility** *noun*; **impossibly** *adverb*.

impost /ˈɪmpəʊst/ *noun* tax, duty.

impostor /ɪmˈpɒstə/ *noun* (also **imposter**) person who assumes false character; swindler.

imposture /ɪmˈpɒstʃə/ *noun* fraudulent deception.

impotent /ˈɪmpət(ə)nt/ *adjective* powerless; (of male) unable to achieve erection of penis or have sexual intercourse. □ **impotence** *noun*.

impound /ɪmˈpaʊnd/ *verb* confiscate; shut up in pound.

impoverish /ɪmˈpɒvərɪʃ/ *verb* make poor. □ **impoverishment** *noun*.

impracticable /ɪmˈpræktɪkəb(ə)l/ *adjective* impossible in practice. □ **impracticability** *noun*; **impracticably** *adverb*.

impractical /ɪmˈpræktɪk(ə)l/ *adjective* not practical; esp. *US* not practicable. □ **impracticality** /-ˈkæl-/ *noun*.

imprecation /ɪmprɪˈkeɪʃ(ə)n/ *noun formal* curse.

imprecise /ɪmprɪˈsaɪs/ *adjective* not precise.

impregnable /ɪmˈpregnəb(ə)l/ *adjective* safe against attack. □ **impregnability** *noun*.

impregnate /ˈɪmpregneɪt/ *verb* (**-ting**) fill, saturate; make pregnant. □ **impregnation** *noun*.

impresario /ɪmprɪˈsɑːrɪəʊ/ *noun* (*plural* **-s**) organizer of public entertainments.

impress ● *verb* /ɪmˈpres/ affect or influence deeply; arouse admiration or respect in; (often + *on*) emphasize; imprint, stamp. ● *noun* /ˈɪmpres/ mark impressed; characteristic quality.

impression /ɪmˈpreʃ(ə)n/ *noun* effect produced on mind; belief; imitation of person or sound, esp. done to entertain; impressing, mark impressed; unaltered reprint of book etc.; issue of book or newspaper etc.; print from type or engraving.

impressionable *adjective* easily influenced.

impressionism *noun* school of painting concerned with conveying effect of natural light on objects; style of music or writing seeking to convey esp. fleeting feelings or experience. □ **impressionist** *noun*; **impressionistic** /-ˈnɪs-/ *adjective*.

impressive /ɪmˈpresɪv/ *adjective* arousing respect, approval, or admiration. □ **impressively** *adverb*.

imprimatur /ɪmprɪˈmɑːtə/ *noun* licence to print; official approval.

imprint ● *verb* /ɪmˈprɪnt/ (often + *on*) impress firmly, esp. on mind; make impression of (figure etc.) on thing; make impression on with stamp etc. ● *noun* /ˈɪmprɪnt/ impression; printer's or publisher's name in book etc.

imprison /ɪmˈprɪz(ə)n/ *verb* (**-n-**) put into prison; confine. □ **imprisonment** *noun*.

improbable /ɪmˈprɒbəb(ə)l/ *adjective* not likely, difficult to believe. □ **improbability** *noun*; **improbably** *adverb*.

improbity /ɪmˈprəʊbɪtɪ/ *noun* (*plural* **-ies**) wickedness; dishonesty; wicked or dishonest act.

impromptu /ɪmˈprɒmptjuː/ ● *adverb & adjective* unrehearsed. ● *noun* (*plural* **-s**) impromptu performance or speech; short, usually solo, musical piece, often improvisatory in style.

improper /ɪmˈprɒpə/ *adjective* unseemly, indecent; inaccurate, wrong. □ **improperly** *adverb*.

impropriety /ɪmprəˈpraɪətɪ/ *noun* (*plural* **-ies**) indecency; instance of this; incorrectness, unfitness.

improve /ɪmˈpruːv/ *verb* (**-ving**) make or become better; (+ *on*) produce something better than; (as **improving** *adjective*) giving moral benefit. □ **improvement** *noun*.

improvident /ɪmˈprɒvɪd(ə)nt/ *adjective* lacking foresight; wasteful. □ **improvidence** *noun*; **improvidently** *adverb*.

improvise /ˈɪmprəvaɪz/ *verb* (**-sing**) compose extempore; provide or construct from materials etc. not intended for the purpose. □ **improvisation** *noun*; **improvisational** *adjective*; **improvisatory** /-ˈzeɪtərɪ/ *adjective*.

imprudent /ɪmˈpruːd(ə)nt/ *adjective* rash, indiscreet. □ **imprudence** *noun*; **imprudently** *adverb*.

impudent /ˈɪmpjʊd(ə)nt/ *adjective* impertinent. □ **impudence** *noun*; **impudently** *adverb*.

impugn /ɪmˈpjuːn/ *verb* challenge; call in question.

impulse /ˈɪmpʌls/ *noun* sudden urge; tendency to follow such urges; impelling; impetus.

impulsive /ɪmˈpʌlsɪv/ *adjective* apt to act on impulse; done on impulse; tending to impel. □ **impulsively** *adverb*; **impulsiveness** *noun*.

impunity /ɪm'pjuːnɪtɪ/ *noun* exemption from punishment or injurious consequences. □ **with impunity** without punishment etc.

impure /ɪm'pjʊə/ *adjective* adulterated; dirty; unchaste.

impurity *noun* (*plural* **-ies**) being impure; impure thing or part.

impute /ɪm'pjuːt/ *verb* (**-ting**) (+ *to*) ascribe (fault etc.) to. □ **imputation** *noun*.

in ● *preposition expressing inclusion or position within limits of space, time, circumstance, etc.*; after (specified period of time); with respect to; as proportionate part of; with form or arrangement of; as member of; involved with; within ability of; having the condition of; affected by; having as aim; by means of; meaning; into (with verb of motion or change). ● *adverb expressing position bounded by certain limits, or movement to point enclosed by them*; into room etc.; at home etc.; so as to be enclosed; as part of a publication; in fashion, season, or office; (of player etc.) having turn or right to play; (of transport) at platform etc.; (of season, harvest, ordered goods, etc.) having arrived or been received; (of fire etc.) burning; (of tide) at highest point. ● *adjective* internal, living etc. inside; fashionable; (of joke etc.) confined to small group. □ **in-between** *colloquial* intermediate; **in-house** within an institution, company, etc.; **ins and outs** (often + *of*) details; **in so far as** to the extent that; **in that** because, in so far as; **in-tray** tray for incoming documents etc.; **in with** on good terms with.

in. *abbreviation* inch(es).

inability /ɪnə'bɪlɪtɪ/ *noun* being unable.

inaccessible /ɪnæk'sesɪb(ə)l/ *adjective* not accessible; unapproachable. □ **inaccessibility** *noun*.

inaccurate /ɪn'ækjʊrət/ *adjective* not accurate. □ **inaccuracy** *noun* (*plural* **-ies**); **inaccurately** *adverb*.

inaction /ɪn'ækʃ(ə)n/ *noun* absence of action.

inactive /ɪn'æktɪv/ *adjective* not active; not operating. □ **inactivity** /-'tɪv-/ *noun*.

inadequate /ɪn'ædɪkwət/ *adjective* insufficient; incompetent. □ **inadequacy** *noun* (*plural* **-ies**); **inadequately** *adverb*.

inadmissible /ɪnəd'mɪsɪb(ə)l/ *adjective* not allowable. □ **inadmissibility** *noun*; **inadmissibly** *adverb*.

inadvertent /ɪnəd'vɜːt(ə)nt/ *adjective* unintentional; inattentive. □ **inadvertence** *noun*; **inadvertently** *adverb*.

inadvisable /ɪnəd'vaɪzəb(ə)l/ *adjective* not advisable. □ **inadvisability** *noun*.

inalienable /ɪn'eɪlɪənəb(ə)l/ *adjective* that cannot be transferred to another or taken away.

inane /ɪ'neɪn/ *adjective* silly, senseless; empty. □ **inanity** /-'næn-/ *noun* (*plural* **-ies**).

inanimate /ɪn'ænɪmət/ *adjective* not endowed with animal life; spiritless, dull.

inapplicable /mə'plɪkəb(ə)l/ *adjective* not applicable; irrelevant. □ **inapplicability** *noun*.

inapposite /ɪn'æpəzɪt/ *adjective* not apposite.

inappropriate /ɪnə'prəʊprɪət/ *adjective* not appropriate. □ **inappropriately** *adverb*; **inappropriateness** *noun*.

inapt /ɪn'æpt/ *adjective* not suitable; unskilful. □ **inaptitude** *noun*.

inarticulate /ɪnɑː'tɪkjʊlət/ *adjective* unable to express oneself clearly; not articulate, indistinct; dumb; not jointed. □ **inarticulately** *adverb*.

inasmuch /ɪnəz'mʌtʃ/ *adverb* (+ *as*) since, because; to the extent that.

inattentive /ɪnə'tentɪv/ *adjective* not paying attention; neglecting to show courtesy. □ **inattention** *noun*; **inattentively** *adverb*.

inaudible /ɪn'ɔːdɪb(ə)l/ *adjective* that cannot be heard. □ **inaudibly** *adverb*.

inaugural /ɪn'ɔːgjʊr(ə)l/ ● *adjective* of inauguration. ● *noun* inaugural speech or lecture.

inaugurate /ɪn'ɔːgjʊreɪt/ *verb* (**-ting**) admit (person) to office; initiate use of or begin with ceremony; begin, introduce. □ **inauguration** *noun*.

inauspicious /ɪnɔː'spɪʃəs/ *adjective* not of good omen; unlucky.

inborn /'ɪnbɔːn/ *adjective* existing from birth; innate.

inbred /ɪn'bred/ *adjective* inborn; produced by inbreeding.

inbreeding /ɪn'briːdɪŋ/ *noun* breeding from closely related animals or people.

Inc. *abbreviation US* Incorporated.

incalculable /ɪn'kælkjʊləb(ə)l/ *adjective* too great for calculation; not calculable beforehand; uncertain. □ **incalculability** *noun*; **incalculably** *adverb*.

incandesce /ɪnkæn'des/ *verb* (**-cing**) (cause to) glow with heat.

incandescent *adjective* glowing with heat, shining; (of artificial light) produced by glowing filament etc. □ **incandescence** *noun*.

incantation /ɪnkæn'teɪʃ(ə)n/ *noun* spell, charm. □ **incantational** *adjective*.

incapable /ɪn'keɪpəb(ə)l/ *adjective* not capable; too honest, kind, etc. to do something; not capable of rational conduct. □ **incapability** *noun*.

incapacitate /ɪnkə'pæsɪteɪt/ *verb* (**-ting**) make incapable or unfit.

incapacity /ɪnkə'pæsɪtɪ/ *noun* inability; legal disqualification.

incarcerate /ɪn'kɑːsəreɪt/ *verb* (**-ting**) imprison. □ **incarceration** *noun*.

incarnate /ɪn'kɑːnət/ *adjective* in esp. human form.

incarnation /ɪnkɑː'neɪʃ(ə)n/ *noun* embodiment in flesh; (**the Incarnation**) embodiment of God in Christ; (often + *of*) living type (of a quality etc.).

incautious /ɪn'kɔːʃəs/ *adjective* rash. □ **incautiously** *adverb*.

incendiary /ɪn'sendɪərɪ/ ● *adjective* (of bomb) filled with material for causing fires; of arson; guilty of arson; inflammatory. ● *noun* (*plural* **-ies**) incendiary person or bomb.

incense[1] /'ɪnsens/ *noun* gum or spice giving sweet smell when burned; smoke of this, esp. in religious ceremonial.

incense[2] /ɪn'sens/ *verb* (**-sing**) make angry.

incentive /ɪn'sentɪv/ ● *noun* motive, incitement; payment etc. encouraging effort in work. ● *adjective* serving to motivate or incite.

inception /ɪn'sepʃ(ə)n/ *noun* beginning.

incessant /ɪn'ses(ə)nt/ *adjective* unceasing, continual; repeated. □ **incessantly** *adverb*.

incest /'ɪnsest/ *noun* crime of sexual intercourse between people prohibited from marrying because of closeness of their blood relationship.

incestuous /ɪn'sestjʊəs/ *adjective* of or guilty of incest; having relationships restricted to a particular group etc.

inch ● *noun* twelfth of (linear) foot (2.54 cm); this as unit of map-scale (e.g. 1 inch to 1 mile) or as unit of rainfall (= 1 inch depth of water). ● *verb* move gradually. □ **every inch** entirely; **within an inch of one's life** almost to death.

inchoate /ɪn'kəʊeɪt/ *adjective* just begun; undeveloped. □ **inchoation** *noun*.

incidence /'ɪnsɪd(ə)ns/ *noun* range, scope, extent, manner, or rate of occurrence; falling of line, ray, particles, etc. on surface; coming into contact with thing.

incident /'ɪnsɪd(ə)nt/ ● noun event, occurrence; violent episode, civil or military; episode in play, film, etc. ● adjective (often + to) apt to occur, naturally attaching; (often + on, upon) (of light etc.) falling.

incidental /ɪnsɪ'dent(ə)l/ adjective (often + to) minor, supplementary; not essential. □ **incidental music** music played during or between scenes of play, film, etc.

incidentally adverb by the way; in an incidental way.

incinerate /ɪn'sɪnəreɪt/ verb (-ting) burn to ashes. □ **incineration** noun.

incinerator noun furnace or device for incineration.

incipient /ɪn'sɪpɪənt/ adjective beginning, in early stage.

incise /ɪn'saɪz/ verb (-sing) make cut in; engrave.

incision /ɪn'sɪʒ(ə)n/ noun cutting, esp. by surgeon; cut.

incisive /ɪn'saɪsɪv/ adjective sharp; clear and effective.

incisor /ɪn'saɪzə/ noun cutting-tooth, esp. at front of mouth.

incite /ɪn'saɪt/ verb (-ting) (often + to) urge on, stir up. □ **incitement** noun.

incivility /ɪnsɪ'vɪlɪtɪ/ noun (plural **-ies**) rudeness; impolite act.

inclement /ɪn'klemənt/ adjective (of weather) severe, stormy. □ **inclemency** noun.

inclination /ɪnklɪ'neɪʃ(ə)n/ noun propensity; liking, affection; slope, slant.

incline ● verb /ɪn'klaɪn/ (-ning) (usually in passive) dispose, influence; have specified tendency; be disposed, tend; (cause to) lean or bend. ● noun /'ɪnklaɪn/ slope.

include /ɪn'kluːd/ verb (-ding) comprise, regard or treat as part of whole. □ **inclusion** /-ʒ(ə)n/ noun.

inclusive /ɪn'kluːsɪv/ adjective (often + of) including; including the limits stated; comprehensive; including all accessory payments. ■ **inclusively** adverb; **inclusiveness** noun.

incognito /ɪnkɒg'niːtəʊ/ ● adjective & adverb with one's name or identity concealed. ● noun (plural **-s**) person who is incognito; pretended identity.

incoherent /ɪnkəʊ'hɪərənt/ adjective unintelligible; lacking logic or consistency; not clear. □ **incoherence** noun; **incoherently** adverb.

incombustible /ɪnkəm'bʌstɪb(ə)l/ adjective that cannot be burnt.

income /'ɪnkʌm/ noun money received, esp. periodically, from work, investments, etc. □ **income tax** tax levied on income.

incoming adjective coming in; succeeding another.

incommensurable /ɪnkə'menʃərəb(ə)l/ adjective (often + with) not comparable in size, value, etc.; having no common factor. □ **incommensurability** noun.

incommensurate /ɪnkə'menʃərət/ adjective (often + with, to) out of proportion; inadequate; incommensurable.

incommode /ɪnkə'məʊd/ verb (-ding) formal inconvenience; trouble, annoy.

incommodious /ɪnkə'məʊdɪəs/ adjective formal too small for comfort; inconvenient.

incommunicable /ɪnkə'mjuːnɪkəb(ə)l/ adjective that cannot be shared or communicated.

incommunicado /ɪnkəmjuːnɪ'kɑːdəʊ/ adjective without means of communication, in solitary confinement in prison etc.

incomparable /ɪn'kɒmpərəb(ə)l/ adjective without an equal; matchless. □ **incomparability** noun; **incomparably** adverb.

incompatible /ɪnkəm'pætɪb(ə)l/ adjective not compatible. □ **incompatibility** noun.

incompetent /ɪn'kɒmpɪt(ə)nt/ adjective inept; (often + to) lacking the necessary skill, not legally qualified. □ **incompetence** noun.

incomplete /ɪnkəm'pliːt/ adjective not complete.

incomprehensible /ɪnkɒmprɪ'hensɪb(ə)l/ adjective that cannot be understood.

incomprehension /ɪnkɒmprɪ'henʃ(ə)n/ noun failure to understand.

inconceivable /ɪnkən'siːvəb(ə)l/ adjective that cannot be imagined. □ **inconceivably** adverb.

inconclusive /ɪnkən'kluːsɪv/ adjective (of argument etc.) not convincing or decisive.

incongruous /ɪn'kɒŋgrʊəs/ adjective out of place; absurd; (often + with) out of keeping. □ **incongruity** /-'gruːɪtɪ/ noun (plural **-ies**); **incongruously** adverb.

inconsequent /ɪn'kɒnsɪkwənt/ adjective irrelevant; not following logically; disconnected. □ **inconsequence** noun.

inconsequential /ɪnkɒnsɪ'kwenʃ(ə)l/ adjective unimportant; inconsequent. □ **inconsequentially** adverb.

inconsiderable /ɪnkən'sɪdərəb(ə)l/ adjective of small size, value, etc.; not worth considering. □ **inconsiderably** adverb.

inconsiderate /ɪnkən'sɪdərət/ adjective not considerate of others; thoughtless. ■ **inconsiderately** adverb; **inconsiderateness** noun.

inconsistent /ɪnkən'sɪst(ə)nt/ adjective not consistent. □ **inconsistency** noun (plural **-ies**); **inconsistently** adverb.

inconsolable /ɪnkən'səʊləb(ə)l/ adjective that cannot be consoled. □ **inconsolably** adverb.

inconspicuous /ɪnkən'spɪkjʊəs/ adjective not conspicuous; not easily noticed. □ **inconspicuously** adverb; **inconspicuousness** noun.

inconstant /ɪn'kɒnst(ə)nt/ adjective fickle; variable. □ **inconstancy** noun (plural **-ies**).

incontestable /ɪnkən'testəb(ə)l/ adjective that cannot be disputed. □ **incontestably** adverb.

incontinent /ɪn'kɒntɪnənt/ adjective unable to control bowels or bladder; lacking self-restraint. □ **incontinence** noun.

incontrovertible /ɪnkɒntrə'vɜːtɪb(ə)l/ adjective indisputable. □ **incontrovertibly** adverb.

inconvenience /ɪnkən'viːnɪəns/ ● noun lack of ease or comfort; trouble; cause or instance of this. ● verb (-cing) cause inconvenience to.

inconvenient adjective causing trouble, difficulty, or discomfort; awkward. □ **inconveniently** adverb.

incorporate ● verb /ɪn'kɔːpəreɪt/ (-ting) include as part or ingredient; (often + in, with) unite (in one body); admit as member of company etc.; (esp. as **incorporated** adjective) constitute as legal corporation. ● adjective /ɪn'kɔːpərət/ incorporated. □ **incorporation** noun.

incorporeal /ɪnkɔː'pɔːrɪəl/ adjective without substance or material existence. □ **incorporeally** adverb.

incorrect /ɪnkə'rekt/ adjective untrue, inaccurate; improper, unsuitable. □ **incorrectly** adverb.

incorrigible /ɪn'kɒrɪdʒɪb(ə)l/ adjective that cannot be corrected or improved. □ **incorrigibility** noun; **incorrigibly** adverb.

incorruptible /ɪnkə'rʌptɪb(ə)l/ adjective that cannot decay or be corrupted. □ **incorruptibility** noun; **incorruptibly** adverb.

increase ● verb /ɪŋ'kriːs/ (-sing) become or make greater or more numerous. ● noun /'ɪnkriːs/ growth, enlargement; (of people, animals, or plants) multiplication; increased amount. □ **on the increase** increasing.

increasingly /ɪn'kriːsɪŋlɪ/ adverb more and more.

incredible /ɪn'kredɪb(ə)l/ *adjective* that cannot be believed; *colloquial* surprising, extremely good. □ **incredibility** *noun*; **incredibly** *adverb*.

incredulous /ɪn'kredjʊləs/ *adjective* unwilling to believe; showing disbelief. □ **incredulity** /ɪn-krɪ'djuːlɪtɪ/ *noun*; **incredulously** *adverb*.

increment /'ɪŋkrɪmənt/ *noun* amount of increase; added amount. □ **incremental** /-'ment(ə)l/ *adjective*.

incriminate /ɪn'krɪmɪneɪt/ *verb* (**-ting**) indicate as guilty; charge with crime. □ **incrimination** *noun*; **incriminatory** *adjective*.

incrustation /ɪnkrʌs'teɪʃ(ə)n/ *noun* encrusting, being encrusted; crust, hard coating; deposit on surface.

incubate /'ɪŋkjʊbeɪt/ *verb* (**-ting**) hatch (eggs) by sitting on them or by artificial heat; cause (bacteria etc.) to develop; develop slowly.

incubation *noun* incubating, being incubated; period between infection and appearance of first symptoms.

incubator *noun* apparatus providing warmth for hatching eggs, rearing premature babies, or developing bacteria.

incubus /'ɪŋkjʊbəs/ *noun* (*plural* **-buses** or **-bi** /-baɪ/) demon or male spirit formerly believed to have sexual intercourse with sleeping women; nightmare; oppressive person or thing.

inculcate /'ɪnkʌlkeɪt/ *verb* (**-ting**) (often + *upon, in*) urge, impress persistently. □ **inculcation** *noun*.

incumbency /ɪn'kʌmbənsɪ/ *noun* (*plural* **-ies**) office or tenure of incumbent.

incumbent /ɪn'kʌmbənt/ ● *adjective* lying, pressing; currently holding office. ● *noun* holder of office, esp. benefice. □ **it is incumbent on a person** (+ *to do*) it is a person's duty.

incur /ɪn'kɜː/ *verb* (**-rr-**) bring on oneself.

incurable /ɪn'kjʊərəb(ə)l/ ● *adjective* that cannot be cured. ● *noun* incurable person. □ **incurability** *noun*; **incurably** *adverb*.

incurious /ɪn'kjʊərɪəs/ *adjective* lacking curiosity.

incursion /ɪn'kɜːʃ(ə)n/ *noun* invasion; sudden attack. □ **incursive** *adjective*.

indebted /ɪn'detɪd/ *adjective* (usually + *to*) owing money or gratitude. □ **indebtedness** *noun*.

indecent /ɪn'diːs(ə)nt/ *adjective* offending against decency; unbecoming; unsuitable. □ **indecent assault** sexual attack not involving rape. □ **indecency** *noun*; **indecently** *adverb*.

indecipherable /ɪndɪ'saɪfərəb(ə)l/ *adjective* that cannot be deciphered.

indecision /ɪndɪ'sɪʒ(ə)n/ *noun* inability to decide; hesitation.

indecisive /ɪndɪ'saɪsɪv/ *adjective* not decisive; irresolute; not conclusive. □ **indecisively** *adverb*; **indecisiveness** *noun*.

indecorous /ɪn'dekərəs/ *adjective* improper, undignified; in bad taste. □ **indecorously** *adverb*.

indeed /ɪn'diːd/ ● *adverb* in truth; really; admittedly. ● *interjection* expressing irony, incredulity, etc.

indefatigable /ɪndɪ'fætɪɡəb(ə)l/ *adjective* unwearying, unremitting. □ **indefatigably** *adverb*.

indefeasible /ɪndɪ'fiːzɪb(ə)l/ *adjective* literary (esp. of claim, rights, etc.) that cannot be forfeited or annulled.

indefensible /ɪndɪ'fensɪb(ə)l/ *adjective* that cannot be defended. □ **indefensibility** *noun*; **indefensibly** *adverb*.

indefinable /ɪndɪ'faɪnəb(ə)l/ *adjective* that cannot be defined; mysterious. □ **indefinably** *adverb*.

indefinite /ɪn'defɪnɪt/ *adjective* vague, undefined; unlimited; (of adjectives, adverbs, and pronouns) not determining the person etc. referred to. □ **indefinite**

article word (*a, an* in English) placed before noun and meaning 'one, some, any'.

indefinitely *adverb* for an unlimited time; in an indefinite manner.

indelible /ɪn'delɪb(ə)l/ *adjective* that cannot be rubbed out; permanent. □ **indelibly** *adverb*.

indelicate /ɪn'delɪkət/ *adjective* coarse, unrefined; tactless. □ **indelicacy** *noun* (*plural* **-ies**); **indelicately** *adverb*.

indemnify /ɪn'demnɪfaɪ/ *verb* (**-ies, -ied**) (often + *against, from*) secure against loss or legal responsibility; (often + *for*) exempt from penalty; compensate. □ **indemnification** *noun*.

indemnity /ɪn'demnɪtɪ/ *noun* (*plural* **-ies**) compensation for damage; sum exacted by victor in war; security against damage or loss; exemption from penalties.

indent ● *verb* /ɪn'dent/ make or impress notches, dents, or recesses in; set back (beginning of line) inwards from margin; draw up (legal document) in duplicate; (often + *for*) make requisition. ● *noun* /'ɪndent/ order (esp. from abroad) for goods; official requisition for stores; indented line; indentation; indenture.

indentation /ɪnden'teɪʃ(ə)n/ *noun* indenting, being indented; notch.

indenture /ɪn'dentʃə/ ● *noun* (usually in *plural*) sealed agreement; formal list, certificate, etc. ● *verb* (**-ring**) *historical* bind by indentures, esp. as apprentice.

independent /ɪndɪ'pend(ə)nt/ ● *adjective* (often + *of*) not depending on authority; self-governing; not depending on another person for one's livelihood or opinions; (of income) making it unnecessary to earn one's livelihood; unwilling to be under obligation to others; not depending on something else for validity etc.; (of institution) not supported by public funds. ● *noun* politician etc. independent of any political party. □ **independence** *noun*; **independently** *adverb*.

indescribable /ɪndɪ'skraɪbəb(ə)l/ *adjective* beyond description; that cannot be described. □ **indescribably** *adverb*.

indestructible /ɪndɪ'strʌktɪb(ə)l/ *adjective* that cannot be destroyed. □ **indestructibility** *noun*; **indestructibly** *adverb*.

indeterminable /ɪndɪ'tɜːmɪnəb(ə)l/ *adjective* that cannot be ascertained or settled.

indeterminate /ɪndɪ'tɜːmɪnət/ *adjective* not fixed in extent, character, etc.; vague. □ **indeterminacy** *noun*.

index /'ɪndeks/ ● *noun* (*plural* **-es** or **indices** /'ɪndɪsiːz/) alphabetical list of subjects etc. with references, usually at end of book; card index; measure of prices or wages compared with a previous month, year, etc.; *Mathematics* exponent. ● *verb* furnish (book) with index, enter in index; relate (wages, investment income, etc.) to a price index. □ **index finger** finger next to thumb; **index-linked** related to value of price index.

Indian /'ɪndɪən/ ● *noun* native or national of India; person of Indian descent; (in full **American Indian**) original inhabitant of America. ● *adjective* of India; of the subcontinent comprising India, Pakistan, and Bangladesh; of the original inhabitants of America. □ **Indian corn** maize; **Indian file** single file; **Indian ink** black pigment, ink made from this; **Indian summer** period of calm dry warm weather in late autumn, happy tranquil period late in life.

indiarubber *noun* rubber, esp. for rubbing out pencil marks etc.

indicate /'ɪndɪkeɪt/ *verb* (**-ting**) point out, make known; show; be sign of; require, call for; state briefly; give as reading or measurement; point by hand; use a vehicle's indicator. □ **indication** *noun*.

indicative /ɪnˈdɪkətɪv/ ● *adjective* (+ *of*) suggestive, giving indications; *Grammar* (of mood) stating thing as fact. ● *noun Grammar* indicative mood; verb in this mood.

indicator *noun* flashing light on vehicle showing direction in which it is about to turn; person or thing that indicates; device indicating condition of machine etc.; recording instrument; board giving current information.

indices *plural of* INDEX.

indict /ɪnˈdaɪt/ *verb* accuse formally by legal process.

indictable *adjective* (of an offence) rendering person liable to be indicted; so liable.

indictment *noun* indicting, accusation; document containing this; thing that serves to condemn or censure.

indifference /ɪnˈdɪfrəns/ *noun* lack of interest or attention; unimportance.

indifferent *adjective* (+ *to*) showing indifference; neither good nor bad; of poor quality or ability. □ **indifferently** *adverb.*

indigenous /ɪnˈdɪdʒɪnəs/ *adjective* (often + *to*) native or belonging naturally to a place.

indigent /ˈɪndɪdʒ(ə)nt/ *adjective formal* needy, poor. □ **indigence** *noun.*

indigestible /ɪndɪˈdʒestɪb(ə)l/ *adjective* difficult or impossible to digest.

indigestion /ɪndɪˈdʒestʃ(ə)n/ *noun* difficulty in digesting food; pain caused by this.

indignant /ɪnˈdɪɡnənt/ *adjective* feeling or showing indignation. □ **indignantly** *adverb.*

indignation /ɪndɪɡˈneɪʃ(ə)n/ *noun* anger at supposed injustice etc.

indignity /ɪnˈdɪɡnɪtɪ/ *noun* (*plural* **-ies**) humiliating treatment; insult.

indigo /ˈɪndɪɡəʊ/ *noun* (*plural* **-s**) deep violet-blue; dye of this colour.

indirect /ɪndaɪˈrekt/ *adjective* not going straight to the point; (of route etc.) not straight. □ **indirect object** word or phrase representing person or thing affected by action of verb but not acted on (see panel at OBJECT); **indirect speech** reported speech; **indirect tax** tax on goods and services, not income. □ **indirectly** *adverb.*

indiscernible /ɪndɪˈsɜːnɪb(ə)l/ *adjective* that cannot be discerned.

indiscipline /ɪnˈdɪsɪplɪn/ *noun* lack of discipline.

indiscreet /ɪndɪˈskriːt/ *adjective* not discreet; injudicious, unwary. □ **indiscreetly** *adverb.*

indiscretion /ɪndɪˈskreʃ(ə)n/ *noun* indiscreet conduct or action.

indiscriminate /ɪndɪˈskrɪmɪnət/ *adjective* making no distinctions; done or acting at random. □ **indiscriminately** *adverb.*

indispensable /ɪndɪˈspensəb(ə)l/ *adjective* that cannot be dispensed with; necessary. □ **indispensably** *adverb.*

indisposed /ɪndɪˈspəʊzd/ *adjective* slightly unwell; averse, unwilling. □ **indisposition** /-spəˈzɪʃ(ə)n/ *noun.*

indisputable /ɪndɪˈspjuːtəb(ə)l/ *adjective* that cannot be disputed. □ **indisputably** *adverb.*

indissoluble /ɪndɪˈsɒljʊb(ə)l/ *adjective* that cannot be dissolved; lasting, stable. □ **indissolubly** *adverb.*

indistinct /ɪndɪˈstɪŋkt/ *adjective* not distinct; confused, obscure. □ **indistinctly** *adverb.*

indistinguishable /ɪndɪˈstɪŋɡwɪʃəb(ə)l/ *adjective* (often + *from*) not distinguishable.

indite /ɪnˈdaɪt/ *verb* (**-ting**) *formal or jocular* put into words; write (letter etc.).

individual /ɪndɪˈvɪdʒʊəl/ ● *adjective* of, for, or characteristic of single person or thing; having distinct character; designed for use by one person; single; particular. ● *noun* single member of class, group, etc.; single human being; *colloquial* person; distinctive person.

individualism *noun* social theory favouring free action by individuals; being independent or different. □ **individualist** *noun*; **individualistic** /-ˈlɪs-/ *adjective.*

individuality /ɪndɪvɪdʒʊˈælɪtɪ/ *noun* individual character, esp. when strongly marked; separate existence.

individualize *verb* (also **-ise**) (**-zing** or **-sing**) give individual character to; (esp. as **individualized** *adjective*) personalize.

individually *adverb* one by one; personally; distinctively.

indivisible /ɪndɪˈvɪzɪb(ə)l/ *adjective* not divisible.

indoctrinate /ɪnˈdɒktrɪneɪt/ *verb* (**-ting**) teach to accept a particular belief uncritically. □ **indoctrination** *noun.*

Indo-European /ɪndəʊjʊərəˈpɪən/ ● *adjective* of family of languages spoken over most of Europe and Asia as far as N. India; of hypothetical parent language of this family. ● *noun* Indo-European family of languages; hypothetical parent language of these.

indolent /ˈɪndələnt/ *adjective* lazy; averse to exertion. □ **indolence** *noun*; **indolently** *adverb.*

indomitable /ɪnˈdɒmɪtəb(ə)l/ *adjective* unconquerable; unyielding. □ **indomitably** *adverb.*

indoor /ˈɪndɔː/ *adjective* done etc. in building or under cover.

indoors /ɪnˈdɔːz/ *adverb* in(to) a building.

indubitable /ɪnˈdjuːbɪtəb(ə)l/ *adjective* that cannot be doubted. □ **indubitably** *adverb.*

induce /ɪnˈdjuːs/ *verb* (**-cing**) prevail on, persuade; bring about; bring on (labour) artificially; bring on labour in (mother); speed up birth of (baby); produce by induction; infer. □ **inducible** *adjective.*

inducement *noun* attractive offer; incentive; bribe.

induct /ɪnˈdʌkt/ *verb* install into office etc.

inductance *noun* property of electric circuit in which variation in current produces electromotive force.

induction /ɪnˈdʌkʃ(ə)n/ *noun* inducting, inducing; act of bringing on (esp. labour) artificially; general inference from particular instances; formal introduction to new job etc.; production of electric or magnetic state by proximity to electric circuit or magnetic field.

inductive /ɪnˈdʌktɪv/ *adjective* (of reasoning etc.) based on induction; of electric or magnetic induction.

indulge /ɪnˈdʌldʒ/ *verb* (**-ging**) (often + *in*) take one's pleasure freely; yield freely to (desire etc.); gratify by compliance with wishes.

indulgence *noun* indulging; thing indulged in; *RC Church* remission of punishment still due after absolution; privilege granted.

indulgent *adjective* lenient; willing to overlook faults; indulging. □ **indulgently** *adverb.*

industrial /ɪnˈdʌstrɪəl/ *adjective* of, engaged in, for use in, or serving the needs of, industry; having highly developed industries. □ **industrial action** strike or disruptive action by workers as protest; **industrial estate** area of land zoned for factories etc. □ **industrially** *adverb.*

industrialism *noun* system in which manufacturing industries predominate.

industrialist *noun* owner or manager in industry.

industrialize *verb* (also **-ise**) (**-zing** or **-sing**) make (nation etc.) industrial. □ **industrialization** *noun.*

industrious /ɪnˈdʌstrɪəs/ *adjective* hard-working. □ **industriously** *adverb.*

industry /'ɪndəstrɪ/ noun (plural **-ies**) branch of trade or manufacture; commercial enterprise; trade or manufacture collectively; concerted activity; diligence.

inebriate ● verb /ɪ'niːbrɪeɪt/ (**-ting**) make drunk; excite. ● adjective /ɪ'niːbrɪət/ drunken. ● noun /ɪ'niːbrɪət/ drunkard. □ **inebriation** noun.

inedible /ɪn'edɪb(ə)l/ adjective not suitable for eating.

ineducable /ɪn'edjʊkəb(ə)l/ adjective incapable of being educated.

ineffable /ɪn'efəb(ə)l/ adjective too great for description in words; that must not be uttered. □ **ineffability** noun; **ineffably** adverb.

ineffective /ɪnɪ'fektɪv/ adjective not achieving desired effect or results. □ **ineffectively** adverb; **ineffectiveness** noun.

ineffectual /ɪnɪ'fektʃʊəl/ adjective ineffective, feeble. □ **ineffectually** adverb.

inefficient /ɪnɪ'fɪʃ(ə)nt/ adjective not efficient or fully capable; (of machine etc.) wasteful. □ **inefficiency** noun; **inefficiently** adverb.

inelegant /ɪn'elɪɡənt/ adjective ungraceful, unrefined. □ **inelegance** noun; **inelegantly** adverb.

ineligible /ɪn'elɪdʒɪb(ə)l/ adjective not eligible or qualified. □ **ineligibility** noun.

ineluctable /ɪnɪ'lʌktəb(ə)l/ adjective inescapable, unavoidable.

inept /ɪ'nept/ adjective unskilful; absurd, silly; out of place. □ **ineptitude** noun; **ineptly** adverb.

inequality /ɪnɪ'kwɒlɪtɪ/ noun (plural **-ies**) lack of equality; variability; unevenness.

inequitable /ɪn'ekwɪtəb(ə)l/ adjective unfair, unjust.

inequity /ɪn'ekwɪtɪ/ noun (plural **-ies**) unfairness, injustice.

ineradicable /ɪnɪ'rædɪkəb(ə)l/ adjective that cannot be rooted out.

inert /ɪ'nɜːt/ adjective without inherent power of action etc.; chemically inactive; sluggish, slow; lifeless.

inertia /ɪ'nɜːʃə/ noun property by which matter continues in existing state of rest or motion unless acted on by external force; inertness; tendency to remain unchanged. □ **inertia reel** reel allowing seat belt to unwind freely but locking on impact; **inertia selling** sending of unsolicited goods in hope of making a sale.

inescapable /ɪnɪ'skeɪpəb(ə)l/ adjective that cannot be escaped or avoided. □ **inescapably** adverb.

inessential /ɪnɪ'senʃ(ə)l/ ● adjective not necessary; dispensable. ● noun inessential thing.

inestimable /ɪn'estɪməb(ə)l/ adjective too great etc. to be estimated. □ **inestimably** adverb.

inevitable /ɪn'evɪtəb(ə)l/ adjective unavoidable; bound to happen or appear; colloquial tiresomely familiar. □ **inevitability** noun; **inevitably** adverb.

inexact /ɪnɪɡ'zækt/ adjective not exact. □ **inexactitude** noun.

inexcusable /ɪnɪk'skjuːzəb(ə)l/ adjective that cannot be justified. □ **inexcusably** adverb.

inexhaustible /ɪnɪɡ'zɔːstɪb(ə)l/ adjective that cannot be used up.

inexorable /ɪn'eksərəb(ə)l/ adjective relentless. □ **inexorably** adverb.

inexpedient /ɪnɪk'spiːdɪənt/ adjective not expedient.

inexpensive /ɪnɪk'spensɪv/ adjective not expensive.

inexperience /ɪnɪk'spɪərɪəns/ noun lack of experience. □ **inexperienced** adjective.

inexpert /ɪn'ekspɜːt/ adjective unskilful.

inexpiable /ɪn'ekspɪəb(ə)l/ adjective that cannot be expiated.

inexplicable /ɪnɪk'splɪkəb(ə)l/ adjective that cannot be explained. □ **inexplicably** adverb.

inexpressible /ɪnɪk'spresɪb(ə)l/ adjective that cannot be expressed. □ **inexpressibly** adverb.

in extremis /ɪn ɪk'striːmɪs/ adjective at point of death; in great difficulties. [Latin]

inextricable /ɪnɪk'strɪkəb(ə)l/ adjective that cannot be separated, loosened, or resolved; inescapable. □ **inextricably** adverb.

infallible /ɪn'fælɪb(ə)l/ adjective incapable of error; unfailing, sure. □ **infallibility** noun; **infallibly** adverb.

infamous /'ɪnfəməs/ adjective notoriously vile, evil; abominable. □ **infamously** adverb; **infamy** noun (plural **-ies**).

infant /'ɪnf(ə)nt/ noun child during earliest period of life; thing in early stage of development; Law person under 18. □ **infancy** noun.

infanta /ɪn'fæntə/ noun historical daughter of Spanish or Portuguese king.

infanticide /ɪn'fæntɪsaɪd/ noun killing of infant, esp. soon after birth; person guilty of this.

infantile /'ɪnfəntaɪl/ adjective of or like infants. □ **infantile paralysis** poliomyelitis.

infantry /'ɪnfəntrɪ/ noun (plural **-ies**) (group of) foot-soldiers. □ **infantryman** soldier of infantry regiment.

infatuate /ɪn'fætjʊeɪt/ verb (**-ting**) (usually as **infatuated** adjective) inspire with intense fondness. □ **infatuation** noun.

infect /ɪn'fekt/ verb affect or contaminate with germ, virus, or disease; imbue, taint.

infection /ɪn'fekʃ(ə)n/ noun infecting, being infected; disease; communication of disease.

infectious adjective infecting; transmissible by infection; apt to spread. □ **infectiously** adverb.

infelicity /ɪnfɪ'lɪsɪtɪ/ noun (plural **-ies**) inapt expression; unhappiness. □ **infelicitous** adjective.

infer /ɪn'fɜː/ verb (**-rr-**) deduce, conclude.

■ **Usage** It is a mistake to use infer to mean 'imply', as in Are you inferring that I'm a liar?

inference /'ɪnfərəns/ noun act of inferring; thing inferred. □ **inferential** /-'ren(ə)l/ adjective.

inferior /ɪn'fɪərɪə/ ● adjective lower in rank etc.; of poor quality; situated below. ● noun inferior person.

inferiority /ɪnfɪərɪ'ɒrɪtɪ/ noun being inferior. □ **inferiority complex** feeling of inadequacy, sometimes marked by compensating aggressive behaviour.

infernal /ɪn'fɜːn(ə)l/ adjective of hell; hellish; colloquial detestable, tiresome. □ **infernally** adverb.

inferno /ɪn'fɜːnəʊ/ noun (plural **-s**) raging fire; scene of horror or distress; hell.

infertile /ɪn'fɜːtaɪl/ adjective not fertile. □ **infertility** /-fə'tɪl-/ noun.

infest /ɪn'fest/ verb overrun in large numbers. □ **infestation** noun.

infidel /'ɪnfɪd(ə)l/ ● noun disbeliever in esp. the supposed true religion. ● adjective of infidels; unbelieving.

infidelity /ɪnfɪ'delɪtɪ/ noun (plural **-ies**) being unfaithful.

infighting noun conflict or competitiveness in organization; boxing within arm's length.

infiltrate /'ɪnfɪltreɪt/ verb (**-ting**) enter (territory, political party, etc.) gradually and imperceptibly; cause to do this; permeate by filtration; (often + into, through) introduce (fluid) by filtration. □ **infiltration** noun; **infiltrator** noun.

infinite /'ɪnfɪnɪt/ adjective boundless; endless; very great or many. □ **infinitely** adverb.

infinitesimal /ɪnfɪnɪ'tesɪm(ə)l/ adjective infinitely or very small. □ **infinitesimally** adverb.

infinitive /ɪnˈfɪnɪtɪv/ ● noun verb-form expressing verbal notion without particular subject, tense, etc. ● adjective having this form.

infinitude /ɪnˈfɪnɪtjuːd/ noun literary infinite number etc.; being infinite.

infinity /ɪnˈfɪnɪtɪ/ noun (plural **-ies**) infinite number or extent; being infinite; boundlessness; infinite distance; Mathematics infinite quantity.

infirm /ɪnˈfɜːm/ adjective weak.

infirmary /ɪnˈfɜːmərɪ/ noun (plural **-ies**) hospital; sickbay in school etc.

infirmity /ɪnˈfɜːmɪtɪ/ noun (plural **-ies**) being infirm; particular physical weakness.

in flagrante delicto /ɪn fləˈɡræntɪ dɪˈlɪktəʊ/ adverb in act of committing offence. [Latin]

inflame /ɪnˈfleɪm/ verb (**-ming**) provoke to strong feeling; cause inflammation in; aggravate; make hot; (cause to) catch fire.

inflammable /ɪnˈflæməb(ə)l/ adjective easily set on fire or excited. □ **inflammability** noun.

■ **Usage** Because *inflammable* could be thought to mean 'not easily set on fire', *flammable* is often used instead. The negative of *inflammable* is *noninflammable*.

---

inflammation /ɪnfləˈmeɪʃ(ə)n/ noun inflaming; disordered bodily condition marked by heat, swelling, redness, and usually pain.

inflammatory /ɪnˈflæmətərɪ/ adjective tending to inflame; of inflammation.

inflatable ● adjective that can be inflated. ● noun inflatable object.

inflate /ɪnˈfleɪt/ verb (**-ting**) distend with air or gas; (usually + *with*; usually in *passive*) puff up (with pride etc.); resort to inflation of (currency); raise (prices) artificially; (as **inflated** adjective) (esp. of language, opinions, etc.) bombastic, exaggerated.

inflation noun inflating, being inflated; general rise in prices, increase in supply of money regarded as cause of such rise. □ **inflationary** adjective.

inflect /ɪnˈflekt/ verb change or vary pitch of (voice); modify (word) to express grammatical relation; undergo such modification.

inflection /ɪnˈflekʃ(ə)n/ noun (also **inflexion**) inflecting, being inflected; inflected form; inflecting suffix etc.; modulation of voice. □ **inflectional** adjective.

inflexible /ɪnˈfleksɪb(ə)l/ adjective unbendable; unbending; unyielding. □ **inflexibility** noun; **inflexibly** adverb.

inflexion = INFLECTION.

inflict /ɪnˈflɪkt/ verb deal (blow etc.); impose. □ **infliction** noun.

inflight adjective occurring or provided during a flight.

inflorescence /ɪnfləˈres(ə)ns/ noun collective flower head of plant; arrangement of flowers on plant; flowering.

inflow noun flowing in; that which flows in.

influence /ˈɪnflʊəns/ ● noun (usually + *on*) effect a person or thing has on another; (usually + *over*, *with*) ascendancy, moral power; thing or person exercising this. ● verb (**-cing**) exert influence on; affect. □ **under the influence** colloquial drunk.

influential /ɪnflʊˈenʃ(ə)l/ adjective having great influence.

influenza /ɪnflʊˈenzə/ noun infectious viral disease with fever, severe aching, and catarrh.

influx /ˈɪnflʌks/ noun flowing in.

inform /ɪnˈfɔːm/ verb tell; (usually + *against*, *on*) give incriminating information about person to authorities.

informal /ɪnˈfɔːm(ə)l/ adjective without formality; not formal. □ **informality** /-ˈmæl-/ noun (plural **-ies**); **informally** adverb.

informant noun giver of information.

information /ɪnfəˈmeɪʃ(ə)n/ noun what is told; knowledge; news; formal charge or accusation. □ **information retrieval** tracing of information stored in books, computers, etc.; **information technology** study or use of processes (esp. computers etc.) for storing, retrieving, and sending information.

informative /ɪnˈfɔːmətɪv/ adjective giving information, instructive.

informed adjective knowing the facts; having some knowledge.

informer noun person who informs, esp. against others.

infraction /ɪnˈfrækʃ(ə)n/ noun infringement.

infra dig /ɪnfrə ˈdɪɡ/ adjective colloquial beneath one's dignity.

infrared /ɪnfrəˈred/ adjective of or using radiation just beyond red end of spectrum.

infrastructure /ˈɪnfrəstrʌktʃə/ noun structural foundations of a society or enterprise; roads, bridges, sewers, etc., regarded as country's economic foundation; permanent installations as basis for military etc. operations.

infrequent /ɪnˈfriːkwənt/ adjective not frequent. □ **infrequently** adverb.

infringe /ɪnˈfrɪndʒ/ verb (**-ging**) break or violate (law, another's rights, etc.); (usually + *on*) encroach, trespass. □ **infringement** noun.

infuriate /ɪnˈfjʊərɪeɪt/ verb (**-ting**) enrage; irritate greatly. □ **infuriating** adjective.

infuse /ɪnˈfjuːz/ verb (**-sing**) (usually + *with*) fill (with a quality); steep or be steeped in liquid to extract properties; (usually + *into*) instil (life etc.).

infusible /ɪnˈfjuːzɪb(ə)l/ adjective that cannot be melted. □ **infusibility** noun.

infusion /ɪnˈfjuːʒ(ə)n/ noun infusing; liquid extract so obtained; infused element.

ingenious /ɪnˈdʒiːnɪəs/ adjective clever at contriving; cleverly contrived. □ **ingeniously** adverb.

■ **Usage** *Ingenious* is sometimes confused with *ingenuous*.

---

ingénue /ˈæʒeɪˈnjuː/ noun artless young woman, esp. as stage type. [French]

ingenuity /ɪndʒɪˈnjuːɪtɪ/ noun inventiveness, cleverness.

ingenuous /ɪnˈdʒenjʊəs/ adjective artless; frank. □ **ingenuously** adverb.

■ **Usage** *Ingenuous* is sometimes confused with *ingenious*.

---

ingest /ɪnˈdʒest/ verb take in (food etc.); absorb (knowledge etc.). □ **ingestion** noun.

inglenook /ˈɪŋɡəlnʊk/ noun space within opening either side of old-fashioned wide fireplace.

inglorious /ɪnˈɡlɔːrɪəs/ adjective shameful; not famous.

ingoing adjective going in.

ingot /ˈɪŋɡət/ noun (usually oblong) mass of cast metal, esp. gold, silver, or steel.

ingrained /ɪnˈɡreɪnd/ adjective deeply rooted, inveterate; (of dirt etc.) deeply embedded.

ingratiate /ɪnˈɡreɪʃɪeɪt/ verb (**-ting**) (**ingratiate oneself**; usually + *with*) bring oneself into favour. □ **ingratiating** adjective.

ingratitude /ɪnˈɡrætɪtjuːd/ noun lack of due gratitude.

ingredient /ɪnˈɡriːdɪənt/ noun component part in mixture.

ingress /'ɪŋgres/ *noun* going in; right to go in.

ingrowing *adjective* (of nail) growing into the flesh.

inhabit /ɪn'hæbɪt/ *verb* (-t-) dwell in, occupy. □ **inhabitable** *adjective*; **inhabitant** *noun*.

inhalant /ɪn'heɪlənt/ *noun* medicinal substance to be inhaled.

inhale /ɪn'heɪl/ *verb* (-ling) breathe in. □ **inhalation** /-hə'leɪʃ(ə)n/ *noun*.

inhaler *noun* device for administering inhalant, esp. to relieve asthma.

inhere /ɪn'hɪə/ *verb* (-ring) be inherent.

inherent /ɪn'herənt/ *adjective* (often + *in*) existing in something as essential or permanent attribute. □ **inherently** *adverb*.

inherit /ɪn'herɪt/ *verb* (-t-) receive as heir; derive (characteristic) from ancestors; derive or take over (situation) from predecessor. □ **inheritor** *noun*.

inheritance *noun* what is inherited; inheriting.

inhibit /ɪn'hɪbɪt/ *verb* (-t-) hinder, restrain, prevent; (as **inhibited** *adjective*) suffering from inhibition; (usually + *from*) prohibit.

inhibition /ɪnhɪ'bɪʃ(ə)n/ *noun* restraint of direct expression of instinct; *colloquial* emotional resistance to thought or action; inhibiting, being inhibited.

inhospitable /ɪnhɒs'pɪtəb(ə)l/ *adjective* not hospitable; affording no shelter.

inhuman /ɪn'hju:mən/ *adjective* brutal, unfeeling, barbarous. □ **inhumanity** /-'mæn-/ *noun* (*plural* -**ies**); **inhumanly** *adverb*.

inhumane /ɪnhju:'meɪn/ *adjective* not humane, callous.

inimical /ɪ'nɪmɪk(ə)l/ *adjective* hostile; harmful.

inimitable /ɪ'nɪmɪtəb(ə)l/ *adjective* that cannot be imitated. □ **inimitably** *adverb*.

iniquity /ɪ'nɪkwɪtɪ/ *noun* (*plural* -**ies**) wickedness; gross injustice. □ **iniquitous** *adjective*.

initial /ɪ'nɪʃ(ə)l/ ● *adjective* of or at beginning. ● *noun* first letter, esp. of person's name. ● *verb* (-**ll**-; *US* -**l**-) mark or sign with one's initials. □ **initially** *adverb*.

initiate ● *verb* /ɪ'nɪʃɪeɪt/ (-**ting**) originate, set going; admit into society, office, etc., esp. with ritual; (+ *into*) instruct in subject. ● *noun* /ɪ'nɪʃɪət/ initiated person. □ **initiation** *noun*; **initiatory** /ɪ'nɪʃjətərɪ/ *adjective*.

initiative /ɪ'nɪʃətɪv/ *noun* ability to initiate, enterprise; first step; (**the initiative**) power or right to begin.

inject /ɪn'dʒekt/ *verb* (usually + *into*) force (medicine etc.) (as) by syringe; administer medicine etc. to (person) by injection; place (quality etc.) where needed in something. □ **injection** *noun*.

injudicious /ɪndʒu:'dɪʃəs/ *adjective* unwise, ill-judged.

injunction /ɪn'dʒʌŋkʃ(ə)n/ *noun* authoritative order; judicial order restraining from specified act or compelling restitution etc.

injure /'ɪndʒə/ *verb* (-ring) hurt, harm, impair; do wrong to.

injurious /ɪn'dʒʊərɪəs/ *adjective* hurtful; defamatory; wrongful.

injury /'ɪndʒərɪ/ *noun* (*plural* -**ies**) physical damage, harm; offence to feelings etc.; *esp. Law* wrongful treatment. □ **injury time** extra time at football match etc. to compensate for that lost in dealing with injuries.

injustice /ɪn'dʒʌstɪs/ *noun* unfairness; unjust act.

ink ● *noun* coloured fluid or paste for writing or printing; black liquid ejected by cuttlefish etc. ● *verb* mark, cover, or smear with ink. □ **ink-jet printer** printing machine firing tiny jets of ink at paper; **inkwell** pot for ink, esp. in hole in desk. □ **inky** *adjective* (-**ier**, -**iest**).

inkling /'ɪŋklɪŋ/ *noun* (often + *of*) hint, slight knowledge or suspicion.

inland ● *adjective* /'ɪnlənd/ remote from sea or border within a country; carried on within country. ● *adverb* /ɪn'lænd/ in or towards interior of country. □ **Inland Revenue** government department assessing and collecting taxes.

in-laws /'ɪnlɔ:z/ *plural noun* relatives by marriage.

inlay ● *verb* /ɪn'leɪ/ (*past & past participle* **inlaid** /ɪn'leɪd/) embed (thing in another); decorate (thing) thus. ● *noun* /'ɪnleɪ/ inlaid material or work; filling shaped to fit tooth-cavity.

inlet /'ɪnlət/ *noun* small arm of sea etc.; piece inserted; way of admission.

inmate /'ɪnmeɪt/ *noun* occupant of house, hospital, prison, etc.

in memoriam /ɪn mɪ'mɔ:rɪæm/ *preposition* in memory of.

inmost /'ɪnməʊst/ *adjective* most inward.

inn *noun* pub, sometimes with accommodation; *historical* house providing lodging etc. for payment, esp. for travellers. □ **innkeeper** keeper of inn; **Inns of Court** 4 legal societies admitting people to English bar.

innards /'ɪnədz/ *plural noun colloquial* entrails.

innate /ɪ'neɪt/ *adjective* inborn; natural. □ **innately** *adverb*.

inner /'ɪnə/ ● *adjective* interior, internal. ● *noun* circle nearest bull's-eye of target. □ **inner city** central area of city, esp. regarded as having social problems; **inner tube** separate inflatable tube in pneumatic tyre. □ **innermost** *adjective*.

innings /'ɪnɪŋz/ *noun* (*plural* same) esp. *Cricket* batsman's or side's turn at batting; term of office etc. when person, party, etc. can achieve something.

innocent /'ɪnəs(ə)nt/ ● *adjective* free from moral wrong; not guilty; guileless; harmless. ● *noun* innocent person, esp. young child. □ **innocence** *noun*; **innocently** *adverb*.

innocuous /ɪ'nɒkjʊəs/ *adjective* harmless.

innovate /'ɪnəveɪt/ *verb* (-**ting**) bring in new ideas etc.; make changes. ● **innovation** *noun*; **innovative** /-vətɪv/ *adjective*; **innovator** *noun*.

innuendo /ɪnjʊ'endəʊ/ *noun* (*plural* -**es** or -**s**) allusive (usually depreciatory or sexually suggestive) remark.

innumerable /ɪ'nju:mərəb(ə)l/ *adjective* countless.

innumerate /ɪ'nju:mərət/ *adjective* not knowing basic mathematics. □ **innumeracy** *noun*.

inoculate /ɪ'nɒkjʊleɪt/ *verb* (-**ting**) treat with vaccine or serum to promote immunity against a disease. □ **inoculation** *noun*.

inoffensive /ɪnə'fensɪv/ *adjective* not objectionable; harmless.

inoperable /ɪ'nɒpərəb(ə)l/ *adjective* that cannot be cured by surgical operation.

inoperative /ɪ'nɒpərətɪv/ *adjective* not working or taking effect.

inopportune /ɪ'nɒpətju:n/ *adjective* not appropriate, esp. as regards time.

inordinate /ɪ'nɔ:dɪnət/ *adjective* excessive. □ **inordinately** *adverb*.

inorganic /ɪnɔ:'gænɪk/ *adjective Chemistry* not organic; without organized physical structure; extraneous.

input /'ɪnpʊt/ ● *noun* what is put in; place of entry of energy, information, etc.; action of putting in or feeding in; contribution of information etc. ● *verb* (**inputting**; *past & past participle* **input** or **inputted**) put in; supply (data, programs, etc.) to computer.

inquest /'ɪŋkwest/ *noun* inquiry held by coroner into cause of death.

inquietude /ɪn'kwaɪɪtju:d/ *noun* uneasiness.

inquire /ɪn'kwaɪə/ *verb* (-**ring**) seek information formally; make inquiry; ask question.

inquiry /ɪn'kwaɪərɪ/ *noun* (*plural* **-ies**) investigation, esp. official; asking; question.

inquisition /ɪnkwɪ'zɪʃ(ə)n/ *noun* investigation; official inquiry; (**the Inquisition**) *RC Church History* ecclesiastical tribunal for suppression of heresy. □ **inquisitional** *adjective*.

inquisitive /ɪn'kwɪzɪtɪv/ *adjective* curious, prying; seeking knowledge. □ **inquisitively** *adverb*; **inquisitiveness** *noun*.

inquisitor /ɪn'kwɪzɪtə/ *noun* investigator; *historical* officer of Inquisition.

inquisitorial /ɪnkwɪzɪ'tɔːrɪəl/ *adjective* inquisitor-like; prying.

inroad *noun* (often in *plural*) encroachment; using up of resources etc.; hostile incursion.

inrush *noun* rapid influx.

insalubrious /ɪnsə'luːbrɪəs/ *adjective* (of climate or place) unhealthy.

insane /ɪn'seɪn/ *adjective* mad; *colloquial* extremely foolish. □ **insanely** *adverb*; **insanity** /ɪn'sænɪtɪ/ *noun* (*plural* **-ies**).

insanitary /ɪn'sænɪtərɪ/ *adjective* not sanitary.

insatiable /ɪn'seɪʃəb(ə)l/ *adjective* that cannot be satisfied; extremely greedy. □ **insatiability** *noun*; **insatiably** *adverb*.

insatiate /ɪn'seɪʃɪət/ *adjective* never satisfied.

inscribe /ɪn'skraɪb/ *verb* (**-bing**) (usually + *in, on*) write or carve (words etc.) on surface; mark (surface) with characters; (usually + *to*) write informal dedication in or on (book etc.); enter on list; *Geometry* draw (figure) within another so that some points of their boundaries coincide.

inscription /ɪn'skrɪpʃ(ə)n/ *noun* words inscribed; inscribing.

inscrutable /ɪn'skruːtəb(ə)l/ *adjective* mysterious, impenetrable. □ **inscrutability** *noun*; **inscrutably** *adverb*.

insect /'ɪnsekt/ *noun* small invertebrate animal with segmented body, 6 legs, and usually wings.

insecticide /ɪn'sektɪsaɪd/ *noun* preparation used for killing insects.

insectivore /ɪn'sektɪvɔː/ *noun* animal or plant that feeds on insects. □ **insectivorous** /-'tɪvərəs/ *adjective*.

insecure /ɪnsɪ'kjʊə/ *adjective* not secure or safe; not feeling safe. □ **insecurity** /-'kjʊr-/ *noun*.

inseminate /ɪn'semɪneɪt/ *verb* (**-ting**) introduce semen into; sow (seed etc.). □ **insemination** *noun*.

insensate /ɪn'senseɪt/ *adjective* without esp. physical sensibility; stupid.

insensible /ɪn'sensɪb(ə)l/ *adjective* unconscious; unaware; callous; imperceptible. □ **insensibility** *noun*; **insensibly** *adverb*.

insensitive /ɪn'sensɪtɪv/ *adjective* not sensitive. □ **insensitively** *adverb*; **insensitiveness** *noun*; **insensitivity** /-'tɪv-/ *noun*.

insentient /ɪn'senʃ(ə)nt/ *adjective* inanimate.

inseparable /ɪn'sepərəb(ə)l/ *adjective* that cannot be separated. □ **inseparability** *noun*; **inseparably** *adverb*.

insert ● *verb* /ɪn'sɜːt/ place or put (thing into another). ● *noun* /'ɪnsɜːt/ thing inserted.

insertion /ɪn'sɜːʃ(ə)n/ *noun* inserting; thing inserted.

inset ● *noun* /'ɪnset/ extra piece inserted in book, garment, etc.; small map etc. within border of larger. ● *verb* /ɪn'set/ (**insetting**; *past & past participle* **inset** or **insetted**) put in as inset; decorate with inset.

inshore /ɪn'ʃɔː/ *adverb & adjective* at sea but close to shore.

inside ● *noun* /ɪn'saɪd/ inner side or part; interior; side of path away from road; (usually in *plural*) *colloquial* stomach and bowels. ● *adjective* /'ɪnsaɪd/ of, on, or in the inside; nearer to centre of games field. ● *adverb* /ɪn'saɪd/ on, in, or to the inside; *slang* in prison. ● *preposition* /ɪn'saɪd/ within, on the inside of; in less than. □ **inside out** with inner side turned outwards; **know inside out** know thoroughly.

insider /ɪn'saɪdə/ *noun* person within organization etc.; person privy to secret.

insidious /ɪn'sɪdɪəs/ *adjective* proceeding inconspicuously but harmfully. □ **insidiously** *adverb*.

insight *noun* capacity for understanding hidden truths etc.; instance of this.

insignia /ɪn'sɪgnɪə/ *plural noun* badges or marks of office etc.

insignificant /ɪnsɪg'nɪfɪkənt/ *adjective* unimportant; trivial. □ **insignificance** *noun*.

insincere /ɪnsɪn'sɪə/ *adjective* not sincere. □ **insincerely** *adverb*; **insincerity** /-'ser-/ *noun*.

insinuate /ɪn'smjʊeɪt/ *verb* (**-ting**) hint obliquely; (usually + *into*) introduce subtly or deviously. □ **insinuation** *noun*.

insipid /ɪn'sɪpɪd/ *adjective* dull, lifeless; flavourless. □ **insipidity** /-'pɪd-/ *noun*; **insipidly** *adverb*.

insist /ɪn'sɪst/ *verb* demand or maintain emphatically. □ **insistence** *noun*; **insistent** *adjective*; **insistently** *adverb*.

in situ /ɪn 'sɪtjuː/ *adverb* in its original place. [Latin]

insobriety /ɪnsə'braɪətɪ/ *noun* intemperance, esp. in drinking.

insole *noun* removable inner sole for use in shoe.

insolent /'ɪnsələnt/ *adjective* impertinently insulting. □ **insolence** *noun*; **insolently** *adverb*.

insoluble /ɪn'sɒljʊb(ə)l/ *adjective* that cannot be solved or dissolved. □ **insolubility** *noun*; **insolubly** *adverb*.

insolvent /ɪn'sɒlv(ə)nt/ ● *adjective* unable to pay debts. ● *noun* insolvent debtor. □ **insolvency** *noun*.

insomnia /ɪn'sɒmnɪə/ *noun* sleeplessness.

insomniac /ɪn'sɒmnɪæk/ *noun* person suffering from insomnia.

insouciant /ɪn'suːsɪənt/ *adjective* carefree, unconcerned. □ **insouciance** *noun*.

inspect /ɪn'spekt/ *verb* look closely at; examine officially. □ **inspection** *noun*.

inspector *noun* official employed to inspect or supervise; police officer next above sergeant in rank. □ **inspectorate** *noun*.

inspiration /ɪnspə'reɪʃ(ə)n/ *noun* creative force or influence; person etc. stimulating creativity etc.; sudden brilliant idea; divine influence, esp. on writing of Scripture.

inspire /ɪn'spaɪə/ *verb* (**-ring**) stimulate (person) to esp. creative activity; animate; instil thought or feeling into; prompt, give rise to; (as **inspired** *adjective*) characterized by inspiration. □ **inspiring** *adjective*.

inspirit /ɪn'spɪrɪt/ *verb* (**-t-**) put life into, animate; encourage.

inst. *abbreviation* instant, of current month.

instability /ɪnstə'bɪlɪtɪ/ *noun* lack of stability.

install /ɪn'stɔːl/ *verb* place (equipment etc.) in position ready for use; place (person) in office with ceremony. □ **installation** /-stə'leɪ-/ *noun*.

instalment *noun* (*US* **installment**) any of several usually equal payments for something; any of several parts, esp. of broadcast or published story.

instance /'ɪnst(ə)ns/ ● *noun* example; particular case. ● *verb* (**-cing**) cite as instance.

instant /'ɪnst(ə)nt/ ● *adjective* occurring immediately; (of food etc.) processed for quick preparation; urgent, pressing; of current month. ● *noun* precise moment; short space of time.

instantaneous /ɪnstən'teɪnɪəs/ *adjective* occurring or done in an instant. □ **instantaneously** *adverb*.

instantly adverb immediately.

instead /ɪn'stɛd/ adverb (+ of) in place of; as substitute or alternative.

instep /'ɪnstɛp/ noun inner arch of foot between toes and ankle; part of shoe etc. fitting this.

instigate /'ɪnstɪgeɪt/ verb (-ting) bring about by persuasion; incite. □ **instigation** noun; **instigator** noun.

instil /ɪn'stɪl/ verb (US **instill**) (-ll-) (often + into) put (ideas etc. into mind etc.) gradually; put in by drops. □ **instillation** noun; **instilment** noun.

instinct /'ɪnstɪŋkt/ noun inborn pattern of behaviour; innate impulse; intuition. □ **instinctive** /-'stɪŋktɪv/ adjective; **instinctively** /-'stɪŋktɪvlɪ/ adverb; **instinctual** /-'stɪŋktjʊəl/ adjective.

institute /'ɪnstɪtjuːt/ ● noun organized body for promotion of science, education, etc. ● verb (-ting) establish; initiate (inquiry etc.); (usually + to, into) appoint (person) as cleric in church etc.

institution /ɪnstɪ'tjuːʃ(ə)n/ noun (esp. charitable) organization or society; established law or custom; colloquial well-known person; instituting, being instituted.

institutional adjective of or like an institution; typical of institutions.

institutionalize verb (also **-ise**) (-zing or **-sing**) (as **institutionalized** adjective) made dependent by long period in institution; place or keep in institution; make institutional.

instruct /ɪn'strʌkt/ verb teach; (usually + to do) direct, command; employ (lawyer); inform. □ **instructor** noun.

instruction /ɪn'strʌkʃ(ə)n/ noun (often in plural) order, direction (as to how thing works etc.); teaching. □ **instructional** adjective.

instructive /ɪn'strʌktɪv/ adjective tending to instruct; enlightening.

instrument /'ɪnstrəmənt/ noun tool, implement; (in full **musical instrument**) contrivance for producing musical sounds; thing used in performing action; person made use of; measuring device, esp. in aircraft; formal (esp. legal) document.

instrumental /ɪnstrə'mɛnt(ə)l/ adjective serving as instrument or means; (of music) performed on instruments.

instrumentalist noun performer on musical instrument.

instrumentality /ɪnstrəmɛn'tælɪtɪ/ noun agency, means.

instrumentation /ɪnstrəmɛn'teɪʃ(ə)n/ noun provision or use of instruments; arrangement of music for instruments; particular instruments used in piece.

insubordinate /ɪnsə'bɔːdɪnət/ adjective disobedient; unruly. □ **insubordination** noun.

insubstantial /ɪnsəb'stænʃ(ə)l/ adjective lacking solidity or substance; not real.

insufferable /ɪn'sʌfərəb(ə)l/ adjective unbearable; unbearably conceited etc. □ **insufferably** adverb.

insufficient /ɪnsə'fɪʃ(ə)nt/ adjective not enough, inadequate. □ **insufficiency** noun; **insufficiently** adverb.

insular /'ɪnsjʊlə/ adjective of or like an island; separated, remote; narrow-minded. □ **insularity** /-'lær-/ noun.

insulate /'ɪnsjʊleɪt/ verb (-ting) isolate, esp. by nonconductor of electricity, heat, sound, etc. □ **insulation** noun; **insulator** noun.

insulin /'ɪnsjʊlɪn/ noun hormone regulating the amount of glucose in the blood, the lack of which causes diabetes.

insult ● verb /ɪn'sʌlt/ abuse scornfully; offend self-respect etc. of. ● noun /'ɪnsʌlt/ insulting remark or action. □ **insulting** adjective; **insultingly** adverb.

insuperable /ɪn'suːpərəb(ə)l/ adjective impossible to surmount; impossible to overcome. □ **insuperability** noun; **insuperably** adverb.

insupportable /ɪnsə'pɔːtəb(ə)l/ adjective unbearable; unjustifiable.

insurance /ɪn'ʃʊərəns/ noun procedure or contract securing compensation for loss, damage, injury, or death on payment of premium; sum paid to effect insurance.

insure /ɪn'ʃʊə/ verb (-ring) (often + against) effect insurance with respect to.

insurgent /ɪn'sɜːdʒ(ə)nt/ ● adjective in revolt; rebellious. ● noun rebel. □ **insurgence** noun.

insurmountable /ɪnsə'maʊntəb(ə)l/ adjective insuperable.

insurrection /ɪnsə'rɛkʃ(ə)n/ noun rising in resistance to authority; incipient rebellion. □ **insurrectionist** noun.

intact /ɪn'tækt/ adjective unimpaired; entire; untouched.

intaglio /ɪn'tɑːlɪəʊ/ noun (plural **-s**) gem with incised design; engraved design.

intake noun action of taking in; people, things, or quantity taken in; place where water is taken into pipe, or fuel or air into engine.

intangible /ɪn'tændʒɪb(ə)l/ adjective that cannot be touched or mentally grasped. □ **intangibility** noun; **intangibly** adverb.

integer /'ɪntɪdʒə/ noun whole number.

integral /'ɪntɪgr(ə)l/ adjective of or essential to a whole; complete; of or denoted by an integer.

▪ **Usage** Integral is often pronounced /ɪn'tɛgr(ə)l/ (with the stress on the -teg-), but this is considered incorrect by some people.

integrate /'ɪntɪgreɪt/ verb (-ting) combine (parts) into whole; complete by adding parts; bring or come into equal membership of society; desegregate (school etc.), esp. racially. □ **integrated circuit** small piece of material replacing electrical circuit of many components. □ **integration** noun.

integrity /ɪn'tɛgrɪtɪ/ noun honesty; wholeness; soundness.

integument /ɪn'tɛgjʊmənt/ noun skin, husk, or other (natural) covering.

intellect /'ɪntəlɛkt/ noun faculty of knowing and reasoning; understanding.

intellectual /ɪntə'lɛktʃʊəl/ ● adjective of, requiring, or using intellect; having highly developed intellect. ● noun intellectual person. □ **intellectualize** verb (also **-ise**) (-zing or **-sing**); **intellectually** adverb.

intelligence /ɪn'tɛlɪdʒ(ə)ns/ noun intellect; quickness of understanding; collecting of information, esp. secretly for military or political purposes; information so collected; people employed in this. □ **intelligence quotient** number denoting ratio of person's intelligence to the average.

intelligent adjective having or showing good intelligence, clever. □ **intelligently** adverb.

intelligentsia /ɪntɛlɪ'dʒɛntsɪə/ noun class of intellectuals regarded as cultured and politically enterprising.

intelligible /ɪn'tɛlɪdʒɪb(ə)l/ adjective that can be understood. □ **intelligibility** noun; **intelligibly** adverb.

intemperate /ɪn'tɛmpərət/ adjective immoderate; excessive in consumption of alcohol, or in general indulgence of appetite. □ **intemperance** noun.

intend /ɪn'tɛnd/ verb have as one's purpose; (usually + for, as, to do) design, destine.

intended ● *adjective* done on purpose. ● *noun colloquial* fiancé(e).

intense /ɪn'tens/ *adjective* (**-r, -st**) existing in high degree; vehement; violent, forceful; extreme; very emotional. □ **intensity** *noun* (*plural* **-ies**); **intensely** *adverb*.

■ *Usage Intense* is sometimes confused with *intensive*, and wrongly used to describe a course of study etc.

intensify *verb* (**-ies, -ied**) make or become (more) intense. □ **intensification** *noun*.

intensive /ɪn'tensɪv/ *adjective* thorough, vigorous; concentrated; of or relating to intensity; increasing production relative to cost. □ **-intensive** making much use of; **intensive care** medical treatment with constant supervision of dangerously ill patient. □ **intensively** *adverb*.

intent /ɪn'tent/ ● *noun* intention; purpose. ● *adjective* (usually + *on*) resolved, bent; attentively occupied; eager. □ **to all intents and purposes** practically. □ **intently** *adverb*.

intention /ɪn'tenʃ(ə)n/ *noun* purpose, aim; intending.

intentional *adjective* done on purpose. □ **intentionally** *adverb*.

inter /ɪn'tɜ:/ *verb* (**-rr-**) bury (corpse etc.).

inter- *combining form* among, between; mutually, reciprocally.

interact /ɪntə'rækt/ *verb* act on each other. □ **interaction** *noun*.

interactive *adjective* reciprocally active; (of computer etc.) allowing two-way flow of information between itself and user. □ **interactively** *adverb*.

interbreed /ɪntə'bri:d/ *verb* (*past & past participle* **-bred**) (cause to) produce hybrid individual.

intercalary /ɪn'tɜ:kələrɪ/ *adjective* inserted to harmonize calendar with solar year; having such addition; interpolated.

intercede /ɪntə'si:d/ *verb* (**-ding**) intervene on behalf of another; plead.

intercept /ɪntə'sept/ *verb* seize, catch, stop, etc. in transit; cut off. □ **interception** *noun*; **interceptor** *noun*.

intercession /ɪntə'seʃ(ə)n/ *noun* interceding. □ **intercessor** *noun*.

interchange ● *verb* /ɪntə'tʃeɪndʒ/ (**-ging**) (of two people) exchange (things) with each other; make exchange of (two things); alternate. ● *noun* /'ɪntətʃeɪndʒ/ reciprocal exchange; alternation; road junction where traffic streams do not cross. □ **interchangeable** *adjective*.

inter-city /ɪntə'sɪtɪ/ *adjective* existing or travelling between cities.

intercom /'ɪntəkɒm/ *noun colloquial* system of intercommunication by telephone or radio.

intercommunicate /ɪntəkə'mju:nɪkeɪt/ *verb* (**-ting**) have communication with each other; (of rooms etc.) open into each other. □ **intercommunication** *noun*.

intercommunion /ɪntəkə'mju:nɪən/ *noun* mutual communion, esp. between religious bodies.

interconnect /ɪntəkə'nekt/ *verb* connect with each other. □ **interconnection** *noun*.

intercontinental /ɪntəkɒntɪ'nent(ə)l/ *adjective* connecting or travelling between continents.

intercourse /'ɪntəkɔ:s/ *noun* social, international, etc. communication or dealings; sexual intercourse.

interdenominational /ɪntədɪnɒmɪ'neɪʃən(ə)l/ *adjective* of or involving more than one Christian denomination.

interdependent /ɪntədɪ'pend(ə)nt/ *adjective* mutually dependent. □ **interdependence** *noun*.

interdict ● *noun* /'ɪntədɪkt/ *formal* prohibition; *RC Church* sentence debarring person, or esp. place, from ecclesiastical functions and privileges. ● *verb* /ɪntə'dɪkt/ prohibit (action); forbid use of; (usually + *from*) restrain (person). □ **interdiction** /-'dɪk-/ *noun*; **interdictory** /-'dɪk-/ *adjective*.

interdisciplinary /ɪntədɪsɪ'plɪnərɪ/ *adjective* of or involving different branches of learning.

interest /'ɪntrəst/ ● *noun* concern, curiosity; quality causing this; subject, hobby, etc., towards which one feels it; advantage; money paid for use of money borrowed etc.; thing in which one has stake or concern; financial stake; legal concern, title, or right. ● *verb* arouse interest of; (usually + *in*) cause to take interest; (as **interested** *adjective*) having private interest, not impartial.

interesting *adjective* causing curiosity; holding the attention. □ **interestingly** *adverb*.

interface /'ɪntəfeɪs/ ● *noun* surface forming common boundary of two regions; place where interaction occurs between two systems etc.; apparatus for connecting two pieces of esp. computing equipment so they can be operated jointly. ● *verb* (**-cing**) connect by means of interface; interact.

interfere /ɪntə'fɪə/ *verb* (**-ring**) (often + *with*) meddle; be an obstacle; intervene; (+ *with*) molest sexually.

interference *noun* interfering; fading of received radio signals.

interferon /ɪntə'fɪərɒn/ *noun* protein inhibiting development of virus in cell.

interfuse /ɪntə'fju:z/ *verb* (**-sing**) mix, blend. □ **interfusion** *noun*.

interim /'ɪntərɪm/ ● *noun* intervening time. ● *adjective* provisional, temporary.

interior /ɪn'tɪərɪə/ ● *adjective* inner; inland; internal, domestic. ● *noun* inner part; inside; inland region; home affairs of country; representation of inside of room etc.

interject /ɪntə'dʒekt/ *verb* make (remark etc.) abruptly or parenthetically; interrupt.

interjection /ɪntə'dʒekʃ(ə)n/ *noun* exclamation.

interlace /ɪntə'leɪs/ *verb* (**-cing**) bind intricately together; interweave.

interlard /ɪntə'lɑ:d/ *verb* mix (speech etc.) with unusual words or phrases.

interleave /ɪntə'li:v/ *verb* (**-ving**) insert (usually blank) leaves between leaves of (book).

interline /ɪntə'laɪn/ *verb* (**-ning**) put extra layer of material between fabric of (garment) and its lining.

interlink /ɪntə'lɪŋk/ *verb* link together.

interlock /ɪntə'lɒk/ ● *verb* engage with each other by overlapping etc.; lock together. ● *noun* machine-knitted fabric with fine stitches.

interlocutor /ɪntə'lɒkjʊtə/ *noun formal* person who takes part in conversation. □ **interlocutory** *adjective*.

interloper /'ɪntələʊpə/ *noun* intruder; person who thrusts himself or herself into others' affairs.

interlude /'ɪntəlu:d/ *noun* interval between parts of play etc., performance filling this; contrasting time, event, etc. in middle of something.

intermarry /ɪntə'mærɪ/ *verb* (**-ies, -ied**) (+ *with*) (of races, castes, families, etc.) become connected by marriage. □ **intermarriage** /-rɪdʒ/ *noun*.

intermediary /ɪntə'mi:dɪərɪ/ ● *noun* (*plural* **-ies**) mediator. ● *adjective* acting as mediator; intermediate.

intermediate /ɪntə'mi:dɪət/ ● *adjective* coming between in time, place, order, etc. ● *noun* intermediate thing.

interment /ɪn'tɜ:mənt/ *noun* burial.

intermezzo /ɪntə'metsəʊ/ *noun* (*plural* **-mezzi** /-sɪ/ or **-s**) *Music* short connecting movement or composition.

interminable /ɪnˈtɜːmɪnəb(ə)l/ *adjective* endless; tediously long. □ **interminably** *adverb*.

intermingle /ɪntəˈmɪŋɡ(ə)l/ *verb* (**-ling**) mix together, mingle.

intermission /ɪntəˈmɪʃ(ə)n/ *noun* pause, cessation; interval in cinema etc.

intermittent /ɪntəˈmɪt(ə)nt/ *adjective* occurring at intervals, not continuous or steady. □ **intermittently** *adverb*.

intermix /ɪntəˈmɪks/ *verb* mix together.

intern ● *noun* /ˈɪntɜːn/ *US* resident junior doctor in hospital. ● *verb* /ɪnˈtɜːn/ confine within prescribed limits. □ **internee** /-ˈniː/ *noun*; **internment** *noun*.

internal /ɪnˈtɜːn(ə)l/ *adjective* of or in the inside of thing; relating to inside of the body; of domestic affairs of country; (of students) attending a university as well as taking its exams; used or applying within an organization; intrinsic; of mind or soul. □ **internal-combustion engine** engine in which motive power comes from explosion of gas or vapour with air in cylinder. □ **internally** *adverb*.

international /ɪntəˈnæʃ(ə)n(ə)l/ ● *adjective* existing or carried on between nations; agreed on by many nations. ● *noun* contest (usually in sports) between representatives of different nations; such representative; (**International**) any of 4 successive associations for socialist or Communist action. □ **internationality** /-ˈnæl-/ *noun*; **internationally** *adverb*.

internationalism *noun* advocacy of community of interests among nations. □ **internationalist** *noun*.

internationalize *verb* (also **-ise**) (**-zing** or **-sing**) make international; bring under joint protection etc. of different nations.

internecine /ɪntəˈniːsaɪn/ *adjective* mutually destructive.

interpenetrate /ɪntəˈpenɪtreɪt/ *verb* (**-ting**) penetrate each other; pervade. □ **interpenetration** *noun*.

interpersonal /ɪntəˈpɜːsən(ə)l/ *adjective* between people.

interplanetary /ɪntəˈplænɪtərɪ/ *adjective* between planets.

interplay /ˈɪntəpleɪ/ *noun* reciprocal action.

Interpol /ˈɪntəpɒl/ *noun* International Criminal Police Organization.

interpolate /ɪnˈtɜːpəleɪt/ *verb* (**-ting**) insert or introduce between other things; make (esp. misleading) insertions in. □ **interpolation** *noun*.

interpose /ɪntəˈpəʊz/ *verb* (**-sing**) insert (thing between others); introduce, use, say, etc. as interruption or interference; interrupt; advance (objection etc.) so as to interfere; intervene. □ **interposition** /-pəˈzɪʃ(ə)n/ *noun*.

interpret /ɪnˈtɜːprɪt/ *verb* (**-t-**) explain the meaning of (esp. words); render, represent; act as interpreter. □ **interpretation** *noun*.

interpreter *noun* person who translates orally.

interracial /ɪntəˈreɪʃ(ə)l/ *adjective* between or affecting different races.

interregnum /ɪntəˈreɡnəm/ *noun* (*plural* **-s**) interval with suspension of normal government between successive reigns or regimes; interval, pause.

interrelated /ɪntərɪˈleɪtɪd/ *adjective* related to each other. □ **interrelation** *noun*; **interrelationship** *noun*.

interrogate /ɪnˈterəɡeɪt/ *verb* (**-ting**) question closely or formally. □ **interrogation** *noun*; **interrogator** *noun*.

interrogative /ɪntəˈrɒɡətɪv/ ● *adjective* of, like, or used in questions. ● *noun* interrogative word.

interrogatory /ɪntəˈrɒɡətərɪ/ ● *adjective* questioning. ● *noun* (*plural* **-ies**) set of questions.

interrupt /ɪntəˈrʌpt/ *verb* break continuity of (action, speech, etc.); obstruct (view etc.). □ **interruption** *noun*.

intersect /ɪntəˈsekt/ *verb* divide by passing or lying across; cross or cut each other.

intersection /ɪntəˈsekʃ(ə)n/ *noun* intersecting; place where two roads intersect; point or line common to lines or planes that intersect.

intersperse /ɪntəˈspɜːs/ *verb* (**-sing**) (usually + *between*, *among*) scatter; (+ *with*) vary (thing) by scattering others among it.

interstate /ˈɪntəsteɪt/ *adjective* existing etc. between states, esp. of US.

interstellar /ɪntəˈstelə/ *adjective* between stars.

interstice /ɪnˈtɜːstɪs/ *noun* gap, chink, crevice.

interstitial /ɪntəˈstɪʃ(ə)l/ *adjective* forming or in interstices.

intertwine /ɪntəˈtwaɪn/ *verb* (**-ning**) (often + *with*) twine closely together.

interval /ˈɪntəv(ə)l/ *noun* intervening time or space; pause; break; *Music* difference of pitch between two sounds. □ **at intervals** here and there, now and then.

intervene /ɪntəˈviːn/ *verb* (**-ning**) occur in meantime; interfere; prevent or modify events; come between people or things; mediate.

intervention /ɪntəˈvenʃ(ə)n/ *noun* intervening; interference; mediation.

interview /ˈɪntəvjuː/ ● *noun* oral examination of applicant; conversation with reporter, for broadcast or publication; meeting of people, esp. for discussion. ● *verb* hold interview with. □ **interviewee** /-vjuːˈiː/ *noun*; **interviewer** *noun*.

interweave /ɪntəˈwiːv/ *verb* (**-ving**; *past* **-wove**; *past participle* **-woven**) weave together; blend intimately.

intestate /ɪnˈtesteɪt/ ● *adjective* not having made a will before death. ● *noun* person who has died intestate. □ **intestacy** /-təsɪ/ *noun*.

intestine /ɪnˈtestɪn/ *noun* (in *singular* or *plural*) lower part of alimentary canal. □ **intestinal** *adjective*.

intimate¹ ● *adjective* /ˈɪntɪmət/ closely acquainted; familiar; closely personal; (usually + *with*) having sexual relations; (of knowledge) thorough; close. ● *noun* intimate friend. □ **intimacy** /-məsɪ/ *noun*; **intimately** *adverb*.

intimate² /ˈɪntɪmeɪt/ *verb* (**-ting**) state or make known; imply. □ **intimation** *noun*.

intimidate /ɪnˈtɪmɪdeɪt/ *verb* (**-ting**) frighten, esp. in order to influence conduct. □ **intimidation** *noun*.

into /ˈɪntʊ, ˈɪntə/ *preposition expressing motion or direction to point within, direction of attention, or change of state*; after the beginning of; *colloquial* interested in.

intolerable /ɪnˈtɒlərəb(ə)l/ *adjective* that cannot be endured. □ **intolerably** *adverb*.

intolerant /ɪnˈtɒlərənt/ *adjective* not tolerant. □ **intolerance** *noun*.

intonation /ɪntəˈneɪʃ(ə)n/ *noun* modulation of voice, accent; intoning.

intone /ɪnˈtəʊn/ *verb* (**-ning**) recite with prolonged sounds, esp. in monotone.

in toto /ɪn ˈtəʊtəʊ/ *adverb* entirely. [Latin]

intoxicant /ɪnˈtɒksɪkənt/ ● *adjective* intoxicating. ● *noun* intoxicating substance.

intoxicate /ɪnˈtɒksɪkeɪt/ *verb* (**-ting**) make drunk; excite or elate beyond self-control. □ **intoxication** *noun*.

intractable /ɪnˈtræktəb(ə)l/ *adjective* not easily dealt with; stubborn. □ **intractability** *noun*.

intramural /ɪntrəˈmjʊər(ə)l/ *adjective* situated or done within walls of institution etc.

intransigent /ɪnˈtrænsɪdʒ(ə)nt/ ● *adjective* uncompromising. ● *noun* such person. □ **intransigence** *noun*.

intransitive /ɪnˈtrænsɪtɪv/ *adjective* (of verb) not taking direct object.

intrauterine /ɪntrəˈjuːtəram/ *adjective* within the womb.

intravenous /ɪntrəˈviːnəs/ *adjective* in(to) vein(s). □ **intravenously** *adverb*.

intrepid /ɪnˈtrepɪd/ *adjective* fearless; brave.

intricate /ˈɪntrɪkət/ *adjective* complicated; perplexingly detailed. □ **intricacy** /-kəsɪ/ *noun* (*plural* **-ies**); **intricately** *adverb*.

intrigue ● *verb* /ɪnˈtriːg/ (**-gues**, **-gued**, **-guing**) carry on underhand plot; use secret influence; rouse curiosity of. ● *noun* /ˈɪntriːg/ underhand plotting or plot; secret arrangement, esp. with romantic associations. □ **intriguing** *adjective*; **intriguingly** *adverb*.

intrinsic /ɪnˈtrɪnzɪk/ *adjective* inherent; essential. □ **intrinsically** *adverb*.

intro /ˈɪntrəʊ/ *noun* (*plural* **-s**) *colloquial* introduction.

introduce /ɪntrəˈdjuːs/ *verb* (**-cing**) make (person) known by name to another; announce or present to audience; bring (custom etc.) into use; bring (bill etc.) before Parliament; (+ *to*) initiate (person) in subject; insert; bring in; usher in, bring forward. □ **introducible** *adjective*.

introduction /ɪntrəˈdʌkʃ(ə)n/ *noun* introducing, being introduced; formal presentation; preliminary matter in book; introductory treatise. □ **introductory** *adjective*.

introspection /ɪntrəˈspekʃ(ə)n/ *noun* examination of one's own thoughts. □ **introspective** *adjective*.

introvert ● *noun* person chiefly concerned with his or her own thoughts; shy thoughtful person. ● *adjective* (also **introverted**) characteristic of an introvert. □ **introversion** /-ˈvɜːʃ(ə)n/ *noun*.

intrude /ɪnˈtruːd/ *verb* (**-ding**) (+ *on, upon, into*) come uninvited or unwanted; force on a person. □ **intruder** *noun*; **intrusion** /-ʒ(ə)n/ *noun*; **intrusive** /-sɪv/ *adjective*.

intuition /ɪntjuːˈɪʃ(ə)n/ *noun* immediate apprehension by mind without reasoning; immediate insight. □ **intuit** /ɪnˈtjuːɪt/ *verb*; **intuitional** *adjective*.

intuitive /ɪnˈtjuːɪtɪv/ *adjective* of, having, or perceived by intuition. □ **intuitively** *adverb*; **intuitiveness** *noun*.

Inuit /ˈɪnjuːɪt/ ● *noun* (*plural* same or **-s**) N. American Eskimo; language of Inuit. ● *adjective* of Inuit or their language.

inundate /ˈɪnʌndeɪt/ *verb* (**-ting**) (often + *with*) flood, overwhelm. □ **inundation** *noun*.

inure /ɪˈnjʊə/ *verb* (**-ring**) habituate, accustom. □ **inurement** *noun*.

invade /ɪnˈveɪd/ *verb* (**-ding**) enter (country etc.) with arms to control or subdue it; swarm into; (of disease etc.) attack; encroach on. □ **invader** *noun*.

invalid¹ /ˈɪnvəlɪd, -liːd/ ● *noun* person enfeebled or disabled by illness or injury. ● *adjective* of or for invalids; sick, disabled. ● *verb* (**-d-**) (often + *out* etc.) remove from active service; disable (person) by illness. □ **invalidism** *noun*; **invalidity** /-ˈlɪd-/ *noun*.

invalid² /ɪnˈvælɪd/ *adjective* not valid. □ **invalidity** /-vəˈlɪd-/ *noun*.

invalidate /ɪnˈvælɪdeɪt/ *verb* (**-ting**) make invalid. □ **invalidation** *noun*.

invaluable /ɪnˈvæljʊəb(ə)l/ *adjective* beyond price, very valuable.

invariable /ɪnˈveərɪəb(ə)l/ *adjective* unchangeable; always the same. □ **invariably** *adverb*.

invasion /ɪnˈveɪʒ(ə)n/ *noun* invading, being invaded. □ **invasive** /-sɪv/ *adjective*.

invective /ɪnˈvektɪv/ *noun* violent attack in words.

inveigh /ɪnˈveɪ/ *verb* (+ *against*) speak or write with strong hostility against.

inveigle /ɪnˈveɪg(ə)l/ *verb* (**-ling**) (+ *into, to do*) entice, persuade by guile. □ **inveiglement** *noun*.

invent /ɪnˈvent/ *verb* create by thought; originate; fabricate. □ **inventor** *noun*.

invention /ɪnˈvenʃ(ə)n/ *noun* inventing, being invented; thing invented; inventiveness.

inventive *adjective* able to invent; imaginative. □ **inventively** *adverb*; **inventiveness** *noun*.

inventory /ˈɪnvəntərɪ/ ● *noun* (*plural* **-ies**) list of goods etc. ● *verb* (**-ies**, **-ied**) make inventory of; enter in inventory.

inverse /ɪnˈvɜːs/ ● *adjective* inverted in position, order, or relation. ● *noun* inverted state; (often + *of*) direct opposite. □ **inverse proportion**, **ratio** relation between two quantities such that one increases in proportion as the other decreases.

inversion /ɪnˈvɜːʃ(ə)n/ *noun* inverting, esp. reversal of normal order of words.

invert /ɪnˈvɜːt/ *verb* turn upside down; reverse position, order, or relation of. □ **inverted commas** quotation marks.

invertebrate /ɪnˈvɜːtɪbrət/ ● *adjective* without backbone. ● *noun* invertebrate animal.

invest /ɪnˈvest/ *verb* (often + *in*) apply or use (money) for profit; devote (time etc.) to an enterprise; (+ *in*) buy (something useful or otherwise rewarding); (+ *with*) endue with qualities etc.; (often + *with, in*) clothe with insignia of office. □ **investor** *noun*.

investigate /ɪnˈvestɪgeɪt/ *verb* (**-ting**) inquire into, examine. □ **investigation** *noun*; **investigative** /-gətɪv/ *adjective*; **investigator** *noun*.

investiture /ɪnˈvestɪtʃə/ *noun* formal investing of person with honours etc.

investment *noun* investing; money invested; property etc. in which money is invested.

inveterate /ɪnˈvetərət/ *adjective* (of person) confirmed in (usually undesirable) habit etc.; (of habit etc.) long-established. □ **inveteracy** *noun*.

invidious /ɪnˈvɪdɪəs/ *adjective* likely to excite ill-will against performer, possessor, etc.

invigilate /ɪnˈvɪdʒɪleɪt/ *verb* (**-ting**) supervise examinees. □ **invigilation** *noun*; **invigilator** *noun*.

invigorate /ɪnˈvɪgəreɪt/ *verb* (**-ting**) give vigour to. □ **invigorating** *adjective*.

invincible /ɪnˈvɪnsɪb(ə)l/ *adjective* unconquerable. □ **invincibility** *noun*; **invincibly** *adverb*.

inviolable /ɪnˈvaɪələb(ə)l/ *adjective* not to be violated. □ **inviolability** *noun*.

inviolate /ɪnˈvaɪələt/ *adjective* not violated; safe (from harm). □ **inviolacy** *noun*.

invisible /ɪnˈvɪzɪb(ə)l/ *adjective* that cannot be seen. □ **invisible exports, imports** items for which payment is made by or to another country but which are not goods. □ **invisibility** *noun*; **invisibly** *adverb*.

invite ● *verb* /ɪnˈvaɪt/ (**-ting**) request courteously to come, to do, etc.; solicit courteously; tend to evoke unintentionally; attract. ● *noun* /ˈɪnvaɪt/ *colloquial* invitation. □ **invitation** /ɪnvɪˈteɪʃ(ə)n/ *noun*.

inviting *adjective* attractive. □ **invitingly** *adverb*.

in vitro /ɪn ˈviːtrəʊ/ *adverb* (of biological processes) taking place in test-tube or other laboratory environment. [Latin]

invocation /ɪnvəˈkeɪʃ(ə)n/ *noun* invoking; calling on, esp. in prayer or for inspiration etc. □ **invocatory** /ɪnˈvɒkətərɪ/ *adjective*.

invoice /ˈɪnvɔɪs/ ● *noun* bill for usually itemized goods etc. ● *verb* (**-cing**) send invoice to; make invoice of.

invoke /ɪnˈvəʊk/ verb (**-king**) call on in prayer or as witness; appeal to (law, authority, etc.); summon (spirit) by charms; ask earnestly for (vengeance, justice, etc.).

involuntary /ɪnˈvɒləntərɪ/ adjective done etc. without exercise of will; not controlled by will. □ **involuntarily** adverb.

involute /ˈɪnvəluːt/ adjective intricate; curled spirally.

involution /ɪnvəˈluːʃ(ə)n/ noun involving; intricacy; curling inwards, part so curled.

involve /ɪnˈvɒlv/ verb (**-ving**) (often + in) cause (person, thing) to share experience or effect; imply, make necessary; (often + in) implicate (person) in charge, crime, etc.; include or affect in its operation; (as **involved** adjective) complicated. □ **involvement** noun.

invulnerable /ɪnˈvʌlnərəb(ə)l/ adjective that cannot be wounded. □ **invulnerability** noun.

inward /ˈɪnwəd/ ● adjective directed towards inside; going in; situated within; mental, spiritual. ● adverb (also **inwards**) towards inside; in mind or soul.

inwardly adverb on the inside; in mind or spirit; not aloud.

inwrought /ɪnˈrɔːt/ adjective (often + with) decorated (with pattern); (often + in, on) (of pattern) wrought (in or on fabric).

iodine /ˈaɪədiːn/ noun black solid halogen element forming violet vapour; solution of this used as antiseptic.

IOM abbreviation Isle of Man.

ion /ˈaɪən/ noun atom or group of atoms that has lost or gained one or more electrons.

ionic /aɪˈɒnɪk/ adjective of or using ions.

ionize verb (also **-ise**) (**-zing** or **-sing**) convert or be converted into ion(s). □ **ionization** noun.

ionosphere /aɪˈɒnəsfɪə/ noun ionized region in upper atmosphere. □ **ionospheric** /-'sfer-/ adjective.

iota /aɪˈəʊtə/ noun ninth letter of Greek alphabet (Ι, ι); (usually with negative) a jot.

IOU /aɪəʊˈjuː/ noun (plural **-s**) signed document acknowledging debt.

IOW abbreviation Isle of Wight.

IPA abbreviation International Phonetic Alphabet.

ipecacuanha /ɪpɪkækjʊˈɑːnə/ noun root of S. American plant used as emetic etc.

ipso facto /ɪpsəʊ ˈfæktəʊ/ adverb by that very fact. [Latin]

IQ abbreviation intelligence quotient.

IRA abbreviation Irish Republican Army.

Iranian /ɪˈreɪnɪən/ ● adjective of Iran (formerly Persia); of group of languages including Persian. ● noun native or national of Iran.

Iraqi /ɪˈrɑːkɪ/ ● adjective of Iraq. ● noun (plural **-s**) native or national of Iraq.

irascible /ɪˈræsɪb(ə)l/ adjective irritable; hot-tempered. □ **irascibility** noun.

irate /aɪˈreɪt/ adjective angry, enraged.

ire /ˈaɪə/ noun literary anger.

iridescent /ɪrɪˈdes(ə)nt/ adjective showing rainbow-like glowing colours; changing colour with position. □ **iridescence** noun.

iris /ˈaɪərɪs/ noun circular coloured membrane surrounding pupil of eye; bulbous or tuberous plant with sword-shaped leaves and showy flowers.

Irish /ˈaɪərɪʃ/ ● adjective of Ireland. ● noun Celtic language of Ireland; (**the Irish**; treated as plural) the Irish people. □ **Irish coffee** coffee with dash of whiskey and a little sugar, topped with cream; **Irishman**, **Irishwoman** native of Ireland; **Irish stew** dish of stewed mutton, onions, and potatoes.

irk verb irritate, annoy.

irksome adjective annoying, tiresome.

iron /ˈaɪən/ ● noun common strong grey metallic element; this as symbol of strength or firmness; tool etc. of iron; implement heated to smooth clothes etc.; golf club with iron or steel head; (in plural) fetters; (in plural) stirrups; (often in plural) leg-support to rectify malformations. ● adjective of iron; robust; unyielding. ● verb smooth (clothes etc.) with heated iron. □ **Iron Age** era characterized by use of iron weapons etc.; **Iron Curtain** historical notional barrier to passage of people and information between Soviet bloc and West; **ironing board** narrow folding table etc. for ironing clothes on; **iron lung** rigid case over patient's body for administering prolonged artificial respiration; **ironmonger** dealer in **ironmongery**, household and building hardware; **iron rations** small emergency supply of food; **ironstone** hard iron ore, kind of hard white pottery.

ironic /aɪˈrɒnɪk/ adjective (also **ironical**) using or displaying irony. □ **ironically** adverb.

irony /ˈaɪrənɪ/ noun (plural **-ies**) expression of meaning, usually humorous or sarcastic, by use of words normally conveying opposite meaning; apparent perversity of fate or circumstances.

irradiate /ɪˈreɪdɪeɪt/ verb (**-ting**) subject to radiation; shine on; throw light on; light up. □ **irradiation** noun.

irrational /ɪˈræʃ(ə)n(ə)l/ adjective unreasonable, illogical; not endowed with reason; Mathematics not expressible as an ordinary fraction. □ **irrationality** /-ˈnæl-/ noun; **irrationally** adverb.

irreconcilable /ɪˈrekənsaɪləb(ə)l/ adjective implacably hostile; (of ideas etc.) incompatible. □ **irreconcilably** adverb.

irrecoverable /ɪrɪˈkʌvərəb(ə)l/ adjective that cannot be recovered or remedied.

irredeemable /ɪrɪˈdiːməb(ə)l/ adjective that cannot be redeemed, hopeless. □ **irredeemably** adverb.

irreducible /ɪrɪˈdjuːsɪb(ə)l/ adjective not able to be reduced or simplified.

irrefutable /ɪrɪˈfjuːtəb(ə)l/ adjective that cannot be refuted. □ **irrefutably** adverb.

irregular /ɪˈregjʊlə/ ● adjective not regular; unsymmetrical, uneven; varying in form; not occurring at regular intervals; contrary to rule; (of troops) not in regular army; (of verb, noun, etc.) not inflected according to usual rules. ● noun (in plural) irregular troops. □ **irregularity** /-ˈlær-/ noun (plural **-ies**); **irregularly** adverb.

irrelevant /ɪˈrelɪv(ə)nt/ adjective not relevant. □ **irrelevance** noun; **irrelevancy** noun (plural **-ies**).

irreligious /ɪrɪˈlɪdʒəs/ adjective lacking or hostile to religion; irreverent.

irremediable /ɪrɪˈmiːdɪəb(ə)l/ adjective that cannot be remedied. □ **irremediably** adverb.

irremovable /ɪrɪˈmuːvəb(ə)l/ adjective not removable. □ **irremovably** adverb.

irreparable /ɪˈrepərəb(ə)l/ adjective that cannot be rectified or made good. □ **irreparably** adverb.

irreplaceable /ɪrɪˈpleɪsəb(ə)l/ adjective that cannot be replaced.

irrepressible /ɪrɪˈpresɪb(ə)l/ adjective that cannot be repressed. □ **irrepressibly** adverb.

irreproachable /ɪrɪˈprəʊtʃəb(ə)l/ adjective faultless, blameless. □ **irreproachably** adverb.

irresistible /ɪrɪˈzɪstɪb(ə)l/ adjective too strong, convincing, charming, etc. to be resisted. □ **irresistibly** adverb.

irresolute /ɪˈrezəluːt/ adjective hesitating; lacking in resolution. □ **irresoluteness** noun; **irresolution** /-ˈluːʃ(ə)n/ noun.

irrespective /ɪrɪˈspektɪv/ adjective (+ of) not taking into account, regardless of.

irresponsible /ɪrɪˈspɒnsɪb(ə)l/ *adjective* acting or done without due sense of responsibility; not responsible. □ **irresponsibility** *noun*; **irresponsibly** *adverb*.

irretrievable /ɪrɪˈtriːvəb(ə)l/ *adjective* that cannot be retrieved or restored. □ **irretrievably** *adverb*.

irreverent /ɪˈrevərənt/ *adjective* lacking in reverence. □ **irreverence** *noun*; **irreverently** *adverb*.

irreversible /ɪrɪˈvɜːsɪb(ə)l/ *adjective* that cannot be reversed or altered. □ **irreversibly** *adverb*.

irrevocable /ɪˈrevəkəb(ə)l/ *adjective* unalterable; gone beyond recall. □ **irrevocably** *adverb*.

irrigate /ˈɪrɪɡeɪt/ *verb* (**-ting**) water (land) by system of artificial channels; (of stream etc.) supply (land) with water; *Medicine* moisten (wound etc.) with constant flow of liquid. □ **irrigable** *adjective*; **irrigation** *noun*; **irrigator** *noun*.

irritable /ˈɪrɪtəb(ə)l/ *adjective* easily annoyed; very sensitive to contact. □ **irritability** *noun*; **irritably** *adverb*.

irritant /ˈɪrɪt(ə)nt/ ● *adjective* causing irritation. ● *noun* irritant substance or agent.

irritate /ˈɪrɪteɪt/ *verb* (**-ting**) excite to anger, annoy; stimulate discomfort in (part of body). □ **irritating** *adjective*; **irritation** *noun*.

Is. *abbreviation* Island(s); Isle(s).

is 3rd singular present of BE.

isinglass /ˈaɪzɪŋɡlɑːs/ *noun* kind of gelatin obtained from sturgeon etc.

Islam /ˈɪzlɑːm/ *noun* religion of Muslims, proclaimed by Prophet Muhammad; the Muslim world. □ **Islamic** /-ˈlæm-/ *adjective*.

island /ˈaɪlənd/ *noun* piece of land surrounded by water; traffic island; detached or isolated thing.

islander *noun* native or inhabitant of island.

isle /aɪl/ *noun literary* (usually small) island.

islet /ˈaɪlɪt/ *noun* small island.

isn't /ˈɪz(ə)nt/ is not.

isobar /ˈaɪsəbɑː/ *noun* line on map connecting places with same atmospheric pressure. □ **isobaric** /-ˈbær-/ *adjective*.

isolate /ˈaɪsəleɪt/ *verb* (**-ting**) place apart or alone; separate (esp. infectious patient from others); insulate (electrical apparatus), esp. by gap; disconnect. □ **isolation** *noun*.

isolationism *noun* policy of holding aloof from affairs of other countries or groups. □ **isolationist** *noun*.

isomer /ˈaɪsəmə/ *noun* one of two or more compounds with same molecular formula but different arrangement of atoms. □ **isomeric** /-ˈmer-/ *adjective*; **isomerism** /aɪˈsɒmərɪz(ə)m/ *noun*.

isosceles /aɪˈsɒsɪliːz/ *adjective* (of triangle) having two sides equal.

isotherm /ˈaɪsəθɜːm/ *noun* line on map connecting places with same temperature. □ **isothermal** /-ˈθɜːm(ə)l/ *adjective*.

isotope /ˈaɪsətəʊp/ *noun* any of two or more forms of chemical element with different relative atomic mass and different nuclear but not chemical properties. □ **isotopic** /-ˈtɒp-/ *adjective*.

Israeli /ɪzˈreɪlɪ/ ● *adjective* of modern state of Israel. ● *noun* (*plural* **-s**) native or national of Israel.

issue /ˈɪʃuː/ ● *noun* giving out or circulation of shares, notes, stamps, etc.; copies of journal etc. circulated at one time; each of regular series of magazine etc.; outgoing, outflow; point in question, essential subject of dispute; result, outcome; offspring. ● *verb* (**issues**, **issued**, **issuing**) go or come out; give or send out; publish, circulate; supply, (+ *with*) supply with equipment etc.; (+ *from*) be derived, result; (+ *from*) emerge.

isthmus /ˈɪsməs/ *noun* (*plural* **-es**) neck of land connecting two larger land masses.

IT *abbreviation* information technology.

it *pronoun* the thing in question; indefinite, undefined, or impersonal subject, action, condition, object, etc.; *substitute for deferred subject or object*; exactly what is needed; perfection; *slang* sexual intercourse, sex appeal. □ **that's it** *colloquial* that is what is required, that is the difficulty, that is the end, enough.

Italian /ɪˈtæljən/ ● *noun* native, national, or language of Italy. ● *adjective* of Italy.

italic /ɪˈtælɪk/ ● *adjective* (of type etc.) of sloping kind; (of handwriting) neat and pointed; (**Italic**) of ancient Italy. ● *noun* (usually in *plural*) italic type.

italicize /ɪˈtælɪsaɪz/ *verb* (also **-ise**) (**-zing** or **-sing**) print in italics.

itch ● *noun* irritation in skin; restless desire; disease with itch. ● *verb* feel irritation or restless desire.

itchy *adjective* (**-ier**, **-iest**) having or causing itch. □ **have itchy feet** *colloquial* be restless, have urge to travel.

it'd /ˈɪtəd/ it had; it would.

item /ˈaɪtəm/ *noun* any one of enumerated things; separate or distinct piece of news etc.

itemize *verb* (also **-ise**) (**-zing** or **-sing**) state by items. □ **itemization** *noun*.

iterate /ˈɪtəreɪt/ *verb* (**-ting**) repeat; state repeatedly. □ **iteration** *noun*; **iterative** /-rətɪv/ *adjective*.

itinerant /aɪˈtɪnərənt/ ● *adjective* travelling from place to place. ● *noun* itinerant person.

itinerary /aɪˈtɪnərərɪ/ *noun* (*plural* **-ies**) route; record of travel; guidebook.

it'll /ˈɪt(ə)l/ it will; it shall.

its *adjective* of belonging to it.

it's /ɪts/ it is; it has.

■ **Usage** Because it has an apostrophe, *it's* is easily confused with *its*. Both are correctly used in *Where's the dog?—It's in its kennel, and it's eaten its food* (= *It is in its kennel, and it has eaten its food.*)

itself /ɪtˈself/ *pronoun: emphatic & reflexive form of* IT.

ITV *abbreviation* Independent Television.

IUD *abbreviation* intrauterine (contraceptive) device.

I've /aɪv/ I have.

ivory /ˈaɪvərɪ/ *noun* (*plural* **-ies**) white substance of tusks of elephant etc.; colour of this; (in *plural*) *slang* things made of or resembling ivory, esp. dice, piano keys, or teeth. □ **ivory tower** seclusion from harsh realities of life.

ivy /ˈaɪvɪ/ *noun* (*plural* **-ies**) climbing evergreen with shiny 5-angled leaves.

jab ● verb (**-bb-**) poke roughly; stab; (+ *into*) thrust (thing) hard or abruptly. ● noun abrupt blow or thrust; *colloquial* hypodermic injection.

jabber ● verb chatter volubly; utter fast and indistinctly. ● noun chatter, gabble.

jabot /'ʒæbəʊ/ noun frill on front of shirt or blouse.

jacaranda /dʒækəˈrændə/ noun tropical American tree with blue flowers or one with hard scented wood.

jacinth /'dʒæsmθ/ noun reddish-orange zircon used as gem.

jack ● noun device for lifting heavy objects, esp. vehicles; lowest-ranking court card; ship's flag, esp. showing nationality; device using single-pronged plug to connect electrical equipment; small white target ball in bowls; (in *plural*) game played with jackstones. ● verb (usually + *up*) raise (as) with jack. □ **jackboot** boot reaching above knee; **jack in** *slang* abandon (attempt etc.); **jack-in-the-box** toy figure that springs out of box; **jack of all trades** person with many skills; **jack plug** electrical plug with single prong; **jackstone** metal etc. piece used in tossing games.

jackal /'dʒæk(ə)l/ noun African or Asian wild animal of dog family.

jackass noun male ass; stupid person.

jackdaw noun grey-headed bird of crow family.

jacket /'dʒækɪt/ noun short coat with sleeves; covering round boiler etc.; outside wrapper of book; skin of potato. □ **jacket potato** one baked in its skin.

jackknife ● noun large clasp-knife. ● verb (**-fing**) (of articulated vehicle) fold against itself in accident.

jackpot noun large prize, esp. accumulated in game, lottery, etc.

Jacobean /dʒækəˈbiːən/ adjective of reign of James I.

Jacobite /'dʒækəbaɪt/ noun *historical* supporter of James II in exile, or of Stuarts.

Jacuzzi /dʒəˈkuːzi/ noun (plural **-s**) *proprietary term* large bath with massaging underwater jets.

jade[1] noun hard usually green stone for ornaments; green colour of jade.

jade[2] noun inferior or worn-out horse.

jaded adjective tired out, surfeited.

jag ● noun sharp projection of rock etc. ● verb (**-gg-**) cut or tear unevenly; make indentations in.

jagged /'dʒægɪd/ adjective unevenly cut or torn. □ **jaggedly** adverb; **jaggedness** noun.

jaguar /'dʒægjʊə/ noun large American spotted animal of cat family.

jail /dʒeɪl/ (also **gaol**) ● noun place for detention of prisoners; confinement in jail. ● verb put in jail. □ **jailbird** prisoner, habitual criminal. □ **jailer** noun.

jalap /'dʒæləp/ noun purgative drug.

jalopy /dʒəˈlɒpi/ noun (plural **-ies**) *colloquial* dilapidated old motor vehicle.

jalousie /'ʒæluːzi/ noun slatted blind or shutter.

jam[1] ● verb (**-mm-**) (usually + *into*, *together*, etc.) squeeze or cram into space; become wedged; cause (machinery) to become wedged and so unworkable, become wedged in this way; block (exit, road, etc.) by crowding; (usually + *on*) apply (brakes) suddenly; make (radio transmission) unintelligible with interference. ● noun squeeze; stoppage; crowded mass,

esp. of traffic; *colloquial* predicament. □ **jam session** (in jazz etc.) improvised ensemble playing.

jam[2] noun conserve of boiled fruit and sugar; *colloquial* easy or pleasant thing.

jamb /dʒæm/ noun side post or side face of doorway or window frame.

jamboree /dʒæmbəˈriː/ noun celebration; large rally of Scouts.

jammy adjective (**-ier**, **-iest**) covered with jam; *colloquial* lucky, profitable.

Jan. abbreviation January.

jangle /'dʒæŋɡ(ə)l/ ● verb (**-ling**) (cause to) make harsh metallic sound. ● noun such sound.

janitor /'dʒænɪtə/ noun doorkeeper; caretaker.

January /'dʒænjʊərɪ/ noun (plural **-ies**) first month of year.

japan /dʒəˈpæn/ ● noun hard usually black varnish. ● verb (**-nn-**) make black and glossy (as) with japan.

Japanese /dʒæpəˈniːz/ ● noun (plural same) native, national, or language of Japan. ● adjective of Japan or its people or language.

jape noun practical joke.

japonica /dʒəˈpɒnɪkə/ noun flowering shrub with red flowers and edible fruits.

jar[1] noun container, usually of glass and cylindrical.

jar[2] ● verb (**-rr-**) (often + *on*) (of sound, manner, etc.) strike discordantly, grate; (often + *against*, *on*) (cause to) strike (esp. part of body) with vibration or shock; (often + *with*) be at variance. ● noun jarring sound, shock, or vibration.

jardinière /ʒɑːdɪˈnjeə/ noun ornamental pot or stand for plants.

jargon /'dʒɑːgən/ noun words used by particular group or profession; debased or pretentious language.

jasmine /'dʒæzmɪn/ noun shrub with white or yellow flowers.

jasper /'dʒæspə/ noun red, yellow, or brown opaque quartz.

jaundice /'dʒɔːndɪs/ ● noun yellowing of skin caused by liver disease, bile disorder, etc. ● verb (as **jaundiced** adjective) affected with jaundice; envious, resentful.

jaunt /dʒɔːnt/ ● noun pleasure trip. ● verb take a jaunt.

jaunty adjective (**-ier**, **-iest**) cheerful and self-confident; sprightly. □ **jauntily** adverb; **jauntiness** noun.

javelin /'dʒævəlɪn/ noun light spear thrown in sport or, formerly, as weapon.

jaw ● noun bony structure containing teeth; (in *plural*) mouth, gripping parts of tool etc.; *colloquial* tedious talk. ● verb *slang* speak at tedious length. □ **jawbone** lower jaw in most mammals.

jay noun noisy European bird of crow family with vivid plumage. □ **jaywalk** walk across road carelessly or dangerously; **jaywalker** person who does this.

jazz noun rhythmic syncopated esp. improvised music of American black origin. □ **and all that jazz** *colloquial* and other related things; **jazz up** enliven.

jazzy adjective (**-ier**, **-iest**) of or like jazz; vivid.

jealous /'dʒeləs/ adjective resentful of rivalry in love; (often + *of*) envious (of person etc.), protective (of rights etc.). □ **jealously** adverb; **jealousy** noun (plural **-ies**).

jeans /dʒiːnz/ *plural noun* casual esp. denim trousers.

Jeep *noun proprietary term* small sturdy esp. military vehicle with 4-wheel drive.

jeer ● *verb* (often + *at*) scoff, deride. ● *noun* taunt.

Jehovah /dʒə'həʊvə/ *noun* (in Old Testament) God. □ **Jehovah's Witness** member of unorthodox Christian sect.

jejune /dʒɪ'dʒuːn/ *adjective* (of ideas, writing, etc.) shallow, naïve, or dry and uninteresting.

jell *verb colloquial* set as jelly; (of ideas etc.) take definite form; cohere.

jellied /'dʒelɪd/ *adjective* (of food etc.) set as or in jelly.

jelly /'dʒelɪ/ *noun* (*plural* **-ies**) (usually fruit-flavoured) semi-transparent dessert set with gelatin; similar preparation as jam or condiment; *slang* gelignite. □ **jelly baby** jelly-like babyshaped sweet; **jellyfish** (*plural* same or **-es**) marine animal with jelly-like body and stinging tentacles.

jemmy /'dʒemɪ/ *noun* (*plural* **-ies**) burglar's crowbar.

jeopardize *verb* (also **-ise**) (**-zing** or **-sing**) endanger.

jeopardy /'dʒepədɪ/ *noun* danger, esp. severe.

jerboa /dʒɜː'bəʊə/ *noun* small jumping desert rodent.

Jeremiah /dʒerɪ'maɪə/ *noun* dismal prophet.

jerk[1] ● *noun* sharp sudden pull, twist, etc.; spasmodic muscular twitch; *slang* fool. ● *verb* move, pull, throw, etc. with jerk. □ **jerky** *adjective* (**-ier**, **-iest**); **jerkily** *adverb*; **jerkiness** *noun*.

jerk[2] *verb* cure (beef) by cutting in long slices and drying in the sun.

jerkin /'dʒɜːkɪn/ *noun* sleeveless jacket.

jeroboam /dʒerə'bəʊəm/ *noun* wine bottle of 4–12 times ordinary size.

jerry-building *noun* building of shoddy houses with bad materials. □ **jerry-builder** *noun*; **jerry-built** *adjective*.

jerrycan *noun* kind of petrol- or water-can.

jersey /'dʒɜːzɪ/ *noun* (*plural* **-s**) knitted usually woollen pullover; knitted fabric; (**Jersey**) dairy cow from Jersey.

Jerusalem artichoke /dʒə'ruːsələm/ *noun* kind of sunflower with edible tubers; this tuber as vegetable.

jest ● *noun* joke; fun; banter; object of derision. ● *verb* joke; fool about. □ **in jest** in fun.

jester *noun historical* professional clown at medieval court etc.

Jesuit /'dʒezjʊɪt/ *noun* member of RC Society of Jesus. □ **Jesuitical** /-'ɪt-/ *adjective*.

jet[1] ● *noun* stream of water, steam, gas, flame, etc. shot esp. from small opening; spout or nozzle for this purpose; jet engine or plane. ● *verb* (**-tt-**) spurt out in jet(s); *colloquial* send or travel by jet plane. □ **jet engine** one using jet propulsion; **jet lag** exhaustion felt after long flight across time zones; **jet plane** one with jet engine; **jet-propelled** having jet propulsion, very fast; **jet propulsion** propulsion by backward ejection of high-speed jet of gas etc.; **jet set** wealthy people who travel widely, esp. for pleasure; **jet-setter** such a person.

jet[2] *noun* hard black lignite, often carved and highly polished. □ **jet black** deep glossy black.

jetsam /'dʒetsəm/ *noun* objects washed ashore, esp. jettisoned from ship.

jettison /'dʒetɪs(ə)n/ *verb* throw (cargo, fuel, etc.) from ship or aircraft to lighten it; abandon; get rid of.

jetty /'dʒetɪ/ *noun* (*plural* **-ies**) pier or breakwater protecting or defending harbour etc.; landing-pier.

Jew /dʒuː/ *noun* person of Hebrew descent or whose religion is Judaism.

jewel /'dʒuːəl/ ● *noun* precious stone; this used in watchmaking; jewelled personal ornament; precious person or thing. ● *verb* (**-ll-**; *US* **-l-**) (esp. as **jewelled** *adjective*) adorn or set with jewels.

jeweller *noun* (*US* **jeweler**) maker of or dealer in jewels or jewellery.

jewellery /'dʒuːəlrɪ/ *noun* (also **jewelry**) rings, brooches, necklaces, etc. collectively.

Jewish *adjective* of Jews or Judaism. □ **Jewishness** *noun*.

Jewry /'dʒʊərɪ/ *noun* Jews collectively.

Jezebel /'dʒezəbəl/ *noun* shameless or immoral woman.

jib ● *noun* projecting arm of crane; triangular staysail. ● *verb* (**-bb-**) (esp. of horse) stop and refuse to go on; (+ *at*) show aversion to.

jibe[1] = GIBE.

jibe[2] *US* = GYBE.

jiffy /'dʒɪfɪ/ *noun* (*plural* **-ies**) (also **jiff**) *colloquial* short time, moment. □ **Jiffy bag** *proprietary term* padded envelope.

jig ● *noun* lively dance; music for this; device that holds piece of work and guides tools operating on it. ● *verb* (**-gg-**) dance jig; (often + *about*) move quickly up and down; fidget.

jigger /'dʒɪgə/ *noun* small glass for measure of spirits.

jiggery-pokery /dʒɪgərɪ'pəʊkərɪ/ *noun colloquial* trickery; swindling.

jiggle /'dʒɪg(ə)l/ ● *verb* (**-ling**) (often + *about*) rock or jerk lightly; fidget. ● *noun* light shake.

jigsaw *noun* (in full **jigsaw puzzle**) picture on board etc. cut into irregular interlocking pieces to be reassembled as pastime; mechanical fine-bladed fret saw.

jihad /dʒɪ'hæd/ *noun* Muslim holy war against unbelievers.

jilt *verb* abruptly reject or abandon (esp. lover).

jingle /'dʒɪŋg(ə)l/ ● *noun* mixed ringing or clinking noise; repetition of sounds in phrase; short catchy verse in advertising etc. ● *verb* (**-ling**) (cause to) make jingling sound.

jingo /'dʒɪŋgəʊ/ *noun* (*plural* **-es**) blustering patriot. □ **jingoism** *noun*; **jingoist** *noun*; **jingoistic** /-'ɪs-/ *adjective*.

jink ● *verb* move elusively; elude by dodging. ● *noun* jinking. □ **high jinks** boisterous fun.

jinnee /dʒi'niː/ *noun* (also **jinn**, **djinn**, **djinn**/) (*plural* **jinn** or **djinn**) (in Muslim mythology) spirit of supernatural power in human or animal form.

jinx *colloquial* ● *noun* person or thing that seems to bring bad luck. ● *verb* (esp. as **jinxed** *adjective*) subject to bad luck.

jitter /'dʒɪtə/ *colloquial* ● *noun* (**the jitters**) extreme nervousness. ● *verb* be nervous; act nervously. □ **jittery** *adjective*.

jive ● *noun* lively dance of 1950s; music for this. ● *verb* (**-ving**) dance to or play jive music. □ **jiver** *noun*.

Jnr. *abbreviation* Junior.

job ● *noun* piece of work (to be) done; paid employment; *colloquial* difficult task; *slang* a crime, esp. a robbery. ● *verb* (**-bb-**) do jobs; do piece-work; buy and sell (stocks etc.); deal corruptly with (matter). □ **jobcentre** local government office advertising available jobs; **job-hunt** *colloquial* seek employment; **job lot** mixed lot bought at auction etc.

jobber /'dʒɒbə/ *noun* person who jobs; *historical* principal or wholesaler on Stock Exchange.

jobbery *noun* corrupt dealing.

jobless *adjective* unemployed. □ **joblessness** *noun*.

job-sharing *noun* sharing of full-time job by two or more people. □ **job-share** *noun & verb*.

jockey /'dʒɒkɪ/ ● *noun* rider in horse races. ● *verb* (**-eys**, **-eyed**) cheat, trick. □ **jockey for position** manoeuvre for advantage.

jockstrap /'dʒɒkstræp/ *noun* support or protection for male genitals worn esp. in sport.

jocose /dʒə'kəʊs/ *adjective* playful; jocular. □ **jocosely** *adverb*; **jocosity** /-'kɒs-/ *noun* (*plural* **-ies**).

jocular /'dʒɒkjʊlə/ *adjective* fond of joking; humorous. □ **jocularity** /-'lær-/ *noun* (*plural* **-ies**); **jocularly** *adverb*.

jocund /'dʒɒkənd/ *adjective literary* merry, cheerful. □ **jocundity** /dʒə'kʌn-/ *noun* (*plural* **-ies**); **jocundly** *adverb*.

jodhpurs /'dʒɒdpəz/ *plural noun* riding breeches tight below knee.

jog ● *verb* (**-gg-**) run slowly, esp. as exercise; push, jerk; nudge, esp. to alert; stimulate (person's memory). ● *noun* spell of jogging; slow walk or trot; push, jerk; nudge. □ **jogtrot** slow regular trot. □ **jogger** *noun*.

joggle /'dʒɒg(ə)l/ ● *verb* (**-ling**) move in jerks. ● *noun* slight shake.

joie de vivre /ʒwɑː də 'viːvrə/ *noun* exuberance; high spirits. [French]

join ● *verb* (often + *to*, *together*) put together, fasten, unite; connect (points) by line etc.; become member of (club etc.); take one's place with (person, group, etc.); (+ *in*, *for*, etc.) take part with (others) in activity etc.; (often + *with*, *to*) come together, be united; (of river etc.) become connected or continuous with. ● *noun* point, line, or surface of junction. □ **join in** take part in (activity); **join up** enlist for military service.

joiner *noun* maker of furniture and light woodwork. □ **joinery** *noun*.

joint ● *noun* place at which two or more things are joined; device for doing this; point at which two bones fit together; division of animal carcass as meat; *slang* restaurant, bar, etc.; *slang* marijuana cigarette. ● *adjective* held by, done by, or belonging to two or more people etc.; sharing with another. ● *verb* connect by joint(s); divide at joint or into joints. □ **joint stock** capital held jointly.

jointure /'dʒɔɪntʃə/ *noun* estate settled on wife by husband for use after his death.

joist *noun* supporting beam in floor, ceiling, etc.

jojoba /həʊ'həʊbə/ *noun* plant with seeds yielding oil used in cosmetics etc.

joke ● *noun* thing said or done to cause laughter; witticism; ridiculous person or thing. ● *verb* (**-king**) make jokes. □ **jokily** *adverb*; **jokiness** *noun*; **jokingly** *adverb*; **jokey**, **joky** *adjective*.

joker *noun* person who jokes; playing card used in some games.

jollification /dʒɒlɪfɪ'keɪʃ(ə)n/ *noun* merrymaking.

jolly /'dʒɒlɪ/ ● *adjective* (**-ier**, **-iest**) cheerful; festive, jovial; *colloquial* pleasant, delightful. ● *adverb colloquial* very. ● *verb* (**-ies**, **-ied**) (usually + *along*) *colloquial* coax, humour. □ **jollity** *noun* (*plural* **-ies**).

jolt ● *verb* shake (esp. in vehicle) with jerk; shock, perturb; move along jerkily. ● *noun* jerk; surprise, shock.

jonquil /'dʒɒŋkwɪl/ *noun* narcissus with white or yellow fragrant flowers.

josh *slang* ● *verb* tease, make fun of. ● *noun* good-natured joke.

joss *noun* Chinese idol. □ **joss-stick** incense stick for burning.

jostle /'dʒɒs(ə)l/ ● *verb* (**-ling**) (often + *against*) knock; elbow; (+ *with*) struggle. ● *noun* jostling.

jot ● *verb* (**-tt-**) (usually + *down*) write briefly or hastily. ● *noun* very small amount.

jotter *noun* small pad or notebook.

joule /dʒuːl/ *noun* SI unit of work and energy.

journal /'dʒɜːn(ə)l/ *noun* newspaper, periodical; daily record of events; diary; account book; part of shaft or axle resting on bearings.

journalese /dʒɜːnə'liːz/ *noun* hackneyed style of writing characteristic of newspapers.

journalism /'dʒɜːnəlɪz(ə)m/ *noun* work of journalist.

journalist /'dʒɜːnəlɪst/ *noun* person writing for or editing newspapers etc. □ **journalistic** /-'lɪs-/ *adjective*.

journey /'dʒɜːnɪ/ ● *noun* (*plural* **-s**) act of going from one place to another; distance travelled, time taken. ● *verb* (**-s**, **-ed**) make journey, travel. □ **journeyman** qualified mechanic or artisan working for another.

joust /dʒaʊst/ *historical* ● *noun* combat with lances between two mounted knights. ● *verb* engage in joust. □ **jouster** *noun*.

jovial /'dʒəʊvɪəl/ *adjective* merry, convivial, hearty. □ **joviality** /-'æl-/ *noun*; **jovially** *adverb*.

jowl /dʒaʊl/ *noun* jaw, jawbone; cheek; loose skin on throat.

joy *noun* gladness, pleasure; thing causing joy; *colloquial* satisfaction. □ **joyride** *colloquial* (go for) pleasure ride in esp. stolen car; **joystick** control column of aircraft, lever for moving image on VDU screen. □ **joyful** *adjective*; **joyfully** *adverb*; **joyfulness** *noun*; **joyless** *adjective*; **joyous** *adjective*; **joyously** *adverb*.

JP *abbreviation* Justice of the Peace.

Jr. *abbreviation* Junior.

jubilant /'dʒuːbɪlənt/ *adjective* exultant, rejoicing. □ **jubilantly** *adverb*; **jubilation** *noun*.

jubilee /'dʒuːbɪliː/ *noun* anniversary (esp. 25th or 50th); time of rejoicing.

Judaic /dʒuː'deɪɪk/ *adjective* of or characteristic of Jews.

Judaism /'dʒuːdeɪɪz(ə)m/ *noun* religion of Jews.

Judas /'dʒuːdəs/ *noun* traitor.

judder /'dʒʌdə/ ● *verb* shake noisily or violently. ● *noun* juddering.

judge /dʒʌdʒ/ ● *noun* public official appointed to hear and try legal cases; person appointed to decide dispute or contest; person who decides question; person having judgement of specified type. ● *verb* (**-ging**) form opinion (about); estimate; act as judge (of); try legal case; (often + *to do*, *that*) conclude, consider.

judgement *noun* (also **judgment**) critical faculty, discernment, good sense; opinion; sentence of court of justice; *often jocular* deserved misfortune. □ **Judgement Day** day on which God will judge humankind. □ **judgemental** /-'men-/ *adjective*.

judicature /'dʒuːdɪkətʃə/ *noun* administration of justice; judge's position; judges collectively.

judicial /dʒuː'dɪʃ(ə)l/ *adjective* of, done by, or proper to court of law; of or proper to a judge; having function of judge; impartial. □ **judicially** *adverb*.

judiciary /dʒuː'dɪʃərɪ/ *noun* (*plural* **-ies**) judges collectively.

judicious /dʒuː'dɪʃəs/ *adjective* sensible, prudent. □ **judiciously** *adverb*.

judo /'dʒuːdəʊ/ *noun* sport derived from ju-jitsu.

jug ● *noun* deep vessel for liquids, with handle and lip; contents of this; *slang* prison. ● *verb* (**-gg-**) (usually as **jugged** *adjective*) stew (hare) in casserole. □ **jugful** *noun* (*plural* **-s**).

juggernaut /'dʒʌgənɔːt/ *noun* large heavy lorry; overwhelming force or object.

juggle /'dʒʌg(ə)l/ ● *verb* (**-ling**) (often + *with*) keep several objects in the air at once by throwing and catching; manipulate or rearrange (facts). ● *noun* juggling; fraud. □ **juggler** *noun*.

jugular /'dʒʌgjʊlə/ ● *adjective* of neck or throat. ● *noun* jugular vein. □ **jugular vein** any of large veins in neck carrying blood from head.

juice /dʒuːs/ *noun* liquid part of vegetable, fruit, or meat; animal fluid, esp. secretion; *colloquial* petrol, electricity.

juicy /ˈdʒuːsɪ/ *adjective* (**-ier, -iest**) full of juice; *colloquial* interesting, scandalous; *colloquial* profitable. □ **juicily** *adverb*.

ju-jitsu /dʒuːˈdʒɪtsuː/ *noun* Japanese system of unarmed combat.

ju-ju /ˈdʒuːdʒuː/ *noun* (*plural* **-s**) charm or fetish of some W. African peoples; supernatural power attributed to this.

jujube /ˈdʒuːdʒuːb/ *noun* flavoured jelly-like lozenge.

jukebox /ˈdʒuːkbɒks/ *noun* coin-operated machine playing records or compact discs.

Jul. *abbreviation* July.

julep /ˈdʒuːlep/ *noun* sweet drink, esp. medicated; *US* spirits and water iced and flavoured.

julienne /dʒuːlɪˈen/ ● *noun* vegetables cut into thin strips. ● *adjective* cut into thin strips.

Juliet cap /ˈdʒuːlɪət/ *noun* small close-fitting cap worn by brides etc.

July /dʒuːˈlaɪ/ *noun* (*plural* **Julys**) seventh month of year.

jumble /ˈdʒʌmb(ə)l/ ● *verb* (**-ling**) (often + *up*) mix; confuse; muddle. ● *noun* confused heap etc.; muddle; articles in jumble sale. □ **jumble sale** sale of second-hand articles, esp. for charity.

jumbo /ˈdʒʌmbəʊ/ *noun* (*plural* **-s**) big animal (esp. elephant), person, or thing. ● **jumbo jet** large airliner for several hundred passengers, esp. Boeing 747.

jump ● *verb* spring from ground etc.; (often + *up, from, in, out,* etc.) rise or move suddenly; jerk from shock or excitement; pass over (obstacle) by jumping; (+ *to, at*) reach (conclusion) hastily; (of train etc.) leave (rails); pass (red traffic light); get on or off (train etc.) quickly, esp. illegally; attack (person) unexpectedly. ● *noun* act of jumping; sudden movement caused by shock etc.; abrupt rise in price, status, etc.; obstacle to be jumped, esp. by horse; gap in series etc. □ **jump at** accept eagerly; **jumped-up** *adjective colloquial* upstart; **jump the gun** start prematurely; **jump-jet** vertical take-off jet plane; **jump-lead** cable for carrying current from one battery to another; **jump-off** deciding round in show-jumping; **jump the queue** take unfair precedence; **jump ship** (of seaman) desert; **jump suit** one-piece garment for whole body; **jump to it** *colloquial* act promptly and energetically.

jumper /ˈdʒʌmpə/ *noun* knitted pullover; loose outer jacket worn by sailors; *US* pinafore dress.

jumpy *adjective* (**-ier, -iest**) nervous, easily startled. □ **jumpiness** *noun*.

Jun. *abbreviation* June; Junior.

junction /ˈdʒʌŋkʃ(ə)n/ *noun* joining-point; place where railway lines or roads meet. □ **junction box** box containing junction of electric cables etc.

juncture /ˈdʒʌŋktʃə/ *noun* point in time, esp. critical one; joining-point.

June *noun* sixth month of year.

jungle /ˈdʒʌŋg(ə)l/ *noun* land overgrown with tangled vegetation, esp. in tropics; tangled mass; place of bewildering complexity or struggle.

junior /ˈdʒuːnɪə/ ● *adjective* (often + *to*) lower in age, standing, or position; the younger (esp. after name); (of school) for younger pupils. ● *noun* junior person.

juniper /ˈdʒuːnɪpə/ *noun* prickly evergreen shrub or tree with purple berry-like cones.

junk[1] ● *noun* discarded articles, rubbish; anything regarded as of little value; *slang* narcotic drug, esp. heroin. ● *verb* discard as junk. □ **junk food** food which is not nutritious; **junk mail** unsolicited advertising sent by post.

junk[2] *noun* flat-bottomed sailing vessel in China seas.

junket /ˈdʒʌŋkɪt/ ● *noun* pleasure outing; official's tour at public expense; sweetened and flavoured milk curds; feast. ● *verb* (**-t-**) feast, picnic.

junkie /ˈdʒʌŋkɪ/ *noun slang* drug addict.

junta /ˈdʒʌntə/ *noun* (usually military) clique taking power after *coup d'état*.

juridical /dʒʊəˈrɪdɪk(ə)l/ *adjective* of judicial proceedings, relating to the law.

jurisdiction /dʒʊərɪsˈdɪkʃ(ə)n/ *noun* (often + *over*) administration of justice; legal or other authority; extent of this.

jurisprudence /dʒʊərɪsˈpruːd(ə)ns/ *noun* science or philosophy of law.

jurist /ˈdʒʊərɪst/ *noun* expert in law. □ **juristic** /-ˈrɪs-/ *adjective*.

juror /ˈdʒʊərə/ *noun* member of jury.

jury /ˈdʒʊərɪ/ *noun* (*plural* **-ies**) group of people giving verdict in court of justice; judges of competition. □ **jury-box** enclosure in court for jury.

just ● *adjective* morally right, fair; deserved; well-grounded; justified. ● *adverb* exactly; very recently; barely; quite; *colloquial* simply, merely, positively. □ **just now** at this moment, a little time ago. □ **justly** *adverb*.

justice /ˈdʒʌstɪs/ *noun* fairness; authority exercised in maintenance of right; judicial proceedings; magistrate, judge. □ **do justice to** treat fairly, appreciate properly; **Justice of the Peace** lay magistrate.

justify /ˈdʒʌstɪfaɪ/ *verb* (**-ies, -ied**) show justice or truth of; (esp. in *passive*) be adequate grounds for, vindicate; *Printing* adjust (line of type) to fill space evenly; (as **justified** *adjective*) just, right. □ **justifiable** *adjective*; **justification** *noun*.

jut ● *verb* (**-tt-**) (often + *out*) protrude. ● *noun* projection.

jute /dʒuːt/ *noun* fibre from bark of E. Indian plant, used for sacking, mats, etc.; plant yielding this.

juvenile /ˈdʒuːvənaɪl/ ● *adjective* youthful; of or for young people; *often derogatory* immature. ● *noun* young person; actor playing juvenile part. □ **juvenile delinquency** offences committed by people below age of legal responsibility; **juvenile delinquent** such offender.

juvenilia /dʒuːvəˈnɪlɪə/ *plural noun* youthful works of author or artist.

juxtapose /dʒʌkstəˈpəʊz/ *verb* (**-sing**) put side by side; (+ *with*) put (thing) beside another. □ **juxtaposition** /-pəˈzɪʃ(ə)n/ *noun*.

K *abbreviation* (also **K.**) kelvin(s); Köchel (list of Mozart's works); (also **k**) 1,000.

k *abbreviation* kilo-; knot(s).

kaftan = CAFTAN.

kaiser /ˈkaɪzə/ *noun historical* emperor, esp. of Germany or Austria.

kale *noun* variety of cabbage, esp. with wrinkled leaves.

kaleidoscope /kəˈlaɪdəskəʊp/ *noun* tube containing angled mirrors and pieces of coloured glass producing reflected patterns when shaken; constantly changing scene, group, etc. □ **kaleidoscopic** /-ˈskɒp-/ *adjective*.

kalends = CALENDS.

kamikaze /kæmɪˈkɑːzɪ/ ● *noun historical* explosive-laden Japanese aircraft deliberately crashed on to target in 1939–45 war; pilot of this. ● *adjective* reckless, esp. suicidal.

kangaroo /kæŋgəˈruː/ *noun* (*plural* **-s**) Australian marsupial with strong hind legs for jumping. □ **kangaroo court** illegal court held by strikers, mutineers, etc.

kaolin /ˈkeɪəlɪn/ *noun* fine white clay used esp. for porcelain and in medicines.

kapok /ˈkeɪpɒk/ *noun* fine cotton-like material from tropical tree, used to stuff cushions etc.

kaput /kəˈpʊt/ *adjective slang* broken, ruined.

karabiner /kærəˈbiːnə/ *noun* coupling link used by mountaineers.

karakul /ˈkærəkʊl/ *noun* (also **caracul**) Asian sheep whose lambs have dark curled fleece; fur of this.

karaoke /kærɪˈəʊkɪ/ *noun* entertainment in nightclubs etc. with customers singing to backing music.

karate /kəˈrɑːtɪ/ *noun* Japanese system of unarmed combat.

karma /ˈkɑːmə/ *noun Buddhism & Hinduism* person's actions in one life, believed to decide fate in next; destiny.

kauri /ˈkaʊrɪ/ *noun* (*plural* **-s**) coniferous NZ timber tree.

kayak /ˈkaɪæk/ *noun* Eskimo one-man canoe.

kazoo /kəˈzuː/ *noun* toy musical instrument into which player sings wordlessly.

KBE *abbreviation* Knight Commander of the Order of the British Empire.

kea /ˈkiːə/ *noun* green and red NZ parrot.

kebab /kɪˈbæb/ *noun* pieces of meat and sometimes vegetables grilled on skewer.

kedge ● *verb* (**-ging**) move (ship) with hawser attached to small anchor. ● *noun* (in full **kedge-anchor**) small anchor for this purpose.

kedgeree /kedʒəˈriː/ *noun* dish of fish, rice, hard-boiled eggs, etc.

keel *noun* main lengthwise member of base of ship etc. ● *verb* (often + *over*) (cause to) fall down or over; turn keel upwards. □ **keelhaul** drag (person) under keel as punishment; **on an even keel** steady, balanced.

keen¹ *adjective* enthusiastic, eager; (often + *on*) enthusiastic about, fond of; intellectually acute; (of knife) sharp; (of price) competitive. □ **keenly** *adverb*; **keenness** *noun*.

keen² ● *noun* Irish wailing funeral song. ● *verb* (often + *over, for*) wail mournfully, esp. at funeral.

keep ● *verb* (*past & past participle* **kept**) have charge of; retain possession of; (+ *for*) retain or reserve (for future); maintain or remain in good or specified condition; restrain; detain; observe or respect (law, secret, etc.); own and look after (animal); clothe, feed, etc. (person); carry on (a business); maintain, guard, protect. ● *noun* maintenance, food; *historical* tower, stronghold. □ **for keeps** *colloquial* permanently; **keep at** (cause to) persist with; **keep away** (often + *from*) avoid, prevent from being near; **keep-fit** regular physical exercises; **keep off** (cause to) stay away from, abstain from, avoid; **keep on** continue, (+ *at*) nag; **keep out** (cause to) stay outside; **keep up** maintain, prevent from going to bed, (often + *with*) not fall behind; **keep up with the Joneses** compete socially with neighbours.

keeper *noun* person who looks after or is in charge of an animal, person, or thing; custodian of museum, forest, etc.; wicket-keeper, goalkeeper; ring holding another on finger.

keeping *noun* custody, charge; (esp. in **in** or **out of keeping with**) agreement, harmony.

keepsake *noun* souvenir, esp. of person.

keg *noun* small barrel. □ **keg beer** beer kept in pressurized metal keg.

kelp *noun* large seaweed suitable for manure.

kelpie /ˈkelpɪ/ *noun Scottish* malevolent water-spirit; Australian sheepdog.

Kelt = CELT.

kelter = KILTER.

kelvin /ˈkelvɪn/ *noun* SI unit of temperature.

ken ● *noun* range of knowledge or sight. ● *verb* (**-nn-**; *past & past participle* **kenned** or **kent**) *Scottish & Northern English* recognize, know.

kendo /ˈkendəʊ/ *noun* Japanese fencing with bamboo swords.

kennel /ˈken(ə)l/ ● *noun* small shelter for dog; (in *plural*) breeding or boarding place for dogs. ● *verb* (**-ll-**; US **-l-**) put or keep in kennel.

Kenyan /ˈkenjən/ ● *adjective* of Kenya. ● *noun* native or national of Kenya.

kept *past & past participle* of KEEP.

keratin /ˈkerətɪn/ *noun* fibrous protein in hair, hooves, claws, etc.

kerb *noun* stone etc. edging to pavement etc. □ **kerb-crawling** *colloquial* driving slowly to pick up prostitute; **kerb drill** rules taught to children about crossing roads.

kerfuffle /kəˈfʌf(ə)l/ *noun colloquial* fuss, commotion.

kermes /ˈkɜːmɪz/ *noun* female of insect with berry-like appearance that feeds on **kermes oak**, evergreen oak; red dye made from these insects.

kernel /ˈkɜːn(ə)l/ *noun* (usually soft) edible centre within hard shell of nut, fruit stone, seed, etc.; central or essential part.

kerosene /ˈkerəsiːn/ *noun esp. US* fuel oil distilled from petroleum etc.; paraffin oil.

kestrel /ˈkestr(ə)l/ *noun* small hovering falcon.

ketch *noun* kind of two-masted sailing boat.

ketchup /ˈketʃəp/ *noun* (US **catsup** /ˈkætsəp/) spicy sauce made esp. from tomatoes.

kettle /ˈket(ə)l/ *noun* vessel for boiling water in. □ **kettledrum** large bowl-shaped drum.

key /kiː/ ● *noun* (*plural* **-s**) instrument for moving bolt of lock, operating switch, etc.; instrument for winding clock etc. or grasping screw, nut, etc.; finger-operated button or lever on typewriter, piano, computer terminal, etc.; explanation, word, or system for understanding list of symbols, code, etc.; *Music* system of related notes based on particular note; roughness of surface helping adhesion of plaster etc. ● *verb* fasten with pin, wedge, bolt, etc.; (often + *in*) enter (data) by means of (computer) keyboard; roughen (surface) to help adhesion of plaster etc. □ **keyed up** tense, excited; **keyhole** hole by which key is put into lock; **keynote** prevailing tone or idea, *Music* note on which key is based; **keypad** miniature keyboard etc. for telephone, portable computer, etc.; **keyring** ring for keeping keys on; **keystone** central principle of policy, system, etc., central stone of arch.

keyboard ● *noun* set of keys on typewriter, computer, piano, etc. ● *verb* enter (data) by means of keyboard. □ **keyboarder** *noun* Computing.

KG *abbreviation* Knight of the Order of the Garter.

kg *abbreviation* kilogram(s).

KGB *noun historical* secret police of USSR.

khaki /'kɑːkɪ/ ● *adjective* dull brownish-yellow. ● *noun* (*plural* **-s**) khaki colour, cloth, or uniform.

khan /kɑːn/ *noun: title of ruler or official in Central Asia.* □ **khanate** *noun.*

kHz *abbreviation* kilohertz.

kibbutz /kɪ'bʊts/ *noun* (*plural* **-im** /-iːm/) communal esp. farming settlement in Israel.

kibosh /'kaɪbɒʃ/ *noun slang* nonsense. □ **put the kibosh on** put an end to.

kick ● *verb* strike, strike out, or propel forcibly with foot or hoof; (often + *at, against*) protest, rebel; *slang* give up (habit); (often + *out*) expel, dismiss; (**kick oneself, could kick oneself**) be annoyed with oneself; score (goal) by kicking. ● *noun* kicking action or blow; recoil of gun; *colloquial* temporary enthusiasm, sharp stimulant effect; (often in *plural*) thrill. □ **kick about** drift idly, discuss informally; **kickback** recoil, payment esp. for illegal help; **kick the bucket** *slang* die; **kick off** *verb* begin football game, remove (shoes etc.) by kicking, *colloquial* start; **kick-off** *noun* start, esp. of football game; **kickstart(er)** (pedal on) device to start engine of motorcycle etc.; **kick up a fuss** *colloquial* create disturbance, object; **kick upstairs** get rid of by promotion.

kid¹ ● *noun* young goat; leather from this; *colloquial* child. ● *verb* (**-dd-**) (of goat) give birth to kid.

kid² *verb* (**-dd-**) *colloquial* deceive, tease. □ **no kidding** *slang* that is the truth.

kidnap /'kɪdnæp/ *verb* (**-pp-**; *US* **-p-**) carry off (person) illegally, esp. to obtain ransom. □ **kidnapper** *noun.*

kidney /'kɪdnɪ/ *noun* (*plural* **-s**) either of two organs serving to excrete urine; animal's kidney as food. □ **kidney bean** red-skinned kidney-shaped bean; **kidney machine** apparatus able to perform function of damaged kidney; **kidney-shaped** having one side concave and the other convex.

kill ● *verb* deprive of life or vitality; end; (**kill oneself**) *colloquial* overexert oneself, laugh heartily; *colloquial* overwhelm with amusement; switch off; pass (time) while waiting; *Computing* delete; *Sport* stop (ball) dead. ● *noun* (esp. in hunting) act of killing, animal(s) killed. □ **killjoy** depressing person; **kill off** destroy completely, bring about death of (fictional character).

killer *noun* person or thing that kills; murderer. □ **killer whale** dolphin with prominent dorsal fin.

killing ● *noun* causing death; *colloquial* great financial success. ● *adjective colloquial* very funny; exhausting.

kiln *noun* oven for burning, baking, or drying esp. pottery.

kilo /'kiːləʊ/ *noun* (*plural* **-s**) kilogram.

kilo- *combining form* one thousand.

kilobyte /'kɪləbaɪt/ *noun* Computing 1,024 bytes as measure of memory size etc.

kilocalorie /'kɪləkælərɪ/ *noun* large calorie (see CALORIE).

kilocycle /'kɪləsaɪk(ə)l/ *noun historical* kilohertz.

kilogram /'kɪləgræm/ *noun* SI unit of mass (2.205 lb).

kilohertz /'kɪləhɜːts/ *noun* 1,000 hertz.

kilolitre /'kɪləliːtə/ *noun* (*US* **-liter**) 1,000 litres.

kilometre /'kɪləmiːtə/ *noun* (*US* **-meter**) 1,000 metres (0.6214 mile).

■ **Usage** *Kilometre* is often pronounced /kɪ'lɒmɪtə/ (with the stress on the *-lom-*), but this is considered incorrect by some people.

kiloton /'kɪlətʌn/ *noun* (also **kilotonne**) unit of explosive power equal to that of 1,000 tons of TNT.

kilovolt /'kɪləvəʊlt/ *noun* 1,000 volts.

kilowatt /'kɪləwɒt/ *noun* 1,000 watts. □ **kilowatt-hour** electrical energy equal to 1 kilowatt used for 1 hour.

kilt ● *noun* pleated skirt usually of tartan, traditionally worn by Highland man. ● *verb* tuck up (skirts) round body; (esp. as **kilted** *adjective*) gather in vertical pleats.

kilter /'kɪltə/ *noun* (also **kelter** /'keltə/) good working order.

kimono /kɪ'məʊnəʊ/ *noun* (*plural* **-s**) wide-sleeved Japanese robe; similar dressing gown.

kin ● *noun* one's relatives or family. ● *adjective* related.

kind /kaɪnd/ ● *noun* species, natural group of animals, plants, etc.; class, type, variety. ● *adjective* (often + *to*) friendly, benevolent. □ **in kind** in same form, (of payment) in goods etc. instead of money.

kindergarten /'kɪndəgɑːt(ə)n/ *noun* class or school for young children.

kind-hearted *adjective* of kind disposition. □ **kind-heartedly** *adverb*; **kind-heartedness** *noun.*

kindle /'kɪnd(ə)l/ *verb* (**-ling**) set on fire, light; inspire; become aroused or animated.

kindling /'kɪndlɪŋ/ *noun* small sticks etc. for lighting fires.

kindly /'kaɪndlɪ/ ● *adverb* in a kind way; please. ● *adjective* (**-ier, -iest**) kind; (of climate etc.) pleasant, mild.

kindred /'kɪndrɪd/ ● *adjective* related, allied, similar. ● *noun* blood relationship; one's relations.

kinetic /kɪ'netɪk/ *adjective* of or due to motion. □ **kinetic energy** energy of motion. □ **kinetically** *adverb.*

king *noun* (as title usually **King**) male sovereign, esp. hereditary; outstanding man or thing in specified field; largest kind of a thing; chess piece which must be checkmated for a win; crowned piece in draughts; court card depicting king; (**the King**) national anthem when sovereign is male. □ **King Charles spaniel** small black and tan kind; **kingcup** marsh marigold; **kingpin** main or large bolt, essential person or thing; **king-size(d)** large. □ **kingly** *adjective*; **kingship** *noun.*

kingdom *noun* state or territory ruled by king or queen; spiritual reign of God; domain; division of natural world. □ **kingdom come** *colloquial* the next world.

kingfisher *noun* small river bird with brilliant blue plumage, which dives for fish.

kink ● *noun* twist or bend in wire etc.; tight wave in hair; mental peculiarity. ● *verb* (cause to) form kink.

kinky *adjective* (**-ier, -iest**) *colloquial* sexually perverted or unconventional; (of clothing) bizarre and sexually provocative. □ **kinkily** *adverb.*

kinship *noun* blood relationship; similarity.

kinsman /'kɪnzmən/ *noun* (*feminine* **kinswoman**) blood relation.

kiosk /'ki:ɒsk/ *noun* open-fronted booth selling newspapers, food, etc.; telephone box.

kip *slang* ● *noun* sleep, bed. ● *verb* (**-pp-**) (often + *down*) sleep.

kipper /'kɪpə/ ● *noun* fish, esp. herring, split, salted, dried, and usually smoked. ● *verb* treat (herring etc.) this way.

kir /kɪə/ *noun* dry white wine with blackcurrant liqueur.

kirk *noun* Scottish & Northern English church. □ **Kirk-session** lowest court in Church of Scotland.

kirsch /kɪəʃ/ *noun* spirit distilled from cherries.

kismet /'kɪzmet/ *noun* destiny.

kiss ● *verb* touch with lips, esp. as sign of love, reverence, etc.; touch lightly. ● *noun* touch of lips; light touch. □ **kiss-curl** small curl of hair on forehead or nape of neck; **kiss of life** mouth-to-mouth resuscitation.

kisser *noun slang* mouth; face.

kissogram *noun* novelty greeting message with kiss.

kit ● *noun* equipment, clothing, etc. for particular purpose; specialized, esp. sports, clothing or uniform; set of parts needed to assemble furniture, model, etc. ● *verb* (**-tt-**) supply; (often + *out*) equip with kit. □ **kitbag** usually cylindrical canvas etc. bag for carrying soldier's etc. kit.

kitchen /'kɪtʃɪn/ *noun* place where food is cooked; kitchen fitments. □ **kitchen garden** garden for growing fruit and vegetables.

kitchenette /kɪtʃɪ'net/ *noun* small kitchen or cooking area.

kite *noun* light framework with thin covering flown on long string in wind; soaring bird of prey.

kith /kɪθ/ *noun* □ **kith and kin** friends and relations.

kitsch /kɪtʃ/ *noun* vulgar, pretentious, or worthless art.

kitten /'kɪt(ə)n/ ● *noun* young cat, ferret, etc. ● *verb* give birth to (kittens).

kittenish *adjective* playful; flirtatious.

kittiwake /'kɪtɪweɪk/ *noun* kind of small seagull.

kitty[1] /'kɪtɪ/ *noun* (*plural* **-ies**) joint fund; pool in some card games.

kitty[2] /'kɪtɪ/ *noun* (*plural* **-ies**) *childish name for* kitten or cat.

kiwi /'ki:wi:/ *noun* flightless NZ bird; (**Kiwi**) *colloquial* New Zealander. □ **kiwi fruit** green-fleshed fruit.

Klaxon /'klæks(ə)n/ *noun proprietary term* horn, warning hooter.

Kleenex /'kli:neks/ *noun* (*plural* same or **-es**) *proprietary term* disposable paper handkerchief.

kleptomania /kleptə'meɪnɪə/ *noun* irresistible urge to steal. □ **kleptomaniac** /-nɪæk/ *adjective & noun*.

km *abbreviation* kilometre(s).

knack /næk/ *noun* acquired faculty of doing something skilfully; habit of action, speech, etc.

knacker /'nækə/ ● *noun* buyer of useless horses for slaughter. ● *verb slang* (esp. as **knackered** *adjective*) exhaust, wear out.

knapsack /'næpsæk/ *noun* soldier's or hiker's bag carried on back.

knapweed /'næpwi:d/ *noun* plant with thistle-like flower.

knave /neɪv/ *noun* rogue, scoundrel; jack (in playing cards). □ **knavery** *noun*; **knavish** *adjective*.

knead /ni:d/ *verb* work into dough, paste, etc., esp. by hand; make (bread, pottery) thus; massage.

knee /ni:/ ● *noun* joint between thigh and lower leg; lap of sitting person; part of garment covering knee. ● *verb* (**knees**, **kneed**, **kneeing**) touch or strike with knee. □ **kneecap** convex bone in front of knee; **knees-up** *colloquial* lively party or gathering.

kneel /ni:l/ *verb* (*past & past participle* **knelt**) rest or lower oneself on knee(s).

kneeler *noun* cushion for kneeling on.

knell /nel/ *noun* sound of bell, esp. for death or funeral; event etc. seen as bad omen.

knelt *past & past participle of* KNEEL.

knew *past of* KNOW.

knickerbockers /'nɪkəbɒkəz/ *plural noun* loose-fitting breeches gathered in at knee. □ **Knickerbocker Glory** ice cream and fruit in tall glass.

knickers /'nɪkəz/ *plural noun* woman's or girl's undergarment for lower torso.

knick-knack /'nɪknæk/ *noun* (also **nick-nack**) trinket, small ornament.

knife /naɪf/ ● *noun* (*plural* **knives**) cutting blade or weapon with long sharpened edge fixed in handle; cutting-blade in machine; (**the knife**) *colloquial* surgery. ● *verb* (**-fing**) cut or stab with knife. □ **knife-edge** edge of knife, position of extreme uncertainty; **knife-pleat** overlapping narrow flat pleat.

knight /naɪt/ ● *noun* man awarded non-hereditary title (*Sir*) by sovereign; *historical* man raised to honourable military rank; *historical* lady's champion in tournament etc.; chess piece usually in shape of horse's head. ● *verb* confer knighthood on. □ **knighthood** *noun*; **knightly** *adjective*.

knit /nɪt/ *verb* (**-tt-**; *past & past participle* **knitted** or **knit**) make (garment etc.) by interlocking loops of esp. wool with knitting-needles or knitting machine; make (plain stitch) in knitting; wrinkle (brow); (often + *together*) make or become close, (of broken bone) become joined. □ **knitwear** knitted garments.

knitting *noun* work being knitted. □ **knitting-needle** thin pointed rod used usually in pairs for knitting.

knob /nɒb/ *noun* rounded protuberance, e.g. door handle, radio control, etc.; small lump (of butter, coal, etc.). □ **knobby** *adjective*.

knobbly /'nɒblɪ/ *adjective* (**-ier**, **-iest**) hard and lumpy.

knock /nɒk/ ● *verb* strike with audible sharp blow; (often + *at*) strike (door etc.) for admittance; (usually + *in*, *off*, etc.) drive by striking; make (hole) by knocking; (of engine) make thumping etc. noise; *slang* criticize. ● *noun* audible sharp blow; rap, esp. at door. □ **knock about**, **around** treat roughly, wander about aimlessly, (usually + *with*) associate socially; **knock back** *slang* eat or drink, esp. quickly; **knock down** *verb* strike (esp. person) to ground, demolish, (usually + *to*) (at auction) sell to bidder, *colloquial* lower price of; **knock-down** *adjective* (of price) very low; **knock knees** legs curved inward at the knee; **knock-kneed** with knock knees; **knock off** strike off with blow, *colloquial* finish work, do or make rapidly, (often + *from*) deduct (amount) from price, *slang* steal, kill; **knock on the head** put end to (scheme etc.); **knock on wood** *US* touch wood; **knock out** *verb* make unconscious by blow to head, defeat (boxer) by knocking down for count of 10, defeat in knockout competition, *colloquial* tire out; **knock-out** *noun* blow that knocks boxer out, competition in which loser of each match is eliminated, *slang* outstanding person or thing; **knock together** construct hurriedly; **knock up** *verb* make hastily, arouse by knock at door, practise tennis etc. before formal game begins, *US slang* make pregnant; **knock-up** *noun* practice at tennis etc.

knocker *noun* hinged metal device on door for knocking with.

knoll /nəʊl/ *noun* small hill, mound.

knot /nɒt/ ● *noun* intertwining of rope, string, etc. so as to fasten; set method of this; tangle in hair, knitting, etc.; unit of ship's or aircraft's speed equal to one nautical mile per hour; hard mass formed in tree trunk where branch grows out; round cross-grained piece in board caused by this; (usually + *of*) cluster. ● *verb* (**-tt-**) tie in knot; entangle. □ **knotgrass** wild plant with creeping stems and pink flowers; **knot-hole** hole in timber where knot has fallen out.

knotty *adjective* (**-ier, -iest**) full of knots; puzzling.

know /nəʊ/ *verb* (*past* **knew** /njuː/; *past participle* **known**) (often + *that, how, what,* etc.) have in the mind, have learnt; be acquainted with; recognize, identify; (often + *from*) be able to distinguish; (as **known** *adjective*) publicly acknowledged. □ **in the know** having inside information; **know-how** practical knowledge or skill.

knowing *adjective* cunning; showing knowledge, shrewd.

knowingly *adverb* in a knowing way; consciously, intentionally.

knowledge /'nɒlɪdʒ/ *noun* (usually + *of*) awareness, familiarity, person's range of information, understanding (of subject); sum of what is known.

knowledgeable *adjective* (also **knowledgable**) well-informed, intelligent. □ **knowledgeably** *adverb*.

known *past participle* of KNOW.

knuckle /'nʌk(ə)l/ ● *noun* bone at finger-joint; knee- or ankle-joint of quadruped; this as joint of meat. ● *verb* (**-ling**) strike, rub, etc. with knuckles. □ **knuckle down** (often + *to*) apply oneself earnestly; **knuckleduster** metal guard worn over knuckles in fighting, esp. to inflict greater damage; **knuckle under** give in, submit.

KO *abbreviation* knockout.

koala /kəʊ'ɑːlə/ *noun* (also **koala bear**) small Australian bearlike marsupial with thick grey fur.

kohl /kəʊl/ *noun* black powder used as eye make-up, esp. in Eastern countries.

kohlrabi /kəʊl'rɑːbɪ/ *noun* (*plural* **-bies**) cabbage with edible turnip-like stem.

kookaburra /'kʊkəbʌrə/ *noun* Australian kingfisher with strange laughing cry.

Koran /kɔː'rɑːn/ *noun* Islamic sacred book.

Korean /kə'riːən/ ● *noun* native or national of N. or S. Korea; language of Korea. ● *adjective* of Korea or its people or language.

kosher /'kəʊʃə/ ● *adjective* (of food or food-shop) fulfilling requirements of Jewish law; *colloquial* correct, genuine. ● *noun* kosher food or shop.

kowtow /kaʊ'taʊ/ ● *noun historical* Chinese custom of touching ground with forehead, esp. in submission. ● *verb* (usually + *to*) act obsequiously; perform kowtow.

k.p.h. *abbreviation* kilometres per hour.

kraal /krɑːl/ *noun South African* village of huts enclosed by fence; enclosure for cattle etc.

kremlin /'kremlɪn/ *noun* citadel within Russian town; (**the Kremlin**) that in Moscow, Russian government.

krill *noun* tiny plankton crustaceans eaten by whales etc.

krugerrand /'kruːgərænd/ *noun* S. African gold coin.

krummhorn /'krʌmhɔːn/ *noun* (also **crumhorn**) medieval wind instrument.

krypton /'krɪptɒn/ *noun* gaseous element used in lamps etc.

Kt. *abbreviation* Knight.

kts. *abbreviation* knots.

kudos /'kjuːdɒs/ *noun colloquial* glory, renown.

kumquat /'kʌmkwɒt/ *noun* (also **cumquat**) small orange-like fruit.

kung fu /kʌŋ 'fuː/ *noun* Chinese form of karate.

kV *abbreviation* kilovolt(s).

kW *abbreviation* kilowatt(s).

kWh *abbreviation* kilowatt-hour(s).

L¹ *noun* (also **l**) (Roman numeral) 50.
L² *abbreviation* Lake. □ **L-plate** sign bearing letter L, attached to vehicle to show that driver is learner.
l *abbreviation* left; line; litre(s).
LA *abbreviation* Los Angeles.
la = LAH.
Lab. *abbreviation* Labour.
lab *noun colloquial* laboratory.
label /'leɪb(ə)l/ ● *noun* piece of paper attached to object to give information about it; classifying phrase etc.; logo, title, or trademark of company. ● *verb* (**-ll-**; *US* **-l-**) attach label to; (usually + *as*) assign to category.
labial /'leɪbɪəl/ ● *adjective* of lips; *Phonetics* pronounced with (closed) lips. ● *noun Phonetics* labial sound.
labium /'leɪbɪəm/ *noun* (*plural* **labia**) each fold of skin of pairs enclosing vulva.
labor etc. *US & Australian* = LABOUR etc.
laboratory /lə'bɒrətərɪ/ *noun* (*plural* **-ies**) place used for scientific experiments and research.
laborious /lə'bɔːrɪəs/ *adjective* needing hard work; (esp. of literary style) showing signs of effort. □ **laboriously** *adverb*.
labour /'leɪbə/ (*US & Australian* **labor**) ● *noun* physical or mental work, exertion; workers, esp. as political force; (**Labour**) the Labour Party; process of giving birth; task. ● *verb* work hard, exert oneself; elaborate needlessly; proceed with difficulty; (as **laboured** *adjective*) done with great effort; (+ *under*) suffer because of. □ **labour camp** prison camp enforcing hard labour; **Labour Exchange** *colloquial or historical* jobcentre; **Labour Party** political party formed to represent workers' interests; **labour-saving** designed to reduce or eliminate work.
labourer *noun* (*US* **laborer**) person doing unskilled paid manual work.
Labrador /'læbrədɔː/ *noun* dog of retriever breed with black or golden coat.
laburnum /lə'bɜːnəm/ *noun* tree with drooping golden flowers and poisonous seeds.
labyrinth /'læbərɪnθ/ *noun* complicated network of passages; intricate or tangled arrangement. □ **labyrinthine** /-'rɪnθaɪn/ *adjective*.
lac *noun* resinous substance from SE Asian insect, used to make varnish and shellac.
lace ● *noun* open patterned fabric or trimming made by twisting, knotting, or looping threads; cord etc. passed through eyelets or hooks for fastening shoes etc. ● *verb* (**-cing**) (usually + *up*) fasten or tighten with lace(s); add spirits to (drink); (+ *through*) pass (shoelace etc.) through. □ **lace-up** shoe fastened with lace.
lacerate /'læsəreɪt/ *verb* (**-ting**) tear (esp. flesh etc.) roughly; wound (feelings etc.). □ **laceration** *noun*.
lachrymal /'lækrɪm(ə)l/ *adjective* (also **lacrimal**) of tears.
lachrymose /'lækrɪməʊs/ *adjective formal* often weeping; tearful.
lack ● *noun* (usually + *of*) deficiency, want. ● *verb* be without or deficient in. □ **lacklustre** (*US* **lackluster**) dull, lacking in vitality etc.
lackadaisical /lækə'deɪzɪk(ə)l/ *adjective* languid; unenthusiastic.
lackey /'lækɪ/ *noun* (*plural* **-s**) servile follower; footman, manservant.

lacking *adjective* undesirably absent; (+ *in*) deficient in.
laconic /lə'kɒnɪk/ *adjective* using few words. □ **laconically** *adverb*.
lacquer /'lækə/ ● *noun* hard shiny shellac or synthetic varnish; substance sprayed on hair to keep it in place. ● *verb* coat with lacquer.
lacrimal = LACHRYMAL.
lacrosse /lə'krɒs/ *noun* hockey-like game played with ball carried in net at end of stick.
lactate /læk'teɪt/ *verb* (**-ting**) (of mammals) secrete milk. □ **lactation** *noun*.
lactic /'læktɪk/ *adjective* of milk.
lactose /'læktəʊs/ *noun* sugar present in milk.
lacuna /lə'kju:nə/ *noun* (*plural* **-s** or **-nae** /-ni:/) missing part, esp. in manuscript; gap.
lacy /'leɪsɪ/ *adjective* (**-ier**, **-iest**) like lace fabric.
lad *noun* boy, youth; *colloquial* man.
ladder /'lædə/ ● *noun* set of horizontal bars fixed at intervals between two uprights for climbing up and down; unravelled stitching in stocking etc.; means of advancement in career etc. ● *verb* cause or develop ladder in (stocking etc.).
lade *verb* (**-ding**; *past participle* **laden**) load (ship); ship (goods); (as **laden** *adjective*) (usually + *with*) loaded, burdened.
la-di-da /lɑːdɪ'dɑː/ *adjective colloquial* pretentious or affected, esp. in manner or speech.
ladle /'leɪd(ə)l/ ● *noun* deep long-handled spoon for serving liquids. ● *verb* (**-ling**) (often + *out*) transfer with ladle.
lady /'leɪdɪ/ *noun* (*plural* **-ies**) woman regarded as having superior status or refined manners; *polite form of address for woman; colloquial* wife, girlfriend; (**Lady**) *title used before name of peeresses, peers' female relatives, wives and widows of knights, etc.*; (**Ladies**) women's public lavatory. □ **ladybird** small beetle, usually red with black spots; **Lady chapel** chapel dedicated to Virgin Mary; **Lady Day** Feast of the Annunciation, 25 Mar.; **ladylike** like or appropriate to lady.
Ladyship *noun* □ **Her** or **Your Ladyship** *title used of or to Lady*.
lag¹ ● *verb* (**-gg-**) fall behind; not keep pace. ● *noun* delay.
lag² *verb* (**-gg-**) enclose (boiler etc.) with heat-insulating material.
lag³ *noun slang* habitual convict.
lager /'lɑːgə/ *noun* kind of light beer. □ **lager lout** *colloquial* youth behaving violently through drinking too much.
laggard /'lægəd/ *noun* person lagging behind.
lagging *noun* insulating material for boiler etc.
lagoon /lə'gu:n/ *noun* salt-water lake separated from sea by sandbank, reef, etc.
lah *noun* (also **la**) *Music* sixth note of scale in tonic sol-fa.
laid *past & past participle* of LAY¹. □ **laid-back** relaxed, easy-going.
lain *past participle* of LIE¹.
lair *noun* wild animal's home; person's hiding place.
laird /'leəd/ *noun Scottish* landed proprietor.
laissez-faire /leɪseɪ'feə/ *noun* (also **laisser-faire**) policy of not interfering. [French]

laity /'leɪtɪ/ *noun* lay people, as distinct from clergy.

lake¹ *noun* large body of water surrounded by land. □ **Lake District** region of lakes in Cumbria.

lake² *noun* reddish pigment originally made from lac.

lam *verb* (**-mm-**) *slang* hit hard, thrash.

lama /'lɑːmə/ *noun* Tibetan or Mongolian Buddhist monk.

lamasery /'lɑːməsərɪ/ *noun* (*plural* **-ies**) lama monastery.

lamb /læm/ ● *noun* young sheep; its flesh as food; gentle, innocent, or weak person. ● *verb* (of sheep) give birth.

lambaste /læm'beɪst/ *verb* (**-ting**) (also **lambast** /-'bæst/) *colloquial* thrash, beat.

lambent /'læmbənt/ *adjective* (of flame etc.) playing on a surface; (of eyes, wit, etc.) gently brilliant. □ **lambency** *noun*.

lambswool *noun* soft fine wool from young sheep.

lame ● *adjective* disabled in foot or leg; (of excuse etc.) unconvincing; (of verse etc.) halting. ● *verb* (**-ming**) make lame, disable. □ **lame duck** helpless person or firm. □ **lamely** *adverb*; **lameness** *noun*.

lamé /'lɑːmeɪ/ *noun* fabric with gold or silver thread woven in.

lament /lə'ment/ ● *noun* passionate expression of grief; song etc. of mourning. ● *verb* express or feel grief for or about; utter lament; (as **lamented** *adjective*) recently dead. □ **lamentation** /læmən-/ *noun*.

lamentable /'læməntəb(ə)l/ *adjective* deplorable, regrettable. □ **lamentably** *adverb*.

lamina /'læmɪnə/ *noun* (*plural* **-nae** /-niː/) thin plate or layer. □ **laminar** *adjective*.

laminate ● *verb* /'læmɪneɪt/ (**-ting**) beat or roll into thin plates; overlay with plastic layer etc.; split into layers. ● *noun* /'læmɪnət/ laminated structure, esp. of layers fixed together. □ **lamination** *noun*.

lamp *noun* device for giving light from electricity, gas, oil, etc.; apparatus producing esp. ultraviolet or infrared radiation. □ **lamppost** post supporting street light; **lampshade** usually partial cover for lamp.

lampoon /læm'puːn/ ● *noun* satirical attack on person etc. ● *verb* satirize. □ **lampoonist** *noun*.

lamprey /'læmprɪ/ *noun* (*plural* **-s**) eel-like fish with sucker mouth.

Lancastrian /læŋ'kæstrɪən/ ● *noun* native of Lancashire or Lancaster. ● *adjective* of Lancashire or Lancaster; of House of Lancaster in Wars of Roses.

lance /lɑːns/ ● *noun* long spear, esp. one used by horseman. ● *verb* (**-cing**) prick or open with lancet. □ **lance-corporal** army NCO below corporal.

lanceolate /'lɑːnsɪələt/ *adjective* shaped like spearhead, tapering to each end.

lancer /'lɑːnsə/ *noun* *historical* soldier of cavalry regiment originally armed with lances; (in *plural*) quadrille.

lancet /'lɑːnsɪt/ *noun* small broad two-edged surgical knife with sharp point.

land ● *noun* solid part of earth's surface; ground, soil, expanse of country; nation, state; landed property; (in *plural*) estates. ● *verb* set or go ashore; bring (aircraft) down; alight on ground etc.; bring (fish) to land; (often + *up*) bring to or arrive at certain situation or place; *colloquial* deal (person etc. a blow etc.); (+ *with*) present (person) with (problem etc.); *colloquial* win (prize, appointment, etc.). □ **landfall** approach to land after sea or air journey; **landfill** waste material used to landscape or reclaim land, disposing of waste in this way; **landlady** woman owning rented property or keeping pub, guest-house, etc.; **landlocked** (almost) enclosed by land; **landlord** man owning rented property or keeping pub, guest-house, etc.;

landlubber person unfamiliar with sea and ships; **landmark** conspicuous object, notable event; **landmine** explosive mine laid in or on ground; **landslide** sliding down of mass of land from cliff or mountain, overwhelming majority in election.

landau /'lændɔː/ *noun* (*plural* **-s**) 4-wheeled enclosed carriage with divided top.

landed *adjective* owning or consisting of land.

landing /'lændɪŋ/ *noun* platform or passage at top of or part way up stairs. □ **landing-craft** craft used for putting troops and equipment ashore; **landing-gear** undercarriage of aircraft; **landing-stage** platform for disembarking passengers and goods.

landscape /'lændskeɪp/ ● *noun* scenery in area of land; picture of it. ● *verb* (**-ping**) improve (piece of land) by **landscape gardening**, laying out of grounds to resemble natural scenery.

lane *noun* narrow road; division of road for one line of traffic; strip of track or water for competitor in race; regular course followed by ship or aircraft.

language /'læŋgwɪdʒ/ *noun* use of words in agreed way as means of human communication; system of words of particular community, country, etc.; faculty of speech; style of expression; system of symbols and rules for computer programs. □ **language laboratory** room with tape recorders etc. for learning foreign language.

languid /'læŋgwɪd/ *adjective* lacking vigour; idle. □ **languidly** *adverb*.

languish /'læŋgwɪʃ/ *verb* lose or lack vitality. □ **languish for** long for; **languish under** live under (depression etc.).

languor /'læŋgə/ *noun* lack of energy; idleness; soft or tender mood or effect. □ **languorous** *adjective*.

lank *adjective* (of grass, hair, etc.) long and limp; thin and tall.

lanky *adjective* (**-ier**, **-iest**) ungracefully thin and long or tall.

lanolin /'lænəlɪn/ *noun* fat from sheep's wool used in cosmetics, ointments, etc.

lantern /'lænt(ə)n/ *noun* lamp with transparent case protecting flame etc.; glazed structure on top of dome or room; light-chamber of lighthouse. □ **lantern jaws** long thin jaws.

lanyard /'lænjəd/ *noun* cord round neck or shoulder for holding knife etc.; *Nautical* short rope.

lap¹ *noun* front of sitting person's body from waist to knees; clothing covering this. □ **lap-dog** small pet dog; **laptop** (microcomputer) suitable for use while travelling.

lap² ● *noun* one circuit of racetrack etc.; section of journey etc.; amount of overlap. ● *verb* (**-pp-**) overtake (competitor in race who is a lap behind); (often + *about*, *around*) fold or wrap (garment etc.).

lap³ ● *verb* (**-pp-**) (esp. of animal) drink by scooping with tongue; (usually + *up*, *down*) drink greedily; (usually + *up*) receive (gossip, praise, etc.) eagerly; (of waves etc.) ripple; make lapping sound against (shore). ● *noun* act or sound of lapping.

lapel /lə'pel/ *noun* part of coat-front folded back.

lapidary /'læpɪdərɪ/ ● *adjective* concerned with stones; engraved on stone; concise, well-expressed. ● *noun* (*plural* **-ies**) cutter, polisher, or engraver of gems.

lapis lazuli /læpɪs 'læzjʊlɪ/ *noun* bright blue gem; its colour.

lapse /læps/ ● *noun* slight error; slip of memory etc.; weak or careless decline into inferior state. ● *verb* (**-sing**) fail to maintain position or standard; (+ *into*) fall back into (inferior or previous state); (of right etc.) become invalid.

lapwing /'læpwɪŋ/ *noun* plover with shrill cry.

larceny /ˈlɑːsənɪ/ noun (plural **-ies**) theft of personal property. □ **larcenous** adjective.

larch noun deciduous coniferous tree with bright foliage; its wood.

lard ● noun pig fat used in cooking etc. ● verb insert strips of bacon in (meat etc.) before cooking; (+ with) embellish (talk etc.) with (strange terms etc.).

larder noun room or cupboard for storing food.

lardy-cake noun cake made with lard, currants, etc.

large adjective of relatively great size or extent; of larger kind; comprehensive. □ **at large** at liberty, as a body or whole; **large as life** in person, esp. prominently. □ **largeness** noun; **largish** adjective.

largely adverb to a great extent.

largesse /lɑːˈʒes/ noun (also **largess**) money or gifts freely given.

largo /ˈlɑːɡəʊ/ Music ● adverb & adjective in slow time and dignified style. ● noun (plural **-s**) largo movement or passage.

lariat /ˈlærɪət/ noun lasso; rope for tethering animal.

lark[1] noun small bird with tuneful song, esp. skylark.

lark[2] colloquial ● noun frolic; amusing incident; type of activity. ● verb (+ about) play tricks.

larkspur noun plant with spur-shaped calyx.

larva /ˈlɑːvə/ noun (plural **-vae** /-viː/) insect in stage between egg and pupa. □ **larval** adjective.

laryngeal /ləˈrɪndʒɪəl/ adjective of the larynx.

laryngitis /lærɪnˈdʒaɪtɪs/ noun inflammation of larynx.

larynx /ˈlærɪŋks/ noun (plural **larynges** /ləˈrɪndʒiːz/ or **-xes**) cavity in throat holding vocal cords.

lasagne /ləˈsænjə/ noun pasta sheets.

lascivious /ləˈsɪvɪəs/ adjective lustful. □ **lasciviously** adverb.

laser /ˈleɪzə/ noun device producing intense beam of special kind of light. □ **laser printer** printing machine using laser to produce image.

lash ● verb make sudden whiplike movement; beat with whip; (often + against, down) (of rain etc.) beat, strike; criticize harshly; rouse, incite; (often + together, down) fasten with rope etc. ● noun sharp blow with whip etc.; flexible part of whip; eyelash. □ **lash out** speak or hit out angrily, colloquial spend money extravagantly.

lashings plural noun colloquial (often + of) plenty.

lass noun esp. Scottish & Northern English or poetical girl.

lassitude /ˈlæsɪtjuːd/ noun languor; disinclination to exert oneself.

lasso /læˈsuː/ ● noun (plural **-s** or **-es**) rope with running noose used esp. for catching cattle. ● verb (**-es**, **-ed**) catch with lasso.

last[1] /lɑːst/ ● adjective after all others; coming at end; most recent; only remaining. ● adverb after all others; on most recent occasion. ● noun last, last-mentioned, or most recent person or thing; last mention, sight, etc.; end; death. □ **at (long) last** in the end, after much delay; **the last straw** slight addition to task etc. making it unbearable.

last[2] /lɑːst/ verb remain unexhausted, adequate, or alive for specified or long time. □ **last out** be sufficient for whole of given period.

last[3] /lɑːst/ noun shoemaker's model for shaping shoe etc. □ **stick to one's last** keep to what one understands.

lasting adjective permanent, durable.

lastly adverb finally.

lat. abbreviation latitude.

latch ● noun bar with catch as fastening of gate etc.; spring-lock as fastening of outer door. ● verb fasten with latch. □ **latchkey** key of outer door; **latch on to** colloquial attach oneself to, understand.

late ● adjective after due or usual time; far on in day, night, period, etc.; flowering, ripening, etc. towards end of season; no longer alive or having specified status; of recent date. ● adverb after due or usual time; far on in time; at or till late hour; at late stage of development; formerly but not now. □ **late in the day** at late stage of proceedings etc. □ **lateness** noun.

lateen sail /ləˈtiːn/ noun triangular sail on long yard at angle of 45° to mast.

lately adverb not long ago; recently.

latent /ˈleɪt(ə)nt/ adjective existing but not developed or manifest; concealed, dormant. □ **latency** noun.

lateral /ˈlætər(ə)l/ ● adjective of, at, towards, or from side(s). ● noun lateral shoot or branch. □ **lateral thinking** method of solving problems by indirect or illogical methods. □ **laterally** adverb.

latex /ˈleɪteks/ noun milky fluid of esp. rubber tree; synthetic substance like this.

lath /lɑːθ/ noun thin flat strip of wood.

lathe /leɪð/ noun machine for shaping wood, metal, etc. by rotating article against cutting tools.

lather /ˈlɑːðə/ ● noun froth made by agitating soap etc. and water; frothy sweat; state of agitation. ● verb (of soap) form lather; cover with lather; colloquial thrash.

Latin /ˈlætɪn/ ● noun language of ancient Rome. ● adjective of or in Latin; of countries or peoples speaking languages developed from Latin; of RC Church. □ **Latin America** parts of Central and S. America where Spanish or Portuguese is main language.

Latinate /ˈlætɪneɪt/ adjective having character of Latin.

latitude /ˈlætɪtjuːd/ noun angular distance N. or S. of equator; (usually in plural) regions, climes; freedom from restriction in action or opinion.

latrine /ləˈtriːn/ noun communal lavatory, esp. in camp.

latter /ˈlætə/ ● adjective second-mentioned of two; nearer the end. ● noun (**the latter**) the latter thing or person. □ **latter-day** modern, contemporary.

latterly adverb recently; in latter part of life or period.

lattice /ˈlætɪs/ noun structure of crossed laths or bars with spaces between, used as fence, screen, etc.; arrangement resembling this. □ **lattice window** one with small panes set in lead. □ **latticed** adjective.

Latvian /ˈlætvɪən/ ● noun native, national, or language of Latvia. ● adjective of Latvia.

laud /lɔːd/ verb praise, extol.

laudable adjective praiseworthy. □ **laudably** adverb.

laudanum /ˈlɔːdənəm/ noun solution prepared from opium.

laudatory /ˈlɔːdətərɪ/ adjective praising.

laugh /lɑːf/ ● verb make sounds etc. usual in expressing amusement, scorn, etc.; express by laughing; (+ at) make fun of, ridicule. ● noun sound or act of laughing; colloquial comical person or thing. □ **laugh off** shrug off (embarrassment etc.) by joking.

laughable adjective amusing; ridiculous. □ **laughably** adverb.

laughing noun laughter. □ **laughing gas** nitrous oxide as anaesthetic; **laughing jackass** kookaburra; **laughing stock** object of general derision. □ **laughingly** adverb.

laughter /ˈlɑːftə/ noun act or sound of laughing.

launch[1] /lɔːntʃ/ ● verb set (vessel) afloat; hurl or send forth (rocket etc.); start or set in motion (enterprise, person, etc.); formally introduce (new product) with publicity; (+ into) make start on; (+ out) make start on new enterprise. ● *noun* launching. □ **launch pad** platform with structure for launching rockets from.

launch² /lɔːntʃ/ *noun* large motor boat.

launder /ˈlɔːndə/ *verb* wash and iron etc. (clothes etc.); *colloquial* transfer (money) to conceal its origin.

launderette /lɔːnˈdret/ *noun* (also **laundrette**) establishment with coin-operated washing machines and driers for public use.

laundress /ˈlɔːndrɪs/ *noun* woman who launders.

laundry /ˈlɔːndrɪ/ *noun* (*plural* **-ies**) place where clothes etc. are laundered; clothes etc. that need to be or have been laundered.

laurel /ˈlɒr(ə)l/ *noun* any of various kinds of shrub with dark green glossy leaves; (in *singular* or *plural*) wreath of bay-leaves as emblem of victory or poetic merit. □ **look to one's laurels** beware of losing one's pre-eminence; **rest on one's laurels** stop seeking further success.

lava /ˈlɑːvə/ *noun* matter flowing from volcano and solidifying as it cools.

lavatorial /lævəˈtɔːrɪəl/ *adjective* of or like lavatories; (esp. of humour) relating to excretion.

lavatory /ˈlævətərɪ/ *noun* (*plural* **-ies**) receptacle for urine and faeces, usually with means of disposal; room etc. containing this.

lave *verb* (**-ving**) *literary* wash, bathe; wash against; flow along.

lavender /ˈlævɪndə/ *noun* evergreen fragrant-flowered shrub; its dried flowers used to scent linen; pale purplish colour. □ **lavender-water** light perfume.

laver /ˈleɪvə/ *noun* kind of edible seaweed.

lavish /ˈlævɪʃ/ ● *adjective* profuse; abundant; generous. ● *verb* (often + *on*) bestow or spend (money, praise, etc.) abundantly. □ **lavishly** *adverb*.

law *noun* rule or set of rules established in a community, demanding or prohibiting certain actions; such rules as social system or branch of study; binding force; (**the law**) legal profession, *colloquial* police; law courts, legal remedy; science or philosophy of law; statement of regularity of natural occurrences. □ **law-abiding** obedient to the laws; **law court** court of law; **Law Lord** member of House of Lords qualified to perform its legal work; **lawsuit** bringing of claim etc. before law court; **lay down the law** give dogmatic opinions; **take the law into one's own hands** get one's rights without help of the law.

lawful *adjective* permitted, appointed, or recognized by law; not illegal. □ **lawfully** *adverb*; **lawfulness** *noun*.

lawless *adjective* having no laws; disregarding laws. □ **lawlessness** *noun*.

lawn¹ *noun* piece of close-mown grass in garden etc. □ **lawnmower** machine for cutting lawns; **lawn tennis** tennis played with soft ball on grass or hard court.

lawn² *noun* kind of fine linen or cotton.

lawyer /ˈlɔɪə/ *noun* person practising law, esp. solicitor.

lax *adjective* lacking care or precision; not strict. □ **laxity** *noun*; **laxly** *adverb*; **laxness** *noun*.

laxative /ˈlæksətɪv/ ● *adjective* helping evacuation of bowels. ● *noun* laxative medicine.

lay¹ ● *verb* (*past & past participle* **laid**) place on surface, esp. horizontally; put or bring into required position or state; make by laying; (of bird) produce (egg); cause to subside or lie flat; (usually + *on*) attribute (blame etc.); make ready (trap, plan); prepare (table) for meal; put fuel ready to light (fire); put down as bet. ● *noun* way, position, or direction in which something lies. □ **lay bare** expose, reveal; **lay-by**

extra strip beside road where vehicles may park; **lay claim to** claim as one's own; **lay down** relinquish, make (rule), store (wine) in cellar, sacrifice (one's life); **lay in** provide oneself with stock of; **lay into** *colloquial* attack violently with blows or verbally; **lay it on thick** or **with a trowel** *colloquial* flatter, exaggerate grossly; **lay off** discharge (workers) temporarily, *colloquial* desist; **lay on** provide, spread on; **lay out** spread, expose to view, prepare (body) for burial, *colloquial* knock unconscious, expend (money); **layout** way in which land, building, printed matter, etc., is arranged or set out; **lay up** store, save (money), (as **laid up** *adjective*) confined to bed or the house; **lay waste** ravage, destroy.

■ **Usage** It is incorrect in standard English to use *lay* to mean 'lie', as in *She was laying on the floor.*

lay² *adjective* not ordained into the clergy; not professionally qualified; of or done by such people. □ **layman**, **laywoman** person not in holy orders, one without professional or special knowledge; **lay reader** lay person licensed to conduct some religious services.

lay³ *noun* short poem meant to be sung; song.

lay⁴ *past of* **LIE¹**.

layer ● *noun* thickness of matter, esp. one of several, covering surface; hen that lays eggs. ● *verb* arrange in layers; propagate (plant) by fastening shoot down to take root.

layette /leɪˈet/ *noun* clothes etc. prepared for newborn child.

lay figure *noun* artist's jointed wooden model of human figure; unrealistic character in novel etc.

laze ● *verb* (**-zing**) spend time idly. ● *noun* spell of lazing.

lazy *adjective* (**-ier**, **-iest**) disinclined to work, doing little work; of or inducing idleness. □ **lazybones** *colloquial* lazy person. □ **lazily** *adverb*; **laziness** *noun*.

lb *abbreviation* pound(s) weight.

■ **Usage** It is a common mistake to write *lbs* as an abbreviation for *pounds. 28 lb* is correct.

l.b.w. *abbreviation* leg before wicket.

l.c. *abbreviation* loc. cit.; lower case.

LCD *abbreviation* liquid crystal display.

L/Cpl *abbreviation* Lance-Corporal.

LEA *abbreviation* Local Education Authority.

lea *noun* *poetical* meadow, field.

leach *verb* make (liquid) percolate through some material; subject (bark, ore, ash, soil) to this; (usually + *away*, *out*) remove (soluble matter) or be removed in this way.

lead¹ /liːd/ ● *verb* (*past & past participle* **led**) conduct, esp. by going in front; direct actions or opinions of; (often + *to*) guide by persuasion; provide access to; pass or spend (life etc.); have first place in; go or be first; play (card) as first player in trick; (+ *to*) result in; (+ *with*) (of newspapers or broadcast) have as main story. ● *noun* guidance, example; leader's place; amount by which competitor is ahead of others; clue; strap etc. for leading dog etc.; *Electricity* conductor carrying current to place of use; chief part in play etc.; *Cards* act or right of playing first. □ **lead by the nose** make (someone) do all one wishes them to; **lead-in** introduction, opening; **lead on** entice dishonestly; **lead up the garden path** *colloquial* mislead; **lead up to** form preparation for, direct conversation towards.

lead² /led/ ● *noun* heavy soft grey metal; graphite used in pencils; lump of lead used in sounding; blank space between lines of print. ● *verb* cover, frame, or space with lead(s). □ **lead-free** (of petrol) without added lead compounds.

leaded /'ledɪd/ *adjective* (of petrol) with added lead compounds; (of window pane) framed with lead.

leaden /'led(ə)n/ *adjective* of or like lead; heavy, slow; lead-coloured.

leader /'liːdə/ *noun* person or thing that leads; leading performer in orchestra, quartet, etc.; leading article. □ **leadership** *noun*.

leading /'liːdɪŋ/ *adjective* chief, most important. □ **leading aircraftman** one ranking just below NCO in RAF; **leading article** newspaper article giving editorial opinion; **leading light** prominent influential person; **leading note** *Music* seventh note of ascending scale; **leading question** one prompting the answer wanted.

■ **Usage** *Leading question* does not mean a 'principal' or 'loaded' or 'searching' question.

leaf ● *noun* (*plural* **leaves**) flat usually green part of plant growing usually on stem; foliage; single thickness of paper, esp. in book; very thin sheet of metal etc.; hinged part, extra section, or flap of table etc. ● *verb* (of plants etc.) begin to grow leaves; (+ *through*) turn over pages of (book etc.). □ **leaf-mould** soil composed chiefly of decaying leaves. □ **leafage** *noun*; **leafy** *adjective* (**-ier**, **-iest**).

leaflet /'liːflɪt/ *noun* sheet of paper, pamphlet, etc., giving information; young leaf.

league¹ /liːg/ ● *noun* people, countries, etc., joining together for particular purpose; group of sports clubs who contend for championship; class of contestants. ● *verb* (**-gues**, **-gued**, **-guing**) (often + *together*) join in league. □ **in league** allied, conspiring; **league table** list in order of success.

league² /liːg/ *noun* *archaic* measure of travelling distance, usually about 3 miles.

leak ● *noun* hole through which liquid etc. passes accidentally in or out; liquid etc. thus passing through; similar escape of electric charge; disclosure of secret information. ● *verb* (let) pass out or in through leak; disclose (secret); (often + *out*) become known. □ **leaky** *adjective* (**-ier**, **-iest**).

leakage *noun* action or result of leaking.

lean¹ ● *verb* (*past & past participle* **leaned** or **leant** /lent/) (often + *across, back, over,* etc.) be or place in sloping position; (usually + *against, on*) rest for support against; (usually + *on, upon*) rely, depend; (usually + *to, towards*) be inclined or partial. ● *noun* inclination, slope. □ **lean on** *colloquial* put pressure on (person) to act in certain way; **lean-to** building with roof resting against larger building or wall.

lean² *adjective* (of person etc.) having no superfluous fat; (of meat) containing little fat; meagre. ● *noun* lean part of meat. □ **lean years** time of scarcity. □ **leanness** *noun*.

leaning *noun* tendency or inclination.

leap ● *verb* (*past & past participle* **leaped** or **leapt** /lept/) jump, spring forcefully. ● *noun* forceful jump. □ **by leaps and bounds** with very rapid progress; **leapfrog** game in which player vaults with parted legs over another bending down; **leap year** year with 29 Feb. as extra day.

learn /lɜːn/ *verb* (*past & past participle* **learned** /lɜːnt, lɜːnd/ or **learnt**) get knowledge of or skill in by study, experience, or being taught; commit to memory; (usually + *of, about*) be told about, find out.

learned /'lɜːnɪd/ *adjective* having much knowledge from studying; showing or requiring learning.

learner *noun* person learning, beginner; (in full **learner driver**) person who is learning to drive but has not yet passed driving test.

learning *noun* knowledge got by study.

lease /liːs/ ● *noun* contract by which owner of land or building allows another to use it for specified time, usually for rent. ● *verb* (**-sing**) grant or take on lease. □ **leasehold** holding of property by lease; **leaseholder** *noun*; **new lease of** (*US* **on**) **life** improved prospect of living, or of use after repair.

leash ● *noun* strap for holding dog(s). ● *verb* put leash on; restrain. □ **straining at the leash** eager to begin.

least ● *adjective* smallest, slightest. ● *noun* least amount. ● *adverb* in the least degree. □ **at least** at any rate; **to say the least** putting the case moderately.

leather /'leðə/ ● *noun* material made from skin of animal by tanning etc.; piece of leather for cleaning esp. windows; *slang* cricket ball, football. ● *verb* beat, thrash; cover or polish with leather. □ **leatherjacket** larva of crane-fly.

leatherette /leðə'ret/ *noun* imitation leather.

leathery *adjective* like leather; tough.

leave¹ *verb* (**-ving**; *past & past participle* **left**) go away (from); cause or allow to remain; depart without taking; cease to reside at, belong to, work for, etc.; abandon; (usually + *to*) commit to another person; bequeath; deposit or entrust (object, message, etc.) to be dealt with in one's absence; not consume or deal with. □ **leave off** come to or make an end, stop; **leave out** omit.

leave² *noun* permission; (in full **leave of absence**) permission to be absent from duty; period for which this lasts. □ **on leave** absent thus; **take one's leave of** say goodbye to.

leaven /'lev(ə)n/ ● *noun* substance used to make dough ferment and rise; transforming influence. ● *verb* ferment (dough) with leaven; permeate, transform.

leavings *plural noun* what is left.

Lebanese /lebə'niːz/ ● *adjective* of Lebanon. ● *noun* (*plural* same) native or national of Lebanon.

lecher /'letʃə/ *noun* lecherous man.

lecherous *adjective* lustful. □ **lecherously** *adverb*; **lechery** *noun*.

lectern /'lekt(ə)n/ *noun* stand for holding Bible etc. in church; similar stand for lecturer etc.

lecture /'lektʃə/ ● *noun* talk giving information to class etc.; admonition, reprimand. ● *verb* (**-ring**) (often + *on*) deliver lecture(s); admonish, reprimand.

lecturer *noun* person who lectures, esp. as teacher in higher education.

lectureship *noun* university post as lecturer.

led *past & past participle* of LEAD¹.

ledge *noun* narrow shelf or projection from vertical surface.

ledger /'ledʒə/ *noun* book in which firm's accounts are kept.

lee *noun* shelter given by neighbouring object; side of thing away from the wind. □ **leeway** allowable deviation, drift of ship to leeward.

leech *noun* bloodsucking worm formerly used medicinally for bleeding; person who sponges on others.

leek *noun* vegetable of onion family with long cylindrical white bulb.

leer ● *verb* look slyly, lasciviously, or maliciously. ● *noun* leering look.

leery *adjective* (**-ier**, **-iest**) *slang* knowing, sly; (usually + *of*) wary.

lees /liːz/ *plural noun* sediment of wine etc.; dregs.

leeward /'liːwəd, *Nautical* 'luːəd/ ● *adjective & adverb* on or towards sheltered side. ● *noun* this direction.

left¹ ● *adjective* on or towards west side of person or thing facing north; (also **Left**) *Politics* of the Left. ● *adverb* on or to left side. ● *noun* left part, region, or direction; *Boxing* left hand, blow with this; (often **Left**)

Politics group favouring socialism, radicals collectively. □ **left-hand** on left side; **left-handed** naturally using left hand for writing etc., made by or for left hand, turning to left, (of screw) turned anticlockwise to tighten, awkward, clumsy, (of compliment etc.) ambiguous; **left-handedness** *noun*; **left-hander** left-handed person or blow; **left wing** more radical section of political party, left side of army, football team, etc.; **left-wing** socialist, radical; **left-winger** member of left wing. □ **leftward** *adjective & adverb*; **leftwards** *adverb*.

left² *past & past participle of* LEAVE¹.

leg *noun* each of limbs on which person or animal walks and stands; leg of animal as food; part of garment covering leg; support of chair, table, etc.; section of journey, race, competition, etc.; *Cricket* half of field behind batsman's back. □ **leg before wicket** *Cricket* (of batsman) declared out for illegal obstruction of ball that would have hit wicket; **leg it (-gg-)** *colloquial* walk or run hard; **leg warmer** either of pair of tubular knitted garments covering leg from ankle to thigh; **pull (person's) leg** deceive playfully. □ **legged** *adjective*.

legacy /ˈlegəsɪ/ *noun* (*plural* **-ies**) gift left by will; anything handed down by predecessor.

legal /ˈliːg(ə)l/ *adjective* of, based on, or concerned with law; appointed, required, or permitted by law. □ **legal aid** state help with cost of legal advice; **legal tender** currency that cannot legally be refused in payment of debt. □ **legality** /lɪˈgælɪtɪ/ *noun*; **legally** *adverb*.

legalize /ˈliːgəlaɪz/ *verb* (also **-ise**) (**-zing** or **-sing**) make lawful; bring into harmony with law. □ **legalization** *noun*.

legate /ˈlegət/ *noun* papal ambassador.

legatee /legəˈtiː/ *noun* recipient of legacy.

legation /lɪˈgeɪʃ(ə)n/ *noun* diplomatic minister and his or her staff; this minister's official residence.

legato /lɪˈgɑːtəʊ/ *Music* ● *adverb & adjective* in smooth flowing manner. ● *noun* (*plural* **-s**) legato passage.

legend /ˈledʒ(ə)nd/ *noun* traditional story, myth; *colloquial* famous or remarkable person or event; inscription; explanation on map etc. of symbols used.

legendary *adjective* existing in legend; *colloquial* remarkable, famous.

legerdemain /ledʒədəˈmeɪn/ *noun* sleight of hand; trickery, sophistry.

leger line /ˈledʒə/ *noun Music* short line added for notes above or below range of staff.

legging *noun* (usually in *plural*) close-fitting trousers for women or children; outer covering of leather etc. for lower leg.

leggy *adjective* (**-ier**, **-iest**) long-legged; long-stemmed and weak.

legible /ˈledʒɪb(ə)l/ *adjective* easily read. □ **legibility** *noun*; **legibly** *adverb*.

legion /ˈliːdʒ(ə)n/ ● *noun* division of 3,000–6,000 men in ancient Roman army; other large organized body. ● *adjective* great in number.

legionary ● *adjective* of legions. ● *noun* (*plural* **-ies**) member of legion.

legionnaire /liːdʒəˈneə/ *noun* member of foreign legion. □ **legionnaires' disease** form of bacterial pneumonia.

legislate /ˈledʒɪsleɪt/ *verb* (**-ting**) make laws. □ **legislator** *noun*.

legislation *noun* making laws; laws made.

legislative /ˈledʒɪslətɪv/ *adjective* of or empowered to make legislation.

legislature /ˈledʒɪsleɪtʃə/ *noun* legislative body of a state.

legitimate /lɪˈdʒɪtɪmət/ *adjective* (of child) born of parents married to one another; lawful, proper, regular; logically admissible. □ **legitimacy** *noun*; **legitimately** *adverb*.

legitimize /lɪˈdʒɪtɪmaɪz/ *verb* (also **-ise**) (**-zing** or **-sing**) make legitimate; serve as justification for. □ **legitimization** *noun*.

legume /ˈlegjuːm/ *noun* leguminous plant; edible part of this.

leguminous /lɪˈgjuːmɪnəs/ *adjective* of the family of plants with seeds in pods, e.g. peas and beans.

lei /ˈleɪ/ *noun* Polynesian garland of flowers.

leisure /ˈleʒə/ *noun* free time, time at one's own disposal. □ **at leisure** not occupied, in an unhurried way; **at one's leisure** when one has time; **leisure centre** public building with sports facilities etc.; **leisurewear** informal clothes, esp. sportswear.

leisured *adjective* having ample leisure.

leisurely ● *adjective* relaxed, unhurried. ● *adverb* without hurry.

leitmotif /ˈlaɪtməʊtiːf/ *noun* (also **leitmotiv**) recurring theme in musical etc. composition representing particular person, idea, etc.

lemming /ˈlemɪŋ/ *noun* Arctic rodent reputed to rush, during migration, in large numbers into sea and drown.

lemon /ˈlemən/ *noun* acid yellow citrus fruit; tree bearing it; pale yellow colour. □ **lemon cheese**, **curd** thick creamy lemon spread. □ **lemony** *adjective*.

lemonade /leməˈneɪd/ *noun* drink made from lemons; synthetic substitute for this, often fizzy.

lemon sole /ˈlemən/ *noun* (*plural* same or **-s**) fish of plaice family.

lemur /ˈliːmə/ *noun* tree-dwelling primate of Madagascar.

lend *verb* (*past & past participle* **lent**) grant temporary use of (thing); allow use of (money) in return for interest; bestow, contribute; (**lend itself to**) be suitable for. □ **lend an ear** listen. □ **lender** *noun*.

length *noun* measurement from end to end; extent in or of time; length of horse, boat, etc. as measure of lead in race; long stretch or extent; degree of thoroughness in action. □ **at length** in detail, after a long time. □ **lengthways** *adverb*; **lengthwise** *adverb & adjective*.

lengthen *verb* make or become longer.

lengthy *adjective* (**-ier**, **-iest**) of unusual length, prolix, tedious.

lenient /ˈliːnɪənt/ *adjective* merciful, not severe, mild. □ **lenience** *noun*; **leniency** *noun*; **leniently** *adverb*.

lens /lenz/ *noun* piece of transparent substance with one or both sides curved, used in spectacles, telescopes, cameras, etc.; combination of lenses used in photography.

Lent *noun* religious period of fasting and penitence from Ash Wednesday to Easter Eve. □ **Lenten** *adjective*.

lent *past & past participle of* LEND.

lentil /ˈlentɪl/ *noun* edible seed of leguminous plant; this plant.

lento /ˈlentəʊ/ *Music* ● *adjective* slow. ● *adverb* slowly. ● *noun* lento movement or passage.

Leo /ˈliːəʊ/ *noun* fifth sign of zodiac.

leonine /ˈliːənaɪn/ *adjective* lionlike; of lions.

leopard /ˈlepəd/ *noun* large animal of cat family with dark-spotted fawn or all black coat, panther.

leotard /ˈliːətɑːd/ *noun* close-fitting one-piece garment worn by dancers etc.

leper /ˈlepə/ *noun* person with leprosy.

leprechaun /ˈleprəkɔːn/ *noun* small mischievous sprite in Irish folklore.

leprosy /'leprǝsɪ/ noun contagious disease of skin and nerves. □ **leprous** adjective.

lesbian /'lezbɪǝn/ ● noun homosexual woman. ● adjective of homosexuality in women. □ **lesbianism** noun.

lesion /'liːʒ(ǝ)n/ noun damage, injury; change in part of body due to injury or disease.

less ● adjective smaller; of smaller quantity; not so much. ● adverb to smaller extent, in lower degree. ● noun smaller amount, quantity, or number. ● preposition minus, deducting.

■ **Usage** The use of less to mean 'fewer', as in There are less people than yesterday, is incorrect in standard English.

lessee /le'siː/ noun (often + of) person holding property by lease.

lessen /'les(ǝ)n/ verb diminish.

lesser adjective not so great as the other(s).

lesson /'les(ǝ)n/ noun period of teaching; (in plural; usually + in) systematic instruction; thing learnt by pupil; experience that serves to warn or encourage; passage from Bible read aloud during church service.

lessor /le'sɔː/ noun person who lets property by lease.

lest conjunction in order that not, for fear that.

let[1] ● verb (**-tt-**; past & past participle **let**) allow, enable, or cause to; grant use of (rooms, land, etc.) for rent or hire. ● auxiliary verb in exhortations, commands, assumptions, etc. ● noun act of letting. □ **let alone** not to mention; **let be** not interfere with; **let down** verb lower, fail to support or satisfy, disappoint; **let-down** noun disappointment; **let go** release, lose hold of; **let in** allow to enter, (usually + for) involve (person, often oneself) in loss, problem, etc., (usually + on) allow (person) to share secret etc.; **let off** fire (gun), cause (steam etc.) to escape, not punish or compel; **let on** colloquial reveal secret; **let out** verb release, reveal (secret etc.), slacken, put out to rent; **let-out** noun colloquial opportunity to escape; **let up** verb colloquial become less severe, diminish; **let-up** noun colloquial relaxation of effort, diminution.

let[2] noun obstruction of ball or player in tennis etc. after which ball must be served again. □ **without let or hindrance** unimpeded.

lethal /'liːθ(ǝ)l/ adjective causing or sufficient to cause death. □ **lethally** adverb.

lethargy /'leθǝdʒɪ/ noun lack of energy; unnatural sleepiness. □ **lethargic** /lɪ'θɑːdʒɪk/ adjective; **lethargically** /lɪ'θɑːdʒɪkǝlɪ/ adverb.

letter /'letǝ/ ● noun character representing one or more of sounds used in speech; written or printed communication, usually sent in envelope by post; precise terms of statement; (in plural) literature. ● verb inscribe letters on; classify with letters. □ **letter bomb** terrorist explosive device sent by post; **letter box** box for delivery or posting of letters, slit in door for delivery of letters; **letterhead** printed heading on stationery; **letterpress** printed words in illustrated book, printing from raised type; **to the letter** keeping to every detail.

lettuce /'letɪs/ noun plant with crisp leaves used in salad.

leucocyte /'luːkǝsaɪt/ noun white blood cell.

leukaemia /luː'kiːmɪǝ/ noun (US **leukemia**) malignant progressive disease in which too many white blood cells are produced.

Levant /lɪ'vænt/ noun (**the Levant**) archaic East-Mediterranean region.

Levantine /'levǝntaɪn/ ● adjective of or trading to the Levant. ● noun native or inhabitant of the Levant.

levee /'levɪ/ noun US embankment against river floods.

level /'lev(ǝ)l/ ● noun horizontal line or plane; height or value reached; position on real or imaginary scale; social, moral, or intellectual standard; plane of rank or authority; instrument giving line parallel to plane of horizon; level surface, flat country. ● adjective flat, not bumpy; horizontal; (often + with) on same horizontal plane as something else, having equality with something else; even, uniform, well-balanced. ● verb (**-ll-**; US **-l-**) make level; raze, completely destroy; (usually + at) aim (gun etc.); (usually + at, against) direct (accusation etc.). □ **do one's level best** colloquial do one's utmost; **find one's level** reach right social, intellectual, etc., position; **level crossing** crossing of road and railway etc. at same level; **level-headed** mentally well-balanced, cool; **level pegging** equality of scores etc.; **on the level** colloquial truthfully, honestly.

lever /'liːvǝ/ ● noun bar pivoted about fulcrum to transfer force; bar used on pivot to prise or lift; projecting handle used to operate mechanism; means of exerting moral pressure. ● verb use lever; lift, move, etc. (as) with lever.

leverage noun action or power of lever; means of accomplishing a purpose.

leveret /'levǝrɪt/ noun young hare.

leviathan /lɪ'vaɪǝθ(ǝ)n/ noun Biblical sea monster; very large or powerful thing.

Levis /'liːvaɪz/ plural noun proprietary term type of (originally blue) denim jeans.

levitate /'levɪteɪt/ verb (**-ting**) (cause to) rise and float in air. □ **levitation** noun.

levity /'levɪtɪ/ noun lack of serious thought; frivolity.

levy /'levɪ/ ● verb (**-ies, -ied**) impose or collect (payment etc.) compulsorily; enrol (troops etc.). ● noun (plural **-ies**) levying; payment etc. or (in plural) troops levied.

lewd /ljuːd/ adjective lascivious, indecent.

lexical /'leksɪk(ǝ)l/ adjective of the words of a language; (as) of a lexicon.

lexicography /leksɪ'kɒgrǝfɪ/ noun compiling of dictionaries. □ **lexicographer** noun.

lexicon /'leksɪkǝn/ noun dictionary.

Leyden jar /'laɪd(ǝ)n/ noun early kind of capacitor.

LF abbreviation low frequency.

liability /laɪǝ'bɪlɪtɪ/ noun (plural **-ies**) being liable; troublesome person or thing; handicap; (in plural) debts for which one is liable.

liable /'laɪǝb(ǝ)l/ adjective legally bound; (+ to) subject to; (+ to do) under an obligation; (+ to) exposed or open to (something undesirable); (+ for) answerable for.

■ **Usage** Liable is often used to mean 'likely', as in It is liable to rain, but this is considered incorrect by some people.

liaise /lɪ'eɪz/ verb (**-sing**) (usually + with, between) colloquial establish cooperation, act as link.

liaison /lɪ'eɪzɒn/ noun communication, cooperation; illicit sexual relationship.

liana /lɪ'ɑːnǝ/ noun climbing plant in tropical forests.

liar /'laɪǝ/ noun person who tells lies.

Lib. abbreviation Liberal.

lib noun colloquial liberation.

libation /laɪ'beɪʃ(ǝ)n/ noun (pouring out of) drink-offering to a god.

libel /'laɪb(ǝ)l/ ● noun Law published false statement damaging to person's reputation, publishing of this; false defamatory statement. ● verb (**-ll-**; US **-l-**) Law publish libel against. □ **libellous** adjective.

liberal /'lɪbǝr(ǝ)l/ ● adjective abundant; giving freely; generous; open-minded; not rigorous; (of studies) for general broadening of mind; Politics favouring moderate reforms. ● *noun* person of liberal views, esp. (**Liberal**) member of a Liberal Party. □ **Liberal Democrat** member of **Liberal Democrats**, UK political party. □ **liberalism** *noun*; **liberality** /-'ræl-/ *noun*; **liberally** *adverb*.

liberalize *verb* (also **-ise**) (**-zing** or **-sing**) make or become more liberal or less strict. □ **liberalization** *noun*.

liberate /'lɪbəreɪt/ *verb* (**-ting**) (often + *from*) set free; free (country etc.) from aggressor; (as **liberated** *adjective*) (of person etc.) freed from oppressive social conventions. □ **liberation** *noun*; **liberator** *noun*.

libertine /'lɪbətiːn/ *noun* licentious person.

liberty /'lɪbəti/ *noun* (*plural* **-ies**) being free, freedom; right or power to do as one pleases; (in *plural*) privileges granted by authority. □ **at liberty** free, (+ *to do*) permitted; **take liberties** (often + *with*) behave in unacceptably familiar way.

libidinous /lɪ'bɪdɪnəs/ *adjective* lustful.

libido /lɪ'biːdəʊ/ *noun* (*plural* **-s**) psychic impulse or drive, esp. that associated with sex instinct. □ **libidinal** /lɪ'bɪdɪn(ə)l/ *adjective*.

Libra /'liːbrə/ *noun* seventh sign of zodiac.

librarian /laɪ'breərɪən/ *noun* person in charge of or assistant in library. □ **librarianship** *noun*.

library /'laɪbrərɪ/ *noun* (*plural* **-ies**) a collection of books, films, records, etc.; room or building etc. where these are kept; series of books issued in similar bindings.

libretto /lɪ'bretəʊ/ *noun* (*plural* **-ti** /-tɪ/ or **-s**) text of opera etc. □ **librettist** *noun*.

lice *plural* of LOUSE.

licence /'laɪs(ə)ns/ *noun* (US **license**) official permit to own, use, or do, something, or carry on trade; permission; excessive liberty of action; writer's etc. deliberate deviation from fact.

license /'laɪs(ə)ns/ ● *verb* (**-sing**) grant licence to; authorize use of (premises) for certain purpose. ● *noun* US = LICENCE.

licensee /laɪsən'siː/ *noun* holder of licence, esp. to sell alcoholic liquor.

licentiate /laɪ'senʃɪət/ *noun* holder of certificate of professional competence.

licentious /laɪ'senʃəs/ *adjective* sexually promiscuous.

lichee = LYCHEE.

lichen /'laɪkən/ *noun* plant composed of fungus and alga in association, growing on rocks, trees, etc.

lich-gate /'lɪtʃɡeɪt/ *noun* (also **lychgate**) roofed gateway of churchyard.

licit /'lɪsɪt/ *adjective* *formal* lawful, permitted.

lick ● *verb* pass tongue over; bring into specified condition by licking; (of flame etc.) play lightly over; *colloquial* thrash, defeat. ● *noun* act of licking with tongue; *colloquial* pace, speed; smart blow. □ **lick one's lips**, **chops** look forward with great pleasure.

licorice = LIQUORICE.

lid *noun* hinged or removable cover, esp. at top of container; eyelid. □ **put the lid on** *colloquial* be the culmination of, put stop to. □ **lidded** *adjective*.

lido /'liːdəʊ/ *noun* (*plural* **-s**) public open-air swimming pool or bathing beach.

lie¹ /laɪ/ ● *verb* (**lying**; *past* **lay**; *past participle* **lain**) be in or assume horizontal position on supporting surface; (of thing) rest on flat surface; remain undisturbed or undiscussed; be kept, remain, or be in specified place etc.; (of abstract things) be in certain relation; be situated or spread out to view etc. ● *noun* way, position, or direction in which something lies. □ **lie in** stay in bed late in morning; **lie-in** *noun*; **lie low** keep quiet or unseen; **lie of the land** state of affairs.

■ **Usage** It is incorrect in standard English to use *lie* to mean 'lay', as in *lie her on the bed*.

lie² /laɪ/ ● *noun* intentional false statement; something that deceives. ● *verb* (**lies**, **lied**, **lying**) tell lie(s); (of thing) be deceptive. □ **give the lie to** show the falsity of.

lied /liːd/ *noun* (*plural* **lieder**) German song of Romantic period for voice and piano.

liege /liːdʒ/ *historical* ● *adjective* entitled to receive, or bound to give, feudal service or allegiance. ● *noun* (in full **liege lord**) feudal superior; (usually in *plural*) vassal, subject.

lien /'liːən/ *noun* Law right to hold another's property till debt on it is paid.

lieu /ljuː/ *noun* □ **in lieu** instead; (+ *of*) in place of.

Lieut. *abbreviation* Lieutenant.

lieutenant /lef'tenənt/ *noun* army officer next below captain; naval officer next below lieutenant commander; deputy. □ **lieutenant colonel**, **commander**, **general** officers ranking next below colonel etc. □ **lieutenancy** *noun* (*plural* **-ies**).

life *noun* (*plural* **lives**) capacity for growth, functional activity, and continual change until death; living things and their activity; period during which life lasts; period from birth to present time or from present time to death; duration of thing's existence or ability to function; person's state of existence; living person; business and pleasures of the world; energy, liveliness; biography; *colloquial* imprisonment for life. □ **life assurance** life insurance; **lifebelt** buoyant ring to keep person afloat; **lifeblood** blood as necessary to life, vital factor or influence; **lifeboat** boat for rescues at sea, ship's boat for emergency use; **lifebuoy** buoyant support to keep person afloat; **life cycle** series of changes in life of organism; **lifeguard** expert swimmer employed to rescue bathers from drowning; **Life Guards** regiment of royal household cavalry; **life insurance** insurance which makes payment on death of insured person; **life-jacket** buoyant jacket to keep person afloat; **lifeline** rope etc. used for life-saving, sole means of communication or transport; **life peer** peer whose title lapses on death; **life sentence** imprisonment for life; **life-size(d)** of same size as person or thing represented; **lifestyle** way of life; **life-support machine** respirator; **lifetime** duration of person's life.

lifeless *adjective* dead; unconscious; lacking movement or vitality. □ **lifelessly** *adverb*.

lifelike *adjective* closely resembling life or person or thing represented.

lifer *noun* *slang* person serving life sentence.

lift ● *verb* (often + *up*, *of*, etc.) raise to higher position, go up, be raised; yield to upward force; give upward direction to (eyes etc.); add interest to; (of fog etc.) rise, disperse; remove (barrier etc.); transport supplies, troops, etc. by air; *colloquial* steal, plagiarize. ● *noun* lifting; ride in another person's vehicle; apparatus for raising and lowering people or things to different floors of building, or for carrying people up or down mountain etc.; transport by air; upward pressure on aerofoil; supporting or elevating influence; elated feeling. □ **lift-off** vertical take-off of spacecraft or rocket.

ligament /'lɪɡəmənt/ *noun* band of tough fibrous tissue linking bones.

ligature /'lɪɡətʃə/ *noun* tie, bandage; Music slur, tie; Printing two or more letters joined, e.g. æ.

■ **Usage** *Ligature*, in the Printing sense, is sometimes confused with *digraph*, which means 'two letters representing one sound'.

light¹ /laɪt/ ● noun electromagnetic radiation that stimulates sight and makes things visible; appearance of brightness; source of light; (often in plural) traffic light; flame, spark, or device for igniting; aspect in which thing is regarded; mental or spiritual illumination; vivacity, esp. in person's eyes. ● verb (past **lit**; past participle **lit** or **lighted**) set burning, begin to burn; (often + up) give light to; make prominent by light; show (person) way etc. with light; (usually + up) (of face or eyes) brighten with pleasure etc. ● adjective well-provided with light, not dark; (of colour) pale. □ **bring** or **come to light** reveal or be revealed; **in the light of** taking account of; **light bulb** glass bulb containing metal filament giving light when current is passed through it; **lighthouse** tower with beacon light to warn or guide ships at sea; **lightship** anchored ship with beacon light; **light year** distance light travels in one year.

light² /laɪt/ ● adjective not heavy; relatively low in weight, amount, density, or intensity; (of railway) suitable for small loads; carrying only light arms; (of food) easy to digest; (of music etc.) intended only as entertainment, not profound; (of sleep or sleeper) easily disturbed; easily done; nimble; cheerful. ● adverb lightly; with light load. ● verb (past & past participle **lit** or **lighted**) (+ on, upon) come upon or find by chance. □ **light-fingered** given to stealing; **light flyweight** amateur boxing weight (up to 48 kg); **light-headed** giddy, delirious; **light-hearted** cheerful; **light heavyweight** amateur boxing weight (75–81 kg); **light industry** manufacture of small or light articles; **light middleweight** amateur boxing weight (67–71 kg); **lightweight** adjective below average weight, of little importance, noun lightweight person or thing, amateur boxing weight (57–60kg); **light welterweight** amateur boxing weight (60–63.5 kg). □ **lightly** adverb; **lightness** noun.

lighten¹ verb make or become lighter in weight; reduce weight or load of.

lighten² verb shed light on, make or grow bright.

lighter¹ noun device for lighting cigarettes etc.

lighter² noun boat for transporting goods between ship and wharf etc.

lightning /'laɪtnɪŋ/ noun flash of light produced by electric discharge between clouds or between clouds and ground. □ **lightning-conductor** metal rod or wire fixed to building or mast to divert lightning to earth or sea.

lights plural noun lungs of sheep, pigs, etc. as food, esp. for pets.

ligneous /'lɪgnɪəs/ adjective of the nature of wood.

lignite /'lɪgnaɪt/ noun brown coal of woody texture.

lignum vitae /lɪgnəm 'vaɪtɪ/ noun a hard-wooded tree.

like¹ ● adjective (**more like, most like**) similar to another, each other, or original; resembling; such as; characteristic of; in suitable state or mood for. ● preposition in manner of, to same degree as. ● adverb slang so to speak; colloquial probably. ● conjunction colloquial as, as if (see note below). ● noun counterpart, equal; similar person or thing.

■ **Usage** It is incorrect in standard English to use like as a conjunction, as in Tell it like it is or He's spending money like it was going out of fashion.

like² ● verb (**-king**) find agreeable or enjoyable; feel attracted by, choose to have, prefer. ● noun (in plural) things one likes or prefers.

likeable adjective (also **likable**) pleasant, easy to like. □ **likeably** adverb.

likelihood /'laɪklɪhʊd/ noun probability.

likely /'laɪklɪ/ ● adjective (**-ier, -iest**) probable; such as may well happen or be true; to be expected; promising, apparently suitable. ● adverb probably. □ **not likely!** colloquial certainly not.

liken verb (+ to) point out resemblance between (person, thing) and (another).

likeness noun (usually + between, to) resemblance; (+ of) semblance, guise; portrait, representation.

likewise adverb also, moreover; similarly.

liking noun what one likes; one's taste; (+ for) fondness, taste, fancy.

lilac /'laɪlək/ ● noun shrub with fragrant pinkish-violet or white flowers; pale pinkish-violet colour. ● adjective of this colour.

liliaceous /lɪlɪ'eɪʃəs/ adjective of the lily family.

lilliputian /lɪlɪ'pjuːʃ(ə)n/ ● noun diminutive person or thing. ● adjective diminutive.

lilt ● noun light springing rhythm; tune with this. ● verb (esp. as **lilting** adjective) speak etc. with lilt.

lily /'lɪlɪ/ noun (plural **-ies**) tall bulbous plant with large trumpet-shaped flowers; heraldic fleur-de-lis. □ **lily of the valley** plant with fragrant white bell-shaped flowers.

limb¹ /lɪm/ noun leg, arm, wing; large branch of tree; branch of cross. □ **out on a limb** isolated.

limb² /lɪm/ noun specified edge of sun, moon, etc.

limber¹ /'lɪmbə/ ● adjective lithe, flexible; agile. ● verb (usually + up) make oneself supple; warm up for athletic etc. activity.

limber² /'lɪmbə/ ● noun detachable front of gun-carriage. ● verb attach limber to.

limbo¹ /'lɪmbəʊ/ noun (plural **-s**) supposed abode of souls of unbaptized infants, and of the just who died before Christ; intermediate state or condition of awaiting decision.

limbo² /'lɪmbəʊ/ noun (plural **-s**) W. Indian dance in which dancer bends backwards to pass under progressively lowered horizontal bar.

lime¹ ● noun white caustic substance got by heating limestone. ● verb (**-ming**) treat with lime. □ **limekiln** kiln for heating limestone. □ **limy** adjective (**-ier, -iest**).

lime² noun round green acid fruit; tree producing this fruit. □ **lime-green** yellowish-green colour.

lime³ noun (in full **lime tree**) tree with heart-shaped leaves and fragrant creamy blossom.

limelight noun intense white light used formerly in theatres; glare of publicity.

limerick /'lɪmərɪk/ noun humorous 5-line verse.

limestone noun rock composed mainly of calcium carbonate.

limit /'lɪmɪt/ ● noun point, line, or level beyond which something does not or may not extend or pass; greatest or smallest amount permitted. ● verb (**-t-**) set or serve as limit to; (+ to) restrict to. □ **limitless** adjective.

limitation /lɪmɪ'teɪʃ(ə)n/ noun limiting, being limited; limit of ability; limiting circumstance.

limn /lɪm/ verb archaic paint.

limousine /lɪmʊ'ziːn/ noun large luxurious car.

limp¹ ● verb walk or proceed lamely or awkwardly. ● noun lame walk.

limp² adjective not stiff or firm; without will or energy. □ **limply** adverb; **limpness** noun.

limpet /'lɪmpɪt/ noun mollusc with conical shell sticking tightly to rocks.

limpid /'lɪmpɪd/ adjective clear, transparent. □ **limpidity** /-'pɪd-/ noun.

linage /'laɪnɪdʒ/ noun number of lines in printed or written page etc.; payment by the line.

linchpin /'lɪntʃpɪn/ noun pin passed through axle-end to keep wheel on; person or thing vital to organization etc.

linctus /ˈlɪŋktəs/ *noun* syrupy medicine, esp. soothing cough mixture.

linden /ˈlɪnd(ə)n/ *noun* = LIME TREE.

line¹ ● *noun* continuous mark made on surface; furrow, wrinkle; use of lines in art; straight or curved track of moving point; outline; limit, boundary; row of persons or things; *US* queue; mark defining area of play or start or finish of race; row of printed or written words; portion of verse written in line; (in *plural*) piece of poetry, words of actor's part; length of cord, rope, etc. serving specified purpose; wire or cable for telephone or telegraph; connection by means of this; single track or branch of railway; regular succession of buses, ships, aircraft, etc., plying between certain places, company conducting this; several generations (of family); stock; manner of procedure, conduct, thought, etc.; channel; department of activity, branch of business; type of product; connected series of military field works, arrangement of soldiers or ships side by side; each of very narrow horizontal sections forming television picture. ● *verb* (**-ning**) position or stand at intervals along. □ **line printer** machine that prints computer output a line at a time; **linesman** umpire's or referee's assistant who decides whether ball has fallen within playing area or not; **line up** *verb* arrange or be arranged in lines, have ready; **line-up** *noun* line of people for inspection, arrangement of team, band, etc.

line² *verb* (**-ning**) apply layer of usually different material to cover inside of (garment, box, etc.); serve as lining for; *colloquial* fill (purse etc.).

lineage /ˈlɪnɪdʒ/ *noun* lineal descent, ancestry.

lineal /ˈlɪnɪəl/ *adjective* in direct line of descent or ancestry; linear. □ **lineally** *adverb*.

lineament /ˈlɪnɪəmənt/ *noun* (usually in *plural*) distinctive feature or characteristic, esp. of face.

linear /ˈlɪnɪə/ *adjective* of or in lines; long and narrow and of uniform breadth.

linen /ˈlɪnɪn/ ● *noun* cloth woven from flax; articles made or originally made of linen, as sheets, shirts, underwear, etc. ● *adjective* made of linen.

liner¹ *noun* ship or aircraft carrying passengers on regular line.

liner² *noun* removable lining.

ling¹ *noun* (*plural* same) long slender marine fish.

ling² *noun* kind of heather.

linger /ˈlɪŋgə/ *verb* stay about; (+ *over, on,* etc.) dally; be protracted; (often + *on*) die slowly.

lingerie /ˈlæʒərɪ/ *noun* women's underwear and nightclothes.

lingo /ˈlɪŋgəʊ/ *noun* (*plural* **-s** or **-es**) *colloquial* foreign language.

lingual /ˈlɪŋgw(ə)l/ *adjective* of tongue; of speech or languages.

linguist /ˈlɪŋgwɪst/ *noun* person skilled in languages or linguistics.

linguistic /lɪŋˈgwɪstɪk/ *adjective* of language or the study of languages. □ **linguistically** *adverb*.

linguistics *noun* study of language and its structure.

liniment /ˈlɪnɪmənt/ *noun* embrocation.

lining *noun* material used to line surface.

link ● *noun* one loop or ring of chain etc.; one in series; means of connection. ● *verb* (+ *together, to, with*) connect, join; clasp or intertwine (hands etc.).

linkage *noun* linking or being linked.

links *noun* (treated as *singular* or *plural*) golf course.

Linnaean /lɪˈniːən/ *adjective* of Linnaeus or his system of classifying plants and animals.

linnet /ˈlɪnɪt/ *noun* brown-grey finch.

lino /ˈlaɪnəʊ/ *noun* (*plural* **-s**) linoleum. □ **linocut** design carved in relief on block of linoleum, print made from this.

linoleum /lɪˈnəʊlɪəm/ *noun* canvas-backed material coated with linseed oil, cork, etc.

linseed /ˈlɪnsiːd/ *noun* seed of flax.

lint *noun* linen or cotton with one side made fluffy, used for dressing wounds; fluff.

lintel /ˈlɪnt(ə)l/ *noun* horizontal timber, stone, etc. over door or window.

lion /ˈlaɪən/ *noun* (*feminine* **lioness**) large tawny flesh-eating wild cat of Africa and S. Asia; brave or celebrated person.

lionize *verb* (also **-ise**) (**-zing** or **-sing**) treat as celebrity.

lip *noun* either edge of opening of mouth; edge of cup, vessel, cavity, etc., esp. part shaped for pouring from; *colloquial* impudent talk. □ **lip-read** understand (speech) by observing speaker's lip-movements; **lip-service** insincere expression of support; **lipstick** stick of cosmetic for colouring lips.

liquefy /ˈlɪkwɪfaɪ/ *verb* (**-ies, -ied**) make or become liquid. □ **liquefaction** /-ˈfækʃ(ə)n/ *noun*.

liqueur /lɪˈkjʊə/ *noun* any of several strong sweet alcoholic spirits.

liquid /ˈlɪkwɪd/ ● *adjective* having consistency like that of water or oil, flowing freely but of constant volume; having appearance of water; (of sounds) clear, pure; (of assets) easily convertible into cash. ● *noun* liquid substance; *Phonetics* sound of *l* or *r*. □ **liquid crystal** liquid in state approaching that of crystalline solid; **liquid crystal display** visual display in some electronic devices.

liquidate /ˈlɪkwɪdeɪt/ *verb* (**-ting**) wind up affairs of (firm etc.); pay off (debt); wipe out; kill. □ **liquidator** *noun*.

liquidation /lɪkwɪˈdeɪʃ(ə)n/ *noun* liquidating, esp. of firm. □ **go into liquidation** be wound up and have assets apportioned.

liquidity /lɪˈkwɪdɪtɪ/ *noun* (*plural* **-ies**) state of being liquid; having liquid assets.

liquidize *verb* (also **-ise**) (**-zing** or **-sing**) reduce to liquid state.

liquidizer *noun* (also **-iser**) machine for liquidizing foods.

liquor /ˈlɪkə/ *noun* alcoholic (esp. distilled) drink; other liquid, esp. that produced in cooking.

liquorice /ˈlɪkərɪs/ *noun* (also **licorice**) black root extract used as sweet and in medicine; plant from which it is obtained.

lira /ˈlɪərə/ *noun* chief monetary unit of Italy (*plural* **lire** /-rɪ/) and Turkey (*plural* **-s**).

lisle /laɪl/ *noun* fine cotton thread for stockings etc.

lisp ● *noun* speech defect in which *s* is pronounced like *th* in *thick* and *z* like *th* in *this*. ● *verb* speak or utter with lisp.

lissom /ˈlɪsəm/ *adjective* lithe, agile.

list¹ ● *noun* number of items, names, etc. written or printed together as record; (in *plural*) palisades enclosing tournament area. ● *verb* arrange as or enter in list; (as **listed** *adjective*) approved for Stock Exchange dealings, (of a building) of historical importance and officially protected. □ **enter the lists** issue or accept challenge.

list² ● *verb* (of ship etc.) lean over to one side. ● *noun* listing position, tilt.

listen /ˈlɪs(ə)n/ *verb* make effort to hear something, attentively hear person speaking; (+ *to*) give attention with ear to, take notice of. □ **listen in** tap telephonic communication, use radio receiving set. □ **listener** *noun*.

listless /'lɪstlɪs/ *adjective* lacking energy or enthusiasm. □ **listlessly** *adverb*; **listlessness** *noun*.

lit *past & past participle of* LIGHT[1,2].

litany /'lɪtənɪ/ *noun* (*plural* **-ies**) series of supplications to God used in church services; (**the Litany**) that in Book of Common Prayer.

litchi = LYCHEE.

liter *US* = LITRE.

literacy /'lɪtərəsɪ/ *noun* ability to read and write.

literal /'lɪtər(ə)l/ *adjective* taking words in their basic sense without metaphor etc.; corresponding exactly to original words; prosaic; matter-of-fact. □ **literalism** *noun*; **literally** *adverb*.

literary /'lɪtərərɪ/ *adjective* of or concerned with or interested in literature.

literate /'lɪtərət/ ● *adjective* able to read and write. ● *noun* literate person.

literati /lɪtə'rɑːtɪ/ *plural noun* the class of learned people.

literature /'lɪtərətʃə/ *noun* written works, esp. those valued for form and style; writings of country or period or on particular subject; *colloquial* printed matter, leaflets, etc.

lithe /laɪð/ *adjective* flexible, supple.

litho /'laɪθəʊ/ *colloquial* ● *noun* lithography. ● *verb* (**-oes, -oed**) lithograph.

lithograph /'lɪθəɡrɑːf/ ● *noun* lithographic print. ● *verb* print by lithography.

lithography /lɪ'θɒɡrəfɪ/ *noun* process of printing from plate so treated that ink sticks only to design to be printed. □ **lithographer** *noun*; **lithographic** /lɪθə'ɡræfɪk/ *adjective*.

Lithuanian /lɪθju:'eɪnɪən/ ● *noun* native, national, or language of Lithuania. ● *adjective* of Lithuania.

litigant /'lɪtɪɡənt/ ● *noun* party to lawsuit. ● *adjective* engaged in lawsuit.

litigate /'lɪtɪɡeɪt/ *verb* (**-ting**) go to law; contest (point) at law. □ **litigation** *noun*; **litigator** *noun*.

litigious /lɪ'tɪdʒəs/ *adjective* fond of litigation; contentious.

litmus /'lɪtməs/ *noun* dye turned red by acid and blue by alkali.

litre /'liːtə/ *noun* (*US* **liter**) metric unit of capacity (1.76 pints).

litter /'lɪtə/ ● *noun* refuse, esp. paper, discarded in public place; odds and ends lying about; young animals brought forth at one birth; vehicle containing couch and carried on men's shoulders or by animals; kind of stretcher for sick and wounded; straw etc. as bedding for form; material for animal's, esp. cat's, indoor toilet. ● *verb* make (place) untidy; give birth to (puppies etc.); provide (horse etc.) with bedding.

little /'lɪt(ə)l/ ● *adjective* (**-r, -st; less** or **lesser, least**) small in size, amount, degree, etc.; short in stature; of short distance or duration; (**a little**) certain but small amount of; trivial; only small amount; operating on small scale; humble, ordinary; young, younger. ● *noun* not much, only small amount; short time or distance. ● *adverb* (**less, least**) to small extent only; not at all. □ **little by little** by degrees, gradually; **the little people** fairies.

littoral /'lɪtər(ə)l/ ● *adjective* of or on the shore. ● *noun* region lying along shore.

liturgy /'lɪtədʒɪ/ *noun* (*plural* **-ies**) fixed form of public worship; (**the Liturgy**) the Book of Common Prayer. □ **liturgical** /-'tɜːdʒ-/ *adjective*.

live[1] /lɪv/ *verb* (**-ving**) have life; be or remain alive; have one's home; (**+ on, off**) subsist or feed on; keep one's position; pass, spend; conduct oneself in specified way; enjoy life to the full. □ **live down**

cause (scandal etc.) to be forgotten through blameless behaviour thereafter; **live it up** *colloquial* live exuberantly and extravagantly.

live[2] /laɪv/ ● *adjective* that is alive, living; (of broadcast, performance, etc.) heard or seen while happening or with audience present; of current interest; glowing, burning; (of match, bomb, etc.) not yet kindled or exploded; charged with electricity. ● *adverb* as live performance. □ **livestock** (usually treated as *plural*) animals kept on farm for use or profit; **live wire** spirited person.

liveable /'lɪvəb(ə)l/ *adjective* (also **livable**) *colloquial* (usually **liveable-in**) (of house etc.) fit to live in; (of life) worth living; *colloquial* (usually **liveable-with**) (of person) easy to live with.

livelihood /'laɪvlɪhʊd/ *noun* means of living; job, income.

livelong /'lɪvlɒŋ/ *adjective* in its entire length.

lively /'laɪvlɪ/ *adjective* (**-ier, -iest**) full of life, energetic; (of imagination) vivid; cheerful; *jocular* exciting, dangerous. □ **liveliness** *noun*.

liven /'laɪv(ə)n/ *verb* (often **+ up**) make or become lively, cheer up.

liver[1] /'lɪvə/ *noun* large glandular organ in abdomen of vertebrates; liver of some animals as food.

liver[2] /'lɪvə/ *noun* person who lives in specified way.

liverish /'lɪvərɪʃ/ *adjective* suffering from liver disorder; peevish, glum.

liverwort *noun* mosslike plant sometimes lobed like liver.

livery /'lɪvərɪ/ *noun* (*plural* **-ies**) distinctive uniform of member of City Company or servant; distinctive guise or marking; distinctive colour scheme for company's vehicles etc. □ **at livery** (of horse) kept for owner at fixed charge; **livery stable** stable where horses are kept at livery or let out for hire.

lives *plural of* LIFE.

livid /'lɪvɪd/ *adjective colloquial* furious; of bluish leaden colour.

living /'lɪvɪŋ/ ● *noun* being alive; livelihood; position held by clergyman, providing income. ● *adjective* contemporary; now alive; (of likeness) exact; (of language) still in vernacular use. □ **living-room** room for general day use; **living wage** wage on which one can live without privation; **within living memory** within memory of living people.

lizard /'lɪzəd/ *noun* reptile with usually long body and tail, 4 legs, and scaly hide.

llama /'lɑːmə/ *noun* S. American ruminant kept as beast of burden and for woolly fleece.

Lloyd's /lɔɪdz/ *noun* incorporated society of underwriters in London. □ **Lloyd's Register** annual classified list of all ships.

lo *interjection archaic* look.

loach *noun* (*plural* same or **-es**) small freshwater fish.

load ● *noun* what is (to be) carried; amount usually or actually carried; burden of work, responsibility, care, etc.; (in *plural*; often **+ of**) plenty; (**a load of**) a quantity of; amount of power carried by electrical circuit or supplied by generating station. ● *verb* put load on or aboard; place (load) aboard ship or on vehicle etc.; (often **+ up**) (of vehicle or person) take load aboard; (often **+ with**) burden, strain, overwhelm; put ammunition in (gun), film in (camera), cassette in (tape recorder), program in (computer), etc. □ **load line** Plimsoll line.

loaded *adjective slang* rich, drunk, *US* drugged; (of dice etc.) weighted; (of question or statement) carrying hidden implication.

loadstone = LODESTONE.

loaf[1] *noun* (*plural* **loaves**) unit of baked bread, usually of standard size or shape; other cooked food in loaf shape; *slang* head.

loaf² *verb* (often + *about*) spend time idly, hang about.

loam *noun* rich soil of clay, sand, and humus. □ **loamy** *adjective*.

loan ● *noun* thing lent, esp. money; lending, being lent. ● *verb* lend (money, works of art, etc.). □ **on loan** being lent.

loath *adjective* (also **loth**) disinclined, reluctant.

loathe /ləʊð/ *verb* (**-thing**) detest, hate. □ **loathing** *noun*.

loathsome /ˈləʊðsəm/ *adjective* arousing hatred or disgust; repulsive.

loaves *plural* of LOAF¹.

lob ● *verb* (**-bb-**) hit or throw (ball etc.) slowly or in high arc. ● *noun* such ball.

lobar /ˈləʊbə/ *adjective* of a lobe, esp. of lung.

lobate /ˈləʊbeɪt/ *adjective* having lobe(s).

lobby /ˈlɒbɪ/ ● *noun* (*plural* **-ies**) porch, ante-room, entrance hall, corridor; (in House of Commons) large hall used esp. for interviews between MPs and the public; (also **division lobby**) each of two corridors to which MPs retire to vote; group of lobbyists. ● *verb* (**-ies, -ied**) solicit support of (influential person); inform (legislators etc.) in order to influence them. □ **lobby correspondent** journalist who receives unattributable briefings from government.

lobbyist *noun* person who lobbies MP etc.

lobe *noun* lower soft pendulous part of outer ear; similar part of other organs. □ **lobed** *adjective*.

lobelia /ləˈbiːlɪə/ *noun* plant with bright, esp. blue, flowers.

lobotomy /ləˈbɒtəmɪ/ *noun* (*plural* **-ies**) incision into frontal lobe of brain to relieve mental disorder.

lobster /ˈlɒbstə/ *noun* marine crustacean with two pincer-like claws; its flesh as food. □ **lobster pot** basket for trapping lobsters.

lobworm *noun* large earthworm used as fishing bait.

local /ˈləʊk(ə)l/ ● *adjective* belonging to, existing in, or peculiar to particular place; of the neighbourhood; of or affecting a part and not the whole; (of telephone call) to nearby place and at lower charge. ● *noun* inhabitant of particular place; (often **the local**) *colloquial* local public house. □ **local authority** administrative body in local government; **local colour** touches of detail in story etc. designed to provide realistic background; **local government** system of administration of county, district, parish, etc. by elected representatives of those who live there. □ **locally** *adverb*.

locale /ləʊˈkɑːl/ *noun* scene or locality of event or occurrence.

locality /ləʊˈkælɪtɪ/ *noun* (*plural* **-ies**) district; thing's site or scene; thing's position.

localize /ˈləʊkəlaɪz/ *verb* (also **-ise**) (**-zing** or **-sing**) restrict or assign to particular place; invest with characteristics of place; decentralize.

locate /ləʊˈkeɪt/ *verb* (**-ting**) discover exact place of; establish in a place, situate; state locality of.

■ **Usage** In standard English, it is incorrect to use *locate* to mean merely 'find' as in *I can't locate my key.*

---

location *noun* particular place; locating; natural, not studio, setting for film etc.

loc. cit. *abbreviation* in the passage cited (*loco citato*).

loch /lɒx, lɒk/ *noun* Scottish lake or narrow inlet of the sea.

lock¹ ● *noun* mechanism for fastening door etc. with bolt requiring key of particular shape; section of canal or river confined within sluice-gates for moving boats from one level to another; turning of vehicle's front wheels; interlocked or jammed state; wrestling hold. ● *verb* fasten with lock; (+ *up*) shut

(house etc.) thus; (of door etc.) be lockable; (+ *up, in, into*) enclose (person, thing) by locking; (often + *up, away*) store inaccessibly; make or become rigidly fixed; (cause to) jam or catch. □ **lockjaw** form of tetanus in which jaws become rigidly closed; **lockkeeper** keeper of river or canal lock; **lock on to** (of missile etc.) automatically find and then track (target); **lock out** *verb* keep out by locking door, (of employer) subject (employees) to lockout; **lockout** *noun* employer's exclusion of employees from workplace until certain terms are accepted; **locksmith** maker and mender of locks; **lock-up** house or room for temporary detention of prisoners, premises that can be locked up. □ **lockable** *adjective*.

lock² *noun* portion of hair that hangs together; (in *plural*) the hair.

locker *noun* (usually lockable) cupboard, esp. for public use.

locket /ˈlɒkɪt/ *noun* small ornamental case for portrait etc., usually on chain round neck.

locomotion /ləʊkəˈməʊʃ(ə)n/ *noun* motion or power of motion from place to place.

locomotive /ləʊkəˈməʊtɪv/ ● *noun* engine for pulling trains. ● *adjective* of, having, or bringing about locomotion.

locum tenens /ləʊkəm ˈtiːnenz/ *noun* (*plural* **locum tenentes** /tɪˈnentiːz/) (also *colloquial* **locum**) deputy acting esp. for doctor or member of clergy.

locus /ˈləʊkəs/ *noun* (*plural* **loci** /-saɪ/) position; place; line or curve etc. made by all points satisfying certain conditions or by defined motion of point, line, or surface.

locust /ˈləʊkəst/ *noun* African or Asian grasshopper migrating in swarms and consuming all vegetation.

locution /ləˈkjuːʃ(ə)n/ *noun* phrase, word, or idiom; style of speech.

lode *noun* vein of metal ore. □ **lodestar** star used as guide in navigation, esp. pole star; **lodestone**, **loadstone** magnetic oxide of iron, piece of this as magnet.

lodge ● *noun* small house, esp. one for gatekeeper at entrance to park or grounds of large house; porter's room etc.; members or meeting-place of branch of society such as Freemasons; beaver's or otter's lair. ● *verb* (**-ging**) reside, esp. as lodger; provide with sleeping quarters; submit (complaint etc.); become fixed or caught; deposit for security; settle, place.

lodger *noun* person paying for accommodation in another's house.

lodging *noun* temporary accommodation; (in *plural*) room(s) rented for lodging in.

loft ● *noun* attic; room over stable; gallery in church or hall; pigeon house. ● *verb* send (ball etc.) high up.

lofty *adjective* (**-ier, -iest**) of imposing height; haughty, aloof; exalted, noble. □ **loftily** *adverb*; **loftiness** *noun*.

log¹ ● *noun* unhewn piece of felled tree; any large rough piece of wood; *historical* floating device for ascertaining ship's speed; record of ship's or aircraft's voyage; any systematic record of experiences etc. ● *verb* (**-gg-**) enter (ship's speed or other transport details) in logbook; enter (data etc.) in regular record; cut into logs. □ **logbook** book containing record or log, vehicle registration document; **log on** or **off**, **log in** or **out** begin or end operations at terminal of esp. multi-access computer.

log² *noun* logarithm.

logan /ˈləʊgən/ *noun* (in full **logan-stone**) poised heavy stone rocking at a touch.

loganberry /ˈləʊgənbərɪ/ *noun* (*plural* **-ies**) dark red fruit, hybrid of blackberry and raspberry.

logarithm /ˈlɒgərɪð(ə)m/ *noun* an arithmetic exponent used in computation. □ **logarithmic** /-ˈrɪðmɪk/ *adjective*.

loggerhead /ˈlɒgəhed/ *noun* □ **at loggerheads** (often + *with*) disagreeing or disputing.

loggia /ˈlɒʊdʒə/ *noun* open-sided gallery or arcade.

logging *noun* work of cutting and preparing forest timber.

logic /ˈlɒdʒɪk/ *noun* science of reasoning; chain of reasoning; use of or ability in argument; inexorable force; principles used in designing computer etc.; circuits based on these. □ **logician** /ləˈdʒɪʃ(ə)n/ *noun*.

logical *adjective* of or according to logic; correctly reasoned, consistent; capable of correct reasoning. □ **logicality** /-ˈkæl-/ *noun*; **logically** *adverb*.

logistics /ləˈdʒɪstɪks/ *plural noun* organization of (originally military) services and supplies. □ **logistic** *adjective*; **logistical** *adjective*; **logistically** *adverb*.

logo /ˈlɒʊgəʊ/ *noun* (*plural* **-s**) organization's emblem used in display material.

loin *noun* (in *plural*) side and back of body between ribs and hip-bones; joint of meat from this part of animal. □ **loincloth** cloth worn round hips, esp. as sole garment.

loiter /ˈlɔɪtə/ *verb* stand about idly; linger. □ **loiter with intent** linger to commit felony.

loll *verb* stand, sit, or recline in lazy attitude; hang loosely.

lollipop /ˈlɒlɪpɒp/ *noun* hard sweet on stick. □ **lollipop man, lady** *colloquial* warden using circular sign on pole to stop traffic for children to cross road.

lollop /ˈlɒləp/ *verb* (**-p-**) *colloquial* flop about; move in ungainly bounds.

lolly /ˈlɒlɪ/ *noun* (*plural* **-ies**) *colloquial* lollipop; ice lolly; *slang* money.

lone *adjective* solitary; without companions; isolated; unmarried. □ **lone hand** hand played or player playing against the rest at cards, person or action without allies; **lone wolf** loner.

lonely /ˈlɒʊnlɪ/ *adjective* (**-ier, -iest**) without companions; sad because of this; isolated; uninhabited. □ **loneliness** *noun*.

loner *noun* person or animal preferring to be alone.

lonesome *adjective esp. US* lonely; causing loneliness.

long¹ *adjective* (**longer** /ˈlɒŋgə/, **longest** /ˈlɒŋgɪst/) measuring much from end to end in space or time; (following measurement) in length or duration; consisting of many items; tedious; of elongated shape; reaching far back or forward in time; involving great interval or difference. ● *noun* long interval or period. ● *adverb* (**longer** /ˈlɒŋgə/, **longest** /ˈlɒŋgɪst/) by or for a long time; (following nouns of duration) throughout specified time; (in *comparative*) after implied point of time. □ **as, so long as** provided that; **before long** soon; **in the long run** eventually; **longboat** sailing ship's largest boat; **longbow** one drawn by hand and shooting long arrow; **long-distance** travelling or operating between distant places; **long face** dismal expression; **longhand** ordinary handwriting; **long johns** *colloquial* long underpants; **long jump** athletic contest of jumping along ground in one leap; **long-life** (of milk etc.) treated to prolong shelf-life; **long odds** chances with low probability; **long-playing** (of gramophone record) playing for about 20–30 minutes on each side; **long-range** having a long range, relating to period of time far into future; **longshore** existing on or frequenting the shore; **long shot** wild guess or venture; **long sight** ability to see clearly only what is comparatively distant; **long-sighted** having long sight, far-sighted; **long-suffering** bearing provocation patiently; **long-term** of or for long period of time; **long-winded** (of speech or writing) tediously long.

long² *verb* (+ *for, to do*) have strong wish or desire for. □ **longing** *noun* & *adjective*; **longingly** *adverb*.

long. *abbreviation* longitude.

longevity /lɒnˈdʒevɪtɪ/ *noun formal* long life.

longitude /ˈlɒŋgɪtjuːd/ *noun* angular distance E. or W. of (esp. Greenwich) meridian.

longitudinal /lɒŋgɪˈtjuːdɪn(ə)l/ *adjective* of or in length; running lengthwise; of longitude. □ **longitudinally** *adverb*.

longways *adverb* (also **longwise**) in direction parallel with thing's length.

loo *noun colloquial* lavatory.

loofah /ˈluːfə/ *noun* rough bath-sponge made from dried pod of type of gourd.

look /lʊk/ ● *verb* (often + *at, down, up,* etc.) use or direct one's eyes; examine; make visual or mental search; (+ *at*) consider; (+ *for*) seek; have specified appearance, seem; (+ *into*) investigate; (of thing) face some direction; indicate (emotion) by looks; (+ *to do*) expect. ● *noun* act of looking; gaze, glance; appearance of face, expression; (in *plural*) personal appearance. □ **look after** attend to; **look back** (+ *on, to*) turn one's thoughts to (something past); **look down (up)on** regard with contempt; **look forward to** await (expected event) eagerly or with specified feelings; **look in** *verb* make short visit; **look-in** *noun colloquial* chance of participation or success; **looking-glass** mirror; **look on** be spectator; **look out** *verb* (often + *for*) be vigilant or prepared; **lookout** *noun* watch, observation-post, person etc. stationed to keep watch, prospect, *colloquial* person's own concern; **look up** search for (esp. information in book), *colloquial* visit (person), improve in prospect; **look up to** respect.

loom¹ /luːm/ *noun* apparatus for weaving.

loom² /luːm/ *verb* appear dimly, esp. as vague often threatening shape.

loon /luːn/ *noun* kind of diving bird; *colloquial* crazy person.

loony /ˈluːnɪ/ *slang* ● *noun* (*plural* **-ies**) lunatic. ● *adjective* (**-ier, -iest**) crazy.

loop /luːp/ ● *noun* figure produced by curve or doubled thread etc. crossing itself; thing, path, etc. forming this figure; similarly shaped attachment used as fastening; contraceptive coil; endless band of tape or film allowing continuous repetition; repeated sequence of computer operations. ● *verb* form or bend into loop; fasten with loop(s); form loop. □ **loop line** railway or telegraph line that diverges from main line and joins it again.

loophole *noun* means of evading rule etc. without infringing it; narrow vertical slit in wall of fort etc.

loopy *adjective* (**-ier, -iest**) *slang* crazy.

loose /luːs/ ● *adjective* not tightly held; free from bonds or restraint; not held together; not compact or dense; inexact; morally lax. ● *verb* (**-sing**) free; untie, detach; release; relax (hold etc.). □ **at a loose end** unoccupied; **let loose** release; **loose cover** removable cover for armchair etc.; **loose-leaf** (of notebook etc.) with pages that can be removed and replaced; **on the loose** escaped from captivity, enjoying oneself freely. □ **loosely** *adverb*.

loosen *verb* make or become loose or looser. □ **loosen up** relax.

loot /luːt/ ● *noun* spoil, booty; *slang* money. ● *verb* rob or steal, esp. after rioting etc.; plunder.

lop *verb* (**-pp-**) (often + *off*) cut or remove (part or parts) from whole, esp. branches from tree; prune (tree).

lope ● *verb* (**-ping**) run with long bounding stride. ● *noun* such stride.

lop-eared *adjective* having drooping ears.

lopsided *adjective* unevenly balanced.

loquacious /ləˈkweɪʃəs/ *adjective* talkative.
□ **loquacity** /-ˈkwæsɪtɪ/ *noun.*

lord ● *noun* master, ruler; *historical* feudal superior, esp. of manor; peer of realm, person with title *Lord*; (**Lord**) (often **the Lord**) God, Christ; (**Lord**) *title used before name of certain male peers and officials*; (**the Lords**) House of Lords. ● *interjection expressing surprise, dismay, etc.* □ **lord it over** domineer; **Lord Mayor** *title of mayor in some large cities*; **Lord's Day** Sunday; **Lord's Prayer** the Our Father; **Lord's Supper** Eucharist.

lordly *adjective* (**-ier, -iest**) haughty, imperious; suitable for a lord.

Lordship *noun* □ **His, Your Lordship** *title used of or to man with rank of Lord.*

lore *noun* body of tradition and information on a subject or held by particular group.

lorgnette /lɔːˈnjet/ *noun* pair of eyeglasses or opera-glasses on long handle.

lorn *adjective archaic* desolate, forlorn.

lorry /ˈlɒrɪ/ *noun* (*plural* **-ies**) large vehicle for transporting goods etc.

lose /luːz/ *verb* (**-sing**; *past & past participle* **lost**) be deprived of; cease to have, esp. by negligence; be deprived of (person) by death; become unable to find, follow, or understand; let pass from one's control; be defeated in; get rid of; forfeit (right to something); suffer loss or detriment; cause (person) the loss of; (of clock etc.) become slow; (in *passive*) disappear, perish. □ **be lost without** be dependent on.

loser *noun* person or thing that loses esp. contest; *colloquial* person who regularly fails.

loss *noun* losing, being lost; what is lost; detriment resulting from losing. □ **at a loss** (sold etc.) for less than was paid for it; **be at a loss** be puzzled or uncertain; **loss-leader** item sold at a loss to attract customers.

lost *past & past participle* of LOSE.

lot *noun colloquial* (**a lot**, or **lots**) large number or amount; each of set of objects used to make chance selection; this method of deciding, share or responsibility resulting from it; destiny, fortune, condition; *esp. US* plot, allotment; article or set of articles for sale at auction etc.; group of associated people or things. □ **draw, cast lots** decide by lots; **the (whole) lot** total number or quantity.

■ **Usage** *A lot of*, as in *a lot of people*, is fairly informal, though acceptable in serious writing, but *lots of people* is not acceptable.

loth = LOATH.

lotion /ˈləʊʃ(ə)n/ *noun* medical or cosmetic liquid preparation applied externally.

lottery /ˈlɒtərɪ/ *noun* (*plural* **-ies**) means of raising money by selling numbered tickets and giving prizes to holders of numbers drawn at random.

lotto /ˈlɒtəʊ/ *noun* game of chance like bingo.

lotus /ˈləʊtəs/ *noun* legendary plant inducing luxurious langour when eaten; kind of water lily. □ **lotus position** cross-legged position of meditation.

loud ● *adjective* strongly audible; noisy; (of colours etc.) gaudy, obtrusive. ● *adverb* loudly. □ **loud-speaker** apparatus that converts electrical signals into sounds. □ **loudly** *adverb*; **loudness** *noun.*

lough /lɒk, lɒx/ *noun Irish* lake, sea inlet.

lounge ● *verb* (**-ging**) recline comfortably; loll; stand or move idly. ● *noun* place for lounging, esp. sitting-room in house; public room (in hotel etc.); place in airport etc. with seats for waiting passengers; spell of lounging. □ **lounge suit** man's suit for ordinary day wear.

lour /laʊə/ *verb* (also **lower** /laʊə/) frown, look sullen; (of sky etc.) look dark and threatening.

louse /laʊs/ ● *noun* (*plural* **lice**) parasitic insect; (*plural* **louses**) *slang* contemptible person. ● *verb* (**-sing**) delouse.

lousy /ˈlaʊzɪ/ *adjective* (**-ier, -iest**) *colloquial* very bad, disgusting, ill; (often + *with*) *colloquial* well supplied; infested with lice.

lout *noun* rough-mannered person. □ **loutish** *adjective.*

louvre /ˈluːvə/ *noun* (also **louver**) each of set of overlapping slats designed to admit air and some light and exclude rain; domed structure on roof with side openings for ventilation etc.

lovable /ˈlʌvəb(ə)l/ *adjective* (also **loveable**) inspiring affection.

lovage /ˈlʌvɪdʒ/ *noun* herb used for flavouring etc.

love /lʌv/ ● *noun* deep affection or fondness; sexual passion; sexual relations; beloved one; sweetheart; *colloquial form of address regardless of affection*; *colloquial* person of whom one is fond; affectionate greetings; (in games) no score, nil. ● *verb* (**-ving**) feel love for; delight in, admire; *colloquial* like very much. □ **fall in love** (often + *with*) suddenly begin to love; **in love** (often + *with*) enamoured (of); **love affair** romantic or sexual relationship between two people; **love-bird** kind of parakeet; **love-in-a-mist** blue-flowered cultivated plant; **lovelorn** pining from unrequited love; **lovesick** languishing with love; **make love** (often + *to*) have sexual intercourse (with), pay amorous attention (to).

loveable = LOVABLE.

loveless *adjective* unloving or unloved or both.

lovely *adjective* (**-ier, -iest**) *colloquial* pleasing, delightful; beautiful. □ **loveliness** *noun.*

lover *noun* person in love with another, or having sexual relations with another; (in *plural*) unmarried couple in love or having sexual relations; person who enjoys specified thing.

loving ● *adjective* feeling or showing love, affectionate. ● *noun* affection. □ **loving cup** two-handled drinking cup passed round at banquets. □ **lovingly** *adverb.*

low¹ /ləʊ/ ● *adjective* not high or tall; not elevated in position; (of sun) near horizon; of humble rank; of small or less than normal amount, extent, or intensity; dejected; lacking vigour; (of sound) not shrill or loud; commonplace; (of opinion) unfavourable; mean, vulgar. ● *noun* low or lowest level or number; area of low pressure. ● *adverb* in or to low position; in low tone, at low pitch. □ **lowbrow** *colloquial* not intellectual or cultured; **Low Church** section of Church of England attaching little importance to ritual, priestly authority, and sacraments; **Low Countries** Netherlands, Belgium, and Luxembourg; **low-down** *adjective* mean, dishonourable, *noun colloquial* (**the lowdown**; usually + *on*) relevant information; **lower case** small letters, not capitals; **low frequency** *Radio* 30–300 kilohertz; **low pressure** low degree of activity, atmospheric condition with pressure below average; **Low Sunday** Sunday after Easter; **low tide, water** time or level of tide at its ebb; **low water mark** level reached at low water.

low² /ləʊ/ ● *noun* sound made by cattle; moo. ● *verb* make this sound.

lower¹ *verb* let or haul down; make or become lower; degrade.

lower² = LOUR.

lowland /ˈləʊlənd/ ● *noun* (usually in *plural*) low-lying country. ● *adjective* of or in lowland. □ **lowlander** *noun.*

lowly *adjective* (**-ier, -iest**) humble; unpretentious. □ **lowliness** *noun.*

loyal /'lɔɪəl/ *adjective* (often + *to*) faithful; steadfast in allegiance etc. □ **loyally** *adverb*; **loyalty** *noun* (*plural* **-ies**).

loyalist *noun* person remaining loyal to legitimate sovereign etc.; (**Loyalist**) supporter of union between Great Britain and Northern Ireland. □ **loyalism** *noun*.

lozenge /'lɒzɪndʒ/ *noun* rhombus; small sweet or medicinal tablet to be dissolved in mouth; lozenge-shaped object.

LP *abbreviation* long-playing (record).

LSD *abbreviation* lysergic acid diethylamide, a powerful hallucinogenic drug.

Lt. *abbreviation* Lieutenant; light.

Ltd. *abbreviation* Limited.

lubber /'lʌbə/ *noun* clumsy fellow, lout.

lubricant /'lu:brɪkənt/ *noun* substance used to reduce friction.

lubricate /'lu:brɪkeɪt/ *verb* (**-ting**) apply oil, grease, etc. to; make slippery. □ **lubrication** *noun*.

lubricious /lu:'brɪʃəs/ *adjective* slippery, evasive; lewd. □ **lubricity** *noun*.

lucerne /lu:'sɜ:n/ *noun* alfalfa.

lucid /'lu:sɪd/ *adjective* expressing or expressed clearly; sane. □ **lucidity** /-'sɪd-/ *noun*; **lucidly** *adverb*.

luck *noun* good or bad fortune; circumstances brought by this; success due to chance.

luckless *adjective* unlucky; ending in failure.

lucky *adjective* (**-ier, -iest**) having or resulting from good luck; bringing good luck. □ **lucky dip** tub containing articles from which one chooses at random. □ **luckily** *adverb*.

lucrative /'lu:krətɪv/ *adjective* profitable. □ **lucratively** *adverb*.

lucre /'lu:kə/ *noun* derogatory financial gain.

ludicrous /'lu:dɪkrəs/ *adjective* absurd, ridiculous, laughable. □ **ludicrously** *adverb*; **ludicrousness** *noun*.

ludo /'lu:dəʊ/ *noun* board game played with dice and counters.

lug ● *verb* (**-gg-**) drag or carry with effort; pull hard. ● *noun* hard or rough pull; *colloquial* ear; projection on object by which it may be carried, fixed in place, etc.

luggage /'lʌgɪdʒ/ *noun* suitcases, bags, etc., for traveller's belongings.

lugger /'lʌgə/ *noun* small ship with 4-cornered sails (**lugsails**).

lugubrious /lu'gu:brɪəs/ *adjective* doleful. □ **lugubriously** *adverb*; **lugubriousness** *noun*.

lukewarm /lu:k'wɔ:m/ *adjective* moderately warm, tepid; unenthusiastic.

lull ● *verb* soothe, send to sleep; (usually + *into*) deceive (person) into undue confidence; allay (suspicions etc.); (of noise, storm, etc.) lessen, fall quiet. ● *noun* temporary quiet period.

lullaby /'lʌləbaɪ/ *noun* (*plural* **-ies**) soothing song to send child to sleep.

lumbago /lʌm'beɪgəʊ/ *noun* rheumatic pain in muscles of lower back.

lumbar /'lʌmbə/ *adjective* of lower back. □ **lumbar puncture** withdrawal of spinal fluid from lower back for diagnosis.

lumber /'lʌmbə/ ● *noun* disused and cumbersome articles; partly prepared timber. ● *verb* (usually + *with*) encumber (person); move in slow clumsy way; cut and prepare forest timber for transporting. □ **lumberjack** person who fells and transports lumber; **lumber-room** room where things in disuse are kept.

lumen /'lu:men/ *noun* SI unit of luminous flux.

luminary /'lu:mɪnərɪ/ *noun* (*plural* **-ies**) *literary* natural light-giving body; wise person; celebrated member of group.

luminescence /lu:mɪ'nes(ə)ns/ *noun* emission of light without heat. □ **luminescent** *adjective*.

luminous /'lu:mɪnəs/ *adjective* shedding light; phosphorescent, visible in darkness. □ **luminosity** /-'nɒs-/ *noun*.

lump¹ ● *noun* compact shapeless mass; tumour; swelling, bruise; heavy ungainly person etc. ● *verb* (usually + *together* etc.) class, mass. □ **lump sugar** sugar in small lumps or cubes; **lump sum** sum including number of items or paid down all at once.

lump² *verb colloquial* (in contrast with *like*) put up with ungraciously.

lumpish *adjective* heavy, clumsy; stupid.

lumpy *adjective* (**-ier, -iest**) full of or covered with lumps. □ **lumpily** *adverb*; **lumpiness** *noun*.

lunacy /'lu:nəsɪ/ *noun* (*plural* **-ies**) insanity; great folly.

lunar /'lu:nə/ *adjective* of, like, concerned with, or determined by the moon. □ **lunar module** craft for travelling between moon and orbiting spacecraft; **lunar month** period of moon's revolution, (in general use) 4 weeks.

lunate /'lu:neɪt/ *adjective* crescent-shaped.

lunatic /'lu:nətɪk/ ● *noun* insane person; wildly foolish person. ● *adjective* insane; very reckless or foolish.

lunation /lu:'neɪʃ(ə)n/ *noun* interval between new moons, about 29½ days.

lunch ● *noun* midday meal. ● *verb* take lunch; provide lunch for.

luncheon /'lʌntʃ(ə)n/ *noun formal* lunch. □ **luncheon voucher** voucher issued to employees and exchangeable for food at restaurant etc.

lung *noun* either of pair of respiratory organs in humans and many other vertebrates.

lunge ● *noun* sudden movement forward; attacking move in fencing. ● *verb* (**-ging**) (usually + *at*) deliver or make lunge.

lupin /'lu:pɪn/ *noun* cultivated plant with long tapering spikes of flowers.

lupine /'lu:paɪn/ *adjective* of or like wolves.

lupus /'lu:pəs/ *noun* inflammatory skin disease.

lurch¹ ● *noun* stagger; sudden unsteady movement or tilt. ● *verb* stagger, move unsteadily.

lurch² *noun* □ **leave in the lurch** desert (friend etc.) in difficulties.

lurcher /'lɜ:tʃə/ *noun* crossbred dog, usually working dog crossed with greyhound.

lure ● *verb* (**-ring**) (usually + *away, into*) entice; recall with lure. ● *noun* thing used to entice, enticing quality (of chase etc.); falconer's apparatus for recalling hawk.

lurid /'ljʊərɪd/ *adjective* bright and glaring in colour; sensational, shocking; ghastly, wan. □ **luridly** *adverb*.

lurk *verb* linger furtively; lie in ambush; (usually + *in, about*, etc.) hide, esp. for sinister purpose; (as **lurking** *adjective*) latent.

luscious /'lʌʃəs/ *adjective* richly sweet in taste or smell; voluptuously attractive.

lush¹ *adjective* luxuriant and succulent.

lush² *noun slang* alcoholic, drunkard.

lust ● *noun* strong sexual desire; (usually + *for, of*) passionate desire for or enjoyment of; sensuous appetite seen as sinful. ● *verb* (usually + *after, for*) have strong or excessive (esp. sexual) desire. □ **lustful** *adjective*; **lustfully** *adverb*.

lustre /'lʌstə/ *noun* (*US* **luster**) gloss, shining surface; brilliance, splendour; iridescent glaze on pottery and porcelain. □ **lustrous** *adjective*.

lusty *adjective* (**-ier, -iest**) healthy and strong; vigorous, lively. □ **lustily** *adverb*.

lute[1] /luːt/ *noun* guitar-like instrument with long neck and pear-shaped body.

lute[2] /luːt/ ● *noun* clay or cement for making joints airtight. ● *verb* (**-ting**) apply lute to.

lutenist /'luːtənɪst/ *noun* lute-player.

Lutheran /'luːθərən/ ● *noun* follower of Martin Luther; member of Lutheran Church. ● *adjective* of Luther, the doctrines associated with him, or the Protestant Reformation. □ **Lutheranism** *noun*.

lux /lʌks/ *noun* (*plural* same) SI unit of illumination.

luxuriant /lʌg'zjʊərɪənt/ *adjective* growing profusely; exuberant, florid. □ **luxuriance** *noun*; **luxuriantly** *adverb*.

■ **Usage** *Luxuriant* is sometimes confused with *luxurious*.

luxuriate /lʌg'zjʊərɪeɪt/ *verb* (**-ting**) (+ *in*) take self-indulgent delight in, enjoy as luxury.

luxurious /lʌg'zjʊərɪəs/ *adjective* supplied with luxuries; very comfortable; fond of luxury. □ **luxuriously** *adverb*.

■ **Usage** *Luxurious* is sometimes confused with *luxuriant*.

luxury /'lʌkʃərɪ/ ● *noun* (*plural* **-ies**) choice or costly surroundings, possessions, etc.; thing giving comfort or enjoyment but inessential. ● *adjective* comfortable, expensive, etc.

LV *abbreviation* luncheon voucher.

lychee /'laɪtʃɪ/ *noun* (also **litchi**, **lichee**) sweet white juicy brown-skinned fruit; tree bearing this.

lych-gate = LICH-GATE.

Lycra /'laɪkrə/ *noun proprietary term* elastic polyurethane fabric.

lye /laɪ/ *noun* water made alkaline with wood ashes; any alkaline solution for washing.

lying *present participle* of LIE[1,2].

lymph /lɪmf/ *noun* colourless fluid from tissues of body, containing white blood cells; this fluid as vaccine.

lymphatic /lɪm'fætɪk/ *adjective* of, secreting, or carrying lymph; (of person) pale, flabby. □ **lymphatic system** vessels carrying lymph.

lynch /lɪntʃ/ *verb* put (person) to death by mob action without legal trial. □ **lynching** *noun*.

lynx /lɪŋks/ *noun* (*plural* same or **-es**) wild cat with short tail, spotted fur, and proverbially keen sight.

lyre /laɪə/ *noun* ancient U-shaped stringed instrument.

lyric /'lɪrɪk/ ● *adjective* (of poetry) expressing writer's emotion, usually briefly; (of poet) writing in this way; meant or fit to be sung; songlike. ● *noun* lyric poem; (in *plural*) words of song.

lyrical *adjective* lyric; resembling, or using language appropriate to, lyric poetry; *colloquial* highly enthusiastic. □ **lyrically** *adverb*.

lyricism /'lɪrɪsɪz(ə)m/ *noun* quality of being lyrical.

lyricist /'lɪrɪsɪst/ *noun* writer of lyrics.

M¹ *noun* (also **m**) (Roman numeral) 1,000.

M² *abbreviation* (also **M.**) Master; *Monsieur*; motorway; mega-.

m *abbreviation* (also **m.**) male; masculine; married; mile(s); metre(s); million(s); minute(s); milli-.

MA *abbreviation* Master of Arts.

ma /mɑː/ *noun colloquial* mother.

ma'am /mæm/ *noun* madam (esp. used in addressing royal lady).

mac *noun* (also **mack**) *colloquial* mackintosh.

macabre /məˈkɑːbr/ *adjective* gruesome, grim.

macadam /məˈkædəm/ *noun* broken stone as material for road-making; tarmacadam. □ **macadamize** *verb* (also **-ise**) **(-zing** or **-sing)**.

macaroni /mækəˈrəʊnɪ/ *noun* pasta tubes.

macaroon /mækəˈruːn/ *noun* biscuit made of ground almonds etc.

macaw /məˈkɔː/ *noun* kind of parrot.

mace¹ *noun* staff of office, esp. symbol of Speaker's authority in House of Commons.

mace² *noun* dried outer covering of nutmeg as spice.

macédoine /ˈmæsɪdwɑːn/ *noun* mixture of fruits or vegetables, esp. cut up small.

macerate /ˈmæsəreɪt/ *verb* **(-ting)** soften by soaking. □ **maceration** *noun*.

machete /məˈʃetɪ/ *noun* broad heavy knife used in Central America and W. Indies.

machiavellian /mækɪəˈvelɪən/ *adjective* unscrupulous, cunning.

machination /mækɪˈneɪʃ(ə)n/ *noun* (usually in *plural*) intrigue, plot.

machine /məˈʃiːn/ ● *noun* apparatus for applying mechanical power, having several interrelated parts; bicycle, motorcycle, etc.; aircraft; computer; controlling system of an organization. ● *verb* **(-ning)** make or operate on with machine. □ **machine-gun** automatic gun that gives continuous fire; **machine-readable** in form that computer can process; **machine tool** mechanically operated tool.

machinery *noun* (*plural* **-ies**) machines; mechanism; organized system; means arranged.

machinist *noun* person who works machine.

machismo /məˈkɪzməʊ/ *noun* being macho; masculine pride.

macho /ˈmætʃəʊ/ *adjective* aggressively masculine.

macintosh = MACKINTOSH.

mack = MAC.

mackerel /ˈmækr(ə)l/ *noun* (*plural* same or **-s**) edible sea fish. □ **mackerel sky** sky dappled with rows of small fleecy white clouds.

mackintosh /ˈmækɪntɒʃ/ *noun* (also **macintosh**) waterproof coat or cloak; cloth waterproofed with rubber.

macramé /məˈkrɑːmɪ/ *noun* art of knotting cord or string in patterns; work so made.

macrobiotic /mækrəʊbaɪˈɒtɪk/ *adjective* of diet intended to prolong life, esp. consisting of wholefoods.

macrocosm /ˈmækrəʊkɒz(ə)m/ *noun* universe; whole of a complex structure.

mad *adjective* **(-dd-)** insane; frenzied; wildly foolish; infatuated; *colloquial* annoyed. □ **madcap** *adjective* wildly impulsive, *noun* reckless person; **madhouse** *colloquial* confused uproar, *archaic* mental home or hospital; **madman**, **madwoman** mad person. □ **madly** *adverb*; **madness** *noun*.

madam /ˈmædəm/ *noun* polite formal address to *woman*; *colloquial* conceited or precocious girl or young woman; woman brothel-keeper.

Madame /məˈdɑːm/ *noun* (*plural* **Mesdames** /meɪˈdɑːm/) *title used of or to French-speaking woman*.

madden *verb* make mad; irritate. □ **maddening** *adjective*.

madder /ˈmædə/ *noun* herbaceous climbing plant; red dye from its root; synthetic substitute for this dye.

made *past* & *past participle* of MAKE.

Madeira /məˈdɪərə/ *noun* fortified wine from Madeira; (in full **Madeira cake**) kind of sponge cake.

Mademoiselle /mædəmwəˈzel/ *noun* (*plural* **Mesdemoiselles** /meɪdm-/) *title used of or to unmarried French-speaking woman*.

Madonna /məˈdɒnə/ *noun* (**the Madonna**) the Virgin Mary; (**madonna**) picture or statue of her.

madrigal /ˈmædrɪɡ(ə)l/ *noun* part-song for several voices, usually unaccompanied.

maelstrom /ˈmeɪlstrəm/ *noun* great whirlpool.

maestro /ˈmaɪstrəʊ/ *noun* (*plural* **maestri** /-strɪ/ or **-s**) eminent musician, esp. teacher or conductor.

Mafia /ˈmæfɪə/ *noun* organized international group of criminals.

Mafioso /mæfɪˈəʊsəʊ/ *noun* (*plural* **Mafiosi** /-sɪ/) member of the Mafia.

mag *noun colloquial* magazine.

magazine /mægəˈziːn/ *noun* periodical publication containing contributions by various writers; chamber containing cartridges fed automatically to breech of gun; similar device in slide projector etc.; store for explosives, arms, or military provisions.

magenta /məˈdʒentə/ *noun* shade of crimson; aniline dye of this colour.

maggot /ˈmæɡət/ *noun* larva, esp. of bluebottle. □ **maggoty** *adjective*.

Magi /ˈmeɪdʒaɪ/ *plural noun* (**the Magi**) the 'wise men from the East' in the Gospel.

magic /ˈmædʒɪk/ ● *noun* art of influencing events supernaturally; conjuring tricks; inexplicable influence. ● *adjective* of magic. □ **magic lantern** simple form of slide projector.

magical *adjective* of magic; resembling, or produced as if by, magic; wonderful, enchanting. □ **magically** *adverb*.

magician /məˈdʒɪʃ(ə)n/ *noun* person skilled in magic; conjuror.

magisterial /mædʒɪˈstɪərɪəl/ *adjective* imperious; authoritative; of a magistrate.

magistracy /ˈmædʒɪstrəsɪ/ *noun* (*plural* **-ies**) magisterial office; magistrates.

magistrate /ˈmædʒɪstreɪt/ *noun* civil officer administering law, esp. one trying minor offences etc.

magnanimous /mæɡˈnænɪməs/ *adjective* nobly generous, not petty in feelings or conduct. □ **magnanimity** /-nəˈnɪm-/ *noun*.

magnate /ˈmæɡneɪt/ *noun* person of wealth, authority, etc.

magnesia /mæɡˈniːʃə/ *noun* magnesium oxide; hydrated magnesium carbonate, used as antacid and laxative.

magnesium /mæg'niːzɪəm/ *noun* silvery metallic element.

magnet /'mægnɪt/ *noun* piece of iron, steel, etc., having properties of attracting iron and of pointing approximately north when suspended; lodestone; person or thing that attracts.

magnetic /mæg'netɪk/ *adjective* having properties of magnet; produced or acting by magnetism; capable of being attracted by or acquiring properties of magnet; very attractive. □ **magnetic field** area of influence of magnet; **magnetic north** point indicated by north end of compass needle; **magnetic storm** disturbance of earth's magnetic field; **magnetic tape** coated plastic strip for recording sound or pictures.

magnetism /'mægnɪtɪz(ə)m/ *noun* magnetic phenomena; science of these; personal charm.

magnetize /'mægnɪtaɪz/ *verb* (also **-ise**) (**-zing** or **-sing**) make into magnet; attract like magnet. □ **magnetization** *noun*.

magneto /mæg'niːtəʊ/ *noun* (*plural* **-s**) electric generator using permanent magnets (esp. for ignition in internal-combustion engine).

magnificent /mæg'nɪfɪs(ə)nt/ *adjective* splendid; imposing; *colloquial* excellent. □ **magnificence** *noun*; **magnificently** *adverb*.

magnify /'mægnɪfaɪ/ *verb* (**-ies**, **-ied**) make (thing) appear larger than it is, as with lens (**magnifying glass**) etc.; exaggerate; intensify; *archaic* extol. □ **magnification** *noun*.

magnitude /'mægnɪtjuːd/ *noun* largeness, size; importance.

magnolia /mæg'nəʊlɪə/ *noun* kind of flowering tree; very pale pinkish colour of its flowers.

magnum /'mægnəm/ *noun* (*plural* **-s**) wine bottle twice normal size.

magpie /'mægpaɪ/ *noun* crow with long tail and black and white plumage; chatterer; indiscriminate collector.

Magyar /'mægjɑː/ ● *noun* member of the chief ethnic group in Hungary; their language. ● *adjective* of this people.

maharaja /mɑːhə'rɑːdʒə/ *noun* (also **maharajah**) *historical title of some Indian princes.*

maharanee /mɑːhə'rɑːniː/ *noun* (also **maharani**) (*plural* **-s**) *historical* maharaja's wife or widow.

maharishi /mɑːhə'rɪʃi/ *noun* (*plural* **-s**) great Hindu sage.

mahatma /mə'hætmə/ *noun* (in India etc.) revered person.

mah-jong /mɑː'dʒɒŋ/ *noun* (also **-jongg**) originally Chinese game played with 136 or 144 pieces.

mahogany /mə'hɒgənɪ/ *noun* (*plural* **-ies**) reddish-brown wood used for furniture etc.; colour of this.

mahout /mə'haʊt/ *noun* elephant driver.

maid *noun* female servant; *archaic* girl, young woman. □ **maidservant** female servant.

maiden /'meɪd(ə)n/ ● *noun* *archaic* girl, young unmarried woman; *Cricket* maiden over. ● *adjective* unmarried; (of voyage, speech by MP, etc.) first. □ **maidenhair** delicate kind of fern; **maiden name** woman's surname before marriage; **maiden over** *Cricket* over in which no runs are scored. □ **maidenly** *adjective*.

mail[1] ● *noun* letters etc. conveyed by post; the post. ● *verb* send by mail. □ **mail order** purchase of goods by post.

mail[2] *noun* armour of metal rings or plates.

maim *verb* cripple, mutilate.

main ● *adjective* chief, principal. ● *noun* principal channel for water, gas, etc., or (usually in *plural*) electricity; (in *plural*) domestic electricity supply as distinct from batteries; *archaic* high seas. □ **in the**

main mostly, on the whole; **mainframe** central processing unit of large computer, large computer system; **mainland** continuous extent of land excluding nearby islands etc.; **mainmast** principal mast; **mainsail** lowest sail or sail set on after part of mainmast; **mainspring** principal spring of watch or clock, chief motive power etc.; **mainstay** chief support; **mainstream** prevailing trend of opinion, fashion, etc.

mainly *adverb* mostly; chiefly.

maintain /meɪn'teɪn/ *verb* keep up; keep going; support; assert as true; keep in repair.

maintenance /'meɪntənəns/ *noun* maintaining, being maintained; provision of enough to support life; alimony.

maiolica /mə'jɒlɪkə/ *noun* (also **majolica**) kind of decorated Italian earthenware.

maisonette /meɪzə'net/ *noun* flat on more than one floor; small house.

maize *noun* N. American cereal plant; cobs or grain of this.

Maj. *abbreviation* Major.

majestic /mə'dʒestɪk/ *adjective* stately and dignified; imposing. □ **majestically** *adverb*.

majesty /'mædʒɪstɪ/ *noun* (*plural* **-ies**) stateliness of aspect, language, etc.; sovereign power; (**His, Her, Your Majesty**) *title used of or to sovereign or sovereign's wife or widow.*

majolica = MAIOLICA.

major /'meɪdʒə/ ● *adjective* greater or relatively great in size etc.; unusually serious or significant; *Music* of or based on scale having semitone next above third and seventh notes; of full legal age. ● *noun* army officer next below lieutenant colonel; person of full legal age; *US* student's main subject or course, student of this. ● *verb* (+ *in*) *US* study or qualify in as a major. □ **major-domo** /-'dəʊməʊ/ (*plural* **-s**) housesteward; **major-general** army officer next below lieutenant general.

majority /mə'dʒɒrɪtɪ/ *noun* (*plural* **-ies**) (usually + *of*) greater number or part; number by which winning vote exceeds next; full legal age.

■ **Usage** *Majority* should strictly be used of a number of people or things, as in *the majority of people*, and not of a quantity of something, as in *the majority of the work*.

make ● *verb* (**-king**; *past & past participle* **made**) construct, frame, create, esp. from parts or other substance; compel; bring about, give rise to; cause to become or seem; write, compose; constitute, amount to; undertake; perform; gain, acquire, obtain as result; prepare for consumption or use; proceed; *colloquial* arrive at or in time for, manage to attend; *colloquial* achieve place in; establish, enact; consider to be, estimate as; secure success or advancement of; accomplish; become; represent as; form in the mind. ● *noun* origin of manufactured goods, brand; way thing is made. □ **make believe** *verb* pretend; **make-believe** *noun* pretence, *adjective* pretended; **make do** (often + *with*) manage (with substitute etc.); **make for** tend to result in, proceed towards; **make good** compensate for, repair, succeed in an undertaking; **make off** depart hastily; **make out** discern, understand, assert, pretend, *colloquial* progress, write out, fill in; **makeshift** (serving as) temporary substitute or device; **make up** *verb* act to overcome (deficiency), complete, (+ *for*) compensate for, be reconciled, put together, prepare, invent (story), apply cosmetics (to); **make-up** *noun* cosmetics, similar preparation used as disguise by actor, person's temperament etc., composition; **makeweight** small quantity added to make full weight; **on the make** *colloquial* intent on gain.

maker *noun* person who makes, esp. (**Maker**) God.

making *noun* (in *plural*) earnings, profit; essential qualities for becoming. □ **be the making of** ensure success of; **in the making** in the course of being made.

malachite /ˈmæləkaɪt/ *noun* green mineral used for ornament.

maladjusted /mælə'dʒʌstɪd/ *adjective* (of person) unable to cope with demands of social environment. □ **maladjustment** *noun*.

maladminister /mæləd'mɪnɪstə/ *verb* manage badly or improperly. □ **maladministration** *noun*.

maladroit /mælə'drɔɪt/ *adjective* bungling, clumsy.

malady /ˈmælədɪ/ *noun* (*plural* **-ies**) ailment, disease.

malaise /mə'leɪz/ *noun* feeling of illness or uneasiness.

malapropism /ˈmæləprɒpɪz(ə)m/ *noun* comical confusion between words.

malaria /mə'leərɪə/ *noun* fever transmitted by mosquitoes. □ **malarial** *adjective*.

Malay /mə'leɪ/ ● *noun* member of a people predominating in Malaysia and Indonesia; their language. ● *adjective* of this people or language.

malcontent /ˈmælkəntent/ ● *noun* discontented person. ● *adjective* discontented.

male ● *adjective* of the sex that can beget offspring by fertilizing; (of plants or flowers) containing stamens but no pistil; (of parts of machinery) designed to enter or fill corresponding hollow part. ● *noun* male person or animal.

malediction /mælɪ'dɪkʃ(ə)n/ *noun* curse. □ **maledictory** *adjective*.

malefactor /ˈmælɪfæktə/ *noun* criminal; evil-doer. □ **malefaction** /-ˈfækʃ(ə)n/ *noun*.

malevolent /mə'levələnt/ *adjective* wishing evil to others. □ **malevolence** *noun*.

malformation /mælfɔː'meɪʃ(ə)n/ *noun* faulty formation. □ **malformed** /-ˈfɔːmd/ *adjective*.

malfunction /mæl'fʌŋkʃ(ə)n/ ● *noun* failure to function normally. ● *verb* function faultily.

malice /ˈmælɪs/ *noun* ill-will; desire to do harm.

malicious /mə'lɪʃəs/ *adjective* given to or arising from malice. □ **maliciously** *adverb*.

malign /mə'laɪn/ ● *adjective* injurious; malignant; malevolent. ● *verb* speak ill of; slander. □ **malignity** /mə'lɪgnɪtɪ/ *noun*.

malignant /mə'lɪgnənt/ *adjective* (of disease) very virulent; (of tumour) spreading, recurring, cancerous; feeling or showing intense ill-will. □ **malignancy** *noun*.

malinger /mə'lɪŋgə/ *verb* pretend to be ill, esp. to escape duty.

mall /mæl, mɔːl/ *noun* sheltered walk; shopping precinct.

mallard /ˈmælɑːd/ *noun* (*plural* same) kind of wild duck.

malleable /ˈmælɪəb(ə)l/ *adjective* that can be shaped by hammering; pliable. □ **malleability** *noun*.

mallet /ˈmælɪt/ *noun* hammer, usually of wood; implement for striking croquet or polo ball.

mallow /ˈmæləʊ/ *noun* flowering plant with hairy stems and leaves.

malmsey /ˈmɑːmzɪ/ *noun* a strong sweet wine.

malnutrition /mælnju:'trɪʃ(ə)n/ *noun* lack of foods necessary for health.

malodorous /mæl'əʊdərəs/ *adjective* evil-smelling.

malpractice /mæl'præktɪs/ *noun* improper, negligent, or criminal professional conduct.

malt /mɔːlt/ ● *noun* barley or other grain prepared for brewing etc.; *colloquial* malt whisky. ● *verb* convert (grain) into malt. □ **malted milk** drink made from

dried milk and extract of malt; **malt whisky** whisky made from malted barley.

Maltese /mɔːl'tiːz/ ● *noun* native, national, or language of Malta. ● *adjective* of Malta. □ **Maltese cross** one with equal arms broadened at ends.

maltreat /mæl'triːt/ *verb* ill-treat. □ **maltreatment** *noun*.

mama /mə'mɑː/ *noun* (also **mamma**) *archaic* mother.

mamba /ˈmæmbə/ *noun* venomous African snake.

mamma = MAMA.

mammal /ˈmæm(ə)l/ *noun* animal of class secreting milk to feed young. □ **mammalian** /-ˈmeɪlɪən/ *adjective*.

mammary /ˈmæmərɪ/ *adjective* of breasts.

Mammon /ˈmæmən/ *noun* wealth regarded as god or evil influence.

mammoth /ˈmæməθ/ ● *noun* large extinct elephant. ● *adjective* huge.

man ● *noun* (*plural* **men**) adult human male; human being, person; the human race; employee, workman; (usually in *plural*) soldier, sailor, etc.; suitable or appropriate person; husband; *colloquial* boyfriend; human being of specified type; piece in chess, draughts, etc. ● *verb* (**-nn-**) supply with person(s) for work or defence. □ **manhole** opening giving person access to sewer, conduit, etc.; **man-hour** work done by one person in one hour; **man in the street** ordinary person; **man-of-war** warship; **manpower** people available for work or military service; **manservant** (*plural* **menservants**) male servant; **mantrap** trap set to catch esp. trespassers.

manacle /ˈmænək(ə)l/ ● *noun* (usually in *plural*) handcuff. ● *verb* (**-ling**) put manacles on.

manage /ˈmænɪdʒ/ *verb* (**-ging**) organize, regulate; succeed in achieving; contrive; succeed with limited resources; cope; succeed in controlling; cope with. □ **managing director** director with executive control or authority. □ **manageable** *adjective*.

management *noun* managing, being managed; administration; people managing a business.

manager *noun* person controlling or administering business etc.; person controlling activities of person, team, etc.; person who manages money etc. in specified way. □ **managerial** /-ˈdʒɪərɪəl/ *adjective*.

manageress /mænɪdʒə'res/ *noun* woman manager, esp. of shop, hotel, etc.

mañana /mæn'jɑːnə/ *adverb & noun* some time in the future. [Spanish]

manatee /mænə'tiː/ *noun* large aquatic plant-eating mammal.

Mancunian /mæŋ'kjuːnɪən/ ● *noun* native of Manchester. ● *adjective* of Manchester.

mandarin /ˈmændərɪn/ *noun* (**Mandarin**) official language of China; *historical* Chinese official; influential person, esp. bureaucrat; (in full **mandarin orange**) tangerine.

mandate /ˈmændeɪt/ ● *noun* official command; authority given by electors to government etc.; authority to act for another. ● *verb* (**-ting**) instruct (delegate) how to act or vote.

mandatory /ˈmændətərɪ/ *adjective* compulsory; of or conveying a command.

mandible /ˈmændɪb(ə)l/ *noun* jaw, esp. lower one; either part of bird's beak; either half of crushing organ in mouth-parts of insect etc.

mandolin /mændə'lɪn/ *noun* kind of lute with paired metal strings plucked with a plectrum.

mandrake /ˈmændreɪk/ *noun* narcotic plant with forked root.

mandrill /ˈmændrɪl/ *noun* large W. African baboon.

mane *noun* long hair on horse's or lion's neck; *colloquial* person's long hair.

manège /mæ'neɪʒ/ noun riding-school; movements of trained horse; horsemanship.

maneuver US = MANOEUVRE.

manful adjective brave, resolute. □ **manfully** adverb.

manganese /'mæŋgəniːz/ noun grey brittle metallic element; black oxide of this.

mange /meɪndʒ/ noun skin disease of dogs etc.

mangel-wurzel /'mæŋg(ə)l wɜːz(ə)l/ noun large beet used as cattle food.

manger /'meɪndʒə/ noun eating-trough in stable.

mangle[1] /'mæŋg(ə)l/ verb (**-ling**) hack, cut about; mutilate, spoil.

mangle[2] /'mæŋg(ə)l/ ● noun machine with rollers for pressing water out of washed clothes. ● verb (**-ling**) put through mangle.

mango /'mæŋgəʊ/ noun (plural **-es** or **-s**) tropical fruit with yellowish flesh; tree bearing it.

mangold /'mæŋg(ə)ld/ noun mangel-wurzel.

mangrove /'mæŋgrəʊv/ noun tropical seashore tree with many tangled roots above ground.

mangy /'meɪndʒɪ/ adjective (**-ier**, **-iest**) having mange; squalid, shabby.

manhandle verb (**-ling**) colloquial handle roughly; move by human effort.

manhood noun state of being a man; manliness; a man's sexual potency; men of a country.

mania /'meɪnɪə/ noun mental illness marked by excitement and violence; (often + for) excessive enthusiasm, obsession.

maniac /'meɪnɪæk/ ● noun colloquial person behaving wildly; colloquial obsessive enthusiast; person suffering from mania. ● adjective of or behaving like maniac. □ **maniacal** /mə'naɪək(ə)l/ adjective.

manic /'mænɪk/ adjective of or affected by mania. □ **manic-depressive** adjective relating to mental disorder with alternating periods of elation and depression, noun person having such disorder.

manicure /'mænɪkjʊə/ ● noun cosmetic treatment of the hands. ● verb (**-ring**) give manicure to. □ **manicurist** noun.

manifest /'mænɪfest/ ● adjective clear to sight or mind; indubitable. ● verb make manifest; (**manifest itself**) reveal itself. ● noun cargo or passenger list. □ **manifestation** noun; **manifestly** adverb.

manifesto /mænɪ'festəʊ/ noun (plural **-s**) declaration of policies.

manifold /'mænɪfəʊld/ ● adjective many and various; having various forms, applications, parts, etc. ● noun manifold thing; pipe etc. with several outlets.

manikin /'mænɪkɪn/ noun little man, dwarf.

Manila /mə'nɪlə/ noun strong fibre of Philippine tree; (also **manila**) strong brown paper made of this.

manipulate /mə'nɪpjʊleɪt/ verb (**-ting**) handle, esp. with skill; manage to one's own advantage, esp. unfairly. □ **manipulation** noun; **manipulator** noun.

manipulative /mə'nɪpjʊlətɪv/ adjective tending to exploit a situation, person, etc., for one's own ends.

mankind noun human species.

manly adjective (**-ier**, **-iest**) having qualities associated with or befitting a man. □ **manliness** noun.

manna /'mænə/ noun food miraculously supplied to Israelites in wilderness.

mannequin /'mænɪkɪn/ noun fashion model; dummy for display of clothes.

manner /'mænə/ noun way thing is done or happens; (in plural) social behaviour; style; (in plural) polite behaviour; outward bearing, way of speaking, etc.; kind, sort.

mannered adjective behaving in specified way; showing mannerisms.

mannerism noun distinctive gesture or feature of style; excessive use of these in art etc.

mannerly adjective well-behaved, polite.

mannish adjective (of woman) masculine in appearance or manner; characteristic of man as opposed to woman.

manoeuvre /mə'nuːvə/ (US **maneuver**) ● noun planned movement of vehicle or troops; (in plural) large-scale exercise of troops etc.; agile or skilful movement; artful plan. ● verb (**-ring**) move (thing, esp. vehicle) carefully; perform or cause to perform manoeuvres; manipulate by scheming or adroitness; use artifice. □ **manoeuvrable** adjective.

manor /'mænə/ noun large country house with lands; historical feudal lordship over lands. □ **manorial** /mə'nɔːrɪəl/ adjective.

mansard /'mænsɑːd/ noun roof with 4 sloping sides, each of which becomes steeper halfway down.

manse /mæns/ noun (esp. Scottish Presbyterian) minister's house.

mansion /'mænʃ(ə)n/ noun large grand house; (in plural) block of flats.

manslaughter noun unintentional but not accidental unlawful killing of human being.

mantel /'mænt(ə)l/ noun mantelpiece, mantelshelf. □ **mantelpiece** structure above and around fireplace, mantelshelf; **mantelshelf** shelf above fireplace.

mantilla /mæn'tɪlə/ noun Spanish woman's lace scarf worn over head and shoulders.

mantis /'mæntɪs/ noun (plural same or **mantises**) kind of predatory insect.

mantle /'mænt(ə)l/ ● noun loose sleeveless cloak; covering; fragile tube round gas jet to give incandescent light. ● verb (**-ling**) clothe; conceal, envelop.

manual /'mænjʊəl/ ● adjective of or done with hands. ● noun reference book; organ keyboard played with hands, not feet. □ **manually** adverb.

manufacture /mænjʊ'fæktʃə/ ● noun making of articles, esp. in factory etc.; branch of industry. ● verb (**-ring**) make, esp. on industrial scale; invent, fabricate. □ **manufacturer** noun.

manure /mə'njʊə/ ● noun fertilizer, esp. dung. ● verb (**-ring**) treat with manure.

manuscript /'mænjʊskrɪpt/ ● noun book or document written by hand or typed, not printed. ● adjective written by hand.

Manx ● adjective of Isle of Man. ● noun Celtic language of Isle of Man. □ **Manx cat** tailless variety.

many /'menɪ/ ● adjective (**more**, **most**) numerous, great in number. ● noun (treated as plural) many people or things; (**the many**) the majority of people.

Maori /'maʊrɪ/ ● noun (plural same or **-s**) member of aboriginal NZ race; their language. ● adjective of this people.

map ● noun flat representation of (part of) earth's surface, or of sky; diagram. ● verb (**-pp-**) represent on map. □ **map out** plan in detail.

maple /'meɪp(ə)l/ noun kind of tree. □ **maple leaf** emblem of Canada; **maple sugar** sugar got by evaporating sap of some kinds of maple; **maple syrup** syrup got from maple sap or maple sugar.

maquette /mə'ket/ noun preliminary model or sketch.

Mar. abbreviation March.

mar verb (**-rr-**) spoil; disfigure.

marabou /'mærəbuː/ noun (plural **-s**) large W. African stork; its down as trimming etc.

maraca /mə'rækə/ noun clublike bean-filled gourd etc., shaken as percussion instrument.

maraschino /mærəˈskiːnəʊ/ noun (plural **-s**) liqueur made from cherries. □ **maraschino cherry** one preserved in maraschino.

marathon /ˈmærəθ(ə)n/ noun long-distance foot race; long-lasting, esp. difficult, undertaking.

maraud /məˈrɔːd/ verb make raid; pillage. □ **marauder** noun.

marble /ˈmɑːb(ə)l/ ● noun kind of limestone used in sculpture and architecture; anything of or like marble; small ball of glass etc. as toy; (in plural; treated as singular) game played with these; (in plural) slang one's mental faculties; (in plural) collection of sculptures. ● verb (**-ling**) (esp. as **marbled** adjective) give veined or mottled appearance to (esp. paper).

marcasite /ˈmɑːkəsaɪt/ noun crystalline iron sulphide; crystals of this used in jewellery.

March noun third month of year. □ **March hare** hare in breeding season.

march[1] ● verb walk in military manner or with regular paces; proceed steadily; cause to march or walk. ● noun act of marching; uniform military step; long difficult walk; procession as demonstration; progress; piece of music suitable for marching to. □ **march past** ceremonial march of troops past saluting point. □ **marcher** noun.

march[2] noun historical boundary (often in plural); tract of (often disputed) land between countries etc.

marchioness /mɑːʃəˈnes/ noun marquess's wife or widow; woman holding rank of marquess.

mare /meə/ noun female equine animal, esp. horse. □ **mare's nest** illusory discovery.

margarine /mɑːdʒəˈriːn/ noun butter substitute made from edible oils etc.

marge /mɑːdʒ/ noun colloquial margarine.

margin /ˈmɑːdʒɪn/ noun edge or border of surface; plain space round printed page etc.; amount by which thing exceeds, falls short, etc. □ **margin of error** allowance for miscalculation or mischance.

marginal adjective written in margin; of or at edge; (of constituency) having elected MP with small majority; close to limit, esp. of profitability; insignificant; barely adequate. □ **marginally** adverb.

marginalize verb (also **-ise**) (**-zing** or **-sing**) make or treat as insignificant. □ **marginalization** noun.

marguerite /mɑːɡəˈriːt/ noun ox-eye daisy.

marigold /ˈmærɪɡəʊld/ noun plant with golden or bright yellow flowers.

marijuana /mærɪˈhwɑːnə/ noun dried leaves etc. of hemp smoked as drug.

marimba /məˈrɪmbə/ noun African and Central American xylophone; orchestral instrument developed from this.

marina /məˈriːnə/ noun harbour for pleasure boats.

marinade /mærɪˈneɪd/ ● noun mixture of wine, vinegar, oil, spices, etc., for soaking fish or meat. ● verb (**-ding**) soak in marinade.

marinate /ˈmærɪneɪt/ verb (**-ting**) marinade.

marine /məˈriːn/ ● adjective of, found in, or produced by, the sea; of shipping; for use at sea. ● noun member of corps trained to fight on land or sea; country's shipping, fleet, or navy.

mariner /ˈmærɪnə/ noun seaman.

marionette /mærɪəˈnet/ noun puppet worked with strings.

marital /ˈmærɪt(ə)l/ adjective of or between husband and wife; of marriage.

maritime /ˈmærɪtaɪm/ adjective connected with the sea or seafaring; living or found near the sea.

marjoram /ˈmɑːdʒərəm/ noun aromatic herb used in cookery.

mark[1] ● noun visible sign left by person or thing; stain, scar, etc; written or printed symbol; number or letter denoting conduct or proficiency; (often + of) sign, indication; lasting effect; target, thing aimed at; line etc. serving to indicate position; (followed by numeral) particular design of piece of equipment. ● verb make mark on; distinguish with mark; correct and assess (student's work etc.); attach price to; notice, observe; characterize; acknowledge, celebrate; indicate on map etc.; keep close to (opposing player) in games; (in passive) have natural marks. □ **mark down** reduce price of; **mark off** separate by boundary; **mark out** plan (course), destine, trace out (boundaries etc.); **mark time** march on spot without moving forward, await opportunity to advance; **mark up** verb increase price of; **mark-up** noun amount added to price by retailer for profit.

mark[2] noun Deutschmark.

marked /mɑːkt/ adjective having a visible mark; clearly noticeable. □ **markedly** /-kɪdlɪ/ adverb.

marker noun thing that marks a position; person or thing that marks; pen with broad felt tip; scorer, esp. at billiards.

market /ˈmɑːkɪt/ ● noun gathering for sale of commodities, livestock, etc.; space for this; (often + for) demand for commodity etc.; place or group providing such demand; conditions for buying and selling; stock market. ● verb (**-t-**) offer for sale; archaic buy or sell goods in market. □ **market garden** place where vegetables are grown for market; **market-place** open space for market, commercial world; **market research** surveying of consumers' needs and preferences; **market town** town where market is held; **market value** value as saleable thing; **on the market** offered for sale. □ **marketing** noun.

marketable adjective able or fit to be sold.

marking noun (usually in plural) identification mark; colouring of fur, feathers, etc.

marksman /ˈmɑːksmən/ noun skilled shot, esp. with rifle. □ **marksmanship** noun.

marl noun soil composed of clay and lime, used as fertilizer.

marlinspike /ˈmɑːlɪnspaɪk/ noun pointed tool used to separate strands of rope or wire.

marmalade /ˈmɑːməleɪd/ noun preserve of oranges or other citrus fruit.

Marmite /ˈmɑːmaɪt/ noun proprietary term thick brown spread made from yeast and vegetable extract.

marmoreal /mɑːˈmɔːrɪəl/ adjective of or like marble.

marmoset /ˈmɑːməzet/ noun small bushy-tailed monkey.

marmot /ˈmɑːmət/ noun burrowing rodent with short bushy tail.

marocain /ˈmærəkeɪn/ noun fabric of ribbed crêpe.

maroon[1] /məˈruːn/ adjective & noun brownish-crimson.

maroon[2] /məˈruːn/ verb put and leave ashore on desolate island or coast; leave stranded.

marquee /mɑːˈkiː/ noun large tent.

marquess /ˈmɑːkwəs/ noun British nobleman ranking between duke and earl.

marquetry /ˈmɑːkɪtrɪ/ noun inlaid work in wood etc.

marquis /ˈmɑːkwɪs/ noun (plural **-quises**) foreign nobleman ranking between duke and count.

marquise /mɑːˈkiːz/ noun marquis's wife or widow; woman holding rank of marquis.

marriage /ˈmærɪdʒ/ noun legal union of man and woman for the purpose of living together; act or ceremony establishing this; particular matrimonial union. □ **marriage certificate, lines** certificate stating that marriage has taken place; **marriage guidance** counselling of people with marital problems.

marriageable adjective free, ready, or fit for marriage.

marrow /'mærəʊ/ noun large fleshy gourd, cooked as vegetable; bone marrow. □ **marrowbone** bone containing edible marrow; **marrowfat** kind of large pea.

marry /'mærɪ/ verb (**-ies, -ied**) take, join, or give in marriage; enter into marriage; (+ *into*) become member of (family) by marriage; unite intimately.

Marsala /mɑːˈsɑːlə/ noun dark sweet fortified wine.

Marseillaise /mɑːseɪˈjeɪz/ noun French national anthem.

marsh noun low watery ground. □ **marsh gas** methane; **marsh mallow** shrubby herb; **marsh-mallow** soft sweet made from sugar, albumen, gelatin, etc. □ **marshy** adjective (**-ier, -iest**).

marshal /'mɑːʃ(ə)l/ ● noun (**Marshal**) high-ranking officer of state or in armed forces; officer arranging ceremonies, controlling procedure at races, etc. ● verb (**-ll-**) arrange in due order; conduct (person) ceremoniously. □ **marshalling yard** yard in which goods trains etc. are assembled.

marsupial /mɑːˈsuːpɪəl/ ● noun mammal giving birth to underdeveloped young subsequently carried in pouch. ● adjective of or like a marsupial.

mart noun trade centre; auction-room; market.

Martello tower /mɑːˈteləʊ/ noun small circular coastal fort.

marten /'mɑːtɪn/ noun weasel-like flesh-eating mammal with valuable fur; its fur.

martial /'mɑːʃ(ə)l/ adjective of warfare; warlike. □ **martial arts** fighting sports such as judo or karate; **martial law** military government with ordinary law suspended.

Martian /'mɑːʃ(ə)n/ ● adjective of planet Mars. ● noun hypothetical inhabitant of Mars.

martin /'mɑːtɪn/ noun bird of swallow family.

martinet /mɑːtɪˈnet/ noun strict disciplinarian.

Martini /mɑːˈtiːnɪ/ noun (plural **-s**) proprietary term type of vermouth; cocktail of gin and vermouth.

martyr /'mɑːtə/ ● noun person who undergoes death or suffering for great cause; (+ *to*) colloquial constant sufferer from. ● verb put to death as martyr; torment. □ **martyrdom** noun.

marvel /'mɑːv(ə)l/ ● noun wonderful thing; (+ *of*) wonderful example of. ● verb (**-ll-**; US **-l-**) (+ *at, that*) feel surprise or wonder.

marvellous /'mɑːvələs/ adjective (US **marvelous**) astonishing; excellent. □ **marvellously** adverb.

Marxism /'mɑːksɪz(ə)m/ noun doctrines of Marx, predicting common ownership of means of production. □ **Marxist** noun & adjective.

marzipan /'mɑːzɪpæn/ noun paste of ground almonds, sugar, etc.

mascara /mæsˈkɑːrə/ noun cosmetic for darkening eyelashes.

mascot /'mæskɒt/ noun person, animal, or thing supposed to bring luck.

masculine /'mæskjʊlɪn/ adjective of men; manly; *Grammar* belonging to gender including words for most male people and animals. □ **masculinity** /-'lɪn-/ noun.

maser /'meɪzə/ noun device for amplifying or generating microwaves.

mash ● noun soft or confused mixture; mixture of boiled bran etc. fed to horses; colloquial mashed potatoes. ● verb crush (potatoes etc.) to pulp.

mask /mɑːsk/ ● noun covering for all or part of face, worn as disguise or for protection, or by surgeon etc. to prevent infection of patient; respirator; likeness of person's face, esp. one made by taking mould from face; disguise. ● verb cover with mask; conceal; protect.

masochism /'mæsəkɪz(ə)m/ noun pleasure in suffering physical or mental pain, esp. as form of sexual perversion. □ **masochist** noun; **masochistic** /-'kɪs-/ adjective.

mason /'meɪs(ə)n/ noun person who builds with stone; (**Mason**) Freemason.

Masonic /məˈsɒnɪk/ adjective of Freemasons.

masonry /'meɪsənrɪ/ noun stonework; mason's work; (**Masonry**) Freemasonry.

masque /mɑːsk/ noun musical drama with mime, esp. in 16th & 17th c.

masquerade /mæskəˈreɪd/ ● noun false show, pretence; masked ball. ● verb (**-ding**) appear in disguise; assume false appearance.

mass¹ ● noun cohesive body of matter; dense aggregation; (in *singular* or *plural*; usually + *of*) large number or amount; (usually + *of*) unbroken expanse (of colour etc.); (**the mass**) the majority; (**the masses**) ordinary people; *Physics* quantity of matter body contains. ● verb gather into mass; assemble into one body. ● adjective of or relating to large numbers of people or things. □ **mass media** means of communication to large numbers of people; **mass production** mechanical production of large quantities of standardized article.

mass² noun (often **Mass**) Eucharist, esp. in RC Church; (musical setting of) liturgy used in this.

massacre /'mæsəkə/ ● noun general slaughter. ● verb (**-ring**) make massacre of.

massage /'mæsɑːʒ/ ● noun kneading and rubbing of muscles etc., usually with hands. ● verb (**-ging**) treat thus.

masseur /mæˈsɜː/ noun (feminine **masseuse** /mæˈsɜːz/) person who gives massage.

massif /'mæsiːf/ noun mountain heights forming compact group.

massive /'mæsɪv/ adjective large and heavy or solid; unusually large or severe; substantial. □ **massively** adverb.

mast¹ /mɑːst/ noun upright to which ship's yards and sails are attached; tall metal structure supporting radio or television aerial; flag-pole.

mast² /mɑːst/ noun fruit of beech, oak, etc., esp. as food for pigs.

mastectomy /mæˈstektəmɪ/ noun (plural **-ies**) surgical removal of a breast.

master /'mɑːstə/ ● noun person having control or ownership; ship's captain; male teacher; prevailing person; skilled workman; skilled practitioner; holder of university degree above bachelor's; revered teacher; great artist; *Chess etc.* player at international level; thing from which series of copies is made; (**Master**) *title prefixed to name of boy.* ● adjective commanding; main, principal; controlling others. ● verb overcome, conquer; acquire complete knowledge of. □ **master-key** one opening several different locks; **mastermind** noun person with outstanding intellect, verb plan and direct (enterprise); **Master of Ceremonies** person introducing speakers at banquet or entertainers at variety show; **masterpiece** outstanding piece of artistry, one's best work; **master-switch** switch controlling electricity etc. supply to entire system.

masterful adjective imperious, domineering; very skilful. □ **masterfully** adverb.

■ **Usage** *Masterful* is normally used of a person, whereas *masterly* is used of achievements, abilities, etc.

masterly adjective very skilful.

■ **Usage** See note at MASTERFUL.

mastery *noun* control, dominance; (often + *of*) comprehensive skill or knowledge.

mastic /'mæstɪk/ *noun* gum or resin from certain trees; such tree; waterproof filler and sealant.

masticate /'mæstɪkeɪt/ *verb* (**-ting**) chew. □ **mastication** *noun*.

mastiff /'mæstɪf/ *noun* large strong kind of dog.

mastodon /'mæstədɒn/ *noun* (*plural* same or **-s**) extinct animal resembling elephant.

mastoid /'mæstɔɪd/ ● *adjective* shaped like woman's breast. ● *noun* (in full **mastoid process**) conical prominence on temporal bone; (usually in *plural*) colloquial inflammation of mastoid.

masturbate /'mæstəbeɪt/ *verb* (**-ting**) produce sexual arousal (of) by manual stimulation of genitals. □ **masturbation** *noun*.

mat[1] ● *noun* piece of coarse fabric on floor, esp. for wiping shoes on; piece of material laid on table etc. to protect surface. ● *verb* (**-tt-**) (esp. as **matted** *adjective*) bring or come into thickly tangled state. □ **on the mat** *slang* being reprimanded.

mat[2] = MATT.

matador /'mætədɔ:/ *noun* bullfighter whose task is to kill bull.

match[1] ● *noun* contest, game; person or thing equal to, exactly resembling, or corresponding to another; marriage; person viewed as marriage prospect. ● *verb* be equal, correspond; be or find match for; (+ *against*, *with*) place in conflict or competition with. □ **matchboard** tongued and grooved board fitting into others; **matchmaker** person who arranges marriages or schemes to bring couples together; **match point** state of game when one side needs only one point to win match; **match up** (often + *with*) fit to form whole, tally; **match up to** be equal to.

match[2] *noun* short thin piece of wood etc., tipped with substance that ignites when rubbed on rough or specially prepared surface. □ **matchbox** box for holding matches; **matchstick** stem of match; **matchwood** wood suitable for matches, minute splinters.

matchless *adjective* incomparable.

mate[1] ● *noun* companion, fellow worker; colloquial *form of address*, esp. *to another man*; each of a breeding pair, esp. of birds; colloquial partner in marriage; subordinate officer on merchant ship; assistant to worker. ● *verb* (**-ting**) come or bring together for breeding.

mate[2] *noun & verb* (**-ting**) checkmate.

material /mə'tɪərɪəl/ ● *noun* that from which thing is made; cloth, fabric; (in *plural*) things needed for activity; person or thing of specified kind or suitable for purpose; (in *singular* or *plural*) information etc. for book etc.; (in *singular* or *plural*) elements. ● *adjective* of matter; not spiritual; of bodily comfort etc.; important, relevant.

materialism *noun* greater interest in material possessions and comfort than in spiritual values; theory that nothing exists but matter. □ **materialist** *noun*; **materialistic** /-'lɪs-/ *adjective*.

materialize *verb* (also **-ise**) (**-zing** or **-sing**) become fact, happen; colloquial appear, be present; represent in or assume bodily form. □ **materialization** *noun*.

maternal /mə'tɜ:n(ə)l/ *adjective* of or like a mother; motherly; related on mother's side.

maternity /mə'tɜ:nɪtɪ/ ● *noun* motherhood; motherliness. ● *adjective* for women in pregnancy or childbirth.

matey *adjective* (also **maty**) (**-tier**, **-tiest**) familiar and friendly. □ **matily** *adverb*.

math *noun* US colloquial mathematics.

mathematics /mæθə'mætɪks/ *plural noun* (also treated as *singular*) science of space, number, and quantity. □ **mathematical** *adjective*; **mathematician** /-mə'tɪʃ(ə)n/ *noun*.

maths *noun* colloquial mathematics.

matinée /'mætɪneɪ/ *noun* (US **matinee**) theatrical etc. performance in afternoon. ● **matinée coat** baby's short coat.

matins /'mætɪnz/ *noun* (also **mattins**) morning prayer.

matriarch /'meɪtrɪɑ:k/ *noun* female head of family or tribe. □ **matriarchal** /-'ɑ:k(ə)l/ *adjective*.

matriarchy /'meɪtrɪɑ:kɪ/ *noun* (*plural* **-ies**) female-dominated system of society.

matrices *plural of* MATRIX.

matricide /'meɪtrɪsaɪd/ *noun* killing of one's mother; person who does this.

matriculate /mə'trɪkjʊleɪt/ *verb* (**-ting**) admit (student) to university; be thus admitted. □ **matriculation** *noun*.

matrimony /'mætrɪmənɪ/ *noun* marriage. □ **matrimonial** /-'məʊnɪəl/ *adjective*.

matrix /'meɪtrɪks/ *noun* (*plural* **matrices** /-si:z/ or **-es**) mould in which thing is cast or shaped; place etc. in which thing is developed; rock in which gems etc. are embedded; *Mathematics* rectangular array of quantities treated as single quantity.

matron /'meɪtrən/ *noun* woman in charge of nursing in hospital; married, esp. staid, woman; woman nurse and housekeeper at school etc.

matronly *adjective* like a matron, esp. portly or staid.

matt *adjective* (also **mat**) dull, not shiny or glossy.

matter /'mætə/ ● *noun* physical substance; thing(s), material; (**the matter**; often + *with*) thing that is amiss; content as opposed to form, substance; affair, concern; purulent discharge. ● *verb* (often + *to*) be of importance. □ **a matter of** approximately, amounting to; **matter of course** natural or expected thing; **matter-of-fact** prosaic, unimaginative, unemotional; **no matter** (+ *when*, *how*, etc.) regardless of.

matting *noun* fabric for mats.

mattins = MATINS.

mattock /'mætək/ *noun* tool like pickaxe with adze and chisel edge as ends of head.

mattress /'mætrɪs/ *noun* fabric case filled with soft or firm material or springs, used on or as bed.

mature /mə'tʃʊə/ ● *adjective* (**-r**, **-st**) fully developed, ripe; adult; careful, considered; (of bill etc.) due for payment. ● *verb* (**-ring**) bring to or reach mature state. □ **maturity** *noun*.

matutinal /mætju:'taɪn(ə)l/ *adjective* of or in morning.

maty = MATEY.

maudlin /'mɔ:dlɪn/ *adjective* weakly sentimental.

maul /mɔ:l/ ● *verb* injure by clawing etc.; handle roughly; damage. ● *noun* *Rugby* loose scrum; brawl; heavy hammer.

maulstick /'mɔ:lstɪk/ *noun* stick held to support hand in painting.

maunder /'mɔ:ndə/ *verb* talk ramblingly.

Maundy /'mɔ:ndɪ/ *noun* distribution of **Maundy money**, silver coins minted for English sovereign to give to the poor on **Maundy Thursday**, Thursday before Easter.

mausoleum /mɔ:sə'li:əm/ *noun* magnificent tomb.

mauve /məʊv/ *adjective & noun* pale purple.

maverick /'mævərɪk/ *noun* unorthodox or independent-minded person; US unbranded calf etc.

maw *noun* stomach of animal.

mawkish /'mɔ:kɪʃ/ *adjective* feebly sentimental.

maxillary /mæk'sɪlərɪ/ *adjective* of the jaw.

maxim /'mæksɪm/ *noun* general truth or rule of conduct briefly expressed.

maxima *plural* of MAXIMUM.

maximal /'mæksɪm(ə)l/ *adjective* greatest possible in size, duration, etc.

maximize /'mæksɪmaɪz/ *verb* (also **-ise**) (**-zing** or **-sing**) make as large or great as possible. □ **maximization** *noun*.

■ **Usage** *Maximize* should not be used in standard English to mean 'to make as good as possible' or 'to make the most of'.

maximum /'mæksɪməm/ ● *noun* (*plural* **maxima**) highest possible amount, size, etc. ● *adjective* greatest in amount, size, etc.

May *noun* fifth month of year; (**may**) hawthorn, esp. in blossom. □ **May Day** 1 May as Spring festival or as international holiday in honour of workers; **mayfly** insect living briefly in spring as adult; **maypole** decorated pole danced round on May Day; **May queen** girl chosen to preside over May Day festivities.

may *auxiliary verb* (*3rd singular present* **may**; *past* **might** /maɪt/) *expressing possibility, permission, request, wish, etc.* □ **be that as it may** although that is possible.

■ **Usage** Both *can* and *may* are used for asking permission, as in *Can I move?* and *May I move?*, but *may* is better in formal English because *Can I move?* also means 'Am I physically able to move?'

maybe /'meɪbi/ *adverb* perhaps.

mayday /'meɪdeɪ/ *noun* international radio distress signal.

mayhem /'meɪhem/ *noun* destruction, havoc.

mayonnaise /meɪə'neɪz/ *noun* creamy dressing of oil, egg yolk, vinegar, etc.; dish dressed with this.

mayor /meə/ *noun* head of corporation of city or borough; head of district council with status of borough. □ **mayoral** *adjective*.

mayoralty /'meərəlti/ *noun* (*plural* **-ies**) office of mayor; period of this.

mayoress /'meərɪs/ *noun* woman mayor; wife or consort of mayor.

maze *noun* network of paths and hedges designed as puzzle; labyrinth; confused network, mass, etc.

mazurka /mə'zɜːkə/ *noun* lively Polish dance in triple time; music for this.

MB *abbreviation* Bachelor of Medicine.

MBE *abbreviation* Member of the Order of the British Empire.

MC *abbreviation* Master of Ceremonies; Military Cross.

MCC *abbreviation* Marylebone Cricket Club.

MD *abbreviation* Doctor of Medicine; Managing Director.

me¹ /miː/ *pronoun used by speaker or writer to refer to himself or herself as object of verb*; *colloquial* I.

■ **Usage** Some people consider it correct to use only *It is I*, but this is very formal or old-fashioned in most situations, and *It is me* is normally quite acceptable. On the other hand, it is not standard English to say *Me and him went* rather than *He and I went*.

me² /miː/ *noun* (also **mi**) *Music* third note of scale in tonic sol-fa.

mead *noun* alcoholic drink of fermented honey and water.

meadow /'medəʊ/ *noun* piece of grassland, esp. used for hay; low ground, esp. near river. □ **meadowsweet** a fragrant flowering plant.

meagre /'miːgə/ *adjective* (*US* **meager**) scanty in amount or quality.

meal¹ *noun* occasion when food is eaten; the food eaten on one occasion. □ **meal-ticket** *colloquial* source of income.

meal² *noun* grain or pulse ground to powder.

mealy *adjective* (**-ier, -iest**) of, like, or containing meal. □ **mealy-mouthed** afraid to speak plainly.

mean¹ *verb* (*past & past participle* **meant** /ment/) have as one's purpose, design; intend to convey or indicate; involve, portend; (of word) have as equivalent in same or another language; (+ *to*) be of specified significance to.

mean² *adjective* niggardly; not generous; ignoble; of low degree or poor quality; malicious; *US* vicious, aggressive. □ **meanness** *noun*.

mean³ ● *noun* condition, quality, or course of action equally far from two extremes; term midway between first and last terms of progression; quotient of the sum of several quantities and their number. ● *adjective* (of quantity) equally far from two extremes; calculated as mean.

meander /mɪ'ændə/ ● *verb* wander at random; wind about. ● *noun* (in *plural*) sinuous windings; circuitous journey.

meaning ● *noun* what is meant; significance. ● *adjective* expressive; significant. □ **meaningfully** *adverb*; **meaningless** *adjective*; **meaninglessness** *noun*.

means *plural noun* (often treated as *singular*) action, agent, device, or method producing result; money resources. □ **means test** inquiry into financial resources of applicant for assistance etc.

meantime ● *adverb* meanwhile. ● *noun* intervening period.

meanwhile *adverb* in the intervening time; at the same time.

measles /'miːz(ə)lz/ *plural noun* (also treated as *singular*) infectious viral disease with red rash.

measly /'miːzlɪ/ *adjective* (**-ier, -iest**) *colloquial* meagre, contemptible.

measure /'meʒə/ ● *noun* size or quantity found by measuring; system or unit of measuring; vessel, rod, tape, etc., for measuring; degree, extent; factor determining evaluation etc.; (usually in *plural*) suitable action; legislative enactment; prescribed extent or amount; poetic metre. ● *verb* (**-ring**) find size, quantity, proportions, etc. of by comparison with known standard; be of specified size; estimate by some criterion; (often + *off*) mark (line etc. of given length); (+ *out*) distribute in measured quantities; (+ *with, against*) bring into competition with. □ **measurable** *adjective*; **measurement** *noun*.

measured *adjective* rhythmical; (of language) carefully considered.

measureless *adjective* not measurable; infinite.

meat *noun* animal flesh as food; (often + *of*) chief part.

meaty *adjective* (**-ier, -iest**) full of meat; fleshy; of or like meat; substantial, satisfying.

Mecca /'mekə/ *noun* place one aspires to visit.

mechanic /mɪ'kænɪk/ *noun* person skilled in using or repairing machinery.

mechanical *adjective* of, working, or produced by, machines or mechanism; automatic; lacking originality; of mechanics as a science. □ **mechanically** *adverb*.

mechanics /mɪ'kænɪks/ *plural noun* (usually treated as *singular*) branch of applied mathematics dealing with motion; science of machinery; routine technical aspects of thing.

mechanism /'mekənɪz(ə)m/ *noun* structure or parts of machine; system of parts working together; process, method.

mechanize /'mekənaɪz/ verb (also **-ise**) (**-zing** or **-sing**) introduce machines in; make mechanical; equip with tanks, armoured cars, etc. □ **mechanization** noun.

medal /'med(ə)l/ noun commemorative metal disc etc., esp. awarded for military or sporting prowess.

medallion /mɪ'dæljən/ noun large medal; thing so shaped, e.g. portrait.

medallist /'medəlɪst/ noun (US **medalist**) winner of (specified) medal.

meddle /'med(ə)l/ verb (**-ling**) (often + with, in) interfere in others' concerns.

meddlesome adjective interfering.

media plural of MEDIUM.

■ **Usage** It is a mistake to use media with a singular verb, as in The media is biased.

mediaeval = MEDIEVAL.

median /'mi:dɪən/ ● adjective situated in the middle. ● noun straight line from angle of triangle to middle of opposite side; middle value of series.

mediate /'mi:dɪeɪt/ verb (**-ting**) act as go-between or peacemaker. □ **mediation** noun; **mediator** noun.

medical /'medɪk(ə)l/ ● adjective of medicine in general or as distinct from surgery. ● noun colloquial medical examination. □ **medical certificate** certificate of fitness or unfitness to work etc.; **medical examination** examination to determine person's physical fitness. □ **medically** adverb.

medicament /mɪ'dɪkəmənt/ noun substance used in curative treatment.

medicate /'medɪkeɪt/ verb (**-ting**) treat medically; impregnate with medicinal substance.

medication /medɪ'keɪʃ(ə)n/ noun medicinal drug; treatment using drugs.

medicinal /mə'dɪsɪn(ə)l/ adjective (of substance) healing.

medicine /'meds(ə)n/ noun science or practice of diagnosis, treatment, and prevention of disease, esp. as distinct from surgery; substance, esp. one taken by mouth, used in this. □ **medicine man** witchdoctor.

medieval /medi'i:v(ə)l/ adjective (also **mediaeval**) of Middle Ages.

mediocre /mi:dɪ'əʊkə/ adjective indifferent in quality; second-rate.

mediocrity /mi:dɪ'ɒkrɪtɪ/ noun (plural **-ies**) being mediocre; mediocre person.

meditate /'medɪteɪt/ verb (**-ting**) engage in (esp. religious) contemplation; plan mentally. □ **meditation** noun; **meditative** /-tətɪv/ adjective.

Mediterranean /medɪtə'reɪnɪən/ adjective of the sea between Europe and N. Africa, or the countries bordering on it.

medium /'mi:dɪəm/ ● noun (plural **media** or **-s**) middle quality, degree, etc. between extremes; environment; means of communication; physical material or form used by artist, composer, etc.; (plural **-s**) person claiming to communicate with the dead. ● adjective between two qualities etc.; average, moderate. □ **medium-range** (of aircraft, missile, etc.) able to travel medium distance.

medlar /'medlə/ noun tree bearing fruit like apple, eaten when decayed; such fruit.

medley /'medlɪ/ noun (plural **-s**) varied mixture.

medulla /mɪ'dʌlə/ noun inner part of certain bodily organs; soft internal tissue of plants. □ **medulla oblongata** /ɒblɒŋ'gɑ:tə/ lowest part of brainstem. □ **medullary** adjective.

meek adjective humble and submissive or gentle. □ **meekly** adverb; **meekness** noun.

meerschaum /'mɪəʃəm/ noun soft white clay-like substance; tobacco pipe with bowl made from this.

meet¹ ● verb (past & past participle **met**) encounter or (of two or more people) come together; be present at arrival of (person, train, etc.); come into contact (with); make acquaintance of; deal with (demand etc.); (often + with) experience, receive. ● noun assembly for a hunt; assembly for athletics.

meet² adjective archaic fitting, proper.

meeting noun coming together; assembly of esp. a society, committee, etc.; race meeting.

mega- combining form large; one million; slang extremely, very big.

megabyte /'megəbaɪt/ noun 2²⁰ bytes (approx. 1,000,000) as unit of computer storage.

megalith /'megəlɪθ/ noun large stone, esp. prehistoric monument. □ **megalithic** /-'lɪθ-/ adjective.

megalomania /megələ'meɪnɪə/ noun mental disorder producing delusions of grandeur; passion for grandiose schemes. □ **megalomaniac** adjective & noun.

megaphone /'megəfəʊn/ noun large funnel-shaped device for amplifying voice.

megaton /'megətʌn/ noun unit of explosive power equal to that of 1,000,000 tons of TNT.

meiosis /maɪ'əʊsɪs/ noun (plural **meioses** /-si:z/) cell division resulting in gametes with half normal chromosome number; ironical understatement.

melamine /'meləmi:n/ noun crystalline compound producing resins; plastic made from this.

melancholia /melən'kəʊlɪə/ noun depression and anxiety.

melancholy /'melənkəlɪ/ ● noun pensive sadness; depression; tendency to this. ● adjective sad; depressing. □ **melancholic** /-'kɒl-/ adjective.

mêlée /'meleɪ/ noun (US **melee**) confused fight or scuffle; muddle.

mellifluous /mɪ'lɪflʊəs/ adjective (of voice etc.) pleasing, musical.

mellow /'meləʊ/ ● adjective (of sound, colour, light, or flavour) soft and rich, free from harshness; (of character) gentle; mature; genial. ● verb make or become mellow.

melodic /mɪ'lɒdɪk/ adjective of melody; melodious.

melodious /mɪ'ləʊdɪəs/ adjective of, producing, or having melody; sweet-sounding. □ **melodiously** adverb.

melodrama /'melədrɑ:mə/ noun sensational play etc. appealing blatantly to emotions; this type of drama. □ **melodramatic** /-drə'mæt-/ adjective.

melody /'melədɪ/ noun (plural **-ies**) arrangement of notes to make distinctive pattern; tune; principal part in harmonized music; tunefulness.

melon /'melən/ noun sweet fleshy fruit of various climbers of gourd family.

melt verb become liquid or change from solid to liquid by action of heat; dissolve; (as **molten** adjective) (esp. of metals etc.) liquefied by heat; soften, be softened; (usually + into) merge; (often + away) leave unobtrusively. □ **melt down** melt (esp. metal) for reuse, become liquid and lose structure; **melting point** temperature at which solid melts; **melting pot** place for mixing races, theories, etc.

member /'membə/ noun person etc. belonging to society, team, group, etc.; (**Member**) person elected to certain assemblies; part of larger structure; part or organ of body, esp. limb.

membership noun being a member; number or group of members.

membrane /'membreɪn/ noun pliable tissue connecting or lining organs in plants and animals; pliable sheet or skin. □ **membranous** /-brən-/ adjective.

memento /mɪ'mentəʊ/ noun (plural **-es** or **-s**) souvenir of person or event.

memo /'meməʊ/ *noun* (*plural* **-s**) *colloquial* memorandum.

memoir /'memwɑː/ *noun* historical account etc. written from personal knowledge or special sources; (in *plural*) autobiography.

memorable /'memərəb(ə)l/ *adjective* worth remembering; easily remembered. □ **memorably** *adverb*.

memorandum /memə'rændəm/ *noun* (*plural* **-da** or **-s**) note or record for future use; informal written message, esp. in business etc.

memorial /mɪ'mɔːrɪəl/ ● *noun* object etc. established in memory of person or event. ● *adjective* commemorative.

memoriam see IN MEMORIAM.

memorize /'meməraɪz/ *verb* (also **-ise**) (**-zing** or **-sing**) commit to memory.

memory /'meməri/ *noun* (*plural* **-ies**) faculty by which things are recalled to or kept in mind; store of things remembered; remembrance, esp. of person etc.; storage capacity of computer etc.; posthumous reputation.

memsahib /'memsɑːb/ *noun historical* European married woman in India.

men *plural* of MAN.

menace /'menɪs/ ● *noun* threat; dangerous thing or person; *jocular* nuisance. ● *verb* (**-cing**) threaten. □ **menacingly** *adverb*.

ménage /meɪ'nɑːʒ/ *noun* household.

menagerie /mɪ'nædʒəri/ *noun* small zoo.

mend ● *verb* restore to good condition; repair; regain health; improve. ● *noun* darn or repair in material etc. □ **on the mend** recovering, esp. in health.

mendacious /men'deɪʃəs/ *adjective* lying, untruthful. □ **mendacity** /-'dæs-/ *noun* (*plural* **-ies**).

mendicant /'mendɪkənt/ ● *adjective* begging; (of friar) living solely on alms. ● *noun* beggar; mendicant friar.

menfolk *plural noun* men, esp. men of family.

menhir /'menhɪə/ *noun* usually prehistoric monument of tall upright stone.

menial /'miːnɪəl/ ● *adjective* (of work) degrading, servile. ● *noun* domestic servant.

meningitis /menɪn'dʒaɪtɪs/ *noun* (esp. viral) infection and inflammation of membranes enclosing brain and spinal cord.

meniscus /mɪ'nɪskəs/ *noun* (*plural* **menisci** /-saɪ/) curved upper surface of liquid in tube; lens convex on one side and concave on the other.

menopause /'menəpɔːz/ *noun* ceasing of menstruation; period in woman's life when this occurs. □ **menopausal** /-'pɔːz(ə)l/ *adjective*.

menses /'mensiːz/ *plural noun* flow of menstrual blood etc.

menstrual /'menstruəl/ *adjective* of menstruation.

menstruate /'menstrueɪt/ *verb* (**-ting**) undergo menstruation.

menstruation *noun* discharge of blood etc. from uterus, usually at monthly intervals.

mensuration /mensjʊə'reɪʃ(ə)n/ *noun* measuring; measuring of lengths, areas, and volumes.

mental /'ment(ə)l/ *adjective* of, in, or done by mind; caring for mental patients; *colloquial* insane. □ **mental age** degree of mental development in terms of average age at which such development is attained; **mental deficiency** abnormally low intelligence; **mental patient** sufferer from mental illness. □ **mentally** *adverb*.

mentality /men'tælɪti/ *noun* (*plural* **-ies**) mental character or disposition.

menthol /'menθɒl/ *noun* mint-tasting organic alcohol found in oil of peppermint etc., used as flavouring and to relieve local pain.

mention /'menʃ(ə)n/ ● *verb* refer to briefly or by name; disclose. ● *noun* reference, esp. by name.

mentor /'mentɔː/ *noun* experienced and trusted adviser.

menu /'menjuː/ *noun* (*plural* **-s**) list of dishes available in restaurant etc., or to be served at meal; *Computing* list of options displayed on VDU.

MEP *abbreviation* Member of European Parliament.

mercantile /'mɜːkəntaɪl/ *adjective* of trade, trading; commercial. □ **mercantile marine** merchant shipping.

mercenary /'mɜːsɪnəri/ ● *adjective* primarily concerned with or working for money etc. ● *noun* (*plural* **-ies**) hired soldier in foreign service.

mercer /'mɜːsə/ *noun* dealer in textile fabrics.

mercerize /'mɜːsəraɪz/ *verb* (also **-ise**) (**-zing** or **-sing**) treat (cotton) with caustic alkali to strengthen and make lustrous.

merchandise /'mɜːtʃəndaɪz/ ● *noun* goods for sale. ● *verb* (**-sing**) trade (in); promote (goods, ideas, etc.).

merchant /'mɜːtʃ(ə)nt/ *noun* wholesale trader, esp. with foreign countries; *esp. US & Scottish* retail trader. □ **merchant bank** bank dealing in commercial loans and finance; **merchantman** merchant ship; **merchant navy** nation's commercial shipping; **merchant ship** ship carrying merchandise.

merchantable *adjective* saleable.

merciful /'mɜːsɪfʊl/ *adjective* showing mercy. □ **mercifulness** *noun*.

mercifully *adverb* in a merciful way; fortunately.

merciless /'mɜːsɪləs/ *adjective* showing no mercy. □ **mercilessly** *adverb*.

mercurial /mɜː'kjʊərɪəl/ *adjective* (of person) volatile; of or containing mercury.

mercury /'mɜːkjʊri/ *noun* silvery heavy liquid metal used in barometers, thermometers, etc.; (**Mercury**) planet nearest to the sun. □ **mercuric** /-'kjʊər-/ *adjective*; **mercurous** *adjective*.

mercy /'mɜːsi/ *noun* (*plural* **-ies**) compassion towards defeated enemies or offenders or as quality; act of mercy; thing to be thankful for. □ **at the mercy of** in the power of; **mercy killing** killing done out of pity.

mere¹ /mɪə/ *adjective* (**-st**) being only what is specified. □ **merely** *adverb*.

mere² /mɪə/ *noun* dialect or poetical lake.

meretricious /merə'trɪʃəs/ *adjective* showily but falsely attractive.

merganser /mɜː'gænsə/ *noun* (*plural* same or **-s**) a diving duck.

merge *verb* (**-ging**) (often + *with*) combine, join or blend gradually; (+ *in*) (cause to) lose character and identity in (something else).

merger *noun* combining, esp. of two commercial companies etc. into one.

meridian /mə'rɪdɪən/ *noun* circle of constant longitude passing through given place and N. & S. Poles; corresponding line on map etc.

meridional /mə'rɪdɪən(ə)l/ *adjective* of or in the south (esp. of Europe); of a meridian.

meringue /mə'ræŋ/ *noun* sugar, whipped egg whites, etc. baked crisp; cake of this.

merino /mə'riːnəʊ/ *noun* (*plural* **-s**) variety of sheep with long fine wool; soft material, originally of merino wool; fine woollen yarn.

merit /'merɪt/ ● *noun* quality of deserving well; excellence, worth; (usually in *plural*) thing that entitles to reward or gratitude. ● *verb* (**-t-**) deserve.

meritocracy /merɪ'tɒkrəsi/ *noun* (*plural* **-ies**) government by those selected for merit; group selected in this way.

meritorious /merɪ'tɔːrɪəs/ *adjective* praiseworthy.

merlin /'mɜːlɪn/ *noun* kind of small falcon.

mermaid /'mɜːmeɪd/ *noun* legendary creature with woman's head and trunk and fish's tail.

merry /'merɪ/ *adjective* (**-ier, -iest**) joyous; full of laughter or gaiety; *colloquial* slightly drunk. □ **merry-go-round** fairground ride with revolving model horses, cars, etc.; **merrymaking** festivity. □ **merrily** *adverb*; **merriment** *noun*.

mésalliance /meɪ'zælɪɑ̃s/ *noun* marriage with social inferior. [French]

mescal /'meskæl/ *noun* peyote cactus. □ **mescal buttons** disc-shaped dried tops from mescal, esp. as intoxicant.

mescaline /'meskəlɪn/ *noun* (also **mescalin**) hallucinogenic alkaloid present in mescal buttons.

Mesdames, Mesdemoiselles *plural of* MADAME, MADEMOISELLE.

mesh ● *noun* network structure; each of open spaces in net, sieve, etc.; (in *plural*) network, snare. ● *verb* (often + *with*) (of teeth of wheel) be engaged; be harmonious; catch in net.

mesmerize /'mezməraɪz/ *verb* (also **-ise**) (**-zing** or **-sing**) hypnotize; fascinate. □ **mesmerism** *noun*.

meso- *combining form* middle, intermediate.

mesolithic /mezəʊ'lɪθɪk/ *adjective* of Stone Age between palaeolithic and neolithic periods.

meson /'miːzɒn/ *noun* elementary particle with mass between that of electron and proton.

Mesozoic /mesəʊ'zəʊɪk/ ● *adjective* of geological era marked by development of dinosaurs. ● *noun* this era.

mess ● *noun* dirty or untidy state; state of confusion or trouble; something spilt etc.; disagreeable concoction; soldiers etc. dining together; army dining-hall; meal taken there; domestic animal's excreta; *archaic* portion of liquid or pulpy food. ● *verb* (often + *up*) make mess of, dirty, muddle; (*+ with*) interfere with; take one's meals; *colloquial* defecate. □ **make a mess of** bungle; **mess about, around** potter.

message /'mesɪdʒ/ *noun* communication sent by one person to another; exalted or spiritual communication.

messenger /'mesɪndʒə/ *noun* person who carries message(s).

Messiah /mɪ'saɪə/ *noun* promised deliverer of Jews; Jesus regarded as this. □ **Messianic** /mesɪ'ænɪk/ *adjective*.

Messieurs *plural of* MONSIEUR.

Messrs /'mesəz/ *plural of* MR.

messy *adjective* (**-ier, -iest**) untidy, dirty; causing or accompanied by a mess; difficult to deal with; awkward. □ **messily** *adverb*.

met *past & past participle of* MEET[1].

metabolism /mɪ'tæbəlɪz(ə)m/ *noun* all chemical processes in living organism producing energy and growth. □ **metabolic** /metə'bɒlɪk/ *adjective*.

metacarpus /metə'kɑːpəs/ *noun* (*plural* **-carpi** /-paɪ/) set of bones forming part of hand between wrist and fingers. □ **metacarpal** *adjective*.

metal /'met(ə)l/ ● *noun* any of class of mainly workable elements such as gold, silver, iron, or tin; alloy of any of these; (in *plural*) rails of railway; road-metal. ● *adjective* made of metal. ● *verb* (**-ll-**; *US* **-l-**) make or mend (road) with road-metal; cover or fit with metal.

metallic /mɪ'tælɪk/ *adjective* of or like metal(s); sounding like struck metal.

metallurgy /mɪ'tælədʒɪ/ *noun* science of metals and their application; extraction and purification of metals. □ **metallurgic** /metə'lɜːdʒɪk/ *adjective*; **metallurgical** /metə'lɜːdʒɪk(ə)l/ *adjective*; **metallurgist** *noun*.

metamorphic /metə'mɔːfɪk/ *adjective* of metamorphosis; (of rock) transformed naturally. □ **metamorphism** *noun*.

metamorphose /metə'mɔːfəʊz/ *verb* (**-sing**) (often + *to, into*) change in form or nature.

metamorphosis /metə'mɔːfəsɪs/ *noun* (*plural* **-phoses** /-siːz/) change of form, esp. from pupa to insect; change of character, conditions, etc.

metaphor /'metəfɔː/ *noun* application of name or description to something to which it is not literally applicable (see panel). □ **metaphoric** /-'fɒr-/ *adjective*; **metaphorical** /-'fɒr-/ *adjective*; **metaphorically** /-'fɒr-/ *adverb*.

metaphysics /metə'fɪzɪks/ *plural noun* (usually treated as *singular*) philosophy dealing with nature of existence, truth, and knowledge. □ **metaphysical** *adjective*.

metatarsus /metə'tɑːsəs/ *noun* (*plural* **-tarsi** /-saɪ/) set of bones forming part of foot between ankle and toes. □ **metatarsal** *adjective*.

mete *verb* (**-ting**) (usually + *out*) *literary* apportion, allot.

meteor /'miːtɪə/ *noun* small solid body from outer space becoming incandescent when entering earth's atmosphere.

meteoric /miːtɪ'ɒrɪk/ *adjective* rapid; dazzling; of meteors.

meteorite /'miːtɪəraɪt/ *noun* fallen meteor; fragment of rock or metal from outer space.

meteorology /miːtɪə'rɒlədʒɪ/ *noun* study of atmospheric phenomena, esp. for forecasting weather. □ **meteorological** /-rə'lɒdʒ-/ *adjective*; **meteorologist** *noun*.

meter[1] /'miːtə/ ● *noun* instrument that measures or records, esp. gas, electricity, etc. used, distance travelled, etc.; parking meter. ● *verb* measure or record by meter.

meter[2] *US* = METRE.

methane /'miːθeɪn/ *noun* colourless odourless inflammable gaseous hydrocarbon, the main constituent of natural gas.

methanol /'meθənɒl/ *noun* colourless inflammable organic liquid, used as solvent.

Metaphor

A metaphor is a figure of speech that goes further than a simile, either by saying that something is something else that it could not normally be called, e.g.

> *The moon was a ghostly galleon tossed upon cloudy seas.*
> *Stockholm, the Venice of the North*

or by suggesting that something appears, sounds, or behaves like something else, e.g.

> *burning ambition*   *blindingly obvious*
> *the long arm of the law*

methinks /mɪˈθɪŋks/ verb (past **methought** /mɪˈθɔːt/) archaic it seems to me.

method /ˈmeθəd/ noun way of doing something; procedure; orderliness.

methodical /mɪˈθɒdɪk(ə)l/ adjective characterized by method or order. □ **methodically** adverb.

Methodist /ˈmeθədɪst/ ● noun member of Protestant denomination originating in 18th-c. Wesleyan evangelistic movement. ● adjective of Methodists or Methodism. □ **Methodism** noun.

methought past of METHINKS.

meths noun colloquial methylated spirit.

methyl /ˈmeθɪl/ noun hydrocarbon radical CH₃. □ **methyl alcohol** methanol.

methylate /ˈmeθɪleɪt/ verb (**-ting**) mix or impregnate with methanol; introduce methyl group into (molecule).

meticulous /məˈtɪkjʊləs/ adjective giving great attention to detail; very careful and precise. □ **meticulously** adverb.

métier /ˈmetjeɪ/ noun one's trade, profession, or field of activity; one's forte. [French]

metonymy /mɪˈtɒnɪmɪ/ noun substitution of name of attribute for that of thing meant.

metre /ˈmiːtə/ noun (US **meter**) SI unit of length (about 39.4 in.); any form of poetic rhythm; basic rhythm of music.

metric /ˈmetrɪk/ adjective of or based on the metre. □ **metric system** decimal measuring system with metre, litre, and gram or kilogram as units of length, volume, and mass; **metric ton** 1,000 kg.

metrical adjective of or composed in metre; of or involving measurement. □ **metrically** adverb.

metronome /ˈmetrənəʊm/ noun device ticking at selected rate to mark musical time.

metropolis /mɪˈtrɒpəlɪs/ noun chief city, capital.

metropolitan /metrəˈpɒlɪt(ə)n/ ● adjective of metropolis; of mother country as distinct from colonies. ● noun bishop with authority over bishops of province.

mettle /ˈmet(ə)l/ noun quality or strength of character; spirit, courage. □ **mettlesome** adjective.

mew¹ ● noun cat's cry. ● verb utter this sound.

mew² noun gull, esp. common gull.

mews /mjuːz/ noun (treated as singular) stabling round yard etc., now used esp. for housing.

mezzanine /ˈmetsəniːn/ noun storey between two others (usually ground and first floors).

mezzo /ˈmetsəʊ/ Music ● adverb moderately. ● noun (in full **mezzo-soprano**) (plural **-s**) female singing voice between soprano and contralto, singer with this voice. □ **mezzo forte** fairly loud(ly); **mezzo piano** fairly soft(ly).

mezzotint /ˈmetsəʊtɪnt/ noun method of copper or steel engraving; print so produced.

mf abbreviation mezzo forte.

mg abbreviation milligram(s).

Mgr. abbreviation Manager; Monseigneur; Monsignor.

MHz abbreviation megahertz.

mi = ME².

miaow /mɪˈaʊ/ ● noun characteristic cry of cat. ● verb make this cry.

miasma /mɪˈæzmə/ noun (plural **-mata** or **-s**) archaic infectious or noxious vapour.

mica /ˈmaɪkə/ noun silicate mineral found as glittering scales in granite etc. or crystals separable into thin plates.

mice plural of MOUSE.

Michaelmas /ˈmɪkəlməs/ noun feast of St Michael, 29 Sept. □ **Michaelmas daisy** autumn-flowering aster.

mickey /ˈmɪkɪ/ noun (also **micky**) □ **take the mickey** (often + out of) slang tease, mock.

micro /ˈmaɪkrəʊ/ noun (plural **-s**) colloquial microcomputer; microprocessor.

micro- combining form small; one-millionth.

microbe /ˈmaɪkrəʊb/ noun micro-organism (esp. bacterium) causing disease or fermentation. □ **microbial** /-ˈkrəʊb-/ adjective.

microbiology /maɪkrəʊbaɪˈɒlədʒɪ/ noun study of micro-organisms. □ **microbiologist** noun.

microchip /ˈmaɪkrəʊtʃɪp/ noun small piece of semiconductor used to carry integrated circuits.

microcomputer /ˈmaɪkrəʊkəmpjuːtə/ noun small computer with microprocessor as central processor.

microcosm /ˈmaɪkrəkɒz(ə)m/ noun (often + of) miniature representation, e.g. humankind seen as small-scale model of universe; epitome. □ **microcosmic** /-ˈkɒz-/ adjective.

microdot /ˈmaɪkrəʊdɒt/ noun microphotograph of document etc. reduced to size of dot.

microfiche /ˈmaɪkrəʊfiːʃ/ noun small flat piece of film bearing microphotographs of documents etc.

microfilm /ˈmaɪkrəʊfɪlm/ ● noun length of film bearing microphotographs of documents etc. ● verb photograph on microfilm.

microlight /ˈmaɪkrəʊlaɪt/ noun kind of motorized hang-glider.

micrometer /maɪˈkrɒmɪtə/ noun gauge for accurate small-scale measurement.

micron /ˈmaɪkrɒn/ noun millionth of a metre.

micro-organism /maɪkrəʊˈɔːgənɪz(ə)m/ noun microscopic organism.

microphone /ˈmaɪkrəfəʊn/ noun instrument for converting sound waves into electrical energy for reconversion into sound.

microphotograph /maɪkrəʊˈfəʊtəgrɑːf/ noun photograph reduced to very small size.

microprocessor /maɪkrəʊˈprəʊsesə/ noun data processor using integrated circuits contained on microchip(s).

microscope /ˈmaɪkrəskəʊp/ noun instrument with lenses for magnifying objects or details invisible to naked eye.

microscopic /maɪkrəˈskɒpɪk/ adjective visible only with microscope; extremely small; of the microscope. □ **microscopically** adverb.

microscopy /maɪˈkrɒskəpɪ/ noun use of microscopes.

microsurgery /ˈmaɪkrəʊsɜːdʒərɪ/ noun intricate surgery using microscopes.

microwave /ˈmaɪkrəʊweɪv/ ● noun electromagnetic wave of length between 1 mm and 30 cm; (in full **microwave oven**) oven using microwaves to cook or heat food quickly. ● verb (**-ving**) cook in microwave oven.

micturition /mɪktjʊəˈrɪʃ(ə)n/ noun formal urination.

mid- combining form middle of. □ **midday** middle of day, noon; **mid-life** middle age; **mid-off, -on** Cricket position of fielder near bowler on off or on side.

midden /ˈmɪd(ə)n/ noun dunghill; refuse heap.

middle /ˈmɪd(ə)l/ ● adjective at equal distance, time, or number from extremities; central; intermediate in rank, quality, etc.; average. ● noun (often + of) middle point, position, or part; waist. □ **in the middle of** in the process of; **middle age** period between youth and old age; **the Middle Ages** period of European history from c. 1000 to 1453; **middle class** noun social class between upper and lower, including professional and business workers; **middle-class** adjective; **the Middle East** countries from Egypt to Iran inclusive; **middleman** trader who handles commodity between producer and consumer; **middleweight** amateur boxing weight (71–75 kg).

middling ● *adjective* moderately good. ● *adverb* fairly, moderately.

midge *noun* gnatlike insect.

midget /'mɪdʒɪt/ *noun* extremely small person or thing.

midland /'mɪdlənd/ ● *noun* (**the Midlands**) inland counties of central England; middle part of country. ● *adjective* of or in midland or Midlands.

midnight *noun* middle of night; 12 o'clock at night. □ **midnight sun** sun visible at midnight during summer in polar regions.

midriff /'mɪdrɪf/ *noun* front of body just above waist.

midshipman /'mɪdʃɪpmən/ *noun* naval officer ranking next above cadet.

midst *noun* middle. □ **in the midst of** among.

midsummer *noun* period of or near summer solstice, about 21 June. □ **Midsummer Day, Midsummer's Day** 24 June.

midwife /'mɪdwaɪf/ *noun* (*plural* **-wives**) person trained to assist at childbirth. □ **midwifery** /-wɪfrɪ/ *noun*.

midwinter *noun* period of or near winter solstice, about 22 Dec.

mien /miːn/ *noun literary* person's look or bearing.

might¹ *past of* MAY.

might² /maɪt/ *noun* strength, power.

mightn't /'maɪt(ə)nt/ might not.

mighty ● *adjective* (**-ier, -iest**) powerful, strong; massive. ● *adverb colloquial* very. □ **mightily** *adverb*.

mignonette /mɪnjə'net/ *noun* plant with fragrant grey-green flowers.

migraine /'miːgreɪn/ *noun* recurrent throbbing headache often with nausea and visual disturbance.

migrant /'maɪgrənt/ ● *adjective* migrating. ● *noun* migrant person or animal, esp. bird.

migrate /maɪ'greɪt/ *verb* (**-ting**) move from one place, esp. one country, to settle in another; (of bird etc.) change habitation seasonally. □ **migration** *noun*; **migratory** /'maɪgrətərɪ/ *adjective*.

mikado /mɪ'kɑːdəʊ/ *noun* (*plural* **-s**) *historical* emperor of Japan.

mike *noun colloquial* microphone.

milch *adjective* (of cow etc.) giving milk.

mild /maɪld/ *adjective* (esp. of person) gentle; not severe or harsh; (of weather) moderately warm; (of flavour) not sharp or strong. □ **mild steel** tough low-carbon steel. □ **mildly** *adverb*; **mildness** *noun*.

mildew /'mɪldjuː/ ● *noun* destructive growth of minute fungi on plants, damp paper, leather, etc. ● *verb* taint or be tainted with mildew.

mile *noun* unit of linear measure (1,760 yds, approx. 1.6 km); (in *plural*) *colloquial* great distance or amount; race extending over one mile. □ **milestone** stone beside road to mark distance in miles, significant point (in life, history, etc.).

mileage *noun* number of miles travelled; *colloquial* profit, advantage.

miler *noun colloquial* person or horse specializing in races of one mile.

milfoil /'mɪlfɔɪl/ *noun* common yarrow.

milieu /mɪ'ljɜː/ *noun* (*plural* **-x** or **-s** /-z/) person's environment or social surroundings.

militant /'mɪlɪt(ə)nt/ ● *adjective* combative; aggressively active in support of cause; engaged in warfare. ● *noun* militant person. □ **militancy** *noun*; **militantly** *adverb*.

militarism /'mɪlɪtərɪz(ə)m/ *noun* aggressively military policy etc.; military spirit. □ **militarist** *noun*; **militaristic** /-'rɪst-/ *adjective*.

military /'mɪlɪtərɪ/ ● *adjective* of or characteristic of soldiers or armed forces. ● *noun* (treated as *singular* or *plural*; **the military**) the army.

militate /'mɪlɪteɪt/ *verb* (**-ting**) (usually + *against*) have force or effect.

■ **Usage** *Militate* is often confused with *mitigate*, which means 'to make less intense or severe'.

militia /mɪ'lɪʃə/ *noun* military force, esp. one conscripted in emergency. □ **militiaman** *noun*.

milk ● *noun* opaque white fluid secreted by female mammals for nourishing young; milk of cows, goats, etc. as food; milklike liquid of coconut etc. ● *verb* draw milk from (cow etc.); exploit (person, situation). □ **milk chocolate** chocolate made with milk; **milk float** small usually electric vehicle used in delivering milk; **milkmaid** woman who milks cows or works in dairy; **milkman** person who sells or delivers milk; **milk run** routine expedition etc.; **milk shake** drink of whisked milk, flavouring, etc.; **milksop** weak or timid man or youth; **milk tooth** temporary tooth in young mammals.

milky *adjective* (**-ier, -iest**) of, like, or mixed with milk; (of gem or liquid) cloudy. □ **Milky Way** luminous band of stars, the Earth's galaxy.

mill ● *noun* building fitted with mechanical device for grinding corn; such device; device for grinding any solid to powder; building fitted with machinery for manufacturing processes etc.; such machinery. ● *verb* grind or treat in mill; (esp. as **milled** *adjective*) produce ribbed edge on (coin); (often + *about, round*) move aimlessly. □ **millpond** pond retained by dam for operating mill-wheel; **mill-race** current of water driving mill-wheel; **millstone** each of two circular stones for grinding corn, heavy burden, great responsibility; **mill-wheel** wheel used to drive watermill.

millennium /mɪ'lenɪəm/ *noun* (*plural* **-s** or **millennia**) thousand-year period; (esp. future) period of happiness on earth. □ **millennial** *adjective*.

miller /'mɪlə/ *noun* person who owns or works mill, esp. corn-mill; person operating milling machine.

millesimal /mɪ'lesɪm(ə)l/ ● *adjective* thousandth; of, belonging to, or dealing with, thousandth or thousandths. ● *noun* thousandth part.

millet /'mɪlɪt/ *noun* cereal plant bearing small nutritious seeds; seed of this.

milli- *combining form* one-thousandth.

millibar /'mɪlɪbɑː/ *noun* unit of atmospheric pressure equivalent to 100 pascals.

milligram /'mɪlɪgræm/ *noun* (also **-gramme**) one-thousandth of a gram.

millilitre /'mɪlɪliːtə/ *noun* (*US* **-liter**) one-thousandth of a litre (0.002 pint).

millimetre /'mɪlɪmiːtə/ *noun* (*US* **-meter**) one-thousandth of a metre.

milliner /'mɪlɪnə/ *noun* maker or seller of women's hats. □ **millinery** *noun*.

million /'mɪljən/ *noun* (*plural* same) one thousand thousand; (**millions**) *colloquial* very large number. □ **millionth** *adjective* & *noun*.

millionaire /mɪljə'neə/ *noun* (*feminine* **millionairess**) person possessing over a million pounds, dollars, etc.

millipede /'mɪlɪpiːd/ *noun* (also **millepede**) small crawling invertebrate with many legs.

millisecond /'mɪlɪsekənd/ *noun* one-thousandth of a second.

milometer /maɪ'lɒmɪtə/ *noun* instrument for measuring number of miles travelled by vehicle.

milt *noun* spleen in mammals; reproductive gland or sperm of male fish.

mime ● *noun* acting without words, using only gestures; performance using mime. ● *verb* (**-ming**) express or represent by mime.

mimeograph /ˈmɪmɪəɡrɑːf/ ● *noun* machine which duplicates from stencil; copy so produced. ● *verb* reproduce in this way.

mimetic /mɪˈmetɪk/ *adjective* of or practising imitation or mimicry.

mimic /ˈmɪmɪk/ ● *verb* (**-ck-**) imitate (person, gesture, etc.), esp. to entertain or ridicule; copy minutely or servilely; resemble closely. ● *noun* person who mimics. □ **mimicry** *noun*.

mimosa /mɪˈməʊzə/ *noun* shrub with globular usually yellow flowers; acacia plant.

Min. *abbreviation* Minister; Ministry.

min. *abbreviation* minute(s); minimum; minim (fluid measure).

minaret /mɪnəˈret/ *noun* tall slender turret next to mosque, used by muezzin.

minatory /ˈmɪnətərɪ/ *adjective formal* threatening.

mince ● *verb* (**-cing**) cut or grind (meat etc.) finely; (usually as **mincing** *adjective*) walk or speak in affected way. ● *noun* minced meat. □ **mincemeat** mixture of currants, sugar, spices, suet, etc.; **mince pie** (usually small) pie containing mincemeat. □ **mincer** *noun*.

mind /maɪnd/ ● *noun* seat of consciousness, thought, volition, and feeling; attention, concentration; intellect; memory; opinion; sanity. ● *verb* object to; be upset; (often + *out*) heed, take care; look after; concern oneself with. □ **be in two minds** be undecided.

minded *adjective* (usually + *to do*) disposed, inclined. □ **-minded** inclined to think in specified way, or with specified interest.

minder *noun* person employed to look after person or thing; *slang* bodyguard.

mindful *adjective* (often + *of*) taking heed or care.

mindless *adjective* lacking intelligence; brutish; not requiring thought or skill. □ **mindlessly** *adverb*; **mindlessness** *noun*.

mine¹ *pronoun* the one(s) belonging to me.

mine² ● *noun* hole dug to extract metal, coal, salt, etc.; abundant source (of information etc.); *military* explosive device placed in ground or water. ● *verb* (**-ning**) obtain (minerals) from mine; (often + *for*) dig in (earth etc.) for ore etc. or to tunnel; lay explosive mines under or in. □ **minefield** area planted with explosive mines; **minesweeper** ship for clearing explosive mines from sea. □ **mining** *noun*.

miner *noun* worker in mine.

mineral /ˈmɪnər(ə)l/ *noun* inorganic substance; substance obtained by mining; (often in *plural*) artificial mineral water or other carbonated drink. □ **mineral water** water naturally or artificially impregnated with dissolved salts.

mineralogy /mɪnəˈrælədʒɪ/ *noun* study of minerals. □ **mineralogical** /-rəˈlɒdʒ-/ *adjective*; **mineralogist** *noun*.

minestrone /mɪnɪˈstrəʊnɪ/ *noun* soup containing vegetables and pasta, beans, or rice.

mingle /ˈmɪŋɡ(ə)l/ *verb* (**-ling**) mix, blend.

mingy /ˈmɪndʒɪ/ *adjective* (**-ier, -iest**) *colloquial* stingy.

mini /ˈmɪnɪ/ *noun* (*plural* **-s**) *colloquial* miniskirt; (**Mini**) *proprietary term* make of small car.

mini- *combining form* miniature; small of its kind.

miniature /ˈmɪnɪtʃə/ ● *adjective* much smaller than normal; represented on small scale. ● *noun* miniature object; detailed small-scale portrait. □ **in miniature** on small scale.

miniaturist *noun* painter of miniatures.

miniaturize *verb* (also **-ise**) (**-zing** or **-sing**) produce in smaller version; make small. □ **miniaturization** *noun*.

minibus /ˈmɪnɪbʌs/ *noun* small bus for about 12 passengers.

minicab /ˈmɪnɪkæb/ *noun* car used as taxi, hireable only by telephone.

minim /ˈmɪnɪm/ *noun Music* note equal to two crotchets or half a semibreve; one-sixtieth of fluid drachm.

minimal /ˈmɪnɪm(ə)l/ *adjective* very minute or slight; being a minimum. □ **minimally** *adverb*.

minimize /ˈmɪnɪmaɪz/ *verb* (also **-ise**) (**-zing** or **-sing**) reduce to or estimate at minimum; estimate or represent at less than true value etc.

minimum /ˈmɪnɪməm/ ● *noun* (*plural* **minima**) least possible or attainable amount. ● *adjective* that is a minimum. □ **minimum wage** lowest wage permitted by law or agreement.

minion /ˈmɪnjən/ *noun derogatory* servile subordinate.

miniskirt /ˈmɪnɪskɜːt/ *noun* very short skirt.

minister /ˈmɪnɪstə/ ● *noun* head of government department; member of clergy, esp. in Presbyterian and Nonconformist Churches; diplomat, usually ranking below ambassador. ● *verb* (usually + *to*) help, serve, look after. □ **ministerial** /-ˈstɪər-/ *adjective*.

ministration /mɪnɪˈstreɪʃ(ə)n/ *noun* (usually in *plural*) help, service; ministering, esp. in religious matters.

ministry /ˈmɪnɪstrɪ/ *noun* (*plural* **-ies**) government department headed by minister; building for this; (**the ministry**) profession of religious minister, ministers of government or religion.

mink *noun* (*plural* same or **-s**) small semi-aquatic stoat-like animal; its fur; coat of this.

minke /ˈmɪŋkɪ/ *noun* small whale.

minnow /ˈmɪnəʊ/ *noun* (*plural* same or **-s**) small freshwater carp.

Minoan /mɪˈnəʊən/ ● *adjective* of Cretan Bronze Age civilization. ● *noun* person of this civilization.

minor /ˈmaɪnə/ ● *adjective* lesser or comparatively small in size or importance; *Music* (of scale) having semitone above second, fifth, and seventh notes; (of key) based on minor scale. ● *noun* person under full legal age; *US* student's subsidiary subject or course. ● *verb US* (+ *in*) study (subject) as subsidiary.

minority /maɪˈnɒrɪtɪ/ *noun* (*plural* **-ies**) (often + *of*) smaller number or part, esp. in politics; smaller group of people differing from larger in race, religion, language, etc.; being under full legal age; period of this.

minster /ˈmɪnstə/ *noun* large or important church; church of monastery.

minstrel /ˈmɪnstr(ə)l/ *noun* medieval singer or musician; musical entertainer with blacked face.

mint¹ *noun* aromatic herb used in cooking; peppermint; peppermint sweet. □ **minty** *adjective* (**-ier, -iest**).

mint² ● *noun* (esp. state) establishment where money is coined; *colloquial* vast sum. ● *verb* make (coin); invent (word, phrase, etc.).

minuet /mɪnjʊˈet/ *noun* slow stately dance in triple time; music for this.

minus /ˈmaɪnəs/ ● *preposition* with subtraction of; less than zero; *colloquial* lacking. ● *adjective Mathematics* negative. ● *noun* minus sign; negative quantity; *colloquial* disadvantage. □ **minus sign** symbol (−) indicating subtraction or negative value.

minuscule /ˈmɪnəskjuːl/ *adjective colloquial* extremely small or unimportant.

minute¹ /ˈmɪnɪt/ ● *noun* sixtieth part of hour; distance covered in minute; moment; sixtieth part of angular degree; (in *plural*) summary of proceedings of meeting; official memorandum. ● verb (-ting) record in minutes; send minutes to. □ up to the minute up to date.

minute² /maɪˈnjuːt/ adjective (-est) very small; accurate, detailed. □ **minutely** adverb.

minutiae /maɪˈnjuːʃɪ/ plural noun very small, precise, or minor details.

minx /mɪŋks/ noun pert, sly, or playful girl.

miracle /ˈmɪrək(ə)l/ noun extraordinary, supposedly supernatural, event; remarkable happening. □ **miracle play** medieval play on biblical themes.

miraculous /mɪˈrækjʊləs/ adjective being a miracle; supernatural; surprising. □ **miraculously** adverb.

mirage /ˈmɪrɑːʒ/ noun optical illusion caused by atmospheric conditions, esp. appearance of water in desert; illusory thing.

mire ● noun area of swampy ground; mud. ● verb (-ring) sink in mire; bespatter with mud. □ **miry** adjective.

mirror /ˈmɪrə/ ● noun polished surface, usually of coated glass, reflecting image; anything reflecting state of affairs etc. ● verb reflect in or as in mirror. □ **mirror image** identical image or reflection with left and right reversed.

mirth noun merriment, laughter. □ **mirthful** adjective.

misadventure /mɪsədˈventʃə/ noun Law accident without crime or negligence; bad luck.

misalliance /mɪsəˈlaɪəns/ noun unsuitable alliance, esp. marriage.

misanthrope /ˈmɪsənθrəʊp/ noun (also **misanthropist** /mɪˈsænθrəpɪst/) person who hates humankind. □ **misanthropic** /-ˈθrɒp-/ adjective.

misanthropy /mɪˈsænθrəpɪ/ noun condition or habits of misanthropy.

misapply /mɪsəˈplaɪ/ verb (-ies, -ied) apply (esp. funds) wrongly. □ **misapplication** /-æplɪˈkeɪ-/ noun.

misapprehend /mɪsæprɪˈhend/ verb misunderstand (words, person). □ **misapprehension** noun.

misappropriate /mɪsəˈprəʊprɪeɪt/ verb (-ting) take (another's money etc.) for one's own use; embezzle. □ **misappropriation** noun.

misbegotten /mɪsbɪˈgɒt(ə)n/ adjective illegitimate, bastard; contemptible.

misbehave /mɪsbɪˈheɪv/ verb (-ving) behave badly. □ **misbehaviour** noun.

miscalculate /mɪsˈkælkjʊleɪt/ verb (-ting) calculate wrongly. □ **miscalculation** noun.

miscarriage /ˈmɪskærɪdʒ/ noun spontaneous abortion. □ **miscarriage of justice** failure of judicial system.

miscarry /mɪsˈkærɪ/ verb (-ies, -ied) (of woman) have miscarriage; (of plan etc.) fail.

miscast /mɪsˈkɑːst/ verb (past & past participle -cast) allot unsuitable part to (actor) or unsuitable actors to (play etc.).

miscegenation /mɪsɪdʒɪˈneɪʃ(ə)n/ noun interbreeding of races.

miscellaneous /mɪsəˈleɪnɪəs/ adjective of mixed composition or character; (+ plural noun) of various kinds. □ **miscellaneously** adverb.

miscellany /mɪˈselənɪ/ noun (plural -ies) mixture, medley.

mischance /mɪsˈtʃɑːns/ noun bad luck; instance of this.

mischief /ˈmɪstʃɪf/ noun troublesome, but not malicious, conduct, esp. of children; playfulness; malice; harm, injury. □ **mischievous** /ˈmɪstʃɪvəs/ adjective; **mischievously** /ˈmɪstʃɪvəslɪ/ adverb.

misconceive /mɪskənˈsiːv/ verb (-ving) (often + of) have wrong idea or conception; (as **misconceived** adjective) badly organized etc. □ **misconception** /-ˈsep-/ noun.

misconduct /mɪsˈkɒndʌkt/ noun improper or unprofessional conduct.

misconstrue /mɪskənˈstruː/ verb (-strues, -strued, -struing) interpret wrongly. □ **misconstruction** /-ˈstrʌk-/ noun.

miscount /mɪsˈkaʊnt/ ● verb count inaccurately. ● noun inaccurate count.

miscreant /ˈmɪskrɪənt/ noun vile wretch, villain.

misdeed /mɪsˈdiːd/ noun evil deed, wrongdoing.

misdemeanour /mɪsdɪˈmiːnə/ noun (US **misdemeanor**) misdeed; historical indictable offence less serious than felony.

misdirect /mɪsdaɪˈrekt/ verb direct wrongly. □ **misdirection** noun.

miser /ˈmaɪzə/ noun person who hoards wealth and lives miserably. □ **miserly** adjective.

miserable /ˈmɪzərəb(ə)l/ adjective wretchedly unhappy or uncomfortable; contemptible, mean; causing discomfort. □ **miserably** adverb.

misericord /mɪˈzerɪkɔːd/ noun projection under hinged choir stall seat to support person standing.

misery /ˈmɪzərɪ/ noun (plural -ies) condition or feeling of wretchedness; cause of this; colloquial constantly grumbling person.

misfire /mɪsˈfaɪə/ ● verb (-ring) (of gun, motor engine, etc.) fail to go off, start, or function smoothly; (of plan etc.) fail to be effective. ● noun such failure.

misfit /ˈmɪsfɪt/ noun person unsuited to surroundings, occupation, etc.; garment etc. that does not fit.

misfortune /mɪsˈfɔːtʃ(ə)n/ noun bad luck; instance of this.

misgiving noun (usually in plural) feeling of mistrust or apprehension.

misgovern /mɪsˈgʌv(ə)n/ verb govern badly. □ **misgovernment** noun.

misguided /mɪsˈgaɪdɪd/ adjective mistaken in thought or action. □ **misguidedly** adverb.

mishandle /mɪsˈhænd(ə)l/ verb (-ling) deal with incorrectly or inefficiently; handle roughly.

mishap /ˈmɪshæp/ noun unlucky accident.

mishear /mɪsˈhɪə/ verb (past & past participle **-heard** /-ˈhɜːd/) hear incorrectly or imperfectly.

mishmash /ˈmɪʃmæʃ/ noun confused mixture.

misinform /mɪsɪnˈfɔːm/ verb give wrong information to, mislead. □ **misinformation** /-fəˈm-/ noun.

misinterpret /mɪsɪnˈtɜːprɪt/ verb (-t-) interpret wrongly. □ **misinterpretation** noun.

misjudge /mɪsˈdʒʌdʒ/ verb (-ging) judge wrongly. □ **misjudgement** noun.

mislay /mɪsˈleɪ/ verb (past & past participle **-laid**) accidentally put (thing) where it cannot readily be found.

mislead /mɪsˈliːd/ verb (past & past participle **-led**) cause to infer what is not true; deceive. □ **misleading** adjective.

mismanage /mɪsˈmænɪdʒ/ verb (-ging) manage badly or wrongly. □ **mismanagement** noun.

misnomer /mɪsˈnəʊmə/ noun wrongly used name or term.

misogyny /mɪˈsɒdʒɪnɪ/ noun hatred of women. □ **misogynist** noun.

misplace /mɪsˈpleɪs/ verb (-cing) put in wrong place; bestow (affections, confidence, etc.) on inappropriate object. □ **misplacement** noun.

misprint ● noun /ˈmɪsprɪnt/ printing error. ● verb /mɪsˈprɪnt/ print wrongly.

mispronounce /mɪsprəˈnaʊns/ verb (-cing) pronounce (word etc.) wrongly. □ **mispronunciation** /-nʌnsɪˈeɪ-/ noun.

misquote /mɪsˈkwəʊt/ verb (-ting) quote inaccurately. □ **misquotation** noun.

misread /mɪsˈriːd/ *verb* (*past & past participle* **-read** /-ˈred/) read or interpret wrongly.

misrepresent /mɪsreprɪˈzent/ *verb* represent wrongly; give false account of. □ **misrepresentation** *noun*.

misrule /mɪsˈruːl/ ● *noun* bad government. ● *verb* (**-ling**) govern badly.

Miss *noun title of girl or unmarried woman.*

miss ● *verb* fail to hit, reach, meet, find, catch, or perceive; fail to seize (opportunity etc.); regret absence of; avoid; (of engine etc.) misfire. ● *noun* failure. □ **give (thing) a miss** *colloquial* avoid; **miss out** omit.

missal /ˈmɪs(ə)l/ *noun* RC Church book of texts for Mass; book of prayers.

misshapen /mɪsˈʃeɪpən/ *adjective* deformed, distorted.

missile /ˈmɪsaɪl/ *noun* object, esp. weapon, suitable for throwing at target or discharging from machine; weapon directed by remote control or automatically.

missing *adjective* not in its place; lost; (of person) not traced but not known to be dead.

mission /ˈmɪʃ(ə)n/ *noun* task or goal assigned to person or group; journey undertaken as part of this; military or scientific expedition; group of people sent to conduct negotiations or to evangelize; missionary post.

missionary /ˈmɪʃənərɪ/ ● *adjective* of or concerned with religious missions, esp. abroad. ● *noun* (*plural* **-ies**) person doing missionary work.

missis = MISSUS.

missive /ˈmɪsɪv/ *noun jocular* letter; official letter.

misspell /mɪsˈspel/ *verb* (*past & past participle* **-spelt** or **-spelled**) spell wrongly.

misspend /mɪsˈspend/ *verb* (*past & past participle* **-spent**) (esp. as **misspent** *adjective*) spend wrongly or wastefully.

misstate /mɪsˈsteɪt/ *verb* (**-ting**) state wrongly or inaccurately. □ **misstatement** *noun*.

missus /ˈmɪsɪz/ *noun* (also **missis**) *colloquial or jocular form of address to woman*; (**the missis**) *colloquial* my or your wife.

mist ● *noun* water vapour in minute drops limiting visibility; condensed vapour obscuring glass etc.; dimness or blurring of sight caused by tears etc. ● *verb* cover or be covered (as) with mist.

mistake /mɪsˈteɪk/ ● *noun* incorrect idea or opinion; thing incorrectly done, thought, or judged. ● *verb* (**-king**; *past* **mistook** /-ˈstʊk/; *past participle* **mistaken**) misunderstand meaning of; (+ *for*) wrongly take (person, thing) for another.

mistaken /mɪˈsteɪkən/ *adjective* wrong in opinion or judgement; based on or resulting from error. □ **mistakenly** *adverb*.

mister /ˈmɪstə/ *noun colloquial or jocular form of address to man.*

mistime /mɪsˈtaɪm/ *verb* (**-ming**) say or do at wrong time.

mistle thrush /ˈmɪs(ə)l/ *noun* large thrush that eats mistletoe berries.

mistletoe /ˈmɪs(ə)ltəʊ/ *noun* parasitic white-berried plant.

mistook *past* of MISTAKE.

mistral /ˈmɪstr(ə)l/ *noun* cold N or NW wind in S. France.

mistreat /mɪsˈtriːt/ *verb* treat badly. □ **mistreatment** *noun*.

mistress /ˈmɪstrɪs/ *noun* female head of household; woman in authority; female owner of pet; female teacher; woman having illicit sexual relationship with (usually married) man.

mistrial /mɪsˈtraɪəl/ *noun* trial made invalid by error.

mistrust /mɪsˈtrʌst/ ● *verb* be suspicious of; feel no confidence in. ● *noun* suspicion; lack of confidence. □ **mistrustful** *adjective*; **mistrustfully** *adverb*.

misty *adjective* (**-ier**, **-iest**) of or covered with mist; dim in outline; obscure. □ **mistily** *adverb*.

misunderstand /mɪsʌndəˈstænd/ *verb* (*past & past participle* **-stood** /-ˈstʊd/) understand incorrectly; misinterpret words or actions of (person). □ **misunderstanding** *noun*.

misuse ● *verb* /mɪsˈjuːz/ (**-sing**) use wrongly; ill-treat. ● *noun* /mɪsˈjuːs/ wrong or improper use.

mite¹ *noun* small arachnid, esp. of kind found in cheese etc.

mite² *noun* small monetary unit; small object or child; modest contribution.

miter US = MITRE.

mitigate /ˈmɪtɪgeɪt/ *verb* (**-ting**) make less intense or severe. □ **mitigation** *noun*.

■ **Usage** *Mitigate* is often confused with *militate*, which means 'to have force or effect'.

mitre /ˈmaɪtə/ (*US* **miter**) ● *noun* bishop's or abbot's tall deeply cleft headdress; joint of two pieces of wood at angle of 90°, such that line of junction bisects this angle. ● *verb* (**-ring**) bestow mitre on; join with mitre.

mitt *noun* (also **mitten**) glove with only one compartment for the 4 fingers and another for thumb; glove leaving fingers and thumb-tip bare; *slang* hand; baseball glove.

mix ● *verb* combine or put together (two or more substances or things) so that constituents of each are diffused among those of the other(s); prepare (compound, cocktail, etc.) by combining ingredients; combine (activities etc.); join, be mixed, combine; be compatible; be sociable; (+ *with*) be harmonious with; combine (two or more sound signals) into one. ● *noun* mixing, mixture; proportion of materials in mixture; ingredients prepared commercially for making cake, concrete, etc.

mixed /mɪkst/ *adjective* of diverse qualities or elements; containing people from various backgrounds, of both sexes, etc. □ **mixed marriage** marriage between people of different race or religion; **mixed-up** *colloquial* mentally or emotionally confused, socially ill-adjusted.

mixer *noun* machine for mixing foods etc.; person who manages socially in specified way; (usually soft) drink to be mixed with spirit; device combining separate signals from microphones etc.

mixture /ˈmɪkstʃə/ *noun* process or result of mixing; combination of ingredients, qualities, etc.

mizen-mast /ˈmɪz(ə)n/ *noun* mast next aft of mainmast.

ml *abbreviation* millilitre(s); mile(s).

Mlle *abbreviation* (*plural* **-s**) Mademoiselle.

MM *abbreviation* Messieurs; Military Medal.

mm *abbreviation* millimetre(s).

Mme *abbreviation* (*plural* **-s**) Madame.

mnemonic /nɪˈmɒnɪk/ ● *adjective* of or designed to aid memory. ● *noun* mnemonic word, verse, etc. □ **mnemonically** *adverb*.

MO *abbreviation* Medical Officer; money order.

mo /məʊ/ *noun* (*plural* **-s**) *colloquial* moment.

moan ● *noun* low murmur expressing physical or mental suffering or pleasure; *colloquial* complaint. ● *verb* make moan or moans; *colloquial* complain, grumble. □ **moaner** *noun*.

moat *noun* defensive ditch round castle etc., usually filled with water.

mob ● *noun* disorderly crowd; rabble; **(the mob)** *usually derogatory* the populace; *colloquial* gang, group. ● *verb* **(-bb-)** crowd round to attack or admire.

mob-cap *noun historical* woman's indoor cap covering all the hair.

mobile /'məʊbaɪl/ ● *adjective* movable; able to move easily; (of face etc.) readily changing expression; (of shop etc.) accommodated in vehicle to serve various places; (of person) able to change social status. ● *noun* decoration that may be hung so as to turn freely. □ **mobility** /mə'bɪl-/ *noun*.

mobilize /'məʊbɪlaɪz/ *verb* (also **-ise)** **(-zing** or **-sing)** make or become ready for (esp. military) service or action. □ **mobilization** *noun*.

mobster /'mɒbstə/ *noun slang* gangster.

moccasin /'mɒkəsɪn/ *noun* soft flat-soled shoe originally worn by N. American Indians.

mock ● *verb* (often + *at*) ridicule, scoff (at); treat with scorn or contempt; mimic contemptuously. ● *adjective* sham; imitation; as a trial run. □ **mock turtle soup** soup made from calf's head etc.; **mock-up** experimental model of proposed structure etc. □ **mockingly** *adverb*.

mockery *noun* (*plural* **-ies)** derision; counterfeit or absurdly inadequate representation; travesty.

mode *noun* way in which thing is done; prevailing fashion; *Music* any of several types of scale.

model /'mɒd(ə)l/ ● *noun* representation in 3 dimensions of existing person or thing or of proposed structure, esp. on smaller scale; simplified description of system etc.; clay, wax, etc. figure for reproduction in another material; particular design or style, esp. of car; exemplary person or thing; person employed to pose for artist or photographer, or to wear clothes etc. for display; (copy of) garment etc. by well-known designer. ● *adjective* exemplary; ideally perfect. ● *verb* **(-ll-;** *US* **-l-)** fashion or shape (figure) in clay, wax, etc.; (+ *after, on,* etc.) form (thing) in imitation of; act or pose as model; (of person acting as model) display (garment).

modem /'məʊdem/ *noun* device for sending and receiving computer data by means of telephone line.

moderate /'mɒdərət/ ● *adjective* avoiding extremes, temperate in conduct or expression; fairly large or good; (of wind) of medium strength; (of prices) fairly low. ● *noun* person of moderate views. ● *verb* /-reɪt/ **(-ting)** make or become less violent, intense, rigorous, etc.; act as moderator of or to. □ **moderately** /-rətlɪ/ *adverb*; **moderation** *noun*.

moderator *noun* arbitrator, mediator; presiding officer; Presbyterian minister presiding over ecclesiastical body.

modern /'mɒd(ə)n/ ● *adjective* of present and recent times; in current fashion, not antiquated. ● *noun* person living in modern times. □ **modernity** /mə'dɜːn-/ *noun*.

modernism *noun* modern ideas or methods, esp. in art. □ **modernist** *noun* & *adjective*.

modernize *verb* (also **-ise)** **(-zing** or **-sing)** make modern; adapt to modern needs or habits. □ **modernization** *noun*.

modest /'mɒdɪst/ *adjective* having humble or moderate estimate of one's own merits; bashful; decorous; not excessive; unpretentious, not extravagant. □ **modestly** *adverb*; **modesty** *noun*.

modicum /'mɒdɪkəm/ *noun* (+ *of*) small quantity.

modify /'mɒdɪfaɪ/ *verb* (**-ies, -ied**) make less severe; make partial changes in. □ **modification** *noun*.

modish /'məʊdɪʃ/ *adjective* fashionable. □ **modishly** *adverb*.

modulate /'mɒdjʊleɪt/ *verb* **(-ting)** regulate, adjust; moderate; adjust or vary tone or pitch of (speaking voice); alter amplitude or frequency of (wave) by using wave of lower frequency to convey signal; *Music* pass from one key to another. □ **modulation** *noun*.

module /'mɒdjuːl/ *noun* standardized part or independent unit in construction, esp. of furniture, building, spacecraft, or electronic system; unit or period of training or education. □ **modular** *adjective*.

modus operandi /məʊdəs ɒpə'rændɪ/ *noun* (*plural* **modi operandi** /məʊdɪ/) method of working. [Latin]

modus vivendi /məʊdəs vɪ'vendɪ/ *noun* (*plural* **modi vivendi** /məʊdɪ/) way of living or coping; compromise between people agreeing to differ. [Latin]

mog *noun* (also **moggie)** *slang* cat.

mogul /'məʊg(ə)l/ *noun colloquial* important or influential person.

mohair /'məʊheə/ *noun* hair of angora goat; yarn or fabric from this.

Mohammedan = MUHAMMADAN.

moiety /'mɔɪətɪ/ *noun* (*plural* **-ies)** half; each of two parts of thing.

moiré /'mwɑːreɪ/ *adjective* (of silk) watered; (of metal) having clouded appearance.

moist *adjective* slightly wet; damp. □ **moisten** *verb*.

moisture /'mɔɪstʃə/ *noun* water or other liquid diffused as vapour or within solid, or condensed on surface.

moisturize *verb* (also **-ise)** **(-zing** or **-sing)** make less dry (esp. skin by use of cosmetic). □ **moisturizer** *noun*.

molar /'məʊlə/ ● *adjective* (usually of mammal's back teeth) serving to grind. ● *noun* molar tooth.

molasses /mə'læsɪz/ *plural noun* (treated as *singular*) uncrystallized syrup extracted from raw sugar; *US* treacle.

mold *US* = MOULD¹,²,³.

molder *US* = MOULDER.

molding *US* = MOULDING.

moldy *US* = MOULDY.

mole¹ *noun* small burrowing animal with dark velvety fur and very small eyes; *slang* spy established in position of trust in organization. □ **molehill** small mound thrown up by mole in burrowing.

mole² *noun* small permanent dark spot on skin.

mole³ *noun* massive structure as pier, breakwater, or causeway; artificial harbour.

mole⁴ *noun* SI unit of amount of substance.

molecule /'mɒlɪkjuːl/ *noun* group of atoms forming smallest fundamental unit of chemical compound. □ **molecular** /mə'lekjʊlə/ *adjective*.

molest /mə'lest/ *verb* annoy or pester (person); attack or interfere with (person), esp. sexually. □ **molestation** *noun*; **molester** *noun*.

moll *noun slang* gangster's female companion; prostitute.

mollify /'mɒlɪfaɪ/ *verb* (**-ies, -ied**) soften, appease. □ **mollification** *noun*.

mollusc /'mɒləsk/ *noun* (*US* **mollusk)** invertebrate with soft body and usually hard shell, e.g. snail or oyster.

mollycoddle /'mɒlɪkɒd(ə)l/ *verb* **(-ling)** coddle, pamper.

molt *US* = MOULT.

molten /'məʊlt(ə)n/ *adjective* melted, esp. made liquid by heat.

molto /'mɒltəʊ/ *adverb Music* very.

molybdenum /mə'lɪbdɪnəm/ *noun* silver-white metallic element added to steel to give strength and resistance to corrosion.

moment /'məʊmənt/ *noun* very brief portion of time; exact point of time; importance; product of force and distance from its line of action to a point.

momentary *adjective* lasting only a moment; transitory. □ **momentarily** *adverb*.

momentous /mə'mentəs/ *adjective* very important.

momentum /mə'mentəm/ *noun* (*plural* **-ta**) quantity of motion of moving body, the product of its mass and velocity; impetus gained by movement or initial effort.

Mon. *abbreviation* Monday.

monarch /'mɒnək/ *noun* sovereign with title of king, queen, emperor, empress, or equivalent. □ **monarchic** /mə'naːk-/ *adjective*; **monarchical** /mə'naːk-/ *adjective*.

monarchist *noun* advocate of monarchy.

monarchy *noun* (*plural* **-ies**) government headed by monarch; state with this.

monastery /'mɒnəstrɪ/ *noun* (*plural* **-ies**) residence of community of monks.

monastic /mə'næstɪk/ *adjective* of or like monasteries or monks, nuns, etc. □ **monastically** *adverb*; **monasticism** /-sɪz(ə)m/ *noun*.

Monday /'mʌndeɪ/ *noun* day of week following Sunday.

monetarism /'mʌnɪtərɪz(ə)m/ *noun* control of supply of money as chief method of stabilizing economy. □ **monetarist** *adjective & noun*.

monetary /'mʌnɪtərɪ/ *adjective* of the currency in use; of or consisting of money.

money /'mʌnɪ/ *noun* (*plural* **-s** or **monies**) coins and banknotes as medium of exchange; (in *plural*) sums of money; wealth. □ **moneylender** person lending money at interest; **money market** trade in short-term stocks, loans, etc.; **money order** order for payment of specified sum, issued by bank or Post Office; **money-spinner** thing that brings in a profit.

moneyed /'mʌnɪd/ *adjective* rich.

Mongol /'mɒŋg(ə)l/ ● *adjective* of Asian people now inhabiting Mongolia; resembling this people. ● *noun* Mongolian.

Mongolian /mɒŋ'gəʊlɪən/ ● *noun* native, national, or language of Mongolia. ● *adjective* of or relating to Mongolia or its people or language.

Mongoloid /'mɒŋgəlɔɪd/ ● *adjective* characteristic of Mongolians, esp. in having broad flat yellowish face. ● *noun* Mongoloid person.

mongoose /'mɒŋguːs/ *noun* (*plural* **-s**) small flesh-eating civet-like mammal.

mongrel /'mʌŋgr(ə)l/ ● *noun* dog of no definable type or breed; any animal or plant resulting from crossing of different breeds or types. ● *adjective* of mixed origin or character.

monies *plural* of MONEY.

monitor /'mɒnɪtə/ ● *noun* person or device for checking; school pupil with disciplinary etc. duties; television set used to select or verify picture being broadcast or to display computer data; person who listens to and reports on foreign broadcasts etc.; detector of radioactive contamination. ● *verb* act as monitor of; maintain regular surveillance over.

monk /mʌŋk/ *noun* member of religious community of men living under vows. □ **monkish** *adjective*.

monkey /'mʌŋkɪ/ ● *noun* (*plural* **-eys**) any of various primates, e.g. baboons, marmosets; mischievous person, esp. child. ● *verb* (**-eys**, **-eyed**) (often + *with*) play mischievous tricks. □ **monkey-nut** peanut; **monkey-puzzle** tree with hanging prickly branches; **monkey wrench** wrench with adjustable jaw.

monkshood /'mʌŋkshʊd/ *noun* poisonous plant with hood-shaped flowers.

mono /'mɒnəʊ/ *colloquial* ● *adjective* monophonic. ● *noun* monophonic reproduction.

mono- *combining form* (usually **mon-** before vowel) one, alone, single.

monochromatic /mɒnəkrə'mætɪk/ *adjective* (of light or other radiation) of single colour or wavelength; containing only one colour.

monochrome /'mɒnəkrəʊm/ ● *noun* photograph or picture in one colour, or in black and white only. ● *adjective* having or using one colour or black and white only.

monocle /'mɒnək(ə)l/ *noun* single eyeglass.

monocular /mə'nɒkjʊlə/ *adjective* with or for one eye.

monody /'mɒnədɪ/ *noun* (*plural* **-ies**) ode sung by one actor in Greek tragedy; poem lamenting person's death.

monogamy /mə'nɒgəmɪ/ *noun* practice or state of being married to one person at a time. □ **monogamous** *adjective*.

monogram /'mɒnəgræm/ *noun* two or more letters, esp. initials, interwoven.

monograph /'mɒnəgrɑːf/ *noun* treatise on single subject.

monolith /'mɒnəlɪθ/ *noun* single block of stone, esp. shaped into pillar etc.; person or thing like monolith in being massive, immovable, or solidly uniform. □ **monolithic** /-'lɪθ-/ *adjective*.

monologue /'mɒnəlɒg/ *noun* scene in drama in which person speaks alone; dramatic composition for one performer; long speech by one person in conversation etc.

monomania /mɒnə'meɪnɪə/ *noun* obsession by single idea or interest. □ **monomaniac** *noun & adjective*.

monophonic /mɒnə'fɒnɪk/ *adjective* (of sound-reproduction) using only one channel of transmission.

monoplane /'mɒnəpleɪn/ *noun* aeroplane with one set of wings.

monopolist /mə'nɒpəlɪst/ *noun* person who has or advocates monopoly. □ **monopolistic** /-'lɪs-/ *adjective*.

monopolize /mə'nɒpəlaɪz/ *verb* (also **-ise**) (**-zing** or **-sing**) obtain exclusive possession or control of (trade etc.); dominate (conversation etc.). □ **monopolization** *noun*; **monopolizer** *noun*.

monopoly /mə'nɒpəlɪ/ *noun* (*plural* **-ies**) exclusive possession or control of trade in commodity or service; (+ *of*, *US on*) sole possession or control.

monorail /'mɒnəʊreɪl/ *noun* railway with single-rail track.

monosodium glutamate /mɒnəʊ'səʊdɪəm 'gluː-təmeɪt/ *noun* sodium salt of glutamic acid used to enhance flavour of food.

monosyllable /'mɒnəsɪləb(ə)l/ *noun* word of one syllable. □ **monosyllabic** /-'læb-/ *adjective*.

monotheism /'mɒnəθiːɪz(ə)m/ *noun* doctrine that there is only one God. □ **monotheist** *noun*; **monotheistic** /-'ɪst-/ *adjective*.

monotone /'mɒnətəʊn/ *noun* sound continuing or repeated on one note or without change of pitch.

monotonous /mə'nɒtənəs/ *adjective* lacking in variety, tedious through sameness. □ **monotonously** *adverb*; **monotony** *noun*.

monoxide /mə'nɒksaɪd/ *noun* oxide containing one oxygen atom.

Monseigneur /mɒnsen'jɜː/ *noun* (*plural* **Messeigneurs** /mesen'jɜː/) *title given to eminent French person, esp. prince, cardinal, etc.* [French]

Monsieur /mə'sjɜː/ *noun* (*plural* **Messieurs** /mes'jɜː/) *title used of or to French-speaking man.*

Monsignor /mɒn'siːnjə/ *noun* (*plural* **-nori** /-'njɔːrɪ/) *title of various RC priests and officials.*

monsoon /mɒn'suːn/ *noun* wind in S. Asia, esp. in Indian Ocean; rainy season accompanying summer monsoon.

monster /'mɒnstə/ ● noun imaginary creature, usually large and frightening; inhumanly wicked person; misshapen animal or plant; large, usually ugly, animal or thing. ● adjective huge.

monstrance /'mɒnstrəns/ noun RC Church vessel in which host is exposed for veneration.

monstrosity /mɒn'strɒsɪtɪ/ noun (plural -ies) huge or outrageous thing.

monstrous /'mɒnstrəs/ adjective like a monster; abnormally formed; huge; outrageously wrong; atrocious. □ **monstrously** adverb.

montage /mɒn'tɑːʒ/ noun selection, cutting, and arrangement as consecutive whole, of separate sections of cinema or television film; composite whole made from juxtaposed photographs etc.

month /mʌnθ/ noun (in full **calendar month**) each of 12 divisions of year; period of time between same dates in successive calendar months; period of 28 days.

monthly ● adjective done, produced, or occurring once every month. ● adverb every month. ● noun (plural -ies) monthly periodical.

monument /'mɒnjumənt/ noun anything enduring that serves to commemorate, esp. structure, building, or memorial stone.

monumental /mɒnju'ment(ə)l/ adjective extremely great; stupendous; massive and permanent; of or serving as monument.

moo ● noun (plural -s) characteristic sound of cattle. ● verb (**moos, mooed**) make this sound.

mooch verb colloquial (usually + about, around) wander aimlessly; esp. US cadge.

mood¹ noun state of mind or feeling; fit of bad temper or depression.

mood² noun Grammar form(s) of verb indicating whether it expresses fact, command, wish, etc.

moody adjective (-ier, -iest) given to changes of mood; gloomy, sullen.

moon ● noun natural satellite of the earth, orbiting it monthly, illuminated by and reflecting sun; satellite of any planet. ● verb (often + about, around) wander aimlessly or listlessly. □ **moonbeam** ray of moonlight; **moonlight** noun light of moon, verb colloquial have other paid occupation, esp. one by night as well as one by day; **moonlit** lit by the moon; **moonshine** foolish or visionary talk, illicit alcohol; **moonshot** launching of spacecraft to moon; **moonstone** feldspar of pearly appearance; **moonstruck** slightly mad.

moony adjective (-ier, -iest) listless; stupidly dreamy.

Moor /mʊə/ noun member of a Muslim people of NW Africa. □ **Moorish** adjective.

moor¹ /mʊə/ noun open uncultivated upland, esp. when covered with heather. □ **moorhen** small waterfowl; **moorland** large area of moor.

moor² /mʊə/ verb attach (boat etc.) to fixed object. □ **moorage** noun.

mooring noun (often in plural) place where boat etc. is moored; (in plural) set of permanent anchors and chains.

moose noun (plural same) N. American deer; elk.

moot ● adjective debatable, undecided. ● verb raise (question) for discussion. ● noun historical assembly.

mop ● noun bundle of yarn or cloth or a sponge on end of stick for cleaning floors etc.; thick mass of hair. ● verb (-pp-) wipe or clean (as) with mop. □ **mop up** wipe with mop, colloquial absorb, dispose of, complete occupation of (area etc.) by capturing or killing enemy troops left there.

mope ● verb (-ping) be depressed or listless. ● noun person who mopes. □ **mopy** adjective (-ier, -iest).

moped /'məʊped/ noun low-powered motorized bicycle.

moquette /mɒ'ket/ noun thick pile or looped material used for upholstery etc.

moraine /mə'reɪn/ noun area of debris carried down and deposited by glacier.

moral /'mɒr(ə)l/ ● adjective concerned with goodness or badness of character or behaviour, or with difference between right and wrong; virtuous in conduct. ● noun moral lesson of story etc.; (in plural) moral principles or behaviour. □ **moral support** psychological rather than physical help. □ **morally** adverb.

morale /mə'rɑːl/ noun confidence, determination, etc. of person or group.

moralist /'mɒrəlɪst/ noun person who practises or teaches morality. □ **moralistic** /-'lɪs-/ adjective.

morality /mə'rælɪtɪ/ noun (plural -ies) degree of conformity to moral principles; moral conduct; science of morals.

moralize /'mɒrəlaɪz/ verb (also **-ise**) (**-zing** or **-sing**) (often + on) indulge in moral reflection or talk. □ **moralization** noun.

morass /mə'ræs/ noun entanglement; literary bog.

moratorium /mɒrə'tɔːrɪəm/ noun (plural -s or **-ria**) (often + on) temporary prohibition or suspension (of activity); legal authorization to debtors to postpone payment.

morbid /'mɔːbɪd/ adjective (of mind, ideas, etc.) unwholesome; colloquial melancholy; of or indicative of disease. □ **morbidity** /-'bɪd-/ noun; **morbidly** adverb.

mordant /'mɔːd(ə)nt/ ● adjective (of sarcasm etc.) caustic, biting; smarting; corrosive, cleansing. ● noun mordant substance.

more /mɔː/ ● adjective greater in quantity or degree; additional. ● noun greater quantity, number, or amount. ● adverb to greater degree or extent; forming comparative of adjectives and adverbs.

morello /mə'reləʊ/ noun (plural -s) sour kind of dark cherry.

moreover /mɔː'rəʊvə/ adverb besides, in addition.

mores /'mɔːreɪz/ plural noun customs or conventions of community.

morganatic /mɔːgə'nætɪk/ adjective (of marriage) between person of high rank and one of lower rank, the latter and the latter's children having no claim to possessions of former.

morgue /mɔːg/ noun mortuary; room or file of miscellaneous information kept by newspaper office.

moribund /'mɒrɪbʌnd/ adjective at point of death; lacking vitality.

Mormon /'mɔːmən/ noun member of Church of Jesus Christ of Latter-Day Saints. □ **Mormonism** noun.

morn noun poetical morning.

morning /'mɔːnɪŋ/ noun early part of day till noon or lunchtime. □ **morning coat** tailcoat with front cut away; **morning dress** man's morning coat and striped trousers; **morning glory** climbing plant with trumpet-shaped flowers; **morning sickness** nausea felt in morning in pregnancy; **morning star** planet, usually Venus, seen in east before sunrise.

morocco /mə'rɒkəʊ/ noun (plural -s) fine flexible leather of goatskin tanned with sumac.

moron /'mɔːrɒn/ noun colloquial very stupid person; adult with mental age of 8–12. □ **moronic** /mə'r-/ adjective.

morose /mə'rəʊs/ adjective sullen, gloomy. □ **morosely** adverb; **moroseness** noun.

morphia /'mɔːfɪə/ noun morphine.

morphine /'mɔːfiːn/ noun narcotic drug from opium.

morphology /mɔːˈfɒlədʒɪ/ noun study of forms of things, esp. of animals and plants and of words and their structure. □ **morphological** /-fəˈlɒdʒ-/ adjective.

morris dance /ˈmɒrɪs/ noun traditional English dance in fancy costume. □ **morris dancer** noun; **morris dancing** noun.

morrow /ˈmɒrəʊ/ noun (usually **the morrow**) literary following day.

Morse /mɔːs/ noun (in full **Morse code**) code in which letters, numbers, etc. are represented by combinations of long and short light or sound signals.

morsel /ˈmɔːs(ə)l/ noun mouthful; small piece (esp. of food).

mortal /ˈmɔːt(ə)l/ ● adjective subject to or causing death; (of combat) fought to the death; (of enemy) implacable. ● noun human being. □ **mortal sin** depriving soul of salvation. □ **mortally** adverb.

mortality /mɔːˈtælɪtɪ/ noun (plural **-ies**) being subject to death; loss of life on large scale; (in full **mortality rate**) death rate.

mortar /ˈmɔːtə/ noun mixture of lime or cement, sand, and water, for bonding bricks or stones; short cannon for firing shells at high angles; vessel in which ingredients are pounded with pestle. □ **mortarboard** stiff flat square-topped academic cap, flat board for holding mortar.

mortgage /ˈmɔːɡɪdʒ/ ● noun conveyance of property to creditor as security for debt (usually one incurred by purchase of property); sum of money lent by this. ● verb (**-ging**) convey (property) by mortgage.

mortgagee /mɔːɡɪˈdʒiː/ noun creditor in mortgage.

mortgager /ˈmɔːɡɪdʒə/ noun (also **mortgagor** /-ˈdʒɔː/) debtor in mortgage.

mortice = MORTISE.

mortician /mɔːˈtɪʃ(ə)n/ noun US undertaker.

mortify /ˈmɔːtɪfaɪ/ verb (**-ies, -ied**) humiliate, wound (person's feelings); bring (body etc.) into subjection by self-denial; (of flesh) be affected by gangrene. □ **mortification** noun; **mortifying** adjective.

mortise /ˈmɔːtɪs/ (also **mortice**) ● noun hole in framework to receive end of another part, esp. tenon. ● verb (**-sing**) join, esp. by mortise and tenon; cut mortise in. □ **mortise lock** lock recessed in frame of door etc.

mortuary /ˈmɔːtjʊərɪ/ ● noun (plural **-ies**) room or building in which dead bodies are kept until burial or cremation. ● adjective of death or burial.

Mosaic /məʊˈzeɪɪk/ adjective of Moses.

mosaic /məʊˈzeɪɪk/ noun picture or pattern made with small variously coloured pieces of glass, stone, etc.; diversified thing.

moselle /məʊˈzel/ noun dry German white wine.

Moslem = MUSLIM.

mosque /mɒsk/ noun Muslim place of worship.

mosquito /mɒsˈkiːtəʊ/ noun (plural **-es**) biting insect, esp. with long proboscis to suck blood. □ **mosquito-net** net to keep off mosquitoes.

moss noun small flowerless plant growing in dense clusters in bogs and on trees, stones, etc.; Scottish & Northern English peatbog. □ **mossy** adjective (**-ier, -iest**).

most /məʊst/ ● adjective greatest in quantity or degree; the majority of. ● noun greatest quantity or number; the majority. ● adverb in highest degree; forming superlative of adjectives and adverbs.

mostly adverb mainly; usually.

MOT abbreviation (in full **MOT test**) compulsory annual test, instituted by Ministry of Transport, of vehicles over specified age.

mot /məʊ/ noun (plural **mots** same pronunciation) (usually **bon mot** /bɔ̃/) witty saying. □ **mot juste** /ˈʒuːst/ most appropriate expression. [French]

mote noun speck of dust.

motel /məʊˈtel/ noun roadside hotel for motorists.

moth /mɒθ/ noun nocturnal insect like butterfly; insect of this type breeding in cloth etc., on which its larva feeds. □ **mothball** ball of naphthalene etc. kept with stored clothes to deter moths; **moth-eaten** damaged by moths, time-worn.

mother /ˈmʌðə/ ● noun female parent; woman or condition etc. giving rise to something else; (in full **Mother Superior**) head of female religious community. ● verb treat as mother does. □ **mother country** country in relation to its colonies; **mother-in-law** (plural **mothers-in-law**) husband's or wife's mother; **motherland** native country; **mother-of-pearl** iridescent substance forming lining of oyster and other shells; **mother tongue** native language. □ **motherhood** noun; **motherly** adjective.

motif /məʊˈtiːf/ noun theme repeated and developed in artistic work; decorative design; ornament sewn separately on garment.

motion /ˈməʊʃ(ə)n/ ● noun moving; changing position; gesture; formal proposal put to committee etc.; application to court for order; evacuation of bowels. ● verb (often + to do) direct (person) by gesture. □ **motion picture** esp. US cinema film. □ **motionless** adjective.

motivate /ˈməʊtɪveɪt/ verb (**-ting**) supply motive to, be motive of; cause (person) to act in particular way; stimulate interest of (person in activity). □ **motivation** noun.

motive /ˈməʊtɪv/ ● noun what induces person to act; motif. ● adjective tending to initiate movement.

motley /ˈmɒtlɪ/ ● adjective (**-lier, -liest**) diversified in colour; of varied character. ● noun historical jester's particoloured costume.

motor /ˈməʊtə/ ● noun thing that imparts motion; machine (esp. using electricity or internal combustion) supplying motive power for vehicle or other machine; car. ● adjective giving, imparting, or producing motion; driven by motor; of or for motor vehicles. ● verb go or convey by motor vehicle. □ **motor bike** colloquial, **motorcycle** two-wheeled motor vehicle without pedal propulsion; **motor car** car; **motorway** fast road with separate carriageways limited to motor vehicles.

motorcade /ˈməʊtəkeɪd/ noun procession of motor vehicles.

motorist noun driver of car.

motorize verb (also **-ise**) (**-zing** or **-sing**) equip with motor transport; provide with motor.

mottle /ˈmɒt(ə)l/ verb (**-ling**) (esp. as **mottled** adjective) mark with spots or smears of colour.

motto /ˈmɒtəʊ/ noun (plural **-es**) maxim adopted as rule of conduct; words accompanying coat of arms; appropriate inscription; joke, maxim, etc. in paper cracker.

mould[1] /məʊld/ (US **mold**) ● noun hollow container into which substance is poured or pressed to harden into required shape; pudding etc. shaped in mould; form, shape; character, type. ● verb shape (as) in mould; give shape to; influence development of.

mould[2] /məʊld/ noun (US **mold**) furry growth of fungi, esp. in moist warm conditions.

mould[3] /məʊld/ noun (US **mold**) loose earth; upper soil of cultivated land, esp. when rich in organic matter.

moulder /ˈməʊldə/ verb (US **molder**) decay to dust; (+ away) rot, crumble.

moulding noun (US **molding**) ornamental strip of plaster etc. applied as architectural feature, esp. in cornice; similar feature in woodwork etc.

mouldy adjective (US **moldy**) (**-ier, -iest**) covered with mould; stale; out of date; colloquial dull, miserable.

moult /məʊlt/ (US **molt**) ● verb shed (feathers, hair, shell, etc.) in renewing plumage, coat, etc. ● noun moulting.

mound /maʊnd/ noun raised mass of earth, stones, etc.; heap, pile; hillock.

mount¹ ● verb ascend; climb on to; get up on (horse etc.); set on horseback; (as **mounted** adjective) serving on horseback; (often + up) accumulate, increase; set in frame etc., esp. for viewing; organize, arrange (exhibition, attack, etc.). ● noun backing etc. on which picture etc. is set for display; horse for riding; setting for gem etc.

mount² noun (poetical except before name) mountain, hill.

mountain /ˈmaʊntɪn/ noun large abrupt elevation of ground; large heap or pile; huge quantity; large surplus stock. □ **mountain ash** tree with scarlet berries; **mountain bike** sturdy bicycle with straight handlebars and many gears.

mountaineer /maʊntɪˈnɪə/ ● noun person practising mountain climbing. ● verb climb mountains as sport. □ **mountaineering** noun.

mountainous adjective having many mountains; huge.

mountebank /ˈmaʊntɪbæŋk/ noun swindler, charlatan.

Mountie /ˈmaʊntɪ/ noun colloquial member of Royal Canadian Mounted Police.

mourn /mɔːn/ verb (often + for, over) feel or show sorrow or regret; grieve for loss of (dead person etc.).

mourner noun person who mourns, esp. at funeral.

mournful adjective doleful, sad. □ **mournfully** adverb.

mourning noun expression of sorrow for dead, esp. by wearing black clothes; such clothes.

mouse /maʊs/ ● noun (plural **mice**) small rodent; timid or feeble person; Computing small device controlling cursor on VDU screen. ● verb (also /maʊz/) (-sing) (of cat etc.) hunt mice. □ **mouser** noun; **mousy** adjective.

mousse /muːs/ noun dish of whipped cream, eggs, etc., flavoured with fruit, chocolate, etc., or with meat or fish purée.

moustache /məˈstɑːʃ/ noun (US **mustache**) hair left to grow on upper lip.

mouth ● noun /maʊθ/ (plural **mouths** /maʊðz/) external opening in head, for taking in food and emitting sound; cavity behind it containing teeth and vocal organs; opening of container, cave, trumpet, volcano, etc.; place where river enters sea. ● verb /maʊð/ (-thing) say or speak by moving lips silently; utter insincerely or without understanding. □ **mouth-organ** harmonica; **mouthpiece** part of musical instrument, telephone, etc., placed next to lips; **mouthwash** liquid antiseptic etc. for rinsing mouth.

mouthful noun (plural -s) quantity of food etc. that fills the mouth; colloquial something difficult to say.

move /muːv/ ● verb (-ving) (cause to) change position, posture, home, or place of work; put or keep in motion; rouse, stir; (often + about, away, off, etc.) go, proceed; take action; (+ in) be socially active in; affect with emotion; (cause to) change attitude; propose as resolution. ● noun act or process of moving; change of house, premises, etc.; step taken to secure object; moving of piece in board game. □ **move in with** start to share accommodation with; **move out** leave one's home. □ **movable** adjective.

movement noun moving, being moved; moving parts of mechanism; group of people with common object; (in plural) person's activities and whereabouts; chief division of longer musical work; bowel motion; rise or fall of stock-market prices.

movie /ˈmuːvɪ/ noun esp. US colloquial cinema film.

moving adjective emotionally affecting.

mow /məʊ/ verb (past participle **mowed** or **mown**) cut (grass, hay, etc.) with scythe or machine. □ **mower** noun.

MP abbreviation Member of Parliament.

mp abbreviation mezzo piano.

m.p.g. abbreviation miles per gallon.

m.p.h. abbreviation miles per hour.

Mr /ˈmɪstə/ noun (plural **Messrs**) title prefixed to name of man or to designation of office etc.

Mrs /ˈmɪsɪz/ noun (plural same) title of married woman.

MS abbreviation (plural **MSS** /em'esɪz/) manuscript; multiple sclerosis.

Ms /mɪz/ noun title of married or unmarried woman.

M.Sc. abbreviation Master of Science.

Mt. abbreviation Mount.

much ● adjective existing or occurring in great quantity. ● noun great quantity; (usually in negative) noteworthy example. ● adverb in great degree; for large part of one's time; often. □ **a bit much** colloquial excessive; **much of a muchness** very nearly the same.

mucilage /ˈmjuːsɪlɪdʒ/ noun viscous substance obtained from plants; adhesive gum.

muck ● noun colloquial dirt, filth; anything disgusting; manure. ● verb (usually + up) colloquial bungle; make dirty; (+ out) remove manure from. □ **muck about, around** colloquial potter or fool about; **muck in** (often + with) colloquial share tasks etc.; **muckraking** seeking out and revealing of scandals etc. □ **mucky** adjective (-ier, -iest).

mucous /ˈmjuːkəs/ adjective of or covered with mucus. □ **mucous membrane** mucus-secreting tissue lining body cavities etc.

mucus /ˈmjuːkəs/ noun slimy substance secreted by mucous membrane.

mud noun soft wet earth. □ **mudguard** curved strip over wheel to protect against mud; **mud-slinging** abuse, slander.

muddle /ˈmʌd(ə)l/ ● verb (-ling) (often + up) bring into disorder; bewilder; confuse. ● noun disorder; confusion. □ **muddle along** progress in haphazard way.

muddy ● adjective (-ier, -iest) like mud; covered in or full of mud; (of liquid, colour, or sound) not clear; confused. ● verb (-ies, -ied) make muddy.

muesli /ˈmjuːzlɪ/ noun breakfast food of crushed cereals, dried fruit, nuts, etc.

muezzin /muːˈezɪn/ noun Muslim crier who proclaims hours of prayer.

muff¹ noun covering, esp. of fur, for keeping hands or ears warm.

muff² verb colloquial bungle; miss (catch etc.).

muffin /ˈmʌfɪn/ noun light flat round spongy cake, eaten toasted and buttered; US similar cake made from batter or dough.

muffle /ˈmʌf(ə)l/ verb (-ling) (often + up) wrap for warmth or to deaden sound.

muffler noun wrap or scarf worn for warmth; thing used to deaden sound.

mufti /ˈmʌftɪ/ noun civilian clothes.

mug¹ ● noun drinking vessel, usually cylindrical with handle and no saucer; its contents; gullible person; slang face, mouth. ● verb (-gg-) attack and rob, esp. in public place. □ **mugger** noun; **mugging** noun.

mug² verb (-gg-) (usually + up) slang learn (subject) by concentrated study.

muggins /ˈmʌgɪnz/ noun (plural same or **mugginses**) colloquial gullible person (often meaning oneself).

muggy /ˈmʌgɪ/ adjective (-ier, -iest) (of weather etc.) oppressively humid.

Muhammadan /məˈhæməd(ə)n/ *noun & adjective* (also **Mohammedan**) Muslim.

■ **Usage** The term *Muhammadan* is not used by Muslims and is often regarded as offensive.

mulatto /mjuːˈlætəʊ/ *noun* (*plural* -**s** or -**es**) person of mixed white and black parentage.

mulberry /ˈmʌlbərɪ/ *noun* (*plural* -**ies**) tree bearing edible purple or white berries; its fruit; dark red, purple.

mulch ● *noun* layer of wet straw, leaves, plastic, etc., put round plant's roots to enrich or insulate soil. ● *verb* treat with mulch.

mule¹ /mjuːl/ *noun* offspring of male donkey and female horse or (in general use) vice versa; obstinate person; kind of spinning machine.

mule² /mjuːl/ *noun* backless slipper.

muleteer /mjuːləˈtɪə/ *noun* mule driver.

mulish *adjective* stubborn.

mull¹ *verb* (often + *over*) ponder.

mull² *verb* heat and spice (wine, beer).

mullah /ˈmʌlə/ *noun* Muslim learned in theology and sacred law.

mullet /ˈmʌlɪt/ *noun* (*plural* same) edible sea fish.

mulligatawny /mʌlɪgəˈtɔːnɪ/ *noun* highly seasoned soup originally from India.

mullion /ˈmʌljən/ *noun* vertical bar between panes in window. □ **mullioned** *adjective*.

multi- *combining form* many.

multicoloured /ˈmʌltɪkʌləd/ *adjective* of many colours.

multifarious /mʌltɪˈfeərɪəs/ *adjective* many and various; of great variety.

multiform /ˈmʌltɪfɔːm/ *adjective* having many forms; of many kinds.

multilateral /mʌltɪˈlætər(ə)l/ *adjective* (of agreement etc.) in which 3 or more parties participate; having many sides. □ **multilaterally** *adverb*.

multilingual /mʌltɪˈlɪŋgw(ə)l/ *adjective* in, speaking, or using many languages.

multinational /mʌltɪˈnæʃən(ə)l/ ● *adjective* operating in several countries; of several nationalities. ● *noun* multinational company.

multiple /ˈmʌltɪp(ə)l/ ● *adjective* having several parts, elements, or components; many and various. ● *noun* quantity exactly divisible by another. □ **multiple sclerosis** see SCLEROSIS.

multiplicand /mʌltɪplɪˈkænd/ *noun* quantity to be multiplied.

multiplication /mʌltɪplɪˈkeɪʃ(ə)n/ *noun* multiplying.

multiplicity /mʌltɪˈplɪsɪtɪ/ *noun* (*plural* -**ies**) manifold variety; (+ *of*) great number.

multiplier /ˈmʌltɪplaɪə/ *noun* quantity by which given number is multiplied.

multiply /ˈmʌltɪplaɪ/ *verb* (-**ies**, -**ied**) obtain from (number) another a specified number of times its value; increase in number, esp. by procreation.

multi-purpose /mʌltɪˈpɜːpəs/ *adjective* having several purposes.

multiracial /mʌltɪˈreɪʃ(ə)l/ *adjective* of several races.

multitude /ˈmʌltɪtjuːd/ *noun* (often + *of*) great number; large gathering of people; (**the multitude**) the common people. □ **multitudinous** /-ˈtjuːdɪnəs/ *adjective*.

mum¹ *noun colloquial* mother.

mum² *adjective colloquial* silent. □ **mum's the word** say nothing.

mumble /ˈmʌmb(ə)l/ ● *verb* (-**ling**) speak or utter indistinctly. ● *noun* indistinct utterance.

mumbo-jumbo /mʌmbəʊˈdʒʌmbəʊ/ *noun* (*plural* -**s**) meaningless ritual; meaningless or unnecessarily complicated language; nonsense.

mummer /ˈmʌmə/ *noun* actor in traditional play or mime.

mummery /ˈmʌmərɪ/ *noun* (*plural* -**ies**) ridiculous (esp. religious) ceremonial; performance by mummers.

mummify /ˈmʌmɪfaɪ/ *verb* (-**ies**, -**ied**) preserve (body) as mummy. ● **mummification** *noun*.

mummy¹ /ˈmʌmɪ/ *noun* (*plural* -**ies**) *colloquial* mother.

mummy² /ˈmʌmɪ/ *noun* (*plural* -**ies**) dead body preserved by embalming, esp. in ancient Egypt.

mumps *plural noun* (treated as *singular*) infectious disease with swelling of neck and face.

munch *verb* chew steadily.

mundane /mʌnˈdeɪn/ *adjective* dull, routine; of this world. □ **mundanely** *adverb*.

municipal /mjuːˈnɪsɪp(ə)l/ *adjective* of municipality or its self-government.

municipality /mjuːnɪsɪˈpælɪtɪ/ *noun* (*plural* -**ies**) town or district with local self-government; its governing body.

munificent /mjuːˈnɪfɪs(ə)nt/ *adjective* (of giver or gift) splendidly generous. □ **munificence** *noun*.

muniment /ˈmjuːnɪmənt/ *noun* (usually in *plural*) document kept as evidence of rights or privileges.

munition /mjuːˈnɪʃ(ə)n/ *noun* (usually in *plural*) military weapons, ammunition, etc.

mural /ˈmjʊər(ə)l/ ● *noun* painting executed directly on wall. ● *adjective* of, on, or like wall.

murder /ˈmɜːdə/ ● *noun* intentional unlawful killing of human being by another; *colloquial* unpleasant or dangerous state of affairs. ● *verb* kill (human being) intentionally and unlawfully; *colloquial* utterly defeat; spoil by bad performance, mispronunciation, etc. □ **murderer, murderess** *noun*; **murderous** *adjective*.

murky /ˈmɜːkɪ/ (-**ier**, -**iest**) *adjective* dark, gloomy; (of liquid etc.) dirty.

murmur /ˈmɜːmə/ ● *noun* subdued continuous sound; softly spoken utterance; subdued expression of discontent. ● *verb* make murmur; utter in low voice.

murrain /ˈmʌrɪn/ *noun* infectious disease of cattle.

Muscadet /ˈmʌskədeɪ/ *noun* dry white wine of France from Loire region; variety of grape used for this.

muscat /ˈmʌskət/ *noun* sweet usually fortified white wine made from musk-flavoured grapes; this grape.

muscatel /mʌskəˈtel/ *noun* muscat wine or grape; raisin made from muscat grape.

muscle /ˈmʌs(ə)l/ ● *noun* fibrous tissue producing movement in or maintaining position of animal body; part of body composed of muscles; strength, power. ● *verb* (-**ling**) (+ *in, in on*) *colloquial* force oneself on others. □ **muscle-bound** with muscles stiff and inelastic through excessive exercise; **muscle-man** man with highly developed muscles.

Muscovite /ˈmʌskəvaɪt/ ● *noun* native or citizen of Moscow. ● *adjective* of Moscow.

muscular /ˈmʌskjʊlə/ *adjective* of or affecting muscles; having well-developed muscles. □ **muscular dystrophy** hereditary progressive wasting of muscles. □ **muscularity** /-ˈlær-/ *noun*.

muse¹ /mjuːz/ *verb* (-**sing**) (usually + *on, upon*) ponder, reflect.

muse² /mjuːz/ *noun Greek & Roman Mythology* any of 9 goddesses inspiring poetry, music, etc.; (usually **the muse**) poet's inspiration.

museum /mjuːˈziːəm/ *noun* building for storing and exhibiting objects of historical, scientific, or cultural interest. □ **museum piece** object fit for museum, *derogatory* old-fashioned person etc.

mush *noun* soft pulp; feeble sentimentality; *US* maize porridge. □ **mushy** *adjective* (-**ier**, -**iest**).

mushroom /'mʌʃrʊm/ ● noun edible fungus with stem and domed cap; pinkish-brown colour. ● verb appear or develop rapidly. □ **mushroom cloud** mushroom-shaped cloud from nuclear explosion.

music /'mjuːzɪk/ noun art of combining vocal or instrumental sounds in harmonious or expressive way; sounds so produced; musical composition; written or printed score of this; pleasant sound. □ **music centre** equipment combining radio, record player, tape recorder, etc.; **music-hall** variety entertainment, theatre for this.

musical ● adjective of music; (of sounds) melodious, harmonious; fond of or skilled in music; set to or accompanied by music. ● noun musical film or play. □ **musicality** /-'kæl-/ noun; **musically** adverb.

musician /mjuː'zɪʃ(ə)n/ noun person skilled in practice of music, esp. professional instrumentalist. □ **musicianship** noun.

musicology /mjuːzɪ'kɒlədʒɪ/ noun study of history and forms of music. □ **musicological** /-kə'lɒdʒ-/ adjective; **musicologist** noun.

musk noun substance secreted by male musk deer and used in perfumes; plant which originally had smell of musk. □ **musk deer** small hornless Asian deer; **muskrat** large N. American aquatic rodent with smell like musk, its fur; **musk-rose** rambling rose smelling of musk. □ **musky** adjective (**-ier**, **-iest**).

musket /'mʌskɪt/ noun historical infantryman's (esp. smooth-bored) light gun.

musketeer /mʌskə'tɪə/ noun historical soldier armed with musket.

musketry /'mʌskɪtrɪ/ noun muskets; soldiers armed with muskets; knowledge of handling small arms.

Muslim /'mʊzlɪm/ (also **Moslem** /'mɒzləm/) ● noun follower of Islamic religion. ● adjective of Muslims or their religion.

muslin /'mʌzlɪn/ noun fine delicately woven cotton fabric.

musquash /'mʌskwɒʃ/ noun muskrat; its fur.

mussel /'mʌs(ə)l/ noun edible bivalve mollusc.

must¹ ● auxiliary verb (3rd singular present **must**; past **had to**) be obliged to; be certain to; ought to. ● noun colloquial thing that should not be missed.

■ **Usage** The negative *I must not go* means 'I am not allowed to go'. To express a lack of obligation, use *I am not obliged to go*, *I need not go*, or *I haven't got to go*.

must² noun grape juice before fermentation is complete.

mustache US = MOUSTACHE.

mustang /'mʌstæŋ/ noun small wild horse of Mexico and California.

mustard /'mʌstəd/ noun plant with yellow flowers; seeds of this crushed into paste and used as spicy condiment. □ **mustard gas** colourless oily liquid whose vapour is powerful irritant.

muster /'mʌstə/ ● verb collect (originally soldiers); come together; summon (courage etc.). ● noun assembly of people for inspection. □ **pass muster** be accepted as adequate.

mustn't /'mʌs(ə)nt/ must not.

musty /'mʌstɪ/ adjective (**-ier**, **-iest**) mouldy, stale; dull, antiquated. □ **mustiness** noun.

mutable /'mjuːtəb(ə)l/ adjective literary liable to change. □ **mutability** noun.

mutant /'mjuːt(ə)nt/ ● adjective resulting from mutation. ● noun mutant organism or gene.

mutate /mjuː'teɪt/ verb (cause to) undergo mutation.

mutation noun change; genetic change which when transmitted to offspring gives rise to heritable variations.

mute /mjuːt/ ● adjective silent; refraining from or temporarily bereft of speech; dumb; soundless. ● noun dumb person; device for damping sound of musical instrument. ● verb (**-ting**) muffle or deaden sound of; (as **muted** adjective) (of colours etc.) subdued. □ **mute swan** common white swan. □ **mutely** adverb.

mutilate /'mjuːtɪleɪt/ verb (**-ting**) deprive (person, animal) of limb etc.; destroy usefulness of (limb etc.); excise or damage part of (book etc.). □ **mutilation** noun.

mutineer /mjuːtɪ'nɪə/ noun person who mutinies.

mutinous /'mjuːtɪnəs/ adjective rebellious.

mutiny /'mjuːtɪnɪ/ ● noun (plural **-ies**) open revolt, esp. by soldiers or sailors against officers. ● verb (**-ies**, **-ied**) engage in mutiny.

mutt noun slang stupid person.

mutter /'mʌtə/ ● verb speak in barely audible manner; (often + *against*, *at*) grumble. ● noun muttered words etc.; muttering.

mutton /'mʌt(ə)n/ noun flesh of sheep as food.

mutual /'mjuːtʃʊəl/ adjective (of feelings, actions, etc.) experienced or done by each of two or more parties to the other(s); colloquial common to two or more people; having same (specified) relationship to each other. □ **mutuality** /-'æl-/ noun; **mutually** adverb.

■ **Usage** The use of *mutual* to mean 'common to two or more people' is considered incorrect by some people, who use *common* instead.

muzzle /'mʌz(ə)l/ ● noun projecting part of animal's face, including nose and mouth; guard put over animal's nose and mouth; open end of firearm. ● verb (**-ling**) put muzzle on; impose silence on.

muzzy /'mʌzɪ/ adjective (**-ier**, **-iest**) confused, dazed; blurred, indistinct. □ **muzzily** adverb.

MW abbreviation megawatt(s); medium wave.

my /maɪ/ adjective of or belonging to me.

mycology /maɪ'kɒlədʒɪ/ noun study of fungi; fungi of particular region.

mynah /'maɪnə/ noun (also **myna**) talking bird of starling family.

myopia /maɪ'əʊpɪə/ noun short-sightedness; lack of imagination. □ **myopic** /-'ɒp-/ adjective.

myriad /'mɪrɪəd/ literary ● noun indefinitely great number. ● adjective innumerable.

myrrh /mɜː/ noun gum resin used in perfume, medicine, incense, etc.

myrtle /'mɜːt(ə)l/ noun evergreen shrub with shiny leaves and white scented flowers.

myself /maɪ'self/ pronoun: emphatic form of I² or ME¹; reflexive form of ME¹.

mysterious /mɪs'tɪərɪəs/ adjective full of or wrapped in mystery. □ **mysteriously** adverb.

mystery /'mɪstərɪ/ noun (plural **-ies**) hidden or inexplicable matter; secrecy, obscurity; fictional work dealing with puzzling event, esp. murder; religious truth divinely revealed; (in plural) secret ancient religious rites. □ **mystery play** miracle play; **mystery tour** pleasure trip to unspecified destination.

mystic /'mɪstɪk/ ● noun person who seeks unity with deity through contemplation etc., or believes in spiritual apprehension of truths beyond understanding. □ **mysticism** /-sɪz(ə)m/ noun.

mystical adjective of mystics or mysticism; of hidden meaning; spiritually symbolic.

mystify /'mɪstɪfaɪ/ verb (**-ies**, **-ied**) bewilder, confuse. □ **mystification** noun.

mystique /mɪs'tiːk/ noun atmosphere of mystery and veneration attending some activity, person, profession, etc.

myth /mɪθ/ *noun* traditional story usually involving supernatural or imaginary people and embodying popular ideas on natural or social phenomena; widely held but false idea; fictitious person, thing, or idea. □ **mythical** *adjective*.

mythology /mɪˈθɒlədʒɪ/ *noun* (*plural* **-ies**) body or study of myths. □ **mythological** /-θəˈlɒdʒ-/ *adjective*; **mythologize** *verb* (also **-ise**) (**-zing** or **-sing**).

myxomatosis /mɪksəməˈtəʊsɪs/ *noun* viral disease of rabbits.

Nn

N *abbreviation* (also **N.**) north(ern).

n *noun* indefinite number.

n. *abbreviation* (also **n**) noun; neuter.

NAAFI /'næfɪ/ *abbreviation* Navy, Army, and Air Force Institutes (canteen for servicemen).

nab *verb* (**-bb-**) *slang* arrest; catch in wrongdoing; grab.

nacre /'neɪkə/ *noun* mother-of-pearl from any shelled mollusc. □ **nacreous** /'neɪkrɪəs/ *adjective*.

nadir /'neɪdɪə/ *noun* point on celestial sphere directly below observer; lowest point; time of despair.

naff *adjective slang* unfashionable; rubbishy.

nag¹ *verb* (**-gg-**) persistently criticize or scold; (often + *at*) find fault or urge, esp. continually; (of pain) be persistent.

nag² *noun colloquial* horse.

naiad /'naɪæd/ *noun* water nymph.

nail ● *noun* small metal spike hammered in to fasten things; horny covering on upper surface of tip of human finger or toe. ● *verb* fasten with nail(s); fix or hold tight; secure, catch (person, thing).

naïve /naɪ'iːv/ *adjective* (also **naive**) innocent, unaffected; foolishly credulous. □ **naïvely** *adverb*; **naïvety** *noun*.

naked /'neɪkɪd/ *adjective* unclothed, nude; without usual covering; undisguised; (of light, flame, sword, etc.) unprotected. □ **nakedly** *adverb*; **nakedness** *noun*.

namby-pamby /næmbɪ'pæmbɪ/ ● *adjective* insipidly pretty or sentimental; weak. ● *noun* (*plural* **-ies**) namby-pamby person.

name ● *noun* word by which individual person, animal, place, or thing is spoken of etc.; (usually abusive) term used of person; word denoting object or class of objects; reputation, esp. good. ● *verb* (**-ming**) give name to; state name of; mention; specify; cite. □ **name-day** feast-day of saint after whom person is named; **namesake** person or thing having same name as another.

nameless *adjective* having, or showing, no name; left unnamed.

namely *adverb* that is to say; in other words.

nanny /'nænɪ/ *noun* (*plural* **-ies**) child's nurse; *colloquial* grandmother; (in full **nanny goat**) female goat.

nano- /'nænəʊ/ *combining form* one thousand millionth.

nap¹ ● *noun* short sleep, esp. by day. ● *verb* (**-pp-**) have nap.

nap² *noun* raised pile on cloth, esp. velvet.

nap³ ● *noun* card game; racing tip claimed to be almost a certainty. ● *verb* (**-pp-**) name (horse) as probable winner. □ **go nap** try to take all 5 tricks in nap, risk everything.

napalm /'neɪpɑːm/ *noun* thick jellied hydrocarbon mixture used in bombs.

nape *noun* back of neck.

naphtha /'næfθə/ *noun* inflammable hydrocarbon distilled from coal etc.

naphthalene /'næfθəliːn/ *noun* white crystalline substance produced by distilling tar.

napkin /'næpkɪn/ *noun* piece of linen etc. for wiping lips, fingers, etc. at table; baby's nappy.

nappy /'næpɪ/ *noun* (*plural* **-ies**) piece of towelling etc. wrapped round baby to absorb urine and faeces.

narcissism /'nɑːsɪsɪz(ə)m/ *noun* excessive or erotic interest in oneself. □ **narcissistic** /-'sɪstɪk/ *adjective*.

narcissus /nɑː'sɪsəs/ *noun* (*plural* **-cissi** /-saɪ/) any of several flowering bulbs, including daffodil.

narcosis /nɑː'kəʊsɪs/ *noun* unconsciousness; induction of this.

narcotic /nɑː'kɒtɪk/ ● *adjective* (of substance) inducing drowsiness etc.; (of drug) affecting the mind. ● *noun* narcotic substance or drug.

nark *slang* ● *noun* police informer. ● *verb* annoy.

narrate /nə'reɪt/ *verb* (**-ting**) give continuous story or account of; provide spoken accompaniment for (film etc.). □ **narration** *noun*; **narrator** *noun*.

narrative /'nærətɪv/ ● *noun* ordered account of connected events. ● *adjective* of or by narration.

narrow /'nærəʊ/ ● *adjective* (**-er**, **-est**) of small width; restricted; of limited scope; with little margin; precise, exact; narrow-minded. ● *noun* (usually in *plural*) narrow part of strait, river, pass, etc. ● *verb* become or make narrower; contract; lessen. □ **narrow boat** canal boat; **narrow-minded** rigid or restricted in one's views, intolerant. □ **narrowly** *adverb*; **narrowness** *noun*.

narwhal /'nɑːw(ə)l/ *noun* Arctic white whale, male of which has long tusk.

nasal /'neɪz(ə)l/ ● *adjective* of nose; (of letter or sound) pronounced with breath passing through nose, e.g. *m*, *n*, *ng*; (of voice etc.) having many nasal sounds. ● *noun* nasal letter or sound. □ **nasally** *adverb*.

nascent /'næs(ə)nt/ *adjective* in act of being born; just beginning to be. □ **nascency** /-ənsɪ/ *noun*.

nasturtium /nə'stɜːʃəm/ *noun* trailing garden plant with edible leaves and bright orange, red, or yellow flowers.

nasty /'nɑːstɪ/ ● *adjective* (**-ier**, **-iest**) unpleasant; difficult to negotiate; (of person or animal) ill-natured, spiteful. ● *noun* (*plural* **-ies**) *colloquial* violent horror film, esp. on video. □ **nastily** *adverb*; **nastiness** *noun*.

Nat. *abbreviation* National(ist); Natural.

natal /'neɪt(ə)l/ *adjective* of or from birth.

nation /'neɪʃ(ə)n/ *noun* community of people having mainly common descent, history, language, etc., forming state or inhabiting territory. □ **nationwide** extending over whole nation.

national /'næʃən(ə)l/ ● *adjective* of nation; characteristic of particular nation. ● *noun* citizen of specified country. □ **national anthem** song adopted by nation, intended to inspire patriotism; **national grid** network of high-voltage electric power lines between major power stations; **National Insurance** system of compulsory payments from employee and employer to provide state assistance in sickness, retirement, etc.; **national service** *historical* conscripted peacetime military service. □ **nationally** *adverb*.

nationalism *noun* patriotic feeling, principles, etc.; policy of national independence. □ **nationalist** *noun*; **nationalistic** /-'lɪs-/ *adjective*.

nationality /næʃə'nælɪtɪ/ *noun* (*plural* **-ies**) membership of nation; being national; ethnic group within one or more political nations.

nationalize /'næʃənəlaɪz/ *verb* (also **-ise**) (**-zing** or **-sing**) take (industry etc.) into state ownership; make national. □ **nationalization** *noun*.

native /'neɪtɪv/ ● *noun* (usually + *of*) person born in specified place; local inhabitant; indigenous animal or plant. ● *adjective* inherent; innate; of one's birth; (usually + *to*) belonging to specified place; born in a place.

nativity /nə'tɪvɪtɪ/ noun (plural **-ies**) (esp. **the Nativity**) Christ's birth; birth.

NATO /'neɪtəʊ/ abbreviation (also **Nato**) North Atlantic Treaty Organization.

natter /'nætə/ colloquial ● verb chatter idly. ● noun aimless chatter.

natty /'nætɪ/ adjective (**-ier, -iest**) trim; smart.

natural /'nætʃər(ə)l/ ● adjective existing in or caused by nature; not surprising; to be expected; unaffected; innate; physically existing; Music not flat or sharp. ● noun colloquial (usually + for) person or thing naturally suitable, adept, etc.; Music sign (♮) showing return to natural pitch, natural note. □ **natural gas** gas found in earth's crust; **natural history** study of animals and plants; **natural number** whole number greater than 0; **natural selection** process favouring survival of organisms best adapted to environment.

naturalism noun realistic representation in art and literature; philosophy based on nature alone. □ **naturalistic** /-'lɪs-/ adjective.

naturalist noun student of natural history.

naturalize verb (also **-ise**) (**-zing** or **-sing**) admit (foreigner) to citizenship; introduce (plant etc.) into another region; adopt (foreign word, custom, etc.). □ **naturalization** noun.

naturally adverb in a natural way; as might be expected, of course.

nature /'neɪtʃə/ noun thing's or person's essential qualities or character; physical power causing material phenomena; these phenomena; kind, class.

naturism noun nudism. □ **naturist** noun.

naught /nɔːt/ archaic ● noun nothing. ● adjective worthless.

naughty /'nɔːtɪ/ adjective (**-ier, -iest**) (esp. of children) disobedient; badly behaved; colloquial jocular indecent. □ **naughtily** adverb; **naughtiness** noun.

nausea /'nɔːsɪə/ noun inclination to vomit; revulsion.

nauseate /'nɔːsɪeɪt/ verb (**-ting**) affect with nausea. □ **nauseating** adjective.

nauseous /'nɔːsɪəs/ adjective causing or inclined to vomit; disgusting.

nautical /'nɔːtɪk(ə)l/ adjective of sailors or navigation. □ **nautical mile** unit of approx. 2,025 yards (1,852 metres).

nautilus /'nɔːtɪləs/ noun (plural **nautiluses** or **nautili** /-laɪ/) kind of mollusc with spiral shell.

naval /'neɪv(ə)l/ adjective of navy; of ships.

nave[1] noun central part of church excluding chancel and side aisles.

nave[2] noun hub of wheel.

navel /'neɪv(ə)l/ noun depression in belly marking site of attachment of umbilical cord. □ **navel orange** one with navel-like formation at top.

navigable /'nævɪgəb(ə)l/ adjective (of river etc.) suitable for ships; seaworthy; steerable. □ **navigability** noun.

navigate /'nævɪgeɪt/ verb (**-ting**) manage or direct course of (ship, aircraft); sail on (sea, river, etc.); fly through (air); help car-driver etc. by map-reading etc. □ **navigator** noun.

navigation noun act or process of navigating; art or science of navigating.

navvy /'nævɪ/ noun (plural **-ies**) labourer employed in building roads, canals, etc.

navy /'neɪvɪ/ noun (plural **-ies**) state's warships with their crews, maintenance systems, etc.; (in full **navy blue**) dark blue colour.

nay ● adverb or rather; and even; archaic no. ● noun 'no' vote.

Nazi /'nɑːtsɪ/ ● noun (plural **-s**) historical member of German National Socialist party. ● adjective of Nazis or Nazism. □ **Nazism** noun.

NB abbreviation note well (nota bene).

NCB abbreviation historical National Coal Board.

NCO abbreviation non-commissioned officer.

NE abbreviation north-east(ern).

Neanderthal /nɪ'ændətɑːl/ adjective of type of human found in palaeolithic Europe.

neap noun (in full **neap tide**) tide with smallest rise and fall.

Neapolitan /nɪə'pɒlɪt(ə)n/ ● noun native of Naples. ● adjective of Naples.

near /nɪə/ ● adverb (often + to) to or at short distance in space or time; closely. ● preposition to or at a short distance from in space, time, condition, or resemblance. ● adjective close (to); not far in place or time; closely related; (of part of vehicle, animal, or road) on left side; colloquial stingy; with little margin. ● verb approach, draw near to. □ **the Near East** countries of eastern Mediterranean; **near-sighted** short-sighted.

nearby ● adjective near in position. ● adverb close.

nearly adverb almost; closely. □ **not nearly** nothing like, far from.

neat adjective tidy, methodical; elegantly simple; brief and clear; cleverly done; dexterous; (of alcoholic liquor) undiluted. □ **neaten** verb; **neatly** adverb; **neatness** noun.

neath preposition poetical beneath.

nebula /'nebjʊlə/ noun (plural **nebulae** /-liː/) cloud of gas and dust seen in night sky, appearing luminous or as dark silhouette. □ **nebular** adjective.

nebulous /'nebjʊləs/ adjective cloudlike; indistinct; vague.

necessary /'nesəsərɪ/ ● adjective requiring to be done; essential; inevitable. ● noun (plural **-ies**) (usually in plural) any of basic requirements of life. □ **necessarily** adverb.

necessitate /nɪ'sesɪteɪt/ verb (**-ting**) make necessary (esp. as result).

necessitous /nɪ'sesɪtəs/ adjective poor, needy.

necessity /nɪ'sesɪtɪ/ noun (plural **-ies**) indispensable thing; pressure of circumstances; imperative need; poverty; constraint or compulsion seen as natural law governing human action.

neck ● noun part of body connecting head to shoulders; part of garment round neck; narrow part of anything. ● verb colloquial kiss and caress amorously. □ **neckline** outline of garment-opening at neck; **necktie** strip of material worn round shirt-collar, knotted at front.

necklace /'nekləs/ noun string of beads, precious stones, etc. worn round neck; South African petrol-soaked tyre placed round victim's neck and lighted.

necromancy /'nekrəʊmænsɪ/ noun divination by supposed communication with the dead; magic. □ **necromancer** noun.

necrophilia /nekrə'fɪlɪə/ noun morbid esp. sexual attraction to corpses.

necropolis /ne'krɒpəlɪs/ noun ancient cemetery.

necrosis /ne'krəʊsɪs/ noun death of tissue. □ **necrotic** /-'krɒt-/ adjective.

nectar /'nektə/ noun sugary substance produced by plants and made into honey by bees; Mythology drink of gods.

nectarine /'nektərɪn/ noun smooth-skinned variety of peach.

NEDC abbreviation National Economic Development Council.

née /neɪ/ adjective (US **nee**) (before married woman's maiden name) born.

need ● *verb* stand in want of; require; (usually + *to do*) be under necessity or obligation. ● *noun* requirement; circumstances requiring action; destitution, poverty; emergency.

needful *adjective* requisite.

needle /'niːd(ə)l/ ● *noun* very thin pointed rod with slit ('eye') for thread, used in sewing; knitting-needle; pointer on dial; any small thin pointed instrument, esp. end of hypodermic syringe; obelisk; pointed rock or peak; leaf of fir or pine. ● *verb* (**-ling**) *colloquial* annoy, provoke. □ **needlecord** fine-ribbed corduroy fabric; **needlework** sewing or embroidery.

needless *adjective* unnecessary. □ **needlessly** *adverb*.

needy *adjective* (**-ier, -iest**) poor, destitute.

ne'er /neə/ *adverb poetical* never. □ **ne'er-do-well** good-for-nothing person.

nefarious /nɪ'feərɪəs/ *adjective* wicked.

negate /nɪ'geɪt/ *verb* (**-ting**) nullify; deny existence of.

negation *noun* absence or opposite of something positive; act of denying; negative statement; negative or unreal thing.

negative /'negətɪv/ ● *adjective* expressing or implying denial, prohibition, or refusal; lacking positive attributes; opposite to positive; (of quantity) less than zero, to be subtracted; *Electricity* of, containing, or producing, kind of charge carried by electrons. ● *noun* negative statement or word; *Photography* image with black and white reversed or colours replaced by complementary ones. ● *verb* (**-ving**) refuse to accept; veto; disprove; contradict; neutralize. □ **negatively** *adverb*.

neglect /nɪ'glekt/ ● *verb* fail to care for or do; (+ *to do*) fail; pay no attention to; disregard. ● *noun* negligence; neglecting, being neglected. □ **neglectful** *adjective*; **neglectfully** *adverb*.

negligée /'neglɪʒeɪ/ *noun* (also **négligé**) woman's flimsy dressing gown.

negligence /'neglɪdʒ(ə)ns/ *noun* lack of proper care or attention; culpable carelessness. □ **negligent** *adjective*; **negligently** *adverb*.

negligible /'neglɪdʒɪb(ə)l/ *adjective* not worth considering; insignificant.

negotiate /nɪ'gəʊʃɪeɪt/ *verb* (**-ting**) confer in order to reach agreement; obtain (result) by negotiating; deal successfully with (obstacle etc.); convert (cheque etc.) into money. □ **negotiable** /-ʃəb-/ *adjective*; **negotiation** *noun*; **negotiator** *noun*.

Negress /'niːgrɪs/ *noun* female Negro.

■ **Usage** The term *Negress* is often considered offensive; *black* is usually preferred.

Negro /'niːgrəʊ/ ● *noun* (*plural* **-es**) member of dark-skinned (originally) African race; black. ● *adjective* of this race; black.

■ **Usage** The term *Negro* is often considered offensive; *black* is usually preferred.

Negroid /'niːgrɔɪd/ ● *adjective* (of physical features etc.) characteristic of black people. ● *noun* black person.

neigh /neɪ/ ● *noun* cry of horse. ● *verb* make a neigh.

neighbour /'neɪbə/ (*US* **neighbor**) *noun* person living next door or nearby; fellow human being. ● *verb* border on, adjoin.

neighbourhood *noun* (*US* **neighborhood**) district; vicinity; people of a district.

neighbourly *adjective* (*US* **neighborly**) like good neighbour, friendly, helpful. □ **neighbourliness** *noun*.

neither /'naɪðə/ *adjective, pronoun & adverb* not either.

nelson /'nels(ə)n/ *noun* wrestling hold in which arm is passed under opponent's arm from behind and hand applied to neck (**half nelson**), or both arms and hands are applied (**full nelson**).

nem. con. *abbreviation* with no one dissenting (*nemine contradicente*). [Latin]

nemesis /'neməsɪs/ *noun* justice bringing deserved punishment.

neo- *combining form* new; new form of.

neolithic /niːə'lɪθɪk/ *adjective* of later Stone Age.

neologism /niː'blədʒɪz(ə)m/ *noun* new word; coining of new words.

neon /'niːɒn/ *noun* inert gas giving orange glow when electricity is passed through it.

neophyte /'niːəfaɪt/ *noun* new convert; novice of religious order; beginner.

nephew /'nefjuː/ *noun* son of one's brother or sister or of one's spouse's brother or sister.

nephritic /nɪ'frɪtɪk/ *adjective* of or in kidneys.

nephritis /nɪ'fraɪtɪs/ *noun* inflammation of kidneys.

nepotism /'nepətɪz(ə)m/ *noun* favouritism to relatives in conferring offices.

nereid /'nɪərɪɪd/ *noun* sea nymph.

nerve ● *noun* fibre or bundle of fibres conveying impulses of sensation or motion between brain and other parts of body; coolness in danger; *colloquial* impudence; (in *plural*) nervousness, mental or physical stress. ● *verb* (**-ving**) (usually **nerve oneself**) brace or prepare (oneself). □ **nerve-cell** cell transmitting impulses in nerve tissue.

nerveless *adjective* lacking vigour.

nervous *adjective* easily upset, timid, highly strung; anxious; affecting the nerves; (+ *of*) afraid of. □ **nervous breakdown** period of mental illness, usually after stress; **nervous system** body's network of nerves. □ **nervously** *adverb*; **nervousness** *noun*.

nervy *adjective* (**-ier, -iest**) *colloquial* nervous; easily excited.

nest ● *noun* structure or place where bird lays eggs and shelters young; breeding-place, lair; snug retreat, shelter; brood, swarm; group or set of similar objects. ● *verb* use or build nest; (of objects) fit one inside another. □ **nest egg** money saved up as reserve.

nestle /'nes(ə)l/ *verb* (**-ling**) settle oneself comfortably; press oneself against another in affection etc.; (+ *in, into*, etc.) push (head, shoulders, etc.) affectionately or snugly; lie half hidden or embedded.

nestling /'nestlɪŋ/ *noun* bird too young to leave nest.

net¹ ● *noun* open-meshed fabric of cord, rope, etc.; piece of net used esp. to contain, restrain, or delimit, or to catch fish; structure with net used in various games. ● *verb* (**-tt-**) cover, confine, or catch with net; hit (ball) into net, esp. of goal. □ **netball** game similar to basketball.

net² (also **nett**) ● *adjective* remaining after necessary deductions; (of price) not reducible; (of weight) excluding packaging etc. ● *verb* (**-tt-**) gain or yield (sum) as net profit.

nether /'neðə/ *adjective archaic* lower.

nett = NET².

netting *noun* meshed fabric of cord or wire.

nettle /'net(ə)l/ ● *noun* plant covered with stinging hairs; plant resembling this. ● *verb* (**-ling**) irritate, provoke. □ **nettle-rash** skin eruption like nettle stings.

network ● *noun* arrangement of intersecting horizontal and vertical lines; complex system of railways etc.; people connected by exchange of information etc.; group of broadcasting stations connected for simultaneous broadcast of a programme;

system of interconnected computers. ● *verb* broadcast on network.

neural /'njʊər(ə)l/ *adjective* of nerve or central nervous system.

neuralgia /njʊə'rældʒə/ *noun* intense pain along a nerve, esp. in face or head. □ **neuralgic** *adjective*.

neuritis /njʊə'raɪtɪs/ *noun* inflammation of nerve(s).

neuro- /'njʊərəʊ/ *combining form* nerve(s).

neurology /njʊə'rɒlədʒɪ/ *noun* study of nerve systems. □ **neurological** /-rə'lɒdʒ-/ *adjective*; **neurologist** *noun*.

neuron /'njʊərɒn/ *noun* (also **neurone** /-rəʊn/) nerve cell.

neurosis /njʊə'rəʊsɪs/ *noun* (*plural* **-roses** /-siːz/) disturbed behaviour pattern associated with nervous distress.

neurotic /njʊə'rɒtɪk/ ● *adjective* caused by or relating to neurosis; suffering from neurosis; *colloquial* abnormally sensitive or obsessive. ● *noun* neurotic person.

neuter /'njuːtə/ ● *adjective* neither masculine nor feminine. ● *verb* castrate, spay.

neutral /'njuːtr(ə)l/ ● *adjective* supporting neither of two opposing sides, impartial; vague, indeterminate; (of a gear) in which engine is disconnected from driven parts; (of colours) not strong or positive; *Chemistry* neither acid nor alkaline; *Electricity* neither positive nor negative. ● *noun* neutral state or person. □ **neutrality** /-'træl-/ *noun*.

neutralize *verb* (also **-ise**) (**-zing** or **-sing**) make neutral; make ineffective by opposite force. □ **neutralization** *noun*.

neutrino /njuː'triːnəʊ/ *noun* (*plural* **-s**) elementary particle with zero electric charge and probably zero mass.

neutron /'njuːtrɒn/ *noun* elementary particle of about same mass as proton but without electric charge.

never /'nevə/ *adverb* at no time, on no occasion; not ever; not at all; *colloquial* surely not. □ **the never-never** *colloquial* hire purchase.

nevermore *adverb* at no future time.

nevertheless /nevəðə'les/ *adverb* in spite of that; notwithstanding.

new *adjective* of recent origin or arrival; made, discovered, acquired, or experienced for first time; not worn; renewed; reinvigorated; different; unfamiliar. □ **New Age** set of alternative beliefs replacing traditional Western culture; **newborn** recently born; **newcomer** person recently arrived; **newfangled** different from what one is used to; **new moon** moon when first seen as crescent; **New Testament** part of Bible concerned with Christ and his followers; **New World** N. & S. America; **New Year's Day**, **Eve** 1 Jan., 31 Dec.

newel /'njuːəl/ *noun* supporting central post of winding stairs; top or bottom post of stair-rail.

newly *adverb* recently; afresh.

news /njuːz/ *plural noun* (usually treated as *singular*) information about important or interesting recent events, esp. when published or broadcast; (**the news**) broadcast report of news. □ **newsagent** seller of newspapers etc.; **newscast** radio or television broadcast of news reports; **newsletter** informal printed bulletin of club etc.; **newspaper** /'njuːs-/ printed publication of loose folded sheets with news etc.; **newsprint** low-quality paper for printing newspapers; **newsreader** person who reads out broadcast news bulletins; **newsreel** short cinema film of recent events; **news room** room where news is prepared for publication or broadcasting; **newsworthy** topical, worth reporting as news.

newsy *adjective* (**-ier**, **-iest**) *colloquial* full of news.

newt /njuːt/ *noun* small tailed amphibian.

newton /'njuːt(ə)n/ *noun* SI unit of force.

next ● *adjective* (often + *to*) being, placed, or living nearest; nearest in time. ● *adverb* (often + *to*) nearest in place or degree, on first or soonest occasion. ● *noun* next person or thing. ● *preposition colloquial* next to. □ **next door** in next house or room; **next of kin** closest living relative(s).

nexus /'neksəs/ *noun* (*plural* same) connected group or series.

NHS *abbreviation* National Health Service.

NI *abbreviation* Northern Ireland; National Insurance.

niacin /'naɪəsɪn/ *noun* nicotinic acid.

nib *noun* pen-point; (in *plural*) crushed coffee or cocoa beans.

nibble /'nɪb(ə)l/ ● *verb* (**-ling**) (+ *at*) take small bites at; eat in small amounts; bite gently or playfully. ● *noun* act of nibbling; very small amount of food.

nice *adjective* pleasant, satisfactory; kind, good-natured; fine, (of distinctions) subtle; fastidious. □ **nicely** *adverb*; **niceness** *noun*.

nicety /'naɪsɪtɪ/ *noun* (*plural* **-ies**) subtle distinction or detail; precision. □ **to a nicety** exactly.

niche /niːʃ/ *noun* shallow recess, esp. in wall; comfortable or apt position in life or employment.

nick ● *noun* small cut or notch; *slang* prison, police station; *colloquial* state, condition. ● *verb* make nick(s) in; *slang* steal, arrest, catch. □ **in the nick of time** only just in time.

nickel /'nɪk(ə)l/ *noun* silver-white metallic element used esp. in magnetic alloys; *colloquial* US 5-cent coin.

nickname /'nɪkneɪm/ ● *noun* familiar or humorous name added to or substituted for real name of person or thing. ● *verb* (**-ming**) give nickname to.

nicotine /'nɪkətiːn/ *noun* poisonous alkaloid present in tobacco.

nicotinic acid /nɪkə'tɪnɪk/ *noun* vitamin of B group.

nictitate /'nɪktɪteɪt/ *verb* (**-ting**) blink, wink. □ **nictitation** *noun*.

niece /niːs/ *noun* daughter of one's brother or sister or of one's spouse's brother or sister.

nifty /'nɪftɪ/ *adjective* (**-ier**, **-iest**) *colloquial* clever, adroit; smart, stylish.

niggard /'nɪgəd/ *noun* stingy person.

niggardly *adjective* stingy. □ **niggardliness** *noun*.

niggle /'nɪg(ə)l/ *verb* (**-ling**) fuss over details, find fault in petty way; *colloquial* nag. □ **niggling** *adjective*.

nigh /naɪ/ *adverb* & *preposition archaic* near.

night /naɪt/ *noun* period of darkness from one day to next; time from sunset to sunrise; nightfall; darkness of night; evening. □ **nightcap** *historical* cap worn in bed, drink before going to bed; **nightclub** club providing entertainment etc. late at night; **nightdress** woman's or child's loose garment worn in bed; **nightfall** end of daylight; **nightjar** nocturnal bird with harsh cry; **night-life** entertainment available at night; **nightmare** terrifying dream or *colloquial* experience; **night safe** safe with access from outer wall of bank for deposit of money when bank is closed; **nightshade** any of various plants with poisonous berries; **nightshirt** long shirt worn in bed.

nightingale /'naɪtɪŋgeɪl/ *noun* small reddish-brown bird, of which the male sings tunefully, esp. at night.

nightly ● *adjective* happening, done, or existing in the night; recurring every night. ● *adverb* every night.

nihilism /'naɪɪlɪz(ə)m/ *noun* rejection of all religious and moral principles. □ **nihilist** *noun*; **nihilistic** /-'lɪs-/ *adjective*.

nil *noun* nothing.

nimble /'nɪmb(ə)l/ *adjective* (**-r**, **-st**) quick and light in movement or function; agile. □ **nimbly** *adverb*.

nimbus /'nɪmbəs/ noun (plural **nimbi** /-baɪ/ or **nim-buses**) halo; rain-cloud.

nincompoop /'nɪŋkəmpuːp/ noun foolish person.

nine adjective & noun one more than eight. □ **ninepins** (usually treated as singular) kind of skittles. □ **ninth** /naɪnθ/ adjective & noun.

nineteen /naɪn'tiːn/ adjective & noun one more than eighteen. □ **nineteenth** adjective & noun.

ninety /'naɪntɪ/ adjective & noun (plural **-ies**) nine times ten. □ **ninetieth** adjective & noun.

ninny /'nɪnɪ/ noun (plural **-ies**) foolish person.

nip[1] ● verb (**-pp-**) pinch, squeeze sharply, bite; (often + off) remove by pinching etc.; colloquial go nimbly. ● noun pinch, sharp squeeze, bite; biting cold. □ **nip in the bud** suppress or destroy at very beginning.

nip[2] noun small quantity of spirits.

nipper noun person or thing that nips; claw of crab etc.; colloquial young child; (in plural) tool with jaws for gripping or cutting.

nipple /'nɪp(ə)l/ noun small projection in mammals from which females milk for young is secreted; teat of feeding-bottle; device like nipple in function; nipple-like protuberance.

nippy adjective (**-ier**, **-iest**) colloquial quick, nimble; chilly.

nirvana /nɪə'vɑːnə/ noun (in Buddhism) perfect bliss attained by extinction of individuality.

nit noun egg or young of louse or other parasitic insect; slang stupid person. □ **nit-picking** colloquial fault-finding in a petty way.

niter US = NITRE.

nitrate /'naɪtreɪt/ noun salt of nitric acid; potassium or sodium nitrate as fertilizer.

nitre /'naɪtə/ noun (US **niter**) saltpetre.

nitric acid /'naɪtrɪk/ noun colourless corrosive poisonous liquid.

nitrogen /'naɪtrədʒ(ə)n/ noun gaseous element forming four-fifths of atmosphere. □ **nitrogenous** /-'trɒdʒɪnəs/ adjective.

nitroglycerine /naɪtrəʊ'glɪsərɪn/ noun (US **nitroglycerin**) explosive yellow liquid.

nitrous oxide /'naɪtrəs/ noun colourless gas used as anaesthetic.

nitty-gritty /nɪtɪ'grɪtɪ/ noun slang realities or practical details of a matter.

nitwit noun colloquial stupid person.

NNE abbreviation north-north-east.

NNW abbreviation north-north-west.

No = NOH.

No. abbreviation number.

no /nəʊ/ ● adjective not any; not a; hardly any; used to forbid thing specified. ● adverb by no amount, not at all. ● interjection expressing negative reply to question, request, etc. ● noun (plural **noes**) utterance of word no, denial or refusal; 'no' vote. □ **no-ball** unlawfully delivered ball in cricket etc.; **no longer** not now as formerly; **no one** nobody; **no way** colloquial it is impossible.

nob[1] noun slang person of wealth or high social position.

nob[2] noun slang head.

nobble /'nɒb(ə)l/ verb (**-ling**) slang try to influence (e.g. judge); tamper with (racehorse etc.); steal; seize; catch.

nobility /nəʊ'bɪlɪtɪ/ noun (plural **-ies**) nobleness of character, birth, or rank; class of nobles.

noble /'nəʊb(ə)l/ ● adjective (**-r**, **-st**) belonging to the aristocracy; of excellent character; magnanimous; of imposing appearance. ● noun nobleman; noblewoman. □ **nobleman** peer; **noblewoman** peeress. □ **nobly** adverb.

noblesse oblige /nəʊbles ɒ'bliːʒ/ noun privilege entails responsibility. [French]

nobody /'nəʊbədɪ/ ● pronoun no person. ● noun (plural **-ies**) person of no importance.

nocturnal /nɒk'tɜːn(ə)l/ adjective of or in the night; done or active by night.

nocturne /'nɒktɜːn/ noun Music short romantic composition, usually for piano; picture of night scene.

nod ● verb (**-dd-**) incline head slightly and briefly; let head droop in drowsiness; be drowsy; show (assent etc.) by nod; (of flowers etc.) bend and sway; make momentary slip or mistake. ● noun nodding of head. □ **nod off** colloquial fall asleep.

noddle /'nɒd(ə)l/ noun colloquial head.

node noun part of plant stem from which leaves emerge; knob on root or branch; natural swelling; intersecting point, esp. of planet's orbit with plane of celestial equator; point or line of least disturbance in vibrating system; point at which curve crosses itself; component in computer network. □ **nodal** adjective.

nodule /'nɒdjuːl/ noun small rounded lump of anything; small tumour, ganglion, swelling on legume root. □ **nodular** adjective.

noggin /'nɒgɪn/ noun small mug; small measure of spirits.

Noh /nəʊ/ noun (also **No**) traditional Japanese drama.

noise /nɔɪz/ ● noun sound, esp. loud or unpleasant one; confusion of loud sounds. ● verb (**-sing**) (usually in passive) make public, spread abroad.

noisome /'nɔɪsəm/ adjective literary harmful, noxious; evil-smelling.

noisy adjective (**-ier**, **-iest**) making much noise; full of noise. □ **noisily** adverb.

nomad /'nəʊmæd/ noun member of tribe roaming from place to place for pasture; wanderer. □ **nomadic** /-'mæd-/ adjective.

nom de plume /nɒm də 'pluːm/ noun (plural **noms de plume** same pronunciation) writer's assumed name. [French]

nomenclature /nəʊ'menklətʃə/ noun system of names for things; terminology of a science etc.

nominal /'nɒmɪn(ə)l/ adjective existing in name only; not real or actual; (of sum of money etc.) very small; of, as, or like noun. □ **nominally** adverb.

nominate /'nɒmɪneɪt/ verb (**-ting**) propose (candidate) for election; appoint to office; appoint (date or place). □ **nomination** noun; **nominator** noun.

nominative /'nɒmɪnətɪv/ Grammar ● noun case expressing subject of verb. ● adjective of or in this case.

nominee /nɒmɪ'niː/ noun person who is nominated.

non- prefix not. For words starting with non- that are not found below, the root-words should be consulted.

nonagenarian /nəʊnədʒɪ'neərɪən/ noun person from 90 to 99 years old.

non-belligerent /nɒnbə'lɪdʒərənt/ ● adjective not engaged in hostilities. ● noun non-belligerent state etc.

nonce /nɒns/ noun □ **for the nonce** for the time being, for the present; **nonce-word** word coined for one occasion.

nonchalant /'nɒnʃələnt/ adjective calm and casual. □ **nonchalance** noun; **nonchalantly** adverb.

non-combatant /nɒn'kɒmbət(ə)nt/ noun person not fighting in a war, esp. civilian, army chaplain, etc.

non-commissioned /nɒnkə'mɪʃ(ə)nd/ adjective (of officer) not holding commission.

noncommittal /nɒnkə'mɪt(ə)l/ adjective avoiding commitment to definite opinion or course of action.

non-conductor /nɒnkən'dʌktə/ noun substance that does not conduct heat or electricity.

nonconformist /nɒnkən'fɔːmɪst/ noun person who does not conform to doctrine of established Church, esp. (**Nonconformist**) member of Protestant sect dissenting from Anglican Church; person not conforming to prevailing principle.

nonconformity /ˌnɒnkənˈfɔːmɪtɪ/ *noun* nonconformists as body; (+ *to*) failure to conform.

non-contributory /ˌnɒnkənˈtrɪbjʊtərɪ/ *adjective* not involving contributions.

nondescript /ˈnɒndɪskrɪpt/ ● *adjective* lacking distinctive characteristics, not easily classified. ● *noun* such person or thing.

none /nʌn/ *pronoun* (often + *of*) not any; no person(s). □ **none the** (+ *comparative*), **none too** not in the least.

■ **Usage** The verb following *none* can be singular or plural when it means 'not any of several', e.g. *None of us knows* or *None of us know.*

nonentity /nɒˈnentɪtɪ/ *noun* (*plural* **-ies**) person or thing of no importance; non-existence; non-existent thing.

nonet /nəʊˈnet/ *noun* musical composition for 9 performers; the performers; any group of 9.

nonetheless /ˌnʌnðəˈles/ *adverb* nevertheless.

non-event /nɒnɪˈvent/ *noun* insignificant event, esp. contrary to hopes or expectations.

non-existent /ˌnɒnɪgˈzɪst(ə)nt/ *adjective* not existing. □ **non-existence** *noun.*

non-fiction /nɒnˈfɪkʃ(ə)n/ *noun* literary work other than fiction.

non-interference /ˌnɒnɪntəˈfɪərəns/ *noun* nonintervention.

non-intervention /ˌnɒnɪntəˈvenʃ(ə)n/ *noun* policy of not interfering in others' affairs.

nonpareil /ˈnɒnpəˈreɪl/ ● *adjective* unrivalled, unique. ● *noun* such person or thing.

non-party /nɒnˈpɑːtɪ/ *adjective* independent of political parties.

nonplus /nɒnˈplʌs/ *verb* (**-ss-**) completely perplex.

nonsense /ˈnɒns(ə)ns/ *noun* (often as *interjection*) absurd or meaningless words or ideas; foolish conduct. □ **nonsensical** /-ˈsen-/ *adjective.*

non sequitur /nɒn ˈsekwɪtə/ *noun* conclusion that does not logically follow from the premisses. [Latin]

non-slip /nɒnˈslɪp/ *adjective* that does not slip; that prevents slipping.

non-smoker /nɒnˈsməʊkə/ *noun* person who does not smoke; train compartment etc. where smoking is forbidden. □ **non-smoking** *adjective.*

non-starter /nɒnˈstɑːtə/ *noun colloquial* person or scheme not worth considering.

non-stick /nɒnˈstɪk/ *adjective* that does not allow things to stick to it.

non-stop /nɒnˈstɒp/ ● *adjective* (of train etc.) not stopping at intermediate stations; done without stopping. ● *adverb* without stopping.

noodle[1] /ˈnuːd(ə)l/ *noun* strip or ring of pasta.

noodle[2] /ˈnuːd(ə)l/ *noun* simpleton.

nook /nʊk/ *noun* corner or recess; secluded place.

noon *noun* 12 o'clock in day, midday. □ **noonday** midday.

noose /nuːs/ ● *noun* loop with running knot; snare. ● *verb* (**-sing**) catch with or enclose in noose.

nor *conjunction* and not.

Nordic /ˈnɔːdɪk/ *adjective* of tall blond Germanic people of Scandinavia.

norm *noun* standard, type; standard amount of work etc.; customary behaviour.

normal /ˈnɔːm(ə)l/ ● *adjective* conforming to standard; regular, usual, typical; *Geometry* (of line) at right angles. ● *noun* normal value of a temperature etc.; usual state, level, etc. □ **normalcy** *noun esp. US*; **normality** /-ˈmæl-/ *noun*; **normalize** *verb* (also **-ise**) (**-zing** or **-sing**); **normally** *adverb.*

Norman /ˈnɔːmən/ ● *noun* (*plural* **-s**) native of medieval Normandy; descendant of people established there in 10th c. ● *adjective* of Normans; of style of medieval architecture found in Britain under Normans.

Norse ● *noun* Norwegian language; Scandinavian language group. ● *adjective* of ancient Scandinavia, esp. Norway. □ **Norseman** *noun.*

north ● *noun* point of horizon 90° anticlockwise from east; corresponding compass point; (usually **the North**) northern part of world, country, town, etc. ● *adjective* towards, at, near, or facing north; (of wind) from north. ● *adverb* towards, at, or near north; (+ *of*) further north than. □ **northbound** travelling or leading north; **north-east**, **-west** point midway between north and east or west; **north-north-east**, **north-north-west** point midway between north and north-east or north-west; **North Star** pole star. □ **northward** *adjective*, *adverb*, & *noun*; **northwards** *adverb.*

northerly /ˈnɔːðəlɪ/ *adjective* & *adverb* in northern position or direction; (of wind) from north.

northern /ˈnɔːð(ə)n/ *adjective* of or in the north. □ **northern lights** aurora borealis. ■ **northernmost** *adjective.*

northerner *noun* native or inhabitant of north.

Norwegian /nɔːˈwiːdʒ(ə)n/ ● *noun* native, national, or language of Norway. ● *adjective* of or relating to Norway.

nose /nəʊz/ ● *noun* organ above mouth, used for smelling and breathing; sense of smell; odour or perfume of wine etc.; projecting part or front end of car, aircraft, etc. ● *verb* (**-sing**) (usually + *about* etc.) search; (often + *out*) perceive smell of, discover by smell; thrust nose against or into; make one's way cautiously forward. □ **nosebag** fodder-bag hung on horse's head; **nosebleed** bleeding from nose; **nose-dive** (make) steep downward plunge.

nosegay *noun* small bunch of flowers.

nosh *slang* ● *verb* eat. ● *noun* food or drink. □ **nosh-up** large meal.

nostalgia /nɒsˈtældʒə/ *noun* (often + *for*) yearning for past period; homesickness. □ **nostalgic** *adjective.*

nostril /ˈnɒstr(ə)l/ *noun* either of two openings in nose.

nostrum /ˈnɒstrəm/ *noun* quack remedy, patent medicine; pet scheme.

nosy *adjective* (**-ier**, **-iest**) *colloquial* inquisitive, prying.

not *adverb* expressing negation, refusal, or denial. □ **not half** *slang* very much, very, not nearly, *colloquial* not at all; **not quite** almost.

notable /ˈnəʊtəb(ə)l/ ● *adjective* worthy of note; remarkable; eminent. ● *noun* eminent person. □ **notability** *noun*; **notably** *adverb.*

notary /ˈnəʊtərɪ/ *noun* (*plural* **-ies**) solicitor etc. who certifies deeds etc. □ **notarial** /-ˈteər-/ *adjective.*

notation /nəʊˈteɪʃ(ə)n/ *noun* representation of numbers, quantities, musical notes, etc. by symbols; set of such symbols.

notch ● *noun* V-shaped indentation on edge or surface. ● *verb* make notches in; (usually + *up*) score, win, achieve (esp. amount or quantity).

note ● *noun* brief written record as memory aid; short letter; formal diplomatic message; additional explanation in book; banknote; notice, attention; eminence; single musical tone of definite pitch; written sign representing its pitch and duration; quality or tone of speaking. ● *verb* (**-ting**) observe, notice; (often + *down*) record as thing to be remembered; (in *passive*; often + *for*) be well known. □ **notebook** book for making notes in; **notecase** wallet for banknotes; **notelet** small folded card for informal letter; **notepaper** paper for writing letters; **noteworthy** worthy of attention, remarkable.

nothing /ˈnʌθɪŋ/ ● *noun* no thing, not anything; person or thing of no importance; non-existence; no amount; nought. ● *adverb* not at all; in no way.

nothingness *noun* non-existence; worthlessness.

notice /ˈnəʊtɪs/ ● *noun* attention; displayed sheet etc. with announcement; intimation; warning; formal declaration of intention to end agreement or employment at specified time; short published review of new play, book, etc. ● *verb* (**-cing**) (often + *that, how,* etc.) perceive, observe. □ **noticeable** *adjective*; **noticeably** *adverb*.

notifiable /ˈnəʊtɪfaɪəb(ə)l/ *adjective* (esp. of disease) that must be notified to authorities.

notify /ˈnəʊtɪfaɪ/ *verb* (**-ies, -ied**) (often + *of, that*) inform, give notice to (person); make known. □ **notification** *noun*.

notion /ˈnəʊʃ(ə)n/ *noun* concept, idea; opinion; vague understanding; intention.

notional *adjective* hypothetical, imaginary. □ **notionally** *adverb*.

notorious /nəʊˈtɔːrɪəs/ *adjective* well known, esp. unfavourably. □ **notoriety** /-təˈraɪətɪ/ *noun*; **notoriously** *adverb*.

notwithstanding /nɒtwɪðˈstændɪŋ/ ● *preposition* in spite of. ● *adverb* nevertheless.

nougat /ˈnuːgɑː/ *noun* sweet made from nuts, egg white, and sugar or honey.

nought /nɔːt/ *noun* digit 0; cipher; *poetical or archaic* nothing.

noun /naʊn/ *noun* word used to name person or thing (see panel).

nourish /ˈnʌrɪʃ/ *verb* sustain with food; foster, cherish (feeling etc.). □ **nourishing** *adjective*.

nourishment *noun* sustenance, food.

nous /naʊs/ *noun colloquial* common sense.

Nov. *abbreviation* November.

nova /ˈnəʊvə/ *noun* (*plural* **novae** /-viː/ or **-s**) star showing sudden burst of brightness and then subsiding.

novel /ˈnɒv(ə)l/ ● *noun* fictitious prose story of book length. ● *adjective* of new kind or nature.

novelette /nɒvəˈlet/ *noun* short (esp. romantic) novel.

novelist /ˈnɒvəlɪst/ *noun* writer of novels.

novella /nəˈvelə/ *noun* (*plural* **-s**) short novel or narrative story.

novelty /ˈnɒvəltɪ/ *noun* (*plural* **-ies**) newness; new thing or occurrence; small toy etc.

November /nəʊˈvembə/ *noun* eleventh month of year.

novena /nəˈviːnə/ *noun RC Church* special prayers or services on 9 successive days.

novice /ˈnɒvɪs/ *noun* probationary member of religious order; beginner.

noviciate /nəˈvɪʃɪət/ *noun* (also **novitiate**) period of being a novice; religious novice; novices' quarters.

now ● *adverb* at present or mentioned time; immediately; by this time: in the immediate past. ● *conjunction* (often + *that*) because. ● *noun* this time; the present. □ **now and again** or **then** occasionally.

nowadays /ˈnaʊədeɪz/ ● *adverb* at present time or age. ● *noun* the present time.

nowhere /ˈnəʊweə/ ● *adverb* in or to no place. ● *pronoun* no place.

nowt *noun colloquial or dialect* nothing.

noxious /ˈnɒkʃəs/ *adjective* harmful, unwholesome.

nozzle /ˈnɒz(ə)l/ *noun* spout on hose etc.

nr. *abbreviation* near.

NSPCC *abbreviation* National Society for Prevention of Cruelty to Children.

NSW *abbreviation* New South Wales.

NT *abbreviation* New Testament; Northern Territory (of Australia); National Trust.

nuance /ˈnjuːɑ̃s/ *noun* subtle shade of meaning, feeling, colour, etc.

nub *noun* point or gist (of matter or story).

nubile /ˈnjuːbaɪl/ *adjective* (of woman) marriageable, sexually attractive. □ **nubility** *noun*.

nuclear /ˈnjuːklɪə/ *adjective* of, relating to, or constituting a nucleus; using nuclear energy. □ **nuclear energy** energy obtained by nuclear fission or fusion; **nuclear family** couple and their child(ren); **nuclear fission** nuclear reaction in which heavy nucleus splits with release of energy; **nuclear fuel** source of nuclear energy; **nuclear fusion** nuclear reaction in which nuclei of low atomic number fuse with release of energy; **nuclear physics** physics of

---

Noun

A noun is the name of a person or thing. There are four kinds:

1 common nouns (the words for articles and creatures), e.g.

shoe	in	*The red shoe was left on the shelf.*
box	in	*The large box stood in the corner.*
plant	in	*The plant grew to two metres.*
horse	in	*A horse and rider galloped by.*

2 proper nouns (the names of people, places, ships, institutions, and animals, which always begin with a capital letter), e.g.

Jane	*USS Enterprise*	*Bambi*
London	*Grand Hotel*	

3 abstract nouns (the words for qualities, things we cannot see or touch, and things which have no physical reality), e.g.

truth	*absence*
explanation	*warmth*

4 collective nouns (the words for groups of things), e.g.

committee	*squad*	*the Cabinet*
herd	*swarm*	*the clergy*
majority	*team*	*the public*

atomic nuclei; **nuclear power** power derived from nuclear energy, country that has nuclear weapons.

nucleic acid /nju:ˈkliːɪk/ noun either of two complex organic molecules (DNA and RNA) present in all living cells.

nucleon /ˈnjuːklɪʊn/ noun proton or neutron.

nucleus /ˈnjuːklɪəs/ noun (plural **nuclei** /-lɪaɪ/) central part or thing round which others collect; kernel; initial part; central core of atom; part of cell containing genetic material.

nude /njuːd/ ● adjective naked, unclothed. ● noun painting etc. of nude human figure; nude person. □ **in the nude** naked. □ **nudity** noun.

nudge ● verb (**-ging**) prod gently with elbow to draw attention; push gradually. ● noun gentle push.

nudist /ˈnjuːdɪst/ noun person who advocates or practises going unclothed. □ **nudism** noun.

nugatory /ˈnjuːɡətərɪ/ adjective futile, trifling; inoperative, not valid.

nugget /ˈnʌɡɪt/ noun lump of gold etc., as found in earth; lump of anything.

nuisance /ˈnjuːs(ə)ns/ noun person, thing, or circumstance causing annoyance.

null adjective (esp. **null and void**) invalid; non-existent; expressionless. □ **nullity** noun.

nullify /ˈnʌlɪfaɪ/ verb (**-ies, -ied**) neutralize; invalidate. □ **nullification** noun.

numb /nʌm/ ● adjective deprived of feeling; paralysed. ● verb make numb; stupefy, paralyse. □ **numbness** noun.

number /ˈnʌmbə/ ● noun arithmetical value representing a quantity; word, symbol, or figure representing this; total number or aggregate; numerical reckoning; quantity; amount; person or thing having place in a series, esp. single issue of magazine, item in programme, etc. ● verb include; assign number(s) to; amount to specified number. ● **number one** colloquial oneself; **number plate** plate bearing number esp. of motor vehicle.

■ **Usage** The phrase a number of is normally used with a plural verb, as in a number of problems remain.

numberless adjective innumerable.

numeral /ˈnjuːmər(ə)l/ ● noun symbol or group of symbols denoting a number. ● adjective of or denoting a number.

numerate /ˈnjuːmərət/ adjective familiar with basic principles of mathematics. □ **numeracy** noun.

numeration /njuːməˈreɪʃ(ə)n/ noun process of numbering; calculation.

numerator /ˈnjuːməreɪtə/ noun number above line in vulgar fraction.

numerical /njuːˈmerɪk(ə)l/ adjective of or relating to number(s). □ **numerically** adverb.

numerology /njuːməˈrɒlədʒɪ/ noun study of supposed occult significance of numbers.

numerous /ˈnjuːmərəs/ adjective many; consisting of many.

numinous /ˈnjuːmɪnəs/ adjective indicating presence of a god; awe-inspiring.

numismatic /njuːmɪzˈmætɪk/ adjective of or relating to coins or medals.

numismatics plural noun (usually treated as singular) study of coins and medals. □ **numismatist** /-ˈmɪzmətɪst/ noun.

nun noun member of community of women living under religious vows.

nuncio /ˈnʌnsɪəʊ/ noun (plural **-s**) papal ambassador.

nunnery noun (plural **-ies**) religious house of nuns.

nuptial /ˈnʌpʃ(ə)l/ ● adjective of marriage or weddings. ● noun (usually in plural) wedding.

nurse /nɜːs/ ● noun person trained to care for sick and help doctors or dentists; nursemaid. ● verb (**-sing**) work as nurse; attend to (sick person); feed or be fed at breast; hold or treat carefully; foster; harbour. □ **nursing home** private hospital or home.

nursemaid noun woman in charge of child(ren).

nursery /ˈnɜːsərɪ/ noun (plural **-ies**) room or place equipped for young children; place where plants are reared for sale. □ **nurseryman** grower of plants for sale; **nursery rhyme** traditional song or rhyme for young children; **nursery school** school for children between ages of 3 and 5.

nurture /ˈnɜːtʃə/ ● noun bringing up, fostering care; nourishment. ● verb (**-ring**) bring up, rear.

nut noun fruit consisting of hard shell or pod around edible kernel or seeds; this kernel; small usually hexagonal flat piece of metal with threaded hole through it for screwing on end of bolt to secure it; slang head; slang crazy person; small lump of (coal etc.). □ **nutcase** slang crazy person; **nutcracker** (usually in plural) device for cracking nuts; **nuthatch** small bird climbing up and down tree trunks; **nuts** slang crazy.

nutmeg /ˈnʌtmeg/ noun hard aromatic seed used as spice etc.; E. Indian tree bearing this.

nutria /ˈnjuːtrɪə/ noun coypu fur.

nutrient /ˈnjuːtrɪənt/ ● noun substance providing essential nourishment. ● adjective serving as or providing nourishment.

nutriment /ˈnjuːtrɪmənt/ noun nourishing food.

nutrition /njuːˈtrɪʃ(ə)n/ noun food, nourishment. □ **nutritional** adjective; **nutritionist** noun.

nutritious /njuːˈtrɪʃəs/ adjective efficient as food.

nutritive /ˈnjuːtrɪtɪv/ adjective of nutrition; nutritious.

nutshell noun hard covering of nut. □ **in a nutshell** in few words.

nutter noun slang crazy person.

nutty adjective (**-ier, -iest**) full of nuts; tasting like nuts; slang crazy.

nux vomica /nʌks ˈvɒmɪkə/ noun E. Indian tree; its seeds, containing strychnine.

nuzzle /ˈnʌz(ə)l/ verb (**-ling**) prod or rub gently with nose; nestle, lie snug.

NW abbreviation north-west(ern).

NY abbreviation US New York.

nylon /ˈnaɪlɒn/ noun strong light synthetic fibre; nylon fabric; (in plural) stockings of nylon.

nymph /nɪmf/ noun mythological semi-divine female spirit associated with rivers, woods, etc.; immature form of some insects.

nymphomania /nɪmfəˈmeɪnɪə/ noun excessive sexual desire in a woman. □ **nymphomaniac** noun & adjective.

NZ abbreviation New Zealand.

Oo

O¹ □ **O level** *historical* ordinary level in GCE exam.

O² /əʊ/ *interjection* = OH; *used before name in exclamation.*

oaf *noun* (*plural* **-s**) awkward lout. □ **oafish** *adjective*; **oafishly** *adverb*; **oafishness** *noun*.

oak *noun* acorn-bearing hardwood tree with lobed leaves; its wood. □ **oak-apple**, **-gall** abnormal growth produced on oak trees by insects.

oakum /'əʊkəm/ *noun* loose fibre got by picking old rope to pieces.

OAP *abbreviation* old-age pensioner.

oar /ɔː/ *noun* pole with blade used to propel boat by leverage against water; rower.

oarsman /'ɔːzmən/ *noun* (*feminine* **-woman**) rower. □ **oarsmanship** *noun*.

oasis /əʊ'eɪsɪs/ *noun* (*plural* **oases** /-siːz/) fertile spot in desert.

oast *noun* hop-drying kiln. □ **oast house** building containing this.

oat *noun* cereal plant grown as food; (in *plural*) grain of this; tall grass resembling this. □ **oatcake** thin oatmeal biscuit; **oatmeal** meal ground from oats, greyish-fawn colour; **sow one's wild oats** indulge in youthful follies before becoming steady. □ **oaten** *adjective*.

oath /əʊθ/ *noun* (*plural* **-s** /əʊðz/) solemn declaration naming God etc. as witness; curse. □ **on**, **under oath** having sworn solemn oath.

ob. *abbreviation* died (*obiit*).

obbligato /ɒblɪ'gɑːtəʊ/ *noun* (*plural* **-s**) *Music* accompaniment forming integral part of a composition.

obdurate /'ɒbdjʊrət/ *adjective* stubborn; hardened. □ **obduracy** *noun*.

OBE *abbreviation* Officer of the Order of the British Empire.

obedient /əʊ'biːdɪənt/ *adjective* obeying or ready to obey; submissive to another's will. □ **obedience** *noun*; **obediently** *adverb*.

obeisance /əʊ'beɪs(ə)ns/ *noun* gesture expressing submission, respect, etc.; homage. □ **obeisant** *adjective*.

obelisk /'ɒbəlɪsk/ *noun* tapering usually 4-sided stone pillar.

obelus /'ɒbələs/ *noun* (*plural* **obeli** /-laɪ/) dagger-shaped mark of reference (†).

obese /əʊ'biːs/ *adjective* very fat. □ **obesity** *noun*.

obey /əʊ'beɪ/ *verb* carry out command of; do what one is told to do.

obfuscate /'ɒbfʌskeɪt/ *verb* (**-ting**) obscure, confuse; bewilder. □ **obfuscation** *noun*.

obituary /ə'bɪtjʊərɪ/ ● *noun* (*plural* **-ies**) notice of death(s); brief biography of deceased person. ● *adjective* of or serving as obituary.

object ● *noun* /'ɒbdʒɪkt/ material thing; person or thing to which action or feeling is directed; thing sought or aimed at; word or phrase representing person or thing affected by action of verb (see panel). ● *verb* /əb'dʒekt/ (often + *to*, *against*) express opposition, disapproval, or reluctance; protest. □ **no object** not an important factor. □ **objector** *noun*.

objectify /əb'dʒektɪfaɪ/ *verb* (**-ies**, **-ied**) present as an object, embody.

objection /əb'dʒekʃ(ə)n/ *noun* expression of disapproval or opposition; objecting; adverse reason or statement.

objectionable *adjective* unpleasant, offensive; open to objection. □ **objectionably** *adverb*.

objective /əb'dʒektɪv/ ● *adjective* external to the mind; actually existing; dealing with outward things uncoloured by opinions or feelings; *Grammar* (of case or word) in form appropriate to object. ● *noun* object or purpose; *Grammar* objective case. □ **objectively** *adverb*; **objectivity** /ɒbdʒek'tɪvɪtɪ/ *noun*.

objet d'art /ɒbʒeɪ 'dɑː/ *noun* (*plural* **objets d'art** same pronunciation) small decorative object. [French]

oblate /'ɒbleɪt/ *adjective* (of spheroid) flattened at poles.

oblation /əʊ'bleɪʃ(ə)n/ *noun* thing offered to a divine being.

obligate /'ɒblɪgeɪt/ *verb* (**-ting**) bind (person) legally or morally.

obligation /ɒblɪ'geɪʃ(ə)n/ *noun* compelling power of law, duty, etc.; duty; binding agreement; indebtedness for service or benefit.

Object

There are two types of object:

1 A direct object is a person or thing directly affected by the verb and can usually be found by asking the question 'whom or what?' after the verb, e.g.

> *The electors chose* Mr Smith.
> *Charles wrote* a letter.

2 An indirect object is usually a person or thing receiving something from the subject of the verb, e.g.

> *He gave* me *the pen.*
> (*me* is the indirect object, and *the pen* is the direct object.)

> *I sent* my bank *a letter.*
> (*my bank* is the indirect object, and *a letter* is the direct object.)

Sentences containing an indirect object usually contain a direct object as well, but not always, e.g.
> *Pay me.*

'Object' on its own usually means a direct object.

obligatory /ə'blɪɡətərɪ/ adjective binding, compulsory. □ **obligatorily** adverb.

oblige /ə'blaɪdʒ/ verb (**-ging**) compel, require; be binding on; do (person) small favour; (as **obliged** adjective) grateful.

obliging adjective helpful, accommodating. □ **obligingly** adverb.

oblique /ə'bliːk/ ● adjective slanting; at an angle; not going straight to the point, indirect; Grammar (of case) other than nominative or vocative. ● noun oblique stroke. □ **obliquely** adverb; **obliqueness** noun; **obliquity** /ə'blɪkwɪtɪ/ noun.

obliterate /ə'blɪtəreɪt/ verb (**-ting**) blot out, leave no clear trace of. □ **obliteration** noun.

oblivion /ə'blɪvɪən/ noun state of having or being forgotten.

oblivious /ə'blɪvɪəs/ adjective unaware or unconscious. □ **obliviously** adverb; **obliviousness** noun.

oblong /'ɒblɒŋ/ ● adjective rectangular with adjacent sides unequal. ● noun oblong figure or object.

obloquy /'ɒbləkwɪ/ noun abuse, being ill spoken of.

obnoxious /əb'nɒkʃəs/ adjective offensive, objectionable. □ **obnoxiously** adverb; **obnoxiousness** noun.

oboe /'əʊbəʊ/ noun double-reeded woodwind instrument. □ **oboist** noun.

obscene /əb'siːn/ adjective offensively indecent; colloquial highly offensive; Law (of publication) tending to deprave and corrupt. □ **obscenely** adverb; **obscenity** /-'sen-/ noun (plural **-ies**).

obscure /əb'skjʊə/ ● adjective not clearly expressed or easily understood; unexplained; dark, indistinct; hidden, undistinguished. ● verb (**-ring**) make obscure or invisible. □ **obscurity** noun.

obsequies /'ɒbsɪkwɪz/ plural noun funeral.

obsequious /əb'siːkwɪəs/ adjective fawning, servile. □ **obsequiously** adverb; **obsequiousness** noun.

observance /əb'zɜːv(ə)ns/ noun keeping or performance of law, duty, etc.; rite, ceremonial act.

observant adjective good at observing. □ **observantly** adverb.

observation /ɒbzə'veɪʃ(ə)n/ noun observing, being observed; comment, remark; power of perception. □ **observational** adjective.

observatory /əb'zɜːvətərɪ/ noun (plural **-ies**) building for astronomical or other observation.

observe /əb'zɜːv/ verb (**-ving**) perceive, become aware of; watch; keep (rules etc.); celebrate (rite etc.); remark; take note of scientifically. □ **observable** adjective.

observer noun person who observes; interested spectator; person attending meeting to note proceedings but without participating.

obsess /əb'ses/ verb fill mind of (person) all the time; preoccupy. □ **obsession** noun; **obsessional** adjective; **obsessive** adjective; **obsessively** adverb; **obsessiveness** noun.

obsidian /əb'sɪdɪən/ noun dark glassy rock formed from lava.

obsolescent /ɒbsə'les(ə)nt/ adjective becoming obsolete. □ **obsolescence** noun.

obsolete /'ɒbsəliːt/ adjective no longer used, antiquated.

obstacle /'ɒbstək(ə)l/ noun thing obstructing progress.

obstetrics /əb'stetrɪks/ plural noun (usually treated as singular) branch of medicine or surgery dealing with childbirth. □ **obstetric** adjective; **obstetrician** /ɒbstə'trɪʃ(ə)n/ noun.

obstinate /'ɒbstɪnət/ adjective stubborn, intractable. □ **obstinacy** noun; **obstinately** adverb.

obstreperous /əb'strepərəs/ adjective noisy, unruly. □ **obstreperously** adverb; **obstreperousness** noun.

obstruct /əb'strʌkt/ verb block up; make hard or impossible to pass along or through; retard or prevent progress of.

obstruction /əb'strʌkʃ(ə)n/ noun obstructing, being obstructed; thing that obstructs; Sport unlawfully obstructing another player.

obstructive adjective causing or meant to cause obstruction.

obtain /əb'teɪn/ verb acquire; get; have granted to one; be prevalent or established. □ **obtainable** adjective.

obtrude /əb'truːd/ verb (**-ding**) (often + on, upon) thrust (oneself etc.) importunately forward. □ **obtrusion** noun.

obtrusive /əb'truːsɪv/ adjective unpleasantly noticeable; obtruding oneself. □ **obtrusively** adverb; **obtrusiveness** noun.

obtuse /əb'tjuːs/ adjective dull-witted; (of angle) between 90° and 180°; blunt, not sharp or pointed. □ **obtuseness** noun.

obverse /'ɒbvɜːs/ noun counterpart, opposite; side of coin or medal that bears head or principal design; front or top side.

obviate /'ɒbvɪeɪt/ verb (**-ting**) get round or do away with (need, inconvenience, etc.).

obvious /'ɒbvɪəs/ adjective easily seen, recognized, or understood. □ **obviously** adverb; **obviousness** noun.

OC abbreviation Officer Commanding.

ocarina /ɒkə'riːnə/ noun egg-shaped musical wind instrument.

occasion /ə'keɪʒ(ə)n/ ● noun special event or happening; time of this; reason, need; suitable juncture, opportunity. ● verb cause, esp. incidentally.

occasional adjective happening irregularly and infrequently; made or meant for, acting on, etc. special occasion(s). □ **occasional table** small table for use as required. □ **occasionally** adverb.

Occident /'ɒksɪd(ə)nt/ noun (**the Occident**) West, esp. Europe and America as distinct from the Orient. □ **occidental** /-'den-/ adjective.

occiput /'ɒksɪpʌt/ noun back of head. □ **occipital** /-'sɪpɪt-/ adjective.

occlude /ə'kluːd/ verb (**-ding**) stop up; obstruct; Chemistry absorb (gases); (as **occluded** adjective) Meteorology (of frontal system) formed when cold front overtakes warm front, raising warm air. □ **occlusion** noun.

occult /ɒ'kʌlt, 'ɒkʌlt/ adjective involving the supernatural, mystical; esoteric. □ **the occult** occult phenomena generally.

occupant /'ɒkjʊpənt/ noun person occupying dwelling, office, or position. □ **occupancy** noun (plural **-ies**).

occupation /ɒkjʊ'peɪʃ(ə)n/ noun profession or employment; pastime; occupying or being occupied, esp. by armed forces of another country.

occupational adjective of or connected with one's occupation. □ **occupational disease, hazard** one to which a particular occupation renders someone especially liable; **occupational therapy** programme of mental or physical activity to assist recovery from disease or injury.

occupier /'ɒkjʊpaɪə/ noun person living in house etc. as owner or tenant.

occupy /'ɒkjʊpaɪ/ verb (**-ies**, **-ied**) live in; be tenant of; take up, fill (space, time, or place); take military possession of; place oneself in (building etc.) without authority as protest etc.; hold (office); keep busy.

occur /ə'kɜː/ verb (**-rr-**) take place, happen; be met with or found in some place or conditions; (+ to) come into one's mind.

occurrence /ə'kʌrəns/ noun happening; incident.

ocean /ˈəʊʃ(ə)n/ *noun* large expanse of sea, esp. one of the 5 named bodies of this, e.g. Atlantic Ocean; (often in *plural*) *colloquial* immense expanse or quantity. □ **oceanic** /əʊʃɪˈænɪk/ *adjective*.

oceanography /əʊʃɪˈnɒɡrəfɪ/ *noun* study of the oceans. □ **oceanographer** *noun*.

ocelot /ˈʊsɪlɒt/ *noun* S. American leopard-like cat.

ochre /ˈəʊkə/ *noun* (*US* **ocher**) earth used as pigment; pale brownish-yellow colour. □ **ochreous** /ˈəʊkrɪəs/ *adjective*.

o'clock /əˈklɒk/ *adverb* of the clock (used to specify hour).

Oct. *abbreviation* October.

octa- *combining form* (also **oct-** before vowel) eight.

octagon /ˈɒktəɡən/ *noun* plane figure with 8 sides and angles. □ **octagonal** /-ˈtæɡ-/ *adjective*.

octahedron /ɒktəˈhiːdrən/ *noun* (*plural* **-s**) solid figure contained by 8 (esp. triangular) plane faces. □ **octahedral** *adjective*.

octane /ˈɒkteɪn/ *noun* colourless inflammable hydrocarbon occurring in petrol. □ **high-octane** (of fuel used in internal-combustion engines) not detonating rapidly during power stroke; **octane number, rating** figure indicating antiknock properties of fuel.

octave /ˈɒktɪv/ *noun Music* interval of 8 diatonic degrees between two notes, 8 notes occupying this interval, each of two notes at this interval's extremes; 8-line stanza.

octavo /ɒkˈteɪvəʊ/ *noun* (*plural* **-s**) size of book or page with sheets folded into 8 leaves.

octet /ɒkˈtet/ *noun* musical composition for 8 performers; the performers; any group of 8.

octo- *combining form* (also **oct-** before vowel) eight.

October /ɒkˈtəʊbə/ *noun* tenth month of year.

octogenarian /ɒktəʊdʒɪˈneərɪən/ *noun* person from 80 to 89 years old.

octopus /ˈɒktəpəs/ *noun* (*plural* **-puses**) mollusc with 8 suckered tentacles.

ocular /ˈɒkjʊlə/ *adjective* of, for, or by the eyes; visual.

oculist /ˈɒkjʊlɪst/ *noun* specialist in treatment of eyes.

OD /əʊˈdiː/ *slang* ● *noun* drug overdose. ● *verb* (**OD's, OD'd, Od'ing**) take overdose.

odd *adjective* extraordinary, strange; (of job etc.) occasional, casual; not normally considered, unconnected; (of numbers) not divisible by 2; left over, detached from set etc.; (added to weight, sum, etc.) rather more than. □ **oddball** *colloquial* eccentric person. □ **oddly** *adverb*; **oddness** *noun*.

oddity /ˈɒdɪtɪ/ *noun* (*plural* **-ies**) strange person, thing, or occurrence; peculiar trait; strangeness.

oddment *noun* odd article; something left over.

odds *plural noun* ratio between amounts staked by parties to a bet; chances in favour of or against result; balance of advantage; difference giving an advantage. □ **at odds** (often + *with*) in conflict; **odds and ends** remnants, stray articles; **odds-on** state when success is more likely than failure; **over the odds** above general price etc.

ode *noun* lyric poem of exalted style and tone.

odious /ˈəʊdɪəs/ *adjective* hateful, repulsive. □ **odiously** *adverb*; **odiousness** *noun*.

odium /ˈəʊdɪəm/ *noun* general dislike or disapproval.

odor *US* = ODOUR.

odoriferous /əʊdəˈrɪfərəs/ *adjective* diffusing (usually pleasant) odours.

odour /ˈəʊdə/ *noun* (*US* **odor**) smell or fragrance; favour or repute. □ **odorous** *adjective*; **odourless** *adjective*.

odyssey /ˈɒdɪsɪ/ *noun* (*plural* **-s**) long adventurous journey.

OED *abbreviation* Oxford English Dictionary.

oedema /ɪˈdiːmə/ *noun* (*US* **edema**) excess fluid in body cavities or tissues.

Oedipus complex /ˈiːdɪpəs/ *noun* attraction of child to parent of opposite sex (esp. son to mother). □ **Oedipal** *adjective*.

oesophagus /iːˈsɒfəgəs/ *noun* (*US* **esophagus**) (*plural* **-gi** /-dʒaɪ/ or **-guses**) passage from mouth to stomach, gullet.

oestrogen /ˈiːstrədʒ(ə)n/ *noun* (*US* **estrogen**) hormone producing female physical characteristics.

oeuvre /ˈɜːvr/ *noun* works of creative artist considered collectively. [French]

of /ɒv/ *preposition* belonging to, from; concerning; out of; among; relating to; *US* (of time in relation to following hour) to. □ **be of** possess, give rise to; **of late** recently; **of old** formerly.

off ● *adverb* away, at or to distance; out of position; loose, separate, gone; so as to be rid of; discontinued, stopped; not available on menu. ● *preposition* from; not on. ● *adjective* further; far; right-hand; *colloquial* annoying; not acceptable; *Cricket* of, in, or into half of field which batsman faces. ● *noun* start of race; *Cricket* the off side. □ **off and on** now and then; **offbeat** unconventional, *Music* not coinciding with beat; **off chance** remote possibility; **off colour** unwell, *US* rather indecent; **offhand** without preparation, casual, curt; **off-licence** shop selling alcoholic drink for consumption away from premises; **offline** *Computing adjective* not online, *adverb* with delay between data production and its processing; **off-peak** (of electricity, traffic, etc.) used or for use at times of lesser demand; **offprint** reprint of part of publication; **offshoot** side-shoot or branch, derivative; **offside** (of player in field game) in position where he or she may not play the ball; **off the wall** *slang* crazy, absurd; **off white** white with grey or yellowish tinge.

offal /ˈɒf(ə)l/ *noun* edible organs of animal, esp. heart, liver, etc.; refuse, scraps.

offence /əˈfens/ *noun* (*US* **offense**) illegal act; transgression; upsetting of person's feelings, insult; aggressive action.

offend /əˈfend/ *verb* cause offence to, upset; displease, anger; (often + *against*) do wrong. □ **offender** *noun*; **offending** *adjective*.

offense *US* = OFFENCE.

offensive /əˈfensɪv/ ● *adjective* causing offence; insulting; disgusting; aggressive; (of weapon) for attacking. ● *noun* aggressive attitude, action, or campaign. □ **offensively** *adverb*; **offensiveness** *noun*.

offer /ˈɒfə/ ● *verb* present for acceptance, refusal, or consideration; (+ *to do*) express readiness, show intention; attempt; present by way of sacrifice. ● *noun* expression of readiness to do or give if desired, or buy or sell; amount offered; proposal, esp. of marriage; bid. □ **on offer** for sale at certain (esp. reduced) price.

offering *noun* contribution, gift; thing offered.

offertory /ˈɒfətərɪ/ *noun* (*plural* **-ies**) offering of bread and wine at Eucharist; collection of money at religious service.

office /ˈɒfɪs/ *noun* room or building where administrative or clerical work is done; place for transacting business; department or local branch, esp. for specified purpose; position with duties attached to it; tenure of official position; duty, task, function; (usually in *plural*) piece of kindness, service; authorized form of worship.

officer /ˈɒfɪsə/ *noun* person holding position of authority or trust, esp. one with commission in armed forces; policeman or policewoman; president, treasurer, etc. of society etc.

official /ə'fɪʃ(ə)l/ ● adjective of office or its tenure; characteristic of people in office; properly authorized. ● noun person holding office or engaged in official duties. □ **official secrets** confidential information involving national security. □ **officialdom** noun; **officially** adverb.

officialese /əfɪʃə'liːz/ noun derogatory officials' jargon.

officiate /ə'fɪʃɪeɪt/ verb (**-ting**) act in official capacity; conduct religious service.

officious /ə'fɪʃəs/ adjective domineering; intrusive in correcting etc. □ **officiously** adverb; **officiousness** noun.

offing /'ɒfɪŋ/ noun □ **in the offing** at hand, ready or likely to happen etc.

offset ● noun side-shoot of plant used for propagation; compensation; sloping ledge. ● verb (**-setting**; past & past participle **-set**) counterbalance, compensate.

offspring noun (plural same) person's child, children, or descendants; animal's young or descendants.

oft adverb archaic often.

often /'ɒf(ə)n/ adverb (**oftener**, **oftenest**) frequently; many times; at short intervals; in many instances.

ogee /'əʊdʒiː/ noun S-shaped curve or moulding.

ogive /'əʊdʒaɪv/ noun pointed arch; diagonal rib of vault.

ogle /'əʊg(ə)l/ ● verb (**-ling**) look lecherously or flirtatiously (at). ● noun flirtatious glance.

ogre /'əʊgə/ noun (feminine **ogress** /-grɪs/) man-eating giant. □ **ogreish**, **ogrish** /'əʊgərɪʃ/ adjective.

oh /əʊ/ interjection (also **O**) expressing surprise, pain, etc.

ohm /əʊm/ noun SI unit of electrical resistance.

OHMS abbreviation On Her or His Majesty's Service.

oho /əʊ'həʊ/ interjection expressing surprise or exultation.

OHP abbreviation overhead projector.

oil ● noun viscous usually inflammable liquid insoluble in water; petroleum. ● verb apply oil to, lubricate; treat with oil. □ **oilcake** compressed linseed etc. as cattle food or manure; **oilfield** district yielding mineral oil; **oil paint** paint made by mixing pigment with oil; **oil painting** use of or picture in oil paints; **oil rig** equipment for drilling an oil well; **oilskin** cloth waterproofed with oil, garment or (in plural) suit of it; **oil slick** patch of oil, esp. on sea; **oil well** well from which mineral oil is drawn.

oily adjective (**-ier**, **-iest**) of, like, covered or soaked with, oil; (of manner) fawning.

ointment /'ɔɪntmənt/ noun smooth greasy healing or cosmetic preparation for skin.

OK /əʊ'keɪ/ (also **okay**) colloquial ● adjective & adverb all right. ● noun (plural **OKs**) approval, sanction. ● verb (**OK's**, **OK'd**, **OK'ing**) approve, sanction.

okapi /əʊ'kɑːpɪ/ noun (plural same or **-s**) African partially striped ruminant mammal.

okay = OK.

okra /'əʊkrə/ noun tall originally African plant with edible seed pods.

old /əʊld/ adjective (**-er**, **-est**) advanced in age; not young or near its beginning; worn, dilapidated, or shabby from age; practised, inveterate; dating from far back; long established; former; colloquial: used to indicate affection. □ **old age** later part of normal lifetime; **old-age pension** state retirement pension; **old-age pensioner** person receiving this; **Old Bill** slang the police; **old boy** former male pupil of school, colloquial elderly man; **old-fashioned** in or according to fashion no longer current, antiquated; **old girl** former female pupil of school, colloquial elderly woman; **Old Glory** US Stars and Stripes; **old guard** original, past, or conservative members of group; **old hand** experienced or practised person; **old hat** colloquial hackneyed; **old maid** derogatory elderly unmarried woman, prim and fussy person; **old man** colloquial one's father, husband, or employer etc.; **old man's beard** wild clematis; **old master** great painter of former times, painting by such painter; **Old Testament** part of Bible dealing with pre-Christian times; **old wives' tale** unscientific belief; **old woman** colloquial one's wife or mother, fussy or timid man; **Old World** Europe, Asia, and Africa. □ **oldish** adjective; **oldness** noun.

olden adjective archaic old, of old.

oldie noun colloquial old person or thing.

oleaginous /əʊlɪ'ædʒɪnəs/ adjective like or producing oil; oily.

oleander /əʊlɪ'ændə/ noun evergreen flowering Mediterranean shrub.

olfactory /ɒl'fæktərɪ/ adjective of the sense of smell.

oligarch /'ɒlɪgɑːk/ noun member of oligarchy.

oligarchy /'ɒlɪgɑːkɪ/ noun (plural **-ies**) government by small group of people; members of such government; state so governed. □ **oligarchic(al)** /-'gɑːk-/ adjective.

olive /'ɒlɪv/ ● noun oval hard-stoned fruit yielding oil; tree bearing this; dull yellowish green. ● adjective olive-green; (of complexion) yellowish-brown. □ **olive branch** gesture of peace or reconciliation.

Olympiad /ə'lɪmpɪæd/ noun period of 4 years between Olympic Games; celebration of modern Olympic Games.

Olympian /ə'lɪmpɪən/ adjective of Olympus; magnificent, condescending; aloof.

Olympic /ə'lɪmpɪk/ ● adjective of the Olympic Games. ● plural noun (**the Olympics**) Olympic Games. □ **Olympic Games** ancient Greek athletic festival held every 4 years, or modern international revival of this.

OM abbreviation Order of Merit.

ombudsman /'ɒmbʊdzmən/ noun official appointed to investigate complaints against public authorities.

omega /'əʊmɪgə/ noun last letter of Greek alphabet (Ω, ω); last of series.

omelette /'ɒmlɪt/ noun beaten eggs fried and often folded over filling.

omen /'əʊmən/ noun event supposedly warning of good or evil; prophetic significance.

ominous /'ɒmɪnəs/ adjective threatening; inauspicious. □ **ominously** adverb.

omit /əʊ'mɪt/ verb (**-tt-**) leave out; not include; leave undone; (+ to do) neglect. □ **omission** /əʊ'mɪʃ(ə)n/ noun.

omni- combining form all.

omnibus /'ɒmnɪbəs/ ● noun formal bus; volume containing several novels etc. previously published separately. ● adjective serving several purposes at once; comprising several items.

omnipotent /ɒm'nɪpət(ə)nt/ adjective all-powerful. □ **omnipotence** noun.

omnipresent /ɒmnɪ'prez(ə)nt/ adjective present everywhere. □ **omnipresence** noun.

omniscient /ɒm'nɪsɪənt/ adjective knowing everything. □ **omniscience** noun.

omnivorous /ɒm'nɪvərəs/ adjective feeding on both plant and animal material; jocular reading everything that comes one's way. □ **omnivore** /'ɒmnɪvɔː/ noun; **omnivorousness** noun.

on ● preposition (so as to be) supported by, covering, attached to, etc.; (of time) exactly at; during; close to, in direction of; at, near, concerning, about; added to. ● adverb (so as to be) on something; in some direction, forward; in advance; with movement; in operation or activity; colloquial willing to participate, approve, bet, etc.; *colloquial* practicable, acceptable; being shown or performed. ● *adjective* Cricket of, in, or into half of field behind batsman's back. ● *noun* Cricket the on side. □ **be on about** *colloquial* discuss, esp. tiresomely; **online** directly controlled by or connected to computer; **onscreen** when being filmed; **on to** to a position on.

■ **Usage** See note at ONTO.

ONC *abbreviation* Ordinary National Certificate.

once /wʌns/ ● *adverb* on one occasion only; at some time in past; ever or at all. ● *conjunction* as soon as. ● *noun* one time or occasion. □ **at once** immediately, simultaneously; **once-over** *colloquial* rapid inspection.

oncology /ɒŋˈkɒlədʒɪ/ *noun* study of tumours.

oncoming *adjective* approaching from the front.

OND *abbreviation* Ordinary National Diploma.

one /wʌn/ ● *adjective* single and integral in number; only such; without others; identical; forming a unity. ● *noun* lowest cardinal numeral; thing numbered with it; unit, unity; single thing, person, or example; *colloquial* drink. ● *pronoun* any person. □ **one-armed bandit** *colloquial* fruit machine with long handle; **one-horse** *colloquial* small, poorly equipped; **one-man** involving or operated by one person only; **one-off** made as the only one, not repeated; **one-sided** unfair, partial; **one-way** allowing movement etc. in one direction only.

oneness *noun* singleness; uniqueness; agreement, sameness.

onerous /ˈəʊnərəs/ *adjective* burdensome. □ **onerousness** *noun*.

oneself *pronoun: emphatic & reflexive form of* ONE. □ **be oneself** act in one's natural manner.

ongoing *adjective* continuing, in progress.

onion /ˈʌnjən/ *noun* vegetable with edible bulb of pungent smell and flavour.

onlooker *noun* spectator. □ **onlooking** *adjective*.

only /ˈəʊnlɪ/ ● *adverb* solely, merely, exclusively. ● *adjective* existing alone of its or their kind. ● *conjunction colloquial* except that; but then. □ **if only** even if for no other reason than, I wish that.

o.n.o. *abbreviation* or near offer.

onomatopoeia /ɒnəmætəˈpiːə/ *noun* formation of word from sound associated with thing named, e.g. *whizz, cuckoo*. □ **onomatopoeic** *adjective*.

onset *noun* attack; impetuous beginning.

onslaught /ˈɒnslɔːt/ *noun* fierce attack.

onto *preposition* = ON TO.

■ **Usage** *Onto* is much used but is still not as widely accepted as *into*. It is, however, useful in distinguishing between, e.g., *We drove on to the beach* (i.e. towards it) and *we drove onto the beach* (i.e. into contact with it).

ontology /ɒnˈtɒlədʒɪ/ *noun* branch of metaphysics concerned with the nature of being. □ **ontological** /-təˈlɒdʒ-/ *adjective*; **ontologically** /-təˈlɒdʒ-/ *adverb*; **ontologist** *noun*.

onus /ˈəʊnəs/ *noun* (*plural* **onuses**) burden, duty, responsibility.

onward /ˈɒnwəd/ ● *adverb* (also **onwards**) advancing; into the future. ● *adjective* forward, advancing.

onyx /ˈɒnɪks/ *noun* semiprecious variety of agate with coloured layers.

oodles /ˈuːd(ə)lz/ *plural noun colloquial* very great amount.

ooh /uː/ *interjection expressing surprised pleasure, pain, excitement, etc.*

oolite /ˈəʊəlaɪt/ *noun* granular limestone. □ **oolitic** /-ˈlɪt-/ *adjective*.

oomph /ʊmf/ *noun slang* energy, enthusiasm; attractiveness, esp. sex appeal.

ooze[1] ● *verb* (**-zing**) trickle or leak slowly out; (of substance) exude fluid; (often + *with*) give off (a feeling) freely. ● *noun* sluggish flow. □ **oozy** *adjective*.

ooze[2] *noun* wet mud. □ **oozy** *adjective*.

op *noun colloquial* operation.

op. *abbreviation* opus.

opacity /əʊˈpæsɪtɪ/ *noun* opaqueness.

opal /ˈəʊp(ə)l/ *noun* semiprecious milk-white or bluish stone with iridescent reflections.

opalescent /əʊpəˈles(ə)nt/ *adjective* iridescent. □ **opalescence** *noun*.

opaline /ˈəʊpəlaɪn/ *adjective* opal-like; opalescent.

opaque /əʊˈpeɪk/ *adjective* (**-r, -st**) not transmitting light; impenetrable to sight; unintelligible; stupid. □ **opaquely** *adverb*; **opaqueness** *noun*.

op. cit. *abbreviation* in the work already quoted (*opere citato*).

OPEC /ˈəʊpek/ *abbreviation* Organization of Petroleum Exporting Countries.

open /ˈəʊpən/ ● *adjective* not closed, locked, or blocked up; not covered or confined; exposed; (of goal etc.) undefended; undisguised, public; unfolded, spread out; (of fabric) with gaps; frank; open-minded; accessible to visitors or customers; (of meeting, competition, etc.) not restricted; (+ *to*) willing to receive, vulnerable to. ● *verb* make or become open or more open; (+ *into* etc.) give access; establish, set going; start; ceremonially declare open. ● *noun* (**the open**) open air; open competition etc. □ **open air** *noun* outdoors; **open-air** *adjective* outdoor; **open day** day when public may visit place normally closed to them; **open-ended** with no limit or restriction; **open-handed** generous; **open-heart surgery** surgery with heart exposed and blood made to bypass it; **open house** hospitality for all visitors; **open letter** one addressed to individual and printed in newspaper etc.; **open-minded** accessible to new ideas, unprejudiced; **open-plan** (of house, office, etc.) having large undivided rooms; **open prison** one with few physical restraints on prisoners; **open question** matter on which different views are legitimate; **open sandwich** one without bread on top; **open sea** expanse of sea away from land. □ **openness** *noun*.

opener *noun* device for opening tins or bottles etc.

opening ● *noun* gap, aperture; opportunity; beginning, initial part. ● *adjective* initial, first.

openly *adverb* publicly, frankly.

opera[1] /ˈɒpərə/ *noun* musical drama with sung or spoken dialogue. □ **opera-glasses** small binoculars for use in theatres etc.; **opera house** theatre for operas.

opera[2] *plural of* OPUS.

operable /ˈɒpərəb(ə)l/ *adjective* that can be operated; suitable for treatment by surgical operation.

operate /ˈɒpəreɪt/ *verb* (**-ting**) work, control (machine etc.); be in action; perform surgical operation(s); direct military etc. action. □ **operating theatre** room for surgical operations.

operatic /ɒpəˈrætɪk/ *adjective* of or like opera.

operation *noun* action, working; performance of surgery on a patient; military manoeuvre; financial transaction. □ **operational** *adjective*; **operationally** *adverb*.

operative /ˈɒpərətɪv/ ● *adjective* in operation; having principal relevance; of or by surgery. ● *noun* worker, artisan.

operator *noun* person operating machine, esp. connecting lines in telephone exchange; person engaging in business.

operetta /ɒpəˈretə/ *noun* light opera.

ophidian /əʊˈfɪdɪən/ ● *noun* member of suborder of reptiles including snakes. ● *adjective* of this order.

ophthalmia /ɒfˈθælmɪə/ *noun* inflammation of eye.

ophthalmic /ɒfˈθælmɪk/ *adjective* of or relating to the eye and its diseases. □ **ophthalmic optician** one qualified to prescribe as well as dispense spectacles.

ophthalmology /ɒfθælˈmɒlədʒɪ/ *noun* study of the eye. □ **ophthalmologist** *noun*.

ophthalmoscope /ɒfˈθælməskəʊp/ *noun* instrument for examining the eye.

opiate /ˈəʊpɪət/ ● *adjective* containing opium; soporific. ● *noun* drug containing opium, usually to ease pain or induce sleep; soothing influence.

opine /əʊˈpaɪn/ *verb* (**-ning**) (often + *that*) express or hold as opinion.

opinion /əˈpɪnjən/ *noun* unproven belief; view held as probable; professional advice; estimation. □ **opinion poll** assessment of public opinion by questioning representative sample.

opinionated /əˈpɪnjəneɪtɪd/ *adjective* unduly confident in one's opinions.

opium /ˈəʊpɪəm/ *noun* drug made from juice of certain poppy, used as narcotic or sedative.

opossum /əˈpɒsəm/ *noun* tree-living American marsupial; *Australian & NZ* marsupial resembling this.

opponent /əˈpəʊnənt/ *noun* person who opposes.

opportune /ˈɒpətjuːn/ *adjective* well-chosen, specially favourable; (of action, event, etc.) well-timed.

opportunism /ɒpəˈtjuːnɪz(ə)m/ *noun* adaptation of policy to circumstances, esp. regardless of principle. □ **opportunist** *noun*; **opportunistic** /-ˈnɪs-/ *adjective*; **opportunistically** /-ˈnɪs-/ *adverb*.

opportunity /ɒpəˈtjuːnɪtɪ/ *noun* (*plural* **-ies**) favourable chance or opening offered by circumstances.

oppose /əˈpəʊz/ *verb* (**-sing**) set oneself against; resist; argue against; (+ *to*) place in opposition or contrast. □ **as opposed to** in contrast with. □ **opposer** *noun*.

opposite /ˈɒpəzɪt/ ● *adjective* facing, on other side; (often + *to, from*) contrary; diametrically different. ● *noun* opposite thing, person, or term. ● *adverb* in opposite position. ● *preposition* opposite to. □ **opposite number** person in corresponding position in another group etc.; **the opposite sex** either sex in relation to the other.

opposition /ɒpəˈzɪʃ(ə)n/ *noun* antagonism, resistance; being in conflict or disagreement; contrast; group or party of opponents; chief parliamentary party, or group of parties, opposed to party in office; act of placing opposite.

oppress /əˈpres/ *verb* govern tyrannically; treat with gross harshness or injustice; weigh down. □ **oppression** *noun*; **oppressor** *noun*.

oppressive *adjective* that oppresses; (of weather) sultry, close. □ **oppressively** *adverb*; **oppressiveness** *noun*.

opprobrious /əˈprəʊbrɪəs/ *adjective* (of language) severely scornful; abusive.

opprobrium /əˈprəʊbrɪəm/ *noun* disgrace; cause of this.

opt *verb* (usually + *for*) make choice; decide. □ **opt out (of)** choose not to take part etc. (in).

optic /ˈɒptɪk/ *adjective* of eye or sight.

optical *adjective* visual; of or according to optics; aiding sight. □ **optical fibre** thin glass fibre used to carry light signals; **optical illusion** image which deceives the eye, mental misapprehension caused by this.

optician /ɒpˈtɪʃ(ə)n/ *noun* maker, seller, or prescriber of spectacles, contact lenses, etc.

optics *plural noun* (treated as *singular*) science of light and vision.

optimal /ˈɒptɪm(ə)l/ *adjective* best, most favourable.

optimism /ˈɒptɪmɪz(ə)m/ *noun* inclination to hopefulness and confidence. □ **optimist** *noun*; **optimistic** /-ˈmɪs-/ *adjective*; **optimistically** /-ˈmɪs-/ *adverb*.

optimize /ˈɒptɪmaɪz/ *verb* (also **-ise**) (**-zing** or **-sing**) make best or most effective use of. □ **optimization** *noun*.

optimum /ˈɒptɪməm/ ● *noun* (*plural* **-ma**) most favourable conditions; best practical solution. ● *adjective* optimal.

option /ˈɒpʃ(ə)n/ *noun* choice, choosing; right to choose; right to buy, sell, etc., on specified conditions at specified time. □ **keep, leave one's options open** not commit oneself.

optional *adjective* not obligatory. □ **optionally** *adverb*.

opulent /ˈɒpjʊlənt/ *adjective* wealthy; luxurious; abundant. □ **opulence** *noun*.

opus /ˈəʊpəs/ *noun* (*plural* **opuses** or **opera** /ˈɒpərə/) musical composition numbered as one of composer's works; any artistic work.

or *conjunction* introducing *alternatives*. □ **or else** otherwise, colloquial: expressing threat.

oracle /ˈɒrək(ə)l/ *noun* place at which ancient Greeks etc. consulted gods for advice or prophecy; response received there; person or thing regarded as source of wisdom etc. □ **oracular** /əˈrækjʊlə/ *adjective*.

oral /ˈɔːr(ə)l/ ● *adjective* spoken, verbal; by word of mouth; done or taken by mouth. ● *noun colloquial* spoken exam. □ **orally** *adverb*.

orange /ˈɒrɪndʒ/ ● *noun* roundish reddish-yellow citrus fruit; its colour; tree bearing it. ● *adjective* orange-coloured.

orangeade /ɒrɪndʒˈeɪd/ *noun* drink made from or flavoured like oranges, usually fizzy.

orang-utan /ɔːræŋuːˈtæn/ *noun* (also **orang-outang** /-uːˈtæŋ/) large anthropoid ape.

oration /ɔːˈreɪʃ(ə)n/ *noun* formal or ceremonial speech.

orator /ˈɒrətə/ *noun* maker of a formal speech; eloquent public speaker.

oratorio /ɒrəˈtɔːrɪəʊ/ *noun* (*plural* **-s**) semi-dramatic musical composition usually on sacred theme.

oratory /ˈɒrətərɪ/ *noun* (*plural* **-ies**) art of or skill in public speaking; small private chapel. □ **oratorical** /-ˈtɒr-/ *adjective*.

orb *noun* globe surmounted by cross as part of coronation regalia; sphere, globe; *poetical* celestial body; *poetical* eye.

orbicular /ɔːˈbɪkjʊlə/ *adjective formal* spherical, circular.

orbit /ˈɔːbɪt/ ● *noun* curved course of planet, comet, satellite, etc.; one complete passage round another body; range or sphere of action. ● *verb* (**-t-**) go round in orbit; put into orbit. □ **orbiter** *noun*.

orbital *adjective* of orbits; (of road) passing round outside of city.

Orcadian /ɔːˈkeɪdɪən/ ● *adjective* of Orkney. ● *noun* native of Orkney.

orchard /ˈɔːtʃəd/ *noun* enclosed piece of land with fruit trees.

orchestra /ˈɔːkɪstrə/ *noun* large group of instrumental performers. □ **orchestra pit** part of theatre where orchestra plays. □ **orchestral** /ɔːˈkestr(ə)l/ *adjective*.

orchestrate /ˈɔːkɪstreɪt/ *verb* (**-ting**) compose or arrange for orchestral performance; arrange (elements) for desired effect.

orchid /'ɔːkɪd/ *noun* any of various plants, often with brilliantly coloured or grotesquely shaped flowers.

ordain /ɔː'deɪn/ *verb* confer holy orders on; decree, order.

ordeal /ɔː'diːl/ *noun* severe trial; painful or horrific experience.

order /'ɔːdə/ ● *noun* condition in which every part, unit, etc. is in its right place; tidiness; specified sequence; authoritative direction or instruction; state of obedience to law, authority, etc.; direction to supply something, thing(s) (to be) supplied; social class or rank; kind, sort; constitution or nature of the world, society, etc.; *Biology* grouping of animals or plants below class and above family; religious fraternity; grade of Christian ministry; any of 5 classical styles of architecture; company of people distinguished by particular honour, etc., insignia worn by its members; stated form of divine service; system of rules etc. (at meetings etc.). ● *verb* command, prescribe; command or direct (person) to specified destination; direct manufacturer, tradesman, etc. to supply; direct waiter to serve; (often as **ordered** *adjective*) put in order; (of God, fate, etc.) ordain. □ **in** or **out of order** in correct or incorrect sequence; **of** or **in the order of** approximately.

orderly ● *adjective* methodically arranged; tidy; not unruly. ● *noun* (*plural* **-ies**) soldier in attendance on officer; hospital attendant. □ **orderly room** room in barracks for company's business.

ordinal /'ɔːdɪn(ə)l/ *noun* (in full **ordinal number**) number defining position in a series; compare CAR-DINAL NUMBER.

ordinance /'ɔːdɪnəns/ *noun* decree; religious rite.

ordinand /'ɔːdɪnænd/ *noun* candidate for ordination.

ordinary /'ɔːdɪnərɪ/ *adjective* normal; not exceptional; commonplace. □ **ordinary level** *historical* lowest in GCE exam; **ordinary seaman** sailor of lowest rank. □ **ordinarily** *adverb*; **ordinariness** *noun*.

ordination /ɔːdɪ'neɪʃ(ə)n/ *noun* conferring of holy orders; ordaining.

ordnance /'ɔːdnəns/ *noun* artillery and military supplies; government service dealing with these. □ **Ordnance Survey** government survey of UK producing detailed maps.

ordure /'ɔːdjʊə/ *noun* dung.

ore *noun* naturally occurring mineral yielding metal or other valuable minerals.

oregano /ɒrɪ'gɑːnəʊ/ *noun* dried wild marjoram as seasoning.

organ /'ɔːgən/ *noun* musical instrument consisting of pipes that sound when air is forced through them, operated by keys and pedals; similar instrument producing sound electronically; part of body serving some special function; medium of opinion, esp. newspaper. □ **organ-grinder** player of barrel organ.

organdie /'ɔːgəndɪ/ *noun* fine translucent muslin, usually stiffened.

organic /ɔː'gænɪk/ *adjective* of or affecting bodily organ(s); (of animals and plants) having organs or organized physical structure; (of food) produced without artificial fertilizers or pesticides; (of chemical compound etc.) containing carbon; organized; inherent, structural. □ **organic chemistry** that of carbon compounds. □ **organically** *adverb*.

organism /'ɔːgənɪz(ə)m/ *noun* individual animal or plant; living being with interdependent parts; system made up of interdependent parts.

organist *noun* player of organ.

organization /ɔːgənaɪ'zeɪʃ(ə)n/ *noun* (also **-isation**) organized body, system, or society; organizing, being organized.

organize /'ɔːgənaɪz/ *verb* (also **-ise**) (**-zing** or **-sing**) give orderly structure to; make arrangements for

(person, oneself); initiate, arrange for; (as **organized** *adjective*) make organic or into living tissue. □ **organizer** *noun*.

orgasm /'ɔːgæz(ə)m/ ● *noun* climax of sexual excitement. ● *verb* have sexual orgasm. □ **orgasmic** /-'gæz-/ *adjective*.

orgy /'ɔːdʒɪ/ *noun* (*plural* **-ies**) wild party with indiscriminate sexual activity; excessive indulgence in an activity. □ **orgiastic** /-'æs-/ *adjective*.

oriel /'ɔːrɪəl/ *noun* window projecting from wall at upper level.

orient /'ɔːrɪənt/ ● *noun* (**the Orient**) the East, countries east of Mediterranean, esp. E. Asia. ● *verb* place or determine position of with aid of compass; find bearings of; (often + *towards*) direct; place (building etc.) to face east; turn eastward or in specified direction.

oriental /ɔːrɪ'ent(ə)l/ (often **Oriental**) ● *adjective* of the East, esp. E. Asia; of the Orient. ● *noun* native of Orient.

orientate /'ɔːrɪənteɪt/ *verb* (**-ting**) orient.

orientation *noun* orienting, being oriented; relative position; person's adjustment in relation to circumstances; briefing.

orienteering /ɔːrɪən'tɪərɪŋ/ *noun* competitive sport of running across rough country with map and compass.

orifice /'ɒrɪfɪs/ *noun* aperture; mouth of cavity.

origami /ɒrɪ'gɑːmɪ/ *noun* Japanese art of folding paper into decorative shapes.

origan /'ɒrɪgən/ *noun* (also **origanum** /ə'rɪgənəm/) wild marjoram.

origin /'ɒrɪdʒɪn/ *noun* source; starting point; (often in *plural*) parentage.

original /ə'rɪdʒɪn(ə)l/ ● *adjective* existing from the beginning; earliest; innate; not imitative or derived; creative not copied; by artist etc. himself or herself. ● *noun* original pattern, picture, etc. from which another is copied or translated. □ **original sin** innate sinfulness held to be common to all human beings after the Fall. □ **originality** /-'næl-/ *noun*; **originally** *adverb*.

originate /ə'rɪdʒɪneɪt/ *verb* (**-ting**) begin; initiate or give origin to, be origin of. □ **origination** *noun*; **originator** *noun*.

oriole /'ɔːrɪəʊl/ *noun* kind of bird, esp. **golden oriole** with black and yellow plumage in male.

ormolu /'ɔːməluː/ *noun* gilded bronze; gold-coloured alloy; articles made of or decorated with these.

ornament ● *noun* /'ɔːnəmənt/ thing used to adorn or decorate; decoration; quality or person bringing honour or distinction. ● *verb* /-ment/ adorn, beautify. □ **ornamental** /-'men-/ *adjective*; **ornamentation** /-men-/ *noun*.

ornate /ɔː'neɪt/ *adjective* elaborately adorned; (of literary style) flowery. □ **ornately** *adverb*.

ornithology /ɔːnɪ'θɒlədʒɪ/ *noun* study of birds. □ **ornithological** /-θə'lɒdʒ-/ *adjective*; **ornithologist** *noun*.

orotund /'ɒrətʌnd/ *adjective* (of voice) full, round; imposing; (of writing, style, etc.) pompous; pretentious.

orphan /'ɔːf(ə)n/ ● *noun* child whose parents are dead. ● *verb* bereave of parents.

orphanage *noun* home for orphans.

orrery /'ɒrərɪ/ *noun* (*plural* **-ies**) clockwork model of solar system.

orris root /'ɒrɪs/ *noun* fragrant iris root used in perfumery.

ortho- *combining form* straight, correct.

orthodontics /ɔːθəˈdɒntɪks/ *plural noun* (usually treated as *singular*) correction of irregularities in teeth and jaws.

orthodox /ˈɔːθədɒks/ *adjective* holding usual or accepted views, esp. on religion, morals, etc.; conventional. □ **Orthodox Church** Eastern Church headed by Patriarch of Constantinople, including Churches of Russia, Romania, Greece, etc. □ **orthodoxy** *noun*.

orthography /ɔːˈθɒgrəfɪ/ *noun* (*plural* **-ies**) spelling, esp. with reference to its correctness. □ **orthographic** /-ˈgræf-/ *adjective*.

orthopaedics /ɔːθəˈpiːdɪks/ *plural noun* (treated as *singular*) (US **-pedics**) branch of medicine dealing with correction of diseased or injured bones or muscles. □ **orthopaedic** *adjective*; **orthopaedist** *noun*.

OS *abbreviation* old style; Ordinary Seaman; Ordnance Survey; outsize.

Oscar /ˈɒskə/ *noun* statuette awarded annually in US for excellence in film acting, directing, etc.

oscillate /ˈɒsɪleɪt/ *verb* (**-ting**) (cause to) swing to and fro; vacillate; *Electricity* (of current) undergo high-frequency alternations. □ **oscillation** *noun*; **oscillator** *noun*.

oscilloscope /əˈsɪləskəʊp/ *noun* device for viewing oscillations usually on screen of cathode ray tube.

osier /ˈəʊzɪə/ *noun* willow used in basketwork; shoot of this.

osmosis /ɒzˈməʊsɪs/ *noun* passage of solvent through semipermeable partition into another solution; process by which something is acquired by absorption. □ **osmotic** /-ˈmɒt-/ *adjective*.

osprey /ˈɒspreɪ/ *noun* (*plural* **-s**) large bird preying on fish.

osseous /ˈɒsɪəs/ *adjective* of bone; bony; having bones.

ossify /ˈɒsɪfaɪ/ *verb* (**-ies**, **-ied**) turn into bone; harden; make or become rigid or unprogressive. □ **ossification** *noun*.

ostensible /ɒˈstensɪb(ə)l/ *adjective* professed; used to conceal real purpose or nature. □ **ostensibly** *adverb*.

ostentation /ɒstenˈteɪʃ(ə)n/ *noun* pretentious display of wealth; showing off. □ **ostentatious** *adjective*.

osteoarthritis /ɒstɪəʊɑːˈθraɪtɪs/ *noun* degenerative disease of the joints. □ **osteoarthritic** /-ˈθrɪt-/ *adjective*.

osteopath /ˈɒstɪəpæθ/ *noun* person who treats disease by manipulation of bones. □ **osteopathy** /-ˈɒp-/ *noun*.

osteoporosis /ɒstɪəʊpəˈrəʊsɪs/ *noun* brittle bones caused by hormonal change or deficiency of calcium or vitamin D.

ostler /ˈɒslə/ *noun historical* stableman at inn.

ostracize /ˈɒstrəsaɪz/ *verb* (also **-ise**) (**-zing** or **-sing**) exclude from society, refuse to associate with. □ **ostracism** /-sɪz(ə)m/ *noun*.

ostrich /ˈɒstrɪtʃ/ *noun* large flightless swift-running African bird; person refusing to acknowledge awkward truth.

OT *abbreviation* Old Testament.

other /ˈʌðə/ ● *adjective* further, additional; different; (**the other**) the only remaining. ● *noun* other person or thing. □ **the other day, week,** etc. a few days etc. ago; **other half** *colloquial* one's wife or husband; **other than** apart from.

otherwise /ˈʌðəwaɪz/ ● *adverb* or else; in different circumstances; in other respects; in a different way; as an alternative. ● *adjective* different.

otiose /ˈəʊtɪəʊs/ *adjective* not required, serving no practical purpose.

OTT *abbreviation colloquial* over-the-top.

otter /ˈɒtə/ *noun* furred aquatic fish-eating mammal.

Ottoman /ˈɒtəmən/ ● *adjective historical* of Turkish Empire. ● *noun* (*plural* **-s**) Turk of Ottoman period; (**ottoman**) cushioned seat without back or arms, storage-box with padded top.

OU *abbreviation* Open University; Oxford University.

oubliette /uːblɪˈet/ *noun* secret dungeon with trapdoor entrance.

ouch /aʊtʃ/ *interjection* expressing sharp or sudden pain.

ought /ɔːt/ *auxiliary verb* expressing duty, rightness, probability, etc.

oughtn't /ˈɔːt(ə)nt/ ought not.

Ouija /ˈwiːdʒə/ *noun* (in full **Ouija board**) *proprietary term* board marked with letters or signs used with movable pointer to try to obtain messages in seances.

ounce /aʊns/ *noun* unit of weight (1/16 lb, 28.35 g); very small quantity.

our /aʊə/ *adjective* of or belonging to us.

ours /aʊəz/ *pronoun* the one(s) belonging to us.

ourselves /aʊəˈselvz/ *pronoun: emphatic form of* WE *or* US; *reflexive form of* US.

ousel = OUZEL.

oust /aʊst/ *verb* drive out of office or power, esp. by seizing place of.

out /aʊt/ ● *adverb* away from or not in place, not at home, office, etc.; into open, sight, notice, etc.; to or at an end; not burning; in error; *colloquial* unconscious; (+ *to do*) determined; (of limb etc.) dislocated. ● *preposition* out of. ● *noun* way of escape. ● *verb* emerge. □ **out for** intent on, determined to get; **out of** from inside, not inside, from among, lacking, having no more of, because of.

■ **Usage** The use of *out* as a preposition, as in *He walked out the room*, is not standard English. *Out of* should be used instead.

---

out- *prefix* so as to surpass; external; out of.

outback *noun Australian* remote inland areas.

outbalance /aʊtˈbæləns/ *verb* (**-cing**) outweigh.

outbid /aʊtˈbɪd/ *verb* (**-dd-**; *past & past participle* **-bid**) bid higher than.

outboard motor *noun* portable engine attached to outside of boat.

outbreak /ˈaʊtbreɪk/ *noun* sudden eruption of emotion, war, disease, fire, etc.

outbuilding *noun* shed, barn, etc. detached from main building.

outburst *noun* bursting out, esp. of emotion in vehement words.

outcast ● *noun* person cast out from home and friends. ● *adjective* homeless; rejected.

outclass /aʊtˈklɑːs/ *verb* surpass in quality.

outcome *noun* result.

outcrop *noun* rock etc. emerging at surface; noticeable manifestation.

outcry *noun* (*plural* **-ies**) loud public protest.

outdated /aʊtˈdeɪtɪd/ *adjective* out of date, obsolete.

outdistance /aʊtˈdɪst(ə)ns/ *verb* (**-cing**) leave (competitor) behind completely.

outdo /aʊtˈduː/ *verb* (**-doing**; *3rd singular present* **-does**; *past* **-did**; *past participle* **-done**) surpass, excel.

outdoor *adjective* done, existing, or used out of doors; fond of the open air.

outdoors /aʊtˈdɔːz/ ● *adverb* in(to) the open air. ● *noun* the open air.

outer *adjective* outside, external; farther from centre or inside. □ **outer space** universe beyond earth's atmosphere. □ **outermost** *adjective*.

outface /aʊtˈfeɪs/ *verb* (**-cing**) disconcert by staring or by confident manner.

outfall *noun* outlet of river, drain, etc.

outfield *noun* outer part of cricket or baseball pitch. □ **outfielder** *noun*.

outfit *noun* set of equipment or clothes; *colloquial* (organized) group or company.

outfitter *noun* supplier of clothing.

outflank /aʊt'flæŋk/ *verb* get round the flank of (enemy); outmanoeuvre.

outflow *noun* outward flow; what flows out.

outgoing ● *adjective* friendly; retiring from office; going out. ● *noun* (in *plural*) expenditure.

outgrow /aʊt'grəʊ/ *verb* (*past* **-grew**; *past participle* **-grown**) get too big for (clothes etc.); leave behind (childish habit etc.); grow faster or taller than.

outgrowth *noun* offshoot.

outhouse *noun* shed etc., esp. adjoining main house.

outing *noun* pleasure trip.

outlandish /aʊt'lændɪʃ/ *adjective* bizarre, strange. □ **outlandishly** *adverb*; **outlandishness** *noun*.

outlast /aʊt'lɑːst/ *verb* last longer than.

outlaw ● *noun* fugitive from law; *historical* person deprived of protection of law. ● *verb* declare (person) an outlaw; make illegal; proscribe.

outlay *noun* expenditure.

outlet *noun* means of exit; means of expressing feelings; market for goods.

outline ● *noun* rough draft; summary; line(s) enclosing visible object; contour; external boundary; (in *plural*) main features. ● *verb* (**-ning**) draw or describe in outline; mark outline of.

outlive /aʊt'lɪv/ *verb* (**-ving**) live longer than, beyond, or through.

outlook *noun* view, prospect; mental attitude.

outlying *adjective* far from centre; remote.

outmanoeuvre /aʊtmə'nuːvə/ *verb* (**-ring**) (*US* **-maneuver**) outdo by skilful manoeuvring.

outmatch /aʊt'mætʃ/ *verb* be more than a match for.

outmoded /aʊt'məʊdɪd/ *adjective* outdated; out of fashion.

outnumber /aʊt'nʌmbə/ *verb* exceed in number.

outpace /aʊt'peɪs/ *verb* (**-cing**) go faster than; outdo in contest.

outpatient *noun* non-resident hospital patient.

outplacement *noun* help in finding new job after redundancy.

outpost *noun* detachment on guard at some distance from army; outlying settlement etc.

outpouring *noun* (usually in *plural*) copious expression of emotion.

output ● *noun* amount produced (by machine, worker, etc.); electrical power etc. supplied by apparatus; printout, results, etc. from computer; place where energy, information, etc., leaves a system. ● *verb* (**-tt-**; *past & past participle* **-put** or **-putted**) (of computer) supply (results etc.).

outrage ● *noun* forcible violation of others' rights, sentiments, etc.; gross offence or indignity; fierce resentment. ● *verb* (**-ging**) subject to outrage; insult; shock and anger.

outrageous /aʊt'reɪdʒəs/ *adjective* immoderate; shocking; immoral, offensive. □ **outrageously** *adverb*.

outrank /aʊt'ræŋk/ *verb* be superior in rank to.

outré /'uːtreɪ/ *adjective* eccentric, violating decorum. [French]

outrider *noun* motorcyclist or mounted guard riding ahead of car(s) etc.

outrigger *noun* spar or framework projecting from or over side of ship, canoe, etc. to give stability; boat with this.

outright ● *adverb* altogether, entirely; not gradually; without reservation. ● *adjective* downright, complete; undisputed.

outrun /aʊt'rʌn/ *verb* (**-nn-**; *past* **-ran**; *past participle* **-run**) run faster or farther than; go beyond.

outsell /aʊt'sel/ *verb* (*past & past participle* **-sold**) sell more than; be sold in greater quantities than.

outset *noun* □ **at, from the outset** at or from the beginning.

outshine /aʊt'ʃaɪn/ *verb* (**-ning**; *past & past participle* **-shone**) be more brilliant than.

outside ● *noun* /aʊt'saɪd, 'aʊtsaɪd/ external surface, outer part(s); external appearance; position on outer side. ● *adjective* /'aʊtsaɪd/ of, on, or nearer outside; not belonging to particular circle or institution; (of chance etc.) remote; greatest existent or possible. ● *adverb* /aʊt'saɪd/ on or to outside; out of doors; not within or enclosed. ● *preposition* /aʊt'saɪd/ not in; to or at the outside of; external to; beyond limits of. □ **at the outside** (of estimate etc.) at the most; **outside interest** hobby etc. unconnected with one's work.

outsider /aʊt'saɪdə/ *noun* non-member of circle, party, profession, etc.; competitor thought to have little chance.

outsize *adjective* unusually large.

outskirts *plural noun* outer area of town etc.

outsmart /aʊt'smɑːt/ *verb* outwit; be too clever for.

outspoken /aʊt'spəʊkən/ *adjective* saying openly what one thinks; frank. □ **outspokenly** *adverb*; **outspokenness** *noun*.

outspread /aʊt'spred/ *adjective* spread out.

outstanding /aʊt'stændɪŋ/ *adjective* conspicuous, esp. from excellence; still to be dealt with; (of debt) not yet settled. □ **outstandingly** *adverb*.

outstation *noun* remote branch or outpost.

outstay /aʊt'steɪ/ *verb* stay longer than (one's welcome etc.).

outstretched /aʊt'stretʃt/ *adjective* stretched out.

outstrip /aʊt'strɪp/ *verb* (**-pp-**) go faster than; surpass in progress, competition, etc.

out-take *noun* film or tape sequence cut out in editing.

out-tray *noun* tray for outgoing documents.

outvote /aʊt'vəʊt/ *verb* (**-ting**) defeat by majority of votes.

outward /'aʊtwəd/ ● *adjective* directed towards outside; going out; physical; external, apparent. ● *adverb* (also **outwards**) in outward direction, towards outside. □ **outwardly** *adverb*.

outweigh /aʊt'weɪ/ *verb* exceed in weight, value, influence, etc.

outwit /aʊt'wɪt/ *verb* (**-tt-**) be too clever for; overcome by greater ingenuity.

outwith /aʊt'wɪθ/ *preposition Scottish* outside.

outwork *noun* advanced or detached part of fortress etc.; work done off premises of shop, factory, etc. supplying it.

outworn /aʊt'wɔːn/ *adjective* worn out; obsolete.

ouzel /'uːz(ə)l/ *noun* (also **ousel**) small bird of thrush family.

ouzo /'uːzəʊ/ *noun* (*plural* **-s**) Greek aniseed-flavoured alcoholic spirit.

ova *plural of* OVUM.

oval /'əʊv(ə)l/ ● *adjective* shaped like egg, elliptical. ● *noun* elliptical closed curve; thing with oval outline.

ovary /'əʊvərɪ/ *noun* (*plural* **-ies**) either of two ovum-producing organs in female; seed vessel in plant. □ **ovarian** /əʊ'veər-/ *adjective*.

ovation /əʊ'veɪʃ(ə)n/ *noun* enthusiastic applause or reception.

oven /'ʌv(ə)n/ *noun* enclosed chamber for cooking food in. □ **ovenproof** heat-resistant; **oven-ready** (of food) prepared before sale for immediate cooking; **ovenware** dishes for cooking food in oven.

over /'əʊvə/ ● *adverb* outward and downward from brink or from erect position; so as to cover whole surface; so as to produce fold or reverse position; above in place or position; from one side, end, etc. to other; from beginning to end with repetition; in excess; settled, finished. ● *preposition* above; out and down from; so as to cover; across; on or to other side, end, etc. of; concerning. ● *noun Cricket* sequence of 6 balls bowled from one end before change is made to other; play during this time. □ **over the way** (in street etc.) facing or across from.

over- *prefix* excessively; upper, outer; over; completely.

overact /əʊvə'rækt/ *verb* act (a role) with exaggeration.

over-active /əʊvə'ræktɪv/ *adjective* too active.

overall ● *adjective* /'əʊvərɔːl/ taking everything into account, inclusive, total. ● *adverb* /əʊvər'ɔːl/ including everything; on the whole. ● *noun* /'əʊvərɔːl/ protective outer garment; (in *plural*) protective trousers or suit.

overarm *adjective & adverb* with arm raised above shoulder.

overawe /əʊvə'rɔː/ *verb* (**-wing**) awe into submission.

overbalance /əʊvə'bæləns/ *verb* (**-cing**) lose balance and fall; cause to do this.

overbearing /əʊvə'beərɪŋ/ *adjective* domineering; oppressive.

overblown /əʊvə'bləʊn/ *adjective* inflated, pretentious; (of flower etc.) past its prime.

overboard *adverb* from ship into water. □ **go overboard** *colloquial* show extreme enthusiasm, behave immoderately.

overbook /əʊvə'bʊk/ *verb* make too many bookings for (aircraft, hotel, etc.).

overcame *past of* OVERCOME.

overcast *adjective* (of sky) covered with cloud; (in sewing) edged with stitching.

overcharge /əʊvə'tʃɑːdʒ/ *verb* (**-ging**) charge too high a price to; put too much charge into (battery, gun, etc.).

overcoat *noun* warm outdoor coat.

overcome /əʊvə'kʌm/ *verb* (**-coming**; *past* **-came**; *past participle* **-come**) prevail over, master; be victorious; (usually as **overcome** *adjective*) make faint; (often + *with*) make weak or helpless.

overcrowd /əʊvə'kraʊd/ *verb* (usually as **overcrowded** *adjective*) cause too many people or things to be in (a place). □ **overcrowding** *noun*.

overdevelop /əʊvədɪ'veləp/ *verb* (**-p-**) develop too much.

overdo /əʊvə'duː/ *verb* (**-doing**; *3rd singular present* **-does**; *past* **-did**; *past participle* **-done**) carry to excess; (as **overdone** *adjective*) overcooked. □ **overdo it, things** *colloquial* exhaust oneself.

overdose ● *noun* excessive dose of drug etc. ● *verb* (**-sing**) take overdose.

overdraft *noun* overdrawing of bank account; amount by which account is overdrawn.

overdraw /əʊvə'drɔː/ *verb* (*past* **-drew**; *past participle* **-drawn**) draw more from (bank account) than amount in credit; (as **overdrawn** *adjective*) having overdrawn one's account.

overdress /əʊvə'dres/ *verb* dress ostentatiously or with too much formality.

overdrive *noun* mechanism in vehicle providing gear above top gear for economy at high speeds; state of high activity.

overdue /əʊvə'djuː/ *adjective* past the time when due or ready; late, in arrears.

overestimate ● *verb* /əʊvər'estɪmeɪt/ (**-ting**) form too high an estimate of. ● *noun* /əʊvər'estɪmət/ too high an estimate. ● **overestimation** *noun*.

overexpose /əʊvərɪk'spəʊz/ *verb* (**-sing**) expose too much to public; expose (film) for too long.

overfish /əʊvə'fɪʃ/ *verb* deplete (stream etc.) by too much fishing.

overflow ● *verb* /əʊvə'fləʊ/ flow over; be so full that contents overflow; (of crowd etc.) extend beyond limits or capacity of; flood; (of kindness, harvest, etc.) be very abundant. ● *noun* /'əʊvəfləʊ/ what overflows or is superfluous; outlet for excess liquid.

overgrown /əʊvə'grəʊn/ *adjective* grown too big; covered with weeds etc. □ **overgrowth** *noun*.

overhang ● *verb* /əʊvə'hæŋ/ (*past & past participle* **-hung**) project or hang over. ● *noun* /'əʊvəhæŋ/ fact or amount of overhanging.

overhaul *verb* /əʊvə'hɔːl/ check over thoroughly and make repairs to if necessary; overtake. ● *noun* /'əʊvəhɔːl/ thorough examination, with repairs if necessary.

overhead ● *adverb* /əʊvə'hed/ above one's head; in sky. ● *adjective* /'əʊvəhed/ placed overhead. ● *noun* /'əʊvəhed/ (in *plural*) routine administrative and maintenance expenses of a business. □ **overhead projector** projector for producing enlarged image of transparency above and behind user.

overhear /əʊvə'hɪə/ *verb* (*past & past participle* **-heard**) hear as hidden or unintentional listener.

overindulge /əʊvərɪn'dʌldʒ/ *noun* (**-ging**) indulge to excess.

overjoyed /əʊvə'dʒɔɪd/ *adjective* filled with great joy.

overkill *noun* excess of capacity to kill or destroy; excess.

overland *adjective & adverb* by land and not sea.

overlap ● *verb* /əʊvə'læp/ (**-pp-**) partly cover; cover and extend beyond; partly coincide. ● *noun* /'əʊvəlæp/ overlapping; overlapping part or amount.

overlay ● *verb* /əʊvə'leɪ/ (*past & past participle* **-laid**) lay over; (+ *with*) cover (thing) with (coating etc.). ● *noun* /'əʊvəleɪ/ thing laid over another.

overleaf /əʊvə'liːf/ *adverb* on other side of page of book.

overlie /əʊvə'laɪ/ *verb* (**-lying**; *past* **-lay**; *past participle* **-lain**) lie on top of.

overload ● *verb* /əʊvə'ləʊd/ load too heavily (with baggage, work, etc.); put too great a demand on (electrical circuit etc.). ● *noun* /'əʊvələʊd/ excessive quantity or demand.

overlook /əʊvə'lʊk/ *verb* fail to observe; tolerate; have view of from above.

overlord *noun* supreme lord.

overly *adverb* excessively.

overman /əʊvə'mæn/ *verb* (**-nn-**) provide with too large a crew, staff, etc.

overmuch /əʊvə'mʌtʃ/ *adverb & adjective* too much.

overnight /əʊvə'naɪt/ ● *adverb* for a night; during the night; suddenly. ● *adjective* for use or done etc. overnight; instant.

over-particular /əʊvəpə'tɪkjʊlə/ *adjective* fussy or excessively particular.

overpass *noun esp. US* bridge by which road or railway line crosses another.

overplay /əʊvə'pleɪ/ *verb* give undue importance or emphasis to. □ **overplay one's hand** act on unduly optimistic estimate of one's chances.

overpower /əʊvə'paʊə/ *verb* subdue, reduce to submission; (esp. as **overpowering** *adjective*) be too intense or overwhelming for.

overproduce /ˌəʊvəprə'djuːs/ verb (**-cing**) produce in excess of demand or of defined amount. □ **overproduction** noun.

overrate /ˌəʊvə'reɪt/ verb (**-ting**) assess or value too highly; (as **overrated** adjective) not as good as it is said to be.

overreach /ˌəʊvə'riːtʃ/ verb (**overreach oneself**) fail by attempting too much.

overreact /ˌəʊvərɪ'ækt/ verb respond more violently etc. than is justified. □ **overreaction** noun.

override ● verb /ˌəʊvə'raɪd/ (**-ding**; past **-rode**; past participle **-ridden**) have priority over; intervene and make ineffective; interrupt action of (automatic device). ● noun /'əʊvəraɪd/ suspension of automatic function.

overrider noun each of pair of projecting pieces on bumper of car.

overrule /ˌəʊvə'ruːl/ verb (**-ling**) set aside (decision etc.) by superior authority; reject proposal of (person) in this way.

overrun /ˌəʊvə'rʌn/ verb (**-nn-**; past **-ran**; past participle **-run**) spread over; conquer (territory) by force; exceed time etc. allowed.

overseas ● adverb /ˌəʊvə'siːz/ across or beyond sea. ● adjective /'əʊvəsiːz/ of places across sea; foreign.

oversee /ˌəʊvə'siː/ verb (**-sees**; past **-saw**; past participle **-seen**) superintend (workers etc.). □ **overseer** noun.

over-sensitive /ˌəʊvə'sensɪtɪv/ adjective excessively sensitive; easily hurt; quick to react. □ **over-sensitiveness** noun; **oversensitivity** /-'tɪv-/ noun.

oversew /verb (past participle **-sewn** or **-sewed**) sew (two edges) with stitches lying over them.

oversexed /ˌəʊvə'sekst/ adjective having unusually strong sexual desires.

overshadow /ˌəʊvə'ʃædəʊ/ verb appear much more prominent or important than; cast into shade.

overshoe noun shoe worn over another for protection in wet weather etc.

overshoot /ˌəʊvə'ʃuːt/ verb (past & past participle **-shot**) pass or send beyond (target or limit); go beyond runway when landing or taking off. □ **overshoot the mark** go beyond what is intended or proper.

oversight noun failure to notice; inadvertent omission or mistake; supervision.

oversimplify /ˌəʊvə'sɪmplɪfaɪ/ verb (**-ies**, **-ied**) distort (problem etc.) by putting it in too simple terms. □ **oversimplification** noun.

oversleep /ˌəʊvə'sliːp/ verb (past & past participle **-slept**) sleep beyond intended time of waking.

overspend /ˌəʊvə'spend/ verb (past & past participle **-spent**) spend beyond one's means.

overspill noun what is spilt over or overflows; surplus population leaving one area for another.

overspread /ˌəʊvə'spred/ verb (past & past participle **-spread**) cover surface of; (as **overspread** adjective) (usually + with) covered.

overstate /ˌəʊvə'steɪt/ verb (**-ting**) state too strongly; exaggerate. □ **overstatement** noun.

overstep /ˌəʊvə'step/ verb (**-pp-**) pass beyond. □ **overstep the mark** go beyond conventional behaviour.

overstrain /ˌəʊvə'streɪn/ verb damage by exertion; stretch too far.

overstrung adjective /ˌəʊvə'strʌŋ/ (of person, nerves, etc.) too highly strung; /'əʊvəstrʌŋ/ (of piano) with strings crossing each other obliquely.

oversubscribe /ˌəʊvəsəb'skraɪb/ verb (**-bing**) (usually as **oversubscribed** adjective) subscribe for more than available amount or number of (offer, shares, places, etc.).

overt /əʊ'vɜːt/ adjective openly done, unconcealed. □ **overtly** adverb.

overtake /ˌəʊvə'teɪk/ verb (**-king**; past **-took**; past participle **-taken**) catch up and pass; (of bad luck etc.) come suddenly upon.

overtax /ˌəʊvə'tæks/ verb make excessive demands on; tax too highly.

over-the-top adjective colloquial excessive.

overthrow ● verb /ˌəʊvə'θrəʊ/ (past **-threw**; past participle **-thrown**) remove forcibly from power; conquer. ● noun /'əʊvəθrəʊ/ defeat; downfall.

overtime ● noun time worked in addition to regular hours; payment for this. ● adverb in addition to regular hours.

overtone noun Music any of tones above lowest in harmonic series; subtle extra quality or implication.

overture /'əʊvətjʊə/ noun orchestral prelude; (usually in plural) opening of negotiations; formal proposal or offer.

overturn /ˌəʊvə'tɜːn/ verb (cause to) fall down or over; upset, overthrow.

overview noun general survey.

overweening /ˌəʊvə'wiːnɪŋ/ adjective arrogant.

overweight ● adjective /ˌəʊvə'weɪt/ above the weight allowed or desirable. ● noun /'əʊvəweɪt/ excess weight.

overwhelm /ˌəʊvə'welm/ verb overpower with emotion; overcome by force of numbers; bury, submerge utterly.

overwhelming adjective too great to resist or overcome; by a great number. □ **overwhelmingly** adverb.

overwork /ˌəʊvə'wɜːk/ ● verb (cause to) work too hard; weary or exhaust with work; (esp. as **overworked** adjective) make excessive use of. ● noun excessive work.

overwrought /ˌəʊvə'rɔːt/ adjective over-excited, nervous, distraught; too elaborate.

oviduct /'əʊvɪdʌkt/ noun tube through which ova pass from ovary.

oviform /'əʊvɪfɔːm/ adjective egg-shaped.

ovine /'əʊvaɪn/ adjective of or like sheep.

oviparous /əʊ'vɪpərəs/ adjective egg-laying.

ovoid /'əʊvɔɪd/ adjective (of solid) egg-shaped.

ovulate /'ɒvjʊleɪt/ verb (**-ting**) produce ova or ovules, or discharge them from ovary. □ **ovulation** noun.

ovule /'ɒvjuːl/ noun structure containing germ cell in female plant.

ovum /'əʊvəm/ noun (plural **ova** /'əʊvə/) female egg cell from which young develop after fertilization with male sperm.

ow /aʊ/ interjection expressing sudden pain.

owe /əʊ/ verb (**owing**) be under obligation to (re)pay or render; (usually + for) be in debt; (usually + to) be indebted to person, thing, etc. for.

owing /'əʊɪŋ/ adjective owed, yet to be paid; (+ to) caused by, because of.

owl /aʊl/ noun night bird of prey; solemn or wise-looking person. □ **owlish** adjective.

owlet /'aʊlɪt/ noun small or young owl.

own /əʊn/ ● adjective (after my, your, etc.) belonging to myself, yourself, etc.; not another's. ● verb have as property, possess; acknowledge as true or belonging to one. □ **come into one's own** achieve recognition, receive one's due; **hold one's own** maintain one's position, not be defeated; **on one's own** alone, independently, unaided; **own goal** goal scored by mistake against scorer's own side, action etc. having unintended effect of harming person's own interests; **own up** confess.

owner noun possessor. □ **owner-occupier** person who owns and occupies house. □ **ownership** noun.

ox *noun* (*plural* **oxen**) large usually horned ruminant; castrated male of domestic species of cattle. □ **ox-eye daisy** daisy with large white petals and yellow centre; **oxtail** tail of ox, often used in making soup.

oxalic acid /ɒkˈsælɪk/ *noun* intensely sour poisonous acid found in wood sorrel and rhubarb leaves.

oxidation /ɒksɪˈdeɪʃ(ə)n/ *noun* oxidizing, being oxidized.

oxide /ˈɒksaɪd/ *noun* compound of oxygen with another element.

oxidize /ˈɒksɪdaɪz/ *verb* (also **-ise**) (**-zing** or **-sing**) combine with oxygen; rust; cover with coating of oxide. □ **oxidization** *noun*.

oxyacetylene /ˌɒksɪəˈsetɪliːn/ *adjective* of or using mixture of oxygen and acetylene, esp. in cutting or welding metals.

oxygen /ˈɒksɪdʒ(ə)n/ *noun* colourless odourless tasteless gaseous element essential to life and to combustion. □ **oxygen tent** enclosure to allow patient to breathe air with increased oxygen content.

oxygenate /ˈɒksɪdʒəneɪt/ *verb* (**-ting**) supply, treat, or mix with oxygen; oxidize.

oyez /əʊˈjes/ *interjection* (also **oyes**) *uttered by public crier or court officer to call for attention.*

oyster /ˈɔɪstə/ ● *noun* bivalve mollusc living on seabed, esp. edible kind. ● *adjective* (in full **oyster-white**) greyish white.

oz *abbreviation* ounce(s).

ozone /ˈəʊzəʊn/ *noun* form of oxygen with pungent odour; *colloquial* invigorating seaside air. □ **ozone-friendly** not containing chemicals destructive to ozone layer; **ozone layer** layer of ozone in stratosphere that absorbs most of sun's ultraviolet radiation.

p *abbreviation* (also **p.**) penny, pence; page; piano (softly). □ **p. & p.** postage and packing.

PA *abbreviation* personal assistant; public address.

pa /pɑː/ *noun colloquial* father.

p.a. *abbreviation* per annum.

pace¹ ● *noun* single step in walking or running; distance covered in this; speed, rate of progression; gait. ● *verb* (**-cing**) walk (over, about), esp. with slow or regular step; set pace for; (+ *out*) measure (distance) by pacing. □ **pacemaker** person who sets pace, natural or electrical device for stimulating heart muscle.

pace² /ˈpɑːtʃeɪ/ *preposition* with all due deference to. [Latin]

pachyderm /ˈpækɪdɜːm/ *noun* large thick-skinned mammal, esp. elephant or rhinoceros. □ **pachydermatous** /-ˈdɜːmətəs/ *adjective*.

pacific /pəˈsɪfɪk/ ● *adjective* tending to peace, peaceful; (**Pacific**) of or adjoining the Pacific. ● *noun* (**the Pacific**) ocean between America to the east and Asia to the west.

pacifist /ˈpæsɪfɪst/ *noun* person opposed to war. □ **pacifism** *noun*.

pacify /ˈpæsɪfaɪ/ *verb* (**-ies**, **-ied**) appease (person, anger, etc.); bring (country etc.) to state of peace. □ **pacification** *noun*.

pack ● *noun* collection of things tied or wrapped together for carrying; backpack; set of packaged items; set of playing cards; *usually derogatory* lot, set; group of wild animals or hounds; organized group of Cub Scouts or Brownies; forwards of Rugby team; area of large crowded pieces of floating ice in sea. ● *verb* put together into bundle, box, etc., fill with clothes etc. for transport or storing; cram, crowd together, form into pack; (esp. in *passive*; often + *with*) fill; wrap tightly. □ **packed out** full, crowded; **packhorse** horse for carrying loads; **pack in** *colloquial* stop, give up; **pack it in, up** *colloquial* end or stop it; **pack up** *colloquial* stop working, break down, retire from contest, activity, etc.; **send packing** *colloquial* dismiss summarily.

package ● *noun* parcel; box etc. in which goods are packed; (in full **package deal**) set of proposals or items offered or agreed to as a whole. ● *verb* (**-ging**) make up into or enclose in package. □ **package holiday, tour**, etc., one with fixed inclusive price. □ **packaging** *noun*.

packet /ˈpækɪt/ *noun* small package; *colloquial* large sum of money; *historical* mail-boat.

pact *noun* agreement, treaty.

pad¹ ● *noun* piece of soft stuff used to diminish jarring, raise surface, absorb fluid, etc.; sheets of blank paper fastened together at one edge; fleshy cushion forming sole of foot of some animals; leg-guard in games; flat surface for helicopter take-off or rocket-launching; *slang* lodging. ● *verb* (**-dd-**) provide with pad or padding, stuff; (+ *out*) fill out (book etc.) with superfluous matter.

pad² ● *verb* (**-dd-**) walk softly; tramp (along) on foot; travel on foot. ● *noun* sound of soft steady steps.

padding *noun* material used to pad.

paddle¹ /ˈpæd(ə)l/ ● *noun* short oar with broad blade at one or each end; paddle-shaped instrument; fin, flipper; board on paddle-wheel or mill-wheel; action or spell of paddling. ● *verb* (**-ling**) move on water or propel (boat etc.) with paddle(s); row gently.

□ **paddle-wheel** wheel for propelling ship, with boards round circumference.

paddle² /ˈpæd(ə)l/ ● *verb* (**-ling**) wade about in shallow water. ● *noun* action or spell of paddling.

paddock /ˈpædək/ *noun* small field, esp. for keeping horses in; enclosure where horses or cars are assembled before race.

paddy¹ /ˈpædɪ/ *noun* (*plural* **-ies**) (in full **paddy field**) field where rice is grown; rice before threshing or in the husk.

paddy² /ˈpædɪ/ *noun* (*plural* **-ies**) *colloquial* rage, temper.

padlock /ˈpædlɒk/ ● *noun* detachable lock hanging by pivoted hook. ● *verb* secure with padlock.

padre /ˈpɑːdrɪ/ *noun* chaplain in army etc.

paean /ˈpiːən/ *noun* (*US* **pean**) song of praise or triumph.

paediatrics /piːdɪˈætrɪks/ *plural noun* (treated as *singular*) (*US* **pediatrics**) branch of medicine dealing with children's diseases. □ **paediatric** *adjective*; **paediatrician** /-əˈtrɪʃ(ə)n/ *noun*.

paedophile /ˈpiːdəfaɪl/ *noun* (*US* **pedophile**) person feeling sexual attraction towards children.

paella /paɪˈelə/ *noun* Spanish dish of rice, saffron, chicken, seafood, etc.

paeony = PEONY.

pagan /ˈpeɪɡən/ ● *noun* heathen, pantheist, etc. ● *adjective* of pagans; heathen; pantheistic. □ **paganism** *noun*.

page¹ ● *noun* leaf of book etc.; each side of this. ● *verb* (**-ging**) number pages of.

page² ● *noun* boy or man employed as liveried servant or personal attendant. ● *verb* (**-ging**) call name of (person sought) in public rooms of hotel etc. □ **page-boy** boy attending bride etc., woman's short hairstyle.

pageant /ˈpædʒ(ə)nt/ *noun* spectacular performance, usually illustrative of historical events; any brilliant show.

pageantry *noun* spectacular show or display.

pager *noun* bleeping device calling bearer to telephone etc.

paginate /ˈpædʒɪneɪt/ *verb* (**-ting**) number pages of (book etc.). □ **pagination** *noun*.

pagoda /pəˈɡəʊdə/ *noun* temple or sacred tower in China etc.; ornamental imitation of this.

pah *interjection expressing disgust*.

paid past & past participle of PAY.

pail *noun* bucket.

pain ● *noun* bodily suffering caused by injury, pressure, illness, etc.; mental suffering; *colloquial* troublesome person or thing. ● *verb* cause pain to. □ **be at** or **take pains** take great care; **in pain** suffering pain; **painkiller** pain-relieving drug.

painful *adjective* causing or (esp. of part of the body) suffering pain; causing trouble or difficulty. □ **painfully** *adverb*.

painless *adjective* not causing pain. □ **painlessly** *adverb*.

painstaking /ˈpeɪnzteɪkɪŋ/ *adjective* careful, industrious, thorough. □ **painstakingly** *adverb*.

paint ● *noun* colouring matter, esp. in liquid form, for applying to surface. ● *verb* cover surface of with paint; portray or make pictures in colours; describe vividly; apply liquid or cosmetic to. □ **paintbox** box holding dry paints for painting pictures; **painted**

lady butterfly with spotted orange-red wings; **paint-work** painted, esp. wooden, surface or area in building etc.

painter[1] *noun* person who paints, esp. as artist or decorator.

painter[2] *noun* rope at bow of boat for tying it up.

painting *noun* process or art of using paint; painted picture.

pair ● *noun* set of two people or things; thing with two joined or corresponding parts; engaged or married or mated couple; two playing cards of same denomination; (either of) two MPs etc. on opposite sides agreeing not to vote on certain occasions. ● *verb* (often + *off*) arrange or unite as pair, in pairs, or in marriage; mate.

Paisley /'peɪzlɪ/ *noun* (*plural* **-s**) pattern of curved feather-shaped figures.

pajamas *US* = PYJAMAS.

Pakistani /pɑːkɪs'tɑːnɪ/ ● *noun* (*plural* **-s**) native or national of Pakistan; person of Pakistani descent. ● *adjective* of Pakistan.

pal *colloquial* ● *noun* friend. ● *verb* (**-ll-**) (+ *up*) make friends.

palace /'pælɪs/ *noun* official residence of sovereign, president, archbishop, or bishop; stately or spacious building.

palaeo- *combining form* (*US* **paleo-**) ancient; prehistoric.

palaeography /pælɪ'ɒɡrəfɪ/ *noun* (*US* **paleography**) study of ancient writing and documents.

palaeolithic /pælɪəʊ'lɪθɪk/ *adjective* (*US* **paleolithic**) of earlier Stone Age.

palaeontology /pælɪɒn'tɒlədʒɪ/ *noun* (*US* **paleontology**) study of life in geological past. □ **palaeontologist** *noun*.

Palaeozoic /pælɪəʊ'zəʊɪk/ (*US* **Paleozoic**) ● *adjective* of geological era marked by appearance of plants and animals, esp. invertebrates. ● *noun* this era.

palais /'pæleɪ/ *noun colloquial* public dance hall.

palanquin /pælən'kiːn/ *noun* (also **palankeen**) Eastern covered litter for one.

palatable /'pælətəb(ə)l/ *adjective* pleasant to taste; (of idea etc.) acceptable, satisfactory.

palatal /'pælət(ə)l/ ● *adjective* of the palate; (of sound) made with tongue against palate. ● *noun* palatal sound.

palate /'pælət/ *noun* roof of mouth in vertebrates; sense of taste; liking.

palatial /pə'leɪʃ(ə)l/ *adjective* like palace, splendid.

palaver /pə'lɑːvə/ *noun colloquial* tedious fuss and bother.

pale[1] ● *adjective* (of complexion etc.) whitish; faintly coloured; (of colour) faint, (of light) dim. ● *verb* (**-ling**) grow or make pale; (often + *before*, *beside*) seem feeble in comparison (with). □ **palely** *adverb*.

pale[2] *noun* pointed piece of wood for fencing etc.; stake; boundary. □ **beyond the pale** outside bounds of acceptable behaviour.

paleo- *US* = PALAEO-.

Palestinian /pælɪ'stɪnɪən/ ● *adjective* of Palestine. ● *noun* native or inhabitant of Palestine.

palette /'pælɪt/ *noun* artist's flat tablet for mixing colours on; range of colours used by artist. □ **palette-knife** knife with long round-ended flexible blade, esp. for mixing colours or applying or removing paint.

palimony /'pælɪmənɪ/ *noun esp. US colloquial* allowance paid by either of a separated unmarried couple to the other.

palimpsest /'pælɪmpsest/ *noun* writing material used for second time after original writing has been erased.

palindrome /'pælɪndrəʊm/ *noun* word or phrase that reads same backwards as forwards. □ **palindromic** /-'drɒm-/ *adjective*.

paling *noun* (in *singular* or *plural*) fence of pales; pale.

palisade /pælɪ'seɪd/ ● *noun* fence of pointed stakes. ● *verb* (**-ding**) enclose or provide with palisade.

pall[1] /pɔːl/ *noun* cloth spread over coffin etc.; ecclesiastical vestment; dark covering. □ **pallbearer** person helping to carry or escort coffin at funeral.

pall[2] /pɔːl/ *verb* become uninteresting.

pallet[1] /'pælɪt/ *noun* straw mattress; makeshift bed.

pallet[2] /'pælɪt/ *noun* portable platform for transporting and storing loads.

palliasse /'pælɪæs/ *noun* straw mattress.

palliate /'pælɪeɪt/ *verb* (**-ting**) alleviate without curing; excuse, extenuate. □ **palliative** /-ətɪv/ *adjective* & *noun*.

pallid /'pælɪd/ *adjective* pale, sickly-looking.

pallor /'pælə/ *noun* paleness.

pally *adjective* (**-ier**, **-iest**) *colloquial* friendly.

palm[1] /pɑːm/ *noun* (also **palm tree**) (usually tropical) treelike plant with unbranched stem and crown of large esp. sickle- or fan-shaped leaves; leaf of this as symbol of victory. □ **Palm Sunday** Sunday before Easter.

palm[2] /pɑːm/ ● *noun* inner surface of hand between wrist and fingers. ● *verb* conceal in hand. □ **palm off** (often + *on*) impose fraudulently (on person).

palmate /'pælmeɪt/ *adjective* shaped like open hand.

palmetto /pæl'metəʊ/ *noun* (*plural* **-s**) small palm tree.

palmist /'pɑːmɪst/ *noun* teller of character or fortune from lines etc. in palm of hand. □ **palmistry** *noun*.

palmy /'pɑːmɪ/ *adjective* (**-ier**, **-iest**) of, like, or abounding in palms; flourishing.

palomino /pælə'miːnəʊ/ *noun* (*plural* **-s**) golden or cream-coloured horse with light-coloured mane and tail.

palpable /'pælpəb(ə)l/ *adjective* that can be touched or felt; readily perceived. □ **palpably** *adverb*.

palpate /'pælpeɪt/ *verb* (**-ting**) examine (esp. medically) by touch. □ **palpation** *noun*.

palpitate /'pælpɪteɪt/ *verb* (**-ting**) pulsate, throb; tremble. □ **palpitation** *noun*.

palsy /'pɔːlzɪ/ ● *noun* (*plural* **-ies**) paralysis, esp. with involuntary tremors. ● *verb* (**-ies**, **-ied**) affect with palsy.

paltry /'pɔːltrɪ/ *adjective* (**-ier**, **-iest**) worthless, contemptible, trifling.

pampas /'pæmpəs/ *plural noun* large treeless S. American plains. □ **pampas grass** large ornamental grass.

pamper /'pæmpə/ *verb* overindulge.

pamphlet /'pæmflɪt/ *noun* small unbound booklet, esp. controversial treatise.

pamphleteer /pæmflɪ'tɪə/ *noun* writer of (esp. political) pamphlets.

pan[1] ● *noun* flat-bottomed usually metal vessel used in cooking etc.; shallow receptacle or tray; bowl of scales or of lavatory. ● *verb* (**-nn-**) *colloquial* criticize harshly; (+ *off*, *out*) wash (gold-bearing gravel) in pan; search for gold in this way. □ **pan out** turn out, work out well or in specified way.

pan[2] ● *verb* (**-nn-**) swing (film-camera) horizontally to give panoramic effect or follow moving object; (of camera) be moved thus. ● *noun* panning movement.

pan- *combining form* all; the whole of (esp. referring to a continent, racial group, religion, etc.).

panacea /pænə'siːə/ *noun* universal remedy.

panache /pə'næʃ/ *noun* assertively flamboyant or confident style.

panama /'pænəmɑː/ *noun* hat of strawlike material with brim and indented crown.

panatella /pænə'telə/ *noun* long thin cigar.

pancake *noun* thin flat cake of fried batter, usually folded or rolled up with filling. □ **Pancake Day** Shrove Tuesday (when pancakes are traditionally eaten); **pancake landing** *colloquial* emergency aircraft landing with undercarriage still retracted.

panchromatic /pænkrəʊ'mætɪk/ *adjective* (of film etc.) sensitive to all visible colours of spectrum.

pancreas /'pæŋkrɪəs/ *noun* gland near stomach supplying digestive fluid and insulin. □ **pancreatic** /-'æt-/ *adjective*.

panda /'pændə/ *noun* (also **giant panda**) large rare bearlike black and white mammal native to China and Tibet; (also **red panda**) racoon-like Himalayan mammal. □ **panda car** police patrol car.

pandemic /pæn'demɪk/ *adjective* (of disease) widespread; universal.

pandemonium /pændɪ'məʊnɪəm/ *noun* uproar; utter confusion; scene of this.

pander /'pændə/ ● *verb* (+ *to*) indulge (person or weakness). ● *noun* procurer, pimp.

pandit = PUNDIT.

pane *noun* single sheet of glass in window or door.

panegyric /pænɪ'dʒɪrɪk/ *noun* eulogy; speech or essay of praise.

panel /'pæn(ə)l/ ● *noun* distinct, usually rectangular, section of surface, esp. of wall, door, or vehicle; group or team of people assembled for discussion, consultation, etc.; strip of material in garment; list of available jurors; jury. ● *verb* (**-ll-**; *US* **-l-**) fit with panels. □ **panel game** broadcast quiz etc. played by panel. □ **panelling** *noun*.

panellist *noun* (*US* **panelist**) member of panel.

pang *noun* sudden sharp pain or distressing emotion.

pangolin /pæŋ'gəʊlɪn/ *noun* scaly anteater.

panic /'pænɪk/ ● *noun* sudden alarm; infectious fright. ● *verb* (**-ck-**) (often + *into*) affect or be affected with panic. □ **panic-stricken**, **-struck** affected with panic. □ **panicky** *adjective*.

panicle /'pænɪk(ə)l/ *noun* loose branching cluster of flowers.

panjandrum /pæn'dʒændrəm/ *noun*: *mock title of great personage.*

pannier /'pænɪə/ *noun* one of pair of baskets or bags etc. carried by beast of burden or on bicycle or motorcycle.

panoply /'pænəplɪ/ *noun* (*plural* **-ies**) complete or splendid array; full armour.

panorama /pænə'rɑːmə/ *noun* unbroken view of surrounding region; picture or photograph containing wide view. □ **panoramic** /-'ræm-/ *adjective*.

pansy /'pænzɪ/ *noun* (*plural* **-ies**) garden plant of violet family with richly coloured flowers.

pant ● *verb* breathe with quick breaths; yearn. ● *noun* panting breath.

pantaloons /pæntə'luːnz/ *plural noun* baggy trousers gathered at ankles.

pantechnicon /pæn'teknɪkən/ *noun* large furniture van.

pantheism /'pænθɪɪz(ə)m/ *noun* doctrine that God is everything and everything is God. □ **pantheist** *noun*; **pantheistic** /-'ɪs-/ *adjective*.

pantheon /'pænθɪən/ *noun* building with memorials of illustrious dead; deities of a people collectively; temple of all gods.

panther /'pænθə/ *noun* leopard, esp. black; *US* puma.

panties /'pæntɪz/ *plural noun colloquial* short-legged or legless knickers.

pantile /'pæntaɪl/ *noun* curved roof-tile.

pantograph /'pæntəgrɑːf/ *noun* instrument for copying plan etc. on any scale.

pantomime /'pæntəmaɪm/ *noun* dramatic usually Christmas entertainment based on fairy tale; *colloquial* absurd or outrageous behaviour; gestures and facial expressions conveying meaning.

pantry /'pæntrɪ/ *noun* (*plural* **-ies**) room in which provisions, crockery, cutlery, etc. are kept.

pants *plural noun* underpants; knickers; *US* trousers.

pap¹ *noun* soft or semi-liquid food; trivial reading matter.

pap² *noun archaic* nipple.

papa /pə'pɑː/ *noun archaic: child's name for* father.

papacy /'peɪpəsɪ/ *noun* (*plural* **-ies**) Pope's office or tenure; papal system.

papal /'peɪp(ə)l/ *adjective* of the Pope or his office.

paparazzo /pæpə'rætsəʊ/ *noun* (*plural* **-zzi** /-tsɪ/) freelance photographer who pursues celebrities to photograph them.

papaya = PAWPAW.

paper /'peɪpə/ ● *noun* substance made in very thin sheets from pulp of wood etc., used for writing, printing, wrapping, etc.; newspaper; (in *plural*) documents; set of exam questions or answers; wallpaper; essay. ● *adjective* not actual, theoretical. ● *verb* decorate (wall etc.) with paper. □ **paper-boy**, **-girl** one who delivers or sells newspapers; **paper-clip** clip of bent wire or plastic for holding sheets of paper together; **paper-knife** blunt knife for opening envelopes etc.; **paper money** banknotes etc.; **paper round** job of regularly delivering newspapers, route for doing this; **paperweight** small heavy object to hold papers down; **paperwork** office record-keeping and administration.

paperback ● *adjective* bound in stiff paper, not boards. ● *noun* paperback book.

papier mâché /pæpɪeɪ 'mæʃeɪ/ *noun* moulded paper pulp used for making models etc.

papilla /pə'pɪlə/ *noun* (*plural* **papillae** /-liː/) small nipple-like protuberance. □ **papillary** *adjective*.

papoose /pə'puːs/ *noun* young N. American Indian child.

paprika /'pæprɪkə/ *noun* ripe red pepper; condiment made from this.

papyrus /pə'paɪərəs/ *noun* (*plural* **papyri** /-raɪ/) aquatic plant of N. Africa; ancient writing material made from stem of this; manuscript written on this.

par *noun* average or normal value, degree, condition, etc.; equality, equal footing; *Golf* number of strokes needed by first-class player for hole or course; face value. □ **par for the course** *colloquial* what is normal or to be expected.

para /'pærə/ *noun colloquial* paratrooper.

para- *prefix* beside, beyond.

parable /'pærəb(ə)l/ *noun* story used to illustrate moral or spiritual truth.

parabola /pə'ræbələ/ *noun* plane curve formed by intersection of cone with plane parallel to its side. □ **parabolic** /pærə'bɒlɪk/ *adjective*.

paracetamol /pærə'siːtəmɒl/ *noun* compound used to relieve pain and reduce fever; tablet of this.

parachute /'pærəʃuːt/ ● *noun* usually umbrella-shaped apparatus allowing person or heavy object to descend safely from a height, esp. from aircraft. ● *verb* (**-ting**) convey or descend by parachute. □ **parachutist** *noun*.

parade /pə'reɪd/ ● *noun* public procession; muster of troops etc. for inspection; parade ground; display, ostentation; public square, row of shops. ● *verb* (**-ding**) march ceremonially; assemble for parade; display ostentatiously. □ **parade ground** place for muster of troops.

paradigm /'pærədaɪm/ *noun* example or pattern, esp. of inflection of word.

paradise /'pærədaɪs/ *noun* heaven; place or state of complete bliss; garden of Eden.

paradox /'pærədɒks/ *noun* seemingly absurd or self-contradictory though often true statement etc. □ **paradoxical** /-'dɒks-/ *adjective*; **paradoxically** /-'dɒks-/ *adverb*.

paraffin /'pærəfɪn/ *noun* inflammable waxy or oily substance got by distillation from petroleum etc., used in liquid form esp. as fuel. □ **paraffin wax** solid paraffin.

paragon /'pærəgən/ *noun* (often + *of*) model of excellence.

paragraph /'pærəgrɑːf/ *noun* distinct passage in book etc. usually marked by indentation of first line; mark of reference (¶); short separate item in newspaper etc.

parakeet /'pærəkiːt/ *noun* small usually long-tailed parrot.

parallax /'pærəlæks/ *noun* apparent difference in position or direction of object caused by change of observer's position; angular amount of this.

parallel /'pærəlel/ ● *adjective* (of lines) continuously equidistant; precisely similar, analogous, or corresponding; (of processes etc.) occurring or performed simultaneously. ● *noun* person or thing analogous to another; comparison; imaginary line on earth's surface or line on map marking degree of latitude. ● *verb* (**-l-**) be parallel or correspond to; represent as similar; compare. □ **parallelism** *noun*.

parallelepiped /pærəlelə'paɪped/ *noun* solid bounded by parallelograms.

parallelogram /pærə'leləgræm/ *noun* 4-sided rectilinear figure whose opposite sides are parallel.

paralyse /'pærəlaɪz/ *verb* (**-sing**) (*US* **-lyze**; **-zing**) affect with paralysis; render powerless, cripple.

paralysis /pə'rælɪsɪs/ *noun* impairment or loss of esp. motor function of nerves, causing immobility; powerlessness.

paralytic /pærə'lɪtɪk/ ● *adjective* affected with paralysis; *slang* very drunk. ● *noun* person affected with paralysis.

paramedic /pærə'medɪk/ *noun* paramedical worker.

paramedical /pærə'medɪk(ə)l/ *adjective* supplementing and supporting medical work.

parameter /pə'ræmɪtə/ *noun Mathematics* quantity constant in case considered, but varying in different cases; (esp. measurable or quantifiable) characteristic or feature; (loosely) boundary, esp. of subject for discussion.

paramilitary /pærə'mɪlɪtərɪ/ ● *adjective* similarly organized to military forces. ● *noun* (*plural* **-ies**) member of unofficial paramilitary organization.

paramount /'pærəmaʊnt/ *adjective* supreme; most important or powerful.

paramour /'pærəmʊə/ *noun archaic* illicit lover of married person.

paranoia /pærə'nɔɪə/ *noun* mental derangement with delusions of grandeur, persecution, etc.; abnormal tendency to suspect and mistrust others. □ **paranoiac** *adjective* & *noun*; **paranoid** /'pærənɔɪd/ *adjective* & *noun*.

paranormal /pærə'nɔːm(ə)l/ *adjective* beyond the scope of normal scientific investigations etc.

parapet /'pærəpɪt/ *noun* low wall at edge of roof, balcony, bridge, etc.; mound along front of trench etc.

paraphernalia /pærəfə'neɪlɪə/ *plural noun* (also treated as *singular*) personal belongings, miscellaneous accessories, etc.

paraphrase /'pærəfreɪz/ ● *noun* restatement of sense of passage etc. in other words. ● *verb* (**-sing**) express meaning of in other words.

paraplegia /pærə'pliːdʒə/ *noun* paralysis below waist. □ **paraplegic** *adjective* & *noun*.

parapsychology /pærəsaɪ'kɒlədʒɪ/ *noun* study of mental phenomena outside sphere of ordinary psychology.

paraquat /'pærəkwɒt/ *noun* quick-acting highly toxic herbicide.

parasite /'pærəsaɪt/ *noun* animal or plant living in or on another and feeding on it; person exploiting another or others. □ **parasitic** /-'sɪt-/ *adjective*; **parasitism** *noun*.

parasol /'pærəsɒl/ *noun* light umbrella giving shade from the sun.

paratroops /'pærətruːps/ *plural noun* airborne troops landing by parachute. □ **paratrooper** *noun*.

paratyphoid /pærə'taɪfɔɪd/ *noun* fever resembling typhoid.

parboil /'pɑːbɔɪl/ *verb* partly cook by boiling.

parcel /'pɑːs(ə)l/ ● *noun* goods etc. packed up in single wrapping; piece of land. ● *verb* (**-ll-**; *US* **-l-**) (+ *up*) wrap into parcel; (+ *out*) divide into portions.

parch *verb* make or become hot and dry; slightly roast.

parchment /'pɑːtʃmənt/ *noun* skin, esp. of sheep or goat, prepared for writing etc.; manuscript written on this.

pardon /'pɑːd(ə)n/ ● *noun* forgiveness; remission of punishment. ● *verb* forgive; excuse; release from legal consequences of offence etc. ● *interjection* (also **pardon me** or **I beg your pardon**) *formula of apology or disagreement; request to repeat something said.* □ **pardonable** *adjective*.

pare /peə/ *verb* (**-ring**) trim or reduce by cutting away edge or surface of; (often + *away*, *down*) whittle away.

parent /'peərənt/ *noun* person who has had or adopted a child; father, mother; source, origin. □ **parent company** company of which others are subsidiaries; **parent-teacher association** social and fund-raising organization of school's teachers and parents. □ **parental** /pə'rent(ə)l/ *adjective*; **parenthood** *noun*.

parentage *noun* lineage, descent from or through parents.

parenthesis /pə'renθəsɪs/ *noun* (*plural* **-theses** /-siːz/) word, clause, or sentence inserted as explanation etc. into passage independently of grammatical sequence; (in *plural*) round brackets used to mark this; interlude. □ **parenthetic** /pærən'θetɪk/ *adjective*.

par excellence /pɑːr eksə'lɑ̃s/ *adverb* superior to all others so called. [French]

parfait /'pɑːfeɪ/ *noun* rich iced pudding of whipped cream, eggs, etc.; layers of ice cream, meringue, etc., served in tall glass.

pariah /pə'raɪə/ *noun* social outcast; *historical* member of low or no caste.

parietal /pə'raɪət(ə)l/ *adjective* of wall of body or any of its cavities. □ **parietal bone** either of pair forming part of skull.

paring *noun* strip pared off.

parish /'pærɪʃ/ *noun* division of diocese having its own church and clergyman; local government district; inhabitants of parish.

parishioner /pə'rɪʃənə/ *noun* inhabitant of parish.

parity /'pærɪtɪ/ *noun* (*plural* **-ies**) equality; equal status etc.; equivalence; being at par.

park ● *noun* large public garden in town; large enclosed piece of ground attached to country house or laid out or preserved for public use; place where vehicles may be parked; area for specified purpose. ● *verb* place and leave (esp. vehicle) temporarily. ☐ **parking-lot** *US* outdoor car park; **parking meter** coin-operated meter allocating period of time for which a vehicle may be parked in street; **parking ticket** notice of fine etc. imposed for parking vehicle illegally.

parka /'pɑːkə/ *noun* jacket with hood, as worn by Eskimos, mountaineers, etc.

parkin /'pɑːkɪn/ *noun* oatmeal gingerbread.

parky /'pɑːkɪ/ *adjective* (**-ier, -iest**) *colloquial or dialect* chilly.

parlance /'pɑːləns/ *noun* way of speaking.

parley /'pɑːlɪ/ ● *noun* (*plural* **-s**) meeting between representatives of opposed forces to discuss terms. ● *verb* (**-leys, -leyed**) (often + *with*) hold parley.

parliament /'pɑːləmənt/ *noun* body consisting of House of Commons and House of Lords and forming (with Sovereign) legislature of UK; similar legislature in other states.

parliamentarian /pɑːləmənˈteərɪən/ *noun* member of parliament.

parliamentary /pɑːləˈmentərɪ/ *adjective* of, in, concerned with, or enacted by parliament.

parlour /'pɑːlə/ *noun* (*US* **parlor**) *archaic* sitting-room in private house; *esp. US* shop providing specified goods or services. ☐ **parlour game** indoor game, esp. word game.

parlous /'pɑːləs/ *adjective archaic* perilous; hard to deal with.

Parmesan /pɑːmɪˈzæn/ *noun* hard Italian cheese usually used grated as flavouring.

parochial /pəˈrəʊkɪəl/ *adjective* of a parish; of narrow range, merely local. ☐ **parochialism** *noun*.

parody /'pærədɪ/ ● *noun* (*plural* **-ies**) humorous exaggerated imitation of author, style, etc.; travesty. ● *verb* (**-ies, -ied**) write parody of; mimic humorously. ☐ **parodist** *noun*.

parole /pəˈrəʊl/ ● *noun* temporary or permanent release of prisoner before end of sentence, on promise of good behaviour; such promise. ● *verb* (**-ling**) put (prisoner) on parole.

parotid /pəˈrɒtɪd/ ● *adjective* situated near ear. ● *noun* (in full **parotid gland**) salivary gland in front of ear.

paroxysm /'pærəksɪz(ə)m/ *noun* (often + *of*) fit (of pain, rage, coughing, etc.).

parquet /'pɑːkeɪ/ ● *noun* flooring of wooden blocks arranged in a pattern. ● *verb* (**-eted** /-eɪd/, **-eting** /-eɪŋ/) floor (room) thus.

parricide /'pærɪsaɪd/ *noun* person who kills his or her parent; such a killing. ☐ **parricidal** /-ˈsaɪd(ə)l/ *adjective*.

parrot /'pærət/ ● *noun* mainly tropical bird with short hooked bill, of which some species can be taught to repeat words; unintelligent imitator or chatterer. ● *verb* (**-t-**) repeat mechanically. ☐ **parrot-fashion** (learning or repeating) mechanically, by rote.

parry /'pærɪ/ ● *verb* (**-ies, -ied**) ward off, avert. ● *noun* (*plural* **-ies**) act of parrying.

parse /pɑːz/ *verb* (**-sing**) describe (word) or analyse (sentence) in terms of grammar.

parsec /'pɑːsek/ *noun* unit of stellar distance, about 3.25 light years.

parsimony /'pɑːsɪmənɪ/ *noun* carefulness in use of money etc.; meanness. ☐ **parsimonious** /-ˈməʊn-/ *adjective*.

parsley /'pɑːslɪ/ *noun* herb used for seasoning and garnishing.

parsnip /'pɑːsnɪp/ *noun* plant with pale yellow tapering root used as vegetable; this root.

parson /'pɑːs(ə)n/ *noun* parish clergyman; *colloquial* any clergyman. ☐ **parson's nose** fatty flesh at rump of cooked fowl.

parsonage *noun* parson's house.

part ● *noun* some but not all; component, division, portion; share, allotted portion; person's share in an action etc.; assigned character or role; *Music* one of melodies making up harmony of concerted music; side in agreement or dispute, (usually in *plural*) region, direction, way; (in *plural*) abilities. ● *verb* divide into parts; separate; (+ *with*) give up, hand over; make parting in (hair). ● *adverb* partly, in part. ☐ **on the part of** made or done by; **part and parcel** (usually + *of*) essential part; **part-exchange** *noun* transaction in which article is given as part of payment for more expensive one, *verb* give (article) thus; **part of speech** grammatical class of words (noun, pronoun, adjective, adverb, verb, etc.); **part-song** song for 3 or more voice parts; **part-time** employed for or occupying less than normal working week etc.; **part-timer** part-time worker.

partake /pɑːˈteɪk/ *verb* (**-king**; *past* **partook**; *past participle* **partaken**) (+ *of, in*) take share of; (+ *of*) eat or drink some of.

parterre /pɑːˈteə/ *noun* level garden space filled with flower-beds etc.; *US* pit of theatre.

partial /'pɑːʃ(ə)l/ *adjective* not total or complete; biased, unfair; (+ *to*) having a liking for. ☐ **partiality** /-ʃɪˈæl-/ *noun*; **partially** *adverb*.

participate /pɑːˈtɪsɪpeɪt/ *verb* (**-ting**) (often + *in*) have share or take part. ☐ **participant** *noun*; **participation** *noun*.

participle /'pɑːtɪsɪp(ə)l/ *noun* word (either **present participle**, e.g. *writing*, or **past participle**, e.g. *written*) formed from verb and used in complex verb-forms or as adjective. ☐ **participial** /-ˈsɪp-/ *adjective*.

particle /'pɑːtɪk(ə)l/ *noun* minute portion of matter; smallest possible amount; minor esp. indeclinable part of speech.

particoloured /'pɑːtɪkʌləd/ *adjective* (*US* **-colored**) of more than one colour.

particular /pəˈtɪkjʊlə/ ● *adjective* relating to or considered as one as distinct from others; special; scrupulously exact; fastidious. ● *noun* detail, item; (in *plural*) detailed account. ☐ **in particular** specifically. ☐ **particularity** /-ˈlær-/ *noun*.

particularize /pəˈtɪkjʊləraɪz/ *verb* (also **-ise**) (**-zing** or **-sing**) name specially or one by one; specify (items). ☐ **particularization** *noun*.

particularly *adverb* very; specifically; in a fastidious way.

parting *noun* leave-taking; dividing line of combed hair.

partisan /pɑːtɪˈzæn/ ● *noun* strong supporter of party, side, or cause; guerrilla. ● *adjective* of partisans; biased. ☐ **partisanship** *noun*.

partition /pɑːˈtɪʃ(ə)n/ ● *noun* structure dividing a space, esp. light interior wall; division into parts. ● *verb* divide into parts; (+ *off*) separate with partition.

partitive /'pɑːtɪtɪv/ ● *adjective* (of word) denoting part of collective whole. ● *noun* partitive word.

partly *adverb* with respect to a part; to some extent.

partner /'pɑːtnə/ ● *noun* sharer; person associated with others in business; either of pair in marriage etc. or dancing or game. ● *verb* be partner of. ☐ **partnership** *noun*.

partridge /'pɑːtrɪdʒ/ *noun* (*plural* same or **-s**) kind of game bird.

parturition /pɑːtjʊˈrɪʃ(ə)n/ *noun formal* childbirth.

party /'pɑːtɪ/ *noun* (*plural* **-ies**) social gathering; group of people travelling or working together; political group putting forward candidates in elections and usually organized on national basis; each side in agreement or dispute. □ **party line** set policy of political party etc., shared telephone line; **party wall** wall common to adjoining rooms, buildings, etc.

parvenu /'pɑːvənjuː/ noun (plural -**s**; feminine **parvenue**, plural -**s**) newly rich social climber; upstart.

pascal /'pæsk(ə)l/ noun SI unit of pressure; (**Pascal** /pæs'kɑːl/) computer language designed for training.

paschal /'pæsk(ə)l/ adjective of Passover; of Easter.

pasha /'pɑːʃə/ noun historical Turkish officer of high rank.

pasque-flower /'pæskflaʊə/ noun kind of anemone.

pass¹ /pɑːs/ ● verb move onward, proceed; go past; leave on one side or behind; (cause to) be transferred from one person or place to another; surpass; go unremarked or uncensured; move; cause to go; be successful in (exam); allow (bill in Parliament) to proceed; be approved; elapse; happen; spend (time etc.); Football etc. kick, hand, or hit (ball etc.) to player of one's own side; (+ into, from) change; come to an end; be accepted as adequate; discharge from body as or with excreta; utter (judgement etc.). ● noun passing, esp. of exam; status of degree without honours; written permission, ticket, or order; Football etc. passing of ball; critical position. □ **make a pass at** colloquial make sexual advances to; **pass away** die; **passbook** book recording customer's transactions with bank etc.; **passer-by** (plural **passers-by**) person who goes past, esp. by chance; **pass for** be accepted as; **passkey** private key to gate etc., master-key; **pass off** fade away, be carried through (in specified way), lightly dismiss, (+ as) misrepresent as something false; **pass on** proceed, die, transmit to next person in a series; **pass out** become unconscious, complete military training; **pass over** omit, overlook, make no remark on, die; **pass round** distribute, give to one person after another; **pass up** colloquial refuse or neglect (opportunity etc.); **password** prearranged word or phrase to secure recognition, admission, etc.

pass² /pɑːs/ noun narrow way through mountains.

passable adjective adequate, fairly good.

passage /'pæsɪdʒ/ noun process or means of passing, transit; passageway; right to pass through; journey by sea or air; transition from one state to another; short part of book or piece of music etc.; duct etc. in body.

passageway noun narrow way for passing along; corridor.

passé /'pæseɪ/ adjective (feminine **passée**) outmoded; past its prime.

passenger /'pæsɪndʒə/ noun traveller in or on vehicle (other than driver, pilot, crew, etc.); colloquial idle member of team etc.

passerine /'pæsəriːn/ ● noun bird able to grip branch etc. with claws. ● adjective of passerines.

passim /'pæsɪm/ adverb throughout. [Latin]

passion /'pæʃ(ə)n/ noun strong emotion; outburst of anger; intense sexual love; strong enthusiasm; object arousing this; (**the Passion**) sufferings of Christ during his last days, Gospel narrative of this or musical setting of it. □ **passion-flower** plant with flower supposed to suggest instruments of Crucifixion; **passion-fruit** edible fruit of some species of passion-flower. □ **passionless** adjective.

passionate /'pæʃənət/ adjective dominated by, easily moved to, or showing passion. □ **passionately** adverb.

passive /'pæsɪv/ adjective acted upon, not acting; submissive; inert; Grammar (of verb) of which subject undergoes action (e.g. was written in it was written by me). □ **passive smoking** involuntary inhalation of

others' cigarette smoke. □ **passively** adverb; **passivity** /-'sɪv-/ noun.

Passover /'pɑːsəʊvə/ noun Jewish spring festival commemorating Exodus from Egypt.

passport /'pɑːspɔːt/ noun official document showing holder's identity and nationality etc. and authorizing travel abroad.

past /pɑːst/ ● adjective gone by; just over; of former time; Grammar expressing past action or state. ● noun past time or events; person's past life or career; past tense. ● preposition beyond. ● adverb so as to pass by. □ **past it** colloquial old and useless; **past master** expert.

pasta /'pæstə/ noun dried flour paste in various shapes.

paste /peɪst/ ● noun any moist fairly stiff mixture; dough of flour with fat, water, etc.; flour and water or other mixture as adhesive; meat or fish spread; hard glasslike material used for imitation gems. ● verb (-**ting**) fasten or coat with paste; slang beat, thrash. □ **pasteboard** stiff substance made by pasting together sheets of paper. □ **pasting** noun.

pastel /'pæst(ə)l/ ● noun pale shade of colour; crayon made of dry pigment-paste; drawing in pastel. ● adjective of pale shade of colour.

pastern /'pæst(ə)n/ noun part of horse's foot between fetlock and hoof.

pasteurize /'pɑːstʃəraɪz/ verb (also -**ise**) (-**zing** or -**sing**) partially sterilize (milk etc.) by heating. □ **pasteurization** noun.

pastiche /pæs'tiːʃ/ noun picture or musical composition made up from various sources; literary or other work imitating style of author or period etc.

pastille /'pæstɪl/ noun small sweet or lozenge.

pastime /'pɑːstaɪm/ noun recreation; hobby.

pastor /'pɑːstə/ noun minister, esp. of Nonconformist church.

pastoral /'pɑːstər(ə)l/ ● adjective of shepherds; of (esp. romanticized) rural life; of pastor. ● noun pastoral poem, play, picture, etc.; letter from bishop or other pastor to clergy or people.

pastrami /pæ'strɑːmɪ/ noun seasoned smoked beef.

pastry /'peɪstrɪ/ noun (plural -**ies**) dough of flour, fat, and water; (item of) food made wholly or partly of this.

pasturage noun pasture land; pasturing.

pasture /'pɑːstʃə/ ● noun land covered with grass etc. for grazing animals; herbage for animals. ● verb (-**ring**) put (animals) to pasture; graze.

pasty¹ /'pæstɪ/ noun (plural -**ies**) pie of meat etc. wrapped in pastry and baked without dish.

pasty² /'peɪstɪ/ adjective (-**ier**, -**iest**) pallid.

pat¹ ● verb (-**tt**-) strike gently with flat palm or other flat surface, esp. in affection etc. ● noun light stroke or tap, esp. with hand in affection etc.; patting sound; small mass, esp. of butter, made (as) by patting.

pat² ● adjective known thoroughly; apposite, opportune, esp. glibly so. ● adverb in a pat way. □ **have off pat** have memorized perfectly.

patch ● noun piece put on in mending or as reinforcement; cover protecting injured eye; large or irregular spot on surface; distinct area or period; small plot of ground. ● verb mend with patch(es); (often + up) piece together; (+ up) settle (quarrel etc.), esp. hastily. □ **not a patch on** colloquial very much inferior to; **patchwork** stitching together of small pieces of differently coloured cloth to form pattern.

patchy adjective (-**ier**, -**iest**) uneven in quality; having patches. □ **patchily** adverb.

pate noun colloquial head.

pâté /'pæteɪ/ *noun* smooth paste of meat etc. □ **pâté de foie gras** /də fwɑː 'grɑː/ pâté made from livers of fatted geese.

patella /pə'telə/ *noun* (*plural* **patellae** /-liː/) kneecap.

paten /'pæt(ə)n/ *noun* plate for bread at Eucharist.

patent /'peɪt(ə)nt, 'pæt-/ ● *noun* official document conferring right, title, etc., esp. sole right to make, use, or sell some invention; invention or process so protected. ● *adjective* /'peɪt(ə)nt/ plain, obvious; conferred or protected by patent; (of food, medicine, etc.) proprietary. ● *verb* obtain patent for (invention). □ **patent leather** glossy varnished leather. □ **patently** *adverb*.

patentee /peɪtən'tiː/ *noun* holder of patent.

paterfamilias /peɪtəfə'mɪliæs/ *noun* male head of family etc.

paternal /pə'tɜːn(ə)l/ *adjective* of father, fatherly; related through father.

paternalism *noun* policy of restricting freedom and responsibility by well-meant regulations. □ **paternalistic** /-'lɪs-/ *adjective*.

paternity /pə'tɜːnɪtɪ/ *noun* fatherhood; one's paternal origin.

paternoster /pætə'nɒstə/ *noun* Lord's Prayer, esp. in Latin.

path /pɑːθ/ *noun* (*plural* **paths** /pɑːðz/) footway, track; line along which person or thing moves. □ **pathway** path, its course.

pathetic /pə'θetɪk/ *adjective* exciting pity, sadness, or contempt. □ **pathetically** *adverb*.

pathogen /'pæθədʒ(ə)n/ *noun* agent causing disease. □ **pathogenic** /-'dʒen-/ *adjective*.

pathological /pæθə'lɒdʒɪk(ə)l/ *adjective* of pathology; of or caused by mental or physical disorder. □ **pathologically** *adverb*.

pathology /pə'θɒlədʒɪ/ *noun* study of disease. □ **pathologist** *noun*.

pathos /'peɪθɒs/ *noun* quality that excites pity or sadness.

patience /'peɪʃ(ə)ns/ *noun* ability to endure delay, hardship, provocation, pain, etc.; perseverance; solo card game.

patient ● *adjective* having or showing patience. ● *noun* person under medical etc. treatment. □ **patiently** *adverb*.

patina /'pætɪnə/ *noun* (*plural* -**s**) film, usually green, on surface of old bronze etc.; gloss produced by age on woodwork etc.

patio /'pætɪəʊ/ *noun* (*plural* -**s**) paved usually roofless area adjoining house; roofless inner courtyard.

patisserie /pə'tiːsərɪ/ *noun* shop where pastries are made and sold; pastries collectively.

patois /'pætwɑː/ *noun* (*plural* same /-wɑːz/) regional dialect differing from literary language.

patriarch /'peɪtrɪɑːk/ *noun* male head of family or tribe; chief bishop in Orthodox and RC Churches; venerable old man. □ **patriarchal** /-'ɑːk-/ *adjective*.

patriarchate /'peɪtrɪɑːkət/ *noun* office, see, or residence of patriarch; rank of tribal patriarch.

patriarchy /'peɪtrɪɑːkɪ/ *noun* (*plural* -**ies**) male-dominated social system, with descent reckoned through male line.

patrician /pə'trɪʃ(ə)n/ ● *noun* person of noble birth, esp. in ancient Rome. ● *adjective* of nobility; aristocratic.

patricide /'pætrɪsaɪd/ *noun* parricide. □ **patricidal** /-'saɪd(ə)l/ *adjective*.

patrimony /'pætrɪmənɪ/ *noun* (*plural* -**ies**) property inherited from father or ancestors; heritage.

patriot /'peɪtrɪət/ *noun* person devoted to and ready to defend his or her country. □ **patriotic** /-'ɒt-/ *adjective*; **patriotism** *noun*.

patrol /pə'trəʊl/ ● *noun* act of walking or travelling round area etc. to protect or supervise it; person(s) or vehicle(s) sent out on patrol; unit of usually 6 in Scout troop or Guide company. ● *verb* (-**ll**-) carry out patrol of; act as patrol. □ **patrol car** car used by police etc. for patrol.

patron /'peɪtrən/ *noun* (*feminine* **patroness**) person who gives financial or other support; customer of shop etc. □ **patron saint** saint regarded as protecting person, place, activity, etc.

patronage /'pætrənɪdʒ/ *noun* patron's or customer's support; right of bestowing or recommending for appointments; condescending manner.

patronize /'pætrənaɪz/ *verb* (also -**ise**) (-**zing** or -**sing**) treat condescendingly; act as patron to; be customer of. □ **patronizing** *adjective*.

patronymic /pætrə'nɪmɪk/ *noun* name derived from that of father or ancestor.

patten /'pæt(ə)n/ *noun* *historical* wooden sole mounted on iron ring for raising wearer's shoe above mud etc.

patter[1] /'pætə/ ● *noun* sound of quick light taps or steps. ● *verb* (of rain etc.) make this sound.

patter[2] /'pætə/ ● *noun* rapid often glib or deceptive talk. ● *verb* say or talk glibly.

pattern /'pæt(ə)n/ ● *noun* decorative design on surface; regular or logical form, order, etc.; model, design, or instructions from which thing is to be made; excellent example. ● *verb* decorate with pattern; model (thing) on design etc.

patty /'pætɪ/ *noun* (*plural* -**ies**) small pie or pasty.

paucity /'pɔːsɪtɪ/ *noun* smallness of number or quantity.

paunch /pɔːntʃ/ *noun* belly, stomach. □ **paunchy** *adjective*.

pauper /'pɔːpə/ *noun* very poor person. □ **pauperism** *noun*.

pause /pɔːz/ ● *noun* temporary stop or silence; *Music* mark denoting lengthening of note or rest. ● *verb* (-**sing**) make a pause; wait.

pavane /pə'vɑːn/ *noun* (also **pavan** /'pæv(ə)n/) *historical* stately dance; music for this.

pave *verb* (-**ving**) cover (street, floor, etc.) with durable surface. □ **pave the way** (usually + *for*) make preparations. □ **paving** *noun*.

pavement *noun* paved footway at side of road. □ **pavement artist** artist who draws in chalk on pavement for tips.

pavilion /pə'vɪljən/ *noun* building on sports ground for spectators or players; summer house etc. in park; large tent; building or stand at exhibition.

pavlova /pæv'ləʊvə/ *noun* meringue dessert with cream and fruit filling.

paw ● *noun* foot of animal with claws; *colloquial* person's hand. ● *verb* touch with paw; *colloquial* fondle awkwardly or indecently.

pawn[1] *noun* chessman of smallest size and value; person subservient to others' plans.

pawn[2] *verb* deposit (thing) as security for money borrowed; pledge. □ **in pawn** held as security; **pawnbroker** person who lends money at interest on security of personal property; **pawnshop** pawnbroker's place of business.

pawpaw /'pɔːpɔː/ *noun* (also **papaya** /pə'paɪə/) pear-shaped mango-like fruit with pulpy orange flesh; tropical tree bearing this.

pay ● *verb* (*past & past participle* **paid**) discharge debt to; give as due; render, bestow (attention etc.); yield adequate return; let out (rope) by slackening it; reward or punish. ● *noun* wages. □ **in the pay of** employed by; **pay-as-you-earn** collection of income tax by deduction at source from wages etc.; **pay-claim** demand for increase in pay; **payday** day on which wages are paid; **pay for** hand over money for, bear cost of, suffer or be punished for; **paying guest** lodger; **payload** part of (esp. aircraft's) load from which revenue is derived; **paymaster** official who pays troops, workmen, etc.; **Paymaster General** Treasury minister responsible for payments; **pay off** pay in full and discharge, *colloquial* yield good results; **pay-off** *slang* payment, climax, end result; **pay phone** coin box telephone; **payroll** list of employees receiving regular pay. □ **payee** /peɪ'iː/ *noun*.

payable *adjective* that must or may be paid.

PAYE *abbreviation* pay-as-you-earn.

payment *noun* paying, amount paid; recompense.

payola /peɪ'əʊlə/ *noun esp. US slang* bribe offered for unofficial media promotion of product etc.

PC *abbreviation* Police Constable; personal computer; politically correct; political correctness; Privy Councillor.

p.c. *abbreviation* per cent; postcard.

pd. *abbreviation* paid.

PE *abbreviation* physical education.

pea *noun* climbing plant bearing round edible seeds in pods; one of its seeds; similar plant. □ **pea-souper** *colloquial* thick yellowish fog.

peace *noun* quiet, calm; freedom from or cessation of war; civil order. □ **peacemaker** person who brings about peace; **peacetime** time when country is not at war.

peaceable *adjective* disposed or tending to peace, peaceful.

peaceful *adjective* characterized by or not infringing peace. □ **peacefully** *adverb*; **peacefulness** *noun*.

peach¹ *noun* roundish juicy fruit with downy yellow or rosy skin; tree bearing it; yellowish-pink colour; *colloquial* person or thing of superlative merit. □ **peach Melba** dish of ice cream and peaches. □ **peachy** *adjective* (**-ier, -iest**).

peach² *verb colloquial* turn informer; inform.

peacock /'piːkɒk/ *noun* (*plural* same or **-s**) male peafowl, bird with brilliant plumage and erectile fanlike tail. □ **peacock blue** bright lustrous greenish blue of peacock's neck; **peacock butterfly** butterfly with eyelike markings resembling those on peacock's tail.

peafowl /'piːfaʊl/ *noun* kind of pheasant, peacock or peahen.

peahen /'piːhen/ *noun* female peafowl.

peak¹ ● *noun* pointed top, esp. of mountain; stiff projecting brim at front of cap; highest point of achievement, intensity, etc. ● *verb* reach highest value, quality, etc.

peak² *verb* waste away; (as **peaked** *adjective*) pinched-looking.

peaky *adjective* (**-ier, -iest**) sickly, puny.

peal ● *noun* loud ringing of bell(s); set of bells; loud repeated sound. ● *verb* (cause to) sound in peal; utter sonorously.

peanut *noun* plant bearing underground pods containing seeds used as food and yielding oil; its seed; (in *plural*) *colloquial* trivial amount, esp. of money. □ **peanut butter** paste of ground roasted peanuts.

pear /peə/ *noun* fleshy fruit tapering towards stalk; tree bearing it.

pearl /pɜːl/ ● *noun* rounded lustrous usually white solid formed in shell of certain oysters and prized as gem; imitation of this; precious thing, finest example. ● *verb poetical* (of moisture) form drops, form drops on; fish for pearls. □ **pearl barley** barley rubbed into small rounded grains; **pearl button** button of (real or imitation) mother-of-pearl.

pearly ● *adjective* (**-ier, -iest**) resembling a pearl; adorned with pearls. ● *noun* (*plural* **-ies**) pearly king or queen; (in *plural*) pearly king's or queen's clothes. □ **Pearly Gates** *colloquial* gates of Heaven; **pearly king, queen** London costermonger, or his wife, wearing clothes covered with pearl buttons.

peasant /'pez(ə)nt/ *noun* (in some countries) worker on land, farm labourer; small farmer; *derogatory* lout, boor. □ **peasantry** *noun* (*plural* **-ies**).

pease-pudding /piːz/ *noun* dried peas boiled in cloth.

peat *noun* vegetable matter decomposed by water and partly carbonized; piece of this as fuel. □ **peatbog** bog composed of peat. □ **peaty** *adjective*.

pebble /'peb(ə)l/ *noun* small stone made smooth by action of water. □ **pebble-dash** mortar with pebbles in it as wall-coating. □ **pebbly** *adjective*.

pecan /'piːkən/ *noun* pinkish-brown smooth nut; kind of hickory producing it.

peccadillo /pekə'dɪləʊ/ *noun* (*plural* **-es** or **-s**) trivial offence.

peck¹ ● *verb* strike, pick up, pluck out, or make (hole) with beak; kiss hastily or perfunctorily; *colloquial* (+ *at*) eat (meal) listlessly or fastidiously. ● *noun* stroke with beak; hasty or perfunctory kiss. □ **pecking order** social hierarchy.

peck² *noun* measure of capacity for dry goods (2 gallons, 9.092 litres).

pecker *noun* □ **keep your pecker up** *colloquial* stay cheerful.

peckish *adjective colloquial* hungry.

pectin /'pektɪn/ *noun* soluble gelatinous substance in ripe fruits, causing jam etc. to set.

pectoral /'pektər(ə)l/ ● *adjective* of or for breast or chest. ● *noun* pectoral fin or muscle.

peculiar /pɪ'kjuːlɪə/ *adjective* odd; (usually + *to*) belonging exclusively; belonging to the individual; particular, special.

peculiarity /pɪkjuːlɪ'ærɪtɪ/ *noun* (*plural* **-ies**) oddity; characteristic; being peculiar.

peculiarly *adverb* more than usually, especially; oddly.

pecuniary /pɪ'kjuːnɪərɪ/ *adjective* of or in money.

pedagogue /'pedəgɒg/ *noun archaic or derogatory* schoolmaster.

pedagogy /'pedəgɒdʒɪ/ *noun* science of teaching. □ **pedagogic(al)** /-'gɒg-/ *adjective*.

pedal /'ped(ə)l/ ● *noun* lever or key operated by foot, esp. in bicycle, motor vehicle, or some musical instruments. ● *verb* (**-ll-;** *US* **-l-**) work pedals (of); ride bicycle. ● *adjective* /'piːd(ə)l/ of foot or feet.

pedant /'ped(ə)nt/ *noun derogatory* person who insists on strict adherence to literal meaning or formal rules. □ **pedantic** /pɪ'dæntɪk/ *adjective*; **pedantry** *noun*.

peddle /'ped(ə)l/ *verb* (**-ling**) sell as pedlar; advocate; sell (drugs) illegally; engage in selling, esp. as pedlar.

peddler *noun* person who sells drugs illegally; *US* = PEDLAR.

pedestal /'pedɪst(ə)l/ *noun* base of column; block on which something stands.

pedestrian /pɪ'destrɪən/ ● *noun* walker, esp. in town. ● *adjective* prosaic, dull. □ **pedestrian crossing** part of road where crossing pedestrians have right of way.

pedicure /'pedɪkjʊə/ *noun* care or treatment of feet, esp. of toenails.

pedigree /'pedɪgriː/ *noun* recorded (esp. distinguished) line of descent of person or animal; genealogical table; *colloquial* thing's history.

pediment /'pedɪmənt/ *noun* triangular part crowning front of building, esp. over portico.

pedlar /'pedlə/ *noun* (*US* **peddler**) travelling seller of small wares.

pedometer /pɪ'dɒmɪtə/ *noun* instrument for estimating distance travelled on foot.

pedophile *US* = PAEDOPHILE.

peduncle /pɪ'dʌŋk(ə)l/ *noun* stalk of flower, fruit, or cluster, esp. main stalk bearing solitary flower.

pee *colloquial* ● *verb* (**pees, peed**) urinate. ● *noun* urination; urine.

peek *noun & verb* peep, glance.

peel ● *verb* strip rind etc. from; (usually + *off*) take off (skin etc.); become bare of bark, skin, etc.; (often + *off*) flake off. ● *noun* rind or outer coating of fruit, potato, etc.

peeling *noun* (usually in *plural*) piece peeled off.

peep¹ ● *verb* look furtively or through narrow aperture; come cautiously or partly into view; emerge. ● *noun* furtive or peering glance; (usually + *of*) first light of dawn. □ **peep-hole** small hole to peep through; **Peeping Tom** furtive voyeur; **peep-show** exhibition of pictures etc. viewed through lens or peep-hole.

peep² ● *verb* cheep, squeak. ● *noun* cheep, squeak; slight sound, utterance, or complaint.

peer¹ *verb* look closely or with difficulty.

peer² *noun* (*feminine* **peeress**) duke, marquis, earl, viscount, or baron; equal (esp. in civil standing or rank). □ **peer group** person's associates of same status.

peerage *noun* peers as a class; rank of peer or peeress.

peerless *adjective* unequalled.

peeve *colloquial* ● *verb* (**-ving**) (usually as **peeved** *adjective*) irritate. ● *noun* cause or state of annoyance.

peevish *adjective* querulous, irritable. □ **peevishly** *adverb*.

peewit /'piːwɪt/ *noun* lapwing.

peg ● *noun* wooden, metal, etc. bolt or pin for holding things together, hanging things on, etc.; each of pins used to tighten or loosen strings of violin etc.; forked wooden peg etc. for hanging washing on line; drink, esp. of spirits. ● *verb* (**-gg-**) (usually + *down, in*, etc.) fix, mark, or hang out (as with peg(s); keep (prices etc.) stable. □ **off the peg** (of clothes) ready-made; **peg away** (often + *at*) work persistently; **pegboard** board with holes for pegs; **peg out** *slang* die, mark out boundaries of.

pejorative /pɪ'dʒɒrətɪv/ ● *adjective* derogatory. ● *noun* derogatory word.

peke *noun colloquial* Pekingese.

Pekingese /piːkɪ'niːz/ *noun* (also **Pekinese**) (*plural* same) dog of small short-legged snub-nosed breed with long silky hair.

pelargonium /pelə'gəʊnɪəm/ *noun* plant with showy flowers; geranium.

pelf *noun* money, wealth.

pelican /'pelɪkən/ *noun* large waterfowl with pouch below bill for storing fish. □ **pelican crossing** road crossing-place with traffic lights operated by pedestrians.

pellagra /pə'lægrə/ *noun* deficiency disease with cracking of skin.

pellet /'pelɪt/ *noun* small compressed ball of a substance; pill; small shot.

pellicle /'pelɪk(ə)l/ *noun* thin skin; membrane; film.

pell-mell /pel'mel/ *adverb* headlong; in disorder.

pellucid /pɪ'luːsɪd/ *adjective* transparent, clear.

pelmet /'pelmɪt/ *noun* hanging border concealing curtain-rods etc.

pelt¹ ● *verb* assail with missiles, abuse, etc.; (of rain) come down hard; run at full speed. ● *noun* pelting.

pelt² *noun* skin of animal, esp. with hair or fur still on it.

pelvis /'pelvɪs/ *noun* lower abdominal cavity in most vertebrates, formed by haunch bones etc. □ **pelvic** *adjective*.

pen¹ ● *noun* implement for writing with ink. ● *verb* (**-nn-**) write. □ **penfriend** friend with whom one communicates by letter only; **penknife** small folding knife; **pen-name** literary pseudonym; **pen-pal** *colloquial* penfriend.

pen² ● *noun* small enclosure for cows, sheep, poultry, etc. ● *verb* (**-nn-**) enclose; put or keep in confined space.

pen³ *noun* female swan.

penal /'piːn(ə)l/ *adjective* of or involving punishment; punishable.

penalize /'piːnəlaɪz/ *verb* (also **-ise**) (**-zing** or **-sing**) subject to penalty or disadvantage; make punishable.

penalty /'penəltɪ/ *noun* (*plural* **-ies**) fine or other punishment; disadvantage, loss, etc., esp. as result of one's own actions; disadvantage imposed in sports for breach of rules etc. □ **penalty area** *Football* area in front of goal within which breach of rules involves award of penalty kick for opposing team; **penalty kick** free kick at goal from close range.

penance /'penəns/ *noun* act of self-punishment, esp. imposed by priest, performed as expression of penitence.

pence *plural* of PENNY.

penchant /'pɑ̃ʃɑ̃/ *noun* (+ *for*) inclination or liking for.

pencil /'pens(ə)l/ ● *noun* instrument for drawing or writing, esp. of graphite enclosed in wooden cylinder or metal case with tapering end; something used or shaped like this. ● *verb* (**-ll-**; *US* **-l-**) write, draw, or mark with pencil.

pendant /'pend(ə)nt/ *noun* ornament hung from necklace etc.

pendent /'pend(ə)nt/ *adjective* formal hanging; overhanging; pending.

pending /'pendɪŋ/ ● *adjective* awaiting decision or settlement. ● *preposition* until; during.

pendulous /'pendjʊləs/ *adjective* hanging down; swinging.

pendulum /'pendjʊləm/ *noun* (*plural* **-s**) body suspended so as to be free to swing, esp. regulating movement of clock's works.

penetrate /'penɪtreɪt/ *verb* (**-ting**) make way into or through; pierce; permeate; see into or through; be absorbed by the mind; (as **penetrating** *adjective*) having or suggesting insight, (of voice) easily heard above other sounds, piercing. □ **penetrable** /-trəb(ə)l/ *adjective*; **penetration** *noun*.

penguin /'peŋgwɪn/ *noun* flightless seabird of southern hemisphere.

penicillin /penɪ'sɪlɪn/ *noun* antibiotic obtained from mould.

peninsula /pɪ'nɪnsjʊlə/ *noun* piece of land almost surrounded by water or projecting far into sea etc. □ **peninsular** *adjective*.

penis /'piːnɪs/ *noun* sexual and (in mammals) urinatory organ of male animal.

penitent /'penɪt(ə)nt/ ● *adjective* repentant. ● *noun* penitent person; person doing penance. □ **penitence** *noun*; **penitently** *adverb*.

penitential /penɪ'tenʃ(ə)l/ *adjective* of penitence or penance.

penitentiary /penɪ'tenʃərɪ/ ● *noun* (*plural* **-ies**) *US* prison. ● *adjective* of penance or reformatory treatment.

pennant /'penənt/ *noun* tapering flag, esp. that at masthead of ship in commission.

penniless /'penɪlɪs/ *adjective* destitute.

pennon /'penən/ noun long narrow triangular or swallow-tailed flag; long pointed streamer on ship.

penny /'penɪ/ noun (plural **pence** or, for separate coins only, **pennies**) British coin worth 1/100 of pound, or formerly 1/240 of pound. □ **penny-farthing** early kind of bicycle with large front wheel and small rear one; **penny-pinching** noun meanness, adjective mean; **a pretty penny** a large sum of money.

pennyroyal /penɪ'rɔɪəl/ noun creeping kind of mint.

penology /piː'nɒlədʒɪ/ noun study of punishment and prison management.

pension¹ /'penʃ(ə)n/ ● noun periodic payment made by government, exemployer, private fund, etc. to person above specified age or to retired, widowed, disabled, etc. person. ● verb grant pension to. □ **pension off** dismiss with pension.

pension² /pɑ̃'sjɔ̃/ noun European, esp. French, boarding house. [French]

pensionable adjective entitled or entitling person to pension.

pensioner noun recipient of (esp. retirement) pension.

pensive /'pensɪv/ adjective deep in thought. □ **pensively** adverb.

pent adjective (often + in, up) closely confined; shut in.

penta- combining form five.

pentacle /'pentək(ə)l/ noun figure used as symbol, esp. in magic, e.g. pentagram.

pentagon /'pentəgən/ noun plane figure with 5 sides and angles; (**the Pentagon**) (pentagonal headquarters of) leaders of US defence forces. □ **pentagonal** /-'tæg-/ adjective.

pentagram /'pentəgræm/ noun 5-pointed star.

pentameter /pen'tæmɪtə/ noun line of verse with 5 metrical feet.

Pentateuch /'pentətjuːk/ noun first 5 books of Old Testament.

pentathlon /pen'tæθlən/ noun athletic contest of 5 events. □ **pentathlete** noun.

Pentecost /'pentɪkɒst/ noun Whit Sunday; Jewish harvest festival 50 days after second day of Passover.

pentecostal /pentɪ'kɒst(ə)l/ adjective (of religious group) emphasizing divine gifts, esp. healing, and often fundamentalist.

penthouse /'penthaʊs/ noun flat on roof or top floor of tall building.

penultimate /pɪ'nʌltɪmət/ adjective & noun last but one.

penumbra /pɪ'nʌmbrə/ noun (plural **-s** or **-brae** /-briː/) partly shaded region round shadow of opaque body; partial shadow. □ **penumbral** adjective.

penurious /pɪ'njʊərɪəs/ adjective poor; stingy.

penury /'penjʊrɪ/ noun (plural **-ies**) destitution, poverty.

peon /'piːən/ noun Spanish-American day-labourer.

peony /'piːənɪ/ noun (also **paeony**) (plural **-ies**) plant with large globular red, pink, or white flowers.

people /'piːp(ə)l/ ● plural noun persons in general; (singular) race or nation; (**the people**) ordinary people, esp. as electorate; parents or other relatives; subjects. ● verb (**-ling**) (usually + with) fill with people; populate; (esp. as **peopled** adjective) inhabit.

PEP /pep/ abbreviation Personal Equity Plan.

pep colloquial ● noun vigour, spirit. ● verb (**-pp-**) (usually + up) fill with vigour. □ **pep pill** one containing stimulant drug; **pep talk** exhortation to greater effort or courage.

pepper /'pepə/ ● noun hot aromatic condiment from dried berries of some plants; capsicum plant, its fruit. ● verb sprinkle or flavour with pepper; pelt with missiles. □ **pepper-and-salt** of closely mingled dark and light colour; **peppercorn** dried

pepper berry, (in full **peppercorn rent**) nominal rent; **pepper-mill** mill for grinding peppercorns by hand.

peppermint noun species of mint grown for its strong-flavoured oil; sweet flavoured with this oil; the oil.

pepperoni /pepə'rəʊnɪ/ noun sausage seasoned with pepper.

peppery adjective of, like, or abounding in pepper; hot-tempered.

pepsin /'pepsɪn/ noun enzyme contained in gastric juice.

peptic /'peptɪk/ adjective digestive. □ **peptic ulcer** one in stomach or duodenum.

per preposition for each; by, by means of, through.

peradventure /pərəd'ventʃə/ adverb archaic perhaps.

perambulate /pə'ræmbjʊleɪt/ verb (**-ting**) walk through, over, or about. □ **perambulation** noun.

perambulator noun formal pram.

per annum /pər 'ænəm/ adverb for each year.

per capita /pə 'kæpɪtə/ adverb & adjective for each person.

perceive /pə'siːv/ verb (**-ving**) become aware of by one of senses; apprehend; understand. □ **perceivable** adjective.

per cent /pə 'sent/ (US **percent**) ● adverb in every hundred. ● noun percentage; one part in every hundred.

percentage noun rate or proportion per cent; proportion.

percentile /pə'sentaɪl/ noun each of 99 points at which a range of data is divided to make 100 groups of equal size; each of these groups.

perceptible /pə'septɪb(ə)l/ adjective that can be perceived. □ **perceptibility** noun; **perceptibly** adverb.

perception /pə'sepʃ(ə)n/ noun act or faculty of perceiving. □ **perceptual** /-'septʃʊəl/ adjective.

perceptive /pə'septɪv/ adjective sensitive; discerning; capable of perceiving. □ **perceptively** adverb; **perceptiveness** noun.

perch¹ ● noun bird's resting-place above ground; high place for person or thing to rest on; historical measure of length (5½ yds). ● verb rest or place on perch.

perch² noun (plural same or **-es**) edible spiny-finned freshwater fish.

perchance /pə'tʃɑːns/ adverb archaic maybe.

percipient /pə'sɪpɪənt/ adjective perceiving; conscious.

percolate /'pɜːkəleɪt/ verb (**-ting**) (often + through) filter gradually; (of idea etc.) permeate gradually; prepare (coffee) in percolator. □ **percolation** noun.

percolator noun apparatus for making coffee by circulating boiling water through ground beans.

percussion /pə'kʌʃ(ə)n/ noun playing of music by striking instruments with sticks etc.; such instruments collectively; gentle tapping of body in medical diagnosis; forcible striking of body against another. □ **percussionist** noun; **percussive** adjective.

perdition /pə'dɪʃ(ə)n/ noun damnation.

peregrine /'perɪgrɪn/ noun (in full **peregrine falcon**) kind of falcon.

peremptory /pə'remptərɪ/ adjective admitting no denial or refusal; imperious. □ **peremptorily** adverb.

perennial /pə'renɪəl/ ● adjective lasting through the year; (of plant) living several years; lasting long or for ever. ● noun perennial plant. □ **perennially** adverb.

perestroika /pere'strɔɪkə/ noun (in former USSR) reform of economic and political system.

perfect ● adjective /'pɜːfɪkt/ complete; faultless; not deficient; very enjoyable; exact, precise; entire, unqualified; Grammar (of tense) expressing completed action. ● *verb* /pə'fekt/ make perfect; complete. ● *noun* /'pɜːfɪkt/ perfect tense. □ **perfect pitch** *Music* ability to recognize pitch of note.

perfection /pə'fekʃ(ə)n/ *noun* being or making perfect; perfect state; perfect person, specimen, etc.

perfectionism *noun* uncompromising pursuit of perfection. □ **perfectionist** *noun*.

perfectly *adverb* quite, completely; in a perfect way.

perfidy /'pɜːfɪdɪ/ *noun* breach of faith, treachery. □ **perfidious** /-'fɪd-/ *adjective*.

perforate /'pɜːfəreɪt/ *verb* (**-ting**) pierce, make hole(s) through; make row of small holes in (paper etc.). □ **perforation** *noun*.

perforce /pə'fɔːs/ *adverb archaic* unavoidably, necessarily.

perform /pə'fɔːm/ *verb* carry into effect; go through, execute; act, sing, etc., esp. in public; (of animals) do tricks etc. □ **performing arts** drama, music, dance, etc. □ **performer** *noun*.

performance *noun* act, process, or manner of doing or functioning; execution (of duty etc.); performing of or in play etc.; *colloquial* fuss, emotional scene.

perfume /'pɜːfjuːm/ ● *noun* sweet smell; fragrant liquid, esp. for application to the body, scent. ● *verb* (**-ming**) impart perfume to.

perfumer /pə'fjuːmə/ *noun* maker or seller of perfumes. □ **perfumery** *noun* (*plural* **-ies**).

perfunctory /pə'fʌŋktərɪ/ *adjective* done merely out of duty; superficial. □ **perfunctorily** *adverb*; **perfunctoriness** *noun*.

pergola /'pɜːgələ/ *noun* arbour or covered walk arched with climbing plants.

perhaps /pə'hæps/ *adverb* it may be, possibly.

perianth /'perɪænθ/ *noun* outer part of flower.

perigee /'perɪdʒiː/ *noun* point nearest to earth in orbit of moon etc.

perihelion /perɪ'hiːlɪən/ *noun* (*plural* **-lia**) point nearest to sun in orbit of planet, comet, etc. round it.

peril /'perɪl/ *noun* serious and immediate danger. □ **perilous** *adjective*; **perilously** *adverb*.

perimeter /pə'rɪmɪtə/ *noun* circumference or outline of closed figure; length of this; outer boundary.

period /'pɪərɪəd/ ● *noun* amount of time during which something runs its course; distinct portion of history, life, etc.; occurrence of menstruation, time of this; complete sentence; *esp. US* full stop. ● *adjective* characteristic of past period.

periodic /pɪərɪ'ɒdɪk/ *adjective* appearing or recurring at intervals. □ **periodic table** arrangement of chemical elements by atomic number and chemical properties. □ **periodicity** /-rɪə'dɪsɪtɪ/ *noun*.

periodical ● *noun* magazine etc. published at regular intervals. ● *adjective* periodic. □ **periodically** *adverb*.

peripatetic /perɪpə'tetɪk/ *adjective* (of teacher) working in more than one establishment; going from place to place; itinerant.

peripheral /pə'rɪfər(ə)l/ ● *adjective* of minor importance; of periphery. ● *noun* input, output, or storage device connected to computer.

periphery /pə'rɪfərɪ/ *noun* (*plural* **-ies**) bounding line, esp. of round surface; outer or surrounding area.

periphrasis /pə'rɪfrəsɪs/ *noun* (*plural* **-phrases** /-siːz/) circumlocution, roundabout speech or phrase. □ **periphrastic** /perɪ'fræstɪk/ *adjective*.

periscope /'perɪskəʊp/ *noun* apparatus with tube and mirrors or prisms for viewing objects otherwise out of sight.

perish /'perɪʃ/ *verb* suffer destruction, die; lose natural qualities; (cause to) rot or deteriorate; (in *passive*) suffer from cold.

perishable ● *adjective* subject to speedy decay; liable to perish. ● *noun* perishable thing (esp. food).

perisher *noun slang* annoying person.

perishing *colloquial* ● *adjective* confounded; intensely cold. ● *adverb* confoundedly.

peritoneum /perɪtə'niːəm/ *noun* (*plural* **-s** or **-nea**) membrane lining abdominal cavity. □ **peritoneal** *adjective*.

peritonitis /perɪtə'naɪtɪs/ *noun* inflammation of peritoneum.

periwig /'perɪwɪg/ *noun historical* wig.

periwinkle[1] /'perɪwɪŋk(ə)l/ *noun* evergreen trailing plant with blue or white flower.

periwinkle[2] /'perɪwɪŋk(ə)l/ *noun* winkle.

perjure /'pɜːdʒə/ *verb* (**-ring**) (**perjure oneself**) commit perjury; (as **perjured** *adjective*) guilty of perjury. □ **perjurer** *noun*.

perjury /'pɜːdʒərɪ/ *noun* (*plural* **-ies**) wilful lying while on oath.

perk[1] *verb* □ **perk up** (cause to) recover courage, smarten up, raise (head etc.) briskly.

perk[2] *noun colloquial* perquisite.

perky *adjective* (**-ier, -iest**) lively and cheerful.

perm[1] ● *noun* permanent wave. ● *verb* give permanent wave to.

perm[2] *colloquial* ● *noun* permutation. ● *verb* make permutation of.

permafrost /'pɜːməfrɒst/ *noun* permanently frozen subsoil, as in polar regions.

permanent /'pɜːmənənt/ *adjective* lasting or intended to last indefinitely. □ **permanent wave** long-lasting artificial wave in hair. □ **permanence** *noun*; **permanently** *adverb*.

permeable /'pɜːmɪəb(ə)l/ *adjective* capable of being permeated. □ **permeability** *noun*.

permeate /'pɜːmɪeɪt/ *verb* (**-ting**) penetrate, saturate, pervade; be diffused. □ **permeation** *noun*.

permissible /pə'mɪsɪb(ə)l/ *adjective* allowable. □ **permissibility** *noun*.

permission /pə'mɪʃ(ə)n/ *noun* consent, authorization.

permissive /pə'mɪsɪv/ *adjective* tolerant, liberal; giving permission. □ **permissiveness** *noun*.

permit ● *verb* /pə'mɪt/ (**-tt-**) give consent to; authorize; allow; give opportunity; (+ *of*) allow as possible. ● *noun* /'pɜːmɪt/ written order giving permission or allowing entry.

permutation /pɜːmjʊ'teɪʃ(ə)n/ *noun* one of possible ordered arrangements of set of things; combination or selection of specified number of items from larger group.

pernicious /pə'nɪʃəs/ *adjective* destructive, injurious. □ **pernicious anaemia** defective formation of red blood cells through lack of vitamin B.

pernickety /pə'nɪkɪtɪ/ *adjective colloquial* fastidious, over-precise.

peroration /perə'reɪʃ(ə)n/ *noun* concluding part of speech.

peroxide /pə'rɒksaɪd/ ● *noun* (in full **hydrogen peroxide**) colourless liquid used in water solution, esp. to bleach hair; oxide containing maximum proportion of oxygen. ● *verb* (**-ding**) bleach (hair) with peroxide.

perpendicular /pɜːpən'dɪkjʊlə/ ● *adjective* (usually + *to*) at right angles; upright; very steep; (**Perpendicular**) of or in style of English Gothic architecture of 15th & 16th c. ● *noun* perpendicular line etc. □ **perpendicularity** /-'lærɪtɪ/ *noun*.

perpetrate /'pɜːpɪtreɪt/ *verb* (**-ting**) commit. □ **perpetration** *noun*; **perpetrator** *noun*.

perpetual /pə'petʃʊəl/ *adjective* lasting for ever or indefinitely; continuous; *colloquial* frequent. □ **perpetually** *adverb*.

perpetuate /pə'petʃʊeɪt/ *verb* (**-ting**) make perpetual; cause to be always remembered. □ **perpetuation** *noun*.

perpetuity /pɜːpɪ'tjuːɪtɪ/ *noun* (*plural* **-ies**) perpetual continuance or possession. □ **in perpetuity** for ever.

perplex /pə'pleks/ *verb* bewilder, puzzle; complicate, tangle. □ **perplexing** *adjective*; **perplexity** *noun*.

per pro. /pɜː 'prəʊ/ *abbreviation* through the agency of (used in signatures) (*per procurationem*). [Latin].

■ **Usage** The abbreviation *per pro.* (or *p.p.*) is frequently written before the wrong name: "T. Jones, *p.p.* P. Smith" means that P. Smith is signing on behalf of T. Jones.

perquisite /'pɜːkwɪzɪt/ *noun* extra profit additional to main income etc.; customary extra right or privilege.

■ **Usage** *Perquisite* is sometimes confused with *prerequisite*, which means 'a thing required as a precondition'.

perry /'perɪ/ *noun* (*plural* **-ies**) drink made from fermented pear juice.

per se /pɜː 'seɪ/ *adverb* by or in itself, intrinsically. [Latin]

persecute /'pɜːsɪkjuːt/ *verb* (**-ting**) subject to constant hostility and ill-treatment; harass, worry. □ **persecution** /-'kjuːʃ(ə)n/ *noun*; **persecutor** *noun*.

persevere /pɜːsɪ'vɪə/ *verb* (**-ring**) continue steadfastly, persist. □ **perseverance** *noun*.

Persian /'pɜːʃ(ə)n/ ● *noun* native, national, or language of Persia (now Iran); (in full **Persian cat**) cat with long silky hair. ● *adjective* of Persia (Iran). □ **Persian lamb** silky curled fur of young karakul.

persiflage /'pɜːsɪflɑːʒ/ *noun* banter; light raillery.

persimmon /pɜː'sɪmən/ *noun* tropical tree; its edible orange tomato-like fruit.

persist /pə'sɪst/ *verb* (often + *in*) continue to exist or do something in spite of obstacles. □ **persistence** *noun*; **persistent** *adjective*; **persistently** *adverb*.

person /'pɜːs(ə)n/ *noun* individual human being; living body of human being; *Grammar* one of 3 classes of pronouns, verb-forms, etc., denoting person etc. speaking, spoken to, or spoken of. □ **in person** physically present.

persona /pə'səʊnə/ *noun* (*plural* **-nae** /-niː/) aspect of personality as perceived by others. □ **persona grata** /'grɑːtə/ (*plural* **personae gratae** /-niː, -tiː/) person acceptable to certain others; **persona non grata** /nɒn/ (*plural* **personae non gratae**) person not acceptable.

personable *adjective* pleasing in appearance or demeanour.

personage *noun* person, esp. important one.

personal /'pɜːsən(ə)l/ *adjective* one's own; individual, private; done etc. in person; directed to or concerning individual; referring (esp. in hostile way) to individual's private life; *Grammar* of or denoting one of the 3 persons. □ **personal column** part of newspaper devoted to private advertisements and messages; **personal computer** computer designed for use by single individual; **personal equity plan** scheme for taxfree personal investments; **personal organizer** means of keeping track of personal affairs, esp. loose-leaf notebook divided into sections; **personal pronoun** pronoun replacing subject, object, etc., of clause etc.; **personal property** all property except land.

personality /pɜːsə'nælɪtɪ/ *noun* (*plural* **-ies**) distinctive personal character; well-known person; (in *plural*) personal remarks.

personalize *verb* (also **-ise**) (**-zing** or **-sing**) identify as belonging to particular person.

personally *adverb* in person; for one's own part; in a personal way.

personification /pəsɒnɪfɪ'keɪʃ(ə)n/ *noun* type of metaphor in which human qualities are attributed to object, plant, animal, nature, etc., e.g. *Life can play some nasty tricks.*

personify /pə'sɒnɪfaɪ/ *verb* (**-ies**, **-ied**) attribute human characteristics to; symbolize by human figure; (usually as **personified** *adjective*) embody, exemplify typically. □ **personification** *noun*.

personnel /pɜːsə'nel/ *noun* staff of an organization; people engaged in particular service, profession, etc. □ **personnel department** department of firm etc. dealing with appointment, training, and welfare of employees.

perspective /pə'spektɪv/ ● *noun* art of drawing so as to give effect of solidity and relative position and size; relation as to position and distance, or proportion between visible objects, parts of subject, etc.; mental view of relative importance of things; view, prospect. ● *adjective* of or in perspective. □ **in** or **out of perspective** according or not according to rules of perspective, in or not in proportion.

Perspex /'pɜːspeks/ *noun proprietary term* tough light transparent plastic.

perspicacious /pɜːspɪ'keɪʃəs/ *adjective* having mental penetration or discernment. □ **perspicacity** /-'kæs-/ *noun*.

perspicuous /pə'spɪkjʊəs/ *adjective* lucid; clearly expressed. □ **perspicuity** /-'kjuː-/ *noun*.

perspire /pə'spaɪə/ *verb* (**-ring**) sweat. □ **perspiration** /pɜːspɪ'reɪʃ(ə)n/ *noun*.

persuade /pə'sweɪd/ *verb* (**-ding**) cause (person) by argument etc. to believe or do something; convince.

persuasion /pə'sweɪʒ(ə)n/ *noun* persuading; conviction; religious belief or sect.

persuasive /pə'sweɪsɪv/ *adjective* able or tending to persuade. □ **persuasively** *adverb*; **persuasiveness** *noun*.

pert *adjective* saucy, impudent; jaunty. □ **pertly** *adverb*; **pertness** *noun*.

pertain /pə'teɪn/ *verb* belong, relate.

pertinacious /pɜːtɪ'neɪʃəs/ *adjective* persistent, obstinate. □ **pertinacity** /-'næs-/ *noun*.

pertinent /'pɜːtɪnənt/ *adjective* relevant. □ **pertinence** *noun*; **pertinency** *noun*.

perturb /pə'tɜːb/ *verb* throw into agitation; disquiet. □ **perturbation** *noun*.

peruke /pə'ruːk/ *noun historical* wig.

peruse /pə'ruːz/ *verb* (**-sing**) read; scan. □ **perusal** *noun*.

pervade /pə'veɪd/ *verb* (**-ding**) spread through, permeate; be rife among. □ **pervasion** *noun*; **pervasive** *adjective*.

perverse /pə'vɜːs/ *adjective* obstinately or wilfully in the wrong; wayward. □ **perversely** *adverb*; **perversity** *noun*.

perversion /pə'vɜːʃ(ə)n/ *noun* perverting, being perverted; preference for abnormal form of sexual activity.

pervert ● *verb* /pə'vɜːt/ turn (thing) aside from proper or normal use; lead astray from right behaviour or belief etc.; (as **perverted** *adjective*) showing perversion. ● *noun* /'pɜːvɜːt/ person who is perverted, esp. sexually.

pervious /'pɜːvɪəs/ *adjective* permeable; allowing passage or access.

peseta /pə'seɪtə/ *noun* Spanish monetary unit.

peso /'peɪsəʊ/ *noun* (*plural* **-s**) monetary unit in several Latin American countries.

pessary /'pesərɪ/ *noun* (*plural* **-ies**) device worn in vagina; vaginal suppository.

pessimism /'pesɪmɪz(ə)m/ *noun* tendency to take worst view or expect worst outcome. □ **pessimist** *noun*; **pessimistic** /-'mɪst-/ *adjective*.

pest *noun* troublesome or destructive person, animal, or thing.

pester /'pestə/ *verb* trouble or annoy, esp. with persistent requests.

pesticide /'pestɪsaɪd/ *noun* substance for destroying harmful insects etc.

pestilence /'pestɪləns/ *noun* fatal epidemic disease, esp. bubonic plague.

pestilent /'pestɪlənt/ *adjective* deadly; harmful or morally destructive.

pestilential /pestɪ'lenʃ(ə)l/ *adjective* of pestilence; pestilent.

pestle /'pes(ə)l/ *noun* instrument for pounding substances in a mortar.

pet[1] ● *noun* domestic animal kept for pleasure or companionship; favourite. ● *adjective* as, of, or for a pet; favourite; *expressing fondness*. ● *verb* (**-tt-**) fondle, esp. erotically; treat as pet.

pet[2] *noun* fit of ill humour.

petal /'pet(ə)l/ *noun* each division of flower corolla.

peter /'piːtə/ *verb* □ **peter out** diminish, come to an end.

petersham /'piːtəʃəm/ *noun* thick ribbed silk ribbon.

petiole /'petɪəʊl/ *noun* leaf-stalk.

petite /pə'tiːt/ *adjective* (of woman) of small dainty build. [French]

petit four /petɪ'fɔː/ *noun* (*plural* **petits fours** /'fɔːz/) very small fancy cake.

petition /pə'tɪʃ(ə)n/ ● *noun* request, supplication; formal written request, esp. one signed by many people, to authorities etc. ● *verb* make petition to; ask humbly.

petit point /petɪ 'pwæ/ *noun* embroidery on canvas using small stitches.

petrel /'petr(ə)l/ *noun* seabird, usually flying far from land.

petrify /'petrɪfaɪ/ *verb* (**-ies, -ied**) paralyse with terror or astonishment etc.; turn or be turned into stone. □ **petrifaction** /-'fækʃ(ə)n/ *noun*.

petrochemical /petrəʊ'kemɪk(ə)l/ *noun* substance obtained from petroleum or natural gas.

petrodollar /'petrəʊdɒlə/ *noun* notional unit of currency earned by petroleum-exporting country.

petrol /'petr(ə)l/ *noun* refined petroleum used as fuel in motor vehicles, aircraft, etc.

petroleum /pɪ'trəʊlɪəm/ *noun* hydrocarbon oil found in upper strata of earth, refined for use as fuel etc. □ **petroleum jelly** translucent solid mixture of hydrocarbons got from petroleum and used as lubricant etc.

petticoat /'petɪkəʊt/ *noun* woman's or girl's undergarment hanging from waist or shoulders.

pettifogging /'petɪfɒgɪŋ/ *adjective* quibbling, petty; dishonest.

pettish *adjective* fretful, peevish.

petty /'petɪ/ *adjective* (**-ier, -iest**) unimportant, trivial; small-minded; minor, inferior. □ **petty cash** money kept for small items of expenditure; **petty officer** naval NCO. □ **pettiness** *noun*.

petulant /'petjʊlənt/ *adjective* peevishly impatient or irritable. □ **petulance** *noun*; **petulantly** *adverb*.

petunia /pɪ'tjuːnɪə/ *noun* cultivated plant with vivid funnel-shaped flowers.

pew *noun* (in church) enclosed compartment or fixed bench with back; *colloquial* seat.

pewter /'pjuːtə/ *noun* grey alloy of tin, antimony, and copper; articles made of this.

peyote /peɪ'əʊtɪ/ *noun* a Mexican cactus; hallucinogenic drug prepared from it.

pfennig /'fenɪg/ *noun* one-hundredth of Deutschmark.

PG *abbreviation* (of film) classified as suitable for children subject to parental guidance.

pH /piː'eɪtʃ/ *noun* measure of acidity or alkalinity of a solution.

phagocyte /'fægəsaɪt/ *noun* blood corpuscle etc. capable of absorbing foreign matter.

phalanx /'fælæŋks/ *noun* (*plural* **phalanxes** or **phalanges** /fə'lændʒiːz/) group of infantry in close formation; united or organized party or company.

phallus /'fæləs/ *noun* (*plural* **phalli** /-laɪ/ or **phalluses**) (esp. erect) penis; image of this. □ **phallic** *adjective*.

phantasm /'fæntæz(ə)m/ *noun* illusion; phantom. □ **phantasmal** /-'tæzm(ə)l/ *adjective*.

phantasmagoria /fæntæzmə'gɔːrɪə/ *noun* shifting scene of real or imaginary figures. □ **phantasmagoric** /-'gɒrɪk/ *adjective*.

phantom /'fæntəm/ ● *noun* spectre, apparition; mental illusion. ● *adjective* illusory.

Pharaoh /'feərəʊ/ *noun* ruler of ancient Egypt.

Pharisee /'færɪsiː/ *noun* member of ancient Jewish sect distinguished by strict observance of traditional and written law; self-righteous person; hypocrite. □ **Pharisaic** /-'seɪɪk/ *adjective*.

pharmaceutical /fɑːmə'sjuːtɪk(ə)l/ *adjective* of pharmacy; of use or sale of medicinal drugs. □ **pharmaceutics** *noun*.

pharmacist /'fɑːməsɪst/ *noun* person qualified to practise pharmacy.

pharmacology /fɑːmə'kɒlədʒɪ/ *noun* study of action of drugs on the body. □ **pharmacological** /-kə-'lɒdʒ-/ *adjective*; **pharmacologist** *noun*.

pharmacopoeia /fɑːməkə'piːə/ *noun* book with list of drugs and directions for use; stock of drugs.

pharmacy /'fɑːməsɪ/ *noun* (*plural* **-ies**) preparation and dispensing of drugs; pharmacist's shop; dispensary.

pharynx /'færɪŋks/ *noun* (*plural* **pharynges** /-rɪndʒiːz/ or **-xes**) cavity behind mouth and nose. □ **pharyngeal** /færɪn'dʒiːəl/ *adjective*.

phase /feɪz/ ● *noun* stage of development, process, or recurring sequence; aspect of moon or planet. ● *verb* (**-sing**) carry out by phases. □ **phase in, out** bring gradually into or out of use.

Ph.D. *abbreviation* Doctor of Philosophy.

pheasant /'fez(ə)nt/ *noun* long-tailed game bird.

phenomenal /fɪ'nɒmɪn(ə)l/ *adjective* extraordinary, remarkable; of or concerned with phenomena. □ **phenomenally** *adverb*.

phenomenon /fɪ'nɒmɪnən/ *noun* (*plural* **-mena**) observed or apparent object, fact, or occurrence; remarkable person or thing.

■ **Usage** It is a mistake to use the plural form *phenomena* when only one phenomenon is meant.

phew /fjuː/ *interjection* expressing disgust, relief, etc.

phial /'faɪəl/ *noun* small glass bottle.

philander /fɪ'lændə/ *verb* flirt or have casual affairs with women. □ **philanderer** *noun*.

philanthropy /fɪ'lænθrəpɪ/ *noun* love of all humankind; practical benevolence. □ **philanthropic** /-'θrɒp-/ *adjective*; **philanthropist** *noun*.

philately /fɪ'lætəlɪ/ *noun* stamp-collecting. □ **philatelist** *noun*.

philharmonic /fɪlhɑː'mɒnɪk/ *adjective* devoted to music.

philippic /fɪ'lɪpɪk/ *noun* bitter verbal attack.

philistine /'fɪlɪstaɪn/ ● *noun* person who is hostile or indifferent to culture. ● *adjective* hostile or indifferent to culture. □ **philistinism** /-stɪn-/ *noun*.

Phillips /ˈfɪlɪps/ *noun proprietary term* □ **Phillips screw, screwdriver** screw with cross-shaped slot, corresponding screwdriver.

philology /fɪˈlɒlədʒɪ/ *noun* study of language. □ **philological** /-ləˈlɒdʒ-/ *adjective*; **philologist** *noun*.

philosopher /fɪˈlɒsəfə/ *noun* expert in or student of philosophy; person who acts philosophically.

philosophical /filəˈsɒfɪk(ə)l/ *adjective* (also **philosophic**) of or according to philosophy; calm under adverse circumstances. □ **philosophically** *adverb*.

philosophize /fɪˈlɒsəfaɪz/ *verb* (also **-ise**) (**-zing** or **-sing**) reason like philosopher; theorize.

philosophy /fɪˈlɒsəfɪ/ *noun* (*plural* **-ies**) use of reason and argument in seeking truth and knowledge, esp. of ultimate reality or of general causes and principles; philosophical system; system for conduct of life.

philtre /ˈfɪltə/ *noun* (*US* **philter**) love potion.

phlebitis /flɪˈbaɪtɪs/ *noun* inflammation of vein. □ **phlebitic** /-ˈbɪt-/ *adjective*.

phlegm /flem/ *noun* bronchial mucus ejected by coughing; calmness; sluggishness.

phlegmatic /flegˈmætɪk/ *adjective* calm; sluggish.

phlox /flɒks/ *noun* (*plural* same or **-es**) plant with clusters of white or coloured flowers.

phobia /ˈfəʊbɪə/ *noun* abnormal fear or aversion. □ **phobic** *adjective & noun*.

phoenix /ˈfiːnɪks/ *noun* bird, the only one of its kind, fabled to burn itself and rise from its ashes.

phone *noun & verb* (**-ning**) *colloquial* telephone. □ **phone book** telephone directory; **phonecard** card holding prepaid units for use with cardphone; **phone-in** broadcast programme in which listeners or viewers participate by telephone.

phonetic /fəˈnetɪk/ *adjective* of or representing vocal sounds; (of spelling) corresponding to pronunciation. □ **phonetically** *adverb*.

phonetics *plural noun* (usually treated as *singular*) study or representation of vocal sounds. □ **phonetician** /fəʊnɪˈtɪʃ(ə)n/ *noun*.

phoney /ˈfəʊnɪ/ (also **phony**) *colloquial* ● *adjective* (**-ier**, **-iest**) false, sham, counterfeit. ● *noun* (*plural* **-eys** or **-ies**) phoney person or thing. □ **phoniness** *noun*.

phonic /ˈfɒnɪk/ *adjective* of (vocal) sound.

phonograph /ˈfəʊnəgrɑːf/ *noun* early form of gramophone.

phonology /fəˈnɒlədʒɪ/ *noun* study of sounds in language. □ **phonological** /fəʊnəˈlɒdʒɪk(ə)l/ *adjective*.

phony = PHONEY.

phosphate /ˈfɒsfeɪt/ *noun* salt of phosphoric acid, esp. used as fertilizer.

phosphorescence /fɒsfəˈres(ə)ns/ *noun* emission of light without combustion or perceptible heat. □ **phosphoresce** *verb* (**-cing**); **phosphorescent** *adjective*.

phosphorus /ˈfɒsfərəs/ *noun* nonmetallic element occurring esp. as waxlike substance appearing luminous in dark. □ **phosphoric** /-ˈfɒrɪk/ *adjective*; **phosphorous** *adjective*.

photo /ˈfəʊtəʊ/ *noun* (*plural* **-s**) photograph. □ **photo finish** close finish of race in which winner is distinguishable only on photograph; **photofit** picture of suspect constructed from composite photographs.

photo- *combining form* light; photography.

photocopier /ˈfəʊtəʊkɒpɪə/ *noun* machine for photocopying documents.

photocopy /ˈfəʊtəʊkɒpɪ/ ● *noun* (*plural* **-ies**) photographic copy of document. ● *verb* (**-ies**, **-ied**) make photocopy of.

photoelectric /fəʊtəʊɪˈlektrɪk/ *adjective* with or using emission of electrons from substances exposed to light. □ **photoelectric cell** device using this

effect to generate current. □ **photoelectricity** /-ˈtrɪsɪtɪ/ *noun*.

photogenic /fəʊtəʊˈdʒenɪk/ *adjective* looking attractive in photographs; producing or emitting light.

photograph /ˈfəʊtəgrɑːf/ ● *noun* picture formed by chemical action of light on sensitive film. ● *verb* take photograph (of). □ **photographer** /fəˈtɒgrəfə/ *noun*; **photographic** /-ˈgræf-/ *adjective*; **photography** /fəˈtɒgrəfɪ/ *noun*.

photogravure /fəʊtəʊgrəˈvjʊə/ *noun* picture produced from photographic negative transferred to metal plate and etched in; this process.

photojournalism /fəʊtəʊˈdʒɜːnəlɪz(ə)m/ *noun* reporting of news by photographs in magazines etc.

photolithography /fəʊtəʊlɪˈθɒgrəfɪ/ *noun* lithography using plates made photographically.

photometer /fəʊˈtɒmɪtə/ *noun* instrument for measuring light. □ **photometric** /fəʊtəʊˈmetrɪk/ *adjective*; **photometry** /-ˈtɒmɪtrɪ/ *noun*.

photon /ˈfəʊtɒn/ *noun* quantum of electromagnetic radiation energy.

Photostat /ˈfəʊtəʊstæt/ ● *noun proprietary term* type of photocopier; copy made by it. ● *verb* (**photostat**) (**-tt-**) make Photostat of.

photosynthesis /fəʊtəʊˈsɪnθəsɪs/ *noun* process in which energy of sunlight is used by green plants to form carbohydrates from carbon dioxide and water. □ **photosynthesize** *verb* (also **-ise**) (**-zing** or **-sing**).

phrase /freɪz/ ● *noun* group of words forming conceptual unit but not sentence (see panel); short pithy expression; *Music* short sequence of notes. ● *verb* (**-sing**) express in words; divide (music) into phrases. □ **phrase book** book listing phrases and their foreign equivalents, for use by tourists etc. □ **phrasal** *adjective*

phraseology /freɪzɪˈɒlədʒɪ/ *noun* (*plural* **-ies**) choice or arrangement of words. □ **phraseological** /-zɪəˈlɒdʒ-/ *adjective*.

phrenology /frɪˈnɒlədʒɪ/ *noun historical* study of external form of cranium as supposed indication of mental faculties etc. □ **phrenologist** *noun*.

phut /fʌt/ *adverb colloquial* □ **go phut** collapse, break down.

phylactery /fɪˈlæktərɪ/ *noun* (*plural* **-ies**) small box containing Hebrew texts, worn by Jewish man at prayer.

phylum /ˈfaɪləm/ *noun* (*plural* **phyla**) major division of plant or animal kingdom.

physic /ˈfɪzɪk/ *noun esp. archaic* medicine; medical art or profession.

physical /ˈfɪzɪk(ə)l/ ● *adjective* of the body; of matter; of nature or according to its laws; of physics. ● *noun US* medical examination. □ **physically** *adverb*.

physician /fɪˈzɪʃ(ə)n/ *noun* doctor, esp. specialist in medical diagnosis and treatment.

physics /ˈfɪzɪks/ *plural noun* (usually treated as *singular*) science of properties and interaction of matter and energy. □ **physicist** *noun*.

physiognomy /fɪzɪˈɒnəmɪ/ *noun* (*plural* **-ies**) features or type of face; art of judging character from face etc.

physiology /fɪzɪˈɒlədʒɪ/ *noun* science of functioning of living organisms. □ **physiological** /-əˈlɒdʒ-/ *adjective*; **physiologist** *noun*.

physiotherapy /fɪzɪəʊˈθerəpɪ/ *noun* treatment of injury or disease by exercise, heat, or other physical agencies. □ **physiotherapist** *noun*.

physique /fɪˈziːk/ *noun* bodily structure and development.

pi /paɪ/ *noun* sixteenth letter of Greek alphabet (Π, π); (as π) symbol of ratio of circumference of circle to diameter (approx. 3.14).

pia mater /paɪə 'meɪtə/ noun inner membrane enveloping brain and spinal cord.

pianissimo /pɪə'nɪsɪməʊ/ Music ● adjective very soft. ● adverb very softly. ● noun (plural -s or -mi /-mɪ/) very soft playing, singing, or passage.

pianist /'pɪənɪst/ noun player of piano.

piano[1] /pɪ'ænəʊ/ noun (plural -s) keyboard instrument with metal strings struck by hammers. □ **piano-accordion** accordion with small keyboard like that of piano.

piano[2] /'pjɑːnəʊ/ Music ● adjective soft. ● adverb softly. ● noun (plural -s or -ni /-nɪ/) soft playing, singing, or passage.

pianoforte /pɪænəʊ'fɔːtɪ/ noun formal or archaic = PIANO[1].

piazza /pɪ'ætsə/ noun public square or market-place.

pibroch /'piːbrɒk/ noun martial or funeral bagpipe music.

picador /'pɪkədɔː/ noun mounted man with lance in bullfight.

picaresque /pɪkə'resk/ adjective (of style of fiction) dealing with episodic adventures of rogues.

piccalilli /pɪkə'lɪlɪ/ noun (plural -s) pickle of chopped vegetables, mustard, and spices.

piccolo /'pɪkələʊ/ noun (plural -s) small high-pitched flute.

pick ● verb select carefully; pluck, gather (flower, fruit, etc.); probe with fingers or instrument to remove unwanted matter; clear (bone etc.) of scraps of meat etc.; eat (food, meal, etc.) in small bits. ● noun picking, selection; (usually + of) best; pickaxe; colloquial plectrum; instrument for picking. □ **pick a lock** open lock with instrument other than proper key, esp. with criminal intent; **pick on** nag at, find fault with, select; **pickpocket** person who steals from pockets; **pick up** take hold of and lift, acquire casually, learn routinely, stop for and take with one, make acquaintance of casually, recover, improve, arrest, detect, manage to receive (broadcast signal etc.), accept responsibility of paying (bill etc.), resume; **pick-up** person met casually, small open truck, part of record player carrying stylus, device on electric guitar etc. that converts string vibrations into electrical signals, act of picking up; **pick-your-own** (of fruit and vegetables) dug or picked by customer at farm etc.

pickaxe /'pɪkæks/ noun (US **pickax**) tool with sharp-pointed iron cross-bar for breaking up ground etc.

picket /'pɪkɪt/ ● noun one or more people stationed to dissuade workers from entering workplace during strike etc.; pointed stake driven into ground; small group of troops sent to watch for enemy. ● verb (-t-) place or act as picket outside; post as military picket; secure with stakes. □ **picket line** boundary established by workers on strike, esp. at workplace entrance, which others are asked not to cross.

pickings plural noun perquisites, gleanings.

pickle /'pɪk(ə)l/ ● noun (often in plural) vegetables etc. preserved in vinegar etc.; liquid used for this; colloquial plight. ● verb (-ling) preserve in or treat with pickle; (as **pickled** adjective) slang drunk.

picky adjective (-ier, -iest) colloquial highly fastidious.

picnic /'pɪknɪk/ ● noun outing including outdoor meal; such meal; something pleasantly or easily accomplished. ● verb (-ck-) eat meal outdoors.

pictograph /'pɪktəgrɑːf/ noun (also **pictogram** /-græm/) pictorial symbol used as form of writing.

pictorial /pɪk'tɔːrɪəl/ adjective of, expressed in, or illustrated with a picture or pictures. □ **pictorially** adverb.

picture /'pɪktʃə/ ● noun painting, drawing, photograph, etc. esp. as work of art; portrait; beautiful object; scene; mental image; cinema film; (**the pictures**) cinema (performance). ● verb (-ring) imagine; represent in picture; describe graphically. □ **picture postcard** postcard with picture on one side; **picture window** large window of one pane of glass.

picturesque /pɪktʃə'resk/ adjective striking and pleasant to look at; (of language etc.) strikingly graphic.

piddle /'pɪd(ə)l/ verb (-ling) colloquial urinate; (as **piddling** adjective) colloquial trivial; work or act in trifling way.

pidgin /'pɪdʒɪn/ noun simplified language, esp. used between speakers of different languages.

pie noun dish of meat, fruit, etc., encased in or covered with pastry etc. and baked. □ **pie chart** diagram representing relative quantities as sectors of circle; **pie-eyed** slang drunk.

piebald /'paɪbɔːld/ ● adjective having irregular patches of two colours, esp. black and white. ● noun piebald animal.

piece /piːs/ ● noun distinct portion forming part of or broken off from larger object; coin; picture, literary or musical composition; example, item; chessman, man at draughts, etc. ● verb (-cing) (usually + together) form into a whole; join. □ **of a piece** uniform or consistent; **piece-work** work paid for according to amount done.

pièce de résistance /pjes də reɪ'ziːstɑ̃s/ noun (plural **pièces de résistance** same pronunciation) most important or remarkable item.

piecemeal ● adverb piece by piece, part at a time. ● adjective gradual; unsystematic.

pied /paɪd/ adjective of mixed colours.

Phrase

A phrase is a group of words that has meaning but does not have a subject, verb, or object (unlike a clause or sentence). It can be:

1 a noun phrase, functioning as a noun, e.g.

I went to see my friend Tom.
The only ones they have are too small.

2 an adjective phrase, functioning as an adjective, e.g.

I was very pleased indeed.
This one is better than mine.

3 an adverb phrase, functioning as an adverb, e.g.

They drove off in their car.
I was there ten days ago.

pied-à-terre /pjeɪdɑːˈteə/ noun (plural **pieds-** same pronunciation) (usually small) flat, house, etc. kept for occasional use. [French]

pier /pɪə/ noun structure built out into sea etc. used as promenade and landing-stage or breakwater; support of arch or of span of bridge; pillar; solid part of wall between windows etc. □ **pier-glass** large tall mirror.

pierce /pɪəs/ verb (**-cing**) go through or into like spear or needle; make hole in; make (hole etc.).

pierrot /ˈpɪərəʊ/ noun (feminine **pierrette** /pɪəˈret/) French white-faced pantomime character with clown's costume; itinerant entertainer so dressed.

pietà /pɪeˈtɑː/ noun representation of Virgin Mary holding dead body of Christ. [Italian]

pietism /ˈpaɪətɪz(ə)m/ noun extreme or affected piety.

piety /ˈpaɪətɪ/ noun piousness.

piffle /ˈpɪf(ə)l/ colloquial ● noun nonsense. ● verb (**-ling**) talk or act feebly.

pig ● noun wild or domesticated animal with broad snout and stout bristly body; colloquial greedy, dirty, obstinate, or annoying person; oblong mass of smelted iron or other metal. ● verb (**-gg-**) colloquial eat (food) greedily. □ **pigheaded** obstinate; **pig-iron** crude iron from smelting-furnace; **pig it** colloquial live in disorderly fashion; **pig out** esp. US slang eat greedily; **pigsty** sty for pigs; **pigtail** plait of hair hanging from back or each side of head.

pigeon /ˈpɪdʒ(ə)n/ noun bird of dove family. □ **pigeon-hole** each of set of compartments in cabinet etc. for papers etc., verb classify mentally, put in pigeon-hole, put aside for future consideration; **pigeon-toed** having toes turned inwards.

piggery noun (plural **-ies**) pig farm; pigsty.

piggish adjective greedy; dirty; mean.

piggy ● noun (plural **-ies**) colloquial little pig. ● adjective (**-ier, -iest**) like a pig; (of features etc.) like those of a pig. □ **piggyback** (a ride) on shoulders and back of another person; **piggy bank** pig-shaped money box.

piglet /ˈpɪglɪt/ noun young pig.

pigment /ˈpɪgmənt/ ● noun coloured substance used as paint etc., or occurring naturally in plant or animal tissue. ● verb colour (as) with natural pigment. □ **pigmentation** noun.

pigmy = PYGMY.

pike noun (plural same or **-s**) large voracious freshwater fish; spear formerly used by infantry. □ **pikestaff** wooden shaft of pike (**plain as a pikestaff** quite obvious).

pilaff = PILAU.

pilaster /pɪˈlæstə/ noun rectangular column, esp. one fastened into wall.

pilau /pɪˈlaʊ/ noun (also **pilaff** /pɪˈlɑːf/) Middle Eastern or Indian dish of rice with meat, spices, etc.

pilchard /ˈpɪltʃəd/ noun small sea fish related to herring.

pile¹ ● noun heap of things laid on one another; large imposing building; colloquial large amount, esp. of money; series of plates of dissimilar metals laid alternately for producing electric current; nuclear reactor; pyre. ● verb (**-ling**) heap; (+ with) load with; (+ in, into, on, out of, etc.) crowd. □ **pile up** accumulate, heap up; **pile-up** colloquial collision of several motor vehicles.

pile² noun heavy beam driven vertically into ground as support for building etc.

pile³ noun soft projecting surface of velvet, carpet, etc.

piles plural noun colloquial haemorrhoids.

pilfer /ˈpɪlfə/ verb steal or thieve in petty way.

pilgrim /ˈpɪlgrɪm/ noun person who journeys to sacred place; traveller. □ **Pilgrim Fathers** English Puritans who founded colony in Massachusetts in 1620.

pilgrimage noun pilgrim's journey.

pill noun ball or flat piece of medicinal substance to be swallowed whole; (usually **the pill**) colloquial contraceptive pill. □ **pillbox** small round shallow box for pills, hat shaped like this, Military small round concrete shelter, mainly underground.

pillage /ˈpɪlɪdʒ/ verb (**-ging**) & noun plunder.

pillar /ˈpɪlə/ noun slender upright structure used as support or ornament; person regarded as mainstay; upright mass. □ **pillar-box** public postbox shaped like pillar.

pillion /ˈpɪljən/ noun seat for passenger behind motorcyclist etc.

pillory /ˈpɪlərɪ/ ● noun (plural **-ies**) historical frame with holes for head and hands, allowing an offender to be exposed to public ridicule. ● verb (**-ies, -ied**) expose to ridicule; historical set in pillory.

pillow /ˈpɪləʊ/ ● noun cushion as support for head, esp. in bed; pillow-shaped support. ● verb rest (as) on pillow. □ **pillowcase**, **pillowslip** washable cover for pillow.

pilot /ˈpaɪlət/ ● noun person operating controls of aircraft; person in charge of ships entering or leaving harbour etc.; experimental or preliminary study or undertaking; guide, leader. ● adjective experimental, preliminary. ● verb (**-t-**) act as pilot to; guide course of. □ **pilot-light** small gas burner kept alight to light another; **pilot officer** lowest commissioned rank in RAF.

pimento /pɪˈmentəʊ/ noun (plural **-s**) allspice; sweet pepper.

pimiento /pɪmɪˈentəʊ/ noun (plural **-s**) sweet pepper.

pimp ● noun person who lives off earnings of prostitute or brothel. ● verb act as pimp, esp. procure clients for prostitute.

pimpernel /ˈpɪmpənel/ noun scarlet pimpernel.

pimple /ˈpɪmp(ə)l/ noun small hard inflamed spot on skin. □ **pimply** adjective.

pin ● noun small thin pointed piece of metal with head, used as fastening; wooden or metal peg, rivet, etc.; (in plural) colloquial legs. ● verb (**-nn-**) fasten with pin(s); transfix with pin, lance, etc.; (usually + on) fix (responsibility, blame, etc.); seize and hold fast. □ **pinball** game in which small metal balls are shot across board and strike obstacles; **pincushion** small pad for holding pins; **pin down** (often + to) bind (person etc.) to promise, arrangement, etc., make (person) declare position or intentions; **pin-money** small sum of money, esp. earned by woman; **pinpoint** noun very small or sharp thing, adjective precise, verb locate with precision; **pinprick** petty irritation; **pins and needles** tingling sensation in limb recovering from numbness; **pinstripe** very narrow stripe in cloth; **pin-table** table used in pinball; **pin-tail** duck or grouse with pointed tail; **pin-tuck** narrow ornamental tuck; **pin-up** picture of attractive or famous person, pinned up on wall etc.; **pinwheel** small Catherine wheel.

pina colada /piːnə kəˈlɑːdə/ noun cocktail of pineapple juice, rum, and coconut.

pinafore /ˈpɪnəfɔː/ noun apron, esp. with bib; (in full **pinafore dress**) dress without collar or sleeves, worn over blouse or jumper.

pince-nez /ˈpænsneɪ/ noun (plural same) pair of eyeglasses with spring that clips on nose.

pincers /ˈpɪnsəz/ plural noun gripping-tool forming pair of jaws; pincershaped claw in crustaceans etc. □ **pincer movement** converging movement by two wings of army against enemy position.

pinch ● *verb* grip tightly, esp. between finger and thumb; constrict painfully; (of cold etc.) affect painfully; *slang* steal, arrest; stint, be niggardly. ● *noun* pinching; (as **pinched** *adjective*) (of features) drawn; amount that can be taken up with fingers and thumb; stress of poverty etc. □ **at a pinch** in an emergency.

pinchbeck /'pɪntʃbek/ ● *noun* goldlike copper and zinc alloy used in cheap jewellery etc. ● *adjective* spurious, sham.

pine¹ *noun* evergreen needle-leaved coniferous tree; its wood. □ **pine cone** fruit of pine; **pine nut**, **kernel** edible seed of some pines.

pine² *verb* (**-ning**) (often + *away*) waste away with grief, disease, etc.; (usually + *for*) long.

pineal /'pɪnɪəl/ *adjective* shaped like pine cone. □ **pineal gland**, **body** conical gland in brain, secreting hormone-like substance.

pineapple /'paɪnæp(ə)l/ *noun* large juicy tropical fruit with yellow flesh and tough skin.

ping ● *noun* abrupt single ringing sound. ● *verb* (cause to) emit ping.

ping-pong *noun colloquial* table tennis.

pinion¹ /'pɪnjən/ ● *noun* outer part of bird's wing; *poetical* wing; flight feather. ● *verb* cut off pinion of (wing or bird) to prevent flight; restrain by binding arms to sides.

pinion² /'pɪnjən/ *noun* small cogwheel engaging with larger.

pink¹ ● *noun* pale red colour; garden plant with clove-scented flowers; (**the pink**) the most perfect condition. ● *adjective* pink-coloured; *colloquial* mildly socialist. □ **in the pink** *colloquial* in very good health. □ **pinkish** *adjective*; **pinkness** *noun*.

pink² *verb* pierce slightly; cut scalloped or zigzag edge on. □ **pinking shears** dressmaker's serrated shears for cutting zigzag edge.

pink³ *verb* (of vehicle engine) emit high-pitched explosive sounds caused by faulty combustion.

pinnace /'pɪnɪs/ *noun* ship's small boat.

pinnacle /'pɪnək(ə)l/ *noun* culmination, climax; natural peak; small ornamental turret crowning buttress, roof, etc.

pinnate /'pɪneɪt/ *adjective* (of compound leaf) with leaflets on each side of leaf-stalk.

pinny /'pɪnɪ/ *noun* (*plural* **-ies**) *colloquial* pinafore.

pint /paɪnt/ *noun* measure of capacity (1/8 gal., 0.568 litre); *colloquial* pint of beer. □ **pint-sized** *colloquial* very small.

pinta /'paɪntə/ *noun colloquial* pint of milk.

pintle /'pɪnt(ə)l/ *noun* bolt or pin, esp. one on which some other part turns.

Pinyin /pɪn'jɪn/ *noun* system of romanized spelling for transliterating Chinese.

pioneer /paɪə'nɪə/ ● *noun* beginner of enterprise etc.; explorer or settler. ● *verb* initiate (enterprise etc.) for others to follow; act as pioneer.

pious /'paɪəs/ *adjective* devout, religious; sanctimonious; dutiful. □ **piously** *adverb*.

pip¹ *noun* seed of apple, pear, orange, etc.

pip² *noun* short high-pitched sound.

pip³ *verb* (**-pp-**) *colloquial* hit with a shot; (also **pip at** or **to the post**) defeat narrowly.

pip⁴ *noun* each spot on dominoes, dice, or playing cards; star on army officer's shoulder.

pip⁵ *noun* disease of poultry etc.; (esp. **the pip**) *colloquial* (fit of) depression, boredom, or bad temper.

pipe ● *noun* tube of earthenware, metal, etc., esp. for carrying gas, water, etc.; narrow tube with bowl at one end containing tobacco for smoking; quantity of tobacco held by this; wind instrument of single tube; each tube by which sound is produced in organ; (in *plural*) bagpipes; tubular organ etc. in body; high note or song, esp. of bird; boatswain's whistle; measure of capacity for wine (105 gals., 477 litres). ● *verb* (**-ping**) convey (as) through pipes; play on pipe; (esp. as **piped** *adjective*) transmit (recorded music etc.) by wire or cable; utter shrilly; summon, lead, etc. by sound of pipe or whistle; trim with piping; furnish with pipe(s). □ **pipeclay** fine white clay for tobacco pipes or for whitening leather etc.; **pipe-cleaner** piece of flexible tuft-covered wire to clean inside tobacco pipe; **pipe down** *colloquial* be quiet; **pipe-dream** extravagant fancy, impossible wish, etc.; **pipeline** pipe conveying oil etc. across country, channel of supply or communication; **pipe up** begin to play, sing, etc.

piper *noun* person who plays on pipe, esp. bagpipes.

pipette /pɪ'pet/ *noun* slender tube for transferring or measuring small quantities of liquid.

piping *noun* ornamentation of dress, upholstery, etc. by means of cord enclosed in pipelike fold; ornamental cordlike lines of sugar etc. on cake etc.; length or system of pipes. □ **piping hot** (of food, water, etc.) very or suitably hot.

pipit /'pɪpɪt/ *noun* small bird resembling lark.

pippin /'pɪpɪn/ *noun* apple grown from seed; dessert apple.

piquant /'pi:kənt/ *adjective* agreeably pungent, sharp, appetizing, stimulating. □ **piquancy** *noun*.

pique /pi:k/ ● *verb* (**piques**, **piqued**, **piquing**) wound pride of; stir (curiosity). ● *noun* resentment; hurt pride.

piquet /pɪ'ket/ *noun* card game for two players.

piracy /'paɪrəsɪ/ *noun* (*plural* **-ies**) activity of pirate.

piranha /pɪ'rɑːnə/ *noun* voracious S. American freshwater fish.

pirate /'paɪərət/ ● *noun* seafaring robber attacking ships; ship used by pirate; person who infringes copyright or regulations or encroaches on rights of others etc. ● *verb* (**-ting**) reproduce (book etc.) or trade (goods) without permission. □ **piratical** /-'ræt-/ *adjective*.

pirouette /pɪrʊ'et/ ● *noun* dancer's spin on one foot or point of toe. ● *verb* (**-tting**) perform pirouette.

piscatorial /pɪskə'tɔːrɪəl/ *adjective* of fishing.

Pisces /'paɪsiːz/ *noun* twelfth sign of zodiac.

piscina /pɪ'siːnə/ *noun* (*plural* **-nae** /-niː/ or **-s**) stone basin near altar in church, for draining water after use.

pistachio /pɪs'tɑːʃɪəʊ/ *noun* (*plural* **-s**) kind of nut with green kernel.

piste /piːst/ *noun* ski run of compacted snow.

pistil /'pɪstɪl/ *noun* female organ in flowers. □ **pistillate** *adjective*.

pistol /'pɪst(ə)l/ *noun* small firearm.

piston /'pɪst(ə)n/ *noun* sliding cylinder fitting closely in tube and moving up and down in it, used in steam or petrol engine to impart motion; sliding valve in trumpet etc. □ **piston rod** rod connecting piston to other parts of machine.

pit¹ ● *noun* large hole in ground; coal mine; covered hole as trap; depression in skin or any surface; orchestra pit; (**the pits**) *slang* worst imaginable place, situation, person, etc.; area to side of track where racing cars are refuelled etc. during race; sunken area in floor of workshop etc. for inspection or repair of underside of vehicle etc. ● *verb* (**-tt-**) (usually + *against*) set (one's wits, strength, etc.) in competition; (usually as **pitted** *adjective*) make pit(s) in; store in pit. □ **pit bull terrier** small American dog noted for ferocity; **pitfall** unsuspected danger or drawback, covered pit as trap; **pit-head** top of shaft of coal mine, area surrounding this; **pit of the stomach** hollow below base of breastbone.

pit² verb (**-tt-**) (usually as **pitted** adjective) remove stones from (fruit).

pita = PITTA.

pit-a-pat /'pɪtəpæt/ (also **pitter-patter** /'pɪtəpætə/) ● adverb with sound as of light quick steps; falteringly. ● noun such sound.

pitch¹ ● verb set up (esp. tent, camp, etc.) in chosen position; throw; express in particular style or at particular level; fall heavily; (of ship etc.) plunge in lengthwise direction; set at particular musical pitch. ● noun area of play in esp. outdoor game; height, degree, intensity, etc.; gradient, esp. of roof; Music degree of highness or lowness of tone; act or process of pitching; colloquial salesman's persuasive talk; place, esp. in street or market, where one is stationed; distance between successive points, lines, etc. □ **pitched battle** vigorous argument etc., planned battle between sides in prepared positions; **pitched roof** sloping roof; **pitchfork** noun fork with long handle and two prongs for tossing hay etc., verb (+ into) thrust forcibly or hastily into office, position, etc.; **pitch in** colloquial set to work vigorously; **pitch into** colloquial attack vigorously.

pitch² ● noun dark resinous tarry substance. ● verb coat with pitch. □ **pitch-black, -dark** intensely dark; **pitch pine** resinous kinds of pine. □ **pitchy** adjective (**-ier, -iest**).

pitchblende /'pɪtʃblend/ noun uranium oxide yielding radium.

pitcher¹ /'pɪtʃə/ noun large jug, ewer.

pitcher² noun player who delivers ball in baseball.

piteous /'pɪtɪəs/ adjective deserving or arousing pity. □ **piteously** adverb; **piteousness** noun.

pith noun spongy tissue in stems of plants or lining rind of orange etc.; chief part; vigour, energy. □ **pith helmet** sun-helmet made from dried pith of plants.

pithy /'pɪθɪ/ adjective (**-ier, -iest**) condensed and forcible, terse. □ **pithily** adverb; **pithiness** noun.

pitiable /'pɪtɪəb(ə)l/ adjective deserving or arousing pity or contempt. □ **pitiably** adverb.

pitiful /'pɪtɪfʊl/ adjective arousing pity; contemptible. □ **pitifully** adverb.

pitiless /'pɪtɪlɪs/ adjective showing no pity. □ **pitilessly** adverb.

piton /'piːtɒn/ noun peg driven in to support climber or rope.

pitta /'pɪtə/ noun (also **pita**) originally Turkish unleavened bread which can be split and filled.

pittance /'pɪt(ə)ns/ noun scanty allowance, small amount.

pitter-patter = PIT-A-PAT.

pituitary /pɪ'tjuːɪtərɪ/ noun (plural **-ies**) (in full **pituitary gland**) small ductless gland at base of brain.

pity /'pɪtɪ/ ● noun sorrow for another's suffering; cause for regret. ● verb (**-ies, -ied**) feel pity for. □ **pitying** adjective.

pivot /'pɪvət/ ● noun shaft or pin on which something turns; crucial person or point. ● verb (**-t-**) turn (as) on pivot; provide with pivot. □ **pivotal** adjective.

pixie /'pɪksɪ/ noun (also **pixy**) (plural **-ies**) fairy-like being.

pizza /'piːtsə/ noun flat piece of dough baked with topping of cheese, tomatoes, etc.

pizzeria /piːtsə'riːə/ noun pizza restaurant.

pizzicato /pɪtsɪ'kɑːtəʊ/ Music ● adverb plucking. ● adjective performed thus. ● noun (plural **-s** or **-ti** /-tɪ/) pizzicato note or passage.

pl. abbreviation plural; place; plate.

placable /'plækəb(ə)l/ adjective easily appeased; mild-tempered. □ **placability** noun.

placard /'plækɑːd/ ● noun large notice for public display. ● verb post placards on.

placate /plə'keɪt/ verb (**-ting**) conciliate, pacify. □ **placatory** adjective.

place ● noun particular part of space; space or room of or for person etc.; city, town, village, residence, building; rank, station, position; building or spot devoted to specified purpose; office, employment; duties of this. ● verb (**-cing**) put or dispose in place; assign rank, order, or class to; give (order for goods etc.) to firm etc.; (in passive) be among first 3 (or 4) in race. □ **in place** suitable, in the right position; **in place of** instead of; **out of place** unsuitable, in the wrong position; **place-kick** Football kick made with ball placed on ground; **place-mat** small mat on table at person's place; **place setting** set of cutlery etc. for one person to eat with; **take place** happen; **take the place of** be substituted for. □ **placement** noun.

placebo /plə'siːbəʊ/ noun (plural **-s**) medicine with no physiological effect prescribed for psychological reasons; dummy pill etc. used in controlled trial.

placenta /plə'sentə/ noun (plural **-tae** /-tiː/ or **-s**) organ in uterus of pregnant mammal that nourishes foetus. □ **placental** adjective.

placid /'plæsɪd/ adjective calm, unruffled; not easily disturbed. □ **placidity** /plə'sɪdɪtɪ/ noun; **placidly** adverb.

placket /'plækɪt/ noun opening or slit in garment, for fastenings or access to pocket.

plagiarize /'pleɪdʒəraɪz/ verb (also **-ise**) (**-zing** or **-sing**) take and use (another's writings etc.) as one's own. □ **plagiarism** noun; **plagiarist** noun; **plagiarizer** noun.

plague /pleɪg/ ● noun deadly contagious disease; (+ of) colloquial infestation; great trouble or affliction. ● verb (**plaguing**) colloquial annoy, bother; afflict, hinder; affect with plague.

plaice /pleɪs/ noun (plural same) marine flatfish.

plaid /plæd/ noun chequered or tartan, esp. woollen, cloth; long piece of this as part of Highland costume.

plain ● adjective clear, evident; readily understood; simple; not beautiful or distinguished-looking; straightforward in speech; not luxurious. ● adverb clearly; simply. ● noun level tract of country; ordinary stitch in knitting. □ **plain chocolate** chocolate made without milk; **plain clothes** ordinary clothes as distinct from esp. police uniform; **plain flour** flour with no raising agent; **plain sailing** simple situation or course of action; **plainsong** traditional church music sung in unison in medieval modes and free rhythm; **plain-spoken** frank. □ **plainly** adverb.

plaint noun Law accusation, charge; literary lamentation.

plaintiff /'pleɪntɪf/ noun person who brings case against another in law court.

plaintive /'pleɪntɪv/ adjective mournful-sounding. □ **plaintively** adverb.

plait /plæt/ ● noun length of hair, straw, etc. in 3 or more interlaced strands. ● verb form into plait.

plan ● noun method or procedure for doing something; drawing exhibiting relative position and size of parts of building etc.; diagram; map. ● verb (**-nn-**) arrange beforehand, scheme; make plan of; design; (as **planned** adjective) in accordance with plan; make plans. □ **plan on** (often + present participle) colloquial aim at, intend. □ **planning** noun.

planchette /plɑːn'ʃet/ noun small board on castors, with pencil, said to write messages from spirits when person's fingers rest on it.

plane¹ ● noun flat surface (not necessarily horizontal); colloquial aeroplane; level of attainment etc. ● adjective level as or lying in a plane.

plane² ● noun tool for smoothing surface of wood by paring shavings from it. ● verb (**-ning**) smooth or pare with plane.

plane³ noun tall spreading broad-leaved tree.

planet /'plænɪt/ noun heavenly body orbiting star. □ **planetary** adjective.

planetarium /plænɪ'teərɪəm/ noun (plural **-s** or **-ria**) building in which image of night sky as seen at various times and places is projected; device for such projection.

plangent /'plændʒ(ə)nt/ adjective literary loudly lamenting; plaintive; reverberating.

plank ● noun long flat piece of timber; item of political or other programme. ● verb provide or cover with planks; (usually + down) colloquial put down roughly, deposit (esp. money).

plankton /'plæŋkt(ə)n/ noun chiefly microscopic organisms drifting in sea or fresh water.

planner noun person who plans new town etc.; person who makes plans; list, table, chart, etc. with information helpful in planning.

plant /plɑːnt/ ● noun organism capable of living wholly on inorganic substances and lacking power of locomotion; small plant (other than trees and shrubs); equipment for industrial process; colloquial thing deliberately placed for discovery, esp. to incriminate another. ● verb place (seed etc.) in ground to grow; fix firmly, establish; cause (idea etc.) to be established, esp. in another person's mind; deliver (blow etc.); colloquial place (something incriminating) for later discovery.

plantain¹ /'plæntɪn/ noun herb yielding seed used as food for birds.

plantain² /'plæntɪn/ noun plant related to banana; banana-like fruit of this.

plantation /plɑːn'teɪʃ(ə)n/ noun estate for cultivation of cotton, tobacco, etc.; number of growing plants, esp. trees, planted together; historical colony.

planter noun owner or manager of plantation; container for house-plants.

plaque /plæk/ noun ornamental tablet of metal, porcelain, etc.; deposit on teeth, where bacteria proliferate.

plasma /'plæzmə/ noun (also **plasm** /'plæz(ə)m/) colourless fluid part of blood etc. in which corpuscles etc. float; protoplasm; gas of positive ions and free electrons in about equal numbers. □ **plasmic** adjective.

plaster /'plɑːstə/ ● noun mixture esp. of lime, sand, and water spread on walls etc.; sticking plaster; plaster of Paris. ● verb cover with or like plaster; apply, stick, etc. like plaster to; (as **plastered** adjective) slang drunk. □ **plasterboard** two boards with core of plaster used for walls etc.; **plaster cast** bandage stiffened with plaster of Paris and wrapped round broken limb etc.; **plaster of Paris** fine white gypsum powder for plaster casts etc. □ **plasterer** noun.

plastic /'plæstɪk/ ● noun synthetic resinous substance that can be given any shape; (in full **plastic money**) colloquial credit card(s). ● adjective made of plastic; capable of being moulded; giving form to clay, wax, etc. □ **plastic arts** those involving modelling; **plastic explosive** putty-like explosive; **plastic surgery** repair or restoration of lost or damaged etc. tissue. □ **plasticity** /-'tɪs-/ noun; **plasticize** /-saɪz/ verb (also **-ise**) (**-zing** or **-sing**); **plasticky** adjective.

Plasticine /'plæstəsiːn/ noun proprietary term pliant substance used for modelling.

plate ● noun shallow usually circular vessel from which food is eaten or served; similar vessel used for collection in church etc.; table utensils of gold,

silver, or other metal; objects of plated metal; piece of metal with inscription, for fixing to door etc.; illustration on special paper in book; thin sheet of metal, glass, etc. coated with sensitive film for photography; flat thin sheet of metal etc.; part of denture fitting to mouth and holding teeth; each of several sheets of rock thought to form earth's crust. ● verb (**-ting**) cover (other metal) with thin coating of silver, gold, etc.; cover with plates of metal. □ **plate glass** thick fine-quality glass for mirrors, windows, etc.; **platelayer** workman laying and repairing railway lines. □ **plateful** noun (plural **-s**).

plateau /'plætəʊ/ ● noun (plural **-x** or **-s** /-z/) area of level high ground; state of little variation following an increase. ● verb (**plateaus, plateaued, plateauing**) (often + out) reach level or static state after period of increase.

platelet /'pleɪtlɪt/ noun small disc in blood, involved in clotting.

platen /'plæt(ə)n/ noun plate in printing press by which paper is pressed against type; corresponding part in typewriter etc.

platform /'plætfɔːm/ noun raised level surface, esp. one from which speaker addresses audience, or one along side of line at railway station; floor area at entrance to bus etc.; thick sole of shoe; declared policy of political party.

platinum /'plætɪnəm/ noun white heavy precious metallic element that does not tarnish. □ **platinum blonde** adjective silvery-blond, noun person with such hair.

platitude /'plætɪtjuːd/ noun commonplace remark. □ **platitudinous** /-'tjuːd-/ adjective.

Platonic /plə'tɒnɪk/ adjective of Plato or his philosophy; (**platonic**) (of love or friendship) not sexual.

platoon /plə'tuːn/ noun subdivision of infantry company.

platter /'plætə/ noun flat plate or dish.

platypus /'plætɪpəs/ noun (plural **-puses**) Australian aquatic egg-laying mammal with ducklike beak.

plaudit /'plɔːdɪt/ noun (usually in plural) round of applause; commendation.

plausible /'plɔːzɪb(ə)l/ adjective reasonable, probable; (of person) persuasive but deceptive. □ **plausibility** noun; **plausibly** adverb.

play ● verb occupy or amuse oneself pleasantly; (+ with) act light-heartedly or flippantly with (feelings etc.); perform on (musical instrument), perform (piece of music etc.); cause (record etc.) to produce sounds; perform (drama, role); (+ on) perform (trick or joke etc.) on; colloquial cooperate, do what is wanted; take part in (game); have as opponent in game; move (piece) in game, put (card) on table, strike (ball), etc.; move about in lively or unrestrained way; (often + on) touch gently; pretend to be; allow (fish) to exhaust itself pulling against line. ● noun recreation; amusement; playing of game; dramatic piece for stage etc.; freedom of movement; fitful or light movement; gambling. □ **play along** pretend to cooperate; **play back** play (what has been recorded); **playback** noun; **play ball** colloquial cooperate; **playbill** poster announcing play etc.; **playboy** pleasure-seeking usually wealthy man; **play by ear** perform (music) without having seen it written down, (also **play it by ear**) colloquial proceed gradually according to results; **play one's cards right** colloquial make best use of opportunities and advantages; **play down** minimize; **playfellow** playmate; **play the game** behave honourably; **playground** outdoor area for children to play in; **playgroup** group of preschool children who play together under supervision; **playhouse** theatre; **playing card** small usually oblong card used in games, one of set of usually 52 divided into 4 suits; **play it cool** *colloquial* appear relaxed or indifferent; **playmate** child's companion in play; **play-off** extra match played to decide draw or tie; **plaything** toy; **play up** behave mischievously, annoy in this way, cause trouble; **play with fire** take foolish risks; **playwright** dramatist. □ **player** *noun*.

playful *adjective* fond of or inclined to play; done in fun. □ **playfully** *adverb*; **playfulness** *noun*.

plc *abbreviation* (also **PLC**) Public Limited Company.

plea *noun* appeal, entreaty; *Law* formal statement by or on behalf of defendant; excuse.

pleach *verb* entwine or interlace (esp. branches to form a hedge).

plead *verb* (+ *with*) make earnest appeal to; address court as advocate or party; allege as excuse; (+ *guilty, not guilty*) declare oneself to be guilty or not guilty of a charge; make appeal or entreaty.

pleading *noun* (usually in *plural*) formal statement of cause of action or defence.

pleasant /ˈplez(ə)nt/ *adjective* (**-er, -est**) agreeable; giving pleasure. □ **pleasantly** *adverb*.

pleasantry *noun* (*plural* **-ies**) joking remark; polite remark.

please /pliːz/ *verb* (**-sing**) be agreeable to; give joy or gratification to; think fit; (in *passive*) be willing, like; *used in polite requests*. □ **pleased** *adjective*; **pleasing** *adjective*.

pleasurable /ˈpleʒərəb(ə)l/ *adjective* causing pleasure. □ **pleasurably** *adverb*.

pleasure /ˈpleʒə/ ● *noun* satisfaction, delight; sensuous enjoyment; source of gratification; will, choice. ● *adjective* done or used for pleasure.

pleat ● *noun* flattened fold in cloth etc. ● *verb* make pleat(s) in.

pleb *noun colloquial* plebeian.

plebeian /plɪˈbiːən/ ● *noun* commoner, esp. in ancient Rome; working-class person (esp. uncultured). ● *adjective* of the common people; uncultured, coarse.

plebiscite /ˈplebɪsaɪt/ *noun* referendum.

plectrum /ˈplektrəm/ *noun* (*plural* **-s** or **-tra**) thin flat piece of plastic etc. for plucking strings of musical instrument.

pledge ● *noun* solemn promise; thing given as security for payment of debt etc.; thing put in pawn; token; drinking of health. ● *verb* (**-ging**) deposit as security, pawn; promise solemnly by pledge; bind by solemn promise; drink to the health of.

Pleiades /ˈplaɪədiːz/ *plural noun* cluster of stars in constellation Taurus.

plenary /ˈpliːnərɪ/ *adjective* (of assembly) to be attended by all members; entire, unqualified.

plenipotentiary /plenɪpəˈtenʃərɪ/ ● *noun* (*plural* **-ies**) person (esp. diplomat) having full authority to act. ● *adjective* having such power.

plenitude /ˈplenɪtjuːd/ *noun literary* fullness; completeness; abundance.

plenteous /ˈplentɪəs/ *adjective literary* plentiful.

plentiful /ˈplentɪfʊl/ *adjective* existing in ample quantity. □ **plentifully** *adverb*.

plenty /ˈplentɪ/ ● *noun* abundance; quite enough. ● *adjective colloquial* plentiful. ● *adverb colloquial* fully.

plenum /ˈpliːnəm/ *noun* full assembly of people or a committee etc.

pleonasm /ˈpliːənæz(ə)m/ *noun* use of more words than are needed. □ **pleonastic** /-ˈnæstɪk/ *adjective*.

plesiosaur /ˈpliːsɪəsɔː/ *noun* large extinct reptile with flippers and long neck.

plethora /ˈpleθərə/ *noun* overabundance.

pleurisy /ˈplʊərəsɪ/ *noun* inflammation of membrane enclosing lungs. □ **pleuritic** /-ˈrɪt-/ *adjective*.

plexus /ˈpleksəs/ *noun* (*plural* same or **plexuses**) network of nerves or blood vessels.

pliable /ˈplaɪəb(ə)l/ *adjective* easily bent or influenced; supple; compliant. □ **pliability** *noun*.

pliant /ˈplaɪənt/ *adjective* pliable. □ **pliancy** *noun*.

pliers /ˈplaɪəz/ *plural noun* pincers with parallel flat surfaces for bending wire etc.

plight[1] /plaɪt/ *noun* unfortunate condition or state.

plight[2] /plaɪt/ *verb archaic* pledge. □ **plight one's troth** promise to marry.

plimsoll /ˈplɪms(ə)l/ *noun* rubber-soled canvas shoe. □ **Plimsoll line, mark** marking on ship's side showing limit of legal submersion under various conditions.

plinth *noun* base supporting column, vase, statue, etc.

plod *verb* (**-dd-**) walk or work laboriously. □ **plodder** *noun*.

plonk[1] ● *verb* set down hurriedly or clumsily; (usually + *down*) set down firmly. ● *noun* heavy thud.

plonk[2] *noun colloquial* cheap or inferior wine.

plop ● *noun* sound of smooth object dropping into water. ● *verb* (**-pp-**) (cause to) fall with plop. ● *adverb* with a plop.

plot ● *noun* small piece of land; plan or interrelationship of main events of tale, play, etc.; secret plan, conspiracy. ● *verb* (**-tt-**) make chart, diagram, graph, etc. of; hatch secret plans; devise secretly; mark on chart or diagram. □ **plotter** *noun*.

plough /plaʊ/ (*US* **plow**) ● *noun* implement for furrowing and turning up soil; similar instrument for clearing away snow etc. ● *verb* (often + *up, out*, etc.) turn up or extract with plough; furrow, make (furrow); (+ *through*) advance laboriously or cut or force way through; *colloquial* fail in exam. □ **plough back** reinvest (profits) in business; **ploughman** user of plough; **ploughman's lunch** meal of bread, cheese, pickles, etc.; **ploughshare** blade of plough.

plover /ˈplʌvə/ *noun* plump-breasted wading bird.

plow *US* = PLOUGH.

ploy *noun* manoeuvre to gain advantage.

pluck ● *verb* pick or pull out or away; strip (bird) of feathers; pull at, twitch; (+ *at*) tug or snatch at; sound (string of musical instrument) with finger or plectrum. ● *noun* courage; twitch; animal's heart, liver, and lungs. □ **pluck up** summon up (one's courage etc.).

plucky *adjective* (**-ier, -iest**) brave, spirited.

plug ● *noun* something fitting into hole or filling cavity; device of metal pins etc. for making electrical connection; spark plug; *colloquial* piece of free publicity; cake or stick of tobacco. ● *verb* (**-gg-**) (often + *up*) stop with plug; *slang* shoot; *colloquial* seek to popularize by frequent recommendation. □ **plug away** (often + *at*) *colloquial* work steadily; **plug-hole** hole for plug, esp. in sink or bath; **plug in** *verb* connect electrically by inserting plug into socket; **plug-in** *adjective* designed to be plugged into socket; **pull the plug** *colloquial* flush toilet; (+ *on*) put an end to by withdrawing resources etc.

plum *noun* roundish fleshy stone fruit; tree bearing this; reddish-purple colour; raisin; *colloquial* prized thing. □ **plum pudding** Christmas pudding.

plumage /ˈpluːmɪdʒ/ *noun* bird's feathers.

plumb /plʌm/ ● *noun* lead ball attached to line for testing water's depth or whether wall etc. is vertical. ● *adverb* exactly; vertically; *US slang* quite, utterly. ● *adjective* vertical. ● *verb* provide with plumbing; fit as part of plumbing system; work as plumber; test with plumb; experience (extreme feeling); learn detailed facts about. □ **plumb line** string with plumb attached.

plumber noun person who fits and repairs apparatus of water supply, heating, etc.

plumbing noun system or apparatus of water supply etc.; plumber's work.

plume /pluːm/ ● noun feather, esp. large and showy one; feathery ornament in hat, hair, etc.; feather-like formation, esp. of smoke. ● verb (**-ming**) furnish with plume(s); (**plume oneself on, upon**) pride oneself on.

plummet /ˈplʌmɪt/ ● noun plumb, plumb line; sounding line. ● verb (**-t-**) fall rapidly.

plummy adjective (**-ier, -iest**) colloquial (of voice) affectedly rich in tone; colloquial good, desirable.

plump¹ ● adjective having full rounded shape; fleshy. ● verb (often + up, out) make or become plump. □ **plumpness** noun.

plump² ● verb (+ for) decide on, choose. ● noun abrupt or heavy fall. ● adverb colloquial with plump.

plunder /ˈplʌndə/ ● verb rob or steal, esp. in war; embezzle. ● noun plundering; property plundered.

plunge ● verb (**-ging**) (usually + in, into) throw forcefully, dive, (cause to) enter into impetuously, immerse completely; move suddenly downward; move with a rush; colloquial run up gambling debts. ● noun plunging, dive; decisive step.

plunger noun part of mechanism that works with plunging or thrusting motion; rubber cup on handle for removing blockages by plunging action.

pluperfect /pluːˈpɜːfɪkt/ Grammar ● adjective expressing action completed prior to some past point of time. ● noun pluperfect tense.

plural /ˈplʊər(ə)l/ ● adjective more than one in number; denoting more than one. ● noun plural word, form, or number.

pluralism noun form of society in which minority groups retain independent traditions; holding of more than one office at a time. □ **pluralist** noun; **pluralistic** /-ˈlɪst-/ adjective.

plurality /plʊəˈrælɪtɪ/ noun (plural **-ies**) state of being plural; pluralism; large number; non-absolute majority (of votes etc.).

pluralize verb (also **-ise**) (**-zing** or **-sing**) make plural; express as plural.

plus ● preposition with addition of; (of temperature) above zero; colloquial having gained. ● adjective (after number) at least, (after grade) better than; Mathematics positive; additional, extra. ● noun plus sign; advantage. □ **plus sign** symbol (+) indicating addition or positive value.

■ **Usage** The use of plus as a conjunction, as in they arrived late, plus they wanted a meal, is considered incorrect except in very informal use.

plush ● noun cloth of silk, cotton, etc., with long soft pile. ● adjective made of plush; colloquial plushy.

plushy adjective (**-ier, -iest**) colloquial stylish, luxurious.

plutocracy /pluːˈtɒkrəsɪ/ noun (plural **-ies**) state in which power belongs to rich; wealthy élite. □ **plutocrat** /ˈpluːtəkræt/ noun; **plutocratic** /-təˈkræt-/ adjective.

plutonium /pluːˈtəʊnɪəm/ noun radioactive metallic element.

pluvial /ˈpluːvɪəl/ adjective of or caused by rain.

ply¹ /plaɪ/ noun (plural **-ies**) thickness, layer; strand.

ply² /plaɪ/ verb (**-ies, -ied**) wield; work at; (+ with) supply continuously or approach repeatedly with; (often + between) (of vehicle etc.) go to and fro.

plywood noun strong thin board made by gluing layers of wood with the direction of the grain alternating.

PM abbreviation prime minister.

p.m. abbreviation after noon (post meridiem).

PMS abbreviation premenstrual syndrome.

PMT abbreviation premenstrual tension.

pneumatic /njuːˈmætɪk/ adjective filled with air or wind; operated by compressed air.

pneumonia /njuːˈməʊnɪə/ noun inflammation of lung(s).

PO abbreviation Post Office; postal order; Petty Officer; Pilot Officer.

po noun (plural **-s**) colloquial chamber pot. □ **po-faced** solemn-faced, humourless, smug.

poach¹ verb cook (egg) without shell in boiling water; cook (fish etc.) by simmering in small amount of liquid. □ **poacher** noun.

poach² verb catch (game or fish) illicitly; (often + on) trespass, encroach; appropriate (another's ideas, staff, etc.). □ **poacher** noun.

pock noun (also **pock-mark**) small pus-filled spot, esp. in smallpox. □ **pock-marked** adjective.

pocket /ˈpɒkɪt/ ● noun small bag sewn into or on garment for carrying small articles; pouchlike compartment in suitcase, car door, etc.; financial resources; isolated group or area; cavity in earth etc. containing ore; pouch at corner or on side of billiard or snooker table into which balls are driven. ● adjective small, esp. small enough for carrying in pocket. ● verb (**-t-**) put into pocket; appropriate; submit to (affront etc.); conceal (feelings). □ **in** or **out of pocket** having gained or lost in transaction; **pocketbook** notebook, folding case for papers, paper money, etc.; **pocket knife** small folding knife; **pocket money** money for minor expenses, esp. given to child.

pod ● noun long seed vessel, esp. of pea or bean. ● verb (**-dd-**) form pods; remove (peas etc.) from pods.

podgy /ˈpɒdʒɪ/ adjective (**-ier, -iest**) short and fat.

podium /ˈpəʊdɪəm/ noun (plural **-s** or **podia**) rostrum.

poem /ˈpəʊɪm/ noun metrical composition; elevated composition in verse or prose; something with poetic qualities.

poesy /ˈpəʊəzɪ/ noun archaic poetry.

poet /ˈpəʊɪt/ noun (feminine **poetess**) writer of poems. □ **Poet Laureate** poet appointed to write poems for state occasions.

poetaster /pəʊɪˈtæstə/ noun inferior poet.

poetic /pəʊˈetɪk/ adjective (also **poetical**) of or like poetry or poets. □ **poetic justice** well-deserved punishment or reward; **poetic licence** departure from truth etc. for effect. □ **poetically** adverb.

poetry /ˈpəʊɪtrɪ/ noun poet's art or work; poems; poetic or tenderly pleasing quality.

pogo /ˈpəʊɡəʊ/ noun (plural **-s**) (also **pogo stick**) stilt-like toy with spring, used to jump about on.

pogrom /ˈpɒɡrəm/ noun organized massacre (originally of Jews in Russia).

poignant /ˈpɔɪnjənt/ adjective painfully sharp, deeply moving; arousing sympathy; pleasantly piquant. □ **poignance** noun; **poignancy** noun; **poignantly** adverb.

poinsettia /pɔɪnˈsetɪə/ noun plant with large scarlet bracts surrounding small yellowish flowers.

point ● noun sharp end, tip; geometric entity with position but no magnitude; particular place; precise moment; very small mark on surface; decimal point; stage or degree in progress or increase; single item or particular; unit of scoring in games etc., or in evaluation etc.; significant thing, thing actually intended or under discussion; sense, purpose, advantage; characteristic; each of 32 directions marked on compass; (usually in plural) pair of tapering movable rails to direct train from one line to another; power point; Cricket (position of) fielder near batsman on off side; promontory. ● verb (usually + to, at) direct (finger, weapon, etc.); direct attention; (+ *at*, *towards*) aim or be directed to; (+ *to*) indicate; give force to (words, action); fill joints of (brickwork) with smoothed mortar or cement; (of dog) indicate presence of game by acting as pointer. □ **at** or **on the point of** on the verge of; **point-blank** at close range, directly, flatly; **point-duty** traffic control by police officer; **point of view** position from which thing is viewed, way of considering a matter; **point out** indicate, draw attention to; **point-to-point** steeplechase for hunting horses; **point up** emphasize.

pointed *adjective* having point; (of remark etc.) cutting, emphasized. □ **pointedly** *adverb*.

pointer *noun* indicator on gauge etc.; rod for pointing at features on screen etc.; *colloquial* hint; dog of breed trained to stand rigid looking at game.

pointless *adjective* purposeless, meaningless; ineffective. □ **pointlessly** *adverb*; **pointlessness** *noun*.

poise /pɔɪz/ ● *noun* composure; equilibrium; carriage (of head etc.). ● *verb* (**-sing**) balance, hold suspended or supported; be balanced or suspended.

poised *adjective* self-assured; carrying oneself with dignity; (often + *for*) ready.

poison /ˈpɔɪz(ə)n/ ● *noun* substance that when absorbed by living organism kills or injures it; *colloquial* harmful influence. ● *verb* administer poison to; kill or injure with poison; treat (weapon) with poison; corrupt, pervert; spoil. □ **poison ivy** N. American climbing plant secreting irritant oil from leaves; **poison-pen letter** malicious anonymous letter. □ **poisoner** *noun*; **poisonous** *adjective*.

poke ● *verb* (**-king**) push with (end of) finger, stick, etc.; (+ *out*, *up*, etc.) (be) thrust forward; (+ *at* etc.) make thrusts; (+ *in*) produce (hole etc.) in by poking; stir (fire). ● *noun* poking; thrust, nudge. □ **poke fun at** ridicule.

poker¹ *noun* metal rod for stirring fire.

poker² /ˈpəʊkə/ *noun* card game in which players bet on value of their hands. □ **poker-face** impassive countenance assumed by poker player.

poky /ˈpəʊkɪ/ *adjective* (**-ier**, **-iest**) (of room etc.) small and cramped.

polar /ˈpəʊlə/ *adjective* of or near either pole of earth etc.; having magnetic or electric polarity; directly opposite in character. □ **polar bear** large white bear living in Arctic.

polarity /pəˈlærɪtɪ/ *noun* (*plural* **-ies**) tendency of magnet etc. to point to earth's magnetic poles or of body to lie with axis in particular direction; possession of two poles having contrary qualities; possession of two opposite tendencies, opinions, etc.; electrical condition of body (positive or negative).

polarize /ˈpəʊləraɪz/ *verb* (also **-ise**) (**-zing** or **-sing**) restrict vibrations of (light-waves etc.) to one direction; give polarity to; divide into two opposing groups. □ **polarization** *noun*.

Polaroid /ˈpəʊlərɔɪd/ *noun proprietary term* material in thin sheets polarizing light passing through it; camera that produces print immediately after each exposure; (in *plural*) sunglasses with Polaroid lenses.

Pole *noun* native or national of Poland.

pole¹ *noun* long slender rounded piece of wood, metal, etc., esp. as support etc.; *historical* measure of length (5½ yds). □ **pole-vault** jump over high bar with aid of pole held in hands.

pole² *noun* each of two points in celestial sphere (in full **north**, **south pole**) about which stars appear to revolve; each end of axis of earth (in full **North**, **South Pole**) or of other body; each of two opposite points on surface of magnet at which magnetic forces are strongest; positive or negative terminal of electric cell, battery, etc.; each of two opposed principles.

□ **pole star** star near N. pole of heavens, thing serving as guide.

poleaxe /ˈpəʊlæks/ (*US* **-ax**) ● *noun historical* battleaxe; butcher's axe. ● *verb* (**-xing**) hit or kill with poleaxe; (esp. as **poleaxed** *adjective*) *colloquial* dumbfound, overwhelm.

polecat /ˈpəʊlkæt/ *noun* small dark brown mammal of weasel family.

polemic /pəˈlemɪk/ ● *noun* verbal attack; controversy; (in *plural*) art of controversial discussion. ● *adjective* (also **polemical**) involving dispute, controversial. □ **polemicist** /-sɪst/ *noun*.

police /pəˈliːs/ ● *noun* (treated as *plural*) civil force responsible for maintaining public order; its members; force with similar functions. ● *verb* (**-cing**) control or provide with police; keep in order, control, administer. □ **police dog** dog used in police work; **police force** body of police of country, district, or town; **policeman**, **policewoman**, **police officer** member of police force; **police state** totalitarian state controlled by political police; **police station** office of local police force.

policy¹ /ˈpɒlɪsɪ/ *noun* (*plural* **-ies**) course of action adopted by government, business, etc.; prudent conduct.

policy² /ˈpɒlɪsɪ/ *noun* (*plural* **-ies**) (document containing) contract of insurance. □ **policyholder** person or body holding insurance policy.

polio /ˈpəʊlɪəʊ/ *noun* poliomyelitis.

poliomyelitis /pəʊlɪəʊmaɪəˈlaɪtɪs/ *noun* infectious viral disease of grey matter of central nervous system, with temporary or permanent paralysis.

Polish /ˈpəʊlɪʃ/ ● *adjective* of Poland. ● *noun* language of Poland.

polish /ˈpɒlɪʃ/ ● *verb* (often + *up*) make or become smooth or glossy by rubbing; (esp. as **polished** *adjective*) refine, improve. ● *noun* substance used for polishing; smoothness, glossiness; refinement. □ **polish off** finish quickly.

polite /pəˈlaɪt/ *adjective* (**-r**, **-st**) having good manners, courteous; cultivated, refined. □ **politely** *adverb*; **politeness** *noun*.

politic /ˈpɒlɪtɪk/ ● *adjective* judicious, expedient; prudent, sagacious. ● *verb* (**-ck-**) engage in politics.

political /pəˈlɪtɪk(ə)l/ *adjective* of state or its government; of public affairs; of, engaged in, or taking a side in politics; relating to pursuit of power, status, etc. □ **political asylum** state protection for foreign refugee; **political correctness** avoidance of language or action which excludes ethnic or cultural minorities; **political economy** study of economic aspects of government; **political geography** geography dealing with boundaries etc. of states; **political prisoner** person imprisoned for political reasons.

politically *adverb* in a political way. □ **politically correct** exhibiting political correctness.

politician /pɒlɪˈtɪʃ(ə)n/ *noun* person engaged in politics.

politicize /pəˈlɪtɪsaɪz/ *verb* (also **-ise**) (**-zing** or **-sing**) give political character or awareness to.

politics /ˈpɒlɪtɪks/ *plural noun* (treated as *singular* or *plural*) art and science of government; political life, affairs, principles, etc.; activities relating to pursuit of power, status, etc.

polity /ˈpɒlɪtɪ/ *noun* (*plural* **-ies**) form of civil administration; organized society, state.

polka /ˈpɒlkə/ ● *noun* lively dance; music for this. ● *verb* (**-kas**, **-kaed** /-kəd/ or **-ka'd**, **-kaing** /-kəɪŋ/) dance polka. □ **polka dot** round dot as one of many forming regular pattern on textile fabric etc.

poll /pəʊl/ ● *noun* (often in *plural*) voting; counting of votes; result of voting, number of votes recorded;

questioning of sample of population to estimate trend of public opinion; head. ● *verb* take or receive vote(s) of, vote; record opinion of (person, group); cut off top of (tree etc.) or (esp. as **polled** *adjective*) horns of (cattle). □ **polling booth** cubicle where voter stands to mark ballot paper; **polling station** building used for voting; **poll tax** *historical* tax levied on every adult.

pollack /'pɒlæk/ *noun* (also **pollock**) (*plural* same or **-s**) edible marine fish related to cod.

pollard /'pɒləd/ ● *noun* hornless animal; tree polled to produce close head of young branches. ● *verb* make pollard of (tree).

pollen /'pɒlən/ *noun* fertilizing powder discharged from flower's anther. □ **pollen count** index of amount of pollen in air.

pollinate /'pɒlɪneɪt/ *verb* (**-ting**) sprinkle (stigma of flower) with pollen. □ **pollination** noun.

pollock = POLLACK.

pollster *noun* person who organizes opinion poll.

pollute /pə'luːt/ *verb* (**-ting**) contaminate; make impure. □ **pollutant** *noun*; **polluter** *noun*; **pollution** *noun*.

polo /'pəʊləʊ/ *noun* game like hockey played on horseback. □ **polo-neck** (sweater with) high round turned-over collar.

polonaise /pɒlə'neɪz/ *noun* slow processional dance; music for this.

poltergeist /'pɒltəɡaɪst/ *noun* noisy mischievous ghost.

poltroon /pɒl'truːn/ *noun* coward. □ **poltroonery** *noun*.

poly- *combining form* many; polymerized.

polyandry /'pɒlɪændrɪ/ *noun* polygamy in which one woman has more than one husband.

polyanthus /pɒlɪ'ænθəs/ *noun* (*plural* **-thuses**) cultivated primula.

polychromatic /pɒlɪkrəʊ'mætɪk/ *adjective* many-coloured.

polychrome /'pɒlɪkrəʊm/ ● *adjective* in many colours. ● *noun* polychrome work of art.

polyester /pɒlɪ'estə/ *noun* synthetic fibre or resin.

polyethylene /pɒlɪ'eθɪliːn/ *noun* polythene.

polygamy /pə'lɪɡəmɪ/ *noun* practice of having more than one wife or husband at once. □ **polygamist** *noun*; **polygamous** *adjective*.

polyglot /'pɒlɪɡlɒt/ ● *adjective* knowing, using, or written in several languages. ● *noun* polyglot person.

polygon /'pɒlɪɡən/ *noun* figure with many sides and angles. □ **polygonal** /pə'lɪɡ-/ *adjective*.

polyhedron /pɒlɪ'hiːdrən/ *noun* (*plural* **-dra**) solid figure with many faces. □ **polyhedral** *adjective*.

polymath /'pɒlɪmæθ/ *noun* person of great or varied learning.

polymer /'pɒlɪmə/ *noun* compound of molecule(s) formed from repeated units of smaller molecules. □ **polymeric** /-'mer-/ *adjective*; **polymerization** *noun*; **polymerize** *verb* (also **-ise**) (**-zing** or **-sing**).

polyp /'pɒlɪp/ *noun* simple organism with tube-shaped body; small growth on mucous membrane.

polyphony /pə'lɪfənɪ/ *noun* (*plural* **-ies**) contrapuntal music. □ **polyphonic** /pɒlɪ'fɒnɪk/ *adjective*.

polypropylene /pɒlɪ'prəʊpɪliːn/ *noun* any of various thermoplastic materials used for films, fibres, or moulding.

polystyrene /pɒlɪ'staɪəriːn/ *noun* kind of hard plastic.

polysyllabic /pɒlɪsɪ'læbɪk/ *adjective* having many syllables; using polysyllables.

polysyllable /'pɒlɪsɪləb(ə)l/ *noun* polysyllabic word.

polytechnic /pɒlɪ'teknɪk/ *noun* college providing courses in esp. vocational subjects up to degree level.

polytheism /'pɒlɪθiːɪz(ə)m/ *noun* belief in or worship of more than one god. □ **polytheistic** /-'ɪst-/ *adjective*.

polythene /'pɒlɪθiːn/ *noun* a tough light plastic.

polyunsaturated /pɒlɪʌn'sætʃəreɪtɪd/ *adjective* (of fat) containing several double or triple bonds in each molecule and therefore capable of combining with hydrogen and not associated with accumulation of cholesterol.

polyurethane /pɒlɪ'jʊərəθeɪn/ *noun* synthetic resin or plastic used esp. in paints or foam.

polyvinyl chloride /pɒlɪ'vaɪnɪl/ *noun* see PVC.

pomade /pə'mɑːd/ *noun* scented ointment for hair.

pomander /pə'mændə/ *noun* ball of mixed aromatic substances; container for this.

pomegranate /'pɒmɪɡrænɪt/ *noun* tropical tough-rinded many-seeded fruit; tree bearing this.

pommel /'pʌm(ə)l/ *noun* knob of sword hilt; projecting front of saddle.

pomp *noun* splendid display, splendour; specious glory.

pom-pom /'pɒmpɒm/ *noun* automatic quick-firing gun.

pompon /'pɒmpɒn/ *noun* (also **pompom**) decorative tuft or ball on hat, shoe, etc.

pompous /'pɒmpəs/ *adjective* self-important, affectedly grand or solemn. □ **pomposity** /-'pɒs-/ *noun* (*plural* **-ies**); **pompously** *adverb*; **pompousness** *noun*.

ponce *slang* ● *noun* man who lives off prostitute's earnings. ● *verb* (**-cing**) act as ponce. □ **ponce about** move about effeminately.

poncho /'pɒntʃəʊ/ *noun* (*plural* **-s**) cloak of rectangular piece of material with slit in middle for head.

pond *noun* small body of still water.

ponder /'pɒndə/ *verb* think over; muse.

ponderable /'pɒndərəb(ə)l/ *adjective* *literary* having appreciable weight.

ponderous /'pɒndərəs/ *adjective* heavy and unwieldy; laborious, dull. □ **ponderously** *adverb*; **ponderousness** *noun*.

pong *noun* & *verb* *colloquial* stink. □ **pongy** *adjective* (**-ier**, **-iest**).

poniard /'pɒnjəd/ *noun* dagger.

pontiff /'pɒntɪf/ *noun* Pope.

pontifical /pɒn'tɪfɪk(ə)l/ *adjective* papal; pompously dogmatic.

pontificate ● *verb* /pɒn'tɪfɪkeɪt/ (**-ting**) be pompously dogmatic. ● *noun* /pɒn'tɪfɪkət/ office of bishop or Pope; period of this.

pontoon¹ /pɒn'tuːn/ *noun* card game in which players try to acquire cards with face value totalling 21.

pontoon² /pɒn'tuːn/ *noun* flat-bottomed boat; boat etc. as one of supports of temporary bridge.

pony /'pəʊnɪ/ *noun* (*plural* **-ies**) horse of any small breed. □ **pony-tail** hair drawn back, tied, and hanging down behind head; **pony-trekking** travelling across country on ponies for pleasure.

poodle /'puːd(ə)l/ *noun* dog of breed with thick curling hair.

pooh /puː/ *interjection* *expressing contempt or disgust*. □ **pooh-pooh** express contempt for, ridicule.

pool¹ *noun* small body of still water; small shallow body of any liquid; swimming pool; deep place in river.

pool² ● *noun* common supply of people, vehicles, etc., for sharing by group; group of people sharing duties etc.; common fund, e.g. of profits or of gamblers' stakes; arrangement between competing parties to fix prices and share business; game like billiards with usually 16 balls; (**the pools**) football pool. ● *verb* put into common fund; share in common.

poop *noun* stern of ship; furthest aft and highest deck.

poor /pʊə/ *adjective* having little money or means; (+ *in*) deficient in; inadequate; inferior; deserving pity; despicable. □ **poor man's** inferior substitute for.

poorly ● *adverb* in poor manner; badly. ● *adjective* unwell.

pop¹ ● *noun* abrupt explosive sound; *colloquial* effervescent drink. ● *verb* (-**pp**-) (cause to) make pop; (+ *in, out, up*, etc.) move, come, or put unexpectedly or suddenly; *slang* pawn. ● *adverb* with the sound pop. □ **popcorn** maize kernels which burst open when heated; **pop-eyed** *colloquial* with eyes bulging or wide open; **popgun** toy gun shooting pellet etc. by compressed air or spring; **popping crease** *Cricket* line in front of and parallel to wicket; **pop-up** involving parts that pop up automatically.

pop² *noun colloquial* (in full **pop music**) highly successful commercial music; pop record or song. □ **pop art** art based on modern popular culture and the mass media; **pop culture** commercial culture based on popular taste; **pop group** ensemble playing pop music.

pop³ *noun esp. US colloquial* father.

popadam = POPPADAM.

pope *noun* (also **Pope**) head of RC Church.

popinjay /'pɒpɪndʒeɪ/ *noun* fop, conceited person.

poplar /'pɒplə/ *noun* slender tree with straight trunk and often tremulous leaves.

poplin /'pɒplɪn/ *noun* closely woven corded fabric.

poppadam /'pɒpədəm/ *noun* (also **poppadom, popadam**) thin crisp spiced Indian bread.

popper *noun colloquial* press-stud; thing that pops.

poppet /'pɒpɪt/ *noun colloquial* (esp. as term of endearment) small or dainty person.

poppy /'pɒpɪ/ *noun* (*plural* **-ies**) plant with bright flowers and milky narcotic juice; artificial poppy worn on Remembrance Sunday. □ **Poppy Day** Remembrance Sunday.

poppycock /'pɒpɪkɒk/ *noun slang* nonsense.

populace /'pɒpjʊləs/ *noun* the common people.

popular /'pɒpjʊlə/ *adjective* generally liked or admired; of, for, or prevalent among the general public. □ **popularity** /-'lærɪtɪ/ *noun*; **popularize** *verb* (also **-ise**) (**-zing** or **-sing**); **popularly** *adverb*.

populate /'pɒpjʊleɪt/ *verb* (**-ting**) form population of; supply with inhabitants.

population /pɒpjʊ'leɪʃ(ə)n/ *noun* inhabitants of town, country, etc.; total number of these.

populous /'pɒpjʊləs/ *adjective* thickly inhabited.

porcelain /'pɔːsəlɪn/ *noun* fine translucent ceramic; things made of this.

porch *noun* covered entrance to building.

porcine /'pɔːsaɪn/ *adjective* of or like pigs.

porcupine /'pɔːkjʊpaɪn/ *noun* large rodent with body and tail covered with erectile spines.

pore¹ *noun* minute opening in surface through which fluids may pass.

pore² *verb* (**-ring**) (+ *over*) be absorbed in studying (book etc.).

pork *noun* flesh of pig used as food.

porker *noun* pig raised for food.

porn (also **porno**) *colloquial* ● *noun* pornography. ● *adjective* pornographic.

pornography /pɔː'nɒgrəfɪ/ *noun* explicit presentation of sexual activity in literature, films, etc., to stimulate erotic rather than aesthetic feelings. □ **pornographic** /-nə'græf-/ *adjective*.

porous /'pɔːrəs/ *adjective* having pores; permeable. □ **porosity** /-'rɒs-/ *noun*.

porphyry /'pɔːfɪrɪ/ *noun* (*plural* **-ies**) hard rock with feldspar crystals in fine-grained red mass.

porpoise /'pɔːpəs/ *noun* sea mammal of whale family.

porridge /'pɒrɪdʒ/ *noun* oatmeal or other cereal boiled in water or milk.

porringer /'pɒrɪndʒə/ *noun* small soupbowl.

port¹ *noun* harbour; town possessing harbour.

port² *noun* strong sweet fortified wine.

port³ ● *noun* left-hand side of ship or aircraft looking forward. ● *verb* turn (helm) to port.

port⁴ *noun* opening in ship's side for entrance, loading, etc.; porthole. □ **porthole** (esp. glazed) aperture in ship's side to admit light.

portable /'pɔːtəb(ə)l/ *adjective* easily movable, convenient for carrying; adaptable in altered circumstances. □ **portability** *noun*.

portage /'pɔːtɪdʒ/ *noun* carrying of boats or goods between two navigable waters.

Portakabin /'pɔːtəkæbɪn/ *noun proprietary term* prefabricated small building.

portal /'pɔːt(ə)l/ *noun* doorway, gate.

portcullis /pɔːt'kʌlɪs/ *noun* strong heavy grating lowered in defence of fortress gateway.

portend /pɔː'tend/ *verb* foreshadow as an omen; give warning of.

portent /'pɔːtent/ *noun* omen, significant sign; marvellous thing.

portentous /pɔː'tentəs/ *adjective* like or being portent; pompously solemn.

porter¹ /'pɔːtə/ *noun* person employed to carry luggage etc.; dark beer brewed from charred or browned malt. □ **porterhouse steak** choice cut of beef.

porter² /'pɔːtə/ *noun* gatekeeper or doorkeeper, esp. of large building.

porterage *noun* (charge for) hire of porters.

portfolio /pɔːt'fəʊlɪəʊ/ *noun* (*plural* **-s**) folder for loose sheets of paper, drawings, etc.; samples of artist's work; list of investments held by investor etc.; office of government minister. ● **Minister without Portfolio** government minister not in charge of department.

portico /'pɔːtɪkəʊ/ *noun* (*plural* **-es** or **-s**) colonnade; roof supported by columns, usually serving as porch to building.

portion /'pɔːʃ(ə)n/ ● *noun* part, share; helping; destiny or lot. ● *verb* divide into portions; (+ *out*) distribute.

Portland /'pɔːtlənd/ *noun* □ **Portland cement** cement manufactured from chalk and clay; **Portland stone** a valuable building limestone.

portly /'pɔːtlɪ/ *adjective* (**-ier, -iest**) corpulent.

portmanteau /pɔːt'mæntəʊ/ *noun* (*plural* **-s** or **-x** /-z/) case for clothes etc., opening into two equal parts. □ **portmanteau word** word combining sounds and meanings of two others.

portrait /'pɔːtrɪt/ *noun* drawing, painting, photograph, etc. of person or animal; description.

portraiture /'pɔːtrɪtʃə/ *noun* portraying; description; portrait.

portray /pɔː'treɪ/ *verb* make likeness of; describe. □ **portrayal** *noun*.

Portuguese /pɔːtʃʊ'giːz/ ● *noun* (*plural* same) native, national, or language of Portugal. ● *adjective* of Portugal.

pose /pəʊz/ ● *verb* (**-sing**) assume attitude, esp. for artistic purpose; (+ *as*) pretend to be; behave affectedly for effect; propound (question, problem); arrange in required attitude. ● *noun* attitude of body or mind; affectation, pretence.

poser *noun* poseur; *colloquial* puzzling question or problem.

poseur /pəʊ'zɜː/ *noun* person who behaves affectedly.

posh *colloquial* ● *adjective* smart; upper-class. ● *adverb* in an upper-class way. □ **poshly** *adverb*; **poshness** *noun*.

posit /'pɒzɪt/ *verb* (**-t-**) assume as fact, postulate.

position /pə'zɪʃ(ə)n/ ● *noun* place occupied by person or thing; way thing is placed; proper place; advantage; mental attitude; situation; rank, status; paid employment; strategic location. ● *verb* place in position. □ **in a position to** able to. □ **positional** *adjective*.

positive /'pɒzɪtɪv/ ● *adjective* explicit, definite, unquestionable; convinced, confident, cocksure; absolute, not relative; *Grammar* (of adjective or adverb) expressing simple quality without comparison; constructive; marked by presence and not absence of qualities; favourable; dealing only with matters of fact, practical; *Mathematics* (of quantity) greater than zero; *Electricity* of, containing, or producing kind of charge produced by rubbing glass with silk; *Photography* showing lights and shades or colours as seen in original image. ● *noun* positive adjective, photograph, quantity, etc. □ **positive discrimination** making distinctions in favour of groups believed to be underprivileged; **positive vetting** inquiry into background etc. of candidate for post involving national security. □ **positively** *adverb*; **positiveness** *noun*.

positivism *noun* philosophical system recognizing only facts and observable phenomena. □ **positivist** *noun & adjective*.

positron /'pɒzɪtrɒn/ *noun* elementary particle with same mass as but opposite charge to electron.

posse /'pɒsɪ/ *noun* strong force or company; group of law-enforcers.

possess /pə'zes/ *verb* hold as property, own; have; occupy, dominate mind of. □ **possessor** *noun*.

possession /pə'zeʃ(ə)n/ *noun* possessing, being possessed; thing possessed; occupancy; (in *plural*) property; control of ball by player.

possessive /pə'zesɪv/ ● *adjective* wanting to retain what one possesses; jealous and domineering; *Grammar* indicating possession. ● *noun Grammar* possessive case or word. □ **possessiveness** *noun*.

possibility /pɒsɪ'bɪlɪtɪ/ *noun* (*plural* **-ies**) state or fact of being possible; thing that may exist or happen; (usually in *plural*) capability of being used.

possible /'pɒsɪb(ə)l/ ● *adjective* capable of existing, happening, being done, etc.; potential. ● *noun* possible candidate, member of team, etc.; highest possible score.

possibly *adverb* perhaps; in accordance with possibility.

possum /'pɒsəm/ *noun colloquial* opossum. □ **play possum** *colloquial* pretend to be unconscious or unaware.

post¹ /pəʊst/ ● *noun* upright of timber or metal as support in building, to mark boundary, carry notices, etc.; pole etc. marking start or finish of race. ● *verb* (often + *up*) display (notice etc.) in prominent place; advertise by poster or list.

post² /pəʊst/ ● *noun* official conveying of parcels, letters, etc.; single collection or delivery of these; letters etc. dispatched; place where letters etc. are collected. ● *verb* put (letter etc.) into post; (esp. as **posted** *adjective*) (often + *up*) supply with information; enter in ledger. □ **postbox** public box for posting mail; **postcard** card for posting without envelope; **postcode** group of letters and figures in postal address to assist sorting; **post-haste** with great speed; **postman**, **postwoman** person who collects or delivers post; **postmark** official mark on letters to cancel stamp; **postmaster**, **postmistress** official in charge of post office; **post office** room or building for postal business; **Post Office** public department or corporation providing postal services.

post³ /pəʊst/ ● *noun* appointed place of soldier etc. on duty; occupying force; fort; paid employment; trading post. ● *verb* place (soldier etc.) at post; appoint to post or command.

post- *prefix* after, behind.

postage *noun* charge for sending letter etc. by post. □ **postage stamp** small adhesive label indicating amount of postage paid.

postal *adjective* of or by post. □ **postal order** money order issued by Post Office.

postdate /pəʊst'deɪt/ *verb* (**-ting**) give later than actual date to; follow in time.

poster *noun* placard in public place; large printed picture. □ **poster paint** gummy opaque paint.

poste restante /pəʊst re'stɑ̃t/ *noun* department in post office where letters are kept till called for.

posterior /pɒ'stɪərɪə/ ● *adjective* later in time or order; at the back. ● *noun* (in *singular* or *plural*) buttocks.

posterity /pɒ'sterɪtɪ/ *noun* later generations; descendants.

postern /'pɒst(ə)n/ *noun archaic* back or side entrance.

postgraduate /pəʊst'grædjʊət/ ● *noun* person on course of study after taking first degree. ● *adjective* relating to postgraduates.

posthumous /'pɒstjʊməs/ *adjective* occurring after death; published after author's death; born after father's death. □ **posthumously** *adverb*.

postilion /pɒ'stɪljən/ *noun* (also **postillion**) rider on near horse of team drawing coach etc. without coachman.

post-impressionism /pəʊstɪm'preʃənɪz(ə)m/ *noun* art intending to express individual artist's conception of objects represented. □ **post-impressionist** *noun & adjective*.

post-industrial /pəʊstɪn'dʌstrɪəl/ *adjective* of society or economy no longer reliant on heavy industry.

post-mortem /pəʊst'mɔːtəm/ ● *noun* examination of body made after death; *colloquial* discussion after conclusion (of game etc.). ● *adverb & adjective* after death.

postnatal /pəʊst'neɪt(ə)l/ *adjective* existing or occurring after birth.

postpone /pəʊst'pəʊn/ *verb* (**-ning**) cause to take place at later time. □ **postponement** *noun*.

postscript /'pəʊstskrɪpt/ *noun* addition at end of letter etc. after signature.

postulant /'pɒstjʊlənt/ *noun* candidate, esp. for admission to religious order.

postulate ● *verb* /'pɒstjʊleɪt/ (**-ting**) (often + *that*) assume or require to be true, take for granted; claim. ● *noun* /'pɒstjʊlət/ thing postulated; prerequisite.

posture /'pɒstʃə/ ● *noun* relative position of parts, esp. of body; bearing; mental attitude; condition or state (of affairs etc.). ● *verb* (**-ring**) assume posture, esp. for effect; pose (person).

postwar /pəʊst'wɔː/ *adjective* occurring or existing after a war.

posy /'pəʊzɪ/ *noun* (*plural* **-ies**) small bunch of flowers.

pot¹ ● *noun* rounded ceramic, metal, or glass vessel; flowerpot, teapot, etc.; contents of pot; chamber pot; total amount bet in game etc.; (usually in *plural*) *colloquial* large sum; *slang* cup as prize. ● *verb* (**-tt-**) plant in pot; (usually as **potted** *adjective*) preserve (food) in sealed pot; pocket (ball) in billiards etc.; abridge, epitomize; shoot at, hit, or kill (animal). □ **go to pot** *colloquial* be ruined; **pot-belly** protuberant belly; **pot-boiler** work of literature etc. done merely to earn money; **pot-herb** herb grown in kitchen garden; **pothole** deep hole in rock, hole in road surface; **potluck** whatever is available; **pot plant** plant grown in flowerpot; **pot roast** piece of braised meat; **pot-roast** braise; **potsherd** broken piece of ceramic material; **pot-shot** random shot. □ **potful** noun (plural **-s**).

pot² noun slang marijuana.

potable /'pəʊtəb(ə)l/ adjective drinkable.

potash /'pɒtæʃ/ noun any of various compounds of potassium.

potassium /pə'tæsɪəm/ noun soft silver-white metallic element.

potation /pə'teɪʃ(ə)n/ noun a drink; drinking.

potato /pə'teɪtəʊ/ noun (plural **-es**) edible plant tuber; plant bearing this. □ **potato crisp** crisp.

poteen /pɒ'tʃiːn/ noun Irish illicit distilled spirit.

potent /'pəʊt(ə)nt/ adjective powerful, strong; cogent; (of male) able to achieve erection of penis or have sexual intercourse. □ **potency** noun.

potentate /'pəʊtənteɪt/ noun monarch, ruler.

potential /pə'tenʃ(ə)l/ ● adjective capable of coming into being; latent. ● noun capability for use or development; usable resources; quantity determining energy of mass in gravitational field or of charge in electric field. □ **potentiality** /-ʃɪ'æl-/ noun; **potentially** adverb.

pother /'pɒðə/ noun literary din, fuss.

potion /'pəʊʃ(ə)n/ noun liquid dose of medicine, poison, etc.

pot-pourri /pəʊ'pʊərɪ/ noun (plural **-s**) scented mixture of dried petals and spices; musical or literary medley.

pottage /'pɒtɪdʒ/ noun archaic soup, stew.

potter¹ /'pɒtə/ verb (US **putter**) (often + about, around) work etc. in aimless or desultory manner; go slowly.

potter² /'pɒtə/ noun maker of ceramic vessels.

pottery /'pɒtərɪ/ noun (plural **-ies**) vessels etc. made of baked clay; potter's work or workshop.

potty¹ /'pɒtɪ/ adjective (**-ier**, **-iest**) slang crazy; insignificant. □ **pottiness** noun.

potty² noun (plural **-ies**) colloquial chamber pot, esp. for child.

pouch ● noun small bag, detachable pocket; baggy area of skin under eyes etc.; baglike receptacle in which marsupials carry undeveloped young, other baglike natural structure. ● verb put or make into pouch; take possession of.

pouffe /puːf/ noun firm cushion as low seat or footstool.

poulterer /'pəʊltərə/ noun dealer in poultry and usually game.

poultice /'pəʊltɪs/ ● noun soft usually hot dressing applied to sore or inflamed part of body. ● verb (**-cing**) apply poultice to.

poultry /'pəʊltrɪ/ noun domestic fowls.

pounce ● verb (**-cing**) spring, swoop; (often + on, upon) make sudden attack, seize eagerly. ● noun act of pouncing.

pound¹ noun unit of weight equal to 16 oz (454 g); (in full **pound sterling**) monetary unit of UK etc.

pound² verb crush or beat with repeated strokes; (+ at, on) deliver heavy blows or gunfire to; (+ along etc.) walk, run, etc. heavily.

pound³ noun enclosure where stray animals or officially removed vehicles are kept until claimed.

poundage noun commission or fee of so much per pound sterling or weight.

-pounder combining form thing or person weighing specified number of pounds; gun firing shell weighing specified number of pounds.

pour /pɔː/ verb (usually + down, out, over, etc.) (cause to) flow in stream or shower; dispense (drink); rain heavily; (usually + in, out, etc.) come or go in profusion or in a rush; discharge copiously.

pout ● verb push lips forward, esp. as sign of displeasure; (of lips) be pushed forward. ● noun pouting expression.

pouter noun kind of pigeon able to inflate crop.

poverty /'pɒvətɪ/ noun being poor, want; (often + of, in) scarcity, lack; inferiority, poorness. □ **poverty-stricken** very poor; **poverty trap** situation in which increase of income incurs greater loss of state benefits.

POW abbreviation prisoner of war.

powder /'paʊdə/ ● noun mass of fine dry particles; medicine or cosmetic in this form; gunpowder. ● verb apply powder to; (esp. as **powdered** adjective) reduce to powder. □ **powder blue** pale blue; **powder-puff** soft pad for applying cosmetic powder to skin; **powder-room** euphemistic women's lavatory. □ **powdery** adjective.

power /'paʊə/ ● noun ability to do or act; mental or bodily faculty; influence, authority; ascendancy; authorization; influential person etc.; state with international influence; vigour, energy; colloquial large number or amount; capacity for exerting mechanical force; mechanical or electrical energy; electricity supply; particular source or form of energy; product obtained by multiplying a number by itself a specified number of times; magnifying capacity of lens. ● verb supply with mechanical or electrical energy; (+ up, down) increase or decrease power supplied to (device), switch on or off. □ **power cut** temporary withdrawal or failure of electric power supply; **powerhouse** power station, person or thing of great energy; **power of attorney** authority to act for another in legal and financial matters; **power point** socket for connection of electrical appliance etc. to mains; **power-sharing** coalition government; **power station** building where electric power is generated for distribution.

powerful adjective having great power or influence. □ **powerfully** adverb; **powerfulness** noun.

powerless adjective without power; wholly unable. □ **powerlessness** noun.

powwow /'paʊwaʊ/ ● noun meeting for discussion (originally among N. American Indians). ● verb hold powwow.

pox noun virus disease leaving pocks; colloquial syphilis.

pp abbreviation pianissimo.

pp. abbreviation pages.

p.p. abbreviation (also **pp**) per pro.

PPS abbreviation Parliamentary Private Secretary; further postscript (postpostscriptum).

PR abbreviation public relations; proportional representation.

practicable /'præktɪkəb(ə)l/ adjective that can be done or used. □ **practicability** noun.

practical /'præktɪk(ə)l/ ● adjective of or concerned with practice rather than theory; functional; good at making, organizing, or mending things; realistic; that is such in effect, virtual. ● noun practical exam. □ **practical joke** trick played on person. □ **practicality** /-'kæl-/ noun (plural **-ies**).

practically adverb virtually, almost; in a practical way.

practice /'præktɪs/ noun habitual action; repeated exercise to improve skill; action as opposed to theory; doctor's or lawyer's professional business etc.; procedure, esp. of specified kind. □ **in practice** when applied, in reality, skilled from recent practice; **out of practice** lacking former skill.

practise /'præktɪs/ verb (**-sing**) (US **-tice**; **-cing**) carry out in action; do repeatedly to improve skill; exercise oneself in or on; (as **practised** adjective) expert; engage in (profession, religion, etc.).

practitioner /præk'tɪʃənə/ *noun* professional worker, esp. in medicine.

praesidium = PRESIDIUM.

praetorian guard /priːˈtɔːrɪən/ *noun* bodyguard of ancient Roman emperor etc.

pragmatic /præg'mætɪk/ *adjective* dealing with matters from a practical point of view. □ **pragmatically** *adverb*.

pragmatism /'prægmətɪz(ə)m/ *noun* pragmatic attitude or procedure; *Philosophy* doctrine that evaluates assertions according to their practical consequences. □ **pragmatist** *noun*.

prairie /'preərɪ/ *noun* large treeless tract of grassland, esp. in N. America.

praise /preɪz/ ● *verb* (**-sing**) express warm approval or admiration of; glorify. ● *noun* praising; commendation. □ **praiseworthy** worthy of praise.

praline /'prɑːliːn/ *noun* sweet made of nuts browned in boiling sugar.

pram *noun* carriage for baby, pushed by person on foot.

prance /prɑːns/ ● *verb* (**-cing**) (of horse) spring from hind legs; walk or behave in an elated or arrogant way. ● *noun* prancing; prancing movement.

prank *noun* practical joke.

prat *noun* slang fool.

prate ● *verb* (**-ting**) talk too much; chatter foolishly. ● *noun* idle talk.

prattle /'præt(ə)l/ ● *verb* (**-ling**) talk in childish or inconsequential way. ● *noun* prattling talk.

prawn *noun* edible shellfish like large shrimp.

pray *verb* (often + *for, to do, that*) say prayers; make devout supplication; entreat.

prayer /preə/ *noun* request or thanksgiving to God or object of worship; formula used in praying; entreaty. □ **prayer book** book of set prayers; **prayer-mat** small carpet on which Muslims kneel when praying; **prayer-shawl** one worn by male Jews when praying.

pre- *prefix* before (in time, place, order, degree, or importance).

preach *verb* deliver (sermon); proclaim (the gospel etc.); give moral advice obtrusively; advocate, inculcate. □ **preacher** *noun*.

preamble /priːˈæmb(ə)l/ *noun* preliminary statement; introductory part of statute, deed, etc.

prearrange /priːəˈreɪndʒ/ *verb* (**-ging**) arrange beforehand. □ **prearrangement** *noun*.

prebend /'prebənd/ *noun* stipend of canon or member of chapter; portion of land etc. from which this is drawn. □ **prebendal** /prɪˈbend(ə)l/ *adjective*.

prebendary /'prebəndərɪ/ *noun* (*plural* **-ies**) holder of prebend; honorary canon.

Precambrian /priːˈkæmbrɪən/ ● *adjective* of earliest geological era. ● *noun* this era.

precarious /prɪˈkeərɪəs/ *adjective* uncertain, dependent on chance; perilous. □ **precariously** *adverb*; **precariousness** *noun*.

precast /priːˈkɑːst/ *adjective* (of concrete) cast in required shape before positioning.

precaution /prɪˈkɔːʃ(ə)n/ *noun* action taken beforehand to avoid risk or ensure good result. □ **precautionary** *adjective*.

precede /prɪˈsiːd/ *verb* (**-ding**) come or go before in time, order, importance, etc.; (+ *by*) cause to be preceded by.

precedence /'presɪd(ə)ns/ *noun* priority; right of preceding others. □ **take precedence** (often + *over, of*) have priority.

precedent ● *noun* /'presɪd(ə)nt/ previous case taken as guide or justification etc. ● *adjective* /prɪˈsiːd(ə)nt/ preceding.

precentor /prɪˈsentə/ *noun* leader of singing or (in synagogue) prayers of congregation.

precept /'priːsept/ *noun* rule for action or conduct.

preceptor /prɪˈseptə/ *noun* teacher, instructor. □ **preceptorial** /priːsepˈtɔːrɪəl/ *adjective*.

precession /prɪˈseʃ(ə)n/ *noun* slow movement of axis of spinning body around another axis; such change causing equinoxes to occur earlier in each successive sidereal year.

precinct /'priːsɪŋkt/ *noun* enclosed area, esp. around building; district in town, esp. where traffic is excluded; (in *plural*) environs.

preciosity /preʃɪˈɒsɪtɪ/ *noun* affected refinement in art.

precious /'preʃəs/ ● *adjective* of great value; much prized; affectedly refined. ● *adverb* colloquial extremely, very.

precipice /'presɪpɪs/ *noun* vertical or steep face of rock, cliff, mountain, etc.

precipitate ● *verb* /prɪˈsɪpɪteɪt/ (**-ting**) hasten occurrence of; (+ *into*) cause to go into (war etc.) hurriedly or violently; throw down headlong; *Chemistry* cause (substance) to be deposited in solid form from solution; *Physics* condense (vapour) into drops. ● *adjective* /prɪˈsɪpɪtət/ headlong; hasty, rash. ● *noun* /prɪˈsɪpɪtət/ solid matter precipitated; moisture condensed from vapour.

precipitation /prɪsɪpɪˈteɪʃ(ə)n/ *noun* precipitating, being precipitated; rash haste; rain, snow, etc., falling to ground.

precipitous /prɪˈsɪpɪtəs/ *adjective* of or like precipice; steep.

précis /'preɪsiː/ ● *noun* (*plural* same /-siːz/) summary, abstract. ● *verb* (**-cises** /-siːz/, **-cised** /-siːd/, **-cising** /-siːŋ/) make précis of.

precise /prɪˈsaɪs/ *adjective* accurately worded; definite, exact; punctilious.

precisely *adverb* in a precise way, exactly; quite so.

precision /prɪˈsɪʒ(ə)n/ ● *noun* accuracy. ● *adjective* designed for or produced by precise work.

preclude /prɪˈkluːd/ *verb* (**-ding**) (+ *from*) prevent; make impossible.

precocious /prɪˈkəʊʃəs/ *adjective* prematurely developed in some respect. □ **precociously** *adverb*; **precociousness** *noun*; **precocity** /-ˈkɒs-/ *noun*.

precognition /priːkɒgˈnɪʃ(ə)n/ *noun* (esp. supernatural) foreknowledge.

preconceive /priːkənˈsiːv/ *verb* (**-ving**) form (opinion etc.) beforehand.

preconception /priːkənˈsepʃ(ə)n/ *noun* preconceived idea; prejudice.

precondition /priːkənˈdɪʃ(ə)n/ *noun* condition that must be fulfilled beforehand.

precursor /priːˈkɜːsə/ *noun* forerunner; person who precedes in office etc.; harbinger.

predate /priːˈdeɪt/ *verb* (**-ting**) precede in time.

predator /'predətə/ *noun* predatory animal; exploiter of others.

predatory /'predətərɪ/ *adjective* (of animal) preying naturally on others; plundering or exploiting others.

predecease /priːdɪˈsiːs/ *verb* (**-sing**) die before (another).

predecessor /'priːdɪsesə/ *noun* previous holder of office or position; ancestor; thing to which another has succeeded.

predestine /priːˈdestɪn/ *verb* (**-ning**) determine beforehand; ordain by divine will or as if by fate. □ **predestination** *noun*.

predetermine /priːdɪˈtɜːmɪn/ *verb* (**-ning**) decree beforehand; predestine.

predicament /prɪˈdɪkəmənt/ *noun* difficult or unpleasant situation.

predicate ● verb /'predɪkeɪt/ (**-ting**) assert (something) about subject of proposition; (+ on) base (statement etc.) on. ● noun /'predɪkət/ Grammar & Logic what is said about subject of sentence or proposition. □ **predicable** adjective; **predication** noun.

predicative /prɪ'dɪkətɪv/ adjective Grammar (of adjective or noun) forming part or all of predicate; that predicates.

predict /prɪ'dɪkt/ verb forecast; prophesy. □ **predictable** adjective; **predictably** adverb; **prediction** noun.

predilection /priːdɪ'lekʃ(ə)n/ noun (often + for) preference, special liking.

predispose /priːdɪs'pəʊz/ verb (**-sing**) influence favourably in advance; (+ to, to do) render liable or inclined beforehand to. □ **predisposition** /-pə'zɪʃ(ə)n/ noun.

predominate /prɪ'dɒmɪneɪt/ verb (**-ting**) (+ over) have control over; prevail; preponderate. □ **predominance** noun; **predominant** adjective; **predominantly** adverb.

pre-eminent /priː'emɪnənt/ adjective excelling others; outstanding. □ **preeminence** noun; **pre-eminently** adverb.

pre-empt /priː'empt/ verb forestall; obtain by pre-emption.

■ Usage Pre-empt is sometimes used to mean prevent, but this is considered incorrect in standard English.

pre-emption /priː'empʃ(ə)n/ noun purchase or taking of thing before it is offered to others.

pre-emptive /priː'emptɪv/ adjective pre-empting; Military intended to prevent attack by disabling enemy.

preen verb (of bird) tidy (feathers, itself) with beak; (of person) smarten or admire (oneself, one's hair, clothes, etc.); (often + on) pride (oneself).

prefab /'priːfæb/ noun colloquial prefabricated building.

prefabricate /priː'fæbrɪkeɪt/ verb (**-ting**) manufacture sections of (building etc.) prior to assembly on site.

preface /'prefəs/ ● noun introduction to book stating subject, scope, etc.; preliminary part of speech. ● verb (**-cing**) (often + with) introduce or begin (as with preface; (of event etc.) lead up to (another). □ **prefatory** adjective.

prefect /'priːfekt/ noun chief administrative officer of district in France etc.; senior pupil in school, authorized to maintain discipline.

prefecture /'priːfektʃə/ noun district under government of prefect; prefect's office or tenure.

prefer /prɪ'fɜː/ verb (**-rr-**) (often + to, to do) like better; submit (information, accusation, etc.); promote (person).

preferable /'prefərəb(ə)l/ adjective to be preferred, more desirable. □ **preferably** adverb.

preference /'prefərəns/ noun preferring, being preferred; thing preferred; favouring of one person etc. before others; prior right.

preferential /prefə'renʃ(ə)l/ adjective of, giving, or receiving preference. □ **preferentially** adverb.

preferment /prɪ'fɜːmənt/ noun formal promotion to higher office.

prefigure /priː'fɪgə/ verb (**-ring**) represent or imagine beforehand.

prefix /'priːfɪks/ ● noun part-word added to beginning of word to alter meaning, e.g. re- in retake, ex- in ex-president; title before name. ● verb (often + to) add as introduction; join (word, element) as prefix.

pregnant /'pregnənt/ adjective having child or young developing in womb; significant, suggestive. □ **pregnancy** noun (plural **-ies**).

preheat /priː'hiːt/ verb heat beforehand.

prehensile /priː'hensaɪl/ adjective (of tail, limb, etc.) capable of grasping.

prehistoric /priːhɪs'tɒrɪk/ adjective of period before written records. □ **prehistory** /-'hɪstərɪ/ noun.

prejudge /priː'dʒʌdʒ/ verb (**-ging**) form premature judgement on (person etc.).

prejudice /'predʒʊdɪs/ ● noun preconceived opinion; (+ against, in favour of) bias; harm (possibly) resulting from action or judgement. ● verb (**-cing**) impair validity of; (esp. as **prejudiced** adjective) cause (person) to have prejudice. □ **prejudicial** /-'dɪʃ-/ adjective.

prelacy /'preləsɪ/ noun (plural **-ies**) church government by prelates; (**the prelacy**) prelates collectively; office or rank of prelate.

prelate /'prelət/ noun high ecclesiastical dignitary, e.g. bishop.

preliminary /prɪ'lɪmɪnərɪ/ ● adjective introductory, preparatory. ● noun (plural **-ies**) (usually in plural) preliminary action or arrangement; preliminary trial or contest.

prelude /'preljuːd/ ● noun (often + to) action, event, etc. serving as introduction; introductory part of poem etc.; Music introductory piece of suite, short piece of similar type. ● verb (**-ding**) serve as prelude to; introduce with prelude.

premarital /priː'mærɪt(ə)l/ adjective occurring etc. before marriage.

premature /'premətʃə/ adjective occurring or done before usual or right time; too hasty; (of baby) born 3 or more weeks before expected time. □ **prematurely** adverb.

premed /priː'med/ noun colloquial premedication.

premedication /priːmedɪ'keɪʃ(ə)n/ noun medication in preparation for operation.

premeditate /priː'medɪteɪt/ verb (**-ting**) think out or plan beforehand. □ **premeditation** noun.

premenstrual /priː'menstrʊəl/ adjective of the time immediately before menstruation.

premier /'premɪə/ ● noun prime minister. ● adjective first in importance, order, or time. □ **premiership** noun.

première /'premɪeə/ ● noun first performance or showing of play or film. ● verb (**-ring**) give première of.

premise /'premɪs/ noun premiss; (in plural) house or other building with its grounds etc.; (in plural) Law previously specified houses, lands, or tenements. □ **on the premises** in the house etc. concerned.

premiss /'premɪs/ noun previous statement from which another is inferred.

premium /'priːmɪəm/ ● noun amount to be paid for contract of insurance; sum added to interest, wages, etc.; reward, prize. ● adjective of best quality and highest price. □ **at a premium** highly valued, above usual or nominal price; **Premium (Savings) Bond** government security not bearing interest but with periodic prize draw.

premonition /premə'nɪʃ(ə)n/ noun forewarning; presentiment. □ **premonitory** /prɪ'mɒnɪtərɪ/ adjective.

prenatal /priː'neɪt(ə)l/ adjective existing or occurring before birth.

preoccupy /priː'ɒkjʊpaɪ/ verb (**-ies**, **-ied**) dominate mind of; (as **preoccupied** adjective) otherwise engrossed. □ **preoccupation** noun.

preordain /priːɔː'deɪn/ verb ordain or determine beforehand.

prep noun colloquial homework; time when this is done.

prepack /priː'pæk/ verb (also **prepackage** /-'pækɪdʒ/) pack (goods) before retail.

preparation /prepə'reɪʃ(ə)n/ *noun* preparing, being prepared; (often in *plural*) thing done to make ready; substance specially prepared.

preparatory /prɪ'pærətərɪ/ ● *adjective* (often + *to*) serving to prepare; introductory. ● *adverb* (often + *to*) as a preparation. □ **preparatory school** private primary or (*US*) secondary school.

prepare /prɪ'peə/ *verb* (**-ring**) make or get ready; get oneself ready.

prepay /priː'peɪ/ *verb* (*past & past participle* **prepaid**) pay (charge) beforehand; pay postage on beforehand. □ **prepayment** *noun*.

preponderate /prɪ'pɒndəreɪt/ *verb* (**-ting**) (often + *over*) be superior in influence, quantity, or number; predominate. □ **preponderance** *noun*; **preponderant** *adjective*.

preposition /prepə'zɪʃ(ə)n/ *noun* word used before noun or pronoun to indicate its relationship to another word (see panel). □ **prepositional** *adjective*.

prepossess /priːpə'zes/ *verb* (usually in *passive*) take possession of; prejudice, usually favourably; (as **prepossessing** *adjective*) attractive. □ **prepossession** *noun*.

preposterous /prɪ'pɒstərəs/ *adjective* utterly absurd; contrary to nature or reason. □ **preposterously** *adverb*.

prepuce /'priːpjuːs/ *noun* foreskin.

Pre-Raphaelite /priː'ræfəlaɪt/ ● *noun* member of group of 19th-c. English artists. ● *adjective* of Pre-Raphaelites; (**pre-Raphaelite**) (esp. of woman) of type painted by Pre-Raphaelites.

pre-record /priːrɪ'kɔːd/ *verb* record in advance.

prerequisite /priː'rekwɪzɪt/ ● *adjective* required as precondition. ● *noun* prerequisite thing.

■ **Usage** *Prerequisite* is sometimes confused with *perquisite* which means 'an extra profit, right, or privilege'.

prerogative /prɪ'rɒɡətɪv/ *noun* right or privilege exclusive to individual or class.

Pres. *abbreviation* President.

presage /'presɪdʒ/ ● *noun* omen; presentiment. ● *verb* (**-ging**) portend; indicate (future event etc.); foretell, foresee.

presbyopia /prezbɪ'əʊpɪə/ *noun* long-sightedness. □ **presbyopic** *adjective*.

presbyter /'prezbɪtə/ *noun* priest of Episcopal Church; elder of Presbyterian Church.

Presbyterian /prezbɪ'tɪərɪən/ ● *adjective* (of Church, esp. Church of Scotland) governed by elders all of equal rank. ● *noun* member of Presbyterian Church. □ **Presbyterianism** *noun*.

presbytery /'prezbɪtərɪ/ *noun* (*plural* **-ies**) eastern part of chancel; body of presbyters; RC priest's house.

prescient /'presɪənt/ *adjective* having foreknowledge or foresight. □ **prescience** *noun*.

prescribe /prɪ'skraɪb/ *verb* (**-bing**) advise use of (medicine etc.); lay down authoritatively.

■ **Usage** *Prescribe* is sometimes confused with *proscribe*, which means 'forbid'.

prescript /'priːskrɪpt/ *noun* ordinance, command.

prescription /prɪ'skrɪpʃ(ə)n/ *noun* prescribing; doctor's (usually written) instruction for composition and use of medicine; medicine thus prescribed.

prescriptive /prɪ'skrɪptɪv/ *adjective* prescribing, laying down rules; arising from custom.

presence /'prez(ə)ns/ *noun* being present; place where person is; personal appearance; person or spirit that is present. □ **presence of mind** calmness and quick-wittedness in sudden difficulty etc.

present[1] /'prez(ə)nt/ ● *adjective* being in place in question; now existing, occurring, or being dealt with etc.; *Grammar* expressing present action or state. ● *noun* (**the present**) now; present tense. □ **at present** now; **for the present** just now; **present-day** of this time, modern.

present[2] /prɪ'zent/ *verb* introduce; exhibit; offer or give (thing) to; (+ *with*) provide (person) with; put (play, film, etc.) before public; reveal; deliver (cheque etc.) for payment etc. □ **present arms** hold rifle etc. in saluting position.

present[3] /'prez(ə)nt/ *noun* gift.

presentable /prɪ'zentəb(ə)l/ *adjective* of good appearance; fit to be shown. □ **presentability** *noun*; **presentably** *adverb*.

presentation /prezən'teɪʃ(ə)n/ *noun* presenting, being presented; thing presented; manner or quality of presenting; demonstration of materials etc., lecture.

presenter *noun* person introducing broadcast programme.

presentiment /prɪ'zentɪmənt/ *noun* vague expectation, foreboding.

presently *adverb* before long; *US & Scottish* at present.

preservative /prɪ'zɜːvətɪv/ ● *noun* substance for preserving food etc. ● *adjective* tending to preserve.

preserve /prɪ'zɜːv/ ● *verb* (**-ving**) keep safe or free from decay; maintain, retain; treat (food) to prevent decomposition or fermentation; keep (game etc.) undisturbed for private use. ● *noun* (in *singular* or *plural*)

Preposition

A preposition is used in front of a noun or pronoun to form a phrase. It often describes the position of something, e.g. *under the chair*, or the time at which something happens, e.g. *in the evening*.

Prepositions in common use are:

about	behind	into	through
above	beside	like	till
across	between	near	to
after	by	of	towards
against	down	off	under
along	during	on	underneath
among	except	outside	until
around	for	over	up
as	from	past	upon
at	in	round	with
before	inside	since	without

preserved fruit, jam; place where game etc. is preserved; sphere of activity regarded by person as his or hers alone. □ **preservation** /prezə'veɪʃ(ə)n/ noun.

preshrunk /priː'ʃrʌŋk/ adjective (of fabric etc.) treated so as to shrink during manufacture and not in use.

preside /prɪ'zaɪd/ verb (**-ding**) (often + at, over) be chairperson or president; exercise control or authority.

presidency /'prezɪdənsɪ/ noun (plural **-ies**) office of president; period of this.

president /'prezɪd(ə)nt/ noun head of republic; head of society or council etc., of certain colleges, or (US) of university, company, etc.; person in charge of meeting. □ **presidential** /-'den-/ adjective.

presidium /prɪ'sɪdɪəm/ noun (also **praesidium**) standing committee, esp. in Communist country.

press¹ ● verb apply steady force to; flatten, shape, smooth (esp. clothes); (+ out, of, from, etc.) squeeze (juice etc.); embrace, caress firmly; (+ on, against, etc.) exert pressure on; be urgent, urge; (+ for) demand insistently; (+ up, round, etc.) crowd; (+ on, forward, etc.) hasten; (+ on, upon) force (offer etc.) on; manufacture (gramophone record, car part, etc.) using pressure. ● noun pressing; device for compressing, flattening, extracting juice, etc.; machine for printing; (**the press**) newspapers; publicity in newspapers; printing house; publishing company; crowding, crowd; pressure of affairs; large usually shelved cupboard. □ **press agent** person employed to manage advertising and press publicity; **press conference** meeting with journalists; **press gallery** gallery for reporters, esp. in legislative assembly; **press release** statement issued to newspapers etc.; **press-stud** small device fastened by pressing to engage two parts; **press-up** exercise in which prone body is raised by pressing down on hands to straighten arms.

press² verb historical force to serve in army or navy; bring into use as makeshift. □ **press-gang** noun historical group of men employed to press men for navy, verb force into service.

pressing ● adjective urgent; insistent. ● noun thing made by pressing, e.g. gramophone record; series of these made at one time; act of pressing. □ **pressingly** adverb.

pressure /'preʃə/ ● noun exertion of continuous force, force so exerted, amount of this; urgency; affliction, difficulty; constraining or compelling influence. ● verb (**-ring**) (often + into) apply pressure to, coerce, persuade. □ **pressure-cooker** pan for cooking quickly under high pressure; **pressure group** group formed to influence public policy.

pressurize verb (also **-ise**) (**-zing** or **-sing**) (esp. as **pressurized** adjective) maintain normal atmospheric pressure in (aircraft cabin etc.) at high altitude; raise to high pressure; pressure (person).

prestidigitator /prestɪ'dɪdʒɪteɪtə/ noun formal conjuror. □ **prestidigitation** noun.

prestige /pres'tiːʒ/ ● noun respect or reputation. ● adjective having or conferring prestige. □ **prestigious** /-'stɪdʒəs/ adjective.

presto /'prestəʊ/ Music ● adverb & adjective in quick tempo. ● noun (plural **-s**) presto movement or passage.

prestressed /priː'strest/ adjective (of concrete) strengthened by stretched wires in it.

presumably /prɪ'zjuːməblɪ/ adverb as may reasonably be presumed.

presume /prɪ'zjuːm/ verb (**-ming**) (often + that) suppose to be true, take for granted; (often + to do) venture; be presumptuous; (+ on, upon) make unscrupulous use of.

presumption /prɪ'zʌmpʃ(ə)n/ noun arrogance, presumptuous behaviour; taking for granted; thing presumed to be true; ground for presuming.

presumptive /prɪ'zʌmptɪv/ adjective giving grounds for presumption.

presumptuous /prɪ'zʌmptʃʊəs/ adjective unduly confident, arrogant. □ **presumptuously** adverb; **presumptuousness** noun.

presuppose /priːsə'pəʊz/ verb (**-sing**) assume beforehand; imply. □ **presupposition** /-sʌpə'zɪʃ(ə)n/ noun.

pre-tax /priː'tæks/ adjective (of income) before deduction of taxes.

pretence /prɪ'tens/ noun (US **pretense**) pretending, make-believe; pretext; (+ to) (esp. false) claim; ostentation.

pretend /prɪ'tend/ ● verb claim or assert falsely; imagine in play; (as **pretended** adjective) falsely claimed to be; (+ to) profess to have. ● adjective colloquial pretended.

pretender noun person who claims throne, title, etc.

pretense US = PRETENCE.

pretension /prɪ'tenʃ(ə)n/ noun (often + to) assertion of claim; pretentiousness.

pretentious /prɪ'tenʃəs/ adjective making excessive claim to merit or importance; ostentatious. □ **pretentiously** adverb; **pretentiousness** noun.

preternatural /priːtə'nætʃər(ə)l/ adjective extraordinary; supernatural.

pretext /'priːtekst/ noun ostensible reason; excuse.

pretty /'prɪtɪ/ ● adjective (**-ier**, **-iest**) attractive in delicate way; fine, good; considerable. ● adverb colloquial fairly, moderately. ● verb (**-ies**, **-ied**) (often + up) make pretty. □ **pretty-pretty** colloquial too pretty. □ **prettify** verb (**-ies**, **-ied**); **prettily** adverb; **prettiness** noun.

pretzel /'prets(ə)l/ noun crisp knot-shaped salted biscuit.

prevail /prɪ'veɪl/ verb (often + against, over) be victorious; be the more usual or predominant; exist or occur in general use; (+ on, upon) persuade.

prevalent /'prevələnt/ adjective generally existing or occurring. □ **prevalence** noun.

prevaricate /prɪ'værɪkeɪt/ verb (**-ting**) speak or act evasively or misleadingly. □ **prevarication** noun; **prevaricator** noun.

■ **Usage** *Prevaricate* is often confused with *procrastinate*, which means 'to defer action'.

prevent /prɪ'vent/ verb (often + from doing) stop, hinder. □ **preventable** adjective (also **preventible**); **prevention** noun.

■ **Usage** The use of *prevent* without 'from' as in *She prevented me going* is informal. An acceptable further alternative is *She prevented my going*.

preventative /prɪ'ventətɪv/ adjective & noun preventive.

preventive /prɪ'ventɪv/ ● adjective serving to prevent, esp. disease. ● noun preventive agent, measure, drug, etc.

preview /'priːvjuː/ ● noun showing of film, play, etc. before it is seen by general public. ● verb view or show in advance.

previous /'priːvɪəs/ ● adjective (often + to) coming before in time or order; colloquial hasty, premature. ● adverb (+ to) before. □ **previously** adverb.

pre-war /priː'wɔː/ adjective existing or occurring before a war.

prey /preɪ/ ● noun animal hunted or killed by another for food; (often + to) victim. ● verb (+ on, upon) seek or take as prey; exert harmful influence.

price ● *noun* amount of money for which thing is bought or sold; what must be given, done, etc. to obtain thing; odds. ● *verb* (**-cing**) fix or find price of; estimate value of. □ **at a price** at high cost; **price tag** label on item showing its price.

priceless *adjective* invaluable; *colloquial* very amusing or absurd.

pricey *adjective* (**pricier, priciest**) *colloquial* expensive.

prick ● *verb* pierce slightly, make small hole in; (+ *off, out*) mark with pricks or dots; trouble mentally; tingle. ● *noun* pricking, mark of it; pain caused by pricking, mental pain. □ **prick out** plant (seedlings etc.) in small holes pricked in earth; **prick up one's ears** (of dog) erect the ears when alert, (of person) become suddenly attentive.

prickle /'prɪk(ə)l/ ● *noun* small thorn; hard-pointed spine; prickling sensation. ● *verb* (**-ling**) cause or feel sensation as of prick(s).

prickly *adjective* (**-ier, -iest**) having prickles; irritable; tingling. □ **prickly heat** itchy inflammation of skin near sweat glands; **prickly pear** cactus with pear-shaped edible fruit, its fruit. □ **prickliness** *noun.*

pride ● *noun* elation or satisfaction at one's achievements, possessions, etc.; object of this; unduly high opinion of oneself; proper sense of one's own worth, position, etc.; group (of lions etc.). ● *verb* (**-ding**) (**pride oneself on, upon**) be proud of. □ **pride of place** most important position; **take (a) pride in** be proud of.

prie-dieu /priː'djɜː/ *noun* (*plural* **-x** same pronunciation) kneeling-desk for prayer.

priest /priːst/ *noun* ordained minister of some Christian churches (above deacon and below bishop); (*feminine* **priestess**) official minister of non-Christian religion. □ **priesthood** *noun;* **priestly** *adjective.*

prig *noun* self-righteous or moralistic person. □ **priggish** *adjective;* **priggishness** *noun.*

prim *adjective* (**-mm-**) stiffly formal and precise; prudish. □ **primly** *adverb;* **primness** *noun.*

prima /'priːmə/ *adjective* □ **prima ballerina** chief female dancer in ballet; **prima donna** chief female singer in opera, temperamental person.

primacy /'praɪməsɪ/ *noun* (*plural* **-ies**) pre-eminence; office of primate.

prima facie /praɪmə 'feɪʃɪ/ ● *adverb* at first sight. ● *adjective* (of evidence) based on first impression.

primal /'praɪm(ə)l/ *adjective* primitive, primeval; fundamental.

primary /'praɪmərɪ/ ● *adjective* of first importance; fundamental; original. ● *noun* (*plural* **-ies**) primary colour, feather, school, etc.; *US* primary election. □ **primary colour** one not obtained by mixing others; **primary education** education for children under 11; **primary election** *US* election to select candidate(s) for principal election; **primary feather** large flight feather of bird's wing; **primary school** school for primary education. □ **primarily** /'praɪmərɪlɪ, praɪ'meərɪlɪ/ *adverb.*

primate /'praɪmeɪt/ *noun* member of highest order of mammals, including apes, man, etc.; archbishop.

prime¹ ● *adjective* chief, most important; of highest quality; primary, fundamental; (of number etc.) divisible only by itself and unity. ● *noun* best or most vigorous state. □ **prime minister** chief minister of government; **prime time** time when television etc. audience is largest.

prime² *verb* (**-ming**) prepare (thing) for use; prepare (gun) for firing or (explosive) for detonation; pour liquid into (pump) to start it working; cover (wood, metal, etc.) with primer; equip (person) with information etc.

primer¹ *noun* substance applied to bare wood, metal, etc. before painting.

primer² *noun* elementary school-book; introductory book.

primeval /praɪ'miːv(ə)l/ *adjective* of first age of world; ancient, primitive.

primitive /'prɪmɪtɪv/ ● *adjective* at early stage of civilization; crude, simple. ● *noun* untutored painter with naïve style; picture by such painter. □ **primitively** *adverb;* **primitiveness** *noun.*

primogeniture /praɪməʊ'dʒenɪtʃə/ *noun* being first-born; first-born's right to inheritance.

primordial /praɪ'mɔːdɪəl/ *adjective* existing at or from beginning, primeval.

primrose /'prɪmrəʊz/ *noun* plant bearing pale yellow spring flower; this flower; pale yellow. □ **primrose path** pursuit of pleasure.

primula /'prɪmjʊlə/ *noun* cultivated plant with flowers of various colours.

Primus /'praɪməs/ *noun proprietary term* portable cooking stove burning vaporized oil.

prince *noun* (as title usually **Prince**) male member of royal family other than king; ruler of small state; nobleman of some countries; (often + *of*) the greatest. □ **Prince Consort** husband of reigning queen who is himself a prince.

princely *adjective* (**-ier, -iest**) of or worthy of a prince; sumptuous, splendid.

princess /prɪn'ses/ *noun* (as title usually **Princess** /'prɪnses/) prince's wife; female member of royal family other than queen.

principal /'prɪnsɪp(ə)l/ ● *adjective* first in importance, chief; leading. ● *noun* chief person; head of some institutions; principal actor, singer, etc.; capital sum lent or invested; person for whom another is agent etc. □ **principal boy** (usually actress playing) leading male role in pantomime. □ **principally** *adverb.*

principality /prɪnsɪ'pælɪtɪ/ *noun* (*plural* **-ies**) state ruled by prince; (**the Principality**) Wales.

principle /'prɪnsɪp(ə)l/ *noun* fundamental truth or law as basis of reasoning or action; personal code of conduct; fundamental source or element. □ **in principle** in theory; **on principle** from moral motive.

principled *adjective* based on or having (esp. praiseworthy) principles of behaviour.

prink *verb* (usually **prink oneself**; often + *up*) smarten, dress up.

print ● *verb* produce by applying inked type, plates, etc. to paper etc.; express or publish in print; (often + *on, with*) impress, stamp; write in letters that are not joined; produce (photograph) from negative; (usually + *out*) produce computer output in printed form; mark (fabric) with design. ● *noun* mark left on surface by pressure; printed lettering, words, or publication (esp. newspaper); engraving; photograph; printed fabric. □ **in print** (of book etc.) available from publisher, in printed form; **out of print** (of book etc.) no longer available from publisher; **printed circuit** electric circuit with thin conducting strips printed on flat sheet; **printing press** machine for printing from type, plates, etc.; **printout** computer output in printed form.

printer ● *noun* person who prints books etc.; owner of printing business; device that prints esp. computer output.

prior /'praɪə/ ● *adjective* earlier; (often + *to*) coming before in time, order, or importance. ● *adverb* (+ *to*) before. ● *noun* (*feminine* **prioress**) superior of religious house; (in abbey) deputy of abbot.

priority /praɪ'ɒrɪtɪ/ *noun* (*plural* **-ies**) thing considered more important than others; precedence in time, rank, etc.; right to do something before other people. □ **prioritize** *verb* (also **-ise**) (**-zing** or **-sing**).

priory /'praɪərɪ/ *noun* (*plural* **-ies**) religious house governed by prior or prioress.

prise /praɪz/ *verb* (also **prize**) (**-sing** or **-zing**) force open or out by leverage.

prism /'prɪz(ə)m/ *noun* solid figure whose two ends are equal parallel rectilinear figures, and whose sides are parallelograms; transparent body of this form with refracting surfaces.

prismatic /prɪz'mætɪk/ *adjective* of, like, or using prism; (of colours) distributed (as if) by transparent prism.

prison /'prɪz(ə)n/ *noun* place of captivity, esp. building to which people are consigned while awaiting trial or for punishment.

prisoner /'prɪznə/ *noun* person kept in prison; person or thing confined by illness, another's grasp, etc.; (in full **prisoner of war**) person captured in war.

prissy /'prɪsɪ/ *adjective* (**-ier**, **-iest**) prim, prudish. □ **prissily** *adverb*; **prissiness** *noun*.

pristine /'prɪstiːn/ *adjective* in original condition, unspoilt; ancient.

privacy /'prɪvəsɪ/ *noun* (right to) being private; freedom from intrusion or publicity.

private /'praɪvət/ ● *adjective* belonging to an individual, personal; confidential, secret; not public; secluded; not holding public office or official position; not supported, managed, or provided by state. ● *noun* private soldier; (in *plural*) *colloquial* genitals. □ **in private** privately; **private detective** detective outside police force; **private enterprise** business(es) not under state control; **private eye** *colloquial* private detective; **private means** unearned income from investments etc.; **private member** MP not holding government office; **private parts** *euphemistic* genitals; **private soldier** ordinary soldier, not officer. □ **privately** *adverb*.

privateer /praɪvə'tɪə/ *noun* (commander of) privately owned and government-commissioned warship.

privation /praɪ'veɪʃ(ə)n/ *noun* lack of comforts or necessities.

privatize /'praɪvətaɪz/ *verb* (also **-ise**) (**-zing** or **-sing**) transfer from state to private ownership. □ **privatization** *noun*.

privet /'prɪvɪt/ *noun* bushy evergreen shrub used for hedges.

privilege /'prɪvɪlɪdʒ/ ● *noun* right, advantage, or immunity belonging to person, class, or office; special benefit or honour. ● *verb* (**-ging**) invest with privilege.

privy /'prɪvɪ/ ● *adjective* (+ *to*) sharing secret of; *archaic* hidden, secret. ● *noun* (*plural* **-ies**) lavatory. □ **Privy Council** group of advisers appointed by sovereign; **Privy Councillor, Counsellor** member of this; **privy purse** allowance from public revenue for monarch's private expenses; **privy seal** state seal formerly affixed to minor documents.

prize¹ ● *noun* reward in competition, lottery, etc.; reward given as symbol of victory or superiority; thing (to be) striven for. ● *adjective* to which prize is awarded; excellent of its kind. ● *verb* (**-zing**) value highly. □ **prizefight** boxing match for money.

prize² *noun* ship or property captured in naval warfare.

prize³ = PRISE.

PRO *abbreviation* Public Record Office; public relations officer.

pro¹ *noun* (*plural* **-s**) *colloquial* professional.

pro² ● *adjective* in favour. ● *noun* (*plural* **-s**) reason in favour. ● *preposition* in favour of. □ **pros and cons** reasons for and against.

proactive /prəʊ'æktɪv/ *adjective* (of person, policy, etc.) taking the initiative.

probability *noun* (*plural* **-ies**) being probable; likelihood; (most) probable event; extent to which thing is likely to occur, measured by ratio of favourable cases to all cases possible. □ **in all probability** most probably.

probable /'prɒbəb(ə)l/ ● *adjective* (often + *that*) that may be expected to happen or prove true; likely. ● *noun* probable candidate, member of team, etc. □ **probably** *adverb*.

probate /'prəʊbeɪt/ *noun* official proving of will; verified copy of will.

probation /prə'beɪʃ(ə)n/ *noun* system of supervising behaviour of offenders as alternative to prison; testing of character and abilities of esp. new employee. □ **probation officer** official supervising offenders on probation. □ **probationary** *adjective*.

probationer *noun* person on probation.

probe ● *noun* investigation; device for measuring, testing, etc.; blunt-ended surgical instrument for exploring wound etc.; unmanned exploratory spacecraft. ● *verb* (**-bing**) examine closely; explore with probe.

probity /'prəʊbɪtɪ/ *noun* uprightness, honesty.

problem /'prɒbləm/ ● *noun* doubtful or difficult question; thing hard to understand or deal with. ● *adjective* causing problems.

problematic /prɒblə'mætɪk/ *adjective* (also **problematical**) attended by difficulty; doubtful, questionable.

proboscis /prəʊ'bɒsɪs/ *noun* (*plural* **-sces**) long flexible trunk or snout, e.g. of elephant; elongated mouth-parts of some insects.

procedure /prə'siːdʒə/ *noun* way of conducting business etc. or performing task; set series of actions. □ **procedural** *adjective*.

proceed /prə'siːd/ *verb* (often + *to*) go forward or on further, make one's way; (often + *with*, *to do*) continue or resume; adopt course of action; go on to say; (+ *against*) start lawsuit against; (often + *from*) originate.

proceeding *noun* action, piece of conduct; (in *plural*) legal action, published report of discussions or conference.

proceeds /'prəʊsiːdz/ *plural noun* profits from sale etc.

process¹ /'prəʊses/ ● *noun* course of action or proceeding, esp. series of stages in manufacture etc.; progress or course; natural or involuntary course of change; action at law; summons, writ; *Biology* natural appendage or outgrowth of organism. ● *verb* subject to particular process; (as **processed** *adjective*) (of food) treated, esp. to prevent decay.

process² /prə'ses/ *verb* walk in procession.

procession /prə'seʃ(ə)n/ *noun* people etc. advancing in orderly succession, esp. at ceremony, demonstration, or festivity.

processional ● *adjective* of processions; used, carried, or sung in processions. ● *noun* processional hymn (book).

processor /'prəʊsesə/ *noun* machine that processes things; central processor; food processor.

proclaim /prə'kleɪm/ *verb* (often + *that*) announce publicly or officially; declare to be. □ **proclamation** /prɒklə-/ *noun*.

proclivity /prə'klɪvɪtɪ/ *noun* (*plural* **-ies**) natural tendency.

procrastinate /prəʊ'kræstɪneɪt/ *verb* (**-ting**) defer action. □ **procrastination** *noun*.

■ **Usage** *Procrastinate* is often confused with *prevaricate*, which means 'to speak or act evasively or misleadingly'.

procreate /'prəʊkrɪeɪt/ verb (**-ting**) produce (offspring) naturally. □ **procreation** noun; **procreative** /-krɪ'eɪ-/ adjective.

proctor /'prɒktə/ noun university disciplinary official. □ **proctorial** /-'tɔːrɪəl/ adjective.

procuration /prɒkjʊ'reɪʃ(ə)n/ noun formal procuring; action of attorney.

procurator /'prɒkjʊreɪtə/ noun agent or proxy, esp. with power of attorney. □ **procurator fiscal** (in Scotland) local coroner and public prosecutor.

procure /prə'kjʊə/ verb (**-ring**) succeed in getting; bring about; act as procurer. □ **procurement** noun.

procurer noun (feminine **procuress**) person who obtains women for prostitution.

prod ● verb (**-dd-**) poke with finger, stick, etc.; stimulate to action. ● noun poke, thrust; stimulus to action.

prodigal /'prɒdɪg(ə)l/ ● adjective wasteful; (+ of) lavish of. ● noun spendthrift. □ **prodigal son** repentant wastrel. □ **prodigality** /-'gæl-/ noun.

prodigious /prə'dɪdʒəs/ adjective marvellous; enormous; abnormal.

prodigy /'prɒdɪdʒɪ/ noun (plural **-ies**) exceptionally gifted person, esp. precocious child; marvellous thing; (+ of) wonderful example of.

produce ● verb /prə'djuːs/ (**-cing**) manufacture or prepare; bring forward for inspection etc.; bear, yield, or bring into existence; cause or bring about; Geometry extend or continue (line); bring (play etc.) before public. ● noun /'prɒdjuːs/ what is produced, esp. agricultural products; amount produced; (often + of) result.

producer noun person who produces goods etc.; person who supervises production of play, film, broadcast, etc.

product /'prɒdʌkt/ noun thing or substance produced, esp. by manufacture; result; Mathematics quantity obtained by multiplying.

production /prə'dʌkʃ(ə)n/ noun producing, being produced; total yield; thing produced, esp. play etc. □ **production line** systematized sequence of operations to produce commodity.

productive /prə'dʌktɪv/ adjective producing, esp. abundantly. □ **productively** adverb; **productiveness** noun.

productivity /prɒdʌk'tɪvɪtɪ/ noun capacity to produce; effectiveness of industry, workforce, etc.

Prof. abbreviation Professor.

profane /prə'feɪn/ ● adjective irreverent, blasphemous; obscene; not sacred. ● verb (**-ning**) treat irreverently; violate, pollute. □ **profanation** /prɒfə-/ noun.

profanity /prə'fænɪtɪ/ noun (plural **-ies**) blasphemy; swear-word.

profess /prə'fes/ verb claim openly to have; (often + to do) pretend, declare; affirm one's faith in or allegiance to.

professed adjective self-acknowledged; alleged, ostensible. □ **professedly** /-sɪdlɪ/ adverb.

profession /prə'feʃ(ə)n/ noun occupation or calling, esp. learned or scientific; people in a profession; declaration, avowal.

professional ● adjective of, belonging to, or connected with a profession; competent, worthy of professional; engaged in specified activity as paid occupation, or (derogatory) fanatically. ● noun professional person. □ **professionally** adverb.

professionalism noun qualities of professionals, esp. competence, skill, etc.

professor /prə'fesə/ noun highest-ranking academic in university department, US university teacher;

person who professes a religion etc. □ **professorial** /prɒfɪ'sɔːrɪəl/ adjective; **professorship** noun.

proffer /'prɒfə/ verb offer.

proficient /prə'fɪʃ(ə)nt/ adjective (often + in, at) adept, expert. □ **proficiency** noun; **proficiently** adverb.

profile /'prəʊfaɪl/ ● noun side view or outline, esp. of human face; short biographical sketch. ● verb (**-ling**) represent by profile. □ **keep a low profile** remain inconspicuous.

profit /'prɒfɪt/ ● noun advantage, benefit; financial gain, excess of returns over outlay. ● verb (**-t-**) be beneficial to; obtain advantage. □ **at a profit** with financial gain; **profit margin** profit after deduction of costs.

profitable adjective yielding profit; beneficial. □ **profitability** noun; **profitably** adverb.

profiteer /prɒfɪ'tɪə/ ● verb make or seek excessive profits, esp. illegally. ● noun person who profiteers.

profiterole /prə'fɪtərəʊl/ noun small hollow cake of choux pastry with filling.

profligate /'prɒflɪgət/ ● adjective recklessly extravagant; licentious, dissolute. ● noun profligate person. □ **profligacy** noun; **profligately** adverb.

pro forma /prəʊ 'fɔːmə/ ● adverb & adjective for form's sake. ● noun (in full **pro forma invoice**) invoice sent in advance of goods supplied.

profound /prə'faʊnd/ adjective (**-er, -est**) having or demanding great knowledge, study, or insight; intense, thorough; deep. □ **profoundly** adverb; **profoundness** noun; **profundity** /-'fʌndɪtɪ/ noun (plural **-ies**).

profuse /prə'fjuːs/ adjective (often + in, of) lavish, extravagant, copious. □ **profusely** adverb; **profusion** noun.

progenitor /prəʊ'dʒenɪtə/ noun ancestor; predecessor; original.

progeny /'prɒdʒɪnɪ/ noun offspring, descendants; outcome, issue.

progesterone /prəʊ'dʒestərəʊn/ noun a sex hormone that helps to initiate and maintains pregnancy.

prognosis /prɒg'nəʊsɪs/ noun (plural **-noses** /-siːz/) forecast, esp. of course of disease.

prognostic /prɒg'nɒstɪk/ ● noun (often + of) advance indication; prediction. ● adjective (often + of) foretelling, predictive.

prognosticate /prɒg'nɒstɪkeɪt/ verb (**-ting**) (often + that) foretell; betoken. □ **prognostication** noun.

programme /'prəʊgræm/ (US **program**) ● noun list of events, performers, etc.; radio or television broadcast; plan of events; course or series of studies, lectures, etc.; (usually **program**) series of instructions for computer. ● verb (**-mm-**; US **-m-**) make programme of; (usually **program**) express (problem) or instruct (computer) by means of program. □ **programmable** adjective; **programmer** noun.

progress ● noun /'prəʊgres/ forward movement; advance, development, improvement; historical state journey, esp. by royalty. ● verb /prə'gres/ move forward or onward; advance, develop, improve. □ **in progress** developing, going on.

progression /prə'greʃ(ə)n/ noun progressing; succession, series.

progressive /prə'gresɪv/ ● adjective moving forward; proceeding step by step; cumulative; favouring rapid reform; modern, efficient; (of disease etc.) increasing in severity or extent; (of taxation) increasing with the sum taxed. ● noun (also **Progressive**) advocate of progressive policy. □ **progressively** adverb.

prohibit /prə'hɪbɪt/ verb (**-t-**) (often + from) forbid; prevent.

prohibition /prəʊhɪˈbɪʃ(ə)n/ noun forbidding, being forbidden; edict or order that forbids; (usually **Prohibition**) legal ban on manufacture and sale of alcohol. □ **prohibitionist** noun.

prohibitive /prəˈhɪbɪtɪv/ adjective prohibiting; (of prices, taxes, etc.) extremely high. □ **prohibitively** adverb.

project ● noun /ˈprɒdʒekt/ plan, scheme; extensive essay, piece of research, etc. by student(s). ● verb /prəˈdʒekt/ protrude, jut out; throw, impel; forecast; plan; cause (light, image, etc.) to fall on surface; cause (voice etc.) to be heard at distance.

projectile /prəˈdʒektaɪl/ ● noun object to be fired (esp. by rocket) or hurled. ● adjective of or serving as projectile; projecting, impelling.

projection /prəˈdʒekʃ(ə)n/ noun projecting, being projected; thing that protrudes; presentation of image(s) etc. on surface; forecast, estimate; mental image viewed as objective reality; transfer of feelings to other people etc.; representation of earth etc. on plane surface.

projectionist noun person who operates projector.

projector /prəˈdʒektə/ noun apparatus for projecting image or film on screen.

prolactin /prəʊˈlæktɪn/ noun hormone that stimulates milk production after childbirth.

prolapse ● noun /ˈprəʊlæps/ (also **prolapsus** /-ˈlæpsəs/) slipping forward or downward of part or organ; prolapsed womb, rectum, etc. ● verb /prəˈlæps/ (**-sing**) undergo prolapse.

prolate /ˈprəʊleɪt/ adjective (of spheroid) lengthened along polar diameter.

prolegomenon /prəʊlɪˈgɒmɪnən/ noun (plural **-mena**) (usually in plural) preface to book etc., esp. discursive or critical.

proletarian /prəʊlɪˈteərɪən/ ● adjective of proletariat. ● noun member of proletariat.

proletariat /prəʊlɪˈteərɪət/ noun working class; esp. derogatory lowest class.

proliferate /prəˈlɪfəreɪt/ verb (**-ting**) reproduce; produce (cells etc.) rapidly; increase rapidly, multiply. □ **proliferation** noun.

prolific /prəˈlɪfɪk/ adjective producing many offspring or much output; (often + of) abundantly productive; copious.

prolix /ˈprəʊlɪks/ adjective lengthy; tedious. □ **prolixity** /-ˈlɪks-/ noun.

prologue /ˈprəʊlɒg/ noun introduction to poem, play, etc.; (usually + to) introductory event.

prolong /prəˈlɒŋ/ verb extend; (as **prolonged** adjective) (tediously) lengthy. □ **prolongation** /prəʊlɒŋˈgeɪʃ(ə)n/ noun.

prom noun colloquial promenade; promenade concert.

promenade /prɒməˈnɑːd/ ● noun paved public walk, esp. at seaside; leisure walk. ● verb (**-ding**) make promenade (through); lead about, esp. for display.

□ **promenade concert** one at which (part of) audience is not seated; **promenade deck** upper deck on liner.

promenader noun person who promenades; regular attender at promenade concerts.

prominent /ˈprɒmɪnənt/ adjective jutting out; conspicuous; distinguished. □ **prominence** noun.

promiscuous /prəˈmɪskjʊəs/ adjective having frequent casual sexual relationships; mixed and indiscriminate; colloquial casual. □ **promiscuously** adverb; **promiscuity** /prɒmɪsˈkjuːɪtɪ/ noun.

promise /ˈprɒmɪs/ ● noun explicit undertaking to do or not to do something; favourable indications. ● verb (**-sing**) (usually + to do, that) make promise; (often + to do) seem likely; colloquial assure.

promising adjective likely to turn out well; hopeful, full of promise. □ **promisingly** adverb.

promissory /ˈprɒmɪsərɪ/ adjective expressing or implying promise. □ **promissory note** signed document containing promise to pay stated sum.

promontory /ˈprɒməntərɪ/ noun (plural **-ies**) point of high land jutting out into sea etc.; headland.

promote /prəˈməʊt/ verb (**-ting**) (often + to) advance (person) to higher office or position; help forward, encourage; publicize and sell. □ **promotion** noun; **promotional** adjective.

promoter noun person who promotes, esp. sporting event, theatrical production, etc., or formation of joint-stock company.

prompt ● adjective acting, made, or done immediately; ready. ● adverb punctually. ● verb (usually + to, to do) incite; supply (actor, speaker) with next words or with suggestion; inspire. ● noun prompting; thing said to prompt actor etc.; sign on computer screen inviting input. □ **promptitude** noun; **promptly** adverb; **promptness** noun.

prompter noun person who prompts actors.

promulgate /ˈprɒmʌlgeɪt/ verb (**-ting**) make known to the public; proclaim. □ **promulgation** noun.

prone adjective lying face downwards; lying flat, prostrate; (usually + to, to do) disposed, liable. □ **-prone** likely to suffer. □ **proneness** noun.

prong noun spike of fork.

pronominal /prəʊˈnɒmɪn(ə)l/ adjective of, concerning, or being a pronoun.

pronoun /ˈprəʊnaʊn/ noun word used as substitute for noun or noun phrase usually already mentioned or known (see panel).

pronounce /prəˈnaʊns/ verb (**-cing**) utter or speak, esp. in approved manner; utter formally; state (as) one's opinion; (usually + on, for, against, etc.) pass judgement. □ **pronounceable** adjective; **pronouncement** noun.

pronounced adjective strongly marked.

pronto /ˈprɒntəʊ/ adverb colloquial promptly, quickly.

Pronoun

A pronoun is used as a substitute for a noun or a noun phrase, e.g.

He *was upstairs.*   *Did you see* that?
Anything *can happen now.*   It's *lovely weather.*

Using a pronoun often avoids repetition, e.g.

I found Jim—he *was upstairs.*
(instead of *I found Jim—Jim was upstairs.*)

Where are your keys?—I've *got* them.
(instead of *Where are your keys?—I've got my keys.*)

pronunciation /prənʌnsɪˈeɪʃ(ə)n/ *noun* pronouncing of word, esp. with reference to standard; act of pronouncing; way of pronouncing words.

proof /pruːf/ ● *noun* fact, evidence, reasoning, or demonstration that proves something; test, trial; standard of strength of distilled alcohol; trial impression of printed matter for correction. ● *adjective* (often + *against*) impervious to penetration, damage, etc. by a specified thing. ● *verb* make proof, esp. against water or bullets. □ **proofread** read and correct (printed proof); **proofreader** person who does this.

prop[1] ● *noun* rigid support; person or thing that supports, comforts, etc. ● *verb* (**-pp-**) (often + *against, up*, etc.) support (as) with prop.

prop[2] *noun colloquial* stage property.

prop[3] *noun colloquial* propeller.

propaganda /prɒpəˈɡændə/ *noun* organized propagation of a doctrine etc.; *usually derogatory* ideas etc. so propagated. □ **propagandist** *noun*.

propagate /ˈprɒpəɡeɪt/ *verb* (**-ting**) breed from parent stock; (often **propagate itself**) (of plant etc.) reproduce itself; disseminate; transmit. □ **propagation** *noun*; **propagator** *noun*.

propane /ˈprəʊpeɪn/ *noun* gaseous hydrocarbon used as fuel.

propel /prəˈpel/ *verb* (**-ll-**) drive or push forward; urge on. □ **propellant** *noun & adjective*.

propeller *noun* revolving shaft with blades, esp. for propelling ship or aircraft.

propensity /prəˈpensɪtɪ/ *noun* (*plural* **-ies**) inclination, tendency.

proper /ˈprɒpə/ *adjective* accurate, correct; suitable; appropriate; decent, respectable; (usually + *to*) belonging, relating; strictly so called, genuine; *colloquial* thorough. □ **proper name, noun** name of person, place, etc. □ **properly** *adverb*.

property /ˈprɒpətɪ/ *noun* (*plural* **-ies**) thing(s) owned; landed estate; quality, characteristic; movable article used on theatre stage or in film.

prophecy /ˈprɒfɪsɪ/ *noun* (*plural* **-ies**) prophetic utterance; prediction; prophesying.

prophesy /ˈprɒfɪsaɪ/ *verb* (**-ies, -ied**) (usually + *that, who*, etc.) foretell; speak as prophet.

prophet /ˈprɒfɪt/ *noun* (*feminine* **prophetess**) teacher or interpreter of divine will; person who predicts; (**the Prophet**) Muhammad.

prophetic /prəˈfetɪk/ *adjective* (often + *of*) containing a prediction, predicting; of prophet.

prophylactic /prɒfɪˈlæktɪk/ ● *adjective* tending to prevent disease etc. ● *noun* preventive medicine or action; *esp. US* condom.

prophylaxis /prɒfɪˈlæksɪs/ *noun* preventive treatment against disease.

propinquity /prəˈpɪŋkwɪtɪ/ *noun* nearness; close kinship; similarity.

propitiate /prəˈpɪʃɪeɪt/ *verb* (**-ting**) appease. □ **propitiation** *noun*; **propitiatory** /-ʃətərɪ/ *adjective*.

propitious /prəˈpɪʃəs/ *adjective* favourable, auspicious; (often + *for, to*) suitable.

proponent /prəˈpəʊnənt/ *noun* person advocating proposal etc.

proportion /prəˈpɔːʃ(ə)n/ ● *noun* comparative part, share; comparative ratio; correct relation between things or parts of thing; (in *plural*) dimensions. ● *verb* (usually + *to*) make proportionate.

proportional *adjective* in correct proportion; comparable. □ **proportional representation** representation of parties in parliament in proportion to votes they receive. □ **proportionally** *adverb*.

proportionate /prəˈpɔːʃənət/ *adjective* proportional. □ **proportionately** *adverb*.

proposal /prəˈpəʊz(ə)l/ *noun* proposing; scheme etc. proposed; offer of marriage.

propose /prəˈpəʊz/ *verb* (**-sing**) put forward for consideration; (usually + *to do*) purpose; (usually + *to*) offer marriage; nominate as member of society etc. □ **propose a toast** ask people to drink to health or in honour of person or thing. □ **proposer** *noun*.

proposition /prɒpəˈzɪʃ(ə)n/ ● *noun* statement, assertion; scheme proposed, proposal; statement subject to proof or disproof; *colloquial* problem, opponent, prospect, etc.; *Mathematics* formal statement of theorem or problem; likely commercial enterprise, person, etc.; sexual proposal. ● *verb colloquial* put (esp. sexual) proposal to.

propound /prəˈpaʊnd/ *verb* offer for consideration.

proprietary /prəˈpraɪətərɪ/ *adjective* of or holding property; of proprietor; held in private ownership; manufactured by one particular firm. □ **proprietary name, term** name of product etc. registered as trade mark.

proprietor /prəˈpraɪətə/ *noun* (*feminine* **proprietress**) owner. □ **proprietorial** /-ˈtɔːr-/ *adjective*.

propriety /prəˈpraɪɪtɪ/ *noun* (*plural* **-ies**) fitness, rightness; correctness of behaviour or morals; (in *plural*) rules of polite behaviour.

propulsion /prəˈpʌlʃ(ə)n/ *noun* driving or pushing forward; force causing this. □ **propulsive** /-ˈpʌlsɪv/ *adjective*.

pro rata /prəʊ ˈrɑːtə/ ● *adjective* proportional. ● *adverb* proportionally. [Latin]

prorogue /prəˈrəʊg/ *verb* (**-gues, -gued, -guing**) discontinue meetings of (parliament etc.) without dissolving (it); be prorogued. □ **prorogation** /prəʊrə-/ *noun*.

prosaic /prəˈzeɪɪk/ *adjective* like prose; unromantic; commonplace. □ **prosaically** *adverb*.

proscenium /prəˈsiːnɪəm/ *noun* (*plural* **-s** or **-nia**) part of theatre stage in front of curtain and enclosing arch.

proscribe /prəˈskraɪb/ *verb* (**-bing**) forbid; denounce; outlaw. □ **proscription** /-ˈskrɪp-/ *noun*; **proscriptive** /-ˈskrɪp-/ *adjective*.

■ **Usage** *Proscribe* is sometimes confused with *prescribe* which means 'to impose'.

prose /prəʊz/ ● *noun* ordinary language not in verse; passage of this, esp. for translation; dullness. ● *verb* (**-sing**) talk tediously.

prosecute /ˈprɒsɪkjuːt/ *verb* (**-ting**) institute legal proceedings against; *formal* carry on (trade etc.). □ **prosecutor** *noun*.

prosecution /prɒsɪˈkjuːʃ(ə)n/ *noun* prosecuting, being prosecuted; prosecuting party.

proselyte /ˈprɒsəlaɪt/ *noun* convert, esp. recent; convert to Jewish faith. □ **proselytism** /-lɪtɪz(ə)m/ *noun*.

proselytize /ˈprɒsələtaɪz/ *verb* (also **-ise**) (**-zing** or **-sing**) (seek to) convert.

prosody /ˈprɒsədɪ/ *noun* science of versification. □ **prosodist** *noun*.

prospect ● *noun* /ˈprɒspekt/ (often in *plural*) expectation; extensive view; mental picture; possible or likely customer etc. ● *verb* /prəˈspekt/ (usually + *for*) explore (for gold etc.). □ **prospector** *noun*.

prospective /prəˈspektɪv/ *adjective* some day to be, expected, future.

prospectus /prəˈspektəs/ *noun* (*plural* **-tuses**) pamphlet etc. advertising or describing school, business, etc.

prosper /ˈprɒspə/ *verb* succeed, thrive.

prosperity /prɒˈsperɪtɪ/ *noun* prosperous state.

prosperous /'prɒspərəs/ adjective successful, rich, thriving; auspicious. ☐ **prosperously** adverb.

prostate /'prɒsteɪt/ noun (in full **prostate gland**) gland secreting component of semen. ☐ **prostatic** /-'stæt-/ adjective.

prostitute /'prɒstɪtjuːt/ ● noun person who offers sexual intercourse for payment. ● verb (**-ting**) make prostitute of; misuse, offer for sale unworthily. ☐ **prostitution** noun.

prostrate ● adjective /'prɒstreɪt/ lying face downwards, esp. in submission; lying horizontally; overcome, esp. exhausted. ● verb /prɒs'treɪt/ (**-ting**) lay or throw flat; overcome, make weak. ☐ **prostration** noun.

prosy /'prəʊzɪ/ adjective (**-ier**, **-iest**) tedious, commonplace, dull.

protagonist /prə'tægənɪst/ noun chief person in drama, story, etc.; supporter of cause.

■ **Usage** The use of protagonist to mean 'a supporter of a cause' is considered incorrect by some people.

protean /'prəʊtɪən/ adjective variable, versatile.

protect /prə'tekt/ verb (often + from, against) keep (person etc.) safe; shield.

protection /prə'tekʃ(ə)n/ noun protecting, being protected, defence; person etc. that protects; protectionism; colloquial immunity from violence etc. by paying gangsters etc.

protectionism noun theory or practice of protecting home industries. ☐ **protectionist** noun & adjective.

protective /prə'tektɪv/ adjective protecting; intended for or giving protection. ☐ **protective custody** detention of person for his or her own protection. ☐ **protectively** adverb; **protectiveness** noun.

protector noun (feminine **protectress**) person or thing that protects; historical regent ruling during minority or absence of sovereign. ☐ **protectorship** noun.

protectorate /prə'tektərət/ noun state controlled and protected by another; such protectorship; historical office of protector of kingdom or state; period of this.

protégé /'prɒtɪʒeɪ/ noun (feminine **protégée** same pronunciation) person under protection, patronage, etc. of another.

protein /'prəʊtiːn/ noun any of a class of nitrogenous compounds essential in all living organisms.

pro tem /prəʊ 'tem/ adjective & adverb colloquial for the time being (pro tempore).

protest ● noun /'prəʊtest/ expression of dissent or disapproval; legal written refusal to pay or accept bill. ● verb /prə'test/ (usually + against, at, about, etc.) make protest; affirm (innocence etc.); write or get protest relating to (bill); US object to. ☐ **protester, protestor** noun.

Protestant /'prɒtɪst(ə)nt/ ● noun member or adherent of any of Churches separated from RC Church in Reformation. ● adjective of Protestant Churches or Protestants. ☐ **Protestantism** noun.

protestation /prɒtɪs'teɪʃ(ə)n/ noun strong affirmation; protest.

proto- combining form first.

protocol /'prəʊtəkɒl/ ● noun official formality and etiquette; draft, esp. of terms of treaty. ● verb (**-ll-**) draft or record in protocol.

proton /'prəʊtɒn/ noun elementary particle with positive electric charge equal to electron's, and occurring in all atomic nuclei.

protoplasm /'prəʊtəplæz(ə)m/ noun viscous translucent substance comprising living part of cell in organism. ☐ **protoplasmic** /-'plæzmɪk/ adjective.

prototype /'prəʊtətaɪp/ noun original as pattern for copy, improved form, etc.; trial model of vehicle, machine, etc. ☐ **prototypic** /-'tɪp-/ adjective; **prototypical** /-'tɪp-/ adjective.

protozoan /prəʊtə'zəʊən/ ● noun (plural **-s**) (also **protozoon** /-'zəʊɒn/, plural **-zoa** /-'zəʊə/) one-celled microscopic organism. ● adjective (also **protozoic** /-'zəʊɪk/) of protozoa.

protract /prə'trækt/ verb (often as **protracted** adjective) prolong, lengthen. ☐ **protraction** noun.

protractor noun instrument for measuring angles, usually in form of graduated semicircle.

protrude /prə'truːd/ verb (**-ding**) thrust forward; stick out. ☐ **protrusion** noun; **protrusive** adjective.

protuberant /prə'tjuːbərənt/ adjective bulging out; prominent. ☐ **protuberance** noun.

proud /praʊd/ adjective feeling greatly honoured; haughty, arrogant; (often + of) feeling or showing (proper) pride; imposing, splendid; (often + of) slightly projecting. ☐ **do (person) proud** colloquial treat with great generosity or honour. ☐ **proudly** adverb.

prove /pruːv/ verb (**-ving**; past participle **proved** or esp. US & Scottish **proven** /'pruːv(ə)n/) (often + that) demonstrate to be true by evidence or argument; (**prove oneself**) show one's abilities etc.; (usually + to be) be found; test accuracy of; establish validity of (will); (of dough) rise. ☐ **provable** adjective.

■ **Usage** The use of proven as the past participle is uncommon except in certain expressions, such as of proven ability. It is, however, standard in Scots and American English.

provenance /'prɒvɪnəns/ noun (place of) origin; history.

provender /'prɒvɪndə/ noun fodder; jocular food.

proverb /'prɒvɜːb/ noun short pithy saying in general use.

proverbial /prə'vɜːbɪəl/ adjective notorious; of or referred to in proverbs. ☐ **proverbially** adverb.

provide /prə'vaɪd/ verb (**-ding**) supply; (usually + for, against) make due preparation; (usually + for) take care of person etc. with money, food, etc.; (often + that) stipulate. ☐ **provided, providing** (often + that) on condition or understanding that.

providence /'prɒvɪd(ə)ns/ noun protective care of God or nature; (**Providence**) God; foresight, thrift.

provident /'prɒvɪd(ə)nt/ adjective having or showing foresight, thrifty.

providential /prɒvɪ'denʃ(ə)l/ adjective of or by divine foresight or intervention; opportune, lucky. ☐ **providentially** adverb.

province /'prɒvɪns/ noun principal administrative division of country etc.; (**the provinces**) whole of country outside capital; sphere of action; branch of learning.

provincial /prə'vɪnʃ(ə)l/ ● adjective of province(s); unsophisticated, uncultured. ● noun inhabitant of province(s); unsophisticated or uncultured person. ☐ **provincialism** noun.

provision /prə'vɪʒ(ə)n/ ● noun providing; (in plural) food and drink, esp. for expedition; legal or formal stipulation. ● verb supply with provisions.

provisional ● adjective providing for immediate needs only, temporary; (**Provisional**) of the unofficial wing of the IRA. ● noun (**Provisional**) member of unofficial wing of IRA. ☐ **provisionally** adverb.

proviso /prə'vaɪzəʊ/ noun (plural **-s**) stipulation; limiting clause. ☐ **provisory** adjective.

provocation /prɒvə'keɪʃ(ə)n/ noun provoking, being provoked; cause of annoyance.

provocative /prə'vɒkətɪv/ adjective (usually + of) tending or intended to provoke anger, lust, etc. ☐ **provocatively** adverb.

provoke /prəˈvəʊk/ verb (**-king**) (often + to, to do) rouse, incite; call forth, cause; (usually + into) irritate, stimulate; tempt.

provost /ˈprɒvəst/ noun head of some colleges; head of cathedral chapter; /prəˈvəʊ/ (in full **provost marshal**) head of military police in camp or on active service.

prow /praʊ/ noun bow of ship; pointed or projecting front part.

prowess /ˈpraʊɪs/ noun skill, expertise; valour, gallantry.

prowl /praʊl/ ● verb (often + about, around) roam, esp. stealthily in search of prey, plunder, etc. ● noun prowling. □ **prowler** noun.

prox. abbreviation proximo.

proximate /ˈprɒksɪmət/ adjective nearest, next before or after.

proximity /prɒkˈsɪmɪtɪ/ noun nearness.

proximo /ˈprɒksɪməʊ/ adjective of next month.

proxy /ˈprɒksɪ/ noun (plural **-ies**) authorization given to deputy; person authorized to deputize; document authorizing person to vote on another's behalf; vote so given.

prude noun excessively squeamish or sexually modest person. □ **prudery** noun; **prudish** adjective; **prudishly** adverb; **prudishness** noun.

prudent /ˈpruːd(ə)nt/ adjective cautious; politic. □ **prudence** noun; **prudently** adverb.

prudential /pruːˈdenʃ(ə)l/ adjective of or showing prudence.

prune¹ noun dried plum.

prune² verb (**-ning**) (often + down) trim (tree etc.) by cutting away dead or overgrown parts; (usually + off, away) remove (branches etc.) thus; reduce (costs etc.); (often + of) clear superfluities from; remove (superfluities).

prurient /ˈprʊərɪənt/ adjective having or encouraging unhealthy sexual curiosity. □ **prurience** noun.

Prussian /ˈprʌʃ(ə)n/ ● adjective of Prussia. ● noun native of Prussia. □ **Prussian blue** deep blue (pigment).

prussic acid /ˈprʌsɪk/ noun highly poisonous liquid.

pry /praɪ/ verb (**pries**, **pried**) (usually + into etc.) inquire impertinently, look inquisitively.

PS abbreviation postscript.

psalm /sɑːm/ noun (also **Psalm**) sacred song; (**the (Book of) Psalms**) book of these in Old Testament.

psalmist /ˈsɑːmɪst/ noun author or composer of psalm(s).

psalmody /ˈsɑːmədɪ/ noun practice or art of singing psalms.

Psalter /ˈsɔːltə/ noun Book of Psalms; (**psalter**) version or copy of this.

psaltery /ˈsɔːltərɪ/ noun (plural **-ies**) ancient and medieval plucked stringed instrument.

psephology /sɪˈfɒlədʒɪ/ noun statistical study of voting etc. □ **psephologist** noun.

pseudo- combining form (also **pseud-** before vowel) false, not genuine; resembling, imitating.

pseudonym /ˈsjuːdənɪm/ noun fictitious name, esp. of author.

psoriasis /səˈraɪəsɪs/ noun skin disease with red scaly patches.

PSV abbreviation public service vehicle.

psych /saɪk/ verb colloquial (usually + up) prepare mentally; (often + out) intimidate; (usually + out) analyse (person's motivation etc.).

psyche /ˈsaɪkɪ/ noun soul, spirit, mind.

psychedelic /saɪkəˈdelɪk/ adjective expanding the mind's awareness, hallucinatory; vivid in colour, design, etc.

psychiatry /saɪˈkaɪətrɪ/ noun study and treatment of mental disease. □ **psychiatric** /-krˈætrɪk/ adjective; **psychiatrist** noun.

psychic /ˈsaɪkɪk/ ● adjective (of person) regarded as having paranormal powers, clairvoyant; of the soul or mind. ● noun psychic person, medium.

psychical adjective concerning psychic phenomena or faculties; of the soul or mind.

psycho- combining form of mind or psychology.

psychoanalysis /saɪkəʊəˈnælɪsɪs/ noun treatment of mental disorders by bringing repressed fears etc. into conscious mind. □ **psychoanalyse** /-ˈænəl-/ verb (**-sing**); **psychoanalyst** /-ˈænəl-/ noun; **psychoanalytical** /-ænəˈlɪt-/ adjective.

psychokinesis /saɪkəʊkɪˈniːsɪs/ noun movement of objects by telepathy.

psychological /saɪkəˈlɒdʒɪk(ə)l/ adjective of the mind; of psychology; colloquial imaginary. □ **psychological block** inhibition caused by emotion; **psychological moment** best time to achieve purpose; **psychological warfare** campaign to reduce enemy's morale. □ **psychologically** adverb.

psychology /saɪˈkɒlədʒɪ/ noun (plural **-ies**) study of human mind; treatise on or theory of this; mental characteristics. □ **psychologist** noun.

psychopath /ˈsaɪkəpæθ/ noun mentally deranged person, esp. with abnormal social behaviour; mentally or emotionally unstable person. □ **psychopathic** /-ˈpæθ-/ adjective.

psychosis /saɪˈkəʊsɪs/ noun (plural **-choses** /-siːz/) severe mental derangement involving loss of contact with reality.

psychosomatic /saɪkəʊsəˈmætɪk/ adjective (of disease) mental, not physical, in origin; of both mind and body.

psychotherapy /saɪkəʊˈθerəpɪ/ noun treatment of mental disorder by psychological means. □ **psychotherapist** noun.

psychotic /saɪˈkɒtɪk/ ● adjective of or suffering from psychosis. ● noun psychotic person.

PT abbreviation physical training.

pt abbreviation part; pint; point; port.

PTA abbreviation parent–teacher association.

ptarmigan /ˈtɑːmɪɡən/ noun bird of grouse family.

Pte. abbreviation Private (soldier).

pteridophyte /ˈterɪdəfaɪt/ noun flowerless plant.

pterodactyl /terəˈdæktɪl/ noun large extinct flying reptile.

PTO abbreviation please turn over.

ptomaine /ˈtəʊmeɪn/ noun any of a group of compounds (some toxic) in putrefying matter.

pub noun colloquial public house.

puberty /ˈpjuːbətɪ/ noun period of sexual maturing.

pubes¹ /ˈpjuːbiːz/ noun (plural same) lower part of abdomen.

pubes² plural of PUBIS.

pubescence /pjuːˈbes(ə)ns/ noun beginning of puberty; soft down on plant or animal. □ **pubescent** adjective.

pubic /ˈpjuːbɪk/ adjective of pubes or pubis.

pubis /ˈpjuːbɪs/ noun (plural **pubes** /-biːz/) front portion of hip bone.

public /ˈpʌblɪk/ ● adjective of the people as a whole; open to or shared by all; done or existing openly; of or from government; involved in community affairs. ● noun (treated as singular or plural) (members of) community as a whole; section of community. □ **go public** (of company) start selling shares on open market, reveal one's plans; **in public** publicly, openly; **public address system** equipment of loudspeakers etc.; **public convenience** public lavatory; **public figure** famous person; **public house** place selling alcoholic drink for consumption on premises; **public lending right** right of authors to payment when their books are lent by public libraries; **public relations** professional promotion of company, product, etc.; **public school** independent fee-paying school; *US, Australian, Scottish, etc.* non-fee-paying school; **public-spirited** ready to do things for the community; **public transport** buses, trains, etc. available for public use on fixed routes; **public utility** organization supplying water, gas, etc. to community. ☐ **publicly** *adverb*.

publican /ˈpʌblɪkən/ *noun* keeper of public house.

publication /pʌblɪˈkeɪʃ(ə)n/ *noun* publishing; published book, periodical, etc.

publicist /ˈpʌblɪsɪst/ *noun* publicity agent, public relations officer.

publicity /pʌbˈlɪsɪtɪ/ *noun* (means of attracting) public attention; (material used for) advertising.

publicize /ˈpʌblɪsaɪz/ *verb* (also **-ise**) (**-zing** or **-sing**) advertise, make publicly known.

publish /ˈpʌblɪʃ/ *verb* prepare and issue (book, magazine, etc.) for public sale; make generally known; formally announce.

publisher *noun* person or firm that publishes books etc.

puce /pjuːs/ *adjective & noun* purplebrown.

puck¹ *noun* rubber disc used in ice hockey.

puck² *noun* mischievous sprite. ☐ **puckish** *adjective*; **puckishly** *adverb*; **puckishness** *noun*.

pucker /ˈpʌkə/ *verb* (often + *up*) gather into wrinkles, folds, or bulges. ● *noun* such wrinkle etc.

pudding /ˈpʊdɪŋ/ *noun* sweet cooked dish; savoury dish containing flour, suet, etc.; sweet course of meal; kind of sausage.

puddle /ˈpʌd(ə)l/ *noun* small (dirty) pool; clay made into watertight coating.

pudenda /pjuːˈdendə/ *plural noun* genitals, esp. of woman.

pudgy /ˈpʌdʒɪ/ *adjective* (**-ier**, **-iest**) *colloquial* plump, podgy.

puerile /ˈpjʊəraɪl/ *adjective* childish, immature. ☐ **puerility** /-ˈrɪl-/ *noun* (*plural* **-ies**).

puerperal /pjuːˈɜːpər(ə)l/ *adjective* of or due to childbirth.

puff ● *noun* short quick blast of breath or wind; sound (as) of this; vapour or smoke sent out in one blast; light pastry cake; gathered material in dress etc.; unduly enthusiastic review, advertisement, etc. ● *verb* emit puff(s); smoke or move with puffs; (usually in *passive*; often + *out*) *colloquial* put out of breath; pant; (usually + *up, out*) inflate; (usually as **puffed up** *adjective*) elate, make boastful; advertise in exaggerated terms. ☐ **puff-adder** large venomous African viper; **puffball** ball-shaped fungus; **puff pastry** pastry consisting of thin layers.

puffin /ˈpʌfɪn/ *noun* N. Atlantic and N. Pacific auk with short striped bill.

puffy *adjective* (**-ier**, **-iest**) swollen, puffed out; *colloquial* short-winded.

pug *noun* (in full **pug-dog**) dog of small breed with flat nose. ☐ **pug-nose** short flat or snub nose.

pugilist /ˈpjuːdʒɪlɪst/ *noun* boxer. ☐ **pugilism** *noun*; **pugilistic** /-ˈlɪs-/ *adjective*.

pugnacious /pʌgˈneɪʃəs/ *adjective* disposed to fight. ☐ **pugnaciously** *adverb*; **pugnacity** /-ˈnæs-/ *noun*.

puissance /ˈpwiːsɑ̃s/ *noun* jumping of large obstacles in showjumping.

puissant /ˈpwiːsɒnt/ *adjective* *literary* powerful; mighty.

puke /pjuːk/ *verb & noun* (**-king**) *slang* vomit. ☐ **pukey** *adjective*.

pukka /ˈpʌkə/ *adjective* *colloquial* genuine; reliable.

pulchritude /ˈpʌlkrɪtjuːd/ *noun* *literary* beauty. ☐ **pulchritudinous** /-ˈtjuːdməs/ *adjective*.

pull /pʊl/ ● *verb* exert force on (thing etc.) to move it to oneself or origin of force; exert pulling force; extract by pulling; damage (muscle etc.) by abnormal strain; proceed with effort; (+ *on*) draw (weapon) against (person); attract; draw (liquor) from barrel etc.; (+ *at*) pluck at; (often + *on, at*) inhale or drink deeply, suck. ● *noun* act of pulling; force thus exerted; influence; advantage; attraction; deep draught of liquor; prolonged effort; handle etc. for applying pull; printer's rough proof; suck at cigarette. ☐ **pull back** retreat; **pull down** demolish; **pull in** arrive to take passengers, move to side of or off road, *colloquial* earn, *colloquial* arrest; **pull-in** roadside café etc.; **pull off** remove, win, manage successfully; **pull oneself together** recover control of oneself; **pull out** take out, depart, withdraw, leave station or stop, move towards off side; **pull-out** removable section of magazine; **pull round, through** (cause to) recover from illness; **pull strings** exert (esp. clandestine) influence; **pull together** work in harmony; **pull up** (cause to) stop moving, pull out of ground, reprimand, check oneself.

pullet /ˈpʊlɪt/ *noun* young hen, esp. less than one year old.

pulley /ˈpʊlɪ/ *noun* (*plural* **-s**) grooved wheel(s) for cord etc. to run over, mounted in block and used to lift weight etc.; wheel or drum mounted on shaft and turned by belt, used to increase speed or power.

Pullman /ˈpʊlmən/ *noun* (*plural* **-s**) luxurious railway carriage or motor coach; sleeping car.

pullover *noun* knitted garment put on over the head.

pullulate /ˈpʌljʊleɪt/ *verb* (**-ting**) sprout; swarm; develop; (+ *with*) abound with. ☐ **pullulation** *noun*.

pulmonary /ˈpʌlmənərɪ/ *adjective* of lungs; having (organs like) lungs; affected with or subject to lung disease.

pulp ● *noun* fleshy part of fruit etc.; soft shapeless mass, esp. of materials for papermaking; cheap fiction. ● *verb* reduce to or become pulp. ☐ **pulpy** *adjective*; **pulpiness** *noun*.

pulpit /ˈpʊlpɪt/ *noun* raised enclosed platform for preaching from; (**the pulpit**) preachers collectively, preaching.

pulsar /ˈpʌlsɑː/ *noun* cosmic source of regular rapid pulses of radiation.

pulsate /pʌlˈseɪt/ *verb* (**-ting**) expand and contract rhythmically; throb, vibrate, quiver. ☐ **pulsation** *noun*.

pulse¹ ● *noun* rhythmical throbbing of arteries; each beat of arteries or heart; throb or thrill of life or emotion; general feeling; single vibration of sound, electromagnetic radiation, etc.; rhythmical (esp. musical) beat. ● *verb* (**-sing**) pulsate.

pulse² *noun* (treated as *singular* or *plural*) (plant producing) edible seeds of peas, beans, lentils, etc.

pulverize /ˈpʌlvəraɪz/ *verb* (also **-ise**) (**-zing** or **-sing**) reduce or crumble to powder or dust; *colloquial* demolish, crush. ☐ **pulverization** *noun*.

puma /ˈpjuːmə/ *noun* large tawny American feline.

pumice /ˈpʌmɪs/ *noun* (in full **pumice stone**) light porous lava used as abrasive; piece of this.

pummel /ˈpʌm(ə)l/ *verb* (**-ll-**; *US* **-l-**) strike repeatedly, esp. with fists.

pump¹ ● *noun* machine or device for raising or moving liquids or gases; act of pumping. ● *verb* (often + *in, out, up*, etc.) raise, remove, inflate, empty, etc. (as) with pump; work pump; persistently question (person) to elicit information; move vigorously up and down. ☐ **pump iron** *colloquial* exercise with weights.

pump² *noun* plimsoll; light shoe for dancing etc.

pumpernickel /ˈpʌmpənɪk(ə)l/ noun wholemeal rye bread.

pumpkin /ˈpʌmpkɪn/ noun large yellow or orange fruit used as vegetable; plant bearing it.

pun ● noun humorous use of word(s) with two or more meanings, play on words. ● verb (-nn-) (usually + on) make pun(s).

Punch noun grotesque humpbacked puppet in *Punch and Judy* shows.

punch¹ ● verb strike with fist; make hole in (as) with punch; pierce (hole) thus. ● noun blow with fist; *colloquial* vigour, effective force; instrument or machine for piercing holes or impressing design in leather, metal, etc. □ **pull one's punches** avoid using full force; **punchball** stuffed or inflated ball used for practice in punching; **punch-drunk** stupefied (as) with repeated punches; **punchline** words giving point of joke etc.; **punch-up** *colloquial* fist-fight, brawl. □ **puncher** noun.

punch² noun hot or cold mixture of wine or spirit with water, fruit, spices, etc. □ **punch-bowl** bowl for punch; deep round hollow in hill.

punchy adjective (-ier, -iest) vigorous, forceful.

punctilio /pʌŋkˈtɪliəʊ/ noun (plural -s) delicate point of ceremony or honour; petty formality.

punctilious /pʌŋkˈtɪliəs/ adjective attentive to formality or etiquette; precise in behaviour. □ **punctiliously** adverb; **punctiliousness** noun.

punctual /ˈpʌŋktʃʊəl/ adjective observing appointed time; prompt. □ **punctuality** /-ˈæl-/ noun; **punctually** adverb.

punctuate /ˈpʌŋktʃʊeɪt/ verb (-ting) insert punctuation marks in; interrupt at intervals.

punctuation noun (system of) punctuating. □ **punctuation mark** any of the marks used in writing to separate sentences, phrases, etc.

puncture /ˈpʌŋktʃə/ ● noun prick, pricking; hole made by this. ● verb (-ring) make or suffer puncture (in); deflate.

pundit /ˈpʌndɪt/ noun (also **pandit**) learned Hindu; expert.

pungent /ˈpʌndʒ(ə)nt/ adjective having sharp or strong taste or smell; biting, caustic. □ **pungency** noun.

punish /ˈpʌnɪʃ/ verb inflict penalty on (offender) or for (offence); tax, abuse, or treat severely. □ **punishable** adjective; **punishment** noun.

punitive /ˈpjuːnɪtɪv/ adjective inflicting or intended to inflict punishment; extremely severe.

punk noun (in full **punk rock**) deliberately outrageous style of rock music; (in full **punk rocker**) fan of this; *esp. US* hooligan, lout.

punkah /ˈpʌŋkə/ noun large swinging fan on frame worked by cord or electrically.

punnet /ˈpʌnɪt/ noun small basket for fruit etc.

punster /ˈpʌnstə/ noun maker of puns.

punt¹ ● noun square-ended flat-bottomed boat propelled by long pole. ● verb travel or carry in punt.

punt² ● verb kick (football) dropped from hands before it reaches ground. ● noun such kick.

punt³ verb *colloquial* bet, speculate in shares etc.; (in some card games) lay stake against bank.

punt⁴ /pʊnt/ noun chief monetary unit of Republic of Ireland.

punter noun *colloquial* person who gambles or bets; customer, client.

puny /ˈpjuːnɪ/ adjective (-ier, -iest) undersized; feeble.

pup ● noun young dog, wolf, rat, seal, etc. ● verb (-pp-) give birth to (pups).

pupa /ˈpjuːpə/ noun (plural **pupae** /-piː/) insect in stage between larva and imago.

pupil¹ /ˈpjuːpɪl/ noun person being taught.

pupil² /ˈpjuːpɪl/ noun opening in centre of iris of eye.

puppet /ˈpʌpɪt/ noun small figure moved esp. by strings as entertainment; person controlled by another. □ **puppet state** country apparently independent but actually under control of another power. □ **puppetry** noun.

puppy /ˈpʌpɪ/ noun (plural -ies) young dog; conceited young man. □ **puppy fat** temporary fatness of child or adolescent; **puppy love** calf love.

purblind /ˈpɜːblaɪnd/ adjective partly blind, dim-sighted; obtuse, dull. □ **purblindness** noun.

purchase /ˈpɜːtʃəs/ ● verb (-sing) buy. ● noun buying; thing bought; firm hold on thing, leverage; equipment for moving heavy objects. □ **purchaser** noun.

purdah /ˈpɜːdə/ noun screening of Muslim or Hindu women from strangers.

pure /pjʊə/ adjective unmixed, unadulterated; chaste; not morally corrupt; guiltless; sincere; not discordant; (of science) abstract, not applied. □ **pureness** noun; **purity** noun.

purée /ˈpjʊəreɪ/ ● noun smooth pulp of vegetables or fruit etc. ● verb (-ées, -éed) make purée of.

purely adverb in a pure way; merely, solely, exclusively.

purgative /ˈpɜːɡətɪv/ ● adjective serving to purify; strongly laxative. ● noun purgative thing.

purgatory /ˈpɜːɡətərɪ/ ● noun (plural -ies) place or state of spiritual cleansing, esp. after death and before entering heaven; place or state of temporary suffering or expiation. ● adjective purifying. □ **purgatorial** /-ˈtɔːrɪəl/ adjective.

purge /pɜːdʒ/ ● verb (-ging) (often + of, from) make physically or spiritually clean; remove by cleansing; rid of unacceptable members; empty (bowels); *Law* atone for (offence). ● noun purging; purgative.

purify /ˈpjʊərɪfaɪ/ verb (-ies, -ied) clear of extraneous elements, make pure; (often + of, from) cleanse. □ **purification** noun; **purificatory** /-fɪkeɪtərɪ/ adjective.

purist /ˈpjʊərɪst/ noun stickler for correctness, esp. in language. □ **purism** noun.

puritan /ˈpjʊərɪt(ə)n/ ● noun (**Puritan**) *historical* member of English Protestant group regarding Reformation as incomplete; purist member of any party; strict observer of religion or morals. ● adjective (**Puritan**) *historical* of Puritans; scrupulous in religion or morals. □ **puritanical** /-ˈtæn-/ adjective; **puritanically** /-ˈtæn-/ adverb; **puritanism** noun.

purl¹ ● noun knitting stitch with needle moved in opposite to normal direction; chain of minute loops. ● verb knit with purl stitch.

purl² verb flow with babbling sound.

purler /ˈpɜːlə/ noun *colloquial* heavy fall.

purlieu /ˈpɜːljuː/ noun (plural -s) person's limits or usual haunts; *historical* tract on border of forest; (in *plural*) outskirts, outlying region.

purlin /ˈpɜːlɪn/ noun horizontal beam along length of roof.

purloin /pəˈlɔɪn/ verb *formal or jocular* steal, pilfer.

purple /ˈpɜːp(ə)l/ ● noun colour between red and blue; purple robe, esp. of emperor etc.; cardinal's scarlet official dress. ● adjective of purple. ● verb (-ling) make or become purple. □ **purplish** adjective.

purport ● verb /pəˈpɔːt/ profess, be intended to seem; (often + that) have as its meaning. ● noun /ˈpɜːpɔːt/ ostensible meaning; tenor of document or statement. □ **purportedly** adverb.

purpose /ˈpɜːpəs/ ● noun object to be attained, thing intended; intention to act; resolution, determination. ● verb (-sing) have as one's purpose, intend. □ **on**

purpose intentionally; **to good, little, no,** etc. **purpose** with good, little, no, etc., effect or result; **to the purpose** relevant, useful.

purposeful *adjective* having or indicating purpose; intentional. □ **purposefully** *adverb*; **purposefulness** *noun*.

purposeless *adjective* having no aim or plan.

purposely *adverb* on purpose.

purposive /'pɜːpəsɪv/ *adjective* having, serving, or done with a purpose; purposeful.

purr /pɜː/ ● *verb* make low vibratory sound of cat (expressing pleasure; (of machinery etc.) run smoothly and quietly. ● *noun* purring sound.

purse /pɜːs/ ● *noun* small pouch for carrying money in; *US* handbag; funds; sum given as present or prize. ● *verb* (**-sing**) (often + *up*) contract (esp. lips); become wrinkled. □ **hold the purse-strings** have control of expenditure.

purser /'pɜːsə/ *noun* ship's officer who keeps accounts, esp. head steward in passenger vessel.

pursuance /pə'sjuːəns/ *noun* (+ *of*) carrying out or observance (of plan, rules, etc.).

pursuant /pə'sjuːənt/ *adverb* (+ *to*) in accordance with.

pursue /pə'sjuː/ *verb* (**-sues, -sued, -suing**) follow with intent to overtake, capture, or harm; proceed along; engage in (study etc.); carry out (plan etc.); seek after; continue to investigate etc.; persistently importune or assail. □ **pursuer** *noun*.

pursuit /pə'sjuːt/ *noun* pursuing; occupation or activity pursued. □ **in pursuit of** pursuing.

purulent /'pjʊərʊlənt/ *adjective* of, containing, or discharging pus. □ **purulence** *noun*.

purvey /pə'veɪ/ *verb* provide or supply food etc. as one's business. □ **purveyor** *noun*.

purview /'pɜːvjuː/ *noun* scope of document etc.; range of physical or mental vision.

pus /pʌs/ *noun* thick yellowish liquid produced by infected tissue.

push /pʊʃ/ ● *verb* exert force on (thing) to move it away, cause to move thus; exert such force; thrust forward or upward; (cause to) project; make (one's way) forcibly or persistently; exert oneself; (often + *to, into, to do*) urge, impel; (often + *for*) pursue (claim etc.) persistently; promote, advertise; *colloquial* sell (drug) illegally. ● *noun* act of pushing; force thus exerted; vigorous effort; determination; use of influence to advance person. □ **give** or **get the push** *colloquial* dismiss, be dismissed; **push-bike** *colloquial* bicycle; **pushchair** child's folding chair on wheels; **push off** *colloquial* go away; **pushover** *colloquial* opponent or difficulty easily overcome.

pusher *noun colloquial* seller of illegal drugs.

pushing *adjective* pushy; *colloquial* having nearly reached (specified age).

pushy *adjective* (**-ier, -iest**) *colloquial* excessively self-assertive. □ **pushily** *adverb*; **pushiness** *noun*.

pusillanimous /pjuːsɪ'lænɪməs/ *adjective formal* cowardly, timid. □ **pusillanimity** /-lə'nɪm-/ *noun*.

puss /pʊs/ *noun colloquial* cat; sly or coquettish girl.

pussy /'pʊsɪ/ *noun* (*plural* **-ies**) (also **pussy-cat**) *colloquial* cat. □ **pussyfoot** *colloquial* move stealthily, equivocate; **pussy willow** willow with furry catkins.

pustulate /'pʌstjʊleɪt/ *verb* (**-ting**) form into pustules.

pustule /'pʌstjuːl/ *noun* pimple containing pus. □ **pustular** *adjective*.

put /pʊt/ ● *verb* (**-tt-**; *past & past participle* **put**) move to or cause to be in specified place, position, or state; (often + *on, to*) impose; (+ *for*) substitute (thing) for (another); express in specified way; (+ *at*) estimate; (+ *into*) express or translate in (words etc.); (+ *into*) invest (money) in; (+ *on*) stake (money) on;

(+ *to*) submit for attention; hurl (shot etc.) as sport. ● *noun* throw of shot. □ **put about** spread (rumour etc.); **put across** make understood, achieve by deceit; **put away** restore to usual place, lay aside for future, imprison, consume (food or drink); **put back** restore to usual place, change (meeting etc.) to later time, move back hands of (clock or watch); **put by** lay aside for future; **put down** suppress, *colloquial* snub, record in writing, enter on list, (+ *as, for*) account or reckon, (+ *to*) attribute to, kill (old etc. animal), pay as deposit; **put in** submit (claim), (+ *for*) be candidate for (election etc.), spend (time); **put off** postpone, evade (person) with excuse, dissuade, disconcert; **put on** clothe oneself with, cause (light etc.) to operate, make (transport) available, stage (play etc.), advance hands of (clock or watch), feign, increase one's weight by (specified amount); **put out** disconcert, annoy, inconvenience, extinguish; **put over** put across; **put through** complete, connect by telephone; **put together** make from parts, combine (parts) into whole; **put up** *verb* build, raise, lodge (person), engage in (fight etc.), propose, provide (money) as backer, display (notice), offer for sale etc.; **put-up** *adjective* fraudulent; **put upon** (usually in *passive*) *colloquial* unfairly burden or deceive; **put (person) up to** instigate him or her to; **put up with** endure, tolerate.

putative /'pjuːtətɪv/ *adjective formal* reputed, supposed.

putrefy /'pjuːtrɪfaɪ/ *verb* (**-ies, -ied**) become or make putrid, go bad; fester; become morally corrupt. □ **putrefaction** /-'fæk-/ *noun*; **putrefactive** /-'fæk-/ *adjective*.

putrescent /pjuː'tres(ə)nt/ *adjective* rotting. □ **putrescence** *noun*.

putrid /'pjuːtrɪd/ *adjective* decomposed, rotten; noxious; corrupt; *slang* contemptible, very unpleasant. □ **putridity** /-'trɪd-/ *noun*.

putsch /pʊtʃ/ *noun* attempt at revolution.

putt /pʌt/ ● *verb* (**-tt-**) strike (golf ball) on putting green. ● *noun* putting stroke. □ **putting green** smooth turf round hole on golf course.

puttee /'pʌtɪ/ *noun historical* long strip of cloth wound round leg for protection and support.

putter¹ *noun* golf club used in putting.

putter² *US* = POTTER¹.

putty /'pʌtɪ/ ● *noun* paste of chalk, linseed oil, etc. for fixing panes of glass etc. ● *verb* (**-ies, -ied**) fix, fill, etc. with putty.

puzzle /'pʌz(ə)l/ ● *noun* difficult or confusing problem; problem or toy designed to test ingenuity etc. ● *verb* (**-ling**) perplex, (usually + *over* etc.) be perplexed; (usually as **puzzling** *adjective*) require much mental effort; (+ *out*) solve using ingenuity etc. □ **puzzlement** *noun*.

PVC *abbreviation* polyvinyl chloride, a plastic used for pipes, electrical insulation, etc.

pyaemia /paɪ'iːmɪə/ *noun* (*US* **pyemia**) severe bacterial infection of blood.

pygmy /'pɪgmɪ/ (also **pigmy**) ● *noun* (*plural* **-ies**) member of dwarf people of esp. equatorial Africa; very small person, animal, or thing. ● *adjective* very small.

pyjamas /pə'dʒɑːməz/ *plural noun* (*US* **pajamas**) suit of trousers and top for sleeping in etc.; loose trousers worn in some Asian countries.

pylon /'paɪlən/ *noun* tall structure esp. as support for electric cables.

pyorrhoea /paɪə'rɪə/ *noun* (*US* **pyorrhea**) gum disease; discharge of pus.

pyramid /'pɪrəmɪd/ *noun* monumental (esp. ancient Egyptian) stone structure with square base and sloping sides meeting at apex; solid of this shape with base of 3 or more sides; pyramid-shaped thing. □ **pyramidal** /-'ræm-/ *adjective*.

pyre /'paɪə/ *noun* pile of combustible material, esp. for burning corpse.

pyrethrum /paɪ'riːθrəm/ *noun* aromatic chrysanthemum; insecticide from its dried flowers.

Pyrex /'paɪəreks/ *noun proprietary term* a hard heat-resistant glass.

pyrites /paɪ'raɪtiːz/ *noun* (in full **iron pyrites**) yellow sulphide of iron.

pyromania /paɪərəʊ'meɪnɪə/ *noun* obsessive desire to start fires. □ **pyromaniac** *noun & adjective.*

pyrotechnics /paɪərəʊ'tekniks/ *plural noun* art of making fireworks; display of fireworks. □ **pyrotechnic** *adjective.*

pyrrhic /'pɪrɪk/ *adjective* (of victory) achieved at too great cost.

python /'paɪθ(ə)n/ *noun* large snake that crushes its prey.

pyx /pɪks/ *noun* vessel for consecrated bread of Eucharist.

Qq

Q *abbreviation* (also **Q.**) question.

QC *abbreviation* Queen's Counsel.

QED *abbreviation* which was to be proved (*quod erat demonstrandum*).

QM *abbreviation* Quartermaster.

qr. *abbreviation* quarter(s).

qt *abbreviation* quart(s).

qua /kwɑː, kweɪ/ *conjunction* in the capacity of.

quack[1] ● *noun* harsh sound made by ducks. ● *verb* utter this sound.

quack[2] *noun* unqualified practitioner, esp. of medicine; *slang* any doctor. □ **quackery** *noun*.

quad /kwɒd/ *colloquial* ● *noun* quadrangle; quadruplet; quadraphonics. ● *adjective* quadraphonic.

quadrangle /ˈkwɒdræŋg(ə)l/ *noun* 4-sided plane figure, esp. square or rectangle; 4-sided court, esp. in college etc. □ **quadrangular** /-ˈræŋgjʊlə/ *adjective*.

quadrant /ˈkwɒdrənt/ *noun* quarter of circle or sphere or of circle's circumference; optical instrument for measuring angle between distant objects.

quadraphonic /kwɒdrəˈfɒnɪk/ *adjective* (of sound reproduction) using 4 transmission channels. □ **quadraphonically** *adverb*; **quadraphonics** *plural noun*.

quadrate ● *adjective* /ˈkwɒdrət/ square, rectangular. ● *noun* /ˈkwɒdrət, -dreɪt/ rectangular object. ● *verb* /kwɒˈdreɪt/ (**-ting**) make square.

quadratic /kwɒˈdrætɪk/ *Mathematics* ● *adjective* involving the square (and no higher power) of unknown quantity or variable. ● *noun* quadratic equation.

quadriceps /ˈkwɒdrɪseps/ *noun* 4-headed muscle at front of thigh.

quadrilateral /kwɒdrɪˈlætər(ə)l/ ● *adjective* having 4 sides. ● *noun* 4-sided figure.

quadrille /kwɒˈdrɪl/ *noun* square dance, music for this.

quadruped /ˈkwɒdrʊped/ *noun* 4-footed animal, esp. mammal.

quadruple /ˈkwɒdrʊp(ə)l/ ● *adjective* fourfold; having 4 parts; (of time in music) having 4 beats in bar. ● *noun* fourfold number or amount. ● *verb* /kwɒˈdruːp(ə)l/ multiply by 4.

quadruplet /ˈkwɒdrʊplɪt/ *noun* each of 4 children born at one birth.

quadruplicate ● *adjective* /kwɒˈdruːplɪkət/ fourfold; of which 4 copies are made. ● *verb* /-keɪt/ (**-ting**) multiply by 4.

quaff /kwɒf/ *verb literary* drink deeply; drain (cup etc.) in long draughts.

quagmire /ˈkwɒgmaɪə, ˈkwæg-/ *noun* muddy or boggy area; hazardous situation.

quail[1] *noun* (*plural* same or **-s**) small game bird related to partridge.

quail[2] *verb* flinch, show fear.

quaint *adjective* attractively odd or old-fashioned. □ **quaintly** *adverb*; **quaintness** *noun*.

quake ● *verb* (**-king**) shake, tremble. ● *noun colloquial* earthquake.

Quaker *noun* member of Society of Friends. □ **Quakerism** *noun*.

qualification /kwɒlɪfɪˈkeɪʃ(ə)n/ *noun* accomplishment fitting person for position or purpose; thing

that modifies or limits; qualifying, being qualified. □ **qualificatory** /ˈkwɒl-/ *adjective*.

qualify /ˈkwɒlɪfaɪ/ *verb* (**-ies**, **-ied**) (often as **qualified** *adjective*) make competent or fit for purpose or position; make legally entitled; (usually + *for*) satisfy conditions; modify, limit; *Grammar* (of word) attribute quality to (esp. noun); moderate, mitigate; (+ *as*) be describable as. □ **qualifier** *noun*.

qualitative /ˈkwɒlɪtətɪv/ *adjective* concerned with quality as opposed to quantity. □ **qualitatively** *adverb*.

quality /ˈkwɒlɪtɪ/ ● *noun* (*plural* **-ies**) excellence; degree of excellence; attribute, faculty; relative nature or character; timbre. ● *adjective* of high quality.

qualm /kwɑːm/ *noun* misgiving; scruple of conscience; momentary faint or sick feeling.

quandary /ˈkwɒndərɪ/ *noun* (*plural* **-ies**) perplexed state; practical dilemma.

quango /ˈkwæŋgəʊ/ *noun* (*plural* **-s**) semi-public administrative body appointed by government.

quanta *plural of* QUANTUM.

quantify /ˈkwɒntɪfaɪ/ *verb* (**-ies**, **-ied**) determine quantity of; express as quantity. □ **quantifiable** *adjective*.

quantitative /ˈkwɒntɪtətɪv/ *adjective* concerned with quantity as opposed to quality; measured or measurable by quantity.

quantity /ˈkwɒntɪtɪ/ *noun* (*plural* **-ies**) property of things that is measurable; size, extent, weight, amount, or number; (in *plural*) large amounts or numbers; length or shortness of vowel sound or syllable; *Mathematics* value, component, etc. that may be expressed in numbers. □ **quantity surveyor** person who measures and prices building work.

quantum /ˈkwɒntəm/ *noun* (*plural* **-ta**) discrete amount of energy proportional to frequency of radiation it represents; required or allowed amount. □ **quantum mechanics**, **theory** theory assuming that energy exists in discrete units.

quarantine /ˈkwɒrəntiːn/ ● *noun* isolation imposed on person or animal to prevent infection or contagion; period of this. ● *verb* (**-ning**) put in quarantine.

quark[1] /kwɑːk/ *noun Physics* component of elementary particles.

quark[2] /kwɑːk/ *noun* kind of low-fat curd cheese.

quarrel /ˈkwɒr(ə)l/ ● *noun* severe or angry dispute; break in friendly relations; cause of complaint. ● *verb* (**-ll-**; *US* **-l-**) (often + *with*) find fault; dispute; break off friendly relations. □ **quarrelsome** *adjective*.

quarry[1] /ˈkwɒrɪ/ ● *noun* (*plural* **-ies**) place from which stone etc. is extracted. ● *verb* (**-ies**, **-ied**) extract (stone etc.) from quarry. □ **quarry tile** unglazed floor-tile.

quarry[2] /ˈkwɒrɪ/ *noun* (*plural* **-ies**) intended victim or prey; object of pursuit.

quart /kwɔːt/ *noun* liquid measure equal to quarter of gallon; two pints (1.136 litre).

quarter /ˈkwɔːtə/ ● *noun* each of 4 equal parts; period of 3 months; point of time 15 minutes before or after any hour; 25 US or Canadian cents, coin worth this; part of town, esp. as occupied by particular class; point of compass, region at this; direction, district; source of supply; (in *plural*) lodgings, accommodation of troops etc.; one-fourth of a lunar month; mercy towards enemy etc. on condition of surrender; grain measure equivalent to 8 bushels, *colloquial* one-fourth of a pound weight. ● *verb* divide into quarters; put (troops etc.) into quarters; provide with lodgings; *Heraldry* place (coats of arms) on 4 quarters of shield. □ **quarterback** player in American football who directs attacking play; **quarter day** day on which quarterly payments are due; **quarterdeck** part of ship's upper deck near stern; **quarter-final** *Sport* match or round preceding semifinal; **quarter-hour** period of 15 minutes; **quartermaster** regimental officer in charge of quartering, rations, etc., naval petty officer in charge of steering, signals, etc.

quarterly ● *adjective* produced or occurring once every quarter of year. ● *adverb* once every quarter of year. ● *noun* (*plural* **-ies**) quarterly journal.

quartet /kwɔːˈtet/ *noun* musical composition for 4 performers; the performers; any group of 4.

quarto /ˈkwɔːtəʊ/ *noun* (*plural* **-s**) size of book or page made by folding sheet of standard size twice to form 4 leaves.

quartz /kwɔːts/ ● *noun* silica in various mineral forms. ● *adjective* (of clock or watch) operated by vibrations of electrically driven quartz crystal.

quasar /ˈkweɪzɑː/ *noun* starlike object with large red shift.

quash /kwɒʃ/ *verb* annul; reject as not valid; suppress, crush.

quasi- /ˈkweɪzaɪ/ *combining form* seemingly, not really; almost.

quaternary /kwəˈtɜːnərɪ/ *adjective* having 4 parts.

quatrain /ˈkwɒtreɪn/ *noun* 4-line stanza.

quatrefoil /ˈkætrəfɔɪl/ *noun* leaf consisting of 4 leaflets; design or ornament in this shape.

quaver /ˈkweɪvə/ ● *verb* (esp. of voice or sound) vibrate, shake, tremble; sing or say with quavering voice. ● *noun Music* note half as long as crotchet; trill in singing; tremble in speech. □ **quavery** *adjective*.

quay /kiː/ *noun* artificial landing-place for loading and unloading ships. □ **quayside** land forming or near quay.

queasy /ˈkwiːzɪ/ *adjective* (**-ier**, **-iest**) (of person) nauseous; (of stomach) easily upset; (of the conscience etc.) overscrupulous. □ **queasily** *adverb*; **queasiness** *noun*.

queen ● *noun* (as title usually **Queen**) female sovereign; (in full **queen consort**) king's wife; woman, country, or thing pre-eminent of its kind; fertile female among bees, ants, etc.; most powerful piece in chess; court card depicting queen; (**the Queen**) national anthem when sovereign is female; *offensive slang* male homosexual. ● *verb* convert (pawn in chess) to queen when it reaches opponent's side of board. □ **queen mother** king's widow who is mother of sovereign; **Queen's Bench** division of High Court of Justice; **Queen's Counsel** counsel to the Crown, taking precedence over other barristers; **the Queen's English** English language correctly written or spoken. □ **queenly** *adjective* (**-ier**, **-iest**).

Queensberry Rules /ˈkwiːnzbərɪ/ *plural noun* standard rules, esp. of boxing.

queer ● *adjective* strange, odd, eccentric; suspect, of questionable character; slightly ill, faint; *offensive slang* (esp. of a man) homosexual. ● *noun offensive slang* homosexual. ● *verb slang* spoil, put out of order. □ **in Queer Street** *slang* in difficulty, esp. in debt.

quell *verb* suppress, crush.

quench *verb* satisfy (thirst) by drinking; extinguish (fire or light); cool, esp. with water; stifle, suppress.

quern *noun* hand mill for grinding corn.

querulous /ˈkwerʊləs/ *adjective* complaining; peevish. □ **querulously** *adverb*.

query /ˈkwɪərɪ/ ● *noun* (*plural* **-ies**) question; question mark. ● *verb* (**-ies**, **-ied**) ask, inquire; call in question; dispute accuracy of.

quest ● *noun* search, seeking; thing sought, esp. by medieval knight. ● *verb* (often + *about*) go about in search of something.

question /ˈkwestʃ(ə)n/ ● *noun* sentence worded or expressed so as to seek information or answer; doubt or dispute about matter, raising of such doubt etc.; matter to be discussed or decided; problem requiring solution. ● *verb* ask questions of; subject (person) to examination; throw doubt on. □ **be just a question of time** be certain to happen sooner or later; **be a question of** be at issue, be a problem; **call in** or **into question** express doubts about; **in question** being discussed or referred to; **out of the question** not worth questioning, impossible; **question mark** punctuation mark (?) indicating question (see panel); **question-master** person presiding over quiz game etc.; **question time** period in Parliament when MPs may question ministers. □ **questioner** *noun*; **questioning** *adjective & noun*; **questioningly** *adverb*.

questionable *adjective* doubtful as regards truth, quality, honesty, wisdom, etc.

questionnaire /kwestʃəˈneə/ *noun* list of questions for obtaining information esp. for statistical analysis.

queue /kjuː/ ● *noun* line or sequence of people, vehicles, etc. waiting their turn. ● *verb* (**-s**, **-d**, **queuing** or **queueing**) (often + *up*) form or join queue. □ **queue-jump** push forward out of turn in queue.

quibble /ˈkwɪb(ə)l/ ● *noun* petty objection, trivial point of criticism; evasion. ● *verb* (**-ling**) use quibbles.

quiche /kiːʃ/ *noun* savoury flan.

quick ● *adjective* taking only a short time; arriving after only a short time, prompt; with only a short interval; lively, alert, intelligent; (of temper) easily roused. ● *adverb* quickly. ● *noun* soft sensitive flesh, esp. below nails or skin; seat of emotion. □ **quicklime** unslaked lime; **quicksand** (often in *plural*) area of loose wet sand that sucks in anything placed on it, treacherous situation etc.; **quickset** (of hedge etc.) formed of cuttings, esp. hawthorn; **quicksilver** mercury; **quickstep** fast foxtrot; **quick-tempered** easily angered; **quick-witted** quick to grasp situation, make repartee, etc.; **quick-wittedness** *noun*. □ **quickly** *adverb*.

Question mark **?**

This is used instead of a full stop at the end of a sentence to show that it is a question, e.g.

Have you seen the film yet?
You didn't lose my purse, did you?

It is **not** used at the end of a reported question, e.g.

I asked you whether you'd seen the film yet.

quicken *verb* make or become quicker, accelerate; give life or vigour to, rouse; (of woman) reach stage in pregnancy when movements of foetus can be felt; (of foetus) begin to show signs of life.

quid[1] *noun slang* (*plural* same) one pound sterling.

quid[2] *noun* lump of tobacco for chewing.

quid pro quo /ˌkwɪd prəʊ ˈkwəʊ/ *noun* (*plural* **quid pro quos**) gift, favour, etc. exchanged for another.

quiescent /kwɪˈes(ə)nt/ *adjective* inert, dormant. □ **quiescence** *noun*.

quiet /ˈkwaɪət/ ● *adjective* with little or no sound or motion; of gentle or peaceful disposition; unobtrusive, not showy; not overt, disguised; undisturbed, uninterrupted; not busy. ● *noun* silence, stillness; undisturbed state, tranquillity. ● *verb* (often + *down*) make or become quiet, calm. □ **be quiet** (esp. in *imperative*) cease talking etc.; **keep quiet** (often + *about*) say nothing; **on the quiet** secretly. □ **quietly** *adverb*; **quietness** *noun*.

quieten *verb* (often + *down*) make or become quiet or calm.

quietism *noun* passive contemplative attitude towards life. □ **quietist** *noun* & *adjective*.

quietude /ˈkwaɪətjuːd/ *noun* state of quiet.

quietus /kwaɪˈiːtəs/ *noun* release from life; death, final riddance.

quiff *noun* man's tuft of hair brushed upwards in front.

quill *noun* (in full **quill-feather**) large feather in wing or tail; hollow stem of this; (in full **quill pen**) pen made of quill; (usually in *plural*) porcupine's spine.

quilt ● *noun* bedspread, esp. of quilted material. ● *verb* line bedspread or garment with padding enclosed between layers of fabric by lines of stitching. □ **quilter** *noun*; **quilting** *noun*.

quin *noun colloquial* quintuplet.

quince *noun* (tree bearing) acid pear-shaped fruit used in jams etc.

quincentenary /ˌkwɪnsenˈtiːnərɪ/ ● *noun* (*plural* **-ies**) 500th anniversary; celebration of this. ● *adjective* of this anniversary.

quinine /ˈkwɪniːn/ *noun* bitter drug used as a tonic and to reduce fever.

Quinquagesima /ˌkwɪŋkwəˈdʒesɪmə/ *noun* Sunday before Lent.

quinquennial /kwɪŋˈkwenɪəl/ *adjective* lasting 5 years; recurring every 5 years. □ **quinquennially** *adverb*.

quintessence /kwɪnˈtes(ə)ns/ *noun* (usually + *of*) purest and most perfect form, manifestation, or embodiment of quality etc.; highly refined extract. □ **quintessential** /-trˈsen-/ *adjective*; **quintessentially** /-trˈsen-/ *adverb*.

quintet /kwɪnˈtet/ *noun* musical composition for 5 performers; the performers; any group of 5.

quintuple /ˈkwɪntjʊp(ə)l/ ● *adjective* fivefold, having 5 parts. ● *noun* fivefold number or amount. ● *verb* (**-ling**) multiply by 5.

quintuplet /ˈkwɪntjʊplɪt/ *noun* each of 5 children born at one birth.

quip ● *noun* clever saying, epigram. ● *verb* (**-pp-**) make quips.

quire *noun* 25 sheets of paper.

quirk *noun* peculiar feature; trick of fate. □ **quirky** *adjective* (**-ier, -iest**).

quisling /ˈkwɪzlɪŋ/ *noun* collaborator with invading enemy.

quit ● *verb* (**-tting**; *past & past participle* **quitted** or **quit**) give up, let go, abandon; *US* cease, stop; leave or depart from. ● *adjective* (+ *of*) rid of.

quitch *noun* couch grass.

quite *adverb* completely, altogether, absolutely; rather, to some extent; (often + *so*) *said to indicate agreement*. □ **quite a**, **quite some** a remarkable; **quite a few** *colloquial* a fairly large number (of); **quite something** *colloquial* a remarkable thing or person.

quits *adjective* on even terms by retaliation or repayment. □ **call it quits** acknowledge that things are now even, agree to stop quarrelling.

quiver[1] /ˈkwɪvə/ ● *verb* tremble or vibrate with slight rapid motion. ● *noun* quivering motion or sound.

quiver[2] /ˈkwɪvə/ *noun* case for arrows.

quixotic /kwɪkˈsɒtɪk/ *adjective* extravagantly and romantically chivalrous. □ **quixotically** *adverb*.

Quotation marks ' ' " "

Also called inverted commas, these are used:

1 round a direct quotation (closing quotation marks come after any punctuation which is part of the quotation), e.g.

> He said, 'That is nonsense.'
> 'That', he said, 'is nonsense.'
> 'That, however,' he said, 'is nonsense.'
> Did he say, 'That is nonsense'?
> He asked, 'Is that nonsense?'

2 round a quoted word or phrase, e.g.

> What does 'integrated circuit' mean?

3 round a word or phrase that is not being used in its central sense, e.g.

> the 'king' of jazz
> He said he had enough 'bread' to buy a car.

4 round the title of a book, song, poem, magazine article, television programme, etc. (but not a book of the Bible), e.g.

> 'Hard Times' by Charles Dickens

5 as double quotation marks round a quotation within a quotation, e.g.

> He asked, 'Do you know what "integrated circuit" means?'

In handwriting, double quotation marks are usual.

quiz ● *noun* (*plural* **quizzes**) test of knowledge, esp. as entertainment; interrogation, examination. ● *verb* examine by questioning.

quizzical /ˈkwɪzɪk(ə)l/ *adjective* mocking, gently amused. □ **quizzically** *adverb*.

quod *noun slang* prison.

quoin /kɔɪn/ *noun* external angle of building; cornerstone; wedge used in printing or gunnery.

quoit /kɔɪt/ *noun* ring thrown to encircle peg; (in *plural*) game using these.

quondam /ˈkwɒndæm/ *adjective* that once was, former.

quorate /ˈkwɔːreɪt/ *adjective* constituting or having quorum.

Quorn /kwɔːn/ *noun proprietary term* vegetable protein food made from fungus.

quorum /ˈkwɔːrəm/ *noun* minimum number of members that must be present to constitute valid meeting.

quota /ˈkwəʊtə/ *noun* share to be contributed to or received from total; number of goods, people, etc. stipulated or permitted.

quotable *adjective* worth quoting.

quotation /kwəʊˈteɪʃ(ə)n/ *noun* passage or remark quoted; quoting, being quoted; contractor's estimate. □ **quotation marks** inverted commas (' ' or " ") used at beginning and end of quotation etc. (see panel).

quote ● *verb* (**-ting**) cite or appeal to as example, authority, etc.; repeat or copy out passage from; (+ *from*) cite (author, book, etc.); (+ *as*) cite (author etc.) as proof, evidence, etc.; (as *interjection*) *used in dictation etc. to indicate opening quotation marks*; (often + *at*) state price of; state (price) for job. ● *noun colloquial* passage quoted; (usually in *plural*) quotation marks.

quoth /kwəʊθ/ *verb* (only in 1st & 3rd persons) *archaic* said.

quotidian /kwɒˈtɪdɪən/ *adjective* occurring or recurring daily; commonplace, trivial.

quotient /ˈkwəʊʃ(ə)nt/ *noun* result of division sum.

q.v. *abbreviation* which see (*quod vide*).

Rr

R *abbreviation* (also **R.**) *Regina*; *Rex*; River; (also ®) registered as trademark. □ **R & D** research and development.

r. *abbreviation* (also **r**) right; radius.

RA *abbreviation* Royal Academy or Academician; Royal Artillery.

rabbet /'ræbɪt/ ● *noun* step-shaped channel cut along edge or face of wood etc. to receive edge or tongue of another piece. ● *verb* (**-t-**) join with rabbet; make rabbet in.

rabbi /'ræbaɪ/ *noun* (*plural* **-s**) Jewish religious leader; Jewish scholar or teacher, esp. of the law. □ **rabbinical** /rə'bɪn-/ *adjective*.

rabbit /'ræbɪt/ ● *noun* burrowing mammal of hare family; its fur. ● *verb* (**-t-**) hunt rabbits; (often + *on, away*) *colloquial* talk pointlessly; chatter. □ **rabbit punch** blow with edge of hand on back of neck.

rabble /'ræb(ə)l/ *noun* disorderly crowd, mob; contemptible or inferior set of people. □ **rabble-rouser** person who stirs up rabble, esp. to agitate for social change.

Rabelaisian /ræbə'leɪzɪən/ *adjective* exuberantly and coarsely humorous.

rabid /'ræbɪd/ *adjective* affected with rabies, mad; violent, fanatical. □ **rabidity** /rə'bɪd-/ *noun*.

rabies /'reɪbiːz/ *noun* contagious viral disease of esp. dogs; hydrophobia.

RAC *abbreviation* Royal Automobile Club.

raccoon /rə'kuːn/ *noun* (also **racoon**) (*plural* same or **-s**) N. American mammal with bushy tail; its fur.

race[1] ● *noun* contest of speed or to be first to achieve something; (in *plural*) series of races for horses etc.; strong current in sea or river; channel. ● *verb* (**-cing**) take part in race; have race with; (+ *with*) compete in speed; cause to race; go at full speed; (usually as **racing** *adjective*) follow or take part in horse racing. □ **racecourse** ground for horse racing; **racehorse** one bred or kept for racing; **race meeting** sequence of horse races at one place; **racetrack** racecourse, track for motor racing; **racing car** one built for racing; **racing driver** driver of racing car.

race[2] *noun* each of the major divisions of humankind, each having distinct physical characteristics; group of people, animals, or plants connected by common descent; any great division of living creatures. □ **race relations** relations between members of different races in same country.

raceme /rə'siːm/ *noun* flower cluster with flowers attached by short stalks at equal distances along stem.

racial /'reɪʃ(ə)l/ *adjective* of or concerning race; on grounds of or connected with difference in race. □ **racially** *adverb*.

racialism *noun* = RACISM. □ **racialist** *noun* & *adjective*.

racism *noun* (prejudice based on) belief in superiority of particular race; antagonism towards other races. □ **racist** *noun* & *adjective*.

rack[1] ● *noun* framework, usually with rails, bars, etc., for holding things; cogged or toothed rail or bar engaging with wheel, pinion, etc.; *historical* instrument of torture stretching victim's joints. ● *verb* inflict suffering on; *historical* torture on rack. □ **rack one's brains** make great mental effort; **rack-rent** extortionate rent.

rack[2] *noun* destruction (esp. in **rack and ruin**).

rack[3] *verb* (often + *off*) draw off (wine etc.) from lees.

racket[1] /'rækɪt/ *noun* (also **racquet**) bat with round or oval frame strung with catgut, nylon, etc., used in tennis etc.; (in *plural*) game like squash but in larger court.

racket[2] ● *noun* uproar, din; *slang* scheme for obtaining money etc. by dishonest means; dodge; sly game; *colloquial* line of business.

racketeer /rækɪ'tɪə/ *noun* person who operates dishonest business. □ **racketeering** *noun*.

raconteur /rækɒn'tɜː/ *noun* teller of anecdotes.

racoon = RACCOON.

racy *adjective* (**-ier**, **-iest**) lively and vigorous in style; risqué; of distinctive quality. □ **raciness** *noun*.

rad *noun* unit of absorbed dose of ionizing radiation.

RADA /'rɑːdə/ *abbreviation* Royal Academy of Dramatic Art.

radar /'reɪdɑː/ *noun* radio system for detecting the direction, range, or presence of objects; apparatus for this. □ **radar trap** device using radar to detect speeding vehicles.

raddled /'ræd(ə)ld/ *adjective* worn out.

radial /'reɪdɪəl/ ● *adjective* of or arranged like rays or radii; having spokes or radiating lines; acting or moving along such lines; (in full **radial-ply**) (of tyre) having fabric layers arranged radially. ● *noun* radial-ply tyre. □ **radially** *adverb*.

radian /'reɪdɪən/ *noun* SI unit of plane angle (about 57°).

radiant /'reɪdɪənt/ ● *adjective* emitting or issuing in rays; beaming with joy etc.; splendid, dazzling. ● *noun* point or object from which heat or light radiates. □ **radiance** *noun*; **radiantly** *adverb*.

radiate /'reɪdɪeɪt/ *verb* (**-ting**) emit rays of light, heat, etc.; be emitted in rays; emit or spread from a centre; transmit or demonstrate.

radiation *noun* radiating; emission of energy as electromagnetic waves; energy thus transmitted, esp. invisibly; (in full **radiation therapy**) treatment of cancer etc. using e.g. X-rays or ultraviolet light. □ **radiation sickness** sickness caused by exposure to radiation such as gamma rays.

radiator *noun* device for heating room etc. by circulation of hot water etc.; engine-cooling device in motor vehicle or aircraft.

radical /'rædɪk(ə)l/ ● *adjective* fundamental; far-reaching, thorough; advocating fundamental reform; forming the basis; primary; of the root of a number or plant. ● *noun* person holding radical views; atom or group of atoms forming base of compound and remaining unchanged during reactions; quantity forming or expressed as root of another. □ **radicalism** *noun*; **radically** *adverb*.

radicchio /rə'diːkɪəʊ/ *noun* (*plural* **-s**) chicory with purplish leaves.

radicle /'rædɪk(ə)l/ *noun* part of seed that develops into root.

radii *plural* of **radius**.

radio /'reɪdɪəʊ/ ● *noun* (*plural* **-s**) transmission and reception of messages etc. by electromagnetic waves of radio frequency; apparatus for receiving, broadcasting, or transmitting radio signals; sound broadcasting (station or channel). ● *verb* (**-es**, **-ed**) send (message) by radio; send message to (person) by radio; communicate or broadcast by radio. □ **radio-controlled** controlled from a distance by radio; **radio telephone** one operating by radio; **radio telescope** aerial system for analysing radiation in the radio-frequency range from stars etc.

radioactive adjective of or exhibiting radioactivity.

radioactivity noun spontaneous disintegration of atomic nuclei, with emission of usually penetrating radiation or particles.

radiocarbon noun radioactive isotope of carbon.

radiogram /'reɪdɪəʊɡræm/ noun combined radio and record player; picture obtained by X-rays etc.; telegram sent by radio.

radiograph /'reɪdɪəʊɡrɑːf/ ● noun instrument recording intensity of radiation; picture obtained by X-rays etc. ● verb obtain picture of by X-rays, gamma rays, etc. □ **radiographer** /-'ɒɡrəfə/ noun; **radiography** /-'ɒɡrəfi/ noun.

radiology /reɪdɪ'ɒlədʒɪ/ noun esp. Medicine study of X-rays and other high-energy radiation. □ **radiologist** noun.

radiophonic adjective of electronically produced sound, esp. music.

radioscopy /reɪdɪ'ɒskəpɪ/ noun examination by X-rays etc. of objects opaque to light.

radiotherapy noun treatment of disease by X-rays or other forms of radiation.

radish /'rædɪʃ/ noun plant with crisp pungent root; this root, esp. eaten raw.

radium /'reɪdɪəm/ noun radioactive metallic element.

radius /'reɪdɪəs/ noun (plural **radii** /-dɪaɪ/ or **-es**) straight line from centre to circumference of circle or sphere; distance from a centre; bone of forearm on same side as thumb.

radon /'reɪdɒn/ noun gaseous radioactive inert element arising from disintegration of radium.

RAF abbreviation Royal Air Force.

raffia /'ræfɪə/ noun palm tree native to Madagascar; fibre from its leaves.

raffish /'ræfɪʃ/ adjective disreputable, rakish; tawdry.

raffle /'ræf(ə)l/ ● noun fund-raising lottery with prizes. ● verb (**-ling**) (often + off) sell by raffle.

raft /rɑːft/ noun flat floating structure of wood etc., used for transport.

rafter /'rɑːftə/ noun any of sloping beams forming framework of roof.

rag¹ noun torn, frayed, or worn piece of woven material; remnant; (in plural) old or worn clothes; derogatory newspaper. □ **rag-bag** miscellaneous collection; **rag doll** stuffed cloth doll; **ragtime** form of highly syncopated early jazz; **the rag trade** colloquial the clothing business; **ragwort** yellow-flowered ragged-leaved plant.

rag² ● noun fund-raising programme of stunts etc. staged by students; prank; rowdy celebration, disorderly scene. ● verb (**-gg-**) tease; play rough jokes on; engage in rough play.

ragamuffin /'rægəmʌfɪn/ noun child in ragged dirty clothes.

rage ● noun violent anger; fit of this. ● verb (**-ging**) be full of anger; (often + at, against) speak furiously; be violent, be at its height; (as **raging** adjective) extreme, very painful. □ **all the rage** very popular, fashionable.

ragged /'rægɪd/ adjective torn; frayed; in ragged clothes; with a broken or jagged outline or surface; lacking finish, smoothness, or uniformity.

raglan /'ræɡlən/ adjective (of sleeve) running up to neck of garment.

ragout /ræ'guː/ noun highly seasoned stew of meat and vegetables.

raid ● noun rapid surprise attack by armed forces or thieves; surprise visit by police etc. to arrest suspects or seize illicit goods. ● verb make raid on. □ **raider** noun.

rail¹ ● noun bar used to hang things on or as protection, part of fence, top of banisters, etc.; steel bar(s) making railway track; railway. ● verb provide or enclose with rail(s). □ **railcard** pass entitling holder to reduced rail fares.

rail² verb (often + at, against) complain or protest strongly; rant.

rail³ noun marsh wading bird.

railing noun (often in plural) fence or barrier made of rails.

raillery /'reɪlərɪ/ noun good-humoured ridicule.

railroad ● noun esp. US railway. ● verb (often + into, through) coerce, rush.

railway /'reɪlweɪ/ noun track or set of tracks of steel rails on which trains run; organization and people required to work such a system. □ **railwayman** male railway employee.

raiment /'reɪmənt/ noun archaic clothing.

rain ● noun condensed atmospheric moisture falling in drops; fall of these; falling liquid or objects; (**the rains**) rainy season. ● verb (after it) rain falls, send in large quantities; fall or send down like rain; lavishly bestow. □ **raincoat** waterproof or water-resistant coat; **rainfall** total amount of rain falling within given area in given time; **rainforest** tropical forest with heavy rainfall; **take a rain check on** reserve right to postpone taking up (offer) until convenient.

rainbow /'reɪnbəʊ/ ● noun arch of colours formed in sky by reflection, refraction, and dispersion of sun's rays in falling rain etc. ● adjective many-coloured. □ **rainbow trout** large trout originally of N. America.

rainy adjective (**-ier, -iest**) (of weather, day, climate, etc.) in or on which rain is falling or much rain usually falls. □ **rainy day** time of need in the future.

raise /reɪz/ ● verb (**-sing**) put or take into higher position; (often + up) cause to rise or stand up or be vertical; increase amount, value, or strength of; (often + up) build up; levy, collect; cause to be heard or considered; bring up, educate; breed; remove (barrier); rouse. ● noun Cards increase in stake or bid; US rise in salary. □ **raise Cain, hell, the roof** be very angry, cause an uproar; **raise a laugh** cause others to laugh.

raisin /'reɪz(ə)n/ noun dried grape.

raison d'être /reɪzɔ̃ 'detr/ noun (plural **raisons d'être** same pronunciation) purpose that accounts for, justifies, or originally caused thing's existence. [French]

raj /rɑːdʒ/ noun (**the raj**) historical British rule in India.

raja /'rɑːdʒə/ noun (also **rajah**) historical Indian king or prince.

rake¹ ● noun implement with long handle and toothed crossbar for drawing hay etc. together, smoothing loose soil, etc.; similar implement. ● verb (**-king**) collect or gather (as) with rake; ransack, search thoroughly; direct gunfire along (line) from end to end. □ **rake in** colloquial amass (profits etc.); **rake-off** colloquial commission or share; **rake up** revive (unwelcome) memory of.

rake² noun dissolute man of fashion.

rake³ ● verb (**-king**) set or be set at sloping angle. ● noun raking position or build; amount by which thing rakes.

rakish adjective dashing, jaunty; dissolute. □ **rakishly** adverb.

rallentando /ˌrælənˈtændəʊ/ *Music* ● *adverb & adjective* with gradual decrease of speed. ● *noun* (*plural* **-s** or **-di** /-dɪ/) rallentando passage.

rally /ˈrælɪ/ ● *verb* (**-ies, -ied**) (often + *round*) bring or come together as support or for action; recover after illness etc., revive; (of prices etc.) increase after fall. ● *noun* (*plural* **-ies**) rallying, being rallied; mass meeting; competition for motor vehicles over public roads; extended exchange of strokes in tennis etc. □ **rallycross** motor racing across country.

RAM *abbreviation* Royal Academy of Music; random-access memory.

ram ● *noun* uncastrated male sheep; (**the Ram**) zodiacal sign or constellation Aries; falling weight of pile-driving machine; hydraulic water pump. ● *verb* (**-mm-**) force into place; (usually + *down, in,* etc.) beat down or drive in by blows; (of ship, vehicle, etc.) strike, crash against. □ **ram-raid** crashing vehicle into shop front in order to steal contents; **ram-raider** *noun*; **ram-raiding** *noun*.

Ramadan /ˈræmədæn/ *noun* ninth month of Muslim year, with strict fasting from sunrise to sunset.

ramble /ˈræmb(ə)l/ ● *verb* (**-ling**) walk for pleasure; talk or write incoherently. ● *noun* walk taken for pleasure.

rambler *noun* person who rambles; straggling or spreading rose.

rambling *adjective* wandering; disconnected, incoherent; irregularly arranged; (of plant) straggling, climbing.

RAMC *abbreviation* Royal Army Medical Corps.

ramekin /ˈræmɪkɪn/ *noun* small dish for baking and serving individual portion of food.

ramification /ˌræmɪfɪˈkeɪʃ(ə)n/ *noun* (usually in *plural*) consequence; subdivision.

ramify /ˈræmɪfaɪ/ *verb* (**-ies, -ied**) (cause to) form branches or subdivisions; branch out.

ramp *noun* slope joining two levels of ground, floor, etc.; stairs for entering or leaving aircraft; transverse ridge in road making vehicles slow down.

rampage ● *verb* /ræmˈpeɪdʒ/ (**-ging**) (often + *about*) rush wildly, rage, storm. ● *noun* /ˈræmpeɪdʒ/ wild or violent behaviour. □ **on the rampage** rampaging.

rampant /ˈræmpənt/ *adjective* unchecked, flourishing excessively; rank, luxuriant; *Heraldry* (of lion etc.) standing on left hind foot with forepaws in air; fanatical. □ **rampancy** *noun*.

rampart /ˈræmpɑːt/ *noun* defensive broad-topped wall; defence, protection.

ramrod *noun* rod for ramming down charge of muzzle-loading firearm; thing that is very straight or rigid.

ramshackle /ˈræmʃæk(ə)l/ *adjective* rickety, tumbledown.

ran *past of* RUN.

ranch /rɑːntʃ/ ● *noun* cattle-breeding establishment, esp. in US & Canada; farm where other animals are bred. ● *verb* farm on ranch. □ **rancher** *noun*.

rancid /ˈrænsɪd/ *adjective* (of fat or fatty foods) smelling or tasting rank and stale. □ **rancidity** /-ˈsɪd-/ *noun*.

rancour /ˈræŋkə/ *noun* (*US* **rancor**) inveterate bitterness; malignant hate. □ **rancorous** *adjective*.

rand *noun* monetary unit of South Africa.

random /ˈrændəm/ *adjective* made, done, etc. without method or conscious choice. □ **at random** without particular aim; **random-access** (of computer memory) having all parts directly accessible. □ **randomly** *adverb*.

randy /ˈrændɪ/ *adjective* (**-ier, -iest**) eager for sexual satisfaction.

ranee /ˈrɑːniː/ *noun* (also **rani**) (*plural* **-s**) *historical* raja's wife or widow.

rang *past of* RING².

range /reɪndʒ/ ● *noun* region between limits of variation, esp. scope of operation; such limits; area relevant to something; distance attainable by gun or projectile, distance between gun etc. and target; row, series, etc., esp. of mountains; area with targets for shooting; fireplace for cooking; area over which a thing is distributed; distance that can be covered by vehicle without refuelling; stretch of open land for grazing or hunting. ● *verb* (**-ging**) reach; extend; vary between limits; (usually in *passive*) line up, arrange; rove, wander; traverse in all directions. □ **rangefinder** instrument for determining distance of object.

ranger *noun* keeper of royal or national park, or of forest; (**Ranger**) senior Guide.

rangy /ˈreɪndʒɪ/ *adjective* (**-ier, -iest**) tall and slim.

rani = RANEE.

rank¹ ● *noun* position in hierarchy; grade of advancement; distinct social class, grade of dignity or achievement; high social position; place in scale; row or line; single line of soldiers drawn up abreast; place where taxis wait for customers. ● *verb* have rank or place; classify, give a certain grade to; arrange in rank. □ **rank and file** (usually treated as *plural*) ordinary members of organization; **the ranks** common soldiers.

rank² *adjective* luxuriant; coarse; choked with weeds etc.; foul-smelling; loathsome; flagrant; gross, complete.

rankle /ˈræŋk(ə)l/ *verb* (**-ling**) cause persistent annoyance or resentment.

ransack /ˈrænsæk/ *verb* pillage, plunder; thoroughly search.

ransom /ˈrænsəm/ ● *noun* sum demanded or paid for release of prisoner. ● *verb* buy freedom or restoration of; hold (prisoner) to ransom; release for a ransom. □ **hold to ransom** keep (prisoner) and demand ransom, demand concessions from by threats.

rant ● *verb* speak loudly, bombastically, or violently. ● *noun* piece of ranting. □ **rant and rave** express anger noisily and forcefully.

ranunculus /rəˈnʌŋkjʊləs/ *noun* (*plural* **-luses** or **-li** /-laɪ/) plant of genus including buttercup.

RAOC *abbreviation* Royal Army Ordnance Corps.

rap¹ ● *noun* smart slight blow; sound of this, tap; *slang* blame, punishment; rhythmic monologue recited to music; (in full **rap music**) style of rock music with words recited. ● *verb* (**-pp-**) strike smartly; make sharp tapping sound; criticize adversely; *Music* perform rap. □ **take the rap** suffer the consequences. □ **rapper** *noun Music*.

rap² *noun* the least bit.

rapacious /rəˈpeɪʃəs/ *adjective* grasping, extortionate, predatory. □ **rapacity** /-ˈpæs-/ *noun*.

rape¹ ● *noun* act of forcing esp. woman or girl to have sexual intercourse unwillingly; (often + *of*) violation. ● *verb* (**-ping**) commit rape on.

rape² *noun* plant grown as fodder and for oil from its seed.

rapid /ˈræpɪd/ ● *adjective* (**-er, -est**) quick, swift. ● *noun* (usually in *plural*) steep descent in river bed, with swift current. □ **rapid eye movement** jerky movement of eyes during dreaming. □ **rapidity** /rəˈpɪd-/ *noun*; **rapidly** *adverb*.

rapier /ˈreɪpɪə/ *noun* light slender sword for thrusting.

rapine /ˈræpaɪn/ *noun rhetorical* plundering.

rapist *noun* person who commits rape.

rapport /ræˈpɔː/ *noun* communication or relationship, esp. when useful and harmonious.

rapprochement /ræˈprɒʃmɑ̃/ *noun* resumption of harmonious relations, esp. between states. [French]

rapscallion /ræp'skæljən/ *noun archaic* rascal.

rapt *adjective* absorbed; intent; carried away with feeling or thought.

rapture /'ræptʃə/ *noun* ecstatic delight; (in *plural*) great pleasure or enthusiasm or expression of it. □ **rapturous** *adjective*.

rare¹ *adjective* (**-r, -st**) seldom done, found, or occurring; uncommon; exceptionally good; of less than usual density. □ **rareness** *noun*.

rare² *adjective* (**-r, -st**) (of meat) underdone.

rarebit *noun* see WELSH RAREBIT.

rarefy /'reərɪfaɪ/ *verb* (**-ies, -ied**) (often as **rarefied** *adjective*) make or become less dense or solid; refine, make (idea etc.) subtle. □ **rarefaction** /-'fækʃ(ə)n/ *noun*.

rarely *adverb* seldom, not often.

raring /'reərɪŋ/ *adjective colloquial* eager (esp. in **raring to go**).

rarity /'reərətɪ/ *noun* (*plural* **-ies**) rareness; uncommon thing.

rascal /'rɑːsk(ə)l/ *noun* dishonest or mischievous person. □ **rascally** *adjective*.

rase = RAZE.

rash¹ *adjective* reckless; hasty, impetuous. □ **rashly** *adverb*; **rashness** *noun*.

rash² *noun* skin eruption in spots or patches; (usually + *of*) sudden widespread phenomenon.

rasher /'ræʃə/ *noun* thin slice of bacon or ham.

rasp /rɑːsp/ ● *noun* coarse file; grating noise or utterance. ● *verb* scrape roughly or with rasp; make grating sound; say gratingly; grate on.

raspberry /'rɑːzbərɪ/ *noun* (*plural* **-ies**) red fruit like blackberry; shrub bearing this; *colloquial* sound made by blowing through lips, expressing derision or disapproval.

Rastafarian /ræstə'feərɪən/ (also **Rasta** /'ræstə/) ● *noun* member of Jamaican sect regarding Haile Selassie of Ethiopia (d. 1975) as God. ● *adjective* of this sect.

rat ● *noun* large mouselike rodent; *colloquial* unpleasant or treacherous person. ● *verb* (**-tt-**) hunt or kill rats; (also + *on*) inform (on), desert, betray. □ **ratbag** *slang* obnoxious person; **rat race** *colloquial* fiercely competitive struggle.

ratable = RATEABLE.

ratatouille /rætə'tuːɪ/ *noun* dish of stewed onions, courgettes, tomatoes, aubergines, and peppers.

ratchet /'rætʃɪt/ *noun* set of teeth on edge of bar or wheel with catch ensuring motion in one direction only; (in full **ratchet-wheel**) wheel with rim so toothed.

rate ● *noun* numerical proportion between two sets of things or as basis of calculating amount or value; charge, cost, or value; measure of this; pace of movement or change; (in *plural*) tax levied by local authorities according to value of buildings and land occupied. ● *verb* (**-ting**) estimate worth or value of; assign value to; consider, regard as; (+ *as*) rank or be considered as; subject to payment of local rate; deserve. □ **at any rate** in any case, whatever happens; **at this rate** if this example is typical; **rate-capping** *historical* imposition of upper limit on local authority rates; **ratepayer** person liable to pay rates.

rateable /'reɪtəb(ə)l/ *adjective* (also **ratable** /'reɪtəb(ə)l/) liable to rates. □ **rateable value** value at which business etc. is assessed for rates.

rather /'rɑːðə/ *adverb* by preference; (usually + *than*) more truly; as a more likely alternative; more precisely; to some extent; /rɑː'ðɜː/ most emphatically.

ratify /'rætɪfaɪ/ *verb* (**-ies, -ied**) confirm or accept by formal consent, signature, etc. □ **ratification** *noun*.

rating /'reɪtɪŋ/ *noun* placing in rank or class; estimated standing of person as regards credit etc.; non-commissioned sailor; (usually in *plural*) popularity of a broadcast as determined by estimated size of audience.

ratio /'reɪʃɪəʊ/ *noun* (*plural* **-s**) quantitative relation between similar magnitudes.

ratiocinate /rætɪ'ɒsɪneɪt/ *verb* (**-ting**) *literary* reason, esp. using syllogisms. □ **ratiocination** *noun*.

ration /'ræʃ(ə)n/ ● *noun* official allowance of food, clothing, etc., in time of shortage; (usually in *plural*) fixed daily allowance of food. ● *verb* limit (food etc. or people) to fixed ration; (usually + *out*) share (out) in fixed quantities.

rational /'ræʃən(ə)l/ *adjective* of or based on reason; sensible; endowed with reason; rejecting what is unreasonable; *Mathematics* expressible as ratio of whole numbers. □ **rationality** /-'næl-/ *noun*; **rationally** *adverb*.

rationale /ræʃə'nɑːl/ *noun* fundamental reason, logical basis.

rationalism *noun* practice of treating reason as basis of belief and knowledge. □ **rationalist** *noun & adjective*; **rationalistic** /-'lɪs-/ *adjective*.

rationalize *verb* (also **-ise**) (**-zing** or **-sing**) (often + *away*) offer rational but specious explanation of (behaviour or attitude); make logical and consistent; make (industry etc.) more efficient by reducing waste. □ **rationalization** *noun*.

ratline /'rætlɪn/ *noun* (also **ratlin**) (usually in *plural*) any of the small lines fastened across ship's shrouds like ladder rungs.

rattan /rə'tæn/ *noun* palm with long thin many-jointed stems; cane of this.

rattle /'ræt(ə)l/ ● *verb* (**-ling**) (cause to) give out rapid succession of short sharp sounds; cause such sounds by shaking something; move or travel with rattling noise; (usually + *off*) say or recite rapidly; (usually + *on*) talk in lively thoughtless way; *colloquial* disconcert, alarm. ● *noun* rattling sound; device or plaything made to rattle. □ **rattlesnake** poisonous American snake with rattling rings on tail. □ **rattly** *adjective*.

rattling ● *adjective* that rattles; brisk, vigorous. ● *adverb colloquial* remarkably (good etc.).

raucous /'rɔːkəs/ *adjective* harsh-sounding; hoarse. □ **raucously** *adverb*; **raucousness** *noun*.

raunchy /'rɔːntʃɪ/ *adjective* (**-ier, -iest**) *colloquial* sexually boisterous.

ravage /'rævɪdʒ/ ● *verb* (**-ging**) devastate, plunder. ● *noun* (usually in *plural*; + *of*) destructive effect.

rave ● *verb* (**-ving**) talk wildly or deliriously; (usually + *about, over*) speak with rapturous admiration; *colloquial* enjoy oneself freely. ● *noun colloquial* highly enthusiastic review; (also **rave-up**) lively party.

ravel /'ræv(ə)l/ *verb* (**-ll-**; *US* **-l-**) entangle, become entangled; fray out.

raven /'reɪv(ə)n/ ● *noun* large glossy black crow with hoarse cry. ● *adjective* glossy black.

ravening /'rævənɪŋ/ *adjective* hungrily seeking prey; voracious.

ravenous /'rævənəs/ *adjective* very hungry; voracious; rapacious. □ **ravenously** *adverb*.

raver *noun colloquial* uninhibited pleasure-loving person.

ravine /rə'viːn/ *noun* deep narrow gorge.

raving ● *noun* (usually in *plural*) wild or delirious talk. ● *adjective colloquial* utter, absolute. ● *adverb colloquial* utterly, absolutely.

ravioli /rævɪ'əʊlɪ/ *noun* small square pasta envelopes containing meat, spinach, etc.

ravish /'rævɪʃ/ *verb archaic* rape (woman); enrapture.

ravishing *adjective* lovely, beautiful. □ **ravishingly** *adverb*.

raw *adjective* uncooked; in natural state, not processed or manufactured; inexperienced, untrained; stripped of skin; unhealed; sensitive to touch; (of weather) cold and damp; crude. □ **in the raw** in its natural state, naked; **raw-boned** gaunt; **raw deal** unfair treatment; **rawhide** untanned hide, rope or whip of this; **raw material** material from which manufactured goods are made.

Rawlplug /'rɔːlplʌg/ *noun proprietary term* cylindrical plug for holding screw in masonry.

ray¹ *noun* single line or narrow beam of light; straight line in which radiation travels; (in *plural*) radiation; trace or beginning of enlightening influence; any of set of radiating lines, parts, or things; marginal part of daisy etc.

ray² *noun* large edible marine fish with flat body.

ray³ *noun* (also **re**) *Music* second note of scale in tonic sol-fa.

rayon /'reɪɒn/ *noun* textile fibre or fabric made from cellulose.

raze *verb* (also **rase**) (**-zing** or **-sing**) completely destroy, tear down.

razor /'reɪzə/ *noun* instrument for shaving. □ **razorbill** auk with sharp-edged bill; **razor-blade** flat piece of metal with sharp edge, used in safety razor; **razor-edge**, **razor's edge** keen edge, sharp mountain ridge, critical situation, sharp line of division.

razzle /'ræz(ə)l/ *noun colloquial* spree. □ **razzle-dazzle** excitement, bustle, extravagant publicity.

razzmatazz /ræzmə'tæz/ *noun* (also **razzamatazz** /ræzə-/) *colloquial* glamorous excitement; insincere activity.

RC *abbreviation* Roman Catholic.

Rd. *abbreviation* Road.

RE *abbreviation* Religious Education; Royal Engineers.

re¹ /riː/ *preposition* in the matter of; about, concerning.

re² = RAY³.

re- *prefix attachable to almost any verb or its derivative, meaning:* once more, anew, afresh; back. For words starting with *re-* that are not found below, the root-words should be consulted.

reach ● *verb* (often + *out*) stretch out, extend; (often + *for*) stretch hand etc.; get as far as, get to or attain; make contact with; pass, hand; take with outstretched hand; *Nautical* sail with wind abeam. ● *noun* extent to which hand etc. can be reached out, influence exerted, etc.; act of reaching out; continuous extent, esp. of river or canal. □ **reach-me-down** *colloquial* ready-made garment. □ **reachable** *adjective*.

react /rɪ'ækt/ *verb* (often + *to*) respond to stimulus; change or behave differently due to some influence; (often + *with*) undergo chemical reaction (with other substance); (often + *against*) respond with repulsion to; tend in reverse or contrary direction.

reaction /rɪ'ækʃ(ə)n/ *noun* reacting; response; bad physical response to drug etc.; occurrence of condition after its opposite; tendency to oppose change or reform; interaction of substances undergoing chemical change.

reactionary ● *adjective* tending to oppose (esp. political) change or reform. ● *noun* (*plural* **-ies**) reactionary person.

reactivate /rɪ'æktɪveɪt/ *verb* (**-ting**) restore to state of activity. □ **reactivation** *noun*.

reactive /rɪ'æktɪv/ *adjective* showing reaction; reacting rather than taking initiative; susceptible to chemical reaction.

reactor *noun* (in full **nuclear reactor**) device in which nuclear chain reaction is used to produce energy.

read ● *verb* (*past & past participle* **read** /red/) reproduce (written or printed words) mentally or (often + *aloud, out, off*, etc.) vocally; (be able to) convert (written or printed words or other symbols) into intended words or meaning; interpret; (of meter) show (figure); interpret state of (meter); study (subject) at university; (as **read** /red/ *adjective*) versed in subject (esp. literature) by reading; (of computer) copy or transfer (data); hear and understand (over radio); substitute (word etc.) for incorrect one. ● *noun* spell of reading; *colloquial* book etc. as regards readability. □ **take as read** treat (thing) as if it has been agreed.

readable *adjective* able to be read; interesting to read. □ **readability** *noun*.

reader *noun* person who reads; book intended for reading pratice; device for producing image that can be read from microfilm etc.; (also **Reader**) university lecturer of highest grade below professor; publisher's employee who reports on submitted manuscripts; printer's proof-corrector.

readership *noun* readers of a newspaper etc.; (also **Readership**) position of Reader.

readily *adverb* without reluctance; willingly; easily.

readiness *noun* prepared state; willingness; facility; promptness in argument or action.

reading *noun* act of reading; matter to be read; literary knowledge; entertainment at which something is read; figure etc. shown by recording instrument; interpretation or view taken; interpretation made (of music etc.); presentation of bill to legislature.

ready /'redɪ/ ● *adjective* (**-ier, -iest**) with preparations complete; in fit state; willing; (of income etc.) easily secured; fit for immediate use; prompt, enthusiastic; (+ *to do*) about to; provided beforehand. ● *adverb* usually in combination beforehand; in readiness. ● *noun slang* (**the ready**) ready money; (**readies**) bank notes. ● *verb* (**-ies, -ied**) prepare. □ **at the ready** ready for action; **ready-made**, **ready-to-wear** (esp. of clothes) made in standard size, not to measure; **ready money** cash, actual coin; **ready reckoner** book or table listing standard numerical calculations.

reagent /riː'eɪdʒ(ə)nt/ *noun* substance used to produce chemical reaction.

real ● *adjective* actually existing or occurring; genuine; appraised by purchasing power. ● *adverb Scottish & US colloquial* really, very. □ **real ale** beer regarded as brewed in traditional way; **real estate** property such as land and houses; **real tennis** original form of tennis played on indoor court.

realism *noun* practice of regarding things in their true nature and dealing with them as they are; fidelity to nature in representation. □ **realist** *noun*.

realistic /rɪə'lɪstɪk/ *adjective* regarding things as they are; based on facts rather than ideals. □ **realistically** *adverb*.

reality /rɪ'ælɪtɪ/ *noun* (*plural* **-ies**) what is real or existent or underlies appearances; (+ *of*) real nature of; real existence; being real; likeness to original. □ **in reality** in fact.

realize *verb* (also **-ise**) (**-zing** or **-sing**) (often + *that*) be or become fully aware of; understand clearly; convert into actuality; convert into money; acquire (profit); be sold for. □ **realizable** *adjective*; **realization** *noun*.

really /'rɪəlɪ/ *adverb* in fact; very; I assure you; *expression of mild protest or surprise*.

realm /relm/ *noun formal* kingdom; domain.

realty /'riːəltɪ/ *noun* real estate.

ream *noun* 500 sheets of paper; (in *plural*) large quantity of writing.

reap *verb* cut (grain etc.) as harvest; receive as consequences of actions. □ **reaper** *noun*.

rear[1] ● *noun* back part of anything; space or position at back. ● *adjective* at the back. □ **bring up the rear** come last; **rear admiral** naval officer below vice admiral. □ **rearmost** *adjective*.

rear[2] *verb* bring up and educate; breed and care for; cultivate; (of horse etc.) raise itself on hind legs; raise, build.

rearguard *noun* troops detached to protect rear, esp. in retreat. □ **rearguard action** engagement undertaken by rearguard, defensive stand or struggle, esp. when losing.

rearm /riː'ɑːm/ *verb* arm again, esp. with improved weapons. □ **rearmament** *noun*.

rearward /'rɪəwəd/ ● *noun* rear. ● *adjective* to the rear. ● *adverb* (also **rearwards**) towards the rear.

reason /'riːz(ə)n/ ● *noun* motive, cause, or justification; fact adduced or serving as this; intellectual faculty by which conclusions are drawn; sanity; sense, sensible conduct; moderation. ● *verb* form or try to reach conclusions by connected thought; (+ *with*) use argument with person by way of persuasion; (+ *that*) conclude or assert in argument; (+ *out*) think out.

reasonable *adjective* having sound judgement; moderate; ready to listen to reason; sensible; inexpensive; tolerable. □ **reasonableness** *noun*; **reasonably** *adverb*.

reassure /riːə'ʃʊə/ *verb* (**-ring**) restore confidence to; confirm in opinion etc. □ **reassurance** *noun*; **reassuring** *adjective*.

rebate[1] /'riːbeɪt/ *noun* partial refund; deduction from sum to be paid, discount.

rebate[2] /'riːbeɪt/ *noun & verb* (**-ting**) rabbet.

rebel ● *noun* /'reb(ə)l/ person who fights against, resists, or refuses allegiance to, established government; person etc. who resists authority or control. ● *verb* /rɪ'bel/ (**-ll-**) (usually + *against*) act as rebel; feel or show repugnance.

rebellion /rɪ'beljən/ *noun* open resistance to authority, esp. organized armed resistance to established government.

rebellious /rɪ'beljəs/ *adjective* disposed to rebel; in rebellion; unmanageable. □ **rebelliously** *adverb*; **rebelliousness** *noun*.

rebound *verb* /rɪ'baʊnd/ spring back after impact; (+ *upon*) have adverse effect on (doer). ● *noun* /'riːbaʊnd/ rebounding, recoil; reaction. □ **on the rebound** while still recovering from emotional shock, esp. rejection by lover.

rebuff /rɪ'bʌf/ ● *noun* rejection of person who makes advances, offers help, etc.; snub. ● *verb* give rebuff to.

rebuke /rɪ'bjuːk/ ● *verb* (**-king**) express sharp disapproval of (person) for fault; censure. ● *noun* rebuking, being rebuked.

rebus /'riːbəs/ *noun* (*plural* **rebuses**) representation of word (esp. name) by pictures etc. suggesting its parts.

rebut /rɪ'bʌt/ *verb* (**-tt-**) refute, disprove; force back. □ **rebuttal** *noun*.

recalcitrant /rɪ'kælsɪtrənt/ *adjective* obstinately disobedient; objecting to restraint. □ **recalcitrance** *noun*.

recall /rɪ'kɔːl/ ● *verb* summon to return; recollect, remember; bring back to memory; revoke, annul; revive, resuscitate. ● *noun* (also /'riːkɔːl/) summons to come back; act of remembering; ability to remember; possibility of recalling.

recant /rɪ'kænt/ *verb* withdraw and renounce (belief or statement) as erroneous or heretical. □ **recantation** /riːkæn'teɪʃ(ə)n/ *noun*.

recap /'riːkæp/ *colloquial* ● *verb* (**-pp-**) recapitulate. ● *noun* recapitulation.

recapitulate /riːkə'pɪtjʊleɪt/ *verb* (**-ting**) summarize, restate briefly. □ **recapitulation** *noun*.

recast /riː'kɑːst/ ● *verb* (*past & past participle* **recast**) cast again; put into new form; improve arrangement of. ● *noun* recasting; recast form.

recce /'rekɪ/ *colloquial* ● *noun* reconnaissance. ● *verb* (**recced, recceing**) reconnoitre.

recede /rɪ'siːd/ *verb* (**-ding**) go or shrink back; be left at an increasing distance; slope backwards; decline in force or value.

receipt /rɪ'siːt/ ● *noun* receiving, being received; written or printed acknowledgement of payment received; (usually in *plural*) amount of money received. ● *verb* place written or printed receipt on (bill). □ **in receipt of** having received.

receive /rɪ'siːv/ *verb* (**-ving**) take or accept (thing offered, sent, or given); acquire; have conferred etc. on one; react to (news etc.) in particular way; stand force or weight of; consent to hear or consider; admit, entertain as guest, greet, welcome; be able to hold; convert (broadcast signals) into sound or pictures; (as **received** *adjective*) accepted as authoritative or true. □ **Received Pronunciation** standard pronunciation of English in Britain (see panel at ACCENT).

receiver *noun* part of telephone containing earpiece; (in full **official receiver**) person appointed to administer property of bankrupt person etc. or property under litigation; radio or television receiving apparatus; person who receives stolen goods.

receivership *noun* □ **in receivership** being dealt with by receiver.

recent /'riːs(ə)nt/ *adjective* not long past, that happened or existed lately; not long established, modern. □ **recently** *adverb*.

receptacle /rɪ'septək(ə)l/ *noun* object or space used to contain something.

reception /rɪ'sepʃ(ə)n/ *noun* receiving, being received; way in which person or thing is received; social occasion for receiving guests, esp. after wedding; place where visitors register on arriving at hotel, office, etc.; (quality of) receiving of broadcast signals. □ **reception room** room for receiving guests, clients, etc.

receptionist *noun* person employed to receive guests, clients, etc.

receptive /rɪ'septɪv/ *adjective* able or quick to receive ideas etc. □ **receptively** *adverb*; **receptiveness** *noun*; **receptivity** /riːsep'tɪv-/ *noun*.

recess /rɪ'ses/ ● *noun* space set back in wall; (often in *plural*) remote or secret place; temporary cessation from work, esp. of Parliament. ● *verb* make recess in; place in recess; *US* take recess, adjourn.

recession /rɪ'seʃ(ə)n/ *noun* temporary decline in economic activity or prosperity; receding, withdrawal.

recessive /rɪ'sesɪv/ *adjective* tending to recede; (of inherited characteristic) appearing in offspring only when not masked by inherited dominant characteristic.

recherché /rə'ʃeəʃeɪ/ *adjective* carefully sought out; far-fetched.

recidivist /rɪ'sɪdɪvɪst/ *noun* person who relapses into crime. □ **recidivism** *noun*.

recipe /'resɪpɪ/ *noun* statement of ingredients and procedure for preparing dish etc.; (+ *for*) certain means to.

recipient /rɪ'sɪpɪənt/ *noun* person who receives something.

reciprocal /rɪˈsɪprək(ə)l/ ● *adjective* in return; mutual; *Grammar* expressing mutual relation. ● *noun Mathematics* function or expression so related to another that their product is unity. □ **reciprocally** *adverb*.

reciprocate /rɪˈsɪprəkeɪt/ *verb* (**-ting**) requite, return; (+ *with*) give in return; interchange; (of machine part) move backwards and forwards. □ **reciprocation** *noun*.

reciprocity /resɪˈprɒsɪtɪ/ *noun* condition of being reciprocal; mutual action; give and take.

recital /rɪˈsaɪt(ə)l/ *noun* reciting, being recited; concert of classical music by soloist or small group; (+ *of*) detailed account of (facts etc.); narrative.

recitation /resɪˈteɪʃ(ə)n/ *noun* reciting; piece recited.

recitative /resɪtəˈtiːv/ *noun* passage of singing in speech rhythm, esp. in narrative or dialogue section of opera or oratorio.

recite /rɪˈsaɪt/ *verb* (**-ting**) repeat aloud or declaim from memory; enumerate.

reckless /ˈreklɪs/ *adjective* disregarding consequences or danger etc. □ **recklessly** *adverb*; **recklessness** *noun*.

reckon /ˈrekən/ *verb* (often + *that*) think, consider; count or compute by calculation; (+ *on*) rely or base plans on; (+ *with*, *without*) take (or fail to take) into account.

reckoning *noun* calculating; opinion; settlement of account.

reclaim /rɪˈkleɪm/ *verb* seek return of (one's property etc.); bring (land) under cultivation from sea etc.; win back from vice, error, or waste condition. □ **reclaimable** *adjective*; **reclamation** /reklə-/ *noun*.

recline /rɪˈklaɪn/ *verb* (**-ning**) assume or be in horizontal or leaning position.

recluse /rɪˈkluːs/ *noun* person given to or living in seclusion. □ **reclusive** *adjective*.

recognition /rekəɡˈnɪʃ(ə)n/ *noun* recognizing, being recognized.

recognizance /rɪˈkɒɡnɪz(ə)ns/ *noun Law* bond by which person undertakes to observe some condition; sum pledged as surety for this.

recognize /ˈrekəɡnaɪz/ *verb* (also **-ise**) (**-zing** or **-sing**) identify as already known; realize or discover nature of; (+ *that*) realize or admit; acknowledge existence, validity, character, or claims of; show appreciation of; reward. □ **recognizable** *adjective*.

recoil ● *verb* /rɪˈkɔɪl/ jerk or spring back in horror, disgust, or fear; shrink mentally in this way; rebound; (of gun) be driven backwards by discharge. ● *noun* /ˈriːkɔɪl/ act or sensation of recoiling.

recollect /rekəˈlekt/ *verb* remember; call to mind.

recollection /rekəˈlekʃ(ə)n/ *noun* act or power of recollecting; thing recollected; person's memory, time over which it extends.

recommend /rekəˈmend/ *verb* suggest as fit for purpose or use; advise (course of action etc.); (of qualities etc.) make acceptable or desirable; (+ *to*) commend or entrust. □ **recommendation** *noun*.

recompense /ˈrekəmpens/ ● *verb* (**-sing**) make amends to; compensate; reward or punish. ● *noun* reward; compensation; retribution.

reconcile /ˈrekənsaɪl/ *verb* (**-ling**) make friendly again after estrangement; (usually **reconcile oneself** or in *passive*; + *to*) make resigned to; settle (quarrel etc.); harmonize; make compatible; show compatibility of. □ **reconcilable** /-ˈsaɪl-/ *adjective*; **reconciliation** /-sɪlɪ-/ *noun*.

recondite /ˈrekəndaɪt/ *adjective* abstruse; obscure.

recondition /riːkənˈdɪʃ(ə)n/ *verb* overhaul, renovate, make usable again.

reconnaissance /rɪˈkɒnɪs(ə)ns/ *noun* survey of region to locate enemy or ascertain strategic features; preliminary survey.

reconnoitre /rekəˈnɔɪtə/ *verb* (US **reconnoiter**) (**-ring**) make reconnaissance (of).

reconsider /riːkənˈsɪdə/ *verb* consider again, esp. for possible change of decision.

reconstitute /riːˈkɒnstɪtjuːt/ *verb* (**-ting**) reconstruct; reorganize; rehydrate (dried food etc.). □ **reconstitution** /-ˈtjuːʃ(ə)n/ *noun*.

reconstruct /riːkənˈstrʌkt/ *verb* build again; form impression of (past events) by assembling evidence; re-enact (crime); reorganize. □ **reconstruction** *noun*.

record ● *noun* /ˈrekɔːd/ evidence etc. constituting account of occurrence, statement, etc.; document etc. preserving this; (in full **gramophone record**) disc carrying recorded sound in grooves, for reproduction by record player; facts known about person's past, esp. criminal convictions; best performance or most remarkable event of its kind. ● *verb* /rɪˈkɔːd/ put in writing or other permanent form for later reference; convert (sound etc.) into permanent form for later reproduction. □ **have a record** have criminal conviction; **off the record** unofficially, confidentially; **on record** officially recorded, publicly known; **recorded delivery** Post Office service in which dispatch and receipt are recorded; **record player** apparatus for reproducing sounds from gramophone records.

recorder /rɪˈkɔːdə/ *noun* apparatus for recording; woodwind instrument; (also **Recorder**) barrister or solicitor serving as part-time judge.

recording /rɪˈkɔːdɪŋ/ *noun* process of recording sound etc. for later reproduction; material or programme recorded.

recordist /rɪˈkɔːdɪst/ *noun* person who records sound.

recount /rɪˈkaʊnt/ *verb* narrate; tell in detail.

re-count ● *verb* /riːˈkaʊnt/ count again. ● *noun* /ˈriːkaʊnt/ re-counting, esp. of votes.

recoup /rɪˈkuːp/ *verb* recover or regain (loss); compensate or reimburse for loss.

recourse /rɪˈkɔːs/ *noun* resort to possible source of help; person or thing resorted to.

recover /rɪˈkʌvə/ *verb* regain possession, use, or control of; return to health, consciousness, or normal state or position; secure by legal process; make up for; retrieve. □ **recoverable** *adjective*.

re-cover /riːˈkʌvə/ *verb* cover again; provide (chairs etc.) with new cover.

recovery *noun* (*plural* **-ies**) recovering, being recovered.

recreant /ˈrekrɪənt/ *literary* ● *adjective* cowardly. ● *noun* coward.

re-create /riːkrɪˈeɪt/ *verb* (**-ting**) create anew; reproduce. □ **re-creation** *noun*.

recreation /rekrɪˈeɪʃ(ə)n/ *noun* (means of) entertaining oneself; pleasurable activity. □ **recreation ground** public land for sports etc. □ **recreational** *adjective*.

recriminate /rɪˈkrɪmɪneɪt/ *verb* (**-ting**) make mutual or counter accusations. □ **recrimination** *noun*; **recriminatory** *adjective*.

recrudesce /riːkruːˈdes/ *verb* (**-cing**) *formal* (of disease, problem, etc.) break out again. □ **recrudescence** *noun*; **recrudescent** *adjective*.

recruit /rɪˈkruːt/ ● *noun* newly enlisted serviceman or servicewoman; new member of a society etc. ● *verb* enlist (person) as recruit; form (army etc.) by enlisting recruits; replenish, reinvigorate. □ **recruitment** *noun*.

rectal /ˈrekt(ə)l/ *adjective* of or by means of rectum.

rectangle /'rektæŋg(ə)l/ *noun* plane figure with 4 straight sides and 4 right angles. □ **rectangular** /-'tæŋgjʊlə/ *adjective*.

rectify /'rektɪfaɪ/ *verb* (**-ies, -ied**) adjust or make right; purify, esp. by repeated distillation; convert (alternating current) to direct current. □ **rectifiable** *adjective*; **rectification** *noun*.

rectilinear /rektɪ'lɪnɪə/ *adjective* bounded or characterized by straight lines; in or forming straight line.

rectitude /'rektɪtjuːd/ *noun* moral uprightness.

recto /'rektəʊ/ *noun* (*plural* **-s**) right-hand page of open book; front of printed leaf.

rector /'rektə/ *noun* incumbent of C. of E. parish where in former times all tithes passed to incumbent; head priest of church or religious institution; head of university or college. □ **rectorship** *noun*.

rectory *noun* (*plural* **-ies**) rector's house.

rectum /'rektəm/ *noun* (*plural* **-s**) final section of large intestine.

recumbent /rɪ'kʌmbənt/ *adjective* lying down, reclining.

recuperate /rɪ'kuːpəreɪt/ *verb* (**-ting**) recover from illness, exhaustion, loss, etc.; regain (health, loss, etc.). □ **recuperation** *noun*; **recuperative** /-rətɪv/ *adjective*.

recur /rɪ'kɜː/ *verb* (**-rr-**) occur again or repeatedly; (+ *to*) go back to in thought or speech; (as **recurring** *adjective*) (of decimal fraction) with same figure(s) repeated indefinitely.

recurrent /rɪ'kʌrənt/ *adjective* recurring. □ **recurrence** *noun*.

recusant /'rekjʊz(ə)nt/ *noun* person refusing submission or compliance, esp. (*historical*) one who refused to attend services of the Church of England. □ **recusancy** *noun*.

recycle /riː'saɪk(ə)l/ *verb* (**-ling**) convert (waste) to reusable material. □ **recyclable** *adjective*.

red ● *adjective* (**-dd-**) of colour from that of blood to deep pink or orange; flushed; bloodshot; (of hair) reddish-brown; having to do with bloodshed, burning, violence, or revolution; *colloquial* Communist. ● *noun* red colour, paint, clothes, etc.; *colloquial* Communist. □ **in the red** in debt or deficit; **red admiral** butterfly with red bands; **red-blooded** virile, vigorous; **redbrick** (of university) founded in the 19th or early 20th c.; **red card** Football card shown by referee to player being sent off; **red carpet** privileged treatment of eminent visitor; **redcoat** *historical* British soldier; **Red Crescent** equivalent of Red Cross in Muslim countries; **Red Cross** international relief organization; **redcurrant** small red edible berry, shrub bearing it; **red flag** symbol of revolution, danger signal; **red-handed** in act of crime; **redhead** person with red hair; **red herring** irrelevant diversion; **red-hot** heated until red, *colloquial* highly exciting or excited, *colloquial* (of news) completely new; **red lead** red oxide of lead as pigment; **red-letter day** joyfully noteworthy or memorable day; **red light** stop signal, warning; **red meat** meat that is red when raw (e.g. beef); **red neck** conservative working-class white in southern US; **red pepper** cayenne pepper, red fruit of capsicum; **red rag** thing that excites rage; **redshank** sandpiper with bright red legs; **red shift** displacement of spectrum to longer wavelengths in light from receding galaxies; **redstart** red-tailed songbird; **red tape** excessive bureaucracy or formality; **redwing** thrush with red underwings; **redwood** tree with red wood. □ **reddish** *adjective*; **redness** *noun*.

redden *verb* make or become red; blush.

redeem /rɪ'diːm/ *verb* recover by expenditure of effort; make single payment to cancel (regular charge etc.); convert (tokens or bonds) into goods or cash; deliver from sin and damnation; (often as **redeeming** *adjective*) make amends or compensate for; save, rescue, reclaim; fulfil (promise). □ **redeemable** *adjective*.

redeemer *noun* one who redeems, esp. Christ.

redemption /rɪ'dempʃ(ə)n/ *noun* redeeming, being redeemed.

redeploy /riːdɪ'plɔɪ/ *verb* send (troops, workers, etc.) to new place or task. □ **redeployment** *noun*.

rediffusion /riːdɪ'fjuːʒ(ə)n/ *noun* relaying of broadcast programmes, esp. by cable from central receiver.

redolent /'redələnt/ *adjective* (+ *of, with*) strongly smelling or suggestive of. □ **redolence** *noun*.

redouble /riː'dʌb(ə)l/ *verb* (**-ling**) make or grow greater or more intense or numerous; double again.

redoubt /rɪ'daʊt/ *noun* Military outwork or fieldwork without flanking defences.

redoubtable /rɪ'daʊtəb(ə)l/ *adjective* formidable.

redound /rɪ'daʊnd/ *verb* (+ *to*) make great contribution to (one's advantage etc.); (+ *upon, on*) come back or recoil upon.

redress /rɪ'dres/ ● *verb* remedy; put right again. ● *noun* reparation; (+ *of*) redressing.

reduce /rɪ'djuːs/ *verb* (**-cing**) make or become smaller or less; (+ *to*) bring by force or necessity; convert to another (esp. simpler) form; bring lower in status, rank, or price; lessen one's weight or size; make (sauce etc.) more concentrated by boiling; weaken; impoverish; subdue. □ **reduced circumstances** poverty after relative property. □ **reducible** *adjective*.

reduction /rɪ'dʌkʃ(ə)n/ *noun* reducing, being reduced; amount by which prices etc. are reduced; smaller copy of picture etc. □ **reductive** *adjective*.

redundant /rɪ'dʌnd(ə)nt/ *adjective* superfluous; that can be omitted without loss of significance; no longer needed at work and therefore unemployed. □ **redundancy** *noun* (*plural* **-ies**).

reduplicate /rɪ'djuːplɪkeɪt/ *verb* (**-ting**) make double; repeat. □ **reduplication** *noun*.

re-echo /riː'ekəʊ/ *verb* (**-es, -ed**) echo repeatedly; resound.

reed *noun* firm-stemmed water or marsh plant; tall straight stalk of this; vibrating part of some wind instruments. □ **reedy** *adjective* (**-ier, -iest**).

reef¹ *noun* ridge of rock or coral etc. at or near surface of sea; lode of ore, bedrock surrounding this.

reef² ● *noun* each of several strips across sail, for taking it in etc. ● *verb* take in reef(s) of (sail). □ **reef-knot** symmetrical double knot.

reefer *noun slang* marijuana cigarette; thick double-breasted jacket.

reek ● *verb* (often + *of*) smell unpleasantly; have suspicious associations. ● *noun* foul or stale smell; *esp. Scottish* smoke; vapour, exhalation.

reel ● *noun* cylindrical device on which thread, paper, film, wire, etc. are wound; device for winding and unwinding line as required, esp. in fishing; lively folk or Scottish dance, music for this. ● *verb* wind on reel; (+ *in, up*) draw in or up with reel; stand, walk, etc. unsteadily; be shaken physically or mentally; dance reel. □ **reel off** recite rapidly and without apparent effort.

re-entrant /riː'entrənt/ *adjective* (of angle) pointing inwards.

re-entry /riː'entrɪ/ *noun* (*plural* **-ies**) act of entering again, esp. (of spacecraft etc.) of re-entering earth's atmosphere.

reeve *noun historical* chief magistrate of town or district; official supervising landowner's estate.

ref¹ *noun colloquial* referee.

ref² *noun colloquial* reference.

refectory /rɪˈfektərɪ/ *noun* (*plural* **-ies**) dining-room, esp. in monastery or college. □ **refectory table** long narrow table.

refer /rɪˈfɜː/ *verb* (**-rr-**) (usually + *to*) have recourse to (some authority or source of information); send on or direct; make allusion or be relevant. □ **referred pain** pain felt in part of body other than actual source. □ **referable** *adjective*.

referee /refəˈriː/ ● *noun* umpire, esp. in football or boxing; person referred to for decision in dispute etc.; person willing to testify to character of applicant for employment etc. ● *verb* (**-rees, -reed**) act as referee (for).

reference /ˈrefərəns/ *noun* referring to some authority; scope given to such authority; (+ *to*) relation, respect, or allusion to; direction to page, book, etc. for information; written testimonial, person giving it. □ **reference book** book for occasional consultation. □ **referential** /-ˈren-/ *adjective*.

referendum /refəˈrendəm/ *noun* (*plural* **-s** or **-da**) vote on political question open to entire electorate.

referral /rɪˈfɜːr(ə)l/ *noun* referring of person to medical specialist etc.

refill ● *verb* /riːˈfɪl/ fill again. ● *noun* /ˈriːfɪl/ thing that refills; act of refilling. □ **refillable** *adjective*.

refine /rɪˈfaɪn/ *verb* (**-ning**) free from impurities or defects; (esp. as **refined** *adjective*) make or become more elegant or cultured.

refinement *noun* refining, being refined; fineness of feeling or taste; elegance; added development or improvement; subtle reasoning; fine distinction.

refiner *noun* person or firm refining crude oil, metal, sugar, etc.

refinery *noun* (*plural* **-ies**) place where oil etc. is refined.

refit ● *verb* /riːˈfɪt/ (**-tt-**) *esp. Nautical* make or become serviceable again by repairs etc. ● *noun* /ˈriːfɪt/ refitting.

reflate /riːˈfleɪt/ *verb* (**-ting**) cause reflation of (currency, economy, etc.).

reflation *noun* inflation of financial system to restore previous condition after deflation. □ **reflationary** *adjective*.

reflect /rɪˈflekt/ *verb* throw back (light, heat, sound, etc.); (of mirror etc.) show image of, reproduce to eye or mind; correspond in appearance or effect to; bring (credit, discredit, etc.); (usually + *on, upon*) bring discredit; (often + *on, upon*) meditate; (+ *that, how,* etc.) consider.

reflection /rɪˈflekʃ(ə)n/ *noun* reflecting, being reflected; reflected light, heat, colour, or image; reconsideration; (often + *on*) thing bringing discredit; (often + *on, upon*) comment.

reflective *adjective* (of surface) reflecting; (of mental faculties) concerned in reflection or thought; thoughtful. □ **reflectively** *adverb*.

reflector *noun* piece of glass or metal for reflecting light in required direction; telescope etc. using mirror to produce images.

reflex /ˈriːfleks/ ● *adjective* (of action) independent of will; (of angle) larger than 180°. ● *noun* reflex action; sign, secondary manifestation; reflected light or image. □ **reflex camera** camera in which image is reflected by mirror to enable correct focusing.

reflexive /rɪˈfleksɪv/ *Grammar* ● *adjective* (of word or form) referring back to subject (e.g. *myself* in I *hurt myself*); (of verb) having reflexive pronoun as object. ● *noun* reflexive word or form.

reflexology /riːflekˈsɒlədʒɪ/ *noun* massage to areas of soles of feet. □ **reflexologist** *noun*.

reform /rɪˈfɔːm/ ● *verb* make or become better; abolish or cure (abuse etc.). ● *noun* removal of abuses, esp. political; improvement. □ **reformative** *adjective*.

reformation /refəˈmeɪʃ(ə)n/ *noun* reforming or being reformed, esp. radical improvement in political, religious, or social affairs; (**the Reformation**) 16th-c. movement for reform of abuses in Roman Church ending in establishment of Reformed or Protestant Churches.

reformatory /rɪˈfɔːmətərɪ/ ● *noun* (*plural* **-ies**) US *historical* institution for reform of young offenders. ● *adjective* producing reform.

reformer *noun* advocate of reform.

reformism *noun* policy of reform rather than abolition or revolution. □ **reformist** *noun & adjective*.

refract /rɪˈfrækt/ *verb* deflect (light) at certain angle when it enters obliquely from another medium. □ **refraction** *noun*; **refractive** *adjective*.

refractor *noun* refracting medium or lens; telescope using lens to produce image.

refractory /rɪˈfræktərɪ/ *adjective* stubborn, unmanageable, rebellious; resistant to treatment; hard to fuse or work.

refrain¹ /rɪˈfreɪn/ *verb* (+ *from*) avoid doing (action).

refrain² /rɪˈfreɪn/ *noun* recurring phrase or lines, esp. at ends of stanzas.

refresh /rɪˈfreʃ/ *verb* give fresh spirit or vigour to; revive (memory). □ **refreshing** *adjective*; **refreshingly** *adverb*.

refresher *noun* something that refreshes, esp. drink; extra fee to counsel in prolonged lawsuit. □ **refresher course** course reviewing or updating previous studies.

refreshment *noun* refreshing, being refreshed; (usually in *plural*) food or drink.

refrigerant /rɪˈfrɪdʒərənt/ ● *noun* substance used for refrigeration. ● *adjective* cooling.

refrigerate /rɪˈfrɪdʒəreɪt/ *verb* (**-ting**) cool or freeze (esp. food). □ **refrigeration** *noun*.

refrigerator *noun* cabinet or room in which food etc. is refrigerated.

refuge /ˈrefjuːdʒ/ *noun* shelter from pursuit, danger, or trouble; person or place offering this.

refugee /refjuˈdʒiː/ *noun* person taking refuge, esp. in foreign country, from war, persecution, etc.

refulgent /rɪˈfʌldʒ(ə)nt/ *adjective literary* shining, gloriously bright. □ **refulgence** *noun*.

refund ● *verb* /rɪˈfʌnd/ pay back (money etc.); reimburse. ● *noun* /ˈriːfʌnd/ act of refunding; sum refunded. □ **refundable** /rɪˈfʌn-/ *adjective*.

refurbish /riːˈfɜːbɪʃ/ *verb* brighten up, redecorate. □ **refurbishment** *noun*.

refusal /rɪˈfjuːz(ə)l/ *noun* refusing, being refused; (in full **first refusal**) chance of taking thing before it is offered to others.

refuse¹ /rɪˈfjuːz/ *verb* (**-sing**) withhold acceptance of or consent to; (often + *to do*) indicate unwillingness; not grant (request) made by (person); (of horse) be unwilling to jump (fence etc.).

refuse² /ˈrefjuːs/ *noun* items rejected as worthless; waste.

refusenik /rɪˈfjuːznɪk/ *noun historical* Soviet Jew refused permission to emigrate to Israel.

refute /rɪˈfjuːt/ *verb* (**-ting**) prove falsity or error of; rebut by argument; deny or contradict (without argument). □ **refutation** /refjʊˈteɪʃ(ə)n/ *noun*.

■ **Usage** The use of *refute* to mean 'deny, contradict' is considered incorrect by some people. *Repudiate* can be used instead.

reg /redʒ/ *noun colloquial* registration mark.

regain /rɪˈgeɪn/ *verb* obtain possession or use of after loss.

regal /ˈriːg(ə)l/ *adjective* of or by monarch(s); magnificent. □ **regality** /rɪˈgæl-/ *noun*; **regally** *adverb*.

regale /rɪˈgeɪl/ *verb* (**-ling**) entertain lavishly with feasting; (+ *with*) entertain with (talk etc.).

regalia /rɪˈgeɪlɪə/ *plural noun* insignia of royalty or an order, mayor, etc.

regard /rɪˈgɑːd/ ● *verb* gaze on; heed, take into account; look upon or think of in specified way. ● *noun* gaze; steady look; attention, care; esteem; (in *plural*) *expression of friendliness in letter etc.* □ **as regards** about, in respect of; **in this regard** on this point; **in, with regard to** in respect of.

regardful *adjective* (+ *of*) mindful of.

regarding *preposition* concerning; in respect of.

regardless ● *adjective* (+ *of*) without regard or consideration for. ● *adverb* without paying attention.

regatta /rɪˈgætə/ *noun* event consisting of rowing or yacht races.

· regency /ˈriːdʒənsɪ/ *noun* (*plural* **-ies**) office of regent; commission acting as regent; regent's or regency commission's period of office; (**Regency**) (in UK) 1811–1820.

regenerate ● *verb* /rɪˈdʒenəreɪt/ (**-ting**) bring or come into renewed existence; improve moral condition of; impart new, more vigorous, or spiritually higher life or nature to; regrow or cause (new tissue) to regrow. ● *adjective* /-rət/ spiritually born again, reformed. ● **regeneration** *noun*; **regenerative** /-rətɪv/ *adjective*.

regent /ˈriːdʒ(ə)nt/ ● *noun* person acting as head of state because monarch is absent, ill, or a child. ● *adjective* (after noun) acting as regent.

reggae /ˈregeɪ/ *noun* W. Indian style of music with strongly accented subsidiary beat.

regicide /ˈredʒɪsaɪd/ *noun* person who kills or helps to kill a king; killing of a king.

regime /reɪˈʒiːm/ *noun* (also **régime**) method of government; prevailing system; regimen.

regimen /ˈredʒɪmən/ *noun* prescribed course of exercise, way of life, and diet.

regiment ● *noun* /ˈredʒɪmənt/ permanent unit of army consisting of several companies, troops, or batteries; (usually + *of*) large or formidable array or number. ● *verb* /-ment/ organize in groups or according to system; form into regiment(s). □ **regimentation** /-men-/ *noun*.

regimental /redʒɪˈment(ə)l/ ● *adjective* of a regiment. ● *noun* (in *plural*) military uniform, esp. of particular regiment.

Regina /rɪˈdʒaɪnə/ *noun* (after name) reigning queen; *Law* the Crown. [Latin]

region /ˈriːdʒ(ə)n/ *noun* geographical area or division, having definable boundaries or characteristics; administrative area, esp. in Scotland; part of body; sphere, realm. □ **in the region of** approximately. □ **regional** *adjective*; **regionally** *adverb*.

register /ˈredʒɪstə/ ● *noun* official list; book in which items are recorded for reference; device recording speed, force, etc.; compass of voice or instrument; form of language used in particular circumstances; adjustable plate for regulating draught etc. ● *verb* set down formally, record in writing; enter or cause to be entered in register; send (letter) by registered post; record automatically, indicate; make mental note of; show (emotion etc.) in face etc.; make impression. □ **registered post** postal procedure with special precautions and compensation in case of loss; **register office** state office where civil marriages are conducted and births, marriages, and deaths are recorded.

registrar /redʒɪˈstrɑː/ *noun* official keeping register; chief administrator in university etc.; hospital doctor training as specialist.

registration /redʒɪˈstreɪʃ(ə)n/ *noun* registering, being registered. □ **registration mark, number** combination of letters and numbers identifying vehicle.

registry /ˈredʒɪstrɪ/ *noun* (*plural* **-ies**) place where registers or records are kept. □ **registry office** register office (the official name).

Regius professor /ˈriːdʒɪəs/ *noun* holder of university chair founded by sovereign or filled by Crown appointment.

regress ● *verb* /rɪˈgres/ move backwards; return to former stage or state. ● *noun* /ˈriːgres/ act of regressing. □ **regression** /rɪˈgreʃ(ə)n/ *noun*; **regressive** /rɪˈgresɪv/ *adjective*.

regret /rɪˈgret/ ● *verb* (**-tt-**) feel or express sorrow, repentance, or distress over (action or loss); say with sorrow or remorse. ● *noun* sorrow, repentance, or distress over action or loss. □ **regretful** *adjective*; **regretfully** *adverb*.

regrettable *adjective* undesirable, unwelcome; deserving censure. □ **regrettably** *adverb*.

regular /ˈregjʊlə/ ● *adjective* acting, done, or recurring uniformly; habitual, orderly; conforming to rule or principle; symmetrical; conforming to correct procedure etc.; *Grammar* (of verb etc.) following normal type of inflection; *colloquial* absolute, thorough; (of soldier etc.) permanent, professional. ● *noun* regular soldier; *colloquial* regular customer, visitor, etc.; one of regular clergy. □ **regularity** /-ˈlærɪtɪ/ *noun*; **regularize** *verb* (also **-ise**) (**-zing** or **-sing**); **regularly** *adverb*.

regulate /ˈregjʊleɪt/ *verb* (**-ting**) control by rule, subject to restrictions; adapt to requirements; adjust (clock, watch, etc.) to work accurately. □ **regulator** *noun*.

regulation ● *noun* regulating, being regulated; prescribed rule. ● *adjective* in accordance with regulations, of correct pattern etc.

regulo /ˈregjʊləʊ/ *noun* (usually + numeral) number on scale denoting temperature in gas oven.

regurgitate /rɪˈgɜːdʒɪteɪt/ *verb* (**-ting**) bring (swallowed food) up again to mouth; reproduce (information etc.). □ **regurgitation** *noun*.

rehabilitate /riːhəˈbɪlɪteɪt/ *verb* (**-ting**) restore to normal life by training, etc. esp. after imprisonment or illness; restore to former privileges or reputation or to proper condition. □ **rehabilitation** *noun*.

rehash ● *verb* /riːˈhæʃ/ put into new form without significant change or improvement. ● *noun* /ˈriːhæʃ/ material rehashed; rehashing.

rehearsal /rɪˈhɜːs(ə)l/ *noun* trial performance or practice; rehearsing.

rehearse /rɪˈhɜːs/ *verb* (**-sing**) practise before performing in public; recite or say over; give list of, enumerate.

Reich /raɪx/ *noun* former German state, esp. Third Reich (1933–45).

reign /reɪn/ ● *verb* be king or queen; prevail; (as **reigning** *adjective*) currently holding title. ● *noun* sovereignty, rule; sovereign's period of rule.

reimburse /riːɪmˈbɜːs/ *verb* (**-sing**) repay (person); refund. □ **reimbursement** *noun*.

rein /reɪn/ ● *noun* (in *singular* or *plural*) long narrow strap used to guide horse; means of control. ● *verb* (+ *back, up, in*) pull back or up or hold in (as) with reins; govern, control.

reincarnate ● *verb* /riːɪnˈkɑːneɪt/ (**-ting**) give esp. human form to again. ● *adjective* /-nət/ reincarnated.

reincarnation /riːɪnkɑːˈneɪʃ(ə)n/ *noun* rebirth of soul in new body.

reindeer /'reɪndɪə/ noun (plural same or **-s**) subarctic deer with large antlers.

reinforce /riːɪn'fɔːs/ verb (**-cing**) support or strengthen, esp. with additional personnel or material. □ **reinforced concrete** concrete with metal bars etc. embedded in it.

reinforcement noun reinforcing, being reinforced; (in plural) additional personnel, equipment, etc.

reinstate /riːɪn'steɪt/ verb (**-ting**) replace in former position; restore to former privileges. □ **reinstatement** noun.

reinsure /riːɪn'ʃʊə/ verb (**-ring**) insure again (esp. of insurer transferring risk to another insurer). □ **reinsurance** noun.

reiterate /riː'ɪtəreɪt/ verb (**-ting**) say or do again or repeatedly. □ **reiteration** noun.

reject ● verb /rɪ'dʒekt/ put aside or send back as not to be used, done, or complied with; refuse to accept or believe in; rebuff. **●** noun /'riːdʒekt/ rejected thing or person. □ **rejection** /rɪ'dʒek-/ noun.

rejoice /rɪ'dʒɔɪs/ verb (**-cing**) feel joy, be glad; (+ in, at) take delight in.

rejoin[1] /riː'dʒɔɪn/ verb join again; reunite.

rejoin[2] /rɪ'dʒɔɪn/ verb say in answer; retort.

rejoinder /rɪ'dʒɔɪndə/ noun reply, retort.

rejuvenate /rɪ'dʒuːvəneɪt/ verb (**-ting**) make (as if) young again. □ **rejuvenation** noun.

relapse /rɪ'læps/ **●** verb (**-sing**) (usually + into) fall back (into worse state after improvement). **●** noun relapsing, esp. deterioration in patient's condition after partial recovery.

relate /rɪ'leɪt/ verb (**-ting**) narrate, recount; (usually + to, with) connect in thought or meaning; have reference to; (+ to) feel connected or sympathetic to.

related adjective connected, esp. by blood or marriage.

relation /rɪ'leɪʃ(ə)n/ noun connection between people or things; relative; (in plural) dealings (with others); narration.

relationship noun state of being related; connection; association; colloquial emotional association between two people.

relative /'relətɪv/ **●** adjective in relation or proportion to something else; implying comparison or relation; (+ to) having application or reference to; Grammar (of word, clause, etc.) referring to expressed or implied antecedent, attached to antecedent by such word. **●** noun person connected by blood or marriage; species related to another by common origin; relative word, esp. pronoun. □ **relative density** ratio between density of substance and that of a standard (usually water or air). □ **relatively** adverb.

relativity /relə'tɪvɪtɪ/ noun relativeness; Physics theory based on principle that all motion is relative and that light has constant velocity in a vacuum.

relax /rɪ'læks/ verb make or become less stiff, rigid, tense, formal, or strict; reduce (attention, efforts); cease work or effort; (as **relaxed** adjective) at ease, unperturbed.

relaxation /riːlæk'seɪʃ(ə)n/ noun relaxing; recreation.

relay /'riːleɪ/ **●** noun fresh set of people etc. to replace tired ones; supply of material similarly used; relay race; device activating electric circuit; device transmitting broadcast; relayed transmission. **●** verb /also rɪ'leɪ/ receive (esp. broadcast message) and transmit to others. □ **relay race** one between teams of which each member in turn covers part of distance.

release /rɪ'liːs/ **●** verb (**-sing**) (often + from) set free, liberate, unfasten; allow to move from fixed position; make (information) public; issue (film etc.) generally. **●** noun liberation from restriction, duty, or

difficulty; handle, catch, etc. that releases part of mechanism; item made available for publication; film, record, etc. that is released; releasing of film etc.

relegate /'relɪɡeɪt/ verb (**-ting**) consign or dismiss to inferior position; transfer (team) to lower division of league. □ **relegation** noun.

relent /rɪ'lent/ verb relax severity; yield to compassion.

relentless adjective unrelenting. □ **relentlessly** adverb.

relevant /'relɪv(ə)nt/ adjective (often + to) bearing on or pertinent to matter in hand. □ **relevance** noun.

reliable /rɪ'laɪəb(ə)l/ adjective that may be relied on. □ **reliability** noun; **reliably** adverb.

reliance /rɪ'laɪəns/ noun (+ in, on) trust or confidence in. □ **reliant** adjective.

relic /'relɪk/ noun object interesting because of its age or associations; part of holy person's body or belongings kept as object of reverence; surviving custom, belief, etc. from past age; (in plural) dead body or remains of person, what has survived.

relict /'relɪkt/ noun object surviving in primitive form.

relief /rɪ'liːf/ noun (feeling accompanying) alleviation of or deliverance from pain, distress, etc.; feature etc. that diversifies monotony or relaxes tension; assistance given to people in special need; replacing of person(s) on duty by another or others; person(s) thus bringing relief; thing supplementing another in some service; method of carving, moulding, etc., in which design projects from surface; piece of sculpture etc. in relief; effect of being done in relief given by colour or shading etc.; vividness, distinctness. □ **relief map** one showing hills and valleys by shading or colouring etc.

relieve /rɪ'liːv/ verb (**-ving**) bring or give relief to; mitigate tedium of; release (person) from duty by acting as or providing substitute; (+ of) take (burden or duty) away from; (**relieve oneself**) urinate, defecate. □ **relieved** adjective.

religion /rɪ'lɪdʒ(ə)n/ noun belief in superhuman controlling power, esp. in personal God or gods entitled to obedience; system of faith and worship.

religiosity /rɪlɪdʒɪ'ɒsɪtɪ/ noun state of being religious or too religious.

religious /rɪ'lɪdʒəs/ **●** adjective devoted to religion, devout; of or concerned with religion; of or belonging to monastic order; scrupulous. **●** noun (plural same) person bound by monastic vows. □ **religiously** adverb.

relinquish /rɪ'lɪŋkwɪʃ/ verb give up, let go, resign, surrender. □ **relinquishment** noun.

reliquary /'relɪkwərɪ/ noun (plural **-ies**) receptacle for relic(s).

relish /'relɪʃ/ **●** noun (often + for) liking or enjoyment; appetizing flavour, attractive quality; thing eaten with plainer food to add flavour; (+ of) distinctive flavour or taste. **●** verb get pleasure out of, enjoy greatly; anticipate with pleasure.

reluctant /rɪ'lʌkt(ə)nt/ adjective (often + to do) unwilling, disinclined. □ **reluctance** noun; **reluctantly** adverb.

rely /rɪ'laɪ/ verb (**-ies, -ied**) (+ on, upon) depend with confidence on; be dependent on.

REM abbreviation rapid eye movement.

remade past & past participle of REMAKE.

remain /rɪ'meɪn/ verb be left over; stay in same place or condition; be left behind; continue to be.

remainder /rɪ'meɪndə/ **●** noun residue; remaining people or things; number left after subtraction or division; (any of) copies of book left unsold. ● *verb* dispose of remainder of (book) at reduced prices.

remains /rɪ'meɪnz/ *plural noun* what remains after other parts have been removed or used; relics of antiquity etc.; dead body.

remake ● *verb* /riː'meɪk/ (**-king**; *past & past participle* **remade**) make again or differently. ● *noun* /'riːmeɪk/ remade thing, esp. cinema film.

remand /rɪ'mɑːnd/ ● *verb* return (prisoner) to custody, esp. to allow further inquiry. ● *noun* recommittal to custody. □ **on remand** in custody pending trial; **remand centre** institution for remand of accused people.

remark /rɪ'mɑːk/ ● *verb* (often + *that*) say by way of comment; (usually + *on, upon*) make comment; *archaic* take notice of. ● *noun* comment, thing said; noticing.

remarkable *adjective* worth notice; exceptional, striking. □ **remarkably** *adverb*.

REME /'riːmi:/ *abbreviation* Royal Electrical and Mechanical Engineers.

remedial /rɪ'miːdɪəl/ *adjective* affording or intended as a remedy; (of teaching) for slow or disadvantaged pupils.

remedy /'remɪdɪ/ ● *noun* (*plural* **-ies**) (often + *for, against*) medicine or treatment; means of removing anything undesirable; redress. ● *verb* (**-ies, -ied**) rectify, make good. □ **remediable** /rɪ'miːdɪəb(ə)l/ *adjective*.

remember /rɪ'membə/ *verb* (often + *to do, that*) keep in the memory; not forget; bring back into one's thoughts; acknowledge in making gift etc.; convey greetings from.

remembrance /rɪ'membrəns/ *noun* remembering, being remembered; recollection; keepsake, souvenir; (in *plural*) greetings conveyed through third person.

remind /rɪ'maɪnd/ *verb* (usually + *of, to do, that*) cause (person) to remember or think of.

reminder *noun* thing that reminds; (often + *of*) memento.

reminisce /remɪ'nɪs/ *verb* (**-cing**) indulge in reminiscence.

reminiscence /remɪ'nɪs(ə)ns/ *noun* remembering things past; (in *plural*) *literary* account of things remembered.

reminiscent *adjective* (+ *of*) reminding or suggestive of; concerned with reminiscence.

remiss /rɪ'mɪs/ *adjective* careless of duty; negligent.

remission /rɪ'mɪʃ(ə)n/ *noun* reduction of prison sentence for good behaviour; remittance of debt etc.; diminution of force etc.; (often + *of*) forgiveness (of sins etc.).

remit ● *verb* /rɪ'mɪt/ (**-tt-**) refrain from exacting or inflicting (debt, punishment, etc.); abate, slacken; send (esp. money); (+ *to*) refer to some authority, send back to lower court; postpone, defer; pardon (sins etc.). ● *noun* /'riːmɪt/ terms of reference of committee etc.; item remitted.

remittance *noun* money sent; sending of money.

remittent *adjective* (of disease etc.) abating at intervals.

remix ● *verb* /riː'mɪks/ mix again. ● *noun* /'riːmɪks/ remixed recording.

remnant /'remnənt/ *noun* small remaining quantity; piece of cloth etc. left when greater part has been used or sold.

remold *US* = REMOULD.

remonstrate /'remənstreɪt/ *verb* (**-ting**) (+ *with*) make protest; argue forcibly. □ **remonstrance** /rɪ'mɒnstrəns/ *noun*; **remonstration** *noun*.

remorse /rɪ'mɔːs/ *noun* bitter repentance; compunction; mercy.

remorseful *adjective* filled with repentance. □ **remorsefully** *adverb*.

remorseless *adjective* without compassion. □ **remorselessly** *adverb*.

remote /rɪ'məʊt/ *adjective* (**-r, -st**) distant in place or time; secluded; distantly related; slight, faint; aloof, not friendly. □ **remote control** (device for) control of apparatus etc. from a distance. □ **remotely** *adverb*; **remoteness** *noun*.

remould ● *verb* /riː'məʊld/ (*US* **remold**) mould again, refashion; reconstruct tread of (tyre). ● *noun* /'riːməʊld/ remoulded tyre.

removal /rɪ'muːv(ə)l/ *noun* removing, being removed; transfer of furniture etc. on moving house.

remove /rɪ'muːv/ ● *verb* (**-ving**) take off or away from place occupied; convey to another place; dismiss; cause to be no longer available; (in *passive*; + *from*) be distant in condition; (as **removed** *adjective*) (esp. of cousins) separated by a specified number of generations. ● *noun* distance, degree of remoteness; stage in gradation; form or division in some schools. □ **removable** *adjective*.

remunerate /rɪ'mjuːnəreɪt/ *verb* (**-ting**) pay for service rendered. □ **remuneration** *noun*; **remunerative** /-rətɪv/ *adjective*.

Renaissance /rɪ'neɪs(ə)ns/ *noun* revival of classical art and literature in 14th–16th c.; period of this; style of art and architecture developed by it; (**renaissance**) any similar revival. □ **Renaissance man** person with many talents.

renal /'riːn(ə)l/ *adjective* of kidneys.

renascent /rɪ'næs(ə)nt/ *adjective* springing up anew; being reborn. □ **renascence** *noun*.

rend *verb* (*past & past participle* **rent**) *archaic* tear or wrench forcibly.

render /'rendə/ *verb* cause to be or become; give in return; pay as due; (often + *to*) give (assistance), show (obedience etc.); present, submit; represent, portray; perform; translate; (often + *down*) melt (fat) down; cover (stone or brick) with plaster. □ **rendering** *noun*.

rendezvous /'rɒndɪvuː/ ● *noun* (*plural* same /-vuːz/) agreed or regular meeting-place; meeting by arrangement. ● *verb* (**rendezvouses** /-vuːz/; **rendezvoused** /-vuːd/; **rendezvousing** /-vuːɪŋ/) meet at rendezvous.

rendition /ren'dɪʃ(ə)n/ *noun* interpretation or rendering of dramatic or musical piece.

renegade /'renɪgeɪd/ *noun* deserter of party or principles.

renege /rɪ'niːg, rɪ'neɪg/ *verb* (**-ging**) (often + *on*) go back on promise etc.

renew /rɪ'njuː/ *verb* make new again; restore to original state; replace; repeat; resume after interruption; grant or be granted continuation of (licence etc.). □ **renewable** *adjective*; **renewal** *noun*.

rennet /'renɪt/ *noun* curdled milk from calf's stomach, or artificial preparation, used in making cheese etc.

renounce /rɪ'naʊns/ *verb* (**-cing**) consent formally to abandon; repudiate; decline further association with.

renovate /'renəveɪt/ *verb* (**-ting**) restore to good condition; repair. □ **renovation** *noun*; **renovator** *noun*.

renown /rɪ'naʊn/ *noun* fame, high distinction. □ **renowned** *adjective*.

rent¹ ● *noun* periodical payment for use of land or premises; payment for hire of machinery etc. ● *verb* (often + *from*) take, occupy, or use for rent; (often + *out*) let or hire for rent; (often + *at*) be let at specified rate.

rent² *noun* tear in garment etc.; gap, cleft, fissure.

rent³ *past & past participle of* REND.

rental /'rent(ə)l/ *noun* amount paid or received as rent; act of renting.

rentier /'rɑ̃tieɪ/ *noun* person living on income from property or investments. [French]

renunciation /rɪnʌnsɪ'eɪʃ(ə)n/ *noun* renouncing, self-denial, giving up of things.

rep¹ *noun colloquial* representative, esp. commercial traveller.

rep² *noun colloquial* repertory; repertory theatre or company.

repair¹ /rɪ'peə/ ● *verb* restore to good condition after damage or wear; set right or make amends for. ● *noun* (result of) restoring to sound condition; good or relative condition for working or using. □ **repairable** *adjective*; **repairer** *noun*.

repair² /rɪ'peə/ *verb* (usually + *to*) resort; go.

reparable /'repərəb(ə)l/ *adjective* that can be made good.

reparation /repə'reɪʃ(ə)n/ *noun* making amends; (esp. in *plural*) compensation.

repartee /repɑː'tiː/ *noun* (making of) witty retorts.

repast /rɪ'pɑːst/ *noun formal* meal.

repatriate /riː'pætrɪeɪt/ *verb* (**-ting**) return (person) to native land. □ **repatriation** *noun*.

repay /rɪ'peɪ/ *verb* (*past & past participle* **repaid**) pay back (money); make repayment to (person); reward (action etc.). □ **repayable** *adjective*; **repayment** *noun*.

repeal /rɪ'piːl/ ● *verb* annul, revoke. ● *noun* repealing.

repeat /rɪ'piːt/ ● *verb* say or do over again; recite, report; recur. ● *noun* repeating; thing repeated, esp. broadcast; *Music* passage intended to be repeated. □ **repeatable** *adjective*; **repeatedly** *adverb*.

repeater *noun* person or thing that repeats; firearm that fires several shots without reloading; watch that strikes last quarter etc. again when required; device for retransmitting electrical message.

repel /rɪ'pel/ *verb* drive back; ward off; be repulsive or distasteful to; resist mixing with; push away from itself. □ **repellent** *adjective & noun*.

repent /rɪ'pent/ *verb* (often + *of*) feel sorrow about one's actions etc.; wish one had not done, resolve not to continue (wrongdoing etc.). □ **repentance** *noun*; **repentant** *adjective*.

repercussion /riːpə'kʌʃ(ə)n/ *noun* indirect effect or reaction following event etc.; recoil after impact.

repertoire /'repətwɑː/ *noun* stock of works that performer etc. knows or is prepared to perform.

repertory /'repətərɪ/ *noun* (*plural* **-ies**) performance of various plays for short periods by one company; repertory theatres collectively; store of information etc.; repertoire. □ **repertory company** one performing plays from repertoire; **repertory theatre** one with repertoire of plays.

repetition /repə'tɪʃ(ə)n/ *noun* repeating, being repeated; thing repeated, copy. □ **repetitious** *adjective*; **repetitive** /rɪ'petətɪv/ *adjective*.

repine /rɪ'paɪn/ *verb* (**-ning**) (often + *at, against*) fret, be discontented.

replace /rɪ'pleɪs/ *verb* (**-cing**) put back in place; take place of, be or provide substitute for; (often + *with, by*) fill up place of.

replacement *noun* replacing, being replaced; person or thing that replaces another.

replay ● *verb* /riː'pleɪ/ play (match, recording, etc.) again. ● *noun* /'riːpleɪ/ replaying of match, recorded incident in game, etc.

replenish /rɪ'plenɪʃ/ *verb* (often + *with*) fill up again. □ **replenishment** *noun*.

replete /rɪ'pliːt/ *adjective* (often + *with*) well-fed; filled or well-supplied. □ **repletion** *noun*.

replica /'replɪkə/ *noun* exact copy, esp. duplicate made by original artist; model, esp. small-scale.

replicate /'replɪkeɪt/ *verb* make replica of. □ **replication** *noun*.

reply /rɪ'plaɪ/ ● *verb* (**-ies, -ied**) (often + *to*) make an answer, respond; say in answer. ● *noun* (*plural* **-ies**) replying; what is replied.

report /rɪ'pɔːt/ ● *verb* bring back or give account of; tell as news; describe, esp. as eyewitness; make official or formal statement; (often + *to*) bring to attention of authorities, present oneself as arrived; take down, write description of, etc. for publication; (+ *to*) be responsible to. ● *noun* account given or opinion formally expressed after investigation; description, reproduction, or summary of speech, law case, scene, etc., esp. for newspaper publication or broadcast; common talk, rumour; repute; periodical statement on (esp. pupil's) work etc.; sound of gun-shot. □ **reportedly** *adverb*.

reporter *noun* person employed to report news etc. for media.

repose¹ /rɪ'pəuz/ ● *noun* rest; sleep; tranquillity. ● *verb* (**-sing**) rest; lie, esp. when dead.

repose² /rɪ'pəuz/ *verb* (**-sing**) (+ *in*) place (trust etc.) in.

repository /rɪ'pɒzɪtərɪ/ *noun* (*plural* **-ies**) place where things are stored or may be found; receptacle; (often + *of*) book, person, etc. regarded as store of information, recipient of secrets etc.

reprehend /reprɪ'hend/ *verb formal* rebuke, blame.

reprehensible /reprɪ'hensɪb(ə)l/ *adjective* blameworthy.

represent /reprɪ'zent/ *verb* stand for, correspond to; be specimen of; symbolize; present likeness of to mind or senses; (often + *as, to be*) describe or depict, declare; (+ *that*) allege; show or play part of; be substitute or deputy for; be elected by as member of legislature etc.

representation /reprɪzen'teɪʃ(ə)n/ *noun* representing, being represented; thing that represents another.

representational *adjective* (of art) seeking to portray objects etc. realistically.

representative /reprɪ'zentətɪv/ ● *adjective* typical of class; containing typical specimens of all or many classes; (of government etc.) of elected deputies or based on representation. ● *noun* (+ *of*) sample, specimen, or typical embodiment of; agent; commercial traveller; delegate or deputy, esp. in representative assembly.

repress /rɪ'pres/ *verb* keep under; put down; suppress (esp. unwelcome thought). □ **repression** *noun*; **repressive** *adjective*.

reprieve /rɪ'priːv/ ● *verb* (**-ving**) remit or postpone execution of; give respite to. ● *noun* reprieving, being reprieved.

reprimand /'reprɪmɑːnd/ ● *noun* official rebuke. ● *verb* rebuke officially.

reprint ● *verb* /riː'prɪnt/ print again. ● *noun* /'riːprɪnt/ reprinting of book etc.; quantity reprinted.

reprisal /rɪ'praɪz(ə)l/ *noun* act of retaliation.

reprise /rɪ'priːz/ *noun Music* repeated passage or song etc.

repro /'riːprəu/ *noun* (*plural* **-s**) *colloquial* reproduction, copy.

reproach /rɪ'prəutʃ/ ● *verb* express disapproval to (person) for fault etc. ● *noun* rebuke, censure; (often + *to*) thing that brings discredit.

reproachful *adjective* full of or expressing reproach. □ **reproachfully** *adverb*.

reprobate /'reprəbeɪt/ *noun* unprincipled or immoral person.

reproduce /riːprə'djuːs/ *verb* (**-cing**) produce copy or representation of; produce further members of same species by natural means; (**reproduce itself**) produce offspring. □ **reproducible** *adjective*.

reproduction /riːprə'dʌkʃ(ə)n/ ● *noun* reproducing, esp. of further members of same species; copy of work of art. ● *adjective* (of furniture etc.) imitating earlier style. □ **reproductive** *adjective*.

reproof /rɪ'pruːf/ *noun formal* blame; rebuke.

reprove /rɪ'pruːv/ *verb* (**-ving**) *formal* rebuke.

reptile /'reptaɪl/ *noun* cold-blooded scaly animal of class including snakes, lizards, etc.; grovelling or repulsive person. □ **reptilian** /-'tɪl-/ *adjective*.

republic /rɪ'pʌblɪk/ *noun* state in which supreme power is held by the people or their elected representatives.

republican ● *adjective* of or characterizing republic(s); advocating or supporting republican government. ● *noun* supporter or advocate of republican government; (**Republican**) member of political party styled 'Republican'. □ **republicanism** *noun*.

repudiate /rɪ'pjuːdɪeɪt/ *verb* (**-ting**) disown, disavow, deny; refuse to recognize or obey (authority) or discharge (obligation or debt). □ **repudiation** *noun*.

repugnance /rɪ'pʌgnəns/ *noun* aversion, antipathy; inconsistency or incompatibility of ideas etc.

repugnant /rɪ'pʌgn(ə)nt/ *adjective* distasteful; contradictory.

repulse /rɪ'pʌls/ *verb* (**-sing**) drive back; rebuff, reject. ● *noun* defeat, rebuff.

repulsion /rɪ'pʌlʃ(ə)n/ *noun* aversion, disgust; *Physics* tendency of bodies to repel each other.

repulsive /rɪ'pʌlsɪv/ *adjective* causing aversion or loathing. □ **repulsively** *adverb*.

reputable /'repjʊtəb(ə)l/ *adjective* of good reputation, respectable.

reputation /repjʊ'teɪʃ(ə)n/ *noun* what is generally said or believed about character of person or thing; credit, respectability.

repute /rɪ'pjuːt/ ● *noun* reputation. ● *verb* (as **reputed** *adjective*) be generally considered. □ **reputedly** *adverb*.

request /rɪ'kwest/ ● *noun* asking for something, thing asked for. ● *verb* ask to be given, allowed, etc.; (+ *to do*) ask (person) to do something; (+ *that*) ask that.

Requiem /'rekwɪəm/ *noun* (also **requiem**) *esp. RC Church* mass for the dead.

require /rɪ'kwaɪə/ *verb* (**-ring**) need; depend on for success etc.; lay down as imperative; command, instruct; demand, insist on. □ **requirement** *noun*.

requisite /'rekwɪzɪt/ ● *adjective* required, necessary. ● *noun* (often + *for*) thing needed.

requisition /rekwɪ'zɪʃ(ə)n/ ● *noun* official order laying claim to use of property or materials; formal written demand. ● *verb* demand use or supply of.

requite /rɪ'kwaɪt/ *verb* (**-ting**) make return for; reward, avenge; (often + *for*) give in return. □ **requital** *noun*.

reredos /'rɪədɒs/ *noun* ornamental screen covering wall above back of altar.

rescind /rɪ'sɪnd/ *verb* abrogate, revoke, cancel. □ **rescission** /-'sɪʒ-/ *noun*.

rescue /'reskjuː/ ● *verb* (**-ues**, **-ued**, **-uing**) (often + *from*) save or set free from danger or harm. ● *noun* rescuing, being rescued. □ **rescuer** *noun*.

research /rɪ'sɜːtʃ, 'riːsɜːtʃ/ ● *noun* systematic investigation of materials, sources, etc. to establish facts. ● *verb* do research into or for. □ **researcher** *noun*.

resemble /rɪ'zemb(ə)l/ *verb* (**-ling**) be like; have similarity to. □ **resemblance** *noun*.

resent /rɪ'zent/ *verb* feel indignation at; be aggrieved by. □ **resentful** *adjective*; **resentfully** *adverb*; **resentment** *noun*.

reservation /rezə'veɪʃ(ə)n/ *noun* reserving, being reserved; thing reserved (e.g. room in hotel); spoken or unspoken limitation or exception; (in full **central reservation**) strip of land between carriageways of road; area reserved for occupation of aboriginal peoples.

reserve /rɪ'zɜːv/ ● *verb* (**-ving**) put aside or keep back for later occasion or special use; order to be retained or allocated for person at particular time; retain, secure. ● *noun* thing reserved for future use; limitation or exception attached to something; self-restraint, reticence; company's profit added to capital; (in *singular* or *plural*) assets kept readily available, troops withheld from action to reinforce or protect others, forces outside regular ones but available in emergency; extra player chosen as possible substitute in team; land reserved for special use, esp. as habitat.

reserved *adjective* reticent, uncommunicative; set apart for particular use.

reservist *noun* member of reserve forces.

reservoir /'rezəvwɑː/ *noun* large natural or artificial lake as source of water supply; receptacle for fluid; supply of facts etc.

reshuffle /riː'ʃʌf(ə)l/ ● *verb* (**-ling**) shuffle again; change posts of (government ministers etc.). ● *noun* reshuffling.

reside /rɪ'zaɪd/ *verb* (**-ding**) have one's home; (+ *in*) (of right etc.) be vested in, (of quality) be present in.

residence /'rezɪd(ə)ns/ *noun* residing; place where one resides; house, esp. large one. □ **in residence** living or working at specified place.

resident /'rezɪd(ə)nt/ ● *noun* (often + *of*) permanent inhabitant; guest staying at hotel. ● *adjective* residing, in residence; living at one's workplace etc.; (+ *in*) located in.

residential /rezɪ'denʃ(ə)l/ *adjective* suitable for or occupied by dwellings; used as residence; connected with residence.

residual /rɪ'zɪdjʊəl/ *adjective* left as residue or residuum.

residuary /rɪ'zɪdjʊərɪ/ *adjective* of the residue of an estate; residual.

residue /'rezɪdjuː/ *noun* remainder, what is left over; what remains of estate when liabilities have been discharged.

residuum /rɪ'zɪdjʊəm/ *noun* (*plural* **-dua**) substance left after combustion or evaporation; residue.

resign /rɪ'zaɪn/ *verb* (often + *from*) give up job, position, etc.; relinquish, surrender; (**resign oneself to**) accept (situation etc.) reluctantly.

resignation /rezɪg'neɪʃ(ə)n/ *noun* resigning, esp. from job or office; reluctant acceptance of the inevitable.

resigned *adjective* (often + *to*) having resigned oneself; resolved to endure; indicative of this. □ **resignedly** /-nɪdlɪ/ *adverb*.

resilient /rɪ'zɪlɪənt/ *adjective* resuming original form after compression etc.; readily recovering from setback. □ **resilience** *noun*.

resin /'rezɪn/ ● *noun* sticky secretion of trees and plants; (in full **synthetic resin**) organic compound made by polymerization etc. and used in plastics. ● *verb* (**-n-**) rub or treat with resin. □ **resinous** *adjective*.

resist /rɪ'zɪst/ *verb* withstand action or effect of; abstain from (pleasure etc.); strive against, oppose; offer opposition. □ **resistible** *adjective*.

resistance /rɪˈzɪst(ə)ns/ *noun* resisting; power to resist; ability to withstand disease; impeding effect exerted by one thing on another; *Physics* property of hindering passage of electric current, heat, etc.; resistor; secret organization resisting regime, esp. in occupied country. □ **resistant** *adjective*.

resistor *noun* device having resistance to passage of electric current.

resit ● *verb* /riːˈsɪt/ (**-tt-**; *past & past participle* **resat**) sit (exam) again after failing. ● *noun* /ˈriːsɪt/ resitting of exam; exam for this.

resoluble /rɪˈzɒljʊb(ə)l/ *adjective* resolvable; (+ *into*) analysable into.

resolute /ˈrezəluːt/ *adjective* determined, decided; purposeful. □ **resolutely** *adverb*.

resolution /rezəˈluːʃ(ə)n/ *noun* resolute temper or character; thing resolved on; formal expression of opinion of meeting; (+ *of*) solving of question etc.; resolving, being resolved.

resolve /rɪˈzɒlv/ ● *verb* (**-ving**) make up one's mind, decide firmly; cause to do this; solve, settle; (+ *that*) pass resolution by vote; (often + *into*) (cause to) separate into constituent parts, analyse; *Music* convert or be converted into concord. ● *noun* firm mental decision; determination. □ **resolved** *adjective*.

resonant /ˈrezənənt/ *adjective* echoing, resounding; continuing to sound; causing reinforcement or prolongation of sound, esp. by vibration. □ **resonance** *noun*.

resonate /ˈrezəneɪt/ *verb* (**-ting**) produce or show resonance; resound. □ **resonator** *noun*.

resort /rɪˈzɔːt/ ● *noun* place frequented, esp. for holidays etc.; thing to which recourse is had, expedient; (+ *to*) recourse to, use of. ● *verb* (+ *to*) turn to as expedient; (+ *to*) go often or in numbers to. □ **in the** or **as a last resort** when all else has failed.

resound /rɪˈzaʊnd/ *verb* (often + *with*) ring, echo; produce echoes, go on sounding, fill place with sound; be much talked of, produce sensation.

resounding *adjective* ringing, echoing; unmistakable, emphatic.

resource /rɪˈzɔːs/ ● *noun* expedient, device; (often in *plural*) means available; stock that can be drawn on; (in *plural*) country's collective wealth, person's inner strength; skill in devising expedients. ● *verb* (**-cing**) provide with resources.

resourceful *adjective* good at devising expedients. □ **resourcefully** *adverb*; **resourcefulness** *noun*.

respect /rɪˈspekt/ ● *noun* deferential esteem; (+ *of*, *for*) heed, regard; detail, aspect; reference, relation; (in *plural*) polite greetings. ● *verb* regard with deference or esteem; treat with consideration, spare. □ **respectful** *adjective*; **respectfully** *adverb*.

respectable *adjective* of acceptable social standing, decent in appearance or behaviour; reasonably good in condition, appearance, size, etc. □ **respectability** *noun*; **respectably** *adverb*.

respecting *preposition* with regard to.

respective /rɪˈspektɪv/ *adjective* of or relating to each of several individually.

respectively *adverb* for each separately or in turn, and in the order mentioned.

respiration /respəˈreɪʃ(ə)n/ *noun* breathing; single breath in or out; plant's absorption of oxygen and emission of carbon dioxide.

respirator /ˈrespəreɪtə/ *noun* apparatus worn over mouth and nose to filter inhaled air; apparatus for maintaining artificial respiration.

respire /rɪˈspaɪə/ *verb* (**-ring**) breathe; inhale and exhale; (of plant) carry out respiration. □ **respiratory** /-ˈspɪr-/ *adjective*.

respite /ˈrespaɪt/ *noun* interval of rest or relief; delay permitted before discharge of obligation or suffering of penalty.

resplendent /rɪˈsplend(ə)nt/ *adjective* brilliant, dazzlingly or gloriously bright. □ **resplendence** *noun*.

respond /rɪˈspɒnd/ *verb* answer, reply; (often + *to*) act etc. in response.

respondent ● *noun* defendant, esp. in appeal or divorce case. ● *adjective* in position of defendant.

response /rɪˈspɒns/ *noun* answer, reply; action, feeling, etc. caused by stimulus etc.; (often in *plural*) part of liturgy said or sung in answer to priest.

responsibility /rɪspɒnsəˈbɪlɪti/ *noun* (*plural* **-ies**) (often + *for*, *of*) being responsible, authority; person or thing for which one is responsible.

responsible /rɪˈspɒnsəb(ə)l/ *adjective* (often + *to*, *for*) liable to be called to account; morally accountable for actions; of good credit and repute; trustworthy; (often + *for*) being the cause; involving responsibility. □ **responsibly** *adverb*.

responsive /rɪˈspɒnsɪv/ *adjective* (often + *to*) responding readily (to some influence); sympathetic; answering; by way of answer. □ **responsiveness** *noun*.

rest¹ ● *verb* cease from exertion or action; be still, esp. to recover strength; lie in sleep or death; give relief or repose to; be left without further investigation or discussion; (+ *on*, *upon*, *against*) place, lie, lean, or depend on; (as **rested** *adjective*) refreshed by resting. ● *noun* repose or sleep; resting; prop or support for steadying something; *Music* (sign denoting) interval of silence. □ **at rest** not moving, not agitated or troubled; **rest-cure** prolonged rest as medical treatment; **rest home** place where elderly or convalescent people are cared for; **rest room** *esp. US* public lavatory; **set at rest** settle, reassure.

rest² ● *noun* (**the rest**) remainder or remaining parts or individuals. ● *verb* remain in specified state; (+ *with*) be left in the charge of. □ **for the rest** as regards anything else.

restaurant /ˈrestərɒnt/ *noun* public premises where meals may be bought and eaten.

restaurateur /restərəˈtɜː/ *noun* keeper of restaurant.

restful *adjective* quiet, soothing.

restitution /restɪˈtjuːʃ(ə)n/ *noun* restoring of property etc. to its owner; reparation.

restive /ˈrestɪv/ *adjective* fidgety; intractable, resisting control.

restless *adjective* without rest; uneasy, agitated, fidgeting. □ **restlessly** *adverb*; **restlessness** *noun*.

restoration /restəˈreɪʃ(ə)n/ *noun* restoring, being restored; model or drawing representing supposed original form of thing; (**Restoration**) re-establishment of British monarchy in 1660.

restorative /rɪˈstɒrətɪv/ ● *adjective* tending to restore health or strength. ● *noun* restorative food, medicine, etc.

restore /rɪˈstɔː/ *verb* (**-ring**) bring back to original state by rebuilding, repairing, etc.; give back; reinstate; bring back to former place, condition, or use; make restoration of (extinct animal, ruined building, etc.). □ **restorer** *noun*.

restrain /rɪˈstreɪn/ *verb* (usually + *from*) check or hold in; keep under control; repress; confine.

restraint /rɪˈstreɪnt/ *noun* restraining, being restrained; restraining agency or influence; self-control, moderation; reserve of manner.

restrict /rɪˈstrɪkt/ *verb* confine, limit; withhold from general disclosure. □ **restriction** *noun*.

restrictive /rɪˈstrɪktɪv/ *adjective* restricting. □ **restrictive practice** agreement or practice that limits competition or output in industry.

result /rɪ'zʌlt/ ● *noun* consequence; issue; satisfactory outcome; answer etc. got by calculation; (in *plural*) list of scores, winners, etc. in sporting events or exams. ● *verb* (often + *from*) arise as consequence; (+ *in*) end in.

resultant ● *adjective* resulting. ● *noun* force etc. equivalent to two or more acting in different directions at same point.

resume /rɪ'zju:m/ *verb* (**-ming**) begin again; recommence; take again or back. □ **resumption** /-'zʌmp-/ *noun*; **resumptive** /-'zʌmp-/ *adjective*.

résumé /'rezjʊmeɪ/ *noun* summary.

resurgent /rɪ'sɜ:dʒ(ə)nt/ *adjective* rising or arising again. □ **resurgence** *noun*.

resurrect /rezə'rekt/ *verb colloquial* revive practice or memory of; raise or rise from dead.

resurrection /rezə'rekʃ(ə)n/ *noun* rising from the dead; revival from disuse or decay etc.

resuscitate /rɪ'sʌsɪteɪt/ *verb* (**-ting**) revive from unconsciousness or apparent death; revive, restore. □ **resuscitation** *noun*.

retail /'ri:teɪl/ ● *noun* sale of goods to the public in small quantities. ● *adjective & adverb* by retail; at retail price. ● *verb* sell by retail; (often + *at, of*) (of goods) be sold by retail; (also /rɪ'teɪl/) recount. □ **retailer** *noun*.

retain /rɪ'teɪn/ *verb* keep possession of, continue to have, use, etc.; keep in mind; keep in place, hold fixed; secure services of (esp. barrister) by preliminary fee.

retainer *noun* fee for securing person's services; faithful servant; reduced rent paid to retain unoccupied accommodation; person or thing that retains.

retake ● *verb* /ri:'teɪk/ (**-king**; *past* **retook**; *past participle* **retaken**) take (photograph, exam, etc.) again; recapture. ● *noun* /'ri:teɪk/ filming, recording, etc. again; taking of exam etc. again.

retaliate /rɪ'tælɪeɪt/ *verb* (**-ting**) repay in kind; attack in return. □ **retaliation** *noun*; **retaliatory** /-'tæljət-/ *adjective*.

retard /rɪ'tɑːd/ *verb* make slow or late; delay progress or accomplishment of. □ **retardant** *adjective & noun*; **retardation** /ri:-/ *noun*.

retarded *adjective* backward in mental or physical development.

retch *verb* make motion of vomiting.

retention /rɪ'tenʃ(ə)n/ *noun* retaining, being retained.

retentive /rɪ'tentɪv/ *adjective* tending to retain; (of memory) not forgetful.

rethink ● *verb* /ri:'θɪŋk/ (*past & past participle* **rethought** /-'θɔ:t/) consider again, esp. with view to making changes. ● *noun* /'ri:θɪŋk/ rethinking, reassessment.

reticence /'retɪs(ə)ns/ *noun* avoidance of saying all one knows or feels; taciturnity. □ **reticent** *adjective*.

reticulate ● *verb* /rɪ'tɪkjʊleɪt/ (**-ting**) divide or be divided in fact or appearance into network. ● *adjective* /rɪ'tɪkjʊlət/ reticulated. □ **reticulation** *noun*.

retina /'retɪnə/ *noun* (*plural* **-s** or **-nae** /-niː/) light-sensitive layer at back of eyeball. □ **retinal** *adjective*.

retinue /'retɪnjuː/ *noun* group of people attending important person.

retire /rɪ'taɪə/ *verb* (**-ring**) leave office or employment, esp. because of age; cause (employee) to retire; withdraw, retreat, seek seclusion or shelter; go to bed; *Cricket* (of batsman) suspend one's innings. □ **retired** *adjective*.

retirement *noun* retiring; period spent as retired person; seclusion. □ **retirement pension** pension paid by state to retired people above certain age.

retiring *adjective* shy, fond of seclusion.

retort¹ /rɪ'tɔ:t/ ● *noun* incisive, witty, or angry reply. ● *verb* say by way of retort; repay in kind.

retort² /rɪ'tɔ:t/ *noun* vessel with long downward-bent neck for distilling liquids; vessel for heating coal to generate gas.

retouch /ri:'tʌtʃ/ *verb* improve (esp. photograph) by minor alterations.

retrace /rɪ'treɪs/ *verb* (**-cing**) go back over (one's steps etc.); trace back to source or beginning.

retract /rɪ'trækt/ *verb* withdraw (statement etc.); draw or be drawn back or in. □ **retractable** *adjective*; **retraction** *noun*.

retractile /rɪ'træktaɪl/ *adjective* retractable.

retread ● *verb* /ri:'tred/ (*past* **retrod**; *past participle* **retrodden**) tread (path etc.) again; (*past & past participle* **retreaded**) put new tread on (tyre). ● *noun* /'ri:tred/ retreaded tyre.

retreat /rɪ'tri:t/ ● *verb* go back, retire; recede. ● *noun* (signal for) act of retreating; withdrawing into privacy; place of seclusion or shelter; period of seclusion for prayer and meditation.

retrench /rɪ'trentʃ/ *verb* cut down expenses; reduce amount of (costs); economize. □ **retrenchment** *noun*.

retrial /ri:'traɪəl/ *noun* retrying of case.

retribution /retrɪ'bju:ʃ(ə)n/ *noun* recompense, usually for evil; vengeance. □ **retributive** /rɪ'trɪb-/ *adjective*.

retrieve /rɪ'tri:v/ *verb* (**-ving**) regain possession of; find again; obtain (information in computer); (of dog) find and bring in (game); (+ *from*) rescue from (bad state etc.); restore to good state; repair, set right. □ **retrievable** *adjective*; **retrieval** *noun*.

retriever *noun* dog of breed used for retrieving game.

retro /'retrəʊ/ *slang* ● *adjective* reviving or harking back to past. ● *noun* (*plural* **retros**) retro fashion or style.

retro- *combining form* backwards, back.

retroactive /retrəʊ'æktɪv/ *adjective* having retrospective effect.

retrod *past* of RETREAD.

retrodden *past participle* of RETREAD.

retrograde /'retrəgreɪd/ ● *adjective* directed backwards; reverting, esp. to inferior state. ● *verb* move backwards; decline, revert.

retrogress /retrə'gres/ *verb* move backwards; deteriorate. □ **retrogression** *noun*; **retrogressive** *adjective*.

retrorocket /'retrəʊrɒkɪt/ *noun* auxiliary rocket for slowing down spacecraft etc.

retrospect /'retrəspekt/ *noun* □ **in retrospect** when looking back.

retrospection /retrə'spekʃ(ə)n/ *noun* looking back into the past.

retrospective /retrə'spektɪv/ ● *adjective* looking back on or dealing with the past; (of statute etc.) applying to the past as well as the future. ● *noun* exhibition etc. showing artist's lifetime development. □ **retrospectively** *adverb*.

retroussé /rə'tru:seɪ/ *adjective* (of nose) turned up at tip.

retroverted /'retrəʊvɜ:tɪd/ *adjective* (of womb) inclining backwards.

retry /ri:'traɪ/ *verb* (**-ies**, **-ied**) try (defendant, law case) again.

retsina /ret'si:nə/ *noun* resin-flavoured Greek white wine.

return /rɪ'tɜ:n/ ● *verb* come or go back; bring, put, or send back; give in response; yield (profit); say in reply; send (ball) back in tennis etc.; state in answer to formal demand; elect as MP etc. ● *noun* coming, going, putting, giving, sending, or paying back; what is returned; (in full **return ticket**) ticket for journey to place and back again; (in *singular* or *plural*) proceeds, profit; coming in of these; formal statement or report; (in full **return match, game**) second game between same opponents; (announcement of) person's election as MP etc. ● **by return (of post)** by the next available post in the return direction; **returning officer** official conducting election in constituency etc. and announcing result.

returnee /rɪtɜːˈniː/ *noun* person who returns home, esp. after war service.

reunify /riːˈjuːnɪfaɪ/ *verb* (**-ies, -ied**) restore to political unity. □ **reunification** *noun*.

reunion /riːˈjuːnjən/ *noun* reuniting, being reunited; social gathering, esp. of former associates.

reunite /riːjuːˈnaɪt/ *verb* (**-ting**) (cause to) come together again.

reuse ● *verb* /riːˈjuːz/ (**-sing**) use again. ● *noun* /riːˈjuːs/ second or further use. □ **reusable** *adjective*.

Rev. *abbreviation* Reverend.

rev *colloquial* ● *noun* (in *plural*) revolutions of engine per minute. ● *verb* (**-vv-**) (of engine) revolve; (often + *up*) cause (engine) to run quickly.

revalue /riːˈvæljuː/ *verb* (**-ues, -ued, -uing**) give different, esp. higher, value to (currency etc.). □ **revaluation** *noun*.

revamp /riːˈvæmp/ *verb* renovate, revise; patch up.

Revd *abbreviation* Reverend.

reveal /rɪˈviːl/ *verb* display, show, allow to appear; (often as **revealing** *adjective*) disclose, divulge.

reveille /rɪˈvælɪ/ *noun* military waking-signal.

revel /ˈrev(ə)l/ ● *verb* (**-ll-**; *US* **-l-**) make merry, be riotously festive; (+ *in*) take keen delight in. ● *noun* (in *singular* or *plural*) revelling. ● **reveller** *noun*; **revelry** *noun* (*plural* **-ies**).

revelation /revəˈleɪʃ(ə)n/ *noun* revealing; knowledge supposedly disclosed by divine or supernatural agency; striking disclosure or realization; (**Revelation** or *colloquial* **Revelations**) last book of New Testament.

revenge /rɪˈvendʒ/ ● *noun* (act of) retaliation; desire for this. ● *verb* (**-ging**) avenge; (**revenge oneself** or in *passive*; often + *on, upon*) inflict retaliation.

revengeful *adjective* eager for revenge.

revenue /ˈrevənjuː/ *noun* income, esp. annual income of state; department collecting state revenue.

reverberate /rɪˈvɜːbəreɪt/ *verb* (**-ting**) (of sound, light, or heat) be returned or reflected repeatedly; return (sound etc.) thus; (of event) produce continuing effect. ● **reverberant** *adjective*; **reverberation** *noun*; **reverberative** /-rətɪv/ *adjective*.

revere /rɪˈvɪə/ *verb* (**-ring**) regard with deep and affectionate or religious respect.

reverence /ˈrevərəns/ ● *noun* revering, being revered; deep respect. ● *verb* (**-cing**) treat with reverence.

reverend /ˈrevərənd/ *adjective* (esp. as title of member of clergy) deserving reverence. □ **Reverend Mother** Mother Superior of convent.

reverent /ˈrevərənt/ *adjective* feeling or showing reverence. □ **reverently** *adverb*.

reverential /revəˈrenʃ(ə)l/ *adjective* of the nature of, due to, or characterized by reverence. □ **reverentially** *adverb*.

reverie /ˈrevərɪ/ *noun* fit of musing; daydream.

revers /rɪˈvɪə/ *noun* (*plural* same /-ˈvɪəz/) (material of) turned-back front edge of garment.

reverse /rɪˈvɜːs/ ● *verb* (**-sing**) turn the other way round or up, turn inside out; convert to opposite character or effect; (cause to) travel backwards; make (engine) work in contrary direction; revoke, annul. ● *adjective* backward, upside down; opposite or contrary in character or order, inverted. ● *noun*

opposite or contrary; contrary of usual manner; piece of misfortune, disaster; reverse gear or motion; reverse side; side of coin etc. bearing secondary design; verso of printed leaf. □ **reverse the charges** have recipient of telephone call pay for it; **reverse gear** gear used to make vehicle etc. go backwards; **reversing light** light at rear of vehicle showing it is in reverse gear. □ **reversal** *noun*; **reversible** *adjective*.

reversion /rɪˈvɜːʃ(ə)n/ *noun* return to previous state or earlier type; legal right (esp. of original owner) to possess or succeed to property on death of present possessor.

revert /rɪˈvɜːt/ *verb* (+ *to*) return to (former condition, practice, subject, opinion, etc.); return by reversion. □ **revertible** *adjective*.

review /rɪˈvjuː/ ● *noun* general survey or assessment; survey of past; revision, reconsideration; published criticism of book, play, etc.; periodical in which events, books, etc. are reviewed; inspection of troops etc. ● *verb* survey, look back on; reconsider, revise; hold review of (troops etc.); write review of (book etc.). □ **reviewer** *noun*.

revile /rɪˈvaɪl/ *verb* (**-ling**) abuse verbally.

revise /rɪˈvaɪz/ *verb* (**-sing**) examine and improve or amend; reconsider and alter (opinion etc.); go over (work etc.) again, esp. for examination. □ **revisory** *adjective*.

revision /rɪˈvɪʒ(ə)n/ *noun* revising, being revised; revised edition or form.

revisionism *noun* often derogatory revision or modification of orthodoxy, esp. of Marxism. □ **revisionist** *noun & adjective*.

revitalize /riːˈvaɪtəlaɪz/ *verb* (also **-ise**) (**-zing** or **-sing**) imbue with new vitality.

revival /rɪˈvaɪv(ə)l/ *noun* reviving, being revived; new production of old play etc.; (campaign to promote) reawakening of religious fervour.

revivalism *noun* promotion of esp. religious revival. □ **revivalist** *noun & adjective*.

revive /rɪˈvaɪv/ *verb* (**-ving**) come or bring back to consciousness, life, vigour, use, or notice.

revivify /rɪˈvɪvɪfaɪ/ *verb* (**-ies, -ied**) restore to life, strength, or activity. □ **revivification** *noun*.

revoke /rɪˈvəʊk/ ● *verb* (**-king**) rescind, withdraw, cancel; *Cards* fail to follow suit though able to. ● *noun* *Cards* revoking. □ **revocable** /ˈrevəkəb(ə)l/ *adjective*; **revocation** /revəˈkeɪʃ(ə)n/ *noun*.

revolt /rɪˈvəʊlt/ ● *verb* rise in rebellion; affect with disgust; (often + *at, against*) feel revulsion. ● *noun* insurrection; sense of disgust; rebellious mood.

revolting *adjective* disgusting, horrible. □ **revoltingly** *adverb*.

revolution /revəˈluːʃ(ə)n/ *noun* forcible overthrow of government or social order; fundamental change; revolving; single completion of orbit or rotation.

revolutionary ● *adjective* involving great change; of political revolution. ● *noun* (*plural* **-ies**) instigator or supporter of political revolution.

revolutionize *verb* (also **-ise**) (**-zing** or **-sing**) change fundamentally.

revolve /rɪˈvɒlv/ *verb* (**-ving**) turn round; rotate; move in orbit; ponder in the mind; (+ *around*) be centred on.

revolver *noun* pistol with revolving chambers enabling user to fire several shots without reloading.

revue /rɪˈvjuː/ *noun* theatrical entertainment of usually comic sketches and songs.

revulsion /rɪˈvʌlʃ(ə)n/ *noun* abhorrence; sudden violent change of feeling.

reward /rɪˈwɔːd/ ● *noun* return or recompense for service or merit; requital for good or evil; sum offered for detection of criminal, recovery of lost property, etc. ● *verb* give or serve as reward to. □ **rewarding** *adjective*.

rewind /riː'waɪnd/ *verb* (*past & past participle* **rewound** /-'waʊnd/) wind (film, tape, etc.) back.

rewire /riː'waɪə/ *verb* (**-ring**) provide with new electrical wiring.

rework /riː'wɜːk/ *verb* revise, refashion, remake. □ **reworking** *noun*.

Rex *noun* (after name) reigning king; *Law* the Crown. [Latin].

rhapsodize /'ræpsədaɪz/ *verb* (also **-ise**) (**-zing** or **-sing**) speak or write rhapsodies.

rhapsody /'ræpsədɪ/ *noun* (*plural* **-ies**) enthusiastic or extravagant speech or composition; melodic musical piece often based on folk culture. □ **rhapsodic** /-'sɒd-/ *adjective*.

rhea /'riːə/ *noun* large flightless S. American bird.

rheostat /'riːəstæt/ *noun* instrument used to control electric current by varying resistance.

rhesus /'riːsəs/ *noun* (in full **rhesus monkey**) small Indian monkey. □ **rhesus factor** antigen occurring on red blood cells of most humans and some other primates; **rhesus-positive, -negative** having or not having rhesus factor.

rhetoric /'retərɪk/ *noun* art of persuasive speaking or writing; language intended to impress, esp. seen as inflated, exaggerated, or meaningless.

rhetorical /rɪ'tɒrɪk(ə)l/ *adjective* expressed artificially or extravagantly; of the nature of rhetoric. □ **rhetorical question** question asked not for information but to produce effect. □ **rhetorically** *adverb*.

rheumatic /ruː'mætɪk/ ● *adjective* of, caused by, or suffering from rheumatism. ● *noun* person suffering from rheumatism; (in *plural*, often treated as *singular*) *colloquial* rheumatism. □ **rheumatic fever** fever with pain in the joints. □ **rheumatically** *adverb*; **rheumaticky** *adjective colloquial*.

rheumatism /'ruːmətɪz(ə)m/ *noun* disease marked by inflammation and pain in joints etc.

rheumatoid /'ruːmətɔɪd/ *adjective* having the character of rheumatism. □ **rheumatoid arthritis** chronic progressive disease causing inflammation and stiffening of joints.

rhinestone /'raɪnstəʊn/ *noun* imitation diamond.

rhino /'raɪnəʊ/ *noun* (*plural* same or **-s**) *colloquial* rhinoceros.

rhinoceros /raɪ'nɒsərəs/ *noun* (*plural* same or **-roses**) large thick-skinned animal with usually one horn on nose.

rhizome /'raɪzəʊm/ *noun* underground rootlike stem bearing both roots and shoots.

rhododendron /rəʊdə'dendrən/ *noun* (*plural* **-s** or **-dra**) evergreen shrub with large flowers.

rhomboid /'rɒmbɔɪd/ ● *adjective* (also **rhomboidal** /-'bɔɪd-/) like a rhombus. ● *noun* quadrilateral of which only opposite sides and angles are equal.

rhombus /'rɒmbəs/ *noun* (*plural* **-buses** or **-bi** /-baɪ/) oblique equilateral parallelogram, e.g. diamond on playing card.

rhubarb /'ruːbɑːb/ *noun* (stalks of) plant with fleshy leaf-stalks cooked and eaten as dessert; *colloquial* indistinct conversation or noise, from repeated use of word 'rhubarb' by stage crowd.

rhyme /raɪm/ ● *noun* identity of sound at ends of verse or verse-lines; (in *singular* or *plural*) rhymed verse; use of rhyme; word providing rhyme. ● *verb* (**-ming**) (of words or lines) produce rhyme; (+ *with*) be or use as rhyme; write rhymes; put into rhyme.

rhythm /'rɪð(ə)m/ *noun* periodical accent and duration of notes in music; type of structure formed by

this; measured flow of words in verse or prose; *Physiology* pattern of successive strong and weak movements; regularly occurring sequence of events. □ **rhythm method** contraception by avoiding sexual intercourse near times of ovulation. □ **rhythmic** *adjective*; **rhythmical** *adjective*; **rhythmically** *adverb*.

rib ● *noun* each of the curved bones joined to spine and protecting organs of chest; joint of meat from this part of animal; supporting ridge, timber, rod, etc. across surface or through structure; combination of plain and purl stitches producing ribbed design. ● *verb* (**-bb-**) provide or mark (as) with ribs; *colloquial* tease. □ **ribcage** wall of bones formed by ribs round chest; **rib-tickler** something amusing. □ **ribbed** *adjective*; **ribbing** *noun*.

ribald /'rɪb(ə)ld/ *adjective* irreverent, coarsely humorous. □ **ribaldry** *noun*.

riband /'rɪbənd/ *noun* ribbon.

ribbon /'rɪbən/ *noun* narrow strip or band of fabric; material in this form; ribbon worn to indicate some honour, membership of sports team, etc.; long narrow strip; (in *plural*) ragged strips. □ **ribbon development** building of houses along main road outwards from town.

riboflavin /raɪbəʊ'fleɪvɪn/ *noun* (also **riboflavine** /-viːn/) vitamin of B complex, found in liver, milk, and eggs.

ribonucleic acid /raɪbəʊnjuː'kliːɪk/ *noun* substance controlling protein synthesis in cells.

rice *noun* (grains from) swamp grass grown esp. in Asia. □ **rice-paper** edible paper made from pith of an oriental tree and used for painting and in cookery.

rich *adjective* having much wealth; splendid, costly; valuable; abundant, ample; (often + *in*, *with*) abounding; fertile; (of food) containing much fat, spice, etc.; mellow, strong and full; highly amusing or ludicrous. □ **richness** *noun*.

riches *plural noun* abundant means; valuable possessions.

richly *adverb* in a rich way; fully, thoroughly.

Richter scale /'rɪktə/ *noun* scale of 0–10 for representing strength of earthquake.

rick[1] *noun* stack of hay etc.

rick[2] (also **wrick**) ● *noun* slight sprain or strain. ● *verb* slightly sprain or sprain.

rickets /'rɪkɪts/ *noun* (treated as *singular* or *plural*) children's deficiency disease with softening of the bones.

rickety /'rɪkɪtɪ/ *adjective* shaky, insecure; suffering from rickets.

rickshaw /'rɪkʃɔː/ *noun* (also **ricksha** /-ʃə/) light two-wheeled hooded vehicle drawn by one or more people.

ricochet /'rɪkəʃeɪ/ ● *noun* rebounding of esp. shell or bullet off surface; hit made after this. ● *verb* (**-cheted** /-ʃeɪd/ or **-chetted** /-ʃetɪd/; **-cheting** /-ʃeɪɪŋ/ or **-chetting** /-ʃetɪŋ/) (of projectile) make ricochet.

ricotta /rɪ'kɒtə/ *noun* soft Italian cheese.

rid *verb* (**-dd-**; *past & past participle* **rid**) (+ *of*) make (person, place) free of.

riddance /'rɪd(ə)ns/ *noun* □ **good riddance** *expression of relief at getting rid of something or someone.*

ridden *past participle* of RIDE.

riddle[1] /'rɪd(ə)l/ ● *noun* verbal puzzle or test, often with trick answer; puzzling fact, thing, or person. ● *verb* (**-ling**) speak in riddles.

riddle[2] /'rɪd(ə)l/ ● *verb* (**-ling**) (usually + *with*) make many holes in, esp. with gunshot; (in *passive*) fill, permeate; pass through riddle. ● *noun* coarse sieve.

ride ● *verb* (**-ding**; *past* **rode**; *past participle* **ridden** /'rɪd(ə)n/) (often + *on*, *in*) travel or be carried on or in (bicycle, vehicle, horse, etc.); be carried or supported by; cross, be conveyed over; float buoyantly; (as **ridden** *adjective*) (+ *by, with*) dominated by or infested with. ● *noun* journey or spell of riding in vehicle, on horse, etc.; path (esp. through woods) for riding on; amusement for riding on at fairground. □ **ride up** (of garment) work upwards when worn; **take for a ride** *colloquial* hoax, deceive.

rider *noun* person riding; additional remark following statement, verdict, etc.

ridge *noun* line of junction of two surfaces sloping upwards towards each other; long narrow hilltop; mountain range; any narrow elevation across surface. □ **ridge-pole** horizontal pole of long tent; **ridgeway** road along ridge.

ridicule /'rɪdɪkjuːl/ ● *noun* derision, mockery. ● *verb* **(-ling)** make fun of; mock; laugh at.

ridiculous /rɪ'dɪkjʊlǝs/ *adjective* deserving to be laughed at; unreasonable. □ **ridiculously** *adverb*; **ridiculousness** *noun*.

riding[1] /'raɪdɪŋ/ *noun* sport or pastime of travelling on horseback.

riding[2] /'raɪdɪŋ/ *noun historical* former division of Yorkshire.

Riesling /'riːzlɪŋ/ *noun* (white wine made from) type of grape.

rife *adjective* widespread; (+ *with*) abounding in.

riff *noun* short repeated phrase in jazz etc.

riffle /'rɪf(ǝ)l/ ● *verb* **(-ling)** (often + *through*) leaf quickly through (pages); shuffle (cards). ● *noun* riffling; *US* patch of ripples in stream etc.

riff-raff /'rɪfræf/ *noun* rabble, disreputable people.

rifle[1] /'raɪf(ǝ)l/ ● *noun* gun with long rifled barrel; (in *plural*) troops armed with these. ● *verb* **(-ling)** make spiral grooves in (gun etc.) to make projectile spin. □ **rifle range** place for rifle practice.

rifle[2] /'raɪf(ǝ)l/ *verb* **(-ling)** (often + *through*) search and rob; carry off as booty.

rift *noun* crack, split; cleft; disagreement, dispute. □ **rift-valley** one formed by subsidence of section of earth's crust.

rig[1] ● *verb* **(-gg-)** provide (ship) with rigging; (often + *out, up*) fit with clothes or equipment; (+ *up*) set up hastily or as makeshift. ● *noun* arrangement of ship's masts, sails, etc.; equipment for special purpose; oil rig; *colloquial* style of dress, uniform. □ **rig-out** *colloquial* outfit of clothes. □ **rigger** *noun*.

rig[2] ● *verb* **(-gg-)** manage or fix fraudulently. ● *noun* trick, swindle.

rigging *noun* ship's spars, ropes, etc.

right /raɪt/ ● *adjective* just, morally or socially correct; correct, true; preferable, suitable; in good or normal condition; on or towards east side of person or thing facing north; (also **Right**) *Politics* of the Right; (of side of fabric etc.) meant to show; *colloquial* real, complete. ● *noun* what is just; fair treatment; fair claim; legal or moral entitlement; right-hand part, region, or direction; *Boxing* right hand, blow with this; (often **Right**) *Politics* conservatives collectively. ● *verb* (often *reflexive*) restore to proper, straight, or vertical position; correct, avenge; set in order; make reparation for. ● *adverb* straight; *colloquial* immediately; (+ *to, round, through*, etc.) all the way; (+ *off, out*, etc.) completely; quite, very; justly, properly, correctly, truly; on or to right side. ● *interjection colloquial: expressing agreement or consent.* □ **by right(s)** if right were done; **in the right** having justice or truth on one's side; **right angle** angle of 90°; **right-hand** on right side; **right-handed** naturally using right hand for writing etc., made by or for right hand, turning to right, (of screw) turning clockwise to tighten;

right-hander right-handed person or blow; **right-hand man** essential or chief assistant; **Right Honourable** *title of certain high officials, e.g. Privy Counsellors*; **right-minded, -thinking** having sound views and principles; **right of way** right to pass over another's ground, path subject to such right, precedence granted to one vehicle over another; **Right Reverend** *title of bishop*; **right wing** more conservative section of political party etc., right side of football etc. team; **right-wing** conservative, reactionary; **right-winger** member of right wing. □ **rightward** *adjective & adverb*; **rightwards** *adverb*.

righteous /'raɪtʃǝs/ *adjective* morally right; virtuous, law-abiding. □ **righteously** *adverb*; **righteousness** *noun*.

rightful *adjective* legitimately entitled to (position etc.); that one is entitled to. □ **rightfully** *adverb*.

rightly *adverb* justly, correctly, properly, justifiably.

rigid /'rɪdʒɪd/ *adjective* not flexible, unbendable; inflexible, harsh. □ **rigidity** /-'dʒɪd-/ *noun*; **rigidly** *adverb*.

rigmarole /'rɪgmǝrǝʊl/ *noun* complicated procedure; rambling tale etc.

rigor *US* = RIGOUR.

rigor mortis /rɪgǝ 'mɔːtɪs/ *noun* stiffening of body after death.

rigorous /'rɪgǝrǝs/ *adjective* strict, severe; exact, accurate. □ **rigorously** *adverb*; **rigorousness** *noun*.

rigour /'rɪgǝ/ *noun* (*US* **rigor**) severity, strictness, harshness; (in *plural*) harsh conditions; strict application or observance etc.

rile *verb* **(-ling)** *colloquial* anger, irritate.

rill *noun* small stream.

rim *noun* edge or border, esp. of something circular; outer ring of wheel, holding tyre; part of spectacle frames around lens. □ **rimless** *adjective*; **rimmed** *adjective*.

rime ● *noun* frost; hoar-frost. ● *verb* **(-ming)** cover with rime.

rind /raɪnd/ *noun* tough outer layer or covering of fruit and vegetables, cheese, bacon, etc.

ring[1] ● *noun* circular band, usually of metal, worn on finger; circular band of any material; line or band round cylindrical or circular object; mark or part etc. resembling ring; ring in cross-section of tree representing one year's growth; enclosure for circus, boxing, betting at races, etc.; people or things arranged in circle, such arrangement; combination of traders, politicians, spies, etc. acting together; gas ring; disc or halo round planet, moon, etc. ● *verb* (often + *round, about, in*) encircle; put ring on (bird etc.). □ **ring-binder** loose-leaf binder with ring-shaped clasps; **ring-dove** woodpigeon; **ring finger** finger next to little finger, esp. on left hand; **ringleader** instigator in crime or mischief etc.; **ringmaster** director of circus performance; **ring-pull** (of tin) having ring for pulling to break seal; **ring road** bypass encircling town; **ringside** area immediately beside boxing or circus ring etc.; **ringworm** skin infection forming circular inflamed patches.

ring[2] ● *verb* (*past* **rang**; *past participle* **rung**) (often + *out* etc.) give clear resonant sound; make (bell) ring; call by telephone; (usually + *with, to*) (of place) resound, re-echo; (of ears) be filled with sensation of ringing; (+ *in, out*) usher in or out with bell-ringing; give specified impression. ● *noun* ringing sound or tone; act of ringing bell, sound caused by this; *colloquial* telephone call; set of esp. church bells; specified feeling conveyed by words etc.. □ **ring back** make return telephone call to; **ring off** end telephone call; **ring up** make telephone call (to), record (amount) on cash register.

ringlet /'rɪŋlɪt/ *noun* curly lock of esp. long hair.

rink noun area of ice for skating, curling, etc.; enclosed area for roller-skating; building containing either of these; strip of bowling green; team in bowls or curling.

rinse ● verb (**-sing**) (often + through, out) wash or treat with clean water etc.; wash lightly; put through clean water after washing; (+ out, away) remove by rinsing. ● noun rinsing; temporary hair tint.

riot /'raɪət/ ● noun disturbance of peace by crowd; loud revelry; (+ of) lavish display of; colloquial very amusing thing or person. ● verb make or engage in riot. □ **run riot** throw off all restraint, spread uncontrolled. □ **rioter** noun; **riotous** adjective.

RIP abbreviation may he, she, or they rest in peace (requiesca(n)t in pace).

rip ● verb (**-pp-**) tear or cut quickly or forcibly away or apart; make (hole etc.) thus; make long tear or cut in; come violently apart, split. ● noun long tear or cut; act of ripping. □ **let rip** colloquial (allow to) proceed or act without restraint or interference; **rip-cord** cord for releasing parachute from its pack; **rip off** colloquial swindle, exploit, steal; **rip-off** noun □ **ripper** noun.

riparian /raɪ'peərɪən/ adjective of or on riverbank.

ripe adjective ready to be reaped, picked, or eaten; mature; (often + for) fit, ready. □ **ripen** verb; **ripe-ness** noun.

riposte /rɪ'pɒst/ ● noun quick retort; quick return thrust in fencing. ● verb (**-ting**) deliver riposte.

ripple /'rɪp(ə)l/ ● noun ruffling of water's surface; small wave(s); gentle lively sound, e.g. of laughter or applause; slight variation in strength of current etc.; ice cream with veins of syrup. ● verb (**-ling**) (cause to) form or flow in ripples; show or sound like ripples.

rise /raɪz/ ● verb (**-sing**; past tense **rose** /rəʊz/; past participle **risen** /'rɪz(ə)n/) come or go up; project or swell upwards; appear above horizon; get up from lying, sitting, or kneeling; get out of bed; (of meeting etc.) adjourn; reach higher level; make social progress; (often + up) rebel; come to surface; react to provocation; ascend, soar; have origin, begin to flow. ● noun rising; upward slope; increase in amount, extent, pitch, etc.; increase in salary; increase in status or power; height of step, incline, etc.; origin. □ **give rise to** cause, induce; **get, take a rise out of** colloquial provoke reaction from; **on the rise** on the increase.

riser noun person who rises from bed; vertical piece between treads of staircase.

risible /'rɪzɪb(ə)l/ adjective laughable, ludicrous.

rising ● adjective advancing; approaching specified age; going up. ● noun insurrection. □ **rising damp** moisture absorbed from ground into wall.

risk ● noun chance of danger, injury, loss, etc.; person or thing causing risk. ● verb expose to risk; venture on, take chances of. □ **at risk** exposed to danger; **at one's (own) risk** accepting responsibility for oneself; **at the risk of** with the possibility of (adverse consequences).

risky adjective (**-ier, -iest**) involving risk; risqué. □ **riskily** adverb; **riskiness** noun.

risotto /rɪ'zɒtəʊ/ noun (plural **-s**) Italian savoury rice dish cooked in stock.

risqué /'rɪskeɪ/ adjective (of story etc.) slightly indecent.

rissole /'rɪsəʊl/ noun fried cake of minced meat coated in breadcrumbs.

ritardando /rɪtɑː'dændəʊ/ adverb, adjective, & noun (plural **-s** or **-di** /-dɪ/) Music = RALLENTANDO.

rite noun religious or solemn ceremony or observance. □ **rite of passage** (often in plural) event marking change or stage in life.

ritual /'rɪtʃʊəl/ ● noun prescribed order esp. of religious ceremony; solemn or colourful pageantry etc.; procedure regularly followed. ● adjective of or done as ritual or rite. □ **ritually** adverb.

ritualism noun regular or excessive practice of ritual. □ **ritualist** noun; **ritualistic** /-'lɪs-/ adjective; **ritualistically** /-'lɪs-/ adverb.

rival /'raɪv(ə)l/ ● noun person or thing that competes with another or equals another in quality. ● verb (**-ll-**; US **-l-**) be rival of or comparable to.

rivalry noun (plural **-ies**) being rivals; competition.

riven /'rɪv(ə)n/ adjective literary split, torn.

river /'rɪvə/ noun large natural stream of water flowing to sea, lake, etc.; copious flow. □ **riverside** ground along riverbank.

rivet /'rɪvɪt/ ● noun nail or bolt for joining metal plates etc. ● verb (**-t-**) join or fasten with rivets; fix, make immovable; (+ on, upon) direct intently; (esp. as **riveting** adjective) engross.

riviera /rɪvɪ'eərə/ noun coastal subtropical region, esp. that of SE France and NW Italy.

rivulet /'rɪvjʊlɪt/ noun small stream.

RLC abbreviation Royal Logistics Corps.

RM abbreviation Royal Marines.

rm. abbreviation room.

RN abbreviation Royal Navy.

RNA abbreviation ribonucleic acid.

RNLI abbreviation Royal National Lifeboat Institution.

roach noun (plural same or **-es**) small freshwater fish.

road noun way with prepared surface for vehicles, etc.; route; (usually in plural) piece of water near shore in which ships can ride at anchor. □ **any road** dialect anyway; **in the** or **one's road** dialect forming obstruction; **on the road** travelling; **roadbed** foundation of road or railway, US part of road for vehicles; **roadblock** barrier on road to detain traffic; **road fund licence** = TAX DISC; **road-hog** colloquial reckless or inconsiderate motorist etc.; **roadhouse** inn etc. on main road; **road-metal** broken stone for road-making; **roadshow** touring entertainment etc., esp. radio or television series broadcast from changing venue; **roadstead** sea road for ships; **road tax** tax payable on vehicles; **road test** test of vehicle's roadworthiness; **roadway** part of road used by vehicles; **roadworks** construction or repair of roads; **roadworthy** (of vehicle) fit to be used on road; **roadworthiness** noun.

roadie noun colloquial assistant of touring band etc., responsible for equipment.

roadster noun open car without rear seats.

roam verb ramble, wander; travel unsystematically over, through, or about.

roan ● adjective (esp. of horse) with coat thickly interspersed with hairs of another colour. ● noun roan animal.

roar /rɔː/ ● noun loud deep hoarse sound as of lion; loud laugh. ● verb (often + out) utter loudly, or make roar, roaring laugh, etc.; travel in vehicle at high speed. □ **roaring drunk** very drunk and noisy; **roaring forties** stormy ocean tracts between latitudes 40° and 50°S; **roaring success** great success; **roaring twenties** decade of 1920s.

roast ● verb cook or be cooked by exposure to open heat or in oven; criticize severely. ● adjective roasted. ● noun (dish of) roast meat; meat for roasting; process of roasting.

rob verb (**-bb-**) (often + of) take unlawfully from, esp. by force; deprive of. □ **robber** noun; **robbery** noun (plural **-ies**).

robe ● noun long loose garment, esp. (often in plural) as indication of rank, office, etc.; esp. US dressing gown. ● verb (**-bing**) clothe in robe; dress.

robin /'rɒbɪn/ *noun* (also **robin redbreast**) small brown red-breasted bird.

Robin Hood *noun* person who steals from rich to give to poor.

robot /'rəʊbɒt/ *noun* automaton resembling or functioning like human; automatic mechanical device; machine-like person. □ **robotic** /-'bɒt-/ *adjective*; **robotize** *verb* (also **-ise**) (**-zing** or **-sing**).

robotics /rəʊ'bɒtɪks/ *plural noun* (usually treated as *singular*) science or study of robot design and operation.

robust /rəʊ'bʌst/ *adjective* (**-er**, **-est**) strong, esp. in health and physique; (of exercise etc.) vigorous; straightforward; (of statement etc.) bold. □ **robustly** *adverb*; **robustness** *noun*.

roc *noun* gigantic bird of Eastern legend.

rock¹ *noun* solid part of earth's crust; material or projecting mass of this; (**the Rock**) Gibraltar; large detached stone; *US* stone of any size; firm support or protection; hard sweet usually as peppermint-flavoured stick; *slang* precious stone, esp. diamond. □ **on the rocks** *colloquial* short of money, (of marriage) broken down, (of drink) served with ice cubes; **rock-bottom** very lowest (level); **rock-cake** bun with rough surface; **rock crystal** crystallized quartz; **rock face** vertical surface of natural rock; **rock-garden** rockery; **rock plant** plant that grows on or among rocks; **rock-salmon** catfish, dogfish, etc.; **rock salt** common salt as solid mineral.

rock² ● *verb* move gently to and fro; set, keep, or be in such motion; (cause to) sway; oscillate; shake, reel. ● *noun* rocking motion; rock and roll, popular music influenced by this. □ **rock and roll**, **rock 'n' roll** popular dance music with heavy beat and blues influence; **rocking-chair** chair on rockers or springs; **rocking-horse** toy horse on rockers or springs.

rocker *noun* device for rocking, esp. curved bar etc. on which something rocks; rocking-chair; rock music devotee, esp. leather-clad motorcyclist.

rockery *noun* (*plural* **-ies**) pile of rough stones with soil between them for growing rock plants on.

rocket /'rɒkɪt/ ● *noun* firework or signal propelled to great height after ignition; engine operating on same principle; rocket-propelled missile, spacecraft, etc. ● *verb* (**-t-**) move rapidly upwards or away; bombard with rockets.

rocketry *noun* science or practice of rocket propulsion.

rocky¹ *adjective* (**-ier**, **-iest**) of, like, or full of rocks.

rocky² *adjective* (**-ier**, **-iest**) *colloquial* unsteady, tottering.

rococo /rə'kəʊkəʊ/ ● *adjective* of ornate style of art, music, and literature in 18th-c. Europe. ● *noun* this style.

rod *noun* slender straight round stick or bar; cane for flogging; fishing-rod; *historical* measure of length (5½ yds.).

rode *past of* RIDE.

rodent /'rəʊd(ə)nt/ *noun* mammal with strong incisors and no canine teeth (e.g. rat, squirrel, beaver).

rodeo /'rəʊdɪəʊ/ *noun* (*plural* **-s**) exhibition of cowboys' skills; round-up of cattle for branding etc.

roe¹ *noun* (also **hard roe**) mass of eggs in female fish; (also **soft roe**) male fish's milt.

roe² *noun* (*plural* same or **-s**) (also **roe-deer**) small kind of deer. **roebuck** male roe.

roentgen /'rʌntjən/ *noun* (also **röntgen**) unit of exposure to ionizing radiation.

rogation /rə'geɪʃ(ə)n/ *noun* (usually in *plural*) litany of the saints chanted on the 3 days (**Rogation Days**) before Ascension Day.

roger /'rɒdʒə/ *interjection* your message has been received and understood; *slang* I agree.

rogue /rəʊg/ *noun* dishonest or unprincipled person; *jocular* mischievous person; wild fierce animal driven or living apart from herd; inferior or defective specimen. □ **roguery** *noun* (*plural* **-ies**); **roguish** *adjective*.

roister /'rɔɪstə/ *verb* (esp. as **roistering** *adjective*) revel noisily, be uproarious. □ **roisterer** *noun*.

role *noun* (also **rôle**) actor's part; person's or thing's function. □ **role model** person on whom others model themselves; **role-playing**, **-play** acting of characters or situations as aid in psychotherapy, teaching, etc.; **role-play** *verb*.

roll /rəʊl/ ● *verb* (cause to) move or go in some direction by turning over and over on axis; make cylindrical or spherical by revolving between two surfaces or over on itself; gather into mass; (often + **along**, **by**, etc.) move or be carried on or as if on wheels; flatten with roller; rotate; sway or rock; proceed unsteadily; undulate, show undulating motion or surface; sound with vibration. ● *noun* rolling motion or gait; undulation; act of rolling; rhythmic rumbling sound; anything forming cylinder by being turned over on itself without folding; small loaf of bread for one person; official list or register. □ **roll-call** calling of list of names to establish presence; **rolled gold** thin coating of gold applied by roller to base metal; **rolled oats** husked and crushed oats; **rolling-mill** machine or factory for rolling metal into shape; **rolling-pin** roller for pastry; **rolling-stock** company's railway or (*US*) road vehicles; **roll-mop** rolled pickled herring fillet; **roll-neck** having high loosely turned-over collar; **roll-on** applied by means of rotating ball; **roll-on roll-off** (of ship etc.) in which vehicles are driven directly on and off; **roll-top desk** desk with flexible cover sliding in curved grooves; **roll-up** hand-rolled cigarette; **strike off the rolls** debar from practising as solicitor.

roller *noun* revolving cylinder for smoothing, flattening, crushing, spreading, etc.; small cylinder on which hair is rolled for setting; long swelling wave. □ **roller bearing** bearing with cylinders instead of balls; **roller coaster** switchback at fair etc.; **roller-skate** noun frame with small wheels, strapped to shoes; boot with small wheels underneath; *verb* move on roller-skates; **roller towel** towel with ends joined.

rollicking /'rɒlɪkɪŋ/ *adjective* jovial, exuberant.

roly-poly /rəʊlɪ'pəʊlɪ/ ● *noun* (*plural* **-ies**) (also **roly-poly pudding**) pudding of rolled-up suet pastry covered with jam and boiled or baked. ● *adjective* podgy, plump.

ROM *noun* *Computing* read-only memory.

Roman /'rəʊmən/ ● *adjective* of ancient Rome or its territory or people; of medieval or modern Rome; Roman Catholic; (**roman**) (of type) plain and upright, used in ordinary print; (of the alphabet etc.) based on the ancient Roman system with letters A–Z. ● *noun* (*plural* **-s**) citizen of ancient Roman Republic or Empire, or of modern Rome; Roman Catholic; (**roman**) roman type. □ **Roman candle** firework discharging coloured sparks; **Roman Catholic** *adjective* of part of Christian Church acknowledging Pope as its head, *noun* member of this; **Roman Catholicism** *noun*; **Roman Empire** *historical* that established in 27 BC and divided in AD 395; **Roman law** law code of ancient Rome, forming basis of many modern codes; **Roman nose** one with high bridge; **roman numerals** numerals expressed in letters of Roman alphabet. □ **romanize** *verb* (also **-ise**) (**-zing** or **-sing**); **romanization** *noun*.

romance /rəʊ'mæns/ ● *noun* (also /'rəʊ-/) idealized, poetic, or unworldly atmosphere or tendency; love affair; (work of) literature concerning romantic love, stirring action, etc.; medieval tale of chivalry; exaggeration, picturesque falsehood. ● adjective (**Romance**) (of a language) descended from Latin. ● verb (**-cing**) exaggerate, fantasize; woo.

Romanesque /rəʊmə'nesk/ ● noun style of European architecture c. 900–1200, with massive vaulting and round arches. ● adjective of this style.

Romanian /rəʊ'meɪnɪən/ (also **Rumanian** /ruː-/) ● noun native, national, or language of Romania. ● adjective of Romania or its people or language.

romantic /rəʊ'mæntɪk/ ● adjective of, characterized by, or suggestive of romance; imaginative, visionary; (of literature or music etc.) concerned more with emotion than with form; (also **Romantic**) of the 18th–19th-c. romantic movement or style in European arts. ● noun romantic person; romanticist. □ **romantically** adverb.

romanticism /rəʊ'mæntɪsɪz(ə)m/ noun (also **Romanticism**) adherence to romantic style in literature, art, etc. □ **romanticist, Romanticist** noun.

romanticize /rəʊ'mæntɪsaɪz/ verb (also **-ise**) (**-zing** or **-sing**) make romantic; exaggerate; indulge in romance.

Romany /'rɒmənɪ/ ● noun (plural **-ies**) Gypsy; language of Gypsies. ● adjective of Gypsies or Romany language.

Romeo /'rəʊmɪəʊ/ noun (plural **-s**) passionate male lover or seducer.

romp ● verb play roughly and energetically; (+ along, past, etc.) colloquial proceed without effort. ● noun spell of romping. □ **romp in, home** colloquial win easily.

rompers plural noun (also **romper suit**) young child's one-piece garment.

rondeau /'rɒndəʊ/ noun (plural **-x** same pronunciation or /-z/) short poem with two rhymes only, and opening words used as refrains.

rondel /'rɒnd(ə)l/ noun rondeau.

rondo /'rɒndəʊ/ noun (plural **-s**) musical form with recurring leading theme.

röntgen = ROENTGEN.

rood /ruːd/ noun crucifix, esp. on rood-screen; quarter-acre. □ **rood-screen** carved screen separating nave and chancel.

roof /ruːf/ ● noun (plural **roofs** /ruːvz/) upper covering of building; top of covered vehicle etc.; top interior surface of oven, cave, mine, etc. ● verb (often + in, over) cover with roof; be roof of. □ **roof of the mouth** palate; **roof-rack** framework for luggage on top of vehicle; **rooftop** outer surface of roof, (in plural) tops of houses etc.

rook[1] /rʊk/ ● noun black bird of crow family nesting in colonies. ● verb colloquial charge (customer) extortionately; win money at cards etc., esp. by swindling.

rook[2] /rʊk/ noun chess piece with battlement-shaped top.

rookery noun (plural **-ies**) colony of rooks, penguins, or seals.

rookie /'rʊkɪ/ noun slang recruit.

room /ruːm/ ● noun space for, or occupied by, something; capacity; part of building enclosed by walls; (in plural) apartments or lodgings. ● verb US have room(s), lodge. □ **room service** provision of food etc. in hotel bedroom.

roomy adjective (**-ier, -iest**) having much room, spacious. □ **roominess** noun.

roost /ruːst/ ● noun bird's perch. ● verb (of bird) settle for rest or sleep.

rooster noun domestic cock.

root[1] /ruːt/ ● noun part of plant below ground conveying nourishment from soil; (in plural) fibres or branches of this; plant with edible root, such root;

(in plural) emotional attachment or family ties in a place; embedded part of hair or tooth etc.; basic cause, source; Mathematics number which multiplied by itself a given number of times yields a given number, esp. square root; core of a word. ● verb (cause to) take root; (esp. as **rooted** adjective) fix or establish firmly; pull up by roots. □ **root out** find and get rid of; **rootstock** rhizome, plant into which graft is inserted, source from which offshoots have arisen; **take root** begin to draw nourishment from the soil, become established. □ **rootless** adjective.

root[2] /ruːt/ verb (often + up) turn up (ground) with snout etc. in search of food; (+ around, in, etc.) rummage; (+ out, up) extract by rummaging; (+ for) US slang encourage by applause or support.

rope ● noun stout cord made by twisting together strands of hemp or wire etc.; (+ of) string of onions, pearls etc.; (**the rope**) (halter for) execution by hanging. ● verb (**-ping**) fasten or catch with rope; (+ off, in) enclose with rope. □ **know, learn,** or **show the ropes** know, learn, show how to do a thing properly; **rope into** persuade to take part (in).

ropy adjective (also **ropey**) (**-ier, -iest**) colloquial poor in quality. □ **ropiness** noun.

Roquefort /'rɒkfɔː/ noun proprietary term soft blue ewe's-milk cheese.

rorqual /'rɔːkw(ə)l/ noun whale with dorsal fin.

rosaceous /rəʊ'zeɪʃəs/ adjective of plant family including the rose.

rosary /'rəʊzərɪ/ noun (plural **-ies**) RC Church repeated sequence of prayers; string of beads for keeping count in this.

rose[1] /rəʊz/ ● noun prickly shrub bearing fragrant red, pink, yellow, or white flowers; this flower; pinkish-red colour or (usually in plural) complexion; rose-shaped design; circular fitting on ceiling from which electric light hangs by cable; spray nozzle of watering-can etc.; (in plural) used to express ease, luck, etc. ● adjective rose-coloured. □ **rosebowl** bowl for cut roses, esp. given as prize; **rosebud** bud of rose, pretty girl; **rose-coloured** pinkish-red, cheerful, optimistic; **rose-hip** fruit of rose; **rose-water** perfume made from roses; **rose-window** circular window with roselike tracery; **rosewood** close-grained wood used in making furniture.

rose[2] past of RISE.

rosé /'rəʊzeɪ/ noun light pink wine. [French]

rosemary /'rəʊzmərɪ/ noun evergreen fragrant shrub used as herb.

rosette /rəʊ'zet/ noun rose-shaped ornament made of ribbons etc. or carved in stone etc.

rosin /'rɒzɪn/ ● noun resin, esp. in solid form. ● verb (**-n-**) rub with rosin.

RoSPA /'rɒspə/ abbreviation Royal Society for the Prevention of Accidents.

roster /'rɒstə/ ● noun list or plan of turns of duty etc. ● verb place on roster.

rostrum /'rɒstrəm/ noun (plural **rostra** or **-s**) platform for public speaking etc.

rosy /'rəʊzɪ/ adjective (**-ier, -iest**) pink, red; optimistic, hopeful.

rot ● verb (**-tt-**) undergo decay by putrefaction; perish, waste away; cause to rot, make rotten. ● noun decay, rottenness; slang nonsense; decline in standards etc. ● interjection expressing incredulity or ridicule. □ **rotgut** slang cheap harmful alcohol.

rota /'rəʊtə/ noun list of duties to be done or people to do them in turn.

rotary /'rəʊtərɪ/ ● adjective acting by rotation. ● noun (plural **-ies**) rotary machine; (**Rotary**; in full **Rotary International**) worldwide charitable society of businessmen.

rotate /rəʊˈteɪt/ verb (**-ting**) move round axis or centre, revolve; arrange or take in rotation. □ **rotatory** /ˈrəʊtətərɪ/ adjective.

rotation noun rotating, being rotated; recurrent series or period; regular succession; growing of different crops in regular order. □ **rotational** adjective.

rote noun (usually in **by rote**) mechanical repetition (in order to memorize).

rotisserie /rəʊˈtɪsərɪ/ noun restaurant etc. where meat is roasted; revolving spit for roasting food.

rotor /ˈrəʊtə/ noun rotary part of machine; rotating aerofoil on helicopter.

rotten /ˈrɒt(ə)n/ adjective (**-er, -est**) rotting or rotted; fragile from age etc.; morally or politically corrupt; slang disagreeable, worthless. □ **rotten borough** historical (before 1832) English borough electing MP though having very few voters. □ **rottenness** noun.

rotter noun slang objectionable person.

Rottweiler /ˈrɒtvaɪlə/ noun black-and-tan dog noted for ferocity.

rotund /rəʊˈtʌnd/ adjective plump, podgy. □ **rotundity** noun.

rotunda /rəʊˈtʌndə/ noun circular building, esp. domed.

rouble /ˈruːb(ə)l/ noun (also **ruble**) monetary unit of Russia etc.

roué /ˈruːeɪ/ noun (esp. elderly) debauchee.

rouge /ruːʒ/ ● noun red cosmetic used to colour cheeks. ● verb (**-ging**) colour with or apply rouge; blush.

rough /rʌf/ ● adjective having uneven surface, not smooth or level; shaggy; coarse, violent; not mild, quiet, or gentle; (of wine) harsh; insensitive; unpleasant, severe; lacking finish etc.; approximate, rudimentary. ● adverb in a rough way. ● noun (usually **the rough**) hardship; rough ground; hooligan; unfinished or natural state. ● verb make rough; (+ out, in) sketch or plan roughly. □ **rough-and-ready** rough or crude but effective, not over-particular; **rough-and-tumble** adjective irregular, disorderly, noun scuffle; **roughcast** noun plaster of lime and gravel, verb coat with this; **rough diamond** uncut diamond, rough but honest person; **rough house** slang disturbance, rough fight; **rough it** colloquial do without basic comforts; **rough justice** treatment that is approximately fair, unfair treatment; **roughneck** colloquial worker on oil rig, rough person; **rough up** slang attack violently. □ **roughen** verb; **roughly** adverb; **roughness** noun.

roughage noun fibrous material in food, stimulating intestinal action.

roughshod /ˈrʌfʃɒd/ □ **ride roughshod over** treat arrogantly.

roulade /ruːˈlɑːd/ noun filled rolled piece of meat, sponge, etc.; quick succession of notes.

roulette /ruːˈlet/ noun gambling game with ball dropped on revolving numbered wheel.

round /raʊnd/ ● adjective shaped like circle, sphere, or cylinder; done with circular motion; (of number etc.) without odd units; entire, continuous, complete; candid; (of voice etc.) sonorous. ● noun round object; revolving motion, circular or recurring course, series; route for deliveries, inspection, etc.; drink etc. for each member of group; one bullet, shell, etc.; slice of bread, sandwich made from two slices, joint of beef from haunch; one period of play etc., one stage in competition, playing of all holes in golf course once; song for unaccompanied voices overlapping at intervals; rung of ladder; (+ of) circumference or extent of. ● adverb with circular motion, with return to starting point or change to opposite position; to, at, or affecting circumference, area, group, etc.; in every direction from a centre;

measuring (specified distance) in girth. ● preposition so as to encircle or enclose; at or to points on circumference of; with successive visits to; within a radius of; having as central point; so as to pass in curved course, having thus passed. ● verb give or take round shape; pass round (corner etc.); (usually + up, down) express (number) approximately. □ **in the round** with all angles or features shown or considered, with audience all round theatre stage; **Roundhead** historical member of Parliamentary party in English Civil War; **round off** make complete or less angular; **round on** attack unexpectedly; **round out** provide with more details, finish; **round robin** petition with signatures in circle to conceal order of writing, tournament in which each competitor plays every other; **Round Table** international charitable association; **round table** assembly for discussion, esp. at conference; **round trip** trip to one or more places and back; **round up** gather or bring together; **round-up** rounding-up, summary.

roundabout ● noun road junction with traffic passing in one direction round central island; revolving device in children's playground; merry-go-round. ● adjective circuitous.

roundel /ˈraʊnd(ə)l/ noun circular mark; small disc, medallion.

roundelay /ˈraʊndɪleɪ/ noun short simple song with refrain.

rounders /ˈraʊndəz/ noun team game in which players hit ball and run through round of bases.

roundly adverb bluntly, severely.

rouse /raʊz/ verb (**-sing**) (cause to) wake; (often + up) make or become active or excited; anger; evoke (feelings). □ **rousing** adjective.

roustabout /ˈraʊstəbaʊt/ noun labourer on oil rig; unskilled or casual labourer.

rout /raʊt/ ● noun disorderly retreat of defeated troops; overthrow, defeat. ● verb put to flight, defeat.

route /ruːt/ ● noun way taken (esp. regularly) from one place to another. ● verb (**-teing**) send etc. by particular route. □ **route march** training-march for troops.

routine /ruːˈtiːn/ ● noun regular course or procedure, unvarying performance of certain acts; set sequence in dance, comedy act, etc.; sequence of instructions to computer. ● adjective performed as routine; of customary or standard kind. □ **routinely** adverb.

roux /ruː/ noun (plural same) mixture of fat and flour used in sauces etc.

rove /rəʊv/ verb (**-ving**) wander without settling, roam; (of eyes) look about.

rover noun wanderer.

row[1] /rəʊ/ noun line of people or things; line of seats in theatre etc. □ **in a row** forming a row, colloquial in succession.

row[2] /rəʊ/ ● verb propel (boat) with oars; convey thus. ● noun spell of rowing; trip in rowing boat. □ **rowing boat** (US **row-boat**) small boat propelled by oars. □ **rower** noun.

row[3] /raʊ/ colloquial ● noun loud noise, commotion; quarrel, dispute; severe reprimand. ● verb make or engage in row; reprimand.

rowan /ˈrəʊən/ noun (in full **rowan tree**) mountain ash; (in full **rowan-berry**) its scarlet berry.

rowdy /ˈraʊdɪ/ ● adjective (**-ier, -iest**) noisy and disorderly. ● noun (plural **-ies**) rowdy person. □ **rowdily** adverb; **rowdiness** noun; **rowdyism** noun.

rowel /ˈraʊəl/ noun spiked revolving disc at end of spur.

rowlock /ˈrɒlək/ noun device for holding oar in place.

royal /ˈrɔɪəl/ ● adjective of, suited to, or worthy of king or queen; in service or under patronage of king or queen; of family of king or queen; splendid, on great scale. ● *noun colloquial* member of royal family. □ **royal blue** deep vivid blue; **Royal Commission** commission of inquiry appointed by Crown at request of government; **royal flush** straight poker flush headed by ace; **royal jelly** substance secreted by worker bees and fed to future queen bees; **Royal Navy** British navy; **royal 'we'** use of 'we' instead of 'I' by single person. □ **royally** *adverb*.

royalist *noun* supporter of monarchy, *esp. historical* of King's side in English Civil War.

royalty *noun* (*plural* **-ies**) being royal; royal people; member of royal family; percentage of profit from book, public performance, patent, etc. paid to author etc.; royal right (now esp. over minerals) granted by sovereign; payment made by producer of minerals etc. to owner of site etc.

RP *abbreviation* Received Pronunciation.

RPI *abbreviation* retail price index.

rpm *abbreviation* revolutions per minute.

RSA *abbreviation* Royal Society of Arts; Royal Scottish Academy; Royal Scottish Academician.

RSC *abbreviation* Royal Shakespeare Company.

RSM *abbreviation* Regimental Sergeant-Major.

RSPB *abbreviation* Royal Society for the Protection of Birds.

RSPCA *abbreviation* Royal Society for the Prevention of Cruelty to Animals.

RSV *abbreviation* Revised Standard Version (of Bible).

RSVP *abbreviation* please answer (*répondez s'il vous plaît*).

Rt. Hon. *abbreviation* Right Honourable.

Rt Revd *abbreviation* (also **Rt. Rev.**) Right Reverend.

rub ● *verb* (**-bb-**) move hand etc. firmly over surface of; (usually + *against, in, on, over*) apply (hand etc.) thus; polish, clean, abrade, chafe, or make dry, sore, or bare by rubbing; (+ *in, into, through, over*) apply by rubbing; (often + *together, against, on*) move with friction or slide (objects) against each other; get frayed or worn by friction. ● *noun* action or spell of rubbing; impediment or difficulty. □ **rub off** (usually + *on*) be transferred by contact, be transmitted; **rub out** erase with rubber; **rub up the wrong way** irritate.

rubato /ruːˈbɑːtəʊ/ *noun Music* (*plural* **-s** or **-ti** /-tɪ/) temporary disregarding of strict tempo.

rubber[1] /ˈrʌbə/ *noun* elastic substance made from latex of plants or synthetically; piece of this or other substance for erasing pencil marks; (in *plural US*) galoshes. □ **rubber band** loop of rubber to hold papers etc.; **rubberneck** *colloquial* (be) inquisitive sightseer; **rubber plant** tropical plant often grown as house-plant, (also **rubber tree**) tree yielding latex; **rubber stamp** device for inking and imprinting on surface, (person giving) mechanical endorsement of actions etc.; **rubber-stamp** approve automatically. □ **rubberize** *verb* (also **-ise**) (**-zing** or **-sing**); **rubbery** *adjective*.

rubber[2] /ˈrʌbə/ *noun* series of games between same sides or people at whist, bridge, cricket, etc.

rubbish /ˈrʌbɪʃ/ ● *noun* waste or worthless matter; litter; trash; (often as *interjection*) nonsense. ● *verb colloquial* criticize contemptuously. □ **rubbishy** *adjective*.

rubble /ˈrʌb(ə)l/ *noun* rough fragments of stone, brick, etc.

rubella /ruːˈbelə/ *noun formal* German measles.

Rubicon /ˈruːbɪkɒn/ *noun* point from which there is no going back.

rubicund /ˈruːbɪkʌnd/ *adjective* ruddy, red-faced.

ruble = ROUBLE.

rubric /ˈruːbrɪk/ *noun* heading or passage in red or special lettering; explanatory words; established

custom or rule; direction for conduct of divine service in liturgical book.

ruby /ˈruːbɪ/ ● *noun* (*plural* **-ies**) crimson or rose-coloured precious stone; deep red colour. ● *adjective* ruby-coloured. □ **ruby wedding** 40th wedding anniversary.

RUC *abbreviation* Royal Ulster Constabulary.

ruche /ruːʃ/ *noun* frill or gathering of lace etc. □ **ruched** *adjective*.

ruck[1] **(the ruck)** main group of competitors not likely to overtake leaders; undistinguished crowd of people or things; *Rugby* loose scrum.

ruck[2] ● *verb* (often + *up*) crease, wrinkle. ● *noun* crease, wrinkle.

rucksack /ˈrʌksæk/ *noun* bag carried on back, esp. by hikers.

ruckus /ˈrʌkəs/ *noun esp. US* row, commotion.

ruction /ˈrʌkʃ(ə)n/ *noun colloquial* disturbance, tumult; (in *plural*) row.

rudder /ˈrʌdə/ *noun* flat piece hinged to vessel's stern or rear of aeroplane for steering. □ **rudderless** *adjective*.

ruddy /ˈrʌdɪ/ *adjective* (**-ier, -iest**) freshly or healthily red; reddish; *colloquial* bloody, damnable.

rude *adjective* impolite, offensive; roughly made; primitive, uneducated; abrupt, sudden; *colloquial* indecent, lewd; vigorous, hearty. □ **rudely** *adverb*; **rudeness** *noun*.

rudiment /ˈruːdɪmənt/ *noun* (in *plural*) elements or first principles of subject, imperfect beginning of something undeveloped; vestigial or undeveloped part or organ. □ **rudimentary** /-ˈmentərɪ/ *adjective*.

rue[1] *verb* (**rues, rued, rueing** or **ruing**) repent of; wish undone or non-existent.

rue[2] *noun* evergreen shrub with bitter strong-scented leaves.

rueful *adjective* genuinely or humorously sorrowful. □ **ruefully** *adverb*.

ruff[1] *noun* projecting starched frill worn round neck; projecting or coloured ring of feathers or hair round bird's or animal's neck; domestic pigeon.

ruff[2] ● *verb* trump at cards. ● *noun* trumping.

ruffian /ˈrʌfɪən/ *noun* violent lawless person.

ruffle /ˈrʌf(ə)l/ ● *verb* (**-ling**) disturb smoothness or tranquillity of; gather into ruffle; (often + *up*) (of bird) erect (feathers) in anger, display, etc. ● *noun* frill of lace etc.

rufous /ˈruːfəs/ *adjective* reddish-brown.

rug *noun* floor-mat; thick woollen wrap or coverlet.

Rugby /ˈrʌgbɪ/ *noun* (in full **Rugby football**) team game played with oval ball that may be kicked or carried. □ **Rugby League** partly professional Rugby with teams of 13; **Rugby Union** amateur Rugby with teams of 15.

rugged /ˈrʌgɪd/ *adjective* (esp. of ground) rough, uneven; (of features) furrowed, irregular; harsh; robust. □ **ruggedly** *adverb*; **ruggedness** *noun*.

rugger /ˈrʌgə/ *noun colloquial* Rugby.

ruin /ˈruːɪn/ ● *noun* wrecked or spoiled state; downfall; loss of property or position; (in *singular* or *plural*) remains of building etc. that has suffered ruin; cause of ruin. ● *verb* bring to ruin; spoil, damage; (esp. as **ruined** *adjective*) reduce to ruins. □ **ruination** *noun*.

ruinous *adjective* bringing ruin; disastrous; dilapidated.

rule ● *noun* compulsory principle governing action; prevailing custom, standard, normal state of things; government, dominion; straight measuring device, ruler; code of discipline of religious order; *Printing* thin line or dash. ● *verb* (**-ling**) dominate; keep under control; (often + *over*) have sovereign control of;

(often + *that*) pronounce authoritatively; make parallel lines across (paper), make (straight line) with ruler etc. □ **as a rule** usually; **rule of thumb** rule based on experience or practice, not theory; **rule out** exclude.

ruler *noun* person exercising government or dominion; straight strip of plastic etc. used to draw or measure.

ruling *noun* authoritative pronouncement.

rum¹ *noun* spirit distilled from sugar cane or molasses. □ **rum baba** sponge cake soaked in rum syrup.

rum² *adjective* (**-mm-**) *colloquial* queer, strange.

Rumanian = ROMANIAN.

rumba /ˈrʌmbə/ *noun* ballroom dance of Cuban origin; music for this.

rumble /ˈrʌmb(ə)l/ ● *verb* (**-ling**) make continuous deep sound as of thunder; (+ *along, by, past,* etc.) (esp. of vehicle) move with such sound; *slang* see through, detect. ● *noun* rumbling sound.

rumbustious /rʌmˈbʌstʃəs/ *adjective colloquial* boisterous, uproarious.

ruminant /ˈruːmɪnənt/ ● *noun* animal that chews the cud. ● *adjective* of ruminants; meditative.

ruminate /ˈruːmɪneɪt/ *verb* (**-ting**) meditate, ponder; chew the cud. □ **rumination** *noun*; **ruminative** /-nətɪv/ *adjective*.

rummage /ˈrʌmɪdʒ/ ● *verb* (**-ging**) search, esp. unsystematically; (+ *up, out*) find among other things. ● *noun* rummaging. □ **rummage sale** *esp. US* jumble sale.

rummy /ˈrʌmɪ/ *noun* card game played usually with two packs.

rumour /ˈruːmə/ (*US* **rumor**) ● *noun* (often + *of, that*) general talk, assertion, or hearsay of doubtful accuracy. ● *verb* (usually in *passive*) report by way of rumour.

rump *noun* hind part of mammal or bird, esp. buttocks; remnant of parliament etc. □ **rump steak** cut of beef from rump.

rumple /ˈrʌmp(ə)l/ *verb* (**-ling**) crease, ruffle.

rumpus /ˈrʌmpəs/ *noun colloquial* row, uproar.

run ● *verb* (**-nn-**; *past* **ran**; *past participle* **run**) go at pace faster than walk; flee; go or travel hurriedly, briefly, etc.; advance smoothly or (as) by rolling or on wheels; (cause) to be in action or operation; be current or operative; (of bus, train, etc.) travel on its route; (of play etc.) be presented; extend, have course or tendency; compete in or enter (horse etc.) in race etc.; (often + *for*) seek election; (cause to) flow or emit liquid; spread rapidly; perform (errand); publish (article etc.); direct (business etc.); own and use (vehicle); smuggle; (of thought, the eye, etc.) pass quickly; (of tights etc.) ladder. ● *noun* running; short excursion; distance travelled; general tendency; regular route; continuous stretch, spell, or course; (often + *on*) high general demand; quantity produced at one time; general or average type or class; point scored in cricket or baseball; (+ *of*) free use of; animal's regular track; enclosure for fowls etc.; range of pasture; ladder in tights etc.; *Music* rapid scale passage. □ **give (person) the run-around** deceive, evade; **on the run** fleeing; **runabout** light car or aircraft; **run across** happen to meet; **run after** pursue; **run away** *verb* (often + *from*) flee, abscond; **runaway** *noun* person, animal, vehicle, etc. running away or out of control; **run down** *verb* knock down, reduce numbers of, (of clock etc.) stop, discover after search, *colloquial* disparage; **run-down** *noun* reduction in numbers, detailed analysis, *adjective* dilapidated, decayed, exhausted; **run dry** cease to flow; **run in** *verb* run (vehicle, engine) carefully when new, *colloquial* arrest; **run-in** *noun colloquial* quarrel; **run into** collide with, encounter, reach as many as; **run low,**

short become depleted, have too little; **run off** flee, produce (copies) on machine, decide (race) after tie or heats, write or recite fluently; **run-of-the-mill** ordinary, not special; **run on** continue in operation, speak volubly, continue on same line as preceding matter; **run out** come to an end, (+ *of*) exhaust one's stock of, put down wicket of (running batsman); **run out on** *colloquial* desert; **run over** (of vehicle) knock down or crush, overflow, review quickly; **run through** *verb* examine or rehearse briefly, deal successively with, spend money rapidly, pervade, pierce with blade; **run-through** *noun* rehearsal; **run to** have money or ability for, reach (amount etc.), show tendency to; **run up** *verb* accumulate (debt etc.), build or make hurriedly, raise (flag); **run-up** *noun* (often + *to*) preparatory period; **run up against** meet with (difficulty etc.); **runway** specially prepared airfield surface for taking off and landing.

rune *noun* letter of earliest Germanic alphabet; similar character of mysterious or magic significance. □ **runic** *adjective*.

rung¹ *noun* step of ladder; strengthening crosspiece of chair etc.

rung² *past participle* of RING².

runnel /ˈrʌn(ə)l/ *noun* brook; gutter.

runner *noun* racer; creeping rooting plant-stem; groove, rod, etc. for thing to slide along or on; sliding ring on rod etc.; messenger; long narrow ornamental cloth or rug; (in full **runner bean**) kind of climbing bean. □ **runner-up** (*plural* **runners-up** or **runner-ups**) competitor taking second place.

running ● *noun* act or manner of running race etc. ● *adjective* continuous; consecutive; done with a run. □ **in** or **out of the running** with good or poor chance of success; **running commentary** verbal description of events in progress; **running knot** one that slips along rope etc. to allow tightening; **running mate** *US* vice-presidential candidate, horse setting pace for another; **running repairs** minor or temporary repairs; **running water** flowing water, esp. on tap.

runny *adjective* (**-ier, -iest**) tending to run or flow; excessively fluid.

runt *noun* smallest pig etc. of litter; undersized person.

rupee /ruːˈpiː/ *noun* monetary unit of India, Pakistan, etc.

rupiah /ruːˈpiːə/ *noun* monetary unit of Indonesia.

rupture /ˈrʌptʃə/ ● *noun* breaking, breach; breach in relationship; abdominal hernia. ● *verb* (**-ring**) burst (cell, membrane, etc.); sever (connection); affect with or suffer hernia.

rural /ˈrʊər(ə)l/ *adjective* in, of, or suggesting country.

ruse /ruːz/ *noun* stratagem, trick.

rush¹ ● *verb* go, move, flow, or act precipitately or with great speed; move or transport with great haste; perform or deal with hurriedly; force (person) to act hastily; attack or capture by sudden assault. ● *noun* rushing; violent advance or attack; sudden flow; period of great activity; sudden migration of large numbers; (+ *on, for*) strong demand for a commodity; (in *plural*) *colloquial* first uncut prints of film. ● *adjective* done hastily. □ **rush hour** time each day when traffic is heaviest.

rush² *noun* marsh plant with slender pith-filled stem; its stem esp. used for making basketware etc.

rusk *noun* slice of bread rebaked as light biscuit, esp. for infants.

russet /ˈrʌsɪt/ ● *adjective* reddish-brown. ● *noun* russet colour; rough-skinned russet-coloured apple.

Russian /ˈrʌʃ(ə)n/ ● *noun* native or national of Russia or (loosely) former USSR; person of Russian descent; language of Russia. ● *adjective* of Russia or (loosely) former USSR or its people; of or in Russian.

□ **Russian roulette** firing of revolver held to one's head after spinning cylinder with one chamber loaded; **Russian salad** mixed diced cooked vegetables with mayonnaise.

rust ● *noun* reddish corrosive coating formed on iron etc. by oxidation; plant disease with rust-coloured spots; reddish-brown. ● *verb* affect or be affected with rust; become impaired through disuse. □ **rustproof** not susceptible to corrosion by rust.

rustic /'rʌstɪk/ ● *adjective* of or like country people or country life; unsophisticated; of rough workmanship; made of untrimmed branches or rough timber; *Architecture* with roughened surface. ● *noun* country person, peasant. □ **rusticity** /-'tɪs-/ *noun*.

rusticate /'rʌstɪkeɪt/ *verb* (**-ting**) expel temporarily from university; retire to or live in the country; make rustic. □ **rustication** *noun*.

rustle /'rʌs(ə)l/ ● *verb* (**-ling**) (cause to) make sound as of dry blown leaves; steal (cattle or horses). ● *noun* rustling sound. □ **rustle up** *colloquial* produce at short notice. □ **rustler** *noun*.

rusty *adjective* (**-ier, -iest**) rusted, affected by rust; stiff with age or disuse; (of knowledge etc.) impaired by neglect; rust-coloured; discoloured by age.

rut¹ ● *noun* deep track made by passage of wheels; fixed (esp. tedious) practice or routine. ● *verb* (**-tt-**) (esp. as **rutted** *adjective*) mark with ruts.

rut² ● *noun* periodic sexual excitement of male deer etc. ● *verb* (**-tt-**) be affected with rut.

ruthless /'ruːθlɪs/ *adjective* having no pity or compassion. □ **ruthlessly** *adverb*; **ruthlessness** *noun*.

RV *abbreviation* Revised Version (of Bible).

rye /raɪ/ *noun* cereal plant; grain of this, used for bread, fodder, etc.; (in full **rye whisky**) whisky distilled from rye.

Ss

S *abbreviation* (also **S.**) Saint; south(ern).

s. *abbreviation* second(s); *historical* shilling(s); son.

SA *abbreviation* Salvation Army; South Africa; South Australia.

sabbath /'sæbəθ/ *noun* religious rest-day kept by Christians on Sunday and Jews on Saturday.

sabbatical /sə'bætɪk(ə)l/ ● *adjective* (of leave) granted at intervals to university teacher for study or travel. ● *noun* period of sabbatical leave.

saber *US* = SABRE.

sable /'seɪb(ə)l/ ● *noun* (*plural* same or **-s**) small dark-furred mammal; its skin or fur. ● *adjective Heraldry* black; *esp. poetical* gloomy.

sabot /'sæbəʊ/ *noun* wooden or wooden-soled shoe.

sabotage /'sæbətɑːʒ/ ● *noun* deliberate destruction or damage, esp. for political purpose. ● *verb* (**-ging**) commit sabotage on; destroy, spoil.

saboteur /sæbə'tɜː/ *noun* person who commits sabotage.

sabre /'seɪbə/ *noun* (*US* **saber**) curved cavalry sword; light fencing-sword. □ **sabre-rattling** display or threat of military force.

sac *noun* membranous bag in animal or plant.

saccharin /'sækərɪn/ *noun* a sugar substitute.

saccharine /'sækəriːn/ *adjective* excessively sentimental or sweet.

sacerdotal /sækə'dəʊt(ə)l/ *adjective* of priests or priestly office.

sachet /'sæʃeɪ/ *noun* small bag or packet containing shampoo, perfumed substances, etc.

sack¹ ● *noun* large strong bag for coal, food, mail, etc.; amount held by sack; (**the sack**) *colloquial* dismissal, *US slang* bed. ● *verb* put in sack(s); *colloquial* dismiss from employment. □ **sackcloth** coarse fabric of flax or hemp.

sack² ● *verb* plunder and destroy (town etc.). ● *noun* such sacking.

sack³ *noun historical* white wine from Spain etc.

sackbut /'sækbʌt/ *noun* early form of trombone.

sacking *noun* sackcloth.

sacral /'seɪkr(ə)l/ *adjective* of sacrum.

sacrament /'sækrəmənt/ *noun* symbolic Christian ceremony, esp. Eucharist; sacred thing. □ **sacramental** /-'men-/ *adjective*.

sacred /'seɪkrɪd/ *adjective* (often + *to*) dedicated to a god, connected with religion; safeguarded or required, esp. by tradition; inviolable. □ **sacred cow** *colloquial* idea or institution unreasonably held to be above criticism.

sacrifice /'sækrɪfaɪs/ ● *noun* voluntary relinquishing of something valued; thing thus relinquished; loss entailed; slaughter of animal or person, or surrender of possession, as offering to deity; animal, person, or thing thus offered. ● *verb* (**-cing**) give up; (+ *to*) devote to; offer or kill (as) sacrifice. □ **sacrificial** /-'fɪʃ-/ *adjective*.

sacrilege /'sækrɪlɪdʒ/ *noun* violation of what is sacred. □ **sacrilegious** /-'lɪdʒəs/ *adjective*.

sacristan /'sækrɪst(ə)n/ *noun* person in charge of sacristy and church contents.

sacristy /'sækrɪstɪ/ *noun* (*plural* **-ies**) room in church for vestments, vessels, etc.

sacrosanct /'sækrəʊsæŋkt/ *adjective* most sacred; inviolable. □ **sacrosanctity** /-'sæŋkt-/ *noun*.

sacrum /'seɪkrəm/ *noun* (*plural* **sacra** or **-s**) triangular bone between hip-bones.

sad *adjective* (**-dd-**) sorrowful; causing sorrow; regrettable; deplorable. □ **sadden** *verb*; **sadly** *adverb*; **sadness** *noun*.

saddle /'sæd(ə)l/ ● *noun* seat of leather etc. fastened on horse etc.; bicycle etc. seat; joint of meat consisting of the two loins; ridge rising to a summit at each end. ● *verb* (**-ling**) put saddle on (horse etc.); (+ *with*) burden with task etc. □ **saddle-bag** each of pair of bags laid across back of horse etc., bag attached to bicycle etc. saddle.

saddler *noun* maker of or dealer in saddles etc. □ **saddlery** *noun* (*plural* **-ies**).

sadism /'seɪdɪz(ə)m/ *noun colloquial* enjoyment of cruelty to others; sexual perversion characterized by this. □ **sadist** *noun*; **sadistic** /sə'dɪs-/ *adjective*; **sadistically** /sə'dɪs-/ *adverb*.

sadomasochism /seɪdəʊ'mæsəkɪz(ə)m/ *noun* sadism and masochism in one person. □ **sado-masochist** *noun*; **sadomasochistic** /-'kɪs-/ *adjective*.

s.a.e. *abbreviation* stamped addressed envelope.

safari /sə'fɑːrɪ/ *noun* (*plural* **-s**) expedition, esp. in Africa, to observe or hunt animals. □ **safari park** area where wild animals are kept in open for viewing.

safe ● *adjective* free of danger or injury; secure, not risky; reliable, sure; prevented from escaping or doing harm; cautious. ● *noun* strong lockable cupboard for valuables; ventilated cupboard for provisions. □ **safe conduct** immunity from arrest or harm; **safe deposit** building containing strong-rooms and safes for hire. □ **safely** *adverb*.

safeguard ● *noun* protecting proviso, circumstance, etc. ● *verb* guard or protect (rights etc.).

safety /'seɪftɪ/ *noun* being safe; freedom from danger. □ **safety-belt** belt or strap preventing injury, esp. seat-belt; **safety-catch** device preventing accidental operation of gun trigger or machinery; **safety curtain** fireproof curtain to divide theatre auditorium from stage; **safety match** match that ignites only on specially prepared surface; **safety net** net placed to catch acrobat etc. in case of fall; **safety pin** pin with guarded point; **safety razor** razor with guard to prevent user cutting skin; **safety-valve** valve relieving excessive pressure of steam, means of harmlessly venting excitement etc.

saffron /'sæfrən/ ● *noun* deep yellow colouring and flavouring from dried crocus stigmas; colour of this. ● *adjective* deep yellow.

sag ● *verb* (**-gg-**) sink or subside; have downward bulge or curve in middle. ● *noun* state or amount of sagging. □ **saggy** *adjective*.

saga /'sɑːgə/ *noun* long heroic story, esp. medieval Icelandic or Norwegian; long family chronicle; long involved story.

sagacious /sə'geɪʃ(ə)s/ *adjective* showing insight or good judgement. □ **sagacity** /-'gæs-/ *noun*.

sage¹ *noun* aromatic herb with dull greyish-green leaves.

sage² ● *noun* wise man. ● *adjective* wise, judicious, experienced. □ **sagely** *adverb*.

Sagittarius /sædʒɪ'teərɪəs/ *noun* ninth sign of zodiac.

sago /'seɪgəʊ/ *noun* (*plural* **-s**) starch used in puddings etc.; (in full **sago palm**) any of several tropical trees yielding this.

sahib /sɑːb/ *noun historical form of address to European men in India.*

said *past & past participle of* SAY.

sail ● *noun* piece of material extended on rigging to catch wind and propel vessel; ship's sails collectively; voyage or excursion in sailing vessel; wind-catching apparatus of windmill. ● *verb* travel on water by use of sails or engine-power; begin voyage; navigate (ship etc.); travel on (sea); glide or move smoothly or with dignity; (often + *through*) *colloquial* succeed easily. □ **sailboard** board with mast and sail, used in windsurfing; **sailcloth** material for sails, kind of coarse linen; **sailing boat, ship,** etc., vessel moved by sails; **sailplane** kind of glider.

sailor *noun* seaman or mariner, *esp.* below officer's rank. □ **bad, good sailor** person very liable or not liable to seasickness.

sainfoin /'sænfɔɪn/ *noun* pink-flowered plant used as fodder.

saint /seɪnt, before a name usually sənt/ ● *noun* holy or canonized person, regarded as deserving special veneration; very virtuous person. ● *verb* (as **sainted** *adjective*) holy, virtuous. □ **sainthood** *noun*; **saintlike** *adjective*; **saintliness** *noun*; **saintly** (**-ier, -iest**) *adjective*.

sake¹ *noun* □ **for the sake of** out of consideration for, in the interest of, in order to please, get, etc.

sake² /'sɑːkɪ/ *noun* Japanese rice wine.

salaam /sə'lɑːm/ ● *noun* (*chiefly as Muslim greeting*) Peace!; low bow. ● *verb* make salaam.

salacious /sə'leɪʃəs/ *adjective* erotic; lecherous. □ **salaciousness** *noun*; **salacity** /-'læs-/ *noun*.

salad /'sæləd/ *noun* cold mixture of usually raw vegetables etc. with dressing. □ **salad cream** creamy salad dressing; **salad days** period of youthful inexperience; **salad dressing** sauce of oil, vinegar, etc. for salads.

salamander /'sæləmændə/ *noun* newtlike amphibian formerly supposed to live in fire; similar mythical creature.

salami /sə'lɑːmɪ/ *noun* (*plural* **-s**) highly-seasoned sausage, originally Italian.

sal ammoniac /sæl ə'məʊnɪæk/ *noun* ammonium chloride.

salary /'sælərɪ/ ● *noun* (*plural* **-ies**) fixed regular payment by employer to employee. ● *verb* (**-ies, -ied**) (usually as **salaried** *adjective*) pay salary to.

sale *noun* exchange of commodity for money etc.; act or instance of selling; amount sold; temporary offering of goods at reduced prices; event at which goods are sold. □ **on, for sale** offered for purchase; **saleroom** room where auctions are held; **salesman, salesperson, saleswoman** person employed to sell goods etc.

saleable *adjective* fit or likely to be sold. □ **saleability** *noun*.

salesmanship *noun* skill in selling.

salient /'seɪlɪənt/ ● *adjective* prominent, conspicuous; (of angle) pointing outwards. ● *noun* salient angle; outward bulge in military line.

saline /'seɪlaɪn/ ● *adjective* containing or tasting of salt(s); of salt(s). ● *noun* salt lake, spring, etc.; saline solution. □ **salinity** /sə'lɪn-/ *noun*.

saliva /sə'laɪvə/ *noun* colourless liquid produced by glands in mouth. □ **salivary** *adjective*.

salivate /'sælɪveɪt/ *verb* (**-ting**) secrete saliva, esp. in excess.

sallow¹ /'sæləʊ/ *adjective* (**-er, -est**) (esp. of complexion) yellowish.

sallow² /'sæləʊ/ *noun* low-growing willow; shoot or wood of this.

sally /'sælɪ/ ● *noun* (*plural* **-ies**) witticism; military rush; excursion. ● *verb* (**-ies, -ied**) (usually + *out, forth*) set out for walk etc., make sally.

salmon /'sæmən/ ● *noun* (*plural* same) large silver-scaled fish with orange-pink flesh. ● *adjective* orange-pink. □ **salmon-pink** orange-pink; **salmon trout** large silver-coloured trout.

salmonella /sælmə'nelə/ *noun* (*plural* **-llae** /-liː/) bacterium causing food poisoning; such food poisoning.

salon /'sælɒn/ *noun* room or establishment of hairdresser, fashion designer, etc.; *historical* meeting of eminent people at fashionable home; reception room of large house.

saloon /sə'luːn/ *noun* large room or hall on ship, in hotel, etc., or for specified purpose; saloon car; *US* drinking bar; saloon bar. □ **saloon bar** more comfortable bar in public house; **saloon car** car with body closed off from luggage area.

salsa /'sælsə/ *noun* dance music of Cuban origin; kind of spicy tomato sauce.

salsify /'sælsɪfɪ/ *noun* (*plural* **-ies**) plant with long fleshy edible root.

salt /sɔːlt/ ● *noun* (also **common salt**) sodium chloride, esp. mined or evaporated from sea water, and used esp. for seasoning or preserving food; *Chemistry* substance formed in reaction of an acid with a base; piquancy, wit; (in *singular* or *plural*) substance resembling salt in taste, form, etc.; (esp. in *plural*) substance used as laxative; (also **old salt**) experienced sailor. ● *adjective* containing, tasting of, or preserved with salt. ● *verb* cure, preserve, or season with salt; sprinkle salt on (road etc.). □ **salt away, down** *slang* put (money etc.) by; **salt-cellar** container for salt at table; **salt-mine** mine yielding rock salt; **salt of the earth** finest or most honest people; **salt-pan** vessel, or hollow near sea, used for getting salt by evaporation; **salt-water** of or living in sea; **take with a pinch** or **grain of salt** be sceptical about; **worth one's salt** efficient, capable.

salting *noun* (esp. in *plural*) marsh overflowed by sea.

saltire /'sɔːltaɪə/ *noun* X-shaped cross.

saltpetre /sɔːlt'piːtə/ *noun* (*US* **saltpeter**) white crystalline salty substance used in preserving meat and in gunpowder.

salty *adjective* (**-ier, -iest**) tasting of or containing salt; witty, piquant. □ **saltiness** *noun*.

salubrious /sə'luːbrɪəs/ *adjective* health-giving. □ **salubrity** *noun*.

saluki /sə'luːkɪ/ *noun* (*plural* **-s**) dog of tall slender silky-coated breed.

salutary /'sæljʊtərɪ/ *adjective* producing good effect.

salutation /sælju:'teɪʃ(ə)n/ *noun* formal sign or expression of greeting.

salute /sə'luːt/ ● *noun* gesture of respect, homage, greeting, etc.; *Military etc.* prescribed gesture or use of weapons or flags as sign of respect etc. ● *verb* (**-ting**) make salute (to); greet; commend.

salvage /'sælvɪdʒ/ ● *noun* rescue of property from sea, fire, etc.; saving and utilization of waste materials; property or materials salvaged. ● *verb* (**-ging**) save from wreck etc. □ **salvageable** *adjective*.

salvation /sæl'veɪʃ(ə)n/ *noun* saving, being saved; deliverance from sin and damnation; religious conversion; person or thing that saves. □ **Salvation Army** worldwide quasi-military Christian charitable organization.

Salvationist *noun* member of Salvation Army.

salve¹ ● *noun* healing ointment; (often + *for*) thing that soothes. ● *verb* (**-ving**) soothe.

salve² *verb* (**-ving**) save from wreck, fire, etc. □ **salvable** *adjective*.

salver /'sælvə/ *noun* tray for drinks, letters, etc.

salvo /'sælvəʊ/ *noun* (*plural* **-es** or **-s**) simultaneous firing of guns etc.; round of applause.

sal volatile /sæl və'lætɪlɪ/ *noun* solution of ammonium carbonate, used as smelling salts.

SAM *abbreviation* surface-to-air missile.

Samaritan /sə'mærɪt(ə)n/ *noun* (in full **good Samaritan**) charitable or helpful person; member of counselling organization.

samba /'sæmbə/ ● *noun* ballroom dance of Brazilian origin; music for this. ● *verb* (**-bas**, **-baed** or **-ba'd** /-bəd/, **-baing** /-bəɪŋ/) dance samba.

same ● *adjective* identical; unvarying; just mentioned. ● *pronoun* (**the same**) the same person or thing. ● *adverb* (**the same**) in the same manner. □ **all** or **just the same** nevertheless; **at the same time** simultaneously, notwithstanding. □ **sameness** *noun*.

samosa /sə'məʊsə/ *noun* Indian fried triangular pastry containing spiced vegetables or meat.

samovar /'sæməvɑː/ *noun* Russian tea-urn.

Samoyed /'sæməjed/ *noun* member of a northern Siberian people; (also **samoyed**) dog of white Arctic breed.

sampan /'sæmpæn/ *noun* small boat used in Far East.

samphire /'sæmfaɪə/ *noun* cliff plant used in pickles.

sample /'sɑːmp(ə)l/ ● *noun* small representative part or quantity; specimen; typical example. ● *verb* (**-ling**) take samples of; try qualities of; experience briefly.

sampler /'sɑːmplə/ *noun* piece of embroidery worked to show proficiency.

samurai /'sæmʊraɪ/ *noun* (*plural* same) Japanese army officer; *historical* member of Japanese military caste.

sanatorium /sænə'tɔːrɪəm/ *noun* (*plural* **-riums** or **-ria**) residential clinic, esp. for convalescents and the chronically sick; accommodation for sick people in school etc.

sanctify /'sæŋktɪfaɪ/ *verb* (**-ies**, **-ied**) consecrate, treat as holy; purify from sin; sanction. □ **sanctification** *noun*.

sanctimonious /sæŋktɪ'məʊnɪəs/ *adjective* ostentatiously pious. □ **sanctimoniously** *adverb*; **sanctimony** /'sæŋktɪmənɪ/ *noun*.

sanction /'sæŋkʃ(ə)n/ ● *noun* approval by custom or tradition; express permission; confirmation of law etc.; penalty or reward attached to law; moral impetus for obedience to rule; (esp. in *plural*) (esp. economic) action to coerce state to conform to agreement etc. ● *verb* authorize, countenance; make (law etc.) binding.

sanctity /'sæŋktɪtɪ/ *noun* holiness, sacredness; inviolability.

sanctuary /'sæŋktʃʊərɪ/ *noun* (*plural* **-ies**) holy place; place where birds, wild animals, etc. are protected; place of refuge.

sanctum /'sæŋktəm/ *noun* (*plural* **-s**) holy place, esp. in temple or church; *colloquial* person's den.

sand ● *noun* fine grains resulting from erosion of esp. siliceous rocks; (in *plural*) grains of sand, expanse of sand, sandbank. ● *verb* smooth or treat with sandpaper or sand. □ **sandbag** *noun* bag filled with sand, esp. for making temporary defences, *verb* defend or hit with sandbag(s); **sandbank** sand forming shallow place in sea or river; **sandblast** *verb* treat with jet of sand driven by compressed air or steam, *noun* this jet; **sandcastle** model castle of sand on beach; **sand-dune, -hill** dune; **sand-martin** bird nesting in sandy banks; **sandpaper** *noun* paper with abrasive coating for smoothing or polishing wood etc., *verb* treat with this; **sandpiper** bird inhabiting wet sandy places; **sandpit** hollow or box containing sand for children to play in; **sandstone** sedimentary rock of compressed sand; **sandstorm** storm with clouds of sand raised by wind.

sandal /'sænd(ə)l/ *noun* shoe with openwork upper or no upper, fastened with straps.

sandal-tree /'sændəltri:/ *noun* tree yielding sandalwood.

sandalwood /'sændəlwʊd/ *noun* scented wood of sandal-tree.

sandwich /'sænwɪdʒ/ ● *noun* two or more slices of bread with filling; layered cake with jam, cream, etc. ● *verb* put (thing, statement, etc.) between two of different kind; squeeze in between others. □ **sandwich-board** each of two advertising boards worn front and back; **sandwich course** course with alternate periods of study and work experience.

sandy *adjective* (**-ier**, **-iest**) containing or covered with sand; (of hair) reddish; sand-coloured.

sane *adjective* of sound mind, not mad; (of opinion etc.) moderate, sensible.

sang *past of* SING.

sang-froid /sɑ̃'frwɑː/ *noun* calmness in danger or difficulty.

sangria /sæŋ'griːə/ *noun* Spanish drink of red wine with fruit etc.

sanguinary /'sæŋgwɪnərɪ/ *adjective* bloody; blood-thirsty.

sanguine /'sæŋgwɪn/ *adjective* optimistic; (of complexion) florid, ruddy.

Sanhedrin /'sænɪdrɪn/ *noun* court of justice and supreme council in ancient Jerusalem.

sanitarium /sænɪ'teərɪəm/ *noun* (*plural* **-s** or **-ria**) *US* sanatorium.

sanitary /'sænɪtərɪ/ *adjective* (of conditions etc.) affecting health; hygienic. □ **sanitary towel** (*US* **sanitary napkin**) absorbent pad used during menstruation. □ **sanitariness** *noun*.

sanitation /sænɪ'teɪʃ(ə)n/ *noun* sanitary conditions; maintenance etc. of these; disposal of sewage, refuse, etc.

sanitize /'sænɪtaɪz/ *verb* (also **-ise**) (**-zing** or **-sing**) make sanitary, disinfect; *colloquial* censor.

sanity /'sænɪtɪ/ *noun* being sane; moderation.

sank *past of* SINK.

Sanskrit /'sænskrɪt/ ● *noun* ancient and sacred language of Hindus in India. ● *adjective* of or in Sanskrit.

Santa Claus /'sæntə klɔːz/ *noun* person said to bring children presents at Christmas.

sap¹ ● *noun* vital juice of plants; vitality; *slang* foolish person. ● *verb* (**-pp-**) drain of sap; weaken. □ **sappy** *adjective* (**-ier**, **-iest**).

sap² ● *noun* tunnel or trench for concealed approach to enemy. ● *verb* (**-pp-**) dig saps; undermine.

sapient /'seɪpɪənt/ *adjective literary* wise; aping wisdom. □ **sapience** *noun*.

sapling /'sæplɪŋ/ *noun* young tree.

sapper *noun* digger of saps; private of Royal Engineers.

sapphire /'sæfaɪə/ ● *noun* transparent blue precious stone; its colour. ● *adjective* (also **sapphire blue**) bright blue.

saprophyte /'sæprəfaɪt/ *noun* plant or micro-organism living on dead organic matter.

saraband /'særəbænd/ *noun* slow Spanish dance; music for this.

Saracen /'særəs(ə)n/ *noun* Arab or Muslim of time of Crusades.

sarcasm /'sɑːkæz(ə)m/ *noun* ironically scornful remark(s). □ **sarcastic** /sɑː'kæstɪk/ *adjective*; **sarcastically** /sɑː'kæstɪkəlɪ/ *adverb*.

sarcophagus /sɑː'kɒfəgəs/ *noun* (*plural* **-gi** /-gaɪ/) stone coffin.

sardine /sɑː'diːn/ *noun* (*plural* same or **-s**) young pilchard etc. tinned tightly packed.

sardonic /sɑːˈdɒnɪk/ adjective bitterly mocking; cynical. □ **sardonically** adverb.

sardonyx /ˈsɑːdənɪks/ noun onyx in which white layers alternate with yellow or orange ones.

sargasso /sɑːˈgæsəʊ/ noun (plural **-s** or **-es**) seaweed with berry-like airvessels.

sarge noun slang sergeant.

sari /ˈsɑːrɪ/ noun (plural **-s**) length of material draped round body, worn traditionally by Hindu etc. women.

sarky /ˈsɑːkɪ/ adjective (**-ier**, **-iest**) slang sarcastic.

sarong /səˈrɒŋ/ noun garment of long strip of cloth tucked round waist or under armpits.

sarsaparilla /sɑːsəpəˈrɪlə/ noun dried roots of esp. smilax used to flavour drinks and medicines and formerly as tonic; plant yielding these.

sarsen /ˈsɑːs(ə)n/ noun sandstone boulder carried by ice in glacial period.

sarsenet /ˈsɑːsnɪt/ noun soft silk fabric used esp. for linings.

sartorial /sɑːˈtɔːrɪəl/ adjective of men's clothes or tailoring. □ **sartorially** adverb.

SAS abbreviation Special Air Service.

sash[1] noun strip or loop of cloth worn over one shoulder or round waist.

sash[2] noun frame holding glass in window sliding up and down in grooves.

sass US colloquial ● noun impudence. ● verb be impudent to. □ **sassy** adjective (**-ier**, **-iest**).

sassafras /ˈsæsəfræs/ noun small N. American tree; medicinal preparation from its leaves or bark.

Sassenach /ˈsæsənæk/ noun Scottish usually derogatory English person.

Sat. abbreviation Saturday.

sat past & past participle of SIT.

Satan /ˈseɪt(ə)n/ noun the Devil.

satanic /səˈtænɪk/ adjective of or like Satan; hellish, evil.

Satanism noun worship of Satan. □ **Satanist** noun.

satchel /ˈsætʃ(ə)l/ noun small bag, esp. for carrying school-books.

sate verb (**-ting**) formal gratify fully, surfeit.

sateen /sæˈtiːn/ noun glossy cotton fabric like satin.

satellite /ˈsætəlaɪt/ ● noun heavenly or artificial body orbiting earth or other planet; (in full **satellite state**) small country controlled by another. ● adjective transmitted by satellite; receiving signal from satellite.

satiate /ˈseɪʃɪeɪt/ verb (**-ting**) sate. □ **satiation** noun.

satiety /səˈtaɪɪtɪ/ noun formal being sated.

satin /ˈsætɪn/ ● noun silk etc. fabric glossy on one side. ● adjective smooth as satin. □ **satinwood** kind of yellow glossy timber. □ **satiny** adjective.

satire /ˈsætaɪə/ noun ridicule, irony, etc. used to expose folly, vice, etc.; literary work using satire. □ **satirical** /səˈtɪrɪk(ə)l/ adjective; **satirically** /səˈtɪrɪkəlɪ/ adverb.

satirist /ˈsætərɪst/ noun writer of satires; satirical person.

satirize /ˈsætəraɪz/ verb (also **-ise**) (**-zing** or **-sing**) attack or describe with satire.

satisfaction /sætɪsˈfækʃ(ə)n/ noun satisfying, being satisfied; thing that satisfies; atonement; compensation.

satisfactory /sætɪsˈfæktərɪ/ adjective adequate; causing satisfaction. □ **satisfactorily** adverb.

satisfy /ˈsætɪsfaɪ/ verb (**-ies**, **-ied**) meet expectations or wishes of; be adequate; meet (an appetite or want); rid (person) of an appetite or want; pay; fulfil, comply with; convince.

satsuma /sætˈsuːmə/ noun kind of tangerine.

saturate /ˈsætʃəreɪt/ verb (**-ting**) fill with moisture; fill to capacity; cause (substance) to absorb, hold, etc. as much as possible of another substance; supply (market) beyond demand; (as **saturated** adjective) (of fat) containing the most possible hydrogen atoms.

saturation noun saturating, being saturated. □ **saturation point** stage beyond which no more can be absorbed or accepted.

Saturday /ˈsætədeɪ/ noun day of week following Friday.

Saturnalia /sætəˈneɪlɪə/ noun (plural same or **-s**) ancient Roman festival of Saturn; (**saturnalia**) (treated as singular or plural) scene of wild revelry.

saturnine /ˈsætənaɪn/ adjective of gloomy temperament or appearance.

satyr /ˈsætə/ noun Greek & Roman Mythology part-human part-animal woodland deity; lecherous man.

sauce /sɔːs/ ● noun liquid or viscous accompaniment to food; something that adds piquancy; colloquial impudence. ● verb (**-cing**) colloquial be impudent to. □ **sauce-boat** jug or dish for serving sauce; **saucepan** cooking vessel usually with handle, used on hob.

saucer /ˈsɔːsə/ noun shallow circular dish, esp. for standing cup on.

saucy adjective (**-ier**, **-iest**) impudent, cheeky. □ **saucily** adverb; **sauciness** noun.

sauerkraut /ˈsaʊəkraʊt/ noun German dish of pickled cabbage.

sauna /ˈsɔːnə/ noun period spent in room with steam bath; this room.

saunter /ˈsɔːntə/ ● verb stroll. ● noun leisurely walk.

saurian /ˈsɔːrɪən/ adjective of or like a lizard.

sausage /ˈsɒsɪdʒ/ noun seasoned minced meat etc. in edible cylindrical case; sausage-shaped object. □ **sausage meat** minced meat for sausages etc.; **sausage roll** sausage meat in pastry cylinder.

sauté /ˈsəʊteɪ/ ● adjective fried quickly in a little fat. ● noun food cooked thus. ● verb (past & past participle **sautéd** or **sautéed**) cook thus.

savage /ˈsævɪdʒ/ ● adjective fierce, cruel; wild, primitive. ● noun derogatory member of primitive tribe; brutal or barbarous person. ● verb (**-ging**) attack and maul; attack verbally. □ **savagely** adverb; **savagery** noun (plural **-ies**).

savannah /səˈvænə/ noun (also **savanna**) grassy plain in tropical or subtropical region.

savant /ˈsæv(ə)nt/ noun (feminine **savante** same pronunciation) learned person.

save[1] verb (**-ving**) (often + from) rescue or preserve from danger or harm; (often + up) keep for future use; relieve (person) from spending (money, time, etc.); prevent exposure to (annoyance etc.); prevent need for; rescue spiritually; Football etc. avoid losing (match), prevent (goal) from being scored. ● noun Football etc. act of saving goal. □ **savable**, **saveable** adjective; **saver** noun.

save[2] preposition & conjunction archaic or poetical except; but.

saveloy /ˈsævəlɔɪ/ noun highly seasoned sausage.

saving ● noun anything saved; an economy; (usually in plural) money saved; act of preserving or rescuing. ● preposition except; without offence to. □ **-saving** making economical use of specified thing; **saving grace** redeeming feature.

saviour /ˈseɪvjə/ noun (US **savior**) person who saves from danger etc.; (**the**, **our Saviour**) Christ.

savoir faire /sævwɑː ˈfeə/ noun ability to behave appropriately; tact. [French]

savory[1] /ˈseɪvərɪ/ noun aromatic herb used in cookery.

savory[2] US = SAVOURY.

savour /'seɪvə/ (*US* **savor**) ● *noun* characteristic taste, flavour, etc.; tinge or hint. ● *verb* appreciate, enjoy; (+ *of*) imply, suggest.

savoury /'seɪvərɪ/ (*US* **savory**) ● *adjective* with appetizing taste or smell; (of food) salty or piquant, not sweet; pleasant. ● *noun* (*plural* **-ies**) savoury dish.

savoy /sə'vɔɪ/ *noun* rough-leaved winter cabbage.

savvy /'sævɪ/ *slang* ● *verb* (**-ies**, **-ied**) know. ● *noun* knowingness, understanding. ● *adjective* (**-ier**, **-iest**) *US* knowing, wise.

saw[1] ● *noun* implement with toothed blade etc. for cutting wood etc. ● *verb* (*past participle* **sawn** or **sawed**) cut or make with saw; use saw; make to-and-fro sawing motion. □ **sawdust** fine wood fragments produced in sawing; **sawfish** (*plural* same or **-es**) large sea fish with toothed flat snout; **sawmill** factory for sawing wood into planks; **sawtooth(ed)** serrated.

saw[2] *past of* SEE[1].

saw[3] *noun* proverb, maxim.

sawyer /'sɔːjə/ *noun* person who saws timber.

sax *noun colloquial* saxophone.

saxe /sæks/ *noun & adjective* (in full **saxe blue**; as *adjective* often hyphenated) light greyish-blue.

saxifrage /'sæksɪfreɪdʒ/ *noun* small-flowered rock-plant.

Saxon /'sæks(ə)n/ ● *noun historical* member or language of Germanic people that occupied parts of England in 5th–6th c.; Anglo-Saxon. ● *adjective historical* of the Saxons; Anglo-Saxon.

saxophone /'sæksəfəʊn/ *noun* keyed brass reed instrument used esp. in jazz. □ **saxophonist** /'sɒfən-/ *noun*.

say ● *verb* (*3rd singular present* **says** /sez/; *past & past participle* **said** /sed/) utter, remark; express; state; indicate; (in *passive*; usually + *to do*) be asserted; (+ *to do*) *colloquial* direct, order; convey (information); adduce, plead; decide; take as example or as near enough; (**the said**) *Law or jocular* the previously mentioned. ● *noun* opportunity to express view; share in decision. □ **say-so** *colloquial* power of decision, mere assertion.

saying *noun* maxim, proverb, etc.

sc. *abbreviation* scilicet.

scab ● *noun* crust over healing cut, sore, etc.; skin disease; plant disease; *colloquial derogatory* blackleg. ● *verb* (**-bb-**) form scab; *colloquial derogatory* act as blackleg. □ **scabby** *adjective* (**-ier**, **-iest**).

scabbard /'skæbəd/ *noun historical* sheath of sword etc.

scabies /'skeɪbiːz/ *noun* contagious skin disease causing itching.

scabious /'skeɪbɪəs/ *noun* plant with pincushion-shaped flowers.

scabrous /'skeɪbrəs/ *adjective* rough, scaly; indecent.

scaffold /'skæfəʊld/ *noun* scaffolding; *historical* platform for execution of criminal.

scaffolding *noun* temporary structure of poles, planks, etc. for building work; materials for this.

scald /skɔːld/ ● *verb* burn (skin etc.) with hot liquid or vapour; heat (esp. milk) to near boiling point; (usually + *out*) clean with boiling water. ● *noun* burn etc. caused by scalding.

scale[1] ● *noun* each of thin horny plates protecting skin of fish and reptiles; thing resembling this; incrustation inside kettle etc.; tartar on teeth. ● *verb* (**-ling**) remove scale(s) from; form or come off in scales. □ **scaly** *adjective* (**-ier**, **-iest**).

scale[2] *noun* (often in *plural*) weighing machine; (also **scale-pan**) pan of weighing-balance. □ **tip**, **turn the scales** be decisive factor, (+ *at*) weigh (specified amount).

scale[3] ● *noun* graded classification system; ratio of reduction or enlargement in map, picture, etc.; relative dimensions; *Music* set of notes at fixed intervals, arranged in order of pitch; set of marks on line used in measuring etc., rule determining distances between these, rod on which these are marked. ● *verb* (**-ling**) climb; represent in proportion; reduce to common scale. □ **scale down**, **up** make or become smaller or larger in proportion; **to scale** uniformly in proportion.

scalene /'skeɪliːn/ *adjective* (of triangle) having unequal sides.

scallion /'skæljən/ *noun esp. US* shallot; spring onion.

scallop /'skæləp/ ● *noun* edible bivalve with fan-shaped ridged shells; (in full **scallop shell**) one shell of this, esp. used for cooking or serving food on; (in *plural*) ornamental edging of semicircular curves. ● *verb* (**-p-**) ornament with scallops.

scallywag /'skælɪwæg/ *noun* scamp, rascal.

scalp ● *noun* skin and hair on head; *historical* this cut off as trophy by N. American Indian. ● *verb historical* take scalp of.

scalpel /'skælp(ə)l/ *noun* small surgical knife.

scam *noun US slang* trick, fraud.

scamp *noun colloquial* rascal, rogue.

scamper /'skæmpə/ ● *verb* run and skip. ● *noun* act of scampering.

scampi /'skæmpɪ/ *plural noun* large prawns.

scan ● *verb* (**-nn-**) look at intently or quickly; (of verse etc.) be metrically correct; examine (surface etc.) for radioactivity etc.; traverse (region) with radar etc. beam; resolve (picture) into elements of light and shade for esp. television transmission; analyse metre of (line etc.); obtain image of (part of body) using scanner. ● *noun* scanning; image obtained by scanning.

scandal /'skænd(ə)l/ *noun* disgraceful event; public outrage; malicious gossip. □ **scandalmonger** /-mʌŋgə/ person who spreads scandal. □ **scandalous** *adjective*; **scandalously** *adverb*.

scandalize *verb* (also **-ise**) (**-zing** or **-sing**) offend morally, shock.

Scandinavian /skændɪ'neɪvɪən/ ● *noun* native or inhabitant, or family of languages, of Scandinavia. ● *adjective* of Scandinavia.

scanner *noun* device for scanning; diagnostic apparatus measuring radiation, ultrasound reflections, etc. from body.

scansion /'skænʃ(ə)n/ *noun* metrical scanning of verse.

scant *adjective* barely sufficient; deficient.

scanty *adjective* (**-ier**, **-iest**) of small extent or amount; barely sufficient. □ **scantily** *adverb*; **scantiness** *noun*.

scapegoat /'skeɪpgəʊt/ *noun* person blamed for others' faults.

scapula /'skæpjʊlə/ *noun* (*plural* **-lae** /-liː/ or **-s**) shoulder blade.

scapular /'skæpjʊlə/ ● *adjective* of scapula. ● *noun* monastic short cloak.

scar[1] ● *noun* mark left on skin etc. by wound etc.; emotional damage. ● *verb* (**-rr-**) (esp. as **scarred** *adjective*) mark with or form scar(s).

scar[2] *noun* (also **scaur**) steep craggy part of mountainside.

scarab /'skærəb/ *noun* kind of beetle; gem cut in form of beetle.

scarce ● *adjective* in short supply; rare. ● *adverb archaic or literary* scarcely. □ **make oneself scarce** *colloquial* keep out of the way, disappear.

scarcely /'skeəslɪ/ *adverb* hardly, only just.

scarcity *noun* (*plural* **-ies**) lack or shortage.

scare /skeə/ ● verb (**-ring**) frighten; (as **scared** adjective) (usually + of) frightened; (usually + away, off, etc.) drive away by frightening. ● noun sudden fright or alarm, esp. caused by rumours. □ **scarecrow** human figure used for frightening birds away from crops, colloquial badly-dressed or tatesque person; **scaremonger** /-mʌŋgə/ person who spreads scare(s).

scarf[1] noun (plural **scarves** /skɑːvz/ or **-s**) piece of material worn round neck or over head for warmth or ornament.

scarf[2] ● verb join ends of (timber etc.) by thinning or notching them and bolting them together. ● noun (plural **-s**) joint made thus.

scarify /'skærɪfaɪ/ verb (**-ies**, **-ied**) make slight incisions in; scratch; criticize etc. mercilessly; loosen (soil). □ **scarification** noun.

scarlatina /skɑːləˈtiːnə/ noun scarlet fever.

scarlet /'skɑːlət/ ● adjective of brilliant red tinged with orange. ● noun scarlet colour, pigment, clothes, etc. □ **scarlet fever** infectious fever with scarlet rash; **scarlet pimpernel** wild plant with small esp. scarlet flowers.

scarp ● noun steep slope, esp. inner side of ditch in fortification. ● verb make perpendicular or steep.

scarper /'skɑːpə/ verb slang run away, escape.

scarves plural of SCARF[1].

scary adjective (**-ier**, **-iest**) colloquial frightening.

scat ● noun wordless jazz singing. ● verb (**-tt-**) sing scat.

scathing /'skeɪðɪŋ/ adjective witheringly scornful. □ **scathingly** adverb.

scatology /skæˈtɒlədʒɪ/ noun preoccupation with excrement or obscenity. □ **scatological** /-təˈlɒdʒ-/ adjective.

scatter /'skætə/ ● verb throw about, strew; cover by scattering; (cause to) flee; (cause to) disperse; (as **scattered** adjective) wide apart, sporadic; Physics deflect or diffuse (light, particles, etc.). ● noun act of scattering; small amount scattered; extent of distribution. □ **scatterbrain** person lacking concentration; **scatterbrained** adjective.

scatty /'skætɪ/ adjective (**-ier**, **-iest**) colloquial lacking concentration. □ **scattily** adverb; **scattiness** noun.

scavenge /'skævɪndʒ/ verb (**-ging**) (usually + for) search for and collect (discarded items).

scavenger /'skævɪndʒə/ noun person who scavenges; animal etc. feeding on carrion.

SCE abbreviation Scottish Certificate of Education.

scenario /sɪˈnɑːrɪəʊ/ noun (plural **-s**) synopsis of film, play, etc.; imagined sequence of future events.

■ **Usage** Scenario should not be used in standard English to mean 'situation', as in It was an unpleasant scenario.

scene /siːn/ noun place of actual or fictitious occurrence; incident; public display of emotion, temper, etc.; piece of continuous action in a play, film, book, etc.; piece(s) of scenery for a play; landscape, view; colloquial area of interest or activity. □ **behind the scenes** out of view of audience, secret, secretly; **scene-shifter** person who moves scenery in theatre.

scenery /'siːnərɪ/ noun features (esp. picturesque) of landscape; backcloths, properties, etc. representing scene in a play etc.

scenic /'siːnɪk/ adjective picturesque; of scenery. □ **scenically** adverb.

scent /sent/ ● noun characteristic, esp. pleasant, smell; liquid perfume; smell left by animal; clues etc. leading to discovery; power of scenting. ● verb discern by smell; sense; (esp. as **scented** adjective) make fragrant.

scepter US = SCEPTRE.

sceptic /'skeptɪk/ noun (US **skeptic**) sceptical person; person who questions truth of religions, or the possibility of knowledge. □ **scepticism** /-sɪz(ə)m/ noun.

sceptical /'skeptɪk(ə)l/ adjective (US **skeptical**) inclined to doubt accepted opinions; critical; in credulous. □ **sceptically** adverb.

sceptre /'septə/ noun (US **scepter**) staff borne as symbol of sovereignty.

schedule /'ʃedjuːl/ ● noun timetable; list, esp. of rates or prices. ● verb (**-ling**) include in schedule; make schedule of; list (building) for preservation. □ **on schedule** at time appointed; **scheduled flight**, **service**, etc., regular public one.

schema /'skiːmə/ noun (plural **schemata** or **-s**) synopsis, outline, diagram.

schematic /skɪˈmætɪk/ ● adjective of or as scheme or diagram. ● noun diagram, esp. of electronic circuit.

schematize /'skiːmətaɪz/ verb (also **-ise**) (**-zing** or **-sing**) put in schematic form.

scheme /skiːm/ ● noun systematic arrangement; artful plot; outline, syllabus, etc. ● verb (**-ming**) plan, esp. secretly or deceitfully. □ **scheming** adjective.

scherzo /'skeətsəʊ/ noun (plural **-s**) Music vigorous and lively movement or composition.

schism /'skɪz(ə)m/ noun division of esp. religious group into sects etc. □ **schismatic** /-ˈmæt-/ adjective & noun.

schist /ʃɪst/ noun layered crystalline rock.

schizo /'skɪtsəʊ/ colloquial ● adjective schizophrenic. ● noun (plural **-s**) schizophrenic person.

schizoid /'skɪtsɔɪd/ ● adjective tending to schizophrenia. ● noun schizoid person.

schizophrenia /skɪtsəˈfriːnɪə/ noun mental disorder marked by disconnection between thoughts, feelings, and actions. □ **schizophrenic** /-ˈfren-/ adjective & noun.

schmaltz /ʃmɔːlts/ noun colloquial sickly sentimentality. □ **schmaltzy** adjective (**-ier**, **-iest**).

schnapps /ʃnæps/ noun any of various spirits drunk in N. Europe.

schnitzel /'ʃnɪts(ə)l/ noun veal escalope.

scholar /'skɒlə/ noun learned person; holder of scholarship; person of specified academic ability. □ **scholarly** adjective.

scholarship noun learning, erudition; award of money etc. towards education.

scholastic /skəˈlæstɪk/ adjective of schools, education, etc.; academic.

school[1] /skuːl/ ● noun educational institution for pupils up to 19 years old or (US) at any level; school buildings, pupils, staff, etc; (time given to) teaching; university department or faculty; group of artists, disciples, etc. following or holding similar principles, opinions, etc.; instructive circumstances. ● verb send to school; discipline, train, control; (as **schooled** adjective) (+ in) educated, trained. □ **schoolboy**, **schoolchild**, **schoolgirl** one who attends school; **school-leaver** person who has just left school; **schoolmaster**, **schoolmistress**, **schoolteacher** teacher in school; **schoolroom** room used for lessons, esp. in private house.

school[2] /skuːl/ noun shoal of fish, whales, etc.

schooling noun education.

schooner /'skuːnə/ noun two-masted fore-and-aft rigged ship; large glass, esp. for sherry; US & Australian tall beer glass.

schottische /ʃɒˈtiːʃ/ noun kind of slow polka.

sciatic /saɪˈætɪk/ adjective of hip or sciatic nerve; of or having sciatica. □ **sciatic nerve** large nerve from pelvis to thigh.

sciatica /saɪˈætɪkə/ noun neuralgia of hip and leg.

science /ˈsaɪəns/ noun branch of knowledge involving systematized observation, experiment, and induction; knowledge so gained; pursuit or principles of this; skilful technique. □ **science fiction** fiction with scientific theme; **science park** area containing science-based businesses.

scientific /saɪənˈtɪfɪk/ adjective following systematic methods of science; systematic, accurate; of or concerned with science.

scientist /ˈsaɪəntɪst/ noun student or expert in science.

sci-fi /ˈsaɪfaɪ/ noun colloquial science fiction.

scilicet /ˈsaɪlɪset/ adverb that is to say.

scimitar /ˈsɪmɪtə/ noun curved oriental sword.

scintillate /ˈsɪntɪleɪt/ (**-ting**) (esp. as **scintillating** adjective) talk or act cleverly; sparkle, twinkle. □ **scintillation** noun.

scion /ˈsaɪən/ noun shoot cut for grafting; young member of family.

scissors /ˈsɪzəz/ plural noun (also **pair of scissors** singular) cutting instrument with pair of pivoted blades.

sclerosis /skləˈrəʊsɪs/ noun abnormal hardening of tissue; (in full **multiple sclerosis**) serious progressive disease of nervous system. □ **sclerotic** /-ˈrɒt-/ adjective.

scoff¹ ● verb (usually + at) speak derisively, mock. ● noun mocking remark, taunt.

scoff² colloquial ● verb eat (food) greedily. ● noun food.

scold /skəʊld/ ● verb rebuke; find fault noisily. ● noun archaic nagging woman.

sconce noun wall-bracket holding candlestick or light-fitting.

scone /skɒn, skəʊn/ noun small cake of flour etc. baked quickly.

scoop /skuːp/ ● noun short-handled deep shovel; long-handled ladle; excavating part of digging machine etc.; device for serving ice cream etc.; quantity taken up by scoop; scooping movement; exclusive news item; large profit made quickly. ● verb (usually + out) hollow out or (usually + up) lift (as) with scoop; forestall (rival newspaper etc.) with scoop; secure (large profit etc.), esp. suddenly.

scoot /skuːt/ verb (esp. in imperative) colloquial shoot along; depart, flee.

scooter noun child's toy with footboard on two wheels and long steering-handle; low-powered motorcycle.

scope noun range, opportunity; extent of ability, outlook, etc.

scorch ● verb burn or discolour surface of with dry heat; become so discoloured etc.; (as **scorching** adjective) colloquial (of weather) very hot; (of criticism etc.) stringent. ● noun mark of scorching. □ **scorched earth policy** policy of destroying everything that might be of use to invading enemy.

scorcher noun colloquial extremely hot day.

score ● noun number of points, goals, etc. made by player or side in game etc.; respective scores at end of game; act of gaining esp. goal; (plural same or **-s**) (set of) 20; (in plural) a great many; reason, motive; Music copy of composition with parts arranged one below another; music for film or play; notch, line, etc. made on surface; record of money owing. ● verb (**-ring**) win, gain; make (points etc.) in game; keep score; mark with notches etc.; have an advantage; Music (often + for) orchestrate or arrange (piece of music); slang obtain drugs illegally, make sexual conquest. □ **keep (the) score** register points etc. as

they are made; **score (points) off** colloquial humiliate, esp. verbally; **scoreboard** large board for displaying score in match etc.

scoria /ˈskɔːrɪə/ noun (plural **scoriae** /-riːiː/) (fragments of) cellular lava; slag.

scorn ● noun disdain, contempt, derision. ● verb hold in contempt; reject or refuse to do as unworthy.

scornful adjective (often + of) contemptuous. □ **scornfully** adverb.

Scorpio /ˈskɔːpɪəʊ/ noun eighth sign of zodiac.

scorpion /ˈskɔːpɪən/ noun lobster-like arachnid with jointed stinging tail.

Scot noun native of Scotland.

Scotch ● adjective Scottish, Scots. ● noun Scottish, Scots; Scotch whisky. □ **Scotch broth** meat soup with pearl barley etc.; **Scotch egg** hard-boiled egg in sausage meat; **Scotch fir** Scots pine; **Scotch mist** thick mist and drizzle; **Scotch terrier** small rough-coated terrier; **Scotch whisky** whisky distilled in Scotland.

■ **Usage** Scots or Scottish is preferred to Scotch in Scotland, except in the compound nouns given above.

scotch verb decisively put an end to; archaic wound without killing.

scot-free adverb unharmed, unpunished.

Scots ● adjective Scottish. ● noun Scottish; form of English spoken in (esp. Lowlands of) Scotland. □ **Scotsman, Scotswoman** Scot; **Scots pine** kind of pine tree.

Scottish ● adjective of Scotland or its inhabitants. ● noun (**the Scottish**) (treated as plural) people of Scotland.

scoundrel /ˈskaʊndr(ə)l/ noun unscrupulous villain; rogue.

scour¹ /skaʊə/ ● verb rub clean; (usually + away, off, etc.) clear by rubbing; clear out (pipe etc.) by flushing through. ● noun scouring, being scoured. □ **scourer** noun.

scour² /skaʊə/ verb search thoroughly.

scourge /skɜːdʒ/ ● noun person or thing regarded as causing suffering; whip. ● verb (**-ging**) whip; punish, oppress.

Scouse /skaʊs/ colloquial ● noun Liverpool dialect; (also **Scouser**) native of Liverpool. ● adjective of Liverpool.

scout /skaʊt/ ● noun person sent out to get information or reconnoitre; search for this; talent-scout; (also **Scout**) member of (originally boys') association intended to develop character. ● verb (often + for) seek information etc.; (often + about, around) make search; (often + out) colloquial explore. □ **Scoutmaster** person in charge of group of Scouts. □ **scouting** noun.

Scouter noun adult leader of Scouts.

scowl /skaʊl/ ● noun sullen or bad-tempered look. ● verb wear scowl.

scrabble /ˈskræb(ə)l/ ● verb (**-ling**) scratch or grope busily about. ● noun scrabbling; (**Scrabble**) proprietary term game in which players build up words from letter-blocks on board.

scrag ● noun (also **scrag-end**) inferior end of neck of mutton; skinny person or animal. ● verb (**-gg-**) slang strangle, hang; handle roughly, beat up.

scraggy adjective (**-ier, -iest**) thin and bony. □ **scragginess** noun.

scram verb (**-mm-**) (esp. in imperative) colloquial go away.

scramble /ˈskræmb(ə)l/ ● verb (**-ling**) clamber, crawl, climb, etc.; (+ for, at) struggle with competitors (for thing or share); mix indiscriminately; cook (eggs) by stirring in heated pan; alter sound frequencies of (broadcast or telephone conversation) so as to make it unintelligible without special receiver; (of fighter aircraft or pilot) take off rapidly. ● *noun* scrambling; difficult climb or walk; (+ *for*) eager struggle or competition; motorcycle race over rough ground; emergency take-off by fighter aircraft.

scrambler *noun* device for scrambling telephone conversations; motorcycle used for scrambles.

scrap¹ ● *noun* small detached piece, fragment; waste material; discarded metal for reprocessing; (with negative) smallest piece or amount; (in *plural*) odds and ends, bits of uneaten food. ● *verb* (**-pp-**) discard as useless. □ **scrapbook** book in which cuttings etc. are kept; **scrap heap** collection of waste material, state of being discarded as useless; **scrapyard** place where (esp. metal) scrap is collected.

scrap² *colloquial* ● *noun* fight or rough quarrel. ● *verb* (**-pp-**) have scrap.

scrape ● *verb* (**-ping**) move hard edge across (surface), esp. to smooth or clean; (+ *away, off*, etc.) remove by scraping; rub (surface) harshly against another; scratch, damage, or make by scraping; draw or move with sound (as) of scraping; produce such sound from; (often + *along, by, through*, etc.) move while (almost) touching; narrowly achieve; (often + *by, through*) barely manage, pass exam etc. with difficulty; (+ *together, up*) provide or amass with difficulty; be economical; make clumsy bow; (+ *back*) draw (hair) tightly back. ● *noun* act or sound of scraping; scraped place, graze; *colloquial* predicament caused by rashness. □ **scraper** *noun*.

scrapie /ˈskreɪpi/ *noun* viral disease of sheep.

scrappy *adjective* (**-ier, -iest**) consisting of scraps; incomplete.

scratch ● *verb* score or wound superficially, esp. with sharp object; scrape with the nails to relieve itching; make or form by scratching; (+ *out, off, through*) erase; withdraw from race or competition; (often + *about, around*, etc.) scratch ground etc. in search, search haphazardly. ● *noun* mark, wound, or sound made by scratching; act of scratching oneself; *colloquial* trifling wound; starting line for race etc.; position of those receiving no handicap. ● *adjective* collected by chance; collected or made from whatever is available; with no handicap given. □ **from scratch** from the beginning, without help; **up to scratch** up to required standard.

scratchy *adjective* (**-ier, -iest**) tending to make scratches or scratching noise; causing itchiness; (of drawing etc.) careless. □ **scratchily** *adverb*; **scratchiness** *noun*.

scrawl ● *verb* write in hurried untidy way. ● *noun* hurried writing; scrawled note. □ **scrawly** *adjective* (**-ier, -iest**).

scrawny /ˈskrɔːni/ *adjective* (**-ier, -iest**) lean, scraggy.

scream ● *noun* piercing cry (as) of terror or pain; *colloquial* hilarious occurrence or person. ● *verb* emit scream; utter in or with scream; move with scream; laugh uncontrollably; be blatantly obvious.

scree *noun* (in *singular* or *plural*) small loose stones; mountain slope covered with these.

screech ● *noun* harsh scream or squeal. ● *verb* utter with or make screech. □ **screech-owl** barn owl.

screed *noun* long usually tiresome letter or harangue; layer of cement etc. applied to level a surface.

screen ● *noun* fixed or movable upright partition for separating, concealing, or protecting from heat etc.; thing used to conceal or shelter; concealing stratagem; protection thus given; blank surface on which images are projected; (**the screen**) cinema industry, films collectively; windscreen; large sieve; system for detecting disease, ability, attribute, etc.

● *verb* shelter, hide; protect from detection, censure, etc.; (+ *off*) conceal behind screen; show (film etc.); prevent from causing, or protect from, electrical interference; test (person or group) for disease, reliability, loyalty, etc.; sieve. □ **screenplay** film script; **screen printing** printing process with ink forced through areas of sheet of fine mesh; **screen test** audition for film part; **screenwriter** person who writes for cinema.

screw /skruː/ ● *noun* cylinder or cone with spiral ridge running round it outside (**male screw**) or inside (**female screw**); (in full **woodscrew**) metal male screw with slotted head and sharp point; (in full **screw-bolt**) blunt metal male screw on which nut is threaded; straight screw used to exert pressure; (in *singular* or *plural*) instrument of torture acting thus; (in full **screw propeller**) propeller with twisted blades; one turn of screw; (+ *of*) small twisted-up paper (of tobacco etc.); oblique curling motion; *slang* prison warder. ● *verb* fasten or tighten (as) with screw(s); (of ball etc.) swerve; (+ *out, of*) extort from; swindle. □ **screwball** *US slang* crazy or eccentric person; **screwdriver** tool for turning screws by putting tool's tip into screw's slot; **screw up** contract, crumple, or contort; summon up (courage etc.), *slang* bungle, spoil, or upset; **screw-up** *slang* bungle.

screwy *adjective* (**-ier, -iest**) *slang* mad, eccentric; absurd. □ **screwiness** *noun*.

scribble /ˈskrɪb(ə)l/ ● *verb* (**-ling**) write or draw carelessly or hurriedly; *jocular* be author or writer. ● *noun* scrawl; hasty note etc.

scribe ● *noun* ancient or medieval copyist of manuscripts; pointed instrument for marking wood etc.; *colloquial* writer. ● *verb* (**-bing**) mark with scribe. □ **scribal** *adjective*.

scrim *noun* open-weave fabric for lining, upholstery, etc.

scrimmage /ˈskrɪmɪdʒ/ ● *noun* tussle, brawl. ● *verb* (**-ging**) engage in scrimmage.

scrimp *verb* skimp.

scrip *noun* provisional certificate of money subscribed to company etc.; extra share(s) instead of dividend.

script ● *noun* text of play, film, or broadcast (see panel at DIRECT SPEECH); handwriting; typeface imitating handwriting; alphabet or other system of writing; examinee's written answer(s). ● *verb* write script for (film etc.). □ **scriptwriter** person who writes scripts for films, etc.

scripture /ˈskrɪptʃə/ *noun* sacred writings; (**Scripture, the Scriptures**) the Bible. □ **scriptural** *adjective*.

scrivener /ˈskrɪvənə/ *noun* *historical* copyist, drafter of documents; notary.

scrofula /ˈskrɒfjʊlə/ *noun* disease with glandular swellings. □ **scrofulous** *adjective*.

scroll /skrəʊl/ ● *noun* roll of parchment or paper; book in ancient roll form; ornamental design imitating roll of parchment. ● *verb* (often + *down, up*) move (display on VDU screen) to view later or earlier material.

scrotum /ˈskrəʊtəm/ *noun* (*plural* **scrota** or **-s**) pouch of skin enclosing testicles. □ **scrotal** *adjective*.

scrounge /skraʊndʒ/ *verb* (**-ging**) obtain (things) by cadging. □ **on the scrounge** scrounging. □ **scrounger** *noun*.

scrub¹ ● *verb* (**-bb-**) clean by hard rubbing, esp. with hard brush; (often + *up*) (of surgeon etc.) clean and disinfect hands etc. before operating; *colloquial* cancel; pass (gas etc.) through scrubber. ● *noun* scrubbing, being scrubbed.

scrub² *noun* brushwood or stunted trees etc.; land covered with this. □ **scrubby** *adjective* (**-ier, -iest**).

scrubber *noun slang* promiscuous woman; apparatus for purifying gases etc.

scruff[1] *noun* back of neck.

scruff[2] *noun colloquial* scruffy person.

scruffy /'skrʌfɪ/ *adjective* (**-ier, -iest**) *colloquial* shabby, slovenly, untidy. □ **scruffily** *adverb*; **scruffiness** *noun*.

scrum *noun* scrummage; *colloquial* scrimmage. □ **scrum-half** *Rugby* half-back who puts ball into scrum.

scrummage /'skrʌmɪdʒ/ *noun Rugby* massed forwards on each side pushing to gain possession of ball thrown on ground between them.

scrumptious /'skrʌmpʃəs/ *adjective colloquial* delicious.

scrumpy /'skrʌmpɪ/ *noun colloquial* rough cider.

scrunch ● *verb* (usually + *up*) crumple; crunch. ● *noun* crunch.

scruple /'skru:p(ə)l/ ● *noun* (often in *plural*) moral concern; doubt caused by this. ● *verb* (**-ling**) (+ *to do*; usually in negative) hesitate owing to scruples.

scrupulous /'skru:pjʊləs/ *adjective* conscientious, thorough; careful to avoid doing wrong; over-attentive to details. □ **scrupulously** *adverb*.

scrutineer /skru:tɪ'nɪə/ *noun* person who scrutinizes ballot papers.

scrutinize /'skru:tɪnaɪz/ *verb* (also **-ise**) (**-zing** or **-sing**) subject to scrutiny.

scrutiny /'skru:tɪnɪ/ *noun* (*plural* **-ies**) critical gaze; close examination; official examination of ballot papers.

scuba /'sku:bə/ *noun* (*plural* **-s**) aqualung. □ **scuba-diving** swimming underwater using scuba.

scud ● *verb* (**-dd-**) move straight and fast; skim along; *Nautical* run before wind. ● *noun* scudding; vapoury driving clouds or shower.

scuff ● *verb* graze or brush against; mark or wear out (shoes etc.) thus; shuffle or drag feet. ● *noun* mark of scuffing.

scuffle /'skʌf(ə)l/ ● *noun* confused struggle or fight at close quarters. ● *verb* (**-ling**) engage in scuffle.

scull ● *noun* each of pair of small oars; oar used to propel boat from stern; (in *plural*) sculling race. ● *verb* propel with scull(s).

scullery /'skʌlərɪ/ *noun* (*plural* **-ies**) back kitchen; room where dishes are washed etc.

sculpt *verb* sculpture.

sculptor /'skʌlptə/ *noun* (*feminine* **sculptress**) person who sculptures.

sculpture /'skʌlptʃə/ ● *noun* art of making 3-dimensional forms by chiselling, carving, modelling, casting, etc.; work of sculpture. ● *verb* (**-ring**) represent in or adorn with sculpture; practise sculpture. □ **sculptural** *adjective*.

scum ● *noun* layer of dirt etc. at surface of liquid; *derogatory* worst part, person, or group. ● *verb* (**-mm-**) remove scum from; form scum (on). □ **scumbag** *slang* contemptible person. □ **scummy** *adjective* (**-ier, -iest**).

scupper[1] /'skʌpə/ *noun* hole in ship's side draining water from deck.

scupper[2] /'skʌpə/ *verb slang* sink (ship, crew); defeat or ruin (plan etc.); kill.

scurf *noun* dandruff. □ **scurfy** *adjective* (**-ier, -iest**).

scurrilous /'skʌrɪləs/ *adjective* grossly or obscenely abusive. □ **scurrility** /skə'rɪl-/ *noun* (*plural* **-ies**); **scurrilously** *adverb*; **scurrilousness** *noun*.

scurry /'skʌrɪ/ ● *verb* (**-ies, -ied**) run hurriedly, scamper. ● *noun* (*plural* **-ies**) scurrying sound or movement; flurry of rain or snow.

scurvy /'skɜ:vɪ/ ● *noun* disease resulting from deficiency of vitamin C. ● *adjective* (**-ier, -iest**) paltry, contemptible. □ **scurvily** *adverb*.

scut *noun* short tail, esp. of hare, rabbit, or deer.

scutter /'skʌtə/ *verb & noun colloquial* scurry.

scuttle[1] /'skʌt(ə)l/ *noun* coal scuttle; part of car body between windscreen and bonnet.

scuttle[2] /'skʌt(ə)l/ ● *verb* (**-ling**) scurry; flee in undignified way. ● *noun* hurried gait; precipitate flight.

scuttle[3] /'skʌt(ə)l/ ● *noun* hole with lid in ship's deck or side. ● *verb* (**-ling**) let water into (ship) to sink it.

scythe /saɪð/ ● *noun* mowing and reaping implement with long handle and curved blade. ● *verb* (**-thing**) cut with scythe.

SDLP *abbreviation* (in N. Ireland) Social Democratic and Labour Party.

SDP *abbreviation* (in UK) Social Democratic Party.

SE *abbreviation* south-east(ern).

sea *noun* expanse of salt water covering most of earth; area of this; large inland lake; (motion or state of) waves of sea; (+ *of*) vast quantity or expanse. □ **at sea** in ship on the sea, confused; **sea anchor** bag to reduce drifting of ship; **sea anemone** polyp with petal-like tentacles; **seabed** ocean floor; **seaboard** coastline, coastal area; **sea dog** old sailor; **seafarer** traveller by sea; **seafood** edible marine fish or shellfish; **sea front** part of seaside town facing sea; **seagoing** designed for open sea; **seagull** = GULL[1]; **sea horse** small fish with head like horse's; **seakale** plant with young shoots used as vegetable; **sea legs** ability to keep one's balance at sea; **sea level** mean level of sea's surface, used in reckoning heights of hills etc. and as barometric standard; **sea lion** large, eared seal; **seaman** person whose work is at sea, sailor, sailor below rank of officer; **seaplane** aircraft designed to take off from and land on water; **seaport** town with harbour; **sea salt** salt got by evaporating sea water; **seascape** picture or view of sea; **seashell** shell of salt-water mollusc; **seashore** land next to sea; **seasick** nauseous from motion of ship at sea; **seasickness** *noun*; **seaside** sea-coast, esp. as holiday resort; **sea urchin** small marine animal with spiny shell; **seaweed** plant growing in sea; **seaworthy** fit to put to sea.

seal[1] ● *noun* piece of stamped wax etc. attached to document or to receptacle, envelope, etc. to guarantee authenticity or security; metal stamp etc. used in making seal; substance or device used to close gap etc.; anything regarded as confirmation or guarantee; decorative adhesive stamp. ● *verb* close securely or hermetically; stamp, fasten, or fix with seal; certify as correct with seal; (+ *off*) prevent access to or from; (often + *up*) confine securely; settle, decide. □ **sealing wax** mixture softened by heating and used for seals.

seal[2] ● *noun* fish-eating amphibious marine mammal with flippers. ● *verb* hunt seals.

sealant *noun* material for sealing, esp. to make watertight.

seam ● *noun* line where two edges join, esp. of cloth or boards; fissure between parallel edges; wrinkle; stratum of coal etc. ● *verb* join with seam; (esp. as **seamed** *adjective*) mark or score with seam. □ **seamless** *adjective*.

seamstress /'si:mstrɪs/ *noun* woman who sews.

seamy *adjective* (**-ier, -iest**) disreputable, sordid; showing seams. □ **seaminess** *noun*.

seance /'seɪɑ̃s/ *noun* meeting at which spiritualist attempts to contact the dead.

sear /sɪə/ *verb* scorch, cauterize; cause anguish to; brown (meat) quickly.

search /sɜ:tʃ/ ● *verb* examine thoroughly to find something; make investigation; (+ *for, out*) look for, seek out; (as **searching** *adjective*) keenly questioning. ● *noun* act of searching; investigation. □ **searchlight** outdoor lamp designed to throw strong beam of light in any direction, light or beam from this; **search party** group of people conducting organized search; **search warrant** official authorization to enter and search building. □ **searcher** noun; **searchingly** adverb.

season /'si:z(ə)n/ ● noun each of climatic divisions of year; proper or suitable time; time when something is plentiful, active, etc.; **(the season)** (also **high season**) busiest period at resort etc.; colloquial season ticket. ● verb flavour with salt, herbs, etc.; enhance with wit etc.; moderate; (esp. as **seasoned** adjective) make or become suitable by exposure to weather or experience. □ **in season** (of food) available plentifully, (of animal) on heat; **season ticket** one entitling holder to unlimited travel, access, etc. in given period.

seasonable adjective suitable to season; opportune.

■ **Usage** *Seasonable* is sometimes confused with *seasonal*.

seasonal adjective of, depending on, or varying with seasons.

■ **Usage** *Seasonal* is sometimes confused with *seasonable*.

seasoning noun salt, herbs, etc. as flavouring for food.

seat ● noun thing made or used for sitting on; buttocks, part of garment covering them; part of chair etc. on which buttocks rest; place for one person in theatre etc.; position as MP, committee member, etc., or right to occupy it; machine's supporting or guiding part; location; country mansion; posture on horse. ● verb cause to sit; provide sitting accommodation for; (as **seated** adjective) sitting; establish in position. □ **seat belt** belt securing seated person in vehicle or aircraft.

seating noun seats collectively; sitting accommodation.

sebaceous /sɪ'beɪʃəs/ adjective fatty; secreting oily matter.

Sec. abbreviation (also **sec.**) secretary.

sec. abbreviation second(s).

sec[1] noun colloquial (in phrases) second, moment.

sec[2] adjective (of wine) dry.

secateurs /sekə'tɜ:z/ plural noun pruning clippers.

secede /sɪ'si:d/ verb (**-ding**) withdraw formally from political or religious body.

secession /sɪ'seʃ(ə)n/ noun seceding. □ **secessionist** noun & adjective.

seclude /sɪ'klu:d/ verb (**-ding**) keep (person, place) apart from others; (esp. as **secluded** adjective) screen from view.

seclusion /sɪ'klu:ʒ(ə)n/ noun secluded state or place.

second[1] /'sekənd/ ● adjective next after first; additional; subordinate; inferior; comparable to. ● noun runner-up; person or thing coming second; second gear; (in plural) inferior goods; colloquial second helping or course; assistant to boxer, duellist, etc. ● verb formally support (nomination, proposal, etc.). □ **second-best** next after best; **second class** second-best group, category, postal service, or accommodation; **second cousin** child of parent's first cousin; **second fiddle** subordinate position; **second-guess** colloquial anticipate by guesswork, criticize with hindsight; **second-hand** (of goods) having had previous owner, (of information etc.) obtained indirectly; **second nature** acquired tendency that has become instinctive; **second-rate** inferior; **second sight** clairvoyance; **second string** alternative course of action etc.; **second thoughts** revised opinion; **second wind** renewed capacity for

effort after breathlessness or tiredness. □ **seconder** noun.

second[2] /'sekənd/ noun SI unit of time (1/60 of minute); 1/60 of minute of angle; colloquial very short time.

second[3] /sɪ'kɒnd/ verb transfer (person) temporarily to another department etc. □ **secondment** noun.

secondary /'sekəndərɪ/ ● adjective coming after or next below what is primary; derived from or supplementing what is primary; (of education etc.) following primary. ● noun (plural **-ies**) secondary thing. □ **secondary colour** result of mixing two primary colours.

secondly adverb furthermore; as a second item.

secrecy /'si:krəsɪ/ noun being secret; keeping of secrets.

secret /'si:krɪt/ ● adjective not (to be) made known or seen; working etc. secretly; liking secrecy. ● noun thing (to be) kept secret; mystery; effective but not widely known method. □ **in secret** secretly; **secret agent** spy; **secret police** police operating secretly for political ends; **secret service** government department concerned with espionage. □ **secretly** adverb.

secretariat /sekrɪ'teərɪət/ noun administrative office or department; its members or premises.

secretary /'sekrɪtərɪ/ noun (plural **-ies**) employee who deals with correspondence, records, making appointments, etc.; official of society etc. who writes letters, organizes business, etc.; principal assistant of government minister, ambassador, etc. □ **secretary bird** long-legged crested African bird; **Secretary-General** principal administrative officer of organization; **Secretary of State** head of major government department, (in US) foreign minister. □ **secretarial** /-'teərɪəl/ adjective.

secrete /sɪ'kri:t/ verb (**-ting**) (of cell, organ, etc.) produce and discharge (substance); conceal. □ **secretory** adjective.

secretion /sɪ'kri:ʃ(ə)n/ noun process or act of secreting; secreted substance.

secretive /'si:krətɪv/ adjective inclined to make or keep secrets, uncommunicative. □ **secretively** adverb; **secretiveness** noun.

sect noun group sharing (usually unorthodox) religious etc. doctrines; religious denomination.

sectarian /sek'teərɪən/ ● adjective of sect(s); bigoted in following one's sect. ● noun member of a sect. □ **sectarianism** noun.

section /'sekʃ(ə)n/ ● noun each of parts into which something is divisible or divided; part cut off; subdivision; US area of land, district of town; surgical separation or cutting; cutting of solid by plane, resulting figure or area of this; thin slice cut off for microscopic examination. ● verb arrange in or divide into sections; compulsorily commit to psychiatric hospital.

sectional adjective of a social group; partisan; made in sections; local rather than general. □ **sectionally** adverb.

sector /'sektə/ noun branch of an enterprise, the economy, etc.; Military portion of battle area; plane figure enclosed between two radii of circle etc.

secular /'sekjʊlə/ adjective not concerned with religion, not sacred; (of clerics) not monastic. □ **secularism** noun; **secularization** noun; **secularize** verb (also **-ise**) (**-zing** or **-sing**).

secure /sɪ'kjʊə/ ● adjective untroubled by danger or fear; safe; reliable, stable, fixed. ● verb (**-ring**) make secure or safe; fasten or close securely; obtain. □ **securely** adverb.

security noun (plural **-ies**) secure condition or feeling; thing that guards or guarantees; safety against espionage, theft, etc.; organization for ensuring this;

thing deposited as guarantee for undertaking or loan; (often in *plural*) document as evidence of loan, certificate of stock, bonds, etc. □ **security risk** person or thing threatening security.

sedan /sɪ'dæn/ *noun* (in full **sedan chair**) *historical* enclosed chair for one person, usually carried on poles by two; *US* saloon car.

sedate /sɪ'deɪt/ ● *adjective* tranquil, serious. ● *verb* (**-ting**) put under sedation. □ **sedately** *adverb*; **sedateness** *noun*.

sedation *noun* treatment with sedatives.

sedative /'sedətɪv/ ● *noun* calming drug or influence. ● *adjective* calming, soothing.

sedentary /'sedəntərɪ/ *adjective* sitting; (of work etc.) done while sitting; (of person) disinclined to exercise.

sedge *noun* grasslike waterside or marsh plant. □ **sedgy** *adjective*.

sediment /'sedɪmənt/ *noun* dregs; matter deposited on land by water or wind. □ **sedimentary** /-'men-/ *adjective*; **sedimentation** *noun*.

sedition /sɪ'dɪʃ(ə)n/ *noun* conduct or speech inciting to rebellion. □ **seditious** *adjective*.

seduce /sɪ'djuːs/ *verb* (**-cing**) entice into sexual activity or wrongdoing; coax or lead astray. □ **seducer** *noun*.

seduction /sɪ'dʌkʃ(ə)n/ *noun* seducing, being seduced; tempting or attractive thing.

seductive /sɪ'dʌktɪv/ *adjective* alluring, enticing. □ **seductively** *adverb*; **seductiveness** *noun*.

sedulous /'sedjʊləs/ *adjective* persevering, diligent, painstaking. □ **sedulity** /sɪ'djuː-/ *noun*; **sedulously** *adverb*.

see¹ *verb* (**sees**; *past* **saw**; *past participle* **seen**) perceive with the eyes; have or use this power; discern mentally, understand; watch; experience; ascertain; imagine, foresee; look at; meet; visit, be visited by; meet regularly; reflect, get clarification; (+ *in*) find attractive in; escort, conduct; witness (event etc.); ensure. □ **see about** attend to, consider; **see off** be present at departure of, *colloquial* get the better of; **see over** inspect, tour; **see red** *colloquial* become enraged; **see through** not be deceived by, support (person) during difficult time, complete (project); **see-through** translucent; **see to** attend to, repair; **see to it** (+ *that*) ensure.

see² *noun* area under (arch)bishop's authority; (arch)bishop's office or jurisdiction.

seed ● *noun* part of plant capable of developing into another such plant; seeds collectively, esp. for sowing; semen; prime cause, beginning; offspring; *Tennis etc.* seeded player. ● *verb* place seed(s) in; sprinkle (as) with seed; sow seeds; produce or drop seed; remove seeds from (fruit etc.); place crystal etc. in (cloud) to produce rain; *Tennis etc.* designate (competitor in knockout tournament) so that strong competitors do not meet each other until later rounds, arrange (order of play) thus. □ **go, run to seed** cease flowering as seed develops, become degenerate, unkempt, etc.; **seed-bed** bed prepared for sowing, place of development; **seed-pearl** very small pearl; **seed-potato** potato kept for planting; **seedsman** dealer in seeds.

seedling *noun* young plant raised from seed.

seedy *adjective* (**-ier, -iest**) shabby; *colloquial* unwell; full of seed.

seeing *conjunction* (usually + *that*) considering that, inasmuch as, because.

seek *verb* (*past & past participle* **sought** /sɔːt/) (often + *for, after*) search, inquire; try or want to obtain or reach; request; endeavour. □ **seek out** search for and find. □ **seeker** *noun*.

seem *verb* (often + *to do*) appear, give the impression.

seeming *adjective* apparent but doubtful. □ **seemingly** *adverb*.

seemly /'siːmlɪ/ *adjective* (**-ier, -iest**) in good taste, decorous. □ **seemliness** *noun*.

seen *past participle* of SEE¹.

seep *verb* ooze, percolate.

seepage *noun* act of seeping; quantity that seeps.

seer /sɪə/ *noun* person who sees; prophet, visionary.

seersucker /'sɪəsʌkə/ *noun* thin cotton etc. fabric with puckered surface.

see-saw /'siːsɔː/ ● *noun* long board supported in middle so that children etc. sitting on ends move alternately up and down; this game; up-and-down or to-and-fro motion, contest, etc. ● *verb* play or move (as) on see-saw; vacillate. ● *adjective & adverb* with up-and-down or to-and-fro motion.

seethe /siːð/ *verb* (**-thing**) boil, bubble; be very angry, resentful, etc.

segment ● *noun* /'segmənt/ part cut off or separable from other parts; part of circle or sphere cut off by intersecting line or plane. ● *verb* /seg'ment/ divide into segments. □ **segmental** /-'ment-/ *adjective*; **segmentation** *noun*.

segregate /'segrɪgeɪt/ *verb* (**-ting**) put apart, isolate; separate (esp. ethnic group) from the rest of the community. □ **segregation** *noun*; **segregationist** *noun & adjective*.

seigneur /sem'jɜː/ *noun* feudal lord. □ **seigneurial** *adjective*.

seine /sem/ ● *noun* large vertical fishing net. ● *verb* (**-ning**) fish with seine.

seismic /'saɪzmɪk/ *adjective* of earthquake(s).

seismograph /'saɪzməɡrɑːf/ *noun* instrument for recording earthquake details. □ **seismographic** /-'græf-/ *adjective*.

seismology /saɪz'mɒlədʒɪ/ *noun* the study of earthquakes. □ **seismological** /-mə'lɒdʒ-/ *adjective*; **seismologist** *noun*.

seize /siːz/ *verb* (**-zing**) (often + *on, upon*) take hold or possession of, esp. forcibly, suddenly, or by legal power; take advantage of; comprehend quickly or clearly; affect suddenly; (also **seise**) (usually + *of*) *Law* put in possession of. □ **seize up** (of mechanism) become jammed, (of part of body etc.) become stiff.

seizure /'siːʒə/ *noun* seizing, being seized; sudden attack of epilepsy, apoplexy, etc.

seldom /'seldəm/ *adverb* rarely, not often.

select /sɪ'lekt/ ● *verb* choose, esp. with care. ● *adjective* chosen for excellence or suitability; exclusive. □ **select committee** parliamentary committee conducting special inquiry. □ **selector** *noun*.

selection /sɪ'lekʃ(ə)n/ *noun* selecting, being selected; person or thing selected; things from which choice may be made; = NATURAL SELECTION.

selective *adjective* of or using selection; able to select; selecting what is convenient. □ **selectively** *adverb*; **selectivity** /-'tɪv-/ *noun*.

selenium /sɪ'liːnɪəm/ *noun* non-metallic element in some sulphide ores.

self ● *noun* (*plural* **selves** /selvz/) individuality, essence; object of introspection or reflexive action; one's own interests or pleasure, concentration on these.

self- *combining form expressing reflexive action, automatic or independent action, or sameness.* □ **self-addressed** addressed to oneself; **self-adhesive** (of envelope etc.) adhesive, esp. without wetting; **self-aggrandizement** enriching oneself, making oneself powerful; **self-assertive** confident or assertive in promoting oneself, one's claims, etc.; **self-assertion** *noun*; **self-assured** self-confident; **self-catering** providing cooking facilities but no food; **self-centred**

preoccupied with oneself; **self-confessed** openly admitting oneself to be; **self-confident** having confidence in oneself; **self-confidence** noun; **self-conscious** nervous, shy, embarrassed; **self-consciously** adverb; **self-contained** uncommunicative, complete in itself; **self-control** control of oneself, one's behaviour, etc.; **self-critical** critical of oneself, one's abilities, etc.; **self-defence** defence of oneself, one's reputation, etc.; **self-denial** abstinence, esp. as discipline; **self-deprecating** belittling oneself; **self-destruct** (of device etc.) explode or disintegrate automatically, esp. when preset to do so; **self-determination** nation's right to determine own government etc., free will; **self-effacing** retiring, modest; **self-employed** working as freelance or for one's own business etc.; **self-employment** noun; **self-esteem** good opinion of oneself; **self-evident** needing no proof or explanation; **self-explanatory** not needing explanation; **self-financing** not needing subsidy; **self-fulfilling** (of prophecy etc.) assured fulfilment by its utterance; **self-governing** governing itself or oneself; **self-government** noun; **self-help** use of one's own abilities etc. to achieve success etc.; **self-image** one's conception of oneself; **self-important** conceited, pompous; **self-importance** noun; **self-indulgent** indulging one's own pleasures, feelings, etc., (of work of art etc.) lacking control; **self-indulgence** noun; **self-interest** one's own interest or advantage; **self-interested** adjective; **self-made** successful or rich by one's own efforts; **self-opinionated** obstinate in one's opinion; **self-pity** pity for oneself; **self-portrait** portrait of oneself by oneself; **self-possessed** unperturbed, cool; **self-possession** noun; **self-preservation** keeping oneself safe, instinct for this; **self-raising** (of flour) containing a raising agent; **self-reliance** reliance on one's own abilities etc.; **self-reliant** adjective; **self-respect** respect for oneself; **self-restraint** self-control; **self-righteous** smugly sure of one's righteousness; **self-righteously** adverb; **self-righteousness** noun; **self-rule** selfgovernment; **self-sacrifice** selflessness, self-denial; **self-satisfied** complacent; **self-satisfaction** noun; **self-seeking** selfish; **self-service** with customers helping themselves and paying cashier afterwards; **self-starter** electric device for starting engine, ambitious person with initiative; **self-styled** called so by oneself; **self-sufficient** capable of supplying one's own needs; **self-sufficiency** noun; **self-willed** obstinately pursuing one's own wishes; **self-worth** self-esteem.

selfish adjective concerned chiefly with one's own interests or pleasure; actuated by or appealing to self-interest. □ **selfishness** noun.

selfless adjective unselfish.

selfsame /'selfseɪm/ adjective (**the selfsame**) the very same, the identical.

sell ● verb (past & past participle **sold** /səʊld/) exchange or be exchanged for money; stock for sale; (+ at, for) have specified price; betray or prostitute for money etc.; advertise, publicize; cause to be sold; colloquial make (person) enthusiastic about (idea etc.). ● noun colloquial manner of selling; deception, disappointment. □ **sell-by date** latest recommended date of sale; **sell off** sell at reduced prices; **sell out** sell (all one's stock or shares etc.), betray, be treacherous; **sell-out** commercial success, betrayal; **sell short** disparage, underestimate; **sell up** sell one's business, house, etc.

seller noun person who sells; thing that sells well or badly as specified. □ **seller's market** time when goods are scarce and expensive.

Sellotape /'seləteɪp/ ● noun proprietary term adhesive usually transparent cellulose tape. ● verb (**sellotape**) (**-ping**) fix with Sellotape.

selvage /'selvɪdʒ/ noun (also **selvedge**) edge of cloth woven to prevent fraying.

selves plural of SELF.

semantic /sɪ'mæntɪk/ adjective of meaning in language.

semantics plural noun (usually treated as singular) branch of linguistics concerned with meaning.

semaphore /'seməfɔː/ ● noun system of signalling with arms or two flags; railway signalling apparatus with arm(s). ● verb (**-ring**) signal or send by semaphore.

semblance /'sembləns/ noun (+ of) appearance, show.

semen /'siːmən/ noun reproductive fluid of males.

semester /sɪ'mestə/ noun half-year term in universities.

semi /'semɪ/ noun colloquial (plural **-s**) semi-detached house.

semi- prefix half; partly.

semibreve /'semɪbriːv/ noun Music note equal to 4 crotchets.

semicircle /'semɪsɜːk(ə)l/ noun half of circle or its circumference. □ **semicircular** /-'sɜːkjʊlə/ adjective.

semicolon /semɪ'kəʊlən/ noun punctuation mark (;) of intermediate value between comma and full stop (see panel).

semiconductor /semɪkən'dʌktə/ noun substance that is a poor electrical conductor when either pure or cold and a good conductor when either impure or hot.

semi-detached /semɪdɪ'tætʃt/ ● adjective (of house) joined to another on one side only. ● noun such house.

semifinal /semɪ'faɪn(ə)l/ noun Sport match or round preceding final. □ **semifinalist** noun.

seminal /'semɪn(ə)l/ adjective of seed, semen, or reproduction; germinal; (of idea etc.) providing basis for future development.

Semicolon ;

This is used:

1 between clauses that are too short or too closely related to be made into separate sentences; such clauses are not usually connected by a conjunction, e.g.

> *To err is human; to forgive, divine.*
> *You could wait for him here; on the other hand I could wait in your place; this would save you valuable time.*

2 between items in a list which themselves contain commas, if it is necessary to avoid confusion, e.g.

> *The party consisted of three teachers, who had already climbed with the leader; seven pupils; and two parents.*

seminar /'semɪnɑː/ *noun* small class for discussion etc.; short intensive course of study; specialists' conference.

seminary /'semɪnərɪ/ *noun* (*plural* **-ies**) training college for priests etc. □ **seminarist** *noun*.

semipermeable /semɪ'pɜːmɪəb(ə)l/ *adjective* (of membrane etc.) allowing small molecules to pass through.

semiprecious /semɪ'preʃəs/ *adjective* (of gem) less valuable than a precious stone.

semi-professional /semɪprə'feʃən(ə)l/ ● *adjective* (of footballer, musician, etc.) paid for activity but not relying on it for living; of semi-professionals. ● *noun* semi-professional person.

semiquaver /'semɪkweɪvə/ *noun* Music note equal to half a quaver.

semi-skimmed /semɪ'skɪmd/ *adjective* (of milk) with some of cream skimmed off.

Semite /'siːmaɪt/ *noun* member of peoples supposedly descended from Shem, including Jews and Arabs.

Semitic /sɪ'mɪtɪk/ *adjective* of Semites, esp. Jews; of languages of family including Hebrew and Arabic.

semitone /'semɪtəʊn/ *noun* half a tone in musical scale.

semivowel /'semɪvaʊəl/ *noun* sound intermediate between vowel and consonant; letter representing this.

semolina /semə'liːnə/ *noun* hard round grains of wheat used for puddings etc.; pudding of this.

Semtex /'semteks/ *noun* proprietary term odourless plastic explosive.

SEN *abbreviation* State Enrolled Nurse.

Sen. *abbreviation* Senior; Senator.

senate /'senɪt/ *noun* upper house of legislature in some countries; governing body of some universities or (*US*) colleges; ancient Roman state council.

senator /'senətə/ *noun* member of senate. □ **senatorial** /-'tɔː-/ *adjective*.

send *verb* (*past & past participle* **sent**) order or cause to go or be conveyed; cause to become; send message etc.; grant, bestow, inflict, cause to be. □ **send away for** order (goods) by post; **send down** rusticate or expel from university, send to prison; **send for** summon, order by post; **send off** dispatch, attend departure of person; **send-off** party etc. at departure of person; **send off for** send away for; **send on** transmit further or in advance of oneself; **send up** *colloquial* ridicule (by mimicking); **send-up** *noun* ● **sender** *noun*.

senescent /sɪ'nes(ə)nt/ *adjective* growing old. □ **senescence** *noun*.

seneschal /'senɪʃ(ə)l/ *noun* steward of medieval great house.

senile /'siːnaɪl/ *adjective* of old age; mentally or physically infirm because of old age. □ **senile dementia** illness of old people with loss of memory etc. □ **senility** /sɪ'nɪl-/ *noun*.

senior /'siːnɪə/ ● *adjective* higher in age or standing; (placed after person's name) senior to relative of same name. ● *noun* senior person; one's elder or superior. □ **senior citizen** old-age pensioner. □ **seniority** /-'ɒr-/ *noun*.

senna /'senə/ *noun* cassia; laxative from leaves and pods of this.

señor /sen'jɔː/ *noun* (*plural* **señores** /-rez/) *title used of or to Spanish-speaking man.*

señora /sen'jɔːrə/ *noun* *title used of or to Spanish-speaking esp. married woman.*

señorita /senjə'riːtə/ *noun* *title used of or to young Spanish-speaking esp. unmarried woman.*

sensation /sen'seɪʃ(ə)n/ *noun* feeling in one's body; awareness, impression; intense feeling, esp. in community; cause of this; sense of touch.

sensational *adjective* causing or intended to cause public excitement etc.; wonderful. □ **sensationalism** *noun*; **sensationalist** *noun & adjective*; **sensationalize** *verb* (also **-ise**) (**-zing** or **-sing**).

sense ● *noun* any of bodily faculties transmitting sensation; sensitiveness of any of these; ability to perceive; (+ *of*) consciousness; appreciation, instinct; practical wisdom; meaning of word etc.; intelligibility, coherence; prevailing opinion; (in *plural*) sanity, ability to think. ● *verb* (**-sing**) perceive by sense(s); be vaguely aware of; (of machine etc.) detect. □ **make sense** be intelligible or practicable; **make sense of** show or find meaning of. □ **sense of humour** see HUMOUR.

senseless *adjective* pointless, foolish; unconscious. □ **senselessly** *adverb*; **senselessness** *noun*.

sensibility *noun* (*plural* **-ies**) capacity to feel; (exceptional) sensitiveness; (in *plural*) tendency to feel offended etc.

■ Usage *Sensibility* should not be used in standard English to mean 'possession of good sense'.

sensible /'sensɪb(ə)l/ *adjective* having or showing good sense; perceptible by senses; (of clothing etc.) practical; (+ *of*) aware of. □ **sensibly** *adverb*.

sensitive /'sensɪtɪv/ *adjective* (often + *to*) acutely affected by external impressions, having sensibility; easily offended or hurt; (often + *to*) responsive to or recording slight changes of condition; Photography responding (esp. rapidly) to light; (of topic etc.) requiring tact or secrecy. □ **sensitively** *adverb*; **sensitiveness** *noun*; **sensitivity** /-'tɪv-/ *noun* (*plural* **-ies**).

sensitize /'sensɪtaɪz/ *verb* (also **-ise**) (**-zing** or **-sing**) make sensitive. □ **sensitization** *noun*.

sensor /'sensə/ *noun* device to detect or measure a physical property.

sensory /'sensərɪ/ *adjective* of sensation or senses.

sensual /'sensjʊəl/ *adjective* of physical, esp. sexual, pleasure; enjoying, giving, or showing this. □ **sensuality** /-'æl-/ *noun*; **sensually** *adverb*.

■ Usage *Sensual* is sometimes confused with *sensuous.*

sensuous /'sensjʊəs/ *adjective* of or affecting senses, esp. aesthetically. □ **sensuously** *adverb*; **sensuousness** *noun*.

■ Usage *Sensuous* is sometimes confused with *sensual.*

sent *past & past participle* of SEND.

sentence /'sent(ə)ns/ ● *noun* grammatically complete series of words with (implied) subject and predicate (see panel); punishment allotted to person convicted in criminal trial; declaration of this. ● *verb* (**-cing**) declare sentence of, condemn.

sententious /sen'tenʃəs/ *adjective* pompously moralizing; affectedly formal; using maxims. □ **sententiousness** *noun*.

sentient /'senʃ(ə)nt/ *adjective* capable of perception and feeling. □ **sentience** *noun*; **sentiently** *adverb*.

sentiment /'sentɪmənt/ *noun* mental feeling; (often in *plural*) opinion; emotional or irrational view(s); tendency to be swayed by feeling; mawkish tenderness.

sentimental /sentɪ'ment(ə)l/ *adjective* of or showing sentiment; showing or affected by emotion rather than reason. □ **sentimentalism** *noun*; **sentimentalist** *noun*; **sentimentality** /-'tæl-/ *noun*; **sentimentalize** *verb* (also **-ise**) (**-zing** or **-sing**); **sentimentally** *adverb*.

sentinel /'sentɪn(ə)l/ *noun* sentry.

sentry /'sentrɪ/ *noun* (*plural* **-ies**) soldier etc. stationed to keep guard. □ **sentry-box** cabin to shelter standing sentry.

sepal /'sep(ə)l/ *noun* division or leaf of calyx.

separable /'sepərəb(ə)l/ *adjective* able to be separated. □ **separability** *noun*.

separate ● *adjective* /'sepərət/ forming unit by itself, existing apart; disconnected, distinct, individual. ● *noun* /'sepərət/ (*in plural*) articles of dress not parts of suits. ● *verb* /'sepəreɪt/ (**-ting**) make separate, sever; prevent union or contact of; go different ways; (esp. as **separated** *adjective*) cease to live with spouse; secede; divide or sort into parts or sizes; (often + *out*) extract or remove (ingredient etc.). □ **separately** *adverb*; **separateness** *noun*; **separator** *noun*.

■ **Usage** *Separate, separation*, etc. are not spelt with an *e* in the middle.

separation /sepə'reɪʃ(ə)n/ *noun* separating, being separated; arrangement by which couple remain married but live apart.

separatist /'sepərətɪst/ *noun* person who favours separation, esp. political independence. □ **separatism** *noun*.

sepia /'siːpɪə/ *noun* dark reddish-brown colour or paint; brown tint used in photography.

sepoy /'siːpɔɪ/ *noun historical* Indian soldier under European, esp. British, discipline.

sepsis /'sepsɪs/ *noun* septic condition.

Sept. *abbreviation* September.

sept *noun* clan, esp. in Ireland.

September /sep'tembə/ *noun* ninth month of year.

septet /sep'tet/ *noun* musical composition for 7 performers; the performers; any group of 7.

septic /'septɪk/ *adjective* contaminated with bacteria, putrefying. □ **septic tank** tank in which sewage is disintegrated through bacterial activity.

septicaemia /septɪ'siːmɪə/ *noun* (*US* **septicemia**) blood poisoning.

septuagenarian /septjʊədʒɪ'neərɪən/ *noun* person between 70 and 79 years old.

Septuagesima /septjʊə'dʒesɪmə/ *noun* third Sunday before Lent.

Septuagint /'septjʊədʒɪnt/ *noun* ancient Greek version of Old Testament.

septum /'septəm/ *noun* (*plural* **septa**) partition such as that between nostrils.

sepulchral /sɪ'pʌlkr(ə)l/ *adjective* of tomb or burial; funereal, gloomy.

sepulchre /'sepəlkə/ (*US* **sepulcher**) ● *noun* tomb, burial cave or vault. ● *verb* (**-ring**) lay in sepulchre.

sequel /'siːkw(ə)l/ *noun* what follows; novel, film, etc. that continues story of earlier one.

sequence /'siːkwəns/ *noun* succession; order of succession; set of things belonging next to one another; unbroken series; episode or incident in film etc.

sequential /sɪ'kwenʃ(ə)l/ *adjective* forming sequence or consequence. □ **sequentially** *adverb*.

sequester /sɪ'kwestə/ *verb* (esp. as **sequestered** *adjective*) seclude, isolate; sequestrate.

sequestrate /'siːkwɪstreɪt/ *verb* (**-ting**) confiscate; take temporary possession of (debtor's estate etc.). □ **sequestration** *noun*.

sequin /'siːkwɪn/ *noun* circular spangle on dress etc. □ **sequined, sequinned** *adjective*.

sequoia /sɪ'kwɔɪə/ *noun* extremely tall Californian conifer.

sera *plural* of SERUM.

seraglio /sə'rɑːlɪəʊ/ *noun* (*plural* **-s**) harem; *historical* Turkish palace.

seraph /'seraf/ *noun* (*plural* **-im** or **-s**) member of highest of 9 orders of angels. □ **seraphic** /sə'ræfɪk/ *adjective*.

Serb ● *noun* native of Serbia; person of Serbian descent. ● *adjective* Serbian.

Serbian /'sɜːbɪən/ ● *noun* Slavonic dialect of Serbs; Serb. ● *adjective* of Serbs or their dialect.

Serbo-Croat /sɜːbəʊ'krəʊæt/ (also **Serbo-Croatian** /-krəʊ'eɪʃ(ə)n/) ● *noun* main official language of former Yugoslavia, combining Serbian and Croatian dialects. ● *adjective* of this language.

serenade /serə'neɪd/ ● *noun* piece of music performed at night, esp. under lover's window; orchestral suite for small ensemble. ● *verb* (**-ding**) perform serenade to.

serendipity /seran'dɪpɪtɪ/ *noun* faculty of making happy discoveries by accident. □ **serendipitous** *adjective*.

serene /sɪ'riːn/ *adjective* (**-r, -st**) clear and calm; placid, unperturbed. □ **serenely** *adverb*; **serenity** /-'ren-/ *noun*.

serf *noun historical* labourer not allowed to leave the land on which he worked; oppressed person, drudge. □ **serfdom** *noun*.

serge *noun* durable woollen fabric.

sergeant /'sɑːdʒ(ə)nt/ *noun* non-commissioned army or RAF officer next below warrant officer; police officer next below inspector. □ **sergeant major** warrant officer assisting adjutant of regiment or battalion.

serial /'sɪərɪəl/ ● *noun* story published, broadcast, or shown in instalments. ● *adjective* of, in, or forming series. □ **serial killer** person who murders repeatedly. □ **serially** *adverb*.

serialize *verb* (also **-ise**) (**-zing** or **-sing**) publish or produce in instalments. □ **serialization** *noun*.

Sentence

A sentence is the basic unit of language in use and expresses a complete thought. There are three types of sentence, each starting with a capital letter, and each normally ending with a full stop, a question mark, or an exclamation mark:

Statement: *You're happy.*
Question: *Is it raining?*
Exclamation: *I wouldn't have believed it!*

A sentence, especially a statement, often has no punctuation at the end in a public notice, a newspaper headline, or a legal document, e.g.

Government cuts public spending

A sentence normally contains a subject and a verb, but may not, e.g.

What a mess!   *Where?*   *In the sink.*

series /'sɪəriːz/ *noun* (*plural* same) number of similar or related things, events, etc.; succession, row, set; *Broadcasting* set of related but individually complete programmes. □ **in series** in ordered succession, (of set of electrical circuits) arranged so that same current passes through each circuit.

serif /'serɪf/ *noun* fine cross-line at extremities of printed letter.

serious /'sɪərɪəs/ *adjective* thoughtful, earnest; important, requiring thought; not negligible, dangerous; sincere, in earnest; (of music, literature, etc.) intellectual, not popular. □ **seriously** *adverb*; **seriousness** *noun*.

serjeant /'sɑːdʒ(ə)nt/ *noun* (in full **serjeant-at-law,** *plural* **serjeants-at-law**) *historical* barrister of highest rank. □ **serjeant-at-arms** official of court, city, or parliament, with ceremonial duties.

sermon /'sɜːmən/ *noun* discourse on religion or morals, esp. delivered in church; admonition, reproof.

sermonize *verb* (also **-ise**) (**-zing** or **-sing**) (often + *to*) moralize.

serous /'sɪərəs/ *adjective* of or like serum, watery; (of gland etc.) having serous secretion.

serpent /'sɜːpənt/ *noun* snake, esp. large; cunning or treacherous person.

serpentine /'sɜːpəntaɪn/ ● *adjective* of or like serpent; coiling, sinuous; cunning, treacherous. ● *noun* soft usually dark green rock, sometimes mottled.

SERPS *abbreviation* State Earnings-Related Pension Scheme.

serrated /sə'reɪtɪd/ *adjective* with sawlike edge. □ **serration** *noun*.

serried /'serɪd/ *adjective* (of ranks of soldiers etc.) close together.

serum /'sɪərəm/ *noun* (*plural* **sera** or **-s**) liquid separating from clot when blood coagulates, esp. used for inoculation; watery fluid in animal bodies.

servant /'sɜːv(ə)nt/ *noun* person employed for domestic work; devoted follower or helper.

serve ● *verb* (**-ving**) do service for; be servant to; carry out duty; (+ *in*) be employed in (esp. armed forces); be useful to or serviceable for; meet needs, perform function; go through due period of (apprenticeship, prison sentence, etc.); go through (specified period) of imprisonment etc.; (often + *up*) present (food) to eat; act as waiter; attend to (customer etc.); (+ *with*) supply with (goods); treat (person) in specified way; *Law* (often + *on*) deliver (writ etc.), (+ *with*) deliver writ etc. to; set (ball) in play at tennis etc.; (of male animal) copulate with (female). ● *noun Tennis etc.* service. □ **serve (person) right** be his or her deserved misfortune. □ **server** *noun*.

service /'sɜːvɪs/ ● *noun* (often in *plural*) work done or doing of work for employer or for community etc.; work done by machine etc.; assistance or benefit given; provision of some public need, e.g. transport or (often in *plural*) water, gas, etc.; employment as servant; state or period of employment; Crown or public department or organization; (in *plural*) the armed forces; ceremony of worship; liturgical form for this; (routine) maintenance and repair of machine etc. after sale; assistance given to customers; serving of food etc., quality of this; nominal charge for this; (in *plural*) motorway service area; set of dishes etc. for serving meal; act of serving in tennis etc., person's turn to serve, game in which one serves. ● *verb* (**-cing**) maintain or repair (car, machine, etc.); provide service for. □ **at (person's) service** ready to serve him or her; **of service** useful; **service area** area near road supplying petrol, refreshments, etc.; **service charge** additional charge for service in restaurant etc.; **service flat** one in which domestic service etc. is provided; **service**

industry one providing services, not goods; **serviceman, servicewoman** person in armed services; **service road** one giving access to houses etc. lying back from main road; **service station** establishment selling petrol etc. to motorists.

serviceable *adjective* useful, usable; durable but plain. □ **serviceability** *noun*.

serviette /sɜːvɪ'et/ *noun* table napkin.

servile /'sɜːvaɪl/ *adjective* of or like slave(s); fawning, subservient. □ **servility** /-'vɪl-/ *noun*.

servitude /'sɜːvɪtjuːd/ *noun* slavery, subjection.

servo- /'sɜːvəʊ/ *combining form* power-assisted.

sesame /'sesəmɪ/ *noun* E. Indian plant with oilyielding seeds; its seeds.

sesqui- /'seskwɪ/ *combining form* one and a half.

sessile /'sesaɪl/ *adjective Biology* attached directly by base without stalk or peduncle; fixed, immobile.

session /'seʃ(ə)n/ *noun* period devoted to an activity; assembly of parliament, court, etc.; single meeting for this; period during which such meetings are regularly held; academic year. □ **in session** assembled for business, not on vacation. □ **sessional** *adjective*.

set ● *verb* (**-tt-**; *past & past participle* **set**) put, lay, or stand in certain position etc.; apply; fix or place ready; dispose suitably for use, action, or display; adjust hands or mechanism of (clock, trap, etc.); insert (jewel) in ring etc.; lay (table) for meal; style (hair) while damp; (+ *with*) ornament or provide (surface) with; bring into specified state, cause to be; harden, solidify; (of sun, moon, etc.) move towards or below earth's horizon; show (story etc.) as happening in a certain time or place; (+ *to do*) cause (person) to do specified thing; (+ *present participle*) start (person, thing) doing something; present or impose as work to be done, problem to be solved, etc.; exhibit as model etc.; initiate (fashion etc.); establish (record etc.); determine, decide; appoint, establish; put parts of (broken or dislocated bone, limb, etc.) together for healing; provide (song, words) with music; arrange (type) or type for (book etc.); (of tide, current, etc.) have a certain motion or direction; (of face) assume hard expression; (of eyes etc.) become motionless; have a certain tendency; (of blossom) form into fruit; (of dancer) take position facing partner; (of hunting dog) take rigid attitude indicating presence of game. ● *noun* group of linked or similar things or persons; section of society; collection of objects for specified purpose; radio or television receiver; *Tennis etc.* group of games counting as unit towards winning match; *Mathematics* collection of things sharing a property; direction or position in which something sets or is set; slip, shoot, bulb, etc. for planting; setting, stage furniture, etc. for play, film, etc.; setting of sun, hair, etc.; = SETT. ● *adjective* prescribed or determined in advance; unchanging, fixed; prepared for action; (+ *on, upon*) determined to get, achieve, etc. □ **set about** begin, take steps towards, *colloquial* attack; **set aside** put to one side, keep for future, disregard or reject; **set back** place further back in space or time, impede or reverse progress of, *colloquial* cost (person) specified amount; **set-back** reversal or arrest of progress; **set down** record in writing, allow to alight; **set forth** begin journey, expound; **set in** begin, become established, insert; **set off** begin journey, detonate (bomb etc.), initiate, stimulate, cause (person) to start laughing etc., adorn, enhance, (+ *against*) use as compensating item against; **set on** (cause or urge to) attack; **set out** begin journey, (+ *to do*) intend, exhibit, arrange; **set piece** formal or elaborate arrangement, esp. in art or literature; **set square** right-angled triangular plate for drawing lines at certain angles; **set to** begin doing something vigorously; **set theory** study or use of sets in mathematics; **set-to** (*plural* **-tos**) *colloquial* fight, argument; **set up** place in position or view, start, establish, equip, prepare, *colloquial* cause (person) to look guilty or foolish; **set-up** arrangement or organization, manner or structure of this, instance of setting person up; **set upon** set on.

sett *noun* (also **set**) badger's burrow, paving-block.

settee /se'ti:/ *noun* sofa.

setter *noun* dog of long-haired breed trained to stand rigid on scenting game.

setting *noun* position or manner in which thing is set; surroundings; period, place, etc. of story, film, etc.; frame etc. for jewel; music to which words are set; cutlery etc. for one person at table; operating level of machine.

settle[1] /'set(ə)l/ *verb* (**-ling**) (often + *down, in*) establish or become established in abode or lifestyle; (often + *down*) regain calm after disturbance, adopt regular or secure way of life, (+ *to*) apply oneself to; (cause to) sit down or come to rest; make or become composed etc.; determine, decide, agree on; resolve (dispute etc.); agree to terminate (lawsuit); (+ *for*) accept or agree to; pay (bill); (as **settled** *adjective*) established; colonize; subside, sink. □ **settle up** pay money owed etc.

settle[2] /'set(ə)l/ *noun* high-backed bench, often with box under seat.

settlement *noun* settling, being settled; place occupied by settlers, small village; political etc. agreement; arrangement ending dispute; terms on which property is given to person; deed stating these; amount or property given.

settler *noun* person who settles in newly developed region.

seven /'sev(ə)n/ *adjective & noun* one more than six. □ **seventh** *adjective & noun*.

seventeen /sevən'ti:n/ *adjective & noun* one more than sixteen. □ **seventeenth** *adjective & noun*.

seventy /'sevəntɪ/ *adjective & noun* (*plural* **-ies**) seven times ten. □ **seventieth** *adjective & noun*.

sever /'sevə/ *verb* divide, break, or make separate, esp. by cutting.

several /'sevr(ə)l/ ● *adjective* a few; quite a large number; *formal* separate, respective. ● *pronoun* a few; quite a large number. □ **severally** *adverb*.

severance /'sevr(ə)ns/ *noun* severing; severed state. □ **severance pay** payment to employee on termination of contract.

severe /sɪ'vɪə/ *adjective* rigorous and harsh; not negligible, worrying; forceful; extreme; exacting; unadorned. □ **severely** *adverb*; **severity** /-'ver-/ *noun*.

sew /səʊ/ *verb* (*past participle* **sewn** or **sewed**) fasten, join, etc. with needle and thread or sewing machine. □ **sewing machine** machine for sewing or stitching.

sewage /'su:ɪdʒ/ *noun* waste matter carried in sewers. □ **sewage farm**, **works** place where sewage is treated.

sewer /'su:ə/ *noun* (usually underground) conduit for carrying off drainage water and waste matter.

sewerage /'su:ərɪdʒ/ *noun* system of or drainage by sewers.

sewing /'səʊɪŋ/ *noun* material or work to be sewn.

sewn *past participle* of SEW.

sex ● *noun* group of males or females collectively; fact of belonging to either group; sexual instincts, desires, activity, etc.; *colloquial* sexual intercourse. ● *adjective* of or relating to sex or sexual differences. ● *verb* determine sex of; (as **sexed** *adjective*) having specified sexual appetite. □ **sex appeal** sexual

attractiveness; **sex life** person's sexual activity; **sex symbol** person famed for sex appeal.

sexagenarian /seksədʒɪ'neərɪən/ *noun* person between 60 and 69 years old.

Sexagesima /seksə'dʒesɪmə/ *noun* second Sunday before Lent.

sexism *noun* prejudice or discrimination against people (esp. women) because of their sex. □ **sexist** *adjective & noun*.

sexless *adjective* neither male nor female; lacking sexual desire or attractiveness.

sextant /'sekst(ə)nt/ *noun* optical instrument for measuring angle between distant objects, esp. sun and horizon in navigation.

sextet /seks'tet/ *noun* musical composition for 6 performers; the performers; any group of 6.

sexton /'sekst(ə)n/ *noun* person who looks after church and churchyard, often acting as bell-ringer and gravedigger.

sextuple /'sekstjʊ:p(ə)l/ *adjective* sixfold.

sextuplet /'sekstjʊplɪt/ *noun* each of 6 children born at one birth.

sexual /'sekʃʊəl/ *adjective* of sex, the sexes, or relations between them. □ **sexual intercourse** insertion of man's penis into woman's vagina. □ **sexuality** /-'æl-/ *noun*; **sexually** *adverb*.

sexy *adjective* (**-ier**, **-iest**) sexually attractive or provocative; *colloquial* (of project etc.) exciting. □ **sexily** *adverb*; **sexiness** *noun*.

SF *abbreviation* science fiction.

Sgt. *abbreviation* Sergeant.

sh *interjection* hush.

shabby /'ʃæbɪ/ *adjective* (**-ier**, **-iest**) faded and worn, dingy, dilapidated; poorly dressed; contemptible. □ **shabbily** *adverb*; **shabbiness** *noun*.

shack ● *noun* roughly built hut or cabin. ● *verb* (+ *up*) *slang* cohabit.

shackle /'ʃæk(ə)l/ ● *noun* metal loop or link closed by bolt, coupling link; fetter; (usually in *plural*) restraint. ● *verb* (**-ling**) fetter, impede, restrain.

shad *noun* (*plural* same or **-s**) large edible marine fish.

shade ● *noun* comparative darkness caused by shelter from direct light and heat; area so sheltered; darker part of picture etc.; a colour, esp. as darker or lighter than one similar; comparative obscurity; slight amount; lampshade; screen moderating light; (in *plural*) *esp. US colloquial* sunglasses; *literary* ghost; (in *plural*; + *of*) reminder of. ● *verb* (**-ding**) screen from light; cover or moderate light of; darken, esp. with parallel lines to represent shadow etc.; (often + *away, off, into*) pass or change gradually. □ **shading** *noun*.

shadow /'ʃædəʊ/ ● *noun* shade; patch of shade; dark shape projected by body blocking out light; inseparable attendant or companion; person secretly following another; (with negative) slightest trace; insubstantial remnant; shaded part of picture; gloom, sadness. ● *verb* cast shadow over; secretly follow and watch. □ **shadow-boxing** boxing against imaginary opponent; **Shadow Cabinet**, **Minister**, etc., members of opposition party holding posts parallel to those of government. □ **shadowy** *adjective*.

shady /'ʃeɪdɪ/ *adjective* (**-ier**, **-iest**) giving or situated in shade; disreputable, of doubtful honesty.

shaft /ʃɑ:ft/ *noun* narrow usually vertical space for access to mine or (in building) for lift, ventilation, etc.; (+ *of*) ray of (light), stroke of (lightning); handle of tool etc.; long narrow part supporting, connecting, or driving thicker part(s) etc.; *archaic* arrow, spear, its long slender stem; hurtful or provocative remark;

each of pair of poles between which horse is harnessed to vehicle; central stem of feather; column, esp. between base and capital.

shag ● *noun* coarse tobacco; rough mass of hair; (crested) cormorant. ● *adjective* (of carpet) with long rough pile.

shaggy *adjective* (**-ier**, **-iest**) hairy, rough-haired; tangled. □ **shaggy-dog story** lengthy 'joke' without funny ending. □ **shagginess** *noun*.

shagreen /ʃæˈɡriːn/ *noun* kind of untanned granulated leather; sharkskin.

shah /ʃɑː/ *noun* historical ruler of Iran.

shake ● *verb* (**-king**; *past* **shook** /ʃʊk/; *past participle* **shaken**) move violently or quickly up and down or to and fro; (cause to) tremble or vibrate; agitate, shock, disturb; weaken, impair; *colloquial* shake hands. ● *noun* shaking, being shaken; jerk, shock; (**the shakes**) *colloquial* fit of trembling. □ **shake down** settle or cause to fall by shaking, become comfortably settled or established; **shake hands** (often + **with**) clasp hands, esp. at meeting or parting or as sign of bargain; **shake off** get rid of, evade; **shake up** mix (ingredients) or restore to shape by shaking, disturb or make uncomfortable, rouse from lethargy etc.; **shake-up** upheaval, reorganization.

shaker *noun* person or thing that shakes; container for shaking together ingredients of cocktails etc.

Shakespearian /ʃeɪkˈspɪəriən/ *adjective* (also **Shakespearean**) of Shakespeare.

shako /ˈʃækəʊ/ *noun* (*plural* **-s**) cylindrical plumed military peaked cap.

shaky *adjective* (**-ier**, **-iest**) unsteady, trembling; infirm; unreliable. □ **shakily** *adverb*; **shakiness** *noun*.

shale *noun* soft rock that splits easily. □ **shaly** *adjective*.

shall *auxiliary verb* (*3rd singular present* **shall**) *used to form future tenses.*

shallot /ʃəˈlɒt/ *noun* onion-like plant with cluster of small bulbs.

shallow /ˈʃæləʊ/ ● *adjective* having little depth; superficial, trivial. ● *noun* (often in *plural*) shallow place. □ **shallowness** *noun*.

sham ● *verb* (**-mm-**) feign; pretend (to be). ● *noun* imposture, pretence; bogus or false person or thing. ● *adjective* pretended, counterfeit.

shamble /ˈʃæmb(ə)l/ ● *verb* (**-ling**) walk or run awkwardly, dragging feet. ● *noun* shambling gait.

shambles *plural noun* (usually treated as *singular*) *colloquial* mess, muddle; butcher's slaughterhouse; scene of carnage.

shambolic /ʃæmˈbɒlɪk/ *adjective colloquial* chaotic, disorganized.

shame ● *noun* humiliation caused by consciousness of guilt or folly; capacity for feeling this; state of disgrace or discredit; person or thing that brings disgrace etc.; wrong or regrettable thing. ● *verb* (**-ming**) bring disgrace on, make ashamed; (+ **into**, **out of**) force by shame into or out of. □ **shamefaced** showing shame, bashful.

shameful *adjective* disgraceful, scandalous. □ **shamefully** *adverb*; **shamefulness** *noun*.

shameless *adjective* having or showing no shame; impudent. □ **shamelessly** *adverb*.

shammy /ˈʃæmɪ/ *noun* (*plural* **-ies**) *colloquial* chamois leather.

shampoo /ʃæmˈpuː/ ● *noun* liquid for washing hair; similar substance for washing cars, carpets, etc. ● *verb* (**-poos**, **-pooed**) wash with shampoo.

shamrock /ˈʃæmrɒk/ *noun* trefoil, as national emblem of Ireland.

shandy /ˈʃændɪ/ *noun* (*plural* **-ies**) beer with lemonade or ginger beer.

shanghai /ʃæŋˈhaɪ/ *verb* (**-hais**, **-haied**, **-haiing**) *colloquial* trick or force (person) to do something, esp. be sailor.

shank *noun* leg, lower part of leg; shaft or stem, esp. joining tool's handle to its working end.

shan't /ʃɑːnt/ shall not.

shantung /ʃænˈtʌŋ/ *noun* soft undressed Chinese silk.

shanty[1] /ˈʃæntɪ/ *noun* (*plural* **-ies**) hut, cabin. □ **shanty town** area with makeshift housing.

shanty[2] /ˈʃæntɪ/ *noun* (*plural* **-ies**) (in full **sea shanty**) sailors' work song.

shape ● *noun* outline; form; specific form or guise; good or specified condition; person or thing seen indistinctly; mould, pattern. ● *verb* (**-ping**) give a certain form to, fashion, create; influence; (usually + **up**) show promise; (+ **to**) make conform to. □ **take shape** assume distinct form, develop.

shapeless *adjective* lacking definite or attractive shape. □ **shapelessness** *noun*.

shapely *adjective* (**-ier**, **-iest**) of pleasing shape, well-proportioned. □ **shapeliness** *noun*.

shard *noun* broken fragment of pottery, glass, etc.

share[1] /ʃeə/ ● *noun* portion of whole given to or taken from person; each of equal parts into which company's capital is divided, entitling owner to proportion of profits. ● *verb* (**-ring**) have or use with another or others; get, have, or give share of; (+ **in**) participate in; (+ **out**) divide and distribute. □ **shareholder** owner of shares in a company; **shareout** division and distribution.

shark *noun* large voracious sea fish; *colloquial* swindler, extortioner. □ **sharkskin** skin of shark, smooth slightly shiny fabric.

sharp ● *adjective* having edge or point able to cut or pierce; tapering to a point or edge; abrupt, steep, angular; well-defined; severe, intense; pungent, acid; shrill, piercing; harsh; acute, sensitive, clever; unscrupulous; vigorous, brisk; *Music* above true pitch, a semitone higher than note named. ● *noun Music* sharp note; sign (♯) indicating this; *colloquial* swindler, cheat. ● *adverb* punctually; suddenly; at a sharp angle; *Music* above true pitch. □ **sharp practice** barely honest dealings; **sharpshooter** skilled marksman; **sharp-witted** keenly perceptive or intelligent. □ **sharpen** *verb*; **sharpener** *noun*; **sharply** *adverb*; **sharpness** *noun*.

sharper *noun* swindler, esp. at cards.

shatter /ˈʃætə/ *verb* break suddenly in pieces; severely damage, destroy; (esp. in *passive*) severely upset; (usually as **shattered** *adjective*) *colloquial* exhaust.

shave ● *verb* (**-ving**); *past participle* **shaved** or (as *adjective*) **shaven**) remove (hair, bristles) with razor; remove hair with razor from (leg, head, etc.) or from face of (person); reduce by small amount; pare (wood etc.) to shape it; miss or pass narrowly. ● *noun* shaving, being shaved; narrow miss or escape.

shaver *noun* thing that shaves; electric razor; *colloquial* young lad.

shaving *noun* (esp. in *plural*) thin paring of wood.

shawl *noun* large usually rectangular piece of fabric worn over shoulders etc. or wrapped round baby.

she *pronoun* (as subject of verb) the female person or animal in question.

s/he *pronoun: written representation of* 'he or she'.

sheaf *noun* (*plural* **sheaves**) bundle of things laid lengthways together and usually tied, esp. reaped corn or collection of papers. ● *verb* make into sheaves.

shear ● *verb* (*past* **sheared**; *past participle* **shorn** or **sheared**) clip wool off (sheep etc.); remove by cutting; cut with scissors, shears, etc.; strip bare, deprive; (often + *of*) distort, be distorted, or break. ● *noun* strain produced by pressure in structure of substance; (in *plural*) (also **pair of shears** *singular*) scissor-shaped clipping or cutting instrument. □ **shearer** *noun*.

sheath /ʃiːθ/ *noun* (*plural* **-s** /ʃiːðz/) close-fitting cover, esp. for blade; condom. □ **sheath knife** dagger-like knife carried in sheath.

sheathe /ʃiːð/ *verb* (**-thing**) put into sheath; encase or protect with sheath.

sheaves *plural of* SHEAF.

shebeen /ʃɪˈbiːn/ *noun esp. Irish* unlicensed drinking place.

shed¹ *noun* one-storeyed building for storage or shelter or as workshop etc.

shed² *verb* (**-dd-**; *past & past participle* **shed**) let, or cause to, fall off; take off (clothes); reduce (electrical power load); cause to fall or flow; disperse, diffuse, radiate; get rid of.

she'd /ʃiːd/ she had; she would.

sheen *noun* lustre, brightness.

sheep *noun* (*plural* same) mammal with thick woolly coat, esp. kept for its wool or meat; timid, silly, or easily-led person; (usually in *plural*) member of minister's congregation. □ **sheep-dip** preparation or place for cleansing sheep of vermin etc.; **sheepdog** dog trained to guard and herd sheep, dog of breed suitable for this; **sheepfold** enclosure for sheep; **sheepshank** knot for temporarily shortening rope; **sheepskin** sheep's skin with wool on.

sheepish *adjective* embarrassed or shy; ashamed. □ **sheepishly** *adverb*.

sheer¹ ● *adjective* mere, complete; (of cliff etc.) perpendicular; (of textile) diaphanous. ● *adverb* directly, perpendicularly.

sheer² *verb* swerve or change course; (often + *away*, *off*) turn away, esp. from person that one dislikes or fears.

sheet¹ ● *noun* rectangular piece of cotton etc. as part of bedclothes; broad thin flat piece of paper, metal, etc.; wide expanse of water, ice, flame, etc. ● *verb* cover (as) with sheet; (of rain etc.) fall in sheets. □ **sheet metal** metal rolled or hammered etc. into thin sheets; **sheet music** music published in separate sheets.

sheet² *noun* rope at lower corner of sail to control it. □ **sheet anchor** emergency anchor, person or thing depended on as last hope.

sheikh /ʃeɪk/ *noun* chief or head of Arab tribe, family, or village; Muslim leader.

sheila /ˈʃiːlə/ *noun Australian & NZ offensive slang* girl, young woman.

shekel /ˈʃek(ə)l/ *noun* chief monetary unit of Israel; *historical* weight and coin in ancient Israel etc.; (in *plural*) *colloquial* money.

shelduck /ˈʃeldʌk/ *noun* (*plural* same or **-s**; *masculine* **sheldrake**, *plural* same or **-s**) brightly coloured wild duck.

shelf *noun* (*plural* **shelves**) wooden etc. board projecting from wall or forming part of bookcase or cupboard; ledge on cliff face etc.; reef, sandbank. □ **on the shelf** (of woman) considered past marriageable age, put aside; **shelf-life** time for which stored thing remains usable; **shelf-mark** code on book to show its place in library.

shell ● *noun* hard outer case of many molluscs, tortoise, egg, nut-kernel, seed, etc.; explosive artillery projectile; hollow container for fireworks, cartridges, etc.; light racing boat; framework of vehicle etc.; walls of unfinished or gutted building etc. ● *verb* remove shell or pod from; fire shells at. □ **come out of one's shell** become less shy; **shellfish** aquatic mollusc with shell, crustacean; **shell out** *colloquial* pay (money); **shell-shock** nervous breakdown caused by warfare; **shell-shocked** *adjective* □ **shell-like** *adjective*.

she'll /ʃiːl/ she will; she shall.

shellac /ʃəˈlæk/ ● *noun* resin used for making varnish. ● *verb* (**-ck-**) varnish with shellac.

shelter /ˈʃeltə/ ● *noun* protection from danger, bad weather, etc.; place providing this. ● *verb* act or serve as shelter to; shield; take shelter.

shelve *verb* (**-ving**) put aside, esp. temporarily; put on shelf; provide with shelves; (of ground) slope.

shelving *noun* shelves; material for shelves.

shepherd /ˈʃepəd/ ● *noun* (*feminine* **shepherdess**) person who tends sheep; pastor. ● *verb* tend (sheep); marshal or guide like sheep. □ **shepherd's pie** minced meat baked with covering of (esp. mashed) potato.

sherbet /ˈʃɜːbət/ *noun* flavoured effervescent powder or drink.

sherd *noun* potsherd.

sheriff /ˈʃerɪf/ *noun* (also **High Sheriff**) chief executive officer of Crown in county, administering justice etc.; *US* chief law-enforcing officer of county; (also **sheriff-depute**) *Scottish* chief judge of county or district.

sherry /ˈʃerɪ/ *noun* (*plural* **-ies**) fortified wine originally from Spain.

she's /ʃiːz/ she is; she has.

Shetland pony /ˈʃetlənd/ *noun* pony of small hardy breed.

shew *archaic* = SHOW.

shiatsu /ʃɪˈætsuː/ *noun* Japanese therapy involving pressure on specific points of body.

shibboleth /ˈʃɪbəleθ/ *noun* long-standing formula, doctrine, phrase, etc. espoused by party or sect.

shied *past & past participle of* SHY².

shield /ʃiːld/ ● *noun* piece of defensive armour held in front of body when fighting; person or thing giving protection; shield-shaped trophy; protective plate or screen in machinery etc.; representation of shield for displaying person's coat of arms. ● *verb* protect, screen.

shier *comparative of* SHY¹.

shiest *superlative of* SHY¹.

shift ● *verb* (cause to) change or move from one position to another; remove, esp. with effort; *slang* hurry; *US* change (gear). ● *noun* shifting; relay of workers; period for which they work; device, expedient, trick; woman's loose straight dress; displacement of spectral line; key on keyboard for switching between lower and upper case etc.; *US* gear lever in motor vehicle. □ **make shift** manage, get along; **shift for oneself** rely on one's own efforts; **shift one's ground** alter stance in argument etc.

shiftless *adjective* lacking resourcefulness; lazy.

shifty *adjective* (**-ier**, **-iest**) *colloquial* evasive, deceitful.

Shiite /ˈʃiːaɪt/ *noun* member of esp. Iranian branch of Islam opposed to Sunnis. ● *adjective* of this branch.

shillelagh /ʃɪˈleɪlɪ/ *noun* Irish cudgel.

shilling /ˈʃɪlɪŋ/ *noun historical* former British coin and monetary unit, worth 1/20 of pound; monetary unit in some other countries.

shilly-shally /ˈʃɪlɪʃælɪ/ *verb* (**-ies**, **-ied**) be undecided, vacillate.

shimmer /ˈʃɪmə/ ● *verb* shine tremulously or faintly. ● *noun* tremulous or faint light.

shin ● *noun* front of leg below knee; cut of beef from this part. ● *verb* (**-nn-**) (usually + *up*, *down*) climb quickly using arms and legs. □ **shin-bone** tibia.

shindig /ˈʃɪndɪg/ noun (also **shindy**) colloquial lively noisy party; brawl, disturbance.

shine ● verb (**-ning**; past & past participle **shone** /ʃɒn/ or **shined**) emit or reflect light, be bright, glow; (of sun, star, etc.) be visible; cause to shine; be brilliant, excel; (past & past participle **shined**) polish. ● noun light, brightness; polish, lustre. □ **take a shine to** colloquial take a liking to.

shiner noun colloquial black eye.

shingle[1] /ˈʃɪŋg(ə)l/ noun small rounded pebbles on seashore. □ **shingly** adjective.

shingle[2] /ˈʃɪŋg(ə)l/ noun rectangular wooden tile used on roofs etc.; archaic shingled hair. ● verb (**-ling**) roof with shingles; archaic cut (woman's hair) short and tapering.

shingles /ˈʃɪŋg(ə)lz/ plural noun (usually treated as singular) painful viral infection of nerves with rash, esp. round waist.

Shinto /ˈʃɪntəʊ/ noun (also **Shintoism**) Japanese religion with worship of ancestors and nature-spirits.

shinty /ˈʃɪntɪ/ noun (plural **-ies**) game resembling hockey; stick or ball for this.

shiny adjective (**-ier, -iest**) having shine; (of clothing) with nap worn off.

ship ● noun large seagoing vessel; US aircraft; spaceship. ● verb (**-pp-**) transport, esp. in ship; take in (water) over ship's side etc.; lay (oars) at bottom of boat; fix (rudder etc.) in place; embark; be hired to work on ship. □ **shipmate** fellow member of ship's crew; **ship off** send away; **shipshape** trim, neat, tidy; **shipwreck** noun destruction of ship by storm or collision etc., ship so destroyed, verb (usually in passive) cause to suffer this; **shipwright** shipbuilder, ship's carpenter; **shipyard** place where ships are built.

shipment noun goods shipped; act of shipping goods etc.

shipper noun person or company that ships goods.

shipping noun transport of goods etc.; ships collectively.

shire /ʃaɪə/ noun county. □ **shire horse** heavy powerful horse.

shirk verb avoid (duty, work, etc.). □ **shirker** noun.

shirr ● noun elasticated gathered threads forming smocking. ● verb gather (material) with parallel threads. □ **shirring** noun.

shirt noun upper-body garment of cotton etc., usually with sleeves and collar. □ **in shirtsleeves** not wearing jacket; **shirt dress**, **shirtwaister** dress with bodice like shirt.

shirty adjective (**-ier, -iest**) colloquial annoyed. □ **shirtily** adverb; **shirtiness** noun.

shish kebab /ʃɪʃ/ noun pieces of meat and vegetables grilled on skewer.

shiver[1] /ˈʃɪvə/ ● verb tremble with cold, fear, etc. ● noun momentary shivering movement; (**the shivers**) attack of shivering. □ **shivery** adjective.

shiver[2] /ˈʃɪvə/ ● noun (esp. in plural) small fragment, splinter. ● verb break into shivers.

shoal[1] ● noun multitude, esp. of fish swimming together. ● verb form shoal(s).

shoal[2] ● noun area of shallow water; submerged sandbank. ● verb (of water) become shallow.

shock[1] ● noun violent collision, impact, etc.; sudden and disturbing emotional effect; acute prostration following wound, pain, etc.; electric shock; disturbance in stability of organization etc. ● verb horrify, outrage; cause shock; affect with electric or pathological shock. □ **shock absorber** device on vehicle etc. for absorbing shock and vibration; **shockproof** resistant to effects of shock; **shock therapy** electroconvulsive therapy; **shock wave** moving region of high air pressure caused by explosion etc.

shock[2] noun unkempt or shaggy mass of hair.

shocker noun colloquial shocking person or thing; sensational novel etc.

shocking adjective causing shock, scandalous; colloquial very bad. ● **shocking pink** vibrant shade of pink. □ **shockingly** adverb.

shod past & past participle of SHOE.

shoddy /ˈʃɒdɪ/ adjective (**-ier, -iest**) poorly made; counterfeit. □ **shoddily** adverb; **shoddiness** noun.

shoe /ʃuː/ ● noun foot-covering of leather etc., esp. one not reaching above ankle; protective metal rim for horse's hoof; thing like shoe in shape or use. ● verb (**shoes, shoeing**; past & past participle **shod**) fit with shoe(s). □ **-shod** having shoes of specified kind; **shoehorn** curved implement for easing heel into shoe; **shoelace** cord for lacing shoe; **shoestring** shoelace, colloquial small esp. inadequate amount of money; **shoe-tree** shaped block for keeping shoe in shape.

shone past & past participle of SHINE.

shoo ● interjection used to frighten animals etc. away. ● verb (**shoos, shooed**) utter such sound; (usually + away) drive away thus.

shook past of SHAKE.

shoot /ʃuːt/ ● verb (past & past participle **shot**) cause (weapon) to discharge missile; kill or wound with bullet, arrow, etc.; send out or discharge rapidly; come or go swiftly or suddenly; (of plant) put forth buds etc., (of bud etc.) appear; hunt game etc. with gun; film, photograph; Football score or take shot at (goal); (often + up) slang inject (drug). ● noun young branch or sucker; hunting party or expedition; land on which game is shot. □ **shooting gallery** place for shooting at targets with rifles etc.; **shooting star** small rapidly moving meteor; **shooting stick** walking stick with foldable seat.

shop ● noun place for retail sale of goods or services; act of shopping; place for making or repairing something; colloquial place of business etc. ● verb (**-pp-**) go to shop(s) to make purchases; slang inform against. □ **shop around** look for best bargain; **shop assistant** person serving in shop; **shop-floor** production area in factory etc., workers as distinct from management; **shopkeeper** owner or manager of shop; **shoplift** steal goods while appearing to shop; **shoplifter** noun; **shop-soiled** soiled or faded by display in shop; **shop steward** elected representative of workers in factory etc.; **shopwalker** supervisor in large shop; **talk shop** talk about one's occupation. □ **shopper** noun.

shopping noun purchase of goods; goods bought. □ **shopping centre** area containing many shops.

shore[1] ● noun land adjoining sea, lake, etc.; (usually in plural) country. □ **on shore** ashore; **shoreline** line where shore meets water.

shore[2] verb (**-ring**) (often + up) support (as if) with prop(s) or beam(s).

shorn past participle of SHEAR.

short ● adjective measuring little from end to end in space or time, or from head to foot; (usually + of, on) deficient, scanty; concise, brief; curt, uncivil; (of memory) unable to remember distant events; (of vowel or syllable) having the lesser of two recognized durations; (of pastry) easily crumbled; (of a drink of spirits) undiluted. ● adverb before the natural or expected time or place; abruptly; rudely. ● noun short circuit; colloquial short drink; short film. ● verb short-circuit. □ **short back and sides** short simple haircut; **shortbread**, **shortcake** rich crumbly biscuit or cake made of flour, butter, and sugar; **shortchange** cheat, esp. by giving insufficient change;

short circuit electric circuit through small resistance, esp. instead of through normal circuit; **short-circuit** cause short circuit in, have short circuit, shorten or avoid by taking short cut; **shortcoming** deficiency, defect; **short cut** path or course shorter than usual or normal; **shortfall** deficit; **shorthand** method of rapid writing using special symbols, abbreviated or symbolic means of expression; **short-handed, -staffed** understaffed; **shorthorn** animal of breed of cattle with short horns; **short list** list of candidates from whom final selection will be made; **short-list** put on short list; **short-lived** ephemeral; **short-range** having short range, relating to immediate future; **short shrift** curt or dismissive treatment; **short sight** inability to focus except at close range; **short-tempered** easily angered; **short-term** of or for a short period of time; **short-winded** easily becoming breathless. □ **shorten** verb.

shortage noun (often + of) deficiency; lack.

shortening noun fat for pastry.

shortly adverb (often + before, after) soon; curtly.

shorts plural noun trousers reaching to knees or higher; US underpants.

short-sighted adjective having short sight; lacking imagination or foresight. □ **short-sightedly** adverb; **shortsightedness** noun.

shot[1] noun firing of gun etc.; attempt to hit by shooting or throwing etc.; single missile for gun etc.; (plural same or **-s**) small lead pellet of which several are used for single charge; (treated as plural) these collectively; photograph, film sequence; stroke or kick in ball game; colloquial attempt, guess; person of specified skill in shooting; heavy metal ball thrown in shot-put; colloquial drink of spirits; injection of drug etc. □ **shotgun** gun for firing small shot at short range; **shotgun wedding** colloquial wedding enforced because of bride's pregnancy; **shot-put** athletic contest in which shot is thrown; **shot-putter** noun.

shot[2] ● past & past participle of SHOOT. ● adjective woven so as to show different colours at different angles.

should /ʃʊd/ auxiliary verb (3rd singular present **should**) used in reported speech; expressing obligation, likelihood, or tentative suggestion; used to form conditional clause or (in 1st person) conditional mood.

shoulder /ˈʃəʊldə/ ● noun part of body to which arm, foreleg, or wing is attached; either of two projections below neck; animal's upper foreleg as joint of meat; (also in plural) shoulder regarded as supportive, comforting, etc.; strip of land next to road; part of garment covering shoulder. ● verb push with shoulder; make one's way thus; take on (burden, responsibility, etc.). □ **shoulder blade** either flat bone of upper back; **shoulder-length** (of hair etc.) reaching to shoulders; **shoulder pad** pad in garment to bulk out shoulder; **shoulder strap** strap going over shoulder from front to back of garment, strap suspending bag etc. from shoulder.

shouldn't /ˈʃʊd(ə)nt/ should not.

shout /ʃaʊt/ ● verb speak or cry loudly; say or express loudly. ● noun loud cry calling attention to or expressing joy, defiance, approval, etc. □ **shout down** reduce to silence by shouting.

shove /ʃʌv/ ● verb (-**ving**) push, esp. vigorously or roughly; colloquial put casually. ● noun act of shoving. □ **shove-halfpenny** form of shoveboard played with coins etc. on table; **shove off** start from shore, mooring, etc.; colloquial in boat, slang depart.

shovel /ˈʃʌv(ə)l/ ● noun spadelike scoop used to shift earth or coal etc. ● verb (-**ll**-; US -**l**-) move (as) with shovel. □ **shovelboard** game played esp. on ship's deck by pushing discs over marked surface.

shoveller /ˈʃʌvələ/ noun (also **shoveler**) duck with shovel-like beak.

show /ʃəʊ/ ● verb (past participle **shown** or **showed**) be, or allow or cause to be, seen; manifest; offer for inspection; express (one's feelings); accord, grant (favour, mercy, etc.); (of feelings etc.) be manifest; instruct by example; demonstrate, make understood; exhibit; (often + in, round, etc.) conduct, lead; colloquial appear, arrive. ● noun showing; spectacle, exhibition, display; public entertainment or performance; outward appearance, impression produced; ostentation, mere display; colloquial undertaking, business. □ **good** (or **bad** or **poor**) **show!** colloquial that was well (or badly) done; **showbiz** colloquial show business; **show business** colloquial the entertainment profession; **showcase** glass case or event etc. for displaying goods or exhibits; **showdown** final test or confrontation; **show house, flat** furnished and decorated new house or flat on show to prospective buyers; **showjumping** competitive jumping on horseback; **show off** display to advantage, colloquial act pretentiously; **show-off** colloquial person who shows off; **show-piece** excellent specimen suitable for display; **showroom** room where goods are displayed for sale; **show trial** judicial trial designed to frighten or impress the public; **show up** make or be visible or conspicuous, expose, humiliate, colloquial appear or arrive; **show willing** show willingness to help etc.

shower /ˈʃaʊə/ ● noun brief fall of rain, snow, etc.; brisk flurry of bullets, dust, etc.; sudden copious arrival of gifts, honours, etc.; (in full **shower-bath**) bath in which water is sprayed from above. ● verb descend, send, or give in shower; take shower-bath; (+ upon, with) bestow lavishly. □ **showery** adjective.

showing noun display; quality of performance, achievement, etc.; evidence; putting of case etc.

shown past participle of SHOW.

showy adjective (-**ier**, -**iest**) gaudy; striking. □ **showily** adverb; **showiness** noun.

shrank past of SHRINK.

shrapnel /ˈʃræpn(ə)l/ noun fragments of exploded bomb etc.

shred ● noun scrap, fragment; least amount. ● verb (-**dd**-) tear, cut, etc. to shreds. □ **shredder** noun.

shrew noun small long-snouted mouse-like animal; bad-tempered or scolding woman. □ **shrewish** adjective.

shrewd adjective astute; clever. □ **shrewdly** adverb; **shrewdness** noun.

shriek ● noun shrill cry or sound. ● verb make a shriek; say in shrill tones.

shrike noun bird with strong hooked beak.

shrill ● adjective piercing and high-pitched. ● verb sound or utter shrilly. □ **shrillness** noun; **shrilly** adverb.

shrimp noun (plural same or -**s**) small edible crustacean; colloquial very small person.

shrine noun sacred or revered place; casket or tomb holding relics.

shrink ● verb (past **shrank**; past participle **shrunk** or (esp. as adjective) **shrunken**) become or make smaller, esp. by action of moisture, heat, or cold; (usually + from) recoil, flinch. ● noun slang psychiatrist. □ **shrink-wrap** wrap (article) in material that shrinks tightly round it.

shrinkage noun process or degree of shrinking; allowance for loss by theft or wastage.

shrivel /ˈʃrɪv(ə)l/ verb (-**ll**-; US -**l**-) contract into wrinkled or dried-up state.

shroud /ʃraʊd/ ● noun wrapping for corpse; something which conceals; rope supporting mast. ● verb clothe (corpse) for burial; cover, disguise.

Shrove Tuesday /ʃrəʊv/ noun day before Ash Wednesday.

shrub *noun* woody plant smaller than tree and usually branching from near ground. □ **shrubby** *adjective*.

shrubbery *noun* (*plural* **-ies**) area planted with shrubs.

shrug ● *verb* (**-gg-**) draw up (shoulders) momentarily as gesture of indifference, ignorance, etc. ● *noun* shrugging movement.

shrunk (also **shrunken**) *past participle* of SHRINK.

shudder ● *verb* shiver from fear, cold, etc.; feel strong repugnance, fear, etc.; vibrate. ● *noun* act of shuddering.

shuffle /'ʃʌf(ə)l/ ● *verb* (**-ling**) drag or slide (feet) in walking; mix up or rearrange (esp. cards); be evasive; keep shifting one's position. ● *noun* shuffling action or movement; change of relative positions; shuffling dance. □ **shuffle off** remove, get rid of.

shufti /'ʃʊftɪ/ *noun* (*plural* **-s**) *colloquial* look, glimpse.

shun *verb* (**-nn-**) avoid, keep clear of.

shunt ● *verb* move (train etc.) to another track; (of train) be shunted; redirect. ● *noun* shunting, being shunted; conductor joining two points in electric circuit for diversion of current; *slang* collision of vehicles.

shush /ʃʊʃ/ *interjection & verb* hush.

shut *verb* (**-tt-**; *past & past participle* **shut**) move (door, window, lid, etc.) into position to block opening; become or be capable of being shut; shut door etc. of; become or make closed for trade; fold or contract (book, hand, telescope); bar access to (place). □ **shut down** close, cease working; **shut-eye** *colloquial* sleep; **shut off** stop flow of (water, gas, etc.), separate; **shut out** exclude, screen from view, prevent; **shut up** close all doors and windows of, imprison, put away in box etc., (esp. in *imperative*) *colloquial* stop talking.

shutter ● *noun* movable hinged cover for window; device for exposing film in camera. ● *verb* provide or close with shutter(s).

shuttle /'ʃʌt(ə)l/ ● *noun* part of loom which carries weft-thread between threads of warp; thread-carrier for lower thread in sewing machine; train, bus, aircraft, etc. used in shuttle service; space shuttle. ● *verb* (**-ling**) (cause to) move to and fro like shuttle. □ **shuttlecock** cork with ring of feathers, or similar plastic device, struck to and fro in badminton; **shuttle diplomacy** negotiations conducted by mediator travelling between disputing parties; **shuttle service** transport system operating to and fro over short distance.

shy[1] ● *adjective* (**-er**, **-est**) timid and nervous in company; self-conscious; easily startled. ● *verb* (**shies**, **shied**) (usually + *at*) (esp. of horse) start back or aside in fright. ● *noun* sudden startled movement. □ **-shy** showing fear or dislike of. □ **shyly** *adverb*; **shyness** *noun*.

shy[2] ● *verb* (**shies**, **shied**) throw, fling. ● *noun* (*plural* **shies**) throw, fling.

shyster /'ʃaɪstə/ *noun colloquial* person who acts unscrupulously or unprofessionally.

SI *abbreviation* international system of units of measurement (*Système International*).

si /siː/ *noun* Music te.

Siamese /saɪəˈmiːz/ ● *noun* (*plural* same) native or language of Siam (now Thailand); (in full **Siamese cat**) cat of cream-coloured dark-faced short-haired breed with blue eyes. ● *adjective* of Siam. □ **Siamese twins** twins joined together at birth.

sibilant /'sɪbɪlənt/ ● *adjective* hissing, sounded with hiss. ● *noun* sibilant speech sound or letter. □ **sibilance** *noun*.

sibling /'sɪblɪŋ/ *noun* each of two or more children having one or both parents in common.

sibyl /'sɪbɪl/ *noun* pagan prophetess.

sic *adverb* used or spelt thus (confirming form of quoted words). [Latin]

sick ● *adjective* vomiting, disposed to vomit; *esp. US* ill, unwell; (often + *of*) *colloquial* disgusted, surfeited; *colloquial* (of humour) cruel, morbid, perverted, offensive. ● *noun colloquial* vomit. ● *verb* (esp. + *up*) *colloquial* vomit. □ **sickbay** place for sick people; **sickbed** invalid's bed; **sick leave** leave granted because of illness; **sick pay** pay given during sick leave.

sicken *verb* make or become sick, disgusted, etc.; (often + *for*) show symptoms of illness; (as **sickening** *adjective*) disgusting, *colloquial* very annoying. □ **sickeningly** *adverb*.

sickle /'sɪk(ə)l/ *noun* short-handled implement with semicircular blade for reaping, lopping, etc.

sickly *adjective* (**-ier**, **-iest**) liable to be ill, weak; faint, pale; causing sickness; mawkish, weakly sentimental.

sickness *noun* being ill; disease; vomiting, nausea.

side ● *noun* each of inner or outer surfaces of object, esp. as distinct from top and bottom or front and back or ends; right or left part of person's or animal's body; part of object, place, etc. that faces specified direction or that is on observer's right or left; either surface of thing regarded as having two; aspect of question, character, etc.; each of sets of opponents in war, game, etc.; cause represented by this; part or region near edge; *colloquial* television channel; each of lines bounding triangle, rectangle, etc.; position nearer or farther than, or to right or left of, dividing line; line of descent through father or mother; spinning motion given to ball by striking it on side; *slang* swagger, assumption of superiority. ● *adjective* of, on, from, or to side; oblique, indirect; subordinate, subsidiary, not main. ● *verb* (**-ding**) take side in dispute etc.; (+ *with*) be on or join same side as. □ **on the side** as sideline, illicitly, *US* as side dish; **sideboard** table or flat-topped chest with drawers and cupboards for crockery etc.; **sideboards**, **sideburns** short side-whiskers; **side by side** standing close together, esp. for mutual encouragement; **sidecar** passenger car attached to side of motorcycle; **side drum** small double-headed drum; **side effect** secondary (usually undesirable) effect; **sidekick** *colloquial* close associate; **sidelight** light from side, small light at side of front of vehicle etc.; **sideline** work etc. done in addition to one's main activity, (usually in *plural*) line bounding side of sports pitch etc., space just outside these for spectators to sit; **side-saddle** *noun* saddle for woman riding with both legs on same side of horse, *adverb* sitting thus on horse; **sideshow** minor show or stall in exhibition, fair, etc.; **sidesman** assistant churchwarden; **sidestep** *noun* step taken sideways, *verb* avoid, evade; **sidetrack** divert from course, purpose, etc.; **sidewalk** *US* pavement; **side-whiskers** hair left unshaven on cheeks; **take sides** support either of (usually) two opposing sides in argument etc.

sidelong ● *adjective* directed to the side. ● *adverb* to the side.

sidereal /saɪˈdɪərɪəl/ *adjective* of or measured or determined by stars.

sideways *adverb & adjective* to or from a side; with one side facing forward.

siding *noun* short track by side of railway line for shunting etc.

sidle /'saɪd(ə)l/ *verb* (**-ling**) walk timidly or furtively.

siege /siːdʒ/ *noun* surrounding and blockading of town, castle, etc. □ **lay siege to** conduct siege of; **raise siege** end it.

siemens /'siːmənz/ *noun* (*plural* same) SI unit of electrical conductance.

sienna /sɪˈenə/ noun kind of earth used as pigment; its colour of reddish- or yellowish-brown.

sierra /sɪˈerə/ noun long jagged mountain chain, esp. in Spain or Spanish America.

siesta /sɪˈestə/ noun afternoon nap or rest in hot countries.

sieve /sɪv/ ● noun utensil with network or perforated bottom through which liquids or fine particles can pass. ● verb (**-ving**) sift.

sift verb separate with or cause to pass through sieve; sprinkle through perforated container; closely examine details of, analyse; (of snow, light, etc.) fall as if from sieve.

sigh /saɪ/ ● verb emit long deep audible breath in sadness, weariness, relief, etc.; yearn; express with sighs. ● noun act of sighing; sound (like that) made in sighing.

sight /saɪt/ ● noun faculty of seeing; seeing, being seen; thing seen; range of vision; (usually in plural) notable features of a place; device assisting aim with gun or observation with telescope etc.; aim or observation so gained; colloquial unsightly person or thing; colloquial great deal. ● verb get sight of; observe presence of; aim (gun etc.) with sight. □ **at first sight** on first glimpse or impression; **on, at sight** as soon as person or thing is seen; **sight-read** read (music) at sight; **sight-screen** Cricket large white screen placed near boundary in line with wicket to help batsman see ball; **sightseer** person visiting sights of place; **sightseeing** noun.

sighted adjective not blind. □ **-sighted** having specified vision.

sightless adjective blind.

sign /saɪn/ ● noun indication of quality, state, future event, etc.; mark, symbol, etc.; motion or gesture used to convey information, order, etc.; signboard; each of the 12 divisions of the zodiac. ● verb write one's name on (document etc.) as authorization; write (one's name) thus; communicate by gesture. □ **signboard** board bearing name, symbol, etc. displayed outside shop, inn, etc.; **sign in** sign register on arrival, get (person) admitted by signing register; **sign language** series of signs used esp. by deaf or dumb people for communication; **sign off** end contract, work, etc.; **sign on** register to obtain unemployment benefit; **sign out** sign register on departing; **signpost** noun post etc. showing directions of roads, verb provide with signpost(s); **sign up** engage (person), enlist in armed forces; **signwriter** person who paints signboards etc.

signal[1] /ˈsɪɡn(ə)l/ ● noun sign, esp. prearranged one, conveying information or direction; message of such signs; event which causes immediate activity; Electricity transmitted impulses or radio waves; sequence of these; device on railway giving instructions or warnings to train drivers etc. ● verb (**-ll-**; US **-l-**) make signal(s) (to); (often + to do) transmit, announce, or direct by signal(s). □ **signal-box** building from which railway signals are controlled; **signalman** railway signal operator.

signal[2] /ˈsɪɡn(ə)l/ adjective remarkable, noteworthy. □ **signally** adverb.

signalize verb (also **-ise**) (**-zing** or **-sing**) make conspicuous or remarkable; indicate.

signatory /ˈsɪɡnətərɪ/ ● noun (plural **-ies**) party that has signed an agreement, esp. a treaty. ● adjective having signed such an agreement.

signature /ˈsɪɡnətʃə/ noun person's name or initials used in signing; act of signing; Music key signature, time signature; section of book made from one sheet folded and cut. □ **signature tune** tune used esp. in broadcasting to announce a particular programme, performer, etc.

signet /ˈsɪɡnɪt/ noun small seal. □ **signet ring** ring with seal set in it.

significance /sɪɡˈnɪfɪkəns/ noun importance; meaning; being significant; extent to which result deviates from hypothesis such that difference is due to more than errors in sampling.

significant /sɪɡˈnɪfɪkənt/ adjective having or conveying meaning, important. □ **significant figure** Mathematics digit conveying information about a number containing it. □ **significantly** adverb.

signify /ˈsɪɡnɪfaɪ/ verb (**-ies**, **-ied**) be sign or symbol of; represent, mean, denote; make known; be of importance, matter. □ **signification** noun.

signor /ˈsiːnjɔː/ noun (plural **-i** /-ˈnjɔːriː/) title used of or to Italian man.

signora /siːˈnjɔːrə/ noun title used of or to Italian esp. married woman.

signorina /siːnjəˈriːnə/ noun title used of or to Italian unmarried woman.

Sikh /siːk/ noun member of Indian monotheistic sect.

silage /ˈsaɪlɪdʒ/ noun green fodder stored in silo; storage in silo.

silence /ˈsaɪləns/ ● noun absence of sound; abstinence from speech or noise; neglect or omission to mention, write, etc. ● verb (**-cing**) make silent, esp. by force or superior argument.

silencer noun device for reducing noise made by gun, vehicle's exhaust, etc.

silent /ˈsaɪlənt/ adjective not speaking; making or accompanied by little or no sound. □ **silently** adverb.

silhouette /sɪluˈet/ ● noun dark outline or shadow in profile against lighter background; contour, outline, profile; portrait in profile showing outline only, usually cut from paper or in black on white. ● verb (**-tting**) represent or show in silhouette.

silica /ˈsɪlɪkə/ noun silicon dioxide, occurring as quartz and as main constituent of sand etc. □ **siliceous** /sɪˈlɪʃəs/ adjective.

silicate /ˈsɪlɪkeɪt/ noun compound of metal(s), silicon, and oxygen.

silicon /ˈsɪlɪkən/ noun non-metallic element occurring in silica and silicates. □ **silicon chip** silicon microchip.

silicone /ˈsɪlɪkəʊn/ noun any organic compound of silicon with high resistance to cold, heat, water, etc.

silicosis /sɪlɪˈkəʊsɪs/ noun lung disease caused by inhaling dust containing silica.

silk noun fine strong soft lustrous fibre produced by silkworms; thread or cloth made from this; (in plural) cloth or garments of silk; colloquial Queen's Counsel. □ **silk-screen printing** screen printing; **silkworm** caterpillar which spins cocoon of silk; **take silk** become Queen's Counsel.

silken adjective of or resembling silk; soft, smooth, lustrous.

silky adjective (**-ier**, **-iest**) like silk in smoothness, softness, etc.; suave. □ **silkily** adverb.

sill noun slab of wood, stone, etc. at base of window or doorway.

silly /ˈsɪlɪ/ ● adjective (**-ier**, **-iest**) foolish, imprudent; weak-minded; Cricket (of fielder or position) very close to batsman. ● noun (plural **-ies**) colloquial silly person. □ **silliness** noun.

silo /ˈsaɪləʊ/ noun (plural **-s**) pit or airtight structure in which green crops are stored for fodder; tower or pit for storage of grain, cement, etc.; underground storage chamber for guided missile.

silt ● noun sediment in channel, harbour, etc. ● verb (often + up) block or be blocked with silt.

silvan = SYLVAN.

silver /ˈsɪlvə/ ● noun greyish-white lustrous precious metal; coins or articles made of or looking like this;

colour of silver. ● *adjective* of or coloured like silver. ● *verb* coat or plate with silver; provide (mirror-glass) with backing of tin amalgam etc.; make silvery; turn grey or white. □ **silver birch** common birch with silvery white bark; **silverfish** (*plural* same or **-es**) small silvery wingless insect, silver-coloured fish; **silver jubilee** 25th anniversary of reign; **silver medal** medal awarded as second prize; **silver paper** aluminium foil; **silver plate** articles plated with silver; **silver-plated** plated with silver; **silver sand** fine pure kind used in gardening; **silver screen** (usually **the silver screen**) cinema films collectively; **silverside** upper side of round of beef; **silversmith** worker in silver; **silver wedding** 25th anniversary of wedding.

silvery *adjective* like silver in colour or appearance; having clear soft ringing sound.

simian /ˈsɪmɪən/ ● *adjective* of anthropoid apes; resembling ape, monkey. ● *noun* ape or monkey.

similar /ˈsɪmɪlə/ *adjective* like, alike; (often + *to*) having resemblance. □ **similarity** /-ˈlær-/ *noun* (*plural* **-ies**); **similarly** *adverb*.

simile /ˈsɪmɪlɪ/ *noun* esp. poetical comparison of two things using *like* or *as* (see panel).

similitude /sɪˈmɪlɪtjuːd/ *noun* guise, appearance; comparison or its expression.

simmer /ˈsɪmə/ ● *verb* be or keep just below boiling point; be in state of suppressed anger or laughter. ● *noun* simmering state. □ **simmer down** become less agitated.

simnel cake /ˈsɪmn(ə)l/ *noun* rich fruit cake, usually with almond paste.

simony /ˈsaɪmənɪ/ *noun* buying or selling of ecclesiastical privileges.

simoom /sɪˈmuːm/ *noun* hot dry dust-laden desert wind.

simper /ˈsɪmpə/ ● *verb* smile in silly affected way; utter with simper. ● *noun* such smile.

simple /ˈsɪmp(ə)l/ *adjective* (**-r, -st**) easily understood or done, presenting no difficulty; not complicated or elaborate; plain; not compound or complex; absolute, unqualified, straightforward; foolish, feeble-minded. □ **simple-minded** foolish, feeble-minded. □ **simpleness** *noun*.

simpleton /ˈsɪmpəlt(ə)n/ *noun* stupid or gullible person.

simplicity /sɪmˈplɪsɪtɪ/ *noun* fact or condition of being simple.

simplify /ˈsɪmplɪfaɪ/ *verb* (**-ies, -ied**) make simple or simpler. □ **simplification** *noun*.

simplistic /sɪmˈplɪstɪk/ *adjective* excessively or affectedly simple. □ **simplistically** *adverb*.

simply *adverb* in a simple way; absolutely; merely.

simulate /ˈsɪmjʊleɪt/ *verb* (**-ting**) pretend to be, have, or feel; counterfeit; reproduce conditions of (situation etc.), e.g. for training. □ **simulation** *noun*; **simulator** *noun*.

simultaneous /sɪməlˈteɪnɪəs/ *adjective* (often + *with*) occurring or operating at same time. □ **simultaneity** /-təˈneɪtɪ/ *noun*; **simultaneously** *adverb*.

sin ● *noun* breaking of divine or moral law; offence against good taste etc. ● *verb* (**-nn-**) commit sin; (+ *against*) offend. □ **sinner** *noun*.

since ● *preposition* throughout or within period after. ● *conjunction* during or in time after; because. ● *adverb* from that time or event until now.

sincere /sɪnˈsɪə/ *adjective* (**-r, -st**) free from pretence, genuine, honest, frank. □ **sincerity** /-ˈser-/ *noun*.

sincerely *adverb* in a sincere way. □ **Yours sincerely** *written before signature at end of informal letter.*

sine *noun* ratio of side opposite angle (in right-angled triangle) to hypotenuse.

sinecure /ˈsaɪnɪkjʊə/ *noun* position that requires little or no work but usually yields profit or honour.

sine die /ˈsaɪneɪ ˈdiːeɪ/ *adverb formal* indefinitely. [Latin]

sine qua non /ˈsaɪneɪ kwɑː ˈnəʊn/ *noun* indispensable condition or qualification. [Latin]

sinew /ˈsɪnjuː/ *noun* tough fibrous tissue joining muscle to bone; tendon; (in *plural*) muscles, strength; framework of thing. □ **sinewy** *adjective*.

sinful *adjective* committing or involving sin. □ **sinfully** *adverb*; **sinfulness** *noun*.

sing *verb* (*past* **sang**; *past participle* **sung**) utter musical sounds, esp. words in set tune; utter (song, tune); (of wind, kettle, etc.) hum, buzz, or whistle; *slang* become informer; (+ *of*) *literary* celebrate in verse. □ **sing out** shout; **singsong** *noun* session of informal singing, *adjective* (of voice) monotonously rising and falling. □ **singer** *noun*.

singe /sɪndʒ/ ● *verb* (**-geing**) burn superficially; burn off tips or edges of (esp. hair). ● *noun* superficial burn.

single /ˈsɪŋg(ə)l/ ● *adjective* one only, not double or multiple; united, undivided; of or for one person or thing; solitary; taken separately; unmarried; (with negative or in questions) even one. ● *noun* single thing, esp. room in hotel; (in full **single ticket**) ticket for one-way journey; pop record with one piece of music on each side; *Cricket* hit for one run; (usually in *plural*) game with one player on each side. ● *verb* (**-ling**) (+ *out*) choose for special attention. □ **single-breasted** (of coat etc.) with only one vertical row of buttons, and overlapping little at the front; **single-decker** bus with only one deck; **single file** line of people one behind another; **single-handed** without help; **single-handedly** *adverb*; **single-minded** intent on only one aim; **single parent** parent bringing up child or children alone. □ **singly** /ˈsɪŋglɪ/ *adverb*.

singlet /ˈsɪŋglɪt/ *noun* sleeveless vest.

Simile

A simile is a figure of speech involving the comparison of one thing with another of a different kind, using *as* or *like*, e.g.

> *The water was as clear as glass.*
> *Cherry blossom lay like driven snow upon the lawn.*

Everyday language is rich in similes:

with *as*:	*as like as two peas*	*as poor as a church mouse*
	as strong as an ox	*as rich as Croesus*
with *like*:	*spread like wildfire*	*run like the wind*
	sell like hot cakes	*like a bull in a china shop*

singleton /'sɪŋgəlt(ə)n/ *noun* player's only card of particular suit.

singular /'sɪŋgjʊlə/ ● *adjective* unique; outstanding; extraordinary, strange; *Grammar* denoting one person or thing. ● *noun Grammar* singular word or form. □ **singularity** /-'lær-/ *noun* (*plural* **-ies**); **singularly** *adverb*.

Sinhalese /sɪnhə'liːz/ ● *noun* (*plural* same) member of a people from N. India now forming majority of population of Sri Lanka; their language. ● *adjective* of this people or language.

sinister /'sɪnɪstə/ *adjective* suggestive of evil; wicked, criminal; ominous; *Heraldry* on left side of shield etc. (i.e. to observer's right).

sink ● *verb* (*past* **sank** or **sunk**; *past participle* **sunk** or (as *adjective*) **sunken**) fall or come slowly downwards; disappear below horizon; go or penetrate below surface of liquid; go to bottom of sea etc.; settle down; decline in strength and vitality; descend in pitch or volume; cause or allow to sink or penetrate; cause failure of; dig (well), bore (shaft); engrave (die); invest (money); cause (ball) to enter pocket at billiards or hole at golf etc. ● *noun* plumbed-in basin, esp. in kitchen; place where foul liquid collects; place of vice. □ **sinking fund** money set aside for eventual repayment of debt.

sinker *noun* weight used to sink fishing or sounding line.

Sino- /'saɪnəʊ/ *combining form* Chinese.

sinology /saɪ'nɒlədʒɪ/ *noun* study of China and its language, history, etc. □ **sinologist** *noun*.

sinuous /'sɪnjʊəs/ *adjective* with many curves, undulating. □ **sinuosity** /-'ɒs-/ *noun*.

sinus /'saɪnəs/ *noun* either of cavities in skull communicating with nostrils.

sinusitis /saɪnə'saɪtɪs/ *noun* inflammation of sinus.

sip ● *verb* (**-pp-**) drink in small mouthfuls. ● *noun* small mouthful of liquid; act of taking this.

siphon /'saɪf(ə)n/ ● *noun* tube shaped like inverted V or U with unequal legs, used for transferring liquid from one container to another by atmospheric pressure; bottle from which fizzy water is forced by pressure of gas. ● *verb* (often + *off*) conduct or flow through siphon, divert or set aside (funds etc.).

sir /sɜː/ *noun* polite form of address or reference to a man; (**Sir**) title used before forename of knight or baronet.

sire ● *noun* male parent of animal, esp. stallion; *archaic form of address to king*; *archaic* father or other male ancestor. ● *verb* (**-ring**) beget.

siren /'saɪərən/ *noun* device for making loud prolonged signal or warning sound; *Greek Mythology* woman or winged creature whose singing lured unwary sailors on to rocks; dangerously fascinating woman.

sirloin /'sɜːlɔɪn/ *noun* best part of loin of beef.

sirocco /sɪ'rɒkəʊ/ *noun* (*plural* **-s**) Saharan simoom; hot moist wind in S. Europe.

sisal /'saɪs(ə)l/ *noun* fibre from leaves of agave.

siskin /'sɪskɪn/ *noun* small songbird.

sissy /'sɪsɪ/ (also **cissy**) *colloquial* ● *noun* (*plural* **-ies**) effeminate or cowardly person. ● *adjective* (**-ier**, **-iest**) effeminate; cowardly.

sister /'sɪstə/ *noun* woman or girl in relation to her siblings; female fellow member of trade union, sect, human race, etc.; member of female religious order; senior female nurse. **sister-in-law** (*plural* **sisters-in-law**) husband's or wife's sister, brother's wife. □ **sisterly** *adjective*.

sisterhood *noun* relationship (as) of sisters; society of women bound by monastic vows or devoting themselves to religious or charitable work; community of feeling among women.

sit *verb* (**-tt-**; *past & past participle* **sat**) support body by resting buttocks on ground, seat, etc.; cause to sit; place in sitting position; (of bird) perch or remain on nest to hatch eggs; (of animal) rest with hind legs bent and buttocks on ground; (of parliament, court, etc.) be in session; (usually + *for*) pose (for portrait); (+ *for*) be MP for (constituency); (often + *for*) take (exam). □ **be sitting pretty** be comfortably placed; **sit back** relax one's efforts; **sit down** sit after standing, cause to sit, (+ *under*) suffer tamely (humiliation etc.); **sit in** occupy place as protest; **sit-in** *noun*; **sit in on** be present as guest etc. at (meeting); **sit on** be member of (committee etc.), *colloquial* delay action about, *slang* repress or snub; **sit out** take no part in (dance etc.), stay till end of, sit outdoors; **sit tight** *colloquial* remain firmly in one's place, not yield; **sit up** rise from lying to sitting, sit firmly upright, defer going to bed, *colloquial* become interested, aroused, etc.; **sit-up** physical exercise of sitting up from supine position without using arms or hands.

sitar /'sɪtɑː/ *noun* long-necked Indian lute.

sitcom /'sɪtkɒm/ *noun colloquial* situation comedy.

site ● *noun* ground chosen or used for town or building; ground set apart for some purpose. ● *verb* (**-ting**) locate, place.

sitter *noun* person who sits for portrait etc.; babysitter.

sitting ● *noun* continuous period spent engaged in an activity; time during which assembly is engaged in business; session in which meal is served. ● *adjective* having sat down; (of animal or bird) still; (of MP etc.) current. □ **sitting-room** room in which to sit and relax.

situ see IN SITU.

situate /'sɪtjʊeɪt/ *verb* (**-ting**) (usually in *passive*) place or put in position, situation, etc.

situation *noun* place and its surroundings; circumstances; position; state of affairs; *formal* paid job. □ **situation comedy** broadcast comedy series involving characters dealing with awkward esp. domestic or everyday situations. □ **situational** *adjective*.

six *adjective & noun* one more than five; *Cricket* hit scoring six runs. □ **hit, knock for six** *colloquial* utterly surprise or defeat.

sixpence /'sɪkspəns/ *noun* sum of 6 (esp. old) pence; *historical* coin worth this.

sixpenny /'sɪkspənɪ/ *adjective* costing or worth 6 (esp. old) pence.

sixteen /sɪks'tiːn/ *adjective & noun* one more than fifteen. □ **sixteenth** *adjective & noun*.

sixth ● *adjective & noun* next after fifth; any of 6 equal parts of thing. □ **sixth form** form in secondary school for pupils over 16; **sixth-form college** separate college for pupils over 16; **sixth sense** supposed intuitive or extrasensory faculty.

sixty /'sɪkstɪ/ *adjective & noun* (*plural* **-ies**) six times ten. □ **sixtieth** *adjective & noun*.

sizable = SIZEABLE.

size¹ ● *noun* relative bigness or extent of a thing; dimensions, magnitude; each of classes into which things are divided by size. ● *verb* (**-zing**) sort in sizes or by size. □ **size up** *colloquial* form judgement of.

size² ● *noun* sticky solution used for glazing paper and stiffening textiles etc. ● *verb* (**-zing**) treat with size.

sizeable *adjective* (also **sizable**) fairly large.

sizzle /'sɪz(ə)l/ ● *verb* (**-ling**) sputter or hiss, esp. in frying. ● *noun* sizzling sound. □ **sizzling** *adjective & adverb*.

SJ *abbreviation* Society of Jesus.

skate¹ ● *noun* ice-skate; roller-skate. ● *verb* (**-ting**) move, glide, or perform (as) on skates; (+ *over*) refer fleetingly to, disregard. □ **skateboard** *noun* short narrow board on roller-skate wheels for riding on standing up, *verb* ride on skateboard. □ **skater** *noun*.

skate² *noun* (*plural* same or **-s**) large edible marine flatfish.

skedaddle /skɪ'dæd(ə)l/ *verb* (**-ling**) *colloquial* run away, retreat hastily.

skein /skeɪn/ *noun* quantity of yarn etc. coiled and usually loosely twisted; flock of wild geese etc. in flight.

skeleton /'skelɪt(ə)n/ ● *noun* hard framework of bones etc. of animal; supporting framework or structure of thing; very thin person or animal; useless or dead remnant; outline sketch. ● *adjective* having only essential or minimum number of people, parts, etc. □ **skeleton key** key fitting many locks. □ **skeletal** *adjective*.

skerry /'skerɪ/ *noun* (*plural* **-ies**) *Scottish* reef, rocky islet.

sketch ● *noun* rough or unfinished drawing or painting; rough draft, general outline; short usually humorous play. ● *verb* make or give sketch of; make sketches.

sketchy *adjective* (**-ier, -iest**) giving only a rough outline; *colloquial* insubstantial or imperfect, esp. through haste. □ **sketchily** *adverb*.

skew ● *adjective* oblique, slanting, set askew. ● *noun* slant. ● *verb* make skew; distort; move obliquely.

skewbald /'skjuːbɔːld/ ● *adjective* (of animal) with irregular patches of white and another colour. ● *noun* skewbald animal, esp. horse.

skewer /'skjuːə/ ● *noun* long pin for holding meat compactly together while cooking. ● *verb* fasten together or pierce (as) with skewer.

ski /skiː/ ● *noun* (*plural* **-s**) each of pair of long narrow pieces of wood etc. fastened under feet for travelling over snow; similar device under vehicle. ● *verb* (**skis; ski'd** or **skied** /skiːd/; **skiing**) travel on skis. □ **skier** *noun*.

skid ● *verb* (**-dd-**) (of vehicle etc.) slide esp. sideways or obliquely on slippery road etc.; cause (vehicle) to skid. ● *noun* act of skidding; runner used as part of landing-gear of aircraft. □ **skid-pan** slippery surface for drivers to practise control of skidding; **skid row** *US slang* district frequented by vagrants.

skiff *noun* light boat, esp. for rowing or sculling.

skilful /'skɪlfʊl/ *adjective* (*US* **skillful**) having or showing skill. □ **skilfully** *adverb*.

skill *noun* practised ability, expertness, technique; craft, art, etc. requiring skill.

skilled *adjective* skilful; (of work or worker) requiring or having skill or special training.

skillet /'skɪlɪt/ *noun* long-handled metal cooking pot; *US* frying-pan.

skim *verb* (**-mm-**) take scum or cream etc. from surface of (liquid); barely touch (surface) in passing over; (often + *over*) deal with or treat (matter) superficially; (often + *over, along*) glide lightly; read or look over superficially. □ **skim, skimmed milk** milk with cream removed.

skimp *verb* (often + *on*) economize; supply meagrely, use too little of.

skimpy *adjective* (**-ier, -iest**) meagre, insufficient.

skin ● *noun* flexible covering of body; skin removed from animal, material made from this; complexion; outer layer or covering; film like skin on liquid etc.; container for liquid, made of animal's skin. ● *verb* (**-nn-**) strip skin from; graze (part of body); *slang* swindle. □ **skin-deep** superficial; **skin-diver** person who swims under water without diving suit; **skin-diving** *noun*; **skinflint** miser; **skin-graft** surgical transplanting of skin, skin thus transferred; **skintight** very closefitting.

skinful *noun colloquial* enough alcohol to make one drunk.

skinny *adjective* (**-ier, -iest**) thin, emaciated.

skint *adjective slang* having no money.

skip¹ ● *verb* (**-pp-**) move along lightly, esp. by taking two hops with each foot in turn; jump lightly esp. over skipping rope; frisk, gambol; move quickly from one subject etc. to another; omit or make omissions in reading; *colloquial* not attend etc.; *colloquial* leave hurriedly. ● *noun* skipping movement or action. □ **skipping-rope** length of rope turned over head and under feet while jumping it.

skip² *noun* large container for refuse etc.; container in which men or materials are lowered or raised in mines etc.

skipjack *noun* (in full **skipjack tuna**) (*plural* same or **-s**) small Pacific tuna.

skipper /'skɪpə/ ● *noun* captain of ship, aircraft, team, etc. ● *verb* be captain of.

skirl ● *noun* shrill sound of bagpipes. ● *verb* make skirl.

skirmish /'skɜːmɪʃ/ ● *noun* minor battle; short argument etc. ● *verb* engage in skirmish.

skirt ● *noun* woman's garment hanging from waist, or this part of complete dress; part of coat etc. that hangs below waist; hanging part at base of hovercraft; (in *singular* or *plural*) border, outlying part; flank of beef etc. ● *verb* go or be along or round edge of. □ **skirting board** narrow board etc. round bottom of room-wall.

skit *noun* light piece of satire, burlesque.

skittish /'skɪtɪʃ/ *adjective* lively, playful; (of horse etc.) nervous, inclined to shy.

skittle /'skɪt(ə)l/ *noun* pin used in game of skittles, in which number of wooden pins are set up to be bowled or knocked down.

skive *verb* (**-ving**) (often + *off*) *slang* evade work; play truant.

skivvy /'skɪvɪ/ *noun* (*plural* **-ies**) *colloquial derogatory* female domestic servant.

skua /'skjuːə/ *noun* large predatory seabird.

skulduggery /skʌl'dʌgərɪ/ *noun* trickery, unscrupulous behaviour.

skulk *verb* lurk or conceal oneself or move stealthily.

skull *noun* bony case of brain; bony framework of head; head as site of intelligence. □ **skull and crossbones** representation of skull over two crossed thigh-bones, esp. on pirate flag or as emblem of death; **skullcap** close-fitting peakless cap.

skunk *noun* (*plural* same or **-s**) black white-striped bushy-tailed mammal, emitting powerful stench when attacked; *colloquial* contemptible person.

sky /skaɪ/ *noun* (*plural* **skies**) (in *singular* or *plural*) atmosphere and outer space seen from the earth. □ **sky blue** bright clear blue; **skydiving** sport of performing acrobatic manoeuvres under free fall before opening parachute; **skylark** *noun* lark that sings while soaring, *verb* play tricks and practical jokes; **skylight** window in roof; **skyline** outline of hills, buildings, etc. against sky; **sky-rocket** *noun* firework shooting into air and exploding, *verb* rise steeply; **skyscraper** very tall building.

slab *noun* flat thickish esp. rectangular piece of solid material; mortuary table.

slack¹ ● *adjective* (of rope etc.) not taut; inactive, sluggish; negligent, remiss; (of tide etc.) neither ebbing nor flowing. ● *noun* slack part of rope etc.; slack period; (in *plural*) casual trousers. ● *verb* slacken; *colloquial* take a rest, be lazy. □ **slack off** loosen; **slack up** reduce level of activity or speed. □ **slackness** *noun*.

slack² *noun* coal dust, coal fragments.

slacken verb make or become slack. □ **slacken off** slack off.

slacker noun shirker.

slag ● noun refuse left after ore has been smelted etc. ● verb (**-gg-**) form slag; (often + off) slang insult, slander. □ **slag-heap** hill of refuse from mine etc.

slain past participle of SLAY.

slake verb (**-king**) assuage or satisfy (thirst etc.); cause (lime) to heat and crumble by action of water.

slalom /ˈslɑːləm/ noun downhill ski-race on zigzag course between artificial obstacles.

slam¹ ● verb (**-mm-**) shut, throw, or put down violently or with bang; slang criticize severely. ● noun sound or action of slamming.

slam² noun winning of all tricks at cards.

slander /ˈslɑːndə/ ● noun false and damaging utterance about person. ● verb utter slander about. □ **slanderous** adjective.

slang ● noun very informal words, phrases, or meanings, not regarded as standard and often peculiar to profession, class, etc. ● verb use abusive language (to). □ **slanging match** prolonged exchange of insults. □ **slangy** adjective.

slant /slɑːnt/ ● verb slope, (cause to) lie or go obliquely; (often as **slanted** adjective) present (news etc.) in biased or particular way. ● noun slope, oblique position; point of view, esp. biased one. ● adjective sloping, oblique.

slantwise adverb aslant.

slap ● verb (**-pp-**) strike (as) with palm of hand; lay forcefully; put hastily or carelessly. ● noun slapping stroke or sound. ● adverb suddenly, fully, directly. □ **slapdash** hasty, careless; **slap-happy** colloquial cheerfully casual; **slapstick** boisterous comedy; **slap-up** colloquial lavish.

slash ● verb cut or gash with knife etc.; (often + at) deliver or aim cutting blows; reduce (prices etc.) drastically; criticize harshly. ● noun slashing cut; Printing oblique stroke; slang act of urinating.

slat noun long narrow strip of wood, plastic, or metal, used in fences, venetian blinds, etc.

slate ● noun fine-grained bluish-grey rock easily split into thin smooth plates; piece of this used esp. in roofing or historical for writing on; colour of slate; list of nominees for office etc. ● verb (**-ting**) roof with slates; colloquial criticize severely; US make arrangements for (event etc.), nominate for office. ● adjective of (colour of) slate. □ **slating** noun; **slaty** adjective.

slattern /ˈslæt(ə)n/ noun slovenly woman. □ **slatternly** adjective.

slaughter /ˈslɔːtə/ ● verb kill (animals) for food etc.; kill (people) ruthlessly or in large numbers; colloquial defeat utterly. ● noun act of slaughtering. □ **slaughterhouse** place for slaughter of animals for food. ● **slaughterer** noun.

Slav /slɑːv/ ● noun member of group of peoples of central and eastern Europe speaking Slavonic languages. ● adjective of the Slavs.

slave ● noun person who is owned by and has to serve another; drudge, very hard worker; (+ of, to) obsessive devotee. ● verb (**-ving**) work very hard. □ **slave-driver** overseer of slaves, hard taskmaster; **slave trade** dealing in slaves, esp. African blacks.

slaver¹ noun historical ship or person engaged in slave trade.

slaver² /ˈslævə/ ● verb dribble; drool. ● noun dribbling saliva; flattery; drivel.

slavery /ˈsleɪvərɪ/ noun condition of slave; drudgery; practice of having slaves.

Slavic /ˈslɑːvɪk/ adjective & noun Slavonic.

slavish /ˈsleɪvɪʃ/ adjective like slaves; without originality. □ **slavishly** adverb.

Slavonic /sləˈvɒnɪk/ ● adjective of group of languages including Russian, Polish, and Czech. ● noun Slavonic group of languages.

slay verb (past **slew** /sluː/; past participle **slain**) kill. □ **slayer** noun.

sleaze noun colloquial sleaziness.

sleazy /ˈsliːzɪ/ adjective (**-ier, -iest**) squalid, tawdry. □ **sleazily** adverb; **sleaziness** noun.

sled noun & verb (**-dd-**) US sledge.

sledge ● noun vehicle on runners for use on snow. ● verb (**-ging**) travel or carry on sledge.

sledgehammer /ˈsledʒhæmə/ noun large heavy hammer.

sleek ● adjective (of hair, skin, etc.) smooth and glossy; looking well-fed and comfortable. ● verb make sleek. □ **sleekly** adverb; **sleekness** noun.

sleep ● noun condition in which eyes are closed, muscles and nerves relaxed, and consciousness suspended; period of this; rest, quiet, death. ● verb (past & past participle **slept**) be or fall asleep; spend the night; provide sleeping accommodation for; (+ with, together) have sexual intercourse; (+ on) defer (decision) until next day; (+ through) fail to be woken by; be inactive or dead; (+ off) cure by sleeping. □ **sleeping bag** padded bag to sleep in when camping etc.; **sleeping car, carriage** railway coach with beds or berths; **sleeping partner** partner not sharing in actual work of a firm; **sleeping pill** pill to induce sleep; **sleeping policeman** ramp etc. in road to slow traffic; **sleepwalk** walk about while asleep; **sleepwalker** noun **sleepless** adjective; **sleeplessness** noun.

sleeper noun sleeping person or animal; beam supporting railway track; sleeping car; ring worn in pierced ear to keep hole open.

sleepy adjective (**-ier, -iest**) feeling need of sleep; quiet, inactive. □ **sleepily** adverb; **sleepiness** noun.

sleet ● noun snow and rain together; hail or snow melting as it falls. ● verb (after it) sleet falls. □ **sleety** adjective.

sleeve noun part of garment covering arm; cover for gramophone record; tube enclosing rod etc. □ **up one's sleeve** in reserve. □ **sleeved** adjective; **sleeveless** adjective.

sleigh /sleɪ/ ● noun sledge, esp. for riding on. ● verb travel on sleigh.

sleight of hand /slaɪt/ noun dexterity, esp. in conjuring.

slender /ˈslendə/ adjective (**-er, -est**) of small girth or breadth; slim; slight, scanty, meagre.

slept past & past participle of SLEEP.

sleuth /sluːθ/ ● noun colloquial detective. ● verb investigate crime etc.

slew¹ /sluː/ ● verb (often + round) turn or swing to new position. ● noun such turn.

slew² past of SLAY.

slice ● noun thin flat piece or wedge cut from something; share; kitchen utensil with thin broad blade; stroke sending ball obliquely. ● verb (**-cing**) (often + up) cut into slices; (+ off) cut off; (+ into, through) cut (as) with knife; strike (ball) with slice.

slick ● adjective colloquial skilful, efficient; superficially dexterous, glib; sleek, smooth. ● noun patch of oil etc., esp. on sea. ● verb colloquial make smooth or sleek. □ **slickly** adverb; **slickness** noun.

slide ● verb (past & past participle **slid**) (cause to) move along smooth surface touching it always with same part; move quietly or smoothly; glide over ice without skates; (often + into) pass unobtrusively. ● noun act of sliding; rapid decline; smooth slope down which people or things slide; track for sliding, esp. on ice; part of machine or instrument that slides; mounted transparency viewed with projector; piece of glass holding object for microscope; hair-slide. □ **let things slide** be negligent, allow deterioration; **slide-rule** ruler with sliding central strip, graduated logarithmically for rapid calculations; **sliding scale** scale of fees, taxes, wages, etc. that varies according to some other factor.

slight /slaɪt/ ● *adjective* small, insignificant; inadequate; slender, frail-looking. ● *verb* treat disrespectfully, ignore. ● *noun* act of slighting. □ **slightly** *adverb*; **slightness** *noun*.

slim ● *adjective* (-mm-) not fat, slender; small, insufficient. ● *verb* (-mm-) (often + *down*) become slim, esp. by dieting etc.; make slim. □ **slimline** of slender design, not fattening. □ **slimmer** *noun*; **slimming** *noun*.

slime *noun* oozy or sticky substance.

slimy *adjective* (-ier, -iest) like, covered with, or filled with slime; *colloquial* disgustingly obsequious. □ **sliminess** *noun*.

sling[1] ● *noun* strap etc. used to support or raise thing; bandage supporting injured arm; strap etc. used to throw small missile. ● *verb* (*past & past participle* **slung**) suspend with sling; *colloquial* throw. □ **sling-back** shoe held in place by strap above heel; **sling one's hook** *slang* go away.

sling[2] *noun* sweetened drink of spirits (esp. gin) with water.

slink *verb* (*past & past participle* **slunk**) (often + *off, away, by*) move stealthily or guiltily.

slinky *adjective* (-ier, -iest) (of garment) close-fitting and sinuous.

slip[1] ● *verb* (-pp-) slide unintentionally or momentarily, lose footing or balance; go with sliding motion; escape or fall because hard to grasp; go unobserved or quietly; make careless or slight mistake; fall below standard; place stealthily or casually; release from restraint or connection; (+ *on, off*) pull (garment) easily or hastily on or off; escape from, evade. ● *noun* act of slipping; careless or slight error; pillowcase; petticoat; (in *singular* or *plural*) slipway; *Cricket* fielder behind wicket on off side, (in *singular* or *plural*) this position. □ **give (person) the slip** escape from, evade; **slip-knot** knot that can be undone by pull, running knot; **slip-on** (of shoes or clothes) easily slipped on or off; **slipped disc** displaced disc between vertebrae; **slip-road** road for entering or leaving motorway etc.; **slipstream** current of air or water driven backwards by propeller etc.; **slip up** *colloquial* make mistake; **slip-up** *noun*; **slipway** ramp for shipbuilding or landing boats.

slip[2] *noun* small piece of paper, esp. for making notes; cutting from plant for grafting or planting.

slippage *noun* act or instance of slipping.

slipper *noun* light loose indoor shoe.

slippery /ˈslɪpərɪ/ *adjective* difficult to grasp, stand on, etc., because smooth or wet; unreliable, unscrupulous. □ **slipperiness** *noun*.

slippy *adjective* (-ier, -iest) *colloquial* slippery.

slipshod *adjective* careless, slovenly.

slit ● *noun* straight narrow incision or opening. ● *verb* (-tt-; *past & past participle* **slit**) make slit in; cut in strips.

slither /ˈslɪðə/ ● *verb* slide unsteadily. ● *noun* act of slithering. □ **slithery** *adjective*.

sliver /ˈslɪvə/ ● *noun* long thin slice or piece. ● *verb* cut or split into slivers.

slob *noun* *colloquial* derogatory lazy, untidy, or fat person.

slobber /ˈslɒbə/ *verb & noun* slaver. □ **slobbery** *adjective*.

sloe *noun* blackthorn; its small bluish-black fruit.

slog ● *verb* (-gg-) hit hard and usually unskilfully; work or walk doggedly. ● *noun* heavy random hit; hard steady work or walk; spell of this.

slogan /ˈsləʊgən/ *noun* catchy phrase used in advertising etc.; party cry, watchword.

sloop /sluːp/ *noun* small one-masted fore-and-aft rigged vessel.

slop ● *verb* (-pp-) (often + *over*) spill over edge of vessel; spill or splash liquid on. ● *noun* liquid spilled or splashed; (in *plural*) dirty waste water, wine, etc.; (in *singular* or *plural*) unappetizing liquid food.

slope ● *noun* inclined position, direction, or state; piece of rising or falling ground; difference in level between two ends or sides of a thing; place for skiing. ● *verb* (-ping) have or take slope, slant; cause to slope. □ **slope off** *slang* go away, esp. to evade work etc.

sloppy *adjective* (-ier, -iest) wet, watery, too liquid; careless, untidy; foolishly sentimental. □ **sloppily** *adverb*; **sloppiness** *noun*.

slosh ● *verb* (often + *about*) splash or flounder; *slang* hit, esp. heavily; *colloquial* pour (liquid) clumsily. ● *noun* slush; act or sound of splashing; *slang* heavy blow.

sloshed *adjective* *slang* drunk.

slot ● *noun* slit in machine etc. for something (esp. coin) to be inserted; slit, groove, etc. for thing; allotted place in schedule. ● *verb* (-tt-) (often + *in, into*) place or be placed (as if) into slot; provide with slot(s). □ **slot machine** machine worked by insertion of coin, esp. delivering small items or providing amusement.

sloth /sləʊθ/ *noun* laziness, indolence; slow-moving arboreal S. American mammal.

slothful *adjective* lazy. □ **slothfully** *adverb*.

slouch /slaʊtʃ/ ● *verb* stand, move, or sit in drooping fashion. ● *noun* slouching posture or movement; *slang* incompetent or slovenly worker etc. ● **slouch hat** hat with wide flexible brim.

slough[1] /slaʊ/ *noun* swamp, miry place. □ **Slough of Despond** state of hopeless depression.

slough[2] /slʌf/ ● *noun* part that animal (esp. snake) casts or moults. ● *verb* (often + *off*) cast or drop as slough.

Slovak /ˈsləʊvæk/ ● *noun* member of Slavonic people inhabiting Slovakia; their language. ● *adjective* of this people or language.

sloven /ˈslʌv(ə)n/ *noun* untidy or careless person.

Slovene /ˈsləʊviːn/ (also **Slovenian** /-ˈviːnɪən/) ● *noun* member of Slavonic people in Slovenia; their language. ● *adjective* of Slovenia or its people or language.

slovenly ● *adjective* careless and untidy, unmethodical. ● *adverb* in a slovenly way. □ **slovenliness** *noun*.

slow /sləʊ/ ● *adjective* taking relatively long time to do thing(s); acting, moving, or done without speed; not conducive to speed; (of clock etc.) showing earlier than correct time; dull-witted, stupid; tedious; slack, sluggish; (of fire or oven) not very hot; (of photographic film) needing long exposure; reluctant. ● *adverb* slowly. ● *verb* (usually + *down, up*) (cause to) move, act, or work with reduced speed or vigour. □ **slowcoach** *colloquial* slow person; **slow motion** speed of film or videotape in which actions etc. appear much slower than usual, simulation of this in real action; **slow-worm** small European legless lizard. □ **slowly** *adverb*; **slowness** *noun*.

sludge *noun* thick greasy mud or sediment; sewage. □ **sludgy** *adjective*.

slug[1] *noun* slimy shell-less mollusc; bullet, esp. irregularly shaped; missile for airgun; *Printing* metal bar for spacing; mouthful of liquor.

slug² US ● verb (**-gg-**) hit hard. ● noun hard blow.

sluggard /'slʌgəd/ noun lazy person.

sluggish adjective inert, slow-moving. □ **sluggishly** adverb; **sluggishness** noun.

sluice /sluːs/ ● noun (also **sluice-gate, -valve**) sliding gate or other contrivance for regulating volume or flow of water; water so regulated; (also **sluiceway**) artificial water-channel; place for or act of rinsing. ● verb (**-cing**) provide or wash with sluice(s); rinse; (of water) rush out (as if) from sluice.

slum ● noun house unfit for human habitation; (often in plural) overcrowded and squalid district in city. ● verb (**-mm-**) visit slums, esp. out of curiosity. □ **slum it** colloquial put up with conditions less comfortable than usual. □ **slummy** adjective.

slumber /'slʌmbə/ verb & noun poetical sleep.

slump ● noun sudden severe or prolonged fall in prices and trade. ● verb undergo slump; sit or fall heavily or limply.

slung past & past participle of SLING¹.

slunk past & past participle of SLINK.

slur ● verb (**-rr-**) sound (words, musical notes, etc.) so that they run into one another; archaic or US put slur on (person, character); (usually + over) pass over lightly. ● noun imputation of wrongdoing; act of slurring; Music curved line joining notes to be slurred.

slurp colloquial ● verb eat or drink noisily. ● noun sound of slurping.

slurry /'slʌrɪ/ noun thin semi-liquid cement, mud, manure, etc.

slush noun thawing snow; silly sentimentality. □ **slush fund** reserve fund, esp. for bribery. □ **slushy** adjective (**-ier, -iest**).

slut noun derogatory slovenly or promiscuous woman. □ **sluttish** adjective.

sly adjective (**-er, -est**) crafty, wily; secretive; knowing, insinuating. □ **on the sly** secretly. □ **slyly** adverb; **slyness** noun.

smack¹ ● noun sharp slap or blow; hard hit; loud kiss; loud sharp sound. ● verb slap; part (lips) noisily in anticipation of food; move, hit, etc. with smack. ● adverb colloquial with a smack; suddenly, violently; exactly.

smack² (+ of) ● verb taste of, suggest. ● noun flavour or suggestion of.

smack³ noun single-masted sailing boat.

smack⁴ noun slang heroin, other hard drug.

smacker noun slang loud kiss; £1, US $1.

small ● adjective not large or big; not great in importance, amount, number, etc.; not much; insignificant; of small particles; on small scale; poor, humble; mean; young. ● noun slenderest part, esp. of back; (in plural) colloquial underwear, esp. as laundry. ● adverb into small pieces. □ **small arms** portable firearms; **small change** coins, not notes; **small fry** unimportant people, children; **smallholding** agricultural holding smaller than farm; **small hours** night-time after midnight; **small-minded** petty, narrow in outlook; **smallpox** historical acute contagious disease with fever and pustules usually leaving scars; **small print** matter printed small, esp. limitations in contract; **small talk** trivial social conversation; **small-time** colloquial unimportant, petty. □ **smallness** noun.

smarmy /'smɑːmɪ/ adjective (**-ier, -iest**) colloquial ingratiating. □ **smarmily** adverb; **smarminess** noun.

smart ● adjective well-groomed, neat; bright and fresh in appearance; stylish, fashionable; esp. US clever, ingenious, quickwitted; quick, brisk; painfully severe, sharp, vigorous. ● verb feel or give pain; rankle; (+ for) suffer consequences of. ● noun sharp bodily or mental pain, stinging sensation. ● adverb

smartly. □ **smartish** adjective & adverb; **smartly** adverb; **smartness** noun.

smarten verb (usually + up) make or become smart.

smash ● verb (often + up) break to pieces; bring or come to destruction, defeat, or disaster; (+ into, through) move forcefully; (+ in) break with crushing blow; hit (ball) hard, esp. downwards. ● noun act or sound of smashing; (in full **smash hit**) very successful play, song, etc. ● adverb with smash. □ **smash-and-grab** robbery with goods snatched from broken shop window etc.

smashing adjective colloquial excellent, wonderful.

smattering /'smætərɪŋ/ noun slight knowledge.

smear /smɪə/ ● verb daub or mark with grease etc.; smudge; defame. ● noun action of smearing; material smeared on microscope slide etc. for examination; specimen of this. □ **smear test** cervical smear. □ **smeary** adjective.

smell ● noun sense of odour perception; property perceived by this; unpleasant odour; act of inhaling to ascertain smell. ● verb (past & past participle **smelt** or **smelled**) perceive or examine by smell; stink; seem by smell to be; (+ of) emit smell of, suggest; detect; have or use sense of smell. □ **smelling salts** sharp-smelling substances sniffed to relieve faintness.

smelly adjective (**-ier, -iest**) strong- or evil-smelling.

smelt¹ verb melt (ore) to extract metal; obtain (metal) thus. □ **smelter** noun.

smelt² past & past participle of SMELL.

smelt³ noun (plural same or **-s**) small edible green and silver fish.

smilax /'smaɪlæks/ noun any of several climbing plants.

smile ● verb (**-ling**) have or assume facial expression of amusement or pleasure, with ends of lips turned upward; express by smiling; give (smile); (+ on, upon) favour. ● noun act of smiling; smiling expression or aspect.

smirch verb & noun stain, smear.

smirk ● noun conceited or silly smile. ● verb give smirk.

smite verb (**-ting**; past **smote**; past participle **smitten** /'smɪt(ə)n/) archaic or literary hit, chastise, defeat; (in passive) affect strongly, seize.

smith noun blacksmith; worker in metal, craftsman.

smithereens /smɪðə'riːnz/ plural noun small fragments.

smithy /'smɪðɪ/ noun (plural **-ies**) blacksmith's workshop, forge.

smitten past participle of SMITE.

smock ● noun loose shirtlike garment, often adorned with smocking. ● verb adorn with smocking.

smocking noun ornamentation on cloth made by gathering it tightly with stitches.

smog noun dense smoky fog. □ **smoggy** adjective (**-ier, -iest**).

smoke ● noun visible vapour from burning substance; act of smoking tobacco etc.; colloquial cigarette, cigar. ● verb (**-king**) inhale and exhale smoke of (cigarette etc.); do this habitually; emit smoke or visible vapour; darken or preserve with smoke. □ **smoke bomb** bomb emitting dense smoke on bursting; **smoke-free** free from smoke, where smoking is not permitted; **smoke out** drive out by means of smoke, drive out of hiding etc.; **smokescreen** cloud of smoke concealing esp. military operations, ruse for disguising activities; **smokestack** funnel of locomotive or steamship, tall chimney.

smoker noun person who habitually smokes tobacco; compartment on train where smoking is permitted.

smoky *adjective* (**-ier**, **-iest**) emitting, filled with, or obscured by, smoke; coloured by or like smoke; having flavour of smoked food.

smolder US = SMOULDER.

smooch /smuːtʃ/ ● *verb* kiss and caress. ● *noun* smooching.

smooth /smuːð/ ● *adjective* having even surface; free from projections and roughness; that can be traversed uninterrupted; (of sea etc.) calm, flat; (of journey etc.) easy; not harsh in sound or taste; conciliatory, slick; not jerky. ● *verb* (often + *out, down*) make or become smooth; (often + *out, down, over, away*) get rid of (differences, faults, etc.). ● *noun* smoothing touch or stroke. □ **smooth-tongued** insincerely flattering. □ **smoothly** *adverb*; **smoothness** *noun*.

smorgasbord /ˈsmɔːɡəsbɔːd/ *noun* Swedish hors d'oeuvres; buffet meal with various esp. savoury dishes.

smote *past of* SMITE.

smother /ˈsmʌðə/ *verb* suffocate, stifle; (+ *in, with*) overwhelm or cover with (kisses, gifts, etc.); extinguish (fire) by heaping with ashes etc.; have difficulty breathing; (often + *up*) suppress, conceal.

smoulder /ˈsməʊldə/ (US **smolder**) ● *verb* burn without flame or internally; (of person) show silent emotion. ● *noun* smouldering.

smudge ● *noun* blurred or smeared line, mark, etc. ● *verb* (**-ging**) make smudge on or with; become smeared or blurred. □ **smudgy** *adjective*.

smug *adjective* (**-gg-**) self-satisfied. □ **smugly** *adverb*; **smugness** *noun*.

smuggle /ˈsmʌɡ(ə)l/ *verb* (**-ling**) import or export illegally, esp. without paying duties; convey secretly. □ **smuggler** *noun*; **smuggling** *noun*.

smut ● *noun* small piece of soot; spot or smudge made by this; obscene talk, pictures, or stories; fungous disease of cereals. ● *verb* (**-tt-**) mark with smut(s). □ **smutty** *adjective* (**-ier**, **-iest**).

snack *noun* light, casual, or hasty meal. □ **snack bar** place where snacks are sold.

snaffle /ˈsnæf(ə)l/ ● *noun* (in full **snaffle-bit**) simple bridle-bit without curb. ● *verb* (**-ling**) *colloquial* steal, seize.

snag ● *noun* unexpected obstacle or drawback; jagged projection; tear in material etc. ● *verb* (**-gg-**) catch or tear on snag.

snail *noun* slow-moving mollusc with spiral shell.

snake ● *noun* long limbless reptile; (also **snake in the grass**) traitor, secret enemy. ● *verb* (**-king**) move or twist like a snake. □ **snakes and ladders** board game with counters moved up 'ladders' and down 'snakes'; **snakeskin** *noun* skin of snake, *adjective* made of snakeskin.

snaky *adjective* of or like a snake; sinuous; treacherous.

snap ● *verb* (**-pp-**) break sharply; (cause to) emit sudden sharp sound; open or close with snapping sound; speak irritably; (often + *at*) make sudden audible bite; move quickly; photograph. ● *noun* act or sound of snapping; crisp biscuit; snapshot; (in full **cold snap**) sudden brief period of cold weather; card game in which players call 'snap' when two similar cards are exposed; vigour. ● *adverb* with snapping sound. ● *adjective* done without forethought. □ **snapdragon** plant with two-lipped flowers; **snap-fastener** press-stud; **snap out of** *slang* get out of (mood etc.) by sudden effort; **snapshot** informal or casual photograph; **snap up** accept (offer etc.) hastily or eagerly.

snapper *noun* any of several edible marine fish.

snappish *adjective* curt, ill-tempered.

snappy *adjective* (**-ier**, **-iest**) *colloquial* brisk, lively; neat and elegant; snappish. □ **snappily** *adverb*.

snare /sneə/ ● *noun* trap, esp. with noose, for birds or animals; trap, trick, temptation; (in *singular* or *plural*) twisted strings of gut, hide, or wire stretched across lower head of side drum to produce rattle; (in full **snare drum**) side drum with snares. ● *verb* (**-ring**) catch in snare, trap.

snarl[1] ● *verb* growl with bared teeth; speak angrily. ● *noun* act or sound of snarling.

snarl[2] ● *verb* (often + *up*) twist, entangle, hamper movement of (traffic etc.), become entangled. ● *noun* tangle.

snatch ● *verb* (often + *away, from*) seize quickly, eagerly, or unexpectedly; steal by grabbing; *slang* kidnap; (+ *at*) try to seize, take eagerly. ● *noun* act of snatching; fragment of song, talk, etc.; short spell of activity etc.

snazzy /ˈsnæzɪ/ *adjective* (**-ier**, **-iest**) *slang* smart, stylish, showy.

sneak ● *verb* go or convey furtively; *slang* steal unobserved; *slang* tell tales; (as **sneaking** *adjective*) furtive, persistent and puzzling. ● *noun* mean-spirited, underhand person; *slang* tell-tale. ● *adjective* acting or done without warning, secret. □ **sneak-thief** person who steals without breaking in. □ **sneaky** *adjective* (**-ier**, **-iest**).

sneaker *noun slang* soft-soled shoe.

sneer ● *noun* derisive smile or remark. ● *verb* (often + *at*) make sneer; utter with sneer. □ **sneering** *adjective*; **sneeringly** *adverb*.

sneeze ● *noun* sudden involuntary explosive expulsion of air from irritated nostrils. ● *verb* (**-zing**) make sneeze. □ **not to be sneezed at** *colloquial* worth having or considering.

snick ● *verb* make small notch or cut in; *Cricket* deflect (ball) slightly with bat. ● *noun* such notch or deflection.

snicker /ˈsnɪkə/ *noun & verb* snigger.

snide *adjective* sneering, slyly derogatory.

sniff ● *verb* inhale air audibly through nose; (often + *up*) draw in through nose; smell scent of by sniffing. ● *noun* act or sound of sniffing. □ **sniff at** show contempt for; **sniffer-dog** *colloquial* dog trained to find drugs or explosives by scent.

sniffle /ˈsnɪf(ə)l/ ● *verb* (**-ling**) sniff repeatedly or slightly. ● *noun* act of sniffling; (in *singular* or *plural*) cold in the head causing sniffling.

snifter /ˈsnɪftə/ *noun slang* small alcoholic drink.

snigger /ˈsnɪɡə/ ● *noun* half-suppressed laugh. ● *verb* utter snigger.

snip ● *verb* (**-pp-**) cut with scissors etc., esp. in small quick strokes. ● *noun* act of snipping; piece snipped off; *slang* something easily done, bargain.

snipe ● *noun* (*plural* same or **-s**) wading bird with long straight bill. ● *verb* (**-ping**) fire shots from hiding usually at long range; (often + *at*) make sly critical attack. □ **sniper** *noun*.

snippet /ˈsnɪpɪt/ *noun* small piece cut off; (usually in *plural*) scrap of information etc., short extract from book etc.

snitch ● *verb slang* steal; (often + *on*) inform on person. ● *noun* informer.

snivel /ˈsnɪv(ə)l/ ● *verb* (**-ll-**; US **-l-**) sniffle; weep with sniffling; show maudlin emotion. ● *noun* act of snivelling.

snob *noun* person who despises people with inferior social position, wealth, intellect, tastes, etc. □ **snobbery** *noun*; **snobbish** *adjective*; **snobby** *adjective* (**-ier**, **-iest**).

snood /snuːd/ *noun* woman's loose hairnet.

snook /snuːk/ *noun slang* contemptuous gesture with thumb to nose and fingers spread. □ **cock a snook (at)** make this gesture (at), show contempt (for).

snooker /'snu:kə/ ● noun game played on oblong cloth-covered table with 1 white, 15 red, and 6 other coloured balls; position in this game where direct shot would give points to opponent. ● verb subject (player) to snooker; (esp. as **snookered** adjective) slang thwart, defeat.

snoop /snu:p/ colloquial ● verb pry into another's affairs; (often + about, around) investigate (often stealthily) transgressions of rules etc. ● noun act of snooping. □ **snooper** noun.

snooty /'snu:tɪ/ adjective (**-ier, -iest**) colloquial supercilious, snobbish. □ **snootily** adverb.

snooze /snu:z/ colloquial ● noun short sleep, nap. ● verb (**-zing**) take snooze.

snore ● noun snorting or grunting sound of breathing during sleep. ● verb (**-ring**) make this sound.

snorkel /'snɔ:k(ə)l/ ● noun device for supplying air to underwater swimmer or submerged submarine. ● verb (**-ll-**; US **-l-**) use snorkel.

snort ● noun explosive sound made by driving breath violently through nose, esp. by horses, or by humans to show contempt, incredulity, etc.; colloquial small drink of liquor; slang inhaled dose of powdered cocaine. ● verb make snort; slang inhale (esp. cocaine); express or utter with snort.

snot noun slang nasal mucus.

snotty adjective (**-ier, -iest**) slang running or covered with nasal mucus; snooty; contemptible. □ **snottily** adverb; **snottiness** noun.

snout /snaʊt/ noun projecting nose (and mouth) of animal; derogatory person's nose; pointed front of thing.

snow /snəʊ/ ● noun frozen vapour falling to earth in light white flakes; fall or layer of this; thing resembling snow in whiteness or texture etc.; slang cocaine. ● verb (after it) snow falls; (+ in, over, up, etc.) confine or block with snow. □ **snowball** noun snow pressed into ball for throwing in play, verb throw or pelt with snowballs, increase rapidly; **snow-blind** temporarily blinded by glare from snow; **snowbound** prevented by snow from going out; **snowcap** snow-covered mountain peak; **snowdrift** bank of snow piled up by wind; **snowdrop** spring-flowering plant with white drooping flowers; **snowed under** overwhelmed, esp. with work; **snowflake** each of the flakes in which snow falls; **snow goose** white Arctic goose; **snowline** level above which snow never melts entirely; **snowman** figure made of snow; **snowplough** device for clearing road of snow; **snowshoe** racket-shaped attachment to boot for walking on surface of snow; **snowstorm** heavy fall of snow, esp. with wind; **snow white** pure white. □ **snowy** adjective (**-ier, -iest**).

SNP abbreviation Scottish National Party.

Snr. abbreviation Senior.

snub ● verb (**-bb-**) rebuff or humiliate in a sharp or cutting way. ● noun snubbing, rebuff. ● adjective (of nose) short and turned up.

snuff¹ ● noun charred part of candle-wick. ● verb trim snuff from (candle). □ **snuff it** slang die; **snuff out** extinguish (candle), put an end to (hopes etc.).

snuff² ● noun powdered tobacco or medicine taken by sniffing. ● verb take snuff.

snuffle /'snʌf(ə)l/ ● verb (**-ling**) make sniffing sounds; speak nasally; breathe noisily, esp. with blocked nose. ● noun snuffling sound or speech.

snug ● adjective (**-gg-**) cosy, comfortable, sheltered; close-fitting. ● noun small room in pub. □ **snugly** adverb.

snuggle /'snʌg(ə)l/ verb (**-ling**) settle or move into warm comfortable position.

so¹ /səʊ/ ● adverb to such an extent, in this or that manner or state; also; indeed, actually; very; thus. ● conjunction (often + that) consequently, in order that; and then; (introducing question) after that. □ **so-and-so** particular but unspecified person or thing, colloquial objectionable person; **so as to** in order to; **so-called** commonly called but often incorrectly; **so long** colloquial goodbye; **so so** colloquial only moderately good or well.

so² = SOH.

soak ● verb make or become thoroughly wet through saturation; (of rain etc.) drench; (+ in, up) absorb (liquid, knowledge, etc.); (+ in, into, through) penetrate by saturation; colloquial extort money from; colloquial drink heavily. ● noun soaking; colloquial hard drinker. □ **soakaway** arrangement for disposal of waste water by percolation through soil.

soaking adjective (in full **soaking wet**) wet through.

soap ● noun cleansing substance yielding lather when rubbed in water; colloquial soap opera. ● verb apply soap to. □ **soapbox** makeshift stand for street orator; **soap opera** domestic broadcast serial; **soap powder** powdered soap usually with additives, for washing clothes etc.; **soapstone** steatite; **soapsuds** suds.

soapy adjective (**-ier, -iest**) of or like soap; containing or smeared with soap; unctuous, flattering.

soar /sɔ:/ verb fly or rise high; reach high level or standard; fly without flapping wings or using motor power.

sob ● verb (**-bb-**) inhale convulsively, usually with weeping; utter with sobs. ● noun act or sound of sobbing. □ **sob story** colloquial story or explanation appealing for sympathy.

sober /'səʊbə/ ● adjective (**-er, -est**) not drunk; not given to drink; moderate, tranquil, serious; (of colour) dull. ● verb (often + down, up) make or become sober. □ **soberly** adverb.

sobriety /sə'braɪtɪ/ noun being sober.

sobriquet /'səʊbrɪkeɪ/ noun (also **soubriquet** /'su:-/) nickname.

Soc. abbreviation Socialist; Society.

soccer /'sɒkə/ noun Association football.

sociable /'səʊʃəb(ə)l/ adjective liking company, gregarious, friendly. □ **sociability** noun; **sociably** adverb.

social /'səʊʃ(ə)l/ ● adjective of society or its organization, esp. of relations of (classes of) people; living in communities; gregarious. ● noun social gathering. □ **social science** study of society and social relationships; **social security** state assistance to the poor and unemployed; **social services** welfare services provided by the State, esp. education, health care, and housing; **social work** professional or voluntary work with disadvantaged groups; **social worker** noun. □ **socially** adverb.

socialism noun political and economic theory advocating state ownership and control of means of production, distribution, and exchange; social system based on this. □ **socialist** noun & adjective; **socialistic** /-'lɪs-/ adjective.

socialite /'səʊʃəlaɪt/ noun person moving in fashionable society.

socialize /'səʊʃəlaɪz/ verb (also **-ise**) (**-zing** or **-sing**) mix socially; make social; organize in a socialistic way.

society /sə'saɪətɪ/ noun (plural **-ies**) organized and interdependent community; system and organization of this; (members of) aristocratic part of this; mixing with other people, companionship, company; association, club. □ **societal** adjective.

sociology /səʊsɪ'ɒlədʒɪ/ noun study of society and social problems. □ **sociological** /-ə'lɒdʒ-/ adjective; **sociologist** noun.

sock¹ *noun* knitted covering for foot and lower leg; insole.

sock² *colloquial* ● *verb* hit hard. ● *noun* hard blow. □ **sock it to** attack or address vigorously.

socket /'sɒkɪt/ *noun* hollow for thing to fit into etc., esp. device receiving electric plug, light bulb, etc.

Socratic /sə'krætɪk/ *adjective* of Socrates or his philosophy.

sod *noun* turf, piece of turf; surface of ground.

soda /'səʊdə/ *noun* any of various compounds of sodium in common use; (in full **soda water**) effervescent water used esp. with spirits etc. as drink. □ **soda fountain** device supplying soda water, shop or counter with this.

sodden /'sɒd(ə)n/ *adjective* saturated, soaked through; stupid, dull, etc. with drunkenness.

sodium /'səʊdɪəm/ *noun* soft silver-white metallic element. □ **sodium bicarbonate** white compound used in baking-powder; **sodium chloride** common salt; **sodium lamp** lamp using sodium vapour and giving yellow light; **sodium nitrate** white powdery compound in fertilizers etc.

sofa /'səʊfə/ *noun* long upholstered seat with raised back and ends. □ **sofa bed** sofa that can be converted into bed.

soffit /'sɒfɪt/ *noun* undersurface of arch, lintel, etc.

soft ● *adjective* not hard, easily cut or dented, malleable; (of cloth etc.) smooth, fine, not rough; mild; (of water) low in mineral salts which prevent lathering; not brilliant or glaring; not strident or loud; sibilant; not sharply defined; gentle, conciliatory, compassionate, sympathetic; feeble, half-witted, silly, sentimental; *colloquial* easy; (of drug) not highly addictive. ● *adverb* softly. □ **have a soft spot for** be fond of; **softball** form of baseball with softer larger ball; **soft-boiled** (of egg) boiled leaving yolk soft; **soft-centred** having soft centre, soft-hearted; **soft drink** non-alcoholic drink; **soft fruit** small stoneless fruit; **soft furnishings** curtains, rugs, etc.; **soft-hearted** tender, compassionate; **soft option** easier alternative; **soft palate** back part of palate; **soft pedal** *noun* pedal on piano softening tone; **soft-pedal** *verb* refrain from emphasizing; **soft sell** restrained salesmanship; **soft soap** *colloquial* persuasive flattery; **soft-spoken** having gentle voice; **soft target** vulnerable person or thing; **soft touch** *colloquial* gullible person, esp. over money; **software** computer programs; **softwood** wood of coniferous tree. □ **softly** *adverb*; **softness** *noun*.

soften /'sɒf(ə)n/ *verb* make or become soft(er); (often + *up*) reduce strength, resistance, etc. of. □ **softener** *noun*.

softie *noun* (also **softy**) (*plural* **-ies**) *colloquial* weak, silly, or soft-hearted person.

soggy /'sɒgɪ/ *adjective* (**-ier**, **-iest**) sodden, water-logged.

soh *noun* (also **so**) *Music* fifth note of scale in tonic sol-fa.

soil¹ *noun* upper layer of earth, in which plants grow; ground, territory.

soil² ● *verb* make dirty, smear, stain; defile; discredit. ● *noun* dirty mark; filth, refuse. □ **soil pipe** discharge-pipe of lavatory.

soirée /'swɑːreɪ/ *noun* evening party.

sojourn /'sɒdʒ(ə)n/ ● *noun* temporary stay. ● *verb* stay temporarily.

sola /'səʊlə/ *noun* pithy-stemmed E. Indian swamp plant. □ **sola topi** sun-helmet made from pith of this.

solace /'sɒləs/ ● *noun* comfort in distress or disappointment. ● *verb* (**-cing**) give solace to.

solan /'səʊlən/ *noun* (in full **solan goose**) large goose-like gannet.

solar /'səʊlə/ *adjective* of or reckoned by sun. □ **solar battery, cell** device converting solar radiation into electricity; **solar panel** panel absorbing sun's rays as energy source; **solar plexus** complex of nerves at pit of stomach; **solar system** sun and the planets etc. whose motion is governed by it.

solarium /sə'leərɪəm/ *noun* (*plural* **-ria**) room with sunlamps, glass roof, etc.

sold *past & past participle of* SELL.

solder /'sɒldə/ ● *noun* fusible alloy used for joining metals, wires, etc. ● *verb* join with solder. □ **soldering iron** tool for melting and applying solder.

soldier /'səʊldʒə/ ● *noun* member of army, esp. (in full **common soldier**) private or NCO; *colloquial* bread finger, esp. for dipping in egg. ● *verb* serve as soldier. □ **soldier on** *colloquial* persevere doggedly. □ **soldierly** *adjective*.

soldiery *noun* soldiers collectively.

sole¹ ● *noun* undersurface of foot; part of shoe, sock, etc. below foot, esp. part other than heel; lower surface or base of plough, golf-club head, etc. ● *verb* (**-ling**) provide with sole.

sole² *noun* (*plural* same or **-s**) type of flatfish.

sole³ *adjective* one and only single; exclusive. □ **solely** *adverb*.

solecism /'sɒlɪsɪz(ə)m/ *noun* mistake of grammar or idiom; offence against etiquette.

solemn /'sɒləm/ *adjective* serious and dignified; formal; awe-inspiring; of cheerless manner; grave. □ **solemness** *noun*; **solemnity** /sə'lem-/ *noun* (*plural* **-ies**) **solemnly** *adverb*.

solemnize /'sɒləmnaɪz/ *verb* (also **-ise**) (**-zing** or **-sing**) duly perform (esp. marriage ceremony); make solemn. □ **solemnization** *noun*.

solenoid /'səʊlənɔɪd/ *noun* cylindrical coil of wire acting as magnet when carrying electric current.

sol-fa /'sɒlfɑː/ *noun* system of syllables representing musical notes.

solicit /sə'lɪsɪt/ *verb* (**-t-**) seek repeatedly or earnestly; (of prostitute) accost (man) concerning sexual activity. □ **solicitation** *noun*.

solicitor /sə'lɪsɪtə/ *noun* lawyer qualified to advise clients and instruct barristers.

solicitous /sə'lɪsɪtəs/ *adjective* showing concern; (+ *to do*) eager, anxious. □ **solicitously** *adverb*.

solicitude /sə'lɪsɪtjuːd/ *noun* being solicitous.

solid /'sɒlɪd/ ● *adjective* (**-er**, **-est**) of firm and stable shape, not liquid or fluid; of such material throughout, not hollow; alike all through; sturdily built, not flimsy; 3-dimensional; of solids; sound, reliable; uninterrupted; unanimous. ● *noun* solid substance or body; (in *plural*) solid food. ● *adverb* solidly. **solid-state** using electronic properties of solids to replace those of valves. □ **solidly** /sə'lɪd-/ *noun*; **solidly** *adverb*; **solidness** *noun*.

solidarity /sɒlɪ'dærɪtɪ/ *noun* unity, esp. political or in industrial dispute; mutual dependence.

solidify /sə'lɪdɪfaɪ/ *verb* (**-ies**, **-ied**) make or become solid.

soliloquy /sə'lɪləkwɪ/ *noun* (*plural* **-quies**) talking without or regardless of hearers; this part of a play. □ **soliloquize** *verb* (also **-ise**) (**-zing** or **-sing**).

solipsism /'sɒlɪpsɪz(ə)m/ *noun* theory that self is all that exists or can be known.

solitaire /'sɒlɪteə/ *noun* jewel set by itself; ring etc. with this; game for one player who removes pegs etc. from board on jumping others over them; *US* card game for one person.

solitary /'sɒlɪtərɪ/ ● *adjective* living or being alone; not gregarious; lonely; secluded; single. ● *noun* (*plural* **-ies**) recluse; *colloquial* solitary confinement.

531

solitude | sortie

□ **solitary confinement** isolation in separate prison cell.

solitude /'sɒlɪtjuːd/ *noun* being solitary; solitary place.

solo /'səʊləʊ/ ● *noun* (*plural* **-s**) piece of music or dance performed by one person; thing done by one person, esp. unaccompanied flight; (in full **solo whist**) type of whist in which one player may oppose the others. ● *verb* (**-es, -ed**) perform a solo. ● *adjective & adverb* unaccompanied, alone.

soloist /'səʊləʊɪst/ *noun* performer of solo.

solstice /'sɒlstɪs/ *noun* either of two times (**summer, winter solstice**) when sun is farthest from equator.

soluble /'sɒljʊb(ə)l/ *adjective* that can be dissolved or solved. □ **solubility** *noun*.

solution /sə'luːʃ(ə)n/ *noun* (means of) solving a problem; conversion of solid or gas into liquid by mixture with liquid; state or substance resulting from this; dissolving, being dissolved.

solve *verb* (**-ving**) answer, remove, or deal with (problem). □ **solvable** *adjective*.

solvency /'sɒlvənsɪ/ *noun* being financially solvent.

solvent /'sɒlv(ə)nt/ ● *adjective* able to pay one's debts; able to dissolve or form solution. ● *noun* solvent liquid etc.

somatic /sə'mætɪk/ *adjective* of the body, not of the mind.

sombre /'sɒmbə/ *adjective* (also *US* **somber**) dark, gloomy, dismal. □ **sombrely** *adverb*; **sombreness** *noun*.

sombrero /sɒm'breərəʊ/ *noun* (*plural* **-s**) broad-brimmed hat worn esp. in Latin America.

some /sʌm/ ● *adjective* unspecified amount or number of; unknown, unspecified; approximately; considerable; at least a small amount of; such to a certain extent; *colloquial* a remarkable. ● *pronoun* some people or things, some number or amount. ● *adverb colloquial* to some extent. □ **somebody** *pronoun* some person, *noun* important person; **someday** at some time in the future; **somehow** for some reason, in some way, by some means; **someone** somebody; **something** unspecified or unknown thing, unexpressed or intangible quantity or quality, *colloquial* notable person or thing; **sometime** at some time, former(ly); **sometimes** occasionally; **somewhat** to some extent; **somewhere** (in or to) some place.

somersault /'sʌməsɒlt/ ● *noun* leap or roll in which one turns head over heels. ● *verb* perform somersault.

somnambulism /sɒm'næmbjʊlɪz(ə)m/ *noun* sleepwalking. □ **somnambulant** *adjective*; **somnambulist** *noun*.

somnolent /'sɒmnələnt/ *adjective* sleepy, drowsy; inducing drowsiness. □ **somnolence** *noun*.

son /sʌn/ *noun* male in relation to his parent(s); male descendant; (+ *of*) male member of (family etc.); male inheritor of a quality etc.; *form of address, esp. to boy*. □ **son-in-law** (*plural* **sons-in-law**) daughter's husband.

sonar /'səʊnɑː/ *noun* system for detecting objects under water by reflected sound; apparatus for this.

sonata /sə'nɑːtə/ *noun* musical composition for one or two instruments in several related movements.

song *noun* words set to music or for singing; vocal music; composition suggestive of song; cry of some birds. □ **for a song** *colloquial* very cheaply; **songbird** bird with musical call; **song thrush** common thrush; **songwriter** writer of (music for) songs.

songster /'sɒŋstə/ *noun* (*feminine* **songstress**) singer; songbird.

sonic /'sɒnɪk/ *adjective* of or using sound or sound waves. □ **sonic bang, boom** noise made by aircraft flying faster than sound.

sonnet /'sɒnɪt/ *noun* poem of 14 lines with fixed rhyme scheme.

sonny /'sʌnɪ/ *noun colloquial familiar form of address to young boy.*

sonorous /'sɒnərəs/ *adjective* having a loud, full, or deep sound; (of speech etc.) imposing. □ **sonority** /sə'nɒr-/ *noun* (*plural* **-ies**).

soon /suːn/ *adverb* in a short time; relatively early; readily, willingly. □ **sooner or later** at some future time. □ **soonish** *adverb*.

soot /sʊt/ *noun* black powdery deposit from smoke.

soothe /suːð/ *verb* (**-thing**) calm; soften, mitigate.

soothsayer /'suːθseɪə/ *noun* seer, prophet.

sooty *adjective* (**-ier, -iest**) covered with soot; black, brownish black.

sop ● *noun* thing given or done to pacify or bribe; piece of bread etc. dipped in gravy etc. ● *verb* (**-pp-**) (+ *up*) soak up.

sophism /'sɒfɪz(ə)m/ *noun* false argument, esp. one meant to deceive.

sophist /'sɒfɪst/ *noun* captious or clever but fallacious reasoner. □ **sophistic** /sə'fɪs-/ *adjective*.

sophisticate /sə'fɪstɪkət/ *noun* sophisticated person.

sophisticated /sə'fɪstɪkeɪtɪd/ *adjective* worldly-wise, cultured, elegant; highly developed and complex. □ **sophistication** *noun*.

sophistry /'sɒfɪstrɪ/ *noun* (*plural* **-ies**) use of sophisms; a sophism.

sophomore /'sɒfəmɔː/ *noun US* second-year university or high-school student.

soporific /sɒpə'rɪfɪk/ ● *adjective* inducing sleep. ● *noun* soporific drug or influence. □ **soporifically** *adverb*.

sopping *adjective* drenched.

soppy *adjective* (**-ier, -iest**) *colloquial* mawkishly sentimental, silly.

soprano /sə'prɑːnəʊ/ ● *noun* (*plural* **-s**) highest singing voice; singer with this. ● *adjective* having range of soprano.

sorbet /'sɔːbeɪ/ *noun* water-ice; sherbet.

sorcerer /'sɔːsərə/ *noun* (*feminine* **sorceress**) magician, wizard. □ **sorcery** *noun* (*plural* **-ies**).

sordid /'sɔːdɪd/ *adjective* dirty, squalid; ignoble, mercenary. □ **sordidly** *adverb*; **sordidness** *noun*.

sore ● *adjective* painful; suffering pain; aggrieved, vexed; *archaic* grievous, severe. ● *noun* sore place, subject, etc. ● *adverb archaic* grievously, severely. □ **soreness** *noun*.

sorely *adverb* extremely.

sorghum /'sɔːɡəm/ *noun* tropical cereal grass.

sorority /sə'rɒrɪtɪ/ *noun* (*plural* **-ies**) *US* female students' society in university or college.

sorrel[1] /'sɒr(ə)l/ *noun* sour-leaved herb.

sorrel[2] /'sɒr(ə)l/ ● *adjective* of light reddish-brown colour. ● *noun* this colour; sorrel animal, esp. horse.

sorrow /'sɒrəʊ/ ● *noun* mental distress caused by loss, disappointment, etc.; cause of sorrow. ● *verb* feel sorrow, mourn. □ **sorrowful** *adjective*.

sorry /'sɒrɪ/ *adjective* (**-ier, -iest**) pained, regretful, penitent; feeling pity; wretched.

sort ● *noun* class, kind; *colloquial* person of specified kind. ● *verb* (often + *out, over*) arrange systematically. □ **of a sort, of sorts** *colloquial* barely deserving the name; **out of sorts** slightly unwell, in low spirits; **sort out** separate into sorts, select from miscellaneous group, disentangle, put into order, solve, *colloquial* deal with or punish.

sortie /'sɔːtiː/ ● *noun* sally, esp. from besieged garrison; operational military flight. ● *verb* (**sortieing**) make sortie.

SOS *noun* (*plural* **SOSs**) international code-signal of extreme distress; urgent appeal for help.

sot *noun* habitual drunkard. □ **sottish** *adjective*.

sotto voce /ˌsɒtəʊ ˈvəʊtʃɪ/ *adverb* in an undertone. [Italian]

sou /suː/ *noun* (*plural* **-s**) *colloquial* very small amount of money; *historical* former French coin of low value.

soubrette /suːˈbret/ *noun* pert maidservant etc. in comedy; actress taking this part.

soubriquet = SOBRIQUET.

soufflé /ˈsuːfleɪ/ *noun* light spongy dish made with stiffly beaten egg white.

sough /saʊ, sʌf/ ● *noun* moaning or rustling sound, e.g. of wind in trees. ● *verb* make this sound.

sought /sɔːt/ *past* & *past participle* of SEEK. □ **sought-after** much in demand.

souk /suːk/ *noun* market-place in Muslim countries.

soul /səʊl/ *noun* spiritual or immaterial part of person; moral, emotional, or intellectual nature of person; personification, pattern; an individual; animating or essential part; energy, intensity; soul music. □ **soul-destroying** tedious, monotonous; **soul mate** person ideally suited to another; **soul music** type of black American music; **soul-searching** introspection.

soulful *adjective* having, expressing, or evoking deep feeling. □ **soulfully** *adverb*.

soulless *adjective* lacking sensitivity or noble qualities; undistinguished, uninteresting.

sound¹ /saʊnd/ ● *noun* sensation produced in ear when surrounding air etc. vibrates; vibrations causing this; what is or may be heard; idea or impression given by words. ● *verb* (cause to) emit sound; utter, pronounce; convey specified impression; give audible signal for; test condition of by sound produced. □ **sound barrier** high resistance of air to objects moving at speeds near that of sound; **sound effect** sound other than speech or music produced artificially for film, broadcast, etc.; **sounding-board** person etc. used to test or disseminate opinion(s), canopy projecting sound towards audience; **sound off** talk loudly, express one's opinions forcefully; **soundproof** *adjective* impervious to sound, *verb* make soundproof; **sound system** equipment for reproducing sound; **soundtrack** sound element of film or videotape, recording of this available separately; **sound wave** wave of compression and rarefaction by which sound is transmitted in air etc.

sound² /saʊnd/ ● *adjective* healthy, not diseased or rotten; uninjured; correct, well-founded; financially secure; undisturbed; thorough. ● *adverb* soundly. □ **soundly** *adverb*; **soundness** *noun*.

sound³ /saʊnd/ *verb* test depth or quality of bottom of (sea, river, etc.); (often + *out*) inquire (esp. discreetly) into views etc. of (person).

sound⁴ /saʊnd/ *noun* strait (of water).

sounding *noun* measurement of depth of water; (in *plural*) region near enough to shore for sounding; (in *plural*) cautious investigation.

soup /suːp/ ● *noun* liquid food made by boiling meat, fish, or vegetables. ● *verb* (usually + *up*) *colloquial* increase power of (engine), enliven. □ **in the soup** *colloquial* in difficulties; **soup-kitchen** place supplying free soup etc. to the poor; **soup-spoon** large round-bowled spoon. □ **soupy** *adjective* (**-ier, -iest**).

soupçon /ˈsuːpsɔ̃/ *noun* small quantity, trace.

sour /saʊə/ ● *adjective* having acid taste or smell (as) from unripeness or fermentation; morose, bitter; unpleasant, distasteful; (of soil) dank. ● *verb* make or become sour. □ **sour grapes** resentful disparagement of something coveted; **sourpuss** *colloquial* bad-tempered person. □ **sourly** *adverb*; **sourness** *noun*.

source /sɔːs/ *noun* place from which river or stream issues; place of origination; person, book, etc. providing information. □ **at source** at point of origin or issue.

souse /saʊs/ ● *verb* (**-sing**) immerse in pickle or other liquid; (as **soused** *adjective*) *colloquial* drunk; (usually + *in*) soak (thing). ● *noun* pickle made with salt; *US* food in pickle; a plunge or drenching in water.

soutane /suːˈtɑːn/ *noun* cassock of RC priest.

south /saʊθ/ ● *noun* point of horizon opposite north; corresponding compass point; (usually **the South**) southern part of world, country, town, etc. ● *adjective* towards, at, near, or facing south; (of wind) from south. ● *adverb* towards, at, or near south; (+ *of*) further south than. □ **southbound** travelling or leading south; **south-east, -west** point midway between south and east or west; **southpaw** *colloquial* left-handed person, esp. boxer; **south-south-east, south-south-west** point midway between south and south-east or south-west. □ **southward** *adjective, adverb,* & *noun*; **southwards** *adverb*.

southerly /ˈsʌðəlɪ/ *adjective* & *adverb* in southern position or direction; (of wind) from south.

southern /ˈsʌð(ə)n/ *adjective* of or in south. □ **Southern Cross** constellation with stars forming cross; **southern lights** aurora australis. □ **southernmost** *adjective*.

southerner *noun* native or inhabitant of south.

souvenir /suːvəˈnɪə/ *noun* memento of place, occasion, etc.

sou'wester /saʊˈwestə/ *noun* waterproof hat with broad flap at back; SW wind.

sovereign /ˈsɒvrɪn/ ● *noun* supreme ruler, esp. monarch; *historical* British gold coin nominally worth £1. ● *adjective* supreme; royal; (of remedy etc.) effective. □ **sovereignty** *noun* (*plural* **-ies**).

Soviet /ˈsəʊvɪət/ *historical* ● *adjective* of USSR. ● *noun* citizen of USSR; (**soviet**) elected council in USSR.

sow¹ /səʊ/ *verb* (*past* **sowed**; *past participle* **sown** or **sowed**) scatter (seed) on or in earth, (often + *with*) plant with seed; initiate.

sow² /saʊ/ *noun* adult female pig.

soy *noun* (in full **soy sauce**) sauce made from pickled soya beans.

soya /ˈsɔɪə/ *noun* (in full **soya bean**) (seed of) leguminous plant yielding edible oil and flour.

sozzled /ˈsɒz(ə)ld/ *adjective colloquial* very drunk.

spa /spɑː/ *noun* curative mineral spring; resort with this.

space ● *noun* continuous expanse in which things exist and move; amount of this taken by thing or available; interval between points or objects; empty area; outdoor urban recreation area; outer space; interval of time; expanse of paper used in writing, available for advertising, etc.; blank between printed, typed, or written words etc.; *Printing* piece of metal separating words etc. ● *verb* (**-cing**) set or arrange at intervals; put spaces between. □ **space age** era of space travel; **space-age** very modern; **spacecraft** vehicle for travelling in outer space; **spaceman, spacewoman** astronaut; **space out** spread out (more) widely; **spaceship** spacecraft; **space shuttle** spacecraft for repeated use; **space station** artificial satellite as base for operations in outer space; **spacesuit** sealed pressurized suit for astronaut in space; **space-time** fusion of concepts of space and time as 4-dimensional continuum.

spacious /ˈspeɪʃəs/ *adjective* having ample space, roomy. □ **spaciously** *adverb*; **spaciousness** *noun*.

spade¹ *noun* long-handled digging tool with rectangular metal blade. □ **spadework** hard preparatory work. □ **spadeful** *noun* (*plural* **-s**).

spade² noun playing card of suit denoted by black inverted heart-shaped figures with short stems.

spaghetti /spə'getɪ/ noun pasta in long thin strands. □ **spaghetti western** cowboy film made cheaply in Italy.

span¹ ● noun full extent from end to end; each part of bridge between supports; maximum lateral extent of aeroplane or its wing or of bird's wing etc.; distance between outstretched tips of thumb and little finger; 9 inches. ● verb (**-nn-**) extend from side to side or end to end of; bridge (river etc.).

span² past of SPIN.

spandrel /'spændrɪl/ noun space between curve of arch and surrounding rectangular moulding, or between curves of adjoining arches and moulding above.

spangle /'spæŋg(ə)l/ ● noun small piece of glittering material, esp. one of many used to ornament dress etc. ● verb (**-ling**) (esp. as **spangled** adjective) cover (as) with spangles.

Spaniard /'spænjəd/ noun native or national of Spain.

spaniel /'spænj(ə)l/ noun dog of breed with long silky coat and drooping ears.

Spanish /'spænɪʃ/ ● adjective of Spain. ● noun language of Spain.

spank verb & noun slap, esp. on buttocks.

spanker noun Nautical fore-and-aft sail on mizen-mast.

spanking ● adjective brisk; colloquial striking, excellent. ● adverb colloquial very. ● noun slapping on buttocks.

spanner /'spænə/ noun tool for turning nut on bolt etc. □ **spanner in the works** colloquial impediment.

spar¹ noun stout pole, esp. as ship's mast etc.

spar² ● verb (**-rr-**) make motions of boxing; argue. ● noun sparring; boxing match. □ **sparring partner** boxer employed to spar with another as training; person with whom one enjoys arguing.

spar³ noun easily split crystalline mineral.

spare /speə/ ● adjective not required for ordinary or present use, extra; for emergency or occasional use; lean, thin; frugal. ● noun spare part. ● verb (**-ring**) afford to give, dispense with; refrain from killing, hurting, etc.; not inflict; be frugal or grudging of. □ **go spare** colloquial become very angry; **spare (person's) life** not kill; **spare part** duplicate, esp. as replacement; **spare-rib** closely trimmed rib of esp. pork; **spare time** leisure; **spare tyre** colloquial roll of fat round waist; **to spare** left over. □ **sparely** adverb; **spareness** noun.

sparing adjective frugal, economical; restrained. □ **sparingly** adverb.

spark ● noun fiery particle of burning substance; (often + of) small amount; flash of light between electric conductors etc.; this for firing explosive mixture in internal-combustion engine; flash of wit etc.; (also **bright spark**) lively or clever person. ● verb emit spark(s); (often + off) stir into activity, initiate. □ **spark plug, sparking plug** device for making spark in internal-combustion engine. □ **sparky** adjective.

sparkle /'spɑːk(ə)l/ ● verb (**-ling**) (seem to) emit sparks; glitter, scintillate; (of wine etc.) effervesce. ● noun glitter; lively quality. □ **sparkly** adjective.

sparkler noun sparkling firework; colloquial diamond.

sparrow /'spærəʊ/ noun small brownish-grey bird. □ **sparrowhawk** small hawk.

sparse /spɑːs/ adjective thinly scattered. □ **sparsely** adverb; **sparseness** noun; **sparsity** noun.

Spartan /'spɑːt(ə)n/ ● adjective of ancient Sparta; austere, rigorous. ● noun native or citizen of Sparta.

spasm /'spæz(ə)m/ noun sudden involuntary muscular contraction; convulsive movement or emotion etc.; (usually + of) colloquial brief spell.

spasmodic /spæz'mɒdɪk/ adjective of or in spasms, intermittent. □ **spasmodically** adverb.

spastic /'spæstɪk/ ● adjective of or having cerebral palsy. ● noun spastic person.

spat¹ past & past participle of SPIT¹.

spat² (usually in plural) historical short gaiter covering shoe.

spate noun river-flood; large amount or number (of similar events etc.).

spathe /speɪð/ noun large bract(s) enveloping flower-cluster.

spatial /'speɪʃ(ə)l/ adjective of space. □ **spatially** adverb.

spatter /'spætə/ ● verb splash or scatter in drips. ● noun splash; pattering.

spatula /'spætjʊlə/ noun broad-bladed implement used esp. by artists and in cookery.

spawn ● verb (of fish, frog, etc.) produce (eggs); be produced as eggs or young; produce or generate in large numbers. ● noun eggs of fish, frogs, etc.; white fibrous matter from which fungi grow.

spay verb sterilize (female animal) by removing ovaries.

speak verb (past **spoke**; past participle **spoken** /'spəʊk(ə)n/) utter words in ordinary way; utter (words, the truth, etc.); converse; (+ of, about) mention; (+ for) act as spokesman for; (+ to) speak with reference to or in support of; deliver speech; (be able to) use (specified language) in speaking; convey idea; (usually + to) affect. □ **speak for itself** be sufficient evidence; **speaking clock** telephone service announcing correct time; **speak out** give one's opinion courageously; **speak up** speak (more) loudly.

speaker noun person who speaks, esp. in public; person who speaks specified language; (**Speaker**) presiding officer of legislative assembly; loudspeaker.

spear ● noun thrusting or hurling weapon with long shaft and sharp point; tip and stem of asparagus, broccoli, etc. ● verb pierce or strike (as) with spear. □ **spearhead** noun point of spear; person(s) leading attack or challenge, verb act as spearhead of (attack etc.); **spearmint** common garden mint.

spec¹ noun colloquial speculation. □ **on spec** as a gamble.

spec² noun colloquial specification.

special /'speʃ(ə)l/ ● adjective exceptional; peculiar, specific; for particular purpose; for children with special needs. ● noun special constable, train, edition of newspaper, dish on menu, etc. □ **Special Branch** police department dealing with political security; **special constable** person assisting police in routine duties or in emergencies; **special effects** illusions created by props, camera-work, etc.; **special licence** licence allowing immediate marriage without banns; **special pleading** biased reasoning. □ **specially** adverb.

specialist noun person trained in particular branch of profession, esp. medicine; person specially studying subject or area.

speciality /speʃɪ'ælɪtɪ/ noun (plural **-ies**) special subject, product, activity, etc.; special feature or skill.

specialize verb (also **-ise**) (**-zing** of **-sing**) (often + in) become or be specialist; devote oneself to an interest, skill, etc.; (esp. in passive) adapt for particular purpose; (as **specialized** adjective) of a specialist. □ **specialization** noun.

specialty /'speʃəltɪ/ noun (plural **-ies**) esp. US speciality.

specie /'spiːʃiː/ noun coin as opposed to paper money.

species /'spiːʃiːz/ noun (plural same) class of things having common characteristics; group of animals or plants within genus; kind, sort.

specific /spə'sɪfɪk/ ● *adjective* clearly defined; relating to particular subject, peculiar; exact, giving full details; *archaic* (of medicine etc.) for particular disease. ● *noun archaic* specific medicine; specific aspect. □ **specific gravity** relative density. □ **specifically** *adverb*; **specificity** /-'fɪs-/ *noun*.

specification /spesɪfɪ'keɪʃ(ə)n/ *noun* specifying; (esp. in *plural*) detailed description of work (to be) done or of invention, patent, etc.

specify /'spesɪfaɪ/ *verb* (**-ies, -ied**) name or mention expressly or as condition; include in specifications.

specimen /'spesmɪn/ *noun* individual or sample taken as example of class or whole, esp. in experiments etc.; *colloquial usually derogatory* person of specified sort.

specious /'spiːʃəs/ *adjective* plausible but wrong.

speck ● *noun* small spot or stain; particle. ● *verb* (esp. as **specked** *adjective*) mark with specks.

speckle /'spek(ə)l/ ● *noun* speck, esp. one of many markings. ● *verb* (**-ling**) (esp. as **speckled** *adjective*) mark with speckles.

specs *plural noun colloquial* spectacles.

spectacle /'spektək(ə)l/ *noun* striking, impressive, or ridiculous sight; public show; object of public attention; (in *plural*) pair of lenses in frame supported on nose and ears, to correct defective eyesight.

spectacled *adjective* wearing spectacles.

spectacular /spek'tækjʊlə/ ● *adjective* striking, impressive, lavish. ● *noun* spectacular performance. □ **spectacularly** *adverb*.

spectator /spek'teɪtə/ *noun* person who watches a show, game, incident, etc. □ **spectator sport** sport attracting many spectators. □ **spectate** *verb* (**-ting**).

specter *US* = SPECTRE.

spectra *plural of* SPECTRUM.

spectral /'spektr(ə)l/ *adjective* of or like spectres or spectra; ghostly.

spectre /'spektə/ *noun* (*US* **specter**) ghost; haunting presentiment.

spectroscope /'spektrəskəʊp/ *noun* instrument for recording and examining spectra. □ **spectroscopic** /-'skɒp/ *adjective*; **spectroscopy** /-'trɒskəpɪ/ *noun*.

spectrum /'spektrəm/ *noun* (*plural* **-tra**) band of colours as seen in rainbow etc.; entire or wide range of subject, emotion, etc.; arrangement of electromagnetic radiation by wavelength.

speculate /'spekjʊleɪt/ *verb* (**-ting**) (usually + *on, upon, about*) theorize, conjecture; deal in commodities etc. in expectation of profiting from fluctuating prices. □ **speculation** *noun*; **speculative** /-lətɪv/ *adjective*; **speculator** *noun*.

sped *past & past participle of* SPEED.

speech *noun* faculty, act, or manner of speaking; formal public address; language, dialect. □ **speech day** annual prize-giving day in school; **speech therapy** treatment for defective speech.

speechify /'spiːtʃɪfaɪ/ *verb* (**-ies, -ied**) *jocular* make speeches.

speechless *adjective* temporarily silenced by emotion etc.

speed ● *noun* rapidity; rate of progress or motion; gear on bicycle; relative sensitivity of photographic film to light; *slang* amphetamine. ● *verb* (*past & past participle* **sped**) go or send quickly; (*past & past participle* **speeded**) travel at illegal or dangerous speed; *archaic* be or make prosperous or successful. □ **speedboat** fast motor boat; **speed limit** maximum permitted speed on road etc.; **speedway** (dirt track for) motorcycle racing, *US* road or track for fast vehicles. □ **speeder** *noun*.

speedometer /spiː'dɒmɪtə/ *noun* instrument on vehicle indicating its speed.

speedwell /'spiːdwel/ *noun* small blue-flowered herbaceous plant.

speedy *adjective* (**-ier, -iest**) rapid; prompt. □ **speedily** *adverb*.

speleology /spiːlɪ'ɒlədʒɪ/ *noun* the study of caves etc.

spell¹ *verb* (*past & past participle* **spelt** or **spelled**) write or name correctly the letters of (word etc.); (of letters) form (word etc.); result in. □ **spell out** make out letter by letter, explain in detail. □ **speller** *noun*.

spell² *noun* words used as charm; effect of these; fascination. □ **spellbound** held as if by spell, fascinated.

spell³ *noun* (fairly) short period; period of some activity or work.

spelling *noun* way word is spelt; ability to spell.

spelt¹ *past & past participle of* SPELL¹.

spelt² *noun* kind of wheat giving very fine flour.

spend *verb* (*past & past participle* **spent**) pay out (money); use or consume (time or energy); use up; (as **spent** *adjective*) having lost force or strength. □ **spendthrift** extravagant person. □ **spender** *noun*.

sperm *noun* (*plural* same or **-s**) spermatozoon; semen. □ **sperm bank** store of semen for artificial insemination; **sperm whale** large whale hunted for spermaceti.

spermaceti /spɜːmə'setɪ/ *noun* white waxy substance used for ointments etc.

spermatozoon /spɜːmətəʊ'zəʊən/ *noun* (*plural* **-zoa**) fertilizing cell of male organism.

spermicide /'spɜːmɪsaɪd/ *noun* substance that kills spermatozoa. □ **spermicidal** /-'saɪd-/ *adjective*.

spew *verb* (often + *up*) vomit; (often + *out*) (cause to) gush.

sphagnum /'sfægnəm/ *noun* (*plural* **-na**) (in full **sphagnum moss**) moss growing in bogs, used as packing etc.

sphere /sfɪə/ *noun* solid figure with every point on its surface equidistant from centre; ball, globe; field of action, influence, etc.; place in society; *historical* each of revolving shells in which heavenly bodies were thought to be set.

spherical /'sferɪk(ə)l/ *adjective* shaped like sphere; of spheres. □ **spherically** *adverb*.

spheroid /'sfɪərɔɪd/ *noun* spherelike but not perfectly spherical body. □ **spheroidal** /-'rɔɪd-/ *adjective*.

sphincter /'sfɪŋktə/ *noun* ring of muscle closing and opening orifice.

Sphinx /sfɪŋks/ *noun* ancient Egyptian stone figure with lion's body and human or animal head; (**sphinx**) inscrutable person.

spice ● *noun* aromatic or pungent vegetable substance used as flavouring; spices collectively; piquant quality; slight flavour. ● *verb* (**-cing**) flavour with spice; enhance.

spick and span *adjective* trim and clean; smart, new-looking.

spicy *adjective* (**-ier, -iest**) of or flavoured with spice; piquant, improper. □ **spiciness** *noun*.

spider /'spaɪdə/ *noun* 8-legged arthropod, many species of which spin webs esp. to capture insects as food. □ **spider plant** house plant with long narrow leaves.

spidery *adjective* elongated and thin.

spiel /ʃpiːl/ *noun slang* glib speech or story, sales pitch.

spigot /'spɪgət/ *noun* small peg or plug; device for controlling flow of liquid in tap.

spike¹ ● *noun* sharp point; pointed piece of metal, esp. forming top of iron railing; metal point on sole of running shoe to prevent slipping; (in *plural*) spiked running shoes; large nail. ● *verb* (**-king**) put spikes on or into; fix on spike; *colloquial* add alcohol to (drink), contaminate. □ **spike (person's) guns** defeat his or her plans.

spike² *noun* cluster of flower heads on long stem.

spikenard /'spaikna:d/ *noun* tall sweet-smelling plant; *historical* aromatic ointment formerly made from this.

spiky *adjective* (**-ier, -iest**) like a spike; having spikes; *colloquial* irritable.

spill¹ ● *verb* (*past & past participle* **spilt** or **spilled**) allow (liquid etc.) to fall or run out of container, esp. accidentally; (of liquid etc.) fall or run out thus; throw from vehicle, saddle, etc.; (+ *into, out,* etc.) leave quickly; *slang* divulge (information etc.); shed (blood). ● *noun* spilling, being spilt; tumble, esp. from horse or vehicle. □ **spill the beans** *colloquial* divulge secret etc. □ **spillage** *noun*.

spill² *noun* thin strip of wood, paper, etc. for lighting candle etc.

spillikin /'spilikin/ *noun* splinter of wood etc.; (in *plural*) game in which thin rods are removed one at a time from heap without disturbing others.

spilt *past & past participle* of SPILL¹.

spin ● *verb* (**-nn-**; *past* **spun** or **span**; *past participle* **spun**) (cause to) turn or whirl round rapidly; make (yarn) by drawing out and twisting together fibres of wool etc.; make (web etc.) by extruding fine viscous thread; (of person's head) be in a whirl; tell or compose (story etc.); toss (coin); (as **spun** *adjective*) made into threads. ● *noun* revolving motion, whirl; rotating dive of aircraft; secondary twisting motion e.g. of ball in flight; *colloquial* brief drive, esp. in car. □ **spin bowler** *Cricket* one who imparts spin to ball; **spin-drier, -dryer** machine for drying clothes by spinning them in rotating drum; **spin-dry** *verb*; **spinning wheel** household implement for spinning yarn, with spindle driven by wheel with crank or treadle; **spin-off** incidental result, esp. from technology; **spin out** prolong; **spin a yarn** tell story.

spina bifida /spaina 'bifidə/ *noun* congenital spinal defect, with protruding membranes.

spinach /'spinidʒ/ *noun* green vegetable with edible leaves.

spinal /'spain(ə)l/ *adjective* of spine. □ **spinal column** spine; **spinal cord** cylindrical nervous structure within spine.

spindle /'spind(ə)l/ *noun* slender rod for twisting and winding thread in spinning; pin or axis on which something revolves; turned piece of wood used as banister etc.

spindly *adjective* (**-ier, -iest**) long or tall and thin.

spindrift /'spindrift/ *noun* spray on surface of sea.

spine *noun* series of vertebrae extending from skull, backbone; needle-like outgrowth of animal or plant; part of book enclosing page-fastening; ridge, sharp projection. □ **spine-chiller** suspense or horror film, story, etc.

spineless *adjective* lacking resoluteness.

spinet /spi'net/ *noun historical* small harpsichord with oblique strings.

spinnaker /'spinəkə/ *noun* large triangular sail used at bow of yacht.

spinner *noun* spin bowler; person or thing that spins, esp. manufacturer engaged in spinning; spin-drier; revolving bait or lure in fishing.

spinneret /'spinəret/ *noun* spinning-organ in spider etc.

spinney /'spini/ *noun* (*plural* **-s**) small wood, thicket.

spinster /'spinstə/ *noun formal* unmarried woman.

spiny *adjective* (**-ier, -iest**) having (many) spines.

spiraea /spai'riːə/ *noun* (US **spirea**) garden plant related to meadowsweet.

spiral /'spaiər(ə)l/ ● *adjective* coiled in a plane or as round a cylinder or cone; having this shape. ● *noun* spiral curve; progressive rise or fall. ● *verb* (**-ll-**; US **-l-**) move in spiral course; (of prices etc.) rise or fall continuously. □ **spiral staircase** circular staircase round central axis.

spirant /'spaiərənt/ ● *adjective* uttered with continuous expulsion of breath. ● *noun* spirant consonant.

spire *noun* tapering structure, esp. on church tower; any tapering thing.

spirea *US* = SPIRAEA.

spirit /'spirit/ ● *noun* person's essence or intelligence, soul; rational being without material body; ghost; person's character; attitude; type of person; prevailing tendency; (usually in *plural*) distilled alcoholic liquor; distilled volatile liquid; courage, vivacity; (in *plural*) mood; essential as opposed to formal meaning. ● *verb* (**-t-**) (usually + *away, off,* etc.) convey mysteriously. □ **spirit gum** quick-drying gum for attaching false hair; **spirit lamp** lamp burning methylated or other volatile spirit; **spirit level** device used to test horizontality.

spirited *adjective* lively, courageous. □ **-spirited** in specified mood. □ **spiritedly** *adverb*.

spiritual /'spiritʃʊəl/ ● *adjective* of spirit; religious, divine, inspired; refined, sensitive. ● *noun* (also **Negro spiritual**) religious song originally of American blacks. □ **spirituality** /-'æl-/ *noun*; **spiritually** *adverb*.

spiritualism *noun* belief in, and practice of, communication with the dead, esp. through mediums. □ **spiritualist** *noun*; **spiritualistic** /-'lis-/ *adjective*.

spirituous /'spiritʃʊəs/ *adjective* very alcoholic; distilled as well as fermented.

spit¹ ● *verb* (**-tt-**; *past & past participle* **spat** or **spit**) eject (esp. saliva) from mouth; do this as gesture of contempt; utter vehemently; (of fire etc.) throw out with explosion; (of rain etc.) fall lightly; make spitting noise. ● *noun* saliva; spitting. □ **spitfire** fiery-tempered person; **spitting distance** *colloquial* very short distance; **spitting image** *colloquial* exact counterpart or likeness.

spit² ● *noun* rod for skewering meat for roasting over fire etc.; point of land projecting into sea; spade-depth of earth. ● *verb* (**-tt-**) pierce (as) with spit. □ **spit-roast** roast on spit.

spite ● *noun* ill will, malice. ● *verb* (**-ting**) hurt, thwart. □ **in spite of** notwithstanding.

spiteful *adjective* malicious. □ **spitefully** *adverb*.

spittle /'spit(ə)l/ *noun* saliva.

spittoon /spi'tuːn/ *noun* vessel to spit into.

spiv *noun colloquial* man, esp. flashily-dressed one, living from shady dealings. □ **spivvish** *adjective*; **spivvy** *adjective*.

splash ● *verb* (cause to) scatter in drops; wet or stain by splashing; (usually + *across, along, about,* etc.) move with splashing; jump or fall into water etc. with splash; display (news) conspicuously; decorate with scattered colour; spend (money) ostentatiously. ● *noun* act or noise of splashing; quantity splashed; mark of splashing; prominent news feature, display, etc.; patch of colour; *colloquial* small quantity of soda water etc. (in drink). □ **splashback** panel behind sink etc. to protect wall from splashes; **splashdown** alighting of spacecraft on sea; **splash down** *verb*; **splash out** *colloquial* spend money freely.

splat *colloquial* ● *noun* sharp splattering sound. ● *adverb* with splat. ● *verb* (**-tt-**) fall or hit with splat.

splatter /'splætə/ *verb & noun* splash, esp. with continuous noisy action, spatter.

splay ● *verb* spread apart; (of opening) have sides diverging; make (opening) with divergent sides.

● *noun* surface at oblique angle to another. ● *adjective* splayed.

spleen *noun* abdominal organ regulating quality of blood; moroseness, irritability.

splendid /'splendɪd/ *adjective* magnificent; glorious, dignified; excellent. □ **splendidly** *adverb*.

splendiferous /splen'dɪfərəs/ *adjective colloquial* splendid.

splendour /'splendə/ *noun* (US **splendor**) dazzling brightness; magnificence.

splenetic /splɪ'netɪk/ *adjective* bad-tempered, peevish.

splenic /'splenɪk/ *adjective* of or in spleen.

splice ● *verb* (**-cing**) join (ropes) by interweaving strands; join (pieces of wood, tape, etc.) by overlapping; (esp. as **spliced** *adjective*) *colloquial* join in marriage. ● *noun* join made by splicing.

splint ● *noun* strip of wood etc. bound to broken limb while it heals. ● *verb* secure with splint.

splinter /'splɪntə/ ● *noun* small sharp fragment of wood, stone, glass, etc. ● *verb* split into splinters, shatter. □ **splinter group** breakaway political group. □ **splintery** *adjective*.

split ● *verb* (**-tt-**; *past & past participle* **split**) break, esp. lengthwise or with grain; break forcibly; (often + *up*) divide into parts, esp. equal shares; (often + *off*, *away*) remove or be removed by breaking or dividing; (usually + *on*, *over*, etc.) divide into disagreeing or hostile parties; cause fission of (atom); *slang* leave, esp. suddenly; (usually + *on*) *colloquial* inform; (as **splitting** *adjective*) (of headache) severe; (of head) suffer severe headache. ● *noun* splitting; disagreement, schism; (in *plural*) feat of leaping or sitting with legs straight and pointing in opposite directions. □ **split hairs** make over-subtle distinctions; **split infinitive** one with adverb etc. inserted between *to* and verb (see note below); **split-level** with more than one level; **split personality** condition of alternating personalities; **split pin** metal cotter with its two ends splayed out after passing through hole; **split second** very short time; **split-second** very rapid, (of timing) very accurate; **split up** separate, end relationship.

■ **Usage** Split infinitives, as in *I want to quickly sum up* and *Your job is to really get to know everybody*, are common in informal English, but many people consider them incorrect and prefer *I want quickly to sum up* or *I want to sum up quickly*. They should therefore be avoided in formal English, but note that just changing the order of words can alter the meaning, e.g. *Your job is really to get to know everybody.*

splodge *colloquial* ● *noun* daub, blot, smear. ● *verb* (**-ging**) make splodge on. □ **splodgy** *adjective*.

splosh *colloquial* ● *verb* move with splashing sound. ● *noun* splashing sound; splash of water etc.

splotch *noun & verb* splodge. □ **splotchy** *adjective*.

splurge *colloquial* ● *noun* sudden extravagance; ostentatious display or effort. ● *verb* (**-ging**) (usually + *on*) make splurge.

splutter /'splʌtə/ ● *verb* speak or express in choking manner; emit spitting sounds; speak rapidly or incoherently. ● *noun* spluttering speech or sound.

spoil ● *verb* (*past & past participle* **spoilt** or **spoiled**) make or become useless or unsatisfactory; reduce enjoyment etc. of; decay, go bad; ruin character of by over-indulgence. ● *noun* (usually in *plural*) plunder, stolen goods; profit or advantages accruing from success or position. □ **spoilsport** person who spoils others' enjoyment; **spoilt for choice** having excessive number of choices.

spoiler *noun* device on aircraft to increase drag; device on vehicle to improve road-holding at speed.

spoilt *past & past participle* of SPOIL.

spoke[1] *noun* each of rods running from hub to rim of wheel. □ **put a spoke in (person's) wheel** thwart, hinder.

spoke[2] *past* of SPEAK.

spoken *past participle* of SPEAK.

spokesman /'spəʊksmən/ *noun* (*feminine* **spokeswoman**) person who speaks for others, representative.

spokesperson /'spəʊkspɜːs(ə)n/ *noun* (*plural* **-s** or **spokespeople**) spokesman or spokeswoman.

spoliation /spəʊlɪ'eɪʃ(ə)n/ *noun* plundering, pillage.

spondee /'spɒndiː/ *noun* metrical foot of two long syllables. □ **spondaic** /-'deɪɪk/ *adjective*.

sponge /spʌndʒ/ ● *noun* sea animal with porous body wall and tough elastic skeleton; this skeleton or piece of porous rubber etc. used in bathing, cleaning, etc.; thing like sponge in consistency, esp. sponge cake; act of sponging. ● *verb* (**-ging**) wipe or clean with sponge; (often + *out*, *away*, etc.) wipe off or rub out (as) with sponge; (often + *up*) absorb (as) with sponge; (often + *on*, *off*) live as parasite. □ **sponge bag** waterproof bag for toilet articles; **sponge cake**, **pudding** one of light spongelike consistency; **sponge rubber** porous rubber.

sponger *noun* parasitic person.

spongy *adjective* (**-ier**, **-iest**) like a sponge, porous, elastic, absorbent.

sponsor /'spɒnsə/ ● *noun* person who pledges money to charity in return for specified activity by someone; patron of artistic or sporting activity etc.; company etc. financing broadcast in return for advertising; person introducing legislation; godparent at baptism. ● *verb* be sponsor for. □ **sponsorship** *noun*.

spontaneous /spɒn'teɪnɪəs/ *adjective* acting, done, or occurring without external cause; instinctive, automatic, natural. □ **spontaneity** /-tə'neɪətɪ/ *noun*; **spontaneously** *adverb*.

spoof /spuːf/ *noun & verb colloquial* parody; hoax, swindle.

spook /spuːk/ ● *noun colloquial* ghost. ● *verb* esp. US frighten, unnerve. □ **spooky** *adjective* (**-ier**, **-iest**).

spool /spuːl/ ● *noun* reel on which something is wound; revolving cylinder of angler's reel. ● *verb* wind on spool.

spoon /spuːn/ ● *noun* utensil with bowl and handle for putting food in mouth or for stirring etc.; spoonful; spoon-shaped thing, esp. (in full **spoon-bait**) revolving metal fish-lure. ● *verb* (often + *up*, *out*) take (liquid etc.) with spoon; hit (ball) feebly upwards. □ **spoonbill** wading bird with broad flat-tipped bill; **spoonfeed** feed with spoon, give help etc. to (person) without demanding any effort from recipient. □ **spoonful** *noun* (*plural* **-s**).

spoonerism /'spuːnərɪz(ə)m/ *noun* (usually accidental) transposition of initial sounds of two or more words.

spoor /spʊə/ *noun* animal's track or scent.

sporadic /spə'rædɪk/ *adjective* occurring only sparsely or occasionally. □ **sporadically** *adverb*.

spore *noun* reproductive cell of ferns, fungi, protozoa, etc.

sporran /'spɒrən/ *noun* pouch worn in front of kilt.

sport ● *noun* game or competitive activity usually involving physical exertion; these collectively; (in *plural*) meeting for competition in athletics; amusement, fun; *colloquial* sportsman, good fellow; person with specified attitude to games, rules, etc. ● *verb* amuse oneself, play about; wear or exhibit, esp. ostentatiously. □ **sports car** low-built fast car; **sports coat**, **jacket** man's informal jacket; **sports ground** piece of land used for sport; **sportswear** clothes for sports, informal clothes.

sporting *adjective* of or interested in sport; generous, fair. ◻ **sporting chance** some possibility of success. ◻ **sportingly** *adverb*.

sportive *adjective* playful.

sportsman /'spɔːtsmən/ *noun* (*feminine* **sportswoman**) person engaging in sport; fair and generous person. ◻ **sportsmanlike** *adjective*; **sportsmanship** *noun*.

sporty *adjective* (**-ier, -iest**) *colloquial* fond of sport; *colloquial* rakish, showy.

spot ● *noun* small mark differing in colour etc. from surface it is on; pimple, blemish; particular place, locality; particular part of one's body or character; *colloquial* one's (regular) position in organization, programme, etc.; *colloquial* small quantity; spotlight. ● *verb* (**-tt-**) *colloquial* pick out, recognize, catch sight of; watch for and take note of (trains, talent, etc.); (as **spotted** *adjective*) marked with spots; make spots, rain slightly. ◻ **in a (tight) spot** *colloquial* in difficulties; **on the spot** at scene of event, *colloquial* in position demanding response or action, without delay, without moving backwards or forwards; **spot cash** money paid immediately after sale; **spot check** sudden or random check; **spotlight** *noun* beam of light directed on small area, lamp projecting this, full publicity, *verb* direct spotlight on; **spot on** *colloquial* precise(ly); **spotted dick** suet pudding containing currants; **spot-weld** join (metal surfaces) by welding at points. ◻ **spotter** *noun*.

spotless *adjective* absolutely clean, unblemished. ◻ **spotlessly** *adverb*.

spotty *adjective* (**-ier, -iest**) marked with spots; patchy, irregular.

spouse /spaʊz/ *noun* husband or wife.

spout /spaʊt/ ● *noun* projecting tube or lip for pouring from teapot, kettle, jug, fountain, roof-gutter, etc.; jet of liquid. ● *verb* discharge or issue forcibly in jet; utter at length or pompously. ◻ **up the spout** *slang* useless, ruined, pregnant.

sprain ● *verb* wrench (ankle, wrist, etc.) causing pain or swelling. ● *noun* such injury.

sprang *past of* SPRING.

sprat *noun* small sea fish.

sprawl ● *verb* sit, lie, or fall with limbs spread out untidily; spread untidily, straggle. ● *noun* sprawling movement, position, or mass; straggling urban expansion.

spray[1] ● *noun* water etc. flying in small drops; liquid intended for spraying; device for spraying. ● *verb* throw as spray; sprinkle (as) with spray; (of tomcat) mark environment with urine to attract females. ◻ **spray-gun** device for spraying paint etc. ◻ **sprayer** *noun*.

spray[2] *noun* sprig with flowers or leaves, small branch; ornament in similar form.

spread /spred/ ● *verb* (*past & past participle* **spread**) (often + *out*) open, extend, unfold, cause to cover larger surface, have wide or increasing extent; (cause to) become widely known; cover; lay (table). ● *noun* act, capability, or extent of spreading; diffusion; breadth; increased girth; difference between two rates, prices, etc.; *colloquial* elaborate meal; paste for spreading on bread etc.; bedspread; printed matter spread over more than one column. ◻ **spread eagle** figure of eagle with legs and wings extended as emblem; **spread-eagle** place (person) with arms and legs spread out, defeat utterly; **spreadsheet** computer program for handling tabulated figures etc., esp. in accounting.

spree *noun colloquial* extravagant outing; bout of drinking etc.

sprig ● *noun* small branch or shoot; ornament resembling this, esp. on fabric. ● *verb* (**-gg-**) ornament with sprigs.

sprightly /'spraɪtlɪ/ *adjective* (**-ier, -iest**) vivacious, lively.

spring ● *verb* (*past* **sprang**; *past participle* **sprung**) rise rapidly or suddenly, leap; move rapidly (as) by action of a spring; (usually + *from*) originate; (cause to) act or appear unexpectedly; *slang* contrive escape of (person from prison etc.); (usually as **sprung** *adjective*) provide with springs. ● *noun* jump, leap; recoil; elasticity; elastic device usually of coiled metal used esp. to drive clockwork or for cushioning in furniture or vehicles; season of year between winter and summer; (often + *of*) early stage of life etc.; place where water, oil, etc. wells up from earth, basin or flow so formed; motive for or origin of action, custom, etc. ◻ **spring balance** device measuring weight by tension of spring; **springboard** flexible board for leaping or diving from, source of impetus; **spring-clean** *noun* thorough cleaning of house, esp. in spring, *verb* clean thus; **spring greens** young cabbage leaves; **spring a leak** develop leak; **spring onion** young onion eaten raw; **spring roll** Chinese fried pancake filled with vegetables etc.; **spring tide** tide with greatest rise and fall; **springtime** season or period of spring.

springbok /'sprɪŋbɒk/ *noun* (*plural* same or **-s**) S. African gazelle.

springer *noun* small spaniel.

springy *adjective* (**-ier, -iest**) elastic.

sprinkle /'sprɪŋk(ə)l/ ● *verb* (**-ling**) scatter in small drops or particles; (often + *with*) subject to sprinkling; (of liquid etc.) fall thus on. ● *noun* (usually + *of*) light shower, sprinkling.

sprinkler *noun* device for sprinkling lawn or extinguishing fires.

sprinkling *noun* small sparse number or amount.

sprint ● *verb* run short distance at top speed. ● *noun* such run; similar short effort in cycling, swimming, etc. ◻ **sprinter** *noun*.

sprit *noun* small diagonal spar from mast to upper outer corner of sail. ◻ **spritsail** /'sprɪts(ə)l/ sail extended by sprit.

sprite *noun* elf, fairy.

spritzer /'sprɪtsə/ *noun* drink of white wine with soda water.

sprocket /'sprɒkɪt/ *noun* projection on rim of wheel engaging with links of chain.

sprout /spraʊt/ ● *verb* put forth (shoots etc.); begin to grow. ● *noun* plant shoot; Brussels sprout.

spruce[1] ● *adjective* of trim appearance, smart. ● *verb* (**-cing**) (usually + *up*) make or become smart. ◻ **sprucely** *adverb*; **spruceness** *noun*.

spruce[2] *noun* conifer with dense conical foliage; its wood.

sprung *past participle of* SPRING.

spry /spraɪ/ *adjective* (**-er, -est**) lively, nimble. ◻ **spryly** *adverb*.

spud *noun colloquial* potato; small narrow spade for weeding. ● *verb* (**-dd-**) (+ *up, out*) remove with spud.

spumante /spuːˈmæntɪ/ *noun* Italian sparkling white wine.

spume /spjuːm/ *noun & verb* (**-ming**) froth, foam. ◻ **spumy** *adjective* (**-ier, -iest**).

spun *past & past participle of* SPIN. ◻ **spun silk** cheap material containing waste silk.

spunk *noun colloquial* mettle, spirit. ◻ **spunky** *adjective* (**-ier, -iest**).

spur ● *noun* small spike or spiked wheel attached to rider's heel for urging horse forward; stimulus, incentive; spur-shaped thing, esp. projection from mountain (range), branch road or railway, or hard projection on cock's leg. ● *verb* (**-rr-**) prick (horse) with spur; incite, stimulate. □ **on the spur of the moment** on impulse.

spurge *noun* plant with acrid milky juice.

spurious /ˈspjʊərɪəs/ *adjective* not genuine, fake.

spurn reject with disdain or contempt.

spurt ● *verb* (cause to) gush out in jet or stream; make sudden effort. ● *noun* sudden gushing out, jet; short burst of speed, growth, etc.

sputnik /ˈspʊtnɪk/ *noun* Russian artificial earth satellite.

sputter /ˈspʌtə/ *verb & noun* splutter.

sputum /ˈspjuːtəm/ *noun* thick coughed-up mucus.

spy ● *noun* (*plural* **spies**) person secretly collecting and reporting information for a government, company, etc.; person watching others secretly. ● *verb* (**spies, spied**) discern, see; (often + *on*) act as spy. □ **spyglass** small telescope; **spyhole** peep-hole; **spy out** explore or discover, esp. secretly.

sq. *abbreviation* square.

Sqn. Ldr. *abbreviation* Squadron Leader.

squab /skwɒb/ ● *noun* young esp. unfledged pigeon etc.; short fat person; stuffed cushion, esp. as part of car-seat; sofa. ● *adjective* short and fat.

squabble /ˈskwɒb(ə)l/ ● *noun* petty or noisy quarrel. ● *verb* (**-ling**) engage in squabble.

squad /skwɒd/ *noun* small group sharing task etc., esp. of soldiers or police officers; team. □ **squad car** police car.

squaddie *noun* (also **squaddy**) (*plural* **-ies**) *slang* recruit, private.

squadron /ˈskwɒdrən/ *noun* unit of RAF with 10–18 aircraft; detachment of warships employed on particular service; organized group etc., esp. cavalry division of two troops. □ **squadron leader** RAF officer commanding squadron, next below wing commander.

squalid /ˈskwɒlɪd/ *adjective* filthy, dirty; mean in appearance.

squall /skwɔːl/ ● *noun* sudden or violent gust or storm; discordant cry, scream. ● *verb* utter (with) squall, scream. □ **squally** *adjective*.

squalor /ˈskwɒlə/ *noun* filthy or squalid state.

squander /ˈskwɒndə/ *verb* spend wastefully.

square /skweə/ ● *noun* rectangle with 4 equal sides; object of (roughly) this shape; open area enclosed by buildings; product of number multiplied by itself; L- or T-shaped instrument for obtaining or testing right angles; *slang* conventional or old-fashioned person. ● *adjective* square-shaped; having or in form of a right angle; angular, not round; designating unit of measure equal to area of square whose side is one of the unit specified; (usually + *with*) level, parallel; (usually + *to*) perpendicular; sturdy, squat; arranged; (also **all square**) with no money owed, (of scores) equal; fair, honest, direct; *slang* conventional, old-fashioned. ● *adverb* squarely. ● *verb* (**-ring**) make square; multiply (number) by itself; (usually + *to*, *with*) make or be consistent, reconcile; mark out in squares; settle (bill etc.); place (shoulders etc.) squarely facing forwards; *colloquial* pay, bribe; make scores of (match etc.) equal. □ **square brackets** brackets of the form [ ] (see panel at BRACKET); **square dance** dance with 4 couples facing inwards from 4 sides; **square deal** fair bargain or treatment; **square leg** *Cricket* fielding position on batsman's leg side nearly opposite stumps; **square meal** substantial meal; **square-rigged** having 4-sided sails set across length of ship; **square root** number that multiplied by itself gives specified number. □ **squarely** *adverb*.

squash¹ /skwɒʃ/ ● *verb* crush or squeeze flat or into pulp; (often + *into*) *colloquial* force into small space, crowd; belittle, bully; suppress. ● *noun* crowd, crowded state; drink made of crushed fruit; (in full **squash rackets**) game played with rackets and small ball in closed court. □ **squashy** *adjective* (**-ier, -iest**).

squash² /skwɒʃ/ *noun* (*plural* same or **-es**) trailing annual plant; gourd of this.

squat /skwɒt/ ● *verb* (**-tt-**) sit on one's heels, or on ground with knees drawn up; *colloquial* sit down; act as squatter. ● *adjective* (**-tt-**) short and thick, dumpy. ● *noun* squatting posture; place occupied by squatter(s).

squatter *noun* person who inhabits unoccupied premises without permission.

squaw *noun* N. American Indian woman or wife.

squawk ● *noun* harsh cry; complaint. ● *verb* utter squawk.

squeak ● *noun* short high-pitched cry or sound; (also **narrow squeak**) narrow escape. ● *verb* emit squeak; utter shrilly; (+ *by*, *through*) *colloquial* pass narrowly; *slang* turn informer.

squeaky *adjective* (**-ier, -iest**) making squeaking sound. □ **squeaky clean** *colloquial* completely clean, above criticism. □ **squeakily** *adverb*; **squeakiness** *noun*.

squeal ● *noun* prolonged shrill sound or cry. ● *verb* make, or utter with, squeal; *slang* turn informer; *colloquial* protest vociferously.

squeamish /ˈskwiːmɪʃ/ *adjective* easily nauseated; fastidious. □ **squeamishly** *adverb*; **squeamishness** *noun*.

squeegee /ˈskwiːdʒiː/ *noun* rubber-edged implement on handle, for cleaning windows etc.

squeeze ● *verb* (**-zing**) (often + *out*) exert pressure on, esp. to extract moisture; reduce in size or alter in shape by squeezing; force or push into or through small or narrow space; harass, pressure; (usually + *out of*) get by extortion or entreaty; press (person's hand) in sympathy etc. ● *noun* squeezing, being squeezed; close embrace; crowd, crowded state; small quantity produced by squeezing; restriction on borrowing and investment. □ **squeeze-box** *colloquial* accordion, concertina.

squelch ● *verb* make sucking sound as of treading in thick mud; move with squelching sound; disconcert, silence. ● *noun* act or sound of squelching. □ **squelchy** *adjective*.

squib *noun* small hissing firework; satirical essay.

squid *noun* (*plural* same or **-s**) 10-armed marine cephalopod.

squidgy /ˈskwɪdʒɪ/ *adjective* (**-ier, -iest**) *colloquial* squashy, soggy.

squiffy /ˈskwɪfɪ/ *adjective* (**-ier, -iest**) *slang* slightly drunk.

squiggle /ˈskwɪg(ə)l/ *noun* short curling line, esp. in handwriting. □ **squiggly** *adjective*.

squint ● *verb* have eyes turned in different directions; (often + *at*) look sidelong. ● *noun* squinting condition; sidelong glance; *colloquial* glance, look; oblique opening in church wall.

squire ● *noun* country gentleman, esp. chief landowner of district; *historical* knight's attendant. ● *verb* (**-ring**) (of man) escort (woman).

squirearchy /ˈskwaɪərɑːkɪ/ *noun* (*plural* **-ies**) landowners collectively.

squirm ● *verb* wriggle, writhe; show or feel embarrassment. ● *noun* squirming movement.

squirrel /ˈskwɪr(ə)l/ ● *noun* bushy-tailed usually tree-living rodent; its fur; hoarder. ● *verb* (**-ll-**; *US* **-l-**) (often + *away*) hoard.

squirt ● *verb* eject (liquid etc.) in jet; be ejected thus; splash with squirted substance. ● *noun* jet of water etc.; small quantity squirted; syringe; *colloquial* insignificant person.

squish *colloquial* ● *noun* slight squelching sound. ● *verb* move with squish; squash. □ **squishy** *adjective* (**-ier, -iest**).

Sr. *abbreviation* Senior.

SRN *abbreviation* State Registered Nurse.

SS *abbreviation* steamship; Saints; *historical* Nazi special police force (*Schutzstaffel*).

SSE *abbreviation* south-south-east.

SSW *abbreviation* south-south-west.

St *abbreviation* Saint.

St. *abbreviation* Street.

st. *abbreviation* stone (weight).

stab ● *verb* (**-bb-**) pierce or wound with knife etc.; (often + *at*) aim blow with such weapon; cause sharp pain to. ● *noun* act or result of stabbing; *colloquial* attempt. □ **stab in the back** *noun* treacherous attack, *verb* betray.

stability /stəˈbɪlɪtɪ/ *noun* being stable.

stabilize /ˈsteɪbɪlaɪz/ *verb* (also **-ise**) (**-zing** or **-sing**) make or become stable. □ **stabilization** *noun*.

stabilizer *noun* (also **-iser**) device to keep aircraft or (in *plural*) child's bicycle steady; food additive for preserving texture.

stable /ˈsteɪb(ə)l/ ● *adjective* (**-r, -st**) firmly fixed or established, not fluctuating or changing; not easily upset or disturbed. ● *noun* building for keeping horses; establishment for training racehorses; racehorses of particular stable; people, products, etc. having common origin or affiliation; such origin or affiliation. ● *verb* (**-ling**) put or keep in stable. □ **stably** *adverb*.

stabling *noun* accommodation for horses.

staccato /stəˈkɑːtəʊ/ *esp. Music* ● *adverb & adjective* with each sound sharply distinct. ● *noun* (*plural* **-s**) staccato passage or delivery.

stack ● *noun* (esp. orderly) pile or heap; haystack; *colloquial* large quantity; number of chimneys standing together; smokestack; tall factory chimney; stacked group of aircraft; part of library where books are compactly stored. ● *verb* pile in stack(s); arrange (cards, circumstances, etc.) secretly for cheating; cause (aircraft) to fly in circles while waiting to land.

stadium /ˈsteɪdɪəm/ *noun* (*plural* **-s**) athletic or sports ground with tiered seats for spectators.

staff /stɑːf/ ● *noun* stick or pole for walking, as weapon, or as symbol of office; supporting person or thing; people employed in a business etc.; those in authority in a school etc.; group of army officers assisting officer in high command; (*plural* **-s** or **staves**) *Music* set of usually 5 parallel lines to indicate pitch of notes by position. ● *verb* provide (institution etc.) with staff. □ **staff nurse** one ranking just below a sister.

stag *noun* male deer; person who applies for new shares to sell at once for profit. □ **stag beetle** beetle with antler-like mandibles; **stag-party** *colloquial* party for men only.

stage ● *noun* point or period in process or development; raised platform, esp. for performing plays etc. on; (**the stage**) theatrical profession; scene of action; regular stopping place on route; distance between stopping places; section of space rocket with separate engine. ● *verb* (**-ging**) put (play etc.) on stage; organize and carry out. □ **stagecoach** *historical* coach running on regular route; **stage direction** instruction in a play about actors' movements, sound effects, etc.; **stage door**

entrance from street to backstage part of theatre; **stage fright** performer's fear of audience; **stage-manage** arrange and control as or like stage manager; **stage manager** person responsible for lighting and mechanical arrangements on stage; **stage-struck** obsessed with becoming actor; **stage whisper** loud whisper meant to be overheard.

stagger /ˈstæɡə/ ● *verb* (cause to) walk unsteadily; shock, confuse; arrange (events etc.) so that they do not coincide; arrange (objects) so that they are not in line. ● *noun* staggering movement; (in *plural*) disease, esp. of horses and cattle, causing staggering.

staggering *adjective* astonishing, bewildering. □ **staggeringly** *adverb*.

staging /ˈsteɪdʒɪŋ/ *noun* presentation of play etc.; (temporary) platform; shelves for plants in greenhouse. □ **staging post** regular stopping place, esp. on air route.

stagnant /ˈstæɡnənt/ *adjective* (of liquid) motionless, without current; dull, sluggish. □ **stagnancy** *noun*.

stagnate /stæɡˈneɪt/ *verb* (**-ting**) be or become stagnant. □ **stagnation** *noun*.

stagy /ˈsteɪdʒɪ/ *adjective* (also **stagey**) (**-ier, -iest**) theatrical, artificial, exaggerated.

staid *adjective* sober, steady, sedate.

stain ● *verb* discolour or be discoloured by action of liquid sinking in; spoil, damage; colour (wood, etc.) with penetrating substance; treat with colouring agent. ● *noun* discoloration, spot, mark; blot, blemish; dye etc. for staining. □ **stained glass** coloured glass in leaded window etc.

stainless *adjective* without stains; not liable to stain. □ **stainless steel** chrome steel resisting rust and tarnish.

stair *noun* each of a set of fixed indoor steps; (usually in *plural*) such a set. □ **staircase** flight of stairs and supporting structure; **stair-rod** rod securing carpet between two steps; **stairway** staircase; **stairwell** shaft for staircase.

stake ● *noun* stout pointed stick driven into ground as support, boundary mark, etc.; *historical* post to which person was tied to be burnt alive; sum of money etc. wagered on event; (often + *in*) interest or concern, esp. financial; (in *plural*) prize-money, esp. in horse race, such race. ● *verb* (**-king**) secure or support with stake(s); (often + *off, out*) mark off (area) with stakes; wager; *US colloquial* support, esp. financially. □ **at stake** risked, to be won or lost; **stake out** *colloquial* place under surveillance; **stake-out** *esp. US colloquial* period of surveillance.

stalactite /ˈstæləktaɪt/ *noun* icicle-like deposit of calcium carbonate hanging from roof of cave etc.

stalagmite /ˈstæləɡmaɪt/ *noun* icicle-like deposit of calcium carbonate rising from floor of cave etc.

stale ● *adjective* not fresh; musty, insipid, or otherwise the worse for age or use; trite, unoriginal; (of athlete or performer) impaired by excessive training. ● *verb* (**-ling**) make or become stale. □ **staleness** *noun*.

stalemate ● *noun* *Chess* position counting as draw in which player cannot move except into check; deadlock. ● *verb* (**-ting**) *Chess* bring (player) to stalemate; bring to deadlock.

Stalinism /ˈstɑːlɪnɪz(ə)m/ *noun* centralized authoritarian form of socialism associated with Stalin. □ **Stalinist** *noun & adjective*.

stalk¹ /stɔːk/ ● *noun* main stem of herbaceous plant; slender attachment or support of leaf, flower, fruit, etc.; similar support for organ etc. in animal.

stalk² /stɔːk/ ● *verb* pursue (game, enemy) stealthily; stride, walk in a haughty way; *formal or rhetorical* move silently or threateningly through (place). ● *noun* stalking of game; haughty gait. □ **stalking-horse**

horse concealing hunter, pretext concealing real intentions or actions.

stall¹ /stɔːl/ ● *noun* trader's booth or table in market etc.; compartment for one animal in stable or cowhouse; fixed, usually partly enclosed, seat in choir or chancel of church; (usually in *plural*) each of seats on ground floor of theatre; stalling of engine or aircraft, condition resulting from this. ● *verb* (of vehicle or its engine) stop because of overload on engine or inadequate supply of fuel to it; (of aircraft or its pilot) lose control because speed is too low; cause to stall. □ **stallholder** person in charge of stall in market etc.

stall² /stɔːl/ *verb* play for time when being questioned etc.; delay, obstruct.

stallion /'stæljən/ *noun* uncastrated adult male horse.

stalwart /'stɔːlwət/ ● *adjective* strong, sturdy; courageous, resolute, reliable. ● *noun* stalwart person, esp. loyal comrade.

stamen /'steɪmən/ *noun* organ producing pollen in flower.

stamina /'stæmɪnə/ *noun* physical or mental endurance.

stammer /'stæmə/ ● *verb* speak haltingly, esp. with pauses or rapid repetitions of same syllable; (often + *out*) utter (words) in this way. ● *noun* tendency to stammer; instance of stammering.

stamp ● *verb* bring down (one's foot) heavily, esp. on ground, (often + *on*) crush or flatten in this way, walk heavily; impress (design, mark, etc.) on surface, impress (surface) with pattern etc.; affix postage or other stamp to; assign specific character to, mark out. ● *noun* instrument for stamping; mark or design made by this; impression of official mark required to be made on deeds, bills of exchange, etc., as evidence of payment of tax; small adhesive piece of paper as evidence of payment, esp. postage stamp; mark, label, etc. on commodity as evidence of quality etc.; act or sound of stamping foot; characteristic mark, quality. □ **stamp duty** duty imposed on certain kinds of legal document; **stamping ground** *colloquial* favourite haunt; **stamp on** impress (idea etc.) on (memory etc.); **stamp out** produce by cutting out with die etc., put end to.

stampede /stæm'piːd/ ● *noun* sudden flight or hurried movement of animals or people; response of many people at once to a common impulse. ● *verb* (**-ding**) (cause to) take part in stampede.

stance /stɑːns/ *noun* standpoint, attitude; position of body, esp. when hitting ball etc.

stanch /stɑːntʃ, stɔːntʃ/ *verb* (also **staunch** /stɔːntʃ/) restrain flow of (esp. blood); restrain flow from (esp. wound).

stanchion /'stɑːnʃ(ə)n/ *noun* upright post or support.

stand ● *verb* (*past & past participle* **stood** /stʊd/) have, take, or maintain upright or stationary position, esp on feet or base; be situated; be of specified height; be in specified state; set in upright or specified position; move to and remain in specified position, take specified attitude; remain valid or unaltered; *Nautical* hold specified course; endure, tolerate; provide at one's own expense; (often + *for*) be candidate (for office etc.); act in specified capacity; undergo (trial). ● *noun* cessation from progress, stoppage; *Military* (esp. in **make a stand**) halt made to repel attack;

resistance to attack or compulsion; position taken up, attitude adopted; rack, set of shelves, etc. for storage; open-fronted stall or structure for trader, exhibitor, etc.; standing-place for vehicles; raised structure to sit or stand on; *US* witness-box; each halt made for performance on tour; group of growing plants. □ **as it stands** in its present condition, in the present circumstances; **stand by** stand nearby, look on without interfering, uphold, support (person), adhere to (promise etc.), be ready for action; **stand-by** (person or thing) ready if needed in emergency etc., readiness for duty etc.; **stand down** withdraw from position or candidacy; **stand for** represent, signify, imply, *colloquial* endure, tolerate; **stand in** (usually + *for*) deputize for; **stand-in** deputy, substitute; **stand off** move or keep away, temporarily dismiss (employee); **stand-off half** *Rugby* half-back forming link between scrum-half and three-quarters; **standoffish** cold or distant in manner; **stand on** insist on, observe scrupulously; **stand out** be prominent or outstanding, (usually + *against*, *for*), persist in opposition or support; **standpipe** vertical pipe rising from water supply, esp. one connecting temporary tap to mains; **standpoint** point of view; **standstill** stoppage, inability to proceed; **stand to** *Military* stand ready for attack, abide by, be likely or certain to; **stand to reason** be obvious; **stand up** rise to one's feet, come to, remain in, or place in standing position, (of argument etc.) be valid, *colloquial* fail to keep appointment with; **stand-up** (of meal) eaten standing, (of fight) violent, thorough, (of collar) not turned down, (of comedian) telling jokes to audience; **stand up for** support, side with; **stand up to** face (opponent) courageously, be resistant to (wear, use, etc.).

standard /'stændəd/ ● *noun* object, quality, or measure serving as basis, example, or principle to which others conform or should conform or by which others are judged; level of excellence etc. required or specified; ordinary procedure etc.; distinctive flag; upright support or pipe; shrub standing without support, or grafted on upright stem and trained in tree form. ● *adjective* serving or used as standard; of normal or prescribed quality, type, or size. □ **standard-bearer** person who carries distinctive flag, prominent leader in cause; **standard English** most widely accepted dialect of English (see panel); **standard lamp** lamp on tall upright with base; **standard of living** degree of material comfort of person or group; **standard time** uniform time established by law or custom in country or region.

standardize *verb* (also **-ise**) (**-zing** or **-sing**) cause to conform to standard. □ **standardization** *noun*.

standing ● *noun* esteem, repute, esp. high; duration. ● *adjective* that stands, upright; established, permanent; (of jump, start, etc.) performed with no run-up. □ **standing order** instruction to banker to make regular payments; **standing orders** rules governing procedure in a parliament, council, etc.; **standing ovation** prolonged applause from audience that has risen to its feet; **standing room** space to stand in.

stank *past* of STINK.

stanza /'stænzə/ *noun* group of lines forming division of poem, etc.

Standard English

Standard English is the dialect of English used by most educated English speakers and is spoken with a variety of accents (see panel at ACCENT). While not *in itself* any better than any other dialect, standard English is the form of English used in all formal written contexts.

staphylococcus /ˌstæfɪləˈkɒkəs/ noun (plural **-cocci** /-kaɪ/) bacterium sometimes forming pus. □ **staphylococcal** adjective.

staple¹ /ˈsteɪp(ə)l/ ● noun shaped piece of wire with two points for fastening papers together, fixing netting to post, etc. ● verb (**-ling**) fasten with staple(s). □ **stapler** noun.

staple² /ˈsteɪp(ə)l/ ● noun principal or important article of commerce; chief element, main component; fibre of cotton, wool, etc. with regard to its quality. ● adjective main, principal; important as product or export.

star ● noun celestial body appearing as luminous point in night sky; large luminous gaseous body such as sun; celestial body regarded as influencing fortunes etc.; conventional image of star with radiating lines or points; famous or brilliant person, leading performer. ● adjective outstanding. ● verb (**-rr-**) appear or present as leading performer(s); mark, set, or adorn with star(s). □ **starfish** (plural same or **-es**) sea creature with 5 or more radiating arms; **star-gazer** colloquial usually derogatory or jocular astronomer or astrologer; **starlight** light of stars; **starlit** lit by stars, with stars visible; **Stars and Stripes** US national flag; **star turn** main item in entertainment etc. □ **stardom** noun.

starboard /ˈstɑːbəd/ ● noun right-hand side of ship or aircraft looking forward. ● verb turn (helm) to starboard.

starch ● noun white carbohydrate obtained chiefly from cereals and potatoes; preparation of this for stiffening fabric; stiffness of manner, formality. ● verb stiffen (clothing) with starch. □ **starchy** adjective (**-ier, -iest**).

stare /steə/ ● verb (**-ring**) (usually + at) look fixedly, esp. in curiosity, surprise, horror, etc. ● noun staring gaze. □ **stare (person) in the face** be evident or imminent; **stare out** stare at (person) until he or she looks away.

stark ● adjective sharply evident; desolate, bare; absolute. ● adverb completely, wholly. □ **starkly** adverb.

starkers /ˈstɑːkəz/ adjective slang stark naked.

starlet /ˈstɑːlɪt/ noun promising young performer, esp. film actress.

starling /ˈstɑːlɪŋ/ noun gregarious bird with blackish speckled lustrous plumage.

starry adjective (**-ier, -iest**) full of stars; starlike. □ **starry-eyed** colloquial romantic but impractical, euphoric.

start ● verb begin; set in motion or action; set oneself in motion or action; (often + out) begin journey etc.; (often + up) (cause to) begin operating; (often + up) establish; give signal to (competitors) to start in race; (often + up, from, etc.) jump in surprise, pain, etc.; rouse (game etc.). ● noun beginning; starting-place of race etc.; advantage given at beginning of race etc.; advantageous initial position in life, business, etc.; sudden movement of surprise, pain, etc. □ **starting block** shaped block against which runner braces feet at start of race; **starting price** odds ruling at start of horse race.

starter noun device for starting vehicle engine etc.; first course of meal; person giving signal to start race; horse or competitor starting in race. □ **for starters** colloquial to start with.

startle /ˈstɑːt(ə)l/ verb (**-ling**) shock, surprise.

starve verb (**-ving**) (cause to) die of hunger or suffer from malnourishment; colloquial feel very hungry; suffer from mental or spiritual want; (+ of) deprive of; compel by starvation. □ **starvation** noun.

stash colloquial ● verb (often + away) conceal, put in safe place; hoard. ● noun hiding place; thing hidden.

state ● noun existing condition or position of person or thing; colloquial excited or agitated mental condition, untidy condition; political community under one government, this as part of federal republic; civil government; pomp; (**the States**) USA. ● adjective of, for, or concerned with state; reserved for or done on ceremonial occasions. ● verb (**-ting**) express in speech or writing; fix, specify. □ **lie in state** be laid in public place of honour before burial; **state of the art** current stage of esp. technological development; **state-of-the-art** absolutely up-to-date; **stateroom** state apartment, large private cabin in passenger ship.

stateless adjective having no nationality or citizenship.

stately adjective (**-ier, -iest**) dignified, imposing. □ **stately home** large historic house, esp. one open to public. □ **stateliness** noun.

statement noun stating, being stated; thing stated; formal account of facts; record of transactions in bank account etc.; notification of amount due to tradesman etc.

statesman /ˈsteɪtsmən/ noun (feminine **stateswoman**) distinguished and capable politician or diplomat. □ **statesmanlike** adjective; **statesmanship** noun.

static /ˈstætɪk/ ● adjective stationary, not acting or changing; Physics concerned with bodies at rest or forces in equilibrium. ● noun static electricity; atmospherics. □ **static electricity** electricity not flowing as current.

statics plural noun (usually treated as singular) science of bodies at rest or forces in equilibrium.

station /ˈsteɪʃ(ə)n/ ● noun regular stopping place on railway line; person or thing's allotted place, building, etc.; centre for particular service or activity; establishment involved in broadcasting; military or naval base, inhabitants of this; position in life, rank, status; Australian & NZ large sheep or cattle farm. ● verb assign station to; put in position. □ **stationmaster** official in charge of railway station; **stations of the cross** RC Church series of images representing events in Christ's Passion; **station wagon** esp. US estate car.

stationary adjective not moving; not meant to be moved; unchanging.

stationer noun dealer in stationery.

stationery noun writing materials, office supplies, etc.

statistic /stəˈtɪstɪk/ noun statistical fact or item.

statistical adjective of statistics. □ **statistically** adverb.

statistics plural noun (usually treated as singular) science of collecting and analysing significant numerical data; such data. □ **statistician** /ˌstætɪsˈtɪʃ(ə)n/ noun.

statuary /ˈstætʃʊərɪ/ ● adjective of or for statues. ● noun statues collectively; making statues.

statue /ˈstætʃuː/ noun sculptured figure of person or animal, esp. life-size or larger.

statuesque /ˌstætʃʊˈesk/ adjective like statue, esp. in beauty or dignity.

statuette /ˌstætʃʊˈet/ noun small statue.

stature /ˈstætʃə/ noun height of (esp. human) body; calibre (esp. moral), eminence.

status /ˈsteɪtəs/ noun rank, social position, relative importance; superior social etc. position. □ **status quo** /ˈkwəʊ/ existing conditions; **status symbol** possession etc. intended to indicate owner's superiority.

statute /ˈstætʃuːt/ noun written law passed by legislative body; rule of corporation, founder, etc., intended to be permanent.

statutory /'stætʃʊtərɪ/ *adjective* required or enacted by statute.

staunch[1] /stɔːntʃ/ *adjective* trustworthy, loyal. □ **staunchly** *adverb*.

staunch[2] = STANCH.

stave ● *noun* each of curved slats forming sides of cask; *Music* staff; stanza, verse. ● *verb* (**-ving**; *past & past participle* **stove** /stəʊv/ or **staved**) (usually + *in*) break hole in, damage, crush by forcing inwards. □ **stave off** (*past & past participle* **staved**) avert or defer (danger etc.).

stay[1] ● *verb* continue in same place or condition, not depart or change; (often + *at, in, with*) reside temporarily; *archaic or literary* stop, check, (esp. in *imperative*) pause; postpone (judgement etc.); assuage (hunger etc.), esp. for short time. ● *noun* act or period of staying; suspension or postponement of sentence, judgement, etc.; prop, support; (in *plural*) *historical* (esp. boned) corset. □ **stay-at-home** (person) rarely going out; **staying power** endurance; **stay the night** remain overnight; **stay put** *colloquial* remain where it is put or where one is; **stay up** not go to bed (until late).

stay[2] *noun* rope supporting mast, flagstaff, etc.; supporting cable on aircraft. □ **staysail** sail extended on stay.

stayer *noun* person or animal with great endurance.

STD *abbreviation* subscriber trunk dialling.

stead /sted/ *noun* □ **in** (person's, thing's) **stead** as substitute; **stand** (person) **in good stead** be advantageous or useful to him or her.

steadfast /'stedfɑːst/ *adjective* constant, firm, unwavering. □ **steadfastly** *adverb*; **steadfastness** *noun*.

steady /'stedɪ/ ● *adjective* (**-ier, -iest**) firmly fixed or supported, unwavering; uniform, regular; constant, persistent; (of person) serious and dependable; regular, established. ● *verb* (**-ies, -ied**) make or become steady. ● *adverb* steadily. ● *noun* (*plural* **-ies**) *colloquial* regular boyfriend or girlfriend. □ **steady state** unvarying condition, esp. in physical process. □ **steadily** *adverb*; **steadiness** *noun*.

steak /steɪk/ *noun* thick slice of meat (esp. beef) or fish, usually grilled or fried. □ **steakhouse** restaurant specializing in beefsteaks.

steal ● *verb* (*past* **stole**; *past participle* **stolen** /'stəʊl(ə)n/) take (another's property) illegally or without right or permission, esp. in secret; obtain surreptitiously, insidiously, or artfully; (+ *in, out, away, up,* etc.) move, esp. silently or stealthily. ● *noun US colloquial* act of stealing, theft; *colloquial* easy task, bargain. □ **steal a march on** gain advantage over by surreptitious means; **steal the show** outshine other performers, esp. unexpectedly.

stealth /stelθ/ *noun* secrecy, secret behaviour.

stealthy *adjective* (**-ier, -iest**) done or moving with stealth. □ **stealthily** *adverb*.

steam ● *noun* gas into which water is changed by boiling; condensed vapour formed from this; power obtained from steam; *colloquial* power, energy. ● *verb* cook (food) in steam; give off steam; move under steam power; (+ *ahead, away,* etc.) *colloquial* proceed or travel fast or with vigour. □ **let off steam** relieve pent-up energy or feelings; **steamboat** steam-driven boat; **steam engine** one worked or propelled by steam; **steam iron** electric iron that emits steam; **steamroller** *noun* heavy slow-moving vehicle with roller, used to flatten new-made roads, crushing power or force, *verb* crush or move forcibly or indiscriminately; **steamship** steam-driven ship; **steam train** train pulled by steam engine; **steam up** cover or become covered with condensed steam, (as **steamed up** *adjective*) *colloquial* angry, excited.

steamer *noun* steamboat; vessel for steaming food in.

steamy *adjective* (**-ier, -iest**) like or full of steam; *colloquial* erotic.

steatite /'stɪətaɪt/ *noun* impure form of talc, esp. soapstone.

steed *noun archaic or poetical* horse.

steel ● *noun* strong malleable low-carbon iron alloy, used esp. for making tools, weapons, etc.; strength, firmness; steel rod for sharpening knives. ● *adjective* of or like steel. ● *verb* harden, make resolute. □ **steel band** band playing chiefly calypso-style music on instruments made from oil drums; **steel wool** fine steel shavings used as abrasive; **steelworks** factory producing steel; **steelyard** balance with graduated arm along which weight is moved.

steely *adjective* (**-ier, -iest**) of or like steel; severe, resolute.

steep[1] ● *adjective* sloping sharply; (of rise or fall) rapid; *colloquial* exorbitant, unreasonable, exaggerated, incredible. ● *noun* steep slope, precipice. □ **steepen** *verb*; **steeply** *adverb*; **steepness** *noun*.

steep[2] ● *verb* soak or bathe in liquid. ● *noun* act of steeping; liquid for steeping. □ **steep in** imbue with, make deeply acquainted with (subject etc.).

steeple /'stiːp(ə)l/ *noun* tall tower, esp. with spire, above roof of church. □ **steeplechase** horse race with ditches, hedges, etc. to jump, cross-country foot race; **steeplejack** repairer of tall chimneys, steeples, etc.

steer[1] *verb* guide (vehicle, ship, etc.) with wheel, rudder, etc.; direct or guide (one's course, other people, conversation, etc.) in specified direction. □ **steer clear of** avoid; **steering column** column on which steering wheel is mounted; **steering committee** one deciding order of business, course of operations etc.; **steering wheel** wheel by which vehicle etc. is steered; **steersman** person who steers ship.

steer[2] *noun* bullock.

steerage *noun* act of steering; *archaic* cheapest part of ship's accommodation.

steering *noun* apparatus for steering vehicle etc.

stegosaurus /stegə'sɔːrəs/ *noun* (*plural* **-ruses**) large dinosaur with two rows of vertical plates along back.

stela /'stiːlə/ *noun* (*plural* **stelae** /-liː/) (also **stele** /'stiːlɪ/) ancient upright slab or pillar, usually inscribed and sculptured, esp. as gravestone.

stellar /'stelə/ *adjective* of star or stars.

stem[1] ● *noun* main body or stalk of plant; stalk of fruit, flower, or leaf; stem-shaped part, e.g. slender part of wineglass; *Grammar* root or main part of noun, verb, etc. to which inflections are added; main upright timber at bow of ship. ● *verb* (**-mm-**) (+ *from*) spring or originate from.

stem[2] *verb* (**-mm-**) check, stop.

stench *noun* foul smell.

stencil /'stensɪl/ ● *noun* thin sheet in which pattern is cut, placed on surface and printed, inked over, etc.; pattern so produced. ● *verb* (**-ll-**; *US* **-l-**) (often + *on*) produce (pattern) with stencil; mark (surface) in this way.

Sten gun *noun* lightweight sub-machine-gun.

stenographer /ste'nɒgrəfə/ *noun esp. US* shorthand typist.

stentorian /sten'tɔːrɪən/ *adjective* loud and powerful.

step ● *noun* complete movement of leg in walking or running; distance so covered; unit of movement in dancing; measure taken, esp. one of several in course of action; surface of stair, stepladder, etc. tread; short distance; sound or mark made by foot in walking etc; degree in scale of promotion, precedence, etc.; stepping in unison or to music; state of conforming

● *verb* (**-pp-**) lift and set down foot or alternate feet in walking; come or go in specified direction by stepping; make progress in specified way; (+ *off*, *out*) measure (distance) by stepping; perform (dance). □ **mind, watch one's step** be careful; **step down** resign; **step in** enter, intervene; **stepladder** short folding ladder not leant against wall etc.; **step on it** *colloquial* hurry; **step out** be active socially, take large steps; **stepping-stone** large stone set in stream etc. to walk over, means of progress; **step up** increase, intensify.

step- *combining form* related by remarriage of parent. □ **stepchild, stepdaughter, stepson** one's husband's or wife's child by previous partner; **stepfather, stepmother, step-parent** mother's or father's spouse who is not one's own parent; **stepbrother, stepsister** child of one's step-parent by previous partner.

stephanotis /stefə'nəʊtɪs/ *noun* fragrant tropical climbing plant.

steppe /step/ *noun* level grassy treeless plain.

stereo /'sterɪəʊ/ ● *noun* (*plural* **-s**) stereophonic sound reproduction or equipment; stereoscope. ● *adjective* stereophonic; stereoscopic.

stereo- *combining form* solid; 3-dimensional.

stereophonic /sterɪəʊ'fɒnɪk/ *adjective* using two or more channels, to give effect of naturally distributed sound.

stereoscope /'sterɪəskəʊp/ *noun* device for producing 3-dimensional effect by viewing two slightly different photographs together. □ **stereoscopic** /-'skɒp-/ *adjective*.

stereotype /'sterɪəʊtaɪp/ ● *noun* person or thing seeming to conform to widely accepted type; such type, idea, or attitude; printing plate cast from mould of composed type. ● *verb* (**-ping**) (esp. as **stereotyped** *adjective*) cause to conform to type, standardize; print from stereotype; make stereotype of.

sterile /'steraɪl/ *adjective* not able to produce crop, fruit, or young, barren; lacking ideas or originality, unproductive; free from micro-organisms etc. □ **sterility** /stə'rɪl-/ *noun*.

sterilize /'sterɪlaɪz/ *verb* (also **-ise**) (**-zing** or **-sing**) make sterile; deprive of reproductive power. □ **sterilization** *noun*.

sterling /'stɜːlɪŋ/ ● *adjective* of or in British money; (of coin or precious metal) genuine, of standard value or purity; (of person etc.) genuine, reliable. ● *noun* British money. □ **sterling silver** silver of 92½% purity.

stern[1] *adjective* severe, grim; authoritarian. □ **sternly** *adverb*; **sternness** *noun*.

stern[2] *noun* rear part, esp. of ship or boat.

sternum /'stɜːnəm/ *noun* (*plural* **-na** or **-nums**) breastbone.

steroid /'stɪərɔɪd/ *noun* any of group of organic compounds including many hormones, alkaloids, and vitamins.

sterol /'sterɒl/ *noun* naturally occurring steroid alcohol.

stertorous /'stɜːtərəs/ *adjective* (of breathing etc.) laboured and noisy.

stet *verb* (**-tt-**) (usually written on proof-sheet etc.) ignore or cancel (alteration), let original stand.

stethoscope /'steθəskəʊp/ *noun* instrument used in listening to heart, lungs, etc.

stetson /'stets(ə)n/ *noun* slouch hat with wide brim and high crown.

stevedore /'stiːvədɔː/ *noun* person employed in loading and unloading ships.

stew ● *verb* cook by long simmering in closed vessel; *colloquial* swelter; (of tea etc.) become bitter or strong

from infusing too long. ● *noun* dish of stewed meat etc.; *colloquial* agitated or angry state.

steward /'stjuːəd/ ● *noun* passengers' attendant on ship, aircraft, or train; official managing meeting, show, etc.; person responsible for supplies of food etc. for college, club, etc.; property manager. □ **stewardship** *noun*.

stewardess /stjuːə'des/ *noun* female steward, esp. on ship or aircraft.

stick[1] *noun* short slender length of wood, esp. for use as support or weapon; thin rod of wood etc. for particular purpose; gear lever, joystick; sticklike piece of celery, dynamite, etc.; (often **the stick**) punishment, esp. by beating; *colloquial* adverse criticism; *colloquial* person, esp. when dull or unsociable. □ **stick insect** insect with twiglike body.

stick[2] *verb* (*past* & *past participle* **stuck**) (+ *in, into, through*) thrust, insert (thing or its point); stab; (+ *in, into, on*, etc.) fix or be fixed (as) by pointed end; fix or be fixed (as) by adhesive etc.; lose or be deprived of movement or action through adhesion, jamming, etc.; *colloquial* put in specified position or place, remain; *colloquial* endure, tolerate; (+ *at*) *colloquial* persevere with. □ **get stuck into** *slang* start in earnest; **stick around** *colloquial* linger; **sticking plaster** adhesive plaster for wounds etc.; **stick-in-the-mud** *colloquial* unprogressive or old-fashioned person; **stick it out** *colloquial* endure to the end; **stick out** (cause to) protrude; **stick out for** persist in demanding; **stick up** be or make erect or protruding upwards, fasten to upright surface, *colloquial* rob or threaten with gun; **stick up for** support, defend; **stuck for** at a loss for, needing; **stuck with** *colloquial* unable to get rid of.

sticker *noun* adhesive label.

stickleback /'stɪkl(ə)lbæk/ *noun* small spiny-backed fish.

stickler /'stɪklə/ *noun* (+ *for*) person who insists on something.

sticky *adjective* (**-ier, -iest**) tending or intended to stick or adhere; glutinous, viscous; (of weather) humid; *colloquial* difficult, awkward, unpleasant, painful. □ **sticky wicket** *colloquial* difficult situation. □ **stickiness** *noun*.

stiff ● *adjective* rigid, inflexible; hard to bend, move, turn, etc.; hard to cope with, needing strength or effort; severe, strong; formal, constrained; (of muscle, person, etc.) aching from exertion, injury, etc.; (of esp. alcoholic drink) strong. ● *adverb colloquial* utterly, extremely. ● *noun slang* corpse. □ **stiffnecked** obstinate, haughty; **stiff upper lip** appearance of firmness or fortitude. □ **stiffen** *verb*; **stiffly** *adverb*; **stiffness** *noun*.

stifle /'staɪf(ə)l/ *verb* (**-ling**) suppress; feel or make unable to breathe easily; suffocate. □ **stifling** *adjective*.

stigma /'stɪgmə/ *noun* (*plural* **-s** or **stigmata** /-mətə or -'mɑːtə/) shame, disgrace; part of pistil that receives pollen in pollination; (**stigmata**) marks like those on Christ's body after the Crucifixion, appearing on bodies of certain saints etc.

stigmatize /'stɪgmətaɪz/ *verb* (also **-ise**) (**-zing** or **-sing**) (often + *as*) brand as unworthy or disgraceful.

stile *noun* set of steps etc. allowing people to climb over fence, wall, etc.

stiletto /stɪ'letəʊ/ *noun* (*plural* **-s**) short dagger; (in full **stiletto heel**) long tapering heel of shoe; pointed implement for making eyelets etc.

still[1] ● *adjective* with little or no movement or sound; calm, tranquil; (of drink) not effervescing. ● *noun* deep silence; static photograph, esp. single shot from cinema film. ● *adverb* without moving; even now, at particular time; nevertheless; (+ *comparative*) even, yet, increasingly. ● verb make or become still, quieten. □ **stillbirth** birth of dead child; **stillborn** born dead, abortive; **still life** painting or drawing of inanimate objects. □ **stillness** noun.

still² noun apparatus for distilling spirits etc.

stilt noun either of pair of poles with foot supports for walking at a distance above ground; each of set of piles or posts supporting building etc.

stilted adjective (of literary style etc.) stiff and unnatural.

Stilton /'stɪlt(ə)n/ noun proprietary term strong rich esp. blue-veined cheese.

stimulant /'stɪmjʊlənt/ ● adjective stimulating esp. bodily or mental activity. ● noun stimulant substance or influence.

stimulate /'stɪmjʊleɪt/ verb (**-ting**) act as stimulus to; animate, excite, rouse. □ **stimulation** noun; **stimulative** /-lətɪv/ adjective; **stimulator** noun.

stimulus /'stɪmjʊləs/ noun (plural **-li** /-laɪ/) thing that rouses to activity.

sting ● noun sharp wounding organ of insect, nettle, etc.; inflicting of wound with this; wound itself, pain caused by it; painful quality or effect; pungency, vigour. ● verb (past & past participle **stung**) wound with sting; be able to sting; feel or cause tingling physical pain or sharp mental pain; (+ into) incite, esp. painfully; slang swindle, charge heavily. □ **stinging-nettle** nettle with stinging hairs; **stingray** broad flatfish with stinging tail.

stingy /'stɪndʒɪ/ adjective (**-ier, -iest**) niggardly, mean. □ **stingily** adverb; **stinginess** noun.

stink ● verb (past **stank** or **stunk**; past participle **stunk**) emit strong offensive smell; (often + out) fill (place) with stink; (+ out etc.) drive (person) out etc. by stink; colloquial be or seem very unpleasant. ● noun strong offensive smell; colloquial loud complaint, fuss. □ **stink bomb** device emitting stink when opened.

stinker noun slang particularly annoying or unpleasant person; very difficult problem etc.

stinking ● adjective that stinks; slang very objectionable. ● adverb slang extremely and usually objectionably.

stint ● verb (often + on) supply (food, aid, etc.) meanly or grudgingly; (often **stint oneself**) supply (person etc.) in this way. ● noun allotted amount or period of work.

stipend /'staɪpend/ noun salary, esp. of clergyman.

stipendiary /star'pendjərɪ/ ● adjective receiving stipend. ● noun (plural **-ies**) person receiving stipend. □ **stipendiary magistrate** paid professional magistrate.

stipple /'stɪp(ə)l/ ● verb (**-ling**) draw, paint, engrave, etc. with dots instead of lines; roughen surface of (paint, cement, etc.). ● noun stippling; effect of stippling.

stipulate /'stɪpjʊleɪt/ verb (**-ting**) demand or specify as part of bargain etc. □ **stipulation** noun.

stir ● verb (**-rr-**) move spoon etc. round and round in (liquid etc.), esp. to mix ingredients; cause to move, esp. slightly; be or begin to be in motion; rise from sleep; arouse, inspire, excite; colloquial cause trouble by gossiping etc. ● noun act of stirring; commotion, excitement. □ **stir-fry** verb fry rapidly while stirring, noun stir-fried dish; **stir up** mix thoroughly by stirring, stimulate, incite.

stirrup /'stɪrəp/ noun support for horse-rider's foot, suspended by strap from saddle. □ **stirrup-cup** cup of wine etc. offered to departing traveller, originally rider; **stirrup-pump** hand-operated water-pump with footrest, used to extinguish small fires.

stitch ● noun single pass of needle, or result of this, in sewing, knitting, or crochet; particular method of sewing etc.; least bit of clothing; sharp pain in side induced by running etc. ● verb sew, make stitches (in). □ **in stitches** colloquial laughing uncontrollably; **stitch up** join or mend by sewing.

stoat noun mammal of weasel family with brown fur turning mainly white in winter.

stock ● noun store of goods etc. ready for sale or distribution; supply or quantity of things for use; equipment or raw material for manufacture, trade, etc.; farm animals or equipment; capital of business; shares in this; reputation, popularity; money lent to government at fixed interest; line of ancestry; liquid made by stewing bones, vegetables, etc.; fragrant garden plant; plant into which graft is inserted; main trunk of tree etc.; (in plural) historical timber frame with holes for feet in which offenders were locked as public punishment; base, support, or handle for implement or machine; butt of rifle etc.; (in plural) supports for ship during building or repair; band of cloth worn round neck. ● adjective kept regularly in stock for sale or use; commonly used, hackneyed. ● verb have (goods) in stock; provide (shop, farm, etc.) with goods, livestock, etc. □ **stockbroker** member of Stock Exchange dealing in stocks and shares; **stock-car** specially strengthened car used in racing where deliberate bumping is allowed; **Stock Exchange** place for dealing in stocks and shares, dealers working there; **stock-in-trade** requisite(s) of trade or profession; **stock market** Stock Exchange, transactions on this; **stockpile** noun reserve supply of accumulated stock, verb accumulate stockpile (of); **stockpot** pot for making soup stock; **stock-still** motionless; **stocktaking** making inventory of stock; **stock up** (often + with) provide with or get stocks or supplies (of); **stockyard** enclosure for sorting or temporary keeping of cattle; **take stock** make inventory of one's stock, (often + of) review (situation etc.).

stockade /stɒ'keɪd/ ● noun line or enclosure of upright stakes. ● verb (**-ding**) fortify with this.

stockinet /stɒkɪ'net/ noun (also **stockinette**) elastic knitted fabric.

stocking /'stɒkɪŋ/ noun knitted covering for leg and foot, of nylon, wool, silk, etc. □ **stocking stitch** alternate rows of plain and purl.

stockist noun dealer in specified types of goods.

stocky adjective (**-ier, -iest**) short and strongly built. □ **stockily** adverb.

stodge noun colloquial heavy fattening food.

stodgy adjective (**-ier, -iest**) (of food) heavy, filling; dull, uninteresting. □ **stodginess** noun.

stoic /'stəʊɪk/ noun person having great self-control in adversity. □ **stoical** adjective; **stoicism** /-sɪz(ə)m/ noun.

stoke verb (**-king**) (often + up) feed and tend (fire, furnace, etc.); colloquial fill oneself with food. □ **stokehold** compartment in steamship containing its boilers and furnace; **stokehole** space for stokers in front of furnace.

stoker noun person who tends furnace, esp. on steamship.

stole¹ noun woman's garment like long wide scarf worn over shoulders; strip of silk etc. worn similarly by priest.

stole² past of STEAL.

stolen past participle of STEAL.

stolid /'stɒlɪd/ adjective not easily excited or moved; impassive, unemotional. □ **stolidity** /-'lɪd-/ noun; **stolidly** adverb.

stomach /'stʌmək/ ● noun internal organ in which food is digested; lower front of body; (usually + for) appetite, inclination, etc. ● verb (usually in negative) endure. □ **stomach-pump** syringe for forcing liquid etc. into or out of stomach.

stomp ● *verb* tread or stamp heavily. ● *noun* lively jazz dance with heavy stamping.

stone ● *noun* solid non-metallic mineral matter, rock; small piece of this; hard case of kernel in some fruits; hard morbid concretion in body; (*plural* same) unit of weight (14 lb, 6.35 kg); precious stone. ● *verb* (**-ning**) pelt with stones; remove stones from (fruit). □ **Stone Age** prehistoric period when weapons and tools were made of stone; **stone-cold** completely cold; **stone-cold sober** completely sober; **stonecrop** succulent rock plant; **stone-dead** completely dead; **stone-deaf** completely deaf; **stone fruit** fruit with flesh enclosing stone; **stoneground** (of flour) ground with millstones; **stone's throw** short distance; **stonewall** obstruct with evasive answers etc., *Cricket* bat with excessive caution; **stoneware** impermeable and partly vitrified but opaque ceramic ware; **stonewashed** (esp. of denim) washed with abrasives to give worn or faded look; **stonework** masonry.

stoned *adjective slang* drunk, drugged.

stony *adjective* (**-ier, -iest**) full of stones; hard, rigid; unfeeling, unresponsive. □ **stony-broke** *slang* entirely without money. □ **stonily** *adverb*.

stood *past & past participle* of STAND.

stooge *colloquial* ● *noun* person acting as butt or foil, esp. for comedian; assistant or subordinate, esp. for unpleasant work. ● *verb* (**-ging**) (+ *for*) act as stooge for; (+ *about, around*, etc.) move about aimlessly.

stool /stuːl/ *noun* single seat without back or arms; footstool; (usually in *plural*) faeces. □ **stool-pigeon** person acting as decoy, police informer.

stoop ● *verb* bend down; stand or walk with shoulders habitually bent forward; (+ *to do*) condescend; (+ *to*) descend to (shameful act). ● *noun* stooping posture.

stop ● *verb* (**-pp-**) put an end to progress, motion, or operation of; effectively hinder or prevent; discontinue; come to an end; cease from motion, speaking, or action; defeat; *colloquial* remain; stay for short time; (often + *up*) block or close up (hole, leak, etc.); not permit or supply as usual; instruct bank to withhold payment on (cheque); fill (tooth); press (violin etc. string) to obtain required pitch. ● *noun* stopping, being stopped; place where bus, train, etc. regularly stops; full stop; device for stopping motion at particular point; change of pitch effected by stopping string; (in organ) row of pipes of one character, knob etc. operating these; (in camera etc.) diaphragm, effective diameter of lens, device for reducing this; plosive sound. □ **pull out all the stops** make extreme effort; **stopcock** externally operated valve regulating flow through pipe etc.; **stopgap** temporary substitute; **stop off, over** break one's journey; **stop press** late news inserted in newspaper after printing has begun; **stopwatch** watch that can be instantly started and stopped, used in timing of races etc.

stoppage *noun* interruption of work due to strike etc.; (in *plural*) sum deducted from pay, for tax, etc.; condition of being blocked or stopped.

stopper *noun* plug for closing bottle etc.

storage /ˈstɔːrɪdʒ/ *noun* storing of goods etc.; method of, space for, or cost of storing. □ **storage battery, cell** one for storing electricity; **storage heater** electric heater releasing heat stored outside peak hours.

store ● *noun* quantity of something kept ready for use; (in *plural*) articles gathered for particular purpose, supply of, or place for keeping, these; department store; *esp.* US shop; (often in *plural*) shop selling basic necessities; warehouse for keeping furniture etc. temporarily; device in computer for keeping retrievable data. ● *verb* (**-ring**) (often + *up, away*) accumulate for future use; put (furniture etc.) in a store; stock or provide with something useful; keep (data) for retrieval. □ **in store** in reserve, to come; (+ *for*) awaiting; **storehouse** storage place; **storekeeper** person in charge of stores, US shopkeeper; **storeroom** storage room.

storey /ˈstɔːrɪ/ *noun* (*plural* **-s**) rooms etc. on one level of building.

stork *noun* long-legged usually white wading bird.

storm ● *noun* violent disturbance of atmosphere with high winds and usually thunder, rain, or snow; violent disturbance in human affairs; (+ *of*) shower of missiles or blows, outbreak of applause, hisses, etc.; assault on fortified place. ● *verb* attack or capture by storm; rush violently; rage, be violent; bluster. □ **storm centre** comparatively calm centre of cyclonic storm, centre round which controversy etc. rages; **storm cloud** heavy rain-cloud; **storm troops** shock troops, *historical* Nazi political militia; **take by storm** capture by direct assault, quickly captivate.

stormy *adjective* (**-ier, -iest**) of or affected by storms; (of wind etc.) violent; full of angry feeling or outbursts. □ **stormily** *adverb*.

story /ˈstɔːrɪ/ *noun* (*plural* **-ies**) account of real or imaginary events; tale, anecdote; history of person, institution, etc.; plot of novel, play, etc.; article in newspaper, material for this; *colloquial* fib. □ **storyteller** person who tells or writes stories, *colloquial* liar.

stoup /stuːp/ *noun* basin for holy water; *archaic* flagon, beaker.

stout /staʊt/ ● *adjective* rather fat, corpulent; thick, strong; brave, resolute, vigorous. ● *noun* strong dark beer. □ **stout-hearted** courageous. □ **stoutly** *adverb*; **stoutness** *noun*.

stove¹ /staʊv/ *noun* closed apparatus burning fuel or using electricity etc. for heating or cooking. □ **stove-pipe** pipe carrying smoke and gases from stove to chimney.

stove² *past & past participle* of STAVE.

stow /staʊ/ *verb* pack (goods, cargo, etc.) tidily and compactly. □ **stow away** place (thing) out of the way, hide oneself on ship etc. to travel free; **stowaway** person who stows away.

stowage *noun* stowing; place for this.

straddle /ˈstræd(ə)l/ *verb* (**-ling**) sit or stand across (thing) with legs wide apart; be situated on both sides of; spread legs wide apart.

strafe /strɑːf/ *verb* (**-fing**) bombard; attack with gunfire.

straggle /ˈstræg(ə)l/ ● *verb* (**-ling**) lack compactness or tidiness; be dispersed or sporadic; trail behind in race etc. ● *noun* straggling group. □ **straggler** *noun*; **straggly** *adjective*.

straight /streɪt/ ● *adjective* not curved, bent, crooked or curly; successive, uninterrupted; ordered, level, tidy; honest, candid; (of thinking etc.) logical; (of theatre, music, etc.) not popular or comic; unmodified, (of a drink) undiluted; *colloquial* (of person etc.) conventional, respectable, heterosexual. ● *noun* straight part, esp. concluding stretch of racetrack; straight condition; *colloquial* conventional person, heterosexual. ● *adverb* in straight line, direct; in right direction; correctly. □ **go straight** (of criminal) become honest; **straight away** immediately; **straight face** intentionally expressionless face; **straight fight** *Politics* contest between two candidates only; **straightforward** honest, frank, (of task etc.) simple; **straight man** comedian's stooge; **straight off** *colloquial* without hesitation. □ **straightness** *noun*.

straighten *verb* (often + *out*) make or become straight; (+ *up*) stand erect after bending.

strain¹ ● *verb* stretch tightly; make or become taut or tense; injure by overuse or excessive demands; exercise (oneself, one's senses, thing, etc.) intensely, press to extremes; strive intensely; distort from true intention or meaning; clear (liquid) of solid matter by passing it through sieve etc. ● *noun* act of straining, force exerted in this; injury caused by straining muscle etc.; severe mental or physical demand or exertion; snatch of music or poetry; tone or tendency in speech or writing.

strain² *noun* breed or stock of animals, plants, etc.; characteristic tendency.

strained *adjective* constrained, artificial; (of relationship) distrustful, tense.

strainer *noun* device for straining liquids.

strait *noun* (in *singular* or *plural*) narrow channel connecting two large bodies of water; (usually in *plural*) difficulty, distress. □ **strait-jacket** strong garment with long sleeves for confining violent prisoner etc., restrictive measures; **strait-laced** puritanical.

straitened /ˈstreɪt(ə)nd/ *adjective* of or marked by poverty.

strand¹ ● *verb* run aground; (as **stranded** *adjective*) in difficulties, esp. without money or transport. ● *noun* foreshore, beach.

strand² *noun* each of twisted threads or wires making rope, cable, etc.; single thread or strip of fibre; lock of hair; element, component.

strange /streɪndʒ/ *adjective* unusual, peculiar, surprising, eccentric; (often + *to*) unfamiliar, foreign; (+ *to*) unaccustomed; not at ease. □ **strangely** *adverb*; **strangeness** *noun*.

stranger *noun* person new to particular place or company; (often + *to*) person one does not know.

strangle /ˈstræŋg(ə)l/ *verb* (**-ling**) squeeze windpipe or neck of, esp. so as to kill; hamper or suppress (movement, cry, etc.). □ **stranglehold** deadly grip, complete control. □ **strangler** *noun*.

strangulate /ˈstræŋgjʊleɪt/ *verb* (**-ting**) compress (vein, intestine, etc.), preventing circulation.

strangulation *noun* strangling, being strangled; strangulating.

strap ● *noun* strip of leather etc., often with buckle, for holding things together etc.; narrow strip of fabric forming part of garment; loop for grasping to steady oneself in moving vehicle. ● *verb* (**-pp-**) (often + *down*, *up*, etc.) secure or bind with strap; beat with strap. □ **straphanger** *slang* standing passenger in bus or train; **straphang** *verb* □ **strapless** *adjective*.

strapping *adjective* large and sturdy.

strata *plural* of STRATUM.

■ **Usage** It is a mistake to use the plural form *strata* when only one stratum is meant.

stratagem /ˈstrætədʒəm/ *noun* cunning plan or scheme; trickery.

strategic /strəˈtiːdʒɪk/ *adjective* of or promoting strategy; (of materials) essential in war; (of bombing or weapons) done or for use as longer-term military policy. □ **strategically** *adverb*.

strategy /ˈstrætɪdʒɪ/ *noun* (*plural* **-ies**) long-term plan or policy; art of war; art of moving troops, ships, aircraft, etc. into favourable positions. □ **strategist** *noun*.

stratify /ˈstrætɪfaɪ/ *verb* (**-ies**, **-ied**) (esp. as **stratified** *adjective*) arrange in strata, grades, etc. □ **stratification** *noun*.

stratosphere /ˈstrætəsfɪə/ *noun* layer of atmosphere above troposphere, extending to about 50 km from earth's surface.

stratum /ˈstrɑːtəm/ *noun* (*plural* **strata**) layer or set of layers of any deposited substance, esp. of rock; atmospheric layer; social class.

straw *noun* dry cut stalks of grain; single stalk of straw; thin tube for sucking drink through; insignificant thing; pale yellow colour. □ **clutch at straws** try any remedy in desperation; **straw vote, poll** unofficial ballot as test of opinion.

strawberry /ˈstrɔːbəri/ *noun* (*plural* **-ies**) pulpy red fruit having surface studded with yellow seeds; plant bearing this. □ **strawberry mark** reddish birthmark.

stray ● *verb* wander from the right place, from one's companions, etc., go astray; deviate. ● *noun* strayed animal or person. ● *adjective* strayed, lost; isolated, occasional.

streak ● *noun* long thin usually irregular line or band, esp. of colour; strain or trait in person's character. ● *verb* mark with streaks; move very rapidly; *colloquial* run naked in public.

streaky *adjective* (**-ier**, **-iest**) marked with streaks; (of bacon) with streaks of fat.

stream ● *noun* body of running water, esp. small river; current, flow; group of schoolchildren of similar ability taught together. ● *verb* move as stream; run with liquid; be blown in wind; emit stream of (blood etc.); arrange (schoolchildren) in streams. □ **on stream** in operation or production.

streamer *noun* long narrow strip of ribbon or paper; long narrow flag.

streamline *verb* (**-ning**) give (vehicle etc.) form which presents least resistance to motion; make simple or more efficient.

street *noun* road in city, town, or village; this with buildings on each side. □ **on the streets** living by prostitution; **streetcar** *US* tram; **street credibility, cred** *slang* acceptability within urban subculture; **streetwalker** prostitute seeking customers in street; **streetwise** knowing how to survive modern urban life.

strength *noun* being strong; degree or manner of this; person or thing giving strength; number of people present or available. □ **on the strength of** on basis of.

strengthen *verb* make or become stronger.

strenuous /ˈstrenjʊəs/ *adjective* using or requiring great effort; energetic. □ **strenuously** *adverb*.

streptococcus /streptəˈkɒkəs/ *noun* (*plural* **-cocci** /-kaɪ/) bacterium causing serious infections. □ **streptococcal** *adjective*.

streptomycin /streptəʊˈmaɪsɪn/ *noun* antibiotic effective against many disease-producing bacteria.

stress ● *noun* pressure, tension; quantity measuring this; physical or mental strain; emphasis. ● *verb* emphasize; subject to stress.

stressful *adjective* causing stress.

stretch ● *verb* draw, be drawn, or be able to be drawn out in length or size; make or become taut; place or lie at full length or spread out; extend limbs and tighten muscles after being relaxed; have specified length or extension, extend; strain or exert extremely; exaggerate. ● *noun* continuous extent, expanse, or period; stretching, being stretched; *colloquial* period of imprisonment etc. □ **at a stretch** in one period; **stretch one's legs** exercise oneself by walking; **stretch out** extend (limb etc.), last, prolong; **stretch a point** agree to something not normally allowed. □ **stretchy** *adjective* (**-ier**, **-iest**).

stretcher *noun* two poles with canvas etc. between for carrying person in lying position; brick etc. laid along face of wall.

strew /struː/ *verb* (*past participle* **strewn** or **strewed**) scatter over surface; (usually + *with*) spread (surface) with scattered things.

'strewth = 'STRUTH.

striated /straɪˈeɪtɪd/ *adjective* marked with slight ridges or furrows. □ **striation** *noun*.

stricken /ˈstrɪkən/ *archaic past participle* of STRIKE. ● *adjective* affected or overcome (with illness, misfortune, etc.).

strict *adjective* precisely limited or defined, without deviation; requiring complete obedience or exact performance. □ **strictly** *adverb*; **strictness** *noun*.

stricture /ˈstrɪktʃə/ *noun* (usually in *plural*; often + *on, upon*) critical or censorious remark.

stride ● *verb* (**-ding**; *past* **strode**; *past participle* **stridden** /ˈstrɪd(ə)n/) walk with long firm steps; cross with one step; bestride. ● *noun* single long step; length of this; gait as determined by length of stride; (usually in *plural*) progress. □ **take in one's stride** manage easily.

strident /ˈstraɪd(ə)nt/ *adjective* loud and harsh. □ **stridency** *noun*; **stridently** *adverb*.

strife *noun* conflict, struggle.

strike ● *verb* (**-king**; *past* **struck**; *past participle* **struck** or *archaic* **stricken**) deliver (blow), inflict blow on; come or bring sharply into contact with; propel or divert with blow; (cause to) penetrate; ignite (match) or produce (sparks etc.) by rubbing; make (coin) by stamping; produce (musical note) by striking; (of clock) indicate (time) with chime etc., (of time) be so indicated; attack suddenly; (of disease) afflict; cause to become suddenly; reach, achieve; agree on (bargain); assume (attitude); find (oil etc.) by drilling; come to attention of or appear to; (of employees) engage in strike; lower or take down (flag, tent, etc.); take specified direction. ● *noun* act of striking; employees' organized refusal to work until grievance is remedied; similar refusal to participate; sudden find or success; attack, esp. from air. □ **on strike** taking part in industrial strike; **strikebreaker** person working or employed in place of strikers; **strike home** deal effective blow; **strike off** remove with stroke, delete; **strike out** hit out, act vigorously, delete; **strike up** start (acquaintance, conversation, etc.), esp. casually, begin playing (tune etc.).

striker *noun* employee on strike; *Football* attacking player positioned forward.

striking *adjective* impressive, noticeable. □ **strikingly** *adverb*.

string ● *noun* twine, narrow cord; length of this or similar material used for tying, holding together, pulling, forming head of racket, etc.; piece of catgut, wire, etc. on musical instrument, producing note by vibration; (in *plural*) stringed instruments in orchestra etc.; (in *plural*) condition or complication attached to offer etc.; set of things strung together; tough side of bean-pod etc. ● *verb* (*past & past participle* **strung**) fit with string(s); thread on string; arrange in or as string; remove strings from (bean-pod etc.). □ **string along** *colloquial* deceive, (often + *with*) keep company (with); **string-course** raised horizontal band of bricks etc. on building; **string up** hang up on strings etc., kill by hanging, (usually as **strung up** *adjective*) make tense.

stringed *adjective* (of musical instrument) having strings.

stringent /ˈstrɪndʒ(ə)nt/ *adjective* (of rules etc.) strict, precise. □ **stringency** *noun*; **stringently** *adverb*.

stringer *noun* longitudinal structural member in framework, esp. of ship or aircraft; *colloquial* freelance newspaper correspondent.

stringy *adjective* (**-ier, -iest**) like string, fibrous.

strip[1] ● *verb* (**-pp-**) (often + *of*) remove clothes or covering from, undress; deprive (person) of property or titles; leave bare; (often + *down*) remove accessory fittings of or take apart (machine etc.); remove old paint etc. from with solvent; damage thread

of (screw) or teeth of (gearwheel). ● *noun* act of stripping, esp. in striptease; *colloquial* distinctive outfit worn by sports team. □ **strip club** club where striptease is performed; **striptease** entertainment in which performer slowly and erotically undresses.

strip[2] *noun* long narrow piece. □ **strip cartoon** comic strip; **strip light** tubular fluorescent lamp; **tear (person) off a strip** *colloquial* rebuke.

stripe *noun* long narrow band or strip differing in colour or texture from surface on either side of it; *Military* chevron etc. denoting military rank. □ **stripy** *adjective* (**-ier, -iest**).

striped *adjective* having stripes.

stripling /ˈstrɪplɪŋ/ *noun* youth not yet fully grown.

stripper *noun* device or solvent for removing paint etc.; performer of striptease.

strive *verb* (**-ving**; *past* **strove** /strəʊv/; *past participle* **striven** /ˈstrɪv(ə)n/) try hard; (often + *with, against*) struggle.

strobe *noun colloquial* stroboscope.

stroboscope /ˈstrəʊbəskəʊp/ *noun* lamp producing regular intermittent flashes. □ **stroboscopic** /-ˈskɒp/ *adjective*.

strode *past* of STRIDE.

stroke ● *noun* act of striking; sudden disabling attack caused esp. by thrombosis; action or movement, esp. as one of series or in game etc.; slightest action; single complete action of moving wing, oar, etc.; whole motion of piston either way; mode of moving limbs in swimming; single mark made by pen, paint brush, etc.; detail contributing to general effect; sound of striking clock; oarsman nearest stern, who sets time of stroke; act or spell of stroking. ● *verb* (**-king**) pass hand gently along surface of (hair, fur, etc.); act as stroke of (boat, crew). □ **at a stroke** by a single action; **on the stroke of** punctually at; **stroke of (good) luck** unexpected fortunate event.

stroll /strəʊl/ ● *verb* walk in leisurely fashion. ● *noun* leisurely walk. □ **strolling players** *historical* actors etc. going from place to place performing.

strong ● *adjective* (**stronger** /ˈstrɒŋgə/, **strongest** /-gɪst/) physically, morally, or mentally powerful; vigorous, robust; performed with muscular strength; difficult to capture, escape from, etc.; (of suspicion, belief, etc.) firmly held; powerfully affecting senses or mind etc.; (of drink, solution, etc.) with large proportion of alcohol etc.; powerful in numbers or equipment etc.; (of verb) forming inflections by vowel change in root syllable. ● *adverb* strongly. □ **come on strong** act forcefully; **going strong** *colloquial* thriving; **strong-arm** using force; **strongbox** strongly made box for valuables; **stronghold** fortress, centre of support for a cause etc.; **strong language** swearing; **strong-minded** determined; **strongroom** strongly built room for valuables; **strong suit** thing in which one excels. □ **strongish** *adjective*; **strongly** *adverb*.

strontium /ˈstrɒntɪəm/ *noun* soft silver-white metallic element. □ **strontium-90** radioactive isotope of this.

strop ● *noun* device, esp. strip of leather, for sharpening razors; *colloquial* bad temper. ● *verb* (**-pp-**) sharpen on or with strop.

stroppy /ˈstrɒpɪ/ *adjective* (**-ier, -iest**) *colloquial* badtempered, awkward to deal with.

strove *past* of STRIVE.

struck *past & past participle* of STRIKE.

structuralism *noun* doctrine that structure rather than function is important. □ **structuralist** *noun & adjective*.

structure /'strʌktʃə/ ● *noun* constructed unit, esp. building; way in which thing is constructed; framework. ● *verb* (**-ring**) give structure to, organize. □ **structural** *adjective*; **structurally** *adverb*.

strudel /'struːd(ə)l/ *noun* thin leaved pastry filled esp. with apple and baked.

struggle /'strʌg(ə)l/ ● *verb* (**-ling**) violently try to get free; (often + *for, to do*) make great efforts under difficulties; (+ *with, against*) fight against; (+ *along, up*, etc.) make one's way with difficulty; (esp. as **struggling** *adjective*) have difficulty in getting recognition or a living. ● *noun* act or period of struggling; hard or confused contest.

strum ● *verb* (**-mm-**) (often + *on*) play on (stringed or keyboard instrument), esp. carelessly or unskilfully. ● *noun* strumming sound.

strumpet /'strʌmpɪt/ *noun archaic* prostitute.

strung *past & past participle* of STRING.

strut ● *noun* bar in framework to resist pressure; strutting gait. ● *verb* (**-tt-**) walk in stiff pompous way; brace with strut(s).

'struth /struːθ/ *interjection* (also **'strewth**) *colloquial* exclamation of surprise.

strychnine /'strɪkniːn/ *noun* highly poisonous alkaloid.

stub ● *noun* remnant of pencil, cigarette, etc.; counterfoil of cheque, receipt, etc.; stump. ● *verb* (**-bb-**) strike (one's toe) against something; (usually + *out*) extinguish (cigarette etc.) by pressing lighted end against something.

stubble /'stʌb(ə)l/ *noun* cut stalks of corn etc. left in ground after harvest; short stiff hair or bristles, esp. on unshaven face. □ **stubbly** *adjective*.

stubborn /'stʌbən/ *adjective* obstinate, inflexible. □ **stubbornly** *adverb*; **stubbornness** *noun*.

stubby *adjective* (**-ier, -iest**) short and thick.

stucco /'stʌkəʊ/ ● *noun* (*plural* **-es**) plaster or cement for coating walls or moulding into architectural decorations. ● *verb* (**-es, -ed**) coat with stucco.

stuck *past & past participle* of STICK². □ **stuck-up** *colloquial* conceited, snobbish.

stud¹ ● *noun* large projecting nail, knob, etc. as surface ornament; double button, esp. for use in shirt-front. ● *verb* (**-dd-**) set with studs; (as **studded** *adjective*) (+ *with*) thickly set or strewn with.

stud² *noun* number of horses kept for breeding etc.; place where these are kept; stallion. □ **at stud** (of stallion) hired out for breeding. **stud-book** book giving pedigrees of horses; **stud-farm** place where horses are bred; **stud poker** poker with betting after dealing of cards face up.

student /'stjuːd(ə)nt/ *noun* person who is studying, esp. at place of higher or further education. □ **studentship** *noun*.

studio /'stjuːdɪəʊ/ *noun* (*plural* **-s**) workroom of sculptor, painter, photographer, etc.; place for making films, recordings, or broadcasts. □ **studio couch** couch that can be converted into a bed; **studio flat** one-roomed flat.

studious /'stjuːdɪəs/ *adjective* diligent in study or reading; painstaking. □ **studiously** *adverb*.

study /'stʌdɪ/ ● *noun* (*plural* **-ies**) acquiring knowledge, esp. from books; (in *plural*) pursuit of academic knowledge; private room for reading, writing, etc.; piece of work, esp. in painting, done as exercise or preliminary experiment; portrayal, esp. in literature, of character, behaviour, etc.; *Music* composition designed to develop player's skill; thing worth observing; thing that is or deserves to be investigated. ● *verb* (**-ies, -ied**) make study of; scrutinize; devote time and thought to understanding subject etc. or achieving desired result; (as **studied** *adjective*) deliberate, affected.

stuff ● *noun* material; fabric; substance or things not needing to be specified; particular knowledge or activity; woollen fabric; nonsense; (**the stuff**) *colloquial* supply, esp. of drink or drugs. ● *verb* pack (receptacle) tightly; (+ *in, into*) force or cram (thing); fill out skin to restore original shape of (bird, animal, etc.); fill (bird, piece of meat, etc.) with mixture, esp. before cooking; (also **stuff oneself**) eat greedily; push, esp. hastily or clumsily; (usually in *passive*; + *up*) block up (nose etc.); *slang derogatory* dispose of. □ **get stuffed** *slang* go away, get lost; **stuff and nonsense** something ridiculous or incredible.

stuffing *noun* padding for cushions etc.; mixture used to stuff food, esp. before cooking.

stuffy *adjective* (**-ier, -iest**) (of room etc.) lacking fresh air; dull, uninteresting; conventional, narrow-minded; (of nose etc.) stuffed up. □ **stuffily** *adverb*; **stuffiness** *noun*.

stultify /'stʌltɪfaɪ/ *verb* (**-ies, -ied**) make ineffective or useless, esp. by routine or from frustration. □ **stultification** *noun*.

stumble /'stʌmb(ə)l/ ● *verb* (**-ling**) accidentally lurch forward or have partial fall; (often + *along*) walk with repeated stumbles; speak clumsily; (+ *on, upon, across*) find by chance. ● *noun* act of stumbling. □ **stumbling block** circumstance causing difficulty or hesitation.

stump ● *noun* part of cut or fallen tree still in ground; similar part (of branch, limb, tooth, etc.) cut off or worn down; *Cricket* each of 3 uprights of wicket. ● *verb* (of question etc.) be too difficult for, baffle; (as **stumped** *adjective*) at a loss; *Cricket* put batsman out by touching stumps with ball while he is out of his crease; walk stiffly or clumsily and noisily; *US* traverse (district) making political speeches. □ **stump up** *colloquial* produce or pay over (money required).

stumpy *adjective* (**-ier, -iest**) short and thick. □ **stumpiness** *noun*.

stun *verb* (**-nn-**) knock senseless; stupefy; bewilder, shock.

stung *past & past participle* of STING.

stunk *past & past participle* of STINK.

stunner *noun colloquial* stunning person or thing.

stunning *adjective colloquial* extremely attractive or impressive. □ **stunningly** *adverb*.

stunt¹ *verb* retard growth or development of.

stunt² *noun* something unusual done to attract attention; trick, daring manoeuvre. □ **stunt man** man employed to take actor's place in performing dangerous stunts.

stupefy /'stjuːpɪfaɪ/ *verb* (**-ies, -ied**) make stupid or insensible; astonish. □ **stupefaction** *noun*.

stupendous /stjuː'pendəs/ *adjective* amazing; of vast size or importance. □ **stupendously** *adverb*.

stupid /'stjuːpɪd/ *adjective* (**-er, -est**) unintelligent, slow-witted; typical of stupid person; uninteresting; in state of stupor. □ **stupidity** /-'pɪd-/ *noun* (*plural* **-ies**); **stupidly** *adverb*.

stupor /'stjuːpə/ *noun* dazed or torpid state; utter amazement.

sturdy /'stɜːdɪ/ *adjective* (**-ier, -iest**) robust; strongly built; vigorous. □ **sturdily** *adverb*; **sturdiness** *noun*.

sturgeon /'stɜːdʒ(ə)n/ *noun* (*plural* same or **-s**) large edible fish yielding caviar.

stutter /'stʌtə/ *verb & noun* stammer.

sty¹ /staɪ/ *noun* (*plural* **sties**) enclosure for pigs; filthy room or dwelling.

sty² /staɪ/ *noun* (also **stye**) (*plural* **sties** or **styes**) inflamed swelling on edge of eyelid.

Stygian /'stɪdʒɪən/ *adjective literary* murky, gloomy.

style /staɪl/ ● *noun* kind or sort, esp. in regard to appearance and form (of person, house, etc.); manner of writing, speaking, etc.; distinctive manner of person, artistic school, or period; correct way of designating person or thing; superior quality; fashion in dress etc.; implement for scratching or engraving; part of flower supporting stigma. ● *verb* (**-ling**) design or make etc. in particular style; designate in specified way.

stylish *adjective* fashionable, elegant. □ **stylishly** *adverb*; **stylishness** *noun*.

stylist /ˈstaɪlɪst/ *noun* designer of fashionable styles; hairdresser; stylish writer or performer.

stylistic /staɪˈlɪstɪk/ *adjective* of literary or artistic style. □ **stylistically** *adverb*.

stylized /ˈstaɪlaɪzd/ *adjective* (also **-ised**) painted, drawn, etc. in conventional non-realistic style.

stylus /ˈstaɪləs/ *noun* (*plural* **-luses**) needle-like point for producing or following groove in gramophone record; ancient pointed writing implement.

stymie /ˈstaɪmɪ/ (also **stimy**) ● *noun* (*plural* **-ies**) Golf situation where opponent's ball lies between one's ball and the hole; difficult situation. ● *verb* (**stymying** or **stymieing**) obstruct, thwart.

styptic /ˈstɪptɪk/ ● *adjective* serving to check bleeding. ● *noun* styptic substance.

styrene /ˈstaɪəriːn/ *noun* liquid hydrocarbon used in making plastics etc.

suave /swɑːv/ *adjective* smooth; polite; sophisticated. □ **suavely** *adverb*; **suavity** *noun*.

sub *colloquial* ● *noun* submarine; subscription; substitute; sub-editor. ● *verb* (**-bb-**) (usually + *for*) act as substitute; sub-edit; lend.

sub- *prefix* at, to, or from lower position; secondary or inferior position; nearly; more or less.

subaltern /ˈsʌbəlt(ə)n/ *noun Military* officer below rank of captain, esp. second lieutenant.

sub-aqua /sʌbˈækwə/ *adjective* (of sport etc.) taking place under water.

subatomic /sʌbəˈtɒmɪk/ *adjective* occurring in, or smaller than, an atom.

subcommittee *noun* committee formed from main committee for special purpose.

subconscious /sʌbˈkɒnʃəs/ ● *adjective* of part of mind that is not fully conscious but influences actions etc. ● *noun* this part of the mind. □ **subconsciously** *adverb*.

subcontinent /sʌbˈkɒntɪnənt/ *noun* large land mass, smaller than continent.

subcontract ● *verb* /sʌbkənˈtrækt/ employ another contractor to do (work) as part of larger project; make or carry out subcontract. ● *noun* /sʌbˈkɒntrækt/ secondary contract. □ **subcontractor** /-ˈtræktə/ *noun*.

subculture /ˈsʌbkʌltʃə/ *noun* social group or its culture within a larger culture.

subcutaneous /sʌbkjuːˈteɪnɪəs/ *adjective* under the skin.

subdivide /sʌbdɪˈvaɪd/ *verb* (**-ding**) divide again after first division. □ **subdivision** /ˈsʌbdɪvɪʒ(ə)n/ *noun*.

subdue /səbˈdjuː/ *verb* (**-dues**, **-dued**, **-duing**) conquer, suppress; tame; (as **subdued** *adjective*) softened, lacking in intensity.

sub-editor /sʌbˈedɪtə/ *noun* assistant editor; person who prepares material for printing. □ **sub-edit** *verb* (**-t-**).

subheading /ˈsʌbhedɪŋ/ *noun* subordinate heading or title.

subhuman /sʌbˈhjuːmən/ *adjective* (of behaviour, intelligence, etc.) less than human.

subject ● *noun* /ˈsʌbdʒɪkt/ theme of discussion, description, or representation; (+ *for*) person, circumstance, etc. giving rise to specified feeling, action, etc.; branch of study; word or phrase representing person or thing carrying out action of verb (see panel); person other than monarch living under government; *Philosophy* thinking or feeling entity, conscious self; *Music* theme, leading motif. ● *adjective* /ˈsʌbdʒɪkt/ (+ *to*) conditional on, liable or exposed to; owing obedience to government etc. ● *adverb* /ˈsʌbdʒɪkt/ (+ *to*) conditionally on. ● *verb* /səbˈdʒekt/ (+ *to*) make liable or expose to; (usually + *to*) subdue (person, nation, etc.) to superior will. □ **subjection** *noun*.

subjective /səbˈdʒektɪv/ *adjective* (of art, written history, opinion, etc.) not impartial or literal; *esp. Philosophy* of individual consciousness or perception; imaginary, partial, distorted; *Grammar* of the subject. □ **subjectively** *adverb*; **subjectivity** /sʌbdʒekˈtɪv-/ *noun*.

subjoin /sʌbˈdʒɔɪn/ *verb* add (illustration, anecdote, etc.) at the end.

sub judice /sʌb ˈdʒuːdɪsɪ/ *adjective Law* under judicial consideration and therefore prohibited from public discussion. [Latin]

subjugate /ˈsʌbdʒʊgeɪt/ *verb* (**-ting**) conquer, bring into subjection. □ **subjugation** *noun*; **subjugator** *noun*.

subjunctive /səbˈdʒʌŋktɪv/ *Grammar* ● *adjective* (of mood) expressing wish, supposition, or possibility. ● *noun* subjunctive mood or form.

sublease ● *noun* /ˈsʌbliːs/ lease granted by tenant to subtenant. ● *verb* /sʌbˈliːs/ (**-sing**) lease to subtenant.

sublet /sʌbˈlet/ *verb* (**-tt-**; *past & past participle* **-let**) lease to subtenant.

sub-lieutenant /sʌblefˈtenənt/ *noun* officer ranking next below lieutenant.

sublimate ● *verb* /ˈsʌblɪmeɪt/ (**-ting**) divert energy of (primitive impulse etc.) into socially more acceptable activity; sublime (substance); refine, purify. ● *noun* /ˈsʌblɪmət/ sublimated substance. □ **sublimation** *noun*.

sublime /səˈblaɪm/ ● *adjective* (**-r**, **-st**) of most exalted kind; awe-inspiring; arrogantly undisturbed. ● *verb* (**-ming**) convert (substance) from solid into vapour by heat (and usually allow to solidify again); make sublime; become pure (as if) by sublimation. □ **sublimely** *adverb*; **sublimity** /-ˈlɪm-/ *noun*.

subliminal /səbˈlɪmɪn(ə)l/ *adjective Psychology* below threshold of sensation or consciousness; too faint or rapid to be consciously perceived. □ **subliminally** *adverb*.

sub-machine-gun /sʌbməˈʃiːngʌn/ *noun* hand-held lightweight machine-gun.

submarine /sʌbməˈriːn/ ● *noun* vessel, esp. armed warship, which can be submerged and navigated under water. ● *adjective* existing, occurring, done, or used below surface of sea. □ **submariner** /-ˈmærɪnə/ *noun*.

submerge /səbˈmɜːdʒ/ *verb* (**-ging**) place, go, or dive beneath water; overwhelm with work, problems, etc. □ **submergence** *noun*; **submersion** *noun*.

submersible /səbˈmɜːsɪb(ə)l/ ● *noun* submarine operating under water for short periods. ● *adjective* capable of submerging.

submicroscopic /sʌbmaɪkrəˈskɒpɪk/ *adjective* too small to be seen by ordinary microscope.

submission /səbˈmɪʃ(ə)n/ *noun* submitting, being submitted; thing submitted; submissive attitude etc.

submissive /səbˈmɪsɪv/ *adjective* humble, obedient. □ **submissively** *adverb*; **submissiveness** *noun*.

submit /səb'mɪt/ verb (-tt-) (often + to) cease resistance, yield; present for consideration; (+ to) subject or be subjected to (process, treatment, etc.); *Law* argue, suggest.

subnormal /sʌb'nɔːm(ə)l/ adjective below or less than normal, esp. in intelligence.

subordinate ● adjective /sə'bɔːdɪnət/ (usually + to) of inferior importance or rank; secondary, subservient. **●** noun /sə'bɔːdɪnət/ person working under authority of another. **●** verb /sə'bɔːdɪneɪt/ (-ting) (usually + to) make or treat as subordinate. □ **subordinate clause** clause serving as noun, adjective, or adverb within sentence. □ **subordination** noun.

suborn /sə'bɔːn/ verb induce esp. by bribery to commit perjury or other crime.

subpoena /sə'piːnə/ **●** noun writ ordering person's attendance in law court. **●** verb (past & past participle **-naed** or **-na'd**) serve subpoena on.

sub rosa /sʌb 'rəʊzə/ adjective & adverb in confidence or in secret. [Latin]

subscribe /səb'skraɪb/ verb (-bing) (usually + to, for) pay (specified sum) esp. regularly for membership of organization or receipt of publication etc.; contribute to fund, for cause, etc.; (usually + to) agree with (opinion etc.). □ **subscribe to** arrange to receive (periodical etc.) regularly.

subscriber noun person who subscribes, esp. person paying regular sum for hire of telephone line. □ **subscriber trunk dialling** making of trunk calls by subscriber without assistance of operator.

subscript /'sʌbskrɪpt/ **●** adjective written or printed below the line. **●** noun subscript number etc.

subscription /səb'skrɪpʃ(ə)n/ noun act of subscribing; money subscribed; membership fee, esp. paid regularly.

subsequent /'sʌbsɪkwənt/ adjective (usually + to) following specified or implied event. □ **subsequently** adverb.

subservient /səb'sɜːvɪənt/ adjective servile; (usually + to) instrumental, subordinate. □ **subservience** noun.

subside /səb'saɪd/ verb (-ding) become tranquil; diminish; (of water etc.) sink; (of ground) cave in. □ **subsidence** /-'saɪd-, 'sʌbsɪd-/ noun.

subsidiary /səb'sɪdɪərɪ/ **●** adjective supplementary; additional; (of company) controlled by another. **●** noun (plural **-ies**) subsidiary company, person, or thing.

subsidize /'sʌbsɪdaɪz/ verb (also **-ise**) (-zing or **-sing**) pay subsidy to; support by subsidies.

subsidy /'sʌbsɪdɪ/ noun (plural **-ies**) money contributed esp. by state to keep prices at desired level; any monetary grant.

subsist /səb'sɪst/ verb (often + on) keep oneself alive; be kept alive; remain in being, exist.

subsistence noun subsisting; means of supporting life; minimal level of existence, income, etc.

□ **subsistence farming** farming in which almost all produce is consumed by farmer's household.

subsoil /'sʌbsɔɪl/ noun soil just below surface soil.

subsonic /sʌb'sɒnɪk/ adjective of speeds less than that of sound.

substance /'sʌbst(ə)ns/ noun particular kind of material; reality, solidity; essence of what is spoken or written; wealth and possessions. □ **in substance** generally, essentially.

substandard /sʌb'stændəd/ adjective of lower than desired standard.

substantial /səb'stænʃ(ə)l/ adjective of real importance or value; large in size or amount; of solid structure; commercially successful; wealthy; largely true; real; existing. □ **substantially** adverb.

substantiate /səb'stænʃɪeɪt/ verb (-ting) support or prove truth of (charge, claim, etc.). □ **substantiation** noun.

substantive /'sʌbstəntɪv/ **●** adjective actual, real, permanent; substantial. **●** noun noun. □ **substantively** adverb.

substitute /'sʌbstɪtjuːt/ **●** noun person or thing acting or serving in place of another; artificial alternative to a food etc. **●** verb (-ting) (often + for) put in place of another; act as substitute for. **●** adjective acting as substitute. □ **substitution** noun.

substratum /'sʌbstrɑːtəm/ noun (plural **-ta**) underlying layer.

subsume /səb'sjuːm/ verb (-ming) (usually + under) include under particular rule, class, etc.

subtenant /'sʌbtenənt/ noun person renting room or house etc. from its tenant. □ **subtenancy** noun (plural **-ies**).

subtend /sʌb'tend/ verb (of line) be opposite (angle, arc).

subterfuge /'sʌbtəfjuːdʒ/ noun attempt to avoid blame etc., esp. by lying or deceit.

subterranean /sʌbtə'reɪnɪən/ adjective underground.

subtext noun underlying theme.

subtitle /'sʌbtaɪt(ə)l/ **●** noun subordinate or additional title of book etc.; caption of cinema film, esp. translating dialogue. **●** verb (-ling) provide with subtitle(s).

subtle /'sʌt(ə)l/ adjective (-r, -st) hard to detect or describe; (of scent, colour, etc.) faint, delicate; ingenious, perceptive. □ **subtlety** noun (plural **-ies**); **subtly** adverb.

subtract /səb'trækt/ verb (often + from) deduct (number etc.) from another. □ **subtraction** noun.

subtropical /sʌb'trɒpɪk(ə)l/ adjective bordering on the tropics; characteristic of such regions.

suburb /'sʌbɜːb/ noun outlying district of city.

suburban /sə'bɜːbən/ adjective of or characteristic of suburbs; derogatory provincial in outlook. □ **suburbanite** noun.

suburbia /sə'bɜːbɪə/ noun usually derogatory suburbs and their inhabitants etc.

Subject

The subject of a sentence is the person or thing that carried out the action of the verb and can be found by asking the question 'who or what?' before the verb, e.g.

The goalkeeper *made a stunning save.*
Hundreds of books *are now available on CD-ROM.*

In a passive construction, the subject of the sentence is in fact the person or thing to which the action of the verb is done, e.g.

I *was hit by a ball.*
Has the programme *been broadcast yet?*

subvention /səb'venʃ(ə)n/ *noun* subsidy.

subversive /səb'vɜːsɪv/ ● *adjective* seeking to over-throw (esp. government). ● *noun* subversive person. □ **subversion** *noun*; **subversively** *adverb*; **subversiveness** *noun*.

subvert /səb'vɜːt/ *verb* overthrow or weaken (government etc.).

subway /'sʌbweɪ/ *noun* underground passage, esp. for pedestrians; *US* underground railway.

subzero /sʌb'zɪərəʊ/ *adjective* (esp. of temperature) lower than zero.

succeed /sək'siːd/ *verb* (often + *in*) have success; prosper; follow in order; (often + *to*) come into inheritance, office, title, or property.

success /sək'ses/ *noun* accomplishment of aim; favourable outcome; attainment of wealth, fame, etc.; successful person or thing. □ **successful** *adjective*; **successfully** *adverb*.

succession /sək'seʃ(ə)n/ *noun* following in order; series of things or people following one another; succeeding to inheritance, office, or esp. throne; right to succeed to one of these, set of people with such right. □ **in succession** one after another; **in succession to** as successor of.

successive /sək'sesɪv/ *adjective* following in succession, consecutive. □ **successively** *adverb*.

successor /sək'sesə/ *noun* (often + *to*) person or thing that succeeds another.

succinct /sək'sɪŋkt/ *adjective* brief, concise. □ **succinctly** *adverb*; **succinctness** *noun*.

succour /'sʌkə/ (*US* **succor**) *archaic or formal* ● *noun* help, esp. in time of need. ● *verb* give succour to.

succulent /'sʌkjʊlənt/ ● *adjective* juicy; (of plant) thick and fleshy. ● *noun* succulent plant. □ **succulence** *noun*.

succumb /sə'kʌm/ *verb* (usually + *to*) give way; be overcome; die.

such ● *adjective* (often + *as*) of kind or degree specified or suggested; so great or extreme; unusually, abnormally. ● *pronoun* such person(s) or thing(s). □ **as such** being what has been specified; **such-and-such** particular but unspecified; **suchlike** *colloquial* of such kind.

suck ● *verb* draw (liquid) into mouth by suction; draw liquid from in this way; roll tongue round (sweet etc.) in mouth; make sucking action or noise; (usually + *down*) engulf or drown in sucking movement. ● *noun* act or period of sucking. □ **suck in** absorb, involve (person); **suck up** (often + *to*) *colloquial* behave in a servile way, absorb.

sucker *noun* person easily duped or cheated; (+ *for*) person susceptible to; rubber etc. cap adhering by suction; similar part of plant or animal; shoot springing from plant's root below ground.

suckle /'sʌk(ə)l/ *verb* (**-ling**) feed (young) from breast or udder.

suckling /'sʌklɪŋ/ *noun* unweaned child or animal.

sucrose /'suːkrəʊz/ *noun* kind of sugar obtained from cane, beet, etc.

suction /'sʌkʃ(ə)n/ *noun* sucking; production of partial vacuum so that external atmospheric pressure forces fluid into vacant space or causes adhesion of surfaces.

Sudanese /suːdə'niːz/ ● *adjective* of Sudan. ● *noun* (*plural* same) native or national of Sudan.

sudden /'sʌd(ə)n/ *adjective* done or occurring unexpectedly or abruptly. □ **all of a sudden** suddenly. □ **suddenly** *adverb*; **suddenness** *noun*.

sudorific /suːdə'rɪfɪk/ ● *adjective* causing sweating. ● *noun* sudorific drug.

suds *plural noun* froth of soap and water. □ **sudsy** *adjective*.

sue *verb* (**sues, sued, suing**) begin lawsuit against; (often + *for*) make application to law court for compensation etc.; (often + *to*, *for*) make plea to person for favour.

suede /sweɪd/ *noun* leather with flesh side rubbed into nap.

suet /'suːɪt/ *noun* hard fat surrounding kidneys of cattle and sheep, used in cooking etc. □ **suety** *adjective*.

suffer /'sʌfə/ *verb* undergo pain, grief, etc.; undergo or be subjected to (pain, loss, punishment, grief, etc.); tolerate. □ **sufferer** *noun*; **suffering** *noun*.

sufferance *noun* tacit permission or toleration. □ **on sufferance** tolerated but not supported.

suffice /sə'faɪs/ *verb* (**-cing**) be enough; meet needs of. □ **suffice it to say** I shall say only this.

sufficiency /sə'fɪʃənsɪ/ *noun* (*plural* **-ies**) (often + *of*) sufficient amount.

sufficient /sə'fɪʃ(ə)nt/ *adjective* sufficing; adequate. □ **sufficiently** *adverb*.

suffix /'sʌfɪks/ ● *noun* letter(s) added to end of word to form derivative. ● *verb* add as suffix.

suffocate /'sʌfəkeɪt/ *verb* (**-ting**) kill, stifle, or choke by stopping breathing, esp. by fumes etc.; be or feel suffocated. □ **suffocating** *adjective*; **suffocation** *noun*.

suffragan /'sʌfrəgən/ *noun* bishop assisting diocesan bishop.

suffrage /'sʌfrɪdʒ/ *noun* right of voting in political elections.

suffragette /sʌfrə'dʒet/ *noun historical* woman who agitated for women's suffrage.

suffuse /sə'fjuːz/ *verb* (**-sing**) (of colour, moisture, etc.) spread throughout or over from within. □ **suffusion** /-ʒ(ə)n/ *noun*.

sugar /'ʃʊgə/ ● *noun* sweet crystalline substance obtained from sugar cane and sugar beet, used in cookery, confectionery, etc.; *Chemistry* soluble usually sweet crystalline carbohydrate, e.g. glucose; *esp. US colloquial* darling (as term of address). ● *verb* sweeten or coat with sugar. □ **sugar beet** white beet yielding sugar; **sugar cane** tall stout perennial tropical grass yielding sugar; **sugar-daddy** *slang* elderly man who lavishes gifts on young woman; **sugar loaf** conical moulded mass of hard refined sugar.

sugary *adjective* containing or resembling sugar; cloying, sentimental. □ **sugariness** *noun*.

suggest /sə'dʒest/ *verb* (often + *that*) propose (theory, plan, etc.); hint at; evoke (idea etc.); (**suggest itself**) (of idea etc.) come into person's mind.

suggestible *adjective* capable of being influenced by suggestion. □ **suggestibility** *noun*.

suggestion /sə'dʒestʃ(ə)n/ *noun* suggesting; thing suggested; slight trace, hint; insinuation of belief or impulse into the mind.

suggestive /sə'dʒestɪv/ *adjective* (usually + *of*) conveying a suggestion; (of remark, joke, etc.) suggesting something indecent. □ **suggestively** *adverb*.

suicidal /suːɪ'saɪd(ə)l/ *adjective* (of person) liable to commit suicide; of or tending to suicide; destructive to one's own interests. □ **suicidally** *adverb*.

suicide /'suːɪsaɪd/ *noun* intentional self-killing; person who commits suicide; action destructive to one's own interests etc.

sui generis /sjuːˈɑːdʒenərɪs/ *adjective* of its own kind, unique. [Latin]

suit /suːt, sjuːt/ ● *noun* set of usually matching clothes consisting usually of jacket and trousers or skirt; clothing for particular purpose; any of the 4 sets into which pack of cards is divided; lawsuit. ● *verb* go well with (person's appearance); meet requirements of; (**suit oneself**) do as one chooses; be in harmony with; make fitting; be convenient; adapt;

(as **suited** *adjective*) appropriate, well-fitted.
□ **suitcase** flat case for carrying clothes, usually
with hinged lid.

suitable *adjective* (usually + *to, for*) well-fitted for
purpose; appropriate to occasion. □ **suitability** *noun*;
suitably *adverb*.

suite /swiːt/ *noun* set of rooms, furniture, etc.; *Music*
set of instrumental pieces.

suitor /ˈsuːtə/ *noun* man who woos woman; plaintiff
or petitioner in lawsuit.

sulfur etc. *US* = SULPHUR etc.

sulk ● *verb* be sulky. ● *noun* (also **the sulks**) fit of
sullen silence.

sulky /ˈsʌlkɪ/ *adjective* (**-ier, -iest**) sullen and unsociable from resentment or ill temper. □ **sulkily**
adverb.

sullen /ˈsʌlən/ *adjective* sulky, morose. □ **sullenly** *adverb*; **sullenness** *noun*.

sully /ˈsʌlɪ/ *verb* (**-ies, -ied**) spoil purity or splendour
of (reputation etc.).

sulphate /ˈsʌlfeɪt/ *noun* (*US* **sulfate**) salt or ester of
sulphuric acid.

sulphide /ˈsʌlfaɪd/ *noun* (*US* **sulfide**) binary compound of sulphur.

sulphite /ˈsʌlfaɪt/ *noun* (*US* **sulfite**) salt or ester of
sulphurous acid.

sulphonamide /sʌlˈfɒnəmaɪd/ *noun* (*US* **sulfon-
amide**) kind of antibiotic drug containing
sulphur.

sulphur /ˈsʌlfə/ *noun* (*US* **sulfur**) pale yellow non-
metallic element burning with blue flame and
stifling smell. □ **sulphur dioxide** colourless pungent gas formed by burning sulphur in air and dissolving it in water.

sulphuric /sʌlˈfjʊərɪk/ *adjective* (*US* **sulfuric**) of or
containing sulphur with valency of 6. □ **sulphuric
acid** dense highly corrosive oily acid.

sulphurous /ˈsʌlfərəs/ *adjective* (*US* **sulfurous**) of or
like sulphur; containing sulphur with valency of 4.
□ **sulphurous acid** unstable weak acid used e.g. as
bleaching agent.

sultan /ˈsʌlt(ə)n/ *noun* Muslim sovereign.

sultana /sʌlˈtɑːnə/ *noun* seedless raisin; sultan's wife,
mother, concubine, or daughter.

sultanate /ˈsʌltəneɪt/ *noun* position of or territory
ruled by sultan.

sultry /ˈsʌltrɪ/ *adjective* (**-ier, -iest**) (of weather) oppressively hot; (of person) passionate, sensual.

sum ● *noun* total resulting from addition; amount of
money; arithmetical problem; (esp. in *plural*) *colloquial*
arithmetic work, esp. elementary. ● *verb* (**-mm-**) find
sum of. □ **in sum** briefly, to sum up; **summing-up**
judge's review of evidence given to jury, recapitulation of main points of argument etc.; **sum
up** (esp. of judge) give summing-up, form or express
opinion of (person, situation, etc.), summarize.

sumac /ˈsuːmæk/ *noun* (also **sumach**) shrub with
reddish fruits used as spice; dried and ground leaves
of this for use in tanning and dyeing.

summarize /ˈsʌməraɪz/ *verb* (also **-ise**) (**-zing** or
-sing) make or be summary of.

summary /ˈsʌmərɪ/ ● *noun* (*plural* **-ies**) brief account
giving chief points. ● *adjective* brief, without details
or formalities. □ **summarily** *adverb*.

summation /səˈmeɪʃ(ə)n/ *noun* finding of total or
sum; summarizing.

summer /ˈsʌmə/ *noun* warmest season of year; (often
+ *of*) mature stage of life etc. □ **summer house**
light building in garden etc. for use in summer;
summer pudding dessert of soft fruit pressed in
bread casing; **summer school** course of lectures

etc. held in summer, esp. at university; **summer
time** period from March to October when clocks etc.
are advanced one hour; **summertime** season or
period of summer. □ **summery** *adjective*.

summit /ˈsʌmɪt/ *noun* highest point, top; highest level
of achievement or status; (in full **summit conference, meeting**, etc.) discussion between heads
of governments.

summon /ˈsʌmən/ *verb* order to come or appear, esp.
in lawcourt; (usually + *to do*) call on; call together;
(often + *up*) gather (courage, resources, etc.).

summons /ˈsʌmənz/ ● *noun* (*plural* **summonses**) authoritative call to attend or do something, esp. to
appear in court. ● *verb* *Law* serve with summons.

sumo /ˈsuːməʊ/ *noun* Japanese wrestling in which
only soles of feet may touch ground.

sump *noun* casing holding oil in internal-combustion
engine; pit, well, etc. for collecting superfluous liquid.

sumptuary /ˈsʌmptʃʊərɪ/ *adjective* *Law* regulating (esp.
private) expenditure.

sumptuous /ˈsʌmptʃʊəs/ *adjective* costly, splendid,
magnificent. □ **sumptuously** *adverb*; **sumptuous-
ness** *noun*.

Sun. *abbreviation* Sunday.

sun ● *noun* the star round which the earth travels
and from which it receives light and warmth; this
light or warmth; any star. ● *verb* (**-nn-**) (often **sun
oneself**) expose to sun. □ **sunbathe** bask in sun,
esp. to tan one's body; **sunbeam** ray of sunlight;
sunblock lotion protecting skin from sun; **sunburn**
inflammation of skin from exposure to sun; **sun-
burnt** affected by sunburn; **sundial** instrument
showing time by shadow of pointer in sunlight;
sundown sunset; **sunflower** tall plant with large
golden-rayed flowers; **sunglasses** tinted spectacles
to protect eyes from glare; **sunlamp** lamp giving
ultraviolet rays for therapy or artificial suntan; **sunlight** light from sun; **sunlit** illuminated by sun; **sun
lounge** room with large windows etc. to receive
much sunlight; **sunrise** (time of) sun's rising; **sun-
roof** opening panel in car's roof; **sunset** (time of)
sun's setting; **sunshade** parasol, awning; **sunshine**
sunlight, area illuminated by it, fine weather, cheerfulness; **sunspot** dark patch on sun's surface; **sunstroke** acute prostration from excessive heat of sun;
suntan brownish skin colour caused by exposure
to sun; **suntrap** sunny place, esp. sheltered from
wind; **sun-up** esp. *US* sunrise.

sundae /ˈsʌndeɪ/ *noun* ice cream with fruit, nuts,
syrup, etc.

Sunday /ˈsʌndeɪ/ *noun* day of week following Saturday; Christian day of worship; *colloquial* newspaper
published on Sundays. □ **month of Sundays** *colloquial* very long period; **Sunday school** religious
class held on Sundays for children.

sunder /ˈsʌndə/ *verb literary* sever, keep apart.

sundry /ˈsʌndrɪ/ ● *adjective* various, several. ● *noun*
(*plural* **-ies**) (in *plural*) oddments, accessories, etc. not
mentioned individually. □ **all and sundry** everyone.

sung *past participle* of SING.

sunk *past* & *past participle* of SINK.

sunken *adjective* that has sunk; lying below general
surface; (of eyes, cheeks, etc.) shrunken, hollow.

Sunni /ˈsʌnɪ/ *noun* (*plural* same or **-s**) one of two main
branches of Islam; adherent of this.

sunny *adjective* (**-ier, -iest**) bright with or warmed by
sunlight; cheerful. □ **sunnily** *adverb*; **sunniness** *noun*.

sup[1] ● *verb* (**-pp-**) drink by sips or spoonfuls; *esp.
Northern English colloquial* drink (alcohol). ● *noun* sip of
liquid.

sup[2] *verb* (**-pp-**) *archaic* take supper.

super /'suːpə/ ● *adjective colloquial* excellent, unusually good. ● *noun colloquial* superintendent; supernumerary.

super- *combining form* on top, over, beyond; to extreme degree; extra good or large of its kind; of higher kind.

superannuate /suːpər'ænjʊeɪt/ *verb* (**-ting**) pension (person) off; dismiss or discard as too old; (as **superannuated** *adjective*) too old for work.

superannuation *noun* pension; payment made to obtain pension.

superb /suːˈpɜːb/ *adjective colloquial* excellent; magnificent. □ **superbly** *adverb*.

supercargo /'suːpəkɑːgəʊ/ *noun* (*plural* **-es**) person in merchant ship managing sales etc. of cargo.

supercharge /'suːpətʃɑːdʒ/ *verb* (**-ging**) (usually + *with*) charge (atmosphere etc.) with energy, emotion, etc.; use supercharger on.

supercharger *noun* device forcing extra air or fuel into internal-combustion engine.

supercilious /suːpə'sɪlɪəs/ *adjective* haughtily contemptuous. □ **superciliously** *adverb*; **superciliousness** *noun*.

supererogation /suːpərerə'geɪʃ(ə)n/ *noun* doing of more than duty requires.

superficial /suːpə'fɪʃ(ə)l/ *adjective* of or on the surface; lacking depth; swift, cursory; apparent, not real; (esp. of person) of shallow feelings etc. □ **superficiality** /-ʃɪ'æl-/ *noun*; **superficially** *adverb*.

superfluity /suːpə'fluːɪtɪ/ *noun* (*plural* **-ies**) being superfluous; superfluous amount or thing.

superfluous /suːˈpɜːflʊəs/ *adjective* more than is needed or wanted; useless.

supergrass /'suːpəgrɑːs/ *noun colloquial* police informer implicating many people.

superhuman /suːpə'hjuːmən/ *adjective* exceeding normal human capacity or power.

superimpose /suːpərɪm'pəʊz/ *verb* (**-sing**) (usually + *on*) place (thing) on or above something else. □ **superimposition** /-pə'zɪʃ(ə)n/ *noun*.

superintend /suːpərɪn'tend/ *verb* manage, supervise (work etc.). □ **superintendence** *noun*.

superintendent /suːpərɪn'tend(ə)nt/ *noun* police officer above rank of chief inspector; person who superintends; director of institution etc.

superior /suːˈpɪərɪə/ ● *adjective* higher in rank, quality, etc.; high-quality; supercilious; (often + *to*) better or greater in some respect; written or printed above the line. ● *noun* person superior to another, esp. in rank; head of monastery etc. □ **superiority** /-'ɒr-/ *noun*.

superlative /suːˈpɜːlətɪv/ ● *adjective* of highest degree; excellent; *Grammar* (of adjective or adverb) expressing highest or very high degree of quality etc. denoted by simple word. ● *noun Grammar* superlative expression or word; (in *plural*) high praise, exaggerated language.

superman *noun colloquial* man of exceptional powers or achievement.

supermarket /'suːpəmɑːkɪt/ *noun* large self-service store selling food, household goods, etc.

supernatural /suːpə'nætʃər(ə)l/ ● *adjective* not attributable to, or explicable by, natural or physical laws; magical; mystical. ● *noun* (**the supernatural**) supernatural forces etc. □ **supernaturally** *adverb*.

supernova /suːpə'nəʊvə/ *noun* (*plural* **-vae** /-viː/ or **-vas**) star that suddenly increases very greatly in brightness.

supernumerary /suːpə'njuːmərərɪ/ ● *adjective* in excess of normal number; engaged for extra work; (of actor) with non-speaking part. ● *noun* (*plural* **-ies**) supernumerary person or thing.

superphosphate /suːpə'fɒsfeɪt/ *noun* fertilizer made from phosphate rock.

superpower /'suːpəpaʊə/ *noun* extremely powerful nation.

superscript /'suːpəskrɪpt/ ● *adjective* written or printed above. ● *noun* superscript number or symbol.

supersede /suːpə'siːd/ *verb* (**-ding**) take place of; put or use another in place of. □ **supersession** /-'seʃ-/ *noun*.

supersonic /suːpə'sɒnɪk/ *adjective* of or having speed greater than that of sound. □ **supersonically** *adverb*.

superstar /'suːpəstɑː/ *noun* extremely famous or renowned actor, musician, etc.

superstition /suːpə'stɪʃ(ə)n/ *noun* belief in the supernatural; irrational fear of the unknown or mysterious; practice, belief, or religion based on this. □ **superstitious** *adjective*.

superstore /'suːpəstɔː/ *noun* very large supermarket.

superstructure /'suːpəstrʌktʃə/ *noun* structure built on top of another; upper part of building, ship, etc.

supertanker /'suːpətæŋkə/ *noun* very large tanker.

supertax /'suːpətæks/ *noun* surtax.

supervene /suːpə'viːn/ *verb* (**-ning**) *formal* occur as interruption in or change from some state. □ **supervention** *noun*.

supervise /'suːpəvaɪz/ *verb* (**-sing**) oversee, superintend. □ **supervision** /-'vɪʒ(ə)n/ *noun*; **supervisor** *noun*; **supervisory** *adjective*.

superwoman *noun colloquial* woman of exceptional ability or power.

supine /'suːpaɪn/ ● *adjective* lying face upwards; inactive, indolent. ● *noun* type of Latin verbal noun.

supper /'sʌpə/ *noun* meal taken late in day, esp. evening meal less formal and substantial than dinner.

supplant /sə'plɑːnt/ *verb* take the place of, esp. by underhand means.

supple /'sʌp(ə)l/ *adjective* (**-r, -st**) easily bent, pliant, flexible. □ **suppleness** *noun*.

supplement ● *noun* /'sʌplɪmənt/ thing or part added to improve or provide further information; separate section of newspaper etc. ● *verb* /'sʌplɪment/ provide supplement for. □ **supplemental** /-'ment(ə)l/ *adjective*; **supplementary** /-'mentərɪ/ *adjective*; **supplementation** *noun*.

suppliant /'sʌplɪənt/ ● *adjective* supplicating. ● *noun* humble petitioner.

supplicate /'sʌplɪkeɪt/ *verb* (**-ting**) *literary* make humble petition to or for. □ **supplicant** *noun*; **supplication** *noun*; **supplicatory** /-kətərɪ/ *adjective*.

supply /sə'plaɪ/ *verb* (**-ies, -ied**) provide (thing needed); (often + *with*) provide (person etc. with something); make up for (deficiency etc.). ● *noun* (*plural* **-ies**) provision of what is needed; stock, store; (in *plural*) provisions, equipment, etc. for army, expedition, etc.; person, esp. teacher, acting as temporary substitute. □ **supply and demand** quantities available and required, as factors regulating price. □ **supplier** *noun*.

support /sə'pɔːt/ ● *verb* carry all or part of weight of; keep from falling, sinking, or failing; provide for; strengthen, encourage; give help or corroboration to; speak in favour of; take secondary part to (actor etc.); perform secondary act to (main act) at pop concert. ● *noun* supporting, being supported; person or thing that supports. □ **in support of** so as to support. □ **supportive** *adjective*; **supportively** *adverb*; **supportiveness** *noun*.

supporter *noun* person or thing that supports particular cause, team, sport, etc.

suppose /sə'pəʊz/ *verb* (**-sing**) (often + *that*) assume, be inclined to think; take as possibility or hypothesis; require as condition; (as **supposed** *adjective*) presumed. □ **be supposed to** be expected or required to; (in negative) ought not, not be allowed to; **I suppose so** *expression of hesitant agreement*.

supposedly /sə'pəʊzɪdlɪ/ *adverb* as is generally believed.

supposition /sʌpə'zɪʃ(ə)n/ *noun* what is supposed or assumed.

suppositious /sʌpə'zɪʃəs/ *adjective* hypothetical.

suppository /sə'pɒzɪtərɪ/ *noun* (*plural* **-ies**) solid medical preparation put into rectum or vagina to melt.

suppress /sə'pres/ *verb* put an end to; prevent (information, feelings, etc.) from being seen, heard, or known; *Electricity* partially or wholly eliminate (interference etc.), equip (device) to reduce interference due to it. □ **suppressible** *adjective*; **suppression** *noun*; **suppressor** *noun*.

suppurate /'sʌpjʊreɪt/ *verb* (**-ting**) form or secrete pus; fester. □ **suppuration** *noun*.

supra- *prefix* above.

supranational /su:prə'næʃən(ə)l/ *adjective* transcending national limits.

supremacy /su:'preməsɪ/ *noun* (*plural* **-ies**) being supreme; highest authority.

supreme /su:'pri:m/ *adjective* highest in authority or rank; greatest, most important; (of penalty, sacrifice, etc.) involving death. □ **supremely** *adverb*.

supremo /su:'pri:məʊ/ *noun* (*plural* **-s**) supreme leader.

surcharge /'sɜːtʃɑːdʒ/ ● *noun* additional charge or payment. ● *verb* (**-ging**) exact surcharge from.

surd ● *adjective* (of number) irrational. ● *noun* surd number.

sure /ʃʊə/ ● *adjective* (often + *of*, *that*) convinced; having or seeming to have adequate reason for belief; (+ *of*) confident in anticipation or knowledge of; reliable, unfailing; (+ *to do*) certain; undoubtedly true or truthful. ● *adverb colloquial* certainly. □ **make sure** make or become certain, ensure; **sure-fire** *colloquial* certain to succeed; **sure-footed** never stumbling; **to be sure** admittedly, indeed, certainly. **sureness** *noun*.

surely *adverb* with certainty or safety; *added to statement to express strong belief in its correctness*.

surety /'ʃʊərətɪ/ *noun* (*plural* **-ies**) money given as guarantee of performance etc.; person taking responsibility for another's debt, obligation, etc.

surf ● *noun* foam of sea breaking on rock or (esp. shallow) shore. ● *verb* engage in surfing. □ **surfboard** long narrow board used in surfing. □ **surfer** *noun*.

surface /'sɜːfɪs/ ● *noun* the outside of a thing; any of the limits of a solid; top of liquid, soil, etc.; outward or superficial aspect; *Geometry* thing with length and breadth but no thickness. ● *verb* (**-cing**) give (special) surface to (road, paper, etc.); rise or bring to surface; become visible or known; *colloquial* wake up, get up. □ **surface mail** mail not carried by air; **surface tension** tension of surface of liquid, tending to minimize its surface area.

surfeit /'sɜːfɪt/ ● *noun* excess, esp. in eating or drinking; resulting fullness. ● *verb* (**-t-**) overfeed; (+ *with*) (cause to) be wearied through excess.

surfing *noun* sport of riding surf on board.

surge ● *noun* sudden rush; heavy forward or upward motion; sudden increase (in price etc.); sudden but brief increase in pressure, voltage, etc.; surging motion of sea, waves, etc. ● *verb* (**-ging**) move suddenly and powerfully forwards; (of sea etc.) swell.

surgeon /'sɜːdʒ(ə)n/ *noun* medical practitioner qualified to practise surgery; naval or military medical officer.

surgery /'sɜːdʒərɪ/ *noun* (*plural* **-ies**) manual or instrumental treatment of injuries or disorders of body; place where or time when doctor, dentist, etc. gives advice and treatment to patients, or MP, lawyer, etc. gives advice.

surgical /'sɜːdʒɪk(ə)l/ *adjective* of or by surgery or surgeons; used for surgery; (of appliance) worn to correct deformity etc.; (esp. of military action) swift and precise. □ **surgical spirit** methylated spirits used for cleansing etc. □ **surgically** *adverb*.

surly /'sɜːlɪ/ *adjective* (**-ier**, **-iest**) bad-tempered, unfriendly. □ **surliness** *noun*.

surmise /sə'maɪz/ ● *noun* conjecture. ● *verb* (**-sing**) (often + *that*) infer doubtfully; suppose; guess.

surmount /sə'maʊnt/ *verb* overcome (difficulty, obstacle); (usually in *passive*) cap, crown. □ **surmountable** *adjective*.

surname /'sɜːneɪm/ *noun* name common to all members of family.

surpass /sə'pɑːs/ *verb* outdo, be better than; (as **surpassing** *adjective*) greatly exceeding, excelling others.

surplice /'sɜːplɪs/ *noun* loose full-sleeved white vestment worn by clergy etc.

surplus /'sɜːpləs/ ● *noun* amount left over when requirements have been met; excess of income over spending. ● *adjective* exceeding what is needed or used.

surprise /sə'praɪz/ ● *noun* unexpected or astonishing thing; emotion caused by this; catching or being caught unawares. ● *adjective* made, done, etc. without warning. ● *verb* (**-sing**) affect with surprise; (usually in *passive*; + *at*) shock, scandalize; capture by surprise; come upon (person) unawares; (+ *into*) startle, betray, etc. (person) into doing something. □ **surprising** *adjective*; **surprisingly** *adverb*.

surreal /sə'rɪəl/ *adjective* unreal; dreamlike; bizarre.

surrealism /sə'rɪəlɪz(ə)m/ *noun* 20th-c. movement in art and literature aiming to express subconscious mind by dream imagery etc. □ **surrealist** *noun* & *adjective*; **surrealistic** /-'lɪs-/ *adjective*; **surrealistically** /-'lɪs-/ *adverb*.

surrender /sə'rendə/ ● *verb* hand over, relinquish; submit, esp. to enemy; (often **surrender oneself** + *to*) yield to habit, emotion, influence, etc.; give up rights under (life-insurance policy) in return for smaller sum received immediately. ● *noun* surrendering.

surreptitious /sʌrəp'tɪʃəs/ *adjective* done by stealth; underhand. □ **surreptitiously** *adverb*.

surrogate /'sʌrəgət/ *noun* substitute; deputy, esp. of bishop. □ **surrogate mother** woman who conceives and gives birth to child on behalf of woman unable to do so. □ **surrogacy** *noun*.

surround /sə'raʊnd/ ● *verb* come or be all round; encircle, enclose. ● *noun* border or edging, esp. area between walls and carpet.

surroundings *plural noun* things in neighbourhood of, or conditions affecting, person or thing; environment.

surtax /'sɜːtæks/ *noun* additional tax, esp. on high incomes.

surtitle /'sɜːtaɪt(ə)l/ *noun* caption translating words of opera, projected on to screen above stage.

surveillance /sə'veɪləns/ *noun* close watch undertaken by police etc., esp. on suspected person.

survey ● *verb* /sə'veɪ/ take or present general view of; examine condition of (building etc.); determine boundaries, extent, ownership, etc. of (district etc.). ● *noun* /'sɜːveɪ/ general view or consideration; surveying of property; result of this; investigation of public opinion etc.; map or plan made by surveying.

surveyor /sə'veɪə/ *noun* person who surveys land and buildings, esp. professionally.

survival /sə'vaɪv(ə)l/ *noun* surviving; relic.

survive /sə'vaɪv/ *verb* (**-ving**) continue to live or exist; live or exist longer than; come alive through or continue to exist in spite of (danger, accident, etc.). □ **survivor** *noun*.

sus = SUSS.

susceptibility *noun* (*plural* **-ies**) being susceptible; (in *plural*) person's feelings.

susceptible /sə'septəb(ə)l/ *adjective* impressionable, sensitive; easily moved by emotion; (+ *to*) accessible or sensitive to; (+ *of*) allowing, admitting of (proof etc.).

suspect ● *verb* /səs'pekt/ be inclined to think; have impression of the existence or presence of; (often + *of*) mentally accuse; doubt innocence, genuineness, or truth of. ● *noun* /'sʌspekt/ suspected person. ● *adjective* /'sʌspekt/ subject to suspicion or distrust.

suspend /səs'pend/ *verb* hang up; keep inoperative or undecided temporarily; debar temporarily from function, office, etc.; (as **suspended** *adjective*) (of particles or body in fluid) floating between top and bottom. □ **suspended animation** temporary death-like condition; **suspended sentence** judicial sentence remaining unenforced on condition of good behaviour.

suspender *noun* attachment to hold up stocking or sock by its top; (in *plural*) *US* pair of braces. □ **suspender belt** woman's undergarment with suspenders.

suspense /səs'pens/ *noun* state of anxious uncertainty or expectation.

suspension /səs'penʃ(ə)n/ *noun* suspending, being suspended; means by which vehicle is supported on its axles; substance consisting of particles suspended in fluid. □ **suspension bridge** bridge with roadway suspended from cables supported by towers.

suspicion /səs'pɪʃ(ə)n/ *noun* unconfirmed belief; distrust; suspecting, being suspected; (+ *of*) slight trace of.

suspicious /səs'pɪʃəs/ *adjective* prone to or feeling suspicion; indicating or justifying suspicion. □ **suspiciously** *adverb*.

suss /sʌs/ *verb* (also **sus**) (**-ss-**) *slang* (usually + *out*) investigate, inspect; understand; work out.

sustain /səs'teɪn/ *verb* bear weight of, support, esp. for long period; encourage, support; endure, stand; (of food) nourish; undergo (defeat, injury, loss, etc.); (of court etc.) decide in favour of, uphold; substantiate, corroborate; keep up (effort etc.). □ **sustainable** *adjective*.

sustenance /'sʌstɪnəns/ *noun* nourishment, food; means of support.

suture /'suːtʃə/ ● *noun* joining edges of wound or incision by stitching; stitch or thread etc. used for this. ● *verb* (**-ring**) stitch (wound, incision).

suzerain /'suːzəreɪn/ *noun* historical feudal overlord; archaic sovereign or state having some control over another state that is internally self-governing. □ **suzerainty** *noun*.

svelte /svelt/ *adjective* slim, slender, graceful.

SW *abbreviation* south-west(ern).

swab /swɒb/ ● *noun* absorbent pad used in surgery; specimen of secretion etc. taken for examination; mop etc. for cleaning or mopping up. ● *verb* (**-bb-**) clean with swab; (+ *up*) absorb (moisture) with swab; mop clean (ship's deck).

swaddle /'swɒd(ə)l/ *verb* (**-ling**) wrap tightly in bandages, wrappings, etc. □ **swaddling-clothes** narrow bandages formerly wrapped round newborn child to restrain its movements.

swag *noun* *slang* thief's booty; *Australian & NZ* traveller's bundle; festoon of flowers, foliage, drapery, etc.

swagger /'swægə/ ● *verb* walk or behave arrogantly or self-importantly. ● *noun* swaggering gait or manner.

swain *noun* archaic country youth; *poetical* young lover or suitor.

swallow[1] /'swɒləʊ/ ● *verb* make or let (food etc.) pass down one's throat; accept meekly or gullibly; repress (emotion); engulf; say (words etc.) indistinctly. ● *noun* act of swallowing; amount swallowed.

swallow[2] /'swɒləʊ/ *noun* migratory swift-flying bird with forked tail. □ **swallow-dive** dive with arms spread sideways; **swallow-tail** deeply forked tail, butterfly etc. with this.

swam *past of* SWIM.

swamp /swɒmp/ ● *noun* piece of wet spongy ground. ● *verb* submerge, inundate; cause to fill with water and sink; overwhelm with numbers or quantity. □ **swampy** *adjective* (**-ier, -iest**).

swan /swɒn/ ● *noun* large web-footed usually white waterfowl with long flexible neck. ● *verb* (**-nn-**) (usually + *about, off,* etc.) *colloquial* move about casually or with superior manner. □ **swansong** person's last work or performance before death, retirement, etc.

swank *colloquial* ● *noun* ostentation, swagger. ● *verb* show off. □ **swanky** *adjective* (**-ier, -iest**).

swap /swɒp/ (also **swop**) ● *verb* (**-pp-**) exchange, barter. ● *noun* act of swapping; thing suitable for swapping.

sward /swɔːd/ *noun* literary expanse of short grass.

swarf /swɔːf/ *noun* fine chips or filings of stone, metal, etc.

swarm[1] /swɔːm/ ● *noun* cluster of bees leaving hive etc. with queen bee to establish new colony; large group of insects, birds, or people; (in *plural*; + *of*) great numbers. ● *verb* move in or form swarm; (+ *with*) be overrun or crowded with.

swarm[2] /swɔːm/ *verb* (+ *up*) climb (rope, tree, etc.) clasping or clinging with arms and legs.

swarthy /'swɔːðɪ/ *adjective* (**-ier, -iest**) dark-complexioned, dark in colour.

swashbuckler /'swɒʃbʌklə/ *noun* swaggering adventurer. □ **swashbuckling** *adjective & noun*.

swastika /'swɒstɪkə/ *noun* ancient symbol formed by equal-armed cross with each arm continued at a right angle; this with clockwise continuations as symbol of Nazi Germany.

swat /swɒt/ ● *verb* (**-tt-**) crush (fly etc.) with blow; hit hard and abruptly. ● *noun* act of swatting.

swatch /swɒtʃ/ *noun* sample, esp. of cloth; collection of samples.

swath /swɔːθ/ *noun* (also **swathe** /sweɪð/) ridge of cut grass, corn, etc.; space left clear by mower, scythe, etc.

swathe /sweɪð/ *verb* (**-thing**) bind or wrap in bandages, garments, etc.

sway ● *verb* (cause to) move unsteadily from side to side; oscillate irregularly; waver; have influence over. ● *noun* rule, government; swaying motion.

swear /sweə/ *verb* (*past* **swore**; *past participle* **sworn**) state or promise on oath; cause to take oath; *colloquial* insist; (often + *at*) use profane or obscene language; (+ *by*) appeal to as witness or guarantee of oath, *colloquial* have great confidence in. □ **swear in** admit to office etc. by administering oath; **swear off** *colloquial* promise to keep off (drink etc.); **swear-word** profane or obscene word.

sweat /swet/ ● *noun* moisture exuded through pores, esp. when one is hot or nervous; state or period of sweating; *colloquial* state of anxiety; *colloquial* effort, drudgery, laborious task or undertaking; condensed

moisture on surface. ● *verb (past & past participle*
sweated or *US* **sweat**) exude sweat; be terrified,
suffer, etc.; (of wall etc.) show surface moisture;
(cause to) toil or drudge; emit like sweat; make
(horse, athlete, etc.) sweat by exercise; (as **sweated**
adjective) (of goods, labour, etc.) produced by or subjected to exploitation. ◻ **no sweat** *colloquial* no bother,
no trouble; **sweat-band** band of absorbent material
inside hat or round head, wrist, etc. to soak up sweat;
sweatshirt sleeved cotton sweater; **sweatshop**
workshop where sweated labour is employed.
◻ **sweaty** *adjective* (**-ier, -iest**).

sweater *noun* woollen etc. pullover.

Swede *noun* native or national of Sweden; (**swede**)
large yellow variety of turnip.

Swedish /'swiːdɪʃ/ ● *adjective* of Sweden. ● *noun* language of Sweden.

sweep ● *verb (past & past participle* **swept**) clean or clear
(room, area, etc.) (as) with a broom; (often + *up*)
collect or remove (dirt etc.) by sweeping; (+ *aside*,
away, etc.) dismiss abruptly; (+ *along, down*, etc.)
drive or carry along with force; (+ *off, away*, etc.)
remove or clear forcefully; traverse swiftly or
lightly; impart sweeping motion to; glide swiftly; go
majestically; (of landscape etc.) be rolling or spacious. ● *noun* act or motion of sweeping; curve in
road etc.; range, scope; chimney sweep; sortie by
aircraft; *colloquial* sweepstake. ◻ **sweep the board**
win all the money in gambling game, win all possible
prizes etc.; **sweepstake** form of gambling on horse
races etc. in which money staked is divided among
those who have drawn numbered tickets for winners.

sweeping *adjective* wide in range or effect; gen-
eralized, arbitrary.

sweet ● *adjective* tasting like sugar, honey, etc.; smelling pleasant like perfume, roses, etc., fragrant;
melodious; fresh; not sour or bitter; gratifying,
attractive; amiable, gentle; *colloquial* pretty; (+ *on*)
colloquial fond of, in love with. ● *noun* small shaped
piece of sugar or chocolate confectionery; sweet dish
forming course of meal. ◻ **sweet-and-sour** cooked
in sauce with sugar, vinegar, etc.; **sweetbread** pancreas or thymus of animal, as food; **sweet-brier**
single-flowered fragrant-leaved wild rose; **sweet-
corn** sweet-flavoured maize kernels; **sweetheart**
either of pair of lovers; **sweetmeat** a sweet, a small
fancy cake; **sweet pea** climbing garden annual with
many-coloured scented flowers; **sweet pepper** fruit
of capsicum; **sweet potato** tropical plant with edible tuberous roots; **sweet-talk** flatter in order to
persuade; **sweet tooth** liking for sweet-tasting
things; **sweet william** garden plant with close clusters of sweet-smelling flowers. ◻ **sweetish** *adjective*;
sweetly *adverb*.

sweeten *verb* make or become sweet(er); make agreeable or less painful. ◻ **sweetening** *noun*.

sweetener *noun* thing that sweetens; *colloquial* bribe.

sweetie *noun colloquial* a sweet; sweetheart.

sweetness *noun* being sweet; fragrance.
◻ **sweetness and light** (esp. uncharacteristic)
mildness and reason.

swell ● *verb (past participle* **swollen** /'swəʊlən/ or **-ed**)
(cause to) grow bigger, louder, or more intense; rise
or raise up; (+ *out*) bulge out; (of heart etc.) feel full
of joy, pride, etc.; (+ *with*) be hardly able to restrain
(pride etc.). ● *noun* act or state of swelling; heaving
of sea etc. with unbreaking rolling waves; crescendo;
mechanism in organ etc. for gradually varying volume; *colloquial* fashionable or stylish person. ● *adjective
colloquial esp. US* fine, excellent.

swelling *noun* abnormally swollen place, esp. on body.

swelter /'sweltə/ ● *verb* be uncomfortably hot. ● *noun*
sweltering condition.

swept *past & past participle* of SWEEP.

swerve ● *verb* (**-ving**) (cause to) change direction,
esp. suddenly. ● *noun* swerving motion.

swift ● *adjective* rapid, quick; prompt. ● *noun* swift-
flying long-winged migratory bird. ◻ **swiftly** *adverb*;
swiftness *noun*.

swig ● *verb* (**-gg-**) *colloquial* drink in large draughts.
● *noun* swallow of liquid, esp. of large amount.

swill ● *verb* (often + *out*) rinse, pour water over
or through; drink greedily. ● *noun* swilling; mainly
liquid refuse as pig-food.

swim ● *verb* (**-mm-**; *past* **swam**; *past participle* **swum**)
propel body through water with limbs, fins, etc.;
perform (stroke) or cross (river etc.) by swimming;
float on liquid; appear to undulate, reel, or whirl;
(of head) feel dizzy; (+ *in, with*) be flooded. ● *noun*
act or spell of swimming. ◻ **in the swim** *colloquial*
involved in or aware of what is going on; **swimming
bath, pool** pool constructed for swimming; **swimming costume** bathing costume; **swimsuit** swimming costume, esp. one-piece for women and girls;
swimwear clothing for swimming in. ◻ **swimmer**
noun.

swimmingly *adverb colloquial* smoothly, without obstruction.

swindle /'swɪnd(ə)l/ ● *verb* (**-ling**) (often + *out of*)
cheat of money etc.; defraud. ● *noun* act of swindling;
fraudulent person or thing. ◻ **swindler** *noun*.

swine *noun* (*plural* same) *formal or US* pig; *colloquial* (*plural*
same or **-s**) disgusting person, unpleasant or difficult
thing. ◻ **swinish** *adjective*.

swing ● *verb (past & past participle* **swung**) (cause to)
move with to-and-fro or curving motion; sway or
hang like pendulum or door etc.; oscillate; move
by gripping something and leaping etc.; walk with
swinging gait; (+ *round*) move to face opposite direction; (+ *at*) attempt to hit; *colloquial* (of party etc.)
be lively; have decisive influence on (voting etc.);
colloquial be executed by hanging. ● *noun* act, motion,
or extent of swinging; swinging or smooth gait,
rhythm, or action; seat slung by ropes, chains, etc.
for swinging on or in, spell of swinging thus; smooth
rhythmic jazz or jazzy dance music; amount by
which votes etc. change from one side to another.
◻ **swing-boat** boat-shaped swing at fairs etc.;
swing-bridge bridge that can be swung aside to let
ships etc. pass; **swing-door** door that swings in
either direction and closes by itself when released;
swings and roundabouts situation allowing equal
gain and loss; **swing-wing** (aircraft) with wings that
can pivot to point sideways or backwards.
◻ **swinger** *noun*.

swingeing /'swɪndʒɪn/ *adjective* (of blow etc.) forcible;
huge, far-reaching.

swipe *colloquial* ● *verb* (**-ping**) (often + *at*) hit hard
and recklessly; steal. ● *noun* reckless hard hit or
attempt to hit.

swirl ● *verb* move, flow, or carry along with whirling
motion. ● *noun* swirling motion; twist, curl. ◻ **swirly**
adjective.

swish ● *verb* swing (cane, scythe, etc.) audibly
through air, grass, etc.; move with or make swishing
sound. ● *noun* swishing action or sound. ● *adjective
colloquial* smart, fashionable.

Swiss ● *adjective* of Switzerland. ● *noun* (*plural* same)
native or national of Switzerland. ◻ **Swiss roll** cylindrical cake, made by rolling up thin flat sponge
cake spread with jam etc.

switch ● *noun* device for making and breaking connection in electric circuit; transfer, changeover, deviation; flexible shoot cut from tree; light tapering
rod; *US* railway points. ● *verb* (+ *on, off*) turn (electrical device) on or off; change or transfer (position,

subject, etc.); exchange; whip or flick with switch. □ **switchback** ride at fair etc. with extremely steep ascents and descents, similar railway or road; **switchboard** apparatus for varying connections between electric circuits, esp. in telephony; **switched-on** colloquial up to date, aware of what is going on; **switch off** colloquial cease to pay attention.

swivel /'swɪv(ə)l/ ● noun coupling between two parts etc. so that one can turn freely without the other. ● verb (-**ll-**; US -**l-**) turn (as) on swivel, swing round. □ **swivel chair** chair with revolving seat.

swizz noun (also **swiz**) colloquial something disappointing; swindle.

swizzle /'swɪz(ə)l/ noun colloquial frothy mixed alcoholic drink, esp. of rum or gin and bitters; slang swizz. □ **swizzle-stick** stick used for frothing or flattening drinks.

swollen past participle of SWELL.

swoon /swuːn/ verb & noun literary faint.

swoop /swuːp/ ● verb (often + down) come down with rush like bird of prey; (often + on) make sudden attack. ● noun act of swooping, sudden pounce.

swop = SWAP.

sword /sɔːd/ noun weapon with long blade for cutting or thrusting. □ **put to the sword** kill; **sword dance** dance with brandishing of swords, or steps about swords laid on ground; **swordfish** (plural same or **-es**) large sea fish with swordlike upper jaw; **swordplay** fencing, repartee, lively arguing; **swordsman** person of (usually specified) skill with sword; **swordstick** hollow walking stick containing sword blade.

swore past of SWEAR.

sworn ● past participle of SWEAR. ● adjective bound (as) by oath.

swot colloquial ● verb (-**tt-**) study hard; (usually + up, up on) study (subject) hard or hurriedly. ● noun usually derogatory person who swots.

swum past participle of SWIM.

swung past & past participle of SWING.

sybarite /'sɪbəraɪt/ noun self-indulgent or luxury-loving person. □ **sybaritic** /-'rɪt-/ adjective.

sycamore /'sɪkəmɔː/ noun large maple tree, its wood; US plane tree, its wood.

sycophant /'sɪkəfænt/ noun flatterer, toady. □ **sycophancy** noun; **sycophantic** /-'fæn-/ adjective.

syllabic /sɪ'læbɪk/ adjective of or in syllables. □ **syllabically** adverb.

syllable /'sɪləb(ə)l/ noun unit of pronunciation forming whole or part of word, usually consisting of vowel sound with consonant(s) before or after (see panel). □ **in words of one syllable** plainly, bluntly.

syllabub /'sɪləbʌb/ noun dessert of cream or milk sweetened and whipped with wine etc.

syllabus /'sɪləbəs/ noun (plural **-buses** or **-bi** /-baɪ/) programme or outline of course of study, teaching, etc.

syllogism /'sɪlədʒɪz(ə)m/ noun form of reasoning in which from two propositions a third is deduced. □ **syllogistic** /-'dʒɪs-/ adjective.

sylph /sɪlf/ noun elemental spirit of air; slender graceful woman. □ **sylphlike** adjective.

sylvan /'sɪlv(ə)n/ adjective (also **silvan**) of the woods, having woods; rural.

symbiosis /sɪmbaɪ'əʊsɪs/ noun (plural **-bioses** /-siːz/) (usually mutually advantageous) association of two different organisms living attached to one another etc.; mutually advantageous connection between people. □ **symbiotic** /-'ɒt-/ adjective.

symbol /'sɪmb(ə)l/ noun thing generally regarded as typifying, representing, or recalling something; mark, sign, etc. representing object, idea, process, etc. □ **symbolic** /-'bɒl-/ adjective; **symbolically** /-'bɒl-/ adverb.

symbolism noun use of symbols; symbols; artistic movement or style using symbols to express ideas, emotions, etc. □ **symbolist** noun.

symbolize verb (also -**ise**) (-**zing** or -**sing**) be symbol of; represent by symbol(s).

symmetry /'sɪmɪtrɪ/ noun (plural **-ies**) correct proportion of parts; beauty resulting from this; structure allowing object to be divided into parts of equal shape and size; possession of such structure; repetition of exactly similar parts facing each other or a centre. □ **symmetrical** /-'met-/ adjective; **symmetrically** /-'met-/ adverb.

sympathetic /sɪmpə'θetɪk/ adjective of or expressing sympathy; likeable, pleasant; (+ to) favouring (proposal etc.). □ **sympathetically** adverb.

sympathize /'sɪmpəθaɪz/ verb (also -**ise**) (-**zing** or -**sing**) (often + with) feel or express sympathy; agree. □ **sympathizer** noun.

sympathy /'sɪmpəθɪ/ noun (plural **-ies**) sharing of another's feelings; (often + with) sharing or tendency to share emotion, sensation, condition, etc. of another person; (in singular or plural) compassion, commiseration, condolences; (often + with) agreement (with person etc.) in opinion or desire. □ **in sympathy** (often + with) having, showing, or resulting from sympathy.

symphony /'sɪmfənɪ/ noun (plural **-ies**) musical composition in several movements for full orchestra. □ **symphony orchestra** large orchestra playing symphonies etc. □ **symphonic** /-'fɒn-/ adjective.

symposium /sɪm'pəʊzɪəm/ noun (plural **-sia**) conference, or collection of essays, on particular subject.

symptom /'sɪmptəm/ noun physical or mental sign of disease or injury; sign of existence of something. □ **symptomatic** /-'mæt-/ adjective.

synagogue /'sɪnəgɒg/ noun building for Jewish religious instruction and worship.

sync /sɪŋk/ (also **synch**) colloquial ● noun synchronization. ● verb synchronize. □ **in** or **out of sync** (often + with) according or agreeing well or badly.

synchromesh /'sɪŋkrəʊmeʃ/ ● noun system of gear-changing, esp. in vehicles, in which gearwheels revolve at same speed during engagement. ● adjective of this system.

Syllable

A syllable is the smallest unit of speech that can normally occur alone, such as *a*, *at*, *ta*, or *tat*. A word can be made up of one or more syllables:

    cat, *fought*, and *twinge* each have one syllable;
    rating, *deny*, and *collapse* each have two syllables;
    excitement, *superman*, and *telephoned* each have three syllables;
    American and *complicated* each have four syllables;
    examination and *uncontrollable* each have five syllables.

synchronize /'sɪŋkrənaɪz/ verb (also **-ise**) (**-zing** or **-sing**) (often + with) make or be synchronous (with); make sound and picture (of film etc.) coincide; cause (clocks etc.) to show same time. □ **synchronization** noun.

synchronous /'sɪŋkrənəs/ adjective (often + with) existing or occurring at same time.

syncopate /'sɪŋkəpeɪt/ verb (**-ting**) displace beats or accents in (music); shorten (word) by omitting syllable or letter(s) in middle. □ **syncopation** noun.

syncope /'sɪŋkəpɪ/ noun Grammar syncopation; Medicine fainting through fall in blood pressure.

syncretize /'sɪŋkrətaɪz/ verb (also **-ise**) (**-zing** or **-sing**) attempt to unify or reconcile differing schools of thought. □ **syncretic** /-'kret-/ adjective; **syncretism** noun.

syndicalism /'sɪndɪkəlɪz(ə)m/ noun historical movement for transferring industrial control and ownership to workers' unions. □ **syndicalist** noun.

syndicate ● noun /'sɪndɪkət/ combination of people, commercial firms, etc. to promote some common interest; agency supplying material simultaneously to a number of periodicals etc.; group of people who gamble, organize crime, etc. ● verb /'sɪndɪkeɪt/ (**-ting**) form into syndicate; publish (material) through syndicate. □ **syndication** noun.

syndrome /'sɪndrəʊm/ noun group of concurrent symptoms of disease; characteristic combination of opinions, emotions, etc.

synod /'sɪnəd/ noun Church council of clergy and lay people.

synonym /'sɪnənɪm/ noun word or phrase that means the same as another (see panel).

synonymous /sɪ'nɒnɪməs/ adjective (often + with) having same meaning; suggestive of; associated with.

synopsis /sɪ'nɒpsɪs/ noun (plural **synopses** /-siːz/) summary; outline.

synoptic /sɪ'nɒptɪk/ adjective of or giving synopsis. □ **Synoptic Gospels** those of Matthew, Mark, and Luke.

syntax /'sɪntæks/ noun grammatical arrangement of words; rules or analysis of this. □ **syntactic** /-'tæk-/ adjective.

synthesis /'sɪnθəsɪs/ noun (plural **-theses** /-siːz/) putting together of parts or elements to make up complex whole; Chemistry artificial production of (esp. organic) substances from simpler ones.

synthesize /'sɪnθəsaɪz/ verb (also **-ise**) (**-zing** or **-sing**) make synthesis of.

synthesizer noun (also **-iser**) electronic, usually keyboard, instrument producing great variety of sounds.

synthetic /sɪn'θetɪk/ ● adjective produced by synthesis, esp. to imitate natural product; affected, insincere. ● noun synthetic substance. □ **synthetically** adverb.

syphilis /'sɪfəlɪs/ noun a contagious venereal disease. □ **syphilitic** /-'lɪt-/ adjective.

Syrian /'sɪrɪən/ ● noun native or national of Syria. ● adjective of Syria.

syringa /sɪ'rɪŋgə/ noun shrub with white scented flowers.

syringe /sɪ'rɪndʒ/ ● noun device for drawing in quantity of liquid and ejecting it in fine stream. ● verb (**-ging**) sluice or spray with syringe.

syrup /'sɪrəp/ noun (US **sirup**) sweet sauce of sugar dissolved in boiling water, often flavoured or medicated; condensed sugar-cane juice; molasses, treacle; excessive sweetness of manner. □ **syrupy** adjective.

system /'sɪstəm/ noun complex whole; set of connected things or parts; organized group of things; set of organs in body with common structure or function; human or animal body as organized whole; method, scheme of action, procedure, or classification; orderliness; (**the system**) prevailing political or social order, esp. seen as oppressive. □ **get (thing) out of one's system** get rid of (anxiety etc.). □ **systems analysis** analysis of complex process etc. so as to improve its efficiency, esp. by using computer.

systematic /sɪstə'mætɪk/ adjective methodical; according to system; deliberate. □ **systematically** adverb.

systematize /'sɪstəmətaɪz/ verb (also **-ise**) (**-zing** or **-sing**) make systematic. □ **systematization** noun.

systemic /sɪ'stemɪk/ adjective Physiology of the whole body; (of insecticide etc.) entering plant tissues via roots and shoots. □ **systemically** adverb.

Synonym

A synonym is a word that has the same meaning as, or a similar meaning to, another word:

  cheerful, happy, merry, and *jolly*

are synonyms that are quite close to each other in meaning, as are

  lazy, indolent, and *slothful*

In contrast, the following words all mean 'a person who works with another', but their meanings vary considerably:

  colleague   *conspirator*
  collaborator   *accomplice*
  ally

Tt

T *noun* □ **to a T** exactly, to a nicety; **T-bone** T-shaped bone, esp. in steak from thin end of loin; **T-junction** junction, esp. of two roads, in shape of T; **T-shirt** short-sleeved casual top; **T-square** T-shaped instrument for drawing right angles.

t. *abbreviation* (also **t**) ton(s); tonne(s).

TA *abbreviation* Territorial Army.

ta /tɑː/ *interjection colloquial* thank you.

tab¹ *noun* small piece of material attached to thing for grasping, fastening, identifying, etc.; *US colloquial* bill; distinguishing mark on officer's collar. □ **keep tabs on** *colloquial* have under observation or in check.

tab² *noun* tabulator.

tabard /ˈtæbəd/ *noun* herald's official coat emblazoned with arms of sovereign; woman's or girl's sleeveless jerkin; *historical* knight's short emblazoned garment worn over armour.

tabasco /təˈbæskəʊ/ *noun* pungent pepper; (**Tabasco**) *proprietary term* sauce made from this.

tabby /ˈtæbɪ/ *noun* (*plural* **-ies**) grey or brownish cat with dark stripes.

tabernacle /ˈtæbənæk(ə)l/ *noun historical* tent used as sanctuary by Israelites during Exodus; niche or receptacle, esp. for bread and wine of Eucharist; Nonconformist meeting-house.

tabla /ˈtæblə/ *noun* pair of small Indian drums played with hands.

table /ˈteɪb(ə)l/ ● *noun* flat surface on legs used for eating, working at, etc.; food provided at table; group seated for dinner etc.; set of facts or figures arranged esp. in columns; multiplication table. ● *verb* (**-ling**) bring forward for discussion at meeting etc.; *esp. US* postpone consideration of. □ **at table** taking a meal; **tablecloth** cloth spread over table; **tableland** plateau; **tablespoon** large spoon for serving etc., (also **tablespoonful**) amount held by this; **table tennis** game played with small bats on table divided by net; **tableware** dishes etc. for meals; **table wine** wine of ordinary quality; **turn the tables** (often + *on*) reverse circumstances to one's advantage.

tableau /ˈtæbləʊ/ *noun* (*plural* **-x** /-z/) picturesque presentation; group of silent motionless people representing stage scene.

table d'hôte /tɑːbl(ə)l ˈdəʊt/ *noun* meal from set menu at fixed price.

tablet /ˈtæblɪt/ *noun* small solid dose of medicine etc.; bar of soap etc.; flat slab of stone etc., esp. inscribed.

tabloid /ˈtæblɔɪd/ *noun* small-sized, often popular or sensational, newspaper.

taboo /təˈbuː/ ● *noun* (*plural* **-s**) ritual isolation of person or thing as sacred or accursed; prohibition. ● *adjective* avoided or prohibited, esp. by social custom. ● *verb* (**-oos, -ooed**) put under taboo; exclude or prohibit, esp. socially.

tabor /ˈteɪbə/ *noun historical* small drum.

tabular /ˈtæbjʊlə/ *adjective* of or arranged in tables.

tabulate /ˈtæbjʊleɪt/ *verb* (**-ting**) arrange (figures, facts) in tabular form. □ **tabulation** *noun*.

tabulator *noun* device on typewriter etc. for advancing to sequence of set positions in tabular work.

tachograph /ˈtækəɡrɑːf/ *noun* device in vehicle to record speed and travel time.

tachometer /təˈkɒmɪtə/ *noun* instrument measuring velocity or rate of shaft's rotation (esp. in vehicle).

tacit /ˈtæsɪt/ *adjective* implied or understood without being stated. □ **tacitly** *adverb*.

taciturn /ˈtæsɪtɜːn/ *adjective* saying little, uncommunicative. □ **taciturnity** /-ˈtɜːn-/ *noun*.

tack¹ ● *noun* small sharp broad-headed nail; *US* drawing-pin; long stitch for fastening materials lightly or temporarily together; (in sailing) direction, temporary change of direction; course of action or policy. ● *verb* (often + *down* etc.) fasten with tacks; stitch lightly together; (+ *to, on, on to*) add, append; change ship's course by turning head to wind, make series of such tacks.

tack² *noun* horse's saddle, bridle, etc.

tack³ *noun colloquial* cheap or shoddy material; tat, kitsch.

tackle /ˈtæk(ə)l/ ● *noun* equipment for task or sport; rope(s), pulley(s), etc. used in working sails, hoisting weights, etc.; tackling in football etc. ● *verb* (**-ling**) try to deal with (problem etc.); grapple with (opponent); confront (person) in discussion; intercept or stop (player running with ball etc.). □ **tackle-block** pulley over which rope runs. □ **tackler** *noun*.

tacky¹ /ˈtækɪ/ *adjective* (**-ier, -iest**) slightly sticky.

tacky² /ˈtækɪ/ *adjective* (**-ier, -iest**) *colloquial* in poor taste; cheap, shoddy.

taco /ˈtækəʊ/ *noun* (*plural* **-s**) Mexican dish of meat etc. in crisp folded tortilla.

tact *noun* adroitness in dealing with people or circumstances; intuitive perception of right thing to do or say. □ **tactful** *adjective*; **tactfully** *adverb*; **tactless** *adjective*; **tactlessly** *adverb*.

tactic /ˈtæktɪk/ *noun* piece of tactics.

tactical *adjective* of tactics; (of bombing etc.) done in immediate support of military or naval operation; adroitly planning or planned. □ **tactically** *adverb*.

tactics /ˈtæktɪks/ *plural noun* (also treated as *singular*) disposition of armed forces, esp. in warfare; procedure calculated to gain some end, skilful device(s). □ **tactician** /-ˈtɪʃ-/ *noun*.

tactile /ˈtæktaɪl/ *adjective* of sense of touch; perceived by touch. □ **tactility** /-ˈtɪl-/ *noun*.

tadpole /ˈtædpəʊl/ *noun* larva of frog, toad, etc. at stage of living in water and having gills and tail.

taffeta /ˈtæfɪtə/ *noun* fine lustrous silk or silklike fabric.

taffrail /ˈtæfreɪl/ *noun* rail round ship's stern.

tag ● *noun* label, esp. to show address or price; metal point of shoelace etc.; loop or flap for handling or hanging thing; loose or ragged end; trite quotation, stock phrase. ● *verb* (**-gg-**) furnish with tag(s); (often + *on, on to*) join, attach. □ **tag along** (often + *with*) go along, accompany passively.

tagliatelle /tæljəˈtelɪ/ *noun* ribbon-shaped pasta.

tail¹ ● *noun* hindmost part of animal, esp. extending beyond body; thing like tail in form or position, esp. rear part of aeroplane, vehicle, etc., hanging part of back of shirt or coat, end of procession, luminous trail following comet, etc.; inferior, weak, or last part of anything; (in *plural*) *colloquial* tailcoat, evening dress with this; (in *plural*) reverse of coin turning up in toss; *colloquial* person following another. ● *verb* remove stalks of (fruit etc.); *colloquial* follow closely. □ **tailback** long queue of traffic caused by obstruction; **tailboard** hinged or removable back of lorry etc.; **tailcoat** man's coat divided at back and cut away in front; **tailgate** tailboard, rear door of estate car; **tail-light, -lamp** US rear light on vehicle etc.; **tail off, away** gradually diminish and cease; **tailpiece** final part of thing, decoration at end of chapter etc.; **tailplane** horizontal aerofoil at tail of aircraft; **tailspin** aircraft's spinning dive, state of panic; **tail wind** one blowing in direction of travel. □ **tailless** adjective.

tail² Law ● noun limitation of ownership, esp. of estate limited to person and his heirs. ● adjective so limited.

tailor /'teɪlə/ ● noun maker of (esp. men's) outer garments to measure. ● verb make (clothes) as tailor; make or adapt for special purpose; work as tailor. □ **tailor-made** made by tailor, made or suited for particular purpose. □ **tailored** adjective.

taint ● noun spot or trace of decay, corruption, etc.; corrupt condition, infection. ● verb affect with taint, become tainted; (+ with) affect slightly.

take ● verb (**-king**; past **took** /tʊk/; past participle **taken**) lay hold of; acquire, capture, earn, win; regularly buy (newspaper etc.); occupy; make use of; be effective; consume; use up; carry, accompany; remove, steal; catch, be infected with; be affected by (pleasure etc.); ascertain and record; grasp mentally, understand; accept, submit to; deal with or regard in specified way; teach, be taught or examined in; submit to (exam); make (photograph); have as necessary accompaniment, requirement, or part. ● noun amount taken or caught; scene or film sequence photographed continuously. □ **take after** resemble (parent etc.); **take against** begin to dislike; **take apart** dismantle, colloquial defeat, criticize severely; **take away** remove or carry elsewhere, subtract; **take-away** (cooked meal) bought at restaurant for eating elsewhere, restaurant selling this; **take back** retract (statement), convey to original position, carry in thought to past time, return or accept back (goods); **take down** write down (spoken words), dismantle (structure), lower (garment); **take-home pay** employee's pay after deduction of tax etc.; **take in** receive as lodger etc., undertake (work) at home, make (garment etc.) smaller, understand, cheat, include; **take off** remove (clothing), deduct, mimic, begin a jump, become airborne, (of scheme etc.) become successful; **take-off** act of mimicking or becoming airborne; **take on** undertake, acquire, engage, agree to oppose at game, colloquial show strong emotion; **take out** remove, escort on outing, get (licence etc.), assume control; **takeover** noun; **take to** begin, have recourse to, form liking for; **take up** adopt as pursuit, accept (offer etc.), occupy (time or space), absorb, (often + on) interrupt or correct (speaker), shorten (garment), pursue (matter). □ **taker** noun.

taking ● adjective attractive, captivating. ● noun (in plural) money taken in business etc.

talc noun talcum powder; translucent mineral formed in thin plates.

talcum /'tælkəm/ noun talc; (in full **talcum powder**) usually perfumed powdered talc for toilet use.

tale noun narrative or story, esp. fictitious; allegation or gossip, often malicious.

talent /'tælənt/ noun special aptitude or gift; high mental ability; people of talent; colloquial attractive members of opposite sex; ancient weight and money unit. □ **talent-scout, -spotter** person seeking new talent, esp. in sport or entertainment. □ **talented** adjective.

talisman /'tælɪzmən/ noun (plural **-s**) thing believed to bring good luck or protect from harm.

talk /tɔːk/ ● verb (often + to, with) converse or communicate verbally; have power of speech; express,

utter, discuss; use (language); gossip. ● noun conversation; particular mode of speech; short address or lecture; rumour or gossip, its theme; colloquial empty boasting; (often in plural) discussions, negotiations. □ **talk down** silence by loud or persistent talking, guide (pilot, aircraft) to landing by radio, (+ to) speak patronizingly to; **talk into** persuade by talking; **talk of** discuss, express intention of; **talk over** discuss; **talk round** persuade to change opinion etc.; **talk to** rebuke, scold. □ **talker** noun.

talkative /'tɔːkətɪv/ adjective fond of talking.

talkie noun colloquial early film with soundtrack.

talking ● adjective that talks or can talk; expressive. ● noun action or process of talking. □ **talking of** while we are discussing; **talking point** topic for discussion; **talking-to** colloquial scolding.

tall /tɔːl/ ● adjective of more than average height; of specified height; higher than surroundings. ● adverb as if tall; proudly. □ **tallboy** tall chest of drawers; **tall order** unreasonable demand; **tall ship** high-masted sailing ship; **tall story** colloquial extravagant tale.

tallow /'tæləʊ/ noun hard (esp. animal) fat melted down to make candles, soap, etc.

tally /'tælɪ/ ● noun (plural **-ies**) reckoning of debt or score; mark registering number of objects delivered or received; historical piece of notched wood for keeping account; identification ticket or label; counterpart, duplicate. ● verb (**-ies, -ied**) (often + with) agree, correspond.

tally-ho /tælɪ'həʊ/ interjection huntsman's cry as signal on seeing fox.

Talmud /'tælmʊd/ noun body of Jewish civil and ceremonial law. □ **Talmudic** /-'mʊd-/ adjective; **Talmudist** noun.

talon /'tælən/ noun claw, esp. of bird of prey.

talus /'teɪləs/ noun (plural **tali** /-laɪ/) ankle-bone supporting tibia.

tamarind /'tæmərɪnd/ noun tropical evergreen tree; its fruit pulp used as food and in drinks.

tamarisk /'tæmərɪsk/ noun seaside shrub usually with small pink or white flowers.

tambour /'tæmbʊə/ noun drum; circular frame for stretching embroidery-work on.

tambourine /tæmbə'riːn/ noun small shallow drum with jingling discs in rim, shaken or banged as accompaniment.

tame ● adjective (of animal) domesticated, not wild or shy; uninteresting, insipid. ● verb (**-ming**) make tame, domesticate; subdue. □ **tamely** adverb; **tameness** noun; **tamer** noun.

Tamil /'tæmɪl/ ● noun member of a people inhabiting South India and Sri Lanka; their language. ● adjective of this people or language.

tam-o'-shanter /tæmə'ʃæntə/ noun floppy woollen beret of Scottish origin.

tamp verb ram down tightly.

tamper /'tæmpə/ verb (+ with) meddle or interfere with.

tampon /'tæmpɒn/ noun plug of cotton wool etc. used esp. to absorb menstrual blood.

tan¹ ● noun suntan; yellowish-brown colour; bark of oak etc. used for tanning. ● adjective yellowish-brown. ● verb (**-nn-**) make or become brown by exposure to sun; convert (raw hide) into leather; slang thrash.

tan² abbreviation tangent.

tandem /'tændəm/ ● noun bicycle with two or more seats one behind another; vehicle driven tandem. ● adverb with two or more horses harnessed one behind another. □ **in tandem** one behind the other, alongside each other, together.

tandoor /'tænduə/ noun clay oven.

tandoori /tæn'dʊərɪ/ *noun* spiced food cooked in tandoor.

tang *noun* strong taste or smell; characteristic quality; part of tool by which blade is held firm in handle. □ **tangy** *adjective* (**-ier, -iest**).

tangent /'tændʒ(ə)nt/ *noun* straight line, curve, or surface touching but not intersecting curve; ratio of sides opposite and adjacent to acute angle in right-angled triangle. □ **at a tangent** diverging from previous course or from what is relevant. □ **tangential** /-'dʒenʃ(ə)l/ *adjective*.

tangerine /tændʒə'riːn/ *noun* small sweet-scented fruit like orange, mandarin; deep orange-yellow colour.

tangible /'tændʒɪb(ə)l/ *adjective* perceptible by touch; definite, clearly intelligible, not elusive. □ **tangibility** *noun*; **tangibly** *adverb*.

tangle /'tæŋg(ə)l/ ● *verb* (**-ling**) intertwine or become twisted or involved in confused mass; entangle; complicate. ● *noun* tangled mass or state. □ **tangly** *adjective*.

tango /'tæŋgəʊ/ ● *noun* (*plural* **-s**) (music for) slow South American ballroom dance. ● *verb* (**-goes, -goed**) dance tango.

tank *noun* large receptacle for liquid, gas, etc.; heavy armoured fighting vehicle moving on continuous tracks. □ **tank engine** steam engine with integral fuel and water containers. □ **tankful** *noun* (*plural* **-s**).

tankard /'tæŋkəd/ *noun* (contents of) tall beer mug with handle.

tanker *noun* ship, aircraft, or road vehicle for carrying liquids, esp. oil, in bulk.

tanner *noun* person who tans hides.

tannery *noun* (*plural* **-ies**) place where hides are tanned.

tannic /'tænɪk/ *adjective* of tan. □ **tannic acid** yellowish organic compound used in cleaning, dyeing, etc.

tannin /'tænɪn/ *noun* any of several substances extracted from tree-barks etc. and used in tanning etc.

Tannoy /'tænɔɪ/ *noun proprietary term* type of public address system.

tansy /'tænzɪ/ *noun* (*plural* **-ies**) aromatic herb with yellow flowers.

tantalize /'tæntəlaɪz/ *verb* (also **-ise**) (**-zing** or **-sing**) torment with sight of the unobtainable, raise and then dash the hopes of. □ **tantalization** *noun*.

tantamount /'tæntəmaʊnt/ *adjective* (+ *to*) equivalent to.

tantra /'tæntrə/ *noun* any of a class of Hindu or Buddhist mystical or magical writings.

tantrum /'tæntrəm/ *noun* (esp. child's) outburst of bad temper or petulance.

Taoiseach /'tiːʃəx/ *noun* prime minister of Irish Republic.

tap¹ ● *noun* device by which flow of liquid or gas from pipe or vessel can be controlled; act of tapping telephone; taproom. ● *verb* (**-pp-**) provide (cask) with tap, let out (liquid) thus; draw sap from (tree) by cutting into it; draw supplies or information from; discover and exploit; connect listening device to (telephone etc.). □ **on tap** ready to be drawn off, *colloquial* freely available; **taproom** room in pub serving drinks on tap; **tap root** tapering root growing vertically downwards.

tap² ● *verb* (**-pp-**) (+ *at, on, against*, etc.) strike or cause to strike lightly; (often + *out*) make by taps; tap-dance. ● *noun* light blow or rap; tap-dancing; metal attachment on dancer's shoe. □ **tap-dance** *noun* rhythmic dance performed in shoes with metal taps, *verb* perform this; **tap-dancer** *noun*; **tap-dancing** *noun*.

tapas /'tæpæs/ *plural noun* small savoury esp. Spanish dishes.

tape ● *noun* narrow woven strip of cotton etc. for fastening etc.; this across finishing line of race; (in full **adhesive tape**) strip of adhesive plastic etc. for fastening, masking, insulating, etc.; magnetic tape; tape recording; tape-measure. ● *verb* (**-ping**) tie up or join with tape; apply tape to; (+ *off*) seal off with tape; record on magnetic tape; measure with tape. □ **have** (**person, thing**) **taped** *colloquial* understand fully; **tape deck** machine for using audiotape (separate from speakers etc.); **tape machine** device for recording telegraph messages, tape recorder; **tape-measure** strip of tape or thin flexible metal marked for measuring; **tape recorder** apparatus for recording and replaying sounds on magnetic tape; **tape-record** *verb*; **tape recording** *noun*; **tapeworm** tape-like worm parasitic in alimentary canal.

taper /'teɪpə/ ● *noun* wick coated with wax etc. for conveying flame; slender candle. ● *verb* (often + *off*) (cause to) diminish in thickness towards one end, make or become gradually less.

tapestry /'tæpɪstrɪ/ *noun* (*plural* **-ies**) thick fabric in which coloured weft threads are woven to form pictures or designs; (usually wool) embroidery imitating this; piece of this.

tapioca /tæpɪ'əʊkə/ *noun* starchy granular foodstuff prepared from cassava.

tapir /'teɪpə/ *noun* small piglike mammal with short flexible snout.

tappet /'tæpɪt/ *noun* lever etc. in machinery giving intermittent motion.

tar¹ ● *noun* dark thick inflammable liquid distilled from wood, coal, etc.; similar substance formed in combustion of tobacco. ● *verb* (**-rr-**) cover with tar.

tar² *noun colloquial* sailor.

taramasalata /tærəməsə'lɑːtə/ *noun* (also **taramosalata**) dip made from roe, olive oil, etc.

tarantella /tærən'telə/ *noun* (music for) whirling Southern Italian dance.

tarantula /tə'ræntjʊlə/ *noun* large hairy tropical spider; large black spider of Southern Europe.

tarboosh /tɑː'buːʃ/ *noun* cap like fez.

tardy /'tɑːdɪ/ *adjective* (**-ier, -iest**) slow to act, come, or happen; delaying, delayed. □ **tardily** *adverb*; **tardiness** *noun*.

tare¹ /teə/ *noun* vetch, esp. as cornfield weed or fodder; (in *plural*) *Biblical* injurious cornfield weed.

tare² /teə/ *noun* allowance for weight of packing around goods; weight of vehicle without fuel or load.

target /'tɑːgɪt/ ● *noun* mark fired at, esp. round object marked with concentric circles; person, objective, or result aimed at; butt of criticism etc. ● *verb* (**-t-**) single out as target; aim, direct.

tariff /'tærɪf/ *noun* table of fixed charges; duty on particular class of goods; list of duties or customs due.

tarlatan /'tɑːlət(ə)n/ *noun* thin stiff muslin.

Tarmac /'tɑːmæk/ ● *noun proprietary term* tarmacadam; area surfaced with this. ● *verb* (**tarmac**) (**-ck-**) lay tarmacadam on.

tarmacadam /tɑːmə'kædəm/ *noun* bitumen-bound stones etc. used as paving.

tarn *noun* small mountain lake.

tarnish /'tɑːnɪʃ/ ● *verb* (cause to) lose lustre; impair (reputation etc.). ● *noun* tarnished state; stain, blemish.

taro /'tɑːrəʊ/ *noun* (*plural* **-s**) tropical plant with edible tuberous roots.

tarot /'tærəʊ/ *noun* (in *singular* or *plural*) pack of 78 cards used in fortune-telling.

tarpaulin /tɑːˈpɔːlɪn/ noun waterproof cloth, esp. of tarred canvas; sheet or covering of this.

tarragon /ˈtærəgən/ noun aromatic herb.

tarry[1] /ˈtɑːrɪ/ adjective (**-ier, -iest**) of or smeared with tar.

tarry[2] /ˈtærɪ/ verb (**-ies, -ied**) archaic linger; stay, wait.

tarsal /ˈtɑːs(ə)l/ ● adjective of the ankle-bones. ● noun tarsal bone.

tarsus /ˈtɑːsəs/ noun (plural **tarsi** /-saɪ/) bones of ankle and upper foot.

tart[1] noun pastry case containing fruit, jam, etc. □ **tartlet** noun.

tart[2] ● noun slang prostitute, promiscuous woman. ● verb (+ *up*) colloquial smarten or dress up, esp. gaudily. □ **tarty** adjective (**-ier, -iest**).

tart[3] adjective sharp-tasting, acid; (of remark etc.) cutting, biting. □ **tartly** adverb; **tartness** noun.

tartan /ˈtɑːt(ə)n/ noun (woollen cloth woven in) pattern of coloured stripes crossing at right angles, esp. denoting a Scottish Highland clan.

Tartar /ˈtɑːtə/ noun member of group of Central Asian people including Mongols and Turks; their Turkic language; (**tartar**) harsh or formidable person. □ **tartar sauce** mayonnaise with chopped gherkins etc.

tartar /ˈtɑːtə/ noun hard deposit that forms on teeth; deposit forming hard crust in wine casks.

tartaric /tɑːˈtærɪk/ adjective of tartar. □ **tartaric acid** organic acid found esp. in unripe grapes.

tartrazine /ˈtɑːtrəziːn/ noun brilliant yellow dye from tartaric acid, used to colour food etc.

task /tɑːsk/ ● noun piece of work to be done. ● verb make great demands on. □ **take to task** rebuke, scold; **task force** specially organized unit for task; **taskmaster, taskmistress** person who makes others work hard.

Tass noun official Russian news agency.

tassel /ˈtæs(ə)l/ noun tuft of hanging threads etc. as ornament; tassel-like flowerhead of plant. □ **tasselled** adjective (US **tasseled**).

taste /teɪst/ ● noun (faculty of perceiving) sensation caused in mouth by contact with substance; flavour; small sample of food etc.; slight experience; (often + *for*) liking, predilection; aesthetic discernment in art, clothes, conduct, etc. ● verb (**-ting**) perceive or sample flavour of; eat small portion of; experience; (often + *of*) have specified flavour. □ **taste bud** organ of taste on surface of tongue.

tasteful adjective done in or having good taste. □ **tastefully** adverb; **tastefulness** noun.

tasteless adjective flavourless; having or done in bad taste. □ **tastelessly** adverb; **tastelessness** noun.

taster noun person employed to test food or drink by tasting; small sample.

tasting noun gathering at which food or drink is tasted and evaluated.

tasty adjective (**-ier, -iest**) of pleasing flavour, appetizing; colloquial attractive. □ **tastiness** noun.

tat[1] noun colloquial tatty things; junk.

tat[2] verb (**-tt-**) do, or make by, tatting.

ta-ta /tæˈtɑː/ interjection colloquial goodbye.

tatter /ˈtætə/ noun (usually in plural) rag, irregularly torn cloth, paper, etc. □ **in tatters** colloquial torn in many places, ruined.

tattered adjective in tatters.

tatting /ˈtætɪŋ/ noun (process of making) kind of handmade knotted lace.

tattle /ˈtæt(ə)l/ ● verb (**-ling**) prattle, chatter, gossip. ● noun gossip, idle talk.

tattoo[1] /təˈtuː/ ● verb (**-oos, -ooed**) mark (skin) by puncturing and inserting pigment; make (design)

thus. ● noun such design. □ **tattooer** noun; **tattooist** noun.

tattoo[2] /təˈtuː/ noun evening signal recalling soldiers to quarters; elaboration of this with music and marching etc. as entertainment; drumming, rapping; drumbeat.

tatty /ˈtætɪ/ adjective (**-ier, -iest**) colloquial tattered; shabby, inferior, tawdry. □ **tattily** adverb; **tattiness** noun.

taught past & past participle of TEACH.

taunt ● noun insult; provocation. ● verb insult; provoke contemptuously.

taupe /təʊp/ noun grey tinged with esp. brown.

Taurus /ˈtɔːrəs/ noun second sign of zodiac.

taut adjective (of rope etc.) tight; (of nerves etc.) tense; (of ship etc.) in good condition. □ **tauten** verb; **tautly** adverb; **tautness** noun.

tautology /tɔːˈtɒlədʒɪ/ noun (plural **-ies**) repetition of same thing in different words. □ **tautological** /-təˈlɒdʒ-/ adjective; **tautologous** /-ləgəs/ adjective.

tavern /ˈtæv(ə)n/ noun archaic or literary inn, pub.

taverna /təˈvɜːnə/ noun Greek restaurant.

tawdry /ˈtɔːdrɪ/ adjective (**-ier, -iest**) showy but worthless; gaudy.

tawny /ˈtɔːnɪ/ adjective (**-ier, -iest**) of orange-brown colour. □ **tawny owl** reddish-brown European owl.

tax ● noun money compulsorily levied by state on person, property, business, etc.; (+ *on, upon*) strain, heavy demand. ● verb impose tax on; deduct tax from; make demands on; (often + *with*) charge, call to account. □ **tax avoidance** minimizing tax payment by financial manoeuvring; **tax-deductible** (of expenses) legally deductible from income before tax assessment; **tax disc** licence on vehicle certifying payment of road tax; **tax evasion** illegal non-payment of taxes; **tax-free** exempt from tax; **taxman** colloquial inspector or collector of taxes; **taxpayer** person who pays taxes; **tax return** declaration of income etc. for taxation purposes.

taxation /tækˈseɪʃ(ə)n/ noun imposition or payment of tax.

taxi /ˈtæksɪ/ ● noun (plural **-s**) (in full **taxi-cab**) car plying for hire and usually fitted with taximeter. ● verb (**taxis, taxied, taxiing** or **taxying**) (of aircraft) go along ground before or after flying; go or carry in taxi. □ **taxi rank** (US **taxi stand**) place where taxis wait to be hired.

taxidermy /ˈtæksɪdɜːmɪ/ noun art of preparing, stuffing, and mounting skins of animals. □ **taxidermist** noun.

taximeter /ˈtæksɪmiːtə/ noun automatic fare-indicator in taxi.

taxon /ˈtæks(ə)n/ noun (plural **taxa**) any taxonomic group.

taxonomy /tækˈsɒnəmɪ/ noun classification of living and extinct organisms. □ **taxonomic** /-səˈnɒm-/ adjective; **taxonomical** /-səˈnɒm-/ adjective; **taxonomist** noun.

tayberry /ˈteɪbərɪ/ noun (plural **-ies**) hybrid fruit between blackberry and raspberry.

TB abbreviation tubercle bacillus; tuberculosis.

tbsp. abbreviation tablespoonful.

te /tiː/ noun (also **ti**) seventh note of scale in tonic sol-fa.

tea noun (in full **tea plant**) Asian evergreen shrub or small tree; its dried leaves; infusion of these leaves as drink; infusion made from other leaves etc.; light meal in afternoon or evening. □ **tea bag** small permeable bag of tea for infusion; **tea break** pause in work for drinking tea; **tea caddy** container for tea; **teacake** light usually toasted sweet bun; **tea chest** light metal-lined wooden box for transporting tea; **tea cloth** tea towel; **tea cosy** cover to keep teapot warm; **teacup** cup from which tea is drunk, amount it holds; **tea leaf** leaf of tea, esp. (in *plural*) after infusion; **teapot** pot with handle and spout, in which tea is made; **tearoom** small unlicensed café; **tea rose** rose with scent like tea; **teaset** set of crockery for serving tea; **teashop** tearoom; **teaspoon** small spoon for stirring tea etc., (also **teaspoonful**) amount held by this; **tea towel** cloth for drying washed crockery etc.; **tea trolley** (*US* **tea wagon**) small trolley from which tea is served.

teach *verb* (*past & past participle* **taught** /tɔːt/) give systematic information, instruction, or training to (person) or about (subject, skill); (*+ to do*) instruct to, *colloquial* discourage from. □ **teachable** *adjective*.

teacher *noun* person who teaches, esp. in school.

teaching *noun* teacher's profession; (often in *plural*) what is taught; doctrine.

teak *noun* a hard durable wood.

teal *noun* (*plural* same) small freshwater duck.

team ● *noun* set of players etc. in game or sport; set of people working together; set of draught animals. ● *verb* (usually + *up*) join in team or in common action; (+ *with*) coordinate, match. □ **team-mate** fellow member of team; **team spirit** willingness to act for communal good; **teamwork** combined effort, cooperation.

teamster /'tiːmstə/ *noun US* lorry driver; driver of team.

tear¹ /teə/ ● *verb* (*past* **tore**; *past participle* **torn**) (often + *up*) pull (apart) with some force; make (hole, rent) thus; undergo this; (+ *away, off, at*, etc.) pull violently; violently disrupt; *colloquial* go hurriedly. ● *noun* hole etc. caused by tearing; torn part of cloth etc. □ **tear apart** search exhaustively, criticize forcefully, divide utterly, distress greatly; **tearaway** *colloquial* unruly young person; **tearing hurry** *colloquial* great hurry; **tear into** *colloquial* severely reprimand, start (activity) vigorously; **tear to shreds** *colloquial* criticize thoroughly.

tear² /tɪə/ *noun* drop of clear salty liquid secreted from eye and shed esp. in grief. □ **in tears** weeping; **teardrop** single tear; **tear duct** drain carrying tears to or from eye; **tear gas** gas causing severe irritation to the eyes.

tearful *adjective* in, given to, or accompanied with tears. □ **tearfully** *adverb*.

tease /tiːz/ ● *verb* (**-sing**) make fun of; irritate; entice sexually while refusing to satisfy desire; pick (wool etc.) into separate fibres; raise nap on (cloth) with teasels etc.; (+ *out*) extract or obtain by careful effort. ● *noun colloquial* person fond of teasing; act of teasing.

teasel /'tiːz(ə)l/ *noun* (also **teazel, teazle**) plant with prickly flower heads, used dried for raising nap on cloth; other device used for this.

teaser *noun colloquial* hard question or problem.

teat *noun* nipple on breast or udder; rubber etc. nipple for sucking milk from bottle.

teazel (also **teazle**) = TEASEL.

TEC /tek/ *abbreviation* Training and Enterprise Council.

tec *noun colloquial* detective.

tech /tek/ *noun* (also **tec**) *colloquial* technical college.

technic /'teknɪk/ *noun* (usually in *plural*) technology; technical terms, methods, etc.; technique.

technical *adjective* of the mechanical arts and applied sciences; of a particular subject, craft, etc.; using technical language; specialized; due to mechanical failure; in strict legal sense. □ **technical knockout**

referee's ruling that boxer has lost because he is unfit to continue. □ **technically** *adverb*.

technicality /teknɪ'kælɪtɪ/ *noun* (*plural* **-ies**) being technical; technical expression; technical point or detail.

technician /tek'nɪʃ(ə)n/ *noun* person doing practical or maintenance work in laboratory; person skilled in artistic etc. technique; expert in practical science.

Technicolor /'teknɪkʌlə/ *noun proprietary term* process of colour cinematography; (usually **technicolour**) *colloquial* vivid or artificial colour.

technique /tek'niːk/ *noun* mechanical skill in art; method of achieving purpose, esp. by manipulation; manner of execution in music, painting, etc.

technocracy /tek'nɒkrəsɪ/ *noun* (*plural* **-ies**) (instance of) rule or control by technical experts.

technocrat /'teknəkræt/ *noun* exponent or advocate of technocracy. □ **technocratic** /-'kræt-/ *adjective*.

technology /tek'nɒlədʒɪ/ *noun* (*plural* **-ies**) knowledge or use of mechanical arts and applied sciences; these subjects collectively. □ **technological** /-nə'lɒdʒ-/ *adjective*; **technologically** /-nə'lɒdʒ-/ *adverb*; **technologist** *noun*.

tectonic /tek'tɒnɪk/ *adjective* of building or construction; of changes in the earth's crust.

tectonics *plural noun* (usually treated as *singular*) study of earth's large-scale structural features.

teddy /'tedɪ/ *noun* (also **Teddy**) (*plural* **-ies**) (in full **teddy bear**) soft toy bear.

Teddy boy /'tedɪ/ *noun colloquial* 1950s youth with Edwardian-style clothing, hair, etc.

tedious /'tiːdɪəs/ *adjective* tiresomely long, wearisome. □ **tediously** *adverb*; **tediousness** *noun*.

tedium /'tiːdɪəm/ *noun* tediousness.

tee¹ *noun* letter T.

tee² ● *noun* cleared space from which golf ball is struck at start of play for each hole; small wood or plastic support for golf ball used then; mark aimed at in bowls, quoits, curling, etc. ● *verb* (**tees, teed**) (often + *up*) place (ball) on tee. □ **tee off** make first stroke in golf, *colloquial* start, begin.

teem¹ *verb* be abundant; (+ *with*) be full of, swarm with.

teem² *verb* (often + *down*) pour (esp. of rain).

teen *adjective* teenage.

teenage /'tiːneɪdʒ/ *adjective* of or characteristic of teenagers. □ **teenaged** *adjective*.

teenager /'tiːneɪdʒə/ *noun* person in teens.

teens /tiːnz/ *plural noun* years of one's age from 13 to 19.

teensy /'tiːnzɪ/ *adjective* (**-ier, -iest**) *colloquial* teeny.

teeny /'tiːnɪ/ *adjective* (**-ier, -iest**) *colloquial* tiny.

teepee = TEPEE.

teeter /'tiːtə/ *verb* totter, stand or move unsteadily.

teeth *plural* of TOOTH.

teethe /tiːð/ *verb* (**-thing**) grow or cut teeth, esp. milk teeth. □ **teething ring** ring for infant to bite on while teething; **teething troubles** initial troubles in an enterprise etc.

teetotal /tiː'təʊt(ə)l/ *adjective* advocating or practising total abstinence from alcohol. □ **teetotalism** *noun*; **teetotaller** *noun*.

TEFL /'tef(ə)l/ *abbreviation* teaching of English as a foreign language.

Teflon /'teflɒn/ *noun proprietary term* non-stick coating for kitchen utensils.

Tel. *abbreviation* (also **tel.**) telephone.

tele- *combining form* at or to a distance; television; by telephone.

telecast /'telɪkɑːst/ ● *noun* television broadcast. ● *verb* transmit by television. □ **telecaster** *noun*.

telecommunication /telɪkəmjuːnɪˈkeɪʃ(ə)n/ noun communication over distances by cable, fibre optics, satellites, radio, etc.; (in plural) technology of this.

telefax /ˈtelɪfæks/ noun fax.

telegram /ˈtelɪgræm/ noun message sent by telegraph.

telegraph /ˈtelɪɡrɑːf/ ● noun (device or system for) transmitting messages to a distance by making and breaking electrical connection. ● verb (often + to) send message or communicate by telegraph. □ **telegraphist** /tɪˈlegrə-/ noun.

telegraphic /telɪˈɡræfɪk/ adjective of or by telegraphs or telegrams; economically worded. □ **telegraphically** adverb.

telegraphy /tɪˈlegrəfɪ/ noun communication by telegraph.

telekinesis /telɪkɑːˈniːsɪs/ noun supposed paranormal force moving objects at a distance. □ **telekinetic** /-ˈnet-/ adjective.

telemessage /ˈtelɪmesɪdʒ/ noun message sent by telephone or telex and delivered in printed form.

telemetry /tɪˈlemətrɪ/ noun process of recording readings of instrument and transmitting them by radio. □ **telemeter** /ˈtelɪ-/ noun.

teleology /tiːlɪˈɒlədʒɪ/ noun (plural -ies) Philosophy explanation of phenomena by purpose they serve. □ **teleological** /-əˈlɒdʒ-/ adjective.

telepathy /tɪˈlepəθɪ/ noun supposed paranormal communication of thoughts. □ **telepathic** /telɪˈpæθɪk/ adjective; **telepathically** /telɪˈpæθ-/ adverb.

telephone /ˈtelɪfəʊn/ ● noun apparatus for transmitting sound (esp. speech) to a distance; instrument used in this; system of communication by network of telephones. ● verb (-ning) send (message) or speak to by telephone; make telephone call. □ **on the telephone** having or using a telephone; **telephone book, directory** book listing telephone subscribers and numbers; **telephone booth, box, kiosk** booth etc. with telephone for public use; **telephone number** number used to call a particular telephone. □ **telephonic** /-ˈfɒn-/ adjective; **telephonically** /-ˈfɒn-/ adverb.

telephonist /tɪˈlefənɪst/ noun operator in telephone exchange or at switchboard.

telephony /tɪˈlefənɪ/ noun transmission of sound by telephone.

telephoto /telɪˈfəʊtəʊ/ noun (plural -s) (in full **telephoto lens**) lens used in telephotography.

telephotography /telɪfəˈtɒɡrəfɪ/ noun photographing of distant object with combined lenses giving large image. □ **telephotographic** /-fəʊtəˈɡræf-/ adjective.

teleprinter /ˈtelɪprɪntə/ noun device for sending, receiving, and printing telegraph messages.

teleprompter /ˈtelɪprɒmptə/ noun device beside esp. television camera that slowly unrolls script out of sight of audience.

telesales /ˈtelɪseɪlz/ plural noun selling by telephone.

telescope /ˈtelɪskəʊp/ ● noun optical instrument using lenses or mirrors to magnify distant objects; radio telescope. ● verb (-ping) press or drive (sections of tube etc.) one into another; close or be capable of closing thus; compress.

telescopic /telɪˈskɒpɪk/ adjective of or made with telescope; (esp. of lens) able to magnify distant objects; consisting of sections that telescope. □ **telescopic sight** telescope on rifle etc. used for sighting. □ **telescopically** adverb.

teletext /ˈtelɪtekst/ noun computerized information service transmitted to subscribers' televisions.

telethon /ˈtelɪθɒn/ noun long television programme to raise money for charity.

televise /ˈtelɪvaɪz/ verb (-sing) transmit by television.

television /ˈtelɪvɪʒ(ə)n/ noun system for reproducing on a screen visual images transmitted (with sound) by radio signals or cable; (in full **television set**) device with screen for receiving these signals; television broadcasting. □ **televisual** /-ˈvɪʒʊəl/ adjective.

telex /ˈteleks/ (also **Telex**) ● noun international system of telegraphy using teleprinters and public telecommunication network. ● verb send, or communicate with, by telex.

tell verb (past & past participle **told** /təʊld/) relate in speech or writing; make known, express in words; (often + of, about) divulge information, reveal secret etc.; (+ to do) direct, order; decide about, distinguish; (often + on) produce marked effect or influence. □ **tell apart** distinguish between; **tell off** colloquial scold; **tell-tale** noun person who tells tales, automatic registering device, adjective serving to reveal or betray something; **tell tales** make known person's faults etc.

teller noun person employed to receive and pay out money in bank etc.; person who counts votes; person who tells esp. stories.

telling adjective having marked effect, striking. □ **tellingly** adverb.

telly /ˈtelɪ/ noun (plural -ies) colloquial television.

temerity /tɪˈmerɪtɪ/ noun rashness, audacity.

temp colloquial ● noun temporary employee, esp. secretary. ● verb work as temp.

temper /ˈtempə/ ● noun mental disposition, mood; irritation, anger; tendency to become angry; composure, calmness; metal's hardness or elasticity. ● verb bring (clay, metal) to proper consistency or hardness; (+ with) moderate, mitigate.

tempera /ˈtempərə/ noun method of painting using emulsion e.g. of pigment with egg.

temperament /ˈtemprəmənt/ noun person's or animal's nature and character.

temperamental /temprəˈment(ə)l/ adjective regarding temperament; unreliable, moody; colloquial unpredictable. □ **temperamentally** adverb.

temperance /ˈtempərəns/ noun moderation, esp. in eating and drinking; abstinence, esp. total, from alcohol.

temperate /ˈtempərət/ adjective avoiding excess, moderate; (of region or climate) mild.

temperature /ˈtemprɪtʃə/ noun measured or perceived degree of heat or cold of thing, region, etc.; colloquial body temperature above normal.

tempest /ˈtempɪst/ noun violent storm.

tempestuous /temˈpestʃʊəs/ adjective stormy, turbulent. □ **tempestuously** adverb.

tempi plural of TEMPO.

template /ˈtemplɪt/ noun thin board or plate used as guide in drawing, cutting, drilling, etc.

temple[1] /ˈtemp(ə)l/ noun building for worship, or treated as dwelling place, of god(s).

temple[2] /ˈtemp(ə)l/ noun flat part of side of head between forehead and ear.

tempo /ˈtempəʊ/ noun (plural -pos or -pi /-piː/) speed at which music is (to be) played; speed, pace.

temporal /ˈtempər(ə)l/ adjective worldly as opposed to spiritual, secular; of time; of the temples of the head.

temporary /ˈtempərərɪ/ ● adjective lasting or meant to last only for limited time. ● noun (plural -ies) person employed temporarily. □ **temporarily** adverb.

temporize /ˈtempəraɪz/ verb (also **-ise**) (**-zing** or **-sing**) avoid committing oneself, so as to gain time; procrastinate; comply temporarily.

tempt verb entice, incite to what is forbidden; allure, attract; risk provoking. □ **tempter** noun; **tempting** adjective; **temptingly** adverb; **temptress** noun.

temptation /temp'teɪʃ(ə)n/ noun tempting, being tempted; incitement, esp. to wrongdoing; attractive thing or course of action.

ten adjective & noun one more than nine. □ **the Ten Commandments** rules of conduct given by God to Moses. □ **tenth** adjective & noun.

tenable /'tenəb(ə)l/ adjective maintainable against attack or objection; (+ for, by) (of office etc.) that can be held for period or by (person etc.). □ **tenability** noun.

tenacious /tɪ'neɪʃəs/ adjective (often + of) keeping firm hold; persistent, resolute; (of memory) retentive. □ **tenaciously** adverb; **tenacity** /-'næs-/ noun.

tenancy /'tenənsɪ/ noun (plural -ies) (duration of) tenant's status or possession.

tenant /'tenənt/ noun person who rents land or property from landlord; (often + of) occupant of place.

tenantry noun tenants of estate etc.

tench noun (plural same) freshwater fish of carp family.

tend¹ verb (often + to) be apt or inclined; be moving; hold a course.

tend² verb take care of, look after.

tendency /'tendənsɪ/ noun (plural -ies) (often + to, towards) leaning, inclination.

tendentious /ten'denʃəs/ adjective derogatory designed to advance a particular cause; biased; controversial. □ **tendentiously** adverb; **tendentiousness** noun.

tender¹ /'tendə/ adjective (**tenderer**, **tenderest**) not tough or hard; susceptible to pain or grief; compassionate; delicate, fragile; loving, affectionate; requiring tact; immature. □ **tenderfoot** (plural -s or -feet) novice, newcomer; **tender-hearted** easily moved; **tenderloin** middle part of loin of pork; **tender mercies** harsh treatment. □ **tenderly** adverb; **tenderness** noun.

tender² /'tendə/ ● verb offer, present (services, resignation, payment, etc.); (often + for) make tender. ● noun offer to execute work or supply goods at fixed price.

tender³ /'tendə/ noun person who looks after people or things; supply vessel attending larger one; truck attached to steam locomotive and carrying fuel etc.

tenderize verb (also **-ise**) (**-zing** or **-sing**) render (meat) tender by beating etc.

tendon /'tend(ə)n/ noun tough fibrous tissue connecting muscle to bone etc.

tendril /'tendrɪl/ noun slender leafless shoot by which some climbing plants cling.

tenebrous /'tenɪbrəs/ adjective literary dark, gloomy.

tenement /'tenɪmənt/ noun room or flat within house or block of flats; (also **tenement house**, **block**) house or block so divided.

tenet /'tenɪt/ noun doctrine, principle.

tenfold adjective & adverb ten times as much or many.

tenner /'tenə/ noun colloquial £10 or $10 note.

tennis /'tenɪs/ noun ball game played with rackets on court divided by net. □ **tennis elbow** sprain caused by overuse of forearm muscles.

tenon /'tenən/ noun wooden projection shaped to fit into mortise of another piece.

tenor /'tenə/ ● noun male singing voice between alto and baritone; singer with this; (usually + of) general purport, prevailing course of one's life or habits. ● adjective having range of tenor.

tenosynovitis /ˌtenəʊsaɪnə'vaɪtɪs/ noun repetitive strain injury, esp. of wrist.

tenpin bowling noun game in which ten pins or skittles are bowled in alley.

tense¹ ● adjective stretched tight; strained; causing tenseness. ● verb (**-sing**) make or become tense. □ **tense up** become tense. □ **tensely** adverb; **tenseness** noun.

tense² noun form of verb indicating time of action etc.; set of such forms for various persons and numbers.

tensile /'tensaɪl/ adjective of tension; capable of being stretched. □ **tensile strength** resistance to breaking under tension.

tension /'tenʃ(ə)n/ noun stretching, being stretched; mental strain or excitement; strained state; stress produced by forces pulling apart; degree of tightness of stitches in knitting and machine sewing; voltage.

tent noun portable shelter or dwelling of canvas etc.

tentacle /'tentək(ə)l/ noun slender flexible appendage of animal, used for feeling, grasping, or moving.

tentative /'tentətɪv/ adjective experimental; hesitant, not definite. □ **tentatively** adverb.

tenterhooks /'tentəhʊks/ plural noun □ **on tenterhooks** in suspense, distracted by uncertainty.

tenuous /'tenjʊəs/ adjective slight, insubstantial; oversubtle; thin, slender. □ **tenuity** /-'juːɪtɪ/ noun; **tenuously** adverb.

tenure /'tenjə/ noun (often + of) holding of property or office; conditions or period of this; guaranteed permanent employment, esp. as lecturer. □ **tenured** adjective.

tepee /'tiːpiː/ noun (also **teepee**) N. American Indian's conical tent.

tepid /'tepɪd/ adjective lukewarm; unenthusiastic.

tequila /tɪ'kiːlə/ noun Mexican liquor made from agave.

tercel /'tɜːs(ə)l/ noun (also **tiercel** /'tɪəs(ə)l/) male hawk.

tercentenary /ˌtɜːsen'tiːnərɪ/ noun (plural -ies) 300th anniversary; celebration of this.

tergiversate /'tɜːdʒɪvəseɪt/ verb (**-ting**) change one's party or principles; make conflicting or evasive statements. □ **tergiversation** noun; **tergiversator** noun.

term ● noun word for definite concept, esp. specialized; (in plural) language used, mode of expression; (in plural) relation, footing; (in plural) stipulations, charge, price; limited period; period of weeks during which instruction is given or during which law court holds sessions; Logic word(s) which may be subject or predicate of proposition; Mathematics each quantity in ratio or series, part of algebraic expression; completion of normal length of pregnancy. ● verb call, name. □ **come to terms with** reconcile oneself to; **in terms of** with reference to; **terms of reference** scope of inquiry etc., definition of this. □ **termly** adjective.

termagant /'tɜːməgənt/ noun overbearing woman, virago.

terminable /'tɜːmɪnəb(ə)l/ adjective able to be terminated.

terminal /'tɜːmɪn(ə)l/ ● adjective (of condition or disease) fatal; (of patient) dying; of or forming limit or terminus. ● noun terminating thing, extremity; bus or train terminus; air terminal; point of connection for closing electric circuit; apparatus for transmission of messages to and from computer, communications system, etc. □ **terminally** adverb.

terminate /'tɜːmɪneɪt/ verb (**-ting**) bring or come to an end; (+ in) end in.

termination noun terminating, being terminated; ending, result; induced abortion.

terminology /ˌtɜːmɪ'nɒlədʒɪ/ noun (plural -ies) system of specialized terms. □ **terminological** /-nə'lɒdʒ-/ adjective.

terminus /'tɜ:mɪnəs/ noun (plural **-ni** /-naɪ/ or **-nuses**) point at end of railway or bus route or of pipeline etc.

termite /'tɜ:maɪt/ noun antlike insect destructive to timber.

tern noun seabird with long pointed wings and forked tail.

ternary /'tɜ:nərɪ/ adjective composed of 3 parts.

terrace /'terəs/ ● noun flat area on slope for cultivation; level paved area next to house; row of houses built in one block of uniform style; terrace house; tiered standing accommodation for spectators at sports ground. ● verb (**-cing**) form into or provide with terrace(s). □ **terrace(d) house** house in terrace.

terracotta /terə'kɒtə/ noun unglazed usually brownish-red earthenware; its colour.

terra firma /terə 'fɜ:mə/ noun dry land, firm ground.

terrain /tə'reɪn/ noun tract of land, esp. in military or geographical contexts.

terra incognita /terə ɪŋ'kɒgnɪtə/ noun unexplored region. [Latin]

terrapin /'terəpɪn/ noun N. American edible freshwater turtle.

terrarium /tə'reərɪəm/ noun (plural **-s** or **-ria**) place for keeping small land animals; transparent globe containing growing plants.

terrestrial /tə'restrɪəl/ adjective of or on the earth; earthly; of or on dry land.

terrible /'terɪb(ə)l/ adjective colloquial very great, bad, or incompetent; causing or likely to cause terror; dreadful.

terribly adverb colloquial very, extremely; in terrible manner.

terrier /'terɪə/ noun small active hardy dog.

terrific /tə'rɪfɪk/ adjective colloquial huge, intense, excellent; causing terror. □ **terrifically** adverb.

terrify /'terɪfaɪ/ verb (**-ies**, **-ied**) fill with terror. □ **terrifying** adjective; **terrifyingly** adverb.

terrine /tə'ri:n/ noun (earthenware vessel for) pâté or similar food.

territorial /terɪ'tɔ:rɪəl/ ● adjective of territory or district. ● noun (**Territorial**) member of Territorial Army. □ **Territorial Army** local volunteer reserve force; **territorial waters** waters under state's jurisdiction, esp. part of sea within stated distance of shore. □ **territorially** adverb.

territory /'terɪtərɪ/ noun (plural **-ies**) extent of land under jurisdiction of ruler, state, etc.; (**Territory**) organized division of a country, esp. if not yet admitted to full rights of a state; sphere of action etc., province; commercial traveller's sales area; area defended by animal or human, or by team etc. in game.

terror /'terə/ noun extreme fear; terrifying person or thing; colloquial troublesome or tiresome person, esp. child; terrorism.

terrorist noun person using esp. organized violence to secure political ends. □ **terrorism** noun.

terrorize verb (also **-ise**) (**-zing** or **-sing**) fill with terror; use terrorism against.

terry /'terɪ/ noun looped pile fabric used for nappies, towels, etc.

terse /tɜ:s/ adjective (**-r**, **-st**) concise, brief; curt. □ **tersely** adverb.

tertiary /'tɜ:ʃərɪ/ adjective of third order, rank, etc.

Terylene /'terɪli:n/ noun proprietary term synthetic polyester textile fibre.

TESL /'tes(ə)l/ abbreviation teaching of English as a second language.

tesla /'tezlə/ noun SI unit of magnetic flux density.

tessellated /'tesəleɪtɪd/ adjective of or resembling mosaic; finely chequered.

tessellation /tesə'leɪʃ(ə)n/ noun close arrangement of polygons, esp. in repeated pattern.

test ● noun critical exam or trial of person's or thing's qualities; means, procedure, or standard for so doing; minor exam; colloquial test match. ● verb put to test; try severely, tax. □ **test card** still television picture outside normal programme hours; **test case** Law case setting precedent for other similar cases; **test drive** noun drive taken to judge vehicle's performance; **test-drive** verb take test drive in; **test match** international cricket or Rugby match, usually in series; **test-tube** thin glass tube closed at one end, used for chemical tests etc.; **test-tube baby** colloquial baby conceived elsewhere than in a mother's body. □ **tester** noun.

testaceous /tes'teɪʃəs/ adjective having hard continuous shell.

testament /'testəmənt/ noun a will; (usually + to) evidence, proof; Biblical covenant; (**Testament**) division of Bible. □ **testamentary** /-'ment-/ adjective.

testate /'testeɪt/ ● adjective having left valid will at death. ● noun testate person. □ **testacy** /-təsɪ/ noun (plural **-ies**).

testator /tes'teɪtə/ noun (feminine **testatrix** /-trɪks/) (esp. deceased) person who has made a will.

testes plural of TESTIS.

testicle /'testɪk(ə)l/ noun male organ that secretes spermatozoa, esp. one of pair in scrotum of man and most mammals.

testify /'testɪfaɪ/ verb (**-ies**, **-ied**) (often + to) bear witness; give evidence; affirm, declare.

testimonial /testɪ'məʊnɪəl/ noun certificate of character, conduct, or qualifications; gift presented as mark of esteem.

testimony /'testɪmənɪ/ noun (plural **-ies**) witness's statement under oath etc.; declaration, statement of fact; evidence.

testis /'testɪs/ noun (plural **testes** /-ti:z/) testicle.

testosterone /tes'tɒstərəʊn/ noun male sex hormone.

testy /'testɪ/ adjective (**-ier**, **-iest**) irascible, short-tempered. □ **testily** adverb; **testiness** noun.

tetanus /'tetənəs/ noun bacterial disease causing painful spasm of voluntary muscles.

tetchy /'tetʃɪ/ adjective (**-ier**, **-iest**) peevish, irritable. □ **tetchily** adverb; **tetchiness** noun.

tête-à-tête /teɪtɑ:'teɪt/ ● noun private conversation between two people. ● adverb privately without third person.

tether /'teðə/ ● noun rope etc. confining grazing animal. ● verb fasten with tether. □ **at the end of one's tether** at the limit of one's patience, resources, etc.

tetra- combining form four.

tetragon /'tetrəgən/ noun plane figure with 4 sides and angles. □ **tetragonal** /tɪ'trægən-/ adjective.

tetrahedron /tetrə'hi:drən/ noun (plural **-dra** or **-s**) 4-sided triangular pyramid. □ **tetrahedral** adjective.

Teutonic /tju:'tɒnɪk/ adjective of Germanic peoples or languages; German.

text noun main part of book; original document, esp. as distinct from paraphrase etc.; passage of Scripture, esp. as subject of sermon; subject, theme; (in plural) books prescribed for study; data in textual form, esp. in word processor. □ **textbook** book used in studying, esp. standard book in any subject; **text editor** computing program allowing user to edit text.

textile /'tekstaɪl/ ● noun (often in plural) fabric, esp. woven. ● adjective of weaving or cloth; woven.

textual /'tekstʃʊəl/ adjective of, in, or concerning a text.

texture /'tekstʃə/ ● noun feel or appearance of surface or substance; arrangement of threads in textile fabric. ● verb (-ring) (usually as **textured** adjective) provide with texture; provide (vegetable protein) with texture like meat. □ **textural** adjective.

Thai /taɪ/ ● noun (plural same or **-s**) native, national, or language of Thailand. ● adjective of Thailand.

thalidomide /θə'lɪdəmaɪd/ noun sedative drug found in 1961 to cause foetal malformation when taken early in pregnancy.

than /ðən/ conjunction introducing comparison.

thane /θeɪn/ noun historical holder of land from English king by military service, or from Scottish king and ranking below earl; clan-chief.

thank /θæŋk/ ● verb express gratitude to; hold responsible. ● noun (in plural) colloquial gratitude; (as interjection) expression of gratitude. □ **thanksgiving** expression of gratitude, esp. to God; **Thanksgiving (Day)** US national holiday on fourth Thurs. in Nov.; **thanks to** as result of; **thank you** polite formula expressing gratitude.

thankful adjective grateful, pleased, expressive of thanks.

thankfully adverb in a thankful way; let us be thankful that.

■ **Usage** The use of thankfully to mean 'let us be thankful that' is common, but it is considered incorrect by some people.

thankless adjective not feeling or expressing gratitude; (of task etc.) unprofitable, unappreciated.

that /ðæt/ ● adjective (plural those /ðəʊz/) used to describe the person or thing nearby, indicated, just mentioned, or understood; used to specify the further or less immediate of two. ● pronoun (plural those /ðəʊz/) that one; the one, the person, etc.; /ðət/ (plural that) who, whom, which (used to introduce a defining relative clause). ● adverb (+ adjective or adverb) to that degree, so, (with negative) colloquial very. ● conjunction /ðət/ used to introduce a subordinate clause expressing esp. a statement, purpose, or result. □ **at that** moreover, then; **that is (to say)** in other words, more correctly or intelligibly.

thatch /θætʃ/ ● noun roofing of straw, reeds, etc. ● verb cover with thatch. □ **thatcher** noun.

thaw /θɔː/ ● verb (often + out) pass from frozen into liquid or unfrozen state; (of weather) become warm enough to melt ice or snow; warm into life, animation, cordiality, etc. ● noun thawing; warmth of weather that thaws.

the /ðɪ, ðə, ðiː/ ● adjective (called the definite article) denoting person(s) or thing(s) already mentioned or known about; describing as unique; (+ adjective) which is, who are, etc.; (with the stressed) best known; used with noun which represents or symbolizes a group, activity, etc. ● adverb (before comparatives in expressions of proportional variation) in or by that degree, on that account.

theatre /'θɪətə/ noun (US **theater**) building or outdoor area for dramatic performances; writing, production, acting, etc. of plays; room or hall for lectures etc. with seats in tiers; operating theatre; scene or field of action.

theatrical /θɪ'ætrɪk(ə)l/ ● adjective of or for theatre or acting; calculated for effect, showy. ● noun (in plural) dramatic performances. □ **theatricality** /-'kæl-/ noun; **theatrically** adverb.

thee /ðiː/ pronoun archaic (as object of verb) you (singular).

theft /θeft/ noun act of stealing.

their /ðeə/ adjective of or belonging to them.

theirs /ðeəz/ pronoun the one(s) belonging to them.

theism /'θiːɪz(ə)m/ noun belief in gods or a god. □ **theist** noun; **theistic** /-'ɪstɪk/ adjective.

them /ðem, ð(ə)m/ ● pronoun (as object of verb) the people or things in question; people in general; people in authority; colloquial they. ● adjective slang or dialect those.

theme /θiːm/ noun subject or topic of talk etc.; Music leading melody in a composition; US school exercise on given subject. □ **theme park** amusement park based on unifying idea; **theme song, tune** signature tune. □ **thematic** /θɪ'mætɪk/ adjective; **thematically** /θɪ'mæt-/ adverb.

themselves /ðəm'selvz/ pronoun: emphatic form of THEY or THEM; reflexive form of THEM.

then /ðen/ ● adverb at that time; after that, next; in that case, accordingly. ● adjective such at that time. ● noun that time. □ **then and there** immediately and on the spot.

thence /ðens/ adverb (also **from thence**) archaic or literary from that place, for that reason. □ **thenceforth, thenceforward** from that time on.

theo- combining form God or god(s).

theocracy /θɪ'ɒkrəsɪ/ noun (plural **-ies**) form of government by God or a god directly or through a priestly order etc. □ **theocratic** /θɪə'krætɪk/ adjective.

theodolite /θɪ'ɒdəlaɪt/ noun surveying instrument for measuring angles.

theology /θɪ'ɒlədʒɪ/ noun (plural **-ies**) study or system of (esp. Christian) religion. □ **theologian** /θɪə'ləʊdʒ-/ noun; **theological** /θɪə'lɒdʒ-/ adjective.

theorem /'θɪərəm/ noun esp. Mathematics general proposition not self-evident but demonstrable by argument; algebraic rule.

theoretical /θɪə'retɪk(ə)l/ adjective concerned with knowledge but not with its practical application; based on theory rather than experience. □ **theoretically** adverb.

theoretician /θɪərə'tɪʃ(ə)n/ noun person concerned with theoretical part of a subject.

theorist /'θɪərɪst/ noun holder or inventor of a theory.

theorize /'θɪəraɪz/ verb (also **-ise**) (**-zing** or **-sing**) evolve or indulge in theories.

theory /'θɪərɪ/ noun (plural **-ies**) supposition or system of ideas explaining something, esp. one based on general principles; speculative view; abstract knowledge or speculative thought; exposition of principles of a science etc.; collection of propositions to illustrate principles of a mathematical subject.

theosophy /θɪ'ɒsəfɪ/ noun (plural **-ies**) philosophy professing to achieve knowledge of God by direct intuition, spiritual ecstasy, etc. □ **theosophical** /θɪə'sɒf-/ adjective; **theosophist** noun.

therapeutic /θerə'pjuːtɪk/ adjective of, for, or contributing to the cure of diseases; soothing, conducive to wellbeing. □ **therapeutically** adverb.

therapeutics plural noun (usually treated as singular) branch of medicine concerned with cures and remedies.

therapy /'θerəpɪ/ noun (plural **-ies**) non-surgical treatment of disease etc. □ **therapist** noun.

there /ðeə/ ● adverb in, at, or to that place or position; at that point; in that respect; used for emphasis in calling attention; used to indicate the fact or existence of something. ● noun that place. ● interjection expressing confirmation, triumph, etc.; used to soothe a child etc. □ **thereabout(s)** near that place, amount, or time; **thereafter** formal after that; **thereby** by that means or agency; **therefore** for that reason, accordingly, consequently; **therein** formal in that place or respect; **thereof** formal of that or it; **thereto** formal to that or it, in addition; **thereupon** in consequence of that, directly after that.

therm /θɜːm/ *noun* unit of heat, former UK unit of gas supplied.

thermal /ˈθɜːm(ə)l/ ● *adjective* of, for, producing, or retaining heat. ● *noun* rising current of warm air. □ **thermal unit** unit for measuring heat. □ **thermally** *adverb*.

thermionic valve /θɜːmɪˈɒnɪk/ *noun* device giving flow of electrons in one direction from heated substance, used esp. in rectification of current and in radio reception.

thermo- *combining form* heat.

thermodynamics /θɜːməʊdaɪˈnæmɪks/ *plural noun* (usually treated as *singular*) science of relationship between heat and other forms of energy. □ **thermodynamic** *adjective*.

thermoelectric /θɜːməʊɪˈlektrɪk/ *adjective* producing electricity by difference of temperatures.

thermometer /θəˈmɒmɪtə/ *noun* instrument for measuring temperature, esp. graduated glass tube containing mercury or alcohol.

thermonuclear /θɜːməʊˈnjuːklɪə/ *adjective* relating to nuclear reactions that occur only at very high temperatures; (of bomb etc.) using such reactions.

thermoplastic /θɜːməʊˈplæstɪk/ ● *adjective* becoming plastic on heating and hardening on cooling. ● *noun* thermoplastic substance.

Thermos /ˈθɜːməs/ *noun* (in full **Thermos flask**) *proprietary term* vacuum flask.

thermosetting /ˈθɜːməʊsetɪŋ/ *adjective* (of plastics) setting permanently when heated.

thermosphere /ˈθɜːməsfɪə/ *noun* region of atmosphere beyond mesosphere.

thermostat /ˈθɜːməstæt/ *noun* device for automatic regulation of temperature. □ **thermostatic** /-ˈstæt-/ *adjective*; **thermostatically** /-ˈstæt-/ *adverb*.

thesaurus /θɪˈsɔːrəs/ *noun* (*plural* **-ri** /-raɪ/ or **-ruses**) dictionary of synonyms etc.

these *plural of* THIS.

thesis /ˈθiːsɪs/ *noun* (*plural* **theses** /-siːz/) proposition to be maintained or proved; dissertation, esp. by candidate for higher degree.

Thespian /ˈθespɪən/ ● *adjective* of drama. ● *noun* actor or actress.

they /ðeɪ/ *pronoun* (as subject of verb) the people or things in question; people in general; people in authority.

they'd /ðeɪd/ they had; they would.

they'll /ðeɪəl/ they will; they shall.

they're /ðeə/ they are.

they've /ðeɪv/ they have.

thiamine /ˈθaɪəmiːn/ *noun* (also **thiamin**) B vitamin found in unrefined cereals, beans, and liver.

thick /θɪk/ ● *adjective* of great or specified extent between opposite surfaces; (of line etc.) broad, not fine; closely set; crowded; (usually + *with*) densely filled or covered; firm in consistency; made of thick material; muddy, impenetrable; *colloquial* stupid; (of voice) indistinct; (of accent) marked; *colloquial* intimate. ● *noun* thick part of anything. ● *adverb* thickly. □ **a bit thick** *colloquial* unreasonable, intolerable; **in the thick of** in the busiest part of; **thickhead** *colloquial* stupid person; **thickheaded** *adjective*; **thickset** heavily or solidly built, set or growing close together; **thick-skinned** not sensitive to criticism; **through thick and thin** under all conditions, in spite of all difficulties. □ **thickly** *adverb*; **thickness** *noun*.

thicken *verb* make or become thick(er); become more complicated.

thickener *noun* substance used to thicken liquid.

thickening *noun* thickened part; = THICKENER.

thicket /ˈθɪkɪt/ *noun* tangle of shrubs or trees.

thief /θiːf/ *noun* (*plural* **thieves** /θiːvz/) person who steals, esp. secretly.

thieve /θiːv/ *verb* (**-ving**) be a thief; steal. □ **thievery** *noun*.

thievish *adjective* given to stealing.

thigh /θaɪ/ *noun* part of leg between hip and knee. □ **thigh-bone** femur.

thimble /ˈθɪmb(ə)l/ *noun* metal or plastic cap worn to protect finger and push needle in sewing.

thimbleful *noun* (*plural* **-s**) small quantity, esp. of drink.

thin /θɪn/ ● *adjective* (**-nn-**) having opposite surfaces close together, of small thickness or diameter; (of line etc.) narrow, fine; made of thin material; lean, not plump; not dense or copious; of slight consistency; weak, lacking an important ingredient; (of excuse etc.) transparent, flimsy. ● *adverb* thinly. ● *verb* (**-nn-**) make or become thin(ner); (often + *out*) make or become less dense, crowded, or numerous. □ **thin on the ground** few; **thin on top** balding; **thin-skinned** sensitive to criticism. □ **thinly** *adverb*; **thinness** *noun*.

thine /ðaɪn/ *archaic* ● *pronoun* yours (singular). ● *adjective* your (singular).

thing /θɪŋ/ *noun* any possible object of thought or perception including people, material objects, events, qualities, ideas, utterances, and acts; *colloquial* one's special interest; (**the thing**) *colloquial* what is proper, fashionable, needed, important, etc.; (in *plural*) personal belongings, clothing, or equipment; (in *plural*) affairs, circumstances. □ **have a thing about** *colloquial* be obsessed by or prejudiced about.

thingummy /ˈθɪŋəmɪ/ *noun* (*plural* **-ies**) (also **thingumabob** /-məbɒb/, **thingumajig** /-mədʒɪg/) *colloquial* person or thing whose name one forgets or does not know.

think /θɪŋk/ ● *verb* (*past & past participle* **thought** /θɔːt/) be of opinion; (+ *of*, *about*) consider; exercise mind; form ideas, imagine; have half-formed intention. ● *noun colloquial* act of thinking. □ **think better of** change one's mind about (intention) after reconsideration; **think out** consider carefully, devise; **think over** reflect on; **think-tank** *colloquial* group of experts providing advice and ideas on national or commercial problems; **think twice** avoid hasty action etc.; **think up** *colloquial* devise.

thinker *noun* person who thinks in specified way; person with skilled or powerful mind.

thinking ● *adjective* intelligent, rational. ● *noun* opinion, judgement.

thinner *noun* solvent for diluting paint etc.

third /θɜːd/ *adjective & noun* next after second; any of 3 equal parts of thing. □ **third degree** severe and protracted interrogation by police etc.; **third man** *Cricket* fielder near boundary behind slips; **third party** another party besides the two principals; **third-party insurance** insurance against damage or injury suffered by person other than the insured; **third-rate** inferior, very poor; **Third World** developing countries of Africa, Asia, and Latin America. □ **thirdly** *adverb*.

thirst /θɜːst/ ● *noun* (discomfort caused by) need to drink; desire, craving. ● *verb* feel thirst.

thirsty /ˈθɜːstɪ/ *adjective* (**-ier**, **-iest**) feeling thirst; (of land, season, etc.) dry, parched; (often + *for*, *after*) eager; *colloquial* causing thirst. □ **thirstily** *adverb*; **thirstiness** *noun*.

thirteen /θɜːˈtiːn/ *adjective & noun* one more than twelve. □ **thirteenth** *adjective & noun*.

thirty /ˈθɜːtɪ/ *adjective & noun* (*plural* **-ies**) three times ten. □ **thirtieth** *adjective & noun*.

this /ðɪs/ ● adjective (plural **these** /ðiːz/) used to describe the person or thing nearby, indicated, just mentioned, or understood; used to specify the nearer or more immediate of two; the present (morning, week, etc.). ● pronoun (plural **these** /ðiːz/) this one. ● adverb (+ adjective or adverb) to this degree or extent.

thistle /'θɪs(ə)l/ noun prickly plant, usually with globular heads of purple flowers; this as Scottish national emblem. □ **thistledown** down containing thistle-seeds. □ **thistly** adjective.

thither /'ðɪðə/ adverb archaic or formal to that place.

tho' = THOUGH.

thole /θəʊl/ noun (in full **thole-pin**) pin in gunwale of boat as fulcrum for oar; each of two such pins forming rowlock.

thong /θɒŋ/ noun narrow strip of hide or leather.

thorax /'θɔːræks/ noun (plural **-races** /-rəsiːz/ or **-raxes**) part of the body between neck and abdomen. □ **thoracic** /-'ræs-/ adjective.

thorn /θɔːn/ noun sharp-pointed projection on plant; thorn-bearing shrub or tree. □ **thornless** adjective.

thorny adjective (**-ier**, **-iest**) having many thorns; (of subject) problematic, causing disagreement.

thorough /'θʌrə/ adjective complete, unqualified, not superficial; acting or done with great care etc. □ **thoroughbred** adjective of pure breed, high-spirited, noun such animal, esp. horse; **thoroughfare** public way open at both ends, esp. main road; **thoroughgoing** thorough, complete. □ **thoroughly** adverb; **thoroughness** noun.

those plural of THAT.

thou¹ /ðaʊ/ pronoun archaic (as subject of verb) you (singular).

thou² /θaʊ/ noun (plural same or **-s**) colloquial thousand; one thousandth.

though /ðəʊ/ (also **tho'**) ● conjunction in spite of the fact that; even if; and yet. ● adverb colloquial however, all the same.

thought¹ /θɔːt/ noun process, power, faculty, etc. of thinking; particular way of thinking; sober reflection, consideration; idea, notion; intention, purpose; (usually in plural) one's opinion.

thought² past & past participle of THINK.

thoughtful adjective engaged in or given to meditation; giving signs of serious thought; considerate. □ **thoughtfully** adverb; **thoughtfulness** noun.

thoughtless adjective careless of consequences or of others' feelings; caused by lack of thought. □ **thoughtlessly** adverb; **thoughtlessness** noun.

thousand /'θaʊz(ə)nd/ adjective & noun (plural same) ten hundred; (**thousands**) colloquial large number. □ **thousandth** adjective & noun.

thrall /θrɔːl/ noun literary (often + of, to) slave; slavery.

thrash /θræʃ/ verb beat or whip severely; defeat thoroughly; move or fling (esp. limbs) violently. □ **thrash out** discuss to conclusion.

thread /θred/ ● noun spun-out cotton, silk, glass, etc.; length of this; thin cord of twisted yarns used esp. in sewing and weaving; continuous aspect of thing; spiral ridge of screw. ● verb pass thread through (needle); put (beads) on thread; arrange (material in strip form, e.g. film) in proper position on equipment; pick (one's way) through maze, crowded place, etc. □ **threadbare** (of cloth) so worn that nap is lost and threads showing, (of person) shabby, (of idea etc.) hackneyed; **threadworm** parasitic threadlike worm.

threat /θret/ noun declaration of intention to punish or hurt; indication of something undesirable coming; person or thing regarded as dangerous.

threaten /'θret(ə)n/ verb use threats towards; be sign or indication of (something undesirable); (+ to do)

announce one's intention to do (undesirable thing); give warning of infliction of (harm etc.); (as **threatened** adjective) (of species etc.) likely to become extinct.

three /θriː/ adjective & noun one more than two. □ **three-cornered** triangular, (of contest etc.) between 3 people etc.; **three-dimensional** having or appearing to have length, breadth, and depth; **three-legged race** race for pairs with right leg of one tied to other's left leg; **threepence** /'θrepəns/ sum of 3 pence; **threepenny** /'θrepənɪ/ costing 3 pence; **three-piece** (suit or suite) consisting of 3 items; **three-ply** (wool etc.) having 3 strands, (plywood) having 3 layers; **three-point turn** method of turning vehicle in narrow space by moving forwards, backwards, and forwards again; **three-quarter** Rugby any of 3 or 4 players just behind half-backs; **the three Rs** reading, writing, and arithmetic.

threefold adjective & adverb three times as much or many.

threesome noun group of 3 people.

threnody /'θrenədɪ/ noun (plural **-ies**) song of lamentation.

thresh verb beat out or separate grain from (corn etc.). □ **thresher** noun.

threshold /'θreʃəʊld/ noun plank or stone forming bottom of doorway; point of entry; limit below which stimulus causes no reaction.

threw past of THROW.

thrice adverb archaic or literary 3 times.

thrift noun frugality, economical management. □ **thrifty** adjective (**-ier**, **-iest**).

thrill ● noun wave or nervous tremor of emotion or sensation; throb, pulsation. ● verb (cause to) feel thrill; quiver or throb (as) with emotion.

thriller noun sensational or exciting play, story, etc.

thrips noun (plural same) insect harmful to plants.

thrive verb (**-ving**; past **throve** or **thrived**; past participle **thriven** /'θrɪv(ə)n/ or **thrived**) prosper; grow vigorously.

thro' = THROUGH.

throat noun gullet, windpipe; front of neck; literary narrow passage or entrance.

throaty adjective (**-ier**, **-iest**) (of voice) hoarsely resonant.

throb ● verb (**-bb-**) pulsate; vibrate with persistent rhythm or with emotion. ● noun throbbing, violent beat or pulsation.

throe noun (usually in plural) violent pang. □ **in the throes of** struggling with the task of.

thrombosis /θrɒm'bəʊsɪs/ noun (plural **-boses** /-siːz/) coagulation of blood in blood vessel or organ.

throne ● noun ceremonial chair for sovereign, bishop, etc.; sovereign power. ● verb (**-ning**) enthrone.

throng ● noun (often + of) crowd, esp. of people. ● verb come in multitudes; fill (as) with crowd.

throstle /'θrɒs(ə)l/ noun song thrush.

throttle /'θrɒt(ə)l/ ● noun (lever etc. operating) valve controlling flow of steam or fuel in engine; throat. ● verb (**-ling**) choke, strangle; control (engine etc.) with throttle. □ **throttle back**, **down** reduce speed of (engine etc.) by throttling.

through /θruː/ (also **thro'**, US **thru**) ● preposition from end to end or side to side of; between, among; from beginning to end of; by agency, means, or fault of; by reason of; US up to and including. ● adverb through something; from end to end; to the end. ● adjective (of journey etc.) done without change of line, vehicle, etc.; (of traffic) going through a place to its destination; (of road) open at both ends. □ **be through** colloquial (often + with) have finished, cease to have dealings; **through and through** thoroughly, completely; **throughput** amount of material put through a manufacturing etc. process or a computer.

throughout /θruːˈaʊt/ ● *preposition* right through; from end to end of. ● *adverb* in every part or respect.

throve *past of* THRIVE.

throw /θrəʊ/ ● *verb* (*past* **threw** /θruː/; *past participle* **thrown**) propel through space; force violently into specified position or state; turn or move (part of body) quickly or suddenly; project (rays, light, etc.); cast (shadow); bring to the ground; *colloquial* disconcert; (+ *on, off*, etc.) put (clothes etc.) carelessly or hastily on, off, etc.; cause (dice) to fall on table etc., obtain (specified number) thus; cause to pass or extend suddenly to another state or position; move (switch, lever); shape (pottery) on wheel; have (fit, tantrum, etc.); give (a party). ● *noun* throwing, being thrown; distance a thing is or may be thrown; (**a throw**) *slang* each, per item. □ **throw away** discard as unwanted, waste, fail to make use of; **throwaway** to be thrown away after (one) use, deliberately underemphasized; **throw back** (usually in *passive*; + *on*) compel to rely on; **throwback** (instance of) reversion to ancestral character; **throw in** interpose (word, remark), include at no extra cost, throw (football) from edge of pitch where it has gone out of play; **throw-in** throwing in of football from edge of pitch; **throw off** discard, contrive to get rid of, write or utter in offhand way; **throw open** (often + *to*) cause to be suddenly or widely open, make accessible; **throw out** put out forcibly or suddenly, discard, reject; **throw over** desert, abandon; **throw up** abandon, resign from, vomit, erect hastily, bring to notice.

thrum ● *verb* (**-mm-**) play (stringed instrument) monotonously or unskilfully; (often + *on*) drum idly. ● *noun* such playing; resultant sound.

thrush[1] *noun* kind of songbird.

thrush[2] *noun* fungus infection of throat, esp. in children, or of vagina.

thrust ● *verb* (*past & past participle* **thrust**) push with sudden impulse or with force; (+ *on*) impose (thing) forcibly on; (+ *at, through*) pierce, stab, lunge suddenly; make (one's way) forcibly; (as **thrusting** *adjective*) aggressive, ambitious. ● *noun* sudden or forcible push or lunge; forward force exerted by propeller or jet etc.; strong attempt to penetrate enemy's line or territory; remark aimed at person; stress between parts of arch etc.; (often + *of*) theme, gist.

thud /θʌd/ ● *noun* low dull sound as of blow on nonresonant thing. ● *verb* (**-dd-**) make thud; fall with thud.

thug /θʌg/ *noun* vicious or brutal ruffian. □ **thuggery** *noun*; **thuggish** *adjective*.

thumb /θʌm/ ● *noun* short thick finger on hand, set apart from other 4; part of glove for thumb. ● *verb* soil or wear with thumb; turn over pages (as) with thumb; request or get (lift) by sticking out thumb. □ **thumb index** set of lettered grooves cut down side of book etc. for easy reference; **thumbnail** *noun* nail of thumb, *adjective* concise; **thumbscrew** instrument of torture for squeezing thumbs; **thumbs up, down** indication of approval or rejection; **under (person's) thumb** dominated by him or her.

thump /θʌmp/ ● *verb* beat heavily, esp. with fist; throb strongly; (+ *at, on*, etc.) knock loudly. ● *noun* (sound of) heavy blow.

thumping *adjective colloquial* huge.

thunder /ˈθʌndə/ ● *noun* loud noise accompanying lightning; resounding loud deep noise; strong censure. ● *verb* sound with or like thunder; move with loud noise, utter loudly; (+ *against* etc.) make violent threats. □ **thunderbolt** flash of lightning with

crash of thunder, unexpected occurrence or announcement, supposed bolt or shaft as destructive agent; **thunderclap** crash of thunder; **thundercloud** electrically charged cumulus cloud; **thunderstorm** storm with thunder and lightning; **thunderstruck** amazed. □ **thunderous** *adjective*; **thundery** *adjective*.

thundering *adjective colloquial* huge.

Thur. *abbreviation* (also **Thurs.**) Thursday.

thurible /ˈθjʊərɪb(ə)l/ *noun* censer.

Thursday /ˈθɜːzdeɪ/ *noun* day of week following Wednesday.

thus /ðʌs/ *adverb formal* in this way, like this; accordingly, as a result or inference; to this extent, so.

thwack ● *verb* hit with heavy blow. ● *noun* heavy blow.

thwart /θwɔːt/ ● *verb* frustrate, foil. ● *noun* rower's seat.

thy /ðaɪ/ *adjective* (also **thine**, esp. before vowel) *archaic* your (singular).

thyme /taɪm/ *noun* herb with aromatic leaves.

thymol /ˈθaɪmɒl/ *noun* antiseptic made from oil of thyme.

thymus /ˈθaɪməs/ *noun* (*plural* **thymi** /-maɪ/) ductless gland near base of neck.

thyroid /ˈθaɪrɔɪd/ *noun* thyroid gland. □ **thyroid cartilage** large cartilage of larynx forming Adam's apple; **thyroid gland** large ductless gland near larynx secreting hormone which regulates growth and development, extract of this.

thyself /ðaɪˈself/ *pronoun archaic: emphatic form of* THOU[1] *or* THEE; *reflexive form of* THEE.

ti = TE.

tiara /tɪˈɑːrə/ *noun* jewelled ornamental band worn on front of woman's hair; 3-crowned diadem formerly worn by pope.

tibia /ˈtɪbɪə/ *noun* (*plural* **tibiae** /-biː/) inner of two bones extending from knee to ankle.

tic *noun* (in full **nervous tic**) spasmodic contraction of muscles, esp. of face.

tick[1] ● *noun* slight recurring click, esp. of watch or clock; *colloquial* moment; small mark (✓) to denote correctness etc. ● *verb* make sound of tick; (often + *off*) mark with tick. □ **tick off** *colloquial* reprimand; **tick over** (of engine) idle, function at basic level; **tick-tack** kind of manual semaphore used by racecourse bookmakers; **tick-tock** ticking of large clock etc.

tick[2] *noun* parasitic arachnid or insect on animals.

tick[3] *noun colloquial* financial credit.

tick[4] *noun* case of mattress or pillow; ticking.

ticker *noun colloquial* heart; watch, *US* tape machine. □ **ticker-tape** paper strip from tape machine, esp. as thrown from windows to greet celebrity.

ticket /ˈtɪkɪt/ ● *noun* piece of paper or card entitling holder to enter place, participate in event, travel by public transport, etc.; notification of traffic offence etc.; certificate of discharge from army or of qualification as ship's master, pilot, etc.; price etc. label; *esp. US* list of candidates put forward by group, esp. political party, principles of party; (**the ticket**) *colloquial* what is needed. ● *verb* (**-t-**) attach ticket to.

ticking *noun* strong usually striped material to cover mattresses etc.

tickle /ˈtɪk(ə)l/ ● *verb* (**-ling**) touch or stroke lightly so as to produce laughter and spasmodic movement; excite agreeably, amuse; catch (trout etc.) by rubbing it so that it moves backwards into hand. ● *noun* act or sensation of tickling.

ticklish /ˈtɪklɪʃ/ *adjective* sensitive to tickling; difficult to handle.

tidal /'taɪd(ə)l/ *adjective* related to, like, or affected by tides. □ **tidal wave** exceptionally large ocean wave, esp. one caused by underwater earthquake, widespread manifestation of feeling etc.

tidbit *US* = TITBIT.

tiddler /'tɪdlə/ *noun colloquial* small fish, esp. stickleback or minnow; unusually small thing.

tiddly[1] /'tɪdlɪ/ *adjective* (**-ier, -iest**) *colloquial* slightly drunk.

tiddly[2] /'tɪdlɪ/ *adjective* (**-ier, -iest**) *colloquial* little.

tiddly-wink /'tɪdlɪwɪŋk/ *noun* counter flicked with another into cup; (in *plural*) this game.

tide ● *noun* regular rise and fall of sea due to attraction of moon and sun; water as moved by this; time, season; trend of opinion, fortune, or events. ● *verb* (**-ding**) (**tide over**) temporarily provide with what is needed. □ **tidemark** mark made by tide at high water, *colloquial* line of dirt round bath, or on person's body between washed and unwashed parts; **tideway** tidal part of river.

tidings /'taɪdɪŋz/ *noun archaic or jocular* (treated as *singular* or *plural*) news.

tidy /'taɪdɪ/ ● *adjective* (**-ier, -iest**) neat, orderly; (of person) methodical; *colloquial* considerable. ● *noun* (*plural* **-ies**) receptacle for odds and ends. ● *verb* (**-ies, -ied**) (often + *up*) make (oneself, room, etc.) tidy; put in order. □ **tidily** *adverb*; **tidiness** *noun*.

tie ● *verb* (**tying**) attach or fasten with cord etc.; form into knot or bow; (often + *down*) restrict, bind; (often + *with*) make same score as another competitor; bind (rafters etc.) by crosspiece etc.; *Music* unite (notes) by tie. ● *noun* cord etc. used for fastening; strip of material worn round collar and tied in knot at front; thing that unites or restricts people; equality of score, draw, or dead heat among competitors; match between any pair of players or teams; rod or beam holding parts of structure together; *Music* curved line above or below two notes of same pitch that are to be joined as one. □ **tie-break, -breaker** means of deciding winner when competitors have tied; **tie-dye** method of producing dyed patterns by tying string etc. to keep dye from parts of fabric; **tie-pin** ornamental pin to hold necktie in place; **tie up** fasten with cord etc., invest (money etc.) so that it is not immediately available for use, fully occupy (person), bring to satisfactory conclusion; **tie-up** connection, association.

tied *adjective* (of dwelling house) occupied subject to tenant's working for house's owner; (of public house etc.) bound to supply only particular brewer's liquor.

tier /tɪə/ *noun* row, rank, or unit of structure, as one of several placed one above another. □ **tiered** *adjective*.

tiercel = TERCEL.

tiff *noun* slight or petty quarrel.

tiger /'taɪgə/ *noun* large Asian animal of cat family, with yellow-brown coat with black stripes; fierce, formidable, or energetic person. □ **tiger-cat** any moderate-sized feline resembling tiger; **tiger lily** tall garden lily with dark-spotted orange flowers.

tight /taɪt/ ● *adjective* closely held, drawn, fastened, fitting, etc.; impermeable, impervious; tense, stretched; *colloquial* drunk; *colloquial* stingy; (of money or materials) not easily obtainable; stringent, demanding; presenting difficulties; produced by or requiring great exertion or pressure. ● *adverb* tightly. □ **tight corner** difficult situation; **tight-fisted** stingy; **tight-lipped** restraining emotion, determinedly reticent; **tightrope** high tightly stretched rope or wire on which acrobats etc. perform. □ **tighten** *verb*; **tightly** *adverb*; **tightness** *noun*.

tights *plural noun* thin close-fitting stretch garment covering legs, feet, and lower torso.

tigress /'taɪgrɪs/ *noun* female tiger.

tilde /'tɪldə/ *noun* mark (˜) placed over letter, e.g. Spanish *n* in *señor*.

tile ● *noun* thin slab of concrete, baked clay, etc. for roofing, paving, etc. ● *verb* (**-ling**) cover with tiles. □ **tiler** *noun*.

tiling *noun* process of fixing tiles; area of tiles.

till[1] ● *preposition* up to, as late as. ● *conjunction* up to time when; so long that.

■ **Usage** In all senses, *till* can be replaced by *until*, which is more formal in style.

till[2] *noun* money-drawer in bank, shop, etc., esp. with device recording amount and details of each purchase.

till[3] *verb* cultivate (land).

tillage *noun* preparation of land for growing crops; tilled land.

tiller /'tɪlə/ *noun* bar by which boat's rudder is turned.

tilt ● *verb* (cause to) assume sloping position or heel over; (+ *at*) thrust or run at with weapon; (+ *with*) engage in contest. ● *noun* tilting; sloping position; (of medieval knights etc.) charging with lance against opponent or mark. □ (**at**) **full tilt** at full speed, with full force.

tilth *noun* tillage, cultivation; cultivated soil.

timber /'tɪmbə/ *noun* wood for building, carpentry, etc.; piece of wood, beam, esp. as rib of vessel; large standing trees; (as *interjection*) tree is about to fall.

timbered *adjective* made (partly) of timber; (of land) wooded.

timbre /'tæmbə/ *noun* distinctive character of musical sound or voice apart from its pitch and volume.

timbrel /'tɪmbr(ə)l/ *noun archaic* tambourine.

time ● *noun* indefinite continuous progress of past, present, and future events etc. regarded as a whole; more or less definite portion of this, historical or other period; allotted or available portion of time; definite or fixed point or portion of time; (**a time**) indefinite period; occasion; moment etc. suitable for purpose; (in *plural*) (after numeral etc.) expressing *multiplication*; lifetime; (in *singular* or *plural*) conditions of life or of period; *slang* prison sentence; apprenticeship; date or expected date of childbirth or death; measured amount of time worked; rhythm or measure of musical composition. ● *verb* (**-ming**) choose time for, do at chosen or appropriate time; ascertain time taken by. □ **at the same time** simultaneously, nevertheless; **at times** now and then; **from time to time** occasionally; **in no time** rapidly, in a moment; **in time** not late, early enough, eventually, following time of music etc.; **on time** punctually; **time-and-motion** measuring efficiency of industrial etc. operations; **time bomb** one designed to explode at pre-set time; **time capsule** box etc. containing objects typical of present time, buried for future discovery; **time-honoured** esteemed by tradition or through custom; **timekeeper** person who records time, watch or clock as regards accuracy; **timekeeping** keeping of time, punctuality; **time-lag** interval between cause and effect; **time off** time used for rest or different activity; **timepiece** clock, watch; **time-server** person who adapts his or her opinions to suit prevailing circumstances; **time-share** share in property under time-sharing scheme; **time-sharing** use of holiday home by several joint owners at different times of year, use of computer by several people for different operations at the same time; **time sheet** sheet of paper for recording hours worked; **time-shift** move from one time to another; **time signal** audible indication of exact time of day; **time signature** *Music* indication of rhythm; **time switch** one operating automatically at preset time;

timetable *noun* table showing times of public transport services, scheme of lessons, etc., *verb* include or arrange in such schedule; **time zone** range of longitudes where a common standard time is used.

timeless *adjective* not affected by passage of time. □ **timelessness** *noun*.

timely *adjective* (**-ier, -iest**) opportune, coming at right time. □ **timeliness** *noun*.

timer person or device that measures time taken.

timid /ˈtɪmɪd/ *adjective* (**-er, -est**) easily alarmed; shy. □ **timidity** /-ˈmɪd-/ *noun*; **timidly** *adverb*.

timing *noun* way thing is timed; regulation of opening and closing of valves in internal-combustion engine.

timorous /ˈtɪmərəs/ *adjective* timid, frightened. □ **timorously** *adverb*.

timpani /ˈtɪmpənɪ/ *plural noun* (also **tympani**) kettledrums. □ **timpanist** *noun*.

tin *noun* silvery-white metal used esp. in alloys and in making tin plate; container of tin or tin plate, esp. for preserving food; tin plate. ● *verb* (**-nn-**) preserve (food) in tin; cover or coat with tin. □ **tin foil** foil of tin, aluminium, or tin alloy, used to wrap food; **tin hat** *colloquial* military steel helmet; **tin-opener** tool for opening tins; **tin-pan alley** world of composers and publishers of popular music; **tin plate** sheet steel coated with tin; **tinpot** cheap, inferior; **tinsnips** clippers for cutting sheet metal; **tin-tack** tack[1] coated with tin.

tincture /ˈtɪŋktʃə/ ● *noun* (often + *of*) slight flavour or tinge; medicinal solution of drug in alcohol. ● *verb* (**-ring**) colour slightly, tinge, flavour; (often + *with*) affect slightly.

tinder /ˈtɪndə/ *noun* dry substance readily taking fire from spark. □ **tinder-box** *historical* box with tinder, flint, and steel for kindling fires.

tine *noun* prong, tooth, or point of fork, comb, antler, etc.

ting ● *noun* tinkling sound as of bell. ● *verb* (cause to) emit this.

tinge /tɪndʒ/ ● *verb* (**-ging**) (often + *with*; often in *passive*) colour slightly. ● *noun* tendency to or trace of some colour; slight admixture of feeling or quality.

tingle /ˈtɪŋg(ə)l/ ● *verb* (**-ling**) feel or cause slight pricking or stinging sensation. ● *noun* tingling sensation.

tinker /ˈtɪŋkə/ ● *noun* itinerant mender of kettles, pans, etc.; *Scottish & Irish* Gypsy; *colloquial* mischievous person or animal. ● *verb* (+ *at, with*) work in amateurish or desultory way; work as tinker.

tinkle /ˈtɪŋk(ə)l/ ● *verb* (**-ling**) (cause to) make short light ringing sounds. ● *noun* tinkling sound.

tinnitus /ˈtɪnɪtəs/ *noun Medicine* condition with ringing in ears.

tinny *adjective* (**-ier, -iest**) like tin; flimsy; (of sound) thin and metallic.

tinsel /ˈtɪns(ə)l/ *noun* glittering decorative metallic strips, threads, etc.; superficial brilliance or splendour. □ **tinselled** *adjective*.

tint ● *noun* a variety of a colour; tendency towards or admixture of a different colour; faint colour spread over surface. ● *verb* apply tint to, colour.

tintinnabulation /tɪntɪnæbjʊˈleɪʃ(ə)n/ *noun* ringing of bells.

tiny /ˈtaɪnɪ/ *adjective* (**-ier, -iest**) very small.

tip[1] ● *noun* extremity, esp. of small or tapering thing; small piece or part attached to end of thing. ● *verb* (**-pp-**) provide with tip. □ **tiptop** *colloquial* first-rate, of highest excellence.

tip[2] ● *verb* (**-pp-**) (often + *over, up*) (cause to) lean or slant; (+ *into* etc.) overturn, cause to overbalance, discharge contents of (container etc.) thus. ● *noun* slight push or tilt; place where refuse is tipped.

tip[3] ● *verb* (**-pp-**) give small present of money to, esp. for service; name as likely winner of race or contest; strike or touch lightly. ● *noun* small present of money given esp. for service; piece of private or special information, esp. regarding betting or investment; piece of advice. □ **tip-off** a hint, warning, etc.; **tip off** give warning, hint, or inside information to.

tippet /ˈtɪpɪt/ *noun* cape or collar of fur etc.

tipple /ˈtɪp(ə)l/ ● *verb* (**-ling**) drink intoxicating liquor habitually or repeatedly in small quantities. ● *noun colloquial* alcoholic drink. □ **tippler** *noun*.

tipster /ˈtɪpstə/ *noun* person who gives tips about horse racing etc.

tipsy /ˈtɪpsɪ/ *adjective* (**-ier, -iest**) slightly drunk; caused by or showing intoxication.

tiptoe /ˈtɪptəʊ/ ● *noun* the tips of the toes. ● *verb* (**-toes, -toed, -toeing**) walk on tiptoe or stealthily. ● *adverb* (also **on tiptoe**) with heels off the ground.

TIR *abbreviation* international road transport (*transport international routier*).

tirade /taɪˈreɪd/ *noun* long vehement denunciation or declamation.

tire[1] /taɪə/ *verb* (**-ring**) make or grow weary; exhaust patience or interest of; (in *passive*; + *of*) have had enough of.

tire[2] *US* = TYRE.

tired *adjective* weary, ready for sleep; (of idea) hackneyed. □ **tiredly** *adverb*; **tiredness** *noun*.

tireless *adjective* not tiring easily, energetic. □ **tirelessly** *adverb*; **tirelessness** *noun*.

tiresome *adjective* tedious; *colloquial* annoying. □ **tiresomely** *adverb*.

tiro /ˈtaɪərəʊ/ *noun* (also **tyro**) (*plural* **-s**) beginner, novice.

tissue /ˈtɪʃuː/ *noun* any of the coherent collections of cells of which animals or plants are made; tissue-paper; disposable piece of thin absorbent paper for wiping, drying, etc.; fine woven esp. gauzy fabric; (often + *of*) connected series (of lies etc.). □ **tissue-paper** thin soft paper for wrapping etc.

tit[1] *noun* any of various small birds.

tit[2] *noun* □ **tit for tat** blow for blow, retaliation.

Titan /ˈtaɪt(ə)n/ *noun* (often **titan**) person of superhuman strength, intellect, or importance.

titanic /taɪˈtænɪk/ *adjective* gigantic, colossal.

titanium /taɪˈteɪnɪəm/ *noun* dark grey metallic element.

titbit /ˈtɪtbɪt/ *noun* (*US* **tidbit**) dainty morsel; piquant item of news etc.

titchy /ˈtɪtʃɪ/ *adjective* (**-ier, -iest**) *colloquial* very small.

tithe /taɪð/ *historical* ● *noun* one-tenth of annual produce of land or labour taken as tax for Church. ● *verb* (**-thing**) subject to tithes; pay tithes.

Titian /ˈtɪʃ(ə)n/ *adjective* (of hair) bright auburn.

titillate /ˈtɪtɪleɪt/ *verb* (**-ting**) excite, esp. sexually; tickle. □ **titillation** *noun*.

titivate /ˈtɪtɪveɪt/ *verb* (**-ting**) *colloquial* smarten; put finishing touches to. □ **titivation** *noun*.

title /ˈtaɪt(ə)l/ *noun* name of book, work of art, etc.; heading of chapter etc.; title-page; caption or credit in film etc.; name denoting person's status; championship in sport; legal right to ownership of property; (+ *to*) just or recognized claim to. □ **title-deed** legal document constituting evidence of a right; **title-holder** person holding (esp. sporting) title; **title-page** page at beginning of book giving title, author, etc.; **title role** part in play etc. from which its title is taken.

titled *adjective* having title of nobility or rank.

titmouse /ˈtɪtmaʊs/ *noun* (*plural* **titmice**) small active tit.

titrate /taɪˈtreɪt/ *verb* (**-ting**) ascertain quantity of constituent in (solution) by adding measured amounts of reagent. □ **titration** *noun*.

titter /ˈtɪtə/ ● *verb* laugh covertly, giggle. ● *noun* covert laugh.

tittle /ˈtɪt(ə)l/ *noun* particle, whit.

tittle-tattle /ˈtɪt(ə)ltæt(ə)l/ *noun & verb* (**-ling**) gossip, chatter.

tittup /ˈtɪtəp/ ● *verb* (**-p-** or **-pp-**) go friskily or jerkily, bob up and down, canter. ● *noun* such gait or movement.

titular /ˈtɪtjʊlə/ *adjective* of or relating to title; existing or being in name only.

tizzy /ˈtɪzɪ/ *noun* (*plural* **-ies**) *colloquial* state of nervous agitation.

TNT *abbreviation* trinitrotoluene.

to /tə, before vowel tʊ, when stressed tuː/ ● *preposition* in direction of; as far as, not short of; according to; compared with; involved in, comprising; *used to introduce indirect object of verb etc., to introduce or as substitute for infinitive, or to express purpose, consequence, or cause.* ● *adverb* in normal or required position or condition; (of door) nearly closed. □ **to and fro** backwards and forwards, (repeatedly) from place to place; **to-do** fuss, commotion; **toing and froing** constant movement to and fro, great or dispersed activity.

toad *noun* froglike amphibian breeding in water but living chiefly on land; repulsive person. □ **toadflax** plant with yellow or purple flowers; **toad-in-the-hole** sausages baked in batter; **toadstool** fungus (usually poisonous) with round top and slender stalk.

toady /ˈtəʊdɪ/ ● *noun* (*plural* **-ies**) sycophant. ● *verb* (**-ies**, **-ied**) (+ *to*) behave servilely to, fawn on. □ **toadyism** *noun*.

toast ● *noun* sliced bread browned on both sides by radiant heat; person or thing in whose honour company is requested to drink; call to drink or instance of drinking thus. ● *verb* brown by heat, warm at fire etc.; drink to the health or in honour of. □ **toasting-fork** long-handled fork for toasting bread etc.; **toastmaster**, **toastmistress** person announcing toasts at public occasion; **toast rack** rack for holding slices of toast at table.

toaster *noun* electrical device for making toast.

tobacco /təˈbækəʊ/ *noun* (*plural* **-s**) plant of American origin with leaves used for smoking, chewing, or snuff; its leaves, esp. as prepared for smoking.

tobacconist /təˈbækənɪst/ *noun* dealer in tobacco.

toboggan /təˈbɒgən/ ● *noun* long light narrow sledge for sliding downhill, esp. over snow. ● *verb* ride on toboggan.

toby jug /ˈtəʊbɪ/ *noun* jug or mug in shape of stout man in 3-cornered hat.

toccata /təˈkɑːtə/ *noun* Music composition for keyboard instrument, designed to exhibit performer's touch and technique.

tocsin /ˈtɒksɪn/ *noun* alarm bell or signal.

today /təˈdeɪ/ ● *adverb* on this present day; nowadays. ● *noun* this present day; modern times.

toddle /ˈtɒd(ə)l/ ● *verb* (**-ling**) walk with young child's short unsteady steps; *colloquial* walk, stroll, (usually + *off*, *along*) depart. ● *noun* toddling walk.

toddler *noun* child just learning to walk.

toddy /ˈtɒdɪ/ *noun* (*plural* **-ies**) sweetened drink of spirits and hot water.

toe ● *noun* any of terminal projections of foot or paw; part of footwear that covers toes; lower end or tip of implement etc. ● *verb* (**toes**, **toed**, **toeing**) touch with toe(s). □ **on one's toes** alert; **toecap** (reinforced) part of boot or shoe covering toes; **toehold** slight foothold, small beginning or advantage; **toe the line** conform, esp. under pressure; **toenail** nail of each toe.

toff *noun slang* upper-class person.

toffee /ˈtɒfɪ/ *noun* firm or hard sweet made of boiled butter, sugar, etc.; this substance. □ **toffee-apple** toffee-coated apple; **toffee-nosed** *slang* snobbish, pretentious.

tofu /ˈtəʊfuː/ *noun* curd of mashed soya beans.

tog¹ *colloquial* ● *noun* (in *plural*) clothes. ● *verb* (**-gg-**) (+ *out*, *up*) dress.

tog² *noun* unit of thermal resistance of quilts etc.

toga /ˈtəʊgə/ *noun historical* ancient Roman citizen's loose flowing outer garment.

together /təˈgeðə/ ● *adverb* in(to) company or conjunction; simultaneously; one with another; uninterruptedly. ● *adjective colloquial* well-organized, self-assured, emotionally stable. □ **togetherness** *noun*.

toggle /ˈtɒg(ə)l/ *noun* short bar used like button for fastening clothes; Computing key or command which alternately switches function on and off.

toil ● *verb* work laboriously or incessantly; make slow painful progress. ● *noun* labour; drudgery. □ **toilsome** *adjective*.

toilet /ˈtɔɪlɪt/ *noun* lavatory; process of washing oneself, dressing, etc. □ **toilet paper** paper for cleaning oneself after using lavatory; **toilet roll** roll of toilet paper; **toilet water** dilute perfume used after washing.

toiletries /ˈtɔɪlɪtriːz/ *plural noun* articles or cosmetics used in washing, dressing, etc.

toilette /twɑːˈlet/ *noun* process of washing oneself, dressing, etc.

toils /tɔɪlz/ *plural noun* net, snare.

token /ˈtəʊkən/ *noun* symbol, reminder, mark; voucher; thing equivalent to something else, esp. money. ● *adjective* perfunctory, chosen by tokenism to represent a group. □ **token strike** brief strike to demonstrate strength of feeling.

tokenism *noun* granting of minimum concessions.

told *past & past participle of* TELL.

tolerable /ˈtɒlərəb(ə)l/ *adjective* endurable; fairly good. □ **tolerably** *adverb*.

tolerance /ˈtɒlərəns/ *noun* willingness or ability to tolerate; permitted variation in dimension, weight, etc.

tolerant /ˈtɒlərənt/ *adjective* disposed to tolerate others; (+ *of*) enduring or patient of.

tolerate /ˈtɒləreɪt/ *verb* (**-ting**) allow the existence or occurrence of without authoritative interference; endure; find or treat as endurable; be able to take or undergo without harm. □ **toleration** *noun*.

toll¹ /təʊl/ *noun* charge to use bridge, road, etc.; cost or damage caused by disaster etc. □ **toll-gate** barrier preventing passage until toll is paid.

toll² /təʊl/ ● *verb* (of bell) ring with slow uniform strokes, ring (bell) thus; announce or mark (death etc.) thus; (of bell) strike (the hour). ● *noun* tolling or stroke of bell.

toluene /ˈtɒljuːiːn/ *noun* colourless liquid hydrocarbon used in manufacture of explosives etc.

tom *noun* (in full **tom-cat**) male cat.

tomahawk /ˈtɒməhɔːk/ *noun* N. American Indian war-axe.

tomato /təˈmɑːtəʊ/ *noun* (*plural* **-es**) glossy red or yellow fleshy edible fruit; plant bearing this.

tomb /tuːm/ *noun* burial-vault; grave; sepulchral monument. □ **tombstone** memorial stone over grave.

tombola /tɒmˈbəʊlə/ *noun* kind of lottery.

tomboy /'tɒmbɔɪ/ *noun* girl who enjoys rough noisy recreations. □ **tomboyish** *adjective*.

tome *noun* large book or volume.

tomfool /tɒm'fuːl/ ● *noun* fool. ● *adjective* foolish. □ **tomfoolery** *noun*.

Tommy /'tɒmɪ/ *noun* (*plural* **-ies**) *colloquial* British private soldier.

tommy-gun /'tɒmɪɡʌn/ *noun* sub-machine-gun.

tomorrow /tə'mɒrəʊ/ ● *adverb* on day after today; in future. ● *noun* the day after today; the near future.

tomtit *noun* tit, esp. blue tit.

tom-tom /'tɒmtɒm/ *noun* kind of drum usually beaten with hands.

ton /tʌn/ *noun* measure of weight equalling 2,240 lb (**long ton**) or 2,000 lb (**short ton**); metric ton; unit of measurement of ship's tonnage; (usually in *plural* *colloquial* large number or amount; *slang* speed of 100 m.p.h., score of 100.

tonal /'təʊn(ə)l/ *adjective* of or relating to tone or tonality.

tonality /tə'nælɪtɪ/ *noun* (*plural* **-ies**) relationship between tones of a musical scale; observance of single tonic key as basis of musical composition; colour scheme of picture.

tone ● *noun* sound, esp. with reference to pitch, quality, and strength; (often in *plural*) modulation of voice to express emotion etc.; manner of expression in writing or speaking; musical sound, esp. of definite pitch and character; general effect of colour or of light and shade in picture; tint or shade of colour; prevailing character of morals, sentiments, etc.; proper firmness of body, state of (good) health. ● *verb* (**-ning**) give desired tone to; alter tone of; harmonize. □ **tone-deaf** unable to perceive differences in musical pitch; **tone down** make or become softer in tone; **tone up** make or become stronger in tone. □ **toneless** *adjective*; **tonelessly** *adverb*; **toner** *noun*.

tongs *plural noun* implement with two arms for grasping coal, sugar, etc.

tongue /tʌŋ/ ● *noun* muscular organ in mouth used in tasting, swallowing, speaking, etc.; tongue of ox etc. as food; faculty or manner of speaking; particular language; thing like tongue in shape. ● *verb* (**-guing**) use tongue to articulate (notes) in playing wind instrument. □ **tongue-in-cheek** ironic(ally); **tongue-tied** too shy to speak; **tongue-twister** sequence of words difficult to pronounce quickly and correctly.

tonic /'tɒnɪk/ ● *noun* invigorating medicine; anything serving to invigorate; tonic water; *Music* keynote. ● *adjective* invigorating. □ **tonic sol-fa** musical notation used esp. in teaching singing; **tonic water** carbonated drink with quinine.

tonight /tə'naɪt/ ● *adverb* on present or approaching evening or night. ● *noun* the evening or night of today.

tonnage /'tʌnɪdʒ/ *noun* ship's internal cubic capacity or freight-carrying capacity; charge per ton on freight or cargo.

tonne /tʌn/ *noun* 1,000 kg.

tonsil /'tɒns(ə)l/ *noun* either of two small organs on each side of root of tongue.

tonsillectomy /tɒnsɪ'lektəmɪ/ *noun* (*plural* **-ies**) surgical removal of tonsils.

tonsillitis /tɒnsə'laɪtɪs/ *noun* inflammation of tonsils.

tonsorial /tɒn'sɔːrɪəl/ *adjective usually jocular* of hairdresser or hairdressing.

tonsure /'tɒnʃə/ ● *noun* shaving of crown or of whole head as clerical or monastic symbol; bare patch so made. ● *verb* (**-ring**) give tonsure to.

too *adverb* to a greater extent than is desirable or permissible; *colloquial* very; in addition; moreover.

took *past of* TAKE.

tool /tuːl/ ● *noun* implement for working on something by hand or by machine; thing used in activity; person merely used by another. ● *verb* dress (stone) with chisel; impress design on (leather); (+ *along*, *around*, etc.) *slang* drive or ride esp. in a casual or leisurely way.

toot /tuːt/ ● *noun* sound (as) of horn etc. ● *verb* sound (horn etc.); give out such sound.

tooth /tuːθ/ *noun* (*plural* **teeth**) each of a set of hard structures in jaws of most vertebrates, used for biting and chewing; toothlike part or projection, e.g. cog of gearwheel, point of saw or comb, etc.; (often + *for*) taste, appetite; (in *plural*) force, effectiveness. □ **fight tooth and nail** fight fiercely; **get one's teeth into** devote oneself seriously to; **in the teeth of** in spite of, contrary to, directly against (wind etc.); **toothache** pain in teeth; **toothbrush** brush for cleaning teeth; **toothpaste** paste for cleaning teeth; **toothpick** small sharp stick for removing food lodged between teeth. □ **toothed** *adjective*; **toothless** *adjective*.

toothsome *adjective* (of food) delicious.

toothy *adjective* (**-ier**, **-iest**) having large, numerous, or prominent teeth.

tootle /'tuːt(ə)l/ *verb* (**-ling**) toot gently or repeatedly; (usually + *around*, *along*, etc.) *colloquial* move casually.

top¹ ● *noun* highest point or part; highest rank or place, person occupying this; upper end, head; upper surface, upper part; cover or cap of container etc.; garment for upper part of body; utmost degree, height; (in *plural*) *colloquial* person or thing of best quality; (esp. in *plural*) leaves etc. of plant grown chiefly for its root; *Nautical* platform round head of lower mast. ● *adjective* highest in position, degree, or importance. ● *verb* (**-pp-**) furnish with top, cap, etc.; be higher or better than, surpass, be at or reach top of; *slang* kill, hit golf ball above centre. □ **on top of** fully in command of, very close to, in addition to; **top brass** *colloquial* high-ranking officers; **topcoat** overcoat, final coat of paint etc.; **top dog** *colloquial* victor, master; **top drawer** *colloquial* high social position or origin; **top dress** apply fertilizer on top of (earth) without ploughing it in; **top-flight** of highest rank of achievement; **top hat** tall silk hat; **top-heavy** overweighted at top; **topknot** knot, tuft, crest, or bow worn or growing on top of head; **topmast** mast on top of lower mast; **top-notch** *colloquial* first-rate; **top secret** of utmost secrecy; **topside** outer side of round of beef, side of ship above waterline; **topsoil** top layer of soil; **top up** complete (amount), fill up (partly empty container); **top-up** addition, amount that completes or quantity that fills something. □ **topmost** *adjective*.

top² *noun* toy spinning on point when set in motion.

topaz /'təʊpæz/ *noun* semiprecious transparent stone, usually yellow.

tope *verb* (**-ping**) *archaic or literary* drink alcohol to excess, esp. habitually. □ **toper** *noun*.

topi /'təʊpɪ/ *noun* (also **topee**) (*plural* **-s**) hat, esp sun-helmet.

topiary /'təʊpɪərɪ/ ● *adjective* of or formed by clipping shrubs, trees, etc. into ornamental shapes. ● *noun* topiary art.

topic /'tɒpɪk/ *noun* subject of discourse, conversation, or argument.

topical *adjective* dealing with current affairs, etc. □ **topicality** /-'kæl-/ *noun*.

topless *adjective* without a top; (of garment) leaving breasts bare; (of woman) bare-breasted; (of place) where women go or work bare-breasted.

topography /tə'pɒgrəfɪ/ *noun* detailed description, representation, etc. of features of a district; such features. □ **topographer** *noun*; **topographical** /tɒpə'græf-/ *adjective*.

topology /tə'pɒlədʒɪ/ *noun* study of geometrical properties unaffected by changes of shape or size. □ **topological** /tɒpə'lɒdʒ-/ *adjective*.

topper *noun colloquial* top hat.

topping *noun* thing that tops, esp. sauce on dessert etc.

topple /'tɒp(ə)l/ *verb* (**-ling**) (often + *over*, *down*) (cause to) fall as if top-heavy; overthrow.

topsy-turvy /tɒpsɪ'tɜːvɪ/ *adverb & adjective* upside down; in utter confusion.

toque /təʊk/ *noun* woman's close-fitting brimless hat.

tor *noun* hill, rocky peak.

torch *noun* battery-powered portable lamp; thing lit for illumination; source of heat, light, or enlightenment. □ **carry a torch for** have (esp. unreturned) love for.

tore *past of* TEAR[1].

toreador /'tɒrɪədɔː/ *noun* bullfighter, esp. on horseback.

torment ● *noun* /'tɔːment/ (cause of) severe bodily or mental suffering. ● *verb* /tɔː'ment/ subject to torment, tease or worry excessively. □ **tormentor** /-'men-/ *noun*.

torn *past participle of* TEAR[1].

tornado /tɔː'neɪdəʊ/ *noun* (*plural* **-es**) violent storm over small area, with whirling winds.

torpedo /tɔː'piːdəʊ/ ● *noun* (*plural* **-es**) cigar-shaped self-propelled underwater or aerial missile that explodes on hitting ship. ● *verb* (**-es**, **-ed**) destroy or attack with torpedo(es); make ineffective. □ **torpedo boat** small fast warship armed with torpedoes.

torpid /'tɔːpɪd/ *adjective* sluggish, apathetic; numb; dormant. □ **torpidity** /-'pɪd-/ *noun*.

torpor /'tɔːpə/ *noun* torpid condition.

torque /tɔːk/ *noun* twisting or rotary force, esp. in machine; *historical* twisted metal necklace worn by ancient Gauls and Britons.

torrent /'tɒrənt/ *noun* rushing stream of liquid; downpour of rain; (in *plural*) (usually + *of*) violent flow. □ **torrential** /tə'ren(t)ʃ(ə)l/ *adjective*.

torrid /'tɒrɪd/ *adjective* intensely hot; scorched, parched; passionate, intense.

torsion /'tɔːʃ(ə)n/ *noun* twisting. □ **torsional** *adjective*.

torso /'tɔːsəʊ/ *noun* (*plural* **-s**) trunk of human body; statue of this.

tort *noun* breach of legal duty (other than under contract) with liability for damages. □ **tortious** /'tɔːʃəs/ *adjective*.

tortilla /tɔː'tiːjə/ *noun* thin flat originally Mexican maize cake eaten hot.

tortoise /'tɔːtəs/ *noun* slow-moving reptile with horny domed shell. □ **tortoiseshell** mottled yellowish-brown turtle-shell, cat or butterfly with markings resembling tortoiseshell.

tortuous /'tɔːtʃʊəs/ *adjective* winding; devious, circuitous. □ **tortuously** *adverb*.

torture /'tɔːtʃə/ ● *noun* infliction of severe bodily pain, esp. as punishment or means of persuasion; severe physical or mental pain. ● *verb* (**-ring**) subject to torture. □ **torturer** *noun*; **torturous** *adjective*.

Tory /'tɔːrɪ/ *colloquial* ● *noun* (*plural* **-ies**) member of Conservative party. ● *adjective* Conservative. □ **Toryism** *noun*.

tosa /'təʊsə/ *noun* dog of a mastiff breed.

tosh *noun colloquial* rubbish, nonsense.

toss ● *verb* throw up, esp. with hand; roll about, throw, or be thrown, restlessly or from side to side; throw lightly or carelessly; throw (coin) into air to decide choice etc. by way it falls, (often + *for*) settle question or dispute with (person) thus; (of bull etc.) fling up with horns; coat (food) with dressing etc. by shaking it. ● *noun* tossing; fall, esp. from horseback. □ **toss one's head** throw it back, esp. in anger, impatience, etc.; **toss off** drink off at a draught, dispatch (work) rapidly or easily; **toss up** *verb* toss coin; **toss-up** *noun* doubtful matter, tossing of coin.

tot[1] *noun* small child; dram of liquor.

tot[2] *verb* (**-tt-**) (usually + *up*) add, mount. □ **tot up to** amount to.

total /'təʊt(ə)l/ ● *adjective* complete, comprising the whole; absolute, unqualified. ● *noun* whole sum or amount. ● *verb* (**-ll-**; *US* **-l-**) (often + *to*, *up to*) amount to; calculate total of. □ **totality** /-'tæl-/ *noun* (*plural* **-ies**); **totally** *adverb*.

totalitarian /təʊtælɪ'teərɪən/ *adjective* of one-party government requiring complete subservience to state. □ **totalitarianism** *noun*.

totalizator /'təʊtəlaɪzeɪtə/ *noun* (also **totalisator**) device showing number and amount of bets staked on race when total will be divided among those betting on winner; this betting system.

totalize /'təʊtəlaɪz/ *verb* (also **-ise**) (**-zing** or **-sing**) combine into a total.

tote[1] *noun slang* totalizator.

tote[2] *verb* (**-ting**) *esp. US colloquial* carry, convey. □ **tote bag** large and capacious bag.

totem /'təʊtəm/ *noun* natural object (esp. animal) adopted esp. among N. American Indians as emblem of clan or individual; image of this. □ **totem-pole** post with carved and painted or hung totem(s).

toto see IN TOTO.

totter /'tɒtə/ ● *verb* stand or walk unsteadily or feebly; shake, be about to fall. ● *noun* unsteady or shaky movement or gait. □ **tottery** *adjective*.

toucan /'tuːkən/ *noun* tropical American bird with large bill.

touch /tʌtʃ/ ● *verb* come into or be in physical contact with; (often + *with*) bring hand etc. into contact with; cause (two things) to meet thus; rouse tender or painful feelings in; strike lightly; (usually in negative) disturb, harm, affect, have dealings with, consume, use; concern; reach as far as; (usually in negative) approach in excellence; modify; (as **touched** *adjective*) *colloquial* slightly mad; (usually + *for*) *slang* request and get money etc. from (person). ● *noun* act of touching; sense of feeling; small amount, trace; (**a touch**) slightly; *Music* manner of playing keys or strings, instrument's response to this; artistic, literary, etc. style or skill; *slang* act of requesting and getting money etc. from person; *Football* part of field outside touchlines. □ **touch-and-go** critical, risky; **touch at** *Nautical* call at (port etc.); **touch down** (of aircraft) alight; **touchdown** *noun*; **touchline** side limit of football etc. pitch; **touch off** explode by touching with match etc., initiate (process) suddenly; **touch on, upon** refer to or mention briefly or casually, verge on; **touch-paper** paper impregnated with nitre for igniting fireworks etc.; **touchstone** dark schist or jasper for testing alloys by marking it with them, criterion; **touch-type** type without looking at keys; **touch-typist** *noun*; **touch up** give finishing touches to, retouch; *slang* molest sexually; **touch wood** touch something wooden to avert ill luck; **touchwood** readily inflammable rotten wood.

touché /tuː'ʃeɪ/ *interjection* acknowledging justified accusation or retort, or hit in fencing. [French]

touching ● *adjective* moving, pathetic. ● *preposition literary* concerning. □ **touchingly** *adverb*.

touchy *adjective* (**-ier**, **-iest**) apt to take offence, over-sensitive. □ **touchily** *adverb*; **touchiness** *noun*.

tough /tʌf/ ● *adjective* hard to break, cut, tear, or chew; able to endure hardship, hardy; stubborn, difficult; *colloquial* acting sternly, (of luck etc.) hard; *colloquial* criminal, violent. ● *noun* tough person, esp. ruffian. □ **toughen** *verb*; **toughness** *noun*.

toupee /'tuːpeɪ/ *noun* hairpiece to cover bald spot.

tour /tʊə/ ● *noun* holiday journey or excursion including stops at various places; walk round, inspection; spell of military or diplomatic duty; series of performances, matches, etc. at different places. ● *verb* (often + *through*) go on a tour; make a tour of (country etc.). □ **on tour** (esp. of sports team, theatre company, etc.) touring; **tour operator** travel agent specializing in package holidays.

tour de force /tʊə də 'fɔːs/ *noun* (*plural* **tours de force** same pronunciation) outstanding feat or performance. [French]

tourer *noun* car or caravan for touring in.

tourism *noun* commercial organization and operation of holidays.

tourist *noun* holiday traveller; member of touring sports team. □ **tourist class** lowest class of passenger accommodation in ship, aeroplane, etc.

tourmaline /'tʊəməliːn/ *noun* mineral with unusual electric properties and used as gem.

tournament /'tʊənəmənt/ *noun* large contest of many rounds; display of military exercises; *historical* pageant with jousting.

tournedos /'tʊənədəʊ/ *noun* (*plural* same /-dəʊz/) small thick piece of fillet of beef.

tourney /'tʊənɪ/ *noun* (*plural* **-s**) tournament. ● *verb* (**-eys, -eyed**) take part in tournament.

tourniquet /'tʊənɪkeɪ/ *noun* device for stopping flow of blood through artery by compression.

tousle /'taʊz(ə)l/ *verb* (**-ling**) make (esp. hair) untidy; handle roughly.

tout /taʊt/ ● *verb* (usually + *for*) solicit custom persistently, pester customers; solicit custom of or for; spy on racehorses in training. ● *noun* person who touts.

tow[1] /təʊ/ ● *verb* pull along by rope etc. ● *noun* towing, being towed. □ **in tow** being towed, accompanying or in the charge of a person; **on tow** being towed; **towpath** path beside river or canal originally for horse towing boat.

tow[2] /təʊ/ *noun* fibres of flax etc. ready for spinning. □ **tow-headed** having very light-coloured or tousled hair.

towards /tə'wɔːdz/ *preposition* (also **toward**) in direction of; as regards, in relation to; as a contribution to, for; near.

towel /'taʊəl/ ● *noun* absorbent cloth, paper, etc. for drying after washing etc. ● *verb* (**-ll-**; *US* **-l-**) rub or dry with towel.

towelling *noun* thick soft absorbent cloth used esp. for towels.

tower /'taʊə/ ● *noun* tall structure, often part of castle, church, etc.; fortress etc. with tower; tall structure housing machinery etc. ● *verb* (usually + *above, up*) reach high, be superior; (as **towering** *adjective*) high, lofty, violent. □ **tower block** tall building of offices or flats; **tower of strength** person who gives strong emotional support.

town /taʊn/ *noun* densely populated area, between city and village in size; London or the chief city or town in area; central business area in neighbourhood. □ **go to town** *colloquial* act or work with energy or enthusiasm; **on the town** *colloquial* enjoying urban night-life; **town clerk** *US & historical* official in charge of records etc. of town; **town gas** manufactured gas for domestic etc. use; **town hall** headquarters of local government, with public meeting rooms etc.; **town house** town residence, esp. one of

terrace; **town planning** planning of construction and growth of towns; **township** *South African* urban area for occupation by black people, *US & Canadian* administrative division of county, or district 6 miles square, *Australian & NZ* small town; **townspeople** inhabitants of town.

townie /'taʊnɪ/ *noun* (also **townee** /-'niː/) *derogatory* inhabitant of town.

toxaemia /tɒk'siːmɪə/ *noun* (*US* **toxemia**) blood poisoning; increased blood pressure in pregnancy.

toxic /'tɒksɪk/ *adjective* poisonous; of poison. □ **toxicity** /-'sɪs-/ *noun*.

toxicology /tɒksɪ'kɒlədʒɪ/ *noun* study of poisons. □ **toxicological** /-kə'lɒdʒ-/ *adjective*; **toxicologist** *noun*.

toxin /'tɒksɪn/ *noun* poison produced by living organism.

toy ● *noun* plaything; thing providing amusement; diminutive breed of dog etc. ● *verb* (usually + *with*) amuse oneself, flirt, move thing idly. □ **toy boy** *colloquial* woman's much younger boyfriend; **toyshop** shop selling toys.

trace[1] ● *verb* (**-cing**) find signs of by investigation; (often + *along, through, to*, etc.) follow or mark track, position, or path of; (often + *back*) follow to origins; copy (drawing etc.) by marking its lines on superimposed translucent paper; mark out, delineate, or write, esp. laboriously. ● *noun* indication of existence of something, vestige; very small quantity; track, footprint; mark left by instrument's moving pen etc. □ **trace element** chemical element occurring or required, esp. in soil, only in minute amounts. □ **traceable** *adjective*.

trace[2] *noun* each of two side-straps, chains, or ropes by which horse draws vehicle. □ **kick over the traces** become insubordinate or reckless.

tracer *noun* bullet etc. made visible in flight by flame etc. emitted; artificial radioisotope which can be followed through body by radiation it produces.

tracery /'treɪsərɪ/ *noun* (*plural* **-ies**) decorative stone openwork, esp. in head of Gothic window; lacelike pattern.

trachea /trə'kiːə/ *noun* (*plural* **-cheae** /-'kiːiː/) windpipe.

tracing *noun* traced copy of drawing etc.; act of tracing. □ **tracing-paper** translucent paper for making tracings.

track ● *noun* mark(s) left by person, animal, vehicle, etc.; (in *plural*) such marks, esp. footprints; rough path; line of travel; continuous railway line; racecourse, circuit, prepared course for runners; groove on gramophone record; single song etc. on gramophone record, CD, or magnetic tape; band round wheels of tank, tractor, etc. ● *verb* follow track of; trace (course, development, etc.) from vestiges. □ **in one's tracks** *colloquial* where one stands, instantly; **make tracks** *colloquial* depart; **make tracks for** *colloquial* go in pursuit of or towards; **track down** reach or capture by tracking; **tracker dog** police dog tracking by scent; **track events** running-races; **track record** person's past achievements; **track shoe** runner's spiked shoe; **track suit** warm outfit worn for exercising etc. □ **tracker** *noun*.

tract[1] *noun* (esp. large) stretch of territory; bodily organ or system.

tract[2] *noun* pamphlet, esp. containing propaganda.

tractable /'træktəb(ə)l/ *adjective* easily managed; docile. □ **tractability** *noun*.

traction /'trækʃ(ə)n/ *noun* hauling, pulling; therapeutic sustained pull on limb etc. □ **traction-engine** steam or diesel engine for drawing heavy load.

tractor /'træktə/ *noun* vehicle for hauling farm machinery etc.; traction-engine.

trad *colloquial* ● *noun* traditional jazz. ● *adjective* traditional.

trade ● *noun* buying and selling; this between nations etc.; business merely for profit (as distinct from profession); business of specified nature or time; skilled handicraft; (**the trade**) people engaged in specific trade; *US* transaction, esp. swap; (usually in *plural*) trade wind. ● *verb* (**-ding**) (often + *in*, *with*) engage in trade, buy and sell; exchange; *US* swap; (usually + *with*, *for*) have transaction. □ **trade in** exchange (esp. used article) in part payment for another; **trade mark** device or name legally registered to represent a company or product, distinctive characteristic; **trade name** name by which a thing is known in a trade, or given by manufacturer to a product, or under which a business trades; **trade off** exchange as compromise; **trade-off** balance, compromise; **trade on** take advantage of; **tradesman**, **tradeswoman** person engaged in trade, esp. shopkeeper; **trade(s) union** organized association of workers in trade, profession, etc. formed to further their common interests; **trade-unionist** member of trade union; **trade wind** constant wind blowing towards equator from NE or SE. □ **trader** *noun*.

tradescantia /ˌtrædɪsˈkæntɪə/ *noun* (usually trailing) plant with large blue, white, or pink flowers.

trading *noun* engaging in trade. □ **trading estate** area designed for industrial and commercial firms; **trading post** store etc. in remote region; **trading-stamp** token given to customer and exchangeable in quantity usually for goods.

tradition /trəˈdɪʃ(ə)n/ *noun* custom, opinion, or belief handed down to posterity; handing down of these.

traditional *adjective* of, based on, or obtained by tradition; (of jazz) in style of early 20th c. □ **traditionally** *adverb*.

traditionalism *noun* respect or support for tradition. □ **traditionalist** *noun* & *adjective*.

traduce /trəˈdjuːs/ *verb* (**-cing**) slander. □ **traducement** *noun*; **traducer** *noun*.

traffic /ˈtræfɪk/ ● *noun* vehicles moving on public highway, in air, or at sea; (usually + *in*) trade, esp. illegal; coming and going of people or goods by road, rail, air, sea, etc.; dealings between people etc.; (volume of) messages transmitted through communications system. ● *verb* (**-ck-**) (often + *in*) deal, esp. illegally; barter. □ **traffic island** raised area in road to divide traffic and provide refuge for pedestrians; **traffic jam** traffic at standstill; **traffic light(s)** signal controlling road traffic by coloured lights; **traffic warden** person employed to control movement and parking of road vehicles. □ **trafficker** *noun*.

tragedian /trəˈdʒiːdɪən/ *noun* author of or actor in tragedies.

tragedienne /trədʒiːdrˈen/ *noun* actress in tragedies.

tragedy /ˈtrædʒɪdɪ/ *noun* (*plural* **-ies**) serious accident, sad event; play with tragic unhappy ending.

tragic /ˈtrædʒɪk/ *adjective* disastrous, distressing, very sad; of tragedy. □ **tragically** *adverb*.

tragicomedy /trædʒɪˈkɒmədɪ/ *noun* (*plural* **-ies**) drama or event combining comedy and tragedy.

trail ● *noun* track or scent left by moving person, thing, etc.; beaten path, esp. through wild region; long line of people or things following behind something; part dragging behind thing or person. ● *verb* draw or be drawn along behind; (often + *behind*) walk wearily; follow trail of, pursue; be losing in contest; (usually + *away*, *off*) peter out; (of plant etc.) grow or hang over wall, along ground, etc.; hang loosely. □ **trailing edge** rear edge of aircraft's wing.

trailer *noun* set of extracts from film etc. shown in advance to advertise it; vehicle pulled by another; *US* caravan.

train ● *verb* (often + *to do*) teach (person etc.) specified skill, esp. by practice; undergo this process; bring or come to physical efficiency by exercise, diet, etc.; (often + *up*, *along*) guide growth of (plant); (usually as **trained** *adjective*) make (mind etc.) discerning through practice etc.; (often + *on*) point, aim. ● *noun* series of railway carriages or trucks drawn by engine; thing dragged along behind or forming back part of dress etc.; succession or series of people, things, events, etc.; group of followers, retinue. □ **in train** arranged, in preparation; **train-bearer** person holding up train of another's robe etc.; **train-spotter** person who collects numbers of railway locomotives. □ **trainee** /-ˈniː/ *noun*.

trainer *noun* person who trains horses, athletes, etc.; aircraft or simulator used to train pilots; soft running shoe.

training /ˈtreɪnɪŋ/ *noun* process of teaching or learning a skill etc.

traipse *colloquial* ● *verb* (**-sing**) tramp or trudge wearily. ● *noun* tedious journey on foot.

trait /treɪ/ *noun* characteristic.

traitor /ˈtreɪtə/ *noun* (*feminine* **traitress**) person guilty of betrayal or disloyalty. □ **traitorous** *adjective*.

trajectory /trəˈdʒektərɪ/ *noun* (*plural* **-ies**) path of object moving under given forces.

tram *noun* (also **tramcar**) electrically powered passenger road vehicle running on rails. □ **tramlines** rails for tram, *colloquial* either pair of parallel lines at edge of tennis etc. court.

trammel /ˈtræm(ə)l/ ● *noun* (usually in *plural*) impediment, restraint; kind of fishing net. ● *verb* (**-ll-**; *US* **-l-**) hamper.

tramp ● *verb* walk heavily and firmly; go on walking expedition; walk laboriously across or along; (often + *down*) tread on, stamp on; live as tramp. ● *noun* itinerant vagrant or beggar; sound of person or people walking or marching; long walk; *slang derogatory* promiscuous woman.

trample /ˈtræmp(ə)l/ *verb* (**-ling**) tread under foot; crush thus. □ **trample on** tread heavily on, treat roughly or with contempt.

trampoline /ˈtræmpəliːn/ ● *noun* canvas sheet connected by springs to horizontal frame, used for acrobatic exercises. ● *verb* (**-ning**) use trampoline.

trance /trɑːns/ *noun* sleeplike state; hypnotic or cataleptic state; such state as supposedly entered into by medium; rapture, ecstasy.

tranny /ˈtrænɪ/ *noun* (*plural* **-ies**) *colloquial* transistor radio.

tranquil /ˈtræŋkwɪl/ *adjective* serene, calm, undisturbed. □ **tranquillity** /-ˈkwɪl-/ *noun*; **tranquilly** *adverb*.

tranquillize *verb* (also **-ise**; *US* also **tranquilize**) (**-zing** or **-sing**) make tranquil, esp. by drug etc.

tranquillizer *noun* (also **-iser**; *US* also **tranquilizer**) drug used to diminish anxiety.

trans- *prefix* across, beyond; on or to other side of; through.

transact /trænˈzækt/ *verb* perform or carry through (business etc.).

transaction /trænˈzækʃ(ə)n/ *noun* piece of commercial or other dealing; transacting of business; (in *plural*) published reports of discussions and lectures at meetings of learned society.

transatlantic /trænzətˈlæntɪk/ *adjective* beyond or crossing the Atlantic; American; *US* European.

transceiver /trænˈsiːvə/ *noun* combined radio transmitter and receiver.

transcend /træn'send/ verb go beyond or exceed limits of; excel, surpass.

transcendent adjective excelling, surpassing; transcending human experience; (esp. of God) existing apart from, or not subject to limitations of, material universe. □ **transcendence** noun; **transcendency** noun.

transcendental /trænsen'dent(ə)l/ adjective a priori, not based on experience, intuitively accepted; abstract, vague. □ **Transcendental Meditation** meditation seeking to induce detachment from problems, anxiety, etc.

transcontinental /trænzkɒntɪ'nent(ə)l/ adjective extending across a continent.

transcribe /træn'skraɪb/ verb (**-bing**) copy out; write out (notes etc.) in full; record for subsequent broadcasting; Music adapt for different instrument etc. □ **transcriber** noun; **transcription** /-'skrɪp-/ noun.

transcript /'trænskrɪpt/ noun written copy.

transducer /trænz'djuːsə/ noun device for changing a non-electrical signal (e.g. pressure) into an electrical one (e.g. voltage).

transept /'trænsept/ noun part of cross-shaped church at right angles to nave; either arm of this.

transfer ● verb /træns'fɜː/ (**-rr-**) convey, remove, or hand over (thing etc.); make over possession of (thing, right, etc.) to person; move, change, or be moved to another group, club, etc.; change from one station, route, etc. to another to continue journey; convey (design etc.) from one surface to another. ● noun /'trænsfɜː/ transferring, being transferred; design etc. (to be) conveyed from one surface to another; football player etc. who is transferred; document effecting conveyance of property, a right, etc. □ **transferable** /-'fɜːrəb(ə)l/ adjective; **transference** /'trænsfərəns/ noun.

transfigure /træns'fɪgə/ verb (**-ring**) change appearance of, make more elevated or idealized. □ **transfiguration** noun.

transfix /træns'fɪks/ verb paralyse with horror or astonishment; pierce with sharp implement or weapon.

transform /træns'fɔːm/ verb change form, appearance, character, etc. of, esp. considerably; change voltage etc. of (alternating current). □ **transformation** /-fə'meɪ-/ noun.

transformer noun apparatus for reducing or increasing voltage of alternating current.

transfuse /træns'fjuːz/ verb (**-sing**) transfer (blood or other liquid) into blood vessel to replace that lost; permeate. □ **transfusion** noun.

transgress /trænz'gres/ verb infringe (law etc.); overstep (limit laid down); sin. □ **transgression** noun; **transgressor** noun.

transient /'trænzɪənt/ adjective of short duration; passing. □ **transience** noun.

transistor /træn'zɪstə/ noun semiconductor device capable of amplification and rectification; (in full **transistor radio**) portable radio using transistors.

transistorize verb (also **-ise**) (**-zing** or **-sing**) equip with transistors rather than valves.

transit /'trænzɪt/ noun going; conveying, being conveyed; passage, route; apparent passage of heavenly body across meridian of place or across sun or planet. □ **in transit** (while) going or being conveyed.

transition /træn'zɪʃ(ə)n/ noun passage or change from one place, state, condition, style, etc. to another. □ **transitional** adjective; **transitionally** adverb.

transitive /'trænsɪtɪv/ adjective (of verb) requiring direct object expressed or understood.

transitory /'trænzɪtərɪ/ adjective not lasting; brief, fleeting.

translate /træn'sleɪt/ verb (**-ting**) (often + into) express sense of in another language or in another form; be translatable; interpret; move or change, esp. from one person, place, or condition to another. □ **translatable** adjective; **translation** noun; **translator** noun.

transliterate /trænz'lɪtəreɪt/ verb (**-ting**) represent (word etc.) in closest corresponding characters of another script. □ **transliteration** noun.

translucent /trænz'luːs(ə)nt/ adjective allowing light to pass through, semi-transparent. □ **translucence** noun.

transmigrate /trænzmaɪ'greɪt/ verb (**-ting**) (of soul) pass into different body. □ **transmigration** noun.

transmission /trænz'mɪʃ(ə)n/ noun transmitting, being transmitted; broadcast programme; device transmitting power from engine to axle in vehicle.

transmit /trænz'mɪt/ verb (**-tt-**) pass or hand on, transfer; communicate or be medium for (ideas, emotions, etc.); allow (heat, light, sound, etc.) to pass through. □ **transmissible** adjective; **transmittable** adjective.

transmitter noun person or thing that transmits; equipment used to transmit radio etc. signals.

transmogrify /trænz'mɒgrɪfaɪ/ verb (**-ies, -ied**) jocular transform, esp. in magical or surprising way. □ **transmogrification** noun.

transmute /trænz'mjuːt/ verb (**-ting**) change form, nature, or substance of; historical change (base metals) into gold. □ **transmutation** noun.

transom /'trænsəm/ noun horizontal bar in window or above door; (in full **transom window**) window above this.

transparency /træns'pærənsɪ/ noun (plural **-ies**) being transparent; picture (esp. photograph) to be viewed by light passing through it.

transparent /træns'pærənt/ adjective allowing light to pass through and giving maximum visibility possible; (of disguise, pretext, etc.) easily seen through; (of quality etc.) obvious; easily understood. □ **transparently** adverb.

transpire /træns'paɪə/ verb (**-ring**) (of secret, fact, etc.) come to be known; happen; emit (vapour, moisture) or be emitted through pores of skin etc. □ **transpiration** /-spɪ-/ noun.

■ **Usage** The use of transpire to mean 'happen' is considered incorrect by some people.

transplant ● verb /træns'plɑːnt/ plant elsewhere; transfer (living tissue or organ) to another part of body or to another body. ● noun /'trænsplɑːnt/ transplanting of organ or tissue; thing transplanted. □ **transplantation** noun.

transport ● verb /træns'pɔːt/ take to another place; historical deport (criminal) to penal colony; (as **transported** adjective) (usually + with) affected with strong emotion. ● noun /'trænspɔːt/ system of transporting, means of conveyance; ship, aircraft, etc. used to carry troops, military stores, etc.; (esp. in plural) vehement emotion. □ **transportable** /-'pɔːt-/ adjective.

transportation /trænspɔː'teɪʃ(ə)n/ noun (system of) conveying, being conveyed; US means of transport; historical deporting of criminals.

transporter noun vehicle used to transport other vehicles, heavy machinery, etc. □ **transporter bridge** bridge carrying vehicles etc. across water on suspended moving platform.

transpose /træns'pəʊz/ verb (**-sing**) cause (two or more things) to change places; change position of (thing) in series or (word(s)) in sentence; Music write or play in different key. □ **transposition** /-pə'zɪʃ(ə)n/ noun.

transsexual /træns'sekʃʊəl/ (also **transexual**) ● adjective having physical characteristics of one sex and psychological identification with the other. ● noun transsexual person; person who has had sex change.

transship /træns'ʃɪp/ verb (-pp-) transfer from one ship or conveyance to another. □ **transshipment** noun.

transubstantiation /trænsəbstænʃɪ'eɪʃ(ə)n/ noun conversion of Eucharistic elements wholly into body and blood of Christ.

transuranic /trænzjʊ'rænɪk/ adjective Chemistry (of element) having higher atomic number than uranium.

transverse /'trænzvɜːs/ adjective situated, arranged, or acting in crosswise direction. □ **transversely** adverb.

transvestite /trænz'vestaɪt/ noun man deriving pleasure from dressing in women's clothes. □ **transvestism** noun.

trap ● noun device, often baited, for catching animals; arrangement or trick to catch (out) unsuspecting person; device for releasing clay pigeon to be shot at or greyhound at start of race etc.; curve in drainpipe etc. that fills with liquid and forms seal against return of gas; two-wheeled carriage; trapdoor; slang mouth. ● verb (-pp-) catch (as) in trap; catch (out) using trick etc.; furnish with traps. □ **trapdoor** door in floor, ceiling, or roof.

trapeze /trə'piːz/ noun crossbar suspended by ropes as swing for acrobatics etc.

trapezium /trə'piːzɪəm/ noun (plural **-s** or **-zia**) quadrilateral with only one pair of sides parallel; US trapezoid.

trapezoid /'træpɪzɔɪd/ noun quadrilateral with no sides parallel; US trapezium.

trapper noun person who traps wild animals, esp. for their fur.

trappings /'træpɪŋz/ plural noun ornamental accessories; (esp. ornamental) harness for horse.

Trappist /'træpɪst/ ● noun monk of order vowed to silence. ● adjective of this order.

trash ● noun esp. US worthless or waste stuff, rubbish; worthless person(s). ● verb slang wreck, vandalize. □ **trash can** US dustbin. □ **trashy** adjective (-ier, -iest).

trauma /'trɔːmə/ noun (plural **traumata** /-mətə/ or **-s**) emotional shock; physical injury, resulting shock. □ **traumatic** /-'mæt-/ adjective; **traumatize** verb (also **-ise**) (-zing or -sing).

travail /'træveɪl/ literary ● noun laborious effort; pangs of childbirth. ● verb make laborious effort, esp. in childbirth.

travel /'træv(ə)l/ ● verb (-ll-; US -l-) go from one place to another; make journey(s), esp. long or abroad; journey along or through, cover (distance); colloquial withstand long journey; act as commercial traveller; move or proceed as specified; colloquial move quickly; pass from point to point; (of machine or part) move or operate in specified way. ● noun travelling, esp. abroad; (often in plural) spell of this; range, rate, or mode of motion of part in machinery. □ **travel agency** agency making arrangements for travellers; **travelling salesman** commercial traveller; **travelsick** nauseous owing to motion in travelling.

travelled adjective (US **traveled**) experienced in travelling.

traveller noun (US **traveler**) person who travels or is travelling; commercial traveller. □ **traveller's cheque** cheque for fixed amount, cashed on signature for equivalent in other currencies; **traveller's joy** wild clematis.

travelogue /'trævəlɒg/ noun film or illustrated lecture about travel.

traverse ● verb /trə'vɜːs/ (-sing) travel or lie across; consider or discuss whole extent of. ● noun /'trævəs/ sideways movement; traversing; thing that crosses another. □ **traversal** noun.

travesty /'trævɪstɪ/ ● noun (plural **-ies**) grotesque parody, ridiculous imitation. ● verb (-ies, -ied) make or be travesty of.

trawl ● verb fish with trawl or seine or in trawler; catch by trawling; (often + for, through) search thoroughly. ● noun trawling; (in full **trawl-net**) large wide-mouthed fishing net dragged by boat along sea bottom.

trawler noun boat used for trawling.

tray noun flat board with raised rim for carrying dishes etc.; shallow lidless box for papers or small articles, sometimes forming drawer in cabinet etc.

treacherous /'tretʃərəs/ adjective guilty of or involving violation of faith or betrayal of trust; not to be relied on, deceptive. □ **treacherously** adverb; **treachery** noun.

treacle /'triːk(ə)l/ noun syrup produced in refining sugar; molasses. □ **treacly** adjective.

tread /tred/ ● verb (past **trod**; past participle **trodden** or **trod**) (often + on) set one's foot down; walk on; (often + down, in, into) press (down) or crush with feet; perform (steps etc.) by walking. ● noun manner or sound of walking; top surface of step or stair; thick moulded part of vehicle tyre for gripping road; part of wheel or sole of shoe etc. that touches ground. □ **treadmill** device for producing motion by treading on steps on revolving cylinder, similar device used for exercise, monotonous routine work; **tread water** maintain upright position in water by moving feet and hands.

treadle /'tred(ə)l/ noun lever moved by foot and imparting motion to machine.

treason /'triːz(ə)n/ noun violation of allegiance to sovereign (e.g. plotting assassination) or state (e.g. helping enemy).

treasonable adjective involving or guilty of treason.

treasure /'treʒə/ ● noun precious metals or gems; hoard of them; accumulated wealth; thing valued for rarity, workmanship, associations, etc.; colloquial beloved or highly valued person. ● verb (-ring) value highly; (often + up) store up as valuable. □ **treasure hunt** search for treasure, game in which players seek hidden object; **treasure trove** treasure of unknown ownership found hidden.

treasurer noun person in charge of funds of society etc.

treasury /'treʒərɪ/ noun (plural **-ies**) place where treasure is kept; funds or revenue of state, institution, or society; (**Treasury**) (offices and officers of) department managing public revenue of a country. □ **Treasury bench** government front bench in parliament; **treasury bill** bill of exchange issued by government to raise money for temporary needs.

treat ● verb act, behave towards, or deal with in specified way; apply process or medical care or attention to; present or handle (subject) in literature or art; (often + to) provide with food, drink, or entertainment at one's own expense; (often + with) negotiate terms; (often + of) give exposition. ● noun event or circumstance that gives great pleasure; meal, entertainment, etc. designed to do this; (**a treat**) colloquial extremely good or well. □ **treatable** adjective.

treatise /'triːtɪz/ noun literary composition dealing esp. formally with subject.

treatment noun process or manner of behaving towards or dealing with person or thing; medical care or attention.

treaty /'tri:tɪ/ *noun* (*plural* **-ies**) formal agreement between states; agreement between people, esp. for purchase of property.

treble /'treb(ə)l/ ● *adjective* threefold; triple; 3 times as much or many; high-pitched. ● *noun* treble quantity or thing; (voice of) boy soprano; high-pitched instrument; high-frequency sound of radio, record player, etc. ● *verb* (**-ling**) multiply or be multiplied by 3. □ **trebly** *adverb*.

tree ● *noun* perennial plant with woody self-supporting main stem and usually unbranched for some distance from ground; shaped piece of wood for various purposes; family tree. ● *verb* (**trees, treed**) cause to take refuge in tree. □ **treecreeper** small creeping bird feeding on insects in tree-bark; **tree-fern** large fern with upright woody stem; **tree surgeon** person who treats decayed trees in order to preserve them.

trefoil /'trefɔɪl/ *noun* plant with leaves of 3 leaflets; 3-lobed ornamentation, esp. in tracery windows.

trek ● *verb* (**-kk-**) make arduous journey, esp. (*historical*) migrate or journey by ox-wagon. ● *noun* such journey; each stage of it. □ **trekker** *noun*.

trellis /'trelɪs/ *noun* (in full **trellis-work**) lattice of light wooden or metal bars, esp. support for climbing plants.

tremble /'tremb(ə)l/ ● *verb* (**-ling**) shake involuntarily with emotion, cold, etc.; be affected with extreme apprehension; quiver. ● *noun* trembling, quiver. □ **trembly** *adjective* (**-ier, -iest**).

tremendous /trɪ'mendəs/ *adjective colloquial* remarkable, considerable, excellent; awe-inspiring, overpowering. □ **tremendously** *adverb*.

tremolo /'tremələʊ/ *noun* (*plural* **-s**) tremulous effect in music.

tremor /'tremə/ *noun* shaking, quivering; thrill (of fear, exultation, etc.); (in full **earth tremor**) slight earthquake.

tremulous /'tremjʊləs/ *adjective* trembling. □ **tremulously** *adverb*.

trench ● *noun* deep ditch, esp. one dug by troops as shelter from enemy's fire. ● *verb* dig trench(es) in; make series of trenches (in) so as to bring lower soil to surface. □ **trench coat** lined or padded waterproof coat, loose belted raincoat.

trenchant /'trentʃ(ə)nt/ *adjective* incisive, terse, vigorous. □ **trenchancy** *noun*; **trenchantly** *adverb*.

trencher /'trentʃə/ *noun historical* wooden etc. platter for serving food.

trencherman /'trentʃəmən/ *noun* eater.

trend ● *noun* general direction and tendency. ● *verb* turn away in specified direction; have general tendency. □ **trend-setter** person who leads the way in fashion etc.

trendy *colloquial often derogatory* ● *adjective* (**-ier, -iest**) fashionable. ● *noun* (*plural* **-ies**) fashionable person. □ **trendily** *adverb*; **trendiness** *noun*.

trepan /trɪ'pæn/ *historical* ● *noun* surgeon's cylindrical saw for making opening in skull. ● *verb* (**-nn-**) perforate (skull) with trepan.

trepidation /trepɪ'deɪʃ(ə)n/ *noun* fear, anxiety.

trespass /'trespəs/ ● *verb* (usually + *on, upon*) enter unlawfully (on another's land, property, etc.); encroach. ● *noun* act of trespassing; *archaic* sin, offence. □ **trespasser** *noun*.

tress *noun* lock of hair; (in *plural*) hair.

trestle /'tres(ə)l/ *noun* supporting structure for table etc. consisting of two frames fixed at an angle or hinged or of bar with two divergent pairs of legs; (in full **trestle-table**) table of board(s) laid on trestles; (in full **trestle-work**) open braced framework to support bridge etc.

trews *plural noun* close-fitting usually tartan trousers.

tri- *combining form* three (times).

triad /'traɪæd/ *noun* group of 3 (esp. notes in chord). □ **triadic** /-'æd-/ *adjective*.

trial /'traɪəl/ *noun* judicial examination and determination of issues between parties by judge with or without jury; test; trying thing or person; match held to select players for team; contest for horses, dogs, motorcycles, etc. □ **on trial** being tried in court of law, being tested; **trial run** preliminary operational test.

triangle /'traɪæŋg(ə)l/ *noun* plane figure with 3 sides and angles; any 3 things not in straight line, with imaginary lines joining them; implement etc. of this shape; *Music* instrument of steel rod bent into triangle, struck with small steel rod; situation involving 3 people. □ **triangular** /-'æŋgjʊlə/ *adjective*.

triangulate /traɪ'æŋgjʊleɪt/ *verb* (**-ting**) divide (area) into triangles for surveying purposes. □ **triangulation** *noun*.

triathlon /traɪ'æθlən/ *noun* athletic contest of 3 events. □ **triathlete** *noun*.

tribe *noun* (in some societies) group of families under recognized leader with blood etc. ties and usually having common culture and dialect; any similar natural or political division; *usually derogatory* set or number of people, esp. of one profession etc. or family. □ **tribesman, tribeswoman** member of tribe. □ **tribal** *adjective*.

tribulation /trɪbjʊ'leɪʃ(ə)n/ *noun* great affliction.

tribunal /traɪ'bju:n(ə)l/ *noun* board appointed to adjudicate on particular question; court of justice.

tribune /'trɪbju:n/ *noun* popular leader, demagogue; (in full **tribune of the people**) *Roman History* officer chosen by the people to protect their liberties.

tributary /'trɪbjʊtərɪ/ ● *noun* (*plural* **-ies**) stream etc. that flows into larger stream or lake; *historical* person or state paying or subject to tribute. ● *adjective* that is a tributary.

tribute /'trɪbju:t/ *noun* thing said or done or given as mark of respect or affection etc.; (+ *to*) indication of (some praiseworthy quality); *historical* periodic payment by one state or ruler to another, obligation to pay this.

trice *noun* □ **in a trice** in an instant.

triceps /'traɪseps/ *noun* muscle (esp. in upper arm) with 3 points of attachment.

triceratops /traɪ'serətɒps/ *noun* large dinosaur with 3 horns.

trichinosis /trɪkɪ'nəʊsɪs/ *noun* disease caused by hairlike worms.

trichology /trɪ'kɒlədʒɪ/ *noun* study of hair. □ **trichologist** *noun*.

trichromatic /traɪkrə'mætɪk/ *adjective* 3-coloured.

trick ● *noun* thing done to deceive or outwit; illusion; knack; feat of skill or dexterity; unusual action learned by animal; foolish or discreditable act; hoax, joke; idiosyncrasy; cards played in one round, point gained in this. ● *verb* deceive by trick; swindle; (+ *into*) cause to do something by trickery; take by surprise.

trickery *noun* deception, use of tricks.

trickle /'trɪk(ə)l/ ● *verb* (**-ling**) (cause to) flow in drops or small stream; come or go slowly or gradually. ● *noun* trickling flow. □ **trickle charger** *Electricity* device for slow continuous charging of battery.

trickster /'trɪkstə/ *noun* deceiver, rogue.

tricky *adjective* (**-ier, -iest**) requiring care and adroitness; crafty, deceitful. □ **trickily** *adverb*; **trickiness** *noun*.

tricolour /'trɪkələ/ *noun* (*US* **tricolor**) flag of 3 colours, esp. French national flag.

tricot /'trɪkəʊ/ noun knitted fabric.

tricycle /'traɪsɪk(ə)l/ noun 3-wheeled pedal-driven vehicle.

trident /'traɪd(ə)nt/ noun 3-pronged spear.

Tridentine /traɪ'dentaɪn/ adjective of traditional RC orthodoxy.

triennial /traɪ'enɪəl/ adjective lasting 3 years; recurring every 3 years.

trifle /'traɪf(ə)l/ ● noun thing of slight value or importance; small amount; (**a trifle**) somewhat; dessert of sponge cakes with custard, cream, etc. ● verb (**-ling**) talk or act frivolously; (+ *with*) treat frivolously, flirt heartlessly with.

trifling adjective unimportant; frivolous.

trigger /'trɪgə/ ● noun movable device for releasing spring or catch and so setting off mechanism, esp. of gun; event etc. that sets off chain reaction. ● verb (often + *off*) set (action, process) in motion, precipitate. □ **trigger-happy** apt to shoot on slight provocation.

trigonometry /trɪgə'nɒmətrɪ/ noun branch of mathematics dealing with relations of sides and angles of triangles, and with certain functions of angles. □ **trigonometric** /-nə'met-/ adjective; **trigonometrical** /-nə'met-/ adjective.

trike noun colloquial tricycle.

trilateral /traɪ'lætər(ə)l/ adjective of, on, or with 3 sides; involving 3 parties.

trilby /'trɪlbɪ/ noun (plural **-ies**) soft felt hat with narrow brim and indented crown.

trilingual /traɪ'lɪŋgw(ə)l/ adjective speaking or in 3 languages.

trill ● noun quavering sound, esp. quick alternation of notes; bird's warbling; pronunciation of letter *r* with vibrating tongue. ● verb produce trill; warble (song); pronounce (*r* etc.) with trill.

trillion /'trɪljən/ noun (plural same) million million; million million million; (**trillions**) colloquial large number. □ **trillionth** adjective & noun.

trilobite /'traɪləbaɪt/ noun kind of fossil crustacean.

trilogy /'trɪlədʒɪ/ noun (plural **-ies**) set of 3 related novels, plays, operas, etc.

trim ● verb (**-mm-**) make neat or tidy or of required size or shape, esp. by cutting away irregular or unwanted parts; (+ *off, away*) cut off; ornament; adjust balance of (ship, aircraft) by arranging cargo etc.; arrange (sails) to suit wind. ● noun state of readiness or fitness; ornament, decorative material; trimming of hair etc. ● adjective (**-mm-**) neat; in good order, well arranged or equipped.

trimaran /'traɪməræn/ noun vessel like catamaran, with 3 hulls side by side.

trimming noun ornamental addition to dress, hat, etc.; (in plural) colloquial usual accompaniments.

trinitrotoluene /traɪnaɪtrə'tɒljuːiːn/ noun (also **trinitrotoluol** /-'tɒljuɒl/) a high explosive.

trinity /'trɪnɪtɪ/ noun (plural **-ies**) being 3; group of 3; (**the Trinity**) the 3 persons of the Christian Godhead. □ **Trinity Sunday** Sunday after Whit Sunday.

trinket /'trɪŋkɪt/ noun trifling ornament, esp. piece of jewellery.

trio /'triːəʊ/ noun (plural **-s**) group of 3; musical composition for 3 performers; the performers.

trip ● verb (**-pp-**) (often + *up*) (cause to) stumble, esp. by catching foot; (+ *up*) (cause to) commit fault or blunder; run lightly; make excursion to place; operate (mechanism) suddenly by knocking aside catch etc.; slang have drug-induced hallucinatory experience. ● noun journey or excursion, esp. for pleasure; stumble, blunder, tripping, being tripped up;

nimble step; slang drug-induced hallucinatory experience; device for tripping mechanism etc. □ **trip-wire** wire stretched close to ground to operate alarm etc. if disturbed.

tripartite /traɪ'pɑːtaɪt/ adjective consisting of 3 parts; shared by or involving 3 parties.

tripe noun first or second stomach of ruminant, esp. ox, as food; colloquial nonsense, rubbish.

triple /'trɪp(ə)l/ ● adjective of 3 parts, threefold; involving 3 parties; 3 times as much or as many. ● noun threefold number or amount; set of 3. ● verb (**-ling**) multiply by 3. □ **triple crown** winning of 3 important sporting events; **triple jump** athletic contest comprising hop, step, and jump. □ **triply** adverb.

triplet /'trɪplɪt/ noun each of 3 children or animals born at one birth; set of 3 things, esp. of notes played in time of two.

triplex /'trɪpleks/ adjective triple, threefold.

triplicate ● adjective /'trɪplɪkət/ existing in 3 examples or copies; having 3 corresponding parts; tripled. ● noun /'trɪplɪkət/ each of 3 copies or corresponding parts. ● verb (**-ting**) /'trɪplɪkeɪt/ make in 3 copies; multiply by 3. □ **triplication** noun.

tripod /'traɪpɒd/ noun 3-legged or 3-footed stand, stool, table, or utensil.

tripos /'traɪpɒs/ noun honours exam for primary degree at Cambridge University.

tripper noun person who goes on pleasure trip.

triptych /'trɪptɪk/ noun picture etc. with 3 panels usually hinged vertically together.

trireme /'traɪriːm/ noun ancient Greek warship, with 3 files of oarsmen on each side.

trisect /traɪ'sekt/ verb divide into 3 (usually equal) parts. □ **trisection** noun.

trite adjective hackneyed. □ **tritely** adverb; **triteness** noun.

tritium /'trɪtɪəm/ noun radioactive isotope of hydrogen with mass about 3 times that of ordinary hydrogen.

triumph /'traɪʌmf/ ● noun state of victory or success; great success or achievement; supreme example; joy at success. ● verb gain victory, be successful; Roman History ride in triumph; (often + *over*) exult.

triumphal /traɪ'ʌmf(ə)l/ adjective of, used in, or celebrating a triumph.

■ **Usage** Triumphal, as in triumphal arch, should not be confused with *triumphant*.

triumphant /traɪ'ʌmf(ə)nt/ adjective victorious, successful; exultant. □ **triumphantly** adverb.

■ **Usage** See note at TRIUMPHAL.

triumvirate /traɪ'ʌmvərət/ noun ruling group of 3 men.

trivalent /traɪ'veɪlənt/ adjective Chemistry having a valency of 3. □ **trivalency** noun.

trivet /'trɪvɪt/ noun iron tripod or bracket for pot or kettle to stand on.

trivia /'trɪvɪə/ plural noun trifles, trivialities.

trivial /'trɪvɪəl/ adjective of small value or importance; concerned only with trivial things. □ **triviality** /-'æl-/ noun (plural **-ies**); **trivially** adverb.

trivialize verb (also **-ise**) (**-zing** or **-sing**) make or treat as trivial, minimize. □ **trivialization** noun.

trochee /'trəʊkiː/ noun metrical foot of one long followed by one short syllable. □ **trochaic** /trə'keɪɪk/ adjective.

trod past & past participle of TREAD.

trodden past participle of TREAD.

troglodyte /'trɒglədaɪt/ noun cave dweller.

troika /'trɔɪkə/ noun Russian vehicle drawn by 3 horses abreast.

Trojan /ˈtrəʊdʒ(ə)n/ ● *adjective* of ancient Troy. ● *noun* native or inhabitant of ancient Troy; person who works, fights, etc. courageously. □ **Trojan Horse** person or device planted to bring about enemy's downfall.

troll¹ /trəʊl/ *noun* supernatural cave-dwelling giant or dwarf in Scandinavian mythology.

troll² /trəʊl/ *verb* fish by drawing bait along in water.

trolley /ˈtrɒlɪ/ *noun* (*plural* **-s**) table, stand, or basket on wheels or castors for serving food, carrying luggage etc., gathering purchases in supermarket, etc.; low truck running along rails; (in full **trolley-wheel**) wheel attached to pole etc. for collecting current from overhead electric wire to drive vehicle. □ **trolley bus** electric bus using trolley-wheel.

trollop /ˈtrɒləp/ *noun* disreputable girl or woman.

trombone /trɒmˈbəʊn/ *noun* brass wind instrument with sliding tube. □ **trombonist** *noun*.

troop /truːp/ ● *noun* assembled company, assemblage of people or animals; (in *plural*) soldiers, armed forces; cavalry unit commanded by captain; artillery unit; group of 3 or more Scout patrols. ● *verb* (+ *in*, *out*, *off*, etc.) come together or move in a troop. □ **troop the colour** transfer flag ceremonially at public mounting of garrison guards; **troop-ship** ship for transporting troops.

trooper *noun* private soldier in cavalry or armoured unit; *Australian & US* mounted or State police officer; cavalry horse; troop-ship.

trope *noun* figurative use of word.

trophy /ˈtrəʊfɪ/ *noun* (*plural* **-ies**) cup etc. as prize in contest; memento of any success.

tropic /ˈtrɒpɪk/ *noun* parallel of latitude 23° 27′ N. (**tropic of Cancer**) or S. (**tropic of Capricorn**) of Equator; (**the Tropics**) region lying between these. **tropical** *adjective* of or typical of the Tropics.

troposphere /ˈtrɒpəsfɪə/ *noun* layer of atmosphere extending from 8 km upwards from earth's surface.

trot ● *verb* (**-tt-**) (of person) run at moderate pace; (of horse) proceed at steady pace faster than walk; traverse (distance) thus. ● *noun* action or exercise of trotting; (**the trots**) *slang* diarrhoea. □ **on the trot** *colloquial* in succession, continually busy; **trot out** *colloquial* introduce (opinion etc.) repeatedly or tediously.

troth /trəʊθ/ *noun archaic* faith, fidelity; truth.

trotter *noun* (usually in *plural*) animal's foot, esp. as food; horse bred or trained for trotting.

troubadour /ˈtruːbədʊə/ *noun* singer, poet; French medieval poet singing of love.

trouble /ˈtrʌb(ə)l/ ● *noun* difficulty, distress, vexation, affliction; inconvenience, unpleasant exertion; cause of this; perceived failing; malfunction; disturbance; (in *plural*) public disturbances. ● *verb* (**-ling**) cause distress to, disturb; be disturbed; afflict, cause pain etc. to; subject or be subjected to inconvenience or unpleasant exertion. □ **in trouble** likely to incur censure or punishment, *colloquial* pregnant and unmarried; **troublemaker** person who habitually causes trouble; **troubleshooter** mediator in dispute, person who traces and corrects faults in machinery etc.

troublesome *adjective* causing trouble, annoying.

trough /trɒf/ *noun* long narrow open receptacle for water, animal feed, etc.; channel or hollow like this; elongated region of low barometric pressure.

trounce /traʊns/ *verb* (**-cing**) inflict severe defeat, beating, or punishment on.

troupe /truːp/ *noun* company of actors, acrobats, etc.

trouper *noun* member of theatrical troupe; staunch colleague.

trousers /ˈtraʊzəz/ *plural noun* two-legged outer garment from waist usually to ankles. □ **trouser suit** woman's suit of trousers and jacket.

trousseau /ˈtruːsəʊ/ *noun* (*plural* **-s** or **-x** /-z/) bride's collection of clothes etc.

trout /traʊt/ *noun* (*plural* same or **-s**) fish related to salmon.

trove /trəʊv/ *noun* treasure trove.

trowel /ˈtraʊəl/ *noun* flat-bladed tool for spreading mortar etc.; scoop for lifting small plants or earth.

troy *noun* (in full **troy weight**) system of weights used for precious metals etc.

truant /ˈtruːənt/ ● *noun* child who does not attend school; person who avoids work etc. ● *adjective* idle, wandering. ● *verb* (also **play truant**) be truant. □ **truancy** *noun* (*plural* **-ies**).

truce *noun* temporary agreement to cease hostilities.

truck¹ *noun* lorry; open railway wagon for freight.

truck² *noun* □ **have no truck with** avoid dealing with.

trucker *noun* esp. *US* long-distance lorry driver.

truckle /ˈtrʌk(ə)l/ ● *noun* (in full **truckle-bed**) low bed on wheels, stored under another. ● *verb* (**-ling**) (+ *to*) submit obsequiously to.

truculent /ˈtrʌkjʊlənt/ *adjective* aggressively defiant. □ **truculence** *noun*; **truculently** *adverb*.

trudge ● *verb* (**-ging**) walk laboriously; traverse (distance) thus. ● *noun* trudging walk.

true ● *adjective* (**-r**, **-st**) in accordance with fact or reality; genuine; loyal, faithful; (+ *to*) accurately conforming to (type, standard); correctly positioned or balanced, level; exact, accurate. ● *adverb archaic* truly; accurately; without variation. □ **out of true** out of alignment.

truffle /ˈtrʌf(ə)l/ *noun* rich-flavoured underground fungus; sweet made of soft chocolate mixture.

trug *noun* shallow oblong garden-basket.

truism /ˈtruːɪz(ə)m/ *noun* self-evident or hackneyed truth.

truly /ˈtruːlɪ/ *adverb* sincerely; really; loyally; accurately. □ **Yours truly** *written before signature at end of informal letter; jocular* I, me.

trump¹ ● *noun* playing card(s) of suit temporarily ranking above others; (in *plural*) this suit; *colloquial* helpful or excellent person. ● *verb* defeat with trump; *colloquial* outdo. □ **come** or **turn up trumps** *colloquial* turn out well or successfully, be extremely successful or helpful; **trump card** card belonging to, or turned up to determine, trump suit, *colloquial* valuable resource; **trump up** fabricate, invent (accusation, excuse, etc.).

trump² *noun archaic* trumpet-blast.

trumpery /ˈtrʌmpərɪ/ ● *noun* worthless finery; rubbish. ● *adjective* showy but worthless, trashy, shallow.

trumpet /ˈtrʌmpɪt/ ● *noun* brass instrument with flared mouth and bright penetrating tone; trumpet-shaped thing; sound (as) of trumpet. ● *verb* (**-t-**) blow trumpet; (of elephant) make trumpet; proclaim loudly. □ **trumpeter** *noun*.

truncate /trʌŋˈkeɪt/ *verb* (**-ting**) cut off top or end of; shorten. □ **truncation** *noun*.

truncheon /ˈtrʌntʃ(ə)n/ *noun* short club carried by police officer.

trundle /ˈtrʌnd(ə)l/ *verb* (**-ling**) roll or move, esp. heavily or noisily.

trunk *noun* main stem of tree; body without limbs or head; large luggage-box with hinged lid; *US* boot of car; elephant's elongated prehensile nose; (in *plural*) men's close-fitting shorts worn for swimming etc. □ **trunk call** long-distance telephone call; **trunk line** main line of railway, telephone system, etc.; **trunk road** important main road.

truss ● *noun* framework supporting roof, bridge, etc.; supporting surgical appliance for hernia etc. sufferers; bundle of hay or straw; cluster of flowers or fruit. ● *verb* tie up (fowl) for cooking; (often + *up*) tie (person) with arms to sides; support with truss(es).

trust ● *noun* firm belief that a person or thing may be relied on; confident expectation; responsibility; *Law* arrangement involving trustees, property so held, group of trustees; association of companies for reducing competition. ● *verb* place trust in, believe in, rely on; (+ *with*) give (person) charge of; (often + *that*) hope earnestly that a thing will take place; (+ *to*) consign (thing) to (person); (+ *in*) place reliance in; (+ *to*) place (esp. undue) reliance on. □ **in trust** (of property) managed by person(s) on behalf of another; **trustworthy** deserving of trust, reliable. □ **trustful** *adjective*.

trustee /trʌsˈtiː/ *noun* person or member of board managing property in trust with legal obligation to administer it solely for purposes specified. □ **trusteeship** *noun*.

trusting *adjective* having trust or confidence. □ **trustingly** *adverb*.

trusty ● *adjective* (**-ier, -iest**) *archaic or jocular* trustworthy. ● *noun* (*plural* **-ies**) prisoner given special privileges for good behaviour.

truth /truːθ/ *noun* (*plural* **truths** /truːðz/) quality or state of being true; what is true.

truthful *adjective* habitually speaking the truth; (of story etc.) true. □ **truthfully** *adverb*; **truthfulness** *noun*.

try ● *verb* (**-ies, -ied**) attempt, endeavour; test (quality), test by use or experiment test qualities of; make severe demands on; examine effectiveness of for purpose; ascertain state of fastening of (door etc.); investigate and decide (case, issue) judicially, (often + *for*) subject (person) to trial; (+ *for*) apply or compete for, seek to attain. ● *noun* (*plural* **-ies**) attempt; *Rugby* touching-down of ball by player behind opposing goal line, scoring points and entitling player's side to a kick at goal. □ **try one's hand** (often + *at*) have attempt; **try it on** *colloquial* test how much unreasonable behaviour etc. will be tolerated; **try on** put (clothes etc.) on to test fit etc.; **try-on** *colloquial* act of trying it on or trying on clothes etc., attempt to deceive; **try out** put to the test, test thoroughly; **try-out** experimental test.

trying *adjective* annoying, exasperating; hard to bear.

tryst /trɪst/ *noun archaic* meeting, esp. of lovers.

tsar /zɑː/ *noun* (also **czar**) (*feminine* **tsarina** /-ˈriːnə/) *historical* emperor of Russia. □ **tsarist** *noun & adjective*.

tsetse /ˈtsetsɪ/ *noun* African fly feeding on blood and transmitting disease.

tsp. *abbreviation* (*plural* **tsps.**) teaspoonful.

TT *abbreviation* teetotal(ler); tuberculin-tested; Tourist Trophy.

tub ● *noun* open flat-bottomed usually round vessel; tub-shaped (usually plastic) carton; *colloquial* bath; *colloquial* clumsy slow boat. ● *verb* (**-bb-**) plant, bathe, or wash in tub. □ **tub-thumper** *colloquial* ranting preacher or orator.

tuba /ˈtjuːbə/ *noun* (*plural* **-s**) low-pitched brass wind instrument.

tubby /ˈtʌbɪ/ *adjective* (**-ier, -iest**) short and fat. □ **tubbiness** *noun*.

tube ● *noun* long hollow cylinder; soft metal or plastic cylinder sealed at one end; hollow cylindrical bodily organ; *colloquial* London underground; cathode ray tube, esp. in television; (**the tube**) *esp. US colloquial* television; *US* thermionic valve; inner tube. ● *verb* (**-bing**) equip with tubes; enclose in tube.

tuber /ˈtjuːbə/ *noun* short thick rounded root or underground stem of plant.

tubercle /ˈtjuːbək(ə)l/ *noun* small rounded swelling on part or in organ of body, esp. as characteristic of tuberculosis. □ **tubercle bacillus** bacterium causing tuberculosis. □ **tuberculous** /-ˈbɜːkjʊləs/ *adjective*.

tubercular /tjʊˈbɜːkjʊlə/ *adjective* of or affected with tuberculosis.

tuberculin /tjʊˈbɜːkjʊlɪn/ *noun* preparation from cultures of tubercle bacillus used in diagnosis and treatment of tuberculosis. □ **tuberculin-tested** (of milk) from cows shown to be free of tuberculosis.

tuberculosis /tjʊbəˌkjʊˈləʊsɪs/ *noun* infectious bacterial disease marked by tubercles, esp. in lungs.

tuberose /ˈtjuːbərəʊz/ *noun* plant with creamy-white fragrant flowers.

tuberous /ˈtjuːbərəs/ *adjective* having tubers; of or like a tuber.

tubing *noun* length of tube; quantity of or material for tubes.

tubular /ˈtjuːbjʊlə/ *adjective* tube-shaped; having or consisting of tubes.

TUC *abbreviation* Trades Union Congress.

tuck ● *verb* (often + *in*, *up*) draw, fold, or turn outer or end parts of (cloth, clothes, etc.) close together, push in edges of bedclothes around (person); draw together into small space; stow (thing) away in specified place or way; make stitched fold in (cloth etc.). ● *noun* flattened fold sewn in garment etc.; *colloquial* food, esp. cakes and sweets. □ **tuck in** *colloquial* eat heartily; **tuck shop** shop selling sweets etc. to schoolchildren.

tucker /ˈtʌkə/ ● *noun Australian & NZ slang* food. ● *verb* (esp. in *passive*; often + *out*) *US & Australian colloquial* tire.

Tudor /ˈtjuːdə/ *adjective* of royal family of England from Henry VII to Elizabeth I; of this period (1485–1603); of the architectural style of this period.

Tues. *abbreviation* (also **Tue.**) Tuesday.

Tuesday /ˈtjuːzdeɪ/ *noun* day of week following Monday.

tufa /ˈtjuːfə/ *noun* porous rock formed round mineral springs; tuff.

tuff *noun* rock formed from volcanic ash.

tuft *noun* bunch of threads, grass, feathers, hair, etc. held or growing together at base. □ **tufted** *adjective*; **tufty** *adjective*.

tug ● *verb* (**-gg-**) (often + *at*) pull hard or violently; tow (vessel) by tugboat. ● *noun* hard, violent, or jerky pull; sudden emotion; (also **tugboat**) small powerful boat for towing ships. □ **tug of war** trial of strength between two sides pulling opposite ways on a rope.

tuition /tjuːˈɪʃ(ə)n/ *noun* teaching; fee for this.

tulip /ˈtjuːlɪp/ *noun* bulbous spring-flowering plant with showy cup-shaped flowers; its flower. □ **tuliptree** tree with tulip-like flowers.

tulle /tjuːl/ *noun* soft fine silk etc. net for veils and dresses.

tumble /ˈtʌmb(ə)l/ ● *verb* (**-ling**) (cause to) fall suddenly or headlong; fall rapidly in amount etc.; roll, toss; move or rush in headlong or blundering fashion; (often + *to*) *colloquial* grasp meaning of; fling or push roughly or carelessly; perform acrobatic feats, esp. somersaults; rumple, disarrange. ● *noun* fall; somersault or other acrobatic feat. □ **tumbledown** falling or fallen into ruin, dilapidated; **tumble-drier, -dryer** machine for drying washing in heated rotating drum; **tumble-dry** *verb*.

tumbler *noun* drinking glass without handle or foot; acrobat; part of mechanism of lock.

tumbrel /ˈtʌmbr(ə)l/ *noun* (also **tumbril**) *historical* open cart in which condemned people were carried to guillotine during French Revolution.

tumescent /tjuːˈmes(ə)nt/ *adjective* swelling. □ **tumescence** *noun*.

tumid /ˈtjuːmɪd/ *adjective* swollen, inflated; pompous. □ **tumidity** /-ˈmɪd-/ *noun*.

tummy /ˈtʌmɪ/ *noun* (*plural* **-ies**) *colloquial* stomach.

tumour /ˈtjuːmə/ *noun* (*US* **tumor**) abnormal or morbid swelling in the body.

tumult /ˈtjuːmʌlt/ *noun* uproar, din; angry demonstration by mob, riot; conflict of emotions etc. □ **tumultuous** /-ˈmʌltʃʊəs/ *adjective*.

tumulus /ˈtjuːmjʊləs/ *noun* (*plural* **-li** /-laɪ/) ancient burial mound.

tun *noun* large cask; brewer's fermenting-vat.

tuna /ˈtjuːnə/ *noun* (*plural* same or **-s**) large edible marine fish; (in full **tuna-fish**) its flesh as food.

tundra /ˈtʌndrə/ *noun* vast level treeless Arctic region with permafrost.

tune ● *noun* melody; correct pitch or intonation. ● *verb* (**-ning**) put (musical instrument) in tune; (often + *in*) adjust (radio etc.) to desired frequency etc.; adjust (engine etc.) to run smoothly. □ **change one's tune** voice different opinion, become more respectful; **tune up** bring instrument(s) to proper pitch; **tuning-fork** two-pronged steel fork giving particular note when struck.

tuneful *adjective* melodious, musical. □ **tunefully** *adverb*.

tuneless *adjective* unmelodious, unmusical. □ **tunelessly** *adverb*.

tuner *noun* person who tunes pianos etc.; part of radio or television receiver for tuning.

tungsten /ˈtʌŋst(ə)n/ *noun* heavy steel-grey metallic element.

tunic /ˈtjuːnɪk/ *noun* close-fitting short coat of police or military uniform; loose often sleeveless garment.

tunnel /ˈtʌn(ə)l/ ● *noun* underground passage dug through hill, or under river, road, etc.; underground passage dug by animal. ● *verb* (**-ll-**; *US* **-l-**) (+ *through, into*) make tunnel through (hill etc.); make (one's way) so. □ **tunnel vision** restricted vision, *colloquial* inability to grasp wider implications of situation etc.

tunny /ˈtʌnɪ/ *noun* (*plural* same or **-ies**) tuna.

tuppence = TWOPENCE.

tuppenny = TWOPENNY.

Tupperware /ˈtʌpəweə/ *noun* proprietary term range of plastic containers for food.

turban /ˈtɜːbən/ *noun* man's headdress of fabric wound round cap or head, worn esp. by Muslims and Sikhs; woman's hat resembling this.

turbid /ˈtɜːbɪd/ *adjective* muddy, thick, not clear; confused, disordered. □ **turbidity** /-ˈbɪd-/ *noun*.

■ **Usage** *Turbid* is sometimes confused with *turgid*.

turbine /ˈtɜːbaɪn/ *noun* rotary motor driven by flow of water, gas, etc.

turbo- *combining form* turbine.

turbocharger /ˈtɜːbəʊtʃɑːdʒə/ *noun* (also **turbo**) supercharger driven by turbine powered by engine's exhaust gases.

turbojet /ˈtɜːbəʊdʒet/ *noun* jet engine in which jet also operates turbine-driven air-compressor; aircraft with this.

turboprop /ˈtɜːbəʊprɒp/ *noun* jet engine in which turbine is used as in turbojet and also to drive propeller; aircraft with this.

turbot /ˈtɜːbət/ *noun* (*plural* same or **-s**) large flatfish valued as food.

turbulent /ˈtɜːbjʊlənt/ *adjective* disturbed, in commotion; (of flow of air etc.) varying irregularly; riotous, restless. □ **turbulence** *noun*; **turbulently** *adverb*.

tureen /tjʊəˈriːn/ *noun* deep covered dish for soup.

turf ● *noun* (*plural* **-s** or **turves**) short grass with surface earth bound together by its roots; piece of this cut from ground; slab of peat for fuel; (**the turf**) horse racing, racecourse. ● *verb* cover (ground) with turf; (+ *out*) *colloquial* expel, eject. □ **turf accountant** bookmaker. □ **turfy** *adjective*.

turgid /ˈtɜːdʒɪd/ *adjective* swollen, inflated; (of language) pompous, bombastic. □ **turgidity** /-ˈdʒɪd-/ *noun*.

■ **Usage** *Turgid* is sometimes confused with *turbid*.

Turk *noun* native or national of Turkey.

turkey /ˈtɜːkɪ/ *noun* (*plural* **-s**) large originally American bird bred for food; its flesh. □ **turkeycock** male turkey.

Turkish ● *adjective* of Turkey. ● *noun* language of Turkey. □ **Turkish bath** hot-air or steam bath followed by massage etc., (in *singular* or *plural*) building for this; **Turkish carpet** thick-piled woollen carpet with bold design; **Turkish delight** kind of gelatinous sweet; **Turkish towel** one made of cotton terry.

turmeric /ˈtɜːmərɪk/ *noun* E. Indian plant of ginger family; its rhizome powdered as flavouring or dye.

turmoil /ˈtɜːmɔɪl/ *noun* violent confusion; din and bustle.

turn ● *verb* move around point or axis, give or receive rotary motion; change from one side to another, invert, reverse; give new direction to, take new direction, aim in certain way; (+ *into*) change in nature, form, or condition to; (+ *to*) set about, have recourse to, consider next; become; (+ *against*) make or become hostile to; (+ *on, upon*) face hostilely; change colour; (of milk) become sour; (of stomach) be nauseated; cause (milk) to become sour or (stomach) to be nauseated; (of head) becon ˙ giddy; translate; move to other side of, go round; pass age or time of; (+ *on*) depend on; send, put, cause to go; remake (sheet, shirt collar, etc.); make (profit); divert (bullet); shape (object) in lathe; give (esp. elegant) form to. ● *noun* turning, rotary motion; changed or change of direction or tendency; point of turning or change; turning of road; change of direction of tide; change in course of events; tendency, formation; opportunity, obligation, etc. that comes successively to each of several people etc.; short walk or ride; short performance on stage, in circus, etc.; service of specified kind; purpose; *colloquial* momentary nervous shock; *Music* ornament of principal note with those above and below it. □ **in turn** in succession; **take (it in) turns** act alternately; **turncoat** person who changes sides; **turn down** reject, reduce volume or strength of (sound, heat, etc.) by turning knob, fold down; **turn in** hand in, achieve, *colloquial* go to bed, incline inwards; **turnkey** *archaic* jailer; **turn off** stop flow or working of by means of tap, switch, etc., enter side road, *colloquial* cause to lose interest; **turn on** start flow or working of by means of tap, switch, etc., *colloquial* arouse, esp. sexually; **turn out** expel, extinguish (light etc.), dress, equip, produce (goods etc.), empty, clean out, (cause to) assemble, prove to be the case, result, (usually + *to be*) be found; **turnout** number of people who attend meeting etc., equipage; **turn over** reverse position of, cause (engine etc.) to run, (of engine) start running, consider thoroughly, (+ *to*) transfer care or conduct of (person, thing) to (person); **turnover** turning over, gross amount of money taken in business, rate of sale and replacement of goods, rate at which people enter and leave employment etc., small pie with pastry folded over filling; **turnpike** *US & historical* road on which toll is charged; **turnstile** revolving gate with arms; **turntable** circular revolving plate or platform; **turn to** begin work; **turn turtle** capsize; **turn up** increase (volume or strength of) by turning knob etc., discover, reveal, be found, happen, arrive, shorten (garment etc.), fold over or upwards; **turn-up** turned-up end of trouser leg, *colloquial* unexpected happening.

turner *noun* lathe-worker.

turnery *noun* objects made on lathe; work with lathe.

turning *noun* road branching off another, place where this occurs; use of lathe; (in *plural*) chips or shavings from this. □ **turning circle** smallest circle in which vehicle can turn; **turning point** point at which decisive change occurs.

turnip /'tɜːnɪp/ *noun* plant with globular root; its root as vegetable.

turpentine /'tɜːpəntaɪn/ *noun* resin from any of various trees; (in full **oil of turpentine**) volatile inflammable oil distilled from turpentine and used in mixing paints etc.

turpitude /'tɜːpɪtjuːd/ *noun formal* depravity, wickedness.

turps *noun colloquial* oil of turpentine.

turquoise /'tɜːkwɔɪz/ ● *noun* opaque semiprecious stone, usually greenish-blue; this colour. ● *adjective* of this colour.

turret /'tʌrɪt/ *noun* small tower, esp. decorating building; usually revolving armoured structure for gun and gunners on ship, fort, etc.; rotating holder for tools in lathe etc. □ **turreted** *adjective*.

turtle /'tɜːt(ə)l/ *noun* aquatic reptile with flippers and horny shell. □ **turtle-neck** high close-fitting neck on knitted garment.

turtle-dove /'tɜːt(ə)ldʌv/ *noun* wild dove noted for soft cooing and affection for its mate.

tusk *noun* long pointed tooth, esp. projecting beyond mouth as in elephant, walrus, or boar. □ **tusked** *adjective*.

tussle /'tʌs(ə)l/ *noun & verb* (**-ling**) struggle, scuffle.

tussock /'tʌsək/ *noun* clump of grass etc.

tut = TUT-TUT.

tutelage /'tjuːtɪlɪdʒ/ *noun* guardianship; being under this; tuition.

tutelary /'tjuːtɪlərɪ/ *adjective* serving as guardian or protector; of guardian.

tutor /'tjuːtə/ ● *noun* private teacher; university teacher supervising studies or welfare of assigned undergraduates. ● *verb* act as tutor (to). □ **tutorship** *noun*.

tutorial /tjuː'tɔːrɪəl/ ● *adjective* of tutor or tuition. ● *noun* period of tuition for single student or small group.

tutti /'tʊtɪ/ *Music* ● *adjective & adverb* with all instruments or voices together. ● *noun* (*plural* **-s**) tutti passage.

tut-tut /tʌt'tʌt/ (also **tut**) ● *interjection expressing rebuke or impatience*. ● *noun* such exclamation. ● *verb* (**-tt-**) exclaim thus.

tutu /'tuːtuː/ *noun* (*plural* **-s**) dancer's short skirt of stiffened frills.

tuxedo /tʌk'siːdəʊ/ *noun* (*plural* **-s** or **-es**) *US* (suit including) dinner jacket.

TV *abbreviation* television.

twaddle /'twɒd(ə)l/ *noun* silly writing or talk.

twain *adjective & noun archaic* two.

twang ● *noun* sound made by plucked string of musical instrument, bow, etc.; nasal quality of voice. ● *verb* (cause to) emit twang. □ **twangy** *adjective*.

tweak ● *verb* pinch and twist; jerk; adjust finely. ● *noun* such action.

twee *adjective* (**tweer** /'twiːə/, **tweest** /'twiːɪst/) *derogatory* affectedly dainty or quaint.

tweed *noun* rough-surfaced woollen cloth usually of mixed colours; (in *plural*) clothes of tweed.

tweedy *adjective* (**-ier, -iest**) of or dressed in tweed; heartily informal.

tweet ● *noun* chirp of small bird. ● *verb* make this noise.

tweeter *noun* loudspeaker for high frequencies.

tweezers /'twiːzəz/ *plural noun* small pair of pincers for picking up small objects, plucking out hairs, etc.

twelfth *adjective & noun* next after eleventh; any of twelve equal parts of thing. □ **Twelfth Night** evening of 5 Jan.

twelve /twelv/ *adjective & noun* one more than eleven.

twenty /'twentɪ/ *adjective & noun* (*plural* **-ies**) twice ten. □ **twentieth** *adjective & noun*.

twerp *noun slang* stupid or objectionable person.

twice *adverb* two times; on two occasions; doubly.

twiddle /'twɪd(ə)l/ ● *verb* (**-ling**) twist or play idly about. ● *noun* act of twiddling. □ **twiddle one's thumbs** make them rotate round each other, have nothing to do.

twig[1] *noun* very small branch of tree or shrub.

twig[2] *verb* (**-gg-**) *colloquial* understand, realize.

twilight /'twaɪlaɪt/ *noun* light from sky when sun is below horizon, esp. in evening; period of this; faint light; period of decline. □ **twilight zone** decrepit urban area, undefined or intermediate area.

twilit /'twaɪlɪt/ *adjective* dimly illuminated (as) by twilight.

twill *noun* fabric woven with surface of parallel diagonal ridges. □ **twilled** *adjective*.

twin ● *noun* each of closely related pair, esp. of children or animals born at a birth; counterpart. ● *adjective* forming, or born as one of, twins. ● *verb* (**-nn-**) join closely, (+ *with*) pair; bear twins; link (town) with one abroad for social and cultural exchange. □ **twin bed** each of pair of single beds; **twin set** woman's matching cardigan and jumper; **twin town** town twinned with another.

twine ● *noun* strong coarse string of twisted strands of fibre; coil, twist. ● *verb* (**-ning**) coil, twist; form (string etc.) by twisting strands.

twinge /twɪndʒ/ *noun* sharp momentary local pain.

twinkle /'twɪŋk(ə)l/ ● *verb* (**-ling**) shine with rapidly intermittent light; sparkle; move rapidly. ● *noun* sparkle or gleam of eyes; twinkling light; light rapid movement. □ **twinkly** *adjective*.

twirl ● *verb* spin, swing, or twist quickly and lightly round. ● *noun* twirling; flourish made with pen.

twist ● *verb* change the form of by rotating one end and not the other or the two ends opposite ways; undergo such change; wrench or distort by twisting; wind (strands etc.) about each other, form (rope etc.) thus; (cause to) take spiral form; (+ *off*) break off by twisting; misrepresent meaning of (words); take winding course; *colloquial* cheat; (as **twisted** *adjective*) perverted; dance the twist. ● *noun* twisting, being twisted; thing made by twisting; point at which thing twists; *usually derogatory* peculiar tendency of mind, character, etc.; unexpected development; (**the twist**) 1960s dance with twisting hips. □ **twisty** *adjective* (**-ier, -iest**).

twister *noun colloquial* swindler.

twit[1] *noun slang* foolish person.

twit[2] *verb* (**-tt-**) reproach, taunt, usually good-humouredly.

twitch ● *verb* quiver or jerk spasmodically; pull sharply at. ● *noun* twitching; *colloquial* state of nervousness. □ **twitchy** *adjective* (**-ier, -iest**).

twitter /'twɪtə/ ● *verb* (esp. of bird) utter succession of light tremulous sounds; utter or express thus. ● *noun* twittering; *colloquial* tremulously excited state.

two /tuː/ *adjective & noun* one more than one. □ **two-dimensional** having or appearing to have length and breadth but no depth, superficial; **two-edged** having both good and bad effect, ambiguous; **two-faced** insincere; **two-handed** with 2 hands, used with both hands or by 2 people; **twopence** /'tʌpəns/ sum of 2 pence, (esp. with negative) *colloquial* thing of little value; **twopenny** /'tʌpənɪ/ costing twopence, *colloquial* cheap, worthless; **two-piece** (suit etc.) comprising 2 matching parts; **two-ply** (wool etc.) having 2 strands, (plywood) having 2 layers; **two-step** dance in march or polka time; **two-stroke** (of internal-combustion engine) having power cycle completed in one up-and-down movement of piston; **two-time** *colloquial* be unfaithful to, swindle; **two-tone** having two colours or sounds; **two-way** involving or operating in two directions, (of radio) capable of transmitting and receiving signals.

twofold *adjective & adverb* twice as much or many.

twosome *noun* two people together.

tycoon /taɪ'kuːn/ *noun* business magnate.

tying *present participle* of TIE.

tyke /taɪk/ *noun* (also **tike**) objectionable or coarse man; small child.

tympani = TIMPANI.

tympanum /'tɪmpənəm/ *noun* (*plural* **-s** or **-na**) middle ear; eardrum; vertical space forming centre of pediment; space between lintel and arch above door etc.

type /taɪp/ ● *noun* sort, class, kind; person, thing, or event exemplifying class or group; *colloquial* person, esp. of specified character; object, idea, or work of art serving as model; small block with raised character on upper surface for printing; printing types collectively; typeset or printed text. ● *verb* (**-ping**) write with typewriter; typecast; assign to type, classify. □ **-type** made of, resembling, functioning as; **typecast** cast (performer) repeatedly in similar roles; **typeface** inked surface of type, set of characters in one design; **typescript** typewritten document; **typesetter** compositor, composing machine; **typewriter** machine with keys for producing printlike characters; **typewritten** produced thus.

typhoid /'taɪfɔɪd/ *noun* (in full **typhoid fever**) infectious bacterial fever attacking intestines.

typhoon /taɪ'fuːn/ *noun* violent hurricane in E. Asian seas.

typhus /'taɪfəs/ *noun* an acute infectious fever.

typical /'tɪpɪk(ə)l/ *adjective* serving as characteristic example; (often + *of*) characteristic of particular person or thing. □ **typicality** /-'kæl-/ *noun*; **typically** *adverb*.

typify /'tɪpɪfaɪ/ *verb* (**-ies, -ied**) be typical of; represent by or as type. □ **typification** *noun*.

typist /'taɪpɪst/ *noun* (esp. professional) user of typewriter.

typo /'taɪpəʊ/ *noun* (*plural* **-s**) *colloquial* typographical error.

typography /taɪ'pɒgrəfɪ/ *noun* printing as an art; style and appearance of printed matter. □ **typographer** *noun*; **typographical** /-pə'græf-/ *adjective*; **typographically** /-pə'græf-/ *adverb*.

tyrannical /tɪ'rænɪk(ə)l/ *adjective* acting like or characteristic of tyrant.

tyrannize /'tɪrənaɪz/ *verb* (also **-ise**) (**-zing** or **-sing**) (often + *over*) treat despotically.

tyrannosaurus /tɪrænə'sɔːrəs/ *noun* (*plural* **-ruses**) very large carnivorous dinosaur with short front legs and powerful tail.

tyranny /'tɪrənɪ/ *noun* (*plural* **-ies**) cruel and arbitrary use of authority; rule by tyrant; period of this; state thus ruled. □ **tyrannous** *adjective*.

tyrant /'taɪərənt/ *noun* oppressive or cruel ruler; person exercising power arbitrarily or cruelly.

tyre /'taɪə/ *noun* (*US* **tire**) rubber covering, usually inflated, placed round vehicle's wheel for cushioning and grip.

tyro = TIRO.

tzatziki /tsæt'siːkɪ/ *noun* Greek dish of yoghurt with cucumber and garlic.

U¹ □ **U-boat** *historical* German submarine; **U-turn** U-shaped turn of vehicle to face in opposite direction, reversal of policy.

U² *abbreviation* (of film classified as suitable for all) universal.

UB40 *abbreviation* card for claiming unemployment benefit; *colloquial* unemployed person.

ubiquitous /juːˈbɪkwɪtəs/ *adjective* (seemingly) present everywhere simultaneously; often encountered. □ **ubiquity** *noun*.

UCCA /ˈʌkə/ *abbreviation* Universities Central Council on Admissions.

UDA *abbreviation* Ulster Defence Association.

udder /ˈʌdə/ *noun* baglike milk-producing organ of cow etc.

UDI *abbreviation* unilateral declaration of independence.

UDR *abbreviation* Ulster Defence Regiment.

UEFA /juːˈeɪfə/ *abbreviation* Union of European Football Associations.

UFO /ˈjuːfəʊ/ *noun* (also **ufo**) (*plural* **-s**) unidentified flying object.

ugh /əx, ʌg/ *interjection expressing disgust etc.*

Ugli /ˈʌglɪ/ *noun* (*plural* **-lis** or **-lies**) *proprietary term* mottled green and yellow citrus fruit.

ugly /ˈʌglɪ/ *adjective* (**-ier**, **-iest**) unpleasant to eye, ear, mind, etc.; discreditable; threatening, dangerous; morally repulsive. □ **ugly duckling** person lacking early promise but blossoming later. □ **uglify** *verb* (**-ies**, **-ied**); **ugliness** *noun*.

UHF *abbreviation* ultra-high frequency.

uh-huh /ˈʌhʌ/ *interjection colloquial* yes.

UHT *abbreviation* ultra heat treated (esp. of milk, for long keeping).

UK *abbreviation* United Kingdom.

Ukrainian /juːˈkreɪnɪən/ ● *noun* native, national, or language of Ukraine. ● *adjective* of Ukraine.

ukulele /juːkəˈleɪlɪ/ *noun* small guitar with 4 strings.

ulcer /ˈʌlsə/ *noun* (often pus-forming) open sore on or in body; corrupting influence. □ **ulcerous** *adjective*.

ulcerate /ˈʌlsəreɪt/ *verb* (**-ting**) form into or affect with ulcer. □ **ulceration** *noun*.

ullage /ˈʌlɪdʒ/ *noun* amount by which cask etc. falls short of being full; loss by evaporation or leakage.

ulna /ˈʌlnə/ *noun* (*plural* **ulnae** /-niː/) longer bone of forearm, opposite thumb; corresponding bone in animal's foreleg or bird's wing. □ **ulnar** *adjective*.

ulster /ˈʌlstə/ *noun* long loose overcoat of rough cloth.

Ulsterman /ˈʌlstəmən/ *noun* (*feminine* **Ulsterwoman**) native of Ulster.

ult. *abbreviation* ultimo.

ulterior /ʌlˈtɪərɪə/ *adjective* not admitted; hidden, secret.

ultimate /ˈʌltɪmət/ ● *adjective* last, final; fundamental, basic. ● *noun* (**the ultimate**) best achievable or imaginable; final or fundamental fact or principle. □ **ultimately** *adverb*.

ultimatum /ʌltɪˈmeɪtəm/ *noun* (*plural* **-s**) final statement of terms, rejection of which could cause hostility etc.

ultimo /ˈʌltɪməʊ/ *adjective* of last month.

ultra /ˈʌltrə/ ● *adjective* extreme, esp. in religion or politics. ● *noun* extremist.

ultra- *combining form* extreme(ly), excessive(ly); beyond.

ultra-high /ʌltrəˈhaɪ/ *adjective* (of frequency) between 300 and 3000 megahertz.

ultramarine /ʌltrəməˈriːn/ ● *noun* (colour of) brilliant deep blue pigment. ● *adjective* of this colour.

ultrasonic /ʌltrəˈsɒnɪk/ *adjective* of or using sound waves pitched above range of human hearing. □ **ultrasonically** *adverb*.

ultrasound /ˈʌltrəsaʊnd/ *noun* ultrasonic waves.

ultraviolet /ʌltrəˈvaɪələt/ *adjective* of or using radiation just beyond violet end of spectrum.

ultra vires /ʌltrə ˈvaɪəriːz/ *adverb & adjective* beyond one's legal power or authority. [Latin]

ululate /ˈjuːljʊleɪt/ *verb* (**-ting**) howl, wail. □ **ululation** *noun*.

um *interjection representing hesitation or pause in speech.*

umbel /ˈʌmb(ə)l/ *noun* flower-cluster with stalks springing from common centre. □ **umbellate** *adjective*.

umbelliferous /ʌmbəˈlɪfərəs/ *adjective* (of plant, e.g. parsley or carrot) bearing umbels.

umber /ˈʌmbə/ ● *noun* (colour of) dark brown earth used as pigment. ● *adjective* umber-coloured.

umbilical /ʌmˈbɪlɪk(ə)l/ *adjective* of navel. □ **umbilical cord** cordlike structure attaching foetus to placenta.

umbilicus /ʌmˈbɪlɪkəs/ *noun* (*plural* **-ci** /-saɪ/ or **-cuses**) navel.

umbra /ˈʌmbrə/ *noun* (*plural* **-s** or **-brae** /-briː/) shadow cast by moon or earth in eclipse.

umbrage /ˈʌmbrɪdʒ/ *noun* offence taken.

umbrella /ʌmˈbrelə/ *noun* collapsible cloth canopy on central stick for protection against rain, sun, etc.; protection, patronage; coordinating agency.

umlaut /ˈʊmlaʊt/ *noun* mark (¨) over vowel, esp. in German, indicating change in pronunciation; such a change.

umpire /ˈʌmpaɪə/ ● *noun* person enforcing rules and settling disputes in game, contest, etc. ● *verb* (**-ring**) (often + *for*, *in*, etc.) act as umpire (in).

umpteen /ˈʌmptiːn/ *adjective & noun colloquial* very many. □ **umpteenth** *adjective & noun*.

UN *abbreviation* United Nations.

un- *prefix added to adjectives, nouns, and adverbs, meaning:* not; non-; reverse of, lack of; *added to verbs, verbal derivatives, etc. to express contrary or reverse action, deprivation of or removal from.* For words starting with *un-* that are not found below, the root-words should be consulted.

unaccountable /ʌnəˈkaʊntəb(ə)l/ *adjective* without explanation, strange; not answerable for one's actions. □ **unaccountably** *adverb*.

unadopted /ʌnəˈdɒptɪd/ *adjective* (of road) not maintained by local authority.

unadulterated /ʌnəˈdʌltəreɪtɪd/ *adjective* pure; complete, utter.

unaffected /ʌnəˈfektɪd/ *adjective* (usually + *by*) not affected; free from affectation. □ **unaffectedly** *adverb*.

unalloyed /ʌnəˈlɔɪd/ *adjective* complete, pure.

un-American /ʌnəˈmerɪkən/ *adjective* uncharacteristic of Americans; contrary to US interests, treasonable.

unanimous /juːˈnænɪməs/ *adjective* all in agreement; (of vote etc.) by all without exception. □ **unanimity** /-nəˈnɪm-/ *noun*; **unanimously** *adverb*.

unannounced /ʌnə'naʊnst/ *adjective* not announced, without warning.

unanswerable /ʌn'ɑːnsərəb(ə)l/ *adjective* that cannot be answered or refuted.

unapproachable /ʌnə'prəʊtʃəb(ə)l/ *adjective* inaccessible; (of person) unfriendly, aloof.

unassailable /ʌnə'seɪləb(ə)l/ *adjective* that cannot be attacked or questioned.

unassuming /ʌnə'sjuːmɪŋ/ *adjective* not pretentious, modest.

unattached /ʌnə'tætʃt/ *adjective* not engaged, married, etc.; (often + *to*) not attached to particular organization etc.

unaware /ʌnə'weə/ ● *adjective* (usually + *of, that*) not aware; unperceptive. ● *adverb* unawares.

unawares /ʌnə'weəz/ *adverb* unexpectedly; inadvertently.

unbalanced /ʌn'bælənst/ *adjective* emotionally unstable; biased.

unbeknown /ʌnbɪ'nəʊn/ *adjective* (also **unbeknownst** /-'nəʊnst/) (+ *to*) without the knowledge of.

unbend /ʌn'bend/ *verb* (*past & past participle* **unbent**) straighten; relax; become affable.

unbending /ʌn'bendɪŋ/ *adjective* inflexible; firm, austere.

unblushing /ʌn'blʌʃɪŋ/ *adjective* shameless; frank.

unbosom /ʌn'bʊz(ə)m/ *verb* disclose (thoughts etc.); (**unbosom oneself**) disclose one's thoughts etc.

unbounded /ʌn'baʊndɪd/ *adjective* infinite.

unbridled /ʌn'braɪd(ə)ld/ *adjective* unrestrained, uncontrolled.

uncalled-for /ʌn'kɔːldfɔː/ *adjective* (of remark etc.) rude and unnecessary.

uncanny /ʌn'kænɪ/ *adjective* (**-ier, -iest**) seemingly supernatural, mysterious. □ **uncannily** *adverb*; **uncanniness** *noun*.

uncapped /ʌn'kæpt/ *adjective* *Sport* (of player) not yet awarded his or her cap or never having been selected to represent his or her country.

unceremonious /ʌnserɪ'məʊnɪəs/ *adjective* abrupt, discourteous; informal. □ **unceremoniously** *adverb*.

uncertain /ʌn'sɜːt(ə)n/ *adjective* not certain; unreliable; changeable. □ **in no uncertain terms** clearly and forcefully. □ **uncertainly** *adverb*; **uncertainty** *noun* (*plural* **-ies**).

uncharted /ʌn'tʃɑːtɪd/ *adjective* not mapped or surveyed.

uncle /'ʌŋk(ə)l/ *noun* parent's brother or brother-in-law. □ **Uncle Sam** *colloquial* US government.

unclean /ʌn'kliːn/ *adjective* not clean; unchaste; religiously impure.

uncomfortable /ʌn'kʌmftəb(ə)l/ *adjective* not comfortable; uneasy. □ **uncomfortably** *adverb*.

uncommon /ʌn'kɒmən/ *adjective* unusual, remarkable. □ **uncommonly** *adverb*.

uncompromising /ʌn'kɒmprəmaɪzɪŋ/ *adjective* stubborn; unyielding. □ **uncompromisingly** *adverb*.

unconcern /ʌnkən'sɜːn/ *noun* calmness; indifference, apathy. □ **unconcerned** *adjective*.

unconditional /ʌnkən'dɪʃən(ə)l/ *adjective* not subject to conditions, complete. □ **unconditionally** *adverb*.

unconscionable /ʌn'kɒnʃənəb(ə)l/ *adjective* without conscience; excessive.

unconscious /ʌn'kɒnʃəs/ ● *adjective* not conscious. ● *noun* normally inaccessible part of mind affecting emotions etc. □ **unconsciously** *adverb*; **unconsciousness** *noun*.

unconsidered /ʌnkən'sɪdəd/ *adjective* not considered; disregarded; not premeditated.

unconstitutional /ʌnkɒnstɪ'tjuːʃən(ə)l/ *adjective* in breach of political constitution or procedural rules.

uncooperative /ʌnkəʊ'ɒpərətɪv/ *adjective* not cooperative.

uncork /ʌn'kɔːk/ *verb* draw cork from (bottle); vent (feelings).

uncouple /ʌn'kʌp(ə)l/ *verb* (**-ling**) release from couples or coupling.

uncouth /ʌn'kuːθ/ *adjective* uncultured, rough.

uncover /ʌn'kʌvə/ *verb* remove cover or covering from; disclose.

uncrowned /ʌn'kraʊnd/ *adjective* having status but not name of.

unction /'ʌŋkʃ(ə)n/ *noun* anointing with oil etc. as religious rite or medical treatment; oil etc. so used; soothing words or thought; excessive or insincere flattery; (pretence of) deep emotion.

unctuous /'ʌŋktʃʊəs/ *adjective* unpleasantly flattering; greasy. □ **unctuously** *adverb*.

uncut /ʌn'kʌt/ *adjective* not cut; (of book) with pages sealed or untrimmed; (of film) not censored; (of diamond) not shaped; (of fabric) with looped pile.

undeniable /ʌndɪ'naɪəb(ə)l/ *adjective* indisputable; certain. □ **undeniably** *adverb*.

under /'ʌndə/ ● *preposition* in or to position lower than, below; beneath; inferior to, less than; undergoing, liable to; controlled or bound by; classified or subsumed in. ● *adverb* in or to lower condition or position. ● *adjective* lower.

underachieve /ʌndərə'tʃiːv/ *verb* (**-ving**) do less well than might be expected, esp. academically. □ **underachiever** *noun*.

underarm *adjective & adverb Cricket etc.* with arm below shoulder level.

underbelly *noun* (*plural* **-ies**) under surface of animal etc., esp. as vulnerable to attack.

underbid /ʌndə'bɪd/ *verb* (**-dd-**; *past & past participle* **-bid**) make lower bid than; *Bridge etc.* bid too little (on).

undercarriage *noun* wheeled retractable landing structure beneath aircraft; supporting framework of vehicle etc.

undercharge /ʌndə'tʃɑːdʒ/ *verb* (**-ging**) charge too little to.

underclothes *plural noun* (also **underclothing**) clothes worn under others, esp. next to skin.

undercoat *noun* layer of paint under another; (in animals) under layer of hair etc.

undercook /ʌndə'kʊk/ *verb* cook insufficiently.

undercover /ʌndə'kʌvə/ *adjective* surreptitious; spying incognito.

undercroft *noun* crypt.

undercurrent *noun* current below surface; underlying often contrary feeling, force, etc.

undercut ● *verb* /ʌndə'kʌt/ (**-tt-**; *past & past participle* **-cut**) sell or work at lower price than; strike (ball) to make it rise high; undermine. ● *noun* /'ʌndəkʌt/ underside of sirloin.

underdeveloped /ʌndədɪ'veləpt/ *adjective* immature; (of country etc.) with unexploited potential.

underdog *noun* oppressed person; loser in fight etc.

underdone /ʌndə'dʌn/ *adjective* undercooked.

underemployed /ʌndərɪm'plɔɪd/ *adjective* not fully occupied.

underestimate ● *verb* /ʌndər'estɪmeɪt/ (**-ting**) form too low an estimate of. ● *noun* /ʌndər'estɪmət/ estimate that is too low. □ **underestimation** *noun*.

underexpose /ʌndərɪk'spəʊz/ *verb* (**-sing**) expose (film) for too short a time. □ **underexposure** *noun*.

underfed /ʌndə'fed/ *adjective* malnourished.

underfelt *noun* felt laid under carpet.

underfloor /ˈʌndəˈflɔː/ adjective (esp. of heating) beneath floor.

underfoot /ˌʌndəˈfʊt/ adverb (also **under foot**) under one's feet; on the ground.

underfunded /ˌʌndəˈfʌndɪd/ adjective provided with insufficient money.

undergarment noun piece of underclothing.

undergo /ˌʌndəˈɡəʊ/ verb (3rd singular present **-goes**; past **-went**; past participle **-gone** /-ˈɡɒn/) be subjected to, endure.

undergraduate /ˌʌndəˈɡrædjʊət/ noun person studying for first degree.

underground ● adverb /ˌʌndəˈɡraʊnd/ beneath the ground; in(to) secrecy or hiding. ● adjective /ˈʌndəɡraʊnd/ situated underground; secret, subversive; unconventional. ● noun /ˈʌndəɡraʊnd/ underground railway; secret subversive group or activity.

undergrowth noun dense shrubs etc., esp. in wood.

underhand adjective secret, deceptive; Cricket etc. underarm.

underlay[1] ● verb /ˌʌndəˈleɪ/ (past & past participle **-laid**) lay thing under (another) to support or raise. ● noun /ˈʌndəleɪ/ thing so laid (esp. under carpet).

underlay[2] past of UNDERLIE.

underlie /ˌʌndəˈlaɪ/ verb (**-lying**; past **-lay**; past participle **-lain**) lie under (stratum etc.); (esp. as **underlying** adjective) be basis of, exist beneath superficial aspect of.

underline /ˌʌndəˈlaɪn/ verb (**-ning**) draw line under (words etc.); emphasize.

underling /ˈʌndəlɪŋ/ noun usually derogatory subordinate.

undermanned /ˌʌndəˈmænd/ adjective having insufficient crew or staff.

undermine /ˌʌndəˈmaɪn/ verb (**-ning**) injure or wear out insidiously or secretly; wear away base of; make excavation under.

underneath /ˌʌndəˈniːθ/ ● preposition at or to lower place than, below; on inside of. ● adverb at or to lower place; inside. ● noun lower surface or part. ● adjective lower.

undernourished /ˌʌndəˈnʌrɪʃt/ adjective insufficiently nourished. □ **undernourishment** noun.

underpants plural noun undergarment for lower part of torso.

underpass noun road etc. passing under another; subway.

underpay /ˌʌndəˈpeɪ/ verb (past & past participle **-paid**) pay too little to (person) or for (thing). □ **underpayment** noun.

underpin /ˌʌndəˈpɪn/ verb (**-nn-**) support from below with masonry etc.; support, strengthen.

underprivileged /ˌʌndəˈprɪvɪlɪdʒd/ adjective less privileged than others; having below average income, rights, etc.

underrate /ˌʌndəˈreɪt/ verb (**-ting**) have too low an opinion of.

underscore /ˌʌndəˈskɔː/ verb (**-ring**) underline.

undersea adjective below sea or its surface.

underseal verb seal underpart of (esp. vehicle against rust etc.).

under-secretary /ˌʌndəˈsekrətərɪ/ noun (plural **-ies**) subordinate official, esp. junior minister or senior civil servant.

undersell /ˌʌndəˈsel/ verb (past & past participle **-sold**) sell at lower price than (another seller).

undershirt noun esp. US vest.

undershoot /ˌʌndəˈʃuːt/ verb (past & past participle **-shot**) land short of (runway etc.).

undershot adjective (of wheel) turned by water flowing under it; (of lower jaw) projecting beyond upper jaw.

underside noun lower side or surface.

undersigned /ˌʌndəˈsaɪnd/ adjective whose signature is appended.

undersized /ˈʌndəˈsaɪzd/ adjective smaller than average.

underspend /ˌʌndəˈspend/ verb (past & past participle **-spent**) spend less than (expected amount) or too little.

understaffed /ˌʌndəˈstɑːft/ adjective having too few staff.

understand /ˌʌndəˈstænd/ verb (past & past participle **-stood**) comprehend, perceive meaning, significance, or cause of; know how to deal with; (often + *that*) infer, take as implied. □ **understandable** adjective; **understandably** adverb.

understanding ● noun intelligence; ability to understand; individual's perception of situation; agreement, esp. informal. ● adjective having understanding or insight; sympathetic. □ **understandingly** adverb.

understate /ˌʌndəˈsteɪt/ verb (**-ting**) express in restrained terms; represent as being less than it really is. □ **understatement** noun.

understudy /ˈʌndəstʌdɪ/ ● noun (plural **-ies**) person ready to take another's role when required, esp. in theatre. ● verb (**-ies**, **-ied**) study (role etc.) for this purpose; act as understudy to.

undersubscribed /ˌʌndəsəbˈskraɪbd/ adjective without sufficient subscribers, participants, etc.

undertake /ˌʌndəˈteɪk/ verb (**-king**; past **-took**; past participle **-taken**) agree to perform or be responsible for; engage in; (usually + *to do*) promise; guarantee; affirm.

undertaker /ˈʌndəteɪkə/ noun professional funeral organizer.

undertaking /ˌʌndəˈteɪkɪŋ/ noun work etc. undertaken; enterprise; promise; /ˈʌn-/ professional funeral management.

undertone noun subdued tone; underlying quality or feeling.

undertow noun current below sea surface contrary to surface current.

underused /ˌʌndəˈjuːzd/ adjective not used to capacity.

undervalue /ˌʌndəˈvæljuː/ verb (**-ues**, **-ued**, **-uing**) value insufficiently; underestimate.

underwater /ˌʌndəˈwɔːtə/ ● adjective situated or done under water. ● adverb under water.

underwear noun underclothes.

underweight /ˌʌndəˈweɪt/ adjective below normal weight.

underwent past of UNDERGO.

underwhelm /ˌʌndəˈwelm/ verb jocular fail to impress.

underworld noun those who live by organized crime; mythical home of the dead.

underwrite /ˌʌndəˈraɪt/ verb (**-ting**; past **-wrote**; past participle **-written**) sign and accept liability under (insurance policy); accept (liability) thus; undertake to finance or support; engage to buy all unsold stock in (company etc.). □ **underwriter** /ˈʌn-/ noun.

undesirable /ˌʌndɪˈzaɪərəb(ə)l/ ● adjective unpleasant, objectionable. ● noun undesirable person. □ **undesirability** noun.

undies /ˈʌndɪz/ plural noun colloquial (esp. women's) underclothes.

undo /ʌnˈduː/ verb (3rd singular present **-does**; past **-did**; past participle **-done**; present participle **-doing**) unfasten; annul; ruin prospects, reputation, or morals of.

undoing noun (cause of) ruin; reversing of action etc.; unfastening.

undone /ʌnˈdʌn/ adjective not done; not fastened; archaic ruined.

undoubted /ʌnˈdaʊtɪd/ adjective certain, not questioned. □ **undoubtedly** adverb.

undreamed /ʌn'driːmd, ʌn'dremt/ adjective (also **undreamt** /ʌn'dremt/) (often + of) not thought of, never imagined.

undress /ʌn'dres/ ● verb take off one's clothes; take clothes off (person). ● noun ordinary dress, esp. as opposed to (full-dress) uniform; naked or scantily clad state.

undressed /ʌn'drest/ adjective no longer dressed; (of food) without dressing; (of leather) untreated.

undue /ʌn'djuː/ adjective excessive, disproportionate. □ **unduly** adverb.

undulate /'ʌndjʊleɪt/ verb (**-ting**) (cause to) have wavy motion or look. □ **undulation** noun.

undying /ʌn'daɪɪŋ/ adjective immortal; never-ending.

unearth /ʌn'ɜːθ/ verb discover by searching, digging, or rummaging.

unearthly /ʌn'ɜːθlɪ/ adjective supernatural; mysterious; colloquial very early.

unease /ʌn'iːz/ noun nervousness, anxiety.

uneasy /ʌn'iːzɪ/ adjective (**-ier**, **-iest**) disturbed or uncomfortable in body or mind. □ **uneasily** adverb; **uneasiness** noun.

unemployable /ʌnɪm'plɔɪəb(ə)l/ adjective unfit for paid employment.

unemployed /ʌnɪm'plɔɪd/ adjective out of work; not used.

unemployment /ʌnɪm'plɔɪmənt/ noun lack of employment. □ **unemployment benefit** state payment made to unemployed worker.

unencumbered /ʌnɪm'kʌmbəd/ adjective (of estate) having no liabilities; free, not burdened.

unequivocal /ʌnɪ'kwɪvək(ə)l/ adjective not ambiguous, plain, unmistakable. □ **unequivocally** adverb.

UNESCO /juː'neskəʊ/ abbreviation (also **Unesco**) United Nations Educational, Scientific, and Cultural Organization.

uneven /ʌn'iːv(ə)n/ adjective not level; of variable quality; (of contest) unequal. □ **unevenly** adverb.

unexceptionable /ʌnɪk'sepʃənəb(ə)l/ adjective entirely satisfactory.

■ **Usage** Unexceptionable is sometimes confused with unexceptional.

unexceptional /ʌnɪk'sepʃən(ə)l/ adjective normal, ordinary.

■ **Usage** Unexceptional is sometimes confused with unexceptionable

unfailing /ʌn'feɪlɪŋ/ adjective not failing, constant, reliable. □ **unfailingly** adverb.

unfaithful /ʌn'feɪθfʊl/ adjective not faithful, esp. adulterous. □ **unfaithfulness** noun.

unfeeling /ʌn'fiːlɪŋ/ adjective unsympathetic, harsh.

unfit /ʌn'fɪt/ adjective (often + for, to do) not fit, unsuitable; in poor health.

unflagging /ʌn'flægɪŋ/ adjective tireless, persistent.

unflappable /ʌn'flæpəb(ə)l/ adjective colloquial imperturbable.

unfledged /ʌn'fledʒd/ adjective inexperienced; not fledged.

unfold /ʌn'fəʊld/ verb open out; reveal; become opened out; develop.

unforgettable /ʌnfə'getəb(ə)l/ adjective memorable, wonderful.

unfortunate /ʌn'fɔːtʃənət/ ● adjective unlucky; unhappy; regrettable. ● noun unfortunate person. □ **unfortunately** adverb.

unfounded /ʌn'faʊndɪd/ adjective (of rumour etc.) without foundation.

unfreeze /ʌn'friːz/ verb (**-zing**; past **unfroze**; past participle **unfrozen**) (cause to) thaw; derestrict (assets etc.).

unfrock /ʌn'frɒk/ verb defrock.

unfurl /ʌn'fɜːl/ verb unroll, spread out.

ungainly /ʌn'geɪnlɪ/ adjective awkward, clumsy.

unget-at-able /ʌnget'ætəb(ə)l/ adjective colloquial inaccessible.

ungodly /ʌn'gɒdlɪ/ adjective impious, wicked; colloquial outrageous.

ungovernable /ʌn'gʌvənəb(ə)l/ adjective uncontrollable, violent.

ungracious /ʌn'greɪʃəs/ adjective discourteous, grudging.

ungrateful /ʌn'greɪtfʊl/ adjective not feeling or showing gratitude. □ **ungratefully** adverb.

ungreen /ʌn'griːn/ adjective harmful to environment; not concerned with protection of environment.

unguarded /ʌn'gɑːdɪd/ adjective incautious, thoughtless; not guarded.

unguent /'ʌŋgwənt/ noun ointment, lubricant.

ungulate /'ʌŋgjʊlət/ ● adjective hoofed. ● noun hoofed mammal.

unhallowed /ʌn'hæləʊd/ adjective unconsecrated; not sacred; wicked.

unhand /ʌn'hænd/ verb rhetorical or jocular take one's hands off, release (person).

unhappy /ʌn'hæpɪ/ adjective (**-ier**, **-iest**) miserable; unfortunate; disastrous. □ **unhappily** adverb; **unhappiness** noun.

unhealthy /ʌn'helθɪ/ adjective (**-ier**, **-iest**) in poor health; harmful to health; unwholesome; slang dangerous. □ **unhealthily** adverb.

unheard-of /ʌn'hɜːdɒv/ adjective unprecedented.

unhinge /ʌn'hɪndʒ/ verb (**-ging**) take (door etc.) off hinges; (esp. as **unhinged** adjective) derange, disorder (mind).

unholy /ʌn'həʊlɪ/ adjective (**-ier**, **-iest**) profane, wicked; colloquial dreadful, outrageous.

unhorse /ʌn'hɔːs/ verb (**-sing**) throw (rider) from horse.

uni /'juːnɪ/ noun (plural **-s**) esp. Australian & NZ colloquial university.

uni- combining form having or composed of one.

Uniate /'juːnɪət/ ● adjective of Church in E. Europe or Near East acknowledging papal supremacy but retaining its own liturgy etc. ● noun member of such Church.

unicameral /juːnɪ'kæmər(ə)l/ adjective having one legislative chamber.

UNICEF /'juːnɪsef/ abbreviation United Nations Children's Fund.

unicellular /juːnɪ'seljʊlə/ adjective consisting of a single cell.

unicorn /'juːnɪkɔːn/ noun mythical horse with single straight horn.

unicycle /'juːnɪsaɪk(ə)l/ noun one-wheeled cycle used by acrobats etc.

unification /juːnɪfɪ'keɪʃ(ə)n/ noun unifying, being unified. □ **Unification Church** religious organization funded by Sun Myung Moon. □ **unificatory** adjective.

uniform /'juːnɪfɔːm/ ● adjective unvarying; conforming to same standard or rule; constant over a period. ● noun distinctive clothing worn by members of same organization etc. □ **uniformed** adjective; **uniformity** /-'fɔːm-/ noun; **uniformly** adverb.

unify /'juːnɪfaɪ/ verb (**-ies**, **-ied**) make or become united or uniform.

unilateral /juːnɪ'lætər(ə)l/ adjective done by or affecting one side only. □ **unilaterally** adverb.

unilateralism *noun* unilateral disarmament. □ **unilateralist** *noun & adjective*.

unimpeachable /ˌʌnɪmˈpiːtʃəb(ə)l/ *adjective* beyond reproach.

uninviting /ˌʌnɪnˈvaɪtɪŋ/ *adjective* unattractive, repellent.

union /ˈjuːnjən/ *noun* uniting, being united; whole formed from parts or members; trade union; marriage; concord; university social club or debating society. □ **Union flag, Jack** national flag of UK.

unionist *noun* member of trade union, advocate of trade unions; (usually **Unionist**) supporter of continued union between Britain and Northern Ireland. □ **unionism** *noun*.

unionize *verb* (also **-ise**) (**-zing** or **-sing**) organize in or into trade union. □ **unionization** *noun*.

unique /juːˈniːk/ *adjective* being the only one of its kind; having no like, equal, or parallel; remarkable. □ **uniquely** *adverb*.

■ **Usage** The use of *unique* to mean 'remarkable' is considered incorrect by some people.

unisex /ˈjuːnɪseks/ *adjective* (of clothing etc.) designed for both sexes.

unison /ˈjuːnɪs(ə)n/ *noun* concord; coincidence in pitch of sounds or notes.

unit /ˈjuːnɪt/ *noun* individual thing, person, or group, esp. for calculation; smallest component of complex whole; quantity chosen as standard of measurement; smallest share in unit trust; part with specified function in complex mechanism; fitted item of furniture, esp. as part of set; subgroup with special function; group of buildings, wards, etc. in hospital; single-digit number, esp. 'one'. □ **unit cost** cost of producing one item; **unit trust** company investing contributions from many people in various securities.

Unitarian /juːnɪˈteərɪən/ *noun* member of religious body maintaining that God is one person not Trinity. □ **Unitarianism** *noun*.

unitary /ˈjuːnɪtərɪ/ *adjective* of unit(s); marked by unity or uniformity.

unite /juːˈnaɪt/ *verb* (**-ting**) join together, esp. for common purpose; join in marriage; (cause to) form physical or chemical whole. □ **United Kingdom** Great Britain and Northern Ireland; **United Nations** (treated as *singular* or *plural*) international peace-seeking organization; **United States** = United States of America.

unity /ˈjuːnɪtɪ/ *noun* (*plural* **-ies**) oneness, being one; interconnecting parts making a whole, the whole made; solidarity, harmony between people etc.; the number 'one'.

universal /juːnɪˈvɜːs(ə)l/ ● *adjective* of, belonging to, or done etc. by all; applicable to all cases. ● *noun* term, characteristic, or concept of general application. □ **universal coupling, joint** one transmitting rotary power by a shaft at any angle; **universal time** Greenwich Mean Time. □ **universality** /-ˈsæl-/ *noun*; **universally** *adverb*.

universe /ˈjuːnɪvɜːs/ *noun* all existing things; Creation; all humankind.

university /juːnɪˈvɜːsɪtɪ/ *noun* (*plural* **-ies**) educational institution of advanced learning and research, conferring degrees; members of this.

unkempt /ʌnˈkempt/ *adjective* dishevelled, untidy.

unknown /ʌnˈnəʊn/ ● *adjective* (often + *to*) not known, unfamiliar. ● *noun* unknown thing, person, or quantity. □ **unknown quantity** mysterious or obscure person or thing; **Unknown Soldier, Warrior** unidentified soldier symbolizing nation's dead in war.

unlawful /ʌnˈlɔːfʊl/ *adjective* illegal, not permissible. □ **unlawfully** *adverb*.

unleaded /ʌnˈledɪd/ *adjective* (of petrol etc.) without added lead.

unleash /ʌnˈliːʃ/ *verb* free from leash or restraint; set free to pursue or attack.

unleavened /ʌnˈlev(ə)nd/ *adjective* made without yeast etc.

unless /ʌnˈles/ *conjunction* if not; except when.

unlettered /ʌnˈletəd/ *adjective* illiterate.

unlike /ʌnˈlaɪk/ ● *adjective* not like, different. ● *preposition* differently from.

unlikely /ʌnˈlaɪklɪ/ *adjective* (**-ier, -iest**) improbable; (+ *to do*) not expected; unpromising.

unlisted /ʌnˈlɪstɪd/ *adjective* not included in list, esp. of Stock Exchange prices or telephone numbers.

unload /ʌnˈləʊd/ *verb* remove load from (vehicle etc.); remove (load) from vehicle etc.; remove ammunition from (gun); *colloquial* get rid of.

unlock /ʌnˈlɒk/ *verb* release lock of; release or disclose by unlocking; release feelings etc. from.

unlooked-for /ʌnˈlʊktfɔː/ *adjective* unexpected.

unlucky /ʌnˈlʌkɪ/ *adjective* (**-ier, -iest**) not fortunate or successful; wretched; bringing bad luck; ill-judged. □ **unluckily** *adverb*.

unman /ʌnˈmæn/ *verb* (**-nn-**) deprive of courage, self-control, etc.

unmannerly /ʌnˈmænəlɪ/ *adjective* ill-mannered.

unmask /ʌnˈmɑːsk/ *verb* remove mask from; expose true character of; remove one's mask.

unmentionable /ʌnˈmenʃənəb(ə)l/ ● *adjective* unsuitable for polite conversation. ● *noun* (in *plural*) *jocular* undergarments.

unmistakable /ʌnmɪˈsteɪkəb(ə)l/ *adjective* clear, obvious, plain. □ **unmistakably** *adverb*.

unmitigated /ʌnˈmɪtɪɡeɪtɪd/ *adjective* not modified; absolute.

unmoved /ʌnˈmuːvd/ *adjective* not moved; constant in purpose; unemotional.

unnatural /ʌnˈnætʃər(ə)l/ *adjective* contrary to nature; not normal; lacking natural feelings; artificial, forced. □ **unnaturally** *adverb*.

unnecessary /ʌnˈnesəsərɪ/ *adjective* not necessary; superfluous. □ **unnecessarily** *adverb*.

unnerve /ʌnˈnɜːv/ *verb* (**-ving**) deprive of confidence etc.

unobjectionable /ʌnəbˈdʒekʃənəb(ə)l/ *adjective* acceptable.

unobtrusive /ʌnəbˈtruːsɪv/ *adjective* not making oneself or itself noticed. □ **unobtrusively** *adverb*.

unofficial /ʌnəˈfɪʃ(ə)l/ *adjective* not officially authorized or confirmed. □ **unofficial strike** strike not ratified by trade union.

unpack /ʌnˈpæk/ *verb* open and empty; take (thing) from package etc.

unpalatable /ʌnˈpælətəb(ə)l/ *adjective* (of food, suggestion, etc.) disagreeable, distasteful.

unparalleled /ʌnˈpærəleld/ *adjective* unequalled.

unparliamentary /ʌnpɑːləˈmentərɪ/ *adjective* contrary to proper parliamentary usage. □ **unparliamentary language** oaths, abuse.

unpick /ʌnˈpɪk/ *verb* undo sewing of.

unplaced /ʌnˈpleɪst/ *adjective* not placed as one of the first 3 in race etc.

unpleasant /ʌnˈplez(ə)nt/ *adjective* disagreeable. □ **unpleasantly** *adverb*; **unpleasantness** *noun*.

unplug /ʌnˈplʌɡ/ *verb* (**-gg-**) disconnect (electrical device) by removing plug from socket; unstop.

unplumbed /ʌnˈplʌmd/ *adjective* not plumbed; not fully explored or understood.

unpopular /ʌn'pɒpjʊlə/ *adjective* not popular, disliked. □ **unpopularity** /-'lær-/ *noun*.

unpractised /ʌn'præktɪst/ *adjective* (*US* **unpracticed**) not experienced or skilled; not put into practice.

unprecedented /ʌn'presɪdentɪd/ *adjective* having no precedent, unparalleled.

unprepossessing /ʌnpri:pə'zesɪŋ/ *adjective* unattractive.

unprincipled /ʌn'prɪnsɪp(ə)ld/ *adjective* lacking or not based on moral principles.

unprintable /ʌn'prɪntəb(ə)l/ *adjective* too offensive or indecent to be printed.

unprofessional /ʌnprə'feʃ(ə)n(ə)l/ *adjective* contrary to professional standards; unskilled, amateurish.

unprompted /ʌn'prɒmptɪd/ *adjective* spontaneous.

unputdownable /ʌnpʊt'daʊnəb(ə)l/ *adjective colloquial* compulsively readable.

unqualified /ʌn'kwɒlɪfaɪd/ *adjective* not qualified or competent; complete.

unquestionable /ʌn'kwestʃənəb(ə)l/ *adjective* that cannot be disputed or doubted. □ **unquestionably** *adverb*.

unquote /ʌn'kwəʊt/ *interjection* used in dictation etc. to indicate closing quotation marks.

unravel /ʌn'ræv(ə)l/ *verb* (**-ll-**; *US* **-l-**) make or become unknitted, unknotted, etc.; solve (mystery etc.); undo (knitted fabric).

unreal /ʌn'rɪəl/ *adjective* not real; imaginary; *slang* incredible.

unreasonable /ʌn'ri:zənəb(ə)l/ *adjective* excessive; not heeding reason. □ **unreasonably** *adverb*.

unregenerate /ʌnrɪ'dʒenərət/ *adjective* obstinately wrong or bad.

unrelenting /ʌnrɪ'lentɪŋ/ *adjective* not abating; merciless.

unreliable /ʌnrɪ'laɪəb(ə)l/ *adjective* erratic.

unrelieved /ʌnrɪ'li:vd/ *adjective* monotonously uniform.

unremarked /ʌnrɪ'mɑːkt/ *adjective* not mentioned or remarked on.

unremitting /ʌnrɪ'mɪtɪŋ/ *adjective* incessant. □ **unremittingly** *adverb*.

unremunerative /ʌnrɪ'mju:nərətɪv/ *adjective* unprofitable.

unrequited /ʌnrɪ'kwaɪtɪd/ *adjective* (of love etc.) not returned.

unreserved /ʌnrɪ'zɜːvd/ *adjective* without reservation. □ **unreservedly** /-vɪdlɪ/ *adverb*.

unrest /ʌn'rest/ *noun* disturbance, turmoil, trouble.

unrivalled /ʌn'raɪv(ə)ld/ *adjective* (*US* **unrivaled**) having no equal.

unroll /ʌn'rəʊl/ *verb* open out from rolled-up state; display, be displayed.

unruffled /ʌn'rʌf(ə)ld/ *adjective* calm.

unruly /ʌn'ru:lɪ/ *adjective* (**-ier, -iest**) undisciplined, disorderly. □ **unruliness** *noun*.

unsatisfactory /ʌnsætɪs'fæktərɪ/ *adjective* poor, unacceptable.

unsaturated /ʌn'sætʃəreɪtɪd/ *adjective Chemistry* (of fat) containing double or triple molecular bonds and therefore capable of combining with hydrogen.

unsavoury /ʌn'seɪvərɪ/ *adjective* (*US* **unsavory**) disgusting; (esp. morally) offensive.

unscathed /ʌn'skeɪðd/ *adjective* uninjured, unharmed.

unschooled /ʌn'sku:ld/ *adjective* uneducated, untrained.

unscientific /ʌnsaɪən'tɪfɪk/ *adjective* not scientific in method etc. □ **unscientifically** *adverb*.

unscramble /ʌn'skræmb(ə)l/ *verb* (**-ling**) decode, interpret (scrambled transmission etc.).

unscreened /ʌn'skri:nd/ *adjective* (esp. of coal) not passed through screen; not checked, esp. for security or medical problems; not having screen; not shown on screen.

unscrew /ʌn'skru:/ *verb* unfasten by removing screw(s), loosen (screw).

unscripted /ʌn'skrɪptɪd/ *adjective* (of speech etc.) delivered impromptu.

unscrupulous /ʌn'skru:pjʊləs/ *adjective* without scruples; unprincipled. □ **unscrupulously** *adverb*; **unscrupulousness** *noun*.

unseasonal /ʌn'si:zən(ə)l/ *adjective* not typical of the time or season.

unseat /ʌn'si:t/ *verb* remove from (esp. parliamentary) seat; dislodge from horseback etc.

unseeing /ʌn'si:ɪŋ/ *adjective* unobservant; blind. □ **unseeingly** *adverb*.

unseemly /ʌn'si:mlɪ/ *adjective* (**-ier, -iest**) indecent; unbecoming.

unseen /ʌn'si:n/ ● *adjective* not seen; invisible; (of translation) to be done without preparation. ● *noun* unseen translation.

unselfish /ʌn'selfɪʃ/ *adjective* concerned about others; sharing. □ **unselfishly** *adverb*; **unselfishness** *noun*.

unsettled /ʌn'set(ə)ld/ *adjective* restless, disturbed; open to further discussion; liable to change; not paid.

unsex /ʌn'seks/ *verb* deprive of qualities of one's (esp. female) sex.

unshakeable /ʌn'ʃeɪkəb(ə)l/ *adjective* firm; obstinate.

unsightly /ʌn'saɪtlɪ/ *adjective* ugly. □ **unsightliness** *noun*.

unskilled /ʌn'skɪld/ *adjective* lacking or (of work) not needing special skills.

unsociable /ʌn'səʊʃəb(ə)l/ *adjective* disliking company.

▪ **Usage** *Unsociable* is sometimes confused with *unsocial*.

unsocial /ʌn'səʊʃ(ə)l/ *adjective* not social; not suitable for or seeking society; outside normal working day; antisocial.

▪ **Usage** *Unsocial* is sometimes confused with *unsociable*.

unsolicited /ʌnsə'lɪsɪtɪd/ *adjective* voluntary.

unsophisticated /ʌnsə'fɪstɪkeɪtɪd/ *adjective* artless, simple, natural.

unsound /ʌn'saʊnd/ *adjective* unhealthy; rotten; weak; unreliable.

unsparing /ʌn'speərɪŋ/ *adjective* lavish; merciless.

unspeakable /ʌn'spi:kəb(ə)l/ *adjective* that words cannot express; indescribably bad. □ **unspeakably** *adverb*.

unstable /ʌn'steɪb(ə)l/ *adjective* (**-r, -st**) likely to fall; not stable emotionally; changeable.

unsteady /ʌn'stedɪ/ *adjective* (**-ier, -iest**) not firm; changeable; not regular. □ **unsteadily** *adverb*; **unsteadiness** *noun*.

unstick /ʌn'stɪk/ *verb* (*past & past participle* **unstuck**) separate (thing stuck to another). □ **come unstuck** *colloquial* fail.

unstinting /ʌn'stɪntɪŋ/ *adjective* lavish; limitless. □ **unstintingly** *adverb*.

unstressed /ʌn'strest/ *adjective* not pronounced with stress.

unstring /ʌn'strɪŋ/ *verb* (*past & past participle* **unstrung**) remove string(s) of (bow, harp, etc.); take (beads etc.) off string; (esp. as **unstrung** *adjective*) unnerve.

unstructured /ʌn'strʌktʃəd/ *adjective* without structure; informal.

unstudied /ʌn'stʌdɪd/ *adjective* easy, natural, spontaneous.

unsung /ʌn'sʌŋ/ *adjective* not celebrated, unrecognized.

unswerving /ʌn'swɜːvɪŋ/ *adjective* constant, steady. □ **unswervingly** *adverb*.

unthinkable /ʌn'θɪŋkəb(ə)l/ *adjective* unimaginable, inconceivable, *colloquial* highly unlikely or undesirable.

unthinking /ʌn'θɪŋkɪŋ/ *adjective* thoughtless; unintentional, inadvertent. □ **unthinkingly** *adverb*.

untidy /ʌn'taɪdɪ/ *adjective* (**-ier, -iest**) not neat or orderly. □ **untidily** *adverb*; **untidiness** *noun*.

until /ən'tɪl/ *preposition & conjunction* = TILL[1].

> ■ **Usage** *Until*, as opposed to *till*, is used especially at the beginning of a sentence and in formal style, as in *Until you told me, I had no idea* or *He resided there until his decease.*

untimely /ʌn'taɪmlɪ/ *adjective* inopportune; premature.

untiring /ʌn'taɪərɪŋ/ *adjective* tireless.

unto /'ʌntʊ/ *preposition* archaic to.

untold /ʌn'təʊld/ *adjective* not told; immeasurable.

untouchable /ʌn'tʌtʃəb(ə)l/ ● *adjective* that may not be touched. ● *noun* Hindu of group believed to defile higher castes on contact.

untoward /ʌntə'wɔːd/ *adjective* inconvenient, unlucky; awkward; refractory; unseemly.

untrammelled /ʌn'træm(ə)ld/ *adjective* not hampered.

untruth /ʌn'truːθ/ *noun* being untrue; lie.

unused *adjective* /ʌn'juːzd/ not in use, never used; /ʌn'juːst/ (+ *to*) not accustomed.

unusual /ʌn'juːʒʊəl/ *adjective* not usual; remarkable. □ **unusually** *adverb*.

unutterable /ʌn'ʌtərəb(ə)l/ *adjective* inexpressible; beyond description. □ **unutterably** *adverb*.

unvarnished /ʌn'vɑːnɪʃt/ *adjective* not varnished; plain, direct, simple.

unveil /ʌn'veɪl/ *verb* uncover (statue etc.) ceremonially; reveal (secrets etc.).

unversed /ʌn'vɜːst/ *adjective* (usually + *in*) not experienced or skilled.

unwarrantable /ʌn'wɒrəntəb(ə)l/ *adjective* (also **unwarranted**) unjustified.

unwashed /ʌn'wɒʃt/ *adjective* not washed or clean. □ **the great unwashed** *colloquial* the rabble.

unwell /ʌn'wel/ *adjective* ill.

unwholesome /ʌn'həʊlsəm/ *adjective* detrimental to moral or physical health; unhealthy-looking.

unwieldy /ʌn'wiːldɪ/ *adjective* (**-ier, -iest**) cumbersome or hard to manage owing to size, shape, etc.

unwilling /ʌn'wɪlɪŋ/ *adjective* reluctant. □ **unwillingly** *adverb*; **unwillingness** *noun*.

unwind /ʌn'waɪnd/ *verb* (*past & past participle* **unwound**) draw out or become drawn out after having been wound; *colloquial* relax.

unwitting /ʌn'wɪtɪŋ/ *adjective* not knowing, unaware; unintentional. □ **unwittingly** *adverb*.

unwonted /ʌn'wəʊntɪd/ *adjective* not customary or usual.

unworldly /ʌn'wɜːldlɪ/ *adjective* spiritual; naïve.

unworthy /ʌn'wɜːðɪ/ *adjective* (**-ier, -iest**) (often + *of*) not worthy or befitting; discreditable, unseemly. □ **unworthiness** *noun*.

unwritten /ʌn'rɪt(ə)n/ *adjective* not written; (of law etc.) based on tradition or judicial decision, not on statute.

up ● *adverb* towards or in higher place or place regarded as higher, e.g. the north, a capital; to or in erect or required position; in or into active condition; in stronger position; (+ *to, till*, etc.) to specified place, person, or time; higher in price; completely; completed; into compact, accumulated, or secure state; having risen; happening, esp. unusually. ● *preposition* upwards and along, through, or into; at higher part of. ● *adjective* directed upwards. ● *noun* spell of good fortune. ● *verb* (**-pp-**) *colloquial* start (abruptly or unexpectedly) to speak or act; raise. □ **on the up (and up)** *colloquial* steadily improving; **up against** close to, in(to) contact with, *colloquial* confronted with; **up-and-coming** *colloquial* (of person) promising, progressing; **up for** available for or standing for (sale, office, etc.); **upstate** *US* (in, to, or of) provincial, esp. northern, part of a state; **upstream** *adverb* against flow of stream etc., *adjective* moving upstream; **up to** until, below or equal to, incumbent on, capable of, occupied or busy with; **uptown** *US* (in, into, or of) residential part of town or city; **upwind** in the direction from which the wind is blowing.

upbeat ● *noun* Music unaccented beat. ● *adjective* colloquial optimistic, cheerful.

upbraid /ʌp'breɪd/ *verb* (often + *with, for*) chide, reproach.

upbringing *noun* child's rearing.

up-country /ʌp'kʌntrɪ/ *adjective & adverb* inland.

update ● *verb* /ʌp'deɪt/ (**-ting**) bring up to date. ● *noun* /'ʌpdeɪt/ updating; updated information etc.

up-end /ʌp'end/ *verb* set or rise up on end.

upfront /ʌp'frʌnt/ *colloquial* ● *adverb* (usually **up front**) at the front; in front; (of payments) in advance. ● *adjective* honest, frank, direct; (of payments) made in advance.

upgrade /ʌp'greɪd/ *verb* (**-ding**) raise in rank etc.; improve (equipment etc.).

upheaval /ʌp'hiːv(ə)l/ *noun* sudden esp. violent change or disturbance.

uphill ● *adverb* /ʌp'hɪl/ up a slope. ● *adjective* /'ʌphɪl/ sloping up; ascending; arduous.

uphold /ʌp'həʊld/ *verb* (*past & past participle* **upheld**) support; maintain, confirm. □ **upholder** *noun*.

upholster /ʌp'həʊlstə/ *verb* provide (furniture) with upholstery. □ **upholsterer** *noun*.

upholstery *noun* covering, padding, springs, etc. for furniture; upholsterer's work.

upkeep *noun* maintenance in good condition; cost or means of this.

upland /'ʌplənd/ ● *noun* (usually in *plural*) higher parts of country. ● *adjective* of these parts.

uplift ● *verb* /ʌp'lɪft/ raise; (esp as **uplifting** *adjective*) elevate morally or emotionally. ● *noun* /'ʌplɪft/ elevating influence; support for breasts etc.

up-market /ʌp'mɑːkɪt/ *adjective & adverb* of or to more expensive sector of market.

upon /ə'pɒn/ *preposition* on.

> ■ **Usage** *Upon* is usually more formal than *on*, but it is standard in *once upon a time* and *upon my word*.

upper /'ʌpə/ ● *adjective* higher in place; situated above; superior in rank etc. ● *noun* part of shoe or boot above sole. □ **on one's uppers** *colloquial* extremely short of money; **upper case** capital letters; **the upper crust** *colloquial* the aristocracy; **uppercut** hit upwards with arm bent; **the upper hand** dominance, control; **Upper House** higher legislative assembly, esp. House of Lords.

uppermost ● *adjective* highest, predominant. ● *adverb* on or to the top.

uppity /'ʌpɪtɪ/ *adjective* (also **uppish**) colloquial self-assertive, arrogant.

upright /'ʌpraɪt/ ● *adjective* erect, vertical; (of piano) with vertical strings; honourable, honest. ● *noun* upright post or rod, esp. as structural support; upright piano.

uprising *noun* insurrection.

uproar *noun* tumult, violent disturbance.

uproarious /ʌp'rɔːrɪəs/ *adjective* very noisy; provoking loud laughter; very funny. □ **uproariously** *adverb*.

uproot /ʌp'ruːt/ *verb* pull (plant etc.) up from ground; displace (person); eradicate.

upset ● *verb* /ʌp'set/ (**-tt-**; *past & past participle* **upset**) overturn; disturb temper, digestion, or composure of; disrupt. ● *noun* /'ʌpset/ disturbance, surprising result. ● *adjective* /ʌp'set, 'ʌp-/ disturbed.

upshot *noun* outcome, conclusion.

upside down /ʌpsaɪd 'daʊn/ *adverb & adjective* with upper and lower parts reversed, inverted; in(to) total disorder.

upstage /ʌp'steɪdʒ/ ● *adjective & adverb* nearer back of theatre stage. ● *verb* (**-ging**) move upstage to make (another actor) face away from audience; divert attention from (person) to oneself.

upstairs ● *adverb* /ʌp'steəz/ to or on an upper floor. ● *adjective* /'ʌpsteəz/ situated upstairs. ● *noun* /ʌp'steəz/ upper floor.

upstanding /ʌp'stændɪŋ/ *adjective* standing up; strong and healthy; honest.

upstart ● *noun* newly successful, esp. arrogant, person. ● *adjective* that is an upstart; of upstarts.

upsurge *noun* upward surge.

upswept *adjective* (of hair) combed to top of head.

upswing *noun* upward movement or trend.

uptake *noun colloquial* understanding; taking up (of offer etc.).

uptight /ʌp'taɪt/ *adjective colloquial* nervously tense, angry; *US* rigidly conventional.

upturn ● *noun* /'ʌptɜːn/ upward trend, improvement. ● *verb* /ʌp'tɜːn/ turn up or upside down.

upward /'ʌpwəd/ ● *adverb* (also **upwards**) towards what is higher, more important, etc. ● *adjective* moving or extending upwards. □ **upwardly** *adverb*.

uranium /jʊ'reɪnɪəm/ *noun* radioactive heavy grey metallic element, capable of nuclear fission and used as source of nuclear energy.

urban /'ɜːbən/ *adjective* of, living in, or situated in city or town. □ **urban guerrilla** terrorist operating in urban area.

urbane /ɜː'beɪn/ *adjective* suave; elegant. □ **urbanity** /-'bæn-/ *noun*.

urbanize /'ɜːbənaɪz/ *verb* (also **-ise**) (**-zing** or **-sing**) make urban, esp. by destroying rural quality of (district). □ **urbanization** *noun*.

urchin /'ɜːtʃɪn/ *noun* mischievous, esp. ragged, child; sea urchin.

Urdu /'ʊəduː/ *noun* Persian-influenced language related to Hindi, used esp. in Pakistan.

urea /jʊə'riːə/ *noun* soluble nitrogenous compound contained esp. in urine.

ureter /jʊə'riːtə/ *noun* duct carrying urine from kidney to bladder.

urethra /jʊə'riːθrə/ *noun* (*plural* **-s**) duct carrying urine from bladder.

urge /ɜːdʒ/ ● *verb* (**-ging**) (often + *on*) drive forcibly, hasten; entreat or exhort earnestly or persistently; (often + *on*, *upon*) advocate (action, argument, etc.) emphatically. ● *noun* urging impulse or tendency; strong desire.

urgent /'ɜːdʒ(ə)nt/ *adjective* requiring immediate action or attention; importunate. □ **urgency** *noun*; **urgently** *adverb*.

uric acid /'jʊərɪk/ *noun* constituent of urine.

urinal /jʊə'raɪn(ə)l/ *noun* place or receptacle for urinating by men.

urinary /'jʊərɪnərɪ/ *adjective* of or relating to urine.

urinate /'jʊərɪneɪt/ *verb* (**-ting**) discharge urine. □ **urination** *noun*.

urine /'jʊərɪn/ *noun* waste fluid secreted by kidneys and discharged from bladder.

urn *noun* vase with foot, used esp. for ashes of the dead; large vessel with tap, in which tea etc. is made or kept hot.

urology /jʊə'rɒlədʒɪ/ *noun* study of the urinary system. □ **urological** /-rə'lɒdʒ-/ *adjective*.

ursine /'ɜːsaɪn/ *adjective* of or like a bear.

US *abbreviation* United States.

us /ʌs, əs/ *pronoun used by speaker or writer to refer to himself or herself and one or more others as object of verb; used for* ME *by sovereign in formal contexts or by editorial writer in newspaper; colloquial* we.

USA *abbreviation* United States of America.

usable /'juːzəb(ə)l/ *adjective* that can be used.

USAF *abbreviation* United States Air Force.

usage /'juːsɪdʒ/ *noun* use, treatment; customary practice, established use (esp. of language).

use ● *verb* /juːz/ (**using**) cause to act or serve for purpose; bring into service; treat in specified way; exploit for one's own ends; (as **used** *adjective*) secondhand. ● *noun* /juːs/ using, being used; right or power of using; benefit, advantage; custom, usage. □ **in use** being used; **make use of** use, benefit from; **used to** /juːst/ *adjective* accustomed to, *verb used before other verb to describe habitual action* (e.g. *I used to live here*); **use up** consume, find use for (leftovers etc.).

■ **Usage** The usual negative and question forms of *used to* are, for example, *You didn't use to go there* and *Did you use to go there?* Both are, however, rather informal, so it is better in formal language to use *You used not to go there* and a different expression such as *Were you in the habit of going there?* or *Did you go there when you lived in London?*

---

useful *adjective* that can be used to advantage; helpful, beneficial; *colloquial* creditable, efficient. □ **usefully** *adverb*; **usefulness** *noun*.

useless *adjective* serving no purpose, unavailing; *colloquial* feeble, ineffectual. □ **uselessly** *adverb*; **uselessness** *noun*.

user *noun* person who uses a thing. □ **user-friendly** (of computer, program, etc.) easy to use.

usher /'ʌʃə/ ● *noun* person who shows people to their seats in cinema, church, etc.; doorkeeper of court etc. ● *verb* act as usher to; (usually + *in*) announce, show in.

usherette /ʌʃə'ret/ *noun* female usher, esp. in cinema.

USSR *abbreviation historical* Union of Soviet Socialist Republics.

usual /'juːʒəl/ *adjective* customary; habitual. □ **as usual** as is (or was) usual. □ **usually** *adverb*.

usurer /'juːʒərə/ *noun* person who practises usury.

usurp /jʊ'zɜːp/ *verb* seize (throne, power, etc.) wrongfully. □ **usurpation** /juːzə'p-/ *noun*; **usurper** *noun*.

usury /'juːʒərɪ/ *noun* lending of money at interest, esp. at exorbitant or illegal rate; interest at this rate. □ **usurious** /juː'ʒʊərɪəs/ *adjective*.

utensil /juː'tens(ə)l/ *noun* implement or vessel, esp. for kitchen use.

uterus /'juːtərəs/ *noun* (*plural* **uteri** /-raɪ/) womb. □ **uterine** /-raɪm/ *adjective*.

utilitarian /juːtɪlɪ'teərɪən/ ● *adjective* designed to be useful rather than attractive; of utilitarianism. ● *noun* adherent of utilitarianism.

utilitarianism *noun* doctrine that actions are justified if they are useful or benefit majority.

utility /ju:ˈtɪlɪtɪ/ ● *noun* (*plural* **-ies**) usefulness; useful thing, public utility. ● *adjective* basic and standardized. □ **utility room** room for domestic appliances, e.g. washing machine, boiler, etc.; **utility vehicle** vehicle serving various functions.

utilize /ˈjuːtɪlaɪz/ *verb* (also **-ise**) (**-zing** or **-sing**) turn to account, use. □ **utilization** *noun*.

utmost /ˈʌtməʊst/ ● *adjective* farthest, extreme; greatest. ● *noun* the utmost point, degree, etc. □ **do one's utmost** do all that one can.

Utopia /juːˈtəʊpɪə/ *noun* imagined perfect place or state. □ **Utopian, utopian** *adjective*.

utter[1] /ˈʌtə/ *adjective* complete, absolute. □ **utterly** *adverb*; **uttermost** *adjective*.

utter[2] /ˈʌtə/ *verb* emit audibly; express in words; *Law* put (esp. forged money) into circulation.

utterance *noun* uttering; thing spoken; power or manner of speaking.

UV *abbreviation* ultraviolet.

uvula /ˈjuːvjʊlə/ *noun* (*plural* **uvulae** /-liː/) fleshy part of soft palate hanging above throat. □ **uvular** *adjective*.

uxorious /ʌkˈsɔːrɪəs/ *adjective* excessively fond of one's wife.

Vv

V¹ *noun* (also **v**) (Roman numeral) 5.

V² *abbreviation* volt(s).

v. *abbreviation* verse; versus; very; verb; *vide.*

vac *noun colloquial* vacation.

vacancy /'veɪkənsɪ/ *noun* (*plural* **-ies**) being vacant; unoccupied post, place, etc.

vacant *adjective* not filled or occupied; not mentally active, showing no interest. □ **vacant possession** ownership of unoccupied house etc. □ **vacantly** *adverb.*

vacate /və'keɪt/ *verb* (**-ting**) leave vacant, cease to occupy.

vacation /və'keɪʃ(ə)n/ *noun* fixed holiday period, esp. in law courts and universities; *US* holiday; vacating, being vacated.

vaccinate /'væksɪmeɪt/ *verb* (**-ting**) inoculate with vaccine to immunize against disease. □ **vaccination** *noun.*

vaccine /'væksiːn/ *noun* preparation used for inoculation, originally cowpox virus giving immunity to smallpox.

vacillate /'væsɪleɪt/ *verb* (**-ting**) fluctuate in opinion or resolution. □ **vacillation** *noun;* **vacillator** *noun.*

vacuous /'vækjʊəs/ *adjective* expressionless; unintelligent. □ **vacuity** /və'kjuːɪtɪ/ *noun;* **vacuously** *adverb.*

vacuum /'vækjʊəm/ ● *noun* (*plural* **-s** or **vacua**) space entirely devoid of matter; space or vessel from which air has been completely or partly removed by pump etc.; absence of normal or previous content; (*plural* **-s**) *colloquial* vacuum cleaner. ● *verb colloquial* clean with vacuum cleaner. □ **vacuum brake** brake worked by exhaustion of air; **vacuum cleaner** machine for removing dust etc. by suction; **vacuum flask** vessel with double wall enclosing vacuum so that contents remain hot or cold; **vacuum-packed** sealed after partial removal of air; **vacuum tube** tube containing near-vacuum for free passage of electric current.

vagabond /'vægəbɒnd/ ● *noun* wanderer, esp. idle one. ● *adjective* wandering, having no settled habitation or home.

vagary /'veɪgərɪ/ *noun* (*plural* **-ies**) caprice, eccentric act or idea.

vagina /və'dʒaɪnə/ *noun* (*plural* **-s** or **-nae** /-niː/) canal joining womb and vulva of female mammal. □ **vaginal** *adjective.*

vagrant /'veɪgrənt/ ● *noun* person without settled home or regular work. ● *adjective* wandering, roving. □ **vagrancy** *noun.*

vague /veɪg/ *adjective* uncertain, ill-defined; not clear-thinking, inexact. □ **vaguely** *adverb;* **vagueness** *noun.*

vain *adjective* conceited; empty, trivial; unavailing, useless. □ **in vain** without result or success, lightly or profanely. □ **vainly** *adverb.*

vainglory /veɪn'glɔːrɪ/ *noun* extreme vanity, boastfulness. □ **vainglorious** *adjective.*

valance /'væləns/ *noun* short curtain round bedstead, above window, etc.

vale *noun* (*archaic* except in place names) valley.

valediction /vælɪ'dɪkʃ(ə)n/ *noun* formal bidding farewell; words used in this. □ **valedictory** *adjective &* *noun* (*plural* **-ies**).

valence /'veɪləns/ *noun* valency.

valency /'veɪlənsɪ/ *noun* (*plural* **-ies**) combining-power of an atom measured by number of hydrogen atoms it can displace or combine with.

valentine /'væləntaɪn/ *noun* (usually anonymous) letter or card sent as mark of love on St Valentine's Day (14 Feb.); sweetheart chosen on that day.

valerian /və'lɪərɪən/ *noun* any of various kinds of flowering herb.

valet /'vælɪt/ ● *noun* gentleman's personal servant. ● *verb* (**-t-**) act as valet (to).

valetudinarian /vælɪtjuːdɪ'neərɪən/ ● *noun* person of poor health or unduly anxious about health. ● *adjective* of a valetudinarian.

valiant /'væljənt/ *adjective* brave. □ **valiantly** *adverb.*

valid /'vælɪd/ *adjective* (of reason, objection, etc.) sound, defensible; legally acceptable, not yet expired. □ **validity** /və'lɪd-/ *noun.*

validate /'vælɪdeɪt/ *verb* (**-ting**) make valid, ratify. □ **validation** *noun.*

valise /və'liːz/ *noun US* small portmanteau.

Valium /'vælɪəm/ *noun proprietary term* the tranquillizing drug diazepam.

valley /'vælɪ/ *noun* (*plural* **-s**) low area between hills, usually with stream or river.

valour /'vælə/ *noun* (*US* **valor**) courage, esp. in battle. □ **valorous** *adjective.*

valuable /'væljʊəb(ə)l/ ● *adjective* of great value, price, or worth. ● *noun* (usually in *plural*) valuable thing.

valuation /væljʊ'eɪʃ(ə)n/ *noun* estimation (esp. by professional valuer) of thing's worth; estimated value.

value /'væljuː/ ● *noun* worth, desirability, or qualities on which these depend; worth as estimated; amount for which thing can be exchanged in open market; equivalent of thing; (in full **value for money**) something well worth money spent; ability of a thing to serve a purpose or cause an effect; (in *plural*) one's principles, priorities, or standards; *Music* duration of note; *Mathematics* amount denoted by algebraic term. ● *verb* (**-ues**, **-ued**, **-uing**) estimate value of; have high or specified opinion of. □ **value added tax** tax levied on rise in value of services and goods at each stage of production; **value judgement** subjective estimate of worth etc. □ **valueless** *adjective.*

valuer *noun* person who estimates or assesses values.

valve *noun* device controlling flow through pipe etc., usually allowing movement in one direction only; structure in organ etc. allowing flow of blood etc. in one direction only; thermionic valve; device to vary length of tube in trumpet etc.; half-shell of oyster, mussel, etc.

valvular /'vælvjʊlə/ *adjective* having valve(s); having form or function of valve.

vamoose /və'muːs/ *verb US slang* depart hurriedly.

vamp¹ ● *noun* upper front part of boot or shoe. ● *verb* (often + *up*) repair, furbish, or make by patching or piecing together; improvise musical accompaniment.

vamp² *colloquial* ● *noun* woman who uses sexual attraction to exploit men. ● *verb* allure or exploit (man).

vampire /'væmpaɪə/ *noun* supposed ghost or re-animated corpse sucking blood of sleeping people;

person who preys on others; (in full **vampire bat**) bloodsucking bat.

van¹ *noun* covered vehicle or closed railway truck for transporting goods etc.

van² *noun* vanguard, forefront.

vanadium /vəˈneɪdɪəm/ *noun* hard grey metallic element used to strengthen steel.

vandal /ˈvænd(ə)l/ *noun* person who wilfully or maliciously damages property. □ **vandalism** *noun*.

vandalize /ˈvændəlaɪz/ *verb* (also **-ise**) (**-zing** or **-sing**) destroy or damage wilfully or maliciously (esp. public property).

vane *noun* weather vane; blade of windmill; ship's propeller, etc.

vanguard /ˈvænɡɑːd/ *noun* foremost part of advancing army etc.; leaders of movement etc.

vanilla /vəˈnɪlə/ *noun* tropical fragrant climbing orchid; extract of its fruit (**vanilla-pod**), or synthetic substitute, used as flavouring.

vanish /ˈvænɪʃ/ *verb* disappear; cease to exist. □ **vanishing point** point at which receding parallel lines appear to meet.

vanity /ˈvænɪtɪ/ *noun* (*plural* **-ies**) conceit about one's attainments or appearance; futility, unreal thing. □ **vanity bag**, **case** woman's make-up bag or case.

vanquish /ˈvæŋkwɪʃ/ *verb literary* conquer, overcome.

vantage /ˈvɑːntɪdʒ/ *noun* advantage, esp. in tennis; (also **vantage point**) place giving good view.

vapid /ˈvæpɪd/ *adjective* insipid, dull, flat. □ **vapidity** /vəˈpɪd-/ *noun*.

vapor *US* = VAPOUR.

vaporize /ˈveɪpəraɪz/ *verb* (also **-ise**) (**-zing** or **-sing**) change into vapour. □ **vaporization** *noun*.

vaporous /ˈveɪpərəs/ *adjective* in the form of or consisting of vapour.

vapour /ˈveɪpə/ *noun* (*US* **vapor**) moisture or other substance diffused or suspended in air, e.g. mist, smoke; gaseous form of substance. □ **vapour trail** trail of condensed water from aircraft etc.

variable /ˈveərɪəb(ə)l/ ● *adjective* changeable, adaptable; apt to vary, not constant; *Mathematics* (of quantity) indeterminate, able to assume different numerical values. ● *noun* variable thing or quantity. □ **variability** *noun*.

variance /ˈveərɪəns/ *noun* (usually after *at*) difference of opinion; dispute; discrepancy.

variant ● *adjective* differing in form or details from standard; having different forms. ● *noun* variant form, spelling, type, etc.

variation /veərɪˈeɪʃ(ə)n/ *noun* varying; departure from normal kind, standard, type, etc.; extent of this; thing that varies from type; *Music* theme in changed or elaborated form.

varicose /ˈværɪkəʊs/ *adjective* (esp. of vein etc.) permanently and abnormally dilated.

variegated /ˈveərɪɡeɪtɪd/ *adjective* with irregular patches of different colours; having leaves of two or more colours. □ **variegation** *noun*.

variety /vəˈraɪətɪ/ *noun* (*plural* **-ies**) diversity; absence of uniformity; collection of different things; class of things differing from rest in same general class; member of such class; (+ *of*) different form of thing, quality, etc.; *Biology* subdivision of species; series of dances, songs, comedy acts, etc.

various /ˈveərɪəs/ *adjective* different, diverse; several. □ **variously** *adverb*.

■ **Usage** *Various* (unlike *several*) is not a pronoun and therefore cannot be used with *of*, as (wrongly) in *Various of the guests arrived late*.

varnish /ˈvɑːnɪʃ/ ● *noun* resinous solution used to give hard shiny transparent coating. ● *verb* coat with

varnish; conceal with deceptively attractive appearance.

varsity /ˈvɑːsɪtɪ/ *noun* (*plural* **-ies**) *colloquial* university.

vary /ˈveərɪ/ *verb* (**-ies**, **-ied**) be or become different; be of different kinds; modify, diversify.

vascular /ˈvæskjʊlə/ *adjective* of or containing vessels for conveying blood, sap, etc.

vas deferens /væs ˈdefərenz/ *noun* (*plural* **vasa deferentia** /veɪsə defəˈrenʃɪə/) sperm duct of testicle.

vase /vɑːz/ *noun* vessel used as ornament or container for flowers.

vasectomy /vəˈsektəmɪ/ *noun* (*plural* **-ies**) removal of part of each vas deferens, esp. for sterilization.

Vaseline /ˈvæsɪliːn/ *noun proprietary term* type of petroleum jelly used as ointment etc.

vassal /ˈvæs(ə)l/ *noun* humble dependant; *historical* holder of land by feudal tenure.

vast /vɑːst/ *adjective* immense, huge. □ **vastly** *adverb*; **vastness** *noun*.

VAT *abbreviation* value added tax.

vat *noun* tank, esp. for holding liquids in brewing, dyeing, and tanning.

Vatican /ˈvætɪkən/ *noun* palace or government of Pope in Rome.

vaudeville /ˈvɔːdəvɪl/ *noun esp. US* variety entertainment.

vault /vɔːlt/ ● *noun* arched roof; vaultlike covering; underground room as place of storage; underground burial chamber; act of vaulting. ● *verb* leap or spring, esp. using hands or pole; spring over in this way; (esp. as **vaulted** *adjective*) make in form of vault, provide with vault(s).

vaunt /vɔːnt/ *verb & noun literary* boast.

VC *abbreviation* Victoria Cross.

VCR *abbreviation* video cassette recorder.

VD *abbreviation* venereal disease.

VDU *abbreviation* visual display unit.

veal *noun* calf's flesh as food.

vector /ˈvektə/ *noun Mathematics & Physics* quantity having both magnitude and direction; carrier of disease.

veer /vɪə/ *verb* change direction, esp. (of wind) clockwise; change in opinion, course, etc.

vegan /ˈviːɡən/ ● *noun* person who does not eat animals or animal products. ● *adjective* using or containing no animal products.

vegetable /ˈvedʒtəb(ə)l/ ● *noun* plant, esp. edible herbaceous plant. ● *adjective* of, derived from, or relating to plant life or vegetables as food.

vegetarian /vedʒɪˈteərɪən/ ● *noun* person who does not eat meat or fish. ● *adjective* excluding animal food, esp. meat. □ **vegetarianism** *noun*.

vegetate /ˈvedʒɪteɪt/ *verb* (**-ting**) lead dull monotonous life; grow as plants do.

vegetation /vedʒɪˈteɪʃ(ə)n/ *noun* plants collectively; plant life.

vegetative /ˈvedʒɪtətɪv/ *adjective* concerned with growth and development rather than sexual reproduction; of vegetation.

vehement /ˈviːəmənt/ *adjective* showing or caused by strong feeling, ardent. □ **vehemence** *noun*; **vehemently** *adverb*.

vehicle /ˈviːɪk(ə)l/ *noun* conveyance used on land or in space; thing or person as medium for thought, feeling, or action; liquid etc. as medium for suspending pigments, drugs, etc. □ **vehicular** /vɪˈhɪkjʊlə/ *adjective*.

veil /veɪl/ ● *noun* piece of usually transparent material attached to woman's hat or otherwise forming part of headdress, esp. to conceal or protect face; piece of linen etc. as part of nun's headdress; thing that hides or disguises. ● *verb* cover with veil; (esp.

as **veiled** adjective) partly conceal. □ **beyond the veil** in the unknown state of life after death; **draw a veil over** avoid discussing; **take the veil** become nun.

vein /veɪn/ noun any of tubes carrying blood to heart; (in general use) any blood vessel; rib of leaf or insect's wing; streak of different colour in wood, marble, cheese, etc.; fissure in rock filled with ore; specified character or tendency, mood. □ **veined** adjective.

Velcro /'velkrəʊ/ noun proprietary term fastener consisting of two strips of fabric which cling when pressed together.

veld /velt/ noun (also **veldt**) South African open country.

veleta /və'liːtə/ noun ballroom dance in triple time.

vellum /'veləm/ noun fine parchment, originally calfskin; manuscript on this; smooth writing paper imitating vellum.

velociraptor /vɪ'lɒsɪræptə/ noun small carnivorous dinosaur with short front legs.

velocity /vɪ'lɒsɪtɪ/ noun (plural **-ies**) speed, esp. of inanimate things.

velour /və'lʊə/ noun (also **velours** same pronunciation) plushlike fabric.

velvet /'velvɪt/ ● noun soft fabric with thick short pile on one side; furry skin on growing antler. ● adjective of, like, or soft as velvet. □ **on velvet** in advantageous or prosperous position; **velvet glove** outward gentleness cloaking firmness or inflexibility. □ **velvety** adjective.

velveteen /velvɪ'tiːn/ noun cotton fabric with pile like velvet.

Ven. abbreviation Venerable.

venal /'viːn(ə)l/ adjective able to be bribed; involving bribery; corrupt. □ **venality** /-'næl-/ noun.

■ Usage *Venal* is sometimes confused with *venial*.

vend verb offer (esp. small wares) for sale. □ **vending machine** slot machine selling small items. □ **vendor** noun.

vendetta /ven'detə/ noun blood feud; prolonged bitter quarrel.

veneer /vɪ'nɪə/ ● noun thin covering of fine wood; (often + of) deceptively pleasing appearance. ● verb apply veneer to (wood etc.).

venerable /'venərəb(ə)l/ adjective entitled to deep respect on account of age, character, etc.; *title of archdeacon*.

venerate /'venəreɪt/ verb (**-ting**) regard with deep respect. □ **veneration** noun.

venereal /vɪ'nɪərɪəl/ adjective of sexual desire or intercourse; of venereal disease. □ **venereal disease** disease contracted by sexual intercourse with infected person.

Venetian /vɪ'niːʃ(ə)n/ ● noun native, citizen, or dialect of Venice. ● adjective of Venice. □ **venetian blind** window-blind of adjustable horizontal slats.

vengeance /'vendʒ(ə)ns/ noun punishment inflicted for wrong to oneself or to one's cause. □ **with a vengeance** to extreme degree, thoroughly, violently.

vengeful /'vendʒfʊl/ adjective seeking vengeance, vindictive.

venial /'viːnɪəl/ adjective (of sin or fault) pardonable, not mortal. □ **veniality** /-'æl-/ noun.

■ Usage *Venial* is sometimes confused with *venal*.

venison /'venɪs(ə)n/ noun deer's flesh as food.

Venn diagram noun diagram using overlapping and intersecting circles etc. to show relationships between mathematical sets.

venom /'venəm/ noun poisonous fluid of esp. snakes; malignity, virulence of feeling, language, or conduct. □ **venomous** adjective; **venomously** adverb.

venous /'viːnəs/ adjective of, full of, or contained in veins.

vent[1] ● noun opening for passage of air etc.; outlet, free expression; anus, esp. of lower animal. ● verb give vent or free expression to.

vent[2] noun slit in garment, esp. in back of jacket.

ventilate /'ventɪleɪt/ verb (**-ting**) cause air to circulate freely in (room etc.); air (question, grievance, etc.). □ **ventilation** noun.

ventilator noun appliance or aperture for ventilating room etc.; apparatus for maintaining artifical respiration.

ventral /'ventr(ə)l/ adjective of or on abdomen.

ventricle /'ventrɪk(ə)l/ noun cavity in body; hollow part of organ, esp. brain or heart.

ventricular /ven'trɪkjʊlə/ adjective of or shaped like ventricle.

ventriloquism /ven'trɪləkwɪz(ə)m/ noun skill of speaking without moving the lips. □ **ventriloquist** noun.

venture /'ventʃə/ ● noun risky undertaking; commercial speculation. ● verb (**-ring**) dare, not be afraid; dare to go, make, or put forward; take risks, expose to risk, stake. □ **Venture Scout** senior Scout.

venturesome adjective disposed to take risks.

venue /'venjuː/ noun appointed place for match, meeting, concert, etc.

Venus fly-trap /'viːnəs/ noun insectivorous plant.

veracious /və'reɪʃəs/ adjective formal truthful, true. □ **veracity** /-'ræs-/ noun.

veranda /və'rændə/ noun (sometimes partly covered) platform along side of house.

verb noun word used to indicate action, event, state, or change (see panel).

verbal adjective of words; oral, not written; of a verb; (of translation) literal. □ **verbally** adverb.

verbalize verb (also **-ise**) (**-zing** or **-sing**) put into words.

verbatim /vɜː'beɪtɪm/ adverb & adjective in exactly the same words.

verbena /vɜː'biːnə/ noun (plural same) plant of genus of herbs and small shrubs with fragrant flowers.

verbiage /'vɜːbɪdʒ/ noun derogatory unnecessary number of words.

verbose /vɜː'bəʊs/ adjective using more words than are needed. □ **verbosity** /-'bɒs-/ noun.

verdant /'vɜːd(ə)nt/ adjective (of grass, field, etc.) green, lush. □ **verdancy** noun.

verdict /'vɜːdɪkt/ noun decision of jury; decision, judgement.

verdigris /'vɜːdɪgriː/ noun greenish-blue substance that forms on copper or brass.

verdure /'vɜːdjə/ noun literary green vegetation or its colour.

verge[1] noun edge, border; brink; grass edging of road etc.

verge[2] verb (**-ging**) (+ on) border on; incline downwards or in specified direction.

verger /'vɜːdʒə/ noun caretaker and attendant in church; officer carrying staff before dignitaries of cathedral etc.

verify /'verɪfaɪ/ verb (**-ies**, **-ied**) establish truth or correctness of by examination etc.; fulfil, bear out. □ **verification** noun.

verily /'verɪlɪ/ adverb archaic truly, really.

verisimilitude /verɪsɪ'mɪlɪtjuːd/ noun appearance of being true or real.

veritable /'verɪtəb(ə)l/ adjective real, rightly so called.

verity /'verɪtɪ/ noun (plural **-ies**) true statement; archaic truth.

vermicelli /vɜːmɪ'tʃelɪ/ noun pasta in long slender threads.

vermicide /'vɜːmɪsaɪd/ noun drug used to kill intestinal worms.

vermiform /'vɜːmɪfɔːm/ adjective worm-shaped. □ **vermiform appendix** small blind tube extending from caecum in man and some other mammals.

vermilion /və'mɪljən/ ● noun brilliant scarlet pigment made esp. from cinnabar; colour of this. ● adjective of this colour.

vermin /'vɜːmɪn/ noun (usually treated as plural) mammals and birds harmful to game, crops, etc.; parasitic worms or insects; vile people.

verminous adjective of the nature of or infested with vermin.

vermouth /'vɜːməθ/ noun wine flavoured with aromatic herbs.

vernacular /və'nækjʊlə/ ● noun language or dialect of country; language of particular class or group; homely speech. ● adjective (of language) of one's own country, not foreign or formal.

vernal /'vɜːn(ə)l/ adjective of or in spring.

vernier /'vɜːnɪə/ noun small movable scale for reading fractional parts of subdivisions on fixed scale of measuring instrument.

veronica /və'rɒnɪkə/ noun speedwell.

verruca /və'ruːkə/ noun (plural **verrucae** /-siː/ or **-s**) wart or similar growth, esp. on foot.

versatile /'vɜːsətaɪl/ adjective turning easily or readily from one subject or occupation to another, skilled in many subjects or occupations; having many uses. □ **versatility** /-'tɪl-/ noun.

verse noun poetry; stanza of poem or song; each of short numbered divisions of Bible.

versed /vɜːst/ adjective (+ in) experienced or skilled in.

versicle /'vɜːsɪk(ə)l/ noun short sentence, esp. each of series in liturgy said or sung by minister or priest, answered by congregation.

versify /'vɜːsɪfaɪ/ verb (**-ies, -ied**) turn into or express in verse; compose verses. □ **versification** noun.

version /'vɜːʃ(ə)n/ noun account of matter from particular point of view; particular edition or translation of book etc.

verso /'vɜːsəʊ/ noun (plural **-s**) left-hand page of open book, back of printed leaf.

versus /'vɜːsəs/ preposition against.

vertebra /'vɜːtɪbrə/ noun (plural **-brae** /-briː/) each segment of backbone. □ **vertebral** adjective.

vertebrate /'vɜːtɪbrət/ ● adjective having backbone. ● noun vertebrate animal.

vertex /'vɜːteks/ noun (plural **-tices** /-tɪsiːz/ or **-texes**) highest point, top, apex; meeting-point of lines that form angle.

vertical /'vɜːtɪk(ə)l/ ● adjective at right angles to horizontal plane; in direction from top to bottom of picture etc.; of or at vertex. ● noun vertical line or plane. □ **vertical take-off** take-off of aircraft directly upwards. □ **vertically** adverb.

vertiginous /vɜː'tɪdʒɪnəs/ adjective of or causing vertigo.

vertigo /'vɜːtɪgəʊ/ noun dizziness.

vervain /'vɜːveɪn/ noun any of several verbenas, esp. one with small blue, white, or purple flowers.

verve noun enthusiasm, energy, vigour.

very /'verɪ/ ● adverb in high degree; (+ own or superlative adjective) in fullest sense. ● adjective real, properly so called etc. □ **very good, well** formula of consent or approval; **very high frequency** 30–300 megahertz (in radio); **Very Reverend** title of dean.

vesicle /'vesɪk(ə)l/ noun small bladder, blister, or bubble.

vespers /'vespəz/ plural noun evening church service.

vessel /'ves(ə)l/ noun hollow receptacle, esp. for liquid; ship or boat, esp. large one; duct or canal holding or conveying blood, sap, etc.

vest ● noun undergarment worn on upper part of body; US & Australian waistcoat. ● verb (+ with) bestow (powers, authority, etc.) on; (+ in) confer (property or power) on (person) with immediate fixed right of future possession. □ **vested interest** personal interest in state of affairs, usually with expectation of gain, Law interest (usually in land or money held in trust) recognized as belonging to person.

Verb

A verb says what a person or thing does, and can describe:

> an action, e.g. run, hit
> an event, e.g. rain, happen
> a state, e.g. be, have, seem, appear
> a change, e.g. become, grow

Verbs occur in different forms, usually in one or other of their tenses. The most common tenses are:

the simple present tense:	The boy walks down the road.
the continuous present tense:	The boy is walking down the road.
the simple past tense:	The boy walked down the road.
the continuous past tense:	The boy was walking down the road.
the perfect tense:	The boy has walked down the road.
the future tense:	The boy will walk down the road.

Each of these forms is a finite verb, which means that it is in a particular tense and that it changes according to the number and person of the subject, as in

> I am   you walk
> we are   he walks

An infinitive is the form of a verb that usually appears with 'to', e.g.

> to wander, to look, to sleep.

vestal virgin /'vest(ə)l/ *noun* virgin consecrated to Vesta, Roman goddess of hearth and home, and vowed to chastity.

vestibule /'vestɪbjuːl/ *noun* lobby, entrance hall.

vestige /'vestɪdʒ/ *noun* trace, evidence; slight amount, particle; *Biology* part or organ now atrophied that was well-developed in ancestors. □ **vestigial** /-'tɪdʒɪəl/ *adjective*.

vestment /'vestmənt/ *noun* ceremonial garment worn by priest etc.

vestry /'vestrɪ/ *noun* (*plural* **-ies**) room or part of church for keeping vestments etc. in.

vet ● *noun colloquial* veterinary surgeon. ● *verb* (**-tt-**) make careful and critical examination of (scheme, work, candidate, etc.).

vetch *noun* plant of pea family largely used for fodder.

veteran /'vetərən/ *noun* old soldier or long-serving member of any group; *US* ex-serviceman or -woman. □ **veteran car** one made before 1905.

veterinarian /vetərɪ'neərɪən/ *noun formal* veterinary surgeon.

veterinary /'vetərɪnərɪ/ *adjective* of or for diseases and injuries of animals. □ **veterinary surgeon** person qualified to treat animals.

veto /'viːtəʊ/ ● *noun* (*plural* **-es**) right to reject measure etc. unilaterally; rejection, prohibition. ● *verb* (**-oes, -oed**) reject (measure etc.); forbid.

vex *verb* annoy, irritate; *archaic* grieve, afflict.

vexation /vek'seɪʃ(ə)n/ *noun* vexing, being vexed; annoying or distressing thing.

vexatious /vek'seɪʃ(ə)s/ *adjective* causing vexation; *Law* lacking sufficient grounds for action and seeking only to annoy defendant.

vexed *adjective* (of question) much discussed.

VHF *abbreviation* very high frequency.

via /'vaɪə/ *preposition* by way of, through.

viable /'vaɪəb(ə)l/ *adjective* (of plan etc.) feasible, esp. economically; (esp. of foetus) capable of living and surviving independently. □ **viability** *noun*.

viaduct /'vaɪədʌkt/ *noun* long bridge carrying railway or road over valley.

vial /'vaɪəl/ *noun* small glass vessel.

viands /'vaɪəndz/ *plural noun formal* articles of food.

viaticum /vaɪ'ætɪkəm/ *noun* (*plural* **-ca**) Eucharist given to dying person.

vibes /vaɪbz/ *plural noun colloquial* vibrations, esp. feelings communicated; vibraphone.

vibrant /'vaɪbrənt/ *adjective* vibrating; resonant; (often + *with*) thrilling; (of colour) bright and striking. □ **vibrancy** *noun*.

vibraphone /'vaɪbrəfəʊn/ *noun* percussion instrument with motor-driven resonators under metal bars giving vibrato effect.

vibrate /vaɪ'breɪt/ *verb* (**-ting**) move rapidly to and fro; (of sound) throb, resonate; (+ *with*) quiver; swing to and fro, oscillate. □ **vibratory** *adjective*.

vibration *noun* vibrating; (in *plural*) mental (esp. occult) influence, atmosphere or feeling communicated.

vibrato /vɪ'brɑːtəʊ/ *noun* tremulous effect in musical pitch.

vibrator *noun* device that vibrates, esp. instrument used in massage or sexual stimulation.

viburnum /vaɪ'bɜːnəm/ *noun* shrub with pink or white flowers.

vicar /'vɪkə/ *noun* incumbent of C. of E. parish where in former times incumbent received stipend rather than tithes; *colloquial* any member of the clergy.

vicarage *noun* vicar's house.

vicarious /vɪ'keərɪəs/ *adjective* experienced indirectly; acting or done etc. for another; deputed, delegated. □ **vicariously** *adverb*.

vice[1] *noun* immoral conduct; particular form of this; bad habit. □ **vice ring** group of criminals organizing prostitution; **vice squad** police department concerned with prostitution.

vice[2] *noun* (*US* **vise**) clamp with two jaws for holding an object being worked on.

vice- *combining form* person acting in place of; person next in rank to.

vice-chancellor /vaɪs'tʃɑːnsələ/ *noun* deputy chancellor (esp. administrator of university).

viceregal /vaɪs'riːg(ə)l/ *adjective* of viceroy.

vicereine /'vaɪsreɪn/ *noun* viceroy's wife; woman viceroy.

viceroy /'vaɪsrɔɪ/ *noun* ruler on behalf of sovereign in colony, province, etc.

vice versa /vaɪs 'vɜːsə/ *adjective* with order of terms changed, other way round.

Vichy water /'viːʃiː/ *noun* effervescent mineral water from Vichy in France.

vicinity /vɪ'sɪnɪtɪ/ *noun* (*plural* **-ies**) surrounding district; (+ *to*) nearness to. □ **in the vicinity (of)** near (to).

vicious /'vɪʃəs/ *adjective* bad-tempered, spiteful; violent; corrupt. □ **vicious circle** self-perpetuating, harmful sequence of cause and effect. □ **viciously** *adverb*; **viciousness** *noun*.

vicissitude /vɪ'sɪsɪtjuːd/ *noun literary* change, esp. of fortune.

victim /'vɪktɪm/ *noun* person or thing destroyed or injured; prey, dupe; creature sacrificed to a god etc.

victimize *verb* (also **-ise**) (**-zing** or **-sing**) single out for punishment or unfair treatment; make (person etc.) a victim. □ **victimization** *noun*.

victor /'vɪktə/ *noun* conqueror, winner of contest.

Victoria Cross /vɪk'tɔːrɪə/ *noun* highest decoration for conspicuous bravery in armed services.

Victorian /vɪk'tɔːrɪən/ ● *adjective* of time of Queen Victoria; prudish, strict. ● *noun* person of this time.

Victoriana /vɪktɔːrɪ'ɑːnə/ *plural noun* articles, esp. collectors' items, of Victorian period.

victorious /vɪk'tɔːrɪəs/ *adjective* conquering, triumphant; marked by victory. □ **victoriously** *adverb*.

victory /'vɪktərɪ/ *noun* (*plural* **-ies**) success in battle, war, or contest.

victual /'vɪt(ə)l/ ● *noun* (usually in *plural*) food, provisions. ● *verb* (**-ll-**; *US* **-l-**) supply with victuals; lay in supply of victuals; eat victuals.

victualler /'vɪtlə/ *noun* (*US* **victualer**) person who supplies victuals; (in full **licensed victualler**) publican licensed to sell alcohol.

vicuña /vɪ'kjuːnə/ *noun* S. American mammal with fine silky wool; cloth made from its wool; imitation of this.

vide /'viːdeɪ/ *verb* (in *imperative*) see, consult. [Latin]

videlicet /vɪ'deliset/ *adverb* that is to say; namely.

video /'vɪdɪəʊ/ ● *adjective* relating to recording or reproduction of moving pictures on magnetic tape; of broadcasting of these. ● *noun* (*plural* **-s**) such recording or broadcasting; *colloquial* video recorder; *colloquial* film on videotape. ● *verb* (**-oes, -oed**) record on videotape. □ **video cassette** cassette of videotape; **video game** computer game played on television screen; **video nasty** *colloquial* horrific or pornographic video film; **video (cassette) recorder** apparatus for recording and playing videotapes.

videotape ● *noun* magnetic tape for recording television pictures and sound. ● *verb* (**-ping**) record on this.

vie /vaɪ/ *verb* (**vying**) (often + *with*) contend, compete, strive for superiority.

Vietnamese /vɪetnəˈmiːz/ ● *adjective* of Vietnam. ● *noun* (*plural* same) native, national, or language of Vietnam.

view /vjuː/ ● *noun* range of vision; what is seen, scene, prospect, picture etc. of this; opinion; inspection by eye or mind. ● *verb* look at; survey visually or mentally; form mental impression or opinion of; watch television. □ **in view of** considering; **on view** being shown or exhibited; **viewdata** news and information service from computer source, connected to TV screen by telephone link; **viewfinder** part of camera showing field of photograph; **viewpoint** point of view; **with a view to** with hope or intention of.

viewer *noun* television-watcher; device for looking at film transparencies etc.

vigil /ˈvɪdʒɪl/ *noun* keeping awake during night etc., esp. to keep watch or pray; eve of festival or holy day.

vigilance *noun* watchfulness; caution. □ **vigilant** *adjective*.

vigilante /vɪdʒɪˈlæntɪ/ *noun* member of self-appointed group for keeping order etc.

vignette /viːˈnjet/ *noun* short description, character sketch; illustration not in definite border; photograph etc. with background shaded off.

vigour /ˈvɪgə/ *noun* (*US* **vigor**) activity and strength of body or mind; healthy growth; animation. □ **vigorous** *adjective*; **vigorously** *adverb*.

Viking /ˈvaɪkɪŋ/ *noun* Scandinavian raider and pirate of 8th–11th c.

vile *adjective* disgusting; depraved; *colloquial* abominably bad. □ **vilely** *adverb*; **vileness** *noun*.

vilify /ˈvɪlɪfaɪ/ *verb* (**-ies**, **-ied**) speak ill of, defame. □ **vilification** *noun*.

villa /ˈvɪlə/ *noun* country house, mansion; rented holiday home, esp. abroad; detached or semi-detached house in residential district.

village /ˈvɪlɪdʒ/ *noun* group of houses etc. in country district, larger than hamlet and smaller than town.

villager *noun* inhabitant of village.

villain /ˈvɪlən/ *noun* wicked person; chief wicked character in play, story, etc.; *colloquial* criminal, rascal.

villainous *adjective* wicked.

villainy *noun* (*plural* **-ies**) wicked behaviour or act.

villein /ˈvɪlɪn/ *noun historical* feudal tenant entirely subject to lord or attached to manor. □ **villeinage** *noun*.

vim *noun colloquial* vigour, energy.

vinaigrette /vɪnɪˈgret/ *noun* salad dressing of oil and wine vinegar.

vindicate /ˈvɪndɪkeɪt/ *verb* (**-ting**) clear of suspicion; establish merits, existence, or justice of. □ **vindication** *noun*; **vindicator** *noun*; **vindicatory** *adjective*.

vindictive /vɪnˈdɪktɪv/ *adjective* tending to seek revenge. □ **vindictively** *adverb*; **vindictiveness** *noun*.

vine *noun* trailing or climbing woody-stemmed plant, esp. bearing grapes.

vinegar /ˈvɪnɪgə/ *noun* sour liquid produced by fermentation of wine, malt, cider, etc. □ **vinegary** *adjective*.

vineyard /ˈvɪnjɑːd/ *noun* plantation of grapevines, esp. for wine-making.

vingt-et-un /væterˈœ̃/ *noun* = PONTOON¹. [French]

vino /ˈviːnəʊ/ *noun slang* wine, esp. of inferior kind.

vinous /ˈvaɪnəs/ *adjective* of, like, or due to wine.

vintage /ˈvɪntɪdʒ/ *noun* season's produce of grapes, wine from this; grape-harvest, season of this; wine of high quality from particular year and district; year etc. when thing was made, thing made etc. in particular year etc. ● *adjective* of high or peak quality; of a past season. □ **vintage car** car made 1917–1930.

vintner /ˈvɪntnə/ *noun* wine merchant.

vinyl /ˈvaɪnɪl/ *noun* any of group of plastics made by polymerization.

viol /ˈvaɪəl/ *noun* medieval stringed instrument similar in shape to violin.

viola¹ /vɪˈəʊlə/ *noun* instrument like violin but larger and of lower pitch.

viola² /ˈvaɪələ/ *noun* any plant of genus including violet and pansy, esp. cultivated hybrid.

viola da gamba /vɪəʊlə də ˈgæmbə/ *noun* viol held between player's legs.

violate /ˈvaɪəleɪt/ *verb* (**-ting**) disregard, break (oath, law, etc.); treat profanely; break in on, disturb; rape. □ **violation** *noun*; **violator** *noun*.

violence /ˈvaɪələns/ *noun* being violent; violent conduct or treatment; unlawful use of force. □ **do violence to** act contrary to, outrage.

violent /ˈvaɪələnt/ *adjective* involving great physical force; intense, vehement; (of death) resulting from violence or poison. □ **violently** *adverb*.

violet /ˈvaɪələt/ ● *noun* plant with usually purple, blue, or white flowers; bluish-purple colour at opposite end of spectrum from red; paint, clothes, or material of this colour. ● *adjective* of this colour.

violin /vaɪəˈlɪn/ *noun* high-pitched instrument with 4 strings played with bow. □ **violinist** *noun*.

violoncello /vaɪələnˈtʃeləʊ/ *noun* (*plural* **-s**) *formal* cello.

VIP *abbreviation* very important person.

viper /ˈvaɪpə/ *noun* small venomous snake; malignant or treacherous person.

virago /vɪˈrɑːgəʊ/ *noun* (*plural* **-s**) fierce or abusive woman.

viral /ˈvaɪər(ə)l/ *adjective* of or caused by virus.

virgin /ˈvɜːdʒɪn/ ● *noun* person who has never had sexual intercourse; (**the Virgin**) Christ's mother Mary. ● *adjective* not yet used etc.; virginal. □ **the Virgin birth** doctrine of Christ's birth from virgin mother. □ **virginity** /vəˈdʒɪn-/ *noun*.

virginal *adjective* of or befitting a virgin. ● *noun* (usually in *plural*) legless spinet in box.

Virginia creeper /vəˈdʒɪnɪə/ *noun* vine cultivated for ornament.

Virgo /ˈvɜːgəʊ/ *noun* sixth sign of zodiac.

virile /ˈvɪraɪl/ *adjective* having masculine vigour or strength; sexually potent; of man as distinct from woman or child. □ **virility** /-ˈrɪl-/ *noun*.

virology /vaɪˈrɒlədʒɪ/ *noun* study of viruses.

virtual /ˈvɜːtʃʊəl/ *adjective* being so for practical purposes though not strictly or in name. □ **virtual reality** computer-generated images, sounds, etc. that appear real to the senses. □ **virtually** *adverb*.

virtue /ˈvɜːtʃuː/ *noun* moral goodness; particular form of this; chastity, esp. of woman; good quality; efficacy. □ **by** or **in virtue of** on account of, because of.

virtuoso /vɜːtʃʊˈəʊsəʊ/ *noun* (*plural* **-si** /-siː/ or **-sos**) highly skilled artist, esp. musician. □ **virtuosity** /-ˈɒs-/ *noun*.

virtuous /ˈvɜːtʃʊəs/ *adjective* morally good; *archaic* chaste. □ **virtuously** *adverb*.

virulent /ˈvɪrʊlənt/ *adjective* poisonous; (of disease) violent; bitterly hostile. □ **virulence** *noun*; **virulently** *adverb*.

virus /ˈvaɪərəs/ *noun* microscopic organism able to cause diseases; computer virus.

visa /ˈviːzə/ *noun* endorsement on passport etc., esp. allowing holder to enter or leave country.

visage /ˈvɪzɪdʒ/ *noun literary* face.

vis-à-vis /viːzəˈviː/ ● *preposition* in relation to; in comparison with. ● *adverb* opposite. [French]

viscera /ˈvɪsərə/ plural noun internal organs of body. □ **visceral** adjective.

viscid /ˈvɪsɪd/ adjective glutinous, sticky.

viscose /ˈvɪskəʊz/ noun viscous form of cellulose used in making rayon etc.; fabric made from this.

viscount /ˈvaɪkaʊnt/ noun British nobleman ranking between earl and baron.

viscountess /ˈvaɪkaʊntɪs/ noun viscount's wife or widow; woman holding rank of viscount.

viscous /ˈvɪskəs/ adjective glutinous, sticky; semi-fluid; not flowing freely. □ **viscosity** /-kɒs-/ noun (plural **-ies**).

visibility /vɪzɪˈbɪlɪtɪ/ noun being visible; range or possibility of vision as determined by light and weather.

visible /ˈvɪzɪb(ə)l/ adjective able to be seen, perceived, or discovered; in sight; apparent, open, obvious. □ **visibly** adverb.

vision /ˈvɪʒ(ə)n/ noun act or faculty of seeing; sight; thing or person seen in dream or trance; thing seen in imagination; imaginative insight; foresight, good judgement in planning; beautiful person etc.; TV or cinema picture, esp. of specified quality.

visionary /ˈvɪʒənərɪ/ adjective given to seeing visions or to fanciful theories; having vision or foresight; not real, imaginary; unpractical. ● noun (plural **-ies**) visionary person.

visit /ˈvɪzɪt/ ● verb (**-t-**) go or come to see (person, place, etc.); stay temporarily with or at; (of disease, calamity, etc.) attack; (often + upon) inflict punishment for (sin). ● noun act of visiting, temporary stay with person or at place; (+ to) occasion of going to doctor etc.; formal or official call.

visitant /ˈvɪzɪt(ə)nt/ noun visitor, esp. ghost etc.

visitation /vɪzɪˈteɪʃ(ə)n/ noun official visit of inspection; trouble etc. seen as divine punishment.

visitor noun person who visits; migrant bird.

visor /ˈvaɪzə/ noun movable part of helmet covering face; shield for eyes, esp. one at top of vehicle windscreen.

vista /ˈvɪstə/ noun view, esp. through avenue of trees or other long narrow opening; mental view of long succession of events.

visual /ˈvɪʒʊəl/ adjective of or used in seeing. □ **visual display unit** device displaying data of computer on screen. □ **visually** adverb.

visualize verb (also **-ise**) (**-zing** or **-sing**) imagine visually. □ **visualization** noun.

vital /ˈvaɪt(ə)l/ ● adjective of or essential to organic life; essential to existence, success, etc.; full of life or activity; fatal. ● noun (in plural) vital organs, e.g. lungs and heart. □ **vital statistics** those relating to number of births, marriages, deaths, etc., jocular measurements of woman's bust, waist, and hips. □ **vitally** adverb.

vitality /vaɪˈtælɪtɪ/ noun animation, liveliness; ability to survive or endure.

vitalize verb (also **-ise**) (**-zing** or **-sing**) endow with life; make lively or vigorous. □ **vitalization** noun.

vitamin /ˈvɪtəmɪn/ noun any of various substances present in many foods and essential to health and growth.

vitaminize verb (also **-ise**) (**-zing** or **-sing**) introduce vitamins into (food).

vitiate /ˈvɪʃɪeɪt/ verb (**-ting**) impair, debase; make invalid or ineffectual.

viticulture /ˈvɪtɪkʌltʃə/ noun cultivation of grapes.

vitreous /ˈvɪtrɪəs/ adjective of or like glass.

vitrify /ˈvɪtrɪfaɪ/ verb (**-ies**, **-ied**) change into glass or glassy substance, esp. by heat. □ **vitrification** noun.

vitriol /ˈvɪtrɪəl/ noun sulphuric acid or sulphate; caustic speech or criticism. □ **vitriolic** /-ˈɒl-/ adjective.

vitro see IN VITRO.

vituperate /vaɪˈtjuːpəreɪt/ verb (**-ting**) criticize abusively. □ **vituperation** noun; **vituperative** /-rətɪv/ adjective.

viva¹ /ˈvaɪvə/ colloquial ● noun (plural **-s**) viva voce. ● verb (**vivas, vivaed, vivaing**) viva-voce.

viva² /ˈviːvə/ ● interjection long live. ● noun cry of this as salute etc. [Italian]

vivacious /vɪˈveɪʃəs/ adjective lively, animated. □ **vivacity** /vɪˈvæsɪtɪ/ noun.

vivarium /vaɪˈveərɪəm/ noun (plural **-ria** or **-s**) glass bowl etc. for keeping animals for scientific study; place for keeping animals in (nearly) their natural conditions.

viva voce /vaɪvə ˈvəʊtʃɪ/ ● adjective oral. ● adverb orally. ● noun oral exam.

viva-voce verb (**-voces, -voceed, -voceing**) examine orally.

vivid /ˈvɪvɪd/ adjective (of light or colour) bright, strong, intense; (of memory, description, etc.) lively, incisive, graphic. □ **vividly** adverb; **vividness** noun.

vivify /ˈvɪvɪfaɪ/ verb (**-ies**, **-ied**) give life to, animate.

viviparous /vɪˈvɪpərəs/ adjective bringing forth young alive.

vivisect /ˈvɪvɪsekt/ verb perform vivisection on.

vivisection /vɪvɪˈsekʃ(ə)n/ noun surgical experimentation on living animals for scientific research. □ **vivisectionist** noun.

vixen /ˈvɪks(ə)n/ noun female fox; spiteful woman.

viz. abbreviation videlicet.

vizier /vɪˈzɪə/ noun historical high official in some Muslim countries.

V-neck noun V-shaped neckline on pullover etc.

vocabulary /vəˈkæbjʊlərɪ/ noun (plural **-ies**) words used by language, book, branch of science, or author; list of these; person's range of language.

vocal /ˈvəʊk(ə)l/ adjective of or uttered by voice; speaking one's feelings freely. □ **vocal cords** voice-producing part of larynx. □ **vocally** adverb.

vocalist noun singer.

vocalize verb (also **-ise**) (**-zing** or **-sing**) form (sound) or utter (word) with voice; articulate, express. □ **vocalization** noun.

vocation /vəʊˈkeɪʃ(ə)n/ noun divine call to, or sense of suitability for, career or occupation; employment, trade, profession. □ **vocational** adjective.

vocative /ˈvɒkətɪv/ ● noun case of noun used in addressing person or thing. ● adjective of or in this case.

vociferate /vəˈsɪfəreɪt/ verb (**-ting**) utter noisily; shout, bawl. □ **vociferation** noun.

vociferous /vəˈsɪfərəs/ adjective noisy, clamorous; loud and insistent in speech. □ **vociferously** adverb.

vodka /ˈvɒdkə/ noun alcoholic spirit distilled esp. in Russia from rye etc.

vogue /vəʊɡ/ noun (**the vogue**) prevailing fashion; popular use. □ **in vogue** in fashion. □ **voguish** adjective.

voice ● noun sound formed in larynx and uttered by mouth, esp. in speaking, singing, etc.; ability to produce this; use of voice, spoken or written expression, opinion so expressed, right to express opinion; Grammar set of verbal forms showing whether verb is active or passive. ● verb (**-cing**) express; (esp. as **voiced** adjective) utter with vibration of vocal cords. □ **voice-over** commentary in film by unseen speaker.

void ● adjective empty, vacant; not valid or binding. ● noun empty space, sense of loss. ● verb invalidate; excrete.

voile /vɔɪl/ noun thin semi-transparent fabric.

vol. abbreviation volume.

volatile /ˈvɒlətaɪl/ *adjective* changeable in mood, flighty; unstable; evaporating rapidly. □ **volatility** /-ˈtɪl-/ *noun.*

vol-au-vent /ˈvɒləʊvɑ̃/ *noun* small round case of puff pastry with savoury filling.

volcanic /vɒlˈkænɪk/ *adjective* of, like, or produced by volcano.

volcano /vɒlˈkeɪnəʊ/ *noun* (*plural* **-es**) mountain or hill from which lava, steam, etc. escape through earth's crust.

vole *noun* small plant-eating rodent.

volition /vəˈlɪʃ(ə)n/ *noun* act or power of willing. □ **of one's own volition** voluntarily.

volley /ˈvɒlɪ/ ● *noun* (*plural* **-s**) simultaneous firing of a number of weapons; bullets etc. so fired; (usually + *of*) torrent (of abuse etc.); *Tennis, Football, etc.* playing of ball before it touches ground. ● *verb* (**-eys, -eyed**) return or send by volley. □ **volleyball** game for two teams of 6 hitting large ball by hand over net.

volt /vəʊlt/ *noun* SI unit of electromotive force. □ **voltmeter** instrument measuring electric potential in volts.

voltage *noun* electromotive force expressed in volts.

volte-face /vɒltˈfɑːs/ *noun* (*plural* **voltes-face** same pronunciation) complete change of position in one's attitude or opinion.

voluble /ˈvɒljʊb(ə)l/ *adjective* speaking or spoken fluently or with continuous flow of words. □ **volubility** *noun;* **volubly** *adverb.*

volume /ˈvɒljuːm/ *noun* single book forming part or all of work; solid content, bulk; space occupied by gas or liquid; (+ *of*) amount or quantity of; quantity or power of sound; (+ *of*) moving mass of (water, smoke, etc.).

voluminous /vəˈluːmɪnəs/ *adjective* (of drapery etc.) loose and ample; written or writing at great length.

voluntary /ˈvɒləntrɪ/ ● *adjective* done, acting, or given willingly; unpaid; (of institution) supported or built by charity; brought about by voluntary action; (of muscle, limb, etc.) controlled by will. ● *noun* (*plural* **-ies**) organ solo played before or after church service. □ **voluntarily** *adverb.*

volunteer /vɒlənˈtɪə/ ● *noun* person who voluntarily undertakes task or enters military etc. service. ● *verb* (often + *to*) undertake or offer voluntarily; (often + *for*) be volunteer.

voluptuary /vəˈlʌptjʊərɪ/ *noun* (*plural* **-ies**) person who seeks luxury and sensual pleasure.

voluptuous /vəˈlʌptjʊəs/ *adjective* of, tending to, occupied with, or derived from, sensuous or sensual pleasure; (of woman) curvaceous and sexually desirable. □ **voluptuously** *adverb.*

vomit /ˈvɒmɪt/ ● *verb* (**-t-**) eject (contents of stomach) through mouth, be sick; (of volcano, chimney, etc.) eject violently, belch forth. ● *noun* matter vomited from stomach.

voodoo /ˈvuːduː/ ● *noun* religious witchcraft as practised esp. in W. Indies. ● *verb* (**-doos, -dooed**) affect by voodoo, bewitch.

voracious /vəˈreɪʃəs/ *adjective* greedy in eating, ravenous; very eager. □ **voraciously** *adverb;* **voracity** /-ˈræs-/ *noun.*

vortex /ˈvɔːteks/ *noun* (*plural* **-texes** or **-tices** /-tɪsiːz/) whirlpool, whirlwind; whirling motion or mass; thing viewed as destructive or devouring.

votary /ˈvəʊtərɪ/ *noun* (*plural* **-ies**, *feminine* **votaress**) (usually + *of*) person dedicated to service of god or cult; devotee of a person, occupation etc.

vote ● *noun* formal expression of choice or opinion by ballot, show of hands, etc.; (usually **the vote**) right to vote; opinion expressed by vote; votes given by or for particular group. ● *verb* (**-ting**) (often + *for, against*) give vote; enact etc. by majority of votes; *colloquial* pronounce by general consent; (often + *that*) suggest, urge. □ **vote down** defeat (proposal etc.) by voting; **vote in** elect by voting; **vote with one's feet** *colloquial* indicate opinion by one's presence or absence.

voter *noun* person voting or entitled to vote.

votive /ˈvəʊtɪv/ *adjective* given or consecrated in fulfilment of vow.

vouch /vaʊtʃ/ *verb* (+ *for*) answer or be surety for.

voucher *noun* document exchangeable for goods or services; receipt.

vouchsafe /vaʊtʃˈseɪf/ *verb* (**-fing**) *formal* condescend to grant; (+ *to do*) condescend.

vow /vaʊ/ ● *noun* solemn, esp. religious, promise. ● *verb* promise solemnly; *archaic* declare solemnly.

vowel /ˈvaʊəl/ *noun* speech sound made by vibrations of vocal cords, but without audible friction; letter(s) representing this.

■ **Usage** The (written) vowels of English are customarily said to be *a, e, i, o,* and *u,* but *y* can be either a consonant (as in *yet*) or a vowel (as in *by*), and combinations of these six, such as *ee* in *keep, ie* in *tied, ou* in *pour,* and *ye* in *rye,* are just as much vowels.

vox pop *noun colloquial* popular opinion as represented by informal comments.

vox populi /vɒks ˈpɒpjʊlaɪ/ *noun* public opinion, popular belief. [Latin]

voyage /ˈvɔɪɪdʒ/ ● *noun* journey, esp. long one by sea or in space. ● *verb* (**-ging**) make voyage. □ **voyager** *noun.*

voyeur /vwɑːˈjɜː/ *noun* person who derives sexual pleasure from secretly observing others' sexual activity or organs; (esp. covert) spectator. □ **voyeurism** *noun;* **voyeuristic** /-ˈrɪs-/ *adjective.*

vs. *abbreviation* versus.

VSO *abbreviation* Voluntary Service Overseas.

VTOL /ˈviːtɒl/ *abbreviation* vertical take-off and landing.

vulcanite /ˈvʌlkənaɪt/ *noun* hard black vulcanized rubber.

vulcanize /ˈvʌlkənaɪz/ *verb* (also **-ise**) (**-zing** or **-sing**) make (rubber etc.) stronger and more elastic by treating with sulphur at high temperature. □ **vulcanization** *noun.*

vulgar /ˈvʌlgə/ *adjective* coarse; of or characteristic of the common people; in common use, prevalent. □ **vulgar fraction** fraction expressed by numerator and denominator (e.g. ½), not decimally (e.g. 0.5); **the vulgar tongue** native or vernacular language. □ **vulgarity** /-ˈgær-/ *noun* (*plural* **-ies**); **vulgarly** *adverb.*

vulgarian /vʌlˈgeərɪən/ *noun* vulgar (esp. rich) person.

vulgarism *noun* vulgar word or expression.

vulgarize /ˈvʌlgəraɪz/ *verb* (also **-ise**) (**-zing** or **-sing**) make vulgar; spoil by popularizing. □ **vulgarization** *noun.*

Vulgate /ˈvʌlgeɪt/ *noun* 4th-c. Latin version of Bible.

vulnerable /ˈvʌlnərəb(ə)l/ *adjective* easily wounded or harmed; (+ *to*) open to attack, injury, or criticism. □ **vulnerability** *noun.*

vulpine /ˈvʌlpaɪn/ *adjective* of or like fox; crafty, cunning.

vulture /ˈvʌltʃə/ *noun* large carrion-eating bird of prey; rapacious person.

vulva /ˈvʌlvə/ *noun* (*plural* **-s**) external female genitals.

vv. *abbreviation* verses.

vying *present participle* of VIE.

Ww

W *abbreviation* (also **W.**) watt(s); west(ern).

w. *abbreviation* wicket(s); wide(s); with.

wacky /'wækɪ/ *adjective* (**-ier, -iest**) *slang* crazy.

wad /wɒd/ ● *noun* lump of soft material to keep things apart or in place or to block hole; roll of banknotes. ● *verb* (**-dd-**) stop up or fix with wad; line, stuff, or protect with wadding.

wadding *noun* soft fibrous material for stuffing quilts, packing fragile articles in, etc.

waddle /'wɒd(ə)l/ ● *verb* (**-ling**) walk with short steps and swaying motion. ● *noun* such walk.

wade ● *verb* (**-ding**) walk through water, mud, etc., esp. with difficulty; (+ *through*) go through (tedious task, book, etc.); (+ *into*) *colloquial* attack (person, task). ● *noun* spell of wading. □ **wade in** *colloquial* make vigorous attack or intervention.

wader *noun* long-legged waterfowl; (in *plural*) high waterproof boots.

wadi /'wɒdɪ/ *noun* (*plural* **-s**) rocky watercourse in N. Africa etc., dry except in rainy season.

wafer /'weɪfə/ *noun* very thin light crisp biscuit; disc of unleavened bread used in Eucharist; disc of red paper stuck on legal document instead of seal. □ **wafer-thin** very thin.

waffle[1] /'wɒf(ə)l/ *colloquial* ● *noun* aimless verbose talk or writing. ● *verb* (**-ling**) indulge in waffle.

waffle[2] /'wɒf(ə)l/ *noun* small crisp batter cake. □ **waffle-iron** utensil for cooking waffles.

waft /wɒft/ ● *verb* convey or be conveyed smoothly (as) through air or over water. ● *noun* whiff.

wag[1] ● *verb* (**-gg-**) shake or wave to and fro. ● *noun* single wagging motion. □ **wagtail** small bird with long tail.

wag[2] *noun* facetious person.

wage ● *noun* (in *singular* or *plural*) employee's regular pay, esp. paid weekly. ● *verb* (**-ging**) carry on (war etc.).

waged *adjective* in regular paid employment.

wager /'weɪdʒə/ *noun* & *verb* bet.

waggish *adjective* playful, facetious. □ **waggishly** *adverb*.

waggle /'wæg(ə)l/ *verb* (**-ling**) *colloquial* wag.

wagon /'wægən/ *noun* (also **waggon**) 4-wheeled vehicle for heavy loads; open railway truck. □ **on the wagon** *slang* abstaining from alcohol; **wagon-load** as much as wagon can carry.

wagoner *noun* (also **waggoner**) driver of wagon.

waif *noun* homeless and helpless person, esp. abandoned child; ownerless object or animal.

wail ● *noun* prolonged plaintive inarticulate cry of pain, grief, etc.; sound resembling this. ● *verb* utter wail; lament or complain persistently.

wain *noun* *archaic* wagon.

wainscot /'weɪnskət/ *noun* (also **wainscoting**) boarding or wooden panelling on room-wall.

waist *noun* part of human body between ribs and hips; narrowness marking this; circumference of waist; narrow middle part of anything; part of garment encircling waist; *US* bodice, blouse; part of ship between forecastle and quarterdeck. □ **waistband** strip of cloth forming waist of garment; **waistcoat** usually sleeveless and collarless waist-length garment; **waistline** outline or size of waist.

wait ● *verb* defer action until expected event occurs; await (turn etc.); (of thing) remain in readiness; (usually as **waiting** *noun*) park briefly; act as waiter or attendant; (+ *on*, *upon*) await convenience of, be attendant to. ● *noun* act or period of waiting; (usually + *for*) watching for enemy; (in *plural*) *archaic* street singers of Christmas carols. □ **waiting-list** list of people waiting for thing not immediately available; **waiting-room** room for people to wait in, esp. at surgery or railway station.

waiter *noun* (*feminine* **waitress**) person who serves at hotel or restaurant tables.

waive *verb* (**-ving**) refrain from insisting on or using.

waiver *noun* *Law* (document recording) waiving.

wake[1] ● *verb* (**-king**; *past* **woke**; *past participle* **woken** /'wəʊk(ə)n/) (often + *up*) (cause to) cease to sleep or become alert; *archaic* (except as **waking** *adjective* & *noun*) be awake; disturb with noise; evoke. ● *noun* (chiefly in Ireland) vigil beside corpse before burial, attendant lamentations and merrymaking; (usually in *plural*) annual holiday in (industrial) N. England.

wake[2] *noun* track left on water's surface by moving ship etc.; turbulent air left by moving aircraft. □ **in the wake of** following, as result of.

wakeful *adjective* unable to sleep; sleepless; vigilant. □ **wakefully** *adverb*; **wakefulness** *noun*.

waken /'weɪkən/ *verb* make or become awake.

walk /wɔːk/ ● *verb* move by lifting and setting down each foot in turn, never having both feet off the ground at once; (of quadruped) go with slowest gait; travel or go on foot, take exercise thus; traverse (distance) in walking; tread floor or surface of; cause to walk with one. ● *noun* act of walking, ordinary human gait; slowest gait of animal; person's manner of walking; distance walkable in specified time; excursion on foot; place or track meant or fit for walking. □ **walkabout** informal stroll by royal person etc., Australian Aboriginal's period of wandering; **walking frame** tubular metal frame to assist elderly or disabled people in walking; **walking stick** stick carried for support when walking; **walk off with** *colloquial* steal, win easily; **walk of life** one's occupation; **walk-on part** short or non-speaking dramatic role; **walk out** depart suddenly or angrily, stop work in protest; **walk-out** *noun*; **walk out on** desert; **walkover** easy victory; **walk the streets** be prostitute; **walkway** passage or path for walking along. □ **walkable** *adjective*.

walker *noun* person etc. that walks; framework in which baby can walk unaided; walking frame.

walkie-talkie /wɔːkɪ'tɔːkɪ/ *noun* portable two-way radio.

Walkman /'wɔːkmən/ *noun* (*plural* **-s**) *proprietary term* type of personal stereo.

wall /wɔːl/ ● *noun* continuous narrow upright structure of usually brick or stone, esp. enclosing or dividing a space or supporting a roof; thing like wall in appearance or effect; outermost layer of animal or plant organ, cell, etc. ● *verb* (esp. as **walled** *adjective*) surround with wall; (usually + *up*, *off*) block with wall; (+ *up*) enclose within sealed space. □ **go to the wall** fare badly in competition; **up the wall** *colloquial* crazy, furious; **wallflower** fragrant garden plant, *colloquial* woman not dancing because partnerless; **wall game** Eton form of football; **wallpaper** *noun* paper for covering interior walls of rooms, *verb* decorate with wallpaper; **wall-to-wall** fitted to cover whole floor, *colloquial* ubiquitous.

wallaby /ˈwɒləbɪ/ *noun* (*plural* **-ies**) small kangaroo-like marsupial.

wallah /ˈwɒlə/ *noun slang* person connected with a specified occupation or thing.

wallet /ˈwɒlɪt/ *noun* small flat case for holding bank-notes etc.

wall-eye *noun* eye with whitish iris or outward squint. □ **wall-eyed** *adjective*.

wallop /ˈwɒləp/ *colloquial* ● *verb* (**-p-**) thrash, beat. ● *noun* whack; beer.

wallow /ˈwɒləʊ/ ● *verb* roll about in mud etc.; (+ *in*) indulge unrestrainedly in. ● *noun* act of wallowing; place where animals wallow.

wally /ˈwɒlɪ/ *noun* (*plural* **-ies**) *slang* foolish or incompetent person.

walnut /ˈwɔːlnʌt/ *noun* tree with aromatic leaves and drooping catkins; its nut; its timber.

walrus /ˈwɔːlrəs/ *noun* (*plural* same or **walruses**) long-tusked amphibious arctic mammal. □ **walrus moustache** long thick drooping moustache.

waltz /wɔːls/ ● *noun* ballroom dance in triple time; music for this. ● *verb* dance waltz; (often + *in*, *out*, *round*, etc.) *colloquial* move easily, casually, etc.

wampum /ˈwɒmpəm/ *noun* strings of shell-beads formerly used by N. American Indians for money, ornament, etc.

wan /wɒn/ *adjective* (**-nn-**) pale, weary-looking. □ **wanly** *adverb*.

wand /wɒnd/ *noun* fairy's or magician's magic stick; staff as sign of office etc.; *colloquial Music* conductor's baton.

wander /ˈwɒndə/ *verb* (often + *in*, *off*, etc.) go from place to place aimlessly; meander; diverge from path etc.; talk or think incoherently; be inattentive or delirious. □ **wanderlust** eagerness to travel or wander, restlessness. □ **wanderer** *noun*.

wane ● *verb* (**-ning**) (of moon) decrease in apparent size; decrease in power, vigour, importance, size, etc. ● *noun* process of waning. □ **on the wane** declining.

wangle /ˈwæŋg(ə)l/ *colloquial* ● *verb* (**-ling**) contrive to obtain (favour etc.). ● *noun* act of wangling.

wannabe /ˈwɒnəbɪ/ *noun slang* avid fan who apes person admired; anyone wishing to be someone else.

want /wɒnt/ ● *verb* (often + *to do*) desire; wish for possession of; need; (+ *to do*) *colloquial* should; (usually + *for*) lack; be without or fall short by; (as **wanted** *adjective*) (of suspected criminal etc.) sought by police. ● *noun* lack, deficiency; poverty, need.

wanting *adjective* lacking (in quality or quantity), unequal to requirements; absent.

wanton /ˈwɒnt(ə)n/ ● *adjective* licentious; capricious, arbitrary; luxuriant, wild. ● *noun literary* licentious person. □ **wantonly** *adverb*.

wapiti /ˈwɒpɪtɪ/ *noun* (*plural* **-s**) large N. American deer.

war /wɔː/ ● *noun* armed hostility, esp. between nations; specific period of this; hostility between people; (often + *on*) efforts against crime, poverty, etc. ● *verb* (**-rr-**) (as **warring** *adjective*) rival, fighting; make war. □ **at war** engaged in war; **go to war** begin war; **on the warpath** going to war, *colloquial* seeking confrontation; **war crime** crime violating international laws of war; **war cry** phrase or name shouted to rally troops, party slogan; **war dance** dance performed by primitive peoples before battle or after victory; **warhead** explosive head of missile; **warhorse** *historical* trooper's horse, *colloquial* veteran soldier; **war memorial** monument to those killed in (a) war; **warmonger** /-mʌŋgə/ person who promotes war; **warpaint** paint put on body esp. by N. American Indians before battle, *colloquial* make-up; **warship** ship used in war.

warble /ˈwɔːb(ə)l/ ● *verb* (**-ling**) sing in a gentle trilling way. ● *noun* warbling sound.

warbler *noun* bird that warbles.

ward /wɔːd/ *noun* separate division or room of hospital etc.; administrative division, esp. for elections; minor etc. under care of guardian or court; (in *plural*) corresponding notches and projections in key and lock; *archaic* guardianship. □ **ward off** parry (blow), avert (danger etc.); **wardroom** officers' mess in warship.

warden /ˈwɔːd(ə)n/ *noun* supervising official; president or governor of institution; traffic warden.

warder /ˈwɔːdə/ *noun* (*feminine* **wardress**) prison officer.

wardrobe /ˈwɔːdrəʊb/ *noun* large cupboard for storing clothes; stock of clothes; theatre's costume department. □ **wardrobe master, mistress** person in charge of theatrical wardrobe.

wardship *noun* tutelage.

ware *noun* things of specified kind made usually for sale; (usually in *plural*) articles for sale.

warehouse ● *noun* building in which goods are stored; wholesale or large retail store. ● *verb* (**-sing**) store in warehouse.

warfare /ˈwɔːfeə/ *noun* waging war, campaigning.

warlike *adjective* hostile; soldierly; military.

warlock /ˈwɔːlɒk/ *noun archaic* sorcerer.

warm /wɔːm/ ● *adjective* of or at fairly high temperature; (of person) with skin at natural or slightly raised temperature; (of clothes) affording warmth; hearty, enthusiastic; sympathetic, friendly, loving; *colloquial* dangerous, hostile; *colloquial* (in game) near object sought, near to guessing; (of colour) reddish or yellowish, suggesting warmth; (of scent in hunting) fresh and strong. ● *verb* make or become warm. ● *noun* act of warming; warmth. □ **warm-blooded** (of animals) having blood temperature well above that of environment; **warm-hearted** kind, friendly; **warming-pan** *historical* flat closed vessel holding hot coals for warming beds; **warm up** make or become warm, prepare for performance etc. by practising, reach temperature for efficient working, reheat (food); **warm-up** *noun*. □ **warmly** *adverb*; **warmth** *noun*.

warn /wɔːn/ *verb* (often + *of*, *that*) inform of impending danger or misfortune; (+ *to do*) advise (person) to take certain action; (often + *against*) inform (person) about specific danger. □ **warn off** tell (person) to keep away (from).

warning *noun* what is said or done or occurs to warn person.

warp /wɔːp/ ● *verb* make or become distorted, esp. through heat, damp, etc.; make or become perverted or strange; haul (ship etc.) by rope attached to fixed point. ● *noun* warped state; mental perversion; lengthwise threads in loom; rope used in warping ship.

warrant /ˈwɒrənt/ ● *noun* thing that authorizes an action; written authorization, money voucher, etc.; written authorization allowing police to carry out search or arrest; certificate of service rank held by warrant officer. ● *verb* serve as warrant for, justify; guarantee. □ **warrant officer** officer ranking between commissioned and non-commissioned officers.

warranty /ˈwɒrəntɪ/ *noun* (*plural* **-ies**) undertaking as to ownership or quality of thing sold etc., often accepting responsibility for repairs needed over specified period; authority, justification.

warren /ˈwɒrən/ *noun* network of rabbit burrows; densely populated or labyrinthine building or district.

warrior /'wɒrɪə/ *noun* person skilled in or famed for fighting.

wart /wɔːt/ *noun* small round dry growth on skin; protuberance on skin of animal, surface of plant, etc. □ **wart-hog** African wild pig. □ **warty** *adjective*.

wary /'weərɪ/ *adjective* (**-ier, -iest**) on one's guard, circumspect; cautious. □ **warily** *adverb*; **wariness** *noun*.

was *1st & 3rd singular past of* BE.

wash /wɒʃ/ ● *verb* cleanse with liquid; (+ *out, off, away*, etc.) remove or be removed by washing; wash oneself or one's hands (and face); wash clothes, dishes, etc.; (of fabric or dye) bear washing without damage; bear scrutiny, be believed or acceptable; (of river etc.) touch; (of liquid) carry along in specified direction; sweep, move, splash; (+ *over*).occur without affecting (person); sift (ore) by action of water; brush watery colour over; *poetical* moisten. ● *noun* washing, being washed; clothes for washing or just washed; motion of agitated water or air, esp. due to passage of vessel or aircraft; kitchen slops given to pigs; thin, weak, inferior, or animals' liquid food; liquid to spread over surface to cleanse, heal, or colour. □ **washbasin** basin for washing one's hands etc.; **washboard** ribbed board for washing clothes, this as percussion instrument; **wash down** wash completely, (usually + *with*) accompany or follow (food); **washed out** faded, pale, *colloquial* exhausted; **washed up** esp. *US slang* defeated, having failed; **wash one's hands of** decline responsibility for; **wash out** clean inside of by washing, *colloquial* cause to be cancelled because of rain; **wash-out** *colloquial* complete failure; **washroom** esp. *US* public toilet; **washstand** piece of furniture for holding washbasin, soap-dish, etc.; **wash up** wash (dishes etc.) after use, *US* wash one's face and hands, (of sea) carry on to shore. □ **washable** *adjective*.

washer *noun* person or thing that washes; flat ring placed between two surfaces or under plunger of tap, nut, etc. to tighten joint or disperse pressure.

washerwoman *noun* laundress.

washing *noun* clothes etc. for washing or just washed. □ **washing machine** machine for washing clothes; **washing powder** soap powder or detergent for washing clothes; **washing-up** washing of dishes etc., dishes etc. for washing.

washy *adjective* (**-ier, -iest**) too watery or weak; lacking vigour.

wasn't /'wɒz(ə)nt/ was not.

Wasp /wɒsp/ *noun* (also **WASP**) *US usually derogatory* middle-class white American [Anglo-Saxon] Protestant.

wasp /wɒsp/ *noun* stinging insect with black and yellow stripes. □ **wasp-waist** very slender waist.

waspish *adjective* irritable, snappish.

wassail /'wɒseɪl/ *archaic* ● *noun* festive drinking. ● *verb* make merry.

wastage /'weɪstɪdʒ/ *noun* amount wasted; loss by use, wear, or leakage; (also **natural wastage**) loss of employees other than by redundancy.

waste ● *verb* (**-ting**) use to no purpose or for inadequate result or extravagantly; fail to use; (often + *on*) give (advice etc.) without effect; (in *passive*) fail to be appreciated or used properly; wear away; make or become weak; devastate. ● *adjective* superfluous, no longer needed; uninhabited, not cultivated. ● *noun* act of wasting; waste material; waste region; diminution by wear; waste pipe. □ **go, run to waste** be wasted; **wasteland** land not productive or developed, spiritually or intellectually barren place or time; **waste paper** used or valueless paper; **waste pipe** pipe carrying off waste material; **waste product** useless by-product of manufacture or organism.

wasteful *adjective* extravagant; causing or showing waste. □ **wastefully** *adverb*.

waster *noun* wasteful person; *colloquial* wastrel.

wastrel /'weɪstr(ə)l/ *noun* good-for-nothing person.

watch /wɒtʃ/ ● *verb* keep eyes fixed on; keep under observation, follow observantly; (often + *for*) be in alert state, be vigilant; (+ *over*) look after, take care of. ● *noun* small portable timepiece for wrist or pocket; state of alert or constant attention; *Nautical* usually 4-hour spell of duty; *historical* (member of) body of men patrolling streets at night. □ **on the watch for** waiting for (anticipated event); **watch-dog** dog guarding property, person etc. monitoring others' rights etc.; **watching brief** brief of barrister who follows case for client not directly concerned; **watchman** man employed to look after empty building etc. at night; **watch out** (often + *for*) be on one's guard; **watch-tower** tower for observing prisoners, attackers, etc.; **watchword** phrase summarizing guiding principle. □ **watcher** *noun* (also *in combination*).

watchful *adjective* accustomed to watching; on the watch. □ **watchfully** *adverb*; **watchfulness** *noun*.

water /'wɔːtə/ ● *noun* transparent colourless liquid found in seas and rivers etc. and in rain etc.; sheet or body of water; (in *plural*) part of sea or river; (often **the waters**) mineral water at spa etc.; state of tide; solution of specified substance in water; transparency and lustre of gem; (usually in *plural*) amniotic fluid. ● *verb* sprinkle or soak with water; supply (plant or animal) with water; secrete water; (as **watered** *adjective*) (of silk etc.) having irregular wavy finish; take in supply of water. □ **make water** urinate; **water-bed** mattress filled with water; **water biscuit** thin unsweetened biscuit; **water buffalo** common domestic Indian buffalo; **water cannon** device giving powerful water-jet to disperse crowd etc.; **water chestnut** corm from a sedge, used in Chinese cookery; **water-closet** lavatory that can be flushed; **water-colour** pigment mixed with water and not oil, picture painted or art of painting with this; **watercourse** stream of water, bed of this; **watercress** pungent cress growing in running water; **water-diviner** dowser; **water down** dilute, make less forceful or horrifying; **waterfall** stream or river falling over precipice or down steep hill; **waterfowl** bird(s) frequenting water; **waterfront** part of town adjoining river etc.; **waterhole** shallow depression in which water collects; **water-ice** flavoured and frozen water and sugar; **watering-can** portable container for watering plants; **watering-place** pool where animals drink, spa or seaside resort; **water jump** jump over water in steeplechase etc.; **water level** surface of water, height of this, water table; **water lily** aquatic plant with floating leaves and flowers; **waterline** line where surface of water touches ship's side; **waterlogged** saturated or filled with water; **water main** main pipe in water supply system; **waterman** boatman plying for hire; **watermark** faint design made in paper by maker; **water-meadow** meadow periodically flooded by stream; **water melon** large dark green melon with red pulp and watery juice; **water-mill** mill worked by waterwheel; **water pistol** toy pistol shooting jet of water; **water polo** game played by swimmers with ball like football; **water-power** mechanical force from weight or motion of water; **waterproof** *adjective* impervious to water, *noun* such garment or material, *verb* make waterproof; **water-rat** water vole; **water rate** charge for use of public water supply; **watershed** line between waters flowing to different river basins, turning point in events; **waterside** edge of sea, lake, or river; **water-ski** ski (esp. one of pair) on which person is towed across water by motor boat; **waterspout** gyrating column of water and spray between sea and cloud; **water table** plane below which ground is saturated with water; **watertight** so closely fastened or fitted that water cannot leak through, (of argument etc.) unassailable; **water tower** tower with elevated tank to give pressure for distributing water; **water vole** aquatic vole; **waterway** navigable channel; **waterwheel** wheel driven by water to drive machinery or to raise water; **water-wings** inflated floats used to support person learning to swim; **waterworks** establishment for managing water supply, *colloquial* shedding of tears, *colloquial* urinary system.

watery *adjective* containing too much water; too thin in consistency; of or consisting of water; vapid, uninteresting; (of colour) pale; (of sun, moon, or sky) rainy-looking; (of eyes) moist.

watt /wɒt/ *noun* SI unit of power.

wattage *noun* amount of electrical power expressed in watts.

wattle[1] /'wɒt(ə)l/ *noun* interlaced rods and sticks used for fences etc.; Australian acacia with fragrant golden yellow flowers. □ **wattle and daub** network of rods and twigs plastered with clay or mud as building material.

wattle[2] /'wɒt(ə)l/ *noun* fleshy appendage hanging from head or neck of turkey etc.

wave ● *verb* (**-ving**) move (hand etc.) to and fro in greeting or as signal; show sinuous or sweeping motion; give such motion to; direct (person) or express (greeting etc.) by waving; give undulating form to, have such form. ● *noun* moving ridge of water between two depressions; long body of water curling into arch and breaking on shore; thing compared to this; gesture of waving; curved shape in hair; temporary occurrence or heightening of condition or influence; disturbance carrying motion, heat, light, sound, etc. through esp. fluid medium; single curve in this. □ **wave aside** dismiss as intrusive or irrelevant; **waveband** radio wavelengths between certain limits; **wave down** wave to (vehicle or driver) to stop; **wavelength** distance between successive crests of wave, this as distinctive feature of radio waves from a transmitter, *colloquial* person's way of thinking.

wavelet *noun* small wave.

waver /'weɪvə/ *verb* be or become unsteady or irresolute, begin to give way.

wavy *adjective* (**-ier, -iest**) having waves or alternate contrary curves. □ **waviness** *noun*.

wax[1] ● *noun* sticky pliable yellowish substance secreted by bees as material of honeycomb; this bleached and purified for candles, modelling, etc.; any similar substance. ● *verb* cover or treat with wax; remove hair from (legs etc.) using wax. □ **waxwork** object, esp. lifelike dummy, modelled in wax, (in *plural*) exhibition of wax dummies.

wax[2] *verb* (of moon) increase in apparent size; grow larger or stronger; become.

waxen *adjective* smooth or pale like wax; *archaic* made of wax.

way ● *noun* road, track, path, street; course, route; direction; method, means; style, manner; habitual course of action; normal course of events; distance (to be) travelled; unimpeded opportunity or space to advance; advance, progress; specified condition or state; respect, sense. ● *adverb colloquial* far. □ **by the way** incidentally; **by way of** by means of, as a form of, passing through; **give way** yield under pressure, give precedence; **in the way, in (person's) way** forming obstruction (to); **lead the way** act as guide or leader; **make one's way** go, prosper; **make way for** allow to pass, be superseded by; **out of the way** not forming obstruction, disposed of, unusual,

remote; **pay its** or **one's way** cover costs, pay one's expenses as they arise; **under way** in motion or progress; **way back** *colloquial* long ago; **wayfarer** traveller, esp. on foot; **waylay** lie in wait for, stop to accost or rob; **way of life** principles or habits governing one's actions; **way-out** *colloquial* unusual, eccentric; **wayside** (land at) side of road.

wayward /'weɪwəd/ *adjective* childishly self-willed; capricious. □ **waywardness** *noun*.

WC *abbreviation* water-closet; West Central.

W/Cdr. *abbreviation* Wing Commander.

we /wiː/ *pronoun used* by speaker or writer to refer to himself or herself and one or more others as subject of verb; used for I by sovereign in formal contexts or by editorial writer in newspaper.

weak *adjective* lacking in strength, power, vigour, resolution, or number; unconvincing; (of verb) forming inflections by suffix. □ **weak-kneed** *colloquial* lacking resolution; **weak-minded** mentally deficient, lacking resolution. □ **weaken** *verb*.

weakling *noun* feeble person or animal.

weakly ● *adverb* in a weak way. ● *adjective* (**-ier, -iest**) sickly, not robust.

weakness *noun* being weak; weak point; self-indulgent liking.

weal[1] ● *noun* ridge raised on flesh by stroke of rod or whip. ● *verb* raise weals on.

weal[2] *noun literary* welfare.

wealth /welθ/ *noun* riches; being rich; abundance.

wealthy *adjective* (**-ier, -iest**) having abundance, esp. of money.

wean *verb* accustom (infant or other young mammal) to food other than mother's milk; (often + *from, away from*) disengage (from habit etc.) by enforced discontinuance.

weapon /'wepən/ *noun* thing designed, used, or usable for inflicting bodily harm; means for gaining advantage in a conflict.

weaponry *noun* weapons collectively.

wear /weə/ ● *verb* (*past* **wore**; *past participle* **worn**) have on one's person as clothing, ornament, etc.; exhibit (expression etc.); *colloquial* (usually in negative) tolerate; (often + *away, down*) damage or deteriorate gradually by use or attrition; make (hole etc.) by attrition; (often + *out*) exhaust; (+ *down*) overcome by persistence; (+ *well* etc.) endure continued use or life; (of time) pass, esp. tediously. ● *noun* wearing, being worn; things worn; fashionable or suitable clothing; (in full **wear and tear**) damage from continuous use. □ **wear out** wear or be used until useless, tire or be tired out. □ **wearer** *noun*.

wearisome /'wɪərɪsəm/ *adjective* tedious, monotonous.

weary /'wɪərɪ/ ● *adjective* (**-ier, -iest**) very tired, intensely fatigued; (+ *of*) tired of; tiring, tedious. ● *verb* (**-ies, -ied**) make or become weary. □ **wearily** *adverb*; **weariness** *noun*.

weasel /'wiːz(ə)l/ *noun* small ferocious reddish-brown flesh-eating mammal.

weather /'weðə/ ● *noun* atmospheric conditions at specified place or time as regards heat, cloudiness, humidity, sunshine, wind, and rain etc. ● *verb* expose to or affect by atmospheric changes, season (wood); be discoloured or worn thus; come safely through (storm etc.); get to windward of. □ **make heavy weather of** *colloquial* exaggerate difficulty of; **under the weather** *colloquial* unwell, depressed; **weather-beaten** affected by exposure to weather; **weatherboard** board attached at bottom of door to keep out rain, each of series of overlapping horizontal boards on wall; **weathercock** weather vane in form of cock, inconstant person; **weather forecast** prediction of likely weather; **weather vane** revolving pointer on church spire etc. to show direction of wind.

weave¹ ● verb (-ving; past **wove** /wəʊv/; past participle **woven**) form (fabric) by interlacing threads, form (threads) into fabric, esp. in loom; (+ into) make (facts etc.) into story or connected whole; make (story etc.) thus. **●** noun style of weaving.

weave² verb (-ving) move repeatedly from side to side; take intricate course.

weaver noun person who weaves fabric; (in full **weaver-bird**) tropical bird building elaborately woven nest.

web noun woven fabric; amount woven in one piece; complex series; cobweb or similar tissue; membrane connecting toes of aquatic bird or other animal; large roll of paper for printing. □ **web-footed** having toes connected by web. □ **webbed** adjective.

webbing noun strong narrow closely woven fabric for belts etc.

weber /'veɪbə/ noun SI unit of magnetic flux.

Wed. abbreviation (also **Weds.**) Wednesday.

wed verb (-dd-; past & past participle **wedded** or **wed**) usually formal or literary marry; unite; (as **wedded** adjective) of or in marriage, (+ to) obstinately attached to (pursuit etc.).

we'd /wiːd/ we had; we should; we would.

wedding /'wedɪŋ/ noun marriage ceremony. □ **wedding breakfast** meal etc. between wedding and departure for honeymoon; **wedding cake** rich decorated cake served at wedding reception; **wedding ring** ring worn by married person.

wedge ● noun piece of tapering wood, metal, etc., used for forcing things apart or fixing them immovably etc.; wedge-shaped thing. **●** verb (-ging) secure or force open or apart with wedge; (+ in, into) pack or force (thing, oneself) in or into. □ **thin end of the wedge** colloquial small beginning that may lead to something more serious.

wedlock /'wedlɒk/ noun married state. □ **born in or out of wedlock** born of married or unmarried parents.

Wednesday /'wenzdeɪ/ noun day of week following Tuesday.

wee adjective (**weer** /'wiːə/, **weest** /'wiːɪst/) esp. Scottish little; colloquial tiny.

weed ● noun wild plant growing where it is not wanted; lanky and weakly person or horse; (**the weed**) slang marijuana, tobacco. **●** verb rid of weeds or unwanted parts; (+ out) sort out and remove (inferior or unwanted parts etc.), rid of inferior or unwanted parts etc.; remove or destroy weeds.

weeds plural noun (in full **widow's weeds**) archaic deep mourning worn by widow.

weedy adjective (**-ier, -iest**) weak, feeble; full of weeds.

week noun 7-day period reckoned usually from Saturday midnight; any 7-day period; the 6 days between Sundays; the 5 days Monday to Friday, period of work then done. □ **weekday** day other than (Saturday or) Sunday; **weekend** Saturday and Sunday.

weekly ● adjective done, produced, or occurring once a week. **●** adverb once a week. **●** noun (plural **-ies**) weekly newspaper or periodical.

weeny /'wiːnɪ/ adjective (**-ier, -iest**) colloquial tiny.

weep ● verb (past & past participle **wept**) shed tears; (often + for) lament over; be covered with or send forth drops; exude liquid; come or send forth in drops; (as **weeping** adjective) (of tree) have drooping branches. **●** noun spell of weeping.

weepie noun colloquial sentimental or emotional film, play, etc.

weepy adjective (**-ier, -iest**) colloquial inclined to weep, tearful.

weevil /'wiːvɪl/ noun destructive beetle feeding esp. on grain.

weft noun threads woven across warp to make fabric.

weigh /weɪ/ verb find weight of; balance in hand (as if) to guess weight of; (often + out) take definite weight of (substance), measure out (specified weight); estimate relative value or importance of; (+ with, against) compare with; be of specified weight or importance; have influence; (often + on) be heavy or burdensome (to); raise (anchor). □ **weighbridge** weighing machine for vehicles; **weigh down** bring down by weight, oppress; **weigh in** (of boxer before contest, or jockey after race) be weighed; **weigh-in** noun; **weigh in with** colloquial advance (argument etc.) confidently; **weigh up** colloquial form estimate of; **weigh one's words** carefully choose words to express something.

weight /weɪt/ **●** noun force on a body due to earth's gravitation; heaviness of body; quantitative expression of a body's weight; scale of such weights; body of known weight for use in weighing or weight training; heavy body, esp. used in mechanism etc.; load, burden; influence, importance; preponderance (of evidence etc.). **●** verb attach a weight to, hold down with a weight; impede, burden. □ **pull one's weight** do fair share of work; **weightlifting** sport of lifting heavy objects; **weight training** physical training using weights. □ **weightless** adjective.

weighting noun extra pay in special cases.

weighty adjective (**-ier, -iest**) heavy; momentous; deserving attention; influential, authoritative.

weir /wɪə/ noun dam across river to retain water and regulate its flow.

weird /wɪəd/ adjective uncanny, supernatural; colloquial queer, incomprehensible. □ **weirdly** adverb; **weirdness** noun.

welch = WELSH.

welcome /'welkəm/ **●** noun kind or glad greeting or reception. **●** interjection expressing such greeting. **●** verb (-ming) receive with welcome. **●** adjective gladly received; (+ to) cordially allowed or invited to. □ **make welcome** receive hospitably.

weld ● verb join (pieces of metal or plastic) using heat, usually from electric arc; fashion into effectual or homogeneous whole. **●** noun welded joint. □ **welder** noun.

welfare /'welfeə/ noun well-being, happiness; health and prosperity (of person, community, etc.); (**Welfare**) financial support from state. □ **welfare state** system of social services controlled or financed by government, state operating this; **welfare work** organized effort for welfare of poor, disabled, etc.

welkin /'welkɪn/ noun poetical sky.

well¹ ● adverb (**better, best**) in satisfactory way; with distinction; in kind way; thoroughly, carefully; with heartiness or approval; probably, reasonably; to considerable extent; slang extremely. **●** adjective (**better, best**) in good health; in satisfactory state or position, advisable. **●** interjection expressing astonishment, resignation, etc., or introducing speech. □ **as well** in addition, advisable, desirable, reasonably; **as well as** in addition to; **well-adjusted** mentally and emotionally stable; **well-advised** prudent; **well and truly** decisively, completely; **well-appointed** properly equipped or fitted out; **well away** having made considerable progress, colloquial fast asleep or drunk; **well-balanced** sane, sensible; **well-being** happiness, health, prosperity; **well-born** of noble family; **well-bred** having or showing good breeding or manners; **well-built** big, strong, and shapely; **well-connected** related to good families; **well-disposed** (often + towards) friendly, sympathetic; **well-earned** fully deserved; **well-founded** based on good evidence; **well-groomed** with carefully tended hair, clothes, etc.; **well-heeled** *colloquial* wealthy; **well-informed** having much knowledge or information; **well-intentioned** having or showing good intentions; **well-judged** opportunely, skilfully, or discreetly done; **well-known** known to many; **well-meaning**, **-meant** well-intentioned; **well-nigh** almost; **well off** rich, fortunately situated; **well-read** having read (and learnt) much; **well-spoken** articulate or refined in speech; **well-to-do** prosperous; **well-tried** often tested with good result; **well-wisher** person who wishes another well; **well-worn** much used, trite.

well² ● *noun* shaft sunk in ground to obtain water, oil, etc.; enclosed space resembling well-shaft, e.g. central space in building for staircase, lift, light, or ventilation; source; (in *plural*) spa; ink-well; railed space in law court. ● *verb* (+ *out, up*) rise or flow as water from well. □ **well-head**, **-spring** source.

we'll /wiːl/ we shall; we will.

wellington /ˈwelɪŋt(ə)n/ *noun* (in full **wellington boot**) waterproof rubber boot usually reaching knee.

welly /ˈwelɪ/ *noun* (*plural* **-ies**) *colloquial* wellington.

Welsh ● *adjective* of Wales. ● *noun* language of Wales; **(the Welsh)** (treated as *plural*) the Welsh people. □ **Welshman**, **Welshwoman** native of Wales; **Welsh rarebit** dish of melted cheese etc. on toast.

welsh *verb* (also **welch** /weltʃ/) (of loser of bet, esp. bookmaker) evade an obligation; (+ *on*) fail to carry out promise to (person), fail to honour (obligation).

welt ● *noun* leather rim sewn to shoe-upper for sole to be attached to; weal; ribbed or reinforced border of garment; heavy blow. ● *verb* provide with welt; raise weals on, thrash.

welter /ˈweltə/ ● *verb* roll, wallow; (+ *in*) be soaked in. ● *noun* general confusion; disorderly mixture.

welterweight /ˈweltəweɪt/ *noun* amateur boxing weight (63.5–67 kg).

wen *noun* benign tumour on skin.

wench *noun jocular* girl, young woman.

wend *verb* □ **wend one's way** go.

went *past of* GO¹.

wept *past & past participle of* WEEP.

were *2nd singular past, plural past,* and *past subjunctive of* BE.

we're /wɪə/ we are.

weren't /wɜːnt/ were not.

werewolf /ˈweəwʊlf/ *noun* (*plural* **-wolves**) *Mythology* human being who changes into wolf.

Wesleyan /ˈwezlɪən/ ● *adjective* of Protestant denomination founded by John Wesley. ● *noun* member of this denomination.

west ● *noun* point of horizon where sun sets at equinoxes; corresponding compass point; (usually **the West**) European civilization, western part of world, country, town, etc. ● *adjective* towards, at, near, or facing west; (of wind) from west. ● *adverb* towards, at, or near west; (+ *of*) further west than. □ **go west** *slang* be killed or wrecked etc.; **westbound** travelling or leading west; **West End** fashionable part of London; **west-north-west**, **west-south-west** point midway between west and north-west or south-west. □ **westward** *adjective, adverb, & noun*; **westwards** *adverb*.

westering /ˈwestərɪŋ/ *adjective* (of sun) nearing the west.

westerly /ˈwestəlɪ/ ● *adjective & adverb* in western position or direction; (of wind) from west. ● *noun* (*plural* **-ies**) wind from west.

western /ˈwest(ə)n/ ● *adjective* of or in west. ● *noun* film or novel about cowboys in western N. America. □ **westernize** *verb* (also **-ise**) (**-zing** or **-sing**); **westernmost** *adjective*.

westerner *noun* native or inhabitant of west.

wet ● *adjective* (**-tt-**) soaked or covered with water or other liquid; (of weather) rainy; (of paint) not yet dried; used with water; *colloquial* feeble. ● *verb* (**-tt-**; *past & past participle* **wet** or **wetted**) make wet; urinate in or on. ● *noun* liquid that wets something; rainy weather; *colloquial* feeble or spiritless person; *colloquial* liberal Conservative; *colloquial* drink. □ **wet blanket** gloomy person discouraging cheerfulness etc.; **wet-nurse** *noun* woman employed to suckle another's child, *verb* act as wet-nurse to, *colloquial* treat as if helpless.

wether /ˈweðə/ *noun* castrated ram.

we've /wiːv/ we have.

Wg. Cdr. *abbreviation* Wing Commander.

whack *colloquial* ● *verb* hit forcefully; (as **whacked** *adjective*) tired out. ● *noun* sharp or resounding blow; *slang* share.

whacking *colloquial* ● *adjective* large. ● *adverb* very.

whale ● *noun* (*plural* same or **-s**) large fishlike marine mammal. ● *verb* (**-ling**) hunt whales. □ **whalebone** elastic horny substance in upper jaw of some whales.

whaler *noun* whaling ship or seaman.

wham *interjection colloquial: expressing forcible impact.*

wharf /wɔːf/ ● *noun* (*plural* **wharves** /wɔːvz/ or **-s**) quayside structure for loading or unloading of moored vessels. ● *verb* moor (ship) at wharf; store (goods) on wharf.

what /wɒt/ ● *interrogative adjective* used in asking someone to specify one or more things from an indefinite number. ● *adjective* (usually in exclamation) how great, how remarkable. ● *relative adjective* the or any … that. ● *interrogative pronoun* what thing(s); what did you say? ● *relative pronoun* the things which; anything that. □ **whatever** anything at all that, no matter what, (with negative or in questions) at all, of any kind; **what for?** *colloquial* for what reason?; **what have you** *colloquial* anything else similar; **whatnot** unspecified thing; **what not** *colloquial* other similar things; **whatsoever** whatever; **know what's what** *colloquial* have common sense, know what is useful or important; **what with** *colloquial* because of.

wheat *noun* cereal plant bearing dense 4-sided seed-spikes; its grain used for flour etc. □ **wheat germ** wheat embryo extracted as source of vitamins; **wheatmeal** flour from wheat with some bran and germ removed.

wheatear /ˈwiːtɪə/ *noun* small migratory bird.

wheaten *adjective* made of wheat.

wheedle /ˈwiːd(ə)l/ *verb* (**-ling**) coax by flattery or endearments; (+ *out*) get (thing) from person or cheat (person) of thing by wheedling.

wheel ● *noun* circular frame or disc revolving on axle and used to propel vehicle or other machinery; wheel-like thing; motion as of wheel; movement of line of men etc. with one end as pivot; (in *plural*) *slang* car. ● *verb* turn on axis or pivot; swing round in line with one end as pivot; (often + *about, around*) (cause to) change direction or face another way; push or pull (wheeled thing, or its load or occupant); go in circles or curves. □ **wheel and deal** engage in political or commercial scheming; **wheelbarrow** small cart with one wheel at front and two handles; **wheelbase** distance between axles of vehicle; **wheelchair** disabled person's chair on wheels; **wheel-spin** rotation of vehicle's wheels without traction; **wheels within wheels** intricate machinery, *colloquial* indirect or secret agencies; **wheelwright** maker or repairer of wheels.

wheelie *noun slang* manoeuvre on bicycle or motorcycle with front wheel off the ground.

wheeze ● verb (**-zing**) breathe or utter with audible whistling sound. ● noun sound of wheezing; colloquial clever scheme. □ **wheezy** adjective (**-ier, -iest**).

whelk noun spiral-shelled marine mollusc.

whelp ● noun young dog, puppy; archaic cub; ill-mannered child or youth. ● verb give birth to puppies.

when ● interrogative adverb at what time. ● relative adverb (time etc.) at or on which. ● conjunction at the or any time that; as soon as; although; after which, and then, but just then. ● pronoun what time; which time. □ **whenever, whensoever** at whatever time, on whatever occasion, every time that.

whence archaic or formal ● interrogative adverb from what place. ● relative adverb (place etc.) from which. ● conjunction to the place from which.

where /weə/ ● interrogative adverb in or to what place; in what direction; in what respect. ● relative adverb (place etc.) in or to which. ● conjunction in or to the or any place, direction, or respect in which; and there. ● interrogative pronoun what place. ● relative pronoun the place in or to which. □ **whereabouts** interrogative adverb approximately where, noun person's or thing's location; **whereas** in contrast or comparison with the fact that, taking into consideration the fact that; **whereby** by what or which means; **wherefore** archaic for what or which reason; **wherein** formal in what or which; **whereof** formal of what or which; **whereupon** immediately after which; **wherever** anywhere at all that, no matter where; **wherewithal** /-wɪðɔːl/ colloquial money etc. needed for a purpose.

wherry /'werɪ/ noun (plural **-ies**) light rowing boat, usually for carrying passengers; large light barge.

whet verb (**-tt-**) sharpen; stimulate (appetite etc.). □ **whetstone** stone for sharpening cutting-tools.

whether /'weðə/ conjunction introducing first or both of alternative possibilities.

whew /hwjuː/ interjection expressing astonishment, consternation, or relief.

whey /weɪ/ noun watery liquid left when milk forms curds.

which ● interrogative adjective used in asking someone to specify one or more things from a definite set of alternatives. ● relative adjective being the one just referred to, and this or these. ● interrogative pronoun which person(s) or thing(s). ● relative pronoun which thing(s). □ **whichever** any which, no matter which.

whiff noun puff of air, smoke, etc.; smell; (+ of) trace of; small cigar.

Whig noun historical member of British political party succeeded by Liberals. □ **Whiggery** noun; **Whiggish** adjective; **Whiggism** noun.

while ● noun period of time. ● conjunction during the time that, for as long as, at the same time as; although, whereas. ● verb (**-ling**) (+ away) pass (time etc.) in leisurely or interesting way. ● relative adverb (time etc.) during which. □ **for a while** for some time; **in a while** soon; **once in a while** occasionally.

whilst /waɪlst/ adverb & conjunction while.

whim noun sudden fancy, caprice.

whimper ● verb make feeble, querulous, or frightened sounds. ● noun such sound.

whimsical /'wɪmzɪk(ə)l/ adjective capricious, fantastic. □ **whimsicality** /-'kæl-/ noun; **whimsically** adverb.

whimsy /'wɪmzɪ/ noun (plural **-ies**) whim.

whin noun (in singular or plural) gorse. □ **whinchat** small songbird.

whine ● noun long-drawn complaining cry (as) of dog or child; querulous tone or complaint. ● verb (**-ning**) emit or utter whine(s); complain.

whinge /wɪndʒ/ verb (**-geing** or **-ging**) colloquial complain peevishly.

whinny /'wɪnɪ/ ● noun (plural **-ies**) gentle or joyful neigh. ● verb (**-ies, -ied**) emit whinny.

whip ● noun lash attached to stick, for urging on or for punishing; person appointed by political party to control its discipline and tactics in Parliament; whip's written notice requesting member's attendance; food made with whipped cream etc.; whipperin. ● verb (**-pp-**) beat or urge on with whip; beat (eggs, cream, etc.) into froth; take or move suddenly or quickly; slang steal, excel, defeat; bind with spirally wound twine; sew with overcast stitches. □ **whipcord** tightly twisted cord; (**the**) **whip hand** advantage, control; **whiplash** sudden jerk; **whipperin** huntsman's assistant who manages hounds; **whipping boy** scapegoat; **whip-round** colloquial informal collection of money among group of people; **whipstock** handle of whip.

whippersnapper /'wɪpəsnæpə/ noun small child; insignificant but presumptuous person.

whippet /'wɪpɪt/ noun crossbred dog of greyhound type, used for racing.

whippoorwill /'wɪpʊəwɪl/ noun N. American nightjar.

whirl ● verb swing round and round, revolve rapidly; (+ away) convey or go rapidly in car etc.; send or travel swiftly in orbit or curve; (of brain etc.) seem to spin round. ● noun whirling movement; state of intense activity or confusion. □ **give it a whirl** colloquial attempt it; **whirlpool** circular eddy in sea, river, etc.; **whirlwind** noun whirling mass or column of air, adjective very rapid.

whirligig /'wɜːlɪgɪg/ noun spinning or whirling toy; merry-go-round; revolving motion.

whirr ● noun continuous buzzing or softly clicking sound. ● verb (**-rr-**) make this sound.

whisk ● verb (+ away, off) brush with sweeping movement, take suddenly; whip (cream, eggs, etc.); convey or go lightly or quickly; wave (object). ● noun whisking movement; utensil for whipping eggs, cream, etc.; bunch of twigs, bristles, etc. for brushing or dusting.

whisker /'wɪskə/ noun (usually in plural) hair on cheeks or sides of face of man; each of bristles on face of cat etc.; colloquial small distance. □ **whiskered** adjective; **whiskery** adjective.

whisky /'wɪskɪ/ noun (Irish & US **whiskey**) (plural **-ies** or **-eys**) spirit distilled esp. from malted barley.

whisper /'wɪspə/ ● verb speak using breath instead of vocal cords; talk or say in barely audible tone or confidential way; rustle, murmur. ● noun whispering speech or sound; thing whispered.

whist noun card game, usually for two pairs of opponents. □ **whist drive** whist-party with players moving on from table to table.

whistle /'wɪs(ə)l/ ● noun clear shrill sound made by forcing breath through lips contracted to narrow opening; similar sound made by bird, wind, missile, etc.; instrument used to produce such sound. ● verb (**-ling**) emit whistle; give signal or express surprise or derision by whistling; (often + up) summon or give signal to thus; produce (tune) by whistling; (+ for) seek or desire in vain. □ **whistle-stop** US small unimportant town on railway, politician's brief pause for electioneering speech on tour.

Whit ● noun Whitsuntide. ● adjective of Whitsuntide. □ **Whit Sunday** 7th Sunday after Easter, commemorating Pentecost.

whit noun particle, least possible amount.

white ● adjective of colour produced by reflection or transmission of all light; of colour of snow or milk; pale; of the human racial group having light-coloured skin; albino; (of hair) having lost its colour; (of coffee) with milk or cream. ● noun white colour, paint, clothes, etc.; (in *plural*) white garments worn in cricket, tennis, etc.; (player using) lighter-coloured pieces in chess etc.; egg white; whitish part of eyeball round iris; white person. □ **white ant** termite; **whitebait** small silvery-white food-fish; **white cell** leucocyte; **white-collar** (of worker or work) non-manual, clerical, professional; **white corpuscle** leucocyte; **white elephant** useless possession; **white feather** symbol of cowardice; **white flag** symbol of surrender; **white goods** large domestic electrical equipment; **white heat** degree of heat making metal glow white, state of intense anger or passion; **white-hot** *adjective*; **white hope** person expected to achieve much; **white horses** white-crested waves; **white lead** mixture containing lead carbonate used as white pigment; **white lie** harmless or trivial untruth; **white magic** magic used for beneficent purposes; **white meat** poultry, veal, rabbit, and pork; **White Paper** government report giving information; **white pepper** pepper made by grinding husked berry; **white sauce** sauce of flour, melted butter, and milk or cream; **white slave** woman entrapped for prostitution; **white spirit** light petroleum as solvent; **white sugar** purified sugar; **white tie** man's white bow tie as part of full evening dress; **whitewash** *noun* solution of chalk or lime for whitening walls etc., means of glossing over faults, *verb* apply whitewash (to), gloss over, clear of blame; **white wedding** wedding where bride wears formal white dress; **whitewood** light-coloured wood, esp. prepared for staining etc. □ **whiten** *verb*; **whitener** *noun*; **whiteness** *noun*; **whitish** *adjective*.

whither /'wɪðə/ *archaic* ● *interrogative adverb* to what place. ● *relative adverb* (place etc.) to which.

whiting[1] /'waɪtɪŋ/ *noun* (*plural* same) small edible sea fish.

whiting[2] /'waɪtɪŋ/ *noun* ground chalk used in white-washing etc.

whitlow /'wɪtləʊ/ *noun* inflammation near fingernail or toenail.

Whitsun /'wɪts(ə)n/ ● *noun* Whitsuntide. ● *adjective* of Whitsuntide.

Whitsuntide *noun* weekend or week including Whit Sunday.

whittle /'wɪt(ə)l/ *verb* (**-ling**) (often + *at*) pare (wood etc.) by cutting thin slices or shavings from surface; (often + *away*, *down*) reduce by repeated subtractions.

whiz (also **whizz**) ● *noun* sound made by object moving through air at great speed. ● *verb* (**-zz-**) move with or make a whiz. □ **whiz-kid** *colloquial* brilliant or highly successful young person.

WHO *abbreviation* World Health Organization.

who /huː/ ● *interrogative pronoun* what or which person(s), what sort of person(s). ● *relative pronoun* (person or persons) that. □ **whoever**, **whosoever** the or any person(s) who; no matter who.

whoa /wəʊ/ *interjection* used to stop or slow horse etc.

who'd /huːd/ who had; who would.

whodunit /huː'dʌnɪt/ *noun* (also **whodunnit**) *colloquial* detective story, play, or film.

whole /həʊl/ ● *adjective* uninjured, unbroken, intact, undiminished; not less than; all, all of. ● *noun* complete thing; all of a thing; (+ *of*) all members etc. of. □ **on the whole** all things considered; **wholefood** food not artificially processed or refined; **whole-hearted** completely devoted, done with all possible effort or sincerity; **wholeheartedly** *adverb*; **whole-meal** meal or flour made from whole grains of wheat.

wholesale /'həʊlseɪl/ ● *noun* selling in large quantities, esp. for retail by others. ● *adjective & adverb* by wholesale; on a large scale. ● *verb* (**-ling**) sell wholesale. □ **wholesaler** *noun*.

wholesome *adjective* promoting physical, mental, or moral health; prudent.

wholly /'həʊllɪ/ *adverb* entirely, without limitation; purely.

whom /huːm/ *pronoun* (as object of verb) who. □ **whomever** (as object of verb) whoever; **whomsoever** (as object of verb) whosoever.

whoop /huːp, wuːp/ ● *noun* cry expressing excitement etc.; characteristic drawing-in of breath after cough in whooping cough. ● *verb* utter whoop. □ **whooping cough** /'huːpɪŋ/ infectious disease, esp. of children, with violent convulsive cough.

whoopee /wʊ'piː/ *interjection expressing wild joy*. □ **make whoopee** /'wʊpɪ/ *colloquial* make merry, make love.

whoops /wʊps/ *interjection colloquial apology for obvious mistake*.

whop *verb* (**-pp-**) *slang* thrash, defeat.

whopper *noun slang* big specimen; great lie.

whopping *adjective colloquial* huge.

whore /hɔː/ *noun* prostitute; *derogatory* promiscuous woman. □ **whorehouse** brothel.

whorl /wɜːl/ *noun* ring of leaves etc. round stem; one turn of spiral.

whortleberry /'wɜːt(ə)lberɪ/ *noun* (*plural* **-ies**) bilberry.

who's /huːz/ who is; who has.

▪ **Usage** Because it has an apostrophe, *who's* is easily confused with *whose*. They are each correctly used in *Who's there?* (= *Who is there?*), *Who's taken my pen?* (= *Who has taken my pen?*), and *Whose book is this?* (= *Who does this book belong to?*).

whose /huːz/ ● *interrogative, pronoun, & adjective* of whom. ● *relative adjective* of whom or which.

why /waɪ/ ● *interrogative adverb* for what reason or purpose. ● *relative adverb* (reason etc.) for which. ● *interjection expressing surprise, impatience, reflection, or protest*. □ **whys and wherefores** reasons, explanation.

WI *abbreviation* West Indies; Women's Institute.

wick *noun* strip or thread feeding flame with fuel.

wicked /'wɪkɪd/ *adjective* (**-er**, **-est**) sinful, immoral; spiteful; playfully malicious; *colloquial* very bad; *slang* excellent. □ **wickedly** *adverb*; **wickedness** *noun*.

wicker /'wɪkə/ *noun* plaited osiers etc. as material for chairs, baskets, etc. □ **wickerwork** wicker, things made of wicker.

wicket /'wɪkɪt/ *noun* Cricket 3 upright stumps with bails in position defended by batsman, ground between the two wickets, state of this, batsman's being got out; (in full **wicket-door**, **-gate**) small door or gate, esp. beside or in larger one. □ **wicket-keeper** fielder close behind batsman's wicket.

wide ● *adjective* having sides far apart, broad, not narrow; (following measurement) in width; extending far, not restricted; liberal, not specialized; open to full extent; (+ *of*) not within reasonable distance of, far from. ● *adverb* to full extent; far from target etc. ● *noun* wide ball. □ **-wide** extending over whole of; **wide awake** fully awake, *colloquial* wary or knowing; **wide ball** Cricket ball judged by umpire to be beyond batsman's reach; **wide-eyed** surprised, naïve; **widespread** widely distributed. □ **widen** *verb*.

widely *adverb* far apart; extensively; by many people; considerably.

widgeon /'wɪdʒ(ə)n/ *noun* (also **wigeon**) kind of wild duck.

widow /'wɪdəʊ/ ● *noun* woman who has lost her husband by death and not married again. ● *verb* make into widow or widower; (as **widowed** *adjective*) bereft by death of spouse. □ **widow's peak** V-shaped growth of hair on forehead. □ **widowhood** noun.

widower /'wɪdəʊə/ noun man who has lost his wife by death and not married again.

width noun measurement from side to side; large extent; liberality of views etc.; piece of material of full width. □ **widthways** adverb.

wield /wiːld/ verb hold and use, control, exert.

wife noun (plural **wives**) married woman, esp. in relation to her husband. □ **wifely** adjective.

wig noun artificial head of hair.

wigeon = WIDGEON.

wiggle /'wɪg(ə)l/ colloquial ● verb (**-ling**) move from side to side etc. ● noun wiggling movement; kink in line etc. □ **wiggly** adjective (**-ier, -iest**).

wight /waɪt/ noun archaic person.

wigwam /'wɪgwæm/ noun N. American Indian's hut or tent.

wilco /'wɪlkəʊ/ interjection colloquial: expressing compliance or agreement.

wild /waɪld/ ● adjective in original natural state; not domesticated, cultivated, or civilized; unrestrained, disorderly; tempestuous; intensely eager, frantic; (+ about) colloquial enthusiastically devoted to; colloquial infuriated; random, ill-aimed, rash. ● adverb in a wild way. ● noun wild place, desert. □ **like wildfire** with extraordinary speed; **run wild** grow or stray unchecked or undisciplined; **wild card** card having any rank chosen by its player, person or thing usable in different ways; **wildcat** noun hot-tempered or violent person, adjective (of strike) sudden and unofficial, reckless, financially unsound; **wild-goose chase** foolish or hopeless quest; **wildlife** wild animals collectively; **Wild West** western US in lawless times. □ **wildly** adverb; **wildness** noun.

wildebeest /'wɪldəbiːst/ noun (plural same or **-s**) gnu.

wilderness /'wɪldənɪs/ noun desert, uncultivated area; confused assemblage.

wile ● noun (usually in plural) stratagem, trick. ● verb (**-ling**) lure.

wilful /'wɪlfʊl/ adjective (US **willful**) intentional, deliberate; obstinate. □ **wilfully** adverb.

will¹ auxiliary verb (3rd singular present **will**) used to form future tenses; expressing request as question; be able to; have tendency to; be likely to.

will² ● noun faculty by which person decides what to do; fixed desire or intention; will-power; legal written directions for disposal of one's property etc. after death; disposition towards others. ● verb try to cause by will-power; intend, desire; bequeath by will. □ **at will** whenever one wishes; **will-power** control by purpose over impulse; **with a will** vigorously.

willing /'wɪlɪŋ/ adjective ready to consent or undertake; given etc. by willing person. □ **willingly** adverb; **willingness** noun.

will-o'-the-wisp /wɪləðə'wɪsp/ noun phosphorescent light seen on marshy ground; elusive person.

willow /'wɪləʊ/ noun waterside tree with pliant branches yielding osiers. □ **willowherb** plant with leaves like willow; **willow-pattern** conventional Chinese design of blue on white china etc.

willowy adjective lithe and slender; having willows.

willy-nilly /wɪlɪ'nɪlɪ/ adverb whether one likes it or not.

wilt ● verb wither, droop; lose energy. ● noun plant disease causing wilting.

wily /'waɪlɪ/ adjective (**-ier, -iest**) crafty, cunning.

wimp noun colloquial feeble or ineffectual person. □ **wimpish** adjective.

wimple /'wɪmp(ə)l/ noun headdress covering neck and sides of face, worn by some nuns.

win ● verb (**-nn-**; past & past participle **won** /wʌn/) secure as result of fight, contest, bet, etc.; be victor, be victorious in. ● noun victory in game etc. □ **win the day** be victorious in battle, argument, etc.; **win over** gain support of; **win through, out** overcome obstacles.

wince ● noun start or involuntary shrinking movement of pain etc. ● verb (**-cing**) give wince.

winceyette /wɪnsɪ'et/ noun lightweight flannelette.

winch ● noun crank of wheel or axle; windlass. ● verb lift with winch.

wind¹ /wɪnd/ ● noun air in natural motion; breath, esp. as needed in exertion or playing wind instrument; power of breathing easily; empty talk; gas generated in bowels etc.; wind instruments of orchestra etc.; scent carried by the wind. ● verb exhaust wind of by exertion or blow; make (baby) bring up wind after feeding; detect presence of by scent. □ **get wind of** begin to suspect; **get, have the wind up** colloquial become, be, frightened; **in the wind** colloquial about to happen; **put the wind up** colloquial frighten; **take the wind out of (person's) sails** frustrate by anticipation; **windbag** colloquial person who talks a lot but says little of value; **windbreak** thing that breaks force of wind; **windcheater** windproof jacket; **windfall** fruit blown down by wind, unexpected good fortune, esp. legacy; **wind instrument** musical instrument sounded by air-current; **wind-jammer** merchant sailing ship; **windmill** mill worked by action of wind on sails, toy with curved vanes revolving on stick; **windpipe** air-passage between throat and lungs; **windscreen** screen of glass at front of car etc.; **windscreen wiper** rubber etc. blade to clear windscreen of rain etc.; **windshield** US windscreen; **wind-sock** canvas cylinder or cone on mast to show direction of wind; **windswept** exposed to high winds; **wind-tunnel** enclosed chamber for testing (models or parts of) aircraft etc. in winds of known velocities.

wind² /waɪnd/ ● verb (past & past participle **wound** /waʊnd/) go in spiral, crooked, or curved course; make (one's way) thus; wrap closely, coil; provide with coiled thread etc.; surround (as) with coil; wind up (clock etc.). ● noun bend or turn in course. □ **wind down** lower by winding, unwind, approach end gradually; **winding-sheet** sheet in which corpse is wrapped for burial; **wind up** verb coil whole of, tighten coiling or coiled spring of, colloquial increase intensity of, colloquial provoke to anger etc., bring to conclusion, arrange affairs of and dissolve (company), cease business and go into liquidation, colloquial arrive finally; **wind-up** noun conclusion, colloquial attempt to provoke.

windlass /'wɪndləs/ noun machine with horizontal axle for hauling or hoisting.

window /'wɪndəʊ/ noun opening, usually with glass, in wall etc. to admit light etc.; the glass itself; space for display behind window of shop; window-like opening; transparent part in envelope showing address; opportunity for study or action. □ **window-box** box placed outside window for cultivating plants; **window-dressing** art of arranging display in shop window etc., adroit presentation of facts etc. to give falsely favourable impression; **window-pane** glass pane in window; **window-seat** seat below window, seat next to window in aircraft etc.; **window-shop** look at goods in shop windows without buying anything.

windsurfing noun sport of riding on water on sailboard. □ **windsurf** verb; **windsurfer** noun.

windward /'wɪndwəd/ ● adjective & adverb on or towards side from which wind is blowing. ● noun this direction.

windy *adjective* (**-ier, -iest**) stormy with or exposed to wind; generating or characterized by flatulence; *colloquial* wordy; *colloquial* apprehensive, frightened. □ **windiness** *noun*.

wine ● *noun* fermented grape juice as alcoholic drink; fermented drink resembling this made from other fruits etc.; colour of red wine. ● *verb* (**-ning**) drink wine; entertain with wine. □ **wine bar** bar or small restaurant where wine is main drink available; **wine cellar** cellar for storing wine, its contents; **wineglass** glass for wine, usually with stem and foot; **winepress** press in which grape juice is extracted for wine; **wine waiter** waiter responsible for serving wine.

wing ● *noun* each of the limbs or organs by which bird etc. flies; winglike part supporting aircraft; projecting part of building; *Football etc.* forward player at either end of line, side part of playing area; (in *plural*) sides of theatre stage; extreme section of political party; flank of battle array; part of vehicle over wheel; air-force unit of several squadrons. ● *verb* travel or traverse on wings; wound in wing or arm; equip with wings; enable to fly, send in flight. □ **on the wing** flying; **take under one's wing** treat as protégé; **take wing** fly away; **wing-case** horny cover of insect's wing; **wing-chair** chair with side-pieces at top of high back; **wing-collar** man's high stiff collar with turned-down corners; **wing commander** RAF officer next below group captain; **wing-nut** nut with projections to turn it by; **wingspan** measurement right across wings. □ **winged** *adjective*.

winger *noun Football etc.* wing player.

wink ● *verb* (often + *at*) close and open one eye quickly, esp. as signal; close eye(s) momentarily; (of light) twinkle; (of indicator) flash on and off. ● *noun* act of winking; *colloquial* short sleep. □ **wink at** purposely avoid seeing, pretend not to notice.

winkle /ˈwɪŋk(ə)l/ ● *noun* edible sea snail. ● *verb* (**-ling**) (+ *out*) extract with difficulty.

winning ● *adjective* having or bringing victory; attractive. ● *noun* (in *plural*) money won. □ **winning post** post marking end of race. □ **winningly** *adverb*.

winnow /ˈwɪnəʊ/ *verb* blow (grain) free of chaff etc.; (+ *out, away, from*, etc.) rid grain of (chaff etc.); sift, examine.

winsome /ˈwɪnsəm/ *adjective* attractive, engaging. □ **winsomely** *adverb*; **winsomeness** *noun*.

winter /ˈwɪntə/ ● *noun* coldest season of year. ● *verb* (usually + *at, in*) spend the winter. □ **winter garden** garden of plants flourishing in winter; **wintergreen** kind of plant remaining green all winter; **winter sports** sports practised on snow or ice; **wintertime** season or period of winter.

wintry /ˈwɪntrɪ/ *adjective* (**-ier, -iest**) characteristic of winter; lacking warmth. □ **wintriness** *noun*.

winy *adjective* (**-ier, -iest**) wine-flavoured.

wipe ● *verb* (**-ping**) clean or dry surface of by rubbing; rub (cloth) over surface; spread (liquid etc.) over surface by rubbing; (often + *away, off*, etc.) clear or remove by wiping; erase, eliminate. ● *noun* act of wiping; piece of specially treated cloth for wiping. □ **wipe out** utterly destroy or defeat, clean inside of; **wipe up** dry (dishes etc.), take up (liquid etc.) by wiping.

wiper *noun* windscreen wiper.

wire ● *noun* metal drawn out into thread or slender flexible rod; piece of this; length of this used for fencing or to carry electric current etc.; *colloquial* telegram. ● *verb* (**-ring**) provide, fasten, strengthen, etc. with wire; (often + *up*) install electrical circuits in; *colloquial* telegraph. □ **get one's wires crossed** become confused; **wire-haired** (of dog) having stiff wiry hair; **wire netting** netting made of meshed wire; **wire-tapping** tapping of telephone wires; **wire wool** mass of fine wire for scouring; **wireworm** destructive larva of a kind of beetle.

wireless *noun* radio; radio receiving set.

wiring *noun* system or installation of electrical circuits.

wiry *adjective* (**-ier, -iest**) sinewy, untiring; like wire, tough and coarse.

wisdom /ˈwɪzdəm/ *noun* experience, knowledge, and the power of applying them; prudence, common sense; wise sayings. □ **wisdom tooth** hindmost molar usually cut at age of about 20.

wise[1] /waɪz/ *adjective* having, showing, or dictated by wisdom; prudent, sensible; having knowledge; suggestive of wisdom; *US colloquial* alert, crafty. □ **be, get wise to** *colloquial* be, become, aware of; **wise-crack** *colloquial noun* smart remark, *verb* make wisecrack; **wise guy** *colloquial* know-all; **wise man** wizard, esp. one of the Magi; **wise up** esp. *US colloquial* inform, get wise. □ **wisely** *adverb*.

wise[2] /waɪz/ *noun archaic* way, manner, degree.

-wise /waɪz/ *combining form* added to nouns to form *adjectives and adverbs:* in the manner or direction of (e.g. *clockwise, lengthwise*); with reference to (e.g. *weatherwise*).

wiseacre /ˈwaɪzeɪkə/ *noun* person who affects to be wise.

wish ● *verb* (often + *for*) have or express desire or aspiration; want, demand; express one's hopes for; *colloquial* foist. ● *noun* desire, request, expression of this; thing desired. □ **wishbone** forked bone between neck and breast of fowl; **wish-fulfilment** tendency of unconscious wishes to be satisfied in fantasy; **wishing-well** well at which wishes are made.

wishful *adjective* (often + *to do*) desiring. □ **wishful thinking** belief founded on wishes rather than facts.

wishy-washy /ˈwɪʃɪwɒʃɪ/ *adjective colloquial* feeble or poor in quality or character; weak, watery.

wisp *noun* small bundle or twist of straw etc.; small separate quantity of smoke, hair, etc.; small thin person. □ **wispy** *adjective* (**-ier, -iest**).

wisteria /wɪˈstɪərɪə/ *noun* (also **wistaria** /-ˈteər-/) climbing plant with purple, blue, or white hanging flowers.

wistful /ˈwɪstfʊl/ *adjective* yearning, mournfully expectant or wishful. □ **wistfully** *adverb*; **wistfulness** *noun*.

wit *noun* (in *singular* or *plural*) intelligence, understanding; (in *singular*) imaginative and inventive faculty; amusing ingenuity of speech or ideas; person noted for this. □ **at one's wit's** or **wits' end** utterly at a loss or in despair; **have** or **keep one's wits about one** be alert; **out of one's wits** mad; **to wit** that is to say, namely.

witch *noun* woman supposed to have dealings with Devil or evil spirits; old hag; fascinating girl or woman. □ **witchcraft** use of magic, bewitching charm; **witch-doctor** tribal magician of primitive people; **witch, wych hazel** N. American shrub, astringent lotion from its bark; **witch-hunt** campaign against people suspected of unpopular or unorthodox views.

witchery /ˈwɪtʃərɪ/ *noun* witchcraft.

with /wɪð/ *preposition expressing instrument or means used, company, parting of company, cause, possession, circumstances, manner, agreement, disagreement, antagonism, understanding, regard*. □ **with it** *colloquial* up to date, alert and comprehending; **with that** thereupon.

withdraw /wɪðˈdrɔː/ *verb* (*past* **-drew**; *past participle* **-drawn**) pull or take aside or back; discontinue, cancel, retract; remove, take away; take (money) out of an account; retire or go apart; (as **withdrawn** adjective) unsociable. □ **withdrawal** noun.

withe = WITHY.

wither /'wɪðə/ verb (often + up) make or become dry and shrivelled; (often + away) deprive of or lose vigour or freshness; (esp. as **withering** adjective) blight with scorn etc. □ **witheringly** adverb.

withers /'wɪðəz/ plural noun ridge between horse's shoulder-blades.

withhold /wɪð'həʊld/ verb (past & past participle **-held**) refuse to give, grant, or allow; hold back, restrain.

within /wɪ'ðɪn/ ● adverb inside; indoors; in spirit. ● preposition inside; not beyond or out of; not transgressing or exceeding; not further off than.

without /wɪ'ðaʊt/ ● preposition not having, feeling, or showing; free from; in absence of; with neglect or avoidance of; archaic outside. ● adverb archaic or literary outside, out of doors.

withstand /wɪð'stænd/ verb (past & past participle **-stood**) oppose, hold out against.

withy /'wɪðɪ/ noun (plural **-ies**) tough flexible shoot, esp. of willow.

witless adjective foolish; crazy.

witness /'wɪtnɪs/ ● noun eyewitness; person giving sworn testimony; person attesting another's signature to document; (+ to, of) person or thing whose existence etc. attests or proves something. ● verb be eyewitness of; be witness to (signature etc.); serve as evidence or indication of; give or be evidence. □ **bear witness to** attest truth of, state one's belief in; **witness-box** (US **-stand**) enclosed space in law court from which witness gives evidence.

witter /'wɪtə/ verb (often + on) colloquial chatter annoyingly or on trivial matters.

witticism /'wɪtɪsɪz(ə)m/ noun witty remark.

wittingly /'wɪtɪŋlɪ/ adverb consciously, intentionally.

witty adjective (**-ier, -iest**) showing verbal wit. □ **wittily** adverb; **wittiness** noun.

wives plural of WIFE.

wizard /'wɪzəd/ ● noun sorcerer, magician; person of extraordinary powers. ● adjective slang wonderful. □ **wizardry** noun.

wizened /'wɪz(ə)nd/ adjective shrivelledlooking.

WNW abbreviation west-north-west.

WO abbreviation Warrant Officer.

woad noun plant yielding blue dye; this dye.

wobble /'wɒb(ə)l/ ● verb (**-ling**) sway from side to side; stand or go unsteadily, stagger; waver, vacillate. ● noun wobbling motion. □ **wobbly** adjective (**-ier, -iest**).

woe noun affliction, bitter grief; (in plural) calamities. □ **woebegone** dismallooking.

woeful adjective sorrowful; causing or feeling affliction; very bad. □ **woefully** adverb.

wok noun bowl-shaped frying-pan used in esp. Chinese cookery.

woke past of WAKE[1].

woken past participle of WAKE[1].

wold /wəʊld/ noun high open uncultivated land or moor.

wolf /wʊlf/ ● noun (plural **wolves** /wʊlvz/) wild animal related to dog; slang man who seduces women. ● verb (often + down) devour greedily. □ **cry wolf** raise false alarm; **keep the wolf from the door** avert starvation; **wolfhound** dog of kind used originally to hunt wolves; **wolfsbane** an aconite; **wolf-whistle** man's whistle to attractive woman. □ **wolfish** adjective.

wolfram /'wʊlfrəm/ noun tungsten; tungsten ore.

wolverine /'wʊlvəriːn/ noun N. American animal of weasel family.

wolves plural of WOLF.

woman /'wʊmən/ noun (plural **women** /'wɪmɪn/) adult human female; the female sex; colloquial wife, girlfriend.

womanhood noun female maturity; womanliness; womankind.

womanish adjective derogatory effeminate, unmanly.

womanize verb (also **-ise**) (**-zing** or **-sing**) (of man) be promiscuous. □ **womanizer** noun.

womankind noun (also **womenkind**) women in general.

womanly adjective having or showing qualities associated with women. □ **womanliness** noun.

womb /wuːm/ noun organ of conception and gestation in female mammals.

wombat /'wɒmbæt/ noun burrowing plant-eating Australian marsupial.

women /'wɪmɪn/ plural of WOMAN. □ **women's libber** colloquial supporter of women's liberation; **women's liberation, lib** colloquial movement for release of women from subservient status; **women's rights** human rights of women giving equality with men.

womenfolk noun women in general; women in family.

won past & past participle of WIN.

wonder /'wʌndə/ ● noun emotion, esp. admiration, excited by what is unexpected, unfamiliar, or inexplicable; strange or remarkable thing, specimen, event, etc. ● adjective having amazing properties etc. ● verb be filled with wonder; (+ that) be surprised to find that, be curious to know. □ **no** or **small wonder** it is not surprising; **wonderland** fairyland, place of surprises or marvels.

wonderful adjective very remarkable or admirable. □ **wonderfully** adverb.

wonderment noun surprise, awe.

wondrous /'wʌndrəs/ poetical ● adjective wonderful. ● adverb wonderfully.

wonky /'wɒŋkɪ/ adjective (**-ier, -iest**) slang crooked; unsteady; unreliable.

wont /wəʊnt/ ● adjective archaic or literary (+ to do) accustomed. ● noun formal or jocular custom, habit.

won't /wəʊnt/ will not.

wonted /'wəʊntɪd/ adjective habitual, usual.

woo verb (**woos, wooed**) court, seek love of; try to win; seek support of; coax, importune.

wood /wʊd/ noun hard fibrous substance of tree; this for timber or fuel; (in singular or plural) growing trees occupying piece of ground; wooden cask for wine etc.; wooden-headed golf club; ball in game of bowls. □ **out of the wood(s)** clear of danger or difficulty; **wood anemone** wild spring-flowering anemone; **woodbine** honeysuckle; **woodchuck** N. American marmot; **woodcock** game bird related to snipe; **woodcut** relief cut on wood, print made from this; **woodcutter** person who cuts timber; **woodland** wooded country; **woodlouse** small land crustacean with many legs; **woodman** forester; **woodpecker** bird that taps tree trunks to find insects; **woodpigeon** dove with white patches round neck; **wood pulp** wood fibre prepared for papermaking; **woodwind** wind instrument(s) of orchestra made originally of wood; **woodwork** making of things in wood, things made of wood; **woodworm** beetle larva that bores in wood, resulting condition of wood.

wooded adjective having woods.

wooden /'wʊd(ə)n/ adjective made of wood; like wood; stiff, clumsy; expressionless. □ **woodenly** adverb; **woodenness** noun.

woody adjective (**-ier, -iest**) wooded; like or of wood.

woof[1] /wʊf/ ● noun gruff bark of dog. ● verb give woof.

woof² /wuːf/ *noun* weft.

woofer /'wuːfə/ *noun* loudspeaker for low frequencies.

wool /wʊl/ *noun* fine soft wavy hair forming fleece of sheep etc.; woollen yarn, cloth, or garments; wool-like substance. □ **wool-gathering** absent-mindedness; **the Woolsack** Lord Chancellor's seat in House of Lords.

woollen /'wʊlən/ (*US* **woolen**) ● *adjective* made (partly) of wool. ● *noun* woollen fabric; (in *plural*) woollen garments.

woolly ● *adjective* (**-ier**, **-iest**) bearing or like wool; woollen; indistinct; confused. ● *noun* (*plural* **-ies**) *colloquial* woollen (esp. knitted) garment.

woozy /'wuːzɪ/ *adjective* (**-ier**, **-iest**) *colloquial* dizzy; slightly drunk.

word /wɜːd/ ● *noun* meaningful element of speech, usually shown with space on either side of it when written or printed; speech as distinct from action; one's promise or assurance; (in *singular* or *plural*) thing said, remark, conversation; (in *plural*) text of song or actor's part; (in *plural*) angry talk; news, message; command. ● *verb* put into words, select words to express. □ **word-blindness** dyslexia; **word for word** in exactly the same words, literally; **the Word (of God)** the Bible; **word of mouth** speech (only); **word-perfect** having memorized one's part etc. perfectly; **word processor** computer software or hardware for storing text entered from keyboard, incorporating corrections, and producing printout; **word-process** *verb*; **word processing** *noun*.

wording *noun* form of words used.

wordy *adjective* (**-ier**, **-iest**) using or expressed in (too) many words.

wore *past of* WEAR.

work /wɜːk/ ● *noun* application of effort to a purpose, use of energy; task to be undertaken; thing done or made by work, result of action; employment, occupation, etc., esp. as means of earning money; literary or musical composition; actions or experiences of specified kind; (in *plural*) operative part of clock etc.; (**the works**) *colloquial* all that is available or needed, full treatment; (in *plural*) operations of building or repair; (in *plural*; often treated as *singular*) factory; (usually in *plural* or *in combination*) defensive structure. ● *verb* be engaged in activity; be employed in certain work; make efforts; be craftsman in (material); operate or function, esp. effectively; operate, manage, control; put or keep in operation or at work, cause to toil; cultivate (land); produce as result; *colloquial* arrange; knead, hammer, bring to desired shape or consistency; do, or make by, needlework etc.; (cause to) make way or make (way) slowly or with difficulty; gradually become (loose etc.) by motion; artificially excite; purchase with labour instead of money; obtain money for by labour; (+ *on*, *upon*) influence; be in motion or agitated, ferment. □ **get worked up** become angry, excited, or tense; **workaday** ordinary, everyday, practical; **workbasket** basket for sewing materials; **workbench** bench for manual work, esp. carpentry; **workbox** box for tools, needlework, etc.; **workday** day on which work is usually done; **work experience** temporary experience of employment for young people; **workforce** workers engaged or available, number of these; **workhouse** *historical* public institution for the poor; **work in** find place for; **workload** amount of work to be done; **workman** man employed to do manual labour, person who works in specified manner; **workmanlike** showing practised skill; **workmanship** degree of skill in doing task or of finish in product; **workmate** person working alongside another; **work off** get rid of by work or activity;

work out *verb* solve (sum) or find (amount) by calculation, understand (problem, person, etc.), be calculated, have result, provide for all details of, engage in physical exercise; **workout** *noun* session of physical exercise; **work over** examine thoroughly, *colloquial* treat with violence; **workshop** room or building in which goods are manufactured, place or meeting for concerted activity; **work-shy** disinclined to work; **workstation** location of stage in manufacturing process, computer terminal; **worktop** flat (esp. kitchen) surface for working on; **work to rule** follow official working rules exactly to reduce efficiency as protest; **work-to-rule** *noun*; **work up** bring gradually to efficient or advanced state, advance gradually, elaborate or excite by degrees, mingle (ingredients), learn (subject) by study.

workable *adjective* that can be worked, will work, or is worth working. □ **workability** *noun*.

worker *noun* manual or industrial etc. employee; neuter bee or ant; person who works hard.

working ● *adjective* engaged in work; while so engaged; functioning, able to function. ● *noun* activity of work; functioning; mine, quarry; (usually in *plural*) mechanism. □ **working capital** capital used in conducting a business; **working class** social class employed for wages, esp. in manual or industrial work; **working-class** *adjective*; **working day** workday, part of day devoted to work; **working knowledge** knowledge adequate to work with; **working lunch** lunch at which business is conducted; **working order** condition in which machine works; **working party** committee appointed to study and advise on some question.

world /wɜːld/ ● *noun* the earth, planetary body like it; the universe, all that exists; time, state, or scene of human existence; (**the, this world**) mortal life; secular interests and affairs; human affairs, active life; average, respectable, or fashionable people or their customs or opinions; all that concerns or all who belong to specified class or sphere of activity; vast amount. ● *adjective* of or affecting all nations. □ **out of this world** *colloquial* extremely good etc.; **think the world of** have very high regard for; **world-class** of standard considered high throughout world; **world-famous** known throughout the world; **world music** pop music incorporating ethnic elements; **world war** one involving many important nations; **world-weary** bored with human affairs; **worldwide** *adjective* occurring or known in all parts of the world; *adverb* throughout the world.

worldly *adjective* (**-ier**, **-iest**) temporal, earthly; experienced in life, sophisticated, practical. □ **worldly-wise** prudent in one's dealings with world.

worm /wɜːm/ ● *noun* any of several types of creeping invertebrate animal with long slender body and no limbs; larva of insect; (in *plural*) internal parasites; insignificant or contemptible person; spiral of screw. ● *verb* crawl, wriggle; (**worm oneself**) insinuate oneself (into favour etc.); (+ *out*) obtain (secret etc.) by cunning persistence; rid (dog etc.) of worms. □ **worm-cast** convoluted mass of earth left on surface by burrowing earthworm; **wormeaten** eaten into by worms, decayed, dilapidated.

wormwood /'wɜːmwʊd/ *noun* plant with bitter aromatic taste; bitter humiliation, source of this.

wormy *adjective* (**-ier**, **-iest**) full of worms; wormeaten.

worn ● *past participle of* WEAR. ● *adjective* damaged by use or wear; looking tired and exhausted.

worry /'wʌrɪ/ ● *verb* (**-ies**, **-ied**) be anxious; harass, importune, be trouble or anxiety to; shake or pull about with teeth; (as **worried** *adjective*) uneasy. ● *noun* (*plural* **-ies**) thing that causes anxiety or disturbs tranquillity; disturbed state of mind, anxiety.

□ **worry beads** string of beads manipulated with fingers to occupy or calm oneself. □ **worrier** noun.

worse /wɜːs/ ● adjective more bad; in or into worse health or worse condition. ● adverb more badly; more ill. ● noun worse thing(s); (**the worse**) worse condition. □ **the worse for wear** damaged by use, injured; **worse off** in a worse (esp. financial) position. □ **worsen** verb.

worship /'wɜːʃɪp/ ● noun homage or service to deity; acts, rites, or ceremonies of this; adoration, devotion; (**His, Her, Your Worship**) title used of or to mayor, magistrate, etc. ● verb (**-pp-**; US **-p-**) adore as divine, honour with religious rites; idolize; attend public worship; be full of adoration. □ **worshipper** noun.

worshipful adjective (also **Worshipful**) archaic honourable, distinguished (esp. in old titles of companies or officers).

worst /wɜːst/ ● adjective most bad. ● adverb most badly. ● noun worst part or possibility. ● verb get the better of, defeat. □ **at (the) worst** in the worst possible case; **do your worst** expression of defiance; **get the worst of it** be defeated; **if the worst comes to the worst** if the worst happens.

worsted /'wʊstɪd/ noun fine woollen yarn; fabric made from this.

wort /wɜːt/ noun infusion of malt before it is fermented into beer.

worth /wɜːθ/ ● adjective of value equivalent to; such as to justify or repay; possessing property equivalent to. ● noun value; equivalent of money etc. in commodity etc. □ **worth it** (colloquial), **worth (one's) while, worthwhile** worth the time or effort spent.

worthless adjective without value or merit. □ **worthlessness** noun.

worthy /'wɜːðɪ/ ● adjective (**-ier, -iest**) deserving respect, estimable; entitled to recognition; (usually + of) deserving; (+ of) adequate or suitable for the dignity etc. of. ● noun (plural **-ies**) worthy person; person of some distinction.

would auxiliary verb (3rd singular present **would**) used in reported speech or to form conditional mood; expressing habitual past action, request as question, or probability. □ **would-be** desiring or aspiring to be.

wouldn't /'wʊd(ə)nt/ would not.

wound[1] /wuːnd/ ● noun injury done by cut or blow to living tissue; pain inflicted on feelings, injury to reputation. ● verb inflict wound on.

wound[2] past & past participle of WIND[2]. □ **wound up** excited, tense, angry.

wove past of WEAVE[1].

woven past participle of WEAVE[1].

wow /waʊ/ ● interjection expressing astonishment or admiration. ● noun slang sensational success. ● verb slang impress greatly.

WP abbreviation word processor.

WPC abbreviation woman police constable.

w.p.m. abbreviation words per minute.

WRAC abbreviation historical Women's Royal Army Corps.

wrack noun seaweed cast up or growing on seashore; destruction.

WRAF abbreviation historical Women's Royal Air Force.

wraith /reɪθ/ noun ghost; spectral appearance of living person supposed to portend that person's death.

wrangle /'ræŋg(ə)l/ ● noun noisy argument or dispute. ● verb (**-ling**) engage in wrangle.

wrap ● verb (**-pp-**) (often + up) envelop in folded or soft encircling material; (+ round, about) arrange or draw (pliant covering) round (person). ● noun shawl, scarf, etc.; wrapper; esp. US wrapping material. □ **under wraps** in secrecy; **wraparound, wrap-round** (esp. of clothing) designed to wrap round,

curving round at edges; **wrap-over** adjective (of garment) overlapping when worn, noun such garment; **wrapped up in** engrossed or absorbed in; **wrap up** colloquial finish off (matter), put on warm clothes.

wrapper noun cover for sweet, book, posted newspaper, etc.; loose enveloping robe or gown.

wrapping noun (esp. in plural) material used to wrap, wraps, wrappers. □ **wrapping paper** strong or decorative paper for wrapping parcels.

wrasse /ræs/ noun (plural same or **-s**) brilliant-coloured edible sea fish.

wrath /rɒθ/ noun literary extreme anger. □ **wrathful** adjective.

wreak verb (usually + upon) give play to (vengeance etc.); cause (damage etc.).

wreath /riːθ/ noun (plural **-s** /riːðz/) flowers or leaves wound together into ring, esp. as ornament for head or door or for laying on grave etc.; curl or ring of smoke, cloud, or soft fabric.

wreathe /riːð/ verb (**-thing**) encircle (as) with or like wreath; (+ round) wind (one's arms etc.) round (person etc.); move in wreaths.

wreck ● noun sinking or running aground of ship; ship that has suffered wreck; greatly damaged building, thing, or person. ● verb seriously damage (vehicle etc.); ruin (hopes etc.); cause wreck of (ship).

wreckage noun wrecked material; remnants of wreck; act of wrecking.

wrecker noun person or thing that wrecks or destroys, esp. (historical) person who tries from shore to bring about shipwreck for plunder or profit.

Wren noun member of WRNS.

wren noun small usually brown short-winged songbird.

wrench ● noun violent twist or oblique pull or tearing off; tool for gripping and turning nuts etc.; painful uprooting or parting etc. ● verb twist or pull violently round or sideways; (often + off, away, etc.) pull with wrench.

wrest verb wrench away from person's grasp; (+ from) obtain by effort or with difficulty.

wrestle /'res(ə)l/ ● noun contest in which two opponents grapple and try to throw each other to ground; hard struggle. ● verb (**-ling**) have wrestling match; (often + with) struggle; (+ with) do one's utmost to deal with. □ **wrestler** noun.

wretch noun unfortunate or pitiable person; reprehensible person.

wretched /'retʃɪd/ adjective (**-er, -est**) unhappy, miserable; unwell; of bad quality, contemptible; displeasing. □ **wretchedly** adverb; **wretchedness** noun.

wriggle /'rɪg(ə)l/ ● verb (**-ling**) twist or turn body with short writhing movements; make wriggling motions; (+ along, through, etc.) go thus; be evasive. ● noun wriggling movement. □ **wriggly** adjective.

wring ● verb (past & past participle **wrung**) squeeze tightly; (often + out) squeeze and twist, esp. to remove liquid; break by twisting; distress, torture; extract by squeezing; (+ out, from) obtain by pressure or importunity. ● noun act of wringing. □ **wringing (wet)** so wet that water can be wrung out; **wring one's hands** clasp them as gesture of grief; **wring the neck of** kill (chicken etc.) by twisting neck.

wringer noun device for wringing water from washed clothes etc.

wrinkle /'rɪŋk(ə)l/ ● noun crease in skin or other flexible surface; colloquial useful hint, clever expedient. ● verb (**-ling**) make wrinkles in; form wrinkles. □ **wrinkly** adjective (**-ier, -iest**).

wrist noun joint connecting hand and forearm; part of garment covering wrist. □ **wrist-watch** small watch worn on strap etc. round wrist.

wristlet noun band or ring to guard, strengthen, or adorn wrist.

writ noun formal written court order to do or not do specified act.

write verb (**-ting**; past **wrote**; past participle **written** /'rɪt(ə)n/) mark paper or other surface with symbols, letters, or words; form or mark (such symbols etc.); form or mark symbols of (word, document, etc.); fill or complete with writing; put (data) into computer store; (esp. in passive) indicate (quality or condition) by appearance; compose for reproduction or publication; (usually + to) write and send letter; convey (news etc.) by letter; state in book etc.; (+ into, out of) include or exclude (character, episode) in or from story. □ **write down** record in writing; **write in** send suggestion etc. in writing, esp. to broadcasting station; **write off** verb cancel (debt etc.), acknowledge as lost, completely destroy, (+ for) order or request by post; **write-off** noun thing written off, esp. vehicle etc. so damaged as not to be worth repair; **write up** verb write full account of; **write-up** noun written or published account, review.

writer noun person who writes, esp. author. □ **writer's cramp** muscular spasm due to excessive writing.

writhe /raɪð/ verb (**-thing**) twist or roll oneself about (as) in acute pain; suffer mental torture.

writing noun written words etc.; handwriting; (usually in plural) writer's works. □ **in writing** in written form.

written past participle of WRITE.

WRNS abbreviation historical Women's Royal Naval Service.

wrong ● adjective mistaken, not true, in error; unsuitable, less or least desirable; contrary to law or morality; amiss, out of order. ● adverb in wrong manner or direction, with incorrect result. ● noun what is morally wrong; unjust action. ● verb treat unjustly; mistakenly attribute bad motives to. □ **go wrong** take wrong path, stop functioning properly, depart from virtuous behaviour; **in the wrong** responsible for quarrel, mistake, or offence; **wrongdoer** person who behaves immorally or illegally; **wrongdoing** noun; **wrong-foot** colloquial catch off balance or unprepared; **wrong-headed** perverse and obstinate; **wrong side** worse or undesirable or unusable side; **wrong way round** in opposite of normal orientation or sequence. □ **wrongly** adverb; **wrongness** noun.

wrongful adjective unwarranted, unjustified. □ **wrongfully** adverb.

wrote past of WRITE.

wroth /rəʊθ/ adjective archaic angry.

wrought /rɔːt/ archaic past & past participle of WORK. □ **wrought iron** form of iron suitable for forging or rolling, not cast.

wrung past & past participle of WRING.

WRVS abbreviation Women's Royal Voluntary Service.

wry /raɪ/ adjective (**-er, -est**) distorted, turned to one side; contorted in disgust, disappointment, or mockery; (of humour) dry and mocking. □ **wryneck** small woodpecker able to turn head over shoulder. □ **wryly** adverb; **wryness** noun.

WSW abbreviation west-south-west.

wt abbreviation weight.

wych hazel /wɪtʃ/ witch hazel.

WYSIWYG /'wɪzɪwɪg/ adjective indicating that text on computer screen and printout correspond exactly (what you see is what you get).

Xx

X¹ *noun* (also **x**) (Roman numeral) 10; first unknown quantity in algebra; unknown or unspecified number, person, etc.; cross-shaped symbol, esp. used to indicate position or incorrectness, to symbolize kiss or vote, or as signature of person who cannot write.
□ **X-ray** *noun* electromagnetic radiation of short wavelength able to pass through opaque bodies, photograph made by X-rays, *verb* photograph, examine, or treat with X-rays.

X² *adjective* (of film) classified as suitable for adults only.

xenophobia /zenəˈfəʊbɪə/ *noun* hatred or fear of foreigners.

Xerox /ˈzɪərɒks/ ● *noun proprietary term* type of photocopier; copy made by it. ● *verb* (**xerox**) make Xerox of.

Xmas /ˈkrɪsməs, ˈeksməs/ *noun colloquial* Christmas.

xylophone /ˈzaɪləfəʊn/ *noun* musical instrument of graduated wooden or metal bars struck with small wooden hammers.

Yy

Y *noun* (also **y**) second unknown quantity in algebra; Y-shaped thing.

yacht /jɒt/ ● *noun* light sailing vessel for racing or cruising; larger usually power-driven vessel for cruising. ● *verb* race or cruise in yacht. □ **yachtsman**, **yachtswoman** person who yachts.

yah /jɑː/ *interjection of derision, defiance, etc.*

yahoo /jɑːˈhuː/ *noun* bestial person.

Yahweh /ˈjɑːweɪ/ *noun* Jehovah.

yak *noun* long-haired Tibetan ox.

yam *noun* tropical or subtropical climbing plant; edible starchy tuberous root of this; *US* sweet potato.

yang *noun* (in Chinese philosophy) active male principle of universe (compare YIN).

Yank *noun colloquial often derogatory* American.

yank *verb & noun colloquial* pull with jerk.

Yankee /ˈjæŋkɪ/ *noun colloquial* Yank; *US* inhabitant of New England or of northern States.

yap ● *verb* (**-pp-**) bark shrilly or fussily; *colloquial* talk noisily, foolishly, or complainingly. ● *noun* sound of yapping.

yard¹ *noun* unit of linear measure (3 ft, 0.9144 m.); this length of material; square or cubic yard; spar slung across mast for sail to hang from; (in *plural*; + *of*) *colloquial* a great length. □ **yard-arm** either end of ship's yard; **yardstick** standard of comparison, rod a yard long usually divided into inches etc.

yard² *noun* piece of enclosed ground, esp. attached to building or used for particular purpose; *US & Australian* garden of house.

yardage *noun* number of yards of material etc.

yarmulke /ˈjɑːməlkə/ *noun* (also **yarmulka**) skullcap worn by Jewish men.

yarn ● *noun* spun thread for weaving, knitting, etc.; *colloquial* story, traveller's tale, anecdote. ● *verb colloquial* tell yarns.

yarrow /ˈjærəʊ/ *noun* perennial plant, esp. milfoil.

yashmak /ˈjæʃmæk/ *noun* veil concealing face except eyes, worn by some Muslim women.

yaw ● *verb* (of ship, aircraft, etc.) fail to hold straight course, go unsteadily. ● *noun* yawing of ship etc. from course.

yawl *noun* kind of sailing boat; small fishing boat.

yawn ● *verb* open mouth wide and inhale, esp. when sleepy or bored; gape, be wide open. ● *noun* act of yawning.

yaws /jɔːz/ *plural noun* (usually treated as *singular*) contagious tropical skin disease.

yd *abbreviation* (*plural* **yds**) yard (measure).

ye /jiː/ *pronoun archaic* (as subject of verb) you (plural).

yea /jeɪ/ *archaic* ● *adverb* yes. ● *noun* 'yes' vote.

yeah /jeə/ *adverb colloquial* yes.

year /jɪə/ *noun* time occupied by one revolution of earth round sun, approx. 365 1/4 days; period from 1 Jan. to 31 Dec. inclusive; period of 12 calendar months; (in *plural*) age, time of life; (usually in *plural colloquial* very long time. □ **yearbook** annual publication bringing information on some subject up to date.

yearling *noun* animal between one and two years old.

yearly ● *adjective* done, produced, or occurring once every year; of or lasting a year. ● *adverb* once every year.

yearn /jɜːn/ *verb* be filled with longing, compassion, or tenderness. □ **yearning** *noun & adjective*.

yeast *noun* greyish-yellow fungus, got esp. from fermenting malt liquors and used as fermenting agent, to raise bread, etc.

yeasty *adjective* (**-ier**, **-iest**) frothy; in ferment; working like yeast.

yell ● *noun* sharp loud cry; shout. ● *verb* cry, shout.

yellow /ˈjeləʊ/ ● *adjective* of the colour of lemons, buttercups, etc.; having yellow skin or complexion; *colloquial* cowardly. ● *noun* yellow colour, paint, clothes, etc. ● *verb* turn yellow. □ **yellow-belly** *colloquial* coward; **yellow card** shown by referee to football-player being cautioned; **yellow fever** tropical virus fever with jaundice etc.; **yellow-hammer** bunting of which male has yellow head, neck, and breast; **Yellow Pages** *proprietary term* telephone directory on yellow paper, listing and classifying business subscribers; **yellow streak** *colloquial* trace of cowardice. □ **yellowish** *adjective*; **yellowness** *noun*; **yellowy** *adjective*.

yelp ● *noun* sharp shrill bark or cry as of dog in excitement or pain. ● *verb* utter yelp.

yen¹ *noun* (*plural* same) chief monetary unit of Japan.

yen² *colloquial* ● *noun* intense desire or longing. ● *verb* (**-nn-**) feel longing.

yeoman /ˈjəʊmən/ *noun esp. historical* man holding and farming small estate; member of yeomanry force. □ **Yeoman of the Guard** member of bodyguard of English sovereign.

yeomanry *noun* (*plural* **-ies**) group of yeomen; *historical* volunteer cavalry force in British army.

yes ● *adverb* indicating affirmative reply to question, statement, request, command, *etc.*; (**yes?**) indeed?, is that so?, what do you want? ● *noun* utterance of word yes. □ **yes-man** *colloquial* weakly acquiescent person.

yesterday /ˈjestədeɪ/ ● *adverb* on the day before today. ● *noun* the day before today.

yesteryear /ˈjestəjɪə/ *noun archaic or rhetorical* last year; the recent past.

yet ● *adverb* up to now or then; (with negative or in questions) so soon as, or by, now or then; again, in addition; in the remaining time available; (+ *comparative*) even; nevertheless. ● *conjunction* but nevertheless.

yeti /ˈjetɪ/ *noun* supposed manlike or bearlike Himalayan animal.

yew *noun* dark-leaved evergreen coniferous tree; its wood.

YHA *abbreviation* Youth Hostels Association.

Yiddish /ˈjɪdɪʃ/ ● *noun* language used by Jews in or from Europe. ● *adjective* of this language.

yield /jiːld/ ● *verb* produce or return as fruit, profit, or result; concede, give up; (often + *to*) surrender, submit, defer; (as **yielding** *adjective*) soft and pliable, submissive; (+ *to*) give right of way to. ● *noun* amount yielded or produced.

yin *noun* (in Chinese philosophy) passive female principle of universe (compare YANG).

yippee /jɪˈpiː/ *interjection expressing delight or excitement.*

YMCA *abbreviation* Young Men's Christian Association.

yob /jɒb/ *noun* (also **yobbo**, *plural* **-s**) *slang* lout, hooligan. □ **yobbish** *adjective*.

yodel /ˈjəʊd(ə)l/ ● verb (**-ll-**; US **-l-**) sing with melodious inarticulate sounds and frequent changes between falsetto and normal voice, in manner of Swiss mountain-dwellers. ● noun yodelling cry.

yoga /ˈjəʊgə/ noun Hindu system of meditation and asceticism; system of physical exercises and breathing control used in yoga.

yoghurt /ˈjɒgət/ noun (also **yogurt**) rather sour semisolid food made from milk fermented by added bacteria.

yogi /ˈjəʊgɪ/ noun (plural **-s**) devotee of yoga.

yoke ● noun wooden crosspiece fastened over necks of two oxen etc. and attached to plough or wagon to be pulled; (plural same or **-s**) pair (of oxen etc.); object like yoke in form or function, e.g. wooden shoulderpiece for carrying pair of pails, top part of garment from which rest hangs; sway, dominion, servitude; bond of union, esp. of marriage. ● verb (**-king**) put yoke on; couple or unite (pair); link (one thing) to (another); match or work together.

yokel /ˈjəʊk(ə)l/ noun country bumpkin.

yolk /jəʊk/ noun yellow inner part of egg.

Yom Kippur /jɒm ˈkɪpə/ noun most solemn religious fast day of Jewish year, Day of Atonement.

yon adjective & adverb literary & dialect yonder.

yonder /ˈjɒndə/ ● adverb over there, at some distance in that direction, in place indicated. ● adjective situated yonder.

yore noun □ **of yore** a long time ago.

york verb Cricket bowl out with yorker.

yorker noun Cricket ball that pitches immediately under bat.

Yorkist /ˈjɔːkɪst/ ● noun historical follower of House of York, esp. in Wars of the Roses. ● adjective of House of York.

Yorkshire pudding /ˈjɔːkʃə/ noun baked batter usually eaten with roast beef.

Yorkshire terrier /jɔːkʃə/ noun small long-haired blue and tan kind of terrier.

you /juː/ pronoun the person(s) or thing(s) addressed; one, a person.

you'd /juːd/ you had; you would.

you'll /juːl/ you will; you shall.

young /jʌŋ/ ● adjective (**younger** /ˈjʌŋgə/, **youngest** /ˈjʌŋgɪst/) not far advanced in life, development, or existence, not yet old; immature, inexperienced, youthful; of or characteristic of youth. ● noun offspring, esp. of animals. □ **youngish** adjective.

youngster noun child, young person.

your /jɔː/ adjective of or belonging to you.

you're /jɔː/ you are.

yours /jɔːz/ pronoun the one(s) belonging to you.

yourself /jɔːˈself/ pronoun (plural **yourselves**): emphatic & reflexive form of YOU.

youth /juːθ/ noun (plural **-s** /juːðz/) being young; early part of life, esp. adolescence; quality or condition characteristic of the young; young man; (treated as plural) young people collectively. □ **youth club** place for young people's leisure activities; **youth hostel** any of chain of cheap lodgings where (esp. young) holiday-makers can stay for the night.

youthful adjective young or still having characteristics of youth. □ **youthfulness** noun.

you've /juːv/ you have.

yowl /jaʊl/ ● noun loud wailing cry (as) of cat or dog in distress. ● verb utter yowl.

yo-yo /ˈjəʊjəʊ/ noun (plural **yo-yos**) toy consisting of pair of discs with deep groove between them in which string is attached and wound, and which can be made to fall and rise.

yr. abbreviation year(s); younger; your.

yrs. abbreviation years; yours.

YTS abbreviation Youth Training Scheme.

yuan /juːˈɑːn/ noun (plural same) chief monetary unit of China.

yucca /ˈjʌkə/ noun white-flowered plant with swordlike leaves, often grown as house plant.

yuck /jʌk/ interjection (also **yuk**) slang expression of strong distaste.

yucky adjective (also **yukky**) (**-ier**, **-iest**) slang messy, repellent; sickly, sentimental.

Yugoslav /ˈjuːgəslɑːv/ historical ● adjective of Yugoslavia. ● noun native or national of Yugoslavia. □ **Yugoslavian** /-ˈslɑːv-/ adjective & noun.

yuk = YUCK.

yukky = YUCKY.

yule noun (in full **yule-tide**) archaic festival of Christmas. □ **yule-log** large log burnt at Christmas.

yummy /ˈjʌmɪ/ adjective (**-ier**, **-iest**) colloquial tasty, delicious.

yuppie /ˈjʌpɪ/ noun (also **yuppy**) (plural **-ies**) colloquial usually derogatory young ambitious professional person working in city.

YWCA abbreviation Young Women's Christian Association.

zabaglione /zæbə'ljəʊnɪ/ *noun* Italian dessert of whipped and heated egg yolks, sugar, and wine.

zany /'zeɪnɪ/ *adjective* (**-ier, -iest**) comically idiotic; crazily ridiculous.

zap *verb* (**-pp-**) *slang* kill, destroy; attack; hit hard.

zeal *noun* fervour, eagerness; hearty persistent endeavour. □ **zealous** /'zeləs/ *adjective*.

zealot /'zelət/ *noun* extreme partisan, fanatic.

zebra /'zebrə, 'ziː-/ *noun* (*plural* same or **-s**) African black and white striped horselike animal. □ **zebra crossing** striped street-crossing where pedestrians have precedence.

Zeitgeist /'tsaɪtgaɪst/ *noun* spirit of times. [German]

Zen *noun* form of Buddhism emphasizing meditation and intuition.

zenith /'zenɪθ/ *noun* point of heavens directly overhead; highest point (of power, prosperity, etc.).

zephyr /'zefə/ *noun literary* mild gentle breeze.

zero /'zɪərəʊ/ ● *noun* (*plural* **-s**) figure 0, nought, nil; point on scale of thermometer etc. from which positive or negative quantity is reckoned; (in full **zero-hour**) hour at which planned, esp. military, operation is timed to begin, crucial moment; lowest or earliest point. ● *adjective* no, not any. ● *verb* (**zeroes, zeroed**) adjust (instrument etc.) to zero. □ **zero in on** take aim at, focus attention on; **zero-rated** on which no VAT is charged.

zest *noun* piquancy; keen interest or enjoyment, relish, gusto; outer layer of orange or lemon peel.

zigzag /'zɪgzæg/ ● *adjective* with abrupt alternate right and left turns. ● *noun* zigzag line, thing having sharp turns. ● *adverb* with zigzag manner or course. ● *verb* (**-gg-**) move in zigzag course.

zilch *noun* esp. US slang nothing.

zillion /'zɪlɪən/ *noun* (*plural* same) *colloquial* indefinite large number; (**zillions**) very large number.

Zimmer frame /'zɪmə/ *noun proprietary term* kind of walking frame.

zinc *noun* greyish-white metallic element.

zing *colloquial* ● *noun* vigour, energy. ● *verb* move swiftly, esp. with shrill sound.

zinnia /'zɪnɪə/ *noun* garden plant with showy flowers.

zip ● *noun* light sharp sound; energy, vigour; (in full **zip-fastener**) fastening device of two flexible strips with interlocking projections, closed or opened by sliding clip along them. ● *verb* (**-pp-**) (often + *up*) fasten with zip-fastener; move with zip or at high speed.

zipper *noun* esp. US zip-fastener.

zircon /'zɜːkən/ *noun* translucent varieties of zirconium silicate cut into gems.

zirconium /zə'kəʊnɪəm/ *noun* grey metallic element.

zither /'zɪðə/ *noun* stringed instrument with flat soundbox, placed horizontally and played by plucking.

zloty /'zlɒtɪ/ *noun* (*plural* same or **-s**) chief monetary unit of Poland.

zodiac /'zəʊdɪæk/ *noun* belt of heavens including all apparent positions of sun, moon, and planets as known to ancient astronomers, and divided into 12 equal parts (**signs of the zodiac**).

zombie /'zɒmbɪ/ *noun* corpse said to have been revived by witchcraft; *colloquial* dull or apathetic person.

zone ● *noun* area having particular features, properties, purpose, or use; well-defined region of more or less beltlike form; area between two concentric circles; encircling band of colour etc.; *archaic* girdle, belt. ● *verb* (**-ning**) encircle as or with zone; arrange or distribute by zones; assign as or to specific area. □ **zonal** *adjective*.

zonked /zɒŋkt/ *adjective slang* (often + *out*) exhausted; intoxicated.

zoo *noun* zoological garden.

zoological /zəʊə'lɒdʒɪk(ə)l, zuː-ə-/ *adjective* of zoology. □ **zoological garden(s)** public garden or park with collection of animals for exhibition and study.

■ **Usage** See note at ZOOLOGY.

zoology /zəʊ'ɒlədʒɪ, zuː'ɒl-/ *noun* scientific study of animals. □ **zoologist** *noun*.

■ **Usage** The second pronunciation given for *zoology, zoological*, and *zoologist* (with the first syllable pronounced as in *zoo*), although extremely common, is considered incorrect by some people.

zoom ● *verb* move quickly, esp. with buzzing sound; cause aeroplane to mount at high speed and steep angle; (often + *in, in on*) (of camera) change rapidly from long shot to close-up (of). ● *noun* aeroplane's steep climb. □ **zoom lens** lens allowing camera to zoom by varying focal length.

zoophyte /'zəʊəfaɪt/ *noun* plantlike animal, esp. coral, sea anemone, or sponge.

zucchini /zuː'kiːnɪ/ *noun* (*plural* same or **-s**) esp. US & Australian courgette.

zygote /'zaɪgəʊt/ *noun Biology* cell formed by union of two gametes.